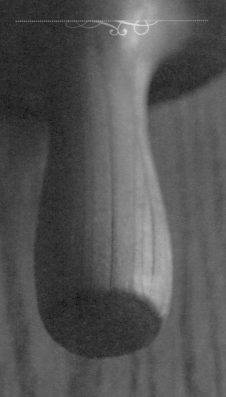

Other books from The Amish Cook

The Amish Cook

The Amish Cook at Home

The Amish Cook's Baking Book

The Amish Cook's Anniversary Book

20 Years of Food, Family, and Faith

LOVINA EICHER with KEVIN WILLIAMS

PHOTOGRAPHY by BETSY DELLAPOSTA

Andrews McMeel
Publishing, LLC
Kansas City • Sydney • London

Andrews McMeel Publishing, LLC
an Andrews McMeel Universal company
1130 Walnut Street, Kansas City, Missouri 64106

www.andrewsmcmeel.com

11 12 13 14 WKT 10 9 8 7 6 5 4 3 2

ISBN: 978-0-7407-9765-1

Library of Congress Control Number: 2010921940

ATTENTION: SCHOOLS AND BUSINESSES
Andrews McMeel books are available at quantity discounts with bulk purchase for educational, business, or sales promotional use. For information, please e-mail the Andrews McMeel Publishing Special Sales Department: specialsales@amuniversal.com

contents

THE AMISH COOK

By Elizabeth Coblentz

a twenty-year journey

The Amish Cook" column started back when I was a teenager living at home. Way back before I had any worries of my own, I remember Mother sitting at the table writing her column. She would sometimes ask my sisters or me to rewrite the column so she'd have her own copy of the column after sending it out to Kevin. I remember doing this for her quite often. I enjoyed rewriting her words, letter for letter. Since writing was something I enjoyed, I received joy from doing this for her. Little did I realize that someday I would be penning this very column. For me, Mother was supposed to live well into her eighties or nineties and still be writing. But God had other plans, taking both my parents suddenly within less than two and a half years. God had once again shown us that He is in control. I knew as a believer in God that He had a purpose for this all. It took prayers, and without God's help it would have been a lot harder. He helped me accept the changes in life. On behalf of my late mother, I would like to thank all of you readers out there. Without you, this column would not have been possible. I also think a great big thank-you should go to my editor, Kevin Williams, for continuing through all these years with many disappointments yet he still did not give up and kept the columns going. My husband, Joe, has always been an encouragement to me. There were times when he rocked our babies to sleep and got everyone settled into bed so I could get the weekly column written. I am writing the column in the early part of our life, whereas Mother wrote it in the latter part of hers. By combining our columns into one book, I hope to give everyone a taste of how all these years have unfolded. I enjoy the journey, and God bless you!

LOVINA EICHER, 2010

etween Lovina's eloquent note and what has been written in our earlier cookbooks, *The Amish Cook at Home* and *The Amish Cook's Baking Book*, I feel like there is little left for me to say. I just never, ever imagined when I met Elizabeth Coblentz quite randomly in her driveway on a warm day in July of 1991 that twenty years later the results of that chance encounter would still be evident. I was young and naive with a full future ahead. In the years since, there have been unimaginable blessings and deep disappointments in my life. It has been an incredible journey, as the Eichers and Coblentzes have both filled my life with a richness and fulfillment that I probably could have never found elsewhere.

The process of syndicating the column has changed. The process of getting "The Amish Cook" column from notebook paper to newspaper used to be much more involved. In the column's first year, back in 1991, I was only eighteen years old and the Internet and e-mail were, for most people, still relegated to geeky corners of universities. In those days, I would use a relatively new device called a fax machine and one-by-one dial "The Amish Cook" to its destination. Fast-forward almost twenty years: What once took two hours now takes two minutes. I simply type in and e-mail the column to newspapers. And my futuristic fax machine sits on a shelf

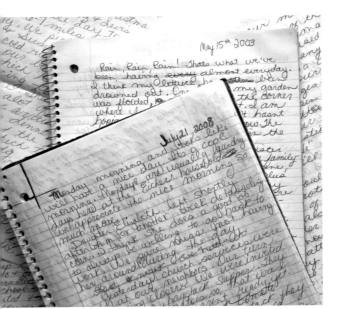

under an inch of dust, long rendered useless by the Internet.

In one of the early columns, Elizabeth mailed her handwritten column to me as usual. Her penmanship, like Lovina's, was typically flawless. But in this column, her recipe for homemade strawberry jam was a little difficult to decipher. And I couldn't just cross-check a similar recipe on the Internet like I can today. Calling Elizabeth was out of the question; for her, the nearest phone was miles away. So I did what any eighteen-year-old might do—I guessed. And so went into the annals of Amish Cook history one of the biggest recipe disasters: What should have said "some" salt I typed in as "epsom salt." Even worse, some readers actually tried the recipe at home.

On another occasion, I erred typing in the column and instead of typing that Elizabeth served "fried chicken" at a wedding, I typed in "fried children," which breezed right through my spell-check, past some copy editors, and onto newspaper pages. There are probably still a few readers who quit reading the column if they believed that was a typical Amish wedding menu.

It was after the epsom salt disaster that I came up with the idea of employing a communications tactic not widely used since World War II: carrier pigeons. I had heard of carrier pigeons' being used to deliver messages to commanders on the front lines. But a few fast phone calls revealed the complexity of such an operation. We would have to have had a colony of pigeons at Elizabeth's and on my end, something I didn't think my parents would have appreciated at the time.

So over the years we've improved our communication without pigeons. Now sometimes Lovina even uses a phone in a milk shed to read the column to me. Unfortunately, as our communications have improved, another kind of communication has not: newspapers. The past twenty years have seen dozens of dailies dim their lights and presses stop. It's sad. Newspapers, I believe, still deserve a prominent place in society as purveyors of opinion and information. There's an intimacy one enjoys with the rough edges of a newspaper that one doesn't get on a sterile screen. I think that is why "The Amish Cook" column is still relevant all these years later. People are searching for a connection somewhere, anywhere, and Lovina, through her simple words and candid thoughts, provides this.

The pages ahead will chronicle the changes experienced by the Coblentzes and Eichers, first in Indiana, and then in Michigan. The writings are authentic, sometimes raw, other times earthy, always sincere. I sincerely hope you enjoy this journey from the Amish Cook's earliest days to Lovina's most recent. And I hope to be penning you all a similar note in twenty years, on our fortieth anniversary! Now, let's go back to the beginning . . .

KEVIN WILLIAMS, EDITOR

1991
a journey begins

AUGUST 1991

This was the first "The Amish Cook" column. We had no idea this was the beginning of a journey that would last more than two decades!

This has been a rushy morning, but enjoyable. We still have five girls here at home yet. Four went to work as usual. They all leave 6:00 to 6:30 A.M. The girls were all busy doing all my cleaning before they left. Working all together like this is what I call real family life. With no boys at home, the girls do the milking and other chores around the barn. We have one daughter and two sons married, and feel lucky to have five grandsons and five granddaughters. Guess we just don't appreciate all our good health enough. The kitchen has the smell of freshly baked pies. There is a tour planning to stop in this afternoon (all senior citizens), so we like to serve them some pie and a drink to the forty or fifty people. It's so good to go in the garden to get rhubarb and get apples from our trees to bake some pies. The pies I baked this morning are three apple, one rhubarb, four lemon, two oatmeal, two blueberry, and I will share the recipes of the oatmeal and apple pie with you readers. I know you'll like it once you give it a try. Looks like my youngest daughter has work for us again. She just picked one bushel of green beans, so we must can them. Good luck!

SEPTEMBER 1991

The columns were considerably shorter in the early days. As you read on, you'll notice that the weekly "letters," as Elizabeth called the columns, grew in length.

I often think how nice we have it now. My great-great-grandfather from Santiglet, Department Dauchs, France, came to America on account of their conscientious objection to compulsory military training in their homeland. It sure must've been sad to leave their friends, loved ones, their families, neighbors, and all acquaintances and all the scenes of their childhood, never to see them again, and go to a land unknown to them, more than three thousand miles across the stormy deep.

The trip they made in five months could now be made in hours by airplane. Their cooking was quite simple compared to ours now. Lots of their food was dried. They didn't have the sewing machines to sew their clothes, as we do now, or washing machines. They had to clear the land to build their house. There weren't mixes of all kinds to bake or prepare a meal.

OCTOBER 1991

This was the first time I had heard the term "nothings," which as a wedding dessert is really something! They are deep-fried circular pastries that also double as wedding decorations. The nothings are stacked on top of one another and serve as edible centerpieces on the wedding tables.

Fall of the year takes many changes. The colors are magnificent, even the bright pumpkins seem faded next to the competing orange leaves. Autumn's crisp air, its sounds and sights. Like nature, I'm ready for a change, too. But it has been good to think of the time I spent putting up the summer harvest for the coming winter. This year, the garden was so plentiful. Do we appreciate it enough?

October is the month our marriage took place. The Asian flu had struck our area that fall, which some of our family members caught. Lo and behold, I was one of the unlucky ones. It was a severe epidemic of influenza that took place in 1957, caused by a virus strain that was thought to have originated in Singapore. Well, we recovered

and prepared food for the wedding. At our weddings (usually on a Thursday), the Tuesday before the wedding some women (immediate family and sometimes some friends) come and help bake pies and "nothings" and are cooks at the wedding, too. Nothings are often prepared for weddings. The Tuesday before the wedding, , we baked eighty-eight cherry, raisin, and pumpkin pies and fifteen batches of nothings.

Dinner and supper are usually served at the home of the bride. When we had the wedding of our daughter in 1981, we served at least 1,000 people that day (dinner and supper). You probably would like to hear of what we serve at our weddings. The menu isn't always the same. Some serve more food and some not so much. Depends, I guess. At our wedding for our daughter, we served 255 pounds of fried chicken, 150 pounds of boneless ham, mashed potatoes, chicken and noodles, gravy, dressing, buttered corn, pork and beans, carrot salad, potato salad, lettuce salad, twenty-four-hour cole slaw, cheese, celery, pickles, fruit salad, tapioca pudding, pie, cake, cookies (baked over 900), nothings, and coffee. Lots of work, but enjoyable.

OCTOBER 1991

This column would begin my years-long education about how the Amish conduct their church services. One of the hallmarks of the Amish religion is their practice of home worship. Amish churches hold worship services every other Sunday. Church members are encouraged to attend neighboring church districts on the "off" Sunday.

Since church services will be held here, Sunday, I must get myself in gear. It's a hustle and bustle at such a time to get your house all cleaned. One way our house gets a thorough cleaning is to hold services there. What a relief! We don't hold church services in a church house. We have it in our homes in the winter or when it's too cold, and in the sheds when the weather is warmer. Each family in the church takes their turn to hold services in their homes. The older ones are excluded to take a turn, as it's too much of a responsibility to have church in their home.

The churches are divided into districts. Each district has four ministers. There are from 20 to 30 families in a church making a total of 150 to 200 or more persons to a district. When it increases in a district too much, finally it is divided. Each district has services every other Sunday, and then some districts have it the next Sunday. So we can attend church every other Sunday if we prefer.

A lunch is served to all who attend church before they leave for home. Lunch usually consists of coffee, bread, cheese, red beets, pickles, the meat usually is bologna, wieners, or ham and various spreads such as peanut butter, jellies and jams, butter, apple butter, and sandwich spread. It just depends, as some serve more and some serve less. In the summertime, you might see sliced tomatoes, radishes, lettuce, and peppers on the lunch menu. At Christmas or Easter, you might find some extra baked goodies being served, also. Two or three tables are set up to each lunch. The young unmarried girls of the church (ages from fourteen and up) take care of the serving of the tables as it has to be reset two or more times. We have a table for the smaller children to help themselves or really cafeteria style. A milk soup is made for the babies and toddlers.

Everyone leaves for home in the afternoon. Sometimes the young unmarried people (sixteen and up) are invited back for the evening meal, which is a good home-cooked meal, and singing is enjoyed by all.

AMISH COOK CLASSIC: CORN RELISH
Makes approximately 10 pints

Corn relish is a favorite in Amish homes, and Elizabeth's recipe is a classic, traditional dish. As the end of the garden draws near in October, relishes are great ways for Amish cooks to use a lot of vegetables. This recipe is provided for canning and cultural insight. The Amish may use ways that are not approved by today's USDA guidelines. Contact your local county extension agent or the USDA.gov for proper canning procedures.

16 cups fresh corn kernels

1 bunch celery, chopped

3 green peppers, finely chopped

1 red pepper, finely chopped

1 tablespoon turmeric powder

1 tablespoon prepared mustard

1 tablespoon all-purpose flour

4 cups white vinegar

1 tablespoon celery seed

1 teaspoon salt

1 cup sugar

In a large pot, combine the corn, celery, and peppers and set aside. In a medium bowl, mix the turmeric powder, mustard, and flour together. Slowly whisk in enough of the vinegar to thoroughly dissolve these ingredients. Once a smooth consistency is reached, whisk in the remaining vinegar and the celery seed, salt, and sugar. Pour this mixture over the vegetables and stir until they are evenly coated. Cook over medium heat for 30 minutes, or until very hot and bubbling. While hot, pack the corn relish into sterilized canning jars and process in a boiling water bath for 10 minutes.

OCTOBER 1991

This column captures the wonderful tradition of autumn apple butter production. Like so many of the old ways, this labor-intensive tradition is slowly vanishing.

The fall harvest has been completed in the fields, so the rush has come to a halt. It reminds me of apple butter cooking at my brother's place. For quite some years, we enjoy an evening and a day or more together. Their family and our family got together sometime, usually in late October, to prepare for the apple butter cooking in a copper kettle. My brother made a stand outside for it. We always hoped for a nice day to cook it, but we got caught with the rain at times. The evening before, we peeled and snitzed (pared) apples, usually thirty gallons or more. Depended on how many gallons we wanted when cooked. The cider was bought, although we also had bought or gathered apples to be put into cider at the cider mill. Such a job!

The next morning, the forty to fifty gallons of cider was to be cooked down in the copper kettle to a certain amount. My brother always had certain marks on a yardstick showing how far the cider is to be cooked down, when the apples are put in, and when the sugar is added. After the sugar was added, it didn't take long anymore to take the copper kettle from the fire. Then we carried the apple butter in by three-gallon stainless steel buckets and then put it into jars to seal. The house usually had the aroma of freshly cooked apple butter. So delicious with home-baked bread. Must say, my brother had the hardest job of us all, as he looked after everything.

NOVEMBER 1991

I got a laugh out of this one. I had always thought the one place safe from things like Stanley or Tupperware parties was an Amish home—but I was wrong! Such events, turns out, are popular among Amish homemakers.

This was what I called an enjoyable day being at a quilting bee. Couple dozen women got together to quilt. Wonder how many stitches are on a quilt like that until it's completed. It'd be remarkable to know, I suppose! It was marked off with a nice quilt pattern of roses and leaves. It's a lot of hard work to have a quilting bee. First to sew the material together after you've bought the material, then to mark it off and put in the quilting frame.

Make sure you have plenty of needles and thread to quilt. Then to prepare a good noon meal. In the forenoon, we were served a cup of coffee and a large doughnut. Ugh. Hard on the waistline. In the afternoon, we were given snacks again. Lots of singing, yodeling, and, of course, gossiping goes on at a day like this. Yet so enjoyable!

At this one place they had a quilting bee, and after dinner the women enjoyed a Stanley bingo. Reckon the Stanley dealer was glad to see so many women present. Terrific! Then afterwards we went back to quilting again. Gave our fingers a rest for a while. A bed comforter was made that day. I would like to do a couple quilts this coming winter. Some women make quilts as they get quilt orders and get paid by how many yards of thread they use.

DECEMBER 1991

Elizabeth's recollections of Christmas were always great reminders about the nonmaterial joys of the special season.

We're looking forward to our 1991 Christmas family gathering again. We always enjoy having our children and grandchildren here for breakfast, dinner, all day. If all goes well, we'll be twenty-nine at the table this year, which includes my aged mother. We set up a long table in our dining room to seat them all and eat breakfast together, also dinner.

Our breakfast usually consists of fried eggs, fried potatoes, ham, bacon, cottage cheese, orange juice, coffee, cinnamon rolls, toast, home-baked bread, and all those Christmas goodies. This only happens once a year. So rejoicing takes place!

Then after breakfast, the dishes are all washed and the table reset for dinner. We all then get settled in the living room to exchange the Christmas-wrapped gifts. It's one anxious moment for the grandchildren to unwrap their gifts.

Then comes the preparing of the great noon meal. The aroma of the stuffed turkey in the oven and the frying of the chicken, plus all other food cooking, makes the kitchen smell great. Making a person hungry again! "The New Year's Song" gets sung several times during the day. The afternoon is spent together playing games, singing Christmas carols, yodeling, visiting, and eating a variety of candies, snacks, and a cheese ball.

After everyone leaves for his or her home in the evening, then comes cleaning up the house, getting everything back in order after a long, enjoyable day.

Liz
Lea
din

the
wh
ten
son
the

ma
co
sliced tomatoes, lettuce salad,
sweet-pepper strips, homemade
bread, crackers with dip, pretzel
sticks, watermelon slices, three
kinds of cake, two kinds of cookies and three kinds of pop.

When the food was ready by
10 a.m., we loaded up the food,
plus paper plates, foam cups, sil-

stu
er.

After
we wash
stainless
tles and
to smal
seemed

It wa
able da
preparin

1992
seeing the sea

JANUARY 1992

I'm sure more than a few people wish they hadn't chosen to read this column while eating breakfast!

The holidays are over now, and the rush has come to a halt. What a relief! What's next on the list to be done in the winter months? Butchering day! Ugh! It's always such a messy and tiresome day. Yet, it's good to have fresh pork, even if we buy some meat from the stores during the year.

Our family comes home early in the morning to help butcher our couple of hogs. The hogs are shot, of course, and then scalded in a butchering tank of hot water, taken out on a butcher table, and what you might call shaven clean. Then the hogs are hung on a scaffold and cut wide open and the stomach, etc., removed. If the intestines get cut, it will look a messy job. The women like to see clean intestines come in as they usually take care of cleaning the stomach and intestines. The intestines are scraped clean and will be stuffed with sausage, which is made with some parts of the meat ground through the grinder.

The hams, bacon, pork chops, or tenderloin, and ribs are all cut out, and later the hams are sugar-cured. Some can it by pressure cooker and fry down the meat. If fried down the next day, it usually goes in a crock and lard is poured over it. After rendering the lard, we'll have those cracklings which some are so fond of. Cracklings are the crisp part remaining after the lard has been removed from hog fat by frying.

Liver pudding is made and then canned. It's made from the head meat, etc., which had been cooked in an iron kettle. At noon, there's usually a good meal to feast on. After all the mess, the iron kettles and butchering items are washed. Greasy, but good eating afterwards. It's just one of those enjoyable days together.

AMISH COOK CLASSIC: HAM SALAD

Serves 8

This dish was a great way to use some of the fresh ham that was harvested during butchering day.

3 cups diced ham	2 hard-boiled eggs, diced
½ cup sweet pickle relish	1 tablespoon lemon juice
2 teaspoons minced onions	¼ teaspoon salt
2 teaspoons prepared mustard	¼ teaspoon pepper
½ cup mayonnaise	1 cup crushed potato chips
1 cup diced celery	

Preheat the oven to 425°F.

In a large bowl, combine all of the ingredients, except for the potato chips. Stir until the mixture is smooth and well combined. Pour the mixture into a 2-quart casserole dish and sprinkle the top with the crushed chips. Cover and bake 20 minutes, or until the top is bubbling and golden.

JANUARY 1992

The older generations of Amish really fascinate me; they have seen the world change so much during their lifetimes. I had the honor of knowing Elizabeth's mother, but, as this column notes, I missed knowing Ben's father by less than a year.

Many of us have experienced quite a bit of cold and snow this winter. Ice and snow bring different activities from what we have other times. For one thing, the snow-covered ground reminds us that we might be able to lure some wild birds close to our house if we would put out some seed. We have a feeder on our board fence close to our house (the feeder is a Christmas gift). So we enjoy watching the birds have a feast. Yesterday, January 29, Mother, us five sisters, and my sister-in-law went to a quilting bee at my other sister's place. Their daughter invited us for her mother's birthday to surprise her. Was she ever surprised to see us all drive in and get out of a van to spend the day there quilting. Her family was also there. Her husband had a nicely decorated birthday cake for her. What a surprise! A good noon meal was enjoyed by all. Well spent! It's been a year now that my husband's father died. He was always such a jolly man even with his lonely, inward feelings. He was noted for his jokes, always having a different one to tell his friends.

FEBRUARY 1992

Elizabeth mentions a "carriage and sleigh" club. This was a group of non-Amish wintersports enthusiasts who liked to tour through the snow countryside in Amish-style sleighs.

Our son and family have just left and I will try to get this column written tonight yet. He was helping my husband today to clear a fence row of eighty rods and in the process to build a new fence. It's quite a job!

It's what you'd call a stormy night with lots of thunder and lightning. We can use the rain to fill up our cistern again. Looks like most of the snow has left us now. The yards and fields look a dirty brown color again with the temperatures in the fifties today, February 18. Warm for February!

Yesterday, my husband had a birthday. So our family enjoyed an evening meal together here in honor of his being sixty-one years old. The married children also brought in food, including homemade ice cream, which seems to go well with a birthday. Also, various cakes and cherry pie were on the menu. The weather was OK to have the grill in gear outside to barbecue steak and ribs. We soon had a well-filled table to feast on and a well-spent evening together. We, also, have a brother-in-law who had a birthday the same day, only a year older than my husband. It was, also, President's Day, so there was no mail delivered.

Our nephew and his wife from Lafayette, Indiana, gave us a surprise visit on Saturday evening, so they enjoyed an evening meal with us. Also, two of our friends from the carriage and sleigh club were our Friday night guests. Quite a surprise to see them come with a nice pony team and a smaller green wagon. They were on their way to the harness shop.

FEBRUARY 1992

I always seemed to drop by at mealtime. I swear it wasn't intentional.

In four years, we'll see February 29 on the calendar again. What will the future hold in the next four years? Only God knows. This is a beautiful day! So many tasks can be done outside. We were surprised to see our friend, Joyce (who sells dry goods), visit with my aged mother about noon. She stopped in for a short visit. Didn't have time to have dinner with us. I had made some cinnamon rolls and was baking bread this morning. Was glad my editor from Middletown got in on the noon meal with us. Then, Saturday evening, I headed for Decatur Hospital with other family members. My aged mother, eighty-seven in April, fell down (she loses her balance at times) while emptying her ash pan from the stove. She received a gash on her forehead and was in awful pain with her shoulders and arms. She was rushed to the hospital by EMS. She had a dislocated shoulder, which was quite painful to get back in place. Lucky no bones were broken, and she was released the same evening.

AMISH COOK CLASSIC: CHEESEBURGER LOAF

Serves 6 to 8

This is one of those hearty, meaty dishes that seems to go perfectly on a cold February night.

2 pounds ground beef

½ cup fresh bread crumbs

1 (10½-ounce) can cream of mushroom soup

1 egg, slightly beaten

3 tablespoons fresh parsley, chopped

1 tablespoon Worcestershire sauce

2 tablespoons chopped onion

1 teaspoon salt

⅛ teaspoon black pepper

1 medium tomato, sliced

1 cup grated mild Cheddar cheese

Preheat the oven to 350°F.

In a large bowl, combine the beef, bread crumbs, soup, egg, parsley, Worcestershire sauce, onion, salt, and pepper. Knead the mixture by hand until it is smooth and uniformly combined. Shape the mixture into a large loaf and place it in a shallow, rimmed baking pan. Bake for 1 hour.

Remove the loaf from the oven and top with the tomato and the Cheddar. Return the loaf to the oven and bake until it is cooked through and the topping is bubbling, 10 to 15 minutes.

FEBRUARY 1992

Dandelions would be a staple of "The Amish Cook" columns in the spring for the next twenty years.

The grass shows spring is here as it greens up, and the first sign is the rebirth of the dandelions, nestled in lawns, pastures, and roadways. Some take the dandelions for weeds, but the sight of early dandelions delights us. We use them as a salad and some wilt them. It's good either way. Dandelions made in a salad for the evening meal really relax a person.

Our family was home to help my husband with our line fence (eighty rods) and have completed it now. What a relief. Putting up a line fence between two woods was quite a job. Guess we can't thank our children enough when in time of need or when they see help is needed. Now they're helping gather, cut, and burn the brush from it. It looks a tiresome job!

We have been trying to get our sewing done before the garden and all that spring rush gets in full gear. I read somewhere that fifty years ago, people finished a day's work and needed rest. Today, they need exercise. Ya reckon?

MARCH 1992

In all the years of "The Amish Cook," this is the only reference ever to a "double wedding." Two Amish cousins of Elizabeth's decided to combine their ceremonies, which meant double the fun for all!

March came in like a lamb, but I'm afraid Mr. Winter will probably show up at the end of the month. Mr. Groundhog saw plenty of his shadow on February 2. Glad we don't have to be in charge of the weather.

Heard some have taken advantage of garden making lately. I put some onions in the garden now (the leftovers of last fall that began to sprout, and became on the soft side), so hopefully we'll be eating onion greens early in the spring. Should get some seeds in for plants, especially hot peppers. Different ones of our friends gave us some last fall, and I guess our family really got addicted to them. The girls like to put some on top of pizza. Makes a good taste!

We are helping our daughter clean their house, as church services are to be held there on Sunday. It's a good time to have it, with early spring cleaning. It's always good to give the house a thorough cleaning, also, before planting the garden. We are looking forward to attending a double wedding on Thursday. I have never been to a double wedding where two couples got married.

It was so nice and warm today, and the girls had the grill in gear tonight. Had barbecued ribs, steak, and hamburgers on the menu.

JULY 1992

This column highlights how Amish families really pitch in to help one another during times of need, even joyous times of need, such as the days after a new life is welcomed into the world.

Friendly greetings to all you readers across the miles. Another day has come and has almost ended. One half of 1992 is now history. Time sure keeps moving along at a brisk pace. This summer was almost a perfect growing season until the rains came. The ground is well soaked. Thousands and thousands of acres are flooded, which were such nice looking crops. We've had downpours of rain which has caused floods in a lot of areas. Rain, floods, high winds, and tornadoes lately have plagued the area. We had four trees downed the other Sunday evening. Lots of our shingles flew off from the barn roof, which needs a new one on the south side now. A barn window had also blown in, which caused a lot of glass over our bales of hay. My husband tried to pick it out of the bales as good as he could so the cows won't get it. Must've been a tornado had touched down.

Our son Albert's had a baby boy born on Albert's birthday, July 15. So they named him Albert Jr. Born at 3:07 A.M. and weighed eight pounds, four ounces. This makes child number four for them. This makes me a grandmother a dozen times: six girls and six boys. Daughters Emma and Susan are taking turns to care for the household duties over at Albert's. Looks like I have to get in on it, too, as the girls have to clean a house the next couple of a days for a good friend of ours.

I also turned a year older, July 18. Daughter Emma turned a year older on July 19. Our family enjoyed a barbecued chicken and steak supper on my birthday. Of course, ice cream and cake had to be on the menu, also. Son Amos and wife Nancy brought it and our daughter Leah brought a skillet and whoopie pies. Susan made zucchini squash bread. ❦

JULY 1992

Elizabeth would occasionally refer to her husband's 1W service, which was an "alternative service" for conscientious war objectors, such as the Amish, Mennonites, and Quakers. During times of war, the Amish have been granted conscientious objector status because of their pacifist beliefs. The Amish are still drafted, though, for service in hospitals and factories. Ben worked at a hospital during the Korean War.

I'm trying to think what would logically be of interest to you readers out there. Well, getting up at four every morning makes a good, long start for the day. Do we appreciate good health enough? My husband usually leaves around 5:30 A.M. for his job as a carpenter. He's been with the Farm Bureau Co-op, Monroe, Indiana, since 1959, just before our oldest was born. At that time, work was hard to pick up. Being out of a job and trying to get one made it hard times. It was a time we won't forget. Ben was in 1W Service at the St. Elizabeth Hospital, Lafayette, Indiana, for two. His brothers Albert Jr. and Andy, also, were in service there. Albert Jr. still works at the hospital and Andy has retired from the post office. Both live in Lafayette and have a family of their own. The family of the late Albert Coblentz Sr. will have their reunion at Robert Coblentz's at Meridian, Mississippi, on Saturday, August 1. So if plans hold out, we plan to attend. My husband is anxious to see where his brother lives in Mississippi.

A local festival is this week in town on Friday and Saturday. People come from far away to be present. Weather seems ideal for it. Talk about weather, it's been a rainy season. Too much for some garden eats. Where water was the most, we can see the cabbage, tomatoes, and carrots look droopy. Just hope they'll perk up yet. But some have lost acres and acres of crops through these heavy rains. ❦

JULY 1992

Elizabeth showed any writer's disdain for deadlines with a big "ugh". She would even occasionally refer to her column as "worthless." This was really just Elizabeth's way of keeping any sense of celebrity in check. Amish writers were very rare in the early 1990s and she didn't want to be seen as feeling "above" anyone because she had the column.

It's 6:30 A.M. and will get myself seated for another letter which was requested for this week. Ugh!

Sounds like a storm is in the air with all my wash on the line. My daughters Verena, Liz, and Lovina left for work at the sewing factory, and Emma left to clean two houses today in town. Susan is at son Albert's to care for the household duties of their new arrival. A sweet little bundle! Naturally, Grandma would think so. Ben has also left for work at 5:30 A.M. So I reckon this just about does it for the rush of the morning in this household. The girls pitched in to have our huge wash on the line. Breakfast dishes were washed and floors swept before they left for work. What a relief! So I must start my sewing after I have this worthless letter written. Always plenty to sew. I can never say that I am caught up. How about you readers out there?

The last two days, I took care of the household duties at son Albert's, as Susan went with Emma to spring clean at a house in town. They have cleaned quite a few houses this year. I also help them sometimes if they need it.

I had quite a surprise when I was at Albert's when I received a birthday cake (10 inches by 14). It was also meant for daughter Emma, as our birthdays were Saturday and Sunday. It came from a friend and was made by Central Pastry Shop of Middletown, Ohio. It was frosted with the picture of the horse and buggy that goes with this column. Good eating! Calories galore!

Well, I had best get my wash off that line. Sounds stormy. We've had lots of that kind of weather lately. Don't like the high winds. The grass and especially weeds in the garden are growing fast.

AMISH COOK CLASSIC: DUTCH COLESLAW

Serves 8 to 10

A nice, cool coleslaw, made from fresh vegetables directly from the garden, was one of Elizabeth's favorite summer menu items.

8 cups shredded green cabbage

1 cup shredded red cabbage

5 cups shredded carrots

1 cup mayonnaise

2 tablespoons white vinegar

½ cup sugar

1 teaspoon salt

¼ teaspoon black pepper

In a large bowl, mix together the cabbage and carrots. Set aside. In a small bowl, combine the mayonnaise, vinegar, sugar, salt, and pepper and stir until smooth and well incorporated. Pour the dressing over the cabbage mixture and toss until the vegetables are evenly coated. Refrigerate the coleslaw overnight before serving.

AUGUST 1992

Some people are surprised when they read about an Amish person staying at a chain motel on a trip, but it really isn't very uncommon.

Susan, Emma, Verena, Alan S. Wickey, Jacob Schwartz Jr., Bill Coblentz, the writer and my husband Ben with Amos and Gyneth Coblentz and children Michael and Heidi left Friday, July 31, at 4:00 A.M. to attend the Coblentz reunion at their brother Robert Coblentz's, Meridian, Mississippi. We arrived at Robert's at 6:25 P.M.

The reunion was held Saturday, August 1, at the Pine Lake Fellowship camp around Meridian. We all slept in cabins Friday and Saturday night at the campgrounds, which was something different on our part. It has seventy-four acres of woods, if I have it straight.

One of my sisters-in-law, Carolyn Coblentz of Lafayette, Indiana, fell in the P.M. and results were a broken ankle. Sunday at 10:38 A.M. we started out for the Gulf of Mexico and arrived at 2:43 P.M. Had supper at Shoney's, which is a good place to eat. Good food! Slept at a motel, Red Carpet Inn along the gulf. We spent Sunday P.M. on the beach at the gulf. Also, everyone enjoyed the water and walking on a pier, probably ½ mile long, except the writer stayed at the starting point. Ha! Was so relaxing at the gulf. Monday we visited our niece, Andrea Wertz, who lives along the gulf, and met her husband at the Ingalls Ship Building at noon, where he is employed. They make war ships, and there are seven thousand employed. We had a nice, enjoyable time and reckon our niece and son enjoyed it, too, with us along the gulf. We took another tour down a pier. It looked better built. Monday evening we slept at Ramada Motel, Nashville, Tennessee, and arrived back home at 3:21 P.M. Tuesday. Daughters Liz and Lovina arrived home soon afterwards from the sewing factory. Good to be together again after such an enjoyable trip. There were eight children of the thirteen children of the late Albert Coblentz present for the reunion, plus some nieces and nephews at Meridian, Mississippi, coming from Berne, Geneva, Lafayette, and Grabill, Indiana, as well as Memphis, Tennessee, and the gulf. We had a very enjoyable, safe trip.

AUGUST 1992

Elizabeth briefly mentions the writing she did for the *Budget*. Elizabeth penned columns regularly for almost forty years before starting her syndicated column.

A nice, cool sunshiny morning with not much of a breeze as yet. Our huge wash is hanging on the line. Results: hopefully it'll be dry. Then comes that huge stack of ironing. Always plenty of that, it seems.

To those who have girls, how often have you heard this: I suppose you don't have to do much with so many around the house? Yes, we've got five girls at home, but where's my help during the day? Three work at the sewing factory, and my two youngest daughters went to clean a house for a good friend of ours. She wanted it cleaned before school starts, as she's a teacher. She taught several of our children years ago. So there you can see what has taken place in this household today. It's a blessing to have them home to help evenings and mornings. I should be weeding and hoeing in the garden now that it's cool, but I can't neglect this column. It must be on its way. It's been forty years that I have written the local news for the *Budget*, a weekly newspaper from Sugarcreek, Ohio.

I made eight batches of rhubarb jam today. It is one of our favorite jams.

We often talk about our trip to Meridian, Mississippi, and to the Gulf of Mexico. Was so interesting! Our daughter Susan and niece Heidi Coblentz kept track of how many different states they could read on car licenses, which we all joined in the fun to see how many states we could see. We saw thirty-eight different states on our trip. Friday evening we had our family, plus two of Ben's brothers, here for an evening meal, plus the editor of this column. This event was in honor of our trip together to Mississippi. Our family got together at our daughter Leah's place on Sunday night in honor of her birthday. We enjoyed a supper plus a lot of salads and goodies.

SEPTEMBER 1992

Elizabeth's trip to Mississippi gave her many memories. It was the only time in her life she saw the ocean.

We are having plenty of rain lately, with at times severe thunderstorms, which I reckon nobody likes to hear or see. We had a severe thunderstorm early this morning. But how thankful when storms come and go without damage. This has been a different summer, it seems, a wet one!

Saturday was a different day of living. We had our full day organized, but how soon all plans are made different. That's what happened on Saturday. Word came that my aged mother of eighty-seven was dying. She just didn't seem well. We thought life had fled, but she was spared to us yet. She seemed somewhat better, so I went home at noon. Verena, Liz, and Lovina had to work in the morning.

When I got back home at noon, we were surprised to see Ben's sisters, Frances and Betty, arrive with their Aunt Amanda from Hartville, Ohio. We hadn't seen her in years. She is seventy-five years old and lives alone. Still does her own cooking and cleaning. So a quick dinner was planned and made. Glad the girls were all home to help with the meal. We had a nice visit together. The Coblentzes got together Sunday for dinner in honor of Aunt Amanda's visit, but we weren't present as we were at mother's bedside.

In my last letter, I had written when we were to Meridian, Mississippi, and Gulf of Mexico, our daughter Susan and cousin Heidi Coblentz were writing down how many different states they could see on the car licenses. Well, I thought it was from thirty-eight different states. But I guess it was from forty-three different states. I wanted to make a correction on that.

Well, I must get into gear, as we're going to cook for Ben and his carpenter crew today. They're not working far from here. So I thought they'd enjoy a cooked meal. My menu will start off with mashed potatoes, fried chicken, gravy, and dressing. So I must get with it.

OCTOBER 1992

This was my first experience with an Amish wedding. A massive amount of preparation goes into such an occasion, which Elizabeth ably describes in this column.

We had such nice weather for the wedding supper of our daughter Liz and Levi Wengerd on October 4. Friday, October 2, we had eighteen women and girls to help bake sixty-one pies (oatmeal, blueberry, and cherry), made ten batches of nothings, which are usually made at weddings, and toasted ten loaves of bread for dressing. The girls were cleaning up for the wedding supper. Daughter Verena barbecued over thirty pounds of chicken for dinner on Friday, so there was plenty left for supper.

On Saturday, October 3, there were six girls came to help us peel four twenty-quart cookers full of potatoes. This made around ten gallons of potato salad. We also washed celery and carrot sticks, cut up onions, carrots, etc., for the dressing, set the table to seat 112 in the living and dining room and forty-six in the washhouse, made carrot salad with twenty boxes of orange and yellow Jell-O, cooked three pounds tapioca with Jell-O, and kept cleaning up for the wedding, Such busy days! Then in the evening, we had some of our friends in to see the tables.

Liz's friend from work helped make her "Good Luck" and "Best Wishes" cakes and help frost her wedding cake. Their help was greatly appreciated.

October 4, Liz and Levi Wengerd were married at John Neuenschwander's in Pennville by Bishop David N. Wengerd, an uncle to the groom. Dinner was at John's and the wedding supper was held here. We served 800 to 900 people. Lots of people here. The menu consisted of: mashed potatoes, chicken and gravy, 250 pounds ham, buttered corn, baked beans, dressing, potato salad, carrot salad, twenty-four-hour cabbage slaw, lettuce salad, celery and carrot sticks, sweet pepper strips, and cheese. Dessert consisted of seventeen different kinds of cakes, sixty-one pies, nothings, puddings, fruit salad, coffee, and jam. We had made three and a half gallons of the twenty-four-hour slaw. There were twenty-three cooks who came in the afternoon to help prepare for the wedding supper. Had more cooks invited to help but some were unable to be present.

Levi and Liz's attendants were daughter Verena and Alan S. Wickey and Daniel Jr. Wengerd and my daughter Susan. They had thirteen couples to wait on tables. Their tablewaiters: Joe C. Eicher and Lovina Coblentz; Jacob B. Schwartz and Emma

Coblentz; Christy Swartzentruber and Annie J. Wengerd; Noah J. Wengerd and Esther C. Eicher; Jacob J. Wengerd and Clara Schwartz; Joe L. Wickey and Elizabeth M. Schwartz; Joe H. Wickey and Lovina Swartzentruber; Melvin M. R. Schwartz and Mary Hilty; Roman Schwartz and Marlene Hilty; Henry Schwartz and Mandy Hilty; Daniel H. B. Schwartz and Lovina C. Graber; LaVern Wickey and Rebecca Wengerd; Kevin Schwartz from Milroy, Indiana, and Barbara Schwartz.

Our friend from Topeka, Indiana, Paul Frys, brought a vanload of friends along for the occasion. ⁥

OCTOBER 1992

And, of course, after the big wedding came the big cleanup!

Well, the weather has stayed nice and warm, although cool nights. Farmers are busy combining soybeans. They sure are having nice fall weather for it. Garden eats are still plentiful and on the menu.

With the wash drying, which seemed like miles of clothesline, the early morning coolness is fading quickly across the clear blue sky. It's what I call a beautiful, cool, and breezy day, lit by clear, bright sunshine. About our wash, there's still a lot to be dried. We hung up over one hundred dish towels and fifty bath and hand towels, washcloths, and dishcloths galore, plus all our other wash, consisting of sheets, pillowcases, blankets, etc. Also, our clothes from our wedding supper Sunday evening of our daughter, Liz and Levi Wengerd. We were blessed with sunshiny weather for the wedding supper of Liz and Levi and since then, too. A lot of cleaning up again. Was a nice evening for it.

Daughters Emma and Susan are assisting the newlyweds today, washing off walls, ceilings, windows, etc. They're preparing to move in the latter part of the week. Me and my girls: Verena, Susan, Emma, and Lovina assisted to help clean their house yesterday and last night. It's a big, new house.

We want to go view Marvin Haines, eighty-two, at the local funeral home. He died so suddenly Monday morning while picking up some walnuts. He leaves to mourn his sorrowing wife, Norma. It was quite a shock to hear the sad news, as daughter Emma

AMISH COOK CLASSIC: CUCUMBER SALAD

Serves approximately 10 to 12 guests

Home canning remains a mainstay in most Amish homemaker's lives. Elizabeth's generation embraced it fully. Home canning will probably slowly fall out of favor as more and more Amish settlements allow gas-powered freezers for food storage.

25 to 30 medium-size cucumbers, peeled and thinly sliced

8 large white onions, chopped

2 large sweet peppers, chopped

½ cup salt

5 cups white vinegar

5 cups sugar

1 teaspoon turmeric powder

½ teaspoon cloves

2 tablespoons mustard seed

In a large bowl, combine the cucumbers, onion, pepper, and salt. Allow to stand for 3 hours and then drain off the liquid.

In a large pot, combine the vinegar, sugar, turmeric, cloves, and mustard seed and bring the mixture to a rapid boil. Add the cucumber mixture to the pot and stir until the vegetables are evenly coated with the vinegar solution. Continue heating over medium heat until the mixture starts to simmer. While the cucumber salad is very hot, pack it into sterilized canning jars and seal immediately.

does weekly cleaning for them. They also are neighbors to our daughter Leah. They are such a nice, wonderful old couple.

Well, I must go and brush some Sunday clothes. It's always work-work-work. ❧

OCTOBER 1992

Elizabeth often included religious references in her column, but subtly so, and I think it resonated with readers.

We had our killing frost this Monday morning, with the temperature at 25°F. As I look out the window, I see the nearby woods in their autumn splendor. Their color of yellow, orange, red against the bright blue October skies reminds us that no artist's paintbrush can quite reproduce the scene produced by the Master Artist, Our Creator. The garden looks droopy right now, although the flowers make a beautiful spot in the garden.

The woodstove was put in gear once more. The cookstove was used often this past summer, as there were a lot of cool, rainy days. I enjoy preparing meals on the range. At the same time, you can have the oven in use to bake, etc. A big meal can be prepared in a hurry on a range.

My aged mother is spending the day here. Glad to have her here again. We had her here the night before daughter Liz got married and took her along to see Liz and Levi get married. Like old people feel sometimes, I guess, she wondered if we wanted to bother with her. We sure did! She enjoyed meeting the people who came to see the wedding tables the evening before.

Daughter Liz and Levi are now settled in their new home, and Liz went back to work at the sewing factory. She's been there over four years now. Sure makes an empty spot in our home. It's been eleven years since we had made the first wedding of our daughter Leah to Paul M. Shetler. Then son Amos was married to Nancy Jean Hilty in '83 and Albert to Sarah Irene Hilty in 1986.

We enjoyed the anniversary card and letter from the *Budget* editor, George R. Smith, who is eighty-five years old. I've been writing for the *Budget* in Sugarcreek, Ohio, since 1952. Life goes on. ❧

1993
lovina gets married

MAY 1993

The brood of grandchildren really began to grow during this period. By the time Elizabeth passed away, nine years after this column was written, she had six grandchildren namesakes. Having so many Elizabeths at family gatherings could get confusing, but it made for a proud grandmother.

We are grandparents for the fifteenth time now. Daughter Liz and Levi had a baby girl, born Monday morning at 7:48 A.M., weighing six pounds and thirteen ounces. This is their first child and, guess what? It was named Elizabeth. Grandma feels proud of that! So the sewing machine has been in gear to sew clothes for the sweet little bundle.

Daughter Susan took over household duties there this week now. Daughter Emma will trade off with Susan to help along, as Emma cleans houses for other people so she's unable to help all week. We are always glad to help out our children when in time of need. So right now, nobody is here to help me with the household duties during the day, although the girls really help in the mornings and evenings when not on their daily jobs.

We had three granddaughters within three weeks. Son Amos had a set of twin girls named Arlene and Marlene. So she must be a busy mother with five girls and one boy to care for. One good thing is when they're all healthy.

Well, I've got nine caps cut out to sew. For you readers who don't know what I mean about sewing a cap, it is a covering the women and girls wear on their heads. For this area, it's to be black in color. Some areas wear the white covering. Then there's a scrap sheet I must complete, which was given to me to do for a neighbor lady who has been very sick. For a shut-in, it's a pastime to see who all got in on it. Someone buys a scrapbook and passes out the sheets to friends and relatives. So it's interesting to read all the different types of sheets with cards, verses, sayings, etc., on it when a shut-in gets the book. The people give the sheets back to the buyer to give the completed book to the sick person or shut-in.

The rain has finally come today. It was beginning to be awfully dry. This will really boost up the garden stuff and crops, also. Should make the hay fields grow.

JULY 1993

According to tradition, Amish weddings are typically announced just a few weeks ahead of time, so much preparation needs to be done for this big event in a very short time.

Well the work is taking place to get ready for my daughter Lovina's wedding. Lots to think and do before the day arrives, which seems to be coming up fast. It takes time and, most of all, money. But it's only once in a lifetime, and that day should really be enjoyed. It is work-work-work. The yellow transparent apples came along this week, and were put into applesauce, and then the green beans are being processed today, Saturday. How lucky or fortunate we should be that our garden has been spared. Some have lost all their gardens through these heavy rains. Our garden was flooded also, but the water receded soon afterwards. Some places were badly flooded, and roads were closed because of high water everywhere. It was the highest some have seen it in this area. Guess we have no control of the weather. Makes one feel helpless when a storm arrives. I have no time to sit here and write this unworthy column with all the work that has to be done, but this is something I can't leave you great readers set out there. This column I can't neglect.

The wedding will be held on son Albert's and grandson Albert Jr.'s birthday, July 15, and then July 18 will be my fifty-seventh birthday.

Well, I need to get in gear. Too much work around here at present.

wedding

by Lovina Eicher

....

In looking back, *it is very hard to believe that so many years have passed since our wedding day. The days before our wedding were busy days of washing walls, ceilings, cleaning closets, cabinets, windows, and everything that goes with a thorough cleaning. Mom would have us girls helping her make homemade noodles for the big event. Another job was collecting Mom's many plates, glasses, bowls, silverware, pots, and pans needed for the wedding meal. Back then, a "wedding wagon" was unheard of. Wedding wagons are portable kitchens that can move from place to place. These kitchens have plenty of utensils, ovens, and staples needed to hold a large gathering. July was a busy time of the year of mowing the grass, weeding the garden, putting up hay, and extra outside chores to get the homestead looking nice for all those visitors. The most popular month for Amish weddings is June. Joe and I, however, chose July for our wedding day since I had a two-week vacation from the sewing factory where I was working. The factory gave a week of extra vacation to anyone getting married, so I had three full weeks to enjoy preparing and cleaning up for the wedding. The day of our wedding was one of the coolest days in July. I am sure the cooks were glad for this, since they fried three hundred pounds of chicken for the noon meal. We had a few sprinkles in the afternoon, otherwise the weather was perfect for a wedding day. As always, God has sent his blessings from above.*

AMISH COOK CLASSIC: SANDWICH SPREAD

Makes 8 pints

This recipe was a summertime staple in Elizabeth's house, adding a tangy touch to meat and cheese sandwiches.

12 green tomatoes, coarsely chopped

12 green peppers, coarsely chopped

12 yellow or red peppers, coarsely chopped

2 large onions, coarsely chopped

1 cup prepared mustard

½ cup sugar

¼ cup salt

1 tablespoon celery seed

4 cups salad dressing, such as Miracle Whip

Run the vegetables through a hand-cranked Victoria strainer until finely ground. (Editor's note: To achieve the fine consistency, the vegetables may be pulsed in an electric food processor instead.)

Put the finely ground vegetables into a large pot. Add the mustard, sugar, salt, and celery seed and stir until the mixture is well combined. Bring the mixture to a boil over medium heat. Reduce the heat and simmer for 15 minutes, stirring frequently. Reduce the heat to a very low setting and add the salad dressing. Stir until smooth in consistency and light yellow in color. While the sandwich spread is very hot, pour it into sterilized canning jars and seal.

JULY 1993

I put on my best dark suit and tie for this wedding and tried to blend in with the crowd. It was an honor to be invited to this wedding by Elizabeth, so I eagerly accepted the invitation.

The weather was ideal for the wedding of daughter Lovina and Joe C. Eicher. Lots of work at such a time.

The Tuesday before the wedding, which was Thursday, July 15, about two dozen women came to help. They baked ninety pies (oatmeal, cherry, raisin, and rhubarb) and made fourteen batches of nothings. Didn't really want that many pies, but that number came upon us before we knew or thought of it. Well, anyways, no worry to run out of pie.

Wednesday about a dozen girls came to peel the potatoes, cut up vegetables for the dressing, and make potato salad, for which I had cooked a twenty-quart cooker full of potatoes. Also the tables were set and the last-minute cleaning done. Our washhouse or shed saw lots of life out there, as all the work was done in there to prepare for the wedding ceremony. Wednesday evening quite a few of our friends came to see the wedding tables, and refreshments were served to the ones who came. It was an enjoyable evening.

Then came the wedding day. We started to fry chicken (three hundred pounds) at 4:15 A.M., which was served for dinner. Had enough for supper, too, and also served boneless ham. Our meals consisted of mashed potatoes, chicken and noodles, gravy, mashed potatoes, dressing, chicken, buttered corn, green beans (which came out of the garden), pork and beans, potato salad, carrot salad, lettuce salad (plenty from the garden), hot peppers, Swiss cheese, fruit salad, tapioca pudding, pies, cakes, nothings, celery sticks, coffee, bread, rhubarb jam, and butter! There were around eighteen skillets used to fry the chicken. We cooked three twenty-quart cookers

of potatoes for dinner for mashed potatoes and two twenty-quart cookers for chicken and noodles. In the afternoon, we again cooked over three twenty-quart cookers of potatoes to be mashed and more chicken and noodles for supper. Also, sixteen quarts of gravy. There were twenty-eight women to prepare the meals. We could seat ninety-eight people in the house and seventy in the washhouse. The toolshed was cleaned out where the wedding services were held and later used to set up a table for the children for the noon and evening meals. We had quite a crowd here for both meals. Well, enough of this for now. What a relief to have it over with. ✑

JULY 1993

Elizabeth playfully called people who shared her birthday—the same day and year—her "twins." She did connect with a few column readers who shared her birthday.

We're canning the rest of our yellow transparent apples into applesauce. I like those apples, as it makes a nice sauce. It's a wonder there's still apples on the trees. With having the wedding here of daughter Lovina and Joe, as there were so many apples laying around in the yard afterwards.

The girls washed off walls, woodwork, etc., since the wedding. They did it before the wedding, but somehow it gets dirty, or so it felt, after the wedding. How clean the house feels again and life goes on. It's easier to get the dishes out of the cupboards than to put them all back in place again.

Sunday, July 18, was my birthday, which makes me another year older. How these years take place! Wonder if I have a twin somewhere out there born July 18, 1936? Meal planning was easier when the children came home for supper. Sunday evening we had plenty of leftovers from the wedding of Lovina. I want to thank you readers out there for sending best wishes to Joe and Lovina and for the encouraging words about my column. Feel unworthy of it all.

The girls are back to work after having two weeks vacation from the sewing factory. Glad for the help.

Garden eats are doing great, although some have lost most of their gardens because of these heavy rains. ✑

JULY 1993

Indiana summers were often broiling hot, but that didn't stop Elizabeth from going outside and working hard in the garden.

The temperature is at 98°F this Wednesday afternoon, with a nice breeze in the air. Looks stormy in the northwest. Emma and Susan are weeding and hoeing the garden, which the weeds had almost taken over since the wedding of daughter Lovina and Joe. The sun is throwing its rays on their weary backs, as they're hoeing through many weeds.

I just picked some sweet corn for our evening meal. Corn on the cob always goes good around here. The ears are well filled out and look a nice yellow color. Green beans were also picked, so they need to be cleaned and washed. We have our canning of green beans completed for the season. Some of our early cabbage got drowned out, but so lucky we didn't lose all of our garden like some did from our recent downpours. Much to be thankful for!

For many of us, spring and summer are very important seasons of the year. It is the time when we are busy planting, nurturing, and caring for our gardens, and also the crops in anticipation of the fall harvest. Long days of toil are put in.

Canning has been on the list. Cherries, green beans, corn, applesauce, etc., have filled those empty jars. How good to see those jars being filled for the long winter months. Daughter Lovina is back to the sewing factory after being off three weeks over her wedding. Verena was on vacation for two weeks and is going on her tenth year at the sewing factory. Lovina is going on her third year. Those three weeks seemed short weeks.

OCTOBER 1993

Elizabeth's aged and beloved mother was written into many columns before she passed away at age ninety-one in 1996.

My mind is wondering to how these years take place. Thirty years ago we moved on this farm. My oldest (Leah) being four years old and Amos turned two years old the next day we moved here. It was hard for him to think why we don't go back home. But they got adjusted to living here. Since living on this farm, we had another boy (Albert) and five more daughters (Verena, Liz, Lovina, Emma, and Susan). The boys and three of the girls are married and have families of their own.

Thinking back then, the land wasn't selling high as it is now, and the wages were low or so it seems now. I guess it's not what you earn, it's what you save. Also, it was hard to find a job when we were first married, thirty-six years ago. Being without a job was tough, especially when those farm payments came along. But somehow, there was always a way, it seemed.

No killing frost as yet. We dug out the flower bulbs that don't survive the cold winter months. Also, the sweet potatoes were dug out and the garden goodies have been taken care of except the lettuce and endive and a few other vegetables remain in the garden. We didn't buy any lettuce from the stores since last spring and it's less than two months from Christmas. Do we appreciate it enough? Canning from the garden is history for 1993.

Well, I had best hurry as I've got the carpenter crew here for dinner today again. Ben's not working too far from here so thought the crew would like a hot meal instead of eating out of their dinner buckets. They're putting up a pole building (54 × 88 foot). We're also getting ready for my mom's reunion on Saturday. We're nearing the four-hundred mark in people expected to come. Mother has more great-grandchildren than grandchildren. Mom is now eighty-eight years old. Lots of work to prepare for the gathering.

Hope you readers are all healthy and want to thank you all who take time to write such encouraging letters or notes. ❦

AMISH COOK CLASSIC: FLORIDA PUDDING
Serves 12

No one seems to know where this recipe gets its name; perhaps it was popular in Florida's Amish settlement as a cool, delicious dessert. Florida's lone Amish settlement is a "melting pot" of plain people from various communities seeking a respite from harsh winter climes for a few weeks. Either way, Elizabeth mentioned this pudding on several occasions in her early columns.

1 (4.6-ounce) box instant pudding mix, any flavor

1 cup all-purpose flour

½ cup walnut pieces

¼ cup margarine, softened

1 cup unsifted powdered sugar

1 cup cream cheese

2 cups whipped cream

Preheat the oven to 350°F. Prepare the instant pudding mix per package directions. Set aside.

In a large bowl, mix the flour, walnut pieces, and margarine until well combined. Press into the bottom of a 9 by 13-inch cake pan. Bake for about 10 minutes, or until lightly browned. Allow to cool completely.

In a separate bowl, mix the powdered sugar and the cream cheese until smooth. Gently fold 1 cup of the whipped cream into the cream cheese mixture. Spread the mixture evenly over the cooled crust, followed by an even layer of the prepared pudding. Top with the remaining whipped cream and sprinkle with additional walnut pieces, if desired. Refrigerate for at least 4 hours before serving.

OCTOBER 1993

This is a wonderful column that describes the celebrations that Amish families mark throughout the year; anniversaries, family reunions, and birthdays are all times for fellowship and food.

Ben and I had quite a surprise Friday evening when all our family gathered here to celebrate our thirty-sixth wedding anniversary, which was on Sunday, October 17. The children decided to have a carry-in supper. My, what a table full of food, which consisted of pizza, fish sticks, mashed potatoes, gravy, macaroni and cheese, pies, corn, mixed vegetables, cheese, cakes, ice cream, cherry delight, potato casserole, pretzels, potato chips, fruit salad, and lettuce salad. Lots more than we could eat for thirty-two of us present. Was an enjoyable evening together! The evening just wasn't long enough.

We are having all of my mother's family here for Saturday dinner, October 30. Eleven years ago, we had the family reunion, which was also on a Saturday, October 30, which was also our oldest son Amos's twenty-first birthday. Was a nice day, as we barbecued chicken that morning. The family has really increased since then, with the nieces and nephews having families of their own.

It'll soon hit the four-hundred mark for Mother's family. It's been four years that father left us for that Great Beyond. Mother is eighty-eight years old, and it

seems the whole family hasn't been together for quite some time. So we decided to take up the task. Boy! How much should I prepare? We're cleaning out our toolshed for the occasion. Also, lots of cleaning, otherwise, has been done. Hoping for a nice, warm day.

Our friends, Lee and Audry DeBolt, had their fortieth anniversary on Sunday, October 17. Their children were celebrating their parents' anniversary with a reception at their church on Sunday from 2:00 P.M. to 4:00 P.M. We had an invitation to attend, but our day had been planned to be at Paul and Leah's house.

We've had sunshiny warm days, giving the farmers a good chance to harvest the crops. The farmers have put in long hours to harvest the crops from the seeds they put in the ground when springtime arrived. The wheat is looking a beautiful green beside the fields that are taking on that dirty brown tinge that will be there till the warmth of spring. The trees are losing their colorful leaves.

A year ago, we had our killing frost, but s'pose one of these days the garden and all those pretty flowers will look bare again. We still have nice oakleaf lettuce to use. Enjoy sharing it with the children. Lots of garden goodies yet.

Well, I must get in gear. Plenty to do before we have the reunion. Want to wash off walls upstairs.

...and she left herself... know.

We arrived home late Wed. eve & to our surprise, our yard... had been rolled & mowed while we were gone. Such a gr... different! Thanks to son-in-law Joe & ... also, to the Hauman's who done the great job for us.

(Enjoy your day, today! What would I do without family? ...Liz called us on the phone, Wed. eve, when we were up... up in the mountains & finally got cut off, which was a comm... thing with the phones in the mountains. Was glad to hear her voice, at least for a while & everything being well at home. Must get to bed & get some shut eyes, as we're all tired. ...glad for the safe & enjoyable trip we all had. Had a good dr... the wheel & reckon he was tired to return back to his home, al... so much traffic on these roads away from home.

1994
"these worthless columns!"

FEBRUARY 1994

Elizabeth really wanted to give each of her sons and daughters keepsake quilts as they moved off into adulthood and married life. She would make four quilts for each of her children. This is a fairly common custom among the Amish. So the winter of 1994 was earmarked to make the quilts. Years later, Elizabeth would often remember this "winter of quilting" fondly.

This about does it for our quilting of quilts. That's all our dining room has seen the last six weeks. We had such cold, snowy weather in all those weeks and how nice to keep busy on making the wedding for the children. We made five quilts (three knotted quilts, and two bed comforters) in these six weeks, in addition to doing our regular daily tasks. With the girls working during the day, the evenings seemed enjoyable with them talking about their workday. Naturally, singing was included. Emma marked off the last two quilts with a four-leaf clover design some call a double wedding ring design. She used one of those Tupperware sauce dishes to mark it off. Lots of stitches on a quilt and we used towards three spools of 750 yards each to make five quilts. Sometimes we would sit down to quilt early in the morning, before the girls went to work when they left at 6:30 A.M., but mostly they leave at 5:30 A.M. Daughters Leah and Liz were home one day to help with the quilting, as they enjoy quilting, also. The last of the quilts went out of frame at 11:00 P.M. last night.

The kitchen has the aroma of home-baked bread now. Made seven loaves today. The children are probably all coming for my husband's birthday, which appeared on the 1994 February calendar. Time has a way of slipping by. You see, time doesn't wait on anyone. Right? My brother-in-law, Emanuel, has a birthday on the same date but is a year older than Ben. Happy birthday goes out to you both, February 17! Ben was enjoying home life on these cold days, but our sons Amos and Albert kept on working (carpenter trade). It was good to have him home to do the barn chores. Otherwise the girls probably would have had to do them. How thankful to have plenty of fuel for our stoves and plenty to eat. Guess we just don't appreciate it enough and then to be in good health.

MARCH 1994

One winter is just ending, but Amish men are already thinking ahead to the next winter and the supply of firewood.

This is a lovely, sunshiny Saturday with the huge wash drying on the clothesline. I enjoy such days.

The girls didn't have to work at the factory today, so lots is getting accomplished. Ben and Joe are back in the woods cutting wood. It's good to have preseasoned wood for the stoves next winter. Lovina and Susan did the wash and now are cleaning up in the washhouse, which gets messy at times. Verena is doing the huge stack of ironing, Emma is at the sewing machine where I was also, but I thought I had best get this column written. Dinner is on the list to do next.

We've been trying to do a lot of our sewing now since the bedding has been completed. It has taken a lot of fuel this cold, snowy winter. Spring is approaching. It'll be good once the woodstoves aren't in gear. Lots more work to see the stoves, stove pipes, and chimneys are in good working order. We keep those wood-boxes full, empty the ash pans constantly, and keep the house dust-free. Lots to do at this time of year.

APRIL 1994

This fascinating column captures the culinary journey many Amish have made from cooking with purely scratch foods to foods that have been store bought. Elizabeth talks of her first encounter with Jell-O and store-bought salad dressing.

The rest have all left for their place of work. The morning work has come to a halt. The breakfast dishes have been washed, the floors swept, etc. So with this quiet, peaceful, relaxing morning, I'll try to give you readers out there another column to read before I start with some other kind of work. Thanks for all those encouraging cards and notes.

Spring has arrived but cold weather remains. Had 24°F yesterday morning and this morning had 29°F, although it's a lovely, sunny, bright, cool, and beautiful day. We're just more ambitious on a nice sunny warm day instead of those cold drear days. It's time to get those seeds around and start off seeds in pots or hotbeds for plants later on. That's on my list today.

Daughter Liz and baby came early with the horse and buggy yesterday morning. She had what I'd call a cold drive, a distance of miles through the cold. After an early dinner, we went over to help my aged mother clean her house, as church services will be held there on Sunday. There we met four of my sisters and some nieces who were cleaning her part of the house. She'll be relaxed when everything has had a good cleaning again. She'll be eighty-nine this month. She's coming here for supper tonight and spent the evening here while sister and family attend a wedding supper. So on the menu I should cook some mush. She likes her mush and milk. I never was too fond of it, but when sliced and fried makes a good breakfast.

I often think how we used to make our own salad dressings, sour creams, and mayonnaises. When milk soured, the cream was taken off the milk and kept for such purposes, and sometimes a little vinegar added to milk to have a sour cream taste. Guess we grew up with it and didn't mind it until salad dressing was put to use. I can remember when I had my first store-bought salad dressing and also Jell-O. We didn't think to buy cake mixes, puddings, etc. It's a good reminder to think of them good ol' days. Well, I had best get to my daily work. Enough written for now. Nobody here to do the work for me.

AMISH COOK CLASSIC: OVERNIGHT SALAD
Serves 8 to 10

Salads that can incorporate many different fresh vegetables from the garden are popular with Amish cooks. This was a favorite in the Coblentz household every summer.

1 large head of lettuce, chopped

1 head of cauliflower, chopped

1 medium onion, chopped

1 pound frozen peas

3 carrots, peeled and chopped (optional)

1 cup salad dressing, such as Miracle Whip

1 cup sugar

1 cup shredded Cheddar cheese

Mix the lettuce, cauliflower, onion, peas, and carrots together in a large bowl. In a separate bowl, combine the salad dressing and the sugar. Stir the dressing mixture until it is smooth and the sugar is well incorporated. Pour the dressing over the vegetables and toss until they are evenly coated. Sprinkle the Cheddar cheese on top of the salad. Cover the bowl and chill the salad overnight in the refrigerator.

JUNE 1994

Elizabeth never understood why her column was so well received. She even called it "worthless," which made me, her editor, cringe. It wasn't very good for marketing! But it really had to do with Elizabeth not wanting to somehow be seen as a celebrity.

The clock shows 8:30 P.M., but I should get this written if the pen stays in gear to write what you might call, just another worthless column. It is bedtime, but now is my chance to do this task.

Daughters Lovina, Susan, Liz, and the writer spent the day at daughter Leah's to assist in making noodles. We used 110 eggs, so they should have plenty of noodles for a while. It is always enjoyable to be working together. It makes life more pleasant. It is so much easier to make noodles with that hand-cranked noodle maker. We used to have to use the rolling pin and cut them with a knife when dry. We tried to make even cuts. On our way to daughter Leah's with the horse and buggy, one horseshoe came off its foot, rolled back to the hind buggy wheel, the wheel caused the horseshoe to flip in the air, and it landed back in the buggy box. Lucky the horseshoe didn't hit anyone in the head. We never seen such a happening. We didn't have to stop the buggy to go pick up the horseshoe as we usually do when the horse loses a shoe. Then on our way home, we stopped at a country store and got stranded there for a while from severe thunderstorms. I was glad to see home again, although we were wet.

Son Albert had church Sunday at their place. We had a nice sunshiny day for it. They served dinner, or as some call it, a lunch, after church. The dinner consisted of coffee, bologna, two kinds of cheese, red beets, pickles, lettuce, bread, margarine, fresh rhubarb jam, hot peppers, peanut butter spread (see page 63), and other snacks.

Sunday morning I was fixing breakfast. As I was frying eggs, I came across what you would call a double egg. To my surprise, it had one yolk and another egg in a shell inside of it. It was an egg within an egg. I broke the little egg and it was just another egg. Never seen such an egg.

How thankful for our much-needed rain. Gives the garden and crops and hay a chance to grow. It should give these seeds a good start to sprout.

JUNE 1994

Although October has increased in popularity among the Amish as a month for weddings, June still wears the crown as the most popular month for this special ceremony.

It is a sunshiny, hot Saturday morning with the temperature at 90°F already. We've experienced some real hot days lately with severe thunderstorms. Rain sure has been appreciated as it seems so dry. Things won't grow well without rain.

Daughters Verena and Emma are at the sewing factory this morning, so I am missing their good help around the house.

Daughter Lovina and her husband Joe, who have been living with us since their wedding, were blessed with a baby girl on Tuesday evening, June 14, born at 9:58 P.M., weighing seven pounds, five ounces and nineteen inches long. So it seems different in this household to have a sweet little bundle in this house again. Last time was when daughter Susan was born eighteen years ago. The name: Elizabeth. I shouldn't forget how it was named.

There's been so many weddings in this month of June in this area. We were at my brother Chris's wedding where their youngest daughter got married. They had a nice day for it. Thursday we also attended a wedding for my cousin's daughter. Looks like we will attend two more weddings this coming week. One is one of my nephews on Tuesday, so Monday we'll go help get ready for the wedding, such as pies, nothings, etc.

Well, this morning we discovered our kerosene tank showed almost empty, and to our luck, the kerosene driver came past with his truck and we got kerosene. We use kerosene for our kerosene cookstoves and for our lamps. The wood cookstove is in use in the wintertime, with the kerosene stoves being in full gear in the summer for cooking, baking, and canning. The kerosene lamps are what we use for our light in the evenings. So you see, no switches in this house. Ha! The lamps have to be kept clean, the wicks trimmed, and the glass globes washed to give us brighter lights. We also have to keep the kerosene stoves clean in the same way, especially the pipeline.

JULY 1994

This column provides some interesting insight into one of the lesser-known customs of the Amish: the surprise twenty-first birthday party.

Ben and I have become grandparents for the seventeenth time, as daughter Liz and her husband Levi gave birth to their second child. This is the second grandchild in the past two weeks to arrive! Liz had an eight-pound baby boy, Levi Jr., named after his father. The sweet little bundle appears to be healthy and has a full head of hair.

Daughters Emma and Verena have taken two weeks of vacation from the sewing factory to help their sisters out with the new arrivals. I will also enjoy having their good help around the house.

This is a month full of birthdays. I will turn fifty-eight this month, and Emma will turn twenty-one this month. Hard to believe how these months melt into years. Many people around here have surprise birthday parties when their children turn the age of twenty-one, if they still are at home and unmarried. They usually try to have a surprise on them before their birthday arrives. The person to be surprised is usually taken somewhere and on their return, the young people of the community are at the house waiting to surprise the unsuspecting, soon-to-be-twenty-one-year-old. Most places, cakes, candy bars, snacks such as potato chips, pretzels, crackers, and pop are served at the parties. Some also serve ice cream. In the evening, the one who turned twenty-one opens his or her many gifts. Also lots of singing and yodeling takes place.

Rising water blocked off the road to daughter Liz's. Our horses plowed right through the water, while some cars were stuck. By late evening when we were returning home from daughter Liz's, the water over the road was too high for even our horses. Ben's good hat fell off and into the water, it sank, so a good hat was lost. A thirty-minute trip took two hours with detours. Still I often think about the floods that hit parts of the Midwest one year ago this month, it makes me sad to think of the lost crops and homes.

1995
writers conference

JANUARY 1995

The Coblentzes often held their annual family Christmas gathering on New Year's Day. With such a large family and so many families to visit on Christmas Day, they thought it would be simpler on everyone's schedules to hold the holiday gathering on New Year's.

The temperature was one below this morning after several months of warm weather. Brrrrr! Following is the account of our interesting New Year's Day.

We started the New Year by going to our son Albert's for breakfast. Biscuits and gravy were on the menu plus other stuff. The table was set when we arrived at 6:00 A.M. and the finishing touches done as to be seated for breakfast. We ate, washed dishes, and headed for our church services, which was a distance of a couple of miles with the horse and buggy. Was such an enjoyable morning. It reminded me of going early on New Year's Day morning to my folks—which is a thing of the past.

Our belated holiday family gathering was held Monday, January 2, and of all things, son Albert left their children here Sunday evening, and around 9:00 P.M. they had an addition to their family. A daughter named Irene was born to them, weighing eight pounds, nine ounces. Was too late to postpone the family gathering again, so we went on as usual, everyone here for breakfast Monday morning. Everyone was present except son Albert and his wife. But on their way home with their new arrival,

Albert and his wife stayed over the noon hour to have dinner with us. We had a bed for the newborn's mother to lay down on and eat a plateful of dinner. So the family was complete again. We are now a total of thirty-five. We have eighteen grandchildren now. Totals are eleven girls to seven boys. We had Albert's four children here for Sunday overnight after the baby was born, plus eight more overnight guests. Had an enjoyable weekend. Somewhat different!

Winter brings with it the woodstove, and there are so many more tasks when you use a woodstove. There might be less dust around, though, as the roads are dusty in summer which causes us to just clean, clean all the time. But in the winter, those ash pans must be emptied from the stoves. Takes more fuel for the lanterns and lamps at this time of year. There is not just a switch we can use to turn on and off our lights. Then there are those wood boxes that have to be filled with wood and the coal buckets for coal. We got our cookstove (Pioneer Maid) in use in the evening of New Year's Day. Now that is something new, to not be using it sooner, but the weather had been on the warm side for so long.

AMISH COOK CLASSIC: HOMEMADE CHEESE SOUP
Serves 4 to 6

This recipe was a favorite of Elizabeth's on cold winter nights. The recipe calls for a bag of frozen mixed vegetables. Elizabeth would use a blend of fresh vegetables from the garden in this recipe, and other home cooks can try the same.

¼ cup (½ stick) butter
¼ cup minced onion
¼ cup all-purpose flour
4 cups milk
1 (10-ounce) bag frozen mixed vegetables
1 cup shredded Cheddar cheese
Salt

In a two-quart pot, melt the butter over medium heat. Add the onion and sauté, stirring frequently, until translucent. Remove the pot from the heat and sprinkle the flour over the cooked onion. Gradually add the milk, whisking constantly, until no lumps remain. Add the frozen mixed vegetables. Cook the mixture over medium heat, stirring constantly, until the soup thickens and coats the back of a spoon. Stir in the Cheddar. Continue heating until the cheese is melted and well combined. Season the soup with salt to taste.

APRIL 1995

I always laughed when I read about a family gathering with three or four hundred people. Elizabeth would act as if it were just another day. Most non-Amish people get stressed out at the thought of entertaining ten or twelve people. Can you imagine having four hundred people over for supper?

This was an enjoyable evening with son Amos and family. We decided to take supper in at Amos's since he is laid up with two breaks in his ankle and one break on his leg. Joe and Lovina's family and son Albert and his family also wanted to go along. So we took potatoes, barbecued pork steak, ham, cottage cheese, and dandelion greens with sour cream and hard-boiled eggs. Joe's took buttered corn, hot peppers, cake, ice cream, and cones, Albert's took macaroni and cheese, deep-fried ham, buttered peas, coleslaw, deviled eggs, and a cherry-covered cake. There was plenty of food! Amos was to the doctor Monday. They took X-rays of his foot and seen the ankle bones weren't in the correct place so two doctors had to twist the foot to get it in place, which I guess was a painful ordeal. They put another cast on. The break in the leg seems to be healing good. They have to go again Wednesday. Just hope for good results. They have six children. A grocery shower was brought to them the evening before from friends of their church. So the people have been very good to them to help them along. They feel so unworthy of it all.

Saturday was the reunion at the home of my sister Lovina in honor of Mother's ninetieth birthday. Around 330 were present with a carry-in meal. Plenty of food! Had a nice day for it. Singing took place in the afternoon. Sister had also invited Mother's remaining family and their live-ins which they're still five sisters and two brothers. So five were present. Most are in their eighties. Mother being ninety now. Lots of work to undertake a huge gathering. They barbecued two hundred pounds of chicken. Was real plenty. The morn of Mother's birthday, April 5, the temperature had dropped to 15°F. Us sisters went to Mother's for a carry-in dinner. Was enjoyable! Will she be with us in a year from now? Good we don't know what the future holds. Right?

Levi Jr., son of daughter Liz and Levi, is now home from the hospital after having pneumonia. He seems his jolly self again. Lots of sickness around it seems. Good when the warm weather arrives once more.

Talking about dandelion greens—it's been on our menu the last week. We're always glad to see the first sign of the rebirth of the dandelion. They're nestled in lawns, gardens, roadways, and pastures. It always delights us to see them grow to have on the menu. We use it as a salad and some wilt them. When they become bigger, it's best to wilt them. Most say it's a good healthy green salad. We make a sour cream to it and add hard-boiled eggs to it. Yum, it's good with potatoes (jackets) and bacon or ham. Makes a good, cheap evening meal. We can always feel good when we eat the dandelion greens in evening, as it relaxes us for a good night's rest.

JUNE 1995

Speaking of large family gatherings, how about eight hundred or one thousand people? That is what the typical wedding attracts. Tradition dictates that the "big day" is on a Thursday in most Amish settlements. This column is also one of several where Elizabeth mentions a "water battle." The Amish enjoy good, clean fun, and nothing feels better on a hot, humid summer day than a good, old-fashioned water fight with buckets full of cool water.

Had ideal weather for daughter Emma and Jacob's wedding on Thursday. The toolshed was cleaned out, where wedding services were to be held, with benches and chairs set up. The other shed (as you might call our washhouse) was used to do the preparing of the noon and evening meals. The house was set up with tables to eat in the dining and living rooms, where we could seat 104 at one time. The kitchen with a folding table in it was used to serve the hot food. The cooks fill those empty bowls for the tablewaiters who kept the food on the tables. After church services, folding tables were set up to serve the children for the noon and evening meals. There were six younger girls who were chosen to keep the food on the table, which included five of my granddaughters. They felt so proud. A good friend of ours from Nappanee, Indiana, who is a bishop, united Emma and Jacob in marriage.

We usually have the women who are cooks at the wedding come on Tuesday to do the baking, and some of the girls come on Wednesday to help with final preparations. But we decided to do everything on Wednesday. It seemed to work out great. The

women baked seventy pies (cherry, raisin, oatmeal, rhubarb). They also made fourteen plates full of "nothings," a traditional Amish wedding pastry. The girls peeled the potatoes (five twenty-quart canners, several sack fulls of potatoes from our garden), washed celery, and washed lettuce from our garden for both meals.

Our girls prepared the wedding tables on Tuesday. For those who may wonder what the wedding tables are: The bride and groom eat their wedding meal and receive visitors while sitting at a table decorated especially for them.

On the noon menu was chicken, mashed potatoes, chicken and noodles, gravy, dressing, frozen mixed vegetables, macaroni and cheese, coleslaw, lettuce salad, cheese, celery, tapioca pudding, fruit salad, various kinds of cake, four kinds of pie, nothings, and coffee. For the evening meal, ham and baked beans were added to the menu. I was glad my aged mother could attend for the whole day. It was quite a week, as Emma's wedding occurred on Thursday and a nephew got married on Saturday. Sunday is the Coblentz family reunion, and it usually ends up with a good water battle.

AUGUST 1995

The Budget, an Amish newspaper in Sugarcreek, Ohio, has periodic picnics where all their writers are invited. It's a great time for food and fellowship. Elizabeth was always proud of her affiliation with the newspaper.

It is a breezy morning as I start writing this. After the 90°F we experienced yesterday, this weather feels refreshing. We could use a good shower again, as this sure is hay fever season. Whoever suffers from it knows what I mean. My husband is bothered with it every year.

Saturday my husband and I attended the big event, which was the *Budget* gathering. The *Budget* (a weekly newspaper) in Sugarcreek, Ohio, is now 105 years old. It carries letters from Amish people all over. Without telephones it is often the sole source of long-distance communication for us. Forty-three years ago, I took up the task of writing for the *Budget*, describing our area news. With Amish people moving to new areas all the time, it has become a big weekly paper. A good dinner was served to all the scribes (scribes are people who write for the weekly paper). The food and fellowship were great.

The meal consisted of mashed potatoes, gravy, fried chicken, roast beef, dressing, corn, salad, pie, Pepsi, coffee, tea, bread and butter. The person writing for the *Budget* the longest was an Amish woman who has been writing for seventy-one years. She is from the state of Delaware and was not able to attend the reunion in Sugarcreek. Around three hundred people attended. The last gathering was five years ago when the newspaper celebrated its centennial. We left at 3:00 A.M. on Saturday morning and were back home by 10:15 P.M. Saturday night. Had an enjoyable day!

You may wonder whether we traveled to Sugarcreek by horse and buggy. No, it would've been too hard on the horse for a whole day. But our brother-in-law once made the three-hundred-mile trip to our place with horse and buggy. They were surprised how many friendly people they met along the way, offering them food and water and feed for their horses. A friend of ours took us in their van to Ohio (Amish people are only allowed to own horse and buggies for travel, but can occasionally be transported in a van by a non-Amish driver). Joe and Lovina and their baby went with us and visited their relatives out there in those hills of Holmes County, Ohio, while we attended the gathering.

SEPTEMBER 1995

This column was a very typical autumn entry from Elizabeth—comforting and simple. It's this simplicity that I believe endeared readers to Elizabeth.

Fall has approached on the 1995 calendar. Autumn brings so many changes: crisp fair, the sounds and sights. But how good it is to think of the time spent putting up the summer harvest for the coming cold when nothing will be grown till spring arrives once more. Daughter Lovina has filled her jars for the coming winter. Was a change for her to be a homemaker now, instead of being an employee of a sewing factory.

Daughter Liz and her children, Lovina and her daughter, Susan and the writer assisted daughter Leah on Tuesday in getting ready for their church services. There's always plenty to do at such a time, that's if you want to give the house a thorough cleaning. What a relief when all is cleaned and back in order again.

Daughter Lovina and I did our wash together in the washhouse this morning. Nice breezy weather will dry it in a hurry. She's baking some chocolate chip cookies for Leah's church services. Cookies and crackers are always passed out to the youngsters in church services in mid-forenoon. Those little ones always look forward to their treat. Well here, Lovina brought me some cookies over, and how good they taste. They're just melting in my mouth now. I must say, they're really good!

I just hope for rain. It's beginning to be quite dry. Garden eats will dry up soon if we don't get rain, as I've planted some late vegetables. The combining of beans and the corn picking have taken place. So the fall harvest is in gear. Nice dry weather for it.

Well, I must get busy as to get ready for my family and some others for supper, tomorrow night. The house needs a cleaning, baking is on the list, and you name it. This writing task, though, can't be neglected. Those encouraging notes and letters from you readers sure keep me to keep on writing. Thank you for all your time and encouragement, greatly appreciated!

AMISH COOK CLASSIC: ZUCCHINI SOUP

Serves 4 to 6

If it's September, it must be zucchini time! Elizabeth could find scores of ways to use this versatile vegetable. A homemade soup was just one recipe featured in the column during the summer of 1995.

2 tablespoons butter

½ cup sliced carrots

½ cup sliced celery

1 small onion, chopped

2 cups chicken broth

2 cups grated zucchini

2 tablespoons chopped fresh parsley

1 small potato, peeled and cubed

¼ teaspoon seasoned salt

Salt and pepper

In a two-quart pot, melt the butter over medium heat, then add the carrots, celery, and onion. Sauté the vegetables, stirring frequently, until the onions become translucent. Add the remaining ingredients and bring the soup to a boil. Reduce the heat and simmer for 30 to 45 minutes, until the vegetables are fork tender.

SEPTEMBER 1995

A good buggy horse is invaluable to the Amish. An emotional attachment grows between equine and owner that is stronger than the one between people and their cars. Whenever a buggy horse reaches the end of its days, there is a sense of sadness.

The first frost brushed the tops of late summer melons with ice. Amazing to have a first frost this early. This week has been full of little problems, but I guess I should not complain. Our health has been good and there is plenty of food for the table. Guess we should thank our Creator for such blessings.

We spent last evening tending to Mae. Mae has been my horse for twenty years. Yesterday she injured her leg while pulling my buggy into town; she twisted her ankle in a rut in the road. She went down fast. Luckily it happened close to home and she was able to limp back. The Amish herb doctor prescribed a mixture of liquid vitamins, hoping that would make her snap out of it. Ben says she'll probably have to be shot. She is suffering, but I hate to see her go; she was such a dependable horse for all these years. I guess life has its share of upsets. So that is taking all the attention around here.

Today, daughter Susan and I were going to put a quilt in frame. Just as we prepared the frame and were going to quilt a peach-colored quilt, we realized that we were out of peach-colored thread. We want to finish a quilt sometime this month. They are so nice and warm for the long winter months ahead.

My aged mother is staying with us this week. She gets very good care when she stays with us. Daughter Emma sewed her a brand-new dress last night, and daughter Lovina is preparing her favorite meals. Mother doesn't eat as much as she used to. Her favorite meals are simple ones—coffee soup and bread soups. She likes to break up bread in a cup and pour coffee over it and eat it.

We get our water from a pump inside a water closet in our kitchen. The water comes from a ground well. The handle on the pump broke yesterday morning. So all the girls had to go outside and wash their hair. It was a little too chilly for that! Ben says it should be fixed by tomorrow morning. We have a water pump outside that is powered by our windmill; that water also comes from a ground well. ❧

NOVEMBER 1995

Elizabeth was happiest when her eight children were all living at home, something she often wistfully reminisced about in her column.

Tuesday was just another one of those days with lots going on. Daughter Emma missed a day from work at the sewing factory as to go along with her husband Jacob to the hospital. Losing his balance, Jacob fell twelve feet off a roof while on construction work the evening before. Results: a broken heel. Gets around with the aid of crutches. So I reckon he won't be climbing up on a roof for some time. Emma and Jacob have lived here with us since their June 15 marriage. Daughters Leah and her children, Liz and her children, and Lovina and her daughter came to spend the day here today. Plans had been made to have a sewing day, but the girls went on with the sewing while I (Jacob's mother also went) along with Jacob and Emma to the hospital. The girls like to sew on my good, old Singer treadle sewing machine, which has been in use for many, many years. We arrived back here from the hospital too late for dinner, but we still got in on the leftovers. The girls had a dinner which consisted of fried chicken, mashed potatoes, gravy, corn, and more. Always tastes better when someone else does the meal. Sister-in-law Betty, who took us to the hospital, also stayed for the late dinner.

It seems impossible that we have seven grandchildren in school now. How these years slip away. We have nineteen grandchildren now, including one set of twin girls. Also, when I took up this task of writing in August of 1991, we had five unmarried girls in our care yet, and two sons and a daughter who were married. Now we still have two unmarried girls here with us.

When you think back, how nice it would be if all eight of our children could still be in our care in these troubled times we are in. Do we appreciate good health enough when you read and hear of so many losing their good health? So, I guess we are just living one day at a time, right?

Well, I must get with it and let you readers out there rest yours eyes until next week if you happen to be reading this column. ✎

1996
secret pals

JANUARY 1996

The Amish often exchange Christmas gifts around the holidays. Their celebration is low-key and the gifts often homemade instead of store bought, but the day is still special.

Now that the rush of the holiday season is over, I thought I would take the time to write about it.

We had a white Christmas for once. Our family gathering was on Christmas Day, with everyone present. The day goes too fast, with our family being a total of thirty-six. All were seated for a breakfast around 7:00 A.M., which included fried eggs and fresh fried potatoes, smoked sausage, ham, bacon, cottage cheese, toast, various kinds of cheese, fruit salad, grape and orange juice, coffee, and all those Christmas goodies. Then dinner was at 11:30 A.M. with a cooked meal of stuffed turkey. Gifts were exchanged; it was exciting to see the children open their gifts.

"The New Year's Song" was sung (a traditional German song celebrating the New Year) at various times. It kind of gives a lonely feeling to think of keeping the traditions of our grandparents and parents. They had the gatherings and the singing of "The New Year's Song." Lots of memories to recall.

My aged mother will be ninety-one in April, so us married children usually have a carry-in supper in an evening in January to get together for the holidays. Lots of bygone family gatherings and memories of when mother and father would have them.

Mother and father had eight married children and eighty-one grandchildren. We have eight children, six married, and nineteen grandchildren.

To the Palmetto, Florida, reader who inquired about a peanut butter–marshmallow creme mixture served at a Sarasota Amish restaurant, see the recipe at the end of this column.

We had church twice in December for us and then it was Joe and Lovina's turn. Last week we butchered our beef, and this week we have been canning beef. Cut up all four quarters on Tuesday. Got around 120 quarts. We chunked a lot of beef and twenty quarts were ground into hamburger. The next day I cooked two pressure cookers of those beef bones and made thirty-three quarts of vegetable soup with the broth and processed it. So a lot of those empty jars were filled once more.

Joe and Lovina, and daughter Liz and her children were here on Tuesday to help, which was great. Even Ben, being home from work, gets in on it. We helped daughter Liz last week with her beef, and the week before we helped son Albert's work up their beef. So it is so nice to work together. It is a mess to go through, but glad to open those cans afterwards.

Happy New Year to all you great readers out there. Often wonder what '96 has in store for us.

AMISH COOK CLASSIC: PEANUT BUTTER SPREAD
Makes 1¾ cups

Although some customs were different in Michigan, one wasn't: Amish peanut butter spread. This sweet favorite is served at after-church meals in most Amish communities. Readers often asked about this recipe because it was mentioned in passing so much in the column. It's an easy recipe, and ingredient amounts can be adjusted to your taste.

½ cup creamy peanut butter
¼ cup marshmallow creme
1 cup light corn syrup

In a medium bowl, combine the peanut butter, marshmallow creme, and corn syrup. Stir with a rubber spatula until the mixture is smooth and evenly combined. Place the mixture in a covered container and refrigerate overnight. Allow the spread to come to room temperature before serving on bread or over ice cream.

FEBRUARY 1996

Elizabeth often wrote about hog butchering, but the family also butchered beef. So this winter featured a change of pace for column readers as she describes the laborious beef butchering process.

The temperature is at −5°F this morning. Winter hangs right in there. Snow-covered ground.

The highlights are: we are grandparents once more, which puts the mark to twenty grandchildren. We have twelve girls and eight boys as grandchildren. Joe and Lovina had a baby girl named Susan J., born on January 24, weighing six pounds and nineteen inches long. She joins a sister, Elizabeth. They live in a trailer across our drive.

Daughter Susan is caring for their household duties now. Seven of the grandchildren are of school age. Baby Susan was born on daughter Liz's twenty-seventh birthday. There are also two of the grandchildren which arrived on daughter Verena's birthday. Son Albert also had their son Albert Jr. born on his birthday and which was the date Joe and Lovina picked for their marriage.

Daughter Lovina cooked some beef bones (two big pressure cookers full) and then took the beef off the bones and we made a vegetable soup out of it. We processed forty-two quarts. She bought several gallons mixed vegetables from the store, and then we added various vegetables to the soup. Well, it looks good in the jars. Good to fill those empty jars, especially for a quick meal when in a busy or late rush. We are feasting on our vegetable soup, which I made and processed thirty-three quarts of it.

We've been having fried what you call "pon hoss" for breakfast every morning the past week, which was done at the butchering of hogs at son Albert's. It's the juice of the cooked head meat, etc., with flour added and some liver pudding and seasoned with salt and pepper. It's cooked in a big iron kettle. Cool, slice, and fry it. We eat ours for breakfast with fried potatoes and eggs, coffee soup, and cheese. Some may ask: What is coffee soup?

Well, it's hot coffee and milk with sugar added to your taste. We use crackers with ours, but some have toasted bread, or cubed bread in it. The liver pudding is made from the bones cooked in the iron kettle. The meat is removed and put through the meat grinder. Some fry it down in an iron kettle and season with salt and pepper.

Well, I had best get busy. Always plenty to do. Just got done with the morning work, washing dishes, sweeping and mopping the floors. So now I could relax when all is clean and in order of the day to write this letter. Looks like daughter Susan is doing a wash at Joe's. I miss her help now. Daughters Verena and Emma are at the sewing factory. Verena is going on her twelfth year at the same place. Emma and Jacob are living here with us since their marriage.

AMISH COOK CLASSIC: SPEEDY CINNAMON ROLLS

Makes approximately 2 dozen rolls

Cinnamon rolls are made from many different recipes passed around Amish settlements. From slow, let-rise-all-day yeasty cinnamon confections to quicker but no less delicious concoctions, cinnamon rolls are a staple of Amish baking. This is a favorite, fast cinnamon roll recipe.

2 cups plus 4½ cups bread flour	2 eggs
2 cups warm water (105° to 115°F)	⅓ cup lard
½ cup granulated sugar	6 tablespoons margarine or butter, softened
1 tablespoon salt	1 cup packed brown sugar
2 packages active dry yeast	1 tablespoon ground cinnamon

In a large bowl, combine 2 cups of the bread flour with the water, sugar, salt, and yeast. Beat the mixture for 2 minutes with a wooden spoon, then add the eggs and the lard. Stir until well blended. Gradually add the remaining 4½ cups bread flour to the mixture and stir until a firm dough is formed. Cover the bowl and set it in a warm area to rest for 20 minutes.

After resting, punch the dough down, divide it in half, and form it into 2 balls. On a floured surface, roll one ball of the dough out as thinly as possible. Brush half of the softened margarine evenly over the dough, then sprinkle with half of the brown sugar and half of the cinnamon. Roll the dough up like a jelly roll. Cut each roll into slices that are ½ to ¾ inch thick. Place the slices ½ inch apart in a buttered jelly roll pan. Repeat with the remaining ball of dough and the remaining margarine, brown sugar, and cinnamon. Place the rolls in a warm area and allow to rise for about 45 minutes, or until doubled in size.

While the rolls are rising, preheat oven to 350°F.

Bake the rolls for 15 to 20 minutes, until they are golden brown. Allow the rolls to cool on wire racks for 15 minutes. If desired, you may spread the rolls with your favorite frosting before serving.

FEBRUARY 1996

Each year, someone would become Elizabeth's "secret pal." Throughout the year, Elizabeth would receive little gifts, mystery notes, and encouragement. Elizabeth would have fun trying to guess who the mystery benefactor was. The identity was often revealed at a surprise breakfast or supper.

It is 23°F this Wednesday morning with snow flurries. It was 70°F yesterday. So quite a change in the weather. No wonder you hear of so much sickness. But glad when everything is well around here again. I must get this written and send it on its way. It's a task that shouldn't be neglected.

We were having company for breakfast, so the girls wanted to have "breakfast pizza" on the menu. So the girls shaped up four of those 7½-ounce biscuit containers on a cookie sheet and put it in the oven to bake. Removed it from the oven and topped it with eight scrambled eggs, a small can of mushrooms, one pound of fried bacon (cut up), and slices of cheese on top then. I fried potatoes and the girls said we could've added the potatoes, too, but the cookie sheet was ready for the oven. Just heat it till the cheese is melted. Then cut it in pieces. So we had breakfast pizza, fried potatoes, apple sauce, oranges, bananas, grapes, hot biscuits, coffee, and jam. Our company enjoyed the breakfast.

The children were here for supper on Friday evening, February 16, in honor of my husband's birthday. Put him up to sixty-five now. Then the next morning (Saturday) we were taken out for breakfast at a restaurant where our "secret pals" of 1995 revealed themselves. Daughter Verena told us we're going out for Dad's birthday, Saturday morning (being his birthday, February 17). We got to the restaurant and were seated, Verena handed us a card, and to our surprise it was daughter Lovina and her husband Joe. Was always teasing Verena all year, telling her that it's her sending all those gifts on special occasions. So it was a great surprise to see who it was—Lovina and Joe. We again have a secret pal for 1996, so I guess we'll keep guessing all year.

FEBRUARY 1996

This column was written when Joe and Lovina were still living on Elizabeth's property in a trailer home. The newlyweds provided a source of company and help for Elizabeth and Ben.

We'd be entering another month tomorrow if it wouldn't be for leap year. So February 29 won't appear on the calendar again till 2000. What is in store for us by then? Only our Heavenly Father knows.

Ben and son-in-law Joe are back in the woods cutting wood again today. We should have plenty of wood to burn for the next coming winter. They've been keeping themselves occupied out there this winter.

We were glad to have Ben's aunt and his cousin and her husband here from Belle Center, Ohio, yesterday. Came for the day. Daughter Liz and her children and Joe's were also here. Had an enjoyable day with singing and yodeling in the afternoon after daughter Verena came home from the factory. Was glad they had supper yet before they left.

It's good to look out and see the windows and curtains are clean once more. It seems the windows in the winter get so filmy looking, probably from snow, rain outside, and then inside by using the stove and especially in the kitchen.

Saturday was such a nice, warm day so we took advantage of it to clean outside. Sunday was also very nice. Our family were all here on Sunday evening, and most of them had supper at Joe's with Verena having the grill in gear. She barbecued chicken, steak, and sausage. Some of the family went somewhere else for supper. So it was good to see the children (two boys and six girls) all on Sunday some time, plus twenty grandchildren.

JUNE 1996

The spring of 1996 brought some change to Elizabeth's homestead. Lovina and her husband, Joe, had lived in a trailer home on the property since they married three years earlier. But now they were moving into their own home about two miles away.

We are well into June, and it really feels like spring. The cold lasted long this year. It has taken plenty of fuel for our stoves to get through the winter and spring. I spent Sunday with mother at her place. She is ninety-one years old. What age can do to these older people! They need their loving care. Daughters Verena and Susan brought dinner over for us all. She was always so fond of dandelion greens made in a salad with hard-cooked eggs, so they brought for dinner dandelion greens made in a salad with hard-cooked eggs. They also brought potatoes, fried chicken, macaroni and cheese, buttered corn, buttered peas, cheese, celery and carrot sticks, peaches, cookies, bread and butter. I kept enough food back for her evening meal, which she enjoyed. I specially learned to enjoy those dandelion greens when we were in her care. At that time, we didn't prepare all kinds of dishes as is done today. It was only a simple well-balanced meal.

In the wintertime, corn meal mush was cooked, which I didn't care for, but mother likes it with milk. What was left, we poured into a pan and then the next morning the cornmeal mush was sliced and fried till golden brown in a skillet. That made a hearty breakfast with fried potatoes. We didn't make all kinds of desserts like we do today. The list of changes in how we eat today could go on and on. The lawn should be mowed, but we've had so much rain, the ground is so soft.

We've helped daughter Lovina clean their house that they recently bought. Lots of cleaning was done. Joe and daughter Susan made four trips back and forth with horse and buggy yesterday, and are at it today again, taking big buggy loads of their household items from the trailer they now live in across our driveway, to their new home a few miles away. A friend helped last night with his van to take some bigger furniture. The trailer is beginning to look empty. It is remarkable how much that trailer held. It is a 14 × 70-foot Holly Park trailer. They have put it up for sale now.

Ben has been helping son Amos the last three weeks with their house remodeling. It is beginning to take shape. They will have lots more room. So it has been busy to help Amos, and also Joe and Lovina to get settled on their property. Will miss Lovina and Joe's two daughters Elizabeth and Susan. It'll be three years this July that they have lived here. So many changes as life goes on.

This is now Saturday morning and I must get my pen in gear to finish this letter. Hope you great readers out there are healthy and happy.

We've experienced a rainy and stormy week. Thanks for all of your interesting and encouraging letters.

JUNE 1996

This was a very happy period for Elizabeth. Two of her daughters still lived at home with her and her other married children lived close by. She spent spring days in the garden, which was a favorite pastime. Time with family was another.

Rain, rain, always more rain for this spring weather. It's been hard for the farmers to get their crops in. Also, many gardens couldn't be completed thus far. I'm one of the unlucky ones, I guess. We are having plenty of onions, radishes, and lettuce on the menu. Rhubarb is doing great. Made seven batches of rhubarb jam. I wanted fresh jam, as church services are to be held here on Sunday.

We have had such a busy spring with son Amos's house being rebuilt and other activities. Joe and Lovina moved about two miles from here, then church services were held here on Sunday and again in two weeks for Jacob and Emma. Lots of cleaning took place. Good to give the entire house a good thorough cleaning.

Paul and Leah's are having a public sale on Saturday, June 15, and will then start the process of moving to their home they bought this spring, about one and a half miles from here, and then Levi and daughter Liz will have church services in their home.

The Coblentz reunion (Ben's family) will be held Saturday, with Ben and his brother, Melvin, of Wisconsin, in charge of it. Daughter Susan helped daughter Liz wash off walls, yesterday. We gave Joe and Lovina's house a thorough cleaning also, before they moved in. Will help daughter Leah, also, before they move in to their house, to clean everything. So the list could go on and on. It's now twelve years since daughter Verena started working at the sewing factory. How those years took way.

We were at Joe and Lovina's for a taco supper, plus other goodies as Ben and son-in-law were helping Joe build a fence for his horses after they came home from work. Work-work-work!

We attended a wedding supper in our area on Thursday evening. Everything was held in a huge tent. They had separate rooms for the cooking, etc. It was a nice day for the wedding after those rainy days before, flooding roads in the area.

Joe and Lovina had all our family invited for her birthday. So we were a total of thirty-six. It seems different not to just walk across our drive to go there, as we need the horse power now to go. They like their new home, but their trailer home stands empty and lonely out there now. ❧

JULY 1996

This column format was always a reader favorite. It read like a diary entry and left many readers marveling at how much Elizabeth could fit into an average day.

4:00 A.M. Time to get up on this nice, breezy morning. Ben and son-in-law Jacob go out to hand milk our five cows and do the rest of the barn work. Daughter Emma and I start breakfast, with the assistance of daughter Susan. Verena gets herself ready to leave for the sewing factory, where she works.

4:50 A.M. We're all seated at the table to feast on breakfast. The menu consists of fried eggs and potatoes, scrambled eggs, coffee soup and crackers, cheese, toast, hot peppers, jam, hot pepper butter, butter, fresh strawberries, coffee, and tea. Some will ask what is coffee soup? It is sweetened hot coffee with milk. You can put crackers or toast in it.

5:00 A.M. Jacob leaves for construction work.

5:30 A.M. Verena leaves for the sewing factory and Ben for his construction work. Ben has been with that company for thirty-seven years. Daughter Verena has been at the sewing factory over twelve years now. Verena got a splinter stuck in the top of her foot while visiting at our son Amos's house on Sunday evening. Ben and I worked so hard to get it removed. Stuck in some way. Hard to remove. Hopefully we got it all out. We soaked her foot every morning and evening with Epsom salt and peroxide

water. And we are keeping it wrapped with a pulling salve. Daughters Emma and Susan are washing the dishes, and I hike out to the garden to hoe. I want to put some more sweet corn and hot peppers in the ground.

6:30 A.M. Daughter Emma is ironing and Susan helps me put out sweet corn and eighteen hot pepper plants.

7:30 A.M. Well, we all get cleaned up to go help daughter Liz clean up from their church services on Sunday, which were held in their home. Always plenty to clean up afterwards.

8:00 A.M. We go to Liz's house. Along the way, we stop to pick up Lovina in her new home, and her two children.

8:30 A.M. We surprise Liz by showing up to help her clean. She is pleasantly surprised!

2:30 P.M. After spending the day helping Liz, we head home. We did a huge amount of laundry, cleaned and mopped the floors, washed and rewashed lots of dishes. Was an enjoyable workday together. She was so glad to see almost everything back in order. They had 135 there for supper Sunday evening.

3:00 P.M. Verena gets home from the sewing factory.

4:30 P.M. Verena prepares a covered skillet casserole for our evening meal. She put a pound of hamburger in a skillet, added a diced up onion, then put the potatoes which were put through the hand-cranked salad maker, then put a can of cream of mushroom soup on top of potatoes and topped it with cheese. It takes an hour in the skillet until it is done.

5:30 P.M. Ben and Jacob get home from work. Go out to do the chores.

Later in the evening: Verena's casserole was good! Son Albert and some of Jacob's friends gave us a visit tonight. Yesterday, daughters Liz, Lovina, Verena, and Susan, and I were at daughter Leah's to help them pack. They are moving to their new home next week, which will bring them lots closer to us (only 1½ miles away). Now it is time to say good night!

OCTOBER 1996

The anniversary of Ben and Elizabeth's marriage was always a special time. Elizabeth joked about the marriage being a "life sentence," but in reality she couldn't imagine life without her beloved Ben. She would only have another three and a half years with him as of this column's writing.

Such a lovely autumn day. This brings back memories of thirty-nine years ago today, when we got what you'd call a life sentence. Ha! Today is Ben and my anniversary. We invited all our family for supper tonight for our wedding anniversary, plus a few more couples who have their anniversary coming up.

The huge wash is drying outside, and the ironing has been completed. I was out in the garden gathering vegetables, as we're going to have a "haystack" for supper for tonight's meal. Some might not know what a haystack is. You put fried hamburger on your plate, then top it with whatever you want and then pour cheese sauce on top.

You soon have a plateful. Some cook rice and mushrooms in with the hamburger. It is a very good meal. So there's to be cut-up lettuce, tomatoes, peppers, celery, carrots, radishes, crushed crackers, and also crushed-up corn chips—all to pile on top of the hamburger. Then pour over the cheese sauce. Also there will be peas, kidney beans, cheese sauce, and hot sauce. As side dishes we will have buttered red beets, green beans, and hot peppers from the garden. How thankful we are for such a plentiful garden. I pickled cucumbers yesterday, our cucumber crop looks like history for 1996. But to think that this is October 17 and no killing frost yet. It'll probably be one of these days soon.

Well, there goes the mailman and really I don't have time to write with all that work ahead. I will write more later. This leaves it later in the evening and all my company has left. Turned out to be stormy and I wonder if any of the children got wet on their way home. We have the open buggies in this area (buggies without a roof). But the umbrella helps a lot. Then winter comes, you just had better bundle up while traveling in the buggy. Winter: I always dread to see that coming up. That means keeping those stoves in high gear once more. They take more work to keep going.

Well, I had best hike to bed. We had forty-nine here for supper. It was good to see all our family together again tonight, plus the others who came. Singing and yodeling took place after supper, which always makes a relaxing feeling. Verena grilled twenty-seven pounds of pork steak for supper, which means leftovers. We had cake and ice cream plus what everyone brought in made more than a table full, which was casserole, salad, pies, brownies, cottage cheese, peas, and fruit salad.

1997
triumph (paul shetler jr.)
and tragedy (mary shetler)

JUNE 1997

June of 1997 was a typical one of early summer fun, reunions, picnics, and getting the garden in gear.

Today was the Coblentz reunion with a good attendance. Lots of food! In the afternoon, the children of Ben's brother Melvin surprised their folks for their thirtieth anniversary. A table was decorated with a three-tier cake, ice cream (mixed with 7UP and pineapple sherbet), and candy. It sure was a great surprise on them. Balloons decorated the table. It looked neat! So we all got in on the cake and ice cream.

We had a severe thunderstorm with hail during the reunion dinner. Son Amos had their new, open two-seater buggy and they didn't bring a canvas to cover it with. The whole buggy, blankets, bonnets, etc., were all wet. The rest of the buggies were well covered, but with such a wind, we were thankful all the canvases covering the buggies stayed on. Some Amish communities have the top buggies (enclosed buggies), but in this area it's an open buggy pulled by a horse. Usually at these hot summer gatherings, the day ends with a water battle, but we had plenty of rain so no one thought of it.

The garden looks wet again. Things are growing well, but some places in the area had so much hail that some of the gardens were ruined. Tomato plants broke, some vegetables were knocked to the ground. Cornfields were stripped. Some people around here used the hail in their yards to fill their ice chests, which are used to keep food during the summer. Ice is usually bought at the ice house, but the hail saved some people the trip. I wonder how we ever did without ice chests years ago. When Ben and I were first married, Ben dug a hole in the ground beside the house and set half of a fifty-gallon barrel in it. Then he made a lid to cover it. There's where we kept our food, as we had no basement. Now, however, we have a nice, cool basement and several ice chests which hold the ice and keep food fresh during the summer.

AUGUST 1997

Elizabeth's grandson Paul Jr. experienced a difficult year in 1997. He was diagnosed with a heart defect that required him to undergo a tricky open-heart surgery. While everyone was concerned Paul Jr. wouldn't make it through the surgery, his older sister unexpectedly died from a diabetic reaction.

Today, Wednesday, was Paul Jr.'s checkup day at Riley's Children's Hospital in Indianapolis, so Ben and I went with daughter Leah and family. It was so good to hear positive reports about him. He seems to be advancing in health. I just think back to the shape he was in. He seems so happy.

A "sunshine box" was taken to Paul and Leah's on Monday evening, which was a day brightener for them. They miss little Mary, but she's at peace. The early report shows that she died of diabetes. They will give more details later this week, and I will share them when I get them. They didn't know Mary was diabetic.

We've been kept busy cleaning the house where Jacob and Emma will be moving. Packing is in full gear. The house will seem empty when they leave. The whole house of Jacob's has been given a thorough cleaning with washing off walls, ceilings, and windows. Makes a good smell now. Emma and Jacob have lived with us since they got married two years ago.

It was a rushy morning, as at 8:00 A.M. a van driver picked us up to take us to Indianapolis for Paul Jr.'s checkup. Before we left, we did a huge amount of laundry. My brother Chris and his wife also went along with us to Indianapolis. It was nice to visit with them as we hardly see them. We used to be together a lot when both our children were young, but both having married children makes it different. We both have families of our own.

Well, I must get this written. Didn't get it finished the other evening. Too tired, I guess. It is Sunday evening now, I have returned from church services. The services were largely attended at one of our friend's in another district. The churches are divided into sections. A good bunch was served at noon. People came to the services from Illinois, Michigan, LaGrange and Milroy, Indiana, and Ohio. Lots of visiting was done after lunch. It was such an enjoyable day.

I am looking for some of my children to come for supper tonight. Jacob and Emma just drove in. They moved on their property yesterday. Was a busy day of moving. The house feels empty without them. But they only live a couple of miles away. Their baby, Elizabeth, will be one year old next month. I missed her this morning as to feed her fried eggs and potatoes. ✂

SEPTEMBER 1997

Paul Jr. showed remarkable resilience in his recovery. Well wishes came from readers throughout the country.

I will try to write a quick column tonight.

Paul Jr. seems to be doing great thus far. He turned two years old on Friday, August 22. That is the same birthday as our daughter Verena, who turned thirty-one. We also have son Albert's daughter Elizabeth's birthday on the same date. Verena planned a taco supper for all the family and some others on her birthday. So our shed was cleaned out and everything was held in there. Was good to all be in one big room together. Then with everyone bringing some food, the big table was well filled.

On August 20, our sweet, loving granddaughter Mary (Paul Jr.'s sister) would've turned six years old. The final report of her death hasn't been fully announced. It must've been a sad time for the family when they spent some time at the grave of Mary on her birthday in the evening. Daughter Leah and her children spent some of the day here, as it seemed such a hard day on them to think of Mary's birthday. It at times seems like a dream. We had Paul and Leah's four children with us for

Amish family suffers through weel

Editor's note to readers: *Elizabeth is taking the week off to care for family members. Her column will return in its regular story and food format next week. The following is a first-hand account of the week's events from Elizabeth's editor, Kevin Williams.*

THE AMISH COOK

It was a dark week for the Coblentz family. But it didn't begin that way. Regular readers of this column have followed Elizabeth's stories over the past five weeks as she has told about her 2-year-old grandson, Paul Jr., undergoing open-heart surgery at Riley's Children's Hospital in Indianapolis.

Paul Jr.'s parents have been deeply touched by the many cards, prayers and well-wishes that have been sent by readers across the country. Leah (Elizabeth's daughter) and Paul spent five long weeks standing vigil by their son as he waged a stoic battle for his life. There were several harrowing moments when doctors thought he would not make it, but Paul Jr. persevered. Doctors called Paul's recovery "miraculous."

Sunday, June 22, brimmed with the excitement of a new beginning. I arrived at Riley's in the afternoon to drive the Shetler family home. A tiny traveling oxygen tank sat alongside Paul Jr. in the car — the only sign of a surgery. He ate Cheerios and grinned as Leah held him on her lap. The two-hour drive back to their eastern Indiana home was filled with happiness, and a little nervousness. After all, Leah was instructed that Paul Jr. would have to have the oxygen tank at all times, receive medicine every four hours, and milk every three. He would need constant care for months as he slowly regained his strength. Still, this was better than being holed up in the hospital. With all its modern conveniences, the hospital was a foreign world to the Shetler family, accustomed to living without plumbing, electricity or cars, according to Amish beliefs.

The reunion between Paul Jr. and his two sisters — Mary and Elizabeth — and two brothers — Ben and Levi — was magical. Colorful, hand-lettered "welcome home" banners greeted the returning trio. Perhaps the person most excited to see Paul Jr. was Mary. With a beaming smile, blond hair covered by a bonnet, and a shy streak, Mary was the closest in age to Paul Jr.

Angelic little Mary — just 5 years old — picked up Paul Jr. and held him in her lap, treating him to one of her heart-melting smiles. She could speak volumes without saying a word.

On my way back to Ohio, I stopped by Elizabeth's daughter Lovina's house. Without phones, communication is slow, so I thought she would appreciate the report that Paul Jr. had arrived home safely. Lovina rewarded me with a juicy T-bone steak for the road. I savored every morsel of the sweet meat as I drove away. I watched the Amish barns silhouetted in the sun disappear in my rearview mirror, and headed back to my life of computers and cars. But images of that wonderful reunion were in my mind. Life was good, for now.

On Wednesday morning I received a message on my answering machine from Elizabeth's daughter Emma (who had run to the nearest pay phone) telling me "bad news, Paul and Leah's daughter Mary died during the night."

Mary?

I replayed my answering machine three times. Yes, she said Mary. Perhaps Emma was confused, maybe she really had meant to say Paul Jr. I jumped into my car for the two-hour trek back to Indiana.

Less than 48 hours after Paul Jr.'s triumphant arrival home, Mary became sick. Late Tuesday night, her fever rose well above 100 degrees. An exhausted Leah — worn out from five restless weeks of waiting at the hospital — alternated between giving treatments to Paul and then cuddling next to Mary on her bed, then back to Paul, and then back to Mary. At midnight, Mary — tortured by a rising fever — asked for some Jell-O. But something was going terribly wrong. Mary's condition was rapidly worsening. A non-Amish neighbor decided to take Mary to the hospital. Leah — who couldn't leave because of Paul Jr. — asked, "Can I at least carry her out to the car?" She cradled her daughter against the humid June night, stroked her blond hair, whispered a loving good-bye, and handed Mary to her husband. Leah went back inside to be with Paul Jr., to begin an uneasy vigil. Paul held Mary in his arms as the neighbor raced toward a nearby Ohio hospital. They never made it. Pulling into an all-night diner, they found someone who could give Mary mouth-to-mouth resuscitation. It was too late; Mary died.

The cozy happiness I had left two days earlier was replaced by shock. Paul and Leah seemed dazed. Numb. But the grieving couldn't get in the way of the constant care still needed for Paul Jr., and the possible threat of an unknown, deadly virus lurking around the house. Dishes were washed and sheets disinfected. There was no time to grieve.

Mary's funeral was at 1 p.m Friday, June 27. Paul and Leah looked to the one man who could provide them with some level of comfort, the one man who could make sense of the senseless: their minister. All in attendance agreed that the minister delivered an uplifting, solid sermon. "We never know who will go next," he said. The 69-year-old minister then stopped mid-sentence and sat down, asked for water, clutched his chest and slumped to the floor. But it was too late; their minister had died of a heart attack. The

# of tragedy

clergyman's brother stoically continued, finishing the sermon to a shaken congregation.

The service was again interrupted, this time by a distant rumble. Although the funeral-goers didn't know it at the time, a cousin of the Shetlers' was cleaning out her kerosene stove when a spark ignited an explosion. The cousin's house was leveled; her body has not been recovered.

The cause of Mary's death has not yet been determined. The coroner is expected to issue an official report this week. The day of Mary's death was to be Paul Shetler's first day back at work in five weeks. Paul and Leah, despite their grief, are persevering. And amid all the tragedy, little Paul Shetler continues to improve. His future prospects brighten with every passing day.

Elizabeth Coblentz *is Old Order Amish. She handwrites this weekly column by lantern light from her Indiana home. Readers with culinary or cultural questions may write to her at: "The Amish cook," c/o Oasis Newsfeatures, P.O. Box 2144, Middletown, Ohio 45042.*

five weeks and four days while Paul Jr. was in the hospital. Often, I think how their three oldest children went to school and Mary was here with me, my daughter Emma and her baby Elizabeth during the day. She must've been lonesome at times, but surely never showed it. She often took care of little Elizabeth. She would often say to me: "Since I can't take care of Paul Jr., I can take care of Elizabeth," which she did. She was such a sweet little girl; I never had to scold her. So easy to care for her.

Now that we think back, she had such heavenly eyes. She was always such a little willing worker and took care of Paul Jr. while daughter Leah did her laundry. I often think back to when the undertaker brought Mary back home to be laid to rest. I put up her hair. It was so fluffy! The same hair I took care of for all those weeks. But I know God knew best for this Angel now in Heaven. How wonderful on her part!

Well I've got tomatoes, pickles, and hot peppers to can. Should pick them tomorrow. I am so glad for daughter Verena's help, as she quit her job at the sewing factory after being there over thirteen years. She says she wants to help me with the work here at home and get a job only a couple of days a week. So it is a change in this household now that Jacob and Emma have moved out and Verena is here during the day. Verena is good help.

Thursday we want to attend a quilting at one of my nieces. She has a quilt in frame to donate at the benefit auction on Saturday, September 14, for Paul and Leah. She told me to bring my girls along, so hopefully we can all go and get some completed for my niece.

Well it is bed time. I need to hike off to bed where everyone else is resting peacefully. Thank you to all those readers for the sympathy cards, encouraging letters, money, that has been sent to us. It has been so comforting to see all those readers with such encouraging letters. A hearty thank-you to you all.

OCTOBER 1997

Most Amish don't carry health insurance. Amish pitch in to help one another when someone in their community is stricken with an illness. So a big benefit auction was held for Paul Jr.'s medical expenses.

The largest benefit auction ever in these parts was held on Saturday, September 13, for Paul and Leah (my daughter) Shelter's two-year-old child, Paul Jr. The auction was to help pay hospital and medical bills resulting from Paul's heart surgeries over the summer. Just the baked and canned goods brought in over $4,000. Paul Neuenschwander of Berne, Indiana, and twelve other area auctioneers donated their time. A hearty thank-you to all!

It started at 9:00 A.M. and sold all day till after 5:30 P.M., with two rings going on. Neuenschwander said this was the largest benefit auction he remembers ever held in the area. The number of items for sale totaled 980 with 266 buy numbers given out. Some of the high-priced items sold included a $900 handmade quilt and a $1,300 grandfather clock. Even two candy suckers were auctioned off at $75. A case of Pepsi sold for $50.

A wide variety of items donated, from livestock to homemade quilts, were auctioned off. Those attending the auction were not asked to pay a specific amount for their meal, but to donate whatever amount of money they chose. This helped raise more than $9,000. There was 800 pounds of barbecued chicken. The soups consisted of chicken noodle, vegetable, and pot pies. Coleslaw, macaroni salad, and lettuce salad were also served, along with ham sandwiches, hot dogs, pickles, catsup, mustard, and sliced tomatoes. There was also a root beer float stand and a lemonade stand. Coffee, pop, chips, and popcorn were also served. Plenty of food everywhere!

Neuenschwander, a well-known auctioneer in the area, has conducted fifteen benefit auctions for the Amish in his fifty-two years as an auctioneer, with this auction being the biggest in terms of profit. He has been inducted into the Reppert Auction Hall of Fame in Indiana. He graduated from Reppert Auctioneering School in 1945.

One of the unique aspects of Phil's auctioneering skills is that he can conduct auctions in both English and Swiss, which is the language of many of the Amish around here. So both Amish and non-Amish were able to participate in this auction. He did a wonderful job to take on this benefit auction for Paul and Leah's family.

It was so good to meet some of my readers of various places, and to think one reader even brought a gift for me. Greatly appreciated. The auction day was so beautiful, couldn't have been nicer. And to top it all off, Paul Jr. seems to be doing better and better. Thanks to God!

It was an early start for a lot of us in the morning of the auction. Baking was done all day Friday and sending help to get ready for the auction. A lot of time was spent filling cups with Jell-O (seventeen boxes). Then Saturday morning was spent making spaghetti and meatballs (twenty-quart and sixteen-quart cookers) and making a big batch of potato salad really put us on the run and the day had just begun.

So the food consisted of soups, crackers, salads, sandwiches, barbecued chicken, sliced tomatoes, home-baked bread buns, a variety of chips, Jell-O, ice cream, popcorn, coffee, pop, pickles catsup, mustard, butter, apple butter, cake, and the beverage stands. Most all was donated, except for some items from the lunch stand.

One item sold was our one-horse mower, which sold for $500. We had a horse which pulled it so well, and every Friday or Saturday I would mow our yard with it. It could get in close corners. That was around twenty-five years ago. I well remember when I was mowing the yard, daughter Leah was baking a birthday cake for my thirty-sixth birthday as to surprise me. Good old days are not forgotten. Leah was twelve years old at the time, being thirteen the next month. She was so happy to surprise me with a cake. Good old memories.

OCTOBER 1997

Elizabeth often recalled the 1957 Asian flu outbreak that struck right around her wedding. The outbreak was especially virulent, killing over seventy thousand Americans that year.

Our fortieth wedding anniversary is now history for 1997. Ben and I celebrated our special day, October 17.

Lots of memories of all those bygone years. There were happy times, and, also, sad times. We are blessed with eight children (two sons and six daughters). We had twenty-three grandchildren, now twenty-two, since the death of granddaughter Mary, who is in such a better place.

All our family (a total of thirty-eight) went out for supper for our anniversary on Friday evening at a place called the East of Chicago Pizza Company, which was planned by the children. Also for our anniversary, daughter Leah had sewed eight pockets on a dishcloth and all eight children were to fill the pockets with money; we received a nice sum. She presented it to us while eating. The owner of the pizza place also gave us a fruit pizza for our fortieth anniversary. The evening was what you would call an enjoyable and relaxing one.

Yes, forty years ago—as I have written about before—was a time when Asian flu struck our area. It was a severe epidemic! My temperature went up to 105 a week before our wedding. All our family came down with the flu except Ben, my dad, and sister. There were so many sick in the area at the time. Mother was still sick the Tuesday before our Thursday wedding. But an Amish lady came by with a home remedy called "tobacco salve" to rub into Mother's chest. It took hold right away and she immediately recovered. I often wonder how the salve was made. You had to watch to not get the salve in the stomach area, only the chest.

Daughter Leah, and her husband, Paul, had all our family invited for the following Sunday evening (October 19) for a barbecue supper, which every one of the family attended. So we all got together on Friday and Sunday evening. Paul Jr. seems to be really improving from open-heart surgery. He was two years old on August 22.

We had a light frost last night. Time of year to expect a killing frost. We still have vegetables and flowers to be taken from the garden. We made twenty-four jars of sauerkraut, a double batch of hot pepper butter, and sandwich spread the other day. We have more cabbage to make more sauerkraut.

NOVEMBER 1997

The arrival a new grandchild was always a blessing that Elizabeth celebrated in her columns. This one announces the arrival of Rosa.

The calendar has turned into November. What is our first thought when we think of November: Thanksgiving Day. Right?

The highlight of our family this week was the birth of a baby daughter to my daughter Liz and her husband, Levi. Rosa A. was born Thursday, October 30, at 7:48 P.M. weighing 7 pounds, length 19 ½ inches. She welcomes a sister, Elizabeth, and brother, Levi. Daughter Verena has been doing the housework duties until Liz recuperates for several days now, in addition to her regular job. I took care of the duties on Friday.

It is a year now that Mother has left us for that Great Beyond. God makes no mistakes. My sister had a quilting bee on Wednesday and Thursday. My folks had lived in a portion of my sister's home in their later years and what a sad feeling not to see how it used to be in the other part of the house where Mother lived. But, I guess, life goes on.

So much going on this week, it seems. Our family got together at son Amos's house on Sunday evening for his birthday. We had a barbecued chicken supper for the occasion. Little Rosa was born on Amos's birthday.

Adding to our busy schedule, daughter Lovina had a Tupperware party on Wednesday evening. And then Thursday we were helping daughter Emma prepare for church services, which is to be held in their home Sunday. Also canned her red beets for her, as red beets and pickles are always on the menu where church services are to be held. Lots of cleaning at such a time. One way the house and everything gets a thorough cleaning. It is good to take the church services in our home, but always glad when it is over again, as next day seems like a clean-up day.

DECEMBER 1997

Elizabeth's husband, Ben, worked as a carpenter for most of his working life, but in his later years he took a job working on a dairy farm.

On Wednesday, December 10, another little one joined our family. My daughter Lovina Eicher and her husband, Joe, became the proud parents of a daughter named Verena J. at 6:32 A.M., weighing seven pounds, one ounce. She joins two sisters, Elizabeth, three; and Susan, one. This put a great smile on my daughter Verena to hear it was named after her. We're helping with the household duties at present. Verena has been there mostly, in addition to working at her regular job.

Brrrr. It is cold this morning with temperatures of 23°F. Ben is at the dairy farm, Verena is at Joe and Lovina's, and Susan is washing off our kitchen walls. They needed a thorough cleaning before the holidays arrive.

Our family gathers during the holidays each year. All our children, and their children come for a day of visiting. This year it will be on January 1. So I will have more to say about our holiday preparations and plans in a later column.

A reader from South Bend, Indiana, recently wrote asking about a sandwich called "Hot Brown." Our local banker's wife saw the column where I mentioned the hot brown request earlier, and she was nice enough to send me this. Hopefully it is what you are looking for. She wrote that her uncle (by marriage) was William Brown and his family owned the Brown Hotel in Louisville, Kentucky, where this sandwich is famous. On a piece of toast, place a slice of roast turkey or ham. If desired, place a slice of tomato or a little mayonnaise. Cover the sandwich with a rich cheese white sauce. You can also place the tomato on top of the white sauce. Top the whole thing with two slices of crisp bacon.

Are you readers out there in the holiday spirit of shopping, baking, and candy making? So much took place this year for us, but much to be thankful for. Do we appreciate it enough? God makes no mistakes. What will 1998 have in store for us? Only our Heavenly Father knows. Right?

1998
a very typical year

JANUARY 1998

Elizabeth was often reflective and pensive at the start of a new year. She continued to mourn the loss of granddaughter Mary at the start of 1998.

As we take another step into the unknown future of '98, what has our Heavenly Father in store for all of us? Only God knows. So many happenings took place in '97 which were sad ones on our part. God makes no mistakes. Only He knows the purpose of it all.

We had our family Christmas gathering on New Year's Day of '98. They all were here for breakfast which count to forty people now. We sure did miss our grandchild, Mary, not being with the family. Paul Jr. was happy and lively to be with us this year as sick as he was and then God took Mary in His care. A healthy, sweet little girl. Death is so final. We all seated to eat together for breakfast. Everyone enjoys spending the morning together. Gifts were exchanged. That's when the grandchildren are ready to open their gifts. It sounds a hustle and bustle. Everyone is excited! Dinner is served with everyone seated at the table. Stuffed turkey and ham was on the menu, plus a lot of leftovers after dinner. The afternoon was spent with a variety of goodies with ham sandwiches also. It's always good to have them all together, but they all look forward to Mother's breakfast. Ha!

Paul's have church services tomorrow, Sunday, and we will have them here on January 11. Son-in-laws Joe and Jacob's are here this Saturday to help clean manure

out of the barn. What a relief to Ben to have help to get everything clean to hold church services.

Also, daughter Emma is here today, so we're doing some preparing for next Sunday. Lots of preparation takes place for church. Paul's were to have church services at their place last Sunday, but due to the death of my uncle, it was postponed for this Sunday. Verena and Emma are preparing pizza for dinner tonight, plus soup, and I reckon leftovers from our New Year's feast. Daughter Lovina didn't come today, as she was here yesterday and helped clean up from New Year's Day. Daughters Verena and Susan had to go on their job of cleaning. Paul's took us along on Christmas Day to reveal their "secret pal" of 1997, which was his folks (two-hour drive). They were so surprised to see us come. Had an enjoyable day. We also have a secret pal for 1997, but they have not revealed themselves to us yet. We can guess and guess and we miss it every year!

Levi's and Joe's both had a daughter in 1997. Such sweet little dolls! Both looked so cute on the bed beside each other on New Year's Day. Levi's had a Rosa and Joe's had a Verena. Amos's little Lovina was walking around the house and Emma's little Elizabeth was trying her best. Albert's little Emma was here also. All the grandchildren seem so precious. Naturally, Grandma would say that.

Happy New Year to all you great readers out there. I am wishing you a happy, healthy year as we enter our unknown future of 1998. You all take care; thank you for your encouraging letters and cards. ❧

FEBRUARY 1998

The big blizzard of '78, as it is referred to in the Midwest, cast a long winter shadow. Even twenty years later, the memories of the event were recalled vividly by Elizabeth.

February is half over. What is becoming of our winter? It's a nice, quiet winter morning at 8:00 A.M. with the temperature at 27°F. The ground looks a bare, brown color with no snow. Thus far, we've had a mild winter and not much of the white stuff on the ground. Our new sleighs are patiently waiting for the snow and so are we.

Twenty years ago, in '78, we could've used the sleighs most of the winter. Being snowbound was OK for several days after the big blizzard, but we were glad when the roads could be plowed open again. Was good to be snowbound together with the family. The snow was so deep, we could walk over the fences and we had a ten-foot drift in front of our shed. We could write our names on the shed roof. Was good to have plenty of fuel and those well-filled jars of food in the cellar. We were lucky that no sickness struck then. We had containers of all kinds filled with milk, as the milk hauler couldn't make it to our house with the snow-covered roads. 1978 is a winter we'll never forget.

1988 brought a drought on us. There wasn't that much from the garden to fill jars with, but we had plenty leftover from the year before. But for some it wasn't much to be thankful for. Verena and Susan went on their cleaning jobs today. Ben is at the dairy farm working. Well, we plan to help daughter Liz get ready for church today and we're ready now to go. Liz will hold services in her home this Sunday. I will finish this later.

Back in the saddle again. Want to finish this letter. We had an enjoyable day at daughter Liz's cleaning. My daughters Emma and Lovina (with their children along) joined me at Liz's to help clean. My daughter Leah wanted to come, but she hated to take Paul Jr. out in the cold. Paul Jr. now takes a couple of steps. He seems such a happy little boy. Remarkable, considering what he went through last summer. (Editor's note: For readers new to this column, Elizabeth's two-and-a-half-year-old grandson, Paul Jr., underwent open-heart surgery last summer.)

Butchering beef and pork is on the usual go at this time of year. I am done for now. After a long day, I'm ready to hit the sack!

MARCH 1998

As editor of the column, I often cringed at the sometimes graphic descriptions Elizabeth included in her writings about hog butchering. Butchering, however, is an important and celebrated custom among the Amish, so I let her write whatever she wished about it.

We had nice weather to butcher seven hogs at son Amos's on Saturday. It was actually for son Amos's and Albert's. It was our annual "butchering day." The hogs were skinned, instead of being scalded as some do it. The hogs were hung on a scaffold and cut wide open, and the stomach was removed. If the intestines get cut it is a messy job. The women like to see clean intestines come in, as they usually take care of cleaning the stomach, intestines, etc. The intestines are scraped clean twice, to be stuffed with sausage, which some parts of the meat were ground through the grinder. The women took care of the intestines, cleaned the stomachs, brains, and tongues, and the girls cut up the fat for the rendering of lard. So many people are fond of the rendering of lard for those delicious "cracklings."

Liver pudding was fried a little in the iron kettle and put in jars to process. The liver pudding is made from the head meat and bones, which were cooked in the iron kettle, and the meat taken from the bones and ground. The juice is made into what you'd call "pon hoss." The juice is cooked with flour, salt, and pepper to thicken. After it's cooled, it can be sliced and fried. This is "pon hoss." Some liver pudding is added to it when it is cooking.

The hams and side meat are usually sugar cured. Some process or fry down some of the meat. My folks would usually fry down stuffed sausage, ribs, and pork chops in an iron kettle the next day and put it in a crock and pour lard over it till covered. When used we'd get the lard-covered meat, heat it, and what we didn't use, pour it into the covered crock. Just so the meat was covered with lard. The morning is spent butchering. Then a noon meal is had and it is usually a good feast for all, with people bringing in a cooked meal for butchering day.

To think seven hogs were butchered on Saturday and really they didn't have that much help there. I must say we were done early, but our sons had an early start on it.

If I have it right, they started at 3:30 A.M. The rendering of lard always has such a good smell when putting through the lard press. ❦

MARCH 1998

Sometimes just for fun, Elizabeth's daughters would plan a "themed" supper for their mother, such as a supper where all the dishes were fried food or meat, or everything was from the garden. In this column, Elizabeth describes a "baked" supper.

We are now well into March. It has been nothing but rain, rain, rain lately. The lowlands are flooded. Everything looks muddy. We need the rain, though. The cisterns should be overflowing by now. We just can't judge the weather. Good thing we can't, I guess. Four of our married children and families arrived here for the Sunday evening meal. The girls suggested a "baked supper." So they had baked beans, baked potatoes, and baked chicken in our wood-burning stove.

They fixed baked chicken by having a pan of melted margarine melted and a pan of Rice Krispies. They dipped the chicken into the margarine and then rolled it in the Rice Krispies to coat it. Then they laid the pieces of chicken on cookie sheets to bake until golden and crispy. That's how they like it when they bake the chicken. It just seemed a different Sunday evening meal for the families, but very enjoyable. We also had buttered corn, peas, lettuce salad, cheese, peaches, applesauce, cake, pie, cookies, and also there was a homemade cheese ball and crackers and brownies.

I don't know what else they ate, but reckon they all got enough, as I wasn't feeling my best. I hurt my leg sometime ago, and it has taken a turn for the worse, so I remained seated. Good I have girls living at home yet at such a time especially.

The three last little babies born to daughters Liz, Lovina, and Emma are doing great so far (Liz has baby Rosa, Lovina baby Verena, and Emma with baby Emma). Paul Jr. is doing well so far. He had a checkup on March 12 and the doctors said he is doing great. Paul's a happy little boy. He can finally walk, just starting to take his first steady steps for the first time in his young life. Paul Jr. is two and a half years old. Who would have thought that he would have pulled through his open-heart surgery last summer at Riley's Children's Hospital in Indianapolis? God was above all. ❦

JULY 1998

Secular holidays like July 4 are observed by the Amish in low-key ways. They generally shy away from overtly patriotic demonstrations (although they are very thankful for the religious freedoms that the United States allows). Summer holidays such as Memorial Day, Independence Day, and Labor Day are spent relaxing and visiting with family.

July 4 was well spent around here. The evening before, five tents were set up in our yard for our visiting children to camp out. Daughter Liz and husband Levi cooked a ham bone and beans on the open fire in an iron kettle. Made one think of years ago when we used to cook potatoes (in their jackets) like that. Cooking outside kept the heat out of the house. Well our fun evening outside ended when a storm came up during the night so everyone took for the house. Twenty-seven in all for lodging for the night was somewhat different, but enjoyable for a holiday.

Coming in the kitchen, it looked like a lot of dishes, but being stormy outside, and us all together, the women washed all those messy containers until 2:00 A.M. The next morning, the morning of July 4, daughter Liz and husband Levi were once again the chief cooks. They made a fire with brick blocks with racks placed on top: eggs, potatoes, toast, bacon, and sausage gravy all made for a delicious breakfast. It looked so neat. Folding tables and benches were set up in the yard and all twenty-seven ate out in the open. I baked forty biscuits and also made a white gravy in the house. There were quite a few other goodies along with the morning meal.

As everyone left, we had happy memories of July 4 even with the rainout of the campout. After breakfast, a water battle took place, which our children enjoy (splashing, spraying with water). On the Fourth of July evening, we enjoyed an evening meal at the dairy farm where my husband works.

Well, I had best get dinner on the table, as I have plenty to do, seventy to eighty people here for supper tonight. Thank you for the birthday cards from you readers. Must hurry. Made some cottage cheese recently. If you have sour milk, heat it till hot—not boiling. Remove from heat. Let cool. Then strain and add salt and pepper to your taste and add some milk or cream. Surprisingly, so many who have tasted this cottage cheese say that they prefer it

SEPTEMBER 1998

"Daily diary" columns were popular with readers, describing the hour-by-hour activities in a busy Amish home. Readers often commented that Elizabeth got more done by 9:00 A.M. than most people got done in a day!

4:00 A.M. Time to get the day started off. Rainy-like outside in these early morning hours. We could use rain. Hopefully enough rain to lay the dust, especially living along a stone road. Gets quite dusty at times.

4:45 A.M. Breakfast is ready and we're seated at the table. Fried potatoes and eggs, bacon, cheese, toast, peaches, marshmallows, sliced tomatoes, hot peppers, coffee and tea (some prefer coffee and some tea), margarine, etc., are on the table.

5:10 A.M. My husband is off to the dairy farm and Susan and I wash dishes and Verena starts ironing the laundry. Plenty of it. This will just be another laundry morning, so I gather the laundry and Susan completed the cleaning.

7:30 A.M. Girls getting ready now for work. Verena quits ironing. Yesterday, they assisted daughter Leah with her cleaning. Paul Jr. seems such a happy boy. He's three years old now. We miss granddaughter Mary not being around. She would have started school this fall, but our Heavenly Father has a purpose for it all.

7:55 A.M. Girls off to work, and I'm about ready to hang the clothes on the clothesline. Looks rainy, but I'll take my try to get it hung out. A little more breezy.

8:50 A.M. The laundry hangs on the clothesline now. The sun is peeping through the clouds. Hopefully the wash will dry. Now here I sit to write this task. Whether it'll be good or bad, is for you to decide. Ha!

Wednesday, daughters Liz, Lovina, Verena, Emma, Susan, and I assisted daughter Leah with her painting, cleaning, and canned around twenty-six quarts of tomato juice. It was an enjoyable day together. Levi's was here for supper then, and Joe's and Jacob's had joined in the evening before. It is always good to see the marrieds come home. Well, this is 12:30 P.M. as I write this and I should get this in the mail today. I hope to beat the mailman to the box.

I want to can some hot peppers this afternoon. It seems such a busy time. Sometimes it's like are you coming or going? The laundry is waiting to be folded and that puts some more ironing on the list. The day has turned out to be a nice, sunshiny day. Much to be thankful for. Anyways, I am glad the laundry has dried as I write this.

OCTOBER 1998

When the first frost of the season was anticipated, Elizabeth and her daughters would harvest the last of the vegetables from the garden. It was always a bittersweet occasion: they were happy at the harvest, but sad that the garden was done for another season.

The morning of Thursday, October 22, was our first frost of the season. The temperature dropped to 33°F. So the leaves keep falling from the trees as I look out the window. I'm admiring those trees in our woods. Colors of all kinds. No artist's paintbrush could quite reproduce the scene produced by our Master Artist, Our Creator.

Yesterday afternoon, in anticipation of the frost, we dug out the carrots, celery, red beets, and picked the tomatoes, mangoes, and hot peppers. So the garden will have a rest till spring. It needs to be plowed now. So many meals that came from the garden. We'll miss those goodies once we run out. Nothing better in taste as when we get it from the garden.

The area farmers are having nice weather, which is letting corn and bean harvesting progress so well. Our crops are all harvested now.

My husband is at the dairy farm and the girls at their jobs. Here I sit to do this task of writing. The girls were home yesterday to help and visit. It always is a good feeling to see them come home. Without the family, life would seem dull. Son-in-law Jacob (daughter Emma) took ladders to the roof and cleaned out both chimneys last night. So glad that's done. Hopefully for most of winter. I'm always afraid of those chimney fires. Good we don't know our future. It seems when in need of help, it usually gets done. So we are thankful for our children and their help.

Daughters Liz and Lovina each came with their horses and buggies for breakfast. Was a chilly drive for them. Emma and her daughters also came for breakfast. We are all going to enjoy breakfast together.

What kind of a winter will we have in store? Cold, snowy? If we have plenty of snow we can go sleighing. The sleighs never were used last winter. Not enough snow.

DECEMBER 1998

This column provides fascinating insight into Amish holiday traditions. The traditions Elizabeth describes are unique to the Swiss Amish settlements near Berne, Indiana.

It is Sunday afternoon and I just got up from a nap and thought I would tackle this task of writing. A nap on a Sunday afternoon always seems good. The girls are gone for the day, so it leaves just my husband and I in this household. The marrieds probably had other plans for the day, as none showed up.

New Year's Day is coming. The children and grandchildren will all arrive here on New Year's Day for breakfast, dinner—all day till they leave for their homes in the evening. They always enjoy Mom's breakfast. Ha!

Years ago, we gathered at Grandpa's on my mom's side for New Year's Day. Memories still linger of those bygone days. They had fourteen children living (one had passed to that Great Beyond), over one hundred grandchildren, and some great-grandchildren. Some went to their house for breakfast, some for dinner. I remember we went once to be there by 4:00 A.M. to sing "The New Year's Song" to Grandpa. Grandma and Grandpa must have been very tired by evening. "The New Year's Song" was sung in various ways.

"The New Year's Song" was brought over from Switzerland and has been sung in my family ever since. My grandparents and parents sang it. On New Year's Day, the young people, sometimes up to twenty horse-drawn buggies, will stop from house to house and sing "The New Year's Song." It is sung in German: "Die Zeit isc Ankommen das friej" are the first words; the song roughly translates into: "The time has come for the New Year, God will give us a good New Year."

There are several variations of the song. We used to stay up until midnight, as my father would blow his big seashell which could be heard for miles away. Guns were also shot to shoot the old year out and shoot the new year in, which is still being done.

At Grandpa's, the grandchildren would all receive a sack of candy and sometimes a hanky or a dish of some kind in the afternoon. Their children received some nice, useful gifts. Now today we give more gifts. Probably we were more satisfied then.

It was a sad New Year's Day when all had gathered at Grandma's when Grandpa left this world. I can remember they used to have one long folding table set to eat and it had to be set and reset so all could eat. The small children ate help-yourself style. As time went on, my parents had us children home on New Year's Day, having the same traditions Grandpa's had. Now, my parents have passed on and we are taking their place to have our children home on New Year's. It's nice to have it on New Year's Day. The day just doesn't seem long enough when we are all together. We eat snacks, sing, yodel, and play games. It is very enjoyable.

1999
corn-husking bees and other occasions

JUNE 1999

The spring of 1999 found Elizabeth's youngest daughter, Susan, laid up with a broken leg. Elizabeth missed her help around the house, but the rest of the siblings pitched in to pick up the slack.

With my daughter Susan laid up because of the tri-break in her leg, I've been without her good help around the homestead. The garden just couldn't get its thorough weeding and care without Susan these past few weeks. Susan, age twenty-three, was usually out there other years, as she likes working outdoors, caring for our garden. Hopefully, one of these days she'll be on the mend.

While I was away at a wedding in Ohio, of all things our married daughters came over to surprise me by completely tending to our garden. It looks so nice! It was quite a surprise. Then one evening, our son-in-law came over and mowed most of the yard. The help of family is so appreciated!

This morning, I am doing laundry. What a good feeling to be doing the laundry out there. Just got done doing a laundry, which we do using a hand-cranked washer. Then it hangs out on the clothesline on this beautiful sunny day. Daughter Verena is completing our weekly cleaning now, and I should be getting dinner ready, but I want to hurry and get this in the mail today. It just really has to be done or I'll be late for this task of writing. But what would we do in life without a family to help us? We

just got behind with our work, but there is so much to be thankful for. Good health means so much.

My husband, Ben, went back to work Tuesday on the dairy farm several miles away. He was out of work for most of the winter with pneumonia. But his journey back to work didn't last long, as the dust, he just couldn't handle it, so it's good he's back home to help with repairs. There's always so much to be done when you live on a farm.

This week has been nice, but chilly, out there. But I like it this way for a change after our hot weather. Nicer to work outside.

The garden gives us easier meal planning with all those vegetables out there to prepare. Soups, salads, and fresh-cooked vegetables are just some of the things we can make when the garden is going good. We put out ten pounds of onions this week. Also, green onions, radishes, lettuce are so good on the menu right now. Later, we planted another couple pounds of onions, so they are coming along nice. This year we're fastening our tomato plants to bamboo sticks to keep them from leaning towards the ground. It seems to be working. This is the first time we have tried this.

AUGUST 1999

Readers of "The Amish Cook" would often send seed samples to Elizabeth, who eagerly tried them out as she writes about in this column.

Sunday, August 15, is when our first newborn, Leah, now Mrs. Paul M. Shetler, was born forty years ago. Then followed two sons and then five girls. For those who write wondering about their ages, it is: Leah, forty; Amos, thirty-eight; Albert, thirty-five; Verena, thirty-three; Liz, thirty; Lovina, twenty-eight; Emma, twenty-six; and Susan, twenty-three. Susan and Verena still live with us at home; the rest have families of their own but all live nearby.

It was hard to see our daughter Leah attend her first year in school, and more yet when our youngest daughter had her last day of school. Those years flew by. But it was enjoyable to attend parties and programs the children would put on at school. Now the grandchildren and all the other children are gearing up for the start of school around here in the coming days.

This morning I have been out in the garden. A reader in Somerset, Pennsylvania, sent me some melon seeds that she said made great big melons. They are doing great so far. The garden has been good, considering the hot, dry weather we have had. We canned some more homemade V8 juice yesterday. I should can pickles or share them with someone, as I really don't need them. We had corn on the cob last night for supper, which I had put out as a second patch. Was good eating. Yummy!

Friday evening we had a belated July birthday supper for the July birthdays. A total of one hundred family members came for a taco supper. Also some other cooked food and desserts were brought. Had such a nice evening.

This morning, daughters Emma, Lovina, and Liz, and nine grandchildren dropped in. They were attending a nearby garage sale. So we had breakfast together—very enjoyable.

Lovina's newborn son, Benjamin, was in the hospital over the weekend from being dehydrated and having gastroenteritis. He seems better now. So while he was in the hospital, we had Lovina and Joe's three little girls with us over the weekend. We took them to church services Sunday and to the hospital in the evening.

AUGUST 1999

This is a fascinating column about a vanishing tradition among the Amish: the corn-husking bee.

I am sitting outside on a beautiful day writing this. I am at my daughter Lovina's and her husband Joe's. The whole family was at Lovina's this morning for breakfast, which consisted of omelettes, bacon, tomatoes, toast, hot peppers, cake, cereal, milk, coffee, tea, and cheese.

The women are washing dishes now. The dishes, of course, are all washed and dried by hand. Makes for a big job in the morning. I am taking a break to write this column. While I am sitting outside writing this, the grandchildren are playing out here in the yard. Reminds me of short years ago when our children were at a tender age. The older grandchildren are in school right now, as the year has begun for them, but it was delayed almost three hours this morning with a thick fog in the area. It has cleared out quite nicely now.

Another memory, with the cornfields being tall this time of year, are corn-husking bees. Who knows what a corn-husking bee is? Well, we used to go to these bees years ago. There are still some people around here who have them, but they aren't as common. Menfolk take the team of horses and wagon to the cornfield when the harvest is ready to be husked. They jerk the ears of corn with the husk on and haul it back to the barn or a shed. This makes a long pile of corn ready to be husked. In the evening, the young people are invited to help husk the corn by lantern light. Benches are set up in front of the corn, so the job can be done sitting down. The husk is sorted. The clean white husk goes into a box and is put into a place to be kept clean. Then the white husk is taken into the house to be put in a big sack (size of a bed) with four openings in it. They stuff the husks inside 'til the sack is full. This is then used as a mattress. There's lots of singing and yodeling going on all evening. After this is completed, everyone goes in the house for soup, sandwiches, or something to drink. There are still corn-husking bees today, but most people use regular store-bought mattresses now—although a few still have the husk-filled ones. Lots easier and less dust with a store-bought one, I'd say.

My children have never been to a corn-husking bee, so all I can do is explain how it was when I used to go to them—it was lots of fun.

SEPTEMBER 1999

Helping family is all in a day's work among the Amish. When Elizabeth's all-important water pump broke, she had no shortage of hands willing to help.

It is Monday morning as I write this. It was a busy weekend that just finished. On Thursday, our water pump stopped on us. It would no longer throw water up from the well. What is it to be without water? So my husband got our five-gallon jug and went over to the neighbors for water. Some of the family said they would come over Friday evening to repair the pump. But, a nice surprise, son-in-law Paul and his son Ben came Friday morning and my husband, Paul, and grandson Ben got it repaired, without pay. So they had a late dinner.

I wanted them to come back here in the evening for supper, but I reckon they were too tired to come back. So the rest showed up in the evening, as promised, to repair the pump but by then it had been fixed. They did stay for supper, though.

Here for supper were: son Albert's, Joe's, and Jacob's families. Joe got the grill in gear for barbecued chicken. Only seasoning salt was added and was so good. Good eating! Then Albert told us to all come to their place on Sunday morning for homemade biscuits and gravy before church.

Amos and Nancy dropped in for Saturday night supper and stayed here for the night. What a treat to see son Amos and Nancy and seven children here for the night. We then all got up early on Sunday morning, got dressed for church services, and went to Albert's for breakfast. It was relaxing to ride in Amos's two-seated buggy on such a beautiful morning and to go to son Albert's for breakfast, where we met Joe's and Jacob's families. Paul and Leah didn't make it. After the biscuit and gravy breakfast, we headed to church, arriving there early. The only bad thing: the weather has been too hot and dry. The gardens could use the rain.

Today, daughter Leah, Lovina, Emma, and their children are here. So daughter Verena made pizza for dinner, topped with sliced tomatoes, sweet peppers, and mashed potatoes and gravy on the side. The list will go on, depending on what food we have.

We're canning tomato juice together today. Keep canning these tomatoes as to not leave them go to waste. So good to fill those jars for the long winter ahead. So glad when the children fill their jars for the winter, also. I think my jars are all full enough now, but I am sharing with children what is from my garden. It just doesn't take as much for us anymore since we are not that many at the table, although the children and their families still come home for meals, which we so enjoy.

I can't believe as I look out the window how the trees are changing color. The leaves look beautiful already. The soybean fields are really turning colors and some are being combined.

Well, dinner is ready and I must meet the rest as my daughters are here. Always good to have them here. ⚓

SEPTEMBER 1999

Elizabeth shares memories of attending public school when she was a child. Although some people unfamiliar with Amish ways may be surprised to hear the Amish Cook talk about attending public schools, it is a very common practice among the Amish. Some Amish communities have their own, private "one-room" country schools, but many send their children to public schools through the eighth or ninth grade. Coblentz attended school through the ninth grade.

It is Sunday morning and our son Albert, his wife, Sarah Irene, and their seven children spent the night here. They had put a treatment on their new floors yesterday, so it left a smell in the house. The children were so glad to have spent a night here. It makes life happier to have our children and families spend a night here.

7:00 A.M. Breakfast was on the list for all of us. We had fried eggs, potatoes, bacon, cheese, toast, cereal, and you name it. Glad when the grandchildren will eat whatever we prepare for a meal.

Noon. More family dropped in, which is a wonderful way to spend a Sunday. A dinner was prepared with barbecued pork chops on the menu. Those here for dinner were Albert's family, Paul and Leah's family, Joe and Lovina's family, and Emma and Jacob's family. Joe and Lovina's little son, Benjamin, seems to be gaining weight now. He was only four pounds, thirteen ounces at birth and later entered the hospital from being dehydrated. They caught it in time. He seems a good baby.

5:30 P.M. It is suppertime and everyone has left, except for Joe's family. We got them to stay for leftovers. So this does it for today, the last Sunday in August. Where did time go? Many happenings have taken place this year: weddings, funerals, birthdays, reunions. Happy and sad events. The grandchildren are once again back to school. We have ten grandchildren of school age. I remember when our daughter Leah started her first day of school. It was a sad feeling to see her go. And it was such a sad feeling many years later when our youngest daughter, Susan, had her last day of school. But they all liked their teachers at the public schools.

When I was at school age, we went to a two-room public school. First to fourth grade were in one room (the little side), and fifth through eighth was called the "big side." A room for lunch buckets and coats divided the two. Then we moved to a different place, which brought us to grade nine and a high school. Was so different from a country school of eight grades. At the high school, they served a noon lunch, but who could afford it? Money just wasn't that plentiful then. I remember this one school, the meal was fifteen cents where we attended, but money wasn't there. So we packed lunch buckets back then, and it wasn't anything fancy. But we enjoyed it just the same, and mother made sure we had plenty to eat. I suppose some children today would turn their nose up if they'd have to eat out of lunch buckets what we used to eat. When our eight children went to public schools where lunch was prepared, I thought it was healthier to let them eat a warm meal at school. Made less work to pack the lunch and keep those buckets clean.

A couple of readers have written to me asking if I have heard of "watermelon preserves." I have not heard of those before. Maybe someone out there has and can share.

Also, a couple of weeks ago I talked about how we drink coffee or tea around here in the morning. I like to make a tea of fresh peppermint. Some have written in asking about how to make that tea. Take leaves from peppermint and pour boiling water over it in a kettle. And turn on very low heat for ten to fifteen minutes. Do not boil. The amount of peppermint you use depends on how strong of a peppermint taste you want.

OCTOBER 1999

I once asked Elizabeth, "If your home caught fire, what is the first thing you'd try to save?" After a short pause, she answered, "The clothing." When all your clothes are made by hand, as the Amish do, the answer makes sense. A lot of labor goes into their clothing, as Elizabeth describes here.

It is a crisp 33°F this beautiful morning, and I must get this written; there's always plenty to do, it seems. Maybe it would be best to take a break from some of this work soon to visit our aged or shut-in neighbors. Good health means so much. This year has been stressful with health problems in the family, but there is also so much to be thankful for. God, the One who makes no mistakes, has a purpose for it all.

Our crops are all harvested now, crops of corn and soybeans out of our fields. Our neighbor has farmed for us since 1958. The years have a way of slipping by. Wonder what the winter will hold. Will it be cold and snowy? With plenty of snow, our horse-drawn sleighs can be used. Being snowbound too long isn't my favorite thing. I often wonder what 2000 holds? God only knows.

Sewing has been our focus the past couple of weeks. As all our clothing is made by hand and it takes a lot of time. My daughter Lovina, her children, Emma and her daughter spent the day here yesterday. Our sewing machines were in gear. The last two weeks, they've made two dresses and aprons for Susan and one outfit, almost completed, for me.

Also, they have made six children's dresses and aprons, and Emma tried her luck with cutting out and sewing a coat. Emma used to work at a sewing factory, so she knows how to put it all together. I am so glad this sewing is getting done. Two men's shirts were also made. While Lovina and Emma have been at the sewing machines working, I usually am in the kitchen preparing meals, washing dishes, and canning. It has been wonderful to spend all this time together.

Well, I must eat some breakfast. Verena has prepared it, and it smells so good. Susan is doing the sweeping. Susan has been unable to work since the tri-break of her ankle May 16, and then an infection set in. Hopefully it will heal completely soon. We just try to take one day at a time.

I continue to harvest late-season goodies from the garden. Turnips and radishes are continuing to go good. A reader in Jacksonville, North Carolina, sent me some turnip

Well, I finally got myself
...ted to write another column.
...anks
...re w
...ep th

The
...rves
...ting
...eat.
...d cr

The
...s id
...l be
...mers
Hor...
...d to
...t-cen
...ish
...ved
...chin
...ugh
...ish
...th a

Am
...der...

The horse-drawn way makes
...much more work, longer and
...re tiring days for the men-
..., but they seem to enjoy the
...shine. Hard work is enjoyed
...all.

Gardens are still doing well in
...s area. One of my nieces dug
... sweet potatoes out of the
...ound recently, and one
...ighed 9 pounds, 2 ounces.
...at giant potato came from a
...nt that I gave her.

That potato wasn't the only
...mple of huge produce from

we had an enjoyable Sunday
dinner at my brother Chris'.
Four of us sisters and our families attended. Our mother, age
82, was also present, as she spent
Saturday night at Chris'.

Barbecued chicken was on
the family-dinner menu — 90
pounds of it — with some left
over. They have a homemade
grill that can cook 30 pounds of
chicken at one time.

Later on, young folks gathered at the Amish bishop's
house for Sunday evening sing-

1/2 cu
4 table
1/2 cu
4 cups
4 cups
1/2 cu
1/2 cu

Cook
and ce
chicke
onion)
bubbly
cheese

Edito
made

ing. T
sip a
Anyo...
tend.

I'll
gathe
you r

Th
ing, a
It fe
chang
ny, w
my v
brief

Ma
cloth...
fore
have
wash
the l
wash
will

seeds earlier this season. They are coming up nicely. A hearty thank-you to people who have sent seeds. There are also a few pumpkins that need to be harvested.

NOVEMBER 1999

The Amish really rally around their own when one is sick, injured, or infirmed. This column illustrates that quality when Susan, Elizabeth's daughter, is visited at her bedside by Amish schoolchildren.

It has been a busy time around here, but when isn't it?

Daughters Lovina and Emma are here today. My husband Ben, Lovina, and daughter Verena are out in our sixteen-acre cornfield picking up corn that was left from the combine when it came through to harvest. A neighbor farms our fields for us. Emma is inside doing some sewing for me.

Daughter Liz and children were here helping yesterday when twenty-six students and two teachers from the local Amish school came in the afternoon to sing for daughter Susan. It was a big, pleasant surprise for her. She received two scrapbooks from the school. It's interesting to see all of the activity ideas one has on each sheet.

Susan hasn't been working since May, when she broke her ankle in three places, and since then infection has set in. But it is looking lots better. I keep telling her to keep looking ahead. Hopefully, she can get back to work soon. The visit from the schoolchildren cheered her up.

In the evening, we went to Lovina and Joe's house. Joe, Jacob (Emma's husband), and Levi (Liz's husband) put up a ceiling at Joe's. It will make it warmer for the winter.

We've had several light frosts recently, so the garden will soon be history for 1999. I dug some of the carrots and was surprised that in the dry and hot weather they did so good. Celery is still out there and some red beets, cabbage, tomatoes, radishes, turnips, and Chinese cabbage. So I must go get these in before our killing frost.

Some readers have asked what Clear Jel is, which I have mentioned in this column. Clear Jel is used around this household as a thickening in salsas, pie fillings, etc. Clear Jel is used in much the same way as cornstarch is, as a thickener. Clear Jel is available at grocery stores.

NOVEMBER 1999

The Amish typically celebrate secular holidays such as Thanksgiving in a subdued way. Still, it's an occasion for a family gathering and a hearty meal, so the day is usually marked in some way.

The highlight of Wednesday, November 17, was when a baby boy was born to daughter Emma and her husband Jacob. He weighed six pounds, ten ounces and arrived at 10:08 P.M. They named the newborn Jacob. He's greeted by two sisters, Elizabeth and Emma. My daughters Verena and Susan are assisting her with household duties, and sometimes so is Grandma. Ha! For us, this makes twelve grandsons, but the girls are still ahead with eighteen. That makes thirty grandchildren, twenty-nine living. Granddaughter Mary is at peace.

What's the next holiday on the calendar? Thanksgiving Day! When I was younger, we always used to recite the poem: "Over the river and through the woods to Grandfather's house we go, the horse knows the way to carry the sleigh over the white and drifted snow." Doesn't this poem sound as if those were the good old days? They were good, although times could have been easier back then.

We have lots to be thankful for when Thanksgiving Day arrives each year. Especially when we think about the struggles those early Pilgrims endured long, long ago. We'll never know the terrors that they braved years and years ago. Shouldn't we be so thankful to our Heavenly Father for our bounteous harvest of 1999? And yet, too often, we forget to be thankful for our plentiful harvest.

On Thanksgiving day, we will have turkey on the menu. Also on the list, chicken and ham, along with sweet potatoes, pumpkin pie and pumpkin bread. Pumpkins are taken from the garden, and they can be cooked and processed. Cookies and bread also can be baked using pumpkin. Sweet potatoes with butter, salt, pepper, and brown sugar are another favorite around here on Thanksgiving day.

Family gatherings or weddings are usually on Thanksgiving day. A twenty-pound stuffed turkey is usually put in the oven for whenever some of the family members come. Often we have our garden plowed on Thanksgiving day, so we'll see what the weather holds. Last year, we attended a wedding at La Grange, Indiana, of the daughter of my niece. It was an enjoyable day, although the garden did not get plowed. It was so good to be with family members that we don't get to see too often. This Thanksgiving Day will be spent with family coming and going from our home. Lots to be thankful for. Lately, I think of what or how one would feel being alone in a house when a partner has gone to that Great Beyond. So we take one day at a time. God makes no mistakes and who will do the judging someday. Right?

I'm wishing all you readers out there a happy Thanksgiving day in 1999 and many more to come. What will 2000 hold? Only God knows. Let's keep Him in our thoughts and prayers. ❧

DECEMBER 1999

A typical day for Elizabeth began at 4:00 A.M., a time that many non-Amish still consider the middle of the night. Elizabeth often got more done by 6:00 A.M. than I'd sometimes get done in an entire day.

It is 4:00 A.M. as I write this, and the thermometer reads 22°F outside. Cold, but we expect all kinds of weather in December. We had snow flurries yesterday.

Thanksgiving day was a workday for us, preparing for having church services here in our home in December. The manure was hauled from the barn to our garden. Trim was put around our new windows. Six old windows were replaced. Still a few windows to have the trim yet, and our garden was plowed for spring of 2000.

Toward evening, our son Albert took our team of horses and manure-spreader to plow their own garden and some of their yard with the assistance of son Amos. We had fried chicken and also chicken and dressing in the oven for both meals on

Thanksgiving day. A change from turkey. Those assisting us on Thanksgiving Day were sons Albert's, Joe's, and Jacob's families. Son Amos's family also came for supper and got in on helping Albert with his plowing. Daughter Leah and her husband Paul were busy, as they were having church services in their home the Sunday after Thanksgiving. He also was occupied with making a new buggy box to be put on our new running gears.

On Sunday, we were able to drive to Paul's for church services in our brand new buggy. Paul put a lot of labor into it. We are so pleased with it. Daughter Liz and husband Levi also were preparing for church services to be at their place the first Sunday in December. So it was a busy Thanksgiving Day!

Levi will be another year older Sunday. Some of the family plans to help with their cleaning today in preparing for church services. So many of the family are having church services in December. Makes for a busy month, so everyone is helping each other clean their houses and prepare food.

Our family Christmas gathering will be held this year on New Year's Day of 2000. That is when the family is together here for breakfast, dinner, and supper—all day. One day of the year we do this and everyone looks forward to it. Tables are set up for the forty-five of us as to eat all at one time for both meals. Yes, we can say forty-five as of now, but lots can take place by then. We've learned to take one day at a time.

To the reader who asked about "schnitz pie," I thought you might be referring to dried apples, sliced thin. Grandpa did this. Out in the orchard, a small tin shanty-like structure with lots of trays in it is where they dried their apples. This was used before any processing in jars was done. I guess back then they dried most of what is processed now.

Several have written asking about homemade V8 juice. We add anything to ours, such as tomatoes, onions, carrots, hot banana peppers and jalapeño peppers, sweet peppers, celery, and cabbage. At times, we add green beans. Season with salt after it is in the jars. I make my own recipe when it comes to V8. Sometimes it is really hot to drink, but good in wintertime when some have colds. If they can drink that hot it makes them feel better. Some process it very hot, others not so hot.

DECEMBER 1999

Although the Amish hold their church services in members' homes, it is not uncommon for people to "swap" service Sundays. For instance, if there is an illness or a new baby, something that would make the hosts unable to hold services that week, they'll simply trade turns with someone else. A "quid pro quo" quickly develops among church members.

This is a cold Wednesday morning, December 23, at 4:00 A.M. The temperature is at eight above right now. I hope it warms up, as we plan to go help at Joe's today. We will wash off walls and floors, and help them get their house ready for church. Church services are to be in their home in January of 2000.

Meanwhile, my daughters Liz, Lovina, and Emma were to our house yesterday to help get ready for church services, which will be here on Sunday, December 26. As I mentioned in last week's column, we are having services here for Emma and Jacob. My daughter Emma and husband Jacob were going to have them in their house this Sunday, but with their new baby, we offered to have it here for them.

By the time you readers read this, Christmas will be over. What will Christmas hold? God only knows. It would be nice to see those snowflakes fall and cover the ground at Christmastime.

On Sunday, we tried our new hand-crank ice-cream freezer, which was a birthday gift to Ben and I. So homemade ice cream was on the menu for supper. The hand-crank ice-cream maker was a gift from Joe's and Jacob's families.

Speaking of Joe, he turned another year older today. So, on Sunday, we were making ice cream in celebration of his birthday. In addition to homemade ice cream, chicken was grilled and barbecued for a special birthday dinner. Also on Sunday, son Albert and his family came here to join us for the occasion. You never know who from the family will arrive. So we had mashed potatoes, gravy, chicken, and the homemade ice cream for dessert.

We had not made homemade ice cream in quite some time. It was delicious, and we plan to make some at our family Christmas gathering. Albert's family and daughter Leah also will bring some homemade ice cream. Everyone thought the ice cream was very yummy, using cream, milk, salt, sugar, and vanilla. It's my own recipe. Our family Christmas gathering is January 1.

The two stoves are in full gear this morning. Several stoves help keep our home warm in the winter. The cookstove takes only wood fuel and is located in our kitchen, and the much larger Hitzer (living room stove) takes wood and coal. So there's extra work with those stoves. You have to keep fuel in them and empty those ash pans. You also have to see that the chimneys are in good working order, as to not have a chimney fire. Those scare me.

Our cookstove ash-pans only have to be emptied about once every five to six weeks when in use. The cookstove does a lot of help in wintertime. You can prepare a meal, you can bake with it, and there is always warm or hot water in its attached tank. The tank needs to be kept filled with water. Our kerosene heater hasn't been in use thus far. We only use it when extra heat is needed.

We had a nice fall and only took a turn for colder weather this week. Last week, it was warm and rainy. The stoves do a good job of keeping the place warm during winter. Well, I must get some breakfast, as the girls are not home. So it's just for hubby and me, which a cup of coffee would do. Ha! Yesterday, daughters Lovina, Emma, and children were here for breakfast and here to help for the day. So the girls made a breakfast casserole and had fried potatoes, oatmeal, toast, bacon, cheese, bananas, and coffee.

2000s

2000
good-bye, ben

JANUARY 2000

With such large families, sudden and tragic funerals are inevitable. In the winter of 2000, one of Elizabeth's nieces was killed in a buggy accident. So she headed to the Amish settlement of Seymour, Missouri, to attend the funeral.

It is Monday morning, January 17, at 8:00 A.M., and we are staying overnight in Greenville, Illinois, as we arrived last evening. We want to attend the funeral tomorrow of my niece, who was killed on Friday. She leaves her husband and a large family behind to mourn in Seymour, Missouri. That is where we are headed. There is a large Amish community there. They moved from our area of Indiana to Seymour around a year ago. It was quite a shock to receive the sad news Friday evening. Death is so final. We will find out more details when we get there later today. Ben is along with me, as is my daughter Verena, two of my sisters, their husbands, and a few others in our extended family.

The weather has been good to travel. Hope it stays this way as we travel back home, either tomorrow night or Wednesday morning. Glad for our van driver, as he seems good at the wheel. One of my daughters (Liz) and family were to start out to Seymour Saturday evening. So we hope to see them when we arrive at the residence of my niece. Jacob's family is staying at our house while we are away to do our barn chores, etc. I reckon my daughter Susan is glad they are staying. When we left yesterday from home on this sad-occasion trip, daughters Leah, son Albert, daughter Lovina, Emma, and all their families were at our home for Sunday dinner.

So plenty of people were there to bid us good-bye. Son Amos's family was at our place Saturday evening, also, before we left. So we quickly had sandwiches, chips, etc., put out before they went home. It was good to see all our children and families before we left.

This will be our first visit to Seymour, Missouri. Ben and I had plans to visit my niece and family some time this year, but didn't expect to make the trip this soon. Our family enjoyed the dinner today our children packed for us before we left. Son-in-law Joe barbecued chicken, ribs, and ham on the grill, while us women prepared mashed potatoes, gravy, dressing, buttered corn, buttered peas, and the list goes on. Thanks goes to Joe for barbecuing the meat.

We'll probably be at the viewing of my niece today. My niece was eighteen years old when she lost her mother (my sister), and now again her oldest daughter is eighteen and now she's gone to that Great Beyond. My niece leaves behind her husband and thirteen children. The two oldest boys are married.

Monday evening I'll quick write a note here and share more next week. But I found out this death could have been prevented. A motorist plowed into my niece's

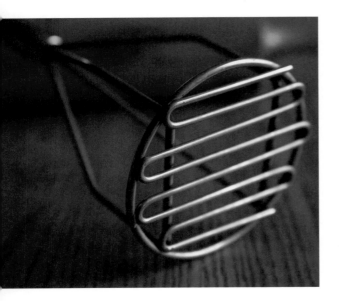

horse-drawn buggy. She was riding in the buggy with her son. Her son received only minor injuries, but the horse also was killed. It happened a short ways from their home. Every Friday she took her boy to a doctor to be treated to help with his muscular dystrophy. Oh! So shocking. She's my oldest niece on my side of the family. But God makes no mistakes. Only He knows the purpose why she's in His care now. She is so badly needed with a large family.

FEBRUARY 2000

Elizabeth writes about the grief brought on by the untimely death of her niece. Elizabeth had no way of knowing when she wrote this that she'd soon be dealing with a deep grief much closer to home.

Last week, I wrote about the untimely death of my niece, who was killed when a motorist struck her buggy outside Seymour, Missouri. She leaves behind a husband and thirteen children. We just got back from Missouri where we attended the funeral. Our thoughts are for the bereaved husband and thirteen children of my niece. She will be badly missed by her friends and relatives. She was a niece who always thought of us by sending a card and letter for Christmas each year and never forgot my birthday. My niece recently told her oldest daughter, age eighteen, "Now you are the age I was when I lost my mother." History repeats itself. A total of eight hundred people attended the funeral. Sixty horse-drawn buggies led a procession to the graveyard. God is never wrong.

FEBRUARY 2000

If it's February, it must be time for another butchering day column!

Butchering of beef and pork seems to make its rounds at this time of year. Butchering our meat is a tough job, but it allows the family to be together for a day of good, hard work. And it provides us with our meat for a long time. It was a time of busy butchering this past week.

We helped our daughter Lovina with cutting up four quarters of beef Thursday. In all, eighty-one quarts of beef were processed, and the rest was put through the grinder for hamburger. Fresh beef can be used for so many things around here. I like to make a beef stew with those leftover bones. It makes such a good stew. The processed beef is great to use for dishes like beef and noodles or beef and gravy. Also, I like to chop up the beef real fine, add ketchup to it, and heat it. This makes such good sandwiches. We like to just heat up the beef chunks for the evening meal with potatoes. It seems a soothing meat, so fresh.

On Saturday, it was pork. We helped our son Albert butcher three hogs with the help of other family members. The men do the cutting, and the women do the cleaning. We used to scald the hogs, but now we skin them. By skinning them, there is no water to be heated in the butchering tank. The hogs are hung on scaffolding and cut wide open to the stomach. It becomes a mess if the intestines are accidentally cut, which then requires washing off the area with water. The women like to see clean intestines, as they will be stuffed with sausage later. The women also cleaned the stomachs, tongues, and brains. Nothing goes to waste.

Rendering lard afterwards, we have those "cracklings," some are so fond of. Liver pudding, produced from the head meat of a hog, is also made. This meat is cooked soft in a big iron kettle. We took the meat off the bones and put it through the grinder. Liver pudding has a good taste; many like it for breakfast.

Then the last of the butchering to be done in the iron kettle is "pon hoss" as we call it. This is made with the juice from the bones that are cooked in the kettle. It is made with a thickening to the juice and some liver pudding added to it. We also season it with salt and pepper. We usually use flour but some use cornmeal. After it is cooked and thickened in the iron kettle, it is put into loaf pans to chill.

When chilled, cut slices and fry in a skillet. At times, a little lard is added if it's not greasy, but at times no lard is added. Fry 'til golden brown. We like ours sliced on the thin side to fry. There are some who put it into jars and process to open later.

The hams, bacon, pork chops, ribs, and tenderloins are taken care of afterward. Some are processed and some sugar-cured. After all the mess is completed, the iron kettles, saws, knives, sausage stuffer, and grinder are washed clean.

Everyone is then rewarded for their work with a delicious, noon meal. After the hog butchering was completed, the menfolk came to the residence to butcher a bull, as we had son Amos's bull here, and also, put Joe's beef through a grinder, as their grinder was not in working order. So this was a long, full day of working together. Sons Amos and Albert each will go in half with the beef. So they will both have lots of beef to care for this week.

Today, February 17, my husband is 3,588 weeks old. Ha! I like to see him when he reads this!

Monday, we attended the funeral of an aged friend. In the afternoon, when we arrived back home, I quick got the laundry done. We had some snowy, icy roads, which were very treacherous on the way to the funeral, but by the way back it had improved.

My grandson Ben, age sixteen, son of Paul and Leah Shetler, is continuing to recover from his broken ankle. This accident could have been prevented. He has endured a lot of pain since. He will be laid up for some time. His younger brother, Paul Jr., seems to be doing well.

Yesterday morning, we had six of our grandchildren here while their mothers went into town. All of them are under age five. I reckon that's what these grandmothers are for: to help these young mothers. They enjoy it here, especially mealtime. Ha!

MARCH 2000

Chimney fires, especially late in the winter, are just one of the many hazards the Amish deal with on a day-to-day basis.

I've got the laundry ready to go onto the clothesline. So hopefully it will dry out nicely, as I want to iron today. I hope everyone out there is in good health. This past Sunday was spent at Joe and Lovina's. Lovina prepared a good noon meal with grilled steak on the menu. Others there were Paul and Leah's family, son Albert's family, and Emma and Jacob's family.

Their evening meal guests were son Amos's family, Levi's family, Jacob's family, Ben and I, and our daughters. It was another good meal. Sons Amos's and Levi's had come to our house for supper and discovered that we were not home. So they went to Joe and Lovina's and found us all gathered there. In fact, Joe's family had all our family there on Sunday at one meal or the other. Grandson Ben, son of Paul's family, gets around with the aid of crutches after having his ankle broken February 4. He had surgery on February 8. I am glad he could be at Joe and Lovina's on Sunday.

Saturday evening, son Albert's family had quite a scare with a chimney fire. Chimney fires are a danger this time of year, as creosote builds up after a long winter. Neighbors had called out the fire department, but the call was canceled as they quickly got it under control. A couple of their neighbors came to their rescue. Some items were already being carried from the house in preparation for fire. Their basement and breezeway got the smoke. But how lucky the house still stands and the smoke mess can be cleaned.

The crocuses have found their way through the ground. A beautiful scene to see that yellow color in the brown-dirty ground. The weather has turned so warm, we were out in the yard without shoes on. It felt so good to be out in that warm air. We took advantage of it and did a huge laundry.

It's amazing how many sympathy cards we have received from readers after the loss of my niece in Seymour, Missouri. I want to thank all you readers out there for sending and taking your time to write. Also, a thank you to the readers who have been sending recipes.

To the Keechobee, Florida, reader (Where is Keechobee?): I have never heard of "Flan with a caramel-flavored juice in the bottom." Sorry!

To the Homosassa, Florida, reader who requested a green tomato pie recipe: I make mine using the following ingredients: 6 green tomatoes, sliced; 1 apple, thinly sliced; 1 cup sugar; ¾ teaspoon cinnamon; 1 tablespoon lemon juice. Arrange half of the fruit in the piecrust. In a separate bowl, mix the other ingredients. Then sprinkle over the fruit in the piecrust. Add the rest of the fruit. Put the top of the piecrust on. Bake at 400°F for 35 minutes. Makes one pie.

To David in Indianapolis about how I make my chili. I put 1 quart or more of canned sausage in a 4-quart kettle and 1 large onion and fry together until golden brown. Then I add 1 pint water and, in a separate bowl, make a thickening of 3 tablespoons flour with water. Add it to the kettle. Add tomato juice and kidney beans as you prefer. Season with salt, pepper, and chili powder to your taste. I also add 1 tablespoon or so of brown sugar. Don't really have a recipe for it. I just sort of make it the way I know how. Everyone in the family seems to eat it very well. They like it with crackers. I like to use the canned sausage better than the hamburger. Good luck!

MAY 2000

Some Amish don't think coloring eggs should be part of Easter, but Elizabeth just viewed it as harmless fun that didn't take away from the religious significance of the day.

It is the last Thursday of April, and it seems to be a nice, sunshiny day so far.

Daughters Lovina and children, and Emma and children, are spending the day here. Yesterday evening, we washed off walls inside and scrubbed the board fence outside. The start of repainting that fence took place. Daughters Liz and Emma and their children spent the day yesterday. Also, we sewed some dresses, and aprons were next on the list. It was a very busy day.

So Emma and Verena are painting the rest of the board fence today, which will make for a better appearance. We had it painted around eight years ago. It must have been good paint as it still didn't look bad as yet.

Lovina is doing some sewing for me now. Lovina and her husband Joe came here after supper last night. Lovina and Joe's three girls fell asleep while they were here, and also Jacob's two oldest girls fell asleep in the evening. So instead of carrying them to the buggy and going home, we decided we would tuck them five girls into bed here. It was cute to see those little girls in a peaceful sleep. They all slept well, being at Grandma and Grandpa's. Everyone enjoyed a good breakfast in the morning.

Daughter Susan went to work today at the factory in the nearby town. Glad she is back to work, as she had a bad 1999 with her broken ankle. She enjoys the work at her place of being employed.

Easter was late this year. Easter was always a time to think of coloring eggs with the children. But that is a thing of the past, now that our children are grown, although I took a notion to color some with the help of Susan this year. We did it for the grandchildren.

Good Friday was spent at Levi's home, so I helped their children with the coloring of eggs. They were so thrilled to color those eggs. Thought we'd color some in case some of the married children would come home for meals over Easter time.

Memories linger of when Mother would fry eggs with the meals when company came on Easter Day. She'd fry eggs for whoever could eat the most, when us children were all at home.

The twins, Arlene and Marlene, daughters of son Amos, turned seven years old this past week. Time has a way of slipping by. I remember well what an exciting morning to receive word to have a set of twins in the family.

Last night, son Albert's and three sons with three of their school buddies took a hike through the woods and came here for a while. It is about one mile across the fields and woods between our houses.

MAY 2000

Buggies aren't much different than cars in that they can experience mechanical mishaps also. Elizabeth describes a frightening one in this column.

This has been such a beautiful day. The day started off with plenty to do. My daughter Verena cleaned all the windows in and out. Susan and I did a big laundry of plenty of bed blankets, all the curtains, five rocking chair covers, bed sheets, pillow cases, and you name it. Being such a drying, sunshiny day outside, we really took advantage of it. We had a late dinner because we were trying to do all we could before noon, and the time just didn't wait on us. Time went on.

In the afternoon, curtains were hung back up, which made for such a good appearance again. The rocking chairs and couch covers were put back on. What a clean feeling to see everything back in its place. Also, the beds were all made, with sheets smelling so crisp and fresh. Some winter coats were washed and will be back in place 'til next winter. The lanterns were given a good washing this morning, which takes some work. And our screens were washed and put on the windows. There are so many spring duties to be done. It seems endless, but how can one complain when in such good health?

It's around 4:00 P.M. as I write this, and we're going to Joe's as they're putting up a fence. So we must get on the road. Will write more later. It's time to go. This is Thursday morning now and soon the mailman will be here and I must finish this so I can beat the mailman to the box. Daughter Liz and children arrived this morning, so it has been nice having them here for a visit. Daughter Lovina and her kids also stopped by. Verena took Lovina's horse-drawn buggy to go after daughter Emma and her children, to bring them here for a visit. But, it so happened about a half mile from here the wheel broke from the axle of the buggy, which keeps the horse under control and the buggy hooked to a pole. It was scary for her. Lucky we have people out there to be helpful at such a time. She was shook up afterwards of the ordeal. She came back home and took daughter Liz's buggy then to get Emma. Glad it didn't happen when Lovina and the children were in the buggy on their way here. It was so good to see that nobody got hurt. The incident disturbed the morning hours, but sewing is taking place now and the sprouts took over with the winter potatoes, so the girls will take care of that project.

Breakfast was served to daughters Liz and Lovina and all their children. It consisted of fried eggs, potatoes, bacon, cereal, toast, cheese, sliced tomatoes, and coffee. The children also always enjoy their soft ice cream, which wasn't all eaten last night, being held in the ice-chest overnight.

may 2000

by Kevin Williams

This was a terribly tough column to write, but I knew Elizabeth was in no position to pen a column during this week.

Benjamin A. "Ben" Coblentz, sixty-nine, passed suddenly from this earth Saturday. Ben's wife, Elizabeth, who pens this weekly column, is still coping with the shock and grief.

I was nineteen years old in 1991, when I first pulled into Elizabeth's driveway one warm July afternoon. From that chance encounter, "The Amish Cook" column was born. I've been Elizabeth's editor ever since, and during that time, the Coblentzes have become practically family. I share in their weddings, births, and, sadly, deaths.

During my years of visiting the Coblentzes, I've been blessed to know Ben. Rare is the couple who remains affectionate and loving after forty-three years of marriage. But Ben and Elizabeth were that living rarity. Ben would affectionately tease Elizabeth (he called her "Lizzie") at the dinner table, and Elizabeth would give back as good as she got. Ben was Elizabeth's calm center. Elizabeth is the emotional one, but she was balanced by Ben's pragmatic peace. They were the perfect balance.

With a long white beard and weathered hands from decades of working as a carpenter, Ben was ever the supportive spouse. In a busy household of children and grandchildren, Ben would sit quietly in his rocker, with a soft smile and gentle demeanor, watching it all.

Ben and I were from two different worlds, yet I felt very close to him. I don't milk cows or cultivate the craft of carpentry as he did. I'm a city boy, more comfortable in my world of computers and cars. Yet we always found things to talk about. We could talk about baseball. We were both avid Cincinnati Reds baseball fans. I would visit with the latest news of trades or home runs and a smile would flicker across his face.

He would show me his purple martin houses or patiently let me follow him into the barn as he did the afternoon chores. It's hard to measure how much any one person impacts our lives. A life is a portrait comprised of brushstrokes from the many people we pass. I look back at the still incomplete portrait of my life, and some of what I am, are the brushstrokes of Ben. For that, I'll always be grateful.

Ben helped teach me to savor simplicity: the pleasure of a purple martin, the quiet calm of sitting on a rocker by a flickering fire or scanning the starlit sky on a crisp, clear January night. In our increasingly material twenty-first-century society, people measure their happiness by tangible things they can touch. For Ben, happiness could be found in the intangibles, in what he could not touch: a bird in flight, a grandchild's innocent heart.

Ben also was my secret ally. Editors often have trouble getting their writers to adhere to deadlines, and, Elizabeth is no different from any other columnist. I like for Elizabeth to send her columns to me on Thursdays. If Thursday morning came, and the column had not been sent, Ben would be nudging Elizabeth out of bed early, envelope and stamp in hand, reminding her to write. Ben was very proud of Elizabeth's column.

The Coblentz farm is my retreat, a place I go to escape the noise of the sometimes rude world we live in. I stand on their porch and savor the pastoral peace of a landscape unbroken by power poles and listen to the rhythmic cadence of a passing horse's hooves. The peace seems to lend itself to infinity, an unchanging land, frozen in another century. If forever exists, it would be found on an Amish farm, where change is glacial. But even on an Amish farm, things change. Quickly.

The Coblentz family has been plunged into sudden sadness with the unexpected passing of Ben from a heart attack. The heart attack followed a small stroke the week before.

Adding insult to injury, Elizabeth, her eight children, and some spouses, were riding in a van to the hospital, following the ambulance, when another van turned into their path. The impact totaled the van and sent Elizabeth into the windshield. Fortunately, no one was seriously injured. Elizabeth is now nursing a broken heart and some bruised ribs.

Ben's gentle soul lives in his sons, Amos and Albert. If the legacy a loved one leaves is his or her children, then Ben can look down from Heaven with happiness. All of his eight children are wonderful. In the baseball terms he loved, he's eight for eight. That's the best average one can ask for.

MAY 2000

This was the second installment in the coverage of Ben's death, which was equally difficult for me to write.

I turned on the emergency flashers and slowed to a crawl. A column of charcoal-black horse-drawn buggies clattered on the road in front of me, moving slowly and solemnly. It was the surreal union of two worlds, as my car joined the funeral procession of buggies. I was honored and deeply touched to be invited to the private cemetery ceremony where Ben A. Coblentz was laid to rest Tuesday, May 23, 2000.

On any other day, I would be tapping my fingers impatiently on the dashboard, waiting for the slow-moving vehicle to get out of my way so I could speed to my destination. Instead, I was forced to take a deep breath and watch the peaceful, pastoral Indiana countryside move by like a slow-motion movie. Century-old barns, gently burbling creeks, and well-manicured meadows were a reminder that there was once another time: a time when things were simpler, were quieter. But it's still there. We just never look.

I originally wanted to write more detail about Ben's funeral. But as I stood in the cemetery, watching the Coblentzes grieve and dealing with my own sadness, it seemed to me these were intensely private moments. It's privacy and anonymity that have helped the Old Order Amish keep the hands of time turned back to a simpler society. So I'll leave the details, if she wishes to share, to Elizabeth when she returns to writing this column.

There was a visitation Monday, May 22, and a funeral Tuesday. My parents came with me to the visitation, as they, too, have grown close to Elizabeth and Ben through the years. I also brought my girlfriend. I was happy to have company, as this would have been a lonely journey without them.

Hundreds of people filed past Ben's open casket, a testimony to how many he touched with his gentle spirit. When the crowd had cleared Monday night, I turned back to say good-bye to Elizabeth one more time and, not watching where I was going, tripped over a chair. Uninjured, but embarrassed, I looked back and saw Elizabeth laugh. It was nice to see her smile. The Coblentzes are accustomed to my clumsiness.

Ben and Elizabeth were inseparable. After forty-three years of marriage, I was in awe of their playful affection and genuine love for one another. Ben delighted in recalling the day they first met on a crowded buggy ride. They both always said how fast those years seem to fly. To them, their wedding seemed like it was last year.

I found the announcement Elizabeth wrote about her own wedding, in her usual simple, no-frills style. The following appeared in an Amish newspaper in 1957:

Oct. 21, 1957: Nice and cool weather. Lots of flu and colds are around. Different schools are closed on account of the flu. Thursday, Oct. 17, was the wedding day of Ben A. Coblentz and Elizabeth Graber (the writer). They were married by Bishop Mose M. Miller from Indiana.

Now it is a funeral being written about.

The funeral service was spoken all in German, so I didn't understand much. Still, it was moving just the same. The crowd was so large that two separate services had to be conducted, one in the Coblentz's home, the other in a shed outside. Elizabeth seemed to be doing very well, surrounded by the support of her family.

I sometimes lie awake at night, wondering what life means, wondering why we are put here on this earth, only to have it one day abruptly end. But I think forty-three years of love and devotion that burns as brightly at the end as it did at the beginning may be much of the meaning. It's one of the best answers I can come up with.

On the way to the visitation, a storm lashed my windshield with driving rains and a wind-whipped westerly. But as the city melted away in my rearview mirror, shafts of sunlight poked through the clouds bathing the surrounding fields in a golden light. Approaching the Coblentz farm, a sea of buggies greeted the eye. Ben would have been amazed. A colorful rainbow arced across the eastern sky. Somewhere, I'm sure, Ben was smiling.

JUNE 2000

This was Elizabeth's first column after her husband's death. It was a touching, teary tribute.

This is a very beautiful, sunshiny Thursday morning, and I guess I should get this column in the mail today.

Daughters Leah, Lovina, Emma, and their lovely children, came for the day today. Now the garden is getting a good weeding. What would I do without my family for support, especially as I write this letter with tear-stained eyes? It's so hard to put this into words, but we must keep our faith from our Heavenly Father above. "He" will help us in such a time of our great loss, very great loss. It just doesn't seem this has taken place with my dear, beloved, calm, patient husband, Ben. Ben's gentle soul lives on in our broken hearts.

Such a wonderful, supportive husband and father to all of us. Lots of memories linger on, as we have to go on. Some readers, who lost spouses, told me in their letters to keep on going: don't sit and think. What would I do without the support of my two daughters, Verena and Susan, here at home? Verena takes over the chores, unless some of our married children are here. Our married children also have been so supportive. Daughter Liz and her children spent the day here yesterday, and son Albert's family was here for supper yesterday. Joe's family came later in the evening and stayed for the night. So we're never alone, as it seems we're overnight someplace or someone in the family stays here overnight. How supportive!

I am so glad Ben didn't have to suffer long. God's ways aren't our ways. He's the One who never made or makes a mistake. He had a purpose to take Ben away from pain and especially, worries, in this troublesome world we have to live in.

On Sunday, May 14, we got up early to start the day off. Ben did the morning chores as usual. And he then got the horse harnessed and hitched up to our new buggy, which he had purchased not too long ago, had breakfast, and then we went on to church services.

At lunch after services, Verena came and said: "Dad doesn't feel too good." So I got up and went to the table of men where he was seated. I asked, "Ben, aren't you feeling good?" And he just mumbled something and we saw right away there was something wrong. Our son Albert and son-in-law Paul got up from the table and carried Ben on a blanket into the yard. Someone else ran to a phone to call for help. Ben was admitted to a hospital, where they determined he had a stroke. But Ben's recovery was quick, and he was able to go home after an overnight stay. He came home and seemed alert. He walked out to the barn on Wednesday morning and again on Thursday morning and was always worried to see that the cow got milked. He was always the one who, at 4:00 A.M., got out of bed to milk the cow. Such a nice week that God spared with us, that final week. Because on Saturday morning, May 20, I fed him two eggs, toast, two cups of homemade garden tea, and some applesauce. He seemed OK. But all at once, he began to breathe hard.

EMS was called again, but life had fled him before they came. So peaceful to see his eyes set on me and feel he was gone. Such a terrible feeling to lose a good husband. So many memories linger on. We had many good days together since we were married on October 17, 1957. Born to this union were eight lovable children: two sons, Amos and Albert; and six daughters, Mrs. Paul (Leah) Shelter, Mrs. Levi (Liz) Wengerd, Mrs. Joe (Lovina) Eicher, Mrs. Jacob (Emma) Schwartz Jr., and Verena and Susan at home with me. How thankful to have them with me.

God has a purpose for it all. We must adjust to a different life. It sure has been different. Can't explain what it's like without my dear husband, Ben. Also, we have twenty-nine grandchildren. We had thirty, but dear little Mary left at five years old for a better home.

The funeral for Ben was on Tuesday, May 23, with around seven hundred people attending. Everyone was invited for a noon lunch as usual. There were twelve tables set up for the lunch at noon in our toolshed. I feel we had so much good help from friends and relatives over this time for the loss of Ben. Thanks goes out to them who helped in our time of great loss.

I should thank all the readers out there for all the cards and gifts since the death of my dear husband, Ben. Words can't express the appreciation to you great readers out there.

On Sunday, this column's editor, Kevin Williams, and his mother brought over one thousand e-mails plus a thirty-two-gallon tub full of cards. The gifts will help with the hospital bills. Thank you all to be so supportive. I won't be able to write everyone to express my appreciation. But I hope this does it.

Good luck to all out there, 'til next time. We never know what the future holds. God only knows.

JUNE 2000

Gradually, Elizabeth's column began to resume a tone of normalcy, but an undercurrent of grief remained in her writing.

I am writing this letter at 4:30 A.M., June 15, here at the desk of Joe's (daughter Lovina's husband) family, as the girls and I spent the night here. Five years ago this morning, we were busy with the wedding of Jacob and my daughter Emma. Today is their anniversary. They are blessed with two little girls and one son. Church services will be in their home June 25, so we've been assisting Emma in getting ready for it. Lots of cleaning to do at such a time.

Last night, it was so stormy. Tornadoes were predicted, and I guess we felt best to go someplace else, which is why we stayed the night at Joe and Lovina's. By staying here, we also got in on Joe's daughter's (little Elizabeth) birthday cake, as she turned six yesterday. Can't imagine her going to school this coming fall.

Seems impossible I will have four grandchildren entering school in September. The twins, Arlene and Marlene, daughters of son Amos and wife Nancy, and Elizabeth, daughter of Liz and Levi, also will be entering school. How these years slip away.

So glad for my eight children and twenty-nine grandchildren who have been so supportive to me, especially since the passing of my dear husband, Ben, last month. Lots of memories linger on. Only those who experience the loss of a life partner know the grief one goes through in this time of sorrow. Friends and relatives have been supportive, and also you readers out there. I want to thank you, and I won't be able to thank you all personally, so I hope this will do. Words can't express the appreciation for all those many cards. My editor has brought a thirty-two-gallon tub full of mail and more than one thousand e-mail letters. I feel so unworthy to receive all this. Maybe someday I'll be able to go through them all again and thank more people. But I must go on and not sit and think. Death is so final, but Ben can now rest, with no more worry or pain, only peace, which he deserved.

JUNE 2000

Columns like this one continued to show Elizabeth in a deep state of mourning following the loss of her husband.

It is a Sunday and such a dreary day.

Jacob and Emma's family were here overnight. Breakfast was prepared for us all. They then left in the morning to go to his folks for noon dinner. We also had a nice noon dinner. The potatoes were peeled and cut up as for the noon meal. Meatloaf was done, also. So we had a head start for dinner. Son Albert and family and Joe (daughter Lovina) and family were our dinner guests. One empty chair remained, without my dear husband Ben. It's not the same, but we must learn to go on in our lives without him. I, at times, do not understand, but God has a purpose for it all. Again, once more, thanks to all you readers out there for all those nice cards and gifts. I feel so unworthy for it all. You readers have been so thoughtful during this time of sorrow. Ben was such a great husband and father, always supportive to all the family.

God's ways aren't our ways. He had a purpose to take Ben in his care. So glad Ben didn't suffer at all. Doctor said he fought to live. How lucky God spared him with us for almost a week after his stroke. Only those with experience know how it is to lose a loved one. Glad he could go before me, as he so relied on me. But it took both of us to go on in life. Death is so final. I must manage to keep looking up. Our children are so supportive. What would I do without my daughters, Verena and Susan, who still live with me at home?

Sunday evening, my sister, who also lost her husband last year, her daughter and family came for a visit. They stayed for supper. Then her other two daughters and families came. My children then began arriving. Paul's (daughter Leah) family, son Albert and family, Levi (daughter Liz) and family, Joe (daughter Lovina) and family, and Jacob (daughter Emma) and family all came here for Sunday supper. So we had around sixty here. Mashed potatoes, gravy, steak, meatloaf, buttered corn, buttered peas, spaghetti and meatballs, lettuce and egg salad, cheese, radishes, carrots, onion greens, cookies, and other baked goods were on the menu.

There was more on the menu, but I can't think of what it was right now. Was good to have them all here, but two were missing: my dear husband and my brother-in-law. They were so badly needed in this troublesome world we have to live in. God, help us in our sorrowing time.

JULY 2000

I remember when Loretta was born. She was Elizabeth's first grandchild to be born after Ben passed away, and I think her arrival was a much-needed tonic for Elizabeth's spirits.

It is 2:30 A.M. on a Thursday morning as I write this column. I forgot it had to be in the mail today. I must get this written and on its way. I'm going to be gone most of the day today, accompanying my daughter Emma and her husband Jacob on errands, as he is off this week on vacation. Some brighter happenings this week as new life came into the family. The highlight of July 1 was another grandchild being born. Joe's (daughter Lovina) family welcomed a new member named Loretta. She was born at 6:28 A.M., weighing six pounds, ten ounces, and is nineteen inches long. Lots of beautiful black hair. She joins three sisters, Elizabeth, Susan, and Verena, and one brother, Benjamin. My daughter Verena is now there to assist with the household duties while Lovina tends to the new baby. This makes thirty living grandchildren. Jacob, Emma, and family are staying here tonight. They came over in the evening to assist with some household chores. I have church services coming up in this home later this month, so there's lots to do to get ready.

Daughter-in-law Sarah Irene (son Albert) and family also came for the day yesterday. So Albert's and Jacob's families were here for supper. What would I do without family? Life must go on without my dear, beloved husband, Ben. We've had so many rains lately. The garden is doing great, as are the surrounding fields of crops, hay, and pastures. Some places it is too wet. My garden isn't completed as yet. I need to put more plants in the garden. Weeds have taken over through this wet weather, but I shouldn't complain. I just need to replant again. There's plenty of garden goodies out there; I just need to get out and weed. Working in the garden is peaceful, and it brings back happy memories of Ben and I putting out the garden together.

Well, maybe I can get some shut-eye now. I can't neglect this writing. Time goes on and life goes on. We must look up to the future. God makes no mistakes. Good luck to all you great readers out there. Your encouragement has meant so much. ❁

JULY 2000

In the aftermath of Ben's death, Elizabeth began to simplify and downsize. In this column, she writes about selling off her last dairy cow. The responsibility of daily milking and care was just too much.

It's a cool, sunshiny Thursday evening. The work of the day took off at an early start. Jacob's (daughter Emma) family was here for the night. Jacob left for work, and Emma started to wash off walls at 6:00 A.M. I really didn't think the walls needed to be washed off again, only the ceilings and woodwork, but she went ahead. Daughters Lovina and Emma were washing off the walls of the dining room and kitchen the day before my dear husband passed away. The day after the funeral, which was May 24, the living room, bedroom, and spare bedroom walls were all washed off before the furniture was put back in place. What a relief when everything feels clean again.

Visiting us today were daughters Leah and Emma. Daughter-in-law Sarah Irene and two boys came in the morning and left after our noon dinner. Everything is clean now: the bedroom, living room, dining room, kitchen, enclosed porch, and our washhouse. The kerosene lamps and dishes look sparkling again. We had the curtains washed and windows cleaned before the death of my husband, so that was one job less to do over the funeral. But then I decided to wash them again, as church services are being conducted here this Sunday. So the curtains and windows again look clean now, also.

My three grandsons Levi, Ben, and Joseph were set to work by weeding my garden today. The weeds had taken over, but that, too, looks nice again. So it was a workday around here. Daughter Verena has been a good help around here. She finally went back to work, where she cleans rooms at a motel in town a couple of days a week. Sounds like they really missed her good work. It seems different not to see a cow in the field and not to have to milk it mornings and evenings. It was always relied on Verena to do the job. This way, by getting rid of the cow, there's no hay to buy, no manure to haul, maybe no vet bill to pay. So it's been a relief not to care for the cow. But she gave a lot of milk, although we didn't use much at times. The cow is in good care, I'd say. A friend of ours bought it, as he milks around two hundred cows. ❦

AUGUST 2000

One way Elizabeth coped her with grief was to stay busy, and that included lots of writing. She wrote her column, cookbooks, and kept contributing to the *Budget*.

It is 4:30 A.M. as I write this column on a clear Thursday morning. We are in need of rain, but we take one day at a time. Even though we need the rain, the gardens have produced great yields this summer. Corn is growing very well in this area, and lots are selling vegetables and fruits.

I've been up for a while now doing writing. I also am a writer for the *Budget*. I've been writing for the *Budget* for some time now, and I also needed to write some for the cookbook that is coming out soon. So it's been write-write-write in these early morning hours. There's a gathering in Sugarcreek, Ohio, soon of all the *Budget* writers. I've attended in the past, but I do not think I will be able to this year. Too much to do around here.

My belated husband, Ben, would always encourage me to keep this "Amish Cook" column going. He'd ask me if I wrote it yet, and if I was writing it, he'd come with an envelope and stamp to get it on its way.

We had church services here on Sunday, July 23. The services went smoothly, with many in attendance. My children were a big help in making sure church went well; these were the first services held in my home since the death of my dear husband two months ago. Time goes on. God has a purpose for everything.

The bench wagon is sitting in our yard now. The bench wagon carries the church benches from place to place wherever church is being held. It will head next to daughter

Lovina's, where she will be holding services soon. We've been helping Joe's (daughter Lovina) family as church services are to be in their home on Sunday, August 6. She is busy caring for a small baby, Loretta, born July 1. Loretta is doing very well, with lots of thick, beautiful black hair. Her siblings have welcomed baby Loretta. Granddaughter Elizabeth, who will begin school in the fall, is always holding and caring for the new baby. The newborn in the family is welcome cheer at this time of year.

We have a wedding to attend in this community on Thursday, August 3. I will be a cook on Tuesday, helping to prepare pies, dinners, and everything else that is needed for the big occasion. My daughter Susan will be a table waiter at the wedding, so that should keep us busy this week, plus preparing for Lovina's church services.

SEPTEMBER 2000

Elizabeth's family was a continual source of happiness for her. Whether it was just dropping in to pitch in with chores or to spend the night, her children were always around in the year 2000.

Lately, with the aid of frequent rains and plenty of sunshine, the garden has done well, and so have the weeds. The weeds have taken over in the garden. We need to spend some time soon getting rid of those weeds.

Some of the children were here Saturday to put a new roof on the south part of my house. The shingles were blowing off from the wind. So it was in a bad state of repair. What would I do without family?

Today, tomato juice was processed, which will taste good when the cold winter months come. It's good to open all kinds of fresh fruits and vegetables during the depths of winter. It provides a splash of cheer to brighten those dreary days. I also hope to process a lot of grape juice this fall. We have a lot of yellow tomatoes this fall, which also need to be harvested. They are ones that Ben and I planted earlier this year. I prefer the red tomatoes, but Ben thought he wanted to try a yellow tomato for this fall.

On Sunday, some of the children were here visiting, and of all things, my two-year-old granddaughter, Verena, daughter of Joe and Lovina, had to be rushed to the hospital. She was badly dehydrated. So while Joe and and Lovina were keeping vigil at the hospital, my daughter Verena (who turned thirty-four last week) went over there to take over their household chores and watch over Joe and Lovina's four other children. What would we do without Verena? Everything appears to be OK with little Verena now, just a bad dehydration.

A reader from Fort Wayne, Indiana, wrote to ask me how I can corn. I usually cut the corn off the cob and put it in quart glass jars. I then put in one teaspoon of salt in four quart jars and fill the jars with water before processing. The same reader also asked how I can tomatoes. I wash the tomatoes and cut them up into chunks. We then put them through a strainer for juice. Put tomatoes in glass jars and add one teaspoon salt to a quart. Process for twenty-five minutes. Same time length applies to corn.

SEPTEMBER 2000

September is the peak of canning season for most Amish homemakers in the Midwest. There's a rush to get the last of the tomatoes canned into sauces, salsas, and juices. September also marks the start of the school year. Most Amish schools typically open their doors after Labor Day, a calendar most public schools have discarded.

This is a nice, sunshiny Thursday morning, with my daughters Leah, Liz, Lovina, and Emma, and their children here today.

Lovina's sweet little girl, Verena, appears to be nicely on the mend from her hospitalization for dehydration a couple of weeks ago. Grandchildren really add life around here. The school-age grandchildren are now in school for the year. Some of the children around here attend public schools, some the one-room Amish schools, and others are homeschooled. My children all attended public schools. It just depends on what the parents prefer. We processed thick and chunky salsa this morning. Many people have written to me asking about what ingredients go into our homemade salsa, which is very popular this time of year with all the vegetables in the garden ripening. Salsas can be used in so many different ways and in so many different dishes. Our salsa takes fourteen pounds of tomatoes (scalded, peeled and cut up), five cups of onions (chopped), ten green peppers (chopped), two ounces or more jalapeño peppers (chopped), one cup vinegar, a half-cup brown sugar, one-fourth cup salt, two teaspoons

oregano flakes, one tablespoon cumin, one tablespoon chili power, one teaspoon garlic powder, and ten teaspoons of Clear Jel (a thickener sold in most supermarkets).

Yesterday afternoon, we had tomatoes here to be used up before they spoil. I hate to see tomatoes go to waste. Thought I had processed enough for the year 2000, but yet we processed thirty-three and a half quarts of V8 tomato juice, which will be good to open when those cold winter months come along. I put in four different colored tomatoes, along with celery, carrots, sweet peppers, banana peppers, jalapeño peppers, and plenty of onions. How relaxing to see my daughter Liz and her husband Levi drive in with their horse-drawn buggy last night while in the midst of making tomato juice. Liz stepped in to help me finish processing the tomato juice. It is hard work to do, such processing. What a surprise to have them stay for the night. It's so good to have family. What would I do without family?

Our drains, that drain away waste water, started to not be in working order, so our son Albert came yesterday. What a mess to go through, but was just glad to see those drains in good working order. Again, it is so nice to have children who come around and are helpful.

On September 4, my son-in-law Joe and my daughter Lovina were here, and with the help of my daughter Verena, the old roof from our barn, which was just replaced, was cleared away. A good meal was served to all after that hard work. The old roof pilings had just been lying on the ground around the barn. The wood had really rotted from the century-old barn roof. It looks very nice with a brand new roof sparkling in the sunshine. The menfolk in our family recently put on the new roof. Now our straw shed, where we keep our straw, needs to be painted next.

OCTOBER 2000

Autumn brings grape-canning duties, and Elizabeth put up plenty of fresh juice for the looming winter.

We're now well into October 2000, and the first chills are in the air. Life goes on. On Thursday, all our four married daughters were home for the day, and all four families were here for supper. It was a wonderful day together, but it feels a lonely feeling after everyone has left for their homes at night. What would I do without family during this time as my husband lies in a peaceful sleep, never to return? Grape time has arrived here. On Monday, we processed our grapes into juice. We worked up ninety-eight quarts of homemade grape juice Monday evening. Since the weather was nice, everything was done outside on the picnic table. Finally, the lantern had to be lit as darkness came upon us. We didn't get all the jars we wanted processed that evening. We took the grapes from their stems and washed them and put them in clean, sterilized canning jars. We process our grape juice for twenty minutes, adding two cups grapes and one-fourth cup sugar to a quart and then three cups grapes and half-cup sugar to a half-gallon jar. I suppose when we open the jars this winter we can dilute it with some water.

I didn't like to add too much sugar to the jars because of blood sugar worries. Sugar can always be added later for the ones with sugar problems. We processed 132 quarts in all. It'll be good, healthy wintertime breakfast drinking. So I must clear space for all those jars to be stored in the cellar.

Daughter Emma found a recipe in a cookbook for grape juice, so she made it that way. That recipe called for five heaping cups of washed grapes and twelve cups of hot water. Let it boil for forty-five minutes. Put through a strainer. Put the juice on the stove and add two and a half cups sugar. Let the juice come to a boil, and then put it in jars and seal. So I guess I'll see how hers tastes and maybe take a try for another year.

Daughter Lovina and children spent the day here, yesterday, and they were all here for supper. We babysat for daughter Emma's two oldest (Elizabeth and Emma) in the afternoon, while Jacob and Emma went to Riley's Children's Hospital in Indianapolis to visit a close relative. So I prepared a fresh vegetable soup for all. I peeled and cut up potatoes and onions and added carrots, corn, peas, and tomato juice, and I got a mango and celery in from the garden to add. I had a big kettle on the stove. I added one quart of our home-canned chunk beef, which made it taste delicious. Everyone seemed to enjoy the soup. That's the way I like to have a fresh soup of garden goodies. We still have tomatoes, sweet peppers, red beets, hot peppers, and celery from the garden as of October 5.

OCTOBER 2000

Elizabeth marked her first wedding anniversary without her husband with sadness.

It is 9:00 A.M. on this Tuesday, October 17, 2000. This is the time of day that wedding services started off when my husband Ben and I were united into marriage in 1957. Lots of memories linger, and who thought a year ago that Ben would not be here for our forty-third anniversary? Only God knows the reason why he is not here.

I can remember that day so clearly: At 4:00 A.M., my sister and I were hard at it frying chicken, which was to be served for the noon meal after our wedding. Many invited guests couldn't attend because of the Asian flu at the time. As I have written about in the past, I also had a severe case of the Asian flu at the time. The week before our wedding, my temperature was up to 105. Being twenty-one years of age, it seemed high enough. Most of our family was down with flu, but everyone was OK, only feeling weak by the wedding day. We caught the flu by visiting someone who had it. It was so catching, but we hadn't realized it. My father, Ben, and one of my sisters never caught it. My mother was still in bed on the Tuesday before our wedding day, which was on a Thursday.

Some women came over on that Tuesday to help bake the pies and make those nothings, which you'll see them on the wedding tables at most weddings around here. At Amish weddings, some serve the cakes from sheet cakes on trays, and others have layer cakes on the cake stands which are cut on the wedding day. It's usually a variety of cakes. The single girls arrive Wednesday to help peel and cut potatoes. Celery also is washed and vegetables diced up for the dressing.

On Thursday, the day of the wedding, carrot salad is made and potato salad is prepared if it is on the menu. In some places, chicken is cut up to be fried on the wedding morning. There are many cooks helping, and the tables are set. Lots of work goes into preparing for a wedding day. With plenty of women for cooks, it makes it easier for

everyone. The waiters are single boys and girls who make sure everyone has enough food. We had seven single couples as waiters at our wedding; some have many more.

There are lots of dishes, kettles, silverware, and pans to get washed for both meals. There is a noon meal right after the wedding and an evening supper for those who stay all day. It always seemed easier to get those dishes out of the cupboards than to put them back in order.

Ben and I then moved onto our current farm March 11, 1958. What a change it made in life. Now we have six girls and two boys and thirty grandchildren (thirty-one, counting Mary Shelter, who passed away). How time flies.

As I look out my window now, the leaves are falling from the trees. They are such beautiful colors of all kinds—beautiful fall weather.

Later in the evening: daughters Liz and children and Emma and children spent the day here. Their husbands joined them here for supper. Son Albert and sons gave me a visit also toward evening. Joe, Lovina, and family also came for supper. Guess what? After supper, dishes were washed by Levi (Liz's husband), with help from Joe and Jacob, who wiped the dishes dry. They were singing while doing it, as the girls put away the food. I guess that was a rare occasion for the men to be seen helping in the kitchen. Ha! What would I do without family?

Ironing was on the list to do today and also canning of green tomato pickles. Never thought I would get those canned as it's such good eating from those jars. A friend of Liz shared the recipe, and now it's in our family to help fill those canning jars for the long winter ahead.

NOVEMBER 2000

The Amish have always displayed a tremendous sense of thrift. This column talks a bit about that virtue.

I am writing this column in the first week of November, and it's just hard to believe that the year 2000 is almost over. We just passed a memorable anniversary in my life. On October 29, 1963, Ben and I moved onto this farm with only two children: Leah and Amos, at the time. Leah was four years old, and Amos was two years old the next day. He couldn't understand why we didn't go back home, but they finally adjusted to their different home. Thinking back, land wasn't selling high as it is now. The wages were low, and it was hard to find a job at the time. I guess we learned to save. Being without a job was tough, especially having bought a farm and those farm payments came along. But somehow there was always a way. Not to say we never worried, but why worry if we can pray?

I guess it's not what you earn, it's what you save. It's a good thing my mother taught us how to save. Mother was a good housekeeper. Lots of memories linger.

Some of the family reminded son Amos Monday evening he was another year older. Granddaughter Rosa (Liz and Levi) also had her third birthday Monday.

We had some trick or treaters last night (Halloween). No tricks, only treats for them little ones. Ha!

It looks like a fall day out there. Daughters Verena and Susan are at work, and I'm waiting to get a ride to attend a Tupperware party at my niece's, and tomorrow my daughter Leah is having a Stanley party.

Well, it is now Thursday, November 2, and I am here at Jacob's (daughter Emma). Some of the family reminded Jacob he is turning another year older, by having a supper last night for the occasion. The girls have left for work, and we're getting ready to attend Leah's party today. So we'll have dinner there, also.

On the breakfast menu here at Jacob's were homemade breakfast sandwiches using shredded potatoes, cheese, scrambled eggs, and home-canned sausage in them and then baked. Home-canned salsa goes good with these sandwiches, plus Emma's home-processed grape juice. She also baked cinnamon rolls and Long John Rolls for Jacob's birthday treat at his place of work.

To the readers who asked about Clear Jel, it can be bought at food stores. It is used as a thickener. Good luck!

2001
mourning and peace

JANUARY 2001

Life's simpler pleasures, like blooming indoor plants and birds feeding in the snow, gave Elizabeth comfort during her first winter as a widow.

Looking out the window on this cold morning, it's a winter scene with the snow-covered ground, and the trees are a Christmassy white. How beautiful!

We've had several mornings of fog. New Year's Day was very bad to drive through that fog. But we got home safely from Levi's (daughter Liz), being there in the assistance of their new arrival, Suzanne. Then a friend of ours took us to son Amos's to spend New Year's Day. They were butchering hogs when daughters Verena and Susan and I arrived. We assisted them with the butchering. Three hogs were butchered and mostly all cut up, and sausage was made. It was an enjoyable New Year's Day at son Amos's. A delicious noon meal was served while we were at Amos's. We left for home around five o'clock. I still admire my blooming Christmas cactus and two poinsettias, which seem so nice. Three years ago, son Amos's gave us one, and two years ago, Jacob's gave us one. They're still such hardy plants. I love flowers, but seems I have too many indoors during the wintertime.

Out my window I can see birds gathering in the snow to eat. The birds enjoy when someone throws feed out for them. That's something Ben always tried to do. He always was a bird watcher at all times. He is still missed, and an empty chair was at the table New Year's Day. Doesn't seem the same.

We've had a cold winter thus far. Hoping for warmer weather. The cold and snow just hangs in here. Sleigh riding goes good on these snow-covered roads. It's taking a lot of fuel to keep these home fires burning.

We spent Christmas Day at Joe's (daughter Lovina), with other family members present. It was an enjoyable day with plenty of food for the meals. What would I do without family? I'm processing meat in those pressure cookers now. Verena hitched the horse to the buggy and left for Jacob's (daughter Emma) to see about their steak to be sliced up for the freezer, and Susan is wrapping gifts for her nieces and nephews. We're just having a late Christmas family gathering this year, January 14. Glad all can be present, hopefully. God only knows what the future holds for 2001.

We'll have lots of delicious desserts and plenty of food at our January 14 family gathering.

JANUARY 2001

Elizabeth Coblentz began her first full year without her husband, Ben, in January 2001. She coped with grief by surrounding herself with family. Much joy was had in spending time with grandchildren.

This seems to be a nice Wednesday evening. The days come and go. We've had plenty of cold days and still there is snow on the ground. Takes plenty of fuel for the home fires this time of year. Daughters Lovina and Emma and children spent the day here. They came last night so I got them to stay for the overnight. Both daughters took each of their husbands, Joe and Jacob, home early in the morning, as to do their chores and be ready to leave for work at 5:30 A.M. Joe and Jacob both work at the same place. Then Lovina and Emma returned, and a breakfast was served. Joe's six-year-old Elizabeth then headed for school, being a kindergartener. Looks so cute to see her go to school with her school bag on her back. Emma and Lovina stayed all day, and Joe and Jacob met them here after work. My daughters were glad to not drive home alone in this cold weather. I must write about what happened in the morning. Three flaps of eggs had been delivered, so daughter Lovina was going to make a run to her house with a horse and buggy to take the eggs home. Verena went outside for a moment with Lovina to help with the buggy. When Verena went back in the house, she discovered Lovina's little eighteen-month-old Benjamin having a ball with those eggs. He had thrown fourteen eggs to the floor and one-year-old Jacob Jr. was playing in it, as he still crawls around. But the mess was soon taken care of. Benjamin had climbed on the step stool and on the sink to the eggs. Lucky he didn't get them all as he'd have had ninety eggs to toss. Ha! Sweet little boy.

This week is going fast. Daughter Leah and children stopped in and had dinner here with us Monday evening. Saturday night was spent at son Albert's, so on Sunday morning we attended church services with them. I was glad our horse was harnessed and hitched to the buggy, so the girls didn't have to do that, as Albert did the duty. Son Albert's, Joe's, and Jacob's families were our Sunday supper guests.

Today, thirty-two years ago, a daughter named Elizabeth was born to Ben and me and goes by the name today of Wengerd (Levi) now. She has three daughters and one son. A baby, Suzanne, was born on December 26, 2000. Her oldest is in first grade in school.

Didn't get to see son Amos over the weekend. Word came that my dad's stepsister, my stepaunt, Elda, died, and the funeral was Friday morning. I still remember as a young girl, she took me along to school one day as a little visitor. I recall that day with her sitting at her desk at a public country school. I will remember her as a great stepaunt.

Brings back memories of those times. I'm so glad to have some of my dad's mom's stainless-steel cookware. She took good care of it. I got the cookware through the children's sale of my deceased folks belongings. Lots of memories. I remember when my dad's mom took us, as young ones, to babysit for us when my folks went to town for only a short while. Grandma would place a cardboard box upside down and put pretzels, etc., on it, and we'd kneel around the box and enjoy the treats. What a treat at that time. She was a great grandma.

Well, I must get back to work.

FEBRUARY 2001

Elizabeth filled her home with grandchildren—the more, the better—during the winter of 2001.

We entered another month today: February. The day looks dreary and damp. Had lots of rain the last couple days. Many were glad for the rain to have water in their cisterns. Some cisterns had gone dry. We have had plenty of snow so far this winter but no rain. We have a big cistern and it seems we don't run out. We used to use the cistern water when Joe's (daughter Lovina) family lived in the trailer home across our driveway and Jacob's (daughter Emma) family lived with us in this household after they married. It took a lot of cistern (soft water) to do laundry, etc.

The highlight of Tuesday, January 30, was another grandchild for me. A baby girl, Leanna, was born to son Albert and Sarah Irene at 1:05 P.M., weighing seven pounds, nine ounces. She joins Elizabeth, Ben, Joseph, Albert Jr., Irene, Emma, and Marvin. So we had all of Albert and Sarah's children in our care until all was over with the baby. They enjoy coming to Grandma's. Daughter Lovina and children were here, also, that day, so it was a full house. Joe's and Levi's families were here for supper also. Son Amos's family spent Saturday here to see what needs to be done, as

church services will be here in the near future. Then Sunday morning, I told Jacob's (daughter Emma) family to drop in for breakfast on their way to his folks' for church. This way, daughter Emma didn't have to mess around for their breakfast. Dishes were washed, and the next thing to do was rest and then think of dinner. Albert's and Joe's (daughter Lovina) families were here for Sunday dinner. Joe's family went after pizza in a nearby town, so pizza was on the menu. We got plenty, just in case some other family members would drop in for dinner. We never know, but always glad to see them come. I suppose they all know they are welcome.

This morning, the girls made omelettes, but made them a different way. They took five eggs, one heaping tablespoon of flour, one teaspoon of salt, a pinch of pepper or to your taste, and two cups of milk, and added shredded cooked potatoes (jackets) and put it in a hot, buttered covered skillet on medium heat. Turn it over and add cheese on top. It was good this way for a change.

Daughters Emma and children are here today. She's helping me with cleaning for church. She's washing off walls, ceilings, etc. It's been a big cleaning day thus far. So glad it's being done. Emma's small daughters Elizabeth and Emma, want to write also, so I gave them paper and pencil to write. They think they're probably helping me with this column. Ha!

MARCH 2001

Elizabeth had already sold the dairy cow but she was still left with several horses to care for. Selling her Belgian horses was difficult for her, but it reduced her workload at home.

On Friday, my sons Amos and Albert, Albert's son Ben, and my daughter Verena went to a horse sale in Shipshewana, Indiana, to see my team of Belgian horses get sold. So I guess they're history now. They were never worked too hard, but they were here when we or one of our children needed them. They would ably perform such tasks as hauling manure, plowing the garden, and getting up wood from the woods. They were a tame team, but were now in their twenties. I really didn't need them anymore, and they were an extra duty to do, to give them water and feed. So the fields behind our barn look empty without them. We still have the horses that pull our buggy. Lots of changes have taken place the past year.

Glad our church services are over for another turn; they were held here Sunday. Lots of cleaning took place before. I was glad for the help of family, including grandchildren, who pitched into assist. Some barn repairs also were done. The Monday after church services, lots of cleaning also is done. We did a lot of laundry Monday.

The Saturday before church services, my son Amos, wife Nancy, and their eight children, plus my daughter Lovina, husband Joe, and their five children were all overnight guests. So it was a full house. Was good to have them here.

Everyone helped with Sunday morning breakfast and then got dressed for church and got everything in order before the first people showed up. Everything was ready in time. Home-baked cookies and crackers were served to the small children in the morning as a treat. And, as usual, a good noon lunch was served to all in attendance at church. We had coffee, ham, two kinds of cheese, lettuce, hot peppers, red beets, pickles, rhubarb jam, margarine, peanut butter spread, home-baked bread, milk, etc. A hot milk soup and crackers were served for the little ones for lunch.

It is now Thursday morning, and I must get this in the mail. We were to Jacob's for supper last night for barbecued pork ribs and stayed for the night. So I am back home now and have completed the chores around here; now I want to help daughter Leah, as Paul's have the next church services in their home.

MAY 2001

In this column, Elizabeth mourns the one-year anniversary of her husband's passing.

This leaves it a Sunday evening, May 20, 2001. It's a year ago now that my dear husband, Ben, was taken to that Heavenly Home. He's in a place where there's no more worry and pain, only peace. But I must go on.

I was glad to see daughter Emma and husband, Jacob, and family coming here last evening, Saturday, as it just made a better feeling to have someone come. They stayed for the night, so this morning we had breakfast together. We didn't know if some other family members would show up for dinner, so we waited to start a dinner. Paul's (daughter Leah), Joe's (daughter Lovina), and Jacob's (daughter Emma) and all their children were our dinner guests. They had dinner here and stayed all day, leaving in the evening. It was a day well spent together with family. Then to my surprise, Ben's sister and husband drove in and gave a visit.

Daughter Lovina will never forget her twenty-ninth birthday last year, May 22, as the funeral of Ben was the next day. So this was a quieter birthday this year.

Now the news of this evening: at 8:30 P.M. a daughter named Laura was born to son Amos and Nancy Jean, weighing nine pounds, eight ounces, and just over twenty-two inches in length. She joins one brother, Ben, and seven sisters: Susan, Elizabeth, Mary Jane, twins Arlene and Marlene, Lovina, and Lisa. I suppose Amos's Ben would have been proud for a brother, but the baby is happy and healthy and that is all that matters. This makes thirty-three grandchildren living, one, Mary Shetler, deceased.

Now it looks a stormy Monday morning and the laundry was hung out on the clothesline early, only to bring the clothes back in because of the rain. I don't like to leave it hang when a storm comes up. It really rained and rained and then quit, so, again, the laundry was hung out and this time it all dried. We are having plenty of rain lately. Had two inches of rain by noon. Verena went over the property she owns to do some cleaning up, and my youngest daughter Susan has been weeding flowers and wherever it needs it. Spring brings many tasks. What would we do without family?

the transition

Elizabeth's sudden passing from an aneurysm at age sixty-six tossed the column's fate into uncertainty. Deciding whether to continue the column was a complicated decision. Readers were really devoted to the column, and that weighed into everything, but that by itself wasn't enough. There had to be a compelling reason to continue. At the end of the day, as editor and creator of the column, I decided that the show must go on. Only weeks before her death, Elizabeth and I had discussed, in passing, what would happen to the column if something ever happened to either of us. It was a plan that neither of us ever thought would need to be implemented, at least not so soon. And we had both reached an understanding that the column would continue. In the event of her passing, one of her daughters would pick up the pen. In the event of mine, my brother would likely have stepped in as editor.

When it was decided that Lovina would be the new Amish Cook, I told her that the audience would stick with her for a while based solely on her mother's memory. But over time, I told Lovina, she'd have to earn the audience herself. And I think she has more than done so. With a mix of candor and calm, Lovina took over the column and made it her own. Occasionally Lovina's daughter, Elizabeth, steps in to write the column, which now means that three generations have picked up the pen to write the column at various times. This makes me feel like an aging editor! ❧

2002
good-bye, elizabeth

OCTOBER 2002

This was Lovina's first column after her mother's death. She eloquently paid homage to her mother and then began a long literary journey of her own.

I am nervous and not sure how to begin this letter. It is very difficult for me to take over this column. I will never be able to write like my dear mother did, but I will try my best. Mother is resting in peace now, but, oh, how we miss her! Life will never be the same without my parents. In less than two and a half years we lost them both. I often think of what Mom would always say: "God makes no mistakes." We must now go on with life and accept the changes that God sends to us. I will always cherish the good memories of my parents. I hope my husband, Joe, and I can raise our children the way they raised us.

My sisters Verena and Susan came home with us the day after Mom's funeral and spent one and a half weeks here. It was nice to be together during this sad time. The home place seems so lonely now. Church services were held here last Sunday, and we'll have them here again next time, the week after next. Mom was greatly missed at services Sunday. Mom always made the coffee for us girls whenever we had church at our house. I am thirty-one and am the sixth of eight children. Joe and I were married on July 15, 1993, and we have six children. Elizabeth is eight and in second grade. Susan is six and in kindergarten. Verena is four and is my little babysitter when the other two are in school. Benjamin is three, Loretta is two, and baby Joseph was born this past summer. Benjamin and Loretta keep me on the go. They are so full of energy, but I am so thankful they are healthy. My husband, Joe, has worked at a furniture factory in town for six years.

I keep very busy just tending to the little ones and trying to keep up with the cleaning, cooking, ironing, laundry, and all that goes with raising a family. There is a lot of work, but I wouldn't want it any other way. My sister Liz and her husband, Levi, have church services at their house this coming Sunday. My sisters Verena, Susan, and Emma and I, and all of our children, spent the day there helping prepare for church. A huge laundry was done (including her curtains). Windows were cleaned and pumpkins were canned, which she had raised in her garden. It was comforting to all be together and talk about the many good memories we have of our parents. That's all we have left now.

NOVEMBER 2002

"The Amish Cook" column took on a livelier, younger feel after Lovina (and her houseful of young children) took over.

This is Sunday evening here at the Eichers. It's bedtime for the children. Morning comes too fast for the school-age girls. They have completed their first semester of school. Time goes too fast!

We had an enjoyable evening. My husband, Joe, and I sang songs with the children. They enjoy that so much! Elizabeth, age eight, and Susan, age six, do a very good job of singing. Three-year-old Benjamin even tries to yodel. It is so cute. Sweet, innocent children. What will they have to face while growing up in this troubled world? Prayers are badly needed for children around the world.

We had an enjoyable day today. Joe and I took the children driving around sightseeing. We drove south from here around eight miles. It brought back memories when we went past the farm where my Uncle Chris and Aunt Lizzie used to live when I was growing up. So many changes . . .

We started out around 9:00 A.M. and arrived back home at 3:00 P.M. We stopped in at a few places to give our horse a rest and so we could also warm up. We have to get used to driving in the cold again. Our buggies are open, with no roof. But we use an umbrella that holds off a lot of the cold wind. It was pretty chilly when we started out, but the sun came out and made it warmer.

We ended up eating lunch at my sister Emma's and Jacob's. They were surprised to see us drive in. Our horse Diamond was glad when we were home again. He is eight and a half years old. We raised him up from a colt. He is a good and safe family horse. We had him vaccinated for the West Nile Virus. Sure would hate to lose him.

A lot of horses died around here this summer from the virus, and Mom's horse had the virus and pulled through OK. He's over twenty years old, so we were surprised he did. My sister Liz and her husband Levi, lost their good horse from it. It was a safe horse that Liz could really drive, so they felt the loss.

The girls played with their dolls this afternoon when we got back, and Benjamin played with his toy horses. His little horses were always breaking through the fence. It's cute to listen to the children while they play. Such big imaginations!

The trees are showing their autumn splendors. We saw a lot of nice scenery today while driving around.

God's wondrous work! The squirrels are busy gathering their nuts for the long winter ahead. We have a lot of trees around here, so there are a lot of leaves that have to be raked up. The girls enjoy doing it, and they also enjoy covering each other up with the leaves.

Joe started coal in the stove yesterday. Coal burns all night and makes a more even heat in the house. It's nice to wake up in the mornings and not have to start up the stove and have a cold house.

So, it's been a long, enjoyable day. Joe has tucked all the children in their beds, and Baby Joseph is almost asleep. It will feel good to retire for the day. Years fly by so fast, and it's nice to enjoy the children. Before we know it, they will all be grown up.

NOVEMBER 2002

Adopting a technique occasionally used by her mother, Lovina's daily diary columns have proved just as popular with readers as Elizabeth's were.

Some people may wonder what a typical day is like around here. Following is the diary of this past Monday:

4:30 A.M. My husband, Joe, starts the woodstove and goes to do the chores. Mornings sure are chilly now. Feels good after it starts warming up in the house. I pack Joe's lunch and get him something for breakfast.

5:15 A.M. Joe is ready for work and is eating his breakfast.

5:30 A.M. Joe leaves for work, and I get daughters Elizabeth and Susan's clothes ready for school.

6:00 A.M. My sisters Verena and Susan are putting water on the stove to heat to do a week's worth of laundry. They came home with us last night from our brother Albert's. Albert's had church services there yesterday. My family and some cousins were there for supper. Our dear mother was greatly missed!

6:30 A.M. Breakfast is ready. On the menu: Egg Dutch (omelette), bacon, cheese, homemade bread, and juice. All the children are awake now except baby Joseph. He usually wakes up to eat around 4:00 A.M. and goes back to sleep. He is three months old now and really starting to make sounds.

7:00 A.M. My daughters Elizabeth and Susan leave for school. My sisters Verena and Susan wash the dishes and sweep the floors, while I sort out the clothes and carry the water to wash.

9:30 A.M. Sister Susan has the wash lines all filled. We'll have to wait to hang out the rest until some of the clothes are dry. I usually wash twice a week and didn't get it done twice last week. Now, today, we have an extra huge wash. Meanwhile, Verena is mixing up a batch of chocolate chip cookies. Yum! My four-year-old daughter Verena is trying to help her. While they were baking the cookies, I rocked three-year-old Benjamin and two-year-old Loretta to sleep. Now they are both taking a nap.

11:30 A.M. Lunch is ready. We have a quick lunch of sandwiches. Sister Verena baked over eighty cookies, and they are delicious! I am sure they won't last too long around here. Benjamin and Loretta are refreshed after their naps.

1:00 P.M. Dishes are washed and put away. Sister Susan is picking marigolds for seed for next year. She's also putting all the weeds on a pile to burn, so the garden will be ready to plow. My sister Verena is mopping all the floors. My daughter Verena is taking a nap, and Benjamin and Loretta are playing outside. Such a nice day to be outdoors. We won't have many days like this left. I get in the clothes that are dry and hang out the rest. My sister Susan comes to help me before heading back out into the garden.

2:30 P.M. Sister Verena and I fold the clothes. There are so many little pieces to fold with six small children in this household. So many little socks to sort. Most of the laundry is dry. It really dried fast with the wind. It feels good to have everything clean again.

3:30 P.M. Girls are home from school and are sampling Verena's chocolate chip cookies.

5:00 P.M. My husband, Joe, is home from work. They are working ten hours a day, and also Saturdays during the forenoon sometimes.

5:30 P.M. Sisters Verena and Susan go home to get some clothes. I prepare a quick supper.

8:00 P.M. Dishes are washed. Everyone is tired and ready for bed. It has been another busy day.

Liz
Lea
din

the
whe
ten
som
the

ma
cor
slic tomatoes, lettuce,
sweet-pepper strips, homemade
bread, crackers with dip, pretzel
sticks, watermelon slices, three
kinds of cake, two kinds of cookies and three kinds of pop.

When the food was ready by
10 a.m., we loaded up the food
plus paper plates, foam cups, silverware and other utensils onto
a two-seated horse and buggy
and headed for the school, which
was a six-mile drive. We left bu

ab
ble

nts
After we g
we washed al
stainless-steel
tles and put th
to smaller c
seemed to be

It was such
able day —
preparing fo
gether on the
The air seem

I will sh

2003
a new amish cook: lovina eicher

Puzzles prove popular during the cold winter months. Children of all ages and adults can get in on the fun!

This is the second day into 2003. My husband, Joe, has left for work, and the children are still asleep. We have no snow here, but ice all over. I do hope there won't be any accidents. Today is the first day of school for the girls after their Christmas break. They are not very excited about ending their vacation. We had a nice time together while they were home from school and Joe off from work.

We have completed the 1,000-piece puzzle we started on Christmas Day. We had one more breakdown with the puzzle when two-year-old Loretta was sitting in the middle of it playing with her dolls. This was the day after her and Benjamin had pulled it off the table, and we had to begin all over. With six children around, it's hard to believe we still had all the pieces. I would like to glue the completed puzzle together sometime.

Last Friday, we helped my sister Liz and husband, Levi, butcher five hogs. It was a lot of hard work. I am sure they were very tired that night, but also glad to have their jars filled again with fresh meat. We also made pon hoss with the juice of the liver pudding, adding flour, salt, pepper, and some liver pudding to it. This is put into containers to cool and harden. Levi's sent some pon hoss and sausage home with us, so we enjoyed it sliced and fried for breakfast. Liz got all or most of her meat processed yet that day. She has a very big pressure cooker that processes eighteen to nineteen quarts at one time. She also had several smaller ones going. I'm sure it was a great relief for her to have it all done that day.

Since there was enough snow, Sister Emma and Jacob, sisters Verena and Susan, and our family took Dad and Mom's bobsled to Levi's. We had our horse and Jacob's horse hitched double. This was the first time any of these horses were hitched double, but they did a real good job of pulling together. It was a cold day, but we kept warm sitting on straw bales covered with blankets.

This is now later, and the girls made it off to school just fine even with the ice. The children have had breakfast and I must get the dishes washed. I hope to get the house cleaned and then start ironing clothes.

APRIL 2003

This column describes the first of several trips the Eichers would make to Michigan to visit family. They found the area to their liking and would ultimately move there.

We are having lovely spring weather this week. Joe worked up the garden tonight, and hopefully I'll be able to get something planted yet this week. I'd like to plant peas, lettuce, radishes, onions, and potatoes soon. Mom was never an early bird with her garden, but she always had the best garden.

We did some cleaning in the front yard. We had ten tree stumps removed, so it looks a mess right now. I will be glad once we get it all straightened out and grass planted. We also had a circle driveway put in, which makes it nicer to get in and out of our place.

We had a nice time in Michigan. We left on Wednesday afternoon and came home around 9:00 P.M. on Friday. Thursday was a very nice day for the wedding of my niece Verena to her husband Melvin. The wedding services were held at the neighbors. The meals were served at Melvin's parents. They could seat around two hundred at one time, so there were a lot of dishes to be washed in between settings. Their menu was mashed potatoes, gravy, meatloaf, ham, dressing, mixed vegetables, taco salad, homemade bread, pies, cakes, fruit, puddings, and ice cream.

I was supposed to go help on Wednesday, as that's when the women and girls get together to bake pies and peel potatoes. So there's not so much to do on the day of the wedding. Some communities do the food preparation on the Tuesday before the Thursday wedding. There is a lot of work in getting ready for a wedding.

On Friday, we stopped at Joe's sister, Carol, husband Pete, and family to see their new house. Then we headed to the hospital around an hour from there yet to visit with Joe's brother. He had a bad accident recently and has a broken arm and leg, two shattered knees, and internal injuries. He wasn't doing too well when we were there. He was in a lot of pain. He is lucky to be alive. God had his protecting hand over him. It took us around three and a half hours to get home from the hospital, so we were a tired bunch. My sisters Verena and Susan went with us, so they spent the night here.

I did a huge laundry on Monday. The clothes dried so nice. I just love wash days like that.

We are enjoying dandelions these last couple of weeks. Also, winter onions. We make a sour cream and pour it over the dandelion greens. Then we put in diced-up hard-boiled eggs. We eat this with cooked potatoes and bacon. My five-year-old daughter, Verena, asked me why I was picking and washing grass to eat.

The rest have all gone to bed, so I think I'll call it a day.

AMISH COOK CLASSIC: RHUBARB CUSTARD PIE

Makes one 9-inch pie

The rhubarb crop was bountiful in the spring of 2003, so items like rhubarb pie were on the menu—and in the column—frequently.

2 cups milk

1 teaspoon all-purpose flour

1 teaspoon water

3 eggs, slightly beaten

½ cup sugar

⅛ teaspoon salt

1 (9-inch) pie shell, unbaked
  (recipe follows)

2 cups finely chopped rhubarb

HOMEMADE PIE DOUGH

3 cups all-purpose flour

1 teaspoon salt

1 cup lard

1 large egg

⅓ cup cold water

1 tablespoon apple cider vinegar

Preheat the oven to 400°F.

In a heavy-bottomed saucepan, heat the milk over medium heat until warm (105° to 110°F). In a small bowl, combine the flour and the water and stir to form a paste. Add the flour mixture to the milk and stir until free of lumps.

In a large bowl, whisk together the eggs, sugar, and salt until well combined. Gradually whisk the warm milk mixture into the egg mixture. Continue whisking until the custard is smooth and all ingredients are evenly incorporated.

Cover the bottom of the unbaked pie shell with the finely chopped rhubarb. Pour the custard mixture over the rhubarb. Bake for 10 minutes, being careful that the custard does not boil. Reduce the heat to 350°F. Continue cooking the pie until the custard is set and the rhubarb is cooked through, about 30 minutes.

TO MAKE THE DOUGH:

In a large bowl, combine the flour and salt. Stir to blend. Add the lard and rub it into the flour with your fingertips until the mixture resembles coarse crumbs. Add the egg, water, and vinegar and stir with a fork until the dry ingredients are moistened. Form the dough into a ball and divide that into three balls. Form a ball into a disk and roll it out to a ⅛-inch thickness on a floured surface.

Fit the dough into a 9-inch pie pan and trim the edges to a 1-inch overhang. Fold the dough under and crimp the edges. If not using now, form the remaining two balls of dough into disks, place each in a resealable plastic bag, and freeze for up to 3 months.

MAY 2003

This column reminds me a lot of Elizabeth's columns. Lovina's own style gradually evolved.

Rain, rain, rain! That's what we've been having almost every day. I think some of my lettuce has been drowned out. One corner of my garden was flooded. Luckily, though, it's the corner where I hadn't planted yet. I am hoping it'll dry up soon. It hasn't dried off for over a week now. The weeds are taking over the garden.

Saturday, May 10, was my sister Susan's twenty-seventh birthday. My family: sister Leah and Paul, brother Albert and Sarah Irene, sister Liz and Levi, sister Emma and Jacob, and Joe and I, plus all our children, spent the day with my sisters Susan and Verena. We were sorting through our parents' belongings. The men were gathering tools, etc., outside. We girls emptied Mom's cupboard, which she had packed with dishes. It was sad to think that Mom was the one to put the dishes in the cupboard. Mom has been gone eight months and dad died three years ago, May 20. Oh, how we miss them! I get such a longing to talk to them once more, but we must leave it all to our Heavenly Father, who doesn't make any mistakes. Someday we'll understand it all. We never know what the next day has in store for us.

My brother Amos and Nancy and family couldn't come help on Saturday, as they were blessed with their tenth child. Baby Samuel was born on May 5. This makes two boys and eight girls for them. I imagine Amos and his son, Ben, age twelve, were excited to see another boy. This is the first grandchild born since Mother died. There are seven grandchildren born since Dad died.

This is our first nice day now for a while. The sun is shining and it's 65°F at 9:00 A.M. Daughter Susan is going on a field trip with her grade, so I'm glad it's nice for them. Daughter Elizabeth has a summer birthday (June 14), so she is treating her class today for her "happy unbirthday." She will bring two of her friends home with her to spend the night with her and then go back to school together tomorrow.

Yesterday I had a bad laundry day. Some of the clothes dried between rain showers but garments I have inside hanging on the rack that I'd like to hang out today now. I have laundry to fold, dishes to wash, floors to mop, so I better get started. Although I don't think my work will run away—sometimes I wish it would. Ha!

JUNE 2003

The Amish commonly rid themselves of loved ones' excess belongings by holding an estate auction. By the spring of 2003, the auction for Elizabeth's estate approached, which brought some sadness.

The sun is shining brightly, which is nice to see after a few cloudy days.

This spring has sure been cool. I'll be glad when it warms up to stay.

I am writing this at Mom's living room table, where she wrote most of her columns. Oh, how I wish she would still be here to do this writing. I will never be able to write like her. She was very special to me and a very good example, so I shall try my best with this column, and hope you readers enjoy it.

We are staying here at Mom and Dad's place for a couple of days, getting ready for the upcoming auction of my parents' 104-acre farm and all their personal property. How sad to see all this take place. I never realized how much work there is in getting ready for an auction. I'm sure sisters Verena and Susan will be glad when it is all over.

After the sale, we'll help Verena and Susan move their belongings to their new home and help them get settled in. The house will be a lot smaller than this one, so I think they'll like it better. Although it'll be a big change on them, as they were born here and have lived here all of their life. Life brings changes and we must go on. God is a great help!

There are three apple trees here in the front yard, which Dad and Mom planted in 1971, the year I was born. They are very nice now and looks like they're loaded with apples. There are so many memories around here, but a place doesn't bring happiness.

There is a new set of buildings going up around the corner from here. It looks like they are making good progress. They have the basement poured and the foundation done for the new barns. There must be a lot of work to building everything new like that.

We spent last Saturday at Joe's uncle Jake's (sister Emma's husband's parents). Joe helped them cement their new barn floor. We drove the twelve miles with horse and buggy. It started raining when we were almost four miles from there. This is when the umbrellas really come in hand. We have a two-seated buggy so we need two umbrellas. Daughter Elizabeth can hold the one in the back. It quit raining after we were there awhile. We stopped in town on the way home for groceries.

Sister Emma was here the last couple of days helping get ready for the auction. They washed off most of the walls and ceilings. The bedroom and porch still have to be done. We would also like to get the grass mowed today. The house is starting to look empty, as some of the furniture has been carried out to the washhouse for the sale. Sister Liz and children just drove in, so we'll have more help today.

Thanks to all you great readers for your encouraging letters and notes.

JUNE 2003

This column was written the day before the estate auction. Elizabeth's house was bought by an Amish family from the area.

We are staying with my sisters Verena and Susan tonight. We have been preparing for the sale of Dad and Mom's place, which is where Verena and Susan have been staying since Mom passed away. All the furniture, dishes, etc., have been carried out to the outbuildings. Tomorrow, Dad and Mom's farm and all their belongings will be sold at public auction. The auctioneers came this forenoon to do the finishing touches.

Sister Emma and children and I and my children spent the day here helping Verena and Susan. There is so much work to do to get ready for an auction. It looks sad to see the house empty. By tomorrow afternoon, we will know who the new owners will be.

Tomorrow, nine years ago, our first child, Elizabeth, was born to us. It doesn't seem that long. Elizabeth was born here in this house, as were six of us children and Jacob and Emma's oldest daughter. Joe and I will have been married ten years on July 15. After we were married, we lived in here with my parents for a year. We then moved into a house trailer across the drive and lived there for eighteen months. My daughter Susan was born in the house trailer. On May 11, 1996, we moved to where we live now, not far away. We missed not living here anymore, but it was nice to have our own place.

While we lived here, Joe would go out every morning at 4:00 A.M. to help Dad milk the cows before they each left for work early. Then every night, the cows had to be milked again. Dad and Joe both worked in the carpenter trade back then.

I remember when Elizabeth was a baby, she would cry a lot during the night. Mom would get up and help me try to settle her down. This was different for Mom to

have a little baby in the house again after almost twenty years. I know I often thought: what would I do without my mother? Time brings changes. But God will not give us a heavier burden than He'll help us carry. Without His help, we couldn't go on.

I made cinnamon rolls today to serve to the auctioneers. As I rolled out the dough, I had to think how often Mom stood by this table to do this. Walking around and looking at the things that will be sold brings back memories. So much farm machinery and all of Dad's tools. I'm not sure how much I will buy tomorrow, but the memories I have of my dear parents are memories that money cannot buy. I am so glad for all the times I came home to spend time with them.

Sunday will be Father's Day and also Jacob and Emma's eighth anniversary. So eight years ago the house was also emptied to set up tables for their wedding. But now this is the last time.

I want to thank all the readers that have written letters and cards of encouragement. It is late already and everyone else has gone to bed, so I better join them.

Joe's sister, Ruth, offered to keep our three youngest children there tomorrow so I won't have my hands so full. I sure do appreciate it. I know they will be in good hands.

NOVEMBER 2003

Eggs are often on the menu in the Eicher household. With several hens and excess eggs, she'll sometimes sell the extras to passersby.

We are in the first week of November and have had splendid weather up until today. It turned cooler, and we had a light rain this morning, though. My husband, Joe, started the coal stove again tonight. We had let it go out last week, as the house was warm enough with our 70°F weather we had last week.

Last week, my sister Verena had a day off from the restaurant where she works, so she spent the day here. We did a big laundry and also all the curtains, then we cleaned all the windows. It was such nice weather to do it, although we had to fight with those ladybugs! It's such a good feeling to see the curtains and windows all clean again. It helped to have my new windows that tilt inward to be washed. We didn't have to go outside and drag the stepladder from window to window.

Tomorrow I will be babysitting for my sisters Liz and Emma's youngest children. I will have four extra children here and they are the same age as my four youngest. I guess it'll be like having four sets of twins for a half day. I'm glad to do it for them. Our children just can't wait until it's time for their cousins to come. I told Liz and Emma to not feed their children, as I need to fix lunch for us anyways. I'll probably make mashed potatoes and beef and noodles. That's a favorite for the children.

The chicks that our two hens hatched this spring are starting to lay eggs, so we now have plenty of eggs for our own use. My four-year-old, Benjamin, does a good job of gathering the eggs every night. Once in awhile, three-year-old Loretta will help him. Benjamin told her to hold the eggs real tight so she won't let them fall. Well, she did hold them tight enough, and when she came in egg yolk was running down her dress. Such a mess to clean!

We had a nice surprise on Sunday evening when Joe's dad from Michigan stopped in for a short visit. He had gotten a ride out here with someone who was coming out here and going back again Sunday evening. I popped popcorn, and we had a nice visit before he had to head back home.

This is now Thursday morning. We are having a light rain and the temperature is around 40°F. Heat feels good in the house. My brother Albert and family stopped in on their way to a wedding and gave us a gallon of apple-pear cider. I know we will enjoy that! They will have a long buggy drive this morning. I think they have around sixteen to eighteen miles to go one way. Hopefully the rain will hold off for them.

AMISH COOK CLASSIC: DELICIOUS OMELETTE

Serves 1 to 2

With fresh eggs so plentiful in the Eicher household, omelettes often find their way onto the family's breakfast menus.

2 teaspoons butter	2 eggs
2 tablespoons chopped onion	2 tablespoons water
¼ cup chopped bell pepper	Pinch of salt and black pepper
¼ cup chopped bacon or ham	¼ cup shredded cheese

In a small nonstick skillet, melt 1 teaspoon of the butter over medium heat. Add the onion and the peppers and cook for 2 minutes, stirring frequently. Add the chopped meat and cook for 2 more minutes. Transfer the cooked filling to a plate and set aside. Wipe the skillet clean with a paper towel.

In a small bowl, beat the eggs, water, and salt and pepper with a fork until well blended. Melt the remaining teaspoon of butter in the skillet over medium heat.

Pour the egg mixture into the skillet and use a spatula to pull the cooked egg toward the center of the pan. Continue to cook the egg, pulling the edges inward, until it is barely moist on top. Sprinkle the shredded cheese over half of the omelette. Top the cheese with the filling mixture. Using a spatula, carefully flip the unfilled half of the omelette over the filled half. When the cheese has melted, run the spatula around the edges of the omelette and slide it onto a plate.

NOVEMBER 2003

Joe had his gallbladder surgery in my hometown, where I knew a surgeon who was a specialist in such procedures. Joe and Lovina stayed at my parents' house while they were in town.

November 25: We are home now after being away for Joe's gallbladder surgery. The surgery went OK, but he still has a lot of pain. It will take time to heal. It's just so nice to be home again after being away from the children for one night and two days. It seemed longer. I knew, though, that they were in good care. My sisters Susan and Emma and her husband, Jacob, had them while we were gone. Jacob took care of our chores and kept the stove going, so we came back to a warm place. My sister Verena went on the journey with Joe and I and stayed with me while Joe was having his surgery. How nice to have family to help. We sure appreciated all the help!

November 26: It is now Wednesday morning. Joe had a rough night, but is feeling a lot better now. The children are so glad to have him home that they don't want to let him rest. But the doctor told Joe that he needs to take it easy and not do a lot of heavy lifting. Joe will be off from work for the next week or so while he recovers. I was teasing Joe that it'll be nice having him around to wipe dishes, sweep floors, and change diapers. Our sixteen-month-old, Joseph, seems so unhappy and can't figure out why he can't jump around on Joe when he holds him. He thinks Joe should pick him up and carry him around. He's just too young to understand. Our oldest daughters, Elizabeth and Susan, are at school now. This is the last day of school for them before the Thanksgiving break. Tomorrow is Thanksgiving day, but we won't go anywhere. Joe will need to take it easy.

Last night, Jacob and Emma and family came over. Jacob did the chores for me. I was glad he did. Verena and Susan had sent over some homemade potato soup and Emma brought some meat, so I heated supper so they could eat with us before they left for home.

I have the laundry all sorted and packed. Sisters Verena and Susan will come get it and wash it for me. I was so glad that they offered to do it. I washed on Thursday of last week, so I have a lot of dirty clothes piled up.

I want to thank the readers who sent Joe "get well" cards. Thank you for your thoughtfulness.

We had some snow flurries on Monday. Enough to get the children excited, but they were disappointed it didn't stick. I told them we'll have more than we want soon enough. They are anxious for sleigh rides again.

Christmas will be tomorrow in four weeks. Time goes so fast. Joe will be thirty-five on December 22. My daughter Verena will be six years old on December 10. She said this morning that it's fourteen days until her birthday. She's so excited that she's counting the days. Happy Thanksgiving to all!

2004
estate sale

FEBRUARY 2004

An alarm clock caused a late morning for Joe. Although Old Order Amish don't have electricity, in some areas they are permitted to have small accessories like battery-powered alarm clocks or small flashlights. Amish children are often fascinated with such electronics, which can result in an erroneous time.

What a morning! We thought our battery-powered alarm clock went off at the usual time of 3:45 A.M., as my husband, Joe, had to leave around 4:30 A.M. for work. Before going outside to do the chores, Joe happened to look at the clock in the living room and it showed 6:15 A.M.

So it was hustle and bustle for a while until Joe found someone to take him to work and the girls were ready for school. Nineteen-month-old Joseph just loves to play with our little alarm clock. I usually set it up higher, but must've forgotten to yesterday. Coming home later last evening, I didn't check to see if the time was right on the clock before setting it. Joseph didn't seem to mind that we all slept a couple hours later. He had the girls laughing before they left for school. He was winking at them and being a little show-off.

This week sure is going fast. Monday I did laundry and hung most of it outside, as the temperature was in the forties most of the day. Everything sure dried nice. By the next morning, the rest was all dry on the clothesline racks. Sure gave me "spring fever" already, although Mr. Groundhog says six more weeks of winter. Let's hope he's wrong!

I guess the main reason I'm hoping for an early spring is that we will be moving to Michigan in April. In our new place, we'll be quite close to Joe's family. It's going to take a lot of packing up with six children. Sisters Verena and Susan bought a house just around the corner from ours in Michigan, so they'll be going with us. We are excited that they found something that close to us.

We will regret pulling the children out of this school they attend now, but after visiting their new school, we were very pleased and the girls are less nervous now about moving. Everyone was very nice and helpful.

There will be many memories to leave behind here in Indiana, but it's a new beginning for us.

Yesterday, sisters Verena and Susan came to help us do some packing. We would like to take a load with things we won't need until we're moved. We'd like to go clean the house and get everything ready for the move. It's a two-and-a-half-hour drive each way, so it's not easy to go clean unless we can go a few days at a time.

FEBRUARY 2004

Lovina's days in Indiana drew to a close by February of 2004. Moving a large household and uprooting a lifetime in the Hoosier State was emotionally and logistically difficult, but also was looked at as an adventure by the Eichers.

It's 4:30 A.M. My husband, Joe, just left for the factory where he has worked for seven and a half years. The children are all still asleep yet, so I want to get this written before they wake up.

Morning came around too fast. We are having another busy week of packing. I wrote last week that we will soon be moving to Michigan. Sisters Susan and Verena will also go. Yesterday sisters Verena, Susan, Emma, and children assisted me in my work, for which I was very grateful to have the help. We put in a full day's work. We packed dishes and utensils. I also emptied my two kitchen cupboards and packed everything carefully. Besides doing all the packing, we also did a huge laundry. All but a few pieces are dry now. I was so glad for such a nice day of weather to do the laundry. It was a great day for the children to play outside, also. They enjoy being outdoors when it's this nice.

Emma's husband, Jacob, helped Joe load up some of the heavy things last night and the night before, also. We borrowed a sixteen-foot, boxed-in trailer for packing and it's surprising how much they have in there already.

We plan to take the load to Michigan on Saturday and Joe wants to see what lumber he'll need to get the barn ready for the horses. He'll have to put up a fence around the pasture field. Everything will take time.

We probably won't get much cleaned in the new house while we are there Saturday. Unloading the trailer will take quite a bit of time. Between unloading and a two-and-a-half-hour journey there and back, it won't give us too much time.

We met one of our new neighbors and she's a very nice lady, which will make moving easier. My daughter Elizabeth, age nine, told me she has our new address in Michigan memorized already. It's going to be different to have a name for our road instead of a number, as we do here in Indiana.

Friday, February 17, would've have been Dad's seventy-third birthday if he was still living. Days like that give a person a longing to see and hear them again. He was a great dad and I'll always have good memories of him. Dad had three sisters and nine brothers, so he had a lot of stories to tell us about his growing up years. With ten boys in the house, I imagine there was not one dull moment.

I hope to get some more things packed today. With ten years of marriage, things accumulate that we don't need. I'm having the girls look through their things they've collected so we can figure out what to take and what not to.

Meanwhile, our ice is finally starting to melt off of our gravel drive. For quite a few weeks now, it has had a layer of ice on it. Makes walking easier for little Joseph and, of course, for me.

MARCH 2004

March 19, 2004, was Lovina and her family's first full day living in Michigan. Lovina and her family hired non-Amish movers to take the bulk of their belongings in a truck. This is common practice among Amish moving long distances.

We headed to Michigan early this morning with another load of hay. My sister Emma, her husband, Jacob, and their son Jacob Jr. went up to Michigan with Joe, little Benjamin, and me. Sisters Verena and Susan kept the other eight children at their house. We started out around 6:00 A.M. and we were home by around 6:30 P.M.

Little Joseph was a lot more contented to stay with Verena and Susan. He just hates sitting in a car seat all the way there and back. I was glad they could stay at Verena and Susan's house. The children enjoyed the day at their house so much that they wanted to spend the night there. We brought them home, though, as I figured Verena and Susan were ready for a break.

In Michigan, Joe and Jacob unloaded the hay, which was a long, hard job. Then a load of lumber we had ordered arrived, so they helped unload that. And while the menfolk were hard at work, Emma and I made chili soup for our lunch, and we all ate our first meal at our new place. The Realtor stopped by, so we made him sit down and eat with us. He sure has been a good help to us already.

Benjamin and Jacob Jr. were quite tired by the time we were ready to go. Four-year-old boys can really get around looking for adventure. They enjoyed being in the haymow with their dads.

Before we started for home we stopped in to see where Mom's cousin and his family live, which is not far from our new place. The boys fell asleep on the way home. They were tired after a full day.

Joe quit his factory job now after being there seven and a half years. With him not working during the day, we hope to have the rest of our belongings loaded up by Thursday afternoon. We want to attend Susan's first-grade musical at school on Thursday afternoon. That will be their last day of school in this school district. We will start out early on Friday morning with the horses and chickens. Verena and Susan will go along. The driver will then come back and pick up Levi, Liz, and children and Jacob, Emma, and children and pull the sixteen-foot enclosed trailer out to Michigan with the rest of our belongings. It will be a busy week!

MARCH 2004

Some readers asked how the heck the Eichers moved everything to Michigan. The answer: just like everyone else. They hired movers. The Amish are allowed to hire others to drive for them, and when moving a family of eight (at the time), that was an absolute necessity.

We have been living at our new place in Michigan for almost two weeks now. So far, we have enjoyed it here.

My husband, Joe, started his construction job yesterday. He really enjoyed his first day on the job. They changed a barn roof, so the work was a lot different than factory work. Seems different to have him leave for work later, but he also comes home later. We have to get adjusted to a different place and different schedule.

Our daughters Elizabeth, nine, Susan, seven, and Verena, six, started school here in Michigan this week. They really seem to like it. Verena only goes a half day, but she likes it so well she would like to go all day.

Benjamin, four, and Loretta, three, miss Verena not being home during the day. Benjamin and Loretta seem lost the last few days since the girls are in school and Joe leaves for work. They had been used to their dad being home from work the past week or so.

Joe was home working on the box stalls for the horses. He got the box stalls done just in time. Our horse, Itty Bit, had a colt March 25. She has a nice-looking filly. The colt is active, always running around the field. Itty Bit had the colt only six days after we brought her here from Indiana, so we are lucky she waited.

The chickens are getting settled into their new place in the barn. Joe had to find a way to keep Benjamin out of the chicken coop. He would keep checking on eggs, bringing one in as soon as it was laid. This was disturbing the hens. Our "little chicks" are now big and starting to lay eggs.

Last Monday afternoon, a few men from this area stopped in to say hi and welcome us to the area. Joe and my brother-in-law, Jacob, were talking with them outside. Jacob's were here for a few days, helping us get unpacked.

Joe was burning trash behind the barn before the men arrived. My sister, Verena, happened to look outside and see that the fire was spreading. We all ran outside to help put it out. The men carried buckets of water while we helped fill them. The fire came very close to our barn, and luckily, the wind was in our favor. We are so thankful there wasn't any damage. A good part of the field behind the barn was burnt and it had started in the cornfield on the dry corn stalks. If we would've been by ourselves, we would probably have lost the barn. So it was a rocky start to our move to Michigan!

We helped sisters Verena and Susan move here to Michigan last Tuesday and Wednesday. They walked over here yesterday and helped me do a big laundry. It's nice having them this close. And now we are even more excited, as sister Emma and Jacob bought a seven-acre farm up here Monday evening. It will be so nice having them in the area. The children miss each other, as they were always together.

MAY 2004

All told, Lovina's two single sisters, Susan and Verena, and her married sister, Emma, made the move to Michigan in the spring of 2004. The rest of their siblings stayed behind in Indiana.

We have already entered the month of May. My sister Susan will turn twenty-eight on May 10. Jacob and Emma's little boy, Benjamin, will be two on May 12. I will turn thirty-three already on May 22.

Then along with all the birthdays coming up in May, we have the sad reminder of the passing away of dear Dad. It will be four long and lonely years on May 20 that he died. God is above and a makes no mistakes, though.

We spent the day at Jacob and Emma's new home here in Michigan yesterday. We spent part of the weekend there unloading all of their belongings. They had all their belongings, plus some hay to unload. It took awhile to get unpacked. The women were washing walls, ceilings, windows, etc., while the men unloaded.

Joe and I plan to go there again today to help them get more organized. Jacob also wants to get a fence up for the horses, so they can go outside. I will help Emma with getting her house organized. I know how it feels to be all disorganized and have to look where everything is. I still haven't unpacked everything, but I have most stuff in

AMISH COOK CLASSIC: POOR MAN'S STEAK
Serves 6

The Eichers may have been in a new state and settlement, but they brought many of their old favorite recipes with them, including this one.

1½ pounds lean ground beef

1 cup dry bread crumbs

1 small onion, chopped

2 eggs

1 teaspoon salt

⅛ teaspoon black pepper

¼ teaspoon garlic powder

1 (10¾-ounce) can cream of mushroom soup

½ cup water

½ cup milk

1 (4-ounce) can sliced mushrooms, drained

Preheat the oven to 350°F. Grease a 9-inch square baking dish and set aside.

In a large bowl, combine the ground beef, bread crumbs, onion, eggs, salt, pepper, and garlic powder. Knead the mixture with your hands until it is smooth and uniformly combined. Shape the meat mixture into a loaf and cut it into nine slices. In a greased skillet, fry the meat slices until browned on each side. Drain off the excess grease and transfer the browned slices to the prepared baking dish. In a medium bowl, combine the mushroom soup, water, and milk. Stir until smooth. Pour the soup mixture evenly over the meat slices and sprinkle with the drained mushrooms. Bake uncovered for 30 to 40 minutes, until the meat slices are cooked through and the sauce is bubbling.

totes with lids, so there is no hurry. My sisters Verena and Susan will help at Jacob's again today, also.

It was nice to see my uncle Joe and aunt Betty, my brother Albert and Sarah Irene, and sister Liz and her daughters, Rosa and Suzanne. They came to Michigan to help Jacob's unload.

Jacob and Emma plan to take their daughters, Elizabeth and Emma, to their new school to enroll them. They are excited and so are our girls to have cousins in the same school again.

It looks like another beautiful day, but the temperature is only 47°F. One morning this week it went down to 32°F and hurt some plants people had out in the gardens. I didn't have any plants out yet, which I was glad for. Hopefully, it'll warm up to stay soon.

It was nice being able to drive to Jacob's with the horse and buggy again. Since we moved on March 19, we were two and a half hours apart, and now it's nice to all be close together, with Verena and Susan just around the corner.

On Friday, May 7, we will head for Indiana again to help prepare for the upcoming sale of our house and some personal property. It will be a great relief to us to have it sold, so we can concentrate fully on getting settled in more around here. Life is just too busy, and I'll be glad when things slow down to a normal pace.

The girls have only three more weeks of school left. I will be glad for their help this summer.

MAY 2004

The arrival of Lovina's new baby caught readers of "The Amish Cook" off guard. Lovina never mentioned her pregnancy during columns. Pregnancy is something most Amish women don't feel comfortable discussing publicly, but the birth was a blessing nonetheless.

As you readers may have heard, we were blessed with a daughter named Lovina on May 18, 2004. She joins siblings Elizabeth, nine; Susan, eight; Verena, six; Benjamin, four; Loretta, three; and Joseph, twenty-two months. She weighed five pounds, fifteen ounces at birth and was over eighteen inches long. She arrived three weeks early, but is doing great so far, which we are thankful for!

I will try to write how everything went. At 3:00 A.M. on May 18, I awoke to very hard pain. I had been having gallbladder attacks throughout this pregnancy and thought it was another attack that would leave in an hour or so, as it usually did. After a couple of hours, my pains got worse and to the point where I could hardly take it anymore. My husband Joe went for my sisters Susan and Verena, who live just around the corner here in Michigan. After they came over, Joe went to our non-Amish neighbor lady and asked if she would take us to the emergency room at the hospital in the nearby town. I had to have help getting out to her car. Susan and Joe went along to the hospital, while Verena stayed here with the children.

They took tests and prepared me for emergency C-section. They discovered I had pancreatitis, which caused me to be put into intensive care for five days. Baby Lovina and I were in the hospital for seven days. I was battling fever and my one lung almost collapsed, so I had to take breathing treatments. The doctor said it could've been too late for both of us had we waited much longer. Joe wanted me to go to the hospital sooner.

It was a relief once I could come home and not be all hooked up to everything. Joe wanted to name the baby after me, as she was born four days before my birthday. I spent my thirty-third birthday in the ICU, but my gift was that I could get moved out of ICU to a regular room that day. I couldn't see the baby for two days because of my fever. Joe would go down to the nursery and feed her and she acted like she knew him already.

Jacob and Emma had their public auction for their property in Indiana on my birthday. Verena and Susan took our six children along to Indiana. I think it was good for them to get away for a day.

I am so glad to be home again. I don't know what we would've done without Verena and Susan's help. The people in the community have been so caring and helpful. I will have to have surgery in several weeks to have my gallbladder removed. It will be a relief when that's over. God was above us and we thank Him for saving us both. Thank you to all the readers for your cards and well wishes.

JUNE 2004

Customs differ from one Amish settlement to the next. One of the differences between Michigan's Amish community and Lovina's former community in Indiana is the use of covered buggies. The buggies in Indiana were open (roofless), which left the riders much more exposed to the elements. Lovina often wrote of this change in the weeks after her move to Michigan.

It's Thursday forenoon and I had better get this written and out in the mailbox before the mailman comes. Time just flies by in the mornings.

My husband, Joe, left at 7:00 A.M. for work. They are doing a lot of roofing jobs, but they also have some pole barns lined up to do. With all the rain lately, they have lost a few days of work.

Joe has been cleaning out the barn. A lot of trash stayed here, so we're gradually trying to get it hauled away.

My daughter Elizabeth had her tenth birthday on June 14. It is so hard to believe that our oldest child is already ten!

Tuesday we went to Indiana to do the closing on our property there. We had it scheduled for May 21, but then I ended up in the hospital, so we had to cancel it until I was able to travel that far. I will probably have my gallbladder surgery in three weeks. I will be so glad to get that over with and hopefully I won't have to be so careful what I eat.

Gardens are starting to look better since we've had a few sunshiny days. My garden needs to be hoed so badly.

Joe didn't come in until 6:30 last night, and we had visitors, so it just hasn't seemed like the nights have been long enough to get everything done lately. Will be glad when I can help with the harder work again.

We took baby Lovina along on Tuesday to Indiana. She did pretty good about traveling. She is sleeping a little longer during the night. I think she had her days and nights mixed up for a while. She would sleep a lot during the day and at night be bright awake.

We have our new covered buggy now. Sunday we went for a ride in it. Sister Emma and Jacob told us to come to their house for dinner. It was nice to get out of the house for a while on such a pleasant day, although I was upset that we missed some visitors from our church who came to see the baby.

Sisters Verena and Susan did my laundry on Monday and swept and mopped the floors. I don't know what I would've done without their help.

Benjamin, Loretta, and Joseph will all have birthdays next month. Joe and I will also have our eleventh wedding anniversary. So July will be a busy month around here.

Little Joseph seems to accept baby Lovina more than he did at first, although it still bothers him at times not to be the baby. We got one of Jacob's puppies, and Joseph just loves that little puppy.

I want to thank all of you readers that have sent baby, birthday, and get-well cards. I appreciate all the good wishes and may God bless each and every one of you for your kindness.

AUGUST 2004

The column became a bit more confusing to follow with the addition of another Lovina!

I will try to get this column written tonight. I am holding baby Lovina, as she is being fussy again. I'm hoping she isn't a "colic" baby. She has a hard time burping after her feeding at night.

Our little Verena was a colic baby, and I remember how often she kept us awake during the night. My husband, Joe, could usually hold her just right and she would settle down. It seems Lovina settles down easier when he holds her.

I remember at the hospital I couldn't see her for two days because I had a fever, so Joe spent more time with baby Lovina than I did. They took me down in a wheelchair to see her after I was feeling better, and as soon as I held her she started crying. Joe took her and she was quiet right away. She must've known who Joe was already.

I was used to having my babies beside me all the time after they were born. But the nurses told me there will be plenty of time for bonding, and they were right! Things have been going pretty smooth since we've been home from the hospital. I want to thank you readers for all your cards and well wishes.

After my gallbladder surgery, I was so tired. Joe would get up and heat Lovina's bottle and feed her. I hated to have him do that and lose sleep, as he had to get to work the next day. But Joe told me that he knows he wouldn't have felt like feeding a baby right after his gallbladder surgery.

Right now Joe is out working in our yard. He hopes to get our hay mowed tomorrow. Hopefully we can get it baled and in the barn before it rains. If it rains, I guess we won't complain, as the other fields need it and also our garden.

Daughter Elizabeth, age ten, is washing supper dishes and Susan, eight, is picking up toys and sweeping floors. I had to hold Lovina, so I figured I might as well write this and get it ready for tomorrow's mail.

Yesterday, July 19, was sister Emma's thirty-first birthday. We surprised her by all getting together for supper. Sisters Verena and Susan were there, also. We had an enjoyable evening and a good meal.

Baby Lovina didn't enjoy her evening, as she was fussy. Maybe we'll have to switch to a different formula. She seems real contented until evening, though.

We had an easy supper tonight—no cooking! Our neighbor lady brought supper in for us. How thoughtful! She was on her way to town and dropped it off. It really gave me a lift, as I was doing some unpacking. I emptied quite a few totes and was just starting to think about what I should fix for supper when she dropped by. I hope I can repay her sometime!

Joe's sister Loretta and husband, Henry, were blessed with a baby girl named Rebecca on Saturday. We would like to go see her sometime. They live in this community. This makes three boys and three girls for them now.

I plan to go spend the day tomorrow at sister Emma's. The children can't wait to visit with their cousins. They always have a fun time playing together. Emma and Jacob are enjoying their new barn, which looks really nice.

SEPTEMBER 2004

This was the Eichers' first trip back to Indiana since their move. They still maintained close ties to their former community, going back for weddings, funerals, or visits with family.

We spent Sunday, August 22, with my brother Albert and Sarah Irene and family in Indiana. My sister Emma, husband Jacob, and their children (plus my sisters Susan and Verena) also went. We hired two vans to take us, as we're a total of seventeen. We started out around 6:00 A.M., after we finally got all the car seats hooked up and the children belted in. That takes awhile just doing that.

My sister Verena's birthday was on Sunday, so she took us all out for breakfast on the way to Indiana. It was a treat to eat out and not do any dishes.

We stopped in at my sister Liz and Levi's on the way to Albert's. She has been busy this summer repainting her bedrooms upstairs and revarnishing the wood floors.

Liz and Levi's decided to join us at Albert's for the day. We were all glad to get to see Albert and Sarah Irene's two-and-a-half-week-old daughter, Susan. She's a sweetie! I didn't realize how my baby Lovina had grown until I saw her beside Susan. They are two and a half months apart.

Albert's family had a big dinner, with the main dish being delicious barbecued chicken.

We all had an enjoyable day together. Albert's oldest daughter, Elizabeth, had her seventeenth birthday on Sunday, as did sister Leah's son Paul Jr. who turned nine. Uncle Joe and Betty Coblentz and a couple of their grandchildren also had dinner with us at Albert's.

Before we started for home, we stopped in for a short visit with my sister Leah and Paul's family. This was the first time they had seen baby Lovina. Leah set some snacks out, and we stayed longer than we had planned to. Leah is preparing for the move to their new fifty-acre farm that they bought nine to ten miles north of them.

After leaving Paul's, we stopped in to say hi to brother Amos, Nancy, and family. They weren't home, so we headed back to Michigan. We arrived back around 9:00 P.M., so we made the children go to bed right away. They had slept on the way home after such a long day. As always, it was good to be back home in Michigan again!

We are trying to get back into a "routine" again as the school year begins. Joe and I now have four children going to school, which is hard to believe. Benjamin only goes half days.

I'm sitting out here on the front steps with Benjamin, Loretta, and Joseph, waiting on the bus to pick up Benjamin. He leaves around 10:25 A.M. So far he seems rarin' to go, so that makes it easier to see him go. Loretta has a paper and pencil and says she's writing a column, too.

I processed nineteen quarts of pickles already and have another bucket yet to go. I made dill, banana, and also some freezer pickles. A lady from the community had extra corn and gave me quite a few bags. It was all bagged and ready. I hadn't met her until Tuesday evening at Joe's sister MaryAnn's. I thought that was so thoughtful for her to do that. It sure means a lot to me.

A friend also gave us a big sack of sweet corn, so I hope to work that up today. I also have green beans to do that I got from Verena and Susan. My hot peppers are also ready to be picked and put into jars, but I'll leave that for next week.

NOVEMBER 2004

A cold, foggy buggy ride is definitely more cozy in a covered buggy. In Indiana, only an umbrella provided protection from the elements.

It turned out to be a warm and beautiful day for a wedding, the wedding of Joe's nephew Emanul. It was very foggy on our way there. It always makes me nervous to drive the buggy through fog. We had our blinking lights on, but I'm always afraid someone won't see us in time. I appreciate the covered buggy even more now with cold weather coming on. The wedding services were held at the bride's neighbors in a big buggy shed.

The meals for those in attendance were served at the bride's home, in a big building where they could seat over a couple hundred people at one time.

In this community, when they have a wedding, they rent a cook wagon and cooler. The wagon has five gas stoves, a sink with hot and cold running water, cabinets, etc. It also has kettles, plates, silverware, bowls, towels, glasses, coffee cups, and just about

AMISH COOK CLASSIC: OVEN OMELETTE

Serves 4 to 6

Egg recipes continued to find their way onto the Eicher menu and into the column, as Lovina's hens were really active!

2 medium onions, diced

2 cups cheese of your choice, shredded

1 (3-ounce) package dried beef, diced

8 eggs

1 cup milk

Salt and black pepper

Preheat the oven to 325°F.

In a buttered 9 by 13-inch pan, layer the onion, cheese, and dried beef. In a large bowl, beat the eggs and the milk together until well combined. Season with the salt and pepper, then pour the egg mixture over the layered ingredients. Bake about 30 minutes, or until the eggs are set.

everything you need to prepare and serve a wedding meal. This makes it so much easier after the wedding not to have all the dishes to put away or return to people.

They assigned us cooks all to specific duties. My job, along with five other women, was to peel potatoes and put them into kettles to cook, then get them all mashed after they were ready. It takes a lot of potatoes on a day like that. It wasn't too bad with all of us to take turns mashing. Some of us had babies to go tend to.

They had women assigned to make homemade gravy, vegetables, chicken, salad dressing, etc.

The cooks and the table waiters (which they choose friends and cousins and assign a boy and girl to every table to wait on) eat before we go over to see the couple get married, which is around noon.

Usually only the cooks that are related to the bride and groom go, and the rest keep watch on the food on the burners. After the couple is united in marriage, everyone comes over to the bride's home to eat.

When Joe and I got married, we had everything (services and meals) all at my parents', which makes it nice.

After everyone was served, dinner dishes were washed, tables set again for supper and the bride and groom opened their many nice wedding gifts. Some singing takes place, also, and then it's time for us cooks to start all over again for supper.

For dinner, they served potatoes, gravy, dressing, corn, baked chicken, salad, bread buns, pudding, fruit, cake, and different kinds of pies. For supper, mashed potatoes, gravy, dressing, mixed vegetables, meatloaf, salad, bread, pies, cake, ice cream, and strawberries were served. Then after every meal they passed a bowl of candy bars around, which I doubt not many people were hungry for until much later.

It was a long day but enjoyable. Was nice to finally climb into bed after a day like that. The children were also tired from a full day of playing with friends and cousins.

DECEMBER 2004

A newborn baby meant Lovina was sometimes up writing the column in the middle of the night as she fed her little namesake.

Today, December 22, is my husband Joe's thirty-sixth birthday. I want to bake a cake for him to mark the occasion. I asked our children yesterday if we want to make him blow out thirty-six candles, and they all thought that it would be fun!

It is 5:00 A.M. now as I write this, and the children are all still asleep. Baby Lovina woke up Joe and I, wanting a bottle. So I decided to write this column while all is quiet.

I don't think we need an alarm clock. For some reason she always knows when 4:30 A.M. comes around. She sleeps all night, though, which I'm glad for.

Baby Lovina gets around everywhere in her walker. We sit her on the floor, but she flops onto her stomach and really gets around. She is now seven months old and such a joy! It's always interesting to see babies learn new things. She likes to tease her two-year-old brother, Joseph, when she's in her walker. She waits until he has all his little horses standing and then she pushes her walker right through them, knocking them all down. Joseph gets so aggravated at her and thinks he has to teach her how to behave. We had a cold weekend, with the temperature going down to 2°F, and it was very windy. It's harder to keep the house cozy when that wind blows. Most of the snow is gone now. I keep hoping we might get just enough snow to cover the ground before Christmas.

I always like to see a white Christmas. I guess we are never satisfied, are we? We should accept the weather however God sends it. Saturday is Christmas Day already.

We will be home and take time to spend the day with the children. Let us take time to thank God for his many, many blessings on this day our dear Savior, Jesus Christ, was born. We wish you all God's blessings throughout the holiday season and in the year 2005.

On Monday morning at 5:00 A.M. we plan to head out to Indiana to sister Leah and Paul's. We will have our family Christmas gathering at their new home. We haven't all been together for a family gathering since Mom died. It will be nice to all get together again, but our dear parents will be greatly missed.

Five of us daughters have moved to different places this year. Six of the oldest grandchildren have a "special" friend now. So along with the two new babies in the family this year, the family is growing in another way. Life goes on and changes are made.

What would we do without our Heavenly Father to guide us through these years? It takes so many prayers. God has been so good to us. We have so many blessings to thank Him for. Do we take enough time for Him in this busy, rushy world?

2005

a fresh start: moving to michigan

This column illustrates a fact of Amish life: buggy rides are just as susceptible to mechanical mishaps as automobiles are!

We are now into the first week of 2005. This morning we awoke to a white world once again. The last snow had melted with the rains we were having off and on.

It is still snowing now, and it makes a person's spirits lift to see it snow after all those dreary days of muddy rain. God is in control of the weather, though, so I should not complain, but be thankful for His many blessings. Our minds go out to the victims of that bad earthquake in Asia. I cannot imagine what those people are going through. Let us remember them in our prayers.

Sunday we were taking Verena and Susan home after having brunch at Jacob and Emma's. While traveling uphill, the bit on our horse, Diamond's, bridle broke and somehow made him lose his footing and fall down. With Verena and Susan along to help, we quickly had all the children out of the buggy. We immediately unhitched Diamond from the buggy, but had to work to get the shaft away. He finally got up, much to our relief. We were afraid he might've broken a leg. Joe walked home to get a new bit for the bridle.

We were fortunate to not be far from home. Diamond was OK, just a little stiff and sore. He is our "Old Faithful"; we raised him form a colt and Joe trained him. He is a trustworthy horse, now almost eleven years old. I told Joe I am glad that bit didn't break on us when we were traveling a busy highway in town. God had his protecting hand over us.

We had Joe's family gathering on New Year's Day. Not everyone made it, but we still had a full house. We decided to empty out our living room and set up three 8-foot tables in there. It was nice to have everything in here and not have so much walking back and forth to our outbuilding where we were going to gather. If I'd have a stove and sink out there, it wouldn't be so bad. Joe grilled forty pounds of chicken for the occasion, and I made mashed potatoes, gravy, ham, dressing, corn, punch, and coffee. The others brought in the salads, pies, cake, puddings, cookies, etc. We had more than enough food, and everyone brought snacks to enjoy while we played games in the afternoon. Before they left, Joe's family carried out the tables and benches and put my furniture back in place.

On Saturday, Joe and Jacob plan to butcher beef. We will go in half and half with each other. We will work up the meat in our pole building next week sometime. I will be glad to get some meat in jars again, as we are all getting low. ❧

MARCH 2005

Lovina's husband, Joe, is a superb horse trainer, but sometimes even the best can be bested by an ornery horse, as this column illustrates.

I now have Benjamin ready for school, and I need to get this written and in today's mail. I have so much work waiting on me, and it would be easy to let this go for now.

It's a relief that the children are all back in school now and feeling better. Only Susan and Benjamin ended up with strep throat. I was so afraid more of the children would catch it. I'll keep my fingers crossed.

My husband, Joe, had a misfortune while training my sister Susan's horse on Friday evening. As Joe was working with her, the horse started kicking while going at a pretty good speed. Joe pulled on the reins and the horse fell, causing Joe to go flying off the cart from the sudden stop. He landed on the horse's head. Joe was in so much pain we figured he might've broken a rib.

After getting it checked out, he found it's badly bruised, but no breaks. He sure is having a rough time getting through each day at work. Because of the bruised rib, Joe hurts so much when he coughs—and he has a bad cough right now. He's using pain relievers, but they don't seem to hold out long. Nights are very miserable for him. Just hope it heals soon.

Joe won't be able to work with the horse for a while, so he asked someone else to finish training her. I am so relieved! There'll be plenty of spring work, and I know he would be pushing it to try and train horses while getting everything else caught up.

Meanwhile, my daughter Elizabeth was washing eggs last week one night. We are getting plenty of eggs from our hen house these days, and it's a chore to wash them all. Elizabeth took a break and joined all of us as we went to the window to watch Joe drive the horse. When we looked back, Joseph, two, was having the time of his life cracking one egg after another onto the countertop. What a mess!

That reminded me of the time when Benjamin was almost eighteen months old, and Jacob and Emma's Jacob was younger and not walking yet. Verena and I had come back to Dad and Mom's with quite a few flats of eggs we had just bought. Verena took the eggs inside and set them on the countertop and came back outside to help me with the horse. When she came back in the house, Benjamin had climbed up on the step stool and was tossing eggs down to Jacob on the floor. They were having a real ball! Eggs are such a mess to clean up, and what a mess that was. There were close to one hundred eggs so, luckily, Verena saw them before they got too far.

We are getting around twenty eggs a day right now from our hens. We are getting stocked up with too many eggs, so I should make homemade noodles soon. Easter is coming up, so that'll use up some when the children color eggs.

AMISH COOK CLASSIC: ASPARAGUS CASSEROLE
Serves 4 to 6

One of the first things Lovina noticed after moving to Michigan was an asparagus patch that had been planted at her new home. Asparagus found its way into casserole, bread, and salad recipes that Lovina shared in her column.

3 tablespoons butter

1 tablespoon grated onion

¼ cup chopped red bell pepper

3 tablespoons all-purpose flour

1 cup milk

1½ teaspoons salt

¼ teaspoon black pepper

3 cups boiled asparagus

3 hard-boiled eggs, sliced

1 cup shredded mild Cheddar cheese

½ cup buttered bread crumbs

Preheat the oven to 350°F. Grease a 9-inch square baking dish and set aside.

In a heavy-bottomed saucepan, melt the butter over medium heat. Add the onion and the bell pepper and sauté until soft. Sprinkle the flour over the mixture, then gradually stir in the milk. Add the salt and the pepper. Continue to cook the sauce, stirring continuously, until thickened.

In the prepared baking dish, alternate layers of the cooked asparagus with the hard-boiled egg slices. Pour the sauce evenly over the layers. Top the casserole with the Cheddar and sprinkle with the bread crumbs. Bake about 25 minutes, or until the sauce is bubbling and the crumbs are golden.

MAY 2005

Baby Lovina turned one year old this month, but had to battle through some illness to get there.

This column is shorter than usual as my husband, Joe, and I are at the local hospital. We've been here since Friday evening with our baby daughter, Lovina. She was badly dehydrated from having diarrhea and vomiting. There seems to be a virus affecting a lot of babies in this community. The doctor thought having her on an IV for a day or two would help get her hydrated again. She'll be a year old already on May 18. It was good Joe and I could both be here, as she would've been a handful for one. She keeps trying to pull out her IV. We had a hard time getting her to settle down, but after that, she slept real good. She's a little fighter and tries to fight the nurses when they come in to take her temperature, etc.

I am trying to help keep her entertained while Joe goes after some breakfast. At the same time, I thought I could write a few lines, but it doesn't seem to be working too well. I'm afraid my editor will have a hard time reading my writing. It's so hard to have a child beg to eat or drink when they aren't allowed. The doctor said we could try food this morning and see if it'll stay down. If it does, hopefully we can go back home by tonight.

Meanwhile, my sisters Verena and Susan have our other six children at their house since last night. What a blessing to have family to help. Jacob will go do our chores.

This is now later and we were allowed to feed Lovina some bananas and applesauce. So far she has kept it down. Joe is trying to settle her down for a nap. I think she misses the other children and all the noise she's used to at home. The doctor hasn't been in yet, so don't know if we'll have to stay or not.

Last week, my sister Emma and I spent the day at Joe's sister Carol's house making noodles from almost one hundred eggs. Joe's sisters MaryAnn, Loretta, and Susan were also there and MaryAnn's married daughter. MaryAnn and her daughter babysit for three children, so all in all there were seven two-year-olds there. The children were all very tired by evening. Mine fell asleep in the buggy on the way home.

MAY 2005

Lovina writes about freezing asparagus in this column. Gasoline-powered freezers, which were not allowed back in Indiana, are permitted by the Amish church in Michigan. Although freezing didn't take the place of the labor-intensive home canning, it provided Lovina with another option.

It is a cool morning, May 12, as I write this. The temperature dipped down to 45°F last night.

Yesterday we had a thunderstorm, which gave us a good, soaking rain. It's been cool ever since.

Today is my sister Emma and husband Jacob's youngest child Benjamin's third birthday. My sister Susan turned twenty-nine on May 10 and my daughter Lovina will be a year old on the eighteenth. Then my birthday will be May 22, making me thirty-four years old.

Lovina ended up being in the hospital for two days and two nights. I ended up taking her to the doctor again, as her fever went up to 105°F. The doctor thinks it's a viral infection. He gave her some medicine, and she seems to be feeling herself again.

I'm so glad all the other children stayed healthy. Lovina is back to crawling around and getting into everything, which is a good sign that she is feeling better. The other children really missed her while she was away.

Our older girls have left for school now, and my four youngest are still sleeping, which is nice for a change. We got to bed later than usual last night, as Joe and I took our oldest daughter, Elizabeth, to the fifth-grade orientation at the school. It is so hard to believe she will be in middle school. The children all read their portfolios to us parents.

We left the other children at Jacob and Emma's and they gave them supper. That sure helped me out to not have to fix supper for everyone. Jacob reshod all of our horses while we were gone. They live within walking distance from school, so we walked, which was nice exercise.

Elizabeth put a vase of fresh lilacs on my desk, and they smell so good. I love smelling lilacs. We have both the purple and white. I'd like to get more started.

I made some coffee and am enjoying a cup while I savor this rare moment of peace and quiet. The birds are singing gaily outside my window. Spring is such a lovely time of the year. Our Creator has given us so many blessings.

Joe is being kept busy taking care of the yard at night. He's feeding the horses the grass clippings, which they really like. As soon as we got our fence up around our pasture field, they will have a lot of good pasture to eat.

I am hoping to finish getting the rest of the garden planted soon. The corn we planted is finally peeping through, and potatoes are coming up nicely and, oh my! Asparagus is shooting up so fast! I'm sharing asparagus with others, as it's way too much for us. I would like to freeze some.

JUNE 2005

One of Lovina's aunts passed away, as described in this column. Lovina's father came from a family of thirteen children; all eventually left the Amish except for Ben, who chose to stay.

We were gone for a couple of days earlier this week to attend the funeral of our aunt Betty Yoder, age sixty-two. It's still so hard to grasp that she's not around anymore. She was an active person and seemed to make everyone laugh. My thoughts and prayers are with the family as they go through this difficult time. It's not easy to lose a parent.

The funeral was largely attended. Betty came from a family of thirteen children and was the third youngest. My grandparents and my dad (her brother) preceded her in death. Dad was the second oldest of the children, ten boys and three girls. I often think Grandma must've really been busy raising ten boys. I got to see a lot of our Coblentz cousins I hadn't seen in awhile. Uncle Andy (Betty's husband) comes from a family of twelve children. I was glad to meet some of his family.

Aunt Catherine, another of Dad's sisters, was still in the hospital recovering from a bad stroke. She was able to come to the funeral, but still looked weak. I hope she keeps improving.

We left for the funeral on Monday. We spent Monday night at my sister Liz and Levi's, near our old home in Indiana. The children were having so much fun that it was hard to get them settled down for bed. My sister Emma, her husband, Jacob, and their children were also staying at Liz's, along with my sisters Verena and Susan. Altogether, there were fifteen children at Liz's that night.

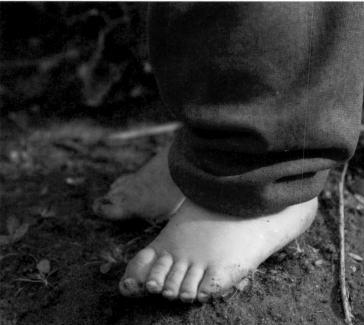

We were all tired and ready for bed when we came home Tuesday night. It just seems to take a lot of packing, even for only one night away. The laundry really added up, so that's what I did yesterday, after unpacking. Now, today, I'd like to get our house organized again. It's been neglected with our leaving too much.

Last night we went to the school for our daughter Verena's kindergarten graduation party. The children all looked so cute.

Everything seems to be growing in the garden. We are enjoying some of the "fruit of our labor," such as fresh green onions, radishes, and lettuce. I had to replant some lettuce, as it came up real spotty. The garden is filled now, but I like to squeeze in a few more rows of radishes somewhere yet. Mom used to plant radishes between the corn rows, as the radishes were usually out before the corn got too big. She could get a lot out of a little space.

Along with all the good stuff growing, so are weeds. We need to get those under control. Joe staked down some cattle panels beside the tomatoes, so that way the tomato plants vine up around those.

JULY 2005

A typical summer at Lovina's house in Michigan is described in this column. By the time this column was written, the Eichers had been settled in their new community for well over a year.

Susan, Verena, and I cleaned out our pole building this morning. It doesn't take much for that building to get disorganized again after cleaning, so we have to stay on top of that.

We also weeded flower beds while my daughter Elizabeth, eleven, was mowing. After lunch we want to get the small building beside the house cleaned out. I am glad to get everything organized before school starts, which is Monday already. Hard to believe the summer went so fast. The basement is almost all cleaned also, which will be nice to have done.

Joe didn't work yesterday, as the factory shut down for a funeral. Our community was deeply saddened by the passing away of a nineteen-year-old Amish boy. The cause of death was ruled an aneurysm. He was with some friends fishing when it happened. What a shock to friends, relatives, and his special friend. Joe worked with him at the factory sometimes. Such a young age! It once again reminds us that God chooses from all ages and we don't have to be old to die.

The community gathered last Saturday (and some on Friday also to prepare) for a "sub drive" to help a young Amish couple with their hospital bills. It is so nice to help each other out in time of need. Volunteers started making submarine sandwiches at 3:00 A.M., and we ready to start delivering to surrounding communities by 7:30 A.M. They made over four thousand subs, which took a lot of willing workers to help.

Saturday we are looking forward to having my oldest sister, Leah, Paul, and family come here to see for the first time where us four sisters moved to. Verena and Susan plan to make a taco dinner for us all before Paul's head on to visit with his parents in a nearby community. Leah turned forty-six on the fifteenth and my sister Verena will be thirty-nine on the twenty-second.

Joe's family from this area enjoyed a good Sunday dinner at his sister, Esther's, house. His sister Ruth, Chris, and family from Berne, Indiana, came to visit Joe's dad. Was nice to get to visit with them again.

Joe's ninety-one-year-old grandmother plans to have a children's sale to get rid of a lot of her belongings. Don't look like we'll be able to go, but sure would be interesting to go. Joe doesn't see his uncles, aunts, and cousins often.

SEPTEMBER 2005

This was the first time Elizabeth Eicher stepped in to write the column for her mother, marking three generations of "The Amish Cook" columnists. Her writing was so clean and so good, it hardly needed any editing, and some readers even questioned whether an eleven-year-old could write this well. She did it completely on her own.

Hi! I'm Lovina's oldest daughter, Elizabeth. I'm eleven years old. I told Mom I would write for her this week, as she's very busy taking care of my new baby brother. Baby Kevin was born at 7:27 A.M., September 2. He weighed eight pounds, four ounces, and was twenty-one inches long. We are very excited to have a new baby again, but we try to give my little sister Lovina extra attention so she doesn't get jealous.

Aunts Susan and Verena took care of us seven children while Mom and Dad were in the hospital. They were there two nights and two days. We were glad when they came back home. Baby Kevin has jaundice and was supposed to stay at the hospital, but they let Dad and Mom bring him home for treatment. We have to keep a light that they call a biliblanket on him. Mom has to switch from back to front every two hours. It keeps her busy. We try to help Mom at nights when we're home from school.

Aunts Verena and Susan came last night to help, and Aunt Emma and Benjamin stayed with Mom, Joseph, Lovina, and baby Kevin while we were in school. Emma will come again today. Our neighbors brought supper in one night, which we really enjoyed.

Mom has to take Kevin to the hospital every day to get a biliruben test on his jaundice. When it gets under 10, Kevin can have the light taken off.

I have to go to bed now so I can get up earlier to help mom pack Dad's lunch and get his breakfast. It is hard to believe Kevin is already six days old. We really enjoy him. I hope I wrote enough! Try this recipe!

AFTER SCHOOL NO-BAKE CHOCOLATE–PEANUT BUTTER CORNFLAKE COOKIES

Makes 16 to 20 bars

Elizabeth also chose a very age-appropriate, kid-friendly recipe with her first column. This is a delicious, easy cookie for kids to make!

½ cup sugar

½ cup light corn syrup

5 tablespoons cocoa powder

1 cup creamy peanut butter

5 cups cornflakes

Lightly grease a 9 by 13-inch pan and set aside.

In a small saucepan, combine the sugar, corn syrup, and cocoa powder. Heat over medium heat, stirring frequently, until the mixture reaches a boil. Immediately remove it from the heat. Add the peanut butter and stir until the mixture is very smooth.

Put the cornflakes in a large bowl. Pour the peanut butter mixture over the cornflakes and stir until evenly coated. Transfer the cookie mixture to the prepared pan and spread evenly. After the mixture has cooled completely, use a knife to cut it into bars.

SEPTEMBER 2005

I was so touched when Lovina gave me my own namesake. Baby Kevin arrived in early September of 2005.

Hello to all you wonderful readers once again. I need to take time this evening to get a column written. It is almost 9:30 P.M. My husband, Joe, and all the children, except Joseph and Elizabeth, are in bed. Three-year-old Joseph is having a hard time settling down for the night in his older brother Benjamin's bedroom. He is going through a stage where he gets scared once it is dark.

Most of you have read by now about the welcome addition of baby Kevin to our family. He is doing good and eats and sleeps most of the time, but he is beginning to be more alert and smiles at us. Such a sweet baby!

I had Kevin by C-section at the hospital, where they also repaired a hernia. I am feeling as good as can be expected after surgery. Although with taking care of eight children, it's hard to get enough rest. Every morning our five school-age children have to be ready by 7:00 A.M., which can make for a rushy morning, especially if Kevin decides he wants to eat right then. We are thankful, though, for all the children's good health and that the surgery went well. Life has so many blessings, and do we thank our Good Lord enough?

Lovina turned sixteen months on Sunday. She's still a baby yet also, but she loves Kevin. I try to give her extra attention and so does everyone else. The last few nights her older sisters Elizabeth and Susan have taken her upstairs with them to bed. She sleeps real good with them. I want to put two and a half bushels of grapes into juice yet this week. What a big job, but I am so glad for the homemade juice. The store-bought is just too sweet.

Kevin will be three weeks old on Friday. He usually wakes up once during the night for his feeding and diaper change. Although, there have been a few nights where he didn't think Mom needed sleep at all. I can't complain, though. On Sunday, Joe took Elizabeth, Benjamin, Loretta, Joseph, and Lovina along to church. My daughters Susan and Verena stayed home with baby Kevin and I. So I got to rest quite a bit. Hopefully next time, we can all go together once again.

Saturday, September 17 has been three long and lonely years that dear mother was laid to rest. It is at times like now with a newborn that I miss her even more. She was there for my first six children's births, doing all she could to help me along. And she was always there to turn to with questions. We must not question why, as we know God makes no mistakes. That is a great help knowing that.

And now it would be also nice to have Mom and Dad hear the news of brother Albert's oldest daughter Elizabeth's wedding coming up in October. This would be my parents' first grandchild getting married. ❧

NOVEMBER 2005

Like many Amish men in Michigan, Joe found work in a factory instead of farming. Factory work in the community was hit hard when the recession of 2009 took hold.

I did laundry today, but it isn't all dry yet. I have some hanging on clothes racks inside since it is wet outside. I should've done the laundry yesterday, but had too many other jobs lined up. One big chore done was defrosting our gas refrigerator, which I let go too long with all that's been going on. It takes longer than cleaning out an ice chest like I had a few years ago, but it's so much easier once it's done.

Saturday we raked and burned a lot of leaves, but we're still far from being done. It was windy on Sunday, so that helped get rid of some more. The children enjoyed making s'mores over the fire Saturday evening after we were done raking. It sure is nice to all go out and work together as a family. We had fun while working, which makes it go a whole lot faster.

Meanwhile, Joseph and Lovina are still feeling OK after their short hospital stay, and are getting back to being ornery. They did their share of getting into trouble while I was outside hanging out the clothes. I kept coming in to check on them. One time they had taken

201

black pepper and sugar and sprinkled it all over the table. Another time they made (Joseph says Lovina did it) a watery mess by the washing machine, playing with the hose. Still, I am just glad they are well again and feel like getting into mischief.

The farmers have harvested the corn beside us and also across the road. With the leaves off the trees, we once again have a lot better view of the surrounding fields. Joe is thinking of trying his luck at hunting deer, which he hasn't done for more than ten years.

4:00 A.M.: My husband Joe left for work fifteen minutes ago. I didn't get this column finished last night due to the children needing help with homework and reading. We are practicing our address with Benjamin and Loretta. It takes a lot of patience to teach a child, but it is so rewarding once they get another task accomplished.

I'm leaving today at 8:15 A.M. to take baby Kevin to the doctor for his two-month checkup. I'll take Joseph and Lovina over to sister Emma's while I am gone. Joseph is so glad that he can go play with Jacob and Emma's Benjamin instead of going along. He doesn't care too much for doctors or nurses since his hospital stay.

I didn't think I had time to get back to bed after Joe left at 3:45 A.M. I have laundry that needs to be folded, floors that need to be swept and breakfast to get for the children before they leave for school. And of course, dishes need to be washed. It is quiet in the morning before the children get up for school.

Friday evening we went to Jacob and Emma's house in honor of Jacob's thirty-third birthday, which was November 1. We decided to wait until Friday when Joe didn't have to get up so early the next morning and the children didn't have school. They prepared a good barbecued steak supper with all the trimmings.

I hope all the readers and editors across the way have a very happy and blessed Thanksgiving holiday with family, friends, and other loved ones. Let's not forget the blessings that He has bestowed upon our country. Let us be thankful for good health. Do we count our blessings enough?

DECEMBER 2005

A new arrival, even in the extended family, is a cause for celebration among the Amish.

Our extended family has grown by one member, so we are all excited. My brother Albert and wife, Sarah Irene, were blessed with their eleventh child. They had a daughter named Sylvia on December 4. This makes six girls and five boys for them, although their oldest child, daughter Elizabeth, has moved to her new home with her husband, Amos. Elizabeth and Amos will spend a few weeks at Albert's, however, helping her mom with the new addition. I'm sure the family is excited to have Elizabeth back home for a while. Sylvia would make grandchild number forty-two for my dear parents, although my niece, Mary, went to her heavenly home eight years ago.

My husband, Joe, is still leaving for work at 3:45 A.M. It is a very cold morning now, with the mercury sitting at −1°F at 5:00 A.M. as I write this. I have fixed Joe his breakfast and gotten him on his way, so it is quiet around here now as I wait for the children to wake up.

We received the sad news yesterday of the death of Joe's uncle LeRoy, sixty-seven, from Milroy, Indiana. He died after a struggle with that dreadful disease: cancer. Our understanding and sympathy goes out to the family. We have plans to start out Friday night for Milroy and stay for the funeral on Saturday. Joe's dad and some of his sisters and husbands, and my sister Emma and husband Jacob (LeRoy was also Jacob's uncle) will set off for Milroy with a hired van driver. It's around a four- to five-hour drive from here. Sisters Verena and Susan will keep our eight children and Jacob's four children at their house while we're gone. I'm so glad they are so willing to put up with twelve children. I'd like to take them along, but with it being so cold and that many hours, it'll be better for them to not go. I will miss them and hope and pray we will have a safe trip.

Our daughter, Verena, will turn eight while we are away. We will have to celebrate her birthday another day. I am sure she'll enjoy her birthday at her aunt's house and also having all her cousins there. Meanwhile, Joe's grandmother will be ninety-two tomorrow. She has been a widow for seventeen years. This is her son-in-law who died.

2006
settling in

MARCH 2006

Elizabeth Eicher once again picked up the pen and wrote a column for her mother. And once again, at the tender age of eleven, she did a sterling job.

I am Elizabeth, age eleven, Lovina's oldest daughter. I am writing this for Mom this week. I should be doing my homework, but I overheard Mom say how much work she has this week, so I decided to write this column and surprise her. The work this week is especially heavy because of an exciting project that Mom and Dad are beginning. They showed us children the plans for our new house, which they are planning to build on our property. It will be exciting to move in when all the work is done in a couple of years!

Mom is outside helping Dad empty an old corncrib building that they plan to tear down where the new house will go. That bad storm last summer really damaged it, but it was already bad to begin with. There is so much junk in there that was here when we moved.

We are also tearing down another older building, and we tore down an old chicken coop. So we have really been busy this week. But it is fun to all work together. And with Mom helping outside a lot, things are getting a little behind in the house. Sister Susan and I want to wash the dishes that Mom didn't get done.

Mom was really thrilled a while ago when our friend brought us a carry-in supper. What a treat that was! Mom thought she had to come in and fix supper yet.

At school we are having "March Reading Month." We all have to read two hundred minutes a week to get our name in the drawing. Two hundred books will be given away in the month of March. I love to read, so I hope I'll win a book.

Uncle Jacob, Aunt Emma, and their family and aunts Verena and Susan came one evening. We all went outside and tore down that old chicken coop. Mom made a haystack supper for them all that night. It helped a lot that they came to help. A haystack supper is a layered dish, that has hamburger, lettuce, and tomatoes in it.

I am watching my little brother Kevin. He is sixth months old and really giggles at us. My one-year-old sister Lovina is also in here, so I rocked her as she is getting grouchy, but she didn't fall asleep. She will be two on May 18. All the other children except my sister Susan are outside. I will copy down the recipe for "world's best sugar cookies." Mom, Susan, and I baked three batches of these on Saturday. We took some to church on Sunday, but the rest have all disappeared. We love them best with homemade, creamy white frosting. Yummy!

If any of you readers know easy-to-make cookie recipes, I would like it if you would send them to us. My sisters and I like mixing up cookies, but Mom still kind of helps us bake them.

WORLD'S BEST SUGAR COOKIES

Makes 4 dozen

Elizabeth called these sugar cookies "the world's best." And judging by how fast they disappear in the Eicher household, perhaps they are!

1 cup powdered sugar

1 cup granulated sugar

1 cup margarine or butter, softened

1 cup vegetable oil

2 teaspoons vanilla extract

2 eggs

5 cups all-purpose flour

1 teaspoon salt

1 teaspoon baking soda

1 teaspoon cream of tartar

Preheat the oven to 350°F.

In a large bowl, cream together the powdered sugar, granulated sugar, margarine, oil, and vanilla until light and fluffy. Add the eggs and beat until evenly incorporated. In another large bowl, sift together the flour, salt, baking soda, and cream of tartar. Gradually add the dry ingredients to the wet mixture, stirring until well combined.

Form the cookie dough into walnut-size balls and place 2 inches apart on ungreased baking sheets. Flatten the balls using the bottom of a glass dipped in sugar. Bake for 10 to 12 minutes, until the edges turn golden brown. Allow the cookies to cool for 2 minutes on the baking sheets before removing. Transfer the cookies to wire racks to cool completely. Cookies may then be frosted, if desired.

APRIL 2006

One of the first things the Eichers had to adjust to when they moved to Michigan was daylight savings time. For years, Indiana was one of the few states to not adopt the time change. Even years later, the time change is a puzzlement to the Eichers.

In past years, Indiana has kept its clocks the same while here in Michigan, we set them forward one hour. But we found out that this year Indiana is also moving its clocks, so I guess we would have had to deal with this daylight savings time one way or another eventually!

While growing up on a farm in Indiana, we used to always get up at 4:00 A.M. to milk the cows by hand. Dad liked to have the cows milked at the same time each day, morning and evening. When my sisters and I would come home from school, we'd go out to milk and do the other evening chores. Dad would come home later in the evening from his work on a construction crew and was always glad when most of the evening chores would already be done.

My husband, Joe, and I had one cow and then later, two, for the first five or six years after we were married, until we moved here. Joe would like to have a cow, now just to have our own milk. With eight children, it takes quite a few gallons a week, and the fresh milk is healthy for them. In this area, they don't have a can truck to sell milk, only a bulk truck. When we had two cows, we sold the extra milk. We were sending two milk cans a day for two cows, which was very good.

Ever since we've been married, Joe has either borrowed a manure spreader or just spread our own manure with a pitchfork. It takes a lot longer that way. So I decided to surprise Joe by getting him a manure spreader of his own. On Saturday, Jacob and Emma went after it. When they came driving in with that new manure spreader, it sure surprised Joe!

A neighbor helped Joe on Saturday in clearing away most of the old corn crib that we're tearing down. But Joe still took time to haul a load of manure out to the field to try out the new spreader. We laughed when one of the girls said that on Sunday morning: "Dad, if you wouldn't have used the manure spreader yet, we could have taken it to church!" I imagine we would have gotten some odd looks to come driving in at church on a manure spreader. Ha!

We are working on getting our last permits for the new house. It looks like we'll be able to get started before too long.

Spring has already arrived and hopefully we'll have nice weather to stay soon. It will be a busy summer. Seems like I finally am settled from the move from Indiana, but I will gladly move again to the new house. I am so limited in storage space, so I'm looking forward to having more space. This house seemed big when we moved here, but with two more children it seems to be getting crowded. I won't know how to act with a new house. We've always lived in older farm houses. The house we are living in now is over one hundred and fifty years old, so it is time for a change.

My daughter Elizabeth wants to thank all the readers that have sent her cookie recipes and for the kind words of encouragement. A special thanks to Annie of Dresden, Ohio, who copied three recipes by hand. She is seventy-eight years old and her hands and body are crippled by arthritis. She is a wheelchair and still does her own work. May God blessed each of you richly for your kindness.

MAY 2006

This column is reminiscent of one her mother wrote (see page 55) about a journey to Sugarcreek, Ohio. This time, the Eichers made the journey to attend a funeral and visit family. Sugarcreek is located in an area that is home to the largest Amish population in the world.

We have been having beautiful spring days, with chilly mornings, but warm afternoons in the sixties and seventies. Our basement for the new house has now been dug out. And in a few days, they will begin to pour the basement walls and floor. It is exciting to see when another step has been accomplished.

The older children have left for school, while Joseph and Lovina are still sleeping, which is unusual. But we went to Jacob's last night for supper and got to bed later than usual, which is why they are still sleeping. Last night, my husband Joe, brother-in-law Jacob, and some of the children went mushroom hunting. They didn't have too much luck, though.

I decided to take advantage of the peace and quiet and get this column written. My dishes aren't washed, floors need to be swept, and the laundry needs to be folded. All that will be easier to do once the children are awake and I can keep an eye on them. It seems like I sweep the floors so much more often since the basement has been dug. The children drag in clumps of dirt on their shoes, in their pockets, etc. I can imagine the fun I'll have once it rains.

As I write this, and the others sleep, little Kevin (eight months) is in his walker. He gets around everywhere. He's already trying to open my cabinet doors. So he needs to be watched more and more.

We started out for Ohio on Wednesday morning. It took us six and a half hours to get to the tiny town of Walhonding, where the viewing was held for Joe's grandmother. She doesn't have to suffer anymore, although she will be greatly missed by all her friends and family.

We then headed for the Sugarcreek, Ohio, area, as the funeral was to be near there the next day. While in the area, we stopped in to visit my aunt Lovina and her husband, Abe Raber. She was surprised to see us and we had a nice, but too short, visit. I hadn't seen Aunt Lovina for almost three years. She is my mom's sister and resembles her a lot. I was named after her. We lived in the same church district while we both lived in Berne, Indiana. My uncle Toby passed away seven years ago from cancer. Lovina married Abe about three years ago. I wished that the time hadn't been too short to visit Lovina's daughters (my cousins) Elizabeth and Lovina and their families and Lovina's son Amos and family, who all live close by her.

Thursday was the funeral in the Sugarcreek area on the place where Joe's grandmother grew up. The funeral was well attended. We saw a lot of Joe's family, uncles, aunts, cousins. I also saw my brother Amos and sister-in-law Nancy there. Joe's grandmother would also have been Nancy's grandmother. I also met a lot of Holmes County readers.

It seemed like a very friendly community.

MAY 2006

This particular column made me feel old. Susan Coblentz was only fifteen when I first met her, and this column chronicles her thirtieth birthday! In this column, Lovina mentions an event that the Amish refer to as a frolic. "Frolic" is a term the Amish use to describe a gathering of volunteers that meet to complete a task, often a barn raising, but in this case, the Eicher's house.

On May 10, my sister Susan celebrated her thirtieth birthday. To mark the occasion, Susan invited us and some others over to her house on Sunday. She served a homemade pizza and ice-cream dinner. In addition to having a good meal, it was also a beautiful day, so the adults did some bicycling and the children were taking pony rides.

My husband Joe gave me a new tribike for my upcoming birthday. I didn't expect a gift with the expense of building our new house. We grew up in a community where the Amish didn't allow bikes. The Amish here in Michigan do allow them. At almost thirty-five years old and after having eight children, I am scared to try a two-wheel bike. I'm afraid I might fall and break a bone. What Joe got me, though, has two wheels in the back and one in front. It really is a smooth-riding bike. We have had lots of fun biking together as a family. It's so relaxing to go for a bike ride after a hard day's work. A person doesn't notice the rolling land until you bike.

On Saturday, we had our frolic. Most of the second floor has now been framed. Also the 20 × 20 foot added-on utility room was framed in.

Now the rafters should be going up this week and maybe the windows. The crew hasn't been here yet this week but they plan to come tomorrow and the rest of the week.

Our neighbor, Marlin, plowed our new garden and now Joe just needs to till it. Maybe I'll get some garden out this week finally, although we have a lot of rocks to pick up first.

On Friday morning we plan to leave at 5:00 A.M. to attend the wedding in Berne, Indiana, for Joe's nephew Clarence. We will come home that evening. I am glad it's on a Friday, as Joe won't have to leave for work the next morning.

Eight-month-old Kevin hasn't been feeling too good this week. He seems to have a bad cold, as does our daughter, Lovina. We will leave them with my sisters, Verena and Susan, while we go to the wedding, as I am afraid they would get worse if we took them. Our children Verena, Benjamin and Loretta decided to also stay at their aunts' house. I'm glad to not have those three missing any more school. Our oldest, Elizabeth and Susan, will go with us to the wedding. It seems they catch up easier with their work. Verena does, too, but she thinks it'll be fun going to her aunts' house. She loves school, so that helps. Little Joseph hasn't decided what he wants to do. I know they are in good care at my sisters' house.

Sister Emma brought us some rhubarb and winter onions so I need to use the rhubarb up yet. And lo and behold, asparagus is now popping up here and there on the dirt piles around the house. They had been buried by dirt from the construction of our new house.

JUNE 2006

The growing Eicher family needed more room by the spring of 2006, so work had begun on building a new home on the same property. The family grew more and more excited as work on the house progressed.

It is so good to see the sun shining once again after having rainy and dreary weather the last week. Yesterday we had only a few sprinkles, but I managed to get most of my laundry dry. I have a basketful that needs to be hung out to finish drying.

Joe and I and our two oldest children, Elizabeth and Susan, went to my nephew Clarence and Marie's wedding. Lovina and Kevin were sick, so we left our six youngest with my sisters Verena and Susan.

It rained most of the day, so I was glad I didn't take Lovina and Kevin to the wedding. We started out about 5:00 A.M. on Friday morning and we arrived back home around 11:45 P.M. We stayed at Verena and Susan's for the night, since the children were all asleep by the time we got there to pick them up.

It was still rainy on Saturday and Sunday. I stayed home from church with Lovina and Kevin so that they could continue to recover. They seem better now, with only a small cold.

But as soon as they began feeling better, I began to feel worse. I think I caught a touch of the flu. I feel a lot better today though. Since I wasn't feeling well last night, Joe and the girls made supper for us all. It's just harder when mother gets sick. Hopefully, no one else in the family will. We went to bed at 8:45 P.M., which is earlier than usual for us. The children asked why we were going to bed when it was still daylight. But I think we all needed a good night's rest.

Once the ground dries up I need to get out into the garden and the grass needs mowed again. Busy, busy springtime!

Our new house is ready for shingles and siding. The windows and doors should be here by next week. The decking is also being put on. Everything takes time and money—nothing is cheap anymore.

Tomorrow will be Lovina's second birthday. I want to make a cake for her. I'll never forget how sick I was when she was born. Do I thank God enough for good health? It's so easy to take our good health for granted until we don't have it anymore.

I will also soon have my thirty-fifth birthday. Time has such a way of slipping by too fast. At this time of year, we are once again reminded of Dad's passing six years ago. We still treasure the precious memories we have of him in our hearts. I know if he'd be living, he'd be here helping us all he could on our new house. He put a lot of labor in helping his children, as did Mother.

Precious memories and how they linger. Our daily wish is to all be reunited in that great kingdom in heaven. How beautiful heaven must be!

JULY 2006

Construction continued on the new home during July, but Lovina also describes a harrowing time caught in their buggy during a menacing thunderstorm.

We are having rain off and on today, which makes it difficult to hang the wash out on the lines. So in between the showers, the clothes have been drying. I don't like to have clothes that are almost dry get wet again. I should've maybe waited to wash the clothes until tomorrow.

With the storms and all the rain we had last night, I thought it might be nicer outside today, but it's still showery. The children and I picked up my sisters Verena and Susan yesterday morning and then headed over to sister Emma's house to help clean. Emma will be holding church services at her house in the near future. We cleaned out closets and washed walls, ceilings, and windows in several bedrooms. Closets are time consuming to clean.

Around 4:30 P.M., we decided to start home, but saw that a storm was brewing in the northwest. We waited at Emma's house a while longer and the storm seemed to just blow over, so we started for home. But we were wrong. Almost halfway home, it started getting very windy and large chunks of hail started hitting our buggy. We put our lights on and I could hardly see where we were going. The horse struggled to keep going. Rain pelted the buggy, and we just all tried to remain calm and hoped our steady horse would get us home. The children were scared. How thankful we were for having a covered buggy, but it was still scary to realize what could happen. We sure were relieved once we arrived home. My husband, Joe, had been worried that we might be in the storm and opened the pole barn door for us to pull into. When we arrived home, several branches were off our trees and my corn was flattened. It is starting to stand up again today. The rest of the garden also looks battered.

Sunday we were surprised to see Joe's dad and his uncle Solomon from Sugarcreek, Ohio, drive in to visit. We made them stay and have dinner with us. Solomon stayed a couple of days and him and Joe's dad came here each day to hang siding on our new house. We sure appreciated their help. There is a little more siding still to do, but that will be a big job to have completed and over with. The boys sure enjoyed being outside with grandpa and Uncle Solomon.

Our blocks came for our chimney on Saturday. Joe, Elizabeth, and I carried some to every level in the house. What a tiring job! Our porch railing should come this week. I'll be relieved once the railing is on. The children like to play on the porch, and I am always afraid they'll fall off. Our porch goes out over our walkout basement, so it's a little higher. We ate quite a few meals out there on the new porch already. It is so nice and breezy under there. I can't wait until we can get a porch swing to hang up.

AMISH COOK CLASSIC: FROSTY STRAWBERRY SQUARES

Makes 10 to 12 squares

Scorching summer days call for cool, refreshing desserts. With a bountiful crop of fresh strawberries, this became a favorite dessert in the Eicher household.

2 egg whites
1 cup sugar
2 cups fresh strawberries, crushed
1 cup whipping cream

In a large bowl, combine the egg whites and the sugar. Beat with a whisk about 10 minutes, or until the mixture has tripled in size. Gently stir the crushed strawberries into the beaten egg mixture. In a separate bowl, beat the whipping cream until stiff peaks form. Carefully fold the whipped cream into the

strawberry mixture until well blended. Pour into a 9 by 13-inch rectangular cake pan. Freeze until firm, at least 6 hours. Cut into squares and serve.

JULY 2006

By the summer of 2006, the Eichers seemed really settled in their new Michigan community. Joe and Jacob spent some days out on the lake fishing, while the children enjoyed a slow-moving summer. Lovina writes about gas lighting in this column. Some Amish churches allow gaslights, others do not. The church district where Lovina lives in Michigan allows gaslights.

We are really enjoying having my husband, Joe, home from the factory this week. It's nice not to have a schedule and not worry about getting up quite so early. Although it hasn't been too relaxing of a vacation for him, with all the work that needs to be done on our new house. Joe is outside working on the house now. There is a little section under the deck going over the walkout basement that needs siding still.

Tomorrow and Saturday, a few men will come help Joe hook up our gas lines into the new house. Our lights will be piped in. That will be so easy not have to fill lanterns, plus they will have self-igniters on them. When we lived in Berne, Indiana, we just had the kerosene lamps. Our next step with the house is to start insulating.

Yesterday, Joe and our two boys, Joseph and Benjamin, hauled quite a few loads of manure. It sure makes it a lot easier with the new manure spreader. Manure makes the best fertilizer. Joe said little Joseph sure tries to get manure into the spreader, even if he doesn't quite get it in. Benjamin does pretty well with it. He sure is excited about turning seven soon.

Joe and Jacob plan to go fishing Friday night. That will at least be one relaxing activity for him on his vacation. Hopefully, he can relax more next year when we should be enjoying our new house.

Meanwhile, I am trying to get some mending done. I cut out and sewed me a new dress and hope to get another one sewn soon. A lady from our community gave me a box of clothes her children had outgrown. It sure helped me out for the children. I really appreciated her thoughtfulness.

My sisters Verena and Susan are on an eight-day trip to the Smoky Mountains with a group of Amish from here. Sounds like they are enjoying their trip. Yesterday, I went over to their garden and picked green beans, peas, and cucumbers. We brought their horse over here to take care of while they are gone.

Earlier this week, Jacob, Emma, and family and our family enjoyed a day at the park. The children enjoyed the swings, slides, merry-go-rounds, etc. We also spent some time with our friends that had the recent house fire. They are still not back in their house.

Brother Amos and Nancy's second oldest daughter is getting married this month. So we'll probably be attending their wedding in Indiana in a couple of weeks.

AUGUST 2006

I didn't realize how frequent mechanical problems were on buggies until I started putting together this column collection. This column features a broken buggy brace.

We continue through the "dog days" of August. Hopefully cooler weather will soon come.

On Monday, my school-age children planned to go canoeing down the river. This was a school-sponsored event for students who wanted to go. The river runs behind the school. I decided to take the children, but we didn't get very far. We had just turned out of our driveway and onto the road when a buggy brace snapped by the shaft. This then left the one end loose from the buggy. I was just ready to urge the horse into a run when I happened to see the shaft coming loose. I tried to get the horse stopped and then jumped off the buggy.

Our horse, Itty Bit, was shook up, as I imagine she knew something wasn't right. I helped her while the children all got off the buggy. Elizabeth and I unhitched her from the buggy and Elizabeth led her to the barn while the other children and I pulled the buggy off the road. It wasn't too easy pulling the buggy with only one side attached.

We were all shook up to think what could've happened had we been going down a hill or out on a busy road. If that had happened on a hill, that could make a horse start kicking, and the buggy could ram into their back.

My husband, Joe, will take our buggy to the buggy shop to have it fixed. He's also going to have brakes put on right away. That will help. If something like that happens again, we will be able to brake the buggy.

On Friday, the school is taking any student who wants to go to the zoo. Ours are going and I am going as a chaperone. I asked if I could bring four-year-old Joseph along and they said yes.

My youngest, Lovina and Kevin, will stay at my sister's that day. Joseph is so excited to get to ride in a school bus and go to the zoo. Every day he asks me if he can still go and asks if he can wear his new pants and shirt.

Sister Emma and her children are going along also. That makes Joseph more excited to have Emma's four-year-old, Benjamin, along. Those two cousins get along so well.

Joseph is such a neat little boy. He won't wear a shirt if a button is missing. He doesn't like it if his pants have a hole in them either. I guess that way I keep getting my mending done sooner. Seven-year-old Benjamin is exactly the opposite. He doesn't care what I give him to wear. It's surprising how siblings can be so different.

Two-year-old Lovina is going through a stage where she repeats everything she hears. Joseph gets so annoyed when she always repeats what he says and does. Now Lovina is starting to complain about her dress when Joseph does about his shirt. Joseph tells her to quit copying him and she just laughs. It is cute to hear them carry a conversation.

Meanwhile, I managed to process fourteen pints of salsa yesterday. I also did twelve quarts of pickles and ten pints of jalapeño peppers this week. Red beets are ready for whenever I decide to do them.

SEPTEMBER 2006

Occasionally, reader mail really piles up. And with eight children at home, answering it all is almost an impossibility for Lovina. Occasionally, she uses her column to talk to readers directly.

It has been a rainy week thus far. I am hoping the rain will hold off just long enough to get my laundry dry. I washed it yesterday and then it started raining, so I left it hanging and now it is all wet again.

Brother Albert, Sarah, and ten children drove the twenty-one miles to our place on Friday evening. Their two oldest boys biked and the rest came in two buggies. Albert Jr. was driving Dad and Mom's open buggy that Albert bought at my parents' estate auction. Albert's family was here for the night and Saturday. Then Saturday evening, they went to Jacob and Emma's for the night. We all had brunch at Jacob's on Sunday. Albert's family started the long ride home around 1:00 P.M.

Jacob's family and Verena and Susan also came here on Saturday to help. We were a total of thirty. We enjoyed eating breakfast and dinner together. A lot more drywall was hung. We sure appreciated all their help; it is nice when family helps each other. Dad and Mom were always willing to lend a hand. May they have their heavenly reward.

Answers to reader questions:

• To Mark from Leipsic, Ohio, on how to get hard-boiled eggs to peel easily: This even works with fresh eggs. It is important to be exact with minutes. Put eggs in a pan and cover with cold water. Bring to a boil for 2 minutes (uncovered). Turn off the heat, cover the pan, and let set for 11 minutes. Then soak the eggs in cold water for 3 to 5 minutes and peel. Good luck!

- Also, about the cucumber salad: I slice cucumbers, dice in some onions, and sprinkle with salt. Add a dressing of your choice.

- To Dorothy from Kewadin, Michigan: This is how I do fried corn—I cut the kernels from fresh corn and fry in butter and season.

- To Shannon from Bourbon, Indiana: This I how I put up my jalapeños—pick jalapeños fresh, wash, and slice or put them whole in clean jars. Measure 3 cups of white vinegar and 3 cups of water and bring to a boil. Then add 1 cup of sugar and ¼ cup of salt. Pour the hot juice over the peppers and tighten the lids. The hot juice will make the lids seal. If you cold pack them, they'll turn soggy.

I have received quite a few requests for my salsa recipe, so I'll share it with you.

THICK AND CHUNKY SALSA
Makes 20 quart jars

14 pounds fresh tomatoes, peeled
and coarsely chopped
5 cups chopped onion
10 green peppers, seeded and
chopped
¼ cup jalapeño pepper, seeded
and chopped
1 cup vinegar, white or apple cider
½ cup brown sugar, packed
¼ cup salt
1 teaspoon garlic powder
2 teaspoons oregano flakes
1 tablespoon ground cumin
3 tablespoons chili powder
10 tablespoons Clear Jel
2 cups water

In a very large stockpot, combine all of the ingredients (except for the Clear Jel and the water) and stir until well combined. Bring the mixture to a boil over medium-high heat. Reduce the heat and allow the salsa to simmer, stirring occasionally, for 45 minutes. In a medium bowl, combine the Clear Jel and the water and stir until smooth. Stir the Clear Jel mixture into the salsa until evenly incorporated. Pour the hot salsa into sterilized canning jars and seal. Process the jars in a boiling water bath for 20 minutes.

NOVEMBER 2006

Baby Kevin suffered health problems during the fall of 2006, but fortunately he was able to battle through them.

This column is a little shorter than usual maybe, because it was an unexpectedly rough week. We had baby Kevin in the hospital over the weekend. He had a respiratory infection and something like an asthma attack.

He started sounded raspy and he cried when he coughed. This continued for a while, so I called the doctor. The doctor heard how fast he was breathing and told us to take him to the emergency room at the local hospital. At first they tested him for RSV, but the test came back negative, which was a relief. So he must have just been congested.

Poor little boy has had his share of sicknesses this last while. After we brought him home, we had to give him mist treatments every six hours. Now I can only do it twice a day. He is feeling much better now.

Joe and I stayed at the hospital all night with Kevin, while sisters Verena and Susan kept our seven other children at their house. Joe came home early Sunday morning to take the children home, since Verena and Susan and Jacob, Emma, and children had plans to attend church services in an Amish community about one and a half hours from here. The services were held at the home of one of Susan's friends. Verena and Susan had a breakfast casserole ready for Joe and the children to take home for breakfast.

About lunch time on Sunday, my uncle Joe and aunt Betty Coblentz from Indiana came to our house for a visit. Joe made them and our children a light lunch of sandwiches. Joe and Betty then came to the hospital to visit with me. While they were there the doctor came and discharged Kevin.

Uncle Joe and Betty brought us home from the hospital. We had to wait on a prescription and arrived home around 4:30 P.M. It was a long, tiring weekend. It was so good to be home again. Joe is now headed for home after a short visit with Verena and Susan. They arrived home shortly before we did.

Since it was such a long day, we all went to bed earlier than usual. We hardly had any sleep at the hospital, as Kevin had to have care every so often. I am so thankful to be back home again.

On a happier note, our biggest thrill lately was to see Kevin taking his first steps and walking short distances. I think he enjoys the attention when everyone in the family oohs and ahhs when he stands up.

Now it is a very beautiful day after a few rainy days, and it has warmed up into the sixties.

Last night, Jacob and Emma brought us supper, which was nice after the stressful weekend. They brought us spaghetti and meatballs, fresh homemade applesauce, and just-baked banana bread. It was such a treat to not have to cook supper. It seems I got behind with my work while Kevin was sick. It could have been worse, and I'm thankful for good health and to just be able to take care of our dear children.

NOVEMBER 2006

The Eichers and I enjoyed a wonderful, quick trip to Kansas to meet readers in the town of Newton. It was great to meet all those that turned out. And the eight Eicher children were so well behaved, it was a terrific journey.

Tomorrow morning, Joe and I will travel with some others from this community to Berne, Indiana. We will attend the funeral for Joe's forty-one-year-old cousin. What a shock it was to the family and everyone!

Her husband awoke the next morning to see his wife had passed away in bed during the night. We didn't hear yet what happened or all the details, although they suspect an aneurysm could be the cause. Our sympathy goes to her husband and four children and also to the extended family. One of her sons is getting married next week.

Once again our Dear Lord has shown us that we never know when our stay here on earth is up. She was only three years older than my husband, Joe. It makes us stop to think about how we should appreciate every day our Heavenly Father gives us together. So often we take life for granted, but the most important part is to be ready to meet our Dear Savior when our time comes.

Along with the sad news, we also received some exciting news. Joe and I are now a great-aunt and -uncle for the first time. My niece Elizabeth and husband, Amos, were blessed with a baby girl named Sarah. This puts brother Albert and Sarah Irene on the grandparents list. Congratulations!

We recently had a chance to travel to Kansas and Missouri with my editor, Kevin Williams, and his special friend, Rachel. Also our eight children and my sisters Verena and Susan were along with us. It was great to see some of the readers of this column in Kansas! I want to thank you for all your kind words of encouragement. May God bless you dearly.

Our highlight on the trip was to go up to the top of the Gateway Arch in St. Louis, Missouri, on the way back home. Four-year-old Joseph thought the whole surrounding city looked like a toy set, and he even asked if he could play with the "little cars" and trucks that he saw when we looked down from the top. It sounded so cute. I had to explain that they were all real, just looked smaller from so far. Another thing that meant a lot to me was to pass through the town in Missouri (Blue Springs) where dear Mother passed away. It gave me a peaceful feeling to finally see where she was when she died.

Kevin was a very good and safe driver and I think he did very well to put up with having eight children along. Rachel was also helpful to have along.

My husband, Joe, is now off for two weeks due to work being slow. Meanwhile, he finds plenty to do here at home with construction continuing on our new house. The insulation for the attic will come tomorrow. On Saturday, several men will come to help blow it into the attic.

Tonight we plan to go to Verena and Susan's for supper. After supper, we will leave our eight children there overnight, as we have to leave at 4:30 A.M. for the funeral. Jacob and Emma will also take their four children to Verena and Susan's, so they will have a total of twelve children for the night. Eight of them will have to be ready for school by 7:00 A.M. Susan and Verena will have their hands full. I do appreciate all that they do and they are always willing to help without complaint.

DECEMBER 2006

While baby Kevin was making mischief, the Eichers were almost done with their new home!

Tomorrow, December 22, is my husband Joe's thirty-eighth birthday. These years fly by so fast! I'm sure we will all celebrate in some way tomorrow in honor of his special day.

Last night, we attended the third- and fourth-grade Christmas program at our school. Daughter Susan, who is in the fourth grade, was in the play. It was interesting and surprising to see the children remember their parts so well.

I made two batches of "speedy cinnamon rolls" (see page 65) yesterday so our children could give each of their teachers a pan for Christmas. I usually put them beside our coal stove to help them rise faster. Luckily, I got fifteen-and-a-half-month-old Kevin to take a nap while they were rising, otherwise he would have been trying to pull them down. He is such a busybody and keeps me on the run. He still notices when someone leaves the bathroom door open. He puts a lot of tissue in the toilet and gets the plunger to try to get it down. He must have seen us do this. I'd rather see him be healthy and ornery than be sick, though.

The painting over at the new house is done now and the floors are also finished. It is starting to take shape, and a little more work and we should be able to move in. It is exciting!

Joe is off work until January 8, so we should get a lot done during this time. He is still battling his cough, but is improving. The schoolchildren will be home until January 3, so the next week or so will be good family time together.

On Saturday, Joe's family gathers at his sister Mary Ann's house for their annual Christmas gathering. Then Sunday after services, our church will have a potluck dinner for the holidays.

On Monday, Christmas Day, we plan to just be at home and spend time together as a family. Family time is so important in these busy, rushy times. We didn't do much in the way of gifts this year. Our new house is our Christmas present. Often the Christmas meaning is forgotten amid all the material things. Let us never forget that we are celebrating the birth of our dear savior, Jesus Christ.

Our thanks goes to the Michigan reader for your very thoughtful gift. May God bless you and all the readers who have sent Christmas cards and encouraging notes.

We sure are having a mild winter so far. We hardly have had much snow. The boys have had their sleds ready for so long, but have not been able to use them. I am sure we will get our share of cold and snowy weather yet. I told Joe it'll probably come about the time we are moving our furniture and belongings into the new house. Such is life.

We want to wish all of you readers a happy New Year!

2007
a houseful of children

JANUARY 2007

The Old Order Amish in Michigan have to pass the same building inspections—plumbing, codes, smoke alarms—that apply to non-Amish before moving into a new home. Unfortunately the plumbing inspectors found some minor flaws, so the Eichers could not yet move into their new home.

It is 2:00 P.M. and the three youngest children are all taking a nap. This rarely ever happens that all three are taking a nap and especially at the same time! I rocked Kevin and Lovina, and meanwhile Joseph fell asleep in his bed. I decided to let my housework wait, as I don't get many quiet moments like this. I feel so tired at night that I usually end up going to bed when Joe and the children do.

Joseph has been a typical four-year-old these last few days, asking me one question after another. He's so enthused about the smoke alarms we put into our new house. They are battery operated and light up when they go off. Before we move in, we need to make sure the children all know our fire plan in case of fire. We hope we'll never have to experience that, but you never know.

Today is our second oldest daughter, Susan's, eleventh birthday. She made cupcakes last night to treat her class. I asked her what she wanted for supper and she said pizza, ice cream, and cupcakes. I will put candles on eleven cupcakes. She also wants a book about tornadoes for her birthday, the same book that Joe and I have been reading (*Devastation in Daviess County*).

Meanwhile, we have our beef all cut up and processed. It makes us feel better to finally have more meat stocked up. I've never been this low on canned meat since Joe and I have been married. Our family grows and I'll need to can extra. I processed thirty-three quarts of beef and thirty-five quarts of hamburger, and also steak and beef for soups. It is nice to have soup ready to just heat and serve on busy days. I cook the meat off the beef bones to make beef stew to add to the vegetables. It's a good, hearty dish for the winter.

We had high hopes of making the move into our new house this week. But the final plumbing inspection did not pass due to some very minor plumbing that wasn't up to code. It's so frustrating and we will be glad once the inspections are done. In the meantime, we are cleaning bathrooms, windows, and getting ready for the move. We've moved quite a few things over already. I've worn a path between both houses forgetting I moved some things over that I still need here.

It is a lot easier to clean since we have the hot and cold water working. A reader asked how we have the bathroom and hot water working without electricity. We have a propane motor in an outside building that pumps water into two pressure tanks. When the pressure gets low the motor automatically will start. Our water heater also runs off propane.

FEBRUARY 2007

Finally, after almost a year of excitement and anticipation, the Eichers were able to move into their new home!

The first of February has arrived and today we plan to move into our new house! The children are all so excited! On Saturday, Jacob, sister Emma and family, and sisters Verena and Susan helped us move most of our furniture, clothes, dishes, and other household belongings over. We still have two beds, a sofa, some chairs, and our stove left to move over. These are all big, heavy items. Verena, Susan, and Jacob's plan to come help us move the rest in today. But tonight we'll all be in our beds over there. So exciting!

I have a bad cold now. I think I am a little drained from the move and the walking back and forth between houses, and this cold isn't helping. This past Monday, we finally got our final inspection and passed it, which was a relief. It has been a long nine and a half months, but whenever I go over to the new house I think it'll be worth all the headaches.

Joe left to go to work around thirty minutes ago. So I decided with everything going on today I better stay up and get this written. I doubt that I'll be able to concentrate later on. The children are all so excited about sleeping in their new bedrooms tonight.

Seven-month-old Kevin loves when we turn him loose in the new house. He'll run around and try to see everything at once. We have to make sure we close all the bathroom doors and put a gate over the stairway. I've caught him running on top of the table a few times. He's full of energy and two-year-old Lovina seems to enjoy helping him get into trouble. She never really got into my things like Kevin does. I think she's trying to get attention. Even though they are sixteen months apart, they are almost the same height, as Lovina is very petite. They almost look like they could be twins. Such sweet little angels. What will life be like when they grow up? It helps to know God has His protecting hand over us.

Jacob's came over one night last week and hung our interior doors before the inspection. That is his job at work. It didn't take him long to have the doors hung.

We are finally having real winter weather. Quite a bit of snow and cold single digit temperatures. Hopefully this cold will put a stop to all the flu and colds going around.

Our thoughts and prayers are also with Joe's ninety-three-year-old grandmother. She had surgery yesterday, as she fell and shattered her upper thigh bone. Doctors don't have hopes that she'll be able to walk again. This will be hard on her, as she was still active.

FEBRUARY 2007

Once again, Elizabeth Eicher, twelve, a year older and wiser than when she wrote last, picked up the pen and shared her feelings about the new house.

On February 1, we spent our first night over in our new house. It was very exciting to wake up and get dressed for school in the morning. I think Mom and Dad are glad to finally be moved.

It was a little hard to find all our clothes since we didn't have everything unpacked yet. Uncle Jacob put rods and shelves in our closets so we have a place to hang our dresses and other clothes.

Today we were home from school because snow drifted over roads. We went to school yesterday, but it was blowing snow all day. It looked like we were having a blizzard! They called off work at the trailer factory where Dad works, too. So we were all home today. It made it seem like it was Saturday. On Friday the sixteenth and Monday the nineteenth, we won't have school because of our midwinter break. That will give us a little more time to help Mom get more organized. We still have some boxes to move over from the old house. So I thought writing the column this week would be a nice help to Mom. We washed clothes today, baked a cake and cupcakes, and also cleaned the new house. We have vinyl floors and I think they are easier to clean than wood floors.

Dad made some wash lines in the basement that will push up when we have church, so they won't be in the way. During the winter, it makes it a lot nicer to wash and hang it up right away, with the stove down there it also helps the clothes dry nicer.

School is going fast this year. Sixth grade doesn't seem too hard for me. We are in the third semester already. There are six girls and eight boys in my grade. My Language Arts teacher is in his upper twenties and fighting a brain tumor. He is a lot of fun and cheerful, even if he probably doesn't always feel well.

Our family is enjoying making homemade ice cream this winter. When everyone takes a turn cranking it doesn't take so long.

I must get ready for bed pretty soon. Dad and Mom like us to get to bed by 8:30 P.M. when we have school the next day. I will share our ice-cream recipe with you. This is for a two-gallon freezer.

HOMEMADE ICE CREAM

Makes about 4 quarts

7 eggs

10 cups whole milk

3½ cups sugar

4 teaspoons vanilla extract

1 teaspoon salt

In a large bowl, beat the eggs with a whisk until light yellow and foamy. Gradually stir in the milk, sugar, vanilla, and salt. Mix until smooth and evenly combined. Freeze according to the manufacturer's instructions for your ice-cream maker.

MARCH 2007

By March, after several weeks of moving boxes and trudging back and forth between the two homes, Lovina was finally beginning to feel settled in. The old house would eventually be sold and trucked off the property.

It has been three weeks now since we have moved into our new house. What a relief it was to finally be able to move in!

I didn't write this column for several weeks, thanks to my editor and my daughter Elizabeth. Time has sped by so fast and we are gradually getting more and more adjusted.

We'll continue to make small improvements and finishing touches to the new house as time goes by. For instance, Joe still wants to build a separate room in the basement for my canning jars. Since we heat from the basement, we need an insulated separate room so the home-canned food stays cool. We still didn't move all the canned food over from the old basement.

We have had some below-zero temperatures since we moved into the new house. We are learning how to adjust our coal stove to heat more when it's that cold. We had a few chilly mornings but it really helped heat when we use our propane lights.

Church services will be held here next month on two separate Sundays, as we skipped our turn last summer. So, along with getting settled, we will start preparing for the services.

Four of our children have had the flu this week, so it was a bit hectic around here. But everyone is back to good health again, except Kevin. He was still feeling sick today. Following the doctor's advice, he has been making improvements, though. Tonight he acts back to normal, which means getting into mischief. He likes checking out my new cabinets. And, of course, we still need to keep our bathroom doors closed.

We have an open stairway, so we use a gate to keep Kevin from climbing up. The minute he discovers the gate open, he climbs those stairs pretty fast. Kevin's OK going up but I still don't trust him coming down.

With the weather warming up again into the forties, the children have been busy making snowmen from the snow still left on the ground. This morning it was really foggy, so the school was on a delay. I'm hoping Joe and his driver make it to work OK, traveling that long distance.

Joe and the boys are starting to work nights on cleaning manure out of the horse stalls. Without gardening and mowing, it'll make it a few less chores while preparing for church services, so in some ways it's easier to hold them during winter, although with the snow melting and the ground softening, we are having our share of mud.

That is when I appreciate my new back entrance area. It's nice to leave boots out there. Four-year-old Joseph came crying to me one day because he caught seven-year-old Benjamin walking across our new floor with his boots on. This was before we had moved in. I thought it was cute that he was so concerned about the new floors.

It is now 9:30 P.M. and everyone has gone to bed. So I will sign off and call it a day, too. Good night and God's blessings to all!

AMISH COOK CLASSIC: BAKED FRENCH TOAST

Serves 4 to 6

Breakfast is an important meal in an Amish home. The meal provides sustenance for the day ahead, but it also needs to be quick and easy amid the bustle of the morning. French toast often fits the bill.

1 cup brown sugar, packed

½ cup butter

2 tablespoons light corn syrup

12 bread slices

½ cup granulated sugar

1 teaspoon ground cinnamon

6 eggs

1½ cups milk

1 teaspoon vanilla extract

Preheat the oven to 350°F.

In a heavy-bottomed saucepan, combine the brown sugar, butter, and corn syrup. Heat the ingredients over medium heat, stirring frequently. When the mixture reaches a boil, remove it from the heat and pour it into the bottom of a 9 by 13-inch glass pan. Layer the bread slices into the glass pan and sprinkle with the sugar and the cinnamon. In a large bowl, whisk the eggs, milk, and vanilla together until smooth and evenly combined. Pour the egg mixture over the bread. Bake 30 to 35 minutes, until puffed and golden.

AUGUST 2007

The summer of 2007 was a bummer for thirteen-year-old Elizabeth Eicher. She had to spend some of her summer on crutches because of a sprained ankle.

All is still quiet and peaceful here at the Eichers' this morning. I decided to write this column before waking the children. My husband, Joe, left for work a few hours ago, so not much activity in the household right now, which is a perfect time for writing.

Daughter Elizabeth—age thirteen—is getting around with crutches since Saturday evening. She has a badly sprained ankle. I was relieved when the X-rays didn't show a break. This is so hard on her, as she is used to being active.

Also on the injured list: my sister Susan was off work for a week after hurting her hand at work. It was infected and swollen. She's still under a doctor's care but has gone back to work.

Last night we had pizza, cupcakes, and root beer floats for son Joseph's fifth birthday. He was proud to get all the extra attention and be able to choose the menu for supper.

Joe and I had our fourteenth anniversary on July 15. How could these years slip by so fast? Mother's seventy-first birthday would have been on July 18. Although she's not here with us anymore, we still will always remember that day. Sister Emma had her thirty-fourth birthday on July 19. We enjoyed a barbecue pork chop supper that evening.

My cousin William and his wife Cathy recently gave us a surprise visit. They live about ninety minutes from here.

On Friday evening, quite a few people from the community gathered to make three thousand pizzas for a fund-raiser. The funds were to a family in our church district to help them along with their hospital bills. There were four assembly lines going with around fifteen people on each line. The "pizza assembly line" was held at the home of a church member. Then there were more people keeping us supplied in the lines with ingredients. I was helping on the "supreme" pizza line but they also did a "meat lovers" pizza. It took between five and a half to six hours to do these, but there was work involved before and after, putting together boxes, and then afterwards cleaning up to do. It was interesting to see how this works and it shows how many hands can make lighter work. It is even nicer to go help when you know its for a good cause.

Saturday was "delivery day" for all those pizzas. There were fifteen drivers hired to go deliver the pizzas in this Amish church district and in other nearby Amish church districts. Daughter Elizabeth went with sister Verena on Saturday to help deliver pizzas. Each van was loaded with two hundred pizzas. Verena and Elizabeth left around 6:00 A.M. and came home around 5:30 P.M. It was after Elizabeth was home that she sprained her ankle. Felt sorry that she had to go through pain after being gone all day doing a good deed, but such is life. It could have been worse and I am thankful it was not a break.

Yesterday the girls and I put up around twenty quarts of pickles. We are enjoying our first tomatoes and sweet corn. We were disappointed to see the raccoons had raided some of our patch already. This is the first year I've had trouble with raccoons. Hopefully we can keep them away from the next batch coming along.

Tomorrow morning at 5:00 A.M., we start out to attend the wedding of niece Susan. God's blessings to all!

AUGUST 2007

The Eichers welcomed a new nephew to the clan with open arms and lots of love. But they also had some scary moments with young Kevin.

We have had an extra full house here the last two evenings because Jacob and Emma's four children have been staying with us. We are all excited to announce the arrival of a five-pound, seven-ounce boy named Steven Jay to Jacob and Emma. He was born by C-section on July 30. He joins siblings Elizabeth, ten; Emma, nine; Jacob, seven; and Benjamin, five. After five years, this is such a welcome addition to the family!

We drove to the hospital with horse and buggy tonight to meet our new nephew and cousin. He is such a cutie! Our little Kevin hesitated about welcoming Steven, since this is "his" Aunt Emma. Our three-year-old Lovina was really proud, and I think she's thinking of the baby as another doll to play with.

I am glad mother and baby seem to be doing fine and plan to be dismissed tomorrow evening. My daughter Elizabeth, thirteen, will help Emma with household duties for a few days. I know she'll do a good job, as she is a big help to me.

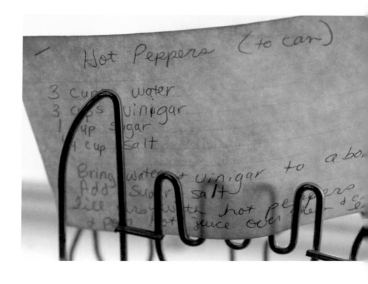

On Saturday, we spent the day helping Jacob and Emma on some various jobs. Kevin fell asleep on the way home after playing hard all day. Daughter Susan carried him and rocked him and I changed his diaper and gave him back to Susan, as he was still sleeping good. Shortly after that, Susan came running to me saying, "Something is really wrong with Kevin!" After not knowing what to do, we had a neighbor call EMS and they arrived quickly. After doing blood tests and X-rays at the hospital, they decided it was a seizure from a fever that had jumped to 106°F in a hurry. The fever was caused from a viral infection. Kevin hadn't acted sick at all so it caught us by surprise. On Monday, I took Kevin back to the doctor for a checkup and he got a clean bill of health.

We were so scared as we never experienced anything like this. How small we felt. We know God was with us but would I have been strong enough in faith if things wouldn't have went the way our prayers went? We need to remember that our Heavenly Father cares for us and will never lay a heavier burden on us than we can carry. My children seem extra special this week.

Thursday we left at 5:00 A.M. to attend niece Susan's wedding. I was one of the cooks, so it was a busy job. They had two delicious meals with fried chicken on the menu.

We ended up back home shortly after 10:00 P.M. I didn't stay to help wash all the dishes. Joe needed to leave for work at 3:45 A.M. Friday morning so we hurried right after the wedding. We missed not having Jacob and Emma at the wedding.

I need to wrap up my writing today, as I would like to can some hot peppers and pickles. My red beets are also ready.

NOVEMBER 2007

In November 2006, the Eichers journeyed to Kansas. This year, they ventured to Wisconsin to attend the wedding of nephew Ben Shetler. Ben lives in the southwestern part of the state, an area that has experienced explosive growth in its Amish population.

Part of our old house is now torn down. Last Friday, Joe and brother-in-law Jacob worked hard to get the windows out, the chimney down, and whatever else needed to be done. Our old house was a split-level, so there were two floors to work on getting taken down.

The one-story part is all that is left now, and that should probably get moved next week by a local Amish couple that wants to convert that portion into a shed. With the house down, I will have a lot better view of the road and surrounding fields. It will be really nice once the basement is filled in and everything is leveled out.

My garden frosted last Friday and now it's history for this year. I need to go out and pick and dry the marigolds and zinnia flowers. These make for cheap but pretty flowers from year to year.

The first really cold mornings also meant that Joe started the coal stove in the house on Tuesday evening. The coal stove, which is in our basement, heats the whole house by moving the warm air upward through ducts into all the rooms. On that cold Tuesday, we had some snow flurries and it was windy. But the house was cozy and it felt good to have the warmth come through the vents from our basement.

We might miss out on seeing the last of our old house being moved, as we plan to leave on Wednesday morning for Wisconsin. This will be a short trip. We'll return home on Friday evening. On Thursday, we will attend nephew Ben and Rose Marie's wedding all day. I will be a cook at the wedding. It'll be a busy day.

I don't know what job I'll be assigned until I get there. Usually at weddings, a paper will be hanging up on the wall telling the cooks what their assignments are. I always like it when they assign all us sisters to the same job. It's more time spent together. It seems like I get a different job at each wedding I go to. One time I got the mashed potatoes, another time the gravy. Other times I've been in charge of the pudding or the salad. Probably the hardest job is frying chicken!

We plan to start out Wednesday morning at 7:30 A.M. Our three other older children will come later in the day in a separate vehicle with my sisters Verena and Susan, and Jacob and Emma and family. This will give the children another half day at school. We plan to all meet back together in Wisconsin Wednesday evening. We hope and pray we'll all make it safe and sound.

We won't start heading back for home until Friday morning. This will give the drivers a good night's rest before starting for home. As far as I know, the rest of my family have plans to go, too. I wish everyone safe travels.

I need to get started packing this weekend. Packing clothes for ten people can be quite a chore, but I enjoy traveling. It's always good to come back to "home sweet home" though.

NOVEMBER 2007

Outsiders are often surprised to find that the Amish stay in modern hotels when traveling. These hotels, of course, are complete with running water, television, and electric lights, all anathema to the Amish at home. But they draw a clear distinction between having technology in the home and using it elsewhere.

We arrived home safe and sound from our Wisconsin trip around 6:30 P.M. Friday evening. We went to Wisconsin to attend the wedding of my nephew, Ben Shetler, and his bride, Rose Marie.

The trip was long, but enjoyable. We started out on Wednesday around 8:30 A.M. It took a long time to get the van loaded and the little ones in their car seats.

Between Albert's and us we had seven children ages one to six in car or booster seats. I thought the little ones did really well to travel that far. We only stopped three times on the way there and two times on the way back home. We had a good driver who knew the way there.

The wedding day was sunny, but cold and windy. The wedding was held in a "bank barn," which is built into a hillside for protection against wind and cold. A back entrance is at the second-floor level. Kerosene heaters also provided some warmth.

My job was to help make the salad for the wedding meal. Two other women were assigned to do that job with me. The salad was a tossed lettuce salad. We used maybe twelve to thirteen big heads of lettuce and diced up a big bowl of tomatoes and had a large kettle of dressing. Other food served at the meal included fried chicken, mashed potatoes, gravy, noodles, dressing, cheese, homemade bread, and vegetables. For dessert, it was pies, puddings, cakes, fruit, and "nothings," which is a popular deep-fried pastry served at weddings back in Indiana.

It was good to return to the warmth of the motel that night. The younger children were tired and fell asleep right away.

The next morning, we took them to the indoor pool and they enjoyed the water. It was interesting to see how much more advanced they were in the water after taking swimming lessons this past summer. Two-year-old Kevin acts afraid of the water, though. Jacob took three-month-old Stephen in the water and he looked like he was enjoying it.

After eating breakfast at the motel, we started loading up for the long trip back home. Our five-year-old, Joseph, and Albert's four-year-old, Andrew, kept us entertained. One minute they were arguing with each other and the next minute they were saying "sorry" and that they liked each other again. If only grown-ups could be like this and forget so soon.

This is now Monday morning, and Joe is back at the neighbor's woods trying his luck with deer hunting. He doesn't have any work this week. We will be glad when things pick up at work.

DECEMBER 2007

The first snow of the season is always a cause of excitement in the Eicher household. It doesn't take long for a frumpy snowman to appear on the lawn. By the end of the winter, the novelty will have worn off and everyone will be ready for warmth.

It snowed enough last evening that we have a nice layer of white on the ground. The children were excited to see it snow.

Eight-year-old Benjamin and five-year-old Joseph were outside after dark, rolling a big ball of snow. They wanted to make a snowman, but the snow was mixed with leaves, making a dirty-looking snowman. Kevin, two, just stood by the window watching the snowflakes falling. The boys were going through my storage totes digging out their snow pants, mittens, and other winter wear. We still don't have enough hooks to hang up all these extra coats. With all the children's coats, we have quite a big collection.

We had a nice Thanksgiving at my sister Susan and Verena's house. They prepared a big turkey stuffed with dressing, mashed potatoes, mixed vegetables, salad, cheese, pickles, tomatoes, sourdough bread roll, cheese ball and crackers, pumpkin roll, pumpkin pie, cake, and ice cream. After our meal, we spent the afternoon playing games.

Jacob, Emma, and family were there also. We had an enjoyable day there together. Let us remember to thank our Heavenly Father for all he does for us not only on Thanksgiving Day, but every day.

Joe has been trying his luck at deer hunting lately. On Saturday morning, when Joe was back in the neighbor's woods hunting, we saw fourteen deer running out of the trees and into our hayfield. We were wondering if Joe had seen them. But it wasn't long before Joe came out and said he shot a deer. We had some pretty excited children. The girls hitched our pony Stormy to the two-wheel cart and Joe and Elizabeth drove to the woods to bring the deer back. Now this afternoon, when Joe gets home from work, we want to cut up the meat.

We are guessing that we'll be able to get around sixty-five to seventy-five pounds of meat from the deer. We need to have about twenty pounds ready for tonight for a man who will make deer sausage out of it for us.

An Amish friend gave me the recipe for how she cans deer meat and makes bologna out of it. It sounds like you can just shake it out of the can and heat it and slice it. If I have enough meat left over, I'd like to have some steaks and then try my luck making deer jerky. I'll let you know how it all turns out.

Benjamin likes to go back in the woods with Joe to help watch for deer. He told Joe not to shoot the little "Bambis," though.

The men are here working on getting the old house ready to move again. It might be able to be moved today yet. It is interesting to see how they go about moving it. It is sitting on skids in our yard.

DECEMBER 2007

Children's birthdays are always celebrated at school. Usually the birthday girl or boy brings in treats for all of her or his classmates. I often wonder why the birthday person gets saddled with the work of supplying the snack, but it's all in good fun!

Monday, December 10, was daughter Verena's birthday. She was excited because she made cupcakes to take to school and treat her classmates. But then school was cancelled due to slick roads, and she was disappointed she couldn't go. I told her she could still take them the next day. The younger children are all bundled up, except two-year-old Kevin, and are having fun sliding down the nearby hill with their sleds. The sleds really slide nicely on this ice and snow.

Last Sunday brother Amos, Nancy, and children and their two married daughters came for the day. Also along with them were brother Albert, Sarah Irene and family, and our sisters Susan, Verena, Emma, and Jacob's and family.

We ended up with about fifty people here for dinner. Joe grilled chicken for everyone, and we also made mashed potatoes, gravy, corn, and peas. Everyone also brought a dish to share, so we had salads and quite a few desserts. It turned out to be a rainy day, so we stayed indoors and played games in the afternoon.

During the visit, I got to meet my new great-niece Lisa. This is brother Amos's first grandchild. This would be Amos's daughter Elizabeth's baby who was born September 18.

We celebrated Verena's birthday on Saturday because we thought she'd be in school today. We fried some deer steak for her birthday. She is the one out of all our children that likes deer meat the best. I fried it like a "poor man's steak," which means I fried it down a little and added cream of mushroom soup and baked it. We also had French fries, ice cream, and cake to celebrate.

My condolences go out to the three Amish widows who lost their husbands in a van crash last week here in Michigan. They will go through some trying times raising their young children by themselves. May God give them the strength to go on.

A person wonders why so many young husbands were taken, but it helps to know that God makes no mistakes and that he has a plan for each of us in life. Our sympathy also goes to the family of Joe's great-uncle Solomon Schwartz. We could not make it to the funeral, but our thoughts were with them just the same.

Our rat terrier dog, Frisco, had four puppies on Friday. Joe fixed a place for her in the pole barn where there is some heat. Joe was afraid it would be too cold for the little puppies without a special spot fixed up for them.

Yesterday we had church services at our neighbor's house. And we all planned for the annual Christmas potluck supper in two weeks. This is something our church does each year. They pass around a tablet while us women are at the table, and we all write what we will bring. Then they make sure we have enough of everything. I am bringing an "overnight salad."

2008
growing up

Although there are many differences between the Amish culture in Michigan versus Indiana, there are also numerous similarities, such as holding church services in one's home. The format is the same: a bench wagon goes from place to place carrying the church benches, and men and women sit in separate aisles.

Church services were held here yesterday, which is always an event that requires a lot of preparation work.

We set up the church benches in our basement for the services. The benches, dishes for meals, and other supplies needed to hold a service are stored in a wagon, which goes from place to place—wherever the services are going to be held.

Services are usually around three hours long. Afterwards, the menfolk set up four tables, with every table sitting sixteen people. Then the women all pitch in and help get the tables set. It is nice to have most of those dishes we need for lunch stored in containers in the bench wagon.

Our menu was coffee, tea, homemade wheat and white bread, bologna, cheese spread, peanut butter spread, dill and sweet pickles, red beets, sweet and hot peppers, butter, homemade jam, and sugar, pumpkin, and butterscotch chip cookies. I also fixed a pot of chicken noodle soup for the younger ones who can't eat sandwiches yet.

All in all, we had about 150 to 175 people show up for services, which is a little lower than usual because some people were gone because of sickness.

After the meal, the men visited with one another while the women helped wash the dishes. Then we served popcorn for a snack.

Midafternoon, everyone went home for a while, but I invited everyone back for supper at 6:00 P.M. We had pizza casserole, tossed salad, homemade bread, pickles, and dressing. For dessert, chocolate pudding, white and chocolate cake, and ice cream were on the menu. We had plenty of food left over.

Quite a few of the families accepted the invitation to come back for supper. We also had the supper in the basement. It sure helps keep the living quarters cleaner when all the church functions can be held in the basement. After supper, the men played games while us women washed dishes. The children played simple games like hide 'n' seek.

We were glad for the cold 30°F weather, even though Joe had to shovel snow. The freezing weather kept the muddiness in the yard down. Our neighbor came and cleaned our drive of snow the day before. He also made a path to the basement door where everyone came in to put their coats and boots and attend services. Now today we want to mop the floors and do the laundry and get back to normal around here.

After Joe gets home from work, he'll stack all the benches back in the bench wagon. I need to clean tablecloths and roll them up so they will be ready to use in two weeks at the next place. Dishes also all have to be packed back in the wagon. Always a relief once everything is back in place, but I enjoy taking our turn to hold church.

I appreciate the bread, cookies, and cakes from the church ladies and my sisters. It takes a lot of the load off me. My neighbor lady offered to make the cheese spread for me, which took another job off my list. And my family here in Michigan helped with the cleaning before church. With everyone pitching in and helping, it made it a lot easier. Now we want to try to return the favor to others in our church when they need us.

Daughter Verena is still on crutches from her fall. The good news is that the bone specialist said there was no break, only a sprain. The ER doctor had thought he had seen a break but there wasn't one. She is having quite a bit of pain since she has fallen on it again. Tomorrow I will take her in for a checkup. Hopefully she has not hurt it worse.

MARCH 2008

Emma and Jacob's newborn, Steven, had to undergo a serious heart procedure. The surgery left everyone concerned, but the little tyke pulled through just fine.

Daughter Lovina is recovering well from her surgery. She had a cyst removed close to her right eyebrow. The doctor did a very good job of hiding the scar under her eyebrow. Lovina had a few painful days when her eyes were swollen shut and bruised. She always called the cyst her "bump." After we were home from the hospital, she said the doctor "took my bump away, but put one on my eye."

Now, Lovina is happier, since she sees the swelling going down. She is back to singing her little songs. Her favorite one now is "This Old Man." In addition to singing songs, she can't wait until her fourth birthday in May. She is a little talker and does all the talking for her and two-year-old Kevin.

This morning, shortly after 6:00 A.M., sister Emma and Jacob dropped their four children off here. They were leaving for the two-hour journey to the hospital for baby Steven's appointment. I fed their children a breakfast of grilled cheese and scrambled eggs. They left here with our five children at 7:00 A.M. to go to school. They were all excited to go to school together!

Steven's heart surgery is still set for Monday, March 3. We hope and pray everything will go well. God is above all and we must accept whatever He wants. We know sometimes we tend to want our way. Prayers do wonders and let us all leave it in His hands.

Jacob's parents, Verena and Susan, and Joe and I, have plans to spend the day at the hospital with Jacob and Emma. The surgery will take four to five hours, so that will be a long wait for them. Jacob and Emma came home from the hospital last weekend and were very happy to be together with their children.

Steven has had a feeding tube on, as he refuses to take a bottle. Emma has her day filled feeding him through the tube eight times a day and breast feeding eight times a day around the clock. Yesterday, my sisters and I gave her a lift by coming over to do her laundry for her. We also washed her kitchen walls and refrigerator and stove.

Meanwhile, we heard the sad news of Mom's cousin Reuben having a massive heart attack at the age of sixty-two. Our sympathy goes to his wife and the family. We never know who God will pick next, so let us all be prepared to meet our maker when our time on earth is done.

I must get back to my work soon. We are getting more snow and ice and have six to eight inches already, but Joe and I still plan to go into town in the buggy to get groceries after he gets home from work. Our horse, which was trained last year, is getting more used to going into town, which is a relief. She hated the white lines at the traffic light at first, but has learned to stop and wait for the signal.

MAY 2008

Once again, Elizabeth does a marvelous job of stepping in for her mother. She's thirteen years old in this column, which means she's been occasionally stepping in for Lovina for two years.

I am giving Mom a break during this busy spring season of readying the garden. The first garden goodies are already coming up. We have peas, lettuce, radishes, onions, and potatoes planted. We were going to plant more on Friday, but it rained and the garden was too wet. The asparagus is starting in and rhubarb is taking over. Mom says she will probably be canning rhubarb juice and jam this week. She made some rhubarb pies this week and they sure didn't last long.

Oh, how wonderful it is to have nice warm days again! This is my favorite season. I love to see all the birds coming back. We have been seeing a lot of beautiful cardinals. Dad put up my bluebird house that I made in third grade at school. Now some bluebirds have made it their home.

Yesterday we spent the day at Uncle Jacob and Aunt Emma's house. Dad, Mom, and some of my brothers and sisters biked the four miles, and so did Aunt Verena and Susan. Since Dad needs to repair the tube in my bike tire, I couldn't bike. So, instead of biking, sister Susan and I took our pony, Stormy, and the pony wagon to Jacob and Emma's. The younger ones who couldn't bike that far also went along. Stormy was rarin' to go after a long rest all winter. It was nice to go for a pony ride again and Kevin and Lovina always enjoy it.

Aunt Emma had a good dinner of homemade French fries, breaded fish, onion rings, white cake, rhubarb pie, ice cream, and peaches. It was all very good. Emma also breaded and deep-fried potato slices and they were good like that.

After dishes were washed, we played kickball. Brother Kevin and cousin Steven, nine months, took a nap while we played. It was fun to all play kickball together and I was on the winning team. We were seventeen total playing, but we let sister Lovina just kick the ball and run around the bases and didn't count her points. Lovina will turn four on May 18. She is excited and keeps asking me how long until her birthday.

Next month on June 14, I will be fourteen. We will have cake and ice cream and family and friends over. Turning fourteen also means that next year is my last year of school, and I am really excited that I will be done. I'm not the only one celebrating fourteen years—our horse Diamond will be fourteen this month. Dad raised him and trained him and he is our best horse and very safe. I am finishing up with my schoolwork for this year. I still have some English and math lessons to do. Reading and spelling are my favorite subjects. Although I miss seeing my friends at school, I enjoyed home schooling. It is more relaxing to do my lessons here at home.

Mom, Susan, and I made this casserole on Saturday for lunch. It is easy to make and we all liked it:

YUMASETTI
Serves 6 to 8

3 pounds ground beef

1 medium onion, chopped

1 (16-ounce) package egg noodles

2 cups peas

2 (10¾-ounce) cans cream of mushroom soup

1 (10¾-ounce) can cream of chicken soup

1 cup sour cream

10 bread slices, toasted and cubed

2 cups shredded cheese of your choice

Preheat the oven to 350°F. Grease a large casserole dish and set aside.

In a large skillet, cook the beef and the onion over medium heat. Remove from the heat when the beef is browned. Drain the grease and transfer the meat mixture to a large bowl. Cook the egg noodles in salted water, per package directions, until tender. Drain well. Add the noodles, peas, mushroom soup, chicken soup, sour cream, and bread to the meat mixture. Stir until all the ingredients are well combined. Transfer the mixture to the prepared casserole dish and top with the shredded cheese. Bake for about 30 minutes, or until the casserole is bubbling and the cheese is melted.

Little ones discover good place to eat some popcorn

By Lovina Eicher
Oasis Newsfeatures

AMISH COOK

Kevin is always excited when Steven comes. I think he likes the idea that he is older and bigger than Steven. Kevin told me Steven sings but that his cousin, baby Marilyn, can't — she just cries. Marilyn is almost 3 months old and is such a little sweetie. She doesn't lack attention when she comes here.

Our annual church potluck Christmas dinner is drawing near. The holidays are coming up way too fast.

Daughter Verena turned 12 years old on Dec. 10.

My husband Joe's grandmother turned 96 on Dec.

evenings rehearsing their lines and practicing scenes. It gets dark so early now, so it is something for them to do. I am looking forward to watching the play and seeing what they came up with this time. Joseph T. told me one evening that he doesn't want to be in the play because Susan is making it too sad, but they talked him into helping them again.

The children are also working on their songs for their school's Christmas program. Lovina S. sings her song to us. It sounds so cute to hear her little voice sing. She is really adjusting well in school.

Last week were the par-

2/3 cup brown sugar

1/2 cup flour

1/2 cup pecans, optional

In a large bowl, mix sweet potatoes, 1/2 cup butter, sugar, vanilla and eggs. Spoon into a 9-inch by 13-inch casserole dish. Then, in a separate bowl, combine brown sugar, flour and the remaining butter. Sprinkle this mixture over the top of potatoes. Sprinkle pecans on top if desired. Bake 30 minutes at 400 degrees. Delicious!

The Amish Cook is a weekly column written by Lovina Eicher, an Old Order Amish woman who lives in Michigan. To comment send mail to Eicher

JUNE 2008

Fishing is a favorite pastime among the Old Order Amish. The activity provides outdoor fun, a self-sufficient food source, and a chance to spend time with family. A buggy pulls the boat to the edge of a pond or lake, the horse is secured to a tree, and the lines are cast!

The 2007–08 school term is now over and this is the children's first day home. We are a little slower today adjusting to our new "summer schedule." Since we had a full weekend, I let the children sleep a little later than usual this morning.

Last week, I had a nice birthday. My husband, Joe, and the children surprised me with a Dairy Queen ice-cream cake. They had a "3" and "7" candle on it, so I only had to blow out two candles.

For my birthday gift, Joe got me a fishing license, fishing pole, and a life jacket. This is the first fishing license I have ever had. I have never taken an interest in fishing, but Joe wants to take me out on the lake fishing to see if he can get me interested. I have never been out on a boat before, and I can't swim, so he wanted me to have a life jacket. Joe and son Benjamin, eight, and brother-in-law Jacob and Jacob Jr., eight, went fishing Saturday. Benjamin has a new pole and was excited to try it out, although he had more fun casting and reeling in his line instead of leaving it out to fish. But that should help get him used to casting better.

Jacob Jr. caught a pretty good-sized bass. Fish makes a very economical, tasty supper. Our children like fish best when I put it in batter and deep-fry it. With meat prices being so high, the more fish we get helps cut down on the grocery bill.

We had an eventful weekend. My sister Liz and family came over Saturday. In honor of their visit, we all gathered at sister Susan and Verena's house for barbecued chicken and hamburgers, plus much more food. Brother Albert and family also came and joined us. Along with them was their oldest daughter Elizabeth and her husband and daughter. They stopped in to see our new house, as Elizabeth hadn't been to Michigan since she was married in 2005.

On Sunday, we all gathered at Albert's for dinner. Albert has plans to move to another place about a mile from where they live now. It is a new house and isn't finished yet. This will give them a lot more room for their family of twelve.

JULY 2008

As the national economy began its downturn in the summer of 2008, fishing became more than just a recreational activity—it also became an important source of food.

With all the nearby lakes here in Michigan, a lot of fishing is being done by people around here during this nice stretch of weather. We have enjoyed quite a few meals of fresh fish and have more in the freezer.

I enjoyed my first time out fishing on the lake. My husband, Joe, took me one evening on his boat. At first I was a little nervous, but I finally got the feel of the boat. It wasn't long before we found a good place to fish. Joe helped me bait my hook, after teaching me how to cast a line. We weren't fishing very long when I caught my first fish; it was a bluegill. Later I almost had a big bass, but it got away before I could pull it into the boat. It was exciting enough, though, to make me want to go again. It was also very relaxing and peaceful out on the water.

Joe told me I did a good job of casting. I think he was a little afraid at first that the worm on my hook would land in his hair. We came home and I helped clean fish for the first time. We then went over to Jacob and Emma's house to meet up with our children. My sisters Verena and Susan had taken the children with them to Jacob's house earlier. We all planned to "camp out" there for the night.

We slept in tents in their yard, which was exciting for the children. The next morning, we cooked breakfast outside. We had bacon, mushrooms, and asparagus on the grill, along with fried potatoes, eggs, biscuits, sausage gravy, cheese, and hot peppers. We also enjoyed chocolate milk, juices, coffee, and fresh tea from the leaves from Emma's tea plants. It was fun to once again cook over an open fire.

My friend Ruth told me how she does her asparagus on the grill. Joe used her method of coating it with olive oil and grilling them. It was very good.

Peas and squash are ready to use now, adding a few more garden goodies to our menu. Also some of my cabbage heads are good-sized and will be ready to use. We like to dip our squash in a batter made of one egg, three-quarter cup flour, one-half cup milk, and one-half teaspoon salt (or choose a seasoning of your choice). Then we deep fry the slices in olive oil. Some of the family like to eat this with bread and salad dressing, adding lettuce and cheese. We also use the batter for onion rings, mushrooms, chicken, or fish.

Meanwhile, we continue to harvest the tea plants from our gardens. Spearmint, peppermint and comfrey are our favorites, but there are quite a few different varieties.

JULY 2008

This column describes a typical Michigan midsummer morning in the Eicher home.

The house seems quiet and very empty this morning. Joe left for work at 3:45 A.M. after being off work for two weeks. Then, at 6:15 A.M., fourteen-year-old daughter Elizabeth left for her summer job helping detassle corn. She enjoys the new friends she is making on the job. Elizabeth is tired when she comes home after walking through the cornfields all day. They certainly put in a lot of miles in a day's work.

At 7:30 this morning, Susan, Verena, Benjamin, and Joseph left for their swimming lessons, which they are taking for the next two weeks. Meanwhile, Lovina and Kevin are still both sleeping. They had a tiring day yesterday. We attended church services in another church district at Joe's nephew's house, which made for a very long, but enjoyable, day.

Son Benjamin turns nine today, which he is pretty excited about. Loretta and Benjamin were both eight years old for two weeks. He is always glad to turn to the next number. Loretta always likes to tease him that she has caught up to his age during the first two weeks in July.

Tomorrow, Joe and I will celebrate fifteen years of marriage. It sure has gone by fast! Joe seems to be doing well with his wisdom teeth out, but he has to be careful until the holes in his mouth grow shut. He isn't supposed to eat popcorn or peanuts for another six weeks. They happen to be some of his favorite snacks.

Friday, Joe and I and drove to Wal-Mart with the horse and buggy, which is probably seven to eight miles from here—about a forty-five-minute ride. He needed to get Lovina and Kevin a life jacket so we could take them out on the boat. Joe and I went to the lake fishing Friday evening, taking Lovina and Kevin along. We just hitch the boat up to the buggy and go to a nearby lake. This was their first time on a boat. Lovina seemed to enjoy it, while Kevin was very scared at first, but gradually loosened up. They enjoyed drinking lemonade and eating crackers while we fished. We caught a few fish, but they were not biting too well.

The next day, Joe and Elizabeth and Susan went fishing, and they had good luck, bringing home quite a few fish. Susan caught a nineteen-inch bass that she thought was going to be a turtle when she felt the weight on her line. The children were really excited to see it after being used to catching the little bluegill we have been reeling in lately. They enjoyed helping with the scaling while Joe filets the fish.

After two weeks of extra activity going on around here, I am kind of enjoying peace and quiet right now. We are still savoring the garden goodies and have added green beans, red beets, and carrots to the menu now. The green peppers are also almost big enough to start using. Corn and tomatoes are not too far from being ready either. Meals are sure easier to make with the garden and sure saves on the grocery bill. All the hoeing and weeding is worth it when you have such a bountiful crop. Most of all, thanks to our heavenly father for sending us sunshine and rain to make it grow!

AUGUST 2008

Many readers inquired about "detasseling" corn. This was Elizabeth Eicher's summer job, and it involves breaking the top off cornstalks to aid in their cross-pollination. It was hard work, but Elizabeth made a lot of new friends.

Today is Elizabeth's last day of corn detasseling for this season. It will be nice to have her home again during the day. I've really missed her help, especially with church services announced to be here in two weeks. We've had a good start in cleaning the house. Sister Emma and children came one day, and we washed some walls, ceilings, and a few windows. We also did a big laundry, washing some curtains, quilts, and so forth. I can see a few busy weeks ahead, but it will be a relief to have everything clean once again. The girls washed off all my kitchen cabinets one day: that is another big job that takes a lot of time.

Meanwhile, Joe and the boys cleaned out our toolshed. With children, it doesn't seem to take long for everything to get disorganized in there. The boys have little hammers, and they seem to want to try them out pounding in nails, although they don't always choose the right place to start pounding.

Along with all the cleaning, canning season is also in full swing. We have peaches, tomatoes, and pickles to do this week.

Another day this week, we helped Jacob and Emma butcher their chickens one evening. The work went fast with everyone pitching in to help. We plucked the chickens by hand, which the children enjoy helping with. After the feathers are off, we gut the chickens and clean them and then cut up the meat really good. We clean the chickens by soaking them in dishpans with water, since there are a lot of little feather pieces to remove. We can usually salvage ten or eleven pieces of chicken from one bird: quarters, breasts, two legs, two thighs, a back piece, and wings, to name a few. Then we pack it in freezer bags. I like white meat and most of my children like white. Emma likes her dark meat. I usually put enough in a freezer bag for a meal.

Benjamin, nine, is outside riding our pony, Stormy. One of our neighbors brought over his saddle for Benjamin to use, but he'd rather ride bareback. Benjamin is a horse lover, and he is always out in the barn with the horses. He made a few "halters" out of baler twine. He was so proud of them that he made a few for his cousin, Jacob Jr. He has a big imagination.

It is dry here and we could use more rain. One day when I drove to town last week, we were about a mile from home and it just poured down rain most of the way into town. When I came home later, Joe said they didn't even have a sprinkle here. It sure made for a cooler ride for our horse, Itty Bit. I like driving her into town, she is safe and makes good time on the road.

Foremost on our minds today is the passing away of Joe's uncle Martin, age sixty-five. He suffered quite a bit from that dreadful cancer. This would also be brother-in-law Jacob's uncle. Our sympathy goes to the family. We hope we will be able to attend his funeral, which is tomorrow.

SEPTEMBER 2008

September brought sadness, as the only brother of the late Elizabeth Coblentz passed away. He was a much-loved uncle to the children.

The Good Lord has once again taken a loved one on before us.

Uncle Chris passed away Monday, August 25, at age seventy. Our deepest sympathy goes to Aunt Lizzie and the family.

I have a lot of childhood memories of times spent with Uncle Chris. One of my best memories is of how we would always get together to make homemade apple butter in a big kettle over an open fire. The evening before, we would go over to Uncle Chris and Aunt Lizzie's to peel bushels of apples, and then go back early the next morning to start cooking them down.

I can still remember the smell of the apples cooking down in the kettle, with Uncle Chris stirring them. Apple butter sandwiches were one of our main snacks when coming home from school as children. We also liked apple butter spread on our fried mush for breakfast.

The taste of apple butter just doesn't seem to go so well with my children, but they never went through the stages of seeing it being made in such huge amounts. After the apple butter was done, it was put into quart jars to process, and we could enjoy it year-round.

Another memory of Uncle Chris is seeing him and his family driving in their bobsled during the winter months. Sometimes they'd pick us up to go on to church or somewhere with them. It was cozy for all of us children to snuggle in the warm buggy robes on top of bales of straw that were used to sit on.

When it was haying time, we'd see them come driving in, and also at hog butchering time. We would also go there whenever they needed help with any chores.

There are lots more memories, and I could go on and on. Uncle Chris is the third of eight children to pass away. He was two years younger than my mother and was her only brother. The funeral will be on Friday in Indiana. This is the second week in a row we will have gone to a funeral in the same community. Once again, our Heavenly Father is warning us to be ready for our Savior when our time on earth here is done.

Jacob and Emma and two of their children, Joe and I and four of our children and brother Albert and Sarah Irene and their youngest child plan to attend the funeral together. Albert and Sarah live in a nearby community, so we will pick them up on the way there.

Meanwhile here in this household, we are trying to get everything clean and done for church services which will be held here on Sunday, so it's a busy time. Jacob and Emma came for a couple of hours tonight to help us with final preparations. Jacob helped Joe set up the church benches in the basement and Emma assisted me with finishing sewing the last of the curtains that I had started.

Saturday daughter Elizabeth will attend the detasseling picnic, so she will be gone for a while. I am sure everyone will be glad once Saturday evening comes and everything is ready for church services on Sunday.

SEPTEMBER 2008

Lovina was the cook at the wedding of her niece. It's always considered an honor to be selected as a cook at a wedding, even though it involves a long day of hard work.

This has been a busy time in the Eicher household!

For starters, we attended the wedding of niece Mary Jane and Amos in Indiana. This is brother Amos and Nancy's third daughter to get married. After having a daughter getting married the last three summers, they should be in good practice.

One outbuilding was set with benches for the wedding service, while another had tables set for the meal. An adjoining building was used for the cooks to prepare food. They served a very delicious meal to all the guests. I was a cook, while my daughter Elizabeth, fourteen, helped wait on the children's table. All the cooks pitched in with different tasks. First I helped with the tapioca pudding, then I worked on the Watergate salad, and then I went in and helped with frying chicken.

We were to wear gray dresses. Elizabeth and I didn't have any that color, so I was extra busy sewing the last few weeks. I also sewed Kevin, three, a new white shirt for the wedding. The men and boys wear white shirts for churches and wedding services. Kevin had outgrown one of his white shirts, and the other was too stained after passing it down from his older brothers, Benjamin and Joseph. On some material the stains are so much easier to get out than others, and it just wouldn't come clean. Although after enjoying his chocolate cake at the wedding, Kevin's new white shirt didn't look very clean anymore.

We cooks fried three hundred pounds of chicken for the noon meal, and there wasn't much left by the time it was all done. Along with chicken, they had mashed potatoes, gravy, noodles, dressing, mixed vegetables, tossed salad, Watergate salad, cheese, mixed fruit, tapioca pudding, a variety of cakes, and plenty of pie, which include the following flavors: pumpkin, cherry, oatmeal, and pecan. We didn't stay all day, so I am not sure what the evening menu was. We were glad we could at least go for the wedding ceremony and the meal afterwards. Meanwhile, we received another wedding invitation, this one from niece Elizabeth and her fiancé, Levi. Their wedding day will be October 16. This is sister Leah and Paul's daughter.

Another excitement for Leah and Paul is that they are now grandparents for the first time. Their son Ben and Rose Marie were blessed with a son September 8 named Ben Jr. While attending the wedding of Mary Jane, I visited with Aunt Lizzie; she is having many lonely days since Uncle Chris's funeral. They were married fifty-one years together.

Another task that has kept us busier than usual is canning grape juice. We canned five bushels of grapes and canned 240 quarts of juice this week. The children are enjoying it already. I think it is a healthy drink for them to enjoy.

Along with everything else, we are helping Emma and Jacob prepare for church services, which will be held at their house next Sunday. We are hoping that things will slow down after that.

Today Emma and Jacob and family were here for the noon meal. We had mashed potatoes, gravy, mixed vegetables, barbecued chicken, cheese, tomatoes, turnips, cole slaw, and cake and ice cream. The chicken was from ones we butchered ourselves. We also had deviled eggs since I have so many eggs on hand. Those are a real treat for everybody. I told them just come over and relax, since preparing for church is so much work, I figured they could use a break!

OCTOBER 2008

More weddings were on the agenda in October of 2008. June is traditionally the month for weddings among the Amish, but the autumn months have been gaining ground in recent years. The harvest is completed and the weather is nice, an important element since at least part of most Amish weddings are held outdoors.

It is 7:00 A.M. and the school-age children have left for the day. Kevin is still eating his breakfast and Lovina, four, is still in bed. Meanwhile, fourteen-year-old daughter Elizabeth is beginning her school lessons for the day. The gaslights make the house feel nice and cozy with the temperatures in the lower forties outside. We are still just relying on the gaslights for heat. With the temperatures dipping lower and lower lately, though, I wouldn't be surprised if we have to start the coal stove soon.

Thursday we attended the wedding of niece Elizabeth and Levi. It was a nice, but chilly day. Three hundred and twenty pounds of chicken were fried for the noon meal. Three twenty-quart kettles of potatoes were cooked for only the noon meal. Gravy, noodles, and mixed vegetables were also made. All of that was served along with lettuce salad, carrot salad, cheese, cakes, pies, tapioca pudding, fresh fruit mixture, and cookies. The same menu was served for the evening meal, with ham and ice cream being added to the offerings.

My job was to help with the dressing. For one meal, we mixed up three thirteen-quart pans of dressing. The bread was toasted and cubed the day before. Also the carrots were shredded and onions were diced the day before, making it easier to mix together.

Friday my husband, Joe, and I, and son Kevin, drove to town with horse and buggy to get some groceries. When I don't need many groceries, we just go to a little store outside of town, making it a ten-mile round-trip.

When we came home, we had out-of-state visitors. My uncle Joe and Betty decided to come for the weekend. While they went to visit with Jacob and Emma, the girls made supper for them and us. We fried chicken and had creamed potatoes, salad, and apple cider. They had to do without dessert, as I had not been prepared for them to come, so I hope they survived. Ha!

The next day, Saturday, the girls and I were cleaning house and Joe and the boys were raking up leaves. Joe and Betty drove in around lunchtime, bringing food for us all. I had already made potato soup and fried hamburgers, so we had plenty of food. Betty brought the children a pack of M&M's, which they divided into eight piles. It reminded me of Grandpa Coblentz when I was a child. Every time Grandpa came, he would bring us a big pack of M&M's and we'd be so excited. We would divide up the pack amongst us children. The M&M's kept Lovina and Kevin occupied for quite a while that evening. They would put theirs all in a row on the table, counting them. Kevin wasn't exactly counting, he was just saying "one, two, three" over and over. Lovina kept telling him, "You forgot four and six because I am four and Joseph is six." It was cute listening to them chatter.

Joe's dad went up to the hospital Friday morning to have some tests done. It ended up he had to stay, and they did some surgery concerning his heart. He is back home again and is doing as well as expected. We were going to visit him yesterday, but I woke up sick in the morning. I am having flulike symptoms; I think I might have chilled myself at the wedding and it is finally getting the best of me.

Uncle Jake and Mary were also planning to be in this area on Wednesday and Thursday. We missed them due to going to the wedding in Indiana.

We were surprised to receive another wedding invitation from one of Joe's cousins in a community about ninety minutes from here. They will exchange their vows on November 6.

2009
much to be thankful for

A baby always brings joy and blessings to the Eicher home. The year 2009 saw the arrival of a new niece for Lovina with the birth of Marilyn to her sister Emma and brother-in-law Jacob.

Yesterday we went to Jacob and Emma's house for a nice Sunday visit. It takes about fifteen to twenty minutes to get there by buggy. We were glad to get to see and hold baby Marilyn again. She is so tiny and so cute.

While visiting we had a delicious meal of mashed potatoes, gravy, barbecued ham and pork chops, corn, coleslaw, cheese, tomatoes, peppers, and homemade pie. Pie flavors were oatmeal, custard, and shoofly. We also enjoyed butterscotch pudding and watermelon.

My husband, Joe, went fishing both Friday and Saturday evening. Saturday they had quite a bit of luck. He went with some friends on a pontoon. Altogether they caught more than forty bluegill and some bass that averaged around sixteen to eighteen inches.

I fix the fish in different ways; sometimes I bread it and deep-fry it, other times I roll it in eggs and flour and fry it. Joe likes it best when I just dip it in eggs, roll the fish in flour, and panfry it. I like it best breaded and deep-fried.

This is the first time Joe has gone bass fishing and he was really excited. I like bass, because it is more of a white meat, while Joe likes the bluegills. We'll have fish one night this week. Our children all like fish so Joe's fishing helps keep the grocery bill down.

Uncle Joe and Aunt Betty were out for a short visit on Friday. Saturday they came again and brought brother Albert and Sarah Irene along and their three youngest children. Joe was fishing so he wasn't home when they came.

The children don't have school today because of the county fair. It is a cloudy and rainy day today so we didn't do laundry. I'd like to make homemade vegetable juice this afternoon. Our last patch of sweet corn is ready so we have been enjoying that.

A lot of the community women will be busy canning grape juice this coming week because the U-pick grapes are ready to be picked. I am not going to do any grape juice this year as I still have enough canned from last year. It is such a good feeling to go to the basement to see all the jars that we have filled. Meanwhile, my cabbage is ready and I am thinking of making sauerkraut with some of it.

This week daughter Elizabeth will be assisting Emma with her household duties. She didn't have to go today as Emma's children are home from school. So I will miss her good help around here this week.

Two weeks ago, I had Joseph, seven, to the doctor as he fell from the pony wagon and hurt his wrist. They took X-rays and could not find a break but put a splint on it for two weeks. I took him back last week for a check-up and they retook the X-rays. The results showed he has two fractured bones by his wrist. Instead of putting on a cast, the doctor put the splint back on because the bone has started to heal anyway. Joseph was disappointed to not be able to get rid of the splint; he'll need another two to three weeks yet. One good thing—it's his left hand so it does not affect his schoolwork.

OCTOBER 2009

October typically marks the end of garden season. The days are shorter, and the last pumpkins and carrots are harvested. The first frost will quash the squash and nip any remaining tomatoes. The soil is soon tilled and will sit dormant awaiting its revival in the spring.

We had our first snow on October 15, which was very early for around here. It didn't stay too long but one of the girls said, "Oh good, now we don't have to rake leaves!"

Our trees are losing leaves fast and once again we are seeing the beautiful artwork of our master artist as the colors really are pretty. Everything is in its autumn splendor.

Our gardens are all tilled up and history for 2009. I still have my carrots in the ground, though. I will just cover them with a pile of leaves and dig them up as I use them. They seem to keep better that way.

Meanwhile, I would like to help sister Emma can her red beets this week and make her cabbage into sauerkraut. These weeks are flying by so fast and time is so limited. Emma and Jacob's baby Marilyn is already five weeks old today. It is a pleasure to hold her when she sleeps and watch her expressions on her face. So far it looks as if her eyes will be blue. It is hard to think of my youngest child, Kevin, being over four. Kevin makes sure we know he is not a baby anymore and he reminds us often that he is older than his cousins Steven and baby Marilyn.

Daughter Lovina, five, left at 7:00 A.M. this morning with the other children. Her classes will now be in the morning instead of the afternoon. She comes home around noon. She is not a morning person but did very well to be ready this morning. I had to tell Benjamin, ten, to quit teasing her as he kept telling her how scary it was to walk to the bus in the dark. Benjamin always enjoys picking on his sisters.

Yesterday we had brunch at Emma and Jacob's house. Brother Albert's family, his daughter Elizabeth, her husband and two children, and Albert's three oldest sons and their special friends all came along. They were also joined by Uncle Joe and Aunt Betty and sisters Susan and Verena.

This gathering was held so Albert's family could meet little Marilyn Jane. Altogether we were a total of forty-one. Needless to say Emma and Jacob had a full house. At least the weather warmed up and the children could enjoy playing outdoors.

On the menu were biscuits and sausage gravy, potatoes, eggs, cheese, hot peppers, cherry pudding, peaches, and apple, pumpkin, and blueberry pies. Beverages included coffee, vegetable juice, and homemade rhubarb juice.

Brother Albert's wife, Sarah Irene, brought us radishes out of her garden. They taste just as fresh and crisp as they do in the spring. Probably with all the cool weather we have this summer it made a good year for radishes all season.

On Friday, Joe and I took our horse and buggy to the children's school as they had "vehicle day." The school had asked if we could bring our buggy so children at the school could also see how the inside of a buggy looks. A lot of the children got inside the buggy to see what it was like to be inside of one. This was a good way to teach young people about safety around buggies since cars and buggies have to share the roads. The school had various other kinds of vehicles there also such as police cars, fire trucks, dump trucks, and bulldozers. It was an interesting hour for all the children.

NOVEMBER 2009

Thanksgiving is a bit more subdued in Amish homes than in many other places, but the day is still marked with a hearty meal that usually includes turkey and trimmings. An Amish man once told me that Thanksgiving isn't celebrated as much in their faith because "every day is Thanksgiving."

It is Monday morning and it is time to start another week.

Today also brings the last day of November. So far we have not received more snow than just some flurries. Sons Benjamin, ten, and Joseph, seven, can't wait until we have that first big snow. Every morning they jump out of bed and look out the window to see if our first snow has arrived. They keep talking about the fun they will have, like hitching our pony, Stormy, to the pony cart and tying the sled behind the cart. The pony will pull them around the field through the snow. Last year that provided hours of fun for them. Everything is always a little bit of a mess when they start pulling out those extra coats, snow pants, boots, gloves, and so forth. The boys are looking forward to the snow a lot more than I am.

We had a very nice Thanksgiving Day with some friends and family over. We set the table using my good china. The girls had fun setting the table and using all the best dishes I have stored away in my cupboard. It was fun for them to use the special dishes and not have to use our everyday dishes. I prepared a twenty-one-pound turkey stuffed with dressing for the Thanksgiving meal. With the food that family and friends brought in, we had quite a big menu. Along with turkey and dressing we had mashed potatoes, gravy, corn, potato salad, cheese, hot peppers, vegetables and dip, homemade bread, butter, rhubarb jam, pumpkin roll, sugar cookies, buttermilk, and sugar cream pies and cherry cheesecake. We had way too much food but leftovers made for easy meals the next day. The afternoon was spent playing board games. And before everyone parted ways and headed for home, root beer floats were served. It was an enjoyable day. We do have so much to be thankful for. I hope all you readers had an enjoyable Thanksgiving Day, too.

My husband, Joe, has still been trying his luck for another deer. He has seen quite a few but they are keeping their distance from his tent. I think today is the last day of shotgun season but I am not sure because I don't get as excited about keeping track of the dates as he does.

With pumpkin still plentiful, I thought I'd share the recipe for my pumpkin roll with you. Be sure to roll up the "short side." You can use fresh pumpkin or canned.

AMISH COOK CLASSIC: PUMPKIN ROLL

PUMPKIN ROLL

Confectioner's sugar, for dusting

3 eggs

1 cup sugar

1 teaspoon lemon juice

⅔ cup pumpkin

¾ cup all-purpose flour

1 teaspoon baking powder

2 teaspoons cinnamon

½ teaspoon salt

½ teaspoon nutmeg

FILLING

8 ounces cream cheese, softened

2 cups confectioner's sugar

4 tablespoons butter, softened

½ teaspoon vanilla extract

Preheat the oven to 375°F. Line a jelly-roll pan with waxed paper and set it aside. On a clean surface, lay out a clean, lint-free dish towel that is slightly larger than the jelly-roll pan. Sift confectioner's sugar over the surface of the towel.

In a large bowl, beat the eggs well. Then add the sugar, lemon juice, and pumpkin and beat well. Then add the flour, baking powder, cinnamon, salt, and nutmeg and beat well until smooth in consistency. Pour the pumpkin mixture into the wax paper–lined jelly-roll pan and bake for 15 minutes, or until set. Remove the pan from the oven and, while it is still hot, flip it over onto the confectioner's sugar–covered dish towel. Peel off the waxed paper and roll the towel and cake together as if rolling up a jelly roll and place it in the refrigerator for 45 minutes to 1 hour, until the towel doesn't feel warm any longer.

While the pumpkin cake is chilling, beat together the cream cheese, butter, confectioner's sugar, and vanilla extract until smooth. When the pumpkin roll is cool, unroll it and remove the towel. Spread the filling over the pumpkin cake, then roll it up and refrigerate at least an hour before slicing and serving.

Rain, Rain, Rain! That's what we'v
been having ~~every~~ almost every
I think my lettuce h...

...to always be willing to go
her around during the day
that ~~night~~ church services
Yesterday ~~neighbors~~
coming closer, neighbors
at our
er a haystack supper
tomatoes so that w
aren't ready

2010
twenty years of
"the amish cook" columns

JANUARY 2010

Michigan winters can plunge the Eicher family into the icebox for a few months. But the children adapt and enjoy all the icy offerings from sledding to snowball fights.

Yesterday morning we had the coldest temperature so far this winter. Our thermometer read zero. It only warmed up to the lower twenties all day. Some of the children still bundled up in the afternoon and took our pony, Stormy, sledding. They hitched him to our two-wheel pony cart and tied three sleds behind that.

Susan, thirteen, is usually the driver and tries to swerve fast enough to empty the sled of its occupants. It looks like fun and it is exciting to watch them from the window. The children tried to talk me into coming out and getting on, but I wasn't quite so eager to go rolling off a sled into the snow. Watching from the warm cozy house suited me just fine.

Kevin is running a low-grade fever and has a chest cold and a cough. My husband, Joe, stayed home yesterday from church with him and a few of the other younger children. Kevin wanted to go outside to get a sled ride so badly. We caught him twice sneaking out of the door with boots, no socks, a thin coat that wasn't even closed, and a hat. Hopefully he will keep getting better and the weather will warm up a bit so he can have another sled ride.

Joe has been enjoying his new hobby of ice fishing. Saturday he went fishing with some friends all day. Another day he took Benjamin and Joseph along. They both enjoyed it. Joseph said it is easier than fishing off the boat because they use small ice-fishing poles. He said you can just drop your line in the hole and pull out a fish. We have had some meals of fresh fish lately and have quite a bit still in the freezer. I think altogether they have brought home more than 200 bluegill in the last week or so.

The house seems extra quiet today. The children went back to school after a two-week holiday break. Joe has also gone back to work. After two quite busy weeks I do treasure the peacefulness around here. It is snowing again this morning. The children made snowmen during their time off. The snow packed really nicely so it was ideal for making snowmen.

On New Year's Eve Jacob and Emma and family stayed here overnight. This was the first time three-and-a-half-month-old Marilyn slept here all night. She is a little sweetie and just smiles and coos. Kevin, four, was so excited to have Steven, two, to stay all night. Kevin told Steven to just wake him up if he needs to go to the bathroom during the night, saying: "I have a flashlight and will shine it for you." The two-year age difference doesn't make any difference when those two boys play together. Kevin does look like he feels proud to be the older one since he is the youngest around here.

We did manage to stay up until midnight playing board games. We adults have a harder time staying up to midnight than the children do. They all did a good job of settling down to sleep once we had everyone situated where they should sleep. Together Jacob's family and ours have fourteen children.

JANUARY 2010

Daily diaries are a favorite format for the column among readers of "The Amish Cook." This diary shows that the rhythm of the Eicher household continues on as usual at the start of a new year.

6:30 A.M. This is Saturday and it was nice not to have to get up at 3:00 A.M. as we do on weekdays. My husband, Joe, and I got up and enjoyed a few minutes of peace and quiet while the children were still asleep. I made Joe some hot chocolate and some coffee for me.

7:00 A.M. We wake up the children and I start breakfast while Joe goes to the basement to refuel the stove with coal. We are having a treat for breakfast: pon hoss. A friend gave us the bones from a hog they butchered. I cooked the meat off the bones and that evening Joe and I made four gallons of pon hoss. I start slicing and frying the pon hoss. Elizabeth and Susan peel potatoes that are still from our garden last summer. We are down to the small size ones and it takes a little more time to peel them. The children all like pon hoss so we fried quite a few pans of it. Pon hoss is made from the juice and meat of pork bones with flour, salt, and pepper added. After this is cooked together we pour it into cake pans. After it is cooled and set it is ready to slice and fry.

8:00 A.M. We are all seated at the table ready to enjoy a breakfast of eggs, fried potatoes, pon hoss, cheese, toast, orange juice, and milk.

9:30 A.M. Joe and children Benjamin, ten; Joseph, seven; Kevin, four; and Lovina, five, all get ready to go outside. Their plans are to clean out the horse stalls and the chicken coop. Lovina is our "fourth little boy" and would rather go out with them instead of staying in the house and helping with indoor chores. Elizabeth, fifteen, and I gather laundry and start filling our Maytag washer with hot water. I have it so much easier to do laundry than when the children were younger before our move to Michigan. It is hard to believe that has almost been six years. Back in Indiana I had to pump all my water from a cistern pump and carry it to a kerosene stove to heat. The big cookers full of hot water then had to be carried to the hand-pump washing machine. Now I have hot and cold running water. I have a hose that reaches the washer and I can just fill it with hot water. While Elizabeth and I are doing laundry, Susan, thirteen, stirs up two batches of brownies. She will be fourteen on the 24th already. After she is done she helps Verena, twelve, and Loretta, nine, do weekly cleaning. They clean the kitchen, dining room, and living room areas.

11:45 A.M. Elizabeth and I are done with the laundry. With it being so cold outside, we hung the clothes all on the lines in the basement. Meanwhile, the girls are done with dishes and cleaning and Joe and the children have come in from the barn. Lovina and Kevin ended up trying to make snowmen instead of helping.

12:15 P.M. We have a light lunch of sandwiches. And, of course, everyone wants to sample Susan's brownies.

1:30 P.M. Joe heads back out to the barn to finish up. He told the boys that they can go play and he will finish up the chores. The boys end up going outside and taking sled rides on the ice. It warmed up enough to make everything icy. Verena and Loretta joined them while Elizabeth and Susan do some cleaning upstairs. I do some mending and ironing.

4:00 P.M. We decide to call it a day and everyone starts getting cleaned up. We have three bathrooms but with ten people getting cleaned up it still takes a little while, especially if we need to let the water heater catch up. I give Kevin a haircut and for once he does better to hold quiet. He almost acted like he could fall asleep. He thinks he is old enough that he should take showers now instead of a bath. We usually plug the drain and let him shower until the tub is half filled and then he usually sits down and plays with his toys. He can spend a long time in there just playing.

7:00 P.M. Everyone is cleaned up and we have potato soup for supper. The girls are washing the dishes. We will take the rest of the day easy until bedtime. A day like today is so precious when everyone pitches in with the work. Working together as a family is always enjoyable and makes memories we will all treasure years from now. The children always seem willing to help out, which makes for a great day. Good night and God's blessings to all.

FEBRUARY 2010

This column refers to a "community center," which is a multipurpose building usually constructed with local materials and by local labor. These are becoming more popular in Amish settlements. The buildings provide a place for potlucks, events, and gatherings. In this case, it was a funeral.

Saturday was the funeral of ninety-year-old Amos Schwartz. He was a member of our church. I will always remember him as a friendly man who always had a smile for everyone. He was a relative to both my grandmothers.

It was a cold morning with the mercury dipping down to a little above zero the day of the funeral, which was held in the local Amish community center.

Once again the community women did a wonderful job of preparing lots of food for the funeral meal. There was more than enough food. Quite a few of the women in our church district gathered at the building around 7:00 A.M. to prepare sandwiches.

It is hard to guess how many to make or how much food is needed for a funeral. Along with the ham sandwiches, chicken noodle soup and casseroles were served, as well as potato salad, cheese, Jell-O, fruit salad, cake, and coffee.

The six scholars have all left for school. Four-year-old Kevin is trying to entertain himself. He makes up imaginary people and makes them talk to one another. It is cute to listen to him; at that age children have such imaginations!

Kevin is already looking forward to noon when Lovina, five, comes home from her half-day of school. One day last week, Lovina's class went on a field trip and they were gone all day. Kevin was disappointed when Lovina didn't come home at noon.

These cold mornings make for a few extra outside chores for daughter Elizabeth, sixteen. The water is usually frozen in the water tanks or in the chicken coop, so she has to break through the top layer of ice with an axe.

I think we are all beginning to look forward to spring weather. We ordered our fourth ton of hard coal. We are hoping that the weather will stay mild and it will be our last one for the winter.

This cold weather keeps the ice frozen for the ice fishermen. So far we haven't had snow as we do other winters.

It would be nice if we could get our butchering done while Joe has a week off from work next week. The factory where Joe works is on reduced hours for a lot of the month. We pray for the continued improvement in the economy. We have been fortunate so far and we can't thank God enough.

Kevin seems extra bored this morning and wants me to read him a book about a bear and a fish. He is eating one of the sugar cookies Elizabeth made last week. She baked several hundred cookies and the sugar cookies are going faster than the chocolate chip. I am hoping they won't disappear too fast, but the children enjoy cookies and milk for an after-school snack.

I need to get busy with household duties. Elizabeth and I hope to get some morning sewing done this week.

epilogue

by Lovina Eicher

My thoughts go back to the time when Mother penned her first "Amish Cook" column. At the time, we were five girls still living at home and three of my siblings were married. Life almost twenty years later has brought a lot of changes. There have been a lot of births in the family and, sadly, a lot of deaths since the column's beginning. Good-byes include my dear parents, my grandmother, Joe's parents, a niece, several uncles and aunts, and a few cousins. We want to strive to all reunite in God's mansion in the sky someday.

There have been so many changes just since I started penning the column in 2002. It is not always easy with a family to take time to write each week. I give it most of my effort in honor of my dear mother who passed away suddenly in 2002, and my father, who passed away so unexpectedly in 2000. This book seems priceless to me. It starts its story back when I was just leaving my teenage years, and then follows the story of Joe and our wedding and each birth of our eight children. The years have flown by so fast and I wonder where the time has gone.

A great big thank-you goes to my husband, Joe, and to each of my eight children: Elizabeth, Susan, Verena, Benjamin, Loretta, Joseph, Lovina, and Kevin. They are all such a blessing to me. Each one seems so precious to me. May God grant us a long and happy life together as a family and if that is not in his plan, may He reward us all and reunite us in his great Heavenly home. Also a big thank-you to my editor Kevin for keeping the column going when it would have been easier to have just given up. I also want to thank our publisher, Andrews McMeel, for giving us a chance to share our story. And last but not least, thank you to all the wonderful readers. Without you, the column would not have been possible. Thanks for all the encouragement by sending all your wishes through the happy and sad times through the twenty-year journey. God bless you.

appendix I: elizabeth's final cookbook

Elizabeth Coblentz and I collaborated on several cookbooks, and at the time of her death we were working on another one. She had completed a table of contents, a rough index, and submitted dozens of recipes for this future, yet-to-be-named project. Unfortunately, her sudden passing in the fall of 2002 prevented this book from ever materializing. As a tribute to this very special woman, we are publishing a few of her previously unpublished recipes and letters here.

AUTUMN SALAD
Serves 4

2 cups peeled and diced apples

1 cup peeled and grated carrots

½ cup raisins

½ cup mayonnaise

In a large bowl, combine the apples, carrots, and raisins. Add the mayonnaise and toss until the ingredients are evenly coated. Chill for 1 hour before serving.

CHRISTMAS HOLLY CANDY
Makes about 3 dozen candies

½ cup (1 stick) margarine

30 large marshmallows

1 teaspoon vanilla extract

2 teaspoons green food coloring

4½ cups cornflakes

1 tablespoon "red hot" cinnamon
   candy

In a large saucepan, melt the margarine over low heat. Add the marshmallows and stir until completely melted. Stir in the vanilla and the food coloring, followed by the cornflakes. Mix until evenly combined. Drop walnut-size mounds of the mixture onto wax paper. Decorate each mound with 3 pieces of the cinnamon candy. Allow to cool until set, about 1 hour.

SAUSAGE GRAVY
Serves 4 to 6

1 pound bulk sausage
¼ cup all-purpose flour
4 cups milk
Salt and black pepper

In a cast-iron skillet, brown the sausage over medium heat. Drain off the grease. Sprinkle in the flour and brown lightly. Gradually add the milk and mix until very smooth. Bring the gravy to a boil, stirring frequently. Reduce the heat and cook until the desired thickness is reached. If gravy becomes too thick, additional milk may be added. Season with salt and pepper to taste and serve over biscuits.

GINGERBREAD COOKIES
Makes 2 to 3 dozen cookies

2 cups all-purpose flour
1 teaspoon baking powder
1 teaspoon baking soda
1 teaspoon ground cinnamon
1 teaspoon ground ginger
⅓ cup sugar
½ cup vegetable shortening
½ cup molasses
3 tablespoons hot water

Preheat the oven to 400°F.

In a large bowl, combine all of the ingredients and stir with a wooden spoon until well blended. Refrigerate the dough for at least 1 hour before handling. On a floured surface, roll the chilled dough to ⅛-inch thickness. Use your favorite cookie cutters to cut shapes from the dough. Place the cookies on ungreased baking sheets. Bake for 8 to 10 minutes, until the edges of the cookies are golden brown. Transfer to wire racks to cool before decorating.

WHOLE WHEAT BATTER BREAD
Makes 1 loaf

1 package active dry yeast

1½ cups warm water (105° to 115°F)

3 tablespoons honey

2 teaspoons salt

1 tablespoon shortening, softened

2 cups bread flour

1 cup whole wheat flour

In a large bowl, dissolve the yeast in the warm water. Add the honey, salt, shortening, and 1 cup of the bread flour. Mix vigorously with a wooden spoon to form a wet batter. Gradually stir in the remaining 1 cup bread flour and the whole wheat flour until evenly combined. Cover the bowl and let the batter rise in a warm place until doubled in size, about 30 minutes. Stir the batter several times, then spread it evenly in a greased 5 by 9-inch loaf pan. Let it rise in a warm place until the batter reaches ½ inch from the top of the pan, about 40 minutes.

While the dough is rising, preheat the oven to 375°F. Bake for about 30 minutes, or until the top is golden and the bread sounds hollow when tapped. After removing the bread from the oven, brush it with butter or margarine for a softer crust. Remove the bread from the pan and cool it on a wire rack.

SOUTHERN CREAM PIE

Serves 6 to 8

⅔ cup sugar
1½ tablespoons all-purpose flour
⅛ teaspoon salt
1 cup light cream
1 teaspoon vanilla extract
1 (8-inch) pie shell, unbaked
Pinch of ground cinnamon

Preheat the oven to 350°F.

In a medium bowl, combine the sugar, flour, and salt. Slowly stir the cream and the vanilla into the dry ingredients. Mix until well combined and smooth. Pour the cream mixture into the unbaked pie shell. Lightly sprinkle the top of the pie with the ground cinnamon. Bake for about 1 hour, until the filling is nearly set. The filling will thicken slightly as the pie cools. Let cool at room temperature before slicing and serving.

COCONUT CREAM PIE

Serves 6 to 8

2 eggs

½ cup sugar

½ cup (1 stick) margarine, softened

½ cup milk

¼ cup all-purpose flour

1 cup shredded sweetened coconut

1 (8-inch) pie shell, unbaked

Preheat the oven to 350°F.

In a large bowl, whisk the eggs and the sugar with a whisk until the mixture is lemon colored. Gradually stir in the margarine, milk, flour, and coconut with a spoon. Mix until well combined. Pour the mixture into the unbaked pie shell. Bake for 45 to 50 minutes, until the filling is set and the crust is golden brown. Let cool at room temperature before slicing and serving.

Good Morn —   8-1-91

you let me know? Really
I don't care to have my name
signed to each issue if that's
okay with you to not have my
name signed to it. Its your
column. Okay? Must get as I have
a tour this P.M. & always plenty

appendix II: letters from the amish cook

hroughout our friendship, Elizabeth would often pen little notes just to me and stick them in with her columns. Some were short and business-like, others longer and more personal.

Elizabeth referred to her columns, at least in the early days, as "letters," and I think her readers looked at them that way, too. I'd set a deadline of Tuesday for her to get her letters in the mail to me so I could send them off the following week. Like a typical writer, she'd wait until the last minute. She was in a good mood when this letter was written, playfully noting the deadlines:

June 6, 1992

Hello—

Tuesday, 11:45 and I just got done with these letters. Lots of writing. I'm here alone so that's what I got done—2 letters. Hope they do! I'm surely running ahead with the letters by now. Ben asked me last night: Do you have your letter written and I said, "No, I'll do it this evening." Was toooooo tired to write last night. I'll try to get these off on a Tuesday. It seemed so hectic for a while. Wasn't feeling my best, I guess . . . Wonder which day you'll be here? I'll try to be home but we never know when we'll have to make a run somewhere. The UPS man was just here. He delivered your letter. So I guess you're still amongst the living. Ha! . . .

I baked some pie for my sister on Saturday, as they had church on Sunday. So I'm tired of seeing pie around here. You probably read in my letters what pies I had baked. Saturday I made four pumpkin pies and two pie shells. I should sew but my, the grass needs to be mowed also. Such nice rains we've had. We have good radishes galore. We sure have feasted on them. Well, I had best get this in the mailbox since it's Tuesday or else Oasis Newsfeatures will close down on me. Ha! Tickles me, Ben keeps reminding me to write letters for Tuesday.

Sometimes I felt like I was getting my own private minicolumn, as in the following letter:

October 12, 1993

Kevin:

It is Tuesday morn and enclosed are two columns. Hope they meet the requirements! OK?? Had unexpected supper guests last night. Thirty-two in all. Ben's brother, Jake's, stopped in here in the A.M. and their plans were to be here for supper. Didn't know what all will drop in then. Had real plenty for all. Had mashed potatoes, gravy, ham, macaroni and cheese, dressing, baked beans, buttered corn, two kinds of cheese, tomatoes, celery, carrot sticks, Waldorf salad, lettuce salad, lettuce, apple crisps, three kinds of cake, one kettle soup, pretzel sticks, potato chips, pop, peaches, pineapples, Jell-O fruit salad, etc. Looked like everyone ate good. Didn't get to town, so I had fix just what I had on hand. Well, I must get in gear. Want to dig up some carrots now.

LIST OF RECIPES

METRIC CONVERSION FORMULAS

TO CONVERT	MULTIPLY
Ounces to grams	Ounces by 28.35
Pounds to kilograms	Pounds by .454
Teaspoons to milliliters	Teaspoons by 4.93
Tablespoons to milliliters	Tablespoons by 14.79
Fluid ounces to milliliters	Fluid ounces by 29.57
Cups to milliliters	Cups by 236.59
Cups to liters	Cups by .236
Pints to liters	Pints by .473
Quarts to liters	Quarts by .946
Gallons to liters	Gallons by 3.785
Inches to centimeters	Inches by 2.54

COMMON INGREDIENTS AND THEIR APPROXIMATE EQUIVALENTS

1 cup all-purpose flour = 140 grams

1 stick butter (4 ounces • ½ cup • 8 tablespoons) = 110 grams

1 cup butter (8 ounces • 2 sticks • 16 tablespoons) = 220 grams

1 cup brown sugar, firmly packed = 25 grams

1 cup granulated sugar = 200 grams

2nd edition

Oxford Textbook of
Geriatric Medicine

Edited by

J. Grimley Evans
Professor of Clinical Geratology, University of Oxford, UK

T. Franklin Williams
Professor of Medicine Emeritus, University of Rochester, New York; formerly Director, National Institute on Aging, National Institutes of Health, Bethesda, Maryland, USA

B. Lynn Beattie
Professor of Medicine, Division of Geriatric Medicine, University of British Columbia, Canada

J-P. Michel
Professor of Geriatric Medicine, University Hospitals of Geneva, Switzerland

G. K. Wilcock
Professor of Care of the Elderly, University of Bristol, UK

OXFORD
UNIVERSITY PRESS

OXFORD
UNIVERSITY PRESS

Great Clarendon Street, Oxford OX2 6DP

Oxford University Press is a department of the University of Oxford.
It furthers the University's objective of excellence in research, scholarship, and
education by publishing worldwide in

Oxford New York

Auckland Bangkok Buenos Aires Cape Town Chennai Dar es Salaam Delhi
Hong Kong Istanbul Karachi Kolkata Kuala Lumpur Madrid Melbourne
Mexico City Mumbai Nairobi Paris São Paulo Singapore Taipei Tokyo Toronto

Oxford is a registered trade mark of Oxford University Press
in the UK and in certain other countries

Published in the United States
by Oxford University Press, Inc., New York

First published 1992
Second edition published 2000
Second edition published in paperback 2003
Reprinted 2003

British Library Cataloguing in Publication Data
Data available

3 5 7 9 10 8 6 4 2

ISBN 0 19 852809 4

Printed in Great Britain
on acid-free paper

Contents

Section 19 Voluntary muscle

Section 20 Psychiatric aspects of the medicine of later life

Section 21 Perioperative assessment and management

Section 22 Legal and ethical issues in geriatric medicine

Section 23 Services

List of Contributors

Ivo L. Abraham Division of Nursing, New York University School of Education, New York, USA

Thurayya Arayssi Clinical Associate, National Institute of Arthritis and Musculoskeletal and Skin Diseases, Bethesda, Maryland, USA

Raymond Auckenthaler Professor of Medicine, Infectious Diseases, University Hospitals of Geneva, Switzerland

Lars Bäckman Department of Psychology, Göteborg University; Department of Clinical Neuroscience and Family Medicine, Karolinska Institute, Stockholm, Sweden

Mary J. Baines Medical Director, The Ellenor Foundation, Livingstone Hospital, Dartford, Kent, UK

Robert C. Baldwin Consultant in Old Age Psychiatry, Manchester Royal Infirmary, Manchester, UK

Arthur K. Balin Clinical Professor of Dermatology; Research Professor of Pathology and Laboratory Medicine, Medical College of Pennsylvania – Hahnemann School of Medicine, Allegheny University of the Health Sciences, Chester, Pennsylvania, USA

John R. Bartlett Consultant Neurosurgeon, King's College Hospital, London, UK

Y. Bashir Department of Cardiology, John Radcliffe Hospital, Oxford, UK

B. Lynn Beattie Professor of Medicine, Division of Geriatric Medicine, University of British Columbia, Canada

David W. Bentley Professor of Medicine, St Louis University School of Medicine, St Louis, Missouri, USA

Thomas P. Beresford Professor of Psychiatry, University of Colorado School of Medicine, Denver, Colorado, USA

Marc R. Blackman Professor of Medicine, Johns Hopkins University; Chief, Division of Endocrinology, and Program Director, General Clinical Research Center, Johns Hopkins Bayview Medical Center, Baltimore, Maryland, USA

Donald L. Bliwise Director, Emory Sleep Disorder Center, Atlanta, Georgia, USA

Julien Bogousslavsky Professor and Chairman, University Department of Neurology; Professor of Cardiovascular Disease, University of Lausanne, Switzerland

Jean-Luc Bosson Université Joseph Fourier, Grenoble, France

Pierre Bouche Hôpital de la Salpêtrière, Paris, France

Alison F. Brading Professor of Pharmacology, University of Oxford, UK

John C.M. Brust Harlem Hospital Center and Columbia University College of Physicians and Surgeons, New York, USA

C.J. Bulpitt Professor of Geriatric Medicine, Department of Medicine, Imperial College School of Medicine, London, UK

Paul Calabresi Rhode Island Hospital, Providence, Rhode Island, USA

Evan Calkins Emeritus Professor of Medicine, State University of New York at Buffalo; Attending Physician, CGF Hospital System, Buffalo, New York, USA

Andrea M. Cannon Specialist Registrar in Urology, Bristol Urological Institute, Bristol, UK

William D. Chey Assistant Professor of Medicine, University of Michigan Medical Center, Ann Arbor, Michigan, USA

William Y. Chey Professor of Medicine, University of Rochester Medical Center, Rochester, New York, USA

John E. Clague Lecturer in Geriatric Medicine; Honorary Consultant, University of Manchester, UK

Daniel O. Clark Assistant Professor of Medicine, Director of Behavioral Sciences, Indiana University Center for Aging Research; Research Scientist, Regenstrief Institute for Health Care, Indianapolis, Indiana, USA

Harvey Jay Cohen Director, Geriatric Research Education and Clinical Center (GRECC), Veterans Administration Medical Center; Director, Center for the Study of Aging; Professor and Chief, Geriatrics Division, Duke University Medical Center, Durham, North Carolina, USA

Kenneth J. Collins Formerly Member of Medical Research Council Staff and Honorary Senior Clinical Lecturer, University College and St Pancras Hospitals, University of London, UK

Gaetano Crepaldi Chief, Department of Internal Medicine, University of Padova, Italy

Richard Curless Consultant Physician, Northumbria Healthcare NHS Trust; Institute for the Health of the Elderly, University of Newcastle upon Tyne, UK

Claire Davey Division of Public Health and Primary Care, University of Oxford, UK

Paul J. Davis Professor and Chairman, Department of Medicine, Albany Medical College; Physician-in-Chief, Albany Medical Center Hospital, Albany, New York, USA

Joy Antonelle deMarcaida Department of Neurology, University of Connecticut School of Medicine, Farmington, Connecticut, USA

Vinod K. Dhawan Chief, Division of Infectious Diseases, Charles R. Drew University of Medicine and Science, Los Angeles, California, USA

Lindsey Dow Consultant Senior Lecturer in Care of the Elderly and General Internal Medicine, University of Bristol, UK

Catherine E. DuBeau Assistant Professor of Medicine, Harvard Medical School; Beth Israel Deaconess Medical Center and the Hebrew Rehabilitation Center for the Aged, Boston, Massachusetts, USA

Andrew Eisen Professor and Head, Division of Neurology, University of British Columbia; Head, Neuromuscular Diseases Unit, Vancouver Hospital, Vancouver, Canada

J.P. Emeriau Hôpital Xavier Amozan, Pessac, France

Pam Enderby Chair of Rehabilitation, University of Sheffield, UK

Ann R. Falsey Department of Medicine, University of Rochester School of Medicine and Dentistry, Rochester, New York, USA

Eleanor E. Faye Ophthalmology Consultant, The Lighthouse Inc., New York, USA

Terry Feest Director, Richard Bright Renal Unit, Southmead Hospital, Bristol; Professor of Clinical Nephrology, University of Bristol, UK

Roger C.L. Feneley Emeritus Consultant Urologist, Bristol Urological Institute, Bristol, UK

Ray Fitzpatrick Division of Public Health and Primary Care, University of Oxford, UK

Alain Franco Professor of Internal Medicine, Université Joseph Fourier, Grenoble, France

Jason Francoeur Faculty of Medicine, University of British Columbia, Vancouver, Canada

Robert P. Friedland Laboratory of Neurogeriatrics, Department of Neurology, Case Western Reserve University School of Medicine, Cleveland, Ohio, USA

Terry Fulmer Division of Nursing, New York University School of Education, New York, USA

Gary Gerstenblith Professor of Medicine, Johns Hopkins University School of Medicine; Director of Clinical Trials Cardiology Division, Baltimore, Maryland, USA

Catherine Goehring Senior Resident, Department of Community Health, University Hospitals of Geneva, Switzerland

Gabriel Gold Consultant Physician, Geriatrics Hospital, University Hospitals of Geneva, Switzerland

Barry J. Goldlist Associate Professor of Medicine, University of Toronto, Canada

Carolyn A. Greig Visiting Lecturer, Queen Margaret University College, Edinburgh, UK

Richard D. Griffiths Reader in Medicine (Intensive Care), University of Liverpool, UK

John Grimley Evans Professor of Clinical Geratology, University of Oxford, UK

A. Julianna Gulya Clinical Professor of Surgery (Otolaryngology – Head and Neck Surgery), George Washington University, Washington, DC, USA

Nortin M. Hadler Professor of Medicine and Microbiology/Immunology, University of North Carolina; Attending Rheumatologist, University of North Carolina Hospitals, Chapel Hill, North Carolina, USA

Ronald C. Hamdy East Tennessee State University, Johnson City, Tennessee, USA

Linda Hands Clinical Reader in Surgery, University of Oxford, UK

S. Mitchell Harman Acting Clinical Director, Chief, Laboratory of Clinical Investigation, National Institute on Aging, National Institutes of Health; Associate Professor of Medicine, Johns Hopkins University, Baltimore, Maryland, USA

Stephen D.R. Harridge Wellcome Trust Research Fellow in Physiology, Royal Free and University College Medical School, University of London, UK

G. Hart Department of Medicine, University of Liverpool, UK

S. Richard Hartson Hôpital Xavier Amozan, Pessac, France

Mujtaba Hasan Senior Lecturer in Geriatric Medicine, University of Wales College of Medicine, Cardiff, UK

Arthur E. Helfand Professor of Community Health and Aging; Chair, Department of Community Health, Aging and Health Policy, Temple University School of Podiatric Medicine, Philadelphia, Pennsylvania, USA

Peter Heywood Department of Neurology, Frenchay Hospital, Bristol, UK

Kossen M.T. Ho Research Urological Registrar, Department of Pharmacology, University of Oxford, UK

Michael A. Horan Professor of Geriatric Medicine, University of Manchester, UK

James Howe Airedale General Hospital, Keighley, UK

Nigel M. Hyman Radcliffe Infirmary NHS Trust, Oxford, UK

D.P. Jewell Reader in Medicine, University of Oxford, UK

Bruce D. Johnson Division of Cardiovascular Diseases, Mayo Clinic and Foundation, Rochester, Minnesota, USA

Alain Junod Chief of Service, Medical Clinic 1, Department of Internal Medicine, University Hospitals of Geneva, Switzerland

Alexandre Kalache Chief, Ageing and Health Programme, World Health Organization, Geneva, Switzerland

Hosam K. Kamel Sub-specialty Resident, Division of Geriatric Medicine, St Louis University Health Sciences Center, St Louis, Missouri, USA

Nicholas Karamitsios Gastroenterology Fellow, Division of Digestive Disease and Nutrition, University of Massachusetts Medical Center, Worcester, Massachusetts, USA

Paul R. Katz Medical Director, Monroe Community Hospital, Rochester; Associate Professor of Medicine, University of Rochester School of Medicine and Dentistry, Rochester, NY, USA

Sarah Keir Senior Registrar in Care of the Elderly and General Medicine, Bristol Royal Infirmary, Bristol, UK

Ingrid Keller Programme Assistant, Ageing and Health Programme, World Health Organization, Geneva, Switzerland

John M. Kellett St George's Hospital Medical School, University of London, UK

R.A. Kenny Professor of Cardiovascular Research; Head of Department of Geriatric Medicine, University of Newcastle upon Tyne, UK

Kay-Tee Khaw Professor of Clinical Gerontology, School of Clinical Medicine, University of Cambridge, UK

S. Khosla Associate Professor of Medicine, Mayo Medical School, Rochester, Minnesota, USA

Kevin Kinsella Study Director, Committee on Population, National Research Council, Washington, DC, USA

Thomas B.L. Kirkwood Department of Geriatric Medicine and School of Biological Sciences, University of Manchester, UK

John H. Klippel Clinical Director, National Institute of Arthritis and Musculoskeletal and Skin Diseases, Bethesda, Maryland, USA

Eric L. Knight Geriatric Medicine Unit, Massachusetts General Hospital, Boston, Massachusetts, USA

K.H. Krause Department of Geriatrics, University Hospitals of Geneva, Switzerland

Mark S. Lachs Associate Professor of Medicine; Chief, Division on Ageing, The New York Hospital – Cornell Medical Center, New York, USA

Edward G. Lakatta Chief, Laboratory of Cardiovascular Science, Intramural Research Program, National Institute on Aging, National Institutes of Health, Baltimore, Maryland, USA

Sarah E. Lamb Co-director of Physiotherapy Research, Physiotherapy Research Unit, Nuffield Hospital NHS Trust, Oxford; Senior Research Fellow, Oxford Centre for Health Care Research and Development, Oxford Brookes University, UK

Peter Langhorne Senior Lecturer in Geriatric Medicine, University of Glasgow, UK

Maria Larsson Department of Clinical Neuroscience and Family Medicine, Karolinska Institute, Stockholm, Sweden

Makau Lee Professor and Director of Digestive Diseases, University of Mississippi Medical Center, Jackson, Mississippi, USA

Bruce Leff Assistant Professor of Medicine, Johns Hopkins University School of Medicine; Assistant Professor of Health Policy Management, Johns Hopkins University School of Hygiene and Public Health, Baltimore, Maryland, USA

Richard W. Lindsay Professor of Internal Medicine; Head, Division of Geriatrics, Department of Internal Medicine, University of Virginia, Charlottesville, Virginia, USA

David A. Lipschitz Professor of Geriatrics; Director, Donald W. Reynolds Department of Geriatrics and Center on Aging, University of Arkansas for Medical Sciences, Little Rock, Arkansas, USA

M. Lutters Department of Geriatrics, University Hospitals of Geneva, Switzerland

Heather MacDonald Geriatrician, Credit Valley Hospital, Toronto; Lecturer, Department of Medicine, University of Toronto, Canada

Graham J. McDougall Division of Nursing, New York University School of Education, New York, USA

Janet E. McElhaney Associate Professor; Director, Clinical Research, The Glennan Center for Geriatrics and Gerontology, Eastern Virginia Medical School, Norfolk, Virginia, USA

W.J. MacLennan Professor Emeritus in Geriatric Medicine, University of Edinburgh, UK

Katie E. Malbut-Shennan Honorary Research Fellow in Geriatric Medicine, Royal Free and University College Medical School, University of London, UK

G.P. Malcolm Department of Neurosurgery, Frenchay Hospital, Bristol, UK

Vincent Marchello Medical Director, Kings Harbor Multicare Center, Bronx, New York, USA

Andrew J. Martin Specialist Registrar in Neurosurgery, King's College Hospital, London, UK

George M. Martin Professor of Pathology; Adjunct Professor of Genetics; Director, Alzheimer's Disease Research Center, University of Washington, Seattle, Washington, USA

Christopher J. Mathias Professor of Neurovascular Medicine, Imperial College School of Medicine at St Mary's Hospital, University of London; University Department of Clinical Neurology, National Hospital and Institute of Neurology, London, UK

L. Joseph Melton III Professor of Epidemiology, Mayo Medical School, Rochester, Minnesota, USA

G.S. Meneilly Professor and Head, Division of Geriatric Medicine, Department of Medicine, University of British Columbia, Vancouver, Canada

B. Robert Meyer Professor of Clinical Medicine, Cornell University Medical College; Director, Cornell Internal Medicine Associates, New York, USA

J.-P. Michel Department of Geriatrics, University Hospitals of Geneva, Switzerland

Kenneth L. Minaker Chief, Geriatric Medicine Unit, Massachusetts General Hospital, Boston, Massachusetts, USA

N. Salles Montaudon Hôpital Xavier Amozan, Pessac, France

John E. Morley Division of Geriatric Medicine, St Louis University Health Sciences Center; Geriatric Research, Education, and Clinical Center, St Louis Veterans Administration Medical Center, St Louis, Missouri, USA

Peter J. Murphy Consultant Physician in Care of the Elderly, United Bristol Hospitals Trust, Bristol, UK

George Myers Emeritus Professor of Sociology, Center for Demographic Studies, Duke University, Durham, North Carolina, USA

Joseph M. Mylotte Professor of Medicine, School of Medicine and Biomedical Sciences, State University of New York, Buffalo, New York, USA

Gary Naglie Associate Professor, Departments of Medicine and Health Administration, University of Toronto; Geriatric Medicine Consultant, University Health Network and Toronto Rehabilitation Institute, Toronto, Canada

Eric A. Newsholme Fellow, Merton College, Oxford, UK

Lindsay E. Nicolle H.E. Sellers Professor and Head, Department of Internal Medicine, University of Manitoba; Health Sciences Centre and St Boniface Hospital, Winnipeg, Canada

Desmond O'Neill Senior Lecturer in Medical Gerontology, Age-Related Health Care, Adelaide and Meath Hospital, Dublin, Ireland

W.P. Orr Department of Cardiology, John Radcliffe Hospital, Oxford, UK

Christopher Patterson Professor, Geriatric Medicine, Faculty of Health Sciences, McMaster University, Hamilton, Ontario, Canada

W. Bradford Patterson Consultant, Dana Farber Cancer Institute, Boston, Massachusetts, USA

Arnaud Perrier Attending Physician, Medical Clinics 1 and 2, Department of Internal Medicine, University Hospitals of Geneva, Switzerland

Norman L. Pflaster South Shore Neurologic Associates, Riverhead, New York, USA

Carol C. Pilbeam Associate Professor of Medicine, University of Connecticut Health Center, Farmington, Connecticut, USA

Jacques J. Proust Professor, Laboratory of the Immunobiology of Aging, Department of Geriatric Medicine, University of Geneva, Switzerland

Nawab Qizilbash Honorary Consultant and Honorary Senior Research Fellow, Oxford Memory Clinic, University of Oxford, UK

Peter V. Rabins Professor of Psychiatry, Johns Hopkins University School of Medicine, Baltimore, Maryland, USA

Lawrence G. Raisz Professor of Medicine, University of Connecticut School of Medicine, Farmington, Connecticut, USA

Shobita Rajagopalan Assistant Professor of Medicine, Division of Infectious Diseases, Department of Internal Medicine, Charles R. Drew University of Medicine and Science, Los Angeles, California, USA

C. Rajkumar Senior Lecturer, Department of Medicine, Imperial College School of Medicine, London, UK

John D. Reinhard Clinical Assistant Professor of Medicine, State University of New York at Buffalo; Physician, Health Care Plan, Buffalo, New York, USA

B. Lawrence Riggs Purvis and Roberta Tabor Professor of Medical Research, Mayo Medical School, Rochester, Minnesota, USA

Jean-Marie Robine Demographer, INSERM, University of Montpelier, France

Kenneth Rockwood Division of Geriatric Medicine, Dalhousie University, Halifax, Nova Scotia, Canada

Dorrie E. Rosenblatt University of Michigan School of Medicine, Ann Arbor, Michigan, USA

John R. Saltzman Assistant Professor of Medicine, Harvard Medical School, Boston, Massachusetts, USA

Michèle J. Saunders Endowed Professor and Chief, Division of Geriatrics and Gerontology, Department of Dental Diagnostic Science; Professor, Department of Medicine, University of Texas Health Science Center at San Antonio; Associate Director, Geriatric Research, Education and Clinical Center, Audie L. Murphy Division, South Texas Veterans Health Care System, San Antonio, Texas, USA

Susan S. Schiffman Professor of Medical Psychology, Duke University Medical School, Durham, North Carolina, USA

Roldano Scognamiglio Professor, Division of Cardiology, Department of Clinical and Experimental Medicine, University of Padova, Italy

J.T. Scott Honorary Consultant Physician, Charing Cross Hospital, London, UK

J.W. Sear Reader in Anaesthetics and Honorary Consultant Anaesthetist, Nuffield Department of Anaesthetics, University of Oxford, UK

W.O. Seiler Chief of the Geriatric Department, Geriatric University Clinic, Cantonal Hospital, Basel, Switzerland

Allison B. Sekuler Department of Psychology, University of Toronto, Ontario, Canada

Robert Sekuler Volen Center for Complex Systems, Brandeis University, Waltham, Massachusetts, USA

J.D. Shearman Senior Registrar in Gastroenterology, Radcliffe Infirmary, Oxford, UK

Kenneth I. Shulman Professor, Department of Psychiatry, University of Toronto, Canada

Peter Singer Professor of Medicine, University of Toronto; Sun Life Chair and Director, University of Toronto Joint Centre for Bioethics; Staff Physician, University Health Network, Toronto, Ontario, Canada

Brent J. Small Department of Clinical Neuroscience and Family Medicine, Karolinska Institute, Stockholm, Sweden

Barry J. Snow Neurologist, Auckland Hospital, Auckland, New Zealand

Diane G. Snustad Associate Professor, Clinical Internal Medicine, University of Virginia Health Services Foundation, Charlottesville, Virginia, USA

Hannes B. Stähelin Professor; Chief, Geriatric University Clinic, University of Basel, Switzerland

Knight Steel Director, Homecare Institute, Hackensack University Medical Center; UMDNJ Endowed Professor of Geriatrics at the New Jersey Medical School, Newark, New Jersey, USA

Richard Suzman Associate Director, Office of Behavioral and Social Sciences Research, National Institute on Aging, National Institutes of Health, Bethesda, Maryland, USA

Christian Swinne Associate Professor, UCL Mont-Godinne, Yvoir, Belgium

Nigel P. Sykes Consultant Physician, St Christopher's Hospice, London, UK

Raymond Tallis Professor of Geriatric Medicine, University of Manchester; Consultant in Health Care of the Elderly, Salford Royal Hospitals Trust, Salford, UK

Irene D. Turpie Professor of Medicine (Geriatrics), McMaster University, Hamilton, Ontario, Canada

N. Vogt Department of Geriatrics, University Hospitals of Geneva, Switzerland

Robert A. Weale Emeritus Professor in Visual Science, King's College London, UK

Charles Weijer Bioethicist and Assistant Professor of Medicine, Dalhousie University, Halifax, Nova Scotia, Canada

Gordon K. Wilcock Professor of Care of the Elderly, University of Bristol, UK

Lyn Williamson Specialist Registrar in Rheumatology, Nuffield Orthopaedic Centre, Oxford, UK

Jonathan P. Willmer Assistant Professor of Medicine (Neurology), University of Ottawa, Ontario, Canada

Rachel Wilson Division of Nursing, New York University School of Education, New York, USA

Leslie Wolfson Professor and Chairman, Department of Neurology, University of Connecticut School of Medicine, Farmington, Connecticut, USA

Ken Woodhouse Professor of Geriatric Medicine, University of Wales College of Medicine, Cardiff, UK

Carole Woodward Université Joseph Fourier, Grenoble, France

Paul Wordsworth Clinical Reader in Rheumatology, University of Oxford, UK

Haruko Yamamoto Stroke Fellow, Department of Neurology, University of Lausanne, Switzerland

Thomas T. Yoshikawa Chair and Professor, Department of Internal Medicine, Charles R. Drew University of Medicine and Science, Los Angeles, California, USA

Archie Young Professor of Geriatric Medicine, University of Edinburgh, UK

Preface to the first edition

There are few diseases or disabilities that are unique to late adult life, and the authors and compilers of a textbook of geriatric medicine must avoid the danger of simply writing a textbook of general medicine. We therefore set out with the explicit intention of compiling a book as a companion volume to a standard textbook of internal medicine. Our authors were asked to start their chapters where the *Oxford Textbook of Medicine* leaves off, to tell our readers the *extra* things that doctors caring for elderly people need to know over and above what their training in general (internal) medicine has taught them.

Our authorship is international but with an inevitable predominance from the United Kingdom which has the longest experience in providing specialist services for an ageing population, and North America which has the greatest output of research in medical geratology (or gerontology to use the established but falsely coined term). We asked our authors to restrict themselves to some 30 references each, either in the form of a bibliography or separately cited items, but to follow whatever style of exposition best suited their disposition and subject matter. With a subject as young and as rapidly developing as geriatric medicine differences of opinion and controversies are inevitable and the reader must not be surprised to find differences of emphasis or even occasional contradictions among the various chapters of this book. In places, typically where practice differs between countries, we have inserted editorial comment in the text but have indicated such interpolations with 'curly' brackets. The authors of the chapters affected may agree or not with our comments and are in no way responsible for them.

We are grateful to our colleagues for their good-natured acceptance of these editorial tyrannies and for the erudition and hard work that have gone into their contributions to this volume. The hope of all of us is that it will contribute to the continuing improvement in the quality of the care and understanding that older people received from their doctors.

J. Grimley Evans
T. Franklin Williams

Preface to the second edition

The responsibilities of a physician caring for older patients are wide indeed. In addition to the traditional concerns of the physician for physical and mental dysfunction, they call for attention to the social, intellectual, and material resources available to patients and their families. In turn, these resources are in part determined by the policies of governments and by economics. Physicians have a duty of advocacy for older people, not in adversarial conflict with other needy groups in society, but in peaceable, albeit determined, pursuit of equity in the allocation of resources in health and social care. Equity implies equal care for equal need. Need is defined in terms of capacity to benefit. Benefit is to be assessed by the individual recipients not by the purveyors of health services. These three assertions define the creed of the modern physician caring for older people. And following the United Nations International Year of Older Persons we are reminded that our responsibilities are worldwide in scope.

All doctors acknowledge a duty to be involved in education—our own continuing professional development, educational support for colleagues in multidisciplinary teams, and education for patients and carers. The technology and practice of medicine continue to advance at a breathless pace that can obscure paradoxes disadvantaging older people. For commercial, regulatory, and practical reasons, new treatments are introduced without adequate evaluation in representative samples of older people. Restricted views of what constitutes the evidence of 'evidence-based medicine' emphasize studies concerned with average effects in samples of patients of uncertain epidemiological provenance and therefore producing results of undefinable generalizability. This may be good enough for health service managers but not for clinicians and their patients. Diversity increases with age but the need to follow up evidence of average effects by identifying the determinants of individuals' outcomes from health-care interventions is often ignored by enthusiasts for evidence-based medicine and by the research funding agencies. All too often the evidence available does not match the needs of patients or doctors. Until these anomalies are addressed, painstaking clinical observation and documentation must protect our older patients from the inadequacies of overviews and meta-analyses.

Herein lies a continued need for textbooks of geriatric medicine. For this second edition of the *Oxford Textbook of Geriatric Medicine* we have enlarged the range of subject matter and authorship and remedied some omissions and imbalances of the first. We have also relaxed the style. For the first edition we asked our authors to start where the *Oxford Textbook of Medicine* left off, but this gave rise to some difficulties and no such restraint has been required on this occasion.

In preparing the book it has been a privilege to work with some of the world's most distinguished scientists and clinicians. We wish to record our admiration for the expertise of our authors and our gratitude for their patience with our editorial intrusions.

J. Grimley Evans   Oxford, UK
T. Franklin Williams   Rochester, USA
B. Lynn Beattie   Vancouver, Canada
J-P. Michel   Geneva, Switzerland
G.K. Wilcock   Bristol, UK
        March 2000

Foreword

Paul B. Beeson

Professor of Medicine Emeritus and VA Distinguished Physician, University of Washington, Seattle, USA

The twentieth century has seen an enormous increase in medical research, in basic sciences as well as in clinical medicine. This has effected substantial alterations in medical education and clinical practice. Some diseases that had been major problems have become far less important. For example, pulmonary tuberculosis, a major problem in the first third of the century which tended to affect persons in early adult life, could only be treated by months of bed rest. Most large cities had special hospitals for the care of such patients. These are no longer needed, because of the availability of specific curative treatment. Similarly, vaccines which prevent the contagious diseases of childhood have come into general use. Effective treatment for other diseases were developed, for example insulin for diabetes and liver extract for pernicious anemia. After about 1920 the clinical manifestations of acute myocardial infarction began to be recognized, and more effective therapy became available. At the beginning of the second third of the century came the sensational discovery of chemotherapy and antibiotic therapy for many infectious diseases, curing severe infections which might have been fatal. Even some neoplastic diseases can now be cured by surgery, radiotherapy, or chemotherapy.

Medical education has changed accordingly. In the first half of the century, although there were full-time salaried teachers for instruction in the basic sciences, clinical teaching was carried out largely as a voluntary contribution by clinicians engaged in private practice, who gave some of their time to the care of indigent people in public hospitals. This was the setting for clinical instruction of medical students. Then, in the second half of the century, there was a huge expansion in research in all branches of medicine. Whereas formerly there were only a few privately funded institutions, such as the Rockefeller Institute, there then came a huge increase in the funding of medical research. Most nations began to support it substantially, as for example the National Institutes of Health in the United States. These agencies not only conducted research in their own laboratories, but also gave large research grants to medical schools.

The sensational progress in the last part of the twentieth century has saved many lives, and thus contributed to a substantial increase in average duration of human life. Accordingly, clinical medicine has found itself engaged more and more in the care of older people, and some physicians have begun to specialize in this field. The term 'geriatrics' and 'gerontology' have come into use. Official recognition of geriatrics as a special branch of clinical medicine first took place in the National Health Service of the United Kingdom. Medical schools everywhere began to include geriatric problems in their courses of instruction. Fellowships and research grants focusing on the ageing process have now been established.

Physicians who have developed a special interest in this kind of practice now hold national meetings, and sponsor publication of journals and books specifically dealing with these subjects. The result has been substantial improvement in the management of some of the disabilities of old people, making this field of practice increasingly attractive. In today's textbooks management of the problems of old age receives increasing emphasis. One would not expect gerontology to splinter into numerous subspecialties, as internal medicine has done; nonetheless we can take satisfaction in the growing interest of the medical profession in the subject of ageing, and the ways in which some of its difficulties can be alleviated.

Geriatric medicine is important, both in the care delivered by geriatrically trained physicians and in contributing to the care of older persons generally through co-operation with, and informing of, physicians in other fields. The second edition of this Textbook should be a valuable resource to help meet the challenges of care in the next century.

Introduction

John Grimley Evans

Ageing, in the sense of senescence, is a progressive loss of adaptability of an individual organism as time passes. As we grow older we become less able to react adaptively to challenges from the external or internal environment. External challenges include injury and infection, and among challenges from the internal environment are arterial occlusion and malignant cell clones. As homeostatic mechanisms become less sensitive, less accurate, slower, and less well sustained, sooner or later we encounter a challenge that we are unable to deal with effectively and we die. Therefore the rise of death rate with age is the hallmark of senescence. In cross-sectional data from developed countries this begins around the age of 12, and except for deviance due to violent deaths in early adult life is broadly exponential thereafter up to old age (Fig. 1). The age of lowest mortality rate curve has been constant for the last 100 years in England and Wales in cross-sectional data (Grimley Evans 1997) but varies in cohort analyses owing to secular variation in social conditions through which younger people have to live. The slowing down in the rate of rise of mortality with age apparent at ages over 80 becomes even more pronounced after the age of 100, perhaps because of the emergence by selective survival of a 'biological elite' (see below).

In order to understand the evolution of senescence (see Chapter 2.1), it is important to bear in mind that even if we did not age we would still die eventually from accident, disease, famine, or warfare, but our risk of dying would be constant with age, or might even fall as natural selection weeded out the weaker members of a population.

Loss of adaptability is also the key concept in medical practice among older people. Older patients will be less able to deal with minor errors in care (e.g. in drug dosage) and will need more help in recovering from disease or injury than will younger patients. The essence of good geriatric medicine is scrupulous and comprehensive attention to detail.

The continuous and broadly exponential increase with age in vulnerability throughout adult life is matched by a similar increase in the use of health services and in the prevalence of chronic disease and disability. There is no discontinuity in later life in any of these aspects of ageing that could provide a biological justification for separating older people from the rest of the adult human race. The arbitrary definition of the state of being 'geriatric' as beginning at age 65 or 75 is a historical accident and, while it may have an administrative convenience, has no basis in biology or epidemiology and may not always be in the best interests of older people. Moreover, the processes that lead to disease and disability in old age are lifelong and can only be understood and modified through a lifelong perspective on ageing.

A model of ageing

Medical students are still taught that in approaching the disability of an old person they should consider whether the problem is due to 'disease' or to 'normal ageing'. Unfortunately for this approach, no one has produced a definition of normal ageing that bears inspection, and disease can be defined in many different ways. In effect students are being asked to separate the undefined from the indefinable. This makes neither for constructive thought nor good medicine, particularly if it is to be inferred that anything characterized as 'normal' is by definition not the proper concern of a doctor.

The question students should be taught to ask when faced with an elderly person with a problem is: 'What can I do to improve the situation?' If this is coupled with a knowledge of the range of therapeutic and prosthetic interventions available, and how to assess their appropriate application, the issue of whether the problem arises from normal ageing or disease is seen to be irrelevant as well as meaningless. However, it is helpful to have some broad model of how age-associated changes come about in order to structure thought about appropriate interventions. Table 1 sets out one such model based on an analysis of the origins of observed differences between the young and older members of a population. The first distinction

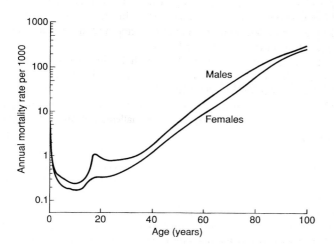

Fig. 1 Age- and sex-specific annual mortality rates, England and Wales, 1988.

Table 1 A model of human ageing: sources of differences between young and old people

Non-ageing	Selective survival
	Differential challenge
	Cohort effects
True ageing	Secondary (reactive)
	Individual
	Species
	Primary
	Intrinsic
	Extrinsic

is between true ageing processes, by which old people have changed from how they were when young, and non-ageing factors, in which the differences between young and old are not due to the old having changed in their lifetime. We will briefly consider each of the processes listed in the table.

Non-ageing

Three phenomena give rise to differences between young and old people which are not due to ageing.

Selective survival

As already noted, those individuals who reach extreme old age, in the ninth and tenth decades of life, are the survivors from their birth cohorts and selected for their greater resistance to whatever mortal challenges their generation had to face. Therefore it is not surprising to find evidence of selection for favourable nuclear and mitochondrial genotypes in comparisons of very old with younger subjects (Takata et al. 1987; Tanaka et al. 1998). This process is sometimes characterized as an emergence of the 'biological elite'. Not surprisingly, there is also selection for lifestyle and environmental factors, for example in the differences in life expectancy between smokers and non-smokers and between social classes. There is also some intriguing evidence for psychological factors having an effect on survival, with the intelligent and those who are determined to stay in control of their own lives likely to enjoy longer survival.

Cohort effects

In changing societies individuals born into successive generations are exposed to different physical and social environments. The effects of these on individuals in their early years may persist throughout the rest of their lives (Riley 1994). The habits of nutrition and food preferences acquired in early life will affect later susceptibility to vascular and other diseases, as will socially determined habits such as smoking and alcohol consumption. Cultural changes will have a major effect on psychological capacity and functioning, through both education and the more subtle influences of the media and government propaganda. The way in which cohort effects can be mistaken for age effects has been

dramatically demonstrated in comparisons of cross-sectional and longitudinal studies of psychological functioning (Schaie and Strother 1968; Schaie 1989). In general, older people subjected to tests devised by (young) psychologists perform less well than younger adults, but when followed up show smaller and later declines with age than the cross-sectional comparisons would predict. Because of cohort effects, we perform better when tested against our own former selves than when tested against other, younger, people born into cohorts increasingly remote from our own.

Differential challenge

If ageing is loss of adaptability, it should only be assessed by exposing individuals at different ages to the same challenge and measuring its effects. In many ways society is organized so that older people are exposed to more severe challenges than are presented to the young, and the differences in outcome are too readily attributed to ageing rather than inequity. The classical example used to be hypothermia in the United Kingdom. Hypothermia is partly due to age-associated deterioration in the ability to maintain body temperature, but 20 years ago it was also due to housing policies which put older people into colder houses and environments (Fox et al. 1973). Sadly, the grossest examples of differential challenge at the present time are to be found in the health services. The quality of medical care which older people receive is often poorer than that offered to the young. There are even attempts to justify this discrimination as legitimate age-based rationing. One of the assumptions underlying explicit or implicit age-based rationing is that older people do not benefit from interventions. In fact, there are many examples of treatments which, in terms of lives saved, may be more effective among the old than among the young. This is true, for example, of thrombolytic therapy in myocardial infarction, in antiplatelet therapy in the secondary prevention of stroke, and in the use of β-blockers following myocardial infarction. However, age-based rationing is only countenanced in societies where there is an ingrained prejudice against older people, and eradicating this form of discrimination is an important long-term task for geriatricians and other decent citizens.

True ageing

True ageing comprises those processes whereby people change as they grow older.

Secondary (reactive) ageing

One of the basic enigmas of ageing is why the body does not detect and repair the ravages of time as well as it deals with some other insults such as minor wounds and infections. This question is dealt with in Section 2, but we need to be aware that the individual may make some adaptive responses to age-associated changes. At the individual level, secondary ageing is more apparent in psychological than in physiological functioning. Individuals may show a range of behavioural adaptations to age-associated impairments in memory and fluid intelligence. Obsessional behaviour is a well-recognized adaptation to unreliable memory and giving up dangerous sports is a sensible adaptation to the slowing of neuromuscular reactions. Professionals caring for older people need to be aware of the possibility of secondary ageing, since attempts to 'normalize' some aspect of physiology or behaviour may do more harm than good if it is compensating for some other underlying impairment.

At a species level, the female menopause is an example of secondary adaptation to the age-associated decline in reproductive efficiency observed in all species. Menopause, defined as a genetically determined total cessation of reproductive capability at an age approximately halfway through the maximum lifespan of the species, is almost exclusively a human and female characteristic. With a family-based social structure and a cumulative culture based on language, there will come a time in a woman's life when in terms of getting her genes into successive generations (the essence of evolutionary success) she will be better engaged in contributing to the survival of her grandchildren, each containing 25 per cent of her genes, than in increasingly dangerous and unsuccessful attempts at producing more children of her own, even though each would contain 50 per cent of her genes. With his much lower biological investment in unsuccessful pregnancies, the male will not be under similar evolutionary pressure to substitute grandparenting for reproduction.

Primary ageing

Primary ageing is due to an interaction between intrinsic (genetic) and extrinsic (environmental and lifestyle) factors. Until recently, the dissection of the intrinsic from the extrinsic components of ageing has been dependent on observations of differing ageing patterns between populations living under different environmental conditions. This epidemiological approach has demonstrated that a number of age-associated changes once thought to be intrinsic have significant extrinsic components. Examples include hypertension, cardiovascular disease, most adult cancers, osteoporotic fractures, and less dramatic but disabling conditions such as high-tone hearing loss (Goycoolea *et al.* 1986) and visual impairments (see Chapters 18.15.1–18.15.3 and 18.16). Epidemiological approaches have also produced evidence that lifelong patterns of physiology and disease may be partly determined by environmental influences acting on the fetus and the infant child (Barker and Robinson 1992). This finding may reflect the existence of 'metabolic switches' which could also underlie other phenomena, such as the effect of caloric restriction in prolonging longevity in rodents (Grimley Evans 1993). In terms of evolutionary biology, the general phenomenon of the adaptation of metabolic pathways to environmental conditions has analogies with the effects of 'thrifty genes', which carry selective advantage in populations undergoing periods of famine but which may confer less than optimal ageing when their possessors come to live under conditions of more than adequate food supply (Neel 1962).

An interaction between specific extrinsic factors and genetically determined individual susceptibility has long been assumed to underlie the link between salt intake and blood pressure (Prior *et al.* 1968), but the new genetics is revealing other examples of individual variation in the metabolism of extrinsically derived chemicals, including drugs and carcinogens. We may perhaps look forward to a time when we can match our individual lifestyles to identified susceptibilities defined by our genomes in order to pursue an ideal of optimal ageing (see below). However, there are also genes with effects on general processes of ageing. Such genes can be pursued by breeding experiments in short-lived lower animals and through comparisons of the genomes of centenarians with those of younger fellow countrymen. It is likely

(see Chapter 2.1) that some at least of these 'longevity assurance genes' will be those which determine processes of damage control by prevention, detection, and repair or replacement, and their balance with reproductive rate.

Variability in ageing

Because of the composite nature of ageing, individuals show wide variation in the pattern and rate of ageing. This means that, for virtually all physiological and psychological variables, the range of differences between individuals increases with age. Medical services need to be sensitive to the greater heterogeneity of individuals in the older age groups. Referring to them collectively as 'the elderly' may inhibit appreciation that older people differ from each other more than do the young. Good science as well as good medicine requires us to respond to older people as individuals and not as uniform members of an arbitrarily defined group.

Optimal ageing

Epidemiological studies of ageing have tended to focus on age-specific means and variances. However, we should not be content with regarding average as a satisfactory attainment. Rowe and Kahn (1998) have proposed a concept of 'successful ageing' characterized by low risk of disease and disease-related disability, high mental and physical function, and active engagement with life. This concept fits well with the context of contemporary North American society, but may not apply so well elsewhere. In particular, engagement in society in old age might be seen as undesirable, and even impious, in some cultures. Even in the United Kingdom, which is culturally close to the United States in many ways, the ideal would be defined as 'healthy ageing', with individuals deciding for themselves what is to constitute 'success'.

In terms of health and abilities, it is possible to view the best currently attained by some as a target for all. Thus 'optimal ageing' might be defined by, perhaps, the top 20 per cent of the distributions in each physiological or psychological variable.

Is it realistic to hope for improvements in the pattern of human ageing without control of intrinsic genetic processes? On average, populations are living longer than they used to, but this could be because people are fitter and therefore are surviving longer, or because ill and frail people are being kept alive longer by modern medical and social services. As a means of distinguishing these two processes, a World Health Organization Scientific Group (1984) proposed that the basic measure of the need for, and success of, health and social services for older people would be measures of disease-free and disability-free life expectancy at later ages as a part of total life expectancy. Undoubtedly, many older people fear disability and the loss of independence that it brings more than they fear death. Few nations collect suitable data for monitoring disease- or disability-free life expectancy. The United States is an exception and there, at least, it seems that the life of older people is being prolonged with an increase in healthy lifespan and a corresponding reduction in the prevalence and duration of disability (Manton *et al.* 1997). This is partly due to improvements in medical knowledge and technology in preventing and reducing disability. However, it also seems that an important factor in this encouraging trend has been the adoption of healthier lifestyles by successive cohorts of older people. Whatever the mechanisms, however, this evidence of change in healthy life expectancy over a short timespan indicates that manipulation of extrinsic factors can improve the trajectory of ageing, and this is an important message for both public health and clinical medicine.

References

Barker, D.J.P. and Robinson R.J. (1992). *Fetal and infant origins of adult disease*. BMJ Publishers, London.

Fox, R.H., Woodward, P.M., Exton-Smith, A.N., and Green, M.F. (1973). Body temperatures in the elderly: a national study of physiological, social and environmental conditions. *British Medical Journal*, i, 200–6.

Goycoolea, M.V., Goycoolea, H.G., Rodriguez, L.G., Martinez, G.C., and Vidal, R. (1986). Effect of life in industrialized societies on hearing in natives of Easter Island. *Laryngoscope*, 9,:1391–6.

Grimley Evans, J. (1993). Metabolic switches in ageing. *Age and Ageing*, 22, 79–81.

Grimley Evans, J. (1997). A correct compassion: the medical response to an ageing society. *Journal of the Royal College of Physicians of London*, 31, 674–84.

Manton, K.G., Corder, L., and Stallard, E. (1997). Chronic disability trends in elderly United States populations 1982–1994. *Proceedings of the National Academy of Sciences of the United States of America*, 94, 2593–8.

Neel, J.V. (1962). Diabetes mellitus: a 'thrifty' genotype made detrimental by progress? *American Journal of Human Genetics*, 14, 353–61.

Riley, M.W. (1994). Aging and society: past, present and future. *Gerontologist*, 34, 436–45.

Rowe, J.W. and Kahn, R.L. (1998). *Successful aging*. Pantheon, New York.

Prior, I.A.M., Grimley Evans, J., Davidson, F., and Lindsay, M. (1968). Sodium intake and blood pressure in two Polynesian populations. *New England Journal of Medicine*, 279, 515–20.

Schaie, M.W. (1989). Perceptual speed in adulthood: cross-sectional and longitudinal studies. *Psychology and Aging*, 4, 443–53.

Schaie, K.W. and Strother, C.R. (1968). A cross-sequential study of age changes in cognitive behaviour. *Psychological Bulletin*, 70, 671–80.

Tanaka, M., Gong, J.-S., Zhang, J., Yoneda, M., and Yagi, K. (1998). Mitochondrial genotype associated with longevity. *Lancet*, 351, 185–6.

Takata, H., Suzuki, M., Ishii, T., Sekiguchi, S., and Iri, H. (1987). Influence of major histocompatibility complex region genes on human longevity among Okinawan-Japanese centenarians and nonagenarians. *Lancet*, ii, 824–6.

World Health Organization Scientific Group on the Epidemiology of Ageing (1984). *The uses of epidemiology in the study of the elderly*, Technical Report Series No. 706. World Health Organization, Geneva.

1

The ageing of populations and communities

1.1 Demography of older populations in developed countries

Kevin Kinsella, Richard Suzman, Jean-Marie Robine, and George Myers

A major success story of the twentieth century has been the extent of population ageing that has resulted from reduced fertility, improved health, and increased longevity. For the first time in history, many societies have the luxury of mass ageing. Accompanying this broad demographic process, however, are other changes (new disease patterns, macroeconomic strains, emergent technologies, changing social norms) that are difficult for societies to plan for. The world's more developed countries, which are the focus of this chapter, face a plethora of sociopolitical issues, ranging from provision of health care to social security to employment rights, that are directly linked to the changing age structure of their populations. As we approach the millennium, many of the debates around these issues will intensify and may well shift from the political to the ethical realm.

There is a growing awareness that the concept of 'elderly' is an inadequate generalization which obscures the heterogeneous nature of a population group that spans more than 50 years of life. 'Elderly' people are at least as diverse as younger age groups in terms of personal and social resources, health, marital status, living arrangements, and social integration. To understand the dynamics of ageing, we need information on older populations from several interrelated perspectives—demographic, medical, social, and economic. In this chapter we seek to lay out the demographic foundation upon which subsequent chapters can build.

Until the mid-1980s, demographic studies of older populations contained largely descriptive analyses of the distribution of those populations by age, sex, marital status, labour-force participation, living arrangements, and causes of death. The analytical tools used were predominantly those of ratios, the life table, and various decompositions. More recently, the field has moved beyond the descriptive phase to probe the causes and consequences of changing age structures in populations. For example, biologically based models have been developed to elucidate and forecast the dynamics underlying the demographic transition in which life expectancy increases before the birth rate falls, and chronic diseases and disabilities become more prevalent. These models describe the transitions as individuals move from independent functioning to dependence, institutionalization, and death. Life tables measuring single unilinear decrements in vital and functional status are giving way to tables that can describe more complex multidirectional changes. Theoretical models are being developed to investigate the deeper structural interrelations between support ratios, intergenerational exchanges, population age structures, and the economics of pension, health, and other social insurance programmes. A new emphasis on longitudinal survey data allows researchers to model and test causality in ways that before could only be roughly approximated.

The 'developed country' category used in this chapter corresponds to the 'more developed' classification employed by the United Nations Statistical Office. Developed countries comprise all nations in Europe (including the following parts of the former Soviet Union: Belarus, Estonia, Latvia, Lithuania, Moldova, Russia, and Ukraine) and North America, plus Australia, Japan, and New Zealand.

Population ageing

The world's elderly population (65 years of age and over) is currently growing at a rate of 2.4 per cent per year, considerably faster than the global total population. In developed countries as a whole, the present elderly population numbers 165 million, and is projected to expand to 257 million by the year 2025. Sweden, with 17.5 per cent of its population aged 65 and over in 1997, has the highest proportion of elderly people of the major countries of the world. Other notably high proportions (in excess of 16 per cent) are found in Italy, Belgium, Greece, and the United Kingdom. Fourteen countries in Table 1 have elderly populations of 2 million or more today; by 2025, six more will have reached this level.

In the simplest terms, population ageing refers to increasing proportions of older people within an overall population age structure. Another way to think of population ageing is to consider a society's median age, the age that divides a population into numerically equal segments of younger and older people. For example, the present median age in Portugal of 36 years indicates that the number of people under the age of 36 equals the number who have already celebrated their thirty-sixth birthday.

With the exception of the low median of 24 years in Albania, today's median age in developed countries ranges from 31 in Ireland to 40 in Japan. The median will rise in every developed country during the next three decades (Fig. 1), and is projected to exceed 50 years in Italy and Germany by the year 2025. Unless birth rates rise unexpectedly in the coming years, these and many other societies

Table 1 Elderly and 'old old' populations in 35 developed countries: 1997 and 2025

Region/country	Elderly (65 +) population (thousands)		Elderly as a percentage of total population		Old old (80 +) as percentage of total population	
	1997	2025	1997	2025	1997	2025
Western Europe						
Austria	1 252	1 888	15.4	24.1	3.6	6.9
Belgium	1 681	2 379	16.5	25.0	3.7	6.7
Denmark	798	1 213	15.0	22.7	4.0	6.4
Finland	747	1 250	14.5	24.9	3.3	6.3
France	9 142	13 694	15.6	23.7	3.8	6.4
Germany	12 956	19 398	15.8	25.7	3.8	7.9
Iceland	31	57	11.6	19.1	2.7	4.5
Ireland	408	688	11.3	17.6	2.6	4.2
Italy	9 841	13 225	17.3	26.3	4.1	8.1
Luxembourg	61	111	14.6	24.8	3.3	6.5
Netherlands	2 100	3 727	13.4	23.5	3.1	5.8
Norway	696	992	15.8	21.6	4.2	5.6
Sweden	1 550	2 083	17.5	22.7	4.9	6.8
Switzerland	1 068	1 787	14.8	25.3	3.9	7.1
United Kingdom	9 270	12 655	15.8	21.1	4.1	5.8
Eastern Europe/Southern Europe						
Albania	193	486	5.9	11.3	0.8	1.9
Belarus	1 378	1 774	13.2	17.3	2.3	3.7
Bulgaria	1 293	1 665	15.6	22.8	2.3	5.9
Czech Republic	1 399	2 227	13.6	22.0	2.5	5.3
Greece	1 715	2 452	16.2	23.4	3.5	6.9
Hungary	1 465	2 068	14.3	22.1	2.6	5.5
Lithuania	462	613	12.8	17.9	2.4	4.6
Poland	4 478	8 017	11.6	20.0	2.0	4.0
Portugal	1 479	2 037	14.9	22.6	3.0	6.3
Romania	2 843	4 170	12.7	19.5	2.0	4.7
Russia	18 350	25 224	12.5	18.2	2.1	3.4
Slovakia	603	1 070	11.2	18.7	1.9	4.0
Slovenia	257	441	13.0	23.7	2.4	6.0
Spain	6 247	8 524	16.0	23.1	3.5	6.7
Ukraine	7 129	8 175	14.1	18.1	2.4	3.9
Other						
Australia	2 270	4 527	12.3	20.4	2.8	5.4
Canada	3 742	7 828	12.3	20.6	2.9	5.1
Japan	19 474	32 169	15.5	26.8	3.3	8.9
New Zealand	416	758	11.6	17.0	2.7	4.3
United States	34 076	61 952	12.7	18.5	3.2	4.3

Data from United States Bureau of the Census (1998).

face a future in which half or more of the citizenry will be over the age of 50 years.

Within an elderly population, different age groups may grow at very different rates. An increasingly important feature of population ageing is the progressive ageing of the older population itself. The fastest growing age segment in many countries is the 'old old', defined here as people aged 80 years and over. This group currently constitutes 22 per cent of the overall elderly population in developed countries, and represents more than 4 per cent of the total population in Scandinavia, Italy, and the United Kingdom. Nine developed nations now have 'old old' populations in excess of 1 million, and four more nations will share this characteristic before the year 2025.

Changes in the age structure of a population result from changes over time in fertility, mortality, and international migration (Myers 1990). Most societies historically have had high levels of both fertility and mortality. As prominent communicable diseases are eradicated and public health measures expand, overall mortality levels decline and life expectancy at birth rises, while fertility tends to remain high. A large proportion of the initial improvement in mortality occurs among infants, so that more babies survive. Consequently, younger population age cohorts grow in size relative to older cohorts, and the population percentage of youths and young adults is relatively high. This is the situation today in many of the world's developing nations.

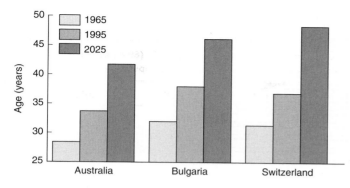

Fig. 1 Median age in three countries: 1965 to 2025.

Populations begin to 'age' only when fertility falls and mortality rates continue to improve or remain at low levels. Countries that have both low fertility and low mortality have completed what demographers call 'the demographic transition', illustrated graphically in Fig. 2. In 1920, the United Kingdom's population age structure had the pyramidal shape common to societies with relatively high fertility and mortality. As early as 1920, however, one can see that fertility was falling significantly; the cohorts aged 0 to 4 and 5 to 9 years were noticeably smaller than those aged 10 to 14 years. By 1970, increases in life expectancy had helped to shift the centre of gravity of the population age structure upwards, and people aged 45 to 64 years were a much greater proportion of the total. As the United Kingdom ages into the twenty-first century, the one-time pyramid will give way to a rectangular shape. By the year 2025, nearly half of the population will be aged 45 years or more, and the ranks of the 'old old' will continue to swell.

The United Kingdom is typical of many European countries which have had low fertility and mortality for decades. Nearly all developed countries now have total fertility rates below the natural replacement level of 2.1 children per woman, with the level in some nations (e.g. Bulgaria, Italy, and Spain) as low as 1.2. Successive small birth cohorts have contributed to the large proportions of elderly people in these societies. Thus we see the importance of understanding past demographic trends, or disruptions thereof, when planning for the future. In spite of the relatively high proportions of elderly people now observed in developed countries, there will be little change in most countries during the next 10 to 15 years, followed by accelerated growth in the second and third decades of the twenty-first century. The lack of change in the near future reflects low fertility during the Second World War and the preceding worldwide economic depression, while the subsequent growth stems from the 'baby boom' that characterized the postwar years in many Western nations. As the large postwar birth cohorts continue to advance in age, the proportions of elderly people will begin to expand noticeably—in the United States, for example, the percentage of elderly people is expected to jump from 13 per cent in the year 2000 to nearly 20 per cent by 2030.

The general similarity in today's level of population ageing in developed countries, however, can mask important current and historical differences. Again, the timing and pace of fertility decline is usually the pre-eminent factor. Table 2 illustrates how rapidly the population of Japan is ageing compared with other developed nations; it took 25 years for Japan to double its proportion of elderly people from 7 to 14 per cent, compared with the 115 years this took for

France. Moreover, by the year 2025, 27 per cent of Japan's population will be 65 years old or over—the highest projected level for any country in the world.

Life expectancy and longevity

The spectacular increases in human life expectancy that began in the mid-1800s and continued during the following century are often ascribed primarily to improvements in medicine. However, the major impact of improvements both in medicine and sanitation did not occur until the late nineteenth century. Earlier and more important factors in lowering mortality were innovations in industrial and agricultural production and distribution, which enabled nutritional diversity and consistency for large numbers of people (Thomlinson 1976). A growing research consensus attributes the gain in human longevity since the early 1800s to a complex interplay of advancements in medicine and sanitation coupled with new modes of familial, social, economic, and political organization (Moore 1993).

Average life expectancy at birth in Japan has now reached 80 years, the highest level of any major country of the world, and several other developed nations (Australia, Sweden, Canada, and Switzerland) have achieved levels of 79 years. Women outlive men in every developed nation (Fig. 3), typically by 5 to 7 years on average. In parts of the former Soviet Union, adult male mortality has increased considerably in recent decades, to the point where the female advantage in life expectancy at birth is as high as 13 years.

Although the effect of fertility decline usually is the driving force behind changing population age structures, changes in mortality assume greater importance as countries reach lower levels of fertility (Caselli *et al.* 1987). Since the beginning of the 1900s, industrialized countries have made enormous strides in extending life expectancy at birth; in the first half of the century, many Western industrialized nations added 20 or more years to their average life expectancies (Table 3). Spain's life expectancy more than doubled between 1900 and 1990.

1. The relative difference among countries has narrowed with time.
2. The pace of improvement has not been linear, especially for males. From the early 1950s to the early 1970s, for example, there was little or no change in male life expectancy in Australia, The Netherlands, Norway, and the United States, while in parts of Eastern Europe and the former Soviet Union, as noted above, male life expectancy has declined during portions of the last three decades;
3. The difference between female and male longevity, which universally has been in favour of women in this century, widened with time.

Given the very low levels of infant mortality found in most developed countries, much of the current gain in life expectancy at birth is attributable to improvement in mortality among the elderly population. Owing in large part to the reduction of heart disease and stroke among middle-aged and older adults, gains in life expectancy at the age of 65 years are now outpacing increases in life expectancy at birth. Many scientists have been surprised at the sustained increases in life expectancy, particularly at older ages. We know very little about the potential for longevity of the human species. This is a domain to which both biology and the demography

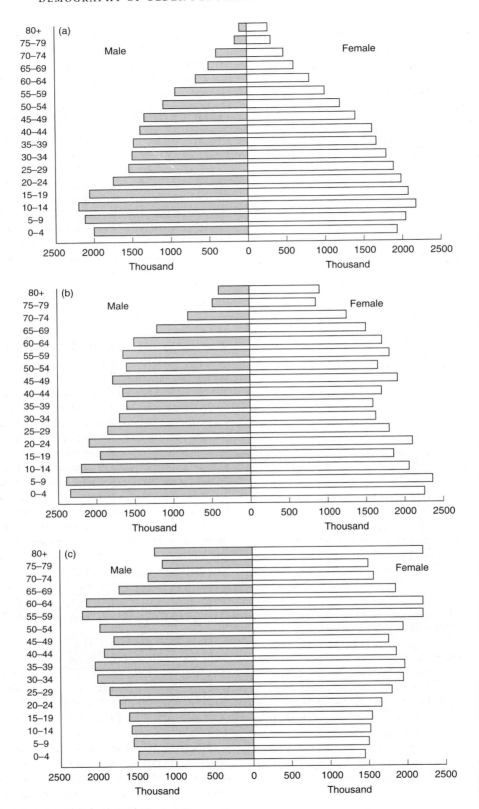

Fig. 2 Total population of the United Kingdom: (a) 1920; (b) 1970; (c) 2025.

Table 2 Speed of population ageing in selected countries

Country	Year in which the proportion of the population aged 65+ years reached or will reach		Number of years required
	7%	**14%**	
France	1865	1980	115
Sweden	1890	1975	85
Australia	1938	2009	71
United States	1944	2013	69
Canada	1944	2010	66
Hungary	1941	1994	53
Poland	1966	2015	49
United Kingdom	1930	1975	45
Spain	1947	1992	45
Japan	1970	1995	25

Data from the United States Bureau of the Census (1998) and country sources.

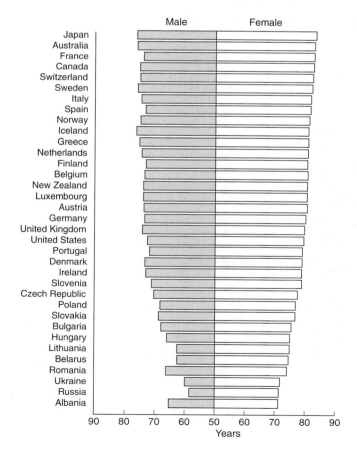

Fig. 3 Life expectancy at birth: 1997.

of ageing can contribute. The fundamental questions relate to mortality at extreme ages and to the variance in the distribution of life duration. At very old ages (85 years and above), mortality rates seem not to increase with age as rapidly as at younger ages. In other words, some researchers (Kannisto 1996; Manton and Stallard 1996; Vaupel 1998) have begun to report a decrease in the rate of increase in mortality at the oldest ages. This may reflect, in part, heterogeneity of the population. Other clues may stem from research now being conducted on old age mortality in non-human species, for example fruit flies (Carey 1997). Changes in very-old-age mortality are dramatically illustrated by the explosion in the number of centenarians seen in many developed countries. In France, for example, where the estimated number of centenarians was about 200 in 1950, their expected future numbers are 8500 in the year 2000, 41 000 in 2025, and 150 000 in 2050 (Dinh 1995). If these demographic projections are indeed realized, the number of centenarians in France will have multiplied by a factor of 750 in one century.

Impact of future mortality rates on population size

The pace at which death rates at advanced ages decline will play a major role in determining future numbers of elderly people and especially of very old individuals. The United States Bureau of the Census, which in 1995 estimated the number of people aged 85 years and over in the United States to be about 3.6 million, has made several projections of the future size of this age segment (Day 1996). The Bureau's middle-mortality series projection suggests that there will be 13.6 million people aged 85 years and over in the year 2040, while their low-mortality (high life expectancy) series projection implies 20.3 million. As those who will be 85 years old and over in the year 2040 are already at least 40 years old, the differences in these projections result almost exclusively from assumptions about adult mortality rates, and are not affected by future birth or infant mortality rates. In the middle-mortality series, the Bureau assumes that average life expectancy at birth will reach 82.0 years in 2050, while in the low-mortality series life expectancy is assumed to reach 89.4 years in 2050.

Alternative projections (Fig. 4), using assumptions of lower death rates and higher average life expectancies, have produced even larger estimates of the future population of the United States aged over 85 years. Simply assuming that death rates will continue falling at about the recent 2 per cent rate results in a projection of 23.5 million aged 85 and over in 2040 (Guralnik *et al.* 1988). Even more optimistic forecasts of future reductions in death rates have been made from mathematical simulations of potential reductions in known risk factors for chronic disease, morbidity, and mortality. Manton *et al.* (1993) have used such a method to generate an extreme 'upper bound' projection for the United States of 54 million people aged 85 and over in 2040. While such projections are not necessarily the most likely, they do illustrate the potential impact of changes in adult mortality on the future size of the extremely old population, and underscore the uncertainty inherent in projections of the size and age composition of older populations.

Table 3 Life expectancy at birth for selected countries: 1900–1997

Region/country	c. 1900		c. 1950		1997	
	Male	Female	Male	Female	Male	Female
Western Europe						
Austria	37.8	39.9	62.0	67.0	74.0	80.5
Belgium	45.4	48.9	62.1	67.4	74.0	80.6
Denmark	51.6	54.8	68.9	71.5	73.4	78.9
France	45.3	48.7	63.7	69.4	74.4	82.5
Germany	43.8	46.6	64.6	68.5	73.6	80.2
Norway	52.3	55.8	70.3	73.8	75.3	81.1
Sweden	52.8	55.3	69.9	72.6	76.4	81.9
United Kingdom	46.4	50.1	66.2	71.1	74.7	80.0
Eastern Europe/Southern Europe						
Czech Republic	38.9	41.7	60.9	65.5	70.5	77.4
Greece	38.1	39.7	63.4	66.7	75.6	80.9
Hungary	36.6	38.2	59.3	63.4	66.1	75.1
Italy	42.9	43.2	63.7	67.2	75.1	81.6
Poland	NA	NA	57.2	62.8	68.3	76.9
Spain	33.9	35.7	59.8	64.3	73.6	81.5
Other						
Australia	53.2	56.8	66.7	71.8	76.7	82.7
Canada	NA	NA	66.4	70.9	75.6	82.5
Japan	42.8	44.3	59.6	63.1	76.8	83.2
New Zealand	NA	NA	67.2	71.3	74.2	80.6
United States	48.3	51.1	66.0	71.7	72.8	79.5

Figures for Germany and the Czech Republic prior to 1995 refer to the former West Germany and Czechoslovakia respectively.
NA, not available.
Data from UNDIESA (1988), Siampos (1990), and United States Bureau of the Census (1998).

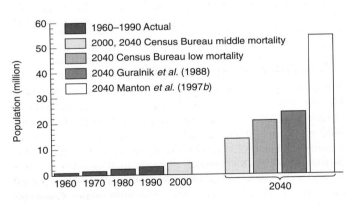

Fig. 4 Forecasts of the American population aged 85 years and over.

Active life expectancy

The extent to which a longer life will be a healthier one rather than one that contains more years of chronic illness or disability will have a potent impact on national health systems, most especially on the demand for long-term care. In 1984, the World Health Organization (WHO) proposed a general model of health transition which distinguished between total survival, disability-free survival, and survival without disabling chronic disease. The relevance of this model lies in its allowing simultaneous estimates of changes in mortality, morbidity, and disability. The evolution of the discrepancies between the three indicators has led to different theories of health change, including (a) a pandemic of chronic disease and disability (Gruenberg 1977; Kramer 1980), (b) a compression of morbidity (Fries 1980), (c) dynamic equilibrium (Manton 1982), and (d) the postponement of all morbid events to older ages (Strehler 1975).

There is considerable controversy over whether the general increase in life expectancy is associated with the compression or expansion of morbidity in later life. To date, empirical assessments have dealt essentially with disability-free life expectancy, often distinguishing between levels of disability (Robine and Ritchie 1991; Suzman *et al.* 1992). Ideally, calculations should be made from longitudinal data by the multistate method, taking into account transitions both from good to bad health and from independence to disability and vice versa as well as transitions from all health statuses towards death (Katz *et al.* 1983; Rogers *et al.* 1989; Crimmins *et al.* 1993; Mathers and Robine 1997). Large longitudinal surveys on population health are rare, and in practice most researchers employ the Sullivan (1971) method which uses prevalence data from cross-sectional studies.

Indices of active life expectancy are increasingly being used to chart the progress and compare the efficacy of health and social systems. However, as international standardization of these measures is only now taking place, and the longitudinal databases on functional status are becoming available for the first time, geographical and

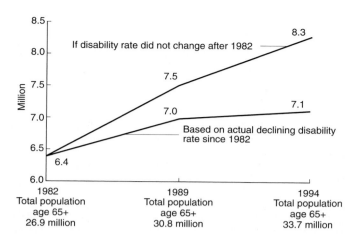

Fig. 5 Estimates of the number of Americans aged 65 years and over with disabilities: 1982 to 1994. (Reproduced with permission from Manton *et al.* (1997*a*).)

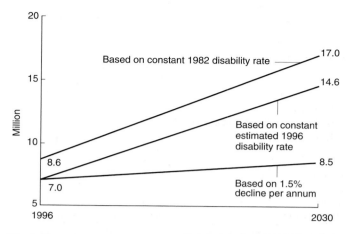

Fig. 6 Illustrative projections of the number of Americans aged 65 years and over with disabilities: 1996 to 2030. (Reproduced with permission from Manton *et al.* (1997*a*).)

time-series comparisons of cross-sectional estimates remain suspect. One general conclusion that has emerged is that, whatever the country considered, the increase in total life expectancy at the age of 65 years does not correspond to an increase in the time lived in severe disability. Some countries even show a dramatic decrease in the number of years lived with severe disabilities; this is the case for the United Kingdom (Bone *et al.* 1995) with regard to the ability to perform basic activities of daily living such as bathing, transferring from bed, feeding, and using a toilet independently. However, when the evolution of total life expectancy is juxtaposed with disability-free life expectancy combining all disability levels, the results are not so homogeneous.

It is not clear how to interpret recorded changes in disability-free life expectancy, and in particular, the decrease in severe disability at the oldest ages which seems to be characteristic of all developed countries with reasonably good data. Several hypotheses have been advanced. Some focus on the efficacy of rehabilitative operations such as extraction of cataracts or hip replacements. Others invoke the use of household equipment which is constantly increasing and which, combined with increasing educational levels, would cause older people now to have, given any impairment or chronic disease, less disability measured in terms of the need for help in performing activities of daily living. Specific studies will be needed to understand these intricate developments and their significance for societies at large, in the manner in which Manton *et al.* (1997*a*) have demonstrated for the American population. Using data from the 1982, 1984, 1989, and 1994 rounds of the United States National Long Term Care Survey, these researchers found that the disability rate among people aged 65 years and over declined by 1.3 per cent per year, resulting in 1.2 million fewer disabled older people in 1994 than would have occurred if the rate had not declined (Fig. 5).

Compounded over long periods of time, such relatively small changes in disability rates at older ages could have a substantial impact on the numbers of dependent older people. For example, if the American disability rate among people aged 65 years and over could be lowered by 1.5 per cent annually for the next 35 years, the increase in the number of dependent older people would be very small even as the elderly population grows significantly (Fig. 6). While

these findings of the decline in the disability rate came as a surprise, it is possible that improvements have been occurring for over a century (Fogel and Costa 1997).

Diversity of the older population

The heterogeneity of the older population is manifested in the diverse demographic, social, and economic characteristics of older people. These are brought about by behavioural features earlier in life, selective survival, and changes that occur in later life. The next sections will examine some important compositional characteristics of the older population, the factors that bring these features about, and their societal consequences.

Urban and rural aged populations

About 70 per cent of people aged 60 years and older in developed countries live in urban areas. As the long-term global trend of urbanization continues, the older population is expected to become even more concentrated in urban areas. Although older women outnumber older men in every national population, the ratio of older men to older women is generally higher in rural areas than in cities. In the rural areas of several countries (e.g. Australia, New Zealand, and Sweden) older men actually outnumber older women. Conversely, elderly women are more likely than elderly men to live in urban areas. The sex difference in residential concentration is probably related to marital status. As discussed below, elderly women are much more likely than elderly men to be widowed, and it may be that urban residence provides widows the benefits of closer proximity to children and social services.

Quality-of-life issues for older populations in rural versus urban areas are beginning to receive additional attention as migration streams increase and the costs of health care and public benefits escalate. Whereas greying rural communities were once associated with negative socio-economic consequences, more recent research has considered positive results that may stem from increased proportions of increasingly affluent elderly people (Bean *et al.* 1994).

Data from Wales (Wenger 1998) suggest that rural dwellers are more likely than their urban counterparts to be involved in community and voluntary activities. Nevertheless, the provision of health and other supportive services to ill and disabled older people in rural areas continues to present special challenges.

Education and income

Education is an important determinant of economic attainment, health, and the ability to participate fully in modern societies. There are notable differences in the educational attainment of older and younger people. While the vast majority of people aged 15 to 34 in most developed countries have completed a primary school education, comparable rates for older people may be less than 60 per cent. Cross-national attainment differences among elderly people often are substantial; in the early 1990s, attainment of a postprimary degree among elderly people was 10 per cent in Spain, 20 per cent in France, 33 per cent in Japan, 41 per cent in Canada, and 64 per cent in the United States. Possession of a postsecondary degree remains relatively uncommon among elderly people everywhere, with proportions well under 10 per cent in almost all nations with available data.

Striking age-cohort differences also appear within populations, and one of the most prominent differences between the young old and old old is the relatively low levels of attainment among the very old. As better educated cohorts reach old age and the oldest cohorts die, the average educational level of an elderly population increases and the age gap narrows. This dynamic and often rapid process of cohort improvement in education is one of the most important changes occurring within older populations, and is likely to have many ramifications for the lifestyles, health status, and use of health care of tomorrow's older cohorts. Education is strongly associated with health. Those with higher education tend to live longer (Land *et al.* 1994). While the precise contributions of each of the many factors that account for this relationship have not been completely determined, it is clear that a well-educated and informed public is more receptive to public health campaigns and is better able to take a large share of responsibility for maintaining personal health.

The absence of adequate longitudinal studies has been, until very recently, a major obstacle to understanding economic status and the dynamics of impoverishment during old age. Relatively little is known with certainty about the income and assets of older populations, their decisions about savings and consumption, and the role of health problems as a factor in impoverishment. However, research is beginning to provide planners with a better basis for policy-making. Data from the Luxembourg Income Study, which afford comparable cross-sectional analyses of various industrialized countries, have shown that household income rises with age of the head of the household until retirement, and then declines. On average, older people who share living arrangements with a spouse and/or others have lower poverty rates than those living alone. Older women are poorer than elderly people in general, and older women living alone are the poorest of elderly people. A nine-nation analysis (T.M. Smeeding and P. Saunders, unpublished data, 1998) concluded that there is more diversity among elderly people in terms of poverty and income distribution than in terms of income sources. Elderly people at low- and middle-income levels rely heavily on social security, while the more well-to-do elderly in all nations benefit proportionally more from earnings, property income, and occupational pensions.

Sex and marital status

Although more male than female babies are born each year, male mortality rates typically are higher than female rates at all ages. Thus as a cohort ages, the proportion of females increases, usually producing a greater proportion of women by the age of 30 or 35 years. The same is true as a population ages, and this trend has become especially pronounced in developed countries. The large differences between female and male life expectancy, and the lingering effects of the Second World War, have resulted in elderly female-to-male ratios that remain as high as 2 to 1 in Russia and other parts of the former Soviet Union. Among the old old (aged 80 years and over), the proportion of females often exceeds 70 per cent (e.g. in Belgium, Germany, and the Ukraine) and has reached 80 per cent in Russia. Hence it can be said that the social, economic, and health problems of elderly people are in large part the problems of elderly women.

The marital status of older people is a central feature of family structure that is closely related to living arrangements, support systems, survival, and economic and psychological wellbeing (Lillard and Waite 1995). Intact husband and wife families provide a continuity of the marital bond established throughout the lifecourse, and thus constitute a multiple support system for spouses in terms of emotional, financial, and social exchanges. Marital status plays a large part in determining the living arrangements of older people, and directly influences the provision of care in coping with ill health and functional disability resulting from chronic disease.

Patterns of marital status are very different among elderly men and women. A compilation of data from the 1990s for 27 industrialized countries (United States Bureau of the Census 1998) shows that the large majority of men aged 65 and over are married, whereas on average about half of all elderly women are widowed. The share of widowers among elderly people in the 27 countries ranged from 14 to 19 per cent, while the comparable share for women ranged from 41 to 59 per cent. Even higher widowhood figures for elderly women are seen in the latest (1989) census data from many countries of the former Soviet Union (e.g. 65 per cent in Belarus and the Ukraine, and 66 per cent in Russia). Figure 7 illustrates the standard pattern for developed countries in which the sex difference in widow/widowerhood increases with age. Among women in the oldest age categories (80 years and over), typically three-quarters or more are widows. Several factors contribute to this sex difference: men marry women younger than themselves, women outlive men on average, and widows are less likely than widowers to remarry. Widowhood frequently results in major declines in the financial status of older women, and is often accompanied by changes in residence and living arrangements.

Changes in marital status over time have occurred slowly, but trends for developed countries indicate that increasing proportions of older people are married, declining proportions are widowed or never married, and the percentage of older people who are divorced or separated is small but steadily rising (Myers 1991). As younger cohorts with higher divorce rates reach old age, the percentage of ever-divorced will increase, along with potential complications implied by blended families, including the complex relationships and responsibilities operating between step-parents and stepchildren. Moreover, there are strong trends emerging amongst younger cohorts towards later ages at first marriage, increased cohabitation, and larger numbers who will never marry. Together with low levels of child

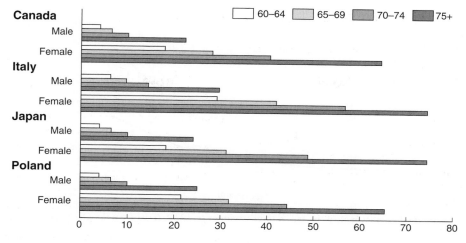

Fig. 7 Percentage widowed at older ages (c. 1990).

bearing, these new trends, if they persist, imply that there will be generations reaching older age in the next century without enduring marital ties and with fewer children to provide supportive services when needed. In countries where fertility rates have been low for many decades, such developments could be felt within the next 10 to 15 years.

Living arrangements

Living arrangements and residential quality are important aspects of the lives of older people, and are determined by a host of factors such as marital, financial, and health status, family size and structure, and cultural traditions including kinship patterns, the value placed upon living independently, availability of social services and social support, and the physical features of housing stock and local communities. In turn, living arrangements affect life satisfaction, health, and, most importantly for those living in the community, the chances of institutionalization.

There are several intersections between living arrangements of older people and general social and economic policies. At the social level, these include broad policies that support the family as well as specific programmes that provide supportive services which permit older people who cannot live independently without personal assistance to remain in the community. Several economic policy issues also can affect living arrangements: increases in benefits that allow older people who wish to live independently of their children to do so, programmes that more easily allow the conversion of housing wealth into income, programmes that encourage the building of elder-friendly housing, and the discouragement of institutionalization through reimbursement disincentives. Data from New Zealand illustrate the interplay of an ageing population and changing social structure. A major change in New Zealand's household structure in recent years has been the growth of one-person households, which accounted for 21 per cent of all households in the 1991 census (up from 12 per cent in 1971). More than half (54 per cent) of the nation's one-person households in 1991 contained a person aged 60 years or older, meaning that 11.3 per cent of all households in New Zealand consisted of an older individual living alone.

Table 4 Percentage of household population aged 65 years and over living alone in 15 developed countries (c. 1991)

Country	Both sexes	Male	Female
Europe			
Czech Republic	36.8	19.0	47.5
Denmark	40.2	23.3	52.0
Finland	36.9	19.5	46.5
France	30.3	15.3	40.2
Greece	16.6	8.7	22.8
Ireland	23.9	18.9	27.7
Norway	34.9	21.3	44.7
Portugal	17.9	9.4	23.9
Romania	23.7	12.4	31.7
Sweden	39.3	25.1	49.9
Other			
Australia	22.6	13.7	29.3
Canada	25.5	14.1	33.7
Japan	11.0	5.2	14.8
New Zealand	29.5	17.8	38.0
United States	28.0	15.1	36.8

Data from United Nations (1997), United States Bureau of the Census (1998), and country sources.

Over the last several decades, most developed countries have experienced large increases in the numbers and proportions of elderly people living alone. In Canada, for instance, the number of elderly women living alone jumped from about 325 000 in 1976 to 620 000 in 1991. Generally, between a fifth and a third of those aged 65 years or older now live alone, with Japan having a very low proportion (11 per cent) and the highest proportions observed in Scandinavian nations and the Czech Republic (Table 4). Because of the longevity and marital status differences described earlier, there are many more older women than men residing singly; the ratio in France exceeds 4 to 1. Living alone increases with advancing age, but around the age of 80 or 85 years, the trend levels off or reverses, especially for women.

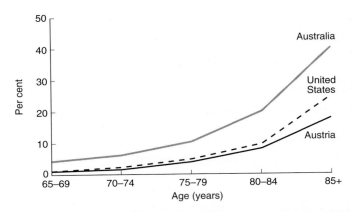

Fig. 8 Proportion of elderly people residing in institutions, by age, in three countries (c. 1990). (Data from the OECD (1996).)

Presumably this occurs as a result of health and/or economic factors that require institutional caretaking, communal living, or sharing of housing costs.

Institutionalization

Rising numbers of elderly individuals living alone have been accompanied by similar increases in the numbers of older people living in institutions. Projections of rapid future growth of this institutionalized population have occasioned intense policy debates about the medical, social, economic, and ethical dimensions of institutionalization. The debates have centred around issues such as the optimal balance between institutional and non-institutional care, the extent to which the family rather than the government should take responsibility for long-term care, and who should pay.

Cross-national comparisons of institutionalized populations are problematic owing to the absence of internationally consistent data, and differences between countries should be considered as indicative of orders of magnitude rather than as precise measurements of variance. In this chapter, institutional living refers to long-term care in either a medically oriented residential facility (e.g. a nursing home) or a non-medical facility (e.g. a home for the aged). The most recent comparative data on institutional care in developed countries show that the proportions of institutionalized people aged 65 and over vary widely, ranging from about 2 per cent in Portugal to more than 10 per cent in Australia. There also has been considerable variation in the relative use of medical and non-medical facilities: Japan, Canada, Australia, and the United States have made greater use of medical care, while an emphasis on non-medical facilities has been more pronounced in Sweden, Switzerland, and Belgium (Doty 1992).

Regardless of national setting, levels of institutionalization are strongly associated with increasing age (Fig. 8). In much of the industrialized world, fewer than 2 per cent of the young old (aged 65 to 69) are in institutions. This level increases fairly slowly until the age of 80, but many nations experience a sharp increase in institutionalization rates among octogenarians. More than half of all Norwegians aged 85 years and over reside in institutions, as do one-third or more of this age group in Australia and New Zealand. Levels are higher for women than for men, consistent with the fact that women in institutions are far more likely than men to be widowed.

Numbers of institutionalized older people are almost certain to increase simply as a correlate of demographic ageing and the fact that proportionally greater numbers of people are living to the oldest ages. Of keen interest to policy-makers and service providers is whether or not the rate of institutionalization will also increase. Many developed countries have tried to dampen rate increases by pursuing policies that allow elderly people to remain in their homes and communities for as long as possible. Such policies may be bearing fruit; an eight-nation study of institutionalization rates among elderly people comparing the 1990s with the 1980s (OECD 1996) showed a decline or essentially no change in seven countries. The only significant increase appeared in the United Kingdom where government policy had made a large subvention from public funds available to the profit-making nursing home industry. The growing use of home help services to support frail elderly people in their own homes is likely to have a corresponding impact on future institutional use. Home help programmes are most widespread in Scandinavian nations; between 14 and 24 per cent of all elderly people receive some home help care in Denmark, Norway, and Finland.

Health expenditure

In 1996, the average total (all ages) of public and private expenditure on health for the 29 Organization for Economic Co-operation and Development (OECD) countries was 8.2 per cent of gross domestic product. In 1960, for a smaller set of 23 countries, average expenditure had been only 3.8 per cent. In spite of this overall increase, the average real growth rate of health expenditures has progressively slowed over the last two decades. Increases in the total size of economies, coupled with attempts to control health costs, have led to stable and even falling fractions of gross domestic product being allocated to health expenditures. There is a strong relationship between national wealth and health expenditures, with wealthier countries spending more per capita on health. In 1996, the United States remained an outlier with 14 per cent of gross domestic product spent on health, with Germany, Switzerland, and Canada falling within the 9 to 10 per cent range, and Turkey, Mexico, South Korea, and Poland spending about 4 to 5 per cent. In 1996, the United States spent about $3898 per capita (in purchasing power parity US dollars) compared with $1317 in the United Kingdom and $232 in Turkey.

A good deal of the difference in expenditure results from differences in private expenditure; in the United States, for example, only 6.3 per cent of gross domestic product went on public expenditure, less than in almost a third of the OECD countries.

Within the older population in the United States, total per capita expenditures increase rapidly with age (Waldo *et al.* 1989). Hospital and nursing home costs account for much of the increase, though acute care costs tend to become lower at extreme ages, perhaps because the increasing numbers and severity of comorbid conditions such as diabetes make intensive treatment more difficult. As an illustration of this relationship, spending by Medicare in America (which does not pay for most nursing home costs) for the last year of life is almost double for those aged 65 to 69 years compared with those aged 90 years and over (Lubitz and Riley 1993).

The dynamic forces that underlie changes in health-care expenditures are only partially understood, and as a result, long-range projections of future health expenditure patterns are controversial. However, population ageing by itself does account for the major share of increased expenditure in industrialized nations. In the 1960s and 1970s, the increase in the coverage of the population eligible for public medical programmes played a significant role, coupled with a growth in real benefits within public schemes. More recently, the rapid and extensive dissemination of new and expensive technologies such as angioplasty, coronary bypass procedures, and hip replacements, has played a major role in the increase in health-care expenditure, at least in the United States. In the space of only 8 years, 1987 to 1995, hip replacements among women in the United States rose from 143 per 100 000 to 1444 per 100 000 (Fuchs 1998). As more efficacious pharmaceuticals and procedures are developed through biomedical research, and as electronic communication becomes more global, it is possible that aspects of American expenditure patterns will become the norm in many societies.

In the first edition of this book, we noted that recent years had witnessed debate about the efficacy of health systems in ageing nations, and that the American system was generally viewed as more expensive and less effective than most European health systems. We questioned whether the standard comparative indicator, life expectancy at birth, was the most appropriate comparative outcome indicator. The finding that, at the age of 80, the American white population had a higher expectation of life than countries such as Japan, Sweden, and Germany, reinforced the need for improved indicators, including ones that measured age-specific health and functional status and expectancy (Manton and Vaupel 1995). The absence of appropriate data from outside the United States has prevented such informed comparisons, and we do not yet know whether the American advantage in life expectancy at age 80 results from the generosity and efficacy of the American Medicare system that does not require age rationing, the American advantage in education levels for older cohort that results in improved health and longevity, or other factors. Despite some unpublished and preliminary attempts, it is debatable whether available data are even adequate to know whether there is any trend in disability at older ages, comparable with the trend of declining disability discovered by Manton *et al.* (1997*a*). Findings from a binational study suggest, for example, that the higher use of surgical procedures for treating coronary artery disease in the United States compared with Canada, which tends to make greater use of medical management, may confer a quality-of-life advantage rather than any improvement in survival. The OECD, sponsored by funding from the National Institute on Aging, is only just embarking on a pilot study to try to find out how a small set of diseases are treated across the older populations of participating countries, at what cost, and with what impact.

Labour force participation, retirement, and pensions

Policy-makers are confronted with several economic questions that arise in ageing societies with changing balances of numbers in different age groups. What kinds of social support will a growing elderly population require, and how much will they cost? Will there be enough younger workers to provide an adequate tax base for this support? Will younger age groups be disadvantaged by an increasing emphasis on the needs of elderly people? How large a proportion of non-workers can a working population support? These questions have come to the fore partly as a result of changes in the economic behaviour of societies.

Declines in retirement age, both statutory and actual, have been observed in many developed countries since 1960 (OECD 1998). The conjunction of trends such as weak economic growth, rising youth unemployment, and the entry of large numbers of women into the labour force, has spurred legislatures and businesses into lowering retirement ages and instituting various early retirement schemes. Concomitantly, rates of participation in the labour force at older ages have dropped, not only in response to these changes, but also because many of today's elderly people are able to afford to stop working. As life expectancy lengthens, individuals spend an increasingly smaller portion of their lives in remunerative work.

Declines in economic activity are especially notable among older men, who greatly outnumber older women in national labour forces. Nearly universal declines have been recorded among men aged 55 and over since the late 1960s, although the decline stopped in some nations (e.g. Australia, Japan, and the United States) in the mid-1980s and may have reversed in the early 1990s. However, in only a few developed nations (e.g. Japan and Portugal) are 20 per cent or more of men aged 65 and over considered to be economically active; in several large industrialized nations (France, Germany, Spain), the rate is 5 per cent or lower.

The female proportion of older workers has been rising in most developed countries since at least 1970. As proportionally greater numbers of younger women enter the labour force, increases in female labour-force participation rates at younger ages 'carry over' into older ages, and to some extent offset declining male participation rates at older ages. As male rates have declined, the labour-force participation rates of older women often have held steady and in some nations increased.

Although the total agricultural labour force has shrunk rapidly in industrialized countries, elderly people who were economically active during the 1980s were more likely to be in agricultural than in other occupations. By the early 1990s, however, service jobs had attained primacy among both younger and older workers, at least at the aggregate level in European Union nations. Two-thirds of economically active older (over 60 years of age) women were engaged in the service sector, compared with just over half of older men. The future occupational structure of older workers is likely to continue to change markedly as more educated and affluent population cohorts reach older age.

Retirement brings economic vulnerability as income from earnings declines and the ability to replace assets is often reduced. Industrialized societies have responded to the increased vulnerability of their elderly citizens with a variety of social insurance programmes and features. The extent to which pensions are financed by contributions from employees, employers, and general tax revenues is different in each nation. However, as demographic ageing has intensified, the cost of social insurance programmes everywhere has risen; pension expenditure, on average, now exceeds 9 per cent of gross domestic product in OECD nations, and represented about 8 per cent of gross domestic product in Eastern Europe in the early 1990s. Rising pension outlay is the result of four major trends in most countries: (a) population ageing and an increasing number of long-lived pension recipients; (b) expanded coverage of population groups once excluded from pension programmes (such as women and the self-employed); (c) legislated increases in the real level of payment per beneficiary; (d) the proliferation of early retirement schemes in both the public and private sectors.

Most industrial nations have financed their pensions on a pay-as-you-go basis. These schemes were popular after the Second World War because of their chain-letter distribution effects, with the earlier beneficiaries receiving far more in benefits than they had paid in contributions. As the schemes reached maturity, they were carried forward with expanded benefits by the strong economic growth of the 1950s and 1960s, combined with increasing numbers of workers. It has been argued that slowing economic growth rates, declining proportions of workers, and increasing proportions of retired people will result in workers paying into actuarially unfavourable plans (World Bank 1994), and that this will strain the implicit contract between generations. Countries throughout the world, including industrialized nations with strong traditions of social insurance, are now exploring a variety of privatization schemes and public pension restructuring which at least partially transfer old-age security provision into the realm of individual decision-making.

A major cross-national study of Canada, France, Germany, Italy, Japan, The Netherlands, Spain, Sweden, the United Kingdom, and the United States (Gruber and Wise 1998) has shown that the structure of public pensions is very powerfully associated with departure from the labour force at older ages. Countries such as Belgium, Italy, The Netherlands, and France that provide generous retirement benefits at relatively early ages exhibit very low levels of labour-force participation after the benefits become available. In essence, countries that 'tax' work so that the added benefit in salary and expected pension income is low for working another year encourage workers to leave far earlier than countries with low rates of 'taxation', such as Japan or, to a somewhat lesser extent, the United States and Sweden. The development of major new longitudinal surveys of health and retirement is permitting, for the first time, studies of the dynamics of interrelated health, family, work, and economic factors that drive the retirement process. Studies such as the Health and Retirement Study (Juster and Suzman 1995) are now being emulated across Europe, opening up new avenues for understanding the determinants and consequences of retirement, and modelling the consequences of, for example, raising the age of early entitlement to public social security benefits.

Conclusion

Concerns have been raised by the perception that, over the last few decades, older citizens have fared better than children in some countries (Richman and Stagner 1986). This debate has occasioned a growing body of research into the nature of intergenerational exchanges and the economic impact of population ageing and changing support ratios. Several tentative conclusions have emerged. Firstly, the future growth rate of the economy overshadows the impact of expected population ageing. Secondly, generations are interdependent, with future older cohorts dependent upon the productivity of the future labour force, which is in turn dependent upon the extent to which older generations are willing to invest in the educational capital of current cohorts of the young. Thirdly, there are modifiable elements; for example, the discovery of the decline in the prevalence of old age disability in the United States provides convincing ground for optimism. The effects of research on the health status and long-term care expenses of future generations of the very old are potentially enormous (Schneider and Guralnik 1990; Suzman et al. 1992; Manton et al. 1997b, 1998). There are also a series of policy options available to slow population ageing and reduce its fiscal impact (Martin 1991). These include pronatalist policies, encouraging immigration, reforming public pensions to ensure fiscal viability, and decreasing early retirement and increasing working life expectancy at older ages. The new findings on the determinants of labour-force participation presented above suggest that policy changes could have a substantial effect on retirement patterns. Finally, although many factors can influence the impact of population ageing in developed nations, there is an irreducible demographic imperative that will result in extensive changes to these societies.

References

Bean, F.D., Myers, G.C., Angel, J.L., and Galle, O.R. (1994). Geographic concentration, migration, and population redistribution among the elderly. In *Demography of aging* (ed. L.G. Martin and S.H. Preston), pp. 319–55. National Academy Press, Washington, DC.

Bone, M.R., Bebbington, A.C., Jagger, C., Morgan, K., and Nicolaas, G. (1995). *Health expectancy and its uses.* Her Majesty's Stationery Office, London.

Carey, J.R. (1997). What demographers can learn from fruit fly actuarial models and biology. *Demography*, 34, 17–30.

Caselli, G., Vallin, J., Vaupel, J.W., and Yashin, A.I. (1987). Age-specific mortality trends in France and Italy since 1900: period and cohort effects. *European Journal of Population*, 3, 33–60.

Crimmins, E., Saito, Y., and Hayward, M.D. (1993). Sullivan and multistate methods of estimating active life expectancy: two methods, two answers. In *Calculation of health expectancies: harmonization, consensus achieved and future perspectives* (ed. J.M. Robine, C.D. Mathers, M.R. Bone, and I. Romieu), pp. 155–60. John Libbey Eurotext, Montrouge.

Day, J.C. (1996). *Population projections of the United States by age, sex, race, and Hispanic origin: 1995 to 2050*, United States Bureau of the Census, Current Population Reports P25-1130. Government Printing Office, Washington, DC.

Dinh, Q.C. (1995). *Projection de la population totale pour la France métropolitaine: Base RP90, Horizons 1990–2050*. Démographie Société No. 44, INSEE, Paris.

Doty, P.J. (1992). The oldest old and the use of institutional long-term care from an international perspective. In *The oldest old* (ed. R.M. Suzman,

D.P. Willis, and K.G. Manton), pp. 251–67. Oxford University Press, New York.

Fogel, R.W. and Costa, D.L. (1997). A theory of technophysio-evolution, with some implications for forecasting population, health care costs, and pension costs. *Demography*, **34**, 49–66.

Fries, J.F. (1980). Aging, natural death, and the compression of morbidity. *New England Journal of Medicine*, **303**, 130–5.

Fuchs, V.R. (1998). *The economics of aging*. Working Paper 6642, National Bureau of Economic Research, Cambridge, MA.

Gruber, J. and Wise, D. (1998). Social security and retirement: an international comparison. *American Economic Review*, **88**, 58–163.

Gruenberg, E.M. (1977). The failures of success. *Milbank Quarterly*, **55**, 3–24.

Guralnik, J.M., Yanagishita, M., and Schneider, E.L. (1988). Projecting the older population of the United States: lessons from the past and prospects for the future. *Milbank Quarterly*, **66**, 283–308.

Juster, F.T. and Suzman, R.M. (1995). An overview of the health and retirement study. *Journal of Human Resources*, **30**, S7–56.

Kannisto, V. (1996). *The advancing frontier of survival. Odense monographs on population aging*, Vol. 2. Odense University, Denmark.

Katz, S., Branch, L.G., Branson, M.H., Papsidero, J.A., Beck, J.C., and Greer, D.S. (1983). Active life expectancy. *New England Journal of Medicine*, **309**, 1218–24.

Kramer, M. (1980). The rising pandemic of mental disorders and associated chronic diseases and disabilities. *Acta Psychiatrica Scandinavica*, **62** (Supplement 285), 282–97.

Land, K.C., Guralnik, J.M., and Blazer, D.G. (1994). Estimating increment-decrement life tables with multiple covariates from panel data: the case of active life expectancy. *Demography*, **31**, 297–319.

Lillard, L.A. and Waite, L.J. (1995). 'Til death do us part': marital disruption and mortality. *American Journal of Sociology*, **100**, 1131–56.

Lubitz, J.D. and Riley, G.F. (1993). Trends in Medicare payments in the last year of life. *New England Journal of Medicine*, **328**, 1092–6.

Manton, K.G. (1982). Changing concepts of morbidity and mortality in the elderly population. *Milbank Quarterly*, **60**, 183–244.

Manton, K.G. and Stallard, E. (1996). Longevity in the United States: age and sex-specific evidence on life span limits from mortality patterns 1960–1990. *Journal of Gerontology*, **51A**, B362–75.

Manton, K.G. and Vaupel, J.W. (1995). Survival after the age of 80 in the United States, Sweden, France, England, and Japan. *New England Journal of Medicine*, **333**, 1232–5.

Manton, K.G., Singer, B.H., and Suzman, R.M. (1993). The scientific and policy needs for improved health forecasting models for elderly populations. In *Forecasting the health of elderly populations* (ed. K.G. Manton, B.H. Singer, and R.M. Suzman), pp. 3–35. Springer-Verlag, New York.

Manton, K.G., Corder, L.S., and Stallard, E. (1997a). Chronic disability trends in the United States elderly population 1982 to 1994. *Proceedings of the National Academy of Sciences of the United States of America*, **94**, 2593–8.

Manton, K.G., Corder, L.S., and Stallard, E. (1997b). Monitoring changes in the health of the United States elderly population: correlates with biomedical research and clinical innovations. *FASEB Journal*, **11**, 923–30.

Manton, K.G., Corder, L.S., and Stallard, E. (1998). Economic effects of reducing disability. Presented at the American Economic Association Annual Meeting, 3–5 January 1998, Chicago, IL.

Martin, L.G. (1991). Population aging policies in East Asia and the United States. *Science*, **251**, 527–31.

Mathers, C. and Robine, J.M. (1997). How good is Sullivan's method for monitoring changes in population health expectancies? *Journal of Epidemiology and Community Health*, **51**, 80–6.

Moore, T.J. (1993). *Lifespan*. Simon and Schuster, New York.

Myers, G.C. (1990). Demography of aging. In *Handbook of aging and the social sciences* (ed. R.H. Binstock and L.K. George), pp. 19–44. Academic Press, New York.

Myers, G.C. (1991). Demographic aging and family support for older persons. In *Family support for the elderly. The international experience* (ed. H. Kendig, A. Hashimoto, and L.C. Coppard), pp. 31–68. Oxford University Press.

OECD (Organization for Economic Co-operation and Development) (1996). *Caring for frail elderly people. Policies in evolution*, Vol. 19. Social Policy Studies, OECD, Paris.

OECD (Organization for Economic Co-operation and Development) (1998). *Maintaining prosperity in an ageing society*. OECD, Paris.

Richman, H. and Stagner, M. (1986). Children in an aging society: treasured resource or forgotten minority? *Daedalus*, **115**, 171–89.

Robine, J.M. and Ritchie, K. (1991). Healthy life expectancy: evaluation of global indicator of change in population health. *British Medical Journal*, **302**, 457–60.

Rogers, A., Rogers, R.G., and Branch, L.G. (1989). A multistate analysis of active life expectancy. *Public Health Reports*, **104**, 222–5.

Schneider, E.L. and Guralnik, J.M. (1990). The aging of America: impact on health care costs. *Journal of the American Medical Association*, **263**, 2335–40.

Siampos, G. (1990). Trends and future prospects of the female overlife by regions in Europe. *Statistical Journal of the United Nations Economic Commission for Europe*, **7**, 13–25.

Strehler, B.L. (1975). Implications of aging research for society. Theoretical concepts of developmental and age changes. *Federation Proceedings*, **34**, 5–8.

Sullivan, D.F. (1971). A single index of mortality and morbidity. *HSMHA Health Report*, **86**, 347–54.

Suzman, R.M., Harris, T., Hadley, E., and Weindruch, R. (1992). The robust oldest old: optimistic perspectives for increasing healthy life expectancy. In *The oldest old* (ed. R.M. Suzman, D.P. Willis, and K.G. Manton), pp. 341–58. Oxford University Press, New York.

Thomlinson, R. (1976). *Population dynamics. Causes and consequences of world demographic change*. Random House, New York.

UNDIESA (United Nations Department of International Economic and Social Affairs) (1988). Sex differentials in survivorship in the developing world: levels, regional patterns and demographic determinants. *Population Bulletin of the United Nations*, **25**, 51–64.

United Nations (1997). *Demographic yearbook 1995*. United Nations, New York.

United States Bureau of the Census (1998). *International Data Base*. International Programs Center, US Bureau of the Census, Washington, DC.

Vaupel, J.W. (1998). Demographic analysis of ageing and longevity. *American Economic Review*, **88**, 242–7.

Waldo, D.R., Sonnefeld, S.T., McCusick, D.R., and Arnett, R.H., III (1989). Health expenditures by age group, 1977 and 1987. *Health Care Financing Review*, **10**, 116–20.

Wenger G.C. (1998). *Aging in rural Wales*. Background document for the program committee meeting for the Rural Aging 2000 International Conference, Morgantown, WV, June 1998.

World Bank (1994). *Averting the old age crisis*. Oxford University Press, New York.

1.2 Social aspects of ageing

Daniel O. Clark

Naturally occurring variability in our social and physical environments has proved ageing to be a highly variable process. Individuals age in many different ways as a result of these complex environments and biology. Identifying variability and determining mutable risk factors raises the potential for positive intervention into the process of ageing. The social environment is particularly influential in the process of ageing, and perhaps most influential in the domain of health-related quality of life (**HRQL**).

The primary objective of this chapter is to present frameworks that can organize discussions of the social distribution of HRQL, and to consider a framework for positive intervention. The discussion of social distribution is limited to age cohort, sex, ethnic, and socio-economic strata, but the frameworks presented offer a structure for investigating social distribution along any strata of interest. Two frameworks have been used to organize this chapter. The first framework provides guidance in the consideration of social strata and the second framework organizes the discussion of HRQL. The frameworks are first presented, and then applied to the discussion of age cohort, sex, and socio-economic and ethnic/racial strata. Finally, a self-care framework is presented as one path to positive intervention.

Social stratification of the life-course

Social experiences over the life-course are highly varied, but common experiences occur as a result of shared social and physical situations. People of the same birth cohort or nationality, for example, share many of the same experiences as they age. Similarly, women have experiences that they hold in common, as do men. This type of classification of experiences can be referred to as social stratification of the life-course. An example of the utility of the stratification perspective can be provided through age stratification, which has received considerable attention of late (Riley 1987). Under the age-stratification perspective, society is stratified by age cohort. Members of a particular cohort have shared historical experiences. Individuals of any given cohort experience historical events at approximately the same stage of the life-course, and that intersection of history and lifestage has considerable implications for the interpretation and impact of events across cohorts. Major sociopolitical events, such as the Great Depression and the Second World War, have profound impacts on all cohorts, but the experience, interpretation, and impact differs with each cohort's lifestage (Elder *et al.* 1984; Wadsworth 1997).

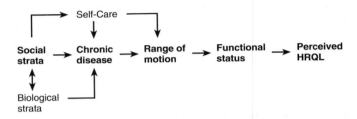

Fig. 1 Social stratification, self-care, and HRQL.

Neither strata, nor classes within strata, are passive. Demographic studies indicate how characteristics of cohorts can lead to profound social change. Large cohorts, such as the 'baby-boomers' born in the years following Second World War, have stretched the capacity of institutions. Early on these cohorts stretched educational facilities and they will soon challenge the capacity of medical facilities. The American civil rights movement is an excellent example of the social and political impact of one minority ethnic class.

To summarize the social stratification of the life-course perspective, classes within strata share events and transitions, and the interpretation and impact of those events and transitions are affected by the stage of the life-course. Importantly, classes within strata are not passive and are themselves often a force in historical events and transitions. Age cohort, sex, and socio-economic and minority status represent common and important characteristics on which strata can be based. These strata are the focus of this chapter.

Health-related quality of life

The HRQL framework is drawn from the Institute of Medicine's report (Institute of Medicine 1990), but can be traced back to Nagi's original work (Nagi 1965). A number of authors have recently expanded on these original writings (Johnson and Wolinsky 1993; Verbrugge and Jette 1994; Wilson and Cleary 1995). Figure 1 contains the HRQL model in the form it will be used here. The model has been expanded from its original form to include social strata, biological strata, and a self-care domain. The self-care domain consists of behaviours practised by individuals that can reduce the likelihood of developing chronic disease, impairment, or disability. Self-care behaviours are an important avenue to interventions for the prevention of declines in HRQL. The concept of self-care will be considered more fully following a review of the social distribution of HRQL. Range of motion includes lower and upper body movements, and functional status includes both traditional activities of daily life (**ADL**) and instrumental activities of daily life (**IADL**). Although not empirically reviewed in this chapter, overall health evaluations or perceived HRQL can be thought of as ultimate outcomes. It is recognized that individuals do not follow the steps of Fig. 1 uniformly (Manton *et al.* 1993; Clark *et al.* 1997*b*), but theoretically the path represents a natural history of HRQL (Wilson and Cleary 1995).

It is worth noting that some social strata also represent biological strata. Sex and age cohort, for example, have both biological and social implications. In fact, it is often the case that social strata have emanated from biological strata. Although we focus here primarily on the central portions of the model (shown in bold type), biological strata are vital to understanding variability in HRQL, particularly in regard to chronic disease and range of motion. The interplay between biological and social strata is complex, and its systematic integration remains a challenge to research on health and ageing.

Measurement issues

A presentation of social aspects of HRQL requires considerable data. The data available to assess the model presented in Fig. 1 are limited in many ways. A majority of the data are based on self-report. This has not emerged as an influential limitation in regard to range motion or functional status (Guralnik *et al.* 1993; Seeman *et al.* 1994), but is quite important in estimates of chronic disease. Survey studies have asked respondents about their disease status in a number of ways, but certain diseases continue to be under-reported, while others may be over-reported. Non-insulin-dependent diabetes mellitus may be the most suspect disease, with up to half of American adults being unaware that they have this condition (Kenny *et al.* 1995). Self-report data are often all that are available, and this can be quite problematic when comparing social strata that may have very different rates of access to health information and care. One partial solution is also to investigate cause of death, although this approach has limitations owing to incomplete and inaccurate death certificates (Manton and Stallard 1984). We will rely on both cause of death and self-report data here.

Reliance on self-report data has also meant that comorbidity and impairment data are lacking. Impairments follow chronic disease in the model of HRQL, but this is not shown in Fig. 1. However, with the exception of self-reported pain (a symptom of impairment) and sensory deficits, epidemiological data on impairment are rarely available. This is particularly true for large-sample panel studies, which have proved critical to estimating prevalence and transition probabilities in HRQL. Similarly, comorbidity plays a critical role in the natural history of HRQL but has been difficult to analyse through self-report epidemiological data (Wallace and Lemke 1991; Boult *et al.* 1994).

Finally, much of the most advanced research into health, social strata, and the life-course has come out of Western European nations, particularly the United Kingdom (Townsend and Davidson 1982; Marmot *et al.* 1991; Davey-Smith and Morris 1994; Wadsworth 1997). However, much of the data on HRQL as a framework has come out of large-scale epidemiological studies in the United States. Thus most of the empirical observations presented here are based on the American population, and the data are mostly based on self-report.

Social strata and health-related quality of life

Although somewhat crude, the social strata discussed in this chapter are presented in perceived order of importance to HRQL. Age cohort may be the most influential. Types and prevalences of disease vary dramatically across age cohorts, as does the technology available for the prevention and treatment of disease. Note that the social dimension of interest here is age cohorts rather than ageing. Chronic disease and range of motion, as well as mortality, vary persistently between the sexes. Socio-economic status is almost always a factor in each of the domains of HRQL, whether in the form of income, education, or occupational class. Minority ethnic and racial status, particularly in the United States, have been important strata, but the impact of minority status seems related most to the adverse exposures and stresses associated with socio-economic status and will be discussed within that context.

Age cohort

Age cohorts are exposed to and create very different environments. The interplay between those environments and stage of the life-course has tremendous implications for HRQL. Although far from numerous, observational studies covering many stages of the life-course have been reported. In general, these studies indicate the importance of a life-course perspective in considering the causes and course of HRQL. Studies indicate, for example, that nutritional deficits during fetal development and early childhood can lead to underdevelopment of critical organs placing individuals at risk for early onset of chronic disease and impairment (Hales *et al.* 1991; Barker *et al.* 1992; Mann *et al.* 1992). In fact, cohort variability in exposures has created tremendous variability in the type and rates of disease. The epidemiological transition from infectious to chronic disease is demonstrated in Table 1 and is brought on largely through changes in exposure to infectious agents combined with improvements in host resistance (McKinlay and McKinlay 1990).

In recent decades, the top five causes of death among elderly people have been cardiovascular disease, cancer, cerebrovascular disease, pneumonia/influenza, and chronic obstructive pulmonary disease. Although these are the leading causes of death, the most costly diseases are those that produce impairment, but rarely lead to death. On self-report, arthritis is the most prevalent chronic condition, and one that causes substantial impairment and disability (Verbrugge and Patrick 1995). High blood pressure, visual impairment, and diabetes are other leading causes of disability, together with cardiovascular disease, chronic obstructive pulmonary disease, and cerebrovascular disease.

Improved management of these conditions can lead to improvements in the prevalence of range of motion and disability over relatively short periods of time. Range of motion limitations, particularly mobility limitations, are the primary cause of ADL and IADL disability (Guralnik *et al.* 1993; Johnson and Wolinsky 1993), but the author is not aware of data that can address age cohort differences in range of motion limitation. As shown in the HRQL model, chronic disease (and lack of self-care) is the primary cause of

Table 1 Top ten causes of death in the United States in 1900 and 1995

Cause of death	1900: % of all deaths	1990: % of all deaths	1900: rate (per 100 000)	1995: rate (per 100 000)
All causes	100.00	100.00	1719	880
Diseases of the heart	11.8	31.9	202	281
Malignant neoplasms	3.7	23.3	64	205
Cerebrovascular disease	6.2	6.8	107	60
Chronic obstructive pulmonary disease	—	4.5	—	39
Accidents	4.2	4.1	72	36
Pneumonia and influenza	11.8	3.6	202	32
Diabetes mellitus	—	2.6	—	23
HIV	—	1.9	—	16
Suicide	—	1.4	—	12
Chronic liver disease	—	1.1	—	10
Tuberculosis	11.3	—	194	—
Diarrhoea	8.3	—	143	—
Senility	6.9	—	118	—
Nephritis	5.2	—	89	—
Diphtheria	2.3	—	40	—

Dash indicates not a top ten cause of death in that year.
Data from National Center for Health Statistics (1986); National Center for Health Statistics (1997).

range of motion limitation. Reductions in the prevalence and impact of chronic disease will lead to reductions in range of motion limitation. In fact, the prevalence of certain chronic conditions, primarily cardio-vascular, have declined in the past decade. Figure 2 shows the prevalence of selected chronic diseases in 1982, 1984, 1989, and 1994 based on self-report data obtained from the National Long-Term

Care Surveys (Manton *et al.* 1993). Heart disease shows a clear decline over the period, while other diseases appear to have held relatively stable.

Recent data from the United States have also shown that rates of ADL and IADL disability have declined across cohorts. These rates have declined for each cohort aged 65 or over in 1982, 1984, or 1989 (Manton *et al.* 1993). This appears to have occurred through reductions in the prevalence of cardiovascular disease (Manton *et al.* 1995). Nonetheless, the rates of ADL and IADL disability remains between 15 and 20 per cent (Clark 1997).

Sex

With the exception of arthritis, chronic disease prevalence is not much higher in women than in men (Verbrugge and Patrick 1995), but older women may be more affected by chronic disease. Women are less likely to die of cardiovascular disease and cancer, but slightly more likely to die of cerebrovascular disease, than men. Based on self-report, the most prevalent chronic disease is arthritis followed by high blood pressure for both men and women. Heart disease is next for men and chronic obstructive pulmonary disease for women. The chronic diseases responsible for the most disability are arthritis and heart disease for both sexes, while high blood pressure is next most significant in women and chronic obstructive pulmonary disease in men.

Many studies have shown that women are more likely than men to have both ADL and IADL disability, which is one of the main

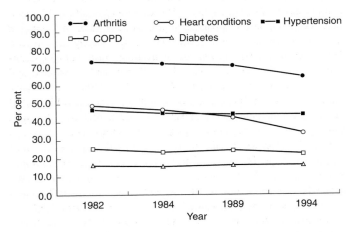

Fig. 2 Prevalence of arthritis, heart conditions, hypertension, diabetes, and chronic obstructive pulmonary disease within older populations in the United States (1982, 1984, 1989, and 1994).

Table 2 Odds ratios and 99 per cent confidence intervals (in parentheses) of onset of lower body range of motion limitation and of ADL disability at 2-year follow-up among American adults aged 70 years and over (baseline sociodemographic characteristics, health behaviours, and medical conditions controlled)

Variable	Onset of lower-body limitation	Onset of ADL disability
Female (relative to male)	1.53 (1.16, 2.02)	0.89 (0.57, 1.38)
Age 85 or over (relative to 70–84 years)	2.38 (1.45, 3.91)	2.37 (1.27, 4.42)
BMI 30 or over (relative to BMI of 19–24)	2.02 (1.33, 3.06)	1.82 (1.09, 3.03)
Lung disease	2.66 (1.66, 4.26)	1.27 (0.80, 2.02)
Arthritis	2.05 (1.44, 2.92)	1.29 (0.89, 1.87)
Depressed	1.38 (0.85, 2.23)	1.87 (1.19, 2.95)
Bothered by pain	1.55 (1.10, 2.17)	1.22 (0.84, 1.76)
N	2857	1871

Race, education, net worth, insurance status, smoking, alcohol intake, high blood pressure, diabetes, cancer, heart disease, stroke, and poor hearing and eyesight were controlled but not statistically significant (odds ratios not shown).
Data are from the 1993 and 1995 Assets and Health Dynamics of the Oldest-Old Study.
BMI, body mass index.

reasons why women are commonly thought to have poorer HRQL. However, recent studies suggest that women are not more likely to have traditional or instrumental activities of daily life disability once range of motion limitation is held constant (Clark *et al.* 1997*b*). In other words, women are more likely to have both ADL and IADL disability in large part because they are more likely to have range of motion limitations, particularly lower-body or mobility limitations. Table 2 shows the odds of onset of mobility limitation (i.e. difficulty walking and/or climbing stairs) among women in comparison with men. Among people with no mobility limitation at baseline, women were 1.5 times more likely than men to have developed a mobility limitation at 2-year follow-up. This odds ratio was obtained after adjusting for demographic characteristics, socio-economic status, chronic conditions, and pain. Among people with no ADL and IADL disability at baseline, women were not more likely to develop disability at 2-years follow-up than men. The largest predictor of disability at 2-years follow-up was mobility limitation at baseline. Thus reductions in sex differences in the rate of ADL and IADL disability would seem to depend on the identification of factors that place women at greater risk of mobility limitation. The differences have been hypothesized to be due to sex differences in the prevalence of certain chronic diseases (Manton 1988). This conclusion is supported by the HRQL model, but disease did not account for the female disadvantage in Table 2 nor has it in similar studies (Wolinsky *et al.* 1996).

Other studies have found socio-economic indicators to account for sex differences in health and functional outcomes (Verbrugge 1989; Maddox and Clark 1992; Ross and Bird 1994). However, each of these studies used different measures of function from that shown in Table 2, and in fact did not distinguish between range of motion and ADL and IADL disability. In fact, Wolinsky *et al.* (1996) used a very similar lower-body difficulty measure to that used here, and showed that females aged 70 and over were more likely than males to experience decline even with sociodemographic, economic, and disease indicators controlled. The considerable reliance on strength

in lower-body range of motion measures may explain differences in the findings of studies relying on lower-body versus ADL measures.

Socio-economic and minority status

It has long been recognized that socio-economic status is an important determinant of health and functional status (Antonovsky 1967). Lower position within a social hierarchy brings about poorer health, presumably through psychosocial stress, environmental conditions, and limited access to valued goods and resources (including information). Each of these may hold direct and indirect consequences for health status. In fact, given the relative nature of social position, elimination of disparities based on social position may be all but impossible (Marmot *et al.* 1991). Indeed, despite considerable recognition of socio-economic disparities in health within Western industrialized nations over the past one to two decades (Townsend and Davidson 1982; United States Department of Health and Human Services 1991), health disparities appear to have widened (Pappas *et al.* 1993; Davey-Smith and Morris 1994). In a widely cited report, Pappas *et al.* (1993) showed that educational disparities in standardized mortality ratios increased by 20 per cent in women and 100 per cent in men between 1960 and 1986. Other studies have shown similar trends (Feldman *et al.* 1989). Preston and Elo (1995) showed that socio-economic disparities in health had increased most among men and older women. Disparities amongst working women appeared to have reduced (Preston and Elo 1995). The increased disparities might be concluded to be due to limited access to health services among the socio-economically disadvantaged, but similar trends have been shown to have occurred in the United Kingdom where access is nearly universal (Davey-Smith and Morris 1994).

Owing in large part to poorer socio-economic status, ethnic and racial minority groups tend to have poorer HRQL than majority groups. This has been particularly apparent in the United States, which has traditionally focused on racial disparities in health rather than socio-economic disparities (Navarro 1990). Despite varying samples and definitions, large-scale surveys in the United States have generally shown older black people and Hispanics to be more likely to have chronic disease, mobility limitations, and disability than older whites (Clark *et al.* 1997*a*). Consistent with trends in socio-economic status and health, the disparity in ADL disability between white and black people of the United States increased over 25 per cent from 1982 to 1989 (Clark 1997). Again, following the HRQL model, much of the greater rate of ADL disability among black people is due to a considerably greater rate of range of motion limitation, which, in turn, is partly determined by chronic disease and impairment.

Whether socio-economic status accounts for greater rates of chronic disease and range of motion limitation within minority classes is not clear. Kingston and Smith (1997) showed that income and education levels accounted for ethnic minority disadvantages in a global functional status measure but chronic disease, particularly diabetes and hypertension, did not. Thus socio-economic status may lead to a greater HRQL impact of chronic disease among minority groups, but may have less significance for the development of chronic disease. However, these authors did not have measures of childhood socio-economic status which may be more important to chronic disease development than current socio-economic position. More complete life-course studies have shown that chronic disease in adulthood is very much related to childhood exposures and deprivations, particularly during the pre- and perinatal periods (Hales *et al.* 1991; Mann *et al.* 1992). In fact, among African-Americans, region of birth affects circulatory disease mortality more than region of death (Schneider *et al.* 1997). Assuming environmental and lifestyle factors vary by region, this is consistent with studies showing the importance of early life stages to chronic disease development in adulthood. Although still under debate, biological factors may also be implicated in the higher rates of hypertension and diabetes among African-Americans in the United States (Andersen *et al.* 1987; Carter *et al.* 1996).

Health-related quality of life and self-care

Approaches to the study of social disparities in health have generally taken two non-mutually exclusive paths. The first is a lifestyle path and concentrates on interventions to improve behaviours that affect the development of chronic disease and impairment. The other is a social structural path and concentrates on the social and economic conditions under which poor health is generated. The lifestyle model is often criticized by proponents of the social structural model for ignoring the root causes of unhealthy lifestyle behaviour (King and Williams 1995), but opportunities for intervention have rarely been identified through the social structural perspective. The lifestyle framework is more amenable to intervention efforts, and the lifestyle perspective can be expanded to incorporate the influences of social structural forces over the life-course. In fact, lifestyle interventions operating within a social structural framework (e.g. identifying and addressing critical aspects of social contexts) may be the most effective for health promotion and disease prevention efforts (Link and Phelan 1995).

Regardless of the emphasis placed on social structure, improved lifestyle self-care behaviour must be a final outcome of a majority of

health promotion and disease prevention studies. Chronic conditions (diseases and impairments) have far surpassed acute, infectious diseases as the most costly conditions of Western developed societies. Chronic conditions consumed 75 per cent of American health-care expenditure in 1990 and afflicted over 45 per cent of the population (Hoffman *et al.* 1996). The prevalence of chronic conditions increases with age, with nearly 90 per cent of adults over the age of 65 years reporting at least one condition. Lifestyle self-care behaviours are the leading actual cause of chronic disease and death in a majority of Western industrialized nations (McGinnis and Foege 1993). Twenty per cent of total American deaths are related to smoking (Novotny 1993), for example, and physical inactivity has been estimated to have a role in over 250 000 deaths each year in the United States (Powell and Blair 1994). In fact, it has been speculated that physical inactivity is the leading actual cause of death among older adults in the United States (Buchner 1997). As shown in Fig. 1, self-care is a primary mechanism through which social strata may affect chronic disease onset and management. Substantial alterations in rates of chronic disease will come primarily through reductions in smoking and obesity, and improved dietary and physical activity habits.

Lifestyle self-care is defined as those behaviours (or lack thereof) intended to prevent primary or secondary disease (Kart and Engler 1994; Ory and Defriese 1997). Many behaviours classified as lifestyle self-care are necessary not only for the prevention of chronic disease, but also for the long-term management of chronic diseases like hypertension and diabetes mellitus. Lifestyle behaviours often have delayed gratification, require regular performance, and may even involve immediate deprivation (e.g. diet) or physical discomfort (e.g. physical activity). Effective public health and behaviour modification campaigns are needed to reduce the prevalence of these self-care risk factors. As the social stratification of the life-course framework suggests, social and individual change can occur within and across strata. Information and resources delivered with attention to the forces of social and economic context may be needed to alter rates of physical inactivity, dietary compliance, and tobacco use among the most vulnerable classes within social strata. Efforts to target vulnerable classes (e.g. less educated, minorities) at critical stages of the life-course have been successful (e.g. prenatal care, childhood nutrition and immunization programmes) and more efforts may lead to efficient gains in HRQL. However, to be maximally effective self-care behaviour interventions should pay careful attention to the role of social and cultural contexts in habit formation and behaviour modification.

Discussion

Chronic diseases generally develop through an accumulation of behavioural risk factors and social and physical exposures over the life-course. The interaction of these with biological factors produces clinically detectable outcomes in middle and later life. This complexity represents a challenge to social and biological scientists who will have to work in concert to understand better the role and interaction of biological and social strata in HRQL. Persistently higher rates of range of motion limitation among women represents an example of the potential importance of such collaboration. Women may be at greater risk for limitation as a result of lower income and social status than men, but studies based on social, economic, and behavioural factors have been unable to show that the considerably greater risk of mobility limitation among women is due to these factors. It is possible that male and female differences in bone structure or muscle strength place women at greater risk for mobility limitation. Given the substantial effect of range of motion limitation on the development of ADL or IADL disability and the tremendous costs of that disability, further efforts to identify the source of sex differences in mobility limitation and possible interventions could be extremely valuable.

There are many risk factors for HRQL decline, and many of these risk factors have self-care behaviour and biological roots. Although not explicitly incorporated into the HRQL model shown in Fig. 1, obesity is another example of a risk factor for mobility limitation and overall HRQL decline that is based in social-behavioural and biological factors. Obesity rates continue to rise (Galuska *et al.* 1996) and effective and practical weight-loss interventions are few (Brown *et al.* 1996). This is particularly true among those with body mass indices of 30 or 35 and over, which is a level of obesity that is strongly associated with chronic disease and mobility limitation (Clark and Mungai 1997). Obesity prevention may be more effective than obesity treatment, and prevention will require an appropriate integration of social structural, behavioural, and biological risk factors targeted at critical stages of the life-course.

HRQL varies substantially between classes within social strata, but a multidisciplinary perspective is necessary to understand the variability and, ultimately, to develop effective interventions. Interventions to affect the disparities cannot be identified without clear understanding of the mechanisms of disparity. The vague conclusions regarding the mechanisms of disparity offered by medical sociological theories, a lack of attention to social structural determinants among behavioural interventionists, and a lack of interaction between basic biologists, psychologists, and sociologists may be hindering improved understanding of HRQL and its determinants. Ultimately, a life-course perspective that merges biological, sociological, and psychological determinants of social disparities in HRQL, as exemplified in the review by Wadsworth (1997), may be necessary to generate opportunities for reductions in HRQL disparities.

References

Andersen, R.M., Mullner, R.M., and Cornelius, L.J. (1987). Black–white differences in health status: methods or substance? *Milbank Quarterly*, **65** (Supplement 1), 72–99.

Antonovsky, A. (1967). Social class, life expectancy and overall mortality. *Milbank Quarterly*, **45**, 31–73.

Barker, D., Meade, C., Fall C., *et al.* (1992). Relation of fetal and infant growth to plasma fibrinogen and factor VII concentrations in adult life. *British Medical Journal*, **304**, 148–52.

Boult, C., Kane, R.L., Louis, T.A., Boult, L., and McCaffrey, D. (1994). Chronic conditions that lead to functional limitation in the elderly. *Journals of Gerontology: Medical Sciences*, **49**, M28–36.

Brown, S.A., Upchurch, S., Anding, R., Winier, M., and Ramirez, G. (1996). Promoting weight loss in type II diabetes. *Diabetes Care*, **19**, 613–24.

Buchner, D.M. (1997). Physical activity and quality of life in older adults. *Journal of the American Medical Association*, **277**, 64–6.

Carter, J.S., Pugh, J.A., and Monterossa, A. (1996). Non-insulin-dependent diabetes mellitus in minorities in the United States. *Annals of Internal Medicine*, **125**, 221–32.

Clark, D.O. (1997). Trends in disability and institutionalization among older blacks and whites. *American Journal of Public Health*, **87**, 438–40.

Clark, D.O. and Mungai, S.M. (1997). The distribution and association of chronic disease and mobility difficulty across four BMI categories of African-American women. *American Journal of Epidemiology*, **145**, 865–75.

Clark, D.O., Mungai, S.M., Stump, T.E., and Wolinsky, F.D. (1997*a*). Prevalence and impact of risk factors for lower body difficulty among Mexican-Americans, African-Americans, and Whites. *Journals of Gerontology: Medical Sciences*, **52A**, M97–105.

Clark, D.O., Stump, T.E., and Wolinsky, F.D. (1997*b*). Predictors of lower body difficulty and recovery among 51 to 61 year-old adults. *American Journal of Epidemiology*, **148**, 63–71.

Davey-Smith, G. and Morris, J. (1994). Increasing inequalities in the health of the nation. *British Medical Journal*, **309**, 1453.

Elder, G.H., Liker, J.R., and Cross, C.E. (1984). Parent–child behaviour in the Great Depression: life course and intergenerational influences. In *Life-span development and behaviour* (ed. P.B. Baltes and O.G. Brim). Academic Press, New York.

Feldman, J.J., Makuc, D.M., Kleinman, J.C., and Cornoni-Huntley, J. (1989). National trends in educational differentials in mortality. *American Journal of Epidemiology*, **129**, 919–33.

Galuska, D.A., Serdula, M., Pamuk, E., Siegel, P.Z., and Byers, T. (1996). Trends in overweight among United States adults from 1987 to 1993: a multi-state telephone survey. *American Journal of Public Health*, **86**, 1729–35.

Guralnik, J.M., Ferrucci, L., Simonsick, R.M., Salive, M.E., and Wallace, R.B. (1993). Lower-extremity function in persons over the age of 70 years as a predictor of subsequent disability. *New England Journal of Medicine*, **332**, 556–61.

Hales, C.N., Barker, D.J.P., Clark, P.M.S., *et al.* (1991). Fetal and infant growth and impaired glucose tolerance at age 64. In *Fetal and infant origins of adult disease* (ed. D.J.P. Barker). BMJ Publications, London.

Hoffman, C., Rice, D., and Sung, H. (1996). Persons with chronic conditions. *Journal of the American Medical Association*, **276**, 1473–9.

Institute of Medicine (1990). *Nutrition during pregnancy*, p. 10. National Academy Press, Washington, DC.

Johnson, R.J. and Wolinsky, F.D. (1993). The structure of health status among older adults: disease, disability, functional limitation, and perceived health. *Journal of Health and Social Behaviour*, **34**, 105–21.

Kart, C.S. and Engler, C.A. (1994). Predisposition to self-health care: who does what for themselves and why. *Journals of Gerontology: Social Sciences*, **49**, S301–8.

Kenny, S.J., Aubert, R.E., and Geiss, L.S. (1995). Prevalence and incidence of non-insulin-dependent diabetes. In *Diabetes in America*, pp. 47–67. NIH Publication No. 95–1468, US Government Printing Office, Washington, DC.

King, G. and Williams, D.R. (1995). Race and health: a multidimensional approach to African-American health. In *Society and health* (ed. B.C. Amick III, S. Levine, A.R. Tarlov, and D.C. Walsh), pp. 93–130. Oxford University Press.

Kington, R.S. and Smith, J.P. (1997). Socio-economic status and racial and ethnic differences in functional status associated with chronic diseases. *American Journal of Public Health*, **87**, 805–10.

Link, B.G. and Phelan, J. (1995). Social conditions as fundamental causes of disease. *Journal of Health and Social Behaviour*, Spec. no. 80–94.

McGinnis, J.M. and Foege, W.H. (1993). Actual causes of death in the United States. *Journal of the American Medical Association*, **270**, 207–12.

McKinlay, J.B. and McKinlay, S.M. (1990). Medical measures and the decline of mortality. In *The sociology of health and illness* (ed. P. Conrad and R. Kern), pp. 10–27. St Martin's Press, New York.

Maddox, G.L. and Clark, D.O. (1992). Trajectories of functional dependence in late life. *Journal of Health and Social Behaviour*, **33**, 114–25.

Mann, S.L., Wadsworth, M.E.J., and Colley, J.R. (1992). Accumulation of factors influencing respiratory illness in members of a national birth cohort and their offspring. *Journal of Epidemiology and Community Health*, **46**, 286.

Manton, K.G. (1988). Planning long-term care for heterogeneous older populations. In *Annual review of gerontology and geriatrics*, Vol. 8 (ed. G.L. Maddox and M.P. Lawton), pp. 217–55. Springer, New York.

Manton, K.G. and Stallard, E. (1984). *Recent trends in mortality analysis*. Academic Press, Orlando, FL.

Manton, K.G., Corder, L.S., and Stallard, E. (1993). Estimates of change in chronic disability and institutional incidence and prevalence rates in the United States elderly population from the 1982, 1984, and 1989 National Long Term Care Survey. *Journals of Gerontology: Social Sciences*, **48**, S153–67.

Manton, K.G., Stallard, E., and Corder, L. (1995). Changes in morbidity and chronic disability in the United States elderly population: evidence from the 1982, 1984, and 1989 national long term care surveys. *Journals of Gerontology: Social Sciences*, **50B**, S194–204.

Marmot, M.G., Davey-Smith, G., Stansfeld, S.A., *et al.* (1991). Health inequalities among British civil servants: the Whitehall II study. *Lancet*, **377**, 1387.

Nagi, S.Z. (1965). Some conceptual issues in disability and rehabilitation. In *Sociology and rehabilitation* (ed. M. Sussman). American Sociological Association, Washington, DC.

National Center for Health Statistics (1986). Births, marriages, divorces, and deaths for 1985. *Monthly Vital Statistics Report*, **34**(12).

National Center for Health Statistics (1997). Report of final mortality statistics for 1995. *Monthly Vital Statistics Report*, **45**(11), Supplement 2.

Navarro, V. (1990). Race or class versus race and class: mortality differentials in the United States. *Lancet*, **336**, 1238–40.

Novotny, T.E. (1993). Tobacco use. In *Chronic disease epidemiology and control* (ed. R.C. Brownson, P.L. Remington, and J.R. Davis), pp. 199–220. American Public Health Association, Washington, DC.

Ory, M.G. and Defriese, G.H. (1997). *Self care in later life: research program and policy perspectives*. Springer, New York.

Pappas, G., Queen, S., Hadden, W., and Fisher, G. (1993). The increasing disparity in mortality between socioeconomic groups in the United States, 1960 and 1986. *New England Journal of Medicine*, **329**, 103–9.

Powell, K.E. and Blair, S.N. (1994). The public health burdens of sedentary living habits: theoretical but realistic estimate. *Medicne and Science in Sports and Exercise*, **26**, 851–6.

Preston, S.H. and Elo, I.T. (1995). Are educational differentials in adult mortality increasing in the United States? *Journal of Aging and Health*, **7**, 476–96.

Riley, M.W. (1987). On the significance of age in sociology. *American Sociological Review*, **52**, 1–14.

Ross, C.E. and Bird, C.E. (1994). Sex stratification and health lifestyle: consequences for men's and women's perceived health. *Journal of Health and Social Behaviour*, **35**, 161–78.

Schneider, D., Greenberg, M.R., and Lu, L.L. (1997). Region of birth and mortality from circulatory diseases among black Americans. *American Journal of Public Health*, **87**, 800–4.

Seeman, T.E., Charpentier, P.A., Berkman, L.F., *et al.* (1994). Predicting changes in physical performance in a high-functioning elderly cohort: MacArthur studies of successful aging. *Journals of Gerontology: Medical Sciences*, **49**, M97–108.

Townsend, P. and Davidson, N. (1982). *Inequalities in health: the black report*. Penguin, Harmondsworth.

Verbrugge, L.M. (1989). The twain meet: empirical explanations of sex differences in health and mortality. *Journal of Health and Social Behaviour*, **30**, 282–304.

Verbrugge, L.M. and Jette, A.M. (1994). The disablement process. *Social Science Medicine*, **38**, 1–14.

Verbrugge, L.M. and Patrick, D.L. (1995). Seven chronic conditions: their impact on United States adults' activity levels and use of medical services. *American Journal of Public Health*, **85**, 173–82.

Wadsworth, M.E.J. (1997). Health inequalities in the life course perspective. *Social Science and Medicine*, **44**, 859–69.

Wallace, R.B. and Lemke, J.H. (1991). The compression of comorbidity. *Journal of Aging and Health*, **3**, 237–46.

Wilson, I.B. and Cleary, P.D. (1995). Linking clinical variables with health-related quality of life. *Journal of the American Medical Association*, **273**, 59–65.

Wolinsky, F.D, Stump, T.E., Callahan, C.M., and Johnson, R.J. (1996). Consistency and change in functional status among older adults over time. *Journal of Aging and Health*, **8**, 155–82.

1.3   Population ageing in developing countries: demographic aspects

Alexandre Kalache and Ingrid Keller

Introduction

In this chapter we address demographic changes in developing countries leading to rapid increases in the relative and absolute numbers of the elderly population. Such changes are commonly referred to as demographic transition, and are essentially due to declining mortality and fertility rates. Recent medical advances are important underlying causes for the rapid 'greying' of the developing world's population.

Table 1 Percentage of persons aged 60 years and over out of total population for selected countries

	1970	1995	2020
Japan	10.6	20.0	31.0
United States	10.6	20.0	31.0
China	6.8	9.3	15.5
Brazil	5.3	7.7	13.5
India	5.9	7.2	11.0
Zimbabwe	4.2	4.3	6.2

Data from United Nations (1995).

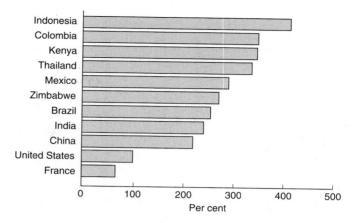

Fig. 1 Percentage increase in elderly populations, 1990 to 2025. (Data from United Nations (1995).)

Policy implications are discussed with special emphasis on the fact that substantial socio-economic changes are now taking place, leading to an erosion of traditional forms of care for older dependent people. Finally, healthy ageing approaches within a life-course perspective, particularly relevant to the developing world, are introduced.

In the 1950s the average life expectancy in the developing world was about 45 years, in 1995 the figure had risen to 64 and it is expected to reach 72 years in 2020. Currently, older people represent 6.4 per cent of the world's population—approximately 370 million people. In 1995, 75 per cent of the world's elderly population were living in the developing world. Currently there is an increase in this age group of about 800 000 per month. This figure is expected to rise to 1.1 million per month in 2010 (Kinsella 1996). The elderly population is currently increasing twice as fast as the general population. Table 1 shows the increase in the proportion of elderly people over the next decades, comparing selected developed and developing countries. These figures indicate the pressing need for drawing the attention of policy- and decision-makers to the ageing of the population. Developing countries will face particular challenges in providing services for their elderly people, given the rapidity of the ageing process paralleled with yet to be solved infrastructural problems.

The demographic transition

The demographic transition can be summarized as a shift from high mortality and high fertility to low mortality and low fertility, thus leading to a high proportion of elderly people. This process of demographic change first started in Europe immediately after the Industrial Revolution and was completed over a long period of time. In France for instance it took 115 years (1865–1980) for the proportion of the elderly population to double from 7 to 14 per cent. The same doubling will be experienced by China in only 27 years (2000–2027). Figure 1 shows that increases of up to 400 per cent of the elderly population in selected countries are expected within the next 30 years, especially in Latin America and South-East Asia. The population pyramid for Latin America shown in Fig. 2 illustrates the changing shape of population composition in the developing world from a pyramid to a bell shape. As a consequence of increases in life expectancy and decreases in fertility, the number of older people increases and that of younger people remains constant or even

decreases. The same phenomenon can be observed in other regions of the developing world.

Increasing life expectancy

In developed countries, mortality rates started to decline throughout the nineteenth and the first half of the twentieth century, reflecting gradual improvements in socio-economic conditions (e.g. improved housing, sanitation, diet, and personal hygiene). As a result, life expectancy gradually increased over a long period of time in comparison with the much faster process currently being observed in developing countries. This can be largely explained by the availability of effective medical technology to control premature death—particularly through vaccines and modern therapy for infectious diseases. Figure 3 shows the changes in causes of death in Mexico between 1951 and 1993.

Declining fertility rates

Total fertility rate is the average number of births each woman between 15 and 49 years of age would have if her lifetime fertility summed the fertility of women of successive ages measured at the same time (WHO 1995). While the worldwide total fertility rate is expected to decline from 4.5 (1970) to 2.4 (2020), some countries experience even greater decreases as shown in Table 2. This will reflect the expected decrease in developing countries. Total fertility rates in developed countries have already reached levels from which further declines are unlikely. Thus, as with global mortality rates, differentials in fertility rates are also rapidly diminishing. In the 1970s, total fertility rates in developing countries were three times higher than those of developed countries. By the year 2020, total fertility rates for most of the developing world are expected to be virtually the same as for industrialized countries.

Previously, declining fertility rates depended upon a high educational level among women and therefore the process was slow. Currently, the availability of highly effective contraceptive methods explain the much faster declines, irrespective of socio-economic factors. In developing countries that are currently experiencing rapid fertility declines, the median population age (i.e. the age that divides a population into numerical equal parts of young and old people) is

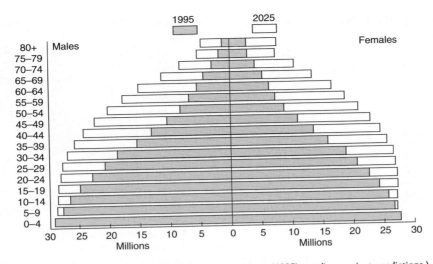

Fig. 2 Population pyramid for Latin America, 1995 and 2025. (Data from United Nations (1995), medium-variant predictions.)

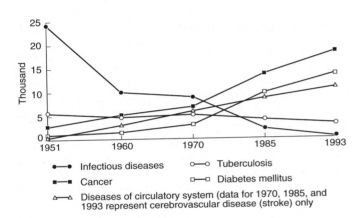

Fig. 3 Changing pattern of causes of death in Mexico; total number of deaths for men. (Data from WHO (1954, 1963, 1973, 1989, 1995).)

Table 2 Total fertility rates[a] for selected countries

	1970	1995	2020
Botswana	6.6	4.5	2.5
Philippines	5.5	3.5	2.1
China	4.7	1.9	2.1
Brazil	4.7	2.6	2.1
France	2.3	1.7	2.0
Japan	2.1	1.5	1.7

[a] The average number of births each woman between 15 and 49 years of age would have if her lifetime fertility summed the fertility of women of successive ages measured at the same time.

Data from United Nations (1995).

Table 3 Support ratio[a] for elderly people aged 65 years and over in selected countries

	1990	2010	2025
Bangladesh	7	7	9
Zimbabwe	7	6	8
Philippines	8	9	13
China	10	14	22
Japan	19	37	49

[a] Support ratio is the number of people aged 65 or over per 100 people of working-age population (20–64 years).

Data from Kinsella and Taeuber (1993).

going to increase substantially in the next few years. For instance, in Cuba and the Republic of Korea, the median age is currently 30 years, expected to increase to 40 and 38 respectively by the year 2020; the corresponding figures for Indonesia are 23 years and 31 years.

Support ratios

Changes in a nation's age structure are also reflected in changing societal support ratios. These ratios indicate either the number of youths (0–19 years of age) or elderly (over 65 years of age) per 100 people of working age population (20–64 years of age).

Developing countries currently have much lower support ratios for the aged population than industrialized countries, usually below 10. Within the next decades, little change is projected for the least developed countries as illustrated in Table 3. Rapidly ageing developing countries like China or Brazil will experience a doubling of the support ratios from 1990 to 2025, but they will still be substantially lower than those for a country such as Japan. Most developed countries already have high support ratios, which are expected to

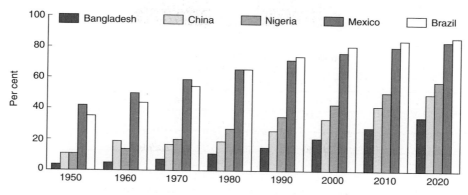

Fig. 4 Increase in urban population in selected countries as a percentage of total population. (Data from United Nations (1995).)

increase further, as a result of continuing low fertility rates and increasing longevity.

It should be noted that not all elderly people require support, and that not all working-age people receive payment for their work. Support from younger to older generations may be direct (e.g. through living arrangements) or through taxation. The numbers given are to be taken as rough indicators for estimating societal expenditure and patterns of social relationships in the future. However, the actual number of elderly people requiring support in the coming decades will very much depend on their health and economic status. It must be borne in mind that older people may also give support to younger generations, for example by child caring.

Other societal changes with implications for ageing

Urbanization

Between 1950 and 1990 the percentage of people living in urban areas in Asia and Africa doubled from roughly 15 to 30 per cent, and in Latin America it increased from 40 to 72 per cent (United Nations 1995). Within the same period the number of cities with a population of over 1 million increased sixfold, from 34 to 213: most of the increase was due to expanding cities in the developing world (Kalache 1998). These trends are expected to continue: by the year 2000, 50 of the 66 largest cities of the world (over 4 million citizens) are projected to be in developing countries. United Nations projections indicate that the process of urbanization throughout the developing world will continue over the next few decades, as shown in Fig. 4.

Urbanization has multiple implications for ageing. The family structure immediately changes from the extended family, which is the norm in rural areas, to the nuclear family, the more common pattern in urban areas. In Table 4 the household composition of elderly people (60 years and over) in urban and rural areas is shown for selected countries. In the late 1980s, about half of the elderly people in urban areas in the Republic of Korea were still living in an extended family household, whereas the proportion of elderly people living in a two- to four-generation household in Brazil was only just over 10 per cent. In the latter country about 25 per cent lived alone, roughly 20 per cent in a conjugal household, suggesting a pattern that is closer to that of fully industrialized societies. In comparison,

in rural Zimbabwe the pattern of household structure for elderly people observed in the late 1980s shows the impact of migration to urban areas. More than one-third of them live in a skip-generation household (grandparents and grandchildren); the middle generation has migrated to urban centres (Hashimoto 1991).

Urbanization first starts with the young moving away from rural areas—often leaving their children behind to be looked after by elderly relatives. As social security schemes providing adequate pensions are rare, such elderly people often depend on financial support from their children living in the city. However, the latter may face poor employment opportunities as unskilled workers. In this case older relatives must finance themselves through farming to supply food for themselves and dependent grandchildren. This is particularly difficult if the older people are disabled and frail.

For those elderly people who move to the city, urban lifestyle is often difficult owing to poor housing and insanitary conditions, an alien environment, drastic changes in societal norms and values (away from the traditional reverence for elderly people observed in rural areas), and total dependence on their children's meagre incomes. Millions of rural migrants are now ageing in urban dwellings without having been fully assimilated into the mainstream of their new environment.

Increasing participation of women in the paid work force

The modernization process leads to an increasing proportion of women entering the paid work force. This is also a reflection of education strategies aimed among other things at decreasing family size. A 15 per cent increase in the number of female students in primary education was observed between 1970 and 1990 in sub-Saharan Africa and South Asia; there was a 25 per cent increase for the same time period in the Middle East and North Africa (World Bank 1993). The increase in the proportion of women participating in the work force is particularly noticeable in middle-income countries; in Mexico, for example, the percentage of women (15 years and over) in the paid work force increased from 19 per cent in 1970 to 30 per cent in 1990. Equivalent increases for Brazil are 24 to 34 per cent, and for Indonesia 30 to 39 per cent (United Nations Development Programme 1997). This suggests that policy-makers will need to seek alternative schemes for caring for older dependent people. Some possible alternatives include a combination of family and community

Table 4 Household composition (per cent) of people aged 60 years and over in selected countries

Household type	Republic of Korea (urban)	Brazil (urban)	Zimbabwe (rural)
One person	7	26	5
Conjugal	11	18	3
Two generations[a]	25	27	10
Two to four generations	51	11	22
Skip generation[b]	2	1	35
Other	4	18	25
Total	100	100	100
Sample size	302	295	300

[a] Elderly and unmarried children.

[b] Grandparents and grandchildren, data for mid-1980s.

Data from Hashimoto (1991).

care, self-care models as well as health promotion and prevention initiatives aimed at extending the healthy life years. Traditional values and financial constraints seem to be outstanding reasons why the proportion of old people living in institutions remains very low in developing countries. In the late 1980s the proportion of people aged 65 years or over and living in institutions was 0.1 per cent in Iran, 0.6 per cent in Botswana, and 1.5 per cent in Brazil, compared with 3.5 per cent in Japan and 7.5 per cent in Switzerland (United Nations 1989). The changes triggered by modernization together with the increasing number of older people in these countries, will continue to lead to pressures towards the institutionalization of dependent elderly people throughout the developing world.

Inadequate social security systems

In most developing countries there is a lack of pension schemes. In part, this is due to the fact that a high proportion of people work in the informal sector and are therefore not participating in social security schemes. Here, the traditional intergenerational 'contract' of caring for each other will continue to be an imperative. In the case of Brazil for example, although there is a minimum age for retirement, the pension schemes for the well off are unrealistically and unfairly generous. Those who enjoy good jobs throughout their working lives cannot only retire early (based on a 'time of service' notion that ordinary workers are not entitled to) but will draw pensions that sometimes are even higher than their last salary. In some Brazilian states, 80 per cent of civil servants are retired before the age of 56 years. As a result of these distortions, the Brazilian Social Security Institute went into deficit in 1996. Future prospects are that the deficit will increase unless drastic reforms are implemented without delay. While in the 1950s eight workers were counted for each pensioner, today the ratio is two to one. Currently the federal government is paying out approximately 17 billion American dollars in pension and social insurance benefits, while receiving only about 2.5 billion in contributions (*Economist* 1997).

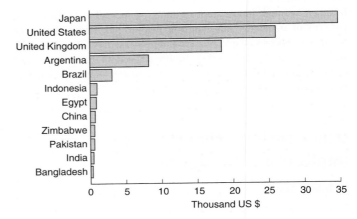

Fig. 5 GNP per capita for selected countries in 1994. (Data from United Nations Development Programme (1997).)

When family bonds are broken, elderly people are left with marginal support from the government or are dependent on themselves. The labour participation of elderly people (aged 60 years or over) in developing countries is significantly higher for elderly men than women; for example, in the mid-1980s, 45 per cent of men and 10 per cent of women in Brazil participated in the labour market, and in Zimbabwe these figures were 69 per cent and 31 per cent respectively (Kinsella and Taeuber 1993).

Health care

Today, looking at industrialized countries attempting to finance advanced health-care policies draws attention to the gross national product per capita (**GNP**) in developing countries. Figure 5 shows the GNP per capita in selected countries; it is evident that most of the countries cannot afford intensive, costly, and technically advanced elderly care systems. It remains a challenge for specialized

Table 5 Percentage of people aged 60 years and over out of total population for selected Eastern European countries and states of the former Soviet Union

	1970	1995	2020
Ukraine	11.2	13.2	20.3
Romania	12.1	15.4	19.6
Poland	12.3	13.5	18.9
Russian Federation	14.1	16.6	21.3
Uzbekistan	5.9	8.4	10.7
Kirghizstan	4.5	5.3	8.5

Data from United Nations (1995).

professionals as well as for other health-care staff and policy-makers to establish an interdisciplinary approach to appropriate health care that is affordable and tailored to individual needs and national traditions.

Medical aspects

The changing pattern of disease is commonly termed the 'epidemiological transition'. Figure 3 shows this epidemiological transition in Mexico, where infectious diseases and tuberculosis showed a rapid decrease as causes of death in the last 35 years, whereas an increase in death due to non-communicable diseases such as cancer, diabetes, and diseases of the circulatory system was observed. Currently, the percentage of deaths in developing countries attributable to communicable and non-communicable diseases is 41.5 per cent and 49.8 per cent respectively (WHO 1996b). By the year 2020 the figures are expected to be 11.7 per cent for communicable diseases and 76.8 per cent for non-communicable diseases. The shift away from infectious diseases towards non-communicable diseases is clearly demonstrated and will become a major concern in developing countries. Furthermore, non-communicable diseases may often be accompanied by long years of disability, when, after a stroke for example, potentially high-cost care can follow. Another example relates to the estimates of cases of age-associated non-insulin-dependent diabetes mellitus. While in 1994 the estimated numbers of cases for Africa and Asia were 6 million and 45 million respectively, projections for 2010 suggest 13 million and 130 million cases (McCarty and Zimmet 1994).

The situation in Eastern Europe

The present situation in countries with economies in transition (Central and Eastern European countries and the former Soviet Union) reveals similar ageing patterns as Western Europe, without the political stability and economic resources. In Table 5 the current percentage of aged people in selected Central and Eastern European countries and states of the former Soviet Union as well as future estimates are given (United Nations 1995). A large difference between the Central Asian states of Kirghizstan and Uzbekistan and Central

and Eastern European countries, including the Russian Federation, is evident.

A moderate decrease in the total fertility rate is projected for all Central and Eastern European countries in the next decades, varying widely among countries in this group. For the Islamic states of the former Soviet Union a significant drop of the total fertility rate is projected between 1970 and 2020—for instance from 4.7 to 2.1 in Kirghizstan and from 6.0 to 2.1 in Uzbekistan. In contrast, slight decreases are projected for Central and Eastern European countries such as Bulgaria (from 2.2 to 1.8), Poland (from 2.2 to 2.1), and Romania (from 2.6 to 1.8) in the same time frame (United Nations 1995).

In terms of life expectancy at birth, the overall increase in life expectancy occurred rapidly after the Second World War in this region, mostly due to improved living conditions and public health policies that produced a large decline in mortality by reducing some major causes of death (e.g. infectious diseases such as tuberculosis. The increase in life expectancy over the last decades in Central and Eastern European countries has occurred more slowly than in the rest of the world and remains smaller than in the rest of Europe. This can be explained in part by an increase in male mortality between 1965 and 1985 due to circulatory diseases. By the mid-1980s circulatory diseases accounted for about half of all male deaths in this region. However, United Nations projections for the year 2020 (compared with 1970) show an increase in male life expectancy at birth from 66 to 69 years in Hungary and from 63 to 69 years in the Russian Federation. Since female life expectancy at birth in expected to increase as well, thereby widening the mortality gap between the sexes, widowhood and loneliness among elderly women are rapidly emerging as important issues.

The causes underlying the demographic transition in the Central and Eastern European countries and the former Soviet Union are manifold. A significant independent cause of this is the decrease in fertility among women age 20 to 29 years, which can be attributed to transition-specific factors including economic insecurity (shrinking of state welfare assistance, inflation, unemployment), weakening administration and institutional infrastructure (including health provision systems), and the deterioration of hygiene and sanitary conditions.

General implications are that regional and subregional differences will occur and the feminization of ageing will be accelerated. Family support will decrease (mostly due to migration and reduction of marriage rates), the probability of widowhood will increase, and insufficient economic support from the government can be expected (United Nations 1997).

Ageing: crisis or opportunity?

So far, this discussion has been based on the assumption that there is a chronological threshold which defines 'old age'—at 60 or 65 years. With respect to the developing countries this definition is inadequate. Individual ageing mainly reflects previous living conditions. What is of major concern in the long run is the quality of life of the survivor and not the number of years lived. Thus it should be considered that the number of 'old' people is underestimated in the developing world when only those aged 60 years and over are included.

Ageing is a natural occurrence; therefore the Ageing and Health Programme of the World Health Organization (**WHO**) strongly emphasizes that ageing is not a disease, but a natural stage of the lifecycle. Each individual should be given the opportunity to age in a healthy and active manner in order, as the United Nations states, 'to add life to years that have been added to life' (United Nations 1997). The greying of the global community should be seen as an opportunity for elderly people to continue as active contributors to society—for example as carers for grandchildren. This has special importance in sub-Saharan Africa, because the HIV/AIDS pandemic is projected to diminish today's adult generation considerably. In developing countries it is particularly essential to provide older people with opportunities for an extended life in good health—meaning physical, social, and mental well being. Therefore, the Ageing and Health Programme focuses on a lifecycle perspective of healthy ageing from early on.

Future implications: healthy ageing

The WHO Health of the Elderly Programme was renamed and reoriented into the Ageing and Health Programme in 1995. The main aim of its multidimensional and intergenerational approach to achieving healthy ageing is to ensure the attainment of the best possible quality of life for as long as possible, for the largest possible number of people.

During the reorientation process in 1995, a Delphi-style study on 'Ageing and Health in Developing Countries' was carried out involving 125 experts in 62 countries from all WHO regions. The results showed that topics related to health promotion (such as community care, multisectoral approaches), ill health (such as measurement of level of independence, identification of the most common causes of disability), and socio-economic as well as family and intergenerational issues are most important for future research. The expert community suggested giving high priority to raising government awareness and preparing policy guidelines for countries with an emphasis on multisectoral policy. Primary health-care workers and policy-makers were the groups identified to be priority target groups for training (WHO 1996a).

For this to be achieved, WHO will be required to advance the current knowledge base of gerontology and geriatrics through research and training efforts. Emphasis is being placed on the unprecedented rates of populations ageing in the developing world, in a context of prevailing poverty and continuing demands arising from problems related to communicable diseases.

The life-course perspective for slowing down functional and mental capacity decline with older age has three key dimensions on which interventions should be focusing. Firstly, health promotion (starting in childhood): promoting a healthy active lifestyle, for example through peer education, social marketing, and mass media. Secondly, disease prevention: the focus has to be on minimizing polyvalent risk factors leading to non-communicable diseases. For example regular physical activity, adapted to individual abilities, plays a significant role in the prevention of cardiovascular diseases, back pain, osteoporosis, and depression. Thirdly, service provision for ageing and elderly people: the need to train primary health-care workers and informal carers in delivering health care to elderly people is of special concern, as community-based care and health maintenance

approaches are more desirable than more expensive in-hospital interventions. The effectiveness of traditional forms of healing and caring should also be considered. Further investigation in this field is needed in order to find appropriate models of good practice.

The WHO Ageing and Health Programme has committed itself to focus on strengthening the information base, policy development, advocacy, community-based programmes, training, and research. Additionally, a WHO global media strategy on healthy ageing is being established. The first step towards achieving political commitment was made with the launching of the Brasilia Declaration on Ageing in July 1996 in a combined effort from the Brazilian government and the WHO Ageing and Health Programme, where a multidisciplinary group of experts identified pressing needs and expressed principles for action.

References

Economist (1997). Inactive workers, inactive congress. *Economist*, 7 June, 60–2.

Hashimoto, A. (1991). Urbanization and changes in living arrangements of the elderly. In *Ageing and urbanization. Proceedings of the UN International Conference on Ageing Populations in the Context of Urbanization, Sendai, Japan, 12–16 September 1988*. United Nations, New York.

Kalache, A. (1998). Future prospects for geriatric medicine in developing countries. In *Geriatric medicine and gerontology* (5th edn) (ed. R. Tallis, W. Fillit, and J.C. Brocklehurst). Churchill Livingstone, Edinburgh.

Kinsella, K. (1996). Demographic aspects. In *Epidemiology in old age* (ed. S. Ebrahim and A. Kalache). BMJ Publishing, London.

Kinsella, K. and Taeuber, C. (1993). *An aging world II*, International Population Reports P95/92–3, US Department of Commerce, Bureau of the Census, Washington, DC.

McCarty, D. and Zimmet, P. (1994). *Diabetes 1994 to 2010: global estimates and projections*. International Diabetes Institute, Melbourne.

United Nations (1993). *Demographic yearbook, special issue: population aging and the situation of elderly persons*. United Nations, New York.

United Nations (1995). *UN population prospectus, 1995 update*. United Nations, New York.

United Nations (1997). *Older persons in countries with economies in transition: designing a policy response*. United Nations, New York.

United Nations Development Programme (1997). *Human development report*. Oxford University Press, New York.

WHO (World Health Organization) (1954). *Annual epidemiological and vital statistics*. WHO, Geneva.

WHO (World Health Organization) (1963). *Annual epidemiological and vital statistics*. WHO, Geneva.

WHO (World Health Organization) (1973). *Annual epidemiological and vital statistics*. WHO, Geneva.

WHO (World Health Organization) (1989). *World health statistics*. WHO, Geneva.

WHO (World Health Organization) (1995). *World health statistics*. WHO, Geneva.

WHO (World Health Organization) (1996a). *Ageing and health programme*. Delphi-style study on Ageing in Developing Countries (unpublished results). WHO, Geneva.

WHO (World Health Organization) (1996b). *Investing in health research and development*. Report of the Ad Hoc Committee on Health Research Relating to Future Intervention Options. WHO, Geneva.

World Bank (1993). *World development report*. Oxford University Press, New York.

2

Biological aspects of ageing

2.1 Biological origins of ageing

Thomas B. L. Kirkwood

Introduction

Ageing, characterized by increasing age-specific mortality, is a general characteristic of mammals, birds, reptiles, and many invertebrates (Comfort 1979; Finch 1990). This broad phylogenetic distribution strongly suggests that ageing long predates the emergence of *Homo sapiens*. Therefore an explanation of the origins of human ageing requires at least two components: firstly, an explanation of why ageing occurs at all, and, secondly, an explanation of the special features of human ageing.

Why should we be interested in these distant origins? The answer is that if we can understand where ageing comes from in evolutionary terms, we shall be better placed to consider the kinds of mechanisms by which our present-day ageing is caused. Medvedev (1990) has catalogued more than 300 different theories of ageing. While many of these so-called theories are unrealistically narrow, it is nevertheless true that the multiple competing hypotheses make ageing a particular challenge for scientific investigation. The evolutionary and comparative approach provides an important tool for gaining insight into the complex nature and causes of the ageing process (Kirkwood 1985; Finch 1990; Kirkwood and Rose 1991; Rose 1991; Partridge and Barton 1993; Holliday 1995).

Three different views of the origins of ageing will be considered in this chapter. The first is that ageing is simply the inevitable price which a higher organism pays for its complexity. In this view there is no requirement to account explicitly for an evolutionary origin of ageing, which is seen simply as a process of biological wear and tear. The other two views both propose evolutionary reasons why ageing occurs, but differ in the type of natural selection thought to have operated. The adaptive evolutionary view suggests that ageing itself is selectively advantageous. This leads to the idea that ageing is a programmed termination of life and that the lifecycle is effectively under genetic control from start to finish. The non-adaptive view suggests that ageing is deleterious, or at best selectively neutral, and that it has evolved as an indirect consequence of the forces shaping life history.

One particular version of the non-adaptive view, the 'disposable soma' theory, suggests that ageing results from natural selection tuning the life history so that fewer resources are invested in somatic maintenance than are necessary for indefinite survival. The disposable soma theory supports the stochastic wear-and-tear concept of ageing, but does so on the basis that wear and tear follows from making the best use of the resources available to the organism rather than from being inevitable.

Before studying these views more closely we need to define ageing in a way that makes it possible to ask questions about its origins. The best definition for this purpose is a population-based definition that ageing is a progressive generalized impairment of function resulting in a loss of adaptive response to stress and in a growing risk of age-associated disease. Individuals may vary in the rate at which specific markers of ageing develop, but the overall effect of these changes is summed up in the increase in the probability of dying—the age-specific mortality—within the population. In humans, cohort mortalities show an approximately exponential rise with increasing chronological age (Fig. 1), noted first by Gompertz (1825). However, there is evidence that the exponential rate of increase in cohort mortalities slows down among centenarians (Smith 1994). It is not known whether this reflects genetic heterogeneity within the population, particularly assiduous medical and social care of the very old, or intrinsic biological processes. Heterogeneity is likely to be at least part of the explanation if, as seems probable, centenarians represent an exceptionally robust subset of the population (Vaupel *et al.* 1979; Schächter *et al.* 1993). When a cohort ages, the frailer individuals die sooner and, as a consequence, the mortality of the survivors is based on a shrinking fraction of the population who may have started their adult lives with intrinsically greater capacity for survival.

Some species, such as sea anemones and hydra, show no increase in age-specific death rate and according to the above definition are

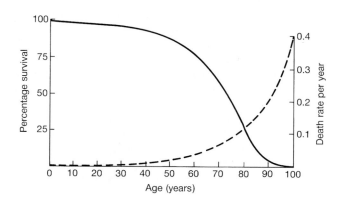

Fig. 1 Age-specific patterns of survival (solid curve) and mortality (broken curve) typical of a population in which ageing occurs. The example is of a human population with well-developed social and medical care. (Reproduced with permission from Kirkwood and Holliday (1986).)

deemed not to age (Comfort 1979; Martinez 1997). Therefore we take the pattern of increasing age-specific death rate as diagnostic of ageing when it is found in a species where death is not linked to some specific stage in the lifecycle, such as the rapid post-spawning death of Pacific salmon. In other words, ageing is the increasing tendency to failure of chronologically older individuals in a population where there is no obvious reason why, if ageing did not occur, the lifecycle of the individual should not extend indefinitely. The exclusion of species which undergo once-only, or semelparous, reproduction is important because in many of these species the commitment to begin the reproductive effort sets in train a specific sequence of physiological events that bring about the postreproductive death of the adult. A discussion of the significance of the differences between post-reproductive death in semelparous species and ageing in repeatedly reproducing, or iteroparous, species can be found elsewhere (Kirkwood 1985).

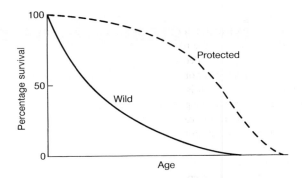

Fig. 2 The survival curve of a wild population tends to show little sign of age-associated mortality, which may become apparent only when the population is transferred to a protected environment.

Wear-and-tear theories

There are many ways in which an organism can be damaged, ranging from a change in a single molecule to the loss of whole organs and structures. It has been suggested that, in a manner similar to the wear and tear of complex machines, these intrinsic processes of biological deterioration present a fundamental barrier to the indefinite survival of higher organisms (Cutler 1978; Sacher 1978). This view finds support in the fact that many of the observable features of the ageing process do indeed resemble wear and tear, and also in the argument that, according to the second law of thermodynamics, ordered systems are intrinsically unstable and tend to give way to disorder.

However, the parallel with inanimate objects fails to allow for the ability of living systems to repair themselves. The second law of thermodynamics tells us only that the degree of disorder, or entropy, increases in closed systems. Organisms are not closed; they take in nutrients from which they extract energy. There is no fundamental reason why this flow of energy into the organism should not be used to maintain the level of entropy at a constant value. Indeed, it must be possible to maintain at least the germ-line in a steady state since, otherwise, species would rapidly become extinct. Furthermore, in the cases of hydra and sea anemone, the powers of maintenance and renewal appear to be sufficient for the entire organism to survive indefinitely without visible deterioration.

To understand the scope and limitations of repair processes requires an analysis that takes account of the potential to evolve new repair mechanisms (Kirkwood 1981). We should not accept that because a particular kind of repair is beyond the capability of an organism in its present form, it is necessarily impossible. The brain is an obvious example of an organ in a higher organism that is vulnerable to irreversible damage because the death of neurones can disrupt the connectivity of its cell networks, and the information represented in these networks is then permanently lost. However, if natural selection had placed sufficiently high importance on it, greater resistance to damage could have been incorporated within these networks, including perhaps the capacity to effect repair. An extreme example, not directly relevant to ageing, emphasizes the point that not all damage which is not repaired is necessarily irreparable. This is the regeneration of amputated limbs, which among vertebrates is

restricted to certain small salamanders (Scadding 1977). While the proximate reason for this difference in regenerative ability between salamanders and other vertebrates depends upon the organization of cells, the ultimate reason depends upon natural selection and the evolutionary balance which must be struck between the costs and benefits of repair. In organisms which are very unlikely to survive during the time period required for a limb to regrow, the force of selection to acquire or retain limb-regenerative ability will be minimal. It may simply be that the salamanders are near to a borderline beyond which the loss of a limb is a sufficiently serious threat to survival and reproduction that it is not worthwhile to retain regenerative ability (Kirkwood 1981).

These considerations tell us that while wear and tear may play a role in ageing, it is not a sufficient explanation of why ageing occurs. This requires that we direct attention to the evolutionary theories.

Adaptive evolutionary theories

The adaptive theories suggest that ageing confers some direct competitive advantage and that senescence is controlled in broadly the same way as development. The attraction of the adaptive theories is that they conform to the way that we tend most easily to think about evolution, namely that new traits emerge because they adapt the genotype in ways that are evidently fitter for survival. In view of the continuing appeal of these theories, it important to be explicit about why they are now thought to be false.

One suggested advantage of ageing is that it prevents old and worn-out individuals from competing for resources with their progeny. This argument is plainly circular, as was pointed out by Medawar (1952), and need be considered no further. Another suggestion is that ageing helps to prevent overcrowding and so lessens the risk of severe depletion of resources (Wynne-Edwards 1962). It is conceivable that ageing could play such a role, but there are two very strong objections to this idea.

The first objection is that there is little evidence from natural populations that ageing is a significant contributor to mortality in the wild. Undoubtedly, an individual that lives long enough to experience senescence becomes more vulnerable to predators and other hazards. However, life tables for wild populations indicate that mortality during the early and middle periods of life is usually so great that few individuals survive long enough for ageing to have a measurable impact on the total death toll (Fig. 2). This means that, in fact, ageing is not needed to prevent overcrowding, nor is it easy to see how natural selection could have directly brought about the evolution of a trait which is so rarely seen under normal conditions.

Some exceptions to the general rule that ageing is rare in the wild may possibly arise in the case of the larger animals. However, even in such species only a minority of individuals survive to old age, and in any case these species evolved from smaller more vulnerable ancestors in which it is reasonable to assume that ageing was already established. Thus the exceptions cannot help us to account for the origins of ageing.

A second objection to the idea that ageing evolved to prevent overcrowding is that the advantage, if it exists, is an advantage for the population rather than the individual. The best course for the individual, if other things are equal, will always be to live as long and reproduce as much as possible. This means that if ageing had evolved as a means to regulate population size, then a mutant in which the ageing process was inactivated would enjoy an advantage and the mutant genotype would spread. For ageing to be stably maintained in the long term, it is necessary that 'group selection' for advantage to the population should outweigh the straightforward selection for advantage to the individual. The requirements for group selection to operate successfully against opposing selection at the level of the individual are very stringent (Maynard Smith 1976), and it is extremely unlikely that they apply to ageing. Briefly, it is necessary that the species is distributed among fairly isolated groups and that the introduction of a non-ageing mutant into a group should rapidly lead to the group's extinction.

Each of the above objections to the adaptive evolution of ageing is forceful in its own right. Taken together, the objections gain extra force because they complement each other. Where one objection applies less strongly, the other is intensified. For example, if ageing does generate significant mortality within a population, so that it is more plausible that it has some role to play, then the disadvantage of ageing to the individual is greater and the group-selection argument is harder to sustain.

One final claim for the adaptive theories is that ageing is necessary for, or helps, evolution to occur (e.g. Libertini 1988). The idea is that since evolution occurs through the operation of natural selection on successive generations, any process that accelerates the turnover of generations may result in a greater ability of a species to adapt to changes in its environment. The various weaknesses in this argument are as follows. Firstly, as discussed above, the generation time in the wild is determined for the most part not by ageing but by environmental hazards. Secondly, the argument assumes that the long-term advantage of adaptability outweighs the short-term disadvantage of reduced lifespan. This depends critically upon the assumed rate of change in the environment, and the argument encounters the same complex difficulties that concern the evolution of sex and the optimal mutation rate (see Maynard Smith 1978). In fact, elevated recombination and/or mutation rates would be an alternative and more direct way to accelerate evolutionary change. Thirdly, for species which spread their reproduction over their lifetime, the critical factor in determining the rate of turnover of generations is not lifespan so much as the age at which individuals become reproductively mature. While there is force to the argument that species with long development times may be limited in their adaptability, the fact that

such species also tend to have long lifespans does not establish that longevity itself poses a disadvantage. This would be true if a long lifespan necessitated slow reproductive maturation, but the causative link is much more likely to be the other way around.

Non-adaptive evolutionary theories

If ageing is not adaptive, then its evolution must be explained through the indirect action of natural selection. The non-adaptive theories of ageing are of two types: (i) ageing occurs because the power of natural selection declines during the lifespan; (ii) ageing occurs as the by-product of selection for some other trait.

Significance of the age-associated decline in the force of natural selection

An important property of any lifecycle in which there is the opportunity for repeated reproduction between maturation and death is that the force of natural selection (i.e. its ability to discriminate between alternative genotypes) weakens with age (Haldane 1941; Medawar 1952; Williams 1957; Hamilton 1966; Charlesworth 1980, 1994). The basic point is that because natural selection operates through the differential effects of genes on reproductive fitness, the force of natural selection must decline in proportion to the decline in the remaining fraction of the organism's total lifetime expectation of reproduction. This is true whether or not the species exhibits ageing, since even if individuals do not age they are nonetheless susceptible to environmental mortality. If a gene effect is expressed early in life, it will influence the reproductive success of a larger proportion of individuals born bearing that gene than if it is expressed late, when many such individuals will already have died.

The attenuation in the force of natural selection with age inevitably means that there is only loose genetic control over the late portions of the lifespan. Indeed, it was suggested by Medawar (1952) that this might be sufficient in itself to account for the origin of ageing. Consider a species in which ageing does not initially occur. If a gene with an age-specific time of expression arises by mutation, and if it is beneficial, then natural selection can be expected to favour bringing forward its time of expression so that more individuals can benefit from it. Conversely, if the gene is harmful, selection would tend to defer its time of expression so that its deleterious effects would be less damaging. Once a harmful gene has been so far delayed that it is expressed at an age when in the wild environment most individuals would have died already, it is beyond the reach of any further opposing selection and can spread to fixation by random drift. Medawar (1952) suggested that, over many generations, there might thus accumulate a miscellaneous collection of late-acting deleterious genes. In the normal environment these genes would only rarely have the opportunity to be expressed. However, in a protected environment survivorship would be greater and a significant fraction of individuals would experience the effects of these genes. The upshot would be that as a result of this process, ageing had appeared in the population.

It is clear that the declining force of natural selection with age is relevant to the origins of ageing, but it is less certain that an accumulation of late-acting deleterious mutations is a complete explanation. An alternative hypothesis forms the basis of the second type of non-adaptive theory, namely that ageing is a by-product of selection for other beneficial traits (Williams 1957). Williams' theory supposes the existence of genes which are pleiotropic, i.e. the same genes are responsible for both good effects early in life and bad effects late in life. Natural selection would favour retention of the genes on the basis of their early benefits, but would defer as far as possible the time of expression of the deleterious effects to ages when survivorship in the wild environment would be low. The decline in the force of natural selection with age would ensure that even quite modest early benefits would outweigh severe harmful side-effects, provided that the latter occurred late enough.

There is now considerable evidence from experiments applying artificial selection to laboratory populations of the fruit fly *Drosophila melanogaster* and other insect species that the general trade-offs implied by the pleiotropic genes theory, also known as antagonistic pleiotropy, do exist (Luckinbill *et al.* 1984; Rose 1984, 1991; Zwaan *et al.* 1995). However, neither Medawar's mutation accumulation theory nor Williams' pleiotropic genes theory specifies which particular genes are likely to have been responsible for the origins of ageing.

Ageing through optimizing the investment in maintenance

In this section, we describe a non-adaptive theory which is more specific about the nature of the genetic processes responsible for ageing. This is the disposable soma theory (Kirkwood 1977, 1981; Kirkwood and Holliday 1979). The disposable soma theory is named for its analogy with disposable goods, which are manufactured with limited investment in durability on the principle that they have a short expected duration of use. The term 'soma' is used in the sense introduced by Weismann (1891) to describe those parts of the body which are distinct from the 'germ-line' that produces the reproductive cells—the sperm and the egg.

We consider how an organism capable of reproducing repeatedly during its lifecycle ought best to allocate energy among the different metabolic tasks it needs to perform. The organism may, in a sense, be viewed as an entity that transforms resources—principally energy in the form of nutrients—from its environment into its progeny. Furthermore, the law of natural selection asserts that those organisms (strictly, the genes that determine the phenotypes of the organisms) which are most efficient in this process are the ones most likely to survive (Townsend and Calow 1981). However, part of the resources must be used for activities such as growth, foraging, defence, and maintenance. As all functions ultimately draw from the same total input of resource, there is an inevitable trade-off (direct or indirect) between the investment that is made in any one function and the investment in others. Note that it is not necessary to assume that energy is in short supply, although this is the case for many species in their natural habitats. Even in populations with abundant energy supplies, those individual genotypes that best utilize the available energy will be the most successful.

As the following argument reveals, the optimum allocation of energy involves a smaller investment in somatic maintenance than would be required for the soma to last indefinitely. Given the continual hazard of accidental death, from which no species is entirely immune, each individual soma can have only a finite expectation of life, even if it were not subject to ageing. When the soma dies, the resources invested in its maintenance are lost. Too low an investment in the

prevention or repair of somatic damage is obviously unsatisfactory because then the soma may disintegrate before it can reproduce. However, too high an investment in maintenance is also wasteful because there is no advantage in maintaining the soma better than is necessary for it to survive its expected lifetime in the wild environment in reasonably sound condition. In the latter case, the 'fitness' of the organism in terms of natural selection, i.e. its ability to compete reproductively, would actually be enhanced by reducing the investment in somatic maintenance and channelling the extra resource into more rapid growth or greater reproductive output.

Therefore fitness is maximized at a level of investment in somatic maintenance which is less than would be required for indefinite somatic survival. The precise optimum investment in maintenance depends on the species' ecological niche. A species subject to high accidental mortality will do better not to invest heavily in each individual soma, but should concentrate instead on more rapid and prolific reproduction. A species which experiences low accidental mortality may profit by doing the reverse. Thus the disposable soma theory not only explains why ageing occurs, but also suggests in broad terms how it is caused. As soon as the division between germ-line and soma evolved, the stage was set for the appearance of ageing.

Implications for genes and mechanisms controlling longevity

As well as explaining the origins of ageing, the evolutionary theories should also account for the divergence of species' lifespans (Table 1). This raises basic questions about the genetic control of ageing. What kinds of genes are involved? How many of them are there? How are they modified by natural selection to produce changes (usually increases) in lifespan?

For the adaptive theories, if we suspend doubts about their plausibility, the control of lifespan is straightforward, but the theories are uninformative about the nature and number of the genes involved. Any gene which has the effect of limiting lifespan might be considered, and there could be any number of them. A single death gene coupled to a suitable biological clock mechanism would suffice and would provide the simplest basis for modifying the lifespan.

For the non-adaptive theories, the kinds of genes proposed have already been considered in the previous section. The general nature of these genes is integral to the theories—late-acting deleterious genes in Medawar's theory, pleiotropic genes with early good effects and late bad effects in Williams' theory, and genes which regulate the levels of somatic maintenance and repair in the disposable soma theory. As regards the numbers of such genes, each of the theories suggests that there are likely to be several, possibly many, genes involved. However, if a very large number of independent genes contribute to ageing, it is difficult to explain how the lifespan can be altered, as modifying the expression of a single gene will do little to alter the rate of ageing and multiple independent changes will be rare. This suggests either that a relatively small number of principal genes are responsible for ageing, or that the expression of the different genes is co-ordinately regulated.

The evolution of increased lifespan in the non-adaptive theories can readily be understood as a consequence of reducing the extrinsic risk of accidental death. An adaptation resulting in lower accidental mortality will reduce the rate of attenuation in the force of natural

Table 1 Maximum recorded lifespans for selected mammals, birds, reptiles, and amphibians

	Scientific name	Common name	Maximum lifespan (years)
Primates	Macaca mulatta	Rhesus monkey	29
	Pan troglodytes	Chimpanzee	44
	Gorilla gorilla	Gorilla	39
	Homo sapiens	Man	115
Carnivores	Felis catus	Domestic cat	28
	Canis familiaris	Domestic dog	20
	Ursus arctos	Brown bear	36
Ungulates	Ovis aries	Sheep	20
	Sus scrofa	Swine	27
	Equus caballus	Horse	46
	Elephas maximus	Indian elephant	70
Rodents	Mus musculus	House mouse	3
	Rattus rattus	Black rat	5
	Sciurus carolinensis	Grey squirrel	15
	Hystrix brachyura	Porcupine	27
Bats	Desmodus rotundus	Vampire bat	13
	Pteropus gianteous	Indian fruit bat	17
Birds	Streptopelia risoria	Domestic dove	30
	Larus argentatus	Herring gull	41
	Aquila chrysaëtos	Golden eagle	46
	Bubo bubo	Eagle owl	68
Reptiles	Eunectes murinus	Anaconda	29
	Macroclemys temmincki	Snapping turtle	58+
	Alligator sinensis	Chinese alligator	52
	Testudo elephantopus	Galapagos tortoise	100+
Amphibians	Xenopus laevis	African clawed toad	15
	Bufo bufo	Common toad	36
	Cynops pyrrhogaster	Japanese newt	25

Reproduced with permission from Kirkwood (1985).

selection at older ages. In Medawar's theory, this will then apply pressure to postpone further the expression of the late deleterious genes. In Williams' theory, the balance between the early beneficial and late harmful effects of the pleiotropic genes will be shifted in favour of reducing the late harmful effects. In the disposable soma theory, the optimum investment in somatic maintenance will be increased. The effect of any of these changes will be to reduce the intrinsic rate of ageing, resulting in increased longevity.

The most explicit predictions follow from the disposable soma theory. In this context, the polygenic nature of senescence is specifically linked to the multiple maintenance and repair systems that protect against accumulation of somatic damage, since the optimality principle that underlies the theory applies equally to each of them. This leads us to expect that, on average, the longevity assured by individual maintenance systems will be similar. This is because if the setting of any one mechanism is unusually low, so that failure occurs chiefly from this cause alone, then selection will tend to increase this setting. Conversely, any mechanism that is set too high may incur disproportionate metabolic costs, and selection will tend to reduce it. Nevertheless, some variation is to be expected. The optimization

process is not exact, and as the optimum is approached the selection differential grows less. Furthermore, there may be gene–environment and other interactions that tend to preserve some polymorphism within the population. The study of the genetic polymorphisms underlying the heritability of human longevity may be particularly informative (Schächter et al. 1993, 1994).

A further implication of the disposable soma theory is that the process of senescence is itself stochastic. The overall rates of accumulation of damage are regulated through genetic settings of the various maintenance functions, but the individual events on which these accumulations are based are random. Stochastic effects will be most apparent where the numbers of initiating events for an age-associated change are small, as in the formation of a tumour, but all stochastic effects will contribute to the intrinsic growth in variability that is one of the hallmarks of senescence.

Lastly, it is suggested that ageing may be to some extent malleable. The idea that senescence results from stochastic accumulation of somatic damage implies that, in principle, aspects of the ageing process may be altered by modifying the exposure to damaging agents and/or enhancing maintenance functions.

Reproductive ageing

So far, we have not specifically considered ageing of the reproductive system, as distinct from generalized aspects of the ageing process. Reproductive ageing is of particular interest because loss of reproductive function will accelerate the decline in the force of natural selection (Partridge and Barton 1996). The reverse is also true. In organisms that continue to grow indefinitely, and in which reproductive output increases with size, the decline in the force of natural selection is slowed. This may explain the considerable longevity of some species of fish (Comfort 1979; Finch 1990).

The reason for leaving reproductive ageing until now is that a circular argument can arise if ageing of the reproductive system is not properly regarded as a feature that logically must follow the origin of ageing more generally. Weismann (1891), for example, originally suggested that ageing was necessary to rid a population of old and worn-out individuals which had produced their required quota of offspring and were of no further reproductive value (but see Kirkwood and Cremer (1982) for the later development of Weismann's views). Similar confusion can arise if the postreproductive death in semelparous species is not treated as distinct from ageing (see Introduction, and Kirkwood (1985)).

After this preamble, it can be seen that although reproductive ageing takes its toll on reproductive function rather than on survival, there is nothing particularly special about it. Once the origin of ageing has been accounted for within an organism whose life history could otherwise extend indefinitely, reproductive ageing can be seen merely as part of the generalized decline in function. In other words, if it does not matter that the organism does not survive indefinitely, then it does not matter that it does not reproduce indefinitely. For most species, reproductive ageing, like other aspects of the ageing process, is probably of little consequence in the wild. The special case of the human menopause is considered in the next section.

One final aspect of reproductive ageing which should be mentioned is the ageing of germ cells. Although the germ-line must, in a sense, be immortal, there is well-documented evidence of maternal and, to a lesser extent, paternal age effects in the frequency of genetic abnormalities (see, for example, Kram and Schneider 1978). The occurrence of age-associated changes in germ cells is not particularly surprising. The increase in abnormal progeny, particularly with maternal age, may either reflect less efficient screening for faults as a general consequence of ageing, or it may be due to the weakness of selection for late reproductive viability. Over a time-scale of generations, however, damage must not be allowed to accumulate in the germ-line, and this may be prevented by any of several mechanisms (Medvedev 1981).

Evolutionary aspects of human ageing

Evolutionary aspects of human ageing have been left until now because (i) human evolution is comparatively recent, and (ii) in human populations certain features of ageing contrast markedly with those in the majority of other animal populations. To pay attention to these features too early could have distorted our understanding of how they must have arisen as modifications of a more general pattern.

First, our species is unique in the high frequency with which individuals survive to show clear signs of ageing, particularly in the more affluent nations. This suggests a challenge to the idea that natural selection will usually operate so that ageing remains a potential rather than an actual phenomenon. The very high incidence of ageing in modern human societies is undoubtedly due to the speed of recent social and cultural evolution, which is likely to have outstripped the potential for natural selection to modify our life history. Nevertheless, ageing is clearly seen, albeit less frequently, in more 'primitive' societies, and mention of it is found in the earliest human records. In terms of the disposable soma theory, it is conceivable that as accidental mortality was progressively reduced under the influence of evolving human intellect and the associated trend to living in more protected social groups, there came a point where it is was no longer selectively worthwhile to increase the investment in somatic maintenance at the cost of further delaying growth and reducing reproduction (Kirkwood and Holliday 1986). Continuing selection pressure for further reduction in accidental mortality would have increased the average lifespan while leaving the underlying rate of ageing unchanged. Therefore more individuals would have begun to live long enough to age.

A second distinctive feature of human ageing is the clearly controlled shutdown of reproductive function that occurs in women at menopause, which happens around the age of 45 to 50 in all regions of the world (Gosden 1985). The proximate cause of the menopause appears to be oocyte depletion, which triggers endocrine changes. Chimpanzees and macaques exhibit similar changes, but these are not so well defined and true menopause is generally thought to be unique to humans, although there is some suggestion that a similar process may occur in female toothed whales (Marsh and Kasuya 1986). All mammals, and many other species, show a decline in fertility with age in females, but this tends to be a more gradual process involving increasing irregularity of cycling rather than a complete shutdown of reproductive function. Fertility in males also declines with age, but does not come to an abrupt halt.

The evolutionary paradox about the menopause is why fertility should cease when a woman is only about half-way through her biological lifespan, and when the impact of senescence on most of her somatic functions is not yet very advanced. It would be expected that natural selection should favour maximum retention of fertility, and assisted-fertilization techniques have recently demonstrated that postmenopausal women can successfully bear children without serious complications.

The menopause is sometimes cited as support for the adaptive theories, since it suggests that a strict genetic control of ageing may exist. A more plausible explanation is as follows. Increased neonatal brain size coupled with the constraint on the birth canal linked to bipedal gait has made giving birth unusually difficult for human females, and the risks of child-bearing would presumably increase steeply if reproduction were to be continued during the later stages of the lifespan. Therefore it makes sense to suppose that the menopause evolved as a means of removing older women from this risk and of preserving them for the important roles of rearing their later-born children and possibly assisting with their grandchildren, as well as sharing their valuable knowledge and experience with their kin group. Seen in this way the menopause is not a primary feature of ageing but a secondary adaptation to lessen its deleterious effects (Medawar 1952; Williams 1957; Hamilton 1966; Kirkwood and Holliday 1986; Hill and Hurtado 1991, 1996; Rogers 1993; Austad 1994; Peccei 1995).

Conclusions

The conclusions we can draw from studying the biological origins of ageing have broad implications for the way we perceive the ageing process. Firstly, ageing needs to be explained in evolutionary terms, as it is not enough to regard it as just due to the inevitability of wear and tear. Secondly, the evolution of ageing as an adaptive process in its own right seems extremely unlikely. Thirdly, the non-adaptive theories in general offer the most plausible explanation for the evolution of ageing and longevity, and these theories make predictions that are amenable to experimental tests (Kirkwood and Rose 1991; Partridge and Barton 1993). Specifically, the disposable soma theory suggests that the efficiencies of somatic maintenance processes are crucial in determining longevity. Molecular studies using either a comparative approach or transgenic animals may serve to identify which of these processes play the most important roles.

A final word should be said about the way in which studies of the evolutionary origins of ageing throw light on the 'programming' of the lifespan. The point of issue between the adaptive and non-adaptive theories is not whether ageing is genetically influenced, as obviously it must be, but why and how this is arranged. This distinction is important as the theories determine the types of mechanism of ageing we are likely to consider as appropriate subjects for research.

References

Austad, S. N. (1994). Menopause: an evolutionary perspective. *Experimental Gerontology*, 29, 255–63.

Charlesworth, B. (1980). *Evolution in age-structured populations.* Cambridge University Press.

Charlesworth, B. (1994). *Evolution in age-structured populations* (2nd edn). Cambridge University Press.

Comfort, A. (1979). *The biology of senescence* (3rd edn). Churchill Livingstone, Edinburgh.

Cutler, R.G. (1978). Evolutionary biology of senescence. In *The biology of ageing* (ed. J.A. Behnke, C.E. Finch, and G.B. Moment), pp. 311–60. Plenum Press, New York.

Finch, C.E. (1990). *Longevity, senescence and the genome.* University of Chicago Press.

Gompertz, B. (1825). On the nature and function expressive of the law of human mortality and on a new mode of determining life contingencies. *Philosophical Transactions of the Royal Society of London*, 115, 513–85.

Gosden, R.G. (1985). *Biology of menopause. The causes and consequences of ovarian ageing.* Academic Press, London.

Haldane, J.B.S. (1941). *New paths in genetics.* Allen and Unwin, London.

Hamilton, W.D. (1966). The moulding of senescence by natural selection. *Journal of Theoretical Biology*, 12, 12–45.

Hill, K. and Hurtado, A.M. (1991). The evolution of premature reproductive senescence and menopause in human females: an evaluation of the 'grandmother hypothesis'. *Human Nature*, 2, 313–50.

Hill, K. and Hurtado, A.M. (1996). *Ache life history: the ecology and demography of a foraging people.* Aldine de Gruyter, New York.

Holliday, R. (1995). *Understanding ageing.* Cambridge University Press.

Kirkwood, T.B.L. (1977). Evolution of ageing. *Nature*, 270, 301–4.

Kirkwood, T.B.L. (1981). Evolution of repair: survival versus reproduction. In *Physiological ecology: an evolutionary approach to resource use* (ed. C.R. Townsend and P. Calow), pp. 165–89. Blackwell Scientific, Oxford.

Kirkwood, T.B.L. (1985). Comparative and evolutionary aspects of longevity. In *Handbook of the biology of ageing* (2nd edn) (ed. C.E. Finch and E.L. Schneider), pp. 27–44. Van Nostrand Reinhold, New York.

Kirkwood, T.B.L. and Cremer, T. (1982). Cytogerontology since 1881: a reappraisal of August Weismann and a review of modern progress. *Human Genetics*, 60, 101–21.

Kirkwood, T.B.L. and Holliday R. (1979). The evolution of ageing and longevity. *Proceedings of the Royal Society of London, Series B*, 205, 531–46.

Kirkwood, T.B.L. and Holliday R. (1986). Ageing as a consequence of natural selection. In *The biology of human ageing* (ed. A.H. Bittles and K.J. Collins), pp. 1–16. Cambridge University Press.

Kirkwood, T.B.L. and Rose, M.R. (1991). Evolution of senescence: late survival sacrificed for reproduction. *Philosophical Transactions of the Royal Society of London, Series B*, 332, 15–24.

Kram, D. and Schneider, E.L. (1978). Parental age effects: increased frequencies of genetically abnormal offspring. In *The genetics of aging* (ed. E.L. Schneider), pp. 225–60. Plenum Press, New York.

Libertini, G. (1988). An adaptive theory of the increasing mortality with increasing chronological age in populations in the wild. *Journal of Theoretical Biology*, 132, 145–62.

Luckinbill, L.S., Arking, R., Clare, M.J., Cirocco, W.C., and Buck, S.A. (1984). Selection of delayed senescence in *Drosophila melanogaster. Evolution*, 38, 996–1003.

Marsh, H. and Kasuya, T. (1986). Changes in the ovaries of the short-finned pilot whale, *Globicephala macrorhynchus*, with age and reproductive activity. In *Reproduction in whales, dolphins and porpoises*, Report of the International Whaling Commission, Special Issue 6 (ed. W.F. Perrin, R.L. Brownell, and D.P. DeMaster), pp. 311–35. International Whaling Commission, Cambridge, MA.

Martinez, D.E. (1997). Mortality patterns suggest lack of senescence in hydra. *Experimental Gerontology*, 33, 217–25.

Maynard Smith, J. (1976). Group selection. *Quarterly Review of Biology*, 51, 277–83.

Maynard Smith, J. (1978). *The evolution of sex.* Cambridge University Press.

Medawar, P.B. (1952). *An unsolved problem of biology.* H.K. Lewis, London. (Reprinted in *The uniqueness of the individual.* Methuen, London, 1957).

Medvedev, Z.A. (1981). On the immortality of the germ line: genetic and biochemical mechanisms—a review. *Mechanisms of Ageing and Development*, 17, 331–59.

Medvedev, Z.A. (1990). An attempt at a rational classification of theories of ageing. *Biological Reviews*, 65, 375–98.

Partridge, L. and Barton, N.H. (1993). Optimality, mutation and the evolution of ageing. *Nature*, 362, 305–11.

Partridge, L. and Barton, N.H. (1996). On measuring the rate of ageing. *Proceedings of the Royal Societ of London, Series B*, 263, 1365–71.

Peccei, J.S. (1995). The origin and evolution of menopause: the altriciality-lifespan hypothesis. *Ethology and Sociobiology*, 16, 425–9.

Rogers, A.R. (1993). Why menopause? *Evolutionary Ecology*, 7, 406–20.

Rose, M.R. (1984). Laboratory evolution of postponed senescence in *Drosophila melanogaster. Evolution*, 38, 1004–10.

Rose, M.R. (1991). *Evolutionary biology of ageing.* Oxford University Press.

Sacher, G.A. (1978). Evolution of longevity and survival characteristics in mammals. In *The genetics of aging* (ed. E.L. Schneider), pp. 151–67. Plenum Press, New York.

Scadding, S.R. (1977). Phylogenic distribution of limb regeneration capacity in adult Amphibia. *Journal of Experimental Zoology*, 202, 57–68.

Schächter, F., Cohen, D., and Kirkwood T.B.L. (1993). Prospects for the genetics of human longevity. *Human Genetics*, 91, 519–26.

Schächter, F., Faure-Delanef, L., Guénot, F., et al. (1994). Genetic associations with human longevity at the *APOE* and *ACE* loci. *Nature Genetics*, 6, 29–32.

Smith, D.W.E. (1994). *Human longevity.* Oxford University Press.

Townsend, C.R. and Calow, P. (1981). *Physiological ecology: an evolutionary approach to resource use.* Blackwell Scientific, Oxford.

Vaupel, J.W., Manton, K.G., and Stallard, E. (1979). The impact of heterogeneity in individual frailty on the dynamics of mortality. *Demography*, 16, 439–54.

Weismann, A. (1891). *Essays upon heredity and kindred biological problems*, Vol. 1 (2nd edn). Clarendon Press, Oxford.

Williams, G.C. (1957). Pleiotropy, natural selection and the evolution of senescence. *Evolution*, 11, 398–411.

Wynne-Edwards, V.C. (1962). *Animal dispersion in relation to social behaviour*. Oliver and Boyd, Edinburgh.

Zwaan, B.J., Bijlsma, R., and Hoekstra, R.F. (1995). Direct selection of lifespan in *Drosophila melanogaster*. *Evolution*, 49, 649–59.

2.2   Biological mechanisms of ageing

George M. Martin

General considerations

Some definitions

Social gerontologists and plant biologists often differentiate between the terms ageing and senescing (or senescence). They use the former to describe all changes in structure and function of an organism from birth (or even fertilization) to death, reserving the term senescence for events that unfold late in the life course and that precede death of tissues, organs, or organisms. However, mammalian bio-gerontologists use the terms ageing and senescence more or less synonymously to describe the structural and functional alterations that appear soon after an organism has completed its development, as defined by the emergence of sexual maturity and (for most mammals) the cessation of major skeletal and organ growth. Some of these alterations involve physiological and behavioural adaptations which compensate for diminished function; one could refer to such compensations as 'sageing', as they reflect the organism's intrinsic and learned wisdom. Inevitably, however, there is a decline in the ability of the organism to maintain homeostasis and to mount a successful reaction to various types of injury. Thermodynamically, there is an inexorable increase in entropy or disorder of molecules and systems. In large populations of mature individuals, one observes an exponential decrease in the probability of survival as a function of chronological time. This is the famous Gompertz relationship, which we now know ceases to hold for exceedingly old members of at least some human populations (Fig. 1). Declines in age-specific death rates at later ages could reflect genetic heterogeneity of human populations. However, even more striking declines in death rates are seen in populations of very old fruit flies from cohorts that are genetically identical. The mechanisms underlying such departures from Gompertz kinetics in very old populations remain unknown. In any case, the ages at which these exponential declines appear and the slopes of these declines are powerfully determined by the constitutional genome, leading to vast differences in the maximum

potential lifespans of different species; among mammalian species, the differences are of the order of 30-fold. However, this is not to deny the important roles of environmental influences in modulating these events, either positively or negatively. To date, however, no environmental agents have been proven to accelerate or decelerate the intrinsic rate of mammalian ageing, or specific aspects of mammalian ageing, with the exception of dietary calories (discussed below).

The term 'age-associated' is non-committal; it includes alterations that are simple functions of chronological time as well as those that are coupled to intrinsic biological ageing. The latter might be diagnosed if it were shown that, among a group of closely related species such as mammals, the ages of onset and the rates of progression of the phenotype of interest were inversely related to the maximum potential lifespan of the species. For example, many age-associated neoplasms appear to be related to intrinsic biological ageing and not simply to chronological time, as their prevalence rises substantially about mid-way through the lifespan (about 2, 4, 8, and 50 years for laboratory mice, white-footed deer mice, dogs, and humans respectively). Figure 2 shows the striking degree of concordance of the scaling of cancers in male beagle dogs and two different populations of human subjects.

Implications of evolutionary theory

The preceding chapter (Chapter 2.1) is of seminal importance in setting the stage for a further analysis of candidate mechanisms of ageing. Therefore let us briefly summarize the major conclusions of evolutionary biologists concerning the natural origins of ageing in age-structured iteroparous animals (animals with repeated episodes of reproduction) such as humans and the vast majority of mammals (Austad 1997). Firstly, there is a consensus supporting non-adaptive evolutionary theories; one would have to invoke group selection as a mechanism for an adaptive evolution of ageing, and there is little support for the importance of group selection as opposed to selection for reproductive fitness at the level of the individual organism. Secondly, two central genetic phenomena appear to have some degree

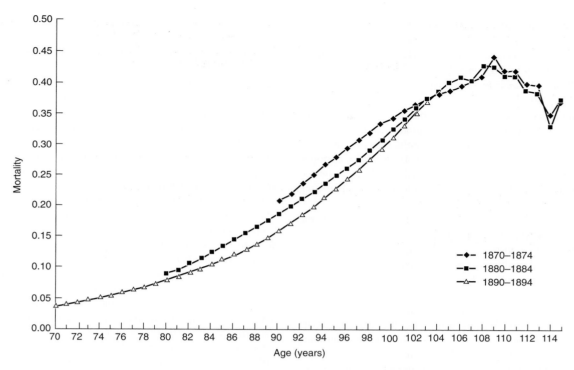

Fig. 1 Age-specific mortality rates for three cohorts of the Caucasian population of the United States (both sexes). (Reproduced with permission from Manton and Stallard (1996).)

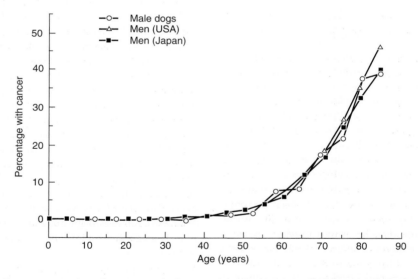

Fig. 2 The cumulative age-specific cancer mortalities (percentage of subjects with cancer) for male beagle dogs, United States males, and Japanese males. The dog data have been normalized to human ages based upon equating 1 dog year to 5.5 human years. (Reproduced with permission from Albert *et al.* (1994).)

of support: (i) the accumulation of germ-line mutations that are expressed relatively late in the life course, when the force of natural selection is weak, and (ii) the principle of antagonistic pleiotropic gene action, whereby selection for alleles that enhance reproductive fitness early in the lifespan exhibit negative effects postreproductively. Perhaps the earliest speculation concerning a concrete example of the latter was made by Williams (1957), who suggested that alleles acting during early phases of the lifespan to enhance calcium uptake, and thus provide sturdy bone structure, did so at the cost of subsequent calcium depositions in arterial walls.

The evolutionary biological theory of ageing has profound implications, as follows.

1. There is no need to invoke primary mechanisms of ageing based upon deterministic 'programmed' gene actions which have, as their direct aim, such outcomes as the 'turning on' of 'killer' genes

or the 'turning off' of essential genes. As a cautionary note, however, it is conceivable that some residue or caricature of such programmes that developed in hypothetical ancestral semelparous species (species with single massive episodes of reproduction) might still be expressed, to some degree, in certain iteroparous species or in particular individuals.

2. There is no reason to believe, *a priori,* that the set of genetic loci of major importance in determining reproductive fitness in one species would be identical to those of another species, although there are likely to be degrees of overlap. Imagine, for example, the striking differences among species as regards loci selected because of behavioural patterns of importance in successful mating behaviour.

3. Just as numerous genetic loci are likely to be involved in the evolution of varying patterns of ageing between species, one would expect plenty of opportunities for different patterns of ageing among individuals within a species, based upon genetic poly-morphisms, mutations, and a complex matrix of genetic–environmental interactions.

4. Although, for any given putative mechanism of ageing, one could entertain a sizeable list of candidate gene loci that might modulate the rate of ageing, the rich variety of loci capable of influencing reproductive fitness or of accumulating mutations would strongly argue against the hypothesis of a single mechanism, process, or theory of ageing. However, this crucial question is by no means settled, as we shall see below.

A few major mechanisms or multiple independent mechanisms of ageing?

While, as indicated above, a polygenic basis for lifespan or for the senescent phenotype does not necessarily obviate the proposal of just a few major mechanisms, or even a single major mechanism, the greater the number of genes shown to be playing a role, the greater is the likelihood that the hypothesis of multiple independent mechanisms is correct. There are as yet no definite estimates in any organism regarding the genetic complexities involved, but a number of lines of evidence point to considerable complexity. In the fruit fly *Drosophila melanogaster,* crosses between comparatively short-lived and long-lived strains (the latter serially selected for high fecundity among females late in the life course) clearly indicate a polygenic determination of lifespan, with genetic loci contributed by each of the three major chromosomes, although with a disproportionately high contribution from chromosome 3 and a relatively minor con-tribution (particularly for males) from chromosome 2 (Luckinbill *et al.* 1988). In the roundworm *Caenorhabditis elegans,* the experimental reassortment of genes from two strains with similar lifespans has produced numerous recombinant inbred lines with striking variations in both mean and maximum lifespans, consistent with a highly polygenic determination (Johnson 1987). However, several single-gene mutations have been associated with substantial increases in the maximum lifespans of *C. elegans.* One of these genes is related to the mammalian insulin receptor family (Kimura *et al.* 1997), raising the question of a major pathway of lifespan regulation in nematodes analogous to what might be induced by caloric restriction.

In higher primates, estimates of the rate of change in cranial capacity of the hominid precursors of humans (which can be stat-istically correlated with potential lifespan) have suggested that some 300 genetic loci might have been involved in the emergence of *Homo sapiens* and its unusually long lifespan (Cutler 1975). However, there are a number of uncertainties in estimates derived from comparisons of lifespans of different species, including the assumption that rates of change of amino acid substitutions in proteins are the appropriate 'molecular clock' for such projections. Other mechanisms, such as chromosomal rearrangements, may be of equal or greater significance; a single such rearrangement could potentially alter the regulation of expression of dozens or hundreds of genes. A study of progeroid mutations of humans gave an estimated upper limit of several thou-sand genetic loci potentially capable of modulating particular aspects of the senescent phenotype, although it was suggested that only a small proportion of these might be of major significance to ageing (Martin 1978). Thus a number of genetic approaches in several species point to a polygenic basis for ageing and hence would suggest caution in embracing a single all-encompassing mechanistic theory of ageing.

In contrast, there is striking evidence, from a wide variety of species (although the most reliable information is confined to rodents), that major (approximately 40 per cent) increases in the maximum lifespans of cohorts of experimental animals (generally consisting of somewhat less than a hundred to a few hundred individuals) can be consistently produced by the simple expedient of restricting the caloric intake to around 60 per cent of that of controls fed *ad libitum* (Weindruch and Walford 1988). The effect is most marked when the caloric restriction (in the face of an otherwise nutritionally sufficient diet) is commenced at weaning, but significant extensions of lifespan are also produced when adults are subjected to caloric restriction. In addition to lifespan, a surprising number (but not all) of the putative biomarkers of ageing examined so far appear to be influenced. There is also a striking retardation of certain diseases commonly observed in ageing rodents, notably chronic nephropathies and neoplasia. While some critics have suggested that the calorically restricted animals should in fact be considered the normal controls (i.e. those fed *ad libitum* may be 'overfed'), such an interpretation does not invalidate the observation of a dramatic effect of calories upon lifespan and a number of age-associated diseases. Thus a detailed understanding of the molecular, cellular, and physiological effects of variations in caloric intake may lead us to a definition of a single predominant mechanism of ageing. If so, then one could envisage interventions less daunting than the rigorous restriction of food. However, it should be em-phasized that there is as yet no good information on the effects of caloric restriction on putative biomarkers of ageing and the lifespans of humans. A modest pilot study in non-human primates by scientists at the United States National Institute on Ageing and at the University of Wisconsin is under way and has provided early evidence indicating that at least some putative biomarkers of ageing (e.g. serum levels of dehydroepiandrosterone sulphate) (Lane *et al.* 1997) are positively influenced by caloric restriction. It will be many years before we know the effects of such caloric restriction on the life-table parameters of these non-human primates.

A sampling of current views on putative mechanisms of ageing

While numerous mechanistic theories of ageing have been proposed, it is fair to say that none of them has as yet been definitively established. It is difficult even to provide a satisfactory system of classifying the diverse ideas, many of which overlap extensively. They also vary substantially in the degree to which fundamental phenomena are invoked, as opposed to restatements of descriptive phenomenology. However, the selected sample discussed below reflects a major segment of current thinking.

Ageing as a by-product of oxidative metabolism (oxidative damage theory)

This theory, which is usually referred to as the free-radical theory of ageing (Harman 1994), is one of the oldest and, in all likelihood, still the most popular single mechanistic theory of ageing.

Chemical free radicals are atoms or group of atoms with an unpaired electron. Consequently they are highly reactive and capable of reacting with a variety of biologically important macromolecules including DNA, protein, and lipid. Some reactive oxygen species, such as single oxygen atoms, are not free radicals but are capable of causing oxidative damage, hence the currently preferred terminology of the oxidative damage (or oxidative stress) theory of ageing. Of special interest are various oxyradicals, mainly partially reduced products of oxygen such as the superoxide radical. Many such substances are likely to have exceedingly short lifespans in biological tissues. For example, the hydroxyl radical may react within a few molecular diameters of its site of formation, with a half-life of the order of a nanosecond. Nevertheless, a variety of lines of evidence indicate that cellular DNA can be readily attacked by the hydroxyl radical, potentially leading to mutagenesis and clastogenesis (chromosome breaks). However, other compounds may be capable of diffusing for substantial distances within a cell before reacting with a suitable substrate (Pryor 1986).

Fortunately, the cytochrome system of respiration developed along with the evolution of aerobic organisms, ensuring that oxygen is largely reduced quadrivalently and thus minimizing the generation of partially reduced products which are highly reactive. However, there is a degree of 'leakiness' in the system, perhaps of the order of a few per cent. Other protective systems, such as the superoxide dismutases, catalase, and glutathione peroxidase, provide a line of defence by enzymatically scavenging partially reduced oxygen products. Moreover, damaged DNA may be repaired by sets of specific enzymes, and altered proteins and lipids may be degraded and replaced, although structural lesions (e.g. the oxidation of amino acid side-chains and cysteine sulphydryl groups (Stadtman and Berlett 1997)) may accumulate in proteins with intrinsically low rates of turnover, such as the lens crystallins and the collagen of connective tissues and blood vessels. The rates of development of such processes might be accelerated by oxidative attacks upon the system of proteases and ancillary proteins that are believed to recognize and preferentially degrade abnormal proteins. Given the large flux of oxygen, some deleterious consequences may occur, depending upon the balance between the rates of generation of the free radicals and the various defence mechanisms in particular tissues. Therefore species-specific lifespans might be attributable to variations in the constitutive baseline efficiencies of the several families of protective enzymes as well as to the rates and levels of induction subsequent to injury; all are under genetic control. Differences in metabolic machinery could also lead to various levels of non-enzymatic scavengers of reactive oxygen species. For example, remarkably high levels of urea are found in certain avian species (Lopez-Torres et al. 1993). This may be one of the reasons that some avian species exhibit such unusually long lifespans despite very high rates of oxidative metabolism (Holmes and Austad 1995). Cultured avian somatic cells have been shown to be intrinsically more resistant than murine cells to various oxidative challenges and to DNA damage (Ogburn et al. 1998).

This, in essence, is the basis for the oxidative stress theory of ageing; it might be regarded as a price we pay for an aerobic lifestyle. In terms of lifestyles, the theory would predict that prolonged and stressful exercise might accelerate rather than retard ageing. Some support for this view comes from experiments in which vigorous exercise (to exhaustion) in rodents was shown to be associated with a three- to fourfold increase in the concentrations of free radicals, an increase in lipid peroxidation (as inferred from the generation of malondialdehyde), and biochemical evidence of mitochondrial damage (Davies et al. 1982). Such alterations are likely to lead to increased depositions of lipofuscin pigments ('ageing pigments'), which are believed to be the products of oxidative attack upon the lipoprotein constituents of cellular organelles. Lipofuscins are one of the few candidates for 'public' biological markers of ageing, as they accumulate in an amazing variety of ageing systems, ranging from fungi undergoing clonal senescence to mammalian myocardium, liver, skeletal muscles, testes, and neuronal subsets (although without any obvious correlation with cellular dysfunction). Moreover, the limited evidence available is consistent with the view that their rates of incorporation are inversely related to the maximum potential lifespans of mammalian species (Martin 1977, 1988).

The notion that ageing may be related, in part, to by-products of oxidative metabolism can be reconciled with evolutionary theory, as one can imagine selection, for reproductive fitness, of alleles at many loci that serve to enhance oxygen flux in various tissues and to accelerate certain other metabolic processes capable of generating free radicals; ageing could emerge as a delayed secondary negative pleiotropic effect. Its fit to the findings on experimental caloric restriction is currently uncertain because in one study of caloric restriction (in rats) there was only a transient lowering of the metabolic rate (oxygen utilization) per unit of lean body mass. However, somewhat different results were found in two other studies (reviewed by Weindruch and Sohal (1997)). It is conceivable that caloric restriction increases the efficiency of the cytochrome system, thereby reducing the extent of univalent reduction of oxygen.

Ageing as a by-product of the flux of reducing sugars

A complex non-enzymatic reaction between a variety of reducing sugars (the most relevant, in terms of concentration, being glucose) and the primary amino group of proteins is one of a growing list of pathways to the production of post-translational alterations of proteins, one of the hallmarks of ageing in a variety of organisms. The resulting altered proteins, if they are long-lived, have complex cross-linked end-products whose structures have not yet been fully elucidated. The initiating reaction is called 'glycation' ('non-enzymatic glycosylation'), and is followed by the formation of labile Schiff base derivatives of proteins, which slowly isomerize to more stable ketoamine adducts via the Amadori rearrangement (see Baynes and Monnier (1989) for an overview of the chemistry and biology).

This proposed molecular mechanism of ageing is supported by the clinical and pathological observations of what appears to be

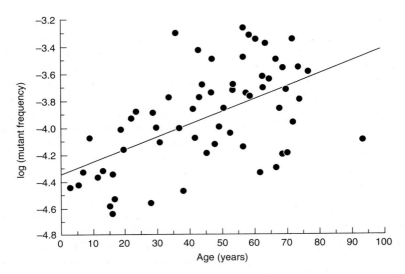

Fig. 3 The age-specific frequencies of HPRT mutations in renal tubular epithelial cells. (Modified with permission from Martin *et al.* (1996), which should be consulted for experimental details.)

premature ageing (or aspects of ageing) in subjects with poorly controlled diabetes mellitus, particularly involving connective tissues and the vasculature. However, there is no correlation between the concentration of blood glucose and the lifespan of a species. This is not a fatal complication for the theory, as one can envisage a number of genetically controlled steps in the determination of the degree to which altered proteins emerge with ageing. One could also reconcile this proposition with evolutionary theories of ageing. It is supported by experiments with caloric restriction which have shown that restricted animals have significantly lower levels of glycated haemoglobin.

Some investigators have attempted to reconcile the oxidative injury and glycation hypotheses by pointing to the possibility of 'auto-oxidative glycation' of proteins. It is also apparent that the glycation idea can be reconciled with genomic instability theories of ageing, as there is evidence that DNA can act as a substrate for glycation and in fact may undergo mutagenesis as a consequence of such reactions.

Ageing as a decline in genomic stability

Many would look to DNA molecules as the ultimate macromolecular targets of ageing, because DNA specifies the information for all metabolic events, including the machinery for its own repair and for the removal of altered proteins. In the case of single-copy sequences specifying critical functions in obligate postreplicative cells, such as neurones, two events (one affecting each of the alleles of the homologous chromosome pair) could result in cell death. In proliferating populations of cells, such events (e.g. the homozygous loss of a tumour suppressor locus) could lead to the emergence of an age-associated neoplasm. Mutations do indeed accumulate in the somatic cells of humans as they age. Only recently has this been shown to be the case for an epithelial cell type (renal tubular epithelial cells) (Martin *et al.* 1996) (Fig. 3). The frequencies of mutations were shown to be about an order of magnitude greater than had previously been observed in lymphocytes and to rise exponentially as functions of donor age. Of course, epithelial cells are the source of most of the cancers that emerge during the latter half of the lifespan. However,

mutations may be the 'tip of the iceberg' in terms of DNA damage. DNA adducts could have deleterious effects on processes such as transcription without resulting in detectable mutations. There is currently a great deal of research on DNA damage and mutation in mitochondrial DNA and the implications for the oxidative damage theory of ageing (Wallace *et al.* 1995). Mitochondria are major sites for the genesis of reactive oxygen species and thus may be particularly vulnerable to mutations, particularly in view of the relative paucity of mechanisms for DNA repair in these organelles. One can expect a mixture of normal and abnormal mitochondria in postreplicative cells such as neurones and skeletal muscle (heteroplasmy), with the potential for the eventual emergence (with ageing) of a predominance of abnormal mitochondria and hence deficiencies in oxidative phosphorylation. This may constitute one pathway towards the development of Parkinson's disease and dementias of the Alzheimer type (Davis *et al.* 1997). It could also contribute to sarcopenia.

Leslie Orgel's protein synthesis error catastrophe theory (Orgel 1963, 1970), which provided a major impetus to the development of molecular gerontology, predicted an exponential rise in the number of point mutations in the somatic cells of ageing organisms towards the latter part of the lifespan. That proposal argued for the primacy, during ageing, of errors in genetic transcription and translation involving proteins that were themselves involved in protein synthesis. Depending upon the efficiencies of the proteases that scavenged the abnormal protein synthesizing machinery, essentially all proteins, including all the enzymes involved in DNA replication and repair would be subject to synthetic errors; hence somatic mutation would be inevitable.

There is now a great deal of evidence arguing against the original form of the Orgel hypothesis. While abnormal proteins are definitely found in ageing organisms, they can be shown to be post-translational in origin rather than the results of errors in synthesis (Warner *et al.* 1987). However, some role for somatic genetic events in the genesis of various aspects of the senescent phenotype seems highly probable, given the substantial degree of genetic plasticity of mammalian somatic cells. The potential mechanisms are numerous in the case of that group of somatic genetic events broadly classified as mutations. These include changes in gene dosage (chromosomal aneuploidy, tandem duplications, deletions, selective gene amplification, and shifts in ploidy), changes in the arrangements of genes (inversions and translocations); and modifications in the primary structure or nucleotide base composition of genes (base substitution, depurinations and depyrimidinations, frameshifts, insertions via transposable elements, mitotic crossing over, gene conversion, and DNA-mediated transformation or transfection).

Much less is known about the molecular basis of changes in gene expression that are not based on alterations in nucleotide sequence or on gene dosage. These events are believed to underlie most developmental and physiological shifts in states of cellular differentiation, with some striking exceptions, such as the loss of the nucleus of mature red blood cells during mammalian erythropoiesis and the rearrangement of immunoglobin and receptor loci of specialized lymphocyte lineages. Inappropriate (i.e. non-adaptive or deleterious) shifts of gene expression are believed to occur during ageing. This idea has been termed 'dysdifferentiation' (Zs-Nagy et al. 1988) or 'epimutation' (Holliday 1987). Its molecular basis is believed to involve changes in states of methylation of the cytosines of DNA and is thought to follow stochastic injurious events, including those resulting from free radicals, although some investigators have also suggested the possibility that changes in methylation at discrete domains of the genome could serve as a deterministic molecular clock.

One special form of change in gene expression involves a battery of genes on the X chromosome that is subject to facultative heterochromatization; this is the basis for the sex chromatin or Barr body. In mice, ageing can reactivate genes within such developmentally 'silenced' DNA, at least for the case of the HPRT gene (hypoxanthine phosphoribosyl transferase, the site of the Lesch–Nyhan mutation); however, this does not occur in humans (Migeon et al. 1988). Recent work on the mechanisms of the reproductive senescence of cultures of Saccharomyces cerevisiae (baker's yeast) has emphasized an important role for alterations in the machinery underlying gene silencing (Smeal et al. 1996).

There is not enough information to decide which of the numerous mechanisms of genomic instability cited above are of the greatest significance for ageing, to what degree such changes are simply related to chronological age, as opposed to intrinsic biological ageing, and to what extent a given pattern is species specific. In the case of certain invertebrates, for example, there is strong evidence against a role for recessive mutations in the determination of lifespan (Maynard Smith 1965).

However, arguments have been made in support of the relative importance of large-scale (chromosomal-type) mutations, at least for the case of proliferative populations of mammalian cells (Martin et al. 1985). It is of interest, for example, that the molecular pathology of the Werner syndrome, perhaps the most striking of the segmental progeroid syndromes of humans (Martin 1978), involves a propensity to undergo relatively large deletions (Fukuchi et al. 1989) that result from mutations in a helicase, a protein that functions to unwind double-stranded nucleic acids (Yu et al. 1996). If this proposition is correct, it points to the special importance of protecting human populations from environmental clastogens (physical, chemical, and viral agents that produce chromosomal mutations). It will also be of considerable conceptual importance to evaluate the role of epimutation in ageing.

As pointed out in Kirkwood's 'disposable' soma concept of ageing (Chapter 2.1), one could reconcile certain pathways of genomic instability to ageing with evolutionary theory, as the energetic investments in preventing and repairing varieties of DNA alteration would be considerable. Compromises in this area of quality control can be envisaged whereby relatively more 'energy' could be devoted to reproduction during the earlier phases of the lifespan. For comparatively long-lived species, one would predict greater fidelity of the enzymes involved in DNA replication and DNA repair, with a decrease in the rate of somatic mutation; this is a basis for the intrinsic mutagenesis theory of ageing (Burnet 1974). Correlations, in mammalian species, between the efficiency of certain methods of DNA repair or certain gene products thought to be of importance to DNA repair (Grube and Burkle 1992) and species lifespan lend some support to that proposal (Hart and Setlow 1974), but as yet there is no systematic evidence pointing to correlations between the maximum potential lifespans of various mammalian species and the rates of accumulation of point mutations.

As yet there is little information on the effects of caloric restriction on various aspects of genomic stability. Restriction does appear to retard the rate of decline in unscheduled DNA synthesis for some tissues of F344 rats (Weraarchakul et al. 1989).

Ageing as a decline in the rate of protein synthesis and turnover

About three-quarters of the large number of studies in various tissues of many organisms have indicated that ageing is associated with a decline in bulk protein synthesis (Richardson 1981). For a limited number of loci so far examined, this appears to be associated with a decline in the rate of gene transcription (Richardson et al. 1987).

The body of knowledge linking ageing to a decline in the rates of protein turnover is more limited (Bienkowski and Baum 1983), but a number of studies (Dubitsky et al. 1985; Goldspink et al. 1985) do indicate such declines. An 'altered protein breakdown' theory of ageing has been proposed whereby compromised lysosomal pathways of protein degradation could result in the accumulation of abnormal proteins in aged cells, with the induction of cytosolic pathways that are presumed to lead to the excessive degradation of normal short-lived proteins with deleterious metabolic effects (Dice and Goff 1987). Rothstein (1982) believes that the numerous post-translationally altered proteins in the tissues of aged animals are the outcome of subtle denaturations that follow from the prolonged 'dwell time' of proteins, the result of decline in the rates of both synthesis and degradation. However, it has yet to be demonstrated that the accumulation of such altered proteins is functionally significant. One should recall that, for the case of heterozygous carriers of numerous recessive inborn errors of metabolism, there is no discernible phenotype, despite the fact that there is typically a reduction by half in the concentrations of the affected enzymes (Pembrey 1987). However, it may be that reductions by half in the concentrations of the functionally active molecules of numerous proteins, particularly if they are parts of some common metabolic pathways, could in fact contribute to the senescent phenotype. Immunological assays for the total populations of such molecules could be misleading, because it has been shown, for enzymes, that there is a decline during ageing in the proportion of enzymatically active molecules in the total of immunologically detectable molecules (Gershon and Gershon 1970).

The observation of a more or less systematic decline in protein synthesis and turnover does not obviously fit with the evolutionary theories discussed above. One possibility is that this represents the extension of a process that begins as growth and becomes down-regulated, permitting more 'resources' to be devoted to reproduction. Once set in motion, such a process could continue throughout later stages of the lifespan. There is some experimental support for this scenario (Swisshelm *et al.* 1990). This would be an example of an antagonistic pleiotropic type of gene action and would then indeed fit the evolutionary biological theory of ageing.

Caloric restriction appears to ameliorate the age-associated decline in protein synthesis and turnover (Holehan and Merry 1986), thus suggesting that these phenomena are fundamental concomitants of ageing.

Ageing as the result of a neuroendocrine 'cascade'

According to this theory (Finch 1976), the peripheral physiological decrements of ageing could be the inevitable by-products of the complex positive and negative feedback systems associated with the neuroendocrine controls of visceral function. The best studied sub-system has been the neuroendocrine reproductive system of the female rodent, in which there is evidence of deleterious feedback effects of oestrogenic substances upon hypothalamic neurones; these effects can be attenuated by oophorectomy (Finch *et al.* 1984; Wise *et al.* 1989)

This model might be regarded as a special case of a more general 'systems analysis' or 'integrative physiology' view of ageing, although modern extensions of this approach introduce thermodynamic concepts of 'physiological noise', lethal fluctuations and catastrophes, non-linear mechanics, and bifurcation theory (Yates 1988), all of which are beyond the scope of this chapter.

One could reconcile these concepts with current evolutionary theory, as the undesirable late effects of feedback are presumably by-products of systems that were selected in order to enhance reproductive fitness. However, some gerontologists regard neuroendocrine theories as examples of 'programmed' ageing in which the 'pacemaker' of ageing is in the central nervous system. Such a view is indeed at variance with the evolutionary theory, although, as indicated earlier, it is conceivable that some evolutionary vestige of a type of 'programmed' ageing, as seen in semelparous organisms, might be operative in mammals.

There is not enough available information to evaluate this theory from the point of view of experimental caloric restriction. On clinical grounds, this theory is of major importance and could underlie human menopause, andropause, and somatopause (Lamberts *et al.* 1997).

Ageing as a decline in proliferative homeostasis

Ageing mammals characteristically have striking multifocal arrays of tissue hyperplasia, often occurring side by side with regions of atrophy. Examples include the following: the proliferation of arterial myointimal cells in atherosclerosis; adipocytes in regional obesity; chondrocytes, osteocytes, and synovial cells in osteoarthrosis; glial cells in regional neuronal atrophy; epidermal basal cells in verruca senilis; epidermal melanocytes in senile lentigo; epidermal squamous cells in senile keratosis; fibroblasts in interstitial fibrosis; fibromuscular

stromal cells and glandular prostatic epithelium in benign prostatic hyperplasia; lymphocytes in ectopic lymphoid tissue; suppressor T cells in immunological deficiency; oral mucosal squamous cells in leucoplakia; ovarian cortical stromal cells in ovarian stromal hyperplasia; pancreatic ductal epithelial cells in ductal hyperplasia and metaplasia; sebaceous glandular epithelium in Fordyce disease (of oral mucosa) and in senile sebaceous hyperplasia (of skin) (Martin 1979).

The underlying mechanisms are unknown, but conceivably could be related to alterations in cell–cell communication, qualitative and/or quantitative changes in cells and/or receptors for various mitogens and cell-cycle inhibitors, or changes in the availability and quality of the effector agents themselves. While there is indeed a large published record pointing to changes in receptors in various types of ageing cells, very little is known about changes in cell–cell communications during ageing. However, it has been speculated that the clonal cell–cell senescence of somatic cells described below could underlie inappropriate hyperplasia through a loss of normal feedback regulation among sets of related cell types (Martin 1979).

Whatever the underlying cellular and molecular mechanisms, one potentially important consequence of these alterations in the control of the mitotic cell cycle is the emergence of benign and malignant neoplasms, as prolonged cell proliferation could allow the expression of initiating events in oncogenesis through the opportunity for selection of secondary and tertiary alterations in the genome which further distance the cell from physiological controls.

Tissue atrophy, presumably due, in part, to the loss of the ability of potential precursor cells to replace effete cells, is the other side of the coin as regards the maintenance of proliferative homeostasis in ageing organisms. However, we have only limited information on this question *in vivo*, particularly in humans. Some experiments with animals have indeed demonstrated a decrease in the baseline and induced proliferative behaviours of various cell types during ageing (Krauss 1981), but there are exceptions (Siemerman *et al.* 1982; Holt and Yeh 1989). Most of our information on the limited replicative potential of normal diploid somatic cells comes from experimental cell and tissue culture. Tissue culture has clearly established that the rate and extent of cellular outgrowth from explants declines as a function of donor age. The outcome of cell culture led to the famous 'Hayflick limit', in which it was quantitatively established by Hayflick and Moorhead (1961) and numerous subsequent workers that mass cultures and individual clones of normal diploid cells from various animal and human tissues eventually cease to replicate unless genetic alterations occur in the cells leading to a 'transformation' to unlimited growth. Many regard such culture systems as models for the study of cellular ageing and have described numerous biochemical and morphological changes associated with the *in vitro* decline in growth potential. A particularly cogent idea (Campisi 1997) is that occasional replicatively senescent cells *in vivo* (Dimri *et al.* 1995) may have broad 'field effects' as a result of the inappropriate overexpression of a variety of gene products. These could include collagenases, elastases, and various cytokines.

The mechanisms underlying the gradual loss of proliferation are unknown. At least four different recessive genetic loci are involved in the escape from the limited lifespan (Pereira-Smith and Smith 1988). One class of hypotheses invokes an active genetically programmed phenomenon (Smith *et al.* 1987), perhaps analogous to the terminal differentiation of stem cell lineages (Martin *et al.* 1975;

Seshadri and Campisi 1990). Any such process should not have escaped the force of natural selection, however, particularly as it is seen in cultures derived from embryos. The process of replicative decline (clonal attenuation) may have evolved as a mechanism to control fetal growth (Martin 1993) or as a tumour suppressor mechanism. The loss of repeat sequences at the ends of chromosomes has also been proposed as a mechanism for exit from the cell cycle (Chiu and Harley 1997). Most normal somatic cells (but not germ-line or many cancer cells) lack an enzyme called telomerase that functions to add such repeat units to chromosome ends. The proliferative span of such cells can be increased by transfection with telomerase (Bodnar et al. 1998). While the process of clonal attenuation could have evolved for adaptive reasons, like other antagonistic pleiotropic types of gene action, there could be deleterious consequences (in this case, loss of proliferative homeostasis) late in the life course. Another class of theories invokes stochastic events, such as the loss of methyl groups in DNA (Holliday 1986) or oxidatively mediated DNA damage (Chen et al. 1995). Finally, it should be noted that caloric restriction (in mice) appears to retard the rate of loss of the replicative potentials of many different somatic cell types (Pendergrass et al. 1995; Wolf et al. 1995).

Ageing as autoimmunity

This is one of the most venerable theories of ageing (Walford 1969) and is based upon a large body of evidence for a rise in the titres of autoantibodies in ageing animals and humans as well as an associated complex series of alterations in the immune system. However, many simple eukaryotic organisms without immune systems undergo biological ageing. While autoimmunity is likely to contribute to the senescent phenotype of mammals, it is unlikely to be the most fundamental underlying mechanism. Moreover, one cannot conclude from the observation of rising titres of antibodies that these are responsible for structural and functional decrements of ageing.

Ageing as the result of mechanical stress

For structures such as teeth, it is clear that mechanical wear and tear can contribute to the phenotype of ageing. However, such effects are likely to be more closely related to chronological time than to intrinsic biological ageing.

Conclusions

We have seen how the concepts of evolutionary biology, as developed in the previous chapter (Chapter 2.1), lead to certain constraints regarding biological mechanisms of ageing. In age-structured populations that reproduce repeatedly, such as human beings and virtually all mammals, there is no theoretical basis for determinative developmentally programmed mechanisms of senescence. There is no evidence of 'killer genes' designed to limit the lifespans of such organisms. A more plausible scenario is that ageing emerges as a by-product of gene action selected on the basis of enhancement of reproductive fitness. Species-specific lifespans and the complex phenotype of senescence appear to be modulated by a large number of genes. Alleles at such loci, acting in concert with numerous

environmental agents, could differentially influence numerous independent and pathogenetically overlapping biological mechanisms of ageing.

The above picture of ageing has important implications for the practice of geriatric medicine. It gives a scientific framework for the common clinical perception that there is enormous individual variation in the patterns of ageing and, consequently, emphasizes the importance of tailoring preventive medicine and management to the unique susceptibilities and strengths of the individual patient. However, the enhancement of longevity via caloric restriction (yet to be confirmed in primates) argues for a major unification of apparently diverse mechanisms of ageing.

Which view is nearer the truth—the evolutionary/genetic view of numerous independent mechanisms, or the caloric restrictionist view of a universal fundamental mechanism of ageing that is yet to be discovered? Perhaps the answer is that there are indeed a few major pathways and numerous minor pathways, all of which are subject to both genetic and environmental controls.

References

Albert, R.E., Benjamin, S.A., and Chukla, R. (1994). Life span and cancer mortality in the beagle dog and humans. *Mechanisms of Ageing and Development*, **74**, 149–59.

Austad, S.N. (1997). *Why we age: what science is discovering about the body's journey throughout life*. Wiley, New York.

Baynes, J.W. and Monnier, V.M. (ed.) (1989). *The Maillard reaction in aging, diabetes, and nutrition*. Liss, New York.

Bienkowski, R.S. and Baum, B.J. (1983). Measurement of intracellular protein degradation. In *Altered proteins and aging* (ed. R.C. Adelman and G.S. Roth), pp. 55–80. CRC Press, Boca Raton, FL.

Bodnar, A.G., Ouelette, M., Frolkis, M., *et al.* (1998). Extension of life-span by introduction of telomerase into normal human cells. *Science*, **279**, 349–52.

Burnet, M. (1974). *Intrinsic mutagenesis: a genetic approach to ageing*. Wiley, New York.

Campisi, J. (1997). Aging and cancer: the double-edged sword of replicative senescence. *Journal of the American Geriatrics Society*, **45**, 482–8.

Chen, Q., Fischer, A. Reagan, J.D., Yan, L.J., and Ames, B.N. (1995). Oxidative DNA damage and senescence of human diploid fibroblast cells. *Proceedings of the National Academy of Sciences of the United States of America*, **92**, 4337–41.

Chiu, C.-P. and Harley, C.B. (1997). Replicative senescence and cell immortality: the role of telomeres and telomerase. *Proceedings of the Society for Experimental Biology and Medicine*, **214**, 99–106.

Cutler, R.G. (1975). Evolution of human longevity and the genetic complexity governing aging rate. *Proceedings of the National Academy of Sciences of the United States of America*, **72**, 4664–8.

Davies, K.J.A., Quintanilha, A.T., Brooks, G.A., and Packer, L. (1982). Free radicals and tissue damage produced by exercise. *Biochemical and Biophysical Research Communications*, **107**, 1198–1205.

Davis, R.E., Miller, S., Herrnstadt, C., *et al.* (1997). Mutations in mitochondrial cytochrome c oxidase genes segregate with late-onset Alzheimer disease. *Proceedings of the National Academy of Sciences of the United States of America*, **94**, 4526–31.

Dice, J.F. and Goff, S.A. (1987). Error catastrophe and aging: future directions of research. In *Aging*, Vol. 31, *Modern biological theories of aging* (ed. H.R. Warner, R.N. Butler, R.L. Sprott, and E.L. Schneider), pp. 155–68. Raven Press, New York.

Dimri, G.P., Lee, X., Basile, G., *et al.* (1995). A biomarker that identifies senescent human cells in culture and in aging skin *in vivo*. *Proceedings of the National Academy of Sciences of the United States of America*, 92, 9363–7.

Dubitsky, R., Bensch, K.G., and Fleming, J.E. (1985). Age-related changes in turnover and concentration of a subset of thorax polypeptides from *Drosophila melanogaster*. *Mechanisms of Ageing and Development*, 32, 311–17.

Finch, C.E. (1976). The regulation of physiological changes during mammalian aging. *Quarterly Review of Biology*, 51, 49–83.

Finch, C.E., Felicio, L.S., Mobbs, C.V., and Nelson, J.F. (1984). Ovarian and steroidal influences on neuroendocrine aging processes in female rodents. *Endocrine Reviews*, 5, 467–97.

Fukuchi, K.-I., Martin, G.M., and Monnat, R.J., Jr (1989). The mutator phenotype of Werner syndrome is characterized by extensive deletions. *Proceedings of the National Academy of Sciences of the United States of America*, 86, 5893–7.

Gershon, H. and Gershon, D. (1970). Detection of inactive enzyme molecules in ageing organisms. *Nature*, 227, 1214–17.

Goldspink, D.F., Lewis, S.E., and Kelly, F.J. (1985). Protein turnover and cathepsin B activity in several individual tissues of fetal and senescent rats. *Comparative Biochemistry and Physiology, Part B*, 82, 849–53.

Grube, K. and Burkle, A. (1992). Poly(ADP-ribose) polymerase activity in mononuclear leukocytes of 13 mammalian species correlates with species-specific life span. *Proceedings of the National Academy of Sciences of the United States of America*, 89, 11 759–63.

Harman, D. (1994). Free-radical theory of aging. Increasing the functional life span. *Annals of the New York Academy of Sciences*, 717, 1–15.

Hart, R.W. and Setlow, R.B. (1974). Correlation between deoxyribonucleic acid excision-repair and life-span in a number of mammalian species. *Proceedings of the National Academy of Sciences of the United States of America*, 71, 2169–73.

Hayflick, L. and Moorhead, P.S. (1961). The serial cultivation of human diploid cell strains. *Experimental Cell Research*, 25, 585–621.

Holehan, A.M. and Merry, E.J. (1986). The experimental manipulation of ageing by diet. *Biological Reviews of the Cambridge Philosophical Society*, 61, 329–68.

Holliday, R. (1986). Strong effects of 5-azacytidine on the *in vitro* lifespan of human diploid fibroblasts. *Experimental Cell Research*, 166, 543–52.

Holliday, R. (1987). The inheritance of epigenetic defects. *Science*, 238, 163–70.

Holmes, D.J. and Austad, S.N. (1995). Birds as animal models for the comparative biology of aging: a prospectus. *Journal of Gerontology: Biological Sciences*, 50A, B59–66.

Holt, P.R. and Yeh, K.Y. (1989). Small intestinal crypt cell proliferation rates are increased in senescent rats. *Journal of Gerontology*, 44, B9–14.

Johnson, T.E. (1987). Aging can be genetically dissected into component processes using long-lived lines of *Caenorhabditis elegans*. *Proceedings of the National Academy of Sciences of the United States of America*, 84, 3777–81.

Kimura, K.D., Tissenbaum, H.A., Liu, Y.X., and Ruvkun, G. (1997). Daf-2, an insulin receptor-like gene that regulates longevity and diapause in *Caenorhabditis elegans*. *Science*, 277, 942–6.

Krauss, S.W. (1981). DNA replication in aging. In *CRC handbook of biochemistry in aging* (ed. J.R. Florini), pp. 3–8. CRC Press, Boca Raton, FL.

Lamberts, S.W.J., van den Beld, A.W., and van der Lely, A.-J. (1997). The endocrinology of aging. *Science*, 278, 419–24.

Lane, M.A., Ingram, D.K., Ball, S.S., and Roth, G.S. (1997). Dehydroepiandrosterone sulfate: a biomarker of primate aging slowed by calorie restriction. *Journal of Clinical Endocrinology and Metabolism*, 82, 2093–6.

Lopez-Torres, M., Perez-Campo, R., Cadenas, S., Rojas, J.C., and Barja, G. (1993). A comparative study of free radicals in vertebrates: II. Non-enzymatic antioxidants and oxidative stress. *Comparative Biochemistry and Physiology, Part B*, 105, 757–63.

Luckinbill, L.S., Graves, I.L., Reed, A.N., and Koetsawang, S. (1988). Localizing genes that defer senescence in *Drosophila melanogaster*. *Heredity*, 60, 367–74.

Manton, K.G. and Stallard, E. (1996). Longevity in the United States: age and sex-specific evidence on life span limits from mortality patterns 1960–1990. *Journal of Gerontology: Biological Sciences*, 51A, B362–75.

Martin, G.M. (1977). Cellular aging–postreplicative cells. A review (Part II). *American Journal of Pathology*, 89, 513–30.

Martin, G.M. (1978). Genetic syndromes in man with potential relevance to the pathobiology of aging. *Birth Defects: Original Article Series*, 14, 5–39.

Martin, G.M. (1979). Proliferative homeostasis and its age-related aberrations. *Mechanisms of Ageing and Development*, 9, 385–91.

Martin, G.M. (1988). Constitutional genetic markers of aging. *Experimental Gerontology*, 23, 257–67.

Martin, G.M. (1993). Clonal attenuation: causes and consequences. *Journal of Gerontology*, 48, B171–2.

Martin, G.M., Sprague, C.A., Norwood, T.A., *et al.* (1975). Do hyperplastoid lines 'differentiate themselves to death'? *Advances in Experimental Medicine and Biology*, 53, 67–90.

Martin, G.M., Fry, M., and Loeb, L.A. (1985). Somatic mutation and aging in mammalian cells. In *Molecular biology of aging: gene stability and gene expression* (ed. R.S. Sohal, L.S. Birnbaum, and R.G. Cutler), pp. 7–21. Raven Press, New York.

Martin, G.M., Ogburn, C.E., Colgin, L.M., Gown, A.M., Edland, S.D., and Monnat, R.J., Jr (1996). Somatic mutations are frequent and increase with age in human kidney epithelial cells. *Human Molecular Genetics*, 5, 215–21.

Maynard Smith, J. (1965). Theories of aging. In *Topics in the biology of aging* (ed. F.L. Krohn), pp. 1–35. Wiley, New York.

Migeon, S.R., Axelman, I., and Beggs, A.N. (1988). Effect of ageing on reactivation of the human X-linked HPRT locus. *Nature*, 335, 93–6.

Ogburn, C.E., Austad, S.N., Holmes, D.J., *et al.* (1998). Cultured renal epithelial cells from birds and mice: enhanced resistance of avian cells to oxidative stress and DNA damage. *Journal of Gerontology: Biological Sciences*, 53A, B287–92.

Orgel, L.E. (1963). The maintenance of the accuracy of protein synthesis and its relevance to ageing. *Proceedings of the National Academy of Sciences of the United States of America*, 6, 517–21.

Orgel, L.E. (1970). The maintenance of the accuracy of protein synthesis and its relevance to ageing: a correction. *Proceedings of the National Academy of Sciences of the United States of America*, 67,1476.

Pembrey, M.E. (1987). Genetic factors in disease. In *Oxford textbook of medicine* (2nd ed.) (ed. D.J. Weatherall, J.G.G. Ledingham, and D.A. Warrell), pp. 4.1–4.47. Oxford University Press.

Pendergrass, W.R., Li, Y., Jiang, D., Fei, R.G., and Wolf, N.S. (1995). Caloric restriction: conservation of cellular replicative capacity *in vitro* accompanies life-span extension in mice. *Experimental Cell Research*, 217, 309–16.

Pereira-Smith, O.M. and Smith, J.R. (1988). Genetic analysis of indefinite division in human cells: identification of four complementation groups. *Proceedings of the National Academy of Sciences of the United States of America*, 85, 6042–6.

Pryor, W.A. (1986). Oxy-radicals and related species: their formation, lifetimes, and reactions. *Annual Review of Physiology*, 48, 657–67.

Richardson, A. (1981). The relationship between aging and protein synthesis. In *CRC handbook of biochemistry in aging* (ed. J. R. Florini), pp. 3–8. CRC Press, Boca Raton, FL.

Richardson, A., Butler, J.A., Rutherford, M.S., *et al.* (1987). Effect of age and dietary restriction on the expression of α2U-globulin. *Journal of Biological Chemistry*, 262, 12 821–5.

Rothstein, M. (1982). *Biochemical approaches to aging*. Academic Press, New York.

Seshadri, T. and Campisi, J. (1990). Repression of c-*fos* transcription and an altered genetic program in senescent human fibroblasts. *Science*, 247, 205–9.

Siemerman, M.B., Weinstein, R., Rowe, I.W., Maciag, T., Fuhro, R., and Gardner, R. (1982). Vascular smooth muscle cell growth kinetics *in vivo* in aged rats. *Proceedings of the National Academy of Sciences of the United States of America*, 79, 3863–6.

Smeal, T., Claus, J., Kennedy, B., Cole, F., and Guarente, L. (1996). Loss of transcriptional silencing causes sterility in old mother cells of *S. cerevisiae*. *Cell*, 84, 633–42.

Smith, J.R., Spiering, A.L., and Pereira-Smith, O.M. (1987). Is cellular senescence genetically programmed? *Basic Life Sciences*, 42, 283–94.

Stadtman, E.R. and Berlett, B.S. (1997). Reactive oxygen-mediated protein oxidation in aging and disease. *Chemical Research in Toxicology*, 10, 485–94.

Swisshelm, K., Distech, C.M., Thorvaldsen, J., Nelson, A., and Salk, D. (1990). Age-related increase in methylation of ribosomal genes and inactivation of chromosome-specific rRNA gene clusters in mouse. *Mutation Research*, 237, 131–46.

Walford, R.L. (1969). *The immunologic theory of aging*. Munksgaard, Copenhagen.

Wallace, D.C., Bohr, V.A., Cortopassi, G., *et al.* (1995). Group Report: The role of bioenergetics and mitochondrial DNA mutations in aging and age-related diseases. In *Molecular aspects of aging* (ed. K. Esser and G.M. Martin), pp. 198–225. Wiley, New York.

Warner, H.R., Butler, R.N., Sprott, R.L., and Schneider, E.L. (ed.) (1987). *Aging*, Vol. 31, *Modern biological theories of aging*. Raven Press, New York.

Weindruch, R. and Sohal, R.S. (1997). Seminars in medicine of the Beth Israel Deaconess Medical Center: caloric intake and aging. *New England Journal of Medicine*, 337, 986–94.

Weindruch, R. and Walford, R.L. (1988). *The retardation of aging and disease by dietary restriction*. Thomas, Springfield, IL.

Weraarchakul, N., Strong, R., Wood, W.G., and Richardson, A. (1989). The effect of aging and dietary restriction on DNA repair. *Experimental Cell Research*, 181, 197–204.

Williams, G.C. (1957). Pleiotropy, natural selection, and the evolution of senescence. *Evolution*, 11, 398–411.

Wise, P. M., Weiland, N.G., Scarbrough, K., Sortino, M.A., Cohen, I.R., and Larson, G.H. (1989). Changing hypothalamopituitary function: its role in aging of the female reproductive system. *Hormone Research*, 31, 39–44.

Wolf, N.S., Penn, P.E., Jiang, D., Fei, R.G., and Pendergrass, W.R. (1995). Caloric restriction: conservation of *in vivo* cellular replicative capacity accompanies life-span extension in mice. *Experimental Cell Research*, 217, 317–23.

Yates, F.E. (1988). The dynamics of aging and time: how physical action implies social action. In *Emergent theories of aging* (ed. J.E. Birren and V.L. Bengtson), pp. 90–117. Springer, New York.

Yu, C.-E., Oshima, J., Fu, Y.H., *et al.* (1996). Positional cloning of the Werner's syndrome gene. *Science*, 272, 258–62.

Zs-Nagy, I., Cutler, R.G., and Semsei, I. (1988). Dysdifferentiation hypothesis of aging and cancer: a comparison with the membrane hypothesis of aging. *Annals of the New York Academy of Sciences*, 521, 215–25.

3

Infections

3.1 Epidemiology of infectious diseases

Ann R. Falsey

Introduction

Infections are among the most common problems of older persons and are a significant cause of morbidity and mortality. Pneumonia and influenza rank fifth and sepsis ranks tenth as leading causes of death in persons aged over 65 (Anonymous 1987). Infections are also among the most frequent reasons for hospital admission of older persons living in the community and are the leading diagnosis necessitating transfer of residents of long-term care facilities to acute care hospitals (Irvine *et al.* 1984; Tresch *et al.* 1985; Ruben *et al.* 1995). Many infectious diseases increase in frequency with age and almost all are associated with increased mortality (Yoshikawa 1994*a*) (Tables 1 and 2).

There are many reasons why older persons are at greater risk for infection and suffer higher complication rates from many infectious processes. Age-associated changes in organ function, such as poor circulation and diminished cough reflex, as well as the presence of comorbid diseases contribute significantly to the risk of infection (Crossley and Peterson 1996). In addition, with the increased use of invasive devices and procedures, such as intravenous and urinary catheters, pacemakers, and defibrillators, modern medicine has both prolonged life and created new risk factors for infection. Ageing itself is associated with a number of changes in immune function which affect both humoral and cellular immunity (Miller 1996). Lastly,

approximately 5 per cent of the elderly population live in long-term care facilities, creating special problems related to living in communal settings (Verghese and Berk 1990).

The incidence of infection in older persons depends on their place of residence and their functional status (Setia *et al.* 1985; Darnowski *et al.* 1991). Although 95 per cent of persons over the age of 65 are living independently in the community, specific data on the epidemiology in this population is scant. However, recent studies indicate that infections are a common problem in this age group. In a 2-year prospective study of 417 non-institutionalized older persons in Pittsburgh, Pennsylvania, investigators found that 494 infections were diagnosed in 224 (54 per cent) subjects. The overall rate of infection was 68.6 infections per 100 person years, and rates were similar for males and females. Respiratory infections were most common (52 per cent), followed by infections of the urinary tract (24 per cent) and skin (18 per cent). Of the 260 hospital admissions which occurred during the 2 years of the study, 100 (35 per cent) involved a diagnosis of infection, yielding an annual hospitalized infection rate of 14.1 per 100 person years (Ruben *et al.* 1995).

Nursing-home populations are strikingly different from community-dwelling older persons. The largest percentage of nursing-home residents are 85 years or older (40 per cent) and are usually female (71 per cent), white (92 per cent), and widowed (61 per cent) (Verghese and Berk 1990). The most common diagnoses of patients

Table 1 Infections showing increased frequency with older age

Urinary tract infections

Pneumonia

Tuberculosis

Skin and soft tissue infection

Herpes zoster

Contiguous focus osteomyelitis

Bacteraemia

Infective endocarditis

Cholecystitis

Diverticulitis

Intra-abdominal abscesses

Table 2 Increased fatality associated with infections in older persons

Infection	Relative risk of fatality of elderly compared with young adults
Pneumonia	3
Pyelonephritis	5–10
Bacteraemia	3
Appendicitis	15–20
Cholecystitis	2–8
Tuberculosis	10
Infective endocarditis	2–3
Bacterial meningitis	3

Adapted with permission from Yoshikawa (1994*a*).

before admission are cardiovascular disease, cerebrovascular disease, and arthritis. However, the three leading diagnoses after admission to the nursing home are urinary tract infection, pneumonia, and decubitus ulcers (Verghese and Berk 1990). Single-day prevalence studies yield highly variable infection rates ranging from 2.7 to 32.7 per cent with an average of 11 per cent (Jackson and Fierer 1985; Setia et al. 1985; Scheckler and Peterson 1986; Magaziner et al. 1991). Incidence rates range from 2.6 to 6.7 infections per 1000 resident days, resulting in approximately 1.5 million nosocomial infections per year in long-term care facilities in the United States (Smith et al. 1991). In addition to the chronic problems of respiratory, urinary tract, and skin infections, nursing homes are prone to epidemics of certain diseases, such as tuberculosis, conjunctivitis, scabies, gastroenteritis, and influenza (Smith et al. 1991). Antibiotic resistance of bacterial pathogens is also a special problem in nursing homes because of frequent use of empirical antibiotics, frequent transfers of residents to acute care facilities, and limited infection-control resources in many institutions (Gaynes et al. 1985; John and Ribner 1991). Older persons have also been shown to be at increased risk of acquiring nosocomial infections during admissions to acute care hospitals (Saviteer et al. 1988; Emori et al. 1991). Infection incidence rates for all categories of nosocomial infections increase significantly per decade of life (Saviteer et al. 1988).

Urinary tract infection

Asymptomatic bacteriuria

Bacteriuria is the most common bacterial infection affecting older persons (Nicolle 1997). The prevalence of bacteriuria in community-dwelling women aged below 60 is less than 5 per cent. This rises to 5 to 10 per cent in women aged 60 to 70 and to 20 to 30 per cent in those aged 80 and over (Boscia et al. 1986; Yoshikawa et al. 1996). Bacteriuria is rare in men aged below 60 (< 1 per cent) but also becomes more common with increasing age. Approximately 1 to 3 per cent of men aged between 60 and 65 will have bacteriuria, and this rises to 10 per cent or more in men aged over 80 (Mims et al. 1990; Nicolle 1994). Bacteriuria is even more common in institutionalized older persons, with prevalence rates of 30 to 50 per cent in women and 20 to 30 per cent in men, and correlates with functional disability (Nicolle et al. 1983; Boscia et al. 1986). High rates of bacteriuria in long-term care facilities are probably related to perineal soiling, incomplete bladder emptying, and more frequent use of bladder catheters (Baldassarre and Kaye 1991). The prevalence of bacteriuria is virtually 100 per cent after 30 days with an indwelling urethral catheter (Warren et al. 1982).

Despite the high prevalence of bacteriuria, most elderly persons, whether in the community or in institutions, are asymptomatic (Boscia et al. 1986; Mims et al. 1990; Nicolle 1994). Defining truly 'asymptomatic' individuals can be somewhat difficult in older persons, since chronic urinary complaints, such as urgency, frequency, and incontinence, are common. The incidence of clinically significant urinary tract infection in subjects with asymptomatic bacteriuria has been reported in relatively few studies. In a study of 61 ambulatory women with untreated bacteriuria, 16.4 per cent became symptomatic during the 6-month follow-up with an incidence of 0.9 per 1000 patient days (Boscia et al. 1987). Among institutionalized elderly people with bacteriuria, asymptomatic infection rates of 0.26 per 1000

patient days in women and 0.34 per 1000 patient days in men have been observed (Nicolle 1994). The contribution of asymptomatic bacteriuria to mortality of older people has been controversial. Early studies from Finland and Greece suggested that ambulatory older persons with bacteriuria showed decreased survival rates (Dontas et al. 1981). Subsequent studies from Sweden and a number of other countries have failed to confirm this observation when death rates were controlled for health status and underlying diseases (Mims et al. 1990; Abrutyn et al. 1994; Nordenstram et al. 1996). In addition, asymptomatic bacteriuria in institutionalized persons is not associated with greater mortality or infectious morbidity (Nicolle 1997). A number of studies have shown that antimicrobial treatment of asymptomatic bacteriuria does not affect mortality and morbidity and is associated with adverse side-effects, emergence of resistant flora, and high relapse rates (Mims et al. 1990; Abrutyn et al. 1994; Nicolle 1994, 1997; Yoshikawa et al. 1996). (See Chapter 15.6 for further discussion.)

Symptomatic urinary tract infection

In contrast with the incidence of asymptomatic bacteriuria, symptomatic urinary tract infection rates are relatively low, although they are a significant source of morbidity in later life. Symptomatic urinary tract infections are the most common nosocomial infections in elderly persons in long-term or acute care hospitals, and they account for approximately 24 per cent of all infections diagnosed in healthy ambulatory persons aged over 65 (Jackson and Fierer 1985; Emori et al. 1991; Ruben et al. 1995). Urinary tract infections are also the most common cause of bacteraemia in both institutionalized and ambulatory elderly populations (Setia et al. 1984; Muder et al. 1992). The use of indwelling urinary catheters has been associated with significantly increased rates of bacteraemia, hospital admission, and mortality (Kunin et al. 1992; Muder et al. 1992).

As in younger persons, Escherichia coli is the most common pathogen in geriatric patients; however, the proportion of infections due to other Gram-negative pathogens, such as Proteus, Klebsiella, Serratia, Enterobacter, and Pseudomonas, is higher (Baldassarre and Kaye 1991). Staphylococcus saprophyticus, a common pathogen in young women, is unusual in older women. Isolates from elderly men are frequently Gram-positive organisms, such as group B streptococci, Enterococcus species, and coagulase-negative staphylococci (Boscia et al. 1986, Nicolle et al. 1983). In chronically catheterized patients, the majority (77 per cent) of bacterial isolates are polymicrobial and are frequently antibiotic resistant (Warren et al. 1982; Gaynes et al. 1985). Urinary tract infection is discussed further in Chapter 15.6.

Respiratory tract infections

Viral respiratory tract infections

Rates of upper respiratory tract infections, the majority of which are caused by viruses, decline with advancing age (Monto and Ullman 1974). Lower rates of infection are presumed to be due to partial immunity and less frequent exposures to viral pathogens. In the Tecumseh study, ambulatory persons aged over 60 had an annual incidence of 1.3 acute respiratory illnesses (Monto and Cavallaro 1971); however, the number of subjects studied was small. Rates of infection depend in large part on where older people reside. Hodder *et al.* (1995) showed that the overall rate of respiratory infections in community residents was 2.5 per 100 person months in contrast with 10.8 per 100 person months in an adult day-care setting (Falsey *et al.* 1995*a*). Rates of infection in nursing homes are variable owing to the epidemic nature of most respiratory viruses, but estimated rates are approximately one to three respiratory infections per resident per year (Scheckler and Peterson 1986; Arroyo *et al.* 1988).

Influenza virus is the best studied of the respiratory viruses and its impact on elderly persons is significant. In studies of non-pandemic influenza, attack rates are 20 to 30 per cent in preschool and school-age children and drop to 10 per cent for older adults (Glezen and Couch 1978). Despite the lower infection rates, complication rates are highest in older persons. During epidemics of influenza H3N2, hospital admission rates are approximately 6 to 15 per 1000 for persons aged over 65 (Glezen 1982; Perrotta *et al.* 1985). Lower respiratory tract involvement with influenza infection also increases with advancing age, rising from 4 to 8 per cent in persons aged between 5 and 50 up to as high as 73 per cent in persons aged over 70 (Betts 1995). Age-associated death rates during influenza epidemics tend to follow hospital admission rates but are approximately 10 to 20 times lower. The likelihood of death from influenza increases 39-fold in the presence of chronic medical conditions such as cardio-vascular disease, diabetes, renal disease, anaemia, or im-munosuppression, and the presence of both pulmonary and cardiovascular disease raises mortality by a factor of 870 (Barber and Mullooly 1982). Influenza is discussed further in Chapter 3.4.

Respiratory syncytial virus is now recognized as a significant respiratory viral pathogen in older persons (Fleming and Cross 1993). A number of respiratory syncytial virus outbreaks in nursing homes have been described, with average attack rates of 20 per cent (Public Health Laboratory Service 1983*b*; Sorvillo *et al.* 1984; Agius *et al.* 1990; Falsey *et al.* 1992). In prospective studies, respiratory syncytial virus accounts for 5 to 27 per cent of wintertime illnesses. Complication rates among frail older people have been variable, with rates of pneumonia ranging from 5 to 67 per cent and death from zero to 53 per cent (Fransen *et al.* 1967; Garvie and Gray 1980; Mather *et al.* 1980; Sorvillo *et al.* 1984; Osterweil and Norman 1990; Falsey *et al.* 1995*b*). Although the precise incidence is unknown, recent studies indicate that respiratory syncytial virus is a cause of excess morbidity and mortality in community-dwelling elderly people at rates similar to influenza (Fleming and Cross 1993; Falsey *et al.* 1995*b*).

Parainfluenza viruses have also been shown to cause outbreaks of respiratory illnesses in nursing homes (Public Health Laboratory Service 1983*a*). Prospective studies of nursing-home residents and community-dwelling older persons show that parainfluenza infections account for 4 to 14 per cent of respiratory infections (Gross *et al.* 1988; Arroyo *et al.* 1988). Other common respiratory viruses such as rhinoviruses and coronaviruses also cause disease in older persons (Falsey *et al.* 1997; Wald *et al.* 1995). Illness appears milder than infection with respiratory syncytial virus or influenza, but prolonged convalescence and complications may occur.

Bacterial respiratory infections

Pneumonia is one of the most important infectious causes of morbidity and mortality in persons of any age, but it is at the extremes of age where its impact is greatest. Whether community, nosocomial, or nursing-home acquired, pneumonia is associated with tremendous expense and morbidity.

Pneumonia is the sixth leading cause of death in the United S (Marrie 1994). In England and Wales, over 25 000 deaths in pe over 65 years in 1990 were attributed to pneumonia, accountin 97 per cent of all deaths due to pneumonia (Woodhead 1994 incidence of pneumonia in adults is fairly constant up to age 5 which there is a steady rise such that the incidence in peo 70 to 79 is 10 times greater than in those aged between 20 (Woodhead 1994). In addition to the overall increase in attac the likelihood of requiring hospital admission for pneumon dramatically with age. The annual incidence of pneumonia r hospital admission is 0.54 cases per 1000 among persons ag 44, whereas the rate is 11.6 cases per 1000 for persons aged (Marrie 1994). The incidence of community-acquired pneum all adult age groups is highest during the winter months probably due to winter respiratory viruses. In a 1-year s respiratory illness in older persons, 53 per cent of patient pneumonia were admitted between December and January katesan *et al.* 1990).

Elderly patients with pneumonia are more likely to develop teraemia, empyema, or meningitis and are more likely to die th their younger counterparts (Verghese and Berk 1983; Finkelstei *al.* 1983). For example, pneumococcal pneumonia led to a 26 cent death rate in those aged over 40 compared with a 4 pe fatality in adults aged under 40 (Sullivan *et al.* 1972). A nu studies have found age to be a risk factor for poor outcome in p with community-acquired pneumonia, yet age alone may not ?? strong independent risk factor for fatality (Granton and Grossma 1993). Elderly persons frequently have comorbid diseases, mal-nutrition, and behavioural and socio-economic factors which also increase the risk of pneumonia-related death. Salive and colleagues found that functional disability, as measured by the Activity of Daily Living Scale, and cognitive impairment were independent risk factors for pneumonia-related mortality in older adults (Salive *et al.* 1993).

Nosocomial pneumonia is the second most frequent cause of hospital-associated infections, but the leading cause of infection-related deaths (Emori *et al.* 1991). Between 1986 and 1990 the National Nosocomial Infection Surveillance System in the United States evaluated more than 100 000 nosocomial infections. Pneumonia accounted for 18 per cent of the infections but was associated with 48 per cent of the deaths (Emori *et al.* 1991). Gross and colleagues found a decade-specific risk of nosocomial infections which increased from a relatively constant rate of 10 per 1000 patients discharged for persons aged below 50, and rose to 100 per 1000 after age 70 (Gross *et al.* 1983). Longer hospital stays may contribute to the risk of nosocomial infection in elderly patients. Saviteer and colleagues found that persons aged over 60 had the highest risk of acquiring pneumonia but that the increased risk did not become apparent until the eighth hospital day (Saviteer *et al.* 1988). Other risk factors associated with nosocomial pneumonia include neurological disease, renal disease, dependency in activities of daily living, difficulty with oropharyngeal secretions, presence of nasogastric tubes, poor nutrition, intubation, and intensive care admission (Harkness *et al.* 1990; Hanson *et al.* 1992).

As in the acute care hospital, pneumonia is the second most common infection in chronic care facilities but remains the most common cause of death (Niederman 1993). The susceptibility to infection correlates strongly with the degree of functional impairment (Alvarez 1990). Accurate rates of pneumonia in residents of chronic

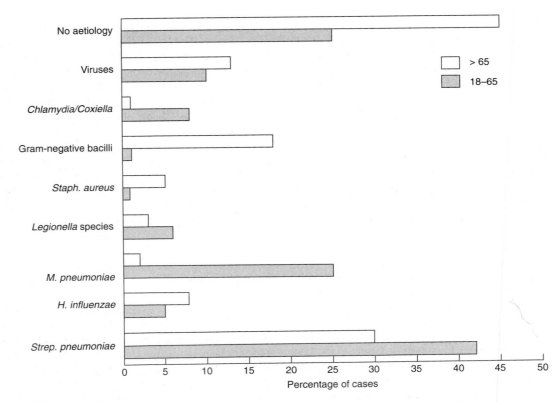

Microbial causes of community-acquired pneumonia in adults: a comparison of those under 65 (shaded bars) (458 patients from three studies) with ... aged 65 years (785 patients from all 11 studies). (Reproduced with permission from Woodhead (1994).)

...ities may be difficult to ascertain as underdiagnosis is common ... of non-specific symptoms, the infrequent use of chest ra-... s, and difficulty obtaining sputum. Prevalence rates of lower ... tract infection in nursing homes range from 1.9 to 2.5 per ... incidence rates of approximately 47 per 100 resident ... Garibaldi et al. 1981; Setia et al. 1985; Scheckler and Peterson ...

...iagnosis of a specific infectious aetiology for pneumonia is ... all ages, but is particularly problematic in elderly persons ... have difficulty in expectorating sputum and may be colonized ...opharynx with Gram-negative bacteria (Marrie et al. 1986). ...trum of pathogens which cause pneumonia in older people ...er than that in young adults (Fig. 1). Nevertheless, Streptococcus ...oniae remains the most common bacterial pathogen, causing ...60 per cent of community-acquired pneumonias. Other bacterial ...ens such as non-typable Haemophilus influenzae, Moraxella ...alis, Staphylococcus aureus are more common in older persons ...1994). Although infection with Gram-negative bacilli occurs ...frequently in older populations, the frequency is probably ...timated because of the poor reliability of sputum samples. ...am-negative bacillary pneumonia is primarily a problem in de-bilitated elderly persons. Legionella should always be considered in the seriously ill patient with pneumonia, although its incidence at older ages appears to vary widely with geographical location. Lastly, the 'atypical' pathogens Mycoplasma pneumoniae and Chlamydia pneumoniae are relatively uncommon in persons aged over 65 (Wood-head 1994).

The aetiologies of pneumonia in nursing homes overlap with the causes of community-acquired pneumonia, but with some important differences. Gram-negative pulmonary infections are more common in nursing-home residents than in community-dwelling elderly people (Garb et al. 1978; Nunley et al. 1990). Garb and colleagues found Klebsiella pneumoniae to be the causative pathogen in 40 per cent of nursing-home residents with pneumonia compared with only 8.6 per cent in the community (Garb et al. 1978). Staph. aureus and Strep. pneumoniae were also common pathogens, found in 26 per cent of cases. E. coli, Enterobacter, Serratia, and Pseudomonas, as well as group B streptococci and anaerobes, are also responsible for pneumonia in chronic care facilities (Nunley et al. 1990; Vankatesan et al. 1990). It is noteworthy that, although the number of Gram-negative pathogens recovered is greater in nursing-home patients than in community-dwelling elderly people, Strep. pneumoniae remains a common cause of nursing-home pneumonia accounting for up to 27 per cent of cases (Garb et al. 1978; Nicolle 1984; Nunley et al. 1990). Lastly, tuberculosis always needs to be considered in the nursing-home resident with pneumonia (see below and Chapter 12.6).

Hospital-acquired pneumonia in older persons is frequently caused by enteric Gram-negative rods and accounts for as many as 60 to 80 per cent of all cases (Niederman 1993). From 1986 to 1990 the National Nosocomial Infection Surveillance study showed nosocomial pneumonia to be due to Pseudomonas in 18 per cent of cases, Enterobacter species in 11 per cent, Klebsiella pneumoniae in 8 per cent, E. coli in 6 per cent, and Staph. aureus in 15 per cent. Mixed and anaerobic infections secondary to aspiration are also considered to be common. Nosocomial *Legionella*, although uncommon, has also been described. The spectrum of pathogens which are isolated from debilitated or chronically ill older persons in many instances reflects the flora of the particular hospital; thus awareness of one's local organisms and resistance patterns is important in diagnosis and treatment.

Tuberculosis

The twentieth century has seen a marked change in the age-specific incidence of tuberculosis. At the turn of the century, tuberculosis was primarily a disease of children and young adults, whereas now its incidence in developed countries is highest in persons aged over 65 (Yoshikawa 1994*b*). In most industrialized countries the incidence of tuberculosis began to decline steadily in the 1960s; however, in the mid-1980s this trend stopped (Dutt and Stead 1991). Several factors such as HIV infection and immigration have influenced the recent trends in the epidemiology of tuberculosis. Elderly people represent an important segment of the population at risk for active disease. In a number of countries, including the United Kingdom, Belgium, Israel, Canada, and the United States, the yearly incidence of tuberculosis in persons aged over 65 is approximately twice to four times greater than in the general population (Van den Brande *et al.* 1990; Macarthur *et al.* 1992; Van Dijk and Rosin 1993; Davies 1994; Duffield *et al.* 1996). Most elderly persons were infected 50 to 70 years ago when 80 per cent of the population aged under 30 became infected. Endogenous reactivation is the primary cause of active disease in later life, although reinfection can occur. A number of factors associated with ageing influence tuberculosis reactivation, such as poor nutrition, diabetes, long-term steroid use, and waning T-cell immunity (Yoshikawa 1994*b*).

In the United States 80 to 90 per cent of tuberculosis cases occur in older people in the community, and persons residing in nursing homes are at an even more increased risk. In the period 1984–1985 the Center for Disease Control in the United States reported a tuberculosis incidence rate of 21.5 per 100 000 population in the elderly living in the community, whereas the rate was 39.2 per 100 000 in nursing-home residents (Yoshikawa 1992).

In nursing homes, tuberculosis is a mixture of reactivation of old lesions with declining resistance and new infection among persons who have lost their immunity and have been exposed to a fellow resident with active disease. Almost all nursing-home residents should be skin-test positive with purified protein derivative (**PPD**) based on previous exposure, but only 15 to 20 per cent are positive on entrance to the institution (Stead *et al.* 1987). The percentage of persons with previously known positive PPDs who remain PPD positive decreases with increasing age and drops from 27 per cent at age 50 to 18 per cent at age 70 and 5 to 10 per cent at age 90. Although most individuals remain immunocompetent, their PPD status reflects 'immunologically forgotten' past infection and thus these individuals are at risk for reinfection. Data from nursing homes in Arkansas show that the number of PPD reactors doubles after 6 months in a nursing home and that men have twice the rate of PPD conversions shown by women. Some cases may represent resolution of anergy with improved nutrition, but others represent reinfection. Epidemics of tuberculosis in nursing homes have been well described. The importance of PPD conversion in nursing-home residents should be stressed, since they are at significantly increased risk for developing active disease (Stead

1981). For those individuals who are PPD positive on admission, only 2 to 3 per cent will develop active tuberculosis, whereas 7.6 per cent of women and 12.7 per cent of men who have a PPD conversion will develop active disease without prophylaxis (Stead *et al.* 1987). The benefit of isoniazid prophylaxis compared with the risk of isoniazid-induced hepatitis even in frail institutionalized elderly people is favourable and is recommended for those with documented PPD conversions (Stead *et al.* 1987).

Persons over 65 with active tuberculosis have a death rate approximately 10 times that of persons aged between 25 and 44. From 1979 to 1989 persons over 65 accounted for 60 per cent of all deaths attributed to tuberculosis in the United States (Yoshikawa 1992). The increased mortality observed in elderly persons may be partly due to atypical presentations which may delay diagnosis and treatment (Alvarez *et al.* 1987).

Infections of the skin and soft tissues

The process of ageing has significant effects on the human skin (Gilchrist 1982). Older skin exhibits increased dryness, loss of glands, decreased elasticity, and poor wound healing. In addition, there may be small-vessel disease due to diabetes or large-vessel atherosclerosis which compromises skin and soft tissue viability. After the urinary and respiratory tracts, the skin is the third most common site of infection in older persons (Alvarez 1990; Ruben *et al.* 1995). The incidence of cellulitis, diabetic foot ulcers, and other cutaneous infections increases with age. In community-dwelling older persons, the incidence for all types of skin infections is 12.7 per 100 person years and the incidence of cellulitis is 3.2 per 100 person years (Ruben *et al.* 1995).

Pressure sores

Skin infections are very common in nursing homes, in part owing to the high prevalence (4–6 per cent) of infected pressure sores (Garibaldi *et al.* 1981; Darnowski *et al.* 1991; Magaziner *et al.* 1991). The incidence of new skin infections in nursing homes is approximately 1.6 per 100 resident months (Scheckler and Peterson 1986). Significant morbidity and mortality are associated with infected decubitus ulcers, and bacteraemia complicates infected pressure sores in up to 80 per cent of cases with fatality rates of approximately 50 per cent (Galpin *et al.* 1976; Chow *et al.* 1977; Bryan *et al.* 1983). Other complications include osteomyelitis, septic arthritis, and tetanus (Bryan *et al.* 1983). In addition to the common skin pathogens *Staph. aureus* and group A streptococci, infected pressure ulcers may contain *Enterococcus* species, group B streptococci, Gram-negative rods, and anaerobes. The majority of infected pressure sores are polymicrobial and include anaerobes and Gram-negative bacilli (Galpin *et al.* 1976; Bryan *et al.* 1983; Setia *et al.* 1985).

Tetanus

In developed countries tetanus is an uncommon infection with an annual incidence of approximately 0.03 per 100 000 and is primarily a disease of older persons, many of whom are not immune (Richardson and Knight 1991). Approximately 70 per cent of recent tetanus cases have been in persons aged over 50 years. In addition, case–fatality rates increase significantly with age. The death rate in cases of tetanus rises from 20 to 30 per cent in the general population to 52 per cent in persons aged 60 and older. Approximately 20 to 30 per cent of tetanus cases are due to chronic wounds such as infected decubitus ulcers or gangrene. Only 54 per cent of community-dwelling elderly people and 29 per cent of those in institutions are immune (Weiss et al. 1983). Elderly women are less likely to be immune than men, particularly those with military service since 1941.

Herpes zoster

Herpes zoster results from the reactivation of latent varicella zoster virus in the dorsal root ganglia. The overall lifetime risk of zoster is approximately 10 to 20 per cent, although the risk increases dramatically with increasing age (Straus et al. 1988). The annual incidence of varicella zoster in the general population is 215 per 100 000, but increases steadily after age 40 reaching 1424 per 100 000 in persons aged over 75 (Donahue 1995). Approximately 1 per cent of persons aged over 80 will develop herpes zoster each year. The risk of postherpetic neuralgia also increases with age (Kost and Straus 1996). Few children have postherpetic neuralgia compared with 47 per cent of adults aged over 60. In addition, the severity and intractability of pain may also increase with age. Pain lasting over a year has been reported in 4 per cent, 22 per cent, and 48 per cent of patients aged under 20, over 55, and over 70 respectively (Kost and Straus 1996). The association of age and risk of herpes zoster is believed to reflect the gradual senescence of cell-mediated immunity (Straus et al. 1988).

Infectious diarrhoea

The importance of diarrhoeal illness among older persons has been increasingly recognized in recent years. Although the overall incidence of diarrhoea in older persons in the general population is not increased, the impact of these illnesses is substantial. In a report from the Center for Disease Control analysing 28 538 diarrhoea-related deaths between 1979 and 1989, the majority (51 per cent) were in adults aged over 74 (Bennett and Greenough 1993). A subsequent study of 87 181 hospital admissions for gastroenteritis found that 85 per cent of the 514 deaths were adults over the age of 60, with a case–fatality rate of 3 per cent in persons aged over 80. Additionally, the World Health Organization found that Japanese adults aged over 75 had a 400-fold increase in mortality due to gastroenteritis. The majority of diarrhoea-related deaths in older persons are presumed to be due to dehydration, leading to organ infarction and failure (Bennett and Greenough 1993).

Age is recognized as a risk factor for many bacterial gastrointestinal pathogens such as Salmonella species, Campylobacter species, and Clostridium difficile (Bennett and Greenough 1993). In addition, older people are more likely to become ill when exposed to pathogens such as cholera, Clostridium perfringens, C. difficile, and toxigenic E. coli. Increased risk for the acquisition of infection is believed to be due to achlorhydria, diminished intestinal mobility, and frequent antibiotic use.

Among older persons, nursing-home residents are at highest risk for developing diarrhoeal illness and outbreaks of diarrhoea occur commonly in long-term care facilities. In addition to outbreaks from common food source exposures, the spread of gastrointestinal pathogens is facilitated by communal activities and faecal incontinence. In 1970 an explosive epidemic of Salmonella occurred in a United States nursing home, with 72 per cent of residents and 29 per cent of staff becoming ill in a 9-day period. Twenty-four per cent of residents died. The presumed source of infection was a common food source, although this was never proved (Bennett 1993). Other reports of Salmonella in nursing homes where epidemics were more prolonged suggest that carrier states and person-to-person spread may be important in the transmission of Salmonella in long-term care facilities. E. coli 0157:H7 has also been implicated in nursing-home outbreaks and is associated with high case–fatality rates (Carter 1987). Outbreaks of rotavirus, Giardia, and cryptosporidiosis have also been reported in chronic care facilities (Cubitt and Holzel 1980; Marrie et al. 1982; Bennett and Greenough 1993).

Lastly, age is also associated with the development of C. difficile diarrhoea in the community, hospital, and nursing-home settings. Clusters of C. difficile have been reported from a number of nursing homes, and control of outbreaks is very difficult because of the prolonged carrier state, hardy spores, and faecal–oral contamination in demented and incontinent patients (Bentley 1990).

Meningitis

The incidence of meningitis is highest among neonates (2 per 10 000 per year); however, a second peak in incidence occurs in persons aged 60 or older (2–9 per 100 000 per year). In the United States approximately 1000 to 3000 cases of meningitis occur in older persons each year (Miller and Choi 1997). Although meningitis is less common in older persons than in young children, the case–fatality rate is higher ranging from 35 to 81 per cent (Behrman et al. 1989; Durand et al. 1993; Miller and Choi 1997).

The spectrum of pathogens which cause meningitis in older persons is somewhat different from that in healthy young adults (Schuchat et al. 1997). Strep. pneumoniae is the single most commonly isolated organism in all studies of elderly adults (32–68 per cent). Listeria monocytogenes, an uncommon pathogen in young adults, accounts for 10 to 25 per cent of cases of meningitis in older people, and H. influenza and Neisseria meningitidis, which are common in children and young adults, are uncommon in older persons (Durand et al. 1993). Gram-negative bacillary meningitis occurs more frequently in older persons (11–25 per cent) and is often associated with urosepsis or head trauma. Staph. aureus meningitis occurs in 4 to 11 per cent of cases, almost always in the presence of disseminated staphylococcal infection. Although tuberculous meningitis is not common at any age, the incidence of active tuberculosis rises with advancing age; therefore tuberculous meningitis should be considered in any older person with 'aseptic' meningitis. Unlike young adults, viral meningitis is relatively uncommon in older adults, accounting for only 2 per cent of cases in one study (Miller and Choi 1997). (See Chapter 18.18 for further discussion.)

Bacteraemia

Both the frequency of and mortality from bacteraemic illnesses appear to increase with advancing age (Richardson et al. 1993). The genitourinary tract is the leading source of bacteraemia in studies of elderly persons and accounts for 24 to 56 per cent of cases of endocarditis. Other common sources include intra-abdominal foci, skin, and the respiratory tract (Esposito *et al.* 1980; Meyers *et al.* 1989; Muder *et al.* 1992; Leibovici *et al.* 1993; Richardson 1993). Gram-negative bacteraemias predominate in most series of older adults. The most frequently isolated species from community-dwelling elderly people are *E. coli* and *Klebsiella* species; other Gram-negative organisms such as *Providencia stuartii*, *Proteus* species, and *Pseudomonas* species are more frequently found in residents of long-term care facilities. *Staph. aureus*, *Enterococcus* species, and *Strep. pneumoniae* are the most common Gram-positive bloodstream isolates. Methicillin-resistant *Staph. aureus* can be a significant problem in long-term care facilities (Muder *et al.* 1992).

Fatality of bacteraemia varies from 9.1 per cent in community-dwelling elderly people with Gram-negative infections to 47.2 per cent in elderly persons with nosocomial bacteraemia (Richardson 1993). Fatality is increased in patients with hospital-acquired bacteraemia, a non-urinary source, respiratory infection, *Staph. aureus* infection, or inappropriate antibiotic treatment.

Infective endocarditis

The epidemiology of infective endocarditis has changed markedly from the preantibiotic area to the present. Prior to 1940 the most common patient with endocarditis was a young person with rheumatic heart disease. Recent reviews of endocarditis show that its incidence is substantially higher in patients over the age of 50, reaching a peak at 70 to 74 years (Terpenning *et al.* 1987; Wells *et al.* 1990; Gleckman 1992; Selton-Suty *et al.* 1997). Age may be a risk factor for endocarditis owing to a number of factors, including a greater prevalence of degenerative valvular disease and prosthetic heart valves (Gleckman 1992). With the decline of rheumatic heart disease, degenerative valvular lesions such as calcified aortic valves and mitral annulus calcification are common predisposing conditions in elderly persons (Thell *et al.* 1975; McKinsey *et al.* 1987). As in younger persons, mitral valve prolapse with redundancy also appears to be a risk factor for infective endocarditis (McKinsey *et al.* 1987). In addition, elderly persons not uncommonly require a prolonged stay in hospital and are subjected to invasive medical procedures causing bacteraemia. Twenty-three per cent of endocarditis cases in elderly adults are considered to be nosocomially acquired (Terpenning *et al.* 1987).

Alpha haemolytic streptococci and *Staph. aureus* remain the most frequently isolated pathogens; however, *Enterococcus* species, *Streptococcus bovis*, and coagulase-negative staphylococci are more common in elderly persons than in younger age groups (Terpenning *et al.* 1987). *Enterococcus* is the third leading cause of endocarditis in elderly patients and tends to occur in elderly men after infections or manipulation of the genitourinary tract (Moellering 1974; Gleckman 1972).

Elderly patients with endocarditis have higher fatality and morbidity than younger persons. The relative risk of dying from endocarditis in persons aged over 60 years was 2.2 in a large study of community-acquired endocarditis from New Zealand (Gleckman 1992). In addition, neurological complications and permanent disability requiring subsequent long-term care are more common in older patients who survive an acute episode of endocarditis (Terpenning *et al.* 1987). (See also Chapter 9.9.)

Conclusion

Older persons represent a rapidly growing segment of the population in the developed world. Not only are many elderly patients more susceptible to infections, but they may have atypical presentations. In addition, they are afflicted by a different spectrum of pathogens compared with younger healthy persons. Because of the increased morbidity and fatality associated with almost every type of infection in the older person, prevention of infection is of utmost importance.

References

Abrutyn, E., Mossey, J., Berlin, J.A, *et al.* (1994). Does asymptomatic bacteriuria predict mortality and does antimicrobial treatment reduce mortality in elderly ambulatory women? *Annals of Internal Medicine*, **120**, 827–33.

Agius, G., Dindinaud, G., Biggar, R.J., *et al.* (1990). An epidemic of respiratory syncytial virus in elderly people: clinical and serological findings. *Journal of Medical Virology*, **30**, 117–27.

Alvarez, S. (1990). Incidence and prevalence of nosocomial infections in nursing homes. In *Infections in nursing homes and long-term care facilities* (ed. A. Verghese and S.L. Berk), pp. 41–54. Karger, New York.

Alvarez, S., Shell, C., and Berk, S.L. (1987). Pulmonary tuberculosis in elderly men. *American Journal of Medicine*, **82**, 602–6.

Anonymous (1990). Hospitalisations for the leading causes of death among the elderly—United States, 1987. *Morbidity and Mortality Weekly Report*, **39**, 777–9.

Arroyo, J.C., Jordan, W., and Milligan, L. (1988). Upper respiratory tract infection and serum antibody responses in nursing home patients. *American Journal of Infection Control*, **16**, 152–8.

Baldassarre, J.S. and Kaye, D. (1991). Special problems of urinary tract infection in the elderly. *Medical Clinics of North America*, **75**, 375–90.

Barker, W.H. and Mullooly, J.P. (1982). Pneumonia and influenza deaths during epidemics. *Archives of Internal Medicine*, **142**, 85–9.

Behrman, R., Meyers, B., Mendelson, M., Sacks, H., and Hirschman, S. (1989). Central nervous system infections in the elderly. *Archives of Internal Medicine*, **149**, 1596–9.

Bennett, R. (1993). Diarrhea among residents of long-term care facilities. *Infection Control and Hospital Epidemiology*, **14**, 397–404.

Bennett, R. and Greenough, W. (1993). Approach to acute diarrhea in the elderly. *Gastroenterology Clinics of North America*, **22**, 517–33.

Bentley, D. (1990). *Clostridium difficile*-associated disease in long term care facilities. *Infection Control and Hospital Epidemiology*, **11**, 434–8.

Betts, R. (1995). Influenza virus. In *Principles and practices of infectious diseases* (4th edn) (ed. G.L. Mandell, J.F. Bennett, and R.Polin), pp. 1546–67. Churchill Livingston, New York.

Boscia, J.A., Kobasa, W.D., Knight, R.A., Abrutyn, E., Levison, M.E., and Kaye, D. (1986). Epidemiology of bacteriuria in an elderly ambulatory population. *American Journal of Medicine*, **80**, 208–14.

Boscia, J.A., Kobasa, W.D., Knight, R.A., Abrutyn, E., Levison, M.E., and Kaye, D. (1987). Therapy vs no therapy for bacteriuria in elderly ambulatory non-hospitalized women. *Journal of the American Medical Association*, **257**, 1067–71.

Bryan, C., Dew, C., and Reynolds, K. (1983). Bacteremia associated with decubitus ulcers. *Archives of Internal Medicine*, **143**, 2093–5.

Carter, A., Borczyk, A., Carlson, J., *et al.* (1987). A severe outbreak of *Escherichia Coli* 0157:H7-associated hemorrhagic colitis in a nursing home. *New England Journal of Medicine*, **317**, 1496–1500.

Chow, A., Galpin, J., and Guze, J. (1977). Clindamycin for treatment of sepsis caused by decubitus ulcers. *Journal of Infectious Diseases*, **135**, S65–8.

Crossley, K.B. and Peterson, P.K. (1996). Infections in the elderly (state-of-the-art clinical article). *Clinical Infectious Diseases*, 22, 209–15.

Cubitt, W.D. and Holzel, H. (1980). An outbreak of rotavirus infection in a long-stay ward of a geriatric hospital. *Journal of Clinical Pathology*, 33, 306–8.

Darnowski, S.B., Gordon, M., and Simon, A.E. (1991). Two years of infection surveillance in a geriatric long-term care facility. *American Journal of Infection Control*, 19, 185–90.

Davies, P.D.O. (1994). Tuberculosis in the elderly. *Journal of Antimicrobial Chemotherapy*, 34 (Supplement A), 93–100.

Donahue, J., Choo, P., Manson, J., and Platt, R. (1995). The incidence of herpes zoster. *Archives of Internal Medicine*, 155, 1605–9.

Dontas, A.S., Kasviki-Charvati, P., Papanayiotou, P.C., and Marketos, S.G. (1981). Bacteriuria and survival in old age. *New England Journal of Medicine*, 304, 939–43.

Duffield, J.S., Adams, W.H., Anderson, M., and Leitch, A.G. (1996). Increasing incidence of tuberculosis in the young and the elderly in Scotland. *Thorax*, 51, 140–2.

Durand, M., Calderwood, S., Weber, D., et al. (1993). Acute bacterial meningitis in adults. *New England Journal of Medicine*, 328, 21–8.

Dutt, A.K. and Stead, W.W. (1991). Tuberculosis in the elderly. In *Respiratory infections in the elderly* (ed. A.K. Dutt and W.W. Stead) pp. 189–205. Raven Press, New York.

Emori, T.G., Banerjee, S.N., Culver, D.H., et al. (1991).Nosocomial infections in elderly patients in the United States, 1986–1990. *American Journal of Medicine*, 91, 289S–93S.

Esposito, A., Gleckman, R., Cram, S., Crowley, M., McCabe, F., and Drapkin, M. (1980). Community-acquired bacteremia in the elderly: analysis of one hundred consecutive episodes. *Journal of the American Geriatrics Society*, 28, 315–19.

Falsey, A.R., Treanor, J.J., Betts, R.F., and Walsh, E.E. (1992). Viral respiratory infections in the institutionalized elderly: clinical and epidemiologic findings. *Journal of the American Geriatrics Society*, 40, 115–19.

Falsey, A.R., McCann, R.M., Hall, W.J., et al. (1995a). Acute respiratory tract infection in daycare centers for older persons. *Journal of the American Geriatrics Society*, 43, 30–6.

Falsey, A.R., Cunningham, C.K., Barker, W.H., et al. (1995b). Respiratory syncytial virus and influenza A infections in the hospitalized elderly. *Journal of Infectious Diseases*, 172, 389–94.

Falsey, A.R., McCann, R.M., Hall, W.J., et al. (1997). The 'common cold' in frail older persons: impact of rhinovirus and coronavirus in a senior daycare center. *Journal of the American Geriatrics Society* , 45, 706–11.

Fein, A.M. (1994). Pneumonia in the elderly. Special diagnostic and therapeutic considerations. *Medical Clinics of North America*, 78, 1015–33.

Finkelstein, M., Petkun, W., and Metal, F. (1983). Pneumococcal bacteremia in adults: age dependent differences in presentation and outcome. *Journal of the American Geriatrics Society*, 31, 19–27.

Fleming, D.M. and Cross, K.W. (1993). Respiratory syncytial virus or influenza? *Lancet*, 342, 1507–10.

Fransen, H., Sterner, G., Forsgren, M., et al. (1967). Acute lower respiratory illness in elderly patients with respiratory syncytial virus infection. *Acta Medica Scandinavica*, 182, 323–9.

Galpin, J., Chow, A., Bayer, A., and Guze, J. (1976). Sepsis associated with decubitus ulcers. *American Journal of Medicine*, 61, 346–50.

Garb, J.L., Brown, R.B., Garb, J.R., and Tuthill, R.W. (1978). Differences in etiology of pneumonias in nursing home and community patients. *Journal of the American Medical Association*, 240, 2169–72.

Garibaldi, R.A., Brodine, S., and Matsumiya, S. (1981). Infections among patients in nursing homes: policies, prevalence and problems. *New England Journal of Medicine*, 305, 731–5.

Garvie, D.G. and Gray, J. (1980). Outbreak of respiratory syncytial virus infection in the elderly. *British Medical Journal*, 281, 1253–4.

Gaynes, R.P., Weinstein, RA., Chamberlin, W., and Kabins, S.A. (1985). Antibiotic-resistant flora in nursing home patients admitted to the hospital. *Archives of Internal Medicine*, 145, 1804–7.

Gilchrest, B. (1982). Age-associated changes in the skin. *Journal of the American Geriatrics Society*, 30, 139–43.

Gleckman, R. (1992). Endocarditis in the elderly. In *Infective endocarditis* (2nd edn) (ed. D. Kaye), pp. 329–43. Raven Press, New York.

Glezen, W.P. (1982). Serious morbidity and mortality associated with influenza epidemics. *Epidemiologic Reviews*, 4, 24–44.

Glezen, W.P. and Couch, R.B. (1978). Interpandemic influenza in the Houston area, 1974–76. *New England Journal of Medicine*, 298, 587–92.

Granton, J.T. and Grossman, R.F. (1993). Community acquired pneumonia in the elderly patient: clinical features, epidemiology, and treatment. *Clinics in Chest Medicine*, 14, 537–53.

Gross, P.A., Rapuano, C., Adrignolo, A., and Shaw, B. (1983). Nosocomial infections: decade-specific risk. *Infection Control*, 4, 145–7.

Gross, P.A., Rodstein, M., LaMontagne, J.R., et al. (1988). Epidemiology of acute respiratory illness during an influenza outbreak in a nursing home. *Archives of Internal Medicine*, 148, 559–61.

Hanson, L.C., Weber, D.J., Rutala, W.A., and Samsa, G.P. (1992). Risk factors for nosocomial pneumonia in the elderly. *American Journal of Medicine*, 92, 161–6.

Harkness, G.A., Bentley, D.W., and Roghmann, K.J. (1990). Risk factors for nosocomial pneumonia in the elderly. *American Journal of Medicine*, 89, 457–63.

Hodder, S.L., Ford, A.B., FitzGibbon, P.A., Jones, P.K., Kumar, M.L., and Mortimer, E.A.J. (1995). Acute respiratory illness in older community residents. *Journal of the American Geriatrics Society*, 43, 24–9.

Irvine, P.W., Van Buren, N., and Crossley, K. (1984). Causes for hospitalization of nursing home residents: the role of infection. *Journal of the American Geriatrics Society*, 32, 103–7.

Jackson, M.M. and Fierer, J. (1985). Infections and infection risk in residents of long-term care facilities: a review of the literature, 1970–1984. *American Journal of Infection Control*, 13, 63–77.

John, J.F.J. and Ribner, B.S. (1991). Antibiotic resistance in long-term care facilities. *Infection Control and Hospital Epidemiology*, 12, 245–50.

Kost, R. and Straus, S. (1996). Postherpetic neuralgia—pathogenesis, treatment, and prevention. *New England Journal of Medicine*, 335, 32–42.

Kunin, C.M., Douthitt, S., Dancing, J., Anderson, J., and Moeschberger, M. (1992). The association between the use of urinary catheters and morbidity and mortality among elderly patients in nursing homes. *American Journal of Epidemiology*, 135, 291–301.

Leibovici, L., Pitlik, S., Konisberger, H., and Drucker, M. (1993). Bloodstream infections in patients older than eighty years. *Age and Ageing*, 22, 431–42.

Macarthur, C., Enarson, D.A., Fanning, E.A., Hessel, P.A., and Newman, S. (1992). Tuberculosis among institutionalized elderly in Alberta, Canada. *International Journal of Epidemiology*, 21, 1175–9.

McKinsey, D., Ratts, T., and Bisno, A. (1987). Underlying cardiac lesions in adults with infective endocarditis. *American Journal of Medicine*, 82, 681–8.

Magaziner, J., Tenney, J.H., DeForge, B., Hebel, R., Muncie, H.L., Jr, and Warren, J.W. (1991). Prevalence and characteristics of nursing home-acquired infections in the aged. *Journal of the American Geriatrics Society*, 39, 1071–8.

Marrie, T.J. (1994). Community-acquired pneumonia. *Clinical Infectious Diseases*, 18, 501–15.

Marrie, T.J., Lee, S., Faulkner, R., Ethier, J., and Young, C. (1982). Rotavirus infection in a geriatric population. *Archives of Internal Medicine*, 142, 313–16.

Marrie, T.J., Durant, H., and Kwan, C. (1986). Nursing home-acquired pneumonia. A case–control study. *Journal of the American Geriatrics Society*, 34, 697–702.

Mather, U., Bentley, D.W., and Hall, C.B. (1980). Concurrent respiratory syncytial virus and influenza A infections in the institutionalized elderly and chronically ill. *Annals of Internal Medicine*, 93, 49–52.

Meyers, B., Sherman, E., Mendelson, M., *et al.* (1989). Bloodstream infections in the elderly. *American Journal of Medicine*, 86, 379–84.

Miller, L. and Choi, C. (1997). Meningitis in older patients: how to diagnose and treat a deadly infection. *Geriatrics*, 52, 43–55.

Miller, R.A. (1996). The aging immune system: primer and prospectus. *Science*, 273, 70–4.

Mims, A.D., Norman, D.C., Yamamura, R.H., and Yoshikawa, T.T. (1990). Clinically inapparent (asymptomatic) bacteriuria in ambulatory elderly men: epidemiological, clinical, and microbiological findings. *Journal of the American Geriatrics Society*, 38, 1209–14.

Moellering, R., Watson, B., and Kunz, L. (1974). Endocarditis due to group D streptococci—comparison of disease caused by *Streptococcus bovis* with that produced by the enterococci. *American Journal of Medicine*, 57, 239–50.

Monto, A.S. and Cavallaro, J.J. (1971). The Tecumseh study of respiratory illness. II. Patterns of occurrence of infection with respiratory pathogens, 1965–1969. *American Journal of Epidemiology*, 94, 280–9.

Monto, A.S. and Ullman, B.M. (1974). Acute respiratory illness in an American community: the Tecumseh study. *Journal of the American Medical Association*, 227, 164–9.

Muder, R.R., Brennen, C., Wagener, M.M., and Goetz, A.M. (1992). Bacteremia in a long-term care facility: A five-year prospective study of 163 consecutive episodes. *Clinical Infectious Diseases*, 14, 647–54.

Nicolle, L.E. (1994). Urinary tract infection in the elderly. *Journal of Antimicrobial Chemotherapy*, 33 (Supplement A), 99–109.

Nicolle, L.E. (1997). Asymptomatic bacteriuria in the elderly. *Infectious Disease Clinics of North America*, 11, 647–62.

Nicolle, L.E., Bjornson, J., Harding, G.K.M., and MacDonell, J.A. (1983). Bacteriuria in elderly institutionalized men. *New England Journal of Medicine*, 309, 1420–5.

Nicolle, L.E., McIntyre, M., Zacharias, H., and MacDonell, J.A. (1984). Twelve-month surveillance of infections in institutionalized elderly men. *Journal of the American Geriatrics Society*, 32, 513–19.

Niederman, M.S. (1993). Nosocomial pneumonia in the elderly patient. Chronic care facility and hospital considerations. *Clinics in Chest Medicine*, 14, 479–90.

Nordenstram, G.R., Brandberg, C.A., Oden, A.S., Svanborg, C.M., and Svanbord, A. (1996). Bacteriuria and mortality in an elderly population. *New England Journal of Medicine*, 314, 1152–6.

Nunley, D., Verghese, A., and Berk, S.L. (1990). Pneumonia in the nursing-home patient. In *Infections in nursing homes and long-term care facilities* (ed. A. Verghese and S.L. Berk), pp. 95–113. Karger, New York.

Osterweil, D. and Norman, D. (1990). An outbreak of an influenza-like illness in a nursing home. *Journal of the American Geriatrics Society*, 38, 659–62.

Perrotta, D.M., Decker, M., and Glezen, W.P. (1985). Acute respiratory disease hospitalisations as a measure of impact of epidemic influenza. *American Journal of Epidemiology*, 122, 468–76.

Public Health Laboratory Service Communicable Disease Surveillance Centre (1983*a*). Parainfluenza infections in the elderly 1976–82. *British Medical Journal*, 287, 1619.

Public Health Laboratory Service Communicable Diseases Surveillance Centre (1983*b*). Respiratory syncytial virus infection in the elderly 1976–1982. *British Medical Journal*, 287, 1618–19.

Richardson, J. (1993). Bacteremia in the elderly. *Journal of General Internal Medicine*, 8, 89–92.

Richardson, J. and Knight, A. (1991). The prevention of tetanus in the elderly. *Archives of Internal Medicine*, 151, 1712–17.

Ruben, F.L., Dearwater, S.R., Norden, C.W., *et al.* (1995). Clinical infections in the non-institutionalized geriatric age group: methods utilized and incidence of infections. The Pittsburgh Good Health Study. *American Journal of Epidemiology*, 141, 145–57.

Salive, M.E., Satterfield, S., Ostfeld, A.M., Wallace, R.B., and Havlik, R.J. (1993). Disability and cognitive impairment are risk factors for pneumonia-related mortality in older adults. *Public Health Reports*, 108, 314–22.

Saviteer, S.M., Samsa, G.P., and Rutala, W.A. (1988). Nosocomial infections in the elderly: increased risk per hospital day. *American Journal of Medicine*, 84, 661–6.

Scheckler, W.E. and Peterson, P.J. (1986). Infections and control among residents of eight rural Wisconsin nursing homes. *Archives of Internal Medicine*, 146, 1981–4.

Schuchat, A., Robinson, K., Wenger, J., *et al.* (1997). Bacterial meningitis in the United States in 1995. *New England Journal of Medicine*, 337, 970–87.

Selton-Suty, C., Hoen, B., Grentzinger, A., *et al.* (1997). Clinical and bacteriological characteristics of infective endocarditis in the elderly. *Heart*, 77, 260–3.

Setia, U., Serventi, I., and Lorenz, P. (1984). Bacteremia in a long-term care facility. *Archives of Internal Medicine*, 144, 1633–5.

Setia, U., Serventi, I., and Lorenz, P. (1985). Nosocomial infections among patients in a long-term care facility: spectrum, prevalence, and risk factors. *American Journal of Infection Control*, 13, 57–62.

Smith, P.W., Daly, P.B., and Roccaforte, J.S. (1991). Current status of nosocomial infection control in extended care facilities. *American Journal of Medicine* 91, 281S–5S.

Sorvillo, F.J., Huie, S.F., Strassburg, M.A., Butsumyo, A., Shandera, W.X., and Fannin, S.L. (1984). An outbreak of respiratory syncytial virus pneumonia in a nursing home for the elderly. *Journal of Infection*, 9, 252–6.

Stead, W.W. (1981). Tuberculosis among elderly persons: an outbreak in a nursing home. *Annals of Internal Medicine*, 94, 606–10.

Stead, W.W., To, T., Harrison, R.W., and Abraham, J.H. (1987). Benefit–risk consideration in preventive treatment for tuberculosis in elderly persons. *Annals of Internal Medicine*, 107, 843–5.

Straus, S., Ostrove, J., Inchauspe, G., *et al.* (1988), Varicella-zoster virus infections. *Annals of Internal Medicine*, 108, 221–37.

Sullivan, R.J., Dowdle, W.R., Marine, W.M., and Hierholzer, J.C. (1972). Adult pneumonia in a general hospital. *Archives of Internal Medicine*, 129, 935–42.

Terpenning, M., Buggy, B., and Kauffman, C. (1987). Infective endocarditis: clinical features in young and elderly patients. *American Journal of Medicine*, 83, 626–34.

Thell, R., Martin, F., and Edwards, J. (1975). Bacterial endocarditis in subjects 60 years of age and older. *Circulation*, 51, 174–82.

Tresch, D.D., Simpson, W.M.J., and Burton, J.R. (1985). Relationship of long-term and acute-care facilities: the problem of patient transfer and continuity of care. *Journal of the American Geriatrics Society*, 33, 819–26.

Van den Brande, P.M., Van de Mierop, F., Verbeken, E.K., and Demedts, M. (1990). Clinical spectrum of endobronchial tuberculosis in elderly patients. *Archives of Internal Medicine*, 150, 2105–8.

Van Dijk, J.M. and Rosin, A.J. (1993). A comparison of clinical features of mycobacterial infections in young and elderly patients. *Netherlands Journal of Medicine*, 42, 12–15.

Vankatesan, P., Gladman, J., Macfarlane, J.T., *et al.* (1990). A hospital study of community acquired pneumonia in the elderly. *Thorax*, 45, 254–8.

Verghese, A. and Berk, S. (1983). Bacterial pneumonia in the elderly. *Medicine*, 62, 271–85.

Verghese, A. and Berk, S. (1990). Introduction and epidemiologic considerations. In *Infections in nursing homes and long term care facilities* (ed. A.Verghese and S. Berk), pp. 1–11. Karger, Basel.

Wald, T.G., Shult, P., Krause, P., Miller, B.A., Drinka, P., and Gravenstein, S. (1995). A rhinovirus outbreak among residents of a long-term care facility. *Annals of Internal Medicine*, 123, 588–93.

Warren, J.W., Tenney, J.H., Hoopes, J.M., Muncie, H.L., and Anthony, W.C. (1982). A prospective microbiologic study of bacteriuria in patients with chronic indwelling urethral catheters. *Journal of Infectious Diseases*, **146**, 719–23.

Weiss, B., Strassburg, M.A., and Feeley, J. (1983). Tetanus and diptheria immunity in an elderly population in Los Angeles County. *American Journal of Public Health*, **73**, 802–4.

Wells, A.U., Fowler, C.C., Pegler-Ellis, R.B., Luke, R., Hannan, S., and Sharpe, D.N. (1990). Endocarditis in the 80's in a general hospital an Auckland, New Zealand. *Quarterly Journal of Medicine*, **76**, 753–62.

Woodhead, M. (1994). Pneumonia in the elderly. *Journal of Antimicrobial Chemotherapy*, **34** (Supplement A), 85–92.

Yoshikawa, T. (1992). Tuberculosis in aging adults. *Journal of the American Geriatrics Society*, **40**, 178–87.

Yoshikawa, T. (1994a). Infectious diseases, immunity, and aging. In *Aging, immunity, and infection* (ed. D. Powers and J. Morley), pp. 1–11. Springer, New York.

Yoshikawa, T. (1994b). The challenge and unique aspects of tuberculosis in older patients. *Infectious Diseases in Clinical Practice*, **3**, 62–6.

Yoshikawa, T., Nicolle, L.E., and Norman, D.C. (1996). Management of complicated urinary tract infections in older patients. *Journal of the American Geriatrics Society*, **44**, 1235–41.

3.2 Infection control

J.-P. Michel, M. Lutters, N. Vogt, and K. H. Krause

Concerns about infectious diseases in elderly people, including cross-infections, are common. With ageing, susceptibility to infections increases owing to a number of physiological factors. These include alteration of skin and mucosal barriers, decrease in lean body mass, reduction of gas exchange surface, increase of pulmonary residual volume, decrease in cardiac adaptability to stress (Vogt 1998), and changes in immunocompetence (Proust *et al.* 1996; Zheng *et al.* 1997) (see Chapter 3.3 for further discussion). In addition, there are risk factors such as relative malnutrition, stress, smoking (Michel 1995), and accumulation of comorbidities (Redelmeier *et al.* 1998).

This increased susceptibility to infectious diseases, particularly in frail elderly people, is compounded by numerous diagnostic and treatment difficulties (Michel *et al.* 1991*a, b*). The clinical diagnosis may be delayed because of the atypical presentation of the infectious disease when the patient has delirium, falls, and urinary incontinence rather than fever. Further, fever, when present, may be a component of a non-infectious process. Microbiological identification and interpretation are difficult because biological samples are scarce and aggressive investigations are not easy to carry out or are associated with potentially serious side-effects. Presence of a urinary catheter, various devices, or previous antibiotic treatment could alter microbiological results. Ecological differences exist between home settings, nursing homes, acute, and medium- and long-stay hospital wards. A 1-day prevalence study performed in 10 geriatric care facilities showed that 16.8 per cent of the 1919 patients over 75 years of age had at least one infectious site (Michel *et al.* 1991*a*). A prospective study in seven nursing homes in the United States showed that the incidence of infections was 5.2 per 1000 days per patient (Lee *et al.* 1992).

As a consequence of the relatively high rate of infection and the difficulties in diagnosis, increased antibiotic usage by geriatric patients, particularly those in hospitals and long-term care facilities, is observed world-wide. A 10-year (1983–1992) retrospective study in the Geneva geriatric hospital showed a doubling in patient daily dose of antimicrobial drugs (Sallin *et al.* 1994). During the study period, the total cost of antibiotics increased from 16 to 36 per cent of the total drug budget of this geriatric hospital (Sallin *et al.* 1994). These data are comparable to antimicrobial drug expenditure in a hospital in Vancouver, Canada, which represented 31 per cent of the total drug expenditure (Frighetto *et al.* 1992). At the same time, antibiotic-resistant strains have emerged. In a prospective survey of seven nursing homes in the United States, 22 per cent of isolated *Pseudomonas* species were gentamicin resistant and 33 per cent were norfloxacine resistant (Lee *et al.* 1992).

The increased use of antibiotics not only increases direct care costs, but also indirect costs which include interventions for adverse reactions to these drugs, increased demands for involvement of the multidisciplinary team, and supply or material use (Michel *et al.* 1994). Conversely, high antibiotic use in geriatric hospital settings does not lead to a decrease in the high mortality rate where infection is the immediate cause of death (McGee 1993).

Infection control programmes can be developed to optimize diagnosis and treatment of infectious diseases in the geriatric population, and to prevent pathogen transmission and cross-infection in the geriatric setting. Individuals with expertise in geriatric infectious diseases and related geriatric infection control programmes should work closely together to optimize geriatric patient care.

Hygiene is essential for geriatric infection control. Seventy per cent of cross-infections can be prevented if basic hygiene rules are obeyed (Brachman 1992). Handwashing is the most important and least expensive measure for preventing transmission of nosocomial infections (Voss and Widmer 1997). Hygiene rules apply not only to hospital patients and staff members, but also to volunteers, visitors, and service personnel (Brachman 1992). Institutional environmental factors such as one-bed or six-bed wards, lavatories inside or outside the ward, air-conditioning or ventilation, and support services including laundry, cleaning, dressing, and cooking processes, as well as disinfection strategies for hands, furniture, sleeping areas, and common rooms, are critical (Veyssier et al. 1997). Unfortunately, up to 30 per cent of cross-infections cannot be prevented and the infection will occur despite all possible precautions (Brachman 1992). In addition, endogenous micro-organisms contribute substantially to nosocomial infections. Thus, despite the importance of preventive measures recommended by geriatric infection control, infection of the institutionalized geriatric patient cannot be completely avoided and optimized patient care requires the availability of expertise in geriatric infectious diseases.

Implementation of an infection control programme is essential to minimize cross-infections in the hospitalized geriatric population by limiting germ reservoirs (patients, staff members, and visitors), controlling the cleanliness of technical areas and procedures, reducing microbe transmission (hand to hand, droplets, fomites), limiting the use of foreign devices (urinary catheters, feeding tubes), increasing host resistance through good nutrition and treatment of comorbidity (Veyssier et al. 1997), and controlling inappropriate antibiotic usage, which is an important aspect of both hospital quality assurance and cost-containment programmes (Coleman et al. 1991).

The comprehensive antimicrobial control programme

The antimicrobial control programme appears to be one of the most cost-beneficial medical interventions of an effective infection control programme (Wenzel 1995). There is continuous development of new agents with expanded antimicrobial activity and improved pharmacokinetic and safety profiles, usually at ever-increasing prices (Crowe and Quintiliani 1995). However, the decision-making capability of practising physicians does not increase at the same rate, and antimicrobial resistance tends to rise (Crowe and Quintiliani 1995). If antibiotic effectiveness is to be maximized, comprehensive antimicrobial control programmes need to be implemented. The comprehensive antimicrobial programme should evolve with a large 'consensus' team composed of practising physicians, infectious diseases specialists, pharmacy directors, nurses, and administrators (Marr and Moffett 1988; Crowe and Quintiliani 1995). This kind of programme develops in stages.

The first stage is infection survey and evaluation (Hirschman et al. 1988; Veyssier et al. 1997). This involves retrospective analysis of infection cases and audits of antibiotic utilization. When an infectious outbreak is detected, strategies are put in place emphasizing daily hygiene processes including reminders about handwashing, patient isolation as required, and restrictions on visitors. Analysis of epidemics must become a routine process to allow prospective audits of infection and to isolate microbes from cultures. Concurrent audit of antibiotic utilization trends is helpful (Marr and Moffett 1988). The evaluation

team may also include an 'antibiotic monitoring programme subcommittee' (Hirschman et al. 1988) which will be responsible for conducting follow-up infection surveys, co-ordinating pharmacy activities, monitoring programme performances, keeping in touch with the infectious diseases division/microbiological laboratory, and communicating new policies to the medical staff (Coleman et al. 1991).

The next stage is the development of guidelines for antibiotic use and control. An antibiotic formulary (Crowe and Quintiliani 1995; Lutters et al. 1998) should be established to ensure that the most efficacious and cost-effective agents within a therapeutic category are readily available (Hess et al. 1990). For this purpose, it is necessary to select drugs appropriate to diagnosis mix and local resistance patterns, minimize drug acquisition costs through competitive bidding and buying alliances, make strong recommendations for the treatment of common infectious diseases seen in geriatric institutions, including oral drugs where appropriate, use oral rather than intravenous antibiotics where possible, and minimize catheter-related infections. It is necessary to establish meaningful restriction policies for broad-spectrum antibiotics, particularly those which may be expensive. Costs should be compared with benefits at all times, and not just the cost of new agents relative to traditional therapies.

A further development may include developing an antimicrobial order sheet (Hess et al. 1990). Two special categories of antimicrobial agent are considered—restricted drugs which require consultation with a geriatric infectious diseases specialist before prescribing because of the potential for inappropriate use, high cost, limited indications, or low therapeutic index, and reserved drugs which are defined as those which are used routinely only for predefined clinical indications. Examples of reserved drugs are cefotetan, cefoxitin, cefuroxime, and ribavirin. Once the guidelines are drafted for the use of each drug, there should a monthly meeting or summary of cases to identify inappropriate uses (Hess et al. 1990).

A dose control and dose interval policy can also be implemented. For example, a dose-exceeding policy could be in place for a patient aged over 80 years with diminished renal function and immunocompetence. Standardized dosing and dose intervals for selected antimicrobial agents may be established for drugs such as ceftriaxone where a 24-h dosing interval suffices for most infections (Hess et al. 1990). Current information on the many therapeutic possibilities is necessary to take advantage of differences in the pharmacokinetics of therapeutically similar compounds in situations where, for example, the route of administration is changed from intravenous to oral as a step-down process (Hirschman et al. 1988; Coleman et al. 1991).

Automatic stop policies minimize inappropriate duration of therapy but may not be acceptable without an adequate understanding of the antibiotic effectiveness (Hirschman et al. 1988). An alert system which automatically prompts a consultation with an infectious diseases expert might be an alternative solution.

Measures that are effective often incorporate other facilitative manoeuvres such as feedback, concurrent review, and concurrent reminder into the drug ordering system (Seto et al. 1996). Evaluation of practices relative to state-of-the-art practices described in authoritative literature is always useful (Marr and Moffett 1988).

Promotional activities include the use of guidelines, handbooks, and educational seminars. The guidelines must include information about how implementation will affect health and the utilization of resources (Brook 1995). Nevertheless, their impact on prescribing behaviour may be minimal or transient (Seto et al. 1996). Monthly meetings of the 'antibiotic monitoring programme subcommittee' with clinicians can help in implementing the antimicrobial agents programme. During such meetings, clinicians must be informed not only about the real cost reductions and cost-avoidance expenses, but also about the decrease in adverse reactions and the absence of an increase in mortality rate (Hirschman *et al.* 1988). Annual meetings are useful to demonstrate the variations in antibiotic usage (calculated on the basis of patient-days) and the patterns of use of antibiotics by medical staff (audit for quality assurance and concurrence review). During these meetings, the trends of susceptibility to micro-organisms by species and site of origin (blood, wound, skin, urinary tract) should be reviewed (Marr and Moffett 1988).

Special concerns related to antibiotic resistance in long-term care facilities

Organisms with antibiotic resistance are becoming increasingly common (Levy 1998; Waldvogel 1999), particularly in long-term care facilities (Yoshikawa 1998). It is known that, given sufficient time and drug use, antibiotic resistance will emerge. The resistance evolves as a progressive phenomenon, first as reduced micro-organism susceptibility and then progressing to high-level resistance organisms that become resistant first to one drug and subsequently to others. Once resistance appears, it is likely to decline slowly if at all. In addition, the presence of antibiotics in the tissue environment may contribute to development of resistance (Waldvogel 1999). Methicillin-resistant *Staphylococcus aureus* (**MRSA**) confers resistance on all penicillinase-resistant penicillins and cephalosporins and requires the a gene that encodes penicillin-binding protein (Lowy 1998). there have also been reports of vancomycin-resistant *Staph. aureus*. Increased cell-wall synthesis and alterations in the cell wall that prevent vancomycin from reaching sites of cell-wall synthesis have been suggested as mechanisms. Smith *et al.* (1999) reported the emergence of vancomycin resistance in *Staph. aureus* and emphasized the need for prudent use of antibiotics, laboratory capacity to identify resistant strains, and the use of infection control precautions to prevent transmission. They noted that adherence to recommended infection control practices may prevent the transmission of *Staph. aureus* from patient to patient and from patient to health-care worker. These practices include those from the Hospital Infection Control Practices Advisory Committee, including situations in which the use of vancomycin should be discouraged and where its use is based on indications, together with the Centers for Disease Control guidelines for preventing the spread of vancomycin-resistant staphylococci (Smith *et al.* 1999). Importantly, the standards adopted in acute care must be modified for long-term care, but consistent infection control practices must be applied.

Rahimi (1998) reported on the cost-effectiveness and validity of aggressive diagnosis and eradication of MRSA colonization. There was no significant correlation between MRSA and active MRSA-related infections. Thus Rahimi recommended that patients colonized by MRSA should not be barred from admission to nursing homes. Universal precautions for infection control were applied and there were no attempts to eradicate MRSA. He concluded that the most effective approach to eliminating risk factors for MRSA was to avoid frequent and prolonged use of antibiotics and to implement simple handwashing techniques.

Brennan *et al.* (1998) described the epidemiology and natural history of colonization with vancomycin-resistant *Enterococcus faecium* (**VREF**) in a long-term care facility They found that long-term care patients have protracted carriage of VREF and the risk of infection is low in this population. Most VREF carriers improve over time, although VREF carriage will be prolonged when antibiotic treatment is undertaken. Importantly, patients in long-term care facilities generally have few risk factors for invasive VREF compared with patients in acute facilities. Reasonable precautions include cohorting colonized patients, handwashing, and donning gowns and gloves before contact with contaminated body substances. Brennan *et al.* (1998) emphasized that patients colonized with VREF should not be denied admission to long-term care and that, if these individuals are admitted to acute care, the receiving institution should be notified of their status.

Yoshikawa (1998) suggested the following principles for minimizing the overall risk of drug-resistant organisms in long-term care facilities.

1. Not all clinical or functional changes in long-term care facility residents should be attributed to infections.
2. Antibiotics should be administered only when there is evidence to indicate potential clinical benefit.
3. Chronic suppressive therapy with antibiotics or antimicrobial chemoprophylaxis should be restricted unless there is documented evidence of clinical efficacy and therapeutic benefit.
4. Continuation of antibiotic therapy beyond standard recommended periods should be discouraged.
5. In circumstances in which a specific pathogen is isolated and antibiotic sensitivity studies are available, the initial broad-spectrum antibiotic should be changed to a narrow-spectrum agent if the organism is susceptible to that agent.
6. Increased education about and stricter practices of infection control in the long-term care facility setting must be mandated.

The practice of glove use and handwashing is pivotal in terms of infection control practices and is crucial for minimizing risk in long-term care facilities. In their study, Thompson *et al.* (1997) showed that glove use and handwashing were markedly deficient and 82 per cent of staff–patient interactions could have resulted in transmission of infectious agents. Consistent performance in this area is mandatory and cost effective.

Another complication of antibiotic therapy is the increasing frequency of *Clostridium difficile* colonization and infection. The normal bowel flora is disrupted by systemic antibiotics and colonization occurs. In some patients toxin will be released causing mucosal damage, and inflammation and infection with the organism may cause diarrhoea, colitis, or both. Individuals may be colonized and not infected. The diagnosis can be made by the sensitive and specific toxin assay, and therapy may be initiated for symptomatic individuals. Recommended therapy is oral metronidazole 250 mg four times daily for 10 days or, if the individual fails to respond, vancomycin 125 mg four times daily. Metronidazole may be given parenterally if indicated.

Conclusion

Comprehensive infection control, including antimicrobial control programmes, is a high priority and should be considered as part of a wider programme including attention to hygiene, particularly handwashing and broader preventive measures such as immunization (see Chapter 3.4). Antibiotic resistance is a continuing problem and procedures must be in place to understand both colonization and infection, particularly for frail elderly people admitted to acute and long-term care facilities.

References

Brachman, P.S. (1992). Epidemiology of nosocomial infections. In *Hospital infections* (3rd edn) (ed. J.V. Benneth and P.S. Brachman), pp. 3–20. Little, Brown, Boston, MA.

Brennan, C., Wagener, M.M., and Muder, R.R. (1998). Vancomycin-resistant *Enterococcus faecium* in a long-term care facility. *Journal of the American Geriatrics Society*, 46, 157–60.

Brook, R.H. (1995). Implementing clinical guidelines. *Lancet*, 346, 132.

Coleman, R.W., Rodondi, L.C., Kaubisch, S., et al. (1991). Cost-effectiveness of prospective and continuous parenteral antibiotic control: experience at the Palo Alto Veterans Affairs Medical centre from 1987 to 1989. *American Journal of Medicine*, 90, 439–44.

Crowe, H.M. and Quintiliani, R. (1995). Antibiotic formulary selection. *Medical Clinics of North America*, 79, 463–75.

Frighetto, L., Nickoloff, D., Martinusen, S.M. et al. (1992). Intravenous-to-oral stepdown program: four years of experience in a large teaching hospital. *Annals of Pharmacotherapy*, 26, 1447–51.

Hess, D.A., Mahoney, C.D., Johnson, P.N., et al. (1990). Integration of clinical and administrative strategies to reduce expenditures for antimicrobial agents *American Journal of Hospital Pharmacy*, 47, 585–91.

Hirschman, S.Z., Meyers, B.R., and Bradbury, K. (1988). Use of antimicrobial agents in a university teaching hospital: evolution of a comprehensive control program. *Archives of Internal Medicine*, 148, 2001–7.

Lee, Y.I., Thrupp, L.D., and Friis, R.H. (1992). Nosocomial infection and antibiotic utilization in geriatric patients: a pilot prospective surveillance program in skilled nursing facilities. *Gerontology*, 38, 223–32.

Levy, S.B. (1998). Multidrug resistance—a sign of the times. *New England Journal of Medicine*, 338, 1376–8.

Lowy, F.D. (1998). Medical progress: *Staphylococcus aureus* infections. *New England Journal of Medicine*, 339, 520–32.

Lutters, M., Herrmann, F., Dayer, P., et al. (1998). Utilisation des antibiotiques dans un hôpital universitaire de gériatrie et formulaires des médicaments. *Schweizerische Medizinische Woschenschrift*, 128, 268–71.

McGee, W. (1993). Causes of death in a hospitalized geriatric population: an autopsy survey of 3000 patients. *Virchows Archiv A Pathological Anatomy and Histopathology*, 423, 343–9.

Marr, J.J. and Moffet, H.L. (1988). Guidelines for improving the use of antimicrobial agents in hospitals: a statement by the Infectious Diseases Society of America. *Journal of Infectious Diseases*, 157, 869–76.

Michel, J.P. (1995). Susceptibilité des personnes âgées aux infections. *Medecine et Maladies Infectieuses*, 25, 962–3.

Michel, J.-P., Lesourd, B., Conne, P., et al. (1991a). Prevalence of infections and their risk factors in geriatric institutions: a one-day multicentre survey. *WHO Bulletin*, 69, 35–41.

Michel, J.-P., Decrey, H., and MacGee, W. (1991b). Infections in the elderly. In *Facts Research in Gerontology* (ed. J.L. Albarède and P. Vellas), pp. 87–95. Serdi, Paris.

Michel, J.-P., Loew, F., Brennensthul, P., et al. (1994). Ethique de l'antibiothérapie en médecine de l'âge avancé. *Schweizerische Medizinische Woschenschrift*, 124, 2220–5.

Proust, J.J., Quadri, R.A., Arbogast, A., et al. (1996). Molecular mechanisms of age-related lymphocyte dysfunction. *Pathologie Biologie*, 44, 729–36.

Rahimi, A.R. (1998). Prevalence and outcome of methicillin-resistant *Staphylococcus aureus* colonization in two nursing centers in Georgia. *Journal of the American Geriatrics Society*, 46, 1555–7.

Redelmeier, D.A., Tan, S.H., and Booth, G.L. (1998). The treatment of unrelated disorders in patients with chronic medical diseases. *New England Journal of Medicine*, 338, 1516–20.

Sallin, M., Zelger, G., and Michel, J. (1994). Antibiotic use in a geriatric hospital: a ten years overview. In *Drug Treatment in the Elderly* (ed. G. Zelger et al.). Reinach.

Seto, W.H., Ching, T.Y., Kou, M., et al. (1996). Hospital antibiotic prescribing successfully modified by 'immediate concurrent feedback'. *British Journal of Clinical Pharmacology*, 41, 229–34.

Smith, T.L., Pearson, M.L., Wilcox, K.R., et al. (1999). Emergence of vancomycin resistance in *Staphylococcus aureus*. *New England Journal of Medicine*, 340, 493–501.

Thompson, B.L., Dwyer, D.M., Ussery, X.T., et al. (1997). Handwashing and glove use in a long-term care facility. *Infection Control and Hospital Epidemiology*, 18, 97–103.

Veyssier, P., Maurice, G., and Meyer, C. (1997). Contrôle et prevention de l'infection dans les services et établissements de long séjour. In *Pathologie infectieuse: infections chez les sujets âgés* (ed. P. Veyssier), pp. 40–59. Ellipses, Paris.

Vogt, N. (1998). Individualiser la pharmacopée en gériatrie. *Schweizerische Medizinische Woschenschrift*, 128, 195–8.

Voss, A. and Widmer, A. (1997). No time for handwashing? Handwashing versus alcoholic rub: can we afford 100 per cent compliance? *Infection Control and Hospital Epidemiology*, 18, 205–8.

Waldvogel, F.A. (1999). New resistance in *Staphylococcus aureus*. *New England Journal of Medicine*, 340, 556–7.

Wenzel, R.P. (1995). The Lowbury Lecture. The economics of nosocomial infections. *Journal of Hospital Infection*, 31, 79–87.

Yoshikawa, T.T. (1998). VRE, MRSA, PRP, and DRGNB in LTCF: lessons to be learned from this alphabet. *Journal of the American Geriatrics Society*, 46, 241–3.

Zheng, B., Han, S., Takahashi, Y., et al. (1997). Immunosenescence and germinal center reaction. *Immunological Reviews*, 160, 63–77.

3.3 Immunity and ageing

Jacques J. Proust

Introduction

Immune senescence is classically viewed as a simple, progressive, and irreversible age-associated decline of the functional capacity of the immunological machinery. Recent observations have shed a new light on the nature of the changes occurring in the immune system with ageing and forced us to revise this canonical concept. More than just a simple waning of activity, immune senescence appears as the result of a true dysfunction of the immune system. The age-associated alterations of the complex network of interactions between various components of the immune system result in the loss of some activities and the simultaneous increase of other activities. On the biological level, the association of these unbalanced and uncoordinated immunological activities results in an inappropriate, inefficient, and sometimes detrimental immune response. On the clinical level, immune senescence is implicated in an ever-growing number of age-associated pathological conditions.

Innate immunity

To cope with pathogenic organisms or cancer cells, the body does not rely solely on the acquired specific immune response but also on innate immunity. Innate immunity provides a rapid but incomplete defence against threatening agents until the slower and more definitive acquired immune response develops. The components of innate immunity usually identify and differentiate potentially noxious organisms from innocuous substances according to their carbohydrate signature.

Dendritic cells

Dendritic cells are the most potent antigen-presenting cells for helper T lymphocytes. Their role is crucial for the initiation of an immune response. Dendritic cells select antigens through specialized receptors that recognize microbial glycoconjugates. Bound molecules are internalized via coated pits and degraded into antigenic peptides. The antigenic peptides associate with newly synthesized major histocompatibility (**MHC**) class II proteins to form a complex subsequently displayed on the cytoplasmic membrane of the dendritic cell. This complex delivers the first activation signal to T lymphocytes. Other signals must also be provided by different molecules expressed on dendritic cells for optimal T-cell activation.

Only a small number of studies have examined the effect of ageing on dendritic cells. Some of these investigations have been confined to thymic dendritic cells or Langerhans cells in the skin. In these studies, simple quantitative comparisons generally show a decreased number of dendritic cells in aged animals and elderly humans (Thiers *et al.* 1984; Nakahama *et al.* 1990).

Other studies performed on the follicular dendritic cells localized in lymph nodes from aged mice demonstrate that antigen-loaded cells do not migrate in the germinal centres as they normally do in young animals. This defect in migration may prevent effective interaction between T and B cells and influence the antibody response (Holmes *et al.* 1984). Moreover, antigens associated with these cells appear less immunogenic than antigens processed and presented by dendritic cells from young controls (Burton *et al.* 1991). Recent reports confirm that the frequencies of dendritic cells as well as their antigen-presenting function is reduced with ageing whereas the expression of MHC class II and intercellular adhesion molecules (**ICAM**) is preserved (Yuan and Baird 1994).

In contrast with the deficiencies observed in cells from aged animals, dendritic cells obtained from the peripheral blood of elderly humans have the same antigen-presenting capacities as similar cells from young individuals. They are equally effective in inducing the proliferation of T-cell clones after antigenic stimulation and present no difference in the expression of surface molecules (Steger *et al.* 1996).

Macrophages

Because macrophages are among the first cells that pathogenic organisms encounter after traversing the epithelial barrier, they are a critical component of the host's response to infection. Macrophages are specialized in phagocytosis and intracellular killing of microorganisms. They demonstrate tumour cytotoxicity following activation by various agents and also function as efficient antigen-presenting cells. These cells are equipped with C-type lectin receptors which allow them to bind soluble glycoconjugates. They also express receptors for lipopolysaccharides, which are constituents of Gram-negative bacterial membranes. Triggering of these receptors induces the synthesis of numerous chemicals and cytokines including interleukins (**IL**) 1, 6, 12, and 15 and tumour necrosis factor-α. These products initiate the acute phase response, enhance the microbiocidal activity of macrophages, stimulate the production of cytokines by other cells, and promote the activation of helper T cells.

Studies concerned with the effect of ageing on the different functions of mononuclear phagocytes have often yielded inconsistent results. Peritoneal macrophages from senescent mice appear to be constitutionally activated and generate large amounts of superoxide (Lavie 1994). Contrasting with this non-specific activation, they exhibit reduced antitumour activity and decreased capacity to produce tumour necrosis factor, IL-1, and nitric oxide which are critical molecules for tumour growth inhibition and tumour cell destruction (Wallace et al. 1995).

Macrophages isolated from the peripheral blood of healthy elderly humans support a normal T-lymphocyte response to specific antigens (tetanus toxoid) but not to mitogens such as phytohaemagglutinin. Following mitogenic activation, their production of cytokines (IL-1, IL-6, and tumour necrosis factor) and their expression of surface molecules (ICAM-1, leucocyte function antigen 3 (**LFA-3**) and HLA DR) are similar to those of young individuals (Rich et al. 1992). In vivo studies performed in elderly humans demonstrate that the rates of macrophage clearance of erythrocytes sensitized by immunoglobulin (**Ig**) G declines notably with advancing age (Melez et al. 1988).

Investigation of the antitumoral properties of aged human monocytes provides results consistent with those obtained in old mice. Activated macrophages purified from elderly donors display a low toxicity against tumour cells. In addition, they show a sharp decrease in the production of IL-1 and nitric oxide (McLachlan et al. 1995). The significant reduction of antitumoral activity of human macrophages with age may contribute to the increased cancer susceptibility of older people.

Natural killer cells

Because natural killer (**NK**) cells are involved in host resistance to a variety of tumours and infectious diseases, they are considered as important players in the innate immune system. NK cells resemble T lymphocytes but do not bear the conventional T-cell antigen receptor. The NK receptor is probably a member of the C-type lectin family, with a broad carbohydrate specificity. NK cells have the ability to kill target cells spontaneously in the absence of any obvious prior activation. It is hypothesized that they scan neighbouring cells for the absence of MHC class I molecules. This recognition of 'non-self' may immediately activate the killing mechanism. NK cells may also kill after they become armed with immunoglobulin bound through Fc receptors on their cell surface.

Reports regarding the effect of ageing on NK-cell activity in different species have been conflicting. In rodents, a marked decline in NK-cell activity, generally assayed in cells purified from the spleen or the lymph nodes of experimental animals, clearly occurs with advancing age (Kiessling et al. 1975; Ho et al. 1990).

In contrast with the studies of murine splenic NK cells, the majority of reports indicate that NK-cell activity derived from human peripheral blood remains unchanged or even increases with age (Bàtori et al. 1981; Krishnaraj 1992). This enhanced activity is usually associated with an increased proportion of cells expressing the NK phenotype.

Interestingly, NK-cell activity recovered from murine peripheral blood does not decline with age (Lanza and Djeu 1982), a finding concordant with the data obtained with human blood. Therefore it is conceivable that the activity of NK cells derived from the spleen and lymph nodes present a similar sensitivity to the ageing process in humans and in mice. The effect of age on human NK cells isolated from internal lymphoid tissues and its potential physiological significance remains to be investigated.

Complement system

Complement, the main soluble effector of innate immunity, consists of approximately 20 interacting plasma proteins constituting a triggered enzyme system. Through cytolysis, opsonization, and activation of inflammation, complement provides a natural and efficient defence system against micro-organisms. The different complement activation pathways (classical, alternative, and lectin pathways) lead to the generation of C3 convertases and subsequent activation of the terminal complement proteins C3 to C9, which are responsible for most of the biological activities of the complement system. Because inherited deficiencies of complement proteins are associated with impaired defence against microbial infection and altered tolerance to self, it is surprising that so few studies have examined complement levels and activity during ageing.

Despite obvious discrepancies between studies, healthy older individuals appear to have slightly higher levels of complement components, including C1q, C3, C4, C5, C9, properdin factor B, and haemolytic complement activity, than do younger persons (Nagaki et al. 1980). Age-associated differences in the level of these acute-phase reactants become more obvious during the course of bacterial infections. Whereas young individuals with acute bacteraemia increase their complement levels dramatically, older individuals do not manifest a significant rise in the concentration of complement proteins. The mechanisms and significance of this age-associated difference are uncertain and could involve decreased complement production as well as increased consumption (Goldberg and Finkelstein 1994).

Given the high degree of polymorphism observed within the complement system, possible association of certain complement phenotypes with particular pathological conditions may convey a biological disadvantage. For instance, the decreased frequency of the C3 phenotype in old persons may be partly explained by the association of the C3F allele with atherosclerosis (Sorensen and Dissing 1975). Similarly, the significant reduction in the prevalence of the null allele of the B gene of C4 reported in older subjects suggests that this allele is associated with increased susceptibility to as yet undefined risk factors, resulting in a shorter life expectancy of the middle-aged carriers (Kramer et al. 1991).

Adaptative immunity

Compared with the relatively rigid structures conveying innate immunity, the acquired immune system supported by T and B lymphocytes appears indefinitely versatile and adaptable. Acquired immunity is largely based on a peptide recognition system which provides a broader range of molecular determinants for immune response than the carbohydrate structures generally recognized by the components of the innate immunity.

Role of thymic involution in immune senescence

The thymus is the primary lymphoid organ where immature bone-marrow-derived precursors are subject to a selection process that allows them to differentiate into functional T lymphocytes. This complex intrathymic event results in the selection of T cells which are able to recognize the MHC class I and II molecules in conditions of affinity such that self-reactivity does not occur. The differentiation process involves the sequential expression of a variety of membrane markers as well as a rearrangement of T-cell receptor genes. Very few cells meet the selection requirements and over 95 per cent of the thymocytes are eliminated *in situ* by an apoptotic mechanism.

In comparison with other organs of the immune system, the thymus appear to undergo premature ageing and the dramatic thymic involution has logically been deemed responsible for the age-associated modification of the T-cell-mediated immune response. The thymus produces a number of immunoregulatory peptides which influence the differentiation of T-lymphocyte precursors and possibly some of the activities of mature B and T cells (Hirokawa and Makinodan 1975). The concentration of thymic hormones decreases with age, and these factors are no longer detected in the plasma of individuals aged over 60 years (Zatz and Goldstein 1985). Some aspects of the age-associated immune dysfunction, including decline in lymphocyte-mediated cytotoxicity, decreased production of high-affinity antibodies, and impaired helper T-cell response, can be improved or prevented by supplementation with certain thymic polypeptides (Bach 1977; Weksler *et al.* 1978; Frasca *et al.* 1982).

Transplantation studies have shown that the capacity of the thymus gland to promote the differentiation of T cells declines rapidly with age. In mice, the rate of export of mature T lymphocytes from the thymus to the periphery decreases by about a factor of 20 between 1 and 6 months of age (Scollay *et al.* 1980). More recent experiments involving thymic transplants into athymic mice indicate that 50 per cent of the capacity of the thymus to support the complete spectrum of T-cell differentiation is lost shortly after birth (Utsuyama *et al.* 1991). However, even in old age, the thymus is capable of supporting some degree of T-cell differentiation. Whether this remaining activity has any physiological significance remains to be demonstrated. The effects of thymectomy in adult life are usually mild and inconsistent (Simpson and Cantor 1975). Moreover, complete structural and functional thymic restoration by growth hormone does not significantly improve the immune response of aged experimental animals (Goya *et al.* 1992).

Contrary to the belief that thymic involution begins at puberty, the regression of the human thymus starts soon after birth and continues at a constant rate until middle age (George and Ritter 1996). The export rate of mature lymphocytes becomes rapidly insufficient to compensate for the high turnover of mature lymphocytes at the periphery and the role of the thymus as a producer of mature cells is progressively taken over by peripheral lymphoid organs. Once the peripheral T-cell pool has been established early in life, the thymus may no longer be needed. Therefore the causative relationship between thymic involution and T-cell immunosenescence is still uncertain.

Changes in T-lymphocyte function

T lymphocytes expressing receptors of adequate affinity are triggered by antigens to proliferate and develop into effector cells. Receptors on T lymphocytes recognize only peptides generated by the breakdown of protein antigens that are bound to MHC class I and II proteins and subsequently displayed on the surface of antigen-presenting cells.

These antigen–MHC product complexes are recognized by class I CD8$^+$-restricted T lymphocytes which differentiate into cytotoxic effectors and by CD4$^+$-restricted T lymphocytes which function as helper cells. Helper T lymphocytes orchestrate the immune response by promoting intracellular killing by macrophages, antibody production by B lymphocytes, and clonal expansion of cytotoxic T lymphocytes.

Together with the T-cell receptor, a second receptor (CD28) must be activated by a specific ligand expressed on the surface of antigen-presenting cells to achieve full activation of helper T cells. Helper T cells responding to antigen express the CD40 ligand, which is a key element in contact-dependent activation of macrophages and B cells bearing the appropriate CD40 receptor.

Naive helper T cells can be induced to differentiate into Th$_1$ or Th$_2$ cells. Th$_1$ cells, through secretion of IL-2, interferon-γ , lymphotoxin, and tumour necrosis factor-α, increase the microbicidal activity of macrophages and cause B cells to switch their immunoglobulin isotypes to IgG$_1$. Th$_2$ cells synthesize IL-4, IL-5, IL-6, IL-10, and IL-13, which collectively mediate the activation of mast cells and eosinophils, direct B-cell immunoglobulin switching to IgE and IgG4, and inhibit macrophage activation. Th$_1$ activities probably evolved to rid the body of intracellular pathogens, whereas Th$_2$-cell functions emerged to promote the destruction of extracellular parasites.

A consensus has emerged that alterations of T-lymphocyte activities underlie much of the age-associated decline in the protective immune response. Indeed, ageing leads to substantial modifications of T-cell function.

Severe age-associated defects in helper T-cell function, attested by a weak allogeneic response, a function primarily attributed to helper T cells (Zharhary and Gershon 1981), or a deficient T-cell-dependent antibody response (Friedman and Globerson 1978; Nicoletti 1994), have been thoroughly documented. T-cell cytotoxicity generated against allogeneic stimulators declines with ageing (Shigemoto *et al.* 1975). The proliferative response of T lymphocytes to mitogenic lectins (Foad *et al.* 1974), monoclonal antibodies directed against components of the T cell receptor complex (Schwab *et al.* 1985), and soluble antigens (Kishimoto *et al.* 1982) decreases significantly in aged humans and rodents. Aged T cells are also hyporesponsive to co-stimulation mediated by the CD28 or CD2 receptors (Engwerda *et al.* 1994; Beckman *et al.* 1995).

In contrast, novel or aberrant characteristics may appear during the course of ageing. For instance, T cells from elderly humans sometimes fail to abide by the obligatory MHC restriction associated with antigen recognition (Schwab *et al.* 1992). Enhanced activity of particular T-cell subpopulations is also observed; the high concentration of IL-6 and IL-10 measured in the serum or in the culture of cells derived from elderly donors (Ershler *et al.* 1993; Cakman *et al.* 1996) indicates that Th$_2$-cell activity increases with age. Mature T cells from aged individuals are also more likely to initiate their apoptotic programme upon activation than are cells from young individuals (Phelouzat *et al.* 1996).

Cellular basis for T-cell dysfunction

At the cellular level, alteration of T-cell-mediated immunity can be partly explained by significant changes in T-lymphocyte populations. The reduction in the generation of helper cell and cytotoxic precursors during ageing (Nordin *et al.* 1983; Miller 1984) undoubtedly influences the corresponding activities. The different distribution of T cells between the CD4$^+$ and CD8$^+$ compartments with advancing age (Nijhuis and Nagelkerken 1992) may also moderately affect the immune response of elderly people. The susceptibility of T-lymphocytes from aged organisms to apoptosis is associated with an increased number of cells expressing the Fas molecule, a receptor specialized in the transmission of death signals (Phelouzat et al. 1997).

Ageing also leads to a dramatic increase in the proportion of antigen-experienced memory T cells associated with a concomitant decrease in naive T lymphocytes (Xu et al. 1993). Although the shift towards memory cells begins rather early in life, the progressive expansion of cells already committed to particular antigens and functionally different from virgin T cells probably accounts for some aspects of the age-associated immune dysfunction. However, recent studies show that naive T lymphocytes also experience intrinsic alterations with ageing (Linton et al. 1996).

T cells, like B cells, can become clonally expanded in most healthy elderly individuals. This mono- or oligoclonal expansion is observed primarily among CD8$^+$ cells and may constitute up to 35 per cent of this cell population (Posnett et al. 1994). Interestingly, the clonally expanded CD8$^+$ cells lack the CD28 surface molecule (Posnett et al. 1994; Batliwalla et al. 1996), a receptor essential for their optimal activation. Although these cells exhibit a high cytotoxic activity (Fagnoni et al. 1996), they have a low proliferative capacity (Batliwalla et al. 1996). The expansion of this particular subset explains the increased frequency of CD8$^+$ CD28$^-$ cells in the peripheral blood of aged persons (Effros et al. 1994; Fagnoni et al. 1996) and probably contributes to the disturbance of their immune response.

Molecular mechanisms of T-cell dysfunction

Because T-lymphocyte activation and entry into the cell cycle is critical for the development of an effective immune response, the age-associated proliferative deficit of T cells has been extensively investigated. Although the molecular mechanisms underlying such a deficit are far from being completely understood, significant progress in their comprehension has been achieved in recent years.

The loss of the proliferative potential of T lymphocytes with ageing was recognized in the early 1970s (Hori et al. 1973; Foad et al. 1974), but it was many years before it became apparent that the mitogen-induced proliferation of T cells depends on their capacity to produce and utilize IL-2. The proliferative impairment of mitogen-stimulated T lymphocytes isolated from aged organisms was then traced to their inability to secrete a sufficient amount of IL-2 (Gillis et al. 1981; Thoman and Weigle 1981). Because mitogenic stimulation induces both the synthesis of IL-2 and the expression of the high-affinity receptor for this lymphokine, the density of IL-2 receptor displayed on the surface of activated T lymphocytes is also logically decreased in advanced age (Negoro et al. 1986; Proust et al. 1988). However, addition of exogenous IL-2 does not fully restore the proliferative capacity of lymphocytes from elderly donors (Gillis et al. 1981) even when these cells are selected for normal expression of their IL-2 receptors (Negoro et al. 1986). This observation suggests that additional molecular events interfere with the mechanisms of cell division during the process of ageing.

Recent studies show that an accumulation of biochemical lesions, which may or may not be located along the pathways leading to IL-2 synthesis, are implicated in the age-associated proliferative defect of T lymphocytes. Initiation of cell division requires delivery of several signals to the cell surface and their intracellular transmission. In cells derived from aged individuals, the signalling cascades may be interrupted at various steps of the signal transmission. For instance, physical and chemical modification of the plasma membranes may prevent adequate signal reception (Stulnig et al. 1995). Additionally, changes in the activities of tyrosine kinase (Patel and Miller 1992; Quadri et al. 1996), phospholipase C-γ (Di Pietro et al. 1993; Grossman et al. 1995), and protein kinase C (Proust et al. 1987; Fulop et al. 1995) combine to block the phosphoinositide pathway. Other modifications impede signal transmission through the Ras (Ghosh and Miller 1995) and mitogen-activated protein kinase (Whisler et al. 1996) pathways.

The solicitation of signalling pathways leads to the activation of a number of genes whose products function as transcription factors regulating the synthesis of lymphokines and entry into the cell cycle. Several defects in gene expression (Nagel et al. 1988; Song et al. 1992), transcription complex formation (Sikora et al. 1992; Pahlavani et al. 1995), and transcription factor DNA binding activity (Whisler et al. 1993) have been reported in T lymphocytes from aged organisms. Some of these defects are related to altered signalling process but others are not. Different mechanisms, such as the progressive loss of telomeric DNA during the successive rounds of cellular replication, may also limit the proliferative potential of T lymphocytes in older people (Hastie et al. 1990; Vaziri et al. 1993).

With a few exceptions, these various molecular mechanisms have been investigated in unselected cell populations. Anomalies observed may in fact reflect the defect of discrete subpopulations of T lymphocytes rather than a general dysfunction. Also, the multiplicity of biochemical alterations detected in lymphocytes from elderly organisms raises the question of their pathogenesis. Interestingly, oxidative stress, a biological phenomenon already strongly implicated in the process of senescence (Harman 1981), is able to interrupt the tyrosine-kinase-mediated signal transmission (Flescher et al. 1994), block the phosphoinositide pathway (Grossman et al. 1995), inhibit the binding of transcription factors to DNA (Flescher et al. 1994), and shorten telomeres (von Zglimicki et al. 1995). The deleterious effect of reactive oxygen species, among other harmful factors, may be a common denominator of the various biochemical alterations implicated in lymphocyte dysfunction during the ageing process.

Changes in B-lymphocyte function

B lymphocytes manufacture antibodies and display them on the cell surface where they serve as receptors for the antigen recognized in its native conformation. In order to express immunoglobulins on their surface, B-cell progenitors must rearrange variable gene segments on the heavy- and light-chain loci. This primary repertoire is further expanded by junctional flexibility, secondary rearrangements, and above all somatic hypermutation, a process unique to the immune system. Specific recognition of foreign antigen by surface immunoglobulin receptors represents the first step in the induction of the humoral response. Helper T lymphocytes recognize the antigenic peptide–MHC product complex and stimulate B-lymphocyte proliferation and differentiation into antibody-secreting cells through interleukin and cell contact signalling.

During the process of senescence, the humoral immune response is generally impaired both quantitatively and qualitatively. After immunization, aged persons produce significantly fewer antibodies than young adults (Burns et al. 1990) and maintain protective titres of serum antibodies for shorter periods (Kishimoto et al. 1980).

Because most B-cell functions are regulated by T lymphocytes or their products, it is difficult to differentiate the age-associated changes in humoral response due to the intrinsic defects of B lymphocytes from those attributable to alteration in T-lymphocyte function. It is possible that much of the decline in humoral immunity observed with ageing is a consequence of the modification of T-cell activities known to promote B-lymphocyte activation and differentiation.

Quantitative modification of the humoral response

The amount of antibody synthesized in response to most foreign antigens decreases with ageing (Rowley et al. 1968). The serum concentration of both anti-blood-group antibodies and other natural antibodies also declines with age (Rowley et al. 1968; Somers and Kuhns 1972).

The age-associated decrease in the total number of circulating B lymphocytes (Utsuyama et al. 1992) and the reduced frequency of antigen-responsive B cells (Zharhary and Klinman 1983) undoubtedly influence the overall production of specific antibodies. However, the amount of antibody synthesized per cell, by responding B lymphocytes, remains unchanged with age (Zharhary and Klinman 1983). This observation suggests that individual B lymphocytes derived from elderly organisms function either optimally or not at all and that the quantitative defect in specific antibody synthesis is essentially due to the presence of non-functional cells.

In contrast with the decline in specific antibody production, the serum concentration of IgA and the IgG$_1$, IgG$_2$, and IgG$_3$ subclasses is usually elevated in humans beyond the seventh decade (Paganelli et al. 1992). The mechanisms underlying the increase in immunoglobulin levels with age are still unclear. A diminished catabolism of immunoglobulin associated with a continuous stimulation of the immune system by iterative exposure to foreign antigens and/or altered autoantigens may partly explain this abnormality. Accordingly, at the cellular level, B lymphocytes from aged animals seem to produce 'non-specific' IgG spontaneously as if they were continuously activated (Glimcher and Cantor 1982).

Qualitative modification of the humoral response

The quality of the humoral response evaluated in terms of affinity and/or avidity is probably more important for immune effectiveness than the quantity of antibodies produced.

A decrease in average serum antibody affinity has been demonstrated in several experimental systems (Goidl et al. 1976; Zharhary et al. 1977). In some instances, passive immunization with antibodies elicited in aged animals show that these specific immunoglobulins are less protective against bacterial infection than those produced in younger animals (Nicoletti et al. 1993). Elderly humans also generate antibodies that typically bind antigens less well than those produced in young individuals (Kishimoto et al. 1980). Evidence for this qualitative change is the failure of the serum of aged individuals immunized with polyvalent pneumococcal vaccine to opsonize pneumococci, despite a high content of antibodies to capsular polysaccharides and phosphorylcholine, the immunodominant epitope of these bacteria (Musher et al. 1986).

The qualitative changes in the antibody response observed with ageing are partly due to alterations in the basic molecular mechanisms responsible for antibody diversity. The antibody repertoire generated by aged animals appears to be different from that of younger controls, as judged by a differential expression of idiotypic markers (Goidl et al. 1980). Sequencing of antibody cDNA suggests that ageing may lead to a repertoire partially dominated by a fairly small number of expanded B-cell clones (Bangs 1991). Recent studies in mice show that, in some cases, B lymphocytes derived from young and aged mice differ in their utilization of IgV genes that encode the antibody molecules (Riley et al. 1989; Nicoletti et al. 1991).

Most importantly, immunoglobulin somatic hypermutation, the basic mechanism that leads to the affinity maturation of serum antibodies through antigen-driven selection of B cells bearing mutated high-affinity receptors, no longer seems to occur in the germinal centre of aged mice (Miller and Kelsoe 1995). These observations indicate that, at least in some instances, B lymphocytes from a senescent immune system produce antibodies that are structurally and functionally different and therefore less protective than those generated in younger organisms.

Autoimmune reactivity

In contrast with the decline in the immune response to exogenous antigens, there is an enhancement of autoimmune reactivity during the ageing process. The percentage of T lymphocytes binding to autologous antigens (Charreire and Bach 1975), the spontaneous expression of autoreactive B lymphocytes (Goidl et al. 1981), the response to altered syngeneic determinant (Naor et al. 1976), and the frequency of autoantibodies directed against a wide variety of organ-specific and non-organ-specific antigens (Goodwin et al. 1982) all increase during senescence, indicating an age-associated propensity to lose self-tolerance.

Apart from their potentially pathogenic properties, some of the autoantibodies generated are involved in immunoregulation. For instance, autoantibodies directed against conformational determinants of immunoglobulins, termed auto-anti-idiotypic antibodies, are produced in large amounts in aged animals and play an important role in the decline of their humoral response (Goidl et al. 1980). Interestingly, the ability to generate large quantities of auto-anti-idiotypic antibodies appears to be an inherent property of B lymphocytes isolated from aged organisms (Goidl et al. 1983).

Our understanding of the autoimmune process, particularly in the field of ageing, remains fragmentary and incomplete. In normal conditions, B cells expressing antibody receptors with high affinity to self will be clonally deleted, rendered silent, or switched to a different specificity. With ageing, particular subsets of B cells may escape deletion or may be unable to revise their receptor and extinguish their high affinity for self. Both the increased percentage representation and the enhanced activity of a distinct subset of B cells expressing the CD5 surface molecule and specialized in autoantibody production (Hu et al. 1993) suggest an age-associated defect in the process of clonal selection and/or receptor editing.

Because, as stated above, antibodies generated by B lymphocytes from aged individuals are structurally and functionally different, they usually show a broad spectrum of cross-reactivity with self and non-self antigens (Borghesi and Nicoletti 1994). The production of such cross-reactive antibodies probably participates in the increased incidence of autoantibodies in older people.

Autoimmunity may also result from a conventional but inappropriate immune response against self-molecules that have either been altered by age-associated processes such as oxidation and/or glycation or released from anatomical sequestration. Polyclonal Band/or T-cell activation by molecules of microbial origin or immunoregulatory disturbances, such as the predominant engagement of Th_2 cells in the immune response of older people, may also be implicated in the aberrant self-recognition characteristic of immune senescence.

Mucosal immunity

Because most pathogens enter the body through mucosal surfaces, mucosal immunity is of prime importance in host defence against infection. In some cases, resistance to infection correlates better with the amount of antibodies present in external secretions than with serum antibody titres. It is usually agreed that the mucosal immune network is structurally and functionally different from the rest of the immune system (Bienenstock 1984). As a corollary, the age-associated changes in various humoral and cell-mediated immunogical activities may not necessarily correlate with those of mucosa-associated lymphoid tissues.

The published data concerning the effects of ageing on mucosal immunity are not always consistent. Studies performed on aged mice generally show that immune competence is preserved in the mucosal compartment (Szewczuk and Campbell 1981), whereas studies of non-human primates indicate that ageing compromises mucosal immunity to the same extent as systemic immunity (Horan 1993).

Available data for elderly humans suggest that mucosal immunosenescence is characterized by deficits in the differentiation and/or migration of IgA-secreting plasma cells and by defects in the initiation and/or regulation of local antibody production (Korsrud and Brnadzaeg 1980; Schmucker et al. 1996).

Allergic reactivity

Allergy is characterized by the enhanced ability of B cells to produce IgE antibodies directed at ubiquitous antigens that activate the immune system after inhalation, ingestion, or penetration through the skin. IgE antibodies bind to high-affinity receptors expressed on the surface of mast cells and basophils. When antigen is reintroduced, IgE-mediated triggering of these receptors initiates the release of vasoactive mediators, chemotactic factors, and cytokines involved in th; allergic cascade. Eosinophils also accumulate at the sites of allergic inflammation and participate in the pathogenesis of allergic reaction by releasing toxic products that contribute to the induction of tissue damage. IgE production is essentially dependent upon the presence of IL-4 released by allergen-activated Th_2 lymphocytes, whereas eosinophils are activated by IL-5.

Although no data are available on the prevalence of allergic reaction in the elderly population, it is usually thought that IgE-mediated hypersensitivity reactions are less frequent and that allergic symptoms tend to improve with age. Several studies provide a biological basis for this assumption. In particular, specific serum IgE production has been shown to decline with age (al-Rayes et al. 1992; Omenaas et al. 1994). This age-associated decrease in IgE synthesis can be traced to a defect in IL-4 production, and the addition of exogenous IL-4 is able to restore normal production of IgE in cell cultures from elderly individuals. The available data point to an impairment in

the transmembrane signalling process as the cause of reduced IL-4 production in old age (al-Rayes et al. 1992).

Whether mast cell function is also impaired with ageing is yet to be demonstrated. However, reactivity to histamine, one of the most potent mediators released during mast cell and basophil degranulation, decreases significantly with age and may account for alleviation of allergic symptomatology in later life (Skassa-Brociek et al. 1987).

Clinical consequences

Age-associated immune dysfunction does not lead to an overt immune deficiency comparable with that observed in AIDS patients. Opportunistic infections usually seen in severely immunocompromised patients do not normally occur in elderly persons. Age-associated immune deficiency develops insidiously and its real impact on health is often revealed under conditions of intense physiological stress (surgery, multiple organ failure, protein-calorie malnutrition, dehydration, etc.). Whereas some pathological conditions are clearly related to specific immune deficits, dysregulation of other immune activities may contribute to a wide range of degenerative diseases associated with ageing but not ordinarily considered immunological in aetiology (Effros 1993).

Infection

While infectious diseases rank low among the various causes of death in adults, they represent a major cause of morbidity and mortality in older people (MacGee 1993).

A causal relationship between immune senescence and infectious diseases has been clearly established with respect to the reactivation of zoster and mycobaterial diseases. The incidence of shingles (late reactivation of a latent varicella zoster infection) increases fivefold between the ages of 45 and 85 and is associated with a loss of cell-mediated immunity to the varicella zoster virus (Berger et al. 1981).

Defects in cell-mediated immunity are also involved in the re-emergence of tuberculosis in old age when this mycobaterial infection occurs frequently (Nagami and Yoskikawa 1983). The same mechanism may explain the endogenous reactivation of latent Epstein–Barr virus infection, usually seen in immunocompromised hosts, in institutionalized elderly adults (Scott et al. 1994).

Quantitative as well as qualitative alterations in specific antibody production partly account for the high incidence and fatality of pneumonia (Yoshikawa 1983), influenza (Barker and Mullooly 1982), infectious endocarditis (Cantrell and Yoshikawa 1983), and tetanus (Schneider 1983) in elderly adults. For similar reasons, increasing age is associated with significantly higher rates of various nosocomial infections; approximately 65 per cent of all nosocomial infections occur in patients over 60 years of age (Gross et al. 1983). Available data indicate that pre-existing immune dysfunction also negatively affects the course of AIDS in older persons (Kendig and Adler 1990).

A limited but compelling body of literature demonstrates a heightened susceptibility to parasitic infection with increasing age. Elderly individuals are particularly vulnerable to metazoan and protozoan parasites. This sensitivity appears to be partly due to a defective production by Th_1 lymphocytes of lymphokines involved in the generation of a specific antibody response against parasitic pathogens (Albright and Albright 1994).

Although there is little doubt that immunosenescence contributes to the increased susceptibility of older people to infection, it is difficult to differentiate the risk attributable to the inadequate immune response from that related to the various pathophysiological modifications of the organism that accompany ageing. Age-associated changes in non-immunological mechanisms of defence as well as the breakdown of natural barriers to infection may lead to increased exposure to pathogens and poor resistance to their dissemination. Structural and functional alterations of different organs probably also determine the specific localization of infections.

Cancer

Age appears to be the most important determinant of cancer risk. The incidence of many cancers rises continuously with age to reach a peak between 75 and 79 years, followed by a decline that may reflect a selection process (Modan *et al.* 1996). Potential age-associated aetiological factors include longer duration of carcinogenic exposure, increased susceptibility to carcinogens, mitochondrial deterioration, DNA mutations, chromosomal breakage and rearrangements, DNA hypomethylation, activation of oncogenes, inactivation of tumour suppressor genes, and diminished efficiency of DNA repair mechanisms (Cohen 1994).

Because effective rejection of tumours requires recruitment of a complex network of participating cells and factors, it is conceivable that the dysregulation of the immune system impairs both the recognition and the elimination of neoplastic cells during the ageing process. Despite numerous attempts to verify this hypothesis, compelling evidence proving that failure of immune surveillance contributes to the increased incidence of cancer in the elderly population is still lacking (Ershler 1993) and will probably await a better comprehension and more precise investigation of the molecular mechanisms underlying cancer immunology.

B-cell chronic lymphocytic leukaemia

Chronic lymphocytic leukaemia is a haematological neoplasm, typically associated with ageing, characterized by a clonal outgrowth of B cells and accompanied by severe immunological disturbances.

Hypogammaglobulinaemia occurs in the majority of patients with chronic lymphocytic leukaemia (Chapel and Bunch 1987) and probably results from the dysfunction of non-clonal B cells. The frequent autoimmune manifestations observed during the course of chronic lymphocytic leukaemia are mainly directed against cells of the haematopoietic system (Hamblin *et al.* 1986). Although most chronic lymphocytic leukaemia B cells are autoreactive, the autoantibodies implicated in the autoimmune phenomena are not secreted by the malignant clone.

Chronic lymphocytic leukaemia appears to be a heterogenous disorder (Kipps *et al.* 1992). Many chronic lymphocytic leukaemia B cells expressing the CD5 molecule and showing no evidence of somatic mutation may represent neoplastic transformation of a relatively immature population of B lymphocytes. Other chronic lymphocytic leukaemia B cells that do not express CD5 but present somatic mutations may originate in a more mature B-cell population. Because the pattern of somatic mutation is compatible with that elicited by antigen selection, antigen-driven expansion may be involved in the development of chronic lymphocytic leukaemia during the course of ageing.

Monoclonal gammopathies

Another consequence of the age-associated immune dysfunction is the emergence of benign monoclonal gammopathy. The frequency of idiopathic paraproteinaemia increases progressively from less than 1 per cent by the age of 50 years to up to 20 per cent in the tenth decade (Radl 1975). An 11-year follow-up study of elderly subjects with idiopathic paraproteinaemia showed that mono- or oligoclonal immunglobulin production does not influence the life expectancy of affected individuals (Axelsson 1977). Homogenous immunoglobulins have also been observed with an increased frequency in aged thymectomized animals, suggesting that altered T-cell function is involved in the pathogenesis of dysglobulinaemia (Radl *et al.* 1980).

Degenerative diseases of ageing

A number of studies now demonstrate a previously unsuspected development of immune activities in relation to structural or functional alterations characteristically associated with the ageing process.

Following the partial discrediting of the immunological theory of ageing proposed in the late 1960s (Walford 1969), the general consensus was that the classically low concentration of age-associated autoantibodies was not pathogenic and should be considered as a simple marker of immune dysfunction. This was reinforced by the observation that, in some cases, ageing organisms are resistant to the induction of experimental autoimmune diseases (Graus *et al.* 1993). However, recent studies show that these autoantibodies tend to rise in the presence of the chronic diseases that accompany ageing (Wolk *et al.* 1993; Potockaplazak *et al.* 1995) and are sometimes associated with either the functional decline of a particular organ (Sundbeck *et al.* 1995) or a specific disease (Fillit and Mulvihill 1993; Xu and Gaskin 1997). The link with various diseases may explain why the presence of autoantibodies in older people is associated with reduced life expectancy (Hooper *et al.* 1972; Mathews *et al.* 1973).

Interestingly, the presence of organ-specific autoantibodies is not detected after the ninth decade (Mariotti *et al.* 1992; Candore *et al.* 1997), suggesting that the absence of autoreactivity represents a survival advantage. The association of organ-specific autoantibodies with age-associated diseases, organic functional decline, or increased mortality, and their absence in healthy centenarians, again raises the question of their real innocuity.

Apart from autoreactivity, other deregulated immunological activities may be implicated in several pathological conditions typically associated with ageing. For instance, activated lymphocytes expressing the elastin–laminin receptor and elastase activities are found in atheromatous lesions and probably participate in the atherosclerotic process (Robert 1996). The presence of T lymphocytes near neuritic plaques and the enhanced expression of immune-system-associated antigens by cells of the central nervous system suggests that some type of immunological response occurs during the course of Alzheimer's disease (Rogers *et al.* 1988). Moreover, the association of complement protein with senile plaques implies that activation of classical complement pathway contributes to neuronal cell death in Alzheimer's disease (Smyth *et al.* 1994). Complement is also involved in the abnormal sequestration of erythrocytes from elderly individuals (Shapiro *et al.* 1993).

The age-associated increase in the synthesis of IL-6, a lymphokine that induces bone resorption, could also be involved in the development of osteoporosis. This hypothesis is substantiated by the observation that IL-6-deficient mice are protected from bone loss caused by oestrogen depletion (Poli *et al.* 1994). Excessive IL-6 production could also be implicated in the pathogenesis of late-life lymphoma, myeloma, and possibly Alzheimer's disease (Ershler *et al.* 1994; Huell *et al.* 1995).

Effectiveness of vaccination

It is generally agreed that antibody response to conventional vaccines declines with age even in healthy individuals. The inadequate production of specific antibody is clearly demonstrated in studies with vaccines containing novel antigens such as tetanus toxoid or hepatitis B virus to which the recipients had no prior immunity induced by natural infection (Cook *et al.* 1987).

With vaccines intended to stimulate an immune system already primed by natural infection or previous vaccination, such as influenza and pneumococcal vaccines, the respective effects of age and pre-existing immunity on the antibody response are more difficult to evaluate. However, reviews of vaccine effectiveness reports reveal that as many as 30 to 40 per cent of healthy elderly persons do not develop protective immunity after immunization with influenza vaccine (Strassburg *et al.* 1986). An even larger percentage of elderly patients with chronic disease do not respond to influenza vaccine by an appropriate antibody response (Gross *et al.* 1989). Pneumoccocal vaccines have also been less effective in preventing illness among high-risk older adults than among healthy young adults (Simberkoff *et al.* 1986).

Although not all aspects of the T-cell response to vaccination have been examined with respect to ageing, it appears that the decreased helper T-cell activity plays a significant role in the reduction of specific antibody production (Kishimoto *et al.* 1982). Both the decline in the cytotoxic activity of influenza-virus-specific T lymphocytes (Powers 1993) and their reduced capacity to synthesize IL-2 in response to the antigenic challenge (McElhaney *et al.* 1990) may also influence the effectiveness of vaccination in older subjects. A detailed discussion of immunization in older persons is given in Chapter 3.4.

Assessment of immunosenescence and prognostic significance

Various immunological parameters have been measured to assess both humoral and cell-mediated immune responses. Some of these indices are thought to reflect the immune status and may serve as indicators of general health and predictors of disease risk and/or survival.

Several prospective studies in elderly humans show that a low responsiveness to skin tests for delayed-type hypersensitivity is a good indicator of mortality over the next few years (Roberts-Thomson *et al.* 1974; Wayne *et al.* 1990). A loss of proliferative potential of T lymphocytes in mitogenic assays is also associated with increased mortality, even when the cause of death does not appear to be directly related to immune senescence (Murasko *et al.* 1988). The total number of circulating lymphocytes may be predictive of mortality. For instance, the development of lymphopenia during bacterial infections in elderly patients is strongly indicative of poor prognosis (Proust *et al.* 1985). A longitudinal survey in apparently healthy elderly men showed that a decline in peripheral blood lymphocyte count is also associated with diminished survival (Bender *et al.* 1986). The presence of

detectable amounts of the cytokine tumour necrosis factor-α in the serum of institutionalized elderly patients is usually correlated with early mortality (Mooradian *et al.* 1991).

In contrast, a combination of different parameters such as a low ratio of CD8 to CD4, a high B-cell number, and a high mitogen-induced T-cell proliferation, may predict the survival of aged individuals (Ferguson *et al.* 1995). In experimental animals selectively bred for differences in humoral response, a high antigen-induced antibody production is associated with increased lifespan (Covelli 1989). Whether high titres of vaccine-induced antibodies represent a survival advantage in later life remains to be confirmed.

Conclusions

Apart from changes brought about by the ageing process, factors such as multiple organ failure, malnutrition, chronic illnesses, sedentary lifestyle, frailty, and depression may adversely affect the immune response and should be carefully considered when attempting to evaluate the degree of immune dysfunction and its potential clinical consequences in old age. Genetic and environmental factors probably also influence the rate of deterioration of the immune function.

In this respect, studying very old people is of major immunological interest because it may help to differentiate innocuous immunological changes from potentially harmful alterations. Centenarians are considered the best example of successful ageing. An appropriate lifestyle combined with a privileged genetic endowment allows them to preserve their immunological defences and to escape major diseases. Interestingly, they present some of the immunological modifications classically associated with ageing in unselected populations, including high levels of immunoglobulins, the presence of non-organ-specific autoantibodies, the clonal expansion of B and T cells, and increased production of IL-6. In contrast, their immunity is characterized by a total absence of organ-specific autoantibodies, a preserved T-cell repertoire, a normal T-cell proliferative response, a high NK cell activity, and an increased resistance of lymphocytes to oxidative stress (Franceschi *et al.* 1995).

Because immune senescence results from a dysregulation of the immunological machinery rather than from a definitive exhaustion of the immune system, it may theoretically be reversed. Already, hormonal and non-hormonal pharmacological interventions have shown promising results. A more complete understanding of the cellular and molecular mechanisms underlying age-associated immune dysregulation should lead to the development of innovative therapeutic strategies designed to promote the restoration of an efficient immune response in older people.

References

Albright, J.W. and Albright, J.F. (1994). Ageing alters the competence of the immune system to control parasitic infection. *Immunology Letters*, **40**, 279–85.

al-Rayes, H., Pachas, W., Mirza, N., Ahern, D.J., Geha, R.S., and Vercelli, D. (1992). IgE regulation and lymphokine patterns in aging humans. *Journal of Allergy and Clinical Immunology*, **90**, 630–6.

Axelsson, U. (1977). An eleven year follow-up on 64 subjects with M components. *Acta Medica Scandinavica*, **201**, 173–5.

Bach, M.A. (1977). Lymphocyte-mediated cytotoxicity: effect of aging, adult thymectomy and thymic factor. *Journal of Immunology*, 119, 641–7.

Barker, W.H., and Mullooly, J.P. (1982). Pneumonia and influenza deaths during epidemics: Implications for prevention. *Archives of Internal Medicine*, 142, 85–9.

Batliwalla, F., Monteiro, J., Serrano, D., and Gregersen, P.K. (1996). Oligoclonality of CD8+ T cells in health and disease: aging, infection, or immune regulation? *Human Immunology*, 48, 1–2.

Bàtori, G., Benczur, M., Varga, M., Garam, T., Onody, C., and Petraniyi, G. (1981). Increased killer cell activity in aged humans. *Immunobiology*, 158, 393–402.

Beckman, I., Sheperd, K., Firgaira, F., and Ahern, M. (1995). Age-related defects in CD2 receptor-induced activation in human T-cell subsets. *Immunology*, 86, 533–6.

Bender, B.S., Nagel, J.E., Adler, W.H., and Andres, R. (1986). A sixteen year longitudinal study of the absolute peripheral blood lymphocyte count and subsequent mortality of elderly men. *Journal of the American Geriatrics Society*, 34, 649–54.

Berger, R., Florent, G., and Just, M. (1981). Decrease of the lymphoproliferative response to varicella-zoster virus antigen in the aged. *Infection and Immunity*, 32, 24–7.

Bienenstock, J. (1984). The mucosal immunologic network. *Annals of Allergy*, 53, 535–40.

Borghesi, C., and Nicoletti, C. (1994). Increase of cross(auto)-reactive antibodies after immunisation in aged mice—a cellular and molecular study. *International Journal of Experimental Pathology*, 75, 123–30.

Burns, E.A., Lum, L.G., Seigneuret, M.C., Giddings, B.R., and Goodwin, J.S. (1990). Decreased specific antibody synthesis in old adults: decreased potency of antigen-specific B cells with aging. *Mechanisms of Ageing and Development*, 53, 229–41.

Burton, G.F., Kosco, M.H., Szakal, A.K., and Tew, J.G. (1991). Iccosomes and the secondary antibody response. *Immunology*, 73, 271–6.

Cakman, I., Rohwer, J., Schutz, R.M., Kirschner, H., and Rink, L. (1996). Dysregulation between TH1 and TH2 T cell population in the elderly. *Mechanisms of Ageing and Development*, 87, 197–209.

Candore, G., Di Lorenzo, G., Mansueto, P., et al. (1997). Prevalence of organ-specific and non-organ-specific autoantibodies in healthy centenarians. *Mechanisms of Ageing and Development*, 94, 183–90.

Cantrell, M., and Yoshikawa, T.T. (1983). Aging and infective endocarditis. *Journal of the American Geriatrics Society*, 31, 216–22.

Chapel, H.M., and Bunch, C. (1987). Mechanisms of infection in chronic lymphocytic leukaemia. *Seminars in Hematology*, 24, 291–6.

Charreire, J. and Bach, J.F. (1975). Binding of autologous erythrocytes to immature T cells. *Proceedings of the National Academy of Sciences of the USA*, 72, 3201–5.

Cohen, H.J. (1994). Biology of aging as related to cancer. *Cancer*, 74 (Supplement 7), 2092–100.

Cook, J.M., Gualde, N., Hessel, L., et al. (1987). Alterations in the human immune response to the hepatitis B vaccine among the elderly. *Cellular Immunology*, 109, 89–96.

Di Pietro, R., Rana, R.A., Sciscio, A., et al. (1993). Age-related events in human active T lymphocytes: changes in the phosphoinositidase C activity. *Biochemical and Biophysical Research Communications*, 194, 566–70.

Effros, R.B. (1993). Immunosenescence-related diseases in the elderly. *Immunology and Allergy Clinics of North America*, 13, 695–712.

Effros, R.B., Boucher, N., Porter, V., et al. (1994). Decline in CD28+ T cells in centenarians and in long-term T cell cultures: a possible cause for both *in vivo* and *in vitro* immunosenescence. *Experimental Gerontology*, 29, 601–9.

Engwerda, C.R., Handwerger, B.S, and Fox, B. (1994). Aged T cells are hyporesponsive to costimulation mediated by CD28. *Journal of Immunology*, 152, 3740–7.

Ershler, W.B. (1993). The influence of an aging immune system on cancer incidence and progression. *Journal of Gerontology*, 48, B3–7.

Ershler, W.B., Sun, W.H., Binkley, N., et al. (1993). Interleukin 6 and aging: blood levels and mononuclear cell production increase with advancing age and *in vitro* production is modifiable by dietary restriction. *Lymphokine and Cytokine Research*, 12, 225–30.

Ershler, W.B., Sun W.H., and Binkley, N. (1994). The role of interleukin-6 in certain age-related diseases. *Drugs and Aging*, 5, 358–65.

Fagnoni, F.F., Vescovini, R., Mazzola, M., et al. (1996). Expansion of cytotoxic CD8+CD28- T cells in healthy ageing people, including centenarians. *Immunobiology*, 88, 501–7.

Ferguson, F.G., Wikby, A., Maxson, P., Olsson, J., and Johansson, B. (1995). Immune parameters in a longitudinal study of a very old population of Swedish people: a comparison between survivors and non-survivors. *Journal of Gerontology, Series A, Biological Science and Medicine*, 50, B378–82.

Fillit, H., and Mulvihill, M. (1993). Association of autoimmunity to vascular heparin sulphate proteoglycan and vascular disease in the aged. *Gerontology*, 39, 177–82.

Flescher, E., Ledbetter, J.A., Schieven, G.L., et al. (1994). Longitudinal exposure of human T lymphocytes to weak oxidative stress suppresses transmembrane and nuclear signal transduction. *Journal of Immunology*, 153, 4880–9.

Foad, B.S.I., Yamaguchi, Y., and Litwin, A. (1974). Phytomitogen responses of peripheral blood lymphocytes in young and older subjects. *Clinical and Experimental Immunology*, 17, 657–61.

Franceschi, C., Monti, D., Sansoni, P., and Cossarizza, A. (1995). The immunology of exceptional individuals: the lesson of centenarians. *Immunology Today*, 16, 12–16.

Frasca, D., Garavini, M., and Doria, G. (1982). Recovery of T cell functions in aged mice injected with synthetic thymosin α-1. *Cellular Immunology*, 72, 384–91.

Friedman, D. and Globerson, A. (1978). Immune reactivity during aging. I. T-helper dependent and independent antibody responses to different antigens, *in vivo* and *in vitro*. *Mechanisms of Ageing and Development*, 7, 289–98.

Fulop, T., Leblanc, C., Lacombe, G., and Dupuis, G. (1995). Cellular distribution of protein kinase C isozymes in CD3-mediated stimulation of human T lymphocytes with aging. *FEBS Letters*, 375, 1–2.

George, A.J.T. and Ritter M.A. (1996). Thymic involution with aging: obsolescence or good housekeeping? *Immunology Today*, 17, 267–72.

Ghosh, J., and Miller, R.A. (1995). Rapid tyrosine phosphorylation of Grb2 and Shc in T cells exposed to anti-CD3, anti-CD4, and anti-CD45 stimuli: Differential effects of aging. *Mechanisms of Ageing and Development*, 80, 171–87.

Gillis, S., Kosak, R., Durante, M., and Weksler, M.E. (1981). Immunological studies of aging: decreased production of and response to T cell growth factor by lymphocytes from aged humans. *Journal of Clinical Investigation*, 67, 937–42.

Glimcher, L.H. and Cantor, H. (1982). T-cell sets that control B-cell secretion of antigen-specific immunoglobulin also control secretion of non-specific immunoglobulin. *Cellular Immunology*, 70, 271–6.

Goidl, E.A., Innes, J.B., and Wecksler, M.E. (1976). Immunological studies of aging. II. Loss of IgG and high affinity plaque forming cells and increased suppressor cell activity in aging mice. *Journal of Experimental Medicine*, 144, 1037–48.

Goidl, E.A., Weksler M.E., Thorbecke, J.G., and Siskind, G.W. (1980). Production of auto-anti-idiotypic antibody during the normal immune response: changes in the auto-anti-idiotypic antibody response and the idiotypic repertoire associated with aging. *Proceedings of the National Academy of Sciences of the USA*, 77, 6788–92.

Goidl, E.A., Michelis, M.A., Siskind, G.W., and Weksler, M.E. (1981). Effect of age on the induction of autoantibodies. *Clinical and Experimental Immunology*, 44, 24–30.

Goidl, E.A., Choy, J.W., Gibbons, J.J., Weksler, M.E., Thorbecke, G.J., and Siskind, G.W. (1983). Production of auto-anti-idiotypic antibodies during the normal immune response. VIII. Analysis of the cellular basis for the increased auto-anti-idiotype antibody production by aged mice. *Journal of Experimental Medicine*, **157**, 1635–45.

Goldberg, T.H. and Finkelstein, M.S. (1994). Diminished complement and elevated cortisol levels in sera from infected elderly patients. *Aging: Immunology and Infectious Disease*, **5**, 99–107.

Goodwin, J.S., Searles, R.P., and Tung, K.S.K. (1982). Immunological responses of a healthy elderly population. *Clinical and Experimental Immunology*, **48**, 403–10.

Goya, R.G., Gagnerault, M.-C., Leite de Morales, M.C., Savino, W., and Dardenne, M. (1992). In vivo effects of growth hormone on thymus function in aging mice. *Brain Behavior and Immunity*, **6**, 341–54.

Graus, Y.M.F., Verschuuren, J.J.G.M., Spaans, F., Jennekens, F., van Breda Vriesman, P.J.C., and De Baets, M.H. (1993). Age-related resistance to experimental autoimmune myasthenia gravis in rats. *Journal of Immunology*, **150**, 4093–103.

Gross, P.A., Rapuano, C., Adrignolo, A., and Shaw, B. (1983). Nosocomial infections: decade-specific risk. *Infection Control*, **4**, 145–7.

Gross, P.A., Quinnan, G.V., Jr, Weksler, M.E., Setia, U., and Douglas, R.J., Jr (1989). Relation of chronic disease and immune response to influenza vaccine in the elderly. *Vaccine*, **7**, 303–8.

Grossman, A., Rabinovitch, P.S., Kavanagh, T.J., et al. (1995). Activation of murine T-cells via phospholipase C gamma 1-associated protein tyrosine phosphorylation is reduced with aging. *Journal of Gerontology, Series A, Biological Science and Medicine*, **50**, B205–12.

Hamblin, T.J., Oscier, D.G., and Young, B.J. (1986). Autoimmunity in chronic lymphocytic leukaemia. *Journal of Clinical Pathology*, **39**, 713–16.

Harman, D. (1981). The aging process. *Proceedings of the National Academy of Sciences of the USA*, **78**, 7124–8.

Hastie, N.D., Dempster, M., Dunlop, M.G., Thompson, A.M., Green, D.K., and Allshire, R.C. (1990). Telomere reduction in human colorectal carcinoma and with aging. *Nature*, **346**, 866–8.

Hirokawa, K., and Makinodan, T. (1975). Thymic involution: effect on T cell differentiation. *Journal of Immunology*, **114**, 1659–64.

Ho, S.-P., Kramer, K.E., and Ershler, W.B. (1990). Effect of host age upon interleukin-2-mediated anti-tumour response in a murine fibrosarcoma model. *Cancer Immunology and Immunotherapy*, **31**, 146–50.

Holmes, K.L., Schnizlein, C.T., Perkins, E.H., and Tew, J.G. (1984). The effect of age on antigen retention in lymphoid follicles and in collagenous tissues in mice. *Mechanisms of Ageing and Development*, **25**, 243–55.

Hooper, B., Wittingham, S., Mathews, J.D., Mackay, I.R., and Curnow, D.H. (1972). Autoimmunity in a rural community. *Clinical and Experimental Immunology*, **12**, 79–87.

Horan, M.A. (1993). Immunosenescence and mucosal immunity. *Lancet*, **341**, 793–4.

Hori, Y., Perkins, E.H., and Halsal, M.K. (1973). Decline in phytohemagglutinin responsiveness of spleen cells from aging mice. *Proceedings of the Society for Experimental Biology and Medicine*, **144**, 48–53.

Hu, A., Ehleiter, D., Benyehuda, A., et al. (1993). Effect of age on the expressed B-cell repertoire—role of B-cell subsets. *Internaional. Immunology*, **5**, 1035–9.

Huell, M., Strauss, S., Volk, B., Berger, M., and Bauer, J. (1995). Interleukin-6 is present in early stages of plaque formation and is restricted to the brains of Alzheimer's disease patients. *Acta Neuropathologica*, **89**, 544–51.

Kendig, N.E. and Adler, W.H. (1990). The implications of the acquired immunodeficiency syndrome for gerontology research and geriatric medicine. *Journal of Gerontology*, **45**, M77–81.

Kiessling, R., Klein, E., Pross, H., and Wigzell, H. (1975). Natural killer cells in the mouse. II. Cytotoxic cells with specificity for mouse Moloney leukaemia cells: characteristics of the killer cells. *Euopean Journal of Immunology*, **5**, 117–21.

Kipps, T.J., Rassenti, L., Duffy, S., et al. (1992). Immunoglobulin V gene expression in CD5 B-cell malignancies. *Annals of the New York Academy of Sciences*, **651**, 373–83.

Kishimoto, S., Tomino, S., Mitsuya, H., Fujiwara, H., and Tsuda, H. (1980). Age-related decline in the *in vitro* and *in vivo* synthesis of anti-tetanus toxoid antibody in humans. *Journal of Immunology*, **125**, 3347.

Kishimoto, S., Tomino, S., Mitsuya, H., and Nishimura, H. (1982). Age-related decrease in frequencies of B-cell precursors and specific helper T cells involved in the IgG anti-tetanus toxoid antibody production in humans. *Clinical Immunology and Immunopathology*, **25**, 1–10.

Korsrud, F.R. and Brnadzaeg, P. (1980). Immune system of human nasopharyngeal and palatine tonsils: histomorphometry of lymphoid components and quantification of immunoglobulin-producing cells in health and disease. *Clinical and Experimental Immunology*, **39**, 361–70.

Kramer, J., Fulop, T., Rajczi, K., et al. (1991). A marked drop in the incidence of the null allele of the B gene of the fourth component of complement (C4B*Q0) in elderly subjects: C4B*Q0 as a probable negative selection factor for survival. *Human Genetics*, **86**, 595–8.

Krishnaraj, R. (1992). Immunosenescence of human NK cells: effects on tumour target recognition, lethal hit, and interferon sensitivity. *Immunology Letters*, **34**, 79–84.

Lanza, E., and Djeu, J.Y. (1982). Age-independent natural killer cell activity in murine peripheral blood. In *NK cells and other natural effector cells* (ed. R.B. Heberman), pp. 335–40. Academic Press, New York.

Lavie, L. (1994). The macrophage in cell biology of aging. *Archives of Gerontology and Geriatrics*, **4** (Supplement), 129–38.

Linton, P.J., Haynes, L., Klinman, N.R., and Schenkman, M.L. (1996). Antigen-independent changes in naive CD4 T cells with aging. *Journal of Experimental Medicine*, **5**, 1891–1900.

McElhaney, J.E., Beattie, B.L., Devine, R., et al. (1990) Age-related decline in IL-2 production in response to influenza vaccine. *Journal of the American Geriatrics Society*, **38**, 652–8.

MacGee, W. (1993). Causes of death in a hospitalised geriatric population: an autopsy study of 3000 patients. *Virchows Archiv. A. Pathological Anatomy and Histopathology*, **423**, 343–9.

McLachlan, J.A., Serkin, C.D., Morrey K.M., and Bakouche, O. (1995). Antitumoral properties of aged human monocytes. *Journal of Immunology*, **154**, 832–43.

Mariotti, S., Sansoni, P., Barbesino, G., et al. (1992). Thyroid and other organ-specific autoantibodies in healthy centenarians. *Lancet*, **339**, 1506–8.

Mathews, J.D., Whittingham, S., Hooper, B.M., et al. (1973). Association of autoantibodies with smoking, cardiovascular morbidity, and death in the Busselton population. *Lancet*, **i**, 754–6.

Melez, K.A., Fries, L.F., Bender, B.S., Quinn, T., and Frank, M.M. (1988). Decline in rates of clearance of IgG-sensitised erythrocytes with increasing age. *Blood*, **71**, 1726–30.

Miller, C. and Kelsoe, G. (1995). Ig V_H hypermutation is absent in the germinal centres of aged mice. *Journal of Immunology*, **155**, 3377–84.

Miller, R.A. (1984). Age-associated decline in precursor frequency from different T cell- mediated reactions, with preservation of helper or cytotoxic effect per precursor cell. *Journal of Immunology*, **132**, 63–8.

Modan, B., Barr, M., Chetrit, A., and Etlin, S. (1996). Cancer in the elderly: an international overview. *International Journal of Oncology*, **9**, 1001–6.

Mooradian, A.D., Reed, R.L., Osterweil, D., and Scuderi, P. (1991). Detectable serum levels of tumour necrosis factor alpha predict early mortality in elderly institutionalised patients. *Journal of the American Geriatrics Society*, **39**, 891–4.

Murasko, D.M., Weiner, P., and Kaye, D. (1988). Association of lack of mitogen-induced lymphocyte proliferation with increased mortality in the elderly. *Aging: Immunology and Infectious Disease*, **1**, 1–6.

Musher, D. M., Chapman, A. J., Goree, A., Jonsson, S., Briles, D., and Baughn, R.E. (1986). Natural and vaccine-related immunity to *Streptococcus pneumoniae*. *Journal of Infectious Diseases*, 154, 245–56.

Nagaki, K., Hiramatsu, S., Inai, S., and Sasaki, A. (1980). The effect of aging on complement activity (CH50) and complement protein levels. *Journal of Clinical and Laboratory Immunology*, 3, 45–50.

Nagami, P.H. and Yoskikawa, T.T. (1983). Tuberculosis in the geriatric patient. *Journal of the American Geriatrics Society*, 31, 356–63.

Nagel, J.E., Chopra, R.K., Chrest, F.J., McCoy, M.T., and Schneider, E.L. (1988). Decreased proliferation, interleukin 2 synthesis, and interleukin 2 receptor expression are accompanied by decreased mRNA expression in phytohemagglutinin-stimulated cells from elderly donors. *Journal of Clinical Investigation*, 81, 1096–1102.

Nakahama, M., Mohri, N., Mori, S., Shindo, G., Yokoi, Y., and Machinami, R. (1990). Immunohistochemical and histometrical studies of the human thymus with special emphasis on age-related changes in medullary epithelial and dendritic cells. *Virchows Archiv. B. Cell Pathology*, 58, 245–51.

Naor, D., Bonavida, B., and Walford, R. L. (1976). Autoimmunity and aging: the age-related response of mice of a long-lived strain to trinitrophenylated syngeneic mouse red blood cells. *Journal of Immunology*, 117, 2204–8.

Negoro, S., Hara, H., Miyata, S., et al. (1986). Mechanisms of age-related decline in antigen-specific T cell proliferative response: IL-2 receptor expression and recombinant IL-2 induced proliferative response of purified TAC-positive T cells. *Mechanisms of Ageing and Development*, 36, 223–41.

Nicoletti, C. (1994). Antibody response in aged C57Bl/6 mice—T helper cells are responsible for the decline of the primary antibody response to bacterial antigen in aging. *Immunobiology*, 190, 1–2.

Nicoletti, C., Borghesi-Nicoletti, C., Yang, X., Schultze, D.H., and Cerny, J. (1991). Repertoire diversity of antibody response to bacterial antigens in aged mice. II. Phosphorylcholine-antibody in young and aged mice differ in both V_H/V_L gene repertoire and in specificity. *Journal of Immunology*, 147, 2750–5.

Nicoletti, C., Yang, X., and Cerny, J. (1993). Repertoire diversity of antibody response to bacterial antigens in aged mice. III. Phosphorylcholine antibody from young and aged mice differ in structure and protective activity against infection with Streptococcus pneumoniae. *Journal of Immunology*, 150, 543–9.

Nijhuis, E.W.P., and Nagelkerken, L. (1992). Age-related changes in immune reactivity: the influence of intrinsic defects and of a changed composition of CD4$^+$ T cell compartment. *Experimental and Clinical Immunogenetics*, 9, 195–202.

Nordin, A.A. and Collins, G.D. (1983). Limiting dilution analysis of alloreactive cytotoxic precursor cells in aging mice. *Journal of Immunology*, 131, 2215–18.

Omenaas, E., Bakke, P., Elsayed, S., Hanoa, R., and Gulsvik, A. (1994). Total and specific serum IgE levels in adults: relationship to sex, age, and environmental factors. *Clinical and Experimental Allergy*, 26, 530–9.

Paganelli, R., Quinti, I., Fagiolo, U., et al. (1992). Changes in circulating B-cells and immunoglobulin classes and subclasses in a healthy aged population. *Clinical and Experimental Immunology*, 90, 351–4.

Pahlavani, M.A., Harris, M.D., and Richardson, A. (1995). The age-related decline in the induction of IL-2 transcription is correlated to changes in the transcription factor NFAT. *Cellular Immunology*, 165, 84–91.

Patel, H.R. and Miller, R.A. (1992). Age-associated changes in mitogen-induced protein phosphorylation in murine T lymphocytes. *European Journal of Immunology*, 22, 253–60.

Phelouzat, M.-A., Arbogast, A., Laforge, T., Quadri, R.A., and Proust, J.J. (1996). Excessive apoptosis of mature T lymphocytes is a characteristic feature of human immune senescence. *Mechanisms of Ageing and Development*, 88, 25–38.

Phelouzat, M.-A., Laforge, T., Arbogast, A., Quadri, R.A., Boutet, S., and Proust, J.J. (1997). Susceptibility to apoptosis of T lymphocytes from

elderly humans is associated with increased *in vivo* expression of functional Fas receptors. *Mechanisms of Ageing and Development*, 96, 35–46.

Poli, V., Balena, R., Fattori, E., et al. (1994). Interleukin-6 deficient mice are protected from bone loss caused by oestrogen depletion. *EMBO Journal*, 13, 1189–96.

Posnett, D.N., Sinha, R., Kabak, S., and Russo, C. (1994). Clonal population of T cells in normal elderly humans—the T cell equivalent to benign monoclonal gammopathy. *Journal of Experimental Medicine*, 179, 609–18.

Potockaplazak, K., Pituchnoworolska, A., and Kocemba, J. (1995). Prevalence of autoantibodies in the very elderly: association with symptoms of ischaemic heart disease. *Aging*, 7, 218–20.

Powers, D.C. (1993). Influenza A virus-specific cytotoxic T lymphocyte activity declines with advancing age. *Journal of the American Geriatrics Society*, 41, 1–5.

Proust, J.J., Rosenzweig, P., Debouzy, C., and Moulias, R. (1985). Lymphopenia induced by bacterial infections in the elderly: a sign of age-related immune dysfunction of major prognostic significance. *Gerontology*, 31, 178–85.

Proust, J.J., Filburn, C.R., Harrison, S.A., Buchholz, M.A., and Nordin, A.A. (1987). Age-related defect in signal transduction during lectin activation of murine T lymphocytes. *Journal of Immunology*, 139, 1472–8.

Proust, J.J., Kittur, D.S., Buchholz, M.A., and Nordin A.A. (1988). Restricted expression of mitogen-induced high affinity IL-2 receptors in aging mice. *Journal of Immunology*, 141, 4902–16.

Quadri, R.A., Plastre, O., Phelouzat, M.-A., Arbogast, A., and Proust , J.J. (1996). Age-related tyrosine-specific protein phosphorylation defect in human T lymphocytes activated through CD3, CD4, CD8 or the IL-2 receptor. *Mechanisms of Ageing and Development*, 88, 125–38.

Radl, J., Sepers, J.M., and Skvaril, F. (1975). Immunoglobin patterns in humans over 25 years of age. *Clinical and Experimental Immunology*, 22, 84–90.

Radl, J., De Glopper, E., Van Den Berg, P., and Van Zwieten, M.J. (1980). Idiopathic paraproteinemia. III. Increased frequency of paraproteinemia in thymectomized aging C57Bl/KalwRij and CBA/BrArRij mice. *Journal of Immunology*, 125, 31–5.

Rich, E.A., Mincek, M.A., Armitage, K.B., et al. (1992). Accessory function and properties of monocytes from healthy elderly humans for T lymphocyte responses to mitogen and antigen. *Gerontology*, 39, 93–108.

Riley, S.C., Froscher, B.G., Linton, P.G., Zharhary, D., Marcu, K., and Klinman, N.R. (1989). Altered V_H gene segment utilisation in response to phosphorylcholine by aged mice. *Journal of Immunology*, 143, 3798–805.

Robert, L. (1996). Aging of the vascular wall and atherogenesis: role of the elastin–laminin receptor. *Atherosclerosis*, 123, 169–79.

Roberts-Thomson, I.C., Wittingham, S., Youngchaiyud, U., and MacKay, I.R. (1974). Aging, immune response and mortality. *Lancet*, ii, 368–70.

Rogers, J., Luber-Narod, J., Styren, S.D., et al. (1988). Expression of immune system-associated antigens by cells of the human central nervous system: relationship to the pathology of Alzheimer's disease. *Neurobiology of Aging*, 9, 339–49.

Rowley, M.J., Buchanan, H., and Mackay, I.R. (1968). Reciprocal change with age in antibody to extrinsic and intrinsic antigens. *Lancet*, ii, 24–6.

Schmucker, D.L., Heyworth, M.F., Owen, R.L., and Daniels, C.K. (1996). Impact of aging on gastrointestinal mucosal immunity. *Digestive Diseases and Sciences*, 41, 1183–93.

Schneider, E.L. (1983). Infectious diseases in the elderly. *Annals of Internal Medicine*, 98, 395–400.

Schwab, R., Hausman, P.B., Rinnooy-Kan, E., and Weksler, M.E. (1985). Immunological studies of aging. X. Impaired T lymphocytes and normal monocytes response from elderly humans to the mitogenic antibodies OKT3 and Leu 4. *Immunology*, 55, 677–84.

Schwab, R., Russo, C., and Wecksler, M.E. (1992). Altered major histocompatibility complex-restricted antigen recognition by T-cells from elderly humans. *European Journal of Immunology*, 22, 2989–93.

Scollay, R.G., Butcher, E.C., and Weissman, I.L. (1980). Thymus cell migration. Quantitative aspects of cellular traffic from the thymus to the periphery in mice. *European Journal of Immunology*, 10, 210–18.

Scott, B.J., Powers, D.C., Johnson, J.E., and Morley, J.E. (1994). Seroepidemiologic evidence of Epstein–Barr virus reactivation in a veterans' nursing home. *Serodiagnosis and Immunotherapy of Infectious Diseases*, 6, 87–92.

Shapiro, S., Kohn, D., and Gershon, H. (1993). A role for complement as the major opsonin in the sequestration of erythrocytes from elderly and young donors. *British Journal of Haematology*, 83, 648–54.

Shigemoto, S., Kishimoto, S., and Yamamura, Y. (1975). Change of cell-mediated cytotoxoxicity with aging. *Journal of Immunology*, 115, 307–9.

Sikora, E., Kaminska, B., Radziszewska, E., and Kaczmarek, L. (1992). Loss of transcription factor AP-1 DNA binding activity during lymphocyte aging *in vivo*. *FEBS Letters*, 312, 179–82.

Simberkoff, M.S., Cross, A.P., Al-Ibrahim, M., *et al.* (1986). Efficacy of pneumococcal vaccine in high risk patients. Results of a Veterans Administration cooperative study. *New Engand Journal of Medicine*, 17, 1318–27.

Simpson, E. and Cantor, H. (1975). Regulation of the immune response by subclasses of T lymphocytes. II. The effect of adult thymectomy upon humoral and cellular responses in mice. *European Journal of Immunology*, 5, 337–43.

Skassa-Brociek, W., Manderscheid, J.C., Michel, F.B., and Bousquet, J. (1987). Skin test reactivity to histamine from infancy to old age. *Journal of Allergy and Clinical Immunology.*, 80, 711–16.

Smyth, M.D., Cribbs, D.H., Tenner, A.J., *et al.* (1994). Decreased levels of C1q in cerebrospinal fluid of living Alzheimer's patients correlate with disease state. *Neurobiology of Aging*, 15, 609–14.

Somers, H. and Kuhns, W.J. (1972). Blood group antibodies in old age. *Proceedings of the Society for Experimental Biology and Medicine*, 141, 1104–7.

Song, L., Stephens, J.M., Kittur, S., *et al.* (1992). Expression of c-fos, c-jun, and Jun B in peripheral blood lymphocytes from young and elderly adults. *Mechanisms of Ageing and Development*, 65, 149–56.

Sorensen, H. and Dissing J. (1975). Association between the C3F gene and atherosclerotic vascular diseases. *Human Heredity*, 25, 279–83.

Steger, M.M., Maczek, C., and Grubeck-Loebenstein, B. (1996). Morphologically and functionally intact dentritic cells can be derived from the peripheral blood of aged individuals. *Clinical and Experimental Immunology*, 105, 544–50.

Strassburg, M.A., Greenland, S., Sorvillo, S.J., Lieb, L.E., and Itabel, L.A. (1986). Influenza in the elderly: report of an outbreak and a review of vaccine effectiveness reports. *Vaccine*, 4, 36–48.

Stulnig, T. M., Buhler, E., Bock, G., Kirchebner, C., Schonitzer, D., and Wick G. (1995). Altered switch in lipid composition during T-cell blast transformation in the healthy elderly. *Journal of Gerontology, Series A, Biological Science and Medicine*, 50, B383–90.

Sundbeck, G., Eden, S., Jagenburg, R., Lundberg, P.A., and Linstedt, G. (1995). Prevalence of serum antithyroid peroxydase antibodies in 85-year-old women and men. *Clinical Chemistry*, 41, 707–12.

Szewczuk, M.R. and Campbell, R.J. (1981). Lack of age-associated auto-anti-idiotypic antibody regulation in mucosal-associated lymph nodes. *European Journal of Immunology*, 11, 650–6.

Thiers, B.H., Maize, J.G., Spice, S.S., and Cantor, A.B. (1984). The effect of aging and chronic sun exposure on human Langerhans cell population. *Journal of Investigative Dermatology*, 82, 223–6.

Thoman, M.L. and Weigle, W.O. (1981). Lymphokines and aging: interleukin-2 production and activity in aged animals. *Journal of Immunology*, 127, 2101–6.

Utsuyama, M., Kasai, M., Kurashima, C., and Hirokawa, K. (1991). Age influence on the thymic capacity to promote differentiation of T cells: induction of different composition of T cell subsets by aging thymus. *Mechanisms of Ageing and Development*, 58, 267–77.

Utsuyama, M., Hirokawa, K., Kurashima, C., *et al.* (1992). Differential age-related changes in the number of CD4$^+$CD45RA$^+$ and CD4$^+$CD29$^+$ T cell subsets in human peripheral blood. *Mechanisms of Ageing and Development*, 63, 57–68.

Vaziri, H., Schächter, F., Uchida, I., *et al.* (1993). Loss of telomeric DNA during aging of normal and trisomy 21 human lymphocytes. *American Journal of Human Genetics*, 52, 661–7.

von Zglimicki, T., Saretzki, G., Docke, W., and Lotze, C. (1995). Mild hyperoxia shortens telomeres and inhibits proliferation of fibroblast: a model for senescence? *Experimental Cell Research*, 220, 186–93.

Walford, R.L. (1969). *Immunologic theory of aging*. Munksgaard, Copenhagen.

Wallace, P.K., Eisenstein, T.K., Meissler, J.J., and Morahan, P.S. (1995). Decreases in macrophage mediated antitumour activity with aging. *Mechanisms of Ageing and Development*, 77, 169–84.

Wayne, S.J., Rhyne, R.L., Garry, P.J., and Goodwin, J.S. (1990). Cell-mediated immunity as a predictor of morbidity and mortality in subjects over 60. *Journal of Gerontology, Series A, Biological Science and Medicine*, 45, M45–8.

Weksler, M.E., Innes, J.B., and Goldstein, G. (1978). Immunological studies of aging. IV. The contribution of thymic involution to the immune deficiencies of aging and reversal with thymopoietin. *Journal of Experimental Medicine*, 148, 996–1006.

Whisler, R.L., Beiqing, L., Wu, L.-C., and Chen, M. (1993). Reduced activation of transcriptional factor AP-1 among peripheral blood T cells from elderly humans after PHA stimulation: restorative effect of phorbol diesters. *Cellular Immunology*, 152, 96–109.

Whisler, R.L., Newhouse, Y.G., and Bagenstose, S.E. (1996). Age-related reductions in the activation of mitogen-activated protein kinases p44(mapk)/ERK1 and p42(mapk)/ERK2 in human T cells stimulated via ligation of the T cell receptor complex. *Cellular Immunology*, 168, 201–10.

Wolk, M., Kieselstein, M., Hamburger, R., and Jaul, E. (1993). Association between high concentration of antibodies to insulin and some diseases common in the elderly. *Gerontology*, 39, 334–7.

Xu, S. and Gaskin, F. (1997). Increased incidence of anti-β-amyloid autoantibodies secreted by Epstein–Barr virus transformed B cell lines from patients with Alzheimer's disease. *Mechanisms of Ageing and Development*, 94, 213–22.

Xu, X.N., Beckman, I., Ahern, M., and Bradley, J. (1993). A comprehensive analysis of peripheral blood lymphocytes in healthy aged humans by flow cytometry. *Immunology and Cell Biology*, 71, 549–57.

Yoshikawa, T.T. (1983). Geriatric infectious diseases: an emerging problem. *Journal of the American Geriatrics Society*, 85 (Supplement 2A), 79–83.

Yuan, A. and Baird, M.A. (1994). Changes in the frequency and function of rat spleen dendritic cells occurs with age. *Aging: Immunology and Infectious Disease*, 5, 121–32.

Zatz, M.M. and Goldstein, A.L. (1985). Thymosins, lymphokines, and the immunology of aging. *Gerontology*, 31, 263–77.

Zharhary, D. and Gershon, H. (1981). Allogeneic T-cytotoxic reactivity of senescent mice: affinity for target cells and determination of cell number. *Cellular Immunology*, 60, 470–9.

Zharhary, D. and Klinman, N.R. (1983). Antigen responsiveness of the mature and generative B cell population of aged mice. *Journal of Experimental Medicine*, 157, 1300–8.

Zharhary, D., Segev, Y., and Gershon, H. (1977). The affinity and spectrum of crossreactivity of antibody production in senescent mice: the IgM response. *Mechanisms of Ageing and Development*, 6, 385–92.

3.4 **Immunization**

Janet E. McElhaney

Introduction

Pneumonia and influenza together represent the fourth leading cause of death in the over-65 population. The increased risk of influenza and pneumococcal disease in older persons is probably due to a combination of the effects of immunosenescence and the chronic diseases which affect 80 to 90 per cent of the over-65 population. The ageing process results in a decline in immunity that largely affects T-cell mediated defence mechanisms. This decline predicts the increased risk of viral infections, particularly influenza, observed in older people. Humoral immunity may also decline with ageing but to a lesser degree, perhaps due to changes in the T-cell function which regulates antibody production (see Chapter 3.3).

Chronic diseases may exaggerate age-associated changes in the immune system as well as cause disease-specific changes in susceptibility to pathogens. Impairments of immunological defence mechanisms and mucosal barrier function, particularly in the lungs, may be compromised. Protection against infectious illnesses, or serious complications of such illnesses, depends on the efficacy of vaccines to compensate for age-associated changes in the immune system and potentially overcome the breakdown in non-specific defence mechanisms. Influenza and pneumococcal infections lead to significant morbidity and mortality that is preventable through vaccination.

A recent analysis of 500 life-saving interventions showed that influenza and pneumococcal vaccinations as well as Pap smears are by far the most cost-effective medical interventions for older people (Tengs *et al.* 1994). Optimizing the effectiveness of immunization in the over-65 population depends on increasing knowledge in terms of how to improve vaccine efficacy (i.e. the ability of the vaccine to protect the host against infection) and vaccine delivery (i.e. programme and policy development to increase vaccination rates).

Impact of influenza and pneumococcal infections

The association between ageing and the risk of serious influenza infections is one of the best-documented effects of immunosenescence. Influenza is estimated to cause 172 000 excess hospital admissions (Barker 1986) and as many as 40 000 excess influenza-associated deaths each year in the United States (Lui and Kendal 1987; Williams *et al.* 1988). Eighty to ninety per cent of the statistics are accounted for by the elderly population. Because of the lack of specific symptoms and the atypical presentations of disease in this age group, these figures probably underestimate the true morbidity and mortality in the older population. In addition, hospital admission and death rates only represent the tip of the iceberg in terms of the cost of functional decline resulting from influenza-related illnesses. Complications of influenza may lead to an irreversible loss of independence and an increased risk of long-term institutionalization of frail elderly people. Therefore projected costs of $10 billion per year in the United States (Williams *et al.* 1988) for a moderately severe influenza outbreak are likely to be gross underestimates of the true cost of this illness when loss of autonomy and quality of life are included.

Pneumococcal pneumonia is another important cause of morbidity and mortality in older people; 10 to 25 per cent of pneumonias are caused by this pathogen and account for 40 000 deaths each year in the United States (Williams *et al.* 1988). Because the data are largely derived from documented pneumococcal bacteraemia rather than pneumonia, for which the rates are three to four times higher (Mufson 1990), the true incidence of pneumococcal-related morbidity and mortality is probably much greater. Therefore it is difficult to determine the true cost, but the fact that 97 per cent of the cost of pneumococcal disease is for hospital care suggests that these infections often cause serious illness.

Vaccination

Influenza vaccines

Rationale

Influenza vaccination represents one of the most important health promotion and disease prevention measures in the elderly population. Vaccination is currently recommended for all persons over the age of 65 (Centers for Disease Control 1987). At highest risk are those elderly individuals with underlying chronic diseases, particularly those with cardiorespiratory disorders as well as those with metabolic or neoplastic diseases. Although influenza vaccination is recognized as perhaps the most cost-effective medical intervention in the elderly population, protection rates are reduced from approximately 90 per cent in younger adults to anywhere between 25 and 44 per cent in the elderly population (Howells *et al.* 1975; Brandiss *et al.* 1981). Vaccination does not change the incidence of upper respiratory tract symptoms, but significantly reduces hospital admission and mortality rates, by 72 per cent and 87 per cent respectively, in community-dwelling elderly people (Barker and Mullooly 1980). The efficacy is greatly reduced in nursing-home residents, who tend to have a greater burden of chronic disease, such that there may be no difference between vaccinated and unvaccinated residents in long-term care. Thus several other strategies should be used in conjunction with vaccination in this setting (Gravenstein *et al.* 1992). Although the antiviral drug amantidine is effective against influenza, adverse effects and drug costs make it unsuitable for mass prophylaxis and limit its use to localized outbreaks. Even with the reduced effectiveness in the elderly population, influenza vaccination represents a cost-saving medical intervention and remains cost-effective when future health care costs for the lives saved are considered (Riddiough *et al.* 1983). Further improvements in the cost–benefit ratio of vaccination programmes will come from a greater understanding of the efficacy of influenza vaccination in different subgroups of the elderly population.

Safety and recommendations

Current vaccines contain an H3N2 and an H1N1 strain of influenza A and a strain of influenza B. Subvirion or whole-killed virus vaccines have generally been administered in the over-65 population, but purified subunit and intranasal attenuated live virus vaccines, as well as some of the newer experimental vaccines, have been used in clinical trials. Owing to the antigenic drift which selects for changes in the surface antigens of the influenza virus, the strains of virus contained in the vaccine are updated annually on the basis of worldwide surveillance for emerging strains of influenza. Vaccination is recommended every autumn for all adults aged over 65 and for all persons with high-risk medical conditions (i.e. cardiac or respiratory diseases, diabetes mellitus, chronic renal failure and neoplastic or haematological disorders). Health care workers who are in close contact with these high-risk patients should also be vaccinated. The only contraindications to vaccination are allergy to eggs or a previous severe reaction to the vaccine (usually related to the preservative in the vaccine). Potential adverse reactions include local swelling and tenderness within 24 to 48 h in 10 to 20 per cent of those vaccinated. Fever, myalgias, and severe local reactions have been reported in less than 2 per cent of cases (Centers for Disease Control 1991). There is no risk of influenza infection through vaccination because whole-virus, subvirion, and subunit vaccines contain inactivated virus. A randomized double-blind placebo-controlled trial showed that only localized tenderness at the site of injection occurred more frequently in the vaccination group; systemic side-effects and a decrease in ability to perform activities of daily living occurred with equal frequency in both groups (Margolis *et al.* 1990).

Immunological responses

Both age and a number of chronic diseases that are commonly associated with ageing increase the risk of influenza viral infections. Immunological defences against influenza may be reduced in the elderly population because of a decline in the immune functions required to prevent serious complications of influenza. In order to gain some insight into the increased risk of influenza and how vaccines may reduce that risk in the elderly population, one must first understand the immunological response to influenza infection

as illustrated in Fig. 1. To summarize, influenza virus infects host cells, typically those lining the respiratory tract, which become factories for viral replication and express viral proteins on the cell surface. Antigen-presenting cells such as macrophages and dendritic cells take up, process, and present viral peptides to helper T cells (T_h); this process leads to virus-specific T-cell activation. Recognition of the antigen–MHC II complex by the T_h receptor stimulates the production of the cytokine interleukin 2 (IL-2). The interaction between IL-2 and its receptor stimulates the clonal expansion of IL-2-secreting antigen-specific activated T_h. Cytokines produced by activated T_h are important for regulation of the immune response to influenza in humans. The production of IL-2 and interferon-γ (IFN-γ) have typically been associated with cell-mediated immunity and have been classified as helper T-cell type 1 (T_h1) cytokines (Mosmann and Coffman 1989). These cytokines, and particularly their effect on stimulating cytotoxic T lymphocytes (CTL), are required for recovery from influenza pneumonia.

T_h2-type cytokines including interleukins 4, 5, and 10, have been associated with the stimulation of B cells resulting in antibody production (Mosmann and Coffman 1989). Circulating antiviral antibodies prevent infections through neutralization of virus on the respiratory epithelium, but T_h2 have not been shown to promote recovery from influenza once tissue invasion has occurred (Graham *et al.* 1994). Antiviral antibodies to influenza are generally strain specific, while T-cell responses tend to be cross-reactive and potentially increase protection against many strains of influenza virus. Thus the regulation of T_h1- and T_h2-type cytokine responses to influenza vaccination may be important in the type of immunity stimulated by these viruses.

Antibody response to influenza

A T_h2-type response to vaccination would stimulate B cells to differentiate and produce antibodies which are specific for the inoculating strain of virus. These strain-specific antibodies bind to the surface glycoproteins, haemagglutinin, and neuraminidase to neutralize the virus on mucosal surfaces of the respiratory tract. The increase in virus strain-specific antibody titres following vaccination lasts for more than 6 months, thus providing protection throughout the influenza season. The protein sequences of haemagglutinin and neuraminidase change as a result of selective pressure by the immune system against the native virus, a phenomenon known as antigenic drift. Mutant viruses thus produced may escape antibody binding owing to changes in the antigenic determinants of the B-cell response. Influenza vaccines must be updated on a yearly basis to include the current circulating strains of virus.

CTL response to influenza

CTLs combat influenza virus infections by recognizing and destroying virus-infected host cells that become the factories for viral replication as illustrated in Fig. 1. Infected cells express on their surfaces internal viral proteins such as nucleoprotein, in combination with major histocompatibility complex class I (MHC I) proteins. Recognition of the MHC I–viral peptide complex by CTL results in the activation of virus-specific CTL. Activated CTLs mediate lysis of virus-infected host cells through binding to the viral peptide–MHC I complex and release of enzymes which lead to apoptosis or programmed cell death of the target cell (Braciale *et al.* 1986). Interferon-γ production by

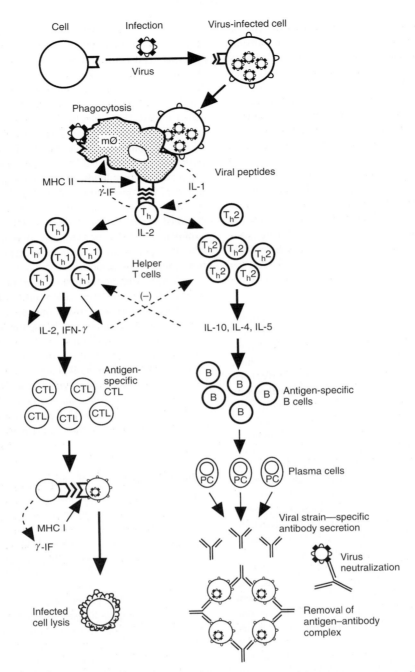

Fig. 1 Immune response to influenza virus by natural infection or vaccination. The two arms of the immune response, which lead to humoral (B-cell-derived) and cell-mediated (T-cell-derived) immunity, are shown. While antibodies prevent invasion of virus at mucosal barriers, CTLs and cytokines are required for clearance of virus from infected lung tissue. Immunosenescence leads to a relatively greater decline in cell-mediated immunity, thus increasing the risk of viral infections such as influenza in the over-65 population.

activated CTLs or other T cells also contributes to the death of virus-infected cells (Ennis and Meager 1981). While antibodies protect against mucosal invasion, activated CTLs are required for effective clearance from infected lung tissue. Therefore T_h-mediated activation of CTLs, which results in the lysis of virus-infected target cells, is likely to be a major determinant of protection against serious influenza infections.

Immunological cross-reactivity and memory

Unlike B-cell-mediated immunity, which is largely strain specific, cell-mediated immunity (T_h and CTL) is much more cross-reactive within the strains of a particular type of influenza (A, B, or C). T_h recognize different portions of the haemagglutinin and neuraminidase molecule than are recognized by B cells. The antigenic determinants of the T_h response are under less pressure from natural selection and are relatively preserved within the strains of influenza A. Therefore T_h-mediated immunity is cross-reactive with many strains of influenza A. Because CTLs mainly recognize internal viral proteins which are highly conserved, CTL responses are cross-reactive across all strains of influenza A (Zweerink *et al.* 1977).

Influenza viral antigens contained in vaccines stimulate a response in both B- and T-cells. Some of these virus-specific lymphocytes remain within the lymphoid circulation to provide a more rapid response to subsequent viral infection, a process called memory. Owing to differences in requirements for antigen presentation between B cells, T_h and CTLs, vaccines may be variably effective in stimulating different components of humoral and cell-mediated immunity. The magnitude and duration of the memory response in each of these immune cell types differs, such that CTL memory generally lasts less than 12 weeks (McMichael *et al.* 1983) and T_h memory is less than 6 months while B-cell memory is lifelong. Thus T-cell mediated immunity provides much broader protection against influenza than humoral immunity, but this memory is of a much shorter duration than B-cell memory.

Immunosenescence and influenza vaccination

Ageing is associated with a decline in T-cell-mediated immunity, while B-cell function is relatively preserved. Thus the transfer of T cells from young to old mice restores the latter's antibody response to normal (Goidl *et al.* 1976). A decline in the antibody response to influenza vaccination has been found in elderly subjects, although the studies to date have not screened study participants to exclude underlying chronic diseases or the effect of previous exposure to the virus through vaccination or natural infection (Levine *et al.* 1987*a*). Poor antibody response to influenza vaccination has also been attributed to chronic stress (Kiecolt-Glaser *et al.* 1996) and correlated with functional decline in older age groups, suggesting that frailty may be another determinant of the observed response (Remarque *et al.* 1996). Increasing the dose of vaccine or the number of doses given does not appear to improve the antibody response (Levine *et al.* 1987*b*; Gross *et al.* 1988). The B-cell response to vaccination may be suppressed owing to poor stimulation of T_h required to 'help' antibody production. The phenomenon of 'original antigenic sin' also appears to produce variable suppression of specific responses to the different subtypes of influenza A; antibody responses to older strains of influenza may be restimulated by new strains of the virus and suppress the primary antibody response to the new viral strain. 'Original antigenic sin' most significantly affects the response to viral strains within the same subtype (H1N1 or H3N2) of viral strains to which one was exposed during childhood (Marine and Thomas 1973). Consequently, vaccination in the current healthy elderly cohort may stimulate the production of antibodies specific for older H1N1 strains to which this cohort was exposed during childhood (McElhaney *et al.* 1993). This secondary response appears to suppress a primary response to the new vaccinating strains of virus, but this explanation remains somewhat controversial (Powers and Belshe 1994). Antibody responses to H3N2 strains to which the elderly cohort would not have been exposed until later on in life (after 1968) are less affected.

Great emphasis has been placed on the antibody response to vaccination as a measure of vaccine efficacy owing to good correlation with protection rates in young adults. Efforts to correlate antibody responses with clinical outcomes in older people have been difficult because studies have failed to exclude individuals with chronic diseases causing immunocompromise or to include the potential effect of previous vaccination and high prevaccination antibody titres (Beyer *et al.* 1989). Antibody responses do not accurately predict immunity in older people, and vaccination may offer protection even in those who do not show a significant rise in antibody titres.

The T-cell-mediated response to vaccination at older ages in terms of cytokine production and CTL activation has been technically much more difficult to measure compared with antibody responses. Thus there are relatively few studies of the cell-mediated response to influenza vaccination in elderly people, and they are often limited to a relatively small number of study subjects limiting the statistical power of the interpretation of results. These assays also depend on studying changes in the *in vitro* response to challenge with influenza virus as a result of vaccination. Current influenza vaccines variably stimulate both cytokine and CTL responses. IL-2 production is often reduced prior to vaccination, but in healthy elderly people increases to levels similar to those in young adults after vaccination (McElhaney *et al.* 1995). The two subtypes of influenza A may select for T_h1 (cell-mediated) versus T_h2 (humoral) responses to vaccination and potentially impact on the clinical outcomes of vaccination. Although influenza vaccines appear to stimulate a CTL response in older and even chronically ill adults (Gorse and Belshe 1990), the CTL response to vaccination appears to be lower in older than in young adults (Mbawuike *et al.* 1993; Powers and Belshe 1993). Also, the degree of cross-reactivity of CTL responses may be less in patients with chronic illness than in healthier older adults (Gorse and Belshe 1990; Powers and Belshe 1993). The magnitude and duration of both T_h and CTL responses in older adults may also be variably affected by the type of vaccine preparation and the viral strains contained in it, as well as by the characteristics of the vaccine recipient including prior vaccination or exposure to the virus, specific rather than all chronic diseases, and the degree of frailty. Currently, the only reliable way to test new influenza vaccines is through large-scale clinical trials which measure clinical endpoints. The aim of further research will be to correlate different T-cell responses with clinical outcomes of vaccination, so that candidate vaccines can be screened by a more cost-effective method before large-scale clinical trials are undertaken.

Effectiveness of vaccination

Vaccine efficacy, as measured by clinical outcomes of vaccination, may vary according to the properties of the vaccine (i.e. different strains or subtypes of influenza contained in the vaccine, or whole-virus versus split-virus vaccines), the attack rates in a particular year (i.e. higher attack rates in the population will more accurately predict the degree of protection through vaccination), and the number of older people included in the study. In a community-based study (Nichol *et al.* 1994), 25 000 people were estimated to be required for sufficient power to detect clinically significant changes in event rates as a result of vaccination). The health status of vaccine recipients is also relevant; vaccination may be ineffective in an institutional setting once an outbreak has occurred. A meta-analysis of a number of studies of clinical outcomes of vaccination showed that vaccination prevents respiratory illness, pneumonia, hospital admission, and death in 56 per cent, 53 per cent, 50 per cent, and 68 per cent of cases respectively (Gross *et al.* 1995). A randomized double-blind placebo-controlled trial also showed at least a 50 per cent reduction in influenza-related illness consistent with the meta-analyses (Govaert *et al.* 1994). Furthermore, a cost–benefit analysis of a large vaccination programme showed a significant reduction in hospital admissions for pneumonia and influenza, all acute and chronic respiratory illnesses, and congestive heart failure. There was an estimated cost-saving of $117 per person vaccinated in a community-based influenza vaccination programme; this may have been an underestimate of the savings due to the exclusion of the reduction in outpatient health care costs that may also have been realized through vaccination (Nichol *et al.* 1994). Savings in health care costs are greatest in the highest-risk older people (i.e. persons with chronic cardiac or respiratory diseases) (Mullooly *et al.* 1994), and repeated vaccination on an annual basis gives more protection than the first dose of vaccine (Ahmed *et al.* 1995). Older people admitted to hospital during the period of influenza vaccination are at highest risk for hospital admission during the subsequent influenza season, but are least likely to receive the vaccine, and should be targeted for influenza vaccination (Fedson *et al.* 1992). Studies have shown that there is no difference in the antibody response to vaccination at hospital discharge compared with 1 month later (Aoki *et al.* 1990); therefore this high-risk group can be targeted for vaccination in hospital. Vaccination rates of 70 to 80 per cent are particularly important for herd immunity in the institutional setting as the individual response to vaccination may be poor in immunocompromised recipients.

Policies and programmes to increase vaccination in developed countries have generally been successful in increasing rates to over 40 per cent. Well-organized programmes for vaccine delivery in high-risk groups have increased rates to 50 to 70 per cent. It has been shown that when physicians recommend vaccination to their patients, 70 to 80 per cent of older people will be vaccinated; without recommendation, less than 10 per cent will be vaccinated, suggesting that the health care provider's recommendation has a much greater impact than personal choice on the ultimate decision regarding vaccination (Centers for Disease Control 1988). However, it has been found that organized programmes are required for effective administration of vaccines and that providing educational material to potential vaccine recipients may be the most cost-effective way of optimizing vaccine delivery in the community (Centers for Disease Control 1989*a*; Fedson 1990).

In Canada, influenza vaccine is generally provided through local Boards of Health but can also be obtained in the family physician's office. The vaccine is given by intramuscular injection (15 µg of each of the three influenza strains in 0.5 ml normal saline), although the subcutaneous route is used in some European countries. There are some data to suggest that the intramuscular route may be more immunogenic. Because influenza vaccine is administered on an annual basis, generally during the months of October and November, programmes for vaccine delivery should be planned in advance. In the institutional setting, this planning includes education of and consent from the vaccinees or their designates so that the vaccine can be administered under a standing order from the medical director. This process maximizes vaccination rates so that levels of over 90 per cent can be achieved.

Future vaccines

Current influenza vaccines are about 50 per cent effective in preventing serious illness but are less effective for preventing respiratory infections in older people than in young adults. Thus the spread of virus may not be well contained through vaccination, particularly in institutional settings. New developments in vaccine technology and different routes of delivery may prove to be exciting advances in vaccines for older people, particularly with respect to stimulating cell-mediated immunity. Combining vaccine adjuvants (Gravenstein *et al.* 1989) or live attenuated nasal vaccines with the standard inactivated parenteral vaccines (Gorse *et al.* 1996) may augment antibody production in older chronically ill people. Peptide vaccines may effectively stimulate isolated components of the immune response without suppressing other immune defence mechanisms (Powers *et al.* 1997). DNA vaccines offer the exciting potential to stimulate long-lasting cell-mediated immunity that may be of greatest benefit in the over-65 population (Ulmer *et al.* 1993). An increased understanding of the type of immunological response which predicts immunity to influenza or improved clinical outcomes through vaccination will also be important for screening and clinical trials of candidate vaccines for older people.

Pneumococcal vaccines

Rationale

In contrast with influenza, pneumococcal disease is a year-round threat to the health of older people. Although it is not transmissible, spread is through human-to-human contact and pneumococci may colonize the respiratory epithelium for extended periods of time before causing illness. Studies of the impact of pneumococcal infections have been largely limited to the documentation of bacteraemic episodes. Despite these limitations, *Pneumococcus* is estimated to cause approximately 40 000 deaths in the over 65-population each year in the United States. Methodological problems have probably led to the inconsistent results obtained in studies of the efficacy of pneumococcal vaccine, but the consensus is that the current 23-valent polysaccharide vaccine is 60 to 70 per cent effective in preventing illness in older people (Centers for Disease Control 1989*b*). The emergence of antibiotic-resistant strains of *Pneumococcus* may increase the perceived need for vaccine prophylaxis in this age group, particularly if older people are found to be carriers of antibiotic-resistant bacteria.

Safety and recommendations

The current pneumococcal vaccine is a 23-valent type-specific polysaccharide antigen derived from the most commonly circulating strains of influenza. The vaccine contains 20 µg of capsular polysaccharide from each of the 23 types of *Pneumococcus* represented in the vaccine. These types account for more than 90 per cent of the circulating *Pneumococcus*. Vaccination is recommended for all persons at least once after age 65. Older people at high risk for pneumococcal infections are similar to those for influenza and include individuals with cardiopulmonary, metabolic, and neoplastic/haematological disorders, in addition to the high-risk groups with functional or anatomical asplenia (Centers for Disease Control 1989*b*). There is additional evidence that vaccination may need to be repeated every 3 to 6 years in older adults owing to a decline in anticapsular antibody titres following vaccination (Mufson *et al.* 1991). Adverse events with vaccination are similar to those for influenza and include a 20 to 30 per cent risk of arm tenderness or soreness and a less than 1 per cent chance of systemic side-effects. The only contraindication is a previous severe reaction to one of the vaccines, and this is usually related to the vaccine preservative.

Immunological responses

Pneumococcus is an extracellular pathogen and disease results from its ability to escape phagocytosis owing to the thick polysaccharide wall covering the bacterium. Lysis of this organism causes intense inflammatory reactions that are potentially linked to various components of the immune response. The major mechanism of immunity to pneumococcal infections is through antibody-mediated activation of complement and complement-dependent opsonization which leads to phagocytosis of the bacterium (Guckian et al. 1980). Pneumococci that are not destroyed by neutrophils and macrophages at the site of inflammation escape into the blood stream causing pneumococcal bacteraemia. Macrophages in the liver and spleen are responsible for ingesting opsonized bacteria. Thus severe pneumococcal infections are associated with disorders of the liver and spleen rather than neutropenia (Johnston 1981). Changes in the dominant infecting strains of Pneumococcus in older adults compared with infants and children (Bruyn et al. 1992) suggest that susceptibility, and hence immunological defence mechanisms against Pneumococcus, change with age.

Immunogenicity of pneumococcal vaccines has largely been determined by the serum antibody response to the type-specific capsular polysaccharides contained in the vaccine. However, contaminating cell wall proteins and polysaccharides contained in the vaccine also stimulate the production of antibodies which are detected in assays of the antibody response but do not contribute to the opsonization of Pneumococcus. Although even low levels of anticapsular antibody seem to be protective, there has been difficulty in standardizing the antibody assay and developing a consensus as to the levels of antibody required for protection (Musher 1995). Chronic illnesses decrease the antibody response, including the duration of the response to vaccination (Kraus et al. 1985), and increase risk of pneumococcal infection, particularly in the older population. Differences in the prevalence rates of different strains of Pneumococcus between children and older adults suggest that there may also be age-associated changes in the need for stimulation of T-cell-dependent mechanisms of protection against Pneumococcus. Although capsular polysaccharide is a T-independent antigen, many other components of Pneumococcus (i.e. pneumolysin, autolysin, and surface protein A) may be involved in stimulating T-cell mediated immunity. Immunoregulation of the inflammatory response by T cells and macrophages may be mediated by these pneumococcal-derived proteins rather than by polysaccharides. Tumour necrosis factor-α and interleukins 1 and 6 are produced in high concentrations mainly by macrophages in response to infection (Perry and Catterall 1994).

Effectiveness of vaccine

Pneumococcal vaccination has been rather controversial in its reported effectiveness. Studies have variably supported the clinical efficacy of pneumococcal vaccination in older people (Centers for Disease Control 1989b). Current policies for pneumococcal vaccination often limit its use to older people with high-risk medical conditions rather than all older people. However, there are no studies in older people that would rationalize the targeting of this vaccine only to groups at very high risk. The current 23-valent polysaccharide vaccine has been found to be cost-effective and perhaps even cost saving in the prevention of disease (Sisk and Riegelman 1986). This vaccine is highly underutilized and vaccination rates in the over-65 population are commonly less than 10 per cent. Therefore a tremendous opportunity exists to enhance vaccine effectiveness through increased vaccine delivery (Fedson and Musher 1994). This will require major

initiatives in terms of programme and policy development to increase vaccination rates.

Pneumococcal vaccine should at least be offered to all older people with high-risk medical conditions. This would include a significant proportion of elderly persons in the institutional setting, and probably all should be considered at high risk because of the opportunity for spread of Pneumococcus. Because vaccination is given once and should probably be repeated at least every 6 years, a database is required to track the individual vaccination records. Pneumococcus vaccine can be administered at any time of the year, including at the time of influenza vaccination, although it should be given as a separate injection. Institutional programmes for vaccine delivery are very important for targeting high-risk older people and may have a role in preventing the emergence of antibiotic-resistant strains of Pneumococcus.

Future vaccine development

Current pneumococcal vaccines containing capsular polysaccharide are inadequate for stimulating the potential T-cell component of the immune response to Pneumococcus. Declining T-cell-mediated immunity may explain the age-associated changes in susceptibility to different serotypes of Pneumococcus. Peptides conjugated to the capsular polysaccharide antigen offer the potential to stimulate both humoral (B-cell) and cell-mediated (T-cell) immunity. These vaccines may prove to be more effective in terms of the spectrum of immunological responses stimulated as well as increasing the duration of the antibody response and T-cell memory for antibody production. Further work on defining protective levels of antibodies and possibly methods of measuring components of the T-cell response to these new vaccines will advance this area of disease prevention.

Tetanus toxoid vaccines

Rationale

Prophylaxis against tetanus is justified on the basis that 60 per cent of reported tetanus cases occur in the over-60 population. However, the overall incidence of tetanus is very low, with only 85 cases being reported in 1989 in the United States (Centers for Disease Control 1990). There are no data on the cost-effectiveness of this vaccine in the over-65 population.

Safety and recommendations

Immunization is recommended for all persons whose immunization status is inadequate or unknown. Three doses of the vaccine are required for primary immunization. Booster immunization should be given routinely every 10 years and after any wound, if the vaccination history is uncertain. This includes lacerations as these wounds are more commonly associated with tetanus in elderly patients. Contraindications to administration of the vaccine include neurological complications or previous hypersensitivity to the toxoid.

Immunological response

Protective levels of antibody are defined as at least 0.01 units/ml. At least 40 per cent of older people living in the community or nursing home have non-protective antibody titres (Bentley 1986). Over 90 per cent of older people develop protective levels of antibody after vaccination. Antitoxin levels decline more rapidly after booster immunization, such that 25 per cent of older people have lower than protective levels after 8 years. This may be an indication to provide booster immunization more frequently than every 10 years.

Effectiveness of vaccine

Because of the low incidence of tetanus, there are no data on the cost-effectiveness of tetanus vaccination in older people. However, immunization is probably effective if protective levels of antibody are maintained.

Summary

Influenza remains the hallmark of disease susceptibility related to a decline in immune function with ageing. Defective cell-mediated immunity increases the risk of viral infections and, in particular, influenza. Current vaccines are effective in reversing age-associated risk for serious complications of influenza infections. There is great potential to optimize vaccine effectiveness through vaccine development and increased vaccination rates in the future.

Pneumococcal vaccination, although cost-effective in older people, is highly underutilized. Major advances in pneumococcal disease prevention will occur through dramatic increases in vaccination rates and improved technologies for the detection of pneumococcal disease. Only then can the real value of vaccination against this pathogen be assessed.

As the population ages and the amount of disability in older people increases, there will be increasing demands on the health care system. Our ability to continue to provide optimal care for the over-65 population will be jeopardized unless major initiatives to support health promotion and disease prevention in this age group are in place. Cost-saving medical interventions such as influenza and pneumococcal vaccinations are critical to the survival of the future health care system, and for the prevention of acute illness and disability in older adults. It will require a collaborative effort between older people, their health care providers, vaccine manufacturers, and public health officials to optimize vaccine effectiveness in the over-65 population.

References

Ahmed, A.E., Nicholson, K.G., and Nguyen-Van-Tam, J.S. (1995). Reduction in mortality associated with influenza vaccine during 1989–90 epidemic. *Lancet*, 346, 591–5.

Aoki, F.Y., Sekla, L.H., Pitch, S., *et al.* (1990). Immunogenicity and acceptability of influenza vaccine (V) administered at hospital discharge (abstract). *Clinical Investigative Medicine*, 13, B58.

Barker, W.H. (1986). Excess pneumonia and influenza associated hospitalisation during influenza epidemics in the United States, 1970–78. *American Journal of Public Health*, 76, 761–5.

Barker, W.H. and Mullooly, J.P. (1980). Influenza vaccination of elderly persons: reduction in pneumonia and influenza hospitalizations and details. *Journal of the American Medical Association*, 244, 2547–9.

Bentley, D.W. (1986). Infectious diseases. In *Clinical geriatrics* (3rd edn) (ed. I. Rossman), pp. 438–71. J.B.Lippincott, Philadelphia, PA.

Beyer, W.E.P., Palache, A.M., Baljet, M., *et al.* (1989). Antibody induction by influenza vaccines in the elderly: a review of the literature. *Vaccine*, 7, 385–94.

Braciale, T.J., Henkel, T.J., Lukacher, A., and Braciale, V.L. (1986). Fine specificity and antigen receptor expression among virus-specific cytolytic T lymphocyte clones. *Journal of Immunology*, 137, 995–1002.

Brandiss, M.W., Betts, R.F., Mathur, U., and Douglas, R.G. (1981). Responses of elderly subjects to monovalent A/USSR/77 (H1N1) and trivalent A/USSR/77 (H1N1), Texas/77 (H3N2), B/Hong Kong/72 vaccines. *American Review of Respiratory Diseases*, 124, 681–4.

Bruyn, G.A.W., Zegers, B.J.M. and van Furth, R. (1992). Mechanisms of host defence against infection with *Streptococcus pneumoniae*. *Clinical Infectious Diseases*, 14, 251–62.

Centers for Disease Control (1987). Recommendations for prevention and control of influenza: recommendations of the immunization practices advisory committee. *Annals of Internal Medicine*, 107, 521–5.

Centers for Disease Control (1988). Adult immunization: knowledge, attitudes, and practices—DeKalb and Fulton counties, Georgia. *Morbidity and Mortality Weekly Report*, 37, 657.

Centers for Disease Control (1989a). Influenza vaccination levels in selected states—behavioural risk factor surveillance system. *Morbidity and Mortality Weekly Report*, 38, 124.

Centers for Disease Control (1989b). Pneumococcal polysaccharide vaccine. *Morbidity and Mortality Weekly Report*, 38, 64–76.

Centers for Disease Control (1990). Summary of notifiable diseases, United States, 1989. *Morbidity and Mortality Weekly Report*, 38.

Centers for Disease Control (1991). Prevention and control of influenza. *Morbidity and Mortality Weekly Report*, 40 (RR-6), 1.

Ennis, F.A. and Meager, A. (1981). Immune interferon produced to high levels of antigenic stimulation of human lymphocytes with influenza virus. *Journal of Experimental Medicine*, 154, 1279–89.

Fedson, D.S. (1990). Influenza vaccination demonstration project: an expanded policy goal. *Infection Control—Hospital Epidemiology*, 11, 357–61.

Fedson, D.S. and Musher, D.M. (1994). Pneumococcal vaccine. In *Vaccines* (ed. S.A. Plotkin and E.A. Mortimer Jr), pp. 517–64. W.B. Saunders, Philadelphia, PA.

Fedson, D.S., Wajda, A., Nichol, J.P., *et al.* (1992). Disparity between influenza vaccination rates and risks of influenza-associated hospital discharge and death in Manitoba in 1982–83. *Annals of Internal Medicine*, 116, 550–5.

Goidl, E.A., Innes, J.B., and Weksler, M.E. (1976). Immunological studies of ageing: II Loss of IgG and high avidity plaque-forming cells and increased suppressor cell activity in ageing mice. *Journal of Experimental Medicine*, 144, 1037–48.

Gorse, G.J. and Belshe, R.B. (1990). Enhancement of anti-influenza A virus cytotoxicity following influenza A virus vaccination in older, chronically ill adults. *Journal of Clinical Microbiology*, 28, 2539–50.

Gorse, G.J., Otto, E.E., Powers, D.C., Chambers, G.W., Eickhoff, C.S., and Newman, F.K. (1996). Induction of mucosal antibodies by live attenuated and inactivated influenza virus vaccines in the chronically ill elderly. *Journal of Infectious Diseases*, 173, 285–90.

Govaert, T.M., Sprenger, M.J.W., Dinant, G.J., Aretz, K., Masurel, N., and Knottnerus, J.A. (1994). Immune response to influenza vaccination of elderly people: a randomized, double-blind, placebo-controlled trial. *Vaccine*, 12, 1185–9.

Graham, M.B., Braciale, V.L., and Braciale, T.J. (1994) Influenza virus-specific CD4+ T helper type 2 T lymphocytes do not promote recovery from experimental virus infection. *Journal of Experimental Medicine*, 180, 1273–82.

Gravenstein, S., Duthie, E.H., Miller, B.A., *et al.* (1989). Augmentation of influenza antibody response in elderly men by thymosin alpha one. A double-blind placebo-controlled clinical study. *Journal of the American Geriatrics Society*, 37, 1–8.

Gravenstein, S., Miller, B.A., and Drinka, P. (1992). Prevention and control of influenza A outbreaks in long-term care facilities (review). *Infection Control and Hospital Epidemiology*, 13, 49–54.

Gross, P.A., Quinnan, G.V., Jr, Weksler, M.E., Gaerlan, P.F., and Denning, C.R. (1988). Immunization of elderly people with high doses of influenza vaccine. *Journal of the American Geriatrics Society*, **36**, 209–12.

Gross, P.A., Hermogenes, A.W., Sacks, H.S., Lau, J., and Levandowski, R.A. (1995). The efficacy of influenza vaccine in elderly persons. *Annals of Internal Medicine*, **123**, 518–27.

Guckian, J.C., Christensen, G.D., and Fine, D.P. (1980). The role of opsonins in recovery from experimental pneumococcal pneumonia. *Journal of Infectious Diseases*, **142**, 175–90.

Howells, C.H.L., Vesselinove-Jenkins, C.M., Evans, A.D., and James, J. (1975). Influenza vaccination and mortality from bronchopneumonia in the elderly. *Lancet*, **i**, 381–3.

Johnston, R.B., Jr (1981). The host response to invasion by *Streptococcus pneumoniae*: protection and the pathogenesis of tissue damage. *Review of Infectious Diseases*, **3**, 282–8.

Kiecolt-Glaser, J.K., Glaser, R., Gravenstein, S., Malarkey, W.B., and Sheridan, J. (1996). Chronic stress alters the immune response to influenza virus vaccine in older adults. *Proceedings of the National Academy of Sciences of the United States of America*, **93**, 3043–7.

Kraus, C., Fisher, S., Ansorg, R., et al. (1985). Pneumococcal antibodies (IgG, IgM) in patients with chronic obstructive lung disease 3 years after pneumococcal vaccination. *Medical Microbiological Immunology*, **174**, 51–8.

Levine, M., Beattie, B.L., McLean, D.M., and Corman, D. (1987a). Characterization of the immune response to trivalent influenza vaccine in elderly men. *Journal of the American Geriatrics Society*, **35**, 609–15.

Levine, M., Beattie, B.L., and McLean, D.M. (1987b). Comparison of one- and two-dose regimens of influenza vaccine in elderly men. *Canadian Medical Association Journal*, **137**, 722–6.

Lui, K.J. and Kendal, A.P. (1987). Impact of influenza epidemics on mortality in the United States from October 1972 to May 1985. *American Journal of Public Health*, **77**, 712–16.

McElhaney, J.E., Meneilly, G.S., Lechelt, K.E., Beattie, B.L., and Bleackley, R.C. (1993). Antibody response to whole-virus and split-virus influenza vaccines in successful ageing. *Vaccine*, **11**, 1055–60.

McElhaney, J.E., Meneilly, G.S., Pinkoski, M.J., Lechelt, K.E., and Bleackley, R.C. (1995). Vaccine-related determinants of the interleukin-2 response to influenza vaccination in healthy young and elderly adults. *Vaccine*, **13**, 6–10.

McMichael, A.J., Dongworth, D.W., Gotch, F.M., Clark, A., and Potter, C.N. (1983). Declining T-cell immunity to influenza. *Lancet*, **ii**, 762–5.

Margolis, K.L., Nichol, K.L., Poland, G.A., et al. (1990). Frequency of adverse reactions to influenza vaccine in the elderly: a randomized, placebo-controlled trial. *Journal of the American Medical Association*, **264**, 1139.

Marine, W.M. and Thomas, J.E. (1973). Age-related response to 1000 CCA units zonally purified, inactivated influenza vaccine in volunteers in the USA. *Postgraduate Medical Journal*, **49**, 164–8.

Mbawuike, I.N., Lange, A.R., and Couch, R.B. (1993). Diminished influenza A virus-specific MHC class I-restricted cytotoxic T lymphocyte activity among elderly persons. *Viral Immunology*, **6**, 55–64.

Mosmann, T.R. and Coffman, R.L. (1989). T_h1 and T_h2 cells: different patterns of lymphokine secretion lead to different functional properties. *Annual Review of Immunology*, **7**, 145–73.

Mufson, M.A. (1990). *Streptococcus pneumoniae*. In *Principles and practice of infectious diseases*. (3rd edn) (ed. G.L. Mandell, R.G. Douglas, and J.E. Bennett), pp. 1539–50. Churchill Livingstone, New York.

Mufson, M.A., Hughey, D.F., Turner, C.E., et al. (1991). Revaccination with pneumococcal vaccine of elderly persons 6 years after primary vaccination. *Vaccine*, **9**, 403–7.

Mullooly, J.P., Bennett, M.D., Hornbrook, M.C., et al. (1994). Influenza vaccination programs for elderly persons: cost-effectiveness in a health maintenance organisation. *Annals of Internal Medicine*, **121**, 947–52.

Musher, D.M. (1995). *Streptococcus pneumoniae*. In *Principles and practice of infectious diseases*. (4th edn) (ed. G.L. Mandell, J.E. Bennett, and R. Dolin), Vol. 2, pp. 1811–26. Churchill Livingstone, New York.

Nichol, K.L., Margolis, K.L., Wuorenma, J., and Von Sternberg, T. (1994). The efficacy and cost effectiveness of vaccination against influenza among elderly persons living in the community. *New England Journal of Medicine*, **331**, 778–84.

Perry, F.E. and Catterall, J.R. (1994). The pneumococcus: host–organism interactions and their implications for immunotherapy and immunoprophylaxis. *Thorax*, **49**, 946–50.

Powers, D. C. and Belshe, R.B. (1993). Effect of age on cytotoxic T lymphocyte memory as well as serum and local antibody responses elicited by inactivated influenza virus vaccine. *Journal of Infectious Diseases*, **167**, 584–92.

Powers, D.C. and Belshe, R.B. (1994). Vaccine-induced antibodies to heterologous influenza A H1N1 viruses: effects of ageing and 'original antigenic sin'. *Journal of Infectious Diseases*, **169**, 1125–9.

Powers, D.C., McElhaney, J.E., Florendo, O.A., Jr, et al. (1997). Humoral and cellular immune responses following vaccination with purified recombinant haemagglutinin from influenza A (H3N2) virus. *Journal of Infectious Diseases*, **175**, 342–51.

Remarque, E.J., Cools, H.J.M., Boere, T.J., van der Klis, R.J., Masurel, N., and Ligthart, G.J. (1996). Functional disability and antibody response to influenza vaccine in elderly patients in a Dutch nursing home. *British Medical Journal*, **312**, 1015.

Riddiough, M.A., Sisk, J.E., and Bell, J.C. (1983). Influenza vaccination: cost-effectiveness and public policy. *Journal of the American Medical Association*, **249**, 3189–95.

Sisk, J.E. and Riegelman, R.K. (1986). Cost effectiveness of vaccination against pneumococcal pneumonia: an update. *Annals of Internal Medicine*, **104**, 79.

Tengs, T.O., Adams, M.E., Pliskin, J.S., et al. (1994). Five-hundred life-saving interventions and their cost-effectiveness. *Risk Analysis*, **15**, 369–90.

Ulmer, J.B., Donelly, J.J., Parker, S.E., et al. (1993). Heterologous protection against influenza by injection of DNA encoding a viral protein. *Science*, **259**, 1745–9.

Williams, W.W., Hickson, M.A., Kane, M.A., et al. (1988). Immunization policies and vaccine coverage among adults. The risk for missed opportunities. *Annals of Internal Medicine*, **108**, 616–25.

Zweerink, H.J., Courtneidge, S.A., Skehel, J.J., et al. (1977). Cytotoxic T-cells kill influenza virus infected cells but do not distinguish between serologically distinct type A viruses. *Nature*, **267**, 354–6.

4

Injuries

4.1 The epidemiology of proximal femoral fracture

John Grimley Evans

Proximal femoral fracture (**PFF**) is a common and disabling injury of later life. In economically advanced countries the cumulative lifetime risk of fracture is now greater than 15 per cent for women and 5 per cent for men (Cummings *et al.* 1989). Around a quarter of the victims die within 6 months and more than half of survivors suffer pain or increased disability.

Fractures of the proximal femur are divided anatomically into intra- and extracapsular for purposes of treatment. It has been claimed that the two forms of fracture differ fundamentally in their epidemiology and aetiology, but much of the difference is attributable to age. Cervical fractures have higher incidence rates than trochanteric fractures in both sexes, and although both show a steep rise in incidence with age over 65, the incidence of trochanteric fractures rises proportionally more steeply than that of cervical fractures. Thus the ratio of cervical to trochanteric fractures falls from approximately 3 at age 60 to 1.3 at age 80 in women. In men the change is less dramatic, falling from 1.9 to 1.2 over the same age range (Alffram 1964). On average, therefore, patients with trochanteric fractures will be older, and frailer, physically and mentally than patients with cervical fracture. There is some evidence that weakness of the trochanteric region is determined largely by trabecular osteoporosis, while the strength of the cervical regions is more dependent on cortical bone. Therefore comparisons of age-matched samples of the two groups show a tendency for trochanteric fracture patients to have had a higher previous incidence of other trabecular bone fractures, for example in the spine and proximal humerus. These considerations aside, the epidemiology of the two types of fracture seems similar and it is customary to treat them as the single entity of PFF.

There are various potential sources of error in the data used for the epidemiological study of PFF and these may affect the numerator or the denominator of calculated incidence rates.

Sources of numerator error

Virtually all cases of PFF are referred to hospital orthopaedic services, but there are problems in the use of routine data for the epidemiological study of PFF. Mortality data based on death certificates giving PFF as the underlying cause of death are unreliable. Patients who die following PFF are often certified as dying from the bronchopneumonia or pulmonary embolism that was the intervening mechanism rather than from the underlying injury. This is more likely the longer the interval between the injury and the death. Data on hospital admissions also have their errors in the handling of interhospital transfers and in the coding of diagnosis, for example where patients are admitted for revision of a prosthesis implanted originally for PFF rather than for a new injury.

Denominator errors

Errors can arise in the use of hospital data if care is not taken over defining the catchment population in terms of geographical area of residence. The aim should be to ensure that the cases of PFF included in the numerator of an incidence rate comprise all and only the cases arising within a geographically defined and enumerated population. Even within a single city hospitals can vary in the selection of cases of PFF that come to them (Grimley Evans *et al.* 1980). This can give rise to misleading differences in clinical outcome as well as distorting the epidemiological picture. An important factor is that although PFF is essentially an injury restricted to old people, there are two sorts of old people at risk. Most obvious is the mentally and physically frail old person who typically breaks her femur in a fall in her own home or while resident in an institution. Such a patient commonly does badly in terms of survival and functional abilities after her fracture. At the other extreme is a busy and active old person who breaks her femur hurrying down a department store escalator in order not to be late to chair the golf club committee. She is often fitter than average for her age and usually does well after fracture. The geographical situation of a hospital within a city will affect the proportions of the two types of patient that are brought to them. This can bias case–control studies and randomized clinical trials based on consecutive admissions to hospital, which is a traditional study design. Such sources of bias probably underlie some of the conflicting results in the literature on PFF, for example whether PFF patients have more or less contact with their general practitioners or take more or less medication than controls.

Age and sex

PFF is rare at ages below 55 and is usually due to serious trauma such as road traffic accidents. Therefore annual incidence rates are low and are higher in men than in women, but they do show a slow rise with age. Fractures in late life are predominantly due to simple falls from a standing position rather than to more severe forms of trauma. From the seventh decade of life incidence rates rise exponentially with age. In the United Kingdom rates rise from approximately 1 to 2 per thousand in women and 0.5 to 1 per thousand in men at age 65, to around 25 per thousand and 10 per thousand respectively by the age of 85. Although all Western populations that have been studied show a higher incidence of PFF in women than in men in old age, some earlier studies found that in other national groups, for example in India, Singapore, and Israel, the sex ratio might be unity or even reversed. A recent study from Beijing also shows slightly higher rates in men than in women (Ling *et al.* 1996). Such sex ratios are only found in regions of low incidence, and it seems that the rise in incidence commonly seen in association with economic development affects women disproportionately. The reasons for this are not known, but changes in levels of physical activity and in cigarette smoking may particularly affect women.

The three-component model of PFF

In economically advanced nations the sex ratio of PFF incidence in later life is similar to that of falls, which also increase with age although less steeply. Over the age range 65 to 85 the annual prevalence of falls increases approximately twofold, but the incidence of PFF increases almost 20-fold. This indicates that the probability of a fall causing a fracture is modulated by other factors that have an increasing effect with age. Osteoporosis is one such factor, but the epidemiology of distal forearm fracture gives a clue to another relevant factor. During the adult years incidence rates of distal forearm fracture are constant until the age of 45 to 60 when, in women but not in men, there is a sharp stepwise increase in incidence rates. This mirrors both the presumed loss of trabecular bone in the early postmenopausal period and an increase in falls among women over the same age range (Winner *et al.* 1989). Thereafter the rates in women show a series of fluctuations but without any general upward trend during old age (Miller and Grimley Evans 1985). There is no increase in incidence in men at any age. This pattern in old age of increasing risk of falls with increasing risk of proximal femoral fracture, but constant rate of distal forearm fracture, suggests that with increasing age a faller is less likely to use his or her arm as a protective response to falling. This is probably due to differences in the direction and nature of falls (tripping forward at younger ages, toppling sideways at older ages) and to the speed of reaction. In addition, some older subjects may be unconscious as they fall owing to some form of syncope (see Chapter 4.4).

Therefore the genesis of PFF in old age lies in the interaction of three components. First is a fall, and hence the various causes in the individual and the environment that lead to falls. Second is the strength of the bone of the femoral neck. Third are protective factors. Some of these are active, such as extension of the arm and other protective responses in falling. Others are passive and include the padding effects of muscle or subcutaneous fat as well as of clothing and floor coverings (Table 1).

Many of the risk factors for PFF are associated with more than one of the three components. Immobility and lack of physical fitness are associated with the risk of falling but also with osteoporosis and possibly with slow protective responses. Cognitive impairment and

Table 1 The pathogenesis of proximal femoral fracture: the three-component model

Bone weakness
Osteomalacia
Osteoporosis
Bone dystrophy
Malignant disease
Paget's disease
Other

Falls
Occurrence
   Environmental hazards
   Drugs
   Sensory impairments
   Motor impairments
   Vestibular or hindbrain function
   Cognitive impairment
   Loss of consciousness
Nature
   Direction (forwards, backwards, sideways)
   Energy (body weight and height, height of fall)

Absence of protective factors in falling
Lack of subcutaneous fat
   Hard floors
Non-protective clothing
Muscle weakness
Slow or inadequate protective responses
   Failure to perceive incipient fall
      Sensory impairment
      Cognitive impairment
      Drugs
   Failure to respond appropriately
      Neurological defect
      Cognitive impairment
      Stiff or immobile joints
      Drugs
      Cold

consumption of long-acting sedative drugs are risk factors for falls but are also likely to impair neuromuscular reactions. Excessive alcohol consumption, which is a cause of falls and impairment of neuromuscular responses in some elderly populations, is also associated with osteoporosis. As a further example, PFF is negatively associated with body weight; this is mediated by both a beneficial effect on bone density (through body weight stimulating bone synthesis and by postmenopausal synthesis of oestrogens in fat tissue) and the cushioning effect of subcutaneous fat preventing bony injury in a fall.

Bone weakness

Some patients with PFF appear not to have broken their femurs in a fall but rather to have fallen because of a spontaneous fracture due to the accumulation of fatigue microtrabecular fractures. Estimates of the frequency of this are unreliable since patients with PFF may be unable to give a clear history of their fall. In one study, 75 per cent of patients were able to give a clear history and of these, 3 per cent (95 per cent confidence limits, 0.5 to 5.5 per cent) might have fallen because of a spontaneous fracture (Grimley Evans et al. 1979).

Pathological fractures of the hip, through metastases, patches of Paget's disease, or areas of bone weakened by other processes, are not very common. In the Newcastle population-based studies the proportion of patients with pathological fractures due to metastatic deposits or Paget's disease was 4 per cent (95 per cent confidence limits, 1.5 to 7 per cent) (Grimley Evans et al. 1979).

Among other causes of bone weakness, mineralization defects and abnormal bone crystal size have been suggested as contributing in a proportion of cases. Microfractures are commonly found in histological studies of patients with PFF and although these might be an indicator of low bone turnover rates, there is no direct evidence of this. The two conditions of most concern in PFF are osteomalacia and osteoporosis.

Osteomalacia

Vitamin D deficiency can cause PFF both by weakening bone and by its neuromyopathic effects which cause proximal muscle weakness and increased risk of falls. The pain of osteomalacia may also impair mobility and co-ordination. Nutritional osteomalacia with radiological changes was not uncommon among older people in the northern parts of the United Kingdom up to the 1970s but is now much rarer. Older people with frank osteomalacia now usually have an underlying cause such as coeliac disease or other malabsorption syndrome. The disappearance of nutritional osteomalacia in the United Kingdom may be due to dietary changes, with more older people now eating vitamin-D-fortified margarine rather than butter.

Low serum vitamin D levels are associated with PFF even in the absence of clinical or histological evidence of osteomalacia. This is because hypovitaminosis D is a marker for being housebound, which in turn is associated with the risk of falls. Because of low dietary intakes and inadequate exposure to ultraviolet light, hypovitaminosis D is common in the older population and its probable contribution to the genesis of osteoporosis is discussed below and, more fully, in Chapters 14.1 and 14.2.

Osteoporosis

A degree of age-associated bone loss is universal in the human species (Garn et al. 1967) and occurred at least as far back as the Bronze Age (Frigo and Lang 1995). Osteoporosis is widely assumed to be the most common cause of bone weakness leading to PFF. However, within Western populations, individuals who suffer fractures are not necessarily more osteoporotic on average than controls. A number of case–control studies have found no significant difference between PFF patients and controls in their average degree of osteoporosis. Some of these studies may have underestimated the significance of osteoporosis by measuring the bone density at sites remote from the femoral neck. Although there is a correlation between osteoporosis assessed at the distal radius or in the vertebral column and osteoporosis in the femoral neck, the relationship is not always close.

There are more pervasive causes of the underestimation of the significance of osteoporosis in PFF. The relative risk of PFF associated with osteoporosis assessed from case–control studies falls with age (e.g. Cooper et al. 1987). This does not necessarily imply, for the

purposes of prevention, that osteoporosis is less important at old ages than at younger. At the age of 65, where the relative risk of PFF associated with severe osteoporosis in women is, say, 50, the annual incidence of the fracture is only 1 to 2 per thousand. At ages 85 and above, where the relative risk has fallen to 5, the annual incidence is 25 per thousand. Even allowing for the different sizes of the populations at these two ages, the actual numbers of excess cases associated with osteoporosis may be higher at the older age than at the younger. This illustrates the well-known epidemiological paradox that in terms of the contribution of a risk factor to the numbers of cases caused (the potential for prevention), it may be more profitable to concentrate on a group where the relative risk is low but the incidence is high than on a group where the relative risk is high but the incidence low.

There is a second reason for care in interpreting the age-associated decline in relative risk of PFF in osteoporosis. It would be possible for osteoporosis to be the chief determinant of PFF in old age and yet for it not to emerge as linked to PFF in case–control studies. It is widely postulated that, in terms of bone strength assessed by measures of osteoporosis, there is a 'fracture threshold' above which fractures due to the forces generated in an average fall are unlikely, and which is independent of age (Riggs and Melton 1986). Since bone mineral content decreases with age in everyone, at extreme old ages, where the incidence of PFF is highest, osteoporosis will not emerge as an important factor in case–control studies because the controls will inevitably be as osteoporotic as the cases. Moreover, the importance of any risk factor for PFF that acts through osteoporosis will also be underestimated by case–control studies among the very old. Technically, this is the problem of 'overmatching' which afflicts case–control studies when matching for one variable, in this case age, also removes the differences in other factors of interest. What will distinguish cases from controls at high ages will be the factors associated with the other two components in fracture genesis—falls and the protective factors in falling.

Falls

The epidemiology of falls reflects interactions between intrinsic factors in individuals and extrinsic factors in their environments. Design of stairs, intensity of lighting, and even styles of decoration may interact with cognitive and motor defects common in later life to cause old people to fall (Archea 1985). Individual risk factors for falling have also been identified in a number of studies (Prudham and Grimley Evans 1981; Tinetti et al. 1988), and are summarized in Table 1 (see also Chapter 4.4). In essence, factors can be classified by their impact on the afferent path, central processor, or efferent path of a homeostatic loop. Examples of afferent impairment include visual and proprioceptive deficits, central processing may be impaired in dementia or intermittently in syncope, and the efferent path is compromised by muscle weakness or motor impairments as in stroke or parkinsonism.

There are many good reasons for trying to reduce the frequency of falls, but identifying old people in the general population who habitually fall may offer little scope for preventing PFF. Although further falls can be prevented by intervention, the cost per injurious fall prevented is high (Tinetti et al. 1994). The majority of fractures occur in a victim's first fall for at least 12 months and the majority of falls cause no fracture.

Other risk factors

A number of risk factors for PFF, which probably exert their effect through several pathways, have been identified from case–control or cohort studies.

Race

There appear to be racial differences in susceptibility to PFF (Griffin *et al.* 1992) but these are often confounded by differences in lifestyle. Rates in white Americans are higher than in Japanese Americans who, despite adopting Western lifestyles, have incidence rates of PFF similar to the low rates observed in Japan (Ross *et al.* 1991). Some apparent racial differences can be attributed at least in part to differences in the prevalence of osteoporosis. Black Americans and New Zealand Polynesians have higher bone densities and lower PFF rates than their European fellow countrywomen. It has been suggested that the femurs of Africans are less liable to fracture owing to a more favorable neck-shaft angle (Walensky and O'Brien 1968), and the levels of physical activity and propensity to falling may also differ between the races.

In contrast with these studies linking PFF incidence with measures of osteoporosis, one study from South Africa found that a higher incidence of PFF among white women than among black women was not matched by a higher prevalence of osteoporosis, assessed by metacarpal cortical thickness (Solomon 1979).

Drugs

As already noted, case–control studies have differed, probably for methodological reasons, in their findings on the association of PFF with consumption of medications. Studies finding that PFF patients consume more medications than controls are matched by other studies showing the opposite. In a large study of Medicaid files which permitted the linking of previous prescriptions to patients with PFF and controls, Ray *et al.* (1989*a*) showed an association of PFF with the use of long-acting, but not short-acting, hypnotics and anxiolytics, and with antipsychotic drugs and tricyclic antidepressants.

Thiazide diuretics apparently protect against osteoporosis and also against PFF (Ray *et al.* 1989*b*). Some studies have shown diuretics to be associated with an increased risk of falls, but this probably reflects a link between cardiovascular disease and falls. It is unlikely to be a causal relationship except for rare instances of iatrogenic hypo-volaemia and hypotension or potassium deficiency.

Oestrogens and the menopause

The effect of oestrogens in retarding the rate of loss of trabecular bone after the menopause is now generally accepted. A large number of studies have found that the use of perimenopausal oestrogens is associated with a lower incidence of osteoporotic fractures. It is assumed that this effect is mediated by postponing the onset of the rapid phase of bone loss that is believed to follow the drop in oestrogen levels at the menopause. It is not known how long, if at all, the effect lasts after the cessation of oestrogen therapy, and few women persist with oestrogen treatment over many years. With some exceptions, most of the reported studies have relied on the accuracy of subjects' recall of medication taken many years earlier. All the studies are susceptible to the criticism that women who demanded or opted for oestrogen replacement therapy may not be comparable

with controls in terms of other risk factors for PFF. In particular, they may be more health conscious, take more exercise, and smoke less (Barrett-Connor 1991). Such bias could only be overcome by long-term randomized controlled trials.

Region

Incidence rates vary between countries; for example, there were higher rates in Norwegians than in white Californians in the early 1980s (Maggi *et al.* 1991). Interpretation of regional variations can be difficult owing to interference from racial and secular differences. Past studies showed a north–south gradient in mortality from falls and fractures in the United Kingdom, but there seems now to be no difference in PFF incidence rates between cities in the North and the Midlands (Grimley Evans 1985). However, in the United States there does seem to be a latitude gradient in standardized hospital admission rates for PFF, with higher rates in the southeast (Jacobsen *et al.* 1990). The reasons are not clear.

Season

In the United Kingdom more cases of PFF occur in the winter months of November to April than in the other 6 months of the year. This is not simply a seasonal effect due, as in distal forearm fracture, to people falling over in the snow and ice since it is also found among those cases of PFF caused by falls indoors. One suggestion has been that thin and undernourished old people may become mildly hypothermic in cold weather and fall over because of the consequent lack of neuromuscular co-ordination (Bastow *et al.* 1983). However, it is not certain that thin patients are hypothermic before they fall rather than becoming so afterwards.

Seasonal variation in vitamin D metabolism is well documented (Hegarty *et al.* 1994). In winter, vitamin D intake and ultraviolet exposure fall, and parathyroid hormone secretion rises (Krall *et al.* 1989). This can lead to a cumulative loss of bone which is potentially preventable by dietary supplements during the winter months (Dawson-Hughes *et al.* 1991). Interventive studies so far reported are promising (see below).

It may be that seasonal variation in PFF incidence is a composite effect of several factors. Extra shopping expeditions for Christmas and the New Year sales may lead to a 'seasonal' increase in outdoor falls leading to PFF. In the Newcastle studies it seemed that the winter peak for fractures occurring out of doors was highest in December and January, when seasonal shopping is at its most intensive, but the peak for fractures incurred indoors was in early spring when vitamin D levels are lowest.

Body weight

As already noted, thinness is a risk factor for PFF through its association with osteoporosis, lack of subcutaneous fat padding, and possibly through predisposition to hypothermia and falls in cold weather. Weight loss after the age of 50 may have an additional effect on the risk of PFF in women (Langlois *et al.* 1996).

Diet

In some studies an inverse relationship between PFF incidence and dietary calcium intake has been found, although in the most widely quoted geographical study there were confounding factors such as differences in energy intake between the populations compared (Matkovic et al. 1977). The link between dietary calcium and osteoporosis is uncertain in Western populations. Little is known about individual variation in the ability to adapt to low-calcium diets, and heterogeneity in this regard among subjects enrolled in interventive studies may underlie the conflicting results reported. Dietary calcium intake might be of more significance in the genesis of osteoporosis in populations in the Far East where the average dietary calcium intake is much lower than in the West (Lau et al. 1992). Other dietary factors thought by some to be involved in the genesis of osteoporosis—high protein intake and deficiency of some micronutrients—are still of uncertain significance for PFF. An association of caffeine intake with osteoporosis and fractures is confounded by smoking.

Experimental studies suggest that bone strength may be weakened by too high or too low a level of dietary fluoride. The conclusion from a review of numerous studies is that fluoride levels of up to 1 ppm in drinking water have no consistent effect on PFF rates (Gordon and Corbin 1992).

Most interest on dietary influences on PFF now focuses on vitamin D. Several trials of supplementation with vitamin D, with or without calcium, have been reported. Two of these involving elderly patients who were in institutions or attending hospital outpatient clinics suggested that vitamin D supplementation reduced the frequency of 'osteoporotic' fractures including PFF. In the study by Chapuy et al. (1994) supplements included calcium, while Heikinheimo et al. (1992) used only vitamin D. The onset of effect was apparently quite rapid in these studies, suggesting that the benefit may have been mediated not through an effect on osteoporosis and bone strength but through a more rapid effect on neuromuscular function and prevention of falls. Unfortunately neither study documented the incidence of falls. However, in a third study (Dawson-Hughes et al. 1997) involving community-dwelling older men and women in which 700 IU of vitamin D and 500 mg of calcium was compared with placebo, a reduction in non-vertebral fractures was seen, again with the difference beginning to emerge within 6 months. In this study it was noted that there was no difference between treatment and placebo groups in the frequency of falls. Only one case of PFF occurred in this study. A fourth study, involving a community-dwelling sample of older people in the Netherlands and testing supplements of 400 IU of vitamin D without calcium, was unable to show any benefit (Lips et al. 1996). The difference between this study and the others may reflect differences in dosage regimes or in the prevalence of individuals sufficiently deficient in vitamin D to benefit from the supplementation.

Synthesis of vitamin D in the skin under the influence of ultraviolet light is an important contributor to body stores of the vitamin, and the annual amount of light of the relevant wavelength diminishes with increasing latitude. However, Jacobsen et al. (1991) were unable to detect any relationship between hospital admission rates for PFF and latitude over a wide range of North America. This also suggests that ambient temperature may not be a powerful factor, although most older people in North America may be more protected by central heating than are their coevals in the United Kingdom.

Physical illness

Several studies have shown that any condition leading to impaired mobility and muscle weakness is associated with a risk of falls, and low levels of habitual physical activity have also been linked to osteoporosis and directly to PFF. Not surprisingly, a number of specific physical illnesses including heart disease, cardiac dysrhythmias, parkinsonism, and stroke have also been shown to be associated with falls. In stroke the hemiplegic leg is more likely to be fractured than the other, and this might reflect both impaired protective responses on that side and disuse osteoporosis. Some studies have found evidence that diabetes mellitus is associated with PFF, but the mechanism is uncertain.

Mental illness

Methods of assessment vary, but about a third of patients with PFF have some degree of cognitive impairment, mostly due to a dementing illness (Grimley Evans et al. 1979). Incidence rates of PFF are high in psychiatric hospitals, and many explanations have been offered for this. Cognitive impairment is a risk factor for falls (Prudham and Grimley Evans 1981), as are long-acting antipsychotic and sedative drugs. Chronic epilepsy used to be associated with drug-induced osteomalacia, but this is now rare. Some elderly demented patients become very thin owing to anorexia and inadequate food intake rather than to any specific effect of dementia on metabolism, and low body weight is a risk factor for PFF. Perhaps the combination of cognitive impairment with restless mobility, which is a common reason for an elderly demented person to be admitted to a psychiatric hospital rather than to a geriatric unit or a residential home, carries a particularly high risk for PFF.

Secular trends

The incidence of PFF has been increasing in the United Kingdom, Sweden, and some other countries, although not apparently the United States, over the last 30 years. In the United Kingdom incidence doubled between the 1950s and the 1980s (Boyce and Vessey 1985). Nothing is known for certain about the causes of the increase, in particular whether it is due to an increase in the prevalence of osteoporosis (as is widely assumed) or to an increase in the frequency of falls or even to changes in the effectiveness of protective factors in falling. A study of skeletons from an eighteenth century London crypt suggested that the prevalence of osteoporosis has increased over the last 200 years, but it is not known when in that period the increase occurred (Lees et al. 1993). A recent analysis of hospital admission data in the United Kingdom suggested the presence of a cohort effect, with successive generations of people born from 1883 up to 1917 reaching later life with an increasing risk of PFF. There was also a strong period effect that was probably due to artefacts from data sampling (Grimley Evans et al. 1997). It is not clear whether incidence rates of PFF have continued to rise since 1979 because reliable national data are no longer available.

Among the suggested explanations for the secular increase are reductions in levels of obesity and in physical exercise during middle life (Boyce and Vessey 1988). It has also been suggested that the increase is due to changes in the characteristics of the elderly population, but unhelpfully it has been attributed both to the elderly becoming more fit and therefore more mobile and liable to falls, and also to their becoming less fit and therefore more liable to falls. There is no good evidence to support either view in general, although there is evidence that patients with dementia are surviving longer now than they used to. Other possible contributing factors include secular increases in height, with taller people being more susceptible to PFF (Hemenway *et al.* 1995), and the associated increase in length of the femoral neck (Reid *et al.* 1994).

Cigarette smoking

Cigarette smoking has been suggested as one of the factors responsible for secular increases in PFF. A series of studies in Newcastle suggested that rates had increased in men before 1971 but have been stable since, while rates in women continued to increase through the 1970s and into the 1980s (Grimley Evans 1985). This pattern is similar to the pattern of cigarette consumption in the general population some 30 years earlier. Cigarette smoking is associated with osteoporosis (Rundgren and Mellstrom 1984), partly through its association with low body weight and partly through an anti-oestrogenic effect in women and by lowering the age of menopause. Cigarette smoking also opposes the effect of postmenopausal oestrogen therapy (Kiel *et al.* 1992). Many case–control studies have failed to identify cigarette smoking as a risk factor for PFF. As noted above, this does not exclude its importance since if it acts through osteoporosis, as is postulated, it may not be detected in case–control studies of very old patients. Cigarette smoking does emerge as a risk factor for PFF in case–control studies of patients aged under 70.

Physical activity

Past physical activity and moderate levels of current activity seem protective against PFF in case–control studies (Law *et al.* 1991). The effect might be mediated through reduced osteoporosis and the prevention of falls. Exercise training has been shown to reduce the incidence of falls in later life (Province *et al.* 1995). Physical activity in childhood may be one of the determinants of the amount of bone tissue laid down early in life (Van den Bergh *et al.* 1995).

Conclusions

Using multiple risk factors, Cummings *et al.* (1995) were able to identify groups of elderly women with a 20-fold difference in risk of PFF. However, it seems unlikely that screening would prove a cost-effective public health approach to controlling the incidence of PFF. A population strategy seems more attractive. Wide variation from place to place and, even more significantly, from time to time in the same place indicates that PFF is not an inevitable consequence of 'normal' or 'intrinsic' ageing but has environmental causes that could presumably offer means of prevention. The amount and therefore the strength of bone tissue in old age is probably determined to an important extent by the amount laid down during childhood and adolescence. Therefore prevention of PFF by an attack on osteoporosis through diet could have a long 'lag period'. Although much of the evidence remains indirect, it seems likely that the abolition of cigarette smoking might reduce the prevalence of osteoporosis and the incidence of PFF.

A recurrent theme in the epidemiology of PFF is that of physical activity which is linked with preventing osteoporosis and may also reduce risk of falling and improve the speed and effectiveness of protective responses in falling. Maintenance of healthy levels of activity into middle age and beyond seems a sensible public health approach. Prevention of falls is unlikely to have a major impact on PFF rates

but is important for other reasons, as is care over the prescription of sedative drugs for old people.

References

Alffram, P.-A. (1964). An epidemiologic study of cervical and trochanteric fractures of the femur in an urban population. Analysis of 1664 cases with special reference to etiologic factors. *Acta Orthopaedica Scandinavica*, **Supplement 65**, 1–109.

Archea, J.C. (1985). Environmental factors associated with stair accidents by the elderly. *Clinics in Geriatric Medicine*, **1**, 555–68.

Barrett-Connor, E. (1991). Postmenopausal estrogen and prevention bias. *Annals of Internal Medicine*, **115**, 455–6.

Bastow, M.D., Rawlings, J., and Allison, S.P. (1983). Undernutrition, hypothermia, and injury in elderly women with fractured femur: an injury response to altered metabolism? *Lancet*, **i**, 143–6.

Boyce, W.J. and Vessey, M.P. (1985). Rising incidence of fracture of the proximal femur. *Lancet*, **i**, 150–1.

Boyce, W.J. and Vessey, M.P. (1988). Habitual physical inertia and other factors in relation to fracture of the proximal femur. *Age and Ageing*, **17**, 319–27.

Chapuy, M.C., Arlot, M.E., Delmas, P.D., and Meunier, P.J. (1994). Effect of calcium and cholecalciferol treatment for three years on hip fractures in elderly women. *British Medical Journal*, **308**, 1081–2.

Cooper, C., Barker, D.J.P., Morris, J., and Briggs, R.S.J. (1987). Osteoporosis, falls and age in fracture of the proximal femur. *British Medical Journal*, **295**, 1327–8.

Cummings, S.R., Black, D.M., and Rubin, S.R. (1989). Lifetime risks of hip, Colles', or vertebral fracture and coronary heart disease among white postmenopausal women. *Archives of Internal Medicine*, **149**, 2445–8.

Cummings, S.R., Nevitt, M.C., Browner, W.S., *et al.* (1995). Risk factors for hip fracture in white women. *New England Journal of Medicine*, **332**, 767–73.

Dawson-Hughes, B., Dallal, G.E., Krall, E.A., Harris, S., Sokoll, L.J., and Falconer, G. (1991). Effect of vitamin D supplementation on wintertime and overall bone loss in healthy postmenopausal women. *Annals of Internal Medicine*, **115**, 505–12.

Dawson-Hughes, B., Harris, S.S., Krall, E.A., and Dallal, G.E. (1997). Effect of calcium and vitamin D supplementation on bone density in men and women 65 years of age or older. *New England Journal of Medicine*, **337**, 670–6.

Frigo, P. and Lang, C. (1995). Osteoporosis in a woman of the early Bronze Age. *New England Journal of Medicine*, **333**, 1468.

Garn, S.M., Rohmann, C.G., and Wagner, B. (1967). Bone loss as a general phenomenon in man. *Federation Proceedings*, **26**, 1729–36.

Gordon, S.L. and Corbin, S.B. (1992). Summary of Workshop on Drinking Water Fluoride Influence on Hip Fracture and Bone Health (National Institutes of Health, 10 April 1991). *Osteoporosis International*, **2**, 109–17.

Griffin, M.R., Ray, W.A., Fought, R.L., and Melton, J. (1992). Black–white differences in fracture rates. *American Journal of Epidemiology*, **136**, 1378–85.

Grimley Evans, J. (1985). Incidence of proximal femoral fracture. *Lancet*, **i**, 925–6.

Grimley Evans, J., Prudham, D., and Wandless, I. (1979). A prospective study of proximal femoral fracture: incidence and outcome. *Public Health*, **93**, 235–41.

Grimley Evans, J., Prudham, D., and Wandless, I. (1980). A prospective study of fractured proximal femur: hospital differences. *Public Health*, **94**, 149–54.

Grimley Evans, J., Seagroatt, V., and Goldacre, M.J. (1997). Secular trends in proximal femoral fracture, Oxford Record Linkage Study area and

England 1968–86. *Journal of Epidemiology and Community Health*, 51, 424–9.

Hegarty, V., Woodhouse, P., and Khaw, K.-T. (1994). Seasonal variation in 25-hydroxyvitamin D and parathyroid hormone concentrations in healthy elderly people. *Age and Ageing*, 23, 478–82.

Heikinheimo, R.J., Inkovaara, J.A., Harju, E.J., *et al.* (1992). Annual injection of vitamin D and fracture of aged bones. *Calcified Tissue International*, 51, 105–10.

Hemenway, D., Feskanich, D., and Colditz, G.A. (1995). Body height and hip fracture: a cohort study of 90 000 women. *International Journal of Epidemiology*, 24, 783–6.

Jacobsen, S.J., Goldberg, J., Miles, T.P., Brody, J.A., Stiers, W., and Rimm, A.A. (1990). Regional variation in the incidence of hip fracture. *Journal of the American Medical Association*, 264, 500–2.

Jacobsen, S.J., Goldberg, J., Miles, T.P., Brody, J.A., Stiers, W., and Rimm, A.A. (1991). Seasonal variation in the incidence of hip fracture among white persons aged 65 years and older in the United States, 1984–1987. *American Journal of Epidemiology*, 133, 996–1004.

Kiel, D.P., Baron, J.A., Anderson, J.J., Hannan, M.T., and Felson, D.T. (1992). Smoking eliminates the protective effect of oral estrogens on the risk for hip fracture among women. *Annals of Internal Medicine*, 116, 716–21.

Krall, E.A., Sahyoun, N., Tannenbaum, S., Dallal, G.E., and Dawson-Hughes, B. (1989). Effect of vitamin D intake on seasonal variation in parathyroid hormone secretion in post-menopausal women. *New England Journal of Medicine*, 321, 1777–83.

Langlois, J.A., Harris, T., Looker, A.C., and Madans, J. (1996). Weight change between age 50 years and old age is associated with risk of hip fracture in white women aged 67 years and older. *Archives of Internal Medicine*, 156, 989–94.

Lau, E.M.C., Woo, J., Leung, P.C., Swaminathan, R., and Leung, D. (1992). The effects of calcium supplementation and exercise on bone density in elderly Chinese women. *Osteoporosis International*, 2, 168–73.

Law, M.R., Wald, N.J., and Meade, T.W. (1991). Strategies for prevention of osteoporosis and hip fracture. *British Medical Journal*, 303, 453–9.

Lees, B., Molleson, T., Arnett, T.R., and Stevenson, J.C. (1993). Differences in proximal femur bone density over two centuries. *Lancet*, 341, 673–5.

Ling, X., Aimin, L., Xieh, Z., Xiaoshu, C., and Cummings, S.R. (1996). Very low rates of hip fracture in Beijing, People's Republic of China. The Beijing Osteoporosis Project. *American Journal of Epidemiology*, 144, 901–7.

Lips, P., Graafmans, W.C., Ooms, M.E., Bezemer, P.D., and Bouter, L.M. (1996). Vitamin D supplementation and fracture incidence in elderly persons. A randomized placebo-controlled clinical trial. *Annals of Internal Medicine*, 124, 400–6.

Maggi, S., Kelsey, J.L., Litvak, J., and Heyse, S.P. (1991). Incidence of hip fractures in the elderly: a cross-national analysis. *Osteoporosis International*, 1, 232–41.

Matkovic, V., Kostial, K., Simonovic, I., Brodarec, A., and Bozina, R. (1977). Influence of calcium intake, age and sex on bone. *Calcified Tissue Research*, 22 (Supplement), 393–6.

Miller, S.W.M. and Grimley Evans, J. (1985). Fractures of the distal forearm in Newcastle: an epidemiological survey. *Age and Ageing*, 14,155–8.

Province, M.A., Hadley, E.C., Hornbrook, M.C., *et al.*, for the FICSIT Group (1995). The effects of exercise on falls in elderly patients. A preplanned meta-analysis of the FICSIT trials. *Journal of the American Medical Association*, 273, 1341–7.

Prudham, D. and Grimley Evans, J. (1981). Factors associated with falls in the elderly: a community study. *Age and Ageing*, 10, 264–70.

Ray, W.A., Griffin, M.R., and Downey, W. (1989a). Benzodiazepines of long and short elimination half-life and the risk of hip fracture. *Journal of the American Medical Association*, 262, 3303–7.

Ray, W.A., Griffin, M.R., Downey, W., and Melton, L.J., III (1989b). Long-term use of thiazide diuretics and risk of hip fracture. *Lancet*, i, 687–90.

Reid, I.R., Chin, K., Evans, M.C., and Jones, J.G. (1994). Relation between increase in length of hip axis in older women between 1950s and 1990s and increase in age specific rates of hip fracture. *British Medical Journal*, 309, 508–9.

Riggs, B.L. and Melton, L.J. (1986). Involutional osteoporosis. *New England Journal of Medicine*, 314, 1676–86.

Ross, P.D., Norimatsu, H., Davis, J.W., *et al.* (1991). A comparison of hip fracture incidence among native Japanese, Japanese Americans, and American Caucasians. *American Journal of Epidemiology*, 133, 801–9.

Rundgren, A. and Mellstrom, D. (1984). The effect of tobacco smoking on the bone mineral content of the ageing skeleton. *Mechanisms of Ageing and Development*, 28, 273–7.

Solomon, L. (1979). Bone density in ageing Caucasian and African populations. *Lancet*, ii, 1326–30.

Tinetti, M.E., Speechley, M., and Ginter, S.F. (1988). Risk factors for falls among elderly persons living in the community. *New England Journal of Medicine*, 319, 1701–7.

Tinetti, M.E., Baker, D.I., McAvay, G., *et al.* (1994). A multifactorial intervention to reduce the risk of falling among elderly people living in the community. *New England Journal of Medicine*, 331, 821–7.

Van den Bergh, M.F.Q., DeMan, S.A., Witteman, J.C.M., Hofman, A., Trouerbach, Th., and Grobbee, D.E. (1995). Physical activity, calcium intake, and bone mineral content in children in The Netherlands. *Journal of Epidemiology and Community Health*, 49, 299–304.

Walensky, N.A. and O'Brien, M.P. (1968). Anatomical factors relative to the racial selectivity of femoral neck fracture. *American Journal of Physical Anthropology*, 28, 93–6.

Winner, S.J., Morgan, C.A., and Grimley Evans, J. (1989). Perimenopausal risk of falling and incidence of distal forearm fracture. *British Medical Journal*, 298, 1486–8.

4.2 Injury in old age

John E. Clague and Michael A. Horan

Introduction

There are many misconceptions about trauma in later life. Trauma is more common among the young, yet in the United States elderly people suffer 25 per cent of injury fatalities despite representing only 11 per cent of the population (Oreskovich *et al.* 1984). Similarly, in England and Wales one-third of deaths due to injury and poisoning occur in the 16 per cent of the population aged over 65 years (Office of Population Censuses and Surveys 1993). In the United States it is estimated that up to one-third of trauma-related hospital costs ($87 billion) are expended on elderly patients. Elderly accident victims have longer stays in hospital and intensive care units (Covington *et al.* 1993), and trauma is the fifth leading cause of death among people aged over 65 years. For any given injury, older people are more likely to die than are younger persons (Oreskovich *et al.* 1984; Finelli *et al.* 1989; Shorr *et al.* 1989).

The true incidence of trauma is likely to be even higher than recorded statistics indicate. Accidental deaths in the United Kingdom are probably under-reported. Deaths occurring late after trauma are commonly certified as being due to a complication which was a consequence of the original trauma (e.g. pulmonary embolism or pneumonia), or a coexisting medical condition is recorded as the cause of death. Only patients presenting for treatment will be included in non-fatal injury statistics. Community surveys suggest that much minor trauma passes unreported (Graham and Firth 1992).

The mechanisms of trauma affecting older people also differ from those common among the young. As people age, falls become an increasingly common cause of injury, and around one-third of people aged over 65 years have at least one fall in a year. In the population aged over 75 years falls are the leading cause of accidental death, and they exceed traffic accidents among those aged 65 to 74 years. Older people account for 70 per cent of all fatal fall injuries. Motor vehicle accidents are less frequent than for younger drivers, but are proportionally higher for the number of miles travelled. Compared with road traffic accidents affecting the younger population, motor vehicle collisions involving older people are more likely to occur in daylight hours, in good weather, and in situations where attention and accurate judgement are required. Accidents involving another vehicle occur more frequently at intersections. Alcohol plays a diminishing role, and accidents are less likely to be attributable to speeding or reckless driving. Medical conditions are significant contributors to accidents where elderly people are deemed at fault (Rehm and Ross 1995). Elderly diabetic patients have been found to have a 2.6 times higher injury risk than non-diabetic controls (Koepsell *et al.* 1994). Cognitive impairment in drivers probably increases accident risk in more severely affected subjects. In postmortem studies of elderly drivers in fatal car accidents, one-third of brains show evidence of Alzheimer's disease (Johansson *et al.* 1997).

Elderly people form the largest group of pedestrian accident victims, reflecting the importance of walking as the favoured mode of travel. They are more likely to be injured at recognized crossing places. Older people are also over-represented in fire fatalities (25 per cent of deaths but only 10 per cent of accidents). Death from fire is the second most common cause of accidental death in later life (Elder *et al.* 1996). Burns are associated with a high fatality rate and are most frequently due to scalds. Non-accidental injury of elderly people by family and carers is a more recently recognized cause of injury (Bennett *et al.* 1997).

The epidemiological data suggest a polarity in causes of trauma in later life. Frail elderly people are at risk of injury because of intrinsic factors making any environment hazardous, but there are also healthy active older people taking the same risks as younger people.

Response to injury

The response to injury is conventionally divided into an initial ebb phase followed by a flow phase (Cuthbertson 1932). The ebb phase is characterized by mobilization of energy substrates, reduction in metabolic rate, and certain neuroendocrine changes—activation of the sympathoadrenal medullary and the pituitary–adrenocortical systems. The flow phase is defined by an increased metabolic rate, catabolism, and fuel utilization. The response of elderly people to injury is similar in many respects to that of the young. Differences have been identified, but the response to injury has yet to be fully evaluated in older patients.

The ebb phase

In the first 24 to 48 h following injury the sympathoadrenal medullary and the pituitary–adrenocortical systems are activated. Concentrations of growth hormone, prolactin, vasopressin, aldosterone, and glucagon are increased. The magnitude of the initial response of the sympathoadrenal medullary system is related to the severity of the injury, whereas for the pituitary–adrenocortical system severity is reflected in the duration of the response. Ageing does not impair the ability of the neuroendocrine systems to respond to injury. Catecholamine levels rise as much in older as in younger subjects.

Breakdown of liver glycogen increases plasma glucose concentrations in proportion to injury severity. No commensurate rise in insulin occurs owing to its suppression by circulating catecholamines. Lactate concentration also rises owing to glycogen breakdown and possibly hypoxia. Plasma glycerol and free fatty acids are also increased soon after injury. These changes do not differ between young and elderly subjects, although older subjects have higher rates of lipolysis and re-esterification of free fatty acids within adipose tissue (Horan et al. 1992).

The flow phase

The increase in metabolic rate is related to the severity of injury. The hypermetabolism is accompanied by a rise in nitrogen excretion due to net muscle protein catabolism. Although not yet intensively studied, older patients show rises in metabolic rate and nitrogen excretion proportional to age-associated changes in body composition. Elderly subjects lose less protein, mainly because of decreased whole-body protein breakdown rate (Jeevanandam et al. 1993). Changes in plasma proteins, including increased acute-phase proteins and reduced albumin, found in young trauma victims have not been studied in elderly subjects, but comparable rises in acute-phase proteins have been found in elderly patients when sepsis is the stimulus.

There is a shift from carbohydrate to fat as the preferred fuel. Blood levels of glucose are high and those of free fatty acids are low. After severe injury, clearance of free fatty acids from the circulation is increased. Glucose clearance is reduced as a consequence of insulin resistance which is exacerbated after injury in elderly people. Endogenous glucose production following injury also increases with age (Watters et al. 1997). In the young, insulin levels may be raised for 2 weeks after injury, but thereafter glucose levels fall to normal. Following injury, glucose intolerance persists in older people and the insulin response to glucose infusion is suppressed (Watters et al. 1994).

Ageing itself is characterized by minor increases in fasting glucose levels and impaired glucose tolerance, but persistent hypercortisolaemia may be the explanation for the insulin resistance seen after injury. Following proximal femoral fracture, cortisol levels tend to remain elevated for at least 2 weeks and high levels may persist for 8 weeks in some cases (Roberts et al. 1990). The reason for this is unclear. It may reflect a failure to downregulate the response rather than indicating persistence of a stimulus. This conjecture is compatible with the observations in old rats of loss of corticosteroid receptors in the hippocampus, thus reducing tonic restraint of the pituitary–adrenocortical system. Impaired dexamethasone suppression is also seen in patients with Alzheimer's disease who have extensive loss of hippocampal neurones. Marked resistance to dexamethasone suppression has been observed in elderly hip fracture patients (Doncaster et al. 1993), possibly indicating degenerative changes in the hippocampus.

It is not known whether the persistent hypercortisolaemia after injury is adaptive or not. In the acute phase of injury, the pituitary–adrenocortical system response helps to defend blood volume by raising blood glucose and supports the compensatory movement of fluid into the intravascular compartment. However, there is little evidence that, once fluid loss has been corrected, an elevated cortisol level is required to maintain blood pressure. If the response is maladaptive, effects such as insulin resistance, muscle proteolysis, impaired wound healing, and immune suppression, as occurs in Cushing's disease, would be seen. If the response is adaptive, evidence of acquired resistance to glucocorticoid effects would be expected. Further work is required to examine the consequences of hypercortisolaemia following injury.

Measuring injury

The term 'injury' generally refers to damage to cells, tissues, and organs, but it is also used in connection with the various physiological responses in the injured subject. Measurement of injury is necessary both to plan management and to evaluate outcome. Injury scoring systems can include an assessment of the anatomical extent of injury, the physiological consequences in the injured subject, or both.

The Injury Severity Score (ISS) is the most widely used anatomical index of injury. In the acute setting it is of limited value as the information necessary for compilation is not all immediately available. It is useful in evaluating trauma systems and in comparative studies of outcome. As with some other scoring systems, it was developed from data collected from young people and so has limitations for older subjects. For example, because of reduced bone mass, the force required to produce a fracture in elderly subjects will be less, and so will be the concomitant soft tissue injury . An anatomical scoring system such as ISS will tend to overestimate the severity of the injury.

Physiologically based systems, such as the Revised Trauma Score, the Simplified Acute Physiology Score (SAPS), the Glasgow Coma Scale (GCS), and the Acute Physiology and Chronic Health Estimate (APACHE), are useful for triage and patient management. Fears that age-associated declines in physiological responses to injury might lead to underestimates on these physiological scoring systems are unfounded. Elderly injured subjects have greater physiological perturbations for all but the most extreme anatomical injury scores (Shabot and Johnson 1995). Age is a poor predictor of survival when physiological perturbations and comorbid factors are taken into account (Knaus et al. 1991).

The Revised Trauma Score plus Injury Severity Score (TRISS) and A Severity Characterization of Trauma (ASCOT), which are commonly used scores combining assessments of extent of injury and physiological consequences, appear to be better predictors of survival, but no scoring system is entirely satisfactory for all purposes. The Geriatric Trauma Survival Score was developed by DeMaria et al. (1987) in an attempt to address the acknowledged deficits of scoring systems for injured elderly people. Although it was 92 per cent accurate in predicting survival, it has not been validated or widely adopted in clinical practice.

Why do elderly trauma victims have a worse outcome?

Apart from age-associated changes placing the subject at greater risk of injury, are there features of ageing which influence outcome? Ageing is characterized by a decreased functional reserve and poorer ability to cope with stressors, thus producing an increased risk of death. We can only speculate on how the age-associated physiological changes might reduce survival following injury. The known changes in myocardial contractility reduce cardiac reserve, and reduced inotropic responsiveness might impair responses to blood loss. Loss of respiratory reserve might predispose to hypoxaemia, and a decline in renal function could impair the ability to cope with haemodynamic disturbance. However, there is little direct evidence that these factors contribute in a major way to injury fatality, and it is more likely that comorbidity and the accumulation of illness through life is the more critical determinant of outcome.

Comorbidity

Many surveys have described the presence of multiple chronic illnesses in community-dwelling elderly subjects. Milzman *et al.* (1992) reported the presence of pre-existing disease in 16 per cent of all trauma victims in a study population of over 7700. This rose to 50 per cent of trauma patients in the 65 to 74 year age group and to 65 per cent of those aged 75. In one study of hip fracture patients, significant comorbidity was found in 78 per cent of patients (Bernadini *et al.* 1995). For all ages, mortalities were three times higher in the presence of premorbid illness. Heart disease, renal disease, and malignancy were particularly associated with increased fatality. Pre-existing disease predicted outcome independently of age and injury severity.

Pre-existing psychological problems which might have been a factor in the injury have also been reported in trauma victims. Such data are reported in studies of patients of all age groups, and the general effect of depression on recovery following injury is well recognized. Comorbidity is associated with a poorer outcome in terms of both fatality rates and functional recovery, although rates of achieving independence vary considerably from the dismal (only 8 per cent achieving independence at 1 year (Oreskovich *et al.* 1984)) to the hopeful (67 per cent independent at least 1 year after discharge (Van Aalst *et al.* 1991)). However, this optimistic finding is misleading as patients aged over 75 had a much worse outcome (88 per cent unacceptable) and other studies confirm that satisfactory functional outcome is less frequent in the very old.

It is easy to see that comorbidity leads to increased fatality. In larger surveys of discharge data, chronic lung disease, ischaemic heart disease, chronic liver disease, diabetes, and coagulopathies have been associated with increased fatality. Hypovolaemia may be poorly tolerated by patients with hypertension and ischaemic heart disease. Medical therapy may interfere with the response to trauma, for example. The use of β-adrenoreceptor antagonists may impair the tachycardia in response to haemorrhage. Underlying chronic lung disease may predispose to infection, respiratory failure, and the need for ventilatory support.

Complications following treatment are recognized as important contributors to poor outcome following injury. Age-associated changes plus comorbidity can explain the increased frequency of complications in elderly patients. Increased ventilator dependence and pneumonia are but two factors leading to increased morbidity in later life.

Common injuries to elderly people

In general, patterns of injury are similar in young and old. Some injuries that are more common or problematic in later life are discussed below.

Chest trauma

Elderly people are at increased risk of morbidity and mortality from injuries that would have insignificant consequences in younger subjects. The chest wall is less elastic and more prone to fracture, but pulmonary contusion is less likely. Older people are more likely to acquire a flail segment. Even without fractures, pain leading to hypoventilation and failure to clear secretions predispose to pneumonia. Adequate analgesia, physiotherapy, and regular assessment of oxygenation are essential to the care of older people with chest injuries.

Abdominal trauma

Abdominal trauma to an elderly patient calls for urgent assessment and treatment. An almost fivefold increase in fatality has been reported in elderly subjects with visceral injury compared with younger patients (Finelli *et al.* 1989). Abdominal trauma is not uncommon, and is reported in up to 35 per cent of older patients with multiple injuries.

Elderly patients are also at increased risk of complications following emergency surgery. As in elective surgical procedures, adequate perioperative evaluation and optimization are desirable. However, there is a dilemma in that delaying surgery in order to achieve cardiovascular stability may result in the development of multiple organ failure from which recovery is rare.

Physical examination alone is thought to be inadequate in the assessment of blunt abdominal trauma. Although diagnostic peritoneal lavage has revolutionized the assessment of abdominal trauma, CT examination of the abdomen is increasingly preferred for preoperative evaluation. It is non-invasive and damage to extraperitoneal structures can be assessed at the same time.

Fractures

Older people are particularly prone to fractures because they have weak bones owing to osteoporosis and are more likely than younger people to fall. Upper-limb fractures are common; falls onto outstretched arms occur most commonly when a person is moving. In contrast, hip fractures more often follow falls from a stationary position or slow locomotion. Long-bone fractures are also reported with no history of falls or trauma and are termed 'minimal trauma fractures'. Severely impaired mobility is the only clearly identified factor in their aetiology.

Three groups of factors are involved in the genesis of a hip fracture. These are the causes of the fall, the determinants of the strength of bone, and the active and passive protective factors that determine how much of the kinetic energy of falling is transmitted to the bone (Grimley Evans 1996). Cadaveric studies indicate that the energy generated in a typical fall is more than sufficient to fracture an old person's hip. Protective factors include stretching out an arm, muscular contractions, and passive energy absorption by soft tissues including subcutaneous fat. Clothing and floor coverings also contribute to energy absorption.

Pelvic fractures have high morbidity and mortality in elderly patients as they may be associated with significant haemorrhage and visceral injury. Fatality rates are as high as 50 per cent in the presence of hypotension and reach 90 per cent if the fracture is open. More typically, falls from a standing height fracture the pubic ramus. The aim of management of this less serious injury is early mobilization through adequate pain control in order to avoid complications of immobility.

The incidence of tibial fracture declines with age in men and remains static in women. Non-operative approaches are not well tolerated. Similarly, ankle fractures are best managed surgically. However, elderly patients enjoy less satisfactory results than their younger counterparts. Ankle fractures are increasing in incidence in older women.

Proximal humerus and distal radius fractures form the bulk of upper-limb injuries. Because of osteoporosis, injuries that might lead to dislocation or ligamentous injury in the young cause fractures in older people. An exception is rotator cuff injury, in that degenerative changes in the tendons make them more prone to injury even with minor trauma.

Soft tissue injury

Many minor injuries do not come to medical attention. Of those that do, pretibial laceration is probably the exemplar of minor injury in elderly people. This injury is rarely seen outside this age group. Age-associated increase in skin fragility plus potential complicating factors such as diabetes or peripheral vascular disease lead to impaired healing. Prolonged bed rest may aid healing but can cause considerable difficulties in restoring independent mobility in one-third of cases.

Head injury

Severe head injury with a GCS score of 8 or less is second only to shock as a predictor of death in elderly patients. In those who do survive (and most studies report fatality following severe brain injury at about 90 per cent), a prolonged hospital stay is frequent and patients are likely to be left with severe deficits.

As the brain ages, the dura become tightly adherent to the skull and therefore extradural haematomas are uncommon. Cerebral atrophy leads to stretching of bridging veins, and this, combined with increased venous fragility and sometimes impaired coagulation, increases the risk of subdural haematomas. Even apparently minor head trauma (high admission GCS score) may have a poor outcome. It had been argued that, because of the dismal prospects of head injury in elderly patients, treatment should be time limited. Why head injury is associated with poor outcome in elderly people is not known, but it has been suggested that the ageing brain is less able to recover from injury.

The optimal treatment of the injured elderly patient

Improvements have occurred in the management of injured elderly patients. In the United States, there was a decline of 63.5 per cent in age-specific mortality from accidental falls between the years 1962 and 1988, reflecting improvements in care rather than changes in the victims or their accidents. Indeed, improvement in survival has been proposed as an ethical justification of the high cost of care of elderly trauma victims.

Inadequate triage of elderly trauma victims has been reported in the United States, possibly indicating suboptimal care. Others have suggested that older patients should be subjected to more intensive

triage in the hope of compensating for their poorer outcome. Attempts have been made to identify the specific components of care that have led to improved survival. The outcome from severe blunt trauma to elderly people has been reported to be improved by avoiding delays in definitive treatment and by the early use of invasive haemodynamic monitoring. It is argued that these approaches reduce the frequency of unrecognized hypoperfusion leading to multiple organ failure, which is invariably associated with extremely high mortality. Whilst the validity of this interpretation is unproven, it is clear that shock may go unrecognized in older patients and is poorly tolerated, and that delays in treatment worsen outcome.

Complications following injury treatment have repeatedly been shown to influence outcome. Some, such as pulmonary infection, may be unavoidable even with optimal care. Aspiration of tube feeds has been reported as a contributor. Pulmonary embolus is perhaps the best recognized cause of avoidable death following trauma, and prophylactic treatment for high-risk patients is mandatory.

Recovery from injury

The aim of trauma therapy is to return the patient to a full and active existence, but the premorbid state of some elderly patients may preclude this even with optimal treatment. Functional outcome depends not only on patient characteristics and the nature of the injury, but also on factors such as the level of social support. As yet, it is not possible to predict outcome for an individual in all situations, but some areas of certainty do exist. As already noted, outcome following severe head injury is invariably poor and in the few survivors function is severely limited. Prompt discussions with family members to explain appropriate limits on care are appropriate.

Our knowledge is probably greatest for factors influencing recovery after hip fracture. Only 40 per cent of patients who were mobile independently prior to injury return to that level of function. Preinjury independence in activities of daily living is a strong predictor of discharge to the usual residence. Comorbid conditions such as depression, dementia, malnutrition, and stroke are associated with poor outcome. Perioperative factors known to influence outcome adversely include delay in surgery. Use of prophylactic antibiotics and anti-coagulants improve outcome. Inadequate nutrition is deleterious and the use of nutritional supplements, by overnight drip feeding through nasogastric tube if necessary, has been shown to improve outcome (Bastow *et al.* 1983; Delmi *et al.* 1990) The importance of 'medical' as distinct from 'surgical' factors in determining outcome has led to the exploration of various models of 'orthogeriatric' care to foster collaboration between orthopaedic surgeons and geriatricians (Briggs 1993). However, the optimal approach to hip fracture rehabilitation has not been defined.

Conclusions

Outcome following injury depends on four main factors: injury severity, physiological reserve, the time to definitive treatment (the 'golden hour'), and the quality of care. Improvements in knowledge and care of injured people have led to significant improvements in survival at all ages including later life. Coupled with this is the increasing recognition of the limits of medical intervention and of the appropriateness of withdrawal of predictably futile treatment. Current knowledge on the factors determining functional recovery of individuals following injury is limited.

References

Bastow, M.D., Rawlings, J., and Alison, S.P. (1983). Benefits of supplementary tube feeding after fractured neck of femur: a randomised controlled trial. *British Medical Journal*, 287, 1589–92.

Bennett, G., Kingston, P., and Penhale, B. (1997). *Dimensions of elder abuse.* Macmillan, London.

Bernadini, B., Meiecke, C., Pagani, M., *et al.* (1995). Comorbidity and adverse clinical events in the rehabilitation of older adults after hip fracture. *Journal of the American Geriatrics Society*, 43, 894–8.

Briggs, R.J. (1993). Orthogeriatric care and its effect on outcome. *Journal of the Royal Society of Medicine*, 86, 560–1.

Covington, D.L., Maxwell, J.G., and Clancy T.V. (1993). Hospital resources used to treat the injured elderly at North Carolina trauma centers. *Journal of the American Geriatrics Society*, 41, 847–52.

Cuthbertson, D.P. (1932). Observations on disturbance of metabolism produced by injury to the limbs. *Quarterly Journal of Medicine*, 25, 233–46.

Delmi, M., Rapin, C.-H., Bengoa, J.-M., Delmas, P.D., Vasey, H., and Bonjour, J.-P. (1990). Dietary supplementation in elderly patients with fractured neck of femur. *Lancet*, 335, 1013–16.

DeMaria, E.J., Kenney, P., Merrian, M.A., Casanova, L.A., and Gann, D.S. (1987). Survival after trauma in geriatric patients. *Annals of Surgery*, 206, 738–43.

Doncaster, H.D., Barton, R.N., Horan, M.A., and Roberts, N.A. (1993). Factors influencing cortisol—adrenocorticotrophin relationships in elderly women with upper femur fractures. *Journal of Trauma*, 34, 49–55.

Elder, A.T., Squires, T., and Bussutil, A. (1996). Fire fatalities in elderly people. *Age and Ageing*, 25, 214–16.

Grimley Evans, J. (1996). Proximal femoral fracture. In *Epidemiology in old age* (ed. S. Ebrahim and A. Kalache), pp. 300–10. BMJ Publishing, London.

Finelli, F.C., Jonsson, J., Champion, H.R., Morelli, S., and Fouty, W.J. (1989). A case control study for major trauma in geriatric patients. *Journal of Trauma*, 29, 541–8.

Graham, H.J. and Firth, J. (1992). Home accidents in older people: role of primary health care team. *British Medical Journal*, 305, 30–2.

Horan, M.A., Roberts, N.A., Barton, R.N., and Little, R.A. (1992). Injury responses in old age. In *Oxford textbook of geriatric medicine* (ed. J. Grimley Evans and T.F. Williams), pp. 88–93. Oxford University Press.

Jeevanandam, M., Petersen, S.R., and Shamos, R.F. (1993). Protein and glucose fuel kinetics and hormonal changes in elderly trauma patients. *Metabolism: Clinical and Experimental*, 42, 1255–62.

Johansson, K., Bogdanovic, N., Kalimo, H., Winblad, B., and Viitanen, M. (1997). Alzheimer's disease and apolipoprotein E$^\epsilon$4 allele in older drivers who died in automobile accidents. *Lancet*, 349, 1143.

Knaus, W.A., Wagner, D.P., Draper, E.A., *et al.* (1991). The APACHE III prognostic system: risk prediction of hospital mortality for critically ill hospitalised adults. *Chest*, 100, 1619–36.

Koepsell, T.D., Wolf, M.E., McCloskey, L., *et al.* (1994). Medical conditions and motor vehicle collision injuries in older adults. *Journal of the American Geriatrics Society*, 42, 695–700.

Milzman, D.P., Boulanger, B.R., Rodriguez, A., Soderstrom, C.A., Mitchell, K.A., and Magnant, C.M. (1992). Pre-existing disease in trauma patients: a predictor of fate independent of age and ISS. *Journal of Trauma*, 32, 236–44.

Office of Population Censuses and Surveys (1993). *1991 Mortality statistics: injury and poisoning: England and Wales*, Series DH4, No. 17. HMSO, London.

Oreskovich, M.R., Howard, J.D., Copass, M.K., and Carrico, C.M. (1984). Geriatric trauma: injury patterns and outcome. *Journal of Trauma*, 24, 565–72.

Rehm, C.G. and Ross, E. (1995). Elderly drivers involved in road crashes: a profile. *American Surgeon*, 61, 435–7.

Roberts, N.A., Barton, R.N., Horan, M.A., and White, A. (1990). Adrenal function after upper femoral fracture in elderly people: persistence of stimulation and the roles of adrenocorticotrophic hormone and immobility. *Age and Ageing*, 12, 70–6.

Shabot, M.M. and Johnson, L.C. (1995). Outcome from critical care in the 'oldest old' trauma patients. *Journal of Trauma*, 39, 254–60.

Shorr, R.M., Rodriguez, A., Indeck, M.C., Crittenden, M.D., Hartunian, S., and Cowley, R.A. (1989). Blunt chest trauma in the elderly. *Journal of Trauma*, 29, 234–7.

Van Aalst, J.A., Morris, J.A., Jr, Yates, H.K., Miller, R.S., and Bass, S.M. (1991). Severely injured geriatric patients return to independent living: a study of factors influencing function and independence. *Journal of Trauma*, 31, 1096–1102.

Watters, J.M., Moulton, S.B., Clancey, S.M., Blakslee, J.M., and Monaghan, R. (1994). Ageing exaggerates glucose intolerance following injury. *Journal of Trauma*, 37, 786–91.

Watters, J.M., Norris, S.B., and Kirkpatrick, S.M. (1997). Endogenous glucose production following injury increases with age. *Journal of Clinical Endocrinology and Metabolism*, 82, 3005–10.

4.3 Pressure ulcers

W. O. Seiler and Hannes B. Stähelin

Introduction

Historical notes

Pressure ulcers, also known as decubitus ulcers or bed sores, have plagued humans since antiquity and have been noted since as far back as ancient Egypt, as exemplified by the large buttock and shoulder ulcers found on the elderly priestess, Amen, of Dynasty XXI (Rowling 1961). Although progress has been made towards understanding the basic pathophysiology and prevention of these ulcers, they remain a very serious health problem, particularly for the elderly population.

Prevalence

Epidemiological studies indicate that approximately 1.5 to 3 million Americans are affected by pressure ulcers. Age and polymorbidity decrease agility and the final result is often immobility, the main risk factor in pressure ulcer formation. The proportions of patients with pressure ulcers in general hospitals (17 per cent), orthopaedic wards (31 per cent), and nursing homes (33 per cent) remain high despite advances in health care. A pressure ulcer will develop during hospital stay in up to 5 per cent of patients admitted to acute care hospitals (Evans *et al.* 1995; Smith 1995).

Economic considerations

The financial cost of pressure ulcers is enormous; for example, in the United States it may exceed $1 billion annually (Maklebust and Sieggreen 1996). Pressure ulcers cause suffering and frustration for patients, their families, and caregivers. More than 17 000 lawsuits related to pressure ulcers are filed annually in the United States, and individual awards have been as high as $4 million (Braun *et al.* 1988).

Physiopathology

Pressure-induced ischaemic skin lesions

All animal biological systems require a continuous and sufficient oxygen supply. The cell's response to a reduction or lack of oxygen depends on its host organ and the location of that organ in the body. Brain and myocardial cells die from lack of oxygen within a few minutes, but skin cells will survive anoxia for about 2 h.

Pressure ulcers are localized necrotic skin lesions caused by a prolonged pressure-induced skin ischaemia when the interface pressure between the patient's body and its supporting surface exceeds the capillary closing pressure. The magnitude and the duration of the interface pressure are the physical determinants in pressure ulcer formation. Prevention strategies focus on these.

Magnitude of the interface pressure

Skin oxygen tension

The pressure on skin areas at which blood flow halts can be demonstrated by means of transcutaneous oxygen tension measurement (Seiler and Stähelin 1979). When the skin site over a bony prominence (e.g. the trochanteric skin area) in a healthy volunteer is loaded by 50 g/cm^2 and 150 g/cm^2, the skin oxygen tension falls from control levels to 50 mmHg (6.6 kPa) and zero respectively. However, if the oxygen tension is measured at a skin site covering a muscle group, it does not fall, even under a load of 175 g/cm^2. Therefore loading the skin area over a bony prominence in healthy subjects to a level exceeding the average capillary pressure of 32 mmHg (4.2 kPa) may lead, after a critical period, to tissue necrosis.

Target interface pressure

The magnitude of the external pressure at which blood flow ceases varies from patient to patient, and within the same patient in different states of health. For example, during dehydration and systemic hypotension, or in frail patients with senile skin atrophy, a smaller amount of interface pressure (<25 mmHg (3.3 kPa)) is sufficient to compress the microcirculation. Therefore the interface pressure of a support system for pressure ulcer prevention in elderly patients should not exceed 25 mmHg (3.3 kPa).

Several factors increase the impact of pressure on the capillaries of the skin microcirculation, including the hardness of the support surface, lack of subcutaneous tissue, site of the pressure, body weight of the patient, nutritional state, and factors affecting skin integrity such as dermatitis or skin atrophy. Among these risk factors only the hardness (Table 1) of the support surface and the site (Table 2) where the pressure impacts on the skin surface are controllable and can be managed for prevention purposes within the necessarily short timespan.

Table 1 Hardness of foam material for pressure ulcer prevention

	CSSC[a]	Interface pressure
Normal hospital mattress	>4.0 kPa	>7.2 kPa (55 mmHg)
Usual foam mattress	>1.8 kPa	>5.6 kPa (43 mmHg)
Special soft foam mattress for prevention purpose	<1.5 kPa	<1.5 kPa (25 mmHg)

[a] Compression stress–strain characteristic (CSSC) according to DIN 53 577 (Anonymous 1989).

To prevent pressure ulcer formation the interface pressure of a patient's support should not exceed 3.3 kPa (25 mmHg) and the CSSC of the mattress should be less than 1.5 kPa. The manufacturers of mattresses for pressure ulcer prevention may indicate these specifications.

Table 2 The five classic pressure ulcer sites and the corresponding causative body position

Ulcer location	Bony prominence	Causative body position[a]
Sacral ulcer	Sacral bone	Supine position
Heel ulcer	Calcanear bone	Supine position
Trochanter ulcer	Trochanteric bone	90° lateral position
Malleolar ulcer	Malleolar bone	90° lateral position
Ischial ulcer	Ischial bone	Sitting position

[a] The location of ulcer formation depends on the body position. Localized pressure is highest on the sacrum and heels in the supine position and on the trochanter in the 90° lateral position. In contrast, none of these five classic ulcer sites is exposed to high interface pressures in the 30° oblique position and skin ischaemia does not occur. Thus the 30° oblique position prevents pressure ulcer formation.

Duration of interface pressure

Normal physiological mobility

The interface pressure has to act for a given time to result in pressure ulcers. The duration of the interface pressure is inversely related to the patient's mobility, and can exceed hours or days in a completely immobile patient. The degree of immobility is not easily recognized or quantified. Mobility is defined as the frequency of voluntary and involuntary movements per unit time. Only the numbers of those spontaneous movements which lead to pressure relief of the sacral skin area (sacral motility score) and the heels are relevant to the prevention of pressure ulcers. The normal physiological motility score of healthy young individuals is approximately four movements per hour during the night, and corresponds to a pressure duration on the sacral area of about 15 min. Each significant body movement interrupts the continuous interface pressure, providing new blood flow to the ischaemic tissue layer. Thus repositioning patients every 15 min avoids pressure ulcer formation even in those at high risk (Seiler *et al.* 1992).

Pathologically decreased mobility

The completely immobile patient does not move during the night, and the sacral motility score is zero movements per 7 h. Thus the interface pressure acts continuously on the same skin area until the patient is mobilized by the nursing staff (e.g. turned into the 30° lateral position). Blood flow ceases in the compressed skin area, producing tissue anoxia and eventually necrosis.

If pressure is continuously applied to skin or soft tissue for a sufficiently long period (normally more than 2 h in healthy subjects) the capillary vessels of the skin microcirculation will collapse and thrombose with fibrin clotting, so that skin ischaemia is irreversible even when the pressure is relieved.

Mobility steadily diminishes with increasing age (Exton-Smith and Sherwin 1961), but the sacral mobility score in healthy elderly people is still sufficiently high (approximately one to two movements per hour) to prevent ulcer formation. Mobility is lowest during sleep when there are no voluntary movements and involuntary movements are significantly reduced. Therefore the risk of formation of decubitus ulcers is significantly increased at night (Seiler *et al.* 1992).

Pressure ulcer risk assessment

Risk factors

Risk factors (predisposing factors) include conditions or diseases which greatly decrease the frequency of voluntary and involuntary movements and which lower the critical arteriolar closing pressure or decrease resistance to interface pressure. Those most frequently seen in elderly patients (Table 3) include fever, coma, cerebrovascular accidents, infections, anaemia, malnutrition, cachexia, oversedation, hypotension, shock, dehydration, surgical intervention, neurological diseases with paralysis, lymphopenia, immobility, decreased body weight, dry sacral skin, and non-blanchable erythema of the sacral skin (Allman *et al.* 1995). Risk factors are the best indicators of risk status. Once they are recognized in a patient, it is crucial to implement a prevention plan without delay.

Pressure ulcer risk assessment scales

Because of the high percentage of elderly patients at risk of pressure ulcers, a formal pressure ulcer risk assessment should be performed on every elderly patient admitted to hospital. Several scales are available to help in identifying a patient's degree of risk for pressure ulcers. Most risk assessment scales are based on the work of Norton (1989). Gosnell (1973) and Braden and Bergstrom (1989) developed risk assessment instruments based on existing scales.

The Norton scale (Norton 1989) consists of five clinical conditions: mental state, physical condition, activity, mobility, and incontinence. Each of the five items is rated and the total score ranges from 5 to 20. The onset of risk is set at a Norton score of 16 or below. The lower the score, the higher is the risk for pressure ulcer formation. The Norton scale is easy to use and serves as a useful documentation of the ulcer risk.

The risk factor tabulation (Table 3), which is based on experience, allows ready identification of patients who are at risk for pressure ulceration.

Table 3 Pressure ulcer risk factors

Immobility[a]
Comatose states
Cerebrovascular accidents
Neurological diseases with paralysis
Surgical intervention, premedication, anaesthesia
Catatonia
Acute depression
Overuse of sedatives and neuroleptics

Arteriolar hypotension[b]
Shock: hypovolaemic, septic, cardiogenic
Dehydration

Oxygen availability[c]
Anaemia, haemoglobin <8 g/dl
Fever >38°C, hypermetabolism
Infections

Malnutrition[d]
Decreased body weight
Cachexia (immobilized by weakness)
Lymphopenia (indicates malnutrition and diminishes immune defence)

Skin conditions[e]
Dry and cracked sacral skin predisposing to skin infections
Moist chapped skin
Non-blanchable erythema of the sacral skin
Senile atrophic skin
Steroid-induced atrophic skin
Microangiopathy in diabetic patients
Skin ischaemia in peripheral vascular disease[b,e]

[a] Risk factors that greatly diminish or prevent involuntary and voluntary bodily movements, thus reducing the patient's mobility score and increasing pressure duration.
[b] Risk factors lowering the threshold of the interface pressure (from 32 mmHg (4.2 kPa) in healthy young subjects to 25 mmHg (3.3 kPa) in the elderly) required to produce anoxia on vulnerable skin areas.
[c] Risk factors that diminish oxygen transport to the cells or increase the metabolic energy requirements of body tissues.
[d] Risk factors that decrease albumin, vitamins, and trace elements which are important in the maintenance of cell resistance to the deleterious effects of pressure.
[e] Risk factors that diminish the resistance of the skin to bacteria, fungi, and infection, thus maintaining bradykinin-induced shunts in the skin microcirculation.

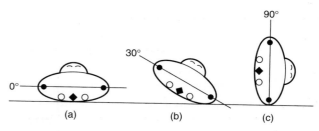

Fig. 1 Optional positioning in pressure ulcer prevention. In the supine position (a) the interface pressure is highest on the skin area over the sacrum (◆) and the heels (○), whereas in the 90° lateral position (c) it is highest on the skin area over the trochanter (●). However, in the 30° oblique position (b) all the sacral, heel, and trochanteric skin areas are pressure relieved.

Ulcer classification

The most widely used classification of pressure ulcers (Table 4) has been proposed by Shea (1975). This classification is easy to learn and has an excellent inter-rater reliability. All stages are based on histopathological studies. Stage I is a non-blanchable erythema of intact skin, the forerunner of skin ulceration. The clinical presentation of stage II also includes epidermal damage ranging from soft tissue swelling, heat, induration, and erythema of unbroken skin to moist, superficial, irregular, or exematous ulceration. Stage III involves full-thickness skin loss associated with extensive tissue necrosis, possibly including damage to muscle or supporting structures such as tendons or joint capsules. In stage IV osteomyelitis is always present.

Prevention

Early identification of risk

Pressure ulcers may form in an elderly patient within 2 h of onset of a risk factor such as a cerebrovascular accident or a fever above 39 °C. The decisive moment to start prevention measures—as soon as risk factors appear—must not be overlooked.

Complete pressure relief: the primary goal

To prevent pressure ulcers in patients at risk, the cause—prolonged continuous pressure localized on skin areas over bony prominences—must be eliminated. This can be achieved by two simple techniques: the static approach of supporting bony prominences on soft foam, and the dynamic approach of 30° oblique positioning (Seiler and Stähelin 1985; Seiler et al. 1986).

The principles of prevention

An effective and timely prevention plan must focus on the mechanisms (the magnitude and duration of the interface pressure) and causes (Table 3). Thus the principles for efficient pressure ulcer prevention are as follows:

(1) managing the magnitude of interface pressure (e.g. reducing the amount of localized pressure on the five classic ulcer sites to below 25 mmHg (3.3 kPa)) by a static prevention method;

Classic ulcer sites

The interface pressure is highest on skin sites over bony prominences. Therefore these sites are the most susceptible to pressure-induced tissue ischaemia and ulcer formation. This was demonstrated using the transcutaneous oxygen tension measurement (Seiler and Stähelin 1979). Thus the classic ulcer sites include the sacral, trochanteric, and ischial bony prominences, the lateral malleolus, and the heels (Table 2). Which of these five skin sites is prone to ulcer formation depends on the body position (Fig. 1); the interface pressure is highest on the sacrum and the heels in the supine position, and on the trochanter in the 90° lateral position. In contrast, none of these five classic ulcer sites is exposed to high interface pressure in the 30° oblique position, and skin ischaemia should not occur (Seiler et al. 1986).

Table 4 Classification of pressure ulcers

Stage I	Non-blanchable erythema of intact skin, considered the precursor of skin ulceration
Stage II	Partial-thickness skin lesion involving the epidermis or dermis or both; the ulcer is superficial and may present clinically as an abrasion, blister, or shallow crater
Stage III	Full-thickness skin loss and damage or necrosis of subcutaneous tissue that may extend to, but not through, underlying fascia, muscles, and tendons but spare the bones
Stage IV	Full-thickness skin loss associated with extensive destruction, tissue necrosis, or damage to muscle, bone, or supporting structures such as tendons or joint capsules; osteomyelitis is present

Based on Shea (1975) and Maklebust and Sieggreen (1996).

(2) managing the duration of interface pressure by frequently turning the patient;

(3) managing additional risk factors by treating or eliminating additional risk factors including malnutrition, fever, infection, dehydration, anaemia, oversedation by neuroleptics or tranquillizers, and serious depression.

A combination of all three methods provides the most effective prevention strategy.

Managing the magnitude of interface pressure

A vast array of aids, special beds, mattresses, and cushions are available to reduce the amount of interface pressure. Pressure-reducing surfaces include foam, gel, water, and air mattresses, alternating pressure pads, low-air-loss, high-air-loss, and oscillating beds, and turning frames and mattresses. However, the usefulness of gel, water, and air mattresses or alternating pressure pads in ulcer healing or for prevention purposes is not certain.

Special beds of the low-air-loss and air-fluidized type are probably the most effective devices for the prevention and treatment of pressure ulcers in selected patients, such as those with large, deep, or multiple sacral ulcers or those undergoing plastic surgery (Evans *et al.* 1995).

Special soft foam material is most frequently used for prevention. The efficacy in preventing ulcer formation depends on the quality of each type of foam mattress. To match a support surface to a particular patient it is necessary to be aware of the special characteristics of each type of pressure-reducing surface (Maklebust and Sieggreen 1996).

Characteristics of special foam material

The hardness of a foam material is quantified using the compression value and the compression stress–strain characteristic (CSSC) according to DIN 53577 (Anonymous 1989) for the hardness testing of foam materials. The standard hospital mattress is generally characterized by a compression value of more than 500 N or a CSSC of more than 4.5 kPa (34.3 mmHg). The interface pressure generated by a standard hospital mattress is greater than 55 mmHg (7.2 kPa) and so easily exceeds the skin arteriolar closing pressure of 25 to 32 mmHg (3.3–4.2 kPa). The transcutaneous oxygen tension of the sacral skin area in a subject lying supine on a standard hospital mattress (Fig. 2) falls to zero (Seiler *et al.* 1983, 1986). Thus the normal hospital mattress induces skin ischaemia in both young and elderly patients. However, ischaemic pain in healthy subjects triggers a spontaneous defence movement, as reflected in the sacral motility score, and protects against ulcer formation. Elderly or sedated patients may not feel the the pain of ischaemia, and the protection provided by spontaneous movement will be inadequate.

The special soft foam mattress for ulcer prevention is characterized by a compression value of less than 200 N and a CSSC of less than 1.5 kPa (11.4 mmHg). The corresponding interface pressure generated by this special foam mattress is less than 25 mmHg (3.3 kPa) and normally will not occlude skin arterioles. To avoid skin ischaemia, even in elderly subjects, the CSSC of a special soft mattress may need to be less than 1.5 kPa (11.4 mmHg). Accordingly, the oxygen tension of the sacral skin area in a subject lying supine on a special soft mattress (Fig. 3) remains normal in about 80 per cent of patients at risk and in nearly 95 per cent of healthy young subjects (Seiler *et al.* 1983, 1986). The remaining 20 per cent of patients with a very high risk for ulceration, i.e. those with polymorbidity and multiple risk factors, are not sufficiently protected by special soft foam supports. To increase the effectiveness of prevention in these patients, the static method has to be combined with the dynamic prevention attained by regular turning.

Managing the duration of interface pressure

Regular turning returns to the patient the benefits of the missing involuntary and voluntary movements. Turning every 2 h reduces the duration of any pressure pattern to below the critical level but places heavy demands on nursing staff. The use of special soft supports or new automatic turning mattresses decreases the frequency of turning required. The frequency of turning should be governed by the appearance of reddened skin areas, which the nursing staff must detect. Manual turning every 2 h places a serious responsibility on staff, as missing just a single turning during the night can initiate a pressure ulcer.

Only the 30° oblique and supine positions should be used; the once common 90° lateral position leads to trochanteric ulcers (Table 2). As already noted, the 30° oblique position relieves pressure on all five classic ulcer sites (sacral, trochanter, heel, ischial, and malleolar) and keeps them normally oxygenated (Seiler *et al.* 1986). The 30° oblique position is well tolerated by elderly patients and can be used in almost any setting.

Continuous automatic turning is easily achieved by using new automatic antidecubitus mattresses. These types of mattresses are useful in situations where the required turning frequency is too high and too time consuming, or when manual turning produces pain or

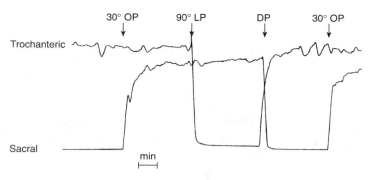

Fig. 2 Transcutaneous oxygen tension as a function of the body position when lying on a normal mattress. The transcutaneous oxygen tension of the sacral skin area rapidly falls to zero when the subject is lying supine (DP) on a normal hospital mattress with a CSSC greater than 4.0 kPa (30.5 mmHg). However, the transcutaneous oxygen tension of the sacral skin area remains normal when the subject is lying in the 30° oblique position (30° OP) even on a normal mattress. The transcutaneous oxygen tension of the trochanteric skin area rapidly falls to zero in the 90° lateral position (90° LP) but remains normal in the supine position (DP) and the 30° oblique position (30° OP).

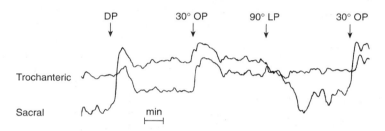

Fig. 3 Transcutaneous oxygen tension as a function of the body position when lying on a special soft mattress. The transcutaneous oxygen tensions of both the sacral skin area and the trochanteric skin area decrease only minimally when the subject is lying supine (DP), in the 30° oblique position (30° OP), or in the 90° lateral position (90° LP) on a special soft mattress with a CSSC less than 1.5 kPa (11.4 mmHg).

interrupts the sleep of high-risk patients. However, turning devices should not be allowed to lull staff into a sense of false security, and nurses must make regular checks to ensure that the equipment is working properly.

Managing additional risk factors

Malnutrition

Malnutrition is documented as promoting ulcer development and impairing wound healing (Pinchcofsky-Devin and Kaminski 1986; Breslow and Bergstrom 1994). It is not easy to measure the nutritional state of patients but the following minimal dataset may be helpful: body mass index, triceps skinfold, leucocyte and lymphocyte counts, haemoglobin, electrolytes, albumin, transferrin, magnesium, zinc, and vitamin B_{12}.

Hypoalbuminaemia, zinc deficiency, and vitamin B12 deficiency are common in acutely ill old people. The plasma albumin level is low in 60 per cent of acutely ill elderly patients and in 85 per cent of polymorbid patients with a pressure ulcer. Hypoalbuminaemia enhances pressure ulcer formation in animal models (Takeda *et al.* 1992).

Zinc deficiency, which slows down wound healing (Agren 1990; Okada *et al.* 1990; Franzen and Ghassemifar 1992; Maitra and Dorani 1992), occurs in 60 per cent of acute elderly patients and in 90 per

cent of patients with a pressure ulcer (Lauber 1995). As a routine procedure, the zinc status in patients with a pressure ulcer should be evaluated and, where appropriate, supplemented.

Vitamin B_{12} deficiency is detectable in about one-third of elderly patients on admission to hospital (Lauber 1995).

Immobility

Immobility, the main cause of ulcer formation, is also a hazard to healing. Therefore it is crucial to mobilize the patient whenever possible. There are several degrees or steps in mobilization including turning every 2 h, sitting in the bed, sitting in a chair, standing beside the bed, and walking.

Treatment

Basis for ulcer therapy

The treatment plan must be based on the pathophysiological findings which impair wound healing (Seiler and Stähelin 1994). Ulcers can only heal if normal physiological wound conditions are restored as far as possible. As healing will not proceed without an adequate blood supply, measures that permit improvement of the microcirculation are crucial. Optimal blood supply to the ulcer tissue is mainly attained

Table 5 Appropriate positioning for therapy of pressure ulcers depending on the ulcer location

Ulcer location	Appropriate positioning	Positioning to avoid
Sacral ulcer	Right 30° oblique position Left 30° oblique position	Supine position 90° lateral positions
Heel ulcer	Right 30° oblique position Left 30° oblique position	Supine position 90° lateral positions
Trochanter ulcer, left side	Right 30° oblique position Supine position	90° lateral position, left 30° oblique position, left
Trochanter ulcer, right side	30° oblique position, left Supine position	90° lateral position, right 30° oblique position, right
Malleolar ulcer, left side	30° oblique position, right Supine position	90° lateral position, left 30° oblique position, left
Malleolar ulcer, right side	30° oblique position, left Supine position	90° lateral position, right 30° oblique position, right
Ischial ulcer	30° oblique position, left 30° oblique position, right Supine position	Sitting position

The position in which the ulcer forms is called the causative body position. It should be avoided in ulcer therapy.

by permanent decompression of the ulcer vasculature. Local infection and necrotic tissue hinder the growth of clean red granulation tissue. Newly formed granulation tissue should be protected from reinfection, desiccation, and trauma during changing of wound dressings. Additional individual risk factors (Table 3) must be treated.

Appropriate positioning for pressure ulcer therapy is shown in Table 5.

Treatment through five therapeutic principles

Based on pathophysiological findings, five treatment principles (Table 6) have been established (Seiler and Stähelin 1989):

(1) complete pressure relief;
(2) debridement of necrotic tissue;
(3) treatment of local infection by systemic antibiotics;
(4) wet wound dressings using Ringer's solution;
(5) elimination of risk factors and evaluation of surgical intervention.

There are two further optional principles:

(6) consideration of plastic surgery in patients with stage III and IV ulcers;
(7) local application of growth factors if their efficacy is proved.

Complete pressure relief

Complete pressure relief is the best way of improving tissue blood supply and oxygenation and is essential for ulcer healing. It can be achieved as described above by using a combination of soft mattresses and regular turning. Specialized beds of the air-loss type are needed in the treatment of stage III and IV ulcers and after plastic surgery.

Debridement

Necrotic tissue should be debrided, except in heel ulcers, by either surgical intervention or enzymatic necrolysis. Necrotic tissue creates favourable conditions for growth of bacteria, specifically anaerobic organisms, and prevents development of granulation tissue. Epithelialization does not occur in the presence of necrotic tissue. A necrotic crust may obscure a purulent infection and penetrate into deeper skin layers causing osteomyelitis, bacteraemia, or sepsis.

Heel ulcers (Fig. 4) with a black necrotic crust need special consideration when a pre-existing arterial obstructive disease impairs the blood circulation. Surgical debridement should not be undertaken before peripheral arterial obstructive disease has been excluded or the arterial blood supply has been improved by surgical intervention.

Managing local infection

Local infection is a frequent complication in ischaemic ulcer tissue. Because bacterial infection delays ulcer healing, its treatment is important. True infection presents with the classic signs including reddening and warmth of the surrounding skin, pain, fever, leucocytosis, and elevated C-reactive protein levels. Bacterial colonization of an ulcer surface is inevitable, and identification of organisms causing surrounding infection may require tissue aspiration or biopsy.

If true infection has been diagnosed, systemic antibiotic treatment may be started based on sensitivity tests. Local disinfectant agents are of no value; they damage the granulation tissue and, at times, impair the body's own immunological defence mechanisms in the locally secreted IgA, lymphocytes, macrophages, leucocytes, and growth factors in the wound fluid. A permanent moist wound dressing is the best method of cleaning the ulcer surface.

Table 6 The five treatment principles[a]

Principle	Aims	Measures
1	Complete pressure relief Interface pressure zero	Positioning on soft supports Turning into the 30° lateral position Turning every 2 h
2	Ulcer cleaning Prevention of infection	Surgical debridement Enzymatic debridement Permanent wet dressing
3	Treatment of local infection Prevention of sepsis	Diagnosis of local infection Systemic antibiotic therapy
4	Permanent wet ulcer surface Ulcer cleaning Enhancement of granulation	Permanent wet dressing Use of Ringer's solution Dressing change three to four times daily
5	Elimination of risk factors	Listing individual risk factors Adequate measures for elimination

[a] There are two additional optional principles: consideration of plastic surgery in patients with Stage III and IV ulcers, and local application of growth factors when their efficacy is proved.

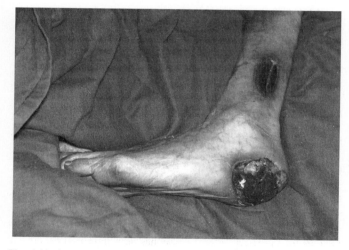

Fig. 4 Heel pressure ulcer with a black necrotic crust. These ulcers need special consideration when a pre-existing arterial obstructive disease impairs the blood circulation. Surgical debridement should not be undertaken before exclusion of a peripheral arterial obstructive disease and improvement of the arterial blood supply by a reconstructive surgical intervention.

Moist wound dressing

Pathophysiological studies of wound healing have demonstrated that wounds heal more rapidly under a suitable moist wound dressing than under the typical dry eschar produced by exposure (Winter 1971), and that wound repair is improved when the ulcer and surrounding tissue can take up oxygen and expel carbon dioxide. These findings indicate that all wound covers should be freely gas permeable. Furthermore, epithelial cells migrate only in a moist environment and achieve optimal mitotic activity under dressing material that maintains a temperature about equal to the body temperature (Lawrence 1982). Therefore the role of a dressing is to protect healing ulcers from mechanical damage, drying and cooling, and external bacterial recontamination. In this setting, there is usually no need for dressings containing potential allergenic agents (e.g. dyes, antibiotics, perfumes, volatile oils) or cytotoxins (e.g. local disinfectants, metals, acidifying agents). Adherent substances (e.g. ointments, powders, pastes) also have no place in decubitus ulcer treatment. At this point in the treatment, which is a long-term process, it is most important not to interfere with normal healing. Ringer's solution (155.5 mmol Na^+, 0.275 mmol Ca^{2+}, 0.4 mmol K^+, 16.35 mmol Cl^-, and 0.1 mmol HCO_3^- per 100 ml) is the most effective of all local treatments. It permits fibroblasts to survive *in vitro* for several days whereas physiological NaCl (0.9 per cent) does not (Kallenberg *et al.* 1970). Dressings kept moist with Ringer's solution create a microclimate-like tissue-culture for new granulation.

The practical management of ulcers deeper than 2 mm includes rinsing with Ringer's solution, inspection for signs of infection, and covering with a thin (2-mm) gauze compress soaked in Ringer's solution. The dressing must always be kept wet. However, if serious infection is present, systemic antibiotic treatment may be started.

Superficial ulcers (less than 2 mm deep) are usually sufficiently revascularized and therefore are clean, granulating, and oxygenated. Here, the role of the dressing is to protect the continuously formed granulations without traumatizing them during dressing changes. This is best achieved by using a very thin paraffin gauze dressing (less than 1 mm thick). Additional measures are not needed, except to check frequently that principles (1), (2), and (3) are being followed.

Elimination of additional risk factors

Patients should be mobilized as much as possible and malnutrition corrected. Almost all patients with a decubitus ulcer have low levels of plasma zinc, albumin, and transferrin. There is often serious vitamin and trace element deficiency. Adequate daily nutrition includes 1.5 g protein per kilogram body weight, 40 cal per kilogram body weight, multivitamins, and trace elements. If dehydration, hypovolaemia, and anaemia are not corrected, wound healing may be hindered.

Optional treatment principles

Plastic surgery is needed in patients with a stage III or IV ulcer, because wound healing may not occur even with the best conservative treatment.

In the future, the topical application of growth factors may be used to enhance wound healing. Transforming growth factor-β seems to be an effective candidate. However, clinical studies confirming the efficacy of growth factors are still needed.

Summary

The number of patients with pressure ulcers in general hospitals (17 per cent), orthopaedic wards (31 per cent), and nursing homes (33 per cent) remains high despite advances in health care that extend life. The magnitude and duration of the interface pressure between the body surface and the supporting surface are the physical determinants in the formation of pressure ulcers. The pressure at which blood flow ceases varies from patient to patient, as well as in the same patient in different states of health. During dehydration and systemic hypotension, or in frail patients with skin atrophy, an interface pressure of less than 25 mmHg (3.3 kPa) is sufficient to compress the microcirculation and cause ulcers. Therefore the interface pressure of a support system for pressure ulcer prevention in elderly patients should not exceed 25 mmHg (3.3 kPa).

The duration of the interface pressure is inversely related to the patient's mobility, and may exceed hours or days in a completely immobile patient. The degree of immobility is not easily recognized or quantified. The normal physiological mobility score of healthy young individuals is approximately four movements per hour during the night, corresponding to a pressure duration on the sacral area of about 15 min. Thus repositioning patients at risk every 15 min absolutely precludes pressure ulcer formation, even in those at high risk. Prolonged continuous pressure localized on skin areas over bony prominences can be eliminated by by using soft foam supports and 30° oblique positioning to reduce both the amount and duration of interface pressure.

Ulcers can heal only if optimal wound conditions are maintained. Five treatment principles have been established: complete pressure relief, debridement of necrotic tissue (except in heel ulcers), treatment of local infection by systemic antibiotics, moist wound dressings using Ringer's solution, and elimination of risk factors and evaluation of surgical intervention.

The pressure ulcer problem is widely overlooked by medical authorities, and therefore the medical field is poorly equipped to handle it. Advances in research and in practicable application of preventive methods are needed, and the findings should be included in teaching manuals for physicians and caregivers.

References

Agren, M.S. (1990). Studies on zinc in wound healing. *Acta Dermato-Venereologica (Supplement)* 154, 1–36.

Allman, R.M., Goode, P.S., Patrick, M.M., Burst, N., and Bartolucci, A. (1995). Pressure ulcer risk factors among hospitalized patients with activity limitation. *Journal of the American Medical Association*, 273, 865–71.

Anonymous (1989). *DIN-Taschenbuch Nr. 235: Schaumstoffe: Prüfung, Anforderung, Anwendung.* Beuth Verlag, Berlin.

Braden, B.J. and Bergstrom, N. (1989). Clinical utility of the Braden scale for predicting pressuure sore risk. *Decubitus*, 2, 44–51.

Braun, J.L., Silvetti, A.N., and Xakellis, G.C. (1988). Decubitus ulcers: what really works? *Patient Care*, 22, 22–34.

Breslow, R.A. and Bergstrom, N. (1994). Nutritional prediction of pressure ulcers. *Journal of the American Dietetic Association*, 94, 1301–4.

Evans, J.M., Andrews, K.L., Chutka, D.S., Fleming, K.C. and Garness, S.L. (1995). Pressure ulcers: prevention and management. *Mayo Clinic Proceedings*, 70, 788–99.

Exton-Smith, A.N. and Sherwin, R.W. (1961). The prevention of pressure sores: the significance of spontaneous bodily movements. *Lancet*, ii, 1124–6.

Franzen, L.E. and Ghassemifar, M.R. (1992). Connective tissue repair in zinc deficiency. An ultrastructural morphometric study in perforated mesentery in rats. *European Journal of Surgery*, 158, 333–7.

Gosnell, D.J. (1973). An assessment tool to identify pressure sore risk. *Nursing Research*, 22, 55–61.

Kallenberg, A., Roth, W., and Ledermann, M. (1970). Experimentelle und bakteriologische Untersuchungen zur Wahl des Spülmuttels für die antibakterielle Spüldrainage. In *Die posttraumatische Osteomyelitis* (ed. G. Hierholzer and J. Rehn), pp. 265–74. Schattauer, New York.

Lauber, C. (1995). Malnutrition in geriatric acute patients. Doctoral Thesis, Medical Faculty, Basel University, Switzerland.

Lawrence, J.C. (1982). What materials for dressings? *Injury*, 13, 500–12.

Maitra, A.K. and Dorani, B. (1992). Role of zinc in post-injury wound healing. *Archives of Emergency Medicine*, 9, 122–4.

Maklebust, J. and Sieggreen, M. (ed.) (1996). *Pressure ulcers. Guidelines for prevention and nursing management.* SN Publications, West Dundee, IL.

Norton, D. (1989). Calculating the risk: reflections on Norton scale. *Decubitus*, 2, 23–31.

Okada, A., Takagi, Y., Nezu, R., and Lee, S. (1990). Zinc in clinical surgery: a research review. *Japanese Journal of Surgery*, 20, 635–44.

Pinchcofsky-Devin, G.D. and Kaminski, M.V. (1986). Correlation of pressure sores and nutritional status. *Journal of the American Geriatrics Society*, 34, 435–40.

Rowling, J.T. (1961). Pathological changes in mummies. *Proceedings of the Royal Society of Medicine*, 54, 409–15.

Seiler, W.O. and Stähelin, H.B. (1979). Skin oxygen tension as a function of imposed skin pressure: implication for decubitus ulcer formation. *Journal of the American Geriatrics Society*, 27, 298–301.

Seiler, W.O. and Stähelin, H.B. (1985). Decubitus ulcers: prevention techniques for the elderly patient. *Geriatrics*, 40, 53–60.

Seiler, W.O. and Stähelin, H.B. (1989). Decubitus ulcers in the elderly. In *Principles and practice of nursing home care* (ed. P.R. Katz and E. Calkins), pp. 328–48. Springer, New York.

Seiler, W.O. and Stähelin, H.B. (1994). Identification of factors that impair wound healing: a possible approach to wound healing research. *Wounds*, 6, 101–6.

Seiler, W.O., Allen, S.R., and Stähelin, H.B. (1983). Decubitus ulcer prevention: new investigative method using transcutaneous oxygen tension measurement. *Journal of the American Geriatrics Society*, 33, 786–9.

Seiler, W.O., Allen, S., and Stähelin, H.B. (1986). Influence of the 30° laterally inclined position and the 'super-soft' 3-piece mattress on skin oxygen tension on areas of maximum pressure. Implications for pressure sore prevention. *Gerontology*, 32, 158–66.

Seiler, W.O., Stähelin, H.B., and Stoffel, F. (1992). Recordings of movement leading to pressure relief of the sacral skin region: identification of patients at risk for pressure ulcer development. *Wounds*, **4**, 256–61.

Shea, J.D. (1975). Pressure sores: Classification and management. *Clinical Orthopaedics and Related Research*, **112**, 90–100.

Smith, D.M. (1995). Pressure ulcers in the nursing home. *Annals of Internal Medicine*, **123**, 433–42.

Takeda, T., Koyama, T., Izawa, Y., Makita, T., and Nakamura, N. (1992). Effects of malnutrition on development of experimental pressure sores. *Journal of Dermatology*, **19**, 602–9.

Winter, G.D. (1971). Healing of skin wounds and the influence of dressings in the repair process. In *Surgical dressings and wound healing* (ed. K.J. Harkiss), pp. 46–60. Bradford University Press–Crosby Lockwood, London.

4.4 Falls and syncope

R. A. Kenny

Introduction

Falls by elderly people primarily occur because increasing frailty and comorbidity make avoidance of extrinsic environmental hazards more difficult. The reported incidence of falls varies with the population studied (community dwelling, hospital patients, or in long-term institutions) and the methods of ascertaining falls. There are also important differences in the frequency of falls in relation to age and sex.

The most important problem concerning falls by elderly people is not simply the high incidence, since young children and athletes suffer a higher incidence of falls than all but the frailest older person, but rather the high incidence together with a high susceptibility to injury. This liability to fall-related injury is due to the high prevalence of clinical diseases such as osteoporosis and of age-associated physiological changes such as slow protective reflexes. Under certain circumstances these make even a mild fall dangerous. Other serious consequences include loss of confidence, functional decline, and institutionalization. If falls are to be prevented, attention must be paid to identifying and reducing fall risk factors as well as providing focused and multidisciplinary assessment and diagnosis.

Epidemiology

In a year, 30 per cent of people aged over 65 years in the community fall; 18 per cent fall once and 12 per cent fall twice or more. Incidence rates are up to 41.4 falls per 1000 person-months (O'Loughlin *et al.* 1993). However, annual incidence rates vary considerably in community-based series, ranging from 217 to 1630 per 1000 persons at risk. Similarly, hospital-based surveys report annual incidence rates varying from 380 to 2900 per 1000 persons at risk in acute and chronic medical and geriatric facilities. This figure increases up to annual rates of 3700 per 1000 persons at risk in psychiatric facilities

for older people (Robbins *et al.*1989). Fall rates are similarly high in institutions, where 10 to 25 per cent will have a serious fall each year (Rubenstein *et al.*1990). The mean incidence is 1.5 falls per bed per year (range 0.2–3.6 falls) (Rubenstein *et al.* 1994).

The variation in fall frequency rates is primarily attributable to methods of ascertainment; for example, regular chart review in a nursing home setting identifies more fall events than appear in incident reports, and both methods give underestimates compared with self-reports of falls (Kantern *et al.* 1993). Self-reporting is also the most accurate method of data ascertainment for hip, wrist, and humeral fractures—the most important fractures caused by falling.

In comparisons of data from patient interviews, staff questionnaires, medical and nursing notes, and accident report forms, patient and staff versions of in-hospital falls often differ widely. In addition, up to 80 per cent of accidents in hospitals and institutions are unwitnessed. Therefore, where possible, the incidence of falls should be based on self-reported events. Even patient recall is not without error; patients recall falls and injuries during the previous 12 months well, but are less accurate for recall periods of 3 and 6 months.

Although the incidence of home accidents is high, few events are reported to medical services (Graham and Firth 1992). Family practitioners are the main contact for patients who report home accidents, and primary care workers have important opportunities for advising elderly people on the prevention of accidents in the home. Awareness of falls can be increased by asking the patient about falls in the previous year and by documenting all reported and recalled falls.

Most falls occur indoors. In institutions over half of falls occur in bedrooms or bathrooms. Apart from ground frost, there is no significant association between prevailing weather conditions and no seasonal variation. In a large series of over 60 000 consecutive adult attendances at an accident and emergency department (Richardson

Table 1 Types of falls by cognitively normal people

Explained fall	Fall resulting from a simple slip, trip, or environmental hazard
Unexplained fall	No apparent cause of the fall
Recurrent fall	Three or more falls (including the index fall) within 2 years
Explained loss of consciousness	Myocardial infarction, stroke, haemorrhage, overdose, status epilepticus, etc.
Unexplained loss of consciousness	Loss of consciousness remains unexplained after routine investigation

et al. 1997) there was no seasonal variation in the proportion presenting with falls; over 85 per cent of falls presented between 8.00 a.m. and 8.00 p.m.

Definition

A fall is an event whereby an individual comes to rest on the ground or another lower level with or without loss of consciousness. Falls have traditionally been described as extrinsic, due to environmental hazards, or intrinsic, due to age-associated physiological changes and/ or clinical disorders. Most falls, particularly of very elderly people, are due to a combination of intrinsic and extrinsic factors. Because presyncope and syncope can cause 'unexplained' falls and because of the frequent overlap of falls and syncope, the presence or absence of loss of consciousness has now been incorporated into the definition.

In patients who are cognitively normal, falls can be classified according to their clinical characteristics. If a patient has tripped or slipped, the fall is 'accidental'. If a patient has fallen and/or lost consciousness for no apparent reason, the episode is described as an 'unexplained' fall. Recurrent falls are defined as three or more falls in the previous 12 months, and intrinsic causes of recurrent and unexplained falls are often similar. Table 1 defines the classification of falls in older adults who are not cognitively impaired.

Causes

There have been many attempts to determine the causes of falling by elderly people. Unfortunately, comparisons between studies are limited because of the differences noted above in the populations examined, the approaches to assessment and investigation, and the definitions of diagnoses.

Multiple pathology and comorbidity are common in later life. There is frequently more than one possible diagnosis for the cause of falls or for a tendency to fall. Therefore it is important to differentiate between an 'attributable diagnosis' and an 'associated diagnosis'. In our studies we have only attributed diagnosis if a specific procedure reproduces symptoms and/or clinical signs or if a specific intervention alleviates the symptoms. If a cause cannot be attributed to a fall, diagnoses are considered to be 'associated'. Rubenstein and Josephson (1996) have reviewed 12 studies, of which six were conducted in institutionalized populations and six in community-dwelling populations. The fall incidence and the distribution of causes of falls clearly differed between the different populations. Frail high-risk populations had a higher incidence of all types of falls,

Table 2 Causes of falls by elderly adults

Cause	Mean (range) (%)	
'Accident'/environment related	31	(1–53)
Gait balance disorders or weakness	17	(4–39)
Dizziness, vertigo	13	(0–30)
Drop attack	9	(0–52)
Confusion	5	(0–14)
Postural hypotension	3	(0–24)
Visual disorder	2	(0–5)
Syncope	0.3	(0–3)
Other specified causes	15	(2–39)
Unknown	5	(0–21)

Data from Rubenstein and Josephson (1996).

particularly those related to disease, than was reported in healthier populations (Table 2).

Environment-related falls are more common in community-living populations than in institutions. The most common environmental factors resulting in falls include poor lighting, ill-fitting carpets and rugs, doorsteps, poorly arranged furniture, children's toys on the floor, and lack of support equipment on the stairs or at the bedside. Accidental falls, which account for 25 to 45 per cent of falls in the community, are due to environmental hazards, sometimes complicated by gait imbalance, poor vision, musculoskeletal abnormalities, impaired postural control, impaired postural reflexes, poor memory, or impaired hearing. Ageing can be associated with impaired responses for adapting to sudden changes in orientation. With advancing years there is a reduction in the ability to adapt to sudden horizontal displacement by rapid adjustment of the hip or by stepping backwards or forwards. Falls may be associated with orthostatic changes (getting out of bed, toileting at night, standing at a wash hand basin, or standing after meals), but it is likely that some of these falls are due to a combination of neurocardiovascular instability and environmental hazards.

Gait disorders can be attributed to age-associated physiological changes and various underlying disorders which increase with ageing

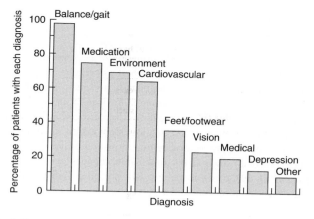

Fig. 1 Proportion of patients with diagnoses which might be attributable causes of falls in cognitively impaired elderly people attending an accident and emergency department because of a fall.

Table 3 Possible causes of unexplained falls or unexplained syncope by adults aged over 50 years attending an accident and emergency department because of a fall ($n = 20\,000$)

Cause	Percentage
Accidental (extrinsic)	38
Medical diagnoses: transient ischaemic attack, stroke, cardiac infarct, epilepsy	25
Cognitive impairment	17
Unexplained	15
Gait/balance	48
Medication	43
Visual impairment	22
Depression	35
Neurocardiovascular instability	82
Carotid sinus syndrome	49
Orthostatic hypotension	15
Vasovagal syndrome	18
Arrhythmia	6

(e.g. stroke, Parkinson's disease, arthritis). Inactivity can cause significant neuromuscular deconditioning. The prevalence of lower-limb weakness increases with advancing years, and has been reported to affect 48 per cent of elderly people in the community, 57 per cent of people in residential facilities (Tinetti *et al.* 1986), and 80 per cent of nursing home residents (Robbins *et al.* 1989). Most studies report an abnormality of gait or balance in 20 to 50 per cent of older patients, with a higher prevalence in fallers (Nevitt *et al.* 1989; Robbins *et al.* 1989).

Gait and balance disorders are an associated diagnosis in 45 per cent of cognitively normal and almost all cognitively impaired adults attending an accident and emergency department because of a fall. Other associated causes are detailed in Fig. 1 (Shaw and Kenny 1997) and Table 3.

An important intrinsic cause of falls, particularly unexplained falls with or without loss of consciousness, is neurocardiovascular instability. The main clinical diagnoses included in this broad category are carotid sinus hypersensitivity, orthostatic hypotension, vasovagal or neurocardiogenic syncope, and postprandial hypotension.

Overlap with syncope

The traditional definitions of syncope and falls treat them as separate conditions with different aetiologies. More recently, evidence has accumulated of an overlap between them. Separation of falls and syncope into two distinct entities relies on an accurate history of the event and an eye-witness account. These are unavailable for at least one-third of older patients who have experienced falls or syncope. In one study of 354 community-dwelling elderly people, of whom 80 per cent were aged between 60 and 80 years and 92 per cent had normal cognitive function, over one-third did not recall having fallen 3 months after a documented fall event. This was despite the event having been reinforced by a health visitor calling shortly afterwards (Cummings *et al.* 1988). Similarly, witness accounts of syncopal events were only available in 40 to 60 per cent of elderly people attending a syncope clinic with recurrent symptoms (McIntosh *et al.* 1993*a*).

The overlap can be demonstrated in young as well as old subjects. In one study (Lempert *et al.* 1994), syncope was induced in 56 of 59 young healthy volunteers by a sequence of hyperventilation, orthostatic change, and Valsalva manoeuvre. Thirteen subjects (25 per cent) fell but preserved consciousness. One subject had amnesia and unresponsiveness without falling. The remainder lost consciousness, fell, had myoclonic activity, and recalled losing consciousness.

An experimental demonstration of the scope for overlap of falls and syncope can be seen in cardio-inhibitory carotid sinus syndrome. Asystole can be induced in patients with a hypersensitive response by carotid sinus massage during head-up tilting. One-third of patients lose consciousness (as witnessed by laboratory staff) during asystole but deny this afterwards, thus demonstrating amnesia for loss of consciousness (Kenny and Traynor 1991). From a review of three studies which included a total of 109 patients for whom cardio-inhibitory carotid sinus syndrome was an attributable cause of falls, 38 per cent of patients presented with falls alone or falls and dizziness but denied syncope. Of the fallers, 51 per cent demonstrated amnesia for loss of consciousness. Two-thirds of patients with orthostatic hypotension as the attributable cause of symptoms also presented with falls only or with falls and dizziness (Ward and Kenny 1996; Stout and Kenny 1998). Of 169 patients who attended a dedicated syncope and falls clinic, over one-third presented with a history of unexplained falls; two-thirds of these had an attributable cardiovascular diagnosis, of which the majority were carotid sinus hypersensitivity, orthostatic hypotension, cardiac arrhythmia, or vasovagal syncope (McIntosh *et al.* 1993*a*).

Drop attacks

Falls are termed drop attacks when the cause is not certain, the event is unexpected, and there is no apparent loss of consciousness. The initial accounts of drop attacks in elderly subjects were detailed by

Sheldon (1960), who noted the dramatic suddenness of the event, without alteration in alertness, an inability to regain upright posture immediately afterwards, and a preponderance of women. Since then, most reports on the epidemiology of falls have included drop attacks as one of the important causes of falls by elderly people.

The incidence of drop attacks increases with age. A survey of 12 studies comprising 3684 falls (Rubenstein and Josephson 1996) estimated that 9 per cent (range 0–52 per cent) were due to drop attacks. In a study of falls among a random sample of elderly subjects aged over 65 years, the proportion due to drop attacks increased from 2 per cent in those aged between 65 and 74 years to 15 per cent in subjects aged over 90 years (Campbell et al. 1981).

Brainstem ischaemia remains the most widely accepted likely pathology for drop attacks, although few studies have reproduced symptoms during ischaemic episodes. Various pathological states which implicate the vertebrobasilar circulation have been causally related to drop attacks. The most important of these are tumours compromising brainstem blood supply, compression of the vertebral arteries by cervical osteophytes in cervical spondylosis, and atherosclerotic vertebrobasilar insufficiency (Kubala and Millikan 1964). In a large series of 1970 patients with cerebrovascular insufficiency, 8 per cent of 373 with intermittent vertebrobasilar disease presented with drop attacks (Meissner et al. 1986).

Amnesia for loss of consciousness may be partially or wholly responsible for syncope presenting as drop attacks in older subjects. The higher incidence with increasing age may be due to altered cerebral autoregulation, reduced cerebral perfusion, and lower thresholds for cerebral hypoperfusion. Absence of a prodrome prior to syncope may further complicate the clinical presentation (Ward and Kenny 1996). The fall in blood pressure may be too fast to produce a prodrome. Interventions which slow down the rate of decline in blood pressure have been shown to convert drop attacks to syncope with a well-recognized prodrome of dizziness (Ward and Kenny 1996).

Transient neuronal dysfunction has also been proposed as a causal factor in some series. Drop attacks in children are typically due to epilepsy, but atypical epilepsy is a rare cause of drop attacks in elderly subjects. Labyrinthine and vestibulo-ocular dysfunction leading to erroneous correction of posture has also been postulated as one of the less likely causes of drop attacks in adults. In the largest series on adult drop attacks (Kubala and Millikan 1964) 64 per cent of 108 cases (mean age 70 years) remained undiagnosed. Most patients who had epilepsy as an attributable cause were aged less than 40. A substantial number of undiagnosed patients had hypertension (41 per cent) and heart disease (25 per cent). This study predated recent publications on the importance of baroreflex control in unexplained falls and standardized tests of baroreflex assessment for patients with drop attacks.

More recently, episodic hypotension and/or bradycardia, mediated by altered baroreflexes, have been reported as common attributable causes of drop attacks in elderly people. These conditions (neurocardiogenic syncope, carotid sinus syndrome, and orthostatic hypotension) produce global cerebral ischaemia and may be manifest as drop attacks rather than as the more classical syncope. In a recent prospective series (Dey et al. 1996), 35 consecutive elderly patients with recurrent drop attacks were investigated in detail, including cardiovascular testing. A diagnosis was attributed to an abnormality only when symptoms were reproduced during investigation and alleviated after specific intervention. Episodic bradycardia or hypotension was diagnosed in 24 patients, carotid sinus syndrome in 18,

orthostatic hypotension in five, and vasovagal syncope in one. Seven of the ten remaining patients for whom no attributable diagnosis was made also had underlying cardiovascular pathology.

Elderly people are particularly prone to syncope because of age-associated physiological changes in cerebral autoregulation, baroreflex sensitivity, intravascular volume regulation, and neurohumoral control. Why elderly patients have amnesia for loss of consciousness is unclear; it may be due to mild cognitive impairment, age-associated impairment of cerebral autoregulation, paradoxical cerebral vasoconstriction during provocative testing, impaired postural control of balance control during mild haemodynamic changes, or other reasons (Lipsitz et al. 1985b). Syncope and falls are often indistinguishable and are manifestations of similar pathophysiological processes.

Syncope

The epidemiology of syncope in old age has not been well studied and accurate estimates of prevalence and incidence are not available. The elucidation of syncope is often complicated by the presence of multiple disorders that may cause it synergistically and by difficulties in determining a relationship between circumstances, medications, and symptoms. Available data suggest that syncope accounts for 3 per cent of emergency room attendances and 1 per cent of medical admissions to a general hospital (Day et al. 1982). In a study of 711 elderly subjects (mean age 87 years) living in a chronic care facility, the prevalence of syncope was reported to be 23 per cent over a 10-year period, with an annual incidence of 6 per cent and a recurrence rate of 30 per cent over a 2-year prospective follow-up (Lipsitz et al. 1985b). This is undoubtedly an underestimate because falls were excluded.

A cause of syncope could not be determined for over 40 per cent of 210 community-dwelling elderly patients (Kapoor et al. 1986). Syncope due to a cardiac cause was associated with higher mortalities irrespective of age. In patients with a non-cardiac or unknown cause of syncope, older age, a history of congestive cardiac failure, and male sex were important predictors of mortality. This study predated the establishment of standardized tests for baroreflex sensitivity, and did not specifically investigate all patients for neurocardiovascular abnormalities.

The temporary cessation of cerebral function that causes syncope results from transient and sudden reduction of blood flow to parts of the brain, such as the reticular activating system of the brainstem, responsible for consciousness. Age-associated physiological impairments in heart rate, blood pressure, and cerebral blood flow, combined with comorbid conditions and concurrent medications, account for the increased prevalence of syncope in elderly subjects. Baroreflex sensitivity is blunted with ageing, manifesting as a reduction in the heart rate response to hypotensive stimuli. Elderly people are prone to reduced blood volume due to excessive salt loss through the kidneys as a result of a decline in plasma renin and aldosterone, a rise in atrial natriuretic peptide, and diuretic therapy. Low blood volume together with age-associated diastolic dysfunction can lead to a low cardiac output which increases susceptibility to orthostatic hypotension and vasovagal syncope. Cerebral autoregulation, which maintains a constant cerebral circulation over a wide range of blood pressure, is altered in the presence of hypertension and possibly by ageing. As a result, sudden mild to moderate declines in peripheral

Table 4 Aetiology of syncope in elderly patients

Cardiac arrhythmia
    Bradyarrhythmia: sick sinus syndrome, high atrioventricular block
    Tachyarrhythmia: supraventricular, ventricular

Neurocardiogenic syncope
    Vasovagal syncope
    Situational syncope
    Micturition syncope
    Defecation syncope
    Cough syncope

Orthostatic hypotension

Carotid sinus syndrome

Drug-induced syncope

Postprandial syncope

Syncope associated with low cardiac output
    Myocardial infarction
    Pulmonary embolism
    Aortic stenosis, mitral stenosis
    Hypertrophic cardiomyopathy
    Pulmonary hypertension

Hyperventilation syncope

Swallow syncope

Glossopharyngeal syncope

Subclavian steal syndrome

Transient ischaemic attack

Epilepsy

blood pressure can affect cerebral blood flow markedly. Causes of syncope are detailed in Table 4.

Carotid sinus syndrome

Carotid sinus syndrome is an important but frequently overlooked cause of syncope and presyncope in elderly people. It is characterized by episodic bradycardia and/or hypotension resulting from exaggerated baroreceptor-mediated reflexes or carotid sinus hypersensitivity. The syndrome is diagnosed in subjects with unexplained symptoms when 5 s of carotid sinus massage produces asystole exceeding 3 s (cardio-inhibitory), or a fall in systolic blood pressure exceeding 50 mmHg (6.6 kPa) in the absence of cardio-inhibition (vasodepressor), or a combination of the two (mixed).

The afferent limb of the carotid sinus reflex terminates at the nucleus of the tractus solitarius in the medulla. The efferent limb comprises the sympathetic nerves supplying the heart, the vasculature, and the cardiac vagus nerve. Physiological rises in arterial blood pressure generate the stretch necessary to activate the reflex. In health, the carotid baroreceptors in conjunction with those of the aortic arch play a major role in the neural control of blood pressure. In patients with carotid sinus syndrome, baroreflex sensitivity, which normally declines with increasing age, is enhanced compared with age-matched

controls (Dehn *et al.* 1984). The site and mechanism of this hypersensitivity are not known, but may be central (O'Mahony 1995).

Atropine in a dose up to 700 μg can abolish bradycardia in all patients. Carotid sinus syndrome and sick sinus syndrome are two separate diagnostic entities, although up to 5 per cent of patients with carotid sinus syndrome can have abnormal intrinsic sinus node function (Morley *et al.* 1983). It is possible that carotid sinus syndrome results from a central abnormality of baroreflex gain. The frequent association of carotid sinus syndrome with atherosclerotic comorbidities has led to speculation that cerebral and/or cardiac ischaemia may play an important role in its pathogenesis (Morley *et al.* 1983).

The prevalence of carotid sinus reflex hypersensitivity in asymptomatic individuals is not known. However, it definitely increases with age and is rare in patients with syncope or falls who are aged less than 50 years. Recent studies suggest that it is not a feature of normal ageing. In a study of 25 healthy elderly subjects, none developed diagnostic or symptomatic cardio-inhibition or vasodepression during carotid sinus massage (McIntosh *et al.* 1994a). In another series, abnormal cardio-inhibition was reported in 2 per cent of 288 healthy subjects (age range 17–84 years) (Brignole *et al.* 1985). Carotid sinus hypersensitivity was demonstrated in 19 per cent of 1000 patients (aged over 50 years) who presented to an accident and emergency department with 'unexplained falls', and the prevalence increased to 21 per cent and to 35 per cent in fallers aged over 65 and over 80 respectively (Fig. 2) (Richardson *et al.* 1997). Abnormal responses to carotid sinus massage are more likely to be observed in asymptomatic individuals with coronary artery disease and those on vasoactive drugs known to influence reflex sensitivity (digoxin, β-blockers, and methyldopa). The prevalence of drug-induced carotid sinus hypersensitivity among elderly fallers is 11 per cent (Richardson *et al.* 1997). Although it is still generally considered as a rare condition, referral centres which routinely perform carotid sinus massage in all older patients presenting with syncope and unexplained falls diagnose carotid sinus syndrome in up to 45 per cent (McIntosh *et al.* 1993a).

Carotid sinus reflex sensitivity is assessed by measuring heart rate and blood pressure responses to carotid sinus massage. In asymptomatic elderly subjects, the normal response is as follows: cardio-inhibition, 1038 ± 195 ms; vasodepression, of 21 ± 14 mmHg (2.8 ± 1.8 kPa) (McIntosh *et al.* 1994a).

Carotid sinus massage is a crude and unquantifiable technique and is prone to both intra- and interobserver variation. More scientific diagnostic methods employing neck chamber suction or drug-induced changes in blood pressure can be used for carotid baroreceptor activation, but neither of these techniques is suitable for routine use. A standardized 5- to 10-s stimulus has been accepted by most current investigators as safe and effective. Over 75 per cent of patients with cardio-inhibitory carotid sinus syndrome respond positively to right-sided carotid sinus massage either alone or combined with left-sided carotid sinus massage (McIntosh *et al.* 1993b).

Complications resulting from carotid sinus massage include cardiac arrhythmias and neurological sequelae. Fatal asystole or ventricular arrhythmias are extremely uncommon and have generally occurred in patients with underlying heart disease undergoing therapeutic rather than diagnostic massage. Digoxin toxicity has been implicated in most cases of ventricular fibrillation. Neurological complications are also uncommon (0.14 per cent) (Munro *et al.* 1994). In a retrospective analysis of 16 000 episodes of carotid sinus massage (Davies and Kenny 1998), only 12 patients developed neurological

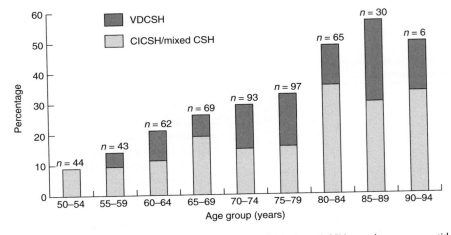

Fig. 2 Prevalence of carotid sinus hypersensitivity in patients with unexplained or recurrent falls: VDCSH, vasodepressor carotid sinus hypersensitivity; CICSH, cardio-inhibitory carotid sinus hypersensitivity.

complications. These resolved within 24 h in eight patients and within 1 week in two patients; neurological deficits persisted in two patients.

It has been suggested that carotid sinus massage should not be performed in patients with known cerebrovascular disease or carotid bruits unless there is a strong indication. It should also be avoided immediately after myocardial infarction when reflex sensitivity may be increased. If there is a significant hypotensive response during the stimulus, it is prudent to rest patients for at least 10 min before allowing them to stand up for other tests. It is not possible to predict from either clinical characteristics or carotid Doppler studies which patients will develop neurological sequelae.

Carotid sinus syndrome should be diagnosed when carotid sinus hypersensitivity is documented in a patient with otherwise unexplained dizziness, falls, or syncope and in whom carotid sinus massage reproduces symptoms. As discussed previously, three subtypes of carotid sinus hypersensitivity or carotid sinus syndrome are currently recognized. The independent vasodepressor response can be confirmed by repeating carotid sinus massage after abolishing significant cardio-inhibition using either atrioventricular sequential pacing or intravenous atropine (Walter *et al.* 1978). Asystole exceeding 1.5 s should be considered 'significant' in this regard.

Symptom reproduction during carotid sinus massage was regarded by early investigators as essential in the diagnosis of carotid sinus syndrome, but it is not always justified in patients with reproducibly abnormal responses. Up to 15 to 30 per cent of patients with unexplained falls only have an abnormal response during upright carotid sinus massage (Kenny and Traynor 1991).

In carotid sinus hypersensitivity, recognized triggers for symptoms are head movement, prolonged standing, postprandial state, straining, looking or stretching upwards, exertion, defecation, and micturition. In a significant number of patients no triggering event can be identified. An abnormal response to carotid sinus massage may not always be reproducible necessitating repetition of the procedure if the diagnosis is strongly suspected.

Carotid sinus hypersensitivity is frequently associated with other hypotensive disorders such as vasovagal syncope and orthostatic hypotension (McIntosh *et al.* 1993*b*), indicating a common pathogenic process. Overlap of hypotensive disorders can make an attributable

diagnosis difficult to identify, but every effort should be made as interventions may vary and assessment of response depends on the initial diagnosis. Approximately half of patients sustain an injury during symptomatic episodes; fractures, particularly of the femoral neck, had been sustained by 25 per cent of patients in one series (McIntosh *et al.* 1993*b*). In a prospective study of falls in nursing home residents, a threefold increase in the fracture rate was observed in those with carotid sinus hypersensitivity (Murphy *et al.* 1986). Indeed, it can be considered as a modifiable risk factor for fractures of the femoral neck (Ward *et al.*, in press). Carotid sinus syndrome is not associated with an increased risk of death. The mortality in patients with carotid sinus syndrome is similar to that in patients with unexplained syncope and the general population matched for age and sex (Brignole *et al.* 1992). Mortality rates are similar for the three subtypes of the syndrome (Brignole *et al.* 1992).

Atrioventricular sequential pacing is the treatment of choice for patients with symptomatic cardio-inhibition (Morley *et al.* 1982). With appropriate pacing, syncope and unexplained falls are abolished in 75 to 90 per cent of patients with cardio-inhibition (Almquist *et al.* 1985). Treatment of vasodepressor carotid sinus syndrome is less successful owing to poor understanding of its pathophysiology. Fludrocortisone, a mineralocorticoid widely employed to treat orthostatic hypotension, is used with good results in the treatment of vasodepressor carotid sinus syndrome, but its longer-term use is limited by adverse effects (da Costa *et al.* 1993).

Orthostatic hypotension

Orthostatic or postural hypotension is arbitrarily defined as a fall of 20 mmHg (2.6 kPa) in systolic blood pressure or 10 mmHg (1.3 kPa) in diastolic blood pressure on assuming an upright posture from a supine position (Mathias and Bannister 1992). Orthostatic hypotension implies abnormal blood pressure homoeostasis and increases in frequency with advancing age. Depending on the methodology used, the prevalence of postural hypotension is found to be between 4 per cent (Lipsitz *et al.* 1985*a*) and 33 per cent (Palmer 1983) in community-dwelling older people. The prevalence and magnitude of falls in systolic blood pressure increase with age and are associated

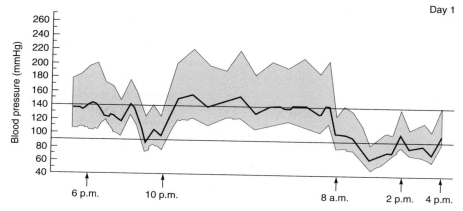

Fig. 3 Twenty-four-hour ambulatory blood pressure profile of a 65-year-old woman with symptomatic orthostatic and postprandial hypotension and supine systolic hypertension who complained of dizziness and unexplained falls.

with general physical frailty and excessive mortality (Masaki *et al.* 1995).

The compensatory response to orthostasis involves activation of the sympathetic nervous system and inhibition of the parasympathetic nervous system, and reflects the integrity of the total arterial baroreflex arc. Orthostatic hypotension results from failure of the arterial baroreflex, which is most commonly due to atherosclerosis plus arterial stiffness or disorders of the autonomic nervous system among community-living elderly people (Bannister and Mathias 1992).

The three phases of heart rate and blood pressure responses to orthostasis—an initial heart rate and blood pressure response, an early phase of stabilization, and a phase of prolonged standing—are all influenced by ageing (Wieling *et al.* 1992). The maximum rise in heart rate and the ratio of the maximum to the minimum heart rate in the initial phase decline with age, implying a relatively fixed heart rate unaffected by posture (Wieling *et al.* 1992). Despite a blunted heart rate response, blood pressure and cardiac output are adequately maintained on standing in active, healthy, well-hydrated, and normotensive elderly subjects. The underlying mechanism involves decreased vasodilatation and reduced venous pooling during the initial phases and increased peripheral vascular resistance after prolonged standing. However, in elderly subjects with hypertension and cardiovascular disease, who are receiving vasoactive drugs, the circulatory adjustments to orthostatic stress are disturbed, predisposing to postural hypotension.

Hypertension and orthostatic hypotension

Ageing is associated with an increased prevalence of hypertension as well as hypotension. Hypertension itself increases the risk of hypotension by impairing baroreflex sensitivity and reducing ventricular compliance. A strong relationship between supine hypertension and orthostatic hypotension has been reported amongst unmedicated institutionalized elderly subjects (Lipsitz *et al.* 1985*b*) (Fig. 3). Hypertension increases the risk of cerebral ischaemia from sudden declines in blood pressure. Elderly hypertensives are more vulnerable to cerebral ischaemic symptoms, even with modest and short-term postural hypotension, as their range of cerebral autoregulation is set at a higher mean level (Strandgaard 1976). In addition, antihypertensive

Table 5 Prevalence of conditions associated with orthostatic hypotension in an elderly population

Associated condition	Prevalence (%)
Drug-induced	28
Autonomic failure	27
Pure autonomic failure	24
Autonomic failure secondary to diabetes mellitus	3
Age-associated	20
Multiple-system atrophy	13
Parkinson's disease with autonomic failure	5
Other cardiovascular disease	5
Unclassified	2

agents impair cardiovascular reflexes and further increase the risk of orthostatic hypotension.

Several pathological conditions are associated with orthostatic hypotension. Autonomic failure (Mathias 1995) (Table 5) and drugs (Table 6) are important causes. In a consecutive series of 70 patients with orthostatic hypotension referred to a dedicated syncope facility, the most common attributable cause of hypotension was medication (Stout and Kenny 1998). Establishing a causal relationship between a drug and orthostatic hypotension requires identification of the responsible medicine, abolition of symptoms by withdrawal of the drug, and rechallenge with the drug to reproduce symptoms. Rechallenge is an important step in the diagnosis but is often omitted in clinical practice in view of potential serious consequences. When several drugs are being taken, the situation is complicated by interactions. A number of non-neurogenic conditions are also associated with postural hypotension. They include myocarditis, atrial myxoma, aortic stenosis, constrictive pericarditis, haemorrhage, diarrhoea, vomiting, ileostomy, burns, haemodialysis, salt-losing nephropathy, diabetes insipidus, adrenal insufficiency, fever, and extensive varicose

Table 6 Commonly used drugs causing orthostatic hypotension

Class of drug	Mechanism of orthostatic hypotension
Antihypertensives	
Calcium-channel-blocking agents	Vasodilatation
Angiotensin-converting enzyme inhibitors	Inhibition of angiotensin II production
Adrenergic nerve blocking agents	α-Adrenergic blockade
α-Adrenoceptor antagonists	α-Adrenergic blockade
Coronary vasodilators	
Nitrates	Vasodilatation
Diuretics	Volume depletion
Psychotropic drugs	
Phenothiazines	α-Adrenergic blockade
Tricyclic antidepressants	α-Adrenergic blockade
Antiparkinsonian drugs	
Levodopa	Not clearly understood
Bromocriptine	Activation of vascular dopaminergic receptors
Central nervous system depressants	
Ethanol	Vasodilatation

veins. In the absence of well-recognized conditions causing primary and secondary autonomic failure (Mathias 1995), ageing can also be considered as a cause.

Primary autonomic failure syndromes

These are discussed more fully in Chapter 18.12. The three main clinical entities are pure autonomic failure, multiple-system atrophy or Shy–Drager syndrome, and autonomic failure associated with idiopathic Parkinson's disease. Pure autonomic failure, a relatively benign entity, was previously known as idiopathic orthostatic hypotension. This condition presents with orthostatic hypotension, defective sweating, impotence, and bowel disturbances. No other neurological deficits are found and resting plasma noradrenaline (norepinephrine) levels are low. Multiple-system atrophy carries the poorest prognosis. Clinical manifestations include features of dysautonomia and motor disturbances due to striatonigral degeneration, cerebellar atrophy, or pyramidal lesions. Resting plasma noradrenaline levels are usually within the normal range but fail to rise on standing or tilting. The prevalence of autonomic failure in Parkinson's disease is not precisely known. Cerebellar and pyramidal signs are not seen. Orthostatic hypotension in Parkinson's disease may be due to factors other than dysautonomia, for example side-effects of drugs, autonomic neuropathy complicating coexisting diabetes mellitus, and confusion with early multiple-system atrophy with predominant Parkinsonian features (Mathias 1995).

The clinical manifestations of orthostatic hypotension are due to hypoperfusion of the brain and other organs. Depending on the degree of fall in blood pressure and cerebral hypoperfusion, symptoms can vary from dizziness to falls to syncope associated with a variety of visual defects ranging from blurred vision to blackout. Other reported ischaemic symptoms of orthostatic hypotension are non-specific lethargy and weakness, suboccipital and paravertebral muscle pain, low backache, calf claudication, and angina (Bleasdale-Barr and Mathias 1994). Several precipitating factors for orthostatic hypotension have been identified, namely speed of positional change, prolonged recumbency, warm environment, raised intrathoracic pressure (coughing, defecation, micturition), physical exertion, and vasoactive drugs.

Orthostatic hypotension is an important cause of unexplained falls and syncope, accounting for 14 per cent of all diagnosed cases in a large series (Kapoor et al. 1986). In a tertiary referral clinic dealing with unexplained syncope, dizziness, and falls, 32 per cent of elderly patients had orthostatic hypotension (McIntosh et al. 1993a). Irrespective of symptoms, orthostatic hypotension increases the risk of falls in the elderly patients. Nineteen per cent of elderly fallers attending an accident and emergency department had a diagnosis of orthostatic hypotension (Moss et al. 1980). Orthostatic hypotension was the cause of drop attacks in 15 per cent of 35 patients aged over 50 years and probably contributed to unexplained falls in a similar proportion of patients.

The diagnosis of orthostatic hypotension involves a demonstration of a postural fall in blood pressure after standing up. Reproducibility of orthostatic hypotension depends on the time of measurement and on autonomic function (Ward and Kenny 1996). The diagnosis may be missed on casual measurement during the afternoon. The procedure should be repeated during the morning after maintaining a supine posture for an adequate period (10 min). Sphygmomanometer measurement is not as sensitive as sophisticated phasic blood pressure measurements, and standing up is as diagnostic as head-up tilting (Ward and Kenny 1996). In patients with unexplained syncope or falls, an attributable diagnosis of orthostatic hypotension depends on reproduction of symptoms where possible.

The aim of therapy for symptomatic orthostatic hypotension is to improve cerebral perfusion. There are several non-pharmacological interventions including avoidance of precipitating factors, elevation of the head of the bed at night, and application of graduated pressure from a support garment to the lower limbs to reduce venous pooling. There are reports suggesting benefit, in a small number of patients, from implantation of cardiac pacemakers to increase heart rate during postural change (Moss et al. 1980; Mathias 1995). However, the effects of tachypacing on improving cardiac output in patients with maximal vasodilatation remains conjectural. Many drugs have been used to raise blood pressure in orthostatic hypotension. The most commonly used of these agents are fludrocortisone, midodrine (an α-agonist), and desmopressin. Patients receiving drug treatment for orthostatic hypotension require frequent monitoring for supine hypertension, electrolyte imbalance, and congestive heart failure.

Neurocardiogenic syncope

The hallmark of neurocardiogenic or vasovagal syncope is hypotension and/or bradycardia sufficiently profound to produce cerebral ischaemia and loss of neural function. Vasovagal syncope has been classified into cardio-inhibitory (bradycardia), vasodepressor (hypotension), and mixed (both) subtypes depending on the blood pressure and heart rate response (Sutton et al. 1992). In most patients, the manifestations occur in three distinct phases: a prodrome or aura, loss of consciousness, and a postsyncopal phase. A precipitating factor or situation is identifiable for most patients. These include emotional stress, anxiety, trauma, physical pain or anticipation of physical pain (e.g. before venesection), sight of blood, accident, warm environment, air travel, and prolonged standing. The most common triggers in older individuals are prolonged standing and vasodilator medication (McIntosh et al. 1993b). In our experience drug-induced falls and syncope in elderly people are more often due to vasovagal syncope than to orthostatic hypotension. Some patients experience symptoms in association with micturition, defecation, or coughing. Prodromal symptoms include extreme fatigue, weakness, sweating, nausea, visual defects, visual and auditory hallucinations, dizziness, vertigo, headache, abdominal discomfort, dysarthria, and paraesthesiae. The duration of prodrome varies from seconds to several minutes, during which some patients take action, such as lying down, to avoid an episode. The syncopal period, during which some patients develop involuntary movements ranging from tonic–clonic movements to myoclonic jerks, is usually brief. Recovery is generally rapid but some patients can experience protracted symptoms such as confusion, disorientation, nausea, headache, dizziness, and a general sense of ill health. The clinical characteristics of neurocardiogenic syncope are similar for young and elderly patients.

The sequence of events leading to neurocardiogenic syncope are not fully understood. The possible mechanism involves a sudden fall in venous return to heart, a rapid fall in ventricular volume, and virtual collapse of the ventricle due to vigorous ventricular contraction (Samoil and Grubb 1992). The net result of these events is stimulation of mechanoreceptors leading to peripheral vasodilatation (hypotension) and bradycardia (Samoil and Grubb 1992).

In comparison with younger adults, healthy elderly subjects are not particularly prone to neurocardiogenic syncope. Owing to an age-associated decline in baroreceptor sensitivity, the paradoxical responses to orthostasis (as in neurocardiogenic syncope) are possibly less marked in elderly subjects. Thus situational syncope is less common in old age. However, in the presence of hypertension and atherosclerotic cerebrovascular disease, excessive loss of baroreflex sensitivity leads to dysautonomic responses to prolonged orthostasis (in which blood pressure and heart rate decline steadily over time) and patients become susceptible to neurocardiogenic syncope. Diuretic- or age-associated contraction of blood volume further increases the risk of syncope.

By using the strong orthostatic stimulus of head-up tilting and maximal venous pooling, reflex neurocardiogenic syncope can be reproduced in a susceptible individual in the laboratory (Kenny et al. 1986). The sensitivity of head-up tilting can be further improved by provocative agents, such as isoprenaline (isoproterenol) and glyceryl trinitrate (nitroglycerin), which accentuate the physiological events leading to vasovagal syncope. Because of the decline in β-receptor sensitivity with age, isoprenaline is less useful as a provocative agent and has a higher incidence of adverse effects. The positivity of head-up tilting can also be enhanced by intravenous cannulation (McIntosh et al. 1994b).

Patient education, involving avoidance of precipitating factors and vasodilator drugs and lying down during prodromal symptoms, has great value in preventing episodes of vasovagal syncope. However, some patients experience symptoms without warning and so need drug therapy. A number of drugs, including β-blockers, disopyramide, transdermal scopolamine, fludrocortisone, fluoxetine, and midodrine, are reported to be useful in alleviating symptoms. Permanent cardiac pacing has been used in some patients, with the dual-chamber mode being preferred (Grubb et al. 1993). However, pacing influences the bradycardia component of the response, but has no effect on the vasodilatation and hypotension which frequently dominate. Its utility is limited in some instances to prolongation of the prodrome in order to allow other evasive action (Grubb et al. 1993).

Postprandial hypotension

In healthy elderly subjects, systolic blood pressure falls by 11 to 16 mmHg (1.4–2.1 kPa) and heart rate rises by 5 to 7 beats/min 60 min after meals (Lipsitz and Fullerton 1986). The change in diastolic blood pressure is not as consistent. In elderly subjects with hypertension, orthostatic hypotension, and autonomic failure, the postprandial blood pressure fall is much greater and without a corresponding rise in heart rate (Jansen et al. 1987). These responses are marked if the energy and simple carbohydrate content of the meal is high. In the majority of elderly subjects, most of these hypotensive episodes go unnoticed. Postprandial physiological changes include increased splanchnic and superior mesenteric artery blood flow at the expense of peripheral circulation, and a rise in plasma insulin levels (Potter et al. 1989) without corresponding rises in sympathetic nervous system activity. The vasodilator effects of insulin (Potter et al. 1989) and other gut peptides such as neurotensin and vasoactive intestinal peptide are thought to be responsible for postprandial hypotension, although the precise mechanism remains uncertain. The clinical significance of a fall in blood pressure after meals is difficult to quantify. However, postprandial hypotension is causally related to recurrent syncope and falls in elderly subjects (Jonsson et al. 1990). In our experience postprandial hypotension occurs in at least 20 per cent of patients with orthostatic hypotension. A reduction in the simple carbohydrate content of food, its replacement with complex carbohydrates, and frequent small meals are effective interventions for postprandial hypotension. Drugs useful in the treatment are indomethacin, octreotide, and caffeine. When given with food, caffeine prevents hypotensive symptoms in both fit and frail elderly subjects (Potter 1996).

Table 7 Important individual risk factors for falls (summary of 16 studies)

Risk factor	Significant total[a]	Mean RR or OR[b]	Range
Weakness	11/11	4.9 (8)[c]	1.9–10.3
Balance deficit	9/9	3.2 (5)	1.6–5.4
Gait deficit	8/9	3.0 (5)	1.7–1.8
Visual deficit	5/9	2.8 (9)	1.1–7.4
Mobility limitation	9/9	2.5 (8)	1.0–5.3
Cognitive impairment	4/8	2.4 (5)	2.0–4.7
Impaired activities of daily living	5/6	2.0 (4)	1.0–3.1
Postural hypotension	2/7	1.9 (5)	1.0–3.4

[a] Number of studies with significant association relative to total number of studies reporting on each factor.
[b] Relative risks (prospective studies) and odds ratios (retrospective studies).
[c] Number in parenthesis indicates the number of studies that reported relative risks or odds ratios.

Data from Rubenstein and Josephson (1996).

Risk factors

A number of risk factors have been identified for falls. They include lower-limb weakness, peripheral neuromuscular dysfunction, gait and balance disturbances, assistive devices, visual defects, stroke disease, self-reported limitations, cognitive impairment, inability to perform activities of daily living, orthostatic hypotension, arthritis, incontinence, and medications. Table 7 lists the major risk factors for falls identified from 16 studies which compared fallers with non-fallers. Risk factors for falls vary according to whether a community, hospital-based, or nursing home population is studied (Rubenstein and Josephson 1996).

Falls during hospital stays are more common in confused patients and those with greater comorbidity. This profile differs from that of fallers in the community, possibly because hospital patients are more ill. Injurious falls are associated with a substantially increased resource utilization, and independently correlated with increased length of stay and, in the United States, with total health-care charges. After adjustment for confounders, fallers in one series stayed in hospital on average 12 days longer and incurred charges over $4000 higher than controls (Bates et al. 1995).

Risk factors for falls in hospitals differ little from those in the nursing home population. Major in-hospital risk factors include congestive cardiac failure, digoxin therapy, benzodiazepine use, and psychoactive agents. Additional risk factors in hospital falls include a history of recent falls, depression, dizziness, and acute confusion.

The presence of impaired orientation, psychoactive drug use, stroke disease, and impaired performance in the 'get up and go' test correctly classified 80 per cent of inpatients into fallers and non-fallers. This is a simple and quick screening test which could be used to identify those at risk of falling in hospital (Lord et al. 1992). Home hazards are frequently cited as risk factors for falls, but, although associated with a higher incidence of hip fracture, they are no more frequent for fallers than for non-fallers (Clemson et al. 1996).

Mobility impairment, including poor gait, poor balance, reduced leg extension strength, abnormal gait and stride length, and abnormal stepping height, is a risk factor for falls, particularly recurrent falls (Graafmans et al. 1996). The loss of postural balance and the inability to recover from an impending fall may be attributed to both abnormal muscle physiology and age-associated delays in central processing.

Four independent predisposing factors for falls (and for incontinence and functional dependence) are slow timed chair-stand (lower extremity impairment), decreased arm strength, decreased vision and hearing, and a high anxiety and depression score. Falls, incontinence, and functional dependence increase as the number of these predisposing factors increases (Tinetti et al. 1995).

Several studies have linked peripheral nerve dysfunction with postural instability and falls by older people. Although the comorbid causes of peripheral neuropathy are themselves often risk factors for falls, peripheral neuropathy appears to stand alone as a risk factor irrespective of associated comorbidity (Richardson and Hurbitz 1995). Sensitivity to foot position declines with age, mainly because of loss of plantar tactile sensation (Robbins et al. 1995). Tripping over an obstacle is a common cause of falls, and both young and old subjects are more likely to fail to avoid an obstacle if their attention is divided, but the effect is much greater in older persons (Chen et al. 1996). Although muscle strength declines with age, and in women begins to decline around the time of the menopause, the use of oestrogen replacement therapy does not appear to influence muscle strength, neuromuscular function, or the incidence of falls (Seeley et al. 1995).

Postural instability is a key feature of many specific neurological disorders such as Parkinson's disease and stroke. Postural instability in Parkinson's disease includes disturbed postural reflexes, poor control of voluntary movement, side-effects of medications (dyskinesias), orthostatic hypotension, gait abnormalities, muscle weakness, and superimposed age-associated changes in peripheral sensation (Bloom 1992).

Falls are the most common single complication following stroke (Dennis et al. 1996), and fall-prevention strategies should be incorporated into stroke rehabilitation programmes (Nyberg and Gustafson 1995). The fear of falling affects both patients and carers (Forster and Young 1995). Falls occur with similar frequency in anticoagulated and non-anticoagulated patients; in hospital patients, the risk of minor injury is similar in the two groups (Stein *et al.* 1995).

Although posturography measurements are useful when elucidating balance problems (Baloh *et al.* 1995), they do not distinguish patients who fall and they do not correlate with other clinical risk factors for falls (Baloh *et al.* 1994). Medications are an often cited risk factor for falls. Common culprit medications include psychotropic drugs, benzodiazepines, antiparkinsonian treatment, and cardiovascular drugs. Psychoactive medication may predispose older patients to falling by impairing important sensorimotor systems which contribute to postural stability (Lord *et al.* 1995). Medication was a possible risk factor for falls in 40 per cent of cognitively normal and 60 per cent of patients with dementia attending an accident and emergency department because of falls (Davies and Kenny 1996; Shaw and Kenny 1997) (Fig. 1 and Table 3).

Cardiovascular medication has been cited as a cause of falls, but there does not appear to be a clear-cut relationship between drug-related orthostatic hypotension and falls (Liu *et al.* 1995). In a cross-sectional study of women using thiazide diuretics over a 10-year period, cases had a higher bone mass but an incidence of falls similar to that of women who had never used thiazide diuretics. The risk of non-spinal osteoporotic fractures was also similar in the two groups, but thiazide users had a trend towards a lower risk of fractures of the hip and the wrist (Cauley *et al.* 1993).

Visual impairment is cited as a major risk factor for falls and recurrent falls. Almost half of all fallers have evidence of visual impairment. In one series (Jack *et al.* 1995), 79 per cent of patients admitted to hospital after a fall had visual impairment including correctable refractory errors (40 per cent), cataract (37 per cent), and senile macular degeneration (14 per cent). The prevalence of visual impairment is higher in fallers admitted to hospital because of a fall than in community-dwelling fallers.

Most falls do not result in serious injury, and even more important than identifying risk factors for falling is identifying risk factors for injurious falls. In nursing home residents, lower-limb weakness, female sex, poor vision and hearing, disorientation, number of previous falls, impaired balance, dizziness, lower body mass and use of mechanical restraints, psychotropic medication, and functional dependence are the major risk factors for injurious falls (Tinetti 1987). Tinnetti *et al.* (1986) found that the risk of injurious falls increased from 27 per cent in patients with one risk factor to 78 per cent in patients with four or more risk factors. Similarly, Nevitt *et al.* (1989) found that the risk of recurrent falls in community-living persons increased from 10 to 69 per cent as the number of risk factors increased from one to four or more.

Investigation of a large series of institutionalized and outpatient populations identified many risk factors associated with falls (Robbins *et al.* 1989). Multivariate analysis enabled simplification of the model so that maximum predictive accuracy could be obtained using only three risk factors: hip weakness, unstable balance, and four or more prescribed medications. With this model the predicted 1-year risk of falling ranged from 12 per cent for persons with no risk factors to 100 per cent for persons with all three.

Use of restraints is uncommon in the United Kingdom. Cotsides (bed rails) were used for 8.4 per cent of one series of acute medical and geriatric patients. For almost all, the reason given for use was prevention of falls (O'Keefe *et al.* 1996). By comparison, in one United States series (Tinetti *et al.* 1992), 31 per cent of nursing home residents who were mobile and unrestrained at baseline had been restrained after 1 year of follow-up, two-thirds intermittently and a third continually. Serious fall-related injuries were more common in the restrained subjects (17 versus 5 per cent). Removing or changing restraints in nursing home patients who are not ambulatory will not increase their mobility. Increased mobility for patients will only be realized if restraint reduction programmes are combined with interventions to improve both mobility and behavioural performance.

Consequences

Forty to eighty per cent of falls by community-dwelling elderly people result in injuries. Most are mild or superficial, but 5 per cent of falls result in fractures and 1 per cent in fractured neck of femur. Eighty per cent of falls in nursing homes result in some injury.

Hip fractures represent one of the most important consequences of falls. Approximately half of previously independent elderly hip-fracture patients become partially dependent and a third ultimately become totally dependent. Hip fractures are associated with a reduction of 12 to 20 per cent in expected survival, with 5 to 20 per cent excess mortality within a year of injury. Age-specific incidence rates have increased in recent years, and in many countries the rise is continuing. Highest incidences have been described in Scandinavia and North America. The average lifetime risk of a hip fracture is 17 per cent in white women and 5 per cent in white men. At the age of 80 one woman in five, and at the age of 90 one woman in two, has suffered a hip fracture. Men also have poor outcomes from fractures; in a population-based series of 131 men in Rochester, only 41 per cent had recovered prefracture functional level and more than half were discharged to nursing homes (Lauritzen 1996).

Half of all attendances by adults aged over 50 years at an inner-city accident and emergency department in the United Kingdom followed a fall, and half of the patients were admitted to hospital (Davies and Kenny 1996; Richardson *et al.* 1997). Up to 50 per cent of the fall-related injuries that required hospital admission resulted in the elderly person being discharged to a nursing home.

Falls are the single most common cause of restricted activity days experienced by community-dwelling older adults and are twice as common a cause of restricted activity as heart disease, arthritis, or hypertension (Kosorok *et al.* 1992). A major consequence of falls is 'fear of falling' and 'post-falling anxiety syndrome'. Being moderately fearful of falling is associated with a decrease of satisfaction with life, increased frailty, and depressed mood, and is further associated with decreased mobility and social activities. This reduction in mobility includes an increase of wheelchair use by ambulant nursing home and residential care subjects (Kutner *et al.* 1994). The negative impact of falls on quality of life, mood, and functional capacity is even more apparent for subjects who experience 'unexplained' or recurrent falls than than for those who have accidental falls (Davies *et al.*, in press).

Intervention

Intervention programmes for falls require detailed assessment and screening for modifiable risk factors. The assessment should include cognitive function, full history of the type and frequency of falls, including whether or not there is associated loss of consciousness and dizziness, and, where possible, a witness account of falls. Details should include associated injuries, comorbidity, and medication use including the timing of doses. A full neurological examination should include assessment of muscle strength in upper and lower limbs, evidence of sensorimotor dysfunction, including tactile sensation and reflexes in the lower limbs, assessment of gait and balance, including posturography, and a search for evidence of Parkinson's disease, stroke, and supranuclear palsy. Cardiovascular assessment should include examination for peripheral vascular disease, cardiac lesions, and arrhythmias. Orthostatic hypotension should be sought in morning supine and upright blood pressures, and postprandial blood pressures should be measured repeatedly.

If falls are unexplained or recurrent, or if some episodes have been associated with loss of consciousness, the heart rate and blood pressure response to both supine and upright carotid sinus stimulation should be determined. If falls remain unexplained or the history suggests neurocardiogenic syncope, prolonged head-up tilt testing is recommended.

Visual assessment should include measurement of visual acuity and examination for cataracts and senile macular degeneration. Other investigations include routine blood screen, incorporating urea and electrolytes, liver function tests, haematology screen, and acute phase protein activity, in addition to chest radiography, and 12-lead surface ECG. Where indicated, patients may require head CT or magnetic resonance imaging scans and ambulatory blood pressure if hypotensive episodes are suspected. Ambulatory ECG monitoring for arrhythmias may be relevant, particularly if the routine ECG is abnormal or there is a history of palpitations associated with falls. Caloric tests and hearing assessment may be necessary if the history suggests vestibular dysfunction.

Post-fall intervention programmes have been developed in many institutions, but possible benefits require further validation in randomized controlled trials. In one nursing home study, a randomized post-fall intervention programme was administered by a nurse practitioner. The group experienced a reduction in hospital admission (26 per cent) and length of hospital stay (62 per cent) compared with controls, but the number of falls was not significantly reduced (Wolf-Klein et al. 1988).

Intervention programmes focusing on specific risk factors (weakness, balance impairments, gait abnormality) are currently under way in the United States (Frailty and Injuries: Co-operative Studies of Intervention Techniques (FICSIT)) and some evidence has emerged of benefits from exercise (Province et al. 1995). Several studies have shown that healthier older adults who engage in intensive exercise can increase lower-limb muscle power; this is so even in frail nursing home patients. Similarly, balance is improved by walking programmes and low-impact aerobic programmes.

Modification of medication can contribute to a reduction in fall rates. Manipulation of cardiovascular medication reduced the incidence of unexplained falls and syncope in a select population of symptomatic patients referred to a specialist syncope facility (McIntosh et al. 1993a). Cardiac pacing intervention is clearly beneficial in reducing syncopal events in older patients with bradyarrhythmia, in particular sinus node disease, atrioventricular conduction disturbances, and carotid sinus syndrome. In one series of patients with cardio-inhibitory carotid sinus syndrome one-third who presented with unexplained falls in addition to syncope were asymptomatic for falls and syncope 1 year after dual-chamber pacing. Randomized control trials of cardiac pacing for unexplained falls are under way.

Both cognitively normal and demented patients comply with environmental home hazard modifications (Chapman et al. 1997). Randomized controlled trials incorporating environmental hazard modification programmes are in progress.

Many fall-assessment tools have been developed for use in hospitals and nursing homes to identify patients at 'high risk of falling'. The 'fall risk' status of a patient is determined by the number of identified risk factors or by a summary score. A nursing care plan is then implemented which includes interventions aimed at injury prevention. Few data support the validity of these assessment tools or the effectiveness of most prevention programmes.

Many devices have been marketed to alert caregivers to patient activity and falls. Alarm systems can deliver earlier assistance systems and may even reduce fall rates. Hip protector pads are currently advocated for use in patients at risk of hip fracture from falls and have been shown to reduce fracture rates (Lauritzen et al. 1993).

Because of the frequent presence of more than one risk factor in patients at most risk of injurious falls, randomized controlled trials of post-fall multi-intervention packages, tailored to individual needs, are required. In our experience, more careful assessment of cardiovascular causes of falls is an important and underutilized component of intervention programmes, particularly for patients with unexplained or recurrent falls.

References

Almquist, A., Gornick, C., and Benson, D.W. (1985). Carotid sinus hypersensitivity: evaluation of the vasodepressor component. *Circulation*, 71, 927–36.

Baloh, R.W, Fife, T.D., Zwerling, L., et al. (1994). Comparison of static and dynamic posturography in young and older normal people. *Journal of the American Geriatrics Society*, 42, 405–12.

Baloh, R.W., Spain, S., Socotch, T.M., Jacobson, K.M., and Bell, T. (1995). Posturography and balance problems in older people. *Journal of the American Geriatrics Society*, 43, 638–44.

Bannister, R. and Mathias, C.J. (1992). Clinical features and manifestations and investigation of primary autonomic failure syndromes. In *Autonomic failure: a textbook of clinical disorders of the autonomic nervous system* (ed. R. Bannister and C.J. Mathias), pp. 531–47. Oxford University Press.

Bates, D.W., Pruess, K., Souney, P., and Platt, R. (1995). Serious falls in hospitalised patients: correlates and resource utilisation. *American Journal of Medicine*, 99, 137–43.

Bleasdale-Barr, K. and Mathias, C.J. (1994). Suboccipital (coat hanger) and other muscular pains—frequency in autonomic failure and other neurological problems, and association with postural hypotension. *Clinical Autonomic Research*, 4, 82–4.

Bloom, B.R. (1992). Postural instability in Parkinson's disease. *Clinical Neurology and Neurosurgery*, 94, S41–5.

Brignole, M., Gigli, G., Altomonte, F., Barra, M., Sartore, B., and Prato, R. (1985). Cardioinhibitory reflex provoked by stimulation of carotid sinus in normal subjects and those with cardiovascular disease. *Giornale Italiano di Cardiologia*, 15, 514–19.

Brignole, M., Oddone, D., Cogorno, S., Menozzi, C., Gianfranchi, L., and Bertulla, A. (1992). Long-term outcome in symptomatic carotid sinus hypersensitivity. *American Heart Journal*, 123, 687–92.

Campbell, A.J, Reinken, J., Allan, B.C., and Martinez, G.S. (1981). Falls in old age: a study of frequency and related clinical factors. *Age and Ageing*, 10, 264–70.

5 Clinical pharmacology and ageing

B. Robert Meyer

The passing of time is obvious: the change from infancy to old age is dramatic. It seems almost ridiculous to suggest that ageing should *not* affect drug responses. Yet 'obvious facts' have a nasty habit of turning into anachronistic nonsense, so that it behooves us to examine critically the evidence on this relationship.

Lasagna (1956)

Introduction

The observations that Lasagna made over 40 years ago about the relationship between age and drug response remain as true today as they were then. The increased interest in geriatrics over this time frame has been accompanied by a significant increase in information about the 'obvious fact' that older individuals may respond to therapy differently from younger individuals. The information that we have gathered in the last four decades allows us to understand better the 'facts' about drug therapy in older patients. In some instances the facts have 'confirmed' the obvious, in others they have clarified the obvious, and in still others they have shown the obvious not to be the case.

The ongoing discussion of drug therapy in the older patient has often been confused by the failure to distinguish consistently between the effects of 'ageing' as a biological process and the facts that confront the clinician when he or she treats an older patient. Most of the studies which have been performed on 'drugs and ageing', and which will be quoted in this chapter, have sought to look at drug effects in healthy volunteers (young and old). Most have self-consciously sought to exclude from their research population those individuals with significant medical illness. The investigators in these studies have proposed thereby to identify the effects of 'ageing' rather than 'disease' on drug pharmacokinetics and pharmacodynamics. This is an important goal, and one that needs to continue to be pursued. It enhances our understanding of both drug therapy and the physiology of ageing.

The practising physician will frequently find that however interesting it may be to differentiate the effects of disease and the effects of the ageing process, this distinction is less relevant to daily practice than the need to know how to treat the geriatric patient 'differently' from the younger patient. Since clinicians treat illness, they will often find the comparison of the healthy older person with the healthy younger person less relevant than the comparison of the 'sick' elderly patient with the 'sick' younger patient. In many situations, the altered responsiveness of older individuals to the effects of drugs may not reflect the effects of the 'ageing' process as much as the effects of the presence of multiple disease processes superimposed upon ageing.

Elderly people tend to take more medication because they have more illnesses. As a population, much of their altered responsiveness to medication may simply reflect the fact that they are, as a population, 'sicker' than younger individuals who are taking the same medication. Unfortunately, there is little quantitative information available on the interactions between severity of illness, age, and altered response to drug therapy.

Geriatric drug use

Individuals over 65 years of age are the greatest consumers of prescription drugs. While the geriatric population comprises between 12 and 15 per cent of the population in most industrialized nations, they consume about 33 per cent of all prescription medications. As the number of older patients grows over the coming decades, it is reasonable to expect that their contribution to prescription drug use will increase in a commensurate fashion.

Reliable information on non-prescription drug use is less easily available, because it usually depends upon self-reporting of use by the individuals involved. Older individuals, like their younger counterparts, are extensive users of over-the-counter drugs. While some reports have suggested that elderly patients were more likely than younger patients to use over-the-counter drugs (Lasilla *et al.* 1996), this finding has not been confirmed in most populations studied (Helling *et al.* 1987; Stoehr *et al.* 1997). In one study (Stoehr *et al.* 1997) the mean number of over-the-counter drugs in use by an older patient at the time of the study was 1.9. In patients over 85 years of age the mean was 2.1. The most common medications used by older patients are analgesics, vitamins, antacids, and laxatives (Hale *et al.* 1987; Helling *et al.* 1987; Lasilla *et al* 1996; Stoehr *et al.* 1997).

For their extensive use of both prescription and non-prescription medications alone, the geriatric population merits special attention

Table 1 Some drugs that are more likely to produce adverse effects in elderly people

Drug	Adverse effect
Benzodiazepines	Sedation, confusion, ataxia
NSAIDs	
Benoxaprofen	Fluid retention
	Peptic ulcer disease
	Toxic hepatitis
Opiate analgesics	Sedation, confusion
	Constipation
Antiarrhythmics	
Lignocaine (lidocaine)	Confusion
Disopyramide	Urinary retention
Major tranquillizers	Malignant hyperthermia
	Tardive dyskinesias
	Confusion, sedation
Diuretics	Dehydration, hyponatraemia
	Carbohydrate intolerance
	Orthostatic hypotension
Isoniazid	Hepatitis
Aminoglycosides	Renal and auditory injury

NSAIDs, non-steroidal anti-inflammatory drugs.

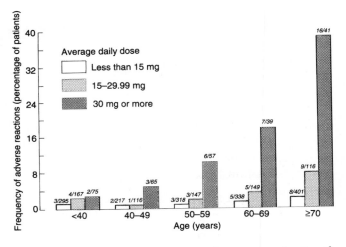

Fig. 1 The frequency of adverse reactions to flurazepam as a function of dose and age. (Reproduced with permission from Greenblatt *et al.* (1977).)

from the medical professional concerned about pharmacological therapy. However, there are many other reasons for paying attention to this population. Older patients are more likely to experience adverse drug reactions, to be taking multiple drugs with potential drug interactions, and to suffer serious and prolonged consequences of the occurrence of adverse effects of drugs.

Despite these compelling reasons for paying attention to drug therapy in older persons, the clinician who is concerned about prescribing a drug for an older patient is less likely to find good information available from formal evaluations of a drug in the geriatric population. In this chapter we provide an overview of what we do (and do not) know about drugs in geriatrics, and give the reader a sense of how far we have (or have not) come since Lasagna's observations four decades ago.

Adverse drug reactions

While the precise incidence of adverse drug reactions will vary according to the definition of an adverse effect and the severity of the reaction that is deemed worthy of documentation, there is agreement that the elderly are more likely than younger individuals to suffer adverse effects from medications.

Age-associated increases in the incidence of adverse reactions have been particularly well described for certain groups of drugs. Some of these are listed in Table 1. The incidence of isoniazid hepatitis increases directly with age. According to data collected by the United States Centers for Disease Control, the incidence of isoniazid hepatitis (not merely transaminase elevation) during the first 3 months of treatment

rises from 0.2 per cent in individuals below 34 years of age to 2.2 per cent in those over 50 years of age. This increasing incidence may be a decisive factor in deciding for or against treatment with isoniazid.

Elderly people are more sensitive than younger people to a variety of drugs acting on the central nervous system. This was first identified with morphine, but has been most extensively described with the benzodiazepines where age-associated changes in sensitivity are well established. In initial large surveillance studies of the use of benzodiazepines, the incidence of side-effects was generally reported to be low. Apart from isolated case reports, no particular comment was made on increased sensitivity in elderly people. Grimley Evans and Jarvis (1972) were the first to report the occurrence of a syndrome of immobility, ataxia, incontinence, and confusion in some of their patients maintained for long periods of time on ordinary therapeutic doses of nitrazepam. They noted that this syndrome was only observed in their elderly patients. Subsequently, the Boston Collaborative Drug Surveillance Program (1973) reviewed the records of patients receiving diazepam and chlordiazepoxide in ordinary therapeutic doses. The reported frequency of drowsiness and excess sedation rose from 4.4 per cent in subjects aged less than 40 years to 10.9 per cent in patients aged over 70. Extension of these observations to patients taking flurazepam showed a similar trend. Adverse effects increased with age and drug dose; 39 per cent of 41 subjects aged over 70 who were taking large doses of the drug (30 mg or more daily) developed adverse effects (predominantly sedation), whereas only 2.7 per cent of 75 subjects who were taking the same dose but were under 40 developed adverse effects (Fig. 1).

Castleden *et al.* (1977) assessed the effects of a single therapeutic dose of nitrazepam upon the performance of a simple test of psychomotor functioning in young and old individuals. Both groups showed impairment of performance. In young individuals, the impairment was not statistically significant. For the older subjects, the effect was significantly different from the control performance for a period of 36 h after a single dose of the drug (Fig. 2). A multidose study by Cook *et al.* (1983) demonstrated that the short-acting benzodiazepine temazepam had prolonged psychometric effects in elderly subjects.

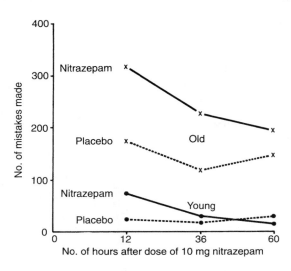

Fig. 2 The total number of mistakes made in a psychomotor test by old and young age groups after receiving nitrazepam 10 mg and placebo. (Reproduced with permission from Castleden et al. (1977).)

Non-steroidal anti-inflammatory drugs are among the most commonly prescribed medications in the world, and elderly individuals comprise a substantial portion of the market for these agents. The propensity of non-steroidal anti-inflammatory drugs to produce gastrointestinal bleeding has been appreciated for many years. This effect has been attributed to local mucosal injury and gastric ulceration. Large studies with a significant percentage of patients under 60 years of age have usually failed to show an association between non-steroidal anti-inflammatory drug use and the occurrence of peptic ulcer disease. However, recent studies focusing on the use of these drugs (particularly aspirin) by elderly people have reported an association with peptic ulcer disease (Somerville et al. 1986). A case–control study of patients enrolled in the Tennessee Medicaid program suggested a substantially increased risk for fatal peptic ulcer disease or upper gastrointestinal haemorrhage relative to controls matched for age, sex, race, calendar year, and nursing home status (Griffin et al. 1988). These authors compared the rates of non-steroidal anti-inflammatory drug use in the 30 days prior to hospital admission for study cases with peptic ulcer disease with their use in the control population over the same period of time. The relative risk ratio for peptic ulcer disease in individuals over the age of 60 using non-steroidal anti-inflammatory drugs in this study was between 4 and 5. Although some investigators have suggested similar results (Faulkner et al. 1988; Griffin et al. 1991; Rodriguez and Jick 1994), other studies have failed to confirm this (Holvoet et al.1991; Laporte et al. 1991). In a recent thoughtful review of this topic, Solomon and Gurwitz (1997) concluded that it had not yet been conclusively demonstrated that the incidence of bleeding induced by non-steroidal anti-inflammatory drugs was higher in older patients. However, these authors also pointed out that, because of their wide prescription for this population and the greater morbidity of any gastrointestinal haemorrhage in this age group, it was clear that elderly patients suffered a disproportionate amount of damage from the use of these drugs.

Hepatic injury has been extraordinarily rare in large populations of individuals taking non-steroidal drugs. However, recent experience demonstrated that the administration of 'routine therapeutic doses' of benoxaprofen to elderly individuals produced significant accumulation of the drug and the occurrence of major hepatotoxic effects. This unexpected event led to the withdrawal of from the market. The hepatotoxicity might have been prevented had dosage been lowered for elderly patients in proportion to their altered elimination of the drug.

The full impact of the adverse effects of medication on elderly individuals is not generally realized. Adverse drug reactions are an important cause of hospital admission of elderly people (more so than in the young) and have a correspondingly greater effect upon the medical costs of this population and their functional status.

The occurrence of traumatic injury is one area where drug therapy may have an important but often under-appreciated impact on elderly people. As a group, the elderly are second only to late adolescents and young adults in the frequency and severity of traumatic injury. Traumatic injury constitutes the sixth leading cause of death in elderly individuals. Between 30 and 40 per cent of individuals over the age of 65 and as many as 50 per cent of individuals over the age of 80 will suffer a fall each year. Women are more likely than men to suffer injury from falls. Approximately a quarter of these falls will result in significant injury and between 5 and 7 per cent of falls results in a fracture (Campbell et al. 1981; Prudham and Grimley Evans 1981).

Impairment of motor and cognitive skills persists for a period of time after the use of many psychoactive drugs. Since elderly people are likely to suffer traumatic injury, take more medications than younger subjects, and have a greater intensity and duration of central nervous system depressant effect from medications, it is reasonable to hypothesize that they are at higher risk for injury induced by the use of psychoactive drugs.

Studies of risk factors for falls have consistently identified psychoactive drug use as an important risk factor. In a study of community-dwelling elderly people over the age of 75 (Tinetti et al. 1988), the most important single risk factor for falls was the use of a sedative drug (defined as a benzodiazepine, a phenothiazine, or an antidepressant). The odds ratio for sedative drug use was an impressive 28.3. Even when corrected for the presence of the next most important individual risk factor (pre-existent cognitive dysfunction), the adjusted odds ratio remained at 2.5. Other studies have found an association between the use of long-acting (but not short-acting) benzodiazepines and falls, and it has also been found that the use of multiple drugs (four or more) is an independent risk factor for falling (Ray et al. 1987; Thapa et al. 1996).

Mechanisms of altered drug response in elderly people

Pharmacokinetics provides quantitative descriptions of the time course of drug absorption, distribution, metabolism, and excretion from the body. Pharmacodynamics examines and describes the magnitude, nature, and the course of drug effects in the body. The altered responsiveness of the older patient to a drug could be the result of alterations in either the pharmacokinetics of the compound in the older individual, or could be due to an altered end-organ response to the drug (pharmacodynamics). These changes occur independently of the presence or absence of pharmacokinetic changes.

Table 2 Some drugs whose absorption is dependent upon gastric pH

Ketoconazole	With achlorhydria give in 4 ml aqueous solution of 0.2 N HCl Use glass to avoid contact with teeth, and follow with a glass of water (*Drug Facts* 1997)
Indomethacin	Mechanism not clear
Fluconazole	Achlorhydria may inhibit absorption (*Drug Facts* 1997)
Tetracyclines	pH-dependent inhibition of dissolution

Table 3 Relationship between pathway for metabolic clearance and age-associated changes in clearance of benzodiazepines

	Mixed-function oxidase	Conjugation (glucuronide)
Diazepam	Clearance decreased	
Chlordiazepoxide	Clearance decreased	
Lorazepam		No change
Oxazepam		No change
Nitrazepam		No change
Temazepam		No change

Pharmacokinetics

There was an early appreciation of the importance of altered pharmacokinetics in older patients. This observation has been repeatedly confirmed over the years. However, there continues to be extensive discussion of the extent to which pharmacokinetic changes observed in older patients are secondary to the process of ageing itself, whether they are the result of the cumulative effects of multiple disease processes, and their effect on drug kinetics.

Oral bioavailability

Altered absorption kinetics has been the area of pharmacokinetics where there has been the least amount of information available. Over 60 years ago Vanzant *et al.* (1932) identified the fact that the incidence of achlorhydria increases with age. According to these admittedly old data, between 20 and 25 per cent of all 80-year-olds have achlorhydria compared with approximately 5 per cent of individuals in their thirties. It would be expected that drugs whose absorption is affected by acid would be more likely to have altered absorption in elderly patients. Drugs fitting this description are listed in Table 2.

In recent years there has been an increasing awareness of the presence of gut-associated cytochrome P-450 enzyme activity. Gut-associated cytochrome activity is critically important in limiting the bioavailability of many drugs after oral dosing. Some of these drugs have very high rates of destruction during absorption and first-pass metabolism in the liver, and therefore would be very sensitive to relatively small changes in bioavailability with ageing. Consider, for example, a drug for which only 5 mg of a 100-mg oral dose escapes destruction during absorption by the gut and first-pass liver metabolism. If the effect of age were to decrease the gut-associated degradation of drug so that 10 mg of the 100-mg dose escaped degradation and was delivered to the systemic circulation, the actual systemic dose of drug administered by the same 100-mg oral dose would be doubled from 5 to 10 mg (100 per cent increase). In contrast, a change of similar magnitude in a drug for which 70 mg of a 100-mg oral dose is bioavailable in younger individuals will produce only a small change in systemic dose from 70 to 75 mg (7 per cent). This 7 per cent change is probably not sufficient to be noticed.

The logical conclusion is that if clinically important changes in oral bioavailability are to be seen in older patients, it is likely that they will be seen with drugs that have high first-pass effect. Preliminary investigations looking at nifedipine and verapamil (drugs which fit this description) appear to confirm this expectation (Robertson *et al.* 1988; Sasaki *et al.* 1993).

Drug distribution

Body composition and protein binding of a drug affect its distribution in the body. Ageing is associated with an increase in the percentage of total body mass that is fat. In young adults, body fat is typically 8 to 20 per cent for males and up to 33 per cent for females. In older individuals, the percentage of body mass that is fat increases to 33 per cent or more in males and to between 40 and 50 per cent in females (Forbes and Reina 1970), and there are corresponding decreases in muscle mass. Total body water also decreases with ageing (Shock *et al.* 1963). These changes will produce alterations in the volume of distribution depending on the distribution characteristics of the drug. Lipid-soluble drugs would be expected to increase their distribution with age, while hydrophilic drugs would be expected to decline in distribution. Again, scattered evidence supports this prediction. There is considerable individual variability in these changes in composition depending upon lifelong body build, lifestyle factors (food intake, exercise), and acquired diseases. When it is clinically critical to know body composition, it may be necessary to make objective determinations.

Changes in serum protein concentrations, most importantly albumin and α_1-acid glycoprotein, could also effect the distribution of drugs. Initial data suggesting that older patients had lower albumin levels now appear to have confounded 'age' and 'illness' effects. The magnitude of the change observed with ageing itself is relatively small. The analysis of the potential impact of protein-binding changes should be similar in nature to the analysis of bioavailability that was given earlier. Given that the overall changes are small, it would be predicted that the effect of age would be important only for drugs in which very extensive protein binding is present. An example of such a drug is naproxen, where as much as a 'doubling' of free drug (from 2 to 4 per cent) has been reported (Upton *et al.* 1984; McVerry *et al.* 1986; van den Ouweland 1988).

Metabolic clearance

Liver metabolism of drugs might be expected to decline with age. The liver decreases in mass after the age of 50, and a decline in liver blood flow with ageing has been well described. However, the actual data in humans have yielded very mixed results. In general, hepatic conjugation reactions (phase 2) appear to be well preserved during ageing. Phase 1 oxidative reactions mediated through the cytochrome P-450 system are potentially affected. Table 3 demonstrates how this generalization is reflected by the analysis of benzodiazepines with either phase 1 or phase 2 clearance mechanisms.

Studies that have demonstrated a decline in the metabolic clearance of drugs in older individuals have generally found that the effects of ageing are significantly less important than the effects of tobacco, alcohol, and other environmental factors known to influence drug clearance. Initial reports suggested that tobacco-induced hepatic enzyme induction was absent in many elderly subjects (Vestal et al. 1979b; Wood 1979; Vestal and Wood 1980). However, recent studies have suggested that this may not be the case. The relative effects of other environmental and/or dietary factors on liver metabolism in elderly compared with younger individuals have not been well studied. The potential effects of altered sex hormone levels in older persons have also been postulated as having a potential impact on hepatic drug clearance (O'Mahony and Woodhouse 1994).

A recent study of antipyrine clearance in liver biopsies from young, middle-aged, and elderly subjects failed to demonstrate a change in cytochrome P-450 content in the samples, but did find a decline in clearance of antipyrine (Sotaniemi et al. 1997). This suggests the possibility of an alteration in affinity or intrinsic activity of cytochrome P-450 for this substrate with age. Our rapidly developing understanding of the complexities of the cytochrome P-450 system has now provided the opportunity to analyse the effects of age on the metabolic capacity of specific enzyme systems within the liver. This effort is just beginning and will provide an opportunity to differentiate the effects of altered total hepatic mass, altered liver blood flow, altered intrinsic activity, and altered inducibility of the individual cytochrome P-450 enzyme systems themselves.

On average, there is a decline in renal function with ageing. However, longitudinal studies show that as many as one-third of people show no decline in function as they age (Lindeman et al. 1985). Serum creatinine concentrations reflect a balance between creatinine production by muscle tissue and creatinine clearance by the kidney. Since creatinine production is decreased in older persons in association with the decrease in their muscle mass, 'normal' serum creatinine concentrations in these patients will not reflect the true decline in renal function. The Cockroft–Gault equation has become a popular and effective technique for correcting for average age-associated changes in creatinine production (Cockroft and Gault 1976):

$$\text{creatinine clearance (men)} = \frac{(140 - \text{age}) \times (\text{weight (kg)})}{72 \times \text{serum creatinine (mg/dl)}}$$

$$\text{creatinine clearance (women)} = 0.85 \frac{(140 - \text{age}) \times (\text{weight (kg)})}{72 \times \text{serum creatinine (mg/dl)}}.$$

Figure 3 shows a graphic representation of this equation for patients of varying ages and sizes with normal or near-normal serum creatinine concentrations. This equation is accurate for individuals without significant oedema or severe cachexia. For drugs substantially excreted through the kidneys, elderly patients need adjustment of dosage based upon glomerular filtration rate, as do younger individuals with a similar degree of renal impairment. There is no unique adjustment in dosing that is specifically related to age, but considerable variability depending upon maintained levels of physical activity and other factors. When the potential impact of any change from 'average' glomerular filtration rate on the effectiveness or toxicity of a given drug is critical, then the actual glomerular filtration rate for the

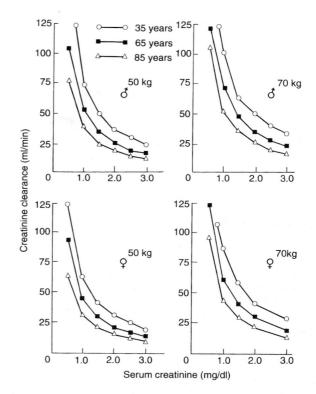

Fig. 3 Relationship of serum creatinine concentration and creatinine clearance to age and body weight for men and women.

patient should be determined rather than relying on averages for age. The glomerular filtration rate can be calculated from measurement of creatinine content in a timed (i.e. 24-h) collection of urine together with serum creatinine concentration.

The renal handling of drugs involves not only glomerular filtration, but also secretion and reabsorption by the renal tubules. Elderly people exhibit alterations in the renal tubular handling of water, salt, and acid, and it would be reasonable to expect similar alterations in renal tubular handling of drugs. However, there are few data on the presence (or absence) of age-related changes in the secretion of compounds by the organic base and acid secretory systems of the renal tubule.

The clinician is often inclined to use drug half-life as a guide to drug dosing. Drug elimination half-life $T_{1/2}$ is related to volume of distribution and clearance by the following formula:

$$T_{1/2} = 0.693 \frac{\text{volume of distribution}}{\text{clearance}}.$$

It follows that changes in drug half-life can be seen as reflections of changes in either the volume of distribution or the clearance. Thus changes in both these parameters may either accentuate or inhibit the changes in $T_{1/2}$. For example, the clearance of antipyrine reduces with age, but its distribution volume decreases. These two changes tend to diminish any changes in $T_{1/2}$ induced by an individual factor alone. In another case, dramatic changes in flurazepam $T_{1/2}$ with age may reflect the occurrence of significant, but smaller, changes in distribution volume (increased) and clearance (decreased).

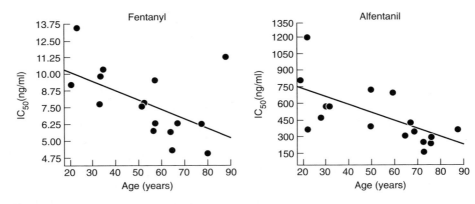

Fig. 4 Inhibitory concentration IC_{50} versus age for fentanyl and alfentanil. The brain sensitivity (IC_{50}) is plotted against the patient's age. The regression lines are shown and have the following equations. Fentanyl: $IC_{50} = -0.0675 \times age + 11.4$ ($P < 0.01$, $r = -0.52$). Alfentanil: $IC_{50} = -7.69 \times age + 886$ ($P < 0.01$, $r = -0.66$). (Reproduced with permission from Scott and Stanski (1986).)

Pharmacodynamics

In addition to pharmacokinetic changes, it is possible that tissue sensitivity to the effects of drugs is altered in elderly subjects. The analysis of pharmacodynamic changes with age is more complicated than that of pharmacokinetic changes, since drug effects are often difficult to quantify and true demonstration of pharmacodynamic differences requires proof of the absence of pharmacokinetic effects. Not surprisingly, therefore, the data on 'dynamic' changes in ageing are more limited.

Reviews of warfarin usage suggest that elderly subjects require lower doses to achieve anticoagulation than do younger individuals. Since no substantive changes in warfarin kinetics have been demonstrated in elderly subjects, the sensitivity observed must reflect altered pharmacodynamic responsiveness. The observed increase in sensitivity may be related to the decreased rates of synthesis of clotting factors seen in older subjects. The effect of age is one of a number of factors that influence warfarin response. In a study by Jones et al. (1980) the effect of age was relatively small and was demonstrable only when other variables were controlled. In a more recent report of a retrospective cohort study (Gurwitz et al. 1992), multivariate analysis suggested that age had a more important effect on anticoagulant response.

The sensitivity of older persons to psychoactive drugs has been noted earlier in this chapter. Altered responsiveness to nitrazepam, as described by Castleden et al. (1977) (Fig. 2), was accompanied by only minimal changes in pharmacokinetics. This suggests that the altered responsiveness observed was due to changes in sensitivity to the drug. Early studies by Reidenberg et al. (1978) demonstrated that elderly subjects given acute intravenous infusions of diazepam prior to endoscopy or cardioversion required less diazepam and achieved higher levels of sedation than younger subjects. Studies with acute infusions of fentanyl and alfentanil have documented very similar findings (Fig. 4) (Scott and Stanski 1987).

In Fig. 2 (Castleden et al. 1977) the older subjects had a higher number of mistakes than the younger individuals at the time of the baseline evaluation. In this case, the number of mistakes on placebo was roughly 15 to 20 times higher in old than in young subjects. The effect of the benzodiazepine was to take an already partially impaired individual and cause further and more dramatic impairment of performance. In this way, the performance of an individual who was well compensated with a mild deficit was impaired further by the drug, and a mild deficit was converted into a severe one.

Recent studies of the ability of young and old subjects to maintain their balance after the administration of the benzodiazepine triazolam conforms to this pattern. Older subjects typically have greater postural sway at baseline, but with considerable variability depending upon maintained levels of physical activity and other factors. The administration of triazolam causes increases in postural sway in all subjects (young and old). The older subjects, whose postural sway is greatest at the start, have the greatest increase in sway after drug therapy. The result is that older subjects are more likely than younger subjects to lose their balance (Robin et al. 1996, Cutson et al. 1997).

The pattern of altered response discussed in the examples above appears to be a useful way of understanding the altered sensitivity of many elderly people. Gurwitz and Avorn (1991) conceptualized this relationship as shown in Fig. 5. Its similarity to Castleden's data is striking. The ordinate represents the baseline functional status of the subject (expressed as level of impairment). The older subject has greater baseline impairment. An equal percentage decline in function as the result of drug effect represents a greater absolute decline for older individuals and, taken with their baseline impairment, is more likely to cause them to cross the hypothetical level at which the impairment of function becomes clinically manifest.

Age-associated changes in sensitivity to drugs affecting the β-adrenergic system are also well established. The reduction of heart rate after propranolol is less in individuals aged between 50 and 65 years than in those aged between 25 and 30. This occurs despite the fact that serum propranolol levels are generally similar to or higher than those in younger patients. This 'pharmacodynamic' insensitivity has been documented by the measurement of the effect of propranolol on isoprenaline (isoproterenol) dose–response curves in young and elderly subjects (Fig. 6). This altered responsiveness appears to be confined to β₁ receptors. Measurements of isoprenaline-induced vasodilation and insulin release (β₂ effects) have failed to show significant changes associated with ageing. The mechanism of altered β₁ sensitivity remains obscure. Initial reports of decreases in the number or density of β-receptors on the lymphocytes of older individuals have not been confirmed. Therefore the observed alteration

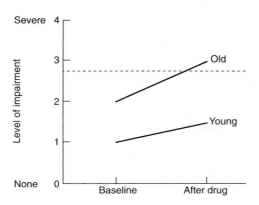

Fig. 5 Interpretation of data from pharmacodynamic studies of drug effects in elderly people. The ordinate shows the level of impairment of any physiological function. The elderly patient has a greater baseline level of impairment. The percentage additional impairment of function induced by a drug is equal for the old and the young. However, the absolute magnitude of effect is greater for the elderly patient because of the baseline difference compared with the young patient. The horizontal line represents a hypothetical threshold level beyond which there is clinical evidence of impairment of function. (Reproduced with permission from Gurwitz and Avorn (1991).)

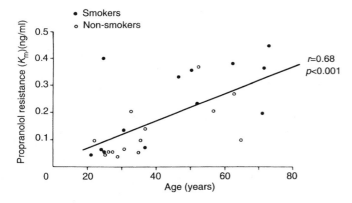

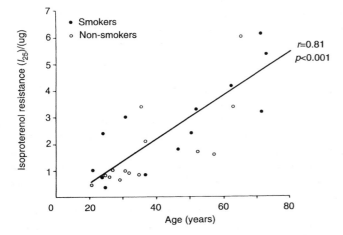

Fig. 6 Relationship between propranolol resistance and age (top panel) and relationship between isoprenaline resistance and age (bottom panel) in smokers. (Reproduced with permission from Vestal et al. (1979b).)

in sensitivity may reflect alterations in postreceptor intracellular events. No alteration in α-adrenergic responsiveness with ageing has been seen (Vestal et al. 1979a).

Compliance

Compliance with a prescribed therapeutic regimen is a necessity for effective pharmacotherapy. Virtually every review of this problem has found that under normal conditions patients frequently fail to follow a doctor's recommendations for therapy. The quoted frequency of non-compliance varies from 10 to 90 per cent. The higher incidence values reflect the compilation and reporting of a large number of trivial errors that are best disregarded. If non-compliance is defined as an alteration in therapy that may impair the likelihood of that therapy being successful, then its probable frequency is between 10 and 50 per cent.

Studies of compliance have shown that the more medications a patient takes, and the longer he or she is asked to take them, the more likely he or she will be to make important errors in administration or to decide to refuse to take the medication. Thus individuals with multiple chronic illnesses taking multiple medications on a chronic basis are those least likely to comply with the full therapeutic regimen. This is often a description of the elderly patient.

Despite the preceding comments (and the common assumption among health-care professionals that older persons are more likely to be non-compliant with therapy), the magnitude of the compliance problem in elderly patients does not appear to be out of proportion to that of younger individuals with comparable levels of medical illness and comparable numbers of medications in their therapeutic regimens.

Whether their compliance with medical therapy is similar to or rather poorer than that of younger individuals, it is clear that elderly patients may well have unique problems in achieving compliance with drug therapy. On average, elderly people in the United States have a lower socio-economic status than the young and spend a higher percentage of their income on health care. A major portion of this expenditure is on prescription medication. Older patients who are taking a variety of different expensive medications over an extended period of time may find that the financial burden is prohibitive. They may either discontinue therapy entirely or consciously adjust the dose of drug downwards in order to stretch their supply of medication over a longer period of time.

Visual impairment may make it difficult for an individual to read prescription labels or to distinguish accurately between different tablets that are similar in appearance. Elderly individuals who were asked to identify paired samples of tablets of a variety of different colours failed to separate different tablets correctly up to 32 per cent of the time (Table 4). Sometimes even the mechanical process of picking up and holding a small pill may be difficult. Childproof containers may also be 'old-person-proof' for many patients. Impaired memory may make it difficult to remember complicated therapeutic regimens.

The physician will be doing elderly patients a service by being aware of these special problems. Specific efforts to communicate with the patient, to simplify medication regimens, to recognize (and to discuss with the patient) the issue of cost of medication, where relevant, to direct the patient to obtaining dispensing systems designed

Table 4 Ageing and ability to discriminate coloured tablets

Colour	Tablets	Percentage correct tablet discrimination
Yellow	Aldomet 250 mg/Inderal 80 mg	77.5
Yellow	Valium 5 mg/Synthroid 0.1 mg	68.5
Yellow	Valium 5 mg/Inderal 80 mg	85.5
Blue	Inderal 20 mg/Hygroton 50 mg	75.0
Blue	Elavil 10 mg/Apresoline 25 mg	90.0
Blue	Valium 10 mg/Apresoline 50 mg	95.0
White	Valium 2 mg/Lanoxin 0.25 mg	75.0
White	Lanoxin 0.25 mg/Lasix 40 mg	55.0

Adapted from Hurd and Blevins (1984).

to maximize compliance, and to use easily opened containers with readable labels will all improve the patient's compliance.

Dosage adjustments for elderly patients

As a rule, elderly individuals should begin drug treatment at a lower dose than younger patients. In the case of drugs with predominantly renal excretion, adjustment according to calculated or measured creatinine clearance provides specific guidance on selection of an appropriate dose. However, when pharmacokinetic parameters such as hepatic clearance are considered, current knowledge provides substantially less precise recommendations on dose adjustment. The possibility of altered pharmacodynamic sensitivity also does not easily lead to precise recommendations on dose adjustment.

Paediatricians have always been trained to adjust dose according to weight. This has never been the practice in internal medicine or geriatrics. As a result, elderly patients with low body weight often receive significantly higher doses of a drug (on a mg/kg basis) than do younger patients. A study of prescriptions for flurazepam, cimetidine, and digoxin filled through the American Association of Retired Persons pharmacy service showed that older patients tended to be smaller, and to receive higher doses of these drugs on a mg/kg basis, than younger patients. On a mg/kg basis, the smallest patients (<50 kg) received a dose of flurazepam that was 88 per cent higher than that given to the largest patients (>90 kg).

The development of dosing guidelines for elderly patients based upon weight is needed. Routine adjustment of dose according to patient weight might well lead to improved prescribing practices and better treatment in this population.

Drug development and elderly people

While older people are major consumers of drugs, until recently they have not participated in the clinical evaluation and development of

Table 5 Basic principles of good prescribing practice

1. Always review the entire medication regimen of the patient whenever you see him or her
2. Consider the use of non-pharmacological rather than pharmacological therapy as an initial management plan
3. Strongly consider discontinuing any drug whose indication for use is no longer clear
4. Always start with the lowest dose that is likely to be successful for this condition in this particular patient
5. Always consider the potential for side-effects and their impact upon the patient
6. When selecting drugs from a particular pharmacological class, consider which member of that class will be best for your particular patient
7. Always look for adverse drug effects, and always consider the possibility of an adverse drug effect as an explanation of symptoms reported by the patient
8. Consider the social and economic issues for a particular patient that will impact upon his or her ability or desire to comply with the prescribed therapy

new chemical entities. In fact, their known sensitivity to a number of drugs has meant that they were routinely excluded from many studies. As the importance of drugs in the geriatric population has been realized, the size of the geriatric population has been recognized, and the potential importance of information on the pharmacokinetic and pharmacodynamic action of drugs in this population has been identified, this policy is slowly changing. It can now be expected that in the United States older persons will have been included in clinical trials of any new drug that has a likelihood of significant use in the geriatric population.

Even as it becomes more common to include individuals aged over 65 in clinical trials, it remains extremely important to continue to increasee the participation of older persons in clinical trials of new pharmacological agents (Avorn 1995). It is particularly important that we improve our ability to collect systematic information on the experience of individuals aged over 75 who are rarely included in systematic clinical trials measuring drug effects. Only in this way can we advance our understanding and provide more definitive recommendations on drug therapy for these patients.

Conclusion

Most discussions of geriatric drug therapy provide a list of 'guidelines for drug therapy in the elderly' (e.g. Stein 1994) A list of such guidelines is given in Table 5. It is not entitled 'Basic principles of good prescribing practice in the elderly', but simply 'Basic principles of good prescribing practice'. These guidelines are not unique or special to geriatrics. No one would advocate that these principles should not apply to any patient for whom a drug is prescribed, regardless of age.

The difference in geriatric drug prescribing does not lie in the principles and policies that should inform clinicians in the selection of therapeutic paths for their patients. Rather, the difference lies in the narrowness of the path that must be followed and the consequences of deviation from that path. Mis-steps in following the path of optimal therapy can lead to dangerous falls, a potential for more serious and persistent injury to the patient, and iatrogenic disease instead of health. The clinician caring for the older patient should (as always) think carefully about his or her therapeutic plan for that patient. For the geriatric patient, the clinician should recall the patient's age, the information contained in books such as this, and then, after careful consideration, . . . should think again.

References

Avorn, J. (1995). Medication use and the elderly: current status and opportunities. *Health Affairs*, 14, 276–86.

Boston Collaborative Drug Surveillance Program (1973). Clinical depression of the central nervous system due to diazepam and chlordiazepoxide in relation to cigarette smoking and age. *New England Journal of Medicine*, 288, 277–80.

Campbell, A.J., Reinken, J., Allan, B.C., et al. (1981). Falls in old age: a study of frequency, and related clinical factors. *Age and Ageing*, 10, 264–70.

Castleden, C.M., George, C.F., Marcer, D., and Hallett, C. (1977). Increased sensitivity to nitrazepam in old age. *British Medical Journal*, i, 10–12.

Cockroft, D.W. and Gault, M.H. (1976). Prediction of creatinine clearance from serum creatinine. *Nephron*, 16, 31–41.

Cook, P.J., Huggett, A., Graham-Pole, R., Savage, I.T., and James, I.M. (1983). Hypnotic accumulation and hangover in elderly in-patients: a controlled double-blind trial of temazepam and nitrazepam. *British Medical Journal*, 286, 100–2.

Cutson, T.M., Gray, S.L., Hughes, M.A., Carson, S.W., and Hanlon, J.T. (1997). Effect of a single dose of diazepam on balance measures in older people. *Journal of the American Geriatrics Society*, 45, 435–550.

Drug Facts and Comparisons (1997). Facts and Comparisons, St Louis, MO.

Faulkner, G., Prichar, P., Somerville, K., and Langman, M.J.S. (1988). Aspirin and bleeding peptic ulcers in the elderly. *British Medical Journal*, 297, 1311–15.

Forbes, G.B. and Reina, J.C. (1970). Adult lean body mass declines with age: some longitudinal issues. *Metabolism: Clinical and Experimental*, 19, 653–63.

Greenblatt, D.J. Allen, M.D., and Shader, R.I. (1977). Toxicity of high-dose flurazepam in the elderly. *Clinical Pharmacology and Therapeutics*, 21, 355–61.

Griffin, M.R., Ray, W.A., and Schaffner, W. (1988). Non-steroidal anti-inflammatory drug use and death from peptic ulcer in elderly persons. *Annals of Internal Medicine*, 109, 359–63.

Griffin, M.R., Piper, J.M., Daugherty, J.R., Snowden, M., and Ray, W.A. (1991). Non-steroidal anti-inflammatory drug use and increased risk for peptic ulcer disease in elderly persons. *Annals of Internal Medicine*, 114, 257–63.

Grimley Evans, J. and Jarvis, E.H. (1972). Nitrazepam and the elderly. *British Medical Journal*, iv, 487.

Gurwitz, J.H. and Avorn, J. (1991). The ambiguous relation between ageing and adverse drug reactions. *Annals of Internal Medicine*, 114, 956–66.

Gurwitz, H.H., Avorn, J., Ross-Degnan, D., Choodnovskiy, I., and Ansell, J. (1992). Ageing and the anticoagulant response to warfarin therapy. *Annals of Internal Medicine*, 116, 901–4.

Hale, W.E., May, F.E., Marks, R.G., et al. (1987). Drug use in an ambulatory elderly population: a five year update. *Drug Intelligence and Clinical Pharmacy*, 21, 530–5.

Helling, D.K., Lemke, J.H., Semla, T.P., et al. (1987). Medication use characteristics in the elderly: the Iowa 65 + rural health study. *Journal of the American Geriatrics Society*, 35, 4–12.

Holvoet, J., Terriere, L., Van Hee, W., et al. (1991). Upper gastrointestinal bleeding in relation to previous use of analgesics and non-steroidal anti-inflammatory drugs and aspirin: a case–control study. *Gut*, 32, 730–4.

Hurd, P.D., and Blevins, J. (1984). Ageing and the color of pills. *New England Journal of Medicine*, 310, 202.

Jones, B.R., Baran, A., and Reidenberg , M.M. (1980). Evaluating patients' warfarin requirements. *Journal of the American Geriatrics Society*, 28, 10–12.

Laporte, J.R., Carne, X., Vidal, X., et al. (1991). Upper gastrointestinal bleeding in relation to previous use of analgesics and non-steroidal anti-inflammatory drugs. *Lancet*, 337, 85–9.

Lasagna, L. (1956). Drug effects as modified by ageing. *Journal of Chronic Diseases*, 3, 567–74.

Lasilla, H.C., Stoehr, G.P., Ganguli, M., et al. (1996). Factors associated with the use of prescription medications in an elderly rural population: the MoVIES Project. *Annals of Pharmacotherapy*, 30, 589–95.

Lindeman, R.D., Tobin, J., and Shock, N. (1985). Longitudinal studies on the rate of decline in renal function with age. *Journal of the American Geriatrics Society*, 33, 278–85.

McVerry, R.M., Lethbridge, J., Martin, N., et al. (1986). Pharmacokinetics of naproxen in elderly patients. *European Journal of Clinical Pharmacology*, 31, 463–8.

Mucklow, J.C. and Fraser, H.S. (1980). The effect of age and smoking on anti-pyrine metabolism. *British Journal of Clinical Pharmacology*, 9, 613–14.

O'Mahony, M.S. and Woodhouse, K.W. (1994). Age, environmental factors and drug metabolism. *Pharmacology and Therapeutics*, 61, 179–87.

Prudham, D. and Grimley Evans, J. (1981). Factors associated with falls in the elderly: a community study. *Age and Ageing*, 10, 141–6.

Ray, W.A., Griffin, M.R., Schaffner, W., Baugh, D.K., and Melton, L.J. (1987). Psychotropic drug use and the risk of hip fracture. *New England Journal of Medicine*, 316, 363–9.

Reidenberg, M.M., Levy, M., Warner, H., Coutinho, C.B., Schwartz, M.A., and Cheripko, Y.G. (1978). Relationship between diazepam dose, plasma level, age and central nervous system depression. *Clinical Pharmacology and Therapeutics*, 23, 371–4.

Robertson, D.R., Waller, D.G., Renwick, A.G., and George, D.F. (1988). Age-related changes in the pharmacokinetics and pharmacodynamics of nifedipine. *British Journal of Clinical Pharmacology*, 25, 297–305.

Robin, D.W., Hasan, S.S., Edeki, T., Lichtenstein, M.J., Shiavi, R.G., and Wood, A.J.J. (1996). Increased baseline sway contributes to increased losses of balance in older people following triazolam. *Journal of the American Geriatrics Society*, 44, 300–4.

Rodriguez, L.A.G. and Jick, H. (1994). Risk of upper gastrointestinal bleeding and perforation associated with individual non-steroidal anti-inflammatory drugs. *Lancet*, 343, 769–92.

Sasaki, M., Tateishi, T., and Ebihara, A. (1993). The effects of age and gender on the stereoselective pharmacokinetics of verapamil. *Clinical Pharmacology and Therapeutics*, 54, 278–85.

Scott, J.C. and Stanski, D.R. (1987). Decreased fentanyl and alfentanil dose requirements with age. A simultaneous pharmacokinetic and pharmacodynamic evaluation. *Journal of Pharmacology and Experimental Therapeutics*, 240, 159–66.

Shock, N.W., Watkin, D.M., Yiengst M.J., et al. (1963). Age differences in water content of the body as related to basal oxygen consumption in males. *Journal of Gerontology*, 18, 1–23.

Solomon, D.H. and Gurwitz, J.H. (1997). Toxicity of non-steroidal anti-inflammatory drugs in the elderly. Is advanced age a risk factor? *American Journal of Medicine*, 102, 208–15.

Sotaniemi, E.A., Arranto, A.J., Pelkonen, O., and Pasanen, M. (1997). Age and cytochrome P450-linked drug metabolism in humans: an analysis of

226 subjects with equal histopathologic conditions. *Clinical Pharmacology and Therapeutics*, **61**, 331–9.

Stein, B.E. (1994). Avoiding drug reactions: seven steps to writing safe prescriptions. *Geriatrics*, **49**, 28–36.

Stoehr, G.P., Ganguli, M., Seaberg, E.C., Echement, D.A., and Belle, S. (1997). Over the counter medication use in an older rural community: the MoVIES Project. *Journal of the American Geriatrics Society*, **45**, 158–65.

Thapa, P.B., Brockman, K.G., Gideon, P., Fought, R.L., and Ray W.A. (1996). Injurious falls in non-ambulatory nursing home residents: a comparative study of circumstances, incidence, and risk factors. *Journal of the American Geriatrics Society*, **44**, 273–8.

Tinetti, M.E., Speechley, M., and Ginter, S.F. (1988). Risk factors for falls among elderly persons living in the community. *New England Journal of Medicine*, **319**, 1701–7.

Upton, R.A., Williams, R.L., Kelly J., and Jones, R.M. (1984). Naproxen pharmacokinetics in the elderly. *British Journal of Clinical Pharmacology*, **18**, 207–14.

van den Ouweland, F.A., Jansen, P.A., Tan, Y., *et al.* (1988). Pharmacokinetics of high-dosage naproxen in elderly patients. *International Journal of Clinical Pharmacology, Therapy, and Toxicology*, **26**, 143–7.

Vanzant, F.R., Alvarez, W.C., Eusterman, G.B., *et al.* (1932). The normal range of gastric acidity from youth to old age. *Archives of Internal Medicine*, **49**, 345–64.

Vestal, R.E. and Wood, A.J. (1980). Influence of age and smoking on drug kinetics in man. *Clinical Pharmacokinetics*, **5**, 309–18.

Vestal, R.E., Wood, A.J., and Shand, D.G. (1979a). Reduced beta-adrenoceptor sensitivity in the elderly. *Clinical Pharmacology and Therapeutics*, **26**, 181–6.

Vestal, R.E., Wood, A.J., Branch, R.A., Shand, D.G., and Wilkinson, G.R. (1979b). Effects of age and cigarette smoking on propranolol distribution. *Clinical Pharmacology and Therapeutics*, **26**, 8–15.

Wood, A.J., Vestal, R.E., Wilkinson, G.R., Branch, R.A., and Shand, D.G. (1979). Effect of ageing and cigarette smoking on anti-pyrine and indocyanine green elimination. *Clinical Pharmacology and Therapeutics*, **26**, 16–20.

6

Nutrition and ageing

controlled trials have failed definitively to prove a beneficial effect of β-carotene in the development of skin cancers (Greenberg *et al.* 1990).

Vitamin D

Recent studies suggest that vitamin D deficiency may be a serious concern in older people. Intakes of the vitamin average 50 per cent of the recommended daily allowance (5 μg/day) in individuals over the age of 50 years (Russell and Suter 1993). Inadequate intake combined with poor absorption leads to osteomalacia and an aggravated risk of fracture in older men and women with age-associated osteopenia. Based on these facts the recommended intake of the vitamin in older people is 10 to 20 μg/day.

In addition to the vitamin's known role in bone metabolism, it also affects macrophage function in general and pulmonary macrophages in particular (Weintraub *et al.* 1989; Winter *et al.* 1989; Crowle and Ross 1990). This has led to the suggestion that vitamin D deficiency increased susceptibility to the development of pulmonary tuberculosis by compromising macrophage function. This has been suggested as contributing to the high prevalence of tuberculosis in nursing home patients in whom deficiencies are common and aggravated by diminished exposure to sunlight (Anonymous 1985). In any patient with severe osteoporosis, fracture, or bone pain, vitamin D-induced osteomalacia must be excluded.

Vitamin E

Vitamin E (α-tocopherol) is abundant in the diet and deficiencies of the vitamin virtually never occur. It is involved in the function of the enzyme glutathione peroxidase which is involved in free-radical scavenging. The vitamin also affects the biophysical properties of the cell membrane reducing the age-associated increase in membrane microviscosity. It also influences immune function and recent evidence indicates that administration of the vitamin enhances immune function in older people and may minimize infectious risk (Meydani *et al.* 1990). Despite these functions, which may be of benefit in improving age-associated declines in cellular function, no good evidence exists indicating a beneficial effect of vitamin E supplementation in subjects of any age.

Vitamin K

This vitamin is essential for the production of a number of factors involved in both the intrinsic and extrinsic clotting cascade. There is evidence that vitamin K administration is beneficial in elderly subjects who have an unexplained prolongation of their prothrombin time. Although dietary intake is adequate, deficiencies can result from the administration of drugs that interfere with the vitamin's absorption or interfere with bacterial flora.

Nutritional assessment

Determining the nutritional status of older people involves an accurate assessment of body composition which is essential to define the presence of obesity and to detect individuals who are significantly underweight. Biochemical and haematological parameters are needed to evaluate visceral protein stores and the functional impact of nutritional deficiencies (Mitchell and Lipschitz 1982b). Nutritional assessment in older people is made difficult because of age-associated alterations in body composition and reductions in immunological function which mimic many of the alterations which occur as a consequence of malnutrition (Table 1).

Anthropometric methods

These include the determination of body composition which involve the comparison of a measured value against a reference standard of height and weight. The alterations in height, weight, postural changes, and mobility that occur with ageing combined with the lack of appropriate standards make the assessment of body composition in elderly people very difficult (Mitchell and Lipschitz 1982b).

In both males and females height decreases by approximately 1 cm per decade after the age of 20 years (Trotter and Gleser 1951). This is caused by vertebral bony loss, increased laxity of vertebral supportive ligaments, reductions in disc spaces, and alterations in posture. Historical examinations of height are also frequently inaccurate in elderly people and its measurement is difficult in bed-ridden patients or in those with significant postural abnormalities. For this reason it has been suggested that alternatives to height should be used in the development of standards for body composition for older people. Options suggested include arm length and knee height measurements (Mitchell and Lipschitz 1982a).

In general a gradual increase in weight occurs with advancing age, peaking in the early forties in males and a decade later in females (Mitchell and Lipschitz 1982b). After the age of 70 years, reductions in weight are not uncommon. Lean body mass decreases by approximately 6.0 per cent per decade after the age of 25 years (Forbes and Reina 1970). By the age of 70 years lean body mass has decreased an average of 5 kg for females and 12 kg for males. Thus, in most elderly people, fat constitutes a far greater percentage of total weight than it does in subjects of younger ages (Fig. 2). Fat distribution also alters with ageing. Truncal and intra-abdominal fat content increase while limb fat is diminished. Skinfold measurements are often employed to estimate fat and muscle stores. Although the triceps skinfold thickness is the most frequently obtained, multiple skin folds are much more reliable than single measurements (Noppa *et al.* 1979). Subscapular and suprailiac skinfolds are the best predictors of fat stores in males, while the triceps skinfold and thigh measurements are of greater value in females. Total body water is also decreased in parallel to decline in lean body mass (see Fig. 2).

Weight is still the most important measure of body composition and a history of recent weight loss is the single most important clue to the presence of a significant nutritional problem. Significant malnutrition can exist in elderly subjects who are overweight, and should be suspected in any subject in whom a significant degree of weight loss has occurred. In sick elderly individuals alterations in fluid balance may make interpretations of weight difficult. However, it is usually easy to identify clinically those patients who are either significantly above or below their ideal body weight.

Although reference tables for nutritional assessment are incomplete and frequently not representative of the entire population, some do exist and these should be employed when anthropometric determinations are obtained in elderly people (Master and Lasser 1960; Buzby and Mullen 1985).

Table 1 Comparison of the effects of ageing and protein energy malnutrition

Ageing	Protein energy malnutrition
Immune function	
↓ T-cell number	↓ T-cell number
↓ T-helper cells	↓ T-helper cells
↑ T-suppressor cells	↑ T-suppressor cells
↓ Blastic response to mitogens	↓ Blastic response to mitogens
Anergy (10%)	Anergy (10%)
↓ B-cell function	B-cell function unaffected
↑ Autoantibody production	Autoantibody production not increased
Natural killer cells normal or ↑	↓ Natural killer cells
Anthropometric measurements	
↓ Lean body mass	↓ Lean body mass
↑ Fat stores	↓ Fat stores
Biochemical measurements	
Serum albumin unchanged	↓ Serum albumin
↓ Transferrin	↓ Transferrin
Haemoglobin unchanged	↓ Haemoglobin
↓ Granulocyte response to infection	↓ Granulocytes response to infection
Drug metabolism	
↓ Drug plasma clearance	↓ Drug plasma clearance
↓ Drug breakdown	↓ Drug breakdown
↓ Excretion	↓ Excretion

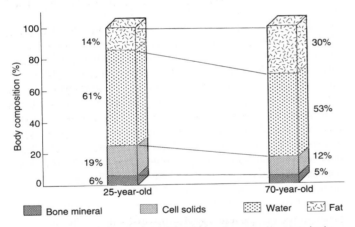

Fig. 2 Diagrammatic comparison of the effect of age on changes in body composition. Note the increased percentage of fat and reduction of body water in the 70-year-old person. This decrease reflects the age-associated decline in lean body mass. (Adapted from Schock *et al.* (1984).)

Biochemical and haematological parameters of nutritional status

Visceral protein stores are best assessed by the determination of serum albumin level. In addition serum transferrin, prealbumin, and retinol-binding protein are also of value (Frisancho 1984). Determination of serum transferrin in older people is complicated by the fact that it varies inversely with tissue iron stores (Lipschitz 1990). As a result of age-associated increases in tissue iron stores, a large fraction of elderly people have transferrin values in a range that may be falsely interpreted as indicating visceral protein store depletion. It must be pointed out that in ambulatory healthy elderly subjects reductions in serum albumin or other measures of visceral protein status are very unusual (Lipschitz 1987).

Protein energy malnutrition is associated with the development of anaemia, accompanied by evidence of iron deficient erythropoiesis and declines in cell-mediated immune function. The nutrition-related alterations in immune and haematopoietic function as a consequence of protein energy malnutrition have similarities to the declines in function which occur as a consequence of ageing. Even in healthy elderly subjects anergy and lymphocytopenia have been reported in approximately 10 per cent of subjects. In addition an unexplained anaemia is not uncommon. For these reasons ascribing declines in immune or haematological function to malnutrition in older individuals must be undertaken with appropriate clinical judgement.

Marasmus

Marasmus is a clinical syndrome characterized by weight loss with is accompanied by marked depletion in both fat stores and muscle mass (McMahon and Bistrian 1990). Serum albumin is normal and visceral organ function remains largely intact. The disorder is caused by an inadequate intake of energy relative to needs. The classic cause is semistarvation as occurs, for example, in anorexia nervosa. Similarly, cachexia associated with cancer, chronic renal, pulmonary, and cardiac failure, and chronic infections presents with the clinical features of marasmus.

Table 2 Common causes of weight loss in older people

Anorexia
Depression
Drugs, e.g. digoxin
Poor dentition

Diseases resulting in anorexia
  Cancer
  Chronic cardiac, renal, and pulmonary failure
  Chronic infections
  Polymyalgia rheumatica and collagen vascular diseases

Single nutrient deficiencies
  Vitamin A
  Zinc

Environmental
Malabsorption   Intestinal ischaemia

Swallowing disorders
  Neurological
  Oesophageal candidiasis

Metabolic   Hyperthyroidism
Decreased activity
Inadequate access to food
Food preferences not met

While as many as 40 per cent of young males and females are overweight, only 10 per cent of subjects over the age of 70 years are obese and 40 per cent are significantly underweight (Sullivan *et al.* 1989). Elderly individuals who fall below the 15th percentile for their ideal body weight can be diagnosed as having marasmus. Although the exact incidence in elderly people is not clear, marasmus is extremely common, particularly in chronically ill, hospital admitted, or institutionalized elderly people. In approximately 75 per cent of patients a cause will be identified (Table 2). Of these causes, anorexia (loss of appetite or desire for food) is a very common component. For further discussion of appetite regulation, anorexia, and protein energy malnutrition, see Chapter 6.3.

The importance of depression and drugs, particularly digitalis, as potentially treatable causes of weight loss cannot be overemphasized. Poor dentition, and loss of taste and smell (dysgeusia) should also be considered in elderly people. In institutionalized and dependent elderly people inadequate access to food, failure to provide desired food choices, and decreased activity, which invariably occurs in recently institutionalized elderly people, are common causes of weight loss. In about 25 per cent of elderly subjects an obvious cause cannot be identified. The aetiology of the weight loss, in these individuals is unknown. Dietary intake data often indicate that energy and protein intake are adequate. It has been suggested that marasmus in the nursing home results largely from anorexia which may be reversible. In these subjects the disorder has been called the 'anorexia of ageing' (see Chapter 6.3).

As indicated above, weight has been shown to decline in subjects over the age of 70 years. It is important to emphasize, however, that at any age, significant recent weight loss of greater than 5 per cent of original weight should never be ascribed to normal ageing. Nor can ageing explain the profound weight loss that characterizes marasmus.

Marasmus is important because underweight older subjects have a marked decrease in reserve capacity and develop serious nutritional problems both rapidly and with relatively minor stress.

Management of weight loss in older people

Weight loss is a major predictor of morbidity and mortality in older people and every effort should be made to identify and correct treatable causes. Of most importance is the correction, if present, of depression, infection, inflammation, or drug-induced anorexia. Every effort should be undertaken to encourage increased intake of a diet high in protein and calories. This can be best achieved by a diet high in protein and fat (eggs, red meat, full cream ice-cream, and so on). Many older people are on overly restricted low-fat diets. In markedly underweight older people, who frequently have low serum cholesterol levels, this is not appropriate. In the very frail it is also important to provide assistance with feeding, to assure that meals are palatable and to provide foods of the appropriate consistency. Frequent small meals are preferable and polymeric dietary supplements should be used only as meal replacements or late night snacks.

To be successful, nutritional therapy must be an integral component of a comprehensive rehabilitation plan that includes physical therapy and exercise, which can help improve physical condition and dependency, and stimulate oral food intake.

For those patients who continue to lose weight and who do not have a terminal illness, feeding via nasogastric tube or percutaneous endoscopic gastrostomy can be considered in full consultation with the patient and family. In general, however, continued weight loss despite correction of all underlying medical conditions carries a very poor prognosis and aggressive nutritional interventions are rarely successful (Sullivan and Lipschitz 1997). A number of appetite stimulants are being studied in older people. These include cyproheptadine, megesterol, growth hormones, and other anabolic steroids (Morley 1997). Although some weight gain can be identified, side-effects are unacceptably high.

Protein energy malnutrition

This disorder may be defined as a metabolic response to a pathological stress that is associated with a significant increase in the protein and energy needs required to maintain homoeostasis (McMahon and Bistrian 1990).

The pathophysiological changes that result in this disorder are illustrated in Fig. 3. The common conditions resulting in protein energy malnutrition are injury, burns, and inflammation (infectious and non-infectious). In the acute setting this response is both physiological and beneficial, and assists in optimizing the body's response to injury. In young individuals the effects of this metabolic response become negative, and significant pathology results if, after a period of approximately 10 days, protein and energy needs are not met. Inadequate nutrient supply primarily affects organ systems with rapid cellular or protein turnover. The disorder is associated with marked depletion of visceral protein stores characterized by the presence of

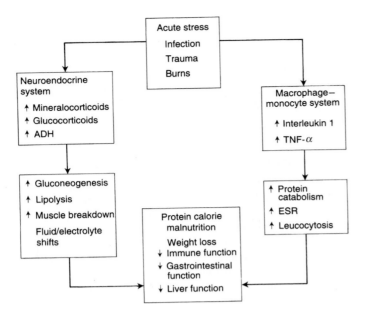

Fig. 3 The pathophysiological responses to stress that result in the development of protein energy malnutrition.

Table 3 Common causes of protein energy malnutrition in older people

Acute infections
Pulmonary
Urinary
Septicaemia
Decubitus ulcer
Acute cardiac or pulmonary failure
Trauma

hypoalbuminaemia. Liver function is impaired, contributing to the low serum albumin. Decreased clearance of drugs and toxins also occurs, increasing the risk of toxicities and adverse drug reactions. The organ systems with the highest turnover of cells are the skin, immunohaematopoietic system, and gastrointestinal tract. Thus protein energy malnutrition is characterized by a dry skin and 'flaky paint' dermatitis. Impaired immune responses lead to compromised host defences increasing the risk of life-threatening infections. Malabsorption also develops as a result of impaired jejunal and ileal mucosal cell proliferation creating a vicious cycle of malnutrition causing malabsorption and worsening malnutrition. As a result of disease and deficiencies of taste-related nutrients anorexia is usually present. The disorder is also referred to as hypoalbuminaemia malnutrition, and is usually diagnosed by the presence of a serum albumin level of less than 3.0 g/dl.

In older people, relatively minor stress of short duration can result in protein energy malnutrition. Thus protein energy malnutrition is common in elderly patients who develop minor pulmonary and urinary infections and is often found soon after an elective surgical procedure (Table 3). The problem of protein energy malnutrition is compounded by the ease with which these patients develop severe dehydration as a consequence of an age-associated decline in thirst drive. This leads to the development of confusion, hypotension, and a vicious cycle in which the patient's overall condition can deteriorate very rapidly. Furthermore, in contrast with younger subjects, the positive benefits of this disorder are limited to a very short period. If nutritional needs are not met within 2 to 3 days of the onset of the acute illness, the declines in immune, hepatic, and gastrointestinal function appear to contribute significantly to increased morbidity, mortality, and prolonged hospital stays.

In the nursing home, protein energy malnutrition should be suspected in any patient who develops an acute decubitus ulcer. Any patient presenting with confusion, lassitude, anorexia, decreased activity, or greater functional dependence, may have developed an acute medical problem such as an infection which, if not treated, will result in the development of significant protein energy malnutrition.

Recent evidence has demonstrated that scant attention is paid to the nutritional status of elderly people in acute hospital wards (Sullivan *et al*. 1989). In a prospective survey of such patients, a high prevalence of malnutrition was documented with 39 per cent having severe protein energy malnutrition and a further 33 per cent being more moderately malnourished. In 17 per cent of patients adequate evaluation of their nutritional status was not possible because of grossly inadequate assessments. In no patient was a diagnosis of malnutrition recorded on the problem chart. In only 10 per cent was any form of intervention attempted and in no circumstance was nutritional intervention adequate. In 20 patients enteral hyperalimentation was attempted. In three of these patients nasogastric feeding was never undertaken. In 80 per cent the tube was removed three or more times. Additional complications included diarrhoea, aspiration, and a fractured wrist in a patient who struggled in an attempt to remove restraints placed to prevent him from removing his nasogastric tube. These data indicate that elderly patients are usually not screened appropriately for protein energy malnutrition, the diagnosis is frequently missed or ignored, and nutrition support therapy is underutilized and often ineffectually managed with a high complication rate. In addition the patient's (and family's) concerns or preferences about intervention are often not sought or ignored. Use of restraints is rarely if ever justifiable.

There is now evidence that inadequate evaluation of a patient's nutritional status may be highly relevant. This is based on data obtained in a recent study which examined the impact of nutritional status on morbidity and mortality in a select population of geriatric rehabilitation patients (Sullivan *et al*. 1990). A prospective evaluation of 110 consecutive admissions to a geriatric rehabilitation hospital revealed a highly significant correlation between parameters which measure nutritional status and risk of developing major infectious and non-infectious complications, as well as mortality. Most importantly, using discriminate function techniques, it was possible to demonstrate that the nutritional impact on outcome was independent of all the other non-nutritional variables that are known to modulate morbidity and mortality. The non-nutritional factors that were important in this regard were functional status, diagnosis, and the number of drugs prescribed. This information is important because it sets the stage for investigations that should be able to determine if aggressive nutritional rehabilitation of selected malnourished geriatric patients decreases morbidity and mortality.

Table 4 Risks of enteral feeding in elderly patients

Side-effects	Corrective actions
Mechanical risks	
Dysphagia	Use pliable non-irritating tubes
Pharyngitis	Feed patient with the upper body elevated
Oesophagitis	
Obstruction	
Pulmonary aspiration	
Gastrointestinal risks	
Nausea and vomiting	Formula dilution
Cramping	Continuous slow infusion
Malabsorption	Formula change
Diarrhoea	Antidiarrhoeal agents
	Lactose-free isotonic formulae
Metabolic risks	
Hyperglycaemia	Monitor carefully
Hyperosmolarity	Appropriate infusion of fluids and electrolytes
Dehydration	
Azotaemia	
Fluid and electrolyte disturbances	
Miscellaneous risks	
Intolerance of nasogastric tube	Consider feeding gastrostomy or jejunostomy
Tube frequently pulled out	Consider peripheral hyperalimentation
	Avoid restraints

Management of protein energy malnutrition

Once a diagnosis of protein energy malnutrition has been made, clinical judgement is extremely important in deciding the appropriate time to commence nutritional support. In the acutely ill patient, attention should first be directed at correcting the major medical abnormalities. Thus, management of infections, control of blood pressure, and the restoration of metabolic, electrolyte, and fluid homoeostasis must assume priority. During this period fluid and nutrient intake should be recorded so that an assessment of future needs can be made. Once the acute process has stabilized, daily calorie counts should be performed and the subjects should be encouraged by the staff to consume as much of their food as possible, with attention to providing for food preferences. If fluid overload is not a major concern, the use of polymeric dietary supplements between meals and in the late evening should be considered. The aim is to achieve a caloric intake of approximately 35 kcal/kg based upon an ideal rather than the actual body weight. It is the author's experience that by encouragement alone only 10 per cent of elderly subjects with protein energy malnutrition can consume sufficient food voluntarily to correct their nutritional deficiency. Thus, most subjects require a more aggressive form of nutritional intervention. Except for those patients with an abnormal gastrointestinal tract the most appropriate method of nutritional correction is enteral hyperalimentation through a small-bore nasogastric polyethylene catheter. These tubes are non-irritating and do not interfere with patient mobility or the ability to swallow food. It is extremely important that after the tube is passed, placement in the stomach be confirmed prior to commencing nutritional feedings. Infusions should begin with an undiluted, commercially available polymeric dietary supplement at a continuous rate of 25 ml/h. The supplement should contain no more than 1 kcal/ml, as caloric-dense fluids are too viscous to pass through the tube with ease. The rate can gradually be increased so that after 48 h the total daily protein and calorie requirements of the patient are met by this route.

Enteral hyperalimentation has major side-effects (Table 4) of which the attending doctor must be aware. One of the most commonly encountered side-effects is excessive fluid retention. When nutritional support begins, weight gain is invariably noted within the first 2 to 3 days. This almost certainly reflects fluid retention, as the weight gain is associated with significant reductions in the serum albumin and haemoglobin levels. The average increase in weight during this time in our patients is 1.3 kg, while the level of serum albumin falls from a mean of 2.8 g/dl in patients prior to nutritional support to a value of 2.3 g/dl at day 3. Occasionally and particularly in elderly subjects with inadequate renal function, excessive retention of fluid can result in peripheral oedema or even heart failure. When this occurs, diuretic therapy can correct the underlying problem or the use of caloric-dense supplements should be considered. Major alterations in circulating electrolytes have also been described. Hyponatraemia and hypocalcaemia occur frequently. In addition, hypophosphataemia and decreased magnesium levels can occur, resulting in worsening confusion and delirium. Hyperglycaemia and glycosuria are occasionally noted, and frank diabetic coma can develop. An additional problem seen occasionally is severe diarrhoea. The risk of diarrhoea can be minimized if supplements are given by slow infusion. Bolus administration of dietary supplements through a nasogastric tube increases the risk of diarrhoea and, particularly in elderly people, enhances the possibility of vomiting and aspiration

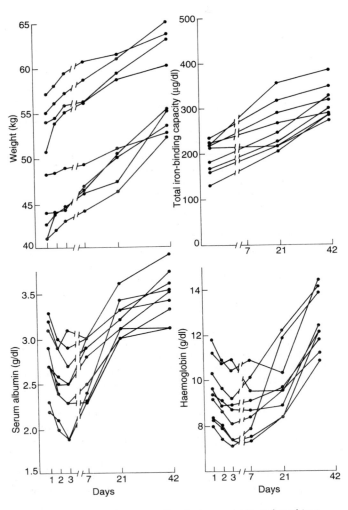

Fig. 4 Changes in weight, serum albumin, haemoglobin, and total iron-binding capacity in nine elderly subjects with severe protein energy malnutrition who received enteral hyperalimentation for 21 days, followed by a further 21 days of intensive nutritional rehabilitation. (Reproduced with permission from Lipschitz and Mitchell (1982).)

pneumonia. Nutritional management requires a great deal of clinical skill, particularly when frail aged subjects are being supported. With suitable training and monitoring, enteral hyperalimentation can be minimized and side-effects easily corrected.

The most difficult aspect of enteral hyperalimentation is intolerance of the tube and this is frequently seen in confused elderly subjects. As indicated above, these patients frequently remove the tube and restraints may be required to prevent this (Sullivan *et al.* 1989). This should be avoided if at all possible. For elderly subjects who are likely to require a prolonged period of enteral hyperalimentation, a feeding jejunostomy or gastrostomy is strongly recommended. For the acutely ill older subject who will require short-term nutritional rehabilitation active attempts at voluntary feeding should be attempted. This is very labour intensive and frequently unsuccessful. A final alternative that may be of great value is the use of short-term peripheral hyper-alimentation by which patients can receive all their protein, car-bohydrate, and fat requirements via a peripheral line. It must be emphasized that older subjects do not tolerate prolonged periods of inadequate nutritional intake. The management of the confused and uncooperative older patient, who has an appropriate indication for nutritional intervention remains a difficult clinical problem requiring a qualified team of health professionals to obtain an adequate clinical outcome.

Although anecdotal evidence has demonstrated that aggressive nutritional intervention can result in weight gain, improved immune and haematological functions as well as the return of serum albumin, transferrin, and other parameters of visceral protein stores to the normal range (Fig. 4), increases in muscle mass, as measured by anthropometric measurements, usually do not occur (Lipschitz and Mitchell 1982). Since a major goal of any geriatric rehabilitation is to improve functional independence and improve strength, strategies aimed at improving muscle mass are particularly important. For this reason the observation that administration of recombinant growth hormone can improve muscle mass and performance in frail elderly people is significant (Rudman *et al.* 1990). A beneficial effect of exercise has also been reported (Fiatarone *et al.* 1990). These studies emphasize the need for a comprehensive approach to the management of elderly malnourished patients. Aggressive nutritional intervention is only a part of a complete strategy aimed at restoring, in the appropriate patient, functional independence.

For further discussion of the management of anorexia and protein energy malnutrition, see Chapter 6.3.

The use of long-term tube feeding

One of the most important and valid indications for long-term tube feeding is a patient who for various reasons is unable to swallow. Patients who have had head and neck surgery or who have swallowing disorders frequently benefit significantly from enteral hyper-alimentation given either via nasogastric tube or percutaneous en-doscopic gastrostomy. Another major site for long-term tube feeding is the nursing home. Here numerous patients with endstage dementia are frequently fed enterally to prevent aspiration and aspiration pneumonia, reduce the risk of pressure ulcers, improve comfort, and prevent dehydration and metabolic abnormalities. Recent reports have questioned the value of enteral hyperalimentation in these patients in whom evidence of improvement or even benefit is minimal (Sheiman 1996). These facts add to the ethical dilemmas involved in the management of patients in the nursing home setting and the role of feeding in either maintaining or prolonging life. In numerous states legal issues prevent families from electing to discontinue tube feeding in patients with limited or no prognosis for meaningful recovery.

In the United States, advance directives by older people, agreed with by family members (or guardian), which explicitly address the issue of when to use or not use enteral feeding, are critical in protecting and honouring the wishes of each person.

In summary, the goal and efforts of nutrition should be to assess, advise, and assist each older person to have and enjoy healthful daily nutrition, with choices in keeping with his or her preferences.

References

Alexander, M.G., Emanuel, G.T., Pinto, J.T., and Rivlin, R.S. (1984). Relation of riboflavin nutriture in healthy elderly to intake of calcium and vitamin supplements: evidence against riboflavin supplementation. *American Journal of Clinical Nutrition*, 39, 540–6.

Allman, R.M. (1989). Pressure sores among the elderly. *New England Journal of Medicine*, 320, 850–3.

Anonymous (1981). *Health and Nutrition Examination Survey*, No. 2. USPHS Division, Hyattsville, MD.

Anonymous (1985). Vitamin D status of the elderly: contributions of sunlight and exposure and diet (lead article). *Nutrition Review*, 43, 78–80.

Birren, J.E. (1950). The relation of structural changes of the eye and vitamin A elevation of the light threshold in later life. *Journal of Experimental Psychology*, 40, 260.

Blumberg, J. and Mayer, J. (1997). Nutritional needs of seniors. *American Journal of Clinical Nutrition*, 16, 517–23.

Bogden, J.D., Oleske, J.M., Munves, E.M., et al. (1987). Zinc and immunocompetence in the elderly: baseline data on zinc nutriture and immunity in unsupplemented subjects. *American Journal of Clinical Nutrition*, 46, 101–9.

Bolsvert, W.A. and Russell, R.M. (1993). Riboflavin requirement of healthy elderly humans and its relationship to micronutrient composition of the diet. *Journal of Nutrition*, 12, 915–25.

Bunker, V.W., Lawson, M.S., Delves, H.T., and Clayton, B.E. (1984). The uptake and excretion of chromium by the elderly. *American Journal of Clinical Nutrition*, 39, 797–802.

Burns, R. and Nichols, L. (1986). Nutritional assessment of community living elderly. *Journal of the American Geriatrics Society*, 34, 781–6.

Buzby, G.P. and Mullen, J.L. (1985). Nutrition assessment. In *Clinical nutrition*, Vol. 1. *Enteral and tube feeding* (ed. J.L. Rombeau and M.D. Caldwell), pp. 127–48. W.B. Saunders, Philadelphia, PA.

Campbell, W.W., Crim, M.C., Dallal, G.E., Young, V.R., and Evans, W.J. (1994). Increased protein requirements in the elderly: new data and retrospective reassessments. *American Journal of Clinical Nutrition*, 60, 501–9.

Carmel, R. (1997). Cobalamin, the stomach and aging. *American Journal of Clinical Nutrition*, 66, 750–9.

Clarkston, W.K., Pantano, M.M., Morley, J.E., Horowitz, M., Littlefield, J.M., and Burton, F.R. (1997). Evidence for the anorexia of aging: gastrointestinal transit and hunger in healthy elderly vs young adults. *American Journal of Physiology*, 272, R243–8.

Crowle, A.J. and Ross, E.J. (1990). Comparative abilities of various metabolites of vitamin D to protect cultured human macrophages against tubercle bacilli. *Journal of Leukaemia and Biology*, 47, 545–50.

Duffy, P.H., Feuers, R.J., Leakey, J.A., Nakamura, K., Turturro, A., and Hart, R.W. (1989). Effect of chronic caloric restriction on physiological variables related to energy metabolism in the male Fischer 344 rat. *Mechanics of Ageing and Development*, 48, 117–33.

Elsborg, L., Lund, V., and Bastrup-Madsen, P. (1976). Serum vitamin B_{12} levels in the aged. *Acta Medica Scandinavica*, 200, 309–14.

Elwood, P.C., Shinton, N.K., Wilson, C.I.D., Sweetnam, P., and Frazier, A.C. (1971). Haemoglobin, vitamin B_{12} and folate levels in the elderly. *British Journal of Haematology*, 21, 557–63.

Fiatarone, M.A., Marks, E.C., Ryan, N.D., Meredith, C.N., Lipsitz, L.A., and Evans, W.J. (1990). High-intensity strength training in nonagenarians. *Journal of the American Medical Association*, 263, 3029–34.

Forbes, G.B. and Reina, J.B. (1970). Adult lean body mass declines with age: some longitudinal observations. *Metabolism*, 19, 653–63.

Frisancho, A.R. (1984). New standards of weight and body composition by frame size and height for assessment of nutritional status of adults and the elderly. *American Journal of Clinical Nutrition*, 40, 808–19.

Garry, P.J. and Hunt, W.C. (1986). Biochemical assessment of vitamin status in the elderly: effects of dietary and supplemental intakes. In *Nutrition and aging* (ed. M. Hutchinson and H.W. Munro), pp. 117–37. Academic Press, New York.

Garry, P.J., Hunt, W.D.C., Bandrofchak, J.L., Vanderjagt, D., and Goodwin, J.S. (1987a). Vitamin A intake and plasma retinol levels in healthy elderly men and women. *American Journal of Clinical Nutrition*, 46, 989–94.

Garry, P.J., Vanderjagt, D.C., and Hunt, W.C. (1987b). Ascorbic acid intakes and plasma levels in healthy elderly. *Annals of the New York Academy of Sciences*, 498, 90–9.

Gebron, R.S., Martinez, O.B., and MacDonald, C. (1985). The zinc, copper and selenium status of a selected sample of Canadian elderly women. *Journal of Gerontology*, 40, 296–302.

Gersovitz, M., Motil, K., Munro, H.N., Scrimshaw, N.S., and Young, V.R. (1982). Human protein requirements: assessment of the adequacy of the current recommended dietary allowance for dietary protein in elderly men and women. *American Journal of Clinical Nutrition*, 35, 6–14.

Greenberg, E.R., Baron, J.A., Stukel, T.H., et al. (1990). A clinical trial of beta carotene to prevent basal and squamous cell cancer of the skin. *New England Journal of Medicine*, 20, 789–95.

Heaney, R.P., Gallagher, J.C., Johnson, C.C., Neer, R., Parfitt, A.M., and Wheedon, G.D. (1982). Calcium nutrition and bone health in the elderly. *American Journal of Clinical Nutrition*, 36, 986–1013.

Iber, F.L., Blass, J.P., Brin, M., and Leevy, C.M. (1982). Thiamin in the elderly—relation to alcoholism and to neurological degenerative disease. *American Journal of Clinical Nutrition*, 36, 1067–82.

Jacob, R.A., Otradovec, D.C.L., Russell, R.M., et al. (1988). Vitamin C status and nutrient interaction in a healthy elderly population. *American Journal of Clinical Nutrition*, 48, 143–4.

Jernigan, J.A. and Gudat, J.C. (1980). Reference values for blood findings in relatively fit elderly persons. *Journal of the American Geriatrics Society*, 28, 308–14.

Koehler, K.M., Pareo-Tubbeh, S.L., Romero, L.J., Baumgartner, R.N., and Garry, P.J. (1997). Folate nutrition and older adults: challenges and opportunities. *Journal of the American Dietetics Association*, 97, 167–73.

Krasinski, S.D., Cohn, J.S., Schaefer, E.J., and Russell, R.M. (1990). Postprandial plasma retinyl ester response is grater in older subjects compared with younger subjects. Evidence for delayed plasma clearance of intestinal lipoproteins. *Journal of Clinical Investigation*, 85, 883–92.

Kritchevsky, D. (1990). Caloric restriction in experimental carcinogenesis. *Basic Life Science*, 52, 171–82.

LaPorte, R.E., Black-Sandler, R., Cauley, J.A., Link, M., Bayles, C., and Marks, B. (1983). The assessment of physical activity in older woman: analysis of the interrelationships and reliability of activity monitoring, activity surveys, and caloric intake. *Journal of Gerontology*, 38, 394–7.

Leupker, R.V. (1988). Detection and treatment of hypercholesterolemia in the older adult. *Geriatric Medicine Today*, 7, 48–50.

Lipschitz, D.A. (1987). Nutrition, aging, and the immunohematopoietic system. *Clinics in Geriatric Medicine*, 3, 319–28.

Lipschitz, D.A. (1990). Anemia in the elderly. In *Principles of geriatric medicine and gerontology* (ed. W.R. Hazzard, R. Andres, E.L. Bierman, and J.P. Blass), pp. 662–8. McGraw-Hill, New York.

Lipschitz, D.A. and Mitchell, C.O. (1982). The correctability of the nutritional, immune and hematopoietic manifestations of protein calorie malnutrition in the elderly. *American Journal of Clinical Nutrition*, 1, 17–25.

Lynch, S.R., Finch, C.A., Morrison, E.R., and Cook, J.D. (1982). Iron status of elderly Americans. *American Journal of Clinical Nutrition*, 36, 1032–45.

McGandy, R.B. (1988). Atherogenesis and aging. In *Health promotion and disease prevention in the elderly* (ed. R. Chernoff and D.A. Lipschitz), pp. 67–75. Raven Press, New York.

McGandy, R.B., Barrows, C.H., Spanias, A., Meredith, A., Stone, J.L., and Norris, A.H. (1966). Nutrient intake and energy expenditure in men of different ages. *Journal of Gerontology*, 21, 581–4.

McGandy, R.B., Russell, R.M., Hartz, S.C., et al. (1986). Nutritional status survey of healthy non-institutionalized elderly: energy and nutrient intakes from 3-day diet records and nutrient supplements. *Nutrition Research*, 6, 785–98.

McMahon, M.M. and Bistrian, B.R. (1990). The physiology of nutritional assessment and therapy in protein calorie malnutrition. *Disease a Month*, 7, 375–417.

Masoro, E.J. (1989). Overview of the effects of food restriction. *Progress in Clinical Biology and Research*, 187, 27–35.

Masoro, E.J. (1990). Physiology of ageing: nutritional aspects. *Age and Ageing*, 19, S5–9.

Masoro, E.J., Katz, M.S., and McMahan, C.A. (1989). Evidence for the glycation hypothesis of aging from the food-restricted rodent model. *Journal of Gerontology*, 44, 20–2.

Master, A. and Lasser, R. (1960). Tables of average weight and height of Americans aged 65–94 years. *Journal of the American Medical Association*, 172, 658–62.

Meydani, S.N., Barklund, M.P., Liu, S., *et al.* (1990). Vitamin E supplementation enhances cell-mediated immunity in healthy elderly subjects. *American Journal of Clinical Nutrition*, 52, 557–63.

Mitchell, C.O. and Lipschitz, D.A. (1982a). Arm length measurement as an alternative to height in nutritional assessment of the elderly. *Journal of Parenteral and Enteral Nutrition*, 6, 226–9.

Mitchell, C.O. and Lipschitz, D.A. (1982b). Detection of protein calorie malnutrition in the elderly. *American Journal of Clinical Nutrition*, 35, 398–406.

Morley, J.E. (1997). Anorexia of aging: physiologic and pathologic. *American Journal of Clinical Nutrition*, 66, 760–73.

Morley, J.E., Silver, A.J., Fiatarone, M., and Mooradian, A.D. (1986). UCLA Grand Rounds: nutrition and the elderly. *Journal of the American Geriatrics Society*, 34, 823–32.

Munro, H.N., Suter, P.M., and Russel, R.M. (1987). Nutritional requirements of the elderly. *Annual Review of Nutrition*, 7, 23–49.

National Center for Health Statistics (1974). *First Health and Nutrition Examination Survey, United States, 1971–1982*. DHEW Publication No. (HRA) 74-1219-1. Health Service Administration, Washington, DC.

Noppa, H., Andersson, M., Bengtsson, C., Bruce, A., and Isaksson, B. (1979). Body composition in middle-aged women with special references to the correlation between body fat mass and anthropometric data. *American Journal of Clinical Nutrition*, 32, 1388–95.

Phillips, P.A., Rolls, B.J., Ledingham, J.G.G., *et al.* (1984). Reduced thirst after water deprivation in healthy elderly men. *New England Journal of Medicine*, 311, 753–6.

Ribaya-Mercado, J.D., Russell, R.M., Sahyoun, N., Morrow, F.D., and Gershoff, S.H. (1991). Vitamin B_6 requirements of elderly men and women. *Journal of Nutrition*, 121, 1062–74.

Roberts, S.B., Fuss, P., Heymann, M.B., *et al.* (1994). Control of food intake in older men. *Journal of the American Medical Association*, 272, 1601–6.

Rudman, E., Feller, A.G., Nagraj, H.S., *et al.* (1990). Effects of human growth hormone in men over 60 years old. *New England Journal of Medicine*, 343, 1–6.

Russell, R.M. and Suter, P.M. (1993). Vitamin requirements of elderly people: an update. *American Journal of Clinical Nutrition*, 58, 4–14.

Russell, R.M., Cox, M.E., and Solomons, N. (1983). Zinc and the special senses. *Annals of Internal Medicine*, 99, 227–39.

Sadowski, J.A. (1992). Riboflavin. In *Nutrition in the elderly. The Boston Nutritional Status Survey* (ed. S.C. Hartz, I.H. Rosenberg, and R.M. Russell), pp. 119–25. Smith-Gordon, London.

Sandstead, H.H., Henriksen, L.K., Greger, J.L., Prasad, A.D., and Good, R.A. (1982). Zinc nutriture in the elderly in relation to taste acuity, immune response and wound healing. *American Journal of Clinical Nutrition*, 36, 1046–59.

Schock, N.W., Greulich, R.C., Andres, R., *et al.* (1984). *Normal human aging; the Baltimore Longitudinal Study of Aging*. NIH Publication No. 84, 2450. United States Department of Health and Human Services, Washington, DC.

Sheiman, S.L. (1996). Tube feeding the demented nursing home resident. *Journal of the American Geriatrics Society*, 44, 1268–70.

Stampfer, M.J., Malinow, M.R., Willett, W.C., *et al.* (1992). A prospective study of plasma homocyst(e)ine and risk of myocardial infarction in US physicians. *Journal of the American Medical Association*, 268, 877–81.

Sullivan, D. and Lipschitz, D.A. (1997). Evaluating and treating nutritional problems in older patients. *Clinics in Geriatric Medicine*, 13, 753–68.

Sullivan, D.A., Moriarty, M.S., Chernoff, R., and Lipschitz, D.A. (1989). An analysis of the quality of care routinely provided to elderly hospitalised veterans. *Journal of Parenteral and Enteral Nutrition*, 13, 249–54.

Sullivan, D.H., Path, G.A., Walls, R.C., and Lipschitz, D.A. (1990). Impact of nutrition status on morbidity and mortality in a select population of geriatric rehabilitation patients. *American Journal of Clinical Nutrition*, 51, 749–58.

Suter, P.M. and Russel, R.M. (1987). Vitamin requirements in the elderly. *American Journal of Clinical Nutrition*, 45, 501–12.

Trotter, M. and Gleser, G. (1951). Anthropometry in the elderly. *American Journal of Physical Anthropology*, 9, 311–24.

Uauy, R., Scrimshaw, N.S., and Young, V.R. (1978). Human protein requirements: nitrogen balance response to graded levels of egg protein in elderly men and women. *American Journal of Clinical Nutrition*, 31, 779–85.

Van Asperen, I.A., Feskens, E.J., Bowles, C.H., and Kromhout, D. (1995). Body iron stores and mortality due to cancer and ischaemic heart disease: a 17-year follow-up study of elderly men and women. *International Journal of Epidemiology*, 24, 665–70.

Vir, S.C. and Love, A.H.G. (1979). Nutritional status of institutionalized and non-institutionalized aged in Belfast, Northern Ireland. *American Journal of Clinical Nutrition*, 32, 1934–47.

Weintraub, S., Winter, C.C., Wahl, S.M., and Wahl, L.M. (1989). Effect of vitamin D deficiency on macrophage and lymphocyte function in the rat. *Calcified Tissue International*, 44, 125–30.,

Whiting, S.J. and Wood, R.J. (1997). Adverse effects of high-calcium diets in humans. *Nutrition Review*, 55, 1–9.

Winter, C.C., Wahl, S.M., and Wahl, L.M. (1989). Effect of vitamin D deficiency on macrophage and lymphocyte function in the rat. *Calcified Tissue International*, 44, 125–30.

Wurtman, J.J., Lieberman, H., Tsay, R., *et al.* (1988). Calorie and nutrient intakes of elderly young subjects measured under identical conditions. *Journal of Gerontology*, 43, B174–80.

Yearick, E.S., Wang, M.S., and Pisias, S.J. (1980). Nutritional status of the elderly: dietary and biochemical findings. *Journal of Gerontology*, 35, 663–71.

6.2 Vitamins

Hannes B. Stähelin

Introduction

Adequate nutrition is essential for maintaining good health in old age and postponing frailty as long as possible. The interrelation between food intake, health, and disease is very complex. Dietary needs depend on many factors such as age, sex, body size and composition, climate, physical activity, intercurrent illness, etc. With advancing age, intake of food, and therefore energy, tends to decrease and thus the risk of undernutrition and selective deficiencies is increased. Consequently, requirements for adequate nutrition are increasingly difficult to meet, and deficiencies become more common in older persons. Food choice and availability are subject to tradition, beliefs, and economic constraints. A highly variable nutrient density offers many opportunities for inadequate daily intake of essential micronutrients. However, ageing *per se* and a number of chronic diseases correlate strongly with the lifelong intake of micronutrients.

On a conceptual basis, we can distinguish the impact of vitamins on (i) the ageing process, (ii) chronic diseases leading to disability, and (iii) deficiency-related morbidity in the elderly patient. Table 1 lists the vitamins and their specific roles in the nutrition of elderly people.

Micronutrients modify the ageing process

Senescence is species-specific; life-span and onset of senescence vary from species to species. Ageing depends among other factors on the capacity to prevent or repair damage to essential structures such as DNA or membranes (Harman 1993). Metabolic processes and exogenous sources continuously generate free oxygen radicals (Halliwell 1994). Increased rate of ageing under oxidative stress and the correlation of antioxidant defences with species-specific life-span are well-known examples of this principle (Pacifici and Davies 1991). Calorie restricted animals extend their life-span via similar mechanisms; their body temperature is lower, which decreases their metabolic rate and their generation of reactive oxygen species. However, in contrast to the 30 per cent calorie reduction, essential nutrients were kept at an optimum in these experiments (Weindruch 1996).

This fact is relevant for older persons, who reduce their caloric intake without maintaining an adequate micronutrient supply in their diet. Micronutrients with antioxidant properties (vitamin C, vitamin E, carotenes, selenium) presumably prevent oxidative stress to cells and delay senescence by diminishing the generation of reactive oxygen species (Sies 1991). Other micronutrients regulate gene expression important in differentiation, and thus maintain cellular homeostasis (vitamin A, vitamin D) and, by slowing the cell-cycle, allow repair processes to take place and suppress proliferation (Sporn and Roberts 1983; Hannah and Norman 1994; Azzi *et al.* 1990; Bässler 1997).

Epidemiological data strongly suggest that bioactive secondary factors from plants such as carotenoids, flavonoids, phenols, phyto-oestrogens, etc, interact with many metabolic processes and enhance or counteract the effects of other micronutrients. Epidemiological evidence also shows that exposure time to an intake pattern correlates with health outcome and ageing (Kühnau 1976).

Micronutrients in the prevention of chronic diseases

Increasing evidence links a high intake of fruit and vegetables to lower rates of atherosclerosis and cancer (Block *et al.* 1992; Gazino *et al.* 1992). Recent reports have extended this link to neurodegenerative diseases (Evans 1993). This protective effect is attributed to antioxidant vitamins and folic acid, but also to an unknown extent to other bioactive nutrients such as flavonoids, phyto-oestrogens, etc. There is no question that dietary habits throughout adult life have a profound impact on the extent and age of onset of manifestations of chronic diseases, and hence contribute substantially to reduction of morbidity and prolonging healthy life expectancy. It is important to emphasize that this effect on morbidity is seen not only in subjects with manifest micronutrient deficiencies, who are rare in the European population, but also in populations which are at the lower end of the micronutrient supply range. However, 'safe plasma levels' have not yet been established. Table 2 gives suggestions put forward by experts (Gey 1998). Given the importance of delaying chronic disease in ageing, we present below a short overview summarizing evidence and current opinions on primary and secondary prevention of atherosclerosis, cancer, and neurodegenerative diseases.

Atherosclerosis

One of the initial events in atherosclerosis is the transformation of macrophages to foam cells. Steinberg *et al.* (1989) found that oxidized low-density lipoproteins are preferred targets for macrophages which incorporate them via the scavenger pathway and transform them to

Table 1 Vitamins: average estimated body store source, and relation to age-associated disorders

Vitamin	Deficiency[a]	Source	Potential problem in geriatric patient
Vitamin A (retinol)	Night vision impairment (1–2 years)	Animal products Plants	Threshold for toxic levels lower
Vitamin D (calciferol)	Osteomalacia Osteoporosis (c. 1 month)	Skin Dairy products Fish	Decreased endocrine production contributes to osteoporosis and secondary hyperparathyroidism
Vitamin E (α-tocopherol)	Neurological deficiencies (c. 1 month)	Plants	Increased risk of atherosclerosis and cancer in subjects with low supply
Vitamin K (phytomenadione, menaquinone)	Coagulation disorder Osteoporosis (c. 1 month)	Green vegetables Cheese Eggs Liver	Deficiencies observed in malnutrition and antibiotic treatment Subclinical deficiency may contribute to osteoporosis
Vitamin B_1 (thiamine)	Wernicke–Korsakow encephalopathy Heart failure (c. 1 week)	Cereals Vegetables Meat	Persons with malnutrition and alcoholism at high risk
Vitamin B_2 (riboflavin)	Pellagra Anaemia (c. 1 month)	Milk Cereals Liver	Skin alterations?
Vitamin B_6 (pyridoxine)	Anaemia Protein metabolism (c. 1 month)	Cereals Meat Liver	Dermatitis around orifice Anaemia Hyper-homocysteinaemia
Folic acid (vitamin B_9)	Anaemia Teratogenicity (c. 3 months)	Vegetables Liver	Hyper-homocysteinaemia Cancer Increased risk of atherosclerosis
Vitamin B_{12} (cyanocobolamin)	Anaemia Neuropathy	Liver Meat Dairy products Eggs	Neuropathy Atherosclerosis Hyper-homocysteinaemia
Vitamin C (ascorbic acid)	Scurvy Cataract Impaired immune function and tissue repair (c. 1 month)	Fruit Vegetables	Malnutrition increases risk for infection, cancer, atherosclerosis, cognitive disorders
Biotin	Ataxia Dermatitis (1 week)	Microbes in gut Eggs Liver	?
Niacin	Pellagra Dermatitis Anaemia (c. 1 month)	Meat	Malnutrition increases risk
Pantothenic acid	Neuropathy Abdominal pain Burning feet (c. 1 week)	Dairy products Liver	Malnutrition increases risk
Carotenoids β-Carotene Provitamin A	(Not established)	Green, yellow, red fruit and vegetables	Low levels of carotenoids associated with atherosclerosis, cancer, poor cognition Correlation independent of provitamin A function

[a] Body store is given in parentheses.

Table 2 Target threshold concentrations of plasma antioxidants

50 µmol/l diet-derived vitamin C
30 µmol/l lipid-standardized vitamin E
0.5 µmol/l diet-derived β-carotene
3.2 µmol/l diet-derived total carotene
0.4 µmol/l lycopene, 0.4 µmol/l lutein>2.0–2.6 µmol/l lipid-standardized vitamin A

Adapted from Gey (1998).

lipid-loaded foam cells. Lipid-soluble antioxidants such as vitamin E protect against oxidation (Esterbauer et al. 1992).

A number of epidemiological studies have found a reduced risk for coronary heart disease and stroke in subjects with a high intake of vitamin E (Rimm et al. 1993). In the Basel Study (Eichholzer et al. 1992), the risk for cardiovascular disease in the 17-year follow-up was increased in subjects with plasma vitamin C and β-carotene levels in the lowest quartile compared with those in higher quartiles (relative risk, 3.32). The relative risk for stroke in the same cohort was 4 (Stähelin 1997). It should be noted that in some cohorts the impact on risk is comparable with or even superior to that of the classical risk factors, such as hypertension, smoking, or hypercholesterolaemia. Indeed, the variation observed in coronary heart disease and stroke throughout Europe is best explained by including antioxidant plasma levels and known risk factors (Gey et al. 1993). These links between antioxidants, oxidative stress, and coronary disease are also found in non-Western populations (Singh et al. 1995).

Based on these experimental and epidemiological studies, a number of intervention trials were started. Vitamins E and C were found to reduce the mortality from coronary heart disease in some, but not all, studies (Azen et al. 1996; Losonczy et al. 1996; Meyer et al. 1996; Rapola et al. 1996; Stephens et al. 1996). The mechanism of action of antioxidants involves lipid oxidation. In addition, vitamin E also affects smooth muscle cell proliferation (Tasinato et al. 1995).

Data from secondary intervention studies suggest that the protective effect is not necessarily a result of lifelong dietary habits, but rather is comparable to a drug action of the ingested micronutrients, since the daily supplementary dosages (α-tocopherol, 100–800 mg; ascorbic acid, 500 mg or more) are far greater than daily intakes with food. Thus the borderline between nutrients and drug treatment with 'nutroceuticals' becomes blurred. Nevertheless, in epidemiological studies addressing primary prevention, a clear-cut effect was seen in subjects not taking supplements (Rimm et al. 1993).

Cancer

The evidence indicates that, although genetics is a factor in the development of cancer, it cannot be explained by heredity alone. Therefore dietary choices become important modifiable determinants of cancer risk (Shibata et al. 1992). Greater consumption of vegetables, fruit, or both has also been consistently associated with lower risk for a number of cancers (Willett 1990).

Vegetables and fruit are complex foods containing a large number of vitamins, minerals, and secondary bioactive non-nutritive compounds (phytochemicals such as phenols, flavonoids, terpenes, sterols, indols, etc.). Thus it is difficult to establish a causal relationship with a given component.

The mechanism protecting the body against carcinogenic factors is believed to be partially mediated by antioxidants. Reactive oxidative species occurring as a result of normal metabolism or induced by other effects are associated with increased cancer risk. It seems likely that no single compound is responsible for the protective effect, but rather that a complex interaction of different micronutrients is essential. For example, the protective effect of vitamin C against stomach cancer could be related to the ability of vitamin C to block the formation of nitrosamine in the stomach. Carotenoids influence the number of gap junctions and hence cell-to-cell signalling (Stahl et al. 1997). Folic acid, which is inversely associated with cancer risk in a number of studies, is necessary for DNA methylation and thus DNA stability (Bässler 1997). The synergistic action of vitamins is reflected in the results of the 17-year follow-up in the Prospective Basel Study (Eichholzer et al. 1996).

The strong and consistent relation between carotenes and lung cancer led to intervention trials with β-carotene and vitamins A and E in high-risk groups (Alpha-Tocopherol, Beta-Carotene Cancer Prevention Study Group 1994; Hennekens et al. 1995; Omenn et al. 1996). Contrary to expectation, β-carotene supplements led to a significantly higher lung cancer mortality. Thus it seems that β-carotene increases the clinical manifestation of cancer in smokers. The paradoxical finding that low carotene intake and plasma levels are associated with increased cancer risk has to be reconciled with the evidence that supplements induce an increased incidence of cancer in high-risk groups. Rapidly growing tissue has a high avidity for micronutrients. Vitamin E concentrations are increased in breast cancer tissue (Gerber and Segala 1992). One explanation based on considerable experimental evidence could be that, in high-risk subjects, supplements protect cells that are already transformed against the body's defence mechanisms, which are partly mediated by oxygen radicals. In practical terms, carotene supplements should not be advocated in persons at risk for lung cancer.

Vitamins, cognition, and neurodegenerative disease

Slowly progressive neurodegenerative processes such as Alzheimer's disease or Parkinson's disease precede clinical manifestation, probably by many years. There is mounting evidence that oxidative stress plays an important role in neurodegeneration. Hence, a high intake of food rich in antioxidant vitamins could diminish oxidative stress on neurones. Epidemiological evidence relating antioxidant vitamins to cognition in older persons is emerging. Analysis of the results of the Basel Study showed that vitamin C and carotene plasma levels obtained prior to and at the time of the cognitive test predicted memory function significantly (Table 3) (Perrig et al. 1997). Similar results were obtained in the Rotterdam Study (Jama et al. 1996) and the SENECA Study (Haller et al. 1996).

Based on the hypothesis that Aβ-amyloid induces oxidative stress and thus becomes neurotoxic, high doses of α-tocopherol were given to subjects with probable Alzheimer's disease (Sano et al. 1997). These findings need confirmation in a larger study but showed that vitamin

Table 3 Basel Longitudinal Study: intercorrelations of various memory functions in 1993 with plasma antioxidant levels, blood pressure, cholesterol, and ferritin measured in 1993 or in the same subjects on entry to the study in 1971

	Priming[a]	WM[b]	Free recall	Recognition	WAIS-R[c]
Vitamin C (1971)	−0.02	0.02	0.01	0.04	0.11*
Vitamin C (1993)	−0.05	0.03	0.10*	0.06	0.16**
β-Carotene (1971)	0.05	0.06	0.05	0.12*	0.10*
β-Carotene (1993)	−0.04	0.00	0.13**	0.22**	0.14**
Vitamin E (1971)	0.06	0.00	−0.02	0.02	0.09
Vitamin E (1993)	0.07	0.05	0.05	0.08	0.04
Systolic blood pressure (1993)	0.04	−0.01	−0.03	0.07	−0.01
Cholesterol (1993)	−0.01	−0.03	0.04	0.13**	−0.02
Ferritin (1993)	0.02	0.00	−0.13**	−0.14**	−0.01

[a] Priming, implicit memory.
[b] WM, working memory.
[c] WAIS-R, semantic memory.

* $p < 0.05$.
** $p < 0.01$.

Reproduced with permission from Perrig et al. (1997).

E significantly slowed down the neurodegenerative process and associated disability. Taken together, a lifelong intake of antioxidant vitamins seems to confer some protection against neurodegenerative disorders. This effect has to be distinguished from impaired cognitive function in subjects with low vitamin B_1 and high alcohol consumption (Wernicke's encephalopathy), or with deficiencies in vitamins B_{12} and B_6 or folic acid (see below). Low antioxidant status is also linked to macular degeneration and cataract.

Summary

There is mounting evidence that a high consumption of fruit and vegetables throughout adulthood significantly lowers the risk of age-associated diseases such as atherosclerosis, cancer, and probably neurodegenerative diseases. The importance of these findings for public health cannot be overestimated. A corollary of this conclusion is that present recommended dietary allowances (**RDAs**) are probably no longer useful guidelines for an optimal nutritional policy.

Vitamins and older people

Old age is associated with increasing morbidity and mortality. Thus, analysing the importance of vitamins for healthy ageing becomes increasingly complex. Is the frequently observed insufficient intake or low plasma level of a given vitamin clinically relevant or merely a reflection of ill health? At what amount and over what time are vitamin supplements protective, and aganst what? In this section we explore our current understanding of these questions.

The first important point is the fact that inadequate energy supply with undernutrition is usually associated with insufficient intake of micronutrients: 'Doctors and nurses frequently fail to recognise undernourishment because they are not trained to look for it' (Lennard-Jones 1992). In a study of home-delivered meals in the United States, 70 per cent had intakes below 66 per cent of the RDA for three or more nutrients (Abasi and Rudman 1994). Deficiencies were particularly noteworthy in the intake of energy, calcium, magnesium, and zinc. A large number of surveys indicate that inadequate intake of vitamins of the B complex, folic acid, and vitamin C is observed under many circumstances. Micronutrient intake from diet records predicts plasma levels. However, important factors affect the plasma concentration of some nutrients. Thus, vitamin C and carotene are lower in smokers than in non-smokers and higher in females than in males (Haller et al. 1996).

Table 4 lists common factors leading to vitamin deficiencies in elderly people.

A large behavioural risk factor survey (21 000 persons) in the United States showed that people with regular physical exercise had a higher intake of fruit and vegetables, were more likely to be non-smokers, and drank less alcohol than subjects with low physical activity. Similarly, the EURONUT–SENECA Study identified four behavioural clusters: 'lean and green eaters' with a high carbohydrate and vitamin C intake, 'gourmands' with a high energy and nutrient intake, 'milk drinkers' with a high intake of calcium and vitamin B_2, and 'small eaters' with marginal energy and nutrient intake (Schroll et al. 1996).

Patients admitted to geriatric wards with an acute illness very frequently suffer from micronutrient deficiencies (Tierney 1996). Among the causes of undernutrition, health factors are prominent. Again, in a survey carried out in England (Lehman 1997), chronic bronchitis and emphysema, cognitive impairment, dysphagia, being housebound, or being edentulous were identified as risk factors for undernutrition. This demonstrates the close connection between

Table 4 Common causes of vitamin deficiencies in old age

Social and psychological
Depression
Eating alone
Impaired mobility
Alcoholism
Elder abuse
Inadequate assistance

Physical
Oral/dental problems, poor hygiene
Neurological deficit leading to impaired chewing/swallowing
Memory disorders
Chronic pulmonary and cardiac disease
Chronic upper gastrointestinal problems (e.g. reflux, atrophic gastritis)
Constipation
Medications

Table 5 Recommended dietary allowances for vitamin intake in the elderly person (over 50)[a]

Vitamin	RDA (women)	RDA (men)
Vitamin A[b]	800 μg	1000 μg
Vitamin D[c]	5 μg	5 μg
Vitamin E[d]	8 mg	10 mg
Vitamin K	65 μg	80 μg
Vitamin C	60 mg	60 mg
Vitamin B_1	1 mg	1.2 mg
Vitamin B_2	1.2 mg	1.4 mg
Vitamin B_6	1.6 mg	2.0 mg
Vitamin B_{12}	2 μg	2 μg
Folic acid	180 μg	200 μg
Niacin[e]	13 mg	15 mg
Biotin	30–100 μg	30–100 μg
Pantothenic acid	4–7 mg	4–7 mg

[a] There is mounting evidence that the RDAs are not sufficiently high for the prevention of certain metabolic disorders and chronic diseases. Furthermore, even the indicated amounts are often difficult for older persons to achieve from food alone.
[b] As retinol equivalent (1 RE = 1 μg retinol = 6 μg β-carotene at 3.33 IU).
[c] Cholecalciferol (5 μg cholecalciferol = 200 IU vitamin D).
[d] 1 mg 1-α-tocopherol equivalent = 1 mg D-α-tocopherol.
[e] As niacin equivalent (1 NE = 1 mg niacin = 60 mg tryptophan).

health factors and social causes of undernutrition. In a large community survey in Boston, Massachusetts, alcohol consumption correlated inversely with riboflavin, copper, and zinc intake (Jacques *et al.* 1989). Supplement use is prevalent in community-dwelling elderly people and is more commonly associated with demographic factors and access to health care than with need (Gray *et al.* 1996). Similarly, low zinc is often encountered in anorexia and could further suppress appetite.

The impact of living arrangements and mobility is probably greatest on vitamin D metabolism. There are numerous surveys showing that housebound persons or patients in long-stay facilities run a far higher risk of vitamin D deficiency and subsequent development of secondary hyperparathyroidism than do mobile free-living elderly subjects. In a survey of 183 nursing home patients (Gloth *et al.* 1995), vitamin D was below 12 ng/l in 86 per cent and parathyroid hormone was elevated in 24 per cent. In a healthy group, vitamin D deficiencies were observed in only 15 per cent and elevated parathyroid hormone in 18 per cent. Vitamin D deficiency in housebound elderly persons was likely to occur despite a relatively high degree of vitamin supplementation, highlighting the critical situation for this vitamin. Similarly, the high frequency of hypovitaminosis D in medical inpatients (Thomas *et al.* 1998) strongly indicates the need for supplements in elderly people.

Among the water-soluble vitamins, the intake of vitamins B_1 and B_6 is two-thirds or less of the RDA in elderly subjects (van der Wielen *et al.* 1995)

A more fundamental question is whether RDAs (Table 5) and plasma levels defined to protect against deficiencies provide an adequate intake to maintain optimal function and prevent chronic disease. This is illustrated by vitamin B_{12}. A plasma concentration of vitamin B_{12} below 220 pmol/l is frequently observed in older adults, and particularly in patients with Alzheimer's disease (Joosten *et al.* 1997; Bottiglieri 1996). Frequently, neurological or haematological signs indicating B_{12} deficiencies are absent. There is still debate in the literature as to whether these low levels indicate true B_{12} deficiency. An important factor may be that elderly subjects with B_{12} below this level score worse in cognitive tests than persons with higher plasma levels (Wahlin *et al.* 1996). Total levels of homocysteine and related

metabolites correlate with low vitamin B_6, vitamin B_{12}, and folate status. Thus the higher total homocysteine levels (6.8–21 μmol/l in old persons versus 5–13.6 μmol/l in younger subjects) could reflect the poorer vitamin B_6, vitamin B_{12}, and folate intake in the older subjects (Selhub *et al.* 1993). Total homocysteine is an important risk factor for vascular disease. There is mounting evidence that higher levels of certain vitamins (e.g. folate) are advisable, even in the healthy adult (Oakley 1998). The higher homocysteine concentration, on average, in elderly subjects suggests inadequate micronutrient intake from food and supports the use of supplements (Rimm *et al.* 1998).

Whether all persons are able to maintain an adequate or even desirably high intake of micronutrients without the use of supplements is still open to debate. Therefore in the next section we examine the controversies surrounding vitamin supplements.

Table 5 gives the RDA levels proposed by the Subcommittee on the Food and Nutrition Board (National Research Council 1989). It is emphasized that no special data or recommendation exist for older persons (≥ 75 years). As outlined above, several lines of evidence suggest that intake from food is inadequate, particularly in frail elderly people, and that intakes above low normal can only be achieved with supplements.

To supplement or not to supplement

Correction of acute deficiencies (e.g. vitamin B_{12} deficiencies) by supplementation is clearly indicated. Certain medical conditions and related therapies may induce deficiencies in water-soluble vitamins very rapidly (see Table 1). Critical reviews have described little if any benefit from supplementation for reasons other than replacement therapy (Buchman 1996).

Multivitamin and micronutrient supplementation in the elderly population at large is more controversial. Chandra (1992) demonstrated that a supplement mixture had significant benefit, with less occurrence of infectious disease and less hospital admission in the supplemented group. However, an English study found no benefit over a 1-month supplementation (Hogarth 1996). Use of supplements is also associated with better education, more health visits, and better self-rated health than in non-users. Thus psychosocial confounding factors again have to be taken into account when evaluating the utility of supplements. Given the likely disease-prevention effect of adequate micronutrient supplementation, a more positive attitude towards large-scale supplementation with multivitamins should be adopted by the medical community and public health authorities.

Vitamins and immune function

Vitamin E (200 mg/day) improved T-cell function by enhancing the response to hepatitis B sixfold, but had no effect on the response to diphtheria toxin (Meydani 1993). Another study found no correlation of the *in vitro* response to T-cell stimulation by phytohaematoglutinin or concanavalin A with plasma levels or intake of zinc, retinol, β-carotene, or α-tocopherol (Gardner *et al.* 1997). In summary, numerous reports show that supplements have an effect on many biological systems, but the clinical impact of these effects remains controversial (Buchman 1996). A short review, ascribing more effect to trace elements than to vitamins, is given by Johnson and Porter (1997).

Vitamins and bone

Probably the best documented case for supplements is the retardation of osteoporosis and related fractures by vitamin D_3 (800 IU/day) and elemental calcium (1 g/day) (Meunier 1996). A Dutch study (Lips *et al.* 1996) in which only 400 IU of vitamin D_3 was given, with no calcium, was negative, indicating, perhaps, that it is necessary to supplement both vitamin D_3 and calcium (Gloth *et al.* 1995).

Vitamin K is important for the carboxylation of glutamic acid residues of osteocalcin. Other well-known proteins with glutamic acid residues are prothrombin and other coagulation factors. Under-carboxylation of osteocalcin, at a level not affecting blood coagulation, is increased in elderly women and correlates strongly with hip fracture risk. Vitamin K levels are lower in elderly women (Hodges *et al.* 1993). It has been shown that administration of vitamin K to postmenopausal women increases bone mass (Maenpaa *et al.* 1989).

A study analysing the association between α-tocopherol and ascorbic acid in the diet found a surprisingly strong link between vitamin E and lung function in elderly persons (Dow *et al.* 1996). For every milligram increase in vitamin E in the daily diet, the forced expiratory volume in 1 s increased by 42 ml and the forced vital capacity increased by 54 ml.

Evidence shows that a lifelong intake of certain vitamins at or above present RDA levels may be effective in preventing a number of chronic diseases associated with ageing (Losonczy *et al.* 1996). Elderly persons are at particular risk for inadequate intake. Ill health is a strong risk factor for deficiencies (Utiger 1998). Despite a relatively high degree of vitamin supplementation (in the United States),

housebound elderly persons are likely to suffer from vitamin D deficiencies (Gloth *et al.* 1995). Undernutrition itself is associated with a high risk of deficiencies in vitamins of the B complex. Evidence is increasing that current RDAs for older people are too low for riboflavin, vitamin B_6, vitamin B_{12}, folic acid, vitamin D, vitamin C, vitamin E, and vitamin K, but too high for retinol (Russell 1997). High intakes and plasma levels of vitamin C and frequent consumption of vegetables may be protective against early mortality and mortality from heart disease (Sahyoun 1996). Thus identification of under-nutrition and/or selective inadequate intake is important. With few exceptions, the value of supplementation with doses several times greater than RDA levels, albeit of great theoretical interest, remains to be established for most micronutrients.

References

Abasi, A.A. and Rudman, D. (1994). Undernutrition in the nursing home: prevalence, consequences, causes and prevention. *Nutrition Review*, 52, 113–22.

Alpha-Tocopherol, Beta-Carotene Cancer Prevention Study Group (1994). The effect of vitamin E and beta carotene on the incidence of lung cancer and other cancers in male smokers. *New England Journal of Medicine*, 330, 1029–35.

Azen, S.P., Qian, D., Mack, W.J., *et al.* (1996). Effect of supplementary antioxidant vitamin intake on carotid arterial wall intima-media thickness in a controlled clinical trial of cholesterol lowering. *Circulation*, 94, 2369–72.

Azzi, A., Boscoboinik, D., Marilley, D., Özer, N., Stäuble, B., and Tasinato, A. (1995). Vitamin E, a sensor and an information transducer of the cell oxidation state. *American Journal of Clinical Nutrition*, 52, 1337S–46S.

Bässler, K.H. (1997). Enzymatic effects of folic acid and vitamin B_{12}. *International Journal for Vitamin and Nutrition Research*, 67, 385–8.

Block, G., Patterson, B., and Subar, A. (1992). Fruit, vegetables, and cancer prevention: a review of the epidemiological evidence. *Nutrition and Cancer*, 18, 1–29.

Bottiglieri, T. (1996). Folate, vitamin B_{12}, and neuropsychiatric disorders. *Nutrition Reviews*, 54, 382–90.

Buchman, A.L. (1996). Vitamin supplementation in the elderly: a critical evaluation. *Gastroenterologist*, 4, 262–75.

Chandra, R.K. (1992). Effect of vitamin and trace-element supplementation on immune responses and infection in elderly subjects. *Lancet*, 340, 1124–7.

Dow, L.,Tracey, M., Villar, A., *et al.* (1996). Does dietary intake of vitamins C and E influence lung function in older people? *American Journal of Respiratory and Critical Care Medicine*, 154, 1401–4.

Eichholzer, M., Stähelin, H.B., and Gey, K.F. (1992). Inverse correlation between essential antioxidants in plasma and subsequent risk to develop cancer, ischaemic heart disease and stroke respectively: 12-year follow-up of the Prospective Basel Study. *Exs*, 62, 398–410.

Eichholzer, M., Stähelin, H.B., Gey, K.F., Ludin, E., and Bernasconi, F. (1996). Prediction of male cancer mortality by plasma levels of interacting vitamins: 17-year follow-up of the prospective Basel study. *International Journal of Cancer*, 66, 45–50.

Esterbauer, H., Gebicki, J., Puhl, H., and Jürgens, G. (1992).The role of lipid peroxidation and antioxidants in oxidative modification of LDL. *Free Radical Biology and Medicine*, 13, 341–90.

Evans, P.H. (1993). Free radicals in brain metabolism and pathology. *British Medical Bulletin*, 49, 577–87.

Gardner, E.M., Bernstein, E.D., Dorfman, M., Abrutyn, E., and Murasko, D.M. (1997). The age-associated decline in immune function of healthy individuals is not related to changes in plasma concentrations of beta-carotene, retinol, alpha-tocopherol or zinc. *Mechanisms of Ageing and Development*, 94, 55–69.

Gazino, J.M., Manson, J.E., Buring, J.E., and Hennekens, C.H. (1992). Dietary antioxidants and cardiovascular disease. *Annals of the New York Academy of Sciences*, 669, 249–59.

Gerber, M. and Segala, C. (1992). Aging and cancer: plasma antioxidants and lipid peroxidation in young and aged breast cancer patients. *Exs*, 62, 235–46.

Gey, K.F. (1998). Vitamin E plus C and interacting conutrients required for optimal health. A critical and constructive review of epidemiology and supplementation data regarding cardiovascular disease and cancer. *Biofactors*, 7, 113–74.

Gey, K.F., Moser, U.K., Jordan, P., Stähelin, H.B., Eichholzer, M., and Lüdin, E. (1993). Increased risk of cardiovascular disease at suboptimal plasma concentrations of essential antioxidants: an epidemiological update with special attention to carotene and vitamin C. *American Journal of Clinical Nutrition*, 57 (Supplement), 787S–97S.

Gloth, F., III., Smith, C.E., Hollis, B.W., and Tobin, J.D. (1995). Functional improvement with vitamin D replenishment in a cohort of frail, vitamin D-deficient older people. *Journal of the American Geriatrics Society*, 43, 1269–71.

Gray, S.L., Hanlon, J.T., Fillenbaum, G.G., Wall, W.J., and Bales, C. (1996). Predictors of nutritional supplement use by the elderly. *Pharmacotherapy*, 16, 715–20.

Haller, J., Weggemans, R.M., Ferry, M., and Guigoz, Y. (1996). Mental health: minimental state examination and geriatric depression score of elderly Europeans in the SENECA Study of 1993. *European Journal of Clinical Nutrition*, 50 (Supplement), S112–16.

Halliwell, B. (1994). Free radicals and antioxidants: a personal view. *Nutrition Reviews*, 52, 253–65.

Hannah, St.S. and Norman, A.W. (1994). $1\alpha25(OH)_2$ Vitamin D_3-regulated expression of the eukaryotic genome. *Nutrition Reviews*, 52, 376–82.

Harman, D. (1993). Free radical involvement in aging. Pathophysiology and therapeutic implications. *Drugs and Aging*, 3, 60–80.

Hennekens, C.H., Gaziano, J.M., Manson, J.E., and Buring, J.E. (1995). Antioxidant vitamin–cardiovascular disease hypothesis is still promising, but still unproven: the need for randomized trials. *American Journal of Clinical Nutrition*, 62 (Supplement 6), 1377S–80S.

Hodges, S.J., Akesson, K., Vergnaud, P., Obrant, K., and Delmas, P.D. (1993). Circulating levels of vitamins K_1 and K_2 decreased in elderly women with hip fracture. *Journal of Bone and Mineral Research*, 8, 1241–5.

Hogarth, M.B., Marshall, P., Lovat, L.B., et al. (1996). Nutritional supplementation in elderly medical in-patients: a double-blind placebo-controlled trial. *Age and Ageing*, 25, 453–7.

Jacques, P.F., Sulsky, S., Hartz, S.C., and Russell, R.M. (1989). Moderate alcohol intake and nutritional status in non-alcoholic elderly subjects. *American Journal of Clinical Nutrition*, 50, 875–83.

Jacques, P.F., Halpner, A.D., and Blumberg, J.B. (1995). Influence of combined antioxidant nutrient intakes on their plasma concentrations in an elderly population. *American Journal of Clinical Nutrition*, 62, 1228–33.

Jama, J.W., Launer, L.J., Witteman, J.C., et al. (1996). Dietary antioxidants and cognitive function in a population-based sample of older persons: the Rotterdam Study. *American Journal of Epidemiology*, 144, 275–80.

Johnson, M.A. and Porter, K.H. (1997). Micronutrient supplementation and infection in institutionalised elders. *Nutrition Reviews*, 55, 400–4.

Joosten, E., Lesaffre, E., Riezler, R., et al. (1993). Is metabolic evidence for vitamin B-12 and folate deficiency more frequent in elderly patients with Alzheimer's disease? *Journal of Gerontology*, 52, M76–9.

Kühnau, J. (1976). The flavanoids: a class of semi-essential food components: their role in human nutrition. *World Review of Nutrition and Dietetics*, 24, 117–20.

Lehman, A.B. (1997). Nutrition and health. What is new? *Reviews of Clinical Gerontology*, 6, 147–68.

Lennard-Jones, J.E. (1992). *A positive approach to nutrition and treatment. Report of a working party*. King's Fund Centre, London.

Lips, P., Graafmans, W.C., Ooms, M.E., Bezemer, P.D., and Bouter, L.M. (1996). Vitamin D supplementation and fracture incidence in elderly persons. A randomized, placebo-controlled clinical trial. *Annals of Internal Medicine*, 124, 400–6.

Losonczy, K.G., Harris, T.B., and Havlik, R.J. (1996). Vitamin E and vitamin C supplement use and risk of all-cause and coronary heart disease mortality in older persons: the Established Populations for Epidemiologic Studies of the Elderly. *American Journal of Clinical Nutrition*, 64, 190–6.

Maenpaa, P.H., Pirhonen, A., Pirskanen, A., et al. (1989). Biochemical indicators related to antioxidant status and bone metabolic activity in Finnish elderly men. *International Journal for Vitamin and Nutrition Research*, 59, 14–19.

Meunier, P. (1996). Prevention of hip fractures by correcting calcium and vitamin D insufficiencies in elderly people. *Scandinavian Journal of Rheumatology, Supplement*, 103, 75–8.

Meydani, S. N. (1993). Vitamin/mineral supplementation, the aging immune response, and risk of infection. *Nutrition Reviews*, 51, 106–9.

Meyer, F., Bairati, I., and Dagenais, G.R. (1996). Lower ischaemic heart disease incidence and mortality among vitamin supplement users. *Canadian Journal of Cardiology*, 12, 930–4.

National Research Council (1989). *Recommended dietary allowances* (10th edn). National Academy Press, Washington, DC.

Oakley, G.P., Jr (1998). Eat right *and* take a multivitamin. *New England Journal of Medicine*, 338, 1060–1.

Omenn, G.S., Goodman, G.E., Thornquist, M.D., et al. (1996). Effects of a combination of beta carotene and vitamin A on lung cancer and cardiovascular disease. *New England Journal of Medicine*, 334, 1150–5.

Pacifici, R.E. and Davies, K.J.A. (1991). Protein, lipid and DNA repair system in oxidative stress: the theory of free radical theory on aging revisited. *Gerontology*, 37, 166–80.

Perrig, W.J., Perrig, P., and Stähelin, H.B. (1997). The relation between antioxidants and memory performance in the old and very old. *Journal of the American Geriatrics Society*, 45, 718–24.

Rapola, J.M., Virtamo, J., Haukka, J.K., et al. (1996). Effect of vitamin E and beta carotene on the incidence of angina pectoris: a randomized, double-blind, controlled trial. *Journal of the American Medical Association*, 275, 693–8.

Rimm, E.B., Stampfer, M.J., Ascherio, A., Giovannucci, E., Colditz, G.A., and Willett, W.C. (1993). Vitamin E consumption and the risk of coronary heart disease in men. *New England Journal of Medicine*, 328, 1444–9.

Rimm, E.B., Willett, W.C., Hu, F.B., et al. (1998). Folate and vitamin B_6 from diet and supplements in relation to risk of coronary heart disease among women. *Journal of the American Medical Association*, 279, 359–64.

Russell, R.M. (1997). New views on the RDAs for older adults. *Journal of the American Dietetic Association*, 97, 515–18.

Sahyoun, N.R., Jacques, P.F., and Russell, R.M. (1996). Carotenoids, vitamins C and E, and mortality in an elderly population. *American Journal of Epidemiology*, 144, 501–11.

Sano, M., Ernesto, C., Thomas, R.G., et al. (1997). A controlled trial of selegiline, alpha-tocopherol, or both as treatment for Alzheimer's disease: the Alzheimer's Disease Cooperative Study. *New England Journal of Medicine*, 336, 1216–22.

Schroll, K., Carbajal, A., Decarli, B., et al. (1996). Food patterns of elderly Europeans. SENECA Investigators. *European Journal of Clinical Nutrition*, 50 (Supplement), S86–100.

Selhub, J., Jacques, P.F., Wilson, P.W., Rush, D., and Rosenberg, I. H. (1993). Vitamin status and intake as primary determinants of homocysteinemia in an elderly population. *Journal of the American Medical Association*, 270, 2693–8.

Shibata, A., Paganini, H.A., Ross, R.K., and Henderson, B.E. (1992). Intake of vegetables, fruits, beta-carotene, vitamin C and vitamin supplements and cancer incidence among the elderly: a prospective study. *British Journal of Cancer*, 66, 673–9.

Sies, H. (ed.) (1991). *Oxidative stress, oxidants and antioxidants*. Academic Press, New York.

Singh, R.B., Ghosh, S., Niaz, M.A., et al. (1995). Dietary intake, plasma levels of antioxidant vitamins, and oxidative stress in relation to coronary artery disease in elderly subjects. *American Journal of Cardiology*, 76, 1233–8.

Sporn, M.B. and Roberts, A.B. (1983). Role of retinoids in differentiation and carcinogenesis. *Cancer Research*, 43, 3034–40.

Stähelin, H.B. (1997). Antioxidants and atherosclerosis. In *Nutrition and stroke* (ed. P. Guesry, M. Hennerici, and G. Sitzer), pp. 75–85. Lippincott–Raven, Philadelphia, PA.

Stahl, W., Nicolai, S., Briviba, K., et al. (1997). Biological activities of natural and synthetic carotenoids: induction of gap junctional communication and singlet oxygen quenching. *Carcinogenesis*, 18, 89–92.

Steinberg, D., Parthasarathy, S., Carew, T.E., Khoo, J.C., and Witzum, J.L. (1989). Beyond cholesterol: modifications of low-density lipoproteins that increase atherogenecity. *New England Journal of Medicine*, 320, 915–24.

Stephens, N.G., Parsons, A., Schofield, P.M., Kelly, F., Cheeseman, K., and Mitchinson, M.J. (1996). Randomised controlled trial of vitamin E in patients with coronary heart disease: Cambridge Heart Antioxidant Study (CHAOS). *Lancet*, 347, 781–6.

Tasinato, A., Boscoboinik, D., Bartoli, G.M., Maroni, P., and Azzi, A. (1995). d-alpha-tocopherol inhibition of vascular smooth muscle cell proliferation occurs at physiological concentrations, correlates with protein kinase C inhibition, and is independent of its antioxidant properties. *Proceedings of the National Academy of Sciences of the United States of America*, 92, 12 190–4.

Thomas, M.K., Lloyd, J.D., Thadhani, R.I., et al. (1998). Hypovitaminosis D in medical inpatients. *New England Journal of Medicine*, 338, 777–83.

Tierney, A.J. (1996). Undernutrition and elderly hospital patients: a review. *Journal of Advanced Nursing*, 23, 228–36.

Utiger, R.D. (1998). The need for more vitamin D. *New England Journal of Medicine*, 338, 828–9.

van der Wielen, R., Lowik, M. R., Haller, J., van den Berg, H., Ferry, M., and van Staveren, W. (1996). Vitamin B-6 malnutrition among elderly Europeans: the SENECA Study. *Journal of Gerontology A*, 51, B100–7.

Wahlin, A., Hill, R.D., Winblad, B., and Backman, L. (1996). Effects of serum vitamin B12 and folate status on episodic memory performance in very old age: a population-based study. *Psychology of Aging*, 11, 487–96.

Weindruch, R. (1996). Caloric restriction and aging. *Scientific American*, 247, 32–8.

Willett, W.C. (1990). Epidemiologic studies of diet and cancer. *Medical Oncology and Tumor Pharmacotherapy*, 7, 93–7.

6.3 Anorexia of ageing

Hosam K. Kamel and John E. Morley

Nutrition is an important factor in many of the physiological and pathological changes associated with ageing. It is estimated that 85 per cent of the chronic diseases and disabilities experienced by older individuals can be prevented or ameliorated by nutritional interventions (Barrocas *et al.* 1995). In many persons, there is a physiological decline in appetite with advancing age. This is known as 'anorexia of ageing' (Morley and Silver 1988). This physiological anorexia counterbalances the decrease in physical activity and resting metabolic rate that accompanies advancing age. This physiological anorexia places older persons at increased risk of protein energy undernutrition, whereupon other factors develop which place them at risk for decreasing food intake or increasing energy expenditure.

Protein energy undernutrition affects up to 15 per cent of community-dwelling and ambulatory elderly persons, 5 to 12 per cent of housebound patients with multiple chronic problems, 35 to 65 per cent of patients acutely admitted to hospital, and 25 to 60 per cent of institutionalized elderly persons (Johnson 1996). In nursing homes, protein energy undernutrition is associated with decubitus ulcers, cognitive impairment, postural hypotension, infections, and anaemia (Morley and Silver 1995). Protein energy undernutrition is also a strong independent risk factor for in-hospital morbidity and early non-elective hospital readmission (Sullivan and Walls 1994). Community-dwelling older persons with protein energy undernutrition may exhibit reduced performance in the basic and instrumental activities of daily living as well as an increased incidence of hip fractures (Wilson and Morley 1995). Despite these well-documented findings, the presence of protein energy undernutrition in older persons is rarely recognized, and even when recognized it is often not treated.

In this chapter we present an overview of appetite regulation and the physiology of the anorexia of ageing. The types and different causes of protein energy undernutrition are discussed. The available screening and assessment tools for protein energy undernutrition are described, and its management is reviewed in depth.

Appetite regulation

The regulation of appetite is a complex process involving both central and peripheral mechanisms. There is evidence that food ingestion is regulated by a central drive that is held in check by a peripheral satiety system (Morley 1980). The central feeding drive system involves a number of anatomical sites such as the paraventricular and ventromedial nuclei of the hypothalamus and structures associated with the fourth ventricle (Morley 1990a). The interaction of a number of neurotransmitters within these sites is believed to be responsible for the generation of the feeding drive.

The major neurotransmitter system involved in the drive to ingest fat is the endogenous opioid system. Among the three opiate receptors in the brain, the K receptor plays a central role in feeding, and its ligand dynorphin is the principle opioid involved in promoting ingestive behaviour (Morley and Levine 1983). The peptide galanin is another neurotransmitter believed to play a central role in driving fat intake (Blundell et al. 1996).

The regulation of carbohydrate ingestion is more complex. There is evidence that neuropeptide Y, a 36-amino-acid peptide, plays a key role in stimulating carbohydrate feeding drive (Schwartz 1992). Noradrenaline (norepinephrine) is also implicated in stimulating carbohydrate ingestion, possibly by modulating the GABA receptor (Leibowitz 1992). Melanin-concentrating hormone increases food intake and has been demonstrated to play a role in the pathogenesis of obesity in rodents (Qu et al.1996).

In contrast to the small number of neurotransmitters that increase feeding, most neurotransmitters appear to inhibit rather than stimulate it. Corticotrophin-releasing factor (CRF) is the major anorexigenic factor. Patients with anorexia nervosa are recognized to have overactive hypothalamic–pituitary–adrenal function, which suggests that the basic defect may be an increase in CRF. Similarly, depressed patients, many of whom are anorexic, also have a nonsuppressible pituitary–adrenal axis, which suggests the possibility of increased CRF function (Morley and Levine 1983). Serotonin (5-hydroxytryptamine) and isatin are other neurotransmitters which appear to play an important role in the inhibition of the central feeding drive (Morley and Silver 1988; Morley et al. 1996).

The peripheral satiation system is largely composed of the gastrointestinal peptide hormones that are released in response to the passage of food through the gut. The best studied of these hormones is cholecystokinin, which is released when fat and protein pass through the gut. It produces its effect on feeding by activating cholecystokinin-A-type receptors in the pyloric region of the stomach. This signal is transmitted via vagal afferent fibres to the nucleus of the tractus solitarius and the hypothalamus, producing physiological termination of a meal. Antagonists of cholecystokinin lead to increased food intake in experimental animals (Silver et al. 1988; Blundell et al. 1996). Amylin is a 37-amino-acid peptide, secreted from the islets of Langerhans in the pancreas in response to oral glucose ingestion, which decreases food intake (Edwards and Morley 1992).

A number of other gastrointestinal and pancreatic hormones, including glucagon, bombesin, and somatostatin, also play a role in producing satisfaction after a meal. Nitric oxide is believed to produce its feeding-enhancing effect by modulating the feeding drive in the central nervous system and by producing increased relaxation of the fundus of the stomach peripherally, thus allowing larger quantities of food to be ingested in a single meal (Morley 1996).

The existence of an adipose-tissue-related satiety mechanism has been postulated to explain the set-point theory of weight control (Weigle 1994). Lipectomy experiments suggest that the adipose tissue mass as a whole is monitored and regulated by the central nervous system (Weigle 1994; Hope et al. 1997). This implies the existence of a satiety signal proportional to the total adipose tissue mass. Substances like satietin, adipsin, and insulin have been proposed as possible indicators of fat stores providing feedback signals to the central nervous system. Human studies have demonstrated that insulin has no effect on food intake when glucose is maintained constant. Recently, the murine obese gene was cloned from fat cells; the secretory product was named leptin (Zhang et al. 1994). Leptin produces a decrease in food intake by complex mechanisms which include inhibiting the release of neuropeptide Y in the hypothalamus (Wolf 1996). In the obese (ob/ob) mouse, leptin is deficient and its administration reduces food intake and makes the obese animal thin (Campfield et al. 1995). In contrast, in the obese (fa/fa) rat, both the circulating leptin levels and the hypothalamic neuropeptide Y content are high (Maffei et al. 1995). A mutation of the hypothalamic leptin receptor gene appears to be responsible for the inability of leptin to act within the hypothalamus to decrease neuropeptide Y levels (Chua 1996; Lida et al. 1996). The situation in obese humans has some similarities to that of the obese fa/fa rat. High plasma leptin levels are also encountered in obese humans, although they cannot yet be ascribed to defects in any isoform of the leptin receptor (Considine et al. 1996a, b). The resistance to leptin action in the human could be due to alterations of leptin effect beyond the leptin receptor site (Jeanrenaud and Jeanrenaud 1996).

Steroid hormones have been implicated in the regulation of food intake. Oestrogen and dehydroepiandrosterone decrease food intake, but testosterone, progesterone, and the glucocorticoids increase it. The mechanism(s) by which steroid hormones modulate food intake is still not clear. Testosterone inhibits leptin (Sih et al. 1997), suggesting a possible mechanism for its action. Males have lower levels of leptin than females. With ageing, leptin levels in males rise as testosterone levels decline, whereas leptin levels decline in older females. Anorexia can also occur secondary to cytokine release (Hori et al. 1991). Cytokines play a role in appetite suppression mainly in pathological states such as cancer, AIDS, and rheumatoid arthritis.

Physiology of the anorexia of ageing

There are several causes of the physiological decrease in food intake (anorexia of ageing) that occurs in older adults (Table 1). The decreased caloric intake in older individuals is a natural physiological response to the decline in resting metabolic rate that occurs with ageing. The resting metabolic rate depends largely on the lean body mass. After about age 30 the lean body mass declines at an average rate of about 5 per cent per decade. At age 80, the lean body mass is only about half that at age 30. This decline is accompanied by a parallel reduction in caloric requirement. The reduction is further compounded by the tendency for less physical activity with advancing

Table 1 Factors involved in the genesis of the anorexia of ageing

Decline in resting metabolic rate

Decreased physical activity

Decline in smell and taste

Deterioration of dental status

Decrease in opioid feeding drive

Increase in the satiety effect of cholecystokinin

Slowing of gastric emptying

Decreased nitric oxide synthase activity in the fundus of the stomach

age (Rudman and Cohn 1992). Other factors involved in the decline of resting metabolic rate with ageing are the reduction in the activity of the Na^+, K^+-ATPase pump, a slight decline in triiodothyronine, and the decrease in food intake.

The sensitivity of the gustatory and olfactory receptors decline in some, but not all, persons with increasing age, reducing the enjoyment of food and the desire to eat (see also Chapter 18.17). The changes in smell are mainly due to the anatomical and physiological changes associated with ageing and are particularly marked in patients with Alzheimer's disease and Parkinson's disease. Elevated threshold levels for recognition of different odours have been documented in older persons. Older adults also have reduced ability to identify odours and are more prone than young adults to olfactory adaptation (Schiffman 1996).

Atrophy of the gustatory papillae has been demonstrated to occur anatomically in humans from middle-age onwards (Aliara 1939).Thresholds for salty, sweet, sour, and bitter tastes tend to increase with advancing age. The elderly also have less ability to discriminate among different intensities of the same substance. Medications and medical disorders contribute substantially to losses in taste sensation (Schiffman 1996). Unlike the olfactory changes, these gustatory changes are subtle and their impact on the production of the anorexia of ageing is uncertain. The desire and ability to eat are further compromised by deterioration in dental status.

Animal studies have demonstrated that ageing affects the basic neurotransmitter mechanisms that regulate appetite. There is a decrease in the endogenous opioid feeding drive with ageing (Gosnell et al. 1983). As the endogenous opioids predominantly drive fat intake, this finding is in keeping with the fact that the decrease in food intake with ageing is due predominantly to a decrease in fat intake. In addition, the satiation effect of cholecystokinin is augmented in older animals (Silver et al. 1990). In humans, cholecystokinin levels have been demonstrated to increase with ageing (Bertelemy 1992).

Slowing of gastric emptying with ageing is another contributory factor to early satiation in older compared with younger individuals (Clarkston et al. 1997). Part of the early satiation in older persons may be due to a decrease in nitric oxide synthase activity in the stomach fundus, resulting in a decrease in adaptive relaxation of the fundus to food in the stomach (Morley 1996). This results in a smaller stomach volume and early satiation, a common problem seen in older persons.

With a lower energy intake, it becomes difficult for the older person to satisfy all his or her micronutrient requirements through diet alone. In addition, the frequent occurrence of achlorhydria contributes to micronutrient deficiency by affecting the absorption of nutrients such as vitamin B_{12}, calcium, and iron. Achlorhydria in older persons may be associated with *Helicobacter pylori* infections. *H. pylori* has been associated with anorexia as well as dyspepsia, and treatment for infection with this bacterium results in restoration of lost weight (Pound and Heading 1995). The potential role of bacterial overgrowth in the small intestine as a contributor to weight loss and micronutrient deficiency has not been determined.

Categories of protein energy undernutrition

Protein energy undernutrition can present in one of three forms: marasmus, kwashiorkor, and mixed marasmus–kwashiorkor. Marasmus is the body's adaptation to insufficient calorie intake, and usually develops slowly over months to years. Patients appear cachectic or wasted with depleted fat stores. Early in the course of marasmus most of the additional calories required come from fat. Once fat stores are depleted, protein (muscle) catabolism increases. Normal serum albumin is maintained until late in the course of the disease; immune status is also maintained until late (Johnson 1996).

If starvation is accompanied by stress (e.g. infection, surgery, trauma), hypoalbuminaemia and kwashiorkor can develop. During stress there is an increased release of catabolic hormones, particularly cortisol, glucagon, and adrenaline (epinephrine). These result in an increase in the metabolic rate and stimulate muscle breakdown, glycolysis, and lypolysis. Various cytokines, including interleukins (**IL**) and tumour necrosis factor, as well as other acute-phase proteins are produced during stress. Hypoalbuminaemia occurs because of downregulation of the gene responsible for albumin synthesis as well as increased albumin catabolism (Johnson 1996). In kwashiorkor weight is preserved but visceral protein stores (albumin, transferrin, and prealbumin) are depleted. This group of patients usually experiences greater morbidity and mortality than patients with marasmus.

When the clinical characteristics of both forms occur simultaneously, the person is said to have marasmus–kwashiorkor. This type of malnutrition usually occurs when the cachectic person is subjected to acute stress and is the most common presentation in elderly persons (Dimaria and Amella 1995). This syndrome has been characterized as the senile rusting syndrome and is closely linked to the development of sarcopenia and frailty in older persons.

Marasmus and protein energy malnutrition are discussed further in Chapter 6.1.

Causes of anorexia and protein energy undernutrition

Anorexia and protein energy undernutrition result from a variety of interacting factors which can be broadly divided into three categories: social, psychological, and medical. The mnemonic MEALS ON WHEELS includes the most common treatable causes of anorexia

Table 2 Common causes of weight loss in older persons

Medications (e.g. digoxin, psychotropics, theophylline)
Emotions (depression)
Anorexia/Alcoholism
Late-life paranoia
Swallowing problems

Oral and dental disorders
No money (poverty)

Wandering (dementia)
Hyperthyroidism/hyperparathyroidism
Enteric problems (malabsorption)
Eating problems
Low-salt low-cholesterol diets
Shopping and food preparation problems

and protein energy undernutrition (Table 2). Table 3 lists the most common causes found in studies of medical outpatients and nursing-home residents.

Social causes

The ability to purchase and prepare food is an essential component of proper nutrition. Therefore poverty, social isolation, and functional impairment can have a significant impact on the older person's nutritional intake. Poverty is the major social cause of weight loss.

In the United States over 12 per cent of the older population live in poverty (Miller and Morley 1995).In addition to being limited in their ability to purchase food, elderly people living in poverty may have inadequate facilities for food preparation and storage or limited access to transportation for shopping (Miller and Morley 1995). Physicians in the United States should be aware that sometimes they induce poverty in their older patients by prescribing expensive drugs. The older person with a limited income often needs to borrow from the food budget to buy the medicine.

As elderly people age and their 'significant other' dies, social isolation becomes an important cause of weight loss. Although some elderly living alone may find it physically difficult to shop or cook, others lack the motivation to prepare food. This is frequently seen after the loss of a spouse, a close friend, or even a pet (Barrocas *et al.* 1995). A social problem directly causing malnutrition in older persons is abuse. Elder abuse or neglect should always be considered in the event of unexplained weight loss (see also Chapter 26.2).

Psychological causes

Depression is an important cause of weight loss in older persons in both the outpatient setting and nursing homes. Weight loss is more likely in depressed older persons than in depressed younger persons (Blazer *et al.* 1987). Two epidemiological studies in nursing homes have found depression to be strongly associated with weight loss (Katz *et al.* 1993; Blaum *et al.* 1995). Depression was found to be the most common cause of weight loss in older persons in both a medical outpatient study (Wilson *et al.* 1998) and a nursing home study

Table 3 Comparison of the causes of anorexia and weight loss

	Thompson and Morris (1991)	Rabinovitz et al. (1986)	Marton et al. (1981)	Morley and Kraenzle (1994)	Wright (1993)
Location	Ambulatory	Hospital	Hospital	Nursing home	Nursing home
No. of patients	45	154	91	36	55
Age (mean or range) (years)	68–83	64.2	59	90.1	85
Causes of anorexia and weight loss (prevalence expressed as a percentage)					
Psychiatric disorders	18	10	9	42	22
Cancer	16	36	19	7	
Gastrointestinal disorders	11	17	14	3	
Medication	9		2	7	
Infection	2	6	3	0	0
Hyperthyroidism	9	3	1	0	
Diabetes mellitus		3	1	0	
Neurological	7		2	3	
Cholesterol phobia	2				
Alcohol	2				
Dementia				12	19
Acute illness					43

Table 4 Mechanisms responsible for the development of protein energy malnutrition in elderly people

	Increased metabolism	Anorexia	Swallowing difficulties	Malabsorption
Pulmonary disease	+	+		
Cardiac disease	+	+		+
Cancer	+	+	+	+
Alcoholism	+	+		+
Infection(s)	+	+	+	+
AIDS	+	+	+	+
Rheumatoid arthritis	+	+		
Tuberculosis	+	+		
Oesophageal candidiasis		+	+	
Gallbladder disease		+		
Endocrine disorders (hyperthyroidism, pheochromocytoma, hypercalcaemia)	+	+		
Parkinson's disease	+			
Essential tremors	+			
Malabsorption syndromes				+

(Morley and Kraenzle 1994). The association between depression and weight loss may be partly due to the elevated levels of CRF, which is a potent anorectic agent (Morley 1996).

Dementia is commonly associated with weight loss. In most cases this is due to forgetting to eat. Excessive wandering, psychotropic medications, depression, and paranoid ideation are other factors contributing to weight loss in demented patients. Some residents with dementia develop apraxia of swallowing and need to be reminded to swallow after each mouthful of food (Morley 1996). Late-life paranoia can lead to weight loss due to decreased food intake because of the belief that the food is being poisoned. In contrast, late-life mania is associated with a rapid pace of life and lack of time to eat, leading to weight loss.

Anorexia nervosa has also been reported in the older population. In some patients it may represent recurrence of a pre-existing condition, but in others anorexia nervosa occurs for the first time later in life, in which case it is termed anorexia tardive. These patients may display certain oral control patterns, such as avoiding eating when hungry (Morley and Silver 1995). Chronic alcoholism is another cause of malnutrition in older persons that is frequently overlooked. Inadequate intake of nutrients in addition to the toxic effect of ethanol and/or its metabolites are the main factors implicated (Gloria *et al.* 1997).

Medical causes

Protein energy undernutrition can be the result of many medical conditions. These can cause weight loss through one or more of the following mechanisms: hypermetabolism, anorexia, swallowing difficulties, and/or malabsorption (Table 4).

Cancer is a common cause of unintentional weight loss, accounting for 16 to 36 per cent of older persons with weight loss (Thompson and Morris 1991). The reasons for weight loss in patients with cancer are multifactorial and include the production of several anorectic substances such as various cytokines (e.g. IL-1 and tumour necrosis factor) (Norton *et al.* 1985) and bombesin, a hormone that produces anorexia by sending satiety messages to the central nervous system (Morley 1990*b*). In addition, abnormalities in taste secondary to the cancer itself, opportunistic infection, radiation therapy, or chemotherapy, together with gastroparesis secondary to autonomic dysfunction in cancer patients (Bruera *et al.* 1986), contribute to anorexia and protein energy undernutrition.

Weight loss occurs in 71 per cent of patients with chronic obstructive pulmonary disease (Vandenbergh *et al.* 1976). Increased utilization of energy due to the use of accessory muscles of respiration is the principal factor involved. Other factors include anorexia induced by drugs (e.g. theophylline, corticosteroids) and by gastric distension secondary to aerophagia. In addition, many of these patients develop severe dyspnea when attempting to eat, which limits the number of calories that can be ingested at a single meal. To overcome this, patients are advised to eat frequent small meals with a high caloric content.

Protein energy undernutrition is a frequent complication in patients with congestive heart failure. This is commonly referred to as cardiac cachexia. Nutritional surveys of hospital inpatients showed that 50 to 68 per cent of patients with congestive heart failure were significantly malnourished (Freeman and Roubenoff 1994). This malnutrition, unlike that seen in simple starvation, preferentially depletes lean body mass. Cardiac cachexia is due to a combination of factors, including anorexia secondary to early satiation (from gut oedema), dyspnoea and medication effects (e.g. digoxin), higher resting metabolic rates (Poehlman *et al.* 1994), impaired fat absorption (King *et al.* 1996), cytokine release (tumour necrosis factor-α and IL-2) (Freeman and Roubenoff 1994), and a protein-losing enteropathy coupled with altered hepatic protein synthesis (Morley 1996).

Metabolic disorders such as hyperthyroidism and hyperparathyroidism are not uncommon causes of weight loss in older persons. They may be overlooked because of unusual presentations in this age group (Morley and Silver 1995). For example, it is not unusual for the older patient with hyperthyroidism to present with weight loss, proximal myopathy, and hyperthyroid cardiac complications (e.g. angina pectoris, congestive heart failure, and atrial fibrillation) and lack the classical symptoms and signs of thyrotoxicosis.

Malabsorption is another cause of protein energy undernutrition in older persons. The differential diagnosis includes late-life onset of gluten enteropathy, particularly in persons with diabetes mellitus and pancreatic insufficiency. In addition, gallbladder disease can result in early satiation which resolves after removal of the gallbladder. Zinc deficiency is associated with anorexia and hypogeusia (diminished taste sensation). It occurs most commonly in persons with cirrhosis of the liver, non-insulin-dependent diabetes mellitus, or lung cancer, and in those taking diuretics.

Patients with rheumatoid arthritis have increased levels of circulating cytokines (tumour necrosis factor and IL-1). These cytokine results in increased resting energy expenditure and decreased serum albumin levels (Roubenoff *et al.* 1995). Older persons with AIDS, like younger patients, develop a wasting syndrome. This is mostly due to decreased food intake secondary to the anorectic effect of circulating cytokines (e.g. IL-1 and tumour necrosis factor). Infection, diarrhoea, and malabsorption are other factors contributing to the wasting syndrome in older patients with AIDS. Martinez *et al.* (1993) reported a series of older patients with severe weight loss and anorexia who did not have an identifiable cause for weight loss. This condition is known as idiopathic pathological senile anorexia. Analysis of the cerebrospinal fluid in these patients revealed increased serotonergic activity, increased levels of cholecystokinin octapeptide and neuropeptide Y, and decreased levels of β-endorphin and tumour necrosis factor.

Polypharmacy is a common cause of malnutrition in the older population. Numerous medications have been linked to the development of anorexia and weight loss in older persons. The most frequently implicated include digoxin, theophylline, non-steroidal anti-inflammatory drugs, iron supplements, antineoplastic drugs, and psychoactive drugs, particularly fluoxetine (Brymer and Winograd 1992), lithium, and the phenothiazines. Inappropriate withdrawal from psychotropic medicines can result in anorexia and weight loss as the only obvious finding associated with the disturbed psychic state (Morley and Kraenzle 1994).

Nutrition assessment

Nutrition assessment is an important component of the comprehensive geriatric assessment. It involves taking a thorough history and physical examination, in conjunction with anthropometric and biochemical measures. A carefully obtained history may be the most valuable tool for identifying persons at risk of malnutrition. One of the most important aspects of the history is weight changes per unit time. There is a broad consensus that an unintentional loss of 4.5 kg or more of body weight in the preceding 6 months is a strong indicator of nutritional risk and morbidity (Rosenberg 1994). A dietary history is best obtained by providing the patient with a simple questionnaire (food diary) that deals with quantity as well as quality of food intake. The history should also ascertain the presence of risk factors for deficient nutrient intake (e.g. poverty, isolation, depression, acute or chronic illness, inability to shop or feed, and history of anorexogenic drugs). The close associates of the patient (spouse, companion, or other caregiver) should be interviewed and often provide the most accurate and useful information.

The physical examination should determine general body habitus, present body weight and height, and the presence of any sign of nutritional deficiency in the skin, hair, nail, eyes, mouth, or muscles. The body mass index (**BMI**) is a very useful tool for assessing the nutritional status and can be calculated using the formula

$$BMI = \frac{weight\ (kg)}{[height\ (m)]^2}.$$

The association between BMI and mortality follows a U-shaped curve, with increased mortality being associated with BMIs both above and below the 'ideal range' (Rosenberg 1994).The nadir of the U-shaped curve, the point associated with minimum mortality, increases with age (Andres 1984). Thus the 'best weight' in terms of mortality for an elderly person is higher than the 'best weight' for a younger person. The desired BMI for older people is 24 to 29, compared with 20 to 24 in younger persons, and a measure below 24 is an indicator of poor nutritional health in an older person (Dimaria and Amella 1995). In addition to the determination of BMI, other anthropometric indicators have been used to elaborate further the information on body composition. These include the determination of mid-arm muscle circumference and triceps skinfold measurements. When compared with age-adjusted standards, these measurements give some indication of relative muscle size and amount of fat (Rosenberg 1994).

Laboratory assessment of malnutrition generally includes determination of albumin, cholesterol, and haemoglobin (to look for nutritionally related anaemia). All these tests are affected by non-nutritional factors, and none alone is adequately sensitive or specific to diagnose malnutrition (Johnson 1996). Serum albumin is the most specific of these markers. The threshold level defining clinically significant hypoalbuminaemia in elderly persons has been debated. Although a serum albumin level below 3.5 g/dl is generally considered a marker of malnutrition, Rudman and Feller (1989) demonstrated increased mortality in nursing home patients with serum albumin levels below 4 g/dl. In our practice we use 4 g/dl as the cut-off point for identifying older persons at risk of malnutrition. However, serum albumin changes with both hydration status and body position; levels decrease by 0.5 g/dl when the patient is in the recumbent position. Furthermore, the specificity of serum albumin measurements as a measure of the nutritional status in acute illness is questionable, since hypoalbuminaemia can be the result of the disease process rather than malnutrition (Dimaria and Amella 1995). As albumin has a half-life of about 21 days, albumin levels respond slowly to either acute starvation or refeeding. Prealbumin, another protein secreted by the liver, has a half-life of 2 days and therefore is more useful for monitoring nutritional interventions and refeeding (Johnson 1996).

Table 5 SCALES: a simple tool for nutritional screening in older adults

Sadness	Yesavage's Geriatric Depression Scale score ≥15
Cholesterol	Less than 4.14 mm/l (160 mg/dl)
Albumin	Less than 4 g/dl
Loss of weight	2.27 kg in 6 months
Eating problems	Cognitive impairment and/or physical limitations
Shopping	Inability to shop or prepare a meal

Total cholesterol level is another measurement that can be used to assess the nutritional status of older persons. Levels below 160 mg/dl are considered markers for malnutrition, perhaps reflecting decreased visceral protein (i.e. carrier lipoprotein), and were associated with increased mortality in a nursing-home population (Barrocas *et al.* 1995). Total lymphocyte count, anergy skin testing, and serum transferrin levels have not proved to be useful as nutritional markers for older persons. Other nutritional markers, such as retinol-binding protein, fibronectin, insulin-like growth factor, and tumour necrosis factor, remain experimental (Johnson 1996).

Three nutritional screening tools have recently become available. The first, developed by the Nutrition Screening Initiative in the United States (White *et al.* 1992), comprises a check list 'DETERMINE your nutritional health', devised for the older person or caregivers of those thought to be at risk of poor nutrition, and aims at enhancing public awareness. The DETERMINE checklist has become a useful tool for surveying and screening. However, it is not a diagnostic tool and should not be used as such (Barrocas *et al.* 1995).It has high sensitivity but poor specificity.

The second tool is identified by the acronym SCALES (Table 5) and was developed by Morley (1991) as a simple screening tool for physicians and dieticians. Indices employed include the individual's mood assessment using Yesavage's Geriatric Depression Scale, cognitive function assessment by the Mini-Mental State Examination, mobility, eating patterns, and socio-economic status. Definite parameters are provided for the diagnosis of significant weight loss. Serum cholesterol and albumin levels are also considered. This instrument is simple to use, cost effective, and easily adaptable to various clinical settings. At present, it is inadequately validated.

The third tool is the Mini Nutritional Assessment (Fig. 1), which is the first scientifically prepared nutritional screening tool for older persons (Guigoz *et al.* 1996). It is composed of 18 simple items, which can be measured rapidly, and can be performed in less than 15 min. It includes a dietary questionnaire, anthropometric measurements, a global assessment, and a subjective assessment of self-perceived quality of health and nutrition. The Mini Nutritional Assessment is the only well-validated instrument presently available for assessing nutritional status in older persons.

Management of anorexia and protein energy undernutrition

Management of protein energy undernutrition entails both early detection and management of treatable disorders. Physicians should be aware of the risk factors of undernutrition. Body weight should be measured monthly, and serum albumin and cholesterol checked at least once a year (Rudman and Cohn 1992). If needed, quantitative evaluation of diet can be carried out in consultation with a dietician. Counselling is mandatory for those patients whose nutritional assessment indicates abnormalities in BMI or nutritional laboratory values. Management of protein energy malnutrition is discussed further in Chapter 6.1.

Special attention should be paid to treating depression and eliminating anorexogenic drugs or unnecessary dietary restrictions. Providing home-delivered meals to housebound elderly people, as well as ensuring assistance with feeding for older persons with functional disabilities, often helps them to gain weight. In institutional settings it is important to pay attention to the ethnic preferences of older residents and to involve the residents in menu revision and food selection. As discussed previously, elderly adults are at risk of not meeting their requirements of certain micronutrients such as vitamin D, vitamin B$_{12}$, folate, calcium, and iron. Elderly persons should be advised to increase their intake of vegetables and fruits. Supplementation with vitamins and minerals should be considered for those who do not consume adequate amounts of nutrients from food sources or show evidence of inadequate intake (Rosenberg 1994).

Dysphagia is a problem for many elderly patients. The presence of dysphagia and the degree of aspiration risk can usually be determined by a bedside swallowing evaluation performed by a speech pathologist or other competent professional. Videofluoroscopic swallowing evaluation is a sensitive tool for assessing aspiration risk and often helps to identify the cause of dysphagia. Persons with dysphagia can be taught the correct swallowing techniques and the appropriate positioning for swallowing safely. Dietary manipulation (e.g. use of thickened liquids) is an important component of the management of dysphagia. (See also Chapter 8.2.)

Nutritional therapy can be administered to elderly patients in one of three forms: oral supplementation, enteral feeding by tube, and parenteral feeding. If the gastrointestinal tract is functioning normally, it should be used for nutrient delivery.

Oral supplements

Elderly patients have a higher incidence of cardiac, renal, liver, and other diseases that require fluid restriction. Thus, when a nutritional supplement is used in patients with these conditions, the total salt and fluid content of the product should be considered. Most supplements that provide 1 cal/cm^3 when taken as directed are equivalent in salt content to a diet containing 2 g of sodium. If additional salt and fluid restriction are needed, supplements containing 1.5 to 2.0 cal/cm^3 are available (Bernard and Rombeau 1986). Older patients with lactase deficiency may benefit from lactose-free supplements. Similarly, older patients with constipation may benefit from supplements with added fibre. Supplements should be given between meals and at least 1 h before the next meal.

The use of oral caloric supplements to improve outcomes in older malnourished persons has been poorly validated by well-controlled trials. However, there is evidence that oral supplementation improves outcome in persons with hip fractures (Bastow *et al.* 1983), pressure ulcers (Breslow *et al.* 1993), and chest infection (Woo *et al.* 1994). Larsson *et al.* (1990) suggested that daily caloric supplementation decreased mortality in both malnourished and non-malnourished older hospital inpatients.

MINI NUTRITIONAL ASSESSMENT
MNA™

ID number _____

Last name: _____ First name: _____ M.I. _____ Sex: _____ Date: _____

Age: _____ Weight (kg): _____ Height (cm): _____ Knee height (cm): _____

Complete the form by writing the numbers in the boxes. Add the numbers in the boxes and compare the total assessment with the Malnutrition Indicator Score.

ANTHROPOMETRIC ASSESSMENT

1. Body mass index (BMI) (weight in kg) / (height in m)^2 **Points**
   (a) BMI <19   = 0 points
   (b) BMI 19 to <21 = 1 point
   (c) BMI 21 to <23 = 2 points
   (d) BMI ≥23   = 3 points
   ☐

2. Mid-arm circumference (MAC) (cm)
   (a) MAC <21   = 0.0 points
   (b) MAC 21≤ 22 = 0.5 points
   (c) MAC >22   = 1.0 points
   ☐.☐

3. Calf circumference (CC) (cm)
   (a) CC <31 = 0 points   (b) CC ≥31 = 1 point
   ☐

4. Weight loss during last 3 months
   (a) Weight loss greater than 3 kg (6.6 lb) = 0 points
   (b) Does not know   = 1 point
   (c) Weight loss between 1 and 3 kg = 2 points
       (2.2 and 6.6 lb)
   (d) No weight loss   = 3 points
   ☐

GENERAL ASSESSMENT

5. Lives independently (not in a nursing home or hospital)
   (a) No = 0 points   (b) Yes = 1 point
   ☐

6. Takes more than 3 prescription drugs per day
   (a) Yes = 0 points   (b) No = 1 point
   ☐

7. Has suffered psychological stress or acute disease in the past 3 months
   (a) Yes = 0 points   (b) No = 2 points
   ☐

8. Mobility
   (a) Bed or chair bound   = 0 points
   (b) Able to get out of bed/chair but does not go out   = 1 point
   (c) Goes out   = 2 points
   ☐

9. Neuropsychological problems
   (a) Severe dementia or depression = 0 points
   (b) Mild dementia   = 1 point
   (c) No psychological problems   = 2 points
   ☐

10. Pressure scores or skin ulcers
    (a) Yes = 0 points   (b) No = 1 point
    ☐

DIETARY ASSESSMENT

11. How many full meals does the patient eat daily?
    (a) 1 meal = 0 points
    (b) 2 meals = 1 point
    (c) 3 meals = 2 points
    ☐

© 1994 Nestac Ltd (Nestlé Research Center)/Clintec Nutritrion Company

12. Selected consumption markers for protein intake
    • At least one serving of dairy products (milk, cheese, yoghurt) per day?   Yes ☐ No ☐
    • Two or more servings of legumes or eggs per week?   Yes ☐ No ☐
    • Meat, fish, or poultry every day ?   Yes ☐ No ☐
    (a) If 0 or 1 yes = 0.0 points
    (b) If 2 yes   = 0.5 points
    (c) If 3 yes   = 1.0 points
    ☐.☐

13. Consumes two or more servings of fruits or vegetables per day?
    (a) No = 0 points   (b) Yes = 1 point
    ☐

14. Has food intake declined over the past 3 months due to loss of appetite, digestive problems, chewing or swallowing difficulties?
    (a) Severe loss of appetite   = 0 points
    (b) Moderate loss of appetite = 1 point
    (c) No loss of appetite   = 2 points
    ☐

15. How much fluid (water, juice, coffee, tea, milk, etc.) is consumed per day? (1 cup = 8 oz)
    (a) Less than 3 cups = 0.0 points
    (b) 3 to 5 cups   = 0.5 points
    (c) More than 5 cups = 1.0 points
    ☐.☐

16. Mode of feeding
    (a) Unable to eat without assistance = 0 points
    (b) Self-fed with some difficulty   = 1 point
    (c) Self-fed without any problem   = 2 points
    ☐

SELF-ASSESSMENT

17. Do they view themselves as having nutritional problems?
    (a) Major malnutrition   = 0 points
    (b) Does not know or moderate malnutrition = 1 point
    (c) No nutrirional problem   = 2 points
    ☐

18. In comparison with other people of the same age, how do they consider their health status?
    (a) Not as good   = 0.0 points
    (b) Does not know = 0.5 points
    (c) As good   = 1.0 points
    (d) Better   = 2.0 points
    ☐.☐

ASSESSMENT TOTAL (max. 30 points): ☐ ☐.☐

MALNUTRITION INDICATOR SCORE

≥ 24 points   Well-nourished   ☐

17–23.5 points   At risk of malnutrition   ☐

<17 points   Malnourished   ☐

Fig. 1 The Mini Nutritional Assessment. (Reproduced with permission from Guigoz et al. (1996).)

Enteral feeding

Enteral tube feeding may be indicated to meet short- and long-term nutritional needs in patients with a functioning gastrointestinal tract. Nutritional intervention is indicated early in an illness to promote healing and to decrease morbidity and mortality. However, there is evidence that tube feedings are often not started soon enough in older hospital inpatients (Rudman and Cohn 1992). A major impact of enteral feeding is the ability to administer long-term nutritional support in the home setting with the help of home care services.

Short-term feeding (less than 6 weeks) can be provided by naso-enteric tubes. Feeding for patients requiring nutritional support for more than 6 weeks can be provided by tube enterostomy. These can be positioned in the stomach, duodenum, or jejunum in the same way as tubes from the nasal route. Gastrostomy tubes can be placed surgically or percutaneously by endoscopic or radiographic techniques. Gastrostomy tubes have not been shown to lower the incidence of aspiration (Rudman and Cohn 1992).

Jejunostomy tubes are used for patients with a high gastrointestinal tract obstruction. They are placed by a surgeon through either a surgical or percutaneous approach. They require a commercially prepared formula delivered by low-volume continuous infusion for adequate absorption (Rudman and Cohn 1992). Recently, gastrostomy–jejunal feeding tubes have become available (Gore et al. 1996). These are primarily used for elderly patients who are at increased risk for aspiration. They have the advantage of allowing feeding into the jejunum with concomitant decompression of the stomach.

Aspiration pneumonia is a common complication of enteral-tube feeding, occurring in up to 36 per cent of patients (Rudman and Cohn 1992). Gastrostomy tubes offer no protection against aspiration, but tubes placed beyond the pylorus decrease its incidence. Diarrhoea is another frequent complication that can be minimized by choosing isotonic formulas for feeding. The use of sorbitol-containing elixir medications (e.g. theophylline) may contribute to diarrhoea in tube-fed patients. Hyponatraemia is a frequent complication because most enteral formulas are relatively low in sodium and high in free-water content. This can be corrected by decreasing the amount of water used to flush the tubing, adding sodium chloride to the tube feeding formula, or switching to a nutrient-dense formula. Leakage of gastric contents around the site of the gastrostomy tube is less frequent with the percutaneous than with the surgical approach. Skin irritation can be treated with cleansing mechanical barriers and H_2 blockers to decrease the acidity of the stomach contents (Rudman and Cohn 1992). Ethical issues regarding the acceptability of long-term tube feeding in older patients should always be discussed with the patient and family before commencing tube feeding (see Chapter 22).

Parenteral feeding

Parenteral nutrition is most appropriately used when the gastro-intestinal tract is inaccessible or not functioning. It involves the parenteral administration of carbohydrates, lipids, amino acids, electrolytes, vitamins, and trace element solutions.

Parenteral nutrition can be administered via a peripheral infusion if a weight-maintenance diet is desired. This route provides only hypocaloric infusions and is acceptable for stable elderly patients who are expected to resume eating an adequate oral diet within a short period of time. We have routinely used this approach for up to 4 to 6 weeks without complications. Parenteral nutrition must be given via the central route if weight gain is desired, since a maximum of 2200 cal/day can be administered peripherally. Older patients receiving parenteral nutrition are prone to developing multiple complications, mostly those related to catheter insertion, volume overload, and electrolyte disturbance. These patients need to be closely monitored by a specialized interdisciplinary team.

Drug treatment

Appetite stimulants have not been very effective. Megestrol acetate may promote weight gain in patients with cancer or AIDS. However, its use in older patients has had inconsistent results and is often complicated by the development of severe constipation The short-term use of human growth hormone, although extremely expensive, may be promising in severely cachectic older patients. Kaiser et al. (1991) demonstrated that a 3-week course of growth hormone therapy in older malnourished patients enhanced weight gain without notable adverse effects. Prolonged administration of growth hormone is complicated by the development of carpal tunnel syndrome, gynaecomastia, and hyperglycaemia (Cohn et al. 1993).

The prokinetic agents metoclopramide and cisapride have been used to treat early satiation and anorexia due to nausea. Metoclopramide was found to stimulate appetite in persons with anorexia caused by the cancer-associated dyspepsia syndrome (Nelson and Walsh 1993), but it can result in dystonic reactions and worsening of parkinsonian symptoms. However, cisapride does not cross the blood–brain barrier and hence appears safe in older persons. Other drugs utilized to improve appetite, such as cyproheptadine (an anti-serotonergic agent) and drobinol (tetrahydrocanabinol), have not been found to be effective in older persons. Magace, although useful in some cancer patients, has been minimally effective in older persons and can be associated with constipation and megacolon.

Conclusion

Over the last few decades, physicians have developed an increased awareness of the prevalence and consequences of malnutrition in elderly patients. This awareness coincides with the development of efficient therapeutic means of reversing malnutrition (Bernard and Rombeau 1986). Older persons experience physiological anorexia in response to decreased metabolism and physical activity. This means that, even in the best of circumstances, they have marginal nutritional health and places them at risk for developing severe anorexia and weight loss when disease occurs (Dimaria and Amella 1995). Depression, poverty, isolation, chronic obstructive pulmonary disease, congestive heart failure, cancer, alcoholism, dementia, and medications account for most cases of anorexia in older adults.

The cornerstone of the management of anorexia and weight loss is early detection and aggressive treatment. The diagnosis of malnutrition should not be based on a single marker. A thorough history and physical examination, in conjunction with anthropometric and biochemical measures, should be utilized. The gastrointestinal tract, if functioning, is the preferred route for nutrient delivery. This can be achieved by oral nutritional supplements or enteral tube feeding if the patient has dysphagia. If the gastrointestinal tract is not functioning or the patient has decreased gastrointestinal motility, parenteral nutrition should be used under the supervision of a specialized team. At present, none of the orexigenic agents available appear to be sufficiently cost effective for routine use.

References

Aliara, E. (1939). Investigations on the human taste organs. I. The structure of taste papillae at various ages. *Archivio Italiano di Anatomia e di Embriologia*, 42, 506–7.

Andres, R. (1984). Mortality and obesity: the rationale for age-specific height–weight tables. In *Principles of geriatric medicine* (ed. R. Andres, E.L. Bierman, and W.R. Hazzard), pp. 311–18. McGraw-Hill, New York.

Barrocas, A., Belcher, D., Champagne, C., and Jastram, C. (1995). Nutrition assessment: practical approaches. *Clinics in Geriatric Medicine*, 11, 675–708.

Bastow, M.D., Rawlings, J., and Allison, S.P. (1983). Benefits of supplementary tube feeding after fractured neck of femur. *British Medical Journal*, 287, 1589–92.

Bernard, M.A. and Rombeau, J.L. (1986). Nutritional support for the elderly patient. In *Nutrition aging, and health* (ed. E.A. Young), pp. 229–58. Liss, New York

Bertelemy, P., Bouisson, M., Vellas, B., *et al.* (1991). Postprandial cholecystokinin secretion in elderly with protein-energy under-nutrition. *Journal of the American Geriatrics Society*, 46, B117–21.

Blaum, C.S., Fries, B.E., and Fiatarone, M.E. (1995). Factors associated with low body mass index and weight loss in nursing home residents. *Journal of Gerontology*, 50, M162–8.

Blazer, D., Bachas, J.R., and Hughes, D.C. (1987). Major depression with melancholia: a comparison of middle aged and elderly adults. *Journal of the American Geriatrics Society*, 35, 927–32.

Blundell, J.E., Lawton, J.R., and MacDiarmid, J.I. (1996). Control of human appetite: implication for the intake of dietary fat. *Annual Review of Nutrition*, 16, 285–319.

Breslow, R.A., Hallfrisch, J., Guy, D.C., Crawley, B., and Goldberg, A.P. (1993). The importance of dietary protein in healing pressure ulcers. *Journal of the American Geriatrics Society*, 41, 357–62.

Bruera, E., Chadwick, S., and Fox, R. (1986). Study of cardiovascular autonomic insufficiency in advanced cancer patients. *Cancer Treatment Reports*, 70, 1383–7.

Brymer, C. and Winograd, C.H. (1992). Fluoxetine in elderly patients: is there cause for concern ? *Journal of the American Geriatrics Society*, 40, 902–5.

Campfield, L.A., Smith, F.J., Gulsez, Y., Devos, R., and Burn, P. (1995). Mouse OB protein: evidence for a peripheral signal linking adiposity and central neural networks. *Science*, 269, 546–9.

Chua, S.C., White, D.W., Wu-Peng, X.S., *et al.* (1996). Phenotype of fatty due to G1n269Pro mutation in the leptin receptor (lepr). *Diabetes*, 45, 1141–3.

Clarkston, W.K., Pantano, M.M., Morley, J.E., Horowitz, M., Littlefield, J.M., and Burton, F.R. (1997). Evidence for the anorexia of ageing: gastrointestinal transit and hunger in healthy elderly vs. young adults. *American Journal of Physiology*, 272, R243–8.

Cohn, L., Feller, A.G., Draper, M.W., Rudman, I.W., and Rudman, D. (1993). Carpal tunnel syndrome and gynecomastia during human growth hormone treatment of elderly men with low circulating IGF-1. *Clinical Endocrinology*, 39, 417–25.

Considine, R.V., Considine, E.L., Williams, C.J., Hyde, T.M., and Caro, J.F. (1996*a*). The hypothalamic leptin receptor in humans: identification of incidental sequence polymorphism and absence of the *db/db* mouse and *fa/fa* rat mutations. *Diabetes*, 19, 92–4.

Considine, R.V., Sinha, M.K., Heiman, M.L., Kriauciunas, A., Stephens, T.W., and Nyce, M.R. (1996*b*). Serum immunorecative-leptin concentrations in normal-weight and obese humans. *New England Journal of Medicine*, 334, 292–5.

Dimaria, R.A. and Amella, E. (1995). Malnutrition in the elderly. In *The encyclopedia of aging* (2nd edn) (ed. G.L. Maddox *et al.*), pp. 599–601. Springer, New York.

Edwards, B.J. and Morley, J.E. (1992). Amylin. *Life Sciences*, 51, 1899–1912.

Freeman, L.M. and Roubenoff, R. (1994). The nutrition implications of cardiac cachexia. *Nutrition Reviews*, 52, 340–7.

Gloria, L., Cravo, M., Camilo, M.E., *et al.* (1997). Nutritional deficiencies in chronic alcoholics: relation to dietary intake and alcohol consumption. *American Journal of Gastroenterology*, 92, 485–9.

Gore, D.C., Delegge, M., Gervin, A., and DeMaria, E.J. (1996). Surgically placed gastro-jejunostomy tubes have fewer complications compared to feeding jejunostomy tubes. *Journal of the American College of Nutrition*, 15, 144–6.

Gosnell, B.A., Levine, A.S., and Morley, J.E. (1983). The effects of ageing on opioid modulation of feeding in rats. *Life Sciences*, 32, 2793–9.

Guigoz, Y., Vellas, B., and Garry, P.J. (1996). Assessing the nutritional status of the elderly: the Mini Nutritional Assessment as part of the geriatric evaluation. *Nutrition Reviews*, 54, S59–65.

Hope, P.J., Wittert, G.A., Horowitz, M., and Morley, J.E. (1997). Feeding patterns of *S. crassicaudate* (*Marsupialia: Dasyuridae*): role of gender, photoperiod, and fat stores. *American Journal of Physiology*, 272, R78–83.

Hori, T., Nakashima, T., Take, S., Kaizuka, Y., Mori, T., and Katafunchi, Y. (1991). Immune cytokines and regulation of body temperature, food intake and cellular immunity. *Brain Research Bulletin*, 27, 309–13.

Jeanrenaud, F.R. and Jeanrenaud, B. (1996). The discovery of leptin and its impact in the understanding of obesity. *European Journal of Endocrinology*, 135, 649–50.

Johnson, L. (1996). Malnutrition. In *Geriatrics review syllabus* (3rd edn) (ed. D.B. Ruben, T.T. Yoshikawa, and R.W. Besdine), pp. 145–52. Kendall Hunt, Des Moines, IA.

Kaiser, F.E., Silver, A.J., and Morley, J. (1991). The effect of recombinant human growth hormone on malnourished older individuals. *Journal of the American Geriatrics Society*, 39, 235–40.

Katz, I.R., Beaston-Wimmer, P., Parmelee, P., *et al.* (1993). Failure to thrive in the elderly : exploration of the concept and delineation of psychiatric components. *Journal of Geriatric Psychiatry and Neurology*, 6, 161–9.

King, D., Smith, M.L., Chapman, T.J., Stockdale, H.R., and Lye, M. (1996). Fat malabsorption in elderly patients with cardiac cachexia. *Age and Ageing*, 52, 144–9.

Larsson, F., Unosson, M., and Ek, A.C. (1990). Effect of dietary supplement on nutritional status and clinical outcome in 501 geriatric patients—a randomized study. *Clinical Nutrition*, 9, 179–84.

Leibowitz, S.F. (1992). Neurochemical–neuroendocrine systems in the brain controlling macronutrient intake and metabolism. *Trends in Neuroscience*, 15, 491–7.

Lida, M., Murakami, T., Ishida, K., Mizuno, A., Kuwajima, M., and Shima, K. (1996). Phenotype-linked amino acid alteration in leptin receptor cDNA from Zucker fatty (*fa/fa*) rat. *Biochemical and Biophysical Research Communications*, 222, 19–26.

Maffei, M., Halaas, J., Ravussin, E., *et al.* (1995). Leptin levels in human and rodents: measurement of plasma leptin and ob RNA in obese and weight-reduced subjects. *Nature Medicine*, 1, 1155–61.

Martinez, M., Hernanzo, A., Gomez-Cerero, J., Pena, J.M., Vazquez, J.J., and Arnalich, F. (1993). Alteration in plasma and cerebrospinal fluid levels of neuropeptides in idiopathic senile anorexia. *Regulatory Peptides*, 44, 109–17.

Marton, K.I., Sox, H.C., Jr, and Krupp, J.R. (1981). Involuntary weight loss: diagnostic and prognostic significance. *Annals of Internal Medicine*, 95, 568–74.

Miller, D.K. and Morley, J.E. (1995). Nutritional epidemiology. *Annual Review of Gerontology*, 15, 20–53.

Morley, J.E. (1980). The neuroendocrine control of appetite: the role of the endogenous opiates, cholecystokinin, TRH, gamma-amino butyric acid and the diazepam receptor. *Life Sciences*, 27, 355–68.

Morley, J.E. (1990a). Appetite regulation by gut peptides. *Annual Review of Nutrition*, **10**, 383–95.

Morley, J.E. (1990b). Anorexia in older patients: its meaning and management. *Geriatrics*, **45**, 59–66.

Morley, J.E. (1991). Why do physicians fail to recognize and treat malnutrition in older persons? *Journal of the American Geriatrics Society*, **39**, 1139–40.

Morley, J.E. (1996). Anorexia in older persons. *Drugs and Aging*, **8**, 134–55.

Morley, J.E. and Kraenzle, D. (1994). Causes of weight loss in a community nursing home. *Journal of the American Geriatrics Society*, **42**, 583–5.

Morley, J.E. and Levine, A.S. (1983). The central control of appetite. *Lancet*, i, 399–401.

Morley, J.E. and Silver, A.J. (1988). Anorexia in the elderly. *Neurobiology of Aging*, **9**, 9–16.

Morley, J.E. and Silver, A.J. (1995). Nutritional issues in nursing home care. *Annals of Internal Medicine*, **123**, 850–9.

Morley, J.E., Farr, S.A., and Flood, JF. (1996). Isatin inhibits food intake in mice. *European Journal of Pharmacology*, **305**, 23–9.

Nelson, K.A. and Walsh, T.D. (1993). Metoclopramide in anorexia caused by cancer-associated dyspepsia syndrome. *Journal of Palliative Care*, **9**, 14–18.

Norton, J.A., Morley, J.F., and Green, M.V. (1985). Parabiotic transfer of cancer anorexia/cachexia in male rats. *Cancer Research*, **45**, 5547–9.

Poehlman, E.T., Scheffers, J., Gottlieb, S.S., Fisher, M.L., and Vaitekevivius, P. (1994). Increased resting metabolic rate in patients with congestive heart failure. *Annals of Internal Medicine*, **121**, 860–2.

Pound, S.E. and Heading, R.C. (1995). Diagnosis and treatment of dyspepsia in the elderly. *Drugs and Aging*, **7**, 347–54.

Qu, D., Ludwig, D.S., Gammeltoft, S., *et al.* (1996). A role for melanin-concentrating hormone in the central regulation of feeding behaviour. *Nature*, **380**, 243–7.

Rabinowitz, M., Pitlik, S.D., Leifer, M., Garty, M., and Rosenfeld, J.B. (1986). Unintentional weight loss. A retrospective analysis of 154 cases. *Archives of Internal Medicine*, **146**, 186–7.

Rosenberg, I.H. (1994). Nutrition and ageing. In *Principles of geriatric medicine and gerontology* (ed. W.R. Hazzard, E.L. Bierman, J.P. Blass, W.H. Ettinger, and J.B. Halter), pp. 49–59. McGraw-Hill, New York

Roubenoff, R., Grimm, L.W., and Roubenoff, R.A. (1995). Albumin, body composition and dietary intake in chronic inflammation. In *Nutritional assessment of the elderly population* (ed. I.M. Rosenberg), pp. 30–9. Raven Press, New York.

Rudman, D. and Cohn, M.E. (1992). Nutrition in the elderly . In *Practice of geriatrics* (2nd edn) (ed. E. Calkins, A.B. Ford, and P. Katz), pp. 19–32. W.B. Saunders, Philadelphia, PA.

Rudman, D. and Feller, A.G. (1989). Protein calorie under-nutrition in the nursing home. *Journal of the American Geriatrics Society*, **37**, 173–83.

Schiffman, S. (1996). Smell and taste. In *Encyclopedia of gerontology* (ed. J.E. Birren), pp. 497–504. Academic Press, San Diego, CA.

Schwartz, M.W., Sipols, A.J., and Marks, J.L. (1992). Inhibition of hypothalamic neuropeptide Y gene expression by insulin. *Endocrinology*, **130**, 3609–16.

Sih, R., Morley, J.E., Kaiser, F.E., Perry, H.M., Patrick, P., and Ross, C. (1997). Testosterone replacement in older hypogonadal men: a 12-month randomized controlled trial. *Journal of Clinical Endocrinology and Metabolism*, **82**, 1661–7.

Silver, A.J. (1990). Aging and risks for dehydration. *Cleveland Clinical Journal of Medicine*, **57**, 341–4.

Silver, A.J., Flood, J.F., and Morley, J.E. (1988). Effects of gastrointestinal peptides on ingestion in old and young mice. *Peptides*, **9**, 221–5.

Sullivan, D.H. and Walls, R.C. (1994). Impact of nutritional status on morbidity in a population of geriatric rehabilitation patients. *Journal of the American Geriatrics Society*, **42**, 471–7.

Thompson, M.P. and Morris, L.K. (1991). Unexplained weight loss in ambulatory elderly. *Journal of the American Geriatrics Society*, **39**, 497–502.

Vandenbergh, E., van de Woestijne, K.P., and Gyselen, A. (1967). Weight changes in the terminal stages of chronic obstructive pulmonary disease: relation to respiratory function and prognosis. *American Review of Respiratory Disease*, **95**, 556–66.

Weigle, D.S. (1994). Appetite and the regulation of body composition. *FASEB Journal*, **8**, 302–10.

White, J.V., Dwyer, J.T., Posner, B.M., Ham, R.J., Lipschitz, D.A., and Wellman, N.S. (1992). Nutrition screening initiative: development and implementations of the public awareness checklist and screening tools. *Journal of the American Dietetic Association*, **92**, 163–6.

Wilson, M.M. and Morley, J.E. (1995). The diagnosis and management of protein energy under-nutrition in older persons. *Annual Review of Gerontology*, **15**, 110–34.

Wilson, M.M., Vaswami, S., Morley, J.E., and Miler K.D. (1998). Prevalence and causes of undernutrition in medical outpatients. *American Journal of Medicine*, **104**, 56–63.

Wolf, G. (1996). Leptin: the weight-reducing plasma protein encoded by the obese gene. *Nutrition Reviews*, **54**, 91–3.

Woo, J., Ho, S.C., Mak, Y.T., Law, L.K., and Cheung, A. (1994). Nutritional status of elderly patients during recovery from chest infection and the role of nutritional supplementation assessed by a prospective randomized single-blind trial. *Age and Ageing*, **23**, 40–8.

Wright, B.A. (1993). Weight loss and weight gain in a nursing home: a prospective study. *Geriatric Nursing*, **14**, 156–9.

Zhang, Y., Proenca, R., Maffei, M., Barone, M., Leopold, L., and Friedman, J.M. (1994). Positional cloning of the mouse obese gene and its human homologue. *Nature*, **372**, 425–32.

7

Endocrine and metabolic disorders

7.1 Disorders of the thyroid gland

Paul J. Davis and Paul R. Katz

Although the physiology of the pituitary–thyroid gland axis is altered in the course of normal ageing of most individuals (Table 1), the ability of the axis to respond to stress is unaltered over the lifespan. Even in healthy centenarians, circulating levels of thyroxine (T4) and free T_4 are supported normally (Mariotti *et al*. 1995). However, there are several changes in pituitary–thyroid axis function with age that must be appreciated in order to interpret serum thyroid function test results correctly in elderly patients.

First, a number of studies have shown that serum levels of tri-iodothyronine (T3) decrease with age (Harman *et al*. 1984). These studies have been difficult to interpret in many cases because of the investigators' failure to exclude important contributions of non-thyroidal illness of various types to serum T_3 concentrations (Chopra 1996; Stockigt 1997). The non-thyroidal illness or euthyroid sick syndrome is mediated by decreased conversion of T_4 to T_3 in non-thyroidal tissues, a change in thyroid hormone metabolism whose mechanism of initiation is unclear but which probably relates in part to actions of cytokines released in response to non-thyroidal illness. The decline in serum T_3 levels with ageing in the most carefully studied healthy aged subjects is very small (Harman *et al*. 1984). It is unlikely that this change is physiologically important. The serum free T_3 concentration may also fall slightly with age (Mariotti *et al*. 1995), and is clearly reduced in healthy centenarians.

The serum T_3 should not be used to screen subjects of any age for the presence of authentic thyroid disease because of the confounding effect of non-thyroidal illness and other factors, such as fasting, on serum T_3 concentration. In patients with thyrotoxicosis and an elevated serum T_4 level, the serum T_3 is sometimes normal or high normal, rather than elevated, because of coincident non-thyroidal illness (e.g. congestive heart failure or systemic infection) that impairs conversion of T_4 to T_3 in tissues other than the thyroid.

However, the measurement of circulating T_3 levels is essential in the clinical setting of T_3 toxicosis, a syndrome of hyperthyroidism due exclusively to increased thyroidal secretion of T_3 that may occur in any age group. Hyperthyroidism may also result from excessive circulating amounts of free T_3; this syndrome of 'free T_3 toxicosis' has been well described in aged subjects (Figge *et al*. 1994).

Second, several changes in the hypothalamic–pituitary gland axis occur that are relevant to thyroid function. In the majority of healthy centenarians the serum thyroid-stimulating hormone (TSH) is decreased (Mariotti *et al*. 1993; Mariotti *et al*. 1995) in the absence of other evidence of thyroid disease. Further, pituitary TSH release in response to systemic administration of thyrotropin-releasing hormone (TRH) is sluggish in elderly men. This finding in normal younger subjects is consistent with hyperthyroidism or hypopituitarism. Its presence in older men is of unknown significance. The administration of TRH was of clinical value in assessing pituitary–thyroid function until the supersensitive TSH radio-immunoassay became available. This assay is able to distinguish low normal from suppressed TSH levels in blood. Thus the change in TRH responsiveness of the pituitary with normal ageing no longer complicates the diagnostic evaluation of elderly men.

Thyroid diseases

Examination of the thyroid gland

Physical examination of the thyroid gland in the elderly subject has several distinctive features. First, localization of the gland on palpation can be difficult. The dorsal kyphosis that is common in ageing can result in seclusion of the lower poles or most of the thyroid gland below the suprasternal notch. The thyroid so affected is described as *en plongeant*. However, visual examination under side-lighting of the pretracheal area, with the patient's neck slightly in extension, can display the anatomy of the slightly enlarged gland very satisfactorily in the elderly patient with symmetrical loss of strap-muscle mass. Second, the prevalence of carotid artery bruits increases with ageing, and these can be misinterpreted to be of thyroid origin. Authentic thyroidal bruits reflect hyperplasia of the gland in the setting of Graves' disease. Careful stethoscopic exploration of the carotid artery and the poles of the thyroid gland with a paediatric bell will usually

Table 1 Human ageing and thyroid hormone economy

Decreased average peripheral turnover (disposal rate) of thyroid hormone

Decreased average thyroidal secretion of thyroid hormone

Normal serum T_4 concentration

Normal or minimally reduced serum T_3 concentration

Normal free thyroid hormone concentration

Normal serum basal TSH concentration

Normal thyroid gland response to exogenous TSH

Decreased pituitary TSH secretory response in men to exogenous TRH

Normal basal metabolic rate (corrected for metabolic cell mass)

disclose the correct origin of the sound. Third, goitre is invariably found in young patients with hyperthyroidism and is also expected in the setting of Hashimoto's thyroiditis in younger subjects. However, goitre should not be expected in elderly hyperthyroid patients (see below). Further, older subjects with Hashimoto's disease and attendant hypothyroidism usually lack goitre.

Goitre

Non-toxic goitre: congenital goitre, endemic goitre, sporadic goitre

Pendred's syndrome (Friis et al. 1988) is the only hereditary defect in thyroid hormonogenesis that is consistent with normal somatic maturation and thus is occasionally first detected in adult patients. This defect in the intrathyroidal metabolism of iodide is associated with goitre, deafness that is usually mild, and eumetabolism or trivial hypothyroidism. Pendred's syndrome has rarely been recognized for the first time in an elderly patient.

Endemic goitre due to iodide lack occurs in younger subjects and does not appear *de novo* in elderly people.

Sporadic goitre may reflect dietary goitrogen content or the use of specific medications, such as lithium or amiodarone, that impair thyroid gland function. Ablative ^{131}I may be useful in achieving a modest reduction in gland size when sporadic goitre in elderly patients affects patency of the upper airway (de Klerk et al. 1997). Thyroiditis is a common cause of sporadic goitre in younger patients (see below). Non-toxic goitres that consist of single or multiple nodules are found with increasing frequency as ageing progresses and are discussed below. Nodules contain cells that when studied *in vitro* usually have abnormalities of hormonogenesis and aberrant responses to TSH. Non-toxic goitre has been reviewed recently (Davis and Davis 1995).

Thyroiditis

Granulomatous thyroiditis ('subacute thyroiditis', de Quervain's thyroiditis) and acute thyroiditis are rare in older patients. Acute thyroiditis is caused by direct spread of viral or bacterial infections from contiguous structures in the tracheopharyngeal region.

In contrast, Hashimoto's thyroiditis (chronic lymphocytic auto-immune throiditis) occurs with appreciable frequency in later life. Serum thyroid antibody titres (antithyroglobulin, antiperoxidase (antimicrosomal)) may be elevated in up to 25 per cent of apparently normal subjects over the age of 60 years. Patients aged 60 or more account for 7 per cent of those with Hashimoto's disease confirmed by needle biopsy of the thyroid (Furszyfer et al. 1970). Autopsy studies have disclosed a similar prevalence. Because goitre may not be prominent in the older subject with lymphocytic thyroiditis, thyroid aspiration or biopsy are less likely to be carried out to confirm the presence of the disease. Thus the discrepancy in the elderly patient population in apparent incidence of thyroiditis (serum thyroid antibody titre versus thyroid biopsy results) cannot be rigorously evaluated.

As in young patients, the significance of Hashimoto's disease in elderly people lies in its progression to hypothyroidism. Agoitrous hypothyroidism in middle-aged and elderly patients is attributable to antecedent lymphocytic thyroiditis. Some elderly patients with Hashimoto's thyroiditis remain eumetabolic and are not treated with thyroid hormone replacement. Appropriate management of

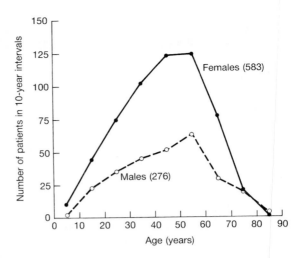

Fig. 1 Age distribution of patients with papillary carcinoma of the thyroid treated at the Mayo Clinic, 1946–1970. (Reproduced with permission from McConahey et al. (1986).)

hypothyroidism, regardless of its origin, is particularly important in the older subject and is discussed below.

Thyroid nodules

Autopsy studies have established that ageing is accompanied by increasing nodularity of several endocrine glands, including the thyroid and adrenal cortex. This tendency to develop nodules in the thyroid is expressed primarily at the subclinical level ('micronodularity'), but the prevalence of macronodules ('nodular goitre'), both multiple and solitary, increases with age (Rojeski and Gharib 1985). The significance of this finding is the risk that such nodules are cancerous (see next section). The risk of thyroidal cysts and sudden haemorrhage into a cyst, with acute appearance of an enlarging nodule, does not appear to increase with patient age. Nodularity sometimes represents localized thyroiditis, but the incidence of this does not rise with age.

Thyroid cancer

In terms of age distribution, the number of cases of thyroid carcinoma peak in the fifth and sixth decades of life (Fig. 1). Case-fatality rates of thyroid cancer increase with age (Fig. 2), despite the fact that the histological appearances of the tumour are identical in young and old subjects. The thyroid cancer with the worst prognosis, regardless of age, is anaplastic; it occurs largely in patients over age 50 years (Nel et al. 1985). Invasive Hurthle cell cancer of the thyroid also has a peak incidence in the sixth decade (Watson et al. 1984). Medullary carcinoma of the thyroid originates in the calcitonin-producing cells of the gland and is usually encountered as a part of multiple endocrine adenomatosis syndrome (MEA type IIa) in younger patients. However, sporadic cases of medullary carcinoma do occur, and the poor prognosis of the sporadic disease is expressed primarily in the elderly patient (Samaan et al. 1988). Thus, regardless of histological type, thyroid cancer has a substantially worse prognosis in old patients. Consistent with this is the specific observation that papillary and follicular carcinomas in elderly people are less responsive to surgical and radio-iodine therapy (Samaan et al. 1983). The presence of

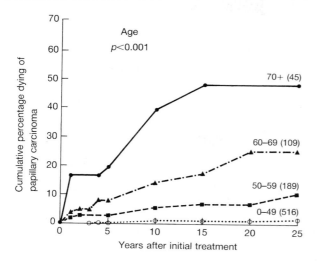

Fig. 2 Cumulative fatality, by age group, of papillary carcinoma of the thyroid evaluated at the Mayo Clinic. (Reproduced with permission from McConahey et al. (1986).)

metastases at the time of presentation of thyroid cancer is higher in younger patients, but the prognosis is better in such individuals than it is in the elderly who present with metastatic thyroid cancer. Five-year survival in patients under age 40 years with a single differentiated distant metastasis is 92 per cent; in patients over 40 it is 8 per cent (Ruegemer et al. 1988). Data for multiple pulmonary metastases from thyroid tumours are similar (Samaan et al. 1985). Local metastatic disease is readily susceptible to resection, with good prognosis in young patients but poor prognosis in the older subject. The explanation for the increased frequency and worsened prognosis of thyroid cancer in older subjects is not known. Of course, longevity increases the potential risk for radiation carcinogensis, but it is not clear that prolonged exposure to very low dose (ambient) radiation promotes thyroid cancer. In contrast, low-dose irradiation of the head and neck delivered on a compressed time basis does heighten the risk of papillary carcinoma of the thyroid gland. This has been documented only in younger patients. It may be speculated that prolonged exposure to natural sources of radiation over the lifespan, in conjunction with a genetic predisposition (e.g. thyroidal *ras* oncogene mutation) (Wright *et al.* 1989), might contribute to the increased risk of thyroid cancer with ageing or with more aggressive tumour behaviour. This possibility remains to be explored.

Whether Hashimoto's thyroiditis is a risk factor for, or is protective against, thyroid cancer is not established. For example, one series describes an incidence of circulating thyroid antibodies in young patients with thyroid cancer that is four to five times that found in elderly patients with such tumours (Pacini *et al.* 1988), whereas data from the Mayo Clinic indicate that the absence of Hashimoto's thyroiditis increases the risk for papillary thyroid cancer in patients over the age of 50 (McConahey *et al.* 1986). Such studies do not permit satisfactory discrimination among such factors as histological typing, antibody type, and tumour behaviour. By 'tumour behaviour' is meant the relatively benign behaviour of metastatic thyroid cancer in young subjects and its aggressive activity in old subjects. There may also be an increased risk of other tumours, such as myelo- and lymphoproliferative disorders and thyroid lymphoma, in patients

with Hashimoto's thyroiditis, but it is not clear that this is age dependent (Holm *et al.* 1985).

Despite its worsening prognosis over the lifespan, thyroid cancer is treated in similar ways (surgery; radio-iodine, where appropriate; chemotherapy of anaplastic and medullary carcinoma) in young and elderly subjects. While the efficacy of the strategy is under review, suppression of endogenous secretion of TSH by administration of exogenous thyroid hormone (L-thyroxine) continues to be endorsed in elderly patients whose thyroid cancers have been managed surgically or with radio-ablation, as it is in younger patients. The reason for this is that TSH is believed to be a permissive factor in the emergence and/or progression of thyroid cancer. Suppression therapy appears to be less effective in elderly patients. A traditional recommendation is that the dose of L-thyroxine selected should be sufficient to reduce the serum concentration of endogenous TSH measured in a supersensitive radio-immunoassay to the lower limit of detectability. Such assays have lower TSH detection limits of 0.01 μU/ml.

Hyperthyroidism

Aetiology

Estimates of the incidence of hyperthyroidism are imprecise (Mogensen and Green 1980), but the disease is acknowledged to be common and, when classically expressed, readily recognized. Twenty per cent of hyperthyroid patients are over the age of 60 years. Subtle or atypical presentations of thyrotoxicosis occur in all age groups and in 25 per cent of affected aged patients (Davis and Davis 1974).

Thyrotoxicosis occurs in patients with diffuse thyroidal hyperplasia (diffuse toxic goitre, Graves' disease), nodular goitre, thyroiditis, or excessive administration of thyroid hormone. Graves' disease is an autoimmune disorder resulting from the production by B lymphocytes of TSH-receptor antibody (human thyroid-stimulating immunoglobulin (hTSIg)) that induces hyperactivity of the gland. Abnormal B-cell activity results from defective suppressor T-cell function. A systematic prospective study of the presence of hTSIg in the serum of elderly patients with hyperthyroidism has not been carried out. The prevalence of diffuse enlargement on palpation or of diffuse radio-iodide uptake on scanning of normal-sized or non-palpable glands in older hyperthyroid patients is 25 to 50 per cent (Nordyke *et al.* 1988). Thus it can be presumed that circulating levels of hTSIg are raised in these patients. The mechanism underlying nodular toxic goitre remains controversial. Elevated levels of hTSIg and other immunoglobulins in this condition have been inconsistently found (Grubeck-Loebenstein *et al.* 1985).

A relatively recently recognized form of hyperthyroidism in younger patients is painless thyroiditis with hypermetabolism. The pathophysiology of this condition involves autoimmune damage to the thyroid, with spillage of iodothyronines into the circulation. The disease is not related to hTSIg, but may be associated with a Hashimoto's thyroiditis-like pattern of serum antibodies to thyroidal antigens. Because hTSIg is absent and endogenous pituitary TSH is suppressed by increased levels of circulating thyroid hormone, the uptake of radio-iodide by the thyroid is very low, in contrast with hTSIg-mediated thyrotoxicosis. Hyperthyroidism associated with painless thyroiditis is a transient form of hypermetabolism, usually requiring minimal symptomatic therapy such as low-dose β-adrenergic blockade. Whether painless thyroiditis with hypermetabolism occurs with appreciable frequency in elderly people has not been specifically determined.

Iodide-induced thyrotoxicosis (Jod-Basedow) is another form of hyperthyroidism associated with little or no uptake of radio-active iodide by the thyroid gland. This usually, but not invariably, occurs in the wake of introduction of iodide to geographical areas of decreased dietary iodide intake. The risk of iodide-induced hyperthyroidism probably increases with age, but the syndrome is rare.

The basis for monosystemic patterns of hyperthyroidism in elderly patients (e.g. clinical presentations limited to the cardiovascular system, gastrointestinal tract or psyche) is unclear, but raises the possibility that peripheral tissue sensitivity to thyroid hormone may be altered with ageing on an organ-specific basis. Studies in experimental animals indicate that iodothyronines have both direct and indirect (catecholamine-mediated, adrenergic-receptor-dependent) effects on the myocardium (Ishac et al. 1983). A modest heightening of the sensitivity of the heart to the action(s) of thyroid hormone could have important clinical effects with relatively small changes in circulating levels of iodothyronines and catecholamines. It has been suggested that older hypothyroid patients require lower doses of thyroid hormone replacement than younger hypothyroid subjects. Recent evidence indicates that, in the past, doses of thyroid hormone replacement in hypothyroid patients of all ages may have been excessive. The indicated replacement therapy for hypothyroidism is L-thyroxine.

Despite studies emphasizing the importance of reducing the dose of thyroid hormone replacement in elderly patients, and despite the impression that sensitivity of tissues to thyroid hormone may be altered with age, it is not clear that iatrogenic hyperthyroidism has occurred with greater frequency in elderly patients during the course of routine management of hypothyroidism or during suppression of endogenous TSH secretion when treating thyroid nodules. However, the consequences of overtreatment of elderly patients with thyroid hormone are more serious than in younger subjects. Exacerbations of heart failure, angina pectoris, or arrhythmias are the most prominent results.

Clinical features

Goitre is an essential feature of hyperthyroidism in younger patients, but may be absent in 50 per cent of elderly thyrotoxic subjects (Nordyke et al. 1988) (Table 2). When the thyroid is not enlarged in older patients with hyperthyroidism, radio-iodine scanning of the thyroid gland usually shows uptake to be uniform; this finding is consistent with diffuse toxic goitre (Graves' disease). The majority of palpably enlarged thyroid glands in older patients with thyrotoxicosis are multinodular or manifest a solitary nodule. The fact that goitre is absent in many elderly thyrotoxic patients sometimes reflects the concomitant presence of kyphosis and age-associated changes in chest diameter that lead to substernal displacement of the thyroid.

Women predominate by a ratio of 5:1 to 10:1 among elderly hyperthyroid individuals. In up to 33 per cent of elderly patients with thyrotoxicosis, the duration of symptoms attributable to thyroid overactivity may be prolonged, often exceeding 1 year. However, the majority of patients come to medical attention within a relatively short time after onset of disease. Whether or not older patients with toxic nodular goitre have a more indolent course than those with Graves' disease remains uncertain.

Table 2 Frequency of signs and symptoms of hyperthyroidism (%)

	Young patients[a] (n = 247)	Elderly patients[b] (n = 85) (60–82 years)	Elderly patients[c] (n = 25) (75–95 years)
Palpitation	89	63	36
Hyperhidrosis	91	38	—
Goitre	100	55	24
Tremor	97	69	8
Weight loss	85	39	44
Atrial fibrillation	10	39	32
Eye signs	71	57	12

[a] Williams (1946); [b] Davis and Davis (1974); [c] Tibaldi et al. (1986).

Many older hyperthyroid patients present with signs and symptoms indistinguishable from those experienced by their younger counterparts. Furthermore, the range of serum T_4 values is similar in young and old thyrotoxic patients (Tibaldi et al. 1986). The presentations of hyperthyroidism due to Graves' disease and to toxic nodular goitre are similar in older people. Although malignant exophthalmos and thyrotoxic dermopathy are exclusive manifestations of Graves' disease, they are infrequently encountered in older hyperthyroid patients.

A large number of older patients suffer from acute or chronic non-thyroidal diseases that often serve to distract the clinician's attention away from the possibility of thyroid disease. Because many of the symptoms reported by older hyperthyroid patients lack specificity, clinicians must have a high index of suspicion if they are to make the diagnosis early. Symptoms such as asthenia, shortness of breath, anxiety or nervousness, and palpitations are frequent in patients with hyperthyroidism, accounting for four of the 20 most commonly reported symptoms mentioned by a sample of euthyroid patients aged 75 years and older during visits to the physician (White et al. 1986). These symptoms in the older hyperthyroid subject may be erroneously attributed to 'normal ageing', as may signs such as thinning of the skin or hair.

Similarly, many older individuals are on multiple medications, some of which may mask symptoms of thyrotoxicosis and further contribute to a delay in diagnosis. For example, β-adrenergic blocking drugs are among the most frequently prescribed class of agents in elderly people and suppress many of the peripheral manifestations of thyroid gland overactivity. Although thyrotoxicosis may be precipitated by the administration of iodinated radiographic dyes or iodine-containing drugs (e.g. amiodarone), this occurs in patients with multinodular glands that are relatively iodine deficient. The likelihood of encountering thyrotoxicosis induced by such drugs is extremely low in developed countries because dietary iodide is sufficient.

Cardiac findings

Although palpitation is commonly reported in elderly hyperthyroid subjects, it is often in the context of other major complaints. In fact, tachycardia is found in only half of older hyperthyroid patients in contrast with its presence in virtually all young thyrotoxic individuals. Even though atrial fibrillation is encountered three to four times more frequently in elderly patients with hyperthyroidism than in younger patients with the disease (Tibaldi *et al.* 1986), it is often associated with normal or even low ventricular response rate in older subjects. This presumably reflects pre-existing disease of the myocardial conduction system. Symptoms of congestive heart failure are common, occurring in up to 60 per cent of the hyperthyroid elderly. In such patients, high-output cardiac failure and normal heart valve function should cause the evaluating physician to consider the possibility of underlying hyperthyroidism. Refractory heart failure and even acute pulmonary oedema are not uncommon. While hyperthyroidism may exacerbate angina pectoris, myocardial infarction in patients with thyrotoxicosis has rarely been documented.

In older patients, there is an increased risk of atrial fibrillation in the setting of low or suppressed serum TSH concentration, but no other serum thyroid function test abnormality (Sawin *et al.* 1994). Caution has been advised in concluding that such patients have incipient or monosystemic cardiac hyperthyroidism (Utiger 1994). However, we have found that some of these patients do respond to a trial of antithyroid therapy (thioamide) by normalizing their serum level of TSH and experiencing a remission of atrial fibrillation. Such patients are considered thyrotoxic and managed as outlined below.

Gastrointestinal findings

In contrast with younger patients, elderly hyperthyroid subjects do not usually manifest hyperphagia. Indeed, anorexia may occur in 30 per cent of older patients with thyrotoxicosis. Surprisingly, constipation is encountered as frequently as diarrhoea or increased stool frequency, and may represent a pre-existing behaviour little affected by thyroid dysfunction. The symptom complex of weight loss, anorexia, and constipation occurs in up to 15 per cent of elderly hyperthyroid individuals, mimicking a malignancy of the gastrointestinal tract (Davis and Davis 1974).

Nutritional state and hyperthyroidism

Nutritional status has not been systematically studied in elderly thyrotoxic patients. In younger patients with hyperthyroidism, the profile of plasma amino acids is normal despite the catabolic nature of the illness. The appreciable frequency of anorexia and decreased caloric intake in older individuals with thyroid hyperfunction encourages speculation that such patients may be inadequately nourished when thyrotoxic. However, anaemia is uncommon in elderly hyperthyroid individuals. Trace metal metabolism is disordered in hyperthyroidism, but it is not clear that the changes are clinically significant in any age group. Metabolic bone disease in hyperthyroidism in all age groups appears to represent loss of bone mass (osteoporosis) in the axial skeleton (Seeman *et al.* 1982). Whether this loss significantly contributes to the progressively increased risk of vertebral crush fracture in ageing is not yet clear. Hypercalcaemia rarely occurs in elderly thyrotoxic patients, but may occasionally be a presenting feature.

Neuromuscular findings

The neuromuscular manifestations of hyperthyroidism in elderly patients are varied and often suggest serious underlying non-endocrine illness. Although usually present in an elderly patient with thyrotoxicosis, tremor is also common in euthyroid older people. When coarse, the tremor may sometimes be confused with that of Parkinson's disease but 'pill-rolling' and rigidity are absent. Thyrotoxicosis may also be associated with weakness of proximal muscles, myalgia, and muscle cramps; these complaints occur with normal or very low levels of serum creatine phosphokinase activity. Whereas myopathy is usually found on careful examination in younger hyperthyroid patients, it is present in about 40 per cent of elderly subjects with thyroid hyperfunction.

Hyperthyroidism may occasionally present as weakness of the bulbar musculature with resulting dysphagia and ptosis. If associated with upper motor neurone signs, these may be misinterpreted as manifestations of cerebrovascular disease. Hyperactive deep tendon reflexes are not prominent in elderly subjects with thyroid overactivity, and the classical rapid relaxation phase after muscle contraction may be present in only 25 per cent of such patients. Seizures may rarely be the presenting manifestation of hyperthyroidism.

Psychiatric findings

In view of the high prevalence of psychiatric illness in the elderly population, the psychiatric findings in older subjects with hyperthyroidism are noteworthy (White *et al.* 1986). Although there is no single and distinctive pattern of symptoms characteristic of thyrotoxicosis, emotional lability, nervousness, and decreased attention span are common. Hyperthyroidism may also present as depression in older patients. In such instances, this is often of the agitated variety and presents in an acute or subacute fashion without antecedent psychiatric illness. At times, hyperthyroidism may present in an apathetic form, in which patients manifest a retarded or stuporous depression. These patients may appear demented (Hall and Beresford 1988). As somatic hyperkinetic features are present in only 25 per cent of elderly thyrotoxic patients, arriving at the correct diagnosis of thyroid disease is fraught with difficulty.

Laboratory findings

The diagnosis of thyrotoxicosis in the elderly patient is confirmed by the finding of an elevated serum T_4 concentration and a fully suppressed serum TSH level, i.e. a TSH value below the limit of detection of the sensitive TSH assay (0.01 µU/ml). A high serum T_4 and normal serum TSH suggest that the principal serum transport protein for thyroid hormone (thyroxine-binding globulin) is elevated. The confounding influence of thyroxine-binding globulin elevation (on a genetic basis or due to oestrogen administration) can be excluded by measurement of the serum free T_4 concentration or free T_4 index. Occasionally, the serum T_4 level may be normal in thyrotoxic patients in whom hypermetabolism is mediated exclusively by high circulating levels of T_3. This state of so-called T_3 toxicosis affects fewer than 5 per cent of elderly hyperthyroid patients. Hyperthyroidism due to isolated increases in free T_3 may also occur. Sometimes the serum T_4 is transiently increased in the presence of acute non-thyroidal illness and returns to normal with successful treatment of the non-endocrine condition.

Highly sensitive immunoradiometric assays for TSH in serum have importantly simplified diagnosis of thyroid disease. Such assays discriminate between low normal and wholly suppressed values of serum TSH; it is the latter that are characteristic of hyperthyroidism. The highly sensitive assay has a lower limit of detection of 0.01 µU/ml. TSH may be undetectable in some patients with autonomously functioning thyroid nodules that have not produced hypermetabolism and in individuals who are taking excessive amounts of L-thyroxine. The ability to recognize TSH suppression has obviated the need to use diagnostic TRH testing.

The thyroidal radio-active iodine uptake test is a reliable confirmatory test in elderly patients with thyrotoxicosis. It may be used to determine the size of the dose of radio-active iodine to ablate the overactive thyroid gland or to determine whether painless thyroiditis (with decreased or absent uptake of iodide by the gland) is present. The uptake test may be misleading when iodine loading of the patient has occurred through diet, medication, or administration of radiographic contrast dyes.

Additional laboratory tests, such as serum cholesterol, calcium, and alkaline phosphatase activity, may be abnormal in hyperthyroidism but have no diagnostic utility.

Treatment

Several options are available for the management of acute thyrotoxicosis and for long-term definitive therapy. Therapeutic decisions should be individualized and based not only on the severity of thyrotoxicosis, but also on concomitant non-thyroidal disease states. For example, the use of β-adrenergic blockade to control symptoms and signs of hypermetabolism in hyperthyroidism is contraindicated in patients with heart failure unless it is clear that a rapid ventricular rate is exacerbating failure.

The mainstays of medical therapy are the thioamides propylthiouracil and methimazole. Carbimazole, a methimazole derivative, is not available in the United States, but is widely used in the United Kingdom and elsewhere. Although their onset of clinical effect is 2 to 4 weeks, they are administered early to inhibit hormonogenesis in the thyroid. This inhibition occurs within 1 to 2 h, but the subsequent process of depletion of hormone stores in the gland, made prior to thioamide treatment, requires several weeks. These agents do not prevent release of thyroid hormone already present in the thyroid gland at the time that therapy is begun. Propylthiouracil also inhibits the conversion of circulating T_4 to the more active T_3 in tissues outside the thyroid. Elderly patients on thioamides should be closely monitored for development of granulocytopenia, since they are more susceptible to bone marrow suppression than are younger patients. Methimazole also presents an increased risk of liver cell damage in older patients. In 20 to 40 per cent of younger patients, a spontaneous remission of Graves' disease may occur after 4 to 12 months of thioamide treatment. The rate of remission during antithyroid therapy has not been rigorously determined in older subjects.

In elderly patients, ablative radio-active iodine (sodium iodide ($Na^{131}I$)) is the preferred treatment. The wisdom of this is particularly clear in patients with other (non-thyroidal) illness and complicated treatment regimens (Griffin and Solomon 1986; Levin 1987). Long-term therapy with thioamide is used when the patient rejects proposed radio-active iodine ablation. In older patients with mild thyrotoxicosis, β-adrenergic blockade may be used alone to control many of the symptoms and signs of hyperthyroidism before, during, or after administration of ablative radio-iodine.

Acute management of severe hyperthyroidism involves specific treatment of tachycardia, congestive heart failure, and body temperature elevation, all of which reflect the effects of thyroid hormone on peripheral tissues. In addition, pharmacological therapy

to inhibit synthesis and release of thyroid hormone is indicated. Rapid achievement of the euthyroid state is particularly desirable in elderly individuals in whom atherosclerotic heart disease is present and the risks of prolonged hypermetabolism are thus significant.

In addition to their other roles in treating thyrotoxicosis, β-adrenergic blocking drugs, carefully titrated against heart rate, are recommended in patients with ventricular rates over 140 beats/min, regardless of whether the underlying rhythm is sinus mechanism or atrial fibrillation. An obvious risk is present when tachycardia is accompanied by congestive heart failure. In this setting, β-adrenergic blockade should be used with caution, but may be a very useful adjunct in the management of heart failure and may be instituted at a low dose in the setting of heart rates of 110 to 140 beats/min.

In infrequent cases of severe hyperthyroidism, inorganic iodide may be used to provide early inhibition of thyroid hormone production within the gland and release of hormone. However, it must be recognized that the use of inorganic iodide precludes the use of therapeutic iodine-131 for some weeks. The onset of iodide action on hormonogenesis and release occurs within hours. Short-term use of corticosteroids is indicated in thyroid storm (fever, tachycardia, exaggerated findings of thyrotoxicosis). Among their many actions, corticosteroids block peripheral conversion of T_4 to T_3, but whether this is clinically important is unclear. β-blockade is the cornerstone of treatment of severe hyperthyroidism, but inorganic iodide and corticosteroids are often prescribed as well.

Iodine-131 therapy is effective and simple to administer, but several points must be kept in mind when treating older patients. It is desirable to control the patient's hyperthyroidism before radio-iodide ablation of the thyroid. Thyroid storm has occurred in patients treated with iodine-131 who were not protected with β-blockade or who had not been returned to the euthyroid state with thioamide. Low-dose β-blockade beginning 1 week before ablative iodine-131 is sufficient to prevent the occasional exacerbation of hyperthyroidism that can occur several days to 2 weeks after administration of the isotope. If thioamide therapy is used as pretreatment, it must be discontinued 3 days before administration of iodine-131. β-blockade has largely replaced thioamide in this role.

Overall, treatment of elderly individuals with ablative radio-iodide is effective and carries very low risk if the precautions mentioned above are taken. More than 60 per cent of elderly hyperthyroid patients are rendered euthyroid or hypothyroid by a single iodine-131 dose of 185 to 230 Mbq. This susceptibility to the effect of radio-active iodide probably reflects a patient subset with toxic diffuse goitre (Graves' disease) and small thyroid glands. Control of toxic nodular goitre usually requires a larger dose of iodine-131 or multiple doses. Many clinicians induce hypothyroidism by intent through the use of a single large dose of radio-iodine. This approach maximizes the therapeutic response to a single dose of iodine-131, but confers the requirement for lifelong thyroid hormone replacement therapy. Follow-up is important, but hypothyroidism after small doses of radio-active iodide appears to develop less frequently in elderly than in young subjects, at least in short-term follow-up (Kendall-Taylor et al. 1984). Thyroidectomy is an acceptable alternative for controlling hyperthyroidism in the older patient. It is infrequently used, but is to be considered in patients with large goitres.

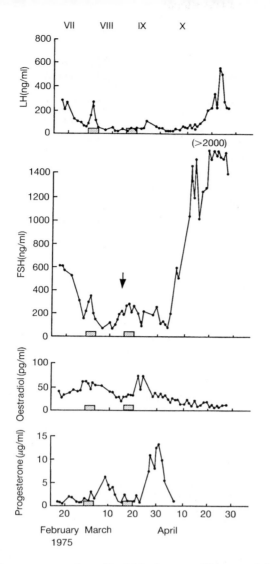

Fig. 2 Serum concentrations of luteinizing hormone, FSH, oestradiol, and progesterone are shown for cycles VII to X (of 10 cycles recorded) of a single 50-year-old woman during the menopausal transition. Date and year are on the x axis. Each shaded block above the x axis indicates a period of vaginal bleeding. Note the decrease in oestradiol and progesterone and the steep rises in luteinizing hormone and FSH at the end of cycle X. (Reproduced with permission from Sherman et al. (1976).)

little or no discomfort. Furthermore, it is not known why some women have a relatively easy time at the menopausal transition, while others experience severe or even disabling symptoms.

Atrophic vaginitis

The vaginal component of the menopausal syndrome results from loss of oestrogen support of the vaginal lining epithelium. The oestrogen-stimulated vaginal lining is a thick multilayered structure with deep papillae descending into the underlying vascular connective tissue, a layer of mitotically active basal cells, mid-level cuboidal cells with abundant stores of glycogen (eventually released into the vaginal lumen), and several layers of squamous cornified cells at the luminal

surface. After the menopause, papillary depth is shallow, glycogen production is nearly absent, and the lining epithelium thins to only a few layers of cells with little or no cornification at the surface. This atrophic lining is often infiltrated with leucocytes. The loss of glycogen leads to an increase in vaginal pH and an alteration of the normal vaginal flora from predominantly acidophilic lactobacilli to a mixed flora of coliforms and other organisms more typical of an alkaline or neutral environment. The thinner lining epithelium and the absent cornified layer provide a less effective barrier against trauma and make the vagina more susceptible to bacterial invasion. In this setting, it is not surprising that many women experience vaginitis. This atrophic vaginitis of menopausal women tends to be resistant to the usual topical or systemic antibacterial or antifungal agents employed for vaginitis in younger women. However, oestrogen therapy is nearly always successful in ameliorating or eliminating the condition. Oestrogen may be applied locally as vaginal cream or suppositories, or given systemically as an oral or transdermal preparation. Many physicians prescribe vaginal oestrogen under the impression that this will avoid exposing the patient to potentially adverse systemic oestrogen effects. However, it has been shown that systemic absorption from vaginal preparations produces biologically significant blood levels of oestrogens. Therefore local oestrogen treatment may have little advantage over oral or transdermal therapy. The comparative effects of the latter two modes of therapy will be discussed below.

Urinary tract infections

The shortening of the urethra, relaxation of pelvic musculature, and altered vaginal flora characteristic of the oestrogen-deficient state also appear to enhance the susceptibility of the postmenopausal female to urinary tract infections. These are similar to urinary tract infections in younger women with the following exceptions: first, they are more frequent and have more tendency to recur; second, because of the age and hormone-deficiency-related relaxation and atrophy of the pelvic musculature, they are more likely to produce urinary incontinence (see below); finally, because ageing is associated with an increase in susceptibility to systemic bacterial infection, probably related to alterations in lymphocyte function (see Chapter 3.3), there is a greater risk in elderly postmenopausal women that a urinary tract infection may develop into pyelonephritis and/or sepsis. For this reason, bladder infections in older women should be treated vigorously with appropriate antibacterial therapy. Initially therapy may be empirical, but it should be modified, if necessary, depending on results of urine culture. Follow-up cultures should always be done within a few days of completing antibacterial therapy to document sterilization of the urine. In the event that persistent bacteriuria or recurrent infection becomes a problem, the chronic daily use of a urinary sterilizing agent, such as metheneamine mandelate (Mandelamine®) or hexamine hippurate, or a combination sulpha drug such as co-trimoxazole may be considered. (In the United Kingdom, however, the Committee on Safety of Medicines recommends that, owing to a risk of side-effects, co-trimoxazole should not be used for urinary tract infections except where specifically indicated, particularly for elderly patients.) In appropriate instances, manipulation of urinary pH by ascorbic acid or potassium citrate may be helpful.

Dyspareunia

Another complaint frequently associated with the menopausal syndrome is the occurrence of discomfort or pain during sexual

Table 1 Plasma concentrations of sex steroids in normal women (ng/dl)

Steroid	Early follicular phase women (18–25 years) (mean value, 15 cycles)	Postmenopausal women (51–65 years)	Ovariectomized women (51–62 years)
Oestrone	5.8 ± 1.6	4.9 ± 0.5	4.8 ± 0.5
Oestradiol	4.0 ± 0.3	2.0 ± 0.1	1.8 ± 0.4
Testosterone	44.0 ± 2.8	29.7 ± 4.0	12.0 ± 2.1
Dihydrotestosterone	33.0 ± 4.0	9.7 ± 2.1	<5
Androstenedione	184.0 ± 16.0	99.0 ± 13.0	64.0 ± 9.0
Dehydroepiandrosterone	550.0 ± 43.0	197.0 ± 43.0	126.0 ± 36.0
Progesterone	31.0 ± 3.0	19.0 ± 3.0	18.0 ± 1.0

Reproduced with permission from Vermeulen (1976).

intercourse (dyspareunia). This problem may or may not occur in association with atrophic vaginitis, and may be of several types. Probably the most common is simple frictional discomfort due to a decrease in normal vaginal lubrication and thinning or inflammation of the vaginal lining. This type of pain is often relieved simply by using aqueous lubricant gel, but treatment with local or systemic oestrogen and, in some cases, antibacterial or antifungal therapy may be necessary to achieve long-term relief. The second type of dyspareunia is due to shortening and loss of elasticity of the vagina, which results in pain on deep penetration. This problem may be relieved by adjusting coital position (and vigour) to reduce depth of penetration. Although ORT helps to prevent this problem if initiated at the onset of the menopause, its value once the condition is established is not certain. Finally, in the case of extreme vaginal atrophy, penetration may not be possible at all because of constriction of the introitus. This situation is most common where there has been a long period of abstinence (i.e. disuse atrophy) followed by an attempt to resume sexual activity. Physical methods, such as gradual stretching of the introitus with a graded series of dilators, can be helpful. The role of ORT, once vaginal constriction has occurred, is not clear. There is some evidence to support the concept that frequent regular sexual intercourse in the postmenopausal period helps to preserve vaginal elasticity as well as the lubrication response and thus may help to prevent the development of dyspareunia.

Hot flushes

In the perimenopausal period, as oestrogen levels fall, many women report the onset of a characteristic complaint which is commonly known as a hot flush (flash). The symptoms vary somewhat, both in their frequency and severity as well as in the particular sensations experienced. Hot flushes usually begin with a sensation of chilliness or even a brief shudder or shivering. This is followed within about a minute by the characteristic intense peripheral flush and a sensation of cutaneous heat, often accompanied by an outbreak of diaphoresis. Symptoms usually last for several minutes and may occur as frequently as every 30 min, but typically are noticed eight to ten times daily at irregular intervals. Although hot flushes occur in as many as 85 per cent of women around the time of the menopause, most women regard them as only a nuisance. However, in about 15 per cent of

women they may be so frequent and severe as to interfere with sleep and normal daily activities.

Prior clinical teaching suggested that hot flushes were a psychological reaction to the subconscious perception of loss of femininity, attractiveness, fertility, etc. engendered by the menopausal transition. The most common treatment was simple reassurance, unfortunately sometimes dispensed in a patronizing manner. More recently, it has become apparent that there is a physiological basis for hot-flush symptoms in that measurable changes in body temperature and blood flow are temporally linked to characteristic hormonal events (Tataryn et al. 1979). In particular, it has been shown that in the perimenopausal period the characteristic secretory pulses of luteinizing hormone and FSH become augmented in amplitude as oestrogen feedback inhibition is reduced. Shortly before such an exaggerated luteinizing hormone pulse begins, there is a brief rise of 1 to 2 °C in core body temperature. It is during this rise that the sensation of chilling may be experienced. This phase is followed by the onset of skin flushing and sweating, during which body temperature returns to normal. During the flush phase there is a decrease in skin resistance and an increase in cutaneous blood flow, which can be metered and recorded by appropriate monitors (Fig. 3). The coupling of physiological events (altered core temperature, reduced skin resistance) with gonadotrophin surges can be seen even during intervals when no subjective hot flush sensations are experienced, but nearly every subjective hot flush is accompanied by measurable physiological changes. The above observations are consistent with the hypothesis that the intermittent hypothalamic neural activity associated with pulsatile neurosecretion of the gonadotrophin-releasing hormone, intensified by loss of negative feedback, spreads into the adjacent hypothalamic thermoregulatory centre, temporarily altering its function to produce an increase in core temperature. The subsequent flushing and sweating is the normal reaction which restores elevated core temperature to normal. Hot flushes may or may not require therapy, depending on the degree to which they elicit discomfort in the individual patient. Fortunately, nearly 100 per cent of patients will obtain significant relief, and in the majority of cases complete alleviation of symptoms, from ORT. Although other forms of therapy have been suggested to be effective, including tranquillizers, α- and β-adrenergic blocking agents, etc., only ORT has been shown to be so that the urethra is shortened and the normal angle between urethra and bladder becomes less acute. Often there will be associated cystocoele or rectocoele and some degree of prolapse of the uterus. In addition to a history of pregnancy and delivery, other contributing factors to this problem may be ageing *per se*, lack of exercise and poor physical conditioning, and loss of oestrogen, all of which contribute to lack of pelvic muscle tone. As has been noted above, oestrogen deficiency also produces vaginal atrophy with an increased risk of vaginitis and cysto-urethritis. Local irritation due to the latter conditions may produce an intense urge for micturition which results in reflex emptying of the bladder if not voluntarily relieved within a short time of its onset. This problem, known as urgency incontinence, may occur independently or in association with stress incontinence. It is important for the physician to differentiate typical stress and urgency incontinence from urinary loss caused by cortical or spinal neuropathy and from the overflow incontinence which occurs with urethral obstruction (see Chapter 15.4).

Postmenopausal patients complaining of urinary incontinence should be questioned regarding symptoms of vaginitis and cystitis, and should be examined for these conditions; a urine culture should be sent. If either or both of the latter diagnoses is positive, appropriate hormonal and antibacterial treatment should be instituted. Whether ORT has a role in the treatment of incontinence beyond its value for relieving atrophic vaginitis is the subject of controversy and continued investigation, but some studies have shown positive effects of oestrogen in patients with stress incontinence. If symptoms are severe or resistant to medical therapy, urological or gynaecological referral is appropriate, particularly since cystometric studies may aid in defining the diagnosis and surgical intervention (bladder resuspension, cystocoele repair, etc.) is helpful in some cases.

Neuroprotective effects of oestrogen

Recently, evidence has been accumulating from a number of epidemiological studies which suggests that women on oestrogen replacement are significantly protected from neurodegenerative disease leading to dementia, in particular Alzheimer's disease (Birge 1996; Paganini-Hill and Henderson 1996). Moreover, experimental studies showing protective effects of oestrogen in neuroblastic cell lines and in animal models of brain damage have provided a scientific underpinning which lends support to this concept. To date, neither the exact mechanism(s) nor the precise degree of protection is known, but clinical intervention studies are underway and additional studies to investigate the extent to which oestrogens may prevent or ameliorate Alzheimer-type dementia are in the planning stage. Thus it seems likely that neuroprotection could be yet another important factor to weigh in constructing risk–benefit analyses for menopausal oestrogen replacement. Again, however, the studies are observational and subject to 'volunteer bias'.

Cosmetic and aesthetic considerations

As noted above, ovarian oestrogens and androgens have peripheral effects on skin and subcutaneous fat distribution which determine female habitus and secondary sex characteristics. The most prominent change, apparent at or shortly after the menopause, is the loss of glandular breast tissue. Although, over a lifetime, gravity and obesity affect breast contour by gradually stretching the supportive ligaments, the atrophy caused by oestrogen deficiency results in relatively rapid loss of the rounded contour of the breast. The flattened atrophic postmenopausal breast is likely to be perceived by both the woman and her consort as less feminine and attractive. In addition, there is withdrawal of subcutaneous fat from breast, hips, buttocks, and the labia majora, all of which may loosen and sag. The labia characteristically gape, exposing the labia minora. In postmenopausal women pubic and axillary hair becomes sparse, grey, and lank. Scalp hair also thins and becomes drier and less lustrous due to decreased oil secretion. In some cases actual male-pattern baldness may appear, probably related to decreased ratios of circulating oestrogen to androgen. The relative extent to which these changes are hormone dependent and hence preventable by oestrogen replacement versus the extent to which they are related to ageing itself and irreversible is not known. Clearly, oestrogen replacement, although it may alleviate or retard some of these changes, does not wholly or indefinitely prevent them. Despite this fact, many women feel that ORT provides significant benefit in terms of their body image and sexual attractiveness. Although this factor is often omitted from discussions of risks and benefits of oestrogen therapy, it is a major consideration for some patients and should not be overlooked.

Oestrogen replacement therapy

Type of oestrogen

Several types of oestrogen preparation are available, and the number will almost certainly increase as oestrogen replacement is more widely prescribed. The traditional and most commonly prescribed preparations, conjugated oestrogens, were originally extracted and purified from the urine of pregnant mares. These extracts are mixtures of oestrone, oestradiol, and reduced oestrogen metabolites conjugated with sulphate and glucuronide (e.g. Premarin®). Currently, there are also pure synthetic conjugated oestrogen preparations, such as oestrone sulphate. Conjugated oestrogens are relatively water soluble compared with native steroid, and hence are well absorbed. Another type of oral oestrogen is micronized oestradiol, which depends for its bioavailability on the very small particle size and hence large surface area for dissolution (e.g. Estrace®). Finally, there are synthetic derivatized oestrogens, such as ethinyloestradiol, which are more potent than the natural compounds and have a prolonged half-life *in vivo*. Oestrogen is also available in transdermal patches and, in some countries, skin creams and pellet implants, all of which supply 17β-oestradiol, the natural ovarian oestrogen. Recently, efforts have been under way to identify and test oestrogenic compounds which would exert protective effects on bone mass and lipid profiles without oestrogenic stimulation of breast or endometrium, thus providing the benefits of ORT without increasing risks of breast or uterine cancer (see below). Two such 'selective oestrogens' on which some clinical data have accumulated are tamoxifen and raloxifene (Delmas *et al.* 1997). While both these drugs remain experimental, and may or may not prove to have the desired clinical risk–benefit ratios, it is likely that oestrogens with selective activities will become important as agents for ORT in the future. (Raloxifene is now approved by the Food and Drugs Administration for use in the United States.)

Oestrogen dose

The amount of oestrogen to be administered depends on the preparation used. The production rate of oestradiol in young women varies from 40 to 200 mg/day depending on the phase of the menstrual cycle, but the average rate is 80 to 100 mg/day. Thus the daily replacement dose of oestrogen should be equivalent to approximately 80 µg of oestradiol in its biological effect. Although normal blood levels of oestradiol are known to average about 100 pg/ml, oral oestrogens do not produce blood oestrogen levels corresponding to the normal physiological pattern and therefore estimates of dose must depend on clinical effects rather than plasma oestradiol measurements. In terms of such measures as vaginal cornification, relief from hot flushes, and urinary calcium excretion, the physiological dose of conjugated oestrogen ranges from 0.625 to 1.25 mg/day. For most women doses of 0.625 mg/day are sufficient to relieve menopausal symptoms and are effective in the prevention of bone loss and fractures as well as cardioprotection. There may be some additional benefit in terms of bone prophylaxis with larger doses (e.g. 1.25 mg/day), but this benefit is marginal and occurs at the expense of a greater risk of adverse effects. The usual doses of micronized oestradiol range from 1 to 2 mg/day, and those of ethinyl oestradiol range from 0.01 to 0.02 mg/day. Transdermal patches which deliver oestradiol doses of 50 or 100 mg/day are available. The higher dose produces oestradiol blood levels in the physiological range and normalizes the clinical indices more completely than does the lower dose. Doses of oestrogen which give adequate clinical effects often do not reduce the blood levels of FSH and luteinizing hormone to premenopausal levels. This may be in part because other hormones (inhibin, androgens, progesterone) normally act in concert with oestrogens to suppress gonadotrophin secretion and in part because pituitary feedback sensitivity to sex steroids may be reduced with age.

Route of administration of oestrogen

As noted above, oral oestrogens are taken up from the intestine into the hepatic portal circulation and hence pass into the liver sinusoids where they act upon and are altered by the hepatocytes. This results in conversion of a large proportion of administered oestradiol to oestrone and a smaller amount to oestrogen conjugates. Thus, with oral oestrogens, the ratio of oestradiol to oestrone is much lower than in premenopausal women, even when pure micronized oestradiol is given. Since oestrone is only about one-third as potent as oestradiol, a greater amount of oestrogen must be given to produce the same physiological effects. The other consequence of this first pass of high concentrations of oestrogen through the liver is the production of an non-physiological degree of oestrogen stimulation of hepatocyte function, including altered protein synthesis and altered bile composition. These effects have implications for alteration of blood pressure, risk of cholelithiasis (see below), and lipoprotein pattern (see above). Thus it has been said that it is not possible to attain truly physiological oestrogen replacement by the oral route. In contrast, transdermal or other parenteral routes of oestradiol replacement have been shown experimentally to approximate a physiological ratio of circulating oestradiol to oestrone and normal levels of heptocyte function.

Use of progestogen

It is now common practice for menopausal women who receive ORT to be treated with a progestogen as well in order to antagonize the effects of oestrogens at the endometrium. Thus oestrogen replacement therapy becomes hormone replacement therapy (**HRT**). The rationale for adding a progestogen is that oestrogen, in the absence of opposing progesterone, causes hyperplasia of the endometrium and, over time, increases the risk of endometrial cancer by a factor of 8 or more. Studies have shown that progestogens cause a loss of oestrogen receptors in endometrial epithelial cells (Whitehead *et al.* 1981) and that women treated cyclically for at least 10 successive days with a progestogen have a rate of endometrial cancer as low as or lower than that of untreated women of comparable age. One study suggests that women so treated may have a lower incidence of breast cancer than the untreated population, but other studies have failed to detect any such effect and one group have even suggested that progestogen treatment may increase breast cancer risk (Bergkvist *et al.*1989). Thus most experts recommend progestogen replacement only for women who have a uterus *in situ*. Although progestogen opposes oestrogen effects on the uterine epithelium and on plasma lipids (see below), it does not appear to do so at bone. In fact, data suggest that some progestogens may be synergistic with oestrogen in preventing bone loss.

Type of progestogen

Progestogens available for use include the 21-carbon compound medroxyprogesterone acetate (Provera®) and a number of more potent orally active steroids derived from 19-nortestosterone and used in oral contraceptive preparations, including levonorgestrel, norethindrone, and ethynodiol. A number of studies have shown that oral 19-nortestosterone-derived progestogens act on the liver to increase LDL and decrease HDL cholesterol, opposing the beneficial effects of oestrogen. Medroxyprogesterone acetate has less of this 'androgenic' effect when given at its effective dose of 10 mg/day. The deleterious lipid effects of the 19-nortestosterone-derived steroids appear to be largely avoided if they are given in low, but still effective, doses (e.g. 250 µg/day for norethindrone or 100 µg/day for levonorgestrel) or if they are administered parenterally (as in an implant). Research is also underway on oral and transdermal preparations of progesterone, the natural human progestogen. Results to date show no negative effects on plasma lipoproteins with such preparations.

Pattern of administration of progestogen

When a progestogen is given cyclically for 10 to 12 days each month and discontinued at the end of each cycle, there is a period of 2 to 5 days of vaginal withdrawal bleeding in most women. Although for some women this event is reassuring proof of continued femininity, many perceive it as an unacceptable nuisance occurring at a time in life when they had anticipated freedom from monthly bleeding. It is possible that a modified cyclic schedule in which progestogen is given for 12 to 14 of each 90 days may be more acceptable for such women. Although such treatment prevents endometrial hyperplasia from building up and hence should lead to avoidance of carcinoma, no data exist on actual cancer risk in women so treated. More recently, an alternative regimen employing continuous low-dose progestogen (e.g. 2.5 mg/day of medroxyprogesterone acetate) has been reported to be effective in preventing endometrial hyperplasia. Such regimens have the advantages of avoiding regular periods of hormone withdrawal with associated bleeding and, in some cases, recurrence of menopausal symptoms. Several studies have shown that this latter mode of therapy results in a quiescent endometrium after approximately 3 to 6 months of treatment; however, during the early phase of combined constant therapy intermittent irregular and sometimes heavy bleeding may occur in a significant minority of women. Again, as for 90-day-interval progestogen treatment, there are currently no data with regard to actual rates of endometrial carcinoma in patients on low-dose constant oestrogen–progestogen regimens.

Duration of therapy

If the purpose of oestrogen treatment is relief of one or more of the acute manifestations of the menopausal syndrome, such as vaginitis or hot flushes, a few weeks to a few months of therapy may suffice. However, if ORT is given for long-term protection against osteoporosis or coronary artery disease, many years of therapy will be required. Formerly, recommendations were for 5 or 10 years of treatment, but it has been shown that whenever ORT is discontinued a period of rapid calcium loss ensues similar to that occurring at the natural menopause. If the object of ORT is prevention of hip fractures, the frequency of which peaks after the age of 70, then 10 years of treatment should delay the peak until approximately age 80. Thus, as life expectancy in women increases past age 80, it may become important to continue ORT for longer periods of time. Theoretically there is no objection to indefinite continuation of ORT, as long as the patient remains comfortable and has no side-effects. There is some evidence that ORT remains effective even when initiated in women over 65. However, one recent epidemiological study showed an apparent diminishing rate of protection against fractures in women treated past 70 years of age. Therefore it is possible that, in extreme old age, beneficial oestrogen effects on bone may be attenuated.

Problems and toxicity of oestrogen replacement

Minor side-effects

Women taking oral oestrogens may complain of nausea or vague abdominal discomfort, only rarely accompanied by vomiting, similar to the gastrointestinal syndrome of pregnancy. Other typical symptoms are bloating and/or fluid retention. With the low doses employed for ORT these symptoms are usually mild, and may remit if therapy is continued for a few more weeks or if doses are lowered temporarily. In studies utilizing transdermal oestradiol the incidence of these symptoms appears to be lower, suggesting that some of them may be mediated by local effects of oestrogen on the upper gastrointestinal tract, first-pass effects of oestrogen on the liver, or oestrogen metabolites produced during first pass through the liver. Women taking oestrogens may develop simple headaches or, on occasion, new onset or exacerbation of severe migraine headaches. The latter event necessitates discontinuation of oestrogen therapy. At initiation of therapy, stimulation of breast tissue may lead to breast pain or tenderness. This usually subsides with continued therapy but may require discontinuation of oestrogen in some patients, particularly those with a past history of painful polycystic breast disease. Finally, oestrogen stimulation of the uterus may cause some intermittent bleeding or spotting, even in women taking cyclic progestogen. This may be due to an inappropriate ratio of oestrogen to progestogen for the particular patient, and may respond to lowering the oestrogen dose or increasing the dose or number of days of treatment with progestogen. Bleeding may also be due to reactivation of a subendometrial uterine leiomyoma, endometrial hyperplasia, or cervical or endometrial cancer. Therefore, if bleeding fails to remit with adjustment of steroid therapy, patients should be evaluated by a gynaecologist.

Hepatic first-pass effects

The prevalence of hypertension and incidence of thromboembolic disease (deep vein thrombophlebitis, pulmonary embolism, and thrombotic stroke) are increased in women taking oral contraceptives. These risks were shown to be related to the oestrogen rather than to the progestogen component, and accordingly the doses of oestrogen in most oral contraceptives were decreased. More recently it has become apparent that these adverse effects of oral oestrogen are mediated by its hepatic first-pass action on the synthesis of a variety of proteins. These include the hormone-binding globulins for sex steroids, cortisol, and thyroid hormones. Oestrogens appear to raise blood pressure by inducing hepatic synthesis of renin substrate (angiotensinogen), resulting in elevated levels of angiotensin. The particular factors responsible for increased intravascular clotting have not been definitively identified, although a number of candidates have been suggested. Studies of women taking the lower doses of oral oestrogens typically given for ORT have not shown detectable increases in clinical hypertension, thrombophlebitis, pulmonary embolus, or stroke, despite measurable increases in binding proteins and renin substrate. Furthermore, measurements of urinary excretion of fibrin breakdown products, an index of subclinical intravascular clot formation, do not increase in women on ORT. Nonetheless, non-oral oestrogen preparations, such as the oestrogen patch, have been devised and marketed based on the concept of avoiding first-pass hepatic effects. With these preparations, there is no increase in any of the hepatic proteins measured and hence, presumably, an even lower risk of thromboembolism and hypertension.

There also appears to be an increase in clinical gallbladder disease in women taking oral oestrogens. This occurs in both women on oral contraceptives and those taking ORT. It is unclear whether this is caused by increased formation of gallstones due to an oestrogen-induced alteration of bile chemistry or by some effect on the gallbladder itself, leading to symptomatic disease in the presence of pre-existing stones. It is also not known whether cholelithiasis can be avoided by a non-oral route of oestrogen administration, although there is reason to presume that this may be so.

Hepatic-mediated effects of oestrogens and progestogens have been discussed above in the section on coronary artery disease. Briefly, data are consistent with the concept that oral oestrogens increase HDL and lower LDL cholesterol, but non-oral oestrogens improve only LDL (which is the fraction that increases when ovarian oestrogen deficiency occurs). Oral progestogens may oppose oestrogen's beneficial effects on HDL and LDL when given at higher doses, but this lipid effect is not evident at low doses or when given parenterally.

Glucose tolerance

Oral contraceptive pills may be associated with decreased glucose tolerance and with onset of diabetes mellitus. It is not clear whether this effect is due to the oestrogen or the progestogen component. Although decreased glucose tolerance has been included as a potential side-effect of oestrogen therapy in older literature, more recent studies have failed to show that this occurs with the lower doses of oestrogen used for postmenopausal ORT. Rather, a neutral effect or even a slight improvement in glucose tolerance in oestrogen-treated women has been demonstrated.

Breast cancer

Many physicians hesitate to prescribe ORT and many women hesitate to accept a prescription for oestrogens because of a fear of inducing carcinoma of the breast. Although some breast cancers are oestrogen responsive, there is no conclusive evidence that postmenopausal ORT is associated with an increased risk of breast cancer, despite numerous studies of this question. The caveat to be considered with regard to most such studies is that their designs and patient populations have been such that a risk ratio of 2.0 or less could not be detected with confidence. This means that women on ORT could have up to twice the incidence of breast carcinoma without these studies showing a statistically significant effect. A few studies have shown an increased risk, a few show a protective effect, and most give risk ratios near 1.0. In one large study, in which oestrogen appeared to increase the risk of breast cancer, this effect disappeared when women having a first-degree relative (mother or sister) with a history of breast cancer were subtracted from the population (Colditz et al. 1990). Thus long-term ORT may be contraindicated in women with a strong family history of breast cancer. The largest rigorous study published so far compared individual data from 52 705 women who developed cancer with data from 108 411 women without breast cancer observed in 51 epidemiological studies in 21 countries (Collaborative Group 1997). This indicated a 2.3 per cent increase in relative risk with each year of use, but with loss of excess risk within 5 years of withdrawal of ORT. In absolute numbers, these results imply an excess of 2, 6, and 12 cancers per 1000 women who started ORT at age 50 after 5, 10, and 15 years of treatment respectively. As with all observational studies, there is the possibility of various forms of bias, and reliable estimates of increased risk (if any) of breast cancer associated with ORT will only be obtained when randomized controlled trials have been completed. The role of progestogen in altering the risk of breast cancer is uncertain, with a single study suggesting a protective effect and another study finding a small increase in risk.

Selection of candidates for therapy

There is no consensus on who should or should not be treated with ORT. Clearly, women with acute symptoms of the menopausal syndrome are candidates for short-term therapy, but controversy continues over which women should be given long-term ORT. Some experts have recommended that any postmenopausal woman without a clear contraindication should be considered a candidate for ORT, but most physicians adopt a more conservative approach.

If ORT is considered as prophylaxis for osteoporosis, then it would be helpful to identify women at high risk for this problem at the time of the menopause. In general, risk factors for osteoporotic bone fractures include family history of osteoporotic fractures, Caucasian race, fair skin, slender stature, sedentary lifestyle, diabetes mellitus, and tobacco and alcohol use. Efforts have been made to devise specific tests or combinations of tests which would reliably predict risk of bone loss. These have included urinary calcium and hydroxyproline, and more recently N-telopeptide excretion, measurements of circulating metabolites of vitamin D, and measurements of bone density by X-rays, by single and dual gamma photon absorption, and by quantitative axial CT. Some of these methods have been highly successful in establishing the diagnosis of osteoporosis, but none has proved sufficiently reliable in predicting it before the fact. There is hope that more objective indices of osteoporosis risk may be devised in the future.

The potential beneficial effects of oestrogen therapy include very significant reduction of coronary artery disease risk, and progestogen treatment essentially eliminates excess risk of endometrial but not breast carcinoma Therefore these factors must also be weighed in the decision as to whom to treat with ORT. A recent paper in which the risks and benefits of HRT were mathematically modelled (Nananda et al. 1997), using assumptions regarding osteoporosis, coronary artery disease, and breast cancer risks based on previously published data, provides some guidance in regard to patient selection. Not surprisingly, these authors found the greatest reduction in risk of overall mortality in women at high risk for cardiovascular disease, as determined by lipid profile and family history, with diminishing benefit as risk for breast cancer increased. Only in the highest breast cancer risk group (defined as two first-degree relatives with breast cancer) did ORT produce net negative effects. In women with one first-degree relative with breast cancer, the degree of benefit varied from neutral to moderately positive, depending on coronary artery disease risk.

If preliminary evidence of a neuroprotective effect of oestrogen preventing or delaying onset of Alzheimer's dementia continues to strengthen as further studies are completed, this factor would also weigh heavily in favour of broader application of ORT. For reasons discussed below, the presence of liver disease or a history of venous thrombosis or thromboembolism should contraindicate use of oral (but not necessarily parenteral) oestrogens. Other relative contraindications to ORT include hypertension, gallbladder disease, and heart or renal failure. Finally, contraindications to oestrogen therapy generally thought to be absolute, such as a history of malignant disease, particularly melanoma and hormone-dependent tumours of breast, ovary, or uterus, are being reconsidered by some experts as possibly not prohibitive in certain cases.

Other problems of postmenopausal women

Vaginal bleeding

In the perimenopausal period irregular vaginal bleeding may merely represent occasional ovarian reactivation due to the presence of a few residual follicles. However, vaginal bleeding by a woman of menopausal age, who has been without menses for 6 months or more and who is not taking ORT, strongly suggests reproductive system pathology such as infections, ulcerations, or tumours of uterus, cervix, or vagina. Thus a woman manifesting postmenopausal bleeding should have an assessment of the vagina, cervix, and uterus, including endometrial biopsy or cytological sampling by some other method such as brushing or washing. Most commonly, only endometrial hyperplasia will be found. This is due to uterine stimulation by unopposed oestrogen. The usual cause is overproduction of oestrogens by peripheral conversion of androgenic precursors, a process that is accelerated in obese women. Other possible causes include granulosa or theca cell tumours of the ovary, adrenal adenoma, and adrenal carcinoma. Thus endocrine evaluation, including measurement of plasma oestradiol, oestrone, and testosterone, and urinary 17-keto-steroids, should be undertaken to localize and define the source of steroid. Further measures would depend on the laboratory findings, but might include various imaging techniques (axial CT, magnetic resonance imaging, angiography, etc.) to define ovarian or adrenal pathology, laparoscopy, and surgical exploration.

Hirsutism and baldness

Some increase in, or darkening and coarsening of, facial and body hair is very common following the menopause. It is usually mild and confined to the moustache, chin, and sideburn area. This is due to the physiological decrease in the oestrogen-to-androgen ratio produced by the reduction of oestrogen secretion by the ovary. For the same reason, those women with a genetic susceptibility to male-pattern baldness may note gradual thinning of hair in the typical frontal and crown areas in their sixties and seventies. If more severe or rapidly progressive hirsutism occurs, with appearance of heavy beard growth or increased chest and abdominal hair, particularly if accompanied by signs of virilization, such as deepening of the voice, clitoromegaly, increased libido, or rapidly progressive hair loss, hyperandrogenism of a pathological type should be suspected. If the testosterone level is high (> 100 ng/dl), ovarian pathology is likely. This may consist of hyperplasia of thecal elements or hilus cells of the ovary or may be due to benign or malignant ovarian tumours. In general, ovarian tumours (whether adenomas or carcinomas) tend to be associated with higher levels of testosterone (> 300 ng/dl), while hyperplastic tissue secretes somewhat less. Tumours of the adrenal gland secrete large amounts of weak androgens (androstenedione, di-hydroepiandrosterone, etc.) and thus can be detected by the increased excretion of urinary 17-ketosteroids or by measurements of the appropriate plasma steroids by radio-immunoassay.

Tumours

Like younger women, postmenopausal women are at risk for neoplasia of the reproductive organs. Certain of these tumours are more common after the menopause. The incidence of endometrial cancer peaks in the sixties, probably because the endometrium of younger women is subject to intermittent maturation and shedding due to cyclic exposure to progesterone. After the menopause, women maintain a low level of tonic oestrogen secretion from the adrenal and ovary which is unopposed by progesterone. This may be sufficient to induce endometrial hyperplasia which can progress to endometrial cancer. Women who are obese are at greater risk for endometrial carcinoma because their oestrogen levels tend to be higher owing to peripheral conversion of steroid precursors to oestrogen by adipose tissue. Vulvar carcinoma is also more common in elderly women. This malignancy of the junctional epithelium is often preceded by a premalignant condition characterized by areas of atrophy and meta-plasia of the vulvar skin known as kraurosis vulvae. The relationship, if any, of this condition to hormone deficiency is unknown. Finally, it should be remembered that ovarian cancer is one of the most common malignancies of women and remains a major cause of death. There does not appear to be any relationship between risk of ovarian cancer and ORT or HRT. Although the incidence of ovarian cancer peaks between the ages of 45 and 55, elderly women remain at risk for this disease.

References

Barrett-Connor, E. (1991). Postmenopausal estrogen and prevention bias. *Annals of Internal medicine*, 115, 455–6.

Barrett-Connor, E. and Bush, T.L. (1991). Estrogen and coronary heart disease in women. *Journal of the American Medical Association*, 265, 1861.

Bergkvist, L., Adami, H.-O., et al. (1989). The risk of breast cancer after estrogen and estrogen-progestin replacement. *New England Journal of Medicine*, 321, 293.

Birge, S.J. (1996). Is there a role for estrogen replacement therapy in the prevention and treatment of dementia? *Journal of the American Geriatrics Society*, 44, 865.

Bush, T.L., Cowan, L.D., Barrett-Connor, E., et al. (1983). Estrogen use and all-cause mortality. *Journal of the American Medical Association*, 249, 903–6.

Cauley, J.A., Seeley, D.G., et al. (1995). Estrogen replacement therapy and fractures in older women. *Annals of Internal Medicine*, 122, 9.

Colditz, G.A, Stampfer, M..J, et al. (1990). Prospective study of estrogen replacement therapy and risk of breast cancer in postmenopausal women. *Journal of the American Medical Association*, 264, 2648.

Collaborative Group on Hormone Factors in Breast Cancer (1997). Breast cancer and hormone replacement therapy: collaborative reanalysis of data from 51 epidemiological studies of 52 705 women with breast cancer and 108 411 women without breast cancer. *Lancet*, 350, 1047–59.

Collins, P. (1996). Vascular aspects of estrogen. *Maturitas*, 23, 217.

Delmas, P.D., Bjarnason, N.H., et al. (1997). Effects of raloxifene on bone mineral density, serum cholesterol concentrations, and uterine endometrium in postmenopausal women. *New England Journal of Medicine*, 337, 1641.

Ettinger, B., Friedman, G.D., et al. (1996). Reduced mortality associated with long-term postmenopausal estrogen therapy. *Obstetrics and Gynecology*, 87, 6.

Fahraeus, L. and Wallentin, L. (1983). High density lipoprotein subfractions during oral and cutaneous administration of 17b-estradiol to menopausal women. *Journal of Clinical Endocrinology and Metabolism*, 56, 797–801.

Gordon, T., Kannel, W.B., Hjortland, M.C., and McNamara, P.M. (1978). Menopause and coronary heart disease, the Framingham Study. *Annals of Internal Medicine*, 89, 157–61.

Grodstein, F., Stampfer, M.J., et al. (1997). Postmenopausal hormone therapy and mortality. *New England Journal of Medicine*, 336, 1769.

Heckbert, S.R., Weiss, N.S., et al. (1997). Duration of estrogen replacement therapy in relation to the risk of incident myocardial infarction in postmenopausal women. *Archives of Internal Medicine*, 157, 1330.

Hillard, T.C., Whitcroft, S.J., et al. (1994). Long-term effects of transdermal and oral hormone replacement therapy on postmenopausal bone loss. *Osteoporosis International*, 4, 341.

Hulley, S., Grady, D., Bush, T., et al., for the Heart and Estrogen/progestin Replacement Study (HERS) Research Group (1998). Randomized trial of estrogen plus progestin for secondary prevention of coronary heart disease in postmenopausal women. *Journal of the American Medical Association*, 280, 605–13.

Jensen, J., Riis, B.J., Strom, V., Nilas, L., and Christiansen, C. (1987). Long-term effects of percutaneous oestrogens and oral progesterone on serum lipoproteins in postmenopausal women. *American Journal of Obstetrics and Gynecology*, 156, 66–71.

Melton, L., Jr (1996). Epidemiology of hip fractures: implications of the exponential increase with age. *Bone*, 18 (Supplement), 121S.

Nananda, F., Eckman, M.H., Karas, R.H., *et al.* (1997). Patient-specific decisions about hormone replacement therapy in postmenopausal women. *Journal of the American Medical Association*, **277**, 1140–7.

National Institutes of Health (1980). *The Lipid Research Clinics*, Vol. I, *The prevalence study*, pp. 70–9. National Institutes of Health, US Department of Health and Human Services, Washington, DC.

Paganini-Hill, A. and Henderson, V.W. (1996). Estrogen replacement therapy and risk of Alzheimer disease. *Archives of Internal Medicine*, **156**, 2213.

Quigley, M.E.T, Martin, P.L., Burnier, A.M., and Brooks, P. (1987). Estrogen therapy arrests bone loss in elderly women. *American Journal of Obstetrics and Gynecology*, **156**, 1516–23.

Sherman, B.M., West, J.H., and Korenman, S.G. (1976). The menopausal transition: Analysis of LH, FSH, estradiol, and progesterone concentrations during the menopausal cycles of older women. *Journal of Clinical Endocrinology and Metabolism*, **42**, 629–36.

Tataryn, I.V., Meldrum, D.R., Lu, K.H, Frumar, A.M., and Judd, H.L. (1979). LH, FSH and skin temperature during the menopausal hot flash. *Journal of Clinical Endocrinology and Metabolism*, **49**, 152–3.

Tikkanen, M.J., Nikkita, E.A., and Vartainen, E. (1978). Natural oestrogens as an effective treatment for type II hyperlipoproteinaemia in postmenopausal women. *Lancet*, **ii**, 490–1.

Vermeulen, A. (1976). The hormonal activity of the postmenopausal ovary. *Journal of Clinical Endocrinology and Metabolism*, **42**, 247–53.

Weiss, N.S., Ure, C.L., Ballard, J.H., Williams, A.R., and Darling, J.R. (1980). Decreased risk of fractures of the hip and lower forearm with postmenopausal use of estrogen. *New England Journal of Medicine*, **303**, 1195–8.

Whitehead, M.I., Townsend, P.T., Pryse-Davies, J., Ryder, T.A., and King, R.J.B. (1981). Effects of oestrogens and progestins on the biochemistry and morphology of the postmenopausal endometrium. *New England Journal of Medicine*, **305**, 1599–1605.

7.4 The hypothalamic–pituitary axes

S. Mitchell Harman and Marc R. Blackman

Introduction

Biological ageing is associated with a progressive loss of functional capacity leading to a decreased ability of the organism to maintain homeostasis initially in the face of stress and later under baseline conditions. Increased understanding of the complexities and heterogeneity of the ageing process has forced revision of the simplistic, but once popular, concept that ageing is a consequence of one or more hormone deficiency states. Rather, ageing results from multiple changes in the molecular, biochemical, and physiological functions of cells, tissues, and organisms (see Chapter 2.2). Sophisticated investigations have produced considerable evidence that (a) characteristic alterations in hormone secretion and action do occur during ageing, in both humans and animals, and (b) certain metabolic and physiological changes associated with normal ageing may actually be secondary phenomena caused wholly or in part by alterations in hormone balance or hormone response.

An important consideration in the study of endocrinology and ageing is the interaction of disease states and hormones. Such interactions have been described for a wide variety of diseases and nearly all the major hormone axes. Because ageing is associated with an increased susceptibility to (and prevalence of) various illnesses, studies of the effects of ageing on hormone balance may be confounded by the effects of coexisting chronic or acute pathology on endocrine function. In addition, the complex interactions of diet, physical activity levels, sleep–wake cycles, body weight and composition, and medications, all of which may vary with the age of the population studied, must be accounted for, as all may affect measurements of hormonal functions.

It should also be borne in mind that, although at its simplest, endocrine function is evaluated by direct measurements (e.g. radioimmunoassay) of hormone concentrations in plasma or urine, there are various complex factors (in addition to disease states, as mentioned above) which modulate and alter the final effects of the hormones measured. First, many hormones are secreted rhythmically with characteristic diurnal and even circannual patterns. For many hormones (e.g. growth hormone), characteristic target organ responses reflect integrated tissue exposure to many hours or days of varying hormone levels and may depend not only on absolute amount, but also on pattern and timing of secretion. Thus hormone concentrations in single, or even a few, blood samples taken at short intervals, may not provide an adequate index of overall hormone activity in the organism. Levels of other hormones (e.g. ACTH) vary rapidly in response to short-term stimuli and tissue response is immediate and short-lived. In these cases, hormone measurements must be interpreted in the context of the relevant physiological states (e.g. stress, blood glucose level, etc.). Other factors which modulate hormone effects include binding of hormones to plasma carrier proteins, in which case biological activity depends mainly on the free hormone fraction, and chemical modifications (such as glycosylation) of the hormone, producing molecular heterogeneity and alterations in the ratio of biological hormone action to hormone concentration as determined by immunoassay.

Finally, hormone measurements must be interpreted in relation to alterations of the following:

(1) rates of hormone secretion, which reflect not only the number of available secretory cells, but also the modulation of their activity by other hormones, neurotransmitters, circulatory factors, and local (paracrine) hormone effects as well as self-modulation (autocrine modulation);

(2) rates of hormone clearance from the plasma, as high blood hormone levels may be due to a reduction in rate of hormone metabolism rather than an increase in secretion;

(3) altered target tissue sensitivity to hormones which may, in turn, reflect changes in hormone receptor number or function, alterations in amount or activity of substances responsible for transduction of receptor signals (e.g. G proteins or phosphokinases), or changes in the cell's internal physiology that limit its capacity to respond to such signals (e.g. altered gene function at the level of transcription, translation, or postsynthetic processing).

Because ageing is such a global process, it is likely that most changes observed in endocrine function with age will result from some combination of the factors reviewed above, rather than from a single cause. Moreover, as noted above, it is typical of the physiology of ageing that basal activities are sustained at normal levels until late in the process. Initial changes tend to reduce the maximum response of which the system is capable (i.e. the reserve capacity), so that the earliest evidence of ageing is seen only when systems are stressed. All the above principles must be considered in a critical review of experimental data pertaining to the effects of ageing on endocrine function.

Effects of ageing on posterior pituitary function

The posterior pituitary gland, or neurohypophysis, is an intrinsic part of the central nervous system, being an embryological outgrowth of the basal hypothalamus. It is connected directly to the base of the brain by the pituitary stalk, with which it is continuous, and contains numerous axon terminals from cells located in the supraoptic and paraventricular nuclei of the hypothalamus. These axons terminate on a network of capillary sinusoids, rather than on other neurones and contain a number of neurotransmitters, of which the most important are the two peptides vasopressin and oxytocin.

Arginine vasopressin (**AVP**), an eight-amino-acid peptide, is also known as antidiuretic hormone (**ADH**). It is the major physiologically active product of the posterior pituitary gland. Although ADH is an arterial vasoconstrictor in high concentrations, its major action is to make the distal tubules and collecting ducts of the renal medulla permeable to water, allowing passage of free water from their lumina back into the interstitial fluid and hence the circulation. When ADH concentrations increase, more water is reabsorbed from the glomerular filtrate, urine volume decreases, and urine concentration and osmolarity increase. In the absence of ADH activity (diabetes insipidus) large volumes (> 10 l/day) of dilute urine are excreted and the individual must either consume large quantities of fluid or rapidly become severely dehydrated.

ADH secretion is normally controlled by two kinds of physiological input. In the usual state, ADH-secreting neurones are regulated by osmoreceptor cells in the central nervous system which detect plasma osmolarity, determined mainly by sodium concentration. Solutes which distribute freely across cell membranes (e.g. urea or glucose) have little or no effect on ADH secretion, although they may contribute to osmolarity as measured by freezing point depression, etc. Increases in plasma osmolarity (i.e. high sodium concentrations) lead to both increased thirst (water intake) and an increase in the rate of ADH secretion (water conservation). A fall in plasma osmolarity, as when large quantities of water are consumed, decrease ADH secretion so that ADH concentrations rapidly fall to a low basal level. The set-point, or level of plasma osmolarity at which ADH secretion begins to increase, varies considerably among individuals and may change from time to time in a single individual depending on a number of factors, including thyroid and glucocorticoid hormone levels, illness, stress, and age. The other factor regulating ADH secretion is blood pressure, as detected by baroreceptors at various sites. This influence is usually less important, but may override osmolar regulation, as when hypotension (e.g. acute haemorrhage) leads to high levels of ADH secretion despite normal osmolarity.

Clinically significant hyponatraemia is more common in older persons. This may be in part because older persons are more prone to illnesses or consume more medications (see below) which cause water retention or sodium loss at the kidney, but they also appear to have a greater likelihood of responding adversely to influences tending to cause haemodilution. However, this tendency to hyponatraemia does not appear to be due mainly to alterations with age in renal function. Although the maximum urinary concentrating ability does tend to diminish with age, this decrease has been shown to be of much smaller magnitude than previously reported; moreover, the renal response to exogenously administered ADH appears to be age invariant. Rather, older people have been shown, on average, to have higher levels of ADH secretion for a given osmolarity, i.e. an alteration downward in their osmolar set-point and higher 'basal' levels of plasma ADH. Nearly three-quarters of patients with the syndrome of inappropriate ADH secretion (**SIADH**) are over 65 years of age (see Chapter 15.1).

Consistent with the observation of higher plasma ADH levels in elderly people, histology of the hypothalamus and neurohypophysis do not show degeneration of neurones or axonal pathways, but rather changes typical of increased hormone synthesis. Similarly, hormone measurements have shown increased hypothalamic ADH content with age. In addition, even when compared with young subjects having similar basal ADH levels, older people demonstrate a 2- to 2.5-fold greater increase in plasma ADH to increases in osmolarity induced by hypertonic saline infusion and less suppression of ADH secretion after ethanol ingestion. Thus, taken together with findings showing no decrease in distribution space or metabolic clearance rate of ADH, available evidence points strongly to a tendency for augmented ADH secretion with age in humans. The exception to the above is the observation that recumbency followed by erect posture leads to a subnormal ADH response in older subjects. Given the brisk secretory response to osmolar stimuli, it is likely that the blunted volume–pressure regulation of ADH secretion with age is due to defects in the baroreceptors or afferent neural pathways, rather than in the neurohypophysis itself.

Clinical hyponatraemia may present in older persons without obvious concomitants, but more commonly it is related to physiological stressors or use of medication(s). It is essential that patients be differentiated as follows:

(1) those with hypervolaemic hyponatraemia (e.g. fluid retention due to heart, liver, or kidney failure);

(2) those with hypovolaemic hyponatraemia (in which increased ADH secretion and water intake are an appropriate response to dehydration and salt loss due to diuretics, mineralocorticoid insufficiency, renal tubular salt wasting, etc.);

(3) those with euvolaemic hyponatraemia (the situation in SIADH).

Although ectopic secretion of ADH by neoplasms (particularly small-cell carcinoma of the lung) must always be considered, the form of ADH excess to which geriatric patients are particularly predisposed is eutopic (i.e. from the pituitary gland). In patients with SIADH, the physician must determine whether predisposing conditions such as cardiac or renal failure, stroke or other central nervous system trauma, medications (particularly sulphonylureas or diuretics), or endocrine disease (hypothyroidism or adrenal failure) are present. Risk factors for SIADH also include surgery or other trauma, anaesthetics, and infections (e.g. pneumonia).

Symptoms of hyponatraemia include weakness, hyporeflexia, muscle cramps, lethargy, disorientation, and, in severe cases, coma and seizures. Mild euvolaemic hyponatraemia can be treated by removal of the offending agent (when possible) and moderate fluid restriction (usually less than 1.5 liters of free water daily). In more severe cases (severe central nervous system symptoms, plasma sodium below 120 mmol/l) infusion of hypertonic saline may be necessary in the acute phase (see Chapter 15.1). This should almost always be done in consultation with an endocrine or renal specialist. The usual recommendation calls for the use of 3 per cent saline given at a rate of about 0.1 ml/kg/min until the plasma sodium reaches 125 mmol/l. In the elderly patient hypertonic saline should be infused more slowly than in younger patients in order to avoid excessive or overly rapid shifting of fluid out of the intracellular compartment (cerebral dehydration) and circulatory overload (congestive failure).

Patients with hyponatraemia require careful and frequent monitoring of fluid intake and output, cardiac status, and plasma sodium until the situation is completely rectified (sodium concentration of 130 mmol/l or more). In certain cases, in which fluid restriction proves inadequate to treat chronic hyponatraemia owing to excessive ADH secretion, oral demeclocycline, a tetracycline derivative which blocks ADH action on the renal tubule, may be useful.

Effects of ageing on anterior pituitary function

The anterior pituitary gland (adenohypophysis) is not a part of the central nervous system, but is derived from an outpouching (Rathke's pouch) of the epithelium of the dorsal pharynx which is sealed off from the digestive tract by formation of the basal cranial bones. It lies in the sella turcica just anterior to and in contact with the neurohypophysis. The adenohypophysis consists of cells of a number of different types, mixed in various proportions throughout the gland. Each type of cell secretes one or more of a family of related protein hormones. These hormones exert a wide variety of effects throughout the body, regulating metabolism, growth, and the thyroid, adrenal, and reproductive functions. The anterior pituitary has been referred to as the 'master gland' because several of its hormones (thyroid-stimulating hormone (TSH), ACTH, and the gonadotrophins luteinizing hormone (LH) and follicle-stimulating hormone (FSH)) stimulate hormone secretion by other endocrine glands (thyroid, adrenal cortex, and gonad). The other anterior pituitary hormones (growth hormone (GH) and prolactin (PRL)) act on non-endocrine target tissues. GH exerts its effects directly at some sites, and indirectly at others by stimulating production of insulin-like growth factor 1 (IGF-1). PRL stimulates its target cells directly without intermediate factors.

Secretion of the anterior pituitary hormones is regulated by specific hypothalamic hormones or neurotransmitters, of which some are stimulatory and others are inhibitory. These factors, all but one of which are peptides, are products of neurosecretion. They are secreted by specialized neurones whose axons terminate on small blood vessels in the median eminence of the hypothalamus (rather than on nerve or muscle cells). These compounds are carried from the median eminence to the anterior pituitary gland via a short network of portal vessels. The response of most kinds of anterior pituitary cells to these hypothalamic factors is further modulated by negative feedback inhibition from the products of their target cells, which reach the pituitary via the systemic circulation. These products may also influence production of the hypophysiotropic neurosecretory factors at the hypothalamic level.

In elderly individuals the anterior pituitary gland tends to be moderately decreased in size. It typically contains areas of fibrosis, local necrosis, and cyst formation. Cells may have extensive deposits of lipofuscin and regional deposits of amyloid are also common. Immunocytochemical investigations have not revealed any prominent age-associated alterations in the relative proportions of different types of pituitary secretory cells. The pituitary content of GH, PRL, and TSH appears to be age invariant, while the LH and FSH contents are somewhat increased in elderly people.

Growth hormone

Native GH is a 191-amino-acid peptide secreted by the somatotropic cells of the pituitary gland. GH is essential for normal growth and development in children, but its role in adult life was long thought to be of little significance. Moreover, until the late 1980s, the expense and limited supply of human GH (hGH) extracted from cadaver pituitaries restricted its use to children with GH deficiency and growth failure. Now that recombinant synthetic hGH is available, it has become possible to assess its potential therapeutic role in adults. Evidence from studies in adult patients with GH deficiency has made it increasingly apparent that GH is an important anabolic hormone which reverses negative nitrogen balance, increases protein synthesis, and causes positive calcium balance and bone growth. It also stimulates lipolysis with concomitant increases in plasma free fatty acids, a reduction in percentage body fat, and improvements in circulating lipoprotein profiles. The fact that normal human ageing is characterized by loss of muscle and bone mass and an increase in percentage body fat suggests that the secretion and/or action of GH may be reduced in elderly persons.

Most peripheral tissue actions of GH are mediated by IGF-1, formerly known as somatomedin-C. The majority of circulating IGF-1 is generated in the liver, but it is also produced at other sites of

GH action, such as osteoblastic cells in bone, where it may act locally. In addition, circulating IGF-1 exerts feedback inhibitory effects on GH secretion by pituitary somatotropic cells. GH secretion is mainly modulated by two hypothalamic peptides released into the pituitary portal circulation. These are GH-releasing hormone, a 44-amino-acid peptide which stimulates GH release, and somatostatin, a peptide found in the hypothalamus and many other tissues, which inhibits GH secretion (as well as the release of various other hormones).

Several GH-releasing peptides and related non-peptide GH secretagogues which exert potent stimulatory effects on pulsatile GH release have recently been synthesized. These GH secretagogues appear to exert their effects by antisomatostatinergic actions which are not mediated via GH-releasing hormone, somatostatin, GH, or opioidergic receptors. An endogenous GH secretagogue receptor has recently been cloned from pituitary and hypothalamic tissue, although the naturally occurring ligand for this receptor has not yet been identified and its precise physiological role in regulating pituitary somatotropic function remains to be elucidated.

The effect of ageing on GH secretion in humans has been evaluated by a number of researchers. Some early studies reported unchanged baseline plasma GH levels. However, GH is normally secreted in rhythmic pulses, with highest frequency and amplitude associated with stage 3 to 4 (slow-wave) sleep. Therefore random single samples do not adequately characterize daily GH secretory dynamics. More recent studies, in which GH was measured in samples taken frequently over a 24-h period, have show a decrease in 24-h integrated GH concentrations and a substantial decrease in the amplitude of GH spontaneous pulses during sleep in elderly men and women. Despite the known alterations of sleep patterns in older people, the decrease in maximum GH secretory activity does not appear to be directly associated with the observed reduction in REM sleep. Another major factor which modulates GH secretion is plasma oestrogen level. It has been demonstrated that GH secretion is significantly greater in females after puberty, but that this difference disappears after the menopause so that elderly people of both sexes exhibit similarly diminished levels of GH. Oral oestrogen treatment appears to augment spontaneous and exercise-induced GH secretion, but simultaneously reduces the blood levels of IGF-1. In contrast, treatment with physiological doses of oestradiol given transdermally to postmenopausal women does not alter basal plasma GH or IGF-1 levels, and may actually decrease the GH secretory response to GH-releasing hormone. The basis for the apparent discrepant effects of oral versus transdermal oestrogens on GH secretion may reside in differential actions on hepatic IGF-1 modulation of the two routes of oestrogen administration.

Responses of GH in elderly people to indirect secretagogues (exercise, L-dopa, arginine, and insulin-induced hypoglycaemia) have been variously reported to show no change or a decrease with ageing. Some investigators have shown that GH responses to direct pituitary stimulation with GH-releasing hormone are present, but significantly reduced, in apparently healthy men and women, whereas others have reported only a non-significant downward trend with age in peak GH response in men. These discrepant findings could be explained by differences among populations studied in a number of important physiological variables which are known to modulate GH secretion. These include adiposity and lean body mass, caloric intake, psychological status (e.g. depression), and levels of sex steroid hormones (particularly oestrogen).

Basal plasma IGF-1 levels have been shown to decrease by 30 to 40 per cent in ageing men and women. Plasma IGF-1 levels correlate well with integrated spontaneous GH secretion and provide a good index of peripheral tissue exposure to GH in young persons. However, these correlations appear to be less reliable in elderly persons, possibly because of age-associated alterations in plasma IGF-binding proteins, the narrowed range of GH secretory variation, or other as yet unidentified factors. Nonetheless, the ability of IGF-1 to respond to GH, whether administered exogenously or incremented endogenously in response to GH-releasing hormone, is preserved in older persons. Therefore it is likely that the observed age-associated decrease in IGF-1 reflects the decrease in circulating GH rather than some acquired tissue resistance to the effects of GH. As far as the actions of IGF-1 are concerned, experiments have shown that cultured human fibroblasts from elderly (and also progeric) donors bind and respond to IGF-1 similarly to those derived from young subjects, but that the synergism between glucocorticoid and IGF-1 in stimulating fibroblast DNA synthesis may be lost in fibroblasts from older donors. The physiological significance of the latter finding is not known.

In studies of GH-deficient non-elderly adults treated with recombinant hGH, increases in plasma IGF-1, nitrogen retention, lean body mass, and basal metabolic rates and decreases in percentage body fat and serum cholesterol have been observed in the short term (4–12 months), with improvements in muscle strength, quality of life, and bone density, and loss of intra-abdominal and total body fat in the longer term (18–24 months). Investigations of the potential value of treatments (e.g. exogenous GH-releasing hormone or GH) to restore GH and IGF-1 in elderly patients to levels characteristic of those in younger people are in their early stages. Short-term treatment (for 7 and 8 days) with recombinant hGH increases circulating levels of IGF-1, improves nitrogen retention, and stimulates bone metabolism in elderly men and women. One study has shown an increase in the strength of some (but not all) muscle groups and an increase in the efficiency of skeletal muscle energy metabolism in elderly men treated with GH-releasing hormone injections for 6 weeks. However, other investigations of hGH treatment over periods varying from 3 months to 1 year in aged men and women have failed to detect significant improvements in bone mass or muscle strength. As noted above, significant improvements in these variables were observed in GH-deficient younger adults only after 18 to 24 months of hGH replacement. Thus additional longer-term studies of GH supplementation (either with hGH or by means of GH secretagogues) may have important implications for age-associated conditions such as osteoporosis, healing of pressure sores or surgical wounds, and restoration of muscle strength, lean body mass, and immune function. Adverse effects of GH treatment of older persons include arthralgias, hyperglycaemia, carpal tunnel syndrome, and fluid retention with peripheral oedema and elevations in blood pressure. In addition, theoretical considerations include a potential for augmentation of tumour cell growth. Therefore, until long-term studies have been completed, treatment regimens optimized, and risk–benefit ratios adequately defined, it is highly inadvisable for older persons to be treated routinely with GH.

Prolactin

Although their absolute number depends on sex, age, and endocrine status (e.g. pregnancy), more than half the secretory cells of the adult pituitary gland are lactotropes, i.e. cells which secrete the 198-amino-acid peptide PRL. Despite this fact, PRL, which stimulates the acinar tissue of the female (oestrogen-conditioned) breast to secrete milk, appears to serve no normal physiological function in the non-lactating adult. Although PRL has considerable structural homology with GH, it neither binds significantly to GH receptors nor exhibits any growth-promoting action. When secreted in excessive amounts, PRL appears to be an 'antireproductive' hormone, suppressing sex steroid production and reducing sexual libido in men and women, and causing impotence in men. These antisexual actions of PRL do not appear to depend entirely on its suppression of androgen production, since exogenous androgen replacement usually fails to restore libido and potency until PRL levels have been reduced.

PRL regulation is unlike that of the other anterior pituitary hormones in that the predominant central nervous system mediated effect on its secretion is inhibitory. Thus disconnection of the anterior pituitary from the hypothalamus leads to increased, rather than diminished, PRL secretion. The hypothalamic PRL inhibitory factor is not a peptide (like the other hypothalamic factors), but has been shown to be dopamine, a catecholamine neurotransmitter, which is secreted into the pituitary portal system at the median eminence. Physiologically important stimulators of pituitary PRL secretion include thyrotrophin-releasing hormone (**TRH**) and oestrogens. Human pituitary PRL content and circulating basal or TRH-stimulated PRL levels are 30 to 50 per cent greater in females than in males at all ages.

Studies of the effects of ageing on PRL secretion have produced varied and contradictory results and no consensus has emerged. Some investigators have reported a decrease in basal PRL levels at the menopause in women, but others have not seen such a change. In older men, basal PRL levels have been reported to be unchanged or increased. Studies of PRL diurnal secretory rhythm have shown both no change and a loss of the normal nocturnal PRL peak in older men. The PRL secretory response to TRH injection has been variously reported to increase, decrease, and remain unchanged with age. Sulpiride, a dopamine receptor antagonist, has been found to produce similar increments of plasma PRL in healthy young and old men.

Given the inconsistency of the experimental findings, it is most likely that alterations in PRL secretions in humans with normal ageing are of small magnitude and probably do not contribute to the observed decrease in sexual activity characteristic of the ageing male. Nonetheless, it should be borne in mind that PRL-secreting adenomas of the pituitary can occur at any age. Moreover, a number of pharmacological agents, including all the major and minor tranquillizers, some antihypertensives, and many antidepressants, have been associated with elevations of PRL, and elderly patients are more likely to be treated with multiple medications. Therefore older patients with reproductive or sexual complaints should have a detailed history of medication use, be examined for galactorrhoea, and have their plasma PRL level measured. If a significantly elevated PRL level is found, subsequent diagnosis and therapy should be directed at eliminating offending medications, if possible, or detecting and treating a PRL-secreting pituitary tumour.

The gonadotrophins

The anterior pituitary secretes two gonadotrophic hormones, LH and FSH. In the male, LH stimulates the interstitial (Leydig) cells of the testis to produce testosterone and FSH initiates and maintains seminiferous tubular function via its action on the Sertoli cells. In the female, LH elicits theca cell production of androgenic steroids (mainly androstenedione), which are converted to oestrogens (mainly oestradiol) by the follicular granulosa cells. In premenopausal females, LH secretion rises to a midcycle peak which activates the ovulatory mechanism, while FSH induces granulosa cell proliferation and follicular maturation. Both LH and FSH are large glycoprotein molecules consisting of two non-covalently bound subunits; the α subunit is common to both LH and FSH (as well as TSH and chorionic gonadotrophin), whereas the β subunit of each molecule is unique and confers both immunological and biological specificity. Central control of gonadotrophin secretion is exercised by gonadotrophin-releasing hormone, a 10-amino-acid peptide secreted into the pituitary portal circulation at the median eminence by axonal terminations of neurosecretory cells located mainly in the arcuate nucleus of the anteromedial hypothalamus. Gonadal steroid hormones exert negative feedback control on both gonadotrophin-releasing hormone and gonadotrophin secretion. An additional peptide factor called inhibin, secreted by Sertoli cells in the male and granulosa cells in the female, feeds back to suppress FSH production.

Most studies of the effects of ageing on gonadal function in men have shown a gradual increase in both LH and FSH after the age of 50. The increase in LH does not appear to be accounted for by a decrease in metabolic clearance of LH; as yet, no data exist for FSH. Although a few men in their eighth or ninth decades may have very high blood levels of FSH and LH, approaching those seen in postmenopausal women, in most the elevations are more modest. The age-associated increase in FSH is disproportionately greater than that of LH, suggesting that ageing has a more prominent effect on seminiferous tubular function (and inhibin secretion) than on gonadal steroid secretion. Consistent with this concept, decreased plasma inhibin levels have been reported in elderly men in parallel with the known decrease in sperm production. Histological examination of testes from aged men have shown varying degrees of tubular involution, hyalinization, and fibrosis, but this tends to be patchy and may be related to local vascular or autoimmune changes. The number of Leydig cells has generally been reported to be normal, with some studies showing increased and a few showing reduced numbers. Total plasma testosterone concentrations in healthy men tend to diminish with age, with the magnitude of decrease depending on the population studies. The decreases observed in most studies have been modest and highly variable, with the majority of men maintaining total testosterone levels within the normal range through the seventh decade. Nearly all such studies have been cross-sectional, but a few sets of longitudinal observations have also shown a modest but steady decline in total testosterone from the third decade on. Because ageing is associated with a significant increase in sex-hormone-binding globulin (with a resultant increase in the fraction of testosterone bound), there is a decrease in plasma free testosterone which is disproportionate to the change in total testosterone but still of only modest magnitude in healthy men. Thus some of the observed increase in LH (and FSH) in men may be due to a decrease in feedback inhibition by free gonadal steroid (i.e. partial Leydig cell failure). This conclusion seems to be supported by data showing a diminished Leydig cell secretory reserve as demonstrated by a reduced response to exogenously administered gonadotrophin. This could be due to altered Leydig cell function, a decrease in Leydig cell number, or both.

There are also data which suggest that the feedback sensitivity of the hypothalamic–pituitary axis to sex steroid inhibition may decrease with age in men. Such a decrease in feedback sensitivity could explain in part the observed increase in plasma FSH and LH levels, despite only a modest change in plasma testosterone. The latter point is controversial, because other investigators, using a somewhat different experimental design, have found greater, rather than lesser, steroid feedback sensitivity in elderly people. Another possible explanation of the increase in gonadotrophins is that ageing results in secretion of gonadotrophins with a decreased bioactivity-to-immunoactivity (**B/I**) ratio. Evidence for altered LH B/I ratio with age has been seen in some, but not all, studies. Similarly, greater charge and size heterogeneity has been observed in FSH extracted from pituitaries of older compared with younger men, and a decrease in the FSH B/I ratio has been reported in one study of elderly men. Thus some available data suggest that the age-associated increases in FSH and LH measured by radio-immunossay may be due in part to altered pituitary processing of the gonadotrophin molecules as a portion of the LH or FSH measured by radio-immunossay is not actually bioactive hormone. Finally, despite the increase in basal concentrations of gonado-trophins, the pituitary LH secretory responses to gonadotrophin-releasing hormone appear to be both delayed and diminished in elderly men, suggesting that there may be some age-associated decrease in pituitary gonadotrophic secretory function. Whether such a change is intrinsic to the pituitary gonadotrophic cells or represents a loss of prior conditioning of such cells due to altered hypothalamic function (e.g. chronic decrease in gonadotrophin-releasing hormone stimulation) has not been determined in humans.

In women, a rise in plasma LH and FSH levels, far greater than that seen in normal male ageing, marks the onset of the menopause, an event related mainly to failure of ovarian secretory as well as germinal function. This subject is covered more thoroughly in Chapter 7.3.

The alteration in gonadotrophic function with age in men is quite subtle and generally has little clinical significance. The physician should be aware that elderly men complaining of symptoms of hypogonadism, particularlyly impotence, may have moderately elevated LH and FSH levels, with 'lower limit of normal' testosterone and free testosterone levels, without any obvious pathology of the reproductive system. However, patients with profound decreases in plasma testosterone (e.g. to levels below 150 ng/dl) should be given the same diagnostic attention as any case of suspected primary hypogonadism. It must be recalled, that serious chronic disease (such as cancer, renal failure, or heart failure), particularly if accompanied by malnutrition and debilitation, may be associated with profound hypogonadism. Hypogonadism induced by concomitant illness may be primary (with elevated gonadotrophin levels), but more often will be found to be secondary (decreased plasma LH and FSH) or mixed (failure of gonadotrophins to increase to compensate for testis failure). Treatment of mildly hypogonadal elderly men with testosterone replacement is con-troversial and at present is not standard medical practice, first because there are no controlled studies which convincingly dem-onstrate beneficial effects and second because prostatic hyperplasia and/or cancer may be induced or exacerbated by androgen treatment.

The pituitary–adrenal axis

The adrenocorticotrophic cells of the anterior pituitary gland syn-thesize a peptide hormone precursor molecule known as pro-opio-melanocortin. This molecule is subsequently processed by peptidases in the secretory cells and, depending on where the peptide chain is severed, may give rise to various combinations of ACTH, α- and β-melanocyte-stimulating hormone, and β-lipotrophin which, by fur-ther cleavage, can release β-endorphin. Pro-opiomelanocortin is se-creted by a number of different cell types besides the pituitary corticotrope, and its postsynthetic processing varies from one location to another. In the anterior pituitary the main products are ACTH, a 39-amino-acid peptide, β-lipotrophin, and α-melanocyte-stimulating hormone. ACTH is the main modulator of adrenocortical function, directly stimulating synthesis of the adrenal cytochrome P-450 en-zymes and dehydrogenases necessary for the production of cortisol, the major adrenal glucocorticoid, from cholesterol.

ACTH secretion is regulated chiefly by corticotrophin-releasing hormone, a 41-amino-acid hypothalamic peptide which stimulates ACTH release, and by glucocorticoids (both natural cortisol and exogenous compounds such as prednisone, dexamethasone, etc.), which inhibit ACTH secretion by the pituitary corticotrope and secretion of corticotrophin-releasing hormone at the hypothalamic level. ACTH and cortisol are normally secreted rhythmically in response to discrete pulses of corticotrophin-releasing hormone re-leased by the hypothalamus into the pituitary portal circulation. These pulses increase to maximum amplitude in the early morning and become smaller and less frequent during the late morning and afternoon, leading to a highly reproducible diurnal secretion pattern for ACTH and cortisol, which has its nadir in the afternoon and evening and peaks between 4.00 and 8.00 a.m. Cortisol is one of the body's major stress hormones, so that any serious stress (traumatic, infectious, or psychological) overrides the normal regulatory mech-anisms and results in hours or even days of much increased ACTH and cortisol secretion. Another important mediator of ACTH secretion is AVP, which is a central nervous system neurotransmitter as well as a neurohormone (as discussed above). AVP appears to have a more prominent role in ACTH secretion during stress than in the basal state.

In the absence of adequate ACTH secretion, secondary adrenal insufficiency develops. Because, without adequate glucocorticoid, or-ganisms succumb to almost any major stress, ACTH (unlike GH, PRL, or the gonadotrophins) is a life-sustaining hormone. Primary (Addison's disease) and secondary glucocorticoid insufficiency are characterized by weight loss, anaemia, hypotension, hyponatraemia, weakness, and fatigue. Glucocorticoid excess is also potentially life threatening. Excessive glucocorticoid produces Cushing's syndrome, which is associated with hypertension, glucose intolerance, centripetal obesity, negative nitrogen balance (loss of muscle mass and strength), loss of calcium from bone (development of osteoporosis), fragility of skin and blood vessels, poor healing of connective tissue, and altered immune function (increased susceptibility to bacterial infection). It should be noted that 'normal' ageing includes changes which, although of lesser degree, are reminiscent of those associated with glucocorticoid excess, such as loss of muscle, increased body fat, and decreased bone calcium. Therefore the characterization of hypothalamic–pituitary–adrenal function with age is of considerable interest.

Early studies in which pituitary–adrenocortical function was de-duced from measurements of random plasma cortisol levels and urinary excretion of 17-hydroxycorticoids, both with and without stimulation of the pituitary–adrenocortical axis (e.g. by insulin hypoglycaemia or metyrapone administration), did not detect systematic age-associated alterations in glucocorticoid levels in plasma, although 24-h urinary excretion of glucocorticoid metabolites was generally reduced. The findings appeared to be explained by a decrease in the metabolic clearance rate of cortisol with a compensatory reduction in secretion rate. Later studies employing sensitive radioimmunoassays for ACTH revealed little change with age in ACTH responses to metyrapone, but suggested altered diurnal rhythmicity of spontaneous ACTH secretion, with a reduction of the overall nadir-to-peak excursion and a shifting of the peak to later morning.

However, other investigators have observed that older patients respond to various stresses (surgery, depression) with greater and more prolonged secretion of cortisol than is seen in younger patients under similar stress. This alteration appears to be of greater duration and magnitude than can be explained by the relatively minor decrease in metabolic clearance rate observed for cortisol. When dexamethasone was used to suppress ACTH and cortisol secretion, there was less of an inhibitory response in healthy elderly subjects or older depressed patients. ACTH and cortisol levels measured in the evening (nadir period) before and after administration of ovine corticotrophin-releasing hormone showed a non-significant but suggestive trend towards higher basal ACTH levels and greater ACTH and cortisol responses to ovine corticotrophin-releasing hormone with age, despite the fact that basal p.m. cortisol levels were higher in the older men. Taken together, these data suggest that ageing may be associated with a tendency for the glucocorticoid negative feedback action on ACTH secretion to diminish with age. Further investigations, using more sensitive methods, should clarify whether a defect in feedback inhibition really exists in humans and whether it may be associated with a subtle, but clinically significant, increase in 24-h integrated exposure to cortisol in older people. The contribution to the putative augmented hypothalamopituitary axis function of the known age-associated increase in AVP secretion (versus altered secretion of or sensitivity to corticotrophin-releasing hormone) has not yet been elucidated.

The pituitary–thyroid axis

Pituitary TSH, also known as thyrotrophin, is, like the gonadotrophins, a large heterodimeric glycoprotein. The TSH α subunit is identical to that of LH and FSH, while specific bioreactivity and immunoreactivity are conferred by the unique β subunit. TSH is the major direct modulator of thyroid function, stimulating uptake and organification of iodine, production and secretion of thyroid hormone(s), and growth and increased vascularity of thyroid tissue. In the absence of TSH, thyroid hormone output becomes insufficient and clinical hypothyroidism occurs. Since thyroid hormones are essential to normal metabolic activity, profound hypothyroidism eventually results in coma, circulatory and respiratory collapse, and death. Therefore TSH, like ACTH, is an essential life-sustaining hormone. TSH synthesis and secretion are stimulated by TRH, which is a cyclic hypothalamic tripeptide. Thyroid hormones feed back to inhibit basal and TRH-stimulated TSH production. When thyroid hormone levels are reduced due to primary thyroid failure, basal TSH levels are very high and TSH responses to TRH are greatly augmented.

In the presence of excess thyroid hormone, TSH blood levels are very low and the TSH response to TRH is absent. New highly sensitive assays for TSH can distinguish between normal and diminished basal plasma levels of TSH and hence can provide reliable information with regard to pituitary thyrotropic function and its modulation by thyroid hormones.

Early studies of the effects of ageing on TSH secretion revealed normal or somewhat elevated levels in otherwise healthy men and women. Large community-based studies sampling TSH in hundreds of subjects found significant elevations in approximately 3 per cent of older men and 8 per cent of older women which were accompanied in some, but not all, by reduced levels of circulating thyroid hormones. These results suggest that undetected primary hypothyroidism is common in older people. It is well known that in early thyroid failure there may be a phase of pituitary compensation evidenced by increased TSH secretion, so that circulating thyroid hormones initially remain within the normal range. This would account for the observation of subjects with high TSH but normal thyroid hormone levels. Another possible explanation for the increase in TSH levels is an age-associated increase in heterotypic autoantibodies which cross-react with the anti-TSH antibodies in the TSH immunoassays.

In studies of healthy ageing men, who had no evidence of hypothyroidism, an ultrasensitive TSH assay has shown a modest but significant age-associated increase in basal TSH levels and concomitant small decreases in free (but not total) thyroxine (T4) and total and free tri-iodothyronine (T3); however, hormone levels were still within the normal range. The latter findings suggest that ageing may be associated with a subtle decrease in thyroid hormone secretion in the absence of identifiable thyroid disease. The TSH secretory response to bolus intravenous TRH administration has been variously reported to be reduced with age in men but not women, decreased in women but not men, and increased in both sexes. Discrepancies in these findings have not been fully resolved and may be related to confounding variables such as the presence of thyroid pathology and non-endocrine concomitant illness in the study populations. Low-dose constant infusion of TRH produces a biphasic TSH response, with early and late peaks. In one study both early and late responses to constant TRH infusion were of similar magnitude, timing, and duration in older and younger men. In this study the expected augmentation of TSH response, in the presence of the significantly lower free thyroid hormone levels observed in the older group, was not evident. Recently 24-h frequent blood sample monitoring of TSH secretion has shown a 50 per cent reduction in spontaneous TSH release in elderly men, despite normal levels of T4 and slightly reduced T3. These latter findings suggest that elderly men may have a subtle decrease in basal TSH secretion relative to the level of thyroid function. (See also Chapter 7.1.)

It should be evident from the above that, despite the frequency of dry skin, cold intolerance, and a general slowing of body processes (and reduced basal metabolic rate) which occur in 'normal ageing', there is no evidence that ageing *per se* is normally a hypothyroid state. The major clinical significance of the physiological changes with age in pituitary–thyroid function relate to the interaction of thyroid function with systemic illness. Both severe acute illness (e.g. sepsis) and less severe chronic illness (e.g. renal or cardiac failure) may be associated with decreases in both total and free plasma T4. This so-called euthyroid sick syndrome is often difficult to differentiate from true hypothyroidism. One method of differentiation is to demonstrate the augmented TSH response to TRH expected in primary thyroid failure. This augmentation is not found in the euthyroid sick syndrome. Studies of TSH secretion in severe illness have suggested that in some patients reduced TSH secretion (the 'sick' thyrotrope) may even be the cause of the euthyroid sick syndrome. Unfortunately, in older persons, particularly elderly men, there is frequently no augmentation of TSH secretion by low levels of T_4. Therefore it is often difficult to distinguish between hypothyroidism and the euthyroid sick syndrome in the elderly patient.

Bibliography

Asnis, G.M., Sachar, E.J., Halbreich, U., et al. (1981). Cortisol secretion in relation to age in major depression. *Psychosomatic Medicine*, 43, 235–42.

Bellantoni, M.F., Vittone, J., Campfield, A.T., Bass, K.M., Harman, S.M., and Blackman, M. (1996). Effects of oral versus transdermal estrogen administration on the GH/IGF-I axis in younger and older postmenopausal women. *Journal of Clinical Endocrinology and Metabolism*, 81, 2848–53.

Blackman, M.R. (1987). Pituitary hormones and ageing. *Endocrinologic and Metabolic Clinics of North America*, 16, 981–94.

Blackman, M.R. (1989). Aging. In *Endocrinology* (ed. L.J. DeGroot et al.), p. 2348. W.B. Saunders, Philadelphia, PA.

Blackman, M.R., Kowatch, M.A., Wehmann, R.E., et al. (1986). Basal serum prolactin levels and prolactin responses to constant infusions of thyrotropin releasing hormone in healthy ageing men. *Journal of Gerontology*, 41, 699–705.

Blackman, M.R., Elahi, D., and Harman, S.M. (1995). Endocrinology and aging. In *Endocrinology* (3rd edn) (ed. L.DeGroot, M. Besser, H.G. Burger, et al.), pp. 2702–30. W.B. Saunders, Philadelphia, PA.

Blichert-Toft, M. (1975). Secretion of corticotrophin and somatotrophin by the senescent adenohypophysis in man. *Acta Endocrinologica*, 195 (Supplement), 13–17.

Burrows, G.N., Wortzman, G., Rewcastle, R.B., et al. (1981). Microadenomas of the pituitary and abnormal sellar tomograms in an unselected autopsy series. *New England Journal of Medicine*, 304, 156–8.

Conover, C.A., Dollar, L.A., Hintz, R.L., et al. (1985). Somatomedin binding and action in fibroblasts from aged and progeric subjects. *Journal of Clinical Endocrinology and Metabolism*, 60, 685–91.

Conover, C.A., Rosenfeld, R.G., and Hintz, R.L. (1985). Aging alters somatomedin-C–dexamethasone synergism in the stimulation of deoxyribonucleic acid synthesis and replication of cultured human fibroblasts. *Journal of Clinical Endocrinology and Metabolism*, 61, 423–8.

Conover, C.A., Rosenfeld, R.G., and Hintz, R.L. (1987). Somatomedin-C/insulin-like growth factor 1 binding and action in human fibroblasts aged in culture: impaired synergism with dexamethasone. *Journal of Gerontology*, 42, 308–14.

Deslypere, J.P. and Vermeulen, A. (1984). Leydig cell function in normal men: effect of age, lifestyle, residence, diet and activity. *Journal of Clinical Endocrinology and Metabolism*, 59, 955–62.

Dilman, V.M., Ostroumova, M.N., and Tsyrlina, E.V. (1979). Hypothalamic mechanisms of aging and of specific age pathology: II. On the sensitivity threshold of hypothalamo-pituitary complex to homeostatic stimuli in adaptive homeostasis. *Experimental Gerontology*, 14, 175–81.

Dudl, J., Ensinck, J., Palmer, E., et al. (1973). Effect of age on growth hormone secretion in man. *Journal of Clinical Endocrinology and Metabolism*, 37, 11–16.

Goldstein, C.S., Braunstein, S., and Goldfarb, S. (1983). Idiopathic syndrome of inappropriate antidiuretic hormone secretion possibly related to advanced age. *Annals of Internal Medicine*, 99, 185–8.

Gregerman, R.I. (1986). Mechanisms of age-related alterations of hormone secretion and action: an overview of 30 years of progress. *Experimental Gerontology*, 21, 345–65.

Harman, S.M. and Nankin, H.R. (1985). Alterations in reproductive and sexual function: male. In *Principles of geriatric medicine* (ed. R. Andes, E.L. Bierman, and W.R. Hazzard), pp. 337–53. McGraw-Hill, New York.

Harman, S.M. and Tsitouras, P.D. (1980). Reproductive hormones in aging men. I. Measurement of sex steroids, basal luteinizing hormone, and Leydig cell response to human chorionic gonadotropin. *Journal of Clinical Endocrinology and Metabolism*, 51, 35–41.

Harman, S.M., Tsitouras, P.D., Costa, P.T., et al. (1982). Reproductive hormones in aging men: II. Basal pituitary gonadotropins and gonadotropin responses to luteinizing hormone-releasing hormone. *Journal of Clinical Endocrinology and Metabolism*, 54, 547–51.

Harman, S.M., Wehmann, R.E., and Blackman, M.R. (1984). Pituitary–thyroid hormone economy in healthy aging men: basal indices of thyroid function and thyrotropin responses to constant infusions of thyrotropin releasing hormone. *Journal of Clinical Endocrinology and Metabolism*, 58, 320–6.

Helderman, J.H. (1982). The impact of normal aging on the hypothalamin–neurohypophyseal–renal axis. In *Endocrine aspects of aging* (ed. S.G. Korenman), pp. 9–32. Elsevier, New York.

Helderman, J.H., Vestal, R.E., Rowe, J.W., et al. (1978). The response of arginine vasopressin to ethanol and hypertonic saline in man: the impact of aging. *Journal of Gerontology*, 33, 39–47.

Ho, K.Y., Evans, W.S., Blizzard, R.M., et al. (1987). Effects of sex and age on the 24 hour profile of growth hormone secretion in man: importance of endogenous estradiol concentrations. *Journal of Clinical Endocrinology and Metabolism*, 64, 51–8.

Hossdorf, T. and Wagner, H. (1980). Secretion of prolactin in healthy men and women of different ages. *Aktuel Gerontologie*, 10, 119–26.

Howard, A.D., Feighner, S.D., Cully, D.F., et al. (1996). A receptor in pituitary and hypothalamus that functions in growth hormone release. *Science*, 273, 974–7.

Johanson, A.J. and Blizzard, R.M. (1981). Low somatomedin-C levels in older men rise in response to growth hormone administration. *Johns Hopkins Medical Journal*, 149, 115–17.

Kalk, W.J., Vinik, A.I., Pimstone, B.L., et al. (1973). Growth hormone responses to insulin hypoglycemia in the elderly. *Journal of Gerontology*, 28, 431–3.

Kirkland, J., Lye, M., Goddard, C., et al. (1984). Plasma arginine vasopressin in dehydrated elderly patients. *Clinical Endocrinology*, 20, 451.

Lang, I., Schernthaner, G., Pietschmann, P., et al. (1987). Effects of sex and age on growth hormone response to growth hormone-releasing hormone in healthy individuals. *Journal of Clinical Endocrinology and Metabolism*, 65, 535–40.

Marcus, R., Butterfield, G., Holloway, L., et al. (1990). Effects of short term administration of growth hormone to elderly people. *Journal of Clinical Endocrinology and Metabolism*, 70, 519–27.

Marrama, P., Montanini, V., Celani, M.F., et al. (1984). Decrease in luteinizing hormone biological activity/immunoreactivity ratio in elderly men. *Maturitas*, 4, 223–31.

Meites, J., Goya, R., and Takahashi, S. (1987). Why the neuroendocrine system is important in aging processes. *Experimental Gerontology*, 22, 1–15.

Minaker, K.L., McNeilly, G.S., and Rowe, J.W. (1985). Endocrine systems. In *Handbook of the biology of aging* (2nd edn) (ed. C.E. Finch and E.L. Schneider), p. 433. Van Nostrand Reinhold, New York.

Pavlov, E.P, Harman, S.M., Chrousos, G.P., et al. (1986). Responses of adrenocorticotropin, cortisol, and dehydroepiandrosterone to ovine corticotropin-releasing hormone in healthy aging men. *Journal of Clinical Endocrinology and Metabolism*, 62, 767–72.

Pavlov, E.P., Harman, S.M., Merriam, G.R., *et al.* (1986). Responses of growth hormone and somatomedin-C to GH-releasing hormone in healthy aging men. *Journal of Clinical Endocrinology and Metabolism*, 62, 595–600.

Tenover, J.S. and Bremner, W.J. (1991). The effects of normal aging on the reponse of the pituitary–gonadal axis to chronic clomiphene administration in men. *Journal of Andrology*, 12, 258–63.

Tenover, J.S., Dahl, K.D., Hsueh, A.J., and Lim, P. (1987). Serum bioactive and immunoreactive follicle-stimulating hormone levels and the response to clomiphene in healthy young and elderly men. *Journal of Clinical Endocrinology and Metabolism*, 64, 1103–8.

Tenover, J.S., McLachlan, R.I., Dahl, D.K., *et al.* (1988). Decreased serum inhibin levels in normal elderly men: evidence for a decline in Sertoli cell function with aging. *Journal of Clinical Endocrinology and Metabolism*, 67, 455–9.

Van Coevorden, A., Laurent, E., Decoster, C., and Kerkhofs, M. (1989). Decreased basal and stimulated thyrotropin secretion in healthy elderly men. *Journal of Clinical Endocrinology and Metabolism*, 69, 177–85.

Winters, S.J. and Troen, P. (1982). Episodic luteinizing hormone (LH) secretion and the response of LH and follicle-stimulating hormone to LH-releasing hormone in aged men. Evidence for coexistent primary testicular insufficiency and an impairment in gonadotropin secretion. *Journal of Clinical Endocrinology and Metabolism*, 55, 560–5.

Winters, S.J., Sherins, R.J., and Troen, P. (1984). The gonadotropin-suppressive activity of androgen is increased in elderly men. *Metabolism*, 33, 1052–9.

Zadik, Z., Chalew, S.A., McCarter, R.J., *et al.* (1985). The influence of age on the 24-hour integrated concentration of growth hormone in normal individuals. *Journal of Clinical Endocrinology and Metabolism*, 60, 513–16.

7.5 Diabetes

G. S. Meneilly

There are two major types of diabetes mellitus: type I or insulin-dependent diabetes mellitus (**IDDM**) and type II or non-insulin-dependent diabetes mellitus (**NIDDM**). Although a small number of elderly patients have profound insulin deficiency similar to patients with IDDM, the vast majority have NIDDM. Multiple studies have evaluated the prevalence of NIDDM in the elderly in diverse population groups (Table 1) (Meneilly and Tessier 1995). In elderly Caucasians the prevalence is approximately 20 per cent, whereas in some ethnic groups the prevalence approaches 50 per cent (Table 1). As many as half of older people with diabetes are unaware that they have the disease (Fig. 1) (Harris 1993). Diabetes appears to be rather more common in women than in men. In view of the increasing numbers of older individuals and the high prevalence of diabetes in this age group, this disease will be a major health problem in the next century.

Pathogenesis

NIDDM in middle-aged subjects is a genetic disease, although the precise genes responsible have yet to be defined (Kahn 1994). Although identical twins of elderly subjects with NIDDM have disordered carbohydrate metabolism, they often do not develop full-blown diabetes. This suggests that, while genetic factors are important, other mechanisms must play a pathogenic role.

There are several potential factors which explain the increasing prevalence of diabetes with age in genetically susceptible individuals (Meneilly and Tessier 1995). Normal age-associated changes in carbohydrate metabolism, including impaired glucose-induced insulin release and resistance to insulin-mediated glucose disposal, contribute to the increasing incidence of diabetes with age. Older people take

Table 1 Prevalence of NIDDM in elderly people

Population	Age (years)	Sex	Prevalence (%)	Criteria
United States				
White	65–74	M	19	NDDG
		F	17	
Black	65–74	M	29	NDDG
		F	24	
Native American	65–94	M	45	NDDG
		F	64	
Finland	70–79	M	35	WHO
		F	37	
Italy	65–80	M	6	NDDG
		F	6	
Micronesia	>60	M	29	WHO
		F	46	

NDDG, National Diabetes Data Group (USA); WHO, World Health Organization.

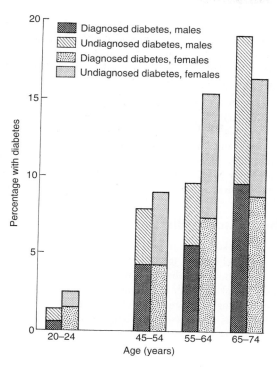

Fig. 1 Percentage of United States population aged 20 to 74 years with diabetes from NHANES II, 1976–1980. (Reproduced with permission from Harris *et al.* (1987).)

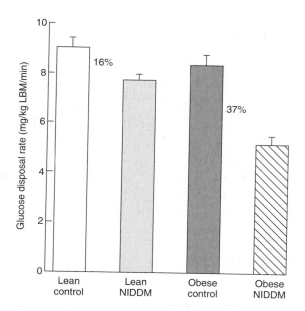

Fig. 2 Comparison of glucose disposal rates: LBM, lean body mass.

multiple drugs which can affect carbohydrate metabolism, particularly thiazides and corticosteroids. A number of lifestyle factors have been associated with an increased prevalence of diabetes in older individuals. These include a low intake of complex carbohydrates, physical inactivity, and obesity, particularly if the distribution of body fat is central in nature.

There appear to be a small percentage of elderly patients who have marked insulin deficiency. These subjects have islet cell antibodies and other autoimmune phenomena suggesting that their diabetes is immune mediated, similar to IDDM in younger subjects. However, the majority of elderly patients have NIDDM. In the last few years, there have been many studies examining changes in glucose metabolism in middle-aged NIDDM patients (DeFronzo 1988). These studies have found that both lean and obese middle-aged patients have resistance to insulin-mediated glucose disposal, a marked impairment in glucose-induced insulin release, and an increase in fasting hepatic glucose output. Recently, investigators have evaluated metabolic alterations in elderly NIDDM patients (Arner *et al.* 1991; Meneilly *et al.* 1996). Unlike middle-aged patients, elderly NIDDM patients have normal fasting hepatic glucose production. In contrast with lean middle-aged NIDDM patients, lean elderly subjects have relatively normal insulin-mediated glucose disposal (Fig. 2). They also have a marked impairment in glucose-induced insulin secretion. Obese elderly subjects have relatively normal glucose-induced insulin secretion but a marked impairment in insulin-mediated glucose disposal (Fig. 2). As will be discussed later, these data have important implications for the management of diabetes in this age group.

A few molecular biological studies have been undertaken in older persons (Meneilly and Tessier 1995). Some elderly subjects have abnormalities in the glucokinase gene, which is the glucose sensor for the β cell. This could explain the alterations in glucose-induced insulin release in these patients. Although insulin receptor numbers appear normal in elderly patients with NIDDM, insulin receptor tyrosine kinase activity is impaired. This abnormality may be the molecular basis for insulin resistance in some patients. Further studies are required to define the molecular defects in elderly NIDDM patients.

Presentation and clinical features

Many elderly patients with diabetes are unaware that they have the disease. Because the renal threshold for glucose commonly increases with age, glucosuria may not develop until the blood sugar is markedly increased, and patients frequently do not have polyuria. The thirst mechanism is also impaired with age, and so polydipsia is not a common presenting symptom. As a result, patients are often asymptomatic at the onset of NIDDM and are diagnosed during an intercurrent illness or as a result of routine blood tests. If patients do have symptoms, they tend to be non-specific or atypical (failure to thrive). Sometimes older patients with diabetes present initially with a complication of the disease (heart attack or stroke).

Few studies have specifically evaluated clinical features in elderly patients with diabetes (Mooradian *et al.* 1988)). Compared with community-dwelling elderly subjects with diabetes, nursing-home patients with this illness tend to have more kidney disease, microvascular disease, and skin infections. Nursing-home patients tend to be leaner, to have lower glycosylated haemoglobin (HbA$_{1c}$) values, and are less likely to be treated with insulin. When elderly nursing-home patients with diabetes are compared with nursing-home residents without diabetes, they are found to have an increased prevalence of neuropathy, macrovascular and microvascular disease, and soft tissue infections. Surveys of community-dwelling elderly subjects with diabetes have found that they have a much higher frequency of chronic disease and use inpatient and outpatient services to a greater extent than age-matched controls without diabetes. These patients are also much more likely to report that the disease has resulted in an impairment in their functional capacity and quality of life. Taken together, the data from nursing-home and community-dwelling elderly subjects indicate that diabetes has a significant effect on morbidity and quality of life in these patients.

Complications

Diabetes is reported as the sixth leading cause of death, yet the mortality rate of elderly patients with diabetes is more than double that of age-matched controls without diabetes (Harris 1990). It is likely that diabetes contributes to many cardiovascular deaths and is underestimated as a contributory cause of death in older persons. The risk of complications is almost as high in elderly patients with undiagnosed diabetes as it is in patients with diagnosed diabetes (Harris 1993). The likelihood of complications increases with both the age of the patient and the duration of diabetes. In epidemiological studies there is a strong correlation between glycaemic control and the risk of complications in the elderly NIDDM patient (Nathan et al. 1986a; Naliboff and Rosenthal 1989), suggesting that improved glycaemic control will reduce the risk of complications in these individuals.

Cardiovascular disease

The risk of cardiovascular disease is about 2.5 times greater in older patients with diabetes than in those without it. Over 70 per cent of older patients with diabetes die from cardiovascular disease, and a substantial percentage are disabled as a result of cardiovascular events. The risk of cardiovascular disease is substantially increased in older patients with diabetes who have poor glycaemic control or other risk factors for cardiovascular disease, including smoking, hypertension, and hyperlipidaemia (Meneilly and Tessier 1995).

The United Kingdom Prospective Diabetes Study trials report clear evidence of benefit from rigorous control of hypertension in patients with NIDDM. A treatment group randomized to control at a mean blood pressure of 144/82 mmHg over 9 years experienced, in comparison with a control group averaging 154/87 mmHg, a 24 per cent lower rate of diabetic complications, a 32 per cent lower rate of death from diabetes-related causes, and a 44 per cent reduction in strokes (UK Prospective Diabetes Study Group 1998a). In a further analysis (UK Prospective Diabetes Study Group 1998b), it was shown that atenolol and captopril were equally effective in reducing the incidence of diabetic complications. It seems reasonable to deduce that the effectiveness of blood pressure control is more important than the nature of the drugs used. There have been some doubts over the safety of calcium-channel blockers for patients with hypertension and diabetes. An analysis of data on diabetic subjects enrolled in the Syst-Eur study of treatment of systolic hypertension in older people

revealed no cause for concern (Tuomilehto et al. 1999). The calcium-channel blocker nitrendipine was at least as effective in reducing total mortality, cardiovascular deaths, and cardiovascular events, including fatal and non-fatal strokes, in diabetic as in non-diabetic subjects.

Lipid values should be measured annually. As yet, there are no specific data on the benefits of treating hyperlipidaemia in older patients with NIDDM. However, epidemiological evidence demonstrates that high lipid values represent as much of a risk in older patients as they do in younger patients with diabetes, suggesting that we should apply similar criteria for treating lipid levels in middle-aged and elderly NIDDM patients. If subjects are still smoking, they should be encouraged to stop.

Cerebral vascular disease

The risk of stroke increases with age and the duration of diabetes. This risk is closely related to glycaemic control, and is twice as great in older patients with diabetes as in age-matched controls without diabetes. The risk of death and disability in older NIDDM patients who suffer a stroke is greater than in age-matched controls who do not have diabetes. Because of the strong association between diabetes and other risk factors and the risk of stroke, aggressive risk factor modification, in particular control of high blood pressure, and optimal glycaemic control in these patients may reduce the incidence of stroke. Many authors recommend the use of prophylactic aspirin in elderly patients with NIDDM who have no neurological or cardiovascular disability in an effort to prevent the development of these complications. The efficacy of prophylactic aspirin therapy in this age group is unknown, and the potential benefits must be weighed against the risk of aspirin-induced gastropathy and bleeding.

Eye disease

The prevalence of diabetic eye disease increases with both age and duration of diabetes and is closely related to glycaemic control and lipid levels. In younger patients with diabetes, diabetic retinopathy is the major cause of impaired vision. In elderly patients with diabetes, other common causes of visual impairment include cataracts, glaucoma, and macular degeneration (Nathan et al. 1986b). Despite the fact that there is a high prevalence of eye disease in older patients with diabetes and effective treatments are available, elderly patients are less likely to be referred to an ophthalmologist. All elderly patients with diabetes should have annual ophthalmological examinations, including assessment of visual symptoms, measurements of visual acuity, thorough retinal examination, and assessment of intraocular pressure. Studies in younger patients suggest that photocoagulation for diabetic retinopathy, cataract surgery, aggressive treatment for glaucoma, and optimal glycaemic control can reduce visual loss. It is presumed that similar interventions will have a benefit in older patients with diabetes.

Kidney disease

A substantial percentage of older people with endstage renal disease have NIDDM. Renal disease is a major cause of morbidity and mortality among older persons (Olivarius et al. 1993). The clinical course of diabetic nephropathy has not been well studied in older patients. Microalbuminuria identifies patients at risk for progression to endstage renal disease and is also a marker for increased risk of cardiovascular morbidity and mortality. The likelihood of developing renal disease is increased in older patients who smoke, have poor glycaemic control, or poorly controlled hypertension. Studies to determine the optimal approach to early diabetic nephropathy have not been conducted in older patients. However, based on studies in middle-aged subjects, glycaemic control should be optimized and hypertension should be aggressively treated with angiotensin-converting enzyme inhibitors. Protein restriction is often used in younger patients with diabetes. As many older patients have inadequate intakes of protein and may be malnourished, protein restriction should be assessed on an individual basis. In order to prevent renal problems in these patients, nephrotoxic drugs and radiographic dye should be avoided if possible. Urinary tract infections should be treated aggressively.

Neuropathy

The prevalence of neuropathy increases with both age and duration of diabetes (Naliboff and Rosenthal 1989). Distal symmetrical polyneuropathy occurs more commonly in men and is also more frequent in patients who consume alcohol, smoke, have high blood pressure, and have poor glycaemic control. Because other causes of peripheral neuropathy are very common in older people, it is extremely important to exclude these causes when evaluating patients. Older patients with diabetes are more likely to develop focal neuropathies associated with diabetes. These generally occur suddenly, are asymmetric, and resolve over several months. The most common focal neuropathies occurring in elderly patients are diabetic ophthalmoploplegia associated with a third-nerve palsy and diabetic amyotrophy. Older patients can also develop diabetic neuropathic cachexia. This syndrome occurs in men and is associated with a painful peripheral neuropathy, depression, anorexia, and weight loss. It resolves within a few months. Normal ageing is characterized by alterations in autonomic nervous system function which can be exacerbated by diabetes (see Chapter 18.12). In particular, older patients with diabetes are more likely than non-diabetic controls to develop orthostatic hypertension and bladder and bowel dysfunction.

Neuropathy is frequently asymptomatic in older individuals. In order to detect this complication, the health care provider should perform an annual neurological examination in all older patients with diabetes, including measurement of orthostatic blood pressure and assessment of reflexes, pinprick, and vibration sense. Patients with peripheral neuropathy should be instructed in proper foot care and footwear. Patients with orthostatic hypotension should take precautions to reduce the risk of falls and may need to be treated with medications. As with other complications, modification of other risk factors and optimal glycaemic control should be attempted.

Foot problems

Because of the high prevalence of peripheral vascular disease and peripheral neuropathy in elderly NIDDM patients as well as their increased susceptibility to infection, the incidence of foot problems increases. The risk of amputation is approximately ten times greater in elderly patients with diabetes than in those who do not have the disease. This risk is increased in men, smokers, and non-white subjects. Although no studies have been performed in elderly subjects, it is likely that multidisciplinary programmes including education, modification of risk factors, and optimization of glycaemic control would reduce the frequency of amputations. Institution of these programmes would seem prudent in the elderly. Elderly patients, caregivers, and health care professionals should inspect the feet frequently, and patients should be advised to seek medical attention immediately if a lesion develops (see also Chapter 13.8.)

Miscellaneous complications

The frequency of periodontal disease is increased in elderly patients with diabetes. Periodontal problems in these patients may alter food choices and contribute to malnutrition. Regular dental care and education regarding effective self-care is essential to maintaining normal dental health in these patients. Malignant otitis externa appears primarily in elderly subjects with diabetes. Diabetes appears to increase the risk of hypothermia in elderly individuals. Intradermal bullae of the feet which resolve spontaneously over a period of several weeks have been described in elderly patients with diabetes. Finally, painful limitation of shoulder movements has been known to occur in elderly NIDDM patients (Meneilly and Tessier 1995).

Hypoglycaemia

The most serious complication associated with the treatment of diabetes in older people is hypoglycaemia. The risk of severe or fatal hypoglycaemia associated with the use of oral agents or insulin increases exponentially with age (Asplund et al. 1983). If an elderly subject presents with hypoglycaemia secondary to a longer-acting sulphonylurea such as glibenclamide or chlorpropamide, glucose may need to be given intravenously for up to 72 h before the episode resolves. The increased frequency of hypoglycaemia in older persons is due to altered release of glucagon, the most important counter-regulatory hormone, impaired awareness of the autonomic warning symptoms of hypoglycaemia, and altered psychomotor performance in response to hypoglycaemia which prevents the patient from taking appropriate steps to return the blood sugar to normal (Meneilly et al. 1994). Animal insulin may be associated with a greater awareness of hypoglycaemic warning symptoms than human insulin in older patients with diabetes, and should be considered for use in elderly patients who have frequent hypoglycaemic episodes or demonstrate hypoglycaemic unawareness when treated with human insulin (Meneilly et al. 1995).

Hyperosmolar non-ketotic coma

Hyperosmolar non-ketotic coma occurs most commonly in NIDDM patients over the age of 50 (Wachtel 1990). Mortality rates as high as 50 per cent have been reported in elderly patients. Survivors often have permanent impairment in their functional status. This syndrome is not uncommonly the first presentation of diabetes in frail multiply impaired older individuals from institutions. Although many factors can precipitate non-ketotic hyperosmolar coma in an elderly person, it is usually caused by an underlying infection, particularly septicaemia. No studies have been conducted to determine the optimal management of these patients. Aggressive replacement of fluid and electrolytes is essential. Invasive monitoring may be required to assess intravascular volume adequately. The dose of insulin employed should be substantially lower than that used for diabetic ketoacidosis. If higher doses of insulin are employed, the likelihood of hypokalaemia and post-treatment hypoglycaemia are increased.

Table 2 Diagnosis of diabetes in elderly people

1. Classic symptoms (thirst, polyuria, weight loss) and random glucose ≥ 11.1 mmol/l (200 mg/dl)

2. Fasting plasma glucose ≥ 7.0 mmol/l (126 mg/dl) on two occasions

3. All plasma glucose values during a 2-h 75-g oral GTT ≥ 11.1 mmol/l (200 mg/dl)

GTT, glucose tolerance test.

Diagnosis of diabetes in older persons

The diagnostic criteria employed for diabetes have recently been revised (Table 2) (American Diabetes Association 1998). As noted previously, classic symptoms (polydipsia, polyphagia, polyuria) are rarely present. The diagnosis is usually made on the basis of two fasting glucose values. It is recognized that many older patients are asymptomatic for many years prior to diagnosis. These patients are still at increased risk for complications, and it has been proposed that screening techniques should be used more widely in elderly individuals who have risk factors for the development of diabetes (family history, hypertension, central obesity, sedentary lifestyle, etc.) (Harris 1993). Currently it is recommended that a fasting glucose measurement be performed every year in elderly patients with the risk factors noted above, and every 3 years in older patients without risk factors.

Reasons to treat older patients patient with diabetes

All clinicians would agree that blood glucose should be sufficiently controlled in elderly patients so that symptoms of hyperglycaemia (polyuria, polydipsia, etc.) do not occur. However, these symptoms are frequently absent. There is less agreement about the optimal degree of glycaemic control in older patients. Observational data suggest that good glycaemic control is important in that older people with poorer control have higher risks of complications and associated disability than do patients with good control. In addition, elderly patients with diabetes show degrees of impairment in cognitive and affective function. The extent of these impairments correlates with the level of HbA$_{1c}$, and improved glycaemic control results in improved cognitive and affective function in older individuals (Tun *et al.* 1990).

However, it is not possible to make a reliable inference of cause and effect from associations noted in observational studies, and randomized controlled trials are essential. The Diabetes Control and Complications Trial in IDDM subjects (DCCT Research Group 1993) and a randomized controlled trial in middle-aged patients with NIDDM (Ohkubo *et al.* 1995) suggested that tight glycaemic control reduced the risk of complications. The United Kingdom Prospective Diabetes Study 33 (UK Prospective Diabetes Study Group 1998*c*) followed 3867 newly diagnosed NIDDM patients over 10 years. Their mean age at entry was 54 years with an interquartile range of 48 to 60 years. Intensive blood glucose control by either sulphonylureas or insulin reduced the risk of microvascular but not macrovascular complications. Among the various specific endpoints, eye complications seemed to show the most benefit. In extrapolating these findings to an older and frailer patient group it should be noted that all intensive treatment increased the risk.

Treatment of diabetes in later life

The management of diabetes in older patients is challenging. These patients frequently take multiple medications, have multiple pathological processes, and have complex social and psychiatric problems which make their management extremely difficult. Because of the complicated nature of these patients and the lifestyle alterations which are necessary, a team approach is essential. A number of studies have suggested that multidisciplinary programmes improve glycaemic control, compliance with therapy, and quality of life of elderly NIDDM patients (Wilson and Pratt 1987; Kronsbein *et al.* 1988; Gilden *et al.* 1989). Education programmes for nursing home staff have also been shown to improve outcome for NIDDM patients in institutions. When designing multidisciplinary programmes for elderly patients, it is important to make sure that written and other educational materials take into account that many of the patients have alterations in their special senses. Any drugs which may be contributing to poor glycaemic control should be stopped if possible. Elderly patients with diabetes and other risk factors have a much higher risk of complications than older patients without these risk factors, and risk factor modification should be an essential part of management.

After modification of risk factors, there are several approaches that are available for the management of diabetes in later life. Pending the results of randomized control trials designed to determine optimal glycaemic control in older patients with diabetes, several recommendations can be made based on the available literature. In an otherwise healthy older patient with diabetes, the fasting glucose should be less than 8 mmol/l (140 mg/dl), the 2-h postmeal glucose level should be less than 11 mmol/l (200 mg/dl), and the HbA$_{1c}$ should be less than 20 per cent above the upper limit of normal for the laboratory. These criteria may be modified if patients are frail and multiply impaired, have frequent hypoglycaemic episodes, or have other comorbid factors.

Exercise

Studies of middle-aged patients with diabetes and elderly subjects with impaired glucose tolerance have shown that exercise programmes can improve insulin sensitivity and glucose tolerance. Only one study has attempted to determine the effects of exercise in elderly patients with diabetes (Skarfors *et al.* 1987). Many patients were excluded from this study because of underlying disease. Of the patients who were enrolled in the study, most withdrew before it could be completed. Although exercise is probably of value in elderly patients with diabetes, further studies are needed to determine who will benefit and how the exercise programme should be modified to achieve maximum benefit with minimal risk of complications.

Diet

Studies of the dietary patterns of older NIDDM patients suggest that they frequently do not comply with a diabetic diet (Horwath 1991). Although patients tend to limit their intake of simple sugars, most

Table 3 Sulphonylureas commonly used to treat diabetes in elderly people

Drug	Daily dose (mg)
Tolbutamide	500–3000
Tolazamide	100–1000
Chlorpropamide	100–750
Acetohexamide	125–1000
Gliclazide	40–320
Glibenclamide	1.25–20
Glipizide	5–40

have diets which are too low in complex carbohydrates and too high in saturated fats. In community-dwelling patients, a multidisciplinary team approach has been shown to improve compliance with dietary therapy and glycaemic control, and weight-loss programmes have been shown to result in substantial improvements in glycaemic control (Reaven *et al.* 1985). However, for frail multiply impaired nursing-home residents, diabetic diets do not appear to result in improved glycaemic control, and they complicate the care and increase the cost of looking after these patients (Coulston *et al.* 1990). Several studies have found that elderly patients with NIDDM are at risk for deficiency of minerals and vitamins. Magnesium, vitamin E and vitamin C supplementation may improve glycaemic control in some patients (Meneilly and Tessier 1995). Zinc supplements may improve wound healing, immune function, and sexual function in selected patients.

Sulphonylureas

As noted earlier, lean elderly NIDDM patients have a marked impairment in glucose-induced insulin release but minimal insulin resistance. Sulphonylureas are the drug of choice in this patient group. Doses of the most commonly used sulphonylureas are shown in Table 3. The kinetics of chlorpropamide, glipizide, and tolbutamide are essentially unchanged with age, but the half-life of glibenclamide is increased (Meneilly and Tessier 1995). Chlorpropamide is more likely than second-generation sulphonylureas to cause the syndrome of inappropriate antidiuretic hormone secretion (**SIADH**). It can cause an antabuse-like affect in the elderly and also interact adversely with the many medications that older people are taking. For these reasons, chlorpropamide is contraindicated in the aged. The second-generation sulphonylureas are free of many of the side-effects of chlorpropamide and are more potent than first-generation agents. However, the frequency of hypoglycaemia in elderly patients appears to be similar with glibenclamide, glipizide, and chlorpropamide (Meneilly and Tessier 1995). Gliclazide (currently not available in the United States) is associated with a lower frequency of hypoglycaemic events than other second-generation sulphonylureas and may be the sulphonylurea of choice in this age group (Tessier *et al.* 1994). Glibenclamide has been shown to reduce insulin requirements in elderly NIDDM patients who are treated concomitantly with insulin (Kyllastinen and Groop 1985).

Metformin

The limited data which are available suggest that metformin is an effective oral hypoglycaemic agent in older patients with NIDDM, particularly obese elderly patients who have relatively normal insulin secretion but resistance to insulin-mediated glucose disposal (Meneilly and Tessier 1995). Based on our clinical experience, about 20 per cent of elderly patients who are poorly controlled on sulphonylureas can be adequately controlled when metformin is added. Patients should be started on 500 mg once daily. The dose can be gradually increased to 1 g three times daily with meals. Introducing metformin gradually reduces the likelihood of gastrointestinal intolerance to the drug. Age is not a risk factor for lactic acidosis during treatment with metformin. Lactic acidosis has not occurred in elderly patients with normal renal and liver function. Metformin should not be given to patients with creatinine values above 180 µmol/l (2.0 mg/dl), chronic liver disease, or congestive heart failure. It should be stopped immediately in patients admitted to hospital with an acute illness that might increase production of lactate (e.g. sepsis).

The United Kingdom Prospective Diabetes Study trial (UK Prospective Diabetes Study Group 1998*d*) reported that intensive glycaemic control with metformin appeared to reduce the frequency of diabetes-related endpoints in overweight diabetic patients, and was associated with less weight gain and fewer hyperglycaemic attacks than were insulin and sulphonylureas. There was a suggestion in the data that patients treated with sulphonylureas and metformin did badly, but there is no collateral evidence of such an effect and it may have been due to chance selection of high-risk patients into the combined therapy group.

Acarbose

Acarbose is an α-glucosidase inhibitor which inhibits the enzymes responsible for the digestion of complex carbohydrates and disaccharides. Data from postmarketing surveillance studies in Europe suggest that this drug will lower Hb_1Ac by approximately 1 per cent in older patients (Spengler and Cagatay 1992), and acarbose appears to be effective in both lean and obese subjects. Acarbose is effective as primary therapy or as an adjunct to sulphonylureas or insulin. The starting dose is 25 mg with the first bite of breakfast. This can be gradually increased to 50 mg three times daily with meals. Doses above 150 mg/day are generally not well tolerated and appear to have little added benefit. A minority of elderly subjects are unable to take the drug because of gastrointestinal side-effects such as bloating and flatulence.

Recently, miglitol (a newer α-glucosidase inhibitor not yet released for use) was compared with glibenclamide in a randomized controlled trial of elderly diabetes patients (Johnston *et al.* 1998). Glycaemic control was better with glibencamide, but patients treated with this drug had more frequent hypoglycaemic events, greater weight gain, and higher incidence of serious cardiovascular events. Thus, while α-glucosidase inhibitors may be less effective than sulphonylureas, they should be considered for use in elderly patients with mild diabetes since they are associated with fewer serious side-effects.

Insulin

It has been demonstrated that elderly patients make substantial errors when trying to mix insulins on their own. The accuracy of insulin injections can be improved if patients are prescribed premixed insulin preparations (Coscelli *et al.* 1992; Brodows and Chessor 1995). There is no evidence that different proportions of insulins (50/50, 70/30, etc.) have any significant effect on glycaemic control in older age groups. Several authors have recommended once-daily insulin injections in older patients because of improved compliance. However, many elderly patients treated with single daily insulin injections need to be switched to two injections a day because of hypoglycaemic episodes. In general, elderly NIDDM patients should be treated with two daily injections of an intermediate-acting insulin. If shorter-acting insulins are required, premixed forms should be used, although the proportion of regular and long-acting insulin does not appear to be critical. For patients who have evidence of hypoglycaemic unawareness or frequent hypoglycaemic episodes, consideration should be given to beef–pork insulin (Meneilly *et al.* 1995).

Other drugs

There are no data as yet on the use of insulin sensitizers such as troglitazone in the management of elderly NIDDM patients. Fluoxetine in large doses has been demonstrated to improve glycaemic control in obese elderly NIDDM patients, presumably because it results in weight loss (Connolly *et al.* 1994).

Monitoring glycaemic control

Because of the increase in the renal threshold for glucose with age, urine glucose testing is not a reliable measure of glycaemic control in elderly subjects. Such patients and/or their caregivers can be taught to self-monitor blood glucose reliably with no adverse affects on quality of life (Gilden *et al.* 1990; Bernbaum *et al.* 1994). HbA_{1c} is the standard measure for long-term glycaemic control in older individuals, although serum fructosamine may eventually prove to be a better marker. In most nursing- home patients a fasting and presupper glucometer once or twice a week coupled with HbA_{1c} every few months should allow adequate assessment of glycaemic control.

Conclusion

We are approaching an epidemic of diabetes among older people in the 21st century. Improving the management of diabetes and vascular risk factor, especially hypertension, will reduce morbidity in these patients and substantially improve their quality of life.

References

American Diabetes Association (1998). Report of the expert committee on the diagnosis and classification of diabetes mellitus. *Diabetes Care*, **21** (Supplement 1), S5–19.

Arner, P., Pollare, T., and Lithell, H. (1991). Different aetiologies of Type 2 (non-insulin-dependent) diabetes mellitus in obese and non-obese subjects. *Diabetologia*, **34**, 483–7.

Asplund, K., Wilholm, B.E., and Lithner, F. (1983). Glibenclamide-associated hypoglycaemia: a report on 57 cases. *Diabetologia*, **24**, 412–17.

Bernbaum, M., Albert, S.G., McGinnis, J., Brusca, S., and Mooradian, A.D. (1994). The reliability of self blood glucose monitoring in elderly diabetic patients. *Journal of the American Geriatrics Society*, **42**, 779–81.

Brodows, R. and Chessor, R. (1995). A comparison of premixed insulin preparations in elderly patients. *Diabetes Care*, **18**, 855–7.

Connolly, V.M., Gallagher, A., and Kesson, C.M. (1994). A study of fluoxetine in obese elderly patients with type 2 diabetes. *Diabetic Medicine*, **12**, 416–18.

Coscelli, C., Calabrese, G., Fedele, D., *et al.* (1992). Use of premixed insulin among the elderly. *Diabetes Care*, **15**, 1628–30.

Coulston, M., Mandelbaum, D., and Reaven, G.M. (1990). Dietary management of nursing home residents with non-insulin-dependent diabetes mellitus. *American Journal of Clinical Nutrition*, **51**, 67–71.

DCCT Research Group (1993). The effect of intensive treatment of diabetes on the development and progression of long-term complications in insulin-dependent diabetes mellitus. *New England Journal of Medicine*, **329**, 977–86.

DeFronzo, R.A. (1988). Lilly Lecture 1987. The triumvirate: β-cell, muscle, liver: a collusion responsible for NIDDM. *Diabetes*, **37**, 667–87.

Gilden, J.L., Hendryx, M., Casia, C., and Singh, S.P. (1989). The effectiveness of diabetes education programs for older patients and their spouses. *Journal of the American Geriatrics Society*, **37**, 1023–30.

Gilden, J.L., Casia, C., Hendryx, M., and Singh, S.P. (1990). Effects of self-monitoring of blood glucose on quality of life in elderly diabetic patients. *Journal of the American Geriatrics Society*, **38**, 511–15.

Harris, M.I. (1990). Epidemiology of diabetes mellitus among the elderly in the United States. *Clinics in Geriatric Medicine*, **6**, 703–19.

Harris, M.I. (1993). Undiagnosed NIDDM: clinical and public health issues. *Diabetes Care*, **16**, 642–52.

Harris, M.I., Hadden, W.C., Knowler, W.C., and Bennett, P.H. (1987). Prevalence of diabetes and impaired glucose tolerance and plasma glucose levels in U.S. population aged 20–74 yr. *Diabetes*, **36**, 530.

Horwath, C.C. (1991). Dietary habits of elderly persons with diabetes. *Journal of the American Dietetic Association*, **91**, 553–7.

Johnston, P.S., Lebovitz, H.E., Coniff, R.F., Simonson, D.C., Raskin, P., and Munera, C.L. (1998). Advantages of α-glucosidase inhibition as monotherapy in elderly type 2 diabetic patients. *Journal of Clinical Endocrinology and Metabolism*, **83**, 1515–22.

Kahn, C.R. (1994). Banting Lecture. Insulin action, diabetogenes, and the cause of type II diabetes. *Diabetes*, **43**, 1066–84.

Kronsbein, P., Mulhauser, I., Venhaus, A., Jorgens, V., Scholz, V., and Berger, M. (1988). Evaluation of a structured treatment and teaching programme on non-insulin-dependent diabetes. *Lancet*, **ii**, 1407–11.

Kyllastinen, M. and Groop, L. (1985). Combination of insulin and glibenclamide in the treatment of elderly non-insulin-dependent (Type 2) diabetic patients. *Annals of Clinical Research*, **17**, 100–4.

Meneilly, G.S. and Tessier, D. (1995). Diabetes in the elderly. *Diabetic Medicine*, **12**, 949–60.

Meneilly, G.S., Cheung, E., and Tuokko, H. (1994). Counterregulatory hormone responses to hypoglycaemia in the elderly patient with diabetes. *Diabetes*, **43**, 403–10.

Meneilly, G.S., Milberg, W.P., and Tuokko, H. (1995). Differential effects of human and animal insulin on the responses to hypoglycaemia in elderly patients with NIDDM. *Diabetes*, **44**, 272–7.

Meneilly, G.S., Elliott, T., Tessier, D., Hards, L., and Tildesley, H. (1996). NIDDM in the elderly. *Diabetes Care*, **19**, 1320–5.

Mooradian, A.D., Osterweil, D., Petrasek, D., and Morley, J.E. (1988). Diabetes mellitus in elderly nursing home patients. A survey of clinical characteristics and management. *Journal of the American Geriatrics Society*, **36**, 391–6.

Naliboff, B.D. and Rosenthal, M. (1989). Effects of age on complications in adult onset diabetes. *Journal of the American Geriatrics Society*, **37**, 838–42.

Nathan, D.M. (1998). Some answers, more controversy, from UKPDS. *Lancet*, **352**, 832–3.

Nathan, D.M., Singer, D.E., Godine, J.E., and Perlmuter, L.C. (1986a) Non-insulin-dependent diabetes in older patients. *American Journal of Medicine*, 81, 837–42.

Nathan, D.M., Singer, D.E., Godine, J.E., Harrington, C.H., and Perlmuter, L.C. (1986b). Retinopathy in older Type II diabetics. *Diabetes*, 35, 797–801.

Ohkubo, Y., Kishikawa, H., Araki, E., *et al.* (1995). Intensive insulin therapy prevents the progression of diabetic neurovascular complications in Japanese patients with non-insulin dependent diabetes mellitus: a randomized prospective 6 year study. *Diabetes Research and Clinical Practice*, 28, 103–17.

Olivarius, N.deF., Andreasen, A.H., Keiding, N., and Mogensen, C.E. (1993). Epidemiology of renal involvement in newly-diagnosed middle-aged and elderly diabetic patients: cross-sectional data from the population-based study 'Diabetes Care in General Practice', Denmark. *Diabetologia*, 36, 1007–16.

Reaven, G.M. and Staff of the Palo Alto GRECC Aging Study Unit (1985). Beneficial effects of weight loss in older patients with NIDDM. *Journal of the American Geriatrics Society*, 33, 93–5.

Skarfors, E.T., Wegener, T.A., Lithell, H., and Selinus, I. (1987). Physical training as treatment for type 2 (non-insulin-dependent) diabetes in elderly men: a feasibility study over 2 years. *Diabetologia*, 30, 930–3.

Spengler, M. and Cagatay, M. (1992). Evaluation of efficacy and tolerability of acarbose by post-marketing surveillance. *Diabetes und Stoffwechsel*, 1, 218–22.

Tessier, D., Dawson, K., Tetrault, J.P., Bravo, G., and Meneilly, G.S. (1994). Glibenclamide vs gliclazide in Type 2 diabetes of the elderly. *Diabetic Medicine*, 11, 974–80.

Tun, P.A., Nathan, D.M., and Perlmuter, L.C. (1990). Cognitive and affective disorders in elderly diabetics. *Clinics in Geriatric Medicine*, 6, 731–46.

Tuomilehto, J., Rastenyte, D., Birkenhäger, W.H., *et al.* (1999). Effects of calcium-channel blockade in older patients with diabetes and systolic hypertension. *New England Journal of Medicine*, 340, 677–84.

UK Prospective Diabetes Study Group (1998a). Tight blood pressure control and risk of microvascular and macrovascular complications in type 2 diabetes: UKPDS 38. *British Medical Journal*, 317, 703–13.

UK Prospective Diabetes Study Group (1998b). Efficacy of atenolol and captopril in reducing risk of microvascular and macrovascular complications in type 2 diabetes: UKPDS 39. *British Medical Journal*, 317, 713–20.

UK Prospective Diabetes Study Group (1998c). Intensive blood-glucose control with sulphonylureas or insulin compared with conventional treatment and risk of complications in patients with type 2 diabetes (UKPDS 33). *Lancet*, 352, 837–53.

UK Prospective Diabetes Study Group (1998d). Effect of intensive blood-glucose control with metformin on complications in overweight patients with type 2 diabetes (UKPDS 34). *Lancet*, 352, 854–65.

Wachtel, T.J. (1990). The diabetic hyperosmolar state. *Clinics in Geriatric Medicine*, 6, 797–806.

Wilson, W. and Pratt, C. (1987). The impact of diabetes education and peer support upon weight and glycaemic control of elderly persons with non-insulin dependent diabetes mellitus (NIDDM). *American Journal of Public Health*, 77, 634–5.

8

Gastroenterology

8.1 Oral health and disease

Michèle J. Saunders

The aims of this chapter are to reacquaint the doctor with information about oral medicine that was once a routine part of general medicine but has been lost as dentistry has become a separate profession, and areas of geriatric oral medicine especially pertinent to the practice of general medicine. We address some of the history of the interrelationship of medicine and dentistry, discuss the importance of oral health to general health, especially for older people, describe the physiological oral changes that occur with ageing and particular oral manifestations of systemic disease in later life, delineate specific oral diseases common in older patients and suggest medical treatment as appropriate, outline standard procedures for oral assessment, and discuss appropriate consultations with, and referrals to, dental professionals.

History

Medicine and dentistry have shared a similar history. In many countries, including Austria, Russia, Italy, Portugal, and Spain, medicine and dentistry have followed an identical path because they were and continue to be the same profession, with dental medicine a subspecialty of medicine and dental training beginning after 5 to 7 years of medical school. In addition, dentistry has made significant contributions to medicine, most notably the use of nitrous oxide as an anaesthetic during surgery, a discovery of dentist Horace Wells in 1844, and the use of ether anaesthesia in 1846 by William T.G. Morton, a dentist who was taking medical classes (Ring 1986). American dentists can still train as anaesthetists without prior medical degrees. More recent contributions have included advances in bone physiology and metabolism research, such as the establishment of an animal model for the bacterial processes initiating the bone loss of periodontitis (Holt *et al.* 1988).

The twentieth century saw tremendous advances in the technologies of both medicine and dentistry, with increasing specialization. Unfortunately, medical education has devoted increasingly less time to oral health and disease, and, until the late 1960s, dentistry education spent a decreasing amount of time focusing on medicine. An example of the former is that, while dentistry's major physical evaluation textbook (Halstead *et al.* 1982) devotes 143 pages to the oral cavity, American medicine's primary physical examination textbook (Bates 1987) devotes slightly more than seven pages to the mouth. Thus, medicine has 'forgotten' most of its dentistry. Likewise, dentists interested in adult medicine have had to specialize in oral medicine or oral surgery, or train in hospital dentistry or geriatrics to gain an adequate medical background to treat patients who are seriously medically compromised.

This lack of cross-reference in education has resulted in a large population of dentists who are oriented towards technique and who selected the field of dentistry because it has become less medically based. It has also resulted in a large population of doctors who no longer appreciate the fact that the mouth is as integral a part of the human body as the pharynx. This has caused medicine to neglect a substantial amount of medical knowledge as it pertains to the diagnosis and treatment of oral manifestations of systemic disease and to the systemic manifestations of oral disease. Both professions often forget that clinical dentistry is a primary care specialty and have overlooked the medical responsibilities such a designation warrants.

Importance of oral health to general health

Dentistry as primary care

International demographics in the early to middle half of the twentieth century reveal reasons why dentistry is often forgotten as a primary care specialty by both medicine and dentistry. A rapidly growing population of young and adult healthy patients appeared to free the dentist from considerations of systemic illness. In addition, in many countries oral health was generally improved with fluoridation of water supplies, and dental specialties flourished together with research and development of dental materials and techniques.

In the early 1960s, an era of increasing awareness of social issues, dentistry began to pay more attention to handicapped, medically compromised, and elderly people. This led to renewed consideration of the importance of the effects of oral health on the rest of physical health and vice versa. The areas of oral medicine, paediatric dentistry, and hospital dentistry burgeoned, with their concentration on treatment of the medically compromised and special care patient. Dentists took the approach that, like the doctor, the dentist has certain 'total body' responsibilities each time he or she uses a syringe, picks up a scalpel, or prescribes medication.

By the late 1960s and early 1970s, several American dental schools had changed their degrees from Doctor of Dental Surgery to Doctor of Dental Medicine, often incorporating lengthy hospital rotations and complete medical history taking and interpretation into the curriculum. A few dental and medical schools even combined their classes for the first 2 years of professional school. Although most dental schools granting the Doctor of Dental Surgery or Doctor of Dental Medicine have now increased the medical portion of their curricula, the depth and amount are by no means uniform. Nevertheless, there has been a steady increase in the numbers of general dentists and oral surgeons with full hospital privileges, taking histories, conducting complete physical examinations, admitting patients, and treating those patients in the operating room.

The elderly patient

More recent demographics indicate a tremendous increase in the number of elderly people, with their accompanying complex medical histories, chronic diseases, functional limitations, medications, and increasing risk for morbidity or mortality from a serious oral problem. For this reason, and because more that 66 per cent of older adults have retained their natural dentition, it is important that adequate training between medicine and dentistry occurs. In 1988, geriatric medicine and dentistry training programmes were developed, with funding by United States congressional mandate, by the Bureau of Health Professions, the Health Resources and Services Administration of the American Public Health Service. Recognizing the need for cross-training between medicine and dentistry, the Bureau of Health Professions formed a doctor–dentist advisory committee to develop a list of learning objectives in geriatric dentistry for doctor fellows. Both medical and dental fellows in these programmes are being cross-trained. The list of learning objectives in geriatric dentistry for doctors appears in Table 1 (Health Resources and Services Administration 1990).

Oral physiology and pathology in elderly people

Physiology of oral ageing

The teeth

No cellular turnover occurs with age in the outer layer, or enamel, of the tooth crown (that portion of the tooth usually exposed to the oral environment above the gingiva in the absence of periodontal disease). Enamel is not a living tissue, but rather a mineralized matrix of hydroxyapatite crystals that undergo surface ion-exchange reactions, for example absorption of fluoride ions. However, there is some cell turnover with ageing in the middle layer, or dentine, of the tooth crown and root(s) as well as in the outside layer of the tooth root(s), or cementum. High cellular turnover remains relatively unchanged with age in the central tooth tissue, the pulp (Ketterl 1983; Mjor 1996).

It is often difficult to differentiate between pathological and physiological changes in the teeth as they age, and many changes occur with prolonged, normal function of the teeth. Age changes in the teeth are therefore loosely defined as 'frequently occurring changes found in functional, intact teeth from older individuals' (Mjor 1996).

Multiple changes in the morphology of the teeth occur with ageing, often resulting in altered coloration of the teeth. The form of the teeth changes over the lifespan due to wear and attrition. Occlusal, incisal, and interproximal wear occur, as well as a loss of anatomical details on the enamel surface. These changes in older teeth result in an apparent change in tooth colour due to a different pattern of light reflection. Dentinal changes also contribute to this colour change. The dentine becomes thicker with age by laying down new dentinal tubules, and the pulpal tissues 'shrink' as the dentine thickens. New dentinal tubules are aligned differently, causing a yellow shading and decreased translucency of the teeth. Other dentinal tubules often become obturated (sclerosed and blocked), resulting in decreased sensitivity in the dentine to discomfort or pain. Further discoloration occurs due to pigmentation of enamel defects and can be exacerbated by poor oral hygiene (Arends et al. 1983; Ketterl 1983; Mjor 1996).

The surface enamel of the tooth is also subject to ion exchange with the oral environment, resulting in chemical changes with ageing, such as a slow build-up in fluoride content from surface contact with fluoridated water, rinses, and toothpastes. The number of cracks in the surface enamel also increases, probably due to the effects of normal tooth function over time.

The primary change that occurs with age in the cementum is a gradual thickening that can be observed radiographically. When the cementum becomes abnormally thick, it is called hypercementosis and is a sign of local or systemic pathology. Usually seen on a radiograph, hypercementosis most often indicates the presence of occlusal trauma, a condition in which the forces of mastication are excessive or are no longer along the long axis of the tooth. It may also occur as a manifestation of systemic disease such as Paget's disease of bone (Ketterl 1983; Mjor 1996).

Pulpal changes with age include a decrease in the number of cells and an increase in the amount of fibrous tissue. The number of blood vessels entering the pulp through the root apices of the teeth also decreases, as does the number of vessel branches. In addition, there is an increase in diffuse mineralization in the pulp. When mineralization occurs in the form of radiographically demonstrable 'stones' in the pulp, it is indicative of oral pathology such as carious lesions, deep restorations, or occlusal trauma (Ketterl 1983; Mjor 1996).

Mucosa and periodontium

The oral mucosa is traditionally divided into three components: the mucosa of the soft palate, cheek, floor of the mouth, and central and lateral surfaces of the tongue; the masticatory mucosa of the hard palate and gingivae; the mucosa of the lips and the dorsum of the tongue. Each of these three components varies in structure to accommodate the amount of functional trauma to which it is exposed. For example, the epithelium of the gingivae and hard palate contains dense collagenous tissue with fibrils binding it to underlying structures, and has relatively little elastic collagen. These properties permit gingival and palatal epithelium to withstand the forces of mastication and to resist movement. In contrast, the epithelium of the lining of the mucosa of the cheek has a less dense lamina propria with more numerous elastin fibres and, therefore, is easily movable (Bottomly 1979; Mackenzie et al. 1996).

The periodontium, the supporting tissues of the teeth, consists of the gingiva, cementum on the roots of the tooth, the alveolar bone surrounding the teeth, the alveolar mucosa covering the alveolar bone, and the periodontal ligament. The primary function of the periodontal ligament, which is not a true ligament, is to connect the teeth to the bone and the gingiva via dense collagenous bundles call Sharpey's fibres (Mackenzie et al. 1996). High turnover of fibroblasts in the periodontal ligament remains relatively unchanged with age.

Whereas early research indicated that oral mucosa ages in parallel with skin, subsequent studies provide conflicting evidence on the

Table 1 Geriatric dentistry objectives for physicians

Didactic

In understanding the role of the dentist and the dental auxiliary as members of the geriatric health-care team, the doctor should be able to describe:
- The scope and content of the training of dentists and their auxiliaries (predoctoral/postdoctoral)
    Basic sciences
    Physical medical pharmacology
    Behavioural sciences
    Clinical sciences
    Requirements for dental specialties
- The normal structures of the oral cavity
    Development
    Maturation
    Ageing
- The specific pathology of the oral cavity (dental caries, periodontal disease, oral cancer)
    Pathology (and natural history where applicable)
    Epidemiology
    Prevention
    Treatment
- Dental care delivery systems
    Types
    Utilization
    Economics
    Ethical/legal aspects
- Preventive care (e.g. prophylaxis for infective endocarditis, and oral hygiene methods, including use of fluoride and chlorhexidine)

Clinical

With regard to direct clinical participation with the dentist and the dental auxiliary as members of the geriatric health-care team, the doctor should:
- Be able to complete an appropriate dental history
- Be able to perform an orofacial examination and functional assessment (including examination for oral cancer, periodontal disease, dental caries, or incorrect fit of dentures)
- Be familiar with appropriate dental treatment plans and preventive regimens for elderly patients
- Be able to interpret the dental record
- Be able to detect clinically the need for dental consultation in ambulatory, inpatient, and long-term care situations
- Understand dental patient management (e.g. management of dental patients exhibiting dementia)
- Be familiar with interdisciplinary consultation and protocols for care (e.g. endstage renal dialysis)

degree of age changes in the oral mucosa and connective tissue of the periodontal ligament. These conflicting data include findings that the cells of the lamina propria of the lining mucosa appear to shrink with age or exhibit no ageing change, the number of fibroblasts in the gingiva and periodontal ligament either increases or remains the same with age, and the orientation of gingival and periodontal ligament collagen fibres is either disrupted or unchanged. Additional research is required to determine whether age-associated changes occur in the functional capacity of oral mucosa and connective tissues (Grant and Bernick 1972; Kydd and Daly 1982; Grove and Klingman 1983; Mackenzie *et al.* 1996). Despite these uncertainties, the clinical appearance of the oral mucosa is recognizably altered in ageing. In elderly patients, for example, the oral mucosa appears to be thinner and more friable.

A number of age-associated changes in the collagenous tissue of the hard palate, gingiva, and periodontal ligament have clearly been identified. To quote a review of the literature (Mackenzie *et al.* 1996): 'The ability of the fibroblasts to synthesize new collagen decreases with age. . . . [T]he collagen fibres appear thicker and coarser. . . . The rate of conversion of soluble collagen to insoluble collagen increases with age and correspondingly, the denaturing temperature is higher. . . .

These changes may affect the functional properties of the periodontal tissues in the aged'.

Salivary glands and secretion

A number of authors erroneously claim that diminished salivary flow is a normal aspect of ageing. This impression is based on studies conducted more than 30 years ago. Studies by Baum (1996) have demonstrated that a dry mouth (xerostomia) is not a physiological concomitant of ageing. In his review of study design and methodologies of the older studies, Baum reveals that the investigators 'frequently compared functional performance in healthy young adults and older, debilitated or infirm patients residing in chronic-care facilities' (Baum 1996). In addition, only whole saliva was studied rather than individual gland function. Therefore the decrease in salivary flow reported in early studies of elderly people was most likely either a result of disease (such as diabetes mellitus, systemic lupus erythematosus, or rheumatoid arthritis) or pharmacologically induced. It is noteworthy that the submandibular glands contribute most of the volume in whole saliva.

However, structural changes in salivary glands do occur with ageing. Baum (1981, 1996) reports that there is some replacement of gland parenchyma with fatty or connective tissue. As it ages, the submandibular gland has an increased percentage of ductal components as opposed to acinar cells. Current evidence is not adequate to determine whether these changes are biologically significant (Bodner and Baum 1984; Heft and Baum 1984).

Studies in rat models, in which morphological changes of ageing in the salivary glands parallel those of humans, report that generalized deterioration of salivary gland function does not occur (Baum 1981; Ito *et al.* 1982). Although *in vitro* secretory events mediated by β-adrenergic receptors do not change with age in the rat, there are changes in secretory events mediated by α-adrenergic receptors. These changes in α-adrenergic-mediated secretory events result in altered electrolyte movement and decreased protein synthesis by the parotid gland (Baum 1981; Ito *et al.* 1981). *In vivo* studies in ageing rat models have shown markedly decreased DNA synthesis by submandibular glands after β-adrenergic receptor stimulation (Baum 1981; Ito *et al.* 1982). Although there was considerable reduction with age in rat parotid salivary flow rates after cholinergic stimulation with pilocarpine, there were no differences between young, adult, and old submandibular gland secretory function after pilocarpine stimulation. Investigation of rat salivary gland function during ageing is ongoing.

The primary role of saliva is protective. Salivary components assist in the maintenance of tissue integrity. These salivary components include antibacterial factors, particularly immunoglobulin G and A, buffers to prevent enamel dissolution by cariogenic bacterial products, lubricating and remineralizing proteins, and a viscous solvent to present foods or liquids to taste-buds and to assist in the formation of a food bolus in preparation for swallowing (Bottomly 1979). Any salivary deficiency that is reported by the patient or observed by the clinician should not be ignored. The aetiology should be determined and the xerostomia treated or managed to avoid severe oral morbidity.

Untreated xerostomia can lead to rampant caries, usually root caries in elderly people. In the absence of salivary remineralizing proteins and antibacterial immunoglobulins, the acid produced by the bacteria in the plaque (food debris, bacteria, bacterial products, and a mucopolysaccharide coating called pellicle) on teeth can demineralize the surface enamel and the softer cementum or dentine of any exposed roots. This demineralization rapidly progresses to caries. The presenting signs and symptoms of, and oral assessment for, xerostomia are discussed below.

Oral manifestations of systemic disease

A number of systemic diseases can result in a variety of oral signs, symptoms, or lesions in people of all ages. The types of systemic conditions with oral manifestations include genetic disease, systemic infections, immunological disorders, malignancies, nutritional disorders, connective tissue disorders, gastrointestinal disease, renal disease, cardiovascular disease, endocrine disease, dermatological disease, skeletal disease, and neurological disorders (Jones and Mason 1980; Shafer *et al.* 1983; Rose and Kaye 1990).

Other conditions that can adversely affect the oral cavity are traumatic injury, drug therapy, infection, psychosomatic disorders, and emotional stress. Oral manifestations of systemic conditions can be found in the dentition, periodontium, and oral mucosa. Manifestations of systemic disease can affect the dentition, and the structure, number, size, and morphology of the teeth. Oral effects of

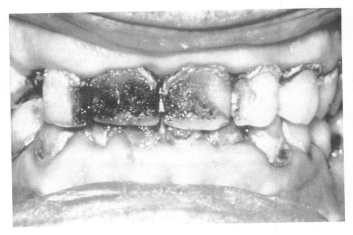

Fig. 1 Elderly patient with Alzheimer's disease.

systemic conditions, for example diabetes, on the periodontium can include an increased prevalence and severity of gingivitis and periodontitis (Jones and Mason 1980).

Poor oral hygiene practices, as a result of debilitating systemic disease, often result in periodontal disease and tooth discoloration. Figure 1 depicts the anterior dentition of an elderly man with Alzheimer's disease. Figure 2 shows the same dentition after a simple professional prophylaxis.

Table 2 illustrates oral manifestations of a number of systemic diseases important in later life (Jones and Mason 1980; Robertson and Greenspan 1988; Darnell and Saunders 1990). Herpetic stomatitis and trigeminal neuralgia are included in this table because of their primary relationship with or effect upon cranial nerves. Some systemic diseases, such as diabetes, Paget's disease, hyperparathyroidism, leukaemia, and AIDS, may first be detected by their oral manifestations. For example, a suspicion of diabetes might first be aroused by gingivitis and/or periodontitis of greater severity than would be warranted by the patient's age and oral hygiene. Alternatively, diabetes can present as delayed healing of a traumatic ulcer, or abnormal bleeding or slow healing after a dental extraction. The doctor who

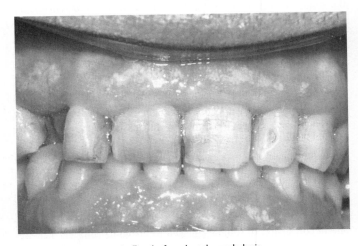

Fig. 2 Same patient as in Fig. 1 after dental prophylaxis.

Table 2 Oral manifestations of selected systemic diseases in elderly people

Systemic disease	Oral manifestation(s)
Neutropenia(s)	• Ulceration and necrosis of gingival margin, associated bleeding; oedematous, hyperaemic, and hyperplastic gingiva with partial desquamation • Deep periodontal pockets and extensive generalized alveolar bone loss
Leukaemia	• Gingival enlargement due to leukaemic cellular infiltration, oedema, and/or hyperplasia; gingival bleeding • Sometimes rapid loss of alveolar bone
Diabetes mellitus	• Exacerbated gingivitis and/or periodontitis (i.e. more rapid loss of periodontal attachment) • Candidiasis (can indicate poor control of disease) • Xerostomia and altered taste; enlarged parotids • Glossopyrosis (burning tongue)
AIDS (10% of all new US cases are in adults over 65 years)	• Oropharyngeal–oesophageal candidiasis • Kaposi's sarcoma • Severe gingivitis and periodontitis
Tuberculosis	• Oral lesions are most often secondary lesions in the posterior of the mouth (primary lesions are not oral) with ulceration and severe pain; or • As primary lesions, are diffuse inflammatory lesions, granulomas, and fissures of tongue, buccal mucosa, gingivae, lips, floor of mouth, and hard and soft palate; mild or absent pain
Vitamin B_1 deficiency	• Exacerbated gingivitis and periodontitis
Folic acid deficiency and/or riboflavin (vitamin B_2) deficiency	• Exacerbated gingivitis and periodontitis • Stomatitis • Angular cheilitis (more common in folic acid deficiency) • Glossitis • Recurrent aphthous ulceration
Vitamin K deficiency	• Gingival bleeding • Postextraction haemorrhage
Vitamin B_6 and/or iron deficiency	• Angular cheilitis • Atrophic glossitis • Generalized stomatitis • Papillary atrophy on dorsum of tongue • Recurrent aphthous ulcers (iron deficiency only)
Vitamin B_{12} deficiency (oral changes may be the only clinical evidence)	• Glossitis initially with oedema and extreme tenderness • Later atrophy of filiform, fungiform, and circumvallate papillae of tongue • Recurrent aphthous ulceration common • No angular cheilitis
Hyperparathyroidism	• Pronounced loss of alveolar bone • Bone cysts in mandible apparent on radiographs
Sjögren's syndrome and rheumatoid arthritis	• Xerostomia • Salivary gland swelling • Temporomandibular joint pain and limitation of jaw movement in up to two-thirds of rheumatoid arthritis cases
Temporal arteritis	• Intense head, face, or jaw ache with tender and inflamed non-pulsing superficial temporal arteries • Possible masseteric pain during mastication or 'intermittent claudication' of jaw or tongue
Chronic renal failure	• Erythemopultaceous stomatitis (thick sticky exudate superimposed on erythematous mucosa) • Ulcerative stomatitis (on gingivae, ventral surface of tongue, floor of mouth) • Oral haemorrhage (especially gingival) • Hyperparakeratosis (looks like hyperkeratosis, distinguishable only by biopsy) • Candidiasis
Paget's disease	• Jaw overgrowth and malocclusion (can be first signs of the disease)

Table 2 *continued*

Systemic disease	Oral manifestation(s)
Metastases (spread intraorally most commonly from the lung, then kidney. Other sites: bone, pharynx, uterus, skin, stomach, intestine, eye, testis, oesophagus, ovary, breast, pancreas, and prostate)	• Oral clinical appearance varies widely • Oral metastasis indicates widespread metastasis and a poor prognosis
Pemphigus vulgaris	• Potentially lethal chronic bullae of stratified squamous mucosa; acanthosis with intraepithelial bullae • 95% have serum IgG, IgM, or IgA autoantibodies to intercellular substances of the suprabasilar epithelium
Benign mucous membrane pemphigoid	• Bullous lesions that heal with scarring • Subepithelial vesicles; IgG, IgA, C_3, and C_4 deposited in basement membrane area
Herpes zoster	• 15% of cases involve trigeminal nerve • Oral lesions common on anterior 12 of tongue, soft palate, buccal mucosa • Severe localized pain precedes vesicular rash • Vesicles break within a few hours and leave painful yellow–grey ulcers with erythematous borders • Rare involvement of cranial nerve VII leads to Ramsay–Hunt syndrome: soft palate, anterior two-thirds of one side of tongue, and unilateral facial muscles are palsied; possible xerostomia. Paralysis can be permanent
Primary herpetic stomatitis (most common oral manifestation of a viral infection)	• Fever, enlarged lymph nodes, painful mouth and throat, followed by • Vesicle development on oral mucosa (most commonly tongue, buccal mucosa, and gingivae), then • Vesicles rupture and form small ulcers with grey–yellow bases and red halos • If gingival herpes, bleeding occurs • If immune suppressed, chronic ulcerative stomatitis develops with 1–1.5 cm painful white shallow ulcers in tongue, buccal mucosa, gingivae, and soft palate • Transmitted via skin contact or saliva
Secondary herpetic stomatitis (30% of those who had primary disease)	• Manifests most often as herpes labialis or 'cold sore' with preliminary prickling or burning sensation, followed by blisters that enlarge, coalesce, rupture, encrust, and then heal • Intraoral lesions occur on gingivae, alveolar ridges, and hard palate as small shallow ulcers with red irregular margins; pain is rare
Trigeminal neuralgia	• Severe intermittent (short) pain in region of maxillary or mandibular branch of cranial nerve V • Can have ache, burning sensation, or constant dull aching pain between attacks • Triggers can include chewing, speaking, yawning, smiling, touching the ala of the nose or outer edge of upper lip, brushing the teeth, hot/cold liquids, sudden noises

Adapted from Jones and Mason (1980).

routinely and carefully examines the patient's mouth for oral manifestations of systemic disease will probably expedite the diagnosis of a variety of illnesses.

In addition, the presence or absence of some oral manifestations can be used to monitor the degree of control of the systemic disease. For example, a diabetic with severe oral candidiasis or another intraoral infection or abscess is likely to be poorly controlled. Also, an elderly patient with controlled chronic renal failure will not manifest erythemopultaceous stomatitis, but might have hyperparakeratosis instead (Table 2). Lastly, some oral manifestations can linger long after the systemic condition resolves; oral lichen planus, for example, can remain up to a year or more after resolution of all other skin lesions. Other oral manifestations can result in permanent scarring, such as benign mucous membrane pemphigoid.

Oral manifestations of drug therapy

The use of medications can result in a number of adverse effects upon the oral mucosa, some of which are listed in Table 3 (Jones and Mason 1980).

Medications can cause other oral manifestations that do not affect the oral mucosa, such as toxic neuritis of trigeminal nerve branches, paraesthesias, tardive dyskinesia, and other dystonias, and tooth discoloration or staining. Of these, probably the most common, and the most important to the doctor, is tardive dyskinesia, an extrapyramidal side-effect of long-term neuroleptics, notably haloperidol, chlorpromazine, and thioridazine. When the first signs of tardive dyskinesia begin, usually as small pursing movements of the lips and short rapid tongue thrusts, it can sometimes be reversed if the dose of the responsible drug is lowered or the medication

Table 3 Adverse effects on the oral mucosa caused by medications

Ulceration	Lichenoid drug eruption
Fixed drug eruptions	Xerostomia
Contact hypersensitivity	Toxic epidermal necrolysis
Erythema multiforme	Oedema
Pigmentation changes	Stomatitis
Exfoliative dermatitis and stomatitis	Disseminated lupus erythematosus-like syndrome
Angular cheilitis	Hypersalivation
Papillary atrophy of the tongue	Salivary gland pain and swelling

changed. If the tardive dyskinesia is not managed immediately, it often progresses to permanent uncontrollable athetoid movements of the lips and tongue.

Table 4 describes the major oral effects of medications commonly affecting older patients and the drugs responsible (Jones and Mason 1980). The doctor who prescribes a medication with pronounced anticholinergic effects would be wise also to prescribe a fluoride gel to be used daily.

Systemic effects of oral disease

The doctor should also be aware of the possible systemic effects of oral disease, particularly infections of dental or periodontal origin. Elderly people with periodontal disease usually have more Gram-negative anaerobic organisms in the periodontal pocket than others without periodontal disease. The sequelae of oral infection can include bacteraemia, septicaemia, infective endocarditis, and occasionally brain abscess (Brewer et al. 1975; Baddour et al. 1979; Mandel et al. 1979; Arseni and Ciurea 1982; Denham 1986; Cuhna 1988; Robertson and Greenspan 1988). These sequelae do not occur with high enough frequency to be of serious concern for most community-dwelling elderly people. Cases are more frequent in nursing facilities, now that more residents who have retained their dentition are being admitted.

The frail medically compromised elderly patient is at highest risk for these sequelae. Both dentists and doctors have a responsibility to minimize this risk (Terezhalmy et al. 1997). Oral and related systemic infections are best prevented by ensuring that nursing staff assist with or provide meticulous oral hygiene for the resident, that oral infections and dental problems such as caries are promptly treated, and that, when indicated, the appropriate prophylactic antibiotic dose is administered before oral treatment. The most recent prophylactic antibiotic regimens recommended by the American Heart Association can be found in Table 5. In the United Kingdom advice on such regimes are regularly updated in the British National Formulary. The American Heart Association recommends the use of (a) the standard regimen, with oral administration of the antibiotic, and (b) the special regimen, with parenteral administration of the antibiotic, for the conditions specified in Table 6.

All dentists should be aware of these American Heart Association recommendations. Dentists will occasionally consult with a patient's doctor for an opinion regarding the need for antibiotic prophylaxis, particularly in those cases where there is an uncertain risk–benefit ratio of prophylaxis (e.g. in mitral valve prolapse, prosthetic joints, or pacemakers). Responses from doctors range from a simple 'yes' or 'no' to directions for a specific regimen, if other than the prescribed regimen of the American Heart Association. If the dentist follows the doctor's advice and prescribes an alternative antibiotic regimen, the dentist is still liable if the patient contracts infective endocarditis. Therefore it is beneficial for both dentist and doctor to know the American Heart Association regimen and to discuss departures from it when appropriate. The dentist will need to know if patients meet the cardiac conditions described in Table 6, which require prophylaxis, such as whether or not a patient with mitral valve prolapse has regurgitation or leaflet damage. Similarly, the use of prophylactic antibiotics for the prevention of prosthetic joint infection has long been a subject of controversy. The latest recommendations of the American Dental Association and the American Academy of Orthopedic Surgeons can be found in Tables 7 and 8. When advising the dentist regarding antibiotic prophylaxis for the prevention of endocarditis or prosthetic joint infection, the doctor should ascertain the extent of the dental procedures to be performed (Table 6) and assess the frailty, burden of disease, and general risk of the elderly patient for infection.

Oral diseases of concern in the older patient

In addition to the oral manifestations of diseases and conditions listed in Table 2, a number of oral and perioral diseases and conditions are of particular concern in elderly people. Table 9 addresses in detail ten of the most significant oral diseases and conditions found in the older adult (Shafer et al. 1983; Lundeen et al. 1985; Glass et al. 1986). Figures 3 to 13 are referenced in Table 9 and illustrate many of these oral and perioral conditions. Most importantly, suggested medical treatments for these conditions are detailed.

The two most significant oral diseases in older people are root caries and periodontal disease. In its national survey of oral health in employed adults and senior citizens carried out between 1985 and 1986, the National Institute of Dental Research found that 67 per cent of older men and 61 per cent of older women had root surface caries (National Institute of Dental Research 1989). The number of carious root surfaces increased with age. This is probably because increasing frailty with age is associated with decreased oral hygiene self-care, and many medications prescribed for age-associated chronic illnesses cause xerostomia. Concomitant periodontal disease (see below) in older people exposes root surfaces to oral bacteria, promoting root caries. In addition, inflammation of periodontal disease causes a decrease in alveolar bone height, leaving the tooth root partially exposed. In the presence of xerostomia, the soft cementum and dentine of the root are an ideal environment for the development of new carious lesions (Fig. 5). Without salivary immunoglobulins (IgG, IgM, and IgA) and the remineralization and buffering capability of saliva, acid produced by oral bacteria promotes caries.

The World Health Organization (WHO) has a global oral data bank which includes epidemiological studies from 1986 to 1996 on non-institutionalized European adults aged 65 to 74 years. Results revealed that 12.8 to 69.6 per cent of subjects were edentulous, the mean number of teeth ranged from 15.1 to 3.8, and the decayed, missing, and filled teeth index ranged from 22.2 to 30.2. This wide range in scores suggests that oral health policies need to be developed and implemented, taking into consideration both geographical and socio-economic differences in populations (Bourgeois *et al.* 1998).

Early periodontal research suggested that older adults lose their teeth because of extractions necessitated by periodontal disease. Results of the National Institute of Dental Research 1985 to 1986 national survey suggest that this tooth loss primarily occurs in the years between 40 and 60, and that tooth loss after 60 is most likely due to caries (National Institute of Dental Research 1989). However, the survey results indicate that periodontal disease is still a serious problem in later life. Seventy-four per cent of the men and 61 per cent of the women surveyed had calculus (calcified plaque), and 98 per cent of the men and 94 per cent of the women had at least one area of over 2 mm loss of periodontal attachment (the distance from the dentinoenamel junction to the margin of the gingiva). These individuals exhibited recession of the gingiva and alveolar bone loss. The mean loss of attachment for men was 3.54 mm and 2.99 mm for women, and 30 per cent of the men and 19 per cent of the women had at least one periodontal pocket depth (distance from the tip of a periodontal explorer placed in the space between the gingiva and

Table 4 Major effects of drugs on the oral mucosa of elderly patients

Effect	Medication(s)
Oral ulceration	Aspirin
	Anti-inflammatories (phenylbutazone)
	Proguanil (antimalarial)
	Emepronium bromide
	Pancreatic extracts
	Isoprenaline (isoproterenol)
	Potassium chloride
	Gentian violet
Fixed drug eruptions (recurrence of the same type of lesion at the same site: ulcers, bullae, erythematous patches, superficial erosions)	Barbiturates
	Chlordiazepoxide
	Phenacetin
	Tetracyclines
	Sulphonamides
	Pyrazolone derivatives
	Phenolphthalein
Lichenoid eruptions (similar to lichen planus; white striations, reticulations or plaques, erosions or ulcerations)	Methyldopa
	Frusemide (furosemide)
	Gold salts
	Tetracycline
	Mercury
	Quinidine
	Phenothiazines
	Tolbutamide
	Chlorothiazide
	Bismuth
	Amiphenazole
	Chloroquine
	Hydroxychloroquine
	Mepacrine
	Chlorpropamide
	Practolol
	Dapsone
	Triprolidine
	Para-aminosalicyclic acid
	Arsenicals
Erythema multiforme (erythematous patches become bullae, then erosions; bloody encrustations on labial erosions)	Sulphonamides
	Penicillins
	Carbamazepine
	Phenylbutazone
	Oxyphenbutazone
	Phenazone
	Chlorpropamide
	Anticonvulsants

Table 4 *continued*

Effect	Medication(s)
Xerostomia	Anticonvulsants
	Antidepressants
	Antihistamines
	Anticholinergics
	Diuretics
	Antihypertensives
	Muscle relaxants
	Narcotics
	Hypnotics
	Minor tranquillizers
	Major tranquillizers
	Sympathomimetics
Salivary gland enlargement and/or pain (can sometimes mimic mumps or Sjögren's syndrome)	Propylthiouracil
	Iodine
	Vincristine
	Clonidine
	Vinblastine
	Penicillamine
	Metronidazole
	Barbiturates
	Griseofulvin
	Lithium carbonate
	Carbimazole

Adapted from Jones and Mason (1980).

Table 5 Prophylactic antibiotic regimens for prevention of bacterial endocarditis: summary of recommended antibiotic regimens for dental procedures in at-risk adults

Standard regimen	
For dental procedures that cause gingival bleeding and oral surgery	Amoxycillin 2.0 g orally 1 h before procedure. For patients unable to take oral medications, 2.0 g of aqueous ampicillin IM or IV within 30 min before procedure
Special regimens	
Oral regimen for penicillin-allergic patients	Clindamycin 600 mg orally 1 h before procedure, *or* Cephalexin or cefadroxil 2.0 g orally 1 h before procedure, *or* Azithromycin or clarithromycin 500 mg orally 1 h before procedure
Parenteral regimen for penicillin-allergic patients	Clindamycin 600 mg IM or IV within 30 min before procedure, *or* Cefazolin 1.0 g IM or IV within 30 min before procedure

IM, intramuscular; IV, intravenous.

Reproduced with permission from Dajani *et al.* (1997).

the tooth to the margin of the gingiva) of 4 mm or more, indicating periodontitis (National Institute of Dental Research 1989).

WHO and Federaçion Dentaire Internationale data on studies conducted in Asia, Africa, and Brazil recognize the excessive burden of oral diseases, especially periodontal disease, in developing countries (Pakhomov 1996; Rana *et al.* 1997; Tapsoba and Deschamps 1997; Pack 1998; van Palenstein Helderman *et al.* 1998). Much research is needed to determine which types of oral health-care delivery systems will work best to address these oral health problems. Meanwhile,

doctors can do much to manage chronic infections of oral origin, which can have profound deleterious effects on general health if left untreated. Doctors can make the case for medically necessary dental care to third-party payers, with regard both to untreated infection and to a patient's inability to maintain adequate nutrition.

Additionally, minority elderly populations, rapidly increasing in number in the United States and elsewhere, have been shown to have more severe caries and periodontal disease than primary populations. This is particularly true of American Hispanics and black people

Table 6 American Heart Association recommendations for prophylactic antibiotics to prevent bacterial endocarditis

Condition	Prophylaxis recommended	Prophylaxis not recommended
High-risk category		
Prosthetic cardiac valves (including biosynthesis and homograft valves)	×	
Surgically constructed systemic pulmonary shunts or conduits	×	
Previous history of bacterial endocarditis	×	
Complex cyanotic congenital cardiac diseases (e.g. single-ventricle states, transposition of the great arteries, tetralogy of Fallot)	×	
Moderate-risk category		
Most congenital cardiac malformations not described above or below		×
Acquired valvular dysfunction (e.g. rheumatic heart disease)	×	
Hypertrophic cardiomyopathy	×	
Mitral valve prolapse *with valvular regurgitation and/or thickened leaflets*	×	
Negligible-risk category (no greater than the general population)		
Isolated secundum atrial septal defect		×
Surgical repair of atrial or ventricular septal defect, or patent ductus arteriosus (without residual beyond 6 months)		×
Previous coronary artery bypass graft surgery		×
Mitral valve prolapse *without valvular regurgitation*		×
Physiological, functional, or innocent heart murmurs		×
Previous Kawasaki disease *without valvular dysfunction*		×
Previous rheumatic fever *without valvular dysfunction*		×
Cardiac pacemakers (intravascular and epicardial) and implanted defibrillators		×
Dental procedures—higher-risk		
Dental extractions	×	
Periodontal procedures including surgery, scaling, and root planing, probing, and recall maintenance	×	
Prophylactic cleaning of teeth and implants where bleeding is expected	×	
Dental implant placement	×	
Endodontic instrumentation or surgery beyond the apex	×	
Subgingival placement of antibiotic fibres or strips	×	
Initial placement of orthodontic bands but not brackets, even for molar uprighting	×	
Intraligamentary local anaesthetic injections	×	
Dental procedures—lower-risk		
Restorative dentistry (operative or prosthodontic) with or without retraction cord (*clinical judgement may indicate antibiotic use in selected circumstances that may create significant bleeding*)		×
Local anaesthetic injections (*except intraligamentary*)		×
Intracanal endodontic treatment, post-placement, and build-up		×
Placement of rubber dam		×
Postoperative suture removal		×
Placement and removal of prosthodontic and orthodontic appliances		×
Making oral impressions		×
Fluoride treatments		×
Taking oral radiographs		×
Orthodontic appliance adjustment		×

Reproduced with permission from Dajani *et al.* (1997).

(National Institute of Dental Research 1989; Watson and Brown 1995). The Oral Health San Antonio Longitudinal Study of Aging is investigating oral health and ageing in a community-based sample of young (aged 35–64 years at baseline in 1993) and older (aged 65–82 years at baseline in 1993) Mexican Americans and European Americans in three socio-economically matched neighbourhoods: an inner-city *barrio*, a transitional neighbourhood, and a suburban neighbourhood in San Antonio, Texas. Preliminary results suggest that the caries and periodontal disease of older Mexican Americans is somewhat worse than the national findings (the water supply in San Antonio is not fluoridated). Elderly people with altered dentition may adapt dietary habits to reflect those of their peers and meet nutrient needs, but these adaptations may limit the variety of foods consumed and impact on quality of life (Mobley *et al.* 1997). More

Table 7 Prophylactic antibiotic regimens for prevention of prosthetic joint infection: summary of recommended antibiotic regimens for dental procedures in at-risk adults[a]

Standard regimen	
For dental procedures that cause gingival bleeding, and oral surgery	Cephalexin, cephradine, or amoxycillin 2.0 g orally 1 h before procedure. For patients unable to take oral medications, 1.0 g of aqueous cefazolin or 2.0 g of aqueous ampicillin IM or IV within 1 h before procedure
Special regimens	
Oral regimen for penicillin-allergic patients	Clindamycin 600 mg orally 1 h before procedure
Parenteral regimen for penicillin-allergic patients	Clindamycin 600 mg IM or IV 1 h before procedure

[a] Not routinely indicated for most patients with total joint replacements. May be considered for a small number of patients at increased risk for potential joint infection. See Table 8.

Reproduced with permission from American Dental Association, American Academy of Orthopedic Surgeons (1997).

Table 8 Recommendations for use of prophylactic antibiotics to prevent prosthetic joint infections[a]

Condition	Prophylaxis recommended	Not recommended
High-risk category		
Immunocompromised/immunosuppressed patients	×	
Inflammatory arthropathies: rheumatoid arthritis, systemic lupus erythematosus	×	
Disease-, drug-, or radiation-induced immunosuppression	×	
Haemophilia	×	
Type 1 diabetes	×	
First 2 years following joint replacement	×	
History of previous joint infection(s)	×	
Malnourished state	×	
No-risk category (joint non-replacements)		
Pins, plates, or screws		×
Dental procedures—higher-risk		
Same as listing in Table 5	×	
Dental procedures—lower-risk		
Same as listing in Table 5		×

[a] Not routinely indicated for most patients with total joint replacements. May be considered for a small number of patients at increased risk for potential joint infection. See Table 7.

Reproduced with permission from American Dental Association, American Academy of Orthopedic Surgeons (1997).

international community-based longitudinal research on the impact of socio-economic status, sex, and cultural factors on oral health in ageing is needed.

When the medical or dental practitioner conducts an oral examination, he or she should screen for periodontal disease. Figure 14 illustrates severe periodontal infection with a gingival abscess. Figure 15 depicts the plaque and gingivitis due to neglect of the affected side in an elderly stroke patient who maintains his own oral hygiene. With reminders and minimal assistance, he could improve his oral status.

Oral assessment of older people

In 1987, the American Congress passed the Omnibus Budget Reconciliation Act (**OBRA**), which requires that nursing facilities participating in the Medicare and/or Medicaid programmes conduct thorough and reproducible assessments of each resident, using a uniform assessment instrument designated by the state. OBRA also requires the nursing facility to be 'directly responsible' for the dental care of its residents. Most states have selected the Minimum Data Set as one of the instruments of choice to conduct the required resident assessments. This instrument was developed for the Health Care Financing Administration and has been adopted by WHO for international use. Currently, the Minimum Data Set has been translated into 18 languages. Table 10 illustrates those sections (E, L, and M) of the Minimum Data Set pertinent to oral health (Health Care Financing Administration 1990).

The Health Care Financing Administration regulations specify that this assessment must be performed on each new resident within 14 days of admission. The oral health assessment will probably be conducted by the doctor or nurse, and referrals for dental care will be made thereafter. The oral part of section E of the form depicts

Table 9 Selected oral diseases of concern in the older adult

Oral disease	Signs	Symptoms	Treatment
Actinic cheilitis (skin degeneration of lip due to sun exposure, usually in older fair-skinned men) (see Fig. 3)	Mild keratosis with subtle blending of vermilion border of lip with contiguous skin. Firm, slightly swollen, and everted appearance, especially lower lip	Usually none	• Should be considered precancerous (with further sun exposure becomes dysplastic and likely to advance to squamous cell carcinoma) • If biopsy shows dysplastic changes, epidermal lip is advised—refer to oral surgeon • Sunscreen is advisable all year round with a sun protection factor of at least 15 (two applications 1 h before sun exposure, then hourly when exposed)
Angular cheilitis (see Fig. 4)	Redness, cracking, or fissuring of the corners of the mouth, lips, or perilabial skin	No discomfort, soreness, or burning sensation depending on severity of lesions	• If due to collapsed vertical height from old worn complete dentures, remake dentures • Determine if aetiology is nutritional deficiency and begin vitamin therapy (usually folic acid, riboflavin, vitamin B_6, or iron) • If candidiasis is superimposed, nystatin ointment 100 000 units/g (apply liberally to affected area three times daily; continue for at least 48 h after lesion has resolved)
Xerostomia (dry mouth)/radiation caries (most likely due to medication, disease, e.g. diabetes, or head and neck radiation for oral cancer, >60 Gy) (see Figs 5 and 6)	Dry smooth shiny mucosa; epithelial atrophy, inflammatory fissuring of tongue; rampant caries, especially at cervical third of teeth on all surfaces and on any exposed root surfaces	Burning, sore tongue and lips; ulcerations; abnormal taste and smell; difficulty swallowing; patient with dentures will claim they do not fit (poor retention because of lack of moisture)	• Bathe tissues frequently with artificial saliva or water; do not use hard sweets (with sugar) to lubricate tissue; humidify air • Avoid spicy food, alcohol, carbonated beverages, tobacco, and caffeine • If teeth are present, stannous fluoride gel 0.4% (After brushing and flossing, apply in flexible tray—made from mouth models/casts of the patient—or brush onto teeth once a day. Leave in mouth for 5 min, expectorate, and do not eat, drink, or rinse for 30 min) • If candidiasis is superimposed, see below
Brown hairy tongue (see Fig. 7)	Elongated and brown–black stained filiform papillae of the tongue, especially the posterior third	Usually none, unless patient complains of bad breath	• If due to antibiotic or other medication allergy or overdose, alter drugs • If due to nicotine or food staining of overgrown papillae, Langlais' Miracle Paste[a] (brush tongue three times daily with paste and stiff brush until overgrowth is removed) • After overgrowth is removed, if candidiasis remains see below

Table 9 *continued*

Oral disease	Signs	Symptoms	Treatment
Candidiasis/denture stomatitis (see Fig. 8)	Acute atrophic candidiasis: erythematous oral/perioral tissues (lips and commissures; lesions can be generalized or patchy; tongue can be red with papillary atrophy)	Generalized burning pain	Prescriptions vary depending on severity and location of lesions and prosthesis. Continue for 48 h after lesions resolve. (If unresolved, consider ketoconazole or fluconazole)
	Acute pseudomembranous candidiasis (thrush): curdy white plaques that can be rubbed off leaving a red bleeding surface	Can be asymptomatic; often discovered by patient or caregiver when bleeding occurs	• Mycostatin ointment 100 000 units/g (apply liberally to affected area three times daily; remove prosthesis first) or
	Chronic atrophic candidiasis (denture sore mouth/stomatitis): swollen erythematous tissue under dentures; rugae lose their anatomy	Often asymptomatic; sometimes burning pain	• Clotrimazole oral troches 10 mg (or use nystatin pastilles): dissolve one troche five times daily as a lozenge for 2 weeks. Remove prosthesis first *and* (if prosthesis)
	Inflammatory papillary hyperplasia/chronic hyperplastic candidiasis: overgrowth of palatal tissue under denture; can have 'pebble' appearance; often red	Asymptomatic	• Mycostatin oral suspension 100 000 units/ml: soak prosthesis overnight with 1 tsp in 8 oz water
			Note: papillary hyperplasia might require surgical removal of excess tissue
Lichen planus: unknown aetiology; older women are particularly prone (see Fig. 9). (Malignant transformation occurs in 1%–10% of oral cases. Evaluate persistent lesions each year and biopsy every 3–5 years)	Erosive lichen planus: superficial ulceration or red atrophic areas of irregular size and shape; lacy white striae (Wickham's) can surround or be adjacent to red component; often bilateral on buccal mucosa	Red lesions are usually painful	• Minor acute episodes are treated with topical corticosteroids: hydrocortisone acetate ointment 0.5% or triamcinolone acetonide ointment 0.1% or betamethasone valerate ointment 0.1% (Dab on oral lesions until ointment adheres, after each meal and at hs. Occlude with gauze until saturated with saliva)
	Hypertrophic lichen planus: lacy white striae that intersect in a reticular pattern	Usually asymptomatic, but can have a burning or dry sensation	• In severe cases, inject lesions with 0.5–1 ml triamcinolone acetonide 10 mg/ml or 0.5 ml methylprednisolone acetate to reduce pain. For severe pain: prednisone 10 mg (four tabs four times daily for 4 days; then decrease by one tab for each of the next 3 days) or dexamethasone elixir 0.5 mg/5 ml (rinse with 1 tsp four times daily for 2 min, then swallow; withdraw gradually)
	Plaque form of lichen planus: presents as white patches (leucoplakia)	Asymptomatic	
	Grinspan's syndrome: diabetes mellitus, hypertension, and lichen planus	Symptomatology reflects type of lichen planus	

Table 9 *continued*

Oral disease	Signs	Symptoms	Treatment
Aphthous ulcer (usually recurrent)	Single or multiple yellow–grey ulcers with red halos. Shape and size varies	Can be very painful ulcers, usually on buccal and labia mucosa and/or dorsum of tongue or floor of mouth	• Supportive and palliative care are indicated, using the same drugs as for lichen planus (above) only if lesions are distinguished from ulcers of herpes, varicella, or Coxsackie viruses. If in doubt, until diagnosis is certain use diphenhydramine hydrochloride elixir 12.5 mg/5 ml (rinse with 1 tbs before each meal and hs)
	Minor aphthae ('canker' sores): single or multiple round to ovoid ulcers <1 cm; heals in 10–14 days with no scarring; variable recurrence		• Tetracycline rinse or systemic drugs can reduce the duration and symptoms: tetracycline HCl 250 mg (two tabs four times daily for 2 days, then one tab four times daily for 3 days) or four times daily, dissolve one tab in 1 tsp water and rinse with suspension for 3–5 min then swallow
	Major aphthae (Sutton's disease, Miculicz's scarring aphthous): multiple ulcers ≥1 cm; heals in 4–6 weeks with scarring; recurs more often		
	Recurrent herpetiform ulcerations: herpetiform-like clusters with no viruses present; very numerous		
Traumatic ulcer (can be caused by sharp restoration, tooth, or prosthesis, or by ill-fitting prosthesis, facial injury, ischaemia at the site of an injection, chemical burn, e.g. aspirin, or food burn, e.g. pizza) (see Fig. 10)	When it is acute, usually a single yellow–grey ulcer with a red halo that pales as it heals. Shape and size vary. Most often found on buccal mucosa, palate, tongue, and floor of the mouth. Should heal in 7–14 days, without secondary infection if source of trauma is eliminated	Depending on the aetiology, might or might not be painful. If it is on the bucca mucosa, patients can bite it accidentally because of the oedema or nervously 'chew' on it making it worse, allowing a secondary infection to develop	• Remove all possible aetiologies: adjust dentures, smooth sharp aspects of teeth, calculus, or restorations
			• Apply topical corticosteroid ointment with a cotton swab to relieve pain and reduce inflammation (see lichen planus)
			• If there is regional lymphadenopathy, secondary infection is likely. Drug of choice is penicillin VK 500 mg (one tab four times daily, 1 h before meals and hs). Treat with erythromycin if patient is allergic to penicillin
			• Consider undiagnosed disease, e.g. diabetes or epidermoid cancer, if lesion does not heal with 7–14 days of treatment

Table 9 *continued*

Oral disease	Signs	Symptoms	Treatment
Epulis fissuratum (aetiology is usually ill-fitting or broken dentures) (see Figs 11 and 12)	Hyperplastic tissue, sometimes erythematous, on the buccal vestibule where the denture is broken or the fit is the poorest. Can be ulcerated under the loose hanging tissue; loose tissue often packs food under it	Patient usually complains about poor fit of denture, or of packing food under denture. If epulis is ulcerated (traumatic ulcer from the denture), patient might complain of pain	• Denture should be relined (additional acrylic placed on tissue surface of denture to improve fit), remade, or repaired if appropriate • If epulis is small, removal of prosthesis, followed by warm salt water rinses three times daily, followed by gentle rubbing of tissue, might reverse condition • If epulis is moderate to large, it will have to be surgically removed by either scalpel or electrosurgery. A soft reline in the denture can serve as a stent until healing is complete and the denture can be remade
Squamous cell carcinoma (most common type of oral cancer) (see Fig. 13)	Often mistaken for traumatic or aphthous ulcer. Appearance can be similar. Usually found on floor of mouth or posterolateral border of tongue	Usually asymptomatic. Patient might see a 'denture ulcer'	• After excisional or incisional biopsy as appropriate confirms diagnosis, refer to dentist for preradiation care (prophylaxis, any urgent restorations or extractions, followed by a rigid daily fluoride regimen and meticulous home care) • Oral cancers are among those with the worst prognosis. Early diagnosis is essential • See xerostomia/radiation caries

tab, tablet; tbs, tablespoon; tsp, teaspoon.

[a] Langlais Miracle Paste, 8 oz pumice and one tube toothpaste mixed to creamy consistency.

Adapted from Lundeen et al. (1985), Glass et al. (1986), and Darnell and Saunders (1990).

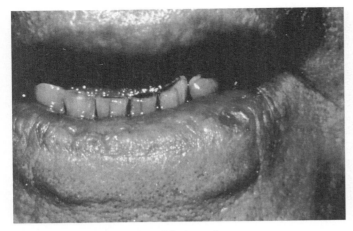

Fig. 3 Actinic cheilitis/keratosis of the lower lip.

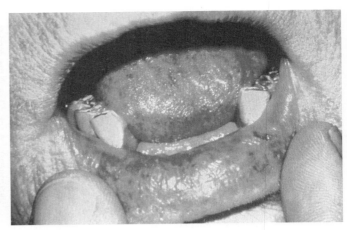

Fig. 6 Soft tissue in a patient with xerostomia.

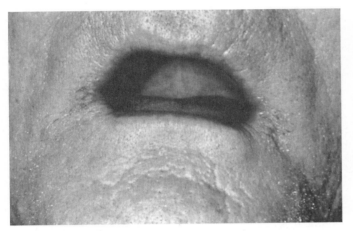

Fig. 4 Angular cheilitis.

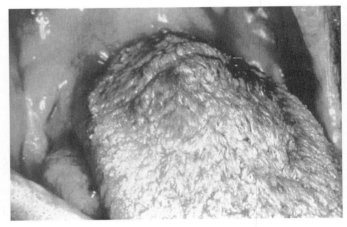

Fig. 7 Brown hairy tongue.

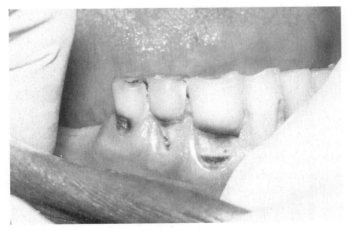

Fig. 5 Root caries in a patient with xerostomia.

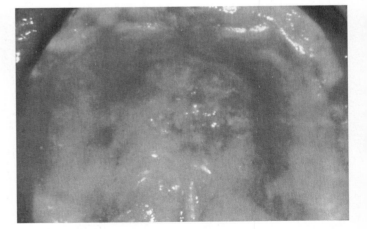

Fig. 8 Candidiasis under denture.

the functional assessment relevant to the resident's ability to perform oral hygiene. Section L includes the characterization of any oral and nutritional problems that might make it difficult to eat (such as the effects of xerostomia). Section M indicates the presence or absence of oral debris, removable prostheses, missing but not replaced teeth, dental problems, soft tissue lesions, or daily oral hygiene care (Table

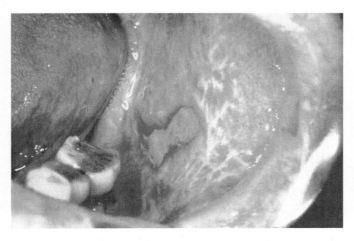

Fig. 9 Oral lichen planus.

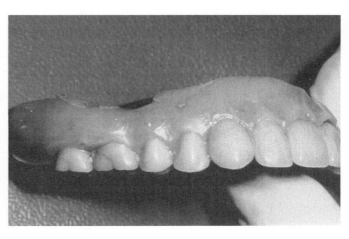

Fig. 12 Broken denture.

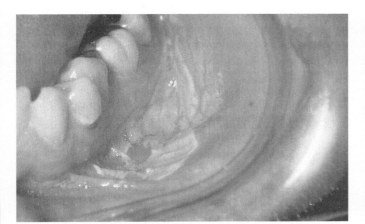

Fig. 10 Aspirin burn.

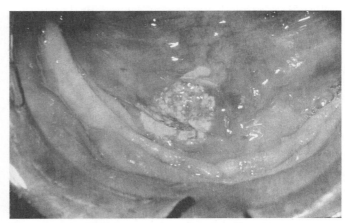

Fig. 13 Squamous cell carcinoma on the floor of the mouth.

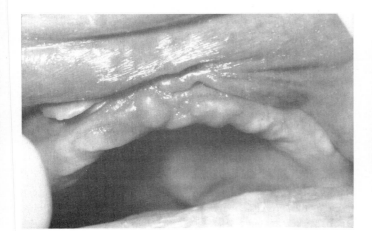

Fig. 11 Epulis fissuratum from loose or broken denture.

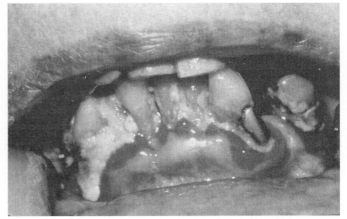

Fig. 14 Severe periodontal infection with gingival abscess.

10). When the Minimum Data Set form indicates that there is a problem with the resident's oral health, the resident should be referred to a dentist for evaluation and necessary treatment.

The OBRA legislation also requires the development of an interdisciplinary care plan for nursing facility residents. By becoming familiar with the full oral assessment, participating non-dental

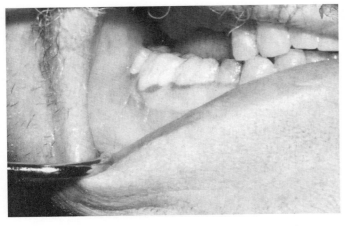

Fig. 15 Plaque and gingivitis due to neglect of the affected side of an elderly stroke patient.

members of the health-care team will understand the oral health needs of the resident and be better able to co-ordinate the dental care with the rest of the resident's treatment.

Preparation for the oral examination

Gloves

The most important first step in preparing for the oral examination is to wear gloves. There are normally a number of cracks in the epidermis of the hands into which bacteria and viruses can pass. Although the primary reason for wearing gloves is to prevent the transmission of the hepatitis B virus, it is also important to wear them when the patient has an obvious herpetic lesion. In addition, it is advisable to wear gloves when there is no lesion, because some patients have active viruses on the epithelial surface before a lesion develops. Figure 16 shows the finger of a gloveless examiner who contracted herpetic whitlow from a patient who had prodromal herpes simplex type 1.

Face and temporomandibular joint

The examination begins with an observation of the face, with special attention to any unusual features, from moles to skeletal asymmetry to enlargement of the parotids (as seen in chronic alcoholism or diabetes). Then, the examiner should palpate the temporomandibular joint bilaterally just anterior to the tragus (the most anterior eminence of the ear), noting any unilateral or bilateral crepitus, subluxation, or discomfort when the patient opens or closes the mouth. These findings might indicate possible arthritic or other temporomandibular joint dysfunction.

Soft tissue examination

The purpose of the soft tissue examination is to screen for soft tissue pathology resulting from diseases described in Tables 2, 4, and 9, most importantly oral cancer. Six per cent of all cancers in men and 3 per cent in women are oral cancers and they are occurring with increasing frequency in older men. The most common sites for oral cancer are the posterolateral borders of the tongue and the floor of the mouth. In a recent report, the United States Centers for Disease Control announced that the oral cancer survival rate has not improved in 16 years and is declining in black Americans (Centers for Disease Control 1990). The Centers for Disease Control has set a goal of reducing oral cancer deaths by 15 per cent by the year 2000. If doctors and nurses would perform oral cancer screening examinations, this goal would be easier to achieve.

In its dental examination training manual for the recently conducted third National Health and Nutrition Examination Survey, the National Institute of Dental and Craniofacial Research (formerly the National Institute of Dental Research) suggests a particular order for the oral soft tissue examination as described below (National Institute for Dental Research 1989). As in any aspect of the physical examination, it is advisable to follow a routine to avoid missing an important finding. The American Cancer Society suggests practitioners look for the following in an intraoral soft tissue examination: 'fleshy looking buds of tissue; a verrucous flat leucoplakic plaque; infiltrated ulcer; scaly looking lesions; small fissures, or induration' (Engleman and Schackner 1966).

Perioral and oral examination

The perioral and oral soft tissue assessment should involve inspection and bidigital and bimanual palpation. Figure 17 illustrates the routine order of the soft tissue assessment (Brunelle 1989) as follows:

A–D	upper then lower lips and labial mucosa
E	right commissure (corner of the mouth)
F	right buccal mucosa
G, H	left commissure, left buccal mucosa
I, J	maxillary right buccal vestibular mucosa, alveolar mucosa, and gingiva
K, L	maxillary anterior buccal vestibular mucosa, alveolar mucosa, and gingiva
M, N	maxillary left buccal vestibular mucosa, alveolar mucosa, and gingiva
O, P	mandibular left buccal vestibular mucosa, alveolar mucosa, and gingiva
Q, R	mandibular anterior buccal vestibular mucosa, alveolar mucosa, and gingiva
S, T	mandibular right buccal vestibular mucosa, alveolar mucosa, and gingiva
U–W	dorsum of tongue, right lateral, and posterolateral border of tongue, left lateral and posterolateral border of tongue
X	floor of the mouth
Y	ventral surface of the tongue

Note that grasping the tip of the tongue with a piece of gauze will facilitate full protrusion and examination of the tongue margins, especially the most posterolateral borders, which are visible only with a point light source such as a pocket light or headlight.

Recorded observations during the soft tissue examination should include abnormalities in colour, size, consistency, texture, and pigmentation, and the presence of swelling, ulceration, vesicles, bullae, coating, or surface abnormalities. Any abnormalities should be described in standard dermatological terms, including size and location (orientation of landmarks).

Table 10 Extracts from the Minimum Data Set sections pertinent to oral health

Section E: Physical functioning and structural problems
1. ADL self-performance (code for resident's performance over all shifts during last 7 days—not including set-up)
   0 Independent No help or oversight *or* help/oversight provided only once or twice during the last 7 days
   1 Supervision Oversight help only provided 3+ times during the last 7 days *or* additional assistance provided only once or twice during the last 7 days
   2 Limited assistance Resident highly involved in process—received physical help in guided manoeuvring of limbs or other non-weight-bearing assistance 3+ times *or* more help provided once or twice during the last 7 days
   3 Extensive assistance While resident performed part of activity over the last 7-day period, help of the following type(s) provided 3 or more times:
      Weight-bearing support
      Full staff performance during part (but not all) of the last 7 days
   4 Total dependence Full staff performance of activity during entire 7 days

2. ADL support provided (code for most support provided over all shifts during the last 7 days regardless of resident's self-performance classification)
   0 No set-up or physical help from staff
   1 Set-up help only
   2 One-person physical assistance
   3 Two+ person physical assistance

g **Personal hygiene**
   How resident maintains personal hygiene, including brushing teeth

4 **Body control problems** (Check all that apply during last 7 days)
   (g) Hand—lack of dexterity (e.g. problem using toothbrush)
   (h) None of the above

Section L: Oral/nutritional status
1. **Oral problems** (Check all that apply)
   (a) Chewing problem
   (b) Swallowing problem
   (c) Mouth pain
   (d) None of the above

1. **Nutritional problems**
   (a) Complaints about the taste of many foods
   (b) Insufficient fluid: dehydrated
   (c) Did not consume all/almost all liquids provided during the last 3 days
   (d) None of the above

2. **Nutritional approaches**
   (b) Feeding tube
   (c) Mechanically altered diet
   (d) None of the above

Section M: oral/dental status
1. **Oral status and disease prevention** (Check all that apply)
   (a) Debris (soft easily movable substances) present in mouth prior to going to bed at night
   (b) Has dentures and/or removable bridge
   (c) Some/all natural teeth lost—does not have or does not use dentures (or partial plates)
   (d) Broken, loose, or carious teeth
   (e) Inflamed gums (gingiva), oral abscesses, swollen or bleeding gums, ulcers, or rashes
   (f) Daily cleaning of teeth/dentures
   (g) None of the above

ADL, activities of daily living.

Reproduced with permission from Health Care Financing Administration (1990).

Salivation

Both parotid glands should be expressed to ensure open ducts, and the sublingual caruncles (openings to the ducts) should be examined. The amount and consistency of the saliva should be observed. Thin, serous fluid is normal. Thick, ropy saliva is suggestive of abnormalities, such as xerostomia from Sjögren's syndrome or other causes, such as diabetes or sinusitis.

Other considerations

The overall clinical impression based on the soft tissue examination

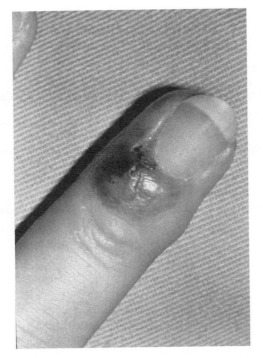

Fig. 16 Whitlow on the finger of an examiner who was gloveless at the time of the examination.

Examination of dentition

The National Institute of Dental Research survey of the oral health status of American adults in 1985 to 1986 found that the number of completely edentulous adults over the age of 65 years is decreasing (National Institute of Dental Research 1987). During the period of 1971 to 1986, the edentulous rate steadily decreased from 55 to 34 per cent, and the decline is expected to continue.

Forensic identification

Cottone and Standish note that there can be 32 teeth present in a given individual's mouth, each with five surfaces, for a total of 160 possible surfaces. This allows for an infinite number of combinations of missing teeth, caries, restorations, and prostheses (Cottone and Standish 1982). Thus, each person has a unique pattern of dentition. When associated with radiographic examination of the teeth and jaws, dental examination of an unknown individual can provide positive identification. In addition, certain dental characteristics are indicative of increased age, for example, more darkly stained teeth, more missing teeth, thickened cementum, more attrition, more periodontal disease, and older restorations. Forensic odontologists often assist medical examiners and coroners in identification efforts, and medical examiners have begun to take courses in forensic odontology.

It is not unusual in a nursing facility for dental prostheses to be lost or taken. When found, prostheses often cannot be returned to the owner because they are not labelled, are often old, and do not fit well. An inexpensive preventive measure is to label each prosthesis, using an emery board, indelible marker, and clear acrylic fingernail polish. The emery board is used to roughen the most posterolateral outside (non-tissue, polished) surface of the maxillary denture, or the most posteromedial outside surface of the mandibular denture.

should also consider other factors, for instance, halitosis and its possible causes (allergies, periodontal disease, or tooth conditions, such as caries or abscess).

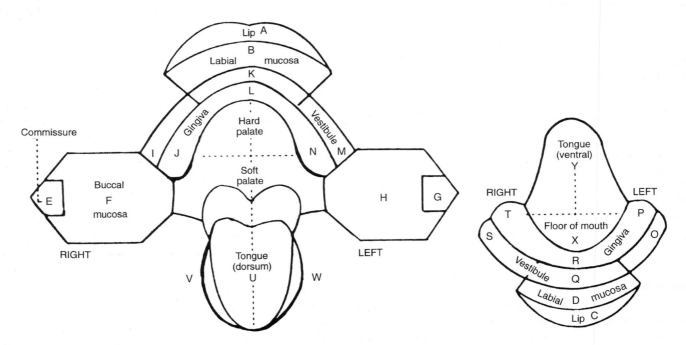

Fig. 17 Routine order of oral soft tissue assessment. (Courtesy of J. Brunelle, National Institute of Dental Research, 1990.)

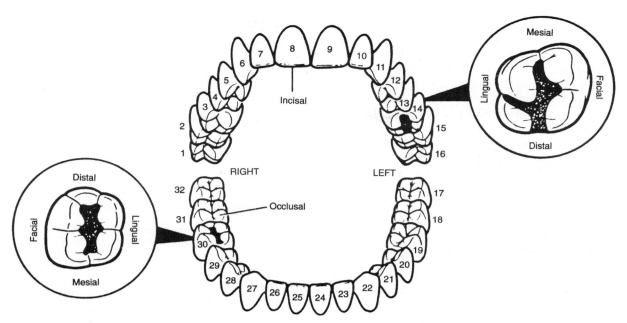

Fig. 18 Universal numbering system and naming of tooth surfaces.

The indelible marker can then be used to label this roughened surface. When the label is dry, one or two coats of the fingernail polish can be applied. This labelling can last up to a year or more (American Society for Geriatric Dentistry and American Dental Association 1977; Saunders and Martin 1993a, b).

Charting the dentition

If the doctor is to conduct oral screening examinations in a nursing facility or other setting, it is helpful if he or she is familiar with dental terminology. There are six anterior teeth in each arch (maxillary and mandibular): two (right and left) central incisors, two lateral incisors, and two cuspid/canines. The ten posterior teeth in each arch are the four premolars (two first bicuspids, and two second bicuspids) and the six molars (two first, two second, and two third molars).

Figure 18 illustrates the universal numbering system for the dentition. Begin with tooth 1 as the most posterior tooth (third molar) in the maxillary right quadrant, count consecutively to the most posterior tooth on the other side of the arch (16), drop to the mandibular leftmost posterior tooth (17), and continue to the most posterior tooth on the mandibular right (32). Note that the third molars are increasingly absent and considered to be unnecessary for the species because of our soft diet. Maxillary and mandibular first bicuspids are often missing in patients who have had full-mouth orthodontics.

Figure 18 also indicates how to name each tooth surface properly. The surface of a tooth that is closest to an imaginary midline drawn vertically in front of the central incisors is termed 'mesial', the surface that is farthest is 'distal', the side closest to the cheeks or lips is 'facial', the side closest to the tongue or palate is 'lingual', the chewing surface of a posterior tooth is 'occlusal', and the biting surface of an anterior tooth is 'incisal'. Restorations are described by the tooth number and surface(s) on which the restorations are placed, using the first letter of each surface to represent that surface. For example,

the black shaded area in the restoration on the right side of the mouth in Fig. 18 is a 30 O amalgam (silver-coloured alloy), while the one on the left is a 14 DOL amalgam. Other possible restorations include crowns, fixed partial dentures (or 'bridges'), tooth-coloured filling materials, and other castings (inlays and onlays).

In an examination of the dentition, missing or defective restorations should be noted, as should missing, carious, fractured, loose, or broken teeth, and the presence or absence of plaque and/or calculus. Particular attention should be paid to any wincing or reported discomfort/pain and the presence of any tardive dyskinesia or other facial tics, tremors, or athetoid movements.

Evaluation of prostheses

Removable complete and removable partial dentures should be evaluated for cleanliness, integrity, fit, stability, and retention. The National Health and Nutrition Examination Survey III instructions provide the basis for the evaluation of prostheses outlined here.

The integrity of the prosthesis is evaluated by removing it from the mouth and inspecting it for fractures, cracks, holes, or other defects of the base material, and missing or chipped prosthetic teeth. Removable partial dentures are also examined for broken clasps or other portions of the framework.

Excessive tooth wear is determined by examining the posterior teeth of the prosthesis. Excessive wear of occlusal surfaces indicates a reduced vertical dimension of occlusion (reduced facial height from nose to chin), and places the patient at risk for angular cheilitis and temporomandibular joint dysfunction.

The inside (tissue surface) of the prosthesis should be examined for the presence of a temporary reline material (usually placed by the patient in an ill-fitting denture to try to improve the fit), tissue conditioner, or denture adhesive. The presence of any of these liners indicates that the prosthesis might not have the proper fit.

The denture is then replaced in the patient's mouth and assessed for its ability to withstand horizontal dislodging forces. Stability of a complete denture is assessed by using the index fingers to apply unilateral alternating forces to the first molar occlusal surface areas (just posterior to the bicuspids/premolars); then by moving the denture laterally without rotating or torquing it. If the prosthesis moves 2 mm or more, the denture lacks stability and probably relates poorly to the underlying bone.

Finally, the denture is evaluated for its ability to withstand vertical dislodging forces by asking the patient to open the mouth comfortably wide, without strain. If the denture dislodges, it lacks retention and probably relates poorly to the underlying soft tissue.

Consultation and referral

If the doctor finds any of the oral problems described in this chapter, a tentative diagnosis should be made, appropriate treatment given, and the patient referred to a dentist for further evaluation, diagnosis, and treatment of any dental problems or oral lesions for which the aetiology or differential diagnosis is uncertain. It is important to refer patients for orodental evaluation in the presence of medical conditions, such as dialysis, chemotherapy, or radiation therapy, associated with oral pathology (Tables 2–9).

It is most important for a patient who will be receiving radiation to the head and neck region for the treatment of cancer to see a dentist at least 2 weeks prior to the radiotherapy. The dentist will develop a plan to reduce the risk for severe sequelae from the radiation. Radiation to the head and neck of over 60 Gy is sufficient to destroy the secretory function of all salivary glands, rendering the patient xerostomic and at high risk for radiation caries. Radiation caries, if not treated promptly, will probably progress and necessitate dental extractions. Postextraction osteoradionecrosis might also result from local ischaemia due to radiation-induced decrease in blood flow to the jaw. Dental referral prior to radiotherapy will provide an oral hygiene regimen (daily brushing, flossing, and topical fluoride treatment) that can prevent the progressive development of radiation caries, extractions, and osteoradionecrosis.

Consultation with the dentist on the use of topical fluorides or chemotherapeutic agents, such as chlorhexidine gluconate (an antimicrobial rinse that has met with some success in limiting periodontal disease), is advisable when the therapy is initiated by the doctor. Chlorhexidine should be considered for all patients with medical conditions that compromise the performance of oral self-care, including Alzheimer's disease, stroke, and parkinsonism.

Dental consultations usually are possible for patients in a variety of both outpatient and inpatient settings, such as a community or hospital clinic, adult day health care, hospice, geriatric assessment units or outpatient clinics, hospital-based home care and other homebound settings, nursing facilities, and respite care settings. In the United States, more dentists are beginning to use portable equipment to treat patients in some of these sites. The number of dentists practising with portable equipment has increased because of the new nursing home law requiring that nursing facilities will be 'directly responsible for the dental care' of their residents. Nursing facilities with at least 200 beds should consider purchasing such equipment and hiring a dentist at least part-time to treat their residents.

When a consultation and/or referral is needed for a patient and there is no dentist of record, alternative services may be available from local dental societies, special interest groups in geriatrics (such as the American Society for Geriatric Dentistry, the American Association of Hospital Dentistry, or the Academy of Dentistry for the Handicapped), contract or consultant dentists to nursing facilities, dental directors of these locations, dental specialists, and dental schools. More dentists are being trained in the principles of geriatric dentistry and are ready to become full members of the geriatric interdisciplinary health-care team.

References

American Dental Association, American Academy of Orthopedic Surgeons (1997). Advisory statement: antibiotic prophylaxis for dental patients with total joint replacements. *Journal of the American Dental Association*, **128**, 1004–8.

American Society for Geriatric Dentistry and American Dental Association (1977). *Oral health for long-term care patients*. American Dental Association, Chicago, IL.

Arends, J., Jongebloed, W.L., and Schutkof, J. (1983). Crystalline diameters of enamel near the anatomical surface. An investigation of mature, deciduous and nonerupted human enamel. *Caries Research*, **17**, 97.

Arseni, C. and Ciurea, A.V. (1982). Rhinogenic cerebral abscesses. *Zentralblatt für Neurochirurgie*, **43**, 129.

Baddour, H.M., Durst, N.L., and Tilson, H.B. (1979). Frontal lobe abscesses of dental origin. *Oral Surgery, Oral Medicine, and Oral Pathology*, **47**, 303.

Bates, B. (1987). *A guide to physical examination and history taking*. J.B. Lippincott, Philadelphia, PA.

Baum, B.J. (1981). Evaluation of stimulated parotid saliva flow rate in different age groups. *Journal of Dental Research*, **60**, 1292.

Baum, B.J. (1996). Age changes in salivary glands and salivary secretion. In *Geriatric dentistry: a textbook of oral gerontology* (2nd edn) (ed. P. Holm-Pedersen and H. Löe). Munksgaard, Copenhagen.

Beck, J.D. and Watkins, C. (1992). Epidemiology of nondental oral disease in the elderly. *Clinics in Geriatric Medicine*, **8**, 461–82.

Bodner, L. and Baum, B.J. (1984). Submandibular gland secretory function in young adult and aging rats. *Comparative Biochemical Physiology*, **77**, 235.

Bottomly, W.K. (1979). Physiology of the oral mucosa. *Otolaryngology Clinics of North America*, **12**, 15.

Bourgeois, D., Nihtila, A., and Mersel, A. (1998). Prevalence of caries and edentulousness among 65–74-year-olds in Europe. *Bulletin of the World Health Organization*, **76**, 413–17.

Brewer, N.S., MacCarty, C.S., and Wellman, W.E. (1975). Brain abscess: a review of recent experience. *Annals of Internal Medicine*, **82**, 571.

Brunelle, J.A. (ed.) (1989). *Dental caries in United States children 1986–87*. NIH publication no. 89-2247. National Institute of Dental Research, National Institutes of Health, Bethesda, MD.

Centers for Disease Control (1990). *Morbidity and mortality weekly report: July 13, 1990*. Centers for Disease Control, Department of Health and Human Services, Atlanta, GA.

Cottone, J.A. and Standish, S.M. (1982). *Outline of forensic dentistry*. Year Book, Chicago, IL.

Cuhna, B.A. (1988). *Infectious diseases in the elderly*. PSG Publishing, Littleton.

Dajani, A.S., Taubert, K.A., Wilson, W., *et al.* (1997). Prevention of bacterial endocarditis: recommendations by the AHA. *Journal of the American Medical Association*, **277**, 1794–801.

Darnell, J.A. and Saunders, M.J. (1990). Oral manifestations in the diabetic patient. *Texas Dental Journal*, **107**, 23.

Denham, M.J. (1986). *Infections in the elderly*. MTP Press, Mystic, CT.

Engleman, M.A. and Schackner, S.J. (1966). *Oral cancer examination procedure*. Publication no. 16-100M-3026-PE. American Cancer Society, New York.

Glass, B.J., Kuhel, R.F., and Langlais, R.P. (1986). The treatment of common orofacial conditions. *Dental Clinics of North America*, October.

Grant, D. and Bernick, S. (1972). The periodontium of aging humans. *Journal of Periodontology*, **43**, 660.

Grove, G.L. and Klingman, A.M. (1983). Age-associated changes in human epidermal cell renewal. *Journal of Gerontology*, **38**, 137.

Halstead, C.L., Blozis, G.G., Drinnan, A.J., and Gier, R.E. (1982). *Physical evaluation of the dental patient*. C.V. Mosby, St Louis, MO.

Health Care Financing Administration (1990). *Minimum data set for nursing facility resident assessment and care screening*. Health Care Financing Administration, Department of Health and Human Services, Baltimore, MD.

Health Resources and Services Administration and Bureau of Health Professions (1990). *Fiscal year 1991 applicant handbook faculty training projects in geriatric medicine and dentistry*, Appendix A. Resource Development Section, Primary Care Medical Education Branch, Division of Medicine, Rockville, MD.

Heft, M.W. and Baum, B.J. (1984). Unstimulated and stimulated parotid salivary flow rate in individuals of different ages. *Journal of Dental Research*, **63**, 1182.

Holt, S.C., Ebersole, J., Felton, J., *et al.* (1988). Implantation of *Bacteroides gingivalis* in nonhuman primates initiates progression of periodontitis. *Science*, **239**, 55.

Ito, H., Baum, B.J., and Roth, G.S. (1981). β-Adrenergic regulation of rat parotid gland exocrine protein secretion during aging. *Mechanisms of Aging and Development*, **15**, 177.

Ito, H., Baum, B.J., Uchida, T., *et al.* (1982). Modulation of rat parotid cell α-adrenergic responsiveness at a step subsequent to receptor activation. *Journal of Biological Chemistry*, **257**, 9532.

Jones, J.H. and Mason, D.K. (ed.) (1980). *Oral manifestations of systemic disease*. W.B. Saunders, Philadelphia, PA.

Ketterl, W. (1983). Age-induced changes in the teeth and their attachment apparatus. *International Dental Journal*, **33**, 262.

Kydd, W.L. and Daly, C.H. (1982). The biologic and mechanical effects of stress on oral mucosa. *Journal of Prosthetic Dentistry*, **47**, 317.

Lundeen, R.C., Langlais, R.P., and Terezhalmy, G.T. (1985). Sunscreen protection for lip mucosa: a review and update for the dentist. *Journal of the American Dental Association*, **111**, 617.

Mackenzie, I.C., Holm-Pedersen, P., and Karring, T. (1996). Age changes in the oral mucous membranes and periodontium. In *Geriatric dentistry: a textbook on oral gerontology* (2nd edn) (ed. P. Holm-Pedersen and H. Löe). Munksgaard, Copenhagen.

Mandel, G.L., Douglas, R.G., and Bennett, J.E. (1979). *Principles and practice of infectious diseases* (2nd edn). Wiley, New York.

Mjor, I.A. (1996). Age changes in the teeth. In *Geriatric dentistry: a textbook of oral gerontology*, (2nd edn), (ed. P. Pedersen and H. Löe). Munksgaard, Copenhagen.

Mobley, C.C., Romeu, J., Cornell, J.E., and Saunders, M.J. (1997). Nutrient profile analysis for elders with removable dental prostheses. *Journal of Dental Research*, **76**, 172.

National Institute of Dental Research (1987). *Oral health of US adults: the national survey of oral health in the US employed adults and seniors, 1985–1986, national findings*. Publication no. 87-2868. National Institute of Dental Research, National Institutes of Health, Bethesda, MD.

National Institute of Dental Research (1989). *National health and nutrition examination survey III (NHANES III) dental examination training manual*. National Institute of Dental Research, National Institutes of Health, Bethesda, MD.

Pack, A.R. (1998). Dental services and needs in developing countries. *International Dental Journal*, **48** (Supplement 1), 239–47.

Pakhomov, G.N. (1996). The World Health Organization's oral health programme (ORH). *FDI World*, **5**, 22–3.

Rana, H., Andersen, R.M., Nakazono, T.T., and Davidson, P.L. (1997). ICS-II USA research design and methodology. *Advances in Dental Research*, **11**, 217–22.

Ring M.E. (1986). *Dentistry: an illustrated history*. H.N. Abrams and C.V. Mosby, St Louis, MO.

Robertson, P.B. and Greenspan, J.S. (1988). *Oral manifestations of AIDS*. Proctor & Gamble, Cincinnati, OH.

Rose, L.F. and Kaye, D. (1990). *Internal medicine for dentistry* (2nd edn). C.V. Mosby, St Louis, MO.

Saunders, M.J. and Martin, W.S. (1993a). *Dental regulations compliance manual for the nursing facility*. American Society for Geriatric Dentistry and South Texas Geriatric Education Center (STGEC), the University of Texas Health Science Center, San Antonio, TX.

Saunders, M.J. and Martin, W.S. (1993b). *Developing a nursing facility dental program: a manual for dental office staff*. American Society for Geriatric Dentistry and South Texas Geriatric Education Center (STGEC), the University of Texas Health Science Center, San Antonio, TX.

Shafer, W.G., Hine, M.K., and Levy, B.M. (1983). *A textbook of oral pathology* (4th edn). W.B. Saunders, Philadelphia, PA.

Ship, J.A. and Puckett, S.A. (1994). Longitudinal study on oral health in subjects with Alzheimer's disease. *Journal of the American Geriatrics Society*, **42**, 57–63.

Tapsoba, H. and Deschamps, J.P. (1997). Promotion of orodental health in adolescents in Africa. *Promotion et Education*, **4**, 26–8 (in French).

Terezhalmy, G.T., Safadi, T.J., Longworth, D.L., and Muehrcke, D.D. (1997). Oral disease burden in patients undergoing prosthetic heart valve implantation. *Annals of Thoracic Surgery*, **63**, 402–4.

van Palenstein Helderman, W. *et al.* (1998). Analysis of epidemiological data on oral diseases in Nepal and the need for a national oral health survey. *International Dental Journal*, **48**, 56–61.

Watson, M.R. and Brown, L.J. (1995). The oral health of United States Hispanics: evaluating their needs and their use of dental services. *Journal of the American Dental Association*, **126**, 789–94.

8.2 Dysphagia

Pam Enderby

The ability to enjoy food and drink in an untroubled and relaxed way contributes to the quality of life of most people. Therefore it is not surprising that swallowing problems can result in a great deal of distress for both patients and their carers.

The oropharyngeal region has evolved multiple co-ordinated functions to ensure that food intake, chewing, and swallowing can be maintained in order to support a healthy life. The functions of the oral cavity—eating, drinking, communicating, swallowing, and smelling—depend upon complex interactions of the muscles of facial expression, the muscles of mastication and deglutition, the oral mucosa, the teeth and periodontal tissues, production and control of saliva, and taste and smell receptors. There is substantial evidence that the prevalence of dysphagia increases with advancing years. Although many of these processes and tissues can remain unaffected in elderly people (Ship *et al.* 1996), ageing may be associated with disease and trauma which, together with their surgical, medical, or radiation therapy, can lead to dysphagia.

An apparent recent increase in the prevalence of dysphagia may be related to better identification. European surveys have suggested that up to 10 per cent of people over 50 years of age experience some difficulty with swallowing (Lindgren and Janzon 1991). A recent study of older patients in long-term care found that the prevalence of undernutrition was close to 50 per cent and was significantly associated with eating and swallowing problems (Keller 1993). In this chapter we focus on dysphagia related specifically to dysfunction of the oral and pharyngeal phases. Dysphagia associated with oesophageal disease is discussed in Chapter 8.3.

Effects of ageing on swallowing

Taste and smell

The evolution of the chemosensory functions of taste and smell was presumably determined by the survival advantages of determining the palatability of foods and drinks, the identification of desirable nutrients, and the detection of toxins. The pleasurable aspects of taste and smell encourage the effort of eating and drinking in sufficient quantities to maintain a healthy diet and support active life. Taste is served by taste buds in the mouth, the pharynx, and the larynx that are innervated by branches of the facial, glossopharyngeal, and vagus nerves (Wysocki and Gilbert 1989). The tactile and temperature sensations in the tongue arise from the lingual branch of the trigeminal nerve, and these perceptions interact in an indistinguishable way with those of taste and smell to produce the composite sensation of flavour (Schiffman 1993). Age-associated changes in taste and smell are discussed in Chapter 18.17.

Chewing

Chewing involves many tissues of the orofacial region, including the teeth, the periodontium, saliva, oral mucosa, and intact neuromuscular co-ordination. Older people are more likely than other age groups to have lost some or all of their teeth, and this will have an effect upon chewing. Evidence indicates that tooth loss affects objective measures of masticatory efficiency (Chauncey *et al.* 1984). There is consensus in recent literature that masticatory efficiency in denture wearers is approximately 75 per cent lower than in people with intact natural dentition. This is due to the reduction in anterior masseter muscle bulk which rapidly follows loss of dentition (Kasai *et al.* 1994). Apart from its association with defective dentition, the influence of age on chewing efficiency is not clear. Older people appear to chew their food for longer and use more chews for each bolus than do younger individuals. One radiological study of 56 elderly people, who were not complaining of swallowing difficulties, found that two-thirds had abnormalities of the oral phase of ingestion (Ekberg and Feinberg 1991). Although sensation of the tip of the tongue remains intact with ageing, there appears to be loss of sensation in the lateral tongue and the floor of the mouth which may be related to the significant prolongation of the oral phase of swallowing in healthy elderly people.

Pharyngo-oesophageal function

The anterior elevation of the larynx, which is important in ensuring the good seal with the epiglottis that prevents aspiration, is reduced and somewhat delayed in normal elderly people. Pharyngeal peristalsis is significantly slowed at ages above 60, but although the cricopharyngeal opening time has been found to be prolonged by some investigators others have found it shortened. There is agreement that the release time is different from that found in younger people (Jaradeh 1994).

The oesophageal phase of swallowing in normal healthy elderly people is delayed because of the longer upper oesophageal sphincter relaxation time, reduced motility, reduced upper oesophageal sphincter pressure (Fulp *et al.* 1990), and less efficient peristalsis (see Chapter 8.3).

The swallowing process

Once food has been taken into the mouth, the lips form a seal and the food is retained in the anterior part of the mouth by the elevation of the tongue and the lowering of the soft palate. This enables the subject to continue breathing at the same time as preparing the bolus for swallowing. The tongue propels the bolus between the teeth and, assisted by pressure from the facial musculature within the cheeks, returns it from the sulcus back into the centre of the mouth. These processes comprise what is known as the preparatory phase and allow the food or liquid to be manipulated prior to the initiation of the swallow. During the preparatory stage many factors are involved in positioning the bolus, including adequate dentition, sufficient masticatory muscle strength, and good labial and buccal tone and strength (in order to retain the bolus within the mouth and avoid leakage) together with appropriate thermal and tactile sensitivity. Once the bolus is prepared it is transported to the back of the tongue in readiness for initiation of the swallow. The transition from the preparatory to the initiation phase has not been well described, but recent reports have suggested that the consistency of the food bolus in the mouth determines when the swallowing reflex will be triggered and concluded that sensory input from the oral cavity receptors may be critical (Palmer et al. 1992). An effective swallow is dependent upon a brisk movement of the back of the tongue energetically propelling the bolus into the pharynx. The method of this propulsion is said to change with age, with some loss of power and efficiency in later life.

During the initiation of the swallow, reflex activity stimulates a complex interdependent series of movements. The soft palate elevates against the forward pressure of the pharyngeal wall, preventing nasal regurgitation, respiration stops, the larynx elevates, the vocal cords adduct, the epiglottis lowers in order to prevent aspiration and creates a patent pathway down into the oesophagus, and the subglottic pressure alters to facilitate the passage of the bolus. With the passage of the bolus through the pharynx, the cricopharyngeal sphincter relaxes so that it can pass into the upper oesophagus. Many studies have suggested that, compared with younger people, normal healthy older subjects have a delayed initiation of the swallow and its related activities. Robbins et al. (1992) reported an increase in the penetration of liquids and solids into the laryngeal vestibule of older subjects, but no aspiration of the bolus below the level of the vocal cords into the trachea in healthy older people. This may be related to a delay in triggering the swallow reflex.

Dysphagic pathologies

The most common causes of oropharyngeal dysphagia in older people are associated with cerebrovascular and neurological diseases, including Parkinson's disease, motor neurone disease, myasthenia gravis, and Alzheimer's disease. Two types of muscular dystrophy may produce dysphagia in later life: myotonic dystrophy (which usually presents before the age of 60) and oculopharyngeal muscular dystrophy. Both are autosomal dominant disorders. They can affect the strength, speed, and co-ordination of the musculature, resulting in effortful, inefficient, or absent ability to eat and swallow. Head and neck cancer can have a dramatic affect on swallowing as a result of surgical resection of structures and radiation, which can destroy salivary glands and cause laryngeal and pharyngeal fibrosis. Other systemic diseases, including arthritis, diabetes, and pulmonary disease, may also be associated with some degree of dysphagia.

Although salivary gland function appears to be unimpaired in healthy older persons (Ship et al. 1995), many medical problems and their treatments (particularly some medications) cause salivary gland dysfunction and dry mouth which can lead to problems with chewing and tasting and particular difficulty in the initiation of swallowing. Patients with xerostomia associated with medications may be at risk of developing aspiration pneumonia (Ship et al. 1996).

Assessment of patients with dysphagia

Specific examination of patients within 24 h of hospital admission for stroke has been associated with an increased detection of dysphagia and reduction in mortality and morbidity (Barer 1989). It has been argued that routine screening for dysphagic problems should be adopted in the clinical assessments of elderly patients with a broader range of presenting problems, as many may have mild to moderate swallowing difficulties which have been undetected for some time. Detection of dysphagic problems can improve therapy and nursing care and prevent impairment of nutritional status, loss of weight, and aspiration pneumonia. There is no inevitable association between consistent aspiration of food or liquid into the airway and aspiration pneumonia, but several studies have shown that patients who continually aspirate are at enhanced risk of pneumonia.

The purpose of assessing oropharyngeal disorders is to diagnose specific swallowing disorders and to inform the choice of treatment programmes. The most common methods of evaluating swallowing competency are the clinical or bedside evaluation, studies using videofluoroscopy or modified barium swallows, and fibre-optic endoscopy. Manometry is useful in research but is not yet a generally valuable investigative technique in oropharyngeal dysphagia, except for the evaluation of cricopharyngeal dysfunction.

Bedside assessment

Swallowing can be disrupted at many different stages, but the following are the most common.

1. Difficulty in retaining the bolus because of poor lip seal leading to dribbling and food escape.
2. Difficulty in chewing the bolus or forming the food into a bolus: the food may be caught in the buccal sulcus or under the tongue. The patient will go on chewing for what appears to be a long time and a swallow may not be triggered.
3. Difficulty in triggering a swallow: the bolus may be formed but the patient is unable to initiate a swallow and the bolus will remain in the mouth.
4. Ineffective swallow reflex: the tongue may be too weak to propel the bolus into the pharynx; the soft palate may not rise efficiently, leading to nasal regurgitation; poor laryngeal elevation will lead to food penetrating to the level of the vocal cords.
5. Inefficient laryngeal protection: unilateral laryngeal elevation or inadequate vocal cord abduction will lead to food penetrating below the level of the vocal cords. This may be silent or can cause coughing and choking.

6. Cricopharyngeal spasm: this will result in the patient trying time and time again to push the bolus into the oesophagus. Patients will complain of a feeling of food being stuck in the throat.

Many different bedside dysphagic assessments are available, as the majority of institutions have designed their own. They frequently include the following:

- taking a careful case history from the patient (including feeding and swallowing function);
- identifying any orofacial abnormalities;
- observing cognitive and behavioural difficulties (the patient needs to be able to pace feeding, sequence, and co-operate with the task);
- noting the vocal quality (a wet, gurgly, weak, or absent voice has been associated with dysphagia);
- observing the ability to produce a voluntary cough;
- observing the patient's alertness and head and trunk posture;
- considering degree of interest in food;
- noting the speed of eating and drinking.

The gag reflex is no longer regarded as having clinical relevance as it has not been found to be indicative of swallowing problems and is absent in almost 20 per cent of normal people (Leder 1996).

The standardized swallow assessment (Fig. 1) is a quick and simple method of identifying the majority of patients who do, or do not, have swallowing problems. The assessment can be carried out by any trained health-care professional, but it is important that he or she understands the implications of the relevant features. For example, it may be necessary to ensure that the examiner understands the term 'wet voice' and can distinguish an effective from an ineffective cough.

For those patients who are able to eat or swallow a little, a timed swallowing test is indicative of swallowing abnormality. The examiner uses 150 ml of tap water in a standard glass, and the neck area of the patient is exposed so that the number of swallows can be counted by observing the thyroid cartilage. The swallowing speed in millilitres per second and the number of swallows for the volume are calculated. In a study by Nathadwarawala et al. (1994), the speed of swallow was found to be significantly slower in patients who either perceived a swallowing problem or who had abnormal symptoms or signs of dysphagia on full evaluation compared with those who did not. Some of the patients in this study who had abnormal signs had not complained of dysphagic symptoms.

Videofluorographic assessment

In many cases it remains difficult to predict the likelihood of aspiration from a patient's clinical signs and symptoms. Many studies have reported previously undetected aspiration in patients evaluated by videofluoroscopic barium swallow examination (Veis and Logemann 1985). Therefore there will be a proportion of patients needing examination with either a modified barium swallow or video-fluoroscopy. These examinations allow dynamic viewing of the oral, pharyngeal, and laryngeal functions in swallowing boluses of various consistencies. It will also demonstrate clearly where there is laryngeal penetration and aspiration. Unfortunately, there are some limitations in using videofluoroscopy with a frail older person. The examination is expensive and is usually only available in environments which can be threatening and intimidating (Wheeler 1995).

Examination requires a degree of co-operation from the patient and is only justifiable if it is likely to lead to changes in the management plan. Although Groher (1994a) calls for a greater use of video-fluoroscopy to inform dysphagia treatment, others have questioned its relevance in the clinical management of stroke patients (Holas et al. 1994) (see below).

The risks of aspiration

Opinions differ on the magnitude of the risk of pneumonia, dehydration, and death associated with aspiration. One study of 114 consecutive stroke patients found that aspiration increased the risk for developing pneumonia by a factor of 6.95 but was not associated with dehydration or death during the subacute phase of stroke (Holas et al. 1994). However, in a study of 121 consecutive patients with acute stroke, patients with absent normal swallow on bedside assessment had significantly higher risk of chest infections, poor nutritional status, death, disability, increased length of hospital stay, and institutional care (Smithard et al. 1996). When other factors were taken into account in this study, dysphagia remained as an independent predictor of outcome only in regard to fatality. This study suggested that the use of videofluoroscopy in detecting aspiration did not add to the value of the bedside assessment and these authors question its value as a routine screening tool.

Patients may aspirate prior to, during, or following a swallow. Aspiration prior to a swallow is usually related to poor tongue control of the bolus. The back of the tongue is normally elevated while the bolus is being prepared so that the airway can remain open and it is possible to continue breathing; this also helps the enjoyment of the taste. If the patient has poor control of the back of the tongue, small particles of food may escape into the open airway while the food is being chewed. This may or may not lead to coughing according to the sensitivity and efficiency of the rest of the swallow mechanism.

Aspiration during the swallow is usually associated with a poor laryngeal seal; either the epiglottis may not be tipping correctly over the laryngeal inlet, or the larynx itself may not elevating symmetrically to form a good seal against the epiglottis. A third possibility is related to mistiming of the epiglottic and laryngeal closure, resulting in part of the bolus escaping into the laryngeal vestibule and part being swallowed normally. Again, the patient may or may not cough depending on the sensitivity and effectiveness of the vocal cord closure.

Aspiration following a swallow may be related to regurgitation into an unprotected airway or associated with a cricopharyngeal spasm such that the bolus is prevented from entering the oesophagus and therefore spills into the larynx.

Management of dysphagia

Dysphagia associated with disorders of the oral motor, sensory, and pharyngeal structures is dealt with here. Dysphagia associated with oesophageal pathology is described in Chapter 8.3.

It is evident from the previous description that the approach to the management of dysphagia must be related to the clinical findings and the underlying disorder.

Conservative management

Conservative management of dysphagia is frequently led by speech and language therapists with dieticians and nurses playing a major

DYSPHAGIA SCREENING TEST
SAFE SWALLOWING ASSESSMENT

Patient's name _____ Ward _____ Consultant _____

Date _____ Time _____ Assessor's name _____

☐ ☐ Please tick large and small boxes

DO NOT ASSESS IF PATIENT
- **HAS WET/GURGLY VOICE AND/OR**
- **IS UNABLE TO CLEAR SECRETIONS FROM MOUTH OR PHARYNX AND/OR**
- **IF YOU SUSPECT THE PATIENT WILL BE UNABLE TO COMPLY WITH THE TEST**

CAN PATIENT MAINTAIN
CONCENTRATION FOR TEST?

SIT PATIENT UPRIGHT

Give one 5-ml teaspoon water → Major problems ☐ → ☐ No attempt to swallow / ☐ Water leaks straight out of mouth → Patient—NBM Refer to S & LT

☐ Some attempt to swallow or no problems

NB Some of the problems listed below may still occur

Give 2nd 5-ml teaspoon water → Problems ☐ → ☐ Coughing/throat clearing / ☐ Choking / ☐ Breathlessness / ☐ Wet/gurgly voice after / ☐ Any other reasons you feel swallowing unsafe → Patient—NBM Refer to S & LT

☐ No problems

Give 3rd 5-ml teaspoon water → Problems ☐ → ☐ Coughing/throat clearing / ☐ Choking / ☐ Breathlessness / ☐ Wet/gurgly voice after / ☐ Any other reasons you feel swallowing unsafe → Patient—NBM Refer to S & LT

☐ No problems

Give half glass water → Problems ☐ → ☐ Coughing/throat clearing / ☐ Choking / ☐ Breathlessness / ☐ Wet/gurgly voice after / ☐ Any other reasons you feel swallowing unsafe → Patient—NBM Refer to S & LT

☐ No problems

Free fluids

Observe patient eating solid food → Problems ☐ → ☐ Coughing/throat clearing / ☐ Very slow eating / ☐ Poor motivation to eat → Refer to S & LT

ALWAYS MAKE SURE
PATIENT IS SITTING
UPRIGHT BEFORE
ATTEMPTING TO EAT

REPEAT ASSESSMENT IF PATIENT DETERIORATES

Be aware that some patients will show no observable sign of aspiration. Chest infections or general deterioration in health may indicate requirement for videofluoroscopy assessment.

Fig. 1 The standardized swallow assessment: NBM, nil by mouth; S&LT, speech and language therapists.

role. Most management strategies comprise all or some of the following approaches.

The correct head and body position should be maintained while feeding. Logemann *et al.* (1989) have established through controlled trials that postural changes or alterations in head or body position during eating are often easy for the patient to implement and can, in certain cases, improve the speed of swallowing and reduce aspiration. In particular, these authors examined the effect of rotating the head to the weaker side, causing the cricopharyngeal anterior–posterior opening diameter to increase so that a greater percentage of the bolus could be swallowed. Other studies have investigated the use of tucking the chin in when swallowing. This head position shifts the tongue base and epiglottis posteriorly, thus narrowing the pharynx and laryngeal entrance. It has been suggested that these changes provided more airway protection from aspiration (Rasley *et al.* 1993).

Modifications to the consistency of food and fluid have been found to be effective. Whereas some patients with cricopharyngeal spasm may find it easier to swallow fluids or slightly thickened fluids, persons with other dysphagic conditions, particularly associated with oral phase problems and with bolus preparation, may benefit from a smooth semisolid diet. It is generally suggested that patients are given moderately sized mouthfuls and encouraged to pause between each mouthful. It is also recommended that patients are given small but frequent meals to avoid fatigue and to ensure that the food remains attractive and at the appropriate temperature.

Increasing the nutrient density of food is a sensible contribution to conservative management of dysphagic patients. Fatigue is known to be associated with a reduction in performance, poor nutrition, and an increased likelihood of aspiration. Therefore high-calorie low-volume foods are valuable.

Experimenting with the placement of food and fluids within the mouth can lead to improvements in swallowing. Some patients respond better if food is placed at the back of the tongue where it is less likely to leak from the lips and is more likely to stimulate a swallow. This is recommended for patients with poor tongue control. The use of special spoons, spouted cups, or syringes to place food accurately have been described (Scott and Austin 1994).

Consideration of the environment associated with mealtimes is sensible. Some patients will be embarrassed by their problems and will eat with greater confidence if they are in a calm and private environment. Unfortunately, many patients are in institutional care where privacy can be difficult to provide. Dysphagic patients will need some personal attention from a competent assistant. At one extreme the patient may need to have every mouthful given to them and their eating routine to be prompted. At the other extreme they may need no more than to be watched for choking or encouraged to persevere (Kayser-Jones 1996).

Thermal stimulation has been suggested as an effective way of increasing the speed and efficiency of the swallow reflex. Rosenbek *et al.* (1991) investigated the effects of stimulating the faucial pillar with a cooled laryngeal mirror on swallowing liquids. They concluded that it was not possible to predict the response to thermal application on baseline testing and although some patients did improve immediately after the delivery of the intervention, these improvements were not maintained at 1-month follow-up.

A review of these and other more unusual conservative approaches to the treatment of oropharyngeal dysphagia has been undertaken by Langmore and Miller (1994) and includes the evaluation of biofeedback approaches, the use of electromyography, and the reduction of oral hypersensivity.

Alternative modes of nutrition

It is not possible to predict which dysphagic people will develop aspiration pneumonia and which will not. Therefore it is difficult to decide who should be left to feed orally and who should be managed by an alternative form of feeding (Groher 1994*b*). Physicians working with older people are frequently confronted with the problem of establishing effective nutrition for frail dysphagic patients at high risk of aspiration. The tradition has been to opt for a nasogastric tube as a short-term solution while natural recovery and the effects of therapy are observed. Use of a percutaneous endoscopically or radiologically placed gastrostomy for long-term nutrition may then be considered. It is possible that nasogastric tubes increase rather than reduce the risk of aspiration. This risk, together with the discomfort of the tube and its cosmetic effect, have led to earlier and more frequent use of a feeding gastrostomy for patients following stroke (Kohli and Bloch 1995). A review of the use of endoscopic gastrostomies in 161 consecutive elderly patients with stroke concluded that it is a useful and generally well-tolerated procedure but that careful patient selection is essential (Raha and Woodhouse 1994). These authors recommended that gastrostomy should be considered for patients with neurological dysphagia, who are likely to need long-term enteral feeding, or for stroke patients who remain dysphagic for more than 3 to 4 weeks after the event. They suggested that patients intolerant of nasogastric tubes soon after stroke should be considered for gastrostomy earlier. However, the use of gastrostomies for very frail older people needs further evaluation and can raise ethical issues (O'Mahony and McIntyre 1995).

Cricopharyngeal myotomy

Cricopharyngeal myotomy is the most common surgical intervention for acquired dysphagia. A literature review suggests a preponderance of favourable outcomes (Bucholz 1995) but, again, patient selection is important. Cricopharyngeal myotomy has been suggested to be appropriate for patients who have an intact voluntary initiation of swallowing and an adequate propulsion of the bolus generated by the tongue and the pharyngeal constrictors but a demonstrated obstruction to the bolus flow at the cricopharyngeal segment. This may identify a specific subgroup of dysphagic patients. Histochemical and biochemical assessment of the cricopharyngeal muscle of 10 elderly patients with swallowing disorders without defined cause revealed inflammatory cell infiltration of connective tissue and degenerative changes of the muscle fibres (Guly *et al.* 1995).

The management of dysphagia is now accepted as being important owing to its close association with morbidity and fatality. Dysphagia has many factors which interplay; these include social and psychological factors, as well as the mechanical and physiological components, and necessitates a multidisciplinary approach to assessment and treatment.

References

Barer, D. (1989). The natural history and functional consequences of dysphasia after hemispheric stroke. *Journal of Neurology, Neurosurgery and Psychiatry*, 52, 236–41.

Buchholz, D.W. (1995). Cricopharyngeal myotomy may be effective treatment for selected patients with neurogenic oropharyngeal dysphagia. *Dysphagia*, 10, 255–8.

Chauncey, H., Muench, M.E., Kapur, K.K., and Wayler, A.H. (1984). The effect of the loss of teeth on diet and nutrition. *International Dental Journal*, 34, 98–104.

Ekberg, O. and Feinberg, M.J. (1991). Altered swallowing function in elderly patients without dysphagia: radiologic findings in 56 cases. *American Journal of Radiology*, 156, 1181–4.

Fulp, S.R., Dalton, C.B., Castell, J.A., and Castell, D.O. (1990). Age related alterations in human upper esophageal sphincter function. *American Journal of Gastroenterology*, 85, 1569–72.

Groher, M.E. (1994a). The detection of aspiration and videofloroscopy (Editorial). *Dysphagia*, 9, 147–8.

Groher, M.E. (1994b). Determination of the risks and benefits of oral feeding. *Dysphagia*, 9, 233–5.

Guly, J.L., Zhang, K.X., Perie, S., Copin, H., Butler-Browne, G., and Barbet, J.P. (1995). Improvement of dysphagia following cricopharyngeal myotomy in a group of elderly patients. *Annals of Otology, Rhinology and Laryngology*, 104, 603–9.

Holas, M.A., DePippo, K., and Reding, M.J. (1994). Aspiration and relative risk of medical complications following stroke. *Archives of Neurology*, 51, 1051–3.

Jaradeh, S. (1994). Neurophysiology of swallowing in the aged. *Dysphagia*, 9, 218–20.

Kasai, K., Richards, L.C., Kanazawa, E., *et al.* (1994). Relationship between attachment of the superficial masseter muscle and the craniofacial morphology in dentate and edentulous humans. *Journal of Dental Research*, 73, 1142–9.

Kayser-Jones, J. (1996). Mealtime in nursing homes: the importance of individualised care. *Journal of Gerontological Nursing*, 22, 26–31.

Keller, H. (1993). Malnutrition and institutionalised elderly; how and why? *Journal of the American Geriatrics Society*, 41, 1212–18.

Kohli, H. and Bloch, R. (1995). Percutaneous endoscopic gastrostomy: a community hospital experience. *American Surgeon*, 61, 191–3.

Langmore, S. and Miller, R. (1994). Behavioural treatment for adults with oropharyngeal dysphagia. *Archives of Physical Medicine and Rehabilitation*, 75, 1154–60.

Leder, S. (1996). Gag reflex and dysphagia. *Head and Neck*, 18, 138–41.

Lindgren, S. and Janzon, L. (1991). Prevalence of swallowing complaints and clinical findings among 50–79 year old men and women in an urban population. *Dysphagia*, 6, 187–92.

Logemann, J.A., Kaharilas, T.G., Kobara, M., and Vakil, N. (1989). The benefit of head rotation on pharyngoesophageal dysphagia. *Archives of Physical Medicine and Rehabilitation*, 70, 767–71.

Nathadwarawala, K.M., McGroary, A., and Wiles, C. (1994). Swallowing in neurological out-patients: use of a timed test. *Dysphagia*, 9, 120–9.

O'Mahony, D. and McIntyre, A.S. (1995). Artificial feeding for elderly patients after stroke. *Age and Ageing*, 24, 533–5.

Palmer, J.B., Rudin, N.J., Gustavo, L., and Crompton, A.W. (1992). Co-ordination of mastication and swallowing. *Dysphagia*, 7, 187–200.

Raha, S.K. and Woodhouse, K. (1994). The use of percutaneous endoscopic gastrostomy (PEG) in 161 consecutive elderly patients. *Age and Ageing*, 23, 162–3.

Rasley, A., Logemann, J.A., Kahrilas, P.J., Rademaker, A.W., Pauloski, B.R., and Dodds, W.J. (1993). Prevention of barium aspiration during videofluoroscopic swallowing studies: value of change in posture. *American Journal of Radiology*, 160, 1005–9.

Robbins, J., Hamilton, J.W., Lof, G.L., and Kempster, G.B. (1992). Oropharyngeal swallowing in normal adults of different ages. *Gastroenterology*, 103, 823–9.

Rosenbek, J.C., Robbins, J., Fishback, B., and Levine, R.L. (1991). Effects of thermal application on dysphagia after stroke. *Journal of Speech and Hearing Research*, 34, 1257–68.

Schiffman, S. (1993). Perception of taste and smell in elderly persons. *Critical Review of Food Sciences Nutrition*, 33, 17–26.

Scott, A.G. and Austin, H.E. (1994). Nasogastric feeding in the management of severe dysphagia in motor neurone disease. *Palliative Medicine*, 8, 45–9.

Ship, J.A., Nolan, N.E., and Puckett, S.A. (1995). Longitudinal analysis of parotid and submandibular salivary flow rates in healthy, different aged, adults. *Journal of Gerontology*, 50, 285–9.

Ship, J.A., Duffy, V., Jones, J.A., and Langmore, S. (1996). Geriatric oral health and its impact on eating. *Journal of the American Geriatrics Society*, 44, 456–64.

Smithard, D., O'Neill, P.A., Park, C., *et al.* (1996). Complications in outcome after acute stroke. Does dysphagia matter? *Stroke*, 27, 1200–4.

Veis, S. and Logemann, J. (1985). Swallowing disorders in patients with cerebro-vascular accident. *Archives of Physical Medicine and Rehabilitation*, 66, 372–5.

Wheeler, D.G. (1995). Communication and swallowing problems in the frail older person. *Topics in Geriatric Rehabilitation*, 11, 11–15.

Wysocki, C.A. and Gilbert, A.N. (1989). National geographic smell survey: effects of age are heterogenous. *Annals of the New York Academy of Sciences*, 561, 12–28.

8.3   **Disorders of the oesophagus**

Richard Curless

Introduction

Problems with swallowing and symptoms related to the oesophagus and upper gastrointestinal tract are common in older people but are often overlooked. Particularly frequent problems include neurological dysphagia, oesophageal strictures and cancer, and atypical presentations of common disorders such as gastro-oesophageal reflux. A few diseases, such as Zenker's diverticulum, cervical osteophytes, and dysphagia aortica, are unique to older age groups. Particular diagnostic care is needed in older people who are more prone to the chronic complications of oesophageal disease such as Barrett's oesophagus and oesophageal adenocarcinoma. Coexisting illness makes the diagnosis of problems such as non-cardiac chest pain more difficult.

Brief overview of functional anatomy and physiology

Pharynx

The function of the pharyngeal cavity is to transfer food and liquid from the mouth to the oesophagus, while safely avoiding aspiration into the larynx. Anatomically, it can be divided into (a) the bony and cartilaginous structures and (b) the striated muscles and their innervation. Alternatively, it can be thought of as three functionally interdependent and communicating spaces: the nasopharynx, the oropharynx, and the hypopharynx.

The pharyngeal striated muscle is densely innervated with a nerve fibre to muscle fibre ratio similar to that of the extraocular muscles, suggesting the need for exceptionally fine motor control. Thirty-one paired striated muscles contribute to the oropharyngeal phases of the swallow. Tongue actions are determined by four intrinsic and four extrinsic muscles supplied by the hypoglossal (XII) and the ansa cervicalis (C1–C2) nerves respectively, except for the palatoglossus (X). The vagus nerve (X) predominantly controls the muscles of the soft palate and pharynx and the intrinsic laryngeal musculature via the recurrent laryngeal nerves. The cell bodies of the motor neurones that innervate the pharyngeal muscles are situated in the nuclei of the trigeminal, facial, and hypoglossal nerves as well as the nucleus ambiguus and spinal segment C1 to C3. The major propulsive muscles of the pharynx are the three paired constrictors: superior, middle, and inferior. Sensory afferents from the larynx travel centrally via the superior laryngeal nerve and from the pharyngeal plexus via the glossopharyngeal nerve. Sensory fibres from the trigeminal, glossopharyngeal, and vagus nerves, which are important in initiating the swallow, converge in the spinal trigeminal system and the tractus solitarius. These afferent swallow pathways finally converge in the medullary swallowing centre.

Oesophagus

Structure and innervation

The oesophageal body is a hollow muscular tube arising as a continuation of the pharynx from the lower border of the cricoid cartilage and ending at the stomach. In clinical practice, measurements of oesophageal length are taken from the upper incisor teeth; the oesophagus commences at 15 cm and the junction with the stomach is at approximately 40 cm. This is a crude estimate of the actual location of the gastro-oesophageal junction.

There are several points of potential constriction in the normal oesophagus which have clinical relevance as sites where food, tablets, or foreign bodies might lodge. They are sited at the cricoid origin, the level of the aortic arch, the crossing of the left main bronchus, the left atrium, and the passage through the diaphragmatic hiatus. In older people, enlargement of the left atrium and the aortic arch determine the two most usual sites.

Detailed descriptions of oesophageal anatomy and physiology can be found elsewhere (Eslami *et al.* 1994; Richards and Sugarbaker 1995). There is little published work to suggest significant anatomical changes with normal ageing. However, studies in which the effect of age on the physiology of swallowing is examined are beginning to appear in the literature. An overview of clinically relevant histology and a description of the normal swallow follows to aid an understanding of problems in disease.

The **gross structure** of the oesophagus is similar to the rest of the gastrointestinal tract, comprising external, muscular, submucosal, and mucosal layers. The muscular layer comprises an outer (longitudinal) and an inner (circular) bundle. The oesophagus is composed of both striated and smooth muscle fibres. The proximal 5 per cent, including the upper oesophageal sphincter, is striated, the middle portion becomes increasingly mixed, and the distal half is entirely smooth muscle.

The **extrinsic innervation** of the oesophagus is from both parasympathetic and sympathetic arms of the autonomic nervous system. Parasympathetic motor outflow to the pharynx and oesophagus is via the glossopharyngeal (IX) and vagal (X) nerves. The upper oesophagus is supplied through branches of the recurrent laryngeal nerve, and the body and distal portions by the vagal nerve itself. The cell bodies of nerves innervating striated muscle are situated in the nucleus ambiguus, whereas smooth muscle fibres are served by the dorsal motor nucleus of the vagus. Sensory afferents from receptors in the mucosa, submucosa, and muscular layers travel via the superior laryngeal, recurrent laryngeal, and vagal nerves. Sympathetic pre-ganglionic fibres arise from cell bodies in the intermediolateral cell column of the fifth and sixth thoracic spinal cord segments to synapse in the cervical, thoracic, and coeliac sympathetic ganglia. Mechanisms of oesophageal pain have been reviewed by Lynn (1992).

Both the striated and smooth muscle portions of the oesophagus contain an **intrinsic innervation**. The myenteric (Auerbach's) plexus is located between the longitudinal and circular muscle layers, whereas the submucosal (Meissner's) plexus lies between the muscularis mucosa and the circular muscle layer. The cell density of both these plexi is much sparser than elsewhere in the gastrointestinal tract.

The **blood supply** to the oesophagus forms a widespread anastomotic network; thus infarction is very rare. Venous drainage of the proximal two-thirds is into the superior vena cava. The lower third and gastric cardia drain via two routes: one to the systemic circulation in branches of the azygos and left inferior phrenic vein, and the other to the portal venous system via the left and short gastric veins. It is this portosystemic anastomosis which leads to the formation of varices in the presence of raised portal pressure.

The **oesophageal mucosa** lies in longitudinal folds in the resting state and comprises epithelium, lamina propria, and muscularis mucosae. It is a non-keratinizing stratified squamous epithelium. About 1 to 2 cm from the gastro-oesophageal junction, a squamo-columnar junction is visible macroscopically as a serrated line (the Z line) where small projections of red gastric epithelium interdigitate with the paler squamous epithelium. Thereafter, the distal 1 to 2 cm of the oesophagus is lined by columnar epithelium. This mucosal junction normally lies within the lower oesophageal sphincter.

The oesophageal sphincters

The **upper oesophageal sphincter** functions as part of both the pharynx and the oesophagus. The sphincteric action arises from striated muscle and depends significantly, but not solely, on the action of cricopharyngeus, with contributions from the cervical oesophagus and the inferior pharyngeal constrictor. A 1-cm zone of maximal intraluminal pressure coincides with the location of the cricopharyngeus. Upper oesophageal sphincter pressure is markedly asymmetric radially and its measurement is significantly influenced by the technique used. Intraluminal upper oesophageal sphincter pressure appears to have two components, one from active contraction of the cricopharyngeus and an additional passive element from tissue elasticity. However, upper oesophageal sphincter tone is neither constant nor continuous. The upper oesophageal sphincter appears to contract in synchrony with inspiration, presumably to prevent entry of air into the oesophagus.

The **gastro-oesophageal junction**, which is the area between the distal oesophagus and the stomach, is complex and important. It contains the physiological lower oesophageal sphincter, the crural diaphragm, and the phreno-oesophageal ligament, and may give rise to oesophageal rings. Manometry demonstrates a physiological sphincter which at rest closes the oesophageal lumen and prevents

reflux of gastric contents. Detailed anatomical studies suggest a corresponding ring of maximal smooth muscle. The exact location of the gastro-oesophageal junction varies with the method used to define it. Physiologically, it can be regarded as the distal part of the lower oesophageal sphincter. Surgeons and endoscopists define the gastro-oesophageal junction in different ways.

The oesophageal phase of swallowing

The oropharyngeal phases of swallowing are dealt with in Chapter 8.2. At rest, both oesophageal sphincters are tonically contracted. Unlike the remainder of the gastrointestinal tract, the oesophagus does not exhibit interprandial contractions. The oesophageal body is flaccid with a small negative pressure which varies with respiration and cardiac contraction. The intraluminal pressure at the gastro-oesophageal junction has components from both the lower oesophageal sphincter and the diaphragmatic crura. The lower oesophageal sphincter is demonstrated manometrically by a 2- to 4-cm zone of occlusion; the basal resting pressure is estimated at 15 to 30 mmHg. The mechanism of tonic contraction of the lower oesophageal sphincter is not clear, but appears to be an intrinsic property of the muscle itself. Many substances, including vasoactive intestinal polypeptide and nitric oxide, have been demonstrated to influence lower oesophageal sphincter pressure.

Once the swallow is initiated, a sequence of involuntary oesophageal contractions and relaxations occurs. Oesophageal peristalsis commences soon after the pharyngeal contraction traverses the upper oesophageal sphincter, moving from the striated to the smooth muscle at 2 to 4 cm/s. Primary peristalsis is initiated by the swallow, whereas secondary peristalsis can be elicited at any oesophageal level by distension. The primary peristaltic wave traverses the length of the oesophagus in 5 to 6 s. The lower oesophageal sphincter starts to relax during this contraction and pressure within the sphincter falls to gastric levels for 5 to 8 s; thus no barrier to the passage of the bolus is offered. There is a brief hypercontraction of about 2 s before basal lower oesophageal sphincter tone returns.

Oesophageal peristalsis is influenced both extrinsically and intrinsically. The control mechanisms governing striated and smooth muscle are distinct. Striated muscle is exclusively vagally innervated, and peristaltic contraction of this segment is a consequence of sequential activation of motor units organized from the medullary swallowing centre (nucleus ambiguus). Vagal control of the oesophageal smooth muscle is more complex. There is evidence for vagal initiation of primary peristaltic activity, at least partially governed by the central swallowing centres (dorsal motor nucleus). However, secondary peristalsis can persist despite vagal denervation, suggesting that intrinsic mechanisms involving the myenteric plexus are important in smooth muscle. The progressive nature of the contraction in oesophageal smooth muscle is programmed by mechanisms residing within the oesophageal wall. A variety of excitatory and inhibitory myenteric neurones and neurotransmitters, including cholinergic and nitric oxide pathways, have been described *in vitro*, but no single substance has been definitively implicated *in vivo*. Currently, there is intense interest in the role of nitric oxide as the main neuromediator of lower oesophageal sphincter relaxation.

Changes with age

The oesophageal phase of swallowing is delayed in older people. There is a longer upper oesophageal sphincter relaxation time, and

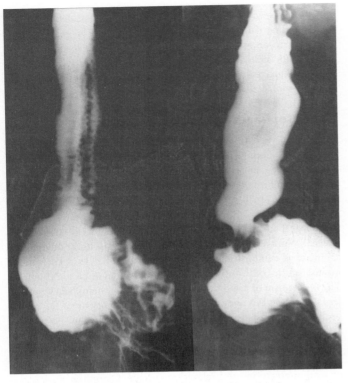

Fig. 1 Tertiary oesophageal contractions above a hiatus hernia as seen on barium swallow. (Courtesy of Dr W. Simpson, Department of Radiology, Newcastle General Hospital.)

Table 1 Percentage prevalence of functional gastrointestinal disorders by age

	15–34	35–44	45 and over
Oesophageal symptoms	48.3	45.8	38.7
Globus	16.4	13.6	10.4
Rumination	14.5	10.6	9.0
Chest pain	18.4	13.9	9.9
Heartburn	30.4	32.9	28.9
Dysphagia	8.4	8.3	6.6
Gastroduodenal symptoms	29.4	25.1	24.0
Bowel symptoms	43.4	44.7	44.3
Chronic abdominal pain	2.3	2.6	1.9
Biliary pain	0.8	1.1	1.9
Anorectal symptoms	28.9	28.5	25.1
All gastrointestinal symptoms	71.9	71.7	67.3

Data from Drossman et al. (1993).

the maximum upper oesophageal sphincter resting pressure appears to decline with age. Data concerning the duration of opening of the upper oesophageal sphincter are conflicting, but there may be a higher proportion of swallows unaccompanied by relaxation (Dejaeger et al. 1994). The amplitude of oesophageal contraction is probably reduced in people aged over 80 years. Evidence for altered primary peristalsis with age is conflicting, whereas secondary peristalsis appears to be provoked less often (Ren et al. 1995). The proportion of tertiary (Fig. 1) and disturbed peristaltic waves increases with age; thus peristalsis may be less efficient. Studies of lower oesophageal sphincter relaxation and basal tone have yielded conflicting results.

The clinical importance of these changes is less clear. For example, a radiological study of asymptomatic elderly people (mean age 83) found that only 16 per cent had a 'normal' swallow as defined for younger patients (Ekberg and Feinberg 1991). Thus a view of dysfunction derived from normative data based on younger people may not be appropriate. There are no data to suggest that swallow efficacy in healthy old age is compromised to a clinically significant extent.

Overview of upper gastrointestinal symptoms

Despite the increasing availability and sophistication of oesophageal investigations, a thorough clinical history remains the cornerstone of diagnosis. Our knowledge of the epidemiology of oesophageal symptoms in the adult population, and in particular older people, is not complete. The variety of symptom definitions and study methods employed has hampered progress. Nonetheless, there is little doubt that symptoms normally attributable to the upper gastrointestinal tract are common and often cannot be explained by structural or biochemical abnormalities. The concept of 'functional gastrointestinal disorders' has become increasingly recognized and diagnostic criteria ('Rome criteria') have been developed for specific anatomical regions—oesophagus, gastroduodenum, biliary tract, intestines, and anorectum (Drossman et al. 1990). The United States Householder Survey (Drossman et al. 1993) suggests that two-thirds of the population had had at least one such symptom in the preceding 3 months (Table 1), that there is considerable overlap of functional gastrointestinal symptoms, and that most people do not consult their doctor. Reported symptom rates, except for incontinence, fall with age. Oesophageal symptoms were reported by 42 per cent of those surveyed.

It should be recognized that these concepts of 'functional disorder' or the 'irritable gut' have developed largely from studies in selected, predominantly young, populations. Thus caution is needed before extrapolating such work to older people in whom serious organic gastrointestinal disease is more common. It is generally held that disease presentation in older people is less specific than in younger adults. Whether this reflects physiological changes in symptom perception (e.g. modification of pain threshold), the effect of concomitant disease, a tendency for old people to attribute symptoms to 'old age', the diligence with which doctors take histories in elderly patients, or simply a lack of published literature directly applicable to older subjects is debatable.

Heartburn, dysphagia, and non-cardiac chest pain

Typically, three clinical presentations of oesophageal disorders are described: heartburn, dysphagia, and non-cardiac chest pain. Heartburn is a retrosternal burning feeling with a tendency to radiate to the mouth, usually occurring an hour or two after meals and exacerbated by bending over or lying recumbent. It is often associated with acid regurgitation, i.e. the effortless entry of small volumes of sour (acid) or bitter (bile) material into the mouth. Acid regurgitation should be distinguished from vomiting, which is the forceful ejection of gastric contents through the mouth as a result of contractions of abdominal muscles. Dysphagia is difficulty in swallowing, usually described as the sensation of food or fluid sticking in its passage from mouth to stomach. It may be associated with odynophagia (a pain felt within 15 s of swallowing), cough after swallowing, hiccough, and belching. Non-cardiac chest pain of oesophageal origin can be severe and mimic cardiac ischaemic pain, leading to intensive cardiac investigations. However, it is increasingly apparent that pharyngeal and oesophageal problems in older people may often present atypically, frequently with respiratory symptoms (Raiha et al. 1992a).

Further confusion stems from the non-specific use of the term dyspepsia to describe a broad spectrum of subjective descriptions of distress believed to emanate from the upper gastrointestinal tract. Only a minority of such people are shown to have endoscopic abnormalities of the upper gastrointestinal tract (such as peptic ulcer), hence the term non-ulcer dyspepsia. It is now suggested that the term dyspepsia be defined specifically as the presence of episodic or persistent pain or discomfort localized to the epigastrium or upper abdomen (Drossman et al. 1990). Subgroups of symptom clusters have also been highlighted: ulcer-like dyspepsia, dysmotility-like dyspepsia, reflux-like dyspepsia, and an unspecified group. An American survey of a randomly selected community sample of 1120 people aged between 30 and 64 years (Talley et al. 1992) identified a prevalence of upper abdominal pain (dyspepsia) within the preceding year of 25.8 per 100 (confidence interval (CI), 22.8–28.8); the subgroup of reflux-like dyspepsia was identified in 9.4 per 100 (CI, 7.4–11.4). One-third of dyspeptics also had irritable bowel symptoms. Other workers suggest a slightly different emphasis based on surveys in Scandinavian populations and describe two dyspeptic syndromes: an upper dyspepsia–heartburn type and an upper dyspepsia–nausea type (Kay and Jorgensen 1996). They suggest that these two symptom complexes are associated with oesophageal and gastroduodenal pathology respectively. Upper dyspeptic symptoms in a random community sample of elderly Scandinavians had a prevalence of up to 10 per cent (Table 2). Incidence rates were of the same magnitude, but disappearance rates over 5 years were higher than 50 per cent (Kay 1994).

Community surveys in the United Kingdom (Jones and Lydeard 1989) suggest that over one-third of people have reported dyspepsia within the previous 6 months, with the frequency appearing to fall with age (24 per cent of women and 15 per cent of men aged over 80). About half of people with dyspepsia reported both heartburn and upper abdominal pain. Only one in four had consulted their general practitioner, with consultation rates increasing with age.

Oesophageal dysphagia

Oropharyngeal dysphagia is dealt with in Chapter 8.2. Difficulty in swallowing should always be taken seriously and investigated to find a cause. True dysphagia has been defined as discomfort, pain, or a sensation of obstruction which develops within 15 s of the pharyngeal movements of swallowing (Edwards 1976). It should be distinguished from two other symptoms that patients may describe: the feeling of a lump or tickle in the throat (globus), and the non-specific feeling of fullness or that food has stuck in the neck or chest that typically develops 10 min or more after eating. 'Cortical inhibition' is a syndrome, encountered particularly in elderly people with dementia, where food is repetitively chewed and then spat out. There is no obstruction and the patient can drink. The problem seems to be one of volition.

Oesophageal dysphagia is a problem of transferring the ingested material down the oesophagus and into the stomach. Broadly, there is either difficulty in luminal flow due to mechanical obstruction (tumours, strictures, rings, extrinsic compression) or abnormal muscular contraction of the oesophageal wall and/or lower oesophageal sphincter (oesophageal motility disorders, scleroderma). Three key elements to the history are useful in oesophageal dysphagia:

(1) whether the dysphagia was initially for food or liquid or both;
(2) whether the dysphagia is intermittent or progressive;
(3) whether there is associated heartburn.

The presence of associated cough or chest pain may be reported. A short and progressive history suggests carcinoma, whereas intermittent difficulties over a longer period are more typical of benign strictures. Webs or rings may cause well-defined episodes of bolus impaction. Difficulties with both liquid and solid boluses from the outset make a motility disorder more likely. Initial dysphagia for solids only suggests a mechanical problem. Chronic heartburn can point to peptic stricture, but is by no means always present. However, these are the classic descriptions of oesophageal dysphagia and less typical presentations are not infrequent. In older people, symptom duration appears to be a less reliable marker for benign as opposed to malignant strictures (Gupta et al. 1987), and the presentation of non-oesophageal lesions such as gastric neoplasia, peptic ulceration, and extrinsic compression with dysphagia has been emphasized (Bannister et al. 1990).

Investigations

Examination

A general physical examination, looking particularly for evidence of neurological and cognitive impairment, combined with a detailed medical, drug, and functional history should allow a provisional diagnosis to be made in the majority of older patients with symptoms of pharyngeal or oesophageal disease and will certainly guide the appropriate use of investigations.

Radiology

A chest radiograph should be performed since it may reveal obvious mediastinal masses, cardiomegaly, retrosternal goitre, or a dilated oesophagus. There may be evidence of aspiration pneumonia, oesophageal air/fluid level, or loss of the gastric air bubble in severe achalasia.

Radiological examination of the upper gastrointestinal tract generally implies examination of the oesophagus, stomach, and duodenum as far as the ligament of Treitz. The oral and pharyngeal

Table 2 Prevalence, incidence, and disappearance rates of upper gastrointestinal symptoms, reported as frequent, in a random sample of elderly people

Symptom	Prevalence (%)	Annual incidence (%)	Disappearance rate (%)
Epigastric pain			
Men	3.9 (2.2–6.2)	2.8 (1.2–5.5)	57.1 (18.4–90.1)
Women	6.9 (4.6–9.9)	9.1 (6.0–13.1)	35.3 (14.2–61.7)
Heartburn			
Men	5.3 (3.4–8.0)	0.8 (0.1–2.7)*	77.8 (52.4–93.6)
Women	7.2 (4.8–10.2)	3.6 (1.8–6.6)	65.2 (42.7–83.6)
Nausea			
Men	1.2 (0.4–2.8)*	0.7 (0.1–2.5)	100 (29.2–100)
Women	3.8 (2.2–6.3)	2.8 (1.2–5.4)	90.0 (55.5–99.7)
Vomiting			
Men	0.2 (0.0–1.3)	0.7 (0.1–2.5)	100 (2.5–100)
Women	1.5 (0.6–3.3)	0.3 (0.0–1.9)	75.0 (19.4–99.4)
Upper dyspepsia			
Men	9.0 (6.4–12.2)	3.1 (1.3–6.0)*	63.6 (40.7–82.8)
Women	12.5 (9.4–16.2)	9.2 (5.9–13.5)	45.7 (28.8–63.4)

95% confidence intervals in parentheses.
* Significant sex difference ($p < 0.05$).
Data from Kay (1994).

phases are only briefly assessed in the conventional examination and, if pathology of the oropharynx (particularly aspiration) is suspected, a detailed examination of this region by videofluoroscopy (see Chapter 8.2) should be specifically requested. The barium examination is tailored to the patient's symptoms, and thus the availability of a history is very important to the radiologist. Double-contrast techniques are usually employed, although single contrast may be useful for anatomical demonstration. Various positional and stress manoeuvres may be needed.

Although difficult for the frail and immobile patient, upper gastrointestinal barium studies are safe, simple, and do not require sedation. The quality of radiographs may decline with older patients, but most still offer considerable diagnostic utility (Hawkins *et al.* 1991; Sangster *et al.* 1992). When dysphagia is the predominant symptom, radiology is always advisable prior to endoscopy.

Endoscopy

Endoscopy combines diagnosis by direct vision and/or biopsy/cytology of the oesophageal mucosa, and the ability to treat or palliate—for example, dilatation of strictures, variceal sclerotherapy, laser therapy, and stenting. Over 90 per cent of upper gastrointestinal endoscopies are for diagnostic purposes; approximately one-third are performed in people over the age of 70 years. One in ten emergency endoscopies are in people over 80 years. Endoscopy is used as the first-line investigation of reflux disease and gastrointestinal bleeding, and should always be performed to confirm the nature of an oesophageal stricture. It has little value in the investigation of motility disorders. Guidelines on appropriate indications for upper gastrointestinal endoscopy have been published (Axon *et al.* 1995). This technique appears to be generally safe as a diagnostic procedure in older people.

Intravenous sedation with a benzodiazepine is used in the majority of procedures in United Kingdom practice. Although the mean dose administered falls with age, there is wide variation and concern that excess dosage may be given to the very old. An opioid analgesic may be added for some therapeutic procedures such as oesophageal dilatation. These drugs, both individually and particularly in combination, can lead to respiratory depression. Cardiopulmonary complications account for over half of all serious adverse events. The overall fatality rate for diagnostic endoscopy has recently been estimated as approximately 1 in 2000 and the morbidity rate as 1 in 200. Adverse outcomes appear to be linked to lack of monitoring and the use of high doses of benzodiazepines. There also appears to be a link between the use of local anaesthetic throat spray and the development of pneumonia. The second most common complication is oesophageal perforation, for which age appears to be a risk factor.

Arterial oxygen desaturation occurs frequently as a result of drug-induced respiratory depression and obstruction of the airway by the endoscope itself. Preoxygenation and supplemental oxygen at flow rates between 2 and 4 l/min via nasal cannulas can largely abolish this. The additional use of pulse oximeters and ECG monitoring is a desirable practice, particularly for patients with cardiopulmonary disease. It has been suggested that older people tolerate endoscopy without sedation and should be offered this choice (Solomon *et al.* 1994). Comprehensive guidelines are available (British Society of Gastroenterology 1991).

Pharyngeal manometry

The recent development of improved solid state transducer systems has fostered renewed interest in the use of manometry in the dysphagic patient. It allows examination of pharyngeal pressures, upper oesophageal sphincter relaxation, and quantitative examination of swallow timings (Castell and Castell 1996). Manometry is likely to develop a clearer role as a complementary investigation to videofluoroscopy.

Oesophageal manometry

Manometry is the most direct method of assessing oesophageal motor function. While it allows measurement of the strength of muscular contractions, it does not directly assess bolus propulsion. Therefore it may need to be combined with radiology or scintigraphy. Advantages of the technique are that it is low risk and does not involve radiation exposure. Disadvantages include equipment cost, invasiveness, and the considerable expertise needed for interpretation.

Oesophageal pressures can be measured by two methods: water-perfused manometric assemblies connected to external pressure transducers or intraluminal transducers with solid state circuitry (Dent and Holloway 1996). Modern assemblies allow recordings to be made simultaneously at multiple levels. The measurement of both upper and lower oesophageal sphincter pressures poses particular problems, because these sphincters have a zone of maximum pressure that is only a few millimetres wide and their positions are mobile compared with the focal pressure sensors. Preliminary studies using ambulatory oesophageal manometry in healthy young and old subjects suggest that physiological motor activity shows significant diurnal variation but is little influenced by age (Adamek et al. 1994).

The clinical role of manometry is limited but it can aid diagnosis of oesophageal motility disorders following radiological and endoscopic investigation (Ergun and Kahrilas 1996). Primary and secondary peristalsis can be successfully evaluated, but lower oesophageal sphincter relaxation poses greater problems. Sensitivity and specificity are high in the diagnosis of achalasia. Manometry assists in the characterization of the hypertensive oesophagus, diffuse oesophageal spasm, and other non-specific motor disorders.

Ambulatory oesophageal pH monitoring

Oesophageal pH monitoring is becoming a more widely established method for the diagnosis of gastro-oesophageal reflux disease. It records spontaneous reflux events and allows direct measurement of the degree of oesophageal acid exposure. Many regard pH monitoring as the gold standard for the diagnosis of gastro-oesophageal reflux disease. Ambulatory pH monitoring equipment is now widely available commercially. The major components are the pH electrode, data storage device, and software.

For standard pH monitoring the electrode is located 5 cm above the proximal margin of the lower oesophageal sphincter, best defined manometrically. The patient is encouraged to pursue normal activities while keeping an accurate symptom diary. The two major elements of analysis are the amount of reflux and the relationship between the patient's symptoms and reflux. Traditionally, a reflux episode is defined when pH falls below 4. Data analysis allows a number of parameters to be calculated. Abnormal reflux is assessed by comparison with normative values for healthy asymptomatic populations. Defining normal values for physiological acid reflux can be difficult; based on relatively small numbers of healthy subjects, it appears that age does not independently influence pH parameters (Richter et al. 1992; Fass et al. 1993). A measure of oesophageal acid exposure that correlates with the severity of oesophagitis is the duration of pH less

than 4, expressed as a percentage of the total recording period. The upper limit of normal is said to be 5 to 7 per cent in younger subjects, but may be up to 12 per cent in older people. However, the level of acid exposure does not indicate whether symptoms are related to acid reflux. Thus a symptom (specificity) index, defined as the percentage of symptom episodes associated with reflux, or a symptom (sensitivity) index, the percentage of reflux episodes associated with symptoms, is calculated.

It is not necessary to monitor pH in all people with suspected gastro-oesophageal reflux disease. In older people, endoscopy to look for moderate to severe oesophagitis and to exclude other pathology, followed by a trial of therapy, is reasonable; pH monitoring is currently reserved for patients with particularly troublesome symptoms in the absence of endoscopic findings and in whom a therapeutic trial has failed, those with atypical symptoms, and assessment of those under consideration for antireflux surgery.

Scintigraphy

The incorporation of a radio-isotope into either a liquid or food bolus allows its passage from oesophagus to stomach to be followed using a gamma camera and data processor. The clinical role of scintigraphy is not clearly established.

Motility disorders of the oesophagus

Primary

The increasing use of manometry, particularly in people with non-cardiac chest pain, has revealed a group of subjects with primary or idiopathic oesophageal motility disorders. Achalasia is the only disorder with a clear pathological basis. If structural cardiac and oesophageal disorders are excluded, about one-third of those with non-cardiac chest pain and two-thirds with dysphagia will have a primary oesophageal motility disorder. Motility is disordered in the sense that it is statistically disparate from that of healthy asymptomatic control populations. The lack of a clear understanding of these primary motility disorders has led to confusing nomenclature. Most of the data are based on young populations; normal ranges for older populations are not well established. Furthermore, similar motility patterns may be seen in some older people without symptoms, and so the relationship between symptoms, radiological and manometric findings, and age-associated changes is unclear. They are broadly grouped under the following headings: diffuse oesophageal spasm, nutcracker oesophagus, hypertensive oesophageal sphincter, and non-specific oesophageal motility disorder.

The term presbyoesophagus was proposed following the demonstration that 15 patients aged over 90 years had motility patterns that were different from those of younger people (Soergel et al. 1964). However, most of these subjects had underlying neurological disorders or diabetes. Subsequent work on patients thoroughly screened for the absence of underlying disease have provided conflicting data about normal ageing and oesophageal motility. In symptomatic patients, radiology suggests that the prevalence of functional motility abnormalities increases with age, but does not correlate well with patients' symptoms (Grishaw et al. 1996). The finding of complete

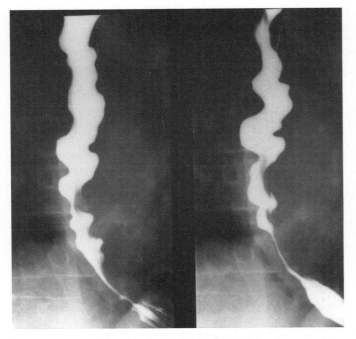

Fig. 2 Barium swallow findings of a 'corkscrew' oesophagus suggesting diffuse oesophageal spasm. (Courtesy of Dr W. Simpson, Department of Radiology, Newcastle General Hospital.)

primary oesophageal aperistalsis is documented more often in symptomatic elderly people (Meshkinpour *et al.* 1994). Until more rigorous data become available, the term presbyoesophagus is best avoided.

No specific symptom pattern allows the diagnosis of primary oesophageal motility disorder to be made. In older people, in particular, cardiac causes of chest pain, structural causes of dysphagia, and gastro-oesophageal reflux disease should be sought first. The diagnosis is usually suggested by barium swallow findings. Accurate classification requires manometry.

Diffuse oesophageal spasm is a syndrome characterized by non-peristaltic contraction of the distal oesophagus following some but not all swallows (>10 per cent). Vigorous contraction waves and abnormalities of basal lower oesophageal sphincter pressure and relaxation are often found radiologically; the 'corkscrew' or 'rosary bead' oesophagus may be described (Fig. 2). 'Nutcracker' oesophagus refers to the manometric finding of average distal oesophageal peristaltic pressures more than two standard deviations above normal. A hypertensive lower oesophageal sphincter is defined as a lower oesophageal sphincter pressure increased by more than two standard deviations with a normal relaxation and peristaltic sequence. Many manometric findings do not fit neatly into the above classification and are regarded as non-specific oesophageal motility disorders.

Achalasia

The characteristics of achalasia are the loss of oesophageal peristalsis and a failure of the lower oesophageal sphincter to open normally in response to swallowing. The aetiology remains unknown. The major differential diagnosis is secondary achalasia due to gastric carcinoma.

Epidemiology

There is a paucity of epidemiological information about this disease. In England, the incidence is probably 0.5 cases per 100 000 per year, while the prevalence is estimated as between 7 and 13 cases per 100 000. Incidence appears to increase with age, but there is no definite sex difference. One-third of cases present over the age of 60. The mean age at death is around 80 years. Geographical variation in the frequency of disease almost certainly exists. Mortality data suggest that it is more common in Ireland, New Zealand, and Sweden.

Pathophysiology

Although achalasia is classically regarded as a primary motor disorder of the oesophagus, emerging evidence points to motor dysfunction in other areas of the gastrointestinal tract, such as stomach and gallbladder. Furthermore, there are suggestions of extra-intestinal autonomic dysfunction in subjects with achalasia. Thus achalasia may be a more generalized neurological disorder expressed predominantly in the oesophagus.

Histologically, there is a loss of ganglion cells within the myenteric plexus, widespread destruction of intrinsic nerves, and variable chronic inflammation (Goldblum *et al.* 1996). This would appear to result in widespread disruption of the neurotransmitter systems. No primary defect of the smooth muscle is recognized. Degenerative changes in the extrinsic nerve supply and dorsal motor nucleus of the vagus have also been described. Whatever the primary lesion, the result of these changes is thought to be loss of intrinsic inhibitory innervation of the lower oesophageal sphincter.

The main manometric findings in achalasia are lack of peristalsis in the oesophageal body, incomplete relaxation of the lower oesophageal sphincter, and raised basal lower oesophageal sphincter tone. Although achalasia is typically considered as a disease affecting the distal oesophagus, it now appears that defects in the upper oesophageal sphincter, pharynx, and proximal oesophagus can also occur.

The aetiology of the damage to the myenteric nerve plexus is not known. Evidence for a substantial genetic element is lacking, except in a particular group with familial pedigrees. The geographical variation in disease frequency supports an environmental agent. A number of infectious agents have been proposed as possible candidates. Many investigators suspect a neurotropic virus, although none has gained particular support. Antimyenteric neuronal antibodies have been described, lending support to an autoimmune mechanism (Verne *et al.* 1997).

Clinical features

The cardinal feature is dysphagia for both liquids and solids, initially intermittent but progressing with time. Patients acquire habits to eat more easily, such as ingesting large quantities of water and the Valsalva manoeuvre. Chest pain is common, but is a less frequent complaint with age. Burning pain or odynophagia suggest secondary oesophagitis due to infection or stasis. As the oesophagus dilates, regurgitation of undigested food may occur. Aspiration with pulmonary symptoms is found in 10 per cent. Weight loss is an indication for treatment. Rapid weight loss should alert the clinician to the possibility of secondary achalasia due to the presence of a carcinoma.

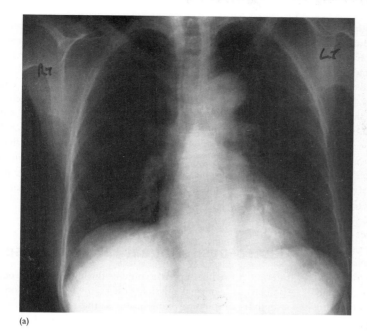

(a)

(b)

Fig. 3 (a) Plain chest radiograph in achalasia with absent gastric air bubble and dilated oesophageal mediastinal outline. (b) Barium swallow with dilatation and tapering of the oesophagus distally at a poorly opening lower oesophageal sphincter. (Courtesy of Dr W. Simpson, Department of Radiology, Newcastle General Hospital.)

Diagnosis

Most patients with achalasia suffer from symptoms for a protracted period (mean 4.7 years) before the diagnosis is made; failure to suspect the diagnosis seems to contribute significantly (Eckardt *et al.* 1997). A plain chest radiograph may reveal a widened mediastinum, air/fluid level, or absence of a gastric air bubble. Barium studies classically demonstrate defective or absent peristalsis in the oesophageal body. Dilatation may become massive with time or residual food debris may be identified. The 'bird's beak' appearance describes the tapering of the distal oesophageal lumen at a poorly opening lower oesophageal sphincter (Fig. 3). Endoscopy will not make the diagnosis, but is essential to exclude secondary causes such as infiltrating carcinoma at the cardia and may reveal the extent of complications. Endoscopic ultrasound may potentially play a useful role.

Manometry is the essential investigation. The typical features will confirm the diagnosis, although manometric recordings are equivocal in some patients. Manometry will distinguish achalasia from other motility disorders but cannot differentiate primary from secondary achalasia. The characteristic features are normal or elevated resting lower oesophageal sphincter pressures, failure of the lower oesophageal sphincter to relax on swallowing, and a lack of oesophageal peristalsis on swallowing. The 'vigorous achalasia' variant is characterized by repetitive simultaneous contractions of relatively high amplitude.

Complications

Infection and stasis can lead to an erosive oesophagitis that may increase the risk of complications. Recent evidence suggests that, contrary to previous belief, gastro-oesophageal reflux disease can occur in subjects with achalasia, leading to a reflux oesophagitis requiring treatment in its own right. The association between achalasia and subsequent carcinoma is controversial. Achalasia has been suggested to be a premalignant condition, with chronic stasis leading to cellular hyperproliferation. The incidence of squamous cell carcinoma is not known, but the risk has been estimated at 14 times that of the normal population (Streitz *et al.* 1995). However, it is not established that treatment of achalasia reduces this risk.

Treatment

The aim of therapy is to reduce pressure at the lower oesophageal sphincter and thereby improve oesophageal emptying, but without causing gastro-oesophageal reflux. Pharmacological (smooth muscle relaxing agents), endoscopic (balloon dilatation or botulinum toxin injection), and surgical (open or laparoscopic myotomy) treatment strategies can be used. The lack of long-term prospective randomized studies means that the optimal approach to management is unclear.

Drug treatment to reduce lower oesophageal sphincter pressure does not appear to be very effective. A variety of agents have been used including nitrates, calcium antagonists, opioid antagonists, and loperamide. They may be useful as a short-term adjunct while awaiting other treatment or in those too frail to undergo other procedures.

Pneumatic dilatation to produce a forceful mechanical disruption of the oesophageal circular muscle at the gastro-oesophageal junction is the most effective non-surgical management. A guide wire is sited endoscopically and dilatation is then carried out with a balloon passed over it. Symptomatic success is reported in 60 to 90 per cent of patients, particularly older subjects and those with longer-standing symptoms. The major immediate complication is of lower oesophageal perforation which occurs in 2 to 4 per cent. Troublesome long-term reflux oesophagitis and peptic stricture formation rates are probably under 1 per cent. The newest approach is that of intrasphincteric endoscopic botulinum toxin injection. Preliminary work is promising although the durability of the response is unknown.

Surgical myotomy seems to carry the greatest success rates (quoted at 90 per cent) but is clearly associated with greater cost and morbidity. Technical improvements, including laparoscopic approaches, have great potential, but identification of the definitive clinical approach awaits large-scale randomized studies of the various modalities emerging. Furthermore, quoted surgical and endoscopic 'success' rates may be overoptimistic. There is little evaluation of long-term quality-of-life issues, but a recent report suggests that two-thirds of patients continue to have some swallowing difficulties and half have dietary restrictions (Meshkinpour *et al.* 1996).

Secondary achalasia

This term refers to the development of achalasia secondary to an underlying malignant disorder. It is found in about 4 per cent of patients, particularly older people. In elderly Western populations, infiltrating gastric carcinoma of the cardia should always be carefully looked for, particularly if the history of dysphagia or weight loss is less than 1 year. Rarely, Chagas' disease, chronic intestinal pseudo-obstruction, amyloidosis, sarcoidosis, and several other neoplasms may give rise to achalasia-like pictures.

Secondary oesophageal motility disorders

These disorders occur as part of a more generalized disease; many also affect oropharyngeal function and have been discussed in Chapter 8.2. Systemic sclerosis is the best studied of the connective tissue disorders involving the gastrointestinal tract, although it is not specifically a disease of older people. The oesophagus is the visceral organ most frequently involved. There is atrophy of oesophageal smooth muscle with collagen replacement. Both chewing difficulties and oesophageal symptoms may be present in roughly 50 per cent of subjects. Peristalsis is disrupted. Lower oesophageal sphincter resting pressure is very low or absent, and this distinguishes it from

achalasia. Symptoms due to gastro-oesophageal reflux predominate. Endoscopically, oesophagitis and strictures may be demonstrated. Treatment is aimed at aggressive management of the reflux and its complications (Lock *et al.* 1997).

Amyloidosis has occasionally caused symptomatic oesophageal problems and may present with an achalasia-like picture or inflammatory erosions. Diabetes mellitus may be associated with diffuse motor disturbances throughout the gastrointestinal tract. Problems are less commonly associated with the oesophagus than the stomach. Although manometric abnormalities have been found in up to half of diabetics with peripheral neuropathy, such patients are not usually symptomatic and other pathologies should be looked for. Alcoholic neuropathy may sometimes cause similar problems.

Gastro-oesophageal reflux disease

Intermittent reflux of gastric contents through the lower oesophageal sphincter is a normal physiological event. If such episodes lead to symptoms or physical complications, the term gastro-oesophageal reflux disease is appropriate. This concept has evolved from initial ideas which attributed reflux symptoms to hiatus hernia (Palmer 1968) through the search for and diagnosis of visible (macroscopic) oesophagitis to the current broader perspective of gastro-oesophageal reflux disease. The spectrum comprises typical symptoms, atypical symptoms, and complications. Physiological reflux in normal people causes neither symptoms nor tissue damage. The physical complications of gastro-oesophageal reflux disease include oesophagitis, strictures, Barrett's metaplasia, bleeding, and pulmonary disease. Significant complications may affect as many as one in five of those with endoscopic oesophagitis. Patients with these problems are at the severe end of the spectrum of those with gastro-oesophageal reflux disease. There have been suggestions that people with symptomatic gastro-oesophageal reflux have an increased risk of oesophageal adenocarcinoma (Lagergen *et al.* 1999).

Hiatus hernia

A hiatus hernia is a protrusion of part of the stomach through the oesophageal hiatus of the diaphragm into the thoracic mediastinum. Three main types are described.

1. Sliding hiatus hernia: this occurs when the oesophagus and gastro-oesophageal junction move easily through the hiatus, with the gastro-oesophageal junction displaced into the thorax. They comprise the majority (90 per cent).
2. Para-oesophageal hiatus hernia: the gastro-oesophageal junction is normally placed but the gastric fundus and greater curvature protrude through the hiatus anteriorly to the oesophagus. Volvulus and strangulation may complicate this type more frequently.
3. Combination hiatus hernia: both the gastro-oesophageal junction and the gastric fundus are displaced.

Radiological hiatus hernia becomes more common with advancing age, and has been described in over 60 per cent of those aged over 70 years in hospital series of symptomatic individuals (Pridie 1966; Stilson *et al.* 1969). Estimates of its prevalence depend upon the vigour and techniques used to search for it. The true prevalence in the community is not known. Most sliding hiatus hernias are asymptomatic, whereas para-oesophageal and combination types may more usually give rise to mechanical effects. Chest tightness, dysphagia, bloating, dyspnoea, and satiety, exacerbated by meals and relieved by vomiting and belching, are described. Whereas para-oesophageal and combination types may warrant surgery, the majority of people with the sliding type are improved or asymptomatic 10 years after its discovery regardless of age (Rex *et al.* 1961). Thus a sliding hiatus hernia in itself should be regarded as a non-pathological finding.

The exact relationship between gastro-oesophageal reflux disease and sliding hiatus hernia remains unclear. Many of the symptoms formerly attributed to hiatus hernia have come to be regarded as due to coexisting gastro-oesophageal reflux. Undoubtedly patients with hiatus hernia are over-represented in groups with gastro-oesophageal reflux disease. The presence of a hiatus hernia appears to predispose to gastro-oesophageal reflux symptoms and exacerbate gastro-oesophageal reflux disease, perhaps by disturbing the action of the lower oesophageal sphincter.

Epidemiology

The prevalence and incidence of gastro-oesophageal reflux disease are not accurately known. Estimated rates vary depending upon whether studies have examined reported symptoms or used investigational methods. Further understanding of the epidemiology has been hampered by the lack of methodologically rigorous studies, using validated survey instruments in true random community samples, and the lack of a gold-standard disease definition. Disease definition has been variable, and the terms hiatus hernia, heartburn, and reflux have been used interchangeably. The increasing availability of oesophageal pH monitoring as the gold standard demonstrates that symptoms do not reliably predict the presence of acid reflux. Thus prevalence rates vary depending upon whether studies are symptom based or rely on supposedly objective measures (usually endoscopy) and the nature of the population surveyed (community versus hospital etc.). Few studies have specifically applied robust survey methods to older populations.

Gastro-oesophageal reflux disease defined by heartburn is extremely common; 44 per cent of adult Americans surveyed by the Gallup Organization experienced it monthly. Recent work based on an age- and sex-stratified random sample of 2200 residents of Olmsted County, Minnesota, aged 25 to 74 years incorporated a valid and reliable self-report questionnaire (Locke *et al.* 1997). The overall age- and sex-adjusted prevalence of any episode of heartburn in the preceding year was 42.4 per cent (95 per cent CI, 39.8–45.1). The proportion with frequent (weekly) heartburn was 17.8 per cent (95 per cent CI, 15.8–19.9). The prevalence of yearly and weekly acid regurgitation was 45.0 per cent (95 per cent CI, 42.3–47.7) and 6.3 per cent (95 per cent CI, 5.0–7.6) respectively. The overall prevalence of gastro-oesophageal reflux disease (defined as either heartburn or acid regurgitation) in the preceding year was 58.7 per cent (95 per cent CI, 56.1–61.3) and for weekly episodes it was 19.8 per cent (95 per cent CI, 17.7–21.9). There were no overall significant differences by age or sex for gastro-oesophageal reflux disease, although heartburn was inversely associated with age. For each symptom, a majority reported its presence for more than the last 5 years and of mild to moderate severity. Only 5.4 per cent of those with heartburn or acid regurgitation in the preceding year had consulted a doctor. Consultation was associated with symptom frequency but not with age or sex.

Table 3 Sex-specific prevalence rates (per cent) of atypical reflux symptoms among Olmsted County residents aged 25 to 74 years

	Men[a]	Women[a]	Overall[b]
NCCP	23.9	22.4	23.1
Dysphagia	12.4	14.6	13.5
Globus	4.9	9.1	7.0
Dyspepsia	9.7	11.5	10.6
Asthma	8.7	9.8	9.3
Bronchitis	13.4	14.6	14.0
Pneumonia	19.9	27.2	23.6
Hoarseness	14.3	15.4	14.8

NCCP, non-cardiac chest pain.
[a] Directly age-adjusted to 1990 white Americans.
[b] Directly age- and sex-adjusted to 1990 white Americans.
Reproduced with permission from Locke *et al.* (1997).

The study also reported prevalence rates within the preceding year for the atypical reflux symptoms of non-cardiac chest pain, dysphagia, globus, dyspepsia, asthma, bronchitis, history of pneumonia, and hoarseness (Table 3). Non-cardiac chest pain was inversely associated with age, whereas there was a direct relationship between age and dysphagia. Of those with dysphagia, 37 per cent reported it for more than 5 years. Bronchitis and a history of pneumonia were associated with increasing age; globus and a history of pneumonia were associated with female sex. With the exception of asthma and a history of pneumonia, the atypical symptoms were each more common in those reporting gastro-oesophageal reflux disease.

Given that the prevalence of hiatus hernia (Stilson *et al.* 1969) and oesophageal dysfunction is believed to increase with age, gastro-oesophageal reflux disease may be thought to be more common in older people. A population-based random sample of 600 non-institutionalized Finns aged 65 years or over suggested an overall prevalence of at least monthly gastro-oesophageal reflux disease (heartburn or regurgitation) of 53.5 per cent in men and 66.2 per cent in women (Raiha *et al.* 1992*a*). There were no significant age trends across 5-year age bands. Again, atypical symptoms (including atypical chest pain, dysphagia, chronic cough, and wheeze) were significantly associated with symptoms of gastro-oesophageal reflux disease. Although community based, the reliability and validity of the survey questionnaire in this population is unclear.

The reporting of typical symptoms does not reliably predict the presence of mucosal abnormalities or pathological acid reflux, nor does their absence exclude them. The prevalence of gastro-oesophageal reflux disease based upon investigations, estimated at 2 per cent for oesophagitis and 5 per cent for reflux disease (Wienbeck and Barnert 1989), is far lower than that based upon symptoms. Again, investigational studies have not focused on older people. A United Kingdom endoscopic series of 8445 symptomatic individuals found overall rates of 22.8 per cent, 3 per cent, and 2.9 per cent for macroscopic oesophagitis, benign oesophageal strictures, and benign oesophageal ulceration respectively. There was an increasing rate of oesophagitis with age, peaking at 26.7 per cent of people in the eighth decade (Stoker *et al.* 1988).

Information about the incidence of gastro-oesophageal reflux disease is scanty. In a report based upon a population of 443 000 people in Northeast Scotland, 100 cases of endoscopically verified severe oesophagitis were found, and suggested an annual incidence rate of 4.5 per 100 000. The incidence of severe oesophagitis increased markedly with age (Brunnen *et al.* 1969).

Pathophysiology

Gastro-oesophageal reflux disease is a consequence of the exposure of the lower oesophageal mucosa to gastric contents, with gastric acid being particularly important. There are four main factors to be considered: a high rate of reflux episodes and consequent excessive mucosal exposure to gastric contents, impaired clearance subsequently of the refluxate back into the stomach, the nature of the refluxate (aggressive factors), and the intrinsic lower oesophageal mucosal protective mechanisms (defensive factors).

Reflux episodes

Dysfunction of the lower oesophageal sphincter is generally accepted as a major part of the mechanism of gastro-oesophageal reflux disease. At rest, lower oesophageal sphincter pressure must be absent for reflux to occur. This may arise because of lowered basal tone or through abnormal patterns of relaxation. The role of transient lower oesophageal sphincter relaxations appears to be central. Ambulatory monitoring suggests that the majority of reflux episodes occur in the postprandial period and that transient lower oesophageal sphincter relaxations are the main underlying mechanism. Swallow-related lower oesophageal sphincter relaxation and persistently absent lower oesophageal sphincter tone are minor components. The neurogenic pathway triggering transient lower oesophageal sphincter relaxations has yet to be fully explained but appears to involve reflex vagal inhibition and to be intimately connected to inhibition of the crural diaphragm (Mittal *et al.* 1995*a, b*).

Impaired clearance

Efficient clearing of refluxed material involves both primary and secondary peristalsis. There is emerging evidence of diminished primary and secondary peristalsis in gastro-oesophageal reflux disease, a consequence of which might be impaired oesophageal acid clearance (Schoeman and Holloway 1995).

Aggressive factors

Gastric acid and pepsin are important in causing oesophageal mucosal damage at low pH values. *In vitro* models have also suggested that bile acids may be harmful, but evidence in humans is less straightforward. The availability of new probes to measure bilirubin concentrations suggests higher rates of duodenal reflux in patients with Barrett's oesophagus and erosive oesophagitis. Thus acid and bile acids may exert a synergistic effect in damaging the oesophageal mucosa (Vaezi *et al.* 1995).

Defensive factors

Oesophageal mucosal defences are believed to play an important role in reducing damage from refluxed gastric contents (Scarpignato *et al.* 1995). The normal oesophageal epithelium maintains its integrity though both structural and functional elements. Structural defences comprise the physical barrier of cell membranes and intercellular junctional complexes. There is a uniform stratified squamous non-keratinized epithelium as far as the gastro-oesophageal junction and oesophageal glands in both lamina propria and submucosa. Mucosal and premucosal functional defences include epithelial repair and cellular defences against acid. The oesophageal glands secrete mucin, alkali bicarbonate ions, and epidermal growth factor. It is now recognized that there is an active immunological barrier from gut-associated lymphoid tissue, which in the oesophagus comprises Langerhans cells and lymphocytes. The nature of the disruption of these defensive processes in gastro-oesophageal reflux disease and the effects of age have yet to be determined.

Clinical features

Most patients with gastro-oesophageal reflux disease have had symptoms for between 1 and 3 years prior to presentation. When heartburn or acid regurgitation clearly dominate, they are specific but insensitive symptoms. It is suggested that elderly patients present in a slightly different manner, with typical symptoms being regurgitation, respiratory problems, and vomiting, rather than heartburn (Raiha *et al.* 1991). However, one-third may have none of these. In addition, at least one-third of elderly people with gastro-oesophageal reflux disease suffer from other conditions which will have a substantial bearing upon management.

Associations between gastro-oesophageal reflux disease and respiratory disease are well established, although their causal nature continues to be debated. Potential mechanisms include direct aspiration of gastric contents and vagally mediated responses to oesophageal acid exposure. Symptoms such as wheeze or cough should prompt a careful evaluation of the likelihood of reflux in an older person. There might be repeated episodes of bronchitis or aspiration pneumonia. A predominantly restrictive ventilatory defect is suggested in older people with gastro-oesophageal reflux disease (Raiha *et al.* 1992*b*). Gastro-oesophageal reflux disease may also present with primarily otolaryngological symptoms such as postnasal drip, hoarseness, neck pain, and dentition problems. Non-cardiac chest pain has been attributed to gastro-oesophageal reflux disease in the majority of cases. Since the chance of coexistent ischaemic heart disease, musculoskeletal disorders, and gastro-oesophageal reflux disease increases with age, diagnosis and management are more complicated for older patients.

The long-term outcome of gastro-oesophageal reflux disease in older patients is unclear. In younger populations, although the severity of symptoms may decline over 10 years or more, pathological reflux still occurs. Quality-of-life scores are worse than in control populations (Isolauri *et al.* 1997). There is no reason to expect a different prognosis in older people.

Investigation

Endoscopy and biopsy

This should be the first line of investigation in older people if uncomplicated gastro-oesophageal reflux disease is suspected and to exclude other serious pathology of the upper gastrointestinal tract. Erosive moderate to severe oesophagitis causes little difficulty and is highly specific for abnormal reflux measured by pH monitoring. However, the sensitivity of endoscopy for milder degrees of oesophagitis and non-erosive disease is low. The use of standard grading

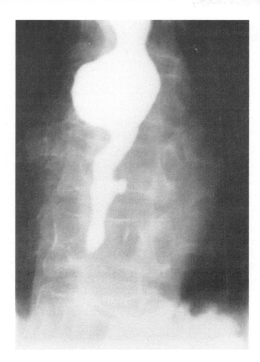

Fig. 4 Barium swallow demonstrating gastro-oesophageal reflux and an oesophageal ulcer. (Courtesy of Dr W. Simpson, Department of Radiology, Newcastle General Hospital.)

scales is to be encouraged, but at least 50 per cent of those with gastro-oesophageal reflux disease disease have a macroscopically normal endoscopy. Histological changes of gastro-oesophageal reflux disease, including basal cell hyperplasia, papillary elongation, and neutrophil/eosinophil infiltration, have been described but do not appear sufficiently robust to be a diagnostic tool in non-erosive disease (Schindlbeck *et al.* 1996). The routine use of random pinch biopsies cannot be recommended for the diagnosis of gastro-oesophageal reflux disease, although a more liberal approach to biopsy seems justified in older people with a higher suspicion of Barrett's metaplasia or early carcinoma.

Barium radiology

In general this has little to offer in the diagnosis of simple gastro-oesophageal reflux disease except where dysphagia is the presenting symptom or in the detection of complications such as severe ulceration or stricture (Fig. 4). The sensitivity and specificity of the barium swallow is insufficient to make it a useful screening test for gastro-oesophageal reflux disease (Johnston *et al.* 1996).

Ambulatory oesophageal pH monitoring

This investigation is generally accepted as the gold standard in the diagnosis of gastro-oesophageal reflux disease. However, this should be viewed with some caution (Ghillebert *et al.* 1995). Not all patients with endoscopic oesophagitis or classical symptoms have abnormal pH studies. The ability of this investigation to differentiate those with symptoms but without oesophagitis from asymptomatic controls may be poor. Its main use is in patients with atypical symptoms and normal endoscopy, and those with respiratory problems thought to be due to acid reflux. It can also aid in the management of those

with continued symptoms despite therapy and prior to antireflux surgery. Newer techniques combining pH with pressure recordings or with bilirubin monitoring have not yet reached routine clinical practice.

Treatment

The aims of therapy should be to relieve the symptoms and avoid the complications of gastro-oesophageal reflux disease. There is evidence to suggest that older persons have more severe mucosal reflux disease but not necessarily reflux symptoms (Collen *et al.* 1995). Thus a more aggressive approach to reflux therapy has been advocated. Such an approach must continue to take into account the overall health and function of the older person (Fig. 5). Recent detailed reviews are available (Galmiche *et al.* 1998; Katz 1998).

Lifestyle modifications

Patients and their relatives should receive education about the nature of gastro-oesophageal reflux disease and simple lifestyle modifications. Elevation of the bed-head, avoiding recumbency for 2 to 3 h after eating, taking smaller meals with reduced fat content, and stopping smoking can all be advised. In older people in particular, a review of medications that might increase reflux should be undertaken. These include anticholinergics, tricyclics, nitrates, calcium antagonists, and theophyllines. However, lifestyle modifications alone rarely suffice.

Medical therapy

Antacids and alginates raise the pH of the refluxed gastric contents and deactivate pepsin. They are more effective than placebo in symptom relief and play a role in self-medication. Sucralfate is a mucosal coating agent which adheres to ulcerated surfaces and may protect against acid and pepsin. Prokinetic agents, such as cisapride, improve lower oesophageal sphincter tone and oesophageal motility, thus reducing reflux and improving luminal clearance. Both sucralfate and cisapride relieve symptoms and promote mucosal healing. This may have a limited role in the treatment of mild to moderate oesophagitis and, perhaps, in combination with other agents.

By far the most effective medical treatment is acid suppression. Gastric acid secretion is inhibited by either antagonizing histamine stimulation of the gastric parietal cell (H_2-receptor antagonists) or by proton pump inhibitors. Both these groups of drugs are widely used and generally well tolerated. The long-term safety of prolonged acid suppression is not known, but no major clinical problems have been reported despite theoretical worries about gastric and oesophageal carcinogenesis, intestinal bacterial overgrowth, and atrophic gastritis (or premalignant condition).

Short-term therapy

The effectiveness of these drugs is directly related to their ability to suppress gastric acid production. Healing of oesophageal lesions requires a greater degree of acid suppression for longer periods than in peptic ulcer disease. Both the H_2-receptor antagonists and proton pump inhibitors have been widely studied as both treatment and maintenance therapies in gastro-oesophageal reflux disease. Unfortunately, the treatment schedules used have varied considerably. Studies suggest mean rates of symptom relief and endoscopic healing with H_2-receptor antagonists of about 60 per cent and 50 per cent respectively. Higher dose regimens than used in standard anti-ulcer

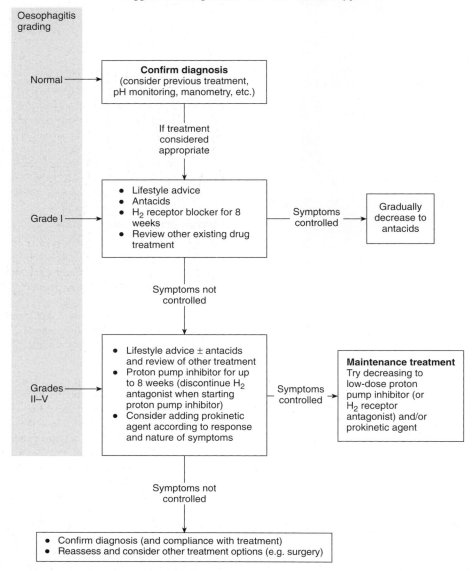

**Gastro-oesophageal reflux disease
Suggested management FOLLOWING endoscopy**

Oesophagitis grading

Normal —

Confirm diagnosis
(consider previous treatment,
pH monitoring, manometry, etc.)

If treatment
considered
appropriate

Grade I —

- Lifestyle advice
- Antacids
- H$_2$ receptor blocker for 8 weeks
- Review other existing drug treatment

Symptoms controlled →

Gradually decrease to antacids

Symptoms not controlled

Grades II–V —

- Lifestyle advice ± antacids and review of other treatment
- Proton pump inhibitor for up to 8 weeks (discontinue H$_2$ antagonist when starting proton pump inhibitor)
- Consider adding prokinetic agent according to response and nature of symptoms

Symptoms controlled →

Maintenance treatment
Try decreasing to low-dose proton pump inhibitor (or H$_2$ receptor antagonist) and/or prokinetic agent

Symptoms not controlled

- Confirm diagnosis (and compliance with treatment)
- Reassess and consider other treatment options (e.g. surgery)

Fig. 5 Suggested approach to the management of gastro-oesophageal reflux disease, after endoscopy, in older people. (Courtesy of Newcastle and North Tyneside Health Authority Drug and Therapeutics Committee.)

treatment are more successful. Consensus has emerged in favour of the use of proton pump inhibitors as first-line therapy to provide rapid symptom relief and mucosal healing in moderate to severe oesophagitis (DeVault and Castell 1995; Boyce 1997; Chiba 1997). Rates of oesophageal healing of over 80 per cent at 4 weeks and over 90 per cent at 8 weeks are typically quoted with proton pump inhibitors. There is little doubt that they are superior to H$_2$-blockers and the advantage is at least as great in elderly patients as for their younger counterparts (James and Parry-Billings 1994). Standard doses of proton pump inhibitors usually suffice, although double-strength dose regimens are used to accelerate healing when standard doses have failed and in particularly severe oesophagitis. In the case of mild oesophagitis, treatment strategies probably depend upon cost

effectiveness; again, the evidence seems to be in favour of proton pump inhibitors (Sridhar *et al.* 1996).

Maintenance therapy

Relapse rates in gastro-oesophageal reflux disease are high (25–85 per cent in various series). Long-term maintenance therapy is desirable both to keep patients symptom free and to reduce complication rates. Again, standard daily doses of proton pump inhibitors restrict relapse rates to between 10 and 20 per cent, and there is preliminary evidence that half-dose regimens may be similarly effective (Bardhan 1995). However, there are few data to demonstrate whether maintenance treatment reduces complications or whether it is cost effective. There is some preliminary evidence that intermittent treatment regimens may help up to 50 per cent of patients' symptoms (Bardhan *et al.* 1999).

Antireflux surgery

Given the effectiveness of proton pump inhibitors, few older patients should require surgery. The introduction of laparoscopic techniques has led some authors to suggest that the threshold for surgery should be lowered in younger people, although the exact technique of fundoplication and long-term outcomes are uncertain (Alderson and Welbourn 1997).

Benign oesophageal strictures

About 80 per cent of benign strictures are believed to be peptic in origin, and perhaps 10 per cent of those with gastro-oesophageal reflux disease severe enough to consult a doctor will suffer from stricture formation. Rarer causes of stricture formation include those that are postoperative, that follow nasogastric intubation, or are due to scleroderma or ingestion of corrosives. Peptic strictures are typically a problem of people in their seventh and eighth decades. Most occur in the distal oesophagus and are 1 to 2 cm long. Those that are more proximal are usually associated with Barrett's oesophagus. Perhaps one-third of patients with Barrett's oesophagus progress to stricture formation.

Dysphagia is the presenting symptom, initially intermittent but typically progressive over a period of 1 to 2 years. An antecedent history of heartburn and acid reflux may be obtained, although in a quarter of those with Barrett's changes no prior history is forthcoming. Patients with dysphagia should have a barium swallow to indicate the length and location of the lesion (Fig. 6). Endoscopy must be performed since about a quarter of radiological strictures have a misleading appearance, with apparently benign strictures being malignant and vice versa. Biopsies and brushings can be taken, allowing a correct histological diagnosis in about 95 per cent of cases.

Therapy aims to relieve dysphagia and prevent recurrence. In elderly people the mainstay of treatment is periodic dilatation of the stricture and acid suppression therapy. Adequate suppressive therapy may reduce the need for dilatation, but up to three-quarters of elderly patients require the procedure at yearly intervals. Patients with a prior history of weight loss who do not report heartburn at initial presentation are more likely to require repeat procedures. The pattern of frequent repeat dilatation for recurrent stricture is established during the first year of follow-up (Agnew *et al.* 1996). Oesophageal dilatation under endoscopic control is now a safe and widely practised procedure. The major complication of perforation should occur in less than 1 per cent of procedures in experienced hands. Conservative management of this complication, undertaken in consultation with an experienced oesophageal surgeon, is often adequate. The indications for surgical treatment of benign oesophageal stricture in older people are now very few indeed. Surgical fatality rates are as high as 15 per cent.

Barrett's oesophagus

The term Barrett's oesophagus or columnar-lined oesophagus is used to describe the condition in which a variable length of the distal

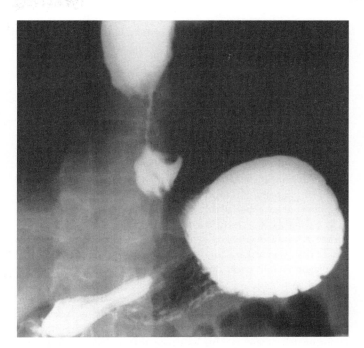

Fig. 6 Sliding hiatus hernia and lower oesophageal peptic stricture. The latter was thought to be malignant on radiology but proved benign after endoscopy and biopsy. (Courtesy of Dr W. Simpson, Department of Radiology, Newcastle General Hospital.)

oesophageal epithelium is replaced by columnar epithelium. It is regarded as a maladaptive response to mucosal injury from gastro-oesophageal reflux whereby the normal stratified squamous epithelium is replaced by a simple columnar metaplastic one. Chronic gastro-oesophageal reflux disease is accepted as the primary risk factor for the development of Barrett's oesophagus. Of greatest clinical concern is the predisposition of 8 to 15 per cent of patients with Barrett's oesophagus to develop adenocarcinoma of the oesophagus and gastric cardia, a risk 30 to 40 times that of the general population. There appears to be aberrant differentiation of oesophageal squamous cells. It is not clear why only a minority of those with reflux develop metaplasia. The severity of reflux damage may be an important factor; acid reflux appears greater in those who develop Barrett's oesophagus. There is considerable interest in the role of duodenogastric reflux. Studies suggest greater bilirubin reflux in those who develop Barrett's oesophagus, and it appears that oesophageal reflux of both acid and duodenal juices is more damaging than either alone. Clearly, the development of Barrett's oesophagus is multifactorial.

The condition appears to have a bimodal age distribution (at least in men), with an overall mean age of 64 years. The male-to-female ratio is estimated at 3:1. The prevalence among individuals with symptoms of gastro-oesophageal reflux disease is around 12 per cent. The population prevalence is not known; autopsy studies suggest that it is about 1 per cent (Cameron *et al.* 1990), more than 20 times higher than clinically based studies. Thus it appears that the majority of cases are clinically undiagnosed. About two-thirds of patients give a preceding history of gastro-oesophageal reflux symptoms. On average, patients with Barrett's oesophagus develop reflux symptoms at a younger age and have a longer duration and severity of symptoms than controls (Eisen *et al.* 1997). In 10 per cent, presentation is with dysphagia secondary to inflammatory stricture. Occasionally, ulcers develop in the columnar epithelium causing chest pain and, rarely, can perforate with severe consequences.

Endoscopic appearances are usually distinctive with a sharp demarcation between pale squamous epithelium and velvety red columnar mucosa. The traditional definition of Barrett's oesophagus requires the replacement of the distal oesophageal lining by 3 cm or more of circumferential columnar epithelium in continuity with the gastric mucosa. This length is purely arbitrary. It has been suggested that the definition should be histologically based; cardia- or junction-type epithelium is not diagnostic, whereas the finding of specialized intestinal epithelium is. Patients who fail to fulfil the traditional definition but have specialized intestinal epithelium have been referred to as having short-segment Barrett's oesophagus. The short-segment variety is easily overlooked at endoscopy but carries an increased cancer risk (Nandurkar et al. 1997). Biopsies are essential to confirm the diagnosis and assess cancer risk. A rigorous systematic biopsy protocol is advised.

Treatment of patients with Barrett's oesophagus aims to control symptoms when present and also to slow down or reverse the potential progression from a metaplastic to a malignant epithelium. Unfortunately, there is little evidence that reducing oesophageal epithelial acid exposure causes significant regression of the metaplasia (Sharma et al. 1997). Where frank carcinoma is arising in metaplastic epithelium, surgery may be successful in appropriately assessed patients. For older people, such a policy needs to be tempered by a general assessment of life expectancy, fitness for surgery, and quality of life. Other strategies to ablate the columnar epithelium, such as photodynamic therapy, laser coagulation, or electrocoagulation, are not yet of proven value.

In view of the risk of the metaplasia–dysplasia–carcinoma sequence, endoscopic screening of patients with gastro-oesophageal reflux disease and surveillance of those with Barrett's oesophagus are potentially attractive. An accumulation of several genetic abnormalities is described during the stepwise neoplastic progression of Barrett's epithelium. They include an increasing proliferation index, p53 overexpression, chromosome loss (17q), and aneuploidy. Overexpression of the oncogene c-erbB-2 may be a late event in the sequence. Patients progress from low- to high-grade dysplasia, with the latter being associated with early invasive cancer in 50 to 66 per cent of cases. High-grade dysplasia is regarded by many as an indication for surgery in younger patients, and resection of high-grade dysplasia or early adenocarcinoma is associated with prolonged survival (Wright 1997). However, there are no data from randomized trials of either screening or surveillance that show a reduction in mortality. The universal adoption of screening programmes cannot yet be justified (van der Burgh et al. 1996).

Non-cardiac chest pain

It is estimated that 20 to 30 per cent of people with angina-like pain have normal coronary angiograms. Despite the exclusion of ischaemic heart disease, many of these people have recurrent disabling symptoms and multiple contacts with health services. Non-cardiac chest pain is an area of increasing interest, but mostly related to middle-aged patients.

Every reasonable effort should be made to exclude cardiac disease. A clinical history is often non-discriminatory in this setting. However, in older people the invasiveness of any further investigations must be tempered by a realistic appraisal of their willingness and suitability to undergo procedures such as exercise testing, angiography, etc. Musculoskeletal disease, peptic ulcer, biliary and pancreatic disease, and depressive illness should be considered as a cause of non-cardiac chest pain in older people.

Oesophageal motility disorders and gastro-oesophageal reflux disease can both be the cause of non-cardiac chest pain. Furthermore, some chest pain episodes in individuals with proven ischaemic heart disease may well be related to oesophageal rather than cardiac dysfunction. The diagnostic value of techniques such as ambulatory pH and manometry in this setting is unclear.

Diverticula, webs, and rings

An oesophageal diverticulum is a pouching of the oesophageal wall that may contain all portions of the wall or lack the muscular coat. Diverticula may arise from pulsion or traction forces. Most are false diverticula, lacking the muscular coat, and result from pulsion forces. Anatomically, they are usually divided into pharyngo-oesophageal, mid-oesophageal, epiphrenic diverticula, and intramural pseudo-diverticulosis.

Pharyngo-oesophageal diverticulum (Zenker's diverticulum)

Zenker's diverticulum is defined as a protrusion of hypopharyngeal mucosa between the oblique fibres of the inferior pharyngeal constrictor and the transverse fibres of the cricopharyngeus. The pathogenesis still remains controversial, but may relate to incomplete opening of the upper oesophageal sphincter due to diminished compliance of the cricopharyngeus.

This is a disorder of people in their seventh and eighth decades. While many are asymptomatic, there may be a presentation of chronic upper dysphagia, regurgitation of undigested food, aspiration, halitosis, or voice changes. Symptoms are progressive as the pouch enlarges (Fig. 7). The most serious complications are the development of squamous carcinoma, fistulas, and aspiration. Diagnosis is made most accurately with barium studies, best seen on lateral films. Endoscopy can be dangerous because of the risk of perforation. Treatment for persistent symptoms is surgical, and cricopharyngeal myotomy seems an important component of any surgical procedure. In very frail elderly people, endoscopic diathermy division of the wall between the oesophagus and the diverticulum may provide symptomatic relief.

Mid-oesophageal diverticula

These arise in the middle third of the oesophagus. They were initially described in relation to traction forces, usually thought to be secondary to mediastinal inflammatory disease such as tuberculosis. More recent systematic studies demonstrate that many appear to arise as a result of pulsion forces secondary to oesophageal motility disorders. They are usually asymptomatic, but may present with dysphagia or chest pain, although these symptoms probably reflect underlying motility

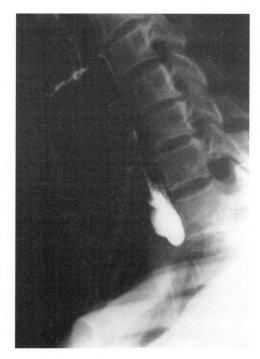

Fig. 7 Barium studies demonstrating a pharyngeal pouch. (Courtesy of Dr W. Simpson, Department of Radiology, Newcastle General Hospital.)

problems. Complications such as perforation are very unusual and active treatment is unnecessary.

Epiphrenic diverticula

These are situated in the distal oesophagus and may be single or multiple. The pathogenesis is most probably secondary to raised intraluminal pressure as a consequence of motility disorders. Again, the majority are probably asymptomatic. Complications and the need for treatment should be assessed on an individual basis.

Pseudodiverticulosis

Oesophageal intramural pseudodiverticulosis due to dilated excretory ducts in the oesophageal mucosal glands is a rare condition predominantly of older people. It is probably secondary to chronic inflammatory change in the ducts of the submucosal glands. Dysphagia for solids is the most usual symptom. This condition is best demonstrated on barium radiology as 'collar stud' lesions. Candidiasis is a complication in about half of cases and should be treated in its own right.

Oesophageal webs and rings

An oesophageal ring is a mucosal structure located at the gastro-oesophageal junction with squamous epithelium on the upper aspect and columnar epithelium on the lower. The term oesophageal web is used for all other ring-like structures throughout the oesophagus and thus covered by squamous epithelium. They are not uncommon and are often coincidental findings by radiology or endoscopy.

Cervical oesophageal webs are found in the postcricoid area. They typically occur in postmenopausal women, and when associated with iron deficiency anaemia have been labelled as the Brown–Kelly–Paterson syndrome (also inappropriately named the Plummer–Vinson syndrome). The incidence of the disorder appears to be falling. Careful radiology or videofluoroscopy of the postcricoid area is needed to make the diagnosis. Diagnostic endoscopy often inadvertently ruptures the web, and sometimes dilatation is needed. They are said to be associated with postcricoid carcinoma; thus regular endoscopic surveillance is advocated.

Lower oesophageal rings (Schatzki's rings) are common (6–14 per cent of barium examinations), but less than 1 per cent are symptomatic. Their aetiology is unclear. Radiology is more sensitive than endoscopy in demonstrating the ring. When sporadic dysphagia is present, simple passage of the endoscope though the ring may suffice.

Mid-oesophageal webs are uncommon but appear to be associated with dermatological problems and graft versus host reactions.

Non-peptic strictures

All oesophageal strictures in older people should be regarded as malignant until proven otherwise. The vast majority of benign strictures are a consequence of reflux disease. Rarely, collagen diseases, infection, Crohn's disease, or caustic injury are implicated. Of particular relevance to older people are strictures secondary to medication. External compression from surrounding mediastinal structures should always be considered as a cause of dysphagic symptoms. Dysphagia aortica as a result of thoracic aortic aneurysm or sclerotic descending aorta, a dilated left atrium, or cervical vertebral osteophytes can give rise to dysphagia. Mediastinal tumours should not be forgotten.

Oesophageal neoplasms
Oesophageal carcinoma

Oesophageal carcinoma is a problem of advancing years; most patients present at ages over 65 years. Cancers of the middle and lower thirds of the oesophagus are most common. The majority are squamous cell carcinoma, although the proportion of adenocarcinoma is worryingly increasing and approaching 50 per cent. Sadly, the outlook remains bleak, with overall 5-year survival rates outside specialist centres of about 5 per cent. Surgical exploration is attempted in under half of patients, of which curative or palliative resection is performed in about three-quarters. Operative fatality rates of 10 to 20 per cent or more are still reported and postoperative morbidity is substantial. Of those who do not proceed to surgery, 10 per cent receive radiotherapy and about half receive palliative intubation. Some encouragement might be taken from reports emanating from specialist centres that suggest recent improvement in both 5-year survival rates (17 per cent) and operative fatality rates (4 per cent) (Thomas *et al.* 1997). Developments in palliative interventions are welcome, although distressing symptoms associated with oesophageal obstruction remain problematic.

Epidemiology

There is considerable geographic and ethnic variation in this disease, suggesting that environmental factors are important. The highest annual incidence rates, exceeding 100 per 100 000, are reported in Iran, China, and parts of Russia, whereas rates in Western Europe and among white Americans are under 10 per 100 000. Higher rates are reported in black Americans. In China, differences of several hundredfold in mortality from squamous carcinoma are found between nearby areas. There has been a dramatic increase in oesophageal adenocarcinoma over recent years (Blot *et al.* 1991), although rates for squamous carcinoma are probably static. Overall, oesophageal cancer is the fourth and fifteenth most common cancer in the developing and the developed worlds respectively.

Several important risk factors for squamous cell carcinoma are recognized, including smoking, alcohol, nitrosamines, and diet. Malnutrition is clearly a risk factor. In the Linxian district of China, where the disease frequency is particularly high, a randomized trial of mineral supplementation with β-carotene, selenium, and α-tocopherol showed a small but significant reduction in 5-year mortality. Achalasia seems to confer a 14- to 17-fold excess risk. Barrett's oesophagus is the major recognized risk factor for adenocarcinoma of the oesophagus. It is increasingly recognized that short segments of Barrett's intestinal metaplasia, which are easily missed at endoscopy, give rise to oesophagogastric junctional adenocarcinoma (Cameron *et al.* 1995). The rare autosomal dominant condition tylosis is associated with a 95 per cent risk of distal oesophageal malignancy by the age of 65. Patients with coeliac disease also have an enhanced risk.

There is some evidence that aspirin and other non-steroidal anti-inflammatory drugs exert protective effects on colorectal and oesophageal mucosa and cancer risk. Definitive data require large randomized controlled trials (Morgan 1996).

Molecular events in oesophageal cancer

Recent work has begun to unravel the sequence of stepwise genetic alterations that activate oncogenes and disable tumour suppressor genes in oesophageal epithelium. Altered cells have a growth advantage and hyperproliferate. When sufficient DNA mutations accumulate, a malignant clone of cells will invade adjacent tissues. Suggested molecular events promoting carcinogenesis include overexpression of the cyclin D1 gene (on chromosome 11q13) and the c-*erbB*-2 gene. Altered expression of the cell adhesion molecule E-cadherin has been observed. Loss of tumour suppressor genes on chromosomes 9q and 3p and abnormalities of the p53 gene on chromosome 17p are described.

Clinical presentation

Dysphagia is the most common symptom, initially for solids but progressing over a few months to liquids and ultimately saliva. Dysphagia does not usually occur until the lumen is at least 60 per cent stenosed and therefore the disease is well advanced. Weight loss may be rapid. Regurgitation, particularly at night, can be troublesome. Pulmonary symptoms result from both aspiration and tracheooesophageal fistula. Odynophagia is not uncommon. Pain may result from invasion of the spine, intercostal nerves, or aorta. Hoarseness occurs if there is recurrent laryngeal nerve involvement. Overt bleeding is unusual; iron deficiency anaemia is more likely. Sudden death due to erosion into the aorta occurs occasionally. Examination may well be unremarkable except for generalized debility and cachexia. When discrete physical signs are present, such as supraclavicular lymphadenopathy, superior vena cava obstruction, cervical masses, stridor,

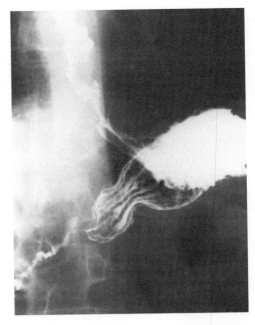

Fig. 8 Barium swallow demonstrating a lower oesophageal carcinoma. (Courtesy of Dr W. Simpson, Department of Radiology, Newcastle General Hospital.)

etc., the disease is considerably advanced. Evidence of ascites and of metastatic spread to the liver should be sought.

The median delay from the onset of symptoms to histological diagnosis in a United Kingdom series was 17.3 weeks (interquartile range 7.3–23.8 weeks) (Martin *et al.* 1997). Delay did not appear to vary with the nature of the presenting symptom. The majority of tumours present in stage 3 or 4 disease, and disease stage is associated with duration of delay.

Investigations

The level of the cancer is initially determined using barium studies (Fig. 8). In the most advanced lesions, the typical 'apple-core' appearance can be seen. Earlier cancers are not so easily identified as malignant. Evidence of a fistula must be distinguished from overspill into the trachea. Endoscopy will normally provide a definitive diagnosis if a combination of multiple biopsies and brushings is employed. Abdominal ultrasound of the liver and coeliac axis should be undertaken. Preoperative staging with CT scanning has relatively low sensitivity for spread to adjacent structures and nodal spread, but is more useful for detecting more distant lung metastases. Bronchoscopy may be employed. Endoscopic ultrasound (endosonography) to assess the depth of invasion through the oesophageal wall and thoracoscopic staging show more promise.

Treatment

The late presentation of the disease remains the limiting factor in therapy. There is no evidence to support the introduction of screening strategies. Surgical resection is the standard approach to early oesophageal carcinoma, although the reality is that only a small minority achieve a cure. Improvements in outcome have occurred, but are predominantly limited to specialist centres. This is a disease of older people and those who are likely to have poorer health status due to smoking, alcohol, and nutritional deficits. Operative fatality and morbidity are crucial considerations. Even in expert hands operative fatality in patients aged over 80 years is more than 40 per cent (Hennessy 1996). Exposing older people to perioperative risks that are of the same magnitude or higher than 5-year survival rates has little merit. Extremely careful assessment and selection is required for older people to benefit from surgery (Adams *et al.* 1996).

Lymph node status is a strong prognostic factor for long-term survival. Unfortunately, the high frequency of microscopic lymph node spread at resection (over 80 per cent) means that preoperative tumour staging can be inaccurate. Favourable outcome is predominantly limited to those with superficial carcinoma. Submucosal cancer should be regarded as an advanced lesion. Surgical 5-year survival in the best hands and carefully selected subjects falls as disease staging worsens (stage I disease, 30–50 per cent; stage IIB, 5–15 per cent). Patterns of treatment failure point to the need for better control of local and distant recurrence with systemic therapy (Ilson and Kelsen 1996).

There has been evaluation of radiotherapy and chemotherapy alone and, increasingly, in combination. Interpretation is hampered by the multiplicity of regimens used, the mixing of the two histological types of oesophageal carcinoma, and the fact that, as usual, many trials excluded people over 70 or 75 years of age. Definitive radiotherapy alone has shown some benefit in patients unsuitable for surgery. Chemotherapy regimens have predominantly incorporated the agents cisplatin, 5-fluorouracil, vindesine, mitomycin, and paclitaxel. Squamous cell oesophageal carcinoma appears to be more chemosensitive than adenocarcinoma. Adjuvant therapy with combined chemoradiation as opposed to surgery alone is increasingly being studied. Multimodal therapy with preoperative radiotherapy and fluorouracil has been shown to be superior to surgery alone in oesophageal adenocarcinoma (3-year survival of 32 per cent versus 5 per cent) (Walsh *et al.* 1996), whereas in squamous carcinoma benefits have been shown only in terms of disease-free survival (Bosset *et al.* 1997). It is recommended that preoperative adjuvant chemoradiotherapy is administered in the context of controlled clinical trials.

Palliative management with the aim of reducing the dysphagia and other symptoms is the realistic option for most patients. Proper evaluation of palliative regimens is still hampered by uncertainty about the robustness of quality-of-life instruments to measure outcome in oesophageal cancer. Palliation is often far from complete, with considerable residual symptoms and dietary modifications still affecting patients.

Although surgery probably provides the most effective palliation, the majority of older subjects are not suitable for surgical treatment. The use of oesophageal stenting for the palliation of malignant oesophageal strictures is an area of continued and active investigation. Expandable metal stents appear to have advantages over conventional rigid systems. The major disadvantages are stent migration and obstruction due to tumour overgrowth. There is a lack of randomized trial information evaluating the numerous technical variations in stent design (Angueira and Kadakia 1997). Complication rates (perforation, 6–8 per cent; dislocation, 1–20 per cent; obstruction, 5–10 per cent) and fatality (about 4 per cent) from these palliative procedures are not negligible. The use of a Nd:YAG laser alone for thermal endoluminal ablation has a complication rate of under 5 per cent, but symptom relief often requires repeat treatments every 4 to 6 weeks. There are early reports that combining laser therapy with palliative radiotherapy reduces the frequency of repeat interventions. Photodynamic therapy is based on the principle that a photosensitive agent selectively accumulates in malignant tissue. Laser therapy activates the photosensitive agent and a non-thermal reaction follows, causing selective damage to malignant tissue. The major disadvantage is accumulation of the agent in the skin, so that sun exposure must be avoided. Therefore it is apparent that well-conducted randomized controlled trials will be vital in determining the most effective palliative management strategies in oesophageal cancer.

Other oesophageal neoplasms

Rare malignant oesophageal neoplasms include histological variants of both squamous cell carcinomas and adenocarcinomas, usually with an even worse outlook. Small-cell carcinomas resembling oat cell tumours of the lung may be seen and have been associated with paraneoplastic syndromes. Carcinoid and sarcoma-like tumours are rare. Non-neoplastic tumours can arise from heterotopias, cysts, or granulomatous deposits. Leiomyoma is the most common benign tumour.

Oesophageal perforation

Spontaneous perforation (Boerhaave's syndrome) follows violent vomiting and, atypically, lesser activities such as straining. The triad of vomiting, lower chest pain, and subcutaneous emphysema is not always present, and delays in diagnosis are potentially fatal. Secondary or traumatic perforation is more common. Instrumental procedures, drug-related or corrosive oesophagitis, and foreign bodies are implicated for older people. Plain chest radiographs are useful and may show pneumomediastinum or loss of contour of the descending aorta at the level of the left diaphragm. Conservative management may be possible in 'clean' perforations, but the involvement of an experienced oesophageal surgeon is crucial.

Oesophageal infections

Infections of the oesophagus are often undiagnosed in frail elderly people and those who are immunocompromised. Inadequate treatment may lead to local and systemic complications. Dysphagia and odynophagia are the typical symptoms, although older people often present non-specifically. Oral examination may show *Candida* or be normal.

Candida albicans is a normal commensal of the digestive tract, thought to be restrained by lactic-acid-producing flora. It is the most prevalent agent causing infectious oesophagitis in older people. Infection is usually associated with breaches of the mucosal surfaces caused by mechanical trauma or obstruction, irradiation, or a defect in systemic immunity (diabetes, malignancy, malnutrition). Broad-spectrum antibiotics are often implicated. Suspicion of the possibility is the key to diagnosis. Barium swallow (Fig. 9) or, preferably, endoscopy with brushings/biopsy will make the diagnosis. Oral systemic therapy with ketoconazole or fluconazole, together with attention to the underlying causes, is usually effective. Viral oesophagitis due to herpes simplex virus, cytomegalovirus, or Epstein–Barr virus

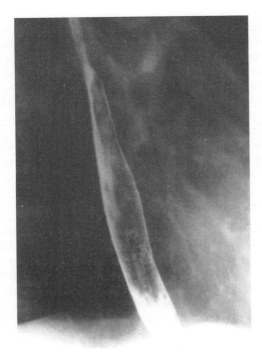

Fig. 9 Barium radiology suggesting oesophageal candidiasis. (Courtesy of Dr W. Simpson, Department of Radiology, Newcastle General Hospital.)

is associated with immune deficiency. HIV infection may occur in older people.

Drugs and the oesophagus

This is an important topic in relation to older people; about half of adverse drug reactions affecting the oesophagus occur in patients aged over 65. Drugs damage the oesophagus either directly by local contact or as a result of systemic absorption.

The normal oesophagus can retain tablets for up to 20 min. Prolonged transit times are more likely in older people. Extrinsic compression which impedes drug passage is more prevalent. Most injuries occur in the mid-lower oesophagus. Gelatin capsule formulations have a particular tendency to remain in the oesophagus of older people. The drugs most often implicated in local injury include slow-release potassium, tetracycline, emepromium bromide, aspirin, non-steroidal anti-inflammatory drugs, and, recently, alendronate. All elderly patients should be advised to take such compounds with plenty of fluids and in the upright position. Liquid formulations may be substituted for tablets.

After systemic absorption some drugs influence oesophageal function by effects on motility and lower oesophageal sphincter pressure. If there is pre-existing disease, symptoms may be exacerbated. Motor stimulation is used therapeutically with prokinetic agents in gastro-oesophageal reflux disease. These should be avoided in oesophageal motility disorders. Drugs which inhibit motor activity and impair lower oesophageal sphincter tone tend to promote gastro-oesophageal reflux disease. These include anticholinergics, nitrates, calcium antagonists, β-blockers, benzodiazepines, and theophyllines.

References

Adamek, R. J., Wegener, M., Wienbeck, M., Gielen, B. (1994). Long-term oesophageal manometry in healthy subjects. Evaluation of normal values and influence of age. *Digestive Diseases and Sciences*, **39**, 2069–73.

Adams, D.J., Craig, S.R., Sang, C.T., Cameron, E.W., Walker, W.S. (1996). Oesophagectomy for carcinoma in the octogenarian. *Annals of Thoracic Surgery*, **61**, 190–4.

Agnew, S.R., Pandya, S.P., Reynolds, R.P.E., and Preiksaitis, H.G. (1996). Predictors for frequent oesophageal dilations of benign peptic strictures. *Digestive Diseases and Sciences*, **41**, 931–6.

Alderson, D. and Welbourn, C.R.B. (1997). Laparoscopic surgery for gastroesophageal reflux disease. *Gut*, **40**, 565–7.

Angueira, C.E. and Kadakia, S.C. (1997). Oesophageal stents for inoperable oesophageal cancer: which top use? *American Journal of Gastroenterology*, **92**, 373–5.

Axon, A.T.R., Bell, G.D., Jones, R.H., Quine, M.A., and McCloy, R.F. (1995). Guidelines on appropriate indications for upper gastrointestinal endoscopy. *British Medical Journal*, **310**, 853–6.

Bannister, P., Stanners, A.J., Mountford, R.A. (1990). Dysphagia in the elderly. *Journal of the Royal Society of Medicine*, **83**, 552–3.

Bardhan, K.D. (1995). The role of proton pump inhibitors in the treatment of gastroesophageal reflux disease. *Alimentary Pharmacological Therapy*, **9** (Supplement 1), 15–25.

Bardhan, K.D., Müller-Lisner, M.A., Bigord, M.A., *et al.* (1999). Symptomatic gastro-oesophageal reflux disease: double blind controlled study of intermittent treatment with omeprazole or ranitidine. *British Medical Journal*, **318**, 502–7.

Blot, W.J., Devesa, S.S., Kneller, R.W., and Fraumeni, J.F. (1991). Rising incidence of adenocarcinoma of the oesophagus and gastric cardia. *Journal of the American Medical Association*, **265**, 1287–9.

Bosset, J.F., Gignoux, M., and Triboulet, J.P. (1997). Chemotherapy followed by surgery compared with surgery alone in squamous-cell cancer of the oesophagus. *New England Journal of Medicine*, **337**, 161–7.

Boyce, H.W. (1997). Therapeutic approaches to healing oesophagitis. *American Journal of Gastroenterology*, **92** (Supplement), 22S–9S

British Society of Gastroenterology (1991). Recommendations for standards of sedation and patient monitoring during gastrointestinal endoscopy. *Gut*, **32**, 823–7.

Brunnen, P.L., Karmody, A.M., Needham, C.D. (1969). Severe peptic oesophagitis. *Gut*, **10**, 831–7.

Cameron, A.J., Zinmeister, A.R., Ballard, D.J., and Carney, J.A. (1990). Prevalence of columnar-lined (Barrett's) oesophagus. Comparison of population-based clinical and autopsy findings. *Gastroenterology*, **99**, 918–22.

Cameron, A.J., Lomboy, C.T., Pera, M., and Carpenter, H.A. (1995). Adenocarcinoma of the oesophagogastric junction and Barrett's oesophagus. *Gastroenterology*, **109**, 1541–6.

Castell, J.A. and Castell, D.O. (1996). Upper oesophageal sphincter and pharyngeal function and oropharyngeal (transfer) dysphagia. *Gastroenterology Clinics of North America*, **25**, 35–50.

Chiba, N., DeCara, C.J., Wilkinson, J.M., and Hunt, R.H. (1997). Speed of healing and symptom relief in grade II to IV gastro-oesophageal reflux: a meta-analysis. *Gastroenterology*, **112**, 1798–810.

Collen, M.J., Abdulian, J.D., and Chen, Y.K. (1995). Gastroesophageal reflux disease in the elderly: more severe disease that requires aggressive therapy. *American Journal of Gastroenterology*, **90**, 1053–7.

Dejaeger, E., Pelemans, W., Bibau, G., and Ponette, E. (1994). Manofluorographic analysis of swallowing in the elderly. *Dysphagia*, **9**, 156–61.

Dent, J. and Holloway, R.H. (1996). Oesophageal motility and reflux testing: state of the art and clinical role in the twenty-first century. *Gastroenterology Clinics of North America*, **25**, 51–73.

DeVault, K.R. and Castell, D.O. (1995). Guidelines for the diagnosis and treatment of gastroesophageal reflux disease. *Archives of Internal Medicine*, 155, 2165–73 .

Drossman, D.A., Funch-Jensen, P., Janssens, J, *et al.* (1990). Identification of subgroups of functional bowel disorders. *Gastroenterology International*, 3, 159–72.

Drossman, D.A., Li, Z., Andruzzi, E., *et al.* (1993). U.S. Householder Survey of functional gastrointestinal disorders: prevalence, sociodemography, and health impact. *Digestive Diseases and Sciences*, 38, 1569–80.

Eckardt, V.F., Köhne, U., Jurginger, T., and Westerneier, T. (1997). Risk factors for diagnostic delay in achalasia. *Digestive Diseases and Sciences*, 42, 580–5.

Edwards, D.A.W. (1976). Discriminatory value of symptoms in the differential diagnosis of dysphagia. *Clinics in Gastroenterology*, 5, 49–57.

Eisen, G.M., Sandler, R.S., Murray, S., and Gottfried, M. (1997). The relationship between gastroesophageal reflux disease and its complications with Barrett's oesophagus. *American Journal of Gastroenterology*, 92, 27–31.

Ekberg, O. and Feinberg, M.J. (1991). Altered swallowing function in elderly patients without dysphagia: radiologic findings in 56 cases. *American Journal of Roentgenology*, 156, 1181–4.

Ergun, G.A. and Kahrilas, P.J. (1996). Clinical applications of oesophageal manometry and pH monitoring. *American Journal of Gastroenterology*, 91, 1077–89.

Eslami, M.H., Richards, W.G., and Sugarbaker, D.J. (1994). Esophageal physiology. *Chest Surgery Clinics of North America*, 4, 635–52.

Fass, R., Sampliner, R.E., Mackel, C., McGee, D., and Rappaport, W. (1993). Age- and gender-related differences in 24 hour oesophageal pH monitoring of normal subjects. *Digestive Diseases and Sciences*, 38, 1926–8.

Galmiche, J.P., Letessier, E., and Scarpignato, C. (1998). Treatment of gastro-oesophageal reflux in adults. *British Medical Journal*, 316, 1720–3.

Ghillebert, G., Demeyere, A.M., Janssens, J., and Vantrappen, G. (1995). How well can quantitative 24 hour intraoesophageal monitoring distinguish various degrees of reflux disease? *Digestive Diseases and Sciences*, 40,1317–24.

Goldblum, J.R., Rice, T.W., and Richter, J.E. (1996). Histopathologic features in esophagomyotomy specimens from patients with achalasia. *Gastroenterology*, 111, 648–54.

Grishaw, E.K., Ott, D.J., Frederick, M.G., Gelfand, D.W., and Chen, M.Y.M. (1996). Functional abnormalities of the esophagus: a prospective analysis of radiographic findings relative to age and symptoms. *American Journal of Roentgenology*, 167, 719–23.

Gupta, S.D., Petrus, L.V., Gibbins, F.J., *et al.* (1987). Endoscopic evaluation of dysphagia in the elderly. *Age and Ageing*, 16, 159–64.

Hawkins, S.P., Rowlands, P.C., and Shorvon, P.J. (1991). Barium meals in the elderly—a quality reassurance. *British Journal of Radiology*, 64, 113–15.

Hennessy, T.P.J. (1996). Cancer of the oesophagus. *Postgraduate Medical Journal*, 72, 458–63.

Ilson, D.H. and Kelsen, D.P. (1996). Management of oesophageal cancer. *Oncology*, 10, 1385–96.

Isolauri, J., Luostarinen, M., Isolauri, E., *et al.* (1997). Natural course of gastroesophageal reflux disease: 17–22 year follow-up of 60 patients. *American Journal of Gastroenterology*, 92, 37–41.

James, O.F.W. and Parry-Billings, K.S. (1994). Comparison of omeprazole and histamine H_2-receptor antagonists in the treatment of elderly and young patients with reflux oesophagitis. *Age and Ageing*, 23, 121–6.

Johnston, B.T., Troshinsky, M.B., Castell, J.A., and Castell, D.O. (1996). Comparison of barium radiology with oesophageal pH monitoring in the diagnosis of gastroesophogeal reflux disease. *American Journal of Gastroenterology*, 91, 1181–5.

Jones, R. and Lydeard, S. (1989). Prevalence of symptoms of dyspepsia in the community. *British Medical Journal*, 298, 30–2.

Katz, P.O. (1998). Gastroesophageal reflux diseases. *Journal of the American Geriatrics Society*, 46, 1558–65.

Kay, L. (1994). Prevalence, incidence and prognosis of gastrointestinal symptoms in a random sample of an elderly population. *Age and Ageing*, 23, 146–9.

Kay, L. and Jorgensen, T. (1996). Redefining abdominal syndromes: results of a population based study. *Scandinavian Journal of Gastroenterology*, 31, 469–75.

Lagergren, J., Bergström, R., Lindgren, A., and Nyren, O. (1999). Symptomatic gastroesophageal reflux as a risk factor for esophageal adenocarcinoma. *New England Journal of Medicine*, 340, 825–31.

Lock, G., Holstege, A., Lang, B., and Scholmerich, J. (1997). Gastrointestinal manifestations of progressive systemic sclerosis. *American Journal of Gastroenterology*, 92, 763–71.

Locke, G.R., Talley, N.J., Fett, S.L., Zinsmeiser, A.R., and Melton, L.J. (1997). Prevalence and clinical spectrum of gastroesophageal reflux: a population-based study in Olmsted County, Minnesota. *Gastroenterology*, 112, 1488–56.

Lynn, R.B. (1992). Mechanisms of esophageal pain. *American Journal of Medicine*, 92, 11S–19S.

Martin, I.G., Young, S., Sue-Ling, H., and Johnston, D. (1997). Delays in the diagnosis of oesophagogastric cancer: a consecutive case series. *British Medical Journal*, 314, 467–71.

Meshkinpour, H., Haghighat, P., and Dutton, C. (1994). Clinical spectrum of oesophageal aperistalsis in the elderly. *American Journal of Gastroenterology*, 89, 1480–3.

Meshkinpour, H., Haghighat, P., and Meshkinpour, A. (1996). Quality of life among patients treated for achalasia. *Digestive Diseases and Sciences*, 41, 352–6.

Mittal, R.K., Holloway, R., and Dent, J. (1995*a*). Effect of atropine on the frequency of reflux and transient lower oesophageal sphincter relaxation in normal subjects. *Gastroenterology*, 109, 1547–54.

Mittal, R.K., Holloway, R.H., Penagini, R., Blackshaw, L.A., and Dent, J. (1995*b*). Transient lower oesophageal sphincter relaxation. *Gastroenterology*, 109, 601–10.

Morgan, G. (1996). Non-steroidal anti-inflammatory drugs and the chemoprevention of colorectal and oesophageal cancers. *Gut*, 38, 646–8.

Nandurkar, S., Talley, N.J., Martin, C.J., Ng, T.H.K., and Adams, S. (1997). Short segment Barrett's oesophagus: prevalence, diagnosis and associations. *Gut*, 40, 710–15.

Palmer, E.D. (1968). The hiatus hernia–esophagitis–esophageal stricture complex: twenty year prospective study. *American Journal of Medicine*, 44, 566–79.

Pridie, R.B. (1966). Incidence and coincidence of hiatus hernia. *Gut*, 7, 188–9.

Raiha, I.J., Hietanen, E., and Sourander, L.B. (1991). Symptoms of gastroesophageal reflux in elderly people. *Age and Ageing*, 20, 365–70.

Raiha, I.J., Impivaara, O., Seppala, M., and Sourander, L.B. (1992*a*). Prevalence and characteristics of symptomatic gastroesophageal reflux disease in the elderly. *Journal of the American Geriatrics Society*, 40, 1209–11.

Raiha, I.J., Ivaska, K., and Sourander, L.B. (1992*b*). Pulmonary function in gastroesophageal reflux disease in elderly people. *Age and Ageing*, 21, 368–73.

Ren, J., Shaker, R., Kusano, M., *et al.* (1995). Effect of aging on the secondary esophageal peristalsis: Presbyesophagus revisited. *American Journal of Physiology*, 268, G772–9.

Rex, J.C., Anderson, H.A., Bartholomew, L.G., and Cain, J.C. (1961). Oesophageal hiatal hernia—a 10 year study of medically treated cases. *Journal of the American Medical Association*, 178, 271–4.

Richards, W.G. and Sugarbaker, D.J. (1995). Neuronal control of oesophageal function. *Chest Surgery Clinics of North America*, 5, 157–71.

Richter, J.E., Bradley, L.A., DeMeester, T.R., and Wu, W. (1992). Normal 24-hr ambulatory oesophageal pH values. Influence of study centre, pH electrode, age, and gender. *Digestive Diseases and Sciences*, 37, 849–56.

Sangster, G., Williams, C.E., Garvey, C.J., and Baldwin, R.N. (1992). Disability and the diagnostic quality of barium meals in elderly patients. *Age and Ageing*, 21, 135–8.

Scarpignato, C., Galmiche, J.P., and Giuli, R. (1995). Esophageal mucosal defence: recent advances. *Digestion*, 56 (Supplement 1), 1–60.

Schindlbeck, N.E., Wiebecke, B., Klauser, A.G., Voderholzer, W.A., and Muller-Lissner, S.A. (1996). Diagnostic value of histology in non-erosive gastroesophageal reflux disease. *Gut*, 39, 151–4.

Schoeman, M.N. and Holloway, R.H. (1995). Integrity and characteristics of secondary oesophageal peristalsis in patients with gastroesophageal reflux disease. *Gut*, 36, 499–504.

Sharma, P., Sampliner, R.E., and Camargo, E. (1997). Normalisation of oesophageal pH with high dose proton pump inhibitor therapy does not result in regression of Barrett's oesophagus. *American Journal of Gastroenterology*, 92, 582–5.

Soergel, K.H., Zhorlaske, F.F., and Amgerg, J.R. (1964). Presbyesophagus: oesophageal motility in nonagenerians. *Journal of Clinical Investigation*, 45, 1472–9.

Solomon, S.A., Kajla, V.Y., and Banerjee, A.K. (1994). Can the elderly tolerate endoscopy without sedation? *Journal of the Royal College of Physicians*, 28, 407–10.

Sridhar, S., Huang, J., O'Brien, B.J., and Hunt, R.H. (1996). Clinical economics review: cost-effectiveness of treatment alternatives for gastroesophageal reflux disease. *Alimentary Pharmacology and Therapeutics*, 10, 865–73.

Stilson, W.L., Sanders, I., Gardiner, G.A., Gorman, H.C., and Lodge, D.F. (1969). Hiatal hernia and gastroesophageal reflux. *Radiology*, 93, 1323–5.

Stoker, D.L., Williams, J.G., Leicester, R.G., and Colin-Jones, D.G. (1988). Oesophagitis—a five year review. *Gut*, 29, A1450.

Streitz, J.M., Jr, Ellis, F.H., Jr, Gibb, S.P., and Heatley, G.M. (1995). Achalasia and squamous cell carcinoma of the esophagus: analysis of 241 patients. *Annals of Thoracic Surgery*, 59, 1604–9.

Talley, N.J., Zinmeister, A.R., Schleck, C.D., and Melton, L.J. (1992). Dyspepsia and dyspepsia subgroups: a population based study. *Gastroenterology*, 102, 1259–68.

Thomas, P., Doddoli, C., Lienne, P., et al. (1997). Changing patterns and surgical results in adenocarcinoma of the oesophagus. *British Journal of Surgery*, 84, 119–25.

Vaezi, M.F., Singh, S., and Richter, J.E. (1995). Role of acid and duodenogastric reflux in oesophageal mucosal injury: a review of animal and human studies. *Gastroenterology*, 108, 1897–1907.

van der Burgh, A., Dees, J., Hop, W.C.J., and van Blankenstein, M. (1996). Oesophageal cancer is an uncommon cause of death in patients with Barrett's oesophagus. *Gut*, 39, 5–8.

Verne, G.N., Sallustio, J.E., and Eaker, E.Y. (1997). Anti-myenteric neuronal antibodies in patients with achalasia. A prospective study. *Digestive Diseases and Sciences*, 42, 307–13.

Walsh, T.N., Noonan, N., Hollywood, D., Kelly, A., Keeling, N., and Hennessy, T.P.J. (1996). A comparison of multimodal therapy and surgery for oesophageal adenocarcinoma. *New England Journal of Medicine*, 335, 462–7.

Wienbeck, M. and Barnert, J. (1989). Epidemiology of reflux disease and reflux oesophagitis. *Scandinavian Journal of Gastroenterology*, 24 (Supplement 156), 7–13.

Wright, T.A. (1997). High grade dysplasia in Barrett's oesophagus. *British Journal of Surgery*, 84, 760–6.

8.4   Disease of the stomach

Makau Lee

The aim of this chapter is to update the status of gastric disease in older persons. First, age-associated changes in gastric physiology are reviewed. Second, current views of the pathogenesis of peptic ulcer disease and therapeutic options are discussed, and finally other gastric disorders that are more prevalent among elderly people are reviewed.

Age-associated changes in the stomach

Recent studies have demonstrated that gastric secretion does not decline with ageing (Collen *et al.* 1994). Seventy-five per cent of older healthy individuals have normal gastric secretion, while the remaining 25 per cent have acid hyposecretion because of atrophic gastritis

(Krasinski *et al.* 1986). Clinically significant reductions in the absorption of iron and vitamin B_{12} may occur in elderly individuals with hypochlorhydria. However, advancing age is associated with significant reductions in gastric pepsin output in humans (Feldman *et al.* 1996). Furthermore, several studies have shown that gastric mucosal prostaglandin content and various mucosal protective mechanisms (such as mucus and bicarbonate production, blood flow, and mucosal proliferation) decline with ageing in both humans and experimental animals (Cryer *et al.* 1992; Lee and Feldman 1994; Lee 1996). These age-associated reductions in gastric mucosal prostaglandins and mucosal defensive factors may predispose elderly people to the development of gastric ulcers from non-steroidal anti-inflammatory drugs (**NSAIDs**). Finally, there are no convincing data to support the notion that gastric emptying is impaired by ageing.

Peptic ulcer disease

Epidemiological studies have consistently demonstrated that the incidence of gastric and duodenal ulcers increases with advancing age (Soll *et al.* 1991; Soll 1993). There have been major changes in our understanding of and practices concerning peptic ulcer disease. We now recognize three major causes of peptic ulcer disease: *Helicobacter pylori*, NSAIDs, and acid hypersecretory states (such as Zollinger–Ellison syndrome). Because *H. pylori* and NSAIDs comprise the aetiological factors for 99 per cent of peptic ulcer disease, they will be reviewed in detail in the following sections.

H. pylori and gastroduodenal disease

H. pylori is a Gram-negative spiral bacterium that colonizes the mucus layer overlying the gastric mucosa and gastric-type epithelium (Graham 1994). *H. pylori* infection is related to age, socio-economic status, and ethnicity, but not to sex (Megraud 1993). In developing countries, approximately 50 per cent of the population is infected by age 10, and the prevalence is about 70 per cent at age 20 (Megraud 1993). In industrialized nations, the prevalence of *H. pylori* infection is less than 5 per cent at age 10, and the infection rates approach 40 per cent by age 50 (Megraud 1993). In the United States, *H. pylori* infection is much more prevalent in the black and Hispanic populations than in white Americans (Megraud 1993). Moreover, *H. pylori* infection is more prevalent in lower socio-economic groups, and the bacterium is transmitted primarily by close contact as reflected in clustering of infection in families and institutions (Duke and Lee 1994).

H. pylori is now accepted as the cause of non-autoimmune chronic gastritis (Peek and Blaser 1996). It is associated with virtually 100 per cent of cases of duodenal ulcers (Megraud 1993; Peek and Blaser 1996). Eradication of *H. pylori* prevents duodenal ulcer relapse and thus cures the disease. It is also strongly associated with gastric ulcers in the absence of NSAID use; nearly 80 per cent of patients with gastric ulcers have had *H. pylori* infection (Megraud 1993; Peek and Blaser 1996). Considerable epidemiological evidence from serological studies suggests that long-standing *H. pylori* infection may increase the risk of subsequent development of gastric malignancies (Nomura *et al.* 1991; Parsonnet *et al.* 1991). However, there is no convincing evidence linking *H. pylori* with non-ulcer dyspepsia (Duke and Lee 1994).

Diagnosis of *H. pylori* infection

The diagnosis of *H. pylori* can be made by various invasive and non-invasive tests (Table 1) (Cerda *et al.* 1994; Duke and Lee 1994). *H. pylori* can be detected in endoscopically obtained biopsy specimens by one of the following methods: histological examination (the gold standard), detection of bacterial urease activity using commercially available diagnostic kits, or culture. Non-invasive tests include serological tests for antibodies to *H. pylori* antigens and breath tests for urease activity using ^{13}C- or ^{14}C-labelled urea. A positive serological test indicates that a patient has been infected with *H. pylori*, while successful *H. pylori* eradication is suggested by a progressive decline in *H. pylori* antibody titre. Breath testing is the best non-invasive method of monitoring *H. pylori* eradication; however, the first-generation breath tests that have been approved for diagnostic use in the United States are quite expensive.

Table 1 Diagnostic tests for *H. pylori*

Test	Sensitivity (%)	Comments
Serology	94–99	Does not differentiate active from past infection
Biopsy urease test	90–98	Test inexpensive, rapid results, requires endoscopy
Histology	90–98	Current gold standard, requires endoscopy
Culture	70–90	Tedious, requires endoscopy, reserved for antibiotic-resistant cases
Breath test	90–95	Simple, useful in follow-up treatment, currently expensive

Adapted from Duke and Lee (1994).

Therapeutic strategies

A United States National Institutes of Health (**NIH**) panel (NIH Consensus Development Panel 1994) has concluded that most cases of peptic ulcer disease can be cured by eradicating *H. pylori* infection, and its recommendations are summarized in Table 2. Patients with proven peptic ulcers and documented *H. pylori* infection should be treated with a standard triple-antibiotic regimen for 14 days in conjunction with a 6-week course of acid-suppression therapy. Alternatively, a 4-week course of omeprazole in conjunction with antibiotics (such as clarithromycin and metronidazole) for the first 14 days can be used. The NIH panel also stressed that empirical treatment for *H. pylori* is inappropriate, and that asymptomatic patients without ulcers, patients with non-ulcer dyspepsia, or ulcer

Table 2 Recommendations for treating *H. pylori* infection

Patient status	Antimicrobial therapy[a]	
	H. pylori negative	*H. pylori* positive
Asymptomatic (no ulcer)	No	No
Non-ulcer dyspepsia	No	No
Gastric ulcer	No	Yes
Duodenal ulcer	No	Yes

[a] Standard therapy: an H_2-receptor antagonist in standard antiulcer doses plus metronidazole (250 mg three times daily) plus bismuth subsalicylate (525 mg four times daily) plus tetracycline or amoxycillin (500 mg four times daily); eradication in 90% of cases. Example of an alternative therapy: omeprazole (40 mg every morning) + clarithromycin (500 mg three times daily) for days 1–14; omeprazole (20 mg every morning) for days 15–28; eradication in about 80% of cases. This is an evolving area, and ongoing studies should provide more precise definition for patient selection and therapeutic regimens. Current regimens are updated regularly in the *British National Formulary*.
Adapted from NIH Consensus Development Panel (1994) and Duke and Lee (1994).

Table 3 Classification of NSAIDs

Acetylated salicylate (e.g. aspirin)

Non-acetylated salicylates (e.g. salsalate, diflunisal)

Fenamates (e.g. meclofenamate)

Indoles (e.g. indomethacin, sulindac, tolmetin)

Naphthylalkanones (e.g. nabumetone)

Oxicams (e.g. piroxicam)

Phenylacetic acids (e.g. diclofenac)

Propionic acids (e.g. ibuprofen, ketoprofen, naproxen)

Pyranocarboxylic acid (e.g. etodolac)

Adapted from Lee (1995).

patients without *H. pylori* infection do not benefit from antimicrobial *H. pylori* eradication (NIH Consensus Development Panel 1994). Finally, follow-up tests are unnecessary in uncomplicated cases of duodenal ulcers, while follow-up endoscopy to document ulcer healing and exclude malignancy is recommended for patients with gastric ulcers (Duke and Lee 1994).

NSAID gastropathy

Aspirin (acetylsalicylic acid) and other NSAIDs are among the most commonly used classes of drugs (Baum *et al.* 1985). Numerous human studies have demonstrated that the use of NSAIDs is associated with various gastroduodenal mucosal lesions, sometimes collectively referred to as NSAID gastropathy (Kendall and Peura 1993; Lee 1995). In this section, the clinical significance, pathophysiology, and therapeutic strategies for treatment and prevention of NSAID gastropathy are reviewed.

Clinical significance and magnitude of NSAID gastropathy

Every year, more than 70 million prescriptions for NSAIDs are written in the United States alone, and the worldwide market for NSAIDs is estimated at $2 billion annually (Lee 1995). A partial list of NSAIDs currently available for therapeutic use is shown in Table 3 (Lee 1995). Aspirin, the prototypical NSAID, is used both therapeutically (to reduce pain, inflammation, and fever) and prophylactically (to prevent thrombotic events). Observational studies also suggest that the use of aspirin and NSAIDs may lead to lower incidence of colonic cancer (Thun *et al.* 1991) and delay the onset of Alzheimer's disease (Breitner *et al.* 1994).

The use of NSAIDs increases the risk of peptic ulcer disease, ulcer complications (haemorrhage and/or perforation), and death from ulcer by a factor of 2 to 4 (Griffin *et al.* 1988, 1991; Bloom 1989; Lee 1995). Most clinical studies have shown that the point prevalence of gastric ulcers among NSAID users varies from 10 to 20 per cent, whereas the prevalence of gastric ulcers among individuals who do not take NSAIDs is approximately 2 per cent (Lee 1995). Endoscopic

studies have shown that gastric ulcers associated with NSAID therapy are three to four times more prevalent than duodenal ulcers. A United States Food and Drug Administration report estimated that approximately 3 per cent of NSAID users develop serious gastrointestinal complications induced by NSAIDs each year, resulting in 200 000 cases of bleeding or perforated ulcers and at least 10 000 deaths annually (US Food and Drug Administration 1988). Moreover, it has been estimated that the average quarterly cost of treating adverse gastrointestinal side effects induced by NSAIDs among arthritic patients is approximately $66 per person (Bloom 1988), while another study estimated that in the United States alone, medical costs attributable to NSAID gastropathy and its complications exceed $4 billion a year (Kendall and Peura 1993).

Although considerable clinical data have been published on the adverse effects of NSAIDs, for several reasons the exact magnitude of the problem is unknown and is probably underestimated (Soll *et al.* 1991; Soll 1993; Lee 1995). First, most studies have been retrospective or uncontrolled. Second, the use of NSAIDs is widespread and frequently under-reported because many preparations are available over the counter without prescription. Third, acute gastric mucosal lesions due to brief exposure to NSAIDs often resolve without any significant clinical sequelae. Fourth, most patients with NSAID gastropathy are asymptomatic, and the occurrence of a life-threatening complication without antecedent symptomatology is frequently the first manifestation in elderly people. Finally, subjective symptomatology in patients taking NSAIDs does not correlate closely with endoscopically observed lesions, and there is no simple non-invasive test for accurately documenting the prevalence of NSAID gastropathy.

Recent studies have also demonstrated that gastrointestinal complications associated with NSAIDs are not limited to the stomach and duodenum. The use of NSAIDs may lead to ulcerations, bleeding and stricture formation in the oesophagus, small bowel, and colon, protein-losing enteropathy, non-specific colitis, and exacerbation of inflammatory bowel disease and diverticular disease of the colon (Allison *et al.* 1992; Bjarnason *et al.* 1993). Furthermore, NSAIDs are an important cause of hepatic injury (Rodriguez *et al.* 1994) and renal toxicity (Verbeeck 1990; Lee 1995).

Pathogenesis of NSAID gastropathy

The mechanisms by which aspirin and other NSAIDs produce acute and chronic gastroduodenal mucosal injury are incompletely understood. Gastric mucosal injury is thought to result when aggressive luminal factors (such as acid and pepsin) overwhelm local mucosal protective factors (Soll *et al.* 1991; Soll 1993; Lee 1995). Results from animal studies suggest that the production of mucosal lesions by aspirin is a result of two independent mechanisms: cyclo-oxygenase inhibition by aspirin, and topical effects induced by salicylate, the product of aspirin deacetylation (Lee 1995). The salicylate-induced toxic effects include changes in transmembrane permeability, electrical activity, metabolism, and ion transport; whereas cyclo-oxygenase inhibition and resultant changes in prostaglandin metabolism may result in alterations or reductions in gastric mucosal defensive functions which include, but are not limited to, bicarbonate and mucus secretion, proliferation and repair, blood flow, and growth factor expression. Cyclo-oxygenase inhibition may also result in an increase in biosynthesis of lipoxygenase products, particularly leukotrienes, which have been shown to play a role in acute gastric mucosal injury in some animal studies (Lee 1995).

Feldman, M. (1990). Prostaglandins and gastric ulcers: from seminal vesicle to misoprostol (Cytotec). *American Journal of Medical Science*, **300**, 116–32.

Feldman, M., Cryer, B., McArthur, K.E., Huet, B.A., and Lee, E. (1996). Effects of aging and gastritis on gastric acid and pepsin secretion in humans: a prospective study. *Gastroenterology*, **110**, 1043–52.

Fries, J.F., Miller, S.R., Spitz, P.W., *et al.* (1989). Toward an epidemiology of gastropathy associated with NSAID use. *Gastroenterology*, **96** (Supplement), 647–55.

Fuchs, C.S. and Mayer, R.J. (1995). Gastric carcinoma. *New England Journal of Medicine*, **333**, 22–7.

Gabriel, S.E., Jaakkimainen, L., and Bombardier, C. (1991). Risk for serious gastrointestinal complications related to use of non-steroidal anti-inflammatory drugs. *Annals of Internal Medicine*, **115**, 787–96.

Glass, G.B.J. and Pitchumoni, C.S. (1975). Atrophic gastritis. *Human Pathology*, **6**, 219–45.

Graham, D.Y. (1994). Evolution of concepts regarding *Helicobacter pylori*. *American Journal of Gastroenterology*, **89**, 469–72.

Graham, D.Y. and Smith, J.L. (1986). Aspirin and the stomach. *Annals of Internal Medicine*, **104**, 390–8.

Graham, D.Y., Schwartz, J.T., Cain, G.D., *et al.* (1982). Prospective evaluation of biopsy number in the diagnosis of oesophageal and gastric carcinoma. *Gastroenterology*, **82**, 228–31.

Graham, D.Y., Smith, J.L., and Dobbs, S.M. (1983). Gastric adaptation occurs with aspirin administration in man. *Digestive Diseases and Sciences*, **28**, 1–6.

Graham, D.Y., Agarwal, N.M., and Roth, S.H. (1988). Prevention of NSAID-induced gastric ulcer with misoprostol: multi-center, double-blind, placebo-controlled trial. *Lancet*, **ii**, 1277–80.

Graham, D.Y., Lidsky, M.D., Cox, A.M., *et al.* (1991). Long-term non-steroidal anti-inflammatory drug use and *Helicobacter pylori* infection. *Gastroenterology*, **100**, 1653–7.

Graham, D.Y., White, R.H., Moreland, L.W., *et al.* (1993). Duodenal and gastric ulcer prevention with misoprostol in arthritis patients taking NSAIDs. *Annals of Internal Medicine*, **119**, 257–62.

Griffin, M.R., Ray, W.A., and Schaffner, W. (1988). Non-steroidal anti-inflammatory drug use and death from peptic ulcer in elderly persons. *Annals of Internal Medicine*, **109**, 359–63.

Griffin, M.R., Piper, J.M., Daughtery, J.R., Snowden, M., and Ray, W.A. (1991). Non-steroidal anti-inflammatory drug use and increased risk for peptic ulcer disease in elderly persons. *Annals of Internal Medicine*, **114**, 257–63.

Haenszel, W., Kurihara, M., Segi, M., and Lee, R.K.C. (1972). Stomach cancer among Japanese in Hawaii. *Journal of the National Cancer Institute*, **49**, 969–88.

Hatfield, A.R.W., Slavin, G., Segal, A.W., *et al.* (1975). Importance of the site of endoscopic gastric biopsy in ulcerating lesions of the stomach. *Gut*, **16**, 884–6.

Hawkey, C.J. (1990). Non-steroidal anti-inflammatory drugs and peptic ulcers. *British Medical Journal*, **300**, 278–84.

Henry, D., Dobson, A., and Turner, C. (1993). Variability in the risk of major gastrointestinal complications from nonaspirin non-steroidal anti-inflammatory drugs. *Gastroenterology*, **105**, 1078–88.

Hollander, D. (1994). Gastrointestinal complications of non-steroidal anti-inflammatory drugs: prophylactic and therapeutic strategies. *American Journal of Medicine*, **96**, 274–81.

Holt, S. and Saleeby, G. (1991). Gastric mucosal injury induced by non-steroidal anti-inflammatory drugs. *Southern Medical Journal*, **84**, 355–60.

Irvin, T.T. and Bridger, J.E. (1988). Gastric cancer: an audit of 122 consecutive cases and the results of R1 gastrectomy. *British Journal of Surgery*, **75**, 106–9.

Johnson, D.A. (1988). Acute and chronic gastritis. In *Manual of clinical problems in gastroenterology* (ed. S.J. Chobanian and M.N. Van Ness), pp. 40–3. Little, Brown, Boston, MA.

Kekki, M., Samloff, I.M., Ihamaki, T., Varis, K., and Siurala, M. (1982). Age- and sex-related behaviour of gastric acid secretion at the population level. *Scandinavian Journal of Gastroenterology*, **17**, 737–43.

Kendall, B.J. and Peura, D.A. (1993). NSAID-associated gastrointestinal damage and the elderly. *Practical Gastroenterology*, **17**, 13–29.

Kim, J.G., Graham, D.Y., and the Misoprostol Study Group (1994). *Helicobacter pylori* infection and development of gastric or duodenal ulcer in arthritic patients receiving chronic NSAID therapy. *American Journal of Gastroenterology*, **89**, 203–7.

Krasinski, S.D., Russell, R.M., Samloff, I.M., *et al.* (1986). Fundic atrophic gastritis in an elderly population. *Journal of the American Geriatrics Society*, **34**, 800–6.

Lanza, F.L. (1984). Endoscopic studies of gastric and duodenal injury after the use of ibuprofen, aspirin, and other non-steroidal anti-inflammatory agents. *American Journal of Medicine*, **77** (Supplement 1), 19–24.

Lee, M. (1995). Prevention and treatment of non-steroidal anti-inflammatory drug-induced gastropathy. *Southern Medical Journal*, **88**, 507–13.

Lee, M. (1996). Age-associated changes in gastric blood flow in rats. *Gerontology*, **42**, 290–3.

Lee, M. and Feldman, M. (1994). Age-associated reductions in gastric mucosal prostaglandin levels increase susceptibility to aspirin-induced injury in rats. *Gastroenterology*, **107**, 1746–50.

Lightdale, C., Botet, J., Brennan, M., *et al.* (1989). Endoscopic ultrasonography compared to computerised tomography for preoperative staging of gastric cancer. *Gastrointestinal Endoscopy*, **35**, 154–56.

McQuaid, K.R. (1997). Alimentary tract. In *Current medical diagnosis and treatment* (ed. L.M. Tierney, S.J. McPhee, and M.A. Papadakis), pp. 519–606. Appleton and Lange, Stamford, CT.

Meddings, J.B., Sutherland, L.R., Byles, N.I., *et al.* (1993). Sucrose: a novel permeability marker for gastroduodenal disease. *Gastroenterology*, **104**, 1619–26.

Megraud, F. (1993). Epidemiology of *Helicobacter pylori* infection. *Gastroenterology Clinics of North America*, **22**, 73–88.

Miller, D.R. (1992). Treatment of non-steroidal anti-inflammatory drug-induced gastropathy. *Clinical Pharmacy*, **11**, 690–704.

Moayyedi, P. and Dixon, M.F. (1997). Significance of *Helicobacter pylori* infection and gastric cancer. *Gastrointestinal Endoscopy Clinics of North America*, **7**, 47–64.

Murphy, J.R. (1996). Gastric adenocarcinoma. In *Consultations in gastroenterology* (ed. W.J. Snape), pp.289–95. W.B. Saunders, Philadelphia, PA.

NIH Consensus Development Panel. (1994). *Helicobacter pylori* in peptic ulcer disease. *Journal of the American Medical Association*, **272**, 65–9.

Nomura, A., Stemmermann, G.N., Chyou, P.H., Kato, I., Perez-Perez, G.I., and Blaser, M.J. (1991). *Helicobacter pylori* infection and gastric carcinoma among Japanese Americans in Hawaii. *New England Journal of Medicine*, **325**, 1132–6.

Parsonnet, J., Friedman, G.D., Vandersteen, D.P., *et al.* (1991). *Helicobacter pylori* infection and the risk of gastric carcinoma. *New England Journal of Medicine*, **325**, 1127–31.

Peek, R.M. and Blaser, M.J. (1996). Pathophysiology of *Helicobacter pylori*-induced gastritis and peptic ulcer disease. *American Journal of Medicine*, **102**, 200–7.

Robinson, M.G., Griffen, J.W., Bowers, J., *et al.* (1989). Effect of ranitidine on gastroduodenal mucosal damage induced by non-steroidal anti-inflammatory drugs. *Digestive Diseases and Sciences*, **34**, 424–8.

Rodriguez, L.A.G., Williams, R., Derby, L.E., *et al.* (1994). Acute liver injury associated with non-steroidal anti-inflammatory drugs and the role of risk factors. *Archives of Internal Medicine*, **154**, 311–16.

Roth, S., Agarwal, N., Mahowald, M., *et al.* (1989). Misoprostol heals gastroduodenal injury in patients with rheumatoid arthritis receiving aspirin. *Archives of Internal Medicine*, **149**, 775–9.

Scheiman, J.M., Behler, E.M., Loeffler, K.M., *et al.* (1994). Omeprazole ameliorates aspirin-induced gastroduodenal injury. *Digestive Diseases and Sciences*, **39**, 97–103.

Silverberg, E., Boring, C.C., and Sauives, T.S. (1990). Cancer statistics. *Cancer Journal for Clinicians*, **40**, 9–26.

Silverstein, F.E., Graham, D.Y., Senior, J.R., *et al.* (1995). Misoprostol reduces serious gastrointestinal complications in patients with rheumatoid arthritis receiving non-steroidal anti-inflammatory drugs. *Annals of Internal Medicine*, **123**, 241–9.

Sipponen, P. (1992). Natural history of gastritis and its relationship to peptic ulcer disease. *Digestion*, **51** (Supplement 1), 70–5.

Soll, A.H. (1993). Gastric, duodenal, and stress ulcer. In *Gastrointestinal Disease* (5th edn) (ed. M. Sleisenger and J. Fordtran), pp. 580–679. W.B. Saunders, Philadelphia, PA.

Soll, A.H., Weinstein, W.M., Kurata, J., and McCarthy, D. (1991). Non-steroidal anti-inflammatory drugs and peptic ulcer disease. *Annals of Internal Medicine*, **114**, 307–19.

Strickland, R.G. and Mackay, I.R. (1973). A reappraisal of the nature and significance of chronic atrophic gastritis. *American Journal of Digestive Disease*, **18**, 426–40.

Thun, M.J., Namboodiri, M.M., and Heath, C.W. (1991). Aspirin use and reduced risk of fatal colon cancer. *New England Journal of Medicine*, **325**, 1593–6.

US Food and Drug Administration (1988). *HHS News*. DHHS Publication No. P88-40. US Department of Health and Human Resources, Rockville, MD.

Verbeeck, R.V. (1990). Pharmacokinetics drug interactions with non-steroidal anti-inflammatory drugs. *Clinical Pharmacokinetics*, **19**, 44–66.

Walan, A., Bader, J.P., Classen, M., *et al.* (1989). Effect of omeprazole and ranitidine on ulcer healing and relapse rate in patients with benign gastric ulcer. *New England Journal of Medicine*, **320**, 69–75.

8.5 Management of gastrointestinal haemorrhage

J. D. Shearman and D. P. Jewell

Introduction

Bleeding from the gastrointestinal tract presents a spectrum of clinical problems in elderly people, ranging from the medical emergency of acute upper gastrointestinal haemorrhage to clinical decisions regarding the thresholds for investigation of patients with iron deficiency anaemia. An increasing proportion of the population is elderly, and an understanding of the possibilities (and limitations) of investigations and treatments in gastrointestinal bleeding in this group of patients is crucial to successful clinical management.

Acute gastrointestinal haemorrhage

Upper gastrointestinal haemorrhage

Presentation

Upper gastrointestinal haemorrhage at any age presents clinically as haematemesis, melaena, or a varying combination of the two. Haematemesis broadly refers to the vomiting of blood, and a clear clinical history is important to distinguish the 'coffee grounds', which may result from any episode of prolonged vomiting, from identifiable

clotted or fresh red blood which heralds a significant upper gastrointestinal bleed. Melaena is similarly difficult to define clinically. The term ought to be reserved to describe a jet-black tarry unformed stool with a very characteristic odour. However, it is often erroneously used to describe any black stool, and care must be taken with patients on oral iron supplements when a Haemoccult test for faecal occult blood will be necessary for the recognition of the presence of haemorrhage. Acute upper gastrointestinal haemorrhage may present as collapse by an elderly patient through its effect on the circulation. Examination of the stool in these circumstances requires awareness and a degree of clinical suspicion.

Incidence

Acute upper gastrointestinal haemorrhage constitutes a significant fraction of acute general medical admissions and an increasing proportion of the patients are elderly. In 1970 an analysis was performed of over 2000 patients presenting with haematemesis and melaena to the Radcliffe Infirmary in Oxford. The overall incidence was 47 admissions per 100 000 adults per year, of whom less than 10 per cent were aged 80 or over (Schiller *et al.* 1970). Nearly 30 years later, the recent national audit of acute upper gastrointestinal haemorrhage in the United Kingdom has demonstrated an increase in the incidence of acute upper gastrointestinal bleeding to 103 per 100 000 adults per

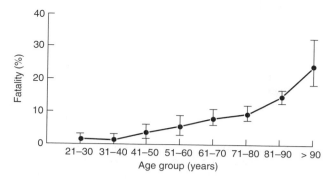

Fig. 1 Hospital fatality rates for emergency admissions with haematemesis and melaena by age group with 95 per cent confidence intervals. (Reproduced with permission from Rockall *et al.* (1995*a*).)

year (Rockall *et al.* 1995*a*). The median age of patients included in this study was 71 years, and the proportion aged over 80 was 27 per cent. This represents a significant increase in the proportion of elderly patients presenting with acute upper gastrointestinal bleeding even compared with data accumulated only a decade previously (Katchinski *et al.* 1989).

Age is an independent risk factor for upper gastrointestinal bleeding, and the annual incidence of haematemesis or melaena in people aged over 75 is 10 times that in patients aged less than 44 (485 per 100 000 compared with 41 per 100 000). The reasons for this are not clear but almost certainly comprise a complex mix of risk factors (including use of non-steroidal anti-inflammatory drugs (NSAIDs)) and the presence of significant comorbidity resulting in an earlier presentation to hospital. Regardless of the underlying epidemiological features, these figures clearly have an impact on the clinical management of elderly patients with acute upper gastrointestinal bleeding.

Fatality and prognosis

Despite the introduction of flexible endoscopy, the overall fatality of upper gastrointestinal haemorrhage has changed very little in the last 30 years (Rockall *et al.* 1995*a*). The changing demography of the population of the United Kingdom and the greater proportion of elderly patients has had a major impact on the fatality of this common medical emergency. In the study performed in 1970, patients aged over 80 experienced a poorer prognosis with a fatality three times that of patients aged less than 60 (Schiller *et al.* 1970). In the recent national audit of acute upper gastrointestinal haemorrhage a clear effect of age on fatality was demonstrated (Fig. 1).

Rockall *et al.* (1995*b*) have formulated a risk score from logistic regression analysis of a range of predictive variables in an attempt to identify the relative effects of different factors on outcome. This score ultimately comprised age, clinical parameters of shock, significant comorbidity, underlying (endoscopic) diagnosis, and the recognition of endoscopic stigmata of recent haemorrhage (Table 1). This scoring system was shown to account for most of the differences in fatality observed between the centres contributing data to the original audit (Rockall *et al.* 1995*a*) and was subsequently validated in a prospective evaluation of a further 1625 cases (Rockall *et al.* 1996).

This scoring system is intended as an epidemiological tool to control for the confounding factors associated with a varying case mix. However, as a semiquantitative formula for the assessment of

risk following a gastrointestinal bleed it helps to identify high-risk patients objectively. The first important general principle of relevance to managing acute haemorrhage in older patients arising from the Rockall scoring system is that the recognition of shock (i.e. tachycardia and/or systolic hypotension) in a patient over the age of 80 years contributes as much to the risk assessment as any single factor that might be identified at endoscopy. The second point is that major organ failure (renal, respiratory, or liver) or disseminated malignancy each contribute more independent risk than any other single factor, and in these circumstances haemorrhage may represent the terminal event.

Beyond the above considerations, patients presenting with a significant gastrointestinal haemorrhage while already in hospital (e.g. following surgery, myocardial infarction, or trauma) have a poor prognosis. Data on this important subgroup are less readily available, and such patients are often excluded from prospective analyses. However, fatality rates in these patients are considerably higher than those in emergency admissions and approach 40 per cent (Rockall *et al.* 1995*a*).

The crucial features in the clinical management of elderly patients with gastrointestinal bleeding are the recognition of those at high risk and early and adequate resuscitation. Interventions such as endoscopy (and indeed surgery) do not universally alter the outcome after a gastrointestinal bleed. These procedures must be considered for elderly patients, as at any other age, but they must be timed with regard to other aspects of resuscitation and viewed with a realistic expectation of their potential contribution to the chances of survival.

Resuscitation

Resuscitation is the primary objective in the clinical management of any acute upper gastrointestinal haemorrhage. This priority is particularly important in elderly patients with significant comorbidity. The first step is to recognize the clinical importance of simple haemodynamic parameters which reliably reflect the severity of a haemorrhage (i.e. pulse rate, blood pressure, and central venous pressure). These parameters may themselves be attenuated by significant cardiovascular comorbidity and concurrent therapies (e.g. β-blockers, diuretics, and vasodilators). A clinical description of postural dizziness, loss of consciousness, or the demonstration of tachycardia or postural (or absolute) systolic hypotension clearly identifies patients at high risk (see Table 1).

Having recognized a haemodynamically significant gastrointestinal haemorrhage, it is imperative to establish good venous access and initiate volume replacement with plasma expanders while whole blood is being cross-matched. The role of central venous pressure monitoring in patients with gastrointestinal bleeding remains contentious. In patients presenting in established hypovolaemic shock, the need for central venous cannulation is often clear if only to provide secure and reliable access to the circulation. The decision whether or not to place a central venous line is more complex in elderly patients with significant comorbidity. No rigid rule can be applied to this common clinical problem, but it should be recognized that central venous pressure monitoring makes volume replacement safer in individuals with heart disease and will also provide the earliest clinical indication of a significant rebleed, which has a major impact on fatality (see below). In such circumstances a urinary catheter is also advisable.

There is no objective evidence that fasting a patient after admission improves outcome. Conversely, many clinicians fear that fasting might

Table 1 Numerical risk scoring system for upper gastrointestinal haemorrhage

Variable	Score			
	0	1	2	3
Age (years)	<60	60–79	⩾80	
Shock	'No shock'	'Tachycardia'	'Hypotension'	
Comorbidity	None		Cardiac failure Ischaemic heart disease Any other major comorbidity	Renal failure Liver failure Disseminated malignancy
Diagnosis	Mallory–Weiss tear, no lesion	All other diagnoses	Malignancy of upper GI tract	
Major SRH	None or dark spot only		Blood in upper GI tract Adherent clot Visible or spurting vessel	

SRH, stigmata of recent bleeding; GI, gastrointestinal.
Maximum additive score prior to diagnosis, 7; maximum additive score following diagnosis, 11.
Reproduced with permission from Rockall *et al.* (1996).

increase gastric acid output and subsequently increase the risk of rebleeding. The only reasons for fasting a patient with a gastrointestinal bleed are to facilitate early endoscopy or if an early surgical intervention is contemplated.

Diagnosis

Endoscopy is both safe and informative in elderly patients; 20 to 30 per cent of procedures performed in those aged over 80 are for the investigation of acute gastrointestinal haemorrhage (Cooper and Neumann 1986; Safe and Owens 1991). However, consideration should be given to the timing of the procedure. Ideally, endoscopy should be performed within 24 h of admission to maximize the diagnostic yield and subsequent prognostic value. This consideration should be balanced against the inherent risks of sedation and other possible complications of performing the procedure as an 'out of hours' emergency in elderly patients with significant comorbidity. Most diagnostic endoscopies can be performed safely in the supervised setting of an endoscopy department the morning after admission.

The spectrum of underlying endoscopic diagnoses accounting for acute upper gastrointestinal haemorrhage in elderly patients differs only slightly from that seen in younger patients (Table 2).

Endoscopic diagnosis provides useful prognostic information in elderly patients following gastrointestinal haemorrhage. Firstly, it will identify those patients who have bled from upper gastrointestinal tumours and varices. In these patients surgery is often best avoided and the prognosis is determined as much by the underlying disease as it is by the haemorrhage itself. The second important role of diagnostic endoscopy is the identification of stigmata of recent haemorrhage. These endoscopic signs (fresh blood clot, visible vessel, etc.) provide very important prognostic information and in particular predict the likelihood of rebleeding which has a significant impact on prognosis (see below).

Therapeutic endoscopy

Patients who have bled from benign peptic ulceration of the upper gastrointestinal tract are candidates for endoscopic therapy. Many different techniques of endoscopic haemostasis have been reported, including diathermy, laser, heater probe, and injection therapy. All have been shown to reduce recurrent or continued bleeding (Sacks *et al.* 1991), although a clear benefit in terms of survival is less certain. Injection of the ulcer with a 1:10 000 dilution of adrenaline remains the simplest of these procedures and is favoured by most endoscopists. Whether the benefit of this procedure is due to vasoconstriction or a physical tamponade is not certain. Although some endoscopists favour circumferential injections around the ulcer as opposed to injection directly into the ulcer base, there is little evidence that one is significantly better than the other and usually the decision is left to the discretion of the endoscopist.

Patients bleeding from oesophageal varices contribute only a small proportion of emergency admissions of elderly people with upper gastrointestinal bleeding. Recognition is important in that such patients require a different emphasis of resuscitation and intervention. Varices should be managed in exactly the same way as in younger patients with early endoscopy and injection sclerotherapy or band ligation (Triger 1992). Prognosis is little different from that of bleeding varices in younger patients and reflects the degree of liver impairment (Bullimore *et al.* 1989).

Surgery

With the advent of flexible endoscopy as a means of early diagnosis and with advances in the medical therapies for peptic ulcer disease, surgery now plays a limited, albeit very important, role in upper gastrointestinal bleeding (Chang *et al.* 1977). Surgery is now largely restricted to patients for whom medical treatment has failed, and so is often performed as an emergency. There are two broad circumstances in which surgical intervention should be considered.

Table 2 Endoscopic diagnoses in patients presenting as emergency admissions with upper gastrointestinal bleeding

Diagnosis	Age <60 (n = 1176)		Age 60–79 (n = 1421)		Age >80 (n = 872)	
	Number (%)	Fatality (%)	Number (%)	Fatality (%)	Number (%)	Fatality (%)
None	23	3	20	13	28	29
Peptic ulcer	29	2	41	9	36	16
Malignancy	1	17	6	34	4	54
Varices	8	13	4	28	1	10
Mallory–Weiss tear	13	0	3	5	2	13
Erosions	13	4	11	1	10	9
Oesophagitis	10	4	11	8	12	7
Other	4	5	6	12	7	18

Modified with permission from Rockall *et al.* (1995*a*).

The first and clearest indication is clinical evidence of continued haemorrhage. In patients in whom it proves impossible to achieve satisfactory resuscitation, emergency endoscopy with a view to early injection therapy is often considered. For elderly patients, this should preferably be undertaken after a consultation with a senior surgeon as in such circumstances endoscopy is most safely performed in an emergency operating theatre with anaesthetic supervision. If bleeding is not controlled by injection therapy, the patient can then quickly be presented for laparotomy.

The second clinical setting in which surgery might be considered following an acute upper gastrointestinal haemorrhage is in patients with evidence of a significant rebleed. This is an important concept in the medical management of patients with acute gastrointestinal bleeding and particularly in patients who have bled from a benign peptic ulcer. A rebleed is defined as further haematemesis or melaena, a continuing fall in haemoglobin, or further cardiovascular instability (i.e. tachycardia and hypotension) without other explanation (Rockall *et al.* 1995*b*). Rebleeding has a significant impact on the fatality of acute upper gastrointestinal haemorrhage, and is associated with at least a doubling of fatality in all risk groups (Rockall *et al.* 1996). Recognition of significant rebleeding often defines a failure of medical treatment and indicates the need for surgical intervention. While surgery might be considered inappropriate in very elderly and physically frail patients with significant comorbidity, it should be recognized that any further endoscopic intervention will be of limited benefit. Age in itself is no contraindication to surgery for acute upper gastrointestinal surgery and older patients fare as well as younger ones (Chang *et al.* 1977; Antler *et al.* 1981).

Eradication of *Helicobacter pylori*

The majority of peptic ulcers are associated with colonization of the stomach by *H. pylori*. In these patients, eradication of the organism results in a significant reduction in the risk of ulcer recurrence. After presentation with a significant upper gastrointestinal haemorrhage from a peptic ulcer, *H. pylori* eradication should be considered (European *Helicobacter pylori* Study Group 1997). Whether or not this should be determined by the demonstration of *H. pylori* infection

is unclear. Many different techniques exist for the demonstration of *H. pylori* infection and each has its limitations. Culture of the organism remains both the gold standard and the least sensitive method for demonstrating infection. Biopsy of the gastric antrum with either conventional histological examination or a test for the presence of bacterial urease will result in a 90 per cent sensitivity. Indirect tests (urease breath test or serology) will similarly miss only a small number of infected patients, but the availability of these tests is limited in some centres. Apart from serological tests, all will have a variable false-negative rate associated with recent use of antibiotics or proton pump inhibitors, both of which are increasingly prescribed for elderly patients.

Most of the currently recommended regimes for *H. pylori* eradication comprise a well-tolerated 1-week course of a combination of two antibiotics and a proton pump inhibitor (European *Helicobacter pylori* Study Group 1997). Treatment of elderly people was not separately addressed in this study but, given that many elderly patients tolerate gastrointestinal haemorrhage poorly, an argument can be made for *H. pylori* eradication treatment in some circumstances regardless of the *H. pylori* status, or even without testing.

Non-steroidal anti-inflammatory drugs

NSAIDs have become one of the most commonly prescribed groups of drugs worldwide and this has been associated with an increasing prevalence of upper gastrointestinal ulceration, particularly in older age groups (Somerville *et al.* 1986; Walt *et al.* 1986; LaPorte *et al.* 1991). As a group of drugs they have combined analgesic and anti-inflammatory actions as a result of their inhibition of cyclo-oxygenase. This has a dual effect on the risk of gastrointestinal bleeding. Firstly, inhibition of platelet cyclo-oxygenase reduces platelet aggregation, causing a mild anticoagulant effect (hence the role of NSAIDs in the secondary prevention of myocardial infarction). Moreover, depletion of gastric mucosal prostaglandins reduces mucosal defence mechanisms and predisposes the patient to epithelial cell damage and ulceration.

Although doubt has been cast on the relative contribution of NSAIDs to upper gastrointestinal bleeding in elderly people (Beard *et al.* 1987), a recent case–control study has suggested that NSAIDs constitute an independent and statistically greater risk than *H. pylori* infection (Pilotto *et al.* 1997), with the presence of the bacteria appearing to protect long-term NSAID users from bleeding. More needs to be learnt about the overlap between these two important cofactors for gastroduodenal ulceration.

In patients who have suffered significant gastrointestinal haemorrhage whilst taking an NSAID, clear guidelines have yet to be established for the subsequent treatment of those who will need to consider restarting the drug. Given the proven association between duodenal ulcer, increased acid secretion, and antral *Helicobacter* infection, patients who have bled from an acute duodenal ulcer may be cautiously restarted on low-dose NSAIDs after *H. pylori* eradication. If ulcer prophylaxis is deemed clinically important, this is probably best provided by effective acid suppression by, for example, a proton pump inhibitor. The underlying pathological mechanisms of gastric ulcers and gastric erosions are subtly different, and deficiencies in mucosal defence may be more important than basal or peak acid output. In view of this observation, synthetic prostaglandins such as misoprostol provide more rational ulcer prophylaxis although their use may be limited by diarrhoea.

In recent years interest has centred on the development of drugs that selectively inhibit the inducible isoform of cyclo-oxygenase (cyclo-oxygenase 2). This isoenzyme appears to account for the majority of the acute inflammatory response whereas the constitutive form (cyclo-oxygenase 1) provides other functions such as the maintenance of mucosal defence. Hence selective cyclo-oxygenase 2 inhibitors are predicted to retain the efficacy of traditional NSAIDs with regard to anti-inflammatory activity without the gastrointestinal side-effects (particularly the risk of gastroduodenal ulceration). The first of these agents, meloxicam, appears to be well tolerated, although rigorous comparative studies of this agent against other NSAIDs are still awaited.

Lower gastrointestinal haemorrhage

Presentation

The incidence of acute lower gastrointestinal bleeding increases with age. Distal colonic haemorrhage presents clinically as fresh blood loss rectally (haematochezia) which is rarely associated with cardiovascular compromise. Bleeding from the proximal colon and distal small bowel may present greater difficulty in confidently excluding an upper gastrointestinal source of bleeding, but true melaena is not characteristic (see also Chapter 8.7)

In the majority of patients with colonic bleeding, haemorrhage stops spontaneously with supportive measures alone (Reinus and Brandt 1990). Identification of the bleeding source may still be considered clinically important for prognostic purposes and subsequent clinical management. In the small proportion of patients in whom bleeding from a distal gastrointestinal source continues, decisions centre largely on the timing of tests and interventions.

Pathology

The most common sources of acute colonic bleeding in older people are diverticular disease and colonic angiodysplasia, which account for over 60 per cent of major bleeding in patients aged over 65 (Boley *et al.* 1979; Smith 1981). Although these conditions are pathologically benign, both may be widespread throughout the colon and the clinical management may be very challenging (Bokari *et al.* 1996).

There are few reliable estimations of the true prevalence of diverticular disease, although it increases with age. Bleeding amounts to approximately a quarter of the complications of this common condition and tends to be sudden and profuse but self-limiting (Meyers *et al.* 1976).

The term angiodysplasia is used to cover a spectrum of clinical conditions ranging from angiographically identifiable arteriovenous malformations to small mucosal telangiectasiae identified at colonoscopy (Kheterpal 1991; Sharma and Gorbien 1995). Some form of vascular malformation has been estimated to occur in as many as 25 per cent of people aged 60 or over, and many of these lesions lie in the proximal colon (Boley *et al.* 1977; Gupta *et al.* 1995). The pathology is degenerative in nature with an age-associated prevalence with some disease associations (heart disease/aortic stenosis, chronic renal failure, collagen vascular disease). The pattern of bleeding from angiodysplasia is varied and although the diagnosis is most commonly considered in patients investigated for iron deficiency anaemia, massive haemorrhage can occur.

Other important pathologies causing acute lower gastrointestinal haemorrhage include colonic cancers, ischaemic colitis, and inflammatory bowel disease. These usually present clinical features that suggest a more significant underlying cause (i.e. subacute obstruction, diarrhoea, and pain).

Management

As with the immediate management of upper gastrointestinal bleeding, resuscitation of patients presenting with rectal bleeding is determined by cardiovascular parameters. However, unlike upper gastrointestinal bleeding, continued haemorrhage from the colon declares itself early and central venous monitoring to detect occult bleeding is not usually necessary.

If there is clinical suspicion that a patient is continuing to bleed from the colon, early surgical referral is recommended as the timing of any subsequent interventions is crucial for successful management.

Mesenteric angiography is potentially the most useful investigation in aiding the management of continued lower intestinal bleeding. However, the utility of this invasive procedure is in part dependent on the correct timing of its use. A negative result does not exclude a significant pathology as bleeding must be continuing at the time of the procedure for a bleeding vessel to be identified. Although the yield of positive results with angiography at any one centre might seem frustratingly low, a positive result might reveal a bleeding lesion amenable to embolization or at least will significantly shorten the duration of any subsequent laparotomy. These two possibilities might prove of great importance in elderly patients with significant comorbidity for whom long periods of general anaesthesia may be costly with respect to long-term survival (Fig. 2).

Many hospitals admitting patients with colonic bleeding do not have access to emergency angiography, and patients who continue to bleed with no source identified on angiography have a poor prognosis (Parkes *et al.* 1993). In such circumstances 'on-table' colonoscopy after colonic lavage may be undertaken at the time of laparotomy if no gross pathology is readily identified by the surgeon. This procedure lengthens the duration of the operation and the diagnostic yield remains limited. In certain circumstances a surgical procedure must be considered without a clearly identified bleeding point. In these cases subtotal colectomy results in

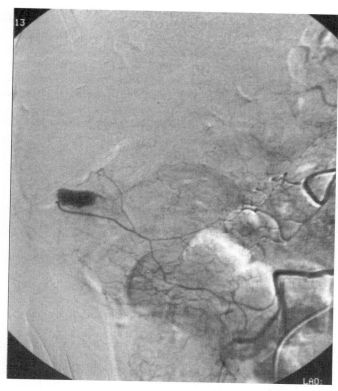

Fig. 2 Mesenteric angiogram performed in an 86-year-old man with acute colonic bleeding. A bleeding point at the hepatic flexure of the colon is demonstrated. At the ensuing laparotomy the bleeding point was found and a right hemicolectomy was completed within 30 min.

both a lower subsequent rebleeding rate and lower mortality compared with segmental resection (Parkes *et al.* 1993).

Bleeding from the small intestine and unidentified sites

A small proportion of the patients presenting with a significant gastrointestinal haemorrhage who settle with conservative management ultimately have no responsible lesion identified after subsequent investigation by endoscopy of either the upper or lower gastrointestinal tract. The value of further investigation in these patients is determined by the severity of the original clinical presentation or the persistent detection of gastrointestinal blood loss. Bleeding sources within the small intestine are very rare, and further investigation by contrast radiology, angiography, or nuclear medicine may be based on associated symptoms or results suggesting the possibility of small bowel disease (see Chapter 8.6). A small bowel barium enema (enteroclysis) demonstrates structural abnormalities of the small intestine such as polyps, leiomyomas, and tumours (e.g. lymphoma). Rarely, elective mesenteric angiography might demonstrate persisting vascular malformations which in themselves may be amenable to embolization. Endoscopic examination of the small intestine (enteroscopy) is increasingly available and may be of value in the further evaluation of structural lesions identified by contrast radiology. Its full utility in the assessment of elderly patients with gastrointestinal bleeding has yet to be defined (see also Chapter 8.6).

Many centres continue to use radiolabelled erythrocyte scanning to detect occult gastrointestinal bleeding sources that are bleeding at a rate slower than that demonstrable by angiography. This technique has greater sensitivity (0.5 ml/min) than visceral angiography, although the resolution of the anatomical location of the bleeding point is often limited.

Identified sources of significant bleeding from the small intestine usually warrant surgical management if they are causing recurrent problems.

Chronic gastrointestinal blood loss

Investigation of iron deficiency

There is no physiological route of iron excretion in humans. In the absence of any other markers of malabsorption, iron deficiency in men and postmenopausal women often signifies chronic intestinal blood loss and, without any intestinal symptoms, this may warrant further gastrointestinal investigation.

Clinical indicators of iron deficiency

The classical hallmark of iron deficiency is microcytic anaemia. However, microcytosis alone may reflect iron deficiency and increasingly it is possible to measure parameters of iron metabolism directly. Of the more specific blood tests, a low level of serum ferritin is a very sensitive marker of iron deficiency. Ferritin is actively secreted into the circulation as part of the 'acute phase' or inflammatory response and it is a less sensitive measure of low iron stores in any condition characterized by acute or chronic inflammation. Transferrin saturation reflects iron transport and this can be calculated from the measurements of serum iron and total iron binding capacity. In inflammatory states resulting in a falsely high ferritin, the transferrin saturation usually falls. Serum iron and total iron binding capacity are often unreliable indices of iron status in older patients, and direct evaluation of bone marrow iron stores by needle aspiration and staining for iron remains the most accurate test of iron deficiency. Whether this will ultimately be replaced by other indirect tests, such as the measurement of serum-soluble transferrin receptor, remains to be seen.

Detection of faecal occult blood

Occult gastrointestinal bleeding can be detected chemically by reaction with guaiac in commercially available test kits such as Haemoccult. These tests are prone to false-positive results caused by the consumption of red meat or even vigorous teeth brushing. Conversely, lesions bleeding intermittently may not be detected in such a way. Even allowing for these exceptions, detection of faecal occult blood is useful in setting an appropriate pace or threshold for subsequent investigation.

Endoscopy and contrast radiology—the pros and cons

In investigating the cause of chronic intestinal blood loss, upper gastrointestinal endoscopy will identify a number of patients with occult gastric or even oesophageal malignancy. Other patients will be found to have benign pathologies such as peptic ulcers and vascular malformations. Beyond these clear aetiologies, the interpretation of other endoscopic findings may be more difficult. In particular the

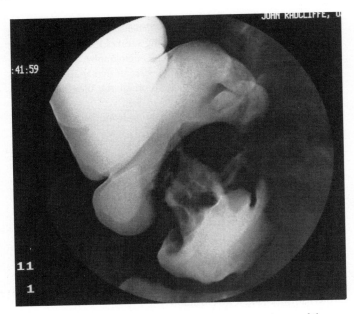

Fig. 3 Single-contrast barium enema demonstrating a carcinoma of the ascending colon in a 93-year-old man presenting with iron deficiency anaemia. The patient subsequently had a successful right hemicolectomy.

identification of gastritis or duodenitis is rarely sufficient to account for anaemia, and in such circumstances consideration should be given to subsequent investigation of the colon.

The choice of investigation of the colon falls between colonoscopy and the barium enema. Each has significant advantages and disadvantages. The advantage of colonoscopy is that tumours can be biopsied and polyps can be snared. Furthermore, a positive diagnosis of colonic angiodysplasia may be made, although a normal examination does not completely exclude it. The disadvantages are largely that the procedure carries a small risk of perforation of the colon (which is potentially greater in patients with diverticular disease), but there is also a risk that the endoscopist will be unable to pass the instrument to the caecum. This is of practical importance in that caecal carcinoma is not uncommon in patients with an asymptomatic anaemia. Barium contrast radiology may demonstrate the right colon in such patients. A practical compromise that will increase the diagnostic yield in elderly patients with an asymptomatic iron deficiency is to perform a limited flexible sigmoidoscopy followed by a barium enema (Fig. 3).

Abdominal CT can detect large colonic tumours in elderly patients who are too frail for more invasive procedures, but this investigation has a low sensitivity and is usually indicated only for patients with gastrointestinal symptoms rather than occult blood loss. There have been promising reports of spiral CT scanning for the detection of colonic tumours, but the place of this investigation is not yet clear.

The effect of anticoagulation

Therapeutic anticoagulation with warfarin is frequently considered in the long-term management of elderly patients with various forms of vascular disease. Other than for very elderly people, age itself appears to be less of a risk for gastrointestinal bleeding than the quality of the control of anticoagulation (Finn *et al.* 1996). In fact, in some cases gastrointestinal bleeding exacerbated by anticoagulation

may be considered advantageous by revealing otherwise unidentified gastrointestinal malignancies (Norton and Armstrong 1997).

There is a significant risk of upper gastrointestinal bleeding from peptic ulcers in patients receiving combination treatment with warfarin and NSAIDs (Shorr *et al.* 1993). Whether or not it is necessary to screen elderly patients for *H. pylori* before starting therapeutic anticoagulation is unproven. As a greater proportion of patients presenting with these common clinical problems are elderly, complex questions such as this will become increasingly important.

References

Antler, A.S., Pitchumoni, C.S., Thomas, E., Orangio, G., and Scanlon, B.C. (1981). Gastrointestinal bleeding in the elderly: morbidity, mortality and cause. *American Journal of Surgery*, **142**, 271–3.

Beard, K., Walker, A.M., Perera, D.R., and Jick, H. (1987). Nonsteroidal anti-inflammatory drugs and hospitalisation for gastroesophageal bleeding in the elderly. *Archives of Internal Medicine*, **147**, 1621–3.

Bokari, M., Vernava, A.M., Ure, T., and Longo, W.E. (1996). Diverticular haemorrhage in the elderly—is it well tolerated? *Diseases of Colon and Rectum*, **39**, 191–5.

Boley, S.J., Sammartano, R.J. Adams, A., DiBiase, A., Kleinhaus, S., and Sprayregen, S. (1977). On the nature and aetiology of vascular ectasias of the colon: degenerative lesions of ageing. *Gastroenterology*, **72**, 650–60.

Boley, S.J., DiBase, A., Brandt, L.J., and Sammartano, R.J. (1979). Lower intestinal bleeding in the elderly. *American Journal of Surgery*, **137**, 57–64.

Bullimore, D.W., Milozewski, K.J., and Losowsky, M.S. (1989). The prognosis of elderly subjects with oesophageal varices. *Age and Ageing*, **18**, 35–8.

Chang, F.C., Drake, J.E., and Farha, G.J. (1977). Massive upper gastrointestinal haemorrhage in the elderly. *American Journal of Surgery*, **134**, 721–3.

Cooper, B.T. and Neumann, C.S. (1986). Upper gastrointestinal endoscopy in patients aged 80 years or more. *Age and Ageing*, **15**, 343–9.

European *Helicobacter pylori* Study Group (1997). Current European concepts in the management of *Helicobacter pylori* infection. The Maastricht Consensus Report. *Gut*, **41**, 8–13.

Finn, S.D., Callahan, C.M., Martin, D.C., McDonell, M.B., Henikoff, J.G., and White, R.H. (1996). The risk for and severity of bleeding complications in elderly patients treated with warfarin. *Annals of Internal Medicine*, **124**, 970–9.

Gupta, N., Longo, W.E., and Vernava, A.M. (1995). Angiodysplasia of the lower gastrointestinal tract: an entity readily diagnosed by colonoscopy and primarily managed nonoperatively. *Diseases of the Colon and Rectum*, **38**, 979–82.

Katchinski, B., Logan, R., Davies, J., and Langman, M. (1989). Audit of mortality in upper gastrointestinal bleeding. *Postgraduate Medical Journal*, **65**, 913–17.

Kheterpal, S. (1991). Angiodysplasia: a review. *Journal of the Royal Society of Medicine*, **84**, 615–18.

LaPorte, J.R., Carne, X., Vidal, X., Moreno, V., and Juan, J. (1991). Upper gastrointestinal bleeding in relation to previous use of analgesics and non-steroidal anti-inflammatory drugs. *Lancet*, **337**, 85–9.

Meyers, M.A., Alonso, D.R., Gray, G.F.J., and Baer, J.W. (1976). Pathogenesis of bleeding colonic diverticulosis. *Gastroenterology*, **71**, 577–83.

Norton, S.A. and Armstrong, C.P. (1997). Lower gastrointestinal bleeding during anticoagulant therapy: a life-saving complication. *Annals of the Royal College of Surgeons of England*, **79**, 38–9.

Parkes, B.M., Obeid, F.N., Sorensen, V.J., Horst, H.M., and Fath, J.J. (1993). The management of massive lower gastrointestinal bleeding. *American Surgeon*, 59, 676–8.

Pilotto, A., Leandro, G., DiMario, F., Franceschi, M., Bozzola, L., and Valerio, G. (1997). Role of *Helicobacter pylori* infection on upper gastrointestinal bleeding in the elderly: a case–control study. *Digestive Diseases and Sciences*, 42, 586–91.

Reinus, J.F. and Brandt, L.J. (1990). Upper and lower gastrointestinal bleeding in the elderly. *Gastroenterology Clinics of North America*, 19, 293–318.

Rockall, T.A., Logan, R.F.A., Devlin, H.B., and Northfield, T.C. (1995a). Incidence of and mortality from acute upper gastrointestinal haemorrhage in the United Kingdom. *British Medical Journal*, 311, 222–6.

Rockall, T., Logan, R., Devlin, H., and Northfield, T. (1995b). Variation in outcome after acute upper gastrointestinal haemorrhage. *Lancet*, 346, 346–50.

Rockall, T., Logan, R., Devlin, H., and Northfield, T. (1996). Risk assessment after acute upper gastrointestinal haemorrhage. *Gut*, 38, 316–21.

Sacks, H.S., Chalmers, T.C., Blum, A.L., Berrier, J., and Pagano, D. (1991). Endoscopic hemostasis—an effective therapy for bleeding peptic ulcers. *Journal of the American Medical Association*, 264, 494–9.

Safe, A.F. and Owens, D. (1991). Upper gastrointestinal endoscopy in octogenarians. *British Journal of Clinical Practice*, 45, 99–101.

Schiller, K., Truelove, S., and Williams, D. (1970). Haematemesis and melaena, with special reference to factors influencing the outcome. *British Medical Journal*, ii, 7–14.

Sharma, R. and Gorbien, M.J. (1995). Angiodysplasia and lower gastrointestinal tract bleeding in elderly patients. *Archives of Internal Medicine*, 155, 807–12.

Shorr, R.I., Ray, W.A., Daugherty, J.R., and Griffen, M.R. (1993). Concurrent use of non-steroidal anti-inflammatory drugs and oral anti-coagulants places elderly persons at high risk for haemorrhagic peptic ulcer disease. *Archives of Internal Medicine*, 153, 1665–70.

Smith, G.W. (1981). Lower GI bleeding in the elderly. Diverticulosis and angiodysplasia as dominant causes. *Postgraduate Medicine*, 69, 36–49.

Somerville, K., Faulkner, G., and Langman, M. (1986). Non-steroidal anti-inflammatory drugs and bleeding peptic ulcer. *Lancet*, i, 462–4.

Triger, D.R. (1992). Bleeding varices in the elderly. *Gut*, 33, 1009–10.

Walt, R., Katschinski, B., Logan, R.. *et al.* (1986). Rising frequency of ulcer perforation in elderly people in the United Kingdom. *Lancet*, ii, 489–92.

8.6 Diseases of the small intestine and pancreas

John R. Saltzman and Nicholas Karamitsios

The small intestine

The overall structure and function of the small intestine seem to be preserved with advancing age. The lack of clinically significant changes in small intestinal function with ageing is attributed to the large reserve capacity of the system. However, disorders of the small intestine are an important cause of morbidity for older people. Bacterial overgrowth of the small intestine is a major cause of occult malabsorption in older persons. Primary disorders of the small intestine such as coeliac disease and Crohn's disease can present for the first time in later life. Gastrointestinal blood loss, both occult and brisk, may originate from the small intestine, and diagnosis and management can be challenging. Small intestinal ischaemia becomes increasingly common with advancing age and must be recognized if its potential morbidity and mortality are to be avoided. Tumours of the small intestine, although rare, may be benign or malignant. It is important for clinicians caring for older persons to be familiar with the disorders that can affect the small intestine.

Changes associated with ageing

Structure

The structure of the small intestine does not seem to be affected by advancing age alone. Although there may be minor microscopic changes in small intestinal structure between young adult and elderly subjects, such as shorter villi in the latter (Webster and Leeming 1975), this has not been consistently demonstrated (Lipski *et al.* 1985).

Function

Specific enzymes may decrease with age, including lactase, deficiency of which causes lactose intolerance. Although lactase activity may decrease with age, human small intestinal maltase and sucrase concentrations are usually preserved. In rat models, there appears to be an age-associated decline in the activity of the sodium–glucose transporter (Lindi *et al.* 1985), but it is not clear whether the same occurs in humans (Vincenzini *et al.* 1989; Wallis *et al.* 1993). There is no clinical evidence of a deficiency syndrome attributable to decreased activity of the sodium–glucose cotransporter.

It is difficult to measure small intestinal motility clinically, but studies have shown essentially intact small intestinal transit times in later life (Husebye and Engedal 1992; Madsen 1992). Diseases that can affect small intestinal motility and are increasingly prevalent in older age groups include diabetes, Crohn's disease, thyroid disorders, and scleroderma. In the absence of such diseases, motility seems to be unaffected by age.

The integrity of the small intestine, as assessed by its permeability, is known to be altered by a variety of diseases such as Crohn's disease and coeliac disease. When small intestinal permeability is altered, there is increased antigen access and, possibly, abnormal nutrient transport. Until recently, there was controversy over whether small intestinal integrity altered with age alone. The ratio of absorption of orally ingested lactulose, a large molecule that is absorbed paracellularly via tight junctions and extrusion zones at villous tips, to mannitol, a relatively small molecule that is absorbed transcellularly through aqueous pores in the cell membrane, is used as a measure of small intestinal permeability. The ratio of absorption of lactulose to mannitol indicates that the small intestinal permeability of adults aged over 60 is similar to that of younger adults (Saltzman *et al.* 1995). While the lactulose–mannitol test measures permeability of the small intestine from the lumen of the gut into the body, the 'leakiness' of the gut from the body into the gut lumen can be measured by the α_1-antitrypsin clearance. There is no significant difference in α_1-antitrypsin clearance between older healthy subjects and younger adults (Saltzman and Russell 1998). Thus small intestinal permeability or integrity does not seem to change with age.

Nutrient absorption

Macronutrient absorption by the small intestine seems to be preserved in healthy older people Carbohydrate absorption at normal intake levels is preserved, but the reserve capacity seems to be diminished in older persons. Absorption may be incomplete when very high carbohydrate loads, such as a 200-g carbohydrate meal, are given (Feibusch and Holt 1982). D-Xylose absorption, which is commonly used clinically to detect altered small intestinal carbohydrate absorption, is preserved in older persons, except perhaps at ages greater than 80 years (Arora *et al.* 1989). However, the urinary excretion of D-xylose decreases with advancing age owing to the age-associated decrease in renal function. As with carbohydrate, fat absorption at normal intake levels is preserved with advancing age (Southgate and Durnin 1970; Arora *et al.* 1989). However, at very high levels of fat intake in debilitated elderly subjects with a body weight 74 per cent of ideal, severe malnourishment, and low visceral protein levels, the reserve capacity for fat absorption can be exceeded and faecal fat content increases (Simko and Michael 1989).

Inadequate dietary intakes are responsible for the majority of instances of poor vitamin status of older people (Suter and Russell 1987). In the absence of small intestinal disease or other specific factors, there are few clinically significant changes in micronutrient absorption associated with age alone. Some of the factors that result in altered small intestinal micronutrient absorption in older persons, in the absence of an overt disease or illness, are atrophic gastritis, causing a lack or reduction of gastric acid secretion, and small intestinal bacterial overgrowth. These conditions can affect absorption of folate, vitamin B_{12}, vitamin K, iron, and calcium.

Disorders of the small intestine

Lactose maldigestion

The most common and best known disorder of intestinal carbohydrate digestion in humans is lactose maldigestion due to reduction or loss of lactase activity in the small intestinal brush border. Most individuals are born with the capacity to digest lactose, but about 75 per cent of adults worldwide have lost this ability and are lactose maldigesters (Scrimshaw and Murray 1988). Owing to the ethnic origins of the population, the prevalence of lactose maldigesters in the United States is much lower, at around 25 per cent of adults. The ability to digest lactose is best preserved in people with an ethnic origin in Northern Europe. Ingestion of lactose by an individual with lactose maldigestion causes symptoms that include abdominal bloating, flatulence, and diarrhoea. In older persons, avoidance of dairy products because of lactose maldigestion is an important problem as it limits intake of vitamin D and calcium and may contribute to the development of osteoporosis.

There are several ways of determining whether an individual is a lactose maldigester. The most common method is a trial of elimination of dairy products from the diet. Although the test is non-specific, resolution of symptoms on a lactose-free diet allows a presumptive diagnosis of lactose intolerance to be made. Other diagnostic tests are the lactose tolerance test and the lactose hydrogen breath test. In each test, a load of lactose is administered to the patient, serial measurements are made, and symptoms are monitored. In the lactose tolerance test, serial serum glucose levels are measured and lactose maldigestion is indicated by a failure of the serum glucose to rise appropriately. In the lactose hydrogen breath test exhaled hydrogen is measured after lactose ingestion; a significant rise in hydrogen excretion is indicative of maldigested lactose reaching the colon where it is broken down by bacteria. Treatment of lactose maldigestion is avoidance of dairy products. It should be noted that many lactose-intolerant individuals can digest lactose contained in yoghurt owing to the presence of live lactose-digesting cultures. There are also varying degrees of lactose maldigestion so that dietary restrictions need to be individualized. Alternatively, lactose-hydrolysed milk can be substituted for conventional milk, although typically only 70 per cent of the lactose content is prehydrolysed. Lactose-hydrolysed milk is more expensive and sweeter than regular milk. Lactase-containing preparations are available in liquid, caplet, capsule, and chewable tablet forms. The liquid preparation can be added to milk and, after incubation for 24 h, 70 to 99 per cent of the lactose will be hydrolysed. These products can also be taken before ingestion of lactose-containing foods and give reasonable control of symptoms.

Small intestinal bacterial overgrowth syndrome

The bacterial overgrowth syndrome is an important clinical entity in later life. Although the small intestine is normally essentially sterile, when it is colonized by organisms there may be malabsorption and clinical symptoms. Usually the upper gastrointestinal tract contains less than 10^3 organisms per millilitre of intestinal secretions. The major factors limiting the growth and survival of organisms in the upper gastrointestinal tract are intestinal motility and gastric acid (Saltzman and Kowdley 1996). Other factors include immunological and bacteriostatic secretions from the intestines, liver, and pancreas.

Any condition that leads to intestinal stasis (e.g. gastrointestinal surgery such as a Billroth II gastrectomy) or disrupts intestinal continuity can lead to pathological bacterial colonization of the small intestine. Any type of stricture or adhesion that results in partial bowel obstruction may lead to abnormal intestinal motility. Jejunal diverticulosis can impair intestinal propulsion and cause stasis. Jejunal diverticula can also become infected and cause small intestinal diverticulitis. Systemic diseases such as scleroderma or diabetes with autonomic neuropathy can cause pseudo-obstruction syndromes with pathological bacterial overgrowth.

Older persons are at higher risk of developing the bacterial overgrowth syndrome owing to reduced or absent gastric acid production as a result of atrophic gastritis or acid-reducing medications. The prevalence of atrophic gastritis in elderly persons ranges from 11 to 50 per cent in various studies, depending on definition, the diagnostic tests utilized, and the population studied (Saltzman 1993; Hurwitz et al. 1997). Although many different classification systems have been used to characterize chronic gastritis, atrophic gastritis is usually categorized into types A and B (Strickland and Mackay 1973). Type A atrophic gastritis occurs in association with autoimmune conditions, such as pernicious anaemia, and predominantly affects the body of the stomach. This condition is found in less than 5 per cent of persons over the age of 60 in the United States (Krasinski et al. 1986). In contrast, type B atrophic gastritis is strongly associated with Helicobacter pylori infection and predominantly affects the antrum of the stomach (Saltzman and Kowdley 1994). It is found in 20 to 30 per cent of persons aged over 60 in the United States (Krasinski et al. 1986). In addition to atrophic gastritis, potent acid-reducing medications such as the proton pump inhibitors, increasingly used by older people, can lead to intestinal bacterial overgrowth (Saltzman et al. 1994).

Clinical manifestations of the bacterial overgrowth syndrome include abdominal pain, bloating, diarrhoea, and weight loss associated with malabsorption, steatorrhoea, and malnutrition. Malabsorption may affect vitamin B_{12} and the fat-soluble vitamins A, D, E, and K in association with general malabsorption of fat (Saltzman and Russell 1994). The symptoms of the bacterial overgrowth syndrome are non-specific and a high index of suspicion must be maintained if it is to be recognized, particularly among older patients who often present with subtle symptoms of bloating or nausea with weight loss and malnutrition.

Non-invasive tests to detect bacterial overgrowth include the glucose and lactulose hydrogen breath tests. However, the sensitivity and specificity of these tests varies and at best is around 80 per cent (King and Toskes 1986; Corazza et al. 1990). The 1-g ^{14}C-xylose breath test is the most sensitive non-invasive test, with a sensitivity of approximately 95 per cent (King and Toskes 1986). However, this test is of limited availability. The gold standard of detection of small intestinal bacterial overgrowth is small intestinal aspiration and quantitative cultures of the aspirate (Corazza et al. 1990). This is usually done by aspiration through a sterile tube placed through an endoscope with immediate setting up of anaerobic and aerobic cultures. The finding of more than 10^5 organisms per millilitre of intestinal contents establishes the diagnosis. Diagnostic tests for the detection of small intestinal bacterial overgrowth are not always available to the clinician, and therapeutic trials of antibiotics are often required.

Treatment of the bacterial overgrowth syndrome is with antibiotics and reversal of predisposing conditions if possible. The antibiotic most widely used has been tetracycline, although other antibiotics including ciprofloxacin and metronidazole, are also appropriate. If underlying conditions cannot be corrected, antibiotics may need to be cycled and given frequently to control the symptoms. For patients with small intestinal motility disorders, prokinetics such as cisapride can be tried. Finally, if nutritional deficiencies are present, nutritional support must be provided (Saltzman and Russell 1994).

Coeliac disease

Coeliac disease (coeliac sprue) causes generalized malabsorption characterized by damage to the epithelial cells of the small intestine induced by ingestion of gliadin-containing gluten. The protein components of gluten are found in wheat, barley, rice, and oats. Although the exact pathogenesis of the disease is unclear, it is known that gliadin initiates an immunological reaction by the enterocyte in persons with a genetic susceptibility. The genetic susceptibility seems to be associated with the histocompatibility antigens HLA B8 and HLA DRw3 which are found in 60 to 90 per cent of persons with coeliac disease compared with 20 to 30 per cent of the general population. Coeliac disease is primarily a disease of the white races, with prevalence rates as high as 1 in 300 in Western Ireland compared with 1 in 2000 in other regions. Coeliac disease is also twice as common in women as in men (Trier 1991).

Symptoms of coeliac disease are classically those of severe malabsorption with diarrhoea, weight loss, abdominal pain, and steatorrhoea. The diagnosis may be suggested by the presence of serum antibodies to gliadin, reticulin, or endomysium. Although the sensitivity and specificity of these tests varies, the immunoglobulin A antiendomysial antibody is the most accurate. The antibodies may decline into the normal range as the disease is treated. Although antibodies are helpful in diagnosis, biopsy of the small intestine is needed for definitive confirmation as treatment has to be lifelong. In addition to malabsorption, coeliac disease may cause dermatitis herpetiformis, which is pruritic, vesicular, and papular. Patients with only dermatitis herpetiformis may have latent coeliac disease. Occult gastrointestinal bleeding may occur in about half of patients with coeliac disease and may contribute to iron deficiency (Fine 1996).

It is important to remember that coeliac disease can present at any time of life. Although symptoms typically begin in early childhood, it is not unusual for them to appear in the third to sixth decades of life. In addition, the presentation of coeliac disease is variable and not all those affected have severe malabsorption. Milder forms can be misdiagnosed as irritable bowel syndrome or remain subclinical. Thus a high index of suspicion is often needed to make a diagnosis of coeliac disease in older patients.

Treatment of coeliac disease is the complete avoidance of dietary gliadin. Wheat, barley, rye, and oats should be avoided, although patients may eat rice and maize. In patients with severe malabsorption, the response to treatment is usually rapid, with improvement often noted within days, although more rarely a full recovery may take months. The usual cause for lack of complete response is an often inadvertent failure to adhere completely to the diet. Rare complications may occur with coeliac disease. Refractory disease can develop in which the patient no longer responds to the diet and needs immunosuppressive medications. This is associated with a poor prognosis. In addition, patients are at increased risk of developing lymphoma and, possibly, adenocarcinoma of the small intestine. These complications should be considered in patients who are compliant with the diet, but who relapse or fail to respond.

Crohn's disease

Inflammatory bowel disease, including Crohn's disease, can present for the first time in later life. One challenge is to distinguish Crohn's disease from other more common disorders in elderly patients such as intestinal ischaemia, diverticulitis, radiation enteritis, infectious gastroenteritis, and ulcerative colitis. Both Crohn's disease and ulcerative colitis are chronic diseases of unknown cause involving both genetic and immunological factors. The body is unable to distinguish foreign antigens from self-antigens and initiates an inflammatory cascade that fails to downregulate the mucosal immune response.

Crohn's disease is characterized by a focal, asymmetric, and transmural inflammatory process that can affect any portion or any combination of areas of the gastrointestinal tract from mouth to anus. Microscopically non-caseating granulomas may be seen, but these are not necessary for the diagnosis. The terminal ileum is most commonly involved, often with simultaneous colonic involvement. However, in about 20 per cent of cases the colon may be the only site of involvement, and, rarely, other areas of the gastrointestinal tract may be the only active site. Owing to the transmural nature of Crohn's disease, fistulas and abscesses may form. Crohn's disease can affect the anorectal region with fissures, fistulas, and perirectal abscesses.

Crohn's disease can occur at any age, but has a peak incidence during the second and third decades of life. However, most epidemiological studies suggest a bimodal incidence with a second later peak, more variable in age, but generally between 50 and 80 years. It is not clear why there is a secondary rise in age-specific incidence, but theories include an environmental cause which manifests in later life, an increased susceptibility to disease with increasing age, ischaemic disease that is mistakenly diagnosed as Crohn's disease, and more careful evaluation of older persons.

Crohn's disease is most common in people from North America and Northern Europe and is rare in the Middle East, Asia, Africa, and Central and South America. Although inflammatory bowel disease can occur in all ethnic groups, there is an increased prevalence in Ashkenazi Jews who originated from Northern Europe.

The clinical signs and symptoms of Crohn's disease are highly variable as they are determined by the site, extent, and activity of disease. Upper gastrointestinal Crohn's disease involving the stomach and upper small intestine can mimic peptic ulcer disease with epigastric pain, nausea, and vomiting. Involvement of the small intestine can lead to diarrhoea, sometimes with bleeding (usually occult), easy fatiguability, abdominal cramping, and tenderness. In older patients the disease can vary from mild to severe in intensity. Chronic Crohn's disease with transmural inflammation leads to narrowing of the intestinal lumen and symptoms of obstruction with abdominal pain that comes in waves, with nausea, vomiting, and decreased stool outputs. Weight loss due to malabsorption or to voluntary limitations on oral intake to reduce symptoms is common. In addition, systemic symptoms may include fever, night sweats, myalgia, and arthralgia.

The nutritional manifestations include those due to malabsorption and protein-losing enteropathy; the latter is characterized by low serum albumin and total protein. Lactose intolerance is also common in active Crohn's disease. Malabsorption involves fats, the fat-soluble vitamins A, D, E, and K, folic acid, vitamin B_{12}, calcium, and iron. Anaemias are common because of iron, folate, and vitamin B_{12} deficiency as well as blood loss from the gastrointestinal tract. During periods of disease activity there may be leucocytosis and thrombocytosis. Nutritional problems may be augmented by extensive bowel resections, and some patients may develop short-bowel syndrome.

Extraintestinal complications may complicate Crohn's disease. Skin and mucous membrane changes are common. Oral aphthous ulcers and fissuring of the mouth and lips may occur, and skin complications include erythema nodosum and pyoderma gangrenosum.

Hepatobiliary complications of Crohn's disease frequently occur. Gallstone formation is common owing to bile salt malabsorption. Bile duct inflammation comprises a spectrum of activity from pericholangitis to primary sclerosing cholangitis and resultant biliary cirrhosis. Pericholangitis is a non-progressive inflammation of the intrahepatic bile ducts and is characterized by minor elevations of the transaminases and serum alkaline phosphatase. In contrast, primary sclerosing cholangitis is a progressive disease of bile duct inflammation that may involve the intrahepatic and/or extrahepatic bile ducts. The serum alkaline phosphatase is typically greatly elevated in this disorder which usually affects males. Biliary strictures may eventually result in cirrhosis, and cholangiocarcinoma may complicate the diagnosis and clinical course.

Other extraintestinal manifestations of Crohn's disease may also occur. Kidney stones composed of calcium oxalate form due to hyperoxaluria. Peripheral or central arthritis may occur. Peripheral arthritis involves the large joints such as the knees, elbows, and ankles in an asymmetrical distribution with inflammation that may parallel the activity of the intestinal inflammation. The central arthritis, which may manifest as ankylosing spondylitis or sacroiliitis, is typically associated with HLA B27 and has a clinical course independent of the activity of the Crohn's disease. Ocular manifestations of inflammatory bowel disease include conjunctivitis, episcleritis, iritis, and uveitis (in association with HLA B27).

The diagnosis of Crohn's disease is primarily clinical; it is based on the overall clinical picture and the evolution of the illness. The are no pathognomonic clinical, endoscopic, or histological features. Colonoscopy can be useful in defining the extent of disease and the pattern of involvement, and provides histological specimens. It is important to try to introduce the colonoscope into the terminal ileum when evaluating for Crohn's disease, but this is possible in only 70 to 80 per cent of patients even for experienced endoscopists. Colonoscopy is equally important in excluding other conditions that may mimic inflammatory bowel disease. Upper endoscopy may be helpful in the evaluation of upper gastrointestinal symptoms, as the differentiation of acid-peptic disease from Crohn's disease may be difficult. Radiographic studies play a central role in diagnosis. A small bowel follow-through or enema (enteroclysis) will demonstrate the extent of small bowel involvement. Air-contrast barium enema studies can evaluate the extent and activity of colonic disease and may allow assessment of the terminal ileum if reflux of the contrast material can be induced. Ultrasonography or CT of the abdomen and pelvis can identify thickened bowel and mesentery as well as abscesses.

The therapy of Crohn's disease depends on the severity of intestinal inflammation and the extent of disease. The mainstays of medical treatment for mild to moderate disease are the 5-aminosalicylate drugs sulphasalazine and mesalazine (mesalamine). Mesalazine is available in several preparations that allow release of the medication directly into the small bowel. In addition to treatment of active disease, there is evidence that mesalazine maintenance therapy may decrease the recurrence of active Crohn's disease. Corticosteroids are effective at managing moderately to severely active Crohn's disease. Treatment with corticosteroids should be tapered off as soon as feasible because of concerns about the development of medication-related side-effects. However, 10 to 15 per cent of patients will experience a flare-up of disease if these drugs are withdrawn. Such patients may be maintained on long-term low-dose corticosteroids but use of other immunosuppressant medications should be considered. Immunosuppressive therapy with azathioprine or 6-mercaptopurine as steroid-sparing agents is helpful in the management of steroid-dependent patients or in addition to other medications in refractory disease. It has recently been recognized that antibiotics may also have an important role in the treatment of active Crohn's disease. Although metronidazole has been used for years as an adjunct for the control of fistulous and perirectal disease, it is now recognized that other antibiotics (ciprofloxacin and clarithromycin) may be beneficial in Crohn's disease, particularly where the terminal ileum is involved. Antibiotics are also important in treating infectious complications of Crohn's disease such as intra-abdominal abscesses. Parenteral hyperalimentation may be needed to rest the gastrointestinal tract, particularly in the management of obstruction and for healing fistulas.

Surgical treatment of Crohn's disease is not primary therapy and is not curative. Rather, surgery is reserved for treatment of the complications of Crohn's disease. During the course of Crohn's disease, approximately 70 per cent of patients will require at least one operation. Extensive resections of the small bowel should be avoided if possible in order to avoid subsequent short-bowel syndrome. The prognosis for older adults with inflammatory bowel disease seems to be better than for younger adults, probably because of earlier recognition of the disease and better therapeutic management (Meuwissen and Seldenrijk 1991).

Bleeding from the small intestine

Gastrointestinal bleeding is an important cause of morbidity and mortality in older persons. Most cases of gastrointestinal blood loss are due to either disorders of the proximal gastrointestinal tract, such as peptic ulcer disease, or colonic sources, such as polyps, cancers, and diverticular disease. Although bleeding from the small intestine is unusual, apart from duodenal ulcer, it is nevertheless a significant problem in the ageing population. We discuss here the main small intestine lesions responsible for haemorrhage in later life. The clinical management of gastrointestinal bleeding in older patients is described in Chapter 8.5.

Non-steroidal agents

Non-steroidal anti-inflammatory drugs (NSAIDs) are important causes of bleeding from the small intestine. With the widespread use of these medications, the epidemiology of peptic ulcer disease has changed in that more elderly patients are presenting with gastrointestinal complications. The gastrointestinal side-effects of NSAIDs are due to a direct topical effect on mucosa, systemic manifestations through effects on prostaglandin metabolism, or, for some drugs, enterohepatic circulation (Wallace 1997).

NSAIDs cause a spectrum of disease of the small intestine, including non-clinically significant disruptions in the mucosa, frank ulcerations, perforation, diaphragm-like stricture formation, altered intestinal permeability, and protein-losing enteropathy (Bjarnason et al. 1993). Although the exact incidence of NSAID-induced ulceration of the small intestine is unclear, autopsy studies have reported non-specific small intestinal ulcerations in 8 per cent of NSAID users (Allison et al. 1992). Bleeding can occur from small erosions in the small intestine and may be made more prominent than the size of the lesions would suggest by the antiplatelet activity of these agents. The treatment of NSAID-induced bleeding from the small intestine requires withdrawal of the responsible drug. There is little to suggest that medications prescribed to treat or prevent gastroduodenal injury from NSAIDs have any useful effect in the small intestine.

Angiodysplasia

Angiodysplasia comprises vascular ectasia and is sometimes regarded as a form of arteriovenous malformation, although, pathologically, arteriovenous malformations are distinct entities. Other gastrointestinal mucosal vascular ectasias occur and may be associated with multisystem diseases (hereditary haemorrhagic telangiectasia or Osler–Weber–Rendu syndrome, CREST syndrome), multiple-haemangioma syndromes (blue rubber bleb naevus syndrome, Klippel–Trenaunay–Weber syndrome, intestinal haemangiomatosis), or other miscellaneous conditions such as pseudoxanthoma elasticum and Ehler–Danlos syndrome. Small bowel angiodysplasia is increasingly recognized as a cause of gastrointestinal bleeding of unclear aetiology. It is now recognized that angiodysplasia may account for up to 24 per cent of obscure upper gastrointestinal bleeding (Clouse et al. 1985). Angiodysplasia is found most commonly in patients aged over 60 years. Angiodysplasia may produce significant morbidity, and the diagnosis and management can be challenging.

The aetiology of angiodysplasia remains uncertain. The lesions are presumed to be acquired since they occur predominantly in an older population. The two leading theories are that angiodysplasia results from either chronic mucosal ischaemia (Baum et al. 1977) or chronic low-grade obstruction of submucosal veins (Boley and Brandt 1986). Other diseases such as chronic renal failure have been associated with angiodysplasia, but no clear cause-and-effect relationship has been established (see also Chapter 8.7).

The only clinical manifestation of angiodysplasia is gastrointestinal bleeding. The bleeding varies in intensity and may present as anaemia of unknown cause or as brisk haemodynamically significant gastrointestinal blood loss. Angiodysplasia is usually present at multiple locations within the gastrointestinal tract, and the clinical presentation varies to some degree on location. The natural history of untreated lesions is unknown, although probably many do not give rise to any problems.

Angiodysplastic lesions are best diagnosed endoscopically. They are 2 to 10 mm in diameter, bright red and flat or slightly raised, and may have a fernlike appearance. They can be easily confused visually with other vascular lesions associated with systemic disease. Endoscopy is both diagnostic and therapeutic, as most treatment strategies have focused on endoscopic obliterative techniques. Cautery devices have been used as well as argon and Nd:YAG lasers. Angiography may reveal lesions not accessible to routine endoscopic examination. Surgical resection can be used as definitive therapy provided that the bleeding lesion can clearly be identified, but this is often difficult in small bowel bleeding with multiple lesions. Medical therapies have been tried with varying success. Oestrogen–progesterone therapy has been the most promising medical therapy, but side-effects are frequent, particularly in male patients, and results have been variable (Van Cutsem et al. 1990; Lewis et al. 1992).

Aortoenteric fistula

Aortoenteric fistulas are rare and life-threatening causes of upper gastrointestinal bleeding. They may be classified as primary or secondary. Secondary fistulas arise following aortic reconstructive surgery and develop in up to 2 per cent of patients approximately 3 to 5 years after surgery (Champion *et al.* 1982). Primary aortoenteric fistulas are rarer and have several possible origins. Before the 1950s, infectious causes, chiefly tuberculosis and syphilis, were the most common, but since the availability of antibiotics, atherosclerosis is the predominant underlying factor (Sweeney and Gadacz 1984).

Clinically, aortoenteric fistulas most commonly present with upper gastrointestinal bleeding which may be massive. However, there may be a 'herald bleed' with an initial bleeding event followed by a period of relative stability before catastrophic haemorrhage occurs. Occasionally there is associated abdominal pain and a palpable pulsatile abdominal mass.

The key to the diagnosis of aortoenteric fistula is considering it as a possibility, which is rarely recognized for patients without a history of aortic reconstructive surgery. Upper endoscopy can help in the diagnosis by excluding other possible causes of upper gastrointestinal bleeding. The diagnosis may indeed be made at the time of endoscopy, but inspection to the fourth portion of the duodenum is necessary and this is beyond the reach of most routine upper endoscopy examinations. Although angiography would potentially be helpful in the diagnosis of aortoenteric fistula, the time required to set up and perform the examination and patient instability often preclude this approach. Urgent laparotomy is the optimal method of diagnosis and treatment. When aortoenteric fistula is suspected, diagnosis and treatment must be carried out urgently.

Small intestinal ischaemia

Small bowel ischaemia is a significant problem in elderly patients owing to the increasing prevalence of atherosclerosis with age. Ischaemia can be classified as acute or chronic, and in the small bowel may be due to arterial or venous disease, and either occlusive (due to an anatomical obstruction to blood flow) or non-occlusive (due to low flow or vasoconstriction). Although the bowel can tolerate a remarkable decrease in blood flow without damage, when it falls below a critical level, oxygen consumption decreases as increased oxygen extraction can no longer compensate for diminished supply.

Acute mesenteric ischaemia is more common than chronic ischaemia, and arterial ischaemia is more common than venous ischaemia. The cause of acute mesenteric ischaemia is arterial mesenteric embolus in 40 to 50 per cent of cases, non-occlusive mesenteric ischaemia in 20 to 30 per cent, superior mesenteric artery thrombosis in 10 per cent, acute mesenteric venous thrombosis in 10 per cent, and focal segmental ischaemia from atheromatous emboli or vasculitides in 5 per cent. Non-occlusive mesenteric ischaemia usually results from splanchnic vasoconstriction following a cardiovascular event such as myocardial infarction or shock.

Typically, acute mesenteric ischaemia presents with severe abdominal pain in a patient with cardiovascular disease, arrhythmia, or hypotension. Initially the pain is out of proportion to physical findings, but over time the abdominal signs evolve to include muscle guarding and rebound tenderness, indicating loss of intestinal viability and bowel infarction. Acute mesenteric venous thrombosis presents in a similar manner but the tempo of the illness is slower. There may be evidence of blood in the stool, but this is more common with colonic

ischaemia. Blood tests may show leucocytosis, metabolic acidaemia, and elevated serum amylase. Plain films of the abdomen are usually normal but may show an ileus, and, when bowel infarction ensues, 'thumbprinting' of the small bowel may be seen.

Where possible, the diagnosis of acute mesenteric ischaemia must be made before intestinal infarction occurs when fatality rises to 70 to 90 per cent. As already noted, plain abdominal radiographs are often unhelpful. In acute mesenteric venous thrombosis, abdominal CT scans or magnetic resonance imaging may demonstrate thrombi in the portal and superior mesenteric veins. Angiography is the principal diagnostic test as it can detect both occlusive and non-occlusive mesenteric ischaemia. Angiography may also be therapeutic as vasodilators such as papaverine can be infused through the superior mesenteric artery.

The initial treatment of patients with suspected acute mesenteric ischaemia includes resuscitation and correction of underlying cardiac arrhythmias and hypotension. Broad-spectrum antibiotics should be started immediately. Papaverine may be infused at the time of angiography. Laparotomy is critical to restore arterial blood flow and/or to resect irreversibly damaged bowel. Anticoagulation is usually started 48 h postoperatively following embolectomy or arterial reconstruction.

Chronic mesenteric ischaemia (abdominal angina) is rare. It is usually due to extensive atherosclerotic disease with narrowing of the abdominal vessels. Although the blood supply is sufficiently compromised to cause ischaemic pain, the vessels are not completely occluded. Typically, pain occurs postprandially, when the metabolic demands of the gut exceed the capacity of its blood supply. Patients experience epigastric or periumbilical cramping, abdominal pain, and weight loss, and occasionally may have malabsorption. The diagnosis can be difficult to make as it has to be based on clinical presentation, angiographic evidence of splanchnic arterial occlusions, and exclusion of other gastrointestinal diseases. Conservative treatment may be tried initially, with small frequent meals to reduce the load on the intestine. A variety of surgical techniques have been used with success to improve the mesenteric blood supply.

Tumours of the small intestine

Benign and malignant tumours may arise from the small intestine. Tumours of the small intestine account for only 1 to 2 per cent of gastrointestinal tumours, although the small intestine provides approximately 90 per cent of the mucosal surface of the gut. It is unclear why tumours of the small intestine, particularly adenocarcinomas, are so rare compared with colonic neoplasms. Rapid transit times with decreased exposure to potential carcinogens and lower numbers of organisms in the small intestine may be responsible. Advancing age does not seem to be a risk factor for small bowel tumours. Patients with chronic diseases of the small intestine, such as Crohn's disease and coeliac disease, suffer a greater than average incidence of small bowel tumours.

Benign tumours of the small intestine include leiomyomas, lipomas, adenomas, and Brunner's gland hamartoma. Malignant tumours include adenocarcinomas, lymphomas, carcinoids, and leiomyosarcomas. Adenocarcinomas are most frequent in the proximal small intestine, and comprise 30 to 50 per cent of malignant small bowel tumours, with a peak incidence in the sixth and seventh decades. Carcinoids and lymphomas are more common in the distal small intestine. Carcinoids comprise 20 to 40 per cent of small intestinal malignancies.

Benign small bowel tumours are clinically asymptomatic in more than half of cases because the contents of the small intestine are liquid and thus the risk of obstruction is low. Large tumours may cause abdominal pain with partial or complete obstruction of the bowel. In addition, tumours may cause intussusception or volvulus. Tumours of the small intestine may also bleed, either at low levels with occult blood loss or occasionally massively, which is typically a feature of leiomyosarcomas. Carcinoid tumours are often found incidentally at unrelated surgery or at autopsy. However, carcinoids may cause obstruction or metastasize to the liver with development of the carcinoid syndrome. Lymphomas may cause fever, weight loss, and malabsorption.

Diagnosis of small bowel tumours can be difficult because of their lack of specific signs or symptoms and their location. Blood tests may reveal a mild iron deficiency anaemia. Carcinoid tumours may cause elevations of plasma serotonin or urinary 5-hydroxyindoleacetic acid. A small bowel follow-through examination or enteroclysis localizes a tumour. Abdominal ultrasonography or CT may demonstrate the tumour and serve to evaluate extraintestinal manifestations such as metastatic involvement of the liver. Endoscopy has a limited role, although enteroscopy will permit inspection of the proximal gastrointestinal tract as far as the proximal jejunum and colonoscopy will often allow visualization of the distal terminal ileum. Rarely, intraoperative endoscopy with advancement of the instrument through the entire small intestine will be required to detect a small bowel tumour.

The primary therapy for symptomatic benign and malignant tumours of the small intestine is surgical removal. Chemotherapy is appropriate for certain tumours, such as extensive small intestinal lymphomas. Radiation therapy is occasionally used in the treatment of bulky tumours or local tumour recurrences.

Pancreas

Pancreatic disease is a common cause of morbidity and mortality in older persons. Acute gallstone pancreatitis and pancreatic cancer are responsible for the great majority of pancreatic disease in this age group. As the percentage of the population that is elderly continues to increase, pancreatic disease will become even more common. Therefore it is important that clinicians caring for older patients are familiar with the clinical presentation and management of this group of disorders.

Age-associated changes

Structure

The anatomy of both the pancreatic parenchyma and the ducts changes with age. The human pancreas, which normally weighs 60 ± 20 g in early adult life, atrophies with advancing age and typically weighs less than 40 g at the age of 85 (Rossle 1921). The average diameter of the pancreatic duct in young adults is 4 mm at the head of the pancreas tapering to 2 mm at the tail. After the age of 50, the pancreatic duct begins to dilate by an average of 8 per cent per decade (Kreel and Sandin 1973). Dilatation occurs proportionally throughout the entire pancreatic duct, and the smooth margins and

tapered appearance of the pancreatic duct are maintained during ageing. Progressive pancreatic duct dilatation correlates with the development of ductular ectasia of the interlobular and intralobular ducts. The ectatic ducts can reach the appearance of cysts, 1 to 2 mm in diameter. These age-associated changes visualized by endoscopic retrograde pancreatography can be misinterpreted as manifestations of chronic pancreatitis (Schmitz-Moormann et al. 1985).

Histologically, the pancreatic parenchyma develops patchy fatty infiltration, lipofuscin deposits, and fibrosis with advancing age (Geokas et al. 1985). In contrast with chronic pancreatitis, age-associated fibrosis does not destroy the parenchyma. The fatty infiltration and fibrosis are both patchy and are responsible for the non-homogenous appearance of the pancreas on CT in older patients. Microscopically, the pancreatic ducts demonstrate proliferation and metaplasia of the ductal epithelial cells (Andrew 1944). The ductal proliferation can lead to lumen expansion, cavitation, and the formation of cysts.

Function

Despite the marked anatomical changes, human studies have failed to show any clinically significant decrease in pancreatic exocrine function with ageing (Gullo et al. 1986). Following pancreatic stimulation, older subjects initially produce pancreatic outputs similar to those of controls, but output is reduced after repeated stimulation (Bartos and Jindrich 1969). The exocrine pancreas has enormous reserve capacity, and clinically apparent malabsorption does not occur until more than 90 per cent of the gland function has been lost (DiMagno et al. 1973). Therefore the failure of human studies to demonstrate any clinically significant decrease in pancreatic exocrine function with ageing is not surprising. Age-associated decreases in secretory volume, bicarbonate, and enzyme outputs in response to an infusion of secretin have been identified (Ishibashi et al. 1991), but are not thought to be clinically significant. The prevalence of fat malabsorption does not increase with ageing.

Disorders of the pancreas

Acute pancreatitis

Acute pancreatitis is a common disorder responsible for 5 to 7 per cent of cases of acute abdominal pain in older persons (Fenyo 1982). The incidence varies geographically depending on the prevalence of the two major causes, ethanol and gallstones. From the 1960s to the 1980s, the annual incidence of pancreatitis in Scotland has increased from 69 to 750 per million females and from 112 to 484 per million males (Wilson and Imrie 1990). This is due to improvements in diagnosis and increased ethanol consumption. Obesity is a risk factor for severe acute pancreatitis and is associated with increased fatality (Funnell et al. 1993). Autopsy data from the United States indicate an overall prevalence of pancreatitis of 0.5 per cent in the general population.

Since Reginald Fitz's classic description of the clinical and pathological features (Fitz 1889), little progress has been made in our understanding of the pathogenesis of acute pancreatitis. The currently most accepted theory indicts intraglandular enzyme activation as the initiating event. The resulting autodigestion stimulates a severe inflammatory reaction which is responsible for the systemic effects of pancreatitis (Dugernier et al. 1996). Past research has focused on the concept of uncontrolled enzyme activation as the major determinant of

Table 1 Causes of pancreatitis

Biliary tract disease (e.g. gallstones)

Idiopathic

Drugs

Alcohol

Traumatic
 Postoperative
 Post-endoscopic (ERCP)
 Blunt abdominal injury

Metabolic
 Hypertriglyceridaemia
 Hyperparathyroidism
 Renal failure

Vascular
 Ischaemia (shock)
 Vasculitis
 Embolic

Infections and infestations
 Ascariasis
 Viral

ERCP, endoscopic retrograde cholangiopancreatography.

Table 2 Drug-induced pancreatitis

Definite association	Probable association	Possible association
Azathioprine	Cyclosporine	Paracetamol (acetaminophen)
Didanosine	6-Mercaptopurine	Amiodarone
Oestrogen	Paracetamol	Atenolol
Frusemide (furosemide)	Rifampicin (rifampin)	Carbamazepine
L-Asparaginase	Steroids	Chlorpromazine
Pentamidine		Cisplatin
Salicylate		Enalapril
Sulphonamide		Lovastatin
Tetracycline		Nitrofurantoin
Thiazides		Procainamide
Valproic acid		

Data from Runzi and Layer (1996).

the severity and course of acute pancreatitis. Experimental and clinical studies assessing the possible benefits of antiprotease supplementation in acute pancreatitis have failed to demonstrate any improvement in morbidity or mortality. Recently, the focus has shifted from enzyme activation towards cytokine activation as the major factor responsible for the multiple-organ damage incurred by patients with severe acute pancreatitis (Rinderknecht 1988). The efficacy of cytokine inhibitors in acute pancreatitis is under investigation.

Gallstones and ethanol account for up to 80 per cent of cases of acute pancreatitis in the general population. The high prevalence of gallstones in later life makes them the most common cause of acute pancreatitis in older people (Table 1). Alcohol is rarely implicated as a cause of acute pancreatitis in older persons, and is surpassed in frequency by both idiopathic and medication-related causes.

Biliary sludge, a suspension of calcium bilirubinate granules and cholesterol monohydrate crystals, has been implicated as a pathogenic factor in up to three-quarters of cases of idiopathic pancreatitis (Lee et al. 1992). In addition, the presence of periampullary extraluminal duodenal diverticula, which are common in older persons, may contribute to idiopathic pancreatitis (Uomo et al. 1996). The prevalence of periampullary extraluminal duodenal diverticula increases with age and they occur in approximately 10 per cent of the population over the age of 60 (Osnes et al. 1981).

Drugs are another important cause of pancreatitis in elderly patients, among whom multiple-drug use is common (Table 2). Most cases are mild to moderate, and withdrawal of the offending medication usually results in a rapid and uneventful recovery. The mechanisms of drug-induced pancreatitis are not well understood, as the associations are often weak and rechallenge is usually contraindicated. Proposed mechanisms include toxic reactions (diuretics

and steroids) or immunological reactions (azathioprine and sulphonamides), with pancreatitis occurring within days to a month of drug exposure. Pentamidine, valproic acid, and didanosine appear to cause pancreatitis through accumulation of a toxic metabolite, with the onset of pancreatitis occurring weeks to months after initial use of the drug (Runzi and Layer 1996).

Cardiovascular disease is common in older persons and can cause ischaemic injury to the pancreas. Ischaemic pancreatitis can result from shock, cardiopulmonary bypass, atheromatous emboli, mesenteric ischaemia, or malignant hypertension (McKay et al. 1958; LeFor et al. 1992; Moolenaar and Lamers 1996). Pancreatitis after cardiopulmonary bypass is rarely severe, and usually manifests as asymptomatic hyperamylasaemia. However, when severe pancreatitis does occur, it is associated with a high fatality (Feiner 1976). In a prospective study of 300 patients undergoing cardiopulmonary bypass, Fernandez-del Castillo et al. (1991) demonstrated that an infusion of more than 800 mg of calcium chloride per square metre of body surface area was an independent risk factor for pancreatic cellular injury during bypass.

Finally, pancreatic carcinoma can present as acute pancreatitis at any age, and is the cause in 1 to 3 per cent of cases (Gambill 1971). Despite this low frequency, the relatively high risk for pancreatic cancer in the elderly requires it to be excluded before an episode of pancreatitis in an older person is deemed idiopathic.

Acute pancreatitis presents similarly in elderly and younger patients. However, older people may exhibit more subtle symptoms and physical findings. As pancreatitis is highly variable, ranging from mild disease to multiple-organ failure, symptoms depend on the disease severity. Abdominal pain is the usual presenting symptom and is typically located in the epigastrium or left upper quadrant, and radiates to the back. The abdomen may be distended, with bowel sounds diminished by ileus, but rigidity and rebound are not common.

Table 3 Non-pancreatic causes of hyperamylasaemia

Renal insufficiency
Diabetic ketoacidosis
Macroamylasaemia
Salivary gland disorders
Mesenteric ischaemia or infarction
Perforated duodenal ulcer
Peritonitis
Chronic liver disease

The pain is usually aggravated by oral intake, and nausea and vomiting are frequently present. In contrast with ulcer disease, vomiting does not usually relieve the pain. The onset of the pain may be gradual or quite sudden, occasionally mimicking a perforated or penetrating duodenal ulcer. In elderly patients who have gallstone pancreatitis, the abdominal pain can be referred to the right upper quadrant owing to concomitant cholangitis. Finally, patients with severe pancreatitis can present with respiratory distress, shock, renal failure, ileus, or ascites.

Diagnosis and differentiation of acute pancreatitis from other abdominal disorders depends on a careful clinical assessment and supportive laboratory and radiological studies. The inability of some elderly patients to describe symptoms accurately, owing to the presence of complicating neurological disorders, calls for even greater reliance on laboratory and imaging studies.

Ever since the association between an elevated serum amylase and acute pancreatitis was discovered by Elman et al. (1929), serum amylase has been the most important laboratory marker for the diagnosis of acute pancreatitis. Increased quantities of pancreatic amylase are found in the bloodstream within hours of the onset of pancreatitis, and return to normal typically within 3 to 5 days. The sensitivity and specificity of serum amylase as a marker of acute pancreatitis is difficult to establish, as not all cases of acute pancreatitis are diagnosed (Wilson and Imrie 1988). In general, a serum amylase greater than three times normal is virtually diagnostic of acute pancreatitis, except where mesenteric ischaemia is present. However, the clinician must be wary of other causes of hyperamylasaemia (Table 3). Unfortunately, in up to 25 per cent of cases of acute pancreatitis serum amylase is normal or only slightly elevated, and amylase levels can normalize within 24 h (Pieper-Bigelow et al. 1990). Furthermore, the degree of serum amylase elevation is not predictive of the severity of the pancreatitis. In acute pancreatitis due to hypertriglyceridaemia, serum amylase levels may be spuriously low.

Serum lipase has shown a greater sensitivity and specificity than serum amylase in the diagnosis of acute pancreatitis (Gumaste et al. 1992), and for many clinicians has become the preferred laboratory test. Lipase levels are high in both alcoholic and non-alcoholic pancreatitis, and the abnormality has a longer half-life than with serum amylase. However, current serum lipase assays are time consuming and have varying sensitivities and specificities depending on the method used (Tietz 1997). This has led to a search for more applicable rapid markers of acute pancreatitis. Recently, the use of a rapid urinary dipstick test for trypsinogen-2 was found to have higher sensitivity (94 per cent) and specificity (95 per cent) than serum and urinary amylase levels in the diagnosis of acute pancreatitis (Kemppainen 1997). Therefore it is hoped that a rapid and more specific and sensitive marker for acute pancreatitis than serum lipase or amylase will be available for routine clinical use in the near future.

Together with laboratory studies, imaging techniques have been crucial in the diagnosis of acute pancreatitis. Plain abdominal radiographs are an initial part of the evaluation of patients with severe abdominal pain. Findings associated with acute pancreatitis include pleural effusions, mostly on the left, an isolated loop (sentinel loop) of small bowel overlying the pancreas, and an ileus pattern.

Ultrasonography has a sensitivity of 67 per cent and a specificity of up to 100 per cent in the diagnosis of acute pancreatitis (Neoptolemos et al. 1984). Ultrasound is superior to CT in imaging the biliary tract, but the evaluation of the pancreas is frequently limited by overlying bowel gas and an inability to detect the presence or absence of pancreatic necrosis. Contrast-enhanced CT is the current imaging method of choice in acute pancreatitis (Chalmers 1997). New helical CT scanners can produce rapid images of the abdomen within a single breath. Rapid images can subsequently be obtained during the administration of intravenous contrast, with non-contrast-enhancing areas of the pancreas reflecting pancreatic necrosis.

Not all patients with acute pancreatitis require an abdominal CT, and up to 15 to 30 per cent of patients with mild pancreatitis may have a pancreas that appears normal on CT (Balthazar 1989). CT is usually indicated when the diagnosis is in doubt, when complications are suspected, or in the assessment of patients with severe acute pancreatitis.

Endoscopic retrograde cholangiopancreatography (**ERCP**) is the current gold standard for the evaluation of common bile duct stones and the pancreatic ductal system. The role of ERCP in the diagnosis of acute pancreatitis is in the evaluation of patients with acute pancreatitis of unknown aetiology (Cotton and Beales 1974). ERCP can determine an aetiology in 30 to 50 per cent of such cases by identifying small pancreatic tumours, choledochocoeles, pancreatic duct strictures, or common bile duct stones and biliary sludge, all of which can pass undetected by non-invasive imaging studies such as CT and ultrasound. Finally, magnetic resonance cholangio-pancreatography is an emerging technique that can provide excellent detail of the biliary and main pancreatic duct anatomy, and may become a non-invasive alternative to diagnostic ERCP.

As previously mentioned, most cases of acute pancreatitis are mild and self-limiting with an overall fatality of 5 per cent. Criteria based on clinical and laboratory data have been developed to predict the severity and fatality of acute pancreatitis. The most commonly used criteria are those of Ranson et al. (1974) and the Glasgow group (Blamey et al. 1984) (Table 4). The greater the number of risk factors, the higher is the fatality. Using Ranson's criteria, patients with only one to two risk factors have a fatality of less than 1 per cent, whereas almost all of those with seven or more risk factors die. A limitation of Ranson's criteria is that a complete risk assessment requires 48 h.

The proportion of pancreatic necrosis has been combined with a grading scale of acute pancreatitis by CT to form a CT severity index. This index, which was developed by Balthazar et al. (1990), correlates with Ranson's criteria for assessing the severity of acute pancreatitis. In this study, a score of 2 was associated with zero fatality, while a score of 7 to 10 was associated with a 17 per cent fatality.

Table 4 Ranson and simplified Glasgow prognostic criteria in acute pancreatitis: risk factors for death

Ranson (on admission)	Simplified Glasgow (within 48 h)
Age >55 years	Age >55 years
WBC >16 000 mm³	WBC >15 000 mm³
LDH >350 IU/l	LDH >600 IU/l
Glucose >200 mg/dl	Glucose >180 mg/dl
AST >250 IU/l	Albumin <3.3 g/dl
	Calcium <8 mg/dl
	Arterial PO_2 <60 mmHg
	BUN >45 mg/dl

Within 48 h
Haematocrit decrease by >10%
BUN increase by >5 mg/dl
Serum calcium <8 mg/dl
Arterial PO_2 <60 mmHg
Base deficit >4 mmol/l
Estimated fluid deficit >6 litres

WBC, white blood cell count; LDH, lactate dehydrogenase; AST, aspartate transaminase; BUN, blood urea nitrogen.
Data from Blamey et al. (1984).

Treatment for acute pancreatitis is largely supportive. Our poor understanding of its pathophysiology has resulted in the lack of any effective specific therapy. Fortunately, most cases of acute pancreatitis (80 per cent) are self-limiting and have an uncomplicated course. Supportive treatment consists of bowel rest (to avoid pancreatic stimulation), intravenous fluids, and analgesics. A nasogastric tube should be placed if nausea and vomiting are prominent. Most patients are able to resume oral intake within a few days, and nutritional support is rarely required.

In the 20 per cent of patients with a more severe clinical course there is often multiple-organ involvement. These patients require nutritional support to offset the hypermetabolic and catabolic inflammatory state that supervenes. Total parenteral nutrition is the usual method of nutritional support in cases of moderate to severe pancreatitis.

In addition to supportive measures, all patients with acute pancreatitis should undergo a thorough investigation to determine the aetiology. This is particularly important in cases due to hypertriglyceridaemia, gallstones/biliary sludge, hypercalcaemia, and drugs, as correction of the precipitating factor usually results in a shortened and less complicated course. Finally, patients with signs of obstructive jaundice, with or without cholangitis, may benefit from an ERCP within 72 h of onset of symptoms (Wilson et al. 1997).

The prophylactic use of antibiotics in severe acute pancreatitis is controversial (Finch and Sawyers 1976; Pederzoli et al. 1993). Infection occurs in 50 to 60 per cent of patients with pancreatic necrosis (Beger et al. 1986) and is responsible for up to 80 per cent of the deaths associated with the disease. When infection complicates an area of pancreatic necrosis, surgical debridement is indicated. The risk of infection increases with the extent of pancreatic necrosis. Most infections occur late, with the peak occurrence at 3 weeks. Recent clinical trials evaluating the efficacy of prophylactic antibiotics in acute pancreatitis have shown a significant decrease in infection rate but with only a trend to improved survival (Sainio et al. 1995; Ho and Frey 1997). Our practice is to administer a course of antibiotics to all patients with severe acute pancreatitis requiring intensive care. Imipenem or a quinolone are our antibiotics of choice for prophylactic treatment, as both can achieve high bactericidal levels in necrotic pancreatic tissue (Bassi et al. 1994).

Complications in acute pancreatitis can be divided into early and late (Steinberg and Tenner 1994). Early complications occur within the first 2 weeks and include multiple-organ failure involving the renal, pulmonary, and cardiovascular systems. Pulmonary dysfunction manifests over a broad range of severity from mild hypoxaemia to full-blown acute respiratory distress syndrome. Renal failure occurs secondary to acute tubular necrosis from hypoperfusion. Some evidence also suggests an ischaemic injury from microthrombi, which arise from the systemic coagulopathy in acute pancreatitis. Cardiovascular collapse can result from fluid sequestration, bleeding, or cytokine-induced vasodilatation. Other early complications of acute pancreatitis include disseminated intravascular coagulation, early infection of pancreatic necrosis, and rupture of the pancreatic duct.

Late complications are defined as those occurring after the second week. Pseudocyst and abscess formation are the more common late complications, and occur in approximately 10 per cent of cases of acute pancreatitis (Ranson and Spencer 1977; Yeo et al. 1990). Pancreatic pseudocysts are collections of pancreatic secretions that occur within or around the pancreas and are surrounded by a non-epithelial fibrous capsule. Pseudocysts should be suspected in patients with severe pancreatitis who have continuing or worsening pain, a palpable abdominal mass, or persistent elevation of serum amylase. Bleeding and infection are the most serious complications of a pseudocyst. Bleeding occurs secondary to erosion of the pseudocyst into a mesenteric artery with pseudoaneurysm formation. It can occur into the pseudocyst, an adjacent viscus such as the stomach, the pancreatic duct, or the retroperitoneum. Another important bleeding complication is the development of gastric varices due to splenic vein thrombosis.

Treatment of pancreatic pseudocysts depends on their size, symptoms, and complications. Six weeks are typically required before any therapy to allow a cyst to mature so that its wall will be able to hold sutures. Pseudocysts can be followed long after 6 weeks, and if they are small (less than 6 cm) and do not increase in size, and patients are able to tolerate oral intake, continued observation is reasonable (Wilson 1997). Treatment of larger or symptomatic pseudocysts requires either external drainage by CT-guided catheter placement, endoscopic cystogastrostomy, or cystoduodenostomy, or surgical internal drainage. Cysts that communicate with the pancreatic duct can be treated with endoscopic transpapillary drainage (Dohmoto and Rupp 1994). Medical therapy with octreotide can also be used to decrease pancreatic secretion (Barkin et al. 1991). If infection of a pseudocyst is suspected, urgent drainage is needed as antibiotics alone are not sufficient.

Chronic pancreatitis

Alcohol is the most common cause of chronic pancreatitis in the West and is responsible for 70 to 80 per cent of cases. As alcohol consumption varies widely among nations, the incidence of chronic pancreatitis is also highly variable. A 1-year prospective study in Denmark revealed an incidence of eight new cases per 100 000 population per year, and a prevalence of 26 cases per 100 000 population (Anonymous 1981). Autopsy data in alcoholics reveal a prevalence of chronic pancreatitis of 50 per cent, which is 50 times greater than in non-alcoholic controls (Clark 1942). Idiopathic causes of chronic pancreatitis are the second most common cause of chronic pancreatitis (20 per cent). Other aetiologies of chronic pancreatitis include hypertriglyceridaemia, hyperparathyroidism, drugs, choledochocoeles, biliary stones, hereditary pancreatitis, and obstruction or disruption of the main pancreatic duct. In older persons, idiopathic causes of chronic pancreatitis predominate, comprising 80 per cent of the cases of chronic pancreatitis. Alcohol-induced chronic pancreatitis is rare after the age of 60, and accounts for less than 5 per cent of cases of chronic pancreatitis in this age group (Ammann 1990).

There are two major forms of chronic pancreatitis, large-duct disease and small-duct disease. The more common large-duct form involves obstruction of the main pancreatic duct by stones, stricture, trauma, or tumour. Duct dilatation occurs proximal to the obstruction, and diffuse or patchy fibrosis and atrophy of the pancreas eventually ensues in the affected proximal areas. Calcifications within the main and major branches of the pancreatic duct develop owing to obstruction of pancreatic secretion, and can at times be identified on a plain abdominal radiograph. In the small-duct form, which is typical of idiopathic chronic pancreatitis, damage occurs directly to the pancreatic parenchyma and small ducts, with sparing of the main pancreatic duct. There is subsequently little or no pancreatic calcification, making the diagnosis more difficult. Chronic small-duct pancreatitis is probably underdiagnosed (Walsh et al. 1992).

The exact pathophysiology by which alcohol and other causes result in chronic pancreatitis is unknown. Nutrition appears to be an important factor in alcoholic chronic pancreatitis, as there are numerous data linking a high-fat high-protein diet to an increased risk of chronic pancreatitis in alcoholics (Durbee and Sarles 1978). Another effect of alcohol that may predispose to chronic pancreatitis is the suppression of lithostatin, a protein found in pancreatic juice which inhibits stone formation (Laugier and Bernard 1996).

Chronic alcoholic pancreatitis is characterized by an initial phase that lasts for several years and manifests as recurrent bouts of abdominal pain. Many of these recurrent bouts are diagnosed as acute alcoholic pancreatitis. Over time there is resolution of pain but loss of glandular function. Symptoms of pancreatic insufficiency are the most common presenting symptom in idiopathic cases of chronic pancreatitis, with abdominal pain being quite uncommon. Thus an elderly patient with alcohol-induced chronic pancreatitis is more likely to have symptoms related to pancreatic gland failure, weight loss, diabetes, and steatorrhoea, rather than abdominal pain.

The diagnosis of chronic pancreatitis should be suspected in any patient with a history of recurrent abdominal pain, weight loss, or diarrhoea. The findings of diffuse pancreatic calcifications on a plain abdominal radiograph are highly suggestive of the diagnosis, but occur in only 30 to 40 per cent of cases. Further testing involves assessing pancreatic structure with CT or ERCP. The sensitivity of ERCP is reported to be over 90 per cent in the diagnosis of chronic pancreatitis, and this technique is considered the gold standard by which other imaging methods are measured (Steer et al. 1995). The limitations of ERCP are in cases of small-duct chronic pancreatitis.

Laboratory studies are very useful in the diagnosis of chronic pancreatitis. The bentiromide test is an indirect measure of pancreatic function. Bentiromide or nitroblue tetrazolium–p-aminobenzoic acid is cleaved by pancreatic chymotrypsin with the release of p-aminobenzoic acid which is subsequently cleared by the kidney and measured in the urine. The amount of p-aminobenzoic acid in the urine is used to calculate the amount of chymotrypsin in the gut, which is a reflection of pancreatic glandular function. However, the best test for the assessment of chronic pancreatitis and pancreatic function is the secretin test which measures pancreatic function directly. A tube is placed in the duodenum and pancreatic secretions are collected after administration of an intravenous dose of secretin. The advantage of the secretin test is that chronic pancreatitis can be diagnosed at an earlier stage than is possible with the bentiromide test, and it is not affected by age or sex (Ammann et al. 1996).

Fat malabsorption is the most common abnormality that occurs when there is loss of pancreatic exocrine function. The treatment of the resulting steatorrhoea is directed at providing adequate quantities of pancreatic enzymes to the intestinal lumen during meals. Approximately 30 000 units of lipase are required with each meal to prevent malabsorption. Commercially available pancreatic enzyme replacement preparations come as enteric and non-enteric coated capsules. The non-enteric coated capsules release lipase into the stomach, resulting in inactivation of lipase if the gastric pH is below 4. Suppression of gastric acid secretion to raise the gastric pH may be warranted if a patient is failing to respond to enzyme therapy or enteric coated preparations are not available.

Management of pain in chronic pancreatitis can be difficult and narcotic addiction is not uncommon. Pancreatic enzymes have been used successfully to provide pain relief in patients with mild to moderate or small-duct pancreatitis (Isaaksson and Ihse 1983; Slaff et al. 1984). The protease component of the enzyme supplements appears to be the active agent and needs to be present in the duodenum; therefore use of non-enteric coated preparations together with gastric acid suppression is required. Other possible methods of pain control include coeliac plexus nerve block performed under CT or endoscopic ultrasound guidance. Coeliac plexus blockade or ablation is used in the relief of pain in pancreatic cancer. Results in chronic pancreatitis have been disappointing, and this method is rarely used (Leung et al. 1983). Octreotide is well tolerated and has shown some promising results in reducing pain (Toskes et al. 1993), but further trials are needed before generalized use of this agent in pain management in chronic pancreatitis can be justified.

Surgery can be an effective treatment for pain in chronic pancreatitis. The presence of a main pancreatic duct dilatation to 7 to 8 mm or more is indicative that surgical decompression is likely to result in substantial relief. The procedure is a longitudinal pancreaticojejunostomy (modified Peustow procedure), and leads to immediate pain relief in up to 75 per cent of patients and long-term pain control in up to 50 per cent (Warshaw 1985). In addition to its effect on pain control, surgical decompression appears to slow the progression of the complications of chronic pancreatitis.

Endoscopic therapy is also an option in the management of patients with major pancreatic duct disease (Burdick and Hogan 1991; Cremer et al. 1991). Removal of obstructing stones, stenting, or dilatation of duct stricture may be performed in an attempt to decrease pancreatic duct pressure, to relieve pain, and to slow the progression of the disease process.

Pseudocysts complicate approximately 10 per cent of cases of chronic pancreatitis, with the majority of the cysts occurring in the body or the tail. Most pseudocysts are asymptomatic, are less than 6 cm in diameter, and require no intervention. Pseudocysts which are greater than 6 cm in diameter or are symptomatic or enlarging should be treated. Treatment options and complications of pseudocysts are the same as those previously described for acute pancreatitis.

Pancreatic cancer

Carcinoma of the pancreas is the fifth leading cause of cancer death in the industrialized world. Age is a major risk factor, with three-quarters of all pancreatic cancers occurring in patients over the age of 60 (MacMahon 1982). Other risk factors for pancreatic cancer include diabetes, cigarette smoking, and chronic pancreatitis. Ninety per cent of the tumours of the pancreas arise from the exocrine pancreas. Islet cell tumours, neuroendocrine tumours, sarcomas, and primary lymphoma of the pancreas are rare.

Adenocarcinoma of the pancreas occurs predominantly in the head of the pancreas (60 to 70 per cent). The most commonly involved site within the pancreatic head is the dorsal pancreas close to the intrapancreatic portion of the common bile duct. Tumours in this region often obstruct the common bile duct and cause jaundice. Tumours in the body and tail are typically larger (5–7 cm on average) than those of the pancreatic head (2.5–3 cm on average) at presentation, as tumours in the head produce symptoms at an earlier stage. The same holds true of tumours of the ampulla of Vater. Carcinomas in this area can cause biliary obstruction at an even earlier stage, and therefore are more amenable to a curative resection (Bakkevold et al. 1992).

The location of a carcinoma within the pancreas predicts the clinical manifestations of the disease. A carcinoma in the pancreatic body and tail would be expected to be relatively large with evidence of spread at initial diagnosis. Tumours in this region of the pancreas can present with obstruction by direct extension of the tumour into the duodenum, upper gastrointestinal haemorrhage secondary to gastric varices from splenic vein thrombosis, symptoms such as mid-back pain due to neural invasion, and abdominal distension due to malignant ascites.

Tumours in the head of the pancreas result in obstructive jaundice in approximately 75 per cent of cases. The onset of the jaundice is usually insidious. Steatorrhoea and malabsorption can occur when there is obstruction of the pancreatic duct. Gastric outlet obstruction and upper gastrointestinal bleeding can occur from direct extension of the tumour into the duodenum. Progressive unremitting abdominal pain that may be aggravated by food, together with anorexia and weight loss are also common in pancreatic cancer. Pain is the presenting symptom in up to 80 per cent of patients, and weight loss of more than 10 per cent of ideal body weight has occurred in almost every patient by the time of diagnosis. The weight loss is due to the combination of decreased caloric intake and malabsorption. Finally, new-onset diabetes can be a presenting symptom of pancreatic cancer. Up to 16 per cent of patients diagnosed with pancreatic cancer have had diabetes for 2 years or less.

The diagnosis of pancreatic cancer is usually made by radiological studies. As patients frequently present with jaundice, an ultrasound or CT scan of the abdomen is usually performed to evaluate the biliary tract, liver, and pancreas. Ultrasound is superior to CT in the evaluation of gallstones and hepatic lesions. However, CT is the imaging study of choice for the pancreas and has a 90 per cent sensitivity and specificity in detecting a pancreatic carcinoma (Freeny et al. 1993). ERCP is the most sensitive diagnostic test for pancreatic cancer (Berland et al. 1981) and is helpful in the small group of patients in whom CT may be inconclusive. In addition, ERCP may be used to decompress the biliary tract and to obtain tissue for histological confirmation of the diagnosis.

Serum markers for pancreatic cancer are also available and are useful in the diagnosis and management of patients with pancreatic cancer. The most commonly used marker is CA 19–9, which has a relatively low specificity (75 per cent) but a high sensitivity (90 per cent) for pancreatic cancer (Steinberg et al. 1986; Pleskow et al. 1989). A level greater than 1000 IU/ml has a specificity of nearly 100 per cent for pancreatic cancer. Elevations in CA 19–9 can occur in other malignancies such as adenocarcinoma of the stomach, colon, or bile ducts. Elevations also occur in benign diseases, such as cirrhosis or cholangitis. CA 19–9 levels are clinically useful in monitoring patients undergoing attempts at curative resection. Maintenance of a normal level postoperatively over time signifies a good prognosis.

Confirmation of a clinical diagnosis of pancreatic cancer requires tissue. In pancreatic cancer this can be done by CT-guided fine-needle aspiration of the pancreas. Alternatively, if ERCP is being performed for relief of biliary obstruction, cytological brushings can be obtained during the procedure. Patients with tumours who are possible candidates for curative resection should not undergo fine-needle biopsy, as the procedure may result in intraperitoneal or needle-tract seeding of tumour.

There has been no progress in the treatment of pancreatic cancer over the past four decades. The mortality is essentially unchanged and, at less than 5 per cent, the disease continues to carry one of the worst 5-year survival rates of all gastrointestinal tumours (Boring et al. 1994). Radiotherapy and chemotherapy do not improve survival. Curative surgical resection is the only option with potential for prolonged survival or cure. Unfortunately, only 10 per cent or less of patients are candidates for surgical resection at the time of diagnosis. Pancreaticoduodenectomy (Whipple procedure) is the procedure performed on tumours in the head of the pancreas. In the past this procedure carried a high fatality (27 per cent), but more recent series demonstrate a mortality of less than 5 per cent (Crist et al. 1987). However, advanced age continues to be associated with increased morbidity and fatality (Lerut et al. 1984).

In the majority of patients with pancreatic cancer, the tumours are not resectable and treatment is palliative. Patients with biliary obstruction can develop hepatic failure, pancreatitis, and cholangitis. Endoscopic placement of a biliary stent is an effective means of relieving the biliary obstruction (Schoeman and Huibregtse 1995). The recent development of self-expanding metallic stents has resulted in improved long-term stent function and a decreased need for restenting in patients with prolonged survival. Alternatively, patients who cannot be stented endoscopically can have percutaneous drainage and stent placement performed. Metal stents for the relief of duodenal obstruction have recently become available, and may obviate the need for gastrointestinal bypass surgery. Patients who do undergo an attempt at resection and are deemed inoperable at the time of laparotomy should undergo a palliative gastrojejunostomy and choledochojejunostomy. Many patients will require more general palliative care (see Chapter 23.8).

Cystic tumours

Cystic tumours of the pancreas are uncommon. They comprise two distinct groups, mucinous and microcystic. Mucinous cystadenoma and cystadenocarcinoma are typically large tumours greater than 5 cm in diameter, with unilobular or multilobulated cysts filled with mucin (Compagno and Oertel 1978b). The cysts are lined by papillary projections of columnar epithelium or invasive carcinoma. In some cases, invasive carcinoma can be found adjacent to normal columnar epithelium. Therefore all mucinous cystadenomas should be considered as possibly malignant, and at the very least as a premalignant lesion. Women are affected more commonly than men with a ratio of 6:1. The age of presentation is usually less than 60 years, and the tumours are more commonly located in the body or tail rather than the head of the pancreas. Unlike adenocarcinoma of the pancreas, all mucinous cystadenomas and cystadenocarcinomas should be resected. The 5-year survival rates with surgery approach 75 per cent (Fernandez-del Castillo and Warshaw 1995).

Microcystic cystadenomas are large benign tumours (mean diameter, 10.8 cm) without malignant potential (Compagno and Oertel 1978a). The cysts are glycogen rich and typically small, and may contain stellate calcifications, in contrast to the curvilinear calcifications on the cyst wall in mucinous cystadenomas. Women and men are affected equally, and the mean age at presentation is 68 years. Differentiating a microcystic cystadenoma from a mucinous cystadenoma or cystadenocarcinoma preoperatively is difficult, as the characteristic stellate (sunburst) calcifications on CT scans are only present in 20 per cent of patients. Therefore resection is usually required to resolve any diagnostic uncertainty. When a lesion is clearly identified as a microcystic cystadenoma, no treatment is required unless the patient is symptomatic.

References

Allison, M.C., Howatson, A.G., Torrance, C.J., Lee, F.D., and Russell, R.I. (1992). Gastrointestinal damage associated with the use of nonsteroidal anti-inflammatory drugs. *New England Journal of Medicine*, 327, 749–54.

Ammann, R.W. (1990). Chronic pancreatitis in the elderly. *Gastroenterology Clinics of North America*, 19, 905–914.

Ammann, S.T., Josephson, S., Forsmark, C.E., Bishop, M., and Toskes, P.P. (1996). Effects of age and gender on pancreatic function: a 10 year experience with the secretin test. *Gastroenterology*, 110, A377.

Andrew, W. (1944). Senile changes in the pancreas of Wistar Institute rats and of man with special regard to the similarity of locule and cavity formation. *American Journal of Anatomy*, 74, 97–127.

Anonymous (1981). Copenhagen Pancreatic Study. An interim report from a prospective epidemiological multi-centre study. *Scandinavian Journal of Gastroenterology*, 16, 305–12.

Arora, S., Kassarjian, Z., Krasinski, S., *et al.* (1989). Effect of age on tests of intestinal and hepatic function in healthy humans. *Gastroenterology*, 96, 1560–65.

Bakkevold, K.E., Arnesj, B., and Kambestad, B. (1992). Carcinoma of the pancreas and papilla of Vater: presenting symptoms, signs, and diagnosis related to stage and tumour site. *Scandinavian Journal of Gastroenterology*, 27, 312–25.

Balthazar, E.J. (1989). CT diagnosis and staging of acute pancreatitis. *Radiology Clinics of North America*, 27, 19–37.

Balthazar, E.J., Robinson, D.L., Megibow, A.J., and Ranson, J.H. (1990) Acute pancreatitis: value of CT in establishing prognosis. *Radiology*, 174, 331–6.

Barkin, J.S., Reiner, D.K., and Deutch, E. (1991). Sandostatin for control of catheter drainage of pancreatic pseudocyst. *Pancreas*, 6, 245–8.

Bartos, V. and Jindrich, G. (1969). The effect of repeated stimulation of the pancreas on the pancreatic secretion in young and aged men. *Gerontology Clinics*, 11, 56–62.

Bassi, C., Pederzoli, P., Vesentini, S., *et al.* (1994). Behaviour of antimicrobials during human necrotizing pancreatitis. *Antimicrobial Agents and Chemotherapy*, 38, 830–6.

Baum, S., Athanasoulis, C.A., Waltman, A.C., *et al.* (1977). Angiodysplasia of the right colon. A cause of gastrointestinal bleeding. *American Journal of Roentgenology*, 129, 789–94.

Beger, H.G., Bittner, R., Block, S., *et al.* (1986). Bacterial contamination of pancreatic necrosis: a prognostic clinical study. *Gastroenterology*, 91, 433–8.

Berland, L.L., Lawson, T.L., Foley, W.D., *et al.* (1981). Computed tomography of the normal and abnormal pancreatic duct: correlation with pancreatic ductography. *Radiology*, 141, 715–24.

Bjarnason, I., Hayllar, J., Macpherson, A.J., and Russell, A.S. (1993). Side effects of nonsteroidal anti-inflammatory drugs on the small and large intestine in humans. *Gastroenterology*, 104, 1832–47.

Blamey, S.L., Imrie, C.W., O'Neill, J., Gilmour, W.H., and Cater, D.C. (1984). Prognostic factors in acute pancreatitis. *Gut*, 25, 1340–6.

Boley, S.J. and Brandt, L.J. (1986).Vascular ectasias of the colon—1986. *Digestive Diseases and Science*, 31 (Supplement 9), 26S–42S.

Boring, C.C., Squires, T.S., Tong, T., *et al.* (1994). Cancer statistics, 1994. *CA*, 44, 7–26.

Burdick, J.S. and Hogan, W.J. (1991). Chronic pancreatitis: selection of patients for endoscopic therapy. *Endoscopy*, 23, 155–9.

Chalmers, A. (1997). The role of imaging in acute pancreatitis. *European Journal of Gastroenterology and Hepatology*, 9, 106–16.

Champion, M., Sullivan, S., Coles, J., *et al.* (1982). Aortoenteric fistula: incidence, presentation, recognition and management. *Annals of Surgery*, 195, 314–17.

Clark, E. (1942). Pancreatitis in acute and chronic alcoholism. *American Journal of Digestive Diseases*, 9, 428–31.

Clouse, R., Costigan, D.J., Mills, B.A., and Zuckerman, G.R. (1985). Angiodysplasia as a cause of upper gastrointestinal bleeding. *Archives of Internal Medicine*, 145, 458–61.

Compagno, J. and Oertel, J.E. (1978a). Microcystic adenomas of the pancreas (glycogen-rich cystadenomas): a clinicopathologic study of 34 cases. *American Journal of Pathology*, 69, 289–298.

Compagno, J. and Oertel, J. E. (1978b). Mucinous cystic neoplasms of the pancreas with overt and latent malignancy (cystadenocarcinoma and cystadenoma): clinicopathologic study of 41 cases. *American Journal of Pathology*, 69, 573–80.

Corazza, G.R., Menozzi, M.G., Strocchi, A., *et al.* (1990). The diagnosis of small bowel bacterial overgrowth. *Gastroenterology*, 98, 302–5.

Cotton, P.B. and Beales, J.S.M. (1974). Endoscopic pancreatography in management of relapsing acute pancreatitis. *British Medical Journal*, i, 608–11.

Cremer, M., Deviere, J., Delhaye, M., Baize, M., and Vandermeeren, A. (1991). Stenting in severe chronic pancreatitis: results of medium-term follow-up in seventy-six patients. *Endoscopy*, 23, 171–6.

Crist, D.W., Sitzmann, J.V., and Cameron, J.L. (1987). Improved hospital morbidity, mortality, and survival rate after the Whipple procedure. *Annals of Surgery*, 206, 358–65.

DiMagno, E.P., Go, V.L.W., and Summerskill, W.H.J. (1973). Relations between pancreatic enzyme outputs and malabsorption in severe pancreatic insufficiency. *New England Journal of Medicine*, 288, 813–15.

Dohmoto, M. and Rupp, K.D. (1992). Endoscopic drainage of pancreatic pseudocysts. *Surgical Endoscopy*, 6, 118–24.

Dugernier, T., Starkel, P., Laterre, P.F., and Reynaert, M.S. (1996) Severe acute pancreatitis: pathophysiologic mechanisms underlying pancreatic necrosis and remote organ damage. *Acta Gastroenterologica Belgica*, 59, 178–85.

Durbee, J.P. and Sarles, H. (1978). Multi-centre survey of the aetiology of pancreatic disease: relationship between the relative risk of developing chronic pancreatitis and alcohol, protein, and lipid consumption. *Digestion*, 18, 337–50.

Elman, R., Arneson, N., and Graham, E.A. (1929). Value of blood amylase estimations in the diagnosis of pancreatic disease: a clinical study. *Archives of Surgery*, 19, 943–67.

Feibusch, J.M. and Holt, P.R. (1982). Impaired absorptive capacity for carbohydrate in the ageing human. *Digestive Diseases and Science*, 27, 1095–1100.

Feiner, H. (1976). Pancreatitis after cardiac surgery. *American Journal of Surgery*, 131, 684–8.

Fenyo, G. (1982). Acute abdominal diseases in the elderly: experience from two series in Stockholm. *American Journal of Surgery*, 143, 751–4.

Fernandez-del Castillo, C. and Warshaw, A.L. (1995). Cystic tumours of the pancreas. *Surgical Clinics of North America*, 75, 1001–15.

Fernandez-del Castillo, C., Harringer, W., Warshaw, A.L., et al. (1991). Risk factors for pancreatic cellular injury after cardiopulmonary bypass. *New England Journal of Medicine*, 325, 382–7.

Finch, W.T. and Sawyers, J.L. (1976). A prospective study to determine the efficacy of antibiotics in acute pancreatitis. *Annals of Surgery*, 183, 667–71.

Fine, K.D. (1996). The prevalence of occult gastrointestinal bleeding in celiac sprue. *New England Journal of Medicine*, 334, 1163–7.

Fitz, R.H. (1889). Acute pancreatitis: a consideration of pancreatic haemorrhage, haemorrhagic, suppurative, and gangrenous pancreatitis, and of disseminated fat-necrosis. *Boston Medical Surgical Journal*, 120, 181–7, 205–7, 229–35.

Freeny, P.C., Traverso, W.L., and Ryan, J.A. (1993). Diagnosis and staging of pancreatic adenocarcinoma with dynamic computed tomography. *American Journal of Surgery*, 165, 600–6.

Funnell, J.C., Bornman, P.C., Weakley, S.P., Terblanche, J., and Marks, I.N. (1993). Obesity: an important prognostic factor in acute pancreatitis. *British Journal of Surgery*, 80, 484–6.

Gambill, E.E. (1971). Pancreatitis associated with pancreatic carcinoma: a study of 26 cases. *Mayo Clinic Proceedings*, 46, 174–7.

Geokas, M.C., Conteas, C.N., and Majumdar, P.N. (1985). The ageing gastrointestinal tract, liver, and pancreas. *Clinics in Geriatric Medicine*, 1, 177–205.

Gullo, L., Ventrucci, M., Naldoni, M., and Pezzilli, R. (1986). Ageing and exocrine pancreatic function. *Journal of the American Geriatrics Society*, 34, 790–2.

Gumaste, V., Dave, P., and Sereny, G. (1992). Serum lipase: a better test to diagnose acute pancreatitis. *American Journal of Medicine*, 92, 239–42.

Ho, H.S. and Frey, C.F. (1997). The role of antibiotic prophylaxis in severe acute pancreatitis. *Archives of Surgery*, 132, 487–93.

Hurwitz, A., Brady, D.A., Schaal, E., Samloff, I.M., Dedon, J., and Ruhl, C.E. (1997). Gastric acidity in older adults. *Journal of the American Medical Association*, 278, 659–62.

Husebye, E. and Engedal, K. (1992). The patterns of motility are maintained in the human small intestine throughout the process of ageing. *Scandinavian Journal of Gastroenterology*, 27, 397–404.

Isaakson, G. and Ihse, I. (1983). Pain reduction by an oral pancreatic enzyme preparation in chronic pancreatitis. *Digestive Diseases and Science*, 28, 97–102.

Ishibashi, T., Matsumoto, S., Harada, H., et al. (1991). Ageing and exocrine pancreatic function evaluated by the recently standardised secretin test. *Japanese Journal of Geriatrics*, 28, 599–605.

Kempainnen, E.A., Hedstrom, J.I., Puolakkainen, P.A., et al. (1997). Rapid measurement of urinary trypsinogen-2 as a screening test for acute pancreatitis. *New England Journal of Medicine*, 336, 1788–93.

King, C.E. and Toskes, P.P. (1986). Comparison of the 1-gram ^{14}C-xylose, 10-gram lactulose and 80-gram glucose H_2 breath tests in patients with small intestinal bacterial overgrowth. *Gastroenterology*, 91, 1447–51.

Krasinski, S., Russell, R., Samloff, M., et al. (1986). Fundic atrophic gastritis in an elderly population. *Journal of the American Geriatric Society*, 34, 800–6.

Kreel, L. and Sandin, B. (1973). Changes in pancreatic morphology associated with ageing. *Gut*, 14, 962–70.

Laugier, R. and Bernard, J.P. (1996). Lithostatine: place in chronic pancreatitis pathogenesis. *Acta Gastroenterologica Belgica*, 59, 188–90.

Lee, S.P., Nicholls, J.F., and Park, H.Z. (1992). Biliary sludge as a cause of acute pancreatitis. *New England Journal of Medicine*, 326, 589–93.

LeFor, A.T., Vuocolo, P., Parker, F.B., Jr, and Sillin, L.F. (1992). Pancreatic complications following cardiopulmonary bypass: factors influencing mortality. *Archives of Surgery*, 127, 1225–31.

Lerut, J.P. Gianello, P.K., Otte, J.B., and Kesters, P.J. (1984). Pancreaticoduodenal resection: surgical experience and evaluation of risk factors in 103 patients. *Annals of Surgery*, 199, 432–7.

Leung, J.W., Bowen-Wright, M., Aveling, W., Shorvon, P.J., and Cotton, P.B. (1983). Coeliac plexus block for pain in pancreatic cancer and chronic pancreatitis. *British Journal of Surgery*, 70, 730–2.

Lewis, B.S., Salomon, P., Rivera-MacMurray, S., Kornbloth, A.A., Wenger, J., and Waye, J.D. (1992). Does hormonal therapy have any benefit for bleeding angiodysplasia? *Journal of Clinical Gastroenterology*, 15, 99–103.

Lindi, C., Marciani, P., Faelli, A., and Esposito, G. (1985). Intestinal sugar transport during ageing. *Biochimica et Biophysica Acta*, 816, 411–14.

Lipski, P.S., Bennett, M.K., Kelly, P.J., and James, O.F.W. (1985). Ageing and duodenal morphometry. *Journal of Clinical Pathology*, 45, 450–2.

McKay, J.W. Baggerstoss, A.H., and Wollaeger, E.E. (1958). Infarcts of the pancreas. *Gastroenterology*, 35, 256–64.

MacMahon, B. (1982). Risk factors for pancreatic cancer. *Cancer*, 50 (Supplement 11), 2676–80.

Madsen, J. (1992). Effects of gender, age, and body mass index on gastrointestinal transit times. *Digestive Diseases and Science*, 37, 1548–53.

Meuwissen, S.G.N. and Seldenrijk, C.A. (1991). Inflammatory bowel disease in the elderly. In *Inflammatory bowel disease* (ed. A.A. Anagnostides, H.J.F. Hodgson, and J.B. Kirsner), pp. 26–38. Chapman & Hall, London.

Moolenaar, W. and Lamers, C.B. (1996). Cholesterol crystal embolization to liver, gallbladder, and pancreas. *Digestive Diseases and Science*, 41, 1819–22.

Neoptolemos, J.P., Hall, A.W., Finlay, D.F., Berry, J.M., Carr-Locke, D.L., and Fossardo, D.P. (1984). The urgent diagnosis of gallstones in acute pancreatitis: a prospective study of three methods. *British Journal of Surgery*, 71, 230–3.

Osnes, M., Lootveit, T., Larsen, S., and Aune, S. (1981). Duodenal diverticula and their relationship to age, sex, and biliary calculi. *Scandinavian Journal of Gastroenterology*, 16, 103–7.

Pederzoli, P., Bassi, C., Vesentini, S., and Campedelli, A. (1993). A randomized multi-center clinical trial of antibiotic prophylaxis of septic complications in acute necrotizing pancreatitis with imipenem. *Surgery, Gynecology and Obstetrics*, 176, 480–3.

Pieper-Bigelow, C., Strocchi, A., and Levitt, M.D. (1990). Where does serum amylase come from and where does it go? *Gastroenterology Clinics of North America*, 19, 793–810.

Pleskow, D.K., Berger, H.J., Gyves, J., et al. (1989). Evaluation of a serological marker, CA 19–9, in the diagnosis of pancreatic cancer. *Annals of Internal Medicine*, 110, 704–9.

Ranson, J.H.C. and Spencer, F.C. (1977). Prevention, diagnosis, and treatment of pancreatic abscess. *Surgery, Gynecology and Obstetrics*, 82, 99–106.

Ranson, J.H.C., Rifkind, K.M., Roses, D.F., Fink, S.D., Eng, K., and Spencer, F.C. (1974). Prognostic signs and the role of operative management in acute pancreatitis. *Surgery, Gynecology and Obstetrics*, 139, 69–81.

Rinderknecht, H. (1988). Fatal pancreatitis, a consequence of excessive leukocyte stimulation? *International Journal of Pancreatology*, 3, 105–12.

Rossle, O. (1921). Beitrage zur Kentniss der gesunden und der kranken Bauchspeicheldruse. *Beitrage zur Pathologischen Anatomie and zur Allgemeinen Pathologie*, 163, 69–79.

Runzi, M. and Layer, P. (1996). Drug-induced pancreatitis: facts and fiction. *Pancreas*, 13, 100–9.

Sainio, V., Kempainnen, E., Puolakkainen, P., *et al.* (1995). Early antibiotic treatment in acute necrotizing pancreatitis. *Lancet*, 346, 663–7.

Saltzman, J.R. (1993). Epidemiology and natural history of atrophic gastritis. In *Chronic gastritis and hypochlorhydria in the elderly* (ed. P.R. Holt and R.M. Russell), pp. 31–47. CRC Press, Boca Raton, FL.

Saltzman, J.R. and Kowdley, K.V. (1994). The consequences of *Helicobacter pylori* infection and gastritis. *Contemporary Internal Medicine*, 6, 7–16.

Saltzman, J.R. and Kowdley, K.V. (1996). Bacterial overgrowth in the elderly. *Facts and Research in Gerontology, Supplement on Digestive Diseases*, pp. 73–85.

Saltzman, J.R. and Russell, R.M. (1994). Nutritional consequences of atrophic gastritis. *Comprehensive Therapy*, 20, 523–30.

Saltzman, J.R. and Russell, R.M. (1998). The ageing gut: nutritional issues. *Gastroenterology Clinics of North America*, 27, 309–24.

Saltzman, J.R., Kowdley, K.V., Pedrosa, M.C., *et al.* (1994). Bacterial overgrowth without clinical malabsorption in elderly hypochlorhydric subjects. *Gastroenterology*, 106, 615–23.

Saltzman, J.R., Kowdley, K.V., Perrone, G., and Russell, R.M. (1995). Changes in small-intestine permeability with ageing. *Journal of the American Geriatrics Society*, 43, 160–4.

Schmitz-Moormann, P., Himmelmann, G.W., Brandes, J.W., *et al.* (1985). Comparative radiological and morphological study of the human pancreas: pancreatitis-like changes in post-mortem ductograms and their morphological pattern. *Gut*, 26, 406–14.

Schoeman, M.N. and Huibregtse, K. (1995). Pancreatic and ampullary carcinoma. *Gastrointestinal Endoscopy Clinics of North America*, 5, 217–36.

Scrimshaw, N. and Murray, E. (1988). Prevalence of lactose maldigestion. *American Journal of Clinical Nutrition*, 48, 1086–98.

Simko, C. and Michael, S. (1989). Absorptive capacity for dietary fat in elderly patients with debilitating disorders. *Archives of Internal Medicine*, 149, 557–60.

Slaff, J., Jacobson, D., Tillman, C.R., *et al.* (1984). Protease-specific suppression of pancreatic exocrine secretion. *Gastroenterology*, 87, 44–52.

Southgate, D.A.T. and Durnin, J.V.G.A. (1970). Calorie conversion factors: an experimental reassessment of the factors used in the calculation of the energy value of human diets. *British Journal of Nutrition*, 24, 517–35.

Steer, M.L., Waxman, I., and Freedman, S. (1995). Chronic pancreatitis. *New England Journal of Medicine*, 332, 1482–90.

Steinberg, W. and Tenner, S. (1994). Acute pancreatitis. *New England Journal of Medicine*, 330, 1198–1210.

Steinberg, W.M.R., Gestund, K.K., Anderson, J.G., *et al.* (1986). Comparison of the sensitivity and specificity of the CA 19–9 and carcinoembryonic antigen assays in detecting cancers of the pancreas. *Gastroenterology*, 90, 343–9.

Strickland, R. and Mackay, I. (1973). A reappraisal of the nature and significance of chronic atrophic gastritis. *Digestive Diseases and Science*, 18, 426–37.

Suter, P.M. and Russell, R.M. (1987). Vitamin requirements of the elderly. *American Journal of Clinical Nutrition*, 45, 501–12.

Sweeney, M.S. and Gadacz, T.R. (1984). Primary aortoenteric fistula: manifestation, diagnosis and treatment. *Surgery*, 96, 492–7.

Tietz, N.W. (1997). Support of the diagnosis of pancreatitis by enzyme tests—old problems, new techniques. *Clinica Chimica Acta*, 257, 85–98.

Toskes, P.P., Forsmark, C.E., Demeo, M.T., *et al.* (1993). A multi-centre controlled trial of octreotide for pain in chronic pancreatitis (abstract). *Pancreas*, 8, 774.

Trier, J.S. (1991). Celiac sprue. *New England Journal of Medicine*, 325, 1709–19.

Uomo, G., Manes, G., Ragozzino, A., Cavallera, A., and Rabitti, P.G. (1996). Periampullary extraluminal duodenal diverticula and acute pancreatitis. *American Journal of Gastroenterology*, 91, 1186–8.

Van Cutsem, E., Rutgeerts, P., and Vantrappen, G. (1990). Treatment of bleeding gastrointestinal vascular malformations with oestrogen–progesterone. *Lancet*, 335, 953–5.

Vincenzini, M.T., Iantomasi, T., Stio, M., *et al.* (1989). Glucose transport during ageing by human intestinal brush-border membrane vesicles. *Mechanisms of Ageing and Development*, 48, 33–41.

Wallace, J.L. (1997). Nonsteroidal anti-inflammatory drugs and gastroenteropathy: the second hundred years. *Gastroenterology*, 112, 1000–16.

Wallis, J.L., Lipski, P.S., Mathers, J., James, O.F.W., and Hirst, B.H. (1993). Duodenal brush-border mucosal glucose transport enzyme activities in ageing man and the effect of bacterial contamination of the small intestine. *Digestive Diseases and Science*, 38, 403–9.

Walsh, T.N., Rode, J., Theis, B.A., and Russell, R.C. (1992). Minimal change chronic pancreatitis. *Gut*, 33, 1566–71.

Warshaw, A.L. (1985). Conservation of pancreatic tissue by combined gastric, biliary, and pancreatic duct drainage for pain from chronic pancreatitis. *American Journal of Surgery*, 149, 563–9.

Webster, S. and Leeming, J. (1975). Effect of ageing on the gastro-intestinal transit of a lactulose-supplemented mixed solid–liquid meal in humans. *Age and Ageing*, 4, 168–74.

Wilson, C. (1997). Management of the later complications of severe acute pancreatitis—pseudocyst, abscess, and fistula. *European Journal of Gastroenterology and Hepatology*, 9, 117–21.

Wilson, C. and Imrie, C.W. (1988). Deaths from acute pancreatitis: why do we miss the diagnosis so frequently? *International Journal of Pancreatology*, 3, 273–81.

Wilson, C. and Imrie, C.W. (1990). Changing patterns of incidence and mortality from acute pancreatitis in Scotland, 1961–1985. *British Journal of Surgery*, 77, 731–4.

Wilson, P.G., Olagunju, O., and Neoptolemos, J.P. (1997). The timing of endoscopic sphincterotomy in gallstone pancreatitis. *European Journal of Gastroenterology and Hepatology*, 9, 137–44.

Yeo, C.J., Bastidas, J.A., Lynch-Nyhan, A., Fishman, E.K., Zinner, M.J., and Cameron, J.L. (1990). The natural history of pancreatic pseudocysts documented by computed tomography. *Surgery, Gynecology and Obstetrics*, 170, 411–17.

8.7 Colonic diseases

William D. Chey and William Y. Chey

Functional colonic diseases

Constipation

Constipation is a common complaint among elderly patients. In the United States, the prevalence of constipation in people aged over 60 years ranges from 4 to 30 per cent. The wide range in prevalence data is in part attributable to how constipation is defined in a given study. The most widely accepted definition is the passage of less than two bowel movements per week.

Constipation is a symptom that can arise as a result of dietary factors, functional abnormalities, perceptual factors, neuromuscular disease, metabolic disease, obstructing lesions, or iatrogenic causes (Table 1). From a physiological standpoint, constipation can be categorized on the basis of slow-transit or disordered defecation. Patients with slow-transit constipation have delayed passage of stool through the colon. In the absence of structural disease, this group can have a generalized delay (colonic inertia) or a delay localized to the left colon (hind-gut pattern).

There are both functional and structural causes of disordered defecation or outlet obstruction. Functional causes include pelvic floor dysynergia (anismus), in which there is a failure to relax the puborectalis and/or the external anal sphincter with defecation, and megarectum, where a dilated inelastic rectum leads to the inability to pass stool. Structural causes of outlet obstruction include rectal prolapse, posterior rectal herniation, and rectocoele.

To patients, the word 'constipation' refers not only to a decreased frequency of bowel movements but also to difficult defecation, incomplete defecation, small stools, or hard stools. This point is highlighted by the fact that geriatric patients often use laxatives despite having a normal frequency of bowel movements. When taking a history it is critical to discuss each of these issues specifically. A recent onset of constipation (within 1–2 years), an abrupt change in bowel pattern, weight loss, or gastrointestinal bleeding should heighten the clinician's concern for malignancy. Issues commonly encountered with elderly patients, such as physical immobility, dietary inadequacies, recent life stress (death of a loved one), dementia, or underlying psychopathology (apathy, depression), should be addressed, as each has been linked with constipation (Merkel *et al.* 1997). In addition, commonly prescribed medications, including calcium-channel blockers, opiates, iron supplements, calcium supplements, calcium- and aluminium-containing antacids, bismuth, and drugs with anticholinergic properties, can cause constipation.

In patients with severe constipation, physical examination can demonstrate abdominal distension. A careful perianal examination

Table 1 Causes of constipation in elderly people

Misperception
Dietary: low fibre or poor fluid intake
Functional
Depression, confusion, inadequate toilet arrangements, weakness, immobility
Neuromuscular disorders
Endocrine diseases: thyroid disease, diabetes mellitus, hyperparathyroidism
Mechanical obstruction: malignancy, ischaemic, diverticular or radiation-induced strictures
Medications: aluminium- or calcium-containing antacids, narcotics, antidepressants, anticholinergics, iron, bismuth, diuretics

Reproduced with permission from Wald (1990).

may reveal an absent anal wink or impaired cutaneous sensation suggestive of underlying neuromuscular disease. Digital rectal examination assesses sphincter tone and helps to exclude faecal impaction or a rectal mass. When asked to strain while the examiner's finger is in the anal canal, patients with pelvic floor dysynergia will sometimes paradoxically contract the external anal sphincter. Bulging of the perineum with straining can be seen with rectal prolapse or a rectocoele. Metabolic causes of constipation, including hypercalcaemia and hypothyroidism, should also be excluded. For an older patient with recent-onset constipation, colonoscopy or a flexible sigmoidoscopy and barium enema should be performed to exclude structural causes of constipation such as malignancy. In addition, endoscopy can reveal melanosis coli in patients with a history of chronic laxative use.

Once structural and metabolic causes have been excluded, patients with constipation should receive counselling on behaviour modification and a therapeutic trial. It is often helpful to have patients try to pass a bowel movement at a specified time each day (typically after breakfast). Initial therapeutic attempts should include an increase in dietary fibre intake (Voderholzer *et al.* 1997). This can be achieved through a high-fibre diet (30 g of dietary fibre or 14 g of crude fibre) or medical supplementation with insoluble fibre (bran) or soluble fibre (psyllium, methylcellulose, or calcium polycarbophil). The total fibre intake should be increased slowly over several weeks to achieve a regular bowel pattern. Patients should be warned that fibre can cause increased flatulence and bloating when first started. These adverse reactions often improve with continued use. Dietary fibre should not be expected to benefit all patients with constipation. In fact, some patients with colonic inertia or outlet obstruction worsen with dietary fibre intake (Devroede 1993).

Faecal incontinence

Elderly patients may suffer from both constipation and faecal incontinence. Faecal incontinence affects up to 1 per cent of people over the age of 65 in the general population living in the community (Tobin and Brocklehurst 1986), 17 to 66 per cent of elderly patients in hospital (Goldstein et al. 1989; Beck 1991–1992; Wald 1993), and 50 per cent of elderly residents in long-term care facilities (Brocklehurst 1951).

Faecal incontinence may be caused by multiple factors. Continence requires the ability to sense rectal filling and to distinguish the nature of the rectal contents (liquid, solid, or gas), the ability of the rectum and distal colon to store faeces for periods of time, and the prevention of unwanted defecation by the internal anal sphincter, a smooth muscle that contracts almost maximally at rest and relaxes with rectal distension, and the external sphincter, a striated muscle that contracts when large volumes enter the rectum (Whitehead et al. 1989). The pelvic floor muscles, in particular the puborectalis, maintain a critical anorectal angle which preserves continence by mechanically retarding the passage of stool. Finally, patients must have the will to maintain continence, an important issue when one is dealing with those afflicted with cognitive dysfunction. Faecal incontinence is most often caused by faecal impaction associated with liquid stool leaking around the faecal mass, and frequently occurs in institutionalized or otherwise physically or mentally impaired patients. In these patients, anal sphincter pressures are generally normal and do not change with disimpaction (Read et al. 1985). In some, the major anorectal abnormality is impairment of anorectal sensation. The cause of faecal incontinence in this group of patients may be the failure to perceive rectal contents in volumes which are sufficiently large to relax the internal anal sphincter, so that they do not consciously contract the external sphincter to prevent soiling (Szurszewski et al. 1989). This may become exacerbated by diminished anal sensation and inability to recognize the nature of rectal contents.

Faecal incontinence in ambulatory non-institutionalized elderly individuals is often associated with abnormal anorectal continence mechanisms (Wald 1990, 1994). Two such abnormalities are recognized: (a) decreased contractile strength; (b) impaired responsiveness of the puborectalis and external anal sphincter muscles to rectal filling. These changes may be caused, in part, by age-associated muscle atrophy and increased proliferation of connective tissue fibres. It has been suggested that there may be partial denervation of these muscles caused by damage to the pudendal nerve. In some women with idiopathic faecal incontinence, the injury to the pudendal nerve may be more severe and characterized by prolonged latency of the pudendoanal reflex, i.e. reflex contraction of the external sphincter after stimulating the dorsal genital nerve (Campbell et al. 1985). It has been suggested that pudendal neuropathy may be caused by repetitive stretching of the nerves with chronic defecatory straining,

hormonal influences, spondylotic compression of nerve roots (Szurszewski et al. 1989), and previous weakening of the muscles from childbirth-associated nerve injury (Snooks et al. 1984; Wald 1993).

Clinical assessment

Incontinent patients should be offered a comprehensive evaluation of their anorectal structure and function using proctosigmoidoscopy, defecography, and anorectal manometry. In addition, pelvic floor neurophysiological studies and endosonography, if available, may be useful in selected patients, particularly those who are candidates for surgery.

Management

The first step in the management of patients with incontinence of liquid stool associated with faecal impaction is manual disimpaction of low-lying stool. If hard stools are beyond reach of the examining finger, repeated tap-water enemas should be administered. After physical disimpaction of stool, oil retention enemas or tap-water enemas should be administered once or twice daily until the bowel is clear. Cathartics such as bisacodyl or polyethylene glycol can be given. When the colon is cleared of stool, patients should undertake a daily bowel programme to prevent recurrence of constipation and faecal impaction.

For patients incontinent of liquid stool, the first step in management is to solidify the stool. This can be achieved with a low dose of a bulking agent (bran or fibre supplement) or an antidiarrhoeal opiate derivative such as loperamide hydrochloride. Patients with incontinence of solid stool benefit from scheduled toileting. A glycerine suppository is inserted into the rectum at a scheduled time after a meal and the patient is encouraged to be mobile. If conservative management does not provide appreciable benefit, biofeedback therapy can be offered to suitably motivated patients. The success rate in these selected patients has been reported to be up to 70 per cent (Wald 1981, 1993; Varma et al. 1988).

When faecal incontinence is associated with rectal prolapse, surgery is the treatment of choice. In other cases, surgery may be offered if other therapy fails to produce satisfactory results.

Irritable bowel syndrome

The term irritable bowel syndrome refers to a heterogeneous group of disorders manifest clinically as abdominal pain and unstable bowel habits. By definition, affected individuals should not have an identifiable structural or metabolic process to explain their symptoms.

Overall, 10 to 15 per cent of the population of the United States has symptoms compatible with the diagnosis of irritable bowel syndrome although only a minority seek medical attention. Despite this, irritable bowel syndrome is one of the most common diagnoses made during physician visits and the second most common cause of absenteeism from work after the common cold. Patients with irritable bowel syndrome incur greater health care expenditures than healthy individuals. Although commonly considered a disease of the young, complaints compatible with irritable bowel syndrome were recently identified in 11 per cent of residents of Olmsted County, Minnesota aged between 65 and 93 years (Talley et al. 1992).

Table 2 Irritable bowel syndrome

Manning criteria
1. Pain eased after a bowel movement
2. Looser stools at onset of pain
3. More frequent bowel movements at onset of pain
4. Abdominal distension

The presence of at least two criteria differentiated those with structural or metabolic disease from those with functional disease

Rome criteria
Continuous or recurrent symptoms for at least 3 months of:
1. Abdominal pain relieved by defecation or associated with a change in frequency or consistency of stool
2. Disturbed defecation at least 25 per cent of the time including:
   (a) Altered stool frequency
   (b) Altered stool form
   (c) Altered stool passage (straining, urgency, tenesmus)
   (d) Passage of mucus
   (e) Abdominal distension

Reproduced with permission from Thompson *et al.* (1989).

As there are currently no reliable physiological markers for irritable bowel syndrome, the diagnosis relies upon symptoms. Until recently, the Manning criteria (Table 2) provided the primary symptom-based definition used to identify patients with irritable bowel syndrome. Talley *et al.* (1990) have found that the sensitivity and specificity for the Manning criteria for functional disease are 58 per cent and 74 per cent respectively. Recognizing the limitations of the Manning criteria, an international panel recently developed the Rome criteria (Table 2) for the diagnosis of irritable bowel syndrome and other functional diseases of the gastrointestinal tract (Thompson *et al.* 1989).

Although the pathophysiology of irritable bowel syndrome remains poorly defined, a number of potential mechanisms have been implicated, including abnormalities in small intestinal and colonic motility, heightened visceral sensation, and psychosocial issues. The importance of psychosocial issues in the pathogenesis of functional bowel disease has been highlighted in the recent literature. Numerous studies have reported an increased incidence of depression, anxiety, hostility, phobia, paranoia, and somatization in patients with irritable bowel syndrome. Patients with functional bowel disease frequently have experienced prior verbal, physical, or sexual abuse (Drossman *et al.* 1997). Underlying psychopathology presumably leads to greater illness behaviour, decreased coping ability, and a greater frequency of physician consultation.

A number of other factors, including carbohydrate (lactose, sorbitol) intolerance, bile salt malabsorption, and coeliac disease, can result in symptoms indistinguishable from those experienced by patients with irritable bowel syndrome. In particular, lactose intolerance increases in frequency with advancing age. In addition, microscopic colitis can also mimic diarrhoea-predominant irritable bowel syndrome.

As the concern for possible colonic malignancy is greater with older patients, the onset of new abdominal pain or a change in bowel habits should prompt an early evaluation including colonoscopy or flexible sigmoidoscopy and a barium enema. The need for further studies is directed by the severity and nature of the individual patient's symptoms. Weight loss in the absence of depression, systemic signs or symptoms (fever, leucocytosis, anaemia, or high sedimentation rate), progressive unrelenting pain, malabsorption, gastrointestinal bleeding, or diarrhoea which occurs at night or does not improve with fasting are not typical of irritable bowel syndrome and should heighten the clinician's suspicion of a malignant or inflammatory process.

Therapy for irritable bowel syndrome can be divided into dietary, psychological, and pharmacological (American Gastroenterological Association 1997). An individualized programme targeted at the patient's predominant symptoms while addressing any concomitant psychosocial stresses will meet with the greatest success. For recommendations regarding the treatment of patients with constipation-predominant irritable bowel syndrome, the reader is referred to the discussion of constipation given previously. Diarrhoea-predominant patients should be carefully questioned about their intake of foods containing poorly absorbed carbohydrates such as lactose, sorbitol, or fructose. The identification and elimination of dietary precipitants can sometimes be facilitated if patients record the contents of their meals and any symptoms they experience for 10 to 14 days. Unfortunately, it is unusual for patients to be able to identify dietary precipitants. In contrast with the constipation-predominant patient, fibre supplementation has not been convincingly proved to benefit patients with diarrhoea predominance. Once organic disease has been satisfactorily excluded, antidiarrhoeal therapy with opiate derivatives such as loperamide or diphenoxylate is a logical choice. Patients with a prominent gastrocolic reflex may benefit from antispasmodic agents such as hyoscamine or dicyclomine. A trial of cholestyramine is another diagnostic and therapeutic option in patients where bile-acid-induced diarrhoea is a consideration; such patients may have a history of terminal ileal resection.

Pain-predominant patients are the most challenging subgroup to treat. The cornerstone of therapy is reassurance and counselling. Narcotics should be avoided because of their potential for dependency. Controlled trials supporting a role for fibre in painful irritable bowel syndrome are lacking. Surprisingly, the same is true for antispasmodic therapy, although these agents are widely used to treat pain in patients with irritable bowel syndrome.

Patients with a significant component of anxiety or depression tend to respond less well to therapy. Tricyclic medications (desipramine, trimipramine, nortriptyline) have been shown to improve both abdominal pain and depressed mood. Side-effects include excessive sedation, disturbances in cardiac conduction, postural hypotension, and anticholinergic effects. These can be avoided by using smaller doses of medication. Serotonin reuptake inhibitors are a potential alternative to tricyclic medications but have not been subjected to randomized trials in patients with irritable bowel syndrome. Patients with significant underlying depression or anxiety may also benefit from psychotherapy.

Colonic vascular diseases

Colonic ischaemia

Colonic ischaemia is primarily a disease of older people. When patients with iatrogenic causes including surgical procedures and drugs are excluded, more than 90 per cent of patients are aged over 60 (Brandt and Boley 1993). The colon is the part of the gastrointestinal

Table 3 Clinical scenarios associated with colonic ischaemia

Non-occlusive

Severe congestive heart failure or cardiac arrhythmia

Hypovolaemia (trauma, sepsis, surgical procedures, long-distance running)

Vasculitis

Drugs (cardiac glycosides, oestrogens, danazol, vasopressin, gold, psychotropic agents)

Occlusive

Aortic surgery

Recent angiographic procedures (cholesterol emboli)

Arterial emboli

Hypercoagulable states (protein C and protein S deficiency, antithrombin III deficiency, factor V Leiden deficiency)

Volvulus

Incarcerated hernia

Necrotizing pancreatitis

tract most frequently injured by ischaemia. The clinical spectrum of colonic ischaemia ranges from mild reversible colonopathy to frank gangrene with or without visceral perforation. The available literature probably underestimates the true incidence of colonic ischaemia (Brandt *et al.* 1981) owing to under-reporting by patients and incomplete evaluation or misdiagnosis by physicians.

In most cases, a specific cause of colonic ischaemia cannot be identified, but atherosclerotic disease is an important contributor in elderly patients. In addition to atherosclerosis, an age-associated change in colonic vasculature consisting of tortuosity of the long colonic arteries has been reported (Bivens and Isaacson 1978). Hypovolaemia (trauma, sepsis, surgical procedures) or severe heart failure can compromise arterial perfusion pressure. Certain drugs (Table 3) can also decrease colonic blood flow. Occlusive causes of colonic ischaemia occur less commonly and include surgical procedures (particularly vascular surgical procedures involving the aorta), thrombotic or cholesterol emboli, volvulus, incarcerated herniation, and necrotising pancreatitis. Hypercoagulable states including deficiencies in protein C and S, anti-thrombin III, or factor V Leiden have also been associated with colonic ischaemia.

Patients usually present with cramping abdominal pain, faecal urgency, and/or haematochezia. Bleeding from colonic ischaemia is rarely severe enough to require transfusion but it can exacerbate underlying haemodynamic instability. Certain clinical situations should heighten the clinician's suspicion for this diagnosis (Table 3). Physical examination usually reveals mild to moderate abdominal discomfort overlying the involved colon. The presence of peritoneal signs should raise concern for transmural involvement or frank perforation.

Unfortunately, routine laboratory studies are usually unhelpful in establishing the diagnosis. Leucocytosis, hyperamylasaemia, and metabolic acidosis can occur but are not specific for colonic ischaemia. The finding of thickened bowel wall by plain film is non-specific and can be seen in ischaemia, infectious colitis, or inflammatory bowel disease. Free intraperitoneal air suggests transmural injury with perforation. CT, when performed in the evaluation of abdominal pain, can reveal non-specific colonic thickening or free intraperitoneal air.

If there is no evidence of peritonitis or perforation, and bleeding is not so brisk as to make the procedure impracticable, colonoscopy is the investigation of choice. Given the transient nature of this disorder, diagnostic studies should be performed within 48 h of symptom onset. Endoscopic findings ranging from bowel wall oedema to extensive ulceration can be indistinguishable from inflammatory bowel disease and some forms of infectious colitis (Brandt *et al.* 1981). Ischaemia can lead to the development of pseudomembranes similar to those seen with *Clostridium difficile* colitis (Robert *et al.* 1993). On rare occasions, areas of inflammation and granulation tissue can mimic colonic malignancy. Flexible sigmoidoscopy with a gentle barium enema is another investigative option for colonic ischaemia but is not as sensitive as colonoscopy. The presence of 'thumbprinting' (prominent mucosal folds) is highly suggestive of colonic ischaemia. As with colonoscopy, mucosal irregularity and/or frank ulceration can also be seen. Some patients present with colonic dilatation at or proximal to the affected colonic segment. Abnormalities associated with mild to moderate ischaemia tend to resolve within a period of 7 to 14 days.

To help distinguish ischaemia from other colitides, understanding the usual distribution of colonic injury is of benefit. The superior mesenteric artery perfuses the caecum, the ascending colon, and much of the transverse colon. The inferior mesenteric artery supplies the descending colon, the sigmoid colon, and part of the rectum. The blood supply of the splenic flexure arises from the arc of Riolan which is derived from the most distal aspect of the superior mesenteric artery and the most proximal part of the inferior mesenteric artery. This unusual blood supply explains the vulnerability of the splenic flexure to ischaemia. The descending and sigmoid colon are also commonly affected. The caecum, ascending colon, and rectum are less frequently involved. Colonic ischaemia is typically segmental but can be universal.

As colonic ischaemia resolves spontaneously in the majority of cases, angiography is seldom necessary although it can be useful in patients where mesenteric ischaemia remains a possibility. Findings at angiography may often not correspond to the distribution of ischaemia found clinically (Robert *et al.* 1993). However, the presence of vascular narrowing, tortuosity, or evidence of fibromuscular dysplasia identifies patients with a higher likelihood of having small vessel disease. Colonic malignancy can serve as the inciting factor for an ischaemic event. If full structural evaluation of the colon has not been done initially, and no obvious precipitant for the development of ischaemia is apparent, older patients should be offered this after resolution of the acute ischaemic injury in order to exclude malignancy.

Half to two-thirds of patients with colonic ischaemia will respond to medical management (Brandt and Boley 1993; Robert *et al.* 1993). Initial treatment should be supportive and include nothing by mouth, volume repletion, serial examinations, and careful monitoring of vital signs and blood counts. Ischaemic injury compromises the ability of the colon to resist invasion by enteric bacteria, and antibiotics that cover colonic flora are appropriate. Measures to improve oxygenation (treatment of underlying lung disease, supplemental oxygen), oxygen-carrying capacity (correcting anaemia), and cardiac output are particularly important in the elderly patient with underlying pulmonary or cardiac disease. Any medications known to impair mesenteric blood flow should be discontinued. Patients with peritoneal signs, with evidence of perforation by plain film or of gangrene by colonoscopy, or

Table 4 Diseases associated with angiodysplasia

Chronic renal failure
Chronic pulmonary disease
Cirrhosis
Systemic sclerosis
Turner's syndrome
von Willebrand's disease
Hereditary haemorrhagic telangiectasia
Aortic stenosis (?)

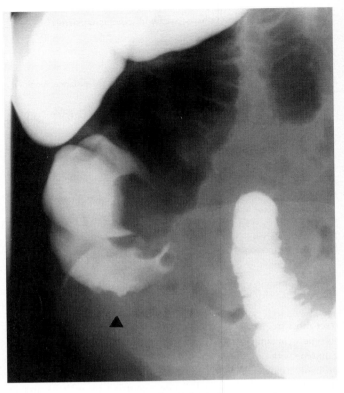

Fig. 1 Characteristic appearance of angiodysplasia.

who deteriorate clinically despite aggressive supportive therapy require surgical intervention with resection of the affected segment.

Late sequelae of colonic ischaemia include non-healing segmental colitis and stricture formation. Patients with chronic segmental colitis and recurrent episodes of pain, fever, unexplained bacteraemia, or bleeding are candidates for elective surgery. Ischaemic strictures most commonly affect the sigmoid colon. Colonic strictures can be asymptomatic, but if signs or symptoms suggestive of obstruction develop, a corrective surgical procedure is indicated.

Angiodysplasia

Angiodysplastic lesions occur in the upper or lower gastrointestinal tract, but in elderly patients are usually found in the colon. Colonic angiodysplasia is a well-established cause of lower gastrointestinal bleeding in individuals aged over 60 years (Sharma and Gorbien 1995).

The prevalence of colonic angiodysplasia is unknown. A recent retrospective study revealed that 8/964 (0.83 per cent) asymptomatic patients who had undergone colonoscopy as screening for colorectal neoplasia had angiodysplasia (Foutch *et al.* 1995). In contrast, the literature suggests that angiodysplasia is more common in patients undergoing evaluation specifically for gastrointestinal bleeding, affecting perhaps 6 per cent (Foutch 1993).

Angiodysplasia in later life probably arises as a consequence of degenerative changes in the submucosal veins, venules, and capillaries (Sharma and Gorbien 1995). It occurs most commonly in the right colon, where the luminal diameter is greatest and wall tension is high, thus increasing the likelihood of submucosal venous obstruction. The resulting local chronic hypo-oxygenation of the submucosal vessels could lead to capillary proliferation, dilatation, and, eventually, discrete vascular lesions. Such a mechanism might explain the increased incidence of angiodysplasia in patients with cardiac, vascular, and pulmonary disease.

The majority of patients with angiodysplasia will have recurrent episodes of painless low-grade blood loss manifest as occult bleeding, melaena, haematochezia, or unexplained iron deficiency anaemia. In a minority of patients, bleeding can be severe enough to cause haemodynamic instability. Bleeding episodes are usually self-limiting. Patients will sometimes have associated medical conditions as outlined in Table 4. The management of gastrointestinal bleeding in older patients is discussed in Chapter 8.5.

At colonoscopy, angiodysplasia appears as slightly raised reddish vascular tufts 5 to 10 mm in diameter. Often, a feeding vessel is apparent (Fig. 1). A barium enema can exclude the presence of structural disease such as malignancy but is not helpful in the evaluation of subtle mucosal or submucosal processes such as angiodysplasia. In addition, a barium enema does not allow biopsy of suspicious lesions or cautery, and is not as sensitive as colonoscopy.

Colonoscopic therapies including electrocautery, injection therapy, heater probe, or laser coagulation have gained popularity for both their effectiveness and their technical ease (Foutch 1993). Hormonal therapy, using oestrogen or oestrogen–progesterone combinations, is another option which has been discussed in the medical literature. A number of small series and case reports have described the benefits of hormonal therapy, but large well-designed trials are needed.

Inflammatory bowel disease

Although inflammatory bowel disease is often considered a disease of young adults, it has been known for many years that it can appear for the first time in the sixth, seventh, or older decades of life. Late-onset ulcerative colitis or Crohn's colitis is becoming increasingly important with the growth in older populations.

Epidemiology

The proportion of patients developing ulcerative colitis after the age of 60 averages about 12 per cent (Grimm and Friedman 1990), and that of patients developing Crohn's disease after the same age averages

Table 5 Extragastrointestinal manifestations of inflammatory bowel disease

Pyoderma gangrenosum
Fatty liver
Erythema nodosum
Chronic active hepatitis
Colitic arthritis
Granulomatous hepatitis
Ankylosing spondylitis
Primary sclerosing cholangitis
Aphthous stomatitis
Cholelithiasis
Amyloidosis
Cholangiocarcinoma
Hypercoagulable states

16 per cent. A bimodal distribution in the age of onset for both ulcerative colitis and Crohn's disease has been reported in several studies (Garland *et al.* 1981). The first peak occurs in the third decade, and the second appears between the ages of 50 and 80. The reason for the bimodal age distribution of inflammatory bowel disease is unknown. Although the second peak has been ascribed to misclassification of clinical conditions simulating inflammatory bowel disease in the elderly, such as ischaemic and infectious colitis (Shapiro *et al.* 1981), the second peak in the incidence of ulcerative colitis has not been affected by exclusion of these conditions.

Clinical features

Ulcerative colitis

Diarrhoea is the main symptom of ulcerative colitis in both older and younger patients. Rectal bleeding or bloody diarrhoea is common, but it has been suggested that non-bloody diarrhoea is not uncommon in late-onset disease (Zimmerman *et al.* 1985). Like young patients, elderly patients may develop extragastrointestinal manifestations of inflammatory bowel disease (Table 5).

Ulcerative colitis tends to be less extensive in elderly than in younger patients (Brust and Bargen 1935; Watts *et al.* 1966). The majority of elderly patients have left-sided disease or proctitis and, in comparison with younger patients, fewer have pancolitis (Sinclair *et al.* 1983). Although older patients are more likely to have limited disease, they tend to present with a severe initial attack and have an increased frequency of toxic megacolon, with correspondingly high fatality (Toghill and Benton 1973; Sinclair *et al.* 1983).

Crohn's disease

As with young patients, typical symptoms include abdominal pain, weight loss, diarrhoea, and, less commonly, fever and rectal bleeding. Extraintestinal manifestations occur with equal frequency in old and young patients (Gupta 1985; Softley *et al.* 1988; Stalnikowicz *et al.*

1989). A higher frequency of diarrhoea has been reported to occur in older than in younger patients (91 versus 61 per cent) (Stalnikowicz *et al.* 1989). In contrast, rectal bleeding occurred in only three of 27 older patients compared with 14 of 15 younger patients. Colitis primarily involving the distal colon and rectum occurred mainly in older patients. The majority of patients with rectosigmoid disease were aged over 45, whereas most of the patients with ileocolonic disease were under 45 (Lockhart-Mummery 1972). Moreover, up to two-thirds of patients with isolated anorectal or distal colonic disease were aged over 50 (Truelove and Pena 1976; Prior *et al.* 1981).

A delay in diagnosis of 6.4 years after the onset of symptoms in elderly patients has been reported, compared with 2.4 years in younger patients (Wald 1994). Of seven patients aged over 70, in whom diagnosis was delayed, five were diagnosed incorrectly before undergoing surgery for an acute complication (Serpell and Johnson 1991). It is likely that a higher frequency of complications in elderly patients with Crohn's disease may reflect a delay in diagnosis or misdiagnosis.

Laboratory abnormalities commonly observed in elderly patients with Crohn's disease are anaemia, leucocytosis, hypoproteinaemia, and elevated erythrocyte sedimentation rate. Pathological features include segmental involvement of the gastrointestinal tract with transmural inflammation which can lead to the formation of deep ulceration, fistulas, and strictures. The rectum is usually spared.

In contrast with ulcerative colitis, mortality from Crohn's disease in older persons is similar to or lower than the average for younger patients (Fleisher *et al.* 1994). The relative risk of dying is highest for those who develop Crohn's disease early in life and decreases with increasing age.

Diagnosis and differential diagnosis

A delay in diagnosis is common in older patients with inflammatory bowel disease and can result in inappropriate treatment and a higher rate of complications. Although clinicians are generally reluctant to perform invasive tests on elderly patients, age alone does not add to the risk from endoscopic procedures. Proctosigmoidoscopy is the first procedure when inflammatory bowel disease is suspected, and this can be particularly important for older patients who may present with atypical symptoms. The differential diagnosis of inflammatory bowel disease in aged patients includes ischaemic colitis, infectious colitis, diverticular disease, microscopic colitis (including lymphocytic colitis and collagenous colitis) radiation enterocolitis, ileocaecal or colorectal carcinoma, lymphoma, carcinoid syndrome, vasculitis, and drug-induced colitis.

Treatment

Medical and surgical therapy for inflammatory bowel disease are the same for older and younger patients. Standard medications are sulphasalazine or 5-aminosalicylic acid (**5-ASA**) preparations and corticosteroids. Corticosteroid or 5-ASA enemas are effective in proctitis or left-sided colitis and have fewer systemic side-effects than oral preparations. Prolonged corticosteroid therapy can become particularly problematic in older patients. Corticosteroids may aggravate or precipitate diabetes, hypertension, congestive heart failure, glaucoma, cataracts, and osteoporosis (see Chapter 14.1). Immunosuppressive drugs should be considered for patients refractory to standard first-line medications and for those intolerant of the side-effects of corticosteroids. Both 6-mercaptopurine and azathioprine have been shown to be effective (Present *et al.* 1980; Present 1989; Jyotheeswaran *et al.* 1995). Either must be given for at least 3 to 6 months to be effective. Cyclosporin and methotrexate can also be used for selected patients.

Elective surgery is well tolerated by older patients with inflammatory bowel disease, and survival rates in ulcerative colitis or Crohn's disease are unaffected by age of onset. Emergency surgery for a complication such as toxic megacolon is poorly tolerated in older patients. Prompt early surgical intervention may be preferable to prolonged attempts at medical management in patients with severe colitis. Total proctocolectomy is preferred in ulcerative colitis. Results with ileoanal anastomosis are less favourable in elderly than in younger patients because of decreased anal sphincter function in some older patients, particularly women (Pemberton *et al.* 1987).

Infectious colitis

Gastrointestinal infections are common in the ageing population. Evidence for infection should be evaluated in all patients with diarrhoea, particularly those with recent onset of symptoms. Laboratory evaluation reveals an infectious cause in as many as 36 per cent of patients with an acute or subacute diarrhoeal illness (Tedesco *et al.* 1983). Routine stool cultures identify typical pathogens such as *Salmonella*, *Shigella*, and *Campylobacter*, as well as *Clostridium difficile*. Special techniques may be required to identify *Yersinia*, *Vibrio* species, and *Escherichia coli* 0157:H7. Blood cultures and faecal examination for ova and parasites may also be indicated in some instances.

E. coli 0157:H7 can cause severe inflammation of the colon resembling ischaemic colitis. Older people seem to be more susceptible to acquiring this infection and are more likely than younger people to experience severe complications. These include haemorrhagic colitis, thrombocytopenic purpura, and death. Patients often experience cramping abdominal pain and tenderness, bloody diarrhoea, and vomiting, but fever and faecal leucocytes are absent. Endoscopy may reveal inflammation with ischaemic-like ulcers, but the rectum is usually spared. A barium enema may demonstrate thumbprinting due to submucosal oedema. The course of illness typically lasts 6 to 8 days and antibiotic therapy is of arguable benefit.

Pseudomembranous colitis affects older persons more frequently and more severely than younger patients. It presents as inflammation and necrosis of the bowel affecting predominantly and primarily the mucosa, but it often extends with varying degrees of severity into the submucosa. Only rarely does it involve other layers of the bowel. Although a history of recent antibiotic use is typical, the onset of symptoms may occur as long as 6 weeks after antibiotics have been discontinued. In addition, pseudomembranous colitis has been reported to occur in the absence of antibiotic exposure, and faecal stasis and hypochlorhydria may play a role.

The causative agent is *C. difficile*, a Gram-positive spore-forming bacillus. It is frequently isolated from the stools of hospital inpatients and the hands of health-care personnel, and is rapidly transmitted among residents of long-term care facilities (Grimm and Friedman 1990). The symptoms of infection include cramping abdominal pain, diarrhoea (usually non-bloody), and leucocytosis. Diagnostic work-up should include demonstration of faecal leucocytes on Gram stain and a positive assay for *C. difficile* cytotoxin. Endoscopic examination of the colon using flexible sigmoidoscopy or colonoscopy reveals numerous pseudomembranes, which are characteristic raised yellow-white plaques adherent to inflamed mucosa. They are found in 80 per cent of patients.

Treatment involves stopping inciting antibiotics if possible, fluid repletion, and vancomycin, metronidazole, or an anion-exchange resin such as cholestyramine. In most patients, metronidazole or vancomycin therapy for 10 to 14 days is effective, but relapse occurs in 10 or 20 per cent of patients for whom prolonged therapy may be needed (LaMont and Tranka 1980).

Colorectal neoplasms

Cancer of the colon or rectum is the most common malignancy of the gastrointestinal tract in older persons, and with lung and breast cancer is one of the three most common malignancies in the Western world. However, the most frequent tumours that occur in the colon and rectum are benign adenomatous polyps.

Colonic polyps

Polyps found during endoscopy or barium enema may be single or multiple, pedunculated or sessile, and sporadic or part of inherited syndrome. They are clinically significant because of bleeding and their potential for malignant transformation. Three types of polyps occur—metaplastic, inflammatory, and neoplastic (adenomatous)—of which the last is the most common. Polyps are most frequently found in the rectum. The prevalence of adenomatous polyps increases with age in countries with a high or intermediate risk for colorectal cancer (they occur in 40 to 50 per cent of people over the age of 60 in the United States), whereas adenomas are uncommon where the incidence of colon cancer is low such as in Japan, Colombia, and the South African black community. The malignancy rate varies from 10 to 40 per cent and differs with the pathology of the polyp. Tubular adenomas have the lowest malignancy, whereas villous adenomas have a malignancy rate of about 40 per cent. Most adenomatous polyps are asymptomatic. Some are diagnosed by detection of occult blood loss in asymptomatic individuals being screened for colon cancer. Diagnosis is usually made by proctosigmoidoscopy, colonoscopy, or double-contrast barium enema. Clinically, adenomas may cause haematochezia and iron deficiency anaemia. Rarely, diarrhoea associated with hypokalaemia may be caused by large villous adenomas. Because adenomatous polyps have the potential to develop into adenocarcinomas, they should be removed endoscopically or surgically. Usually polyps of diameter 3 cm or less are endoscopically removed using an electrocautery snare. Polyps over 3 cm in diameter are more safely removed surgically.

Adenocarcinoma

In Western populations, colorectal carcinoma is the most common malignancy in older persons except for prostatic carcinoma in men. It varies widely in frequency in different parts of the world, occurring much more commonly in North America, northwestern Europe, and New Zealand than in South America, southwestern Asia, equatorial Africa, and India. The annual incidence ranges from 3.5 per 100 000 in India to 32.3 per 100 000 in Connecticut.

Table 6 Risk factors for colorectal cancer

Age over 40 years in Western world
Associated disease
Ulcerative colitis
Crohn's disease
Personal history
Colorectal cancer
Colorectal adenomas
Female genital or breast cancer
Family history
Familial polyposis syndrome
Hereditary non-polyposis colorectal cancer (Lynch syndromes)

Table 7 Final diagnosis in 235 admissions for acute lower gastrointestinal bleeding

	Number (percentage) of patients
Colonic diverticulosis	91 (41.6)
Colorectal malignancy	20 (9.1)
Ischaemic colitis	19 (8.7)
Acute colitis, unknown cause	11 (5.0)
Haemorrhoids	10 (4.6)
Postpolypectomy haemorrhage	9 (4.1)
Colonic angiodysplasia	6 (2.7)
Crohn's disease	5 (2.3)
Other	22 (10.1)
Unknown	26 (11.9)
Total	219 (100)

Reproduced with permission from Longstreth (1997).

Risk factors are listed in Table 6. The major symptoms include rectal bleeding, pain, and change in bowel habit. Unexplained iron deficiency in older persons, particularly men, always requires a thorough evaluation to exclude gastrointestinal cancers, particularly of the right colon or caecum.

Diagnosis is made by a careful history, physical examination, and judicious use of investigations such as flexible sigmoidoscopy or colonoscopy and/or radiological investigation including double-contrast barium enema or CT scan of the abdomen. Spiral CT is a promising newer technique. Colonoscopy is more sensitive than double-contrast barium enema, particularly in detecting small adenomas and cancers, and is also of value in evaluating patients who have an abnormal barium enema finding. Moreover colonoscopy allows polypectomy and biopsy or cytology sampling of suspected cancers. Endoscopic ultrasonography is increasingly being used to help in the staging of rectal cancers.

The therapeutic approach requires consideration of both the immediate clinical management and a long-term plan for the patient. Management may include postoperative adjuvant treatment, plans for future assessment for local recurrence or distant metastasis, and screening family members at increased risk (Table 6).

The most important goal of treatment for primary malignancies of the colon and rectum is complete surgical removal. Surgery may also be required for palliation. The standard approach for anal cancers is to utilize a combination of radiation and chemotherapy, which will usually shrink or obliterate the tumour. Surgical resection is usually reserved for recurrent lesions or those which are unresponsive to chemoradiation. Radiation therapy plays an important role in the postoperative management of rectal cancer, and the combination of radiation and 5-fluorouracil chemotherapy is now a standard treatment. The survival of patients with resected colonic cancer but lymph node spread may be improved by treatment with a combination of 5-fluorouracil and levamisole for a period of 1 year. For patients with metastatic spread, a combination of 5-fluorouracil and leucovorin shrinks tumours more than 5-fluorouracil alone.

Other diseases of the colon

Diverticular disease

Diverticulosis

The prevalence of diverticulosis rises with age to over 50 per cent by 70 years in Westernized societies. Although the vast majority of affected individuals remain asymptomatic, approximately 20 per cent develop symptomatic diverticular disease (Naitove and Smith 1993). The sigmoid is most commonly affected, probably because of its greater wall thickness and low luminal radius, resulting in high intraluminal pressures.

The most common symptom associated with uncomplicated diverticulosis is pain which is typically colicky and left-sided, lasts for hours to days, is exacerbated by eating, and improved by the passage of a bowel movement or flatus. Symptoms are sometimes associated with a change in bowel habit. As the clinical features of painful diverticulosis are similar to those reported by patients with the irritable bowel syndrome, it has been suggested that the two diseases are related pathogenetically.

Physical examination is non-specific but can reveal a tender sigmoid loop with or without distension. Fever, leucocytosis, an elevated sedimentation rate, or faecal occult blood are not features of uncomplicated diverticulosis. The new onset of abdominal pain or altered bowel habits in an older patient should only be attributed to painful diverticulosis after a thorough structural evaluation to exclude an inflammatory or malignant process.

Dietary fibre supplementation is the mainstay of therapy for patients with painful diverticulosis. Fibre increases stool mass, decreases intraluminal pressure, and improves symptoms. Although some sources suggest that antispasmodics are helpful, these agents have not been carefully evaluated in controlled trials.

Diverticular bleeding

Diverticulosis is the most common cause of massive lower gastrointestinal bleeding (Table 7) in older persons (Longstreth 1997). Diverticular haemorrhage accounts for up to 25 per cent of all complications in patients with diverticulosis. Overall, 3 to 5 per cent with diverticulosis will develop significant lower gastrointestinal bleeding.

Seventy per cent of diverticular haemorrhages originate in the right colon and involve a single non-inflamed diverticulum. Histology from surgical specimens reveals rupture of intramural arterial branches adjacent to the diverticular lumen (Naitove and Smith 1993). The presence of diverticular haemorrhage and diverticulitis are nearly mutually exclusive, with fewer than 5 per cent having both processes simultaneously.

Clinical features include lower abdominal cramping followed by the urge to defecate and the passage of frank red blood, clots, maroon stool, or, less often, melaena. Diverticular haemorrhage is rarely a cause of occult gastrointestinal bleeding. Bleeding ceases spontaneously in 80 per cent of cases but recurs in 20 to 25 per cent. After a second haemorrhage, further bleeding recurs in around 50 per cent of cases (Naitove and Smith 1993).

The general management of lower gastrointestinal bleeding is discussed in Chapter 8.5. In the 20 per cent of patients with diverticular haemorrhage who experience persistent bleeding, angiography can offer therapeutic options including intra-arterial vasopressin infusion and embolization. Surgical therapy is reserved for refractory or recurrent bleeding.

Diverticulitis

Diverticulitis is the most common complication of diverticulosis, occurring in 10 to 20 per cent of patients. Those with numerous or widely distributed diverticula, early onset of diverticula, or a history of diverticula for more than 10 years are at higher risk for developing diverticulitis (Naitove and Smith 1993). Diverticulitis tends to occur in a single diverticulum, most commonly in the descending sigmoid colon.

Fever and subumbilical abdominal pain are the two most common presenting complaints, although presentation in older patients may be subtle and can include bacteraemia and its complications. Anorexia and a change in bowel pattern are also common. Dysuria and frequency are suggestive of inflammatory involvement of the bladder. Pneumaturia and faeculent vaginal discharge indicate fistulas. A palpable abdominal mass suggests abscess or phlegmon formation. Approximately 20 to 25 per cent of patients with diverticulitis will have faecal occult blood on digital examination, although frank haemorrhage is rare. Laboratory examination tends to be non-specific; the most common abnormality is leucocytosis.

Plain abdominal films can demonstrate free intraperitoneal air suggestive of perforation, air bubbles outside the bowel suggestive of abscess, air in the bladder suggestive of colovesical fistula, or a reactive pleural effusion. The barium enema has traditionally been the imaging study of choice for diverticulitis. The most specific finding of diverticulitis on barium enema study is extravasation of barium at the tip of a diverticulum (Pohlman 1988). A barium enema can also exclude other structural abnormalities such as neoplasm. However, as raising colonic intraluminal pressure may increase the risk of frank perforation, some have questioned the wisdom of performing a barium enema during the acute illness. Most now believe that it should be delayed in favour of other imaging studies such as CT, which has largely supplanted the barium enema as the investigation of choice for diverticulitis (Cho et al. 1990). CT is non-invasive and allows evaluation of extracolonic structures. Unfortunately, CT findings, including oedema of pericolonic fat, thickened bowel wall, pericolonic fluid collections, soft-tissue stranding, and gas, are indicative but not diagnostic of diverticulitis. CT offers therapeutic options including percutaneous abscess drainage. In one series, this method was successful as a primary therapy in more than 50 per cent of patients with diverticular abscess (Van Sonnenberg et al. 1984). More often, CT-directed percutaneous drainage serves as a bridge to surgical intervention. Complications of diverticulitis include phlegmon or frank abscess formation, fistula formation (colovesical fistulas are most common, but vaginal, enteric, and cutaneous fistulas also occur), bowel obstruction, stricture formation, and peritonitis.

Medical management produces improvement in 75 to 80 per cent of patients with diverticulitis (Naitove and Smith 1993). In approaching the patient with diverticulitis, the clinician should first gauge the severity of illness and decide upon the necessity of hospital admission. Those with severe pain, systemic signs such as high fever or marked leucocytosis, or evidence of a complication (peritoneal signs, abdominal mass, marked nausea and vomiting, abdominal distension, pneumaturia, etc.) should be admitted for inpatient evaluation and therapy. Once admitted, patients should be given nothing by mouth but receive adequate parenteral fluid resuscitation. Blood cultures should be obtained prior to the institution of parenteral antibiotics. Antibiotic therapies proposed for diverticulitis include clindamycin and an aminoglycoside, cefotetan or another second- or third-generation cephalosporin with anaerobic activity, ampicillin–sulbactam with or without metronidazole, or imipenem (Rogers and Green 1994). Whatever antibiotics are chosen, they should be active against Gram-negative enteric flora and anaerobes. In the absence of an abscess, antibiotic therapy should be administered for 7 to 10 days. Clinical response can be expected within 3 to 4 days. Persistent symptoms or a delayed response to adequate medical therapy should raise suspicion of a complication and prompt more detailed investigation.

A small percentage of patients with diverticulitis will not respond to standard medical therapy. Indications for surgical intervention include failure of medical therapy, uncontrolled sepsis, perforation, obstruction, failure of percutaneous abscess drainage, persistent fistulas, and uncontrolled haemorrhage (Floch 1993).

Microscopic colitis

Microscopic colitis includes collagenous and lymphocytic forms, which present with a broadly similar clinical picture .Typically, patients continuously experience unexplained diarrhoea but both barium enema and colonoscopy reveal no colonic mucosal abnormality. Colorectal mucosal biopsies are necessary to establish the diagnosis which can otherwise be mistaken for irritable bowel syndrome.

Collagenous colitis predominantly affects elderly women. Laboratory tests for chronic diarrhoea are usually negative. Interestingly, several immune-related disorders, including enteropathic arthritis and thyroid disease, are reported as occurring in association with collagenous colitis (Giradiello 1993). Histologically, there is a band-like deposition of collagen under the surface epithelium and inflammatory infiltrate, primarily of lymphocytes and plasma cells, in the lamina propria. The lesion may be patchy and multiple biopsy specimens from different regions may be required for diagnosis. Although the pathogenesis of collagenous colitis is unknown, diarrhoea appears to result from increased colonic fluid secretion worsened by eating.

Lymphocytic colitis also usually presents later in life, but both men and women are affected equally. Microscopic examination reveals increased intraepithelial lymphocytes, surface epithelial damage, and

for these differences, including age-associated changes in response to stress and alterations in immunological competence or drug metabolism (Lind *et al.* 1989).

Alcoholic liver disease

Although wide geographical variation is reported, several studies suggest that a significant proportion of patients with alcoholic liver disease not only present in old age but are also more likely to have severe disease at the time of presentation (Hislop *et al.* 1983). In a British study, 28 per cent of patients presented for the first time at ages over 60 (Potter and James 1987). Similarly, a large French study reported that nearly 20 per cent of patients were above the age of 70 years at presentation, and in an American study the peak decade for presentation with cirrhosis was the seventh (Aron *et al.* 1979; Garagliano *et al.* 1979). Alcoholic liver disease in older individuals presents with symptoms and signs suggestive of severe liver disease. However, no age-associated differences have been described in clinical findings or in pathological changes. Potter and James (1987) found that nearly all patients aged over 70 had cirrhosis compared with only about 50 per cent of patients presenting at ages less than 60. Prognosis is also age associated, with studies reporting a 3-year mortality of more than 50 per cent in patients aged over 60 at presentation (Potter and James 1987; Bouchier *et al.* 1992).

It is unclear why older patients have more severe disease and a worse prognosis than younger ones (Schenker 1984). The disparities cannot be explained by drinking habits, as studies have reported no significant difference in mean daily alcohol intake between older and younger patients with alcoholic liver disease (Potter and James 1987). Possible explanations include differences in referral patterns or the natural history of the disease or an increased susceptibility of the livers of older adults to the toxic effects of alcohol (James *et al.* 1986)

Investigation

All patients with suspected alcoholic liver disease should be investigated with liver function tests, serum albumin, blood film, and full blood count including mean corpuscular volume, clotting screen, and random blood or urine ethanol estimations. Liver biopsy has important prognostic value, but may be contraindicated by marked ascites, impaired clotting, or a reduced platelet count. Estimation of serum α-fetoprotein may be indicated if hepatocellular carcinoma is suspected in cases of advanced alcoholic cirrhosis.

Treatment

As the long-term prognosis in patients with alcoholic liver disease is largely dependent upon alcohol consumption, the importance of abstinence cannot be overemphasized (Galambos 1974). However, abstinence may not be easy and its achievement will depend on, among other things, the support that patients receive from health professionals.

Patients with acute alcohol withdrawal will require chlormethiazole or benzodiazepines which should be discontinued before hospital discharge. The β-blocker atenolol in a dose of 50 mg daily for the first week in hospital has been shown to reduce the peripheral manifestations of alcohol withdrawal such as anxiety and tremor (Kraus *et al.* 1985).

There is no specific therapy for alcoholic liver disease. Several hepatoprotective agents have been tested but have proved disappointing. However, the use of corticosteroids has shown some promise; a meta-analysis of trials has demonstrated that treatment with steroids can reduce short-term mortality (Imperiale and McCullough 1990).

Regular follow-up of patients with established alcoholic liver disease is advisable, as the severity of medical illness has been shown to be the critical factor in the decision to stop drinking (Patek and Hermos 1981). Abstinence should be encouraged and complications of both the illness and the therapy should be monitored. Malnutrition is common and always merits attention. Adequate calories should be provided together with high-protein and vitamin supplements.

Infective diseases

Viral hepatitis

The most important causes of viral hepatitis are the five hepatotrophic viruses, termed hepatitis A, B, C, D, and E. Other viruses, including Epstein–Barr virus and cytomegalovirus, have also been implicated in acute hepatitis, particularly in immunocompromised individuals. The clinical presentation of viral hepatitis is similar in old and young patients, but the illness is said to be more cholestatic and recovery slower in elderly people (Goodson *et al.* 1982). Cellular dysfunction, including reduced expression of heat-shock protein and diminished responsiveness to epithelial growth factor, may result in impairment of the ability of hepatocytes to regenerate (Heydari *et al.* 1993).

Hepatitis A

With improvement in socio-economic conditions and sanitation, exposure to hepatitis A and infection with the virus have declined in the developed countries (Floreani and Chiaramonte 1994). Therefore many more people are surviving into old age without acquiring immunity. This may result in increasing numbers of sporadic cases of hepatitis A in older people in the future.

Although death from hepatitis A is uncommon, the ratio of deaths to notifications rises steadily with age. Data from the United Kingdom show that this ratio increased from seven per 10 000 in those aged 15 to 24, to 400 per 10 000 in those aged 65 or over (Forbes and Williams 1988). The disease is more severe in elderly patients and runs a more protracted course. The currently available hepatitis A vaccine is immunogenic in older people and is well tolerated.

Hepatitis B

Sporadic cases of acute hepatitis B are now uncommon in the West. Also, elderly people appear considerably less at risk of contracting the disease as majority of them do not indulge in high-risk activities such as intravenous drug abuse and promiscuous homosexual practices. The illness behaves in a similar fashion to hepatitis A (Chiaramonte *et al.* 1982) , but is more cholestatic and runs a rather protracted course (Goodson *et al.* 1982). Although the clearance of hepatitis B surface antigen (**HBsAg**) may be delayed in old age, this has not been shown to have an adverse effect on prognosis (Laverdant *et al.* 1989).

Older people do not respond as well as younger individuals to the hepatitis B virus (**HBV**) vaccine. This results from a lack of antibody-producing B cells which may be a reflection of an age-associated failure of the immune response (Cook *et al.* 1987). However, the third-generation HBV vaccine has been reported to produce a better antibody response.

Chronic liver disease has not infrequently been reported in elderly patients with hepatitis B, particularly in those who are HBsAg positive but early-antigen negative and early-antibody positive (Dusheiko and Hoofnagle 1991). Such patients are not very infectious. Patients with chronic liver disease due to chronic HBV infection do not differ in presentation, complications, or management from patients with chronic liver disease due to other causes. As the role of any specific antiviral therapy in patients with cirrhotic HBV infection remains uncertain, symptomatic and supportive measures are the mainstay of treatment. However, there is some evidence that treatment with interferon in the acute phase of the illness may prevent progression to the chronic stage (Thomas 1992). Primary hepatocellular carcinoma is the most important complication of chronic HBV infection in elderly patients, particularly men (Melia *et al.* 1984).

Hepatitis C

The molecular cloning of the virus responsible for most cases of post-transfusion non-A non-B hepatitis was reported in 1989 (Kuo *et al.* 1989). This RNA virus is now known as the hepatitis C virus (HCV). Serological testing has shown a high prevalence of anti-HCV in patients with chronic active hepatitis and/or cirrhosis considered to be caused by non-A non-B hepatitis (Anonymous 1990). Non-A non-B (mostly HCV) is now regarded as the most common cause of acute sporadic viral hepatitis in elderly people, with the majority being secondary to blood transfusion (Laverdant *et al.* 1989; Sonnenblick *et al.* 1988). However, recent studies indicate that modern hygienic and sanitation measures have significantly controlled exposure to HCV in all age groups, and the risk of contracting the virus will remain low in both young and elderly people (Chiaramonte *et al.* 1996). A recent study from Northeast England reported a low prevalence of antibody to HCV with liver disease (Brind *et al.* 1990). It is conceivable that this reduction in prevalence may also have resulted from widespread screening of blood products before transfusion.

The acute disease is often asymptomatic and unnoticed, and may frequently be followed by a carrier state. The main symptoms include abdominal pain, fever, and jaundice. In common with other viral hepatitides, cholestasis is a prominent feature. A common sequela is the development of chronic hepatitis C which usually runs a protracted and asymptomatic course. The long-term prognosis of chronic hepatitis C varies, but progression to cirrhosis occurs in 20 per cent of patients within 5 to 10 years (Dusheiko 1992).

As delay in diagnosis frequently occurs, all elderly patients presenting with jaundice or abnormal liver function tests should be screened for acute or chronic infections with the specific serological tests. Liver biopsy should also be performed in patients with chronic hepatitis C infection. There is no recognized treatment for hepatitis C infection. In recent trials, interferon has reduced the incidence of progression to chronic infection in patients with acute hepatitis C (Dusheiko 1992), but its role in elderly patients with chronic hepatitis C remains unclear.

Hepatitis D

Hepatitis D (delta) virus (**HDV**) infection can only take place in conjunction with HBV. It occurs either simultaneously with HBV (coinfection) or in addition to HBV infection in a HBV carrier (superinfection). The virus is rare in developed countries where infection occurs mainly in drug addicts, haemophiliacs, and institutionalized persons. The association of HDV with HBV is said to result in more virulent attacks of HBV (Rizzetto and Verme 1985). Although there are no investigations of HDV specifically in elderly populations, studies in individuals resident in nursing homes suggest that the risk of parenterally transmitted hepatitis viruses, including HBV, HBC, and HDV, will be low provided that hygienic standards are maintained (Floreani and Chiaramonte 1994). Serological tests are available for the diagnosis of HDV.

Hepatitis E

An enterically transmitted epidemic form of hepatitis, originally termed epidemic non-A, non-B hepatitis, is now known as hepatitis E (Krawczynski 1993). Epidemics of hepatitis E have been observed in the Third World and developing countries. Sporadic cases have been seen among returning travellers in developed countries. It is usually self-limiting and does not progress to chronic infection. There are no studies of hepatitis E in the elderly population.

Bacterial infections

Pyogenic liver abscess

The incidence of liver abscess has been reported to increase with age in developed countries, with more than 50 per cent of all cases occurring in patients over 60 years of age. Liver abscess is usually secondary to biliary tract disease and ascending cholangitis, with *Escherichia coli* being the most commonly isolated organism (Greenstein *et al.* 1984). However, in a large proportion of the cases no cause is found. Patients with diabetes mellitus and metastatic cancer are said to be at increased risk of developing liver abscesses (Barnes *et al.* 1987).

As most patients present with non-specific clinical features and there are no pathognomonic changes in liver function tests, the diagnosis is not uncommonly delayed or missed (Beaumont and Davis 1985; Sridharan *et al.* 1990). A high index of suspicion, combined with early ultrasound scanning, will establish the diagnosis in this potentially-life threatening condition. Treatment consists of ultrasound- or CT-guided percutaneous needle aspiration followed by the placement of a percutaneous catheter for continued drainage (Bertel *et al.* 1986). In addition, antibiotic therapy is given, initially intravenously, and continued for several weeks. Ultrasound examinations should be performed at regular intervals in order to monitor the progress of treatment.

Systemic bacterial infections and liver abnormalities

It is not uncommon to find abnormal liver function tests in association with many forms of systemic infection. Such abnormalities have also been shown to occur in patients with non-hepatic infections even in absence of any evidence of bacteraemia. Non-hepatic infections, including diverticulitis, renal abscess, soft tissue abscess, or endocarditis, have been found to be responsible for abnormal liver function tests in almost 15 per cent of hospital admissions (Parker *et al.* 1986).

It is not clear why hepatic dysfunction occurs in patients with systemic infections. Possible explanations include direct bacterial toxicity to the liver, endotoxaemia, or underlying but undetected liver disease. As the abnormalities in hepatic function improve with the treatment of the systemic infection, no further hepatic investigations are required unless abnormal liver function tests persist after the resolution of the infective illness.

Autoimmune liver disease

A number of autoimmune hepatic disorders, including primary biliary cirrhosis, chronic hepatitis, and primary sclerosing cholangitis, occur in older people. The first two are not uncommon in later life, but primary sclerosing cholangitis is extremely rare in older individuals.

Primary biliary cirrhosis

Primary biliary cirrhosis is primarily a disease of middle-aged and older women. The average age at presentation is 55 to 60 years, but about 25 per cent of patients present at ages above 65 years (Almdal et al. 1991). Its prevalence in women aged over 50 has been found to be 1 in 1500 in parts of Europe including the United Kingdom (Myszor and James 1990).

Population studies have revealed that the illness displays a wide variation in clinical features at the onset—a third of patients have no symptoms, about half present with the features of chronic liver disease, and the remainder present with the complications of portal hypertension (Myszor and James 1990). Asymptomatic disease is increasingly being recognized because of the wide availability of the immunological antimitochondrial antibody (AMA) test (Christensen et al. 1980). In women over age 50 with raised serum alkaline phosphatase and positive AMA the diagnosis of primary biliary cirrhosis is very likely. However, diagnosis requires histopathological confirmation by liver biopsy. As the prognosis for such patients does not differ from that of normal age-matched controls, no intervention is recommended in asymptomatic individuals (Mitchison et al. 1990).

The common presenting features in patients with symptomatic primary biliary cirrhosis include pruritus, upper abdominal pain, malaise, and jaundice. Characteristically, liver function tests show cholestasis, immunoglobulin M may be elevated, and AMA is positive in almost every case. There are several types of AMA, of which the serum anti-M2 is the most specific for primary biliary cirrhosis (Leung et al. 1992). The other antibodies include anti-M9 which is associated with early primary biliary cirrhosis and can be found in healthy relatives of sufferers and in technicians handling primary biliary cirrhosis sera. Anti-M4 and anti-M8 are seen in those who are anti-M2 positive and may be associated with more progressive disease. Antibodies to M3, M6, and M5 are thought to be related to drug reactions, iproniazid, and collagen disease respectively. About 10 to 15 per cent of the normal population are anti-M9 positive (Sherlock and Dooley 1997).

The diagnosis should be confirmed by liver biopsy. Age has been found to be an adverse prognostic factor, and other indicators include serum bilirubin, the presence of cirrhosis, low serum albumin, and the presence of portal hypertension (Grambsch et al. 1989). About 50 per cent of primary biliary cirrhosis patients who are symptomatic will be dead within 5 years. Death usually results from the complications of portal hypertension and hepatic failure (Kaplan 1987).

The aim of medical treatment in patients with symptomatic primary biliary cirrhosis is to prevent the onset of worsening symptoms, deteriorating liver function, and the complications of cirrhosis. Several agents have been evaluated, but none has been shown to be of great benefit. Poupon et al. (1991) have provided evidence in support of the role of bile acids, particularly in symptomatic patients

Table 1 Types of autoimmune chronic hepatitis (based on the pattern of circulating autoantibodies)

Type	Antibodies
I	ANA/DNA, SMA
IIa	LKM1
IIb (HCV)	LKM1, anti-HCV

ANA, antinuclear antibody; SMA, smooth muscle antibody; LKM, liver/kidney microsome antibody.

with precirrhotic liver histology. Liver transplantation is now the standard treatment for patients with complications of cirrhosis, but this is yet to be offered to patients above the age of 65.

Chronic hepatitis

Chronic hepatitis, which is a histological diagnosis, is increasingly being recognized in elderly patients (Almadal et al. 1991). It may result from a variety of insults, including hepatitis B (and delta), hepatitis C, and hepatotoxic drugs. However, it is most commonly described in association with autoimmune changes, particularly the presence of positive antinuclear antibody and/or smooth muscle antibody. The illness is insidious in onset, developing over a period of few weeks or months. The main symptoms are fatigue, fluid retention, and jaundice. Although the physical signs of chronic hepatitis are very variable in older individuals, they are similar to those of other chronic liver diseases. The disease may be associated with arthralgia, haemolytic anaemia, or glomerulonephritis. Biochemical abnormalities include elevated transaminases and reduced serum albumin. Immunoglobulins are also greatly increased. Autoantibodies as well as viral markers have been found to be negative in a small proportion of elderly individuals who otherwise appear to have typical features of autoimmune chronic hepatitis. A classification of autoimmune chronic hepatitis, based on the pattern of circulating autoantibodies, is shown in Table 1.

The diagnosis of autoimmune chronic hepatitis is established, after excluding drugs, viral hepatitis, and other causes of chronic liver disease, by demonstrating the presence of smooth muscle antibody and/or antinuclear antibody in the patient's serum together with liver histology compatible with chronic hepatitis . The prognosis is reported to be grave, with 60 per cent dying within 5 years without treatment. Treatment with steroids, usually in combination with azathioprine, has improved this to 80 per cent 5-year survival. Treatment usually needs to be maintained for several years. A trial of steroids is also recommended in patients without autoantibodies, but treatment should be discontinued if there is no response in 3 months.

Primary sclerosing cholangitis

This disease, with a mean age of onset around 40 years, is rare in people aged over 65 (Larusso and Weisner 1990), and. is usually associated with ulcerative colitis. It has a similar clinical course to primary biliary cirrhosis. The diagnosis requires demonstration by endoscopic retrograde cholangiopancreatography (ERCP) of the typical irregular and beaded appearance of the intrahepatic biliary tree together with cholestatic changes in liver function tests and compatible liver histology. Prognosis has been reported to be good in those elderly patients who show no evidence of cirrhosis on liver biopsy.

Cryptogenic liver disease

The availability of modern diagnostic techniques, including serological and immunological tests, has greatly reduced the proportion of patients seen as suffering from cryptogenic liver disease. However, it has been suggested that there may be a specific form of senile cryptogenic cirrhosis. In a large study from the Mayo Clinic, 77 patients over the age of 70 out of a total of 33 500 autopsies were found to have cryptogenic cirrhosis not recognized during life (Ludwig and Baggenstoss 1970). Such patients appear to have a poor prognosis and often present with portal hypertension or occasionally hepatocellular carcinoma (Johnson et al. 1989).

Inherited hepatic disease

Haemochromatosis

Haemochromatosis, an autosomal recessive condition, results from an abnormally increased absorption of iron with an enhanced uptake by the liver from transferrin. The responsible gene is situated on the short arm of chromosome 6, in close proximity to the histocompatibility antigen A3 (Bassett et al. 1981). Although the mean age at presentation is around 50 years, a number of individuals with no previous family history may present at age 70 or older. Typically, elderly patients with haemochromatosis have established chronic liver disease at presentation (Tavill and Bacon 1990). Non-hepatic manifestations include heart failure and diabetes, which develop in about half of the patients. Diagnostic studies should include measurement of serum ferritin and liver biopsy with histological assessment of liver iron stores and measurement of hepatic iron concentration.

Treatment is by venesection with removal of about 500 ml of blood at fortnightly intervals until serum ferritin returns to normal. Venesection prevents progression to cirrhosis, and reduces the incidence of hepatocellular failure in patients with the cirrhosis already present in most elderly patients. However, the development of hepatocellular carcinoma is not prevented in patients with established cirrhosis. It is essential to screen the families of patients with the diagnosis of haemochromatosis.

α_1-Antitrypsin deficiency

The liver is the main source of α_1-antitrypsin which is an inhibitor of protease. A single autosomal dominant gene on the long arm of chromosome 14 controls its secretion. In patients with α_1-antitrypsin deficiency resulting in chronic liver disease, periportal hepatocytes have been shown to accumulate granules of abnormal α_1-antitrypsin in the form of a diastase-resistant material with a positive periodic acid–Schiff reagent stain. The collection of these granules is thought to result from a failure of the cellular transport mechanism.

Most people with ZZ homozygote phenotype status do not survive into old age as they die of severe emphysema or cirrhosis in childhood. In contrast, the outcome of individuals with the Z heterozygote phenotype, which is present in about 3 per cent of West Europeans, remains uncertain (Brind et al. 1990).

Hepatocellular carcinoma

In developed countries, primary hepatocellular carcinoma is predominantly a disease of older people, with more than 50 per cent of patients being aged over 60 years and more than 40 per cent over 70 years at presentation (Stevens et al. 1984; Cobden et al. 1986). Cirrhosis of the liver is the most important risk factor. Melia et al. (1984) have suggested that the length of the time for which a patient has cirrhosis is the key factor in determining the development of malignant change. Elderly patients with cirrhosis who deteriorate suddenly should be investigated for hepatocellular carcinoma. In Europe and North America the main predisposing factors for the development of hepatocellular carcinoma are previous infection with hepatitis B and C viruses or alcoholic cirrhosis or a combination of these (Zaman et al. 1985; Liaw et al. 1986; Dazza et al. 1990).

Hepatocellular carcinoma in older individuals often presents either with the complications of cirrhosis, such as bleeding varices, ascites, or hepatic encephalopathy, or with the symptoms of the tumour itself which include abdominal pain, weight loss, hepatic enlargement, and abdominal swelling. Bone pain from skeletal metastases may also occur.

A rise in the level of serum α-fetoprotein above 500 ng/ml in patients with cirrhosis is highly suggestive of hepatocellular carcinoma. Imaging techniques, such as CT, preferably with angiography, or magnetic resonance imaging, are employed to assess the size, extent, and number of tumours. Histological confirmation should always be obtained by ultrasound- or CT-guided needle biopsy. As the prognosis is dependent to a large extent on the size of tumour at the time of detection, screening of all elderly patients with known cirrhosis for the development of hepatocellular carcinoma is now recommended. Although a number of treatment strategies have been implemented, the overall prognosis remains extremely poor with mean survival from presentation being less than 6 months (Kasugai et al. 1989; Taniguchi et al. 1989; Fortner and Lincer 1990).

Biliary disease

Gallstones

The prevalence of cholelithiasis increases with age, and by 70 years around 30 per cent of women and 19 per cent of men have gallstones (Jorgenssen et al. 1990). Most are asymptomatic, but some subjects will develop biliary pain and complications from stones in the common bile duct (O'Mahony and Schmucker 1994).

Several age-associated factors, including decreased bile acid production and increased hepatic cholesterol secretion resulting in increased cholesterol saturation of bile, are responsible for the high prevalence of gallstones in the elderly population (Einarsson et al. 1985). There is also reduced sensitivity of the gallbladder to cholecystokinin with diminished gallbladder contraction after a meal (Poston et al. 1990), and an increase in the number of duodenal diverticula producing biliary stasis (Grace et al. 1990). Other predisposing factors include drugs (i.e. clofibrate, oestrogen), ileal disease or resection, cirrhosis, and obesity.

Ultrasonography is the investigation of choice in patients with symptomatic gallstones. It can visualize both the contents of the gallbladder and the biliary tract. The diameter of the bile ducts can be measured. ERCP or percutaneous transhepatic cholangiography may be required to outline the biliary tree in the presence of obstructive jaundice. It must be remembered that gallstones are not always detected by ultrasonography.

Choice of treatment depends on the presentation of gallstones (Krasman *et al.* 1991),. and in later life no treatment is recommended for patients with asymptomatic gallstones. Patients who develop complications such as acute cholecystitis, cholangitis, or obstructive jaundice from choledocholithiasis require urgent intervention. The mortality following urgent cholecystectomy in elderly patients with acute cholecystitis is not significantly higher than in young individuals (Hidalgo *et al.* 1989). However, the majority of patients present with occasional upper abdominal pain (biliary colic) or nausea, and ultrasonography reveals stones limited to gallbladder. Although as a general rule gallstones that are symptomatic should be removed, deciding when the stones are symptomatic can be a difficult task.

There are several treatment options once it is established that the gallstones have become symptomatic. Elective cholecystectomy may be offered. Percutaneous laparoscopic cholecystectomy is now routinely carried out in many centres and has become the operative treatment of choice (Cuschieri *et al.* 1989). In experienced hands, the perioperative fatality and morbidity of this form of cholecystectomy are lower than with traditional forms of surgical intervention (Wetter and Way 1991). Patients who have predominantly cholesterol stones and a patent cystic duct may have their stones dissolved by extracorporeal shock-wave lithotripsy which is a safe and effective technique (Sackmann *et al.* 1988). This works best in patients with a solitary stone of diameter less than 30 mm and when combined with oral bile acids given for several months. Chemical dissolution of gallstones by oral bile acids gives poor results and is now seldom done.

Cholecystitis

Cholecystitis is usually associated with gallstones, but about 5 per cent of patients do not have any evidence of stones in the gallbladder. This acalculous cholecystitis occurs in patients with other serious illness, particularly following trauma or major surgery (Ullman *et al.* 1984). The main presenting symptoms of acute cholecystitis include fever, right upper quadrant abdominal pain, and tenderness with nausea and vomiting. Blood cultures frequently grow Gram-negative organisms. The mainstay of treatment is surgery (Ingbar and Jacobson 1990). All patients should receive broad-spectrum antibiotics and supportive measures. Urgent surgical intervention is currently favoured (Hidalgo *et al.* 1989). However, in extremely ill and frail individuals a more conservative approach carries a low mortality and should be preferred.

Cancer of the gallbladder

Carcinoma of the gallbladder is a disease of old age, with the majority of patients being in their seventies at presentation. Although the carcinoma is usually associated with gallstones (Diehl 1983), it is not clear whether the link is strong. The neoplasm is four times more common in women than in men. The disease is often mistaken for some other hepatobiliary problem (Richard and Cantin 1976). Main presenting symptoms include upper abdominal pain, weight loss, a right upper abdominal mass, and jaundice. In patients with no spread beyond the confines of the gallbladder, the tumour may be resectable. However, in the majority of patients the disease has already spread beyond the gallbladder area by the time it presents, and all that can

be offered is palliation. The prognosis of gallbladder cancer is poor with a 1-year survival of less than 10 per cent (Foster 1987).

References

Almdal, T.P., Sorensen, T.I.A., and the Danish Association for the Study of the Liver (1991). Incidence of parenchymal liver disease in Denmark, 1981 to 1985: analysis of hospitalisation registry data. *Hepatology*, 13, 650–5.

Andrew, W. (1971). *The anatomy of aging in man and animals*. Grune and Stratton, New York.

Anonymous (1990). Hepatitis C virus upstanding (editorial). *Lancet*, i, 1431–2.

Aron, E., Dupin, M., and Jobard, P. (1979). Les cirrhosis du troisieme age. *Annales de Gastroenterologie et d'Hepatologie*, 14, 558–63.

Barnes, P.F., DeCock, K.M., Reynolds, T.N., *et al.* (1987). A comparison of amoebic and pyogenic abscess in the liver. *Medicine (Baltimore)*, 66, 472–81.

Bassett, M.L., Halliday, J.W., and Powell, L.W. (1981). HLA typing in idiopathic haemochromatosis: distinction between homozygotes and heterozygotes with biochemical expression. *Hepatology*, 1, 120–7.

Beaumont, D.M. and Davis, M. (1985). Clinical presentation of pyogenic liver abscess in the elderly. *Age and Ageing*, 14, 339–44.

Bertel, C.R., Van Heerden J.A., and Sheedy, P.F. (1986). Treatment of pyogenic hepatic abscess: surgical vs. percutaneous drainage. *Archives of Surgery*, 121, 554–62.

Bouchier, I.A.D., Hislop, W.S., and Prescott, R.J. (1992). A prospective study of alcoholic liver disease and mortality. *Journal of Hepatology*, 16, 290–7.

Brind, A.M., Codd, A.A., Cohen, D.J., *et al.* (1990). Low prevalence of antibody to hepatitis C virus in North East England. *Journal of Medical Virology*, 32, 243–8.

Chan-Yeung, M., Feneira, P., Frohlich, J., *et al.* (1981). The effects of age, smoking, and alcohol on routine laboratory tests. *American Journal of Clinical Pathology*, 75, 320–6.

Chiaramonte, M., Floreani, A., and Naccarato, R. (1982). Hepatitis B infection in homes for the aged. *Journal of Medical Virology*, 9, 247–55.

Chiaramonte, M., Stroffolini, T., Lorenzoni, U., *et al.* (1996). Risk factors in community acquired chronic hepatitis C virus infection: a case–control study in Italy. *Journal of Hepatology*, 24, 129–34.

Christensen, E., Crow, J., Doniach, D., *et al.* (1980). Clinical pattern and course of disease in primary biliary cirrhosis based on an analysis of 236 patients. *Gastroenterology*, 78, 236–46.

Cobden, I., Bassendine, M.F., and James, O.F.W. (1986). Hepatocellular carcinoma in North East England: importance of hepatitis B infection and ex-tropical military service. *Quarterly Journal of Medicine*, 60, 855–63.

Cook, J.M., Gaulde, M., Hessel, L., *et al.* (1987). Alterations in human immune response to the hepatitis B vaccine among the elderly. *Cellular Immunology*, 109, 89–96.

Cuschieri, A., El Ghanny, A.A.B., and Holley, M.P. (1989). Successful chemical cholecystectomy: a laparoscopic guided technique. *Gut*, 30, 1786–94.

Dazza, M.C., *et al.* (1990). Hepatitis C virus antibody and hepatocellular carcinoma. *Lancet*, i, 1216.

Diehl, A.K. (1983). Gallstone size and risk of gallbladder cancer. *Journal of the American Medical Association*, 250, 2323–6.

Dusheiko, G.M. (1992). Hepatitis C virus. In *Recent advances in gastroenterology* (9th edn) (ed. R.E. Pounder), pp. 195–216. Churchill Livingstone, Edinburgh.

Dusheiko, G.M. and Hoofnagle, J.H. (1991). Hepatitis B. In *Oxford textbook of clinical hepatology* (ed. N. McIntyre, J. Benhamou, J. Bircher, *et al.*), pp. 571–92. Oxford University Press.

Eastwood, H.D.H. (1971). Causes of jaundice in the elderly. *Gerontologia Clinica*, 13, 69–81.

Einarsson, K., Nilsell, K., Leijd, B., and Angelin, B. (1985). Influence of age on secretion of cholesterol and synthesis of bile acids by the liver. *New England Journal of Medicine*, 313, 277–82.

Floreani, A. and Chiaramonte, M. (1994). Hepatitis in nursing homes: incidence and management strategies. *Drugs and Aging*, 5, 96–101.

Forbes, A. and Williams, R. (1988). Increasing age—an important adverse prognostic factor in hepatitis A virus infection. *Journal of the Royal College of Physicians of London*, 22, 237–9.

Fortner, J.G., and Lincer, R.M. (1990). Hepatic resection in the elderly. *Annals of Surgery*, 211, 141–5.

Foster, J. (1987). Carcinoma of the gallbladder. In *Surgery of the gallbladder and bile ducts* (ed. L.W. Way and C.A. Pellegrini), pp. 471–90. W.B. Saunders, Philadelphia, PA.

Friis, H. and Andreasen, P.B. (1992). Drug induced hepatic injury: an analysis of 1100 cases reported to the Danish Committee on Adverse Drug Reactions between 1978 and 1987. *Journal of Internal Medicine*, 232, 133–8.

Galambos, J. (1974). Alcoholic hepatitis. In *The liver and its diseases* (ed. F. Schaffner, S. Sherlock, and C. Leevy), pp. 244–80. Intercontinental Medical Books, New York.

Gambert, S.R., *et al.* (1982). Interpretation of laboratory results in the elderly. 1. A clinician's guide to hematologic and hepatorenal function tests. *Postgraduate Medicine*, 2, 147–52.

Garagliano, C.F., Lillenfield, A.M., and Mendelhof, A.I. (1979). Incidence rates of liver cirrhosis and related diseases in Baltimore and selected areas of the United States. *Journal of Chronic Diseases*, 32, 543–54.

Goodson, J.D., Taylor, P.A., Campion, E.W., *et al.* (1982). The clinical course of acute hepatitis in the elderly patient. *Archives of Internal Medicine*, 142, 1485–8.

Grace, P.A., Poston, G.J., and Williamson, R.C.A. (1990). Biliary motility. *Gut*, 31, 571–82.

Grambsch, P.M., Dickson, E.R., Kaplan, M.M., *et al.* (1989). Extramural cross validation of the Mayo PBC model. *Hepatology*, 10, 846–50.

Grasedyck, K., Jahnke, M., Friedrich, O., *et al.* (1980). Aging of liver: morphological and biochemical changes. *Mechanisms of Aging and Development*, 14, 435–42.

Greenblatt, D.J., Sellers, E.M., and Shader, R.I. (1982). Drug disposition in old age. *New England Journal of Medicine*, 306, 1081–8.

Greenstein, A.J., Lowenthal, D., Hammer, G.S., *et al.* (1984). Continuing changing patterns of disease in pyogenic liver abscess: a study of 38 patients. *American Journal of Gastroenterology*, 79, 217–21.

Heydari, A.R., Wu, B., Takahashi, R., *et al.* (1993). Expression of heat shock protein 70 is altered by age and diet at the level of transcription. *Molecular and Cellular Biology*, 13, 2909–18.

Hidalgo, L.A., Capella, G., Pi-Figueras, J., *et al.* (1989). Influence of age on early surgical treatment of acute cholecystitis. *Surgery, Gynecology and Obstetrics*, 169, 393–6.

Hislop, W.S., Bouchier, I.A.D., Allan, J.G., *et al.* (1983). Alcoholic liver disease in Scotland and North East England: presenting features in 510 patients. *Quarterly Journal of Medicine*, 52, 232–43.

Imperiale, T.F. and McCullough, A.J. (1990). Do corticosteroids reduce mortality from alcoholic hepatitis? A meta-analysis of the randomised trials. *Annals of Internal Medicine*, 113, 299–307.

Ingbar, S. and Jacobson, I.M. (1990). Biliary and pancreatic disease in the elderly. *Gastroenterology Clinics of North America*, 19, 433–57.

James, O.F.W. (1985). Drugs and the ageing liver. *Journal of Hepatology*, 1, 431–5.

James, O.F.W., Bridgewater, R., Gilder, F., *et al.* (1986). Alcoholism, alcoholic liver disease and its mortality among the elderly in England. In *Liver and aging* (ed. K. Kitani, pp. 359–70. Elsevier, Amsterdam.

Johnson, P., Hayllar, K., Metivier, E., *et al.* (1989). Survival in cirrhosis: importance of age as an indicator of disease duration (abstract). *Journal of Hepatology*, 9: 546.

Jorgensen, T., Kay, L., and Schultz-Larsen, K. (1990). The epidemiology of gallstones in a 70 year old Danish population. *Scandinavian Journal of Gastroenterology*, 25, 335–40.

Kaplan, M.M. (1987). Primary biliary cirrhosis. *New England Journal of Medicine*, 316, 521–7.

Kasugai, H., Kojima, J., Tatsuta, M., *et al.* (1989). Treatment of hepatocellular carcinoma by transcatheter arterial embolisation combined with intraarterial infusion of a mixture of cisplatin and ethiodized oil. *Gastroenterology*, 97, 965–71.

Kitani, K. (1988). Bile acids in aging. In *Aging in liver and gastrointestinal tract; Falk Symposium 47* (ed. L. Bianchi, P. Holt, O.F. James, and R.N. Butler), pp. 169–80. MTP Press, Lancaster.

Kitani, K. (1990). Ageing and the liver. *Progress in Liver Diseases*, 9, 603–23.

Kopanoff, D.E., Snider, D.E., Jr., and Caras, G.J. (1978). Isoniazid related hepatitis. *American Review of Respiratory Disease*, 117, 991–1001.

Krasman, M.L., Gracie, W.A., and Strasius, S.R. (1991). Biliary tract disease in the aged. *Clinics in Geriatric Medicine*, 7, 347–70.

Kraus, M.L., Gottlieb, L.D., Horwitz, R.I., *et al.* (1985). Randomised clinical trial of atenolol in patients with alcohol withdrawal. *New England Journal of Medicine*, 313, 905–9.

Krawczynski, K. (1993). Hepatitis E. *Hepatology*, 17, 932–41.

Kuo, G., Choo, Q.L., Alter, H.J., *et al.* (1989). An assay for circulating antibodies to a major aetiologic virus of human non-A, non-B hepatitis. *Science*, 244, 362–4.

LaRusso, N.F. and Weisner, R.H. (1990). The syndrome of primary cholangitis. *Progress in Liver Diseases*, 9, 555–66.

Laverdant, C., Algayres, J.P., Daly, J.P., *et al.* (1989). Les hépatites virales après 60 ans: aspects cliniques, étiologiques et évolutifs. *Gastroenterologie Clinique et Biologique*, 13, 499–504.

Leung, P.S.C., Iwayama. T., Prindiville, T., *et al.* (1992). Use of designer recombinant mitochondrial antigens in the diagnosis of primary biliary cirrhosis. *Hepatology*, 15, 367–72.

Liaw, Y.F., Tai, D.I., Chu, C.M., *et al.* (1986). Early detection of hepatocellular carcinoma in patients with chronic type B hepatitis: a prospective study. *Gastroenterology*, 90, 263–7.

Lind, R.C., Gandolfi, A.J., and Hall, P.M. (1989). Age and gender influence halothane associated hepatotoxicity in strain 13 guinea pigs. *Anesthesiology*, 71, 878–84.

Ludwig, J. and Baggenstoss, A.H. (1970). Cirrhosis of the aged and senile cirrhosis—are there two conditions? *Journal of Gerontology*, 25, 244–8.

Marchesini, G., Bua, V., Brunori, A., *et al.* (1988). Galactose elimination capacity and liver volume in ageing man. *Hepatology*, 8, 1079–83.

Marchesini, G., Bianchi, G.P., Fabbri, A., *et al.* (1990). Synthesis of urea after a protein rich meal in normal man in relation to ageing. *Age and Ageing*, 19, 4–10.

Melia, W.M., Wilkinson, M.L., Portmann, B.C., *et al.* (1984). Hepatocellular carcinoma in Great Britain: influence of age, sex, HBsAg status and aetiology of underlying cirrhosis. *Quarterly Journal of Medicine*, 53, 391–400.

Mitchison, H.C., Lucey, M.R., Kelley, P.J., *et al.* (1990). Symptom development and prognosis in primary biliary cirrhosis. *Gastroenterology*, 99, 778–84.

Moss, D. (1994). Liver function tests. *Medicine International*, 22, 425–31.

Myszor, M. and James, O.F.W. (1990). The epidemiology of primary biliary cirrhosis in North East England. *Quarterly Journal of Medicine*, 75, 377–85.

Neuberger, J. and Williams, R. (1984). Halothane anaesthesia and liver damage. *British Medical Journal*, **289**, 1136–9.

O'Mahony, M.S. and Schmucker, D.L. (1994). Liver disease in the elderly. *Seminars in Gastrointestinal Disease*, **5**, 197–206.

Parker, S.G., James, O.F.W., and Young, E.T. (1986). Causes of raised serum alkaline phosphatase in elderly patients. *Modern Trends in Aging Research*, **147**, 153–7.

Patek, A.J. and Hermos, J.A. (1981). Recovery from alcoholism in cirrhotic patients: a study of 45 cases. *American Journal of Medicine*, **70**, 783–5.

Popper, H. (1986). Aging and the liver. *Progress in Liver Diseases*, **8**, 659–83.

Poston, G.J., Draviam, E.J., Yao, C.Z., *et al.* (1990). Effect of age and sensitivity to cholecystokinin on gallstone formation in the guinea pig. *Gastroenterology*, **98**, 993–9.

Potter, J.R. and James, O.F.W. (1987). Clinical features and prognosis of alcoholic liver disease in respect of advancing age. *Gerontology*, **33**, 380–7.

Poupon, R.E., Balkau, B., Eschwege, E., Poupon, R., and the UDCA-PBC Study Group (1991). A multicentre, controlled trial of Ursodiol for the treatment of primary biliary cirrhosis. *New England Journal of Medicine*, **324**, 1548–54.

Richard, P.F. and Cantin, J. (1976). Primary carcinoma of gall bladder: study of 108 cases. *Canadian Journal of Surgery*, **19**, 27–32.

Rizzetto, M. and Verme, G. (1985). Delta hepatitis: present status. *Journal of Hepatology*, **1**, 187–9.

Sackmann, M., *et al.* (1988). Shock wave lithotripsy of gallbladder stones: the first 175 patients. *New England Journal of Medicine*, **318**, 393–7.

Sato, T. and Tauchi, H. (1975). The formation of enlarged and giant mitochondria in the aging process of human hepatic cells. *Acta Pathologica Japonica*, **25**, 403–12.

Sato, T., Cespedes, R.F., Goyenaga, P.H., *et al.* (1979). Age changes in the livers of Costa Ricans. *Mechanisms of Ageing and Development*, **11**, 171–8.

Schenker, S. (1984). Alcoholic liver disease: evaluation of natural history and prognostic factors. *Hepatology*, **4** (Supplement), 36S–43S.

Schmucker, D.L., Woodhouse, K.W., and Wang, R. (1990). Effect of age and gender on *in vitro* properties of human liver mocrosomal monooxygenases. *Clinical Pharmacology and Therapeutics*, **48**, 365–74.

Sherlock, S. and Dooley, J. (1997). Primary biliary cirrhosis. In *Diseases of liver and biliary system* (10th edn) (ed. S. Sherlock and J. Dooley), pp. 239–52. Blackwell Scientific, Oxford.

Shetty, H.G.M. and Woodhouse, K.W. (1992). Use of amiodarone for elderly patients. *Age and Ageing*, **21**, 233–6.

Sonnenblick, M., Uren, R., and Tur-Kaspa, R. (1988). Non-A, non-B hepatitis in the aged (abstract). *Hepatology*, **8**, 1060.

Sridharan, G.V., Wilkinson, S.P., and Primrose, W.R. (1990). Pyogenic liver abscess in the elderly. *Age and Ageing*, **19**, 199–203.

Stevens, R.G., Merkle, E.J., and Lustbader, E.D. (1984). Age and cohort effects in primary liver cancer. *International Journal of Cancer*, **33**, 453–8.

Taniguchi, H., Takahashi, T., Yamaguchi, T., *et al.* (1989). Intraarterial infusion chemotherapy for metastatic liver tumours using multiple anti-cancer agents suspended in a lipid contrast medium. *Cancer*, **64**, 2001–6.

Tavill, A.S. and Bacon, B.R. (1990). Haemochromatosis: iron metabolism and the iron overload syndromes. In *Hepatology: a textbook of liver disease* (2nd edn) (ed. D. Zakim and T.D. Boyer), pp. 1273–99. W.B. Saunders, Philadelphia, PA.

Thomas, H.C. (1992). Management of chronic hepatitis B virus infection. In *Therapy in liver diseases* (ed. J. Rodes and V. Arroyo), pp. 242–7. Doyma, Barcelona.

Ullman, M., Hasselgren, P.O., and Tveit, E. (1984). Post traumatic and postoperative acute acalculous cholecystitis. *Acta Chirurgica Scandinavica*, **150**, 507–10.

Vestal, R.E. (1989). Aging and determinants of hepatic drug clearance. *Hepatology*, **9**, 331–4.

Wetter, L.A. and Way, L.W. (1991). Surgical therapy of gallstone disease. *Seminars in Gastrointestinal Disease*, **2**, 241–9.

Woodhouse, K.W. and James, O.F.W. (1990). Hepatic drug metabolism and ageing. *British Medical Journal*, **46**, 22–35.

Woodhouse, K.W., Mortimer, O., and Wiholm, B.E. (1986). Hepatic adverse drug reaction: the effect of age. In *Liver and ageing* (ed. K. Kitani), pp. 75–80. Elsevier, Amsterdam.

Wynne, H.A., Cope, E., Mutch, E., *et al.* (1989). The effect of age upon liver volume and applied liver blood flow in healthy men. *Hepatology*, **9**, 297–301.

Zaman, S.N., Melia, W.M., Johnson, R.D., *et al.* (1985). Risk factors in development of hepatocellular carcinoma in cirrhosis: prospective study of 613 patients. *Lancet*, **i**, 1357–60.

9

Cardiovascular disorders

9.1 Cardiovascular disorders

Edward G. Lakatta and Gary Gerstenblith

Ageing and cardiovascular structure and function

In so far as atherosclerosis, hypertension, stroke, and heart failure reach epidemic proportions among older members of our society, ageing *per se* is a major risk factor for these diseases. Quantitative information on age-associated alterations in cardiovascular structure and function in health is essential in order to define and target the specific characteristics of cardiovascular ageing that render it a risk factor for these diseases. Such information is also required to differentiate limitations on an elderly individual that relate to disease from those limitations that may fall within expected normal limits. However, defining the effects of ageing *per se* on cardiovascular structure and function is not an easy task, because it is difficult to separate ageing influences from those of lifestyle (e.g. physical activity, smoking, personality characteristics, etc.) and disease (Fig. 1). The interactions among these can have a substantial impact on cardiovascular structure and function, and can alter the manifestations of 'pure' ageing effects on the cardiovascular system.

Occult disease and lifestyle changes that occur with ageing can cause severe functional impairments. Occult disease is particularly pertinent to investigation of age effects on cardiovascular function in humans because coronary atherosclerosis is present in an occult form in at least as large a number of elderly persons as the overt form of the disease (Elveback and Lie 1984). Regular physical activity affects both the structure and function of the cardiovascular system. It has been well established in unselected populations that the average daily level of physical activity declines progressively with age (Lakatta 1985). Genetic components of ageing, disease, and lifestyle (Fig. 1) further complicate the picture, and at present remain largely unknown.

Over the past two decades, a sustained effort has been made to characterize the multiple effects of ageing in health on cardiovascular structure and function in a single study cohort, the Baltimore Longitudinal Study on Ageing (**BLSA**) (Shock *et al.* 1984) In these studies, community-dwelling volunteer participants were rigorously screened to detect both clinical and occult cardiovascular disease and characterized with respect to lifestyle (e.g. exercise habits) in an attempt to deconstruct the interactions depicted in Fig. 1. Some specific

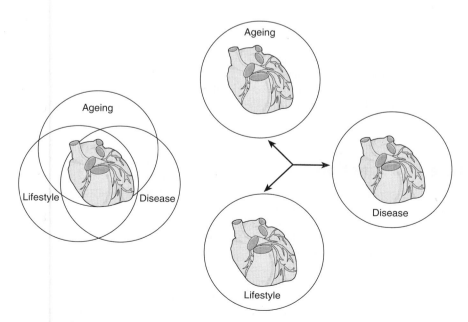

Fig. 1 Interactions between ageing, specific diseases, and lifestyle traits determine cardiovascular structure and function. Each of these factors probably also has a genetic component. In order to determine the importance of these interactions each component must be isolated and characterized.

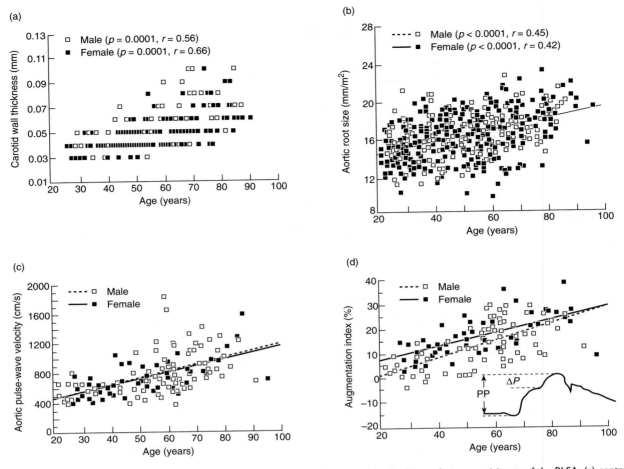

Fig. 2 Age-associated changes in central vascular structure and function in healthy community-dwelling sedentary participants of the BLSA: (a) control intimal–medial carotid wall thickness measured using echo Doppler techniques; (b) aortic root diameter measured using M-mode echocardiography; (c) aortic pulse-wave velocity, an index of aortic stiffness; (d) augmentation index (AGI) (inset) of the carotid pulse pressure due to a late peak in systolic pressure. This late augmentation of systolic pressure in older individuals is attributable to early reflected pulse waves caused by the increased stiffness of large vessels. (Reproduced with permission from Lakatta (1994).)

changes in cardiovascular structure and function that occur with advancing age in these healthy humans are identified and summarized below. Some relevant observations from other human study populations and mechanistic approaches applied to experimental animal models of ageing are also described.

Vascular structure and function

Vascular changes occur with ageing among individuals otherwise considered to be healthy. The large elastic arteries exhibit an increase in wall thickness (Fig. 2(a)) and become dilated (Fig. 2(b)). The increased wall thickness is due to an increase in the thickness of the vascular intima, believed to herald preclinical features of the atherosclerotic process (Markus *et al.* 1997). The thicker-walled dilated conduit arteries of older individuals also become stiffer, as indexed by an increased pulse-wave velocity (Fig. 2(c)). However, these age-associated vascular changes fall below our present 'clinical threshold' for classification as risks for disease, and thus, somewhat surprisingly, are characterized as 'normal'. Stiffening of arteries throughout the body with ageing is not universal, however, as an age-associated increase in stiffness is not observed in the more distal arteries (Boutouyrie *et al.* 1992).

A change in the shape of the pressure pulse contour (Fig. 2(d)) occurs with ageing in otherwise healthy individuals. In younger individuals, the peak systolic pressure occurs at about the time of peak blood flow. In older individuals, pulse waves reflected from the periphery return to the base of the aorta before closure of the aortic valve, because the aorta is stiffer and the forward and reflected pulse waves travel faster. The result of early reflected waves is a late peak in systolic central arterial pressure. As a result of arterial stiffening, the average systolic blood pressure within a population increases (within the normal range) with ageing, whether measured in a cross-sectional study design (Fig. 3(a)) or longitudinally (Fig. 3(b)). It is noteworthy that in the BLSA population shown in Fig. 3 the initial blood pressure level explained little of the variance in the 10-year rate of change in blood pressure, except for a modest relationship for systolic pressure in men. It is also noteworthy that many individuals show little or no longitudinal increase in systolic pressure. Thus age-associated increases in blood pressure are neither universal nor inevitable.

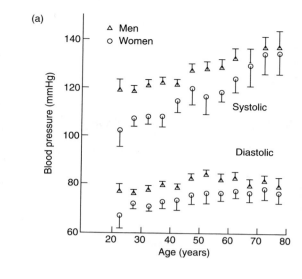

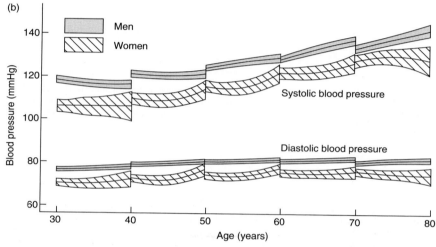

Fig. 3 (a) Observed cross-sectional average (with 95 per cent confidence intervals) systolic and diastolic blood pressure for the BLSA dataset screened for health problems or medications that affect blood pressure. Circles represent the average blood pressure for women, and diamonds represent the mean blood pressure for men. (b) Average (with 95 per cent confidence intervals) systolic and diastolic blood pressure levels estimated from a mixed-effects model for 10-year longitudinal follow-up in healthy BLSA men and women. (Reproduced with permission from Pearson *et al.* (1997).)

The average increase in diastolic pressure with ageing is modest, appears to reach a plateau around mid-life, and is not as marked as the average increase in systolic pressure (Fig. 3). Diastolic pressure in large part reflects the peripheral vascular resistance. In carefully screened healthy BLSA subjects, resting peripheral vascular resistance increases minimally with ageing in men and moderately in women (Fleg *et al.* 1995).

Cardiac structure and function

At rest

Overall cardiac function in most older humans who do not have clinical or occult cardiac disease is adequate to meet the body's requirements at rest (Fig. 4). To sustain a normal left ventricular ejection in the presence of the higher arterial pressure and arterial stiffness, the left ventricular wall, as assessed by echocardiography, thickens slightly (Fig. 5(a)). This is due in a large part to an increase

in cardiac myocyte size (Lakatta 1993*b*). The ability of the myocardium to bear force in late systole is increased, manifested by a lower isovolumic relaxation time. Studies in rat myocardium indicate that this may be attributable to characteristic age-associated changes in cardiac excitation–contraction coupling mechanisms. The transmembrane action potential (Fig. 6(a)), the myoplasmic Ca^{2+} transient that initiates contraction (Fig. 6(c)), and the resultant contraction (Fig. 6(b)) are of longer duration in heart muscle of senescent rats than in young adult rats. The prolonged Ca^{2+} elevation is due to a reduced rate of Ca^{2+} sequestration into its intracellular storage site, the sarcoplasmic reticulum (Fig. 6(d)). This in turn is due to down-regulation of expression of the gene coding for the Ca^{2+} pump protein (Lakatta 1993*b*). The altered pattern of Ca^{2+} regulation shown in Fig. 6 allows the myocardium of older hearts to generate force for a longer time following excitation. This enables the continued ejection of blood during late systole, a beneficial adaptation with respect to enhanced vascular stiffness and early reflected pulse waves (Fig. 2).

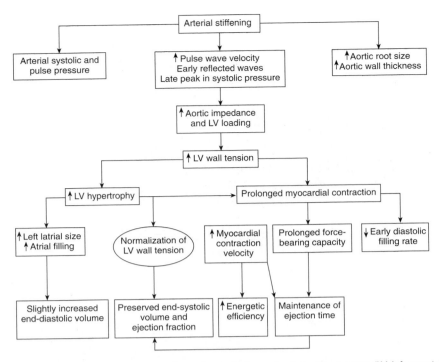

Fig. 4 Structural and functional changes that occur in the heart and vasculature during ageing in healthy humans (LV, left ventricle). These age-associated changes are currently not considered as diseases. However, the altered cardiovascular structure and function due to these changes interact with pathophysical mechanisms of specific cardiovascular (CV) diseases to reduce the threshold and enhance the severity of clinical manifestations of these diseases in older individuals. (Reproduced with permission from Lakatta (1993b).)

In humans, prolonged myocardial contraction and changes in the cardiac matrix appear to underlie the 50 per cent decline in the left ventricular early diastolic filling rate between the ages of 20 and 80 years (Fig. 5(b)). However, an enhanced atrial contribution to ventricular filling (Fig. 4) prevents a reduction in end-diastolic volume. Left ventricular end-systolic volume and ejection fraction at rest are unchanged with ageing (Fig. 4). The cardiac index at seated rest does not vary with age in males (Fleg *et al.* 1995) but is achieved with a slightly lower heart rate and a slightly higher stroke volume. Resting cardiac index appears to decline with age in healthy females, but the sex difference may, in part, be an artefact of normalization of cardiac output to body surface area, as the proportion of body fat increases with age in women to a greater extent than it does in men.

Postural change and exercise

In response to an orthostatic stress, i.e. assumption of the sitting from the supine position, peripheral vascular resistance is equally maintained in individuals of all ages but the heart rate increase is blunted in older compared with younger individuals. However, the expected left ventricular end-diastolic volume reduction is less in older than in younger individuals, and left ventricular stroke volume is better preserved (Rodefeffer *et al.* 1986).

Aerobic capacity during cycle exercise, measured as the maximum work rate or oxygen consumption (Fig. 7), declines with advancing age in healthy sedentary BLSA men and women. Longitudinal analysis reveals that the rate of oxygen consumption (Vo_2) decline varies

among individuals and is influenced by physical activity habits. Oxygen consumption is determined by the oxygen delivery (cardiac output) to and the oxygen utilization (arterial minus venous O_2 content) of the body tissues. Figure 7 shows that, during upright cycle exercise, the approximate 50 per cent decline in oxygen consumption in healthy individuals between the ages of 20 and 80 years is attributable to approximate declines of 30 per cent in cardiac output and 20 per cent in oxygen utilization. The age-associated decline in oxygen utilization can, in part, be attributed to a decrease in skeletal muscle mass with age (Fleg and Lakatta 1988). Despite a decline in muscle mass, body mass may remain constant owing to an increase in body fat, not only subcutaneously, but also intraperitoneally and intramuscularly.

The age-associated decrease in cardiac output during upright cycle exercise at exhaustion (Fig. 7) is due entirely to a reduction in heart rate(Fig. 8(a)), as the stroke volume does not decline with age in either men or women (Fig. 8(b)). However, the manner in which stroke volume is achieved during exercise varies dramatically with ageing. Age-associated changes occur in the rate and extent of cardiac filling in the diastolic interval. While the rate at which the left ventricle fills with blood increases during exercise in individuals of all ages, the early ventricular filling remains blunted in older individuals (Fig. 5(b)). Despite this, the end-diastolic filling volume, i.e. the effective preload determinant of myocardial function and stroke volume, is larger in older than in younger individuals (Fig. 8(c). Thus a 'stiff heart' that prohibits sufficient filling between beats during exercise does not characterize ageing in healthy individuals.

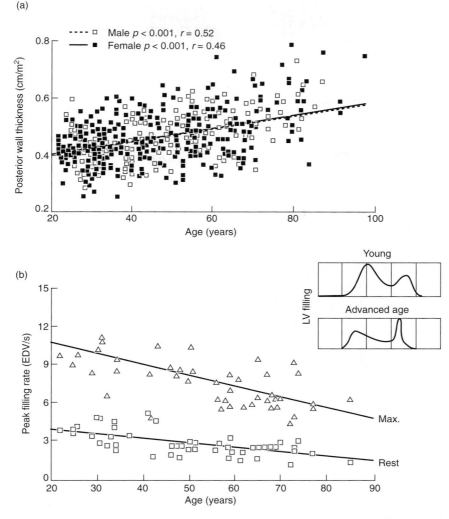

Fig. 5 (a) The left ventricular posterior wall thickness, measured by M-mode echocardiography, increases with age in healthy BLSA men and women. (Reproduced with permission from Gerstenblith *et al.* (1977).) (b) The peak filling rate of the left ventricle (LV) declines at rest and during upright cycle exercise at exhaustion in healthy older BLSA individuals (EDV, end-diastolic volume). (Reproduced with permission from Schulman *et al.* (1992).)

Maintenance of stroke volume by ventricular dilation at end-diastole is through utilization of the Frank–Starling mechanism (Plotnick *et al.* 1986). Figure 9 depicts the utilization of this mechanism in younger and older individuals at rest and over a wide range of exercise work loads. The increase in end-diastolic volume in healthy older individuals during vigorous exercise is due in part to a longer diastolic interval (heart rate is reduced) (Fig. 8(a)) and to an increase in the amount of blood remaining in the heart at end-systole (Fig. 8(d)). The inability of the older heart to empty to the same extent as the younger heart during exercise is one of the most prominent characteristics of cardiac ageing in health (Fig. 8(d)) and leads to a reduction in the maximum ejection fraction (Fig. 8(e)). This relative inability of the aged heart to empty completely during each cardiac cycle during exercise is, in part, attributable to an increased vascular afterload, a reduction of intrinsic myocardial contractility, and a reduction in the β-adrenergic modulation of both myocardial contractility and afterload (Lakatta 1993*b*). The main effects of β-adrenergic modulation of cardiovascular function during

exercise are to enable the heart to beat rapidly and to maintain a small ventricular cavity size in response to enhanced return of venous blood due to the exercise-associated muscular action and reduced peripheral vascular resistance. A small ventricular cavity size is maintained by both an increased heart rate and an augmentation of myocardial contractile strength. Healthy older individuals fail to increase heart rate to the same extent as younger individuals. The lower maximum heart rate and the cardiac dilation at end-diastole and end-systole in older individuals (Fig. 8) are manifestations of deficient β-adrenergic modulation with ageing. This age-associated haemodynamic profile during stress occurs in the presence of enhanced cardiac (Esler *et al.* 1995) as well as whole-body (Fleg *et al.* 1985) noradrenaline spill-over into plasma. Thus the age-associated deficit in the effectiveness of cardiac β-adrenergic control in healthy humans is largely postsynaptic in nature, and probably not the result of lesser neural activation. Thus, in the basal state, infusions of β-adrenergic agonists elicit smaller increases in heart rate, left ventricular ejection fraction, cardiac output, isolated cardiac muscle function,

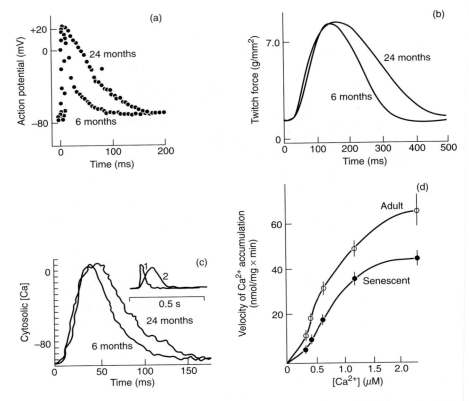

Fig. 6 Representative data depicting differences in various aspects of excitation–contraction coupling mechanisms measured between adult (6 and 9 months) and senescent (24–26 months) rat hearts. (a) Transmembrane action potential. (Reproduced with permission from Wei *et al.* (1984).) (b) Isometric contraction. (Reproduced with permission from Wei *et al.* (1984).) (c) Cytosolic calcium transient, measured by a change in the luminescence of aequorin which has been injected into several cells comprising the muscle preparation. (Reproduced with permission from Orchard and Lakatta (1985).) (d) Sarcoplasmic reticulum Ca^{2+} uptake rate. (Reproduced with permission from Froehlich *et al.* (1978).)

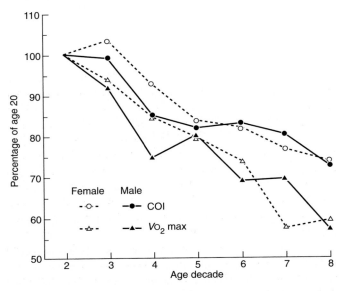

Fig. 7 Oxygen consumption and cardiac output (COl) in healthy sedentary BLSA participants during seated upright exercise on a bicycle ergometer. (Reproduced with permission from Fleg *et al.* (1997).)

and reduced vasodilatory responses in older than in younger sedentary men (Lakatta 1993*a*). In general, the magnitude of the age-associated reduction of cardiac and vascular responses to β-adrenergic stimulation ranges from 30 to 50 per cent of that observed in younger sedentary control subjects (Yin *et al.* 1978; van Brummelen *et al.* 1981; Pan *et al.* 1986; White *et al.* 1994; Davies *et al.* 1996). β-Adrenergic blockade during exercise abolishes the age-associated reductions in exercise heart rate and early diastolic filling rate (Fig. 10), and the age-associated increase in end-diastolic volume (Fig. 9), and thus makes the cardiovascular response of younger individuals to exercise appear similar to that of older subjects.

Intrinsic myocardial contractility is difficult to assess *in vivo* owing to its interactions with preload, afterload, and autonomic modulation. However, best estimates or indices of contractility have been developed. One method of estimating contractility is to determine the extent to which the left ventricle dilates in response to a pressure load in the presence of β-adrenergic blockade. Figure 11(a) shows that the end-diastolic dimension increases in older individuals when confronted with 30-mmHg pressor stress in the presence of β-blockade (with propranolol), but does not change in younger subjects (Yin *et al.* 1978). This decrease in the intrinsic contractility of the heart in otherwise healthy older sedentary subjects becomes evident only after blockade of the sympathetic nervous system (Yin *et al.* 1978). Owing to its deficiency in intrinsic contractility, the heart of

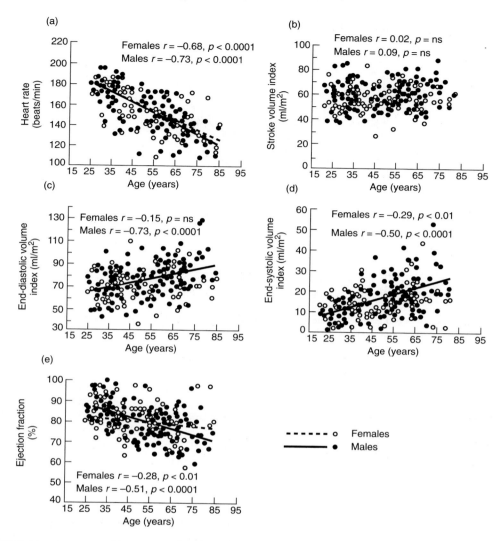

Fig. 8 Least-squares linear regression on age of heart rate and cardiac volumes in healthy sedentary BLSA participants. (Reproduced with permission from Fleg *et al.* (1995).)

the older individual dilates more during a pressor stress, thus utilizing the Frank–Starling mechanism to preserve or augment stroke volume, as is the case during postural changes from the supine position and during upright dynamic exercise (Fig. 9). An additional index of intrinsic myocardial contractility, derived from the ratio of systolic arterial pressure to left ventricular end systolic volume, while not reduced with age at rest, increases less in older than in younger individuals during exercise (Fig. 11(b)).

Impact of lifestyle on age-associated changes in cardiovascular structure and function

There is some evidence to indicate that diet and exercise habits affect both the heart and blood vessels of older individuals. Some clues come from cross-cultural studies. Figure 12(a) shows the mean aortic pressure and pulse-wave velocity, an index of aortic stiffness, in two populations, citizens of Beijing in Northern China and of Guanzhou

Province in Southern China (Avolio *et al.* 1983). The former population is more sedentary than the latter and consumes twice the dietary NaCl. Many epidemiologists believe that a difference in dietary NaCl accounts for at least some of the differences in blood-pressure changes with ageing observed in different populations (Fig. 12(b)). However, this is a very difficult hypothesis to test experimentally over the long term. Still, chronic consumption of the 'usual' salt diet might contribute to the stiffening of the arteries and increase in systolic pressure with ageing that is observed in otherwise healthy members of industrialized societies. In this regard, it has been demonstrated that the salt sensitivity of arterial pressure regulation, measured by first administering a salt-and-water load and then depleting salt and water, increases with ageing in both patients with hypertension and normotensive individuals (Weinberger and Finberg 1991; Overlack *et al.* 1995). However, in an Australian study population in which dietary salt was reduced, the expected age-associated increase in the index of aortic stiffening was not observed (Avolio *et al.* 1986).

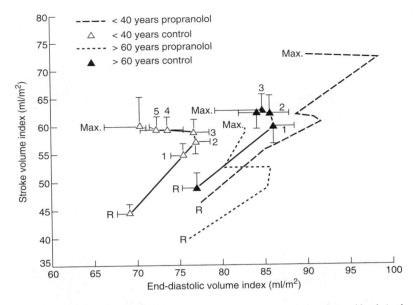

Fig. 9 Stroke volume index as a function of end-diastolic volume index at rest (R) and during graded cycle workloads in the upright seated position in healthy BLSA men in the presence and absence of β-adrenergic blockade. (Data from Fleg *et al.* (1994, 1995).)

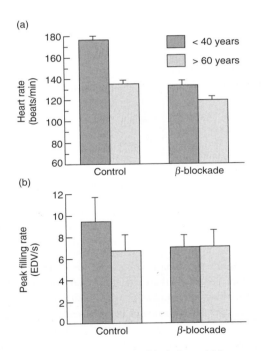

Fig. 10 The effect of acute β-adrenergic blockade on (a) heart rate and (b) peak diastolic filling rate during exhaustive upright cycle exercise in healthy BLSA men. (Reproduced with permission from Fleg *et al.* (1994).)

Physical conditioning also appears to lessen the vascular stiffening associated with ageing. Figure 13(a) indicates that the augmentation of the late systolic peak in arterial pressure, an index of arterial stiffness, is inversely related to aerobic capacity in sedentary individuals (Vaitkevicius *et al.* 1993). Figure 13(b) shows that this arterial stiffness index increases only about half as much in senior endurance-trained

athletes as it does in sedentary controls. Therefore, like chronic NaCl intake, regular exercise may exert a modulatory effect on stiffening of the large arteries with ageing.

Physical conditioning can improve the aerobic capacity of older individuals. The improvement is attributable to increases in both cardiac output and oxygen utilization (Lakatta 1993b) (Fig. 14(a)). Exercise conditioning improvements in cardiac output are derived only from increases in stroke volume, as the age-associated reduction in the maximum heart rate persists following conditioning, even in well-trained athletes (Fig. 14(a)). The improvement in stroke volume derived from conditioning is due largely to an increase in the ability to eject blood from the heart, as reflected in a reduction of end-systolic volume (Fig. 14(b)) and increased ejection fraction. The improvement in ejection of blood from the heart derived from physical conditioning in older individuals appears to be attributable to an augmentation in intrinsic myocardial contractility and a re-duction in vascular afterload, attributable in part at least to a reduction in aortic stiffness, as noted above. The impaired communication between the brain and heart with ageing, i.e. diminished effects of β-adrenergic stimulation on the heart and blood vessels, appears not to change with exercise conditioning (Stratton *et al.* 1992).

Summary

In summary, there is an age-associated increase in vascular afterload on the heart which is due to arterial stiffening and is reflected in the age-associated modest increase in systolic blood pressure. In healthy individuals, these vascular changes are compensated for, in large part, by the age-associated changes in the architecture and contractile properties of the heart which, despite reductions in aortic distensibility, allow the aged heart to pump a normal quantity of blood. In the seated upright position at rest, the heart rate decreases with ageing and ventricular preload (diastolic volume) increases modestly, although the early rapid filling rate is slowed. The fraction of end-diastolic volume

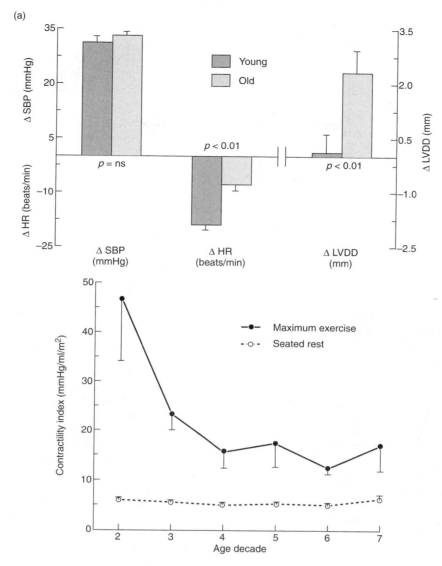

Fig. 11 (a) Heart rate and ventricular dimension measured by M-mode echocardiography in response to a pressor stress in healthy BLSA men in the presence of β-adrenergic blockade. (Reproduced with permission from Yin *et al.* (1978).) (b) Left ventricular contractility at rest and during upright exercise in BLSA men. (Reproduced with permission from Fleg *et al.* (1995).)

ejected with each beat (ejection fraction) does not decline with age. Major age-associated alterations in the cardiovascular response to exercise are evident: There is a striking age-associated decrease in the maximum heart rate; however, the maximum stroke volume is not reduced in older individuals. The main mechanism used to maintain stroke volume in older individuals is the Frank–Starling mechanism. The extent to which the end-systolic volume shrinks and the ejection fraction increases at peak exercise is reduced with ageing, and these deficits probably result from deficient intrinsic myocardial performance to an augmented afterload, both due in part to a deficiency in β-adrenergic stimulation to enhance myocardial contractility or reduce the pulsatile components of vascular afterload. A decrease in the maximum capacity for physical work with ageing is due to both diminished cardiac (heart rate) and peripheral factors. Alterations in cardiac function that exceed the identified limits for ageing changes

for healthy elderly individuals are most likely to be manifestations of the interaction between excessive physical deconditioning and cardiovascular disease, which are, unfortunately, so prevalent within economically developed populations.

It is most remarkable that high levels of cardiac output can be maintained at rest and during exercise in the community-dwelling sedentary aged individual who is highly motivated. Thus age-associated changes in cardiovascular structure and function, as noted above, do not *per se* cause clinical cardiovascular disease in older individuals. However, specific cardiovascular diseases (atherosclerosis and hypertension) that lead to heart failure and stroke occur in advanced age, and their clinical manifestations become altered (lower threshold for clinical symptoms, greater severity, and poorer prognosis) due to interactions (Fig. 1) between age-associated changes that occur in health and the specific pathophysiological mechanisms

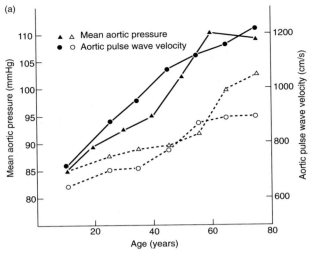

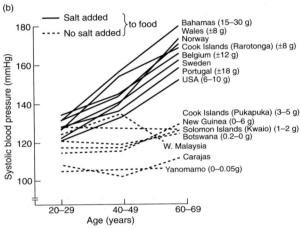

Fig. 12 (a) Mean arterial pressure and pulse-wave velocity in two Chinese populations (solid symbols, urban Beijing; open symbols, rural Guanzhou). (Reproduced with permission from Avolio *et al.* (1983).) (b) Systolic arterial pressure as a function of age and NaCl added to food in several cultures. (Reproduced with permission from MacGregor (1985).)

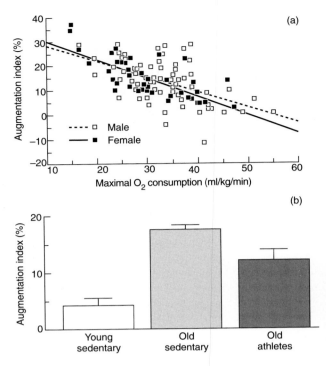

Fig. 13 (a) Carotid augmentation index, a measure of the magnitude of early reflections of the pulse wave which itself is an index of aortic stiffness, is inversely related to V_{O_2}max, an index of aerobic fitness, in healthy sedentary BLSA participants aged between 20 and 80. This inverse relationship between V_{O_2}max and stiffness is significant over and above the effect of age on both parameters. (b) The increase in carotid augmentation index in highly trained older men (60–85 years) is only about half of that expected on the basis of age. Reproduced with permission from Vaitkevicius *et al.* (1993).)

that underlie a given disease. In this regard, cardiovascular changes that occur during ageing in health ought not to be considered to reflect a 'normal process'; rather, these specific age-associated changes must be construed as specific 'risk factors' for the diseases and ought to become targets of interventions designed to prevent the epidemic of cardiovascular disease in later life. Such a strategy would advocate preventive treatment for what is now considered to be 'normal cardiovascular ageing'. Lifestyle changes have already been shown to be effective in the regard; improvements in specific aspects of cardiac function (enhanced ejection capability) and vascular function (reduced arterial stiffness) are affected by regular vigorous exercise.

Cardiovascular disease in elderly individuals

More successful recognition and treatment of cardiovascular risk factors and diseases continue to decrease age-adjusted cardiovascular

mortality (Gillum 1993) and to increase the number and proportion of the cardiac patient population who are considered 'elderly'. In the United States, cardiovascular disease is the leading cause of mortality, accounting for over 40 per cent of deaths in those aged 65 years and above. Over 80 per cent of all cardiovascular deaths occur in the same age group (National Center for Health Statistics 1991). These data indicate that age is the major risk factor for cardiovascular disease. The physiological changes described above alter the substrate upon which specific pathological conditions are imposed and therefore the diagnosis and management of heart disease, as well as its response to therapy.

Ischaemic heart disease

The chief cause of death in later years, as well as in middle age, is atherosclerosis. The diagnosis of ischaemic heart disease in older persons is often obscured by age-associated changes in physical activity status, associated medical conditions, and the increased likelihood of atypical presentations. These probably result in the finding that the prevalence of classic symptomatic disease is less than 50 per cent of the true prevalence of disease as determined by autopsy studies (Tejada *et al.* 1968). These studies indicate that there is a dramatic age-associated increase in the prevalence of significant disease, reaching as high as 50 to 60 per cent in men at the age of 60 years (Fig. 15)

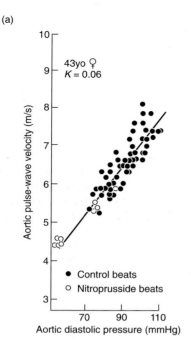

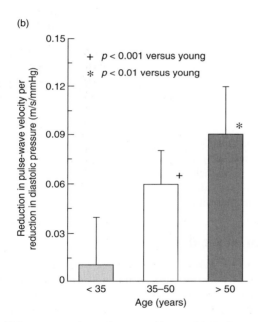

Fig. 19 (a) Improvement in maximum aerobic capacity, cardiac output, and oxygen utilization with physical conditioning. (Reproduced with permission from Carroll *et al.* (1991).) (b) The change in aortic pulse-wave velocity per unit decrease in diastolic pressure in three age groups of patients with dilated cardiomyopathy. The change in those over 50 years of age is significantly greater than in those under 35.

walls, and a low ejection fraction. Those with a predominant diastolic abnormality will have a normal cavity size, often thick walls, and a normal ejection fraction, but delayed indices of diastolic filling. For the patient presenting with worsening symptoms, a search for precipitating factors including medication or dietary non-compliance and a superimposed illness should be pursued.

Treatment of the older patient with heart failure can begin with the underlying aetiology. Thus repeated ischaemic and hypertensive insults should be avoided to the extent possible with appropriate therapy. In the selection of antihypertensive and anti-ischaemic agents in patients with predominant diastolic dysfunction, those which decrease cell calcium loading, enhance left ventricular relaxation, prolong diastolic filling time, reduce left ventricular mass, and decrease deposition of interstitial connective tissue may be particularly useful. In those with associated ischaemic disease, anti-ischaemic interventions may improve function, as well as ischaemic symptoms in patients who have 'hibernating' myocardium. Otherwise, diuretics are useful, particularly in patients with stiff central vascular and ventricular properties, since significant reductions in pressure, and therefore congestive symptoms, can be achieved with modest reductions in intravascular volume. However, in patients with diastolic dysfunction, excessive preload reduction may compromise diastolic filling in those who need high pressures to fill the stiff ventricle. Digitalis should be avoided in patients with predominant diastolic dysfunction unless it is used for its rate-slowing properties in patients with supraventricular arrhythmias. In those with predominant systolic dysfunction, digitalis may improve signs and symptoms of heart failure with a neutral effect on overall survival (Digitalis Group 1997). The steady state plasma concentration of digoxin for any given dosage is increased in many older patients because of the reduced volume of distribution and decline in creatinine clearance. Therefore it is recommended that, in general, the maintenance dose should be reduced to 0.125 mg daily or less in older patients.

Angiotensin-converting enzyme inhibitors are a cornerstone of therapy in patients with symptomatic and asymptomatic systolic dysfunction in whom there is no contraindication to their use, and improve survival and symptoms as well as decrease hospital admission rates (SOLVD Investigators 1991, 1992). Enalapril reduced fatality by 27 per cent in a group of individuals with severe congestive heart failure whose mean age was 70 years (Consensus Trial Study Group 1987). A recent study demonstrated that the benefits of losartan, an angiotensin II type I receptor antagonist, are equal, or superior, to those of captopril in the treatment of elderly individuals with symptomatic heart failure and left ventricular systolic dysfunction (Pitt *et al.* 1997). In this trial of 722 patients aged 65 years or more, all-cause mortality was 4.8 per cent in the losartan group versus 8.7 per cent in those treated with captopril. There was also a significant decrease in those admitted to the hospital for any reason and in those who discontinued therapy due to adverse events.

It is possible to identify older patients who are at increased risk of early hospital admission for congestive heart failure. In such a population, Rich *et al.* (1995) demonstrated that patient education, close monitoring, and early intervention can reduce heart failure readmissions and medical costs, and improve quality of life. Although all patients with congestive heart failure benefit by close follow-up and by a careful explanation of the disease, of symptoms to expect with worsening, and of the importance of dietary and medical compliance, the use of these strategies may be particularly useful for the older population and their caregivers.

particularly relevant in the older population because up to 40 per cent of those who present with failure will have normal systolic function (Wong *et al.* 1989). The two cannot be distinguished on the basis of history, physical examination, or chest radiograph, but can be differentiated by echocardiographic study. The patient with a predominant systolic problem will often have a dilated cavity, thin

Arrhythmias (see also Chapter 9.6)

Age-associated histological changes occur throughout most of the cardiac impulse and conduction system. Most hearts from elderly individuals show a decrease in the number of sinus node pacemaker cells. There are also several age-associated changes in the bundle of His. These include a loss of muscle cells, an increase in fibrous and adipose tissue, and amyloid infiltration. There is also a decrease in the number of cells in the fascicle connecting the main bundle of His to the left bundle. Idiopathic bundle-branch fibrosis is the most common cause of chronic atrioventricular block in patients over 65 years of age. Although sinus bradycardia is frequently present in older persons, the heart rate increases in response to exercise or pharmacological interventions. However, the maximum heart rate achieved decreases with age. The prevalence of ectopic activity increases with age in both non-selected populations and those free from cardiovascular disease. In 98 elderly disease-free participants of the BLSA, 24-h electrocardiographic recordings disclosed more than 100 supraventricular and ventricular premature beats in 25 per cent and 17 per cent respectively of the sample during the monitoring period (Fleg and Kennedy 1982). Thirty-five per cent had multiform ventricular ectopic beats. The prevalence of ventricular tachycardia was 4 per cent, and that of couplets was an additional 11 per cent. In an unselected population (Frishman *et al.* 1996), 5.7 per cent of those aged between 75 and 85 years of age had more than 100 premature ventricular contractions per hour and 5 per cent had ventricular tachycardia. In this population, transient atrioventricular block and sinus bradycardia were independent predictors of stroke, and non-sustained ventricular tachycardia was a predictor of death. The incidence of exercise-induced ventricular ectopy also increases with age in otherwise healthy individuals, although short-term follow-up has not shown any subsequent increase in cardiac events.

Prolongation of the PR interval to 220 or 240 ms frequently occurs with advanced age and is not considered pathological. A leftward shift in the QRS axis also occurs with ageing in Westernized populations and may be related to fibrotic changes in the anterior superior division of the left bundle or in the myocardium, mild left ventricular hypertrophy, or a change in the spatial orientation of the heart in the chest. However, the leftward axis shift was not present in a population with a low prevalence of hypertension and coronary disease (Grimley Evans *et al.* 1982).

Atrial fibrillation is common in older persons (see also Chapter 9.6). In the Cardiovascular Health Study population, atrial fibrillation was present in 4.8 per cent of women and 6.2 per cent of men over 65 years of age (Furberg *et al.* 1994). Its diagnosis does not differ markedly in the older population, although it should be remembered that significant carotid stenoses and sensitivity to carotid sinus massage increase with age. Elderly individuals may also be more prone to atrioventricular block with adenosine (Cerqueira *et al.* 1994). Elderly patients with atrial fibrillation should be evaluated for hyperthyroidism because cardiac signs and symptoms may be the presenting and major manifestations of this disorder (see Chapter 7.1) In the Framingham population, low thyrotrophin levels predicted the development of atrial fibrillation in those over 60 years of age (Sawin *et al.* 1994).

Atrial fibrillation is associated with an increased risk of embolic stroke, and this is particularly true in the older population. In the Framingham Study, the risk of stroke increased from 7.3 per cent for those in the seventh decade to 30.8 per cent for those in the ninth decade, after adjustment for blood pressure (Wolf *et al.* 1987). The risk of stroke can be significantly decreased by anticoagulation with warfarin designed to achieve an INR of 2.0 to 3.0 (Atrial Fibrillation Investigators 1994; European Atrial Fibrillation Trial Study Group 1995). In those who cannot take warfarin, aspirin should be used as meta-analysis of the AFASK and SPAF studies demonstrates a decreased risk of stroke and the combined outcomes of stroke, systemic embolism, and death. The benefit of aspirin was particularly noted in those with a history of hypertension. However, the benefits of aspirin therapy are less significant and consistent than those of warfarin (Atrial Fibrillation Investigators 1994).

In addition to stroke prevention, another aim of therapy is rate control in symptomatic patients. In patients without systolic dysfunction, rate control with verapamil, diltiazem, and β-blockers should be considered, whereas in those with systolic dysfunction digitalis can be used (Prystowski *et al.* 1996). In patients who are intolerant of medical therapy, or in whom that therapy is ineffective, radiofrequency catheter ablation of the atrioventricular node with pacemaker insertion improves symptoms (Kay *et al.* 1988). Radio frequency catheter ablation may also be used to prevent other supraventricular tachycardias in older patients (Epstein *et al.* 1994). The question of whether restoration of sinus rhythm should also be considered an aim of therapy in patients with atrial fibrillation is currently being evaluated in a randomized trial (Planning and Steering Committees of the AFFIRM Study 1997).

The experience with pacemaker therapy in elderly patients is good, and the long-term survival of elderly patients with pacemakers is identical with that of an age-matched population without pacemakers (Siddons 1974). The models which programme atrial and ventricular contractions may be particularly useful in this age group as diastolic filling and cardiac output may be more dependent on a properly timed atrial systole in an older and stiffer left ventricle. In an observational study in the Medicare population, dual-chamber, as compared with single-chamber, pacemaker selection was associated with improved 1- and 2-year survival after controlling for potentially confounding patient and hospital characteristics (Lamas *et al.* 1995).

Valvular heart disease

As age increases, there is a shift in the underlying condition responsible for mitral valve abnormalities from mitral stenosis due to rheumatic disease primarily to mitral insufficiency related to ischaemic disease, but also to degenerative changes in the mitral valve apparatus. The physical signs of mitral stenosis are sometimes obscured in those with mitral disease of rheumatic origin, and at times mitral stenosis is a surprise diagnosis in the older woman with chronic 'pulmonary' disease. There are no unusual findings on auscultation but, as in younger patients, the diastolic rumble and accentuated S1 may be less intense when cardiac output is diminished. The systolic murmur of mitral regurgitation may also be present but assigned less significance than a similar murmur found in a younger individual because of the increased prevalence of other systolic murmurs in older patients. The most important determinants of prognosis are the presence of failure and the atrial rhythm. Perhaps because of the stiffer left ventricle, which increases dependence on atrial systole, the development of atrial fibrillation is an important unfavourable prognostic sign. Calcification of the mitral annulus, also usually asymptomatic, is most frequently diagnosed by the inverted C shape of calcium deposition present on the chest radiograph, or by heavy calcification in the mitral area on echocardiography. The usual murmur is related to mitral insufficiency, but stenosis may also occur. Complications include endocarditis and extension of the calcification into the bundle of His and peripheral bundle branches, resulting in conduction disturbances.

Significant aortic stenosis is not infrequent in older persons and the disease is often rapidly progressive (Iivanainen *et al.* 1996). The most important signs are the extension of the murmur into late systole, a low pulse pressure, and a slowly rising carotid pulse. However, these may not be present, even in the setting of severe stenosis, because of age-associated increased stiffness of the central arteries. Echocardiographic and electrocardiographic evidence of left ventricular hypertrophy is helpful. Although echocardiographically determined thickness of the left ventricular wall increases with age, the change is minimal when compared with pathological states. Heavy calcification of the aortic valve on the echocardiogram also suggests significant obstruction. The main differentials are idiopathic hypertrophic subaortic stenosis, which can be diagnosed with echocardiography, and valvular sclerosis, which can be distinguished by the cardiac examination. Doppler echocardiography may also be particularly useful in establishing the severity of valvular stenosis.

Medical treatment of valvular disease in elderly patients is similar to that in younger patients, although the comments above about the use of digitalis and diuretics should be kept in mind. The fatality among those aged 65 years or more undergoing aortic and mitral valve replacement is generally low (Elayda *et al.* 1993; Logeais *et al.* 1994; Davis *et al.* 1996). Percutaneous balloon valvuloplasty for mitral stenosis may compare favourably with surgical replacement in the appropriate patient because it eliminates the need for thoracotomy and usually results in a shorter hospital stay (Reyes *et al.* 1994). Because of poor long-term results with aortic valvuloplasty (Litvack *et al.* 1988; Eltchaninoff *et al.* 1995), this should be considered as only palliative in patients with definite contraindications to surgery, which is the preferred treatment.

Hypertension (see also Chapter 9.5)

Hypertension is the most important reversible risk factor for myocardial infarction, congestive heart failure, stroke, and overall cardiovascular mortality in older persons. It is also known that treatment of hypertension decreases the risk of many of these outcomes in this age group (Insua *et al.* 1994). Therefore diagnosis, evaluation, and appropriate therapy are important considerations in the medical care of older individuals (Bennet 1994).

Diagnosis

A careful definition of hypertension has assumed more importance with the realization that treatment of even mild elevations in diastolic pressure, i.e. in the range of 90 to 104 mmHg, results in significant improvements in cardiovascular outcomes. The efficacy of therapy for isolated systolic hypertension has now been established (SHEP Cooperative Research Group 1991). The Joint National Committee on the Detection, Evaluation, and Therapy of Hypertension recommends that treatment be considered in individuals over 60 years of age who have a systolic pressure of more than 160 mmHg in the presence of a diastolic pressure of less than 90 mmHg. Two or more readings are required and should be obtained with the patient's arm at heart level and using a cuff that has a circumference two-thirds that of the patient's arm.

The phenomenon of 'white-coat' hypertension, i.e. hypertension only in a medical setting, is more common in the younger age group, but it might be useful to obtain readings either at home or at work to confirm the diagnosis if no evidence of target organ damage is present. The prevalence of 'pseudohypertension' may be more common in older persons. In this condition, the blood pressure reading is falsely elevated due to incompressibility of the brachial artery. Palpability of the brachial or radial artery when the cuff is inflated above the systolic pressure suggests this condition. Certainty requires measurement of intra-arterial pressure. It is also important to measure pressures when the individual is standing before beginning or increasing therapy because an orthostatic fall in pressure is more common in this age group. If the pressure is normal when the patient is upright, further therapy may result in compromise of cerebral flow. Postprandial falls in blood pressure should also be considered when titrating therapy.

Evaluation

Evaluation of the older individual should focus on three areas: the presence or absence of target organ damage, any reversible factors, and other risk factors for atherosclerosis. Renal impairment and left ventricular hypertrophy indicate the need for vigorous therapy and may also affect the choice of therapy. The presence of ischaemic heart disease or other known risk factors also makes careful control of blood pressure more important and influences the therapeutic agent chosen. Reversible causes include hyperthyroidism, which commonly presents in older patients with cardiovascular manifestations, and stenosis of the renal artery due to atherosclerosis. Severe diastolic elevations, the presence of a renal bruit, associated renal dysfunction, and poor response to medical therapy suggest this diagnosis (Derkx and Schalekamp 1994).

Treatment

Non-pharmacological measures can be used to begin treatment in patients with isolated systolic and mild diastolic hypertension and as an adjunct to pharmacological agents in patients with moderate elevations of blood pressure. These include salt restriction, decreasing alcohol intake, and aerobic exercise. Weight reduction lowers pressure as well as left ventricular mass in young hypertensives, and may do so in older patients as well. Even if these measures are not entirely successful in controlling pressure, they decrease the amount of medication that the patient requires and therefore the expense, inconvenience, and side-effects of the therapy. If pharmacological therapy is begun, it is important to use low doses and to increase the dosage slowly. Older individuals may be prone to the hypotensive effects of these agents because of pre-existing decreased plasma volume, diminished responsiveness of baroreceptor, incompetent venous valves, and alterations in the autoregulation of cerebral blood flow.

The choice of which agent to use should be based on several factors (see also Chapter 9.5). One is the pathophysiology, which in older individuals is more likely to be decreased central vascular compliance and increased systemic vascular resistance. Frayed and decreased elastin, increased collagen, and altered vascular response to neurohormonal stimuli may all contribute to the high incidence of isolated systolic hypertension in this population. Therapy directed at slowing or reversing these vascular pathologies may be particularly beneficial in the older population.. Another consideration is the increasing likelihood of coexisting disease. In the presence of ischaemic heart disease, for example, it is often useful to choose an anti-hypertensive drug which also has anti-ischaemic properties. If patients have congestive heart failure, an angiotensin-converting enzyme inhibitor may favourably influence prognosis. Other conditions, such as pulmonary disease or gout, which are more common in older persons may render them more prone to suffer adverse effects of some antihypertensives. Left ventricular hypertrophy increases the risk for the development of coronary disease in older individuals independent of the risk associated with elevation of blood pressure *per se* (Levy *et al.* 1989). Therefore the choice of an antihypertensive that also has antihypertrophic properties should be considered when left ventricular hypertrophy is present (Schulman *et al.* 1990). Further considerations include the potential for adverse effects on lipid and glucose metabolism, and the cost and convenience of the therapy. Considerations of cost include not only that of the medication itself but also the number of medical visits required and the expense of tests used to monitor for efficacy and any adverse effects. (See also Chapter 9.5.)

References

Aguirre, P.V., McMahon, R.P., Mueller, H., *et al.* (1994). Impact of age on clinical outcome and postlytic management strategies in patients treated with intravenous thrombolytic therapy. Results from the TIMI II study. *Circulation*, 328, 673–9.

Anthopoulos, L.P., Bonou, M.S., Kardars, F.G., *et al.* (1996). Stress echocardiography in elderly patients with coronary artery disease. Applicability, safety and prognostic value of dobutamine and adenosine echocardiography in elderly patients. *Journal of the American College of Cardiology*, 28, 52–9.

Atrial Fibrillation Investigators (1994). Risk factors for stroke and efficacy of antithrombotic therapy in atrial fibrillation. Analysis of pooled data from five randomized controlled trials. *Archives of Internal Medicine*, 154, 1449–57.

Avolio, A.P., Chen, S.G., and Wang, R.P. (1983). Effects of ageing on changing arterial compliance and left ventricular load in a northern Chinese urban community. *Circulation*, 68, 50–8.

Avolio, A.P., Clyde, K.M., and Beard, T.C. (1986). Improved arterial distensibility in normotensive subjects on a low salt diet. *Arteriosclerosis*, 6, 166–9.

Bateman, T.M. and O'Keefe, J.H. (1992). Pharmacological (stress) perfusion scintigraphy: methods, advantages, and applications. *American Journal of Cardiac Imaging*, 6, 3–15.

Baudhuin, T., Marwick, T., Melin, J., Wijns, W., D'Hondt, A.-M., and Detry, J.-M. (1993). Diagnosis of coronary artery disease in elderly patients: safety and efficacy of dobutamine echocardiography. *European Heart Journal*, 14, 799–803.

Bennet, N.E. (1994). Hypertension in the elderly. *Lancet*, 344, 447–9.

Beta-Blocker Heart Attack Study Group (1981). The beta-blocker heart attack trial. *Journal of the Medical Association*, 246, 3073–4.

Boutouyrie, P., Laurent, S., Benetos, A., *et al.* (1992). Opposing effects of ageing on distal and proximal large arteries in hypertensives. *Journal of Hypertension*, 10, 587–91.

Carroll, J.D., Schroff, S., Wirsh, P. Halstedd, M., and Rajfer, S.I. (1991). Arterial mechanical properties in dilated cardiomyopathy. Ageing and the response to nitroprusside. *Journal of Clinical Investigation*, 87, 1002–9.

Cerqueira, M.D., Verani, M.S., Schwaiger, M., Heo, J., Iskandrian, A.S., and the Investigators of the Multicenter Adenoscan Trial. (1994). Safety profile of adenosine stress perfusion imaging: results from the Adenoscan Multicenter Trial registry. *Journal of the American College of Cardiology*, 23, 384–9.

Ciaroni S., Delonca, J., and Righetti, A. (1993). Early exercise testing after acute myocardial infarction in the elderly: Clinical evaluation and prognostic significance. *American Heart Journal*, 126, 304–11.

Consensus Trial Study Group (1987). Effects of enalapril on mortality in severe congestive heart failure. *New England Journal of Medicine*, 316, 1429–35.

Corti, M.-C., Guralnik, J.M., Salive, M.E., *et al.* (1997). Clarifying the direct relation between total cholesterol levels and death from coronary heart disease in older persons. *Annals of Internal Medicine*, 126, 753–60.

Curtis, J.J., Walls, J.T., Boley, T.M., Schmaltz, R.A., Demmy, T.L., and Salam, N. (1994). Coronary revascularization in the elderly: determinants of operative mortality. *Annals of Thoracic Surgery*, 58, 1069–72.

Davies, C.H., Ferrara, N., and Harding, S.E. (1996). β-Adrenoceptor function changes with age of subject in myocytes from non-failing human ventricle. *Cardiovascular Research*, 31, 152–6.

Davis, E.A., Greene, P.S., Cameron, D.E., *et al.* (1996). Bioprosthetic versus mechanical prostheses for aortic valve replacement in the elderly. *Circulation*, 94 (Supplement II), II-121–5.

Derkx, F.H.M. and Schalekamp, M.A.D.H. (1994). Renal artery stenosis and hypertension. *Lancet*, 344, 237–9.

Digitalis Group (1997). The effect of digoxin on mortality and morbidity in patients with heart failure. *New England Journal of Medicine*, 336, 525–33.

Elayda, M.A., Hall, R.J., Reul, R.M., *et al.* (1993). Aortic valve replacement in patients 80 years and older: operative risks and long-term results. *Circulation* (Supplement II), 88, II-11–16.

Eltchaninoff, H., Cribier, A., Tron, C., *et al.* (1995). Balloon aortic valvuloplasty in elderly patients at high risk for surgery, or inoperable: intermediate and mid-term results. *European Heart Journal*, 16, 1079–84.

Elveback, L. and Lie, J.T. (1984). Continued high incidence of coronary artery disease at autopsy in Olmstead County, Minnesota, 1950–1979. *Circulation*, 70, 345–9.

Epstein, L.M., Chiesa, N., Wong, M.N., *et al.* (1994). Radiofrequency catheter ablation in the treatment of supraventricualr tachycardia in the elderly. *Journal of the American College of Cardiology*, 23, 1356–62.

Esler, M.D., Turner, A.G., Kaye, D.M., *et al.* (1995). Ageing effects on human sympathetic neuronal function. *American Journal of Physiology*, 268, R278–85.

European Atrial Fibrillation Trial Study Group (1995). Optimal oral anticoagulant therapy in patients with nonrheumatic atrial fibrillation and recent cerebral ischemia. *New England Journal of Medicine*, 333, 5–10.

Every, N.R., Parsons, L.S., Hlatky, M., Martin, J.S., and Weaver, W.D. (1996). A comparison of thrombolytic therapy with primary coronary angioplasty for acute myocardial infarction. *New England Journal of Medicine*, 335, 1253–60.

Fleg, J.L. and Kennedy, H.L. (1982). Cardiac arrhythmias in a healthy elderly populatio: detection by 24-h ambulatory electrocardiography. *Chest*, 81, 302–7.

Fleg, J.L. and Kennedy, H.L. (1992). Long-term prognostic significance of ambulatory electrocardiographic findings in apparently healthy subjects > 60 years of age. *American Journal of Cardiology*, 70, 748–51.

Fleg, J.L., and Lakatta, E.G. (1988). Role of muscle loss in the age-associated reduction in Vo2max. *Journal of Applied Physiology*, 65, 1147–51.

Fleg, J.L., Tzankoff, S.P., and Lakatta, E.G. (1985). Age-related augmentation of plasma catecholamines during dynamic exercise in healthy males. *Journal of Applied Physiology*, 59, 1033–9.

Fleg, J.L., Das, D.N., Wright, J., and Lakatta, E.G. (1990*a*). Age-associated changes in the components of atrioventricular conduction in apparently healthy volunteers. *Journal of Gerontology: Medical Science*, 45, M95–100.

Fleg, J.L., Gerstenblith, G., Zonderman, A.B., *et al.* (1990*b*). Prevalence and prognostic significance of exercise-induced silent myocardial ischemia detected by thallium scintigraphy and electrocardiography in asymptomatic volunteers. *Circulation*, 81, 428–36.

Fleg, J., Schulman, S.P., Gerstenblith, G., Becker, L.C., O'Connor, F.C., and Lakatta, E.G. (1993). Additive effects of age and silent myocardial ischemia on the left ventricular response to upright cycle exercise. *Journal of Applied Physiology*, 75, 499–504.

Fleg, J.L., Schulman, S., O'Connor, F., *et al.* (1994). Effects of acute β-adrenergic receptor blockade on age-associated changes in cardiovascular performance during dynamic exercise. *Circulation*, 90, 2333–41.

Fleg, J.L., O'Connor, F.C., Gerstenblith, G., *et al.* (1995). Impact of age on the cardiovascular response to dynamic upright exercise in healthy men and women. *Journal of Applied Physiology*, 78, 890–900.

Fleg, J.L., O'Connor, F.C., Becker, L.C., Gerstenblith, G., and Lakatta, E.G. (1997). Cardiac versus peripheral contributions to the age-associated decline in aerobic capacity. *Journal of the American College of Cardiology*, 29, 269A.

Folson, A.R., Kaye, S.A., Sellers, T.A., *et al.* (1993). Body fat distribution and 5-year risk of death in older women. *Journal of the American Medical Association*, 269, 483–7.

Forman, D.E., Bernal, J.L., and Wei, J.Y. (1992). Management of acute myocardial infarction in the very elderly. *American Journal of Medicine*, 93, 315–26.

Frishman, W.H., Heiman, M., Karpenos, A., *et al.* (1996). Twenty-four-hour ambulatory electorcardiography in elderly subjects: prevalence of various arrhythmias and prognostic implications (report from the Bronx Longitudinal Ageing Study). *American Heart Journal*, 132, 297–302.

Froehlich, J.P., Lakatta, E.G., Beard, E., Spurgeon, H.A., Weisfeldt, M.L., and Gerstenblith, G. (1978). Studies of sacroplasmic reticulum function and contraction duration in young and aged rat myocardium. *Journal of Molecular and Cellular Cardiology*, 10, 427–38.

Furberg, C.D., Psaty, B.M., Manolio, T.A., Gardin, J.M., Smith, V.E., and Rautaharju, P.M. (1994). Prevalence of atrial fibrillation in elderly subjects (the Cardiovascular Health Study). *American Journal of Cardiology*, 74, 236–41.

Gerstenblith, G., Frederiksen, J., Yin, F.C.P., *et al.* (1977). Echocardiographic assessment of a normal adult ageing population. *Circulation*, 56, 273–8.

Gillum, R.F. (1993). Trends in acute myocardial infarction and coronary heart disease death in the United States. *Journal of the American College of Cardiology*, 23, 1271–7.

Grimley Evans, J., Prior, I.A.M., and Tunbridge, W.M.G. (1982). Age-associated changes in the QRS axis: intrinsic or extrinsic ageing? *Gerontology*, 28, 132–7.

Grines, C.L., Browne, K.F., Marco, J., *et al.* (1993). A comparison of immediate angioplasty with thrombolytic therapy for acute myocardial infarction. *New England Journal of Medicine*, 328, 673–9.

Gurwitz, J.H., Gore, J.M., Goldberg, R.J., Rubison, M., Chandra, N., and Rogers, W.J. (1996). Recent age-related trends in the use of thrombolytic therapy in patients who have had acute myocardial infarction. *Annals of Internal Medicine*, 124, 283–91.

Heath, G.W., Hagberg, J.M., Ehsani, A.A., and Holloszy, J.O. (1981). A physiological comparison of young and older endurance athletes. *Journal of Applied Physiology*, 51, 634–40.

Ho, K.K.L., Pinsky, J.L., Kannel, W.B., and Levy, D. (1993). The epidemiology of heart failure: the Framingham Study. *Journal of the American College of Cardiology*, 22 (Supplement A), 6A–13A.

Iivanainen, A.M., Lindroos, M., Tilvis, R., Heikkila, J., and Kupari, M. (1996). Natural history of aortic valve stenosis of varying severity in the elderly. *American Journal of Cardiology*, 78, 97–101.

Insua, J.T., Sacks, H.S., Lau, T.-S., *et al.* (1994). Drug treatment of hypertension in the elderly: a meta-analysis. *Annals of Internal Medicine*, 121, 355–62.

Katz, E.S., Tanick, P.A., Rusinek, H., Ribakove, G., Spencer, F.C., and Kronzon, I. (1992). Protruding atheromas predict stroke in elderly patients undergoing cardiopulmonary bypass: a review of our experience with intraoperative transoesophageal echocardiography. *Journal of the American College of Cardiology*, 20, 70–7.

Kay, G.N., Bubien, R.S., Epstein, A.E., and Plumb, V.J. (1988). Effect of catheter ablation of the atrioventricular junction on quality of life and exercise tolerance in paroxysmal atrial fibrillation. *American Journal of Cardiology*, 62, 741–4.

Krumholz, H.M., Radford, M.J., Ellerbeck, E.F., *et al.* (1996). Aspirin for secondary prevention after acute myocardial infarction in the elderly: prescribed use and outcomes. *Annals of Internal Medicine*, 124, 292–8.

Kushi, L.H., Folson, A.R., Prineas, R.J., Mink, P.J., Wu, Y., and Bostick, R.M. (1996). Dietary antioxidant vitamins and death from coronary heart disease in postmenopausal women. *New England Journal of Medicine*, 334, 1156–62.

LaCroix, A.Z., Lang, J. Sherr, P., *et al.* (1991). Smoking and mortality among older men and women in three communities. *New England Journal of Medicine*, 324, 1619–25.

Lakatta, E.G. (1985). Health, disease, and cardiovascular ageing. In *Health in an older society* (ed. Institute of Medicine and National Research Council, Committee on an Ageing Society), pp. 73–104. National Academy Press, Washington, DC.

Lakatta, E.G. (1987). Cardiac muscle changes in senescence. *Annual Review of Physiology*, 49, 519–31.

Lakatta, E.G. (1993*a*). Deficient neuroendocrine regulation of the cardiovascular system with advancing age in healthy humans (point of view). *Circulation*, 87, 631–6.

Lakatta, E.G. (1993*b*). Cardiovascular regulatory mechanisms in advanced age. *Physiological Reviews*, 73, 413–67.

Lakatta, E.G. (1994). Ageing effects on the vasculature in health: risk factors for cardiovascular disease. *American Journal of Geriatric Cardiology*, 3, 11–17, 50.

Lam, J.Y.T., Chaitman, B.R., Glaenzer, M., *et al.* (1988). Safety and diagnostic accuracy of dipyridamole-thallium imaging in the elderly. *Journal of the American College of Cardiology*, 11, 585–9.

Lamas, G.A., Pashos, C.L., Norman, S.-L. T., and McNeil, B. (1995). Permanent pacemaker selection and subsequent survival in elderly Medicare pacemaker recipients. *Circulation*, 91, 1063–9.

Lee, K.L., Woodlief, L.H., Topol, E.J., *et al.* (1995). Predictors of 30-day mortality in the era of reperfusion for acute myocardial infarction. Results from an international trial of 41,021 patients. *Circulation*, 91, 1659–68.

Levy, D., Garrison, R.J., Savage, D.D., Kannel, W.B., and Castelli, W.P. (1989). Left ventricular mass and incidence of coronary heart disease in an elderly cohort. *Annals of Internal Medicine*, 110, 101–7.

Lipsitz, L.A., Connelly, C.M., Kelley-Gagnon, M., Kiely, D.K., Abernethy, D., and Waksmonski, C. (1996). Cardiovascular adaptation to orthostatic stress during vasodilator therapy. *Clinical Pharmacology and Therapeutics*, 60, 461–71.

Litvack, F., Jakubowski, A.T., Buchbinder, N.A., and Eigler, N. (1988). Lack of sustained clinical improvement in an elderly population after percutaneous aortic valvuloplasty. *American Journal of Cardiology*, 62, 270–5.

MacGregor, G.A. (1985). Sodium is more important than calcium in essential hypertension. *Hypertension*, 7, 628–37.

Maggioni, A.P., Maseri, A., Fresco, C., *et al.* (1993). Age-related increase in mortality among patients with first myocardial infarctions treated with thrombolysis. *New England Journal of Medicine*, 329, 1442–8.

Markus, R.A., Mack, W.J., Azen, S.P., and Hodis, H.N. (1997). Influence of lifestyle modification on atherosclerotic progression determined by ultrasonographic change in the common carotid intima–media thickness. *American Journal of Clinical Nutrition*, 65, 1000–4.

Montamat, S.C., Cusack, B.J., and Vestal, R.E. (1989). Management of drug therapy in the elderly. *New England Journal of Medicine*, 321, 303–9.

Morrison, D.A., Bies, R.D., and Sacks, J. (1997). Coronary angioplasty for elderly patients with 'high risk' unstable angina: short-term outcomes and long-term survival. *Journal of the American College of Cardiology*, 29, 339–44.

National Center for Health Statistics (1991). *Vital statistics of the United States, 1988*, Vol. II, *Mortality*, Part A, Tables 1-27, 1-29. National Center for Health Statistics, Rockville, MD.

O'Keefe, J.H., Sutton, M.B., McCallister, B.D., et al. (1994). Coronary angioplasty versus bypass surgery in patients > 70 years old matched for ventricular function. *Journal of the American College of Cardiology*, 24, 425–30.

Orchard, C.H. and Lakatta, E.G. (1985). Intracellular calcium transients and developed tensions in rat heart muscle: a mechanism for the negative interval–strength relationship. *Journal of General Physiology*, 86, 637–51.

Overlack, A., Ruppert, M., Kolloch, R., Kraft, K., and Stumpe, K.O. (1995). Age is a major determinant of the divergent blood pressure responses to varying salt intake in essential hypertension. *American Journal of Hypertension*, 8, 829–36.

Pan, H.Y., Hoffman, B.B., Pershe, R.A., et al. (1986). Decline in beta adrenergic receptor-mediated vascular relaxation with ageing in man. *Journal of Pharmacology and Experimental Therapeutics*, 239, 802–7.

Pearson, J.D., Morrell, C.H., Brant, L.J., Landis, P.K., and Fleg, J.L. (1997). Age-associated changes in blood pressure in a longitudinal study of healthy men and women. *Journal of Gerontology*, 52, M177–83.

Peterson, E.D., Jollis, J.G., Bebechuk, J.D., et al. (1994). Changes in mortality after myocardial revascularization in the elderly: the national Medicare experience. *Annals of Internal Medicine*, 121, 919–27.

Pfeffer, M.A., Braunwald, E., Moye, L.A., et al. (1992). Effect of captopril on mortality and morbidity in patients with left ventricular dysfunction after myocardial infarction. *New England Journal of Medicine*, 327, 669–77.

Pitt, B., Segal, R., Martinez, F.A., et al. (1997). Randomized trial of losartan versus captopril in patients over 65 with heart failure (evaluation of losartan in the elderly study, ELITE). *Lancet*, 349, 747–52.

Planning and Steering Committees of the AFFIRM Study (1997). Atrial fibrillation follow-up investigation of rhythm management—the AFFIRM study design. *American Journal of Cardiology*, 79, 1198–1202.

Plotnick, G.D., Becker, L., Fisher, M.L., et al. (1986). Use of the Frank–Starling mechanism during submaximal versus maximal upright exercise. *American Journal of Physiology*, 251, H1101–5.

Prystowsky, E.N., Benson, D.W., Fuster, V., et al. (1996). Management of patients with atrial fibrillation. A statement for healthcare professionals from the Subcommittee on Electrocardiography and Electrophysiology, American Heart Association. *Circulation*, 93, 1262–77.

Reis, S.E., Gloth, S.T., Blumenthal, R.S., et al. (1994). Ethinyl estradiol acutely attenuates abnormal coronary vasomotor responses to acetylcholine in postmenopausal women. *Circulation*, 89, 52–60.

Retchin, S.M. and Brown, B. (1991). Elderly patients with congestive heart failure under prepaid care. *American Journal of Medicine*, 90, 236–42.

Reyes, V.P., Raju, B.S., Wynne, J., et al. (1994). Percutaneous balloon valvuloplasty compared with open surgical commissurotomy for mitral stenosis. *New England Journal of Medicine*, 331, 961–7.

Rich, M.W., Beckham, V., Wittenberg, C., Leven, C.L., Freedland, K.E., and Carney, R.M. (1995). A multidisciplinary intervention to prevent the readmission of elderly patients with congestive heart failure. *New England Journal of Medicine*, 333, 1190–5.

Rodefeffer R.J., Gerstenblith, G., Beard, E., et al. (1986). Postural changes

in cardiac volumes in men in relation to adult age. *Exerimental Gerontology*, 21, 367–78.

Sawin, C.T., Geller, A., Wolf, P.A., et al. (1994). Low serum thyrotropin concentrations as a risk for atrial fibrillation in older persons. *New England Journal of Medicine*, 331, 1249–52.

Scandinavian Simvastatin Survival Study Group (1994). Randomized trial of cholesterol lowering in 4444 patients with coronary heart disease: the Scandinavian Simvastatin Survival Study (4S). *Lancet*, 344, 1383–9.

Schulman, S.P., Weiss, J.L., Becker, L.C., et al. (1990). The effects of antihypertensive therapy on left ventricular mass in elderly patients. *New England Journal of Medicine*, 322, 1350–6.

Schulman, S.P., Lakatta, E.G., Fleg, J.L., Lakatta, L., Becker, L.C., and Gerstenblith, G. (1992). Age-related decline in left ventricular filling at rest and exercise. *American Journal of Physiology*, 263, H1932–8.

Schulman, S.P., Fleg, J.L., Goldberg, A.P., et al. (1996). Continuum of cardiovascular performance across a broad range of fitness levels in healthy older men. *Circulation*, 94, 359–67.

SHEP Cooperative Research Group (1991). Prevention of stroke by antihypertensive drug treatment in older persons with isolated systolic hypertension: final results of the Systolic Hypertension in the Elderly Program (SHEP). *Journal of the American Medical Association*, 265, 3255–64.

Shock, N.W., Greulich, R.C., Andres, R., et al. (1984). *Normal human ageing: the Baltimore Longitudinal Study of Aging*. NIH Publication 84-2450. US Government Printing Office, Washington, DC.

Simoons, J.L., Maggioni, A.P., Knatterud, G., et al. (1993). *Lancet*, 342, 1523–8.

SOLVD Investigators (1991). Effect of enalapril on survival in patients with reduced left ventricular ejection fractions and congestive heart failure. *New England Journal of Medicine*, 235, 293–302.

SOLVD Investigators (1992). Effect of enalapril on mortality and the development of heart failure in asymptomatic patients with reduced left ventricular ejection fraction. *New England Journal of Medicine*, 327, 685–91.

Soumerai, S.B., McLaughlin, T.J., Spiegelman, D., Hertzmark, E., Thhibault, G., and Goldman, L. (1997). Adverse outcomes of underuse of beta blockers in elderly survivors of acute myocardial infarction. *Journal of the American Medical Association*, 277, 115–21.

Stampfer, M.J., Coldtiz, G.A., Willett, S.C., et al. (1991). Postmenopausal oestrogen therapy and cardiovascular disease. Ten year follow-up from the Nurses' Health Study. *New England Journal of Medicine*, 325, 756–62.

Stone, P.H., Thompson, B., Anderson, H.V., et al. (1996). Influence of race, sex, and age on management of unstable angina and non-Q wave myocardial infarction. The TIMI III Registry. *Journal of the American Medical Association*, 275, 1104–12.

Stratton, J.R., Cerquerira, M.D., Schwartz, R.S., et al. (1992). Differences in cardiovascular responses to isoproterenol in relation to age and exercise training in healthy men. *Circulation*, 86, 504–12.

Tan, K.H., Sulke, N., Taub, J., Karani, S., and Sowton, E. (1995). Percutaneous transluminal coronary angioplasty in patients 70 years of age or older: 12 years' experience. *British Heart Journal*, 74, 310–17.

Tejada, C., Strong, J.P., Montenegro, M.R., et al. (1968). Distribution of coronary and aortic atherosclerosis by geographic location, race and sex. *Laboratory Investigation*, 18, 509–26.

ten Berg, J.M., Voors, A.A., Suttorp, M.J., et al. (1996). Long-term results after successful percutaneous transluminal coronary angioplasty in patients over 75 years of age. *American Journal of Cardiology*, 77, 690–5.

Thompson, R.C., Holmes, D.R., Jr, Grill, D.E., Mock, M.B., and Bailey, K.R. (1996). Changing outcome of angioplasty in the elderly. *Journal of the American College of Cardiology*, 27, 8–14.

Vaitkevicius, P.V., Fleg, J.L., and Engel, J.H. (1993). Effects of age and aerobic capacity on arterial stiffness in healthy adults. *Circulation*, 88, 1456–62.

van Brummelen, P., Buhler, F.R., Kiowski, W., et al. (1981). Age-related decrease in cardiac and peripheral vascular responsiveness to isoprenaline: studies in normal subjects. *Clinical Science*, 60, 571–7.

Vestal, R.E., Woods, A.J.J., and Shand, D.G. (1979). Reduced beta-adrenoreceptor sensitivity in the elderly. *Clinical Pharmacology and Therapeutics*, 26, 181–6.

Waller, B.F. and Roberts, W.C. (1983). Cardiovascular disease in the very elderly. Analysis of 40 necropsy patients aged 90 years or over. *American Journal of Cardiology*, 51, 403–21.

Weaver, W.D., Litwin, P.E., Martin, J.S., et al. (1991). Effect of age on use of thrombolytic therapy and mortality in acute myocardial infarction. *Journal of the American College of Cardiology*, 18, 657–62.

Wei, J.Y., Spurgeon, H.A., and Lakatta, E.G. (1984). Excitation–contraction in rat myocardium: alterations with adult ageing. *American Journal of Physiology*, 246, H784–91.

Weinberger, M.H. and Fineberg, N.S. (1991). Sodium and volume sensitivity of blood pressure: age and pressure change over time. *Hypertension*, 18, 67–71.

White, H.D., Barbash, G.I., Califf, R.M., et al. (1996). Age and outcome with contemporary thrombolytic therapy. Results from the GUSTO-1 trial. *Circulation*, 94, 1826–33.

White, M., Roden, R., Minobe, W., et al. (1994). Age-related changes to β-adrenergic neuroffector systems in the human heart. *Circulation*, 90, 1255.

Wolf, P.A., Abbott, R.D., and Kannel, W.B. (1987). Atrial fibrillation: a major contributor to stroke in the elderly. The Framingham Study. *Archives of Internal Medicine*, 155, 469–73.

Wong, W.F., Gold, S., Fukuyama O., et al. (1989). Diastolic dysfunction in elderly patients with congestive heart failure. *American Journal of Cardiology*, 63, 1526–8.

Yin, F.C., Raizes, G.S., Guarnieri, T., et al. (1978). Age-associated decreases in ventricular response to haemodynamic stress during beta-adrenergic blockade. *British Heart Journal*, 40, 1349–55.

9.2 Peripheral arterial disease

Linda Hands

Atherosclerosis is an age-associated disease but its appearance and progression can be accelerated by factors other than age, in particular smoking, hypertension, diabetes, and a raised serum cholesterol. However, in the very old (those over 90 years of age) atherosclerosis may become evident in the absence of these predisposing factors.

Atherosclerosis seems to be an almost inevitable consequence of time. Once it is established, life continues in the balance between disability and durability as the disease threatens a terminal myocardial infarction, renal failure, or stroke. This balance has to be considered when contemplating medical or surgical interventions for patients with atherosclerosis.

1. Do the likely benefits of reduced disability outweigh the risks to life of the procedure itself?

2. Will the benefits conferred by intervention be masked by the burden of other disease? The patient with angina or limiting dyspnoea may receive little benefit from interventions for claudication and a patient with a dense hemiplegia may not be helped by treatment of a toe with dry gangrene.

3. Is life expectancy so limited that, once recovered from the intervention, the patient will have little time left to enjoy its benefits? Many older people do not cope well with general anaesthesia, surgical trauma, and prolonged immobilization. Chest infection, joint stiffness, pressure sores, and depression may make for a stormy and prolonged recovery period.

These considerations have stimulated the search for 'minimally invasive' interventions which carry less of an immediate risk to life and offer the patient a quicker recovery. Almost inevitably, such interventions confer a lower quality and duration of benefit than do the more invasive procedures, but may be more appropriate for patients with limited activity requirements and life expectancy.

The points raised so far should not be interpreted as precluding surgical intervention in older people. They need to be considered but do not apply to all. The patient who has survived to 80 years of age before developing symptoms of atherosclerotic disease is probably made of sterner stuff, both physically and mentally, than the physiologically older patient of 50 who smokes heavily, has diabetes and hypertension, and presents with endstage generalized atherosclerosis.

Carotid disease

Symptomatic disease

Disease in the internal carotid artery can cause a stroke or a transient ischaemic attack, usually by embolization but occasionally through hypoperfusion. Clinically these events commonly manifest as a focal neurological deficit affecting motor or sensory function or speech, or causing transient (amaurosis fugax) or permanent monocular blindness. The patient is at risk of significant cerebral infarction from the same source, particularly when the internal carotid artery is still patent and capable of shedding further debris into the brain.

The stenosis commonly lies at or near the origin of the internal carotid artery and is accessible for surgical correction by carotid endarterectomy. Two large studies (Medical Research Council European Carotid Surgery Trial 1991; North American Symptomatic Carotid Endarterectomy Trial 1991) have demonstrated convincingly that surgical correction of 70 to 80 per cent diameter (depending on the method of measurement) or greater stenosis, associated with an ipsilateral non-disabling stroke, transient ischaemic attack, or amaurosis fugax, confers a significant benefit by reducing the number of subsequent strokes, despite the risk of stroke associated with the surgery itself. These were large multicentre randomized trials. In the North American Study there was an upper age limit of 79 years, but in the European Study all ages were included. Patients were randomized to either best available medical treatment (which usually included aspirin) or to best medical treatment plus carotid endarterectomy. The North American Study was highly selective in its surgeons, and this ensured a lower perioperative major stroke or death rate of 2.1 per cent compared with the European Study where the equivalent figure was 3.7 per cent. Those patients randomized to medical treatment alone had a subsequent stroke rate (major or minor) of 21 to 26 per cent over the next 2 to 3 years. Carotid endarterectomy reduced this rate to between 9 and 12 per cent including the events that occurred in the perioperative period. Most of the severe strokes in the medical group occurred within a year of the initial event and it is probable that surgery needs to be undertaken within this time window if it is to be beneficial.

The same studies also looked at lesser degrees of symptomatic stenoses. They showed that, in general, medical treatment was preferable to surgery if the carotid stenosis was less than 70 per cent.

Thus patients with symptomatic stenosis of 70 per cent or more should be considered for carotid endarterectomy. Those with symptomatic stenosis less than 70 per cent are currently treated with aspirin but if they have recurrent symptoms carotid endarterectomy should be considered.

Therefore it is essential to detect and establish the degree of carotid stenosis in any patient presenting with non-disabling carotid territory stroke, transient ischaemic attack, or amaurosis fugax, provided that there is no major contraindication to surgery. Carotid bruits become more common with increasing age but not all denote internal carotid disease; some are transmitted from proximal vessels and others originate in the external carotid artery. Conversely, a very tight or occluded internal carotid artery will be silent. Carotid duplex examination is a non-invasive low-risk means of detecting and measuring carotid stenosis. In expert hands it provides an accurate assessment without the need for confirmatory angiography. Occasionally there are technical difficulties with duplex assessment, especially with calcified arteries, and intra-arterial angiography is required. This investigation carries at least a 1 per cent risk of stroke in such patients. Magnetic resonance angiography carries a much lower risk but in its current form does not provide a reliable assessment of the degree of stenosis. However, it is useful in differentiating between very tight stenosis (amenable to surgery) and complete occlusion (not amenable to surgery) where duplex assessment sometimes has difficulties.

Although it is important to recognize carotid artery disease as a cause of cerebral ischaemic episodes, it remains a relatively uncommon cause of such episodes. The Lausanne Stroke Registry (Bogousslavsky et al. 1988) assessed 1000 sequential stroke patients. Eighty-nine per cent had cerebral infarction, of which 68 per cent were in the carotid territory and of these only 34 per cent had more than 50 per cent ipsilateral carotid stenosis, 7 per cent had greater than 75 per cent stenosis, and 18 per cent had complete occlusion. Thus less than 30 per cent of the original group presenting with stroke had an associated potentially correctable carotid lesion and 11 per cent had progressed to occlusion and were beyond surgical salvage.

Even though surgery has a part to play in patients with ischaemic deficits related to carotid disease, over 70 per cent of patients with significant carotid disease have no subsequent cerebral events in the 2 to 3 years following presentation. Factors such as plaque morphology may play a part in determining susceptibility, but as yet there are no means of identifying the patients most at risk within this group.

Asymptomatic disease

If a carotid duplex examination happens to show disease in the internal carotid artery, yet the patient is asymptomatic, what should be done?

Norris et al. (1991) followed nearly 700 patients aged 45 to 90 years of age with asymptomatic carotid stenosis for a mean time of 3.5 years and found that the annual cerebrovascular accident rate was 1.3 per cent if the initial stenosis was less than 75 per cent and 3.3 per cent if it was greater than 75 per cent. Older patients tended to have severer stenosis but age itself did not contribute to outcome.

The Asymptomatic Carotid Atherosclerosis Study (1995) randomized 1662 patients aged 40 to 79 years of age with asymptomatic internal carotid artery stenosis greater or equal to 60 per cent to aspirin or aspirin with carotid endarterectomy and showed a small but significant reduction with surgery in the ipsilateral stroke rate from 6.2 to 4 per cent over a median of 2.7 years follow-up, extrapolated to 11 and 5 per cent, respectively, at 5 years. The perioperative stroke or death rate was 2.3 per cent overall but higher in women, which eradicated any advantage to surgery in them. These were patients selected on the basis of a low perioperative stroke or death risk, operated on by highly selected surgeons. Extrapolation of the results to higher-risk patients and less able surgeons would inevitably abolish much of the benefit of surgery and to date there is reluctance in the United Kingdom to embrace surgery for asymptomatic carotid stenosis. At present there is little point in referring asymptomatic patients with carotid bruits for carotid duplex studies.

Lower-limb vascular disease

Occlusive disease of the lower limbs has an insidious onset and, in a patient whose exercise is limited by angina or dyspnoea, may not become apparent until quite advanced. The Edinburgh Study assessed over 1500 patients aged 55 to 74 registered with general practices within the city and found that 18.5 per cent had evidence of lower-limb arterial disease, often asymptomatic, with an ankle-to-brachial index of less than 0.9 (Fowkes et al. 1991). This is a particularly high prevalence compared with other similar population studies, but obviously populations vary. The Hoorn study of Dutch Caucasian subjects aged 50 to 74 years found only 9.4 per cent with an ankle-to-brachial index less than 0.9 (Beks et al. 1995). Such differences reflect variations in risk factor prevalence.

In the Edinburgh Study major lower-limb arterial disease (ankle-to-brachial index less than 0.9 and a drop of over 20 per cent with reactive hyperaemia or an ankle-to-brachial index less than 0.7 or a drop with reactive hyperaemia of over 35 per cent) was much more common in current smokers (17.8 per cent) than in ex-smokers (12.3 per cent) or in those who had never smoked (5.7 per cent) (Fowkes et al. 1995). Those with disease despite never smoking tended to be older and female, with a higher body mass index, cholesterol, and blood pressure.

In the Hoorn Study the prevalence of lower-limb disease (ankle-to-brachial index less than 0.9) in diabetics was 21 per cent compared with 7 per cent in non-diabetics. In the Edinburgh and other studies, male sex was also associated with an increased prevalence of an ankle-to-brachial index less than 0.9.

Claudication

The first symptom of vascular disease of the legs is often a cramping pain in the calves or buttocks felt with exercise. The overall prevalence of claudication in the Edinburgh Study was 4.6 per cent and increased with age (Fowkes et al. 1991). The same study found an equal prevalence of claudication in men and women, a surprising finding since many other studies have found it to be more common in men (Schroll and Munck 1981; Criqui et al. 1985).

In most cases claudication is a benign disease. Two-thirds of those affected will remain stable or improve, and only a third will deteriorate (Silbert and Zazeela 1958; Bloor 1961). Most changes in the severity of symptoms occur within the first year of claudication. It is possible to predict progressive disease in some patients. Silbert and Zazeela (1958) followed up patients with claudication for over 14 years and found that whereas one-third of the non-diabetic patients had increasing symptoms, two-thirds of the diabetic patients deteriorated and four times as many came to amputation. Smoking also plays a role; Silbert and Zazeela (1958) reported that patients with claudication who continued smoking were twice as likely to need amputation as those who stopped smoking. Jonason and Ringqvist (1985) reported an 8 per cent risk of rest pain at 6 years in non-diabetic patients who had either never smoked or stopped within a year of presentation but a 21 per cent risk in those who continued to smoke a year after presentation.

The cohort of claudicating patients who experience progressive disease have generalized 'severe' atherosclerosis. Although less than a third of this group undergo amputation (Bloor 1961) the remainder avoid it by dying from cardiac or cerebrovascular disease (see below) (Naschitz et al. 1988).

The standard conservative management of claudication is advice to stop smoking, lose weight, and exercise—advice which is easy to give, but more difficult to follow. Nevertheless the first stricture is particularly important not only because those who continue to smoke are much more likely to deteriorate but if intervention is required those who smoke have twice the risk of graft occlusion of those who do not (Wiseman et al. 1989).

If claudication imposes a significant restriction in lifestyle, a variety of interventions may be possible. A programme of supervised exercise sessions at least twice a week for 6 months leads to a significant increase in claudication distance even in those restricted by other disease, such as arthritis or angina (Gardner and Poehlmann 1995).

This a low-risk strategy which offers benefits in terms of cardio-respiratory function as well as leg symptoms, but it requires dedication on the part of the patient and this may be lacking.

If the results of exercise prove disappointing, percutaneous trans-luminal balloon angioplasty under local anaesthetic in the radiology department may be feasible. An isolated stricture of less than 10 cm in length or a short occlusion in an artery above knee level is often amenable to dilatation. The results of this procedure above the groin are good—90 per cent patency at 5 years (Insall et al. 1993). When performed below the groin only half remain patent at 5 years (Hunink et al. 1993; Jeans et al. 1994). Dilatation below knee level has an even poorer patency rate. Thus in patients with buttock pain on walking and reduced volume femoral pulses or femoral bruits, suggestive of aortoiliac disease, angiography is well worthwhile; if balloon angio-plasty is feasible, the results are durable. If no pulses are found below the groin, again angiography with a view to angioplasty is worthwhile although less durable. However, if the popliteal pulse is present, angioplasty is unlikely to confer much benefit and surgery is unlikely to be justified for claudication alone, so the risks of angiography are probably not worth taking. The advice of a vascular surgeon should be sought before embarking on angiography: it is not without risk and occasionally precipitates vascular damage and limb loss.

If angiography demonstrates arterial disease beyond the reach of angioplasty, bypass grafting may be feasible. However, the risks of operative intervention restrict its use to those with short distance claudication who are otherwise reasonably healthy (see next section).

Rest pain, ulceration, and gangrene

Those who have developed these features have a particularly 'aggressive' form of atherosclerosis likely, without treatment, to progress to limb loss, unless death from myocardial infarction or stroke intervenes.

Rest pain manifests as foot pain, exacerbated by raising the leg, particularly in bed at night. As a result patients may prefer to sleep in a chair rather than retiring to bed. Rest pain can follow claudication, but if the patient was restricted by angina or dyspnoea, claudication may not have been apparent. Ischaemic ulceration and gangrene occur in the periphery of the circulation, for instance in the toes, but also over pressure areas such as the heel or ankle (Fig. 1). If the patient also has significant venous disease, venous ulcers which have previously healed become resistant to treatment with the advent of arterial disease (Fig. 2). Indeed the use of compression bandaging or compression hose in the presence of arterial disease can lead to gangrene by further impeding arterial inflow.

Exercise is not an option in advanced ischaemia. Stopping smoking is rarely possible when pain is severe. When the patient reaches this stage more aggressive treatment becomes mandatory unless life expectancy is such that morphine is the only alternative. Balloon angioplasty may be feasible and in the frail patient dilatation of long segments of diseased artery are worthwhile: the success rate may be low but the alternatives hold much greater risk.

If the patient has disease above the knee then surgical re-vascularization is almost always technically possible, but may carry a major risk to life. Diabetic patients and the very old often have occlusive disease below the knee. Provided there are reasonable vessels in the foot then femorodistal bypass grafting is feasible but if no major pedal vessels are patent this option disappears.

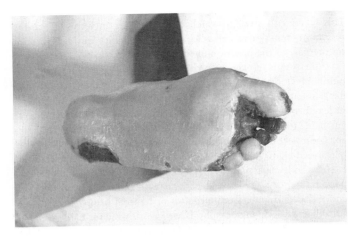

Fig. 1 Gangrene of the forefoot and pressure areas.

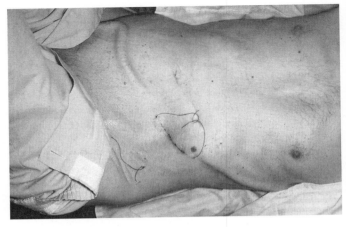

Fig. 3 Extra-anatomical axillobifemoral bypass graft.

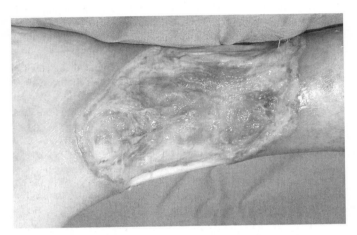

Fig. 2 Ankle ulceration due to both venous and arterial disease.

Aortobifemoral grafting for disease above the groin carries a fatality of about 5 per cent overall, increasing with age. For the older patient, lower risk extra-anatomical bypass grafts, such as femorofemoral crossover or axillobifemoral grafting, may be possible, taking donor blood from the other groin or the axillary artery to the femoral artery via a subcutaneous synthetic graft (Fig. 3).

Nehler *et al.* (1993), found that grafts performed predominantly for limb salvage in patients aged over 80 years resulted in an operative fatality of 6 per cent, an 18-day in-hospital stay, and limb salvage of 91 per cent over 3 years in those who survived that long. Eighty-five per cent of these grafts were infrainguinal and 15 per cent extra-anatomical. Seventy-one per cent of patients remained mobile and at home 3 years after such surgery, but two-thirds of those whose grafts failed, leading to amputation, needed to move into a nursing home. Perler (1994) reports the results of revascularization in patients aged over 80 years of age, with an operative fatality of 7 per cent, and a 50 to 80 per cent 3- to 5-year limb salvage rate. These reports are encouraging but there is no doubt that these patients were selected for a favourable outcome; the number of patients who were offered only amputation is unreported.

Thompson *et al.* (1995) looked at the quality of life of patients 18 months after either infrainguinal revascularization or amputation and found that the first group had a significantly better mobility, social function, and less depression, even if further surgery was required to maintain graft patency.

Those patients unsuitable or unfit for vascular reconstruction may be helped by percutaneous phenol lumbar sympathectomy which occasionally relieves rest pain, improves perfusion, and leads to ulcer healing.

Amputation is a therapeutic manoeuvre in terms of pain relief and should not be regarded as a failure provided that all other treatment options have been considered. Those patients bed-bound by stroke with flexion contraction of a useless limb will not gain a useful limb with surgical revascularization and, if in pain, may be better off with amputation. However, the fatality of amputation is 10 to 14 per cent reflecting the general state of health of the patients. It may be worth considering balloon angioplasty or sympathectomy as a lower risk alternative to relieve rest pain, even if the limb remains useless.

When amputation is chosen, it is important to take steps to have the stump fitted with a leg/foot prosthesis, and the patient enrolled in a skilled rehabilitation programme to build up strength to wear and learn to walk with the prosthesis, together with use of cane or crutch as needed. Many elderly patients are too frail to use their prosthesis in walking far, but it is helpful in transferring and when standing to urinate. Even when the patient is not able to learn to walk using the prosthesis, for cosmetic reasons and sense of identity, it is usually helpful to wear the prosthesis and to dress normally.

Acute leg ischaemia

Sudden onset of pain, pallor, and occasionally paraesthesia and paralysis, in a limb which examination reveals to be cold and pulseless, denotes acute critical ischaemia. This is a medical emergency, particularly if sensation and movement are acutely impaired. Unless the limb is reperfused within 6 h of the onset of symptoms, it may be beyond salvage.

In the older patient common causes include the following:

When rupture occurs

Sudden onset of back, loin, or abdominal pain, often associated with transient or persistent hypotension, announces aneurysm rupture. In patients not known to have an aneurysm, alternative diagnoses of renal colic, pancreatitis, or myocardial infarction may be considered. If an aneurysm is already recorded or subsequently noted, a rupture must be assumed unless evidence of other pathology is overwhelming. Speed is of the essence if survival is the goal. Time taken checking serum amylase, performing an intravenous urogram, or obtaining a CT scan to exclude rupture usually imposes an unacceptable delay unless diagnosis is seriously in doubt. An ultrasound scan, although sometimes quicker, can only confirm the presence of an aneurysm and will not give secure evidence of the presence or absence of a leak. Rapid transfer should take place to a surgical centre where repair can be performed. When feasible an intravenous infusion is helpful in resuscitation during transfer, but efforts to push the blood pressure up to 'normal' levels will only lead to increased bleeding. Fluid transfusion should be restricted to a rate which maintains the systolic pressure at 90 or 100 mmHg until the aorta is clamped in theatre.

A recent prospective study of ruptured aneurysm repair in the north of England demonstrated a 47 per cent fatality in those patients under 80 years and 70 per cent in those over 80 years (Berridge et al. 1995). Similar survival figures were found by Akkersdijk et al. (1994) who studied 115 patients aged 80 to 89 years of age undergoing repair of a ruptured aneurysm. Some authors have shown a rather better survival rate in those over 80 years, but these were much smaller studies. There is no doubt that the patients documented in such reports are highly selected but the results show that, in such a group, survival is not out of the question.

Aune et al. (1995) studied longer-term survival in those undergoing repair of a symptomatic aneurysm (ruptured or acutely expanding). Those over the median age of 72 years had a 6-year postoperative survival, similar to that of sex- and age-matched population data, but for younger patients 20 per cent fewer than expected for the population survived for 6 years. Given the association with cardiac disease and hypertension, a poorer survival might have been expected in both groups. However, only the very fittest patients amongst the elderly population are selected for such surgery.

Distal embolization

The classical 'blue toe' with intact pedal pulses is usually caused by embolization. The heart is the most common source of emboli but occasionally an aortic aneurysm is responsible. Thus an ultrasound scan of the aorta should complement the echocardiogram. Treatment with aspirin is appropriate unless the aneurysm is of a significant size, likely to rupture, or otherwise symptomatic. If this fails to prevent further embolization, the choice lies between aneurysm repair and anticoagulation, and the risks of each have to be assessed. Anticoagulation in the presence of an aneurysm might seem hazardous, but if the aneurysm is small, the risk of rupture is low and anticoagulation is a reasonable option. Even with larger aneurysms, there is no evidence to suggest that those patients who are anticoagulated when their aneurysm ruptures fare any worse. It is unlikely that formation of a clot makes any difference to the rate of leak once the aneurysm is breached; tamponade in the retroperitoneal space is much more important.

Thrombosis

Very occasionally aortic aneurysms thrombose. This usually presents as acute aortic occlusion with lower-limb ischaemia in a previously asymptomatic patient, but the diagnosis is often not made until surgery or thrombolysis (see Chapter 9.2).

Screening for aortic aneurysms

As with all screening programmes, proposals for a national aortic aneurysm screening programme generate enormous controversy related to practical, ethical, and financial issues.

The target populations for pilot studies are usually male, aged between 55 and 74 years, and sometimes hypertensive. The detection rate is only about 5 to 8 per cent, of which relatively few are of sufficient size to merit surgery (Collin et al. 1988; O'Kelly and Heather 1989; Scott et al. 1995).

There are ethical dilemmas in extending screening to older subjects. Older people are more likely to have aneurysms but less likely to be fit for surgery. The fatality of rupture in the very old is extremely high compared with that of elective surgery. Considerable psychological morbidity is engendered by making subjects aware of a potentially lethal disease yet precluding cure because of the risks of elective surgery.

Scott et al. (1995) have performed the only controlled study of the benefit of screening. Over 15 000 subjects in the south of England aged 65 to 80 years were randomized into two groups: one was screened, and the other was not. Any aneurysms in the screened group had follow-up surveillance if not repaired initially. Surgery was considered in those with aneurysms reaching 6 cm, expanding at a rate over 1 cm/year, or becoming symptomatic. This policy led to operation in 16 per cent of the 218 aneurysms in the screened group and reduced the rupture rate by 55 per cent and the mortality by 42 per cent compared with the unscreened group.

Management of known aortic aneurysms

A 4-cm aortic aneurysm in a person aged 80 years or more can be ignored. It is unlikely to reach a size where rupture is probable within a timescale in which the patient could still derive benefit from surgery. Therefore repeated surveillance in such cases is pointless and serves only to cause patient anxiety. There is little point in informing the patient of the aneurysm's existence.

An aneurysm of greater than 6 cm in diameter in an 80-year-old person should be considered for repair if the patient does not have cardiac or other disease likely to cause serious limitation of life expectancy or quality. Under the age of 80 years repair should certainly be considered when aneurysms reach 6 cm in diameter, but cardiac work-up to exclude, or at least define the extent of, any impairment is required. The risks of rupture then need to be balanced against the risk of surgery.

Small aneurysms in younger fit subjects and larger aneurysms in older and less fit subjects can be monitored at regular intervals by ultrasound. However, continued surveillance is only sensible if the subject is a potential candidate for surgery should the aneurysm reach a sufficient size or expansion rate. If the decision is taken not to operate at a certain aneurysm size in an individual, one must decide whether that only holds with the current size and with its current risk of rupture, in which case the risks need to be 'rebalanced' if significant expansion occurs. If elective repair appears inappropriate whatever the size, is there any place for emergency repair if the aneurysm ruptures? Should a primary care doctor send the patient to hospital when such an event occurs, or make him or her comfortable at home? Death without surgery is inevitable, and so perhaps even high-risk emergency surgery should be attempted although few will survive. However, this approach brings significant emotional and physical trauma to the patient and distress to relatives, apart from the possible financial implications. Death in an expensive intensive care unit bed a day or two after hopeless surgery helps no one and wastes resources. A relatively rapid death in a supportive environment at home must surely be preferable. Provided that the patient has been adequately investigated to assess the risk of surgery, those with a poor chance of survival should be cared for at home if rupture occurs, if the resources are available. The decision with regard to surgery is usually made by a vascular surgeon, but it is important that it is conveyed to all those involved in the care of the patient so that management is appropriate when rupture occurs. For obvious reasons, careful consideration may need to be given to what is best for the patient to be told in such circumstances. It may be possible to work out an advanced directive with the patient him- or herself (see Chapter 9.11).

Other aneurysms

A patient prone to aneurysmal disease may develop aneurysms at more than one site. Iliac, femoral, and popliteal aneurysms occur less commonly than those of aorta. Each poses a range of threats similar to that of the aortic aneurysm, i.e. rupture, embolization, and thrombosis, but with smaller vessels the relative risk of rupture declines and that of thrombosis increases. A ruptured iliac aneurysm presents in much the same way as an aortic aneurysm. A thrombosed popliteal aneurysm causes acute limb ischaemia in a previously asymptomatic leg. The aneurysm will usually not be palpable, having lost its pulse. The clue lies in the aneurysmal popliteal artery of the other leg or the aortic aneurysm, for these patients often have aneurysmal disease elsewhere.

Management of iliac aneurysms is similar to that of aortic aneurysms. Asymptomatic popliteal aneurysms pose a dilemma. Surgical intervention in the form of femoropopliteal bypass grafting carries an inevitable morbidity and occasional mortality, although low. There is no evidence that small asymptomatic popliteal aneurysms inevitably thrombose or embolize. Even if thrombosis does occur, prompt recognition and thrombolysis combined with bypass grafting may salvage the situation. Surgical centres vary in their approach, but in our centre only the larger or symptomatic popliteal aneurysms are considered for surgery.

References

Akkersdijk, G.J.M., van Der Graaf, Y., Van Bockel, J.H., de Vries, A.C., and Eikelboom, B.C. (1994). Mortality rates associated with operative treatment of infra-renal abdominal aortic aneurysm in The Netherlands. *British Journal of Surgery*, 81, 706–9.

Allardice, J.T., Allwright, G.J., Wafula, J.M.C., and Wyatt, A.P. (1988). High prevalence of abdominal aortic aneurysm in men with peripheral vascular disease: screening by ultrasonography. *British Journal of Surgery*, 75, 240–2.

Auerbach, O. and Garfinkel, L. (1980) Atherosclerosis and aneurysm of aorta in relation to smoking habits and age. *Chest*, 78, 805–9.

Aune, S., Amundsen, S.R., Evjensvold, J., and Trippestad, A. (1995). The influence of age on operative mortality and long-term relative survival following emergency abdominal aortic aneurysm operations. *European Journal of Vascular and Endovascular Surgery*, 10, 338–41.

Bengtsson, H.Y., Norrgard, O., Angquist, K.A., Ekberg, O., Oberg, L., and Bergqvist, D. (1989). Ultrasonographic screening of the abdominal aortic aneurysm among siblings of patients with abdominal aortic aneurysms. *British Journal of Surgery*, 76, 589–91.

Berridge, D.C., Chamberlain, J., Guy, A.J., and Lambert, D. (1995). Prospective audit of abdominal aortic aneurysm surgery in the northern region from 1988 to 1992. *British Journal of Surgery*, 82, 906–10.

Bussutil, R.W., Abou-Zamzam, A.M., and Madchleder, H.I. (1980). Collagenase activity of human aorta. A comparison of patients with and without abdominal aortic aneurysms. *Archives of Surgery*, 115, 1373–8.

Collin, J., Walton, J., Araujo, L., and Lindsell, D. (1988). Oxford screening programme for abdominal aortic aneurysm in men aged 65 to 74 years. *Lancet*, i, 613–15.

Cronenwett, J.L., Murphy, T.F., Zelenock, G.B., et al. (1985). Actuarial analysis of variables associated with rupture of small abdominal aortic aneurysms. *Surgery*, 98, 3472–83.

Dean, R.H., Woody, J.D., Enarson, C.E., Hansen, K.J., and Plonk, G.W. (1993). Operative treatment of abdominal aortic aneurysms in octogenarians. When is too much too late? *Annals of Surgery*, 217, 721–28.

Johansson, G. and Swedenborg, J. (1986). Ruptured abdominal aortic aneurysms: a study of incidence and mortality. *British Journal of Surgery*, 73, 101–13.

Johnston, K.W. (1994). Non-ruptured abdominal aortic aneurysm: six-year follow-up results from the multicentre prospective Canadian aneurysm study. *Journal of Vascular Surgery*, 20, 163–70.

Magee, T.R., Scott, D.J., Dunkley A., et al. (1992). Quality of life following surgery for abdominal aortic aneurysm. *British Journal of Surgery*, 79, 1014–16.

Nasim, A., Thompson, M.M., Sayers, R.D., Bolia, A., and Bell, P.R.F. (1996). Endovascular repair of abdominal aortic aneurysm: an initial experience. *British Journal of Surgery*, 83, 516–19.

Nevitt, M.P., Ballard, D.J., and Hallett, J.W. (1989). Prognosis of abdominal aortic aneurysms. *New England Journal of Medicine*, 321, 1009–14.

Ogren, M., Bengtsson, H., Bergqvist, D., Ekberg, O., Hedblad, B., and Janzon, L. (1996). Prognosis in elderly men with screening-detected abdominal aortic aneurysm. *European Journal of Vascular and Endovascular Surgery*, 11, 42–7.

O'Hara, P.J., Hertzer, N.R., Krajewski, L.P., Tan, M., Xiong, X., and Beven, E.G. (1995). Ten-year experience with abdominal aortic aneurysm repair in octogenarians: early results and late outcome. *Journal of Vascular Surgery*, 21, 830–37.

O'Kelly, T.J. and Heather, B.P. (1988). The feasibility of screening for abdominal aortic aneurysms in a district general hospital. *Annals of the Royal College of Surgeons of England*, 70, 197–9.

O'Kelly, T.J. and Heather, B.P. (1989). General practice-based population screening for abdominal aortic aneurysms: a pilot study. *British Journal of Surgery*, 76, 479–80.

Paty, P.S.K., Lloyd, W.E., Chang, B.B., Darling, R.C., Leather, R.P., and Shah, D.M. (1993). Aortic replacement for abdominal aortic aneurysm in elderly patients. *American Journal of Surgery*, 166, 191–3.

Pleumeekers, H.J.C.M., Hoes, A.W., van der Does, E. et al. (1995). Aneurysms of the abdominal aorta in older adults. The Rotterdam study. *American Journal of Epidemiology*, 142, 1291–9.

Scott, R.A.P., Wilson, N.M., Ashton, H.A., and Kay, D.N. (1993). Is surgery necessary for abdominal aortic aneurysms less than 6 cm in diameter? *Lancet*, **342**, 1395–6.

Scott, R.A.P., Wilson, N.M., Ashton, H.A., and Kay, D.N. (1995). Influence of screening on the incidence of ruptured abdominal aortic aneurysm: 5-year results of a randomised controlled study. *British Journal of Surgery*, **82**, 1066–70.

Strachan, D.P. (1991). Predictors of death from aortic aneurysm among middle aged men: the Whitehall study. *British Journal of Surgery*, **78**, 401–4.

Webster, M.W., Ferrell, R.E., St Jean, P.L., Majumder, P.P., Fogel, S.R., and Steed, D.L. (1991). Ultrasound screening of first-degree relatives of patients with abdominal aortic aneurysm. *Journal of Vascular Surgery*, **13**, 9–14.

9.4 Venous diseases

Alain Franco, Jean-Luc Bosson, and Carole Woodward

Acute venous diseases

Acute deep venous thrombosis

Acute deep venous thrombosis (**DVT**) of the legs is inextricably linked with its immediate complication—pulmonary embolism. This association justifies the concept of venous thromboembolic disease. Both DVT and pulmonary embolism increase in incidence with age (Kniffin *et al.* 1994). Acute DVT carries an immediate potentially lethal risk of pulmonary embolism, and more than 80 per cent of pulmonary embolisms are due to inferior limb DVT. Untreated venous thromboembolic disease has a fatality rate of 30 per cent. After an acute episode, consequent morbidity is much more often due to the development of a postphlebitic syndrome than to the rare but disabling pulmonary hypertension from recurrent embolism (Wood 1996).

Estimates of the incidence of DVT are very imprecise owing to the lack of reliable diagnostic methods, with even postmortem diagnosis being a subject of discussion. In the United States, it is estimated that there are about 2 million cases of DVT annually and that 600 000 patients develop pulmonary embolism, 30 per cent of which lead to death. In France, the annual number of cases of DVT is between 50 000 and 100 000, accounting for between 5000 and 10 000 deaths. A regular increase in the prevalence of thromboembolic disease had been noted up to the 1970s, followed by a slight decrease. This decline is only seen in surgical wards, whereas in the medical setting there is an important increase in the prevalence of this pathology because of the increasing number of elderly patients in medical units. This trend is expected to continue in the future (Diebold and Lösrh 1991).

Pathology

The thrombus starts in a valvular nest. It is then asymptomatic and can remain so for a few days. When the patient's physiological capacity for containment is exceeded, there is a risk of upstream and, more frequently, downstream extension of a non-adherent thrombus. This extension rapidly reaches the first venous confluent, the adjacent vein flux initially limiting extension at this level. Then the thrombus sticks to the wall of the vein and completely occludes the vascular lumen. The upstream (distal) pressure then increases, generating pain, oedema, and the development of a superficial collateral system. This situation evolves within a few weeks or months towards a more or less complete recanalization and the development of a venous collateral circulation. Thrombus lysis can be accompanied by destruction of the valves included in the thrombus. The resulting valvular incompetence is responsible for post-thrombotic disease.

Thromboembolic migration mainly involves the proximal part of the thrombus which, after having passed through the inferior cava system and the right heart cavities, stops in the pulmonary arterial tree. At the time of diagnosis, there are often many emboli of different age, size, and site.

Aetiology

Venous thromboembolic disease is usually a comorbidity as it occurs as a complication of another disease, either medical or surgical. Therefore it is frequent after hospital admission. One-year fatality of patients presenting with pulmonary embolism or DVT has been reported as 53 per cent and 15 per cent respectively (Heit *et al.* 1999), with age- and sex-adjusted death rates being higher than the population average. Aetiological factors are summed up in the Virchow triad of a vascular parietal factor, increased blood coagulability, and venous stasis. Acute DVT is usually the result of an interaction between a precipitating factor and the background susceptibility of the patient. The principal aetiological factors are listed in Table 1. Blood homocysteine levels seem to be linked to the risk of DVT as to the risk of arterial disease (den Heijer *et al.* 1996). This may contribute to the rising incidence with age, as blood homocysteine levels increase with age in Western populations, probably due in

Table 1 Aetiology of thromboembolic disease in elderly people

Precipitating factors	Level of risk
Surgery	Orthopaedics, brain surgery, multiple trauma, urology, gynaecology, general surgery
Trauma and vascular area	Indwelling catheters and upper-limb thrombosis
Acute venous stasis	Prolonged bed rest, fracture cast, travel, unusual exercise
Risk factors	
Age	Risk $\times 2.5$ after the age of 60 years
History of venous thromboembolic disease	Risk $\times 2$–3 after the age of 60 years
Varicose veins	Risk
Obesity	Risk
Hormone replacement therapy	Risk $\times 2$–4 after the age of 60 years
Smoking	? Increased risk of postoperative DVT
Diseases frequently complicated with venous thromboembolic disease	Cancer, cardiac failure, paralysis, etc.
Immune system pathologies	Systemic lupus erythematosus, antiphospholipid syndrome
Haemostatic abnormalities	AT-III, protein C or S, or fibrinolysis deficiency, resistance to activated protein C
Hyperhomocysteinaemia	Risk
Local stasis, upper limb	Thoracic outlet syndrome
Local stasis, lower limb	May–Cockett syndrome (compression of the left iliac vein by the right iliac artery which can be responsible for a chronic venous thrombosis)

part to a relative dietary deficiency of folate and other B vitamins (Moustapha and Robinson 1999).

An increased risk of venous thromboembolic disease among women taking the contraceptive pill has been recognized for some time. It is now clear that there is also a two- to fourfold risk of the disease in postmenopausal women taking oestrogen or progestogen–oestrogen hormone replacement therapy (Vandenbroucke and Helmerhorst 1996). This needs to be considered in instituting antithrombotic prophylaxis for such women who have to undergo elective surgery or periods of bedrest predisposing to DVT. Short-term suspension of hormone replacement therapy is probably not effective, and may precipitate acute menopausal symptoms.

There is an association between DVT and occult cancer. In unselected patients with DVT around 10 per cent are diagnosed as having cancer over the subsequent 6 months. This represents a relative risk of around 2.5, which declines to normal after 6 months. Cancers can occur at any site (Prandoni *et al.* 1992), although in one series cancers of the gallbladder, liver, and pancreas were over-represented (Nordström *et al.* 1994). The number of cancer cases among patients with DVT increases with age but the risk ratio diminishes. Therefore, for the older patient, there is little justification for intensive investigation if a careful history and examination reveal no indication of an underlying neoplasm. In a Swedish study of 1300 patients with DVT, only 11 patients of all ages with non-metastatic cancer would have been identified by intensive investigation and only two would have benefited (Nordström *et al.* 1994). In addition to thorough clinical evaluation and pelvic digital examination, routine blood tests, chest radiography, and abdominal ultrasound scan are appropriate

for a patient with no specific indicators of underlying neoplastic disease. The relative risk of cancer is thought to be higher for patients with no precipitating factor for thromboembolism and for those with recurrent thrombosis or migratory thrombophlebitis.

Diagnostic features

The diagnosis of thromboembolic disease is pursued when DVT is suspected, during prospective screening of high-risk patients (e.g. postoperatively), and in the context of evaluating possible pulmonary embolism.

Clinical features

Pain, either spontaneous or triggered by palpation, is present in 60 per cent of cases. Oedema is firm and often does not pit. Typically, it is associated with a rise of cutaneous temperature and a slight fever (Wells *et al.* 1995). Most frequently, DVT involves the sural veins (40 per cent of cases). When the occlusion is proximal, involving popliteal, femoral, iliac, and/or caval veins, the oedema involves the entire inferior limb. In the case of iliac thrombosis, which is predominantly left-sided, oedema is observed at the top of the thigh and pain is inguinal. A proximal venous collateral circulation is then formed at both the inguinal and pubic regions (Cockett's syndrome of thrombosis of the left iliac vein) (Fig. 1).

One important clinical form to recognize is the phlegmasia caerulea dolens in which obstruction of the vein by the thrombus is so severe that it causes a circulatory blockage with limb ischaemia. This is a surgical emergency. The differential diagnosis includes oedema from

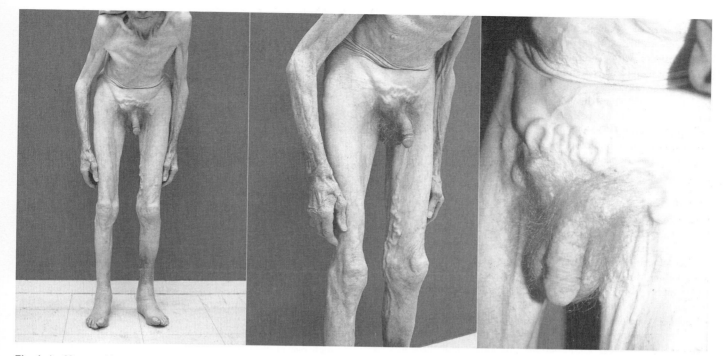

Fig. 1 An 83-year-old patient who had chronic thrombosis of the left iliac vein for 60 years (Cockett's syndrome). (a) Cutaneous pigmentation and distal trophic abnormalities are related to the chronic venous insufficiency. (b, c) Post-thrombotic varicosities of the long saphenous vein and the spontaneous suprapubic left-to-right bypass between the femoral veins.

other causes, either local or general. Lymphoedema occurs progressively, either spontaneously or after an attack of lymphangitis. It is a painless oedema without signs of venous stasis or changes of pigmentation. The swelling usually starts in the toes and the back of the foot, and then progresses proximally.

In the acute situation, other causes of painful legs have to be considered. A ruptured popliteal (Baker's) cyst leads to a severe pain in the popliteal region and the use of calf duplex ultrasonography has revealed the high frequency of this pathology. However, recognition of a Baker's cyst does not exclude the presence of a DVT as well. Other diagnoses that may need consideration are sciatica, haematoma, neuritis, or even acute ischaemia. Clinical signs of DVT are not reliable; sensitivity has been reported to range from 60 to 88 per cent with a specificity of 30 to 72 per cent (Anand *et al.* 1998). When a diagnosis of DVT is suspected, it will normally need to be confirmed by further investigation, but information from both clinical evaluation and investigation should be used in forming a diagnosis (Wells *et al.* 1995; Halkin *et al.* 1998).

Diagnostic techniques

Diagnostic tests should be performed as soon as possible. Ascending phlebography allows visualization of the entire deep venous system. It is the reference diagnostic standard but is invasive and requires an iodine injection with a risk of iodine intolerance and renal failure.

Duplex ultrasonography with or without colour is the preferred diagnostic test for symptomatic patients and gives topographic as well as haemodynamic data. It must be conducted by experienced staff according to a strict protocol of venous compression by the probe and complete examination of the lower-limb venous system from both legs up to the vena cava. The criteria for diagnosing venous

thrombosis are non-compressibility of the venous lumen under gentle probe pressure and presence of direct signs such as a hyperechogenic signal in the vascular lumen and the development of a collateral venous circulation. Compared with contrast venography, the sensitivity of ultrasonography is 98 per cent and the specificity is 97 per cent for thrombosis of the proximal deep veins (Elias *et al.* 1987). It is unhelpful for thrombi confined to the calf veins.

Impedance plethysmography allows the venous obstructive syndrome to be defined and quantified. It is also useful during patient follow-up.

Measurement of accumulation of radioactivity in the legs after administration of radio-iodine-labelled fibrinogen has been used as a research technique, but has no clinical application.

D-Dimers are breakdown products of cross-linked fibrin and elevated titres are found in patients with acute thrombosis. When measured by enzyme-linked immunosorbent assay (**ELISA**), rather than the quicker but less sensitive latex method, D-dimers offer a sensitive but non-specific indicator of thrombosis. Therefore a normal test is useful for excluding the diagnosis of DVT (Bounameaux *et al.* 1997).

CT can distinguish between acute and chronic occlusion of the large veins (vena cava, pelvis, and thigh) and identify associated abnormalities. Magnetic resonance venography can also detect calf vein thrombosis. Neither technique is yet widely used in the diagnosis of venous thrombosis.

Therapy

Treatment during the acute phase

It is generally agreed that DVT in or proximal to the popliteal vein should be treated. Opinions differ on whether DVT restricted to the calf veins can be safely left untreated on the ground that the risks of treatment are higher than the benefits. Cogo *et al.* (1998) studied 1702 patients with clinically suspected DVT, withholding anticoagulant therapy where popliteal compression ultrasonography was normal. The ultrasound examination was repeated 1 week after presentation. The cumulative 6-month rate of thromboembolic complications was only 0.7 per cent but included one fatal pulmonary embolism. Nothing is known of the effect of non-treatment of distal DVT on post-thrombotic complication rates. For distal DVT, it seems that the balance of benefits, risks and inconvenience of therapy needs to be evaluated by patient and doctor in each individual case.

Treatment aims at hastening resorption of the thrombus. Thrombolytic agents, systemically or by local catheter infusion, would seem a logical approach to rapid removal of the venous obstruction and the prevention of valvular damage associated with recanalization. A meta-analysis of studies comparing streptokinase followed by heparin with heparin alone showed that thrombolysis was associated with a 60 per cent lower incidence of post-thrombotic changes but a 3.8 times higher risk of major haemorrhagic complications (Ng and Rivera 1998). For uncomplicated DVT in older patients the risk of immediate haemorrhagic side-effects will often outweigh the long-term benefits of thrombolysis (O'Meara *et al.* 1994). However, thrombolysis may be called for in serious pulmonary embolism and in phlegmasia caerulea dolens.

If used, anticoagulation should be introduced as soon as possible. The classical method is continuous intravenous heparin starting with a loading dose adapted to the weight of the patient. The dosage then varies depending upon the partial thromboplastin time, which should be kept between 1.5 and 2.5 times the control time. Low-molecular-weight heparin has been shown to be as effective as unfractionated heparin (Lensing *et al.* 1995). The advantages of low-molecular-weight heparin include a longer half-life and higher bioavailability after injection. It can be administered subcutaneously, and will produce sustained and predictable effects on once-daily dosage, so obviating the need for anticoagulant monitoring. An economic analysis of a randomized controlled trial of low-molecular-weight heparin showed it to be at least as effective and safe as conventional heparin but less costly (Hull *et al.* 1997). In that study, 37 per cent of patients were considered to have been suitable for outpatient treatment, which would have reduced hospital costs even further. In some centres, measurement of anti-Xa activity is considered advisable 3 h after the injection on day 2, particularly when renal insufficiency is present. If heparin therapy has to be prolonged, the risk of thrombocytopenia calls for platelet count monitoring twice weekly.

Oral anticoagulants such as warfarin should be started simultaneously, in the absence of contraindications, during the first days of treatment (days 1 to 5) (Hull *et al.* 1990). Heparin is discontinued when a satisfactory level of anticoagulation is achieved; two consecutive international normalized ratio measurements with a reading between 2 and 3 must be obtained within a 24-h interval before discontinuing heparin.

Elastic compression, initially by elastic bandage and then by stockings, should ensure a rapid improvement of the symptoms and limit the risk of developing postphlebitic syndrome. During the acute stage, the limb must be monitored and the elastic compression regularly replaced every 8 h, from the foot to the garter for sural DVT, and up to the top of the thigh for proximal DVT. Preventive compression of the unaffected leg is also advisable until mobility is re-established.

Bed rest is the rule during the initial stage, except for calf vein DVT, although this must not exceed 2 to 3 days. Immediate mobilization is possible if the thrombus appears to be adherent at duplex ultrasonography examination and if there are no important painful or inflammatory processes.

The objectives of physiotherapy for DVT are to increase the rate of venous functional recovery and to limit after-effects. This involves gentle mobilization initially, followed by more active exercise to strengthen the muscles. In some cases of severe obstructive thrombosis, local massage may diminish pain and enhance venous bloodflow (Richaud *et al.* 1995).

Complementary treatments

The following complementary measures may need to be considered.

1. Partial interruption of the inferior vena cava can be achieved by the transcutaneous placement of a filter in the vena cava just below the renal veins. The migration of the emboli is interrupted by the endocaval filter which submits them to the fibrinolytic activity of the caval blood flow. This procedure is applied to patients with recurrent pulmonary embolism for whom anticoagulation treatment fails or when there is a contraindication or a complication of anticoagulation. More rarely, in cases of DVT with a high risk of pulmonary embolism or in a particular pathological context, such as when follow-up of the anticoagulation would prove difficult, a vena cava filter should be discussed, irrespective of patient age (Magnant *et al.* 1992).

2. A venous thrombectomy may be necessary in cases of phlegmasia caerulea dolens.

3. In the case of an extensive superficial thrombosis of the long saphenous vein, ligation may be considered if proximal extension of the thrombus cannot be prevented by other means.

Duration of treatment

In determining the duration of anticoagulant treatment it is necessary to recognize that a proportion of patients with DVT are at risk of recurrence for constitutional or other reasons, such as thrombophilia, venous abnormalities or chronic immobility. It is also necessary to consider how long a time-limited cause for an isolated DVT, such as surgery or a long air flight, continues to exert an influence. Schulman *et al.* (1995) compared 6 weeks with 6 months of anticoagulant treatment for patients following a first episode of DVT. They observed a twofold higher incidence of recurrent events in the 6-week group, and the extra events occurred between 6 weeks and 6 months of follow-up. This finding suggests that, for a proportion of patients, whatever mechanisms initiated their DVT continued to act over most of the 6 months of follow-up. Anticoagulant treatment for patients who suffer a second episode of thromboembolism should, where feasible, be offered indefinitely (Schulman *et al.* 1995), although the risk of haemorrhagic complications also continues indefinitely. Some of these patients, particularly the younger ones, will have some form of thrombophilia (Simioni *et al.* 1997). Shorter periods of treatment (4–6 weeks) may be sufficient for patients with postoperative DVT with no continuing risk factors, but better evidence on this is required (Diuguid 1997). The extent of the thrombosis is also a clinical consideration, with shorter courses of treatment thought to carry less risk in patients with distal rather than proximal thrombosis (Hirsh 1995). It is not now considered necessary to taper off anticoagulant treatment. The impression of 'rebound' hypercoagulability from earlier studies was due to too short a period of treatment, revealing the underlying continued effect of prothrombotic mechanisms.

It is customary to maintain elastic compression for as long as anticoagulant treatment is continued. If there is evidence of continued venous obstruction thereafter, long-term wearing of elastic stockings may help to prevent post-thrombotic complications, but there is little evidence on this point. Frail older people may have difficulty in putting the stockings on.

Prophylactic measures against thromboembolic diseases

The use of prophylactic anticoagulant therapy at the time of surgery has been shown to be effective in some circumstances but remains a matter for surgical judgement. Postoperatively, prophylactic measures to avoid DVT involve early standing and rapid mobilization by the patient, and maintaining muscular and articular activity, elevating the legs when possible, elastic compression, and respiratory exercises (see also Chapter 21). Wearing elastic compression stockings or bandages reduces the incidence of postoperative thrombosis by more than 50 per cent. According to the individual risk of venous thromboembolic disease, a drug treatment can be added (Gallus *et al.* 1994). At present, the preferred method consists of a daily injection of low-molecular-weight heparin, with the dosage being adapted to the risk of DVT (Nurmohamed *et al.* 1992; Palmer *et al.* 1997). Minor doses of oral anticoagulation seem to have a similar efficacy at a lower cost. Prophylactic protocols include precise recommendations in surgery.

In medical and geriatric wards, apart from certain pathological situations such as hemiplegia, cardiac insufficiency, and metastatic malignancy, the risk of venous thromboembolic disease is not well known. Thus the risk must be regularly evaluated for each patient in order to assess the necessity of prophylactic treatment, taking into account the risk and cost of such treatments (Clagett *et al.* 1995).

Superficial venous thrombosis

Three types of superficial venous pathology have been identified: varicose vein thrombosis, superficial phlebothrombosis not associated with varicose veins, and phlebitis.

Varicose vein thrombosis

Varicose thrombosis is a complication of existing varicose veins in elderly patients. It occurs secondarily to a precipitating factor such as trauma, prolonged bed rest, local or distant inflammatory problems, or dehydration. A duplex ultrasound scan is useful if propagation of the thrombus to the deep venous system is suspected. Treatment is directed at local measures, involving anti-inflammatory agents, elevation of the legs, and the careful use of removable elastic compression bandages. If the thrombus is thick or very painful, it can be removed by means of a small incision in the vein. This measure instantly relieves the pain and reduces the length of the evolution. Anticoagulants are only indicated when there is deep venous system propagation, thrombosis of the long saphenous vein, or as prophylaxis for patients at risk of DVT.

Superficial phlebothrombosis not associated with varicose veins

Superficial phlebothrombosis unrelated to varicose veins, whether single or multiple (Mondor's disease), can be a sign of immune system disease, blood dyscrasia, or cancer (Trousseau's sign).

Phlebitis

Chemical phlebitis occurs as a consequence of direct endothelial injury by perfusion fluid or a catheter. It is a painful and sometimes extensive inflammation of the vascular wall but is not accompanied by a generalized thrombotic tendency.

Chronic venous diseases

Chronic venous insufficiency (Carpentier and Priollet 1994) is secondary to chronic insufficiency of venous drainage, resulting in venous hypertension. It is particularly frequent in elderly patients, and the tissues of the distal part of the limb, where the venous pressure is highest, are most often affected. The clinical features of chronic venous insufficiency are oedema, pain which is always worse at the end of the day, and the development of trophic disturbances such as subcutaneous fibrosis and cutaneous pigmentation. These trophic changes occur on the medial aspect of the lower leg where venous stasis and hypertension are concentrated. If treatment is not instituted to reduce venous pressure, non-healing leg ulcers are likely to develop.

Post-thrombotic syndrome

When a DVT occurs, the vein involved is usually completely occluded. The blood is then forced to follow abnormal pathways to return to the heart. This leads to an obstructive syndrome secondary to the extension of the thrombosis, and to residual chronic obstruction and reflux syndrome due to the destruction of the valves in the deep and perforating veins.

When the occlusion involves the femoroiliac segment, clinical features include oedema, cyanosis, and pain in the thigh on walking (venous claudication). This pain usually only occurs during strenuous effort. Therefore it is not a common problem for elderly people who rarely engage in the level of exercise necessary to trigger the symptom.

A more frequent problem reflects the development of valvular incompetence in the popliteal and distal veins secondary to sclerosis and retraction of the valves that become glued together in re-canalization of the thrombus. There is a reflux of blood during calf muscle contraction with retrograde venous hypertension, which is increased by erect posture and the presence of post-thrombotic varicose veins.

Chronic functional venous insufficiency

Walking and exercise activate the calf muscular pump and reduce venous stasis pressure. In many elderly patients this pump is not activated owing to lack of physical exercise. Neurological or orthopaedic problems, as well as fear of walking and falling, may confine the patient to a sitting position or to shuffling. These situations favour chronic high venous pressure. Elderly patients should be encouraged to walk as much as possible. This enables the muscle pump to drain the venous system effectively, thus reducing venous pressure. Conversely, shuffling or prolonged sitting will lead to adverse effects due to the persistence of venous stasis.

Varicose veins

Primary (or essential) varicose veins are rarely seen before adulthood and their prevalence increases with age. Hereditary factors, such as female sex, growth, pregnancy, multiparity, being overweight, and prolonged standing position, are significant risk factors. It is a disease of modern civilization, and a factor in the development of varicosities seems to be increased intra-abdominal pressure which is secondary to low-fibre diets (inducing constipation) and tight clothing, and may be associated with low vitamin E intake (Carpentier and Priollet 1994). Varicose veins can be secondary to DVT, where the destruction of deep, perforating, or superficial valves causes reflux leading to venous hypertension.

Tolerance for varicose veins varies considerably. Very old patients are often found with enormous varicose veins that have not been treated. Cultural change and easier access to therapy are likely to reduce the prevalence of the condition in future generations of older people.

Varicose veins should be treated, irrespective of age, if they are responsible for tissue damage. Surgical and medical methods must be considered, according to the type of pathology and to patient characteristics. Stripping of the saphenous veins, ligation of the perforating veins, ambulatory phlebectomy, and sclerotherapy may be considered.

Leg ulcers

Leg ulcers are a common complication of chronic venous insufficiency in elderly people. The typical venous ulcer is on the medial side of the lower leg, and is associated with thinning and pigmentation of the surrounding skin. The differential diagnosis includes arterial ulcers, which are more common on the foot or on the lateral side of the leg. Mixed forms are also common, and it is important to recognize the presence of arterial insufficiency if compression treatment for a venous ulcer is contemplated. In there is doubt, Doppler ultrasonography or other methods of assessing arterial sufficiency should be used.

Local treatments for the ulcer should be limited when possible to wound washing, antiseptic care, and petroleum jelly dressings. The use of topical dressings should be avoided as the risk of sensitization is high. So-called 'phlebotonic' drugs are traditionally prescribed in France, but there is no good evidence of their efficacy. The surface of leg ulcers is invariably colonized by a variety of bacteria, but antibiotics should only be used where there is spreading cellulitis.

A variety of methods of applying compressive therapy have been described, including short-stretch bandages, multiple-layer bandaging, and the Unna's boot system favoured in the United States. A systematic overview (Cullum et al. 1998) concluded that compression therapy is effective in promoting healing of venous ulcers, and high pressure is better than lower, provided that there is no significant arterial disease. There is little evidence at present that one method of compression is better than another. Clinical experience indicates that nursing skill and experience in the rigorous application of pressure bandaging is important, and in the United Kingdom special community-based clinics have been found effective.

Skin grafting can be effective in healing leg ulcers where the surrounding tissues are healthy and well perfused, but the patient must be regarded as at continuing risk of recurrence and should take especial care to avoid trauma to the grafted site

After an ulcer has healed, compression should be continued by using adapted compression stockings (strength varying between 10 and 30 mmHg) from the foot to the thigh, tailored if necessary. Patients usually need help to put them on, but it is important that they are worn for long periods. The assistance of a physiotherapist, qualified in vascular rehabilitation, can be extremely useful.

References

Anand, S.S., Wells, P.S., Hunt, D., Brill-Edwards, P., Cook, D. and Ginsberg, J.S. (1998). Does this patient have deep vein thrombosis? *Journal of the American Medical Association*, **279**, 1094–99.

Bounameaux, H., de Moerloose, P., Perrier, A., and Miron, M.J. (1997). D-dimer testing in suspected venous thromboembolism: an update. *Quarterly Journal of Medicine*, **90**, 437–42.

Carpentier, P. and Priollet, P. (1994). Epidemiology of chronic venous insufficiency. *Presse Medicale*, **23**, 197–201.

Clagett, P., Anderson, F., Heit, J., Levine, M., and Wheeler B.H. (1995). Prevention of venous thromboembolism. Fourth ACCP Consensus Conference on Antithrombotic Therapy. *Chest*, **108** (Supplement 4), 312–34.

Cogo, A., Lensing, A.W.A.., Koopman, M.M.W., *et al.* (1998). Compression ultrasonography for diagnostic management of patients with clinically suspected deep vein thrombosis: prospective cohort study. *British Medical Journal*, **316**, 17–20.

Cullum, N., Fletcher, A.W., Nelson, E.A., and Sheldon, T.A. (1998). Compression bandages and stockings in the treatment of venous leg ulcers. *Cochrane Library*, Issue 4.

den Heijer, M., Koster, T., Blom H.J., *et al.* (1996). Hyperhomocysteinemia as a risk factor for deep-vein thrombosis. *New England Journal of Medicine*, **334**, 759–62.

Diebold, J. and Lösrh, U. (1991). Venous thrombosis and pulmonary embolism. A study of 5039 autopsies. *Pathology Research and Practice*, **187**, 260–6.

Diuguid, D.L. (1997). Oral anticoagulant therapy for venous thromboembolism. *New England Journal of Medicine*, **336**, 433–4.

Elias, A., Le Corff, G., Bouvier, J.L., Benichou, M., and Serradimgni, A. (1987). Value of real time B mode ultrasound imaging in the diagnosis of deep vein thrombosis of the lower limbs. *International Angiology*, **6**, 175–82.

Gallus, A.S., Salzman, E.W., and Hirsh, J. (1994). Prevention of venous thromboembolism. In *Haemostasis and thrombosis: basic principles and clinical practice* (3rd edn) (ed. R.W. Colman, J. Hirsh, V.J. Marder, and E.W. Salzman), pp. 1331–45. J.B. Lippincott, Philadelphia, PA.

Halkin, A., Reichman, J., Schwaber, M., Paltiel, O., and Brezis, M. (1998). Likelihood ratios: getting diagnostic testing into perspective. *Quarterly Journal of Medicine*, **91**, 247–58.

Heit, J.A., Silverstein, M.D., Mohr, D.N., Petterson, T.M., O'Fallon, W.M., and Melton, L.J. (1999). Predictors of survival after deep vein thrombosis and pulmonary embolism: a population-based study. *Archives of Internal Medicine*, **159**, 445–53.

Hirsh, J. (1995). The optimal duration of anticoagulant therapy for venous thrombosis. *New England Journal of Medicine*, **332**, 1710–11.

Hull, R.D., Raskob, G.E., Rosenbloom, D., *et al.* (1990). Heparin for 5 days as compared with 10 days in the initial treatment of proximal venous thrombosis. *New England Journal of Medicine*, **322**, 1260–4.

Hull, R.D., Raskob, G.E., Rosenbloom, D., *et al* (1997). Treatment of proximal vein thrombosis with subcutaneous low-molecular-weight heparin vs intravenous heparin. *Archives of Internal Medicine*, **157**, 289–94.

Kniffin, W.D., Baron, J.A., Barrett, J., Birkmeyer, J.D., and Anderson, F.A. (1994). The epidemiology of diagnosed pulmonary embolism and deep venous thrombosis in the elderly. *Archives of Internal Medicine*, **154**, 861–6.

Rajkumar, C., Cameron, J.D., Christophidis, et al. (1997a). Reduced systemic arterial compliance is associated with left ventricular hypertrophy and diastolic dysfunction in older people. *Journal of the American Geriatrics Society*, 45, 803–8.

Rajkumar, C., Kingwell, B.A., Cameron, J.D., et al. (1997b). Hormonal therapy increases arterial compliance in postmenopausal women. *Journal of the American College of Cardiology*, 30, 350–6.

Rutan, G.H., Kuller, L.H., Neaton, J.D., et al. (1988). Mortality associated with diastolic hypertension and systolic hypertension among men screened for the Multiple Risk Factor Intervention trial. *Circulation*, 77, 504–14.

Safar, M. (1988). Therapeutic trials and large arteries in hypertension. *American Heart Journal*, 115, 702–10.

SHEP Co-operative Research Group (1991). Prevention of stroke by antihypertensive drug treatment in older persons with isolated systolic hypertension. *Journal of the American Medical Association*, 265, 3255–64.

Staessen, J., Amery, A., and Fagard, R. (1990). Isolated systolic hypertension in the elderly. *Journal of Hypertension*, 8, 393–405.

Staessen, J.A., Fagard, R., Thijs, L., et al. (1997). Randomised double-blind comparison of placebo and active treatment for older patients with isolated systolic hypertension. The Systolic Hypertension in Europe (Syst-Eur) Trial Investigators. *Lancet*, 350, 757–64.

Ueda, K., Omae, T., Hasuo, Y., et al. (1988). Prognosis and outcome of elderly hypertensives in the Japanese community: results from long term prospective study. *Journal of Hypertension*, 6, 991–7.

Vanhanen, H., Thijs, L., and Birkenhager, W. (1996). Associations of orthostatic blood pressure in older patients with isolated systolic hypertension. *Journal of Hypertension*, 14, 943–9.

9.6 Cardiac arrhythmias

W. P. Orr and Y. Bashir

Introduction

The incidence of cardiac arrhythmias rises steeply with age, partly as a manifestation of hypertension, ischaemic heart disease, and other cardiovascular pathology, but also in apparently healthy subjects. The principles of diagnosis and treatment do not differ fundamentally from other age groups, but present particular challenges. Arrhythmias can result in diverse and often vague clinical presentations in elderly patients which may be difficult to distinguish from other common disorders (particularly neurological). The problem is accentuated by the high prevalence of asymptomatic abnormalities (conduction defects, ventricular arrhythmias, atrial fibrillation (AF), sinus node dysfunction, etc.) incidentally detected by standard and ambulatory ECG in this age group, which often turn out to be unrelated to the patient's symptoms. Antiarrhythmic drug treatment may be hampered by compliance problems, unpredictable pharmacokinetics, drug interactions resulting from polypharmacy, and increased susceptibility to proarrhythmia and other side-effects such as orthostatic hypotension. Recent advances in non-pharmacological therapy (catheter ablation, complex pacemakers, and implantable cardiac defibrillators) offer dramatic benefits in resistant cases, but are often overlooked because of the expense and reduced priority accorded to elderly patients, or because of concerns (usually unfounded) about the ability of older people to tolerate invasive procedures. Finally, with increasing emphasis on evidence-based clinical practice, we are confronted by the difficulties of extrapolating the findings from randomized trials that exclude elderly patients, exemplified by the issue of stroke prevention in non-rheumatic AF where both the risks and benefits of antithrombotic therapy may differ dramatically from those in the younger trial population.

In this chapter, the common clinical presentations of cardiac arrhythmias and their differential diagnosis are described, followed by a discussion of the available investigations and management of individual arrhythmias.

Clinical presentations

Syncope

Syncope is due to an abrupt reduction of cerebral perfusion, and is almost always followed by rapid recovery, in contrast with other common causes of loss of consciousness such as stroke, epilepsy, and overdose. The reported annual incidence in elderly people is up to 6 per cent (Lipsitz et al. 1985), with as many as half of those affected suffering serious injury (McIntosh et al. 1993). Retrograde amnesia is common, and patients will sometimes deny having lost consciousness despite collapsing. An accurate history is important, particularly regarding the circumstances, possible triggering factors, and associated symptoms, as well as any background of prior episodes. Wherever possible, an eye-witness account of the attacks should be obtained, whereupon differentiation from neurological conditions such as epilepsy may be straightforward. However, in many cases no description is available. Physical examination for evidence of structural cardiac abnormalities, postural hypotension, and carotid bruits, backed up

Table 1 Causes of syncope in four published series

	McIntosh et al. (1993)	Fitzpatrick et al. (1991a)	Kapoor (1990)	Day et al. (1982)
Number	65	322	433	198
Mean age (years)	78	76.3	56	44
Atrioventricular block (%)		34.5	2.5	1.0
Sinoatrial disease (%)	21	21.1	4.4	1.5
Tachyarrhythmias (%)		5.6	13.2	2.5
Neurocardiogenic syncope (%)	43	16.5	28.4	33.3
Carotid sinus syncope (%)	45	9.9	1.2	—
Other cardiopulmonary cause (%)	—	—	4.2	3.5
Non-cardiovascular cause (%)	27.5	—	4.8	45.5
Unexplained (%)	7.7	12.4	41.3	12.6

by appropriate investigations, can provide essential diagnostic information. The causes include bradyarrhythmias (atrioventricular (AV) block or sinoatrial disease), tachyarrhythmias, neurocardiogenic syncope and associated disorders, carotid sinus hypersensitivity, postural hypotension, and mechanical obstruction (e.g. aortic stenosis). However, the relative frequency of these conditions varies markedly between published series, and syncope remains unexplained in a significant proportion of cases despite investigation (Table 1). The presence of structural heart disease adversely influences prognosis, with annual mortality rates of 18 to 33 per cent compared with zero to 12 per cent for patients with syncope but no heart disease (Day et al. 1982; Silverstein et al. 1982; Kapoor et al. 1983; Eagle and Black 1983; Martin et al. 1984; Eagle et al. 1985; Kapoor 1990).

All patients should have a 12-lead ECG and ideally an echocardiogram to look for structural abnormalities. Carotid sinus massage should be performed routinely (see notes below). Ambulatory ECG monitoring is a standard investigation, but the diagnostic yield is disappointing although it can be increased by recording for periods of 48 h or longer (Bass et al. 1990). If these investigations are negative, head-up tilt testing may be helpful to establish a diagnosis of neurocardiogenic syncope, particularly in elderly patients where the associated vagal symptoms may be absent. The overall yield of positive tests is low, but may be up to 75 per cent in older patients with recurrent syncope (Fitzpatrick et al. 1991b). The 'sensitivity' can be further enhanced by the use of provocative agents such as isoprenaline or nitrates (Aerts et al. 1997), although at the expense of more false-positive results (Table 2). Intracardiac electrophysiological studies have been shown to be of very limited value in unexplained syncope, except among patients with structural heart disease where ventricular tachycardia is more likely (Kapoor 1992).

Often the cause of syncope remains unclear despite extensive investigation and there is little choice but to await a recurrence of the symptoms. Traditionally it has been difficult to obtain ECG documentation during syncopal episodes unless these are occurring very frequently. The recent advent of implantable subcutaneous ECG monitoring devices may offer an elegant solution to this problem in recurrent unexplained syncope (Fig. 1) (Leitch et al. 1992; Krahn et al. 1995). An algorithm summarizing the investigation of syncope is shown in Fig. 2 (see also Chapter 4.4).

Palpitation

Palpitation is a common presenting symptom in primary care (Kroenke and Mangelsdorff 1989) and is reported by more than 8 per cent of elderly subjects (Lok and Lau 1996). This patient population represents an extremely heterogenous group. In a recent prospective study, the major causes were cardiac or psychosomatic, but no explanation was found in a significant minority (Barsky et al. 1996).

Benign causes of palpitation (mainly ectopy and sinus tachycardia) can usually be differentiated from pathological tachyarrhythmias on the basis of the history, although occasionally ECG documentation during symptoms is required (see below). If there is no history of angina or syncope, no clinical evidence of heart disease, and the 12-lead ECG is normal, no further investigation of these patients is required and they should be reassured.

Patients with a history suggestive of paroxysmal tachycardia (AF, supraventricular tachycardia, ventricular tachycardia, etc) should be further investigated with a 12-lead ECG to check for pre-excitation and with echocardiography (and other investigations as clinically indicated) to look for underlying heart disease. ECG documentation of the arrhythmia should also be obtained. Depending on the frequency and duration of attacks, this may be achieved by Holter monitoring, transtelephonic ECG monitoring with a patient-activated device, or by asking the patient to attend the emergency department for an ECG during an episode. In most cases the diagnosis can be obtained by these non-invasive methods and appropriate antiarrhythmic therapy prescribed. Invasive electrophysiological testing may be required in a few patients, particularly if there is structural heart disease and/or suspicion of ventricular tachycardia.

Narrow-complex tachycardia

Regular tachycardia with narrow QRS complexes is a common arrhythmia in the emergency department. The normal QRS duration

Table 2 Yield of head-up tilt (HUT) tests in patients with syncope of unknown aetiology

Study	n	Percentage of patients with positive HUT (range)	Percentage of controls with positive HUT (range)
Tilt only	422	47 (26–75)	4 (0–7)
Tilt + isoprenaline	184	66 (60–87)	25 (0–45)

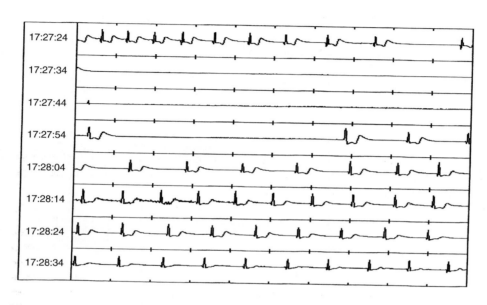

Fig. 1 Syncope due to sinus arrest revealed by a subcutaneous implantable loop recorder.

implies a supraventricular origin with rapid depolarization of both ventricles occurring via the His–Purkinje system. Traditionally, narrow-complex tachycardias have been classified as junctional tachyarrhythmias, where the AV node/junction is an obligatory part of the re-entrant circuit, or intra-atrial tachyarrhythmias, where the arrhythmia arises entirely within atrial tissue and the AV junction acts merely as a bystander. The distinction is important with respect to both diagnosis and treatment. Vagal manoeuvres and intravenous adenosine (Camm and Garratt 1991), by blocking AV nodal conduction, will terminate junctional tachycardia but will cause only transient slowing of the ventricular rate in atrial tachyarrhythmias (Fig. 3). Similarly, drugs which affect AV nodal conduction, such as verapamil and digoxin, may be effective for long-term suppression of junctional tachycardia, whereas atrial tachyarrhythmias can only be prevented by drugs which act directly on the atrial myocardium, particularly class I or class III agents (Vaughan Williams Classification). Atrial tachyarrhythmias account for a higher proportion of supraventricular tachycardia cases in an elderly population because of their association with underlying heart disease and hypertension.

Junctional tachyarrhythmias

The common forms are AV nodal re-entrant tachycardia and AV re-entrant tachycardia. In the former the re-entry circuit consists of two or more pathways within the AV junction, whereas in the latter the AV node acts as the antegrade limb and an accessory pathway as the retrograde limb (Fig. 4). If the accessory pathway can only conduct in the retrograde ventricle–atrium direction, the QRS complexes will be normal both in sinus rhythm and AV re-entrant tachycardia. If the pathway can also conduct in the antegrade atrium–ventricle direction, the ECG in sinus rhythm will show pre-excitation (i.e. Wolff–Parkinson–White syndrome), although the delta wave disappears during AV re-entrant tachycardia when the pathway is used in the retrograde direction.

Atrial tachyarrhythmias

These include atrial flutter and atrial tachycardia. Atrial flutter is most commonly due to a macro re-entrant circuit within the right atrium resulting in continuous depolarization and a sawtooth baseline pattern on the ECG, although atypical forms are also seen. Atrial tachycardia arises from a discrete focus in either atrium and can be due to an automatic or re-entrant mechanism, resulting in well-defined P waves separated by an isoelectric baseline. Although AF is much the most common arrhythmia arising at atrial level, its presentation is quite distinct with irregular tachycardia and so has been dealt with separately (see below).

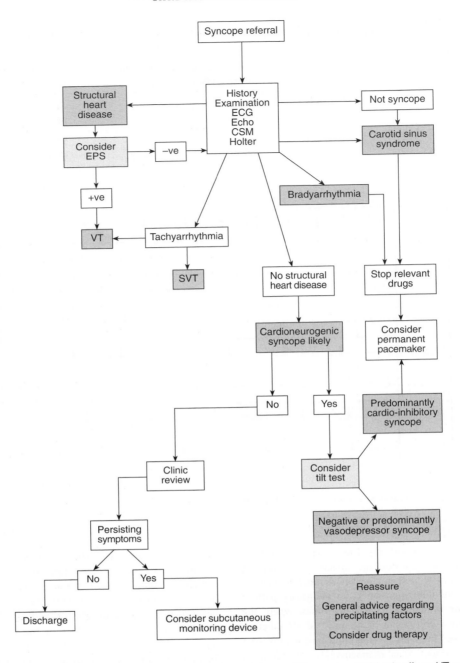

Fig. 2 Algorithm for investigation and management of syncope: CSM, carotid sinus massage; EPS, extrapyramidal side-effects; VT, ventricular tachycardia; SVT, supraventricular tachycardia.

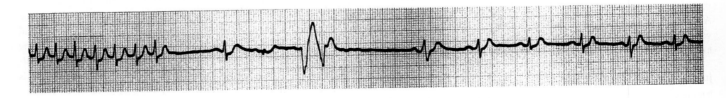

Fig. 3 The effects of adenosine on supraventricular tachycardias.

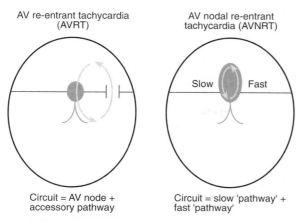

AV re-entrant tachycardia
(AVRT)

AV nodal re-entrant
tachycardia (AVNRT)

Slow Fast

Circuit = AV node +
accessory pathway

Circuit = slow 'pathway' +
fast 'pathway'

Fig. 4 Anatomical pathways of supraventricular tachycardias.

Broad-complex tachycardia

Sustained regular tachycardia with broad QRS complexes (i.e. > 120 ms) usually presents as an acute medical emergency but may be found by ambulatory ECG monitoring in patients with episodic palpitation, syncope, or presyncope. QRS prolongation implies that some or all of the ventricular myocardium is not being depolarized via the specialized His–Purkinje network. Most broad-complex tachycardias are ventricular in origin. The main differential diagnosis is supraventricular tachycardia with aberrant conduction from either pre-existing or 'functional' bundle branch block. Functional block is usually due to repetitive concealed penetration of the bundle (not rate related) and spontaneous ectopic beats may cause switching between broad- and narrow-complex tachycardia or even alternating left and right bundle branch block. Broad-complex tachycardia also occurs in the Wolff–Parkinson–White syndrome owing to antegrade activation of the ventricles via the bypass tract in pre-excited AF/flutter or the antidromic form of AV re-entrant tachycardia.

Clinical criteria such as severity of symptoms and haemodynamic stability are a poor guide to the origin of the tachycardia, but in almost all cases the correct diagnosis can be obtained from the history, 12-lead ECG, and adenosine testing.

History

Various studies including multivariate analysis have shown that an antecedent history of ischaemic heart disease, particularly past myocardial infarction, is a powerful predictor of ventricular tachycardia (VT) (Griffith *et al.* 1991, 1994) (Table 3).

Twelve-lead ECG

Definite evidence of ventriculo-atrial dissociation (independent P waves, fusion or capture beats) is pathognomonic of ventricular tachycardia, but absence of ventriculo-atrial dissociation does not exclude it. The P waves may be hidden within the QRS complexes or T waves (particularly at fast rates), or associated one-to-one with the QRS complexes due to retrograde ventriculo-atrial conduction, or absent completely (as in underlying AF). Otherwise, diagnosis depends on analysis of QRS morphology which should fit a classical left or right bundle branch block pattern in supraventricular tachycardia with aberration but not in ventricular tachycardia (Kindwall

Table 3 Diagnostic role of clinical history in 150 patients with broad complex tachycardia

	VT	SVT
Previous MI	100	2
No previous MI	22	26

Sensitivity, 82%: specificity, 92%: positive predictive accuracy, 98%.
MI, myocardial infarction; VT, ventricular tachycardia; SVT, supraventricular tachycardia.

Reproduced with permission from Akhtar *et al.* (1988).

et al. 1988). Various algorithms have been devised based on the specific morphologies of V1 and V6 but these are cumbersome and difficult for inexperienced clinicians to apply in the acute setting. Greater emphasis should be placed on simpler morphological criteria such as abnormal frontal axis, ventricular concordance, and marked QRS prolongation (> 160 ms) all of which are easy to interpret and favour the diagnosis of ventricular tachycardia (Table 4 and Fig. 5).

Adenosine

Intravenous adenosine has proved invaluable for differentiating ventricular tachycardia and supraventricular tachycardia if the diagnosis is uncertain from the history and ECG alone. Its electrophysiological actions include transient depression of AV nodal conduction. Thus a junctional supraventricular tachycardia involving the AV node as part of the re-entrant circuit will be interrupted by adenosine, and an atrial tachyarrhythmia will be transiently slowed (see under narrow-complex tachyacardia) but ventricular tachycardia will be unaffected. The rapid circulatory clearance (half-life less than 10 s) makes adenosine very safe to use even in sick patients. Incremental bolus administration of up to 0.25 mg/kg of adenosine in broad-complex tachycardia will discriminate ventricular tachycardia with 89 per cent sensitivity, 94 per cent specificity, and 92 per cent positive predictive

Table 4 ECG criteria for diagnosis of ventricular tachycardia

Evidence of VA dissociation
P waves
Fusion beats
Capture beats

QRS morphology—simple criteria
Abnormal axis
Width >160 ms
Concordance

QRS morphology—complex criteria
LBBB
    V1/2: rS or QS patterns, <70 ms to S-wave nadir
    V6: R wave with no Q wave
RBBB
    V1/2: rSR′ with R′>r
    V6: RS pattern with R>S, Q wave <40 ms and <2 mm

VA, ventriculo-atrial; LBBB, left bundle branch block; RBBB, right bundle branch block.

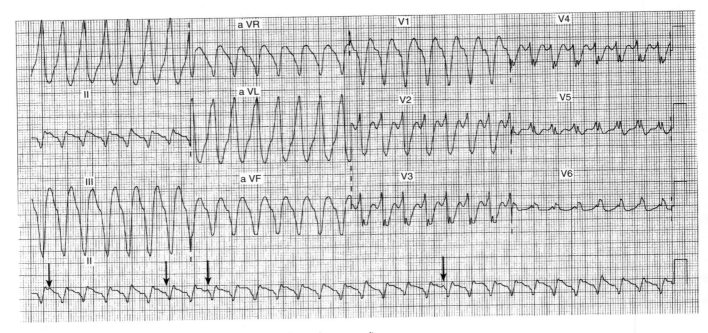

Fig. 5 ECG evidence of ventriculo-atrial dissociation in broad-complex tacycardia.

accuracy (Griffith *et al.* 1988). It is important to appreciate the need to use adequate doses and that a negative adensoine test must be taken as presumptive evidence of ventricular tachycardia.

In general, the tendency has been to over diagnose supraventricular tachycardia, sometimes with disastrous results. Ventricular tachycardia should always be regarded as the default diagnosis of broad-complex tachytachcardia if there is uncertainty.

Atrial fibrillation

AF is the most common sustained arrhythmia in clinical practice, affecting 1 to 2 per cent of the population by the age of 65 years (Boysen *et al.* 1988) and steadily rising to over 10 per cent in the ninth decade (Lake *et al.* 1989). This high prevalence of AF among elderly people reflects increased rates of underlying heart disease as well as age-associated changes in cardiac electrophysiology due to myocardial fibrosis. Associated cardiac conditions include hypertension, coronary artery disease, valvular disease, and cardio-myopathies. It is also seen in association with thyrotoxicosis, chronic lung disease, and excess alcohol consumption. The pathophysiology involves several (typically five to seven) macro re-entrant circuits within the atria. These circuits depend on abnormal areas of slow conduction, most commonly resulting from degenerative fibrosis, possibly accentuated by electrolyte imbalance, ischaemia, and certain antiarrhythmic drugs. Changes in sympathetic and parasympathetic tone can also facilitate re-entry and development of AF by shortening atrial refractoriness.

Clinical consequences

Symptoms

The symptoms associated with AF vary considerably depending on a number of factors including heart rate, underlying cardiac disease, and ventricular function. In some cases loss of AV synchrony is more important than a rapid ventricular rate. At one extreme many patients are completely asymptomatic, but others may experience palpitation, dizziness, lassitude, dyspnoea, and, in some cases, heart failure.

Systemic emboli

Compared with sinus rhythm, permanent AF increases the risk of stroke sixfold (Wolf *et al.* 1987, 1991; Atrial Fibrillation Investigators 1997*a,b*), resulting in an annual average incidence of 7 per cent per annum (Stroke Prevention in Atrial Fibrillation Investigators 1991; Atrial Fibrillation Investigators 1994). However, the absolute rate of stroke varies from 1 to 20 per cent depending on age and the presence of associated risk factors including hypertension, heart failure, prior history of cerebral emboli, diabetes, and echocardiographic evidence of impaired left ventricular function or left atrial enlargement. This predisposition to thromboembolism is the result of both atrial stasis and an associated poorly understood hypercoagulable state (Kumagai *et al.* 1990; Lip *et al.* 1995, Mitusch *et al.* 1996).

Rate-related cardiomyopathy

Poor rate control (usually above 120 beats/min) may result in progressive decline in ventricular function over a period of months, even if the patient is initially well with no adverse haemodynamic effects (Packer *et al.* 1986).

Paroxysmal versus chronic atrial fibrillation

Paroxysmal AF may last from a few seconds to several days before terminating spontaneously. In contrast with sustained (or chronic) AF, which can often be asymptomatic, the abrupt change from sinus rhythm usually leads to prominent and often incapacitating symptoms of palpitation, breathlessness, tiredness, and light-headedness. Patients with paroxysmal AF are generally younger, less likely to have associated structural heart disease, and at lower risk of thromboembolism than patients with chronic AF. At younger ages, it may be a distinct entity, as only a minority of patients convert to sustained AF during long-term follow-up (Stroke Prevention in Atrial Fibrillation Investigators 1991). In some cases paroxysmal AF may be the initial presentation of sinoatrial disease.

Investigation

AF may occur in the absence of underlying heart disease, but such patients are in the minority at later ages. In addition to a 12-lead ECG, all patients should undergo measurement of thyroid function, serum electrolytes, and renal function. A chest radiograph may provide evidence of cardiac enlargement or heart failure. Ideally, all patients with AF should be evaluated by echocardiography to look for associated structural abnormalities (e.g. mitral valve disease or left ventricular dysfunction), to assist with stratifying the long-term risk of thromboembolic complications (left atrial size and left ventricular function), and to help assess the chances of successful cardioversion (greater in the absence of structural abnormalities or left atrial enlargement). Holter ECG monitoring is indicated in patients with paroxysmal AF if sinoatrial disease is suspected because of marked sinus bradycardia or a history of syncope/presyncope. Formal exercise testing may be appropriate in patients who give a clear history of angina or exercise-induced AF.

Investigation of cardiac arrhythmias

Documentation of arrhythmias

Symptoms are frequently a poor guide to the underlying cardiac rhythm and ECG documentation of the rhythm during symptomatic episodes is of vital importance if an accurate diagnosis is to be made.

Resting ECG

The ECG will only reveal the arrhythmia if it is of a persistent nature, but it may demonstrate underlying abnormalities such as frequent atrial or ventricular ectopic beats, abnormal P-wave morphology, pre-excitation, bundle branch block, or markers of underlying ventricular pathology.

Ambulatory ECG monitoring

Ambulatory (Holter) ECG monitoring is conventionally conducted over a 24-h period and therefore its ability to detect serious arrhythmias in patients with intermittent symptoms is limited. The diagnostic yield may be usefully increased by prolonging the recording period to 48 h (Bass *et al.* 1990). Signs of low-grade conducting tissue disease or other early markers of arrhythmia, such as frequent atrial or ventricular ectopics, may be seen even if the patient remains asymptomatic.

Transtelephonic ECG monitoring

Patients with infrequent symptoms, which require ECG documentation but are unlikely to coincide with a 24- to 48-h period of Holter monitoring, may be investigated with a patient-activated ECG recording device. These are available in two main formats: the ECG recorder is applied and activated by the patient at the onset of symptoms, or it is worn continuously and activated immediately after a symptomatic episode. The latter device permanently monitors the

ECG with a loop facility, storing data from the previous loop when activated, and is particularly useful in patients with transient palpitation or syncope. In either format the recording is downloaded transtelephonically for printout in the ECG department.

Implantable loop recorders

Subcutaneously implanted loop recording devices have recently been developed which allow long-term (up to 12–14 months) continuous ECG monitoring and can be activated by the patient with a telemetry wand to store an episode up to 40 min after the onset of symptoms. The major application is investigation of recurrent unexplained syncope (Leitch *et al.* 1992; Krahn *et al.* 1995) (see above and Table 1).

Provocation of arrhythmias

Carotid sinus massage

Carotid sinus massage may be part of the examination of a patient presenting with syncope (see also Chapter 4.4). The patient should be supine with the neck slightly extended. With continuous ECG and blood pressure monitoring, the point of maximum carotid pulsation, medial to the sternomastoid and level with the upper border of the thyroid cartilage, is massaged for 5 s on right side with repetition after 1 min on the left. If necessary, the procedure can be repeated with the patient tilted upright at 70°. Carotid sinus hypersensitivity is diagnosed if stimulation provokes asystole exceeding 3 s (cardio-inhibitory), a decrease in systolic blood pressure exceeding 50 mmHg (vasodepressor), or a combination of the two (mixed response) (Kenny and Traynor 1991).

Exercise testing

Patients giving a history of exercise-related symptoms can be investigated by conventional treadmill or bicycle exercise stress tests. Apart from arrhythmia provocation and investigation of underlying ischaemic heart disease, exercise testing is also useful for assessing chronotropic competence in sinus node disease.

Tilt testing

Tilt testing can be used to confirm a predisposition to neuro-cardiogenic syncope. Continuous ECG and arterial pressure monitoring are performed during a 15-min supine rest period followed by a 60° head-up tilt for up 45 min. The test is considered positive if the patient develops presyncopal or syncopal symptoms accompanied by a fall in mean arterial pressure of more than 30 per cent compared with baseline levels (Fig. 6). Administration of intravenous isoprenaline and/or edrophonium (Fitzpatrick *et al.* 1996), or sublingual nitrate (Aerts *et al.* 1997), may increase the sensitivity of the test but at the expense of specificity.

Intracardiac electrophysiological study

This involves transvenous introduction of multipolar electrode catheters for programmed stimulation and recording from several endocardial sites. The major indication is to assess the anatomy and mechanism of re-entrant arrhythmias or discrete arrhythmogenic foci as a prelude to catheter ablation. Other uses include assessment of drug therapy, risk stratification in coronary artery disease, and evaluation of AV conduction disorders. Occasionally the technique is used

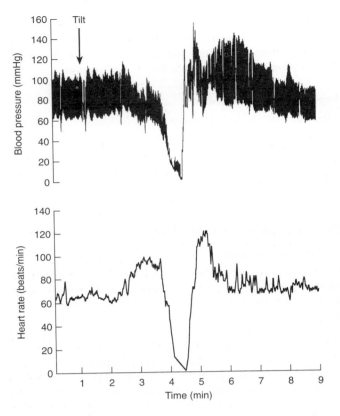

Fig. 6 Positive head-up tilt test.

diagnostically in patients with syncope or paroxysmal tachycardia but no ECG documentation.

Management

Bradyarrhythmias

Elderly patients generally exhibit significantly reduced haemodynamic stability because of diastolic dysfunction due to increased ventricular stiffness as well as more complex alterations in vasomotor regulation (Gribbin *et al.* 1971). Bradyarrhythmias increase in prevalence in later life because of age-associated fibrotic change and the frequent presence of structural heart disease, and are due to either failure of depolarization of the sinoatrial nodal tissue or impairment of conduction of these impulses to the ventricles via the AV node or the His–Purkinje system.

Sinoatrial disease

This is usually caused by idiopathic degeneration of the sinoatrial nodal tissue but occasionally develops secondary to ischaemic heart disease; some commonly prescribed drugs may also exacerbate sinus node dysfunction (Table 5). It can result in a wide range of rhythm disturbances including sinus bradycardia, sinus arrest, sinoatrial exit block, AF, atrial flutter, or combinations (tachy-brady syndrome). Sinoatrial disease may be asymptomatic and only detected incidentally by ambulatory ECG monitoring, or it may present with presyncope

Table 5 Drugs causing sinus node dysfunction or AV block

Digoxin
β-Blockers
Calcium-channel blockers (verapamil, diltiazem)
Class I antiarrhythmics
Psychotropics (tricyclics, lithium, phenothiazines)

or syncope (bradyarrhythmias) or episodic palpitation (atrial tachyarrhythmias). Although the diagnosis is often straightforward, in some cases the abnormalities of sinus node function are remarkably ephemeral and may not be disclosed by repeated ambulatory ECG recordings despite recurrent syncope with no alternative explanation. Invasive electrophysiological testing has proved of limited value in this setting, but much more encouraging results have been achieved with patient-activated implantable subcutaneous ECG monitoring devices (see section on syncope).

Sinoatrial disease has traditionally been regarded as a relatively benign disorder with no associated increase in short-term mortality. Permanent pacing is recommended for symptomatic bradycardia or to enable introduction of antiarrhythmic drug therapy in patients with tachy-brady syndromes. Ventricular-demand (VVI) pacing is associated with a significant incidence of pacemaker syndrome due to retrograde AV nodal conduction and an atrial (AAI) or dual-chamber (DDD) system is the treatment of choice (DDD will be required if there is coexistent AV conduction disease). More recently, retrospective studies and a prospective randomized trial have shown that, in comparison with VVI pacing, atrial pacing of patients with sinoatrial disease also decreases long-term progression to AF, with concomitant reductions in mortality and incidence of stroke (Andersen *et al.* 1994).

Atrioventricular conduction block

High-grade AV block often results from idiopathic conduction tissue fibrosis, but also occurs during acute myocardial ischaemia and in association with calcific aortic stenosis (particularly postoperatively) and heart muscle diseases such as dilated cardiomyopathy, sarcoidosis, rheumatoid disease, and some hereditary neuromuscular disorders. Toxicity from drugs, particularly digoxin, is another important cause (Table 5). The conduction abnormality may be chronic or intermittent, and various grades of AV block are commonly observed in the same individual. Patients can present with syncope or presyncope or with symptoms of low cardiac output or heart failure, but often the conduction disorder is discovered incidentally. In contrast with sinoatrial disease, high-grade AV block may, depending on the site of block, put the patient at risk of sudden death. Proximal block at the level of the AV node is usually benign and often asymptomatic because of the ability of junctional cells beyond the site of block to act as a subsidiary pacemaker, generating stable escape rhythms at around 50 to 60 beats/min, typically with narrow QRS complexes. Distal or infranodal block is more dangerous, with less stable escape rhythms arising from the bundle branch Purkinje network at around 20 to 40 beats/min exhibiting broad QRS complexes and a propensity to degenerate to asystole or ventricular fibrillation. Second-degree block at the level of the AV node almost invariably exhibits Mobitz I or Wenckebach periodicity, whereas with distal block the Mobitz II pattern is more common.

The major management issue is in determining the need for temporary or permanent cardiac pacing (Gregoratos et al. 1998). Patients presenting with bradycardia-related cerebral symptoms and chronic or intermittent high-grade AV block (including the Mobitz I pattern), but with no reversible cause such as drug therapy, should be offered permanent pacing as a matter of urgency. Fibrotic degeneration of the conduction system is generally progressive and there is a risk of sudden death. Interim temporary cardiac pacing is advisable in patients with syncope and chronic complete heart block, particularly with slow broad-complex escape rhythms. Awareness of the progressive nature of AV conduction disease and the prognostic benefits of permanent pacing in symptomatic patients has encouraged a trend towards prophylactic pacing in asymptomatic patients incidentally found to have second- or third-degree Mobitz II block. AV block developing during acute inferior myocardial infarction is usually proximal with a stable escape rhythm and in most cases resolves within a few days. Ischaemically mediated adenosine release may be the principal mechanism and normal conduction can sometimes be restored by administration of theophyllines. Temporary cardiac pacing can be avoided in most cases and a permanent pacemaker is only indicated if there is no recovery within 10 to 14 days. In anterior myocardial infarction, AV block develops distally due to damage of the bundle branches, usually as part of an extensive infarct with cardiogenic shock. Temporary pacing is always required but the prognosis is dismal, with in-hospital fatality greater than 75 per cent.

The choice of pacemaker system in AV block is less clear cut than for patients with sinoatrial disease. Small crossover studies have shown that both dual-chamber (DDD) and rate-adaptive (VVIR) modes improve functional capacity in physically active patients compared with traditional VVI pacing (Payne and Skehan 1994). The costs and benefits of different pacing modalities in elderly patients are being compared in a large prospective randomized trial (Toff et al. 1997).

Neurocardiogenic syncope

This is a heterogenous group of disorders characterized by multiple episodes of loss of consciousness, often recurring periodically throughout the patient's lifetime sometimes in response to specific trigger (e.g. venepuncture) or circumstances (e.g. prolonged standing) (Benditt et al. 1997). In a typical case, syncope is preceded by a short prodrome of feeling hot and light-headed, with profuse sweating, nausea, and visual disturbance. Consciousness returns rapidly on falling to a horizontal position but, in contrast with Stokes–Adams attacks, the vasodilatation and autonomic symptoms persist for some minutes and prevent the patient from being able to stand immediately. Although traditionally regarded as a condition primarily affecting adolesecents and young adults, it is now recognized that the tendency to neurocardiogenic syncope is bimodally distributed. This may be a common cause of unexplained blackouts and falls in elderly people in that the diagnosis is often obscured by blunting or absence of autonomic symptoms, as well as retrograde amnesia for attacks (see Chapter 4.4).

The syndromes share a final common pathway in the medullary vasodepressor region of the brain stem, arising from the various afferent pathways, in particular left ventricular mechanoreceptors. Once triggered, medullary efferents mediate a surge in vagal activity

with vasodilatation and bradycardia, resulting in hypotension and syncope. The relative contribution of bradycardia (cardio-inhibitory reaction) and vasodilatation (vasodepressor reaction) varies between cases and can be assessed using upright tilt testing with beat-to-beat monitoring of the blood pressure and the ECG. Patients with a predominantly cardio-inhibitory component can obtain partial benefit from pacemaker therapy, usually a reduction in symptom severity rather than prevention of attacks. This requires dual-chamber pacemakers equipped with hysteresis or 'rate-drop' algorithms to enable pacing intervention at supranormal rates (> 100 beats/min) to compensate for the vasodepressor component of the reaction. However, pacemaker therapy is not applicable to the majority of patients in whom the vasodepressor reaction is dominant. Medical management of these cases is problematic and involves general advice to avoid potential triggers and reduce the risk of injury. Numerous pharmacological agents have been tried to reduce the frequency of syncope in patients with disabling symptoms, including β-blockers, disopyramide, anticholinergics, vasoconstrictors, theophyllines, fludrocortisone, and fluoxetine, but with generally disappointing results.

Carotid sinus syncope

This condition is characterized by syncopal episodes in patients with demonstrable carotid sinus hypersensitivity (see above and Chapter 4.4) and in whom the symptoms are actually reproduced by carotid sinus massage (McIntosh et al. 1994). Only a minority (5–10 per cent) of patients with carotid sinus hypersensitivity experience spontaneous syncope and it can be difficult to confirm a cause–effect relationship. Classically, symptoms are triggered by a tight shirt collar, shaving, or abrupt neck movements, but in most cases no specific precipitant can be identified. The pathophysiology of carotid sinus hypersensitivity is unclear, but it is associated with ageing, hypertension, and ischaemic heart disease, and should be considered as a clinical marker of widespread arteriosclerotic disease rather than as a distinct disease entity. Dual-chamber (DDD) pacemaker therapy with hysteresis/rate-drop algorithms may be effective for patients with a predominantly cardio-inhibitory reaction, but the vasodepressor component is difficult to treat.

Supraventricular tacharrhythmias

Junctional supraventricular tachycardia

Acute episodes of paroxysmal supraventricular tachycardia can usually be terminated by vagal manoeuvres or intravenous adenosine up to 0.25 mg/kg. If these fail, intravenous verapamil 2.5 to 10 mg by slow injection can be used provided that there are no contraindication such as prior β-blocker therapy. D.C. cardioversion is seldom required. If there is no evidence of major structural heart disease or preexcitation, further management depends on the frequency and severity of attacks. Many patients suffer infrequent episodes that are well tolerated and either self-limiting or terminable by vagal manoeuvres, and for these individuals no maintenance antiarrhythmic therapy is required. If the symptoms are more obtrusive, the preferred pharmacological options are verapamil or digoxin (both AV nodal blocking agents) or β-blockers. Combination of verapamil plus digoxin is worth trying in difficult cases. Class I drugs such as disopyramide, quinidine, and flecainide are effective for junctional supraventricular tachycardia but are associated with some risk of serious proarrhythmia, particularly in elderly patients in whom associated structural heart disease is more likely. For refractory cases, amiodarone is another possibility although, in view of the side-effects, referral for curative ablation may be preferable (see below). Patients with Wolff–Parkinson–White syndrome should generally be referred for electrophysiological assessment, even if their symptoms are mild, because some are at risk of sudden cardiac death from degeneration of rapid pre-excited AF into ventricular fibrillation, and may need catheter ablation of the pathway on prognostic grounds.

For patients in whom drug therapy is ineffective or not tolerated, percutaneous catheter-based techniques for ablation of the arrhythmia substrate now offer the possibility of long-term cure (Zipes 1994). This method involves transcatheter delivery of radiofrequency current to generate discrete myocardial lesions by resistive heating at the electrode–tissue contact (effectively a form of electrocautery). These lesions must be critically placed to abolish part of the re-entrant circuit. In AV re-entrant tachycardia the target site is the accessory pathway (Fig. 4), identified by intracardiac electrophysiological mapping, whereas in AV nodal re-entrant tachycardia the most popular technique is to ablate or modify the posterior 'slow-pathway' component of AV nodal conduction whilst preserving antegrade conduction over the anterior 'fast pathway'. The overall success rate of catheter ablation is around 95 per cent with a low risk of serious complications in experienced hands, although AV nodal modifications for AV nodal re-entrant tachycardia carry a 1 to 2 per cent chance of complete heart block requiring a permanent pacemaker. The procedure is performed under sedation with local anaesthesia and patients are usually discharged within 24 h. As with other invasive cardiac procedures, the operative risks are only slightly increased for elderly patients.

Atrial tachyarrhythmias

Atrial tachycardia and flutter commonly present in elderly patients in association with an acute illness such as pneumonia, pulmonary embolism, or thyroid disease. Immediate restoration of sinus rhythm using d.c. cardioversion may be successful, but the risk of relapse is high without treatment of the underlying problem. Rate control with digoxin or verapamil may stabilize the situation and allow time for investigation and treatment before elective d.c. cardioversion. Pharmacological suppression of recurrent attacks requires agents active on atrial myocardium and is often disappointing. Sotalol and β-blockers are relatively safe but not particular effective. Class I agents can be used but carry some risk of serious proarrhythmia, particularly if there is associated structural disease, and may need to be combined with digoxin to avoid one-to-one conduction and paradoxical acceleration of the ventricular rate. Amiodarone is generally the most effective antiarrhythmic agent in this setting.

In drug-refractory cases, there may be a role for catheter ablation (Zipes 1994). Typical atrial flutter can be interrupted by linear ablation of the isthmus between the tricuspid annulus and the inferior vena cava, and intra-atrial tachycardia can be tackled by direct ablation if there is a single ectopic focus. If these direct approaches fail, patients may benefit from ablation of the AV node and insertion of a VVIR pacemaker to control the heart rate.

Ventricular tacharrhythmias

Acute management

Acute management of sustained monomorphic ventricular tachycardia depends on the haemodynamic status. If the patient is unconscious or severely compromised with hypotension and/or pulmonary oedema, immediate d.c. cardioversion under sedation or general anaesthesia is indicated. Otherwise it is reasonable first to attempt pharmacological conversion with an intravenous antiarrhythmic agent. Lignocaine (lidocaine) is still the most widely used agent (Josephson 1996). It is cleared fairly quickly and causes little haemodynamic depression, and so does not preclude the use of a second drug. However, recent studies suggest that it converts fewer than 30 per cent of cases and may be less effective than alternatives such as sotalol (Ho et al. 1994) or procainamide (Gorgels et al. 1996). Intravenous amiodarone is not useful for acute termination. If episodes of sustained ventricular tachycardia recur frequently, a temporary pacing catheter should be inserted for overdrive pacing. This consists of pacing the ventricles at 20 to 30 beats/min faster than the tachycardia to depolarize the excitable gap of the re-entrant circuit and terminate the ventricular tachycardia. If effective, this can easily be repeated as often as necessary, although there is a small risk of degeneration to ventricular fibrillation requiring a d.c. shock.

Prevention of recurrent episodes

Monomorphic ventricular tachycardia is usually due to re-entry in a fixed electrical substrate involving the border zone of established infarcts. It tends to be recurrent and is seldom triggered by acute myocardial ischaemia which more typically causes polymorphic ventricular tachycardia or ventricular fibrillation. Ischaemically triggered arrhythmias are often self-limiting (in the aftermath of acute myocardial infarction) but otherwise control of recurrent episodes involves β-blockers, antithrombotic agents, and sometimes revascularization. In contrast, suppression of monomorphic ventricular tachycardia requires antiarrhythmic drug therapy. Sotalol and amiodarone are now the principal agents used in this setting; class I agents have largely been abandoned because of compelling evidence of their poor efficacy and adverse impact on survival in patients with coronary artery disease (Echt et al. 1991). Sotalol has to be used at high doses ($\geq$ 320 mg/day) to achieve class III activity in addition to β-blockade and may not be tolerated. Amiodarone is probably the most potent agent with the least risk of causing proarrhythmia. The intravenous preparation can be used in patients with frequent episodes causing haemodynamic collapse for up to 72 h, but otherwise a standard oral loading regime of 0.6 g/day for 7 to 14 days is adequate. Adjunctive β-blockade appears to be highly effective in amiodarone-resistant cases and is well tolerated if introduced cautiously, even in patients with poor left ventricular function (Campbell 1996). Apart from specific antiarrhythmic therapy, attention should be paid to modulating factors such as electrolyte imbalance, arrhythmogenic drugs, and decompensated heart failure, all of which affect the tendency to ventricular tachycardia.

Recent advances in non-pharmacological therapy for drug-refractory cases include implantable cardiac defibrillators and catheter ablation. The implantable cardiac defibrillator consists of a transvenous lead system and generator with the capability of automatic detection and treatment of ventricular tachyarrhythmias by anti-tachycardia pacing, cardioversion, or defibrillation (Fig. 7). Recent trials have shown that, compared with medical therapy, these devices prolong survival in patients at high risk of sudden death, particularly after cardiac arrest or syncopal ventricular tachycardia (AVID Investigators 1997; Mushlin et al. 1998). Their use to benefit elderly patients has been primarily constrained by economic rather than

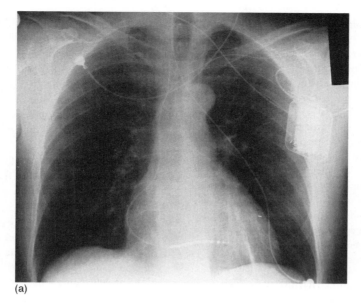

(a)

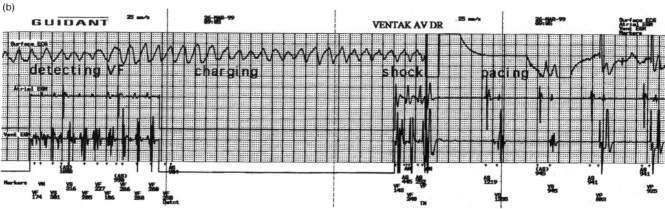

(b)

Fig. 7 Automatic implantable cardioverter defibrillator: (a) radiograph; (b) ECG traces.

clinical considerations. Catheter ablation of ventricular tachycardia in patients with coronary artery disease is technically challenging because of the complexity of the electrical substrate and is usually reserved for cases where the arrhythmia is incessant but haemodynamically stable.

Management of associated cardiac disease

Ventricular tachyarrhythmias commonly occur in association with structural heart disease, and in many patients prognosis is determined by the severity of coronary artery disease or left ventricular dysfunction rather than the arrhythmia itself. All cases should be carefully evaluated, including echocardiography and often coronary angiography, to assess the need for aspirin, statins, angiotensin-converting enzyme inhibitors, myocardial revascularization, etc.

Chronic atrial fibrillation

With established AF of more than 48 to 72 h duration, the major management issues are rate control, antithrombotic prophylaxis, and restoration and maintenance of sinus rhythm.

Rate control

This is usually achieved by digitalization alone, but in resistant cases it may be necessary to add a β-blocker or verapamil. In patients with severely impaired left ventricular function adjunctive treatment with amiodarone may be safer. Although there has been some dispute about the optimal heart rate in AF, there is general agreement that it should at least be slowed to below 100 beats/min at rest. If this cannot be achieved with pharmacological therapy, consideration should be given to catheter ablation of the AV node and implantation of a VVIR pacemaker, particularly if the patient remains symptomatic or there is evidence of rate-related cardiomyopathy.

Antithrombotic prophylaxis

Randomized controlled trials have clearly shown that the overall 5 to 6 per cent annual risk of stroke in non-rheumatic AF can be reduced by approximately two-thirds by long-term anticoagulation with warfarin (Atrial Fibrillation Investigators 1994; Prystowsky *et al.* 1996) with an annual incidence of serious haemorrhagic complications of less than 1.5 per cent. The SPAF III trial has confirmed that this is much greater protection than afforded by aspirin and/or low-intensity anti-coagulation (Cowburn and Cleland 1996). However, these were highly selected populations with over 95 per cent of eligible patients excluded from some of the trials, many because of concerns about the safety of anticoagulants on psychosocial grounds. Few patients above 75 years were randomized, and the haemorrhagic risks of warfarin therapy increase steeply in this age group unless special care is taken. It is unlikely that such favourable results could be achieved by blanket application of anticoagulant therapy to an elderly AF population. Most current guidelines advocate an individualized approach based on stratifying the relative risk of ischaemic stroke versus major haemorrhage in each patient before selecting the most appropriate antithrombotic therapy. In general, most patients without medical or psychosocial contra-indications to anticoagulation should receive warfarin (see Chapter 11.2). Others should receive aspirin where possible. Various guidelines have been issued, but those which embody age limitations should be treated as controversial (Prystowsky et al. 1996).

Restoration and maintenance of sinus rhythm

The rationale for cardioversion is primarily to improve symptoms and functional status in patients who remain limited despite satisfactory ventricular rate control. A secondary consideration is that restoration of sinus rhythm may obviate the need for continued anticoagulation, particularly where there are concerns about the safety of long-term warfarin. The disadvantages are that anticoagulant therapy is still required for at least 8 weeks (2–5 per cent risk of embolic complication without anticoagulation), the cardioversion may fail altogether, and antiarrhythmic agents are often required to maintain sinus rhythm (over 70 per cent of patients revert to AF within 12 months of successful d.c. cardioversion without antiarrhythmic drugs). Furthermore, it is at present not proved that restoration of sinus rhythm will provide the same protection against systemic thromboembolism as anticoagulation and without exposing the patient to risks from the antiarrhythmic therapy (e.g. amiodarone). This is being tested in several large randomized controlled trials (Atrial Fibrillation Investigators 1997a; Hohnloser and Kuck 1997). In general, cardioversion is most likely to succeed in patients with recent onset of AF (less than 12 months), particularly if there was an acute precipitant such as a respiratory tract infection. The absence of severe structural heart disease or marked left atrial enlargement (> 5.0 cm) are also favourable features. Patients should be fully anticoagulated for 3 to 4 weeks beforehand and, even if sinus rhythm is restored, for a month afterwards because restoration of atrial mechanical function is delayed. Indeed, there may be an initial period of 'stunning' during which mechanical function of the left atrium and appendage paradoxically deteriorate and favour formation of new thrombi. Consideration should be given to long-term antiarrhythmic therapy to maintain sinus rhythm, particularly if the patient has undergone cardioversion in the past. In most cases the choice rests between sotalol or ami-odarone. The use of class I agents is now discouraged in the light of evidence that these may increase cardiac mortality (Coplen et al. 1990). If cardioversion fails or the patient later reverts to AF, a strategy of rate control and long-term antithrombotic therapy (as above) would be required.

Paroxysmal atrial fibrillation

Antiarrhythmic drug therapy is unnecessary in a substantial pro-portion of patients with mild infrequent attacks. Digoxin is often prescribed for this condition but has little effect on the frequency of attacks. The major antiarrhythmic agents for suppressing paroxysmal AF are as follows.

1. β-Blockers are particularly indicated if there is any history of adrenergic triggering (e.g. during exercise) or coexisting cardiac disease such as angina or hypertension. Although relatively ineffective as antifibrillatory agents, their main advantage is long-term safety and so they are often used as first-line treatment.

2. Sotalol acts as a β-blocker at low dosage, but above 120 to 160 mg twice daily there is also class III activity. It is important to monitor and treat any hypokalaemia to reduce the risks of torsades de pointes.

3. Amiodarone is the most potent antifibrillatory agent currently available and probably the safest in patients with structural heart disease. Although extracardiac toxicity has been extensively doc-umented, problems are relatively uncommon at a maintenance dose of 200 mg/day. In some cases, side-effects can be further limited by reducing the dose to 100 mg/day.

4. The newer class Ic agents such as flecainide or propafenone are amongst the most potent antifibrillatory agents currently available, but their use is associated with significant risk of proarrhythmia in elderly patients with structural heart disease, particularly ischaemic heart disease with impaired left ventricular function (Echt et al. 1991). Similar reservations apply to the older class Ia agents such as quinidine and disopyramide.

Some patients with drug-refractory paroxysmal AF may benefit from AV nodal ablation and a mode-switching dual-chamber pace-maker, particularly if the attacks are associated with a rapid ventricular rate.

With regard to antithrombotic therapy, the considerations are broadly similar to chronic AF except that the absolute risk of stroke is lower (Lip et al. 1996). It may be reasonable to avoid full anticoagulation in many patients, particularly if the episodes of PAF can be suppressed by antiarrhythmic drug therapy.

References

Aerts, A., et al. (1997). Sublingual nitrates during head-up tilt testing for the diagnosis of vasovagal syncope. *American Heart Journal*, 1997. 133(5): p. 504–507.

Akhtar, M., et al. (1988). Wide QRS complex tachycardia. Reappraisal of a common clinical problem. *Annals of Internal Medicine*, 109, 905–12.

Andersen, H.R., et al. (1994). Prospective randomised trial of atrial versus ventricular pacing in sick-sinus syndrome. *Lancet*, 344, 1523–8.

Atrial Fibrillation Investigators (1994). Risk factors for stroke and efficacy of antithrombotic therapy in atrial fibrillation. Analysis of pooled data from five randomized controlled trials. *Archives of Internal Medicine*, 154, 1449–57, 2254(erratum).

Atrial Fibrillation Investigators (1997a). Atrial fibrillation follow-up investigation of rhythm management – the AFFIRM study design. The Planning and Steering Committees of the AFFIRM study for the NHLBI AFFIRM investigators. *American Journal of Cardiology*, 79, 1198–2002.

Atrial Fibrillation Investigators (1997b). The efficacy of aspirin in patients with atrial fibrillation. Analysis of pooled data from 3 randomized trials. *Archives of Internal Medicine*, 157, 1237–40.

AVID (Antiarrhythmics versus Implantable Defibrillators) Investigators (1997). A comparison of antiarrhythmic-drug therapy with implantable defibrillators in patients resuscitated from near-fatal ventricular arrhythmias. *New England Journal of Medicine*, **337**, 1576–83.

Barsky, A.J., *et al.* (1996). Somatized psychiatric disorder presenting as palpitations. *Archives of Internal Medicine*, **156**, 1102–8.

Bass, E.B., *et al.* (1990). The duration of Holter monitoring in patients with syncope. Is 24 h enough? *Archives of Internal Medicine*, **150**, 1073–8.

Benditt, D.G., Gammage, M.D., Sutton, R., Erickson, M., and Markowitz, T. (1997). Neurocardiogenic Syncope. Proceedings of an International Symposium, Lansdowne, Virginia, 27–29 September 1996. *Pacing and Clinical Electrophysiology*, **20**, 751–860.

Boysen, G., *et al.* (1988). Stroke incidence and risk factors for stroke in Copenhagen. *Stroke*, **19**, 1345–53.

Camm, A.J. and C.J. Garratt (1991). Adenosine and supraventricular tachycardia [see comments]. *New England Journal of Medicine*, **325**, 1621–9.

Campbell, T.J. (1996). Beta-blockers for ventricular arrhythmias: have we underestimated their value? *Australian and New Zealand Journal of Medicine*, **26**, 689–96.

Coplen, S.E., *et al.* (1990). Efficacy and safety of quinidine therapy for maintenance of sinus rhythm after cardioversion. A meta-analysis of randomized control trials. *Circulation*, **82**, 1106–16; **83**, 714 (erratum).

Cowburn, P. and Cleland, J.G. (1996). SPAF-III results. *European Heart Journal*, **17**, 1129.

Day, S.C., *et al.* (1982). Evaluation and outcome of emergency room patients with transient loss of consciousness. *American Journal of Medicine*, **73**, 15–23.

Eagle, K.A. and Black, H.R. (1983). The impact of diagnostic tests in evaluating patients with syncope. *Yale Journal of Biology and Medicine*, **56**, 1–8.

Eagle, K.A., *et al.* (1985). Evaluation of prognostic classifications for patients with syncope. *American Journal of Medicine*, **79**, 455–60.

Echt, D.S., *et al.* (1991). Mortality and morbidity in patients receiving encainide, flecainide, or placebo. The Cardiac Arrhythmia Suppression Trial. *New England Journal of Medicine*, **324**, 781–8.

Fitzpatrick, A.P., *et al.* (1991*a*) The incidence of malignant vasovagal syndrome in patients with recurrent syncope. *European Heart Journal*, **12**, 389–94.

Fitzpatrick, A.P., *et al.* (1991*b*) Methodology of head-up tilt testing in patients with unexplained syncope. *Journal of the American College of Cardiology*, **17**, 125–30.

Fitzpatrick, A.P., *et al.* (1996). Effect of patient characteristics on the yield of prolonged baseline head-up tilt testing and the additional yield of drug provocation. *Heart*, **76**, 406–11.

Gorgels, A.P., *et al.* (1996). Comparison of procainamide and lidocaine in terminating sustained monomorphic ventricular tachycardia. *American Journal of Cardiology*, **78**, 43–6.

Gregoratos, G., *et al.* (1998). ACC/AHA guidelines for implantation of cardiac pacemakers and antiarrhythmia devices: a report of the American College of Cardiology/American Heart Association Task Force on Practice Guidelines (Committee on Pacemaker Implantation). *Journal of the American College of Cardiology*, **31**, 1175–1209.

Gribbin, B., *et al.* (1971). Effect of age and high blood pressure on baroreflex sensitivity in man. *Circulation Research*, **29**, 424–31.

Griffith, M.J., *et al.* (1988). Adenosine in the diagnosis of broad complex tachycardia. *Lancet*, **i**, 672–5.

Griffith, M.J., *et al.* (1991). Multivariate analysis to simplify the differential diagnosis of broad complex tachycardia. *British Heart Journal*, **66**, 166–74.

Griffith, M.J., *et al.* (1994). Ventricular tachycardia as default diagnosis in broad complex tachycardia. *Lancet*, **343**, 386–8.

Ho, D.S., *et al.* (1994). Double-blind trial of lignocaine versus sotalol for acute termination of spontaneous sustained ventricular tachycardia. *Lancet*, **344**, 18–23.

Hohnloser, S.H. and Kuck, K.H. (1997). Atrial fibrillation: maintaining stability of sinus rhythm or ventricular rate control? The need for prospective data: the PIAF trial. *Pacing and Clinical Electrophysiology*, **20**, 1989–92.

Josephson, M.E. (1996). Lidocaine and sustained monomorphic ventricular tachycardia: fact or fiction (editorial). *American Journal of Cardiology*, **78**, 82–3.

Kapoor, W.N. (1990). Evaluation and outcome of patients with syncope. *Medicine (Baltimore)*, **69**, 160–75.

Kapoor, W.N. (1992). Evaluation and management of the patient with syncope. *Journal of the American Medical Association*, **268**, 2553–60.

Kapoor, W.N., *et al.* (1983). A prospective evaluation and follow-up of patients with syncope. *New England Journal of Medicine*, **309**, 197–204.

Kenny, R.A. and Traynor, G. (1991). Carotid sinus syndrome–clinical characteristics in elderly patients. *Age and Ageing*, **20**, 449–54.

Kindwall, K.E., Brown, J., and Josephson, M.E. (1988). Electrocardiographic criteria for ventricular tachycardia in wide complex left bundle branch block morphology tachycardias. *American Journal of Cardiology*, **61**, 1279–83.

Krahn, A.D., *et al.* (1995). The etiology of syncope in patients with negative tilt table and electrophysiological testing. *Circulation*, **92**, 1819–24.

Kroenke, K. and Mangelsdorff, A.D. (1989). Common symptoms in ambulatory care: incidence, evaluation, therapy, and outcome. *American Journal of Medicine*, **86**, 262–6.

Kumagai, K., *et al.* (1990). Increased intracardiovascular clotting in patients with chronic atrial fibrillation. *Journal of the American College of Cardiology*, **16**, 377–80.

Lake, F.R., *et al.* (1989). Atrial fibrillation and mortality in an elderly population. *Australian and New Zealand Journal of Medicine*, **19**, 321–6.

Leitch, J., *et al.* (1992). Feasibility of an implantable arrhythmia monitor. *Pacing and Clinical Electrophysiology*, **15**, 2232–5.

Lip, G.Y., *et al.* (1995). Increased markers of thrombogenesis in chronic atrial fibrillation: effects of warfarin treatment. *British Heart Journal*, **73**, 527–33.

Lip, G.Y., *et al.* (1996). Fibrinogen and fibrin D-dimer levels in paroxysmal atrial fibrillation: evidence for intermediate elevated levels of intravascular thrombogenesis. *American Heart Journal*, **131**, 724–30.

Lipsitz, L.A., Wei, J.Y., and Rowe, J.W. (1985). Syncope in an elderly, institutionalised population: prevalence, incidence, and associated risk. *Quarterly Journal of Medicine*, **55**, 45–54.

Lok, N.S. and Lau, C.P. (1996). Prevalence of palpitations, cardiac arrhythmias and their associated risk factors in ambulant elderly. *International Journal of Cardiology*, **54**, 231–6.

McIntosh, S., Da Costa, D., and Kenny, R.A. (1993). Outcome of an integrated approach to the investigation of dizziness, falls and syncope in elderly patients referred to a 'syncope' clinic. *Age and Ageing*, **22**, 53–8.

McIntosh, S.J., Lawson, J., and Kenny, R.A. (1994). Heart rate and blood pressure responses to carotid sinus massage in healthy elderly subjects. *Age and Ageing*, **23**, 57–61.

Martin, G.J., *et al.* (1984). Prospective evaluation of syncope. *Annals of Emergency Medicine*, **13**, 499–504.

Mitusch, R., *et al.* (1996). Detection of a hypercoagulable state in nonvalvular atrial fibrillation and the effect of anticoagulant therapy. *Thrombosis and Haemostasis*, **75**, 219–23.

Mushlin, A.I., *et al.* (1998). The cost-effectiveness of automatic implantable cardiac defibrillators: results from MADIT. Multicenter Automatic Defibrillator Implantation Trial. *Circulation*, **97**, 2129–35.

Packer, D.L., *et al.* (1986). Tachycardia-induced cardiomyopathy: a reversible form of left ventricular dysfunction. *American Journal of Cardiology*, **57**, 563–70.

Payne, G.E. and Skehan, J.D. (1994). Issues in cardiac pacing: can ageism be justified? (editorial). *British Heart Journal*, **72**, 102–3.

Prystowsky, E.N., *et al.* (1996). Management of patients with atrial fibrillation. A Statement for Healthcare Professionals from the Subcommittee on Electrocardiography and Electrophysiology, American Heart Association. *Circulation*, **93**, 1262–77.

Silverstein, M.D., *et al.* (1982). Patients with syncope admitted to medical intensive care units. *Journal of the American Medical Association*, **248**, 1185–9.

Stroke Prevention in Atrial Fibrillation Investigators (1991). Stroke Prevention in Atrial Fibrillation Study: final results. *Circulation*, **84**, 527–39.

Toff, W.D., *et al.* (1997). The United Kingdom Pacing and Cardiovascular Events (UKPACE) trial. *Heart*, **78**, 221–3.

Wolf, P.A., Abbott, R.D., and Kannel, W.B. (1987). Atrial fibrillation: a major contributor to stroke in the elderly. The Framingham Study. *Archives of Internal Medicine*, **147**, 1561–4.

Wolf, P.A., Abbott, R.D., and Kannel, W.B. (1991). Atrial fibrillation as an independent risk factor for stroke: the Framingham Study. *Stroke*, **22**, 983–8.

Zipes, D.P. (ed.) (1994). *Catheter ablation of arrhythmias*, p.342. Futura, Armonk, NY.

9.7 Atrial fibrillation and anticoagulation

J. P. Emeriau, S. Richard Hartson, and N. Salles Montaudon

Anticoagulation has been used for 40 years for various indications including coronary disease, heart failure, arterial embolism, phlebitis, and prevention of thromboembolic complications. In this area, the risk of peripheral arterial embolism, and particularly of cerebral embolism, is a serious complication in patients with atrial fibrillation. The risk of supraventricular arrhythmias, and particularly atrial fibrillation, increases with age. Anticoagulants are thus commonly indicated for elderly patients, but the treatment increases the risk of haemorrhage, particularly in the presence of certain other medications which older people may also be taking. For this reason, advanced age has long been considered as a contraindication for anticoagulants. A succession of interventional trials performed and published at the beginning of the 1990s has allowed the specification of the indications for and limitations on anticoagulant therapy for elderly patients with atrial fibrillation.

Epidemiology of atrial fibrillation in elderly people (see Chapter 9.1)

The prevalence of atrial fibrillation increases rapidly with age: it is reported with a rate of less than 1 per cent in the 40 to 65 year age group, of 2 to 5 per cent of the 65 to 74 year age group, and more than 5 per cent in patients over 75 years old. In the United States, approximately 50 per cent of patients with atrial fibrillation are over 75 years of age, and atrial fibrillation is the most common arrhythmia in elderly patients. In the Cardiovascular Health Study (Furberg *et al.* 1994), a representative sample of the general population of the United States with 5201 men and women aged over 65 years living at home, 4.8 per cent of women and 6.2 per cent of men had atrial fibrillation. A community study in the United Kingdom found a prevalence of 3.4 per cent of men and 1.9 per cent of women at ages 65 to 74 years, rising to 9.2 per cent and 3.8 per cent respectively at ages over 75 years (Grimley Evans 1985) (Fig. 1).

Atrial fibrillation is easy to diagnose when chronic and permanent. However, it can also occur paroxysmally during physical exercise or at rest. Exercise-induced atrial fibrillation can be screened for by an exercise test. In the Baltimore Longitudinal Study of Aging, the prevalence of exercise-induced supraventricular tachycardia during the initial treadmill exercise test was a function of age and sex. Among the 1383 apparently healthy volunteers, the prevalence of exercise-induced supraventricular tachycardia strikingly increased with age in men but not in women (Maurer *et al.* 1995). Atrial fibrillation can be intermittent and paroxysmal at rest. In the Cardiovascular Health Study, 2.7 per cent of men and 2.4 per cent of women had paroxysmal atrial fibrillation (Manolio *et al.* 1994). In the Framingham Study, as shown in Table 1, the incidence of paroxysmal atrial fibrillation increased exponentially with age (Kannel *et al.* 1983).

The prevalence of atrial fibrillation is correlated with that of associated pathological conditions. In the Cardiovascular Health Study, the prevalence of atrial fibrillation was independently associated with a history of congestive heart failure, valvular heart disease and stroke, echocardiographic evidence of enlarged left atrium, an abnormal mitral and aortic valve function, treated hypertension, and advanced age. Nevertheless, the low prevalence of atrial fibrillation in the absence of clinical and subclinical cardiovascular disease calls into question the existence and the clinical usefulness of the concept

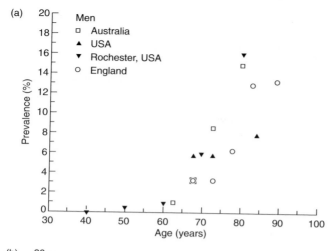

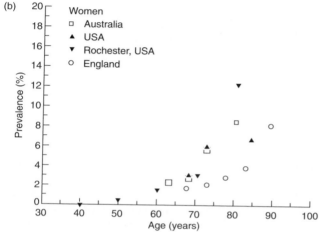

Fig. 1 Prevalence of atrial fibrillation at various ages in Western Australia (Lake *et al.* 1989), a national American population sample (Furberg *et al.* 1994), Rochester, Minnesota (Phillips *et al.* 1990), and Whickham in northeast England (Grimley Evans 1985)

Table 1 Two-year incidence (per thousand) of transient atrial fibrillation

Age (years)	Women per 1000	Men per 1000
30–39	0.0	0.0
40–49	0.4	0.5
50–59	0.6	0.5
60–69	1.9	4.8
70–79	9.2	12.7

Data from Kannel *et al.* (1983).

Different predictive factors for ischaemic stroke were identified in different studies: previous myocardial infarction (Petersen *et al.* 1989); advanced age, angina, and clinical heart disease (Boston Area Anticoagulation Trial for the Atrial Fibrillation Investigators 1990); history of thromboembolism, hypertension, recent heart failure, diabetes, diuretic use, or systolic blood pressure over 160 mmHg (Stroke Prevention in Atrial Fibrillation Investigators 1994); angina or smoking (Ezekowitz *et al.* 1992) (Table 2).

The different risk factors were 'tested' with a multivariate analysis in a meta-analysis combining the data from the five original trials of stroke prevention in atrial fibrillation (Atrial Fibrillation Investigators 1994). Four independent clinical features were identified: previous transient ischaemic attack, diabetes mellitus, hypertension, and advanced age. Patients with any of these untreated risk factors had an estimated annual risk of stroke of 4 per cent. Patients with cardiac disorders such as congestive heart failure and coronary artery disease showed a rate of stroke three times higher than that for patients without any risk factors. In the 60- to 69-year-old patients with lone atrial fibrillation, the incidence of stroke was 1.6 per cent. In the 70- to 79-year-old group, the incidence of stroke was 2.1 per cent.

As well as cardiac failure and symptomatic ischaemic heart disease (Atrial Fibrillation Investigators 1994), fibrillation-related thromboembolism is associated with intra-atrial haemodynamic stasis which predisposes to atrial thrombosis and subsequent embolization. The causal link between the fibrillating atrium and stroke is challenged by the low rate of stroke among patients with lone atrial fibrillation. An enlarged left atrium may contribute to an increased risk of atrial thrombi and thromboembolism in patients with atrial fibrillation. An enlarged left atrium has also been associated with spontaneous echo contrast on transoesophageal echocardiography, consisting of a smoke-like appearance of blood in the atria, suggestive of sluggish flow. Spontaneous echo contrast is associated with left atrial intracardiac thrombi, thromboembolism, and stroke. Left atrial spontaneous echo contrast in non-rheumatic atrial fibrillation indicates the turbulences which predispose patients to intra-atrial thrombosis (Tsai *et al.* 1997). In addition, atrial fibrillation may confer a hypercoagulable state indicated by raised plasma concentrations of fibrin D-dimer β-thromboglobulin (Lip *et al.* 1996). These abnormalities become more pronounced as episodes of paroxysmal atrial fibrillation lengthen (Sohara *et al.* 1997).

of so-called 'lone atrial fibrillation' in older people (Furberg *et al.* 1994).

Thromboembolic risk associated with atrial fibrillation

Heart failure and thromboembolic disease are the most common complications seen in patients with atrial fibrillation. In at least 50 per cent of instances, thromboembolic complications include a stroke. Non-rheumatic atrial fibrillation increases the risk of stroke to 5 per cent per year and accounts for 15 per cent of cases of stroke (Wolf *et al.* 1991). The risk is increased in both paroxysmal and chronic atrial fibrillation (Atrial Fibrillation Investigators 1994; Roy *et al.* 1996). Embolic complications remain rare in patients with lone paroxysmal atrial fibrillation in whom the incidence of embolism is under 2 per cent per year (Petersen *et al.* 1989). In the absence of associated diseases, the risk of thromboembolic disease rises from 1.6 to 3.0 per cent during the seventh to ninth decades of life (Lip 1996).

Table 2 Univariate analysis of predictors of stroke in control patients

Variables identified	All five studies		
	n	Risk ratio	95% confidence interval
AFASAK			
History of myocardial infarction	217	1.7	(1.1–2.7)
BAATAFI			
Increasing age		1.4	(1.1–1.8)
Heart disease	657	3.6	(1.1–2.3)
Angina	363	1.5	(1.0–2.2)
SPAF			
History of stroke or transient ischaemic attack	101	3.1	(1.9–5.2)
History of hypertension	750	1.9	(1.3–2.8)
History of congestive heart failure	349	1.7	(1.1–2.5)
SPINAF			
History of angina	363	1.5	(1.0–2.2)
Current smoker	158	0.4	(0.2–0.96)

AFASAK: Petersen *et al.* (1989).
BAATAFI: Boston Area Anticoagulation Trial for the Atrial Fibrillation Investigators (1990).
SPAF: Stroke Prevention in Atrial Fibrillation Investigators (1994).
SPINAF: Ezekowitz *et al.* (1992).

A history of stroke, transient ischaemic attack, or other embolic events, increases the risk of stroke and mortality in atrial fibrillation. In the Oxfordshire Community Stroke Project, the prevalence of atrial fibrillation was 17 per cent in the overall types of stroke. Patients with cerebral infarction showed a significantly higher 30-day case fatality rate with atrial fibrillation (23 per cent) than with sinus rhythm (8 per cent). In patients who survived at least 30 days, the average annual risk of recurrent stroke was 8.2 per cent with sinus rhythm and 11.0 per cent with atrial fibrillation (Sandercock *et al.* 1992).

In patients with atrial fibrillation, the left atrium is not responsible for all strokes. When the mechanism of stroke is ascertained, only 65 per cent have a cardioembolic origin, arising not only from a dilated left atrium, but also from the aorta, carotids, or cerebral arteries (Miller *et al.* 1993). As well as stroke, atrial fibrillation can be associated with cognitive defects due to silent small deep lacunar infarcts. Finally, inattention and impairments of memory and language have been reported in elderly patients with no clinical or CT scan evidence of cerebral ischaemia (Farina *et al.* 1996). The last question about atrial fibrillation and stroke concerns the onset of atrial fibrillation. In the Framingham Study, atrial fibrillation was present at the time of stroke in 24 per cent of the subjects, and about one-third of the strokes associated with atrial fibrillation occurred within 6 months of the onset of arrhythmia. In addition, a further stroke within 6 months of the first one may be more common in patients with continuous atrial fibrillation.

Anticoagulation and the prevention of thromboembolic complications

Between 1986 and 1996, the results of five randomized controlled trials evaluating the efficacy of warfarin in the primary prevention of

stroke in patients with atrial fibrillation were published (Petersen *et al.* 1986; Boston Area Anticoagulation Trial for the Atrial Fibrillation Investigators 1990; Ezekowitz *et al.* 1992; European Atrial Fibrillation Trial Study Group 1993; Stroke Prevention in Atrial Fibrillation Investigators 1996*a*). Two studies also randomized patients to receive aspirin (Petersen *et al.* 1989; Stroke Prevention in Atrial Fibrillation Investigators 1996*b*). However, many questions about antithrombotic therapy cannot be answered by the results of these five trials considered separately. The five study groups co-operated to pool individual patient data to address these questions (Atrial Fibrillation Investigators 1994). The mean age of patients in the studies was 69 years; almost half had a history of hypertension, about 20 per cent had a history of heart failure, 23 per cent had a history of angina, and 14 per cent had a history of diabetes.

In multivariate analysis, four independent risk factors for stroke were identified: increasing age, previous stroke or transient ischaemic attack, history of hypertension, and diabetes. The presence or absence of these risk factors could be used to divide patients into two different categories of risk. The annual risk of stroke in control patients varied from 1 per cent in patients under 65 years of age without any other risk factor, to 8.1 per cent in patients over 75 years of age with at least one other risk factor than ageing (Table 3).

Warfarin appeared to decrease the rate of stroke in all subgroups of patients, except those under 65 years with no other risk factors. In this group, the risk of stroke was low. Overall, warfarin decreased the frequency of all the strokes by 68 per cent (95 per cent confidence intervals, 50–79 per cent) with a total annual reduction of 3.1 per cent (*p* < 0.001). The incidence of stroke with residual deficit was decreased by 68 per cent (95 per cent confidence intervals, 39–83 per cent) with a total annual reduction of 1.4 per cent (*p* < 0.001).

Another problem concerns the risk of recurrent vascular events in patients with a recent transient ischaemic attack or minor ischaemic

Table 3 Annual event rates by age group and risk factors

Risk categories	Placebo		Warfarin	
	Event rate (%)	95% confidence intervals	Event rate (%)	95% confidence intervals
Age <65 years				
No risk factors	1.0	(0.3–3.1)	1.0	(0.3–3.0)
One or more risk factors	4.9	(3.0–8.1)	1.7	(0.8–3.9)
Age 65–75 years				
No risk factors	4.3	(2.7–7.1)	1.1	(0.4–2.8)
One or more risk factors	5.7	(3.9–8.3)	1.5	(0.9–3.4)
Age >75 years				
No risk factors	3.5	(1.6–7.7)	1.7	(0.5–5.2)
One or more risk factors	8.1	(4.5–13.9)	1.2	(0.3–5.0)

Data from Atrial Fibrillation Investigators (1994).

stroke and non-rheumatic atrial fibrillation. For these patients, anti-coagulant therapy halves the risk of vascular complications (European Atrial Fibrillation Trial Study Group 1993). The risk of recurrent stroke is decreased by two-thirds. The most important difference between primary and secondary prevention studies is the much higher absolute risk of recurrent stroke: 12 per cent in the placebo group of the European Atrial Fibrillation Trial and 3 to 4 per cent in the primary prevention studies.

Anticoagulant-related complications

The risk associated with anticoagulants has been known ever since they were first used. Incidents are considered as minor or major depending on whether they put the patient's life at risk or not. Minor incidents include bruising and subcutaneous or muscular haematomas. Major incidents are exemplified by lesions such as retroperitoneal or gastrointestinal bleeding or, in particular, sub-arachnoid or intracerebral haemorrhage. Various risk factors of bleeding have been identified. Two of them are particularly important: the degree of anticoagulation and age.

Degree of anticoagulation

The rational use of anticoagulants, especially among older patients, has to balance antithrombotic efficacy against the risk of haemorrhage, particularly intracranial haemorrhage, but it is difficult to estimate the risks and benefits. To assess the risk of intracranial haemorrhage, it is possible to analyse the results of the different trials with warfarin in the prevention of non-rheumatic atrial fibrillation complications. Intracranial haemorrhage assumes a great importance because it is comparable in clinical significance to the thromboembolic events that anticoagulants prevent. The absolute rate of anticoagulant-related intracranial haemorrhage ranges from 0.3 per cent per year, as observed in the first five trials in non-rheumatic atrial fibrillation, to approximately 2.0 per cent per year (Landefeld and Goldman 1989). The results were similar in the Stroke Prevention in Atrial Fibrillation

Study II for patients aged over 75 years (Stroke Prevention in Atrial Fibrillation Investigators 1991). In two recent observational studies carried out in anticoagulant therapy units with a detailed follow-up, the rates of haemorrhage were 0.5 and 0.6 per cent per year. To overcome the problem of the low absolute rate of intracranial haemorrhage, Hylek et al. (1996) chose a case–control design with 121 cases and 363 controls. The dominant independent risk factor was prothrombin time ratio. For each 0.5 increase in prothrombin time ratio, the risk of intracranial bleeding doubled. For subdural haemorrhage, the risk was unchanged between prothrombin time ratios ranging from 1 to 2, but rose dramatically above 2 (in the report, the prothrombin time ratio threshold of 2.0 corresponds to an international normalized ratio (INR) range of 3.7–4.3). The degree of anticoagulation is certainly the most important risk factor for intracranial haemorrhage. The association between INR and intra-cranial haemorrhage is stronger. Anticoagulation with an INR between 2 and 3 may combine an optimal therapeutic effect with the lowest risk of bleeding (European Atrial Fibrillation Trial Study Group 1995).

Age

Studies have reported conflicting conclusions with regard to age. Finh et al. (1993) found a reduced risk of complications of anticoagulation for people over 65 years of age (risk ratio 0.8), whereas Landefeld and Goldman (1989) found a highly significantly increased risk (risk ratio 3.2). In the Stroke Prevention in Atrial Fibrillation Trial II (Stroke Prevention in Atrial Fibrillation Investigators 1996b), the intracranial haemorrhage rate was 1.8 per cent per year for patients aged over 75 years compared with 0.5 per cent per year for younger patients. The reasons for the difference between the Stroke Prevention in Atrial Fibrillation Trial II and the other studies may be due to the difference in anticoagulation intensity (Conolly et al. 1991). Hylek et al. (1996) found that age was a strong independent risk factor for subdural haemorrhage, but was of only borderline statistical significance for intracerebral haemorrhage. The incidence rates of intracranial haemorrhage in patients not taking warfarin also rise with age (Broderick et al. 1993).

Table 4 Oral anticoagulation and atrial fibrillation: stratification with age

Age (years)	Risk factors	Recommendations
≤65	Yes	Warfarin INR 2–3
	No	Aspirin or nothing
65–75	Yes	Warfarin INR 2–3
	No	Warfarin or aspirin
≥75		Warfarin INR 2–3

Data from Laupacis et al. (1995).

The different solutions

In order to avoid major haemorrhages and to prevent complications induced by non-rheumatic atrial fibrillation, two approaches can be considered: the administration of the lowest effective degree of anticoagulation or aspirin.

Lowest effective degree of anticoagulation

One approach, especially for higher-risk patients, could be an adjusted warfarin dose. Hylek et al. (1996) attempted to identify the lowest effective degree of anticoagulation for the prevention of ischaemic stroke in patients with atrial fibrillation. In that study, the case subjects were patients with atrial fibrillation who had ischaemic strokes despite receiving anticoagulants. The INR was a powerful determinant for the risk of stroke, with the risk rising steeply as the INR values fell below 2.0. In comparison with patients with an INR of 2.0, those with values of 1.7 had nearly double the risk of stroke, those with values of 1.5 had a risk nearly three times higher, and those with values of 1.3 had a sevenfold higher risk. There were similar results in two other randomized trials (Petersen et al. 1989; Stroke Prevention in Atrial Fibrillation Investigators 1996a).

Aspirin

In the studies investigating stroke prevention with anticoagulants, 53 to 93 per cent of eligible patients had to be excluded because of the risk of bleeding. For patients for whom anticoagulation is contraindicated, aspirin is the only alternative that has been intensively investigated as a means of preventing embolism in atrial fibrillation. In the AFASAK Study (Petersen et al. 1989) a daily dose of 75 mg of aspirin was associated with a non-significant 14 per cent reduction in stroke incidence. The Stroke Prevention in Atrial Fibrillation Study (Stroke Prevention in Atrial Fibrillation Investigators 1991) employed a daily aspirin dose of 325 mg and observed a significant 42 per cent stroke reduction, corresponding to a reduction of 15 to 20 strokes per 1000 patients treated per year. However, the incidence of bleeding was not significantly lower than with warfarin.

The Stroke Prevention in Atrial Fibrillation Study II (Stroke Prevention in Atrial Fibrillation Investigators 1994) aimed to assess the differential effects of warfarin and aspirin according to age, and was designed to detect a 4 per cent reduction in ischaemic strokes or systemic emboli in patients aged over 75 years. Among older patients, warfarin decreased the absolute rate of primary events by 1.2 per cent per year; the primary event rate was 3.6 per cent with warfarin and 4.8 per cent with aspirin (risk ratio 0.73, $p = 0.39$). However, in the older group, the rate of all strokes with long-lasting deficit (ischaemic or haemorrhagic) was 4.3 per cent per year with aspirin and 4.6 per cent per year with warfarin (risk ratio 1.1). Warfarin may be more effective than aspirin in the prevention of ischaemic stroke, but in the oldest group of patients the rate of stroke was substantially diminished by either agent. The conclusions of Stroke Prevention in Atrial Fibrillation Trial II are that aspirin could be a safer and easier alternative to warfarin for patients with atrial fibrillation. However, another question concerns the efficacy of aspirin in patients who are at high risk of thromboembolism, especially for those who are older and who have one or more of the following risk factors: congestive heart failure or ventricular fractional shortening of 25 per cent or less, previous thromboembolism, hypertension, or women aged over 75 years. In the Stroke Prevention in Atrial Fibrillation Study III (Stroke Prevention in Atrial Fibrillation Investigators 1996a), 1044 patients with atrial fibrillation plus at least one of these thromboembolic risk factors were assigned to either a combination of low-degree fixed-dose warfarin (INR 1.2–1.5) and aspirin (325 mg/day) or adjusted-dose warfarin (INR 2.0–3.0). The trial was stopped when the rate of ischaemic stroke and systemic embolism in patients given combination therapy was significantly higher (7.9 per cent per year) than in those given adjusted-dose warfarin (1.9 per cent per year). These results correspond to a total reduction of 6 per cent per year by adjusted-dose warfarin.

The annual rates of disabling strokes (5.6 versus 1.7 per cent) and of primary event or vascular death (11.8 versus 6.4 per cent) were also higher with combination therapy. The rates of major bleeding were similar in the treatment groups.

Albers (1994) has pooled the results of two of the primary prevention studies (AFASAK and Stroke Prevention in Atrial Fibrillation Trial II) and one of the secondary prevention studies (European Atrial Fibrillation Trial Study Group 1993) to compare the efficacy of aspirin and warfarin for stroke prevention in patients with atrial fibrillation. The combined results indicate that anticoagulation is approximately twice as effective as aspirin, as confirmed by Stroke Prevention in Atrial Fibrillation III. Aspirin is justified for patients with very low stroke risk and for those with contraindications to warfarin. Aspirin may be a safe and reasonably effective option when episodes of paroxysmal atrial fibrillation are very infrequent, and for patients aged under 75 years with no structural heart disease. For patients over 75 years, with structural heart disease and frequent paroxysms, warfarin is recommended (Lip 1997).

Indications for anticoagulants

General indications

Oral anticoagulation is effective in decreasing the risk of stroke in patients with atrial fibrillation and, for this purpose, is more effective than aspirin (Table 4). The majority of patients with atrial fibrillation aged over 75 years have one or more risk factors for stroke but the risk of intracranial haemorrhage associated with oral anticoagulant increases with age. In patients aged over 75 years, the risk of stroke when not receiving oral anticoagulation appears greater than the risk of intracranial haemorrhage when receiving oral anticoagulants. Therefore advanced age should not be a contraindication to oral anticoagulation. The recommendations of the Fourth American College of Chest Physicians Conference on Antithrombotic Therapy indicate that: 'In patients older than 75, oral anticoagulation is recommended because of their high risk of stroke (level I evidence) with anticoagulation at the lower end of the therapeutic range of INR 2.0 to 3.0 which might be appropriate in these patients (grade C recommendation)' (Laupacis et al. 1995).

The French guidelines concerning anticoagulation in patients with atrial fibrillation are consistent with the American College of Chest Physicians consensus, especially in elderly patients (Steg 1997). However, the risk of complications is so high for elderly patients that a very cautious attitude is necessary and the target INR range should be between 2 and 3. The efficacy of anticoagulant treatment must be controlled by a regular monitoring of the INR every 2 weeks. Furthermore, an elderly patient treated by anticoagulants needs regular clinical assessment, especially for blood pressure, risk of falls, and use of prescribed or over-the-counter drugs. Non-steroidal anti-inflammatory drugs, aspirin, and antibiotics are among the agents that increase the risk of bleeding.

Anticoagulants and cardioversion

Atrial fibrillation of unknown or long duration

Before elective cardioversion, anticoagulation should be given for 3 weeks. After cardioversion, long-term anticoagulation is indicated if atrial fibrillation recurs, or in the presence of one or more risk factors (Steg 1997).

Atrial fibrillation of short duration

The role of anticoagulation in this situation is controversial owing to the possibility that there has been insufficient time for thrombus formation in the atria. No reliable data have yet been published which justify not giving anticoagulants in this situation. In individuals with impaired ventricular function, an urgent trial of electrical or pharmacological cardioversion could be indicated. Heparin therapy followed by short-term oral anticoagulation may be indicated in three circumstances: acute haemodynamic instability, recurrent atrial fibrillation, and spontaneous echo contrast in the left atrium (Steg 1997).

References

Albers, G.W. (1994). Atrial fibrillation and stroke: three new studies, three remaining questions. *Archives of Internal Medicine*, 154, 1443–8.

Atrial Fibrillation Investigators (1994). Risk factors for stroke and efficacy of antithrombotic therapy in atrial fibrillation: analysis of pooled data from five randomised trials. *Archives of Internal Medicine*, 154, 1449–57.

Boston Area Anticoagulation Trial for Atrial Fibrillation Investigators (1990). The effect of low-dose warfarin on the risk of stroke in patient with non-rheumatic atrial fibrillation. *New England Journal of Medicine*, 323, 1505–11.

Broderick, J., Brott, T., Tomsick, T., and Leach, A. (1993). Lobar haemorrhage in the elderly. The undiminishing importance of hypertension. *Stroke*, 24, 49–51.

Conolly, S.J., Laupacis, A., and Gent, M. (1991). Canadian Atrial Fibrillation Anticoagulation (CAFA) Study. *Journal of the American College of Cardiology*, 18, 349–55.

European Atrial Fibrillation Trial Study Group (1993). Secondary prevention in non-rheumatic atrial fibrillation after transient ischaemic attack or minor stroke. *Lancet*, 342, 1255–62.

European Atrial Fibrillation Trial Study Group (1995). Optimal oral anticoagulant therapy in patients with non-rheumatic atrial fibrillation and recent cerebral ischaemia. *New England Journal of Medicine*, 333, 5–10.

Ezekowitz, M.D., Bridgers, S.L., and James, K.E. (1992). Warfarin in the prevention of stroke associated with nonrheumatic atrial fibrillation. *New England Journal of Medicine*, 327, 1406–12.

Farina, E., Di Lauro, L., Magny, E. Ambrosini, S., Sina, C., and Mariani C. (1996). Neuropsychological deficit in atrial fibrillation: subclinical cognitive defects in atrial fibrillation. *Neurology*, 46, A139.

Finh, S.D., McDonell, M., Martin, D., Henlkoff, J., Vermes, D., and Kent, D. (1993). Risk factors for complications of chronic anticoagulation. *Annals of Internal Medicine*, 118, 511–520.

Furberg, C.D., Psaty, B.M., and Manolio, T.A. (1994). Prevalence of atrial fibrillation in elderly subjects (the Cardiovascular Health Study). *American Journal of Cardiology*, 74, 236–41.

Grimley Evans, J. (1985). Risk factors for stroke in the elderly. MD thesis. University of Cambridge.

Hylek, E.M., Skates, S.J., Sheehan, M.A., and Singer, D.E. (1996). An analysis of the lowest effective intensity of prophylactic anticoagulation for patients with non-rheumatic atrial fibrillation. *New England Journal of Medicine*, 355, 540–6.

Kannel, W.B., Abott, R.D., Savage, D.D., and McNamara, P.M. (1983). Coronary heart disease and atrial fibrillation: the Framingham Study. *American Heart Journal*, 106, 389–96.

Lake, F.R., McGall, M.G., and Cullen, K.J. (1989) Atrial fibrillation and mortality in an elderly population. *Australian and New Zealand Journal of Medicine*, 19, 321–26.

Landefeld, C.S. and Goldman, L. (1989). Major bleeding in outpatients treated with warfarin: incidence and prediction by factors known at the start of outpatient therapy. *American Journal of Medicine*, 87, 144–52.

Laupacis, A., Albers, G., Dalen, J., Dunn, M., Feinberg, W., and Jacobson, A. (1995). Antithrombotic therapy in atrial fibrillation. *Chest*, 108, 352S–9S.

Lip, G.Y. (1996). Antithrombotic treatment for atrial fibrillation. *British Medical Journal*, 312, 45–9.

Lip, G.Y. (1997). Does paroxysmal atrial fibrillation confer a paroxysmal thromboembolic risk? *Lancet*, 349, 1565–6.

Lip, G.Y., Lip, P.L., and Zarifis, J. (1996). Fibrin D-dimer and β-thromboglobulin as markers of thrombogenesis and platelet activation in atrial fibrillation: effects of introducing ultra-low-dose warfarin and aspirin. *Circulation*, 94, 425–31.

Manolio, T.A., Furberg, C.D., and Rautaharju, P.M. (1994). Cardiac arrhythmias on 24-h ambulatory electrocardiography in older women and men: the Cardiovascular Health Study. *Journal of the American College of Cardiology*, 23, 916–25.

Maurer, M.S., Schefrin, E.A., and Fleg J.L. (1995). Prevalence and prognostic significance of exercise-induced supra-ventricular tachycardia in apparently healthy volunteers. *American Journal of Cardiology*, 75, 788–92.

Miller, V.T. Rothrock, J.F., Pearce, L.A., Feinberg, W.M., Hart, R.G., and Anderson, D.C. (1993). Stroke prevention in Atrial Fibrillation Investigators; ischaemic stroke in patients with atrial fibrillation: effects of aspirin according to stroke mechanism. *Neurology*, 43, 32–6.

Petersen, P. and Godtfredsen, J. (1986). Embolic complications in paroxysmal atrial fibrillation. *Stroke*, 17, 622–6.

Petersen, P., Boysen, G., Godtfredsen, J., Andersen, E., and Andersen, B. (1989). Placebo-controlled, randomised trial of warfarin and aspirin for prevention of thromboembolic complications in chronic atrial fibrillation: the Copenhagen AFASAK Study. *Lancet*, i, 175–9.

Phillips, S.J., Whisnant, J.P., and O'Fallon, W.M. (1990) Prevalence of cardiovascular disease and diabetes in residents of Rochester, Minnesota. *Mayo Clinic Proceedings*, 65, 344–59.

Roy, D., Marchand, E., Gagné, P., Chabot, M., and Cartier, R. (1996). Usefulness of anticoagulant therapy in the prevention of embolic complications of atrial fibrillation. *American Heart Journal*, 112, 1039–43.

Sandercock, P., Bamford, J., Dennis, M., *et al.* (1992). Oxfordshire Community Stroke Project. Atrial fibrillation and stroke—prevalence in different types of stroke and influence on early and long term prognosis. *British Medical Journal*, 305, 1460–5.

Sohara, H., Amitani, S., Kurose, M., and Myahara, K. (1997). Atrial fibrillation activates platelets and coagulation in a time-dependent manner: a study in patients with paroxysmal atrial fibrillation. *Journal of the American College of Cardiology*, 29, 106–12.

Steg, P.G. (1997). Recommandations de la Société Française de Cardiologie concernant les indications et la surveillance du traitement anticoagulant oral. *Archives des Maladies du Coeur et des Vaisseaux*, 90, 1289–305.

Stroke Prevention in Atrial Fibrillation Investigators (1991). Stroke Prevention in Atrial Fibrillation Study: final results. *Circulation*, 84, 527–39.

Stroke Prevention in Atrial Fibrillation Investigators (1994). Warfarin versus aspirin for prevention of thromboembolism in atrial fibrillation: the Stroke Prevention in Atrial Fibrillation II Study. *Lancet*, 343, 687–91.

Stroke Prevention in Atrial Fibrillation Investigators (1996a). Adjusted-dose warfarin versus low-intensity, fixed-dose warfarin plus aspirin for high-risk patients with atrial fibrillation: Stroke Prevention in Atrial Fibrillation III randomised clinical trial. *Lancet*, 348, 633–8.

Stroke Prevention in Atrial Fibrillation Investigators (1996b). Bleeding during antithrombotic therapy for atrial fibrillation. *Archives of Internal Medicine*, 156, 409–16.

Tsai, L.M., Chen, J.H., Lin, L.J., and Teng, J.K. (1997). Natural history of left atrial spontaneous echo contrast in non-rheumatic atrial fibrillation. *American Journal of Cardiology*, 80, 897–900.

Wolf, P.A., Bott, R.D., and Kannel, W.B. (1991). Atrial fibrillation as an independent risk factor for stroke: the Framingham Study. *Stroke*, 22, 983–8.

9.8 Cardiovascular disease risk factors

Kay-Tee Khaw

Cardiovascular disease is the leading cause of death for older people, accounting for about half of deaths in people aged 65 years and older in most developed countries. Of the specific causes, ischaemic heart disease or coronary heart disease are the most common, followed by stroke in northern Europe and North America; this pattern is reversed in some countries such as Japan. Cardiovascular disease also encompasses other conditions such as peripheral arterial disease and aortic aneurysms, which are also more common with increasing age.

Although much is already understood about the prevention of cardiovascular disease, and the major burden of cardiovascular disease is in older people, prevention has been generally neglected for older people both in terms of research and practice. This has probably been based on the belief that maintaining quality of life is a more important goal than prevention of mortality in older people. However, men and women aged 65 years in the United Kingdom in 2001 can on average expect to live a further 16 years and 20 years respectively, and at age 75 a further 9 years and 12 years respectively. Cardiovascular disease is also a leading cause of major disability in later life, so that measures that reduce incidence or postpone the onset of stroke or ischaemic heart disease may help to reduce the period of disability at the end of life; indeed, there is evidence that there is a vascular component to other disabling conditions such as some forms of dementia and retinopathy. The shortening of the period of disability by postponing or preventing its onset could contribute much to improving quality towards the end of life.

The three classical established independent cardiovascular risk factors are raised blood pressure, raised blood cholesterol, and tobacco smoking (Neaton and Wentworth 1992). Numerous other risk factors for cardiovascular disease have been documented; apart from age, sex, and family history which are non-modifiable, these include diabetes, raised homocysteine levels, raised levels of haemostatic factors, infection and inflammation, obesity, low physical activity, and psychosocial stress. The major issues for prevention are (a) whether or not risk factors predict cardiovascular disease, (b) whether or not reduction of risk factor levels reduces cardiovascular disease occurrence, and (c) the overall risk–benefit balance.

There are many reasons why older people may differ from younger people. Physiological measures such as blood pressure and cholesterol may be markers of different processes in older compared with younger people; for example, ill health in older people may cause changes in blood lipids and blood pressure levels rather than vice versa, older people may represent resistant survivors in that selective mortality of susceptible people occurs at younger ages, and older people also have different rates and patterns of disease from younger people so that risk–benefit balances, and how they are evaluated, vary considerably. People aged 65 years and older are not a homogeneous group, and those in their ninth decade may differ as much from those in their seventh decade as they in turn differ from those in their fifth. Additionally, life experiences vary such that successive birth cohorts may also differ substantially with respect to health characteristics. Thus, although some early reports from cohort studies (Welborn and Wearne 1979) reported that classical cardiovascular disease risk factors such as blood cholesterol level did not predict cardiovascular disease in people aged over 60 years, this pattern appears to be changing. Later reports from Framingham and elsewhere now report that cardiovascular risk factors have effects well into old age (Barrett-Connor *et al.* 1984; Castelli *et al.* 1989; Benfante and Reed 1990), although the relationships beyond the age of 85 years are less clear. In particular, U-shaped relationships of cardiovascular disease risk factors with total mortality after the age of 85 years have been reported (Mattila *et al.* 1988; Weverling-Rijnsburger *et al.* 1997). Although such relationships may reflect confounding due to existing illnesses, the paucity of evidence at the extremes of old age means that most of the relevant evidence, and thence discussion, applies to people aged 65 to 84 years.

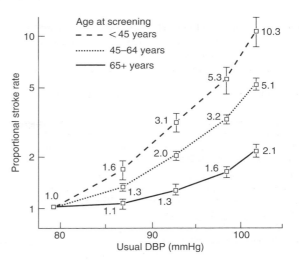

Fig. 1 Relative risks for stroke by age and usual diastolic blood pressure. (Reproduced with permission from Prospective Studies Collaboration (1995).)

Risk factors and cardiovascular disease

Blood pressure (see Chapters 9.1 and 9.5)

Perhaps the best documented risk factor in later life is blood pressure. Raised blood pressure predicts stroke, coronary heart disease, and total cardiovascular disease incidence and mortality at all ages; the relationship is continuous and graded throughout the whole range of blood pressure. The relationship is strongest for stroke. A review of 45 prospective cohorts from around the world estimated that there is about an 80 per cent increase in stroke risk for every 10-mmHg increase in usual diastolic blood pressure (Prospective Studies Collaboration 1995). The relative risk increase was greatest in younger people with a 10-fold increase in stroke risk for those with diastolic pressures above 100 mmHg compared with those with diastolic pressures of less than 80 mmHg for people aged less than 45 years; for people aged over 65 years, the relative risk for those with diastolic blood pressure over 100 mmHg compared with those with diastolic blood pressure less than 80 was 2.1. However, because the absolute risk of stroke is greater in older people, a decrease in blood pressure from the top to the bottom category (diastolic pressure more than 100 to less than 80 mmHg) was associated with a reduction of eight events in those aged over 65 years but of only two events in those aged less than 45 years (Figs 1 and 2).

For coronary heart disease, a review of nine prospective studies estimated the effect at a 29 per cent increase in coronary heart disease risk for every 7.5-mmHg increase in diastolic blood pressure (MacMahon *et al.* 1990*a*). Although the relative impact of raised blood pressure on increasing coronary risk is less than that for stroke, because of the high rates of coronary heart disease at later ages, the absolute impact of a reduction in blood pressure for coronary heart disease is substantial.

Numerous treatment trials have conclusively demonstrated the cardiovascular benefits of blood pressure reduction with an estimated impact of 42 per cent stroke reduction and 14 per cent coronary heart disease reduction for a 5 to 6 mmHg reduction in diastolic blood pressure (MacMahon *et al.* 1990*b*). While most studies have focused on diastolic blood pressure, systolic blood pressure is also a strong predictor of cardiovascular disease in elderly people and trials

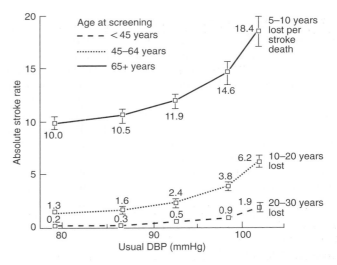

Fig. 2 Absolute risks for stroke by age and usual diastolic blood pressure. (Reproduced with permission from Prospective Studies Collaboration (1995).)

have now established conclusively the benefits of a reduction of both systolic and diastolic blood pressure even at advanced ages. An analysis of the 16 or so trials conducted in people aged 60 years and older (mean age 70, oldest 94 years) reported an average reduction due to active treatment of 19 mmHg in systolic pressure and 9 mmHg in diastolic pressure associated with a 20 per cent reduction in coronary heart disease incidence, a 36 per cent reduction in stroke incidence, and a 12 per cent reduction in all-cause mortality with an average of 4 years of follow-up. To prevent one stroke event, 22 people needed to be treated for 5 years; for coronary heart disease the corresponding number was 45. These were between two and four times lower than the equivalent number needed to be treated to prevent one event in young adults (Sanderson 1996). The Systolic Hypertension in the Elderly Programme (SHEP Cooperative Research Group 1991) and

Table 1 Major hypertension treatment trials in elderly people and effects on coronary heart disease and stroke events and all-cause mortality

Trial	Mean age	Percentage change in event rate in active compared with placebo treatment group		
		Coronary heart disease	Stroke	All-cause mortality
EWHPE (Amery 1985)	72	−29	−34	−11
Coope and Warrender (1986)	69	+1	−45*	−5
STOP-H (Dahlof et al. 1991)	76	−3	−46*	−44*
SHEP (SHEP Cooperative Research Group 1991)	72	−28	−36*	−13
MRC (MRC Working Group 1992)	70	−29	−25*	−4
Syst-Eur (Staessen et al. 1997)	70	−26*	−42*	−14

EWHPE, European Working Party on High Blood Pressure in the Elderly; SHEP, Systolic Hypertension in Elderly Programme; MRC, Medical Research Council; Syst-Eur, Systolic Hypertension in Europe.
* $p < 0.05$.

the Systolic Hypertension in Europe (Staessen et al. 1997) trials have specifically examined and confirmed the cardiovascular benefits of the treatment of isolated systolic hypertension. The Systolic Hypertension in Europe trial reported that to prevent stroke or major cardiovascular endpoints, 33 and 20 people respectively need to be treated for 5 years. All the major trials apart from the Systolic Hypertension in Europe trial used diuretics as first-line hypertensive agents, alone or in combination with other drugs such as β-blockers; in the Systolic Hypertension in Europe trial calcium-channel blockade was used as a first-line therapy. Detailed quality-of-life assessments undertaken in individual trials also show no significant adverse effects of treatment in older patients. Table 1 shows results from some major hypertension trials in elderly people.

Blood cholesterol

The value of blood total cholesterol measurement in predicting coronary heart disease is well established in middle-aged men and women, with a 10 per cent increase in blood cholesterol level being associated with a 20 to 30 per cent increase in coronary heart disease risk, but the association has been questioned in older men and women. A National Heart, Lung and Blood Institute workshop analysed data from 25 populations and reported that serum total cholesterol and low-density lipoprotein cholesterol levels predicted fatal coronary heart disease in both men and women over 65 years of age although the strength and consistency of the relationship in older women were diminished. The relative risks of fatal coronary heart disease associated with cholesterol levels of 6.2 mmol/l or higher compared with levels of less than 5.17 mmol/l were 1.73 and 1.32 for men aged under 65 years and men aged 65 years or more respectively, and 2.44 and 1.12 for women aged under 65 years and women aged 65 years or more respectively (Manolio et al. 1992). However, as with blood pressure, absolute rates of coronary heart disease are greater in older people so that the absolute impact of cholesterol reduction on coronary risk is greater for older than for younger people (Gordon

and Rifkind 1989; Khaw and Rose 1989). In contrast, cholesterol level does not appear to predict stroke (Prospective Studies Collaboration 1995). This may be because stroke comprises both haemorrhagic and thrombotic events, and cholesterol level may relate in different ways to these processes.

Most of the trials of treatment of high cholesterol levels on coronary heart disease have been conducted in middle-aged men and relatively few have included women or elderly people in sufficient numbers for separate analyses. The Scandinavian Simvastatin Survival study, a secondary prevention trial, reported a relative reduction of 39 and 29 per cent in major coronary events and of 37 and 27 per cent in total mortality for those aged under 60 years and those aged 60 years and over respectively (Scandinavian Simvastatin Survival Study Group 1994). In the small number of women in the trial, the relative risks were 0.65 for coronary events and 1.12 for total mortality. Based on evidence to date, lowering blood cholesterol with statin drugs would appear to confer clear benefits for coronary heart disease incidence as well as total mortality in men at all ages in communities in which coronary heart disease is common. For women, who have lower rates of coronary heart disease, the risk–benefit balance is less well documented. Intriguingly, an overview of 16 trials published up to 1995 of cholesterol lowering with statin drugs also indicated significant reductions in stroke of 29 per cent and reductions in total mortality of 22 per cent (Hebert et al. 1997). Table 2 shows results from four major trials. Since cholesterol level per se is not related to stroke in prospective observational studies, it is not clear whether the stroke benefits are due to cholesterol lowering and generalizable to other cholesterol-lowering drugs, or due to some other effect of statin drugs independent of cholesterol lowering such as an alteration of endothelial function or antioxidant activity. Nevertheless, it is no longer a major concern that reduction of cholesterol levels of elderly people might increase their risk of stroke, at least in Western populations where thrombotic strokes predominate. Indeed, much as blood pressure reduction reduces both stroke and coronary heart

Table 2 Major cholesterol-lowering trials using statin drugs and effects on coronary and stroke events and total mortality

Trial	Mean age	Percentage change in event rate in active compared with placebo treatment group		
		Coronary heart disease	Stroke	All-cause mortality
Scandinavian Simvastatin Survival Study Group 1994[a]	59	−34*	−28*	−30
WOSCOP (Shepherd 1995)	55	−31	−10	−22
CARE (Sacks 1996)[a]	59	−24*	−31*	−9
LIPID 1998[a]	62	−24*	−19*	−22

* $p<0.05$.
[a] Secondary prevention trial.

disease risk, so cholesterol lowering with statins appears to reduce both coronary heart disease and stroke risk.

Smoking

The adverse effects of cigarette smoking on cardiovascular disease are substantial. Habitual cigarette smoking increases the risk of coronary heart disease and stroke three- to fourfold in men and women below the age of 65 years. The relative risks for coronary heart disease and stroke for men and women aged 65 years and over are lower (about 1.5), but since the absolute rates of stroke and coronary heart disease are greater in older people, the absolute increase in risk is much greater for those aged 65 years and over. Assessment of the effects of stopping smoking are more difficult since people stop for many reasons, some because they are ill, and there are no randomized trials of smoking cessation on cardiovascular disease in older people. However, stopping smoking even at older ages is associated with improvements in survival. Jaijich *et al.* (1984) reported that current smokers aged 65 to 74 years had 50 per cent excess coronary heart disease mortality; ex-smokers had rates similar to non-smokers. The CASS study (Hermanson *et al.* 1988) reported that the relative risk of myocardial infarction or death in those who continued smoking compared with those who stopped was 2.9 for those aged 70 to 74 years and 1.5 for those aged 55 to 59 years. Doll *et al.* (1994), reporting on 40 years of follow-up from the British Doctors Study, compared survival of cigarette smokers who stopped smoking at different ages with that of non-smokers and those who continued to smoke. Those who stopped before 35 years of age had a pattern of survival that did not differ significantly from that of non-smokers; even those who stopped at 65 to 74 years of age (mean age 71 years) had age-specific mortality rates beyond the age of 75 years appreciably lower than those who continued.

Other risk factors

Many other risk factors have been implicated in cardiovascular disease risk in younger cohorts, and it is likely that they also have effects at older ages. For example, diabetes, glucose intolerance, or hyper-insulinaemia are important risk factors for coronary heart disease in men and women aged over 65 years (Castelli *et al.* 1989; Benfante

and Reed 1990; Feskens and Kromhout 1994). However, for most risk factors there is often a paucity of data in older people. Nevertheless, since the levels and prevalence of most of these risk factors tend to increase with increasing age, as does cardiovascular disease, they may also be of substantial clinical importance in older people. For example, mean levels of homocysteine, haemostatic factors such as fibrinogen, and central obesity, all of which generally increase with increasing age, are associated with increased cardiovascular risk. The potential impact of reducing these levels through interventions, for example folate supplementation to reduce homocysteine levels, could be substantial for older people. Other risk factors include physical activity, infection, psychosocial stress, environmental pollution, and temperature. However, there is as yet insufficient trial evidence on the effects of interventions although they may offer much potential benefit.

Interventions in later life

Prevention strategies

There are two complementary strategies for prevention: the high-risk approach, which aims to identify and treat individuals at high risk (for example, those with raised levels of blood pressure or cholesterol), and the population approach, which aims to reduce risk factor levels in the population as a whole (for example, by changes in diet or physical activity). The latter approach would also reduce the prevalence of high-risk people (Rose 1992). The levels at which individuals are deemed high risk, warranting treatment, depends on judgements about the potential benefits of intervention, which differ in different age groups and populations. The population approach has much greater potential for reducing the incidence in the population as a whole but requires an understanding of the effects of general environmental or lifestyle changes.

Treatment of high-risk individuals: absolute versus relative risk

Cardiovascular disease risk increases continuously with increasing level of blood pressure and blood cholesterol throughout the whole

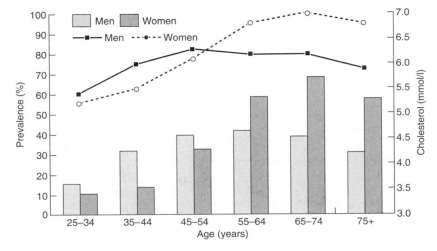

Fig. 3 Mean cholesterol level (lines) and prevalence (bars) of cholesterol levels of 6.5 mmol/l or greater in men and women by age group. (Data from Colhoun *et al.* (1996) given in Table 3.)

range. The threshold for intervention depends on a judgement of the risk–benefit balance. For a given change in risk factor level, the relative increase in risk is generally smaller in older people. However, since the rate of cardiovascular disease increases exponentially with increasing age, the absolute risk associated with a given level of risk factor is much greater in the old. Thus the potential absolute benefit of risk reduction in individual clinical terms is substantially greater in older people, at least in terms of number of events prevented or postponed (Khaw and Rose 1989), and several reviews have indicated the importance of risk factor reduction in elderly people (Wilhelmsen 1988; Stamler 1988). Conversely, the life-years gained may not be greater, and other issues such as general state of health and quality of life may be differently weighted in older and younger people. Since absolute rates of coronary heart disease and stroke differ not only by age but also by sex, presence or absence of other risk factors, and in different communities, and judgements about risk–benefit balances also differ, thresholds for treatment are not easily generalizable. Nevertheless, given the trial evidence, people aged over 65 years are, if anything, likely to derive greater cardiovascular benefit from treatment of hypertension, and men over 65 years from treatment of hypercholesterolaemia, than are younger people. The results of cholesterol-lowering statin treatment for stroke are also promising, but need to be confirmed for women.

Population approach: reduction of risk factor levels in the community as a whole

In most communities, mean levels of risk factors such as blood pressure and cholesterol, and thus prevalence of hypertension and hypercholesterolaemia, increase with increasing age. Figures 3 and 4 illustrate 1994 data for the United Kingdom (Health Survey for England 1996) (shown in Tables 3 and 4). Thus a larger proportion of older people than of younger people have elevated risk factor levels. However, such changes are not necessary concomitants of ageing since many communities have been documented worldwide which have low levels of blood pressure and cholesterol throughout life, as well as low rates of cardiovascular disease. Interventions which

reduce levels of risk factors or mitigate the increases with age in the population as a whole will have a substantial potential impact on cardiovascular disease. For example, reduction of mean systolic blood pressure by 2 mmHg in the whole population might reduce ischaemic heart disease rates by 5 per cent and stroke rates by 13 per cent (Rose 1992). Others have estimated that reduction of the population mean cholesterol level by 0.5 mmol/l could reduce ischaemic heart disease rates by 20 per cent (Khaw and Rose 1989). Many lifestyle factors such as diet and physical activity have a substantial impact on cardiovascular risk factor levels, as well as cardiovascular risk. In contrast with common belief, older people may in fact be more rather than less susceptible to the effects of changes in such lifestyle factors.

Modifiable determinants of classical risk factor levels

Nutrition

Epidemiological studies have long indicated that high dietary sodium intake is related to higher blood pressure levels and, in particular, to the rise of blood pressure with increasing age. The Intersalt Study of 52 communities worldwide estimated that a reduction of 100 mmol sodium daily is associated with a decrease of 5 to 10 mmHg in systolic blood pressure; the lower the average sodium intake in communities, the lower is the rise of blood pressure with age (Intersalt Cooperative Research Group 1988). Older people appear to be more sensitive to the blood-pressure-raising effects of sodium (Khaw and Barrett-Connor 1988). Trials confirm these effects; a trial of modest reduction of salt intake from 10 to 5 g daily in elderly men aged 60 to 78 years reported systolic blood pressure reduced by 7 mmHg and diastolic blood pressure by 3 mmHg; similar changes were observed in normotensive and hypertensive participants (Cappuccio 1997). Other nutritional factors which have been reported to be associated with lower blood pressure levels include high potassium, calcium, magnesium, and dietary fibre intake (generally from fruit and vegetables) and low

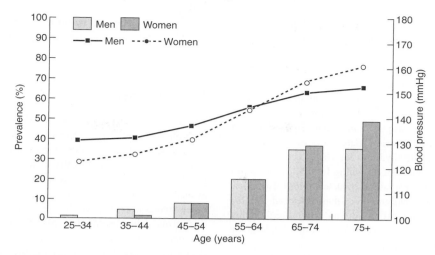

Fig. 4 Mean systolic blood pressure level (lines) and prevalence (bars) of systolic blood pressure of 160 mmHg or greater in men and women by age group. (Data from Colhoun et al. (1996) given in Table 4.)

Table 3 Mean cholesterol level and prevalence of cholesterol levels of 6.5 mmol/l or greater in men and women by age group

	16–24	25–34	35–44	45–54	55–64	65–74	75 +
Men							
Mean cholesterol (mmol/l)	4.7	5.4	6.0	6.3	6.2	6.2	5.9
Percentage with cholesterol ⩾ 6.5 mmol/l	4.0	15.0	31.0	39.0	41.0	38.0	30.0
Women							
Mean cholesterol (mmol/l)	5.0	5.2	5.5	6.1	6.8	7.0	6.8
Percentage with cholesterol ⩾ 6.5 mmol/l	4.0	10.0	13.0	32.0	58.0	68.0	57.0

Data from Colhoun et al. (1996).

Table 4 Mean systolic and diastolic blood pressure and prevalence of systolic blood pressure of 160 mmHg or greater and diastolic blood pressure of 95 mmHg or greater in men and women by age group

	16–24	25–34	35–44	45–54	55–64	65–74	75 +
Men							
Mean SBP (mmHg)	130	131	132	136	144	150	152
Percentage with SBP ⩾ 160 mmHg	1	1	4	7	19	34	34
Mean DBP (mmHg)	64	71	76	81	83	82	81
Percentage with DBP ⩾ 95 mmHg	0	1	4	11	15	15	12
Women							
Mean SBP (mmHg)	121	122	125	132	143	154	160
Percentage with SBP ⩾ 160 mmHg	0	0	1	7	19	36	48
Mean DBP (mmHg)	64	68	71	75	77	79	80
Percentage with DBP ⩾ 95 mmHg	0	1	1	5	5	12	14

SBP, systolic blood pressure; DBP, diastolic blood pressure.
Data from Colhoun et al. (1996).

fat intakes, and some of these have also been related to subsequent cardiovascular disease events (Khaw and Barrett-Connor 1987; Gillman et al. 1995).

The Seven Countries Study was one of the first to implicate high dietary saturated fat intake, and to a lesser extent dietary cholesterol, as strong determinants of blood cholesterol levels and coronary heart disease (Keys et al. 1986). Communities where cholesterol levels are low and do not increase with age are those in which dietary saturated fat intakes are also low. In metabolic ward trials, isocaloric replacement of saturated fats by complex carbohydrates for 10 per cent of dietary calories result in blood total cholesterol falling by 0.52 mmol/l and low-density lipoprotein cholesterol falling by 0.36 mmol/l. Isocaloric replacement of complex carbohydrates by polyunsaturated fats for 5 per cent of dietary calories resulted in total cholesterol falling by 0.13 mmol/l and low-density lipoprotein cholesterol falling by 0.11 mmol/l, but mono-unsaturated fats appear to have no significant effect. A reduction of 200 mg/day in dietary cholesterol further decreases total blood cholesterol by 0.13 mmol/l and low-density lipoprotein cholesterol by 0.10 mmol/l (Clarke et al. 1997). Reduction of the saturated fat intake in the average British diet from 16 per cent of calories to the feasible 8 per cent or less in typical Mediterranean or Japanese diets would reduce blood cholesterol by about 0.8 mmol/l, associated with about a 30 per cent decrease in coronary disease risk.

Alcohol has a more complex relationship with cardiovascular disease and risk factors. Alcohol intake increases systolic blood pressure by about 1 mmHg per daily unit (about 10 g) but also increases levels of high-density lipoprotein cholesterol; it appears to have vasodilating effects at low doses but pressor effects at high doses. While an alcohol intake of about 1 or 2 units/day appears protective for coronary heart disease and possibly stroke, the risk of hypertension and stroke is increased with higher levels of alcohol intake (Marmot and Brunner 1991).

There are many other dietary components such as antioxidants (vitamins E and C) and fatty acids (e.g. ω-3 fatty acids) which affect cardiovascular risk (Committee on Medical Aspects of Food Policy 1994). Some secondary prevention trials indicate substantial benefits of dietary interventions; advice to eat fatty fish twice weekly was associated with a 30 per cent reduction in cardiac and all-cause mortality, while an α-linolenic-rich Mediterranean diet was associated with 70 per cent decrease in cardiovascular disease and all-cause of mortality (Burr et al. 1989; de Lorgeril et al. 1994). Their effects appear to be mediated through mechanisms independent of blood pressure and cholesterol.

The link between obesity, in particular central adiposity, and hypertension and hyperlipidaemia is well established. While average central adiposity, as indicated by waist-to-hip ratio, continues to increase with increasing age, average body mass index does not change much after the age of 65 years. Some of the effects of obesity may reflect physical activity patterns.

Physical activity

Physical activity is beneficially related to both blood pressure and blood lipid levels, as well as heart disease and stroke, although most evidence is based on men with few data for women (National Institutes of Health Consensus Development Panel 1996). While benefits are related to vigorous exercise in younger men, more moderate levels (e.g. walking) appear to be protective against cardiovascular disease as well as death in older men and women (LaCroix et al. 1996).

Conclusion

The classical cardiovascular disease risk factors—raised blood pressure, raised blood cholesterol, and cigarette smoking—predict subsequent cardiovascular disease at older ages, at least up to 85 years. Substantial trial evidence also indicates that reduction of blood pressure reduces the incidence of cardiovascular disease. Although fewer data are available for cholesterol lowering in older people, available evidence using statins also indicates benefits for both ischaemic heart disease and stroke. The absolute benefits of risk factor reduction are larger in older people who have higher cardiovascular disease rates, although decisions to treat rest on judgements of the individual risk–benefit balance. The prevalence of elevated risk factor levels increases with age; primary prevention or reduction of elevated risk factor levels in the general population through lifestyle changes such as reduction of dietary sodium and saturated fat, and increasing fruit and vegetable intake, has been shown to be feasible and effective. Although there is still a dearth of evidence in older people, it is likely that the other risk factors documented in younger cohorts will have effects in the elderly and offer future possibilities for interventions. In the interim, the profound international variation and secular trends in risk factor levels and cardiovascular disease rates, even at older ages, indicate substantial potential for the prevention of a large proportion of cardiovascular disease in elderly people.

References

Amery, A., Birkenhager, W., Brixko, P., et al. (1985). Mortality and morbidity results from the European Working Party on High Blood Pressure in the Elderly trial. Lancet, i, 1349–54.

Barrett-Connor, E., Suarez, L., and Khaw, K.-T. (1984). Ischemic heart disease risk factors over age 50. Journal of Chronic Disease, 37, 903–8.

Benfante, R. and Reed, D. (1990). Is elevated serum cholesterol level a risk factor for coronary heart disease in the elderly? Journal of the American Medical Association, 263, 393–6.

Burr, M.L., Fehily, A.M., Gilbert, J.F., et al. (1989). Effects of changes in fat, fish and fibre intakes on death and myocardial infarction. Lancet, ii, 757–61.

Cappuccio, F., Markandu, N.D., Carney, C., Sagnella, G.A., and MacGregor, G.A. (1997). Double blind randomised trial of modest sodium restriction in older people. Lancet, 350, 850–4.

Castelli, W.P., Wilson, P.W.F., Levy, D., and Anderson, K. (1989). Cardiovascular risk factors in the elderly. American Journal of Cardiology, 63, 12H–19H.

Clarke, R., Frost, C., Collins, R., Appleby, P., and Peto, R. (1997). Dietary lipids and blood cholesterol: quantitative meta-analysis of metabolic ward studies. British Medical Journal, 314, 112–17.

Colhoun, H., Prescott-Clarke, P., Dong, W., Hedges, B., Lampe, F., and Taylor, A. (1996). Health Survey for England 1994. Her Majesty's Stationery Office, London.

Committee on Medical Aspects of Food Policy (1994). Nutritional aspects of cardiovascular disease. Report of the Cardiovascular Review Group Committee on medical aspects of food policy. Department of Health, Her Majesty's Stationery Office, London.

Coope, J. and Warrender, T.S. (1986). Randomised trial of treatment of hypertension in elderly patients in primary care. *British Medical Journal*, **294**, 1145–51.

Dahlof, B., Lindholm, L.H., Hannson, L., Bengt, S., Ekbom, T., and Wester, P.O. (1991). Morbidity and mortality in the Swedish trial in old patients with hypertension (STOP-Hypertension). *Lancet*, **338**, 1281–5.

de Lorgeril, M., Renaud, S., Mamelle, S., et al. (1994). Mediterranean α-linolenic acid rich diet in secondary prevention of coronary heart disease. *Lancet*, **343**, 1454–9.

Doll, R., Peto, P., Wheatley, K., Gray, R., and Sutherland, I. (1994). Mortality in relation to smoking: 40 years' observations on male British doctors. *British Medical Journal*, **309**, 901–11.

Feskens, E.J.M. and Kromhout, D. (1994). Hyperinsulinaemia, risk factors and coronary heart disease. *Arteriosclerosis and Thrombosis*, **14**, 1641–7.

Gillman, M.W., Cupples, L.A., Gagnon, D., et al. (1995). Protective effect of fruits and vegetables on development of stroke in men. *Journal of the American Medical Association*, **273**, 1113–17.

Gordon, D.J. and Rifkind, B.M. (1989). Treating high blood cholesterol in the older patient. *American Journal of Cardiology*, **63**, 48H–52H.

Health Survey for England (1996). Colhoun, H., Prescott-Clarke, P., Dong, W., Hedges. B., Lampe, F., Taylor, A. HMSO, London.

Hebert, P.R., Gaziano, J.M., Chan, K.S., and Hennekens, C.H. (1997). Cholesterol lowering with statin drugs, risk of stroke and total mortality. *Journal of the American Medical Association*, **278**, 313–21.

Hermanson, B., Omenn, G.S., Kronmal, R.A., et al. (1988). Beneficial 6-year outcome of smoking cessation in older men and women with coronary artery disease: results from the CASS Registry. *New England Journal of Medicine*, **319**, 1365–9.

Intersalt Cooperative Research Group (1988). Intersalt: an international study of electrolyte excretion and blood pressure. Results for 24 hour urinary sodium and potassium excretion. *British Medical Journal*, **297**, 319–28.

Jajich, C.L., Ostfeld, A.M., and Freeman, D.H. (1984). Smoking and coronary heart disease mortality in the elderly. *Journal of the American Medical Association*, **252**, 2831–4.

Keys, A., Menotti, A., Karvonen, M.J., et al. (1986). The diet and 15-year death rate in the Seven Countries Study. *American Journal of Epidemiology*, **124**, 903–15.

Khaw, K.T. and Barrett-Connor, E. (1987). Dietary potassium and stroke associated mortality. A 12-year prospective population study. *New England Journal of Medicine*, **316**, 235–40.

Khaw, K.T. and Barrett-Connor, E. (1988). The association between blood pressure, age, and dietary sodium and potassium: a population study. *Circulation*, **77**, 53–61.

Khaw, K.-T. and Rose, G. (1989). Cholesterol screening programmes: how much potential benefit? *British Medical Journal*, **299**, 606–7.

LaCroix, A.Z., Leveille, S.G., Hecht, J.A., Grothaus, L.C., and Wagner, E.H. (1996). Does walking decrease the risk of cardiovascular hospitalizations and death in older adults? *Journal of the American Geriatrics Society*, **44**, 113–20.

LIPID (Long-term Intervention with Pravastatin in Ischaemic Disease) Study Group (1998). Prevention of cardiovascular events and death with pravastatin in patients with coronary heart disease and a broad range of initial cholesterol levels. *New England Journal of Medicine*, **339**, 1349–57.

MacMahon, S., Peto, R., Cutler, J., et al. (1990a). Blood pressure, stroke and coronary heart disease. Part 1. *Lancet*, **335**, 765–74.

MacMahon, S., Peto, R., Cutler, J., et al. (1990b). Blood pressure, stroke and coronary heart disease. Part 2. *Lancet*, **335**, 827–38.

Manolio, T.A., Pearson, T.A., Wenger, N.K., Barrett-Connor, E., Payne, G.H., and Harlan, W.R. (1992). Cholesterol and heart disease in older persons and women. *Annals of Epidemiology*, **2**, 161–76.

Marmot, M. and Brunner, E. (1991). Alcohol and cardiovascular disease: the status of the U-shaped curve. *British Medical Journal*, **303**, 565–8.

Mattila, K., Haavisto, M., Rajala, S., and Heikinheimo, R. (1988). Blood pressure and 5-year survival in the very old. *British Medical Journal*, **296**, 887–9.

Medical Research Council Working Party (1992). Medical Research Council trial of treatment of hypertension in older adults: principal results. *British Medical Journal*, **304**, 405–12.

National Institutes of Health Consensus Development Panel on Physical Activity and Cardiovascular Health (1996). Physical activity and cardiovascular health. *Journal of the American Medical Association*, **276**, 241–6.

Neaton, J.D. and Wentworth, D. (1992). Serum cholesterol, blood pressure, cigarette smoking, and death from coronary heart disease. *Archives of Internal Medicine*, **152**, 56–64.

Prospective Studies Collaboration (1995). Cholesterol, diastolic blood pressure and stroke: 13 000 strokes in 450 000 people in 45 prospective cohorts. *Lancet*, **346**, 1647–53.

Rose, G. (1982). *The strategy of preventive medicine*. Oxford University Press.

Sanderson, S. (1996). Hypertension in the elderly: pressure to treat? *Health Trends*, **28**, 117–21.

Scandinavian Simvastatin Survival Study Group (1994). Randomised trial of cholesterol lowering in 4444 patients with coronary heart disease: the Scandinavian Simvastatin Survival Study (4S). *Lancet*, **344**, 1383–9.

SHEP Cooperative Research Group (1991). Prevention of stroke by antihypertensive drug treatment in older persons with isolated systolic hypertension. Final results of the Systolic Hypertension in the Elderly Program (SHEP). *Journal of the American Medical Association*, **265**, 3255–64.

Staessen, J.A., Fagard, R., Thijs, L., et al. (1997). Randomised double blind comparison of placebo and active treatment for older patients with isolated systolic hypertension. *Lancet*, **350**, 757–64.

Stamler, J. (1988). Risk factor modification trials: implications for the elderly. *European Heart Journal*, **9** (Supplement D), 9–53.

Welborn, T.A. and Wearne, K. (1979). Coronary heart disease incidence and cardiovascular mortality in Busselton with reference to glucose and insulin concentrations. *Diabetes Care*, **2**, 154–60.

Weverling-Rijnsburger, A.W.E., Blauw, G.J., Lagaay, A.M., Knook, D.L., Meinders, A.E., and Westendorp, R.G.J. (1997). Total cholesterol and risk of mortality in the oldest old. *Lancet*, **350**, 1119–23.

Wilhelmsen, L. (1988) Trials in coronary heart disease and hypertension with special reference to the elderly. *European Heart Journal*, **9**, 207–14.

9.9 Myocardial infarction

Gaetano Crepaldi and Roldano Scognamiglio

An increasing proportion of the population is reaching advanced age, and those aged 80 years or older form the most rapidly expanding subgroup. The implications for the prevalence of cardiovascular disease are enormous. A post-mortem study in community-dwelling very old people found one or more major atherosclerotic occlusions in at least one coronary artery in 70 per cent of subjects (Waller and Roberts 1983); moreover, approximately 40 per cent of all octogenarians have symptomatic cardiovascular disease (Wei and Gersh 1987).

Despite an overall decline in cardiovascular disease mortality, heart disease remains a common and serious medical problem for older people; ischaemic disease itself is responsible for over half the deaths and for the vast majority of patients with congestive heart failure and cardiac disability. In fact, age is an independent risk factor for cardiac death; adults aged 65 years or older constitute only about 12 per cent of the population, but 80 per cent of all deaths due to acute myocardial infarction occur in people aged 65 years or older, and 60 per cent of myocardial infarction deaths occur in patients aged 75 years or older (Gurwitz *et al.* 1991).

Thus myocardial infarction can be considered the major identifiable clinical entity of coronary artery disease and has been shown to be highly associated with poor outcome in both the acute and the long-term setting. Awareness of the propensity for atypical presentations, serious complications, and reduced survival in older patients mandates prompt diagnosis and careful management decisions.

Clinical characteristics and outcome

Unrecognized myocardial infarction and atypical presentation (Fig. 1)

Myocardial infarction in older people often has an atypical presentation, with the classic description of retrosternal chest pain, with pressure or tightness often absent. Atypical symptoms of myocardial infarction can include nausea and vomiting, dyspnoea, or mental status alterations related to decreased cardiac output (see Chapter 9.10).

Atypical presentations are more common in patients with hypertension and severe mental deterioration or an impaired mental score (Rodstein 1956; Black 1987; Nadelmann *et al.* 1990). The classic triad of chest pain, ECG changes, and elevated cardiac enzymes occurs in only a minority of these patients presenting with acute myocardial infarction, while confusion, vomiting, syncope, and shortness of

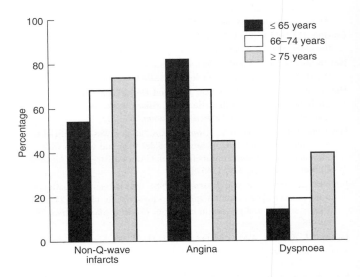

Fig. 1 Comparison of infarct presentation in young, middle-aged, and elderly patients.

breath are reported to be more likely as the presenting complaints. The relative frequency of predominant symptoms for myocardial infarction is reported in Fig. 2.

It is not uncommon for older patients to dismiss these atypical symptoms or not have any detectable symptoms, and therefore not to seek medical attention. Reports of coronary thrombosis without pain have been described as far back as 1912 (Roseman 1954). In the earliest studies (predominantly autopsy studies with an incomplete retrospective review of clinical history) estimates of the proportion of unrecognized myocardial infarction ranged from zero to 61 per cent. In more recent studies, the proportion of unrecognized myocardial infarction has averaged 30 to 40 per cent (Roseman 1954; Rodstein 1956; Johnson *et al.* 1959; Rosenman *et al.* 1967; Kannel and Abbott 1984; Nadelmann *et al.* 1990). A number of theories have been proposed to explain why silent or painless myocardial infarctions occur in older people. A defective myocardial ischaemia and infarction warning system (Cohn 1980) or an increased pain threshold have been suggested as mechanisms to explain silent myocardial ischaemia.

Older individuals with myocardial infarction (about 20 per cent of those over 70 years) are also more likely to have an elevated Mallory body fraction (MB isoenzyme) in the presence of a normal

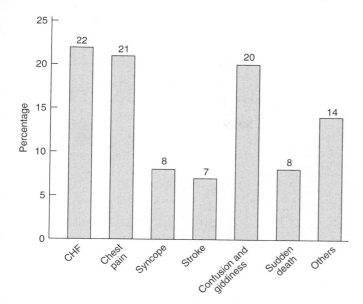

Fig. 2 Prevalence of the symptoms of myocardial infarction in elderly patients (CHF, congestive heart failure).

total creatine kinase. In addition, older patients are more likely to evolve non-Q-wave infarcts because extensive collaterals protect against transmural infarction, and this may mask ECG findings.

Risk factors for coronary disease (see also Chapter 9.4)

Systolic and diastolic blood pressure have been recognized as important risk factors. A systolic blood pressure greater than 160 mmHg, even with a normal diastolic pressure, has to be treated in individuals over 60 years of age (Joint National Committee on the Detection, Evaluation and Treatment of High Blood Pressure 1988; SHEP 1991) (see also Chapter 9.8). Moreover, a U-shaped relationship between diastolic blood pressure and cardiac mortality in patients with known ischaemic disease has been described (Cruickshank *et al.* 1987); those patients whose diastolic pressure is lowered to the 85- to 90-mmHg range have the lowest mortality, while mortality actually increases if diastolic pressure is lowered below 85 mmHg. This relationship may depend on the fact that most coronary flow occurs in diastole, so that a low diastolic pressure can compromise coronary flow in elderly patients with obstructive lesions.

Cigarette use is another important risk factor determining an increased risk of cardiac mortality in elderly people. The effects of smoking cessation have been evaluated in a subset of older participants in the CASS Registry (Hermanson *et al.* 1988). The relative risk of myocardial infarction or death over a 6-year period for those who continued to smoke compared with those who stopped was about threefold.

Elevated total serum cholesterol increases risk for myocardial infarction in men over 65 years of age (Castelli *et al.* 1986; Benfante and Reed 1990). The Framingham Study has also reported that in women and men aged 50 to 82 years there is a significant inverse relationship between high-density lipoprotein cholesterol and the development of coronary disease and myocardial infarction, and a positive relationship between low-density lipoprotein cholesterol and

the risk of developing coronary disease and myocardial infarction (Gordon *et al.* 1977*a*, *b*). Unlike studies in middle-aged men, however, there are no data indicating that treating elevated low-density lipoprotein cholesterol in older people decreases their risk.

Regarding obesity, some studies indicate that an increase in ideal body weight of over 20 per cent is associated with an independent risk of developing coronary artery disease (Hubert *et al.* 1983; Higgins *et al.* 1987).

Diagnostic techniques

The resting ECG may be used in older patients to diagnose acute or old myocardial infarction, whether silent or symptomatic. Ischaemic ST-T wave changes (Fig. 3), as well as arrhythmias and conduction defects that may occur secondary to coronary artery disease, can be diagnosed with the resting ECG. In addition, ECG findings may be predictive of future coronary events, including death. Aronow and coworkers demonstrated that older patients with ST depression greater than 1.0 mm were three times more likely to develop new coronary events (Goldberg *et al.* 1989).

Echocardiography (Fig. 4) can be a useful procedure in the diagnosis of myocardial infarction in older patients in whom atypical presentation is frequent. Detection of wall motion abnormalities is strongly diagnostic of an acute myocardial infarction. Moreover, echocardiography is very useful for the recognition of mechanical complications of myocardial infarction such as rupture of the septum or left ventricular free wall, and acute mitral insufficiency. Left ventricular aneurysm and intraventricular thrombus can be easily recognized.

Left ventricular end-diastolic volume, ejection fraction, and myocardial hypertrophy are findings that can be calculated by two-dimensional echocardiography and can predict future cardiac events and long-term prognosis in older patients.

Prognosis in patients with acute myocardial infarction

Older patients with acute myocardial infarction have significantly higher morbidity and mortality than younger patients (Harris and Piracha 1970; Latting and Silverman 1980). Studies prior to the use of thrombolytic therapy have reported hospital mortality rates of 3.4 to 7.7 per cent in patients younger than 65 years compared with rates of 12.2 to 18.1 per cent in patients aged 66 to 75 years and 17.8 to 33 per cent in patients over 75 years of age. The specific factors involved in this increased mortality rate have not been clearly identified. This difference in outcome between the age groups are probably multifactorial, related to the following:

(1) a more extensive underlying coronary disease;

(2) increased frequency of pre-existing cardiovascular diseases;

(3) myocardial damage from prior infarcts;

(4) decreased ability on the part of the non-infarcted areas to compensate for the myocardium lost as a result of the infarction;

(5) altered healing response following the event;

(6) significantly higher incidence of serious complication of the infarct, including congestive heart failure and rupture;

(7) more comorbidity in older patients often leading to contraindications to thrombolytic therapy;

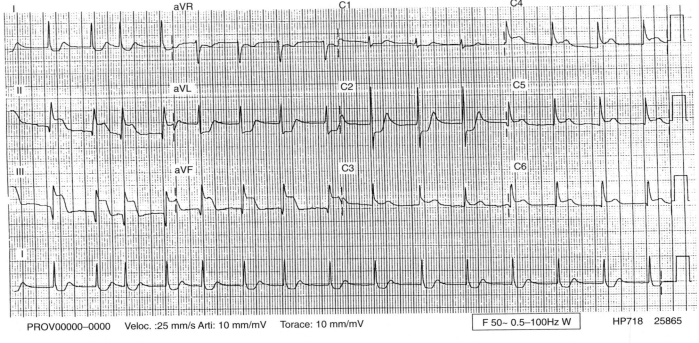

I aVR C1
II aVL C2
III aVF C3
C4
C5
C6
I

PROV00000—0000   Veloc. :25 mm/s Arti: 10 mm/mV   Torace: 10 mm/mV   F 50~ 0.5–100Hz W   HP718   25865

Fig. 3 Ischaemic ST-T wave change in acute inferior myocardial infarction (ECG).

(8) the underuse of therapies in older patients, especially thrombolytic, β-blocker, and aspirin therapy and myocardial revascularization procedures.

Moreover, despite the frequent history of coronary artery disease and the high prevalence of ischaemic chest pain, older patients with myocardial infarction delayed longer in seeking medical assistance than younger patients.

Ageing itself may be associated with significant structural and functional changes in the cardiovascular system; these changes, by decreasing cardiac performance and blunting the compensatory responses, may lead the aged heart to develop heart failure after myocardial infarction and thereby to a higher in-hospital mortality (see Chapter 9.1). Several of these factors need to be examined closely.

Pathophysiology of acute coronary artery occlusion

Rupture of the surfaces of an atherosclerotic plaque with subsequent exposure of thrombogenic factors is the key event in the initiation of thrombosis within coronary arteries. Plaque rupture and thrombus formation are the main factors conditioning the evolutive aspect of acute myocardial infarction. Another mechanism that may alter the balance between myocardial oxygen supply and demand is coronary vasoconstriction at the site of atherosclerotic involvement. This may be the result of a dysfunction in endothelial-dependent dilatation mechanisms or of a platelet-dependent vasoconstriction mediated by serotonin and thromboxane A_2.

In non-Q-wave myocardial infarction several factors are important in preventing the formation of transmural necrosis by limiting the duration of myocardial ischaemia, such as the resolution of vasospasm and spontaneous thrombolysis. Moreover, in a large number of

patients with non-Q-wave myocardial infarction the distal myocardial territory is usually supplied by collaterals.

Q-wave myocardial infarction is the result of an abrupt cessation of perfusion for more than 1 h as a consequence of a fixed and persistent occlusive thrombus. Also in these patients, changes in vascular tone and presence of collateral circulation are factors limiting the extension of myocardial necrosis.

Age-associated structural and functional changes in the myocardium

A constellation of age-associated changes in the senescent heart impact on the management and outcome of myocardial infarction. Some of these changes alter the substrate upon which the disease is superimposed and therefore the presentation and diagnosis of ischaemia (see Chapter 9.1).

The most important changes occurring in the aged heart are as follows.

1. A diminished response to β-adrenergic stimulation in terms of inotropic (Lakatta *et al.* 1975; Kuramoto *et al.* 1978; Guarnieri *et al.* 1980), chronotropic (Yin *et al.* 1979), and vasodilating effects (Pam *et al.* 1986).

2. An impaired diastolic performance with prolonged relaxation, even in the absence of myocardial hypertrophy (Wei *et al.* 1984; Manning *et al.* 1991); several changes at subcellular level may contribute to a delayed myocardial relaxation such as a prolonged cytosolic calcium transport, a decrease in the velocity of calcium accumulation by sarcoplasmic reticulum, and a decrease in the percentage of myosin isozyme with the most rapid adenosine triphosphate hydrolytic rate. Age-associated alterations in measures of left ventricular diastolic performance have been reported using

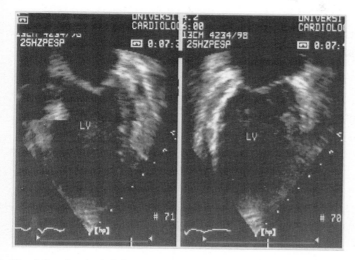

Fig. 4 Septal and apical akinesia in acute anterior myocardial infarction (two-dimensional echocardiogram).

pulsed Doppler echocardiography to assess the pattern of transmitral flow velocity. Abnormalities of left ventricular filling associated with age in subjects without cardiovascular disease may be demonstrated as a decreased early diastolic velocity as well as reduction of early diastolic deceleraton (E wave), associated with increase of late diastolic velocity (A wave). Therefore the relative contribution of atrial contraction to total filling is increased (Fig. 5) (Lakatta and Yin 1982; Walsh 1987).

3. An increase in afterload, as the ascending aorta becomes stiffer and the cross-sectional area of the peripheral vascular bed is reduced (Yin 1980).

These age-associated changes may predispose the heart to ischaemia, with the increased afterload resulting in increased oxygen consumption, and the impaired diastolic relaxation resulting in higher end-diastolic filling pressures and reduced endocardial perfusion.

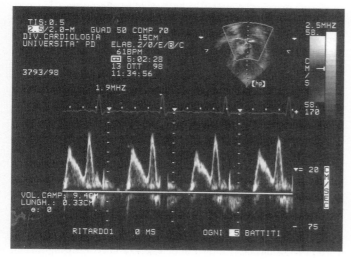

Fig. 5 Reduction of E wave associated with increase of A wave in a patient without coronary artery disease (pulsed Doppler echocardiogram).

Therefore older individuals may be more likely than younger patients to experience dyspnoea for any given ischaemic insult.

Additional factors are important in determining the susceptibility to ischaemia of heart myocardium in older patients.

1. Atherosclerotic coronary lesions tend to become more diffuse and calcified with age, and patients are more likely to have multivessel disease (Waller and Roberts 1983; Lie and Hammond 1988).

2. Changes in vascular reactivity occur, leading to a failure of the coronary bed to dilate commensurately with oxygen demand (reduced 'coronary reserve') and thus compounding the predisposition to ischaemia.

Preconditioning and ischaemic myocardial damage

Pump failure is more frequently encountered in older people, but is not necessarily due to a large infarct or to a different distribution of infarct type and location. This implies that myocardial infarction is less well tolerated by older patients. Experimental studies have shown that an episode of myocardial ischaemia determines a more severe contractile dysfunction, and that the recovery after a period of myocardial ischaemia is more blunted in the senescent than in the adult heart (Frolkis et al. 1991; Ataka et al. 1992). One hypothesis (Abete et al. 1996) is that some endogenous mechanisms involved in the protection of the heart against ischaemia–reperfusion injury may decrease progressively with age. The discovery of the phenomenon of ischaemic preconditioning has focused attention on the heart's capacity to protect itself. Brief periods of ischaemia ('preconditioning') induce intrinsic myocardial changes that are able to protect the heart from longer and sustained ischaemic aggression. This ischaemic preconditioning significantly reduces electromechanical postischaemic dysfunction in adult but not in senescent hearts (Abete et al. 1996). Thus ischaemic preconditioning is missing in older patients, probably because of the absence of a mediator (noradrenaline (norepinephrine), adenosine) that triggers this protective endogenous mechanism against myocardial ischaemia.

Sex and outcome

The relation of sex to the outcome of myocardial infarction is still controversial. Although early studies suggested similar or even better prognosis for women than for men (Norris et al. 1969, 1970), most of the latest studies conclude that women have higher unadjusted fatality and morbidity rates after myocardial infarction in both short-term and long-term follow-ups (Pauletti et al. 1984; Robinson et al. 1988; Greenland et al. 1991; Lincoff et al. 1993). However, when differences in baseline characteristics are taken into account, analyses often reveal relatively similar outcomes in men and women. Therefore the independent role of sex in the outcome after myocardial infarction remains unclear.

Several investigations observed that the women studied were older than the men, and some studies attributed the worse prognosis observed in women to their older ages (Robinson et al. 1988). A sex bias in admission has to be excluded (Behar et al. 1994). A recent report indicated that late arrival is the first cause of ineligibility for thrombolytic therapy in women. Diabetes mellitus alters the perception of symptoms related to myocardial ischaemia and might contribute to a delay in seeking medical care owing to the difficulty

Table 1 Killip classification of acute myocardial infarction patients

Class	Clinical characteristics	% of AMI	% early mortality
1	No signs of heart failure	40–50	6
2	Third heart sound, gallop rhythm	30–40	17
3	Acute pulmonary oedema	10–15	38
4	Cardiogenic shock	5–10	81

AMI, acute myocardial infarction.

in recognizing the acute event (Soler *et al.* 1975; Uretsky *et al.* 1977; Meischke *et al.* 1993). This difficulty might be aggravated in older patients in whom atypical presentation of myocardial infarction is also more frequent (Pathy 1967; Day *et al.* 1987). Women have a higher prevalence of diabetes mellitus and so may have longer delays in arrival and/or emergency room stay—admission time delay is directly associated to mortality. Women also have a tendency to suffer mechanical complications more often than men. The higher prevalence of hypertension may contribute to these complications, particularly to the higher occurrence of cardiac rupture (Pollak *et al.* 1993).

Diabetic and hypertensive patients present not only involvement of epicardial coronary vessels but also small-vessel and myocardial interstitium disease, which lead to an increase in left ventricular stiffness and delayed relaxation. Diabetes mellitus, even in small infarcts, is known to be associated with worse prognosis after myocardial infarction, related to the greater risk of developing heart failure (Jaffe *et al.* 1984; Savage *et al.* 1988). Thus diabetes mellitus and hypertension contribute to the worse outcome through more extensive myocardial damage in the aged females that causes a higher degree of left ventricular systolic and diastolic dysfunction.

Postinfarction risk stratification

After the acute phase of myocardial infarction, risk stratification is based on the same factors as those in the younger patient: left ventricular function, frequency and complexity of ventricular arrhythmias, and subjective or objective evidence of recurrent ischaemia. Killip class (Table 1) is the most powerful predictor of survival in patients aged 65 years or more (Weintraub *et al.* 1983).

Patients at high risk because of poor left ventricular function may be particularly likely to benefit from revascularization procedures like percutaneous transluminal coronary angioplasty (**PTCA**) or bypass surgery if viable myocardium is demonstrable in the context of asynergic areas by low-dose dobutamine infusion or postextrasystolic potentiation.

Patients with recurrent symptoms of ischaemia or with a positive ECG on stress testing are at increased risk of recurrent infarction or death over the first year. They are, generally, considered for more aggressive diagnostic evaluation by cardiac catheterization and coronary angiography, in order to assess the suitability for myocardial revascularization.

Management of acute myocardial infarction

Application of effective preventive and treatment measures might be associated with large survival benefits because older patients are at a greater risk of death related to myocardial infarction (risk increases sixfold for people 75 to 84 years of age and 15-fold for those aged 85 years and older compared with people aged 55 to 64 years).

In the past decade, collaborative research has developed a large and compelling database supporting the survival benefit of thrombolytic and antiplatelet therapies in acute myocardial infarction. Benefit was seen regardless of age, sex, blood pressure, heart rate, or history of myocardial infarction or diabetes and was greater the earlier treatment was begun.

Aspirin

The Second International Study of Infarct Survival (Second International Study of Infarct Survival Collaborative Group 1988), involving more than 17 000 cases, demonstrated the important role of antiplatelet therapy with aspirin. When aspirin was added to streptokinase, the reduction in odds of vascular death increased from 25 to 42 per cent. Moreover, when both drugs were given within 4 h of symptom onset, the odds of death were reduced by 53 per cent. Aspirin also reduced (by 49 per cent) the incidence of early recurrent non-fatal reinfarction.

Moreover, mortality after hospital discharge for an acute myocardial infarction increases dramatically with advancing age; in the second Gruppo Italiano per lo Studio della Sopravivenza nell'Infarto Miocardico (GISSI-2) (Maggioni *et al.* 1993), mortality from hospital discharge to 6 months of follow-up was 4 per cent for patients aged 66 to 70 years, 5 per cent for patients aged 71 to 75 years, 9 per cent for patients aged 76 to 80 years, and 12 per cent for patients older than 80 years of age. Thus secondary prevention, which is designed to reduce mortality, morbidity, and recurrent events in patients who have had an acute myocardial infarction, has an important role in older survivors.

Aspirin may provide the best opportunity for secondary prevention after acute myocardial infarction because of its effectiveness, low cost, safety profile, and lack of strong contraindications. Long-term therapy after myocardial infarction has been shown to be of benefit; placebo-controlled trials demonstrated a 25 per cent reduction in vascular events (mortality reduction, 13 per cent; rate of non-fatal reinfarction, 31 per cent; rate of non-fatal stroke, 42 per cent) (Antiplatelet Trialists' Collaboration 1988). These data provide a strong rationale for the long-term use of aspirin after myocardial infarction in doses as small as 80 to 325 mg/day. The use of aspirin in randomized trials is associated with an odds ratio of 1.5 to 2.0 for all categories of gastrointestinal bleeding, although fatal bleeding is rare (Roderick *et al.* 1993). These data are based on the use of large aspirin doses, commonly in excess of 100 mg/day.

Thrombolytic therapy

Thrombolysis has been shown to be effective in recanalizing infarct-related arteries, salvaging myocardium, preserving left ventricular function, and reducing mortality from acute myocardial infarction

(Rude *et al.* 1981), particularly in patients presenting within 6 h of the onset of symptoms (Yusuf *et al.* 1988*a*).

Gurwitz *et al.* (1996) demonstrated that thrombolytic therapy was indeed used less frequently in the older patients. After adjustment for baseline factors, these authors showed that age itself did affect treatment decisions and substantial differences persist in the proportion of older and younger patients receiving treatment. These differences may not be completely explained by the degree to which older patients do not meet conventional ECG and time-to-presentation criteria for thrombolytic therapy. An important factor seems to be the doctor's reluctance to undertake thrombolytic therapy in older myocardial infarction patients.

Some clinicians believe that the potential haemorrhage risk is greater than the therapeutic benefits of thrombolysis for the older patients. However, age does not represent an adequate criterion by which to judge risk from thrombolysis. GISSI-1, the Anglo-Scandinavian Study of Early Thrombolysis, and AIMS are well-known randomized placebo-controlled mortality trials of thrombolytic therapy that have contributed to our understanding of the relative merits of this therapy in aged myocardial infarction patients. In none of these trials was there an increased incidence of either stroke or bleeding with advancing age. Moreover, thrombolytic therapy reduced mortality in older patients. In the Second International Study of Infarct Survival (Gerstenblith *et al.* 1983), mortality was significantly reduced in older patients treated with thrombolysis; a 15.7 per cent reduction in mortality in those 70 years or older and a 41.2 per cent reduction in those 80 years or older has been demonstrated. Similarly, both the Anglo-Scandinavian Study of Early Thrombolysis (Wilcox *et al.* 1988, 1990) and the APSAC Intervention Mortality Study (AIMS 1988, 1990) showed improved survival in the older subgroups treated with thrombolysis.

Percutaneous transluminal coronary angioplasty and bypass surgery

PTCA and coronary artery bypass graft are the most common mechanical revascularization treatment options for patients with myocardial infarction. In the older patient the high prevalence of comorbidity as well as multivessel disease, increased vessel tortuosity, calcifications, and impaired left ventricular function complicates the issue of revascularization. Many studies have shown the efficacy of emergency PTCA (Holland *et al.* 1989; O'Keefe *et al.* 1989; Lee *et al.* 1990) as well as elective PTCA in the preinfarct period (Myler *et al.* 1991; Thompson *et al.* 1991). Although procedure-related complications are increased relative to young adults, successful revascularization rates are similar (Holt *et al.* 1988; Forman *et al.* 1992). The efficacy of PTCA is particularly compelling since it represents an alternative strategy for older patients for whom thrombolytic agents are frequently contraindicated.

Elective coronary artery bypass is generally well tolerated in the older patient with good short- and long-term outcome (Gersh *et al.* 1983; Rahimtoola *et al.* 1986). Improving surgical technique is contributing to this trend. Elective coronary artery bypass has an important place in the therapeutic armamentarium for the very old in whom the vasculature is not amenable to PTCA. Moreover, patients with multivessel disease or a low ejection fraction often do better with surgery compared with medical or angioplasty revascularization (McCallister *et al.* 1983). However, coronary artery bypass is associated

with high mortality in patients whose condition is unstable (Gersh *et al.* 1983), and the incidence of surgical complications is high.

β-Blockers

Despite the blunted β-responsiveness that occurs in ageing which might presumably protect the older patients from autonomic instability, ischaemia has been shown to reverse β-receptor desensitization in animals, possibly creating a dangerous rebound effect (Strasser *et al.* 1988). Several trials showed the efficacy of β-blockers for older patients by reducing infarct size, sudden death, reinfarction, and overall mortality. In the Beta-Blocker Heart Trial (Beta-Blocker Heart Attack Trial Research Group 1982; Goldstein *et al.* 1983), propranolol was started 5 to 21 days after infarction; mortality decreased by 33.7 per cent in patients aged 60 to 69 years. In the Norwegian Timolol Trial (Pedersen 1983), mortality diminished by 47.8 per cent by timolol. The Metoprolol in Acute Myocardial Infarction (MIAMI) Trial showed a 1.8 per cent reduction in mortality with metoprolol (Schwartz *et al.* 1992). Despite the demonstrated benefits of β-blockers for older patients after myocardial infarction, there is evidence that they are less likely to be given them than younger patients (Soumerai *et al.* 1997).

Calcium-channel antagonists

The efficacy of diltiazem in patients with myocardial infarction has been suggested by two trials. Diltiazem, started between 24 and 72 h after the onset of infarction, reduced the overall 1-year mortality rate from 15 to 9 per cent in older patients with normal left ventricular ejection fraction (Gibson *et al.* 1986). However, 61 per cent of the patients were also receiving β-blockers, and this can significantly confound any meaningful interpretation of the data.

Lower 16-month reinfarction and mortality rates in non-Q-wave and Q-wave myocardial infarction patients treated with verapamil has been demonstrated in the Danish Verapamil Infarction Trial II (Danish Study Group on Verapamil in Myocardial Infarction Trial 1990). About 30 per cent of patients were older than 65 years and β-blocker therapy was used as exclusion criteria. An analysis of the older population has yet to be published.

Nitrates

Several studies suggest the efficacy of intravenous nitrates in acute myocardial infarction (Flaherty *et al.* 1983; Yusuf *et al.* 1988*b*), showing a 33 per cent reduction in fatality. Even though older patients may be more vulnerable to some haemodynamic actions of nitrates (such as reduction in coronary blood flow secondary to hypotension and exacerbation of clinical status by decreasing preload and cardiac output), no studies have actually demonstrated greater adverse effects in older patients with myocardial infarction compared with younger patients.

Angiotensin-converting enzyme inhibitors

Prospective studies have shown that captopril may attenuate progressive left ventricular enlargement after myocardial infarction (Ertl *et al.* 1982; Pfeffer *et al.* 1988). Moreover, the Survival and Ventricular Enlargement (SAVE) trial showed a beneficial effect on survival (Moye *et al.* 1994). Other angiotensin-converting enzyme inhibitors may be similarly beneficial. These studies on ventricular remodelling after myocardial infarction have not focused specifically on older patients.

Conclusion

Choices for optimal treatment of myocardial infarction in older people are not simple, but an aggressive intervention seems to be an appropriate option to consider. Age-associated myocardial structural and functional changes predispose older people to significant morbidity and mortality from myocardial infarction. Thus advanced age has to be a stimulus to perform early and interventional therapy rather than a reason to avoid it. Unfortunately, clinicians are often reluctant to use an interventional approach in older patients even if they may obtain greater benefit from aggressive therapy than younger adults for whom prognosis is often less devastating.

References

Abete, P., Ferrara, N., Cioppa, A., Ferrara, P., and Bianco, S. (1996). Preconditioning does not prevent postischemic dysfunction in aging heart. *Journal of the American College of Cardiology*, 27, 1777–86.

AIMS Trial Study Group (1988). Effect of intravenous APSAC on mortality after acute myocardial infarction: preliminary report of a placebo-controlled clinical trial. *Lancet*, 2, 545–9.

AIMS Trial Study Group (1990). Long-term effects of intravenous anistreplase in acute myocardial infarction: final report of the AIMS Study. *Lancet*, 335, 427–31.

Antiplatelet Trialists' Collaboration (1988). Secondary prevention of vascular disease by prolonged antiplatelet treatment. *British Medical Journal*, 296, 320–31.

Ataka, K., Chen, D., Levitsky, S., Jimenez, E., and Feinberg, H. (1992). Effect of aging on intracellular Ca^{2+}, pH_i and contractility during ischaemia and reperfusion. *Circulation*, 86 (Supplement II), 371–6.

Behar, S., Gottlieb, S., Hod, H., et al. (1994). Influence of gender in the therapeutic management of patients with acute myocardial infarction in Israel. *American Journal of Cardiology*, 73, 438–443.

Benfante, R. and Reed, D. (1990). Is elevated serum cholesterol level a risk factor for coronary heart disease in the elderly? *Journal of the American Medical Association*, 263, 393–6.

Beta-Blocker Heart Attack Trial Research Group (1982). A randomized trial of propranolol in patients with acute myocardial infarction. I. Mortality results. *Journal of the American Medical Association*, 247, 1707–14.

Black, D.A. (1987). Mental state and presentation of myocardial infarction in the elderly. *Age and Ageing*, 16, 125–7.

Castelli, W.P., Garrison, R.J., Wilson, P.W., et al. (1986). Incidence of coronary heart disease and lipoprotein cholesterol levels. The Framingham Study. *Journal of the American Medical Association*, 256, 2835–8.

Cohn, P.F. (1980). Silent myocardial ischemia in patients with a defective anginal warning system. *American Journal of Cardiology*, 45, 697–702.

Cruickshank, J.M., Thorp, J.M., and Zacharias, F.J. (1987). Benefits and potential harm of lowering high blood pressure. *Lancet*, 282, 581–4.

Danish Study Group on Verapamil in Myocardial Infarction Trial II (DAVIT II) (1990). Effect of verapamil on mortality and major events after acute myocardial infarction. *American Journal of Cardiology*, 66, 779–85.

Day, J.J., Bayer, A.J., Pathy, M.S., and Chadha, J.S. (1987). Acute myocardial infarction: diagnostic difficulties and outcome in advanced old age. *Age and Ageing*, 16, 239–43.

Ertl, G., Kloner, R.A., Alexander, R.W., and Braunwald, E. (1982). Limitation of experimental infarct size by an angiotensin-converting enzyme inhibitor. *Circulation*, 65, 40–8.

Flaherty, J.T., Becker, L.C., Bulkley, B.H., et al. (1983). A randomized prospective trial of intravenous nitroglycerin in patients with acute myocardial infarction: benefits of early treatment. *Circulation*, 68, 576–88.

Forman, D.E., Berman, A., McCabe, C.H., Baim, D.S., and Wei, J.Y. (1992). PTCA in the elderly: the 'young old' versus the 'old old'. *Journal of the American Geriatrics Society*, 40, 19–22.

Frolkis, V.V., Frolkis, R.A., Mkhitarian, L.S., and Fairfeld, V.E. (1991). Age-dependent effects of ischemia and reperfusion on cardiac function and Ca^{2+} transport in myocardium. *Gerontology*, 37, 233–9.

Gersh, B.J., Kronmal, R.A., Frye, R.L., et al. (1983). Coronary arteriography and coronary artery bypass surgery: morbidity and mortality in patients aged 65 years or older. *Circulation*, 67, 483–91.

Gerstenblith, G., Fleg, J.L., Becker, L.C., et al. (1983). Maximum left ventricular filling rate in healthy individuals measured by gated blood pool scans: effects of age. *Circulation*, 68 (Supplement III), 101.

Gibson, R.S., Boden, W.E., Theroux, P., et al. (1986). Diltiazem and reinfarction in patients with non Q-wave myocardial infarction. *New England Journal of Medicine*, 315, 423–9.

Goldberg, R.J., Gore, J.M., Gurwitz, J.H., et al. (1989). The impact of age on the incidence and prognosis of initial acute myocardial infarction: the Worcester Heart Attack Study. *American Heart Journal*, 117, 543–9.

Goldstein, S. and the Beta-Blocker Heart Attack Trial Research Group (1983). Propranolol therapy in patients with acute myocardial infarction: the Beta-Blocker Heart Attack Trial. *Circulation*, 67, 153–6.

Gordon, T., Castelli, W.P., and Hjortland, M.C. (1977a). High density lipoprotein as a protective factor against coronary heart disease. The Framingham Study. *American Journal of Medicine*, 62, 707–14.

Gordon, T., Castelli, W.P., Hjortland, M.C., Kannel, W.B., and Dawber, T.R. (1977b). Predicting coronary heart disease in middle-aged and older persons. The Framingham Study. *Journal of the American Medical Association*, 238, 497–9.

Greenland, P., Reicher-Reiss, H., Goldbourt, U., and Behar, S. (1991). In-hospital and 1-year mortality in 1524 women after myocardial infarction, comparison with 4315 men. *Circulation*, 83, 484–91.

Guarnieri, T., Filburn, C.R., Zitnik, G., Roth, G.S., and Lakatta, E.G. (1980). Contractile and biochemical correlates of β-adrenergic stimulation of the aged heart. *American Journal of Physiology*, 239, H501–8.

Gurwitz, J.H., Osganian, V., Goldberg, R.J., Chen, Z., Gore, J.M., and Alpert, J.S. (1991). Diagnostic testing in acute myocardial infarction: does patient age influence utilization patterns? *American Journal of Epidemiology*, 134, 948–57.

Gurwitz, J.H., Gore, J.M., Goldberg, R.J., et al. (1996). Recent age-related trends in the use of thrombolytic therapy in patients who have had acute myocardial infarction. *Annals of Internal Medicine*, 124, 292–8.

Harris, R. and Piracha, A.R. (1970). Acute myocardial infarction in the aged: prognosis and management. *Journal of the American Geriatrics Society*, 18, 893–904.

Hermanson, B., Omenn, G.S., Kronmal, R.A., and Gersh, B.J. (1988). Beneficial 6-year outcome of smoking cessation in older men and women with coronary artery disease. Results from the CASS registry. *New England Journal of Medicine*, 319, 1365–9.

Higgins, M., Kannel, W., Garrison, R., Pinsky, J., and Stokes, J. (1987). Hazards of obesity. The Framingham experience. *Acta Medica Scandinavica*, 723 (Supplement III), 23–36.

Holland, K.J., O'Neill, W.W., Bates, E.R., Pitt, B., and Topol, E.J. (1989). Emergency percutaneous transluminal coronary angioplasty during acute myocardial infarction for patients more than 70 years of age. *American Journal of Cardiology*, 63, 399–403.

Holt, G.W., Sugrue, D.D., Bresnahan, J.F., *et al.* (1988). Results of percutaneous transluminal coronary angioplasty for unstable angina pectoris in patients 70 years of age and older. *American Journal of Cardiology*, **61**, 994–7.

Hubert, H.B., Feinleib, M., McNamara, P.M., and Castelli, W.P. (1983). Obesity as an independent risk factor for cardiovascular disease: a 26-year follow-up of participants in the Framingham Heart Study. *Circulation*, **67**, 698–977.

Jaffe, A.S., Spadaro, J.J., Schetchman, K., *et al.* (1984). Increased congestive heart failure after myocardial infarction of modest extent in patients with diabetes mellitus. *American Heart Journal*, **108**, 31–7.

Johnson, W.J., Achor, R.W.P., Burchell, H.B., and Edwards, J.E. (1959). Unrecognized myocardial infarction. *Archives of Internal Medicine*, **103**, 253–61.

Joint National Committee on the Detection, Evaluation and Treatment of High Blood Pressure (1988). The 1988 report of the Joint National Committee on the Detection, Evaluation and Treatment of High Blood Pressure. *Archives of Internal Medicine*, **148**, 1023–38.

Kannel, W.B. and Abbott, R.D. (1984). Incidence and prognosis of unrecognized myocardial infarction. An update on the Framingham Study. *New England Journal of Medicine*, **311**, 1144–7.

Kuramoto, K., Matsushita, S., Mifune, J., Sakai, M., and Murakami, M. (1978). Electrocardiographic and hemodynamic evaluations of isoproterenol test in elderly ischemic heart disease. *Japanese Circulation Journal*, **42**, 955–60.

Lakatta, E.G. and Yin, F.C. (1982). Myocardial aging: functional alterations and related cellular mechanisms. *American Journal of Physiology*, **242**, H927–31.

Lakatta, E.G., Gerstenblith, G., Angell, C.S., Shock, N.W., and Weisfeldt, M.L. (1975). Diminished inotropic response of aged myocardium to catecholamines. *Circulation Research*, **36**, 262–9.

Latting, C.A. and Silverman, M.E. (1980). Acute myocardial infarction in hospitalized patients over age 70. *American Heart Journal*, **100**, 311–18.

Lee, T.C., Laramee, L.A., Rutherford, B.D., *et al.* (1990). Emergency percutaneous transluminal coronary angioplasty for acute myocardial infarction in patients 70 years of age and older. *American Journal of Cardiology*, **66**, 663–7.

Lie, J.T. and Hammond, P.I. (1988). Pathology of the senescent heart: anatomic observations on 237 autopsy studies of patients 90–105 years old. *Mayo Clinic Proceedings*, **63**, 552–64.

Lincoff, A.M., Califf, R.M., Elli, S.G., *et al.* (1993). Thrombolytic therapy for women with myocardial infarction: is there a gender gap? *Journal of the American College of Cardiology*, **22**, 1780–7.

McCallister, B.D., Hartzler, G.O., Reed, W.A., and Johnson, T.W. (1983). Percutaneous transluminal coronary angioplasty in elderly patients, a comparison with coronary artery bypass surgery (abstract). *Journal of the American College of Cardiology*, **1**, 656.

Maggioni, A.P., Maseri, A., Fresco, C., *et al.* (1993). Age-related increase in mortality among patients with first myocardial infarctions treated with thrombolysis. The Investigators of the Gruppo Italiano per lo Studio della Sopravivenza nell'Infarto Miocardico (GISSI-2). *New England Journal of Medicine*, **329**, 1442–8.

Manning, W.J., Shannon, R.P., Santinga, J.A., *et al.* (1991). Reversal of changes in left ventricular diastolic filling associated with normal aging using diltiazem. *American Journal of Cardiology*, **67**, 894–6.

Meischke, H., Eisenberg, M.S., and Larsen, M.P. (1993). Prehospital delay interval for patients who use emergency medical services: the effect of heart-related medical conditions and demographic variables. *Annals of Emergency Medicine*, **22**, 1597–601.

Moye, L.A., Pfeffer, M.A., Wun, C.C., *et al.* (1994). Uniformity of captopril benefit in the SAVE study: subgroup analysis. Survival and Ventricular Enlargement Study. *European Heart Journal*, **15** (Supplement B), 2–8.

Myler, R.K., Webb, J.G., Nguyen, K.P., *et al.* (1991). Coronary angioplasty in octogenerians: comparisons to coronary bypass surgery.

Catheterization and Cardiovascular Diagnosis, **23**, 3–9.

Nadelmann, J., Frishman, W.H., Ooi, W.L., *et al.* (1990). Prevalence, incidence and prognosis of recognized and unrecognized myocardial infarction in persons aged 75 years or older: the Bronx Aging Study. *American Journal of Cardiology*, **66**, 533–7.

Norris, R.M., Brandt, P.W., Cughey, D.O., Lee, A.J., and Scott, P.J. (1969). A new coronary prognostic index. *Lancet*, **i**, 274–8.

Norris, R.M., Caughey, D.E., Deeming, L.W., Mercer, C.J., and Scott, P.J. (1970). Coronary prognostic index for predicting survival after recovery from acute myocardial infarction. *Lancet*, **ii**, 485–8.

O'Keefe, J.H., Rutherford, B.D., McConahay, D.R., *et al.* (1989). Early and late results of coronary angioplasty without antecedent thrombolytic therapy for acute myocardial infarction. *American Journal of Cardiology*, **64**, 1221–9.

Pam, H.Y., Hoffman, R.R., Perskin, R.A., *et al.* (1986). Decline in beta adrenergic receptors mediated vascular relaxation with aging in man. *Journal of Pharmacology and Experimental Therapy*, **239**, 802–7.

Pathy, M.S. (1967). Clinical presentation of myocardial infarction in the elderly. *British Heart Journal*, **29**, 190–9.

Pauletti, M., Sunseri, L., Curione, M., Erba, S.M., and Borgia, C. (1984). Acute myocardial infarction: sex-related differences in prognosis. *American Heart Journal*, **108**, 63–6.

Pedersen, T.R. (1983). The Norwegian Multicenter Study of timolol after myocardial infarction. *Circulation*, **67**, 149–52.

Pfeffer, M.A., Lamas, G.A., Vaughan, D.E., Parisi, A.F., and Braunwald, E. (1988). Effect of captopril on progressive ventricular dilatation after anterior myocardial infarction. *New England Journal of Medicine*, **319**, 80–6.

Pollak, H., Diez, W., Spiel, R., Enenkel, W., and Mlczoch, J. (1993). Early diagnosis of subacute free wall rupture complicating acute myocardial infarction. *European Heart Journal*, **14**, 640–8.

Rahimtoola, S.H., Grunkemeier, G.L., and Starr, A. (1986). Ten year survival after coronary artery bypass surgery for angina in patients aged 65 years and older. *Circulation*, **74**, 509–17.

Robinson, K., Conroy, R.M., Mulcahy, R., and Hickey, N. (1988). Risk factors and in-hospital course of first episode of myocardial infarction or acute coronary insufficiency in women. *Journal of the American College of Cardiology*, **11**, 932–6.

Roderick, P.J., Wilkes, H.C., and Meade, T.W. (1993). The gastrointestinal toxicity of aspirin, an overview of randomised controlled trials. *British Journal of Clinical Pharmacology*, **35**, 219–26.

Rodstein, M. (1956). The characteristics of nonfatal myocardial infarction in the aged. *Archives of Internal Medicine*, **98**, 84–90.

Roseman, M.D. (1954). Painless myocardial infarction, a review of the literature and analysis of 220 cases. *Annals of Internal Medicine*, **41**, 1–8.

Rosenman, R.H., Friedman, M., Jenkins, C.D., *et al.* (1967). Clinically unrecognized myocardial infarction in the Western Collaborative Group Study. *American Journal of Cardiology*, **19**, 776–82.

Rude, R.E., Muller, J.E., and Braunwald, E. (1981). Efforts to limit the size of myocardial infarcts. *Annals of Internal Medicine*, **95**, 736–61.

Savage, M.P., Krolewski, A.S., Kenien, G.G., *et al.* (1988). Acute myocardial infarction in diabetes mellitus and significance of congestive heart failure as a prognostic factor. *American Journal of Cardiology*, **62**, 665–9.

Schwartz, P.J., La Rovere, M.T., and Vanoli, E. (1992). Autonomic nervous system and sudden cardiac death: experimental basis and clinical observations for post-myocardial infarction risk stratification. *Circulation*, **85**, 77–91.

Second International Study of Infarct Survival (ISIS-2) Collaborative Group (1988). Randomized trial of intravenous streptokinase, oral aspirin, both, or neither among 17 187 cases of suspected myocardial infarction. *Lancet*, **ii**, 349–60.

SHEP Cooperative Research Group (1991). Prevention of stroke by antihypertensive drug treatment in older persons with isolated systolic hypertension. Final results of the Systolic Hypertension in the Elderly Program (SHEP). *Journal of the American Medical Association*, 265, 3255–64.

Soler, N., Bennet, M., Pentecost, B., Fitzgerald, M., and Malins, J. (1975). Myocardial infarction in diabetics. *Quarterly Journal of Medicine*, 173, 125–32.

Soumerai, S.B., McLaughlin, T.J., Spiegelman, D., Hertzmark, E., Thibault, G., and Goldman, L. (1997). Adverse outcomes of underuse of β-blockers in elderly survivors of acute myocardial infarction. *Journal of the American Medical Association*, 277, 115–21.

Strasser, R.H., Krimmer, J., and Marquetant, R. (1988). Regulation of beta-adrenergic receptors, impaired desensitization in myocardial ischemia. *Journal of Cardiovascular Pharmacology*, 12, S15–24.

Thompson, R.C., Holmes, D.R., Gersh, B.J., Mock, M.B., and Bailey, K.R. (1991). Percutaneous transluminal coronary angioplasty in the elderly, early and long-term results. *Journal of the American College of Cardiology*, 17, 1245–50.

Uretsky, B.F., Farquhar, D., Berezin, A., and Hood, W. (1977). Symptomatic myocardial infarction without chest pain, prevalence and clinical course. *American Journal of Cardiology*, 40, 498–503.

Waller, F. and Roberts, W.C. (1983). Cardiovascular disease in the very elderly, analysis of 40 necropsy patients aged 90 years or over. *American Journal of Cardiology*, 51, 403–22.

Walsh, R.A. (1987). Cardiovascular effects of the aging process. *American Journal of Medicine*, 82 (Supplement 1B), 34–40.

Wei, J.H., Spurgeon, H.A., and Lakatta, E.G. (1984). Excitation–contraction in rat myocardium, alterations with adult aging. *American Journal of Physiology*, 246, H784–91.

Wei, J.Y. and Gersh, B.J. (1987). Heart disease in the elderly. In *Current problems in cardiology* (ed. R.A. O'Rourke and M.H. Crawford), pp. 7–65. Year Book Medical Publishers, Chicago, IL.

Weintraub, R.M., Thurer, R.L., Wei, J., and Aroesty, J.M. (1983). Repair of postinfarction ventricular septal defect in the elderly. Early and long-term results. *Thoracic and Cardiovascular Surgery*, 85, 191–6.

Wilcox, R.G., Olsson, C.G., Skene, A.M., von der Lippe, G., Jensen, G., and Hampton, J.R. (1988). Trial of tissue plasminogen activator for mortality reduction in acute myocardial infarction, Anglo-Scandinavian Study of Early Thrombolysis (ASSET). *Lancet*, ii, 525–30.

Wilcox, R.G., von der Lippe, G., Olssoh, C.G., *et al.* (1990). Effects of alteplase in acute myocardial infarction, 6-month results from the ASSET Study. *Lancet*, 335, 1175–8.

Yin, F.C. (1980). The aging vasculature and its effects on the heart. In *The aging heart* (ed. M.L. Weisfeldt), pp. 137–214. Raven Press, New York.

Yin, F.C., Spurgeon, H.A., Greene, H.L., Lakatta, E.G., and Weisfeldt, M.L. (1979). Age-associated decrease in heart rate response to isoproterenol in dogs. *Mechanics of Ageing and Development*, 10, 17–25.

Yusuf, S., Collins, R., MacMahon, S., and Peto, R. (1988a). Effect of intravenous nitrates on mortality in acute myocardial infarction, an overview of the randomized trials. *Lancet*, i, 1088–92.

Yusuf, S., Wittes, J., and Friedman, L. (1988b). Overview of results of randomized clinical trials in heart disease. I. Treatments following myocardial infarction. *Journal of the American Medical Association*, 260, 2088–93.

9.10 Angina

G. Hart

Mortality from coronary heart disease is falling in most Western countries. However, the proportion of older people in the population is rising, which means that the clinical and economic burden of coronary heart disease will continue to increase for many years. More than 70 per cent of the population have coronary atheroma by the age of 70, although clinical evidence of coronary disease is present in only one-third to half of these people. Coronary artery disease is the most common cause of death in persons over the age of 65 (Castelli 1993). The proportion of women affected is much greater than in the younger age groups, so that, at age 75, coronary morbidity is equal for men and women. Clinical studies of coronary artery disease have concentrated on middle-aged men and there is a lack of research into coronary disease in the older age groups, particularly among women.

Clinical presentation

Coronary artery disease is less likely to present as classical angina in older people than it is in middle age. A significant coronary stenosis in a younger person is more likely to present as typical angina, whereas the same degree of stenosis in older people is often not associated with characteristic effort-related chest pain. Reasons for the higher angina threshold in older people are unclear, but possible mechanisms include a reduced sensitivity to pain and a better coronary collateral supply. The symptom of angina, when it is present, appears to have similar characteristics in all age groups. The sensation of angina is usually experienced as a 'discomfort' rather than as a pain. It is located typically in the central, middle, and lower chest with radiation to the arms (the left more often than the right), the neck, the throat, the jaws, and occasionally the upper back. Anginal discomfort is usually experienced at a consistent site in a given individual. Pain which is felt at different sites in the body, on different occasions, is not likely to be caused by cardiac ischaemia.

Typically, angina is induced by effort and relieved by rest. The threshold for angina may be reduced after food and on exposure to cold, which may result in angina on minimal exertion. The first awareness of discomfort in elderly people often gives rise to consideration of alternative disorders such as indigestion or arthritis, particularly if the discomfort is not severe. Mild discomfort, of short duration, does not alert patients to the possibility of a cardiac cause for their symptom. Mild discomfort at rest, in an atypical site such as the back of the neck, may be the first symptom of unstable angina in an older person. Therefore complaints of discomfort in the upper part of the body in older people should be treated seriously.

Older people often complain of effort intolerance and shortness of breath as a result of coronary stenoses. These symptoms may be regarded as 'angina equivalent' when they are associated with objective evidence of inducible cardiac ischaemia, in the absence of anginal chest pain. Pulmonary oedema may be the first manifestation of coronary artery disease in older people. Cardiac hypertrophy from hypertension or reduced arterial compliance is commonly found in these patients. Hypertrophy causes impaired diastolic filling of the left ventricle. An episode of cardiac ischaemia, which results in further elevation of the left atrial pressure, may be sufficient to trigger overt pulmonary oedema. Ischaemia may trigger atrial fibrillation, which in turn can present as pulmonary oedema. Older people with severe coronary artery disease may experience recurrent pulmonary oedema but nevertheless may have normal left ventricular systolic function. Clinical studies have shown that diastolic left ventricular function is usually abnormal at rest and deteriorates during recurrent ischaemic episodes (Siegel et al. 1991).

Diagnostic evaluation

Objective evidence of ischaemia should be sought in all patients complaining of possible anginal chest pain or angina equivalent, so that anti-anginal treatment may be given appropriately. Estimates of the severity of inducible ischaemia, and of left ventricular function at rest and during ischaemia, are useful in determining whether a medical or a surgical approach is appropriate. Prognostic assessment may not be done routinely in older people with coronary disease, largely because of economic constraints, but there is no evidence to adopt such an approach on the grounds of age alone. Contributing conditions should be excluded, and the presence of associated disease should be sought. The impact of the condition on patients' lifestyles and on their families should be assessed. (See also Chapter 9.1.)

Examination of the heart may be normal in patients with severe coronary artery disease and good left ventricular systolic function, but evidence should be sought of more generalized vascular disease by palpation of the peripheral pulses, and by auscultation for renal and carotid artery bruits. Cardiac hypertrophy is often detectable as a sustained apex beat in older patients with coronary disease and hypertension. A fourth heart sound may indicate impaired diastolic function.

Aortic stenosis often presents with angina and effort intolerance, and physical examination may reveal an ejection systolic murmur.

Evidence of left heart failure may be present in the form of a displaced apex beat, a third heart sound, and basal crepitations. Peripheral oedema and an elevated jugular venous pressure demand explanations other than coronary disease if left heart failure is not also present. Ambulatory blood pressure monitoring should be undertaken if the arterial pressure is elevated; the presence of associated hypertension may affect the choice of anti-anginal medication.

Angina may be the first indication that an older person is anaemic and a full blood count should be performed in all cases. The symptom of angina may be improved or eliminated by restoration of a normal haemoglobin concentration.

Electrocardiography

The resting ECG is often abnormal in older people. Evidence of previous infarction, whether transmural or partial-thickness, may be visible. Resting ST-segment depression greater than 0.1 mV in amplitude, and attributable to myocardial ischaemia, is associated with a greater than threefold increase in the likelihood of new cardiac events (myocardial infarction, primary ventricular fibrillation, and sudden cardiac death) in elderly people (Aronow 1989). Conduction defects such as left bundle branch block and first-degree atrioventricular block may be present. These are also associated with a higher incidence of new cardiac events in older people.

Stress testing

Exercise testing is a very useful way of obtaining objective evidence of ischaemia in older people and is at least as sensitive for diagnosing the presence of significant coronary stenoses as it is in younger age groups, possibly because coronary disease is more severe in older people. However, the positive predictive value of the test is reduced because of the higher prevalence of coronary disease in older people (Chaitman et al. 1981). A proportion of older patients cannot manage to perform a treadmill test because of ancillary disabilities such as arthritis, neurological disease, or peripheral vascular disease. Older people are less used to taking exercise, and physical deconditioning may lead to termination of the test on account of breathlessness before a conclusive answer can be obtained. Atrial fibrillation is much more common in older people, and stress testing is less useful in the context of this arrhythmia because the heart rate increment is altered and because of associated repolarization abnormalities, particularly if digoxin is being taken.

The time at which symptoms develop on the treadmill should be noted, and correlation should be sought between symptoms and ST-segment changes. A test can be considered positive for electrical evidence of ischaemia if ST-segment depression greater than 0.1 mV in amplitude develops at any time during the test. The test is negative if the age-related target heart rate is exceeded without the test becoming positive. Any other endpoint must be considered indeterminate. The most common cause of an indeterminate test result is failure to achieve a sufficient heart rate increment, which may be attributable, for example, to treatment with β-blocking drugs, poor left ventricular function, or physical disability or deconditioning. Significant ST-segment depression has been correlated, in older people, with increased mortality at 2 years (Glover et al. 1984). Other adverse prognostic indicators include failure of the blood pressure to rise during the test and high-grade ventricular arrhythmias requiring termination of the test.

Interpretation of a stress test result should be made in conjunction with an estimate of left ventricular function, particularly after myocardial infarction when ST-segment depression *per se* carries less prognostic significance. For example, an exercise test may become positive at an easy workload in a patient with two-vessel disease and good left ventricular function. In contrast, a patient with proximal three-vessel disease and substantial impairment of ventricular function may generate less ST-segment depression, but could stand to benefit from coronary artery surgery more than the patient with the clearly positive result. Adverse prognostic features for a low-level exercise test after myocardial infarction in the older patient include failure to exercise for 6 min, absence of a rise in arterial pressure, ventricular arrhythmias and angina during the test.

Other forms of stress testing may be as applicable in the older patient as in younger age groups. Stress thallium scintigraphy is useful for risk stratification in older patients. The stress may be applied by exercise (Iskandrian *et al.* 1988) or by using intravenous agents such as adenosine or dipyridamole (Lam *et al.* 1988).

Echocardiography

Echocardiography is a valuable non-invasive test for the older patient with angina. If the examination window is favourable, which may not be the case in patients with significant chest disease or obesity, echocardiography provides anatomical detail and allows measurement of the function of the cardiac chambers and valves. Echocardiography is more sensitive than the ECG in detecting left ventricular hypertrophy. This adaptive response is an independent risk factor for mortality whether or not structural coronary disease is present, and older patients with angina have a worse prognosis if left ventricular hypertrophy is also present (Tresch and Aronow 1994). Previous myocardial infarction, which is another adverse prognostic sign in older people with angina, may be detectable as regional wall motion abnormalities on the echocardiogram. Valve abnormalities, including aortic stenosis, may be identified and gradients may be estimated using Doppler flow measurements. Abnormal diastolic function may be predicted from prolongation of the flow of blood through the mitral valve.

Coronary arteriography

If surgical intervention is contemplated, cardiac catheterization and coronary arteriography will be required. These investigations are technically more difficult in older people because of tortuosity and atheroma of the iliofemoral tree, and unfolding and atheroma of the aorta. The brachial approach may be better for patients receiving warfarin treatment and for those with aortic valve disease. Loss of connective tissue support in older patients predisposes to a higher rate of bleeding complications, particularly when a percutaneous approach is used. Stroke is an uncommon complication but the incidence is higher in the elderly patient undergoing cardiac catheterization.

Management of the patient with angina

Reversible factors such as anaemia and congestive heart failure should receive appropriate treatment. Treatment of hypertension (Joint National Committee 1993), angiotensin-converting enzyme inhibitor treatment for left ventricular dysfunction (Pfeffer *et al.* 1992), reduction of elevated plasma cholesterol (Sacks *et al.* 1996), and stopping smoking (LaCroix *et al.* 1991) have all been shown to reduce cardiovascular mortality in older patients. Appropriate support should be arranged if angina is interfering with the patient's lifestyle and ability to care for him- or herself.

Drug treatment for angina

The basic principles of drug treatment for angina are the same for older people as for younger age groups. However, the drugs may be less effective in relieving symptoms and less well tolerated, and side-effects may be more difficult to avoid than with younger patients.

Aspirin

Low-dose aspirin reduces the frequency of unstable angina and improves the prognosis after myocardial infarction, although controlled data on older patients have not been obtained. All patients with atheromatous vascular disease should receive low-dose aspirin unless there is a contraindication or non-steroidal anti-inflammatory drugs are being taken on a regular basis for other purposes. Enteric-coated preparations are useful when conventional aspirin causes gastric irritation.

Nitrates

Nitrate administered through the buccal mucosa from sublingual tablets or a spray is useful in terminating anginal attacks not rapidly relieved by rest, and in prophylactic treatment when a known quantity of effort is likely to result in angina. A suitable preparation should be carried by all patients with effort symptoms from coronary artery disease. Careful instruction in the use of rapidly available nitrate preparations minimizes the occurrence of headache as a side-effect and improves patient compliance. Sublingual tablets deteriorate in the bottle and a fresh supply should be obtained every 3 months.

Nitrate preparations are often used as first-line oral treatment for angina in elderly patients. Mononitrates offer better bio-availability than dinitrates, which have to undergo first-pass metabolism in the liver, and dose titration is more predictable. Many preparations are available with different half-life characteristics. An important principle in treating patients with oral nitrates is to prescribe the drug at such intervals that the patient's plasma is free of administered nitrate for at least 8 h per day. Otherwise, tolerance is liable to develop and the efficacy of subsequent nitrate doses is reduced. A twice-daily regime of isosorbide mononitrate given in the morning and early afternoon is satisfactory for most people. If nocturnal angina is a problem it may be necessary for the patient to accept a nitrate-free period during the day, and to take one of the doses of nitrate on retiring to bed.

β-Blocking drugs

The primary trigger for anginal pain is an increase in myocardial energy demand. Inhibition of cardiac β-receptors causes a reduction in heart rate and cardiac work, which are the principal factors determining oxygen consumption by the heart. Therefore, β-blocking drugs have become the gold standard for the medical treatment of angina in younger people. These compounds remain just as effective in older patients, but they must be used carefully because side-effects and contraindications are more common. The older patient is more likely to have impaired left ventricular function from previous infarction and cardiac hypertrophy. Consequently, pulmonary venous pressure is elevated, which predisposes to overt pulmonary congestion following administration of β-blocking drugs. First-degree heart block is not a contraindication to β-blocking drugs, but higher degrees of heart block, which are more common in older people, preclude their use. Conduction disturbances, including sinoatrial disease, must be excluded before these compounds are given to older people. β-Blocking drugs are contraindicated in asthmatics because of their propensity to cause bronchospasm. They may exacerbate symptoms of claudication in patients with peripheral vascular disease. Because they may mask symptoms of hypoglycaemia, β-blockers are generally not suitable for diabetic patients taking hypoglycaemic medication.

One of the main factors determining which β-blocker to choose is the propensity of the lipid-soluble compounds, such as propranolol, to cross the blood–brain barrier and to give rise to central nervous system side-effects such as insomnia, bad dreams, and depression. Therefore the predominantly water-soluble β-blockers such as atenolol are better tolerated. However, the bio-availability of the water-soluble compounds is lower and less predictable than that of the lipid-soluble drugs, as it is determined largely by gastrointestinal absorption; the plasma half-life is longer and excretion takes place mainly via the kidney. Atenolol is a water-soluble β-blocker which is widely used. A starting dose of 25 mg daily may be appropriate in older patients, particularly if renal function is impaired.

Calcium-channel blockers

Calcium entry through L-type calcium channels promotes contraction in cardiac myocytes and in vascular smooth muscle cells. Three categories of calcium-channel-blocking drugs are available for clinical use, each having different relative affinities for the receptors in vascular and in cardiac muscle. The phenylalkylamine group, represented by verapamil, exerts a depressant action on sinoatrial node automaticity and on atrioventricular conduction. Drugs of this group are the most negatively inotropic of the calcium-channel blockers. Although verapamil is effective in treating angina and hypertension, its use in older people is limited by a higher incidence of cardiac conduction disturbances and gastrointestinal side-effects. Verapamil is not appropriate for patients who have substantial impairment of left ventricular function, or for those who are also receiving β-blocking drugs.

The dihydropyridine group contains widely prescribed drugs such as nifedipine, which exert a much greater relaxing effect on vascular smooth muscle than on cardiac muscle. The dihydropyridines, when used alone, cause marked peripheral vasodilatation. Secondary sympathetic activation and the reflex tachycardia may aggravate cardiac ischaemia. Therefore the dihydropyridine compounds are best used together with a β-blocking drug, and this combination has been shown to bring about a further reduction in the incidence of anginal episodes. The side-effect of peripheral oedema is more common in older people, but cardiac conduction disturbances are not induced by dihydropyridines. These compounds are best administered as twice-daily sustained-release preparations. Newer derivatives such as amlodipine have a longer half-life and may be given once daily for angina.

Diltiazem represents the benzothiazepine group of calcium-channel-blocking drugs. It has properties which are intermediate between the phenylalkylamine and the dihydropyridine groups in that a reflex tachycardia is not produced and its action on cardiac conduction is mild. Diltiazem is very useful for the treatment of angina in patients who cannot tolerate β-blocking drugs or in whom these drugs are contraindicated. It may be combined with a β-blocking drug, but if on this combination a patient's resting heart rate is consistently below 50 beats/min, diltiazem should be discontinued and a dihydropyridine compound substituted.

Other vasodilator compounds

Nicorandil blocks the potassium channel which is opened by low intracellular concentrations of ATP. It is a nitrate compound and a vasodilator. Clinical studies have shown it to be effective in the treatment of angina, but its role is not clear for patients who can tolerate nitrates and calcium-channel-blocking drugs.

Management strategies for patients with angina

The choice of drug treatment is determined by the frequency of a patient's symptoms, the findings from cardiac investigation, and the presence of coexisting disease in other systems. If a patient's angina is infrequent, it may be sufficient to prescribe low-dose aspirin and a readily available nitrate preparation. Daily angina justifies prophylactic oral medication. In patients with previous myocardial infarction a β-blocker may be appropriate. A calcium antagonist would be favoured in those patients who have a history of bronchospasm, peripheral claudication, or diabetes mellitus. Patients who continue to experience symptoms on a daily basis may require a combination of drugs such as an oral nitrate plus a β-blocker, or a β-blocker plus a dihydropyridine compound.

Unstable angina

Unstable angina is an umbrella term which is used to denote angina of duration less than 3 months, a reduction in the threshold of previously stable angina, unpredictable angina, and rest (and especially nocturnal) angina. Unpredictable or rest angina requires hospital treatment in all age groups. Bed rest is appropriate until 24 h after the pain has settled. Sublingual or intravenous nitrates are used when pain is present. Aspirin reduces mortality and progression to infarction, and should be given unless there is a contraindication. β-Blockers improve prognosis in patients with unstable angina. There is less evidence in favour of using calcium-channel blockers, but diltiazem may be worthwhile if a β-blocker cannot be used. Intravenous anticoagulation, to keep the thromboplastin time between two and three times control, is indicated until the patient has begun to mobilize.

Unstable angina which does not settle after medical treatment for 24 to 48 h carries a high mortality. Patients with unstable angina should be considered for diagnostic coronary angiography with a view to percutaneous transluminal coronary angioplasty (PTCA) or coronary bypass surgery. Even though the presence of complicating factors will have been identified prior to angiography, a final decision about the suitability or otherwise of mechanical intervention can only be made once the angiographic appearances are known.

Medical management of refractory angina

The older patient who continues to be severely limited with angina, and who is unsuitable for (further) mechanical intervention, poses a considerable challenge for the physician. Often several combinations of anti-anginal drugs have been tried without success. These patients should be carefully evaluated with the aim of optimizing their haemodynamic state by the appropriate use of drugs. There is little evidence that a combination of three oral agents is more effective than two in the treatment of angina. The patient's symptoms may improve after one or more categories of drug is withdrawn, particularly if their filling pressures were high and the arterial pressure relatively low. The dose–response relationship for dihydropyridines in the treatment of angina is non-linear. Increasing the dose above an optimum level, which must be sought on an individual basis, may increase the frequency of attacks. Angiotensin-converting enzyme inhibitors have been shown to reduce cardiac ischaemia and, if left ventricular function is impaired, angina frequency may improve with these compounds. It is good practice to ask the patient to keep an angina diary when treatment is being altered. In the United Kingdom, perhexilene maleate may be used on a named-patient basis in resistant cases.

Surgical treatment

Older people are more likely to have three-vessel coronary disease and impaired left ventricular function than younger people. They have a lower exercise capability and a higher angina threshold than younger people. When older people first present with symptoms of coronary disease they tend to have more severe coronary lesions, and their symptoms may be correspondingly more limiting. Therefore a 'wait and see' policy involving changes of medication may be disappointing in such patients. There are good reasons to avoid invasive investigation in some elderly people, for example when other serious disease is present. However, it may be logical and rewarding to consider a more aggressive approach earlier in those patients in whom it is appropriate.

Selection criteria for surgery for older people

In most centres the criteria for surgical treatment for angina in older people differ from those for younger age groups, but there is a lack of controlled evidence for many of the decisions. Symptomatic limitation is the predominant criterion for a surgical approach to the treatment of angina at all ages. Angina which interferes with ordinary activities, such as shopping, housework, and recreation, should prompt consideration of whether operative treatment may be appropriate. Unstable angina is often associated with more severe disease, progression of coronary atheroma, and an adverse prognosis, and represents an indication for diagnostic arteriography. A proportion of younger patients who are not limited by angina receive operative treatment based on increased risk, such as in the presence of left main-stem disease, proximal three-vessel disease with impaired left ventricular function, proximal disease of the left anterior descending coronary artery, and adverse results from the non-invasive tests. These criteria are applied less frequently in older people, although there is little evidence to support an approach which ignores prognostic indicators in patients aged over 70 years.

Patients who have had successful PTCA in the preceding months should be given priority for diagnostic angiography, because repeat PTCA carries a high chance of success after restenosis. Patients who have had coronary bypass surgery, often some years previously, constitute a more difficult category to manage because repeat coronary surgery carries a higher risk in later life, with a much lower chance of complete relief of angina than after the first operation. Nevertheless, PTCA may be possible either to one or more of the grafts or to the native coronary vessels, and often produces worthwhile symptom relief.

Percutaneous transluminal coronary angioplasty

Coronary angioplasty on vessels which are not totally occluded carries a primary success rate of 70 to 90 per cent in older people. The primary success rate for multivessel PTCA is similar to that in younger people (Little et al. 1991). Lindsay and colleagues reported primary success rates for multivessel PTCA of 77 per cent in the age group 70 to 92 years, and 85 per cent in the age group 40 to 69 years (Lindsay et al. 1994). The in-hospital fatality rate for PTCA in older people is between zero and 4 per cent (Shimshak and McCallister 1994). Major complications of myocardial infarction, emergency coronary surgery, and stroke occur in 5 to 10 per cent of cases, and are more likely to result in death in older people. There is a higher incidence of local vascular complications such as severe haemorrhage, dissection, aneurysm formation, and arterial occlusion than in younger patients.

Selection bias operates in the older age group to increase the proportion of patients with more severe coronary disease and other complicating factors (including more unstable angina, worse left ventricular function, and a higher proportion of women). One study found that the number of diseased vessels is more important than age per se in predicting death, myocardial infarction, and recurrence of angina (Thompson et al. 1993). However, the Washington Study demonstrated that the risk of in-hospital death increases by 5 per cent per year of age, and that of non-fatal myocardial infarction increases by 10 per cent per year (Lindsay et al. 1994). The fatality rate is very high if PTCA is attempted in the setting of acute myocardial infarction. Success and complication rates for PTCA are similar when the procedure is performed for post-infarct angina and for chronic stable angina in patients with good left ventricular function (Iniguez et al. 1994).

Ongoing symptomatic benefit is present at 1 year in 70 to 90 per cent of older people after PTCA. The angiographic restenosis rate of 30 to 40 per cent compares favourably with the results in the younger age groups. In approximately half of these patients restenosis is not associated with any reported change in symptoms. Recurrent symptoms usually appear within 3 months following the procedure, and approximately 15 per cent of patients of all age groups will require repeat PTCA within 1 year.

Coronary artery surgery

Coronary artery surgery provides an increasingly safe and worthwhile option for the older patient whose symptoms cannot be controlled by drugs and who is unsuitable for PTCA. Symptomatic results are comparable with data for younger people (Kallis et al. 1993; Shimshak and McCallister 1994).

The operative fatality rate is between 2.5 and 5 times that in younger age groups. It is related to the priority category which the physician chooses for the patient. Elective cases carry a 4 per cent death rate, urgent cases a 6.7 per cent death rate, and emergency cases a 13.7 per cent death rate. The categories are determined by the patient's symptomatic status and the severity of their coronary disease. Determinants of outcome in 663 patients aged over 75 years were compared with those in 1464 patients under 65 years of age in the period 1982 to 1990 (Khan *et al.* 1992). The older group contained a higher proportion of women, who fare less well than men partly because they have smaller coronary arteries, and of patients with unstable angina, prior infarction, and hypertension. The mean in-patient fatality rate was 7.5 per cent in the older group compared with 1.8 per cent in the younger cohort. Factors associated with death included age, prior coronary surgery, congestive heart failure, left main-stem disease, functional class, hypertension, prior myocardial infarction, and preoperative atrial fibrillation. Much work remains to be done on investigating the mechanisms by which age gives rise to a higher operative mortality and morbidity. The perioperative mortality is increased approximately threefold in older patients; death is associated with stroke, myocardial infarction, and renal failure. The inpatient stay of older people is longer.

Few studies have been carried out comparing the results of PTCA with coronary bypass surgery in older people, and no randomized trials exist for this group. A study conducted in Holland compared 93 patients aged 75 to 84 who underwent PTCA for severe angina with 81 patients who were treated with coronary bypass surgery (Bonnier *et al.* 1993). The categories were reasonably well matched but bias was likely in the selection of treatment. More coronary vessels were dealt with in the patients undergoing bypass surgery, 77 per cent of whom received three or four bypass grafts compared with 72 per cent of the PTCA group who received dilatation to a single vessel. The primary success rate was 84 per cent in the PTCA group and 63 per cent in the coronary surgery group, and the operative fatality rate was three times higher in the group who underwent thoracotomy. Actuarial 10-year survival was 92 per cent in the PTCA group and 91 per cent in the coronary surgery group. The symptomatic benefit was closely similar in both groups, with 69 per cent being free of angina at 8 years after PTCA and 70 per cent after coronary surgery. A larger case–control study from the United States demonstrated significantly higher complication rates after coronary bypass surgery compared with PTCA in older patients (O'Keefe *et al.* 1994). At follow-up, the surgical group had less recurrent angina and fewer Q-wave infarcts compared with the PTCA group.

These studies would justify an approach favouring PTCA rather than bypass surgery in older people if the coronary anatomy is suitable, even if complete revascularization is not attempted. A pragmatic approach in those who have significant disease of more than one vessel is to carry out PTCA on the 'culprit' lesion, which may be identifiable from the leads in which ECG changes have taken place either spontaneously or on exercise, or from other tests of ischaemia such as exercise nuclear studies. If other vessels bear lesions which are amenable to PTCA, these may be dealt with at the first operation, or it may be reasonable to evaluate the patient symptomatically before deciding on the need for a further procedure. The unstable component of angina is often best dealt with in older people by single-vessel PTCA to the 'culprit' lesion.

References

Aronow, W.S. (1989). Correlation of ischemic ST-segment depression on the resting electrocardiogram with new cardiac events in 1106 patients over 62 years of age. *American Journal of Cardiology*, **64**, 232–3.

Bonnier, H., de Vries, C., Michels, R., and el Gamal, M. (1993). Initial and long-term results of coronary angioplasty and coronary bypass surgery in patients of 75 or older. *British Heart Journal*, **70**, 122–5.

Castelli, W.P. (1993). Risk factors in the elderly: a view from Framingham. *American Journal of Geriatric Cardiology*, **2**, 8–19.

Chaitman, B.R., Bourassa, M.G., Davis, K., *et al.* (1981). Angiographic prevalence of high-risk coronary artery disease in patient subsets (CASS). *Circulation*, **64**, 360–7.

Glover, D.R., Robinson, C.S., and Murray, R.G. (1984). Diagnostic exercise testing in 104 patients over 65 years of age. *European Heart Journal*, **5** (Supplement E), 59–61.

Iniguez, A., Macaya, C., Hernandez, R., *et al.* (1994). Long-term outcome of coronary angioplasty in elderly patients with post-infarction angina. *European Heart Journal*, **15**, 489–94.

Iskandrian, A.S., Heo, J., Decoskey, D., Askenase, A., and Segal, B.L. (1988). Use of exercise thallium-201 imaging for risk stratification of elderly patients with coronary artery disease. *American Journal of Cardiology*, **61**, 269–72.

Joint National Committee on Detection, Evaluation, and Treatment of High Blood Pressure (1993). The fifth report (JNC V). *Archives of Internal Medicine*, **153**, 154–83.

Kallis, P., Unsworth-White, J., Munsch, C., *et al.* (1993). Disability and distress following cardiac surgery in patients over 70 years of age. *European Journal of Cardiothoracic Surgery*, **7**, 306–12.

Khan, S.S., Kupfer, J.M., Matloff, J.M., Tsai, T.P., and Nessim, S. (1992). Interaction of age and preoperative risk factors in predicting operative mortality for coronary bypass surgery. *Circulation*, **86** (Supplement II), II-186–90.

LaCroix, A.Z., Lang, J., Scherr, P., *et al.* (1991). Smoking and mortality among older men and women in three communities. *New England Journal of Medicine*, **324**, 1619–25.

Lam, J.Y.T., Chaitman, B.R., Glaenzer, M., *et al.* (1988). *Journal of the American College of Cardiology*, **11**, 585–9.

Lindsay, J., Reddy, V.M., Pinnow, E.E., Little, T., and Pichard, A.D. (1994). Morbidity and mortality rates in elderly patients undergoing percutaneous coronary transluminal angioplasty. *American Heart Journal*, **128**, 697–702.

Little, T., Milner, M., Pichard, A.D., Mukherjee, D., and Lindsay, J. (1991). A comparison of multi-lesion percutaneous transluminal coronary angioplasty in elderly patients (greater than 70 years) and younger subjects. *American Heart Journal*, **122**, 628–30.

O'Keefe, J.H., Sutton, M.B., McCallister, B.D., *et al.* (1994). Coronary angioplasty versus bypass surgery in patients >70 years old matched for ventricular function. *Journal of the American College of Cardiology*, **24**, 425–30.

Pfeffer, M.A., Braunwald, E., Moye, L.A., *et al.* (1992). Effect of captopril on mortality and morbidity in patients with left ventricular dysfunction after myocardial infarction. *New England Journal of Medicine*, **327**, 669–77.

Sacks, F.M., Pfeffer, M.A., Moye, L.A., *et al.* (1996). The effect of pravastatin on coronary events after myocardial infarction in patients with average cholesterol levels. *New England Journal of Medicine*, **335**, 1001–9.

Shimshak, T.M. and McCallister, B.D. (1994). Coronary artery bypass surgery and percutaneous transluminal coronary angioplasty in the elderly patient with ischemic heart disease. In *Cardiovascular disease in the elderly patient* (ed. D.D. Tresch and W.S. Aronow), pp. 323–44. Dekker, New York.

Siegel, R., Clemens, T., Wingo, M., and Tresch, D.D. (1991). Acute heart failure in the elderly: another manifestation of unstable 'angina'. *Journal of the American College of Cardiology*, **17**, 149A.

Thompson, R.C., Holmes, D.R., Gersh, B.J., and Bailey, K.R. (1993). Predicting early and intermediate outcome of coronary angioplasty in the elderly. *Circulation*, **88**, 1579–87.

Tresch, D.D. and Aronow, W.S. (1994). Recognition and diagnosis of coronary artery disease in the elderly. In *Cardiovascular disease in the* *elderly patient* (ed. D.D. Tresch and W.S. Aronow), pp. 285–304. Dekker, New York.

9.11 Cardiopulmonary resuscitation

J. W. Sear

The use of techniques of ventilation and cardiac massage to revive the 'apparently dead' is not new. Among the earliest references is that in 2 Kings 4: 34–5.

> And he [Elijah] went up, and lay upon the child, and put his mouth upon his eyes, and his hands upon his hands; and he stretched himself upon the child; and the flesh of the child waxed warm.
>
> Then he returned, and walked in the house to and fro; and went up, and stretched himself upon him: and the child sneezed seven times, and the child opened his eyes.

Although the introduction of the use of bellows to ventilate the lungs is attributed to Paracelsus (1493–1541), the modern history of resuscitation began in the mid-eighteenth century, with the formation in Amsterdam in 1767 of the Society for the Recovery of Drowned Persons, while the Humane Society (later the Royal Humane Society) was established in London by William Hawes in 1771. Artificial ventilation of the lungs was first advocated by Marshall Hall in 1856; he described the technique of rotating the patient's body combined with pressure to the back to aid expiration. In 1858, Silvester described the technique of chest-pressure arm-lift ventilation, which was later modified by Holger Nielsen who reported the use of a back-pressure arm-lift technique (cited by Safar *et al.* 1958). The introduction of positive-pressure ventilation as the *modus operandi* of modern resuscitation was first reported by Safar (1958).

Reports of deaths during anaesthesia in the years immediately following the introduction of diethyl ether and chloroform led to anaesthetists showing an interest in the study of cardiac arrest, with the first successful internal cardiac massage procedure probably being performed in Norway in 1901. The first case of cardiac massage in the United Kingdom was attributed to Starling in 1902. Defibrillation arrived on the scene much later, with the first successful defibrillation of the human heart reported by Beck in 1937. External cardiac massage (the mainstay of modern techniques) was made popular in the 1960s by the work of Kouwenhoven (Kouwenhoven *et al.* 1960).

Cardiac arrest (the cessation of effective contraction of the heart) can arise from two different mechanisms—cardiac asystole and ventricular fibrillation. However, a third mechanism (electromechanical dissociation) is equally important and associated with a greater fatality (see below). The exact aetiology of a cardiac arrest cannot be differentiated by clinical observation, but only by electrocardiography or direct inspection of the heart. In asystole the heart is relaxed, soft, blue, and motionless, with the coronary veins tense and prominent, while in ventricular fibrillation there are fine or coarse irregular twitchings of the heart which is pale and cyanotic. During ventricular fibrillation metabolism continues at the usual rate for the heart, thus rendering the heart acidotic and more resistant to the action and effects of drugs used to stimulate it and restore normal excitation–contraction coupling.

Brain ATP is depleted after 4 to 6 min of no blood flow, although normal values return within 6 min of starting cardiopulmonary resuscitation (CPR). Recent animal studies have suggested that good neurological outcome can be seen if an adequate circulation is restored within 10 to 15 min of a cardiac arrest, although only if there has been good cerebral perfusion up to the time of the arrest (Angelos *et al.* 1991; Kern *et al.* 1991). However, in humans there are a large number of other factors that may influence recovery from cardiac arrest, including the time before CPR is commenced, prolonged ventricular fibrillation without definitive therapy, and inadequate coronary and cerebral perfusion during cardiac massage. Thus, in the out-of-hospital scenario, the outcome of cardiac arrest may be improved if CPR is started early by bystanders while awaiting medical or paramedical support.

Aetiology of cardiac arrest

There are many causes of cardiac arrest including the following.

1. Vagal reflex mechanisms following stimulation of the rectum, the uterus and cervix, the throat, the glottis and bronchial tree, the bladder and urethra, the mesentery, and the carotid sheath, and traction of the extraocular muscles.

2. Electrolyte abnormalities, especially hyperkalaemia and hypercalcaemia.

3. Hypoxia and anoxia (although the brain is more sensitive to a lack of oxygen than the heart).

4. Hypercapnia, which in turn results in increased serum concentrations of circulating catecholamines, increased serum potassium levels, prolongation of the period of asystole due to vagal stimulation, and depression of conductivity and contractility secondary to the resulting acidosis.

5. Increased circulating levels of either endogenous or exogenous catecholamines. Many of the older gaseous anaesthetic agents (chloroform, halothane, cyclopropane, and trichloroethylene) sensitize the myocardium to the effects of catecholamines, especially in the presence of accompanying hypoxia.

6. Effects of large doses (or overdoses) of non-anaesthetic drugs (e.g. digitalis, quinidine, and procainamide).

7. Air embolism.

8. Haemorrhage.

9. Fainting.

10. Cardiac disease: acute circulatory obstruction (e.g. atrial myxoma or ball-valve thrombus, pulmonary embolism), in conditions with low cardiac output and where the patient cannot compensate for the fall in systemic vascular resistance seen in response to exercise or anaesthesia, and in cardiomyopathies.

11. Cardiac catheterization and angiocardiography.

12. Coronary occlusion.

13. Electrocution.

14. Drowning.

15. Hypothermia.

16. Anaesthetic drugs, often secondary to errors in technique, overdosage, or hypoxia. Examples of the various causes include the following:

- direct myocardial depression
- vagotonic effect
- sympathetic stimulation
- increased excitability of ventricular muscle
- hypotension
- hypoxia
- hypercapnia associated with respiratory depression.

Techniques of cardiac resuscitation

The protocol approach to CPR is divided into three distinct phases.

1. Basic life support:
   - airway control
   - breathing support
   - circulatory support.

2. Advanced life support:
   - drugs and fluids
   - ECG
   - defibrillation.

3. Postarrest life support.

A major development in resuscitation following cardiac arrest in the United Kingdom (and in other European countries) has been the acceptance by the Resuscitation Council (UK) of new guidelines proposed by the International Liaison Committee on Resuscitation.

Prior to these, the majority of medical and paramedical professionals had adopted the guidelines published by the European Resuscitation Council in 1992 (Guidelines for Advanced Life Support 1992). These new guidelines were formally accepted at the Biannual Meeting of the European Resuscitation Council in June 1998. (Detailed information on the new guidelines and subsequent updates is available from the Resuscitation Council on the Internet at http://www. resus.org.uk, or in a leaflet describing the 1997 Guidelines published by the Resuscitation Council (UK), 9 Fitzroy Square, London W1P 5AH.)

Basic and advanced life support

Basic life support

This describes the sequence of assessment, airway maintenance, breathing, and chest compression. The technique emphasizes that it can be carried out without equipment. However, various adjuncts can be used to improve the quality or efficacy of basic life support (these include endotracheal airway, orolaryngeal airway, or other modalities such as the oesophageal obturator and laryngeal mask airway). The general algorithm for basic life support is shown in Fig. 1.

The aim of basic life support is to produce an artificial circulation to oxygenate the vital organs of the body (heart, kidney, brain, etc.) until definitive advanced care is available. In the case of a cardiac arrest due to cardiac pathology, there is usually also a need for electrical defibrillation to reverse the non-output-producing arrhythmias of pulseless ventricular tachycardia or fibrillation. If the circulation is not restored within about 4 min, brain injury occurs. This timespan may be reduced in elderly patients with cerebrovascular disease. Furthermore, the longer the delay in providing this artificial circulation and starting ventilation, the lower the success rate.

Cardiac massage

The physiology of cardiac compression has recently been re-examined. The concept that the forward flow of blood is achieved by compressing the heart between the sternum and spinal column has been partially discredited. Echocardiography has shown that the cardiac valves are incompetent during resuscitation, and hence flow would occur in both directions. It is now believed, therefore, that the effect of sternal compression is to increase the intrathoracic pressure, squeezing blood out of the thorax in an antegrade manner because the increased intrathoracic pressure itself will also lead to occlusion of the veins at the thoracic inlet, so preventing any retrograde flow. Thus the whole of the thoracic cage acts as the pump, and not just the heart.

The rate of compression is also important, as the 'thoracic pump' part of cardiac output depends on the time available for heart refilling as well as the time to refill the thoracic venous system. Thus, the 1997 guidelines advocate that compression occurs at a rate of about 100 per minute, and this is the same for all age groups. Other aspects of basic life support are unaltered—namely 15 compressions to two ventilations for the single-handed operator, or five compressions to each ventilation where there are two or more operators. In adults the aim of cardiac massage should be to achieve sternal compression by about 4 to 5 cm, while in children the optimal compression is to a depth of about one-third of the chest depth (whatever the child's age).

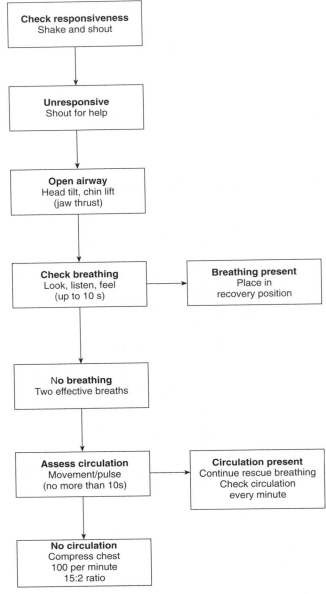

Fig. 1 The algorithms for basic life support. (Reproduced with permission of the Resuscitation Council.)

Because of the difficulty in accurately assessing the carotid pulse especially by non-medically trained personnel, it has now been superseded by the recommendation that the operator looks for signs of adequate circulation (such as patient colour, presence or absence of ventilation, and, by professionals only, evidence of the presence or absence of a central pulse).

Ventilation

There are a number of different approaches to the provision of artificial breathing during cardiopulmonary arrest. These include mouth-to-mouth ventilation, mouth-to-mask ventilation, and mechanical ventilation via an endotracheal tube.

The advantages of mouth-to-mouth ventilation over alternative manual methods has long been recognized as it is easier to maintain the patency of the airway and to deliver positive-pressure ventilation by this technique. Furthermore, the low ventilatory pressure achieved by this method will tend to limit gastric insufflation. However, the use of expired air requires the administration of large tidal volumes in order to maintain adequate oxygenation and ventilation. The use of airway adjuncts (such as the S-tube—two Guedel airways connected at their proximal ends) avoids direct patient contact, but carries the risk of pharyngeal stimulation leading to laryngospasm and induction of vomiting.

Bag–valve–mask ventilation may be preferred, but its main limitation is the achievement of a good mask seal by an operator who has limited training, and the ability to deliver 100 per cent oxygen during CPR is contingent upon the use of a reservoir bag of appropriate size and sufficient gas flow to keep it filled.

Intermittent positive-pressure ventilation is the principal modern method of artificial respiration. Many of these techniques apply a degree of positive end-expiratory pressure to the airway. As hypoxaemia is frequently seen before cardiac arrest and during resuscitation, it can be argued for the value of positive end-expiratory pressure. However, this may both augment or depress cardiac output (Rudikoff *et al.* 1980). Nevertheless if pulmonary oedema occurs during resuscitation, it may limit its effectiveness (Ornato *et al.* 1985). During cardiac resuscitation only basal oxygen requirements and carbon dioxide removal are needed, and so smaller tidal volumes than were previously recommended are employed (400–500 ml for an average adult).

With effective basic life support regimens and immediate response, initial resuscitation success rates will be around 40 per cent, and survival rates to hospital discharge will be 10 to 15 per cent for out-of-hospital arrests, with better figures following in-hospital arrests.

Advanced life support

Again there have been changes in the advanced life support techniques with a simpler algorithm that is applicable to operators using manual, semimanual, or automatic defibrillators (Fig. 2). It is assumed that basic life support will have already been started before the advanced life support algorithm is commenced. The initial precordial thump can be regarded as a low-energy manual defibrillation.

The new algorithm divides resuscitation according to whether the mechanism of arrest is ventricular fibrillation–pulseless ventricular tachycardia or non-ventricular fibrillation–pulseless ventricular tachycardia. In adults, ventricular fibrillation or pulseless ventricular tachycardia is the most common presentation, and most survivors will come from this group.

Ventricular fibrillation

The use of immediate defibrillation at 200 J is recommended, and if there is no response to a repeat shock at that charge, increase to 360 J. If this is still unsuccessful, the pathway should be repeated after the administration of 1 mg adrenaline (epinephrine). Resuscitation should not be interrupted for more than 10 s except for episodes of defibrillation. Once effective cardiac output has been achieved, the myocardium and the circulation in general may need to be supported by an infusion of an inotrope (for example, adrenaline 1 to 10 mg/h). Thus, adrenaline has become a first-line drug in the treatment of cardiac arrest.

Asystolic arrest

The initial treatment in CPR is 1 mg adrenaline followed by 3 mg atropine. If these two drugs do not re-establish ventricular fibrillation or another rhythm, then the use of isoprenaline may be indicated if P waves are present.

Electromechanical dissociation

This is defined as 'QRS complexes without effective ventricular contractions'. Again, the initial treatment is CPR plus 1 mg adrenaline, with correction of any hypovolaemia, and consideration of other causes of the problem—namely pneumothorax, haemothorax, cardiac tamponade, and, especially in a postoperative patient, pulmonary embolism.

Drug administration during cardiac resuscitation

Adrenaline

There have been a number of developments in the use of adrenaline during cardiac resuscitation, as gross changes in peripheral vascular resistance will have a major effect on blood flow.

Adrenaline produces its beneficial effects in the CPR patient principally because of α-adrenergic properties which increase myocardial and cerebral blood flow. The β-adrenergic effects of adrenaline are more controversial as they may increase myocardial work and so reduce subendocardial perfusion. If the operator gives drugs that increase the difference between aortic and right atrial pressure between compressions and so improve coronary blood flow during resuscitation, this might in theory best be accomplished by raising the aortic pressure or lowering right atrial pressure. Aortic pressure between compressions is increased by greater backflow from the extrathoracic arterial bed to the central aorta on release of compression, and by having this backflow occur into a stiffer aorta. This approach to improving both coronary blood flow and overall resuscitation would call for higher doses of adrenaline. This, in turn, would increase coronary flow by its vasoconstrictor properties, making the aorta smaller and stiffer so that any backflow from the periphery will cause a greater increase in aortic pressure. In addition, adrenaline-induced vasoconstriction will reduce flow to non-essential vascular beds. This will result in a decrease in cardiac output but an increase in brain flow, and also an increase in aortic backflow between compressions. The increased backflow into the stiffer aorta would therefore augment aortic pressure and coronary blood flow between compressions.

This controversy has led various groups to investigate whether a standard dosage of 1 mg adrenaline (irrespective of body weight) was correct. Kosnick *et al.* (1985) found that larger doses of adrenaline were needed to prevent a drop in aortic diastolic pressure, while Lindner *et al.* (1991) demonstrated that increasing doses of adrenaline led to increased coronary perfusion pressures.

However, four studies have failed to show an increased survival following cardiac arrest treated with higher doses of adrenaline (Lindner *et al.* 1991; Brown *et al.* 1992; Callaham *et al.* 1992; Stiell *et al.* 1992). There was an increase in the rate of return of spontaneous circulation, with no detrimental outcome overall, and an increased number of survivors in one study where adrenaline was used in the

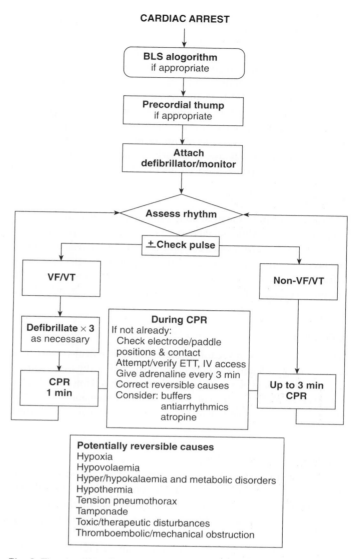

Fig. 2 The algorithms for advanced life support. (Reproduced with permission of the Resuscitation Council.)

treatment of electromechanical dissociation and asystole. Furthermore, in one of the studies the standard dose of adrenaline (1 mg) was better in the treatment of patients aged over 65 years.

Thus there are sufficient data to recommend that the currently used dose of 1 mg intravenous be the initial dose in patients with ventricular fibrillation, but that it is given every 3 to 5 min instead of every 5 min, and that higher doses should not be discouraged. Other drugs (such as atropine, lignocaine (lidocaine), and bretylium) should continue to be used, depending on the experience of the operator and the clinical situation, but probably have no major influence on initial outcome.

Other drugs

Sodium bicarbonate

The use of sodium bicarbonate during resuscitation was based on the theoretical notion that acidosis lowered the fibrillation threshold, and respiratory acidosis impaired the physiological response to catecholamines. Although one animal study showed an improved success of resuscitation from prolonged ventricular fibrillation when bicarbonate was given with adrenaline (Babbs 1980), this has not been supported in human studies (Minuck and Sharma 1977; Guerci *et al.* 1986; Federiuk *et al.* 1991; Vukmir *et al.* 1992).

Bicarbonate is therefore no longer recommended as part of the protocol for cardiac arrest. However, after prolonged CPR, intravenous doses of bicarbonate of up to 50 mmol may be given if there is a persistent metabolic acidosis, a hyperkalaemic arrest, or arrest secondary to tricyclic or phenobarbitone overdose.

Atropine

This acts to enhance sinoatrial node automaticity and atrioventricular node conduction. Although there is no evidence of improved outcome following cardiac arrest when atropine is given during resuscitation, it has been recommended as a second-line drug in ventricular fibrillation refractory to adrenaline, when it can be given as 1 mg intravenous increments every 3 to 5 min up to a full vagolytic dose of 0.04 mg/kg.

Calcium salts

These act to increase myocardial contractility and enhance ventricular automaticity. Calcium was previously advocated as the treatment for asystolic arrest and electromechanical dissociation. However, this has not been supported by recent animal studies (Niemann *et al.* 1985) or clinical trials (Harrison and Amey 1983, 1984; Stuevan *et al.* 1983, 1984, 1985*a,b*).

Lignocaine and bretylium

These antiarrhythmic drugs have been used to aid successful defibrillation when ventricular fibrillation is refractory to shock therapy. A randomized controlled trial in out-of-hospital ventricular fibrillation cardiac arrest failed to demonstrate any effect of these drugs on resuscitative success or survival (Haynes *et al.* 1981; Olson *et al.* 1984). Because the side-effects of bretylium include initial hypertension, tachycardia, and increased contractility followed by hypotension, lignocaine is preferred.

Airway adjuncts

In addition to those already mentioned, there are a number of other aids to airway management, including the oesophageal obturator airway (Combitube®) and the laryngeal mask airway. In a modified form, the oesophageal obturator allows gastric decompression through a separate tube, but it still does not give definitive airway control, and its use has been associated with a significant incidence (up to 3 per cent) of unrecognized airway intubation (Gertler *et al.* 1985). There are presently no data on outcome following cardiac arrest where there has been delayed intubation with a possible contribution to morbidity and mortality; however, aspiration is common with these adjuncts and may prove a fatal complication (Lawes and Baskett 1987).

In the United Kingdom there has been recent interest in the role of the laryngeal mask airway in resuscitation. Its use allows more efficient and easier ventilation than can be achieved by the traditional bag and facemask, and its insertion can be easily taught to nurses, paramedics, and doctors. Although use of the laryngeal mask airway has been described in both hospital and out-of-hospital cardiac arrests (Baskett 1994; Kokkinis 1994), until there are randomized controlled trials of its efficacy, it should be considered as an initial temporary measure rather than as a replacement for endotracheal intubation.

Aetiology of cardiac arrest in elderly patients

This is most frequently connected with myocardial infarction, although in the perioperative period it may often be associated with reduced ventilation, hypotension, or acute drug overdose. In the orthopaedic patient, cardiac arrest may also occur at the time of insertion of acrylic bone cement for fixation of prostheses (Duncan 1989).

Treatment of cardiac arrest in elderly patients

As in younger patients, the airway–breathing–circulation (ABC) approach to the management of cardiac arrest is paramount. The recently revised standards and guidelines of the European Resuscitation Council should be adopted (see above), although there may be some anatomical or pathological problems that make resuscitation difficult in an older patient. These include poor external cardiac compression due to the inelasticity of the chest wall, and the effects of emphysema and thoracic deformities on cardiac massage and gas exchange.

Ventilation should be through an endotracheal tube or a facemask and Ambu Bag®. The ratio of cardiac compressions to ventilation should be about 5:1 with a compression rate of 60 to 100 beats/min. The efficacy of CPR is difficult to define, but the presence of an intra-arterial pressure waveform offers a good indication of some measure of cardiac output, while an end-tidal carbon dioxide of over 15 mmHg indicates efficient resuscitation with a probable favourable outcome— but an end-tidal carbon dioxide concentration of less than 11 mmHg usually predicts a poor result. An ideal goal for the end-tidal carbon dioxide for favourable outcome would be of the order of 20 to 30 mmHg (Sanders *et al.* 1989; Callaham and Barton 1990; Levine *et al.* 1997).

Outcome from cardiac resuscitation of elderly patients

There have been a number of studies investigating outcome following resuscitation in the elderly patient. Murphy *et al.* (1989) studied the outcomes of cardiac arrests in 503 patients aged over 70 years. Of these, 259 occurred in hospital, the remainder in the community. They found that a successful outcome was achieved in about 20 per cent of patients following in-hospital cardiac arrest, but only 3.8 per cent (19 patients) survived to leave hospital. Most of the survivors were from the in-hospital arrest group. A significant number of those who were discharged had a marked neurological deficit necessitating institutional care. These data suggested that resuscitation was rarely effective in elderly patients if the arrest occurred out of hospital, if the arrest was not witnessed (and hence the start of resuscitation was delayed), and where there was asystole or electromechanical dissociation. In contrast, most of the survivors had abnormalities of ventricular arrhythmias and underwent rapid defibrillation.

However, another study by Tresch *et al.* (1989) showed greater hope for the outcome of cardiac arrest in elderly patients. In a series of 214 patients (112 aged over 70 years of age), the discharge rates from hospital were 47 per cent in the younger age group, and 28.6 per cent in those aged over 70 years. Although this difference in discharge rate is significant ($p < 0.001$), many of the elderly patients were effectively resuscitated. Tresch *et al.* (1989) also found no differences in the incidence of ventricular fibrillation or asystolic arrest between the groups, although again electromechanical dissociation was five times more common in the older group. The occurrence of a cardiac arrest was more commonly associated with acute myocardial infarction in the younger patients (33 per cent versus 16 per cent), while in the elderly patients there was more likely to be a history of congestive cardiac failure (42 per cent versus 20 per cent), and the patients were more frequently on digitalis and diuretic therapy. O'Keeffe *et al.* (1991) reported a survival to discharge of 19.2 per cent in hospital patients aged 70 years or less, but only 3.4 per cent in the population over 70 years.

Overall, the percentage of elderly patients (over 65 years of age) who underwent a cardiac arrest and were subsequently discharged from hospital ranges between 3.8 and 17.1 per cent (Taffet *et al.* 1988).

More recent figures support the efficacy of CPR for elderly people, while examining more closely the comorbidity that may follow. The major cause of death in the postarrest period is acute cerebral damage due to hypoxia, and age-associated chronic disease processes of the cardiovascular, respiratory, and cerebrovascular systems add to the severity of the problem. Murphy *et al.* (1989) identified a number of factors that appeared to be associated with a poorer outcome:

- presence of significant chronic disease
- persistent asystolic arrest
- resuscitation lasting more than 15 min.

O'Keeffe *et al.* (1991) found that the best results were achieved if the patient suffered a witnessed cardiac arrest, if the aetiology was secondary to a ventricular arrhythmia, and if resuscitation lasted less than 5 min. However, using multivariate analysis of their 274 patients, these authors still found an inverse relationship between survival and age.

Carlen and Gordon (1995) have studied the fatality and neurological complications in 774 patients suffering cardiac arrest. In patients aged 45 years or less, the 6-month fatality was 68 per cent, while for the elderly group (aged 80 years or older) fatality was 94 per cent. However, there was good neurological function in the survivors of both groups with an institution-independent existence in 27 per cent, and no significant difference between the two age groups.

Out-of-hospital cardiac arrest

In this situation, the patient is dependent on the skills of a bystander in instituting early basic life support-type resuscitation. There have been a number of reports on outcomes for elderly patients following out-of-hospital arrest. Longstreth *et al.* (1990) evaluated outcomes of 3029 patients (1405 aged more than 70 years). As their data summarized in Table 1 show, poorer outcome was associated with an initial rhythm other than ventricular fibrillation; age itself had no influence.

In a prospective study by Bonnin *et al.* (1993), 1228 consecutive out-of-hospital patients (under or over 70 years of age) were enrolled and, after exclusions, the results of 986 patients were analysed (Table 2). There was no difference in survival for young and elderly patients where the arrhythmia was ventricular fibrillation or ventricular tachycardia. However, there were differences in the aetiology of the arrest, with 48 per cent (young) versus 32 per cent (elderly) being due to ventricular fibrillation or ventricular tachycardia ($p < 0.00001$), 18 per cent versus 27 per cent electromechanical dissociation ($p < 0.001$), and 33 per cent versus 41 per cent asystole ($p < 0.02$).

Comparison of the in-hospital and out-of-hospital outcomes can be made from the United Kingdom BRESUS study (Tunstall-Pedoe *et al.* 1992). Data from 12 hospitals over a period of 15.5 hospital years included 3765 arrests, of which 927 had occurred out of hospital. The main survival indicator was proportion alive at 1 year (Table 3).

Out of hospital, elderly patients who are successfully resuscitated do as well as younger ones, but in hospital there is a better outcome for the younger patients. However, initially successful treatment of cardiac arrest in older patients will often result in the need for admission to an intensive therapy unit with a subsequent prolonged period of mechanical ventilation and circulatory support. This requirement is always associated with increased fatality regardless of the age of the patient. Campion *et al.* (1981) found fatality rates of about 78 per cent in patients aged 55 to 64 years, 89 per cent in the 65 to 74 year old age group, and 73 per cent in those patients aged over 75 years.

There are also some data on outcome following cardiac arrest in nursing homes. In general, survival to subsequent hospital discharge is low (0–5 per cent compared with 6–11 per cent for out-of-hospital arrests) despite the shorter response times to the onset of CPR. Many nursing-home patients (80–85 per cent) fail to survive transfer to the emergency departments of local hospitals. These poor survival figures reflect several features of nursing-home patients—older age group, a lower incidence of use of external defibrillation at an early stage during resuscitation compared with out-of-hospital arrests, and a greater incidence of significant associated comorbidity (Applebaum *et al.* 1990; Benkendorf *et al.* 1997).

Conclusion

Overall the outcome following resuscitation after cardiac arrest is poor, with 20 to 50 per cent of the adult population suffering from neurological disabilities (Eleff and Hanley 1996). These range from slight disturbance of cognitive function to a persistent vegetative state. There is little difference between younger and elderly patients in this regard.

Therefore there is much concern over 'do-not-resuscitate' guidelines for both the in-hospital and prehospital settings, as well as involvement of patients in informed discussion of decisions about resuscitation or withholding it. The widespread application and implication of such directives are outside the remit of this chapter, but a number of excellent reviews are available (Mohr and Kettler 1997; Gorman 1997).

Policy and practice with regard to CPR vary between countries and facilities. Explicit guidelines should be available for staff and

Table 1 The influence of age and type of cardiac arrest on the response to immediate treatment and discharge from hospital

	<70 years	>70 years	Died in field or emergency room		Discharged	
			<70 years	>70 years	<70 years	>70 years
Ventricular fibrillation	639	493	285	196	174	102*
Asystole and electromechanical dissociation	985	912	865	823	21	10

* $p<0.01$.

Adapted from Longstreth et al. (1990).

Table 2 The numbers (and percentages) of patients who were initially successfully resuscitated, with the numbers (and percentages) of survivors to 12 months

Age group (years)	n	Successful resuscitation	Survivors at 12 months
Under 70	619	160 (25.8%)	73 (11.8%)
70+	367	81 (22.1%)	24 (6.5%)

Adapted from Bonnin et al. (1993).

Table 3 The survival of patients 1 year after a cardiac arrest based on the site of the initial arrest (outside or inside hospital)

Site of cardiac arrest	Age <65 years	Age >65 years
Outside hospital	24/431 (5.6%)	17/496 (3.4%) NS
In hospital	209/1063 (19.7%)	166/1775 (9.4%)*

* $p<0.001$.
Adapted from Tunstall-Pedoe et al. (1992).

patients in health-care facilities. An example of a guideline for a policy for CPR is given below (adapted with permission from Patient Care Guidelines, Vancouver Hospital and Health Sciences Centre, Vancouver, BC, Canada).

Guideline for cardiopulmonary resuscitation

This guideline relates to the provision of withholding of CPR. The guideline is intended to assist physicians, nurses, and other health professionals to bridge the gap between what they feel they should do and what they feel they are obliged to do for patients at the end of life. The intention is to help physicians and other care providers to make appropriate decisions and to have them feel strongly supported in making the appropriate decisions by the hospital community.

It is emphasized that a decision not to attempt resuscitation means the acceptance, without intervention, of death if and when it occurs, and that **this does not imply a restriction of any other potential form of treatment** unless specified.

There are conditions of ill health where an attending physician's decision that no resuscitation attempts should be made on a patient is clinically appropriate and ethically acceptable. Except in specific circumstances, resuscitation attempts may have little or no chance of success while causing great distress and suffering.

Policy

Terminology

- The standard order about resuscitation that will be used is **DNACPR** (Do Not Attempt Cardiopulmonary Resuscitation) in order to avoid confusion between CPR and other forms of therapy.
- A DNACPR order should be included in the management of a patient having compassionate terminal care.
- A DNACPR order must not affect the provision of any other form of treatment or care that is appropriate for the patient.

Patient and family discussion and education

- CPR should be discussed with:
  - all competent patients with chronic disease or disability
  - all patients for whom death in hospital is expected or probable
  - next of kin or legal guardian for incompetent patients in the above two circumstances.

Appropriate response for different patients

There is no legal or ethical obligation for a physician to offer CPR to a patient if, in the opinion of the physician, this is contraindicated on the balance of very small potential for benefit and very great potential for harm.

For the purpose of discussion about CPR, patients fall into one of the following groups.

- The patient is expected to be successfully treated and leave hospital:
  - there must be a presumption in favour of full life support at the onset of life-threatening illness or an emergency situation.
- Little or nothing is known about the expected outcome of the patient's illness:

- at the time of arrest there is also a presumption in favour of full life support at the onset of life-threatening illness or an emergency, but the situation should be reassessed as soon as information becomes available, and the appropriateness of resuscitation intervention reconsidered.

- The patient is at or near the endstage of a chronic irremediable disease process or the patient is dying from an acute disease process known to be unresponsive to CPR attempts:
  - for a *competent* patient, where there is no reasonable expectation of a successful outcome from CPR attempts, a DNACPR order should be written after discussion with the patient (and family, as appropriate);
  - where a *competent* patient wishes CPR to be attempted after full information and discussion, even when this is deemed to be contraindicated by the physician, then a second opinion should be obtained;
  - in the case of an *incompetent* patient, where there is no reasonable expectation of a successful outcome, a DNACPR order should be written and the family fully informed about the indications for and the results of CPR.

Who may write a DNACPR order

All licensed physicians, whether attending staff or residents (house officers) may write a DNACPR order, where appropriate. A resident should always discuss such an order with the attending physician in advance, where possible.

Guidelines for the appropriate application of CPR

The practice of responding to a cardiac arrest with a 'slow code' (not attending to the arrest in a timely fashion) is wholly unethical and not acceptable in any circumstance.

- In a patient who does not have a DNACPR order written and who suffers an unwitnessed cardiac arrest, CPR should be commenced but, if a perfusing rhythm is not established after one resuscitation cycle, then CPR attempts should be discontinued.
- If asystole is determined to be the cause as opposed to ventricular fibrillation, one cycle of resuscitation should be applied and then attempts discontinued in the absence of either fibrillation or restored heart action.
- In the absence of any evidence of a perfusing rhythm, CPR attempts should not be continued for longer than 20 min unless there are exceptional circumstances.

Advance directives

Any advance directive from a patient requesting no resuscitation, whether expressed verbally or in writing, should be translated without delay by the attending physician or resident into a DNACPR order. When it is in writing, a copy of the advance directive should be in the chart.

Advance directives requesting that CPR should not be attempted must be obeyed by all health-care providers.

CPR and the health-care team

There is no obligation on any health-care professional to undertake CPR in circumstances where the guidelines suggest that it is not indicated.

- The attending physician must discuss with other members of the care team his or her wishes concerning the resuscitation order status for all patients.
- When there is any difference of opinion, members of the health-care team should discuss the indications or contraindications for CPR and attempt to reach a consensus.
- An ethics consultation should be sought if consensus cannot be reached and if time permits.
- Any professional member of the health-care team may initiate an ethics consultation in the event that consensus cannot be reached on the indications for a DNACPR order.
- If the ethics consultation is initiated by a member of the team other than the attending physician, then the other members of the team must be informed.

References

Angelos, M., Safar, P., and Reich, H. (1991). A comparison of cardiopulmonary resuscitation with cardiopulmonary bypass after prolonged cardiac arrest in dogs. Reperfusion pressures and neurologic recovery. *Resuscitation*, 21, 121–35.

Applebaum, G.E., King, J.E., and Finucane, T.E. (1990). The outcome of CPR initiated in nursing homes. *Journal of the American Geriatrics Society*, 39, 197–200.

Babbs, C.F. (1980). New versus old theories of blood flow during CPR. *Critical Care Medicine*, 8, 191–5.

Baskett, P.J.F. (co-ordinator) (1994). Results of a multicentre trial. The use of the laryngeal mask airway by nurses during cardiopulmonary resuscitation. *Anaesthesia*, 49, 3–7.

Benkendorf, R., Swor, R.A., Jackson, R., Rivera-Rivera, E.J., and Demrick, A. (1997). Outcomes of cardiac arrest in the nursing home: destiny or futility? *Prehospital Emergency Care*, 1, 68–72.

Bonnin, M.J., Pepe, P.E., and Clark, P.S. (1993). Survival in the elderly after out-of-hospital cardiac arrest. *Critical Care Medicine*, 21, 1645–51.

Brown, C.G., Martin, D.R., Pepe, P.E., *et al.* and the High-dose Epinephrine Study Group (1992). A comparison of standard-dose and high-dose epinephrine in cardiac arrest outside the hospital. *New England Journal of Medicine*, 327, 1051–5.

Callaham, M. and Barton, C.W. (1990). Prediction of outcome of cardiopulmonary resuscitation from end-tidal carbon dioxide concentration. *Critical Care Medicine*, 18, 358–62.

Callaham, M., Madsen, C.D., Barton, C.W., Saunders, C.E., and Pointer, J. (1992). A randomized clinical trial of high-dose epinephrine and norepinephrine vs. standard-dose epinephrine in pre-hospital cardiac arrest. *Journal of the American Medical Association*, 268, 2667–72.

Campion, E.W., Mulley, A.G., Goldstein, R.L., Barnett, G.O., and Thibault, G.E. (1981). Medical intensive care for the elderly: a study of current use, costs and outcomes. *Journal of the American Medical Association*, 246, 2052–6.

Carlen, P.L. and Gordon, M. (1995). Cardiopulmonary resuscitation and neurological complications in the elderly. *Lancet*, 345, 1253–4.

Duncan, J.A.T. (1989). Intra-operative collapse or death related to the use of acrylic cement in hip surgery. *Anaesthesia*, 44, 149–53.

Eleff, S.M. and Hanley, D.F. (1996). Post-resuscitation prognostication and declaration of brain death. In *Cardiac arrest: the science and practice of resuscitation medicine*, (ed. N.A. Paradis, H.R. Halperin, and R.M. Nowak), pp. 910–22. Williams and Wilkins, Baltimore, MD.

Federiuk, C.S., Sanders, A.B., Kern, K.B., Nelson, J., and Ewy, G.A. (1991). The effect of bicarbonate on resuscitation from cardiac arrest. *Annals of Emergency Medicine*, 20, 1173–7.

Gertler, J.P., Cameron, D.E., Shea, K., and Baker, C.C. (1985). The esophageal obturator airway: obturator or obtundator? *Journal of Trauma*, 25, 424–6.

Gorman, J.L. (1997). Conflicts in resuscitation: ethical dilemmas. *Ulster Medical Journal*, 66, 80–5.

Guerci, A.D., Chandra, N., Johnson, E., et al. (1986). Failure of sodium bicarbonate to improve resuscitation from ventricular fibrillation in dogs. *Circulation*, 74 (Supplement IV), 75–9.

Guidelines for Advanced Life Support (1992). A statement by the Advanced Life Support Working Party of the European Resuscitation Council. *Resuscitation*, 24, 111–21.

Harrison, E.E. and Amey, B.D. (1983). The use of calcium in cardiac resuscitation. *American Journal of Emergency Medicine*, 1, 267–73.

Harrison, E.E. and Amey, B.D. (1984). Use of calcium in electromechanical dissociation. *Annals of Emergency Medicine*, 13, 844–5.

Haynes, R.E., Chinn, T.L., Copass, M.K., and Cobb, L.A. (1981). Comparison of bretylium tosylate and lidocaine in management of out of hospital ventricular fibrillation: a randomized clinical trial. *American Journal of Cardiology*, 48, 353–6.

Kern, K.B., Sanders, A.B., Janas, W., et al. (1991). Limitations of open-chest cardiac massage after prolonged untreated cardiac arrest in dogs. *Annals of Emergency Medicine*, 20, 761–7.

Kokkinis, T.I. (1994). The use of the laryngeal mask airway in CPR. *Resuscitation*, 27, 9–12.

Kosnik, J.W., Jackson, R.E., Keats, S., Tworek, R.M., and Freeman, S.B. (1985). Dose-related response of centrally administered epinephrine on the change in aortic diastolic pressure during closed-chest massage in dogs. *Annals of Emergency Medicine*, 14, 204–8.

Kouwenhoven, W.B., Jude, J.R., and Knickerbocker, G.G. (1960). Closed-chest cardiac massage. *Journal of the American Medical Association*, 173, 1064–7.

Lawes, E.G. and Baskett, P.J. (1987). Pulmonary aspiration during unsuccessful cardiopulmonary resuscitation. *Intensive Care Medicine*, 13, 379–82.

Levine, R.L., Wayne, M.A., and Miller, C.C. (1997). End-tidal carbon dioxide and outcome of out-of-hospital cardiac arrest. *New England Journal of Medicine*, 337, 301–6.

Lindner, K.H., Ahnefeld, F.W., and Prengel, A.W. (1991). Comparison of standard and high-dose adrenaline in the resuscitation of asystole and electromechanical dissociation. *Acta Anaesthesiologica Scandinavica*, 35, 253–6.

Longstreth, W.T., Cobb, L.A., Fahrenbruch, C.E., and Copass, M.K. (1990). Does age affect outcome of out-of-hospital cardiopulmonary resuscitation? *Journal of the American Medical Association*, 264, 2109–10.

Minuck, M. and Sharma, G.P. (1977). Comparison of THAM and sodium bicarbonate in resuscitation of the heart after ventricular fibrillation in dogs. *Anesthesia and Analgesia*, 56, 38–45.

Mohr, M. and Kettler, D. (1997). Ethical aspects of resuscitation. *British Journal of Anaesthesia*, 79, 253–9.

Murphy, D.J., Murray, A.M., Robinson, B.E., and Campion, E.W. (1989). Outcomes of cardiopulmonary resuscitation in the elderly. *Annals of Internal Medicine*, 111, 199–205.

Niemann, J.T., Adomian, G.E., Garner, D., and Rosborough, J.P. (1985). Endocardial and transcutaneous cardiac pacing, calcium chloride, and epinephrine in post-countershock asystole and bradycardias. *Critical Care Medicine*, 13, 699–704.

O'Keeffe, S., Redahan, C., Keane, P., and Daly, K. (1991). Age and other determinants of survival after in-hospital cardiopulmonary resuscitation. *Quarterly Journal of Medicine*, 81, 1005–10.

Olson, D.W., Thompson, B.M., Darin, J.C., and Milbrath, M.H. (1984). A randomized comparison study of bretylium tosylate and lidocaine in resuscitation of patients from out-of-hospital ventricular fibrillation in a paramedic system. *Annals of Emergency Medicine*, 13, 807–10.

Ornato, J.P., Ryschon, T.W., Gonzalez, E.R., and Bredthauer, J.L. (1985). Rapid change in pulmonary vascular hemodynamics with pulmonary edema during cardiopulmonary resuscitation. *American Journal of Emergency Medicine*, 3, 137–42.

Rudikoff, M.T., Maughan, W.L., Effron, M., Freund, P., and Weisfeldt, M.L. (1980). Mechanisms of blood flow during cardiopulmonary resuscitation. *Circulation*, 61, 345–52.

Safar, P. (1958). Ventilatory efficacy of mouth-to-mouth artificial respiration. Airway obstruction during manual and mouth-to-mouth respiration. *Journal of the American Medical Association*, 167, 335–41.

Safar, P., Escarraga, L.A., and Elam, J.O. (1958). A comparison of the mouth-to-mouth and mouth-to-airway methods of artificial ventilation in the chest-pressure armlift methods. *New England Journal of Medicine*, 258, 671–7.

Sanders, A.B., Kern, K.B., Otto, C.W., Milander, M.M., and Ewy, G.A. (1989). End-tidal carbon dioxide monitoring during cardiopulmonary resuscitation: a prognostic indicator for survival. *Journal of the American Medical Association*, 262, 1347–51.

Stiell, I.B., Hebert, P.C., Weitzman, B.N., et al. (1992). High-dose epinephrine in adult cardiac arrest. *New England Journal of Medicine*, 327, 1045–50.

Stueven, H.A., Thompson, B.M., Aprahamian, C., and Darin, J. (1983). Use of calcium in pre-hospital cardiac arrest. *Annals of Emergency Medicine*, 12, 136–9.

Stueven, H.A., Thompson, M.B., Aprahamian, C., et al. (1984). Calcium chloride: reassessment of use in asystole. *Annals of Emergency Medicine*, 13, 820–2.

Stueven, H.A., Thompson, B.M., Aprahamian, C., et al. (1985a). The effectiveness of calcium chloride in refractory electromechanical dissociation. *Annals of Emergency Medicine*, 14, 626–9.

Stuevan, H.A., Thompson, B.M., Aprahamian, C., et al. (1985b). Lack of effectiveness of calcium chloride in refractory asystole. *Annals of Emergency Medicine*, 14, 630–2.

Taffet, G.E., Teasdale, T.A., and Luchi, R.J. (1988). In-hospital cardiopulmonary resuscitation. *Journal of the American Medical Association*, 260, 2069–72.

Tresch, D.D., Thakur, R.K., Hoffmann, R.G., Olson, D., and Brooks, H.L. (1989). Should the elderly be resuscitated following out-of-hospital cardiac arrest? *American Journal of Medicine*, 86, 145–50.

Tunstall-Pedoe, H., Bailey, L., Chamberlain, D.A., Marsden, A.K., Ward, M.E., and Zideman, D.A. (1992). Survey of 3765 cardiopulmonary resuscitations in British Hospitals (the BRESUS study): methods and overall results. *British Medical Journal*, 304, 1347–51.

Vukmir, R.B., Bircher, N.G., Radovsky, A., Menegazzi, J., and Safar, P. (1992). Sodium bicarbonate in cardiac arrest (abstract). *Critical Care Medicine*, 20, S86.

9.12 Heart failure

Christian Swinne

Heart failure is a clinical syndrome of breathlessness, fluid retention, and fatigue due to the inability of the heart to deliver oxygen and nutrients required for resting and exercise metabolic needs, and to the inability to fulfil this function with normal cardiac filling pressures. When the heart is failing, reduction of cardiac output and/or elevation of the filling pressures result in a series of metabolic, cellular, and neurohormonal adaptations which give the clinical picture of the syndrome. Thus heart failure is not a disease but a syndrome deriving from different cardiocirculatory diseases and marking the last step of their natural history. Because of the high prevalence of these diseases in old age, the condition of heart failure is very common in elderly people.

The group of old and very old patients with heart failure is not only large but also different in many respects from the younger group. In old age, the physiopathology of heart failure is influenced by the ageing process. In addition, the functional consequences of heart failure may be added to an already frail and deconditioned older person in whom symptoms are often atypical or absent. Because of the latter effects combined with the selective survival of older patients with less severe syndrome, the proportion of elderly patients with heart failure but preserved ejection fraction is higher than in younger groups. These differences have clinical and prognostic implications. As in younger patients, the natural course of heart failure in older persons is characterized by a poor prognosis. Therefore it is encouraging to note that current therapeutic schedules are able not only to improve this prognosis but also to relieve the symptoms and to allow a good quality of life to be achieved.

Because heart failure is a chronic condition, follow-up strategies are important and have been demonstrated to improve functional status and to produce substantial reductions in complications and the rate of hospital readmission. These advances in the management of heart failure have economic implications, because the syndrome is still one of the main diagnoses leading to hospital admission of older patients. Therefore congestive heart failure can be considered as a true geriatric problem and a challenge for geriatricians and geriatric teams.

Epidemiology (see also Chapter 9.1)

The number of patients with heart failure increases exponentially with age, as does the number of newly diagnosed cases. After the age of 60 years, heart failure, which is the final stage of many cardiovascular diseases, becomes a common problem. This is in part the result of the recent decline in mortality from heart disease at younger ages. It is also a consequence of the better management of acute coronary events, allowing more people to survive for longer although functional impairments are present. Even so, 50 per cent of deaths in old age are related to cardiovascular diseases.

The prevalence of heart failure in the Framingham population between the sixth and the ninth decade of life ranged from 0.5 to 5.5 per cent in men and from 0.3 to 8.5 per cent in women (Kannel and Belanger 1991). Some mild to moderate forms escaped detection and thus the true frequency was probably higher, ranging from 1 to 10 per cent in the same decades in both men and women. The annual incidence of heart failure in the Framingham Study was 4 per 1000 in men and 3 per 1000 in women aged between 55 and 64 years, and 54 per 1000 in men and 85 per 1000 in women aged 85 to 94 years. In a population survey of 30 000 persons in the London area (Sutton 1990), all the patients taking diuretics because of evidence of heart failure were identified (prevalence, 0.4 per cent). Using such diagnosis of heart failure, the prevalence was 0.06 per cent below the age of 65 and 2.8 per cent above this age. Extrapolation of the rate of hospital admissions for heart failure in this survey would give 120 000 admissions per year in the United Kingdom. This figure is comparable with the United States figure of 585 000 hospital discharges annually with the principal diagnosis of heart failure (Gillium 1987). Congestive heart failure is one of the main causes of hospital admission of elderly people and accounts for a substantial proportion of days spent in acute hospitals for people of this age. The majority of patients (80 per cent) admitted for heart failure are elderly, their average stay is 17 days, and they are often readmitted after a short period (Parameshwar et al. 1992). The last trend continues to increase, making proper management of patients with heart failure a matter of urgency.

Ageing and pathophysiology of heart failure

Up to a few decades ago, many clinicians considered that age per se was a possible cause of heart decompensation through a cardiomyopathy of the senescent heart. Cardiac output was also thought to decline with increasing age (Brandfonbrener et al. 1955). There is now much evidence against this view, and it is currently well known that cardiac output is maintained at rest and during exercise in normotensive elderly persons free from heart disease (see Chapter 9.1). Other evidence against a pure age effect is that supporting the role of cardiac

Table 3 Precipitating factors for congestive heart failure

Myocardial ischaemia	Atypical myocardial infarction
Anaemia	Atrial fibrillation
Bradycardia	Fever
Overperfusion	Volume overload (renal failure)
Pressure overload (hypertensive)	Pulmonary infection
Pulmonary embolism	Adverse drug reaction: NSAIDs, steroids, eye drops (Monane *et al.* 1994)
Thyrotoxicosis (Aronow 1995)	Poor compliance with medication (Ghali *et al.* 1994)

NSAID, non-steroidal anti-inflammatory drug.

Myocardial infarction is not always typical in elderly patients. In a series of 110 older patients with overt myocardial infarction, the symptoms leading to the diagnosis were dyspnoea in 35 per cent, thoracic pain in 22 per cent, neurological symptoms in 18 per cent, gastrointestinal symptoms in 4 per cent, and ECG findings in 22 per cent (Kannel and Abbott 1984). Since angina is also often atypical in older patients, it is not uncommon to discover a severe coronary artery disease at the stage of heart failure without any pre-existing history or previous typical symptoms. Silent ischaemia seems to be more frequent with advancing age (Fleg *et al.* 1990; Nadelman *et al.* 1990). This possible cause of heart failure should be considered as a possible cause of nocturnal orthopnoea.

The prevalence and incidence of both chronic and paroxysmal atrial fibrillation increase exponentially with age (Patel 1977). This arrhythmia is poorly tolerated by older people because of the importance of the atrial filling fraction in generating the stroke volume (Myatake *et al.* 1984). Loss of the pump function of the atrium results in a fall in output associated with an increase in atrial pressure leading to pulmonary congestion. Therefore paroxysmal atrial fibrillation is often the cause of pulmonary oedema in older patients, and establishment of fixed atrial fibrillation is a frequent cause of worsening heart failure in elderly patients.

Table 4 Boston group score for congestive heart failure

		Score
I Dyspnoea	At rest	4
	Orthopnoea	4
	Paroxysmal nocturnal	3
	On exertion	2
	On uphill exercise	1
II Physical signs	Jugular pressure >6 cmH$_2$O	2
	Jugular pressure >6 cmH$_2$O and ankle oedema and hepatojugular reflux	3
	Basal crepitation	1
	Diffuse crepitation	2
	Wheezing	3
	Gallop S3	3
	Tachycardia >100 beats/min	1
III Chest radiography	Alveolar oedema	4
	Interstitial oedema	3
	Bilateral pleural effusion	3
	Cardiothoracic ratio >0.5	3
	Apical vascularization	2

Score >8, certain; 5–7, probable; <5, low probability. Maximum 4 points per category.

Clinical diagnosis of heart failure

Elderly patients with heart failure may present atypically and often late in the course of the disease. This is because of their already reduced functional abilities. Therefore, and because the condition is frequent, it is essential for the clinician to keep the possible diagnosis of heart failure in mind.

As in younger adults, the diagnosis of heart failure in elderly patients is essentially clinical. When there is a previous history of heart disease, the combination of a comprehensive history, a clinical examination, and a chest radiograph provide an accurate index of suspicion for the syndrome. The Boston Group Score (Carlson *et al.* 1985; Marantz *et al.* 1988) is a combination of rated subjective, clinical, and radiological signs (see Table 4) which gives a good level of probability for the diagnosis of congestive heart failure. Nevertheless, in the practice of geriatrics, the confounding effects of associated diseases, the atypical manifestations of diseases, and the

frequency of complications substantially modify the basic clinical reasoning and the interpretation of data.

The clinical history and symptoms reported by the patient often emphasize the severity of the syndrome because they are influenced by the self-limitation of physical activity (Noble and Rothbaum 1982). Dyspnoea is common; it is often related to pulmonary disease but may also be related to ischaemia-related transient diastolic dysfunction. Exertional dyspnoea is not experienced by deconditioned older patients. Therefore other signs, such as an abnormally rapid and otherwise unexplained weight gain or a dramatic weight loss in response to diuretics, are of interest for the diagnosis of heart failure. Less specific symptoms (fatigue, bowel discomfort, anorexia, cachexia, delirium) may also be associated. Thus there is further potential for underdiagnosing the condition; atypical symptoms due to congestive heart failure may be attributed to other common geriatric problems.

Table 7 Therapeutic differences according to the ejection-fraction-based types of heart failure

	Poor ejection fraction	Preserved ejection fraction
Digitalis	+ + +	− (+)[a]
Nitrates	+ + +	+[b]
Vasodilators	+ + +	+[b]
Diuretics	+ + +	+[b]
Angiotensin-converting enzyme inhibitors	+ + +	+ + +
Calcium-channel inhibitors	−	+ +
β-Blockers	+[c]	+ +

[a] Only in atrial fibrillation.
[b] Useful in the initial congestive phase; careful use in the chronic phase.
[c] Recent evidence (CIBIS II Investigators and Committees 1999) supports benefits for survival in patients aged 18–80 years.

the related functional impairments are less apparent in deconditioned frail elderly patients. In addition, common non-specific symptoms of heart failure, such as fatigue, anorexia, dyspnoea, and oedema, are frequently attributed to other conditions also prevalent in the elderly. Thus proper diagnosis, treatment, and long-term management of heart failure are important challenges for the geriatrician and the geriatric teams. Moreover, when diagnosed and appropriately treated, the improvement in the quality of life of these patients is often excellent. Otherwise, the prognosis of heart failure in the elderly remains poor with a hospital mortality of 10 to 30 per cent, and an annual mortality as high as 60 per cent in severe cases.

References

Adkins, M.S., Amalfitano, D., Harnum, N.A., Laub, G.W., and McGrath, L.B. (1995). Efficacy of combined coronary revascularization and valve procedures in octogenarians. *Chest*, **108**, 927–31.

Aronow, W.S. (1994). Echocardiography should be performed in all elderly patients with congestive heart failure. *Journal of the American Geriatrics Society*, **42**, 1300–2.

Aronow, W.S. (1995). The heart and thyroid disease. *Clinics in Geriatric Medicine*, **11**, 219–29.

Aronow, W.S. and Kronzon, I. (1987). Correlation of prevalence and severity of valvular aortic stenosis determined by continuous-wave Doppler echocardiography with physical signs of aortic stenosis in patients aged 62 to 100 years with aortic systolic ejection murmurs. *American Journal of Cardiology*, **60**, 399–401.

Aronow, W.S. and Kronzon, I. (1993). Effect of enalapril on congestive heart failure treated with diuretics in elderly patients with prior myocardial infarction and normal left ventricular ejection fractions. *American Journal of Cardiology*, **71**, 602–4.

Aronow, W.S., Ahn, C., and Kronzon, I. (1990). Prognosis of congestive heart failure in elderly patients with normal versus abnormal ventricular systolic function associated with coronary artery disease. *American Journal of Cardiology*, **66**, 1257–9.

Bolling, S.F., Deeb, G.M., and Bach, D.S. (1996). Mitral valve reconstruction in elderly, ischaemic patients. *Chest*, **109**, 35–40.

Boon, N.A. (1991). New deals for old hearts. Age alone should be no barrier to treatment. *British Medical Journal*, **303**, 70.

Brandfonbrener, M., Landowne, M., and Shock, N.W. (1955). Changes in cardiac output with age. *Circulation*, **12**, 557–66.

Caird, F.I. (1976). Clinical examination and investigation of the heart. In *Cardiology in old age* (ed. F.I. Caird, J.L.C. Dall, and R.D. Kennedy), p.128. Plenum Press, New York.

Cargill, R.I., Barr, C.S., Coutie, W.J., Struthers, A.D., and Lipworth, B.J. (1994). C-type natriuretic peptide levels in cor pulmonale and in congestive heart failure. *Thorax*, **49**, 1247–9.

Carlson, K.J., Lee, D.C., Gorell, A.H., *et al.* An analysis of physician's reasons for prescribing long-term digitalis therapy in outpatients. *Journal of Chronic Diseases*, **38**, 733–9.

CIBIS-II Investigators and Committees (1999). The Cardiac Insufficiency Bisoprolol Study II (CIBIS-II): a randomised trial. *Lancet*, **353**, 9–13.

Cody, R.J. (1993). Physiological changes due to age. Implications for drug therapy of congestive heart failure. *Drugs and Aging*, **3**, 320–34.

Cohn, J.N., Johnson, G., and Veterans Administration Co-operative Study Group. (1990). Heart failure with normal ejection fraction. The V-HeFT study. *Circulation*, **81** (Supplement III), III-48–53.

CONSENSUS Trial Study Group (1987). Effects of enalapril on mortality in severe heart failure. *New England Journal of Medicine*, **316**, 1429–35.

Cornwell C.G., Murdoch, W.L., Kyle, R.A., Westermark, P., and Pitkanen, P. (1983). Frequency and distribution of senile cardiovascular amyloid. A clinicopathologic correlation. *American Journal of Medicine*, **75**, 618–23.

Coughlin, S.S., Tefft, M.C., Rice, J.C., Gerone, J.L., and Baughman, K.L. (1996). Epidemiology of idiopathic dilated cardiomyopathy in the elderly: pooled results from two case-control studies. *American Journal of Epidemiology*, **143**, 881–8.

De Bock, V., Mets, T., Romagnoli, M., and Derde, M.P. (1994). Capopril treatment of chronic heart failure in the very old. *Journal of Gerontology*, **49**: M148–52.

Devereux, R.B., Hawkins, I., Kramer-Fox, R., *et al.* (1986). Complications of mitral valve prolapse. Disproportionate occurrence in men and older patients. *American Journal of Medicine*, **81**, 751–8.

Digitalis Investigation Group (1997). The effect of digoxin on mortality and morbidity in patients with heart failure. *New England Journal of Medicine*, **336**, 525–33.

Dougherty, A.H., Naccarelli, G.V., Gray, E.L., Hicks, C.H., and Goldstein, R.A. (1984). Congestive heart failure with normal systolic function. *American Journal of Cardiology*, **54**, 778–82.

Echeverria, H.H., Bilsker, M.S., Myerburg, R.J., and Kessler, K.M. (1983). Congestive heart failure: echocardiographic insights. *American Journal of Medicine*, **75**, 750–5.

Enright, P.L., Ward, B.J., Tracy, R.P., and Lasser, E.C. (1996). Asthma and its association with cardiovascular disease in the elderly. The Cardiovascular Health Study Research Group. *Journal of Asthma*, 33, 45–53.

Ensor, R.E., Fleg, J.L., Kim, Y.C., De Leon, E.F., and Goldman, S.M. (1983). Longitudinal chest X-ray changes in normal men. *Journal of Gerontology*, 38, 307–14.

Fleg, J.L. (1986). Alterations in cardiovascular structure and function with advancing age. *American Journal of Cardiology*, 57, 33c–44c.

Fleg, J.L. (1994). The effect of normative ageing on the cardiovascular system. *American Journal of Geriatric Cardiology*, 3, 25–31.

Fleg, J.L., Gerstenblith, G., Zonderman, A.B., et al. (1990). Prevalence and prognostic significance of exercise-induced silent myocardial ischaemia detected by thallium scintigraphy and electrocardiography in asymptomatic volunteers. *Circulation*, 81, 428–36.

Furberg, C.D., Manolio, T.A., Psaty, B.M., et al. (1992). Major electrocardiographic abnormalities in persons aged 65 years and older (the Cardiovascular Health Study). *American Journal of Cardiology*, 69, 1329–35.

Furberg, C.D., Psaty, B.M., Manolio, T.A., Gardin, J.M., Smith, V.E., and Rautaharju, P.M. (1994). Prevalence of atrial fibrillation in elderly subjects (the Cardiovascular Health Study). *American Journal of Cardiology*, 74, 236–41.

Gales, B.J. and Menasrd, S.M. (1995). Relationship between the administration of selected medications and falls in hospitalized elderly patients. *Annals of Pharmacotherapy*, 29, 354–8.

Ghali, J.K. (1994). Heart failure and non-compliance in the elderly. *Archives of Internal Medicine*, 154, 2109–10.

Gillium, R.F. (1987). Heart failure in the United States 1970–1985. *American Heart Journal*, 113, 1043–5.

Haffner, C.A., Kendall, M.J., Struthers, A.D., Bridges, A., and Stott, D.J. (1995). Effects of captopril and enalapril on renal function in elderly patients with chronic heart failure. *Postgraduate Medical Journal*, 71, 287–92.

Hawkins, C.M., Richardson, D.W., and Vokonas, P.S. (1983). Effect of propanolol in reducing mortality in older myocardial infarction patients. The beta-blocker heart attack trial experience. *Circulation*, 67 (Supplement I), I-94–I-7.

Hubbell, F.A., Ziemba, S.E., Fine, M.J., and Burns, M.J. (1993). The value of baseline chest radiograph reports in the care of elderly patients in an emergency department. *American Journal of Medical Science*, 305, 145–9.

Jacobson, D.R., Pastore, R.D., Yaghoubian, R., et al. (1997). Variant-sequence *trans* thyretin (isoleucine 122) in late-onset cardiac amyloidosis in black Americans. *New England Journal of Medicine*, 336, 466–73.

Kannel, W.B. and Abbott, R.D. (1984). Incidence and prognosis of unrecognised myocardial infarction: an update on the Framingham Study. *New England Journal of Medicine*, 311, 1144–7.

Kannel, W.B. and Belanger, A.J. (1991). Epidemiology of heart failure. *American Heart Journal*, 121, 951–7.

King, D. (1996). Diagnosis and management of heart failure in the elderly. *Postgraduate Medical Journal*, 72, 577–80.

Kornowski, R., Zeeli, D., Averbuch, M., et al. (1995). Intensive home-care surveillance prevents hospitalisation and improves morbidity rates among elderly patients with severe congestive heart failure. *American Heart Journal*, 129, 762–6.

Kunis, R., Greenberg, H., Bor Yeoh, C., et al. (1985). Coronary revascularization for recurrent pulmonary oedema in elderly patients with ischaemic heart disease and preserved ventricular function. *New England Journal of Medicine*, 313, 1207–10.

Kwok, T., Falconer-Smith, J.F., Potter, J.F., and Ives, D.R. Thiamine status of elderly patients with cardiac failure. *Age and Ageing*, 21, 67–71.

Lakatta, E.G. (1986). Diminished beta-adrenergic modulation of cardiovascular function in advanced age. *Cardiology Clinics*, 4, 185–200.

Lechat, P., Packer, M., Chalon, S., Cucherat, M., Arab, T., and Boissel, J.-P. (1998). Clinical effects of β-adrenergic blockade in chronic heart failure. A meta-analysis of double-blind, placebo-controlled randomised trials. *Circulation*, 98, 1184–91.

Lever, H.M., Karam, R.F., Currie, P.J., and Healy, B.P. (1989). Hypertrophic cardiomyopathy in the elderly. Distinction from the young based on cardiac shape. *Circulation*, 79, 580–9.

Luchi, R.J., Snow, E., Luchi, J.M., Nelson, C., and Pircher, F.J. (1982). Left ventricular function in hospitalised geriatric patients. *Journal of the American Geriatrics Society*, 30, 700–5.

Marantz, P.R., Tobin, J.N., Wassertheil-Smoller, S., et al. (1988). The relationship between left ventricular systolic function and congestive heart failure diagnosed by clinical criteria. *Circulation*, 77, 607–12.

Marantz, P.R., Tobin, J.N., Derby, C.A., and Cohen, M.V. (1994). Age-associated changes in diastolic filling: Doppler *E/A* ratio is not associated with congestive heart failure in the elderly. *Southern Medical Journal*, 87, 728–35.

Milne, J.S. and Laure, I.J. (1974). Heart size in older people. *British Heart Journal*, 36, 352–6.

Modena, M.G. (1993). Different aspects of left ventricular hypertrophy in the elderly. *Cardiology in the Elderly*, 1, 417–22.

Monane, M., Bohn, R.L., Gurwitz, J.H., Glynn, R.J., Choodnovskiy, I., and Avorn, J. (1994). Topical glaucoma medications and cardiovascular risk in the elderly. *Clinical Pharmacology and Therapeutics*, 55, 76–83.

Myiatake, K., Okamoto, M., Kinoshita, N., et al. (1984). Augmentation of atrial contribution to ventricular inflow with ageing as assessed by intracardiac Doppler flowmetry. *American Journal of Cardiology*, 53, 586–9.

Nadelman, J., Frishman, W.H., Ooi, W.L., et al. (1990). Prevalence, incidence and prognosis of recognized and unrecognized myocardial infarction in persons aged 75 years or older. The Bronx Aging Study. *American Journal of Cardiology*, 66, 533–7.

Nichol, K.L., Margolis, K.L., Wuorenma, J., and Von Sternberg, T. (1994). The efficacy and cost effectiveness of vaccination against influenza among elderly persons living in the community. *New England Journal of Medicine*, 331, 778–84.

Noble, R.J. and Rothbaum, D.A. (1982). History and physical examination. *Cardiovascular Clinics*, 12, 55–64.

Olson, L.J., Gertz, M.A., Edwards, W.D., et al. (1987). Senile cardiac amyloidosis with myocardial dysfunction. Diagnosis by endomyocardial biopsy and immunohistochemistry. *New England Journal of Medicine*, 317, 738–42.

Parameshwar, J., Shackell, M.M., Richardson, A., Poole-Wilson, P.A., and Sutton, G.C. (1992). Prevalence of heart failure in three general practices in North West London. *British Journal of General Practice*, 42, 287–9.

Patel, K.P. (1977). Electrocardiographic abnormalities in the sick elderly. *Age and Ageing*, 6, 163–7.

Peeters, P. and Mets, T. (1996). The 6 minute walk as an appropriate exercise test in elderly patients with chronic heart failure. *Journal of Gerontology A*, 51, M147–51.

Petrin, T.J. and Tavel, M.E. (1979). Idiopathic hypertrophic subaortic stenosis as observed in a large community hospital: relation to age and history of hypertension. *Journal of the American Geriatrics Society*, 27, 43–6.

Pomerance, A. (1968). Cardiac pathology and systolic murmurs in the elderly. *British Heart Journal*, 30, 687–9.

Pomerance, A. (1981). Cardiac pathology in the elderly. *Cardiovascular Clinics*, 12, 9–54.

Pritchett, G., Cohen, H.J., Rao, K.M., Cobb, F., Sullivan, M., and Currie, M.S. (1995). Tumour necrosis factor, natural killer activity and other measures of immune function and inflammation in elderly men with heart failure. *Gerontology*, 41, 45–56.

Proctor, E.K., Morrow-Howell, N., and Kaplan, S.J. (1996). Implementation of discharge plans for chronically ill elders discharged home. *Health and Social Work*, 21, 30–40.

Puisieux, F., de Groote, P., Lemaire, J.B., Chamas, E., Houdas, Y., and Dewailly, P. (1995). Congestive heart failure in the elderly. Value of Doppler echocardiography. *Revue de Medecine Interne*, 16, 595–601.

Rich, M.W., Beckham, V., Wittenberg, C., Level, C.L., Freedland, K.E., and Carney, R.M. (1995). A multidisciplinary intervention to prevent the readmission of elderly patients with congestive heart failure. *New England Journal of Medicine*, 333, 1190–5.

Rich, M.W., Shah, A.S., Vinson, J.M., Freedland, K.E., Kuru, T., Sperry, J.C. (1996). Iatrogenic congestive heart failure in older adults; clinical course and prognosis. *Journal of the American Geriatrics Society*, 44, 638–43.

Robinson, T., Gariballa, S., Francourt, G., Potter, J., and Castleden, M. (1994). The acute effects of a single dopamine infusion in elderly patients with congestive cardiac failure. *British Journal of Clinical Pharmacology*, 37, 261–3.

Rodeheffer, R.J., Gerstenblith, G., Becker, L., Fleg, J.L., Weisfeldt, M.L., and Lakatta, E.G. (1984). Exercise cardiac output is maintained on advancing age in healthy human subjects: cardiac dilatation and increased stroke volume compensate for diminished heart rate. *Circulation*, 69, 203–13.

Sagie, A., Benjamin, E.J., Galderisi, M., *et al.* (1993). Reference values for Doppler indexes of left ventricular diastolic filling in the elderly. *Journal of the American Society of Echocardiography*, 6, 570–6.

Setaro, J.F., Soufer, R., Remetz, M.S., Perlmutter, R.A., and Zaret, B.L. (1992). Long-term outcome in patients with congestive heart failure and intact systolic left ventricular performance. *American Journal of Cardiology*, 69, 1212–16.

SOLVD Investigators (1991). Effect of enalapril on survival in patients with reduced left ventricular ejection fractions and congestive heart failure. *New England Journal of Medicine*, 325, 293–302.

Soufer, R., Wohlgelernter, D., Vita, D., *et al.* (1985). Intact left systolic ventricular function in clinical congestive heart failure. *American Journal of Cardiology*, 55, 1032–6.

Soumerai, S.B., McLaughlin, T.J., Spiegelman, D., Hertzmark, E., Thibault, G., and Goldman, L. (1997). Adverse outcomes of underuse of β-blockers in elderly survivors of acute myocardial infarction. *Journal of the American Medical Association*, 277, 115–21.

Spodick, D.H. and Quarty-Pigott, V.M. (1973). The fourth heart sound as a normal finding in older persons. *New England Journal of Medicine*, 288, 140–1.

Stone, G.W., Griffin, B., Shah, P.K., *et al.* (1991). Prevalence of unsuspected mitral regurgitation and left ventricular diastolic dysfunction in patients with coronary artery disease and acute pulmonary oedema associated with normal or depressed left ventricular systolic function. *American Journal of Cardiology*, 67, 37–41.

Sutton, G.C. (1990). Epidemiologic aspects of heart failure. *American Heart Journal*, 120, 1538–40.

Swinne, C.J., Shapiro, E.P., Jamart, J.A., and Fleg, J.L. (1996). Age-associated changes in left ventricular outflow tract geometry in normal subjects. *American Journal of Cardiology*, 78, 1070–3.

Topol, E.J., Traill, T.A., and Fortuin, N.J. (1985). Hypertensive hypertrophic cardiomyopathy of the elderly. *New England Journal of Medicine*, 312, 277–83.

Vandewerf, F., Geboers, J., Kesteloot, H., De Geest, H., and Barrios, L. (1986). The mechanisms of disappearance of the physiologic third heart sound with age. *Circulation*, 73, 877–84.

Wallen, T., Landahl, S., Hedner, T., Hedner, J., and Hall, C. (1993). Atrial peptides ANP(1–98) and ANP (96–126) in health and disease in an elderly population. *European Heart Journal*, 14, 1508–13.

Waller, B.F. (1988). Hearts of the oldest old. *Mayo Clinic Proceedings*, 63, 625–7.

Waller, B.F. and Roberts, W.C. (1983). Cardiovascular disease in the very elderly. Analysis of 40 necropsy patients aged 90 years or over. *American Journal of Cardiology*, 51, 403–21.

Wofford, J.L. and Ettinger, W.H. (1991). Risk factors and manifestations of digoxin toxicity in the elderly. *American Journal of Emergency Medicine*, 9, 11–15.

Wong, W.F., Gold, S., and Fukuyama, O. (1989). Diastolic dysfunction in elderly patients with congestive heart failure. *American Journal of Cardiology*, 63, 1526–8.

Yusuf, S. and Furberg, C.D. (1991). Are we biased in our approach to treating elderly patients with heart disease? *American Journal of Cardiology*, 68, 954–6.

9.13 Infective endocarditis

Raymond Auckenthaler

Infective endocarditis has remained a challenging infection for both clinicians and medical researchers since Sir William Osler described the microbiological origin of infective endocarditis in 1885 (Contrepois 1995). Infective endocarditis has been increasing among elderly patients with the expanding lifespan of the population, advances in the field of cardiothoracic surgery, and decline in the incidence of acute rheumatic carditis in developing countries. During recent decades a progressive shift of the maximal incidence of infective endocarditis in young patients to patients above 70 years old has been observed (Terpenning *et al.* 1987; van der Meer *et al.* 1992; Werner *et al.* 1996). Diagnosis of endocarditis in older patients has been more difficult because of atypical presentation and the lack of classic clinical findings, both leading to delayed diagnosis and mismanagement (Habte-Gabr *et al.* 1973; Tenenbaum and Kaplan 1984; Gantz 1991). Today the diagnostic sensitivity for bacterial endocarditis has been greatly improved by better blood culture techniques (Weinstein 1996), transthoracic and transoesophageal echocardiography (Werner *et al.* 1996), and the acceptance of standardized clinical criteria (Durack *et al.* 1994). Rational antimicrobial therapy and surgery of infected or uninfected valves has contributed to a better prognosis of infective endocarditis mainly in older patients (Wilson *et al.* 1995; Antunes and Franco 1996).

Pathogenesis and pathophysiology

The cardiac valves are the main site of infective endocarditis. The pathophysiology is based on (a) predisposing factors of the host, (b) the characteristics of the infective micro-organism, and (c) the risk of transient bacteraemia. Studies in experimental animals have shown that the haemodynamic exposure to high-velocity blood stream with turbulence and other factors modify and damage the endothelial monolayer of valves. Local lesions trigger the deposition of platelets and fibrin leading to sterile vegetations and non-bacterial thrombotic endocarditis (Gould *et al.* 1975). Pre-existing valvular disease, calcifications, and insufficiency of mitral and aortic valve contribute to sterile vegetations in the elderly patient. Any trauma of a mucosal surface associated with dental, gastrointestinal, or genitourinary manipulation or the use of intravascular devices can produce transient bacteraemias and colonization of the vegetations with micro-organisms. Transient bacteraemia is usually of low grade and short duration, and can also occur spontaneously during chewing, tooth brushing, and other normal activities. Thus prophylactic measures during dental intervention only marginally affect the overall frequency of infective endocarditis and good dental hygiene is probably more important (van der Meer *et al.* 1992). The hydrodynamic flow through an orifice from a high-pressure to a low-pressure site favours the deposition of bacteria immediately beyond the low-pressure side of the orifice or at the site where a jet stream strikes the opposing endocardial surface. Thus, in mitral insufficiency, the atrial surface of the mitral valve is involved. In aortic insufficiency it is the ventricular surface of the aortic valve which is typically involved, and the chordae tendineae may also become infected. Endocarditis is much less common in association with low-pressure flow abnormalities such as pure mitral valve stenosis. The ability of bacteria to adhere via specific adhesions to fibrin or other proteins of the extracellular matrix (Baddour 1994; Moreillon *et al.* 1995) explains the variable propensity to develop infection. Once the vegetations are colonized, the bacteria are covered by fibrin and platelets and multiply, thus further contributing to the growth of the vegetations. Progressive destruction of the valve leads to haemodynamic insufficiency and rupture of vegetations with peripheral emboli in any organ. Infective endocarditis also causes continuous stimulation of both humoral and cellular immunity, with systemic manifestations due to circulating immune complexes and rheumatoid factor.

Epidemiology

The exact incidence of infective endocarditis is difficult to determine because diagnostic criteria for endocarditis vary (Steckelberg *et al.* 1990). In developed countries the incidence is less than 4 per 100 000 person-years (Griffin *et al.* 1985). Before 1970 the mean age for infective endocarditis was 32 years and the proportion of patients more than 60 years old was only 5 per cent (Cantrell and Yoshikawa 1983). In the late 1980s this proportion has increased to more than 50 per cent (Terpenning *et al.* 1987; van der Meer *et al.* 1992; Watanakunakorn and Burkert 1993; Werner *et al.* 1996). Many factors contribute to the higher incidence of infective endocarditis in older people. Firstly, the decline of rheumatic fever has resulted in fewer cases of rheumatic heart disease in younger people. Secondly, demographic changes with older populations increases the number of people with degenerative valve disease and calcifications. Up to 30 to 40 per cent of infective endocarditis are linked to calcifications of the mitral valves, nodular calcifications, or a secondary thrombus after myocardial infarction (Scheld and Sande 1995). Thirdly, the advances in the field of cardiothoracic surgery with prosthetic valve replacement at an older age is steadily increasing and contributes to a greater number

Table 1 Duke criteria for diagnosis of infective endocarditis

Definite infective endocarditis

Pathological criteria

Micro-organisms: demonstrated by culture or histology in a vegetation, *or* in a vegetation that has embolized, *or* in an intracardiac abscess, *or*

Pathological lesions: vegetation or intracardiac abscess present, confirmed by histology showing active endocarditis

Clinical criteria, using specific definitions listed in Table 2

Two major criteria, *or*

One major and three minor criteria, *or*

Five minor criteria

Possible infective endocarditis

Findings consistent with infective endocarditis that fall short of 'definite', but not 'rejected'

Rejected

Firm alternative diagnosis for manifestations of endocarditis, *or*

Resolution of manifestations of endocarditis, with antibiotic therapy for 4 days or less, *or*

No pathological evidence of infective endocarditis at surgery or autopsy, after antibiotic therapy for 4 days or less

---

of patients at high risk of infective endocarditis (Werner *et al.* 1996; Selton-Suty *et al.* 1997). Fourthly, new invasive procedures or management of severely ill patients with impaired immune systems contribute to an increasing number of nosocomial acquired bacteraemias and infective endocarditis with a high mortality (Terpenning *et al.* 1987). An increasing frequency of infective endocarditis has also been observed in patients with intracardiac pacemakers (Klug *et al.* 1997). Age-adjusted annual incidence of bacterial endocarditis in men below 40 years of age was 19.6 per million people per year, in contrast with 67.5 per million people per year in men above 70 years (van der Meer *et al.* 1992). It is not known why men remain two to three times more prone to infective endocarditis overall (van der Meer *et al.* 1992), even though the male to female ratio is lower in older people (Selton-Suty *et al.* 1997).

Clinical presentation

The diagnosis of infective endocarditis is not difficult, when presenting with the classic Oslerian manifestations including fever, new significant regurgitant heart murmur, small and large vessel emboli, immunological phenomena, and several positive blood cultures containing streptococci from the viridans group. However, the clinical manifestations are often scarce and non-specific, particularly in older people, and the diagnosis of infective endocarditis is difficult to establish with certainty. Therefore over- or underdiagnosis of infective endocarditis is common (Chassagne *et al.* 1996).

To overcome these difficulties Van Reyn *et al.* (1981) established criteria to classify patients with suspected endocarditis into risk groups based on histopathological, microbiological, and clinical parameters. These criteria were not widely accepted because of their retrospective nature, the lack of prospective validation, and inclusion of echocardiographic findings, and the requirement of histopathology to confirm a definite case of infective endocarditis.

Duke criteria

More recently new diagnostic criteria have been proposed by investigators from Duke University Medical Centre, Durham, North

Carolina (Durack *et al.* 1994) who incorporated two-dimensional echocardiographic findings (Krivokapich and Child 1996) in their classification. These new criteria categorize patients with endocarditis into definite diagnoses based on pathological or clinical criteria, possible, and rejected cases. The criteria are modelled on the Jones criteria for the diagnosis of acute rheumatic fever using major and minor criteria as shown in Tables 1 and 2. The major criteria of the Duke system includes a minimal number of positive blood cultures with typical micro-organisms as well as ECG abnormalities typical of endocarditis. Minor criteria include non-specific findings such as predisposition, fever, or vascular, immunological, and microbiological phenomena. In their study including 405 consecutive cases of suspected infective endocarditis in 353 patients Durack *et al.* (1994) showed that clinically definite cases almost doubled compared with the rate obtained using the Van Reyn *et al.* (1981) criteria. This was mainly due to the introduction of the echocardiographic data in the new schema. The same findings were observed for operated as well as non-operated patients.

The Duke criteria have been evaluated and shown to be superior to the Van Reyn *et al.* criteria in five studies summarized by Bayer and coworkers (Bayer 1993; Bayer *et al.* 1994) and confirmed by Heiro *et al.* (1998). In these studies, the sensitivity of the Duke criteria was found to be about twice as high as that obtained with the Van Reyn *et al.* criteria, thus confirming the importance of echocardiographic findings. It was also noted that only few patients had clinically definite infective endocarditis based on minor criteria only.

The negative predictive value of the Duke criteria for excluding infective endocarditis has been evaluated (Dodds 1996) because of the risk of incorrectly rejecting patients with true infective endocarditis. Of 52 episodes in which the diagnosis had been rejected, patients were followed for at least 3 months. Only in three patients was the diagnosis reclassified to possible endocarditis. Of the remaining 49 episodes, 31 (63 per cent) had a firm alternative diagnosis other than endocarditis, 17 (35 per cent) had resolution of the original clinical syndrome, and a single patient had no evidence of endocarditis at surgery. The negative predictive value of a rejected case of infective endocarditis based on the Duke criteria appeared to be at least 92 per cent.

Table 2 Terminology used in the Duke criteria

Major criteria

Positive blood culture for infective endocarditis

(a)   Typical micro-organism for infective endocarditis from two separate blood cultures
- Viridans streptococci[a], *Strep. bovis*, HACEK group, *or*
- Community-acquired *Staph. aureus* or enterococci, in the absence of a primary focus, *or*

(b)   Persistently positive blood culture[b], defined as recovery of a micro-organism consistent with infective endocarditis from:
- blood cultures drawn more than 12 h apart, *or*
- all of three or a majority of four or more separate blood cultures, with first and last drawn at least 1 h apart

Evidence of endocardial involvement

(a)   Positive echocardiogram for infective endocarditis
- Oscillating intracardiac mass, on valve or supporting structures, or in the path of regurgitant jets, or on implanted material, in the absence of an alternative anatomical explanation, *or*
- Abscess, *or*
- New partial dehiscence of prosthetic valve, *or*

(b)   New valvular regurgitation (increase or change in pre-existing murmur not sufficient)

Minor criteria

- Predisposition: predisposing heart condition or intravenous drug use
- Fever: >38.0°C (100.4°F)
- Vascular phenomena: major arterial emboli, septic pulmonary infarcts, mycotic aneurysm, intracranial haemorrhage, conjunctival haemorrhages, Janeway lesions
- Immunological phenomena: glomerulonephritis, Osler's nodes, Roth spots, rheumatoid factor
- Microbiological evidence: positive blood culture but not meeting major criterion as noted previously or serological evidence of active infection with organism consistent with infective endocarditis
- Echocardiogram: consistent with infective endocarditis but not meeting major criterion as noted previously

[a] Including nutritional variant strains.
[b] Excluding single positive cultures for coagulase-negative staphylococci and organisms that do not cause endocarditis.

The specificity of the Duke criteria was evaluated by Hoehn *et al.* (1996) on a group of patients with acute fever or fever of unknown origin. Of 100 patients with rejected endocarditis according the Duke criteria 23 had a firm alternate diagnosis, 39 resolution of symptoms without antibiotics, and 38 both. Only one patient with a firm, alternate diagnosis, namely a urinary tract infection, was reclassified as clinically definite blood-culture-negative endocarditis based on one major and three minor criteria. Therefore, the specificity of the Duke criteria for clinically diagnosing infective endocarditis is 99 per cent.

In summary, a large number of studies have now clearly established the sensitivity and specificity of the Duke criteria for the diagnosis of infective endocarditis (Sandre and Shafran 1996: Sekeres *et al.* 1997). They are widely accepted and should be used whenever evaluating patients with suspected infective endocarditis. However, it must be emphasized that these studies were not performed in homogeneous patient groups according to risk, age, foreign body, and so on, and that the results might be influenced by a referral bias (Steckelberg *et al.* 1990). The appropriateness of Duke criteria in elderly patients with or without prosthetic valves has not yet been fully validated.

Clinical symptoms and signs of infective endocarditis have been extensively reviewed and described (Scheld and Sande 1995). In elderly people clinical manifestations are known to be protean but only two studies have addressed this problem systematically (Terpenning *et al.* 1987; Selton-Suty 1997). In 53 episodes of endocarditis in patients over the age of 60 years (Terpenning *et al.* 1987), it was observed that elderly patients reported fever because of lack of perception less

frequently in comparison with younger patients and that confusion as a presenting sign was common. New heart murmurs or changing murmurs were heard less frequently and were often neglected because discrete heart murmurs are frequent in elderly people. Errors in diagnosis occurred in two-thirds of the patients over 60 years of age. The non-specific complaints including anorexia, fatigue, and weakness coupled with confusion commonly seen at admission appeared to contribute to frequent diagnoses such as fever of unknown origin, stroke, heart failure, and syncope in elderly patients. Appropriate antibiotic therapy was more often delayed in this group and the fatality was significantly higher (45 per cent) than in middle-aged patients (32 per cent).

Duke criteria have been applied in older patients only by Selton-Suty *et al.* (1997). In this study 25 patients over 70 years of age and 89 under 70 years of age were compared. Surprisingly, location of infective endocarditis and clinical signs and symptoms were similar in both groups, except for a significantly lower occurrence of embolic episodes in those aged above 70 years. This study supports the idea of also applying the Duke criteria to older patients where objective and comparable criteria are more difficult to obtain.

Laboratory work-up

Abnormal haematological parameters are frequent but non-specific in infective endocarditis. Anaemia as observed in any chronic disease is nearly always present. Thrombocytopenia and leucocytosis are less frequent. The sedimentation rate is nearly always elevated, sometimes accompanied with hypergammaglobulinaemia, a positive rheumatoid factor, and circulating immune complexes. C-reactive protein concentrations may be useful to monitor therapy. The urinalysis frequently shows proteinuria, microscopic hematuria sometimes with red cell casts, and other abnormalities.

Microbiological work-up

Blood cultures are the most important laboratory test to confirm a suspected infective endocarditis. Detection of bacteraemia and fungaemia has been greatly improved in microbiological laboratories over recent decades (Weinstein 1996). Three blood cultures within a 24-h period are sufficient in routine conditions. Each culture (one aerobic and one anaerobic bottle) should be taken before administration of antibiotics by separate venepuncture at different sites. The cultures should be drawn at intervals of at least 2 h to document the continuous bacteraemia characteristic of endovascular infections. Three sets should be sufficient to identify more than 95 per cent of bacteria causing endocarditis within 24 to 48 h. If the first sets of cultures remains negative, an additional set of three cultures might be drawn and the laboratory should be immediately contacted for the use of special media when suspecting rare or fastidious organisms such as *Brucella* species, the *Haemophilus–Actinobacillus–Cardiobacterium–Eikenella–Kingella* (HACEK) group of bacteria, *Campylobacter* species, or nutritionally variant streptococci (*Streptococcus defectivus, Streptococcus adjacens*). In acute cases two culture sets can be drawn by separated venepunctures within minutes. Separate venepunctures are essential to suspect contaminants in positive cultures. Blood cultures should not be drawn from intravascular catheters for the same reason.

In patients with remaining negative blood cultures despite optimal blood cultures, serology for *Chlamydia* species, *Brucella* species, *Coxiella burnetii, Legionella* species, *Rochalimaea* species, and perhaps viruses should be performed. In specialized centres amplification methods can be used to detect organisms that are difficult to grow. In any case the conservation of a frozen serum sample is advisable.

Patients with infective endocarditis can present with acute embolic peripheral ischaemia necessitating surgery. In these cases the embolus should be submitted to the laboratory for immediate microscopic examination (Gram, acridine, and fungal stains) and appropriate cultures. Resected heart valves or prostheses should be treated similarly. If the classical microbiological investigations based on cultures remain negative and there is a high degree of suspicion of infective endocarditis, electronic microscopy, amplification methods (polymerase chain reaction), or *in situ* hybridization should be performed (Goldenberger *et al.* 1997). Because these methods are difficult to perform once the material has been processed for culturing, deep-frozen original material should always be kept from tissue or prostheses obtained from a patient with infective endocarditis of unclear aetiology.

Echocardiography

Echocardiography is a cornerstone for the diagnosis of infective endocarditis according to the Duke criteria (Durack *et al.* 1994).

Therefore it should be performed by an experienced operator in all patients with suspected endocarditis. Echocardiography should be first transthoracic and, at least if negative or equivocal, completed with a transoesophageal examination. Transthoracic echocardiography is less sensitive in patients with lung emphysema, deformation of the thorax, or adipose tissue. In contrast, transoesophageal echocardiography is more sensitive (Taams *et al.* 1990; Werner *et al.* 1996) and safe (Daniel *et al.* 1991*a*) for the detection of complications of endocarditis such as abscesses, valve perforation, and for the observation of heart valve prosthesis (Daniel *et al.* 1991*b*). The risk of the transoesophageal procedure is comparable with that of a gastroscopy and is well tolerated in elderly people (Ofili *et al.* 1990).

Major criteria of echocardiographic findings according to the Duke criteria (Durack *et al.* 1994) include oscillating intracardiac mass on valves or supporting structures in the path of regurgitant jets of blood passing through incompetent valves or septal defects. Abscess within the paravalvular tissue or new or increasing partial dehiscence of a prosthetic valve are also major criteria. Minor criteria include abnormalities consistent with infective endocarditis including non-oscillating targets, new valvular fenestration, and nodular thickening.

Cardiac valvular vegetations or non-bacterial thrombotic endocarditis can be observed in cancer patients (Edoute *et al.* 1997). Sterile vegetations are found mainly on the mitral or aortic valve although any valve can be affected. They are most common in patients with solid tumours including carcinoma of the lung, lymphoma, and other cancers (except brain tumours).

Microbiological features

Interpretation of blood cultures with likely pathogens responsible for infective endocarditis is based on all sets of bottles positive with the same micro-organism, for example the viridans group streptococci, *Streptococcus bovis*, the HACEK group, staphylococci, or enterococci. When grown in several blood cultures coagulase-negative staphylococci, *Corynebacterium* species, and *Propionibacterium* species should not be discarded as contaminants in the presence of a prosthetic heart valve, pacemaker, or intravascular device. Primary endocarditis with *Staphylococcus epidermidis* has also been observed without the presence of a foreign body. When suspecting infective endocarditis any organism isolated should be identified to the species level and susceptibility tests performed. In streptococci minimum inhibitory concentration should be determined at least for penicillin and ceftriaxone. Determination of low-level (less than 500 mg/l) or high-level resistance to streptomycin and gentamicin in enterococci is necessary to determine if synergy can be achieved, when used in association with β-lactam antibiotics. All micro-organisms isolated should be kept frozen when suspecting endocarditis or intravascular infections.

Microbiological findings were compared in young and old age groups in three studies (Terpenning *et al.* 1987; Werner *et al.* 1996; Selton-Sutty *et al.* 1997). Staphylococci and group viridans streptococci were the most frequent organisms isolated (over 50 per cent) without statistical difference between both age groups. Only *Strep. bovis* belonging to the group D streptococci and enterococci were isolated more frequently in older patients. Gram-negative bacteria concerned mainly the HACEK group including *Actinobacillus actinomycetemcomitans, Cardiobacterium hominis, Eikenella corrodens,* and *Kingella kingae* amongst others. Yeasts were exceptional.

Blood culture-negative endocarditis in elderly patients vary from 2 to 14 per cent (Terpenning *et al.* 1987; Werner *et al.* 1996; Selton-Suty *et al.* 1997). Previous partial treatment or inadvertent administration of antibiotics for other reasons should be looked for. If so, blood cultures should be repeated after a 2-week interval without antibiotics or if fever reappears. Patients with culture-negative endocarditis need special investigations to be defined in collaboration with the microbiologist according to the patient's history. They include special media and staining, serology, and eventually use of amplification methods (Goldenberger *et al.* 1997).

Treatment

Basic principles

The antimicrobial treatment of infective endocarditis needs special attention. Although micro-organisms have often low minimum inhibitory concentration against antibiotics their elimination needs prolonged bactericidal treatments and relapses are not rare. The reason for this is the impaired local host resistance within vegetations usually containing 10^9 to 10^{10} micro-organisms. In these conditions bacteria have a low metabolic activity with impaired growth capacity which explains the poor killing activity of cell wall active antibiotics. The importance of the local penetration of antibiotics into the vegetations is controversial, but dosing and duration of antibiotic treatment are essential for the cure of endocarditis.

Antimicrobial agents

The correct treatment of infective endocarditis is based on culture results, correct identification, and susceptibility testing. Widely accepted antibiotic regimens either single or in combination are based on *in vitro* killing curves, the animal model of infective endocarditis, and large clinical trials. Intravenous treatment should be the rule in order to achieve high and constant serum levels. Empirical treatment should be started only in acute endocarditis or unstable patients and after an adequate number of blood cultures have been drawn (Table 3). Whenever possible specific treatment adapted to the identified micro-organism with known minimum inhibitory concentration should be initiated (Wilson *et al.* 1995) (Table 4).

Classical regimens are based on hospital treatment and parenteral antibiotic for 4 to 6 weeks according to the micro-organism. The exact determination of the minimum inhibitory concentration for penicillin and/or gentamicin is essential for the choice of the optimal treatment (see Table 4). If a combination therapy is necessary aminoglycosides should be administered three times daily. Regimens with ceftriaxone for 4 weeks have been successfully used in patients with streptococci of the viridans group or with *Haemophilus* species. These treatments can be ambulatory but should not be introduced in patients with cardiovascular risk factors including heart failure, severe aortic insufficiency, or conductive disorders (Francioli *et al.* 1992). More recently, treatments for 2 weeks have been successfully introduced in patients with right-side endocarditis observed in drug addicts or in patients without risks and streptococci with a minimum inhibitory concentration of less than 0.2 mg/l to penicillin (Francioli *et al.* 1995). In these cases the period of hospital admission can be shortened or even changed to an ambulatory treatment. These treatments are based on more bactericidal combinations including β-lactam antibiotics and aminoglycosides. They have not been studied in elderly people, have a lower success rate in left-heart endocarditis and should be used, if at all, with caution in older patients even without renal impairment or defective function of the eighth cranial nerve.

Monitoring

Monitoring the patient with infective endocarditis is important. Daily clinical controls include temperature, heart rate, signs of cardiac insufficiency, new regurgitant murmur, and peripheral emboli. Laboratory control includes blood cultures performed after 3 and 7 days or in cases of insufficient clinical response. Blood cultures should be sterile after 1 week of treatment. Haemoglobin, leucocytes, thrombocytes, C-reactive protein, immune complexes, and urinalysis to exclude nephritis should be performed regularly; ECG and eventually echocardiography should be performed according to the clinical findings. When aminoglycosides are used trough serum levels should be monitored after 2 to 3 days of starting treatment and doses adapted if necessary. Determination of serum bactericidal titre is controversial and is not recommended routinely.

Fever should be monitored carefully. In a study of 200 patients 50 per cent were afebrile after 3 days, 75 per cent after 7 days, and 90 per cent only after 14 days (Ledermann *et al.* 1992). In this study delayed disappearance of fever was linked to *Staphylococcus aureus*, *Pseudomonas aeruginosa*, culture-negative endocarditis, embolization of large vessels, and microvascular lesions (splinter haemorrhages, petechiae, Osler nodes, Janeway and Roth spots). In persistent fever complications should be excluded, including nosocomial infections (phlebitis, urinary tract infection, drug side-effects) and complications of endocarditis.

Complications of endocarditis

Heart failure is a frequent complication of infective endocarditis and must be monitored carefully. It is due to myocarditis, conduction defects, or valve dysfunction. Infective endocarditis is dangerous because of possible rapidly lethal complications needing immediate surgical intervention. Impaired atrioventricular conduction is due to extension of the infection into the interventricular septum, in general by contiguity from an infected aortic valve. Septum perforation is located between the ventricles or between the left ventricle and the right atrium. It leads to rapid cardiac insufficiency, should be confirmed by echocardiography, and followed by immediate surgical intervention. The sudden rupture of an infectious aneurysm from the sinus of Valsalva into the right cavities is characterized by a continuous murmur and cardiac decompensation. Annular or para-annular abscesses are more frequent in prosthetic valves leading to their desinsertion and rapid cardiac decompensation. Repeated systemic emboli or persistence of large and mobile vegetations observed by echocardiography also need rapid surgical intervention (Acar and Michel 1993; Millaire *et al.* 1997).

Role of surgery

The impressive advances in surgical treatment of acquired valvular heart disease have abolished the initial controversy between medical

Table 3 Initial treatment of endocarditis with unknown micro-organisms

Situation	Suspected micro-organism	Antimicrobial (dose)
Acute endocarditis	Staph. aureus Group A/B streptococci Gram-negative bacteria	Flucloxacillin 2 g/4 h IV with gentamicin 1 mg/kg IM/IV every 8 h[a]
Subacute endocarditis	Streptococci, viridans group Enterococcus species Haemophilus species	Penicillin G 5 million units/6 h IV with gentamicin 1 mg/kg IM/IV every 8 h[a]
Prosthetic heart valve (postoperative <1 year)	Staph. aureus Staphylococci, coagulase-negative	Vancomycin[b] 1 g/12 h IV with gentamicin 1 mg/kg IM/IV every 8 h[a] and rifampicin 300 mg/8 h by mouth
Prosthetic heart valve (postoperative ≥1 year)	Streptococci, viridans group Enterococcus species Staphylococci, coagulase-negative	Vancomycin[b] 1 g/12 h IV with gentamicin 1 mg/kg IM/IV every 8 h[a]

IV, intravenous; IM, intramuscular.

[a] Preferentially gentamicin should be used. In case of high-level resistance to gentamicin (>500 mg/l) the micro-organism is resistant to all aminoglycosides (tobramycin, netilmicin, sisomicin, amikacin) and the possible susceptibility to streptomycin alone must be tested.

[b] Dosage of vancomycin and aminoglycosides should be adapted to body weight and renal clearance and monitored carefully.

and surgical therapy (Antunes and Franco 1996). The fatality of uncomplicated cases in older patients is now similar to that observed for younger patients (Aranki *et al.* 1994; Colombo *et al.* 1994). The most important strategic consideration is the evaluation of myocardial function because it determines the prognosis. The optimal time of intervention must be adapted to the clinical situation. When valve replacement is performed too early, the risk for a recurrence of infection or a paravalvular leak is great. In contrast, too late an intervention carries the risk of lethal heart failure. As a rule, valve replacement should be performed only after 1 week of antibiotic therapy (Aranki *et al.* 1994). The duration of postoperative therapy should be adapted to the culture results of the operated valve. If the culture is positive, the antimicrobial treatment should be conducted for an additional 6 weeks. If the culture remains negative, the full course of antibiotic treatment can be limited to 6 weeks.

The decision for surgical intervention must consider the haemodynamic tolerance of the cardiopathy, evolution of the infectious state, occurrence of complications and specific risks linked to the aetiology, and location of the infective endocarditis. Early and close collaboration between the physician, the infectious disease specialist, and the cardiovascular surgeon is essential. Early surgery is mandatory in progressive or significant heart failure which does not resolve with medical therapy, persistent bacteraemia and/or endocarditis due to *Staph. aureus*, Gram-negative bacteria or fungi, or relapse of infection. In acute complications including the development of persistent heart block or bundle branch block, septum perforation, sudden rupture of Valsalva aneurysm, annular or para-annular abscesses, repeated large systemic emboli, or persistence of large and mobile vegetations, surgical intervention should be immediate (Acar and Michel 1993). The surgical approach includes implantation of mechanical valves, bioprosthesis, or more recently, reconstruction of the valve with a lower hospital fatality and an improved long-term survival (Dreyfus *et al.* 1990; Helft *et al.* 1995; Kalangos *et al.* 1995; Muehrcke *et al.* 1997).

Special cases

Pacemaker endocarditis

Pacemaker infection is a common complication with an estimated incidence of 0.1 to 20 per cent. This great variability of infection rate is due to the heterogeneous definitions in the literature and the continuous surgical improvement of implantation and antibiotic prophylaxis. Two types of infection can be distinguished: the more frequent and early infection of the battery pouch, or the rare (0.15 to 1.2 per cent) infection of the pacemaker lead which appears more than 1 month after insertion. The infection can develop either by continuity of a pouch infection or can follow bacteraemia. In more than 75 per cent of cases staphylococci are involved with a predominance of coagulase-negative staphylococci followed by enterococci, streptococci, and rarely Gram-negative bacteria, *Mycobacterium avium* complex, yeasts, or fungi. Diagnosis is based on positive blood cultures, and transoesophageal, eventually endovascular, echocardiography. Complications are frequent with myocardial abscess, wall perforation, pleural or bronchial fistula, infection of mural thrombus, or septic thrombophlebitis. Endocarditis of the tricuspid valve has a fatality of 34 per cent. Treatment includes not only appropriate antibiotic administration for 4 weeks but also the complete removal of the pacemaker wire. Endovascular extraction by an experienced operator is possible in the majority of cases with a specially designed device (Colavita *et al.* 1993); if this approach is not possible surgical removal of the wire and the adjacent infected and fibrous intracardiac tissue is necessary (Arber *et al.* 1994). In relapsing endocarditis after the removal of a pacemaker the surgical removal of infected tissue and appropriate antibiotics are obligatory to cure the infection (Rutschmann *et al.* 1997).

Prosthetic valve endocarditis

Prosthetic valve endocarditis can occur as early or late onset (over 12 months) after implantation and is more frequent in patients with

Table 4 Treatment of endocarditis with known micro-organisms

Micro-organism	Susceptibility	Antimicrobial (dose)	Duration (weeks)	Remarks
Staphylococcus species	Methicillin sensitive	Flucloxacillin 2 g/4 h IV with optional gentamicin 1 mg/kg IM/IV every 8 h[a,b]	4–6	Aminoglycosides may be added for the first 3–5 days in severe cases
		Vancomycin 15 mg/kg every 12 h IV	4–6	For patients allergic to β-lactam antibiotics
	Methicillin resistant	Vancomycin 15 mg/kg every 12 h IV with optional rifampicin 300 mg every 8 h by mouth	4–6	In prosthetic valve endocarditis rifampicin and gentamicin 1 mg/kg IM/IV every 8 h should be added
Strep. viridans group or *Strep. bovis*	Penicillin susceptible (MIC ≤ 0.1 mg/l)	Penicillin G 2–3 million units every 4 h IV	4	Preferred in patients >65 years or in those with impairment of the eighth cranial nerve or renal function
		Ceftriaxone 2 g every 24 h IM/IV	4	
		Pencillin G 2–3 million units every 4 h IV with gentamicin 1 mg/kg IM/IV every 8 h[a,b]	2	Preferred in patients less than 65 years old with normal renal function
		Ceftriaxone 2 g every 24 h IM/IV with gentamicin 1 mg/kg IM/IV every 8 h[a,b]	2	
		Vancomycin 15 mg/kg every 12 h IV	4	For patients allergic to β-lactam antibiotics
Strep. viridans group or *Strep. bovis* or nutritionally variant streptococci	Penicillin resistant (MIC >0.1 and <0.5 mg/l)	Penicillin G 2–3 million units every 4 h IV	4–6	First-generation cephalosporin may be substituted for patients whose penicillin hypersensitivity is not of the immediate type
		With gentamicin 1 mg/kg IM/IV every 8 h[b]	2	
		Vancomycin 15 mg/kg every 12 h IV	4	For patients allergic to β-lactam antibiotics
Group A or B streptococci		Penicillin G 2–3 million units every 4 h IV	4	
Enterococcus species or penicillin-resistant *Streptococcus* species (MIC ≥ 0.5 mg/l)	Gentamicin low level (MIC <500 mg/l)	Pencillin G 3–4 million units every 4 h IV	4–6	4 weeks therapy for patients with symptoms <3 months
		With gentamicin 1 mg/kg IM/IV every 8 h[b]	4–6	6 weeks therapy for patients with symptoms >3 months
		Ampicillin 12 g every 24 h either continuously or divided in 6 doses	4–6	
		Vancomycin 15 mg/kg every 12 h IV with gentamicin 1 mg/kg IM/IV every 8 h[b]	4–6	For patients allergic to β-lactam antibiotics
Haemophilus species	All, with/without β-lactamase	Ceftriaxone 2 g every 24 h IM/IV	4	

IV, intravenous; IM, intramuscular; MIC, minimal inhibitory concentrations.

[a] Preferentially gentamicin should be used. In case of high-level resistance to gentamicin (>500 mg/l) the micro-organism is resistant to all aminoglycosides (tobramycin, netilmicin, sisomicin, amikacin) and the possible susceptibility to streptomycin alone must be confirmed.

[b] Dosage of vancomycin and aminoglycosides should be adapted to body weight and renal clearance and monitored carefully: trough level of vancomycin should be 5–10 mg/l, trough level of gentamicin should be <1 mg/l.

previous endocarditis or multiple valve replacement. Early-onset endocarditis occurs in 0.4 to 3 per cent within 2 to 12 months and is due to peroperative or immediately postoperative contamination. The infection rate is similar for mechanical or bioprosthetic valves and is independent of localization. It is due to coagulase-negative staphylococci or *Staph. aureus* (40 to 60 per cent), Gram-negative bacteria (10 to 30 per cent), or streptococci, *Corynebacterium* species, yeasts, or other rare organisms (Maroni *et al.* 1994).

Late-onset endocarditis occurs in less than 1 per cent per year and is due to bacteraemia as observed in patients without prosthetic valves. Predominant organisms include streptococci (30 to 50 per cent), coagulase-negative streptococci (20 to 30 per cent), *Staph. aureus*, Gram-negative bacilli, yeasts, and *Corynebacterium* species. The fatality is 20 to 40 per cent owing to complications including destruction of the adjacent tissue and dehiscence of the valve, cardiac insufficiency, and embolization of the central nervous system. During the last decade the fatality rate has diminished with better surveillance and early surgical intervention.

Echocardiography is necessary to localize and measure the size of the vegetations, to recognize aortic abscesses, or to remove the prosthetic valve with evaluation of the paraprosthetic regurgitation. This dysfunction leads to rapid cardiac insufficiency and needs early adequate symptomatic treatment. Impaired atrioventricular conductivity is often linked to an abscess of the septum and needs immediate surgical intervention (Wolff *et al.* 1995). Thromboembolic phenomena are observed in 20 to 60 per cent of patients despite anticoagulant therapy.

In infectious prosthetic endocarditis surgical replacement of the valve is mandatory with the exception of late endocarditis without complications due to streptococci. The intervention should be performed once the diagnosis is established irrespective of the duration of the preceding antimicrobial therapy. With this approach the prognosis of infective prosthetic endocarditis has been improved (Maroni *et al.* 1994).

Prophylaxis

It is important to take steps to prevent the development of bacterial endocarditis in people at high risk, for example those with valvular or vascular conditions subject to becoming infected, whenever treatment is being undertaken for dental or other oral, genitourinary, gastrointestinal, or respiratory conditions. The American Heart Association has prepared guidelines for the choice of appropriate antibiotic regimens (Dajani *et al.* 1990). In general, amoxycillin orally is the first choice unless there are contraindications such as allergy or suspicion of risk for an amoxycillin-resistant infection. For example, if a genitourinary intervention is undertaken for a patient with infected urine it is wise for antibiotic prophylaxis to reflect the sensitivities of the infecting organisms.

References

Acar, J. and Michel, P.L. (1993). Chirurgie de l'endocardite bactérienne, quand? *Archives Maladies du Coeur*, 86, 1863–7.

Antunes, M.J. and Franco, C.G. (1996). Advances in surgical treatment of acquired valve disease. *Current Opinion in Cardiology*, 11, 139–54.

Aranki, S.F., Santini, F., Adams, D.H., *et al.* (1994). Aortic valve endocarditis: determinance of early survival and late morbidity. *Circulation*, 90 (Part 2), II-275–82.

Arber, N., Pras, E., Copperman, Y., *et al.* (1994). Pacemaker endocarditis: report of 44 cases and review of the literature. *Medicine*, 73, 299–305.

Baddour, L.M. (1994). Virulence factors among Gram-positive bacteria in experimental endocarditis. *Infection and Immunity*, 62, 2143–8.

Bayer, A.S. (1993). Infective endocarditis. *Clinical Infectious Diseases*, 17, 313–22.

Bayer, A.S., Ward, J.I., Ginzton, L.E., and Shapiro, S.M. (1994). Evaluation of new clinical criteria for the diagnosis of infective endocarditis. *American Journal of Medicine*, 96, 211–19.

Cantrell, M. and Yoshikawa, T.T. (1983). Aging and infective endocarditis. *Journal of the American Geriatrics Society*, 31, 216–22.

Chassagne, P., Perol, M.B., Doucet, J., *et al.* (1996). Is presentation of bacteremia in the elderly the same as in younger patients? *American Journal of Medicine*, 100, 65–7.

Colavita, P.G., Zimmern, S.H., Gallagher, J.J., Fedor, J.M., Austin, W.K., and Smith, H.J. (1993). Intravascular extraction of chronic pacemaker leads: efficacy and follow-up. *Pacing and Clinical Electrophysiology*, 16, 2333–36.

Colombo, T., Lanfranci, M., Passini, L., *et al.* (1994). Active infective endocarditis: surgical approach. *European Journal of Cardiothoracic Surgery*, 8, 15–24.

Contrepois, A. (1995). Notes on the early history of infective endocarditis and the development of an experimental model. *Clinical Infectious Diseases*, 20, 461–6.

Dajani, A.S., *et al.* (1990). Prevention of bacterial endocarditis. Recommendations of the American Heart Association. *Journal of the American Medical Association*, 264, 2919.

Daniel, W.G., Erbel, R., Kasper, W., *et al.* (1991a). Safety of transesophageal echocardiography. A multicenter survey of 10 419 examinations. *Circulation*, 83, 817–21.

Daniel, W.G., Mügge, A., Martin, R.P., *et al.* (1991b). Improvement in the diagnosis of abscesses associated with endocarditis by transesophageal echocardiography. *New England Journal of Medicine*, 324, 795–800.

Dodds III, G.A., Sexton, D.J., Durack, D.T., Bashore, T.M., Corey, G.R., Kisslo, J., and the Duke Endocarditis Service (1996). Negative predictive value of the Duke criteria for infective endocarditis. *American Journal of Cardiology*, 77, 403–7.

Dreyfus, G., Serraf, A., Jebara, V.A., *et al.* (1990). Valve repair in acute endocarditis. *Annals of Thoracic Surgery*, 49, 706–13.

Durack, D.T., Lukes, A.S., Bright, D.D., and the Duke Endocarditis Service (1994). New criteria for diagnosis of infective endocarditis: utilization of specific echocardiographic findings. *American Journal of Medicine*, 96, 200–9.

Edoute, Y., Haim, N., Rinkevich, D., Brenner, B., and Reisner, S. A. (1997). Cardiac valvular vegetations in cancer patients: a prospective echocardiographic study of 200 patients. *American Journal of Medicine*, 102, 252–8.

Francioli, P., Etienne, J., Hoigné, R., Thys, S.P., and Gerber, A. (1992). Treatment of streptococcal endocarditis with a single daily dose of ceftriaxone sodium for 4 weeks. *Journal of the American Medical Association*, 267, 264–7.

Francioli, P., Ruch, W., Stamboulian, D., and the International Infective Endocarditis Study Group (1995). Treatment of streptococcal endocarditis with a single daily dose of ceftriaxone and netilmicin for 14 days: a prospective multicenter study. *Clinical Infectious Diseases*, 21, 1406–10.

Gantz, N.M. (1991). Geriatric endocarditis: avoiding the trend toward mismanagement. *Geriatrics*, 46, 66–8.

Goldenberger, D., Künzli, A., Vogt, P., Zbinden, R., and Altwegg, M. (1997). Molecular diagnosis of bacterial endocarditis by broad-range PCR amplification and direct sequencing. *Journal of Clinical Microbiology*, 35, 2733–9.

Gould, K., Ramirez-Ronda, C.H., Homes, R.K., and Sanford, J.P. (1975). Adherence of bacteria to heart valves *in vitro*. *Journal of Clinical Investigation*, 56, 1364–70

Griffin, M.R., Wilson, W.R., Edwards, W.D., *et al.* (1985). Infective endocarditis. Olmsted county, Minnesota, 1950–1981. *Journal of the American Medical Association*, 254, 1199–2202.

Habte-Gabr, E., January, L.E., and Smith, I.M. (1973). Bacterial endocarditis: the need for early diagnosis. *Geriatrics*, 28, 164–7.

Heiro, M., Nikoskelainen, J., Hartiala, J.J., Saraste, M.K., and Kotilainen, P.M. (1998). Diagnosis of infective endocarditis. *Archives of Internal Medicine*, 158, 18–24.

Helft, G., Tabone, X., Georges, J.L., et al. (1995). Bioprosthetic valve replacement in the elderly. *European Heart Journal*, 16, 529–33.

Hoen, B., Béguinot, I., Rabaud, C., et al. (1996). The Duke criteria for diagnosing infective endocarditis are specific: analysis of 100 patients with acute fever or fever of unknown origin. *Clinical Infectious Diseases*, 23, 298–302.

Kalangos, A., Vuille, C., Pretre, R., Lerch, R., and Faidutti, B. (1995). Chirurgie reconstructive de la valve mitrale en phase aiguë d'endocardite bactérienne. *Schweizerische Medizinische Wochenschrift*, 125, 1592–6.

Klug, D., Lacroix, D., Savoye, C., et al. (1997). Systemic infection related to endocarditis on pacemaker leads. Clinical presentation and management. *Circulation*, 95, 2098–107.

Krivokapich, J. and Child, J.S. (1996). Role of transthoracic and transesophageal echocardiography in diagnosis and management of infective endocarditis. *Cardiology Clinics*, 14, 363–82.

Ledermann, M.M., Sprangue, L., Wallis, R.S., and Ellner, J.J. (1992). Duration of fever during treatment of infective endocarditis. *Medicine*, 71, 52–7.

Maroni, G.P., Terdjman, M., Montély, J.M., and Hanania, G. (1994). L'endocardite infectieuse sur prothèse valvulaire: problèmes actuels. *Archives Maladies du Coeur*, 87, 1837–43.

Millaire, A., Leroy, O., Gaday, V., et al. (1997). Incidence and prognosis of embolic events and metastatic infections in infective endocarditis. *European Heart Journal*, 18, 677–84.

Moreillon, P., Entenza, J.M., Francioli, P., et al. (1995). Role of *Staphylococcus aureus* coagulase and clumping factor in pathogenesis of experimental endocarditis. *Infection and Immunity*, 63, 4738–43.

Muehrcke, D.D., Cosgrove III, D.M., Lytle, B.W., et al. (1997). Is there an advantage to repairing infected mitral valves? *Annals of Thoracic Surgery*, 63, 1718–24.

Ofili, E.O., Rich, M.W., with the technical assistance of Peggy Brown and Jean Lewis (1990). Safety and usefulness of transesophageal echocardiography in persons aged > 70 years. *American Journal of Cardiology*, 66, 1279–80.

Rutschmann, O.T., Auckenthaler, R., Frei, R., Stoermann-Chopard, C., and Pittet, D. (1997). Infections de pacemaker: à propos d'un cas et revue de la littérature. *Médecine et Maladies Infectieuses*, 27, 874–7.

Sandre, R.M. and Shafran, S.D. (1996). Infective endocarditis: review of 135 cases over 9 years. *Clinical Infectious Diseases*, 22, 276–86.

Scheld, W.M. and Sande, M.A. (1995). Endocarditis and intravascular infections. In *Principles and practice of infectious diseases*, (ed. G.L. Mandell, J.E. Bennett, and R. Dolin), pp. 740–83. Churchill Livingstone, Edinburgh.

Sekeres, M.A., Abrutyn, E., Berlin, J.A., et al. (1997). An assessment of the usefulness of the Duke criteria for diagnosing active infective endocarditis. *Clinical Infectious Diseases*, 24, 1185–90.

Selton-Suty, C., Hoen, B., Grentzinger, A., et al. (1997). Clinical and bacteriological characteristics of infective endocarditis in the elderly. *Heart*, 77, 260–3.

Steckelberg, J.M., Melton, III, L.J., Ilstrup, D.M., Rouse, M.S., and Wilson, W.R. (1990). Influence of referral bias on the apparent clinical spectrum of infective endocarditis. *American Journal of Medicine*, 88, 582–8.

Taams, M.A., Gussenhoven, E.J., Bos, E., et al. (1990). Enhanced morphological diagnosis in infective endocarditis by transoesophageal echocardiography. *British Heart Journal*, 63, 109–13.

Tenenbaum, M.J. and Kaplan, M.H. (1984). Infective endocarditis in the elderly: and update. *Geriatrics*, 39, 121–7.

Terpenning, M.S., Buggy, B.P., and Kauffman, C.A. (1987). Infective endocarditis: clinical features in young and elderly patients. *American Journal of Medicine*, 83, 626–34.

van der Meer, J.T.M., Thompson, J., Valkenburg, H.A., and Michel, M.F. (1992). Epidemiology of bacterial endocarditis in The Netherlands. I. Patients characteristics. *Archives of Internal Medicine*, 152, 1863–8.

Van Reyn, C.F, Levy, B.S.D., Arbeit, R.D., Friedland, G., and Crumpacker, C.S. (1981). Infective endocarditis: an analysis based on strict case definitions. *Annals of Internal Medicine*, 94, 505–17.

Watanakunakorn, C. and Burkert, T. (1993). Infective endocarditis at large community teaching hospital, 1980–1990, a review of 210 episodes. *Medicine*, 72, 90–102.

Weinstein, M.P. (1996). Current blood culture methods and systems: clinical concepts, technology and interpretation of results. *Clinical of Infectious Diseases*, 23, 40–6.

Werner, G.S., Schulz, R., Fuchs, J.B., et al. (1996). Infective endocarditis in the elderly in the era of transesophageal echocardiography: clinical features and prognosis compared with younger patients. *American Journal of Medicine*, 100, 90–7.

Wilson, W.R., Karchmer, A.W., Dajani, A.S., et al. (1995). Antibiotic treatment of adults with infective endocarditis due to streptococci, enterococci, staphylococci, and HACEK microorganisms. *Journal of the American Medical Association*, 274, 1706–13.

Wolff, M., Witchitz, S., Chastang, C., Régnier, B., and Vachon, F. (1995). Prosthetic valve endocarditis in the ICU. Prognostic factors of overall survival in a series of 122 cases and consequences for treatment decision. *Chest*, 108, 688–94.

10

Cancer: an overview

W. Bradford Patterson and Paul Calabresi

When someone survives to join the group that we call 'older', cancer has become well known from experience within the family or at least among acquaintances. Cancer is infrequent prior to age 35, despite the public interest and sympathy for children and young adults who are occasionally struck down. In later years, the overall incidence rises rapidly in both men and women (Fig. 1). In the United States the median age of cancer patients is now 70 years. These age-associated increases are seen worldwide, although there are large variations in specific cancers in different countries.

'Is cancer becoming a more common disease?' is a question asked by laymen and medically trained persons alike. In fact, not all types of cancer are increasing, although there is an overall absolute increased incidence. Thus several readily identifiable reasons make cancer a more common and familiar disease than it was in the past.

1. The ageing of populations increases the proportion at risk, so that both cancer incidence and prevalence are on the rise around the world.

2. The incidence of smoking-related cancers, particularly lung cancer, has been rising rapidly for the past 60 years. Since lung cancers make up a large portion of the total in many advanced countries, this particular cancer has a great impact on total incidence, masking a decreased rate in some other cancers such as those of the stomach and cervix. The effect of increased cigarette smoking in Third World countries will not be seen immediately in mortality statistics.

3. Cancer has only been acceptable as a topic for public discussion for the last few decades. In earlier years, a diagnosis of cancer was often kept secret and was certainly never listed in an obituary or in the media. In many cultures today, the prevention, treatment, costs, and pain of cancer are a common topic of conversation.

4. Increased use of cancer screening tests and examinations has contributed to a spurt of new 'early' cases which many experts believe will be a transient phenomenon, particularly for breast and prostate cancer.

It should also be noted that in the United States an overall decline in cancer death rates for both sexes became evident in about 1990 and has continued. While the reasons for this trend cannot be stated with confidence, some cancers are now being prevented by lifestyle changes, more cancers are found at curable stages through early detection programmes, and other cancer deaths are averted by improved treatment.

This overview will selectively address topics that are germane to physicians in their diagnosis and treatment of cancer in older age groups. This important topic has been the subject of a number of recent reviews, to which the reader is referred (Akerley and Calabresi 1994; Balducci *et al.* 1998; Kennedy 1997). For those readers wishing a more detailed description of cancer management, many recent texts are available (Calabresi and Schein 1993; DeVita *et al.* 1997; Holland and Frei 1997).

Causes of cancer in older persons

A major conceptual step forward in our understanding of cancer occurred when oncologists began to recognize and speak of it as a group of diseases, with a few characteristics in common but with many different causes, many different natural histories, and posing very different problems in management and prognosis.

The causes of cancer are almost always multiple. It has been suggested that up to 70 per cent of cancers are due to environmental and lifestyle factors, including tobacco use, high-fat diets, alcohol abuse, excessive sun exposure, and specific carcinogens. This figure may be higher for those cancers appearing in older persons and is

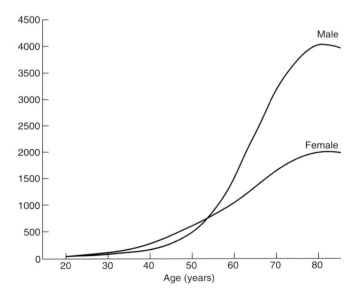

Fig. 1 Cancer incidence by age and sex. (Data from NIA Presentation–Cancer Burden in the Aged, 1997, and NCI SEER Data 1989–1993.)

helpful in dispelling the notion that the causes of cancer are unknown. Understanding cancer causation becomes particularly important when considering appropriate cancer prevention measures.

Why cancer and ageing are so closely related is a question about which scientists have speculated for years. The issue is beyond the scope of this overview, but one recent hypothesis is so provocative that it will be mentioned. Campisi has suggested the possible importance of 'replicative senescence' in linking ageing and cancer (Campisi 1997). This is a term used to describe the fact that all cells have a built-in mechanism which allows for only a predetermined number of cell divisions prior to permanent arrest. Some of these senescent non-replicating cells have altered functions with potentially deleterious effects on tissues, of which basement membranes are one example. Since some senescent cells accumulate during later life, the mechanism of replicative senescence may contribute to tumour inhibition in the early life of an organism but may act as a tumour promoter when the same organism is aged.

The burgeoning field of cancer genetics (Lynch et al. 1995; American Cancer Society 1997) deserves special attention, although until recently genetic predisposition in the Mendelian sense has been considered a cause of cancer in only 15 to 20 per cent of cases. Rapid advances in molecular genetics are providing an increasing number of associations between genes and different types of cancer. Specifically, inherited susceptibility genes (i.e. germ-line abnormalities carried in ova and sperm) have been discovered for breast cancer (BRCA1 and BRCA2), colon cancer (MSH2/MLH1), and melanoma. Not only do these advances raise possibilities for improved screening programmes, but many investigators anticipate that they will lead to new preventive and therapeutic strategies. Investigations to identify these genes begin with chromosomal mapping and analysis of cancer cells taken from many different individuals with the same type of cancer. Chromosomal abnormalities are sought that are common to all or a significant proportion of these cancers. A great deal of knowledge is being collected on specific oncogenes and, more recently, on the role of tumour suppressor genes (p53, RB, BRCA1, BRCA2, etc.) whose malfunction can render normal cells defenceless against the neoplastic process. Knowledge about the clinical significance of these molecular abnormalities is still lacking, and many investigators are attempting to relate the specific genetic changes to the natural history of the cancer—for example, which changes predict for rapid progression versus an indolent course? Others are studying the presence of molecular markers that predict for susceptibility to specific chemotherapeutic agents. Research also involves the study of normal tissues, dysplastic but non-neoplastic tissues, and benign lesions such as colonic polyps that are known to be associated with a higher incidence of neoplasia in the same organ, all with the aim of identifying genetic markers associated with the progression from benign to malignant. In some models, such as the conversion of a benign polyp in the large bowel to a metastatic carcinoma of the colon, it has been documented that a cascade of genetic alterations occurs, involving activation of selected oncogenes and failure of specific tumour suppressor genes (Kinzler and Vogelstein 1996; Lee and Wei 1997). It is too soon to predict when these investigations will bear fruit for the clinician, but it is certain that revolutionary changes will occur in our ability to identify those subjects who are at greater risk for particular cancers and to individualize intervention and treatment more effectively.

Table 1 Relationship of stage at diagnosis of common cancers to increasing patient age

Site	Stage at diagnosis	
	Holmes and Hearne (1981)	Goodwin et al. (1986)
Breast	Increase	Increase
Cervix	Increase	Increase
Colon	—	Neutral
Colorectum	Neutral	—
Endometrium	Increase	Increase
Gallbladder/liver	—	Neutral
Kidney	Increase	Neutral
Lung	Decrease	Decrease
Melanoma	—	Increase
Ovary	Increase	Increase
Pancreas	—	Decrease
Prostate	—	Neutral
Rectum	—	Decrease
Stomach	—	Decrease
Thyroid	—	Increase
Urinary bladder	Increase	Increase

Reproduced with permission from Holmes (1989).

Natural history

The term cancer covers a broad spectrum of disease types, from one with sudden onset and rapid lethal outcome to an indolent series of manageable lesions that require treatment but pose little threat to life.

There is conflicting evidence as to whether the natural history of cancer varies with age. Doubling times of cancer cells are one index of clinical behaviour, but there is such marked variation in doubling time among cancers of the same type (e.g. ductal carcinoma of the breast) that differences based on patient age tend to become a minor variable. Survival rates after diagnosis can be considered as an indicator of natural history, but this criterion ignores the effects of the treatment itself, of treatment choices, and of individual tolerance to treatment, all of which can be major variables when assessing the effects of age. Table 1, taken from a review of many types of cancer, shows the marked variation in the effect of age on stage at diagnosis, which relates closely to survival rates. Clinicians should not consider a patient's age in predicting the rate of progression of a particular cancer. Other factors, including histology, stage at presentation, and observation for even a limited period of time, are much better guides to prognosis than age alone.

It is of interest that in most cases invasion and metastasis, which are hallmarks of the neoplastic process, may be unaffected by age.

Basal cell cancers of skin erode locally, even if neglected, in young and old alike, while a small cancer of the lung that is hardly distinguishable on a chest radiograph may first present clinically as a brain metastasis causing a seizure, also irrespective of the patient's age. Yet sometimes there are significant variations with age. There have been indications that the process of angiogenesis may be less effective in some older individuals, which may inhibit the development of metastases. This and other pathophysiological mechanisms may explain why some older patients experience a more indolent course of their disease (Valentinis *et al.* 1991; Nixon *et al.* 1994).

However, there is also considerable evidence that certain neoplasms, including acute myelogenous leukaemia, Hodgkin's disease and non-Hodgkin's lymphoma, and ovarian carcinoma, may be more aggressive and have a much poorer prognosis in older individuals than in younger patients with similar diagnoses (International Non-Hodgkin's Lymphoma Prognostic Factors Project 1993; Extermann 1997; O'Reilly *et al.* 1997; Thigpen 1998).

Table 2 Cancers that may be prevented

Cancer site	Prevention
Skin	Avoid excessive actinic exposure and use sun-screens
Lung, oral cavity, larynx, oesophagus, bladder	Avoid use of cigarettes or any tobacco products
Oral cavity, oesophagus, liver	Limit alcohol intake Anti-hepatitis vaccine
Breast, endometrium	Reduce saturated fats in diet Exercise
Colon and rectum	Increase fibre and antioxidant vitamins Take one aspirin daily Have colorectal polyps removed
Cervix	Periodic vaginal examination with cervical smear

Response to treatment

Older persons respond as well to treatment as younger patients. This concept is of great importance, having been well documented for a range of cancers and for the common modalities of treatment, which include surgery, radiation therapy, and chemotherapy or hormonal therapy. While there are exceptions, they are much less important than the general rule. Comorbid illness, rather than age itself, is usually the principal factor that makes a patient ineligible for a surgical procedure or for more intensive regional or systemic therapy.

Surgeons have discovered that careful techniques of patient selection, preoperative assessment, safe anaesthesia with attention to tissue oxygenation and blood pressure, together with meticulous postoperative care, permit cancer operations of all types to be carried out at any age with acceptably low fatality and morbidity rates. These techniques are no different from those used with younger patients and for non-neoplastic conditions. While radiotherapy may appear to be safer and less traumatic than a surgical operation for the treatment of cancer in an elderly patient, complications occur with both modalities, and sometimes a 3-h operation is better tolerated than 6 weeks of daily visits for radiotherapy, with the attendant travel and continued stress of a challenging experience. Excellent outcomes for radiotherapy, whether curative or palliative, are not prevented by advancing age if attention is given to patient selection, technique, and physical and psychosocial support during and after treatment (Brady and Markoe 1986).

Hormonal therapy is a particularly important modality for older patients with cancer of the breast, uterus, and prostate. While this treatment is palliative and not curative, the distinction is often blurred in the old and frail person when death from non-cancer causes is not a surprise. For example, the anti-oestrogen tamoxifen can even be employed as primary treatment in place of surgery or radiotherapy for localized breast cancer in older women who are extremely frail or have a very limited life expectancy. For endometrial cancer, progesterone has for many years played an important role in the management of metastatic disease. Metastatic cancer of the prostate in older men responds to treatment with anti-oestrogenic agents such as leuprorelin (leuprolide), flutamide, and bicalutamide, and their

effectiveness can be monitored by periodic determination of prostate-specific antigen levels in the blood.

Prior to about 1980, the toxicity of chemotherapy discouraged its aggressive use for palliation of older patients. Also, some of the most common cancers occurring in people aged over 65 years (lung, colorectal and prostate) did not respond well, or for very long, to any chemotherapeutic agents. Breast cancer has been a gratifying exception, often responding well to chemotherapy. During the past two decades, new agents, including growth factors (such as granulocyte colony-stimulating factor and granulocyte–macrophage colony stimulating factor) and cytoprotective agents (such as dexrazoxane and amifostine), as well as improved techniques of chemotherapeutic administration and supportive care have made it possible to employ a wide range of drugs that can yield worthwhile benefit in selected older patients. Many of these patients are very ready to accept some risk and discomfort for the chance of more effective palliation and perhaps several more years of life.

Two major advances in cancer treatment have occurred in the last quarter-century. One is pretreatment staging, a term used by clinicians to describe tests that assess the extent to which cancer has spread, prior to formulating a therapeutic plan. The other advance is multi-disciplinary management, which brings together the useful characteristics of the major treatment modalities in order to improve results and reduce side-effects.

Cancer prevention, screening, and early detection

Prevention

Older persons should be looked upon as excellent candidates for interventions designed to prevent cancer or to find it early (Warnecke 1989). Table 2 lists the cancers occurring in older persons for which there is evidence that preventive measures are useful. Tobacco products, whether smoked or chewed, represent a major preventable cause of large numbers of cancer cases worldwide, primarily in people over

65 years old. A reduction in smoking and chewing tobacco would lead to a substantial reduction in the incidence of and deaths from cancer of the oral cavity, larynx, lung, oesophagus, pancreas, and bladder. In the United States, cigarette consumption is falling and the annual male death rate from cancer of the lung is declining. Unfortunately, this is not the case in women in whom mortality from lung cancer is still rising and has surpassed that of breast cancer. Deplorably, the export of American cigarettes to Asia and Africa is increasing, and consumption of tobacco products on these continents remains high or is rising.

Clinicians do have the power to influence their older patients to stop smoking. Research has demonstrated that when physicians discuss health risks with patients who smoke, and when information and help about cessation techniques are provided, a quit rate of 10 per cent or greater measured at 1 year can be anticipated. Since it is now known that most smokers who quit are successful only after several tries, repeated attempts by physicians are indicated, and this may make the cumulative cessation rate much higher. A review of many clinical trials that tested smoking cessation interventions showed certain criteria common to the successful methods. These include the provision of information and personalized advice using a variety of formats and communication techniques, and reinforcement through repeated sessions (Kottke et al. 1988; Abrams et al. 1996). Special techniques such as hypnotism are useful for some but not others. The use of nicotine skin patches to counteract the addictive potential of nicotine in cigarettes is clearly useful, particularly with those smokers whose withdrawal symptoms are so strong that they cannot tolerate even a few hours without a cigarette. For older persons, the knowledge that cancer risks can be lowered even after a long history of chronic smoking needs to be emphasized in order to counteract the erroneous belief that irreversible damage has already occurred.

The media and the public often focus on research that supports dietary modification and avoidance of sun exposure as keys to cancer prevention for adults. Without belittling their importance, a reduction of cancer incidence in humans by control of dietary factors is still unproven, and most of the skin cancers that relate to excessive exposure to ultraviolet sunlight, i.e. basal cell and squamous cancers, are non-lethal and easily treated by simple techniques. The development of melanoma appears to be related to sunburn and excess ultraviolet exposure during youth rather than to chronic exposure later in life.

Recently, the relatively new approach of chemoprevention has received increasing attention. A number of agents have demonstrated significant protective effects, such as retinoids for oral neoplasms and aspirin or other non-steroidal anti-inflammatory drugs for colorectal cancer (Giovannucci et al. 1994). Others are the subjects of large randomized clinical trials, such as the study of tamoxifen in women at high risk of developing breast cancer by the National Surgical Adjuvant Breast Project or the national trial of finasteride, a 5-α-reductase inhibitor, for the prevention of prostate cancer (Minton and Shaw 1998).

Screening and early detection

The effect of early detection in reducing morbidity and death has been most obvious with cancer of the cervix and melanoma. Widespread application of cervical cytology (Pap smears) as a screening test in women of all ages has led to the earlier diagnosis of cervical cancer, often in the *in situ* stage when treatment is simpler and usually curative. Unfortunately, the percentage of older women who have never had a Pap smear remains high in populations such as the indigent and ethnic minorities.

Although the incidence of melanoma is rising markedly, early lesions can be detected by careful examination of the skin by a practitioner who has learned the characteristic changes of pigmented skin lesions that signify malignancy. This kind of early detection works for adults of any age and has been largely responsible for the great improvement in control of melanomas, which are now regularly cured in a high percentage of subjects.

Since mammography has been improved in sensitivity and made widely available, a reduction in deaths from breast cancer of up to 35 per cent should now be possible (Feig 1988). In the earliest trials mortality appeared to be improved only in women at about menopausal age, but newer trials show improvement for both younger and older women.

Currently, the screening test most hotly debated involves measurement of prostate-specific antigen to screen asymptomatic men with prostate glands normal to examination. Despite high sensitivity, the test does not have high specificity. In addition, it is not proved that such early detection leads to a survival benefit after aggressive therapy, as described later.

For cancer of the colon and rectum, clinical trials have now provided persuasive evidence that annual faecal occult blood testing combined with internal examination of the colon endoscopically or radiographically every 3 to 5 years will lower mortality from these cancers. The disadvantage of such a policy is the very significant cost of flexible sigmoidoscopy or colonoscopy, which in most patients will be normal, and the slight risk to patients of these invasive procedures. Clinicians should seek patients at high risk, such as those with strong family histories, if they wish to perform truly effective screening.

For basal and squamous cancers of the skin and mucous membranes (oral, vaginal, and anal), finding smaller asymptomatic cancers during a physical examination can lead to less extensive treatment with improved survival. Other common cancers, such as those of the lung and pancreas, do not merit aggressive attempts at early detection, either because trials have not shown such efforts to be effective, or because the treatment of lesions, even when early, has a low cure rate. In the future, we can hope that gene testing will identify subjects at high risk and permit more precise screening of selected individuals.

A distinction should be made between advising physicians to be alert and informed so that uncommon neoplastic lesions will be recognized on physical examination while still 'early', and advising against the routine use of expensive cancer tests that will have a disappointing and almost useless payoff. One is good; the other is not. A uniform policy regarding screening for cancer in asymptomatic older persons cannot be recommended.

The individual asking for a 'cancer check-up' deserves a thorough examination and appropriate tests. One set of recommendations, that of the American Cancer Society, is listed in Table 3. For a chronic smoker, chest radiography and perhaps sputum cytology should be performed, despite the knowledge that finding a lung cancer on that radiograph may not lead to a better outcome than if one waited until symptoms developed. Not to include a radiograph when the patient asks for a cancer examination is hardly defensible. However, when physicians establish policies about what tests to perform regularly for their patients who are over 65, annual chest radiography cannot be

the controversy centres on whether radical perineal prostatectomy or radiation therapy offers the best chance of control at the least risk to the patient. The operation can be performed with relative safety, but with incontinence and impotence as frequently encountered complications. Radiation therapy, however, avoids an operation, has a lower rate of these complications, and may provide as good local control as surgery. Although approximately 15 per cent of patients fail initial treatment with either approach, about half of these (50 per cent) can be salvaged by the subsequent use of the other modality.

There is less debate about advanced but still regional prostatic cancer, since operation is not indicated and radiotherapy can be important in preventing further local spread, with its pain and obstruction. In the presence of metastases, the decision to treat or not to treat depends on the presence or absence of symptoms. Controlled trials have shown no survival advantage when immediate hormonal therapy is used compared with delaying therapy until symptoms appear, which may be much later. Symptomatic metastases may be treated by radiotherapy, orchidectomy or administration of hormone ablating agents, and chemotherapy.

Conclusions

Cancer in older persons should never be regarded as hopeless or unmanageable. Rather, physicians should remember that great variability is a characteristic not only of older people but also of cancer. Thus the range of preventive and therapeutic approaches needs to be broad, more so than in young adults, and participation by the patient, with his or her support system, gains in importance.

Prevention and early detection do not lose their usefulness when people pass the age of 65, although a decrease in frequency of some cancer screening tests may be possible if a series of normal tests has been recorded in previous years. Also, older persons do not lose their ability to resist cancer or to respond to treatment, despite the evidence for deterioration in certain immune functions and alteration of some pharmacokinetic and pharmacodynamic factors as ageing occurs (Vestal and Calabresi 1997).

As general guides to treatment decisions, physicians are urged to keep the following points in mind.

1. Chronological age is of minor importance in selecting treatment, when compared with comorbid illness and patient choice. Average life expectancy for the 80-year-old patient is still about 8 years, and even at 90, 5 years or more of life may be anticipated.

2. Symptomatic cancer deserves treatment at any age, but appropriate treatment may involve only symptom control and not cancer-directed therapy.

3. During the course of advanced cancer, therapeutic decisions that involve new interventions or discontinuation of ongoing efforts almost always require consultation among the family and friends of the patient, and should entail repeated discussions rather than requiring an abrupt decision that may be heart-rending.

References

Abrams, D.B., Orleans, C.T., Niaura, R.S., Goldstein, M.G., Prochaska, J.O., and Velicer, W. (1996). Integrating individual and public health perspectives for treatment of tobacco dependence under managed health care: a combined stepped-care and matching model. *Annals of Behavioral Medicine*, 18, 290–304.

Akerley, W.L., III and Calabresi, P. (1994). Advanced cancer treatment of the elderly. In *The rational use of advanced medical technology with the elderly* (ed. F. Homburger), pp. 236–49. Springer, New York.

American Cancer Society (1997). American Cancer Society Workshop on Heritable Cancer Syndromes and Genetic Testing. *Cancer* (Supplement), 80.

Balducci, L., Lyman, G.H., and Ershler, W.B. (ed.) (1998). *Comprehensive geriatric oncology*. Hardwood Press, London.

Brady, J.W. and Markoe, A.M. (1986). Radiation therapy in the elderly patient. *Frontiers of Radiation Therapy and Oncology*, 20, 80–92.

Calabresi, P. and Schein, P.S. (ed.) (1993). *Medical oncology* (2nd edn). McGraw-Hill, New York.

Campisi, J. (1997). Ageing and cancer: the double-edged sword of replicative senescence. *Journal of the American Geriatrics Society*, 45, 482–8.

DeVita, V.T., Hellman, S., and Rosenberg, S.A. (1997). *Cancer: principles and practice of oncology* (5th edn). Lippincott–Raven, Philadelphia, PA.

Early Breast Trialists' Collaborative Group (1992). Systemic treatment of early breast cancer by hormonal, cytotoxic, or immune therapy. *Lancet*, 339, 1–15.

Extermann, M. (1997). Acute leukaemia in the elderly. *Clinics in Geriatric Medicine*, 13, 227–44.

Feig, S.A. (1988). Decreased breast cancer mortality through mammographic screening: results of clinical trials. *Radiology*, 167, 659–65.

Fuchs, C.S. and Mayer, R.J. (1995). Adjuvant chemotherapy for colon and rectal cancer. *Seminars in Oncology*, 22, 472–87.

Giovannucci, E., Rimm, E.B., Stampfer, M.J., Colditz, G.A., Ascherio, A., and Willett, W.C. (1994). Aspirin use and the risk for colorectal cancer and adenoma in male health professionals. *Annals of Internal Medicine*, 121, 241–6.

Goodwin, J.S., Samet, J.M., Kay, C.R., Humble, C., Kutvirt, D., and Hunt, C. (1986). Stage at diagnosis of cancer varies with the age of the patient. *Journal of the American Geriatrics Society*, 34, 20–6.

Holland, J.F. and Frei, E.F., III (1997). *Cancer medicine* (4th edn). Williams and Wilkins, Baltimore, MD.

Holmes, F.F. (1989). Clinical evidence for a change in tumour aggressiveness with age. *Seminars in Oncology*, 16, 34–40.

Holmes, F. and Hearne, E. (1981). Cancer stage-to-age relationship: implications for cancer screening in the elderly. *Journal of the American Geriatrics Society*, 29, 1001–14.

International Non-Hodgkin's Lymphoma Prognostic Factors Project (1993). A predictive model for aggressive non-Hodgkin's lymphoma. *New England Journal of Medicine*, 329, 987–94.

Kennedy, B.J. (1997). Aging and cancer: geriatric oncology—keynote address to Integrating Geriatrics into Oncology Education. *Cancer*, 80, 1270–2.

Kinzler, K.W. and Vogelstein, B. (1996). Lessons from hereditary colorectal cancer. *Cell*, 87, 159–70.

Kottke, T.E., Battista, R.N., DeFriese, G.H., and Brekke, M.L. (1988). Attributes of successful smoking cessation interventions in medical practice: a meta-analysis of 39 controlled trials. *Journal of the American Medical Association*, 5, 2882–9.

Lee, S.W. and Wei, J.Y. (1997). Molecular interactions of ageing and cancer. *Clinics in Geriatric Medicine*, 13, 69–77.

Lynch, H.T., Fusaro, R.M., and Lynch, J. (1995). Hereditary cancer in adults. *Cancer Detection and Prevention*, 19, 219–33.

Minton, S.E. and Shaw, G.L. (1998). Chemoprevention of cancer in the elderly. In *Comprehensive geriatric oncology* (ed. L. Balducci, G.H. Lyman, and W.B. Ershler), pp. 307–24. Hardwood Press, London.

Nixon, A.J., Neuberg, D., Hayes, D.F., *et al.* (1994). Relationship of patient age to pathologic features of the tumour and prognosis for patients with Stage I or II breast cancer. *Journal of Clinical Oncology*, 12, 888–94.

O'Reilly, S.E., Connors, J.M., Macpherson, N., Klasa, R., and Hoskins, P. (1997). Malignant lymphomas in the elderly. *Clinics in Geriatric Medicine*, 13, 251–63.

Patterson, W.B. (1989). Surgical issues in geriatric oncology. *Seminars in Oncology*, 16, 57–65.

Thigpen, J.T. (1998). Gynecologic cancers. In *Comprehensive geriatric oncology* (ed. L. Balducci, G.H. Lyman, and W.B. Ershler), pp. 721–32. Hardwood Press, London.

Thune, I., Brenn, T., Lund, E., and Gaard, M. (1997). Physical activity and the risk of breast cancer. *New England Journal of Medicine*, 336, 1269–75.

Valentinis, B., Silvestrini, R., Daidone, M.G., *et al.* (1991). ^{3}H-thymidine labeling index, hormone receptors, and ploidy in breast cancers from elderly patients. *Breast Cancer Research and Treatment*, 20, 19–24.

Vestal, R.E. and Calabresi, P. (1997). Geriatric clinical pharmacologist and medical oncologist: a new partnership? *Clinical Pharmacology and Therapeutics*, 62, 361–4.

Walsh, S.J., Begg, C.B., and Carbone, C.C. (1989). Cancer chemotherapy in the elderly. *Seminars in Oncology*, 16, 66–75.

Walsh, T.D. (1987). Control of pain and other symptoms in advanced cancer. *Oncology*, 1, 5–9.

Warnecke, R.B. (1989). The elderly as a target group for prevention and detection of cancer. In *Cancer in the elderly: approaches to early detection and treatment* (ed. R. Yancik and J. Yates), pp. 3–14. Springer, New York.

11

Stroke

The epidemiology of stroke

Haruko Yamamoto and Julien Bogousslavsky

Stroke is not only one of the leading causes of death in developed countries but is also a major cause of disability leading to impaired quality of life, particularly for elderly people. Since stroke is potentially preventable, understanding the epidemiology of stroke may provide clues for its prevention.

Stroke incidence, mortality, and secular trends

According to the World Health Organization MONICA study, the age-standardized annual incidence of stroke is 100 to 280 per 100 000 in men and 50 to 220 per 100 000 in women in populations in Europe, with the incidence tending to be lower in Western Europe than in Eastern Europe (Thorvaldsen *et al.* 1995). The mortality rate also tends to be higher in Eastern Europe and the former USSR. The incidence rate rises steeply with age in all populations, being 11 to 97 per 100 000 in men and 8 to 55 per 100 000 in women aged 35 to 44 years, but 231 to 639 per 100 000 in men and 111 to 434 per 100 000 in women aged of 55 to 64 years. Mortality rates show a similar trend. In the United Kingdom in 1992, the stroke mortality per 100 000 was seven for both men and women aged 35 to 44 years, but it increased to 291 in men and 230 in women aged 65 to 74 years and to 1351 in men and 1438 in women aged 75 years or more (Khaw 1996). Although men tend to have a slightly higher mortality rate than women, the pronounced male excess of coronary heart disease is not present. Figure 1 shows time trends and international comparisons in stroke mortality from 1950 to 1989 (Khaw 1996). In most of the countries included in the figure, mortality rates decreased by about 30 per cent to 60 per cent in the timespan shown; however, these declines do not necessarily indicate a decline of incidence. In the Framingham Study, incidence rates of stroke were almost the same in men in the three decades which began in 1953, 1963, and 1973, while incidence rates of transient ischaemic attack definitely increased in the same period (Wolf *et al.* 1992*b*). In the Rochester Study, after a 45 per cent decline between 1945 and 1979, incidence rates of stroke increased slightly in both men and women of almost all age groups (Brown *et al.* 1996). The increasingly ageing population and improved detection of minor strokes may keep incidence rates unchanged. Better survival after stroke can be attributed to better diagnoses of milder forms of stroke, better management of risk factors with decreased stroke severity at onset, and improved patient management in the acute phase.

Risk factors

Inherent biological traits

Age

Age is an important risk factor for stroke. Less than 15 per cent of stroke patients are aged less than 45, and at least two-thirds are over 60 (Mas and Zuber 1991). In a 12-year follow-up of the Oslo Study, age was an independent risk factor for first stroke incidence; other risk factors were diastolic blood pressure, presence or absence of cigarette smoking, and amount of physical activity at leisure (Haheim *et al.* 1993).

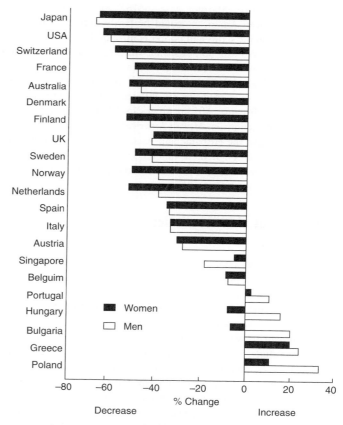

Fig. 1 Changes in age-standardized mortality rates from stroke in men and women in selected countries between 1960 and 1964 and between 1985 and 1989. (Reproduced with permission from Khaw (1996).)

Family history

Although a family history of stroke is believed to be a risk factor, there has not been definitive confirmation by epidemiological study. Maternal history of death from stroke was significantly and independently related to stroke incidence in a cohort study of Swedish men born in 1913 (Welin *et al.* 1987). One study using offspring of the original Framingham Study cohort members showed that both paternal (relative risk 2.4) and maternal (relative risk 1.4) histories of stroke or transient ischaemic attack were associated with an increased risk of stroke (Kiely *et al.* 1993).

Sex

Stroke incidence rates are generally higher in men than women except for subarachnoid haemorrhage, which has an incidence 1.77 times higher in women (Davis 1994). One study showed that carotid stenosis and internal carotid artery wall thickening were greater in men than in women at all ages (O'Leary *et al.* 1992). Women have a lower incidence of transient ischaemic accident and of stroke after transient ischaemic attack compared with men (Davis 1994). These differences may contribute to a lower incidence of stroke.

Ethnic group

It is true that the incidence of stroke is different among human races, but it may be greatly affected by sociocultural and socio-economic differences. For example, after migration to the United States, Japanese men experienced stroke incidence similar to that of Caucasian men in the United States (Marmot *et al.* 1975). An excess of stroke incidence in African Americans could be partly explained by their lower socio-economic status and poorer control of the cardiovascular risk factors compared with non-Hispanic whites (Gillum 1988). Stroke mortality in Asian Indian men in England and Wales has been reported to be higher than the average for men in those countries (Balarajan 1991). In a study of six different ethnic groups (non-Hispanic white, Hispanic, African American, Chinese, Japanese, and Asian Indian) in California, African Americans had the highest death rate for stroke, and the Hispanic and Asian Indian populations had the lowest rates, although these differences were most marked for women and younger age groups, and differences decreased in older age groups (Wild *et al.* 1995).

Physiological characteristics

Blood pressure

Hypertension is the major treatable risk factor for stroke (see also Chapter 11.2). Most prospective studies observed increased incidence of stroke with increased blood pressure, both systolic and diastolic, without threshold (Khaw 1996). In the Framingham Study, the relative risk of stroke in hypertensive patients was 3.1 in men, 2.9 in women, and 1.5 in patients with borderline hypertension (Wolf *et al.* 1992a). In the same study, 56.4 per cent of stroke in men and 66.1 per cent in women was estimated to be reduced if hypertension was effectively treated. Isolated systolic hypertension, which is increasingly prevalent, particularly in the elderly, also increases the risk of stroke. The final results of the Systolic Hypertension in the Elderly Program (SHEP Cooperative Research Group 1991) showed that antihypertensive stepped-care drug treatment reduced the incidence of total stroke by 36 per cent, as well as reducing major cardiovascular events in people with isolated systolic hypertension who were aged 60 years or more. Although systolic blood pressure exerts a greater impact on stroke incidence, diastolic blood pressure level is independently related to risk of stroke. In a meta-analysis of the results from 45 prospective cohorts, relative risks of stroke in the highest diastolic blood pressure category were tenfold, fivefold, and twofold in patients aged below 45 years, 45 to 64 years, and 65 years or more respectively, compared with a combination of the lowest two blood pressure categories (Prospective Studies Collaboration 1995). The presence of adverse effects of lowering blood pressure (the J-shaped curve) is controversial and may not be an excuse for not treating hypertension in the elderly. The impact of hypertension as a risk factor for stroke decreases with age. Some studies have shown that the incidence of stroke in the hypertensive group was 10 times greater at the age of 45 to 54 years; however, it decreased to twice greater in group aged over 65 (Curb *et al.* 1996). These findings may not indicate that hypertension is not a large risk for stroke, but rather that even normotensives have a higher stroke incidence as elderly persons.

Blood cholesterol

Several prospective studies have shown that a low blood cholesterol level is a risk factor for haemorrhagic stroke in Japanese populations, Japanese men living in Hawaii, white men and women, and men aged 65 years or more (Iribarren *et al.* 1996). This adverse effect is seen in very low serum cholesterol categories (less than 180 mg/dl, and particularly less than 160 mg/dl), and some investigators have hypothesized that very low serum cholesterol levels weaken the endothelium of intracerebral arteries, resulting in haemorrhagic stroke in the presence of hypertension. As for ischaemic stroke, however, it remains equivocal whether hypercholesterolaemia is a risk factor. No clear influence of total cholesterol on atherothrombotic brain infarction was observed in the 36-year follow-up data in the Framingham Study (Wolf *et al.* 1992a), but the Honolulu Heart Program demonstrated a relative risk of 1.6 of elevated serum cholesterol for thromboembolic stroke in Japanese Hawaiian men aged 60 to 74 years but not in those aged 51 to 59 years (Benfante *et al.* 1994). A meta-analysis of the results of tests on 45 prospective cohorts did not show a positive relationship between stroke incidence and serum cholesterol level. However, since episodes of ischaemic stroke were not separated from those of haemorrhagic stroke, a positive association with ischaemic stroke could be counterbalanced by a negative association with haemorrhagic stroke (Prospective Studies Collaboration 1995). Several studies using ultrasonography showed that serum lipid levels are related to extracranial carotid artery atherosclerosis and internal carotid artery wall thickness. Autopsy studies have also shown a relationship between atherosclerosis in the circle of Willis and serum lipid levels. The data concerning each lipid subtype are few and inconsistent.

Diabetes mellitus

Glucose intolerance raises the risk of thromboembolic but not haemorrhagic stroke. In the Honolulu Heart Program, relative risks of thromboembolic stroke were 2.5 for patients with diabetes and 1.4 for subjects with high plasma glucose levels without a known history of diabetes, after adjustment for other risk factors (Burchfiel *et al.* 1994). A prospective study in a Finnish cohort of 1298 subjects aged 65 to 74 years showed that fasting and 2-h glucose and glycosylated haemoglobin A_1c predicted stroke events in all study subjects, as well

disease are at higher than average risk for coronary heart disease and vice versa. In epidemiological studies there appears to be no association of total cholesterol with stroke in later life, although in a large systematic review (Fig. 3) there was a trend of a positive association in subjects screened before age 45 (Prospective Studies Collaboration 1995). It is possible that a positive association of serum cholesterol with occlusive stroke is being masked by a negative association with haemorrhagic stroke (Iso *et al.* 1989). Recent overviews of the effects of treatment of patients with ischaemic heart disease with statins show a 29 per cent reduction in stroke (Hebert *et al.* 1997). However, the patients enrolled in the reviewed trials were young (average age under 65). Again, the burden of proof lies with those who assume that the findings would not apply to older people.

References

Amery, A., Birkenhäger, W., Brixko, R., *et al.* (1985). Mortality and morbidity results from the European Working Party on High Blood Pressure in The Elderly trial. *Lancet*, i, 1349–54.

Antiplatelet Trialists' Collaboration (1994). Collaborative overview of randomised trials of antiplatelet therapy. I. Prevention of death, myocardial infarction, and stroke by prolonged antiplatelet therapy in various categories of patients. *British Medical Journal*, 308, 81–106.

Atrial Fibrillation Investigators (1994). Risk factors for stroke and efficacy of anti-thrombotic therapy in atrial fibrillation. Analysis of pooled data from 5 randomised controlled trials. *Archives of Internal Medicine*, 154, 1449–57.

Brennan, P.J., Greenberg, G., Miall, W.E., and Thompson, S.F. (1982). Seasonal variation in arterial blood pressure. *British Medical Journal*, 285, 919–23.

Camargo, C.A. (1989). Moderate alcohol consumption and stroke. The epidemiological evidence. *Stroke*, 20, 1611–26.

CAPRIE Steering Committee (1996). A randomised, blinded, trial of clopidogrel versus aspirin in patients at risk of ischaemic events (CAPRIE). *Lancet*, 348, 1329–39.

CAST (Chinese Acute Stroke Trial) Collaborative Group (1997). CAST: randomised placebo-controlled trial of early aspirin use in 20 000 patients with acute ischaemic stroke. *Lancet*, 349,1641–9.

Collins, R. and MacMahon, S. (1994). Blood pressure, antihypertensive drug treatment and the risks of stroke and of coronary heart disease. *British Medical Bulletin*, 50, 272–98.

Collins, R., Peto, R., MacMahon, S., *et al.* (1990). Blood pressure, stroke, and coronary heart disease. Part 2, Short term reductions in blood pressure: overview of randomised drug trials in their epidemiological context. *Lancet*, 335, 827–38.

Croog, S.H., Levine, S., Sudilovsky, A., Baume, R.M., and Clive, J. (1988). Sexual symptoms in hypertensive patients: a clinical trial of anti-hypertensive medications. *Archives of Internal Medicine*, 148, 78–94.

Diener, H.C., Cunha, L., Forbes, C., Sivenius, J., Smets, P., and Lowenthal, A. (1996). European Stroke Prevention Study 2. Dipyridamole and acetylsalicylic acid in the secondary prevention of stroke. *Journal of Neurological Sciences*, 143, 1–13.

Doll, R., Peto, R., Hall, E., Wheatley, K., and Gray R (1994a). Mortality in relation to smoking: 13 years' observations on male British doctors. *British Medical Journal*, 309, 901–11.

Doll, R., Peto, R., Hall, E., Wheatley, K., and Gray, R (1994b). Mortality in relation to consumption of alcohol: 13 years' observations on male British doctors. *British Medical Journal*, 309, 911–18.

European Carotid Surgery Trialists' Collaborative Group (1991). MRC European Carotid Surgery Trial: interim results for symptomatic patients with severe (70–90 per cent) or with mild (0–29 per cent) carotid stenosis. *Lancet*, 337, 1235–43.

European Carotid Surgery Trialists' Collaborative Group (1998). Randomised trial of endarterectomy for recently symptomatic carotid stenosis: final results of the MRC European Carotid Surgery Trial (ECST). *British Medical Journal*, 315, 1571–7.

Gill, J.S., Davies, P., Ill, S.K., and Beevers, D.G. (1988). Wind-chill and the seasonal variation of cerebrovascular disease. *Journal of Clinical Epidemiology*, 41, 225–30.

Green, C.J., Hadorn, D., and Kazanjian, A. (1995). *Anticoagulation for stroke prevention in chronic non-valvular atrial fibrillation*. Discussion Paper Series BCOHTA95: 2D, BCC Office of Health Technology Assessment, Vancouver. Centre for Health Services and Policy Research, University of British Columbia, Vancouver.

Grimley Evans, J. (1987). Blood pressure and stroke in an elderly English population. *Journal of Epidemiology and Community Health*, 41, 275–82.

Grimley Evans, J., Prudham, D., and Wandless, I. (1980). Risk factors for stroke in the elderly. In *The ageing brain: neurological and mental disturbances* (ed. G. Barbagallo-Sangiori and A.N. Exton-Smith), pp. 113–26. Plenum Press, London.

Hart, R.G. and Halperin, J.L. (1994). Atrial fibrillation and stroke: revisiting the dilemmas. *Stroke*, 25, 1337–41.

Hart, R.G., Boop, B.S., and Anderson, D.C. (1995). Oral anticoagulants and intracranial haemorrhage. Facts and hypotheses. *Stroke*, 25, 1471–7.

He, J., Whelton, P.K., Vu, B., and Klag, M.J. (1998). Aspirin and risk of hemorrhagic stroke. A meta-analysis of randomized controlled trials. *Journal of the American Medical Association*, 280, 1930–5.

Hebert, P.R., Gaziano, M., Chan, K.S., and Hennekens, C.H. (1997). Cholesterol lowering with statin drugs, risk of stroke, and total mortality. *Journal of the American Medical Association*, 278, 313–21.

Hermanson, B., Omenn, G.S., Kronmal, R.A., *et al.* (1988). Beneficial six-year outcome of smoking cessation in older men and women with coronary heart disease. Results from the CASS registry. *New England Journal of Medicine*, 319, 1365–9.

Howard, G., Wagenknecht, L.E., Burke, G.L. *et al.* (1998). Cigarette smoking and progression of atherosclerosis. The Atherosclerosis Risk in Communities (ARIC) Study. *Journal of the American Medical Association*, 279, 119–124.

Iso, H., Jacobs, D.R., Wentworth, D., Neaton, J., and Cohen, J.D. (1989). Serum cholesterol levels and six-year mortality from stroke in 350 977 men screened for the multiple risk factor intervention trial. *New England Journal of Medicine*, 320, 904–10.

Jackson, R., Barham, P., Bills, J., *et al.* (1993). Management of raised blood pressure in New Zealand. *British Medical Journal*, 307, 107–10.

Kerdiles, Y., Lucas, A., Podeur, L., Ferte, P., and Cardon, A. (1997). Results of carotid surgery in elderly patients. *Journal of Cardiovascular Surgery (Torino)*, 38, 327–34.

Kirkendall, W.M. (1988). Comparative assessment of first-line agents for treatment of hypertension. *American Journal of Medicine*, 84 (Supplement 3B), 32–41.

Koudstaal, P.J. (1995). Secondary prevention following stroke or transient ischaemic attack in patients with nonrheumatic atrial fibrillation: anticoagulants versus antiplatelet therapy. In *The Cochrane database of systematic reviews 1995 (Issue 1)* (ed. C. Warlow, J. van Gijn, and P. Sandercock). BMJ Publishers, London.

Langhorne, P., Williams, B.O., Gilchrist, W., and Howie, K. (1993). Do stroke units save lives? *Lancet*, 342, 392–8.

MacMahon, S. (1987). Alcohol consumption and hypertension. *Hypertension*, 9, 525–8.

Miall, W.E. and Brennan, P.J. (1981). Hypertension in the elderly. In *Hypertension in the young and old* (ed. G. Onesti and K.E. Kimm), pp. 277–83. Grune and Stratton, New York.

Moreyra, E., Omron, E.M., Jeffrey, M., and Katz, R. (1995). Treatment of atrial fibrillation: European versus US practice—are we oceans apart? *British Journal of Cardiology*, 2-3, 73–76.

Perry, I.J., Refsum, H., Morris, R.W., Ebrahim, S.B., Ueland, P.M., and Shaper, A.G. (1995). Prospective study of serum total homocysteine concentration and risk of stroke in middle-aged British men. *Lancet*, 346, 1395–8.

Prospective Studies Collaboration (1995). Cholesterol, diastolic blood pressure, and stroke: 13 000 strokes in 450 000 people in 45 prospective cohorts. *Lancet*, 346, 1647–53.

Prystowsky, E.N., Benson, D.W., Fuster, V., *et al.* (1996). management of patients with atrial fibrillation. a statement for healthcare professionals from the Subcommittee on Electrocardiography and Electrophysiology, American Heart Association. *Circulation*, 93, 1262–77.

Qizilbash, N. (1995). Fibrinogen and cerebrovascular disease. *European Heart Journal*, 16 (Supplement A), 42–6.

Qizilbash, N., Jones, L., Warlow, C., and Mann, J. (1991). Fibrinogen and lipid concentrations as risk factors for transient ischaemic attacks and minor ischaemic strokes. *British Medical Journal*, 303, 6605–9.

Qizilbash, N., Duffy, S.W., Prentice, C.R.M., Boothby, M., and Warlow, C. (1997). Von Willebrand factor and risk of ischaemic stroke. *Neurology*, 49, 1552–6.

Ray, W.A., Griffin, M.R., Downey, W., and Melton, L.J. (1989). Long term use of thiazide diuretics and risks of hip fracture. *Lancet*, i, 687–90.

Ridker, P.M., Hennekens, C.H., Stampfer, M.J., Manson, J.E., and Vaughan, D.E. (1994). Prospective study of endogenous tissue plasminogen activator and risk of stroke. *Lancet*, 343, 940–3.

Rose, G. (1992). *The strategy of preventive medicine*. Oxford University Press.

Rothwell, P.M., Wroe, S.J., Slattery, J., *et al.* (1996). Is stroke incidence related to season or temperature? *Lancet*, 347, 934–6.

Sandercock, P.A.G., Bamford, J., Dennis, M., *et al.* (1992). Atrial fibrillation and stroke: prevalence in different stroke types and influence on early and long term prognosis (Oxfordshire Community Stroke Project). *British Medical Journal*, 305, 1460–5.

SHEP Cooperative Research Group (1991). Prevention of stroke by antihypertensive drug treatment in older patients with isolated systolic hypertension: final results of the Systolic hypertension in the Elderly Program (SHEP). *Journal of the American Medical Association*, 265, 3255–64.

Staessen, J., Fagard, R., Van Hoof, R., and Amery, A. (1988). Mortality in various intervention trials: a review. *European Heart Journal*, 9, 215–22.

Van Ruiswyk, J., Noble, H., and Sigmann, P. (1990). The natural history of carotid bruits in elderly persons. *Annals of Internal Medicine*, 112, 340–3.

Wardlaw, J.M., Warlow, C.P., and Counsell, C. (1997). Systematic review of evidence on thrombolytic therapy for acute ischaemic stroke. *Lancet*, 350, 607–14.

Weil, J., Colin-Jones, D., Langman, M., *et al.* (1995) Prophylactic aspirin and risk of peptic ulcer bleeding. *British Medical Journal*, 310, 827–30.

Whisnant, J.P. (1976). A population study of stroke and TIA: Rochester, Minnesota. In *Stroke* (ed. F.J. Gillingham, C. Mawdsley, and A.E. Williams), pp. 21–39. Churchill Livingstone, Edinburgh.

Wilhelmsen, L., Svardsudd, K., Korsan-Bengsten, K., Larsson, B., Welin, L., and Tibblin, G. (1984). Fibrinogen as a risk factor for stroke and myocardial infarction. *New England Journal of Medicine*, 311, 501–5.

Wolf, P.A., Abbott, R.D., and Kannel, W.B. (1991). Atrial fibrillation as an independent risk factor for stroke: the Framingham Study. *Stroke*, 22, 983–8.

Woodhouse, P.R., Khaw, K.T., Plummer, M., Foley, A., and Meade, T.W. (1994). Seasonal variations of plasma fibrinogen and factor VII activity in the elderly: winter infections and death from cardiovascular disease. *Lancet*, 343, 435–9.

11.3 Pathology of stroke

Nigel M. Hyman

The pathology of stroke is essentially the study of cerebral arterial disease. The two major pathological processes causing stroke are infarction, in which brain tissue is deprived of blood supply, and haemorrhage.

Roughly 85 per cent of acute strokes are due to occlusion of a cerebral artery causing cerebral infarction. The remaining 15 per cent are due to either primary intracerebral haemorrhage or haemorrhage secondary to aneurysmal rupture. Of the cases of cerebral infarction, 75 per cent occur in the territory of the middle cerebral artery, 15 per cent in the vertebrobasilar territory, and 10 per cent in the border zones between the territories of two major arteries. Cerebral infarction may be due to primary thrombosis in an artery or may be secondary to occlusion of the vessel by an embolus.

Atherosclerosis is the principal arterial disease causing occlusive stroke in elderly people. The distribution of the atheroma reflects sites of turbulent blood flow and mechanical stresses on the vessel wall. Extracranially, the three most important sites are the bifurcation of the common carotid and the origins of both the common carotid and vertebral arteries. Intracranially, important sites include the vertebral and basilar arteries, the carotid siphon, and the first parts of both the middle cerebral and posterior cerebral arteries.

Thrombosis or embolism

The proportion of cerebral infarcts due to embolism is uncertain but is probably of the order of 50 per cent (Table 1). Difficulties in this

Table 1 Main causes of cerebral arterial embolism in elderly people

Principal sites of extracranial arterial atheroma
Common carotid bifurcation
Origins of the common carotid
Vertebral arteries

Principal sites of intracranial arterial atheroma
Carotid siphon
Vertebral arteries near junction with basilar artery
Basilar artery itself

Cardiac origin
Left atrium: thrombi or myxoma
Mitral valve: vegetation in bacterial and marantic endocarditis; prosthesis; mitral annulus calcification
Left ventricle: mural thrombi from myocardial infarction
Aortic valve: sclerosis and calcification; prosthesis; vegetations in bacterial and marantic endocarditis

Trauma
Direct trauma to neck
Cervical fracture–dislocation

Table 2 Main causes of cerebral arterial thrombosis in elderly people

Atheroma	
Vasculitis	Giant cell (temporal) arteritis
	Polyarteritis nodosa
	Endarteritis obliterans due to tuberculosis
	Syphilis
Haematological disorders	Polycythaemia rubra vera
	Essential thrombocythaemia
	Hyperviscosity syndromes, e.g. myeloma

differential diagnosis at a pathological level arise for several reasons. Firstly, a recent embolus is softer than an *in situ* thrombus and is usually relatively free from the vessel wall but an old lesion may be incorporated into the arterial wall and indistinguishable microscopically. Secondly, a source of embolism, for example from the heart, may be found in association with occlusion of the middle cerebral artery but this relationship could be coincidental rather than causal. About one-third of cerebral emboli arise from the carotid arteries, principally the bifurcation of the common carotid (Fig. 1).

Fig. 1 Atheroma at the origin of the internal carotid artery causing severe stenosis.

Cardiac sources include rheumatic valvular disease, prosthetic mitral valves, and both infective and non-infective valve vegetations. The latter, marantic endocarditis, is an underdiagnosed cause of stroke disease in patients with associated neoplasia. Mitral annulus calcification is common in elderly subjects but the precise association with stroke is unclear. Left ventricular mural thrombi are a source of embolic stroke, particularly complicating full-thickness myocardial infarction.

Although atheroma is by far the most common cause of thrombo-occlusive stroke in elderly people, there are other causes that remain important in view of their therapeutic implications (Table 2).

Rarely, giant cell arteritis can involve the extracranial vertebral arteries to produce a completed brainstem infarction. Polyarteritis nodosa characteristically causes multiple infarcts and haemorrhages in the cortex, white matter, basal ganglia, and brainstem. Systemic lupus erythematosus is a rare disease in elderly people but can cause stroke, particularly in association with the lupus anticoagulant (Mueh *et al.* 1980). Endarteritis obliterans (a reaction of arteries to systemic bacterial infection) can complicate meningovascular syphilis and both pyogenic and tuberculous meningitis. Primary angiitis of the central nervous system (Calabrese and Mallek 1988) occurs in all age groups and can cause stroke, although headache and dementia are more common. The risk of cerebral infarction is increased in polycythaemia, either primary or secondary, essential thrombocythaemia, and chronic myeloid leukaemia with very high white cell counts. Thrombotic arterial lesions are described in hyperviscosity syndromes, particularly Waldenström's macroglobulinaemia and multiple myeloma.

Cerebral infarction

A cerebral infarct is an area of brain in which the blood flow has fallen below the critical level necessary to maintain the viability of the tissue. Early infarction of a major vascular territory is reflected grossly at autopsy by a swollen softened area of brain, which may be more easily detected by palpation than seen with the naked eye. It may be impossible to detect very recent infarction (less than 8 h) until a microscopic examination is made. The separation of infarcted tissue from adjacent relatively normal tissue takes 48 h, and by 3 to 4 days the lesion is well defined and the swelling is greatest. The boundaries of older infarcts are altogether crisper. A cavity 1 cm in diameter is thought to take 3 months to form and very large infarctions may never completely cavitate.

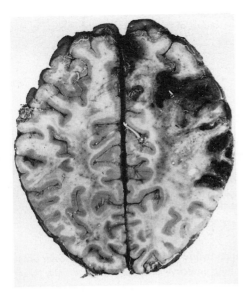

Fig. 2 Haemorrhagic infarction in distribution of both the anterior and middle cerebral arteries.

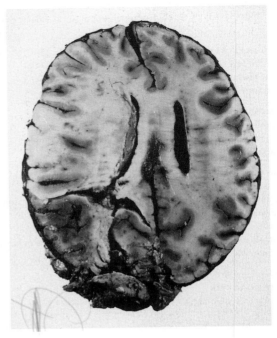

Fig. 3 Massive infarction of the left hemisphere with haemorrhagic infarction of the occipital lobe (see text).

Microscopically the earliest changes include an increase in interstitial fluid within the white matter. Neurones develop ischaemic necrosis with nuclear pyknosis and there is necrosis of glial cells, capillaries, arterioles, and venules, swelling of axons, and pallor of myelin. In pale infarcts there is little or no extravasation of red cells into the lesion but in haemorrhagic infarction the capillary and venular extravasation produces either discrete petechiae, confluent purpura, or frank haemorrhage. The distinction between pale and haemorrhagic infarction is probably unimportant in mild cases as nearly all infarcts show a few petechiae, particularly at the margins. Nevertheless, roughly 30 per cent of cerebral infarcts examined at autopsy are termed haemorrhagic. In those strokes thought to have an embolic basis, at least half are haemorrhagic (Fig. 2). The mechanism of haemorrhagic infarction is complex and may not be due to a single cause. The endothelium of the obstructed blood vessel becomes ischaemic, without vessel rupture, and as the embolus fragments and passes more distally blood seeps through the vessel wall into the adjacent brain substance. Another important factor, subsequent to the lysis of the embolus, is the sudden restoration of blood through the now patent vessel. The ischaemic capillaries rupture and there is secondary irrigation with consequent haemorrhage, particularly involving the cortex. Haemorrhagic infarction is very common in cardioembolic infarcts and less common in watershed infarcts and when infarction complicates vasospasm after subarachnoid haemorrhage.

Within the first week, after both pale and haemorrhagic infarction, capillary hyperplasia and microglial infiltration occur. Eventually the infarcted area shrinks and larger lesions show cavitation traversed by septa. As the lesion shrinks there may be compensatory enlargement of an adjacent ventricle and depression of the cortical surface.

A gradient of blood flow exists after complete occlusion of an artery, and consequently there is absence of flow in the central zone of a vessel's territory and normal or increased flow at the periphery of the territory. It is suggested that this peripheral zone, which is ischaemic and swollen, has not reached a state of irreversible infarction.

The 'ischaemic penumbra' hypothesis is attractive as a rationale for specific forms of treatment for acute stroke but remains controversial, largely because of variable results in animal experiments.

Brain swelling after stroke

Most deaths directly due to acute ischaemic strokes occur within the first 7 days after the onset and are secondary to a complication of cerebral oedema. The latter has two components: (a) 'cytotoxic' oedema due to water entering the cells and producing astrocytic swelling; (b) 'vasogenic' oedema at the periphery of the ischaemic lesion, which causes breakdown in the blood–brain barrier and allows extravasation of proteins into the extracellular space. The rise in oncotic pressure increases water entry into the ischaemic area, which in turn adds to the degree of swelling of the infarct. The oedema reaches a peak 2 to 7 days after the onset and in the case of major infarction in the territory of the middle cerebral artery there is herniation of the ipsilateral cingulate gyrus beneath the free edge of the falx. More importantly there is downward displacement of the brain through the tentorial notch with compression of the diencephalon and adjacent midbrain and subsequent brainstem haemorrhages. Another complication of transtentorial herniation is compression of the posterior cerebral vessels with infarction of the ipsilateral occipital lobe (Fig. 3). Such lesions are usually haemorrhagic and may reflect venous rather than arterial occlusion.

Topography of cerebral infarctions

Variations in individual anastomotic pathways, in association with the degree of atheromatous disease and the speed of occlusion, all

Table 5 Baseline investigations for an elderly stroke patient

Full blood count

Erythrocyte sedimentation rate (and/or C-reactive protein)

Plasma glucose

Plasma urea, creatinine, and electrolytes

Urine analysis

ECG

Chest radiograph

Thyroid function tests (if in atrial fibrillation)

CT or MRI scan (where diagnosis is uncertain or antiplatelet, thrombolytic, or anticoagulant therapy is under consideration)

causes include jugular venous catheterization and drugs such as oestrogens and androgens.

Subarachnoid haemorrhage

Subarachnoid haemorrhage in older patients is more often due to aneurysms than to arteriovenous malformations. Cerebral amyloid angiopathy is also a recognized cause, as are mycotic aneurysms from infective endocarditis.

Clinical assessment

If patients are to be considered for thrombolytic therapy speed is of the essence and initial clinical assessment may be directed simply at establishing the diagnosis of stroke, checking exclusion criteria, and ensuring respiratory function and cardiovascular stability before CT scanning. Once such urgencies have been discharged, or where thrombolytic therapy is not under consideration, a calmer and more comprehensive assessment is required to identify any specific needs for care and to establish a baseline of disability for future measurements of progress. Table 5 outlines baseline investigations that will normally be required for an older stroke patient. Other investigations may be indicated by features in the history or clinical examination.

The unconscious patient

The chief prognostic factors for early death in stroke are level of consciousness and the presence of eye signs suggestive of brainstem involvement. In the individual case, however, progress may be better than initial assessments suggest, and so changes in the level of consciousness and in brainstem signs need to be monitored over at least 24 h before views are formed over prognosis and whether treatment should be purely palliative. It is obviously crucial to be sure that the unconsciousness is due only to stroke and that there is no possibility of a drug overdose.

The level of consciousness should be measured, and the Glasgow Coma Scale (see Chapter 27) is useful. Pupil size and reactivity should be noted, as should eye position. If spontaneous eye movements are not occurring, the doll's eye manoeuvre should be performed. Caloric tests are not usually indicated at this stage but may be needed later if it is necessary to establish brainstem death for legal purposes, for

organ donation, or to clarify the situation for concerned family members.

If the patient shows no improvement, or shows a deterioration in conscious level over 48 h, prospects of useful recovery become more remote and it is usual to review the patient's resuscitation status at this stage. If it is decided that attempts at resuscitation would be futile or undesirable and the patient should be allowed to die, local custom and the sensitivities of the patient's relatives should be consulted over issues of continuing intravenous fluids or other forms of nutrition. Scrupulous general nursing care should continue. The focus of concern may shift at this stage from the patient to his or her relatives, and palliative treatment given for features of the patient that might distress relatives. A common example is the use of hyoscine, and perhaps morphia, to relieve noisy breathing due to the accumulation of pharyngeal secretions. Relatives are often uncertain over their proper role, and their own mental and physical health may suffer from excessive attendance at hospital. They may be helped by some fairly directive advice from the patient's doctor about sharing the bedside vigil, and by confidence in the nurses' commitment to contacting family members if the patient's condition deteriorates.

Swallowing

Dysphagia occurs in around a third of patients with acute stroke and can occur in unilateral cortical lesions (Hamdy *et al.* 1997). Owing to the risk of inhalational pneumonia, stroke patients should be formally assessed for the presence of dysphagia before feeding is allowed. The presence or absence of the gag reflex is not a good guide to the risk of inhalation, and a more elaborate assessment is required (see Chapter 8.2). Although assessment of swallowing is increasingly being undertaken by speech therapists, it is a skill that can usefully be acquired by all doctors and nurses looking after stroke patients. There is as yet no agreed practice with regard to managing the nutrition of stroke patients affected by dysphagia. Percutaneous gastrostomy (placed endoscopically or radiologically) is being used more often but opinions differ over how long a patient should be given for recovery of swallowing before the operation is considered. A randomized trial demonstrated the superiority of gastrostomy over nasogastric feeding for patients who were still dysphagic 14 days after stroke (Norton *et al.* 1996). Some older stroke patients are poorly nourished at the time of admission and might benefit from earlier gastrostomy feeding. There are, however, ethical issues involved in the timing of gastrostomy for severely disabled patients or those who are unable to give informed consent. It has to be recognized that although gastrostomy solves the problem of nutrition it may not prevent pneumonia due to aspiration of saliva or regurgitated stomach contents. Opinions also differ on the use of nasogastric tubes; some clinicians consider that they impair the recovery of swallowing and make aspiration more rather than less likely. Some relevant clinical trials are in progress, but in the meantime there may be virtue in ward teams agreeing on local guidelines.

Motor features

Detailed assessment of motor function may be difficult in a patient who is confused, dysphasic, or unconscious. Paralysis may have to be inferred in the last case by asymmetry in tone between limbs. Usually in acute stroke, the affected limbs are flaccid, with increase in tone and reflexes appearing later. Increased tone does not always occur, however, and flaccid paralysis of limbs may continue. Examination of the cranial nerves is important if hindbrain ischaemia or haemorrhage is suspected; cerebellar features may not be apparent in the unconscious patient.

Neurological causes of resistance of limbs to passive movement in older patients with cerebrovascular disease include rigidity and *gegenhalten* ('holding against'), as well as spasticity. In the rigidity of parkinsonism the resistance is constant throughout the range of movement and is unaffected by the force applied. This 'lead-pipe' rigidity may be modified by a superimposed tremor to produce the well-known pattern of cog-wheel rigidity. In uncomplicated spasticity, increased force may lead to sudden loss of resistance in the 'clasp-knife' pattern, although it may not be appropriate to try to elicit this effect in a frail older patient. In *gegenhalten* the resistance to movement increases with increases in the force applied. This usually indicates frontal lobe damage.

Sensory features

Patients may not recognize that they have a visual field defect, as the brain 'fills in' the missing part of the field. It may also be difficult to test for in an uncooperative patient, but behavioural clues may be present. A patient may look to a person on his right when spoken to from his left for example. Visual inattention (neglect) is common, particularly in non-dominant hemisphere strokes. In this condition the patient can perceive a visual or tactile stimulus on either side of the body when only one side is tested, but perceives only on one side when both are stimulated simultaneously. This is relevant in rehabilitation since important environmental stimuli such as door-posts are symmetrical. Inattention may be overlooked by the examining clinician if it is not routinely looked for in testing a stroke patient's visual fields and limb sensation. It may or may not be associated with more general features of contralateral neglect. These may range from complete loss of awareness of a hemiparetic side of the body and of the same side of space, to minor abnormalities such as finger agnosia.

Speech

It is surprising how often a stroke patient's aphasia may be unrecognized or mistaken for some other syndrome such as delirium, depression, or dementia. There is also a common tendency for carers to overestimate an aphasic patient's ability to comprehend speech, and this can be important where understanding has to be assured for legal or ethical reasons, for example in giving consent to treatment or in drawing up a power of attorney. The Frenchay Aphasia Screening Test (Enderby *et al.* 1987) is a useful brief screening instrument for aphasia in patients with stroke (see Chapter 27).

There have been many classifications of dysphasia, but none has proved universally useful in clinical practice. A simple classification into receptive, motor, and mixed helps in explaining a patient's difficulties to family and friends, and guides professional staff in their approach to a patient. For a patient with receptive difficulties it is sometimes valuable to test reading, as a more reliable mode of communication, but use of pictures may be of more practical use. Aphasias have also been classified into fluent and non-fluent but this is less useful clinically. In general non-fluency implies motor difficulties, while fluency, for example in the more dramatic variant of jargon dysphasia, indicates sensory problems in that the patient does not recognize that what he is saying does not make sense.

'Higher-order' defects

These comprise agnosias and apraxias. In agnosia an object may be seen but not recognized for what it is, or a patient cannot form a coherent cognitive construct from sensory data. A patient with apraxia is unable to carry out tasks even though he is physically capable of the individual motor components of the task. It is important to recognize such defects as they impede rehabilitation and can cause problems with carers who suspect the patient of 'playing up' or being overdependent. A typical situation is of a patient with 'dressing apraxia' (usually, in fact, a mixed motor and sensory higher-order defect) whose exasperated wife complained that 'he can move his arms and see his coat, why does he need me to put it on him all the time?' Some of the more bizarre agnosias are well known as clinical curiosities. Anosagnosia in which the patient with a severe hemiplegia (usually on the left in a right-handed patient) who denies any impairment and never gains insight into his difficulties. Prosopagnosia in which the patient fails to recognize faces can be particularly distressing to friends and relatives, until the problem is explained and they learn always to give the patient a chance to recognize them by their voices. Agnosia can be disabling in the activities of daily life, for a patient who cannot recognize a telephone or a kettle for example.

Investigations

General

The investigations set out in Table 5 should usually be requested for a patient with suspected stroke in order to alert the clinician to additional or alternative diagnoses.

Radiology of stroke

In the acute stroke, radiology may be required to confirm the diagnosis and, where thrombolytic or antiplatelet therapy is being considered, to ensure that no haemorrhage is present. CT scanning is widely available and commonly the first recourse in this situation. The period after the onset of ischaemic stroke is the crucial interval for thrombolytic therapy; no brain changes are detectable on CT scanning. Indeed, if changes are visible, there is a high risk that thrombolytic therapy will induce haemorrhage into the infarct. The sensitivity of CT scanning to such changes varies with the sophistication of the equipment, and this can be a source of error in the assessment of patients for thrombolytic treatment. CT scanning may also reveal thrombi in intracranial vessels as hyperdense lesions, although the presence of calcium in vessel walls may mislead. CT scanning is not reliable for detecting lesions in the brainstem and hindbrain, and small lesions in the basal ganglia may be undetectable. MRI can detect ischaemic lesions earlier than CT through its sensitivity to oedema and it will also give good pictures of the brainstem and hindbrain. More sophisticated radiological techniques are under development.

CT is a sensitive method for detecting cerebral haemorrhage. In monitoring haemorrhage, for example in following a minor cerebellar haemorrhage, MRI may be more sensitive (Gilman 1998). CT is the investigation of choice for the initial diagnosis of subarachnoid haemorrhage, although sensitivity is less than 100 per cent. If the clinical picture is typical and CT is negative, lumbar puncture should be performed and the cerebrospinal fluid inspected for blood and xanthochromia, and analysed spectrophotometrically for haemoglobin and derivatives. Both CT and cerebrospinal fluid usually return to normal within 2 to 3 weeks after a subarachnoid haemorrhage.

instruments relevant to patients with stroke is available (Wade 1992). A minimal requirement would be some form of mental function score and some measure of activities of daily living. In geriatric practice in the United Kingdom the two most widely used scores for clinical purposes are the Abbreviated Mental Test Score (AMTS) and the Barthel Activities of Daily Living Score (see Chapter 27). A wide range of rating scales for rehabilitation is available, and geriatrics teams and the social service teams with which they engage, are well advised to agree on a small number of specific measures they are going to use. Ease of administration is important for measures that are to be used routinely. In addition to ensuring that measures are adequately assessed for validity, reliability, and sensitivity, teams should be sure that the range of the measures is appropriate and that ceiling and floor effects will not be troublesome. The AMTS, for example, is suitable only for the range of mental impairments to be encountered in geriatric or psychogeriatric units. The Mini Mental State Examination (see Chapter 27) is more suitable for detecting smaller degrees of impairment.

Preparing the home

The aim of rehabilitation is to reduce the ecological gap between what a person's environment demands and what he or she is capable of doing. This is achieved by therapeutic interventions to improve the patient and by prosthetic interventions to reduce the demands of the environment. The ultimate prosthesis is institutional care but the aim of the rehabilitation team is to help the patient avoid this if possible. Part of the skill in stroke rehabilitation is to conduct both processes simultaneously so that at the point that the patient is fit to return home any necessary modifications have been carried out and necessary equipment is in place. This can be facilitated by home visits by members of the rehabilitation team to discuss the practicalities with the main carer. This can be done as soon as it becomes possible to judge the patient's future abilities, typically at 4 to 6 weeks from the onset of a moderate or severe stroke. It may or may not be appropriate to take the patient on this first visit, depending on his likely response to it. He may be encouraged by the sign of progress, alternatively he may become depressed at the difficulties ahead, or may refuse to return to hospital. A predischarge visit within 2 weeks of the discharge date and when the apparatus for aftercare is already in place can provide a final and useful check on its adequacy.

The main responsibility at this stage falls on the occupational therapist to determine what is needed and on the social worker to help with organizing and funding it and to ensure that the carers' needs, as well as those of the patient are met. In the most extreme case the patient and main carer may need rehousing, although this is rarely an easy option. Modifications of the home and provision of equipment will deal with most situations. Mobility within and outside the house needs to be provided for; handrails may need to be provided on stairways and in toilets. Beds may have to be moved downstairs. If the patient is to spend part or all of his time in a wheelchair, doorways may have to be widened, ramps provided for outdoor access, table and bed heights modified and bathrooms and kitchens reconfigured. Toilet and bath aids may need to be provided, as may adapted clothing and utensils. Additional help for the carer in the form of bath attendants and nursing aides may be required. Rotas of help from neighbours and relatives may be negotiated.

Follow-up

At the time of discharge arrangements should be in place for follow-up. Most of the aftercare will be supervised by the primary care team but, at the least, the hospital team should arrange some contact to ensure that the care package is working as intended. Respite care in a day hospital or residential institution may need to be provided, and there may be ongoing medical problems such as blood pressure control that need to be supervised in the outpatient clinic or day hospital. Rehabilitation after stroke should not be regarded as a once-and-forever intervention. A patient's functional level may decline over a period at home, and repeated short periods of day hospital rehabilitation may be needed indefinitely.

Prognosis

In a community-based prospective study in Oxford, United Kingdom, 19 per cent of stroke patients were dead at 1 month and 34 per cent at 1 year (Bamford et al. 1990). The outlook for survival was worse for patients with haemorrhagic strokes than for those with ischaemic strokes. In community-based studies from Auckland, New Zealand, and Perth, Western Australia, approximately one-quarter of patients were dead within a month (Bonita et al. 1994).

Case fatality rates will be determined by the selection of patients included, and series restricted to hospital admissions will have been selected to a variable degree for severity. In the Oxford study, 46 per cent of patients were not admitted to hospital compared with 22 per cent in Perth and 28 per cent in Auckland. Racial differences in survival have also been reported (Bonita et al. 1997). The main determinants of survival, and of functional outcome, is the severity of the stroke. Impairment of consciousness, pupillary abnormalities, and urinary incontinence are early signs of severity. Later in the course of rehabilitation specific defects such as unilateral neglect can have a significant effect on functional capabilities.

It can be counterproductive to attempt to make a prognosis for an individual patient too early. In particular, a poor prognosis can become a self-fulfilling prophesy since patients who are expected to do badly are at risk of receiving less than optimal treatment. There is also a paradox that patients who survive a cerebral haemorrhage sometimes do surprisingly well, presumably because part of their initial disability was due to pressure effects rather than destruction of neural tissue. Recovery from stroke can continue for 2 years, but on average around 90 per cent of eventual recovery is apparent by 6 weeks. In an ideal stroke service, a decision that an individual is unable to return home should not normally be made until a 6-week trial of rehabilitation has been undertaken.

Guidelines and guidance

Many patients with stroke are cared for outside specialist stroke units. Guidelines can be valuable to ensure that expertise developed in specialist units can be influential elsewhere. There is also a widespread need for readable and practical guides for non-professional people called upon to help care for a family member or friend afflicted by stroke. Guidelines on stroke rehabilitation for professionals with a companion guide for consumers have been produced by the United States Department of Health and Human Services Agency for Health Care Policy and Research (Gresham and Duncan 1995a, b). Given the variations in organization of services for stroke patients, supplementary guides for consumers may need to be prepared locally.

References

Adams, H.P., Brott, T.G., Furlan, A.J., *et al.* (1996). Guidelines for thrombolytic therapy for acute stroke: supplement to the guidelines for the management of patients with acute ischemic stroke. A statement for healthcare professionals from a special writing group of the Stroke Council, American Heart Association. *Circulation*, 9, 1167–74.

Allen, C.M.C. (1983). Clinical diagnosis of the acute stroke syndrome. *Quarterly Journal of Medicine*, 52, 205–11.

Bamford, J., Sandercock, P., Dennis, M., Burn, J., and Warlow, C. (1990). A prospective study of acute cerebrovascular disease in the community; the Oxfordshire Community Stroke Project, 1981–1986. 2. Incidence, case fatality rates and overall outcome at 1 year of cerebral infarction, primary intracerebral haemorrhage and subarachnoid haemorrhage. *Journal of Neurology, Neurosurgery and Psychiatry*, 53, 16–22.

Bamford, J., Sandercock, P., Dennis, M., Burn, J., and Warlow, C. (1991). Classification and natural history of clinically identifiable subtypes of cerebral infarction. *Lancet*, 337, 1521–6.

Barker, F.G. and Ogilvy, C.S. (1996). Efficacy of prophylactic nimodipine for delayed ischemic deficit after subarachnoid hemorrhage: a meta-analysis. *Journal of Neurosurgery*, 84, 405–14.

Bhakta, B.B., Cozens, J.A., Bamford, J.M., and Chamberlain, M.A. (1996). Use of botulinum toxin in stroke patients with severe upper limb spasticity. *Journal of Neurology, Neurosurgery and Psychiatry*, 61, 30–5.

Bonita, R., Anderson, C.S., Broad, J.B., Jamrozik, K.D., Stewart-Wynne, E.G., and Anderson, N.E. (1994). Stroke incidence and case fatality in Australasia. A comparison of the Auckland and Perth population-based stroke registers. *Stroke*, 25, 552–7.

Bonita, R., Broad, J.B., and Beaglehole, R. (1997). Ethnic differences in stroke incidence and case fatality. *Stroke*, 28, 758–61.

Burn, J., Dennis, M., Bamford, J., Sandercock, P., Wade, D., and Warlow, C. (1997). Epileptic seizures after a first stroke: the Oxfordshire community stroke project. *British Medical Journal*, 315, 1582–7.

CAST (Chinese Acute Stroke Trial) Collaborative Group (1997). CAST: randomised placebo-controlled trial of early aspirin use in 20 000 patients with acute ischaemic stroke. *Lancet*, 349, 1641–9.

Darowski, A., Najim, Z., Weinberg, J., and Guz, A. (1991). The febrile response to mild infections in elderly hospital inpatients. *Age and Ageing*, 20, 193–8.

del Zoppo, G.J., Wagner, S., and Tagaya, M. (1997). Trends and future developments in the pharmacological treatment of acute ischaemic stroke. *Drugs*, 54, 9–38.

Enderby, P.M., Wood, V.A., Wade, D.T., and Langton Hewer, R. (1987). The Frenchay Aphasia Screening Test: a short, simple test for aphasia appropriate for non-specialists. *International Rehabilitation Medicine*, 8, 166–70.

Findlay, J.M. (1997). Current management of aneurysmal subarachnoid hemorrhage guidelines from the Canadian Neurosurgical Society. *Canadian Journal of Neurological Science*, 24, 161–70.

Gebel, J.M., Sila, C.A., Sloan, M.A., *et al.* (1998). Thrombolysis-related intracranial haemorrhage. A radiographic analysis of 244 cases from the GUSTO-1 trial with clinical correlation. *Stroke*, 29, 563–9.

Gilman, S. (1998). Imaging the brain. *New England Journal of Medicine*, 338, 812–20.

Gresham, G.E. and Duncan, P.W. (ed.) (1995*a*). *Post-stroke rehabilitation.* Clinical Practice Guideline. US Department of Health and Human Services Agency for Health Care Policy and Research, Washington, DC.

Gresham, G.E. and Duncan, P.W. (ed.) (1995*b*). *Recovery after a stroke.* US Department of Health and Human Services Agency for Health Care Policy and Research, Washington, DC.

Grimley Evans, J. (1990). Transient neurological dysfunction and risk of stroke in an elderly English population: the different significance of vertigo and non-rotatory dizziness. *Age and Ageing*, 19, 43–9.

Hamdy, S., Aziz, Q., Rothwell, J.C., *et al.* (1997). Explaining oropharyngeal dysphagia after unilateral hemiplegic stroke. *Lancet*, 350, 686–92.

Hankey, G.J. and Hon, C. (1997). Surgery for primary intracerebral haemorrhage: is it safe and effective? A systematic review of case series and randomized trials. *Stroke*, 28, 2126–32.

Heiskanen, O. (1993). Treatment of intracerebral and intracerebellar hemorrhages. *Stroke*, 24 (Supplement 12), 194–5.

Herrmann, N., Black, S.E., Lawrence, J., Szekely, C., and Szalai, J.P. (1998). The Sunnybrook Stroke Study. A prospective study of depressive symptoms and functional outcomes. *Stroke*, 29, 618–24.

Hinge, H.H., Jensen, T.S., Kjaer, M., and Marquardsen, J. (1986). The prognosis of transient global amnesia. *Archives of Neurology*, 43, 673–767.

International Stroke Trial Collaborative Group (1997). The International Stroke Trial (IST): a randomised trial of aspirin, subcutaneous heparin, both, or neither among 19 435 patients with acute ischaemic stroke. *Lancet*, 349, 1569–81.

Kay, R., Wong, K.S., Yu, Y.L., *et al.* (1995). Low-molecular-weight heparin for the treatment of acute ischemic stroke. *New England Journal of Medicine*, 333, 1588–93.

Miller, J.W., Petersen, R.C., Metter, R.J., Millikan, C.H., and Yanagihara, T. (1987). Transient global amnesia: clinical characteristics and prognosis. *Neurology*, 37, 733–7.

Norton, B., Homer-Ward, M., Donnelly, M.T., Long, R.G., and Homes, G.K.T. (1996). A randomised prospective comparison of percutaneous endoscopic gastrostomy and nasogastric tube feeding after acute dysphagic stroke. *British Medical Journal*, 312, 13–16.

O'Dwyer, N.J., Ada, L., and Neilson, P.D. (1996). Spasticity and muscle contracture following stroke. *Brain*, 119, 1737–49.

Rowe, J.G., Molyneux, A.J., Byrne, J.V., Renowden, S., and Aziz, T.Z. (1996). Endovascular treatment of intracranial aneurysms: a minimally invasive approach with advantages for elderly patients. *Age and Ageing*, 25, 372–6.

Solomon, N.A., Glick, H.A., Russo, C.J., Lee, J., and Schulman, K.A. (1994). Patient preferences for stroke outcomes. *Stroke*, 25, 1721–5.

Stachniak, J.B., Layon, A.J., Day, A.L., and Gallagher, T.J. (1996). Craniotomy for intracranial aneurysm and subarachnoid haemorrhage. Is course, cost, or outcome affected by age? *Stroke*, 27, 276–81.

Wade, D.T. (1992). *Measurement in neurological rehabilitation.* Oxford University Press.

Wardlaw, J.M., Warlow, C.P., and Counsell, C. (1997). Systematic review of evidence on thrombolytic therapy for acute ischaemic stroke. *Lancet*, 350, 607–14.

Zorzon, M., Antonutti, L., Mase, G., Biasutti, E., Vitrani, B., and Cazzato, G. (1995). Transient global amnesia and transient ischemic attack. Natural history, vascular risk factors, and associated conditions. *Stroke*, 26, 1536–42.

12

The ageing respiratory system

Age-associated changes in pulmonary reserve

Bruce D. Johnson

Introduction

The respiratory system is an integrative system composed of the extrathoracic airways (nose, pharynx, larynx), intrathoracic airways (trachea, bronchi, alveoli), vasculature (pulmonary and bronchiole circulations), pulmonary lymphatics (maintaining lung fluid balance), respiratory muscles (those involved in regulation of the depth and frequency of breathing through the generation of pleural pressure), and the central nervous system (controlling the rhythmicity of breathing and gas exchange homoeostasis through the activation of the respiratory muscles). From birth to maturity large structural changes occur in the respiratory system (Polgar and Weng 1979). For example, there is an increase in the number of alveoli from approximately 24 to about 300 million, resulting in an increase in lung surface area from 2.8 m² at birth to between 40 and 120 m² at adulthood (Schoenberg *et al.* 1978; Polgar and Weng 1979). There is a corresponding increase in the surface area of the pulmonary vasculature with a doubling of the capillary bed, even after the age of 8 years (Polgar and Weng 1979). Vital capacity (**VC**) increases from approximately 40 ml/kg in the infant to 66 ml/kg in the adult, and contractile proteins of the respiratory muscles shift their composition from slower to faster isoforms with a subsequent increase in the ability to generate respiratory muscle force (Johnson *et al.* 1994). By maturity, the design of the respiratory system results in a capacity for increasing pleural pressure, increasing alveolar ventilation, maintaining pulmonary end-capillary oxygen partial pressure (P_{O_2}), and CO_2 elimination that far exceeds typical demands (except perhaps in the highly fit endurance athlete or in unique environments) (Dempsey 1986; Johnson *et al.* 1992).

The large capacities of the respiratory system allow for a significant erosion in function between maturity and senescence with minimal impact on normal breathing. Only during heavy exercise does it appear that age-associated changes significantly impact on normal breathing, and then primarily through an effect on the breathing strategy, work, and cost of breathing rather than on alveolar to arterial gas exchange (Johnson 1991*a*, *b*). The focus of this chapter is on general structural and functional changes in the respiratory system with ageing that alter pulmonary reserve, and the impact of these changes on the response to exercise.

Structural and functional changes with ageing

There are many structural and functional changes in the respiratory system that have been reported to occur with senescence that affect lung and chest wall function, gas exchange, and, potentially, ventilatory control. The most common of these age-associated changes are summarized in Table 1.

Changes in pulmonary mechanics with ageing

Several factors appear to influence lung volumes, flow rates, and pulmonary mechanics with ageing. The most dominant changes include a stiffening of the chest wall (Rizzato and Marazzini 1970; Morris *et al.* 1971), a decrease in intervertebral spaces (Edge *et al.* 1964; McElvaney *et al.* 1989), an apparent loss of respiratory muscle strength (Black and Hyatt 1969), and a loss of elastic recoil of the lung tissue (Pierce 1965; Pierce and Ebert 1965; Islam 1980). The impact of weight, particularly an increase in abdominal and thoracic weight, on the changes in lung volumes and flow rates associated with ageing remains controversial. Several studies have suggested an increase in fat distribution in these regions with ageing, particularly in Westernized countries (Going *et al.* 1995).

Loss of elastic recoil

Many studies have determined that the dominant influence affecting lung volumes, flow rates, and possibly gas exchange with ageing is the loss of lung elastic recoil (Turner *et al.* 1968; Johnson and Dempsey 1991). This has classically been demonstrated by a shift in the pressure–volume relationship of the lung to the left, as shown in Fig. 1, typically becoming steeper near the mid lung volumes (Gibson *et al.* 1976). Data by Hartung (1957) and Turner *et al.* (1968) have shown that at mid-lung volumes (approximately 50 per cent of total lung capacity (TLC)) deflation transpulmonary pressure falls off at the rate of 0.57 to 0.65 cmH₂O/year. However, subsequent studies have suggested that the loss in static recoil pressure is of the order of 0.1 to 0.2 cmH₂O/year at the higher lung volumes (Murray 1986; Pack and Millman 1988; Knudson 1991).

The basis for the alteration in lung recoil with age remains unclear (Andreottie *et al.* 1983; Eyre *et al.* 1984; Last *et al.* 1990). Elastin and collagen fibres are major elements of the connective tissue network within the lungs (Reiser *et al.* 1987). Because of the stretchable

Table 1 Summary of age-associated changes that influence lung and chest wall function, gas exchange, and ventilatory control

Lung and chest wall function	Gas exchange	Ventilatory control
↓ Lung elastic recoil	↓ Lung elastic recoil	↓ Responsiveness to hypoxia and hypercapnia
↑ Chest wall stiffness	↓ Pulmonary capillary blood volume	↓ Sensitivity to elastic and resistive loads
↓ Respiratory muscle strength	↓ Distensibility of the pulmonary arterial vasculature	↓ Protective reflexes in the airways
↓ Intervertebral space (↓ height, ↑ anteroposterior diameter)	↓ Lung surface area	

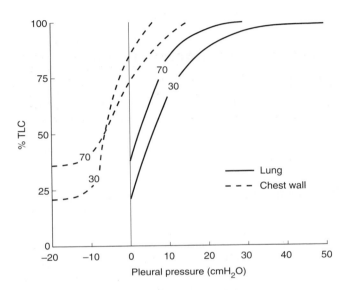

Fig. 1 Pressure–volume characteristics of the lung (solid curves) and chest wall (broken curves) in young (age 30) and older (age 70) adults. (Data from Johnson and Dempsey (1991), Johnson et al. (1992), and Turner et al. (1968).)

properties of the elastin-containing fibres and the non-distensible character of straight collagen fibres, it has been suggested that elastin-containing fibres account for lung compliance changes occurring in the normal breathing range, whereas collagen, a less distensible connective tissue element, limits lung expansion at the higher lung volumes (Mead 1961). Most studies have not demonstrated a change in elastin and collagen content but rather suggest a change in cross-linkage and rearrangement of the collagen fibrils and elastin with ageing (Schofield 1979; Palecek and Jezova 1988). This rearrangement probably explains the increased static compliance with loss of lung tensile strength; however, other tissues are present in the lung and may also contribute to changes in lung compliance. Examples include smooth muscle, pulmonary blood, and bronchial mucus.

Surface-active forces also play a role in the recoil properties of the lung. Studies have demonstrated an increase in alveolar dimensions showing a progressive increase throughout life (Hieronymi 1961). The larger radii of curvature of older alveoli imply a reduced contribution of surface forces to elastic retraction. Weibel (1963) has also demonstrated a disproportionate increase in the alveolar ducts with

ageing, contributing a greater percentage to total lung volume than ducts in the younger lungs. To date, modification of surfactant in the ageing lung appears to be minimal (Yasuoka et al. 1977; Shimura et al. 1986). Data on lung dry weight are somewhat controversial but generally demonstrate little change or a small decrease with ageing (Hieronymi 1961) suggesting the increase in lung volume at a given inflation pressure is not related to a change in total lung area. Additional evidence from Hartung (1957) from postmortem lungs showed a progressive increase in minimal air (that is volume of gas in the freely collapsed lung) with increasing age.

Chest wall compliance

In contrast with the increased compliance of the lung with ageing, there is a significant reduction in compliance of the chest wall, also shown in Fig. 1 (Rizzato and Marazzini 1970; Muiesan et al. 1971). This is thought to be primarily due to a calcification of the costal cartilages. However, early studies suggested that the compliance of the chest wall measured in conscious subjects who attempted to relax were systematically lower than values obtained in the same subjects while anaesthetized and paralysed (Van Lith et al. 1967). This suggests that muscle activity which may not be under voluntary control contributes to chest wall compliance in the conscious state.

Lung volume changes

Figure 2(a) shows the changes in lung volumes and flow rates in an average 30-year-old compared with the average 70-year-old person. Table 2 lists common predicted equations describing the association of age with lung volumes and flow rates and maximal pressures. Most studies have shown little change in TLC and only a small rise in functional residual capacity (**FRC**) with ageing (Crapo et al. 1982a). Those studies which have demonstrated a change in TLC have generally found lower values in the older subjects. In cross-sectional studies, this may be due to a birth cohort effect whereas in longitudinal studies, this is consistent with a decrease in intervertebral spaces and a decalcification of the vertebrae leading to a decrease in total height. Ware et al. (1990) observed a height loss in longitudinal studies of approximately 3 cm from the age of 25 to 75 years with the majority of the decline occurring after the age of 50 years. Cross-sectional data over the same age range demonstrated a loss of 7 cm. It is estimated that the normal height loss with ageing may account for a 10 per cent reduction in TLC; however, there may be some compensation by an increase in anterior to posterior chest wall diameter. In some older subjects, a decrease in the respiratory muscle force production may also result in a decrease in TLC (see below).

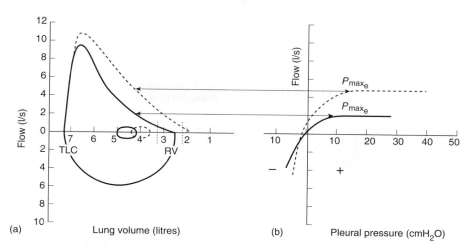

Fig. 2 Changes in lung mechanics with age. (a) Maximum flow volume envelope (MFVL) for 29 older subjects (average age, 70 $\pm$ 2 years) (solid curve) versus the maximal flow–volume envelope for height- and weight-matched 30-year-olds (predicted, Knudson et al. 1983) (broken curve). The smaller loops represent the resting tidal loops for the older and younger subjects placed at their respective FRC values. The dotted vertical lines represent the closing capacity in each age group, with the line at the highest lung volume representing the older subjects. (b) Flow and pleural pressure relationship at a single lung volume of 60 per cent of TLC in a 70-year-old (solid curve) and 30-year-old (broken curve) subjects (isovolume, pressure flow curves). Maximal effective pressure ($P_{max\,e}$) occurred at 12 cmH$_2$O versus 21 cmH$_2$O in the older and younger subjects respectively. Note the evidence for reduced lung elastic recoil in the older fit subject: elevated FRC and closing capacity, reduced maximal expiratory flow, and lower expiratory pressure (and higher lung volume) at which airways are dynamically compressed and flow rate becomes independent of effort.

Table 2 Predicted equations for lung volumes, flow rates, and maximal pressures relative to age

TLC	0.0760 (ht, cm) − 6.69	M (Miller et al. 1983)
	0.0646 (ht, cm) − 5.44	F (Miller et al. 1983)
FVC	0.0844 (ht, cm) − 8.7818 − 0.0298 (age, years)	M (Knudson et al. 1983)
	0.0427 (ht, cm) − 2.9001 − 0.734 (age, years)	F (Knudson et al. 1983)
RV	0.0216 (ht, cm) + 0.0207 (age, years) − 2.840	M (Crapo et al. 1982a)
	0.0197 (ht, cm) + 0.0201 (age, years) − 2.421	F (Crapo et al. 1982a)
FEV$_1$	0.0665 (ht, cm) − 6.5147 − 0.0292 (age, years)	M (Knudson et al. 1983)
	0.0309 (ht, cm) − 1.4050 − 0.0201 (age, years)	F (Knudson et al. 1983)
FEF$_{50}$	0.0684 (ht, cm) − 5.5409 − 0.0366 (age, years)	M (Knudson et al. 1983)
	0.0268 (ht, cm) + 0.6088 − 0.0289 (age, years)	F (Knudson et al. 1983)
MIPS (P_m)	143 − 0.55 (age)	M (Black and Hyatt 1969)
	104 − 0.51 (age)	F (Black and Hyatt 1969)
MEPS (P_m)	268 − 1.03 (age)	M (Black and Hyatt 1969)
	170 − 0.53 (age)	F (Black and Hyatt 1969)

FEV$_1$, forced expiratory volume in 1 s; FEV$_{50}$, flow at 50 per cent of forced expiratory volume; FVC, forced vital capacity; MEPS (P_m), maximum expiratory pressure (mouth); MIPS (P_m), maximum inspiratory pressure (mouth); RV, residual lung volume; TLC, total lung capacity.

FRC is a balance between the inward recoil of the lungs versus the outward recoil of the chest wall. The combination of a small decrease in lung elastic recoil combined with the greater stiffness of the chest wall results in an increase in FRC from 3 to 16 ml/year from maturity to senescence (Crapo et al. 1982a; Knudson 1991).

VC has been reported to fall at the rate of 27 to 41 ml/year in cross-sectional studies, while some longitudinal studies have reported significantly lower rates of decline from 6 to 12 ml/year (Glindmeyer et al. 1982; Knudson et al. 1983; Vollmer et al. 1988). Since TLC

changes little with age, the main reason for the decrease in VC is a rise in residual volume. In the young, the residual volume is the volume at which the outward static recoil pressure of the respiratory system is counterbalanced by the maximal pressure of the expiratory muscles (Knudson 1991). At residual volume the chest wall is the major contributor to the recoil pressure of the respiratory system. In older subjects, expiratory flow may never fall to zero owing to a slower alveolar emptying, so residual volume may not be static (Anthonisen 1986). Therefore the rise in residual volume is probably

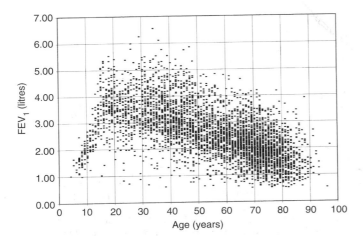

Fig. 3 Age-associated changes in the forced expiratory volume in 1 s (FEV$_1$). Data from non-smoking males and females ($n = 9000$) referred for screening pulmonary function tests. Linear regression (beyond the age of 20): $y = -0.0344$ (age) $+ 4.5332$. (Data from the Mayo Clinic Pulmonary Laboratory.)

secondary to the loss of lung elastic recoil and air trapping; however, the decreased chest wall compliance and potential for decreased expiratory muscle strength could also account for this rise (Leith and Mead 1967). Chest wall strapping studies performed on older and younger adults tend to favour the loss of elastic recoil as the major mechanism for the rise in residual volume (Islam 1980).

Expiratory flow rates and maximal effective pressure generation

The expiratory boundary of the maximal flow–volume envelope declines significantly with ageing, particularly over the lower lung volumes (Knudson et al. 1983; Knudson 1991). The initial portion of a forced expiration from a full lung inflation (over 70 to 75 per cent of TLC) is dependent primarily on the positive pressures produced by the expiratory muscles as well as the recoil forces of the lung and to a lesser extent the diameter of the airways. Thus, this portion of expiration has been termed the effort-dependent portion of the maximal flow–volume envelope. Most studies have demonstrated a non-linear fall in peak expiratory flow rate with ageing (Nunn and Gregg 1989). An average decline of 35 and 25 ml/s/year has been reported for men and women, respectively, becoming most evident after the age of 45 to 50 years (Knudson 1976).

Similar to peak expiratory flow, the forced expiratory volume after 1 s (FEV$_1$) also declines with age in men and women. Work by Ware et al. (1990) suggests that the decline accelerates with increasing years and may occur more rapidly in males, taller people, people with greater than predicted initial values, and individuals with allergies or exposure to environmental influences. The rate of decline in FEV$_1$ ranges from 21 to 51 ml/year; however, some longitudinal studies have suggested a much lower rate of decline of 6 to 12 ml/year (Glindmeyer et al. 1982; Vollmer et al. 1988). FEV$_1$ as a fraction of VC appears to stay quite constant with age. Cross-sectional data from the author's pulmonary function laboratory on FEV$_1$ with ageing is shown in Fig. 3 for non-smoking males and females. Beyond the age of 20 years, an age-associated decline of 33 ml/year was found in

FEV$_1$. The large variability in FEV$_1$ for a given age is in part due to differences in sex and height.

The lower portion of the expiratory boundary of the maximum flow–volume envelope, less than 70 to 75 per cent of TLC, is less dependent on effort (pressure) and is limited mainly by the characteristics of the airways (recoil). As one exhales forcefully, the pressure created outside the lung in the thoracic cavity causes large increases in air flow. The recoil pressure within the airways maintains airway pressure above the thoracic pressures and keeps the airway open. The recoil pressure is reduced as lung volume falls during expiration. The radius of the airways and turbulent flow cause a resistance to air flow, which also causes airway pressure to fall as air is exhaled. At the 'equal pressure point' (i.e. the point where airway pressure equals thoracic pressure), expiratory air flow becomes independent of effort and any additional pressure generated by expiratory muscles is ineffective. The older adult reaches the equal pressure point at a higher lung volume than a younger adult because the recoil pressure within the airway is reduced from the start of an exhalation. Figure 2(b) demonstrates the relationship of pressure to flow during expiration at a lung volume of 60 per cent of the TLC in young adults aged 30 versus 70-year-old subjects. At this lung volume, flow increases linearly with pressure until flow levels off despite further increases in pleural pressure generation. This occurs at approximately 12 cmH$_2$O pleural pressure in the older adult versus 21 cmH$_2$O in the young adults. A family of isovolume pressure–flow relationships can be obtained to describe the pressures at which flow becomes limited for a given lung volume ($P_{max\,e}$). The equations obtained from young adults (Johnson et al. 1992) and the older adults (Johnson et al. 1991b) demonstrates the relationship of effective pressure generation to lung volume (LV) in each age group:

$$-48.5 + 1.022(\text{LV, \%TLC}) \text{ at age } 70$$
$$-34.40 + 0.930(\text{LV, \%TLC}) \text{ at age } 26.$$

Inspiratory flow rates

The ability to generate inspiratory flow is dependent primarily on the pressure generated by the inspiratory muscles (see the discussion of respiratory muscles below), although airway diameter also clearly contributes to the flows obtained (Kelso et al. 1990). Tests of inspiratory flow are thus more motivationally dependent than are those of expiration. Data suggest that maximal inspiratory flows at 50 per cent of the VC may decrease with age at the rate of 26 ml/s/year or decline approximately 15 to 20 per cent from the age of 20 to 60 years (Bass 1973). Since airway diameter does not decrease with ageing, this may largely reflect changes in respiratory muscle structure and function.

Maximal voluntary ventilation

Maximal voluntary ventilation is classically used as an index of ventilatory capacity. Factors influencing it include the available maximal flow rates, VC, and respiratory muscle strength and endurance. Typically, maximal voluntary ventilation is performed over a 12- to 15-s time period and is highly dependent on motivation. It is also well appreciated that the mechanics of breathing (i.e. breathing pattern, pressure generation, end-expiratory lung volume) differ markedly from what is achieved during heavy exercise, when ventilation is involuntarily (reflex) driven (Klas and Dempsey 1989). Thus, the use of maximal voluntary ventilation as an index of ventilatory capacity has been questioned, and other methods have been adopted to estimate ventilatory capacity as it relates to exercise (Johnson *et al.* 1995). With ageing, maximal voluntary ventilation falls in a manner similar to the FEV_1 and VC, suggesting a primary influence of flow and volume changes with ageing rather than changes in muscle function or motivation (Clausen 1982).

Respiratory muscles

The primary inspiratory muscles consist of the diaphragm, scalenes, and parasternal intercostals. The primary expiratory muscles include the abdominal muscles (rectus abdominis, external oblique, internal oblique, and transversus abdominis), and the interosseous intercostals. Expiration at rest is primarily a passive process although studies have shown that the expiratory intercostal muscles of the lower rib cage are electrically active during normal breathing (DeTroyer and Sampson 1982). During the hyperpnoea of exercise, the abdominal muscles become active as do inspiratory accessory muscles (for example the sternocleidomastoids, pectoralis major, pectoralis minor, and the trapezius may also be recruited during exercise to aid in the generation of mechanical pressure).

Indices of respiratory muscle function in humans

Maximal respiratory pressures

The majority of studies assessing respiratory muscle strength with ageing have used mouth (P_m), oesophageal (P_e), or transdiaphragmatic (P_{di}) pressures as indices of muscle force generation. Typically, subjects are asked to perform maximal inspiratory or expiratory efforts against an occluded airway while the corresponding pressure is determined. The simplest and most widely evaluated is mouth pressure against an occluded valve (i.e. maximum inspiratory and maximum expiratory pressure). The majority of studies examining inspiratory muscle pressures have shown a small decline with ageing (Black and Hyatt 1969; Enright *et al.* 1994). However, there is a great deal of overlap at all ages and some studies have not observed significant age-associated changes (Black and Hyatt 1969; McElvaney *et al.* 1989).

As lung volume increases (greater percentage of TLC) and as flow rate increases (velocity of muscle shortening), the ability to generate inspiratory pleural pressure declines. The author tested the influence of lung volume and flow rate on the ability of young and older adults to generate pleural pressure (as inferred from an oesophageal balloon). As shown in Fig. 4, although there was a tendency for a reduction in pressure at the lower lung volumes and flow rates in the older subjects, no significant differences were observed between groups and the decline in oesophageal pressure with increasing lung volume and flow rates was similar.

Tolep *et al.* (1995) measured diaphragm muscle strength when comparing young adults of low normal fitness (average age 24 years, range 19–29) with older adults of above average fitness (average age 68 years, range 65–74). Diaphragm muscle strength was estimated by the measurement of maximal transdiaphragmatic pressure (gastric pressure minus oesophageal pressure) achieved with the combined expulsive and Mueller manoeuvre against an occluded airway (Laporta and Grassino 1985). Although significant overlap between groups was observed and numbers were small, Tolep *et al.* (1995) observed a 25 per cent reduction in the maximal transdiaphragmatic pressure in the older subjects. The reduction in transdiaphragmatic pressure was observed across several lung volumes.

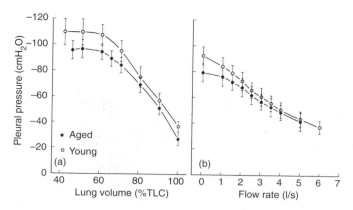

Fig. 4 The effect of (a) lung volume (muscle length) and (b) flow rate (velocity of shortening) on pleural pressure (force) development by inspiratory muscles in older ($n = 12$, age $= 70 \pm 2$ years) and younger ($n = 8$, age $= 26 \pm 2$ years) subjects. The effect of lung volume is shown from values obtained during occlusion (zero flow) and the effect of flow rate is shown from values obtained at 70 per cent TLC. No significant differences were noted between groups ($P < 0.05$). (Reproduced with permission from Johnson *et al.* (1991*b*, 1992).)

Respiratory muscle endurance capacity

Respiratory muscle endurance has been assessed in many ways with increasing levels of sophistication. Several studies have had subjects perform maximal sustained voluntary ventilation until exhaustion, or when a target ventilation can no longer be maintained (Shepard 1967; Martin and Stager 1981). Other studies have had subjects achieve a target mouth, pleural, or transdiaphragmatic pressure to task failure (McCool *et al.* 1986; Aaron *et al.* 1992). To date, few data exist from these types of techniques to describe respiratory muscle endurance with ageing in humans. Minimal data by Morrison *et al.* (1989) combined with data by Martyn *et al.* (1987) suggest that older people can sustain maximal inspiratory pressures (mouth pressures) similar to the young adult (i.e. 79 and 77 per cent of the maximal inspiratory pressure for older and younger subjects respectively). In addition, older adults tested in the author's laboratory achieved higher inspiratory pressures during exercise relative to their inspiratory muscle capacity ($P_{cap\ i}$) than fitness-matched young adults without evidence of an inadequate ventilatory response (Johnson *et al.* 1991*b*, 1992). These studies suggest that there is little change in respiratory muscle endurance capacity with ageing in humans.

Gas exchange

Age-associated changes in the respiratory system which may alter gas exchange include the loss of lung elastic recoil (Holland *et al.* 1968; Anthonisen *et al.* 1970), a decreased surface area of the lung (Thurlbeck 1980), decreased pulmonary capillary blood volume (Crapo 1982*b*), increased dead-space ventilation (Martin *et al.* 1979), and a decreased distensibility of the pulmonary arterial vasculature (Reeves *et al.* 1989). Table 3 lists normative equations for various gas-exchange-related variables in relation to age.

Closing volume

Closing volume is typically determined after a slow inspiration of 100 per cent oxygen from residual volume to TLC followed by a slow controlled expiration back to residual volume. Near the end of the

Table 3 Predicted equations for gas exchange measurements and pulmonary vascular pressure in relation to age

PaO_2	$109.0 - 0.43$ (age)	MF (Sorbini *et al.* 1968)
	$103.7 - 0.24$ (age)	MF (Raine and Bishop 1963)
$P(A-a)DO_2$	0.36 (age) $- 4.3$	MF (Raine and Bishop 1963)
V_d/V_t (%)	0.4 (age) $+ 5.1$	Supine (Raine and Bishop 1963)
	0.1 (age) $+ 20.6$	Sitting (Raine and Bishop 1963)
Closing volume	$-4.0 + 0.46$ (age)[a]	MF (Begin *et al.* 1975)
(% vital capacity)	$-0.22 + 0.44$ (age)[b]	MF (Begin *et al.* 1975)
P_{pa}	0.975 (age) $+ 13.038$[c]	Ekelund 1967*a, b*; Ehrsam 1983; Reeves *et al.* 1989
P_{pw}	0.0175 (age) $+ 9.3042$[c]	Ekelund 1967*a, b*; Ehrsam 1983; Reeves *et al.* 1989
DLco(SB)	0.1646 (ht, cm) $- 0.2290$ (age) $+ 12.9$	M (Miller *et al.* 1983)
	0.1602 (ht, cm) $- 0.1111$ (age) $+ 12.9$	F (Miller *et al.* 1983)

[a] At a controlled expired rate of 0.5 l/s.
[b] At a controlled expired rate of 1.0 l/s.
[c] Rest only.

DLCO(SB), diffusing capacity of the lung for carbon monoxide; $P(A-a)DO_2$, difference of partial pressure of oxygen between alveoli and arterial blood; PaO_2, partial pressure of oxygen in arterial blood; P_{pa}, mean pulmonary artery pressure; P_{pw}, mean pulmonary wedge pressure; V_d/V_t (%), ratio of dead-space to tidal volume.

expiration, the concentration of nitrogen rapidly increases as small airways in the lower zones of the lungs begin to close (Knudson 1991). The closing volume is the volume of air expired after the rapid increase in nitrogen (phase IV). The closing volume is usually less than 10 per cent of the VC in young adults and is less than the FRC. With ageing, the closing volume increases, and may occur at a lung volume which approaches the subject's FRC (Levitzky 1984). Closing volume as a percentage of VC increases approximately 0.46 per cent annually or approximately 20 per cent from age 25 to 70 years (Anthonisen *et al.* 1970; Begin *et al.* 1975). Since small airways depend on lung elastic recoil for their external support, loss of lung recoil with ageing would result in the airways closing at higher lung volumes. A consequence of the increase in closing volume with ageing is the potential for airway closure within the tidal breathing range. If this occurs, it is likely to cause ventilation–perfusion inhomogeneities and thereby increase the alveolar to arterial oxygen difference. It remains unclear if airways actually close at the onset of phase IV or if this represents asynchronous flow limitation due to dynamic compression of airways. Thus other factors may occur with ageing that cause the closing volume to increase.

Ventilation distribution

The loss of elastic recoil in the lung not only affects lung volumes and maximal expiratory flow rates but also affects how ventilation is distributed (Wagner *et al.* 1974; Harf and Hughes 1978). As the lung ages, the decline in recoil is not uniform throughout. The reason for this is unclear, but may relate to variability in particles, whether they be allergens or pollutants, and exposure of these particulates throughout a lifetime. The non-uniformities result in regions of the lungs that may be more or less compliant than other regions, which causes areas of unequal mechanical time constants, so that distribution of a breath is not as uniform as in youth. Topographically, at rest in the normal tidal breathing range, ventilation in an older person may not be preferential to the lower regions of the lung as in the young

adult (Edelman *et al.* 1968). This is presumably due to airway narrowing or closure in these dependent areas of the lung. These topographical differences with age are made worse with a forced expiration (dynamic compression) preceding the measurement of ventilation distribution and abolished with augmented inspiratory flow rates as occur during exercise (Edelman *et al.* 1968).

The alveolar plateau phase using the single-breath oxygen test (similar to the test performed for closing volume) is an estimate of ventilation distribution (Begin *et al.* 1975). Using this technique, the slope of change in nitrogen has been shown to be increased with ageing, but still considered within the normal range (Begin *et al.* 1975).

Matching of ventilation to perfusion

Blood flow to the apex of the lung is higher in older than in younger adults; however, as in younger adults, the majority of blood flow in the older adult is still directed to the lung base (Holland *et al.* 1968; Kronenberg *et al.* 1972). The multiple inert gas technique (**MIGET**) quantifies the intraregional distribution of alveolar ventilation-to-perfusion ratio. To date, a small number of measurements in a few older, healthy, adults showed a greater non-uniformity of alveolar ventilation-to-perfusion ratio relative to the young (Wagner *et al.* 1974). However, in no case was the alveolar ventilation-to-perfusion ratio distribution abnormal (i.e. markedly skewed to extremely low or high alveolar ventilation-to-perfusion ratio) as occurs with some disease states.

Alveolar capillary surface area

Gillooly and Lamb (1993) examined the air space wall surface area per unit volume of lung tissue in a sample of 38 subjects (15 male and 23 female non-smokers) and found a significant negative relationship (-0.78, $p < 0.001$) between area per unit of volume of lung tissue and age. This implies that alveolar wall surface area is

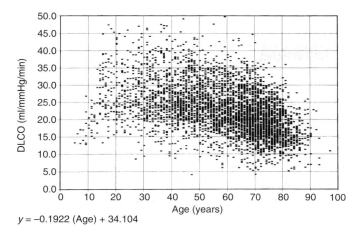

$$y = -0.1922\,(\text{Age}) + 34.104$$

Fig. 5 Age-associated changes in DLco. Cross-sectional data on non-smokers ($n = 9000$). DLco tends to plateau through the age of 50 years, followed by a significant decline. Linear regression beyond the age of 20 results in an annual decline of 0.2 ml/min/mmHg/year. (Data from the Mayo Clinic Pulmonary Laboratory.)

reduced with increasing age and air space size is increasing with age. The relationship found by these investigators implied a decrease of 0.09 mm²/mm³ per year, or a reduction of 30 per cent between the ages of 21 and 93 years. Interestingly there was no difference in the decline in area per unit of volume of lung tissue between the sexes. Similar findings were also reported in an earlier study by Thurlbeck (1967).

The decrease in alveolar septa accounting for these changes in air space wall surface area and an increase in alveolar duct diameter lead to a decrease in total alveolar capillary surface area from approximately 75 m² in the 20-year-old to 60 m² in the 70-year-old, a decrease of 0.3 m²/year. The result of the loss of surface area is a decreased area for diffusion of gases into the pulmonary capillaries. Although change in lung weight with ageing is somewhat controversial, some studies have demonstrated that the lungs are as much as 20 per cent lighter in the older adult (Krumpe et al. 1985). The decreased surface area results in a decrease in lung diffusion capacity for carbon monoxide (DLco), which is a measure of effective alveolar–capillary interface, by approximately 4 to 8 per cent per decade or a decrease of about 0.21 to 0.32 ml/min/mmHg/year for men and 0.06 to 0.18 ml/min/mmHg/year for women (Crapo and Forster 1989). As with other indices of pulmonary function, the decrease in DLco with age may not be linear, with an increased slope of decline after the ages of 40 to 50 years (Muiesan et al. 1971; Georges et al. 1978). The author's cross-sectional data on over 9000 subjects referred for single-breath measurements of DLco demonstrated a greater decline beyond the ages of 50 to 60 years as shown in Fig. 5. Although again there is considerable individual variability, the linear regression results in a decline of 0.2 ml/min/mmHg/year beyond the age of 20 to 25 years.

Pulmonary capillary blood volume

With the reduction in pulmonary alveolar–capillary interface as well as a stiffening of the pulmonary arteries and capillaries, there is a resultant age-associated decrease in pulmonary capillary blood volume (Crapo et al. 1982b). However, the decline appears to be small, resulting in a fall of approximately 2 to 5 ml/decade. Pulmonary capillary blood volume averages 75 ml in the normal young adult, and 50 to 65 ml in the 70-year-old adult. Georges et al. (1978) did not observe a significant decrease until after the age of 50 years.

Dead-space ventilation

There appears to be a slight but significant age-associated rise in dead-space ventilation at rest in the older adult, which has been attributed to the increased diameter of the large airways (anatomical dead-space) as well as to increases in the areas of the lung that are overventilated, i.e. high ventilation-to-perfusion regions (physiological dead-space) (Tenney and Miller 1956). Raine and Bishop (1963) found a larger increase in dead-space expressed as a percentage of the tidal volume in the supine position relative to the sitting position; however, in both conditions the change with ageing was small accounting for an increase of approximately 0.4 per cent/year from the age of 20 to 60 years in the supine position and an increase of 0.1 per cent/year in the sitting position over the same age span. In the author's group of older relatively fit subjects (aged 70 years) the ratio of dead-space to tidal volume (V_d/V_t) was found to be 25 to 30 per cent higher than a group of young endurance athletes (aged 30 years), an increase of 0.6 per cent/year (Dempsey et al. 1993).

Alveolar and arterial oxygenation

Multiple regression equations have been published which describe an age-associated decrease in arterial oxygen tension (Pao_2) and the resulting widening of the alveolar to arterial oxygen difference ($P(A–a)o_2$) (Mellemgaard 1966; Bachofen et al. 1973; Neufeld et al. 1973). Age-associated changes in alveolar oxygen tensions do not occur (Raine and Bishop 1963). Average values observed by Raine and Bishop (1963) for alveolar to arterial oxygen difference were 5.9 and 6.4 mmHg (sitting and supine respectively) for subjects less than 40 years of age, and 16.7 and 15.6 (sitting and supine respectively) for subjects over 40 years of age. However, the change in partial pressure of oxygen in the arterial blood with age appears to be variable, ranging from very little change (less than 1 mmHg per decade) to substantial declines (over 5 mmHg per decade). Reasons for the discrepancies among studies are undetermined but may be because many of the studies were not controlled for body position, smoking, and general health status of the subjects (Ward et al. 1966). In addition these studies were cross-sectional in nature. The small decrease in Pao_2 is probably related to the small increase in in-homogeneities in ventilation-to-perfusion rates. Other possible factors (for example shunt and diffusion limitations) are unlikely candidates for the drop in Pao_2 (Raine and Bishop 1963; Sue et al. 1987).

Pulmonary vascular pressures

Several structural changes with age in the pulmonary vasculature have been reported, including intimal fibrosis and increased wall thickness in the muscular pulmonary arteries (Heath 1964). However, this has not been a consistent finding and the collagen and elastin content of the pulmonary artery does not appear to show significant age-associated changes (Hosoda et al. 1984). Abnormalities in aortic distensibility which increase aortic impedance have been shown to be age associated. Similar changes in the pulmonary circulation appear to be of a smaller magnitude than those in the aorta (Gozna et al. 1974; Murgo and Westerhof 1984). The relative change in pulmonary vascular resistance to systemic vascular resistance has been shown to increase with age (Spirito and Maron 1988), suggesting that the haemodynamic influence of ageing is proportionately greater in the pulmonary than in the systemic vascular bed. It is likely that the increased stiffness of the pulmonary vasculature with age as well as an age-associated change in diastolic heart function has a mild effect (increased slightly) on pulmonary arterial pressure at rest (Ekelund 1967b; Ehrsam et al. 1983). This small increase in pulmonary arterial pressure could account for the increased perfusion to the apex of the lung that has been reported in older people. Changes in pulmonary vascular pressures in relation to age are shown in Table 3.

Control of breathing

Whether the healthy elderly adult has an altered ventilatory control at rest remains controversial (Cameron 1975; Rubin et al. 1982). Several studies have suggested a reduced responsiveness to hypoxic and/or hypercapnic gas mixtures (Altose et al. 1977; Peterson et al. 1981). Peterson et al. (1981) demonstrated a 50 per cent decline in the ventilatory responses to both hypercapnia and hypoxia. The differences were not thought to be related to alterations in pulmonary mechanics or chemoreception, but to a reduction in neuromuscular inspiratory output. Other studies have suggested that the perceptual sensitivity to inspiratory and expiratory resistive and elastic loads is less in older than in young persons (Tack et al. 1981, 1982). Reasons for the altered responsiveness to these two types of loads remain unclear, although it has been hypothesized that there is an age-associated change in the integration of sensory inputs within the central nervous system. Early work by Pontoppidan and Beecher (1960) suggested that with ageing there may be a decrease in the protective reflexes in the airway (that is cough) as well. This was demonstrated by the threshold response to the administration of 1.6 per cent of ammonia gas. The findings demonstrated a sixfold increase in the threshold for a response from the second to the eighth and ninth decades of life. It should be noted, however, that the tests of ventilatory drive are extremely variable within a subject and from subject to subject, and large numbers of individuals have not been thoroughly tested. Perhaps the best test of the adequacy of ventilatory control is the ventilatory response to progressive exercise. To date, in most studies examined, the adequacy of the ventilatory response to exercise in later life is quite similar to that of young adults (i.e. arterial Po_2 remains similar to resting and CO_2 elimination is reduced below resting values) (Johnson and Dempsey 1991; Johnson et al. 1991b).

Impact of age-associated changes on the response to exercise

Table 4 summarizes the impact of age-associated changes in pulmonary mechanics, gas exchange, and ventilatory control on the response to exercise in the healthy, active, older adult.

Pulmonary mechanics

With the decline in pulmonary function, older subjects have a reduced ability to increase tidal volume and to increase flow rates. In the average 70-year-old subject, the reduction amounts to a 30 per cent loss in VC and FEV_1 relative to the 20-year-old adult. The relative reduction in flow rates is particularly great over the lower lung volumes (FRC and below) and thus limits the ability of the older adult to increase flow over this range of lung volumes. Interestingly, with age ventilatory demand tends to fall commensurately with the decline in metabolic demand so that the relative demand–capacity balance may be similar to that of the average fit young adult. It is this relationship of demand to capacity that in part determines the adequacy of the ventilatory compensation to exercise in the older adult. Much of the data presented in this section, examining exercise responses, will be from older fit subjects ($n = 29$, age $= 70$, peak oxygen consumption (Vo_2) $= 44$ ml/kg/min, 199 per cent of age predicted) relative to averagely fit (Vo_2 matched) young adults and/or the young highly trained athletes ($n = 8$, age $= 25$, peak $Vo_2 = 73$ ml/kg/min, 155 per cent of age predicted) studied in the author's laboratory (Johnson et al. 1991a, b, 1992).

Ventilatory demand

Ventilatory demand (V_E) is dependent foremost on metabolic demand, but also on the dead-space ventilation and regulation of arterial CO_2 levels. This relationship is summarized in the following equation:

$$V_E = \frac{K \times V_{CO_2}}{Pa_{CO_2}(1 - V_d/V_t)}$$

where V_d is the dead-space volume, V_t is the tidal volume, and $K = 0.863$ is a constant representing the factor needed to transform fractional gas concentration to partial pressure and to express gas volumes at body temperature and pressure saturated with water vapour. Many studies have evaluated changes in maximal oxygen consumption with ageing, and most demonstrate an annual decline of approximately 0.4 to 0.6 per cent beyond the age of 30 to 35 years and attribute it primarily to a reduced cardiac output as a result of a decrease in heart rate (Bruce et al. 1973; Jones et al. 1985). Thus the average 25 to 30-year-old may have a peak exercise Vo_2 of 45 ml/kg/min and that of the average 70-year-old may be 25 ml/kg/min. This results in a comparable decline in carbon dioxide production (Vco_2) and thus it can be predicted that the peak ventilation necessary for maintaining normal alveolar oxygen levels during peak exercise (assuming a similar V_d/V_t) will fall by approximately 30 to 40 per cent or decrease from 120 l/min for the average fit 30-year-old to 70 l/min for the average 70-year-old adult. However, given the increase in dead-space ventilation with ageing, it is expected the decline in ventilatory demand for the average older individual will only be 25 to 30 per cent.

Breathing pattern

The typical response to exercise is to increase both the frequency of breathing and tidal volume. Most studies have demonstrated a primary increase in tidal volume early in exercise in healthy adults followed by a primary frequency response, especially in heavy and maximal exercise. Older people tend to achieve a tidal volume that reaches a greater percentage of their VC than their younger counterparts.

Several factors determine the peak tidal volume during exercise. McParland et al. (1991) studied the effects of adding dead-space during exercise and found that most subjects will attempt to preserve gas exchange (eliminate CO_2 and maintain alveolar O_2) by increasing the tidal breath. Conversely, lung inflation, detected by stretch receptors in the lung and inspiratory elastic load activating chest wall receptors, may cause restriction of the tidal breath so that the work slightly elevated in the older adults as are pulmonary wedge pressures and the estimated pulmonary vascular resistance. To increase blood flow through the lung, one must increase vascular driving pressure from the pulmonary artery to the left atrium. During heavy exercise in the older subjects, the pulmonary arterial pressure increases (i.e. 100 per cent from rest) out of proportion to those determined at a similar Vo_2 and cardiac output in younger adults (50 per cent). Similarly, pulmonary wedge pressure increases by 120 per cent in the older subjects compared with only 25 per cent in the younger adults. The pressure difference ($P_{pa} - P_{wp}$) was similar in both groups and therefore pulmonary vascular resistance was similar. Although the older adults were more hypertensive than the younger ones at a given oxygen consumption and cardiac output, the younger adults were able to achieve much higher metabolic work rates and therefore reach pulmonary arterial pressures and pulmonary wedge pressures similar to those achieved in the older adults at lower work loads (Reeves et al. 1989).

Scaling of demand to capacity

It is interesting that maximal oxygen consumption, cardiac output, FEV_1, and lung diffusion surface area, appear to decline at similar annual rates with ageing. All of these physiological measurements probably represent a general effect of ageing. As a result, maximal metabolic demands generally do not exceed capacities. Only when the ageing process is accelerated by disease or when demand is exceedingly high, does the ageing pulmonary system appear to alter its response to exercise. Within the older subjects studied, several did truly reach the limits of the lung and respiratory muscles for producing flow, volume, and pressure; and as previously noted, there were several subjects who also demonstrated significantly reduced arterial oxygen tensions with progressive exercise, at metabolic loads where this is rarely observed in the young adult. The upper panels of Fig. 11 show an example of an extremely fit older subject ($Vo_2 = 215$ per cent of age predicted) with normal pulmonary function for age. In this particular subject, ventilation did not increase over the final two exercise loads or with an increased inspired CO_2. The $D(A–a)o_2$ widened, primarily due to a drop in Pao_2. $Paco_2$ actually began to increase over the final work load as would be expected if the ventilatory response was not adequate. The other extreme is shown in the lower panels of Fig. 11 where fitness was average for age, but lung function had declined at faster than the normal rate so that FEV_1 was 50 per cent of age predicted. This subject also reaches the mechanical limits of the lung and chest wall, but due to the low capacity rather than the accentuated demand.

Conclusion

Demand and capacity appear to fall together with ageing so that the response to exercise is generally adequate. It does appear that the loss in lung mechanics may have a more profound effect on exercise performance relative to gas exchange, as even ventilations of 40 to 70 l/min will result in significant expiratory flow limitation, large increases in the work of breathing, and the potential for significant blood flow competition between the locomotor muscles and respiratory muscles. Although arterial hypoxaemia occurs in the older adults, the incidence does not appear to be enhanced in healthy fit older adults, but does occur at lower work loads than typically observed in the young athlete.

References

Aaron, E.A., Johnson, B.D., Seow, K.C., and Dempsey, J.A. (1992). Oxygen cost of exercise hyperpnea: implications for performance. Journal of Applied Physiology, 72, 1818–25.

Altose, M.D., McCauley, W.C., Kelsen, S.G., and Cherniack, N.S. (1977). Effects of hypercapnia and inspiratory flow resistive loading on respiratory activity in chronic airways obstruction. Journal of Clinical Investigation, 59, 500–7.

Andreotti, L., Bussotti, A., Cammelli, D., Aiello, E., and Sampognaro, S. (1983). Connective tissue in aging lung. Gerontology, 29, 377–87.

Anthonisen, N.R. (1986). Tests of mechanical function. In Handbook of physiology, Section 3. The respiratory system, Volume III. Mechanics of breathing, Part 2, pp. 753–84. American Physiological Society, Bethesda, MD.

Anthonisen, N.R., Danson, J., Roberton, P.C., and Ross, W.R.D. (1970). Airway closure as a function of age. Respiratory Physiology, 8, 58–65.

Bachofen, H., Hobi, H.J., and Scherrer, M. (1973). Alveolar-arterial N_2 gradients at rest and during exercise in healthy men of different ages. Journal of Applied Physiology, 34, 137–42.

Bass, H. (1973). The flow volume loop: normal standards and abnormalities in chronic obstructive pulmonary disease. Chest, 63, 171–6.

Begin, R., Renzetti, A.D., Bigler, A.H., and Watanabe, S. (1975). Flow and age dependence of airway closure and dynamic compliance. Journal of Applied Physiology, 38, 199–207.

Black, L.F. and Hyatt, R.E. (1969). Maximal respiratory pressures: normal values and relationship to age and sex. American Review of Respiratory Disease, 99, 696–702.

Bruce, R.A., Kusumi, F., and Hosmer, D. (1973). Maximal oxygen intake and nomographic assessment of functional aerobic impairment in cardiovascular disease. American Heart Journal, 85, 546–62.

Cameron, I.R. (1975). Hypercapnic drive: assessment and interpretation. Proceedings of the Royal Society of Medicine, 68, 242.

Clausen, J.L. (ed.) (1982). Pulmonary function testing guidelines and controversies: equipment, methods, and normal values. In Pulmonary function testing guidelines and controversies; equipment, methods and normal values, pp. 71–5. Academic Press, New York.

Crapo, R.O. and Forster, R.E. II (1989). Carbon monoxide diffusing capacity. Clinical Chest Medicine, 10, 187–98.

Crapo, R.O., Morris, A.H., Clayton, P.D., and Nixon C.R. (1982a). Lung volumes in healthy nonsmoking adults. Bulletin Europeen de Physiopathologie Respiratoire, 18, 419–25.

Crapo, R.O., Morris, A.H., and Gardner, R.M. (1982b). Reference values for pulmonary tissue volume, membrane diffusing capacity and pulmonary capillary blood volume. Clinical Respiratory Physiology, 18, 893–9.

Dempsey, J.A. (1986). Is the lung built for exercise? Medicine and Science in Sports and Exercise, 18, 143–55.

Dempsey, J.A., Johnson, B.D., Pegelow, D., Reddan, W.D., and Badr, S. (1993). Aging effects on exercise-induced arterial hypoxaemia and expiratory flow limitation. Medicine and Science in Sports and Exercise, 25, S184.

DeTroyer, A. and Sampson, M. (1982). Activation of the parasternal intercostals during breathing efforts in human subjects. Journal of Applied Physiology, 52, 524–9.

Edelman, N.H., Mittman, C., Norris, A.H, and Shock, N.W. (1968). Effects of respiratory pattern on age differences in ventilation uniformity. Journal of Applied Physiology, 24, 49–53.

Edge, J.R., Millard, F.J., Reid, L., and Simon, G. (1964). The radiographic appearance of the chest in persons of advanced age. *British Journal of Radiology*, 37, 769.

Ehrsam, R.E., Perruchoud, A., Oberholzer, M., Burkhart, F., and Herzog, H. (1983). Influence of age on pulmonary hemodynamics at rest and during supine exercise. *Clinical Science*, 65, 653–60.

Ekelund, L.G. (1967a). Circulatory and respiratory adaptation during prolonged exercise. *Acta Physiologica Scandinavica*, 292 (Supplement), 1–38.

Ekelund, L.G. (1967b). Circulatory and respiratory adaptation during prolonged exercise of moderate intensity in the sitting position. *Acta Physiologica Scandinavica*, 69, 332–9.

Enright, P.L., Kronmal, T.A., Manolio, T.A., Schenker, M.B., and Hyatt, R.E. (1994). Respiratory muscle strength in the elderly: correlates and reference values. *American Journal of Respiratory Critical Care Medicine*, 149, 430–8.

Eyre, D.R., Paz, M.A., and Gallop, P.M. (1984). Crosslinks in elastin and collagen. *Annual Review of Biochemistry*, 53, 717–48.

Georges, R., Saumon, G., and Loiseau, A. (1978). The relationship of age to pulmonary membrane conductance and capillary blood volume. *American Review of Respiratory Disease*, 117, 1069–78.

Gibson, G.J., Pride, N.B., O'Cain, C., and Quagliato, R. (1976). Sex and age differences in pulmonary mechanics in normal nonsmoking subjects. *Journal of Applied Physiology*, 41, 20–5.

Gillooly, M. and Lamb, D. (1993). Airspace size in lungs of lifelong non-smokers: effect of age and sex. *Thorax*, 48, 39–43.

Glindmeyer, H.W., Diem, J.E., Jones, R.N., and Weill, H. (1982). Noncomparability of longitudinally and cross-sectionally determined annual change in spirometry. *American Review of Respiratory Disease*, 125, 544–8.

Going, S., Williams, D., and Lohman, T. (1995). Aging and body composition: biological changes and methodological issues. *Exercise and Sport Sciences Reviews*, 23, 411–58.

Gozna, E.R., Marble, A.E., Shaw, A., and Holland, J.G. (1974). Age-related changes in the mechanics of the aorta and pulmonary artery of man. *Journal of Applied Physiology*, 36, 407–11.

Harf, A. and Hughes, J.M.B. (1978). Topographical distribution of VA/Q in elderly subjects using krypton-81m. *Respiratory Physiology*, 34, 319–27.

Hartung, W. (1957). Die Altersveraderungen der Lungenelastizitat nach Messungen an isolierten Leichenlungen. *Beitrage Zur Pathologishen Anatomie und allgemeinen Pathologie*, 118, 368–89.

Heath, D. (1964). Structural changes in the pulmonary vasculature associated with aging. In *Aging of the lung*, (ed. L. Carder and J.H. Moyer), pp. 70–6. Grune and Stratton, New York.

Hieronymi, G. (1961). On the change in the morphology of the human lung due to aging. *Ergebnisse der allgemeinen Pathologie und Pathologischen Anatomie*, 41, 1–62.

Holland, J., Milic-Emili, J., Macklem, P.T., and Bates, D.V. (1968). Regional distribution of pulmonary ventilation and perfusion in elderly subjects. *Journal of Clinical Investigation*, 47, 81–92.

Hosoda, Y., Kawano, K., Yamasawa, F., Ishii, T., Shibata, T., and Inayama, S. (1984). Age-dependent changes of collagen and elastin content in human aorta and pulmonary artery. *Angiology*, 10, 615–21.

Islam, M.S. (1980). Mechanism of controlling residual volume and emptying rate of the lung in young and elderly healthy subjects. *Respiration*, 40, 1–8.

Johnson, B.D. and Dempsey, J.A. (1991). Demand vs. capacity in the aging pulmonary system. In *Exercise and sports science reviews* (ed. J.O. Holloszy), pp. 171–210. Williams and Wilkins, Baltimore.

Johnson, B.D., Seow K.C., Pegelow D.F., and Dempsey, J.A. (1990). Adaptation of the inert gas FRC technique for use in heavy exercise. *Journal of Applied Physiology*, 68, 802–9.

Johnson, B.D., Reddan, D.F., Pegelow, K.C., Seow, K.G., and Dempsey, J.A. (1991a). Flow limitation and regulation of functional residual capacity during exercise in a physically active aging population. *American Review of Respiratory Disease*, 143, 960–7.

Johnson, B.D., Reddan, D.F., Seow, K.G., and Dempsey, J.A. (1991b). Mechanical constraints on exercise hyperpnea in a fit aging population. *American Review of Respiratory Disease*, 143, 968–77.

Johnson, B.D., Saupe, K.W., and Dempsey, J.A. (1992). Mechanical constraints on exercise hyperpnea in endurance athletes. *Journal of Applied Physiology*, 73, 874–86.

Johnson, B.D., Wilson, L.E., Zhan, W.Z., Watchko, J.F., Daood, M.J., and Sieck, G.C. (1994). Contractile properties of the developing diaphragm correlate with myosin heavy chain phenotype. *Journal of Applied Physiology*, 77, 481–7.

Johnson, B.D., Scanlon, P.D., and Beck, K.C. (1995). Regulation of ventilatory capacity during exercise in asthmatics. *Journal of Applied Physiology*, 79, 892–901.

Jones, N.L., Makrides, L., Hitchcock, C., Chypchar, T., and McCartney, N. (1985). Normal standards for an incremental progressive cycle ergometer test. *American Review of Respiratory Disease*, 131, 700–8.

Kelso, J.M., Enright, P.L., Scanlon, P.D., O'Connoll, E.J., and Sachs, M.I. (1990). Effect of inhaled methacholine on inspiratory flow. *Chest*, 98, 1426–9.

Klas, J.V. and Dempsey, J.A. (1989). Voluntary versus reflex regulation of maximal exercise flow: volume loops. *American Review of Respiratory Disease*, 139, 150–6.

Knudson, R.J. (1976). The maximum expiratory flow–volume curve. Normal standards, variability, and effects of age. *American Review of Respiratory Disease*, 113, 587–600.

Knudson, R.J. (1991). Physiology of the aging lung. In *The lung*, (ed. R.G. Crystal and J.B. West), pp. 1749–59. Lippincott-Williams and Wilkins, Scranton, PA.

Knudson, R.J., Lebowitz, M.D., Holberg, C.J., and Burrows, B. (1983). Changes in the normal maximal expiratory flow–volume curve with growth and aging. *American Review of Respiratory Disease*, 127, 725–34.

Kronenberg, R.S., L'Heurex, P.O., and Ponto, R.A. (1972). The effect of aging on lung-perfusion. *Annual Internal Medicine*, 76, 413–21.

Krumpe, P.E., Knudson, R.J., Parsons, G., and Reiser, K. (1985). The aging respiratory system. *Clinics in Geriatric Medicine*, 1, 143–75.

Laporta, D. and Grassino, A. (1985). Assessment of transdiaphragmatic pressure in humans. *Journal of Applied Physiology*, 58, 1469–76.

Last, J.A., King, T.E. Jr, Nerlich, A.G., and Reiser, K.M. (1990). Collagen cross-linking in adult patients with acute and chronic fibrotic lung disease. *American Review of Respiratory Disease*, 141, 307–13.

Leith, D.E. and Mead, J. (1967). Mechanisms determining residual volume of the lungs in normal subjects. *Journal of Applied Physiology*, 23, 221–7.

Levitzky, M.G. (1984). Effects of aging on the respiratory system. *Physiologist*, 27, 102–6.

McCool, F.D., McCann, D.R., Leith, D.E., and Hoppin, F.G. Jr (1986). Pressure–flow effects on endurance of inspiratory muscles. *Journal of Applied Physiology*, 60, 299–303.

McElvaney, G., Blackie, S., Morrison, J., Wilcox, P.G, Fairbarn, M.S., and Pardy, R.L. (1989). Maximal static respiratory pressures in the normal elderly. *American Review of Respiratory Disease*, 39, 277–81.

McParland, C., Mink, J., and Gallagher, C.G. (1991). Respiratory adaptations to dead space loading during maximal incremental exercise. *Journal of Applied Physiology*, 70, 55–62.

Martin, B.J. and Stager, J.M. (1981). Ventilatory endurance in athletes and nonathletes. *Medicine and Science in Sports and Exercise*, 13, 21–8.

Martin, C.J., Das, S., and Young, A.C. (1979). Measurement of the dead space volume. *Journal of Applied Physiology*, 47, 319–24.

Martyn, J.B., Moreno, R.H., Pare, P.D., and Pardy, R.L. (1987). Measurement of inspiratory muscle performance with incremental threshold loading. *American Review of Respiratory Disease*, 135, 919–23.

Mead, J. (1961). Mechanical properties of lungs. *Physiology Review*, 41, 281–330.

Mellemgaard, K. (1966). The alveolar-arterial oxygen difference: its size and components in normal man. *Acta Physiologica Scandinavia*, **67**, 10.

Miller, A., Thornton, J.C., Warshaw, R., Anderson, H., Teirstein, A.S., and Selikoff, I.J. (1983). Single breath diffusing capacity in a representative sample of the population of Michigan, a large industrial state. *American Review of Respiratory Disease*, **127**, 270–7.

Morris, J.G., Koski, A., and Johnson, L.C. (1971). Spirometric standards for healthy nonsmoking adults. *American Review of Respiratory Disease*, **103**, 57–67.

Morrison, N.J., Richardson, J., Dunn, L., and Pardy, R.L. (1989). Respiratory muscle performance in normal elderly subjects and patients with COPD. *Chest*, **95**, 90–4.

Muiesan, B., Sorbini, C.A., and Grassi, V. (1971). Respiratory function in the aged. *Bulletin Physio-Pathology Respiratory*, **7**, 973–1003.

Murgo, J.P. and Westerhof, H. (1984). Input impedance of the pulmonary arterial system in normal man. Effects of respiration and comparison to systemic impedance. *Circulation Research*, **54**, 666–73.

Neufeld, O., Smith, J.R., and Goldman, S.L. (1973). Arterial oxygen tension in relation to age in hospital subjects. *Journal of American Geriatric Society*, **21**, 4–9.

Nunn, A.J. and Gregg, I. (1989). New regression equations for predicting peak expiratory flow in adults. *British Medical Journal*, **298**, 1068–70.

Pack, A.I. and Millman, R.P. (1988). The lungs in later life. In *Pulmonary diseases and disorders*, (ed. A.P. Fishman), pp. 79–90. McGraw-Hill, New York.

Palecek, F. and Jezova, E. (1988). Elastic properties of the rat respiratory system related to age. *Physiologia Bohemoslovaca*, **37**, 39–48.

Peterson, D.D., Pack, A.I., Silage, D.A., and Fishman, A.P. (1981). Effects of aging on ventilatory and occlusion pressure responses to hypoxia and hypercapnia. *American Review of Respiratory Disease*, **124**, 387–91.

Pierce, J.A. (1965). Tensile strength of the human lung. *Journal of Clinical Investigation*, **66**, 652–8.

Pierce, J.A. and Ebert, R.V. (1965). Fibrous network of the lung and its change with age. *Thorax*, **20**, 469–76.

Polgar, G. and Weng, T.R. (1979). The functional development of the respiratory system. From the period of gestation to adulthood. *American Review of Respiratory Disease*, **120**, 625–95.

Pontoppidan, H. and Beecher, H.K. (1960). Progressive loss of protective reflexes in the airway with the advance of age. *Journal of the American Medical Association*, **174**, 2209–13.

Raine, J.M., and Bishop, J.M. (1963). A-a difference in O_2 tension and physiological dead space in normal man. *Journal of Applied Physiology*, **18**, 284–8.

Reeves, J.T., Dempsey, J.A., and Grover, R.F. (1989). Pulmonary circulation during exercise. In *Pulmonary vascular physiology and pathophysiology*, (ed. E.K. Weir and J.T. Reeves), pp. 107–33. Marcel Dekker, New York.

Reiser, K.M., Hennessy, S.M., and Last, J.A. (1987). Analysis of age-associated changes in collagen crosslinking in the skin and lung in monkeys and rats. *Biochemical and Biophysical Acta*, **926**, 339–48.

Rizzato, G. and Marazzini, L. (1970). Thoracoabdominal mechanics in elderly men. *Journal of Applied Physiology*, **28**, 457–60.

Road, J.D., Newman, S., Derenne, J.P., and Grassino, A. (1986). The *in vivo* length–force relationship of the canine diaphragm. *Journal of Applied Physiology*, **60**, 63–70.

Rubin, S., Tack, M., and Cherniack, N.S. (1982). Effect of aging on respiratory responses to CO_2 and inspiratory resistive loads. *Journal of Gerontology*, **37**, 306–12.

Saltin, B. (1986). The aging endurance athlete. In *Sports medicine for the mature athlete*, pp. 59–80. (ed. J.R. Sutton and R.M. Brock). Benchmark Press, Indianapolis.

Schoenberg, J.B., Beck, G.T., and Bouhuys, A. (1978). Growth and decay of pulmonary function in healthy blacks and whites. *Respiratory Physiology*, **33**, 367–93.

Schofield, J.D. (1979). Connective tissue aging: differences between mouse tissues in age-related changes in collagen extractability. *Experimental Gerontology*, **15**, 113–19.

Shepard, R.J. (1967). The maximum sustained voluntary ventilation in exercise. *Clinical Science*, **32**, 167–76.

Shimura, S., Boatman, E.S., and Martin, C.J. (1986). Effects of aging on the alveolar pores of Kohn and on the cytoplasmic components of alveolar type II cells in monkey lungs. *Journal of Pathology*, **148**, 1–11.

Sorbini, C.A., Grassi V., Solinas, E., and Muiesan, G. (1968). Arterial oxygen tension in relation to age in healthy subjects. *Respiration*, **25**, 3–13.

Spirito, P. and Maron, B.J. (1988). Influence of ageing on Doppler echocardiographic indexes of left ventricular diastolic function. *British Heart Journal*, **59**, 672–9.

Sue, D.Y., Oren, A., Hansen, J.E., and Wasserman, K. (1987). Diffusing capacity for carbon monoxide as a predictor of gas exchange during exercise. *New England Journal of Medicine*, **316**, 1301–6.

Tack, M., Altose, M.D., and Cherniack, N.S. (1981). Effect of aging on respiratory sensations produced by elastic loads. *Journal of Applied Physiology*, **50**, 844–50.

Tack, M., Altose, M.D., and Cherniack, N.S. (1982). Effect of aging on the perception of resistive ventilatory loads. *American Review of Respiratory Disease*, **126**, 463–7.

Tenney, S.M. and Miller, R.M. (1956). Dead space ventilation in old age. *Journal of Applied Physiology*, **9**, 321–7

Thurlbeck, W.M. (1967). The internal surface area of non-emphysematous lungs. *American Review of Respiratory Disease*, **95**, 765–73.

Thurlbeck, W.M. (1980). The effect of age on the lung. *Aging—its chemistry*, (ed. A.A. Dietz), pp. 88–109. Association for Clinical Chemistry, Washington.

Tolep, K., Higgins, N., Muza, S., Criner, G., and Kelsen, S.G. (1995). Comparison of diaphragm strength between healthy adult elderly and young men. *American Journal of Respiratory Critical Care Medicine*, **152**, 677–82.

Turner, J.M., Mead, J., and Wohl, M.E. (1968). Elasticity of human lungs in relation to age. *Journal of Applied Physiology*, **25**, 664–71.

Van Lith, P.F., Johnson, N.P., and Sharp, J.T. (1967). Respiratory elastances in relaxed and paralyzed states in normal and abnormal men. *Journal of Applied Physiology*, **23**, 475–86.

Vollmer, W.M., Johnson, L.R., McCamant, L.E., and Buist, A.S. (1988). Longitudinal versus cross-sectional estimation of lung function decline-further insights. *Statistics in Medicine*, 7, 685–96.

Wagner, P., Laravuso, R., Uhl, R., and West, J.B. (1974). Continuous contributions of ventilation–perfusion ratios in normal subjects breathing air at 100 per cent O_2. *Journal of Clinical Investigation*, **54**, 54–68.

Ward, R.J.,. Tolas, A.G., Benveniste, R.J., Hansen, J.M., and Bonica, J.J. (1966). Effect of posture on normal arterial blood gas tensions in the aged. *Geriatrics*, **21**, 139–43.

Ware, J.H., Dockery, D.W., Louis, T.A. Xiping, X., Ferris, B.G. Jr, and Speizer, F.E. (1990). Longitudinal and cross-sectional estimates of pulmonary function decline in never-smoking adults. *American Journal of Epidemiology*, **132**, 685–700.

Weibel, E.R. (1963). *Morphometry of the human lung*. Academic Press, New York.

Yasuoka, S., Manabe, H., Oaki, T., and Tsubura, E. (1977). Effect of age on the saturated lecithin contents of human and rat lung tissues. *Journal of Gerontology*, **32**, 387–91.

12.2   **Respiratory infections**

Joseph M. Mylotte and David W. Bentley

Introduction

Respiratory infections result in substantial morbidity and mortality, and contribute to the increasing costs of health care. Among older people admitted to hospital in 1988 in the United States, pneumonia was the fourth leading principal discharge diagnosis (May *et al.* 1991). From 1979 to 1994, overall crude death rates for pneumonia and influenza increased by approximately 60 per cent which was primarily due to a 45 per cent increase in mortality among those 65 years of age and older (Centers for Disease Control and Prevention 1995). In addition, rates of tuberculosis are highest among older people, especially those in nursing homes. This chapter addresses the major types of respiratory infections occurring in elderly people including bacterial pneumonia in the three settings of community, nursing home, and hospital, tuberculosis, and viral respiratory infections.

Community-acquired pneumonia

Epidemiology

The annual incidence of community-acquired pneumonia is substantially higher (approximately 35 per 1000) in older people, especially in elderly males (approximately 65 per 1000) (Jokinen *et al.* 1993). Community-acquired pneumonia case fatality rates increase with age from about 6 per cent in those aged 60 to 74 years to about 17 per cent in those 75 years and older (Jokinen *et al.* 1993). For people admitted to hospital with community-acquired pneumonia, approximately 60 per cent of all deaths occur among those over 70 years of age (Marrie 1990). Age over 65 also predicts a complicated course among patients with community-acquired pneumonia who are initially not admitted to hospital (Fine *et al.* 1990) and is an important prognostic factor among patients with community-acquired pneumonia (Gilbert and Fine 1994).

Risk factors

Factors in men predictive of hospital admission for pneumonia are current smoking, chronic lung disease, and history of myocardial infarction; the predictors in women are primarily chronic lung disease, hypertension, and diabetes (Lacroix 1989). Physical disability and cognitive impairment among community-residing older people are predictors of pneumonia-related mortality (Salive *et al.* 1993).

Aetiology

The aetiology of community-acquired pneumonia in older people remains poorly defined, but some general concepts include the following: (a) *Streptococcus pneumoniae* is the most frequently identified respiratory pathogen; (b) 30 to 50 per cent of the time (even in patients admitted to hospital) no aetiological agent is identified; (c) there is considerable geographic variation in the aetiological agents identified and their rank order; (d) *Mycoplasma pneumoniae* and *Legionella* species are uncommon causes; (e) the role of *Chlamydia pneumoniae* remains to be defined as better diagnostic methods become available (Granton and Grossman 1993; MacFarlane 1994).

Gram-negative bacilli, such as *Haemophilus influenzae*, *Moraxella* (formerly *Branhamella*) *catarrhalis*, and *Enterobacteriaceae*, are often recovered from expectorated sputum from older people with community-acquired pneumonia. However, these same respiratory pathogens often colonize the oropharynx, which adds to the difficulty in identifying the aetiological agents (Valenti *et al.* 1978). In studies with strict definitions for defining the aetiology of community-acquired pneumonia, the prevalence of Gram-negative organisms was less than 15 per cent (Granton and Grossman 1993).

Clinical manifestations

The 'classic' presentation of bacterial pneumonia—cough, fever, chills, pleuritic pain, and lobar consolidation on chest radiograph—is often absent in older people (Bentley 1984). This is especially true for frail elderly people with impaired cognition and functional status. Instead, non-specific findings or a change in the patient's 'baseline' status, for example increasing confusion, lethargy, loss of appetite, or falls, should prompt an investigation for possible infection, including pneumonia. This variability in the presentation of pneumonia in the more debilitated older person often delays diagnosis and leads to increased mortality. In the independent elderly population, however, the signs and symptoms of community-acquired pneumonia are similar to younger people (Marrie 1995).

Diagnosis

The type and extent of diagnostic testing depends, for the most part, on where one decides to treat the elderly person with community-acquired pneumonia, i.e. as an outpatient or in the hospital. If the patient is treated in the outpatient setting, a chest radiograph should be obtained to document the extent of the pneumonia. Sputum cultures are not necessary because they are usually unreliable, and the results are not available when starting treatment. If the person is admitted to hospital, initial evaluation should include a chest radiograph, blood cultures, and sputum Gram stain and culture for common bacterial pathogens. Testing for atypical causes of pneumonia (e.g. *Mycoplasma*, *Legionella*, *Chlamydia*, or viruses) should not be performed routinely because the yield is low, results are not available in time to affect therapy decisions, and the cost of care is increased unnecessarily.

Treatment

The American Thoracic Society has provided guidelines for the empirical treatment of community-acquired pneumonia based primarily on two factors: (a) severity of illness at the time of presentation and the presence of underlying illness; (b) advanced age (over 60 years old) (Niederman *et al.* 1993). For elderly patients treated in the community, recommendations include an oral second-generation cephalosporin (e.g. cefuroxime axetil or oral trimethoprim–sulphamethoxazole) or an oral β-lactam–β-lactamase inhibitor (e.g. amoxycillin–clavulanic acid). There is the option to add erythromycin or some other macrolide for atypical micro-organisms but this should not be necessary routinely. These recommendations should also be appropriate for older people in congregated living units such as assisted-living units, retirement communities, etc. For patients who are more severely ill and treated in the hospital, the recommendation is a parenteral second- or third-generation cephalosporin or parenteral β-lactam–β-lactamase inhibitor with the same considerations for erythromycin. These recommendations are appropriate for older people with community-acquired pneumonia, but may need revision as diagnostic tests become available for atypical organisms or antibiotic resistance becomes more problematic (Finch 1995). Moreover, medical outcomes were similar, but cost of therapy was increased, when elderly outpatients with community-acquired pneumonia were treated with regimens consistent with the American Thoracic Society guidelines versus other regimens (Gleason 1996). These findings (Gleason 1996) suggest the need for further studies of these guidelines in elderly people with community-acquired pneumonia before they are accepted as the standard of care.

The British Thoracic Society guidelines for the treatment of patients admitted to hospital with community-acquired pneumonia recommend a penicillin for most episodes; erythromycin or a second- or third-generation cephalosporin are considered alternative agents (British Thoracic Society 1993). For patients with severe pneumonia of unknown aetiology, high-dose erythromycin intravenously plus a second- or third-generation cephalosporin is recommended. A recent review of community-acquired pneumonia makes recommendations similar to the British Thoracic Society for the treatment of elderly patients (Bartlett and Mundy 1995).

Prevention

All community-residing older people should receive annual influenza vaccine and one dose of pneumococcal vaccine because of the high morbidity and mortality associated with influenza infection and the frequent occurrence of pneumonia caused by *S. pneumoniae*. Revaccination with pneumococcal vaccine is recommended if people received the vaccine over 5 years previously and were aged up to 65 years at the time of the primary vaccination. Elderly people with unknown vaccination status should be administered one dose of pneumococcal vaccine (Centers for Disease Control and Prevention 1997c).

Nursing-home-acquired pneumonia

Epidemiology

Pneumonia is the most important infection occurring in the nursing home with an incidence of about 260 per 1000 resident-years and a case fatality rate of approximately 50 per 1000 resident-years (Bentley *et al.* 1981). Among patients discharged from a nursing home because of infection, about 65 per cent will have pneumonia, with a mortality of about 35 per cent or 1.3 times greater than patients without pneumonia (Beck-Sague *et al.* 1993)

Risk factors

Compared with those patients admitted to hospital with community-acquired pneumonia, elderly residents admitted to hospital with nursing-home-acquired pneumonia have more underlying dementia and cardiovascular disease and a significantly higher fatality (Marrie *et al.* 1986). Other risk factors include difficulty with oropharyngeal secretions, deteriorating health, the occurrence of an unusual event—new confusion, agitation, a fall, or wandering (Harkness 1990)—as well as the presence of a tracheostomy or feeding tubes, bedridden status, and underlying lung disease (Magaziner *et al.* 1991).

Aetiology

The aetiology of nursing-home-acquired pneumonia is also problematic because of the reliance on sputum cultures. Other invasive methods of obtaining respiratory secretions, (e.g. transtracheal aspirates) are not appropriate for the nursing home setting, and blood cultures are infrequently positive when residents with pneumonia are admitted to hospital.

Studies requiring radiographic confirmation and 'scoring' of Gram-stained respiratory secretions for squamous epithelial cells and white blood cells per 100 times microscopic field indicate the following: (a) *S. pneumoniae*—the most frequently identified respiratory pathogen, approximately 30 per cent; (b) *H. influenzae* (non-typable strains) with or without *S. pneumoniae*, about 10 per cent; (c) Gram-negative aerobic bacilli (e.g. *Klebsiella pneumoniae*), about 15 per cent; (d) 'mixed flora' with two or more respiratory pathogens or upper respiratory tract commensals suggesting aspiration of oropharyngeal secretions (Bentley *et al.* 1981). Aetiological agents associated with 'atypical' pneumonia (e.g. *Legionella*, *Mycoplasma*, and *C. pneumoniae*) appear to be very uncommon causes of pneumonia in the nursing home setting (Drinka *et al.* 1994).

Clinical manifestations

The onset of pneumonia in the nursing home resident is often insidious and non-specific with changes in eating habits, development or worsening of incontinence, weight loss, falls, and acute confusion. Occasionally, there is sudden deterioration of an existing underlying disease or slow response to treatment of the disease, for example stroke or congestive heart failure. Fever and cough may be absent in about 25 per cent of elderly residents with pneumonia and complaints of chills are even less common. Tachypnoea (respiratory rate over 25 breaths/min) may be present for 24 to 48 h before other signs develop. On chest examination, crepitation is non-specific, but dullness to percussion is usually present even with dehydration. Evidence of consolidation on physical examination or chest radiograph is usually absent.

Diagnosis

For the reasons noted above, the clinical and aetiological diagnosis of nursing-home-acquired pneumonia remains problematic. This concern may be further compounded by lack of an on-site doctor's evaluation. Recommendations for diagnostic work-up of suspected pneumonia in nursing home residents include:

(1) written documentation of relevant symptoms in the resident or relevant symptoms and signs in the facility staff;

(2) written documentation of relevant physical findings;

(3) monitoring of vital signs, pulse, respiratory rate, and blood pressure, every 8 h during the acute phase of the illness;

(4) obtaining a sputum or nasopharyngeal aspirate specimen, if possible, for Gram stain and culture prior to initiating therapy, along with a white blood cell count, with differential and a chest radiograph.

However, diagnostic criteria for nursing-home-acquired pneumonia may need to be modified depending on the resources for obtaining specimens and laboratory testing (Zimmer et al. 1986).

Treatment

Most residents with nursing-home-acquired pneumonia are treated in the nursing home with oral antibiotics (Warren et al. 1991). Cotrimoxazole is frequently recommended, although there is concern because of increasing resistance among pneumococcal isolates. Second-generation cephalosporins (e.g. cefuroxime axetil) are an effective alternative. Treatment with oral ciprofloxacin is usually effective, but there is concern regarding the reduced Gram-positive activity compared with β-lactams or cotrimoxazole. The resident in hospital with nursing-home-acquired pneumonia can be treated empirically with a β-lactam–β-lactamase inhibitor such as ampicillin–sulbactam or ceftriaxone. In the resident with penicillin allergy, ceftriaxone can usually be used safely but ciprofloxacin intravenously is a reasonable alternative (Mylotte et al. 1994). However, there has been increasing interest in using parenteral antibiotic therapy in the nursing home setting to avoid the stress related to hospital admission.

A major decision concerns whether or not the resident with suspected pneumonia should be admitted to hospital. Although there is limited information, it appears that the 30-day fatality of nursing-home-acquired pneumonia is similar whether treated in the nursing home or in hospital, with approximately 20 per cent of the residents initially treated in the nursing home subsequently requiring hospital admission. Objective factors associated with significantly higher oral antibiotic treatment failure rates and hospital admission or death within 30 days include (a) temperature over 38°C, (b) mechanically altered diet or altered medication, (c) respiratory rate up to 30 breaths/min, (d) pulse up to 90 beats/min, and (e) dependence in feeding. One additional factor associated with reduced treatment failure (in about 15–35 per cent of cases) was a doctor or nurse practitioner

visit within 72 h of onset of pneumonia. How the information collected at the bedside by doctor (or nurse practitioner) observation and lung auscultation can influence treatment success needs further study (Degelau et al. 1995).

Prevention

Recent reports in the United States of outbreaks of pneumococcal pneumonia, including secondary bacteraemia with multidrug resistant *S. pneumoniae*, among unvaccinated residents in chronic care facilities warrants rigorous implementation of recommendations previously noted for pneumococcal vaccine (Centers for Disease Control and Prevention 1997a). This vaccine can be administered simultaneously with influenza vaccine during annual influenza vaccination programmes.

Hospital-acquired pneumonia

Epidemiology

Hospital-acquired pneumonia is a frequent and serious event for older people; about 55 per cent of all nosocomial infections occur in people 65 years of age and older and about 20 per cent of the infections are pneumonias (Emori et al. 1991). Those cases who are 60 years of age and older have about a twice greater likelihood of developing hospital-acquired pneumonia compared with those under 60 years old (Saviteer et al. 1988).

Risk factors

Independent risk factors for hospital-acquired pneumonia in older people include (a) increasing age, (b) difficulty with oropharyngeal secretions, (c) the presence of a nasogastric tube, (d) poor nutrition (low albumin), (e) neuromuscular disease, and (f) intubation (Celis et al. 1988; Harkness et al. 1990).

Aetiology

The most frequent pathogens causing hospital-acquired pneumonia are *Pseudomonas aeruginosa*, *S. aureus* (including methicillin-resistant strains), *Acinetobacter baumannii*, and *K. pneumoniae* (Craven and Steger 1995). Overall, about 50 per cent of cases are caused by Gram-negative aerobic bacilli. There is considerable variation in the frequency with which these organisms cause hospital-acquired pneumonia from hospital to hospital. These variations are due to differences in case mix, that is severity of illness, and the intensity of diagnostic efforts employed to identify a causative agent.

Clinical manifestations/diagnosis

In the intensive care setting, the diagnosis of pneumonia in ventilated patients (regardless of age) is based on the presence of new or progressive lung infiltrate on chest radiograph, fever, leucocytosis, and purulent tracheal secretions. Although these criteria are quite sensitive, they are very non-specific with many non-infectious processes having a similar presentation, for example atelectasis, pulmonary embolism, heart failure, and gastric content aspiration (Niederman et al. 1993). When quantitative bacteriological techniques are used in conjunction with clinical criteria to identify patients with ventilator-associated pneumonia, about 33 per cent of patients with clinical criteria will have the diagnosis supported by bacteriological criteria (Fagon *et al.* 1989). The diagnosis of pneumonia in elderly patients on the hospital ward is problematic because the main clinical features (e.g. fever and leucocytosis) may be absent (Niederman *et al.* 1993).

Many diagnostic approaches have been evaluated regarding the identification of patients with ventilator-associated pneumonia. Most of these approaches, e.g. bronchoscopy with bronchoalveolar lavage or protected specimen brush, require invasive procedures to obtain specimens for quantitative microbiology. Because these approaches have low sensitivity and specificity, patients with pneumonia are often not treated expeditiously because they do not meet the bacteriological criteria for pneumonia (Niederman *et al.* 1994). Moreover, there is little evidence that these invasive diagnostic approaches improves the outcome of elderly patients compared with clinical diagnostic criteria alone. Frequently the information from quantitative bronchoalveolar lavage cultures is not available soon enough to influence survival; only appropriate antibiotic therapy, initiated at the time of the clinical diagnosis of pneumonia, appears to reduce mortality (Luna *et al.* 1997).

Treatment

Supportive therapy is critical and includes replacement of insensible water losses associated with fever, intubation, and hyperventilation. Chest physiotherapy with suctioning and frequent turning can help clear secretions, especially in older people with depressed cough reflexes.

Empirical antibiotic therapy of hospital-acquired pneumonia in the elderly patient includes an agent(s) with activity for both Gram-positive and Gram-negative aerobic bacteria. In the non-intubated patient, in whom *P. aeruginosa* is an unlikely pathogen, several antibiotic regimens are effective, including ceftriaxone, a third-generation cephalosporin, or ampicillin–sulbactam or piperacillin–tazobactam. Combination regimens, e.g. clindamycin plus an aminoglycoside, can be used in the patient with an allergy to β-lactams.

If the patient is on mechanical ventilation, cultures of tracheal secretions obtained within a few days of onset of the pneumonia can be used to guide empirical antibiotic therapy. However, if there is no recent culture, blood cultures and a culture and a Gram stain of tracheal secretions should be obtained before starting empirical treatment guided by the Gram-stain results. If Gram-negative organisms are seen, empirical treatment should emphasize *P. aeruginosa* because it is the most antibiotic resistant and has the worst prognosis of all the Gram-negative organisms causing ventilator-associated pneumonia. Depending on the antibiotic-resistant patterns in the community, treatment is often initiated with an antipseudomonal β-lactam (piperacillin or ceftazidime) plus an aminoglycoside. Monotherapy of ventilator-associated pneumonia with an antibiotic active against aerobic Gram-negative organisms including *P. aeruginosa* (e.g. imipenem–cilastatin) remains controversial. If Gram-positive organisms in clusters are present on the Gram stain, *S. aureus* is likely. If methicillin-resistant *S. aureus* is not a concern, piperacillin–tazobactam plus an aminoglycoside would be appropriate. If methicillin-resistant *S. aureus* is a concern, vancomycin should be added

to the β-lactam–aminoglycoside. Adjustments to these empirical regimens may be necessary as bacteriological data become available (Chastre *et al.* 1995).

Prevention

The Centers for Disease Control and Prevention in the United States have recently published guidelines for the prevention of nosocomial pneumonia (Tablan *et al.* 1994). This comprehensive two-part document is an excellent resource on the techniques that have been documented to be of value in preventing or reducing the risk of nosocomial pneumonia. However, many of the preventive measures that have been advocated in the literature, such as selective digestive decontamination, remain of unproven value in the absence of outbreaks of ventilatory-associated pneumonia.

Tuberculosis (see also Chapter 12.5)

Epidemiology

Despite the impact of HIV infection on the epidemiology of tuberculosis, older people continue to be a major reservoir for tuberculous infection and disease, especially in nursing homes (Dutt and Stead 1992). In the United States in 1984 to 1985, the incidence of tuberculosis among nursing home residents aged 65 years and older was about 40 cases per 100 000 population per year compared with about 20 cases per 100 000 for community-dwelling people aged 65 years and older, and about 10 cases per 100 000 for community-dwelling people aged between 15 and 64 years (Hutton *et al.* 1993).

The epidemiology of tuberculosis in the high-risk setting of the nursing home has been extensively studied in the United States (Stead and To 1987). Sporadic cases of tuberculosis develop primarily among tuberculin reactors; these cases represent reactivation of dormant infection and often are the 'index' cases in nursing homes. Secondary cases of tuberculosis occur among untreated people whose tuberculin skin test converts to positive, and may present as progressive primary tuberculosis with lower lobe disease or intrathoracic adenopathy. The proportion of nursing home residents with positive tuberculin skin tests tends to increase with increasing duration of stay. This increase in positive tuberculin tests is related to (a) more rapid death of some tuberculin-negative residents (negative skin test in these individuals is a 'marker' of a debilitated host), (b) improvement in nutrition (and cell-mediated immune response) in survivors, and (c) unidentified spread of tuberculosis. The risk of developing tuberculosis is higher among those with tuberculin skin test conversion (converters) after admission to the nursing home than those with a positive test of unknown duration on admission to the home (reactors).

Risk factors

The factors predisposing elderly people to develop tuberculosis at higher rates than other groups include (a) underlying diseases that cause debilitation or immunosuppression, (b) use of immunosuppressive drugs, (c) decline in nutritional status, and (d) the natural senescence of the immune system which may play a role in predisposing individuals to reactivation of dormant infection or rapid progression to active disease after infection.

Tuberculin skin test

Tuberculin skin testing is the only method available for detecting tuberculous infection. The Mantoux method is the preferred testing technique and consists of an intradermal injection of 5 tuberculin units of purified protein derivative. The criterion for defining a positive test depends on the population being tested (American Thoracic Society/Centers for Disease Control and Prevention 1990):

- over 5 mm or more of induration at the injection site 48 to 72 h after administration for a high-risk person (e.g. HIV infection) or close contacts of infectious cases and those with fibrotic lesions on chest radiograph;
- over 10 mm for other risk factors (see preventive therapies below);
- over 15 mm in people without a risk factor.

The tuberculin skin test has many limitations that must be understood in order to interpret test results correctly. These limitations include variations in test administration, reading of the test, false positive results, and false negative tests due to immunosuppression by old age, medications, or disease.

Immunity to *M. tuberculosis* may wane with time, especially in the absence of re-exposure to the organism. This waning immunity is particularly common in older people who may have been infected early in life, developed an immune response but were not re-exposed. This may result in a negative tuberculin skin test when tested later in life, for example at the time of admission to a nursing home. However, if the purified protein derivative skin test with 5 tuberculin units is repeated within 1 to 3 weeks of the first test, some patients will now have a positive test (over 10 mm of induration). This sequence of a negative skin test that becomes positive on repeat testing after a short interval is referred to as the 'booster' phenomenon, and the technique used to detect this is called the two-step tuberculin test. People who have a booster reaction should be classified as reactors, not converters. This form of testing should be considered for all older people, especially for all nursing home residents on admission (Finucane 1988), where about 5 per cent of residents will demonstrate the booster phenomenon when retested within 30 days of admission (Stead and To 1987).

Distinguishing between nursing home residents who are tuberculin skin test reactors and versus converters (over 15 mm increase in induration within 2 years) is important because it is predictive of the resident's risk of developing tuberculosis. Depending on sex, only 2 to 4 per cent of residents who are tuberculin reactors will develop active tuberculosis on follow-up, whereas 8 per cent of female residents and 12 per cent of male residents who are tuberculin converters will develop active tuberculosis on follow-up (Stead and To 1987). The high rate of active disease among tuberculin converters argues strongly for an active surveillance programme to identify residents with new tuberculous infection in the nursing home setting.

Clinical manifestations

The clinical diagnosis of tuberculosis is especially difficult in the nursing home population. Cases are often missed either because of atypical presentations or the inability of the older person to communicate their complaints. Reactivation of dormant infection in the lung often presents with non-specific findings including fatigue, anorexia, weight loss, and night sweats with or without fever. There is usually a deterioration of clinical status without explanation. A productive cough may be a late manifestation and is often labelled as 'bronchitis'. The chest radiograph is usually abnormal and demonstrates fibronodular infiltrates in the upper lobes of the lung with or without cavitation; these radiograph changes are often mistaken for cancer.

Nursing home residents with recent exogenous reinfection may present with progressive primary pulmonary tuberculosis (Dutt and Stead 1992). The chest radiograph may demonstrate infiltrates in the lower lobes of the lung with or without hilar and mediastinal lymphadenopathy. The clinical picture is often mistaken for bacterial pneumonia because of the lower lobe involvement and the resident may undergo several courses of antibiotic treatment. Thus, pulmonary tuberculosis should be considered in any nursing home resident with a history of 'recurrent' or 'unresolving' pneumonia. Pleural effusion may be the presenting sign of primary tuberculosis and may be confused with congestive heart failure.

Diagnosis

Early diagnosis of pulmonary tuberculosis depends on the clinician's awareness, especially with the atypical presentations. Once the diagnosis is considered, the patient in hospital or nursing home resident should be placed under respiratory precautions in a negative-pressure room to prevent possible transmission. A chest radiograph is obtained, and the radiologist is informed that tuberculosis is a possible diagnosis. The bacteriological diagnosis of tuberculosis in the older person is problematic because of the difficulty in obtaining appropriate specimens for staining and culture. The standard approach for identifying pulmonary tuberculosis is to obtain three expectorated sputum samples on three separate days (preferably early morning samples). In the absence of expectorated sputum samples, other collection methods may be needed, including nasopharyngeal aspirates, gastric aspirates, or fibreoptic bronchoscopy. The tuberculin skin test is not a useful diagnostic test because false negative reactions can occur in up to 30 per cent. In addition, three negative sputum smears for acid–fast bacilli does not exclude the diagnosis as the sensitivity of this test is only about 60 per cent among people with positive sputum cultures for *M. tuberculosis*.

Treatment

The American Thoracic Society (1994) has developed recommendations for treatment (and prevention) of tuberculosis in the United States. The 6-month treatment regimen of isoniazid (300 mg/day) plus rifampicin (rifampin) (600 mg/day) plus pyrazinamide (25 mg/kg body weight/day) daily for 2 months followed by isoniazid (300 mg) and rifampicin (600 mg) daily is often recommended to promote increased compliance. However, this triple-drug regimen is often difficult for older people. Moreover, drug-resistant tuberculosis has not been a problem, in general, in older people because the disease is usually caused by an infection acquired many years ago. Therefore an alternative regimen is 9 months of isoniazid (300 mg/day) and rifampicin (600 mg/day).

There are two major concerns regarding the chemotherapy of tuberculosis in elderly people: drug interactions and drug toxicity. Drug interactions can be effectively handled if they are recognized prior to initiating therapy. Major drug toxicity, including hepatitis and haematological abnormalities, occurs in less than 5 per cent of elderly patients. All patients should have a complete blood count and liver function test performed before therapy is initiated. Although there is some debate, older people probably should be seen monthly for the first 3 months of therapy for clinical evaluation and laboratory tests for a possible hepatic toxicity. Asymptomatic elevations of serum aminotransferase levels (up to threefold increases from baseline) occur frequently during therapy but usually resolve with no adverse consequences. If nausea, vomiting, anorexia, or jaundice develops, patients should be instructed to discontinue therapy immediately and be seen for diagnostic studies (American Thoracic Society 1994).

Preventive therapy

Preventive therapy is usually not recommended for elderly tuberculin reactors with no risk conditions, because the risk of hepatic toxicity (about 5 per cent) is about the same as the risk for subsequently developing tuberculosis (Stead and To 1987). Preventive therapy is indicated for high-risk older people (see skin test section) and for others with medical conditions increasing the risk of tuberculosis such as diabetes mellitus, adrenocorticosteroid therapy or other immunosuppressive therapy, intravenous drug users, haematological and reticuloendothelial malignancies, endstage renal disease, and marked weight loss. Preventive therapy consists of a single daily dose of isoniazid (300 mg) for 6 to 9 months; people with HIV infection should receive 12 months of therapy. Drug-induced hepatitis requires close monitoring for symptoms of hepatitis as noted above. The caveats about monitoring serum aminotransferase levels during therapy of tuberculosis apply for preventive therapy as well (American Thoracic Society 1994).

Viral respiratory infections

Epidemiology

Viral respiratory infections are increasingly recognized as an important cause of morbidity and mortality in older people. Although surveillance studies in the general population, both in the United States and Europe, indicate that viral respiratory infections occur less frequently (between one and two illnesses per year) with increasing age (Monto and Sullivan 1993; Lina et al. 1996), studies focused on older people note rates ranging from 3 per 100 person-months in the community to 11 per 100 person-months in senior day-care programmes with substantial rates of hospital admission (6 per cent) and death (3 per cent) in the latter setting (Falsey 1995b). Viral respiratory infections account for between 30 and 40 per cent of respiratory infections in nursing home residents, with rates as high as one illness per bed per annum and complications, including treatment with antibiotics (50–90 per cent), pneumonias (10–25 per cent), and deaths (5 per cent) (Falsey et al. 1992; Nicholson et al. 1990).

The seasonal occurrence of viral respiratory infections in older people reflects the occurrence of specific viral pathogens in the community and general population. In the northern hemisphere disease patterns are as follows: parainfluenza peaks in autumn to early winter, adenovirus from autumn to late winter, respiratory syncytial virus in early winter and throughout the influenza season, influenza in late winter to early spring (note that 'out of season' influenza outbreaks do occur in nursing homes (Kohn et al. 1995)),

coronaviruses in late autumn to late winter, and rhinoviruses throughout the year (Lina et al. 1996; Monto and Sullivan 1993). Usually several viral agents are co-circulating simultaneously, especially during the early and late winter months, which can lead to problems in diagnosis, treatment, and prevention (Falsey et al. 1992).

Viral respiratory infections are frequently transmitted to older people from family and other community-based people, for example day-care, nursing home, or hospital staff. Most viral respiratory pathogens are spread by close hand-to-hand contact or by fomites, with hand-washing the single most important infection control measure. Influenza and adenovirus are also transmitted by inhalation of small-particle aerosols, requiring the use of masks by staff and visitors who have contact with ill people and by ill people who are transported out of their rooms. Additional infection control measures during outbreaks in hospitals or nursing homes include single rooms for people suspected of influenza or adenovirus (or cohorting if no single rooms are available), cohort staff, limiting visitors with respiratory symptoms, and avoiding admissions of high-risk people (Graman and Hall 1989).

Influenza virus

Influenza virus infections are the most serious viral respiratory infections. The rates of community-acquired infection are relatively low (about 5 per cent) but are substantial for nursing home residents (between 20 and 35 per cent). Complications associated with underlying chronic conditions, especially cardiopulmonary diseases, occur frequently; hospital admission rates range from 150 to 700 per 100 000 people and deaths from 10 to 400 per 100 000 people, with the highest rates in nursing home residents (Barker and Mullooly 1980, 1982). Clusters or outbreaks of influenza occur frequently in nursing homes and other long-term care facilities.

Influenza viruses belong to the Orthomyxoviridae family, which contains two genera: influenza virus types A and B. Influenza A viruses, the primary cause of severe illness, are classified into subtypes on the basis of haemagglutinin (H) and neuraminidase (N) antigens. Significant antigenic variation or 'drift' with the same subtype, e.g. A/Texas/77 (H_3N_2) and A/Bangkok/79 (H_3N_2), may occur over time so that infection or immunization with one strain may not induce immunity to distant-related strains. Major antigenic 'shifts' of H and N proteins can lead to large-scale epidemics, such as the shift in 1957 from H_1N_1 to H_2N_2 influenza B virus.

The clinical manifestations of uncomplicated influenza are similar in both younger and older people. After an incubation period of 18 to 36 h, there is an abrupt onset of a febrile systemic illness characterized by chilliness or rigors, headache, myalgias, and malaise. Fever ranges from 37.8 to 40°C. Local respiratory signs and symptoms, that is cough, nasal obstruction and sore throat, predominate over the next 3 to 5 days and can persist for 2 to 4 weeks together with malaise. Ocular symptoms, including photophobia, tearing, or painful eye movements, are helpful additional clues to distinguish milder cases from rhinovirus (common colds). In influenza outbreaks in nursing homes, a milder illness may be indistinguishable from respiratory syncytial virus or influenza B infections. Complications include tracheobronchitis, bacterial pneumonia, primary influenza pneumonia, and, rarely, myocarditis, myositis, or encephalitis. Laboratory findings include an elevated peripheral white blood count (10 000–12 000/mm^3 with predominance of polymorphonuclear leucocytes) which changes within a few days to a normal white blood cell count with predominant mononuclear cells. In patients with uncomplicated influenza, the Gram stain of the sputum contains few white blood cells, and the chest radiograph often demonstrates increased interstitial markings without an infiltrate.

The diagnosis of influenza viral infection is frequently based on clinicoepidemiological findings during a community outbreak. However, additional diagnostic efforts are warranted because of the increased frequency of non-influenza respiratory viral infections in older people, especially in nursing homes and day-care centres, and the effectiveness of viral chemotherapy (amantadine or rimantadine) limited to influenza A virus only. Influenza virus is best isolated by obtaining separate swabs of the throat and nasopharynx within 24 to 48 h of the onset of clinical illness. The swabs are combined in a single tube containing viral transport media and carried to an experienced laboratory for virus isolation and rapid diagnostic testing. The virus can be isolated in the majority of specimens within 3 days of inoculation but may take as long as 5 to 7 days. Rapid detection, for example using enzyme immunoassay and direct or indirect immunofluorescence assay, can identify influenza A viral antigen in clinical specimens within 24 h with sensitivities and specificities as high as 90 and 98 per cent, respectively (Leonardi et al. 1994). Although not helpful in the acute illness, a four-fold or greater rise in complement-fixing antibody titres from serum obtained within 7 days of the acute illness (acute phase titre) and 2 to 3 weeks later (convalescent phase titre) are considered diagnostic.

Symptomatic treatment of influenza infection includes bed rest, adequate fluids, paracetamol (acetaminophen), and the use of nasal sprays or drops and cough syrups as required. Therapy for bronchospasm is often required, including inhaled bronchodilators and steroids, theophylline, and intravenous steroids. Empirical antibiotic treatment is indicated for postinfluenza purulent tracheobronchitis or suspected bacterial pneumonia (see above).

Specific antiviral therapy consists of amantadine hydrochloride or rimantadine hydrochloride (a structural analogue); both are symmetric tricyclic amines that specifically inhibit the replication of influenza A viruses but not influenza B viruses (Mahmood and Sacks 1995). Despite the similarities in chemical structure, spectrum of activity, and mechanism of action, the pharmacokinetics of amantadine and rimantadine differ markedly. Amantadine is excreted unmetabolized in the urine with the plasma half-life increased two-fold in healthy older people and even longer in those with impaired renal function. Dose reductions are recommended for amantadine based on alterations in renal function, beginning with 100 mg/day for people with estimated creatinine clearances above 80 ml/min and additional reductions with decreased renal function (Gomolin et al. 1995). Amantadine is available as 100 mg capsules and a more expensive syrup (50 mg/5 ml) for tube-fed patients; both formulations are available generically. In contrast, approximately 75 per cent of rimantadine is metabolized in the liver with a plasma half-life twice as long than amantadine (Mahmood and Sacks 1995). The usual dose of this proprietary drug is 100 mg twice a day for healthy older people with a dose reduction to 100 mg/day for elderly nursing home residents or those experiencing possible side-effects when taking 200 mg/day (Centers for Disease Control and Prevention 1997b).

Adverse reactions occur more frequently in older people receiving amantadine (40 per cent) or rimantadine (30 per cent) than in young healthy adults (10 and 5 per cent, respectively) (Patriarca et al. 1984; Strange et al. 1991; Centers for Disease Control and Prevention

1997b). The most frequent (20 per cent) and serious adverse reactions of amantadine involve the central nervous system and include light-headedness or dizziness, difficulty concentrating, depression, delirium, anxiety (30 per cent rimantadine), insomnia, auditory and visual hallucinations, and seizures (3 per cent) (Strange et al. 1991). These adverse reactions are often associated with high plasma concentrations of amantadine or rimantadine, especially in older people who have renal insufficiency or are receiving over 100 mg per daily dose (Patriarca et al. 1984; Degelau et al. 1990). There is an increase in falls (10 per cent with amantadine) associated with light-headedness, dizziness, and ataxia, especially among ambulatory nursing home residents. Amantadine (or rimantadine) should be discontinued in patients who experience seizures at the 100 mg daily dose. Options for patients with a history of seizures include no dose adjustment beyond those for renal function, further dose reduction, or withholding amantadine or rimantadine (Gomolin et al. 1995). If either drug is used, anticonvulsive therapy should be restarted in patients with a history of major motor seizure disease who have had treatment withdrawn. Other adverse reactions (20 per cent) include gastrointestinal (anorexia, nausea, vomiting, diarrhoea) and anticholinergic (dry mouth, blurred vision, urinary retention, constipation) effects. These adverse reactions are usually mild and can decrease or disappear after the first week despite continuing the drug. Drug–drug interactions with amantadine or rimantadine are most likely to occur with central nervous system stimulants, antihistamines, or anticholinergic drugs (Centers for Disease Control and Prevention 1997b).

Both amantadine and rimantadine are effective symptomatic treatment for uncomplicated influenza A infections when begun within 48 h following the onset of illness. Based on favourable outcome studies (including reduced duration of fever, symptoms, and viral shedding) in younger adults, empirical treatment is recommended for 3 to 5 days in older people with febrile influenza-like illnesses when influenza A is documented in the community or strongly suspected. People in the community who are treated for over 5 days with either drug may shed amantadine- or rimantadine-resistant viruses (Hayden et al. 1989, 1991). Therefore, people being treated for influenza should avoid contact with uninfected people, and treatment should be discontinued as soon as signs and symptoms are reduced, generally after 3 to 5 days of treatment. It is not known whether treatment prevents or reduces morbidity and mortality associated with influenza-related complications in high-risk older people or whether treatment is effective in patients with established infections of the lower respiratory tract.

Prevention of influenza by yearly vaccination with inactivated vaccines is currently the most cost-effective available measure for reducing the impact of influenza in older people (Patriarca et al. 1987). These vaccines contain both killed A- and B-type viruses. Recent reviews provide details regarding formulation dosage, adverse reactions, immunogenicity, efficacy recommendations and strategies for implementing recommendations, and newer approaches (Betts 1995; Bentley 1996). Annual vaccination programmes, beginning in October to mid-November in the northern hemisphere, should be targeted towards all people 65 years of age and older, especially those with chronic pulmonary and cardiovascular diseases and other comorbidities that require regular medical follow-up or hospital admission. Comparable efforts should be directed towards groups of people who can transmit influenza to older people, including doctors, nurses, and other personnel who provide direct patient care in hospitals, nursing homes, ambulatory care settings, and the home.

Chemoprophylaxis with amantadine or rimantadine is effective in preventing (or reducing the severity of) clinical illness and can limit the spread of influenza A outbreaks in nursing homes (Patriarca *et al.* 1987; Gomolin *et al.* 1995). However, it is not a substitute for vaccination. Moreover, influenza A viruses resistant to both amantadine and rimantadine have been recovered in nursing homes in both infected residents treated with one of these drugs (Mast *et al.* 1991), in uninfected contacts who have not received these drugs (Degelau *et al.* 1992), or during the early period of chemoprophylaxis (Houck *et al.* 1995). The clinical importance of amantadine and rimantadine resistance is uncertain, but measures should be implemented to reduce contact between uninfected residents and staff and those residents and staff receiving treatment or chemoprophylaxis.

Recommendations for chemoprophylaxis for residents and staff in nursing homes include the following.

1. Before the outbreak when influenza A virus is in the community:

   (a) as an adjunct to late immunization of high-risk people (duration of chemoprophylaxis is 2 weeks to develop protective serum antibody levels postvaccination);

   (b) as the only preventive measure for the few high-risk people for whom vaccination is contraindicated (duration is the duration of peak influenza season, usually about 12 weeks).

2. When the influenza virus outbreak is detected in the nursing home:

   (a) as an adjunct to late immunization of high-risk people (duration is 2 weeks);

   (b) as an additional margin of protection for those highest-risk residents who were vaccinated over 3 months earlier (duration is until outbreak subsides, usually about 2–3 weeks).

Recommended dosages for chemoprophylaxis with amantadine or rimantadine are the same as those for treatment (Centers for Disease Control and Prevention 1997*b*).

Respiratory syncytial virus

Respiratory syncytial virus is a single-stranded RNA paramyxovirus consisting of two antigenically distinct groups (A and B). Although a well-known respiratory pathogen causing bronchiolitis and pneumonia in infants and young children, respiratory syncytial virus is increasingly being recognized as an important cause of severe illness in older people. It accounts for about 25 per cent of acute respiratory illnesses in nursing home residents (Falsey *et al.* 1992) and about 10 per cent of hospital admissions for elderly people with acute cardiopulmonary conditions or influenza-like illnesses (Falsey *et al.* 1995*a*). Complications vary, depending on the severity of comorbid illnesses, with pneumonia rates approximately 5 to 65 per cent and death rates up to 55 per cent. Outbreaks of respiratory syncytial virus in nursing homes, often concurrent with influenza viruses, occur regularly during the winter seasons in the United States, United Kingdom, and Europe (Falsey 1991; Potter *et al.* 1997).

The clinical manifestations of uncomplicated respiratory syncytial virus infection are similar to any upper respiratory tract infection with fever, nasal congestion, or rhinorrhoea. Although clinically similar, the presence of the latter and the absence or rigors may be helpful in suspecting early respiratory syncytial virus from influenza virus infections (Mathur *et al.* 1980). The presence of nausea, vomiting, and diarrhoea may suggest influenza virus infections (Wald *et al.*

1995). Lower respiratory tract involvement includes persistent fever and cough, wheezing, bronchitis, and exacerbations of asthma, chronic obstructive pulmonary disease, or worsening of cardiac conditions. Nursing home residents experience substantial morbidity with about half suffering prolonged malaise and anorexia lasting 4 weeks or more (Osterweil and Norman 1990). Similar to hospital admission for influenza A, respiratory syncytial virus infections incur substantial morbidity, including prolonged hospital stays (16 days), high intensive care admissions (about 20 per cent), and ventilatory support (about 10 per cent).

The diagnosis of respiratory syncytial virus in older people is problematic. Virus cultures are obtained by the double-swab technique (see above) because nasal washes are poorly tolerated by older people. The virus is labile and difficult to isolate even under optimal conditions using the more rigorous nasal wash technique. Commercial rapid antigen tests (successful in children using nasal washes), are not as sensitive in older people. Thus virus isolation or antigen detection alone will underestimate the true incidence of respiratory syncytial virus infection. Serological techniques, such as enzyme-linked immunosorbent assay or complement fixation, are available for retrospective diagnosis (Falsey *et al.* 1996).

Symptomatic treatment for respiratory syncytial virus infection and the use of empirical antibiotics is as described for influenza virus infections above. Specific antiviral chemotherapy with ribavirin aerosol is approved in the United States only for respiratory syncytial virus-associated bronchitis and pneumonia in infants and children in hospital (Mahmood and Sacks 1995). Ribavirin aerosols have been used in uncontrolled studies in immunocompromised adults (Englund *et al.* 1988) but no studies are available in older people. There is no role for vaccination or chemoprophylaxis.

Other respiratory viruses

As noted in the section above on epidemiology, there are several other respiratory viruses that cause illnesses in older people, including outbreaks in the community as well as in elderly day-care programmes and nursing homes. These viruses include rhinovirus, coronavirus, and adenovirus. The reader is referred to two excellent recent reports for additional discussion regarding these viruses (Nicholson *et al.* 1996; Falsey *et al.* 1997).

References

American Thoracic Society (1994). Treatment of tuberculosis and tuberculous infection in adults and children. *American Journal of Respiratory and Critical Care Medicine*, **149**, 1359–74.

American Thoracic Society/Centers for Disease Control and Prevention (1990). Diagnostic standards and classification of tuberculosis. *American Review of Respiratory Disease*, **142**, 725–35.

Barker, W.H. and Mullooly, J.P. (1980). Impact of epidemic type A influenza in a defined adult population. *American Journal of Epidemiology*, **112**, 798–813.

Barker, W.H. and Mullooly, J.P. (1982). Pneumonia and influenza deaths during epidemics; implications for prevention. *Archives of Internal Medicine*, **142**, 85–9.

Bartlett, J.G. and Mundy, L.M. (1995). Community-acquired pneumonia. *New England Journal of Medicine*, **333**, 1618–24.

Beck-Sague, C., Banerjee, S., and Jarvis, W.R. (1993). Infectious diseases and mortality among US nursing home residents. *American Journal of Public Health*, **83**, 1739–42.

Bentley, D.W. (1984). Bacterial pneumonia in the elderly: clinical features, diagnosis, aetiology, and treatment. *Gerontology*, 30, 297–307.

Bentley, D.W. (1996). Immunizations in older adults. *Infectious Diseases in Clinical Practice*, 5, 490–7.

Bentley, D.W., Ha, K., Mamot, K., et al. (1981). Pneumococcal vaccine in the institutionalized elderly: design of a non-randomized trial and preliminary results. *Reviews of Infectious Diseases*, 3, S71–81.

Betts, R.F. (1995). Vaccines in the prevention of viral pneumonia. *Seminars in Respiratory Infections*, 10, 282–7.

British Thoracic Society (1993). Guidelines for the management of community-acquired pneumonia in adults admitted to hospital. *British Journal of Hospital Medicine*, 49, 346–50.

Celis, R., Torrez, A., Gatell, J.M., Almela, M., Rodriguez-Roisin, R., and Agusti-Vidal, A. (1988). Nosocomial pneumonia. A multivariate analysis of risk and prognosis. *Chest*, 93, 318–24.

Centers for Disease Control and Prevention (1995). Pneumonia and influenza death rates—United States, 1979–1994. *Morbidity and Mortality Weekly Report*, 44, 535–7.

Centers for Disease Control and Prevention (1997a). Outbreaks of pneumococcal pneumonia among unvaccinated residents in chronic-care facilities—Massachusetts, October 1995, Oklahoma, February 1996, and Maryland, May–June 1996. *Morbidity and Mortality Weekly Report*, 46, 60–1.

Centers for Disease Control and Prevention (1997b). Prevention and control of influenza. Recommendations of the Advisory Committee on Immunisation Practices (ACIP). *Morbidity and Mortality Weekly Report*, 46 (RR-9), 1–24.

Centers for Disease Control and Prevention (1997c). Prevention of pneumococcal disease. Recommendations of the Advisory Committee on Immunisation Practices (ACIP). *Morbidity and Mortality Weekly Report*, 46 (RR-8), 1–24.

Chastre, J., Fagon, J.-Y., and Trouillet, J.L. (1995). Diagnosis and treatment of nosocomial pneumonia in patients in intensive care units. *Clinical Infectious Diseases*, 21, S226–37.

Craven, D.E. and Steger, K.A. (1995). Epidemiology of nosocomial pneumonia. New perspectives on an old disease. *Chest*, 108, 1S–16S.

Degelau, J., Somani, S., Cooper, S.L., and Irvine, P.W. (1990). Occurrence of adverse effects and high amantadine concentrations with influenza prophylaxis in the nursing home. *Journal of the American Geriatrics Society*, 38, 428–32.

Degelau, J., Somani, S.K., Cooper, S.L., Guay, D.R.P., and Crossley, K.B. (1992). Amantadine-resistant influenza in a nursing facility. *Archives of Internal Medicine*, 152, 390–2.

Degelau, J., Guay, D., Straub, K., and Luxenberg, M.G. (1995). Effectiveness of oral antibiotic treatment in nursing home-acquired pneumonia. *Journal of the American Geriatrics Society*, 43, 245–51.

Drinka, P.J., Gauerke, C., Voeks, S., Miller, J., Schultz, S., Krause, P., and Golubjatnikov, R. (1994). Pneumonia in a nursing home. *Journal of General Internal Medicine*, 9, 650–2.

Dutt, A.K. and Stead, W.W. (1992). Tuberculosis. *Clinical Geriatric Medicine*, 8, 761–75.

Emori, T.G., Banerjee, S.N., Culver, D.H., et al. (1991). Nosocomial infections in elderly patients in the United States, 1986–1990. *American Journal of Medicine*, 91, 289S–93S.

Englund, J.A., Sullivan, C.J., Jordan, M.C., Dehner, L.P., Vercellotti, G.M., and Balfour, H.H., Jr (1988). Respiratory syncytial virus infection in immunocompromised adults. *Annals of Internal Medicine*, 109, 203–8.

Fagon, J.Y., Chastre, J., Domart, Y., et al.(1989). Nosocomial pneumonia in patients receiving continuous mechanical ventilation: prospective analysis of 52 episodes with use of a protected specimen brush and quantitative culture techniques. *American Review of Respiratory Diseases*, 139, 877–84.

Falsey, A.R. (1991). Non-influenza respiratory virus infection in long-term care facilities. *Infection Control and Hospital Epidemiology*, 12, 602–8.

Falsey, A.R., Treanor, J.J., Betts, R.F., and Walsh, E.E. (1992). Viral respiratory infections in the institutionalized elderly: clinical and epidemiologic findings. *Journal of the American Geriatrics Society*, 40, 115–19.

Falsey, A.R., Cunningham, C.K., Barker, W.H., et al. (1995a). Respiratory syncytial virus and influenza A infections in the hospitalised elderly. *Journal of Infectious Diseases*, 172, 389–94.

Falsey, A.R., McCann, R.M., Hall, W.J., et al. (1995b). Acute respiratory tract infection in day-care centers for older persons. *Journal of the American Geriatrics Society*, 43, 30–6.

Falsey, A.R., McCann, R.M., Hall, W.J., and Criddle, M.M. (1996). Evaluation of four methods for the diagnosis of respiratory syncytial virus infection in older adults. *Journal of the American Geriatrics Society*, 44, 71–3.

Falsey, A.R., McCann, R.M., Hall, W.J., et al. (1997). The 'common cold' in frail older persons: impact of rhinovirus and coronavirus in a senior day-care center. *Journal of the American Geriatrics Society*, 45, 706–11.

Finch, R.C. (1995). Pneumonia: the impact of antibiotic resistance on its management. *Microbial Drug Resistance*, 1, 149–58.

Fine, M.J., Smith, D.N., and Singer, D.E. (1990). Hospitalisation decision in patients with community-acquired pneumonia. A prospective cohort study. *American Journal of Medicine*, 89, 713–21.

Finucane, T.E. (1988). The American Geriatrics Society statement on two-step PPD testing for nursing home patients on admission. *Journal of the American Geriatrics Society*, 36, 77–8.

Gilbert, K. and Fine, M.J. (1994). Assessing prognosis and predicting patient outcomes in community-acquired pneumonia. *Seminars in Respiratory Infections*, 9, 140–52.

Gleason, P.P., Kapoor, W.N., Stone, R.A., et al. (1997). Medical outcomes and antimicrobial costs with the use of the American Thoracic Society guidelines for outpatients with community-acquired pneumonia. *Journal of the American Medical Association*, 278, 32–9.

Gomolin, I.H., Leib, H.B., Arden, N.H., and Sherman, F.T. (1995). Control of influenza outbreaks in the nursing home: guidelines for diagnosis and management. *Journal of the American Geriatrics Society*, 43, 71–4.

Graman, P.S. and Hall, C.B. (1989). Epidemiology and control of nosocomial viral infections. *Infectious Disease Clinics of North America*, 3, 815–41.

Granton, J.T. and Grossman, R.F. (1993). Community-acquired pneumonia in the elderly patient. Clinical features, epidemiology, and treatment. *Clinical Geriatric Medicine*, 14, 537–53.

Harkness, G.A., Bentley, D.W., and Roghmann, K.J. (1990). Risk factors for nosocomial pneumonia in the elderly. *American Journal of Medicine*, 89, 457–63.

Hayden, F.G., Belshe, R.B., Clover, R.D., Hay, A.J., Oakes, M.G., and Soo, W. (1989). Emergence and apparent transmission of rimantadine-resistant influenza A virus in families. *New England Journal of Medicine*, 321, 1696–702.

Hayden, F.G., Sperber, S.J., Belshe, R.B., Clover, R.D., Hay, A.J., and Pyke, S. (1991). Recovery of drug-resistant influenza A virus during therapeutic use of rimantadine. *Antimicrobial Agents and Chemotherapy*, 85, 1741–7.

Houck, P., Hemphill, M., LaCroix, S., Hirsh, D., and Cox, N. (1995). Amantadine-resistant influenza A in nursing homes. *Archives of Internal Medicine*, 155, 533–7.

Hutton, M.D., Cauthen, G.M., and Bloch, A.B. (1993). Results of a 29-state survey of tuberculosis in nursing homes and correctional facilities. *Public Health Report*, 108, 305–14.

Jokinen, C., Heiskanen, L., Juvonen, H., et al. (1993). Incidence of community-acquired pneumonia in the population of four municipalities in eastern Finland. *American Journal of Epidemiology*, 137, 977–88.

Kohn, M.A., Farley, T.A., Sundin, D., Tapia, R., McFarland, L.M., and Arden, N.H. (1995). Three summertime outbreaks of influenza type A. *Journal of Infectious Diseases*, 172, 246–9.

LaCroix, A.Z., Lipson, S., Miles, T.P., and White, L. (1989). Prospective study of pneumonia hospitalizations and mortality of United States older people: the role of chronic conditions, health behaviors, and nutritional status. *Public Health Report*, 104, 350–60.

Leonardi, G.P., Leib, H., Birkhead, G.S., Smith, C., Costello, P., and Conron, W. (1994). Comparison of rapid detection methods for influenza A virus and their value in health care management of institutionalized geriatric residents. *Journal of Clinical Microbiology*, 32, 70–4.

Lina, B., Valette, M., Foray, S., *et al.* (1996). Surveillance of community-acquired viral infections due to respiratory viruses in Rhone-Alpes (France) during winter 1994 to 1995. *Journal of Clinical Microbiology*, 34, 3007–11.

Luna, C.M., Vujacich, P., Niederman, M.S., *et al.* (1997). Impact of BAL data on the therapy and outcome of ventilator-associated pneumonia. *Chest*, 111, 676–85.

MacFarlane, J. (1994). Adult community-acquired pneumonia—a review. *Seminars in Respiratory Infections*, 9, 153–65.

Magaziner, J., Tenney, J.H., DeForge, B., Hebel, J.R., Muncie, H.L. Jr, and Warren, J.W. (1991). Prevalence and characteristics of nursing home-acquired pneumonia in the aged. *Journal of the American Geriatric Society*, 39, 1071–8.

Mahmood, W. and Sacks, S.L. (1995). Anti-infective therapy for viral pneumonia. *Seminars in Respiratory Infections*, 10, 270–81.

Marrie, T.J. (1990). Epidemiology of community-acquired pneumonia in the elderly. *Seminars in Respiratory Infections*, 5, 260–8.

Marrie, T.J. (1995). Management of community-acquired pneumonia in elderly patients. *Infectious Disease Clinical Practice*, 4, 373–7.

Marrie, T.J., Durant, H., and Kwan, C. (1986). Nursing home-acquired pneumonia: a case–control study. *Journal of the American Geriatric Society*, 34, 697–702.

Mast, E.E., Harmon, M.W., Gravenstein, S., *et al.* (1991). Emergence and possible transmission of amantadine-resistant viruses during nursing home outbreaks of influenza A (H3N2). *American Journal of Epidemiology*, 134, 988–97.

Mathur, U., Bentley, D.W., and Hall, C.B. (1980). Concurrent respiratory syncytial virus and influenza A infections in the institutionalized elderly and chronically ill. *Annals of Internal Medicine*, 93, 49–52.

May, D.S., Kelly, J.J., Mendlein, J.M., and Garbe, P.L. (1991). Surveillance of major causes of hospitalisation among the elderly. *Morbidity and Mortality Weekly Report*, 40 (SS-1), 1–22.

Monto, A.S. and Sullivan, K.M. (1993). Acute respiratory illness in the community. Frequency of illness and the agents involved. *Epidemiology and Infection*, 110, 145–60.

Mylotte, J.M., Ksiazek, S., and Bentley, D.W. (1994). Rational approach to the antibiotic treatment of pneumonia in the elderly. *Drugs and Aging*, 4, 21–33.

Nicholson, K.G., Baker, D.J., Farquhar, A., Hurd, D., Kent, J., and Smith, S.H. (1990). Acute upper respiratory tract viral illness and influenza immunisation in homes for the elderly. *Epidemiology and Infection*, 105, 609–18.

Nicholson, K.G., Kent, J., Hammersley, V., and Cancio, E. (1996). Risk factors for lower respiratory complications of rhinovirus infections in elderly people living in the community: prospective cohort study. *British Medical Journal*, 313, 1119–23.

Niederman, M.S., Bass, J.B., Campbell, G.D., *et al.* (1993). Guidelines for the initial management of adults with community-acquired pneumonia: diagnosis, assessment of severity, and initial antimicrobial therapy. *American Review of Respiratory Diseases*, 148, 1418–26.

Niederman, M.S., Torres, A., and Summer, W. (1994). Invasive diagnostic testing is not needed routinely to manage suspected ventilator-associated pneumonia. *American Journal of Respiratory and Critical Care Medicine*, 150, 565–69.

Osterweil, D. and Norman, D. (1990). An outbreak of an influenza-like illness in a nursing home. *Journal of the American Geriatric Society*, 38, 659–62.

Patriarca, P.A., Kater, N.A., Kendal, A.P., *et al.* (1984). Safety of prolonged administration of rimantadine hydrochloride in the prophylaxis of influenza A virus infections in nursing homes. *Antimicrobial Agents and Chemotherapy*, 26, 101–3.

Patriarca, P.A., Arden, N.H., Koplan, J.P., and Goodman, R.A. (1987). Prevention and control of type A influenza infections in nursing homes. Benefits and costs of four approaches using vaccination and amantadine. *Annals of Internal Medicine*, 107, 732–40.

Potter, J., Stott, D.J., Roberts, M.A., *et al.* (1997). Influenza vaccination of health care workers in long-term care hospital reduces the mortality of elderly patients. *Journal of Infectious Diseases*, 175, 1–6.

Salive, M.E., Satterfield, S., Ostfeld, A.M., Wallace, R.B., and Havlik, R.J. (1993). Disability and cognitive impairment are risk factors for pneumonia-related mortality in older adults. *Public Health Report*, 108, 314–22.

Saviteer, S.M., Samsa, G.P., and Rutala, W.A. (1988). Nosocomial infections in the elderly. *American Journal of Medicine*, 84, 661–6.

Stead, W.A. and To, T. (1987). The significance of the tuberculin skin test in elderly persons. *Annals Internal Medicine*, 107, 837–42.

Strange, K.C., Little, D.W., and Blatnik, B. (1991). Adverse reactions to amantadine prophylaxis of influenza in retirement home. *Journal of the American Geriatrics Society*, 33, 700–5.

Tablan, O.C., Anderson, L.J., Arden, N.H., *et al.* (1994). Guidelines for prevention of nosocomial pneumonia. *Infection Control and Hospital Epidemiology*, 15, 587–637.

Valenti, W.M., Trudell, R.G., and Bentley, D.W. (1978). Factors predisposing to oropharyngeal colonization with Gram-negative bacilli in the aged. *New England Journal of Medicine*, 298, 1108–11.

Wald, T.G., Miller, B.A., Shult, P., Drinka, P., Langer, L., and Gravenstein, S. (1995). Can respiratory syncytial virus and influenza A be distinguished clinically in institutionalized older persons? *Journal of the American Geriatrics Society*, 43, 170–4.

Warren, J.W., Palumbo, F.B., Fitterman, L., and Speedie, S.M. (1991). Incidence and characteristics of antibiotic use in aged nursing home patients. *Journal of the American Geriatrics Society*, 39, 963–72.

Zimmer, J.G., Bentley, D.W., Valenti, W.M., and Watson N.M. (1986). Antibiotic use in nursing homes. A quality assessment. *Journal of the American Geriatrics Society*, 34, 703–10.

12.3   Asthma and chronic obstructive pulmonary disease

Sarah Keir and Lindsey Dow

Introduction

On an international scale, asthma and chronic obstructive pulmonary disease (**COPD**) are common causes of respiratory symptoms, physical disability, and impaired quality of life in elderly people. Furthermore, exacerbations of these diseases are a costly and frequent cause of general practitioner contact and emergency hospital admission, and in the older patient in particular may result in death (Mafreda *et al.* 1989). With the rising number of older people in most developed and developing countries, these diseases have great significance from the public health perspective.

Definitions and pathology of asthma and COPD

Asthma

The American Thoracic Society defines asthma as a disease characterized by increased responsiveness of the bronchi to various stimuli, manifested by widespread narrowing of the airways that changes in severity either spontaneously or as a result of treatment (American Thoracic Society 1962). As early as 1892, Osler recognized that airway inflammation was the pathological hallmark of asthma (Osler 1892). Marked changes of airway inflammation are found on bronchial biopsy even in mild asthmatics (Beasley *et al.* 1989). The typical changes found in the large and small airways of asthmatics include airway smooth muscle hypertrophy, thickening of the basement membrane as a consequence of collagen deposition, changes in the epithelial cell lining with loss of cells, and increased fragility, mast cell degranulation, and inflammatory cell infiltrate within the walls and lumen. The inflammatory cells are multicellular, composed mainly of eosinophils but also neutrophils, lymphocytes, and mononuclear cells. Histological changes in non-smoking older asthmatics appear to be similar to those found in young patients (Aoki *et al.* 1995).

COPD

COPD is a heterogeneous disorder characterized by reduced expiratory flow and slow forced emptying of the lungs; these features show minimal change over several months (American Thoracic Society 1995). Most of the air-flow limitation is slowly progressive and irreversible. The air-flow limitation is due to varying combinations of airways disease and emphysema. The airway component consists mainly of decreased luminal diameters caused by various combinations of increased wall thickening, excess mucus, and changes in the lining of the small airways. The definition of COPD includes chronic bronchitis, emphysema, and small airways disease. These three conditions may coexist in tobacco smokers.

Chronic bronchitis is diagnosed when a patient describes the presence of cough productive of phlegm for at least 3 months in two successive years (Medical Research Council 1965) which cannot be explained by another cause such as bronchietasis. Histologically, chronic bronchitis is characterized by enlargement of bronchial mucous glands with dilatation of gland ducts and excess mucus production that primarily affects the central airways. The pathological changes of chronic bronchitis are reversible, if subjects stop smoking tobacco.

Emphysema is a condition of abnormal irreversible enlargement of air spaces distal to the terminal bronchioles. An important pathological feature of this condition is the destruction of lung parenchyma and elastic supporting tissue. Three types of emphysema can be distinguished: centriacinar emphysema (associated with long-standing cigarette smoking), panacinar emphysema (type usually seen in homozygous α-antitrypsin deficiency), and paraseptal emphysema.

Small or peripheral airways disease is characterized by an increase in goblet cell numbers, excess mucus which plugs the airways and an influx of inflammatory cells within the lumen, and the presence of inflammatory cells and fibrosis within the walls (Cosio *et al.* 1978). The 'small' airways are those with a diameter less than 2 mm.

The cellular changes of COPD are much less well described than those of asthma. Whereas the T lymphocytes and eosinophils are considered as the most important cells in asthma, the neutrophil is mainly incriminated in COPD. Tobacco smoking causes an influx of inflammatory cells into the airways and the predominant cell types are the neutrophil and macrophage. The degree of impairment of lung function in tobacco smokers correlates with blood and sputum neutrophilia (Stanescu *et al.* 1985). The cellular changes in COPD can show similarities with asthma in that activated eosinophils, mast cells, and T lymphocytes can be found in and around the airways.

The structural basis of air-flow limitation in COPD lies in and around the small airways (Bosken *et al.* 1990). Lung elastic recoil is

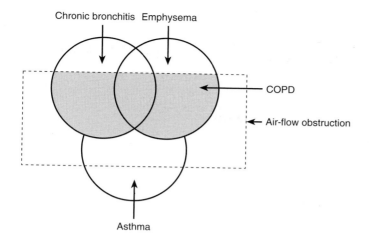

Fig. 1 Interrelationship of diseases of the airways. (Reproduced with permission from Celli *et al.* (1995).)

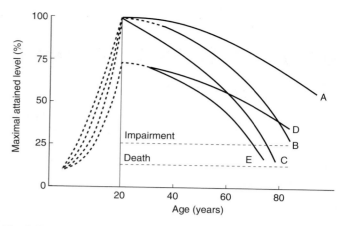

Fig. 2 Theoretical model of lung development and decline. The upper three curves represent patterns of growth in adults who achieve their predicted lung volumes. The top curve represents individual A, a healthy non-smoker with a normal age-associated decline in ventilatory function assessed by forced expiratory volume in 1 s. Individuals B and C represent accelerated decline of ventilatory function which differs on account of factors such as smoking history and inherent susceptibility. The lower two curves D and E represent subjects who did not reach maximum ventilatory capacity, one with moderate subsequent decline and one with steep decline, which may for example be explained by the presence of severe asthma throughout life with or without exposure to other factors such as tobacco smoking or occupational agents known to be toxic to the airways. (Reproduced with permission from Rijcken *et al.* (1991).)

reduced and airways resistance is increased. In addition to the structural changes, bronchoconstriction is usually present but its degree varies between patients and in the same patient over time. During single reversibility testing, up to one-third of patients with COPD will show significant change in forced expiratory volume in 1 s (**FEV1**) and as many as two-thirds will show significant reversibility following repeated testing (Anthonisen and Wright 1986).

In practice, as Fig. 1 illustrates, there is overlap between the clinical features of asthma and COPD and this becomes more marked in older people (Celli *et al.* 1995). One reason for greater overlap between asthma and COPD with ageing is that in the older patient with new onset asthma, the diagnosis may have been delayed for over 5 years and a degree of irreversible air-flow limitation may have developed (Burrows *et al.* 1991). A second reason is that many elderly asthmatics who have had disease since childhood or young adulthood will not have had the benefits of disease-modifying anti-inflammatory drugs such as corticosteroids and as a consequence many will have a degree of irreversible air-flow limitation. A third reason is that since the majority of men aged 65 years and over have a smoking history, some asthmatics will also have smoking-related COPD.

Epidemiology of airways disease

Risk factors for asthma and COPD

Although asthma and COPD are associated with distinct patterns of pathology, they share functional impairment within the airways. The FEV$_1$ and the forced vital capacity are the most practical indicators of lung function in population studies and have been invaluable in determining extrinsic and intrinsic risk factors associated with asthma and COPD or the preceding situation of subclinical impairment of airway function (Fig. 2). As asthma and COPD are so common in older people, identification of reversible risk factors is important in the development of public health policies that aim to increase the proportion of healthy and physically active elderly people. Achieving lung health in older people requires interventions on risk factors throughout life.

Factors known to influence airway function are relevant to asthma and COPD in that they may relate to the development of disease, trigger exacerbations, or influence growth or decline in lung function with time. Risk factors for impaired FEV$_1$ are listed in Table 1. The most obvious determinants of asthma are allergy and bronchial hyper-responsiveness, but their relevance in late-onset asthma is less clear. Tobacco smoking is by far the most important risk factor linked with COPD and reduced lung function in population studies. Tobacco smoking impairs lung growth in younger individuals, and speeds up lung function decline in adulthood (Burrows *et al.* 1977).

Over the past decade, the effect of early-life influences on lung disease in later life have become apparent. Nutrition during pregnancy and infection in the first year of life may affect lung development. Barker showed an association between birth weight and height and age-corrected FEV$_1$ in men aged 59 to 70 years (Barker *et al.* 1991). Mean corrected FEV$_1$ rose by 0.06 litre for each 0.45 kg (1 lb) increase in birth weight. Two or more episodes of respiratory infection during the first few years of life may prevent children reaching their predicted levels of lung function in early adulthood. Documented episodes of respiratory infection during infancy correlate with increased risk of respiratory symptoms and reduced FEV$_1$ in adults aged over 50 years (Barker and Osmond 1986).

Respiratory symptoms in older people

More than half of adults aged over 60 years in population studies in America, Europe, and Finland admit to at least one respiratory symptom (Milne and Williamson 1972; Lebowitz *et al.* 1975; Dow *et al.* 1991; Horsley *et al.* 1991; Ishoaho *et al.* 1994; Nejjari *et al.* 1996; Renwick and Connolly 1996). The severity of these symptoms is less

Table 1 Population risk factors for reduced FEV$_1$

Risk factor	Evidence	Other associations
Environment		
Tobacco smoking		
Active	Definite	COPD causation; exacerbates asthma and COPD
Passive	Possible	Exacerbates asthma
Occupational		
Dust/minerals	Definite	COPD causation; exacerbates asthma
Organic and non-organic compounds	Definite	Asthma causation; exacerbates asthma
Diet		
Reduced antioxidants	Putative	
Excess alcohol	Putative	
Impaired glucose tolerance	Putative	
Air pollution	Possible	Exacerbates asthma and COPD
Host factors		
Atopy	Definite	Asthma causation
Hyper-responsiveness	Definite	Asthma causation; exacerbates asthma and COPD
α-Antitrypsin deficiency	Definite	COPD causation
Low birth weight	Possible	COPD causation
Maternal smoking	Possible	?Asthma causation
Childhood respiratory infection	Possible	?COPD causation

clearly defined, as most questionnaires used in surveys structure the questions to indicate a particular respiratory symptom as being present if it was experienced at any time within the preceding year. A positive response may identify subjects who are symptomatic every day as well as subjects who have experienced the symptom on only one day in a year. The frequency of respiratory symptoms in different epidemiological studies in older people is outlined in Table 2.

Although symptoms such as wheeze or episodic breathlessness are associated with impairment of lung function, they are poorly predictive of asthma or COPD in epidemiological studies, particularly in the older patient. The differential diagnosis of older patients presenting with respiratory symptoms mostly lies within the cardiopulmonary systems and emphasizes the importance of investigations of respiratory and cardiac function as well as chest radiography in determining diagnosis and treatment.

Prevalence of asthma and COPD in older people

Burr *et al.* (1979) investigated a random population sample of 418 subjects over 70 years of age and demonstrated a prevalence of asthma of 2.9 per cent. A quarter of the adults with asthma were undiagnosed and one-third were on appropriate treatment but were unaware that they were asthmatic. A diagnosis of asthma was made if the patients admitted to attacks of breathlessness and wheezing and showed reversibility following trials of bronchodilators and corticosteroids.

These criteria are considered strict in that older people may not present with a typical history of attacks of breathlessness and wheeze.

Lee and Stretton have shown that late-onset asthma can present with a history of paroxysmal nocturnal dyspnoea or cough and phlegm in the absence of wheezing (Lee and Stretton 1972). Too lenient criteria may overestimate asthma prevalence. One survey of 199 subjects aged 55 years and over attending day hospital or living in residential accommodation found that 41 per cent increased their pre-bronchodilator peak expiratory flow by 15 per cent or more (Banerjee *et al.* 1987). A proportion of these subjects may have had asthma or COPD. However, increases in measurements of lung function in subjects unfamiliar with such tests may arise from learning effect or from variability in the measurement itself (Tweedale *et al.* 1984). Other population studies in Europe and the United States indicate that about 5 per cent of over 60-year-olds have asthma; Table 2 summarizes some of these studies. Overlap between asthma and COPD is inevitable as spirometry with measurement of the bronchodilator response will not discriminate between asthma and COPD. It is unclear whether asthma prevalence is rising in older people as it has been found in younger age groups. Mortality from asthma in old age has been considered to be still rising even though asthma mortality in other age groups has levelled out fallen or dropped. However, a recent survey of the accuracy of death certification in deaths in older 'asthmatics' in Northern Ireland indicated that a proportion of these deaths were related to other cardiac and pulmonary causes and not to asthma (Smyth *et al.* 1996).

The prevalence of COPD in America, Europe, and Finland has ranged from 7 to 34 per cent (Lebowitz *et al.* 1975; Ishoaho *et al.* 1994; Renwick and Connolly 1996). Prevalences are higher in the

Table 2 Frequency of selected respiratory symptoms, asthma, and COPD in different population studies of subjects at least 60 years or older

Symptom prevalence	Study sample	Reference

Wheeze (28.4%)
Phlegm (21.6%)
Attacks of breathlessness
    Daytime (20.6%)
    Night-time (9.5%)
Asthma (7.8%)
	Southern England
	Random sample
		Dow et al. (1991)

Asthma (8.4%) Chronic bronchitis (16.4%)	Southern England Random sample	Horsley et al. (1991)
Wheeze (29%) Phlegm (32% men, 4% women)	Edinburgh, Scotland Random sample, 487 subjects	Milne and Williamson (1972)
Current asthma (2.5%) Past asthma (3.6%)	Southwest France Random sample, 2406 subjects	Nejjari et al. (1996)
Asthma (7.3%)	Manchester, UK Random sample, 893 subjects	Connolly et al. (1996)
COPD (12.5% men, 3% women)	Finland Random sample	Ishoaho et al. (1994)

United Kingdom than in other developed countries, and higher in industrialized areas than in rural communities. In Finland, Ishoaho et al. (1994) examined all subjects 65 years and over in a small community and found 12.5 per cent of men and 3 per cent of women had chronic air-flow limitation as defined by an FEV_1 to forced vital capacity ratio of less than 65 per cent. The prevalence of chronic air-flow limitation unresponsive to β_2-agonists was 9.2 per cent in men and 1.3 per cent in women. With the decline in tobacco smoking in subjects who are currently in their twenties and thirties, it is likely that there will be a much lower prevalence of smoking-induced COPD in 30 years time.

Underdiagnosis of asthma and COPD in older people

Asthma and COPD continue to be underdiagnosed or associated with significant delays in diagnosis in older people. The reasons why older people with airways disease are not all diagnosed are unclear. Previous studies on asthma underdiagnosis in children indicate opportunities for improvement in medical care (Gellert et al. 1990). However, improved medical care may not be the only answer. Variations in how patients respond when they have a disease and the way in which they use the health services may contribute. Ageing is associated with a decline in the ability to perceive bronchoconstriction so that older people will not appreciate the same degree of symptoms as a younger person does for equal degrees of air-flow limitation (Connolly et al. 1992a). Knowledge of illnesses and expectations of how doctors and therapy can help may influence whether a patient who develops respiratory symptoms seeks medical advice. Elderly people may feel that being breathless is part of normal ageing and there is little that can be done. Mental health problems have been found to be important in influencing admissions to hospital with asthma and may affect whether or not subjects obtain a label of asthma (Bosley et al. 1996). Cognitive impairment will affect history taking and interfere with the

ability to carry out diagnostic tests of lung function and may result in asthma being overlooked.

Clinical evaluation of the older patient with respiratory symptoms

General considerations

Individual respiratory symptoms or patterns of symptoms are not specific for asthma or COPD and may relate to an entirely different diagnosis such as ischaemic heart disease with left ventricular impairment (Dow et al. 1992). Although it is more typical of airways disease that breathlessness and wheeze may be triggered by cold air, tobacco smoke, exercise, and car fumes, this is common to both asthma and COPD (Table 3).

An adequate drug history is essential in patients suspected of having asthma or COPD since airways obstruction may develop or worsen in relation to the side-effects of several groups of drugs, all more commonly prescribed in old age. Both oral and ocular β-blockers can cause bronchospasm. There is a high hepatic first-pass metabolism with oral β-blockers which is partly bypassed by ocular drugs. Following topical administration, high concentrations reach the lung and bronchoconstriction may result particularly if patients have a history of respiratory symptoms such as wheeze (Diggory et al. 1994). Angiotensin-converting enzyme inhibitors are commonly recognized as causing a dry cough but may induce asthma in a small proportion of patients (Lunde et al. 1994). Aspirin and other non-steroidal anti-inflammatory drugs can cause hypersensitivity reactions associated with bronchospasm.

Physical examination may be diagnostic, inconclusive, or even misguided. For example, in a patient who seeks medical advice on account of attacks of breathlessness and wheeze, the findings of atrial fibrillation and mild basal crepitations on chest auscultation may not

Table 3 Important causes of respiratory symptoms in older people

Pulmonary causes	Asthma
	COPD
	Bronchiectasis
	Pulmonary emboli
	Pulmonary fibrosis
	Pneumonia, bronchitis
	Pleural effusion
	Pneumothorax
	Malignant disease
Cardiac causes	Arrhythmias
	Ischaemic heart disease
	Valvular heart disease
	Cardiomyopathies
	Pericardial disease
Neurological causes	Respiratory muscle weakness
	Cerebrovascular disease (e.g.
	Cheyne–Stokes respiration)

Table 4 Investigations important in the diagnosis of the older patient with respiratory symptoms

Indication	Investigation
Baseline	FEV_1, FVC, PEF
	Chest radiography
	Electrocardiogram
Normal FEV_1/FVC	PEF variability for 2–4 weeks
	ECG
Air-flow limitation	Bronchodilator response
	Corticosteroid response
FEV_1 <69% predicted	Oximetry
Oxygen saturation on oximetry <95%	Arterial gases
Assessment of emphysematous bullae	CT scan
Breathlessness not explained by FEV_1/FVC, ECG, or chest radiography	Maximum respiratory pressures Ventilation–perfusion lung scan

FEV_1, forced expiratory volume in 1 s; FVC, forced vital capacity; PEF, peak expiratory flow.

imply that the underlying problem is heart failure since 5 per cent of adults aged 65 years and over have atrial fibrillation (Wolf *et al.* 1978), and mild basal crepitations on chest auscultation may be found in older people incidentally (Connolly *et al.* 1992*b*). Consequently lung function tests are essential in every patient with respiratory symptoms even in the presence of a diagnosis of heart disease as both airways disease and heart disease may coexist particularly if the patient has a tobacco smoking history.

Investigations appropriate to older patients with chronic respiratory symptoms are listed in Table 4 and are adapted from American and European guidelines for assessing patients with airways disease (American Thoracic Society 1995; Siafakas *et al.* 1995). Compared with younger patients, this list is more extensive in keeping with the larger and more serious differential diagnosis. Once air-flow limitation has been detected, it is standard practice that spirometry is repeated following trials of treatment. As will be discussed, treatment trials are more difficult to interpret in the older patient. Measurement of lung volumes when vital capacity is known and measurement of carbon monoxide diffusing capacity is generally not recommended routinely, but is useful when the degree of respiratory symptoms is out of proportion to the severity of air-flow limitation. Arterial gases should be measured in patients if the FEV_1 to forced vital capacity ratio is less than 50 per cent of the predicted value as once disease is moderate or severe, arterial gases are more likely to be abnormal.

According to American Thoracic Society guidelines, chest radiography is not considered essential in all patients undergoing outpatient evaluation of COPD. However, unless the disease is definite and mild, chest radiography is an important investigation in the older patient in a search for heart disease, or other lung diseases and to look for complications of COPD such as bullae. Skin tests to common aeroallergens and total serum immunoglobulin E are not necessary in the routine assessment of patients with asthma or COPD as they rarely influence clinical management.

Bronchial challenge to non-specific bronchoconstrictor drugs such as histamine are infrequently performed as bronchial hyper-responsiveness can be found in asthma, COPD, heart failure, and healthy individuals. Current interest is focusing on sputum cell content as a means of differentiating asthma from COPD (Ronchi *et al.* 1996). Neutrophil-rich sputum correlates with COPD and eosinophil-rich sputum with asthma. However, there is significant overlap in the cell profiles of sputum in asthma and COPD.

Lung function testing

Identifying air-flow limitation

As discussed above, lung function testing with spirometry is the most important component in the diagnostic process of evaluating the older patient with respiratory symptoms. In contrast with younger subjects with asthma or COPD, older patients will always reveal abnormal spirometry. The majority of unselected people aged 65 years and over can perform reliable spirometry such that the FEV_1 in three spirograms varies by less than 5 per cent (Dow *et al.* 1992).

Opinions differ over what level of lung function should be taken to indicate air-flow limitation (Anthonisen and Wright 1986; Brand *et al.* 1992). Examples include an ratio of FEV_1 to forced vital capacity ratio of 60 per cent or less, an FEV_1 60 per cent or less of the predicted value, or an FEV_1 of 1.5 litres or less. Definitions based on predicted ranges of lung function are often used in younger subjects. In older people there is much less information about normal values for FEV_1, forced vital capacity, and peak expiratory flow, with reference values for subjects aged 75 years and over being extrapolated from lung function measurements in younger subjects or based on samples containing too few older subjects. Criteria based on absolute values tend to overselect short, female, and older adults as they have a low FEV_1. Criteria that use only FEV_1 or peak expiratory flow are at risk of including people with moderate or severe restrictive lung disease who have some reduction in FEV₁ or peak expiratory flow as well as a severe reduction in vital capacity.

At present, the best criterion to define air-flow limitation in the older patient is a ratio of FEV_1 to forced vital capacity of less than 60 per cent. In younger adults, a cut-off point for the definition for air-flow limitation is 70 per cent; however, it has been shown that a ratio of 70 per cent can be found in adults over 65 years who are free of respiratory symptoms (Schmidt *et al.* 1973).

Individuals with normal or minimally reduced spirometry when first seen can be tested for variability of air-flow obstruction by instructing them to perform peak expiratory flow recordings twice daily and at times of respiratory symptoms for 2 to 4 weeks. Variation in peak expiratory flow of the order of 20 per cent or more between the mean morning and mean evening recordings is diagnostic of asthma. It would be expected that significant diurnal variability should be present on at least 2 days of 14. Since many elderly people have impaired visual acuity, it is important to check that they can read the meter correctly in order to ensure this test is performed accurately. In addition, some patients are not able to provide recordings within the prescribed reliability of 5 per cent for three consecutive blows. Since deep inspiration may induce reflex broncho-constriction in asthmatics, a rest of about 1 min between blows may be necessary in some subjects. If subjects remain unable to produce consistent blows with sufficient rest and adequate instruction, then this test should not be carried out as it is likely to lead to a false result.

Reversibility testing: general considerations

If a patient has air-flow limitation, the next step is to try to determine the degree to which the air-flow limitation reverses with broncho-dilators and corticosteroids. Interpretation of the results of reversibility testing is more likely to be difficult in the older patient as fixed air-flow limitation or irreversibility is often present and the improvement in lung function following trials of treatment may only be small. Respiratory clinicians vary with respect to doses of bronchodilators, timing of remeasurement of lung function, doses of corticosteroids, and whether or not the corticosteroid trial should be 2 or 4 weeks. Furthermore, the precise way of defining what represents clinically 'significant' improvement in lung function or other variables such as exercise capacity are numerous. What follows is an attempt at describing why certain methods are more suitable for older patients.

It is not practical to expect patients being assessed for their first time to master the techniques of different inhaler delivery devices. Bronchodilators should be administered through a metered dose inhaler attached to a volume-spacer device or a nebulizer. In both asthma and COPD, there is intersubject variability in the quantity of β₂-agonist or anticholinergic required for maximum broncho-dilatation. Taking this into account suitable doses of bronchodilator are 400 µg salbutamol, 80 µg ipratropium bromide via a spacer or 2.5 to 5 mg salbutamol or 250 to 500 µg ipratropium bromide via the nebulizer. In most subjects, maximal improvement in lung function occurs 15 to 20 min after salbutamol or 30 to 40 min after ipratropium bromide.

Particularly in older subjects, the airway response must be assessed to both groups of bronchodilators. They are best performed on separate occasions. With ageing there is a gradual decrease in β₂-receptor responsiveness as the sensitivity of the adrenoceptors declines (Connolly *et al.* 1994) and the anticholinergic response becomes relatively more important than in younger patients (Van Schaycker *et al.* 1991). A smoking history or features of COPD identifies subjects more likely to respond to anticholinergics whereas an allergic history or a typical history of asthma are more likely to be β₂-agonist responders.

Following bronchodilator studies, the next step is to assess whether subjects respond to corticosteroids. The presence or absence of bronchodilator response has little relation to the corticosteroid response (Nisar *et al.* 1990). Corticosteroid trials are performed in order to identify subjects more likely to respond to maintenance therapy with corticosteroids, and as a method of identifying each asthmatic's best possible lung functions. Corticosteroid trials are usually carried out using prednisolone at a dosage of 30 to 40 mg daily for between 2 to 4 weeks. Trials can be carried out using high-dose inhaled corticosteroids but they do not identify as many subjects considered to be corticosteroid responsive as oral trials (Weir *et al.* 1990). For corticosteroid trials to be safe, it is important to avoid carrying them out in patients in whom high-dose corticosteroids would be dangerous, for instance patients with uncontrolled diabetes mellitus. Since impaired glucose tolerance may be unrecognized in older patients, a capillary or blood glucose is essential before such trials. For a corticosteroid trial to be effective, patients should not have had an exacerbation of airways disease or prior high-dose corticosteroids in the preceding 4 weeks.

What about patients who fail to respond to bronchodilators and corticosteroids on single testing? It is important that these tests are repeated as the proportion of patients defined as reversible to one or both drug groups increases with repeated testing. With COPD, one-third of individuals will demonstrate reversibility to bronchodilators on first testing and this will double by testing on a repeat occasion.

Interpretation and definition of a significant change following reversibility testing

What degree of change in lung function following trials of treatment should be regarded as significant? Assessing the degree of improvement in FEV₁ or peak expiratory flow as a percentage of the pretreatment value is the most commonly used method but is often inaccurate, particularly in the older patient whose FEV₁ is more likely to be severely impaired. The blow-to-blow variability of the FEV₁ in subjects with obstructive or restrictive lung function is 160 ml, so that a significant increase in FEV₁ in absolute terms is considered to be 200 ml (Tweedale *et al.* 1987). Hence expressing the bronchodilator response as a percentage of the pretreatment value becomes more accurate if the increase is only described as significant if it represents at least 15 per cent change and the absolute increase in FEV₁ exceeds 200 ml.

A significant change that differentiates reversibility from irreversibility with a mini-Wright peak flow meter is about 60 ml (Dekker *et al.* 1992); however, in COPD, use of peak expiratory flow alone to measure change in lung function following trials of treatment is not appropriate as it does not reflect what is going on in the smaller airways.

Other methods of interpreting the results of reversibility trials make use of the predicted values and one example is the absolute increase in FEV₁ following bronchodilators or corticosteroids expressed as a percentage of the predicted value for the FEV₁. If the result is in excess of 20 per cent, this is more consistent with asthma than COPD and a more favourable response is likely to occur following prolonged treatment. Predicted values are less reliable in older people, and so the authors recommend that the following criteria are preferential for use in interpreting reversibility trials in older people: significant reversibility is present when the pretreatment FEV_1 increases by at least 15 per cent provided that this includes an increase of FEV_1 of at least 200 ml.

The use of the FEV_1 alone may fail to identify subjects with COPD with small airways disease who show significant increases in other variables such as the vital capacity or exercise tolerance when little change has been demonstrated with the FEV_1 (Butland et al. 1982; Gerard and Light 1984). Therefore it is important to measure vital capacity changes as well as the FEV_1 and if neither indicator has altered, an exercise test should be performed. The most valid way of assessing exercise tolerance in treatment trials is the shuttle walking test of disability (Singh et al. 1992). The protocol for this test requires the patient to walk around cones separated by a distance of 10 m. At regular intervals in the test, patients increase their walking speed until all 12 levels are completed or they have to stop on account of breathlessness. The test has reasonable reproducibility. Previous methods such as the 6-min walking test, which assessed the total distance a subject could walk along the flat, were less reproducible and more subject to bias than the shuttle walking test.

Staging and prognosis of COPD

The severity of COPD is staged on the degree of air-flow limitation as a percentage of predicted values (American Thoracic Society 1995). Stage I is an FEV_1 50 per cent or more of predicted value, in stage II the FEV_1 is 35 to 49 per cent of predicted value, and in stage III the FEV_1 is less than 35 per cent of predicted value. The majority of patients are in stage I and the disease has little impact on quality of life and demands for health care are minimal. Most patients will be cared for in the community. These are the patients most likely to achieve benefit from risk factor reduction. Stages II and III represent the moderate and severe grades with physical disability and impaired quality of life. With greater impairment of lung function, more complications are evident. Predictors of mortality in COPD are advanced age, undernutrition, the degree of impairment of lung function, the presence of irreversibility, and the degree of hypoxia and hypercapnia on arterial gas assessment. In patients with an FEV_1 less than or equal to 0.75 l, 30 per cent will have died within the following year and 95 per cent will have died after 10 years.

Complications of asthma and COPD

General considerations

A number of complications may arise in the natural history of asthma and COPD. Acute exacerbations are among the most serious, and may be caused by a variety of different triggers as described below. In COPD, complications are usually only seen in patients with moderate to severe disease. As indicated at the beginning of this chapter, severe asthma in older patients may be associated with irreversible air-flow limitation, and when this becomes more marked, patients will have features in keeping with COPD.

Pneumothorax

In both asthma and COPD, patients are at risk of developing pneumothoraces. It is essential that all patients admitted to hospital with acute exacerbations should have a chest radiograph. In moderate or severe asthma or COPD, a pneumothorax small enough to be easily missed may none the less be responsible for significant deterioration in a patient's condition. Depending on the size of the pneumothorax and the impact it has on respiratory status, treatment may consist of aspiration, a chest drain, or conservative management. Patients with recurrent pneumothorax should be referred for consideration for surgery.

Hypoxaemic lung disease and cor pulmonale

Impairment of gaseous exchange arises from abnormally increased airways resistance and mismatch of the ventilation–perfusion ratio. Hypoxaemia is defined as partial pressure of oxygen in arterial blood (Pao_2) of 7.3 kPa (55 mmHg) or less (corresponding to oxygen saturation of 88 per cent or less). Hypoxaemia provokes a number of physiological responses that are initially protective but which have deleterious effects in the long term. Stimulation of ventilatory drive produces a higher partial pressure of oxygen (Po_2) and lower partial pressure of carbon dioxide (Pco_2); dilatation of the vascular beds supplying hypoxic tissue results in a compensatory tachycardia and increased cardiac output; constriction of the pulmonary vasculature leads to an improvement in ventilation and perfusion matching; and renal erythropoietin production leads to increased production of red blood cells and thus oxygen delivery. Long-term hypoxaemia unless corrected with oxygen therapy will eventually lead to pulmonary hypertension and right-sided heart failure.

Undernutrition

Undernutrition is a common finding in patients with moderate to severe COPD and is a marker for a poor prognosis. Undernutrition is an independent risk factor for mortality in COPD and is associated with impaired respiratory muscle strength and increased susceptibility to infection. Weight loss arises from increased energy requirements of ventilation in the presence of severe air-flow limitation and reduced nutritional intake.

Respiratory muscle weakness

Impairment of respiratory muscle strength is a feature of severe COPD and can contribute to perception of breathlessness, reduced exercise tolerance, alveolar hypoventilation, and abnormal arterial gases. Abnormal function of respiratory muscles arise from hyperinflation of the chest, undernutrition, physical deconditioning, chronic high-dose corticosteroid therapy, and hypoxia.

Psychosocial problems

Anxiety and depression are common in asthma and COPD, and may contribute to worsening symptoms, impaired quality of life, poor compliance with medication, and increased frequency of hospital admission (Bosley et al. 1996). Many older people are socially isolated, and becoming housebound due to chronic lung disease will add to their psychological stress.

Osteoporosis

Long-term oral corticosteroid therapy at doses higher than 7.5 mg of prednisolone daily may produce osteoporosis. Ali et al. (1991)

have demonstrated that high-dose inhaled corticosteroid therapy may increase biochemical markers of bone turnover but it remains unclear whether this form of therapy is also an independent risk factor for osteoporosis. The most commonly affected site for osteoporosis-related fracture secondary to corticosteroid use is within the vertebral column, and if it progresses to vertebral collapse in the thoracic area may worsen lung disease as it reduces vital capacity and lung expansion. If long-term high-dose steroids are required for asthma or COPD, steps should be taken to prevent osteoporosis.

Exacerbations of asthma and COPD

Acute exacerbations of asthma and COPD in older people are a frequent cause of general practitioner contact and hospital admission. Usually symptoms worsen over a few days but may occasionally be of abrupt onset due to exposure to pollutants or allergens, or because of a pneumothorax. Viral infections are implicated in many exacerbations of asthma. The British Thoracic Society (1997) and the National Asthma Education and Prevention Programme (1996) in America have published guidelines for the assessment and treatment of acute asthma and COPD.

The warning signs of a severe exacerbation of airways disease include breathlessness at rest, a respiratory rate greater than 25 breaths/min, inability to complete a sentence in a single breath on account of breathlessness, cyanosis, 'flap' due to carbon dioxide retention, and tachycardia. Bilateral polyphonic wheeze will usually be present but with life-threatening disease, the chest may become quiet as air flow diminishes. Pulsus paradoxus is not considered important as a measure of severity as it adds nothing to the above criteria and is less reliably detectable in older patients (Petheram et al. 1982). Severe exacerbations of air-flow obstruction in younger patients are usually accompanied by peak expiratory flow less than 50 per cent of predicted values. Many older patients with asthma or COPD have severely impaired lung function between exacerbations, and peak expiratory flow is only of value if the pre-existing levels are known.

Arterial gases should be measured in most older patients admitted to hospital with an exacerbation of airways disease. In younger subjects with asthma, this test is recommended only if oxygen saturations are less than 92 per cent. In older patients, significant carbon dioxide retention may be found even though the oxygen saturation is greater than 91 per cent.

Indications for assisted ventilation include worsening of peak expiratory flow and arterial gases despite full treatment with corticosteroids and bronchodilators; exhaustion, confusion, and respiratory arrest. Decisions over whether to provide assisted ventilation to a patient with known moderate or severe incapacitaty from COPD have become easier with the development of non-invasive ventilation techniques that can be implemented on respiratory wards. Ventilation will be inappropriate for a substantial number of older patients admitted to hospital with severe COPD. Inappropriate treatment, as well as stressful decision-making by junior medical staff, can be avoided by patients making advance directives, in discussion with their families and general practitioners, about the level of care they wish to receive in a severe exacerbation of disease.

Therapeutics of asthma and COPD

There are biological changes with ageing that affect respiratory function, but the commonest reason for varying the standard approach to asthma or COPD for older patients is interaction with other diseases and the drugs given to treat them. For example, dementia may affect the ability of the breathless patient to give a history, carry out essential diagnostic tests, and comply with complicated inhalers.

The aims of treatment of asthma and COPD in the older patient are as follows:

(1) to develop patient and carer understanding and skills necessary to manage asthma/COPD effectively;
(2) to minimize symptoms and physical disability, and to increase quality of life;
(3) to remove or reduce complications of the underlying disease.

Patient and carer education

Patient and carer education is a vital part of treating asthma or COPD. Investing time in explaining what asthma or COPD is and how the different therapies work is essential. Many patients prescribed bronchodilators and corticosteroids do not appreciate the different roles of these two groups of drugs. Many people with asthma and COPD feel that nebulizers are the solution for poorly controlled asthma or COPD when other factors such as persistent smoking or poor inhaler technique are more relevant. Educational leaflets are available from national organizations such as the National Asthma Campaign or the British Lung Foundation to back-up advice from health professionals.

Health professionals need to teach patients and carers the skills required in effectively managing asthma and COPD. This includes not only more obvious skills such as how to work an inhaler, but also how to recognize the signs of an exacerbation and the markers of a severe attack that requires urgent medical attention. Self-management plans have been studied mostly in relation to asthma and will be appropriate for many patients. The complexity of the plan will vary with individual patients. For instance, self-management plans that include home peak flow monitoring with written information about when to increase inhaled corticosteroids, when to take oral corticosteroids, and when to seek medical help, has been shown to improve asthma control in highly motivated patients.

A common area of neglect in education in asthma and COPD is for patients who live in residential or nursing homes. Such patients may not be under regular follow-up and lack access to information. Furthermore, staff working in homes caring for elderly people may be isolated from the usual educational meetings and have inadequate knowledge and skills to manage a patient with asthma or COPD. Homes may not have policies about smoking in the day areas and not allow patients with normal cognitive function to manage their own drugs. Trained respiratory nurses working in primary care or hospital may be an effective way of providing education and support to staff working in these homes.

Corticosteroids

Glucocorticoids are of undoubted benefit in asthma and reduce airways hyper-responsiveness and air-flow limitation, primarily through their effects on inflammation. The role of corticosteroids in COPD is less clear, although in current clinical practice they are used where significant reversibility has been shown in a therapeutic trial (Postma 1991). Unfortunately, maintenance therapy in patients with

COPD who have exhibited significant reversibility following a short-term corticosteroid trial does not guarantee a reduction in symptoms, or improvement in lung function or exercise tolerance.

It is possible that corticosteroids can slow down the decline in lung function that is more rapid in patients with COPD than in asthmatics or individuals with normal lungs. Preliminary studies have suggested that corticosteroids, in combination with regular bronchodilators, reduce decline in lung function in at least a subgroup of patients with COPD (Renkema 1990; Kerstjens et al. 1991).

Inhaled corticosteroid should be advised for asthmatic patients who need to use relief bronchodilators at least once daily. The dosage is based initially on the severity of disease and reviewed every 3 to 6 months. Patients may start with a minimum of 100 to 400 μg beclomethasone or budesonide, or fluticasone 50 to 200 μg daily or a maximum of beclomethasone 2000 μg daily or equivalent in conjunction with oral prednisolone. If the patient is improving, a stepwise reduction in treatment may be possible every few months. With motivated patients, particularly early on in treatment when stability may not be reached, disease monitoring may be enhanced by peak flow measurements to assess diurnal variability. Similar dosage recommendations apply also for patients with COPD who have shown a steroid response, although the role of corticosteroids is less well defined.

Increased doses of inhaled therapy or courses of oral prednisolone may be required in acute exacerbations of asthma. Increased inhaled therapy is as effective as oral prednisolone in mild exacerbations of asthma in the community (Griffiths 1996). Oral prednisolone is low in cost, whilst inhaled therapy is substantially more expensive. As with younger patients, tailored self-management plans developed together with the general practitioner can be effective in improving overall asthma control and reducing the frequency of oral courses of prednisolone. Patients with moderate to severe asthma may need high doses of inhaled corticosteroid (in excess of beclomethasone 1.5–2 mg daily or equivalent) or occasionally in elderly as in younger asthmatics, oral corticosteroids may be needed continually.

Corticosteroid side-effects are dose related. Side-effects with low-dose inhaled corticosteroids consist of dysphonia, thrush, and skin changes. The more dangerous side-effects are only seen with oral use in excess of 7.5 mg of prednisolone daily on a chronic basis and include impaired glucose tolerance, osteoporosis, and hypertension. In elderly patients, the most common problems with corticosteroid use in asthma or COPD affect the skin. 'Senile' purpura, and a greater susceptibility to lacerations with poor healing, due to exposure to ultraviolet radiation, are characteristic of skin ageing but are made worse by corticosteroids. Even in younger adults, skin changes are noted on doses of inhaled beclomethasone as low as 400 μg daily (Capewell et al. 1989). The long-term risks of high-dose inhaled corticosteroids are uncertain; the main concern is over effects on bone, as they increase biochemical markers of bone turnover (Ali et al. 1991).

The side-effects of inhaled corticosteroids can be reduced by the use of volume-spacer devices and postinhalation gargling and spitting to avoid swallowing pharyngeal deposit (Selroos and Halme 1991). Budesonide has a better risk–benefit ratio than beclomethasone on account of its faster metabolism to an inactive compound once systemically absorbed (Brown et al. 1993). Recently, a corticosteroid preparation, fluticasone has become available which has significantly less gastrointestinal absorption but whether it has an advantage over budesonide with regard to long-term side-effects is uncertain. Dose for dose, fluticasone has twice the potency of beclomethasone and because it has almost negligible oral bioavailability, side-effects are less frequent. The potential for side-effects still remains, however, as systemic absorption takes place through the lung.

Bronchodilators

Use in asthma and COPD

Inhaled bronchodilators offer immediate relief therapy for asthma and COPD. Among younger patients, who are easier to identify as having asthma or COPD, the asthmatics will show greatest response to β_2-agonists which are therefore first-line bronchodilator therapy. Anticholinergics will be added as maintenance therapy at a later stage if asthma becomes moderate or severe. Patients with COPD, may respond to either β_2-agonists or anticholinergic drugs and may be given one or both depending on their response. With acute exacerbations of asthma or COPD requiring hospital admission, older patients are treated with high doses of both groups via a nebulizer for the first few days.

β_2-Agonists

β_2-Agonists such as salbutamol, terbutaline, and salmeterol remain the most frequently prescribed inhaled bronchodilator drugs for asthma and COPD. They produce their rapid bronchodilator effect by interaction with specific receptors on the cell membrane. As salbutamol and terbutaline have a short duration of action, longer acting inhaled preparations have now been developed such as salmeterol and formoterol. There is some evidence that longer acting inhaled and oral bronchodilators have a very small effect on the inflammatory response in asthma. The effect, if detectable clinically, is minimal in comparison with that of corticosteroids which remain the mainstay disease suppressant in asthma, and corticosteroid-responsive COPD.

One characteristic seen with many membrane receptor systems is that of desensitization and downregulation after repeated exposure to the agonist (Cockcroft and Swystun 1996). This can result in the tolerance that has been demonstrated with the shorter-acting β_2-agonists. In patients receiving bronchodilators regularly, there is a reduction in the bronchodilator response which can lead to a shorter duration of action. The effect develops over a number of weeks and then stabilizes and is seen in both asthmatics and patients with COPD. The significance of this subsensitivity may be small if a good functional response still remains.

Tachyphylaxis to the protective effects of β_2-agonists on bronchial responsiveness has been demonstrated in a number of studies of asthmatics using non-specific bronchoconstrictor challenges (Sears et al. 1990). Furthermore, rebound increases in bronchial responsiveness may occur when regular β_2-agonists have been stopped abruptly. Some studies have suggested that regular, rather then 'as required' use of β_2-agonists may lead to an increase in exacerbations of asthma.

Dosage regimens

The standard 'as required' dosage of salbutamol through the metered dose inhalers is 100 to 200 μg up to four to six times in 24 h, or nebulized salbutamol 2.5 to 5 mg at the same frequency. The longer acting drugs such as salmeterol are currently recommended in asthma when there are persisting or nocturnal symptoms in spite of regular inhaled corticosteroid and a relief bronchodilator. Longer acting inhaled β_2-agonists are now being used in COPD when an adjunct to short-acting bronchodilators is required for symptomatic relief, and this may remove the need for oral bronchodilators.

In more severe asthma and COPD, it may be necessary to prescribe higher doses of short-acting β_2-agonists. This is only safe if preventive therapy with corticosteroids is appropriately prescribed. Before increasing doses of β_2-agonists, a formal trial using lung function testing should be carried out to identify whether higher doses of β_2-agonists or anticholinergics are most appropriate. Doubling or tripling the dose of salbutamol in conjunction with the use of a volume-spacer device may be sufficient rather than switching to much higher doses which require a nebulizer. Since the side-effects of these drugs is dose dependent, there is a real risk that in a small proportion of older patients with moderate to severe heart disease, the doses used in a nebulizer may exacerbate ischaemic heart disease or tachyarrythmias (Neville et al. 1982).

Should β_2-agonists be prescribed for patients who have irreversible air-flow limitation? A proportion of patients with relatively 'fixed' air-flow limitation may show improvements in symptoms, exercise capacity, and lung function tests that are statistically significant when on short- or long-acting β_2-agonists compared with placebo but do not fulfil the clinical definitions of reversibility. It may be that with higher doses of short-acting bronchodilators or with repeated trials, reversibility would be demonstrated. Whatever the explanation, such patients should be prescribed β_2-agonists and followed to review outcome over a period of months.

Anticholinergic agents

Anticholinergic drugs are principally used in COPD, but may be useful to augment the bronchodilation from β_2-agonists in acute and chronic severe asthma. In COPD, anticholinergic agents are as effective as β_2-agonists, but some patients may show a small increase in FEV_1 with an anticholinergic and a larger increase with a β_2-agonists or vice versa. The presence of a smoking history is a marker of greater likelihood of a response following anticholinergic agents.

Cholinergic nerves are the dominant neural bronchoconstrictor pathways in humans. In COPD, the main reversible component is vagal tone whereas in asthmatics, although vagal bronchoconstrictor tone is enhanced, the predominant cause of airway narrowing is through other mechanisms such as chemical mediators (Barnes 1986). Anticholinergic drugs, such as ipratropium and oxitropium bromide, exert their bronchodilator effect by competitive antagonism predominantly on the muscarinic M3 receptor. Although such receptors are also found on the cells of glands in the submucosa, there is no evidence that anticholinergic drugs have any clinically beneficial effect on mucus secretion or viscosity.

Ipratropium and oxitropium bromide are the most commonly prescribed anticholinergic drugs. They are poorly absorbed from the airways and largely devoid of the widespread systemic effects of older anticholinergics such as atropine. Side-effects may be seen in the higher doses used with nebulizers, and include dry mouth, irritation of the nose and throat, and occasionally blurring of vision. Although glaucoma is not a contraindication to their use, when employing a nebulizer, inhalation via a mouthpiece as opposed to a mask is recommended to minimize ocular exposure. Oxitropium bromide has a longer duration of action than ipratropium bromide allowing it to be taken 8-hourly rather than 6-hourly.

The doses of ipratropium bromide are 20 to 40 µg 6-hourly, or 250 to 500 µg via nebulizer 6-hourly. Oxitropium bromide is prescribed in doses of 200 µg between two to three times daily. In the management of COPD, the conventional dose of ipratropium bromide (20–40 µg) may not be enough to elicit optimal clinical benefit. Up to four times that of the standard dose may be required to achieve maximal bronchodilation (Ikeda et al. 1996). As with higher dose β_2-agonist therapy, prior to longer term prescription of increased doses, benefit should be demonstrated.

Should patients with COPD or severe asthma be automatically prescribed both β-agonist and anticholinergic to maximize bronchodilator effect? Currently, clinical practice varies, but many clinicians prefer to document an improvement in lung function additional to that obtained from a β-agonist before adding an anticholinergic. If the first bronchodilator is already prescribed in a 'high dose', for example 800 µg salbutamol or 120 µg ipratropium bromide, then giving both bronchodilators in COPD appears to offer little or no additional benefit. However, there is lack of agreement about this approach and some studies indicate that combination therapy achieves greater bronchodilation than single-drug therapy. It is up to the patient and the clinician to decide between (a) increasing the dose of a single bronchodilator, (b) using both bronchodilators in separate delivery devices, which is logical as the drugs differ in their onset and durations of action, or (c) combining bronchodilators in one inhaler. Having a single inhaler for bronchodilation is simple, may improve compliance, and in the case of a combination inhaler halves the chlorofluorocarbon release.

Oral and intravenous bronchodilators

Oral bronchodilators are potentially dangerous drugs, and as advancing age is the main determinant of toxicity, they should only be used in elderly patients with moderate or severe asthma or COPD. Indications for their use are largely similar to the indications for longer acting inhaled β_2-agonists, that is persistent symptoms (particularly at night) despite adequate inhaled bronchodilators and corticosteroids. In this respect, much of the use of oral agents has been replaced by the safer longer acting inhaled β_2-agonists. In acute exacerbations of asthma or COPD, bronchodilation is not increased when high-dose nebulized bronchodilators and corticosteroids are already prescribed (Self et al. 1990; Zainudin et al. 1994). The use of intravenous theophyllines or β_2-agonists in this situation will definitely increase the risk of cardiac arrhythmias. In acute exacerbations of COPD or asthma, if theophyllines are to be used and patients are already on oral theophyllines, intravenous theophyllines may raise serum concentrations to dangerously high levels. To avoid this, boluses of theophyllines must not be given and intravenous therapy titrated against measurement of serum levels.

There are many different preparations of theophylline many of which are slow release. The therapeutic range for theophylline is 50 to 110 µmol/l. Doses of oral or intravenous preparations are titrated to maintain serum concentrations within this range, but theophylline may exert its maximal therapeutic effect at serum concentrations near the lower end of the range. Factors known to influence theophylline metabolism, and hence the risk of toxicity, are shown in Table 5 (Shannon 1993). At lower serum concentrations, the most common side-effects of theophylline are nausea, insomnia, and headaches. As serum concentrations increase, effects include seizures, encephalopathy, and cardiac arrythmias, as well as hypokalaemia and

Table 5 Factors important in influencing the metabolism and side-effect profile of theophyllines in old age

Decreased plasma theophylline	Increased plasma theophylline
Cigarette smoking	Obesity
Rifampicin (rifampin)	Hepatic dysfunction
Phenytoin	Congestive cardiac failure
Phenobarbitone (phenobarbital)	Respiratory infection
Carbamazepine	Septicaemia
Aminoglutethimide	Febrile illness
	Cimetidine
	Fluvoxamine
	Erythromycin/clarithromycin
	Ciprofloxacin
	Methotrexate
	Diltiazem, verapamil

hypotension. Elderly people seem to be at the greatest risk of toxicity owing to a greater prevalence of infection, the presence of other interacting drugs, and concomitant liver and renal impairment, all of which interfere with drug metabolism and elimination.

Drug delivery devices: inhalers and nebulizers

The choice of the drug delivery device is particularly important for older patients who may have difficulties with using inhalers. The questions that the patient and doctor need to consider with each device are how easy is it to use and how well the properties of the device match those of the drugs it is to deliver (Pedersen 1996).

There are four main delivery systems: the conventional metered dose inhaler, the metered dose inhaler attached to a spacer device, dry powder inhalers, and nebulizers. These systems differ in their general properties, for instance the metered dose inhaler attached to volume-spacer devices will usually deposit more drug in the lung than a metered dose inhaler alone. With a metered dose inhaler, only about 12 per cent of the drug is delivered to the lungs, the rest is deposited in the mouth, pharynx, and larynx; a significant amount is swallowed and absorbed (Barry and O'Callaghan 1996). A metered dose inhaler in association with an appropriate volume-spacing device can improve delivery to the lungs by up to 24 per cent and thereby reduce systemic absorption. Minimizing upper airway deposition and systemic absorption are particularly important considerations with corticosteroids.

Drugs used with the volume-spacer device differ in the proportion that enters the lung. Only 7 per cent of terbutaline delivered from a metered dose inhaler with a volume-spacing device reaches the lung whereas salbutamol and fenoterol through the same system result in 12 and 21 per cent lung deposition, respectively (Matthys 1990). Some of the more recently developed small volume-spacer devices have not been adequately studied and may not improve drug delivery at all and may in fact reduce it compared with a metered dose inhaler alone. Older large volume-spacer devices with the appropriate metered dose inhaler can be as effective as a nebulizer, and considerably cheaper.

A metered dose inhaler alone may not be effective for older people as a high of degree of dexterity is required. A substantial number of patients, most notably those with arthritis, incordination, tremor, or weakness of the hands, may have considerable difficulty with a metered dose inhaler. For patients with arthritis, devices fitted to the metered dose inhaler can ease activation, for example the Haleraid® which allows the inhaler to be activated by an easier pincer movement (Allen and Harries 1989).

Moderate or severe cognitive impairment may impair the ability of an inhaler user. To use a metered dose inhaler correctly, it is necessary for the patient to have an abbreviated mental test score of at least 7/10 (Allen and Prior 1986). Devices which require multiple separate steps for delivery of drug into the lung will cause the greatest challenge for cognitively impaired patients. A metered dose inhaler requires five separate steps prior to the drug entering the lung, and four steps when attached to the spacer device. A breath-activated device is simplest of all in that it only requires three steps and can be successfully used by 50 per cent of patients with a mental test score down to 5 out of 10 (Allen 1997). The doctor must spend time finding the most suitable device for each patient and the choice should be reassessed following repeated demonstrations by the patient. It may not be essential that the patient should use the inhaler independently and a carer will often find that a metered dose inhaler attached to a spacer is most suitable. Tidal-breathing can be used for inhalation of the drug and the spacer is an efficient way of delivering high doses during an acute attack of asthma or COPD. A single puff of salbutamol into the volume spacer followed by inspiration without delay results in better bronchodilation than multiple puffs or a prolonged delay prior to inspiration (Clark and Lipworth 1996).

The degree of bronchodilation following inhaled drugs is strongly influenced by the electrostatic charge of the plastic spacer lining; the higher the electrostatic charge, the more of the drug that sticks to the inner lining and the less that reaches the lung. All new plastic volume spacers have a high electrostatic charge and this can be reduced by washing in water, priming with 15 puffs of inhaled drug, or coating with an ionic detergent (Clark and Lipworth 1996).

Other devices such as the Rotahaler®, Turbohaler®, Spinhaler®, and Diskhaler® may be preferred by some patients. However, they do involve multiple steps like the metered dose inhaler alone, and offer little practical advantage. An important environmental advantage of dry powder devices is that they are free of chlorofluorocarbons.

Nebulizers may be necessary when patients are unable to cope with any other device or when high-dose therapy is required. Where longer-term use of a nebulizer is being planned, it is essential that patients and carers instructed in using the device, and given written information about the maximum number of repeated doses they can use. It is also important that the device is regularly serviced. Regular follow-up by respiratory specialists may also be appropriate as it is likely that patients requiring nebulizers have complex disease.

Non-drug approaches in asthma and COPD

Smoking cessation

Advice and support in smoking cessation is essential in the management of asthma and COPD. Compared with non-smokers, tobacco smokers have substantially higher risks of death from lung cancer and respiratory failure secondary to COPD. It has been shown that smoking cessation, even in later life, improves life expectancy and slows the rate of decline of FEV_1 (Xu et al. 1992).

Antismoking advice from a family doctor will persuade 3.5 per cent of patients to stop smoking permanently, rising to 5.5 per cent if the advice is accompanied by antismoking literature (Russell *et al.* 1979). The addition of transdermal nicotine significantly enhances the ability of long-term smokers to stop and become long-term ex-smokers, provided that the transdermal nicotine is used as an adjunct rather than substitute for counselling and support in primary care or hospital outpatient departments (Campbell *et al.* 1996).

Long-term oxygen therapy

Long-term oxygen improves survival in patients with chronic hypoxic cor pulmonale (Nocturnal Oxygen Therapy Trial Group 1980). Many patients with COPD are denied the benefits of long-term oxygen therapy as they are not adequately assessed. Before prescribing domiciliary oxygen for a patient, hypoxaemia should be confirmed by arterial blood gas analysis when the patient is in a stable state and has been free of exacerbation for at least 4 weeks. Randomized controlled trials indicate that the criteria for long-term oxygen therapy in hypoxic COPD are that patients should have had one or more episodes of peripheral oedema and their lung function and arterial gases are as follows: Po_2 less than 7.3 kPa; Pco_2 over 6.0 kPa; FEV_1 less than 1.5 litre; forced vital capacity less than 2.0 litre.

Patients who fulfil these criteria should have their arterial gases reassessed after short trials of inspired oxygen to identify those who are dependent on hypoxic drive to maintain ventilation and would develop worsening respiratory failure with prolonged oxygen therapy. Since oxygen therapy is a fire hazard, it must not be prescribed for patients unless they abstain from smoking.

The benefit of domiciliary oxygen in such patients is mediated by its effect in lowering pulmonary arterial pressure. To be effective in improving survival, patients must be able to take continuous oxygen therapy for longer than 15 h/day at an intake sufficient to raise the Po_2 above 8 kPa. Oxygen therapy may be able to improve quality of life and capacity to exercise.

Oxygen can be delivered via a mask or nasal cannulas from cylinders of compressed gas, or from an oxygen concentrator, a device which separates oxygen from atmospheric air. Oxygen concentrators are initially more expensive, but are in the long term more cost-effective and the best option for patients requiring oxygen for long periods of the day. Nasal cannulas lead to better compliance than masks in delivering oxygen, and cannulas can deliver much higher than expected quantities of oxygen in patients who are hypoventilating. Masks provide controlled oxygen delivery and therefore should always be used in patients with hypoventilation, carbon dioxide retention, and reliance on hypoxic drive for respiration. In such patients, new prescriptions of sedatives such as benzodiazepines should be avoided as they can precipitate worsening respiratory failure (Davies and Hopkin 1989).

It is vital that all patients receiving oxygen therapy for hypoxic COPD are regularly reviewed by a respiratory nurse or clinician. At follow-up, undercorrection of oxygen saturations can be identified and treated.

Influenza and pneumococcal vaccination

Influenza and pneumococcal infections are important and avoidable causes of mortality and morbidity in older people particularly those with chronic lung disease. Yearly vaccination for influenza of older people with asthma or COPD will reduce the severity of illness, risk of hospital admission, and death (Wilson 1994). Clinical studies do not support the idea that influenza vaccination causes exacerbations of air-flow obstruction in asthmatics (Watson *et al.* 1997).

Pneumococcal vaccination with the multivalent vaccine has an efficacy of between 50 and 80 per cent in older people (Fedson *et al.* 1994). The vaccination is safe and does not need to be repeated yearly as does vaccination for influenza. Many older people are unaware of the risks of pneumococcal infection and the benefits of pneumococcal vaccination. In a study of British general practice, only 3.6 per cent of older people clinically appropriate for pneumococcal vaccination had been vaccinated. Such low uptake can be improved with a public health campaign (McDonald *et al.* 1997)

Nutritional support

Patients with moderate or severe COPD have increased energy output despite reduced levels of physical activity. Weight loss is inevitable as disease progresses and results from dietary intake that is inadequate in relation to energy needs. Oral supplementation may increase weight provided total energy intake increases by at least 50 per cent (Efthimiou *et al.* 1988). A balance of carbohydrate and fat is sufficient as patients with COPD and undernutrition achieve a positive nitrogen balance and do not normally require extra protein in their daily diet (Fitting 1992).

Pulmonary rehabilitation

Most older patients with moderate or severe COPD, in spite of maximal medical therapy, will continue to experience physical, social, and psychological limitations. Pulmonary rehabilitation has become more widespread and has similarities in approach to stroke rehabilitation in that it is multidisciplinary in its approach and aims to improve functional independence. Many of the aspects already mentioned such as education, nutrition, and oxygen therapy form part of the rehabilitation approach. Exercise is a key feature of pulmonary rehabilitation. Exercise training does nothing to reverse the basic disease process in COPD since resting lung mechanics and gas exchange efficiency do not improve. An exercise programme should be tailored to the individual capabilities of each patient and will include measures aimed at strengthening the upper limbs and body (unweighted arm raises, inflating balloons), lower limbs (walking, step-ups, or cycling), or exercises specifically aimed at breathing. Pursed lip breathing for instance aims to slow respiratory rate and reduce small airway collapse during periods of dyspnoea. Methods designed to reduce anxiety and depression and encourage social integration should also be included. Pulmonary rehabilitation can be carried out in hospital, in the community, or within the home.

A recent meta-analysis of pulmonary rehabilitation trials supported the conclusion that these approaches improve dyspnoea and ability to cope with the condition, quality of life, and, possibly, functional exercise capacity (Lacasse *et al.* 1996).

Ventilatory therapy

Deaths of patients with moderate or severe COPD, and to a lesser extent asthma, are commonly due to respiratory failure. Until recently, ventilatory failure was treated with intravenous respiratory stimulants such as doxapram or mechanical ventilation through an endotracheal tube. Exacerbations of COPD or asthma result in physical fatigue so that a respiratory stimulant may be ineffective in reversing respiratory failure and can pose other risks such as convulsions, agitation, and confusion. Intubation with mechanical ventilation is invasive and may be associated with complications such as tracheal and laryngeal injury, pneumothoraces, or nosocomial infection. Mechanical ventilation requires admission to an intensive care unit, to which access may be limited. For the asthmatic patient with respiratory failure, it remains the appropriate choice as recovery is likely to be more prompt and complete. In COPD, weaning off mechanical ventilation may be difficult, and nasal intermittent positive pressure ventilation has become more popular as first-line therapy in ventilatory failure and is carried out on general medical wards where there is appropriate medical and nursing expertise.

The treatment of patients in hospital with the acute on chronic respiratory failure of COPD now represents the main indication for nasal intermittent positive pressure ventilation. In order to be successful, nasal intermittent positive pressure ventilation needs to be started early in the course of the admission. This method is used in conjunction with other therapies for acute exacerbations such as bronchodilators, corticosteroids, and oxygen. During an acute exacerbation, it may be possible to wean many patients off nasal intermittent positive pressure ventilation after 24 to 72 h whereas others may require longer periods (Branthwaite 1991).

Some patients with severe COPD who are chronically hypoxic and hypercapnic throughout the whole day or at night may benefit from domiciliary nasal intermittent positive pressure ventilation. This method may confer benefit additional to that of long-term oxygen therapy. In order to be considered for a trial of domiciliary nasal intermittent positive pressure ventilation, patients should have daytime hypercapnia and documented nocturnal hypoventilation that can be reversed by ventilation. Some patients experience significant improvements in quality of life when nasal intermittent positive pressure ventilation is combined with long-term oxygen, a result rarely seen with long-term oxygen therapy alone. Nasal intermittent positive pressure ventilation is quite a cumbersome procedure that requires perseverance from the patient and some fail to tolerate it. Therefore, as with long-term oxygen therapy, education, encouragement, and long-term specialist follow-up are essential.

Lung volume reduction surgery

In small and uncontrolled trials, the removal of lung tissue has been found to benefit a proportion of patients with severe 'endstage' COPD. If successful, this operation can improve symptoms, exercise tolerance, quality of life, and FEV_1 (Dantzer and Scharf 1996). 'End-stage COPD' implies patients who are markedly symptomatic and restricted by their disease in spite of maximal therapy. Previously, the only surgical option for such patients was lung transplant, but the lack of organs and the presence of concomitant medical problems often made this an unrealistic option.

As the lungs of a patient with emphysematous COPD become more hyperinflated, the skeletal muscles of inspiration become shortened and progressively less able to generate force. The diaphragm becomes flattened, reducing its ability to contribute to inspiration, and at very large lung volumes it moves paradoxically upwards on inspiration. Reducing lung volume would theoretically increase the resting length of inspiratory muscle and return the diaphragm to its normal dome shape, allowing it to contribute more effectively to respiration.

References

Allen, S.C. (1997). Competence thresholds for the use of inhalers in people with dementia. *Age and Ageing*, 26, 83–6.

Allen, S.C. and Harries, D. (1989). Which inhaler for the elderly asthmatic? *Geriatric Medicine*, 19, 61–3.

Allen, S.C. and Prior, A. (1986). What determines whether an elderly patient can use a metered dose inhaler correctly? *British Journal of Diseases of the Chest*, 80, 45–9.

Ali, N.J., Capewell, S., and Ward, M.J. (1991). Bone turnover during high dose inhaled corticosteroid treatment. *Thorax*, 46, 160–4.

American Thoracic Society (1962). Definitions and classification of chronic bronchitis, asthma and emphysema. *American Review of Respiratory Diseases*, 85, 762–8.

American Thoracic Society (1995). Standards for the diagnosis and care of patients with chronic obstructive pulmonary disease (COPD). *European Respiration Journal*, 8, 1398–420.

Anthonisen, N.R., Wright, E.C., and IPPB Trial Group (1986). Bronchodilator response in chronic obstructive pulmonary disease. *American Review of Respiratory Diseases*, 133, 814–19.

Aoki, K., Ohtsubo, K., Yoshimura, K., Saiki, S., Tai, H., and Okano, H. (1995). Histological evaluation of bronchial tissue from elderly individuals with bronchial asthma. *Japanese Journal of Thoracic Diseases*, 33, 1421–9.

Banerjee, D.K., Lee, G.S., Malik, S.K., and Daly, S. (1987). Underdiagnosis of asthma in the elderly. *British Journal of Diseases of the Chest*, 81, 23–9.

Barker, D.J.P. and Osmond, C. (1986). Childhood respiratory infection and adult chronic bronchitis in England and Wales. *British Medical Journal*, 293, 1271–5.

Barker, D.J.P., Godfrey, K.M., Fall, C., Osmond, C., Winter, P.D., and Shaheen, S.O. (1991). Relation of birthweight and childhood respiratory infection to adult lung function and death from chronic obstructive airways disease. *British Medical Journal*, 303, 671–5.

Barnes. P.J. (1986). Neural control of the airways in health and disease. *American Review of Respiratory Diseases*, 134, 1289–314.

Barry, P.W. and O'Callaghan, C. (1996). Inhalational delivery from seven different spacer devices. *Thorax*, 51, 835–40.

Beasley, R., Roche, W.R., Roberts, J.A., *et al.* (1989). Cellular events in the bronchi in mild asthma and after bronchial provocation. *American Review of Respiratory Diseases*, 139, 806–17

Bosken, C.H., Wiggs, B.R., Pare, P.D., and Hogg, J.C. (1990). Small airway dimensions in smokers with obstruction to airflow. *American Journal of Critical Care Medicine*, 142, 563–70.

Bosley, C.M., Corden, Z.M., and Cochrane, G.M. (1996). Psycho-social factors and asthma. *Respiratory Medicine*, 90, 453–7.

Brand, P.L.P., Quanjer, P.H., Postma, D.S., *et al.* and the Dutch Chronic Non-specific Lung Disease (CNSLD) Study Group (1992). Interpretation of bronchodilator response in patients with obstructive airways disease. *Thorax*, 47, 429–35.

Branthwaite, M.A. (1991). Assisted ventilation 6. Non-invasive and domiciliary ventilation: positive pressure techniques. *Thorax*, 46, 208–12.

British Thoracic Society (1997). British guidelines on asthma management. *Thorax*, 52 (Supplement 1), S1–21.

Brown, P.H., Matusiewicz, S.P., Shearing, C., Tibi, L., Greening, A.P., and Crompton, G.K. (1993). Systemic effects of high dose inhaled steroids: comparison of beclomethasone diproprionate and budesonide in healthy subjects. *Thorax*, 48, 967–73.

Burr, M.L., Charles, T.J., Roy, K., and Seaton, A. (1979). Asthma in the elderly: an epidemiological survey. *British Medical Journal*, 1, 1041–4.

Burrows, B., Knudson, R.J., Cline, M.G., and Lebowitz, M.D. (1977). Quantative relationships between cigarette smoking and ventilatory function. *American Review of Respiratory Diseases*, 115, 195–205.

Burrows, B., Lebowitz, M.D., Barbee, R.A., and Cline, M.G. (1991). Findings before diagnoses among the elderly in a longitudinal study of a general population sample. *Journal of Allergy and Clinical Immunology*, **88**, 870–7.

Butland, R.J.A., Pang, J., Gross, E.R., Woodcock, A.A., and Geddes, D.M. (1982). Two, 6 and 12 min walking tests in respiratory disease. *British Medical Journal*, **284**, 1607–8.

Campbell, I.A., Prescott, R.J., and Tjeder-Burton, S.M. (1996). Transdermal nicotine plus support in patients attending hospital with smoking-related diseases: a placebo-controlled study. *Respiratory Medicine*, **90**, 47–51.

Capewell, S., Reynolds, S., Shuttleworth, D., Edwards, C., and Finlay, A.Y. (1989). Purpura and dermal thinning associated with high dose inhaled corticosteroids. *British Medical Journal*, **300**, 1548–51

Celli, B.R., Snider, G.L., Heffner, J., *et al.* (1995). Standards for the diagnosis and care of patients with chronic obstructive pulmonary disease. *American Journal of Respiratory and Critical Care Medicine*, **152**, S78–121.

Clark, D.J. and Lipworth, B.J. (1996). Effect of multiple actuations, delayed inhalation and antistatic treatment on the lung bioavailability of salbutamol via a spacer device. *Thorax*, **51**, 981–4.

Cockcroft, D.W. and Swystun, V.A. (1996). Functional antagonism: tolerance produced by inhaled beta-agonists. *Thorax*, **51**, 1051–6.

Connolly, M., Crowley, J.J., Charan, N.B., Nielson, C.P., and Vestal, R.E. (1992*a*). Reduced subjective awareness of bronchoconstriction provoked by methacholine in elderly asthmatic and normal subjects as measured on a simple awareness scale. *Thorax*, **47**, 410–13.

Connolly, M.J., Crowley, J.J., and Vestal, R.E. (1992*b*). Clinical significance of crepitations in elderly patients following acute hospital admission. A prospective study. *Age and Ageing*, **21**, 43–8.

Connolly, M.J., Crowley, J.J., Nielson, C.P., Charan, N.B., and Vestal, R.E. (1994). Peripheral mononuclear leucocyte β adrenoceptors and non-specific bronchial responsiveness to methacholine in young and elderly normal subjects and asthmatic patients. *Thorax*, **49**, 26–32.

Cosio, M.G., Ghezzo, H., Hogg, J.C., *et al.* (1978). The relationship between structural changes in small airways and pulmonary function changes. *New England Journal of Medicine*, **298**, 1277–81.

Dantzker, D.R. and Scharf, S.M. (1996). Surgery to reduce lung volume. *New England Journal of Medicine*, **334**, 1128–9.

Davies, R.J. and Hopkin, J.M. (1989). Nasal oxygen in exacerbations of ventilatory failure—under appreciated risk. *British Medical Journal*, **299**, 43–5.

Dekker, F.W., Schrier, A.C., Sterk, P.J., and Dijkman, J.H. (1992). Validity of peak expiratory flow measurement in assessing reversibility of airflow obstruction. *Thorax*, **47**, 162–6.

Diggory, P., Heyworth, P., Chau, G., McKenzie, S., and Sharma, A. (1994). Unsuspected bronchospasm in association with topical timolol—a common problem in elderly people: can we easily identify those affected and do cardio-selective agents lead to improvement? *Age and Ageing*, **23**, 17–21.

Dow, L., Coggon, D., Osmond, C., and Holgate, S.T. (1991). A population survey of respiratory symptoms in the elderly. *European Respiratory Journal*, **4**, 267–72.

Dow, L., Coggon, D., and Holgate, S.T. (1992). Respiratory symptoms as predictors of airways lability in an elderly population. *Respiratory Medicine*, **86**, 27–32.

Efthimiou, J., Fleming, J., Gomes, C., and Spiro, S.G. (1988). The effect of supplementary oral nutrition in poorly nourished patients with chronic obstructive pulmonary disease. *American Review Respiratory Disease*, **137**, 1075–82.

Fedson, D.S., Shapiro, M.D., LaForce, F.M., *et al.* (1994). Pneumococcal vaccine after 15 years of use. Another view. *Archives of Internal Medicine*, **154**, 2531–5.

Fitting, J.-W. (1992) Nutritional support in chronic obstructive lung disease. *Thorax*, **47**, 141–2.

Gellert, A.R., Gellert, S.L., and Iliffe, S.R. (1990). Prevalence and management of asthma in a London inner city general practice. *British Journal of General Practice*, **301**, 771–2.

Gerard, W.M. and Light, R.W. (1984). Should the FVC be considered in evaluating response to bronchodilator? *Chest*, **84**, 87–9.

Griffiths, C. (1996). Steroids in exacerbations of asthma: tablets or inhalers. *Thorax*, **51**, 1071–2.

Horsley, J.R., Sterling, I.J.N., Waters, W.E., and Howell, J.B.L. (1991). Respiratory symptoms among elderly people in the New Forest area as assessed by a postal questionnaire. *Age and Ageing*, **20**, 325–31.

Ikeda, A., Nishimura, K., Koyama, H., Tsukino, M., Mishima, M., and Izumi, T. (1996). Dose–response study of ipratropium bromide aerosol on maximum exercise performance in stable patients with chronic obstructive pulmonary disease. *Thorax*, **51**, 48–53.

Ishoaho, R., Puolijoki, H., Huhti, E., Kivela, S.-L., Laippala, P., and Tala, E. (1994). Prevalence of chronic obstructive pulmonary disease in elderly Finns. *Respiratory Medicine*, **88**, 571–80.

Kerstjens, H.A.M., Brand, P.L.P., Hughes, M.D., Postma, D.S., Quanjer, P.H., Sluiter, H.J., the Dutch CNSLD Study Group (1991). Double-blind 2.5 years prospective study of anti-inflammatory and bronchodilator therapy in obstructive airways disease: first results. *American Review of Respiratory Disease*, **143**, A454.

Lacasse, Y., Wong, E., Guyatt, G.H., King, D., Cook, D.J., and Goldstein, R.S. (1996). Meta-analysis of respiratory rehabilitation in chronic obstructive pulmonary disease. *Lancet*, **348**, 1115–19

Lebowitz, M.D., Knudson, R.J., and Burrows, B. (1975) Tucson epidemiological study of obstructive lung diseases. I Methodology and prevalences of diseases. *American Journal of Epidemiology*, **2**, 137–52.

Lee, H.Y. and Stretton, T.B. (1972). Asthma in the elderly. *British Medical Journal*, **4**, 93–5.

Lunde, H., Hedner, T., Samuelsson, O., *et al.* (1994). Dyspnoea, asthma and bronchospasm in relation to treatment with angiotensin converting enzyme inhibitors. *British Medical Journal*, **308**, 18–21.

McDonald, P., Friedman, E.H.I., Banks, A., Anderson, R., and Carman, V. (1997). Pneumoccal vaccine campaign in general practice. *British Medical Journal*, **314**, 1094–8.

Mafreda, J., Mas, Y., and Litven, W. (1989). Morbidity and mortality from chronic obstructive pulmonary disease. *American Review of Respiratory Disease*, **140**, S19–26.

Matthys, H. (1990). Inhalational delivery of asthma drugs. *Lung*, **168**, 645–52.

Medical Research Council (1965). Definition and classification of chronic bronchitis, clinical and epidemiological purposes; a report to the Medical Research Council by their committee on the aetiology of chronic bronchitis. *Lancet*, i, 775–80.

Milne, J.S. and Williamson, J. (1972). Respiratory symptoms in older people with age and sex differences. *Respiration*, **29**, 359–70.

National Asthma Education and Prevention Programme (1996). *NIH considerations for diagnosing and managing asthma in the elderly*. NIH Publication No. 96-3662.

Nejjari, C., Tessier, J.F., Letenneur, L., *et al.* (1996). Prevalence of self-reported asthma symptoms in French elderly sample. *Respiratory Medicine*, **90**, 401–8.

Neville, E., Corris, P.A., Vivian, J., Narimen, S., and Gibson, G.J. (1982). Nebulised salbutamol and angina. *British Medical Journal*, **285**, 796–7.

Nisar, M., Walshaw, E., Earis, J.E., Pearson, M.G., and Calverley, P.M.A. (1990). Assessment of reversibility of airways obstruction in patients with chronic obstructive airways disease. *Thorax*, **45**, 190–4.

Nocturnal Oxygen Therapy Trial Group (1980). Continuous or nocturnal oxygen therapy in hypoxaemic chronic obstructive lung disease: a clinical trial. *Annals of Internal Medicine*, **93**, 391–8.

Osler, W. (1892). Bronchial asthma. In *Principles and practice of medicine*, (ed. W. Osler). Appleton, New York.

Pedersen, S. (1996). Inhalers and nebulisers: which to choose and why. *Respiratory Medicine*, **90**, 69–77.

Petheram, I.S., Jones, D.A., and Collins, J.V. (1982). Assessment and management of acute asthma in the elderly: a comparison with younger asthmatics. *Postgraduate Medicine Journal*, **58**, 149–51.

Postma, D.S. (1991). Inhaled therapy in COPD: what are the benefits? *Respiratory Medicine*, **85**, 447–9.

Renkema, T.E.J. (1990). A two-year prospective study on the effect of inhaled and inhaled plus oral corticosteroids in chronic airflow obstruction. *American Review of Respiratory Disease*, **141**, A468.

Renwick, D.S. and Connolly, M.J. (1996). Prevalence and treatment of chronic airways obstruction in adults over the age of 45. *Thorax*, **51**, 164–8.

Ronchi, M.C., Piragino, C., Rosi, E., Amendola, M., Duranti, R., and Scano, G. (1996). Role of sputum differential cell count in detecting airway inflammation in patients with bronchial asthma or COPD. *Thorax*, **51**, 1000–4.

Russell, M.A.H., Wilson, C., and Taylor, C. (1979). Effect of General Practitioner advice against smoking. *British Medical Journal*, **2**, 231–5.

Schmidt, O., Dickman, M.L., Gardner, R.M., and Brough, F.K. (1973). Spirometric standards for healthy men and women: 532 subjects ages 55 through 94 years. *American Review of Respiratory Disease*, **108**, 933–9.

Sears, M., Taylor, D.R., Print, C.G., *et al.* (1990) Regular inhaled beta-agonist treatment in bronchial asthma. *Lancet*, **336**, 1391–6.

Self, T.H., Abou-Shala, N., Burns, R., *et al.* (1990). Inhaled albuterol and oral prednisone therapy in hospitalised adult asthmatics. Does aminophylline add any benefit? *Chest*, **98**, 1317–21.

Selroos, O. and Halme, M. (1991). Effect of volumatic spacer and mouth rinsing on systemic absorption of inhaled corticosteroids from a metered dose inhaler and dry powder inhaler. *Thorax*, **46**, 891–4.

Shannon, M. (1993). Predictors of major toxicity after theophylline overdose. *Annals of Internal Medicine*, **119**, 1161–7.

Siafakas, N.M., Vermeire, P., Pride, N.B., *et al.* (1995). Optimal assessment and management of chronic obstructive pulmonary disease (COPD):

The European Respiratory Society Task Force. *European Respiratory Journal*, **8**, 1398–420.

Singh, S.J., Morgan, M.D.L., Scott, S., Walters, D., and Hardman, A.E. (1992). Development of a shuttle walking test of disability in patients with chronic airways obstruction. *Thorax*, **47**, 1019–24.

Smyth, E.T., Wright, S.C., Evans, A.E., Sinnamon, D.G., and MacMahon, J. (1996). Death from airways obstruction. Accuracy of death certification in Northern Ireland. *Thorax*, **51**, 293–7.

Stanescu, D., Sanna, A., Veriter, C., *et al.* (1985). Effect of cigarette smoking on the pulmonary function of children and adolescents. *American Review of Respiratory Disease*, **131**, 752–9.

Tweedale, P.M., Alexander, F., and McHardy, G.J.R. (1984). Short-term variability in FEV_1: relation to pre-test activity, level of FEV_1 and smoking habits. *Thorax*, **39**, 928–32.

Tweedale, P.M., Alexander, F., and McHardy, G.J.R. (1987). Short-term variability in FEV_1 and bronchodilator responsiveness in patients with obstructive ventilatory defects. *Thorax*, **43**, 487–90.

Van Schaycker, C.P., Folgering, H., Harbers, H., Maas, K.L., and van Weel, C. (1991). Effects of allergy and age on responses to salbutamol and ipratropium bromide in moderate asthma and chronic bronchitis. *Thorax*, **46**, 355–9.

Watson, J.M., Cordier, J.F., and Nicholson, K.G. (1997). Does influenza immunisation cause exacerbations of chronic airflow obstruction or asthma? *Thorax*, **52**, 190–4.

Weir, D.C., Gove, R.I., Robertson, A.S., and Burge, P.S. (1990). Corticosteroid trials in non-asthmatic chronic airflow obstruction: a comparison of oral prednisolone and inhaled beclomethasone dipropionate. *Thorax*, **45**, 112–17.

Wilson, R. (1994). Influenza vaccination. *Thorax*, **49**, 1079–80.

Wolf, P.A., Dawber, T.R., Thomas, H.E., and Kannel, W.B. (1978). Epidemiological assessment of chronic atrial fibrillation and risk of stroke: the Framingham Study. *Neurology*, **28**, 973–7.

Xu, X., Dockery, D.W., Ware, J.H., Speizer, F.E., and Ferris, B.G. (1992). Effects of cigarette smoking or rate of loss of pulmonary function in adults: a longitudinal assessment. *American Review of Respiratory Disease*, **146**, 1345–8.

Zainudin, B.M.Z., Ismail, O., and Yusoff, K. (1994). Effect of adding aminophylline infusion to nebulised salbutamol in severe acute asthma. *Thorax*, **49**, 267–9.

12.4 Pulmonary embolism

Arnaud Perrier, Catherine Goehring, and Alain Junod

Definition

Pulmonary embolism results from the migration of a venous thrombus into the pulmonary circulation, most frequently from the deep veins of the lower limbs. Hence pulmonary embolism is predominantly a complication of deep venous thrombosis. Moreover, both disorders share a common pathogenesis and treatment, so that they are increasingly considered as the single pathological entity, venous thromboembolism (Moser 1990). However, pulmonary embolism is potentially fatal and requires specific diagnostic strategies, and so it will be considered separately in this chapter.

Table 1 Incidence of pulmonary embolism with increasing age

Age (years)	Incidence (rate/1000 person-years)
65–69	1.2
70–74	1.7
75–79	2.2
80–84	2.6
85–89	2.8

Data from Kniffin et al. (1994).

Incidence

Pulmonary embolism is a common disorder, and its incidence increases with age because of modifications of haemostasis and increasing frequency of predisposing factors, such as immobilization, surgery, or cancer. In a recent epidemiological study (Kniffin et al. 1994), the incidence of pulmonary embolism increased from 1.2 to 2.8 per 1000 people per year at ages 65 and 85 years, respectively (Table 1). Moreover, both the short- and long-term case-fatality rates are higher in older people. The 30-day case-fatality rate is approximately 13 per cent in elderly patients when pulmonary embolism is the primary diagnosis, and rises to approximately 30 per cent for a secondary diagnosis of pulmonary embolism (Siddique et al. 1996). Overall, 39 per cent of patients aged 65 years or more die during the year following an episode of pulmonary embolism (Kniffin et al. 1994), probably owing to an increased prevalence of comorbidities. Finally, pulmonary embolism is often not recognized before death, as consistently revealed by autopsy studies. In a recent survey from a general hospital (Stein et al. 1995), pulmonary embolism was found in 59 of 404 autopsies (14.6 per cent), and was the likely cause of death in 20, although it had been suspected antemortem in only seven of the 59 patients. Similar observations have been made for 30 years.

Pathogenesis

Pulmonary embolism is caused by the formation of a thrombus in the venous circulation, and 90 per cent of thrombi arise from the deep veins of the lower limbs. Other possible sources are the pelvic veins (particularly after gynaecological or prostatic surgery), the upper extremity, or the right heart. The formation of thrombi is generally due to a combination of factors, most importantly venous stasis and a congenital or, more frequently, acquired, hypercoagulable state. The role of endothelial injury is of less importance, since direct trauma to the endothelium of the affected veins is rare. Venous stasis may result from a number of conditions frequently present in later life, such as venous insufficiency, congestive heart failure, immobilization, or previous deep venous thrombosis. Moreover, ageing is associated with a change in the balance between procoagulant and anticoagulant activities towards thrombus formation. With age, blood levels of fibrinogen and most clotting factors increase, whereas fibrinolytic activity and antithrombin levels decrease (Hager et al. 1989). Other

acquired causes of hypercoagulability include surgery, trauma, malignancy, and high oestrogen states. Congenital deficiencies of coagulation inhibitors (antithrombin III, proteins C and S) or resistance to activated protein C, are less frequent causes of thrombosis in later life.

Physiological consequences

Although pulmonary embolism affects gas exchange to an extent, pulmonary embolism causes death through its haemodynamic effects. The pulmonary vascular bed is a low-pressure high-capacitance system. The acute obstruction of more than 50 per cent of the pulmonary vascular bed results in acute pulmonary hypertension, although pulmonary embolism of smaller size may also provoke an elevation of pulmonary artery pressure, probably through endothelial secretion of vasoconstrictor wall stress substances. The thin wall of the right ventricle may be unable to adjust to the wall stress generated by the high afterload, becomes ischaemic and dyskinetic, and fails despite increasing filling pressures. The mortality associated with this situation is high. Right ventricular dyskinesia, as assessed by echocardiography, has recently been identified as an independent predictor of higher mortality (Goldhaber et al. 1993).

Hypoxaemia and respiratory alkalosis are present in the majority of patients with pulmonary embolism. Hypoxaemia is usually explained by ventilation–perfusion mismatch. Physiological dead space is increased because of high ventilation–perfusion ratios in the embolized zones. However, an increase in total alveolar ventilation is usually sufficient to restore a normal arterial CO_2 pressure. Indeed, hypocapnia is generally present, secondary to the direct stimulation of parenchymal lung receptors by the embolus. Hypoxaemia is thought to result from physiological shunting (low ventilation–perfusion alveolar units). Several mechanisms have been postulated: (a) blood flow through atelectatic zones, surfactant production being impaired in the embolized regions; (b) redistribution of blood flow towards perfused zones of the lung with low ventilation–perfusion ratios; and (c) bronchoconstriction, either reflex or mediated by the release of bronchoconstrictor substances. Whatever the mechanism, hypoxaemia is generally easy to correct by the administration of oxygen via a face mask, and intubation is rarely required because of gas exchange impairment, even in massive pulmonary embolism.

Clinical manifestations and laboratory findings

Symptoms and signs

Symptoms of pulmonary embolism are non-specific. In 50 per cent of patients, the presenting complaint is pleuritic pain, with or without dyspnoea. In another 30 per cent of patients, progressive or acute dyspnoea without chest pain is the only complaint. Cardiovascular collapse or haemoptysis are rare presentations of pulmonary embolism (10 per cent). These symptoms are present with similar frequency in patients suspected of pulmonary embolism in whom the disease is ultimately ruled out. Hence, the clinician usually suspects pulmonary embolism whenever one of these complaints occurs in a patient with

Table 2 Signs, symptoms, and laboratory findings in acute pulmonary embolism

	≥ 70 years	<70 years
Symptoms (%)		
Dyspnoea	78	80
Pleuritic pain	51	60
Cough	35	55
Leg swelling	35	57
Haemoptysis	8	11
Signs		
Tachypnoea (respiratory rate ≥ 20 breaths/min)	74	72
Rales (crackles)	65	56
Tachycardia (heart rate >100 beats/min)	29	27
Increased pulmonary component of the second heart sound	15	23
Signs of deep vein thrombosis	15	15
Chest radiography		
Normal	4	9
Atelectasis or parenchymal abnormality	71	68
Pleural effusion	57	46
Elevated diaphragm	28	25
Electrocardiogram		
Normal	21	20
ST- or T-wave changes	56	41
Signs of right ventricular strain	2–7	2–8

Data from Stein *et al.* (1991).

risk factors for venous thromboembolism, and no obvious alternative diagnosis.

The most common finding on physical examination is tachypnoea (respiratory frequency > 20 breaths/min). Crepitations are often present, but tachycardia is absent in 70 per cent of patients. An increased intensity of the pulmonary component of the second heart sound is infrequent, and signs of deep vein thrombosis are absent in the majority of cases. The mode of presentation of pulmonary embolism appears to be identical in elderly and younger patients (Table 2) (Stein *et al.* 1991).

Chest radiography

Chest radiography is often abnormal in pulmonary embolism. The most common findings are plate-like atelectasis, pleural effusion (usually small), and/or elevation of a hemidiaphragm. Wedge-shaped pleural-based infiltrates are rare and represent pulmonary infarction. Unilateral oligaemia (Westermark's sign) may be present but is more often due to technical artefacts such as the patient not being positioned square on to the X-ray beam. None of these findings is diagnostic of pulmonary embolism, and their usefulness is limited. However, a completely normal chest radiography slightly reduces the probability of pulmonary embolism. Moreover, a chest radiograph is necessary for the interpretation of a lung scan.

Arterial blood gases

A typical pattern combines respiratory alkalosis and hypoxaemia. However, 10 to 20 per cent of patients with documented pulmonary embolism have a normal arterial oxygen pressure (Pao_2), and a normal alveolar-arterial oxygen gradient ($D(A-a)o_2$). Thus, a normal Pao_2 or $D(A-a)o_2$ does not exclude pulmonary embolism, but renders it less likely.

Electrocardiography

The ECG is abnormal in approximately 80 per cent of patients, whether aged more than 70 years or younger (Stein *et al.* 1991). The most common abnormalities are non-specific ST-segment or T-wave changes. The classical, but non-specific, findings of S_1Q_3 pattern, right bundle branch block, pulmonary P waves, elevated right ventricular ST segments, or right axis deviation are seldom observed.

Clinical probability of pulmonary embolism

None of the symptoms, signs, or laboratory findings reflecting pulmonary embolism are sensitive or specific when taken singly. However, their combination allows the clinician to make a global assessment of the likelihood of pulmonary embolism in a given patient. The chest radiograph, blood gases, and ECG are included in the clinical evaluation, since they are readily available. The presence of risk factors for venous thromboembolism is important as the prevalence of pulmonary embolism in patients suspected of the diagnosis increases with the number of risk factors present. Several studies have shown that clinicians are able to classify patients into three categories with reasonable accuracy: low (0–20 per cent), intermediate (21–79 per cent), and high (80–100 per cent) clinical probability of pulmonary embolism. The prevalence of pulmonary embolism in each category is shown in Table 3. Age does not influence the accuracy of clinical probability assessment (Stein *et al.* 1991), although the prevalence of

Table 3 Prevalence of pulmonary embolism (PE) according to clinical probability as assessed empirically by the clinician

	PIOPED study[a] (n)	Geneva study[b] (n)
Clinical probability of PE		
Low (0–20%)[c]	9% (21/228)	9% (15/174)
Intermediate (21–79%)	30% (170/569)	32% (138/432)
High (80–100%)	68% (61/90)	67% (43/64)

[a] Prospective Investigation of Pulmonary Embolism Diagnosis Investigators (1990) (PIOPED).
[b] Perrier et al. (1997).
[c] Low clinical probability was defined as 0–19% in the PIOPED study and 0–20% in the Geneva study.

pulmonary embolism in patients with suspected pulmonary embolism is higher in patients aged over 60 years than in younger patients (40 compared with 20 per cent) (Sackett *et al.* 1991). However, this probably reflects the higher prevalence of risk factors for pulmonary embolism in the older age groups.

The probability of pulmonary embolism after any one of the diagnostic tests discussed below (post-test probability) depends, by Bayes' theorem, both on the test's performance (sensitivity and specificity) and on the pretest probability (Sackett *et al.* 1991). Figure 1 illustrates this relationship, using lung scanning as an example. Consequently, the diagnostic strategy for pulmonary embolism varies according to the clinical or pretest probability (see below).

Diagnostic tests for pulmonary embolism

Ventilation–perfusion lung scan

The ventilation–perfusion lung scan was the first non-invasive test available for diagnosing pulmonary embolism and has been extensively studied. Perfusion scan is obtained by injecting macroaggregates of radiolabelled albumin (usually labelled with technetium) into the

Table 4 Criteria for the interpretation of a lung scan

Normal
Normal perfusion lung scan

Very low probability
Heterogeneous distribution of tracer activity (perfusion phase) or small non-segmental defects

Low probability
Multiple matched V/Q defects or non-segmental mismatched defect(s) or single mismatched perfusion defect

Intermediate probability
Multiple matched V/Q defects with matching radiograph abnormality or associated with a severe chronic obstructive pulmonary disease

High probability
Multiple mismatched V/Q segmental defects

V/Q, ventilation–perfusion.

peripheral venous circulation. Owing to their size, the aggregates are trapped in the precapillary pulmonary vessels. Less than 1 per cent of the vessels are blocked by the aggregates, rendering the procedure safe even in patients with pulmonary hypertension. The distribution of ventilation in the lungs is studied by giving the patient an inert radioactive gas ([131]Xe or Technegas®) to inhale. Images are obtained with a gamma camera. A good quality scan consists of a minimum of six incidences in the perfusion phase and three in the ventilation phase. The rationale for perfusion imaging is self-evident: pulmonary embolism provokes 'cold' spots, so-called perfusion defects. Conversely, ventilation imaging is expected to enhance specificity, since a number of diseases predominantly affecting the lung air spaces, such as pneumonia, are also associated with reduced perfusion. Therefore a mismatched ventilation and perfusion defect, i.e. a perfusion defect with a normal ventilation in the affected zone, should be specific for pulmonary embolism, whereas a matched ventilation and perfusion defect might be seen in a number of conditions, including pulmonary embolism. Hence, the interpretation of the lung scan is complex, and results are given in terms of categories of probability of pulmonary embolism (normal, very low, low, intermediate, and high probability) according to predefined patterns of lung scan findings (Table 4).

Lung scanning is highly sensitive for pulmonary embolism, and so the absence of any perfusion abnormality (normal lung scan)

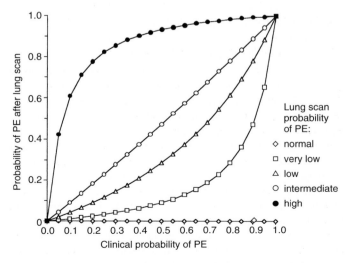

Fig. 1 Relationship between pretest (clinical) probability of pulmonary embolism (PE) and probability of pulmonary embolism after lung scan.

Table 5 Prevalence of pulmonary embolism (PE) according to lung scan result and clinical probability of PE

Clinical probability of PE	Lung scan probability of PE			
	Very low (%)	Low (%)	Intermediate (%)	High (%)
Low (0–20%)	2	4	16	56
Intermediate (21–79%)	6	16	28	88
High (80–100%)	—	40	66	96

Data from Prospective Investigation of Pulmonary Embolism Diagnosis Investigators (1990).

virtually rules out pulmonary embolism. The risk of venous thrombo-embolism during a 3-month follow-up in patients with a normal scan is only 0.4 per cent (Kipper *et al.* 1982; Hull *et al.* 1990). Pulmonary embolism is also highly unlikely when there is a very low probability scan, and most experts accept it as sufficient evidence of the absence of pulmonary embolism, provided the patient does not have a high clinical probability of pulmonary embolism. A high probability lung scan pattern corresponds to multiple mismatched perfusion defects and is highly suggestive of pulmonary embolism, as confirmed by angiography in approximately 90 per cent of patients with such a scan result (Prospective Investigation of Pulmonary Embolism Diagnosis 1990). Low or intermediate probability lung scans should be considered non-diagnostic, as the prevalence of pulmonary embolism in these categories varies between 4 and 66 per cent. A non-diagnostic scan should be followed by other tests or combined with clinical probability to determine the diagnosis. Overall, lung scan establishes a definitive diagnosis in approximately 30 to 50 per cent of patients. This proportion is not affected by age, although older people tend to have a higher proportion of high probability and a lower proportion of normal scans.

Combining lung scan and clinical probability of pulmonary embolism

Combining clinical probability of pulmonary embolism with the ventilation–perfusion scan results enhances the diagnostic efficacy of the scan. As shown in Fig. 1, the probability of pulmonary embolism after lung scan depends on the pretest or clinical probability of pulmonary embolism. In a patient with an intermediate clinical probability of pulmonary embolism (50 per cent) and a low probability lung scan, the probability of pulmonary embolism remains quite high (approximately 30 per cent), and further investigations are warranted. Conversely, with the same lung scan result but a low clinical probability (15 per cent), pulmonary embolism is much less likely (post-test probability 6 per cent). These theoretical data have been confirmed by the Prospective Investigation of Pulmonary Embolism Diagnosis Study. In this series, when both the clinical probability and the lung scan probability were low, the prevalence of pulmonary embolism was only 4 per cent (Table 5). Hence, pulmonary embolism may be ruled out in the subgroup of patients presenting with a low clinical probability (0–20 per cent) and a low probability lung scan, a combination found in approximately 25 per cent of patients with non-diagnostic scans (Perrier *et al.* 1996).

Lower-limb venous compression ultrasonography

Autopsy studies have demonstrated that pulmonary embolism arises from a deep vein thrombosis of the lower limbs in 90 per cent of patients. However, when phlebography is systematically performed in patients with angiographically confirmed pulmonary embolism, deep vein thrombosis is found in only 70 per cent of cases, probably because the clot has entirely embolized to the lung. Nevertheless, the search for residual deep vein thrombosis is rational, since the demonstration of a clot in the lower limbs of a patient suspected of pulmonary embolism warrants anticoagulant treatment, and could thus spare the patient further, possibly invasive, diagnostic procedures.

A number of instruments have been used to this end over the years. Impedance plethysmography was very popular in North America, because of its simplicity and low cost (Hull *et al.* 1985). Its principle rests on the detection of volume changes of the lower extremity. The volume is measured before and after inflation of a cuff applied to the thigh. The cuff is then deflated and the rapidity with which the lower-limb volume returns to the baseline is used as an index of venous patency. Impedance plethysmography was deemed to have a high sensitivity and specificity for symptomatic proximal deep vein thrombosis compared with phlebography. More recent data, however, have shown a lower sensitivity (approximately 60 per cent), possibly due to an increase in the frequency of non-occlusive thrombi (Ginsberg *et al.* 1994). Moreover, a direct comparison of plethysmography and compression ultrasonography showed ultrasonography to be more sensitive (Heijboer *et al.* 1993).

Lower-limb real-time B-mode compression ultrasonography allows the direct visualization of the femoral and popliteal veins and their compression by the ultrasound probe. A normal vein should collapse completely during the manoeuvre, so the finding of a non-compressible or only partially compressible vein is direct evidence of the presence of a luminal clot. Doppler scanning, often associated with compression ultrasonography, may be helpful to identify the vein, but is not essential. The sensitivity and specificity of compression ultrasonography for diagnosing proximal deep vein thrombosis are very high in symptomatic patients, 95 and 98 per cent, respectively (Becker *et al.* 1989). In patients with pulmonary embolism, a majority of which have no symptoms or signs of deep vein thrombosis, ultrasonography shows a deep vein thrombosis in approximately 50 per cent of patients (Perrier *et al.* 1996). Although the specificity of ultrasonography in patients with pulmonary embolism has not been established, it is probably high, as it is in other groups, such as orthopaedic patients being screened for venous thromboembolism after hip surgery (Agnelli *et al.* 1992). The diagnostic usefulness of ultrasonography may be greater in older than in younger patients; in our population, the sensitivity of ultrasonography in patients aged over 60 years with pulmonary embolism was 60 to 70 per cent, compared with 30 to 40 per cent in younger patients.

In summary, ultrasonography reveals a deep vein thrombosis in 50 per cent of patients with pulmonary embolism and establishes the diagnosis of venous thromboembolism. Conversely, the absence of deep vein thrombosis on ultrasonography does not rule out pulmonary embolism, even though it probably identifies a subgroup of patients at lower risk of recurrent venous thromboembolism in the absence of anticoagulant treatment (see below).

Plasma D-dimer measurement

Biological markers for venous thromboembolism have been intensively researched during the past few decades. Among them, the most promising is undoubtedly D-dimer, a product of the degradation of cross-linked fibrin by plasmin that can be detected in blood or plasma by immunological methods. The activation of the coagulation and fibrinolytic systems associated with venous thromboembolism results in the elevation of plasma D-dimer levels. Numerous studies have confirmed the very high sensitivity of D-dimer for acute deep vein thrombosis and pulmonary embolism (Bounameaux *et al.* 1997). When measured by an enzyme-linked immunosorbent assay method, a D-dimer plasma level above 500 µg/l is observed in 97 per cent of patients with acute venous thromboembolism. So a normal D-dimer level (below 500 µg/l) may be reasonably interpreted as excluding pulmonary embolism. However, owing to the variety of conditions other than venous thromboembolism which may be associated with some degree of clotting and fibrinolysis (infectious or malignant diseases, inflammatory states, myocardial infarction, for example), the specificity of D-dimer measurement is low, and depends further on the characteristics of the patient population to which it is applied. In an outpatient population, D-dimer levels are normal, excluding pulmonary embolism, in approximately 50 per cent of patients without the disease (Perrier *et al.* 1996, 1999). In contrast, in patients admitted to hospital for conditions other than venous thromboembolism, the proportion of patients with normal D-dimer levels may be as low as 10 to 20 per cent, owing to the frequency of comorbid conditions (Raimondi *et al.* 1993). Moreover, it is known that D-dimer levels increase with age. In the authors' experience, the specificity of D-dimer decreases steadily with age, from approximately 60 per cent between 20 and 50 years of age, to 32 per cent between 60 and 69, 22 per cent between 70 and 79, and 9 per cent over 80, limiting the usefulness of this test in elderly subjects, even in outpatients (Perrier *et al.* 1997). Finally, the enzyme-linked immunosorbent assay technique is cumbersome and ill-suited to emergency use, and first-generation latex tests were not sensitive enough to rule out pulmonary embolism safely. Future advances reside in the validation of new automated quantitative D-dimer tests (de Moerloose *et al.* 1996; Perrier *et al.* 1999). Newer whole-blood latex tests are not sufficiently sensitive (Ginsberg *et al.* 1998).

Spiral CT

A recent advance in CT technology, the helical or spiral CT scan, allows better visualization of the pulmonary vessels. With this technique, pulmonary emboli appear as filling defects in the arterial lumen, surrounded by a thin contrast film. The sensitivity and specificity of such a finding seems high (more than 95 per cent) for proximal (central or lobar) pulmonary embolism, and acceptable (more than 90 per cent) at the segmental level. At the subsegmental level, however, both sensitivity and specificity are probably much lower, and depend on the radiologist's experience and the quality of the scanner's reconstruction algorithm (van Rossum *et al.* 1996). Moreover, this technique has been investigated only in a small number of patients, and trials incorporating spiral CT in global diagnostic strategies are still under way. The two currently investigated avenues are the use of CT in patients with non-diagnostic lung scans, or as a substitute for a lung scan, since CT is becoming rapidly more widely available than lung scanning. The relative cost-effectiveness of these approaches also needs to be studied.

Magnetic resonance imaging

The role of magnetic resonance imaging (MRI) in the diagnosis of pulmonary embolism is under evaluation (Meaney *et al.* 1997). One potential advantage over CT scanning lies in the avoidance of radiation exposure.

Echocardiography

Echocardiography is especially useful in patients with suspected pulmonary embolism and haemodynamic consequences such as hypotension or cardiovascular collapse. Indeed, the echocardiographic manifestations of pulmonary embolism are mostly indirect, reflecting the existence of pulmonary arterial hypertension. These signs include tricuspid regurgitation (the Doppler measurement of the regurgitation velocity allowing an accurate estimation of the systolic pulmonary arterial pressure), enlargement of right atrium and ventricle, dyskinetic wall motion of the free portion of the right ventricle, and deformation of the interventricular septum which may even bulge in the left ventricle (Come 1992). The sensitivity of these findings in unselected patients with suspected pulmonary embolism is unknown. However, in patients with suspected massive pulmonary embolism, pulmonary hypertension is almost always present and sensitivity of echocardiography is probably high. Moreover, in such patients, echocardiography yields important additional information, allowing the exclusion of tamponade or cardiogenic shock and, using transoesophageal echocardiography, aortic dissection. The specificity of echocardiography in the context of clinically suspected pulmonary embolism is probably high, except in patients with pulmonary hypertension from other causes. The demonstration of thrombi in the right heart chambers or in the pulmonary trunk is exceptional with transthoracic echocardiography, but may be more frequent than originally thought with transoesophageal echocardiography.

In summary, an echocardiogram showing signs of pulmonary hypertension and right ventricular strain in a haemodynamically compromised patient with suspected pulmonary embolism and no other causes of pre-existing pulmonary hypertension, is sufficient evidence of pulmonary embolism to warrant anticoagulation or, where indicated, thrombolytic treatment. In contrast, a normal echocardiogram does not exclude pulmonary embolism, particularly in a patient with non-massive pulmonary embolism.

Pulmonary angiography

Pulmonary angiography remains the gold standard for the diagnosis of pulmonary embolism, but several limitations should be kept in mind. Angiography is an invasive procedure, and carries a significant rate of morbidity and fatality. Major complications of angiography, such as renal failure requiring dialysis, cardiac arrest, respiratory failure (usually pulmonary oedema) requiring intubation, or major haemorrhage at the puncture site, occur in 1 to 3 per cent of patients. The fatality rate varies between 0.2 and 0.5 per cent in various series. The higher figure (0.5 per cent) seems more realistic, since it comes from the only multicentre study (Stein *et al.* 1992). Death from angiography seems to occur only in very ill patients. In the multicentre study, all the angiographic deaths happened in haemodynamically unstable patients admitted to hospital in an intensive care unit (Stein *et al.* 1992). Major complications from angiography do not appear to be more frequent in elderly patients, except for renal failure, which occurs in 3 per cent of patients aged over 70 years compared with 0.7 per cent in younger individuals (Stein *et al.* 1991). Moreover, pulmonary angiography is difficult to interpret. In the Prospective Investigation of Pulmonary Embolism Diagnosis Study (1990), experts disagreed on the presence of pulmonary embolism in 8 per cent, and on the absence of pulmonary embolism in 17 per cent of angiograms. When the controversial angiograms were adjudicated by an expert panel, 3 per cent were still considered equivocal. This may result in both false positive and false negative angiograms, a fact that is often overlooked. Lastly, angiography is costly. For all these reasons, angiography should be performed only in patients in whom non-invasive and cheaper tests have been inconclusive. The purpose of all recently proposed diagnostic strategies for pulmonary embolism is to reduce the requirement for angiography to a minimum.

Diagnostic strategies

Most diagnostic strategies combine non-invasive tests with pulmonary angiography for patients with an inconclusive non-invasive work-up. The cost-effectiveness of various combinations and sequences of tests is currently under investigation. Adding ultrasonography to lung scan and angiography is cost-effective (Oudkerk *et al.* 1993). D-Dimer may also be cost-effective in selected patients. Lung scan is traditionally held as the first test in the diagnostic sequence, although this limits the capacity of institutions without nuclear medicine facilities to investigate suspected pulmonary embolism. Starting the investigation with D-dimer or ultrasonography, depending on the local availability of these tests may be at least as cost-effective (Perrier *et al.* 1997b). The strategy used in the authors' institution is illustrated in Fig. 2 and has recently been validated in a management trial (Perrier *et al.* 1999). Accepted diagnostic criteria for pulmonary embolism are summarized in Table 6.

Patients with adequate cardiorespiratory reserve, that is without haemodynamic compromise or significant chronic heart or respiratory failure, may be managed entirely without angiography, using lung scan and serial lower-limb examination (plethysmography or venous ultrasonography) (Hull *et al.* 1994). Patients with a non-diagnostic scan undergo a lower-limb examination, and this discloses a deep vein thrombosis in approximately 10 per cent. Those with no deep vein thrombosis are not anticoagulated and submitted to serial plethysmography or ultrasonography. The rationale for serial testing

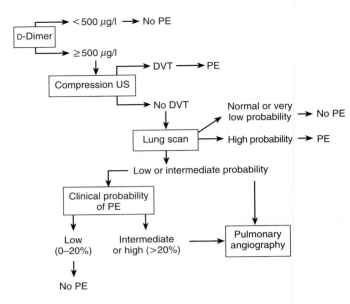

Fig. 2 Diagnostic strategy for pulmonary embolism (PE): DVT, deep vein thrombosis; US, ultrasonography.

Table 6 Recognized diagnostic criteria for pulmonary embolism (PE)

PE
High-probability lung scan
Deep vein thrombosis shown by ultrasonography and clinical suspicion of PE
Angiogram showing PE

No PE
Normal lung scan
Plasma D-dimer below 500 μg/l
Low clinical probability of PE and non-diagnostic lung scan
Normal pulmonary angiogram

is the detection of proximal extension of a calf thrombus. Indeed, calf clots are often not shown by plethysmography or ultrasonography, both procedures having very low sensitivity for detecting distal thrombi. Serial testing discloses a proximal deep vein thrombosis in an additional 2 per cent of patients, warranting anticoagulant treatment. The frequency of serial testing is controversial. The most important series (Hull *et al.* 1994) proposed the repetition of the lower-limb examination on days 3, 5, 7, 10, and 14. A single second examination after 7 days may be a valid and less cumbersome alternative.

Treatment

Death from pulmonary embolism in patients who survived a first episode is most commonly caused by recurrence. Preventing the extension of venous thrombosis by anticoagulants is remarkably effective in reducing recurrence and fatality rates. In the classical and single prospective trial which compared heparin treatment and no treatment in acute pulmonary embolism, fatality was reduced from 30 per cent to approximately 8 per cent by heparin (Barritt *et al.* 1960). When treatment is started with oral anticoagulants alone, the recurrence rate is unacceptably high (Brandjes *et al.* 1992), so treatment should begin with the parenteral administration of unfractionated heparin because of its immediate onset of action. Heparin, a glycosaminoglycan, acts by catalysing the effect of antithrombin, a plasma coagulation inhibitor, causing antithrombin to combine with and inhibit thrombin, factor Xa, and factor IXa more effectively. The biological effect of heparin is monitored by the activated partial thromboplastin time test, or by directly measuring the blood heparin levels by the protamine titration method. The recommended therapeutic range is 0.2 to 0.4 IU/ml, a heparin level sufficient to block thrombus propagation in animal experiments. This usually corresponds to an activated partial thromboplastin time value 1.5 to 2.5 times the control value, although variations may be observed in the function of the thromboplastin used. A sufficient dose of heparin should be given during the first 24 to 48 h to prevent recurrence, and a number of algorithms have been published to ensure that the target activated partial thromboplastin time be reached as quickly as possible (Hyers *et al.* 1995). Alternatively, the risk of recurrence seems low provided the starting dose of heparin is higher than 30 000 IU/24 h (Anand *et al.* 1996). Heparin can also be administered subcutaneously, but the required dose is usually higher. Heparin may be discontinued as soon as oral anticoagulation is effective, that is after 4 to 7 days if oral anticoagulants are started on the first hospital day. Low-molecular-weight heparins are very attractive for the treatment of the acute phase of pulmonary embolism, because of their ease of administration. Since the response to low-molecular-weight heparins is more predictable than to unfractionated heparin, the dose is determined by body weight and no laboratory monitoring is required. This can permit early hospital discharge. Low-molecular-weight heparins have been shown to be at least as effective and safe as unfractionated heparin in the treatment of pulmonary embolism (Simonneau *et al.* 1997; COLUMBUS Investigators 1997).

Oral anticoagulants are chemical derivatives of 4-hydroxycoumarin. They act by inhibiting vitamin K dependent synthesis of coagulant proteins in the liver (factors II, VII, IX, and X). The most commonly used compounds are warfarin and acenocoumarol. Their onset of action is delayed until the normal coagulation factors are cleared from the plasma, a process which takes from 24 h (factor VII) to 3 or 4 days (factor II). The synthesis of two anticoagulant proteins (proteins C and S) is also inhibited by oral anticoagulants. Owing to its short half-life, the plasma level of protein C falls more rapidly than that of the coagulant factors after the administration of warfarin, transiently shifting the balance towards a hypercoagulable state for 24 to 48 h. Administrating large loading doses of oral anticoagulants may exaggerate this phenomenon, and should be avoided. The efficacy of oral anticoagulation is monitored by the international normalized ratio (**INR**), a standardized expression of the prothrombin time, with a target INR of 2.0 to 3.0.

The major side-effect of anticoagulant treatment is bleeding. Risk factors for haemorrhage include past bleeding (particularly gastrointestinal bleeding), cerebrovascular disease, serious heart disease, and renal insufficiency. Whether elderly patients have a higher risk of bleeding remains controversial. A recent study showed that the risk of minor and serious haemorrhages during warfarin treatment was not influenced by age, whereas life-threatening or fatal bleeds were significantly more common in patients over 80 years of age (Fihn *et al.* 1996). The rate of major bleeding in patients treated by intravenous heparin for venous thromboembolism is less than 5 per cent, with a median rate of 1.9 per cent (Hyers *et al.* 1995). Major bleeding occurs in less than 4 per cent of patients during a 3-month treatment with oral anticoagulants, with a median rate of 0.9 per cent (Hyers *et al.* 1995). The fatality associated with a combined short-term heparin and 3-month oral anticoagulant treatment does not exceed 0.5 per cent.

There is no universal recommendation for the duration of oral anticoagulation after a first episode of acute pulmonary embolism. Recent studies highlight the fact that anticoagulation should be tailored to the individual patient's risk of recurrence and of bleeding complications. Patients with venous thromboembolism without an obvious precipitating factor (so-called idiopathic venous thromboembolism) are at higher risk of recurrence than patients with transient risk factors such as surgery. A 3-month treatment period is probably adequate for patients with idiopathic thrombosis and a standard bleeding risk. Patients with persisting risk factors such as malignant disease, prolonged immobilization, or congenital hypercoagulable states may benefit from a longer course of treatment. Finally, recent data suggest that a shorter course of anticoagulants (4–6 weeks) may suffice for patients with postoperative venous thromboembolism and no other risk factor, a finding that awaits further confirmation (British Thoracic Society 1992).

Patients with an absolute contraindication to anticoagulant treatment or a proven recurrent pulmonary embolism while effectively treated with anticoagulants may be managed by the insertion of a filter in the inferior vena cava. Fatal pulmonary embolism occurs in less than 1 per cent of patients with a vena cava filter. However, filters do not prevent small pulmonary emboli or local extension of thrombosis in the lower limbs, and filters cannot be removed. The reported frequency of significant symptomatic post-thrombotic syndrome in patients carrying a filter is 5 to 10 per cent. Concomitant anticoagulant treatment is recommended whenever possible (Becker *et al.* 1992).

Management of massive pulmonary embolism

Massive pulmonary embolism, defined as pulmonary embolism provoking acute right heart failure, systemic hypotension and eventually cardiovascular collapse, is a life-threatening emergency. As such, it requires a different diagnostic approach and therapy. The clinical presentation associates signs of right heart failure (elevated jugular pressure, third heart sound), tachycardia and peripheral hypoperfusion, cyanosis, and hypotension. The principal differential diagnoses are pericardial tamponade, cardiogenic shock, and aortic dissection. However, such a clinical picture in a patient with risk factors for venous thromboembolism (e.g. surgery) is highly suggestive. The most effective screening test is echocardiography, which should demonstrate signs of pulmonary hypertension and right ventricular strain, while yielding useful differential diagnostic information. Moreover, it is usually easy to obtain in the emergency ward and does not require transporting the patient. If echocardiography and clinical presentation are compatible with massive pulmonary embolism and the patient is haemodynamically unstable, thrombolytic treatment

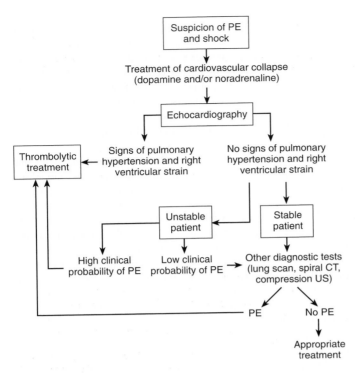

Fig. 3 Management of suspected massive pulmonary embolism: US, ultrasonography.

may be undertaken without performing any other tests (Fig. 3). Diagnostic confirmation may be obtained at a later stage by lung scan, lower-limb compression ultrasonography, or spiral CT. Pulmonary angiography is rarely necessary to confirm the diagnosis and should be done exceptionally, since it carries a higher risk in these patients.

Indications for thrombolytic treatment in pulmonary embolism are controversial because no study comparing heparin and various thrombolytic agents has been able to demonstrate a reduction of fatality by thrombolysis. However, thrombolytic agents improve haemodynamic parameters such as pulmonary artery pressure and pulmonary vascular resistance more rapidly than heparin alone. Moreover, in a trial comparing recombinant tissue plasminogen activator and heparin (Goldhaber *et al.* 1993) there was a trend towards significantly worse prognosis in patients treated with heparin alone. Of the 46 patients treated with recombinant tissue plasminogen activator, none had recurrent venous thromboembolism, compared with five of the 55 treated with heparin, of which two died. Interestingly, recurrence and death occurred only in the patients whose baseline echocardiogram showed signs of right ventricular strain. Therefore most authorities agree that patients with massive pulmonary embolism and haemodynamic compromise should receive thrombolytic treatment. Whether patients without overt haemodynamic consequences of pulmonary embolism, but with signs of right ventricular hypokinesis shown by echocardiography will also benefit from thrombolysis awaits further study.

Thrombolytic agents act by directly dissolving the clot, through activation of plasminogen. Available thrombolytic agents for pulmonary embolism are streptokinase, urokinase, and recombinant tissue plasminogen activator. The best studied agent is recombinant tissue plasminogen activator, which can be given as a short 2-h 100 mg

intravenous infusion, or even as a reduced-dose bolus injection (0.6 mg/kg, maximal dose 50 mg). Although recombinant tissue plasminogen activator selectively attacks the clot-associated plasminogen and is thus more fibrin specific than urokinase and streptokinase, the rate of bleeding complications is similar for all three thrombolytic agents. A notable exception is intracranial haemorrhage, which occurs significantly more frequently with recombinant tissue plasminogen activator (approximately 1–2 per cent versus 0.5–1 per cent with other thrombolytic agents). The risk of major bleeding in more recent studies of thrombolysis in pulmonary embolism is approximately 5 to 10 per cent and may be further reduced by rigorous patient selection and avoiding pulmonary angiography, the groin puncture site being a frequent site of major haemorrhage (Levine *et al.* 1995). Absolute contraindications to thrombolysis include active bleeding sites and central nervous system disease within the previous 3 to 6 months. Old age is associated with an increased risk of intracranial bleeding with thrombolytic treatment (Levine *et al.* 1995), but not of major bleeding from other sources. In a recent series, the efficacy of thrombolysis was similar in patients older than 75 and in younger patients (Gisselbrecht *et al.* 1996).

Patients with massive pulmonary embolism and shock not responding to thrombolytic therapy, or in whom thrombolysis is absolutely contraindicated, should undergo emergency surgical embolectomy. The fatality associated with this procedure is high (up to 50 per cent or more), reflecting the very severe haemodynamic status of patients coming to surgery.

Prevention

The prevention of pulmonary embolism starts with the prevention of deep vein thrombosis. High-risk situations and appropriate prophylaxis are summarized in Table 7. The incidence of deep vein thrombosis in high-risk conditions varies between 25 and 40 per cent, and the various preventive measures reduce this risk by 30 to 70 per cent. After general surgery, for example, the overall incidence of deep vein thrombosis is 25 per cent. The incidence of proximal deep vein thrombosis is lower, approximately 7 per cent. Pulmonary embolism could occur in 1.6 per cent of patients, and cause death in 0.9 per cent, a figure that could be reduced to 0.2 per cent by appropriate prophylaxis (Clagett *et al.* 1995).

A number of pharmacological and mechanical means may be used. Heparin may be given subcutaneously, either at a fixed low dose of 5000 IU every 8 to 12 h, or the dose may be adjusted to maintain the activated partial thromboplastin time at the upper range of normal values. Although the latter regimen is more efficient than fixed low-dose heparin in orthopaedic surgery, it is cumbersome and therefore seldom used. Low-molecular-weight heparins, though more expensive, are effective almost in all clinical settings. Low-dose or low-molecular-weight heparins do not increase the risk of major bleeding in surgical patients. Aspirin has marginal efficacy, if any, in the prophylaxis of venous thromboembolism and should not be used for this purpose. Low-intensity oral anticoagulation (target INR 2.0–3.0) is effective, but associated with an increased frequency of haemorrhages, and should thus be reserved for use in very high-risk situations such as orthopaedic surgery. Mechanical devices such as intermittent pneumatic compression or graded compression elastic

Table 7 High-risk situations for venous thromboembolism and appropriate prophylactic measures

Situation	Low-dose heparin[a]	LMWH	Low-intensity oral anticoagulants[b]	IPC or ES
General surgery	+	+	+	+
Elective hip replacement	±	+	+	+
Elective knee replacement	−	+	−	+
Hip fracture	+	+	+	?
Myocardial infarction	+	+	+	?
Stroke	+	+	?	?
General medical patients	+	+	?	?

[a] Unfractionated subcutaneous heparin, 5000 IU every 8 or 12 h.
[b] Target international normalized ratio, 2.0–3.0.

ES, graded compression elastic stockings; IPC, intermittent pneumatic compression; LMWH, low-molecular-weight heparins.

stockings are effective in reducing the frequency of deep vein thrombosis in surgical situations, but they have not been evaluated in medical patients. In high-risk situations, it is usually advised to combine pharmacological with mechanical preventive measures (Clagett *et al.* 1995).

References

Agnelli, G., Volpato, R., Radicchia, S., *et al.* (1992). Detection of asymptomatic deep vein thrombosis by real-time B-mode ultrasonography in hip surgery patients. *Thrombosis and Haemostasis*, **68**, 257–60.

Anand, S., Ginsberg, J.S., Keavon, C., Gent, M., and Hirsh, J. (1996). The relation between the activated partial thromboplastin time response and recurrence in patients with venous thrombosis treated with continuous intravenous heparin. *Archives of Internal Medicine*, **156**, 1677–81.

Barritt, D.W. and Jordan, S.C. (1960). Anticoagulant drugs in the treatment of pulmonary embolism. *Lancet*, i, 1309–12.

Becker, D.M., Philbrick, J.T., and Abbitt, P.L. (1989). Real-time ultrasonography for the diagnosis of lower extremity deep venous thrombosis. The wave of the future? *Archives of Internal Medicine*, **149**, 1731–4.

Becker, D.M., Philbrick, J.T., and Selby, J.B. (1992). Inferior vena cava filters. Indications, safety, effectiveness. *Archives of Internal Medicine*, **152**, 1985–94.

Bounameaux, H., de Moerloose, P., Perrier, A., and Miron, M.J. (1997). D-Dimer testing in suspected venous thromboembolism: an update. *Quarterly Journal of Medicine*, **90**, 437–42.

Brandjes, D.P.M., Heijboer, H., Büller, H.R., *et al.* (1992). Acenocoumarol and heparin compared with acenocoumarol alone in the initial treatment of proximal-vein thrombosis. *New England Journal of Medicine*, **327**, 1485–9.

British Thoracic Society, Research Committee (1992). Optimum duration of anticoagulation for deep-vein thrombosis and pulmonary embolism. *Lancet*, **340**, 873–6.

Clagett, G.P., Anderson, F.A., Heit, J., Levine, M.N., and Wheeler, H.B. (1995). Prevention of venous thromboembolism. *Chest*, **108**, 312S–34S.

COLUMBUS Investigators (1997). Low-molecular-weight heparin in the treatment of patients with venous thromboembolism. *New England Journal of Medicine*, **337**, 657–62.

Come, P.C. (1992). Echocardiographic evaluation of pulmonary embolism and its response to therapeutic interventions. *Chest*, **101**, 151S–62S.

de Moerloose, P., Desmarais, S., Bounameaux, H., *et al.* (1996). Contribution of a new rapid, individual and quantitative automated D-dimer ELISA to exclude pulmonary embolism. *Thrombosis and Haemostasis*, **75**, 11–13.

Fihn, S.D., Callahan, C.M., Martin, D.C., McDonell, M.B., Henikoff, J.G., and White, R.H. (1996). The risk for and severity of bleeding complications in elderly patients treated with warfarin. The National Consortium of Anticoagulation. *Annals of Internal Medicine*, **124**, 970–9.

Ginsberg, J.S., Wells, P.S., Hirsh, J., *et al.* (1994). Re-evaluation of the sensitivity of impedance plethysmography for the detection of proximal deep vein thrombosis. *Archives of Internal Medicine*, **154**, 1930–3.

Ginsberg, J.S., Wells, P.S., and Brill-Edwards, P. (1995). Application of a novel and rapid whole blood assay for D-dimer in patients with clinically suspected pulmonary embolism. *Thrombosis and Haemostasis*, **73**, 379–86.

Gisselbrecht, M., Diehl, J.L., Meyer, G., Collignon, M.A., and Sors, H. (1996). Clinical presentation and results of thrombolytic therapy in older patients with massive pulmonary embolism: a comparison with non-elderly patients. *Journal of the American Geriatrics Society*, **44**, 189–93.

Goldhaber, S.Z., Haire, W.D., Feldstein, M.L., *et al.* (1993). Alteplase versus heparin in acute pulmonary embolism: randomized trial assessing right-ventricular function and pulmonary reperfusion. *Lancet*, **341**, 507–11.

Hager, K., Setzer, J., Vogl, T., *et al.* (1989). Blood coagulation factors in the elderly. *Archives of Gerontology and Geriatrics*, **9**, 277–82.

Heijboer, H., Büller, H.R., Lensing, A.W.A., Turpie, A.G.G., Colly, L.P., and ten Cate, J.W. (1993). A comparison of real-time compression ultrasonography with impedance plethysmography for the diagnosis of deep-vein thrombosis in symptomatic outpatients. *New England Journal of Medicine*, **329**, 1365–9.

Hull, R.D., Hirsh, J., Carter, C.J., *et al.* (1985). Diagnostic efficacy of impedance plethysmography for clinically suspected deep-vein thrombosis. *Annals of Internal Medicine*, **102**, 21–8.

Hull, R.D., Raskob, G.E., Coates, G., and Panju, A.A. (1990). Clinical validity of a normal perfusion lung scan in patients with suspected pulmonary embolism. *Chest*, **97**, 23–6.

Hull, R.D., Raskob, G.E., Ginsberg, J.S., *et al.* (1994). A non-invasive strategy for the treatment of patients with suspected pulmonary embolism. *Archives of Internal Medicine*, **154**, 289–97.

Hyers, T.M., Hull, R.D., and Weg, J.G. (1995). Antithrombotic therapy for venous thromboembolic disease. *Chest*, **108**, 335S–51S.

Kipper, M.S., Moser, K.M., Kortman, K.E., and Ashburn, W.L. (1982). Long-term follow-up of patients with suspected pulmonary embolism and a normal lung scan. *Chest*, **82**, 411–15.

Kniffin, W.D., Baron, J.A., Barrett, J., Birkmeyer, J.D., and Anderson, F.A. (1994). The epidemiology of diagnosed pulmonary embolism and deep venous thrombosis in the elderly. *Archives of Internal Medicine*, 154, 861–6.

Levine, M.N., Goldhaber, S.Z., Gore, J.M., Hirsh, J., and Califf, R.M. (1995). Hemorrhagic complications of thrombolytic therapy in the treatment of myocardial infarction and venous thromboembolism. *Chest*, 108, 291S–301S.

Meaney, J.F.M., Weg, J.G., Chenevert, T.L., Stafford-Johnson, D., Hamilton, B.H., and Prince, M.R. (1997). Diagnosis of pulmonary embolism with magnetic resonance angiography. *New England Journal of Medicine*, 336, 1422–7.

Moser, K.M. (1990). Venous thromboembolism. *American Review of Respiratory Disease*, 141, 235–49.

Oudkerk, M., van Beek, J.R., van Putten, W.L.J., and Büller, H.R. (1993). Cost-effectiveness analysis of various strategies in the diagnostic management of pulmonary embolism. *Archives of Internal Medicine*, 153, 947–54.

Perrier, A., Bounameaux, H., Morabia, A., *et al.* (1996). Diagnosis of pulmonary embolism by a decision analysis-based strategy including clinical probability, D-dimer levels, and ultrasonography: a management study. *Archives of Internal Medicine*, 156, 531–6.

Perrier, A., Desmarais, S., Goehring, C., *et al.* (1997a). D-dimer testing for suspected pulmonary embolism in outpatients. *American Journal of Respiratory and Critical Care Medicine*, 156, 492–6.

Perrier, A., Buswell, L., Bounameaux, H., *et al.* (1997b). Cost-effectiveness of noninvasive diagnostic aids in suspected pulmonary embolism. *Archives of Internal Medicine*, 157, 2309–16.

Perrier, A., Desmarais, S., Miron, M.J., *et al.* (1999). Noninvasive diagnosis of venous thromboembolism. *Lancet*, 353, 190–5.

Prospective Investigation of Pulmonary Embolism Diagnosis Investigators (1990). Value of the ventilation–perfusion scan in acute pulmonary embolism. *Journal of the American Medical Association*, 263, 2753–9.

Raimondi, P., Bongard, O., de Moerloose, P., Reber, G., Waldvogel, F., and Bounameaux, H. (1993). D-dimer plasma concentration in various clinical conditions: implications for the use of this test in the diagnostic approach of venous thromboembolism. *Thrombosis Research*, 69, 125–30.

Sackett, D.L., Haynes, R.B., Guyatt, G.H., and Tugwell, P. (1991). *Clinical epidemiology. A basic science for clinical medicine* (2nd edn). Little, Brown, Boston, MA.

Siddique, R.M., Siddique, M.I., Connors, A.F., and Rimm, A.A. (1996). Thirty-day case-fatality rates for pulmonary embolism in the elderly. *Archives of Internal Medicine*, 156, 2343–7.

Simonneau, G., Sors, H., Charbonnier, B., *et al.* (1997). A comparison of low-molecular-weight heparin with unfractionated heparin for acute pulmonary embolism. The THESEE Study Group. Tinzaparine ou Heparine Standard: Evaluations dans l'Embolie Pulmonaire. *New England Journal of Medicine*, 337, 663–9.

Stein, P.D. and Henry, J.W. (1995). Prevalence of acute pulmonary embolism among patients in a general hospital and at autopsy. *Chest*, 108, 978–81.

Stein, P.D., Gottschalk, A., Saltzman, H.A., and Terrin, M.L. (1991). Diagnosis of acute pulmonary embolism in the elderly. *Journal of the American College of Cardiology*, 18, 1452–7.

Stein, P.D., Athanasoulis, C., Alavi, A., *et al.* (1992). Complications and validity of pulmonary angiography in acute pulmonary embolism. *Circulation*, 85, 462–8.

van Rossum, A.B., Treurniet, F.E., Kieft, G.J., Smith, S.J., and Schepers-Bok, R. (1996). Role of spiral volumetric computed tomographic scanning in the assessment of patients with clinical suspicion of pulmonary embolism and an abnormal ventilation/perfusion lung scan. *Thorax*, 51, 23–8.

12.5 **Tuberculosis**

Shobita Rajagopalan and Thomas T. Yoshikawa

In the future the battle against this plague of mankind [tuberculosis] will not just be concerned with an uncertain something but with tangible parasite, about whose characteristics a great deal is known and can be explored. (Robert Koch 1882)

Introduction

Tuberculosis remains, among infectious diseases, in John Bunyan's words of 1680, 'the captain of all these men of death'. After a steady decline for the past 70 years, there has been a resurgence in the incidence of tuberculosis in North America, Western Europe, and several developing nations. Much of this rise is attributed to several factors including (a) the ability of *Mycobacterium tuberculosis* to escape immune surveillance at the earliest stages of immunocompromise, (b) complex socio-economic factors including an increasing homeless population, (c) international migration, (d) lifestyle habits, (e) changing medical conditions, and (f) demographic variations (Yoshikawa 1992). Particularly ominous is the emergence of multidrug-resistant strains of *M. tuberculosis*, which result in disease refractory to the available antituberculous drugs. Older people among all racial and ethnic groups are at particular risk for infection with *M. tuberculosis*

Table 3 Criteria for positive tuberculin reaction

Skin test criteria (mm induration)	Population at risk
≥5 mm	People with known or suspected HIV infection[a]
	Close contacts of people with infectious tuberculosis[a]
	People with chest radiographs consistent with tuberculosis (e.g. fibrotic changes)[a]
≥10 mm	Recent converters (≥10 mmol/l with ≥6 mmol/l increase within 2 years; ≥15 mmol/l for those aged ≥35 years)[a]
	Intravenous drug users known to be HIV-seronegative[a]
	People with certain risk factors: silicosis; gastrectomy; jejunoileal bypass; ≥10% below ideal body weight; chronic renal failure; diabetes mellitus; corticosteroid and other immunosuppressive therapy; haematological and other malignancies[a]
	Foreign-born from country with high tuberculosis prevalence[b]
	Medically underserved low-income populations (homeless, black people, Hispanics, Native Americans)[b]
	Residents of long-term care facilities (nursing home, correctional institutions)[b]
≥15 mm	None of the above factors[b]

[a] Chemoprophylaxis recommended for all people regardless of age.
[b] Chemoprophylaxis recommended for people less than 35 years of age.

Data from Centers for Disease Control (1994).

Laboratory diagnosis

Clinical specimens from suspected cases of tuberculosis are initially examined by smear and subsequently cultured for *M. tuberculosis*. The standard laboratory procedure for the definitive diagnosis of tuberculosis is isolation of *M. tuberculosis* by culture of suspected clinical specimens. Smear tests for *M. tuberculosis* are used primarily as a screening tool for tuberculosis and are designed to detect acid-fast bacilli. Smear tests require the presence of a minimum of 10^4 to 10^5 acid-fast bacilli per millilitre of the specimen in order to be visualized by light microscopy; the best yield is with sputum specimens which generally have the highest concentration of organisms (Hanna 1996). The acid-fast staining methods most frequently used include the carbolfuchsin and fluorochrome; Ziehl–Neelsen and Kinyoun procedures use the carbolfuchsin method while auramine–rhodamine dyes apply the fluorochrome method. Auramine–rhodamine is the preferred staining procedure to identify mycobacteria in tissue specimens. In the case of pulmonary tuberculosis and genitourinary tuberculosis, three consecutive early morning sputum or urine specimens respectively are recommended for routine mycobacteriological studies (Krasnow and Wayne 1969; Dutt *et al.* 1989). Induced sputum or bronchoscopic specimens may be needed in patients who are unable to expectorate sputum (Van Den Brande *et al.* 1990). Previously, *M. tuberculosis* was classically isolated using Lowenstein–Jensen medium with an average reporting time for culture of 44.5 days; more recently, the radiometric method (medium containing ^{14}C) for isolation of *M. tuberculosis* has been shown to decrease the reporting time for *M. tuberculosis* culture to an average of 17.3 days. Sterile body fluids and tissues can be inoculated into a liquid medium such as the oleic acid–albumin broth of Dubros and Middlebrook, which also allows growth and detection of *M. tuberculosis* 7 to 10 days earlier than the solid medium techniques.

Histological examination of tissue from sites such as the liver, lymph nodes, bone marrow, pleura, or synovium may show the typical tissue reaction (caseous necrosis with granuloma formation) with or without acid-fast bacilli, which would also strongly support the diagnosis of tuberculous disease.

Advances in molecular mycobacteriology for *M. tuberculosis* are beginning to prove useful in the diagnosis, epidemiology, and clinical management of tuberculosis. The ability of polymerase chain reaction to detect very small numbers of organisms by DNA amplification is expected to increase the sensitivity of diagnosis significantly. In one study, 31 of 117 (26.5 per cent) of specimens were positive by polymerase chain reaction compared with 17 of 117 (14.5 per cent) by culture (Daniel and Debanne 1987; Brisson-Noel *et al.* 1989; Shankar *et al.* 1991). This polymerase chain reaction technique, as well as other tests that detect mycobacterial antigens by particle agglutination and inhibition enzyme-linked immunosorbent assay (Good 1989), may be especially useful in the diagnosis of tuberculous meningitis (Daniel 1987). Similar techniques and the use of DNA probe technology can be used to track the spread of the organism in epidemiological studies and may be used to predict drug resistance before standard results are available; such methods are being currently used in some laboratories. In 1996, the United States Food and Drug Administration approved a nucleic acid amplification test for *M. tuberculosis* complex for use on clinical specimens in conjunction with routine culture. This test uses transcription-mediated amplification to detect *M. tuberculosis* complex ribosomal RNA (Centers for Disease Control and Prevention 1996). Measurement of tuberculostearic acid using gas chromatography mass spectrometry on sputum or bronchial washings and aspirates is more rapid, sensitive, and specific for the detection of *M. tuberculosis* than conventional acid-fast bacilli smears and culture but requires expensive equipment that is not available in most laboratories (French *et al.* 1987; Pang *et al.* 1989). Serological tests detecting antibodies against mycobacterial antigens, have not been refined sufficiently for routine clinical use.

Table 4 Treatment regimens for tuberculosis

	Frequency	Drugs
Option 1	Daily	Isoniazid, rifampicin, pyrazinamide, and ethambutol or streptomycin for 8 weeks[a]
	Daily or 2–3 times weekly[b]	Isoniazid and rifampicin for 16 weeks
Option 2	Daily	Isoniazid, rifampicin, pyrazinamide, and ethambutol or streptomycin[a] for 2 weeks
	Twice weekly[b]	Same drugs for 6 weeks[a]
	Twice weekly[b]	Isoniazid and rifampicin for 16 weeks
Option 3	Three times weekly[b]	Isoniazid, rifampicin, pyrazinamide, and ethambutol or streptomycin for 24 weeks

[a] In areas where primary isoniazid resistance is less than 4%, omit fourth drug.
[b] Intermittent dosing should be directly observed.

Data from Centers for Disease Control (1994).

Treatment

Drug regimens

Presumptive therapy for tuberculosis is often necessary while diagnostic studies are under way because the diagnosis of active tuberculosis can often be challenging and time consuming. Drug therapy requires a multidrug regimen with agents active against the clinical isolate. Susceptibility testing of initial isolates should always be obtained. The American Thoracic Society and the Centers for Disease Control and Prevention recommend that, for most patients, initial therapy should involve four drugs: isoniazid 300 mg, rifampicin (rifampin) 600 mg, pyrazinamide 15 to 30 mg/kg, and ethambutol 15 to 25 mg/kg or streptomycin 15 mg/kg (Table 4) (American Thoracic Society 1994). In areas where the prevalence of primarily isoniazid-resistant isolates is less than 4 per cent, the fourth drug (ethambutol or streptomycin) may be omitted. Since most older people are likely to have acquired their M. tuberculosis infection prior to the availability of antituberculous drugs such as isoniazid and rifampicin, primary drug resistance in this population should be relatively low. Antituberculous therapy in most ageing adults consists of a 6-month or 9-month regimen for most cases of pulmonary or extrapulmonary tuberculosis. The 6-month regimen consists of an intensive phase of therapy for 2 months with isoniazid (300 mg), rifampicin (600 mg), and pyrazinamide (15–30 mg/kg or a maximum of 2 g/day), followed by a continuation phase of daily isoniazid and rifampicin (same dose as the intensive phase) of twice weekly isoniazid (15 mg/kg or a maximum of 900 mg per dose) and rifampicin (10 mg/kg or a maximum of 600 mg per dose) for 4 months. The 9-month regimen is initiated with an intensive therapy phase with daily isoniazid and rifampicin for 1 to 2 months or until smears are negative (same doses as in the intensive phase of the 6-month regimen), followed by the continuation phase of either the daily or twice weekly regimen of isoniazid and rifampicin (doses as outlined in the continuation phase of the 6-month regimen). Intermittent regimens are well tolerated and equally effective as daily regimens (Cohn *et al.* 1990). Use of intermittent regimens makes directly observed therapy more feasible and cost-efficient. Several recent studies have demonstrated that directly observed therapy is more effective than self-administered therapy, and results in lower rates of relapse, emergence of drug resistance, and in HIV-seropositive patients, death. Elderly patients, and those with diabetes mellitus, uraemia, poor nutrition, alcoholism, and seizure disorder who are on treatment with isoniazid should receive daily pyridoxine (vitamin B_6) 50 mg to minimize the risk of peripheral neuropathy associated with isoniazid (American Thoracic Society 1994).

Prevention

Chemoprophylaxis

Tuberculosis chemoprophylaxis is not primary prevention (preventing disease in people previously without this condition) but is secondary prevention (preventing disease in people with subclinical infection). Preventive therapy, according to the criteria outlined in Table 2, with isoniazid should be considered for people at high risk for active tuberculosis who have a positive tuberculin skin test but are asymptomatic and have no radiological evidence of active infection. Such high-risk conditions include known or suspected HIV infection, intravenous drug use with a negative HIV serology, close contact with a known infected case of tuberculosis, chest radiographic evidence of inactive or 'old' tuberculosis, recent tuberculin conversion, or certain medical conditions. These latter include silicosis, diabetes mellitus, lymphoreticular and other haematological malignancies, head and neck malignancies, prolonged corticosteroid therapy, other immunosuppressive therapy, endstage renal disease, intestinal bypass or gastrectomy, chronic malabsorption syndromes, and decrease in body weight to less than 90 per cent of ideal body weight. In these circumstances isoniazid prophylaxis is indicated regardless of age (American Thoracic Society 1994). Many doctors believe that in nursing home residents who represent a high-risk group for tuberculosis, the benefits of isoniazid prophylaxis for a positive tuberculin reaction outweighs the risk of drug toxicity; the Centers for Disease Control and Prevention, however, maintains that individuals 35 years or older with no risk factors and a positive tuberculin skin test of 15 mm or more induration do not require isoniazid chemoprophylaxis.

The standard isoniazid prophylaxis regimen consists of 300 mg daily for 6 months (65 per cent effective) to 12 months (90 per cent effective); 12 months is usually considered in HIV-positive people with a positive purified protein derivative skin test or any person with abnormal chest radiographic evidence of past untreated tuberculosis (Centers for Disease Control and Prevention 1994). Several other regimens are under investigation such as isoniazid in a 900 mg twice weekly dose, rifampicin for 4 months, isoniazid and rifampicin for 4 months, and rifampicin and pyrazinamide for 2 months. Elderly people receiving chemoprophylaxis should be carefully monitored for evidence of isoniazid-associated hepatitis and peripheral neuropathy.

Monitoring of drug therapy

Patients with active pulmonary tuberculosis should have monthly sputum examinations until cultures become negative. Non-compliance or drug resistance should be suspected if sputum cultures remain positive beyond 3 months. Such patients should have a repeat sputum culture and susceptibility and be placed on directly observed therapy pending the results of these data. Most elderly patients should have a chest radiograph 1 to 2 months after drug treatment is initiated; more frequent radiographs are indicated if the clinical condition deteriorates despite treatment, drug resistance is discovered, or if a coexisting lung disorder is suspected. During therapy, liver enzymes, specifically serum glutamate oxaloacetate transaminase should be monitored in all elderly patients on isoniazid, owing to an increased risk of isoniazid induced hepatitis. In 10 to 20 per cent of all patients, regardless of age, a mild elevation of serum glutamate oxaloacetate transaminase occurs within the first 6 months and returns to normal on therapy (American Thoracic Society 1994). Although in younger individuals routine laboratory analysis of liver function is not indicated after an initial baseline study, monthly measurement of serum glutamate oxaloacetate transaminase is recommended in elderly people receiving isoniazid. Development of clinical evidence of hepatitis with a rise of serum glutamate oxaloacetate transaminase five times above normal necessitates cessation of isoniazid and rifampicin. The drug(s) may subsequently be resumed at a lower dose and gradually advanced to the full dose as tolerated, with simultaneous and careful monitoring of serum glutamate oxaloacetate transaminase. In addition to its association with hepatitis, rifampicin also causes orange discoloration of body fluids (Girling 1982; Yoshikawa and Nagami 1982). Ethambutol may cause the loss of colour discrimination, diminished visual acuity, and central scotomas; older people receiving this drug should have frequent evaluation of visual acuity and colour discrimination. Streptomycin is associated with irreversible auditory and vestibular damage and generally should not be prescribed for elderly patients. Adverse effects associated with pyrazinamide include hyperuricaemia, hepatitis, arthralgias, and flushing. Dose adjustments of antituberculous drugs are necessary with streptomycin in the presence of renal impairment, but no adjustment is needed for isoniazid, rifampicin, or pyrazinamide for most elderly patients.

Infection control issues

The Advisory Committee for Elimination of Tuberculosis of the Centers for Disease Control and Prevention has established recommendations for the surveillance, control, and reporting of tuberculosis in long-term care facilities and acute care institutions (Centers for Disease Control and Prevention 1990a, 1994). Prevention of tuberculosis transmission in health-care settings is of utmost importance for patients and health-care workers. All health-care professionals in the United States, including those involved in the care of elderly people in long-term care facilities, should be aware of the recommendations which are also available in summary form (Yoshikawa 1991). Specific requirements and recommendations for the control of tuberculosis will apply in other countries.

References

Alvarez, S.Z. and Carpio, R. (1983). Hepatobiliary tuberculosis. *Digestive Disease Science*, **28**, 193–200.

Alvarez, S. and McCabe, W. (1984). Extrapulmonary tuberculosis revisited: a review of experience at Boston City and other hospitals. *Medicine*, **63**, 25–55.

Alvarez, S., Kasprzyk, D.R., and Freundl, M. (1987a). Two-stage skin testing for tuberculosis in a domicilary population. *American Review of Respiratory Disease*, **136**, 1193–6.

Alvarez, S., Shell, C., and Berk, S.L. (1987b). Pulmonary tuberculosis in elderly men. *American Journal of Medicine*, **82**, 602–6.

American Thoracic Society (1994). Treatment and prevention of tuberculosis in adults and children. *American Journal of Respiratory and Critical Care Medicine*, **149**, 1359–74.

Barry, M.A., Regan, A.M., Kunches, L.M., Harris, M.E., Bunce, S.A., and Craven, D.E. (1987). Two stage tuberculin testing with control antigens in patients residing in two chronic disease hospitals. *Journal of the American Geriatrics Society*, **35**, 147–53.

Bass, J.B. Jr (1990). Tuberculin test, preventive therapy and elimination of tuberculosis. *American Review of Respiratory Disease*, **141**, 812–13.

Battershill, J.H. (1980). Cutaneous testing in the elderly patient with tuberculosis. *Chest*, **77**, 188–9.

Bender, B.S., Nagel, J.E., and Adler, W.H. (1986). Absolute peripheral lymphocyte count and subsequent mortality of elderly males: the Baltimore Longitudinal Study of Ageing. *Journal of the American Geriatrics Society*, **34**, 649–54.

Bloom, B.R. (1994). *Tuberculosis pathogenesis, protection and control: immune mechanisms of protection*, pp. 389–415. American Society for Microbiology Press, Washington DC.

Bloom, B.R. and Murray, C.J.L. (1992). Tuberculosis: commentary on a re-emergent killer. *Science*, **257**, 1055–63.

Bobrowitz, I.D. (1982). Active tuberculosis undiagnosed until autopsy. *American Journal of Medicine*, **12**, 650–8.

Brashear, H.R. and Rendleman, D.A. (1978). Pott's paraplegia. *Southern Medical Journal*, **71**, 1379–82.

Brennen, C., Muder, R.R., and Muraca, P.W. (1988). Occult endemic tuberculosis in a long-term care facility. *Infection Control and Hospital Epidemiology*, **9**, 548–52.

Brisson-Noel, A., Giquel, B., Lecossier, D., Levy-Frebault, V., Nassif, X., and Hance, A.J. (1989). Rapid diagnosis of tuberculosis by amplification of mycobacterial DNA in clinical specimens. *Lancet*, **ii**, 1069–71.

Castle, S.C., Norman, D.C., Perls, T.T., Chang, M.P., Yoshikawa, T.T., and Makinodan, T. (1990). Analysis of cutaneous delayed-type hypersensitivity reaction and T cell proliferative response in elderly nursing home patients: an approach to identifying immunodeficient patients. *Gerontology*, **36**, 217–29.

Cauthen, G.M. and Snider, D.E. Jr (1986). Delayed tuberculin boosting in the older population. *American Review of Respiratory Diseases*, **134**, 857–8.

Centers for Disease Control (1988). Advisory Committee for Immunization Practices (ACIP). Use of BCG vaccines in the control of tuberculosis: a joint statement by the ACIP and the Advisory Committee for Elimination of Tuberculosis. *Morbidity and Mortality Weekly Report*, **37**, 663–5.

Centers for Disease Control (1989). A strategic plan for the elimination of tuberculosis in the United States. *Morbidity and Mortality Weekly Report*, **38** (Supplement 3), 1–25.

Centers for Disease Control (1990*a*). Prevention and control of tuberculosis in facilities providing long-term care to the elderly. Recommendations of the Advisory Committee for Elimination of Tuberculosis. *Morbidity and Mortality Weekly Report*, **39** (No. RR-10), 7–20.

Centers for Disease Control (1990*b*). Screening for tuberculosis and tuberculous infection in high-risk populations: recommendations of the Advisory Committee for Elimination of Tuberculosis. *Morbidity and Mortality Weekly Report*, **39** (RR-8), 1–7.

Centers for Disease Control (1990*c*). *US fact book FY*. Department of Health and Human Services, Atlanta, Georgia.

Centers for Disease Control (1991). *1989 tuberculosis statistics in the United States*. Department of Health and Human Services, HHS Publication No. (CDC) 91-8322.

Centers for Disease Control (1994). Division of Tuberculosis Elimination. *Core curriculum on tuberculosis: what a clinician should know* (3rd edn), pp. 8–9. Department of Health and Human Services, Atlanta, Georgia.

Centers for Disease Control (1996). Nucleic acid amplification tests for tuberculosis. *Morbidity and Mortality Weekly Report*, **45**, 950–2.

Chang, S.-C., Lee, P.-Y., and Perng, R.-P. (1990). Lower lung field tuberculosis. *Chest*, **91**, 230–2.

Chaparas, S.D. (1982). Immunity in tuberculosis. *Bulletin of the World Health Organization*, **60**, 447–62.

Cohn, D.L., Catlin, B.J., Peterson, K.L., Judson, F.L., and Shabaro, J.A. (1990). A 62-dose, 6-month therapy for pulmonary and extrapulmonary tuberculosis. A twice-weekly, directly observed, and cost-effective regimen. *Annals of Internal Medicine*, **112**, 407–15.

Committee on Chemotherapy of Tuberculosis (1985). Standard therapy for tuberculosis. *Chest*, **2** (Supplement), 117S–24S.

Communicable Disease Reports (1994). *Notifiable Diseases Annual Summary 1992*, **20** (Supplement 1), 88.

Counsell, S.R., Tan, J.S., and Dittus, R.S. (1989). Unsuspected pulmonary tuberculosis in a community teaching hospital. *Annals of Internal Medicine*, **149**, 1274–8.

Creditor, M.C., Smith, E.C., Gallai, J.B., Baumann, M., and Nelson, K.T. (1988). Tuberculosis, tuberculin reactivity, and delayed cutaneous hypersensitivity in nursing home residents. *Journal of Gerontology*, **43**, M97–100.

Daniel, T.M. (1987). New approaches to the rapid diagnosis of tuberculous meningitis. *Journal of Infectious Diseases*, **155**, 599–602.

Daniel, T.M. and Debanne, S.M. (1987). The serodiagnosis of tuberculosis and other mycobacterial diseases by enzyme-linked immunosorbent assay. *American Review of Respiratory Disease*, **135**, 1137–51.

Davies, P.D.O. (1994). Tuberculosis in the elderly. *Journal of Antimicrobial Chemotherapy*, **34** (Supplement A), 93–100.

Davies, P.D.O., Humphries, M.J., Byfield, S.P., *et al.* (1984). Bone and joint tuberculosis. A survey of notifications in England and Wales. *Journal of Bone and Joint Surgery*, **66B**, 326–30.

Donath, J. and Khan, F.A. (1984). Tuberculous and postuberculous bronchopleural fistula. Ten years clinical experience. *Chest*, **86**, 697–703.

Dorken, E., Grzybowski, S., and Allen, E.A. (1987). Significance of the tuberculin test in the elderly. *Chest*, **92**, 237–40.

Dubrow, E.L. (1976). Reactivation of tuberculosis: a problem of ageing. *Journal of the American Geriatrics Society*, **11**, 481–7.

Dutt, A.K., Moers, D., and Stead, W.W. (1989). Smear and culture negative pulmonary tuberculosis; four month short course chemotherapy. *American Review of Respiratory Disease*, **139**, 867–70.

Edlin, G.P. (1976). Active tuberculosis unrecognised until necropsy. *Lancet*, i, 650–2.

Edwards, D. and Kirkpatrick, C.H. (1986). The immunology of mycobacterial diseases. *American Review of Respiratory Disease*, **134**, 1062–71.

Essop, A.R., Posen, J.A., Hodkinson, J.H., and Segal, I. (1984). Tuberculous hepatitis: a clinical review of 96 cases, *Quarterly Journal of Medicine*, **53**, 465–77.

Evanchick, C.C., Davis, D.E., and Harrington, T.M. (1986). Tuberculosis of peripheral joints: an often missed diagnosis. *Journal of Rheumatology*, **13**, 187–9.

Fancourt, G.J., Ebden, P., Garner, P., Cookson, J.B., Wales, J.M., and Stoyle, T.F. (1986). Bone tuberculosis: results and experience in Leicestershire. *British Journal of Diseases of the Chest*, **80**, 265–72.

French, G.L., Chan, C.Y., Cheung, S.W., and Oo, K.T. (1987). Diagnosis of pulmonary tuberculosis by detection of tuberculostearic acid in sputum using gas chromatography-mass spectrometry with selected ion monitoring. *Journal of Infectious Diseases*, **156**, 356–62.

Gardner, I.D. and Remington, J.S. (1977). Age-related decline in the resistance of mice to infection with intracellular pathogens. *Infection and Immunity*, **16**, 593–8.

Girling, D.J. (1982). Adverse effects of antituberculous drugs. *Drugs*, **23**, 56–74.

Good, R.C. (1989). Serologic methods for diagnosing tuberculosis. *Annals of Internal Medicine*, **110**, 97–9.

Gordin, F.M., Perez-Stable, E.F., Flaherty, D., *et al.* (1988). Evaluation of a third sequential tuberculin skin test in a chronic care population. *American Review of Respiratory Diseases*, **137**, 153–7.

Gorse, G.J., Pais, M.J., Kusske, J.A., and Cesario, T.C. (1983). Tuberculous spondylitis. A report to six cases and review of the literature. *Medicine*, **62**, 178–93.

Gryzbowski, S. (1983). Tuberculosis. A look at the world situation. *Chest*, **84**, 756–61.

Haas, E.J., Madhavan, T., Quinn, E., *et al.* (1977). Tuberculous meningitis in urban general hospital. *Archives of Internal Medicine*, **137**, 1518–21.

Hanna, B.A. (1996). Diagnosis of tuberculosis by microbiologic techniques. In *Tuberculosis* (ed. W.N. Rom and S.M. Garay), pp. 149–59. Little, Brown, Boston, MA.

Hsu, L.C.S. and Yeong, J.C.Y. (1984). Tuberculosis of the lower cervical spine (C2 to C7): a report on 40 cases. *Journal of Bone and Joint Surgery*, **66B**, 1–5.

Katz, P.R., Reichman, W., Dube, D., *et al.* (1987). Clinical features of pulmonary tuberculosis in young and old veterans. *Journal of the American Geriatrics Society*, **35**, 512–15.

Kelly, P.J. and Karlson, A.G. (1969). Musculoskeletal tuberculosis. *Mayo Clinic Proceedings*, **44**, 73–80.

Klein, N.C., Damsker, B., and Hirschman, S.Z. (1985). Mycobacterial meningitis. Respective analysis from 1973 to 1983. *American Journal of Medicine*, **79**, 29–34.

Klofkorn, R.W. and Steigerwald, J.C. (1976). Carpal tunnel syndrome as the initial manifestation of tuberculosis. *American Journal of Medicine*, **60**, 583–6.

Kollins, S.A., Hartman, G.W., Carr, C.T., Segura, J.W., and Hattery, R.R. (1974). Roentgenographic findings of urinary tract tuberculosis. *American Journal of Medicine*, **121**, 487–99.

Krasnow, I. and Wayne, L.G. (1969). Comparison of methods for tuberculous etiology. *Applied Microbiology*, **18**, 915–19.

Lai, K.K., Stottmeier, K.D., Sherman, I.H., and McCabe, W.R. (1984). Mycobacterial cervical lymphadenopathy. Relation of etiologic agents to age. *Journal of the American Medical Association*, **251**, 1286–8.

McGuiness, G. and Naidich, D.P. (1996). Radiology of tuberculosis. In *Tuberculosis* (ed. W.N. Rom and S.M. Garay), pp. 413–41. Little, Brown, New York.

Mackay, A.D. and Dole, R.B. (1984). The problem of tuberculosis in the elderly. *Quarterly Journal of Medicine*, **53**, 497–510.

Makinodan, T., James, D.J., Inamizu, T., and Chang, M.P. (1984). Immunologic basis for susceptibility to infection in the aged. *Gerontology*, **30**, 279–89.

Mason, J.O. (1986). Opportunities for the elimination of tuberculosis. *American Review Respiratory Disease*, 134, 201–3.

Medical Research Council Cardiothoracic Epidemiology Group (1992). National survey of notifications of tuberculosis in England and Wales. *Thorax*, 47, 770–5.

Miller, R.A. (1989). The cell biology of ageing: immunological models. *Journal of Gerontology*, 44, B4–8.

Molavi, A. and LeFrock, J.L. (1985). Tuberculous meningitis. *Medical Clinics of North America*, 69, 315–31.

Montz, F.J. and DiZerega, G.S. (1985). Genital tuberculosis in an elderly woman with the primary symptoms of pelvic prolapse: case report. *American Journal of Obstetrics and Gynecology*, 152, 42–3.

Morris, C.D.W. (1989). The radiography, haematology and bronchoscopy of pulmonary tuberculosis in the aged. *Quarterly Journal of Medicine*, 71, 529–36.

Morris, C.D.W. and Nell, H. (1988). Epidemic pulmonary tuberculosis in geriatric homes. *South African Medical Journal*, 74, 117–20.

Nagami, P. and Yoshikawa, T.T. (1983). Tuberculosis in the geriatric patient. *Journal of the American Geriatrics Society*, 31, 356–63.

Narain, J., Lofgren, J., Warren, E., and Stead, W.W. (1985). Epidemic tuberculosis in a nursing home: a retrospective cohort study. *Journal of the American Geriatrics Society*, 33, 258–63.

Nash, D.R. and Douglass, J.E. (1980). Anergy in active pulmonary tuberculosis. A comparison between positive and negative reactors and an evaluation of 5 TU and 250 TU skin test doses. *Chest*, 77, 32–5.

Nisar, M., Williams, C.S.D., Ashby, D., and Davies, P.D. (1993). Tuberculin testing in residential homes for the elderly. *Thorax*, 48, 1257–60.

Orme, I.M. (1987). Ageing and immunity to tuberculosis: increases susceptibility of old mice reflects a decreased capacity to generate mediator T lymphocytes. *Journal of Immunology*, 138, 4414–15.

Pang, J.A., Chan, H.S., Chan, C.Y., Cheung, S.W., and French, G.L. (1989). A tuberculosteatic acid assay in the diagnosis of sputum smear-negative pulmonary tuberculosis. A prospective study of bronchoscopic aspirate and lavage specimens. *Annals of Internal Medicine*, 111, 650–4.

Patel, P.J. (1981). Ageing and cellular defence mechanisms: age-related changes in resistance of mice to *Listeria monocytogenes*. *Infection and Immunity*, 32, 557–62.

Paus, B. (1977). The changed pattern of bone and joint tuberculosis in Norway. *Acta Orthopedica Scandinavia*, 48, 277–9.

Proudfoot, A.T., Aktar, A.J., Douglas, A.C., and Horne, N.W. (1969). Miliary tuberculosis in adults. *British Medical Journal*, 2, 273–6.

Quinn, W. (1984). Genitourinary tuberculosis: a study of 1117 cases over a period of 34 years. *British Journal of Urology*, 56, 449–55.

Rich, A.R. and McCordock, H.A. (1933). The pathogenesis of tuberculous meningitis. *Bulletin of the Johns Hopkins Hospital*, 52, 5–37.

Rieder, H.L., Cauthen, G.M., Kelly, G.D., Bloch, A.B., and Snider, D.E. Jr (1989). Tuberculosis in the United States. *Journal of the American Medical Association*, 262, 385–9.

Riley, R.L., Wills, E.F., and Mill, C.M. (1957). Air hygiene and tuberculosis: quantitative studies of infectivity and control in a pilot ward. *American Review of Tuberculosis and Pulmonary Diseases*, 75, 420–31.

Rooney, J.J., Crocco, J.A., and Lyons, H.A. (1970). Tuberculous pericarditis. *Annals of Internal Medicine*, 72, 73–81.

Rudd, A. (1985). Tuberculosis in a geriatric unit. *Journal of the American Geriatrics Society*, 33, 566–9.

Sahn, S.A. and Neff, T.A. (1974). Miliary tuberculosis. *American Journal of Medicine*, 56, 495–505.

Schulze, K., Warner, H.A., and Murray, D. (1977). Intestinal tuberculosis. Experiences at a Canadian teaching hospital. *American Journal of Medicine*, 63, 735–45.

Shankar, P., Manjuath, N., Mohan, K.K., *et al.* (1991). Rapid diagnosis of tuberculous meningitis by polymerase chain reaction. *Lancet*, 337, 5–7.

Simon, J.A., McVicker, S.J., Ferrell, C.R., and Payne, C.B. Jr (1983). Two step tuberculin testing in a veterans domiciliary population. *Southern Medical Journal*, 76, 866–72.

Slavin, R.E., Walsh, T.J., and Pollack, A.D. (1980). Late generalized tuberculosis. *Medicine*, 59, 352–66.

Spencer, D., Yagan, R., Blinkhorn, R., and Spagnuolo, P.J. (1990). Anterior segment upper lobe tuberculosis in the adult. Occurrence in primary and reactivation disease. *Chest*, 97, 384–8.

Stead, W.W. (1965). Pathogenesis of tuberculosis among older persons. *American Review of Respiratory Disease*, 91, 811–22.

Stead, W.W. (1981). Tuberculosis among elderly persons: an outbreak in a nursing home. *Annals of Internal Medicine*, 94, 606–10.

Stead, W.W. (1987). Why does tuberculosis remain so common among the elderly? *Hospital Practice*, 22, 9–10.

Stead, W.W. and Dutt, A.K. (1991). Tuberculosis in elderly persons. *Annual Reviews in Medicine*, 42, 267–76.

Stead, W.W. and To, T. (1987). The significance of the tuberculin skin test in elderly persons. *Annals of Internal Medicine*, 107, 837–42.

Stead, W., Lofgren, J., Warren, E., and Thomas, C. (1985). Tuberculosis as an endemic and nosocomial infection among the elderly in nursing homes. *New England Journal of Medicine*, 312, 1483–7.

Thompson, N.J., Glassroth, J.L., Snider, D.E. Jr, and Farer, L.S. (1979). The booster phenomenon in serial tuberculin testing. *American Review of Respiratory Disease*, 119, 587–97.

Tuli, S.M. (1975). Results of treatment of spinal tuberculosis by 'middle path' regime. *Journal of Bone and Joint Surgery*, 57, 13–23.

Tytle, T.L. and Johnson, T.H. (1984). Changing patterns in pulmonary tuberculosis. *Southern Medical Journal*, 77, 1223–5.

Umeki, S. (1989). Comparison of young and elderly patients with pulmonary tuberculosis. *Respiration*, 55, 75–83.

Van Den Brande, P.M., Vande Mierop, F., Verbeken, E.K., and Demedts, M. (1990). Clinical spectrum of endobronchial tuberculosis in elderly patients. *Archives of Internal Medicine*, 150, 2105–8.

Waldorf, D.S., Wilkens, R.F., and Decker, J. (1968). Impaired delayed hypersensitivity in an ageing population. Association with antinuclear reactivity and rheumatoid factor. *Journal of the American Medical Association*, 203, 831–4.

Weekly Epidemiology Report (1994). Tuberculosis. *Weekly Epidemiology Report*, 69, 77–80

Weekly Epidemiology Report (1996). Tuberculosis. *Weekly Epidemiology Report*, 71, 65–69.

Weir, M.R. and Thornton, G.F. (1985). Extrapulmonary tuberculosis. Experience of a community hospital and review of the literature. *American Journal of Medicine*, 79, 467–78.

Weksler, M.E. (1983). Senescence of the immune system. *Medical Clinics of North America*, 67, 263–72.

Welty, C., Burstin, S., Muspratt, S., *et al.* (1985). Epidemiology of tuberculous infection in a chronic care population. *American Review of Respiratory Disease*, 132, 133–6.

Wiegeshaus, E., Balasubramanian, V., and Smith, D.W. (1989). Immunity to tuberculosis from the perspective of pathogenesis. *Infection and Immunity*, 57, 3671–6.

World Health Organization (1992). Office of Information. *Tuberculosis notification rates in industrialized countries press release*. WHO, Geneva, June, 40.

Yoshikawa, T.T. (1984). Ageing and infectious diseases: state of the art. *Gerontology*, 30, 275–8.

Yoshikawa, T.T. (1990). Tuberculosis in an ageing population. *Ageing Immunology and Infectious Disease*, 2, 63–7.

Yoshikawa, T.T. (1991). Elimination of tuberculosis from the United States. *Journal of the American Geriatrics Society*, 39, 312–14.

Yoshikawa, T.T. (1992). Tuberculosis in ageing adults. *Journal of the American Geriatrics Society*, 40, 178–87.

Yoshikawa, T.T. (1994). The challenge and unique aspects of tuberculosis in older patients. *Infectious Disease in Clinical Practice*, 3, 62–6.

Yoshikawa, T.T. and Nagami, P.H. (1982). Adverse drug reactions in tuberculosis therapy: risks and recommendations. *Geriatrics*, 37, 61–8.

Yoshikawa, T.T. and Norman, D.C. (1987). *Ageing and clinical practice: infectious diseases. Diagnosis and treatment*, pp. 127–39. Igaku-Shoin, New York.

Yu, Y.L., Chow, W.H., Humphries, M.J., Wong, R.W., and Gabriel, M. (1986). Cryptic miliary tuberculosis. *Quarterly Journal of Medicine*, 59, 421–8.

13

Joints and connective tissue

Table 3 Differential diagnosis of rheumatoid arthritis and osteoarthritis

	Rheumatoid arthritis	Osteoarthritis
Time of day when symptoms are most severe	Morning	Evening
Morning stiffness	Almost always present; duration 1–5 h or all day	May be present; duration up to 45 min
Constitutional symptoms	Usually present	Absent, unless patient has concomitant systemic disease
Radiography	Hand involvement focuses on MCP and PIP joints and wrists Juxta-articular osteoporosis, localized thinning, or loss of cortex, and subcortical bone loss leading to cysts; may be a 'double line' surrounding interphalangeal joints	Hand involvement focuses on DIP and PIP joints; wrists are not usually involved Loss of joint space, subchondral 'condensation' (bone thickening), osteophytes, and poorly defined cysts
Joint fluid	White cell count increased (3000–20 000), chiefly polymorphonuclear cells; fluid watery; mucin clot poor	White cell count <3000, mainly mononuclear cells or macrophages; fluid normally viscous; look for crystals; good mucin clot

DIP, distal interphalangeal; MCP, metacarpophalangeal; PIP, proximal interphalangeal.

The radiological changes are best ascertained on radiographs of the hand, where the multiplicity of joints and the closeness of the structures to the radiology film enable identification of subtle changes (Fuchs *et al.* 1989). Optimal definition will be obtained through the use of fine-grain film. The 'double line' surrounding an inflamed joint is due to the differential radiolucency of the synovial tissue and other subcutaneous tissues (Fig. 1). Other radiological features characteristic of rheumatoid arthritis include diffuse periarticular osteoporosis, loss of joint space, poor definition of cortex, subcortical demineralization, and early cystic change, most evident on the radial surface of the metacarpal and medial surface of the metatarsal bones (Figs 1 and 2). In osteoarthritis, in which there is also loss of joint space, there is increased density of juxta-articular bone, large poorly defined subchondral cysts, and osteophytes.

The diagnostic assessment of all patients with arthritis, accompanied by synovial effusion, should also include analysis of the synovial fluid for a total cell count and differential and examination for crystals. An estimation of joint viscosity and/or nature of the 'clot', on dropping a few drops of synovial fluid into a Petri dish of dilute acetic acid, is a useful and inexpensive test (see Table 3). A joint which is chronically involved by rheumatoid arthritis or osteoarthritis has an increased likelihood of serving as the focus for septic arthritis and gout (Lally *et al.* 1989). It is not always easy to detect the presence of septic arthritis in a person with a background of inflammatory changes in many joints. The chief clue is the presence of a degree of inflammation in a single joint which is out of proportion to the involvement in other joints. In this situation, a joint aspiration is mandatory. As a general rule, culture should always be included in the diagnostic assessment of synovial fluid which is cloudy and has decreased viscosity.

Calcium pyrophosphate deposition disease is extremely common amongst older people (Fam *et al.* 1981). The condition may be suspected clinically by the presence of a slight haziness of the articular cartilage, visible with careful study of a radiograph. Confirmation is achieved by demonstrating the typical rhomboid-shaped crystals in

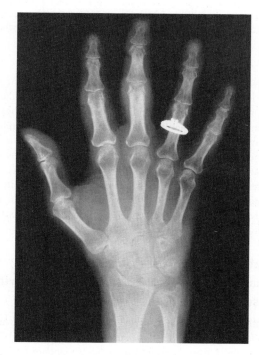

Fig. 1 Posteroanterior radiograph of the hand of a patient with early rheumatoid arthritis. Note the juxta-articular loss of mineral, and the soft tissue swelling adjacent to several metacarpophalangeal joints, especially the third. Reflecting swelling of the synovium, this creates the characteristic 'double line'. The film also exhibits soft tissue swelling over the ulnar styloid head, a change which is especially characteristic of rheumatoid arthritis. Possible erosions should be looked for at the radial side of the metacarpal heads (however, this patient, with very early disease, shows marked thinning of the cortex in this area, but has not yet developed erosions). It is important to obtain a posteroanterior view, individually, of each hand, flat on the film, to avoid rotation of the distal radius and ulna. The film should include a view of the distal radius and ulna. (Courtesy of Dr D. Berens.)

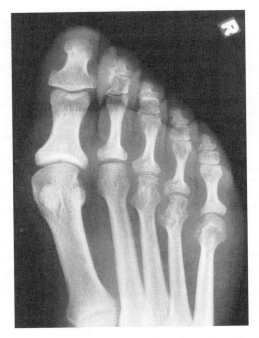

Fig. 2 Anteroposterior radiograph of the foot of a patient with advanced rheumatoid arthritis exhibiting loss of the cortex on the medial surface of the metatarsal heads, together with large erosions of the third, fourth, and to a lesser extent, fifth metatarsal heads. (Courtesy of Dr D. Berens.)

the synovial fluid. Patients with this disorder may exhibit sudden bursts of joint inflammation similar to those seen in gout. Treatment with non-steroidal anti-inflammatory drugs or other anti-inflammatory agents may lead to some symptomatic relief. Alternatively, intra-articular steroid injection will usually end an attack. Colchicine 0.6 mg/day may prevent the acute exacerbations of joint inflammation.

In assessing patients with preponderant joint symptoms in a single joint, one must remember that the symptoms in one joint may, in fact, be referred from another area. A familiar example is that the pain of hip disease may be referred to the knee.

The patient with long-standing crippling rheumatoid arthritis who has grown old with the disease

These patients present a challenge to the best that geriatric medicine has to offer. Let us consider the example of a patient aged 70 years who has suffered from continuously active rheumatoid arthritis for the past 40 years. In most such cases, the activity of the rheumatoid process will finally have subsided, but sequelae remain in the form of severe deformities of the hands and wrists, and destructive changes in the hips, knees, and possibly temporomandibular joints. Of particular importance, if anaesthesia for surgery is a possibility, is identification of the presence of any atlantoaxial instability, which can be a complication of rheumatoid arthritis. The patient may also exhibit residua of previous treatment, particularly decreased bone mass secondary to a decade or more of low-dose prednisone therapy, complicated by physical inactivity (Garton and Reid 1993). The patient may also have accrued renal damage secondary to large doses

of non-steroidal anti-inflammatory drugs, a scarred duodenum also secondary to non-steroidal anti-inflammatory drugs, and, in sero-positive patients, possible scleromalacia. To this are added sequelae of age-associated diseases which occur independently of the rheumatoid process.

Functional assessment

When a patient like this is first referred, an initial step is a comprehensive functional assessment to determine his or her capacity in the various activities of daily living (Katz *et al.* 1970) and instrumental activities of daily living (Lawton and Brody 1969). Objective questionnaires should be utilized to assess the possible presence of depression (Morgan *et al.* 1987) and cognitive deficiency (Folstein *et al.* 1975). A comprehensive assessment of this sort provides essential grounds for the development of a multifaceted plan for management and support, ideally including the co-ordinating role of a care manager.

Comorbid disease

A key issue in the assessment of people with long-standing rheumatoid arthritis relates to the continued threat of independent or related intercurrent disease. As discussed above, musculoskeletal pain, weakness and fatigue, and an elevated sedimentation rate resembling that seen in rheumatoid arthritis, may be due to a range of disorders not usually regarded as rheumatic in nature. Examples include lympho-proliferative disorders, metastatic carcinoma, tuberculosis, sarcoidosis, hypothyroidism, calcium pyrophosphate deposition disease, and osteoporosis. Therefore it is important not only to differentiate these entities from rheumatoid arthritis, but also to be aware of patients who may suffer simultaneously from rheumatoid arthritis and a second disease. An example might be a patient with long-standing rheumatoid arthritis with well-established chronic changes in the joints, who suddenly develops generalized weakness and fatigue, an elevated erythrocyte sedimentation rate, and weight loss. Are these manifestations due to reactivation of the rheumatoid process, or to coincidental presence of another disease? One clue in this differential lies in proportionality. If the increased constitutional manifestations are not matched by a comparable increase in pain, swelling, and tenderness of the joints and in the duration of morning stiffness, one must seek the coincidental presence of a second constitutional illness. In addition, an acutely inflamed joint in such a patient needs to be aspirated to rule out infection before any other therapy is undertaken.

The differential diagnosis between rheumatoid arthritis and gout also commands attention among older patients. In young people, the articular manifestations of gout are usually localized to a single joint, frequently the first metatarsophalangeal joint. This is less apt to be true with older people, in whom the gouty manifestations may occur in several joints, especially the wrists, and sometimes the metacarpophalangeal or proximal interphalangeal joints (Campbell 1988). Although classic rheumatologists previously disagreed, patients, especially in the older group, may suffer simultaneously from both rheumatoid arthritis and gout. In suspected cases, demonstration of urate crystals in the synovial fluid will clarify the diagnosis. Although gouty arthritis will respond well to appropriate treatment, the agents (colchicine, large doses of non-steroidal anti-inflammatory drugs, or adrenocorticotrophic hormone) are toxic in older people and it is important to be certain about the diagnosis.

Table 4 Work-up of a patient suspected of having rheumatoid arthritis

History

Obtain a lifetime history of the patient's musculoskeletal complaints, starting with earliest onset and including response to previous therapy

Obtain a general medical history; document other illnesses and current treatment programme

Determine extent and duration of morning stiffness, fatigue, and other constitutional symptoms

Ascertain ease or difficulty in activities of daily living

Explore possible evidence of depression, cognitive deficiency, or severe anxiety. Use established scales as appropriate. Ask about alcohol consumption

Social aspects: learn about patient's social situation, degree of isolation, and fears and concerns

Establish good doctor–patient relationship

Physical examination

General physical examination, including examination of all joints, with special attention to neurological system, possible enlargement of liver and spleen, possible presence of nodules, also evidence of comorbid cardiovascular or other disease

Document functional limitations; assess range of motion of major joints, presence of crepitus, abnormalities of joint alignment, and possible subluxation. Assess balance, gait, and performance of simple tasks (such as climbing on the examination table)

Assess swelling, tenderness, warmth, possible effusion, and pain on motion of all joints of hands and feet, large joints, and spine

Schirmer's test, if patient complains of dry eyes and mouth

Laboratory

Complete blood cell count, urinalysis, and blood chemistries, including serum creatinine, calcium, uric acid, liver, and thyroid profiles

Erythrocyte sedimentation rate, rheumatoid factor, antinuclear antibody, possibly HLA typing

Radiography: PA of hands; AP of feet. If appropriate: AP of knees, standing, plus lateral; AP of hips and pelvis, and radiographs of spine

Synovial fluid analysis, if effusion is present; obtain culture if one or two joints exhibit disproportionate inflammation

AP, anteroposterior; PA, posteroanterior.

Assessment and management

The work-up of the older patient seriously suspected of having rheumatoid arthritis is summarized in Table 4. The importance of most of the components cited in this table derives logically from the earlier sections on differential diagnosis. Importantly, the design of therapy needs to be tailored to the individual patient, each of whom has a unique social situation, specific limitations of physical function, array of comorbid conditions (both physical and psychological), and fears and concerns about the implications of the illness. The importance of a trusting relationship between the doctor and patient, and emergence of a sense of shared responsibility for the treatment and its outcome, provides an essential cornerstone for effective management.

Especially important in this initial assessment is the need for the doctor to establish clearly whether the patient is suffering from one of the more benign forms of polyarthritis, referred to above, or from true rheumatoid arthritis with its serious implications for loss of physical function and decreased life expectancy (Pincus and Callahan 1986, 1993). It is now widely accepted that the ravages of the disease, especially the destructive changes in joint structure and function, can be attenuated by a comprehensive programme of therapy, including appropriate use of anti-inflammatory, cytotoxic, and/or immunoregulatory agents. There is also increasing agreement that the appropriate time to institute 'disease-modifying' therapy is in the initial phase of the illness, before the destructive changes become well established. Balanced against this is the fact that all of the agents used have varying degrees of potentially serious toxicity—of concern in all patients, but especially in older people. Therefore the 'matching' of appropriate pharmacological therapy with reasonable understanding of the patient's prognosis, if the process is left to pursue its own course,

becomes an increasingly important component in the management of this disease.

There are six components of therapy with rheumatoid arthritis:

(1) comprehensive conservative management;

(2) non-steroidal anti-inflammatory drugs, including acetylsalicylic acid;

(3) relatively safe disease-modifying agents, appropriate for use by primary care doctors;

(4) highly toxic but quite effective disease-modifying agents, most appropriately given by people with extensive experience in their use;

(5) corticosteroids, both oral and intra-articular;

(6) surgery.

All patients should receive the basic components of comprehensive arthritis management. On the initial encounter, an effort should be made to deal with joint inflammation and related symptoms. This can sometimes be achieved through the use of non-steroidal anti-inflammatory drugs. However, there are some patients in whom these symptoms are so distressing and limiting of function that low-dose corticosteroid therapy may be introduced to achieve comfort and improved function. Often patients need to move on to stronger agents which have a positive effect on the disease (Fries *et al.* 1996). These are referred to as disease-modifying agents. In the above list, these are divided into two categories: those that can be employed in the primary care setting (hydrochloroquine, sulphasalazine, and methotrexate), and those which are more powerful and require special expertise (gold salts, cyclosporin A, and experimental agents). All patients with rheumatoid arthritis who are receiving systemic corticosteroid therapy should also be receiving one or several of the disease-modifying agents, and efforts should be made to discontinue corticosteroids when a good response to these agents has been achieved.

Comprehensive management

The multiple components of conservative comprehensive care, which have provided the essential basis of management of this disease for many decades, are still important and should be addressed in every patient with active rheumatoid arthritis (Podgorski and Edmonds 1985; American College of Rheumatology *Ad Hoc* Committee on Clinical Guidelines 1996*a*). The principles are rest, exercise, appropriate use of heat or cold, judicious use of splints, attention to psychosocial needs, and antirheumatic medications. Rheumatoid arthritis is a constitutional illness and leads to increased fatigue. The daily programme, tailored to each patient, should include sufficient rest to avoid fatigue and this should be specified by the doctor. Rest, unaccompanied by some form of exercise, quickly leads to inanition, deconditioning, and flexion contractures of inflamed joints. Therefore, even during periods of acute inflammation, the patient should be instructed in modest range of motion and isometric muscle conditioning exercises, to be conducted over the course of 10 to 15 min, twice daily. Initially, these exercises should be conducted in bed or on an exercise table; later, exercise in a therapeutic pool is particularly effective. The possibility of decreased range of motion or flexion deformity in actively involved joints is a continuing threat and the patient should be instructed in appropriate efforts through exercises, swimming, or other selected physical activities, to limit potential deformities before they become established.

It is also important to restore muscle function to a normal or close to normal level, and maintain it at that level. Muscle and ligaments are essential, not only for joint motion, but also for maintenance of alignment and stability of a given joint. Even in the presence of considerable destruction of the joint surface, patients can retain surprisingly good function if they are able to maintain relatively strong muscle and ligamentous support. Conversely, even with minimal joint damage, malalignment of a joint or inappropriate stress placed on a joint, such as a knee, by an inadequately supported foot, will lead to a greater loss of function than would otherwise be the case.

The close association between emotional factors and musculoskeletal symptoms needs no emphasis. 'He is a pain in the neck' or 'Oh, my aching back' are familiar examples (Lichtenberg *et al.* 1986). It has long been appreciated that patients with rheumatoid arthritis who are resentful, angry, or exhibit marked dependency needs will fare less well than those with a more positive attitude towards life (Bradley 1989). The doctor should ensure that the patient receives adequate social support and that high degrees of anxiety or depression are appropriately treated, especially during periods of active disease. The element of depression commands particular attention. Pain, fatigue, loss of physical function, and uncertain implications for one's future clearly evoke an emotional response. Arthritis is a depressing illness. It is important to differentiate a minor depression or discouragement, a normal result of the pain and functional incapacity of chronic arthritis, from a major depression, which should be treated appropriately.

Non-steroidal anti-inflammatory agents

The choice of drug depends on each individual. Patients who experience tinnitus with aspirin will do better on one of the other non-steroidal anti-inflammatory drugs. However, use of these drugs in the older population presents significant risk of gastropathy (see Chapter 8.4) as well as fluid retention and renal disease. Some agents are more toxic than others (Singh *et al.* 1994). The characteristics of patients with a particularly high risk for non-steroidal anti-inflammatory drug-related gastropathy have been identified (Janssen *et al.* 1994); such patients should be treated with special caution and consideration should be given to the simultaneous admission of misoprostol (Graham *et al.* 1988; Silverstein *et al.* 1995). The recently developed selective COX-2 inhibitors show great promise for providing effective anti-inflammatory action with minimal gastrointestinal toxicity (Vain 1994). The first of these agents to become available clinically is celecoxib (Celebrex). Initial experience is very encouraging.

Prophylactic treatment with antacids and H_2-receptor antagonists is of questionable value in the prevention of gastritis and gastric ulcer (Singh *et al.* 1996), but will decrease the frequency of duodenal ulcers related to non-steroidal anti-inflammatory drugs. Non-steroidal anti-inflammatory drugs should always be taken with food. A detailed review of the toxic effects of all currently available antirheumatic drugs, and appropriate monitoring strategies, has been developed by the American College of Rheumatology *Ad Hoc* Committee on Clinical Guidelines (1996*b*). Although not directed specifically towards older patients, in whom toxic reactions are much more frequent, the report makes reference to the older population in a number of its recommendations and includes a full bibliography.

Relatively safe disease-modifying agents

The two disease-modifying agents most commonly used in the United Kingdom for patients with moderate degrees of disease activity are hydroxychloroquine and sulphasalazine.

Hydroxychloroquine

Hydroxychloroquine is prescribed in an initial dose of 200 mg twice daily. Because of the remote possibility of accumulation of the drug in the cornea, or, less likely, damage to the retina, its use should be preceded by an ophthalmological examination, and this should be repeated in 6 months or 1 year, and then each year that the patient remains on therapy. Should corneal deposits appear, they will be resorbed following discontinuation of the agent. Retinal damage is probably irreversible, but initial changes can be detected by an ophthalmologist before there is any change in visual acuity and, in that instance, the drug should be discontinued. However, both these complications are extremely rare and hydroxychloroquine is probably the least toxic of all the antirheumatic drugs. Demonstration of its effectiveness as an antirheumatic agent, by means of a randomized blinded controlled trial, using pre-established objective criteria, was one of the first such studies undertaken in the field of rheumatology (Cohen and Calkins 1958). Despite its effectiveness in reducing joint inflammation, there is little evidence that it alters the destructive joint changes (van der Heijde 1989). The dose should be reduced to 200 mg/day following 6 or 8 months at the higher dose level. If this causes a disease flair, the dose can be increased again to 400 mg/day. Hydroxychloroquine fits in well with other antirheumatic agents, especially prednisone and methotrexate, and does not contribute to cumulative toxicity.

Sulphasalazine

Sulphasalazine is probably the antirheumatic drug which is most frequently used in the United Kingdom. Therapy is initiated with low doses, such as 500 mg twice or three times daily, and gradually increased as tolerated to 3 or 4 g daily (van de Putte and Weinblatt 1994; Capell 1995). The toxic effects are nausea, vomiting, and epigastric distress. If these occur, the dose should be lowered, and then increased again gradually. Complete blood cell counts and liver enzymes should be assayed periodically. In contrast to most of the so-called 'remittive' or slow-acting antirheumatic drugs, clinical benefit usually becomes evident within a few weeks, although a longer period of time may be necessary to achieve the desired effectiveness. The drug has been shown to have a synergistic effect when combined with methotrexate, and simultaneous use of sulphasalazine, methotrexate, and hydroxychloroquine has provided encouraging results (O'Dell et al. 1996). When combined with corticosteroids, however, there is no increase in the effectiveness of either drug alone.

Methotrexate

In the authors' practice, methotrexate provides the cornerstone of pharmacotherapy for patients with severe potentially destructive arthritis (Willkens 1990). Controlled studies have confirmed the effectiveness of this agent in reducing the inflammatory symptoms in the majority of cases (Hanrahan et al. 1989) and the drug is well tolerated by most patients, including those in the older age group (Wolfe and Cathey 1991). For many years there was controversy as to whether use of this agent actually decreased the destructive changes of rheumatoid arthritis, or merely exhibited an anti-inflammatory effect. Recent evidence suggests that, instituted early in the disease, use of methotrexate will decrease the progression of the disease and reduce long-term disability (Hanrahan et al. 1989; Fries et al. 1996). However, there are serious potential toxic effects, notably liver toxicity (Walker et al. 1993), leucopenia or pancytopenia (Doolittle et al. 1989; MacKinnon et al. 1985), and occasionally acute pneumonitis or pulmonary fibrosis (Green et al. 1988).

Following explanation to the patient of the benefits and potential toxicity of the drug, an initial baseline chest radiograph, complete blood count, and liver profile (liver enzymes and serum albumin) are obtained. Repeat blood tests are scheduled initially at monthly intervals, then reduced in 4 to 6 months to intervals of 6 weeks. Serum creatinine concentration should be assessed at least twice yearly, and more frequently if the patient is also receiving non-steroidal anti-inflammatory drugs since a change in renal function may lead to methotrexate toxicity. The drug is initially prescribed in a dose of 7.5 mg once a week. Folic acid should also be prescribed, either 1 mg/day for 5 days of the week or 5 mg once a week (Morgan et al. 1994). In most cases, a decrease in joint discomfort and physical evidence of inflammation will occur by the end of 2 months. If it has not occurred by that time, the drug should be increased to around 10 or 12.5 mg weekly and, if no response ensues, increased further to but not exceeding 20 mg weekly (Furst et al. 1989). The baseline programme of rest, exercise, localized heat, and aspirin or one of the other non-steroidal anti-inflammatory drugs should be continued during this process. A decrease in serum albumin concentration provides an early note of caution that the patient may have liver disease, either secondary to the methotrexate or due to an independent condition. In either instance, the risk of further liver damage is significantly increased. Modest increases in aspartate aminotransferase

and alanine aminotransferase are frequently seen. If the aspartate aminotransferase reaches twice the normal range on two or three successive occasions, especially in the presence of decreased serum albumin, the drug should be discontinued. Alcohol consumption is strictly forbidden and patients with previously known liver disease should not be treated.

Under certain circumstances, calcium folinate (calcium leucovorin) in a dose of 2.5 or 5 mg, given 24 h after the methotrexate, can be substituted for the folic acid. This may be helpful in patients who experience gastrointestinal symptoms, mucosal ulcers, and minor transaminase elevations, without altering the effectiveness of the agent. Although the possibility of serious pancytopenia secondary to methotrexate is real, it is very rarely seen with these doses. However, in patients who exhibit a modest decrease in the white cell count, substitution of calcium folinate 5 mg 24 h after intake of methotrexate, for folic acid supplementation, may attenuate further decline. If the need for methotrexate is strong, in the face of a declining white cell count, the drug can be continued cautiously while increasing the dose of calcium folinate to 10 or 15 mg and repeating the white cell count at weekly intervals. However, one must bear in mind that increased doses of calcium folinate may attenuate the effectiveness of methotrexate (Shiroky et al. 1993). A decrease in the white cell count to 3000 or less is grounds for stopping the drug. If active disease is not controlled by methotrexate at a dose of 20 mg/week orally, or if there are gastrointestinal side-effects, a favourable response is often achieved by giving the drug intramuscularly in the same dose.

The toxic effect to methotrexate which gives most concern is that of pulmonary alveolitis, which may be followed by fibrosis (Green et al. 1988; Golden et al. 1995). This provides the reason for the baseline chest radiograph. Clinically, the pulmonary change secondary to methotrexate is most frequently evidenced by a persistent nagging cough, often associated with low-grade fever and malaise. If repeat radiographs show increased markings indicative of alveolitis, the drug should be discontinued and the patient treated with a brief course of high-dose corticosteroids. Although the alveolitis is usually reversible, it may progress to fibrosis, which is irreversible.

Methotrexate is often given in concert with other antirheumatic agents, frequently a combination of low-dose prednisone and hydroxychloroquine. Alternatively, it may be combined with sulphasalazine either alone or together with hydroxychloroquine (as noted above, the combination of sulphasalazine and low-dose prednisone does not appear to produce a summative effect). Alternatively, if methotrexate, in combination with these other agents, is not effective, the addition of cyclosporin A has been shown to be beneficial by investigators in Europe and Canada.

Highly toxic but quite effective disease-modifying agents

Gold salts have been shown to be effective in reducing the inflammatory changes associated with rheumatoid arthritis and also inhibiting the destructive effects of the disease on joint structures (Epstein et al. 1991). However, they are extremely toxic, with a high frequency of dermatitis, stomatitis, renal damage, and occasionally thrombocytopenia. A complete blood cell count including platelets, and urinalysis should be obtained within 24 h prior to a given injection. Occasionally, an injection will be followed by weakness, dizziness, nausea, and vomiting, and the presence of these symptoms, even to a mild degree, may serve as a warning that more serious side-effects will occur following succeeding doses. In view of its toxicity, the drug is best administered in a well-established specialty clinic accustomed to following numerous patients with this form of therapy.

Cyclosporin A

Cyclosporin A has been used in humans since 1978, primarily in conjunction with organ transplantation. Although in the United States the drug has been approved by the Federal Drug Administration for use in transplantation, it has not yet achieved approval for wider use. However, rapidly growing experience in Europe and Canada has indicated its effectiveness in a variety of autoimmune diseases, especially rheumatoid arthritis, and it is beginning to be used in the United States for serious cases (Pinayi and Tugwell 1993). Controlled studies have shown that the drug, in addition to decreasing inflammatory manifestations, results in a halting of the progress of radiographic changes in the hand, and have confirmed its effectiveness as a supplement to methotrexate in patients in whom the initial response to the latter drug has become attenuated.

The main toxicity associated with the agent, which is very serious, is renal failure. Patients with abnormal renal function should not be considered as candidates for therapy, and the use of other drugs, known to affect renal function, such as non-steroidal anti-inflammatory drugs, should be discontinued if possible. Exclusions include patients who have a malignancy, either present or in the recent past, or a premalignant condition, and patients suffering from cardiac, lung, or liver disease.

Therapy is commenced in a dose of 2.5 mg/kg/day taken orally twice daily. If there is no clinical response in 4 to 8 weeks, the dose is increased in a stepwise fashion towards but not exceeding 5 mg/kg/day. Blood pressure and serum creatinine values should be obtained every 2 weeks for 3 months, and monthly thereafter. If serum creatinine increases by more than 30 per cent, the dose should be decreased and, if the creatinine elevation persists, it should be discontinued. Other indices to be monitored include liver enzymes, serum protein concentration, magnesium concentration, fasting lipids, and urinary protein.

Many investigators, especially in Europe, currently regard initiation of cyclosporin therapy as the optimal step for patients whose disease cannot be controlled with methotrexate, assuming that the appropriate precautions and exclusions are honoured. However, because of the drug's extreme toxicity, it is strongly recommended that patients receiving it should be followed in a clinic staffed by personnel who have had experience with its use. As a general rule, the less toxic remittive agents mentioned above should be tried first. If the patient fails to respond within 4 to 6 months, consideration should be given to the use of the more potent but toxic agents. This may require referral to an arthritis specialist.

Two powerful new disease-modifying anti-inflammatory drugs, leflunomide (Arava) and etanercept (Enbril), became available in late 1998. Leflunomide is an agent that inhibits *de novo* pyrimidine synthesis and exhibits an antiproliferative effect on the lymphocytes. Initial studies show that it is effective in slowing or arresting the destructive changes accompanying rheumatoid arthritis. It may be given either as the sole disease-modifying agent or in combination with methotrexate or other agents (Mladenovic *et al.* 1995). More experience is required to define its potential toxicity fully. Etanercept is the first of a new class of drugs that targets tumour necrosis factor,

a naturally occurring cytokine which, if produced in excess, stimulates a cascade of inflammatory reactions in the joint. The drug is given by subcutaneous injection twice weekly. It is recommended for use in patients with severely active rheumatoid arthritis who have had an inadequate response to other disease-modifying agents. It can be used in combination with methotrexate in patients who have not responded adequately to methotrexate alone. The drug is very expensive and no long-term experience is available yet.

With the development of the selective COX-2 inhibitors and these two new antirheumatic agents, pharmaceutical therapy for rheumatoid arthritis is entering an exciting new era.

Corticosteroids

For older patients who experience significant loss of physical function secondary to rheumatoid arthritis, low-dose prednisone or prednisolone provides a major source of relief (Cohen and Conn 1997). This is especially important in older people whose capacity for independence or relative independence is threatened by their reduced ability to conduct the activities of daily living. Prednisone or prednisolone, at a dose of 7 or at most 8 mg/day, usually provides significant symptomatic relief and enhanced functional capacity, with little or no initial effect on blood pressure or glucose metabolism. It has recently been shown that the administration of low-dose corticosteroids to patients receiving other antirheumatic agents, results in a slight decrease in joint destruction (Kirwan 1995).

The toxic effect of systemic corticosteroids that causes most serious concern is enhancement of osteoporosis, which is already present in most patients with rheumatoid arthritis owing to physical inactivity and other factors (Dykman *et al.* 1985). It has been shown that prednisone doses as low as 7.5 mg/day will have a negative effect on skeletal density, starting during the first few months of therapy (Laan *et al.* 1993). A loss of even 10 per cent of bone mass, which frequently occurs in patients receiving prednisone, will lead to a doubling of the fracture rate. In patients receiving corticosteroid therapy, calcium 1200 to 1500 mg/day with vitamin D 800 IU/day (often combined with the calcium) is always indicated. Oestrogen replacement will significantly decrease or ablate corticosteroid-induced osteopenia. If the patient will not accept or tolerate oestrogens, use of alendronate or another suitable bisphosphonate is recommended. Guidelines for the control of steroid-induced osteoporosis have been developed by the American College of Rheumatology (American College of Rheumatology *Ad Hoc* Committee on Clinical Guidelines 1996*b*) (Table 5). A combination of 5- and 1-mg tablets of prednisone should be used to permit titration of dosage to the minimal level consistent with the desired effect, thus assisting in the gradual withdrawal of the agent.

Although the osteopenic effect of prednisone can usually be offset by the measures cited above, long-term corticosteroid therapy, even at low doses, has been shown to be associated with increased debility, decreased response to infection, and an increased tendency to diabetes mellitus and hypertension (Ramos-Remus and Russell 1997). Prednisone should always be given in association with one or several other antirheumatic drugs in the expectation that, as they establish their effectiveness in combating active disease, it will be possible gradually to reduce the prednisone dose and, where possible, discontinue it.

Table 5 American College of Rheumatology guidelines for the prevention and management of corticosteroid-induced osteoporosis

Maintain the dose of steroid at the minimal effective level. Alternate day administration does not offer protection against bone loss

Make major effort to cease smoking and limit alcohol consumption

Participate in weight-bearing exercise 30–60 min daily

Maintain calcium intake of 1500 mg/day through food or supplements

Give vitamin D (800 IU/day)

Monitor serum calcium levels and urinary calcium excretion periodically. If patient excretes more than 300 mg calcium over a 24-h period consider low-dose thiazide diuretic with potassium supplement as needed. Monitor serum calcium carefully regarding hypercalcaemia

For postmenopausal women, provide oestrogen supplementation unless contraindicated. Consider obtaining serum testosterone levels in men and, if low, provide testosterone supplementation

Consider use of bisphosphonate (alendronate 5 or 10 mg daily with full glass of water, sitting erect, 30 min before breakfast) in all older patients receiving long-term prednisolone therapy

For patients who exhibit unstable balance or gait abnormalities, or are at high risk for falls, balance and gait training is recommended

Intra-articular corticosteroid injection

One way of avoiding the systemic toxicity of corticosteroids is to administer them intra-articularly. This is particularly effective if one or two large joints are involved, but may also be performed on small joints (Doherty *et al.* 1992). Infection of the joint should be considered and excluded before corticosteroid is administered. Injection of tri-amcinolone hexacetonide may lead to significant relief, lasting for many months. There is a difference of opinion concerning the frequency with which injections may be undertaken, and the total duration of this form of therapy. Some rheumatologists recommend that the injections should be limited to no more than three in a year, and that the course of injections should not extend beyond 1.5 or 2 years, because of possible steroid-induced destructive changes. Others believe that, if the injections yield considerable symptomatic improvement, the course can be continued safely for many years. There are no objective data to support either contention.

Surgery

Of all the advances in therapy of rheumatoid arthritis over the past 30 years, the developments in orthopaedic surgery have been amongst the most spectacular (Bentley and Dowd 1986). Surgery of the hand, hips, and knees has been the most widely developed. Hand surgery, involving tendon transplants, artificial joints, and other aspects of joint reconstruction has become an integral part of the management of patients with deformities secondary to rheumatoid arthritis— especially older patients with long-standing disease. For patients who experience sudden onset of 'dropped fingers' due to tendon rupture, repairs should be undertaken at the earliest possible opportunity. Reconstruction of the feet can lead to symptomatic relief and enhanced ambulation in people who have difficulty in walking and putting their shoes on. This should be undertaken by an orthopaedist with special interest in the field. At a lesser level, appropriate shoes and orthotic foot support will contribute substantially to a patient's ability to walk and maintain independence.

For patients with advanced disease of the hips or knees, joint replacement has assumed an important role in the maintenance of good musculoskeletal function. The timing of these replacements involves a collaborative decision on the part of the patient, doctor, and orthopaedist. The expected duration of effective use of a hip replacement is approximately 15 years, and that for a knee replacement is slightly less. Subsequent replacement of an appliance which has become loose or damaged is fairly satisfactory for hip prostheses, but less well developed for knees. Thus hip replacements are appropriately considered in patients in their mid-fifties and older. For knees, however, it is best to defer the procedure, ideally until the mid-seventies.

These concepts need to be modified for individual situations. Steps essential for the preservation or restoration of reasonable function in an older person are worth undertaking despite reasonable risk, both immediate and long term. The success of these orthopaedic procedures is equally good, and probably better, for patients with rheumatoid arthritis than for those with osteoarthritis. Patients with long-standing rheumatoid arthritis have learnt how to maximize function despite limitations, and gratefully accept ability to maintain a relatively active life, doing chores about the house, maintaining a relatively sedentary job, and enjoying social opportunities, without the need to undertake major sports or labour-intensive work. The need for patients with joint replacements to take antibiotics, in conjunction with dental, urological, or rectal procedures, has been well accepted. One frequently employed regimen is gentamicin 1 h before the procedure.

Finally, the topic of patient and family education deserves special emphasis. Controlled studies have shown that well-designed educational programmes have contributed substantially to better outcomes for patients with rheumatoid arthritis (Lorig *et al.* 1993). Evaluation of group-oriented classes of older patients with rheumatoid and other forms of arthritis, emphasizing patient education, exercise, and social support, has shown significant benefits in terms of function, balance, and general health status. Follow-up of patients by means of routine telephone calls has resulted in improved outcome and decreased utilization of more elaborate (and expensive) interventions (Maisiak *et al.* 1996).

Conclusion

The prevalence of rheumatoid arthritis increases with age. Older patients may present with new-onset disease, or the residue of long-standing arthritis. Differential diagnosis includes a consideration of osteoarthritis, polymyalgia rheumatica, undifferentiated polyarthritis, fibromyalgia, dermatomyositis, other autoimmune rheumatic diseases, and musculoskeletal manifestations of systemic illnesses not usually regarded as rheumatic in nature. Most of these entities occur more frequently in older than in younger people, and several may be present simultaneously. Because a patient has the clinical stigmata or history of one of these diseases does not mean that all symptoms are due to that disorder.

Treatment of rheumatoid arthritis involves a multifaceted approach which works best if it is taken seriously by the doctor, developed jointly with the patient, specified in detail, and supported by an appropriate team of health professionals. Components include rest, exercise, psychosocial support, surgery if indicated, and use of one or several of a wide range of drugs, many of which entail major risks of toxicity. The therapeutic goal may be quite different for older people than for young or middle-aged patients. In the older years, the chief goals are often preservation of function and comfort. Steps to achieve these goals should be undertaken in a proactive fashion, even if they involve both short- and long-terms risks. Properly employed, they will permit older patients with rheumatoid arthritis to achieve satisfying and effective lives.

References

American College of Rheumatology *Ad Hoc* Committee on Clinical Guidelines (1996*a*). Guidelines for the management of rheumatoid arthritis. *Arthritis and Rheumatism*, 39, 713–22.

American College of Rheumatology *Ad Hoc* Committee on Clinical Guidelines (1996*b*). Guidelines for monitoring drug therapy in rheumatoid arthritis. *Arthritis and Rheumatism*, 39, 723–31.

American College of Rheumatology Task Force on Osteoporosis Guidelines (1996). Recommendations for the prevention and treatment of glucocorticoid induced osteoporosis. *Arthritis and Rheumatism*, 39, 1791–1801.

Arnett, F.C., Edworthy, S.M., Bloch, D.A., *et al.* (1988). The American Rheumatism Association 1987 revised criteria for the classification of rheumatoid arthritis. *Arthritis and Rheumatism*, 31, 315–24.

Bentley, G. and Dowd, G.S. (1986). Surgical treatment of arthritis in the elderly. *Clinics in Rheumatic Diseases*, 12, 291–327.

Bergstrom, G., Bjelle, A., Sorensen, L.B., Sundh, V., and Svanborg, A.P. (1986). Prevalence of rheumatoid arthritis, osteoarthritis, chondrocalcinosis and gouty arthritis at age 79. *Journal of Rheumatology*, 13, 527–34.

Bou-Holaigah, I., Rowe, P.C., Kan, J., and Calkins, H. (1995). The relationship between neurally mediated hypotension and the chronic fatigue syndrome. *Journal of the American Medical Association*, 274, 961–7.

Bradley, L.A. (1989). Psychosocial factors and disease outcomes in rheumatoid arthritis: old problems, new solutions, and a future agenda. *Arthritis and Rheumatism*, 32, 1611–14.

Calin, A. and Marks, S.H. (1981). The case against seronegative arthritis. *American Journal of Medicine*, 70, 992–4.

Campbell, S.M. (1988). Gout: how presentation, diagnosis, and treatment differ in the elderly. *Geriatrics*, 43, 71–7.

Capell, H.A. (1995). Clinical efficacy of sulphasalazine—a review. *British Journal of Rheumatology*, 34 (Supplement 2), 35–9.

Cerhan, J.R., Wallace, R.B., el-Khoury, G.Y., Moore, T.E., and Long, C.R. (1995). Decreased survival with increasing prevalence of full-body radiographically defined osteoarthritis in women. *American Journal of Epidemiology*, 141, 225–34.

Chaun, H., Robinson, C.E., Sutherland, W.H., and Dunn, W.L. (1984). Polyarthritis associated with gastric carcinoma. *Canadian Medical Association Journal*, 131, 909–11.

Chuang, T.Y., Hunder, G.G., Ilstrup, D.M., and Kurland, L.T. (1982). Polymyalgia rheumatica: a 10-year epidemiologic and clinical study. *Annals of Internal Medicine*, 97, 672–80.

Cohen A.S. and Calkins E. (1958). A controlled study of chloroquine as an antirheumatic agent. *Arthritis and Rheumatism*, 1, 297–312.

Cohen, M.D. and Conn, D.L. (1997). Benefits of low dose corticosteroids in rheumatoid arthritis. *Bulletin on the Rheumatic Diseases*, 46, 4–7.

DeVere, R. and Bradley, W.G. (1975). Polymyositis: its presentation, morbidity, and mortality. *Brain*, 98, 637–66.

Doherty, M., Hazelman, B.L., Hutton, C.W., Maddison, P.H. and Perry, J.D. (1992). *Rheumatology examination and injection techniques*. W.B. Saunders, London.

Doolittle, G.C., Simpson, K.M., and Lindsley, H.B. (1989). Methotrexate-associated, early-onset pancytopenia in rheumatoid arthritis. *Archives of Internal Medicine*, 149, 1430–1.

Dykman, T.R., Gluck, O.S., Murphy, W.A., Hahn, T.J., and Hahn, B.H. (1985). Evaluation of factors associated with glucocorticoid-induced osteopenia in patients with the rheumatic diseases. *Arthritis and Rheumatism*, 28, 361–8.

Epstein, W.V., Henke, C.J., Yelin, E.H., and Katz, P.P. (1991). Effect of parenterally administered gold therapy on the course of adult rheumatoid arthritis. *Annals of Internal Medicine*, 114, 437–44.

Fam, A.G., Topp, J.R., Stein, H.B., and Little, A.H. (1981). Clinical and roentgenographic aspects of pseudogout: a study of 50 cases and a review. *Canadian Medical Association Journal*, 124, 545–51.

Folstein, M.F., Folstein, S.E., and McHugh, P.R. (1975). 'Mini-Mental State'. A practical method for grading the cognitive state of patients for the clinician. *Journal of Psychiatric Research*, 12, 189–98.

Fries, J.F., Williams, C.A., Morfeld, D., Singh, G., and Sibley, J. (1996). Reduction in long term disability in patients with rheumatoid arthritis by disease-modifying antirheumatic drug-based treatment strategies. *Arthritis and Rheumatism*, 39, 616–22.

Fuchs, H.A., Kaye, J.J., Callahan, L.F., Nance, E.P., and Pincus, T. (1989). Evidence of significant radiographic damage in rheumatoid arthritis within the first 2 years of disease. *Journal of Rheumatology*, 16, 585–91.

Furst, D.E., Koehnke, R., Burmeister, L.F., Kohler, J., and Cargill, I. (1989). Increasing methotrexate effect with increasing dose in the treatment of resistant rheumatoid arthritis. *Journal of Rheumatology*, 16, 313–20.

Garton, M. and Reid, D. (1993). Bone mineral density of the hip and the anteroposterior and lateral dimensions of the spine in men with rheumatoid arthritis. Effects of low-dose corticosteroids. *Arthritis and Rheumatism*, 36, 222–8.

Girdwood, R.H. (1974). Death after taking medicaments. *British Medical Journal*, 1, 501–4.

Golden, M.R., Katz, R.S., Balk, R.A., and Golden, H.E. (1995). The relationship of pre-existing lung disease to the development of methotrexate pneumonitis in patients with rheumatoid arthritis. *Journal of Rheumatology*, 22, 1043–7.

Graham, D.Y., Agrawal, N.M., and Roth, S.H. (1988). Prevention of NSAID-induced gastric ulcer with misoprostol: multicentre, double-blind, placebo-controlled trial. *Lancet*, ii, 1277–80.

Green, L., Schattner, A. and Berkenstadt, H. (1988). Severe reversible interstitial pneumonitis induced by low dose methotrexate: report of a case and review of the literature. *Journal of Rheumatology*, 15, 110–12.

Griffin, E.R., Pipper, J.M., Dougherty, J.R., Showden, M., and Ray, W.A. (1991). Nonsteroidal antiinflammatory drug use and increased risk for peptic ulcer disease in elderly persons. *Annals of Internal Medicine*, 114, 255–63.

Hallgren, H.M., Buckley, C.E. III, Gilbertsen, V.A., and Yunis, E.J. (1973). Lymphocyte phytohemagglutinin responsiveness, immunoglobulins and autoantibodies in aging humans. *Journal of Immunology*, 111, 1101–7.

Hanrahan, P.S., Scrivens, G.A., and Russell, A.S. (1989). Prospective long term follow-up of methotrexate therapy in rheumatoid arthritis: toxicity, efficacy and radiological progression. *British Journal of Rheumatology*, 28, 147–53.

Harris, E.D. Jr (1997). Clinical features of rheumatoid arthritis. In *Textbook of rheumatology* (5th edn) (ed. W.N. Kelley, E.D. Harris Jr, S. Ruddy, and C.B. Sledge), pp. 898–932. W.B. Saunders, Philadelphia.

Hayes, G.S. and Stinson, I.N. (1976). Erythrocyte sedimentation rate and age. *Archives of Ophthalmology*, 94, 939–40.

Healey, L.A. (1997). Case management study: an elderly patient with muscle pain. *Bulletin on the Rheumatic Diseases*, 46, 7–8.

Janssen, M., Dijkman, B.A.C., Lamers, C.B., Zwonderman, A.H., and Vandenbroucke, J.P. (1994). A gastroscopic study of the predicative value of risk factors for non-steroid anti-inflammatory drug-associated ulcer disease in rheumatoid arthritis patients. *British Journal of Rheumatology*, 33, 449–54.

Katz, S., Downs, T.D., Cash, H.R., and Grotz, R.C. (1970). Progress in the development of ADL. *Gerontologist*, 10, 20–30.

Kavanaugh, A.F. (1997). Rheumatoid arthritis in the elderly: is it a different disease? *American Journal of Medicine*, 103, 40S–48S.

Kirwan, J.R. and the Arthritis and Rheumatism Council Low Dose Glucocorticoid Study Group (1995). The effect of glucocorticoids on joint destruction in rheumatoid arthritis. *New England Journal of Medicine*, 333, 142–6.

Laan, R.F., van Reil, P.L., van de Putte, L.B., van Erning, L.J., van't Hof, M.A., and Lemmens, J.A. (1993). Low-dose of prednisone induces rapid reversible axial bone loss in patients with rheumatoid arthritis: a randomised, controlled study. *Annals of Internal Medicine*, 119, 963–8.

Lally, E.V., Zimmerman, N.B., Ho, G.J., and Kaplan, S.R. (1989). Urate-mediated inflammation in nodal osteoarthritis: clinical and roentgenographic correlations. *Arthritis and Rheumatism*, 32, 86–90.

Lawrence, J.S. and Bennett, P.H. (1960). Benign polyarthritis. *Annals of the Rheumatic Diseases*, 19, 20–30.

Lawton, M.P. and Brody, E.M. (1969). Assessment of older people: self maintaining and instrumental activities of daily living. *Gerontologist*, 9, 179–86.

Lichtenberg, P.A., Swenson, C.H., and Skehan, M.W. (1986). Further investigation of the role of personality, lifestyle and arthritic severity in predicting pain. *Journal of Psychosomatic Research*, 30, 327–37.

Linos, A., Worthington, J.W., O'Fallon, W.M., and Kurland, L.T. (1980). The epidemiology of rheumatoid arthritis in Rochester, Minnesota: a study of incidence, prevalence, and mortality. *American Journal of Epidemiology*, 111, 87–98.

Lorig, K.R., Mazonson, P.D., and Holman, H.R. (1993). Evidence suggesting that health education for self-management in patients with chronic arthritis has sustained health benefits while reducing health care costs. *Arthritis and Rheumatism*, 36, 439–46.

McCarty, G.A. (1986). Autoantibodies and their relation to rheumatic diseases. *Medical Clinics of North America*, 70, 237–61.

MacFarlane, D.G. and Dieppe, P.A. (1983). Pseudo-rheumatoid deformity in elderly osteoarthritic hands. *Journal of Rheumatology*, 10, 489–90.

MacKinnon, S.K., Starkelbaum, G., and Willkens, B.F. (1985). Pancytopenia associated with low dose pulse methotrexate in the treatment of rheumatoid arthritis. *Seminars in Arthritis and Rheumatism*, 15, 119–26.

Maddison, P.J. (1987). Systemic lupus erythematosus in the elderly. *Journal of Rheumatology*, 14 (Supplement 13), 182–7.

Maisiak, R., Austin, J., and Heck, L. (1996). Health outcomes of two telephone interventions for patients with rheumatoid arthritis or osteoarthritis. *Arthritis and Rheumatism*, 39, 1391–9.

Mladenovic, V., Domijan, Z., Rozman, B., et al. (1995). Safety and effectiveness of leflunomide in the treatment of patients with active rheumatoid arthritis: results of a randomized, placebo-controlled phase II study. *Arthritis and Rheumatism*, 38, 1595–603.

Morgan, K., Dallosso, H.M., Arie, T., Byrne, E.J., Jones, R., and Waite, J. (1987). Mental health and psychological well-being among the old and the very old living at home. *British Journal of Psychiatry*, 150, 801–7.

Morgan, S.L., Baggott, J.E., Vaughn, W.H., et al. (1994). Supplementation with folic acid during methotrexate therapy for rheumatoid arthritis. A double-blind, placebo controlled trial. *Annals of Internal Medicine*, 121, 833–41.

National Center for Health Statistics (1986). Current Estimate from the National Health Interview Survey. *United States, Vital and Health Statistics Series 10*, No. 164. DHHS Publication No. (PHS) 07-1592. National Center for Health Statistics, Washington, DC.

O'Dell, J.R., Haire, C.E., Erikson, N., et al. (1996). Treatment of rheumatoid arthritis with methotrexate alone, sulfasalazine and hydroxychloriquine, or a combination of all three medications. *New England Journal of Medicine*, 334, 1287–91.

Pinayi, G.S. and Tugwell, P. (ed.) (1993). An international consensus report: the use of cyclosporin A in rheumatoid arthritis. Proceedings of an international consensus meeting, Marlow, Buckinghamshire, United Kingdom, 19–20 July 1992. *British Journal of Rheumatology*, 32 (Supplement 1), 1–78.

Pincus, T. and Callahan, L.F. (1986). Taking mortality in rheumatoid arthritis seriously—predictive markers, socio-economic status and comorbidity. *Journal of Rheumatology*, 13, 841–5.

Pincus, T. and Callahan, L.F. (1993). What is the natural history of rheumatoid arthritis? Controversies in clinical rheumatology. *Rheumatic Disease Clinics of North America*, 19, 123–51.

Podgorski, M.N. and Edmonds, J. (1985). Non-pharmacological treatment of patients with rheumatoid arthritis. *Medical Journal of Australia*, 143, 511–16.

Ramos-Remus, C. and Russell, A.S. (1997). Dangers of low dose corticosteroid therapy in rheumatoid arthritis. *Bulletin on the Rheumatic Diseases*, 46, 1–4.

Ropes, M.W., Bennett, G.A., Cobb, S., Jacox, R., and Jessar, R.A. (1958). 1958 Revision of diagnostic criteria for rheumatoid arthritis. *Bulletin on the Rheumatic Diseases*, 9, 175–6.

Shiel, W.C. Jr and Jason, M. (1989). The diagnostic associations of patients with antinuclear antibodies referred to a community rheumatologist. *Journal of Rheumatology*, 16, 782–5.

Shiroky, J.B., Neville, C., Esdaile, J.M., et al. (1993). Low dose methotrexate with leucovorin (folinic acid) in the management of rheumatoid arthritis. Results of a multicenter randomised double-blind placebo-controlled trial. *Arthritis and Rheumatism*, 36, 795–803.

Silverstein, F.E., Graham, D.Y., Senior, J.R., et al. (1995). Misoprostol reduces serious gastrointestinal complications in patients with rheumatoid arthritis receiving nonsteroidal anti-inflammatory drugs. A randomised, double-blind, placebo-controlled trial. *Annals of Internal Medicine*, 123, 241–9.

Singh, G., Ramey, D.R., Morfeld, D., and Fries, J.F. (1994). Comparative toxicity of non-steroidal anti-inflammatory agents. *Pharmacology and Therapeutics*, 62, 175–91.

Singh, G., Ramey, D.R., Morfeld, D., Shi, H., Hatoum, H.T., and Fries, J.F. (1996). Gastrointestinal tract complications of nonsteroidal anti-inflammatory drug treatment in rheumatoid arthritis: a prospective observational cohort study. *Archives of Internal Medicine*, 156, 1530–6.

Solenger, A.M. (1988). Drug-related lupus. Clinical and etiologic considerations. *Rheumatic Diseases Clinics of North America*, 1, 187–202.

Strand, V. and Talal, N. (1980). Advances in the diagnosis and concept of Sjögren's syndrome: autoimmune exocrinopathy. *Bulletin on the Rheumatic Diseases*, 30, 1046–52.

Tan, E.M., Cohen, A.S., Fries, J.F., *et al.* (1982). The 1982 revised criteria for the classification of systemic lupus erythematosus. *Arthritis and Rheumatism*, 25, 1271–7.

Thomas, C. and Robinson, J.A. (1993). The antinuclear antibody test: when is a positive result clinically relevant? *Postgraduate Medicine*, 94, 55–8, 63, 66.

van de Putte, L.B.A. and Weinblatt, M.E. (ed.) (1995). Radical interventions in early rheumatoid arthritis. The case for enteric-coated sulphasalizine, methotrexate and combined regimines. A workshop held in Camagli, Italy, September, 1994. *British Journal of Rheumatology*, 34 (Supplement 2).

van der Heijde, D.M. (1995). Joint erosions on patients with early rheumatoid arthritis. *British Journal of Rheumatology*, 34 (Supplement 2), 74–8.

van der Heijde, D.M., Gribnau, F.W., van Reil, P.L., Nuver-Zwart, I.H., and van Putte, L.B. (1989). Effect of hydroxychloroquine and sulphaslazine on progression of joint damage in rheumatoid arthritis. *Lancet*, i, 1036–8.

Vane, J.R. (1994). Toward a better aspirin. *Nature*, 367, 215–16.

Walker, A.M., Funch, D., Dreyer, N.A., *et al.* (1993). Determinants of serious liver disease among patients receiving low dose methotrexate for rheumatoid arthritis. *Arthritis and Rheumatism*, 36, 329–35.

Waller, M., Toone, E.C., and Vaughan, J. (1964). Study of rheumatoid factor in an older population. *Arthritis and Rheumatism*, 7, 513–20.

Ward, M.M. and Polisson, R.P. (1989). A meta-analysis of the clinical manifestations of older onset systemic lupus erythematosus. *Arthritis and Rheumatism*, 32, 1226–32.

Willkens, R.F. (1990). Resolve: methotrexate is the drug of choice after NSAIDs in rheumatoid arthritis. *Seminars in Arthritis and Rheumatism*, 20, 76–80.

Wolfe, F. and Cathey, M.A. (1991). The effect of age on methotrexate efficacy and toxicity. *Journal of Rheumatology*, 18, 973–7.

Wolfe, R., Smythe, H.A., Yunus, M.B., *et al.* (1990). The American College of Rheumatology 1990 criteria for the classification of fibromyalgia: report of the Multicenter Criteria Committee. *Arthritis and Rheumatism*, 33, 160–72.

Wolfe, R., Mitchell, D.M., Sibley, J.T., *et al.* (1994). The mortality of rheumatoid arthritis. *Arthritis and Rheumatism*, 37, 481–94.

Zeidler, H. and Hulsemann, J.L. (1989). Benign polyarthritis and undifferentiated arthritis. An epidemiological terra incognita. *Scandinavian Journal of Rheumatology*, 79 (Supplement), 15–20.

13.2 Back pain

Nortin M. Hadler

Regional back pain is the rubric used to denote the low back pain experienced by working age individuals who are otherwise well, who have experienced neither extraordinary biomechanical demands nor violent precipitants, and who have no important neurological signs. This regional back pain has left a great imprint on the industrialized world, far more lasting than it has left on its citizens who suffer the remittent and intermittent episodes of pain. Regional back pain has spawned industries devoted to removing hazards, providing remedies, and indemnifying disability. It is possible to synthesize this experience, and the voluminous literature it has engendered, and allow for more productive and reasoned remedies (Hadler 1999). None of this will occupy us here.

Owing to the previous focus on the worker with regional back pain, the causes in those with regional backache who are beyond working age has only been looked at in the past two decades (Williams and Hadler 1983) and causes in those confronting the end of gainful employment more recently than that (Hadler 1997*a*). This chapter focuses on the former, whilst the little that is known of the latter will only be mentioned briefly.

The predicament of elderly people with backache

Backache colours the daily lives of so many elderly people that it is paradoxical to label the condition 'abnormal'. When community-dwelling septuagenarians were questioned in Gothenberg (Bergstrom *et al.* 1986), nearly half of the women and a quarter of the men had pain at the time. The point prevalence was considerably less for septuagenarians in Iowa, but impressive nonetheless (Lavasky-Shulan *et al.* 1985); nearly a quarter of these people had suffered memorable backache in the preceding 12 months and half were in pain at the time of the survey. They described their pain as intermittent over days if not constant, mild to moderate in severity, and limiting the ease if not the effectiveness with which they accomplished many of the activities of daily living.

For those of working age, backache is an intermittent and remittent problem (Hadler and Carey 1998). For older people, backache is an expected part of life and the ramifications for public health are substantial, and this issue is discussed below. The doctor–patient relationship will be considered first.

The elderly patient with back pain

No elderly patient has as a chief complaint 'My back hurts'. The chief complaint should be heard as 'My back hurts but now I can't cope on my own'. The differential diagnosis relates not to the presence of back pain but to the impairment of coping. Two features of back pain are likely to be responsible: the pain seems qualitatively different from what has been customary, or it is quantitatively different. The latter is far more prevalent as a reason for becoming a patient. However, the former will seem more consonant with the reductionistic Western approach to medicine that has been taught for most of this century.

Atypical back pain

Back pain that is so qualitatively different as to cause the sufferer to seek care is defined a priori by the sufferer. Doctors have learnt to dissect several distinctive causes of this circumstance based on the quality of the experience.

Systemic backache

Systemic backache is an important consideration. Most patients with back pain feel as well as usual were it not for the backache. It is important to distinguish the elderly patient who has back pain and feels poorly beyond the pain, particularly if he or she is anorectic or losing weight. These patients may simply have confounding coincident illnesses, but the back pain may also be due to systemic disease. If the pain makes the patient move, awakens them, and is relieved by moving about, then multiple myeloma and metastatic neoplasms should be considered. If the symptoms are accompanied by fever, then septic discitis or even epidural abscess are urgent possibilities.

If the pain makes them writhe, it is important to consider the vascular system: dissecting or rupturing aneurysms present in this way. Posterior penetrating ulcers and pancreatitis present as back pain but the patient avoids motion preferring to remain still—seated in the case of pancreatitis.

Systemic back pain is more important to consider in elderly people than in the working age population. Its likelihood depends on referral biases; in a general medical clinic it is a rare occurrence. It should engender appropriate diagnostic studies including magnetic resonance imaging (MRI) which is highly sensitive to neoplastic or infectious involvement of the spine. However, even though there are symptoms that suggest systemic disease, atypical presentations of regional disorders are more likely. A thorough diagnostic work-up is necessary, otherwise the coping skills that were affected enough to make the patient seek help may be irreparably harmed.

Other forms of back pain

There are forms of back pain that are sufficiently unusual and distinctive at presentation to cause the elderly patient to seek help but that do not render elderly people systemically ill.

The radiculopathies

In the radiculopathies, the pain is in the extremity, often without axial pain, and seems to defy comprehension. Given the architecture of neural foramina and the likelihood of spondylotic changes, it is remarkable that radiculopathies are not more common, especially in later life. It is even more remarkable that most radiculopathies are intermittent and remittent illnesses implying that some component(s) of the spondylotic process is reversible. However, in contrast to regional spine pain, far fewer people are at risk. There are two major reasons for considering radiculopathy as a separate clinical issue: one benefits the doctor and the other the patient. For the doctor, there is the intellectual satisfaction of 'localization'—we may not be able to define the pathophysiology but at least we know its anatomical source with some reliability. For the patient, radiculopathy portends peripheral damage, provokes a special anxiety, since the experience of referred pain appears to defy reason, and offers some specific therapeutic options.

Localization Table 1 presents the usual symptoms and signs associated with damage to each cervical root and Table 2 presents those for the lumbar radiculopathies. The categorization is clinically useful but far from completely valid or reliable. Generalization of symptoms, and even signs, beyond a single root is not unusual and probably reflects some multiplicity of innervation peripherally and dispersion of input at the level of the cord. In the case of cervical radiculopathies, even more than lumbar, the pain tends to be paraspinal while the paraesthesiae tend to be distal in the distribution noted in Table 2. Some presentations are confounded by coincidental neuropathies. For example, nearly 10 per cent of elderly people lack at least one Achilles reflex further compromising the specificity of this neurological sign for radiculopathy.

Nonetheless, localization is possible from careful elicitation of symptoms, inspection for focal atrophy, muscle and reflex testing, and discernment of sensory deficits. For lumbar radiculopathies, there are also 'tension signs' (see below). However, performing a musculoskeletal examination in an elderly patient, particularly one who is already in pain, calls for gentleness, compassion, and humility. There is nothing gained by increasing their discomfort, and many a 'finding' could well predate the presenting illness. Few elderly people have a mobile spine, so it should not be tested. Gait disorders and some neurological signs, such as absent deep tendon reflexes, diminished sensation in the feet, and altered bowel and bladder function, can be unrelated to the presenting illness. Hip and knee disorders can be confounders which can be identified by a gentle examination that isolates their range of motion with the patient recumbent.

Tension or stretch signs can be elicited in the lower extremity and are probably more sensitive to radiculopathy than the signs listed in Table 2. Straight leg raising takes up the slack on lower lumbar roots that contribute to the sciatic nerve; by 30°, the nerve is taut. The normal nerve can withstand further flexion at the hip with the knee extended. Resistance to such movement beyond 30° (no need to confirm that few elderly patients tolerate more) is the traditional Lesegue sign for sciatica. Many variations, dating back to Imhotep in 1600 BC Egypt (Brandt-Rauf and Brandt-Rauf 1987), have proponents, but none pertain to elderly people. The other commonly employed stretch test is the femoral stretch accomplished by flexing the knee with the patient prone, assuming the elderly patient in pain can assume the prone position. This tests for involvement of the roots contributing to the femoral nerve. It also offers an opportunity to assess hip motion in extension, a posture that isolates the hips and

Table 1 Signs and symptoms of cervical radiculopathies

Root	Pain, numbness	Sensory loss	Motor loss	Reflex loss
C3	Occipital region	Occiput	None	None
C4	Back of neck	Back of neck	None	None
C5	Neck to outer shoulder and arm	Over shoulder	Deltoid	Biceps, supinator
C6	Outer arm to thumb and index fingers	Thumb and index fingers	Biceps (triceps) and wrist extensors	Triceps, supinator biceps
C7	Outer arm to middle finger	Index and middle fingers	Triceps	Triceps
C8	Inner arm to fourth and fifth fingers	Fourth and fifth fingers	Intrinsics, extrinsics	None

Table 2 Signs and symptoms of lumbar radiculopathies

Root	Pain, numbness	Sensory loss	Motor loss	Reflex loss
L4	Anterior thigh and medial leg	Medial leg to medial malleolus	Tibialis anterior	Patellar
L5	Lateral leg and dorsum of the foot	Lateral leg and dorsum of the foot	Extensor hallucis longus	Achilles
L6	Lateral foot	Lateral foot	Peroneus longus and brevis	Achilles

can offer reassurance about their integrity even in the setting of radiculopathy.

Therapeutic implications of radiculopathy Beyond the intellectual satisfaction that the doctor derives from 'localization', the exercise offers a modicum of benefit to the patient. Firstly, there is something baffling and anxiety-provoking about the experience of referred pain. Localization allows the doctor to discuss a 'pinched nerve' with more confidence than any explanation for low back pain can deserve. But confidence wavers with any attempt to explain beyond 'pinched nerve'. For 50 years the disc has been seen as pivotal in the pathogenesis of sciatica, other radiculopathies, and even back pain itself. It has proved impossible to define specific disc pathology that is necessary and sufficient to account for the illness (Ito *et al.* 1998). It may be time to expunge discal explanations from the clinical repertoire, certainly from the repertoire of geriatric medicine. After all, few lumbar discs survive the journey to the last decades of life intact. Something else is 'pinching' the nerve.

Localization, unfortunately, does not alter therapeutic considerations from those that pertain to neck and low back pain without radiculopathy. The one exception may be the surgical option, if one is willing to extrapolate from the experience in younger patients and if it is certain that there is nucleus pulposus in some site beyond the annulus that might be the cause. The former is tenuous; the latter is rare. Even if both occur, and the radiculopathy is sufficiently severe that motor impairment is an issue, defining a threshold for surgical intervention is still not straightforward. The L5–S1 radiculopathy can progress from leg pain to loss of Achilles reflex to reduced strength at the forefoot or ankle. The loss of the reflex has no functional implications. However, a weak distal leg does: surgery even in this setting is not predictably successful and spontaneous remission remains a likelihood. The answer is made at the bedside, involving input from all parties including the patient. For the far less frequent L3–4 radiculopathy, quadriceps power can be at risk with even more potential for functional impairment. Since the experience with this radiculopathy is limited, the tendency is to choose the surgical option more readily. Surgical success even in this setting is often elusive which calls into question the appropriateness of the surgical procedures currently in vogue, or the pathophysiology that underlies their design.

The evidence that surgical intervention to remove extruded nucleus pulposus benefits the sufferer with a lumbar radiculopathy derives from semi-systematic experiences in younger patients; it is far from cogent (Weber 1983; Alaranta *et al.* 1990). However, this benefit has not been demonstrable for acute illness (less than 6 weeks) or for chronic illness (greater than 6 months), nor do the data necessarily apply to an elderly population. Furthermore, the benefit is demonstrable at 6 months after which the patients who were treated conservatively merge with those who submitted to surgery in terms of all functional and symptomatic outcomes (Hoffman *et al.* 1993). This leaves little rationale for recommending surgery; no benefit can be shown for back pain and minor benefit for leg pain. Backache is not a surgical disease; sciatica is, but on rare occasions.

Lumbar spinal stenosis

Lumbar spinal stenosis is a rare condition afflicting older people. It is a topic surrounded with a good deal of controversy. Some would take issue with this introduction; if it is indeed 'rare', why is the rate of surgery for the condition in elderly patients soaring (Chiol et al. 1996)? There is even controversy regarding diagnostic criteria (Katz et al. 1995). The cardinal symptom of lumbar spinal stenosis is neurogenic claudication. This is the experience of aching pain, with or without paraesthesiae, in the buttock and/or posterior thigh and/ or calf precipitated by walking or even assuming an erect posture. Typically, the symptoms are bilateral and sphincter function is not impaired. Characteristically, the sufferer assumes a bent gait, the so-called simian stance, to postpone the onset of symptoms with walking. Often they will choose to walk with the assistance of a shopping cart (many eschew the stigma of a walking frame) over which they can stoop without falling forward. Likewise, sitting is more likely to offer rapid palliation than recumbency. It is because this symptom complex is so distinctive that lumbar stenosis survives as a clinical entity. The differential diagnosis is limited to atypical presentations of vascular claudication and, more remotely, mass lesions encroaching on the cauda equina. Spinal stenosis seldom provokes the cramping pain that is the hallmark of vascular claudication.

There have been attempts to use the difference in pathogenesis between neurogenic and vascular claudication to construct a provocative test; one would predict that while both might be precipitated by ambulation, only vascular claudication would be precipitated by operating a bicycle, though this is not clinically useful (Dong and Porter 1989). The neurological examination seldom proves definitive. Nearly half of patients with symptomatic stenosis have a reduced or absent Achilles reflex, a third have objective lower extremity weakness, and around 20 per cent have diminished or absent knee jerk(s). Whether these signs are part of lumbar spinal stenosis or represent a confounding polyradiculopathy is often not clear. Imaging the spine offers information that is no more specific than the neurological examination. The syndrome was first described in the setting of midline disc protrusions into a narrowed canal, hence the term lumbar spinal 'stenosis'. But the presence of degenerative changes, including some degree of reduction in the dimensions of the lumbar canal, is nearly ubiquitous in later life. The false-positive rate for images of the lumbar spine in diagnosing stenosis varies from 9 to 35 per cent depending on the criteria employed.

In view of these considerations, the diagnosis of lumbar stenosis as a cause of low back pain is based on the stereotypical nature of the symptoms (O'Duffy 1997). It is not an anatomical diagnosis; nor is its pathophysiology certain. About a third of patients improve spontaneously and another third do not progress beyond their status at presentation (Swezey 1996; O'Duffy, 1997). Furthermore, the experience following surgical decompression of the cord is anything but impressive (Turner et al. 1992; Katz et al. 1996); around a third of patients subjected to these extensive procedures do benefit. Far more commonly, pain and neurogenic claudication persist as does the misconception that surgery holds the solution, which often leads to multiple operations. Perioperative complications are frequent for elderly patients, and sometimes catastrophic. The sufferer needs a thoughtful and circumspect assessment; surgery is an option of desperation. Prior to surgery myelographic documentation of complete or near-complete obstruction of the caudal subarachnoid space is prudent.

Insufficiency fractures

Insufficiency fractures are a major issue for older patients. The most frequent location is the bodies of the lumbar vertebrae. These 'compression fractures' are discussed in greater detail in Chapter 14.1. Fractures of other bones in osteopenic bone disease are now recognized as a frequent cause of back pain in elderly people. Insufficiency fractures are spontaneous linear disruptions of cortical and subjacent trabecular bone without displacement. The classic example is the 'march' or stress fracture of the metatarsal in the healthy foot thought to reflect forces in usage that exceed the resilience of the bone. However, almost exclusively in elderly or osteoporotic patients, pelvic structures are similarly susceptible (Renner 1990; Dasgupta et al. 1998). Spontaneous fractures of the pubic rami (and the ribs) are well described and are common in the setting of steroid-induced osteoporosis where they may be asymptomatic, and heal with exuberant callus formation. They also occur without hypercorticism and without exuberant callus. Such fractures are being recognized more frequently in the setting of bone pain; aching pain, prominent at rest and with exacerbation with weight bearing more than with movement. The pubic rami, sacrum, and iliac wings are all susceptible (as are tibial plateaux). The fractures, particularly at the sacrum and iliac wings, are typically subradiograhic raising the possibility of other causes of bone pain including neoplasia. However, they are often demonstrable by scintiscanning although this technique has limited specificity. MRI is particularly sensitive and specific. In practice, insufficiency fractures are diagnosed by exclusion of other possibilities and by the natural history, which unfortunately measures healing in terms of months.

Myelopathy and cauda equina syndrome

Myelopathy and cauda equina syndrome, while infrequent, can be tragic. There are systemic diseases, and even some regional diseases, of the spine that can involve the contents of the canal. When this occurs in the cervical spine, myelopathy can result. Caudal to L1, the cauda equina is at risk. The consequences can be dramatic if not disastrous so that awareness of the clinical presentation and appreciation of the possibilities for intervention are important.

Cervical myelopathy Neither neck pain nor radiculopathy are prerequisites for the clinical presentation of cervical myelopathy: the presentation is often pain free and insidious. An acute or painful onset suggest such processes as central discal herniation, epidural abscess, metastasis, or a vascular catastrophe. The usual patient presents with complaints of diminished dexterity and/or a gait disorder. With higher cervical involvement, above C5, upper extremity paraesthesiae and impaired dexterity are common complaints. But high cervical presentations are less common so that upper extremity symptoms are usually less prominent than those referable to the lower extremity. Gait is often broad based and balance compromised. There may be abnormalities of sphincter function, usually presenting as incontinence.

The findings on examination are of lower motor neurone damage at the level of the lesion and upper motor neurone disease distally. It is the latter finding, usually bilateral hyperreflexia in the lower extremities and Babinski reflexes, that drives the diagnostic work-up. There is often a sensory level, though light touch may be preserved after temperature and proprioception are diminished. The differential diagnosis when lower extremity signs and symptoms predominate include amyotrophic lateral sclerosis, normal pressure hydrocephalus, and multiple strokes. Syringomyelia and neoplastic or other cervical space-occupying lesions can mimic the presentation, including at the

outpatient setting. A hospital bed is also used to facilitate coping and a place where one might gather one's psychological resources while enjoying the privileges and submitting to the constraints of the sick role. This use of an expensive resource is no longer acceptable in most countries and almost no indications remain for hospital admission for regional backache (Cherkin and Deyo 1993). However, hospital admission in the United States for backache still outstrips that in Canada and every other country (Larvis *et al.* 1998). Surgical intervention in the United States in more popular than in any other country. However, there are regional variations in the United States (Volinn 1994).

The elderly person with usual back pain

For the elderly patient with usual back pain, it is important to be aware of what *not* to do. This is not to say that the best management is to do nothing. If sufferers could cope on their own, they would not become patients. Patients need to understand that natural history is on their side; the challenge is how to cope more effectively until remission supervenes. Some of this challenge is met with the insights on palliation and biomechanics discussed above. But much more of this challenge can be met by returning to the pivotal question raised above, of why the patient could not cope with this episode of usual backache.

Rarely is the intensity of regional musculoskeletal pain, or even the impairment of physical function, sufficient to drive someone to seek the help of others. Psychosocial confounders contribute and often predominate. The pain is rendered less tolerable if the rest of life is not in order. People cease persisting and seek help because they can no longer cope on their own. This is certainly the most likely reason for an elderly person to choose to be a patient with knee pain (Hadler 1992). This assertion also applies to backache. Biering-Sorensen *et al.* (1989) were among the first to document this phenomenon. A cohort of 928 of the men and women, aged 30, 40, 50, and 60 years, living in a suburb of Copenhagen were recruited. These people gave an extensive history and had a physical examination at entry into the study, and completed a questionnaire 1 year later. The baseline information included documentation of health, occupational, social, and leisure variables. Regional back pain, termed 'low back trouble' by these investigators, was suffered by 413 of these people during the year and had afflicted another 214 in the year before the study. None of the physical baseline variables, other than previous back pain, correlated with the occurrence of regional back pain. The major finding was that individuals who experienced regional low back pain had 'more health problems and probably a higher psychosocial pressure'. This does not mean there are no other, and possibly remediable risk factors for regional back pain. It means that if they exist, they cannot be discerned because they are overwhelmed by the other risk factors that determine ability to cope with regional back pain. This inference, derived by studying regional back pain as it affects people in a community, reiterates that derived from studies of the illness experienced by patients; the pain is rendered more memorable and less tolerable when the rest of life is not in order.

For elderly people past working age, social isolation tends to be the confounder most likely to render regional back pain intolerable. For those still working, job dissatisfaction and disaffection in the workplace tend to be the confounders for coping successfully with the next episode of back pain (Hadler 1997*a*). This was illustrated by data from the South Manchester Back Pain Study (Papageorgiou *et al.* 1997). A cohort of 1412 working adults who had no recall of backache in the prior month was established. They were assessed at baseline for social class, general health status, and psychological distress. After 1 year, a follow-up questionnaire was administered to those who had not sought care for back pain asking whether they recalled backache 'lasting for 1 day or more'. Of 784 respondents, 247 (32 per cent) reported backache for which they had not consulted a doctor; the remainder, who did not recall backache, were the referent group. Those who were markedly dissatisfied with work at baseline were more likely to recall backache. If dissatisfied because of a perception that they were dreadfully underpaid, they were more likely to have complained of back pain to their general practitioner. But if they felt good about these aspects of their working life, they were less likely to complain of or even recall the episodes of backache that each of them almost certainly faced that year and that were likely to be as painful and biomechanically limiting as that faced by people in the other groups (Hadler 1996). It is the good fortune of the 'referents' that the context in which they suffered back pain so facilitated coping that the episode was forgettable. But for the disaffected worker, particularly the disaffected aged and ageing worker, there is little recourse but to find the next regional backache to be the 'straw that breaks the camel's back'. Recourse to insurance may seem the ready salve although all too often it is disappointing (Hadler 1997*b*).

Clearly regional backache that drives an elderly person, working or not, to the doctor is a reproach to the public health agenda. There may be something to be gained by modifying the biomechanical demands placed on the ageing population at home and at work so that back pain might be less limiting. But such gains pale in comparison with the palliation that might follow if there were attention to the psychosocial confounders that render backache less tolerable. Medicine may have a role in creating awareness and calling for progress. However, there is no doubt that doctors who want to intervene on behalf of an elderly patient with intolerable back pain can no longer avoid an assessment of the psychosocial factors that are likely to be doing harm to the patient's ability to cope.

References

Alaranta, H., Hurme, M., and Einola, S. (1990). A prospective study of patients with sciatica. A comparison between conservatively treated patients who have undergone operation. II. Results after 1 year follow-up. *Spine*, **15**, 1345–9.

Bergstrom, G., Bjelle, A., Sundh, V., and Svanborg, A. (1986). Joint disorders at age 70, 75 and 79 years—a cross-sectional comparison. *British Journal of Rheumatology*, **25**, 333–41.

Biering-Sorensen, F., Thomsen, C.E., and Milden, J. (1989). Risk indicators for low back trouble. *Scandinavian Journal of Rehabilitation Medicine*, **21**, 151–7.

Bigos, S., Bowyer, O.R., Braen, G.R., *et al.* (1994). *Acute low back problems in adults: clinical practice guidelines, no. 14*. AHCPR publication 95-0642. United States Department of Health and Human Services, Public Health Service, Agency for Health Care Policy and Research, Rockville, MD.

Brandt-Rauf, P.W. and Brandt-Rauf, S.I. (1987). History of occupational medicine: relevance of Imhotep and the Edwin Smith papyrus. *British Journal of Industrial Medicine*, **44**, 68–70.

Carette, S., Leclaire, R., Marcoux, S., *et al.* (1997). Epidural corticosteroid injections for sciatica due to herniated nucleus pulposus. *New England Journal of Medicine*, **336**, 1634–40.

Cherkin, D.C. and Deyo, R.A. (1993). Nonsurgical hospitalization for low-back pain. *Spine*, **18**, 1728–35.

Chiol, M.A., Deyo, R.A., Howell, E., and Kreis, S. (1996). An assessment of surgery for spinal stenosis: time trends, geographic variation, complications and reoperations. *Journal of the American Geriatrics Society*, **44**, 285–90.

Dans, P.E. (1994). Credibility, cookbook medicine, and common sense: guidelines and the college. *Annals of Internal Medicine*, **120**, 966–8.

Dasgupta, B., Shah, N., Brown, H., Gordon, T.E., Tanqueray, A.B., and Mellor, J.A. (1988). Sacral insufficiency fractures: an unsuspected cause of low back pain. *British Journal of Rheumatology*, **37**, 789–93.

Deyo, R.A. (1991). Fads in the treatment of low back pain. *New England Journal of Medicine*, **325**, 1039–40.

Dong, G.X. and Porter, R.W. (1989). Walking and cycling tests in neurogenic and intermittent claudication. *Spine*, **14**, 965–9.

Ernst, E. (1997). Acupuncture as a symptomatic treatment of osteoarthritis. *Scandinavian Journal of Rheumatology*, **26**, 444–7.

Hadler, N.M. (1992). Knee pain is the malady—not osteoarthritis. *Annals of Internal Medicine*, **116**, 598–9.

Hadler, N.M. (1996). Regional back pain: predicament at home, nemesis at work. *Journal of Occupational and Environmental Medicine*, **38**, 973–8.

Hadler, N.M. (1997*a*). Plaint of the aged worker. *Journal of Occupational and Environmental Medicine*, **39**, 1141–3.

Hadler, N.M. (1997*b*). Workers with disabling back pain. *New England Journal of Medicine*, **337**, 34–3.

Hadler, N.M. (1999). *Occupational musculoskeletal disorders*, pp. 1–416. Lippincott–Williams and Wilkins, Philadelphia, PA.

Hadler, N.M. and Carey, T.S. (1998). Low back pain: an intermittent and remittent predicament of life. *Annals of the Rheumatic Diseases*, **57**, 1–2.

Hoffman, R.M., Wheeler, K.J., and Deyo, R.A. (1993). Surgery for herniated lumbar discs: a literature synthesis. *Journal of General Internal Medicine*, **8**, 487–96.

Ito, M., Incorvata, K.M., and Yu, S.F. (1998). Predictive signs of discogenic lumbar pain on magnetic resonance imaging with discography correlation. *Spine*, **23**, 1252–60.

Katz, J.N., Dalgas, M., Stucki, G., Katz, N.P., Bayley, J., and Fossel, A.H. (1995). Degenerative lumbar spinal stenosis: diagnostic value of the history and physical examination. *Arthritis and Rheumatism*, **38**, 1236–41.

Katz, J.N., Lipson, S.J., Chang, L.C., Levine, S.A., Fossel, A.H., and Liang, M.H. (1996). Seven- to 10-year outcome of decompressive surgery for degenerative lumbar stenosis. *Spine*, **21**, 92–7.

Kostuik, J.P., Harrington, I., Alexander, D., Rand, W., and Evans, D. (1986). Cauda equina syndrome and lumbar disc herniation. *Journal of Bone and Joint Surgery*, **68A**, 386–91.

Lavis, J.N., Malter, A., Anderson, G.M., *et al.* (1988). Trends in hospital use for mechanical neck and back problems in Ontario and the United States: discretionary care in different health care systems. *Canadian Medical Association Journal*, **158**, 29–35

Lavsky-Shulan, M., Wallace, R.B., Kohout, F.J., Lemke, J.H., Morris, M.C., and Smith, I.M. (1985). Prevalence and functional correlates of low back pain in the elderly: the Iowa 65 + rural health study. *Journal of the American Geriatrics Society*, **33**, 23–8.

Lees, F. and Turner, J.W.A. (1963). Natural history and prognosis of cervical spondylosis. *British Medical Journal*, **2**, 1607–19.

O'Duffy, J.D. (1997). Spinal stenosis. Development of the lesion, clinical classification, and presentation. In *The adult spine* (2nd edn) (ed. J.W. Frymoyer, T.B. Ducker, N.M. Hadler, *et al.*), pp. 769–79. Raven Press, New York.

Papageorgiou, A.C., MacFarlane, G.J., Thomas, E., Croft, P.R., Jayson, M.I.V., and Silman, A.J. (1997). Psychosocial factors in the workplace—do they predict new episodes of low back pain? *Spine*, **22**, 1137–42.

Quebec Task Force on Spinal Disorders (1987). Scientific approach to the assessment and management of activity-related spinal disorders. *Spine*, **12** (Supplement 1), S1–S59.

Renner, J.B. (1990). Pelvic insufficiency fractures. *Arthritis and Rheumatism*, **33**, 426–30.

Revel, M., Payan, D., Vallee, C., *et al.* (1993). Automated percutaneous lumbar discectomy versus chemonucleolysis in the treatment of sciatica. *Spine*, **18**, 1–7.

Sox, H.C. (1994). Practice guidelines: 1994. *American Journal of Medicine*, **97**, 205–7.

Spaccarelli, K.C. (1996). Lumbar and caudal epidural corticosteroid injections. *Mayo Clinical Proceedings*, **71**, 169–78.

Suarez-Almazor, M.E., Belseck, E., Russell, A.S., and Mackel, J.V. (1997). Use of lumbar radiographs for the early diagnosis of low back pain. *Journal of the American Medical Association*, **277**, 1782–6.

Swezey, R.L. (1996). Outcomes for lumbar stenosis. *Journal of Clinical Rheumatology*, **2**, 129–34.

Taylor, J., Johnston, R.A., and Caird, F.I. (1991). Surgical treatment of cervical spondylotic myelopathy in elderly patients. *Age and Ageing*, **20**, 407–12.

Trojan, D.A., Pouchot, J., Pokrupa, R., *et al.* (1992). Diagnosis and treatment of ossification of the posterior longitudinal ligament of the spine: report of eight cases and literature review. *American Journal of Medicine*, **92**, 296–306.

Turner, J.A., *et al.* (1992). Surgery for lumbar spinal stenosis. Attempted meta-analysis of the literature. *Spine*, **17**, 1–8.

Turner, J.A., LeResche, L., Von Korf, M., and Ehrlich, K. (1998). Back pain in primary care. Patient characteristics, content of initial visit and short-term outcomes. *Spine*, **23**, 463–9.

van Tulder, M.W., Assendelft, W.J.J., Koes, B.W., and Bouter, L.M. (1997). Conservative treatment of acute and chronic nonspecific low back pain. *Spine*, **22**, 2128–56.

Volinn, E. (1994). Why does geographic variation in health care practices matter? *Spine*, **19**, 2092S–2100S.

Von Korff, M., Barlow, W., Cherkin, D., and Deyo, R.A. (1994). Effects of practice style in managing back pain. *Annals of Internal Medicine*, **121**, 187–95.

Weber, H. (1983). Lumbar disc herniation. A controlled, prospective study with 10 years observation. *Spine*, **8**, 131–40.

Williams, M.E. and Hadler, N.M. (1983). The illness as the focus of geriatric medicine. *New England Journal of Medicine*, **308**, 1357–60.

13.3 Osteoarthritis

Lyn Williamson and Paul Wordsworth

Introduction

Osteoarthritis is the most common disease of joints and the most important cause of pain and disability in elderly people. In the ageing population it is a growing public health problem with increasing direct costs from drugs, physical therapies, and surgery as well as costs upon the lives of carers.

Definition

The term osteoarthritis describes a heterogeneous group of conditions which share common radiographic and pathological features. There is no consensus about its definition because there are constantly changing concepts of osteoarthritis. A satisfactory working definition is a disorder of synovial joints characterized by loss of articular cartilage and a periarticular bone response.

Epidemiology

Osteoarthritis occurs throughout the world (Cooper 1994). Prevalence data come from autopsy studies, radiographic studies, and clinical surveys. Most epidemiological studies quote radiographic data which vary depending on which joints have been radiographed and which populations studied. However, rates in Europe and the United States are similar, with radiographic changes of osteoarthritis in hands varying between studies from 60 to 70 per cent at the age of 65 years, and increasing to 85 per cent by the age of 80 years. The sex ratio (female to male) varies from 1.5:1 to 4:1. Knee and hand disease are more frequent in women, and hip disease has roughly equal frequency. Prevalence is greatest in the hands and affects the spine, feet, knees, and hips in decreasing order of frequency.

There is poor correlation between radiographic changes and symptoms, with less than 30 per cent of patients experiencing symptoms from the joints exhibiting radiographic changes of osteoarthritis. Symptoms are three times more common in women than men for similar radiographic changes. The exception is the hip where there is good correlation between radiographic changes and symptoms.

Disability is related to symptoms and not to radiographic changes. However, in the absence of other objective markers of disease, most clinical studies have used radiographic changes as surrogate markers for clinical change. This may substantially overestimate the size of the clinical problem.

Table 1 Risk factors for osteoarthritis

Increasing age
Female sex
Obesity
Genetic predisposition
Previous trauma
Occupation (e.g. farmers, miners)
Prior inflammatory joint disease
Congenital and developmental bone and joint disorders
Metabolic disorders (e.g. calcium pyrophosphate deposition disease, haemochromatosis)

In general the prevalence of osteoarthritis is remarkably similar in most populations. However, there are certain exceptions including (a) a lower prevalence of hip osteoarthritis in black and Oriental populations than Caucasians, and (b) lower frequency of polyarticular osteoarthritis of the hands in Africans than in Europeans. In certain areas of the world endemic forms of osteoarthritis exist for which no clear explanation has been found. A range of possible explanations (mycotoxins, abnormalities of trace elements, genetic factors) have been advanced to explain the early onset of widespread osteoarthritis of Kashin–Beck disease in Siberia and northern China, and Mseleni disease of the hip in Natal. There may be important clues to be found in these unusual populations but a number of risk factors for osteoarthritis have already been identified (Table 1).

Risk factors

The development of osteoarthritis at a particular joint site depends upon a generalized predisposition to the condition and biomechanical abnormalities that act at specific joints. These effects are frequently synergistic.

Increasing age

This is the most powerful risk factor. There is a progressive increase in the prevalence rates with increasing age so that osteoarthritis affecting at least one joint is almost universal by the age of 75 years. By the fourth decade up to one-third of individuals will demonstrate radiographic osteoarthritis in at least one joint, but polyarticular disease is rare before the age of 45 years.

Female sex

There is marked female preponderance, particularly in polyarticular osteoarthritis which presents after the menopause. Women who have undergone hysterectomy also have an increased incidence of osteoarthritis. Unfortunately, attempts to retard the development of osteoarthritis by postmenopausal hormonal replacement therapy have been unsuccessful.

Genetic factors

Familial clustering of generalized osteoarthritis is well recognized and highlights the importance of genetic factors. In the 1950s Stecher suggested that nodal osteoarthritis was a dominant trait in women and recessive in men (Stecher 1955). A more likely explanation is polygenic inheritance of susceptibility interacting with non-genetic influences.

Certain forms of monogenic disease affecting the components of articular cartilage (chondrodysplasia) can cause severe and premature osteoarthritis. In some of these the nature of the underlying mutations has been elucidated: multiple epiphyseal dysplasia (type IX collagen and cartilage oligomeric matrix protein), spondyloepiphyseal dysplasia (type II and XI collagen), metaphyseal dysplasia of the Schmid type (type X collagen), and Stickler's syndrome (type II and XI collagen). In addition other rare familial forms of osteoarthritis have been described with very mild evidence of underlying dysplasia and linkage to the cartilage collagen gene COL2AI. How relevant these observations are to sporadic and familial osteoarthritis is not yet clear. However, an important genetic component can be inferred from twin studies which suggest that 39 to 65 per cent of osteoarthritis in the general population can be attributed to genetic factors (Spector et al. 1996). In large-joint osteoarthritis affecting the hips or knees and requiring total joint replacement, it has been estimated that the risk of siblings of affected patients requiring similar surgery is three times that of the age- and sex-matched general population.

Obesity

There is a strong link between obesity and osteoarthritis of the knee and, to a lesser extent, of the hip and fingers. The Framingham Study showed that obesity predicted the development of osteoarthritis, both symptomatic and asymptomatic, up to 30 years later. Those in the highest quintile for body mass index at baseline examination had a 1.9 (male) to 3.2 (female) relative risk of developing severe osteoarthritis in the ensuing 30 years. Moreover, the same group have shown a reduction in the progression of osteoarthritis after weight reduction in women (Felson et al. 1992). As the prevalence of knee and hand osteoarthritis is higher in women it is not yet known whether the association is due to excess mechanical loading or unknown metabolic factors or, more likely, a combination of both.

Major joint trauma

Osteoarthritis of the knee is a common consequence of ligament damage, meniscal tears, or meniscectomy. Major injury, particularly

fractures, alter mechanical function and may predispose to osteoarthritis of affected joints. Most commonly, fractures of the femoral shaft, tibia, humerus, and scaphoid lead to osteoarthritis of the hip, ankle, shoulder, and wrist respectively. Progression to osteoarthritis of the knee following meniscectomy is most pronounced in those who additionally exhibit nodal osteoarthritis in the hands, highlighting the interaction between genetic predisposition and extrinsic factors.

Occupation

Occupations requiring repetitive use of particular joint groups lead to a high incidence of osteoarthritis in those joints. Cotton workers in the United States develop hand osteoarthritis, miners and workers in other occupations that involve regular knee bending develop knee osteoarthritis, ballet dancers develop ankle osteoarthritis, and boxers develop metocarpophalangeal joint osteoarthritis. Many studies have found a strong association between farmers and hip osteoarthritis with up to a tenfold increased prevalence compared with the general male population of similar age. Croft et al. (1992) found other heavy manual workers who regularly lifted weights of more than 25 kg daily had increased risk of isolated hip osteoarthritis. Interestingly, the risk was not as great as found in farmers and the reason for this is unclear.

Hypermobility

Hypermobility, both in the presence and absence of an identifiable collagen abnormality, leads to a wide variety of overuse injuries as well as osteoarthritis, although the strength of the association is not well characterized. Joint deformities and periarticular pain are common in Ehlers–Danlos syndrome but this correlates poorly with osteoarthritic changes in the joints.

Other diseases

Diabetes, hypertension, and hyperuricaemia are all associated with increased osteoarthritis independently of obesity. In addition there is an increased prevalence of diffuse idiopathic skeletal hyperostosis in diabetics.

Cigarette smoking

There may be a negative association between cigarette smoking and osteoarthritis, even after adjusting for body weight.

Osteoporosis

It is intriguing that at the hip, but not at other joints, there is a negative association between osteoporosis and osteoarthritis. Again the underlying mechanism is unknown, although the opposite effects of obesity on osteoarthritis and osteoporosis may contribute and it has been suggested that buttressing of the femoral neck by bony hypertrophy of osteoarthritis may be relevant. A negative association between fractures of the femoral neck and hip osteoarthritis has been suspected for some time although bone mineral density studies have produced conflicting results. Another possible explanation might be that weak less rigid bone may protect the joint from excessive impact loading.

Classification

It is helpful to classify osteoarthritis both by pattern of joint involvement and aetiology.

Primary (idiopathic) osteoarthritis

It is not known whether these are separate diseases or whether they represent a spectrum of severity of the same disease entity.

Localized osteoarthritis

This affects one or two joint sites, typically the distal interphalangeal joints of the hands, the thumb base, knees, hips, and intervertebral facet joints.

Generalized osteoarthritis (primary generalized osteoarthritis; generalized nodal osteoarthritis)

This presents predominantly in middle-aged women, characteristically affecting three or more joint groups; distal interphalangeal joints are counted as one group. There is often a stuttering onset with the appearance of Heberden's and Bouchard's nodes as posterolateral outgrowths from the distal interphalangeal and proximal interphalangeal joints respectively. These can be painful and inflamed as they form, but become painless with time. Inflammation may be episodic, associated with hyaluronate-rich periarticular cysts in the early phase. There is a strong familial association and later in life affected women often develop osteoarthritis of the knees.

Erosive (inflammatory) osteoarthritis

This condition also affects middle-aged women. It presents with an acute inflammatory arthritis in the finger interphalangeal joints associated with erosions and osteophytes, and must be distinguished from rheumatoid arthritis. Symptoms settle spontaneously over the course of a few years often leaving residual joint deformity and ankylosis (Cobby *et al.* 1990).

Secondary osteoarthritis

Virtually any joint insult can be complicated by the development of secondary osteoarthritis. The same clinical features occur as in primary osteoarthritis but with an identifiable cause and possibly a different distribution of joint involvement. Atypical joint involvement should prompt a search for underlying disease processes such as gout or haemochromatosis which may require specific treatment. Secondary osteoarthritis accounts for less than 20 per cent of osteoarthritis. Patients are on average 10 years younger than those with primary osteoarthritis. Important secondary causes to consider are included in Table 2.

Pathogenesis

Osteoarthritis affects the whole joint, but primarily the articular cartilage and subchondral bone, with mild inflammation of the synovial membrane. It is not known whether the initial abnormality in primary osteoarthritis occurs in the cartilage or bone. In most cases of secondary osteoarthritis the primary defect is in the cartilage.

Table 2 Classification of primary (idiopathic), secondary, and neuropathic osteoarthritis

Primary (idiopathic)

Localized
Hands: Heberden's nodes, Bouchard's nodes, first CMC joint
Feet: hallux valgus, hammer toes, talonavicular arthritis
Knees: medial, lateral, patellofemoral compartments
Hips: superior, medial, and concentric cartilage loss
Spine: apophyseal joints, intervertebral discs (spondylitis)

Generalized
Including three or more of the above sites

Erosive (inflammatory)
Middle-aged women: inflammatory arthritis or interphalangeal joints; erosions and osteophytes on radiographs

Secondary

Mechanical
Obesity
Previous trauma
Congenital or developmental disorders, e.g. Perthes' disease
Genetic defects, e.g. epiphyseal dysplasias, Stickler's syndrome
Occupation, e.g. farmers (hip), coal miners (knee)
Leg length discrepancy
Hypermobility

Previous inflammatory bone or joint disease
Rheumatoid arthritis
Infection
Paget's disease
Gout

Metabolic and endocrine
CPPD (knees, wrists)
Haemochromatosis (second and third MCP, wrist, knee, hip, ankle, shoulder)
Hyperparathyroidism (cysts): associated with chronic renal failure
Hypothyroidism: associated with CPPD
Diabetes
Acromegaly

Neuropathic
Diabetes
Syphilis
Peripheral neuropathy/spinal cord trauma
Leprosy
Syringomyelia

CMC, carpometacarpal; CPPD, calcium pyrophosphate deposition disease; MCP, metacarpophalangeal.

Defects have been studied at macroscopic, microscopic, and biochemical levels. Currently much research is directed at the biochemistry of osteoarthritis in the hope of developing new therapies at this level.

Osteoarthritis reflects a disturbance in the homeostasis of synthesis and degradation of articular cartilage. Cartilage consists mainly of collagen (chiefly type II), highly charged proteoglycan molecules, and chondrocytes. Type II collagen accounts for 50 per cent of the dry weight of cartilage protein. The collagen provides a tight three-dimensional framework for the highly hydrophilic proteoglycan molecules. The swelling pressure of the proteoglycans coupled with the tensile strength of the collagen fibres give articular cartilage its unique combination of shock-absorbing and stress-bearing functions. Chondrocytes are secretory cells which can be induced into either anabolic or catabolic pathways by cytokines. In addition their metabolism can be modulated by direct mechanical loading.

In osteoarthritis the earliest macroscopic changes in cartilage is an increase in water content, associated with weakening of the surface type II collagen network which may be due to factors such as ageing, trauma, biomechanical alterations, ligamentous damage and muscle atrophy, or inherent collagen weakness. This leads to a decrease in the proteoglycan concentration and changes in the biomechanical properties of the cartilage, increased permeability to water, and decreased ability to rebound from a deforming load. Remodelling of the subchondral bone leads to advancement of the region of calcified cartilage, and decrease in volume of articular cartilage. Proliferation of cartilage at the joint margins followed by enchondral ossification leads to osteophyte formation.

The chondrocytes, under cytokine stimulation, chiefly interleukin 1 and tumour necrosis factor, increase synthesis of degradative enzymes, which include matrix metalloproteinases (collagenase, gelatinase, stromolysin) and aggrecanase. These enzymes degrade the structural components of articular cartilage. This destructive activity is limited by at least two inhibitors: tissue inhibitor of metalloproteinase and plasminogen activator inhibitor-1. Both inhibitors are synthesized by the chondrocyte under the stimulation of growth factors, primarily transforming growth factor-β.

The chondrocytes in osteoarthritic cartilage become very active metabolically, producing increasing quantities of collagen and proteoglycans. The half-life of proteoglycan is a few weeks, but that of type II collagen is many years. Normal reparative synthesis increases initially and these homeostatic mechanisms maintain reasonable joint function for years. Eventually, however, the system fails, proteoglycan synthesis tails off, cartilage becomes irreparably damaged, and osteoarthritis develops.

Macroscopic changes reflect those seen on radiographs which are still the most widely used way of following progress in osteoarthritis. The articular cartilage softens, and the surface fibrillates, fissures, thins, and develops focal erosions. These become more diffuse and finally there is complete denudation of the cartilage (joint space narrowing). At the base of the fissures and erosions there is new cartilage and new bone formation (subchondral sclerosis). Extrusion of synovial fluid under pressure between the cartilage clefts leads to formation of subchondral bone cysts. Osteophytes form in non-weight-bearing areas at the joint margins. They are outgrowths of cartilage covered in bone which reflect the repair and remodelling process taking place.

Clinical features

History

Pain

Osteoarthritic joints are frequently asymptomatic but pain is the most common presenting complaint. This is usually of insidious onset with an aching quality, localized to the involved joint. Initially it occurs after activity, but rest and night pain occur as the disease progresses.

Age, sex, joint site involved, and psychological factors influence the reporting of pain in osteoarthritis. For given radiographic changes, women are three times more likely than men to suffer pain. Lawrence *et al.* (1966) found that almost all patients with radiographic hip osteoarthritis experience pain, compared with 40 per cent of those with radiographic knee osteoarthritis and 25 per cent with hand osteoarthritis. Summers *et al.* (1988) found severity of pain correlated with level of depression in patients with hip or knee osteoarthritis. Since articular cartilage is aneural, the joint pain in osteoarthritis must arise from other structures.

Bone pain could arise from several causes: microfractures in the subchondral bone, stretching of nerves in the periosteum covering osteophytes, and also intraosseous hypertension. This last factor is thought to be caused by venous outflow obstruction from thickened subchondral trabeculae.

Muscle pain with weakness, aching, and tenderness of the muscles which serve the affected joints is common. Pain from the damaged joint may be referred to the muscles around the joint. Conversely, muscle strengthening exercises relieve pain which suggest that muscular dysfunction may be an important cause of osteoarthritis pain.

Synovitis, particularly in advanced osteoarthritis, may be due to phagocytosis of shards of cartilage and bone fragments, soluble matrix macromolecules (proteoglycans), or crystals (calcium pyrophosphate and calcium hydroxyapatite). It is typically mild and may make only a small overall contribution to pain in osteoarthritis.

Central pain mechanisms are relevant to all chronic pain syndromes. The association of pain and depression is important when considering treatment for elderly patients among whom depression is not uncommonly masked.

Associated syndromes, including fibromyalgia and chronic ligamentous injuries, commonly coexist with osteoarthritis.

Stiffness

In contrast with rheumatoid arthritis, morning stiffness with osteoarthritis is typically short-lived. There is often brief stiffness after periods of immobility such as rising from a chair ('gelling'). There are no systemic symptoms.

Loss of movement

Movement of the joints may be restricted by pain, muscle spasm, or by mechanical obstruction due to joint incongruity, osteophytes, or loose bodies. Contracture of the joint capsule and the surrounding soft tissues may also contribute in more long-standing cases.

Instability

Many patients complain that they feel unsteady and are afraid to go out because the affected joint has 'given way' on them. This usually reflects arthrogenous inhibition of muscle contraction (see Chapter 19.1) or muscle wasting rather than ligamentous instability or joint damage.

Examination

1. Joint tenderness associated with bony or soft tissue swelling. Tenderness may be demonstrated along the joint line or in association with periarticular structures such as tendons and ligaments.

2. Crepitus (the sensation of roughened articular bone surfaces rubbing against each other on movement of the joint).

3. Gross deformity, instability, and subluxation may be present in the later stages.

4. Ankylosis (bony fusion) may occur.

5. Periarticular muscle atrophy may result from chronic disuse due to pain.

6. Signs of inflammation are often not present and synovitis is uncommon.

Natural history

The condition evolves slowly and there have been few prospective studies of outcome. Progression is neither linear nor inevitable, and there is wide variation between patients and between different joints of the same patient. In most people the disease evolves over many years with remissions and exacerbations. There can be periods of months or years with few or no symptoms punctuated by 'flares' which sometimes mimic other forms of acute inflammation such as gout, sepsis, or rheumatoid arthritis. Flares can last days, weeks, or months. Symptomatic as well as radiographic improvement have been demonstrated in both hip and finger osteoarthritis.

Rapidly destructive osteoarthritis, in which joint changes occur in months rather than years, affects a minority of patients, and there is often an identifiable underlying cause such as a crystal arthropathy.

Investigation

Blood tests

In primary osteoarthritis, blood tests, including erythrocyte sedimentation rate and rheumatoid factor, are normal but it must be remembered that a proportion of healthy people aged over 65 years have a weakly positive rheumatoid factor. Spector *et al.* (1997), using monoclonal antibody immunoassay for C-reactive protein and measuring in what has previously been considered the normal range, found modestly raised levels in women with early osteoarthritis. The higher levels predicted those whose disease progressed over the subsequent 4 years, suggesting low-grade inflammation even in early disease.

In secondary osteoarthritis, a few specific blood tests are available to help identify causes: raised iron and ferritin in haemochromatosis; raised calcium and parathyroid hormone in hyperparathyroidism; raised serum urate in gout; low thyroxine and raised thyroid-stimulating hormone in hypothyroidism; abnormal glucose tolerance, low vitamin B_{12}, or positive syphilis serology with neuropathic joints.

Synovial fluid

This is sterile, highly viscous, clear, and yellow with a white cell count of less than $2000/mm^2$. In elderly people, osteoarthritis can be complicated by attacks of gout or pseudogout. During such attacks, synovial fluid contains urate or calcium pyrophosphate dihydrate crystals as well as large numbers of polymorphonuclear cells.

Cartilage degradation products such as keratan sulphate and pyridinoline cross-links are increased in synovial fluid and urine but are too non-specific and variable to be used for diagnosis or to follow progression.

Imaging

There have been many advances in imaging technology which can be divided into those which demonstrate anatomy (plain radiographs, CT, and ultrasound) and those, such as magnetic resonance imaging (MRI), which show both anatomical and physiological features.

As radiographic changes are common in the healthy elderly population, it is important to look for changes of coexistent disease such as rheumatoid arthritis or fracture. As already emphasized, radiographic changes do not always correlate well with symptoms. None the less, plain radiographs are readily available and fairly inexpensive and remain the most widely used investigation for diagnosis and following disease progression. At the hip, two main radiographic patterns are described: 'hypertrophic', where there is joint space narrowing, extensive subchondral sclerosis, and marked osteophyte formation, and 'atrophic', where there is joint space narrowing and destruction of subchondral bone in association with a much smaller bone response and few osteophytes.

CT is very useful for visualizing joints whose axes lie in the axial plain such as intervertebral facet joints, shoulders, and some of the small joints in the wrist. Three-dimensional images can be reconstructed from multiple scans and are particularly useful for demonstrating fractures.

Ultrasound is useful for visualizing joint effusions, synovitis, and periarticular structures such as tendons, bursae, and Baker's cysts at inaccessible sites such as the hip, especially if aspiration and injection are required.

MRI has many advantages over other forms of imaging as it can produce high-resolution images in any spatial plain with both anatomical and physiological information. It is the investigation of choice when evaluating internal joint derangement (knee, hip, shoulder), bone and joint infection, rotator cuff lesions, and other periarticular disorders.

Specific joint features

Hands

Fingers

The distal interphalangeal joints are most commonly affected but similar swellings appear at the proximal interphalangeal joints (Fig. 1). The superolateral bony outgrowths (Heberden's nodes and Bouchard's nodes respectively) are seen four times more commonly in women than in men. They may be tender and inflamed as they form and can be associated with cysts which contain a thick colourless fluid rich in hyaluron. Later the swellings become painless but may be associated with some loss of flexion, medial or lateral angulations, and occasionally interphalangeal joint fusion. Patients have difficulties with activities which require fine finger movements but rarely complain of severe pain.

Thumb

The first carpometacarpal joint is the second most commonly affected joint and often the first to be painful. The thumb has a limited range of movement with an associated tender prominence (osteophyte) at the base of the metacarpus which leads to 'squaring' of the hand. Patients complain both of pain around the wrist and difficulty with

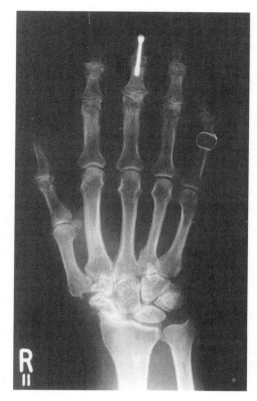

Fig. 1 Generalized nodal osteoarthritis with (a) surgical fusion of painful interphalangeal joints, (b) first carpometacarpal joint osteoarthritis with 'squaring' of the base of the thumb, and (c) osteoarthritis of the radiocarpal joint secondary to an old scaphoid fracture.

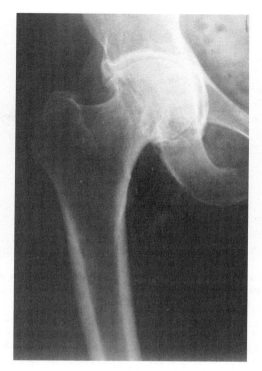

Fig. 2 Concentric osteoarthritis of the hip with marginal osteophyte formation and subchondral sclerosis

opening jars and other activities involving a pinch grip. If the trapezioscaphoid joint is also involved the pain and swelling is often felt on the volar aspect of the wrist.

Hip

Hip osteoarthritis has a roughly equal sex incidence and develops over a wide age range, depending upon aetiology. By the age of 80 years, 10 per cent of the population have radiographic osteoarthritis of the hip. In the younger age group, predisposing factors include congenital dislocation of the hip, Perthes' disease, acetabular dysplasia, and leg length discrepancies. In older people, except where previous femoral shaft fracture or occupational exposure are factors, hip osteoarthritis is usually idiopathic.

Three patterns of hip osteoarthritis are described: superolateral (60 per cent), medial pole (25 per cent), and concentric (15 per cent) (Fig. 2). There is much research into the biomechanics of the hip joint and the extent to which minor changes of the neck–shaft angle can predispose to the different types of osteoarthritis. It is difficult to explain but interesting that hip osteoarthritis is much less associated with obesity than is knee osteoarthritis.

Pain on walking is the major symptom from hip osteoarthritis. It is typically felt in the groin or inner thigh but may also be felt over the greater trochanter or buttock, in which case it must be distinguished from trochanteric bursitis and lumbar spondylosis or sacroiliitis. Twenty per cent of patients feel pain on the medial knee, anterior thigh, or buttocks.

On examination there is decreased range of movement, initially affecting internal rotation. With disease progression all movements are affected but flexion is relatively well preserved until late. There is associated muscle wasting around the joint and patients have an antalgic gait, and the pelvis dips down when attempts are made to stand on the affected leg. There can be both true (bone and cartilage loss) and apparent (flexion contracture) shortening of the affected leg. Patients frequently limp thereby placing excess stress on other lower limb joints (most commonly knees) or back.

The natural history of hip osteoarthritis is very variable, most patients progressing slowly. There is a small subset of patients with aggressive disease who progress from a near normal situation to severe joint destruction in a matter of months. Conversely, spontaneous healing has been demonstrated in up to 5 per cent of patients awaiting arthroplasty. Concentric disease and a hypertrophic pattern are associated with a better prognosis than other forms of disease.

Knee

Osteoarthritis can affect the medial and lateral tibiofemoral compartments and the patellofemoral joint (Fig. 3). Each area can be affected alone or in any combination, with isolated medial compartment being the most common followed by medial plus patellofemoral disease.

Examination shows deformity, crepitus on movement, and quadriceps wasting. In the later stages, bony destruction, ligamentous, and capsular damage may lead to instability. Weight-bearing radiographs will demonstrate cartilage loss. Bilateral medial compartment disease

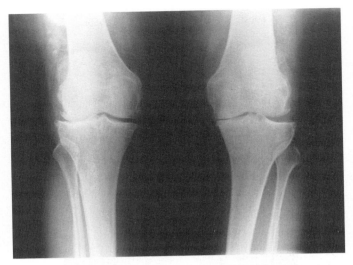

Fig. 3 Severe osteoarthritis of both knees with large osteophytes and synovial enchondromatosis.

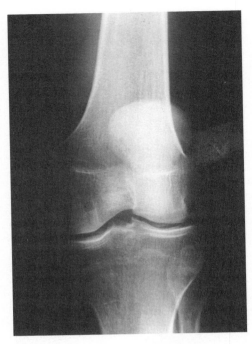

Fig. 4 Chondrocalcinosis in the knee secondary to moderate osteoarthritis.

leads to a progressive varus deformity (bow legs) but valgus deformity can also occur. Once a varus or valgus angulation has developed, significant mechanical strain will be imposed on the corresponding compartment, exacerbating the damage.

Patellofemoral disease can occur in isolation and causes difficulty kneeling, rising from chairs, and climbing stairs. It may only be seen on the lateral radiograph or sky-line views.

A rare complication of both hip and knee osteoarthritis is osteonecrosis which is associated with a sudden increase in severe pain and subsequent collapse of the femoral head and femoral condyles, respectively. Joint sepsis and tibial fracture should be considered in all patients with acutely worsening pain. 'Pseudogout' (calcium pyrophosphate deposition disease) also often affects the osteoarthritic knee and can in turn cause secondary osteoarthritis. Conversely, osteoarthritis can lead to calcium deposition (chondrocalcinosis) (Fig. 4) which is often asymptomatic.

Spine

Degeneration occurs both at the facet joints which are true synovial joints and in the discs and vertebral bodies (spondylosis) (Fig. 5). The processes are closely linked and usually coexist in the same areas of the spine. Radiographic changes of degenerative disc disease are very common and there is little correlation between symptoms and radiographic changes. The cervical spine (especially around C5) and the lumbar spine (L3–5) are most frequently affected. Prior trauma can predispose to severe spinal osteoarthritis and disc degeneration at the site of damage.

Low back pain is frequently exacerbated by standing, repeated bending and lifting, and other specific activities. Acute disc prolapse with nerve root entrapment is uncommon in individuals older than 60 years, but degenerative changes in the disc and facet joints may combine to produce spinal stenosis. This may be central, affecting the spinal cord or cauda equina, or lateral in which case the nerve roots may be compromised in the neural exit foramina. Spinal stenosis may cause myelopathy or radicular symptoms which may be exacerbated by posture or exercise and mimic peripheral vascular

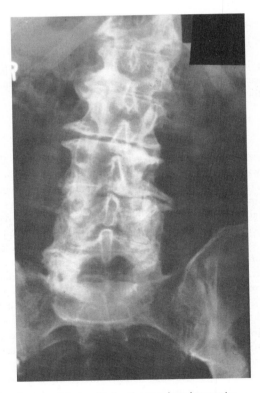

Fig. 5 Lumbar spondylosis with florid osteophyte buttressing.

Table 3 Management of osteoarthritis

Non-pharmacological measures
Patient education
Weight loss
Occupational therapy: footwear, walking aids, home aids
Range of motion and strengthening exercises
Aerobic exercises
Acupuncture

Pharmacological measures
Simple analgesics (paracetamol, codeine)
Topical analgesics (0.025% capsaicin cream)
Oral non-steroidal anti-inflammatory drugs
Intra-articular steroid injections
Closed tidal joint lavage

Surgery
Arthroscopic debridement and joint lavage
Osteotomy (joint realignment: upper tibia)
Total joint arthroplasty (hip and knee)
Resection arthroplasty (first MTP joint, trapeziumectomy)
Arthrodesis (ankle and mid-foot)

MTP, metatarsophalangeal.

Table 4 Management of osteoarthritis in elderly patients

Correct hearing and visual problems
Warm clothing
Use walking stick at correct height with correct hand
Light-weight knee support
Rubber grip at base of walking stick
Heel raise
Wide-fitting shoes with shock-absorbing insoles
Cushioned training shoes for early osteoarthritis
Helpful well-informed carer
Note early asymptomatic osteoarthritis in daughter
Encourage weight loss if necessary
Regular enjoyable aerobic exercise

disease (neurogenic intermittent claudication). Nocturnal pain in the legs in the early hours, waking the subject and eased by walking about, can also be a feature of lumbar spinal stenosis.

Diffuse idiopathic skeletal hyperostosis (Forrestier's disease)

This is a bone-forming condition in which ossification occurs at skeletal sites subjected to stress (Resnick *et al.* 1978). Diffuse idiopathic skeletal hyperostosis occurs in 12 per cent of people over 65 years and is associated with diabetes, obesity, hypertension, and gout. It occurs most frequently in the thoracic spine where it can lead to symptoms of pain and decreased movement. Spinal stiffness may be severe but the condition can be distinguished from ankylosing spondylitis by the absence of sacroiliitis. Rarely in the cervical spine it can cause dysphagia.

Radiographic changes show 'flowing' ossification of the anterior longitudinal ligament connecting at least four contiguous vertebrae, often more prominent on the right-hand side. Bone mineralization is normal. Ossification can also occur at multiple tendinous or ligamentous sites (entheses) in the appendicular skeleton.

Management

Osteoarthritis has an unpredictable, variable outcome. Treatment is aimed at reducing pain, maintaining mobility, minimizing disability, and, if possible, limiting progression of the disease (Hochberg *et al.* 1995) (Tables 3 and 4).

Education

Education of patients and their families, friends, and carers is important and has been found to be cost effective in the treatment of significant osteoarthritis. Lorig *et al.* (1993) found that patients who attended self-management programmes reported decreased pain, fewer visits to the doctor, and an improvement in overall quality of life. Weinberger *et al.* (1993) demonstrated that a bimonthly telephone call from a trained lay interviewer was as effective as a non-steroidal anti-inflammatory drug in reducing joint pain. Both studies underline the importance of psychosocial factors in the cause of chronic osteoarthritic pain.

General measures

The general health and social support of the patient should be optimized. Obese patients should be encouraged to lose weight. Vision and hearing should be corrected as far as possible. Depression should be identified and treated. Any unnecessary medication should be stopped.

Physical measures

1. Local application of heat reduces pain and stiffness and a hot bath or shower is often the most convenient and effective way of applying heat.

2. Occupational therapy assessment and provision of aids may be valuable in reducing the patient's functional limitations which are likely to include problems with toileting, walking, dressing, and bathing.

3. Instability and malalignment of joints probably accelerate the progression of disease and should be corrected where possible (e.g. with wedged insoles or knee supports with three-point fixation).

4. Patients with knee and hip osteoarthritis should avoid prolonged kneeling, standing, or squatting.

5. Shock-absorbing insoles or cushioned training shoes help to reduce the pain of knee, hip, and spinal osteoarthritis.

6. Joint splints may decrease pain and thereby improve function.

7. Walking sticks, crutches, and frames used correctly greatly aid mobility and improve patient confidence as well as safety. Walking sticks should be at the correct height (handle level with the wrist) and held in the correct hand—the contralateral hand for hip osteoarthritis and the ipsilateral hand in knee osteoarthritis. Patients with bilateral disease of the knee and/or hip may need to use crutches or a walking frame.

Physical therapies

Non-exercise physiotherapy using diathermy, ultrasound, and laser treatment has been shown to be no more effective than placebo.

Isometric exercise

Exercises designed to maintain range of motion, and strengthen muscles surrounding a joint, have been shown to improve pain and function. In a randomized controlled trial of patients with knee osteoarthritis, strengthening the quadriceps and hamstrings by an isometric programme decreased joint pain by an amount comparable with that achieved by non-steroidal anti-inflammatory drugs. The control group performed isotonic 'range-of-motion' exercises, had no gains in muscle strength, and their knee pain worsened during the 12-week study period (Feinberg et al. 1992).

Aerobic exercise

Minor (1994) found that patients with lower-limb osteoarthritis (feet, hip, and/or knee) showed significant improvement in pain, 50-ft walking time, depression, anxiety, and aerobic capacity after a 12-week period of aerobic walking and aerobic aquatics. It is important that individual patients select an exercise programme that they find enjoyable, and easy to accomplish.

Transcutaneous electrical nerve stimulation

Transcutaneous electrical nerve stimulation may be useful for short-term pain control, particularly for low back pain caused by osteoarthritis of the lumbar spine.

Acupuncture

Acupuncture may be useful in controlling osteoarthritic pain, particularly knee osteoarthritis. In a controlled study of patients waiting for knee arthroplasty, Christensen (1992) showed acupuncture improved pain in the treatment group compared with controls. Monthly treatments maintained pain control for at least a year to such a degree that 25 per cent of patients withdrew their names for surgery after 1 year of treatment. The treatment is safe and simple and needs to be studied further, especially for elderly patients who may have problems with drug treatment and interactions.

Drugs

First-line treatment is paracetamol (acetaminophen) which Bradley et al. (1991) showed to be as effective as ibuprofen in controlling pain. Paracetamol should be used in a dose of up to 4 g daily.

Non-steroidal anti-inflammatory drug toxicity (gastrointestinal haemorrhage, renal failure, heart failure) account for 15 per cent of acute medical admissions of elderly people and so should be used with caution. At present the choice of non-steroidal anti-inflammatory drug is largely determined by cost and side-effect profile. Ibuprofen has the best gastrointestinal side-effect profile and sulindac the best renal side-effect profile. Non-steroidal anti-inflammatory drugs may be appropriate in patients with a significant inflammatory component, but are best avoided if there is a history of renal impairment or gastrointestinal symptoms.

Capsaicin cream which depletes the local sensory nerves of substance P may reduce joint pain and tenderness when applied topically by patients with hand and knee osteoarthritis (Altman et al. 1994).

Intra-articular steroids can improve pain in selected patients but is less effective than in inflammatory arthropathies. Treatment can be repeated at 4- to 6-monthly intervals since there is no good evidence that it accelerates articular cartilage breakdown. Pain from associated soft tissue periarticular lesions may be amenable to treatment with physical measures or local corticosteroid injection (e.g. trochanteric bursitis and hip osteoarthritis, chronic knee medial collateral ligament strain).

Surgery

Tidal irrigation

This can be performed by either arthroscopy or needle lavage. Ike et al. (1992) showed an improvement in symptoms of pain for up to 14 weeks after arthroscopic tidal irrigation, compared with controls given standard medical treatment.

Arthroscopy

Arthroscopic removal of loose cartilage fragments can relieve pain and prevent joint locking. Chang et al. (1993) found that arthroscopic lavage and debridement was no better than closed-needle tidal irrigation at improving pain and function in knee osteoarthritis.

Joint replacement surgery

Joint replacement surgery has transformed the lives of patients with advanced hip and knee osteoarthritis but should be reserved for those in whom medical treatment has failed. In these patients, pain relief and a satisfactory functional result is obtained in 90 to 95 per cent undergoing primary arthroplasty. In advanced disease total hip replacement is the most cost-effective treatment for improving quality of life. Failure rates after total joint replacement are variable and occur in 10 to 30 per cent after 10 years. In general, revision arthroplasties are technically more difficult and less successful than primary joint replacements.

References

Altman, R.D., Anen, A., Holmburg, C.E., et al. (1994). Capsaicin cream 0.025 per cent as monotherapy for osteoarthritis: a double-blind trial. *Seminars in Arthritis and Rheumatology*, 23 (Supplement 3), 25–33.

Bradley, J.D., Brandt, K.D., Katz, B.P., et al. (1991). Comparison of an anti-inflammatory dose of ibuprofen, and analgesic dose of ibuprofen and acetominophen in the treatment of patients with osteoarthritis of the knee. *New England Journal of Medicine*, 325, 87.

Chang, R.W., Falconer, J., Stulberg, S.D., Arnold, W.J., Manheim, L.M., and Dyer, A.R. (1993). A randomised, controlled trial of arthroscopic surgery versus closed-needle lavage for patients with osteoarthritis of the knee. *Arthritis and Rheumatology*, 36, 289–96.

Christensen, B.V., Iuhl, I.U., Vilbek, H., *et al.* (1992). Acupuncture treatment of severe knee osteoarthrosis—a long term study. *Acta Anaesthesiologica Scandinavica*, 36, 519–25.

Cobby, M., Cushnaghan, J., Creamer, P., Dieppe, P., and Watt, I. (1990). Erosive OA—is it a separate disease entity? *Clinical Radiology*, 42, 258–63.

Cooper, C. (1994). The epidemiology of osteoarthritis. In *Rheumatology* (ed. J. Klippel and P. Dieppe), pp. 1–4. Mosby, New York.

Croft, P., Cooper, C., Wickham, C., and Coggon, D. (1992). Osteoarthritis of the hip and occupational activity. *Scandinavian Journal of Work, Environment and Health*, 18, 59–63.

Feinberg, J., Marzouk, D., Sokolek, C., Katz, B., Bradley, J., and Brandt, K. (1992). Effects of isometric versus range of motion exercise on joint pain and function in patients with knee osteoarthritis (abstract). *Arthritis and Rheumatology*, 35 (Supplement 5), R28.

Felson, D.T., Zhang, U., Anthony, J.M., *et al.* (1992). Weight loss reduces the risk for knee osteoarthritis in women. The Framingham Study. *Annals of Internal Medicine*, 116, 535–9.

Hochberg, M.C., Altman, R.D., Brandt, K.D., *et al.* (1995). Guidelines for the medical management of osteoarthritis. Parts 1 and 2. Osteoarthritis of the hip and knee. *Arthritis and Rheumatology*, 38, 1535–46.

Ike, R.W., Arnold, W.J., Rothschild, E.W., and Shaw, H.L. (1992). Tidal irrigation versus conservative management in patients with osteoarthritis of the knee: a prospective randomized study. *Journal of Rheumatology*, 19, 772–9.

Lawrence, J.S., Bremner, J.M., and Bier, F. (1966). Osteoarthritis: prevalence in the population and relationship between symptoms and X-ray changes. *Annals of Rheumatology Disease*, 25, 1–24.

Lorig, K.R., Mazonson, P.D., and Holman, H.R. (1993). Evidence suggesting that health education for self-management in patients with chronic arthritis has sustained health benefits while reducing health care costs. *Arthritis and Rheumatology*, 36, 439–46.

Minor, M.A. (1994). Exercise in the management of OA of the knee and hip. *Arthritis Care Research*, 7, 198–204.

Resnick, D., Shapiro, R.F., Weisner, K.B., *et al.* (1978). Diffuse idiopathic skeletal hypertrophy (DISH). *Seminars in Arthritis and Rheumatology*, 7, 153.

Spector, T.D., Cicuttini, F., Baker, J., Loughlin, J., and Hart, D. (1996). Genetic influences on osteoarthritis in women: a twin study. *British Medical Journal*, 312, 940–4.

Spector, T.D., Hart, D.J., Nandra, D., *et al.* (1997). Low-level increases in serum C-reactive protein are present in early osteoarthritis of the knee and predict progressive disease. *Arthritis and Rheumatology*, 40, 723–7.

Stecher, R.M. (1955). Heberden's nodes: a clinical description of osteoarthritis of the finger joint. *Annals of the Rheumatic Diseases*, 14, 1–10.

Summers, M.N., Haley, W.E., Reveille, J.O., and Alarcon, G.S. (1988). Radiographic assessment and psychological variables as predictors of pain and functional impairment in osteoarthritis of the hip or knee. *Arthritis and Rheumatology*, 31, 204–9.

Weinberger, M., Tierney, W.M., Cowper, P.A., Katz, B.P., and Booher, P.A. (1993). Cost-effectiveness of increased telephone contact for patients with osteoarthritis: a randomised, controlled trial. *Arthritis and Rheumatology*, 36, 243–6.

13.4 Gout and other crystal arthropathies

J. T. Scott

Mineral deposition often occurs in joints, especially with advancing years. Metabolic disturbances and tissue damage are predisposing factors. Deposits can occur in articular cartilage, synovial membrane, and periarticular structures.

Gout is the best known of these arthropathies, with the crystal concerned being monosodium urate monohydrate. Calcium pyrophosphate dihydrate may be laid down in articular cartilage (chondrocalcinosis), while hydroxyapatite and other basic calcium phosphates are also deposited in relation to joints, characteristically in periarticular tissues.

Gout

Gout is a disease with a strong familial tendency; it is seen predominantly in adult men, and is characterized by episodes of acute arthritis, and later also by chronic damage to joints and other structures. It is caused essentially by hyperuricaemia, an excess of urate in blood and tissues, which in some people (but not all) leads to the deposition of crystals of sodium urate in the joints and elsewhere. These crystalline deposits are now recognized as the cause of the acute gouty attack, and further accumulations of crystalline and amorphous urate form the tophi (Latin *tofus*, porous stone) which are a feature of the advanced, untreated disease.

With increasing knowledge of uric acid metabolism it has now become evident that there are many factors which can influence the development of hyperuricaemia and hence of gout. Gouty arthritis may therefore be regarded as the end result of a number of different biochemical processes. The term primary gout is used when hyperuricaemia is due principally to an inherited metabolic abnormality, and secondary gout when it is largely the result of an acquired disease

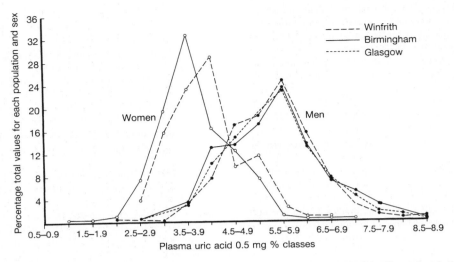

Fig. 1 Distribution curves of serum uric acid concentrations in three normal populations in the United Kingdom. (Reproduced with permission from Sturge *et al.* (1977).)

or some environmental factor. However, in most patients with gout a combination of inherited and environmental influences—particularly food (with regard to both its purine and calorie content), alcohol, and diuretic drugs—appears to be operating.

The pathology and clinical features of gout are described in standard texts, together with accounts of purine metabolism, causes of hyperuricaemia, factors influencing urate crystal deposition and the inflammatory response, and methods of treatment (Scott 1986; Nuki 1987). The striking advances which have occurred during the second half of the present century have recently been reviewed (Scott 1996).

Age and sex

Blood levels of uric acid are generally higher in men than in women because of differences in renal clearance (Fig. 1), and this is reflected in the predominance of gouty arthritis among men. However, after middle age levels in women rise to approach those of men, and gout in elderly women becomes less uncommon (Fig. 2).

A survey of 354 patients with gout (Grahame and Scott 1970) has shown that the peak age of onset lies in the fifth decade in men and the sixth decade in women, with 12 per cent of the total series experiencing their first attack of clinical gout after the age of 60 years. The proportion of women after the age of 60 was 29 per cent compared with only 7 per cent below that age. Other features of gout starting in old age were a somewhat increased incidence of an underlying haematological disorder, an absence of the predilection for higher social strata seen in the younger onset group, and a lower frequency of a positive family history.

Diuretics and gout

Most environmental factors contributing to hyperuricaemia and gout, namely purine intake, calorie consumption with consequent obesity, and regular alcohol ingestion, appear to be of no greater importance in elderly than in younger patients with gout, and perhaps less so. However, special mention must be made of diuretic-induced gout,

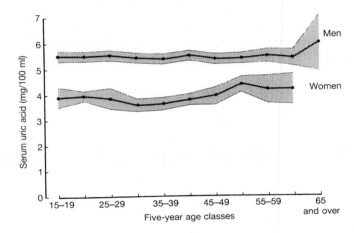

Fig. 2 Mean serum uric levels by 5-year age groups from the combined populations shown in Fig. 1, totalling 1103 subjects. Stippled area is 2 SE on either side of mean. There is a significant rise in uric acid in women occurring at the fifth decade. The rise seen in old men does not reach significance because of the small number of subjects examined at this age. (Reproduced with permission from Sturge *et al.* (1977).)

which has been seen with increasing frequency over the past decade.

The hyperuricaemic action of thiazides and other diuretics, such as frusemide (furosemide), ethacrynic acid, and chlorthalidone, is frequently encountered in clinical practice. The pathogenesis is complex; whether this is due mainly to inhibition of tubular secretion of urate or to more avid resorption, it appears to be dependent upon contraction of extracellular volume (Manuel and Steele 1974).

A study of gout in general practice showed that in 10 per cent of 966 cases the condition was believed to be secondary, with induction of diuretics being the most frequent cause (Currie 1979). It has become apparent that this type of gout is particularly prevalent among elderly women who have been taking diuretics for several years. In a study by MacFarlane and Dieppe (1985), nine of 60 cases of gout

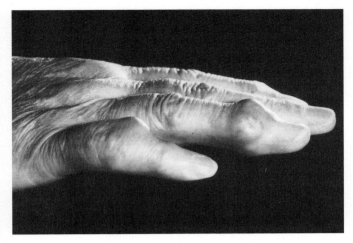

Fig. 3 Urate deposition in a Heberden node at the distal interphalangeal joint in the right ring finger of an elderly woman. There is a similar lesion in the proximal interphalangeal joint of the little finger.

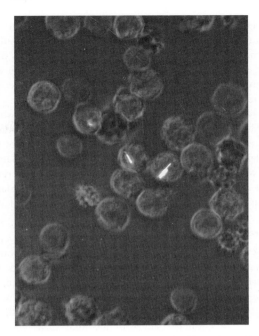

Fig. 4 Intracellular urate crystals seen in joint fluid by polarized light microscopy.

were in women, all of whom had been taking long-term diuretics, whereas only one-third of the men with gout had done so. The men had a mean age of onset of gout of 46 years compared with 77 years for the women. There are similar data from other countries; for example, the striking increase in the prevalence of gout in Finland is partly attributable to diuretics (Isomaki *et al.* 1979).

Therefore a history of diuretic medication is an important factor in the assessment of the patient with gout. It must be remembered, however, that hyperuricaemia is a multifactorial condition and further investigation of an individual patient may reveal other contributory factors, such as inheritance (indicated by a positive family history), renal functional impairment, or occasionally a proliferative haematological disorder, as well as the environmental factors mentioned above (Scott and Higgens 1992).

Clinical features and diagnosis

Attacks of gout in elderly people may resemble those at younger ages, usually occurring in a single joint with the metatarsophalangeal joint of the great toe being involved in 70 per cent of cases. The classical picture is one of a reddened, shiny, swollen, and exquisitely tender joint with distension of superficial veins, an appearance which is typical but which can be mimicked by infection or pyrophosphate arthropathy (see below).

Less typical modes of onset can be more deceptive. The inflammatory episode is sometimes much less acute, and a swollen joint such as a knee can easily be misdiagnosed as rheumatoid arthritis or osteoarthritis, especially if the condition is polyarticular.

A striking presentation, extremely rare in younger adults but not at all uncommon in older people, is where tophaceous deposits are formed in the absence of any history of acute attacks. This is found particularly in women with diuretic-induced gout where urate is deposited in pre-existing Heberden's nodes. The hard swollen distal interphalangeal joints of the fingers result from a combination of osteoarthritis and chronic tophaceous gout (Fig. 3). Of course, such lesions can also be the site of very painful acute attacks.

The diagnosis of gout is primarily clinical but must be checked by estimation of the serum uric acid, which is always raised (above 420 µmol/l, 7 mg%) unless it has been recently lowered by drug treatment. Absolute confirmation of gouty arthritis is provided by the demonstration of urate crystals in synovial fluid or from a tophus; crystals of sodium urate are needle-shaped, between 2 and 20 µm in length (Fig. 4), and show strong, negative birefringence by polarizing microscopy. Fluid is easily examined when an effusion is present in a large joint such as the knee, but a few drops obtained (with adequate local anaesthesia) from a small joint in a toe or finger can be enough to confirm the diagnosis.

Treatment

Acute gout

Treatment of acute gout is directed solely towards relief of inflammation as rapidly as possible. Lowering the levels of uric acid (a process which may well prolong the episode) plays no part at this stage.

Colchicine is the time-honoured remedy; the usual dose is 1.0 mg followed by 0.5 mg every 2 h until the attack subsides. The most frequent toxic effect is diarrhoea, but this does not usually occur until a total dose of 5 to 6 mg has been taken. However, there is a considerable variation in individual sensitivity, and sometimes diarrhoea, nausea, or vomiting preclude the use of colchicine; such symptoms are especially troublesome in older people.

Phenylbutazone is highly effective in a dose of 200 mg four times daily until the attack is relieved. Because of the risk of marrow suppression (minuscule when the drug is given for only a few days), the drug has been withdrawn from prescription in the United Kingdom except for patients with ankylosing spondylitis, although some patients with gout express a strong individual preference for it.

Indomethacin in a dose of 50 mg four times daily is also useful, as is naproxen 250 mg three times daily; indeed therapeutic effect has been shown with most of the other non-steroidal anti-inflammatory drugs such as fenoprofen, ketoprofen, fenbufen, and piroxicam. Azapropazone in a dose of 300 mg three times daily has both anti-inflammatory and uricosuric properties, although whether such a combination of effects is a significant therapeutic advance remains to be confirmed.

Non-steroidal anti-inflammatory drugs must be used with great care in elderly patients. Side-effects such as gastrointestinal intolerance and skin rashes are not infrequent, while fluid retention and a fall in glomerular filtration rate are also documented. Renal damage in patients with normal renal function is rare, but existing renal impairment can be aggravated, owing to the effect of prostaglandin inhibition upon renal blood flow (Carmichael and Shankel 1985).

Long-term management

After just one or two attacks, with only a moderately elevated uric acid, there is little to be lost in awaiting the course of events. Regular prophylactic colchicine, given in a dose of 0.5 to 1.0 mg daily, can prevent recurrences of acute articular gout, but antihyperuricaemic agents are surely more satisfactory. They are certainly indicated in the presence of chronic changes in the joint or tophi, frequent acute attacks, evidence of renal damage, or gout accompanied by a considerably elevated serum uric acid of 480 µmol/l or over.

The drug most commonly used in the United Kingdom to lower serum concentrations of uric acid is the xanthine oxidase inhibitor allopurinol. The final maintenance dose depends upon estimations of serum uric acid, but usually lies in the region of 300 mg daily. Older people tolerate the drug well enough, but severe reactions (exfoliative dermatitis, vasculitis, or bone marrow depression) have occurred, usually in patients with reduced renal function, which must therefore be carefully assessed. Lower doses of allopurinol may be adequate (Cameron and Simmonds 1987).

Uricosuric drugs, such as probenecid, which lower the serum level of uric acid by increasing renal excretion, are generally less effective than allopurinol, and may produce renal deposition of urate. Therefore they should only be used when there are adverse reactions to allopurinol.

Pyrophosphate arthropathy (chondrocalcinosis)

Calcium pyrophosphate dihydrate is produced in large amounts but is normally rapidly hydrolysed to orthophosphate by abundant pyrophosphatase enzymes. Crystallization can occur in cartilage that has been damaged in some way, but other mechanisms are incompletely understood. Deposition takes place initially in the mid-zone of hyaline cartilage around chondrocytes, and also in fibrocartilage. Shedding into joint fluid is associated with crystal-induced inflammation.

Apart from rare familial types and those with defined metabolic associations, the common sporadic cases are found exclusively in elderly people of both sexes (Hamilton 1986). Chondrocalcinosis is rare under the age of 50 years, but has been found in nearly 50 per cent of people over the age of 90 years.

Pyrophosphate is deposited in both fibrous and hyaline cartilage. The most common site is the meniscus of the knee (Fig. 5); the

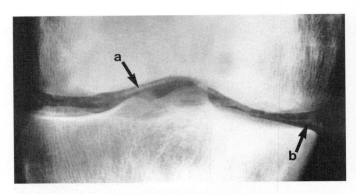

Fig. 5 Radiograph of knee joint showing chondrocalcinosis: deposition of calcium pyrophosphate is seen in (a) hyaline articular cartilage and (b) fibrocartilage of the meniscus.

triangular ligament of the wrist joint and the symphysis pubis can also be involved. These radiological features are critical in diagnosis, together with the demonstration of pyrophosphate crystals when joint fluid is obtained for microscopic examination; the crystals are more pleomorphic than the fine needles of sodium urate and are positively birefringent under the polarizing microscope.

There are several patterns of joint involvement which may occur independently or, at different times, in association with one other.

1. **Asymptomatic chondrocalcinosis** This has been demonstrated in various radiological and autopsy surveys of elderly people.

2. **Acute pyrophosphate arthropathy ('pseudogout')** The affected joint becomes suddenly painful, warm, swollen, tender, and often red. The knee is the most common site, but other joints, especially the wrist, elbow, and ankle, are not infrequently involved, occasionally more than one simultaneously. Unlike urate gout, the great toe is only rarely affected. Attacks last for a few days or several weeks and, as with urate gout, they may follow trauma, surgery, or acute illness. Fever, leucocytosis, and a raised sedimentation rate can occur, but there are usually no biochemical abnormalities. The acute attack can be treated by aspiration of joint fluid and injection of corticosteroid, together with administration of a non-steroidal anti-inflammatory drug. Colchicine is effective but less so than with urate gout.

3. **Osteoarthritis** This is a common association; about half of patients with pyrophosphate arthropathy having some degree of osteoarthritis. It is seen most frequently in the knee joint but may involve sites that are not normally liable to osteoarthritis, such as the wrists, metacarpophalangeal joints, elbows, and shoulders. There is no doubt that pyrophosphate can lead to degenerative changes, but there can also be the opposite sequence of events in which joints with advanced osteoarthritis become the site of crystal deposition.

4. **Chronic destructive arthropathy** Pyrophosphate crystals can also produce a much more severe destructive arthritis, most commonly in the knee, hip, and shoulder joints.

Apart from situations where pyrophosphate is laid down in a joint which is already abnormal (e.g. in hypermobile joints), after menisectomy, and in neuropathic joints, there are several conditions where an association with chondrocalcinosis has been demonstrated.

1. **Hyperparathyroidism** The relation here is presumably with sustained hypercalcaemia. Pyrophosphate arthropathy is sometimes the presenting feature of hyperparathyroidism and a serum calcium is a necessary investigation in all patients with chrondrocalcinosis, though it is nearly always found to be normal.

2. **Gout** There is an association between these two forms of crystal arthritis, patients with gout showing a higher prevalence of chondrocalcinosis than controls. Urate crystals may enhance nucleation of calcium pyrophosphate.

3. **Haemochromatosis** Acute and chronic forms of pyrophosphate arthropathy are found in about half of cases, superimposed on the characteristic degenerative arthritis, which affects first the small joints of the hands and later larger joints. It is likely that iron salts act as nucleating agents for crystal formation.

4. **Hypothyroidism** There are several reports of this association.

5. **Hypophosphatasia** These rare patients have very low levels of alkaline phosphatase and an association with chondrocalcinosis is well documented. Inorganic pyrophosphate is a natural substrate for alkaline phosphatase.

6. **Hypomagnesaemia** Pyrophosphate deposition has been described in some patients with low magnesium levels.

Associations have also been claimed with amyloidosis, diabetes, ochronosis, Wilson's disease, and Paget's disease of the bone, but the lack of controlled observations makes evaluation of these difficult. Again, it should be stressed that, although the possibility of such associations should be borne in mind when chondrocalcinosis is diagnosed, they are not found in the great majority of cases.

Hydroxyapatite and joint disease

Calcium apatite is commonly deposited in soft tissues related to joints, sometimes in well-defined sites such as the supraspinatus tendon or subdeltoid bursa. It is demonstrable by radiographs and is often asymptomatic but may produce local pain, sometimes severe (acute calcific periarthritis). Local injection with lignocaine (lidocaine) and corticosteroid is usually effective.

Apatite crystals have been found in osteoarthritic joints. They can be demonstrated by staining with alizarin red (Paul *et al.* 1983), but this merely confirms the calcific nature of the material. More specific identification depends upon sophisticated techniques such as scanning and transmission electron microscopy. Moreover, the extent to which their presence is causative or merely the result of damage to the joint is debatable. However, there does appear to be an apatite-associated arthropathy in which phagocytosis of crystals leads to the release of proteases and collagenases. A striking example is the 'Milwaukee shoulder' (McCarty 1983), in which destruction of the glenohumeral joint is accompanied by a characteristic upward subluxation of the humeral head.

References

Cameron, J.S. and Simmonds, H.A. (1987). Use and abuse of allopurinol. *British Medical Journal*, **294**, 1504–5.

Carmichael, J. and Shankel, S.W. (1985). Effects of non-steroidal anti-inflammatory drugs on prostaglandins and renal function. *American Journal of Medicine*, **78**, 992–1000.

Currie, W.J.C. (1979). Prevalence and incidence of the diagnosis of gout in Great Britain. *Annals of the Rheumatic Diseases*, **38**, 101–6.

Grahame, R. and Scott, J.T. (1970). Clinical survey of 354 patients with gout. *Annals of the Rheumatic Diseases*, **29**, 461–8.

Hamilton, E.B.D. (1986). Pyrophosphate arthropathy. In *Copeman's textbook of the rheumatic diseases* (ed. J.T. Scott), pp. 938–49. Churchill Livingstone, Edinburgh.

Isomaki, H., von Essen, R., and Ruutsalo, H.M. (1979). Gout, particularly diuretics-induced, is on the increase in Finland. *Scandinavian Journal of Rheumatology*, **6**, 213–16.

McCarty, D.J. (1983). Crystals, joints and consternation. *Annals of the Rheumatic Diseases*, **42**, 243–53.

MacFarlane, D.G. and Dieppe, P.A. (1985). Diuretic-induced gout in elderly women. *British Journal of Rheumatology*, **24**, 155–7.

Manuel, M.A. and Steele, T.H. (1974). Changes in renal urate handling after prolonged thiazide treatment. *American Journal of Medicine*, **57**, 741–6.

Nuki, G. (1987). Disorders of purine metabolism. In *Oxford textbook of medicine* (2nd edn) (ed. D.J. Weatherall, J.G.G. Ledingham, and D.A. Warrell), Section 9, p. 123. Oxford University Press.

Paul, H., Reginato, A.J., and Schumacher, H.R. (1983). Alizarin red S-staining as a screening test to detect calcium compounds in synovial fluid. *Arthritis and Rheumatism*, **26**, 191–200.

Scott, J.T. (1986). Gout. In *Copeman's textbook of the rheumatic diseases* (6th edn) (ed. J.T. Scott), pp. 883–937. Churchill Livingstone, Edinburgh.

Scott, J.T. (1996). Gout: the past 50 years. *Journal of the Royal Society of Medicine*, **89**, 634–7.

Scott, J.T. and Higgens, C.S. (1992). Diuretic-induced gout: a multifactorial condition. *Annals of the Rheumatic Diseases*, **51**, 259–61.

Sturge, R.A., Scott, J.T., Kennedy, A.C., Hart, D.P., and Watson Buchanan, W. (1977). Serum uric acid in England and Scotland. *Annals of the Rheumatic Diseases*, **36**, 420–7.

13.5 Polymyalgia rheumatica and giant cell arteritis

John H. Klippel and Thurayya Arayssi

Polymyalgia rheumatica and giant cell arteritis are systemic inflammatory syndromes which share common clinical pathogenetic features. They are generally considered to constitute a disease spectrum, ranging from the constitutional and musculoskeletal symptoms of polymyalgia rheumatica at one end, to vasculitis of the aortic arch and its branches in giant cell arteritis at the other. The diseases are largely confined to the elderly population and are among the more common of the rheumatic syndromes seen in older people.

Variant presentations include 'steroid-responsive anaemia of the elderly' in which specific symptoms are minimal and the illness is dominated by constitutional features and an anaemia, usually normocytic but occasionally microcytic. Giant cell arteritis without localizing features is also a cause of the syndrome of 'fever of unknown origin' in older people.

Epidemiology

Prospective studies of polymyalgia rheumatica and giant cell arteritis have revealed annual incidence rates of 20 to 30 new cases per 100 000 people (Salvarani *et al.* 1995; Schaufelberger *et al.* 1995). The diseases are distinctly uncommon below the age of 50 years with peak disease incidence rates in the age group 70 to 79 years; they occur more commonly in women than in men (4:1). Racial factors appear to be important and the diseases are seen almost exclusively in Caucasians of northern European, particularly Scandinavian, descent. Familial aggregation and clustering of cases in time and space suggest that genetic and environmental factors are important in pathogenesis.

Polymyalgia rheumatica

Polymyalgia rheumatica is a systemic illness with prominent constitutional and musculoskeletal symptoms. The diagnosis is entirely based on the clinical history, physical examination, the findings of non-specific evidence of inflammation on laboratory testing, and prompt response to treatment with corticosteroids (Table 1).

Musculoskeletal manifestations

Symmetrical pain and stiffness of the neck, shoulders, low back, and pelvic girdle are the clinical hallmarks of polymyalgia rheumatica. In

Table 1 Clinical and laboratory characteristics of polymyalgia rheumatica

Age greater than 50 years
Symmetrical pain and stiffness of shoulder and hip/thigh musculature
Constitutional symptoms including weight loss, anorexia, and fever
Transient synovitis of small and large joints
Elevation of erythrocyte sedimentation rate by over 50 mm/h Westergren
Rapid relief with low-dose corticosteroids

some patients, the onset is dramatic and acute so that the exact date, or even hour, of initial symptoms can be recalled. However, in many patients the process is more insidious and evolves over weeks to months. The stiffness and pain are typically worse after periods of inactivity and particularly prominent in the morning. Movement during sleep often produces pain that awakens the patient and sleep disturbances are common. In severe cases, patients may be unable to get out of bed or have difficulties arising from a chair or bath or climbing stairs.

On physical examination, tenderness and limited range of motion of the neck, shoulders, and hips are typically evident. Muscle atrophy, joint contractures, and immobile 'frozen' joints may develop. Because of pain, muscle strength is difficult to evaluate although it is generally normal. Serum muscle enzymes such as the creatine phosphokinase and aldolase are not elevated, and no abnormalities are detected by electromyographic studies or muscle biopsy.

Synovitis of both large and small peripheral joints can be found in about one-third of patients; involvement of knees, wrists, and sternoclavicular joints is most common (Al-Hussaini and Swannell 1985). Median nerve compression and carpal tunnel syndrome from wrist synovitis has been reported. The extent of synovial involvement may be documented with technetium-99 scans in which increased uptake in axial and peripheral joints may be found. The synovitis is considered to be responsible for most of the musculoskeletal complaints.

Analysis of synovial fluid reveals mild inflammatory changes with leucocyte counts in the range of 300 to 3000/mm³, mostly mononuclear cells. Standard joint radiographs demonstrate only soft tissue swelling without cartilage loss or bone erosions. On arthroscopy, vascular dilatation and perivascular oedema can be demonstrated. The histology of the synovium reveals non-specific mild inflammation with proliferation of synovial cells and scattered infiltration of lymphocytes and plasma cells (Chou and Schumacher 1984). The cellular infiltrate is neither organized into lymphoid follicles nor concentrated around synovial vessels; findings of pannus, vasculitis, giant cells, or granuloma formation are notably absent.

Constitutional symptoms

Indications of a systemic illness may be a prominent feature of polymyalgia rheumatica. These include high fevers, occasionally with shaking chills and night sweats (15 per cent), weight loss (20 per cent), anorexia (20 per cent), and malaise and asthenia (25 per cent) (Salvarani et al. 1987).

Laboratory abnormalities

Elevation of the erythrocyte sedimentation rate (ESR) is seen in the majority of patients with polymyalgia rheumatica. Elevations of the Westergren ESR, often greater than 100 mm/h, are typical. Elevations of other acute phase serum proteins such as haptoglobin and C-reactive protein are also seen (Pountain et al. 1994).

Additional laboratory abnormalities that may be noted include a normochromic, normocytic anaemia, mild elevations of serum liver chemistries, particularly the alkaline phosphatase, thyroid function abnormalities, and thrombocytosis. Abnormalities such as antinuclear antibody and rheumatoid factor are absent or found in low titres. Elevations of anticardiolipin antibody have been noted and may be associated with an increased risk of developing giant cell arteritis (Charkravarty et al. 1995).

Response to corticosteroids

Prompt and dramatic improvement in symptoms with low doses of prednisone (10–15 mg daily) is often used as a test for the diagnosis of polymyalgia rheumatica. However, the clinical response to corticosteroids must be interpreted with caution because many of the inflammatory, or even non-inflammatory, conditions that might be confused with polymyalgia rheumatica improve with corticosteroids. Conversely, the failure of the patient to have substantial improvement with corticosteroids argues strongly against the diagnosis of polymyalgia rheumatica.

Differential diagnosis

The differential diagnosis of polymyalgia rheumatica is extensive and includes giant cell arteritis, acute and chronic infectious processes, metabolic abnormalities, neoplastic diseases, and various other rheumatic conditions. For prognostic and therapeutic reasons, it is important to identify patients with coexistent polymyalgia rheumatica and giant cell arteritis. Although opinions vary, there is probably little justification for routine temporal artery biopsy in patients with uncomplicated polymyalgia rheumatica. However, in patients with suspected vasculitis based on symptoms (headache, visual disturbances, jaw claudication, and so on) or abnormal physical findings (vascular bruits or absent pulses), a temporal artery biopsy should

be performed. The finding of a negative biopsy, in general, is associated with a low risk for the subsequent development of giant cell arteritis (Hall et al. 1983).

The characteristic major organ involvement of the connective tissue diseases such as systemic lupus erythematosus, polymyositis, and scleroderma along with the high incidence of antinuclear antibodies seen in these diseases generally allow for easy differentiation of polymyalgia rheumatica from these conditions. The rheumatic conditions that provide the most difficulty are fibromyalgia, palindromic rheumatism, and, in particular, seronegative rheumatoid arthritis. The diffuse rather than girdle distribution of pain and tenderness, presence of trigger points, absence of synovitis, normal ESR, and failure to respond to corticosteroids are helpful in identifying the patient with fibromyalgia (Buchwald et al. 1988). In patients with synovitis, distinguishing polymyalgia rheumatica from seronegative rheumatoid arthritis is much more problematic (Healey and Sheets 1988) and often passage of time is required before a clear diagnosis is certain. Not surprisingly, a change in the original diagnosis of polymyalgia rheumatica to rheumatoid arthritis in patients with a disease characterized by persistent synovitis is not an uncommon occurrence (Palmer et al. 1986). In patients with early disease, findings more suggestive of rheumatoid arthritis would include clinical involvement of the metatarsophalangeal joints, erosions of bone and cartilage, subcutaneous nodules, and an incomplete response to treatment with low doses of corticosteroids.

Treatment

Untreated, polymyalgia rheumatica is a chronic self-limiting disease with the potential for the progression to giant cell arteritis. The aim of treatment is to relieve symptoms and prevent vascular complications arising from an underlying vasculitis. Low-dose corticosteroids, typically prednisone 10 to 15 mg daily, are the standard treatment for patients with polymyalgia rheumatica (Kyle and Hazleman 1989). Clinical improvement with low-dose prednisone is prompt and dramatic, and most symptoms resolve entirely within several days. Some patients may need higher doses for a short time to bring the disease under control. The correction of laboratory abnormalities, particularly the elevated ESR, occurs much more slowly over a period of several weeks or more. The clinical response to non-steroidal anti-inflammatory drugs is less complete; however, these drugs may be useful in patients with very mild symptoms or in combination with corticosteroids.

Gradual slow reductions of corticosteroids in the range of 2.5 mg prednisone every several weeks may be begun following 4 to 6 weeks of therapy. Where possible the dosage should be monitored by the ESR rather than the symptoms. Recurrence of clinical symptoms during corticosteroid reduction is an indication for dosage increases. Most patients require low-dose maintenance therapy (5.0–7.5 mg prednisone) for a period of 6 to 12 months or longer. In a large series of patients with polymyalgia rheumatica, the median duration of prednisone therapy was approximately 3 years; one-third of the patients were able to discontinue prednisone by 16 months. The relapse rate with discontinuation of prednisone is reported to be in the range of 20 per cent (Ayoub et al. 1985). Relapses are most likely in the first 18 months of treatment, but can occur even after successful treatment when corticosteroids have been discontinued.

Side-effects from corticosteroids are related to both peak and cumulative doses and duration of treatment. The most common of Scandinavian backgrounds. Several studies have shown an increased frequency of HLA *DR4* alleles in patients with giant cell arteritis (Weyand *et al.* 1994).

References

Achkar, A.A., Lie, J.T., Hunder, G.G., O'Fallon, W.M., and Gabriel, S.E. (1994). How does previous corticosteroid treatment affect the biopsy findings in giant cell (cranial) arteritis? *Annals of Internal Medicine*, **120**, 987–92.

Al-Hussaini, A.S. and Swannell, A.J. (1985). Peripheral joint involvement in polymyalgia rheumatica: a clinical study of 56 cases. *British Journal of Rheumatology*, **24**, 27–30.

Ayoub, W.T., Franklin, C.M., and Torretti, D. (1985). Polymyalgia rheumatica. Duration of therapy and long-term outcome. *American Journal of Medicine*, **79**, 309–15.

Bosley, T.M., Savino, P.J., Eagle, R.C., Sandy, R., and Gee, W. (1989). Ocular pneumoplethysmography can help in the diagnosis of giant cell arteritis. *Archives of Ophthalmology*, **107**, 379–81.

Buchwald, D., Sullivan, J.E., Leddy, S., and Komaroff, A.L. (1988). 'Chronic Epstein–Barr virus infection' syndrome and polymyalgia rheumatica. *Journal of Rheumatology*, **15**, 479–82.

Caselli, R.J., Hunder, G.G., and Whisnant, J.P. (1988*a*). Neurologic disease in biopsy-proven giant cell (cranial) arteritis. *Neurology*, **38**, 352–9.

Caselli, R.J., Daube, J.R., Hunder, G.G., and Whisnant, J.P. (1988*b*). Peripheral neuropathic syndromes in giant cell (cranial) arteritis. *Neurology*, **38**, 685–9.

Charkravarty, K., Pountain, G., Merry, P., Byron, M., Hazleman, B., and Scott, D. (1995). A longitudinal study of anticardiolipin antibody in polymyalgia rheumatica and giant cell arteritis. *Journal of Rheumatology*, **33**, 550–4.

Chemnitz, J., Christensen, B.C., Christoffersen, P., Garbarsch, C., Hansen, T.M., and Lorenzen, I. (1987). Giant cell arteritis. Histological, immunohistochemical and electronmicroscopic studies. *Acta Pathologica, Microbiologica, et Immunologica Scandinavica*, **95**, 251–62.

Chou, C.T. and Schumacher, H.R. Jr (1984). Clinical and pathologic studies of synovitis in polymyalgia rheumatica. *Arthritis and Rheumatism*, **27**, 1107–17.

Delecoeuillerie, G., Joly, P., Cohen-de-Lara, A., and Paolaggi, J.B. (1988). Polymyalgia rheumatica and cranial arteritis: a retrospective analysis of prognostic features and different corticosteroid regimens (11 year survey of 210 patients). *Annals of the Rheumatic Diseases*, **47**, 733–9.

Evans, J.M., O'Fallon, W.M., and Hunder, G.G. (1995). Increased incidence of aortic aneurysm and dissection in giant cell (cranial) arteritis: a population-based study. *Annals of Internal Medicine*, **122**, 502–7.

Ferraccioli, G., Salaffi, F., De Vita, S., Casatta, L., and Bartoli, E. (1996). Methotrexate in polymyalgia rheumatica: preliminary results of an open, randomised study. *Journal of Rheumatology*, **23**, 624–8.

Hall, S., Persellin, S., Kurland, L., O'Brien, P.O., and Under, G.G. (1983). The therapeutic impact of temporal artery biopsy. *Lancet*, **ii**, 1217–20.

Healey, L.A. and Sheets, P.K. (1988). The relation of polymyalgia rheumatica to rheumatoid arthritis. *Journal of Rheumatology*, **15**, 750–2.

Hunder, G.G., Block, D.A., Michel, B.H., *et al.* (1990). The American College of Rheumatology 1990 criteria for the classification of giant cell arteritis. *Arthritis and Rheumatism*, **33**, 1122–8.

Kyle, V. and Hazleman, B.L. (1989). Treatment of polymyalgia rheumatica and giant cell arteritis. I. Steroid regimens in the first 2 months. *Annals of the Rheumatic Diseases*, **48**, 658–61.

Machado, E.B., Michet, C.J., Ballard, D.J., Hunder, G.G., Beard, C.M.P., and O'Fallon, W.M. (1988). Trends in incidence and clinical presentation of cranial arteritis in Olmstead County, Minnesota, 1950–1985. *Arthritis and Rheumatism*, **31**, 745–9.

Mehler, M.F. and Rabinowich, L. (1988). The clinical neuro-ophthalmologic spectrum of cranial arteritis. *American Journal of Medicine*, **85**, 839–44.

Palmer, R.G., Prouse, P.J., and Gumpel, J.M. (1986). Occurrence of polymyalgia rheumatica in rheumatoid arthritis. *British Journal of Medicine*, **292**, 867.

Pascuzzi, R.M., Roos, K.L., and Davis, T.E. (1989). Mental status abnormalities in cranial arteritis: a treatable cause of dementia in the elderly. *Arthritis and Rheumatism*, **32**, 1308–11.

Perruquet, J.L., Davis, D.E., and Harrington, T.M. (1986). Aortic arch arteritis in the elderly. An important manifestation of giant cell arteritis. *Archives of Internal Medicine*, **146**, 289–91.

Pountain, G., Calvin, J., and Hazelman, B. (1994). α1 antichymotripsin, C-reactive protein and erythrocyte sedimentation rate in polymyalgia rheumatica/giant cell arteritis. *British Journal of Rheumatology*, **33**, 550–4.

Salvarani, C., Macchioni, P.L., Tartoni, P.L., *et al.* (1987). Polymyalgia rheumatica and giant cell arteritis: a 5-year epidemiologic and clinical study in Reggio Emilia, Italy. *Clinical and Experimental Rheumatology*, **5**, 205–15.

Salvarani, C., Gabriel, S.E., O'Fallon, W.M., and Hunder, G.G. (1995). The incidence of giant cell arteritis in Olmstead County, Minnesota: apparent fluctuations in a cyclic pattern. *Annals of Internal Medicine*, **23**, 192–4.

Save-Soderbergh, J., Malmvall, B.E., Andersson, R., and Bengtsson, B.A. (1986). Giant cell arteritis as a cause of death. Report of nine cases. *Journal of the American Medical Association*, **255**, 493–6.

Schaufelberger, C., Bengtsson, B.A., and Andersson, R. (1995). Epidemiology and mortality in 220 patients with polymyalgia rheumatica. *British Journal of Rheumatology*, **34**, 261–4.

Van der Veen, M.J., Dinant, H.J., van Booma-Frankfort, C., van Albada-Kuipers, A., and Bijlsma, J.W.J. (1996). Can methotrexate be used as a steroid sparing agent in the treatment of polymyalgia rheumatica and giant cell arteritis? *Annals of the Rheumatic Diseases*, **55**, 218–23.

Vilasega, J., Gonzalez, A., Cid, M.C., Lopez-Vivancos, J., and Ortega, A. (1987). Clinical usefulness of temporal artery biopsy. *Annals of the Rheumatic Diseases*, **26**, 282–5.

Weyand, C.M. and Goronzy, J.J. (1995). Giant cell arteritis as an antigen-driven disease. *Rheumatic Disease Clinics of North America*, **21**, 1027–39.

Weyand, C.M., Hunder, N.H., Hicok, K., Hunder, G.G., and Goronzy, J.J. (1994). HLA-DRB1 alleles—polymyalgia rheumatica, giant cell arteritis, and rheumatoid arthritis. *Arthritis and Rheumatism*, **37**, 514–20.

Wong, R.L. and Korn, J.H. (1986). Cranial arteritis without an elevated erythrocyte sedimentation rate. Case report and review of the literature. *American Journal of Medicine*, **80**, 959–64.

13.6 **Connective tissue disorders**

John H. Klippel and Thurayya Arayssi

The term connective tissue disorders is used to describe a group of chronic inflammatory and degenerative rheumatic syndromes of unknown aetiology. Common features of disease pathogenesis of the connective tissue disorders is thought to involve genetic predisposition, vascular injury, and immune-mediated inflammation. Autoantibodies, particularly antinuclear antibodies, develop in most patients. In several of the syndromes, relatively disease-specific antibodies have been identified.

The connective tissue disorders pose particular problems in the elderly population. Clinical presentation and disease course may be substantially different from descriptions in younger patients. Effects of ageing on the immune system and influences of endocrine changes associated with ageing are thought to contribute to the observed differences. The atypical clinical presentations combined with the often prominent non-specific constitutional symptoms may cause long delays in diagnosis. In particular, differentiation from malignant processes, chronic infections, or other rheumatic diseases is often difficult.

Antinuclear antibodies

The majority of patients with connective tissue disorders have antinuclear antibodies, typically in high titre. However, it is important to bear in mind that there are many possible causes of antinuclear antibodies besides the connective tissue diseases (Table 1). Antinuclear antibodies secondary to drugs (see drug-induced lupus below) and as an accompaniment of normal ageing are important considerations in elderly patients. It is estimated that approximately one-quarter of healthy individuals over the age of 60 years have low titres of antinuclear antibodies. Thus, there is a reasonably high likelihood of uncovering an antinuclear antibody on routine laboratory screening.

In general, patients with connective tissue disorders have readily recognizable clinical signs and symptoms, and the antinuclear antibody serves only to help confirm the diagnosis. In perplexing patients with ill-defined symptoms, subtypes of antinuclear antibodies that are disease specific may be helpful in diagnosis. Examples include antibodies to double-stranded DNA and Sm (Smith) in systemic lupus erythematosus, antibodies to histones in drug-induced lupus, antibodies to histadyl t-RNA synthetase (Jo-1) in myositis, and antibodies to topoisomerase I (Scl-70) in diffuse scleroderma and to centromere proteins in limited scleroderma.

In patients in whom antinuclear antibodies are found in the absence of clinical suspicion of a rheumatic disease, it is important to consider the many other causes of antinuclear antibodies.

Systemic lupus erythematosus

Systemic lupus erythematosus is a chronic relapsing and remitting inflammatory syndrome that typically involves multiple organs (Boumpas *et al.* 1995*a*, *b*). The most notable pathological feature is the deposition of circulating antigen–antibody complexes and complement along the vascular basement membranes of target organs. Organs commonly affected include the skin, joints, serosal surfaces, kidneys, heart, lungs, and central nervous system.

The epidemiology and clinical features of systemic lupus erythematosus developing in older people differ substantially from descriptions in younger patients. Instead of a female predominance, men and women are equally affected, presumably a consequence of the diminished influence of oestrogens on the disease after the menopause. Moreover, the clinical disease tends to be mild and often of insidious onset with a relative lack of involvement of major organs such as the kidneys and central nervous system (Maddison 1987; Ward and Polisson 1989).

A genetic susceptibility to lupus is strongly suggested by familial aggregation and twin concordance studies. First-degree relatives have a 10 per cent chance of developing systemic lupus erythematosus which is a 100-fold greater risk than that found in the general population. In twin studies, disease concordance is observed in 25 to 50 per cent of monozygotic twins and 5 per cent of dizygotic twins. In extended families systemic lupus erythematosus may coexist with other autoimmune conditions such as haemolytic anaemia, thyroiditis, rheumatoid arthritis, and insulin-dependent diabetes so as to suggest so-called 'autoimmune genes'. In systemic lupus erythematosus, however, the pattern of inheritance does not follow simple genetic patterns such as autosomal recessive, autosomal dominant, or sex-linked recessive.

Clinical features

A similarity between the atypical lupus syndrome in older people and Sjögren's syndrome with systemic disease manifestations has been noted (Bell 1988). Debilitating constitutional symptoms such as fatigue, anorexia, weight loss, and fever may be common and, in the

Table 1 Causes of antinuclear antibodies

Rheumatic diseases	Systemic lupus erythematosus Sjögren's syndrome Inflammatory myopathies Scleroderma Vasculitis Rheumatoid arthritis
Normal healthy individuals	Females>males Prevalence increases with age Relatives of patients with rheumatic disease
Drug-induced	Chlorpromazine, D-penicillamine, ethosuximide, hydralazine, isoniazid, methyldopa, phenytoin, practolol, procainamide, propylthiouracil, quinidine, sulphasalazine, trimethadione
Hepatic diseases	Chronic active hepatitis Primary biliary cirrhosis Alcoholic liver disease
Pulmonary diseases	Idiopathic pulmonary fibrosis Asbestos-induced fibrosis Primary pulmonary hypertension
Chronic infections	Subacute bacterial endocarditis Osteomeyelitis Tuberculosis
Malignancies	Lymphoma Leukaemia Melanoma Solid tumours (breast, ovary, lung, kidney)
Haematological disorders	Idiopathic thrombocytopenic purpura Autoimmune haemolytic anaemia
Miscellaneous	Endocrine disorders (type 1 diabetes mellitus, Graves' disease) Neurological diseases (multiple sclerosis) Endstage renal failure Following organ transplantation

absence of more classic clinical signs of lupus, cause a long delay in diagnosis (Baer and Pincus 1983).

Transient peripheral symmetrical polyarthritis combined with severe limb girdle pain and stiffness may mimic polymyalgia rheumatica (Hutton and Maddison 1986). The joint involvement is typically not chronic and rarely, if ever, produces cartilage loss, subchondral cystic changes, or bone erosions. The development of persistent synovitis in a single joint suggests a superimposed complication such as septic arthritis or osteonecrosis. Periarticular structures, particularly tendon sheaths, may be involved. Chronic inflammation of tendons and capsular structures may produce joint laxity with rheumatoid-like hand deformities (Fig. 1). Acute tendon involvement may result in tendon rupture, most commonly of the Achilles or patellar tendons. A proximal inflammatory myopathy, often with normal serum levels of creatine phosphokinase, may cause weakness, pain, and muscle wasting.

A wide variety of mucocutaneous lesions may be seen. The erythematous maculopapular facial rash ('butterfly rash') and the atrophic hyperkeratotic lesions of discoid lupus are the best known. However, a spectrum of skin manifestations including acute vasculitic rashes of the trunk and upper extremities, psoriasis-like patches,

bullae, urticarial eruptions, and angioedema may be observed. Many of the skin rashes are worsened by exposure to ultraviolet light. Superficial ulcerations of oral and genital mucosa are typically painless and often go undetected. Ulcerations of the nasal mucosa can lead to epistaxis or perforation of the nasal septum. Diffuse or patchy alopecia in the absence of scarring of the scalp from discoid disease are generally entirely reversible. The regrown hair is often brittle, with a short stubby appearance.

Sterile pleuritis, pericarditis, or peritonitis develop from inflammation of serosal surfaces. Fluid accumulation is usually modest, although on occasion massive ascites or pericardial tamponade may occur. Typically, the fluid has a low white cell count, 3000 cells/mm^3 or less, predominantly made up of mononuclear cells. Reduced levels of complement and lupus erythematosus cells formed *in vivo* may be seen on analysis of the fluid.

Pulmonary manifestations, particularly interstitial lung diseases, are seen with increased frequency in older patients with lupus (Catoggio *et al.* 1984). Acute transient basilar pneumonic infiltrates ('lupus pneumonitis') with non-productive cough, hypoxaemia, and dyspnoea must be distinguished from infective causes. Rare serious pulmonary complications include alveolar haemorrhage with rapid

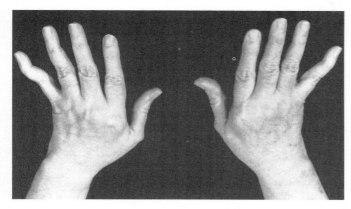

Fig. 1 Lupus arthropathy (Jaccoud's): reversible rheumatoid-like deformities of the hands may develop in the absence of cartilage or bone destruction on radiography.

obliteration of the lung fields and massive haemoptysis and pulmonary hypertension with cor pulmonale.

Non-infective vegetations may develop on the ventricular surfaces of heart valve leaflets (Libman–Sacks endocarditis). The vegetations are a potential nidus for superimposed bacterial infection and antibiotic prophylaxis for dental or other surgical procedures is advised. An inflammatory myocarditis may lead to ventricular arrhythmias, conduction abnormalities, or intractable congestive heart failure. Ischaemic heart disease from coronary arteritis or, more commonly, atherosclerotic disease may be responsible for angina or myocardial infarction.

Gastrointestinal complaints are infrequent; pain from peritonitis is perhaps the most common. Both acute and chronic pancreatitis have been described. Hepatitis when found is typically secondary to the use of salicylates or other non-steroidal anti-inflammatory drugs. Primary biliary cirrhosis has been reported to be increased in lupus. Vasculitis of mesenteric and intra-abdominal organs may produce an acute abdomen that requires surgical exploration.

Clinical evidence of significant renal involvement is considered to be infrequent in older patients. Urine sediment, particularly red blood cells and red cell casts, is indicative of active glomerular inflammation. Proteinuria, often in large amounts and resulting in the nephrotic syndrome, may be seen with lupus membranous nephropathy. Loss of renal function may be acute, similar to that of rapidly progressive nephritis, or, more typically, involve a slowly progressive rise of serum creatinine over the course of many months or years. Renal function is a poor guide to the actual severity of renal involvement since a substantial proportion of nephrons must be destroyed before functional impairment develops. In patients with persistent evidence of nephritis, renal biopsy is advised to determine the type and severity of renal pathology. Hypercellularity may be confined to the mesangium or involve the glomerular capillaries in a focal segmental or diffuse distribution. Extensive glomerular sclerosis is generally recognized as a pathological feature associated with a poor renal outcome (Austin et al. 1994).

Various forms of neurological and psychiatric manifestations may develop (West 1994). Disturbances of mental function range from states of mild confusion with memory deficits and impairments of orientation and perception to major psychiatric disturbances of delirium, hypomania, or psychosis. Seizures are typically of the grand mal type, although petit mal, focal, and temporal lobe epilepsy have been described. Severe headaches with scotomas typical of the fortification spectra of migraines are increased. Less common neurological disturbances include cranial neuropathies, transverse myelopathy, pseudotumour cerebri, chorea and hemiballismus, parkinsonism-like tremors, and both sensory and motor peripheral neuropathies. Conventional studies to evaluate the central nervous system are frequently normal. The cerebrospinal fluid may show mild elevations of protein and immunoglobulin G, oligoclonal bands on electrophoresis, and pleocytosis. Diffuse or focal changes may be found on electroencephalography. Arteriographic studies rarely demonstrate evidence of vasculitis. Magnetic resonance imaging is generally considered to be valuable in the detection of pathological abnormalities associated with central nervous system lupus. However, abnormalities, particularly of white matter, appear to be a common finding in older patients and must be interpreted with caution (Kent et al. 1994).

Drug-induced lupus

Autoimmune syndromes induced by drugs are a very important consideration, particularly in the older population. Numerous drugs have been reported to be associated with the development of antinuclear antibodies (see Table 1). Although the majority of patients with drug-induced antinuclear antibodies are asymptomatic, diseases that are clinically indistinguishable from connective tissue disorders, including systemic lupus erythematosus and polymyositis, may develop in the course of drug administration. By far the two most common drugs responsible for the drug-induced lupus syndromes are procainamide and hydralazine. Prospective studies have documented that between 50 and 75 per cent of patients treated with these agents develop antinuclear antibodies, but only a fraction of these patients have clinical symptoms. The lupus syndrome that develops from drugs, particularly procainamide, is characterized by fever, myalgias, arthralgias, and a high incidence of pleural and pulmonary symptoms. Although involvement of major organs, such as by glomerulonephritis, has been described as part of drug-induced lupus, it is distinctly uncommon. The principal differential diagnosis of drug-induced lupus involves viral syndromes or infectious diseases that may be associated with fever, arthralgias, pleuropericarditis, and antinuclear antibodies such as bacterial endocarditis or tuberculosis. Dressler's syndrome (postpericardiotomy syndrome) should be considered in appropriate cardiac patients who are often simultaneously treated with cardiac drugs associated with the induction of lupus. Other diagnoses to be considered in the appropriate setting include underlying malignancy, adverse or hypersensitivity drug reactions, and graft-versus-host disease.

Characteristically, symptoms subside or completely resolve with discontinuation of the offending drug. However, treatment with anti-inflammatory drugs, including corticosteroids, may be indicated for acute, severe manifestations. Conversely, antinuclear antibodies may remain present for months, or even years, after the drug has been discontinued.

Treatment

Anti-inflammatory agents are often useful in the treatment of minor lupus manifestations such as fatigue, fever, and joint symptoms. Enteric-coated aspirin in moderate doses is generally well tolerated and effective. Patients with active lupus seem more prone to the development of salicylate-induced hepatitis with increases in serum transaminase levels and transient impairments of renal function. These abnormalities are readily reversible upon stopping the salicylate. Non-salicylated non-steroidal anti-inflammatory agents such as ibuprofen, naproxen, tolmetin, and others are similarly useful in the management of mild lupus and are often better tolerated than salicylates. Adverse side-effects of non-steroidal anti-inflammatory drugs are more common in elderly people, and some may be easily confused with manifestations of active lupus such as skin rashes, fluid retention, impairment of renal function, and aseptic meningitis.

Antimalarial drugs have an important adjunctive role in the treatment of mild systemic disease features, especially for the management of mucocutaneous manifestations. The daily dose of antimalarials should not exceed 400 mg hydroxychloroquine, 250 mg chloroquine, or 100 mg quinicrine. At these low doses, the risks of retinal toxicity are extremely small. However, as a precaution, eye examinations for disturbances in colour vision and retinal changes should be undertaken every 6 to 12 months during drug treatment. Additional complications of antimalarial drugs include gastrointestinal complaints, rashes, photosensitivity, and pigmentary changes of the skin and hair.

Adrenal corticosteroids should be reserved for patients who fail to respond to conservative drug therapy or those who have serious disease manifestations. Daily corticosteroids, occasionally needed in divided doses, are generally superior to alternate-day regimens. Manifestations such as fever, fatigue, polyarthritis, or serositis typically respond to treatment with low doses of prednisone of 10 to 20 mg daily. Acute severe or life-threatening manifestations such as pericarditis, myocarditis, acute glomerulonephritis, or central nervous system disease are indications for higher doses of 60 mg prednisone daily or more. Bolus intravenous methylprednisolone (1 g or 15 mg/kg) is an alternative to conventional high-dose oral corticosteroids. The dose of oral corticosteroids should be kept constant until the inflammation is well under control. At that point, a cautious reduction in dose should be undertaken.

Cytotoxic or antimetabolic drugs, such as azathioprine and cyclophosphamide, are generally reserved for patients with serious forms of lupus who have failed conservative therapies, including high-dose corticosteroids. The drugs have been best studied in lupus nephritis with controlled trials clearly showing that cytotoxic agents preserve renal function and reduce the likelihood of endstage renal failure (Gourley et al. 1996).

Sjögren's syndrome

Sjögren's syndrome is a chronic inflammatory disease characterized by lymphocytic infiltration of exocrine glands (Fox 1996). The most prominent symptoms result from dysfunction of the major and minor salivary glands of labial, nasal, and hard palate mucosa. However, diffuse involvement of glands of the upper and lower respiratory tracts, gastrointestinal tract, pancreas, vagina, and skin may produce clinical symptoms. The syndrome may occur alone (primary Sjögren's syndrome) or in association with other rheumatic diseases, particularly rheumatoid arthritis, systemic lupus erythematosus, scleroderma, and inflammatory myopathies (secondary Sjögren's syndrome).

Recent surveys of elderly populations suggest a high prevalence of primary Sjögren's syndrome. In a study of 103 elderly Caucasian women, 40 complained of sicca symptoms, and two patients (2 per cent) with definite primary Sjögren's syndrome were identified (Strickland et al. 1987). In a separate study focal lymphoid aggregates of minor salivary glands that were compatible with the pathology of Sjögren's syndrome were detected in eight of 62 (13 per cent) elderly individuals (Drosos et al. 1988).

Clinical features

Sjögren's syndrome is a chronic disease with a wide clinical spectrum. Most patients present with non-specific symptoms and follow a slow and benign course over a period of 8 to 10 years before development of the full-blown syndrome.

Dry eyes (xerophthalmia) and dry mouth (xerostomia) are the clinical hallmarks of Sjögren's syndrome. Eye symptoms are often insidious and generally involve complaints of a gritty, sandy, 'foreign body' sensation. The conjunctiva may become markedly injected. Accumulations of thick, ropy strands or crusted matter at the inner canthus may be noted on first arising in the morning. Ocular complications of advanced Sjögren's syndrome include corneal ulcerations, vascularization, and opacification.

Periodontal disease with gingivitis leading to accelerated caries formation is a frequent and major complication of oral dryness. Dysfunction of salivary and oesophageal glands leads to chewing and swallowing difficulties. Dry foods such as crackers or biscuits are particularly troublesome. Defects of both taste and smell may be noted. Deep fissures and ulcerations of the tongue and buccal mucosa as well as angular stomatitis may develop.

Enlargement of parotid and salivary glands may be episodic and associated with fever, tenderness, and erythema. Careful consideration must be given to other causes of parotid and salivary gland enlargement and dysfunction (Table 2). Secondary infection from obstruction of the gland ducts by inspissated matter must be considered with acute, inflammatory changes of glands, particularly with unilateral involvement. Conversely, rapidly growing, hard, or nodular glands should suggest malignant change.

Dryness of the oral pharynx, larynx, and tracheobronchial tree may cause hoarseness, recurrent otitis media and conduction deafness, or epistaxis. Involvement of the lower respiratory tract may be associated with recurrent bronchitis, non-productive cough, and an increased frequency of pulmonary infectious complications. In females, involvement of the glands of the vaginal mucosa leads to intense dryness of the vaginal membranes with pruritus and dyspareunia.

In the majority of older patients, Sjögren's syndrome is confined to ocular and oral pathology. However, on rare occasions serious multisystem disease may occur (Table 3). The similarity between systemic Sjögren's syndrome and the other connective tissue disorders, particularly lupus (Bell 1988), has been noted.

Diagnosis

Biopsy of minor salivary glands is the most specific and definitive procedure for diagnosis; biopsy of major salivary glands is indicated only if there is a suspicion of malignancy. Classical pathology of Sjögren's syndrome is characterized by infiltration of the gland with multiple aggregates of lymphocytes, plasma cells, and occasionally macrophages. Destruction and atrophy of the acinar tissue and replacement with fat is an end result of the inflammation. The epithelial and ductal lining cells may become hyperplastic so as to

Table 2 Causes of parotid or salivary gland enlargement or dysfunction

Anticholinergic drugs
Sedatives
Hypnotics
Narcotics
Phenothiazines
Atropine
Antihistamines

Infiltrative disorders
Sarcoidosis
Amyloidosis
Haemochromatosis
Lymphoma
Leukaemia
Primary neoplasms of parotid

Systemic diseases
Cirrhosis
Diabetes mellitus
Hyperlipoproteinaemias
Obesity
Cushing's disease

Infections
Viral (coxsackie virus, mumps, cytomegalic inclusion disease)
Bacterial (staphylococcal organisms typically secondary to obstruction of duct)
Fungal (actinomycosis or histoplasmosis)

Nutritional deficiency
Starvation
Vitamin deficiency (B$_6$, C, and A)

Table 3 Features of systemic Sjögren's syndrome

Gastrointestinal	Oesophageal stenosis, gastric hyposecretion, atrophic gastritis, pancreatitis, malabsorption
Pulmonary	Lymphocyte interstitial pneumonitis, pseudolymphoma, interstitial fibrosis
Renal	Tubular dysfunction, particularly type I renal tubular acidosis and hyposthenuria, Fanconi's syndrome
Myopathy	Interstitial and perivascular fibrosis, inflammatory infiltrates, or both
Vasculitis	Cutaneous, mononeuritis multiplex, axonal neuropathy
Bone marrow	Thrombocytopenia
Nervous system	Cerebrovascular accidents, spinal cord syndromes, psychiatric or cognitive dysfunction, peripheral or cranial (trigeminal) neuropathies

obliterate the lumen. However, the stroma and lobular architecture of the gland are generally preserved. Caution must be used in the interpretation of pathology of minor salivary glands in elderly individuals. Well-recognized changes associated with ageing include acinar atrophy, fibrosis and ductal dilatation, and hyperplasia. In addition, focal aggregates of lymphocytes and plasma cells compatible with findings in Sjögren's syndrome have also been described (DeWilde et al. 1986).

Measurements of the function and imaging of the anatomy of the major salivary glands are non-invasive procedures that may be helpful in monitoring the course of Sjögren's pathology. The flow of saliva from the parotid gland may be directly quantified. Structural abnormalities of acinar tissue and ductal atrophy can be demonstrated by injection of radio-opaque dye into the parotid duct system. The uptake, concentration, and excretion of ^{99}Tc^{m}-pertechnetate by the parotid glands may be measured by sequential scintophotographic techniques.

Several tests may be used to evaluate lachrymal function and ocular pathology. Schirmer's test involves the placement of a narrow strip of No. 41 filter paper in the lower lid and measurement of the amount of wetness that occurs over a period of 5 min. Normally 15 mm, or more, of wetness develops; less than 5 mm is generally considered abnormal. On rose bengal staining or slit-lamp examination, superficial erosions and punctate or filamentous keratitis (keratoconjunctivitis sicca) may be seen.

Sjögren's syndrome and cancer

An increased incidence of lymphomas, particularly of B-cell lineage, has been observed in patients with Sjögren's syndrome. The pathology within the salivary and lymphoid tissues is thought to involve a continuum from benign lymphoid hyperplasia with polyclonal hypergammaglobulinaemia at one end to malignant proliferation at the other (de Vita et al. 1997). An intermediate stage, termed pseudolymphoma, involves extraglandular extension of lymphoproliferation that is clinically and histologically benign. Clinical and laboratory findings associated with an increased risk of lymphoid malignancies include parotid enlargement, splenomegaly, lymphadenopathy and unexplained anaemia, hypogammaglobulinaemia, and a reduction in the titre of rheumatoid factor.

Treatment

The management of Sjögren's syndrome is largely symptomatic and consists of topical fluid replacement to prevent complications of dryness. Artificial tear preparations must be used on a regular basis. In addition to various eye drops, a slow-release capsule containing a polymer of hydroxyproline is available that can be inserted beneath the inferior tarsal margin. Patients who wear contact lens must follow meticulous hygiene practices to avoid infection. Frequent small fluid intake is important; most patients learn on their own to carry a bottle of water with them at all times and to keep a glass of water at their bedside. The use of sugarless tart sweets or lemon-flavoured drops to stimulate saliva secretion is of benefit in some patients. Drugs with anticholinergic properties should be avoided. Measures to prevent dental caries formation are of particular importance. Brushing and flossing for plaque control should be a part of the daily routine. In addition, topical stannous fluoride should be applied to the teeth nightly to promote mineralization and retard tooth damage. Saline nasal sprays and the use of humidifiers aid in reducing nasal and oropharyngeal dryness. Application of lubricants to vulvar and vaginal membranes relieve pruritus and dyspareunia.

Table 4 Causes of muscle weakness in elderly people

Electrolyte disturbances	Hypokalaemia, hypocalcaemia, hypomagnesaemia, hypophosphataemia
Drugs and toxins	Alcohol, D-penicillamine, colchicine, clofibrate, others
Endocrine diseases	Hyperthyroidism, hypothyroidism, Cushing's or Addison's syndrome
Rheumatic diseases	Polymyalgia rheumatica, arthropathies of shoulders, hips, or knees, overlap syndromes
Neurological diseases	Myasthenia gravis, Guillain–Barré, lumbar or cervical cord syndromes
Infections	Bacterial (*Rickettsia*, mycobacteria) Parasites (*Toxoplasma*, *Trichinella*) Viruses (coxsackie virus, echovirus, influenza, HIV, hepatitis B)
Infiltrative disorders	Amyloidosis

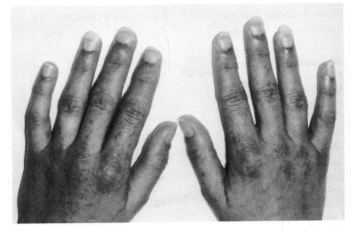

Fig. 2 Dermatomyositis affecting the hands. Erythematous, scaly lesions are present over the metacarpophalangeal joints of both hands. In addition, capillary dilatation is evident in the periungual nail beds.

There is a very limited role for drugs in the management of patients with Sjögren's syndrome. Corticosteroids and cytotoxic drugs should be reserved for patients with life-threatening complications such as vasculitis or central nervous system disease. Topical corticosteroids to the eye accelerate corneal thinning and are contraindicated.

Inflammatory myopathies

Several forms of chronic inflammatory and degenerative adult muscle syndromes are recognized (Dalakas 1991). Polymyositis and dermatomyositis are the most common types. Inclusion body myositis, a relatively recently recognized variant of inflammatory myopathy, is an important consideration in older patients with distinctive clinical and, in particular, pathological features. Inflammatory myopathies may be part of several connective tissue disorders including systemic lupus erythematosus, scleroderma, and Sjögren's syndrome ('overlap syndromes') or occur in association with malignancies.

The peak incidence of adult inflammatory myopathies is in the fourth to sixth decades. A female predominance of the disease is evident in most types except for inclusion body myositis which is characteristically a disease of men. There is no striking familial predisposition to any of the forms of inflammatory myopathy.

Clinical features

The differential diagnosis of muscle pain and weakness is extensive (Table 4). Of importance in the elderly population are electrolyte disturbances, endocrine abnormalities, particularly hypothyroidism, and drug-induced myopathic syndromes.

The clinical presentation of inflammatory myopathy may be either with acute pain and tenderness or, more typically, insidious weakness. Muscle involvement is very symmetrical in distribution. The proximal muscles are affected to a far greater degree than distal muscle groups; inclusion body myositis is an exception in that distal muscle involvement is typical. Common complaints related to lower-extremity involvement include difficulty getting out of a chair, climbing stairs, rising from the bath, or falling while walking. Weakness in the upper extremity typically presents with difficulty performing tasks requiring hand movements above the shoulders such as shaving, combing the hair, or reaching items from a high shelf. Pharyngeal muscles may be affected leading to difficulty in swallowing or hoarseness. In advanced disease, the accessory muscles of the neck may be involved so that patients are unable to raise their heads from the pillow. Muscles of the face, including extraocular muscles, are virtually never involved.

A diagnosis of dermatomyositis is made for patients who have an inflammatory myopathy in association with several distinct types of cutaneous lesions. Perhaps most common are raised violaceous scaly eruptions over the metacarpophalangeal and proximal interphalangeal joints (Gottron's papules) (Fig. 2). This same rash may be seen on the extensor surfaces of the knees and elbows or the malleolar surfaces of the ankles. A somewhat different scaly hyperkeratotic rash may be seen along the radial aspects of the digits and pads of the fingers. Darkened pigmentary changes in the depths of the fissures gives the appearance of the calloused hands of a manual labourer ('mechanic's hands'). A bluish discoloration of the upper eyelid with periorbital oedema (heliotrope rash) may be seen. Erythematous rashes of the face and V-region of the neck may be similar to those seen with systemic lupus. Involvement of the nasolabial folds, present in myositis and absent in lupus, may be a helpful differential point. Finally, various non-specific vascular changes of the periungual capillaries, including erythema, telangiectasias, and nailfold infarcts, may be seen.

The typical clinical presentation of inclusion body myositis is a painless proximal muscle weakness of insidious onset (Lotz *et al.* 1989). Symptoms are often present for several years or more, and prominent atrophy of proximal muscles, often asymmetrical, and some degree of distal muscle involvement is usually evident on clinical examination. Depression or loss of reflexes, particularly of the patellar or biceps tendons, may be an early clue to the diagnosis. In some patients, the disease continues a slow steady progression. In others, it seems to plateau, leaving the patient with fixed weakness and atrophy of the involved musculature.

Signs of systemic and multisystem illness may be a prominent component of the inflammatory myopathies and may confuse diagnostic efforts. High spiking fevers, anorexia, and weight loss may initially suggest an infectious or malignant aetiology. Gastrointestinal symptoms are common and stem from oesophageal dysfunction, reduced motility of the small bowel, and malabsorption. The development of cardiac or pulmonary involvement is the most serious of the systemic features of the inflammatory myopathies. Abnormalities of the cardiac conduction system or actual cardiomyopathy may lead to congestive heart failure, arrhythmias, or sudden death. Progressive dyspnoea from pulmonary involvement may develop from muscular involvement of the diaphragm or intercostal musculature, or, more commonly, from fibrosing alveolitis.

Diagnosis

Muscle inflammation results in increases in the serum levels of enzymes contained in muscle cells. Elevations of creatine phosphokinase and aldolase are commonly used to detect inflammatory muscle disease, elevations of various transferases, and lactate dehydrogenase are less specific. Serum myoglobin and creatine levels may also be elevated; myoglobinuria may be detected as haemoglobin on urine dipstick. Elevations of acute-phase serum proteins leads to increases in the erythrocyte sedimentation rate. Antibodies against several t-RNA transferase enzymes are unique to patients with polymyositis and dermatomyositis. The most common of these antibodies, anti-Jo-1, occurs in a subset of myositis patients with pulmonary fibrosis, Raynaud's disease, and arthritis (Love et al. 1991).

A number of abnormalities may be detected on electromyography. The electromyogram is perhaps most useful in differentiating inflammatory from neuropathic (denervation) myopathies. Findings considered to be characteristic of muscle inflammation include insertional irritability, repetitive, spontaneous discharges, and small amplitude, short, polyphasic motor unit potentials.

The most definitive procedure for documenting muscle inflammation is muscle biopsy. Typically, the biopsy is obtained from the quadriceps or biceps brachii muscles. Since the insertion of needles as part of the electromyographic study may produce pathological changes in the muscle, the biopsy site should be as far as possible from a site where an electromyogram has been recorded. The basic pathology of the inflammatory myopathies consists of inflammatory cell infiltrates and evidence of muscle cell degeneration and regeneration. The cellular infiltrate is predominantly lymphocytes, plasma cells, and macrophages; polymorphonuclear leucocytes are distinctly unusual. Both type I and II muscle fibres are involved and reveal variability in the size of individual muscle fibres.

Variations in pathology among the various types of inflammatory myopathies may be seen. In polymyositis, the inflammatory reaction occurs primarily within fascicles. Necrotic fibres may by scattered or isolated and perifascicular atrophy is not found. By contrast, in dermatomyositis, the inflammatory infiltrates are predominantly perivascular or in septa and perifascicular atrophy is rather characteristic. Necrosis and phagocytosis of muscle fibres tends to be more localized. In inclusion body myositis, myofibre vacuoles within the nucleus and cytoplasm may be seen on trichrome stain of frozen sections and electron microscopy. The vacuoles may be rimmed by basophilic granular material. A characteristic membranous whorl pattern is seen on electron microscopy.

Myositis and cancer

On rare occasions, malignancies have been seen in association with inflammatory myopathies (Sigurgeirsson et al. 1992; Airio et al. 1995), most commonly within a year of each other. Although typically the malignancy antecedes the recognition of muscle disease, cases of simultaneous and late malignancies have been documented. From a practical clinical standpoint, malignancies in patients with myositis are apparent on careful history and physical examination combined with routine laboratory studies and chest radiography. In the absence of clinical suspicion of pathology, there is no justification for exhaustive searches involving various imaging studies.

Treatment

High-dose corticosteroids are generally recognized as the standard drug treatment for patients with acute inflammatory myopathy. Therapy should be initiated with prednisone (or equivalent) at a dose of 1 mg/kg daily. The response to corticosteroids is typically not dramatic, and weeks or more often months are required before convincing evidence of improvement is apparent. Once the disease process is under control, or unacceptable side-effects develop, efforts to reduce the dose of corticosteroids slowly should be initiated. There is some indication that elderly patients require more therapy than younger patients (McKendry 1987). Patients who fail to respond to corticosteroids, or develop unacceptable side-effects, are candidates for cytotoxic drug therapy such as oral azathioprine (2–3 mg/kg daily) or low-dose oral (7.5–15 mg weekly) or intramuscular (0.5–0.8 mg/kg weekly) methotrexate. Hydroxychloroquine (200–400 mg daily) can be used to treat cutaneous lesions of dermatomyositis, although it has no recognizable effects on the myositis. High-dose intravenous immune globulin has been shown to be effective in patients with treatment-resistant dermatomyositis (Dalakas et al. 1993). The role of drug treatment in inclusion body myositis is unclear; in general it is regarded as the least responsive of the inflammatory myopathies (Leff et al. 1993).

Physical therapy plays an important role in the rehabilitation of patients with inflammatory myopathy. Bed rest combined with passive range of motion exercises to maintain joint mobility and prevent contractures is important during periods of severe, active muscle inflammation. With improvement, therapy should include active-assisted and then active exercises.

Scleroderma

The terms scleroderma and systemic sclerosis are used interchangeably to describe a degenerative and inflammatory condition that eventuates in fibrosis. Skin thickening is most commonly confined to the distal extremities, but involvement of proximal extremities, the face, and the trunk may be seen with advanced disease. In addition, vasospasm and fixed structural vascular disease with intimal hyperplasia accounts for internal organ involvement of the gastrointestinal tract, lungs, heart, and kidneys.

The slight female predominance of scleroderma is less apparent in older age groups. The 10-year survival of the disease is estimated to be in the range of 60 to 70 per cent. Diffuse rapidly progressive scleroderma with involvement of the lungs, heart, or kidneys is associated with a poor prognosis.

Clinical features

Two clinical forms of scleroderma are recognized, diffuse and limited. Limited scleroderma is also referred to as the CREST syndrome (calcinosis, Raynaud's disease, oesophageal dysmotility, sclerodactyly, and telangiectasia). These types of scleroderma differ in modes of presentation, evolution of disease course, and autoantibodies (Mitchell et al. 1997).

Skin changes are typically first noted in the hands and fingers, with diffuse non-pitting swelling and puffiness. Over a period of several weeks to months the skin becomes thickened, hard, and shiny in appearance. Additional skin changes include loss of skinfolds and hair, dryness from loss of sebaceous glands, the development of punctate telangiectasias, and pigmentary changes. The skin involvement may be confined to the hands (sclerodactyly) or may spread centrally to affect the forearms, arms, face, anterior chest, and abdomen. Skin thinning, particularly over joints and malleolar surfaces, may lead to ulcer formation. Subcutaneous deposits of hydroxyapatite crystals form at sites of repeated trauma such as elbows, knees, and fingers. The subcutaneous masses may ulcerate to extrude white chalky material and become secondarily infected.

Cold-induced vasospasm (Raynaud's disease) is observed in essentially all patients with scleroderma. It may be the presenting manifestation of disease and long antedate the actual development of other features of scleroderma by many years. Structural abnormalities of nailfold capillaries may be evident grossly or by capillary microscopy. Ischaemia from severe and prolonged Raynaud's disease may lead to painful digits, pitting scars of the digital pulp, or rarely frank gangrene of the distal fingers.

Polyarthralgias and non-specific symmetrical polyarthritis may be seen early. There is little actual bone or joint destruction except for osteolysis of the distal phalanx. Involvement of the synovial lining of tendon sheaths is particularly common, leading to crepitus and palpable coarse leathery friction rubs over flexor tendon sheaths of fingers, knees, and ankles. Fibrosis of the tendons and joint capsule combined with overlying changes in the skin may lead to flexion contractures.

Gastrointestinal symptoms are common, particularly in patients with severe Raynaud's disease. Hypomotility of the distal oesophagus leads to dysphagia especially for solid foods. In addition, incompetence of the gastro-oesophageal sphincter may be associated with reflux, oesophagitis, and strictures. Metaplastic changes of the distal oesophagus are associated with an increased incidence of adenocarcinoma. Loss of smooth muscle of the proximal and distal intestine causes hypomotility with abdominal distension and bloating and pseudo-obstruction. Weakening of the bowel wall leads to the formation of wide-mouthed diverticula of the large bowel, particularly the transverse and descending colon, as well as the jejunum and ileum. Malabsorption and diarrhoea may occur from inadequate mixing of bowel contents and bacterial overgrowth. The appearance of intraperitoneal air by dissection through atrophic mucosa and muscular layers (pneumatosis intestinalis) is a rare complication of scleroderma bowel disease.

Abnormalities on pulmonary function testing, particularly reduction in diffusion capacity, can be demonstrated in most patients with scleroderma. Studies have shown that the abnormalities worsen on exposure to cold, suggesting a Raynaud-like vasospastic process within the pulmonary vasculature. On physical examination and chest radiography, bibasilar interstitial disease with linear or nodular fibrosis is a frequent finding. Progression of the fibrosis with the development of respiratory insufficiency is one of the more serious consequences of scleroderma. In addition, patients with pulmonary fibrosis are at increased risk for the development of alveolar cell carcinoma.

Involvement of the kidneys is the most serious organ complication of scleroderma. On urinalysis, microscopic haematuria and low-grade proteinuria may be seen. Renal involvement is associated with the development of malignant hypertension. Prompt and aggressive medical treatment of the hypertension is critical to prevent rapidly progressive renal failure.

Treatment

The management of scleroderma is largely symptomatic. Prophylactic measures to minimize Raynaud's disease by wearing mittens, avoidance of undue cold exposure, or the use of vasodilating drugs, such as prazosin or nifedipine, relieves the symptoms and complications of vasospasm. Non-steroidal anti-inflammatory drugs and physical therapy are helpful in the treatment of musculoskeletal complications, with the latter being particularly important for joint contractures. Conservative management of skin ulcerations and necrotic digits with occlusive sterile dressings and immobilization promotes healing and prevents secondary infections. Broad-spectrum antibiotics such as tetracycline are helpful in patients with steatorrhoea or other signs of intestinal malabsorption.

There is a very limited role for drugs in the primary management of scleroderma. Low-dose corticosteroids may be valuable in the management of acute inflammatory manifestations such as acute oedematous skin disease, acute pericarditis, or myositis. Colchicine, immunosuppressive agents, cyclosporin A, and D-penicillamine have all been reported to be of benefit, although none has been rigorously studied.

References

Airio, A., Pukaala, E., and Isomaki, A. (1995). Elevated cancer incidence in patients with dermatomyositis: a population based study. *Journal of Rheumatology*, 22, 1300–3.

Austin, H.A., Boumpas, D.T., Vaughan, E.M., and Balow, J.E. (1994). Predicting renal outcomes in severe lupus nephritis: contributions of clinical and histologic data. *Kidney International*, 45, 544–50.

Baer, A.N. and Pincus, T. (1983). Occult systemic lupus erythematosus in elderly men. *Journal of the American Medical Association*, 249, 3350–2.

Bell, D.A. (1988). Systemic lupus erythematosus in the elderly—is it really systemic lupus erythematosus or systemic Sjögren's syndrome? *Journal of Rheumatology*, 5, 723–4.

Boumpas, D.T., Austin, H.A., Fessler, B.J., et al. (1995a). Systemic lupus erythematosus: emerging concepts. Part 1: Renal, neuropsychiatric, cardiovascular, pulmonary, and hematologic disease. *Annals of Internal Medicine*, 122, 940–50.

Boumpas, D.T., Fessler, B.J., Austin, H.A., et al. (1995b). Systemic lupus erythematosus: emerging concepts. Part 2: Dermatologic and joint disease, the antiphospholipid antibody syndrome, pregnancy and hormonal therapy, morbidity and mortality, and pathogenesis. *Annals of Internal Medicine*, 123, 42–53.

Catoggio, L.J., Skinner, R.P., Smith, G., and Maddison, P.J. (1984). Systemic lupus erythematosus in the elderly: clinical and serological characteristics. *Journal of Rheumatology*, 11, 175–81.

Dalakas, M.C. (1991). Polymyositis, dermatomyositis, and inclusion body myositis. *New England Journal of Medicine*, 325, 1487–98.

Dalakas, M.C., Illa, I., Dambrosia, J.M., *et al.* (1993). A controlled trial of high-dose intravenous immune globulin infusions as treatment for dermatomyositis. *New England Journal of Medicine*, 329, 1993–2000.

De Vita, S., Boiocchi, M., Sorrentino, D., *et al.* (1997). Characterization of prelymphomatous stages of B cell lymphoproliferation in Sjögren's syndrome. *Arthritis and Rheumatism*, 40, 318–31.

De Wilde, P.C.M., Baak, J.P.A., van Houwelingen, J.C., Kater, L., and Slootweg, P.J. (1986). Morphometric study of histological changes in sublabial salivary glands due to ageing process. *Journal of Clinical Pathology*, 39, 406–17.

Drosos, A.A., Andonopoulos, A.P., Costopoulos, J.S., Papadimitriou, C.S., and Moutsopoulos, H.M. (1988). Prevalence of primary Sjögren's syndrome in an elderly population. *British Journal of Rheumatology*, 27, 123–7.

Fox, R.I. (1996). Clinical features, pathogenesis, and treatment of Sjögren's syndrome. *Current Opinion in Rheumatology*, 8, 438–45.

Gourley, M.F., Austin, H.A., Scott, D., *et al.* (1996). Methylprednisolone and cyclophosphamide, alone or the combination, in patients with lupus nephritis. A randomised, controlled trial. *Annals of Internal Medicine*, 125, 549–57.

Hutton, C.W. and Maddison, P.J. (1986). Systemic lupus erythematosus presenting as polymyalgia rheumatica in the elderly. *Annals of the Rheumatic Diseases*, 45, 641–4.

Kent, D.L., Haynor, D.R., Longstreth, W.T., and Larson, E.B. (1994). The clinical efficacy of magnetic resonance imaging in neuroimaging. *Annals of Internal Medicine*, 120, 856–71.

Leff, R.L., Miller, F.W., Hicks, J., Frazer, D.D., and Plotz, P.H. (1993). The treatment of inclusion body myositis: a retrospective review and a randomized, prospective trial of immunosuppressive therapy. *Medicine*, 72, 225–35.

Lotz, B.P., Engel, A.G., Nishino, H., Stevens, J.C., and Lichy, W.J. (1989). Inclusion body myositis. Observations in 40 patients. *Brain*, 112, 727–47.

Love, L.A., Leff, R.L., Fraser, D.D., *et al.* (1991). A new approach to the classification of idiopathic inflammatory myopathy: myositis-specific antibodies define useful homogeneous patient groups. *Medicine*, 70, 360–74.

McKendry, R.J. (1987). Influence of age at onset on the duration of treatment in idiopathic adult polymyositis and dermatomyositis. *Archives of Internal Medicine*, 147, 1989–91.

Maddison, P.J. (1987). Systemic lupus erythematosus in the elderly. *Journal of Rheumatology*, 14 (Supplement 13), 182–7.

Mitchell, H., Bolster, M.B., and Le Roy, E.C. (1997). Scleroderma and related conditions. *Medical Clinics of North America*, 81, 129–49.

Sheibani, K., Burke, J.S., Swartz, W.G., Nademanee, A., and Winberg, C.D. (1988). Monocytoid B-cell lymphoma. Clinicopathologic study of 21 cases of a unique type of low-grade lymphoma. *Cancer*, 62, 1531–8.

Sigurgeirsson, B., Lindelöf, B., Edhag, O., and Allander, E. (1992). Risk of cancer in patients with dermatomyositis or polymyositis. A population-based study. *New England Journal of Medicine*, 326, 363–7.

Strickland, R.W., Tesar, J.T., Berne, B.H., Hobbs, B.R., Lewis, D.M., and Welton, R.C. (1987). The frequency of sicca syndrome in an elderly female population. *Journal of Rheumatology*, 14, 766–71.

Ward, M.M. and Polisson, R.P. (1989). A meta-analysis of the clinical manifestations of older-onset systemic lupus erythematosus. *Arthritis and Rheumatism*, 32, 1226–32.

West, S.G. (1994). Neuropsychiatric lupus. *Rheumatic Disease Clinics of North America*, 20, 129–58.

13.7 Soft tissue rheumatism

Thurayya Arayssi and John H. Klippel

Generalized or regional pain is one of the most common complaints of elderly people. Diagnosis and management is challenging since older persons commonly have comorbid conditions which may be responsible for the pain or complicate management or have abnormal radiographs and laboratory findings that may be unrelated to their symptoms. In this chapter we discuss common soft tissue and periarticular rheumatic conditions and their management.

Fibromyalgia

Fibromyalgia is a poorly understood disorder manifested by generalized pain and associated with characteristic tender points (Fig. 1) on physical examination. It has been referred to by many different names such as muscular rheumatism, fibrositis, fibromyositis, and psychogenic rheumatism. It can be a primary disorder or associated with a variety of other rheumatic illnesses, endocrinopathies, malignancies, and infectious diseases (Table 1).

Clinical features

Patients typically complain of generalized aches often associated with morning stiffness. The symptoms wax and wane, and tend to be worsened by excessive emotional or physical stress, poor sleep, or exacerbation of an underlying disease. Other common symptoms include fatigue, feeling of swelling in the hands without objective evidence of synovitis, symptoms of irritable bowel syndrome,

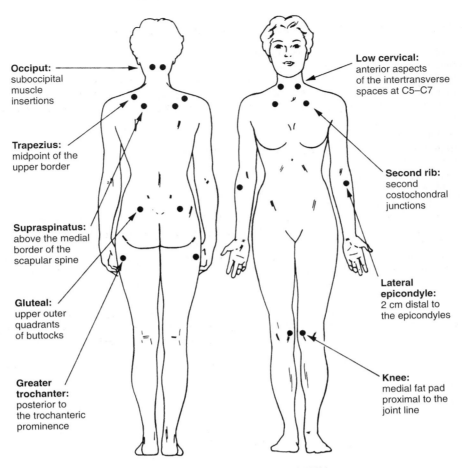

Fig. 1 Tender points in fibromyalgia. (Reproduced with permission from Schumacher *et al.* (1993).)

Table 1 Differential diagnosis of fibromyalgia

Rheumatic diseases
Rheumatoid arthritis
Polymyalgia rheumatica
Systemic lupus erythematosus
Polymyositis
Sjögren's syndrome

Endocrinopathies
Hypothyroidism
Hyperthyroidism
Hypoparathyroidism
Hyperparathyroidism
Osteomalacia
Paget's disease

Infections
Parvovirus B19
HIV
Subacute infective endocarditis
Viral hepatitis

Malignancies
Lymphomas
Multiple myeloma
Carcinomatosis

paraesthesiae, tension headaches, genitourinary symptoms, and affective disorders (Clauw 1995).

Diagnostic criteria for fibromyalgia have been established by the American College of Rheumatology (Wolfe *et al.* 1990) and require the presence of pain in all four quadrants of the body along with 11 of 18 tender points (Table 2). These criteria have been developed to help facilitate research of the disorder and, although helpful for clinical diagnosis, they should not be used rigidly for the purposes of making a clinical diagnosis in individual patients. Diagnosis is usually made by a typical history of generalized pain in association with a normal physical examination except for the presence of tender points. Other secondary causes such as thyroid disease should be excluded before making the diagnosis. Laboratory tests should be limited to a complete blood count, erythrocyte sedimentation rate, and thyroid and blood chemistry screens. Other blood or radiological tests should only be performed if the history or physical examination are suggestive of another disease.

Pathophysiology

The aetiology of fibromyalgia is unknown. Tender points have been biopsied, but no changes have been seen when compared with controls (Yunus and Kaylan-Raman 1989). Various biochemical and neurotransmitter abnormalities have been described. Substance P has been found to be elevated in the cerebrospinal fluid, and serotonin, a neurotransmitter involved with pain, sleep, and mood, has been

Table 2 The American College of Rheumatology 1990 criteria for the classification of fibromyalgia

History of widespread pain

Definition: Pain is considered widespread when all of the following are present: pain in the left side of the body, pain in the right side of the body, pain above the waist and pain below the waist. In addition, axial skeletal pain (cervical spine, anterior chest, thoracic spine, or low back) must be present. In this definition, shoulder and buttock pain is considered as pain for each involved side. 'Low back' pain is considered lower segment pain

Pain in 11 of 18 tender sites on digital palpation

Definition: Pain on digital palpation must be present in at least 11 of the following 18 tender point sites

- Occiput: bilateral, at the suboccipital muscle insertions
- Low cervical: bilateral, at the anterior aspects of the intertransverse spaces at C5–C7
- Trapezius: bilateral, at the midpoint of the upper border
- Supraspinatus: bilateral, at origins, above the scapula spine near the medial border
- Second rib: bilateral, at the second costochondral junctions, just lateral to the junctions on upper surfaces
- Lateral epicondyle: bilateral, 2 cm distal to the epicondyles
- Gluteal: bilateral, in upper outer quadrants of buttocks in anterior fold of muscle
- Greater trochanter: bilateral, posterior to the trochanteric prominence
- Knee: bilateral, at the medial fat pad proximal to the joint line

Digital palpation should be performed with an approximate force of 4 kg. For a tender point to be considered 'positive' the subject must state that the palpation was painful. 'Tender' is not to be considered 'painful'. For classification purposes, patients will be said to have fibromyalgia if both criteria are satisfied. Widespread pain must have been present at least 3 months. The presence of a second clinical disorder does not exclude the definition of fibromyalgia

---

found to be low in fibromyalgia. Insulin-like growth factor 1, a hormone produced in the liver in response to growth hormone, has been shown to be decreased in the majority of patients (Clauw 1995). Fibromyalgia patients have been shown to have abnormalities in the hypothalamopituitary–adrenal axis (Russell 1989), but such findings are also seen in patients with other rheumatic illnesses. Sleep disturbances in the non-rapid eye movement stage may also play a role in the pathogenesis of fibromyalgia (Moldofsky 1989).

Treatment

The mainstay of therapy is education about the disease and its prognosis. Patients should be informed that fibromyalgia is not a deforming or life-threatening illness and that, although it is frequently a chronic problem, effective treatments are available. Patients should be taught healthy sleeping habits which include advice on the importance of sleeping at regular times and avoiding caffeinated beverages near bedtime.

Tricyclic antidepressants (Goldenberg *et al.* 1986) and cyclobenzaprine (Bennet *et al.* 1988) are the most extensively studied drugs for the management of fibromyalgia. These medications should be started at a low dose (as 5–10 mg of either amitriptyline or cyclobenzaprine for example), and increased slowly to a maximum of 80 mg of amitriptyline or 40 mg of cyclobenzaprine. Improvements are usually seen after 4 to 6 weeks of therapy. If anticholinergic side-effects become troublesome, a change to a medication with a lower anticholinergic side-effect profile such as desipramine should be considered.

Studies on selective serotonin reuptake inhibitors (fluoxetine, sertraline) are controversial. Either independently or in combination with tricyclic antidepressants, they may be helpful in selected patients, particularly in those with concomitant depression. Non-steroidal anti-inflammatory medications, narcotics, and benzodiazepines have not been proved to be helpful.

Low-impact aerobic exercise can improve the symptoms of fibromyalgia. Patients should be instructed to start slowly and gradually increase and not get easily discouraged since benefit may not be apparent for several months.

Periarticular syndromes

Shoulder

The shoulder joint is a complex structure consisting of three joints—the sternoclavicular, acromioclavicular, and glenohumeral articulations—which allow the shoulder extensive mobility. The rotator cuff muscles insert adjacent to the glenohumeral joint reinforcing the glenohumeral capsule and holding the humeral head aligned in the glenoid cavity when the arm is lifted. The rotator cuff muscles aid in abduction (supraspinatus), internal rotation (subscapularis), and external rotation (infraspinatus and teres minor) (Fig. 2). The subacromial bursa lies beneath the acromion and the deltoid muscle and, together with the rotator cuff tendons and the long head of the biceps tendon, is the most vulnerable periarticular structure of the shoulder for injury (Table 3).

Rotator cuff tendinitis and subacromial bursitis

With advancing age and repeated stress, the supraspinatus tendon undergoes fissuring and fraying at its distal hypovascularized end, making it more highly prone to injury than the other rotator cuff tendons. Because of the anatomical proximity of the rotator cuff

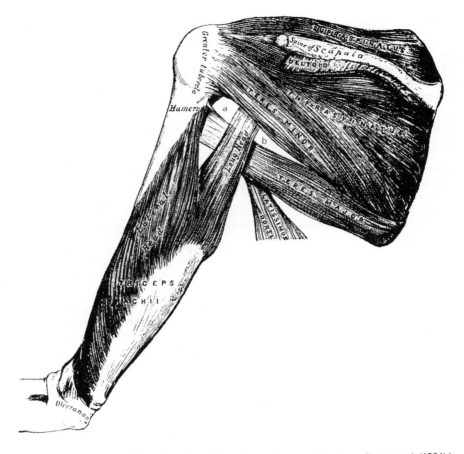

Fig. 2 Posterior view of the shoulder showing the rotator cuff muscles. (Reproduced with permission from Sheon *et al.* (1996).)

Table 3 Differential diagnosis of shoulder pain

Anterior shoulder pain
Bicipital tendinitis
Adhesive capsulitis
Glenohumeral arthritis
Referred pain[a]

Lateral shoulder pain
Rotator cuff tendinitis
Subacromial bursitis
Impingement syndrome
Adhesive capsulitis
Glenohumeral arthritis
Referred pain[a]

Superior shoulder pain
Cervical spine disease
Acromioclavicular arthritis
Referred pain[a]

[a] Causes of referred pain include cervical root compression, thoracic outlet syndrome, reflex sympathetic dystrophy, diaphragmatic irritation, phrenic nerve irritation, coronary artery disease, dissecting aortic aneurysm, and carcinoma of the lung.

tendons to the subacromial bursa, patients with pathologies affecting these structures present with the same complaints and are managed similarly.

The most common complaint is that of a dull ache in the deltoid area that worsens at night, preventing the patient from lying on that side. Occasionally, patients may have pain and difficulty raising the arm above the head or putting on a coat. If the pain is more posterior in position, then involvement of the teres minor or the infraspinatus tendon should be suspected.

On physical examination, the pain can be reproduced by passively abducting the arm above the acromium. This manoeuvre compresses the rotator cuff tendons and the subacromial bursa beneath the greater tuberosity of the humerus and the acromium thus reproducing the pain. One can further distinguish between involvement of the subacromial bursa and the different rotator cuff tendons by applying resistance to active range of motion. Pain on resisted abduction suggests supraspinatus tendinitis, pain on resisted external rotation indicates teres minor or supraspinatus tendinitis, and pain with abduction that is not increased with resisted movement implies subacromial bursitis. Radiological evaluation is not necessary unless there is a history of trauma or the patient does not respond to appropriate therapy.

Treatment of rotator cuff tendinitis includes the use of non-steroidal anti-inflammatory drugs and local corticosteroid and anaesthetic injections. The efficacy of local steroid injections is controversial, but may be preferred to non-steroidal anti-inflammatory

Table 4 Differential diagnosis of frozen shoulder

Unilateral frozen shoulder
Osteoarthritis
Fracture
Calcific tendinitis
Chondrocalcinosis
Milwaukee shoulder
Avascular necrosis
Dislocation
Malignancy

Bilateral frozen shoulder
Rheumatoid arthritis
Polymyalgia rheumatica
Diabetes
Hypothyroidism
Hyperparathyroidism

drugs for an elderly patient with concomitant medical problems. Referral to physical therapy for range of motion exercises may provide additional benefits.

Rotator cuff tears

Rotator cuff tears can vary from a minimal tear affecting a few fibres to full thickness of the cuff resulting in communication between the glenohumeral joint and the subacromial bursa. It usually occurs in the absence of a history of significant trauma, and risk factors include arthritis of the shoulder, systemic corticosteroids, and chronic haemodialysis.

Patients typically present with symptoms similar to those of rotator cuff tendinitis. Passive abduction is possible, but cannot be actively maintained (drop arm sign). Diagnosis is clinical and can be confirmed by an arthrogram or magnetic resonance imaging (**MRI**). The only proven successful therapy is surgical repair. In an elderly patient, where the surgery is difficult, the decision to perform surgery needs to be considered in the context of the patient's other medical problems and level of activity. If surgery is contraindicated, local corticosteroid injections for pain relief and referral to physical therapy are generally beneficial.

Adhesive capsulitis

Adhesive capsulitis or frozen shoulder refers to generalized pain around the shoulder associated with loss of active and passive motion in all directions. It rarely occurs before the age of 50 years and can develop after any type of shoulder disease and immobility. In addition it is described to occur with diabetes and after stroke, myocardial infarction, and trauma. However, many cases are idiopathic (Sheon et al. 1996).

Diagnosis is mostly clinical after excluding other conditions mimicking frozen shoulder (Table 4). Radiological examination is helpful to rule out a fracture. Arthrography can differentiate frozen shoulder from rotator cuff tear, but should only be done if repair of a rotator cuff tear is contemplated. Management of frozen shoulder involves treatment with non-steroidal anti-inflammatory drugs, glucocorticoid injections in the glenohumeral joint and subacromial bursa, and

pendulum and wall-climbing exercises (Fig. 3). Manipulation under anaesthesia is only indicated for those patients whose symptoms have failed to respond to other treatments.

Thoracic outlet syndrome

Compression of the neurovascular bundle where the brachial plexus, subclavian vein, and artery exit beneath the clavicle and the subclavius muscle is called the thoracic outlet syndrome. Clinical presentation depends on whether the obstruction affects predominantly the neural or the vascular bundle. Isolated neurogenic or vascular types are rare. The overlapping type of neurogenic and vascular symptoms without objective findings is more common, but its presence is widely disputed (Sheon et al. 1996).

The predominant symptoms in patients with this syndrome include numbness and pain, typically radiating from the neck and the shoulder to the arm and the hand in an ulnar distribution affecting the ring and the fifth finger. Weakness and intrinsic muscle atrophy can occur late in the disease. Vascular symptoms can accompany the neurological features and consist of discoloration and sensations of cold swelling of the hand, especially in the morning.

The most common causes of thoracic outlet syndrome are sagging shoulder musculature, obesity, and, in women, heavy breasts. People in occupations requiring hyperabduction, such as painting and welding, are at increased risk as well. Anatomical abnormalities such as cervical ribs, elongation of a cervical transverse process, hypertrophy of the omohyoid or the scalene muscles, or poststenotic aneurysms of the subclavian artery are also implicated in thoracic outlet syndrome.

The most important part of the physical examination is to observe the patient for any postural problems in a comparison of one side with the other. Manoeuvres that can be helpful include the Adson test, the hyperabduction manoeuvre, and the costoclavicular manoeuvre. All tests can be positive in asymptomatic people and need to be interpreted in the context of the history (Rayan and Jones 1995).

Management should be directed towards eliminating any aggravating factors identified. Exercises to strengthen and correct the postural deficits are of paramount importance and may be helpful in 50 to 90 per cent of the cases. Surgery is necessary in less than 5 per cent of the cases and should not be attempted unless conservative therapy has failed and other aetiologies for the patient's symptoms (such as a supraclavicular mass or carpal tunnel syndrome) have been excluded.

Elbow

The elbow is a hinge joint that allows flexion and extension of the forearm with some degree of pronation and supination. The majority of elbow pain is caused by involvement of the periarticular structures. Rarely, elbow pain is caused by an intra-articular disorder such as rheumatoid arthritis or crystalline disease, in which case features in the history and physical examination are helpful.

Ulnar nerve entrapment

Ulnar nerve entrapment is a compression neuropathy in the cubital tunnel where the nerve passes the aponeurosis of origin of the flexor carpi ulnaris. External compression, previous fracture or scarring, recurrent subluxation of the nerve, and entrapment distal to the

Dupuytren's contracture

Dupuytren's contracture is a nodular fibrosing lesion of the palmar fascia ultimately leading to contracture of one or more fingers at the metacarpophalangeal joints. It is more common in Caucasians, with the incidence rising with age. Men are more often affected than are women in a ratio of 5:1. Familial clustering is common with a suggestion of an autosomal dominant pattern with variable penetrance (Wurster-Hill *et al.* 1988). The condition can also coexist with other fibrosing diseases such as Peyronie's disease, nodular plantar fibromatosis, and nodular fasciitis of the popliteal fascia (Wooldridge 1988).

The aetiology of the disease is unknown, but it has been related to cigarette smoking (An *et al.* 1988), epilepsy, use of barbiturates, alcoholism, diabetes mellitus, chronic obstructive pulmonary disease, and reflex sympathetic dystrophy (Lynch and Jayson 1979); repetitive trauma is not thought to play a role (French *et al.* 1990). Dupuytren's contracture needs to be distinguished from other similar conditions such as diabetic cheiroarthropathy, fibrosing palmar tenosynovitis, inflammatory arthritis, and traumatic scars.

Patients typically present with painless contractures of the ulnar side of one or both hands with the fourth finger affected earliest followed by the fifth, third, and second. Patients usually cannot place their hands flat on the table (positive table top test) owing to fixed flexion at the metacarpophalangeal joints. The process may remain stable for years or rapidly progress to produce severe deformity and loss of hand function.

Treatment for mild disease involves heat therapy and stretching exercises. Intralesional corticosteroids may be used to control pain. Limited or total fasciectomy should be reserved for those patients with significant impairment (Ketchum and Hixson 1987).

Trigger finger

Trigger finger, also known as snapping finger or stenosing digital tenosynovitis, typically results from repetitive movements of the fingers. Patients usually present with intermittent locking of the thumbs or the fingers upon awakening in the morning. Anatomically, tenosynovitis of the flexor tendons occurs resulting in fibrosis and occasionally the formation of a tendon nodule (Canoso 1990).

Although repetitive trauma is the most common cause of this condition, it has also been described with rheumatoid arthritis (Gray and Gottlieb 1977), psoriatic arthritis, diabetes, amyloidosis, hypothyroidism, sarcoidosis, and tuberculosis.

Treatment consists of local heat, use of non-steroidal anti-inflammatory drugs, and splinting of the finger during sleep to avoid flexion. Intralesional corticosteroids are effective and occasionally curative. Patients more likely to need surgery are those with significant triggering, duration longer than 6 months, and involvement of many fingers (Patel and Bassini 1992).

Knee

The knee is one of the largest joints in the body and the most commonly injured and affected by inflammatory diseases. The cartilaginous medial and lateral menisci protect the tibial plateau and the femoral condyles and distribute forces across the area. The medial and lateral collateral ligaments and the anterior and posterior cruciate

ligament provide stability to the knee. External to the capsule are several bursae that are frequently involved with inflammatory processes. Those include the suprapatellar, prepatellar, infrapatellar, and an adventitious cutaneous bursa in the anterior knee region, the gastrocnemius and the semimembranosus in the posterior region, and the sartorius and anserine bursae which lie medially. Three bursae lie in the lateral region of the knee and anterior to the medial collateral ligament is the 'no name, no fame' bursa of Stuttle (Sheon *et al.* 1996).

Bursitis

The most commonly affected bursae of the knee are the prepatellar bursa, infrapatellar bursa, and anserine bursa. The prepatellar bursa is a superficial bursa that is easily affected by trauma and infections. If infected, patients typically present with sudden onset of pain, swelling, and erythema. Diagnosis of the infection is by culture of aspirated fluid, and treatment is by repeated aspiration and appropriate antibiotics. Recurrent kneeling with forward-leaning posture may lead to chronic inflammation in this bursa, hence the name housemaid's knee. Treatment for chronic bursitis consists of protecting the knee from the trauma. The infrapatellar bursa is located between the patellar tendon and the tibia, and can become chronically inflamed by kneeling in an upright posture (clergyman's knee). Like the prepatellar bursa, it can be affected by trauma and infection and is then treated similarly.

The anserine bursa is located in the medial aspect of the knee under the tendons of the sartorius, gracilis, and semitendinosus as they attach to the medial aspect of the tibia. Anserine bursitis is seen most commonly in obese women with osteoarthritis of the knees. Patients typically complain of pain on climbing the stairs or when their knees touch each other at night. Examination reveals exquisite tenderness over the bursa. Therapy involves rest, stretching of the quadriceps and adductor muscles, and local corticosteroid injection.

Popliteal cysts

Popliteal cysts (Baker's cysts) are common in osteoarthritis but may occur with any condition associated with fluid in the knee. Patients typically complain of fullness in the back of the knee aggravated by walking. If the pain extends into the calf and is associated with swelling and erythema, rupture of the cyst should be suspected.

Physical examination usually reveals swelling of the popliteal fossa. Foucher's sign (tensing of the cyst on extension and softening on semiflexion) is positive and differentiates Baker's cyst from an aneurysm. Occasionally, the cyst may rupture leading to symptoms suggestive of acute thrombophlebitis. Both MRI and ultrasound can be used to differentiate pseudothrombophlebitis from thrombophlebitis, although MRI is more sensitive. Treatment is based on treating the underlying cause and corticosteroid injections into the knee joint.

Hip

The hip joint serves an important role in both locomotion and weight bearing and is subject to frequent mechanical stress. Hip pain is the most common symptom of hip diseases and is a major source of disability for the affected individual. Causes of hip pain include

Table 6 Differential diagnosis of hip pain

Anterior thigh and groin pain
Osteoarthritis
Avascular necrosis
Iliopsoas bursitis
Referred pain
Hip fracture

Lateral hip pain
Trochanteric bursitis
Fascia lata syndrome

Posterior hip pain
Ischial bursitis
Sacroiliitis
Radiculopathy
Tumours

fractures, osteoarthritis, inflammatory synovitis, tendinitis, and bursitis (Table 6). Hip fractures should always be considered in an elderly individual with hip pain and an abnormal gait.

Trochanteric bursitis

Trochanteric bursitis occurs more commonly in women and predominantly in middle-aged or elderly individuals. Patients typically complain of pain along the lateral aspect of the hips exacerbated by lying on that side, walking, and rising from a chair (Toohey et al. 1990). On physical examination, pain may be reproduced by palpating the trochanteric area. In addition, pain may be exacerbated by external rotation against resistance. Other conditions that may contribute to trochanteric bursitis include osteoarthritis of the hip or the spine, scoliosis, leg-length discrepancy, and obesity. Treatment includes local injection with corticosteroids, heat, rest, and stretching exercises of the gluteus medius muscle and the iliotibial band.

Iliopsoas bursitis

The iliopsoas bursa lies between the iliopsoas muscle and the joint capsule. It is uncommonly affected except in association with underlying hip pathology. Patients typically present with anterior thigh and groin pain. They may also hold the hip in flexion and external rotation to eliminate pain and limp to prevent hyperextension. Examination usually reveals tenderness over the involved area. A cystic mass is present in the groin in 30 per cent of cases and in this situation other causes of groin masses should be excluded. Treatment should be directed at the underlying hip pathology. Corticosteroid injection might be helpful and may need to be done with the help of a radiologist. With recurrence of the bursitis, surgical excision may be necessary.

Ischial bursitis

Ischial bursitis (weaver's bottom) refers to inflammation of the bursa overlying the ischial tuberosity. It is usually caused by sitting on hard surfaces for prolonged periods of time. Pain can be severe when sitting or lying down and can radiate to the back of the thigh.

Examination usually shows point tenderness over the ischial tuberosity. Local corticosteroid injections, use of cushions, and knees-to-chest exercises are helpful. In cases resistant to therapy, other causes of buttock pain such as prostatitis or sacroiliitis should be considered (Sheon et al. 1996).

Piriformis syndrome

The piriformis muscle occupies the greater sciatic notch. Patients typically present with pain over the buttocks radiating down to the back of the leg, occasionally associated with a limp. Women are typically more affected than men and history of trauma to the buttock area is common. Examination reveals tenderness of the muscle on rectal or vaginal examination that is exacerbated by resisted internal rotation, abduction, or external rotation (Wyant 1979). Glucocorticosteroid injection in the muscle is usually helpful in alleviating the symptoms.

References

An, H.S., Southworth, S.R., Jackson, W.T., and Russ, B. (1988). Cigarette smoking and Dupuytren's contracture of the hand. *Journal of Hand Surgery*, **13**, 772–4.

Bennett, R.M., Gatter, R.A., Campbell, S.M., Andrews, R.P., Clark, S., and Scarola, J.A. (1988). A comparison of cyclobenzaprine and placebo in the management of fibrositis: a double-blind controlled study. *Arthritis and Rheumatism*, **31**, 1535–42.

Canoso, J.J. (1990). Bursitis, tenosynovitis, ganglions, and painful lesions of the wrist, elbow and hand. *Current Opinion in Rheumatology*, **2**, 276–81.

Clauw, D.J. (1995). Fibromyalgia: more than just a musculoskeletal disease. *American Family Physician*, **52**, 843–51.

Dawson, D.M. (1993). Entrapment neuropathies of the upper extremities. *New England Journal of Medicine*, **329**, 2013–18.

Franklin, G.M., Haug, J., Heyer, N., Checkoway, H., and Peck, N. (1991). Occupational carpal tunnel syndrome in Washington State, 1984–1988. *American Journal of Public Health*, **81**, 741–6.

French, P.D., Kitchen, V.S., and Harris, J.R.W. (1990). Prevalence of Dupuytren's contracture in patients infected with HIV. *British Medical Journal*, **301**, 967.

Goldenberg, D.L., Felson D.T., and Dinerman, H. (1986). A randomized controlled trial of amitriptyline and naproxen in the treatment of patients with fibromyalgia. *Arthritis and Rheumatism*, **29**, 1371–7.

Goroll, A.H., May, L.A., and Mulley, A.G. Jr (ed.) (1995). *Primary care medicine*, pp. 760–1. J.B. Lippincott, Philadelphia, PA.

Gray, R.G. and Gottlieb, N.L. (1977). Hand flexor tenosynovitis in rheumatoid arthritis. Prevalence, distribution, and associated rheumatic features. *Arthritis and Rheumatism*, **20**, 1003–8.

Harvey, F.J., Harvey, P.M., and Horsley, M.W. (1990). de Quervain's disease: surgical or nonsurgical treatment. *Journal of Hand Surgery*, **15**, 83–7.

Katz, J.N., Stirrat, C.R., and Larson, M.G. (1990). A self administered hand symptom diagram for the diagnosis and epidemiologic study of carpal tunnel syndrome. *Journal of Rheumatology*, **17**, 1495–8.

Ketchum, L.D. and Hixson, F.P. (1987). Dermofasciectomy and full thickness grafts in the treatment of Dupuytren's contracture. *Journal of Hand Surgery*, **12**, 659–63.

Kruger, V.L., Kraft, G.H., and Dietz, J.C. (1991). Carpal tunnel syndrome: objective measures and splint use. *Archives of Physical Medicine and Rehabilitation*, **72**, 517–20.

Lynch, M. and Jayson, M.V. (1979). Fasciitis and fibrosis. *Rheumatic Diseases Clinics of North America*, **5**, 833–55.

Moldofsky, H. (1989). Sleep and fibrositis syndrome. *Rheumatic Diseases Clinics of North America*, 15, 90–103.

Omer, G.E. Jr (1992). Median nerve compression at the wrist. *Hand Clinics*, 8, 317–24.

Patel, M.R. and Bassini, L. (1992). Trigger fingers and thumb: when to splint, inject or operate. *Journal of Hand Surgery*, 117, 110–13.

Rayan, G.M. and Jensen, C. (1995). Thoracic outlet syndrome: provocative examination manoeuvres in a typical population. *Journal of Shoulder and Elbow Surgery*, 4, 113–17.

Russell, I.J. (1989). Neurohormonal aspects of fibromyalgia syndrome. *Rheumatic Diseases Clinics of North America*, 15, 149–68.

Schumacher, H.R., Klippel, J.H., and Koopman, W.J. (ed.) (1993). *Primer on the rheumatic diseases*, p. 247. Arthritis Foundation, Atlanta, GA.

Sheon, R.P., Moskowitz, R.W., and Goldberg, V.M. (ed.) (1996). *Soft tissue rheumatic pain. Recognition, management and prevention* (3rd edn). Williams and Wilkins, Baltimore, MD.

Spinner, R.J., Bachman, J.W., and Amadio, P.C. (1989). The many faces of carpal tunnel syndrome. *Mayo Clinic Proceedings*, 64, 829–35.

Stevens, J.C., Sun, S., Beard, C.M., O'Fallon, W.M., and Kurband, L.T. (1988). Carpal tunnel syndrome in Rochester, Minnesota, 1961 to 1980. *Neurology*, 329, 2013–18.

Toohey, A.K., Lasalle T.L., Martinez S., and Polisson, R.P. (1990). Iliopsoas bursitis: clinical features, radiographic findings, and disease associations. *Seminars of Arthritis and Rheumatism*, 20, 41–7.

Wolfe, F., Smythe, H.A., Yunus, M.B., et al. (1990). The American College of Rheumatology 1990 Criteria for the classification of fibromyalgia. Report of the Multicenter Criteria Committee. *Arthritis and Rheumatism*, 33, 160–72.

Wooldridge, W.E. (1988). Four related fibrosing diseases. When you find one, look for another. *Postgraduate Medicine*, 84, 269–74.

Wurster-Hill, D.H., Brown, F., Park J.P., and Gibson S.H. (1988). Cytogenetic studies in Dupuytren's contracture. *American Journal of Human Genetics*, 43, 285–92.

Wyant, G.M. (1979). Chronic pain syndromes and their treatment. III. The piriformis syndrome. *Canadian Anaesthesia Society Journal*, 26, 305–8.

Yunus, M.B. and Kaylan-Raman, U.P. (1989). Muscle biopsy findings in primary fibromyalgia and other forms of nonarticular rheumatism. *Rheumatic Diseases Clinics of North America*, 15, 115–33.

13.8 Foot problems

Arthur E. Helfand

Foot problems represent one of the most distressing and disabling afflictions associated with old age. A key factor in an older person's ability to remain active is the ability to walk effectively and comfortably.

Changes in the foot in relation to age

There are many factors which contribute to the development of foot problems in an older person. Of primary concern are age-associated changes and the presence of multiple chronic diseases. Other significant factors include the amount of walking, limitation in activity, length of any preceding time in hospital or other institutional care, degree of social isolation, emotional adjustments to disease and life in general, and the effects of multiple medications for multiple chronic diseases. Optimal management of foot problems in the older patient requires a comprehensive team approach.

The skin is usually one of the first structures to show change. There is usually a loss of hair below the knee joint and on the dorsum of the foot, with atrophy of the skin giving a parchment-like appearance. Brownish pigmentation is common and related to the deposition of haemosiderin. Hyperkeratosis may be present due to dysfunctional keratinization, as a residuum of pressure and atrophy

of the subcutaneous soft tissue, and as a space replacement as the body adjusts to the changing stress placed on the foot.

The toenails undergo degeneration and may have thickening and longitudinal ridging related to repetitive small injuries and nutritional impairment. Deformities of the toenails become more pronounced and complicated by changes in the periungual nailfolds, such as onychophosis (hyperkeratosis) and tinea unguium (onychomycosis) which are common and usually chronic in older people. Onychomycosis is a constant focus of infection.

There is commonly progressive loss of muscle mass and atrophy of tissue due to decreased activity, which increases the susceptibility of the foot to injury; thus even minor trauma can result in a fracture or rupture of ligaments or tendons.

Impact of disease

Many chronic diseases also produce degenerative changes in the foot. Examples include diabetes mellitus with neuropathy or angiopathy, rheumatoid arthritis, osteoarthritis, gout, and various neuromuscular diseases.

Peripheral arterial insufficiency produces trophic changes, rest pain, intermittent claudication, coldness, and colour changes such as rubor and cyanosis. The presence of haemorrhage subungually or beneath hyperkeratotic tissue, particularly in the diabetic patient, demonstrates angiopathy, which can be an early finding in diabetic patients who are also developing retinal or renal disease.

These changes in the feet predispose the patient to infection, necrosis, and tissue loss if care, which must include education, is not provided in a comprehensive and active manner.

Biomechanical aspects

The feet are fairly rigid structures which must carry heavy physical workloads, both static and dynamic, throughout life. The foot itself is in the shape of a modified rectangle and bears static forces in a triangular pattern. The transmission of weight and force starts at heel strike, and proceeds anteriorly along the lateral segment of the foot and medially across the metatarsal heads to the first metatarsal segment for the push-off phase of the gait cycle. The varied activities of life produce many variations in both the structure and function of the foot, as the body adapts to the stress placed upon it. Flat and hard floor surfaces force the foot to absorb shock, creating prolonged periods of repetitive microtrauma, with the risk of inflammatory changes in bone and soft tissue.

Principles of treatment

Treatment should be directed towards eliminating the cause of trauma and redistributing weight to non-painful areas of the foot. The aims of treatment are to relieve pain and to restore and maintain maximum function.

Foot problems of a mechanical nature typically arise from the interaction between normal morphological variations, the capacity to adapt to stress, and the stressors acting on the foot. Morphological variations may be intrinsic to the foot itself, or extrinsic, such as those arising from changes in the legs, knees, thigh, hip, and back on the human foot. The common intrinsic changes include elements such as a hypermobile segment, pes cavus, atrophy of the interossei muscles producing digiti flexus (hammer toes), and the development of hallux valgus or the so-called 'bunion deformity'.

The foot must be considered as a total end-organ of locomotion; changes in any part of the body that affect the foot are usually the result of a chain of events of a chronic and progressive nature. Once a link in the chain breaks, every effort must be made to prevent further damage and minimize associated complications.

Identifying complicating foot problems

The management of foot problems in the older patient requires early recognition of their aetiological factors, the complaints and symptoms of the patient, physical signs, and the clinical manifestations of disease and degenerative change, which may be local in origin or a complication of a related systemic or functional disease.

Comprehensive assessment

A key component in the management of older patients with foot problems is assessment. This must take into consideration complex and atypical presentations, multiple pathology, multiple drug usage, cognitive impairment, the significance of laboratory results, and

Table 1 Common disorders predisposing to foot problems in elderly patients

Diabetes mellitus
Arteriosclerosis
Buerger's disease
Peripheral neuropathies associated with:
Malnutrition
Alcohol abuse
Malabsorption
Pernicious anaemia
Cancer
Diabetes mellitus
Drugs and toxins
Hereditary disorders
Leprosy
Neurosyphilis
Uraemia
Injury
Peripheral vascular disease
Raynaud's disease
Amyotrophic lateral sclerosis
Lymphoedema or persistent oedema
Arteritis
Chronic venous insufficiency
Coronary artery disease
Arthropathies
Mental illness, dementia, and learning disabilities
Thyroid disease
Stroke
Coagulation deficits (including anticoagulant therapy)
Sickle cell disease
Chronic obstructive pulmonary disease
Obesity
Chronic skin disease (e.g. psoriasis)
Parkinson's disease
Other forms of disability

decreased organ reserve. In addition there is a need to know the premorbid functional status of the patient, the relationship of family and/or community support, the psychosocial impact of illness and/or trauma, and the availability of preventive services. It is also important to assess the activities and instrumental activities of daily living of the patient, foot pain or discomfort and the relationship to ambulatory dysfunction and deconditioning, and the outcomes of immobility. Systemic diseases which place the patient at greatest risk must also be taken into account. Examples are listed in Table 1.

Table 2 Common abnormalities of the feet of elderly patients

Plantar fasciitis
Spur formation
Calcaneal spurs
Periostitis
Decalcification
Stress fractures
Tendinitis
Tenosynovitis
Pes planus
Pes valgo planus
Pes cavus
Hallux valgus
Hallux limitus
Hallux rigidus
Atrophy of the plantar fat pad
Metatarsal prolapse
Metatarsalgia
Hammer toes
Morton's syndrome
Rotational digital deformities
Joint swelling
Bursitis
Haglund's syndrome
Entrapment syndromes

Table 3 Foot abnormalities in rheumatoid arthritis

Hallux limitus
Hallux rigidus
Hallux valgus
Hallux abducto valgus
Cystic erosion
Sesamoid erosion
Sesamoid displacement
Metatarsophalangeal subluxation
Metatarsophalangeal dislocation
Interphalangeal subluxation
Interphalangeal dislocation
Hammer toe
Ankylosis
Phalangeal resorption
Talonavicular arthritis
Extensor tenosynovitis
Rheumatoid nodules
Bowstring extensor tendons
Tendon displacement
Ganglions
Subcalcaneal bursitis
Retrocalcaneal bursitis
Retroachillal bursitis
Calcaneal spur
Prolapsed metatarsal heads
Atrophy of the plantar fat pad
Varus deformity of the little toe
Bunion

Joint disease

Degenerative joint diseases in the elderly foot, as a result of acute or repetitive and chronic microtrauma, strain, obesity, and/or osteoporosis, may present with a variety of changes as listed in Table 2. These changes may result in pain, limited motion and impaired walking, and ambulatory dysfunction, which reduces the quality of life. Gout may present as episodes of acute gouty arthritis and result in chronic manifestations of painful joints, stiffness, soft tissue tophi, a loss of bone substance, gouty arthritis, and joint deformity.

Chronic rheumatoid arthritis may lead to the manifestations listed in Table 3. Early morning stiffness, pain, fibrosis, ankylosis, contracture, deformity, and impaired walking are characteristic effects in the foot.

The principles of management include appropriate imaging and radiographic studies (weight-bearing and non-weight-bearing) for diagnostic impressions, the use of aspirin and related non-steroidal anti-inflammatory drugs for acute pain, and local steroid injections. Management also includes physical modalities such as superficial and deep heat, although these should be used with caution, ultrasound,

muscle stimulation, transcutaneous electrical nerve stimulation, hydrotherapy, and exercise. Shoe changes and shoe modifications (internal and external) should be assessed, as should the need for special shoes, such as Extra-Depth, custom-moulded, and Thermoldable shoes. The need for orthoses for weight diffusion, weight dispersion, support, and dynamics should also be assessed.

Other syndromes

Morton's syndrome (Table 2) is anterior foot pain due to a 'neuroma' (actually a thickening of the perineurium induced by chronic pressure) of the interdigital nerves between the metatarsal heads. The pain is typically sharp and cramping, and may be associated with pain or paraesthesiae in the corresponding toe cleft. The pain can be provoked

Table 4 Features of ischaemic disease of the feet

Amputation of the whole foot or skeletal portion
Absent foot pulses
Advanced trophic changes
Nail changes: thickening
Pigmentary changes: discoloration
Skin texture: thin and shiny
Skin colour: rubor or cyanosis
Claudication or rest pain
Poor capillary return
Cold feet
Paraesthesiae
Oedema
Ulceration
Gangrene

Table 6 Neurological modalities to be tested

Achilles reflex
Plantar reflex
Vibratory sensation
Joint position sense
Sharp and blunt discrimination
Check for presence of paraesthesiae

Table 7 Neurosensory risk stratification

0	No sensory loss
1	Sensory loss
2	Sensory loss and foot deformity
3	Sensory loss and foot deformity with a history of ulceration

by pressure over the intermetatarsal space. Conservative treatment may be beneficial but surgical excision of the 'neuroma' is often required.

Haglund's syndrome consists of a painful swelling of the bursae around the insertion of the Achilles tendon. It is often due to abnormalities of the calcaneum, either a prominent posterior superior ridge or plantar outgrowths affecting the angle between the bone and Achilles tendon. Treatment is usually surgical but relief may be obtained by shoe heel elevation to prevent pressure between the tendon and shoe edge.

Vascular insufficiency

Arterial insufficiency in the legs and feet may present with the clinical findings listed in Table 4 and graded according to Table 5. The hypertensive patient may have pulsations that are a false reflection of the vascular supply. The foot usually shows colour changes, i.e. pallor, rubor, or cyanosis; it is usually cool with skin dry and atrophic. Superficial infections are common and may be painful.

The neurological assessment may identify changes in the clinical fields outlined in Table 6 with risk stratification as indicated in Table 7.

Table 5 Vascular risk stratification

0	No change
1	Mild claudication
2	Moderate claudication
3	Severe claudication
4	Ischaemic rest pain
5	Minor tissue loss
6	Major tissue loss

The toenails demonstrate onychopathy as a result of nutritional changes, repetitive trauma, and vascular disease; this includes discoloration, onycholysis (loosening) with onychauxis (thickening), onychogryphosis (thickening with deformity), onychorrhexis (longitudinal striations), subungual keratosis, splinter haemorrhage and subungual haematoma, and deformity. Oedema may be present in the toes and surrounding nailfolds as demonstrated by a loss of joint lines. Vascular blebs are common in the later stages of local arterial occlusion. When necrosis and gangrene are present, the results of further diagnostic studies, particularly oscillometric studies, Doppler measurements, arteriography, plethysmography, and computed tomographic angiography can help assess the potential for surgical intervention to revascularize the extremity. Preventive measures and early intervention are essential to avoid loss of tissue and threats to continued independent functioning.

Diabetes mellitus

The older diabetic patient presents a special challenge in relation to foot health. It has been projected that half to three-quarters of all amputations in diabetic patients could be prevented by early intervention where disease is found, improved health education, periodic and prophylactic screening and evaluation, and lifelong surveillance, prior to the onset of symptoms. A summary of primary risk factors, symptoms, and clinical findings are listed in Table 8. Table 9 lists the items that should be considered in screening for foot problems in diabetic patients, and Table 10 summarizes the management approach to the prevention of diabetic foot problems.

For the older diabetic, the multiple system involvement, comorbid conditions, and the changes associated with ageing, especially residual deformity and atrophy of soft tissues, add complicating factors and potentiate the social restrictions related to these multiple clinical conditions.

Hyperkeratotic lesions form as space replacements and provide a focus for ulceration due to increased pressure on the soft tissues

Table 8 Risk factors for diabetic foot problems

Age

Smoking

Diabetes present for more than 10 years

Decreased peripheral arterial pulses

Decreased peripheral sensation

Deformities
    Hallux valgus
    Hammer toes
    Prominent metatarsal heads
    Atrophy of plantar fat pad
    Metatarsal head prolapse

History of foot ulcer

Peripheral neuropathy

Peripheral vascular disease

Diabetic neuropathy

Limited joint mobility

Visual impairment

History of alcohol abuse

Inability to bend easily

Patient lives alone

Other specific disease-related risk factors
    Parkinson's disease
    Arthritis
    Renal impairment
    Mental disorders

with an associated localized avascularity from direct pressure and counterpressure. When ulceration is present, the base is usually covered by keratosis which retards and may prevent healing.

Radiographic findings in older diabetic patients usually demonstrate thin trabeculae, decalcification, joint changes, osteophytic formation, osteolysis, deformities, and osteoporosis.

The general principles of the management of foot problems in older diabetics are summarized in Table 10 and include a reduction in local trauma by the use of orthotics, shoe modifications, specialized footwear, and the maximization of weight diffusion and dispersal. After adequate vascular evaluation, physical exercise can be used to improve the vascular supply to the foot together with oxpentifylline (pentoxifylline). Consideration should also be given to appropriate invasive techniques such as surgical revascularization. Ulcers usually require some debridement and treatment with antiseptic compresses, antibiotics as indicated, and appropriate methods to reduce weight to the ulcerative site. Radiographs and bone scans should be obtained early to detect bone change. Aggressive systemic antibiotic therapy and hospital admission may be necessary to prevent a possible amputation and adequately manage the patient.

Asymptomatic older diabetic patients should be evaluated as noted in Tables 8 to 10 so that potential problems are identified in their earliest phase, thus embracing the concept of secondary prevention.

Patients with foot conditions requiring primary management should be followed every 4 to 9 weeks, depending on the extent of complications. A multidisciplinary team is essential, including the primary care doctor and endocrinologist, podiatrist, nurse, educator, and, as necessary, the vascular surgeon, orthopaedic surgeon, social worker, pharmacist, physical therapist, and orthotist.

Psychological aspects of foot health

With depressive states and dementias common in the older patient, ability to maintain the basic and instrumental activities of daily living are significantly related to mobility and walking. The foot is more than a single-purpose locomotor accessory. From a psychosocial point of view, it is clearly utilized to demonstrate hostility, such as kicking an individual or object. It may also be the site of unconsciously chosen expressions of deeper emotional feelings and inadequacies. In addition, the foot, and primarily the musculoskeletal structures, are often a focus for psychosomatic problems associated with depression, loneliness, and so on. For example, suggesting to an older patient with emotional problems that, considering the condition of her feet, one cannot understand how she can walk, may inhibit ambulation and lead to social dependence.

The most common primary physical manifestations of the foot associated with emotional disorders in older people include hysterical paralysis, psychogenic tremors, localized neurodermatitis, pruritus, and hyperhidrosis. Pre-existing conditions that are secondarily affected by emotional disorders resulting in an exacerbation of the disease or disorder, with pedal manifestations, include gout, diabetes mellitus, obesity, vascular insufficiency, psoriasis, urticaria, and atopic dermatitis.

When an older patient presents with inappropriate clinical complaints and symptoms that are not demonstrable as an actual foot disorder or as a manifestation of organic pathology, the potential for emotional transfer must be considered. The foot may provide more than a primary focus for an emotional or psychiatric disorder, it may prove to be exclusive. The older patient may be utilizing his or her foot complaint as a means to seek attention, expecting relief through some form of physical treatment. When such treatment fails to bring relief, the patient usually reacts emotionally by blaming the doctor or other professional staff, feeling hopeless, dejected, and even hostile. The patient may also react somatically, by increasing symptoms and complaints. Foot problems with psychogenic components usually represent some form of anxiety neurosis. They can also present as a manifestation of neurotic or psychotic depression, schizophrenia, involutional psychosis, or dementia. In addition, with our changing society and longevity, the potential to manage foot problems associated with mental retardation, and drug and alcohol abuse, must be considered in planning for foot care for older people in mental health programmes.

Primary foot problems and their management

The management of localized foot problems in the older patient requires a review of aetiological factors, the symptoms presented by the patient, physical signs and clinical manifestations, and the

Table 9 Diabetic foot screen

Change since last evaluation	**Vascular findings**
Current or prior foot ulcer	Cold feet
Change in foot shape or size	Intermittent claudication involving the calf or foot
Weakness	Pain at rest, especially nocturnal, relieved by dependency
Thickened nails with or without subungual haematoma	Dry atrophic skin
Callus with or without haematoma	Rubor of toes
Pre-ulcer signs	Dystrophic toenails
Sensory changes and levels	Prolonged capillary filling time
Skin changes: redness, swelling, warmth, dryness, or maceration	Absent pedal, popliteal, or femoral pulses
Footwear appropriate to risk category	Femoral bruits
Clinical foot care needs	Dependent rubor with plantar pallor on elevation
	Decreased skin temperature

Dermatological findings

Painful or painless wounds
Slow healing or non-healing wounds
Skin colour changes
    Cyanosis
    Redness
Chronic itching, scaling, or dryness
Recurrent infections
    Paronychia
    Tinea pedis
Keratotic lesions with or without haemorrhage, either plantar or digital
Trophic ulcers
Trophic nail changes
Onychomycosis
Onychodystrophy
Onychocryptosis

Neurological findings

Sensory
    Burning
    Tingling
    Clawing sensations
    Pain
    Hypersensitivity
    Sensory deficits
    Loss of vibration sense
    Proprioceptive loss
    Pain
    Impaired temperature perception
    Hyperaesthesia
Motor
    Weakness and foot drop
    Diminished to absent deep tendon reflexes, Achilles then patellar, and weakness
Autonomic
    Diminished sweating
    Hypohidrosis
    Well-perfused, warm, and apparently healthy foot on initial inspection
    Foot pulses palpable with prominent dorsal foot veins
    Diabetic dermopathy or pretibial lesions
    Dry thickened skin
    Xerosis
    Calluses under high-pressure area

Musculoskeletal findings

Gradual change in foot shape or size
Sudden painless change in foot shape with swelling, without a history of trauma
Cavus feet with claw toes
Drop foot
'Rocker-bottom foot' (Charcot's foot)
Neuropathic arthropathy

appropriate diagnostic studies. Complications, sequelae, relevant treatment, prognosis, and overall management of the older patient should reflect a reasonable approach that will reduce pain, improve functional capacity, maintain restored function, and provide for the comfort of the patient in his or her activities of daily living.

Toenails

Changes in the toenails, which commonly occur in older people may be the result of new or long-standing disease, injury, and/or functional abnormality. The primary clinical entities are listed in Table 11. Onychia is an inflammation involving the posterior nail wall and bed. It may be precipitated by local trauma or pressure, or manifest as a complication of systemic disease, such as diabetes mellitus, and is an early sign of a developing infection. Mild erythema, swelling, and pain are the most common findings. Treatment should be directed to removing all pressure from the area and the use of tepid saline compresses for 15 min, three times a day. Appropriate antibiotics

should be considered for patients at particular risk for paronychia and cellulitis. Lamb's wool, tube foam, or modification of the shoe should also be considered to reduce pressure to the toe and nail. If the onychia is not treated early, paronychia may develop with infection and abscess of the posterior nail wall. This may progress proximally and deeper structures may become involved. The potential for osteomyelitis, necrosis, and gangrene is obviously greater in the presence of diabetes and vascular insufficiency. Management includes establishing drainage, microbiological culture, appropriate antibiotics, radiographs and scans (if there is suspicion of bony involvement), compresses, and early follow-up.

Deformities of the toenails result from repetitive microtrauma, degenerative changes, or disease. For example, the continued rubbing of the toenails against the inferior toe box of the shoe is sufficient to produce change. The initial thickening is termed onychauxis. Onychorrhexis with accentuation of normal ridging, trophic changes, and longitudinal striations may reflect systemic disease and/or nutritional imbalance.

Table 10 Risk categories related to management

General principles	**Goals in management**
Key issues of preventive strategies	Relieve areas of excessive plantar pressure
Peripheral neuropathy	Reduce shock pressures
Peripheral vascular disease	Reduce shear
Limited joint mobility	Accommodate deformities
Elevated plantar pressures	Stabilize and support deformities
Bony deformities	Limit joint motion
Hyperkeratosis	Weight diffusion
Diabetic onychopathy/onychodystrophy	Weight dispersion
Prior ulceration	

Management by risk category	
Risk category 0	*Management*
Has a disease that leads to insensitivity	Examine feet at each visit or at least four times per year
Has protective sensation	Clinical care annually as needed
Has not had a plantar ulcer	Patient education
Risk category 1	*Management*
Does not have protective sensation	Examine feet at each visit or at least four times per year
Has not had a plantar ulcer	Clinical care every 6 months as needed
Does not have foot deformity	Soft orthotics/insoles, Plastazote, etc.
	Patient education
Risk category 2	*Management*
Does not have protective sensation	Examine feet at each visit or at least four times per year
Has not had a plantar ulcer	Comprehensive assessment
Does have foot deformity	Custom-moulded orthotics/insoles
	Prescription footwear
	Patient education
Risk category 3	*Management*
Does not have protective sensation	Examine feet at each visit or at least four times per year
Has a history of plantar ulcer	Clinical care every 1 or 2 months as needed
	Custom-moulded shoes as needed
	Prescription footwear with appropriate orthotics/insoles
	Patient education

When debridement is not effected periodically, the nail structure becomes hypertrophic, continues to thicken and is deformed by pressure from the shoe. Onychogryphosis or 'ram's horn nail' is usually complicated by fungal infection. The resultant disability can prevent an older person from wearing shoes. Pain is usually associated with shoe pressure and the deformity. In addition, a traumatic avulsion of the nail is more frequent with this condition. The exaggerated curvature may even lead to penetration of the skin; with resultant infection and ulceration. Management should be directed towards periodic debridement of the nail both in length and thickness, with as little trauma as possible. The extent of onycholysis (loosening of the nail from the anterior edge) and onychoschizia (splitting), help to determine the amount of debridement. With the excess pressure and deformity, the nail grooves become onychophosed (keratotic). This can be treated by debridement and the use of mild keratolytics and emollients, such as 12 per cent ammonium lactate solution and 10 to 20 per cent urea preparations, at home. With onycholysis, subungual debris and keratosis develop, which increases discomfort and may generate pain. However, in diabetes, or other conditions that reduce sensation, the sense of pain may be lost, which tends to delay care until some complicating condition occurs.

The older diabetic usually exhibits some form of onychopathy or nail change, such as onychorrhexis, onychophosis, deformity, hypertrophy, incurvation or involution, subungual haemorrhage not associated with trauma, onycholysis, onychomadesis, autoavulsion, and mycotic infections. Similar changes can be demonstrated in vascular insufficiency. Other diseases such as haemophilia, coronary artery disease, chronic renal failure and chronic obstructive pulmonary disease also place patients at risk for significant complications. Non-traumatic subungual splinter haemorrhages or haematomas may be the earliest sign of other organ complications and should be considered as an indicator for additional assessment.

The most common non-bacterial infection of the toenails is onychomycosis, a chronic and communicable infection. It may cause distal subungual, white superficial, proximal subungual, or total dystrophic changes. The pathogenic agent is usually a dermatophyte or, less frequently, *Candida*. In the superficial variety, the changes appear on the superior surface of the toenail and generally do not invade the deeper structures. In both the distal and proximal manifestations, the nailbed as well as the nailplate are infected. There is usually some degree of onycholysis and subungual keratosis.

turnover. Because of the age-associated defect in osteoblast function, increased turnover would lead to increased bone loss (Riggs and Melton 1992). Finally, recent studies indicate that both the abnormalities in PTH secretion and the resultant increase in bone resorption are reversible by sufficient increases in calcium intake (McKane *et al.* 1996).

Menopause

Women who have undergone oophorectomy in young adulthood have a lower bone density in later life than non-oophorectomized women of the same age. Surgical menopause accelerates bone loss, and oestrogen replacement prevents or slows this loss in both the appendicular and the axial skeletons (Lindsay *et al.* 1980). Epidemiological studies have shown that postmenopausal administration of oestrogen decreases the occurrence of vertebral and hip fractures by about 50 per cent (Grady *et al.* 1992). Thus oestrogen deficiency at the menopause is an important cause of bone loss and subsequent fractures. Men do not undergo the equivalent of menopause, but gonadal function decreases in some older men and overt male hypogonadism is often associated with vertebral fractures (Orwoll and Klein 1995).

The accelerated phase of postmenopausal bone loss in women decreases exponentially after menopause and becomes asymptotic with the slow phase after 5 to 10 years. It is associated with a high rate of bone turnover; more osteoclasts are present and each of them creates a deeper resorption cavity. As assessed by studies of radiocalcium kinetics, there is an increase in bone accretion but an even greater increase in bone resorption (Eastell *et al.* 1988). The primary effect of oestrogen is to decrease bone resorption. Although it was formerly believed that the action of oestrogen on bone was indirect, it has now been conclusively demonstrated that normal human bone cells contain sex steroid receptors and respond directly to treatment with these steroids (Eriksen *et al.* 1988). While the precise mediators of oestrogen action on the skeleton have not been defined, it appears likely that oestrogen deficiency is associated with increased local skeletal production of a number of bone-resorbing cytokines, such as interleukin 1, interleukin 6, and tumour necrosis factor-α, and decreased production of other factors, such as transforming growth factor-β, that inhibit osteoclastic bone resorption (Pacifici 1992; Turner *et al.* 1994; Manolagas and Jilka 1995). Moreover, while the major effects of oestrogen are on the skeleton, it is becoming clear that oestrogen deficiency is associated with a number of extraskeletal abnormalities in calcium metabolism, such as impaired intestinal and renal tubular calcium absorption, that contribute to the negative calcium balance following the menopause (Gennari *et al.* 1990; McKane *et al.* 1995, 1997; Khosla *et al.* 1997).

Sporadic factors

Certain medical diseases, surgical procedures, and medications may be associated with the development of osteoporosis. Bone loss resulting from the presence of these factors is additive to the age-associated slow bone loss that occurs universally and to the accelerated phase of bone loss that occurs postmenopausally in women. One or more of these sporadic factors can be identified in about 20 per cent of women and about 40 per cent of men who present with vertebral or hip fractures (Khosla *et al.* 1995) (Table 1).

Table 1 Causes of secondary osteoporosis

Hypercortisolism
Hypogonadism
Hyperthyroidism
Hyperparathyroidism
Seizure disorder (anticonvulsants)
Malabsorption syndrome
Rheumatoid arthritis
Connective tissue disease
Chronic neurological disease
Chronic obstructive lung disease
Malignancy

Modified with permission from Khosla *et al.* (1995).

In addition, a sedentary life style, cigarette smoking, an excessive ethanol intake (more than two drinks daily), and very low calcium intake (<500 mg/day) may contribute to bone loss.

Trauma

Because the risk of fracture increases as bone density decreases with ageing, older persons with decreased bone density are uniquely subject to fractures from moderate trauma of the sort that rarely causes injury in young people. The most common cause of fracture among older persons is a 'simple' fall from a standing height or less, although a few hip fractures may be spontaneous and vertebral fractures frequently result from lifting or straining. The risk of falling increases with age, and at least a third of community-dwelling older people experience one or more falls annually with an even higher rates among institutionalized persons (Melton and Riggs 1985; Tinetti *et al.* 1988). The pathophysiology of and risk factors for falling are discussed in Chapter 18.11.

It is important to note that the majority of falls do not result in specific injury, even among older persons, although fear of a subsequent fall may become disabling. In most studies, a fifth to a third of the documented falls led to a medically attended injury; only about 1 per cent of these falls resulted in hip fracture. Thus additional risk factors are needed to account for the full spectrum of fall outcomes. These factors are even less completely known than the risk factors for falling *per se*, but it is generally believed that older persons are less able to break the impact of a fall because of decreases in their strength and reaction time. In addition, an age-associated decrease in soft tissue over the proximal femur leads to an increase in the forces on the hips resulting from a fall.

Clinical heterogeneity

The available evidence suggests that there are at least two distinct syndromes of involutional osteoporosis that differ with respect to

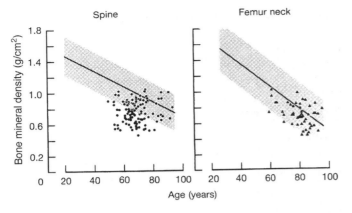

Fig. 3 Bone mineral density values for vertebrae (left) and femoral neck (right) plotted as a function of age in 111 patients with vertebral fractures and 49 patients with hip fractures. The line represents the regression on age; the shaded area represents the 90 per cent confidence limits for 166 normal women. (Reproduced with permission from Riggs and Melton (1986).)

clinical presentation and to relationship of the disease with menopause and age (Riggs and Melton 1990).

Type I (postmenopausal) osteoporosis

This syndrome characteristically affects women within 15 to 20 years after menopause and results from an exaggeration of the post-menopausal phase of accelerated bone loss. Much less commonly, a form of osteoporosis that is similar clinically to that in postmenopausal women occurs in men of the same age. Type I osteoporosis is characterized by a disproportionate loss of trabecular bone (Fig. 3), which results in fractures of the vertebrae and distal forearm (Colles' fracture). The vertebral fractures are usually the 'crush' type associated with deformation and pain. Also, there is an increase in the incidence of ankle fractures and in the rate of tooth loss. These skeletal sites all contain large amounts of trabecular bone.

During the accelerated phase of bone loss, there is increased bone turnover. With its greater surface area, trabecular bone has a rate of loss that is three times normal, but the rate of loss in cortical bone is only slightly greater than normal in patients with type I osteoporosis. The deeper resorption cavities lead to trabecular plate perforation and loss of structural trabeculae, which weakens the bones. The vertebrae are particularly predisposed to acute collapse. However, by the time of clinical presentation tetracycline-labelled iliac crest biopsies may show bone turnover to be high, normal, or low. Thus some osteoporotic patients may have reached a 'burnt-out' stage and will have little further loss of trabecular bone.

Only a subset of postmenopausal women develop type I osteoporosis, although all postmenopausal women have low oestrogen levels. Serum sex steroid levels are similar in postmenopausal women with and without type I osteoporosis. Thus one or more additional causal factors are present in postmenopausal osteoporotic women and interact with oestrogen deficiency to determine individual susceptibility. The possibilities include impaired coupling of formation to resorption, increased local production of cytokines or other factors that increase bone resorption, prolongation of the phase of accelerated

bone loss, low bone density at the inception of menopause, or some combination of these (Riggs and Melton 1990).

Type II (age-associated) osteoporosis

This occurs predominantly in older men and women and results from continuation of the slow age-associated phase of bone loss. It is manifested mainly by hip and vertebral fractures, although fractures of the proximal humerus, proximal tibia, and pelvis are also common. The trabecular thinning associated with the slow phase of bone loss is responsible for gradual, usually painless, vertebral deformities. In contrast with the findings in type I osteoporosis, these deformities are often of the multiple wedge type, leading to dorsal kyphosis (dowager's hump). Bone density values for the proximal femur, vertebrae, and sites in the appendicular skeleton are usually in the lower part of the normal range adjusted for age and sex (Fig. 3). This suggests proportionate losses of cortical and trabecular bone, and a rate of loss that is only slightly more than that in age-matched peers. Therefore the process causing type II osteoporosis may affect virtually the entire population of ageing men and women and, as the slow phase of bone loss progresses, more and more of them will have bone density values in the osteoporotic range (Riggs and Melton 1990).

The two most important age-associated factors are decreased osteoblast function and the age-associated factors leading to secondary hyperparathyroidism. However, the effects of all risk factors for bone loss encountered over a lifetime are cumulative. Thus the residual effects of menopausal bone loss many years before may help to explain why elderly women have a twofold greater incidence of hip fractures than elderly men, even though the rates of slow bone loss are similar. In addition, recent data indicate that oestrogen deficiency may continue to play a significant role even in late (>20 years postmenopause) bone loss in postmenopausal women and perhaps also in men (Khosla *et al.* 1997; McKane *et al.* 1997; Riggs *et al.* 1998).

Diagnosis

The major diagnostic advance in recent years has been the development of practical methods for measuring bone density at the actual sites of the clinically important fractures. Three techniques are generally available: dual-photon absorptiometry, dual-energy X-ray absorptiometry, and quantitative CT using single-energy scanning (for a review see Genant *et al.* (1996)). Ultrasonic techniques are likely to be increasingly used for scanning purposes in the future.

Dual-photon absorptiometry uses transmission scanning with an isotope source (usually ^{153}Gd) that emits two energy peaks, thereby providing a bone density measurement that can be corrected for soft-tissue thickness and composition. This technique has largely been replaced by dual-energy X-ray absorptiometry, a major technological improvement. In principle, dual-energy X-ray absorptiometry is similar to dual-photon absorptiometry but uses an X-ray tube rather than an isotope to produce the photons of two energies. This technique has excellent reproducibility (1 to 2 per cent), low radiation exposure (<3 mrem), and a shorter scan time (5 to 10 min). Both dual-photon absorptiometry and dual-energy X-ray absorptiometry measure the entire vertebra, which is about 70 per cent trabecular bone, and both are sensitive to the effects of dystrophic calcification and vertebral compression in the scanning area. When osteoarthritis of the spine

Table 2 WHO diagnostic criteria for osteoporosis

Normal	BMD within 1 SD of young adult reference mean
Low bone mass (osteopenia)	BMD between 1.0 and 2.5 SD below young adult reference mean
Osteoporosis	BMD 2.5 SD or more below the young adult reference mean
Severe (established) osteoporosis	Osteoporosis as above with one or more fragility fractures

BMD, bone mineral density.

Table 3 Biochemical markers of bone remodelling

Bone formation (serum)
Osteocalcin
Bone-specific alkaline phosphatase
Carboxy-terminal extension peptide of type I procollagen

Bone resorption (urine)
Pyridinoline
Deoxypyridinoline
N-telopeptide of the cross-links of collagen
C-telopeptide of the cross-links of collagen

or calcification of spinal ligaments and aorta is present, dual-energy X-ray absorptiometry may give misleading results for bone density of the lumbar spine in persons over age 70. Dual-energy X-ray absorptiometry can also be used to assess bone density in the proximal femur.

Quantitative CT can provide a measurement limited exclusively to the trabecular bone in the centre of the vertebral body. When it is carefully performed as a research procedure, a reproducibility of 2 to 3 per cent can be achieved but the reproducibility for multi-use instruments may be as poor as 6 to 10 per cent. Accuracy is poor (12–30 per cent), mainly because of the confounding effect of marrow fat, and the radiation exposure is high (200–1000 mrem, depending on the quality of the scanner and the expertise of the operator). Nonetheless quantitative CT can provide useful information and, in contrast with dual-photon absorptiometry and dual-energy X-ray absorptiometry, can be used to evaluate trabecular bone loss in the vertebrae of elderly patients. Methods such as single-photon absorptiometry that measure only the appendicular skeleton are of limited use in the evaluation of osteoporosis, a disease in which the major fractures occur in the axial skeleton.

Because of the low radiation exposure and excellent reproducibility, dual-energy X-ray absorptiometry is increasingly being used to diagnose osteoporosis in the preclinical phase of the disease, before the onset of fracture. Indeed, the main purpose of measuring bone density is to predict the risk of fracture, since every standard deviation decrease in bone density approximately doubles the risk of fracture (an estimate based on data from a number of prospective studies). In order to evaluate more fully the prevalence and incidence of osteoporosis worldwide, the WHO convened an expert panel to define osteoporosis on the basis of bone mass measurements. The definition is based on T scores, or the number of standard deviation units that a given individual is below the young adult reference mean (Table 2). Using these criteria, a diagnosis of osteoporosis can now be made solely on the basis of a low bone density, even in the absence of fragility fractures (Kanis et al. 1994).

Recently, a number of biochemical markers for bone resorption and formation have become available (Table 3) which have the potential to provide prognostic information on rates of bone loss (Delmas 1995). Thus, while measuring the bone density remains the method of choice for making a diagnosis of osteoporosis, it represents a static measurement and cannot predict the rate at which a given individual may lose bone. It appears that increased levels of resorption and formation markers are predictive of increased rates of bone loss when groups of individuals are studied; however, the ability of these markers to provide an accurate prediction of rates of bone loss for the individual patient remains to be established. Several studies now also indicate that increased levels of bone turnover may predict an increased risk of fracture, independently of the level of bone density. At present, however, the most practical use of these markers is to monitor the response to therapy. Thus changes in markers after just 3 months of therapy have been shown to correlate with changes in bone mass after 2 years of therapy. In addition, while the change in bone resorption markers occurs within weeks or a few months of initiating therapy, the changes in bone density may not be discernible for 1 to 2 years after initiating therapy.

Treatment

General measures

Acute back pain from vertebral collapse responds to analgesics, heat, and gentle massage to alleviate muscle spasm. Sometimes a brief period of bed rest is required. Chronic back pain is often caused by spinal deformity and is difficult to relieve completely. Instruction in posture and gait and institution of regular back extension exercises to strengthen the paravertebral muscles are usually beneficial. Occasionally, an orthopaedic back brace is needed. All patients with osteoporosis should have a diet adequate in calcium, protein, and vitamins, should give up smoking and excessive alcohol consumption, and should be reasonably active physically, avoid heavy lifting, and take precautions to prevent falls.

Drug therapy

The drugs currently approved by the United States Food and Drug Administration (FDA) for the treatment of osteoporosis (calcium, oestrogen, calcitonin, the bisphosphonate alendronate, and, more recently, the selective oestrogen receptor modulator raloxifene) act by decreasing bone resorption. Calcium, which may act by decreasing PTH secretion, is safe, well tolerated, and inexpensive. The effect of oestrogen on bone may be mediated by decreasing the production of bone-resorbing cytokines, increasing the production of factors inhibiting bone resorption and/or decreasing skeletal responsiveness to circulating PTH. Nonetheless, numerous studies have now established that, in general, oestrogen increases mean vertebral bone mass by more than 5 per cent and reduces the vertebral fracture rate by half

(Ettinger *et al.* 1985; Lufkin *et al.* 1992). For the individual patient, the benefits of oestrogen replacement therapy should be weighed against the possible risks. For women with an intact uterus, the potential increased risk of endometrial cancer is eliminated by the concurrent administration of a progestogen, either cyclically or on a continuous basis. There is now little doubt that oestrogen therapy is associated with a small increase in the risk of breast cancer. The risk has been calculated as an excess of 2, 6, and 12 cases per 1000 women for 5, 10, and 15 years of continuous use of hormone replacement therapy after the age of 50 (Collaborative Group on Hormonal Factors in Breast Cancer 1997). The excess risk reduces after cessation of hormone therapy and has largely disappeared after 5 years. Clearly, the decision regarding oestrogen replacement therapy needs to be individualized in the light of the beneficial effects of oestrogen replacement in terms of the skeleton and, possibly, cardiovascular disease. So far there has been no randomized trial evidence that oestrogen reduces the incidence of cardiovascular disease; case–control and cohort studies which suggest benefit are all subject to bias because women who opt for hormone replacement therapy are also at lower risk of cardiovascular disease for other reasons (Barrett-Connor 1991).

Tamoxifen is a partial oestrogen agonist/antagonist that functions as an antioestrogen in breast tissue, but appears to have an oestrogen-agonist effect on bone (Love *et al.* 1992). However, the use of tamoxifen is limited because of its side-effects, which include a partial agonist effect on the uterus. Another oestrogen analogue, raloxifene, which was recently approved by the FDA for use in osteoporosis, appears to have oestrogen-agonistic effects on bone with anti-oestrogenic effects on breast and uterine tissue (Black *et al.* 1994; Draper *et al.* 1996; Delmas *et al.* 1997). Thus it could be given without a progestin, and may become a useful alternative to oestrogen in the management of patients with osteoporosis.

The mechanism of action of androgens and synthetic anabolic agents is probably similar to that of oestrogen, although some data suggest a weak stimulation of bone formation. However, because of their masculinizing and hyperlipidaemic effects, androgens and anabolic agents have a limited role in therapy.

Calcitonin is also an option for the patient in whom oestrogen is contraindicated or who is unwilling to take oestrogen. The disadvantages of calcitonin have been the expense and the requirement for parenteral administration. However, intranasally administered calcitonin has recently been approved for the treatment of osteoporosis, and is now available at a significantly lower cost than the parenteral preparation.

Calcitonin has been shown to cause a transient increase in vertebral bone mass in women with postmenopausal osteoporosis, particularly those with increased rates of bone turnover (Overgaard *et al.* 1992; Reginster *et al.* 1994). In addition, calcitonin appears to have significant analgesic effects. Side-effects include nausea and flushing. Some patients may develop resistance to calcitonin because of the development of neutralizing antibodies. Also, in contrast with oestrogen and alendronate, nasal spray calcitonin is much less effective in retarding cortical bone loss than cancellous bone loss. Because of the possibility of inducing secondary hyperparathyroidism, calcium supplements should always be given with calcitonin.

Bisphosphonates are carbon-substituted analogues of pyrophosphate which are potent inhibitors of bone resorption. These drugs are possible alternatives to oestrogen for women in whom oestrogen is either contraindicated or for those who are intolerant

of the side-effects of oestrogen therapy. The first bisphosphonate to be used in the treatment of osteoporosis was etidronate. Initial data indicated that the intermittent use of etidronate (400 mg daily for 2 weeks followed by 11 to 13 weeks of calcium supplementation) decreased vertebral fracture rate (Storm *et al.* 1990; Watts *et al.* 1990). Because of the potential for large doses of etidronate to impair mineralization and the long retention of bisphosphonates in bone, there is concern that etidronate could have adverse long-term effects such as increasing the incidence of hip fracture. Second- and third-generation bisphosphonates such as tiludronate, alendronate, and risidronate are much more potent and have a greater therapeutic window between inhibition of bone resorption and inhibition of mineralization than does etidronate. Alendronate is the first of these second-generation bisphosphonates to be approved for the treatment of osteoporosis. In a large-scale clinical trial, there was a progressive increase in spine and hip bone mineral density during 3 years of daily therapy with alendronate at a dose of 10 mg/day. This, in turn, resulted in significantly fewer spinal fractures in patients receiving alendronate compared with those on placebo (Liberman *et al.* 1995). Recent data also indicate that alendronate therapy may decrease the rate of hip fracture (Black *et al.* 1996). The drug is generally well tolerated, although there does appear to be a low but significant rate of gastrointestinal side-effects, including gastro-oesophageal discomfort and, of greater concern, extensive oesophageal ulcerations in some patients. Thus pre-existing upper-gastrointestinal symptoms are a relative contraindication to use of the drug. In addition, the absorption of most bisphosphonates is very poor, and the drug needs to be administered at least 30 min before breakfast or other medications are taken, with the patient instructed to remain upright and not to go back to bed after taking the drug.

In the United Kingdom, cyclical etidronate remains the most widely used bisphosphonate for treatment of osteoporosis because of its low cost (a half to a third of that of alendronate) and the low incidence of significant side-effects and because there has not been a direct comparison with newer bisphosphonates to justify their higher costs.

Sodium fluoride is the only formation-stimulating drug that has been widely tested. In two major adequately controlled clinical trials, fluoride at a dose of 75 mg/day substantially increased bone mass but did not significantly decrease the rate of vertebral fractures (Riggs *et al.* 1990; Kleerekoper *et al.* 1991). In contrast, recent studies using a lower dose (50 mg/day) in a delayed-release form did indicate a reduction in vertebral fracture rates (Pak *et al.* 1994), although another study using the same dose but without the delayed-release formulation failed to confirm these results. Further, direct studies of bone from patients treated with a dose of 50 mg/day indicate increased fragility of the fluoride-treated bone (Sogaard *et al.* 1994). Thus the future role of sodium fluoride in the treatment of osteoporosis remains unclear at present.

Several studies suggest that the intermittent use of low doses of PTH may be anabolic for bone. In addition, several growth factors with potential anabolic effects on bone, such as the insulin-like growth factors I and II and transforming growth factor-β, are available in highly purified or recombinant form. Although theoretically attractive, clinical application of these agents in the treatment of osteoporosis remains investigational at this point (Riggs and Melton 1992).

Treatment of the individual patient

Therapy for patients with type I osteoporosis should be individualized. For patients with mild disease, only calcium supplementation (1.0–1.5 g/day) need be used. For more severe disease, low-dose oestrogen therapy (such as cyclic doses of 0.625 mg of conjugated oestrogen daily or 0.025 mg of ethynyl oestradiol daily) should be given. Because unopposed oestrogen therapy poses the risk of endometrial hyperplasia, and therefore of carcinoma, concomitant progestogen therapy (5 mg of medroxyprogesterone acetate daily during the last 14 days of each cycle or 2.5 mg daily on a continuous basis) should be given. The side-effects of excessive hepatic production of coagulation factors, renin substrate, and bile cholesterol (which produce an increased risk of venous thrombosis, hypertension, and cholelithiasis respectively) are due to exposure of the liver to a bolus of oestrogen in the first pass after oral administration. These problems can be decreased or eliminated by giving oestrogen via a transdermal patch (0.05 mg of 17β-oestradiol daily). If bone loss or fractures continue on hormone therapy, the oestrogen dosage should be doubled. For those women either intolerant of the side-effects of oestrogen or unable to take oestrogen because of a history of breast cancer, a bisphosphonate or raloxifene are viable options. In general, calcitonin can be used as another option when oestrogen is contra-indicated, or in older women with painful vertebral fractures who may not accept menses with oestrogen or rigid dosing schedules with a bisphosphonate.

Treatment with pharmacological dosages of vitamin D or active vitamin D metabolites should be reserved for patients with documented or suspected impairment of calcium absorption. Impaired calcium absorption can be inferred from a relatively low urinary calcium excretion (<75 mg/day), particularly if this does not increase substantially during oral calcium supplementation.

An important aspect of therapy of all patients with osteoporosis is protection against falls. Potential household hazards such as freshly waxed floors, loose rugs, and raised edges of carpets tacked to the floor should be eliminated. Patients should be encouraged to wear simple Oxford-style shoes and to avoid using shoes with high heels. They should leave a light on at night so that they need not walk in the dark for nocturnal trips to the bathroom, and should be extremely careful when walking on ice and snow. Patients at particularly high risk can be offered hip protectors (Lauritzen et al. 1993).

Prevention

In view of the magnitude of the problem, prevention is the only cost-effective approach. Use of metabolic balance techniques to determine the level of calcium intake required to prevent negative calcium balance has given conflicting results, and population studies have not generally demonstrated a strong relationship between calcium intake and bone loss. Based on the available evidence, recent recommendations for optimal calcium intakes from a National Institutes of Health Consensus Development Conference on Calcium are as follows: 800 to 1000 mg/day during childhood, 1200 to 1500 mg/day from age 12 to 24, 1000 mg/day from age 25 to time of menopause or age 65 (if on oestrogen replacement therapy), and 1500 mg/day after age 65 (NIH Consensus Development Panel 1994). Recommended intakes of calcium are lower in the United Kingdom, where the Reference Nutrient Intake for adults is 700 mg/day.

Adequate vitamin D intake is also important because there is an age-associated decrease in the ability of the skin to synthesize vitamin D and, possibly, in the ability of the intestine to absorb it. Thus, house-bound elderly persons are prone to vitamin D deficiency, particularly when they do not take supplementary vitamins and are consuming a diet with marginal vitamin D content. Indeed, a French study noted a significant reduction in hip fracture rates in elderly women treated with 800 IU of vitamin D daily and 1.2 g of elemental calcium (Chapuy et al. 1992), although this effect was not seen in a subsequent study where the population may not have been as deficient in vitamin D (Lips et al. 1996). In the United States, 10 per cent of an unselected group of elderly patients undergoing bone biopsy at the time of hip fracture were found to have subclinical osteomalacia. In the United Kingdom, osteomalacic changes were common in bone biopsies of patients with proximal femoral fractures in the 1970s but are now much rarer (Compston et al. 1991). This is possibly partly due to older people changing from butter to vitamin-D-fortified margarine in their diet. In the United Kingdom the Reference Nutrient Intake for vitamin D is 10 µg (400 IU) daily.

Physical activity should be encouraged and bone toxins, such as cigarettes and heavy alcohol consumption, should be eliminated. It is well established that skeletal stresses from weight-bearing and muscle contraction stimulate osteoblast function. Muscle mass and bone mass are directly correlated. Moreover, several recent prospective trials in postmenopausal women have shown that an experimental group enrolled in a regular exercise programme gained bone, whereas sedentary controls lost bone (Kohrt et al. 1995).

Because the postmenopausal phase of accelerated bone loss can be prevented by oestrogen replacement, the most effective way of decreasing the incidence of future fractures is to give oestrogen replacement therapy to women at menopause. Women with premature surgical or natural menopause should have oestrogen replacement therapy at least until the usual age of menopause. At menopause, all women should be counselled about the risks and benefits of oestrogen replacement and urged to make a choice. The recent availability of raloxifene will allow women the additional option of taking this selective oestrogen analogue for the prevention of osteoporosis. Alternatively, low-dose alendronate (5 mg/day) and cyclical etidronate have been approved for osteoporosis prevention. However, unless they choose oestrogen therapy for its other benefits, it is probably unwise to treat all perimenopausal women with oestrogen just to prevent osteoporosis because of the side-effects of treatment and the high cost of follow-up. Thus, in order to select those perimenopausal women who would benefit most from treatment, bone density measurements of the lumbar spine or hip should be made. Those women whose bone densities are normal (i.e. within 1 SD of the young normal mean) need not be treated with oestrogen replacement therapy unless they wish to take it for other reasons such as possible cardiovascular benefit or reduction of hot flushes. Those with bone densities in the osteoporotic range (≥2.5 SD below the young normal mean) are at high risk of fracture and should be treated with oestrogen or an alternative therapy. Those with bone densities in the low normal range (between 1 and 2.5 SD below the young normal mean) should be offered oestrogen; if they defer therapy, they should have a repeat bone density measurement in 2 to 3 years and considered for treatment if there has been substantial additional bone loss.

Steroid therapy

Old people are particularly vulnerable to osteoporosis as a side-effect of steroids given as therapy for conditions such as giant-cell arteritis or asthma. Elderly patients who are to be started on steroids at doses above 7.5 mg a day that are likely to be continued for more than 3 weeks should be assessed for bone-protective therapy. The American College of Rheumatology (1996) has published guidelines which are discussed in Chapter 13.1. Some geriatricians starting old and frail patients on long-term treatment with high-dose steroids will initiate bone-protective therapy with biphosphonates and calcium with vitamin D supplements, without subjecting the patients to formal assessment of risk for osteoporosis, but this approach has not been validated.

Conclusions

Enormous strides have been made in recent years in understanding how bone loss develops, how bone turnover is regulated physiologically, and how changes in bone cell activity can be manipulated pharmacologically. Even greater progress is expected in the immediate future. Thus there is every reason to be optimistic that this enormous public health problem can begin to be brought under control within the coming decade.

References

Akerstrom, G., Rudberg, C., Grimelius, L., et al. (1986). Histologic parathyroid abnormalities in an autopsy series. Human Pathology, 17, 520–7.

American College of Rheumatology Taskforce on Osteoporosis Guidelines (1996). Recommendations for the prevention and treatment of glucocorticoid-induced osteoporosis. Arthritis and Rheumatism, 39, 1791–1801.

Barrett-Connor, E. (1991). Postmenopausal estrogen and prevention bias. Annals of Internal Medicine, 115, 455–6.

Black, D.M., Cummings, S.R., Karpf, D.B., et al. (1996). Randomised trial of effect of alendronate on risk of fracture in women with existing vertebral fractures. Lancet, 348, 1535–41.

Black, L.J., Sato, M., Rowley, E.R., et al. (1994). Raloxifene (LY139481 HCI) prevents bone loss and reduces serum cholesterol without causing uterine hypertrophy in ovariectomized rats. Journal of Clinical Investigation, 93, 63–9.

Chapuy, M.C., Arlot, M.E., Duboeuf, F., et al. (1992). Vitamin D$_3$ and calcium to prevent hip fractures in elderly women. New England Journal of Medicine, 327, 1637–42.

Collaborative Group on Hormonal Factors in Breast Cancer (1997). Breast cancer and hormone replacement therapy: collaborative reanalysis of data from 51 epidemiological studies of 52 705 women with breast cancer and 108 411 women without breast cancer. British Medical Journal, 350, 1047–59.

Compston, J.E., Vedi, S., and Croucher, P.I. (1991). Low prevalence of osteomalacia in elderly patients with hip fractures. Age and Ageing, 20, 132–4.

Cooper, G.S. and Umbach, D.M. (1996). Are vitamin D receptor polymorphisms associated with bone mineral density? A meta-analysis. Journal of Bone and Mineral Research, 11, 1841–9.

Delmas, P.D. (1995). Biochemical markers for the assessment of bone turnover: clinical use in osteoporosis. In Osteoporosis: etiology, diagnosis, and management (2nd edn) (ed. B.L. Riggs and L.J. Melton), pp. 319–33. Raven Press, New York.

Delmas, P.D., Bjarnason, N.H., Mitlak, B.H., et al. (1997). Effects of raloxifene on bone mineral density, serum cholesterol concentrations, and uterine endometrium in postmenopausal women. New England Journal of Medicine, 337, 1641–7.

Draper, M.W., Flowers, D.E., Huster, W.J., Neild, J.A., Harper, K.D., and Arnaud, C. (1996). A controlled trial of raloxifene (LY139481) HCl: impact on bone turnover and serum lipid profile in healthy postmenopausal women. Journal of Bone and Mineral Research, 11, 835–42.

Eastell, R., Delmas, P.D., Hodgson, S.F., Eriksen, E.F., Mann, K.G., and Riggs, B.L. (1988). Bone formation rate in older normal women: concurrent assessment with bone histomorphometry calcium kinetics, and biochemical markers. Journal of Clinical Endocrinology and Metabolism, 67, 741–8.

Eastell, R., Yergey, A.L., Vieira, N., Cedel, S.L., Kumar, R., and Riggs, B.L. (1991). Interrelationship among vitamin D metabolism, true calcium absorption, parathyroid function and age in women: evidence of an age-related intestinal resistance to 1,25(OH)$_2$D action. Journal of Bone and Mineral Research, 6, 125–32.

Epstein, S., Bryce, G., Hinman, J.W., Miller, O.N., Riggs, B.L., and Johnston, C.C. (1986). The influence of age on bone mineral regulating hormones. Bone, 7, 421–5.

Eriksen, E.F., Colvard, E.F., Berg, D.S., et al. (1988). Evidence of estrogen receptors in normal human osteoblast-like cells. Science, 241, 84–6.

Ettinger, B., Genant, H.K., and Cann, C.E. (1985). Long-term estrogen replacement therapy prevents bone loss and fractures. Annals of Internal Medicine, 102, 319–24.

Forero, M.S., Klein, R.F., Nissenson, R.A., et al. (1987). Effect of age on circulating immunoreactive and bioactive parathyroid hormone levels in women. Journal of Bone and Mineral Research, 2, 363–6.

Genant, H.K., Engelke, K., Fuerst, T., et al. (1996). Non-invasive assessment of bone mineral and structure: state of the art. Journal of Bone and Mineral Research, 11, 707–30.

Gennari, C., Agnusdei, D., Nardi, P., and Civitelli, R. (1990). Estrogen preserves a normal intestinal responsiveness to 1,25-dihydroxyvitamin D$_3$ in oophorectomized women. Journal of Clinical Endocrinology and Metabolism, 71, 1288–93.

Grady, D., Rubin, S.N., Petitti, D.B., et al. (1992). Hormone therapy to prevent disease and prolong life in postmenopausal women. Annals of Internal Medicine, 117, 1016–37.

Heaney, R.P., Gallagher, J.C., Johnston, C.C., Neer, R., Parfitt, A.M., and Whedon, G.D. (1982). Calcium nutrition and bone health in the elderly. American Journal of Clinical Nutrition, 36, 986–1013.

Johnston, C.C., Miller, J.Z., Slemenda, C.W., et al. (1992). Calcium supplementation and increases in bone mineral density in children. New England Journal of Medicine, 327, 82–7.

Kanis, J.A., Melton, L.J., Christiansen, C., Johnston, C.C., and Khaltaev, N. (1994). The diagnosis of osteoporosis. Journal of Bone and Mineral Research, 9, 1137–41.

Khosla, S., Riggs, B.L., and Melton, L.J. (1995). Clinical spectrum. In Osteoporosis: etiology, diagnosis, and management (2nd edn) (ed. B. L. Riggs and L. J. Melton), pp. 205–23. Lippincott–Raven, Philadelphia, PA.

Khosla, S., Atkinson, E.J., Melton, L.J., III, and Riggs, B. L. (1997). Effects of age and estrogen status on serum parathyroid hormone levels and biochemical markers of bone turnover in women: a population based study. Journal of Clinical Endocrinology and Metabolism, 82, 1522–7.

Kleerekoper, M., Peterson, E.L., Nelson, D.A., et al. (1991). A randomized trial of sodium fluoride as a treatment for postmenopausal osteoporosis. Osteoporosis International, 1, 155–61.

Kohrt, W.M., Snead, D.B., Slatopolsky, E., and Birge, S.J. (1995). Additive effects of weight-bearing exercise and estrogen on bone mineral density in older women. Journal of Bone and Mineral Research, 10, 1303–11.

Lauritzen, J.B., Petersen, M.M., and Lund, B. (1993). Effect of external hip protectors on hip fractures. *Lancet*, 341, 11–13.

Ledger, G.A., Burritt, M.F., Kao, P.C., *et al.* (1994). Abnormalities of parathyroid hormone secretion in elderly women that are reversible by short term therapy with 1,25-dihydroxyvitamin D$_3$. *Journal of Clinical Endocrinology and Metabolism*, 79, 211–16.

Ledger, G.A., Burritt, M.F., Kao, P.C., O'Fallon, W.M., Riggs, B.L., and Khosla, S. (1995). Role of parathyroid hormone in mediating nocturnal and age-related increases in bone resorption. *Journal of Clinical Endocrinology and Metabolism*, 80, 3304–10.

Liberman, U.A., Weiss, S.R., Broll, J., *et al.* (1995). Effect of oral alendronate on bone mineral density and the incidence of fractures in postmenopausal osteoporosis. *New England Journal of Medicine*, 333, 1437–43.

Lindsay, R., Hart, D.M., Forrest, C., and Baird, C. (1980). Prevention of spinal osteoporosis in oophorectomized women. *Lancet*, ii, 1151–4.

Lips, P., Graafmans, W.C., Ooms, M.E., Bezemer, P.D., and Bouter, L.M. (1996). Vitamin D supplementation and fracture incidence in elderly persons. A randomized, placebo-controlled clinical trial. *Annals of Internal Medicine*, 124, 400–6.

Looker, A.C., Johnston, C.C., Wahner, H.W., *et al.* (1995). Prevalence of low femoral bone density in older US women from NHANES III. *Journal of Bone and Mineral Research*, 10, 796–802.

Love, R.R., Mazess, R.B., Barden, H.S., *et al.* (1992). Effects of tamoxifen on bone mineral density in postmenopausal women with breast cancer. *New England Journal of Medicine*, 326, 852–6.

Lufkin, E.G., Wahner, H.W., O'Fallon, W.M., *et al.* (1992). Treatment of postmenopausal osteoporosis with transdermal estrogen. *Annals of Internal Medicine*, 117, 1–9.

McKane, W.R., Khosla, S., Burritt, M.F., *et al.* (1995). Mechanism of renal calcium conservation with estrogen replacement therapy in women in early postmenopause—a clinical research center study. *Journal of Clinical Endocrinology and Metabolism*, 80, 3458–64.

McKane, W. R., Khosla, S., Egan, K. S., Robins, S. P., Burritt, M. F., and Riggs, B. L. (1996). Role of calcium intake in modulating age-related increases in parathyroid function and bone resorption. *Journal of Clinical Endocrinology and Metabolism*, 81, 1699–703.

McKane, R.W., Khosla, S., Risteli, J., Robins, S.P., Muhs, J.M., and Riggs, B.L. (1997). Role of estrogen deficiency in pathogenesis of secondary hyperparathyroidism and increased bone resorption in elderly women. *Proceedings of the Association of American Physicians*, 109, 174–80.

Manolagas, S.C. and Jilka, R.L. (1995). Bone marrow, cytokines, and bone remodelling: Emerging insights into the pathophysiology of osteoporosis. *New England Journal of Medicine*, 332, 305–11.

Melton, L.J., III (1995). How many women have osteoporosis now? *Journal of Bone and Mineral Research*, 10, 175–7.

Melton, L.J., III, and Riggs, B.L. (1985). Risk factors for injury after a fall. *Clinics in Geriatric Medicine*, 1, 525–39.

Melton, L.J., III, Kan, S.H., Wahner, H.W., and Riggs, B.L. (1988). Lifetime fracture risk: an approach to hip fracture risk assessment based on bone mineral density and age. *Journal of Clinical Epidemiology*, 41, 985–94.

Melton, L.J., Thamer, M., Ray, N.F., *et al.* (1997). Fractures attributable to osteoporosis: report from the National Osteoporosis Foundation. *Journal of Bone and Mineral Research*, 12, 16–23.

Morrison, N.A., Qi, J.C., Tokita, A., *et al.* (1994). Prediction of bone density from vitamin D receptor alleles. *Nature*, 367, 284–7.

Morrison, N.A., Qi, J.C., Tokita, A., *et al.* (1997). Prediction of bone density from vitamin D receptor alleles. *Nature*, 387, 106.

NIH Consensus Development Panel (1994). Optimal calcium intake. *Journal of the American Medical Association*, 272, 1942–8.

Orwoll, E.S. and Klein, R.F. (1995). Osteoporosis in men. *Endocrine Reviews*, 16, 87–116.

Overgaard, K., Hansen, M.A., Jensen, S.B., and Christiansen, C. (1992). Effect of salcatonin given intranasally on bone mass and fracture rates in established osteoporosis: a dose-response study. *British Medical Journal*, 305, 556–61.

Pacifici, R. (1992). Is there a causal role for IL-1 in postmenopausal bone loss? *Calcified Tissue International*, 50, 295–9.

Pak, C.Y.C., Sakhaee, K., Piziak, V., *et al.* (1994). Slow-release sodium fluoride in the management of postmenopausal osteoporosis. *Annals of Internal Medicine*, 120, 625–32.

Raisz, L.G. (1988). Local and systemic factors in the pathogenesis of osteoporosis. *New England Journal of Medicine*, 318, 818–28.

Ray, N.F., Chan, J.K., Thamer, M., and Melton, L.J., III (1997). Medical expenditures for the treatment of osteoporotic fractures in the United States in 1995: report from the National Osteoporosis Foundation. *Journal of Bone and Mineral Research*, 12, 24–35.

Reginster, J.Y., Denis, D., Deroisy, R., *et al.* (1994). Long-term (3 years) prevention of trabecular postmenopausal bone loss with low-dose intermittent nasal salmon calcitonin. *Journal of Bone and Mineral Research*, 9, 69–73.

Riggs, B.L. and Melton, L.J. (1986). Medical progress series: involutional osteoporosis. *New England Journal of Medicine*, 314, 1676–86.

Riggs, B.L. and Melton, L.J. (1990). Clinical heterogeneity of involutional osteoporosis: implications for preventive therapy. *Journal of Clinical Endocrinology and Metabolism*, 70, 1229–32.

Riggs, B.L. and Melton, L.J. (1992). The prevention and treatment of osteoporosis. *New England Journal of Medicine*, 327, 620–7.

Riggs, B.L., Wahner, H.W., Dunn, W.L., Mazess, R.B., Offord, K.P., and Melton, L.J., III (1981). Differential changes in bone mineral density of the appendicular skeleton with ageing: relationship to spinal osteoporosis. *Journal of Clinical Investigation*, 67, 328–35.

Riggs, B.L., Hodgson, S.F., O'Fallon, W.M., *et al.* (1990). Effect of fluoride treatment on the fracture rate in postmenopausal women with osteoporosis. *New England Journal of Medicine*, 332, 802–9.

Riggs, B.L., Nguyen, T.V., Melton, L.J., *et al.* (1995). The contribution of vitamin D receptor gene alleles to the determination of bone mineral density in normal and osteoporotic women. *Journal of Bone and Mineral Research*, 10, 991–6.

Riggs, B.L., Khosla, S., and Melton, L.J. (1998). A unitary model for involutional osteoporesis: estrogen deficiency causes both type I and type II osteoporosis in postmenopausal women and contributes to the continuous phase of bone loss in aging men. *Journal of Bone and Mineral Research*, 13, 763–73.

Silverman, S.L. and Madison, R.E. (1988). Decreased incidence of hip fracture in Hispanics, Asians, and Blacks: California hospital discharge data. *American Journal of Public Health*, 98, 1482–3.

Slemenda, C.W., Turner, C.H., Peacock, M., *et al.* (1996). The genetics of proximal femur geometry, distribution of bone mass and bone mineral density. *Osteoporosis International*, 6, 178–82.

Sogaard, C.H., Mosekilde, L., Richards, A., and Mosekilde, L. (1994). Marked decrease in trabecular bone quality after five years of sodium fluoride therapy—assessed by biochemical testing of iliac crest bone biopsies in osteoporotic women. *Bone*, 15, 393–9.

Storm, T., Thamsborg, G., Steiniche, T., Genant, H.K., and Sorensen, O.H. (1990). Effect of intermittent cyclical etidronate therapy on bone mass and fracture rate in women with postmenopausal osteoporosis. *New England Journal of Medicine*, 322, 1265–71.

Tinetti, M.E., Speechley, M., and Ginter, S.F. (1988). Risk factors for falls among elderly persons living in the community. *New England Journal of Medicine*, 319, 1701–7.

Tsai, K., Heath, H., III, Kumar, R., and Riggs, B.L. (1984). Impaired vitamin D metabolism with ageing in women: possible role in pathogenesis of senile osteoporosis. *Journal of Clinical Investigation*, 73, 1668–72.

Turner, R.T., Riggs, B.L., and Spelsberg, T.C. (1994). Skeletal effects of estrogen. *Endocrine Reviews*, 15, 274–300.

Watts, N.B., Harris, S.T., Genant, H.K., *et al.* (1990). Intermittent cyclical etidronate treatment of postmenopausal osteoporosis. *New England Journal of Medicine*, **323**, 73–9.

Young, G., Marcus, R., Minkoff, J.R., Kim, L.Y., and Segre, G.V. (1987). Age-related rise in parathyroid hormone in man: the use of intact and midmolecule antisera to distinguish hormone secretion from retention. *Journal of Bone and Mineral Research*, **2**, 367–74.

14.2 Osteomalacia

Carol C. Pilbeam and Lawrence G. Raisz

Osteomalacia is a metabolic bone disease characterized by impaired mineralization of newly formed bone matrix in mature lamellar bone. Although relatively uncommon compared with osteoporosis, it is important to recognize because treatment is often effective. Left untreated, osteomalacia can lead to weakened bones with fractures and skeletal deformities and can cause bone pain and proximal muscle weakness. It is particularly important to think of the diagnosis when treating older persons who are at increased risk for both osteoporosis and osteomalacia.

Osteomalacia in older persons usually results from decreased vitamin D availability and/or impaired conversion of vitamin D to its active form. A few cases are attributable to chronic hypophosphataemia and to drugs that inhibit mineralization such as bisphosphonates and fluoride. Two of the organs responsible for the synthesis of vitamin D, skin and kidney, as well as the two major target systems, intestine and skeleton, show age-associated changes which affect vitamin D metabolism and action. In most older persons, the changes are not great enough to cause clear-cut impairment of mineralization, but they may be sufficient to contribute to the severity of age-associated bone loss and osteoporosis.

Vitamin D metabolism and actions

Many of the features of the vitamin D hormone system have now been elucidated. Vitamin D_3 can be obtained from the diet, but its major source is the skin, where it is produced by the action of ultraviolet light on 7-dehydrocholesterol. The belief that vitamin D_3 was a 'vitamin' and not a hormone derived in part from the circumstances of industrialized society in northern climates where exposure to the necessary ultraviolet irradiation can be so diminished that adequate amounts of vitamin D_3 are not formed in the skin and supplementation is necessary. Because there are only a few foods rich in vitamin D_3 (oily fish, eggs, chicken liver), some countries fortify foods with vitamin D (milk in the United States, margarine in the United Kingdom). The dietary supplement and food additive used to be vitamin D_2, which is synthesized *in vitro* by ultraviolet photolysis

of ergosterol, but it is now being replaced by synthesized vitamin D_3. Like other fat-soluble substances, both dietary vitamin D_2 and vitamin D_3, hereafter called vitamin D, are absorbed in the upper small intestine and enter the circulation primarily through lymphatic channels.

Vitamin D is bound to vitamin D binding protein and carried to the liver where it is hydroxylated to 25-hydroxyvitamin D (**25(OH)D**), the major circulating metabolite. 25(OH)D circulates tightly bound to vitamin D binding protein at concentrations of 10 to 50 ng/ml (25–125 nmol/l) and has a long half-life of about 15 days. Liver hydroxylation is not closely regulated, and the circulating 25(OH)D level largely reflects the vitamin D reserve. 25(OH)D levels in healthy ambulatory older people are generally lower than in younger people, primarily owing to low exposure to sunlight and decreased dietary intake of vitamin D (Fig. 1). Although age-associated changes in liver metabolism occur, the liver reserve is so large that vitamin D metabolism is usually unaffected. There is an age-associated decline in the ability of the skin to make vitamin D_3 (Holick 1995). 25(OH)D levels in older persons may increase less on ultraviolet irradiation

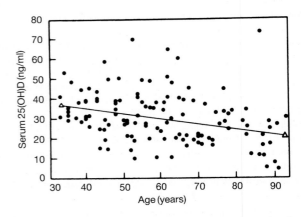

Fig. 1 Distribution of serum 25(OH)D levels by age for a sample of women in Rochester, Minnesota. (Reproduced with permission from Tsai et al. (1987).)

than in younger persons, but regular exposure to sunlight can still maintain them (Reid *et al.* 1986). There may be some decrease in vitamin D absorption with age, but large doses of vitamin D seem to be equally well absorbed by both young and old (Clemens *et al.* 1986).

The kidney is the site of the hydroxylation of 25(OH)D to 1,25-dihydroxyvitamin D (1,25(OH)$_2$D), the most active vitamin D metabolite, which circulates at concentrations of 20 to 60 pg/ml (50–150 pmol/l) with a half-life of about 15 h. This activation step is stimulated by parathyroid hormone (**PTH**) and low phosphate concentration and inhibited by high calcium. With vitamin D deficiency, the stimulation by increased PTH and decreased serum phosphate can maintain levels of 1,25(OH)$_2$D, and hence measurement of 1,25(OH)$_2$D is not a reliable indicator of substrate deficiency. The ability of PTH to increase renal 1α-hydroxylase may diminish with age, possibly owing to diminished renal mass, and may account in part for the age-associated increase in PTH. Some studies have found a decrease in 1,25(OH)$_2$D levels with age which may partially explain the well-documented decrease in calcium absorption in older persons. Some of the decline in 1,25(OH)$_2$D levels after menopause may be secondary to oestrogen withdrawal, since oestrogen replacement in postmenopausal women can increase both total and free 1,25(OH)$_2$D levels. Other studies have found that 1,25(OH)$_2$D levels increase or remain unchanged with age, suggesting that intestinal resistance to vitamin D action might explain the decrease in calcium absorption with ageing. However, a recent study found that older women have normal intestinal responsiveness to vitamin D (Ebeling *et al.* 1994).

The kidney also synthesizes 24,25(OH)$_2$D, and it is not clear whether this is a biologically active compound. There is some evidence that 24,25(OH)$_2$D can stimulate cartilage growth, but it does not appear to be necessary for mineralization. The vitamin D receptor has a high affinity for 1,25(OH)$_2$D but can bind 25(OH)D and 24,25(OH)$_2$D at much higher concentrations. The binding of 25(OH)D may be important in exogenous vitamin D intoxication when 25(OH)D levels are very high but 1,25(OH)$_2$D levels are not.

The major actions of 1,25(OH)$_2$D in calcium homeostasis are to increase calcium and phosphate absorption in the intestine and to increase bone resorption. It is generally agreed that the predominant role of vitamin D on bone mineralization is indirect, i.e. a consequence of the role that vitamin D plays in maintaining the extracellular calcium–phosphate product. For example, the impairment of mineralization seen in vitamin D deficiency in animal models can be reversed by normalizing the serum concentrations of calcium and phosphate. However, 1,25(OH)$_2$D may also have direct effects on osteoblasts to enhance their ability to differentiate and to enable the cells to synthesize a mineralizable matrix. In addition, 1,25(OH)$_2$D can increase the production of the calcium-binding protein osteocalcin by bone cells.

Levels of 25(OH)D vary seasonally, with the nadir at the end of winter months, reflecting the importance of the endogenous photosynthesis of vitamin D (Lund and Sorenson 1979; Dattani *et al.* 1984; van der Wielen *et al.* 1995). These short periods of low vitamin D stores can produce secondary hyperparathyroidism and increase bone turnover, and may aggravate age-associated bone loss; hence they clearly warrant treatment. However, a sustained period of low vitamin D is necessary to cause osteomalacia. The precise relationship of 25(OH)D levels to the development of osteomalacia

is unknown, but values below 10 ng/ml (25 nmol/l) are considered to place individuals at high risk for osteomalacia.

Pathophysiology

After synthesis of matrix by osteoblasts, there is a period of 1 to 2 weeks during which this matrix, or osteoid, matures before mineralization begins. In osteomalacia, mineralization is impaired and wide seams of osteoid accumulate. However, increased osteoid alone is not diagnostic, since this can occur in other conditions where bone matrix formation is rapid and mineralization is normal, such as hyperparathyroidism, hyperthyroidism, and Paget's disease. Definitive diagnosis requires a dynamic measure of the mineralization rate, which can be achieved by double labelling of the mineralization fronts with tetracycline or other calcium-binding compounds before bone biopsy (Parfitt 1990). The absence of tetracycline labels or the finding of a broad diffuse band rather than a well-defined mineralization front are the diagnostic features of osteomalacia. In hypovitaminosis D, secondary hyperparathyroidism precedes the development of severe osteomalacia. Increased bone turnover is evident, with increased numbers of resorption lacunae and often quite irregular trabecular bone structure. These structural abnormalities, coupled with decreased mineralized bone, can lead to deformity and fracture. In advanced cases of osteomalacia, particularly in older persons, the osteoblasts may become flattened and stop forming new matrix. While the severe case of osteomalacia is clearly recognizable, mild degrees of impairment of mineralization can occur in which there is only a small increase in the width of osteoid seams and a partial loss of mineralization fronts. Such mild or intermediate forms may be relatively common in elderly people and therapy may still be beneficial.

Causes of osteomalacia

Vitamin D deficiency

While severe nutritional deficiency of vitamin D is relatively rare, older persons worldwide are a group at increased risk (McKenna 1992). As noted above, 25(OH)D levels fall with age (Fig. 1). Levels in older persons vary with season and sun exposure and also with vitamin D intake. The relative importance of diet will depend on season, form of dress, health status, and mobility. Latitude is also important because the appropriate spectral range of ultraviolet radiation for skin production of vitamin D is not available in northern latitudes (above 40° N) during winter months. Studies in the United States and United Kingdom have found that up to 15 per cent of free-living elderly people have hypovitaminosis D (<15 ng/ml or 37.5 nmol/l) (Omdahl *et al.* 1982). The lowest levels of 25(OH)D are seen among housebound and institutionalized elderly people (Fig. 2). As many as 15 to 35 per cent in the United States and 50 to 60 per cent in Europe and Australia of institutionalized or housebound elderly people who are not taking vitamin D supplements may be deficient (Davies *et al.* 1986; O'Dowd *et al.* 1993; Gloth *et al.* 1995; Stein *et al.* 1996).

Malabsorption

Patients with malabsorption due to gluten-sensitive enteropathy, gastric surgery, bowel resection, or intestinal bypass operations, as

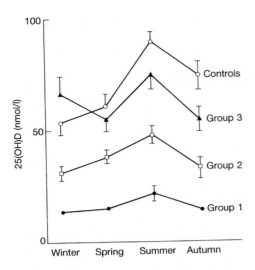

Fig. 2 Serum 25(OH)D levels in three groups of elderly people (65–80 years) and a young adult control group (30–50 years) in Finland: group 1, long-stay (sick and immobile) geriatric patients; group 2, residents at an old people's home; group 3, healthy ambulatory elderly persons living in their own homes. (Reproduced with permission from Lamberg-Allardt (1984).)

well as individuals with impaired fat absorption due to biliary or pancreatic disease, can develop osteomalacia. This occurs not only because of decreased absorption of exogenous vitamin D and increased loss of 25(OH)D from disruption of the enterohepatic circulation but also because of decreased calcium absorption. The calcium may be bound to fats in the intestinal lumen and thus unavailable, or the calcium transport systems in the intestine may be impaired and less responsive to 1,25(OH)$_2$D.

Renal disease

Although chronic renal disease produces impairment of 1α-hydroxylation, this does not lead to osteomalacia in the majority of patients because the calcium–phosphate product remains high as a result of the phosphate retention associated with decreased glomerular filtration. Patients with endstage renal disease on maintenance dialysis generally have uraemic osteodystrophy which is characterized by histological lesions varying from predominant osteitis fibrosa, due to secondary hyperparathyroidism, to predominant osteomalacia. Osteomalacia is more likely to be the more prominent lesion in patients whose dialysates contain large concentrations of aluminum or who take large amounts of aluminum hydroxide gels. This is probably caused by both the depletion of phosphate, which is bound to the aluminum hydroxide gel, and the direct inhibitory effect of aluminum on mineralization. Osteomalacia due to renal tubular disorders is rare in older persons, although occasionally such patients with acidosis, hypophosphataemia, and osteomalacia are encountered.

Other causes

Patients taking anticonvulsants, such as phenytoin, carbamazepine, and phenobarbitone (phenobarbital), can develop osteomalacia probably owing to a combination of impaired metabolism of 25(OH)D

and a direct inhibition of calcium absorption in the intestine. This problem can generally be overcome by a moderate increase in vitamin D intake, and those at high risk (e.g. institutionalized elderly people) should be given prophylactic doses of 800 IU (20 μg) daily or 50 000 IU (1250 μg) monthly.

Tumour-induced osteomalacia may occur in elderly people. This syndrome is characterized by renal phosphate wasting and low serum 1,25(OH)$_2$D levels, and is associated with a variety of benign or malignant tumours occurring primarily in bone or soft tissue. The mechanism is not clear, but it is thought that the tumours secrete factors which inhibit renal tubular reabsorption of phosphate and impair the conversion of 25(OH) to 1,25(OH)$_2$D (Lyles 1996). The syndrome disappears on removal of the tumour.

Although one might expect to see osteomalacia in patients with chronic liver disease owing to failure of synthesis of 25(OH)D, this is not common. Most patients with chronic liver disease have osteoporosis and normal levels of 25(OH)D. Even if 25(OH)D levels are somewhat low, patients often fail to respond to vitamin D administration.

The congenital forms of rickets, such as X-linked hypo-phosphataemic rickets, are not ordinarily encountered in older people because they are diagnosed and treated earlier in life. However, some affected individuals may be unaware of their condition and untreated, even at a late age. Some families with a mild defect in renal tubular transport of phosphate and vitamin D activation have been encountered who develop osteomalacia only late in life (Econs *et al.* 1994).

Osteomalacia can occur with some drugs that are used most frequently by elderly people. In particular, fluoride, used to treat osteoporosis, and bisphosphonates, used to treat Paget's disease and osteoporosis, can inhibit mineralization when taken chronically in large doses. However, the newer bisphosphonates are less likely to cause osteomalacia than the first-generation drugs. It is recommended that patients be given prophylactic doses of 400 to 800 IU (10–20 μg) vitamin D, as well as an adequate intake of calcium, during treatment with these drugs.

Mixed osteomalacia

Osteomalacia in elderly individuals is likely to have a multifactorial aetiology. Poor intake of vitamin D, reduced exposure to sunlight, loss of renal 1α-hydroxylase, and impaired intestinal absorption of calcium can all contribute. Some patients may be phosphate deficient because of decreased intake or the use of diuretics, laxatives, or antacids. Before the calcium deficit associated with vitamin D deficiency results in osteomalacia, individuals develop secondary hyperparathyroidism with increased bone turnover and bone loss. Hence elderly individuals with osteomalacia are likely to have osteoporosis as well.

Hip fracture

One area of particular concern is the relationship between osteomalacia and fracture of the proximal femur. Low levels of 25(OH)D have been found in many patients with hip fracture (Fig. 3). Some studies have reported a high frequency of osteomalacia in patients

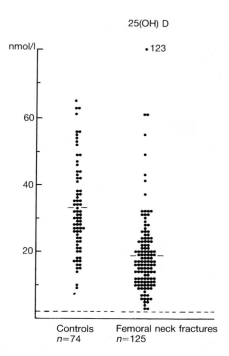

Fig. 3 Concentrations of 25(OH)D in patients with femoral neck fracture and control subjects of the same age. The broken line marks the detection limits of the assay. (Reprinted with permission from Lips *et al.* (1982).)

density in elderly Dutch people (Ooms *et al.* 1995*b*) but did not decrease the incidence of hip fractures (Lips *et al.* 1996). However, in another study of ambulatory elderly French women living in nursing homes, supplementation with both 1.2 g of calcium and 800 IU (20 mg) of vitamin D daily significantly decreased the incidence of hip fractures (Chapuy *et al.* 1992; Chapuy and Meunier 1996). Another study found that the use of vitamin D supplements decreased the risk of hip fracture only in frail women aged over 80 years (Ranstam and Kanis 1995).

Clinical features

Patients with osteomalacia often have generalized bone pain and tenderness, and may have a variety of psychological symptoms, particularly depression. Skeletal deformities develop and there is an increased incidence of fracture. Weakness of the proximal muscles is common. This may be a consequence of secondary hyperparathyroidism or of the deficiencies of vitamin D, calcium, and phosphate. In addition to true fractures, patients with osteomalacia can develop pseudofractures (Looser's zones) in which there is a loss of mineral which appears as a discontinuity of the bone on radiographs. This may be associated with marked local tenderness. Bowing of the limbs and kyphosis can occur in elderly patients with osteomalacia. It is important to look for signs of underlying disorders such as anaemia, steatorrhoea, and polyuria and polydipsia, and to check for previous gastrointestinal surgery.

Biochemical changes

It is possible to have osteomalacia with normal serum calcium, phosphate, alkaline phosphatase, and urine calcium. However, in most patients one or more of these values is abnormal. The combination of a mildly decreased serum calcium, a low serum phosphate, and a markedly low urine calcium with elevation of plasma alkaline phosphatase strongly suggests osteomalacia. However, alkaline phosphatase values are often elevated in older persons for other reasons. Total plasma calcium can be low because of low albumin, and phosphate can be low because of low intake, both of which are common in the older patient. Low urinary calcium is also relatively common. Thus a normal chemical pattern does not exclude, and an abnormal pattern does not establish, the diagnosis of osteomalacia. In patients with vitamin D deficiency, the most important measurement is the serum 25(OH)D level. Serum 1,25(OH)$_2$D levels, which are regulated by PTH, may not be low in patients with vitamin D deficiency but are low in patients with renal failure or renal tubular defects in 1,25(OH)$_2$D synthesis. Renal failure can be detected by measurement of blood urea nitrogen and creatinine or creatinine clearance, and systemic acidosis can be detected by measurement of electrolytes. Acidosis due to a distal tubular defect should be considered if morning urine pH is consistently 6.5 or higher.

with femoral neck fractures (Hoikka *et al.* 1982), while others have found little or no osteomalacia (Lips *et al.* 1982; Compston *et al.* 1991). However, the diagnosis of osteomalacia in these studies was generally based on measurement of osteoid seams in samples obtained at surgery for hip fracture, without tetracycline labelling, and hence there was no definite evidence of impaired mineralization. In addition, several studies have suggested that there is a poor correlation between the blood levels of vitamin D and the presence or absence of increased osteoid on biopsies from hip fracture patients.

It seems most likely that a correlation between low levels of 25(OH)D and increased hip fracture incidence results from increased bone loss associated with secondary hyperparathyroidism. Low levels of 25(OH)D lead to decreased production of 1,25(OH)$_2$D and, consequently, to impaired intestinal calcium absorption and secondary hyperparathyroidism. Vitamin D supplementation of 400 IU (10 mg) daily can decrease parathyroid function in older persons with vitamin D deficiency or hypovitaminosis (Lips *et al.* 1988). However, serum PTH and 25(OH)D levels have been found to be inversely related at 25(OH)D levels up to 44 ng/ml (110 nmol/l) (Dawson-Hughes *et al.* 1997). Serum 25(OH)D levels below 12 ng/ml (30 nmol/l) have been associated with both secondary hyperparathyroidism and increased bone turnover (Ooms *et al.* 1995*a*). Even short periods of low vitamin D stores during the winter can produce secondary hyperparathyroidism and increase bone turnover in healthy older persons which may aggravate age-associated bone loss (Chapuy *et al.* 1996), and hence even these short periods should be avoided.

Whether or not supplementation with vitamin D can decrease risk of hip fracture in older persons probably depends on concomitant calcium supplementation and degree of frailty. Vitamin D supplementation of 400 IU (10 mg) increased femoral neck bone mineral

Radiological changes

In contrast with rickets in children, in which enlargement of the growth plate and cupping of the metaphyses are pathognomonic changes due to cartilage overgrowth in response to impaired mineralization, the radiological changes of osteomalacia in adults are largely non-specific. The one exception is the pseudofracture or Looser zone. This localized area of demineralization can be seen in the long bones, in the pubic rami of the pelvis, in the ribs, and on the lateral margins of the scapula. The vertebrae may show collapse or become biconcave (codfish vertebrae) and decreased mineralization may be detected radiologically, but this occurs in osteoporosis as well as osteomalacia. Coarse trabecular markings have been described in osteomalacic bone but are certainly not diagnostic. In renal osteodystrophy an alternation of dense and lucent areas in the vertebral body can produce the so-called 'rugger jersey' spine.

Bone biopsy

The definitive diagnosis of osteomalacia can only be made by bone biopsy. Bone biopsy may be justified in patients who have bone pain and a presentation which is atypical for osteoporosis, particularly if serum calcium, phosphate, alkaline phosphatase, and urinary calcium are normal. However, a patient with a low 25(OH)D and one or more appropriate biochemical changes might be treated without bone biopsy on the presumption that osteomalacia is responsible, at least in part, for the metabolic bone disease.

Differential diagnosis

In addition to assessing the component of osteoporosis that is likely to coexist with osteomalacia in elderly patients, it is important to consider other causes of proximal muscle weakness and bone pain. Rheumatological disorders, thyrotoxic myopathy, polymyositis, and occasionally lymphoma may mimic osteomalacia. Many patients are thought to have rheumatic disease and are treated with non-steroidal anti-inflammatory agents for long periods before the diagnosis of osteomalacia is made.

Treatment

Hypovitaminosis, which may place an individual at risk for increased bone turnover and bone loss, is not well defined. In theory, hypovitaminosis is present if $1,25(OH)_2D_3$ levels markedly increase following ultraviolet irradiation or a large dose of vitamin D, indicating that the PTH stimulation of $1,25(OH)_2D_3$ production has been limited by substrate availability. In practice, hypovitaminosis is considered to be a 25(OH)D level less than 15 ng/ml (37.5 nmol/l). 25(OH)D levels less than 10 ng/ml (25 nmol/l) are considered to place an individual at high risk for osteomalacia and are equated with vitamin D deficiency. Adequate levels of 25(OH)D can usually be maintained, even in debilitated older persons, with a daily dose of 400 to 800 IU (10–20 μg) of vitamin D, equivalent to one or two multivitamin tablets (Webb et al. 1990). When compliance is a problem, an alternative is to give a single dose of 50 000 IU (1250 μg) every 2 to 3 months, or monthly during the winter months, or a single dose of 100 000 IU (2500 μg) twice a year (Byrne et al. 1995).

Osteomalacia due to vitamin D deficiency will respond rapidly to vitamin D supplementation. Patients can be given 50 000 IU (1250 μg)

weekly for 3 to 5 weeks with subsequent replacement determined by serum levels of 25(OH)D. There may be some justification for using 25(OH)D (calcifidiol, calcidiol) in patients with malabsorption, because it is usually rapidly absorbed and one can measure the serum value after therapy to be certain that the desired level has been reached. However, this medication is much more expensive than vitamin D. 25(OH)D is absorbed in the intestine better than vitamin D itself. Indeed, in elderly patients with gastrointestinal disease, vitamin D may not be absorbed at all. Some patients have been given intramuscular vitamin D to overcome this problem. In patients with severe gastrointestinal disease, oral 25(OH)D may be reasonably well absorbed, but the blood level should still be checked. Patients with gluten-sensitive enteropathy will respond to a gluten-free diet. This diagnosis is sometimes difficult to make because steatorrhoea and other typical features may not be present, and the diagnosis can only be made by jejunal biopsy. Therapy with calcifidiol should begin with the lowest dose of 20 μg daily.

Patients with impaired renal function and low $1,25(OH)_2D$ levels should be treated with $1,25(OH)_2D$ (calcitriol). Since the active hormonal form is being used, the margin of safety is narrower, and hypercalcaemia or hypercalciuria often develops when the dose is increased. This is particularly dangerous when serum phosphorus is high, since this will increase the likelihood of soft-tissue damage and worsening of renal function. Thus serum and urine calcium and phosphorus and renal function should be monitored in patients on calcitriol therapy. Therapy should begin with the lowest dose of 0.25 mg daily. Serum calcium levels should be measured twice weekly, and the dose adjusted in increments of 0.25 mg over 2 to 4 weeks.

Vitamin D toxicity can also be a problem when the prohormone is used, particularly because vitamin D is stored in soft tissue and can accumulate. Thus if toxicity occurs, its course may be quite prolonged. Vitamin D intoxication has been encountered in elderly patients taking doses equal to or greater than 50 000 IU (1250 μg) per week. These large amounts may be necessary in patients with malabsorption, but 25(OH)D levels in the blood should be carefully monitored.

References

Byrne, P.M., Freaney, R., and McKenna, M.J. (1995). Vitamin D supplementation in the elderly: review of safety and effectiveness of different regimes. *Calcified Tissue International*, **56**, 518–20.

Chapuy, M.C. and Meunier, P.J. (1996). Prevention of secondary hyperparathyroidism and hip fracture in elderly women with calcium and vitamin D3 supplements. *Osteoporosis International*, **6** (Supplement 3), S60–3.

Chapuy, M.C., Arlot, M.E., Duboeuf, F., et al. (1992). Vitamin D3 and calcium to prevent hip fractures in the elderly women. *New England Journal of Medicine*, **327**, 1637–42.

Chapuy, M.C., Schott, A.M., Garnero, P., Hans, D., Delmas, P.D., and Meunier, P.J. (1996). Healthy elderly French women living at home have secondary hyperparathyroidism and high bone turnover in winter. EPIDOS Study Group. *Journal of Clinical Endocrinology and Metabolism*, **81**, 1129–33.

Clemens, T.L., Zhou, X.Y., Myles, M., Endres, D., and Lindsay, R. (1986). Serum vitamin D2 and vitamin D3 metabolite concentrations and absorption of vitamin D2 in elderly subjects. *Journal of Clinical Endocrinology and Metabolism*, **63**, 656–60.

Compston, J.E., Vedi, S., and Croucher, F.I. (1991). Low prevalence of osteomalacia in elderly patients with hip fractures. *Age and Ageing*, 20, 132–4.

Dattani, J.T., Exton-Smith, A.N., and Stephen, J.M.L. (1984). Vitamin D status of the elderly in relation to age and exposure to sunlight. *Human Nutrition, Clinical Nutrition*, 38C, 131–7.

Davies, M., Mawer, E.B., Hann, J.T., and Taylor, J.L. (1986). Seasonal changes in the biochemical indices of vitamin D deficiency in the elderly: a comparison of people in residential homes, long-stay wards and attending a day hospital. *Age and Ageing*, 15, 77–83.

Dawson-Hughes, B., Harris, S.S., and Dallal, G.E. (1997). Plasma calcidiol, season, and serum parathyroid hormone concentrations in healthy elderly men and women. *American Journal of Clinical Nutrition*, 65, 67–71.

Ebeling, P.R., Yergey, A.L., Viera, N.E., *et al.* (1994). Influence of age on effects of endogenous 1,25-dihydroxyvitamin D on calcium absorption in normal women. *Calcified Tissue International*, 55, 330–4.

Econs, M.J., Samsa, G.P., Monger, M., Drezner, M.K., and Freussner, J.R. (1994). X-linked hypophosphatemic rickets: a disease often unknown to affected patients. *Bone and Mineral*, 24, 17–24.

Gloth, F.M., Gundberg, C.M., Hollis, B.W., Haddad, J.G., and Tobin, J.D. (1995). Vitamin D deficiency in homebound elderly persons. *Journal of the American Medical Association*, 274, 1683–6.

Hoikka, V., Alhava, E.M., Savolainen, K., and Parvianinen, M. (1982). Osteomalacia in fractures of the proximal femur. *Acta Orthopaedica Scandinavica*, 53, 255–60.

Holick, M. (1995). Environmental factors that influence the cutaneous production of vitamin D. *American Journal of Clinical Nutrition*, 61 (Supplement), 638S–45S

Lamberg-Allardt, C. (1984). Vitamin D intake, sunlight exposure and 25-hydroxyvitamin D levels in the elderly during one year. *Annals of Nutrition and Metabolism*, 28, 144–50.

Lips, P., Netelenbos, J.C., Jongen, M.N.M., *et al.* (1982). Histomorphometric profile and vitamin D status in patients with femoral neck fracture. *Metabolic Bone Disease and Related Research*, 4, 85–93.

Lips, P., Wiersinga, A., van Ginkel, F.C., *et al.* (1988). The effect of vitamin D supplementation on vitamin D status and parathyroid function in elderly subjects. *Journal of Clinical Endocrinology and Metabolism*, 67, 644–50.

Lips, P., Graafmans, W.C., Ooms, M.E., Bezemer, P.D., and Bouter, L.M. (1996). Vitamin D supplementation and fracture incidence in elderly persons. A randomized, placebo-controlled l trial. *Annals of Internal Medicine*, 124, 400–6.

Lund, B. and Sorensen, O.H. (1979). Measurement of 25-hydroxyvitamin D in serum and its relation to sunshine, age and vitamin D intake in the Danish population. *Scandinavian Journal of Clinical and Laboratory Investigation*, 39, 23–30.

Lyles, K.W. (1996). Oncongenic osteomalacia. In *Principles of bone biology* (ed. J.P. Bilezikian, L.G. Raisz, and G.A. Rodan), pp. 935–40. Academic Press, New York.

McKenna, M.J. (1992). Differences in vitamin D status between countries in young adults and in the elderly. *American Journal of Medicine*, 93, 69–77.

O'Dowd, K.J., Clemens, T.L., Kelsey, J.L., and Lindsay, R. (1993). Exogenous calciferol (vitamin D) and vitamin D endocrine status among elderly nursing home residents in the New York City area. *Journal of the American Geriatrics Society*, 41, 414–21.

Omdahl, J.L., Garry, P.J., Hunsaker, L.A., Hunt, W.C., and Goodwin, J.S. (1982). Nutritional status in a healthy elderly population: vitamin D. *American Journal of Clinical Nutrition*, 36, 1225–33.

Ooms, M.E., Lips, P., Roos, J.C., *et al.* (1995a). Vitamin D status and sex hormone binding globulin: determinants of bone turnover and bone mineral density in elderly women. *Journal of Bone and Mineral Research*, 10, 1177–84.

Ooms, M.E., Roos, J.C., Bezemer, P.D., van der Vijgh, W.J.F., Bouter, L.M., and Lips, P. (1995b). Prevention of bone loss by vitamin D supplementation in elderly women: a randomized double-blind trial. *Journal of Clinical Endocrinology and Metabolism*, 80, 1052–8.

Parfitt, A.M. (1990). Osteomalacia and related disorders. In *Metabolic bone diseases and clinically related disorders* (2nd edn) (ed. L.V. Avioli and S.M. Krane), pp. 329–96. W. B. Saunders, Philadelphia, PA.

Ranstam, J. and Kanis, J.A. (1995). Influence of age and body mass on the effects of vitamin D on hip fracture risk. *Osteoporosis International*, 5, 450–4.

Reid, I.R., Gallagher, D.J.A., and Bosworth, J. (1986). Prophylaxis against vitamin D deficiency in the elderly by regular sunlight exposure. *Age and Ageing*, 15, 35–50.

Stein, M.S., Schere, S.C., Walton, S.L., *et al.* (1996). Risk factors for secondary hyperparathyroidism in a nursing home population. *Clinical Endocrinology*, 44, 375–83.

Tsai, K.-S., Wahner, H.W., Offord, K.P., Melton, L.J., III, Kumar, R., and Riggs, B.L. (1987). Effect of ageing on vitamin D stores and bone density in women. *Calcified Tissue International*, 40, 241–3.

van der Wielen, R.P., Lowik, M.R., van den Berg, H., *et al.* (1995). Serum vitamin D concentrations among elderly people in Europe. *Lancet*, 346, 207–10.

Webb, A.R., Pilbeam, C.C., Hanifin, N., and Holick, M.A. (1990). An evaluation of the relative contributions of exposure to sunlight and diet on the circulating concentrations of 25-OH-D in an elderly population in Boston. *American Journal of Clinical Nutrition*, 51, 1075–81.

14.3   Paget's disease of bone

Ronald C. Hamdy

Introduction

Paget's disease is a localized bone disorder that goes through phases of activity and quiescence. During active phases, the bone turnover rate and blood flow are substantially increased at the site of the lesion. The disease may be monostotic, when only one bone, or more commonly one part of a bone, is affected; or it may be polyostotic, when several bones are affected, in which case the distribution of the disease is usually asymmetrical. Any part of the skeleton may be affected; the most frequently involved bones include the pelvis (72 per cent of cases), the lumbar vertebrae (58 per cent), the femora (55 per cent), the thoracic vertebrae (45 per cent), the sacrum (43 per cent), the skull (42 per cent), the tibia (35 per cent), the humerus (31 per cent), and cervical spine (11 per cent) (Meunier 1994).

The natural history of the disease is not clearly defined, and although many lesions tend to progress and invade adjacent bone, the rate of progress is by no means uniform. Even within the same patient, different lesions may progress at different rates, and some may be quiescent while others are active.

Aetiology

Paget's disease of bone is triggered by a very localized overactivity of the osteoclasts. It is still not known why in many cases the disease remains so patchy and localized to individual bones or, as is often the case, to parts of individual bones. It is also not clear why some bones are commonly affected by the disease, while others are usually spared. Several hypotheses have been put forward. These include the following.

Inherited disorder

The higher prevalence of Paget's disease in families suggests that it has a genetic component and is inherited as an autosomal dominant characteristic. There is an increased frequency of HLA-DQw-1 antigen in patients with Paget's disease (Siris 1996). The genetic phenotype may result in an elevated c-*fos* gene expression in the osteoclasts (Hoyland and Sharpe 1994), and an altered interleukin 6 (IL-6) production (Hoyland *et al.* 1994).

However, few cases have been reported among identical twins suggesting that, although there may be a genetically determined predisposition to Paget's disease, some other factors need to be present for the disease to manifest itself.

Viral aetiology

A growing body of evidence supports the hypothesis that Paget's disease has a viral aetiology. First, inclusion bodies characteristic of viral infections can be seen in the nuclei and cytoplasm of osteoclasts in bones affected by Paget's disease (Siris 1996). Second, these para-crystalline inclusion bodies exhibit viral characteristics (Abe *et al.* 1995). Third, marrow mononuclear cells from patients with Paget's disease express measles virus nucleocapsid mRNA (Reddy *et al.* 1995). Fourth, when osteoclasts from embryonic chick tibiae are experimentally infected with canine distemper or measles virus, the rate of bone resorption is greatly increased (Shepard *et al.* 1996). Finally, the experimental infection of osteoclasts with canine distemper virus induces these cells to produce IL-6 and c-*fos* mRNA, in a manner similar to that of osteoclasts of patients with Paget's disease (Mee *et al.* 1995).

Several viruses have been implicated in Paget's disease (Siris 1996) including the measles virus, canine distemper virus, respiratory syncytial virus, paramyxoviruses, and mutations of these viruses.

However, this evidence is circumstantial and reflects only the acute changes induced by the experimental infection of osteoclasts with viruses. It does not explain why it takes such a long time for the disease to manifest itself, the peculiar geographical distribution of the disease, or the patchy and localized nature of the disease in the skeleton. Therefore other factors would need to be present to allow viral infection of osteoclasts to lead to Paget's disease.

Trauma

Trauma may play a role in the localization of Paget's disease. Weight-bearing bones and those exposed to repeated trauma are more susceptible to developing the disease than the rest of the skeleton.

However, trauma *per se* cannot explain the geographical distribution of the disease or the presence of inclusion bodies in the osteoclast. It is possible that trauma acts as a localizing factor for the disease to develop in certain bones or parts of bones rather than others, but there must be some other factor, such as a viral infection in an already genetically predisposed individual, for the disease to manifest itself.

Epidemiology

Paget's disease of bone affects predominantly the older population. It is rare before the age of 40 years, although sporadic cases have been described in very young adults. Most series indicate a slight male predominance.

The peculiar geographical distribution of the disease remains enigmatic (Siris 1996). It is more common in northern Europe and the United States than the rest of the world. However, there is a great deal of variability within these regions. In Europe, for instance, the highest prevalence is seen in England, where about 4.6 per cent of the population over the age of 55 years is affected. The prevalence then decreases from north to south with 2.4 per cent in France, 1.3 per cent in Germany, 1.3 per cent in Spain, 0.3 per cent in Italy, and 0.3 per cent in Greece. The disease is rare in the Scandinavian countries (0.3 per cent), and there are pockets of high prevalence in England (8.3 per cent in Yorkshire), France, and Spain. In the United States, the prevalence also appears to be higher in northern than in southern states. For instance, the disease is twice as common in New York City as in Atlanta. In Australia and New Zealand, it is more common among British descendants than among aborigines or other immigrants. Paget's disease is rare in the Arab Middle East, China, and Japan.

Pathophysiology

Paget's disease of bone is a focal disorder characterized by a localized overactivity of the osteoclasts. Unlike other conditions with osteoclastic hyperactivity, such as hyperparathyroidism, the osteoclasts in Paget's disease are abnormal in appearance. Their numbers are increased, and they are larger than normal, multinucleated, and have many nucleoli. Their pseudopodia and ruffled borders invade the adjacent bone surface and resorb it at an accelerated rate. The resorption cavities are irregular, and their scalloped edges contribute to the 'mosaic appearance' of Paget's disease. Intracytoplasmic and intranuclear inclusion bodies can be seen by electron microscopy.

The osteoclastic hyperactivity is usually, but not always, accompanied by an overactivity of the osteoblasts. The number of osteoblasts is increased, but unlike the osteoclasts their appearance is essentially normal, even though a large number can be seen lining the osteoid surface. It is probable that the increased number and activity of osteoblasts is secondary to the osteoclast abnormalities.

The newly formed bone is architecturally abnormal. Microscopically, it appears as a disorganized mosaic of woven and lamellar bone. Collagen fibres are deposited in a haphazard and random manner. Spatial disorientation and irregular cement lines contribute to the mosaic appearance characteristic of Paget's disease. The vascularity of the bone, bone marrow, and adjacent tissues is increased during the active phase.

Clinical manifestations

Most patients with Paget's disease of bone are asymptomatic and the disease is commonly discovered accidentally during a routine laboratory screen or while investigating some other unrelated disease. The signs and symptoms of Paget's disease vary according to the site of the lesion and its activity.

The two cardinal manifestations are pain and deformities (Hamdy 1994). Most other manifestations are due to complications of the pagetic process. They are often erroneously attributed to the 'ageing process' because of their insidious onset and slow rate of progress (Hamdy et al. 1993a).

Pain

Pain is usually constant and deep-seated, and it often has a nagging character. It tends to be worse at night when the patient lies in a warm bed. It is not worsened by weight bearing or exercise, and may occasionally be relieved by exercise. Pain is more common when the lesion is active. There is little correlation between the radiological appearances of the lesion and the extent of the pain, although radiolucent lesions are more often associated with pain than are dense lesions. Painful Paget's disease lesions usually exhibit an increased uptake of radioactive material on bone scans.

In about two-thirds of cases the pain is due to the disease itself or to compression of the expanding bone by a neighbouring nerve, and in about one-third of the cases it is due to associated osteoarthritis (Hamdy et al. 1993a). Pain may be due to a number of causes including distension of the periosteum associated with the increased vascular flow through the affected bones, an increased intramedullary pressure resulting from an increased bone vascularity, hyperaemia of the marrow cavity, which may stimulate the adjacent nerve endings, and microfractures, particularly in weight-bearing bones. The pain associated with osteosarcomatous change is excruciating and is usually resistant to ordinary analgesics.

It is often difficult to differentiate pain due to Paget's disease from that due to an associated or complicating osteoarthritis. This is particularly the case when a vertebra is affected and the patient complains of back pain. Although a good response to non-steroidal anti-inflammatory drugs suggests an arthropathy, it does not exclude Paget's disease as the cause of the pain. A good response to specific antipagetic therapy is more suggestive of Paget's disease being responsible for the pain than an arthropathy. The intra-articular injection of lignocaine (lidocaine) is sometimes useful for differentiating pain due to osteoarthritis from that due to Paget's disease (Altman 1994).

Deformities

Deformities are the result of the enlarging and mechanically weaker bone. Deformities of the long bones are governed by forces of gravity, mechanical stress, and lines of muscle pull (Hamdy 1981). They are particularly noticeable in long bones and when the skull is affected. Characteristically, the long bones become larger and develop bowing, the tibia anteriorly and the femur anterolaterally.

When the head is affected, it becomes larger and the skull may acquire a corrugated appearance. The face becomes triangular in shape with the base of the triangle on the forehead. If the mandible is also affected, the face becomes rectangular in shape. Dental problems often complicate Paget's disease of the mandible or maxilla. When the base of the skull is affected, it is no longer able to support the weight of the head and becomes invaginated by the cervical vertebrae; this condition is known as platybasia. Patients appear to have a short neck with the chin lying on the chest. These patients are likely to develop a number of neurological complications.

Increased temperature of the skin overlying bone lesions

The skin overlying affected bones is often warmer than that on healthy bones. Differences as high as 5 °C have been reported. In severe cases, the blood supply to the skin may be interfered with and patients may develop ischaemic ulcers which are difficult to heal.

Complications

The complications of Paget's disease depend on the site of the lesion.

Long bones

Fractures are often preceded by fissure fractures, which produce pain at their site. Fractures often follow trivial trauma. No prospective data on the incidence of fractures in patients with Paget's disease are available, but estimates range from 1.5 to 6.6 fractures per 100 patient years (Kanis 1991).

Fractures present difficult management problems. Blood loss may be extensive during surgery, and specific antipagetic therapy before surgery may be recommended to reduce the vascularity of the lesion. Fractures are difficult to heal. Non-union occurs in about 10 per cent of the cases, and the fatality at 3 months is about 18 per cent (Dove 1980). The ultimate outcome of fractures complicating Paget's disease differs according to the site of the fracture (Bradley and Nade 1992).

Results of total hip arthroplasty in patients with Paget's disease of the pelvis or femoral head are not significantly different from those for patients without the disease (Ludowski and Wilson-McDonald 1990).

The skull

Nerves passing through narrow foramina are susceptible to compression by the expanding bone of Paget's disease. Cranial nerves VIII, II, V, and VII are likely to be compressed, and the patient may develop hearing loss, visual disturbances or even unilateral blindness, various degrees of atypical trigeminal neuralgia depending on which branch of the trigeminal nerve is affected, and facial palsy. Changes in olfactory acuity have been reported (Wheeler et al. 1995).

Occasionally hearing loss is associated with a roaring noise in the ear, probably due to the increased blood flow through the petrous bone. Hearing loss may also be due to involvement of the middle-ear ossicles by Paget's disease or invasion of the inner ear by pagetic tissue. Changes in bone density, mass, and form may dampen the finely tuned motion mechanics of the middle and inner ear and lead to hearing impairment (Monsell et al. 1995).

Platybasia may be complicated by involvement of the long tracts in the spinal cord, lower cranial nerve involvement, and hydrocephalus resulting from the obliteration of the flow of the cerebrospinal fluid through the narrow and easily deformed aqueduct of Sylvius connecting the third and fourth ventricles. Patients with hydrocephalus may present with the characteristic triad of rigid gait, urinary incontinence, and mental impairment.

Patients with extensive disease of the head may present with mental impairment and confusion, perhaps resulting from a shunt of blood flow from the internal to the external carotid circulations through the bones of the skull.

Vertebrae

The expanding vertebrae may encroach on the neighbouring nerves or their increased vascularity may cause ischaemia of the nervous structures by shunting the blood flow from the nerves to the hypervascular bone, thus producing a vascular steal (Yost et al. 1993). Cases of paraparesis and even paraplegia complicating Paget's disease of the vertebrae have been reported.

Neoplastic changes

Osteosarcoma is a rare but very serious complication of Paget's disease, affecting less than 1 per cent of patients (Hadjipavlou et al. 1992). It is associated with a very poor prognosis, with about 50 per cent of victims dying within the first 6 months of the diagnosis and only about 10 per cent of the patients surviving for 5 years (Frassica et al. 1991). The patient's age, increased vascularity of the lesion which favours early blood-borne spread, multicentric malignant transformation, involvement of surgically inoperable sites, and early fractures are factors worsening the prognosis of osteosarcoma.

Osteosarcomas are usually heralded by very severe pain in the affected bone and are often associated with a soft-tissue swelling. In most instances neoplastic changes are associated with a reduced uptake of technetium-99m, but an increased uptake of gallium. The characteristic radiological features of osteosarcomas are not usually present and often the diagnosis has to be confirmed by biopsy.

Generalized Paget's disease

Easy fatiguability, lethargy, and apathy are not uncommon in generalized Paget's disease (Hamdy et al. 1993a) and are probably due to the increased cardiac output resulting from the increased bone vascularity. Aortic valve calcification and arteriosclerosis are also more common in patients with Paget's disease. High-output heart failure is rare, but its incidence has often been exaggerated in the past.

Diagnosis

When diagnosing Paget's disease three questions should be addressed. Is the condition Paget's disease? How extensive is the disease? How active are the various lesions?

Biochemical diagnosis

During the active phase biochemical indices of bone turnover are elevated. These elevated levels are proportional to the size of the lesion, so that if the lesion is small, but active, the elevated levels of these various indices may still be within the normal range.

Urinary hydroxyproline excretion rate

The 24-h urinary hydroxyproline excretion rate reflects the degree of bone resorption and therefore osteoclastic activity (Patel et al. 1995a). Because the collection of a 24-h urine specimen is tiresome and often inaccurate, a 2-h specimen is often used to calculate the excretion rate. Diet may interfere with the urinary hydroxyproline levels. Galactosyl hydroxylysine is less affected by diet, but is less sensitive than hydroxyproline (Michalsky et al. 1995).

Serum alkaline phosphatase

The bone isoenzyme of the serum alkaline phosphatase reflects the activity of the osteoblasts, and therefore the activity of the lesion (Patel *et al.* 1995*a*). Its diagnostic accuracy is higher than that of the total serum alkaline phosphatase (84 per cent compared with 78 per cent) (Alvarez *et al.* 1995) but, in the absence of liver disease, it is a good indicator of the rate of bone formation.

Urinary pyridium cross-links or *N*-telopeptides

The urinary pyridoline and deoxypyridinoline excretion rates reflect the degree of bone resorption. A 2-h urine sample is often used. However, these measurements have little advantage over the determination of the urinary hydroxyproline levels (Hamdy *et al.* 1993*b*).

Serum osteocalin

The serum osteocalin or bone γ-carboxyglutamic acid containing protein level reflects the activity of the osteoblasts. However, its diagnostic accuracy is low (35 per cent) (Alvarez *et al.* 1995).

Other markers

Serum bone sialoprotein (Seibel *et al.* 1996), and several other biochemical markers are being investigated as monitors of the rate of bone turnover.

Radiological diagnosis

The radiological features of Paget's disease are so characteristic that in most instances the diagnosis is easy (Mirra *et al.* 1995). The earliest lesion may be a characteristic arrow-shaped zone of demineralization spreading along the bone. Multiple areas of bone resorption and bone deposition are obvious. There is little correlation between the radiographic appearances and the symptoms of the lesions. CT and magnetic resonance imaging are useful for assessing nerve compression and neurological symptoms.

Long bones

In long bones the lesion usually starts in one epiphysis and may gradually spread along the shaft of the bone. The lesions so rarely start in the diaphysis that when this is seen, the diagnosis should be questioned. The demarcation between affected and healthy bone is clear cut. The cortex of the affected long bones is irregularly thickened. Later, the bone is enlarged and may be bowed, with fissure fractures sometimes obvious along the convex border of the deformed bone.

The skull

When the skull is affected, in addition to the areas of bone resorption and bone formation, the diploic space is widened and the tables are indistinguishable from each other. Frontal bones are affected more frequently than the rest of the skull. Occasionally there is no evidence of bone formation and the lesion appears as a radiolucent area known as osteoporosis circumscripta. When the base of the skull is affected, platybasia may be present.

The vertebrae

Affected vertebrae appear larger than the adjacent healthy ones. The trabeculae are coarser and the cortices thickened, giving the appearance of a 'picture frame' (Klein and Norman 1995).

The pelvis

In addition to the characteristics areas of bone resorption and bone formation with coarsening of the trabecular pattern, the heads of the femur may invaginate the mechanically weakened bone and produce protrusio acetabuli. The iliopectineal line is usually prominent.

Radio-isotope scanning

Radio-isotope studies are useful for determining the extent of the disease, the activity of individual lesions, and the response to treatment (Patel *et al.* 1995*b*). Technetium-99 is avidly retained by pagetic lesions; the more active the lesion, the higher is the uptake. If the lesion becomes sarcomatous, the technetium uptake is reduced. Quiescent lesions may not show up on the scan (but are obvious radiologically). [^{67}Ga]citrate and [^{18}F]polyphosphonate are sometimes used. The uptake of the former is increased when the lesion becomes osteosarcomatous.

Treatment of Paget's disease

The majority of patients with Paget's disease do not require specific antipagetic treatment as the disease is usually asymptomatic and the likelihood of complications low. The main aim for treatment should not be to suppress abnormal biochemical, radiological, or scintigraphic findings, but to control the pain and other symptoms, and to treat or prevent the complications associated with the disease. Therefore, before embarking on any specific line of therapy, it is imperative to evaluate the extent of the disease and the activity of the various lesions. These are the main factors that should determine whether or not a patient will be actively treated.

Bisphosphonates

Bisphosphonates reduce bone resorption by inhibiting bone crystal dissolution, inhibiting mature osteoclasts, inhibiting osteoclast formation from precursors, and possibly inducing osteoclast apoptosis (Hughes *et al.* 1995). The suppression of bone resorption is dose dependent, is seen within days of administration, and is manifested by a reduction in the levels of alkaline phosphatase and urinary hydroxyproline levels, as well as by a reduced uptake of radioactive material by the affected bones and a return of the bone histology towards normality. Because of the close coupling between bone formation and bone resorption, the rate of new bone formation is also decreased and the bone blood flow is decreased. Newly formed bone is normal (Meunier and Vignot 1995). The effect of bisphosphonates is long lasting and may persist for several years after discontinuation.

Most bisphosphonates share common features. First, their low bioavailability when administered orally necessitates their intake while the patient is fasting. Second, their uptake by bones is dependent on the bone blood flow, and therefore higher concentrations will reach bones which have a higher blood flow. This targeting effect has obvious advantages in sparing non-affected bones. However, in patients with extensive Paget's disease, a smaller amount of bisphosphonates will reach all affected bones than if the patient had a more localized disease. This may explain the better response to bisphosphonates of patients with localized rather than generalized disease. Third, bisphosphonates are excreted unchanged in the urine and consideration should be given to reducing the dose in patients with renal impairment. Fourth, bisphosphonates are retained by the bones for a long period, and it is recommended not to prescribe them for courses lasting more than 6 months at a time. Subsequent retreatment with bisphosphonates yields good results as evidenced by the reduction in serum alkaline phosphatase and urinary hydroxyproline levels.

Several bisphosphonates have been used in the management of Paget's disease, including: etidronate, alendronate, tiludronate, pamidronate, and clodronate.

Etidronate

The recommended dose in Paget's disease is 5 to 10 mg/kg daily for 3 to 6 months (Dunn *et al.* 1994). Higher doses, such as 20 mg/kg daily, for shorter periods suppress the activity of the disease for a longer time, but may interfere with the mineralization of normal bone and result in histological appearances of osteomalacia and fractures of the healthy bones. Etidronate-induced 'osteomalacia' is not reversed by 1-α-hydroxycholecalciferol. The incidence of osteomalaciac histology is much lower when doses between 5 and 10 mg/kg daily are used.

Extensive osteolytic disease of long bones, particularly the weight-bearing ones, is regarded by many as a contraindication to the use of etidronate because of a possible increased risk of further bone demineralization (Kanis 1991).

The main side-effects of etidronate include intestinal upset and diarrhoea. The effect is dose dependent and can be managed by dividing the dose into two equal portions given at different times of the day. About 5 to 10 per cent of patients treated with etidronate complain of the onset of new bone pain or an exacerbation of pain at a site known to be affected by Paget's disease. The incidence of bone pain is dose related.

Etidronate induces a rise in serum phosphate level which is also dose dependent and is due to the increased renal tubular reabsorption of phosphate. This is particularly the case with doses exceeding 10 mg/kg daily. This hyperphosphataemia can be used to monitor the patient's compliance when higher doses are given (Kanis 1991). If hyperphosphataemia occurs with the regular dose of 5 mg/kg daily, it may indicate that this particular patient is taking or absorbing too much of the bisphosphonate and the dose may have to be reduced.

Alendronate

The recommended dose for Paget's disease is 40 mg daily for 6 months. Alendronate is more effective than etidronate at controlling the activity of Paget's disease (Siris 1996), and is not associated with mineralization problems (Reid *et al.* 1996). The main adverse effect is oesophagitis, which can be avoided by ensuring passage of the tablet into the stomach by taking it with plenty of water and as directed in the packet insert (de Groen *et al.* 1996).

Tiludronate

The recommended dose for Paget's disease is 400 mg daily for 3 months. It is more effective than etidronate (Roux 1995) and is well tolerated (McClung *et al.* 1995). The main adverse effects include diarrhoea, nausea, vomiting, flatulence, and peripheral oedema.

Pamidronate

Pamidronate is available in an injectable form. Various regimens have been proposed, including three daily infusions of 30 mg in 500 ml of saline or 5 per cent dextrose, a weekly infusion of 60 mg until a total dose of 240 to 480 mg is administered, or just a single 60-mg infusion (Pepersack *et al.* 1994). Because of its rapid onset of action, pamidronate is particularly useful in patients with neurological complications or severe lytic lesions, in those resistant to treatment, and prior to surgery on an affected bone (Siris 1996).

The main adverse effects include a low-grade fever, influenza-like symptoms, nausea, abdominal discomfort, mild leukopenia, transient hypocalcaemia, hypophosphataemia, transient proteinuria, ototoxicity (Reid *et al.* 1995), uveitis, and episcleritis (O'Donnell *et al.* 1995). Demineralization defects have also been reported (Adamson *et al.* 1993).

Calcitonin

Calcitonin specifically inhibits the activity of the osteoclasts and reduces their number. It reduces the rate of bone resorption, and therefore the activity of Paget's disease.

Following the acute administration of calcitonin, the osteoclasts detach themselves from the resorption surface of the bone and their nuclearity is decreased. The new bone formed under the influence of calcitonin is more lamellar than woven in structure. Calcitonin also reduces the bone blood flow and may have an analgesic effect.

Following the administration of calcitonin, a rapid decrease in the urine hydroxyproline and serum alkaline phosphatase levels can be observed. Typically these values are reduced to about 50 per cent of the pretreatment values and then tend to settle at these levels. Increasing the dose of calcitonin has little effect on these values, but the addition of another antipagetic agent is likely to induce a further reduction of the biochemical indices. In some instances the stabilization of the biochemical indices is due to an acquired resistance to calcitonin, and may herald the rebound or escape phenomenon when the biochemical markers increase despite continuation of calcitonin therapy.

In contrast with the bisphosphonates, the action of calcitonin is short lived; when treatment is stopped, the activity of the disease rapidly increases and a complete relapse may occur within a few months of discontinuing the therapy. These relapses are usually more difficult to treat and tend to be more resistant to repeated courses of calcitonin. This is a major disadvantage of the use of calcitonin for the long-term control of Paget's disease.

Several types of calcitonin (salmon, porcine, human, and eel) are commercially available. Salmon and eel calcitonin are more potent than equivalent doses of the porcine and human types. These differences may be due to differences in receptor binding affinity or to the rate of metabolic clearance.

There is still no consensus of opinion on the dosage of calcitonin. Doses range from 50 IU three times a week to 100 IU daily (Hamdy 1995). Higher and more frequent doses are associated with a more rapid suppression of bone turnover. Patients with more extensive disease require larger doses of calcitonin.

Resistance to calcitonin develops in about 25 to 45 per cent of treated patients (Grauer *et al.* 1995). In some, but not all, cases resistance to calcitonin therapy is due to the development of antibodies to calcitonin (Grauer *et al.* 1995). In these cases the serum levels of antibodies are elevated and the administration of another type of calcitonin is followed by improvement in the levels of the biochemical indices of disease activity. In many instances, however, antibodies are present but do not interfere with the action of calcitonin (Grauer *et al.* 1995). Resistance to calcitonin in the absence of antibodies is probably due to a downregulation of the calcitonin receptors.

Side-effects associated with calcitonin therapy are more inconvenient than serious, and most are dose dependent. Transient nausea occurring about 2 to 3 h following the parenteral administration of calcitonin is usually self-limiting but affects about a third of patients. However, most patients tolerate this side-effect, particularly if they self-administer the calcitonin on retiring to bed. Other side-effects include flushing, vomiting, diarrhoea, and local pain at the site of the injection. Most of these side-effects are also self-limiting and tend to decrease in severity and disappear as treatment is continued.

Human calcitonin is associated with more side-effects than salmon calcitonin. Flushing in particular may be a severe problem. Patients who develop unacceptable side-effects with one type of calcitonin may tolerate other types.

The intranasal administration of calcitonin is more convenient and is associated with fewer adverse systemic effects but may cause rhinitis.

Plicamycin

Plicamycin (Mithracin®) is a cytotoxic agent inhibiting RNA synthesis. Its main indication in the management of Paget's disease is when a rapid response is needed, as may occur with neurological complications of acute onset. It has to be administered intravenously and is associated with a number of adverse effects including hypocalcaemia, thrombocytopenia, hepatotoxicity, renal impairment, nausea, vomiting, and diarrhoea. It induces long-lasting remissions, but is rarely used because of its adverse effects.

Orthopaedic surgery

Orthopaedic surgery may be indicated for the management of complications interfering with the patient's level of independence or associated with pain which is difficult to control (Kaplan 1994). Specific antipagetic therapy is often recommended before surgery to reduce the vascularity of the lesion.

References

Abe, S., Ohno, T., Park, P., Higaki, S., Unno, K., and Tateishi, A. (1995). Viral behavior of paracrystalline inclusions in osteoclasts of Paget's disease of bone. *Ultrastructural Pathology*, 19, 455–61.

Adamson, B.B., Gallacher, S.J., Byars, J., and Ralston, S.H. (1993). Mineralisation defects with pamidronate therapy for Paget's disease. *Lancet*, 342, 1459–60.

Altman, R.D. (1994). Articular complications of Paget's disease of bone. *Seminars in Arthritis and Rheumatism*, 23, 248–9.

Alvarez, L., Guanabens, N., Peris, P., *et al.* (1995). Discriminative value of biochemical markers of bone turnover in assessing the activity of Paget's disease. *Journal of Bone and Mineral Research*, 10, 458–65.

Bradley, C.M. and Nade, S. (1992). Outcome after fractures of the femur in Paget's disease. *Australia and New Zealand Journal of Surgery*, 62, 39–44.

de Groen, P.C., Lubbe, D.F., Hirsch, L.J., *et al.* (1996). Esophagitis associated with the use of alendronate. *New England Journal of Medicine*, 335, 1016–21.

Dove, J. (1980). Complete fractures of the femur in Paget's disease of bone. *Journal of Bone and Joint Surgery*, 62B, 12–17.

Dunn, C.J., Fitton, A., and Sorkin, E.M. (1994). Etidronic acid. A review of its pharmacological properties and therapeutic efficacy in resorptive bone disease. *Drugs and Aging*, 5, 446–74.

Frassica, F.J., Sim, F.H., and Frassica, D.A. (1991). Survival and management considerations in postirradiation osteosarcoma and Paget's osteosarcoma. *Clinical Orthopaedics*, 270, 120–7.

Grauer, A., Ziegler, R., and Raue, F. (1995). Clinical significance of antibodies against calcitonin. *Experimental and Clinical Endocrinology and Diabetes*, 103, 345–51.

Hadjipavlou, A., Lander, P., and Srolovitz, H. (1992). Malignant transformation in Paget's disease of bone. *Cancer*, 70, 2802–8.

Hamdy, R.C. (1981). *Paget's disease of bone*. Praeger, Eastbourne, Sussex.

Hamdy, R.C. (1994). Paget's disease of bone. *Geriatric Medicine Clinics of North America*, 10, 719–35.

Hamdy, R.C. (1995). Clinical features and pharmacologic treatment of Paget's disease. *Endocrinology and Metabolism Clinic of North America*, 24, 421–36.

Hamdy, R.C., Moore, S.W., and LeRoy, J. (1993a). Clinical presentation of Paget's disease of the bone in older patients. *Southern Medical Journal*, 86, 1097–1100.

Hamdy, N.A., Papapoulos, S.E., Colwell, A., Eastell, R., and Russell, R.G. (1993b). Urinary collagen crosslink excretion: a better index of bone resorption than hydroxyproline in Paget's disease of bone? *Bone and Mineral Research*, 22, 1–8.

Hoyland, J. and Sharpe, P.T. (1994). Upregulation of c-*fos* protooncogene expression in pagetic osteoclasts. *Journal of Bone and Mineral Research*, 9, 1191–4.

Hoyland, J.A., Freemont, A.J., and Sharpe, P.T. (1994). Interleukin-6, IL-6 receptor, and IL-6 nuclear factor gene expression in Paget's disease. *Journal of Bone and Mineral Research*, 9, 75–80.

Hughes, D.E., Wright, K.R., Uy, H.L., *et al.* (1995). Bisphosphonates promote apoptosis in murine osteoclasts *in vivo* and *in vitro*. *Journal of Bone and Mineral Research*, 10, 1478–87.

Kanis, J.A. (1991). *Pathophysiology and treatment of Paget's disease of bone*. Carolina Academic Press, Durham, NC.

Kaplan, F.S. (1994). Paget's disease of bone: orthopaedic complications. *Seminars on Arthritis and Rheumatism*, 23, 250–2.

Klein, R.M. and Norman, A. (1995). Diagnostic procedures for Paget's disease. Radiologic, pathologic and laboratory testing. *Endocrinology and Metabolism Clinics of North America*, 24, 437–50.

Ludowski, P. and Wilson-MacDonald, J. (1990). Total arthroplasty in Paget's disease of the hip: a clinical review and review of the literature. *Clinical Orthopaedics*, 255, 160–7.

McClung, M.R., Tou, C.K., Goldstein, N.H., and Picot, C. (1995). Tiludronate therapy for Paget's disease of bone. *Bone*, 17 (Supplement 5), 493S–6S.

Mee, A.P., Hoyland, J.A., Baird, P., Bennett, D., and Sharpe, P.T. (1995). Canine bone marrow cell cultures infected with canine distemper virus: an *in vivo* model of Paget's disease. *Bone*, 17 (Supplement 4), 461S–6S.

Meunier, P.J. (1994). Bone histomorphometry and skeletal distribution of Paget's disease of bone. *Seminars in Arthritis and Rheumatism*, 23, 219–21.

Meunier, P.J. and Vignot, E. (1995). Therapeutic strategy in Paget's disease of bone. *Bone*, 17 (Supplement 5), 489S–91S.

Michalsky, M., Stepan, J.J., Wilczek, H., Formankova, J., and Moro, L. (1995). Galactosyl hydroxylysine in assessment of Paget's bone disease. *Clinical Chemistry Acta*, **234**, 101–8.

Mirra, J.M., Brien, E.W., and Tehranzadeh, J. (1995). Paget's disease of bone: review with emphasis on radiologic features. Parts I and II. *Skeletal Radiology*, **24**, 163–84.

Monsell, E.M., Bone, H.G., Cody, D.D., *et al.* (1995). Hearing loss in Paget's disease of bone: evidence of auditory nerve integrity. *American Journal of Otology*, **16**, 27–33.

O'Donnell, N.P., Rao, G.P., and Aguis-Fernandez, A. (1995). Paget's disease: ocular complications of disodium pamidronate treatment. *British Journal of Clinical Practice*, **49**, 272–3.

Patel, S., Coupland, C.A., Stone, M.D., and Hosking, D.J. (1995*a*). Comparison of methods of assessing response of Paget's disease to bisphosphonate therapy. *Bone*, **16**, 193–7.

Patel, S., Pearson, D., and Hosking, D.J. (1995*b*). Quantitative bone scintigraphy in the management of monostotic Paget's disease of bone. *Arthritis and Rheumatism*, **38**, 1506–12.

Pepersack, T., Karmali, R., Gillet, C., Francois, D., and Fuss, M. (1994). Paget's disease of bone: five regimens of pamidronate treatment. *Clinical Rheumatology*, **13**, 39–44.

Reddy, S.V., Singer, F.R., and Roodman, G.D. (1995). Bone marrow mononuclear cells from patients with Paget's disease contain measles virus nucleocapsid messenger ribonucleic acid that has mutations in a specific region of the sequence. *Journal of Clinical Endocrinology and Metabolism*, **80**, 2108–11.

Reid, I.R., Mills, D.A., and Wattie, D.J. (1995). Ototoxicity associated with intravenous bisphosphonate administration. *Calcified Tissue International*, **56**, 584–5.

Reid, I.R., Nicholson, G.C., Weinstein, R.S., *et al.* (1996). Biochemical and radiologic improvement in Paget's disease of bone treated with alendronate: a randomized, placebo-controlled trial. *American Journal of Medicine*, **101**, 341–8.

Roux, C. (1995). The methodology of clinical trials of oral tiludronate in Paget's disease of bone. *Bone*, **17** (Supplement 5), 497S–9S.

Seibel, M.J., Woitge, H.W., Pecherstorfer, M., *et al.* (1996). Serum immunoreactive bone sialoprotein as a new marker of bone turnover in metabolic and malignant bone disease. *Journal of Clinical Endocrinology and Metabolism*, **81**, 3289–94.

Shepard, S.L., Cooper, R.J., and McClure, J. (1996). The effect on chick osteoclasts of infection with paramyxoviruses. *Journal of Pathology*, **179**, 448–52.

Siris, E.S. (1996). Paget's disease of bone. In *Primer on the metabolic bone diseases and disorders of mineral metabolism* (3rd edn) (ed. M.J. Favus), pp. 409–19. Lippincott–Raven, Philadelphia, PA.

Wheeler, T.T., Alberts, M.A., Dolan, T.A., and McGorray, S.P. (1995). Dental, visual, auditory and olfactory complications in Paget's disease of bone. *Journal of the American Geriatrics Society*, **43**, 1384–91.

Yost, J.H., Spencer-Green, G., and Krant, J.D. (1993). Vascular steal mimicking compression myelopathy in Paget's disease of bone: rapid reversal with calcitonin and systemic steroids. *Journal of Rheumatology*, **20**, 1064–65.

14.4 Infections of bone

Vinod K. Dhawan and Thomas T. Yoshikawa

Introduction

Bone infections in elderly people are of paramount importance since their prompt recognition and appropriate therapy during the acute stage are critical to preventing the devastating sequelae of chronicity. Osteomyelitis is considered to be acute if it is newly recognized; the relapse of a previously treated or untreated infection is considered to be chronic osteomyelitis (Lew and Waldvogel 1997). Bone necrosis, the hallmark of chronic osteomyelitis, is more likely if clinical signs of bone infection persist for over 10 days (Mader *et al.* 1992). Bone infections in elderly people may begin in one of two ways: metastatic seeding of bone during a bacteraemic episode (haematogenous osteomyelitis), or direct spread of infection from a contiguous focus. The spectrum of osteomyelitis has changed over the years in that haematogenous osteomyelitis has decreased in overall frequency In older people; nowadays, haematogenous osteomyelitis is often seen in association with prosthetic joint infections (Waldvogel and Vasey

1980). However, the incidence of contiguous focus osteomyelitis has increased over the years owing to more frequent trauma and placement of prosthetic bone and joint devices. Also, the prevalence of Gram-negative bacilli, anaerobes, and mixed organisms has increased in patients with osteomyelitis (Gentry 1987). The unique features of bone infection in older age groups are summarized in Table 1.

Pathogenesis

Haematogenous osteomyelitis results from the bacteraemic seeding of bone tissue, most commonly in the metaphysis. The metaphyseal location of osteomyelitis is explained by local factors, such as its sluggish arterial circulation and the absence of phagocytic cells in its vascular lining. Haematogenous osteomyelitis, while common in the long bones in children, usually involves the vertebrae of elderly patients. However, an active distant focus of infection is clearly

Table 1 Characteristic features of osteomyelitis in older patients

Site of involvement	Vertebral localization is more common during haematogenous seeding of bones; peripheral vascular insufficiency leads to frequent involvement of bones of the feet
Type of osteomyelitis	Contiguous focus osteomyelitis is common in elderly patients owing to prosthetic joint surgery, frequent fractures, and pressure ulcers
Clinical presentation	Febrile response may be blunted in an elderly patient with acute osteomyelitis; vertebral osteomyelitis is often mistaken for compression fractures due to osteoporosis, resulting in delayed diagnosis
Microbiology	Gram-negative bacilli are a more common cause of osteomyelitis in older than in younger patients

identified in only 10 to 40 per cent of cases of haematogenous osteomyelitis and commonly includes soft tissue, urinary tract, and pulmonary infections. The presence of growth cartilage in children prevents the intra-articular spread of infection, while the loosely anchored periosteum facilitates the spread of infection to a subperiosteal location and thus the involucrum is formed. In contrast, in older patients, the resorption of growth cartilage and the firmly attached periosteum serve to direct the infectious process away from the subperiosteal space and towards the subarticular space. The attachment of organisms such as *Staphylococcus aureus* to bone and cartilage is facilitated by the presence of receptors for fibronectin, laminin, collagen, and bone sialoglycoprotein (Hermann *et al.* 1988). Once attached, the organisms resist antimicrobial killing (Chuard *et al.* 1991). *Staph. aureus* may survive intracellularly in the bone as a small-colony variant, resulting in persistent bone infection (Proctor *et al.* 1995). Osteolysis occurs through the generation of cytokines such as interleukins 1, 6, and 11 by the inflammatory cells (Manolagas and Jilka 1995). In addition, proteolytic enzymes and toxic oxygen radicals released by phagocytes and the bacterial components may result in osteolysis (Nair *et al.* 1996). Prostaglandin E_2, released in response to fracture, is also an osteoclast agonist. Increased intraosseous pressure produced by the inflammatory exudate causes vascular compromise, bone necrosis, and bone infarction (sequestrum formation).

Infection of bone due to contiguous focus infection is seen in the setting of fractures, orthopaedic surgery, and soft-tissue infections of hands and feet. Total hip replacement surgery, a procedure commonly performed for older people, is complicated by infection in 0.5 to 2 per cent of patients. Pressure ulcers, seen frequently in the United States nursing home population, infect the underlying bone by contiguous spread (Sugarman *et al.* 1983). Patients with peripheral vascular insufficiency are predisposed to infection because of the blunted local inflammatory response. Osteomyelitis associated with vascular insufficiency is common in older people and is seen almost exclusively in the bones of the lower extremities (Caputo *et al.* 1994).

Microbiology

The microbiology of osteomyelitis varies with the type of osteomyelitis and the underlying host factors. Acute haematogenous osteomyelitis is usually monomicrobial and most frequently due to *Staph. aureus*. In contrast, osteomyelitis due to a contiguous focus of infection is frequently polymicrobial in aetiology. While *Staph. aureus* is recovered most frequently, Gram-negative bacilli and anaerobes are also common. Coagulase-negative staphylococci are particularly common in bone infections associated with prosthetic joints and fracture-fixation devices. Gram-negative aerobic bacilli are more common as a cause of osteomyelitis in older than in younger adults, and mycobacteria and fungi may be the responsible organisms in some elderly patients. In a study of vertebral osteomyelitis due to *Candida* species, the mean age of patients (excluding intravenous drug abusers) was 67 years (Friedman and Simon 1987).

Clinical features

Acute osteomyelitis in most older patients manifests clinically as localized bone pain, malaise, fever, and chills. Swelling and tenderness may be present at the site of involvement. In contrast, chronic osteomyelitis presents most often with recurrent or persistent bone drainage. Osteomyelitis following bone surgery causes bone pain with poor wound healing and persistent wound drainage. Prosthetic joint infections produce fever, joint pain, and loosening of the prosthesis. Most prosthetic joint infections are delayed in onset, occurring months after surgery. However, a virulent pathogen may produce clinical disease sooner after surgery.

The recognition and diagnosis of vertebral osteomyelitis is frequently delayed with an elderly patient because of subtlety of clinical features; the vague symptoms and signs are often attributed to non-infectious aetiologies, particularly compression fractures caused by osteoporosis. Vertebral osteomyelitis typically involves the adjacent vertebrae and their intervening disk. The lumbar, thoracic, and cervical spine are involved in descending order of frequency. Backache and localized vertebral tenderness are often present, but low-grade fever is noted inconstantly. There may be a history of prior urinary tract instrumentation in about one-third of patients, and of antecedent skin infections in about 10 per cent. Bone infections may also follow enemas or rectocolonic endoscopy. Extension of vertebral osteomyelitis may result in paravertebral abscesses and epidural space infection, which may threaten the integrity of the spinal cord. Vertebral osteomyelitis should be considered in all elderly patients with severe back pain, particularly in the presence of an ongoing or recent infection (Norman and Yoshikawa 1994).

Osteomyelitis in the setting of peripheral vascular insufficiency typically occurs in the foot bones of diabetic patients and in elderly patients with atherosclerosis. If not treated promptly, infections of traumatic ulcers of the feet may lead to underlying osteomyelitis by contiguous spread. Foot ulcers are complicated by osteomyelitis in 30 to 68 per cent of diabetics. Hypoalgesia due to peripheral neuropathy is responsible for inattention to foot injuries by elderly diabetics.

Diagnosis

The clinical diagnosis of osteomyelitis is often imprecise and needs histological and microbiological confirmation. If a surgical probe can be advanced into the bone at the site of infection, osteomyelitis is considered to be present. Leucocyte counts may be elevated in the acute disease but are usually normal in chronic osteomyelitis. A normocytic normochromic anaemia is present in patients with long-standing bone infection. The erythrocyte sedimentation rate, while non-specific, is almost always elevated, and may be useful in monitoring the therapy of osteomyelitis. Blood cultures are positive for the putative organism in about half of patients with acute haematogenous osteomyelitis, but in less than 10 per cent of other forms of osteomyelitis. Cultures of swabs from ulcers or fistulas are often misleading owing to surface contamination and should not be relied upon to determine antibiotic therapy (Mackowiak et al. 1978). Aspiration of the adjacent joint, if involved, will often reveal the offending pathogen. Needle aspiration from the site of osteomyelitis provides the definitive diagnosis when blood cultures are negative. Ideally, microbiological studies should precede institution of antimicrobial therapy. The diagnostic yield of needle aspiration of bone is approximately 60 per cent (Dich et al. 1975). Open biopsy may be necessary if the needle aspiration is non-diagnostic or non-feasible, the antibiotic response is suboptimal, or atypical pathogens (e.g. fungi, mycobacteria) are suspected. Microbiological diagnosis can be made by an open surgical biopsy in about 90 per cent of patients with osteomyelitis.

Histopathological findings in osteomyelitis include infiltration of polymorphonuclear leucocytes, vascular congestion, vascular thrombosis, and micro-organisms. Special stains and cultures for mycobacterial and fungal pathogens should be performed when an indolent bone infection is suspected to be due to such organisms.

Routine radiographs are insensitive for the early diagnosis of bone infection. Radiological evidence of osteopenia may not be seen until 30 to 50 per cent of the involved bone has been resorbed (Gold et al. 1991; Manion and LaValley 1995). Such changes may take 3 to 4 weeks to manifest. When present, radiological findings in patients with osteomyelitis include soft-tissue swelling, periosteal elevation, periosteal thickening, cortical irregularity, sequestrum formation, and new bone formation (involucrum). In vertebral osteomyelitis, disc-space narrowing and mottled destruction of the adjacent vertebral plateaux may be noted.

Magnetic resonance imaging (MRI) is highly sensitive and is the preferred imaging modality for the diagnosis of osteomyelitis, but is precluded in the presence of ferromagnetic material. However, most orthopaedic devices use titanium, which does not cause any problems with MRI. Focal marrow abnormality with decreased signal intensity on T_1-weighted images and increased signal intensity on T_2-weighted images are suggestive of osteomyelitis. Fat-suppressed contrast-enhanced MRI decreases the bright signal of fat and increases the detection of water, thereby facilitating early detection of osteomyelitis (Morrison et al. 1993). MRI is particularly useful in the evaluation of vertebral osteomyelitis and its related complications.

[99mTc]methyl diphosphonate is useful for nuclear imaging of suspected bone infection (Tumeh and Tohmeh 1991). These scans may be positive as early as 48 h from the onset of osteomyelitis (Treves et al. 1976). However, technetium-99m scans may be falsely positive in the presence of osteoblastic bone tumours or osteonecrosis as in sickle cell disease, recent fractures, arthritis, and soft-tissue abscess. Moreover, technetium-99m bone scans remain positive for an extended period after the eradication of bone infection, precluding their utility in guiding therapy.

CT of bone is prone to artefacts caused by the bone and any metallic material present. Gallium-67 scanning is more specific but less sensitive than technetium-99m bone scanning (Shauwecker et al. 1984). ^{111}In-labelled white cells, ^{111}In-labelled human polyclonal IgG, and ^{111}In-labelled monoclonal antibody against neutrophils have all been used for the evaluation of osteomyelitis (Oyen et al. 1990; Newman et al. 1992).

The degree of vascular compromise in patients with osteomyelitis can be assessed by transcutaneous oximetry, measurement of pulse pressure with Doppler ultrasound, and arteriography.

Treatment

Precise microbiological diagnosis is mandatory for rational antibiotic therapy of osteomyelitis. With diverse aetiological possibilities and varying antimicrobial susceptibilities of responsible pathogens, the empirical use of prolonged courses of antibiotics is rarely justifiable. The cure of acute osteomyelitis is contingent upon timely therapy with appropriate antimicrobial agents administered for 4 to 6 weeks. Shorter courses of treatment may fail to cure acute osteomyelitis. Studies have shown a much higher rate of chronicity of osteomyelitis (19 per cent versus 2 per cent) if treatment of less than 21 days is used compared with treatment for longer than 3 weeks (Dich et al. 1975). The antibiotic regimens recommended for the commonly encountered causes of osteomyelitis are summarized in Table 2. The antimicrobial agent should initially be administered intravenously for 3 to 4 weeks. Therapy may then be continued with a suitable oral alternative (if one is available). The early (after a few days) switch from intravenous to oral antibiotics which has been prescribed in children has not been extensively studied in older patients (Nelson 1996). Outpatient antibiotic therapy of osteomyelitis, using tunnel lines for intravenous administration of antibiotics if necessary, has become popular.

Infections related to prostheses or other devices in the hip may occasionally be cured by treatment with oral quinolones and rifampicin (rifampin) for several months (Widmer et al. 1992; Drancourt et al. 1993). Quinolone therapy, with its well-documented efficacy in Gram-negative aerobic bacillary osteomyelitis, is inadequate for the treatment of osteomyelitis due to Gram-positive cocci such as Staph. aureus. Serum concentration of antibiotics should be optimized for adequate bone penetration and therapeutic levels at the site of infection. Trough serum bactericidal activity at 1:2 titre correlates with high rates of cure of osteomyelitis, although this has not been extensively examined in elderly patients. Treatment of osteomyelitis due to methicillin-resistant staphylococci requires a prolonged course of glycopeptide antibiotics, i.e. vancomycin or teicoplanin (Schaad et al. 1994; Graninger et al. 1995). Fungal osteomyelitis due to Candida species should be treated with about 2 g of amphotericin B. Fluconazole may be an option in some patients. Tubercular osteomyelitis should be treated with antituberculous therapy, as used in patients with pulmonary tuberculosis.

The duration of therapy of chronic osteomyelitis has not been well defined. Surgical debridement of necrotic bone is a critical component of management. Antibiotic therapy is generally administered for 3 to 6 months. There is no proven superiority of local instillation of antibiotics. The use of antibiotic-impregnated beads at the site of chronic osteomyelitis has not been evaluated by randomized prospective studies.

Table 2 Antibiotic treatment of osteomyelitis in older patients

Micro-organisms isolated	Initial intravenous antibiotic therapy	Oral alternative after initial therapy
Staph. aureus		
Penicillin-sensitive	Benzylpenicillin[a] (penicillin G) (4 million units every 6 h)	Phenoxymethylpenicillin (penicillin V) (500 mg every 6 h)
	Cephazolin (cefazolin) (2 g every 6 h)	Clindamycin (300 mg every 6 h)
	Clindamycin (600 mg every 6 h)	Cephalexin (500 mg every 6 h)
	Vancomycin (1 g every 12 h)	
Penicillin-resistant	Nafcillin[a] (2 g every 6 h)	Dicloxacillin (500 mg every 6 h)
	Cephazolin (2 g every 6 h)	Clindamycin (300 mg every 6 h)
	Clindamycin (600 mg every 6 h)	Cephalexin (500 mg every 6 h)
	Vancomycin (1 g every 12 h)	
Methicillin-resistant	Vancomycin[a] (1 g every 12 h)	None
	Teicoplanin (400 mg every 24 h, first day every 12 h)	
Various streptococci (group A or B β-haemolytic or *Streptococcus pneumoniae*)	Benzylpenicillin[a] (4 million units every 6 h)	Phenoxymethylpenicillin (500 mg every 6 h)
	Clindamycin (600 mg every 6 h)	Clindamycin (300 mg every 6 h)
	Erythromycin (500 mg every 6 h)	Cephalexin (500 mg every 6 h)
	Vancomycin (1 g every 12 h)	
	Ceftriaxone (2 g once daily)	
Enteric Gram-negative rods	Ciprofloxacin[a,b] (750 mg every 12 h)	Ciprofloxacin (750 mg every 12 h)
	Ceftriaxone (2 g every 24 h)	
Serratia marcescens or *Pseudomonas aeruginosa*	Ceftazidime[a] (2 g every 8 h) (with aminoglycosides for at least the first 2 weeks)	Ciprofloxacin (750 mg every 12 h)
	Ciprofloxacin (750 mg every 12 h)	
	Imipenem (500 mg every 6 h)	
	Piperacillin–tazobactam (4 g and 0.5 g respectively every 6 h)	
Anaerobes	Clindamycin[a] (600 mg every 6 h)	Co-amoxiclav (amoxicillin–clavulanic acid) (2.0 g and 0.2 g respectively every 8 h)
	Ampicillin–sulbactam (3.0 g and 0.5 g respectively every 8 h)	Metronidazole (500 mg every 8 h)
	Metronidazole (500 mg every 8 h)	
Mixed aerobic and anaerobic micro-organisms	Ampicillin–sulbactam[a] (3.0 g and 0.5 g respectively every 8 h)	Co-amoxiclav (2.0 g and 0.2 g respectively every 8 h)
	Imipenem (500 mg every 6 h)	
	Ticarcillin–clavulanic acid (3.0 g and 0.1 g respectively every 4 h)	

[a] Treatment of first choice.
[b] Ciprofloxacin can be used orally as it is completely absorbed from the gastrointestinal tract.

Strict immobilization of the site of osteomyelitis does not appear to be critical in the management. Moreover, prolonged immobilization risks complications such as thrombophlebitis, pressure ulcers, and physical deconditioning (and hence functional disabilities). There is no proven beneficial role of hyperbaric oxygen therapy in osteomyelitis. Prolonged suppressive antibiotic therapy may be the only option in an occasional patient when medical therapy is not curative and surgical debridement is not feasible.

Role of surgery

Surgical intervention may be necessary for an elderly patient with osteomyelitis (Eckardt *et al.* 1994; Reese and Barrio 1995). Although surgery may often be the only option for curing a bone infection, clinicians must weigh the potential impact of surgery on the functional capacity of elderly patients. Timely and appropriate rehabilitation, including occupational and physical therapy, will be crucial in yielding a good surgical outcome in older patients.

In acute osteomyelitis, surgical decompression will release intramedullary or subperiosteal pus. In chronic osteomyelitis, debridement of devitalized bone and soft tissue is mandatory. The dead-space created by debridement requires bone grafting. Revascularization of tissue reduces the rate of recurrent osteomyelitis and may be accomplished with pedicle muscle flap or myocutaneous flap (Mathes 1982). In patients with vertebral osteomyelitis, timely drainage of epidural abscess is necessary to prevent neurological complications. Surgery is also indicated to stabilize the spine and to drain paravertebral abscesses.

Osteomyelitis associated with vascular insufficiency is a surgical disease; the impaired tissue perfusion precludes access of antibiotics to the site of infection resulting in failure of medical therapy. Surgical treatment of diabetic foot osteomyelitis with peripheral vascular insufficiency depends on oxygen tension at the site of infection, potential for revascularization, extent of local infection, and the patient's preference (Eckman *et al.* 1995). In the presence of adequate oxygen tension and an identified pathogenic organism, debridement of osteomyelitic bone coupled with 4 to 6 weeks of antibiotics may be curative. With digital resection, transmetatarsal amputation, and disarticulation at mid-foot, the patient can walk without a prosthesis.

Osteomyelitis in the presence of orthopaedic hardware is often difficult to eradicate with antibiotic therapy alone. The slime layer formed on the surface of hardware provides a sanctuary for microbes, leading to persistent osteomyelitis. Surgical removal of foreign material is often necessary for cure of infection. In patients where removal of hardware may jeopardize bone stability, this procedure may be postponed until after bone union. Antibiotic therapy is continued during this period of bone healing and for about 4 weeks after removal of hardware. Prosthetic joint infection is generally treated by removal of prosthesis, debridement of the surrounding infected tissue, and intravenous antibiotics therapy for about 4 weeks, followed by placement of a new prosthesis (two-stage exchange arthroplasty). Some orthopaedic surgeons replace the infected prosthesis at the same time as the infected prosthesis is removed (one-stage arthroplasty). The risk of recurrent infection after one-stage arthroplasty is minimized by the use of antibiotic cement during surgery, but the rate of infection still exceeds that of the two-stage procedure.

Complications

The most worrying complication of acute osteomyelitis is the development of chronic osteomyelitis. Secondary amyloidosis, as a complication of chronic osteomyelitis, has become rare in the antibiotic era. Epidermoid carcinoma at the site of chronic osteomyelitis develops at the rate of 0.2 to 1.5 per cent after a mean of 34 years (West *et al.* 1970).

Prevention

Owing to the potentially devastating consequences of prosthetic joint infections, perioperative antimicrobial chemoprophylaxis has become standard care (Dellinger *et al.* 1988; Norden 1991; Classen *et al.* 1992). Antibiotics directed at staphylococci (e.g. cefazolin) should be administered 30 min to 1 h prior to surgery and continued for no longer than 24 h. Meticulous preoperative cleansing of the surgical site, rigorous adherence to aseptic technique, and the use of surgical suites with laminar airflow help to minimize postoperative infections. Similarly, infections following surgery for closed fractures can be reduced by perioperative administration of semisynthetic penicillins or cephalosporins (Boxma *et al.* 1996). Antibiotics may also be useful if administered within 6 h of sustaining an open fracture and given for a day (Patzakis *et al.* 1974). Prevention of pressure ulcers will reduce the incidence of complicating osteomyelitis. Careful and regular foot care, tight control of hyperglycaemia, and early treatment

of soft-tissue infection can reduce the incidence of diabetic foot osteomyelitis.

Conclusion

Osteomyelitis in an elderly patient is challenging for both prevention and management. With the increasing trend for prosthetic joint replacement and use of prosthetic material in reconstructive orthopaedic surgery, osteomyelitis due to contiguous focus will continue to remain a risk for older patients. An aggressive diagnostic approach to the precise microbiology of acute osteomyelitis and its prompt antibiotic therapy for 4 to 6 weeks should prevent osteomyelitis from becoming chronic. The development of better surgical techniques, the use of perioperative antibiotic prophylaxis, and early preventive intervention should reduce the incidence of osteomyelitis.

References

Boxma, H., Broekhuizen, T., Parka, P., and Oosting, H. (1996). Randomised controlled trial of single-dose antibiotic prophylaxis in surgical treatment of closed fractures: the Dutch trauma trial. *Lancet,* 347, 1133–7.

Caputo, G.M., Cavanagh, P.R., Ulbrecht, J.S., Gibson, G.W., and Karchmer, A.W. (1994). Assessment and management of foot disease in patients with diabetes. *New England Journal of Medicine,* 331, 854–60.

Chuard, C., Lucet, J.C., Rohner, P., *et al.* (1991). Resistance of *Staphylococcus aureus* recovered from infected foreign body *in vivo* to killing by antimicrobials. *Journal of Infectious Diseases,* 163, 1369–73.

Classen, D.C., Evans, R.S., Pestotnik, S.L., Horn, S.D., Menlove, R.L., and Burke, J.P. (1992). The timing of prophylactic administration of antibiotics and the risk of surgical-wound infection. *New England Journal of Medicine,* 326, 281–6.

Dellinger, E.P., Caplan, E.S., Weaver, L.D., *et al.* (1988). Duration of preventive antibiotic administration for open extremity fractures. *Archives of Surgery,* 123, 333–9.

Dich, V.Q., Nelson, J.D., and Haltalin, K.C. (1975). Osteomyelitis in infants and children. *American Journal of Diseases of Children,* 129, 1273–8.

Drancourt, M., Stein, A., Argenson, J.N., Zannier, A., Curvale, G., and Raoult, D. (1993). Oral rifampin plus ofloxacin for treatment of *Staphylococcus*-infected orthopaedic implants. *Antimicrobial Agents and Chemotherapy,* 37, 1214–18.

Eckardt, J.J,. Wirganowicz, P.Z., and Mar, T. (1994). An aggressive surgical approach to the management of chronic osteomyelitis. *Clinical Orthopedics,* 298, 229–39.

Eckman, M.H., Greenfield, S., Mackey, W.C., *et al.* (1995). Foot infections in diabetic patients: decision and cost-effectiveness analyses. *Journal of American Medical Association,* 273, 712–20.

Friedman, B.C. and Simon, G.L. (1987). *Candida* vertebral osteomyelitis: report of three cases and a review of the literature. *Diagnostic Microbiology and Infectious Disease,* 8, 31–6.

Gentry, L.O. (1987). Overview of osteomyelitis. *Orthopaedic Reviews,* 16, 255–8.

Gold, R.H., Hawkins, R.A., and Katz, R.D. (1991). Bacterial osteomyelitis: findings on plan radiography, CT, and scintigraphy. *American Journal of Roentgenology,* 157, 365–70.

Graninger, W., Wenisch, C., Wiesinger, E., Menschik, M., Karimi, J., and Presterl, E. (1995). Experience with outpatient intravenous teicoplanin therapy for chronic osteomyelitis. *European Journal of Clinical Microbiology and Infectious Diseases,* 14, 643–7.

Hermann, M., Vaudaux, P.E., Pittet, D., Auckenthacher-Perdreau, F., Peters, G., and Waldvogel, F.A. (1988). Fibronectin, fribrinogen and laminin act as mediators of adherence of clinical staphylococcal isolates to foreign material. *Journal of Infectious Diseases*, 158, 693–701.

Lew, D.P. and Waldvogel, F.A. (1997). Osteomyelitis. *New England Journal of Medicine*, 336, 999–1007.

Mackowiak, P.A., Jones, S.R., and Smith, J.W. (1978). Diagnostic value of sinus-tract cultures in chronic osteomyelitis. *Journal of American Medical Association*, 239, 2772–5.

Mader, J.T., Norden, C., Nelson, J.D., and Calandra, G.B. (1992). Evaluation of anti-infective drugs for the treatment of osteomyelitis in adults: Infectious Diseases Society of America and the Food and Drug Administration. *Clinical Infectious Diseases*, 15 (Supplement 1),155–61.

Manion, S.S. and LaValley, A.L. (1995). Radiographic diagnosis of bone and joint infection In *Diagnosis and management of bone infections* (ed. L.E. Jauregui), pp. 325–72. Dekker, New York.

Manolagas, S.C. and Jilka, R.L. (1995). Bone marrow, cytokines, and bone remodelling: emerging insights into the pathophysiology of osteoporosis. *New England Journal of Medicine*, 332, 305–11.

Mathes, S.J. (1982). The muscle flap for management of osteomyelitis. *New England Journal of Medicine*, 306, 294–5.

Morrison, W.B., Schweitzer, M.E., Bock, G.W., *et al.* (1993). Diagnosis of osteomyelitis: utility of fat-suppressed contrast-enhanced MR imaging. *Radiology*, 189, 251–7.

Nair, S.P., Meghji, S., Wilson, M., Reddi, K., White, P., and Henderson, B. (1996). Bacterially induced bone destruction: mechanisms and misconceptions. *Infection and Immunity*, 64, 2371–80.

Nelson, J.D. (1996). A critical review of the role of oral antibiotics in the management of hematogenous osteomyelitis. In *Current clinical topics in infections disease*, Vol. 4 (ed. R.S. Remington and M.N. Swartz), pp. 64–74. McGraw-Hill, New York.

Newman, L.G., Waller, J., Palestro, C.J., *et al.* (1992). Leukocyte scanning with [111] In is superior to magnetic resonance imaging in diagnosis of clinically unsuspected osteomyelitis in diabetic foot ulcers. *Diabetes Care*, 15, 1527–30.

Norden, C.W. (1991). Antibiotic prophylaxis in orthopaedic surgery. *Reviews of Infectious Diseases* 13 (Supplement 10), S842–6.

Norman, D.C. and Yoshikawa, T.T. (1994). Infections of the bone, joint, and bursa. *Clinics in Geriatric Medicine*, 10, 703–18.

Oyen, W.J., Clessens, R.A., van Horn, J.R., van der Meer, J.W., and Corstens, F.H. (1990). Scintigraphic detection of bone and joint infections with indium-111-labelled non-specific polyclonal human immunoglobulin G. *Journal of Nuclear Medicine*, 31, 403–12.

Patzakis, M.J., Harvey, J.P., Jr, and Ivler, D. (1974). The role of antibiotics in the management of open fractures. *Journal of Bone and Joint Surgery of America*, 56, 532–41.

Proctor, R.A., van Langevalde, P., Kristjansson, M., Maslow, J.N., and Arbeit, R.D. (1995). Persistent and relapsing infections associated with small-colony variants of *Staphylococcus aureus*. *Clinical Infectious Diseases*, 20, 95–102.

Reese, J.H. and Bario, J. (1995). Surgical approaches to the management of osteomyelitis. In: *Diagnosis and management of bone infections* (ed. L.E. Jauregui), pp. 425–9. Dekker, New York.

Schaad, H.J., Chuard, C., Vandaux, P., Waldvogel, F.A., and Lew, D. P. (1994). Teicoplanin alone or combined with rifampin compared with vancomycin for prophylaxis and treatment of experimental foreign body infection by methicillin-resistant *Staphylococcus aureus*. *Antimicrobial Agents and Chemotherapy*, 38, 1703–10.

Shauwecker, D.S., Park, H., Mock, B.H., *et al.* (1984). Evaluation of complicating osteomyelitis with Tc-99m MDP In-111 granulocyte and Ga-67 citrate. *Journal of Nuclear Medicine*, 25, 849–53.

Sugarman, B., Hawes, S., Musher, D.M., Klein, M., Young, E.J., and Pircher, F. (1983). Osteomyelitis beneath pressure sores. *Archives of Internal Medicine*, 143, 683–8.

Treves, S., Khettry, J., Broker, F.H., Wilkinson, R.H., and Watt, H. (1976). Osteomyelitis: early scintigraphic detection in children. *Pediatrics*, 57, 173–86.

Tumeh, S.S. and Tohmeh, A. G. (1991). Nuclear medicine techniques in septic arthritis and osteomyelitis. *Rheumatic Disease Clinic of North America*, 17, 559–83.

Waldvogel, F.A. and Vasey, H. (1980). Osteomyelitis: the past decade. *New England Journal of Medicine*, 303, 360–70.

West, W.F., Kelly, P., and Martin ,W.J. (1970). Chronic osteomyelitis. I. Factors affecting the results of treatment in 186 patients. *Journal of the American Medical Association*, 213, 1837–42.

Widmer, A.F., Gaechter, A., Ochsner, P.E., and Zimmerli, W. (1992). Antimicrobial treatment of orthopaedic implant-related infections with rifampin combinations. *Clinical Infectious Diseases*, 14, 1251–3.

15

Nephrology and the genitourinary system

15.1 Disorders of fluid and electrolyte balance

Eric L. Knight and Kenneth L. Minaker

Introduction

Disorders of fluid and electrolyte balance are very common in older individuals. These disorders are usually treatable if they are approached in a careful, logical manner. The most morbid disorders of fluid and electrolyte balance include dehydration, hypernatraemia and hyponatraemia. Dehydration is listed as one of the diagnoses in approximately 7 per cent of hospital admissions for individuals greater than 65 years old in the United States (Warren *et al.* 1994). The mean length of stay for patients in the United States with a primary diagnosis of dehydration is 14 days (United States Department of Health and Human Services 1988). Hypernatraemia is present in approximately 1 per cent of patients in hospital over the age of 60 years and is associated with a mortality rate greater than 40 per cent (Snyder *et al.* 1987). A study by Weinberg *et al.* (1994*a*) found that among febrile nursing home residents, 60 per cent had hypernatraemia or an elevated ratio of blood urea nitrogen (**BUN**) to creatinine, or both, compared with 5 per cent in a control population. In febrile nursing home residents with impaired oral intake the incidence of laboratory evidence of dehydration was 82 per cent. Hyponatraemia is also very common in older individuals and has been reported to occur in 11 per cent of older patients in hospital (Kleinfield *et al.* 1979). In a study of hospital mortality, hyponatraemia on admission was associated with a doubling of the risk of death (Terzian *et al.* 1994). In a study of nursing home patients, over a 1-year period, 53 per cent had at least one episode of hyponatraemia (Miller *et al.* 1995).

In order to treat disorders of fluid and electrolyte balance appropriately in older patients, an understanding of the underlying physiological changes that predispose older individuals to these disorders is necessary. In general, the homoeostatic reserve decreases with age. Specifically, there is a decrease in thirst in response to hypovolaemia and hyperosmolality. There is, on average, a decrease in glomerular filtration rate and a decrease in renal concentrating ability. There are generalized decreases in renin and aldosterone. There is an impaired renal responsiveness to vasopressin. As a final example of altered physiological mechanisms affecting fluid and electrolyte balance, there is commonly an increase in the level of atrial natriuretic peptide (**ANP**).

Thirst

Thirst sensation is decreased in older individuals. This was first demonstrated in 1984 (Phillips *et al.* 1984). After 24 h of fluid deprivation older volunteers had no change in thirst whereas younger volunteers had increased thirst. Then, when given full access to water, older volunteers drank less than the young. Similar deficits in fluid ingestion were seen when older individuals were infused with hypertonic saline (Dyke *et al.* 1997). This study isolated hyperosmolality as the stimulus for thirst (as hypovolaemia does not occur in this setting). Young and older volunteers were given a 2-h hypertonic saline infusion. Cumulative water intake was measured in the older volunteers compared with the young volunteers (Dyke *et al.* 1997) (Fig. 1). The young were able to defend against increased serum osmolality by increasing their fluid ingestion, but older individuals drank less and had higher serum osmolalities.

The sensation of thirst is mediated by osmoreceptors (which detect changes in osmolality) and by baroreceptors (which detect changes

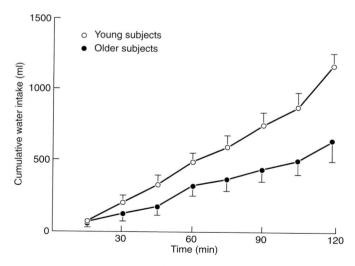

Fig. 1 Cumulative water intake during 2-h hypertonic saline infusion in young and older subjects. Cumulative water intake was less in the older than the younger subjects (1176 ± 86 versus 648 ± 145, $p < 0.01$). (Reproduced with permission from Dyke *et al.* (1997).)

in pressure or volume). Osmoreceptors are located in the brainstem. Low-pressure baroreceptors are located in the cardiac atria and high-pressure baroreceptors are located in the carotid sinus and aortic arch. These receptors project to the hypothalamus and then to the cortex. There is some evidence that the impairment in thirst seen with age may be due to a deficit in the opioid drinking drive (Silver and Morley 1992). Thirst may also be affected by psychological factors, concomitant food ingestion, the temperature of food and liquids, glossopharyngeal reflexes, and many other factors. Unfortunately, the pathophysiology of the thirst deficit seen in older people is poorly understood. The clinical relevance of these observations is that water needs to be a prescription in dehydrated elderly patients as thirst cannot be relied on to compensate for water deficits.

Changes in renal function with age

With age there is a variable decline in renal function. The average weight of the kidneys declines with age. The average renal plasma flow decreases by half from young adulthood to age 80 years. However, there is a lot of individual variability. This decline is highest in individuals with hypertension (Lindeman *et al.* 1984). The fall in creatinine clearance with age is not associated with an increase in serum creatinine because there is decreased production of creatinine secondary to a decrease in muscle mass with age. Therefore, serum creatinine alone is not an accurate estimation of glomerular filtration rate in older individuals. The Cockcroft–Gault formula has been devised to estimate creatinine clearance, which is an estimate of glomerular filtration rate, and takes into account the effects of age, weight, and sex (Cockcroft and Gault 1976; Gault *et al.* 1992). The formula for men is

$$\text{creatinine clearance (ml/min)}$$
$$= \frac{(140 - \text{age}) \times \text{body weight (kg)}}{\text{serum creatinine } (\mu\text{mol/l})} \times 1.23.$$

For women, owing to a higher ratio of fat to muscle for a given weight, the formula is multiplied by 0.85. However, this formula is only an estimate. Therefore, if knowledge of the creatinine clearance is critical, a 24-h urine collection for creatinine should be obtained.

In addition to changes in creatinine clearance, there are other significant changes in renal function. Renin and aldosterone levels are decreased under basal and stimulated conditions. Basal renin levels are diminished by 30 to 50 per cent in older people and are associated with similar declines in aldosterone secretion. These hormonal changes result in impaired sodium conservation. Also, older individuals have an impaired renal concentrating ability. This is thought to be due to at least two major factors. Firstly, there is a relative increase in medullary blood flow secondary to preferential loss of cortical glomeruli. This results in a 'washout' of medullary hypertonicity and a decreased concentrating ability. Decreased NaCl transport in the ascending loop of Henle may also contribute to this concentrating defect. Secondly, there may be an impaired renal responsiveness to vasopressin which may result in excessive water losses.

Conversely, volume expansion may be a significant problem in older individuals. This is mostly explainable on the basis of a decreased glomerular filtration rate as mentioned earlier. For example, it takes older individuals almost twice as long as younger individuals to

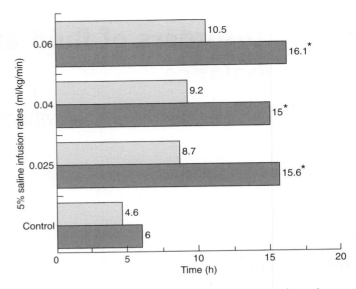

Fig. 2 Time to excrete 50 per cent of sodium load: young subjects (grey bars) versus older subjects (black bars). The time to excrete 50 per cent of the sodium load was significantly longer in the older subjects across all hypertonic sodium loads (*$p < 0.05$). Control infusion, 0.45 per cent saline at 100 ml/h for 2 h. (Reproduced with permission from Fish *et al.* (1995).)

excrete an acute sodium load. A study in which hypertonic saline was infused at different rates in young and older volunteers demonstrated the vulnerability of older individuals to sodium overload (Fish *et al.* 1995). There was a prolonged time required for sodium excretion and a decrease in peak sodium excretion rates (Fig. 2). Impairment in sodium excretion in older individuals is compounded by the high prevalence of congestive heart failure in this population.

Vasopressin

Vasopressin increases water permeability in the collecting tubule of the kidney. It acts through stimulation of adenylyl cyclase. Vasopressin also acts at the ascending loop of Henle to stimulate NaCl reabsorption. Studies in laboratory animals have shown that cyclic adenosine monophosphate generation, a measure of adenylyl cyclase activity, decreases with age (Beck and Yu 1982). This may contribute to the impairment seen in renal concentrating ability with age. There may also be a change in the diurnal variation of vasopressin levels with age (Asplind and Aberg 1991). Normally, in younger individuals, vasopressin levels increase at night. In older individuals this variability may be lost resulting in increased urinary output at night.

There is considerable controversy about vasopressin levels in older people versus younger people. Gender differences in vasopressin have also been reported. Most studies suggest that older people have normal or elevated vasopressin levels compared with the young. There are also some interesting reports that patients with Alzheimer's disease and some neurological diseases may have inappropriately low vasopressin levels for a given serum osmolality (Albert *et al.* 1989; Sonnenblick and Algur 1993). This may predispose this subset of patients to dehydration in addition to other practical considerations such as impairment in the ability to request and access water. (For a further discussion of vasopressin and the syndrome of inappropriate antidiuretic hormone secretion see the section on euvolaemic hyponatraemia below.)

Atrial natriuretic peptide

ANP is an important hormone in volume regulation. The physiological effects of ANP are important to understand because of its role in volume regulation. ANP is a 126-amino-acid polypeptide that is released from the cardiac artria in response to increased atrial stretch. It circulates as an N-terminal and a C-terminal peptide. ANP causes diuresis by reducing sodium reabsorption in the collecting tubules of the kidney and by increasing glomerular filtration rate. It also has other physiological roles including direct vasodilatation and inhibitory effects on renin, angiotensin II, aldosterone, and vasopressin. Older individuals have higher basal levels of ANP than younger individuals (Davis *et al.* 1996). However, under stimulated conditions, such as hypervolaemia, younger individuals are able to generate a significant increase in ANP level whereas older individuals do not (Clark *et al.* 1991). In older individuals the increased basal ANP levels may predispose to dehydration. There is no evidence for a change in the end-organ binding of ANP with age, but there may be a decreased renal haemodynamic response to ANP with age (Mulkerrin *et al.* 1993; Tan *et al.* 1993).

Recognizing dehydration in elderly people

Disorders of volume regulation in older individuals often present with non-specific signs and symptoms. The most specific clinical sign that can be evaluated is acute weight loss. Generally, a loss of over 3 per cent of body weight is considered significant. It is particularly important to identify weight loss in the old because they have a greater proportion of fat relative to lean muscle mass compared with the young. Therefore, since there is less water in fat than in muscle, older individuals have a greater loss of water compared with the young for a given decrease in body weight.

Obtaining an accurate weight may be difficult. In addition, many other clinical signs and symptoms of dehydration may be unreliable. One study of emergency department patients aged 60 years and older found tongue dryness, mouth dryness, upper body muscle weakness, confusion, speech difficulty, and sunkenness of the eyes to be associated with severity of dehydration (Gross *et al.* 1992). However, many of these signs are non-specific. For example, mouth dryness may be caused by mouth breathing or anticholinergic medication, muscle weakness may be due to disuse and atrophy, and confusion may be due to a variety of causes. More objective clinical signs that may be helpful in identifying dehydration include orthostatic hypotension, an elevated BUN-to-creatinine ratio, and an elevated serum osmolality. However, all these signs are non-specific. It may be helpful to compare the objective signs of dehydration with baseline values. Weinberg *et al.* (1994*b*) found no significant changes over 6 months in baseline serum sodium, BUN-to-creatinine ratio, or weight in nursing home residents.

Attempts have been made to identify individuals at risk for dehydration given the non-specific presentation. This is especially true of the oldest people and those individuals living in life care facilities. The United States Omnibus Budget Reconciliation Act

Table 1 The United States Omnibus Budget Reconciliation Act 1987/1990 Minimum Data Set: dehydration/fluid maintenance triggers and additional risk factors for dehydration among residents of long-term care facilities[a]

Dehydration/fluid maintenance triggers

Deterioration in cognitive status, skills, or abilities in last 90 days
Failure to eat or take medication(s)
Urinary tract infection in last 30 days
Current diagnosis of dehydration (ICD-9 code 276-5)
Diarrhoea
Dizziness/vertigo
Fever
Internal bleeding
Vomiting
Weight loss (>5% in last 30 days, or 10% in last 180 days)
Insufficient fluid intake (dehydrated)
Did not consume all/almost all liquids provided during last 3 days
Leaves 25% food uneaten at most meals
Requirement for parenteral (intravenous) fluids

Additional potential risk factors

Hand dexterity/body control problems
Use of diuretics
Abuse of laxatives
Uncontrolled diabetes mellitus
Swallowing problems
Purposeful restriction of fluids
Patients on enteral feedings (need free water in addition to feedings)
History of previous episodes of dehydration
Comprehension/communication problems

ICD-9, *International Classification of Diseases* (9th edn).
[a] Omnibus Budget Reconciliation Act of 1987 and 1990 (Federal, United States of America).

Reproduced with permission from Weinberg *et al.* (1995).

1990 Minimum Data Set identified several potential risk factors for dehydration (Weinberg *et al.* 1995) (Table 1).

A study of 339 hospital admissions from nursing homes analysed odds ratios for risk factors for dehydration (Lavizzo-Mourrey *et al.* 1988). They identified the following risk factors for dehydration: female sex, age over 85 years, over four chronic conditions, over four medications, bedridden status, laxative use, and chronic infections.

Classification of dehydration

Dehydration can be classified on the basis of serum sodium level and serum osmolality. Hypertonic dehydration is characterized by high serum sodium levels (over 145 mmol/l) and elevated serum osmolality (over 295 mosmol/l). The underlying source of dehydration in hypertonic dehydration is water loss disproportionate to sodium loss.

Isotonic dehydration is characterized by normal serum sodium levels (135–145 mmol/l) and normal serum osmolality (280–295 mmol/l). Isotonic dehydration results from both water and sodium losses. Hypotonic dehydration is characterized by low serum sodium levels (less than 135 mmol/l) and low serum osmolality (less than 280 mosmol/l).

There are many causes of dehydration in elderly people. These causes can be classified according to whether they result in increased

Table 2 Causes of increased fluid loss by elderly people

Chronic or acute infections

Excessive urinary losses
Diuretic misuse
Glycosuria
Hypercalciuria
Mannitol
Radiographic contrast agents
Elevated blood urea nitrogen
Diabetes insipidus
   Central (pituitary)
   Nephrogenic
Hypoaldosteronism
   Addison's disease
   Hyporeninaemic hypoaldosteronism
Suppressed vasopressin
   Phenytoin
   Ethanol
   After atrial tachyarrhythmia

Postobstructive diuresis

Gastrointestinal losses
Upper gastrointestinal tract
   Vomiting
   Nasogastric damage
   Enteral alimentation with hypertonic fluids
Lower gastrointestinal tract
   Laxative abuse/bowel preparations
   Infectious/secretory
   Surgical bypass/fistulas
   Ischaemic bowel
   Colectomy

Excessive blood loss

Environment-related fluid loss
Heat wave
Hypothermia

Compartmental fluid shifts
Hypoalbuminaemia
Pancreatitis
Ascites
Anaphylaxis
Burns
Hypertonic peritoneal dialysate

Reproduced with permission from Minaker (1995).

Table 3 Causes of decreased fluid intake by elderly people

Limited access to fluids
Physical restraints
Mobility restriction
Poor visual acuity

Fluid restriction
Preprocedure
Prevention of incontinence/nocturia/aspiration
Therapy for oedema or hyponatraemia

Altered sensorium
Decreased consciousness level
   Sedatives, neuroleptics, narcotics
   Structural and metabolic central nervous system insults
   Febrile illness
Decreased level of awareness
   Dementia, delirium
   Mania, psychosis, depression

Gastrointestinal disorders
Swallowing disorders
Bowel obstruction
   Mechanical
   Metabolic
   Ischaemic
Anticholinergic medication

Alteration in thirst mechanism
Primary adipsia
Medication-related
   Cardiac glycosides
   Amphetamines
Associated with focal central nervous system pathology

Reproduced with permission from Minaker (1995).

fluid loss or decreased fluid intake. Table 2 lists causes of increased fluid loss in elderly people (Minaker 1995). Infections such as pneumonia and urinary tract infections are very common in older individuals and account for a disproportionate amount of dehydration. The resulting fever may cause excessive water loss from sweating and tachypnoea. Excessive urinary fluid losses may also result from diuretic use, hyperglycaemia, hypercalcaemia, mannitol use, and radiographic contrast material use. Other causes of excessive urinary fluid losses include diabetes insipidus, hypoaldosteronism, and suppressed vasopressin. Losses of fluid from the gastrointestinal tract are important in older individuals. One common cause of gastrointestinal fluid loss

that is often overlooked is laxative use. This may result in an increase in fluid loss from the gastrointestinal tract. The gastrointestinal tract is responsible for the majority of fluid absorption in the body. Older patients may also lose a significant amount of fluids during bowel-cleansing regimens for severe constipation or other procedures. Infectious diarrhoea, especially diarrhoea due to *Clostridium difficile*, may also be an important cause of fluid losses. Environment-related fluid losses are also very important. This is especially true during the summer months. Older people are more vulnerable to dehydration during high temperatures than younger people. This is often compounded by lack of access to appropriate cooling devices such as air conditioning.

Table 3 lists the causes of decreased fluid intake (Minaker 1995). Older people may have limited access to fluids secondary to restricted mobility restriction and poor vision. Decreased fluid intake may also be iatrogenically induced by the use of physical restraints or by the use of aggressive fluid restriction. Older patients may also consciously reduce their fluid intake to prevent urinary incontinence. Swallowing problems may also contribute to poor fluid intake. Finally, patients with dementia or altered sensoria are at the highest risk for dehydration secondary to decreased fluid intake.

Unfortunately, dehydration in older people is often multifactorial secondary to decreased functional reserve and significant comorbidity. Patients may have significant physical frailty and cognitive impairment. Initially, it is important to identify the type of dehydration so that appropriate therapy may be instituted. Then, the specific causes of decreased fluid intake and increased fluid losses should be determined so that appropriate preventive measures may be instituted.

Treatment of dehydration

If a patient has had an acute fluid loss then the fluid deficit can be estimated by subtracting the current weight from the baseline weight. Since 1 litre of water weighs 1 kg, the difference in weight approximates the fluid loss. For example, if a 60-kg female becomes dehydrated and loses 2 kg then the water deficit can be determined as follows: 60 kg − 58 kg = 2 kg, 2 kg = 2.0 litre or 2000 ml fluid deficit. However, this formula does not help with determining the type of fluid replacement needed nor does it take maintenance fluid replacement into consideration.

Oral rehydration

Oral rehydration is the least invasive, and preferred, route of rehydration. The type of rehydration fluid indicated depends on the type of dehydration. In hypertonic dehydration the preferred fluid is water or a low-sodium rehydration solution. Fruit juices such as orange, apple, and grape may also be used in this setting. Isotonic dehydration is treated with water and sodium supplementation. This can be accomplished by rehydration with water and solute supplementation (e.g. high-sodium broths and tomato juice) or through isotonic commercial solutions. Hypotonic dehydration is treated as above except that more sodium replacement is required.

Intravenous rehydration

Intravenous rehydration is the fastest way to replete fluid deficits and is indicated when there is significant hypotension, orthostasis, or decreased urine output secondary to dehydration. During acute haemodynamic compromise normal saline is the fluid of choice. Otherwise, the type of fluid therapy is guided by the type of dehydration. For example, hypertonic dehydration may be treated with half-normal saline and isotonic dehydration with normal saline.

Subcutaneous fluid administration

Subcutaneous fluid administration (hypodermoclysis) has been used effectively in the long-term care setting. Hypodermoclysis may be used when oral rehydration is not an option and intravenous rehydration is unobtainable or undesirable. Absorption of normal saline with subcutaneous fluid administration is comparable with intravenous administration (Challiner et al. 1994).

Hypernatraemia

Hypernatraemia is seen in approximately 1 per cent of patients in hospital (Snyder et al. 1987). Approximately half of these cases develop hypernatraemia in the hospital. Older individuals are especially prone to this condition because of many of the physiological changes outlined above. Two of the major factors that contribute to hypernatraemia in older patients are impaired thirst and decreased access to water

secondary to mobility or swallowing impairment. Older individuals are also vulnerable to hypernatraemia in some settings because of delayed excretion of sodium.

Causes of hypernatraemia can be divided into sodium retention or water loss. The former is relatively rare and is usually caused by administration of hypertonic saline.

However, there are many causes of excessive fluid losses. These are outlined above. Snyder et al. (1987) found the following factors to be associated with hypernatraemia in older individuals (listed in descending order of importance): febrile illness, infirmity, surgery, nutritional supplementation, intravenous solutes, diabetes, diarrhoea, gastrointestinal bleeding, diuretics, diabetes insipidus, and dialysis.

Patients with dementia may be especially prone to hypernatraemia because of decreased thirst, an impaired ability to ask for water, and, perhaps, inappropriately low levels of vasopressin. Another important cause of hypernatraemia in older individuals is hypercalcaemia. Hypercalcaemia may cause damage to cells in the loop of Henle and may interfere with vasopressin at the level of the collecting tubule (Rose 1994). Significant hypokalaemia may also cause hypernatraemia by impairing the countercurrent function of the kidney through interference with tubular reabsorption of sodium and by interfering with vasopressin at the level of the collecting tubule (Rose 1994).

The treatment of hypernatraemia is replacement of fluid losses or, in the case of excessive sodium administration, stopping sodium administration. General guidelines for the replacement of fluid losses are outlined above. If fluid losses are primarily water, the fluid deficit can be estimated as follows:

$$\text{fluid deficit} = \text{desired TBW} - \text{current TBW}$$
$$\text{desired TBW} = \frac{\text{measured serum Na} \times \text{current TBW}}{140}$$
$$\text{current TBW (men)} = 0.5 \times \text{body weight (kg)}$$
$$\text{current TBW (women)} = 0.45 \times \text{body weight (kg)}$$

where TBW is the total body water. This formula gives a result in kilograms which can be directly translated into litres of water.

It is important in high-risk individuals to provide adequate hydration to prevent hypernatraemia and its sequelae which include neurological injury, coma, and death. It is also important to search carefully for causes of excess water loss and decreased water intake.

Hyponatraemia

Hyponatraemia is the most common electrolyte abnormality in older individuals as they are predisposed to this condition for many reasons. Firstly, there is a decline in the maximum diluting ability of the kidney with increasing age. This results in excessive sodium losses. Secondly, there may be, although this is controversial, an enhanced vasopressin response to hyperosmolality seen with increasing age. Thirdly, and perhaps most importantly, older individuals are more likely to take medications that cause hyponatraemia or to have diseases associated with hyponatraemia.

Symptoms of hyponatraemia are vague and unreliable. They include lethargy, confusion, agitation, weakness, and anorexia. These symptoms depend on the severity of the hyponatraemia and the rapidity of its development.

A detailed approach to hyponatraemia can be found in standard medical textbooks. A common approach is as follows. Initially, measure the serum osmolality. A normal serum osmolality in the context

Table 4 Aetiology of SIADH

Ectopic ADH production by tumours
Lung, pancreas, duodenum, ureter, nasopharynx, leukaemia, Hodgkin's disease, thymoma

Central nervous system disorders
Brain tumour, encephalitis, meningitis, brain abscess, head injury, subarachnoid haemorrhage, Guillain–Barré syndrome, systemic lupus erythematosus, acute intermittent porphyria

Pulmonary diseases
Pneumonia, tuberculosis, fungal infections, lung abscess, acute respiratory failure, asthma

Endocrine disorders
Hypothyroidism, glucocorticoid deficiency

Drug-induced[a]
Vasopressin, desmopressin, oxytocin, cyclophosphamide, vincristine, vinblastine, chlorpropamide, carbamazepine, nicotine, morphine, non-steroidal anti-inflammatory drugs(?)

[a] Some authorities exclude endocrine disorders and drug-induced hyponatraemia as causes of SIADH.

Reproduced with permission from Sterns and Spital (1990).

of hyponatraemia suggests hyperlipidaemia or hyperproteinaemia. A high serum osmolality is often seen with hyperglycaemia or hypertonic infusions. If the osmolality is low, one should assess the volume status of the patient. Unfortunately, this can be very challenging in older patients. Traditional clinical estimates of dehydration should be employed as outlined above.

Hypovolaemic hyponatraemia

If hypovolaemic hyponatraemia is suspected, urine sodium measurement may be helpful. A low urine sodium will be seen with causes of extrarenal sodium loss such as skin losses and gastrointestinal losses. A high urine sodium may be seen with causes such as renal disease, diuretic use, and hypoaldosteronism. The importance of thiazide diuretic use causing hypovolaemic hyponatraemia in older individuals cannot be overemphasized. In a review of cases of diuretic-induced hyponatraemia, Sonnenblick et al. (1993) found thiazide diuretics were associated with hyponatraemia in 94 per cent of cases. Excess water intake, hypokalaemia and excess vasopressin activity were also associated with hyponatraemia. Thiazide diuretics act at the distal tubule of the kidney and impair sodium transport. This can result in sodium loss in excess of water loss. This may be compounded by age-associated failure of volume- and pressure-mediated vasopressin release (Rowe et al. 1982).

Euvolaemic hyponatraemia

Euvolaemic hyponatraemia may be seen in common conditions such as the syndrome of inappropriate antidiuretic hormone secretion (SIADH) and reset osmostat. Common causes of SIADH in older patients include infections, subdural haematomas, medications, pulmonary disease, and cancer to name just a few. Table 4 provides an abbreviated list of the aetiologies of SIADH (Sterns and Spital 1990).

The acute treatment of SIADH consists of water restriction and sodium replacement. Loop diuretics may be used as an adjunctive agent. Loop diuretics impair water transport in the thick ascending loop of Henle and therefore deliver more water to the distal nephron for excretion. Chronic therapy consists of water restriction and increased salt ingestion. The phenomenon of reset osmostat occurs when the threshold of ADH release is decreased. Usually, the patient has a low stable hyponatraemia.

Hypervolaemic hyponatraemia

Hypervolaemia is suggested by the presence of weight gain and oedema. The most common cause of hypervolaemic hyponatraemia in an older population is congestive heart failure. These patients usually have a very gradual onset of hyponatraemia. Generally, they have increased thirst and it is very difficult for them to reduce water intake. Other causes of hypervolaemic hyponatraemia include nephrotic syndrome and hepatic cirrhosis. The treatment of choice in these settings is water restriction.

Treatment of hyponatraemia

General treatment guidelines for specific types of hyponatraemia are outlined above. The amount of sodium required to correct a sodium deficit to 120 mmol can be estimated as follows (Rose 1994):

$$\text{sodium deficit (men)} = [0.6 \times \text{lean body weight (kg)}] \times (120 - \text{plasma sodium})$$
$$\text{sodium deficit (women)} = [(0.5 \times \text{lean body weight (kg)}] \times (120 - \text{plasma sodium}).$$

However, this formula does not estimate iso-osmotic fluid losses.

The rate of correction of hyponatraemia should depend on the severity of symptoms and the degree of hyponatraemia. A safe sodium level to achieve acutely may be 120 mmol/l followed by more gradual replacement, but no absolutely safe recommendation can be given. The correction of hyponatraemia should be kept at a rate of less than 10 mmol/l in any 24-h period (Laureno and Karp 1997). The major danger of rapid replacement is the precipitation of myelinolysis which may result in paraparesis or quadraparesis, pseudobulbar palsy, and coma. It is most commonly seen in the treatment of chronic hyponatraemia. In this setting the brain has adapted to hyponatraemia by losing solutes. Sodium administration in this setting may result in cerebral dehydration and neurological damage. However, the exact physiological mechanism of this damage is not completely understood.

Conclusions

In summary, older individuals are at high risk for disorders of fluid and electrolyte balance. Physiological changes that occur with ageing predispose older individuals to dehydration and other disorders of fluid balance. These changes include decreased thirst, decreased renal function, decreases in renin and aldosterone, an impaired renal responsiveness to vasopressin, and increased ANP levels. In caring for older patients, one must understand how these changes affect volume regulation. In addition, it is important to be vigilant about detecting early changes in volume status and electrolyte balance in older individuals in order to prevent dehydration, hypernatraemia, and hyponatraemia.

References

Albert, S.G., Nakra, B.R.S., Grossberg, G.T., and Caminal, E.R. (1989). Vasopressin response to dehydration in Alzheimer's disease. *Journal of the American Geriatrics Society*, 37, 843–7.

Asplind, R. and Aberg, H. (1991). Diurnal variations in the levels of antidiuretic hormone in the elderly. *Journal of Internal Medicine*, 229, 131–4.

Beck, N. and Yu, B.P. (1982). Effect of ageing on urinary concentrating mechanism and vasopressin-dependent cAMP in rats. *American Journal of Physiology*, 243, F121–5.

Challiner, Y.C., Jarrett, D., Hayward, M.J., al-Jabouri, M.A., and Julious, S.A. (1994). A comparison of intravenous and subcutaneous hydration in elderly acute stroke patients. *Postgraduate Medical Journal*, 70, 195–7.

Clark, B.A., Elahi, D., Fish, L., *et al.* (1991). Atrial natriuretic peptide suppresses osmostimulated vasopressin release in young and elderly humans. *American Journal of Physiology*, 261, E252–6.

Cockcroft, D.W. and Gault, M.H. (1976). Prediction of creatinine clearance from serum creatinine. *Nephron*, 66, 13.

Davis, K.M., Fish, L.C., Minaker, K.L., and Elahi, D. (1996). Atrial natriuretic peptide levels in the elderly: differentiating normal ageing changes from disease. *Journal of Gerontology: Medical Sciences*, 51A, M95–101.

Dyke, M.M., Davis, K.M., Clark, B.A., Fish, L.C., Elahi, D., and Minaker, K.L. (1997). Effects of hypertonicity on water intake in the elderly: an age-related failure. *Geriatric Nephrology and Urology*, 7, 11–16.

Fish, L.C., Murphy, D.J., Elahi, D., and Minaker, K.L. (1995). Renal sodium excretion in normal ageing: decreased excretion rates lead to delayed handling of sodium loads. *Geriatric Nephrology and Urology*, 4, 145–51.

Gault, M.H., Langerich, L.L., Hamelt, J.D., and Weslowski, C. (1992). Predicting glomerular function from adjusted serum creatinine. *Nephron*, 62, 249.

Gross, C.R., Lindquist, R.D., Woolley, A.C., Granieri, R., Allard, K., and Webster, B. (1992). Clinical indicators of dehydration severity in elderly patients. *Journal of Emergency Medicine*, 10, 267–74.

Kleinfeld, J., Casimir, M., and Bona, S. (1979). Hyponatremia as observed in a chronic disease facility. *Journal of the American Geriatrics Society*, 27, 156–61.

Laureno, R. and Karp, B.I. (1997). Myelinolysis after correction of hyponatremia. *Annals of Internal Medicine*, 126, 57–62.

Lavizzo-Mourrey, R., Johnson, J., and Stalley, P. (1988). Risk factors for dehydration among elderly nursing home residents. *Journal of the American Geriatrics Society*, 36, 213–18.

Lindeman, R.D., Tobinm, J.D., and Shock, N.W. (1984). Association between blood pressure and the rate of decline in renal function with age. *Kidney International*, 26, 861–8.

Miller, M., Morley, J.E., and Rubenstein, L.Z. (1995). Hyponatremia in a nursing home population. *Journal of the American Geriatrics Society*, 43, 1410–13.

Minaker, K.L. (1995). *Care of the elderly—clinical aspects of ageing*, (4th edn), (ed. W. Reichel), pp. 252–68. Williams and Wilkins, Baltimore, MD.

Mulkerrin, E.C., Brain, A., Hampton, D., *et al.* (1993). Reduced renal haemodynamic response to atrial natriuretic peptide in elderly volunteers. *American Journal of Kidney Diseases*, 22, 538–44.

Phillips, P.A., Rolls, B.J., Ledingham, J.G.G., *et al.* (1984). Reduced thirst after water deprivation in healthy elderly men. *New England Journal of Medicine*, 311, 753–9.

Rose, B.D. (1994). *Clinical physiology of acid–base and electrolyte disorders* (4th edn), pp. 676–704. McGraw-Hill, New York.

Rowe, J.W., Minaker, K.L., Sparrow, D., and Robertson, G.L. (1982). Age-related failure of volume pressure-mediated vasopressin release. *Journal of Clinical Endocrinology and Metabolism*, 54, 661–4.

Silver, A.J. and Morley, J.E. (1992). Role of the opioid system in the hypodipsia associated with ageing. *Journal of the American Geriatrics Society*, 40, 556–60.

Snyder, N.A., Feigal, D.W., and Arieff, A.I. (1987). Hypernatremia in elderly patients. *Annals of Internal Medicine*, 107, 309–19.

Sonnenblick, M. and Algur, N. (1993). Hypernatremia in the acutely ill elderly patient: role of impaired arginine vasopressin secretion. *Minerals, Electrolytes and Metabolism*, 19, 32–5.

Sonnenblick, M., Friedlander, Y., and Rosin, A.J. (1993). Diuretic-induced severe hyponatremia. Review and analysis of 129 reported patients. *Chest*, 103, 601–6.

Sterns, R.H. and Spital, A. (1990). *Fluids and electrolytes*, (2nd edn), (ed. J.P. Kokko and R.L. Tannen), p. 153. W.B. Saunders, New York.

Tan, A.C.I.T.L., Jansen, T.L.T.A., Thien, T., Kloppenborg, P.W.C., and Benraad, T.J. (1993). Comparison of cyclic guanosine monophosphate response to infusion of atrial natriuretic peptide in young and elderly subjects. *Journal of the American Geriatrics Society*, 41, 1241–4.

Terzian, C., Frye, E.B., and Piotrowski, Z.H. (1994). Admission hyponatremia in the elderly: factors influencing prognosis. *Journal of General Internal Medicine*, 9, 89–91.

United States Department of Health and Human Services (1988). *Medicare and Medicaid data book*. Health Care Financing Administration Publication 0334, Vol. 37. Office of Research and Demonstration, United States Department of Health and Human Services, Baltimore, MD.

Warren, J.L., Bacon, W.E., Harris, T., McBean, A.M., Foley, D.J., and Phillips, C. (1994). The burden and outcomes associated with dehydration among United States elderly, 1991. *American Journal of Public Health*, 84, 1265–9.

Weinberg, A.D., Pals, J.K., Levesque, P.G., Beal, L.F., Cunningham, T.J., and Minaker, K.L. (1994a). Dehydration and death during febrile episodes in the nursing home. *Journal of the American Geriatrics Society*, 42, 968–71.

Weinberg, A.D., Pals, J.K., McGlinchey-Berroth, R., and Minaker, K.L. (1994b). Indices of dehydration among frail nursing home patients: highly variable but stable over time. *Journal of the American Geriatrics Society*, 42, 1070–3.

Weinberg, A.D., Minaker, K.L. and the Council on Scientific Affairs, American Medical Association (1995). Dehydration evaluation and management in older adults. *Journal of the American Medical Association*, 274, 19.

15.2 Renal disease

Terry Feest

There has been a widespread misconception that renal disease is more common in the young than in elderly people. This was generated by low treatment rates of elderly people with endstage renal failure. In the early 1980s in the United Kingdom and some other countries people over 50 years were rarely offered dialysis therapy. Since then there has been a progressive increase in the acceptance rate for dialysis throughout Europe (Valderrabano 1995) and the United States (Held *et al.* 1997), the main change being a greater acceptance of elderly people. This is not due to a major change in the incidence of renal disease, but to changing attitudes of doctors towards offering treatment. Like most disorders, renal failure is more common in elderly people. There is a need to focus more on the problems of elderly people with renal disease.

Incidence of renal failure in elderly people

Community-based surveys conducted in the United Kingdom in the late 1980s demonstrated the dramatic increase in the incidence of severe chronic and acute renal failure with advancing age (Feest *et al.* 1990, 1993; McGeown 1990) (Fig. 1). After excluding people with other terminal diseases, the incidence of chronic renal failure was around 140 per million population per year. This rises 10-fold with age, from 60 per million per year for those in their third decade to over 600 per million per year for those over 80 years of age. The incidence of acute renal failure shows an even greater relative rise in older age groups.

Referral of those with chronic renal failure for a specialist opinion varies with age. In one study all patients under the age of 60 years were referred, but up to half of those over 60 years were not (Feest *et al.* 1990). There is even greater discrimination against elderly people in health districts distant from a renal unit. Nephrologists assessed the case histories of 23 patients between 65 and 80 years of age who were not referred and judged that they would have offered dialysis to 14, all of whom died quickly without therapy. The low treatment rates in elderly patients were due less to the attitudes of nephrologists than to the unwillingness of other doctors to refer them for specialist advice.

The overall annual acceptance rate for endstage renal failure therapy for adults in the United Kingdom has risen from 19.1 new patients per million population in 1982 (Wing *et al.* 1983) to 82 per million population in 1995 in England (Roderick *et al.* 1998). The proportion over 65 years of age is now 40 per cent (Roderick *et al.* 1998), similar to Europe, but less than the 47 per cent seen in the United States (Held *et al.* 1997). It is higher for men (38 per cent) than women (25 per cent). As the United Kingdom treatment rate has progressively risen (Fig. 2), the major increase has been in elderly and diabetic patients. If all patients up to the age of 80 years are to be treated it has been estimated that in a white Western community at least 80 patients per million per year will need to start renal replacement therapy (Feest *et al.* 1990; McGeown 1990). As

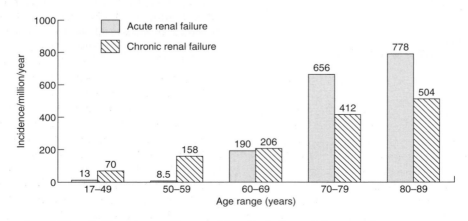

Fig. 1 Age-specific incidence of renal failure (incidence is per million population alive in the quoted age range).

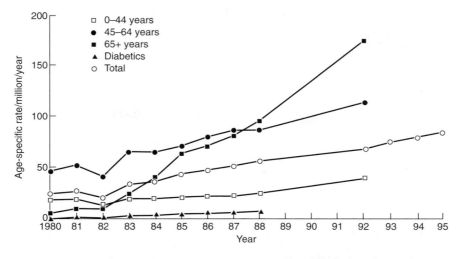

Fig. 2 Patients accepted for renal replacement therapy in the United Kingdom between 1980 and 1995.

many patients over 80 years of age are now offered therapy even more treatment will be needed. Like Europe, the United States (Held *et al.* 1997), Canada (Fenton *et al.* 1995), and Australia (Disney 1995) are experiencing rising dialysis acceptance rates, with almost all the increase amongst elderly people. The current United Kingdom acceptance rate of older patients is 200 per million per year compared with an estimated minimum need of about 400 per million per year. In most countries acceptance rates for renal replacement therapy still fall below the predicted need, and the greatest gap is in those over 60 years of age.

The ageing kidney

Nephrons start to decline in numbers during the third decade of life. Postmortem studies have suggested a loss of renal mass by the eighth decade ranging from 19 per cent in men and 9 per cent in women in Caucasians (Wald 1937) up to 32 per cent and 43 per cent respectively in Japanese (Tauchi *et al.* 1971), with a reduction in renal length of up to 2 cm.

Changes start in the outer cortex with hyalinization and collapse of glomeruli, leading to glomerulosclerosis; these changes are similar to those observed in hypertension (Oliver 1952; Kaplan *et al.* 1975). Tubular degeneration follows, with interstitial fibrosis related to the degenerating nephrons. Surviving nephrons hypertrophy to compensate for the lost nephrons. Thus in ageing kidneys, sclerosed glomeruli exist alongside healthy glomeruli with hypertrophied nephrons.

Compensatory hypertrophy may ameliorate the decline in creatinine clearance until the sixth or seventh decade of life, but a progressive decline is often found with age. By the age of 70 years half of the original nephron complement of around 1.2 million may have been lost (Moore 1931) with development of small superficial punctate scars over the surface of the kidney.

During the period in which creatinine clearance declines the ageing subject is losing muscle mass and so produces less creatinine each day. As a result plasma creatinine may remain stable, masking the underlying progressive loss of renal function. Thus in elderly individuals with low muscle mass and poor nutrition serum creatinine may be a misleading guide to renal function. An approximate calculation of creatinine clearance can be attempted from the plasma creatinine with a correction for age and body weight as follows (Cockroft and Gault 1976):

$$\text{creatinine clearance (ml/min)} = \frac{(140 - \text{age}) \times \text{body weight (kg)} \times K}{\text{serum creatinine (μmol/l)}}$$

where K is 1.23 for men and 1.04 for women. Unfortunately, this calculation is unreliable in very old people (Friedmann *et al.* 1989) and a timed creatinine clearance may be necessary. It may be difficult to obtain accurate urine collections in elderly people, and radioisotope techniques may prove easier and more reliable.

Thus in many elderly people there is significant loss of renal function. By the age of 80 years creatinine clearance may fall to between 40 and 75 ml/min (Kampmann *et al.* 1974) and plasma creatinine may be as high as 140 μmol/l in the absence of overt renal disease.

With ageing, the primary renal lesion is probably vascular (Oliver 1952; McLahan 1978). Above the age of 20 years intimal thickening of renal arterioles is seen, often with subintimal hyaline deposits and thickening and reduplication of the elastic lamina. The elderly renal vessels become tortuous, irregular, and less elastic. Thus they are more susceptible to diminished perfusion.

The renal tubules also undergo age-associated changes. Multiple diverticula develop (McLahan 1978) which may be responsible for the increased incidence of pyelonephritis in elderly people. There is also peritubular fibrosis and loss of urinary concentration, acidification, and toxin secretion. Thus in addition to renovascular vulnerability, elderly people when undergoing metabolic stress usually become dehydrated and acidotic, and accumulate drugs, on a background of already reduced renal function. Therefore the high incidence of acute renal failure in older people is not surprising.

Table 1 Common renal diseases in elderly people

Preventable/treatable
Prostatic obstruction
Renovascular disease
Acute interstitial nephritis/drug-induced disease
Vasculitis
Myeloma

Possibly preventable/treatable
Diabetes type II
Membranous nephropathy
Cholesterol emboli

Common renal disorders of elderly people

The range of diseases causing renal failure in older people is different from that found in younger patients. It is difficult to determine the contribution of different disorders to the overall incidence of renal failure in the whole community, as many elderly patients are not referred for a specialist opinion. In one study up to 70 per cent did not receive an underlying renal diagnosis compared with only 16 per cent of those under 70 years of age (Feest 1996), rendering interpretation of the relative contribution of different diseases to renal failure impossible. Better information is available from those patients starting dialysis, although these are a selected group. Of 200 consecutive dialysands starting dialysis in Bristol in 1993–1994, 42 per cent of those over 65 years of age did not have a firm renal diagnosis. This appears higher than the proportion of undiagnosed older patients reported by the European Dialysis and Transplant Association (Valderrabano et al. 1995), but there are methodological differences and figures are similar if firm rather than presumptive diagnoses are accepted. In the United States around 8.9 per cent of elderly patients starting dialysis do not have a certain diagnosis recorded (Held et al. 1997).

Reviewing the diagnoses made in Europe over the last 20 years glomerulonephritis is now found in a lower proportion of those starting renal replacement therapy, and the proportion with undiagnosed disorders, diabetes, and renovascular disorders has risen (Valderrabano et al. 1995). This does not indicate a reduction in the incidence of glomerulonephritis, but reflects the changing pattern of acceptance for treatment for renal failure. As increasing numbers of older patients are treated there are more patients with diabetes, vascular disease, and no diagnosis; glomerulonephritis has not reduced in total numbers.

It is disappointing that so many potentially treatable disorders feature as causes of endstage renal failure in elderly people (Table 1). Of older patients in the United Kingdom about 10 per cent are men with prostatic obstruction, accounting for nearly 20 per cent of all older men with chronic renal failure. The obstructive causes of renal failure in younger patients were congenital lesions and, rarely, renal stones. There is still a significant proportion of patients (8 per cent in the elderly group) in whom renal failure is attributed to hypertension. In the United States many black people are said to have hypertensive renal disease but the diagnosis is usually presumptive, and

diabetes is more common, especially in this group (Held et al. 1997). Until recently in Europe many diabetics have been refused treatment, although treatment rates are currently increasing.

Not all renal disorders cause endstage renal failure, especially if diagnosed and treated early. Furthermore, nephrotic syndrome is common in elderly people. Some common potentially treatable renal diseases of elderly people are listed in Table 1.

Renovascular disease

Renal failure due to renovascular disease is being diagnosed with increased frequency in the United Kingdom and Europe, where in 1992 it was the cause of renal failure in 17 per cent of patients starting renal replacement therapy (Valderrabano et al. 1995). It is less frequently diagnosed in the United States (Held et al. 1997), but in North Carolina Appel et al. (1995) found critical renovascular disease in 22 per cent of 53 consecutive patients over 50 years of age starting renal replacement therapy. Incidence was 40 per cent in white patients, and even higher in white smokers. It is almost certainly underdiagnosed and may account for a significant proportion of undiagnosed elderly patients with renal failure.

Interest in this condition was stimulated by the occurrence of acute renal failure in patients with bilateral atheromatous renal artery disease when given angiotensin-converting enzyme inhibitors (Hricik et al. 1983). Awareness of the possibility of renal ischaemia in elderly arteriopaths is especially important as this impairment is not always reversible. As type II diabetics have a high incidence of vascular disease special care is needed when treating them with angiotensin-converting enzyme inhibitors.

The majority of patients with renal ischaemia, possibly 90 per cent, have evidence of arteriosclerotic disease elsewhere (Meyrier et al. 1996). Conversely, nearly 40 per cent of patients undergoing arteriography for other forms of arterial disease have severe renal artery stenosis (Olin et al. 1990). There is a close association with abdominal aortic disease and lower extremity occlusive disease, especially in diabetics. The presence of hypertension and decline of renal function are further strong indicators but hypertension is present in only 50 per cent of cases. In patients undergoing coronary angiography who have hypertension and/or chronic renal failure, renal artery stenosis is present in 23 per cent, including 75 per cent of patients who have both hypertension and renal failure (Vetrovec et al. 1989).

The diagnosis of renal ischaemia can be difficult. In any elderly patient with renal failure who does not have heavy proteinuria, renal ischaemia should be considered, especially if renal ultrasound suggests a difference of 1 cm or more in length between the two kidneys. Poorly functioning kidneys take up radioisotopes slowly, and in such circumstances isotope renography is rarely able to provide a diagnosis. The gold standard for investigation, renal arteriography, is an invasive technique which may also cause cholesterol embolism and transient renal failure, but as yet no other widely reliable technique is available.

In an excellent literature review Rimmer and Gennari (1993) note the paucity of prospective studies of patients with renal ischaemia. Mortality rates on dialysis therapy are greater than 50 per cent in 3 years. Their interpretation of the literature is that surgery and angioplasty may delay or prevent the need for dialysis in some cases, but not all series show this. These patients are frail and have widespread arterial disease; it is desirable to avoid operative intervention. This makes percutaneous transluminal renal angioplasty an attractive therapy. There are several optimistic publications on this, one reporting

48 per cent of patients showing long-lasting improvement (Losinno et al. 1994), but such improvements are not universal experience (Zuccala and Zucchelli 1995). Experience with surgical intervention is similarly varied. Overall, with intervention, improvement is more likely if there is rapid preoperative decline of glomerular filtration rate. When kidneys are smaller than 8 cm in length recovery is infrequent.

Renal arterial stenosis causing renal dysfunction in elderly people is common, frequently unrecognized, and increasing in prevalence (Greco and Breyer 1996). Greater awareness and willingness to undertake appropriate investigation is important as therapeutic interventions would appear to be beneficial in many patients.

Cholesterol emboli

Cholesterol embolic disease is often associated with vascular disease. It is almost exclusively a condition of the elderly arteriopath, predominantly male (Vidt 1997). It is recognized with increasing frequency (Scolari et al. 1996) and may account for up to 10 per cent of acute renal failure cases (Mayo and Swartz 1996). It is associated with multiorgan dysfunction. There are usually cutaneous features including widespread livedo reticularis, digital infarcts, and a rash mimicking vasculitis which is particularly common in the lower limb. There may be infarcts in the spleen, cerebrum, gut, and other organs and there is frequently renal involvement. The erythrocyte sedimentation rate is elevated with eosinophilia in up to 70 per cent of patients. A false-positive antineutrophil cytoplasmic antibody test may lead to a mistaken diagnosis of systemic vasculitis. The urine usually contains microscopic haematuria and a little protein. There is frequently pre-existing hypertension, vascular disease, or a degree of renal dysfunction (Fine et al. 1987; Scolari et al. 1996). Of those needing dialysis only 20 per cent recover renal function. In up to 30 per cent of patients there is an immediate precipitating factor, most commonly vascular radiology (Thadhani et al. 1995). Anticoagulation and other operative procedures, especially vascular, also precipitate this condition.

Acute interstitial nephritis and drug reactions

Acute interstitial nephritis and other drug-induced diseases are predominantly diseases of those over 65 years of age, perhaps because they are the group taking most medication. Drug-induced nephropathy should be considered in any patient with renal dysfunction and a relatively inactive urine deposit with little proteinuria, especially if the kidneys are of normal size. Acute interstitial nephritis is nearly always a drug reaction and is most commonly seen with penicillins, analgesics, and diuretics, but almost every drug has been implicated at some time. If it is recognized before there is advanced fibrosis, and the offending drug is stopped, there is an excellent chance of recovery. Occasionally steroids are given to try to hasten recovery although there is no definite evidence of their effectiveness.

Some specific renal drug interactions are important. Angiotensin-converting enzyme inhibitors have already been discussed. The nephrotoxicity of non-steroidal anti-inflammatory drugs is widely recognized. Elderly patients, especially those known to have a degree of renal dysfunction starting these drugs, should have their renal function closely monitored. Non-steroidal anti-inflammatory drugs are often given for older patients with painful non-inflammatory conditions (Phillips et al. 1997) when simple pain killers may be effective. Concomitant use of misoprostol may protect against renal dysfunction (Phillips et al. 1997). A risk–benefit assessment (Ailabouni and Eknoyan 1996) concluded that cautious use of these drugs in elderly people, with monitoring of renal function in those at known potential risk of acute renal failure, is justified.

Radiocontrast-induced nephropathy is also common in elderly people, especially if the plasma creatinine is at all elevated. The risk is greatly reduced if good hydration is maintained (Porter 1994) and low osmolality contrast media are used (Louvel et al. 1996).

Vasculitis in the kidney

Wegener's arteritis and microscopic polyarteritis (polyangiitis) are renal disorders which are most common in middle-aged and elderly patients, with a slight male predominance (Garrett et al. 1992; Pettersson et al. 1995). These conditions frequently present with renal manifestations. In microscopic polyangiitis systemic symptoms are mild or absent in many elderly patients, the disease being limited to the kidney. In Wegener's disease elderly patients are more likely to present with renal dysfunction and often develop pulmonary lesions, but have fewer other systemic symptoms (Vassallo et al. 1997). Renal biopsy shows segmental necrotizing glomeruli and in active cases epithelial crescents are present (Heptinstall et al. 1983). The kidneys may be destroyed within a few days, and so rapid diagnosis and initiation of treatment are essential. Treatment is only effective if given in this early phase. Such disorders should be suspected in any elderly patient with unexplained advancing renal failure and heavy proteinuria with microscopic haematuria. Occasionally an immunologically mediated rapidly progressive glomerulonephritis may present similarly. Immediate renal biopsy is indicated.

In the majority of cases with microscopic vasculitis or Wegener's disease serum antineutrophil cytoplasmic antibodies of various types are present (Amico et al. 1996), with a raised white count and a raised C-reactive protein. Antineutrophil cytoplasmic antibody is not usually present in larger vessel vasculitides. The overall predictive value of antineutrophil cytoplasmic antibodies testing is not high, and false positives and negatives are found (Davenport et al. 1996). In long-term follow-up serial antineutrophil cytoplasmic antibodies alone may also be unreliable in assessing disease activity.

Therapy is with prednisolone and cyclophosphamide. In rapidly advancing cases intravenous pulse methylprednisolone 500 to 1000 mg daily for 3 days is indicated, followed by prednisolone 60 mg daily in a slowly tapering dose (Amico et al. 1996). Cyclophosphamide is given orally at 2 to 3 mg/kg/day in older people, usually with conversion to azathioprine at 3 to 6 months if the disease seems quiescent. Before the introduction of aggressive immunosuppressive therapy mean survival was only 5 months (Walton 1958). In very rapidly progressive cases plasma exchange may be added to the standard therapy, especially when patients are dialysis dependent. No controlled trial of plasma exchange versus intravenous methylprednisolone is available except in dialysis-dependent patients where it has been shown to be of benefit (Pusey et al. 1991). After survival for 1 year the prognosis is excellent with only a slow death rate thereafter. With modern therapy a 5-year survival of such patients may be as good as 70 per cent, and although it is probably lower in elderly people (Pettersson et al. 1995; Vassallo et al. 1997) therapy for these conditions is indicated and worthwhile.

Diabetes

As more elderly patients are accepted for dialysis the proportion with diabetes has grown. In Germany and some Scandinavian countries diabetes is the cause of endstage renal failure in nearly 30 per cent of those starting renal replacement therapy (Valderrabano et al. 1995). In the United States the figure is 33.9 per cent of those over 64 years of age starting dialysis, with type II diabetics outnumbering type I by 2 to 1 (Held et al. 1997). In Europe, of those diabetics starting renal replacement therapy, 56 to 66 per cent of the older patients and 40 per cent of the younger ones have type II diabetes (Catalano and Marshall 1992). The importance of type II diabetes as a cause of renal failure is often underestimated. Although renal failure may occur in fewer type II than type I diabetics the incidence of diabetes in elderly people is so high that total renal deaths in elderly people outnumber the young by 1.7 to 1 (Knowles 1974). If type II diabetics are followed for similar periods of time the cumulative incidence of renal dysfunction is similar to that in type I diabetics (Catalano and Marshall 1992). Many centres underestimate the number of type II diabetics by wrongly classifying those using insulin as type I.

Renal histology in type II diabetics may reveal classical diabetic nephropathy, but in many patients a less specific picture resembling chronic ischaemia is found (Fioretto et al. 1996), emphasizing the important role vascular disease plays in this disorder.

Nephrotic syndrome

Nephrotic syndrome is the most common indication for renal biopsy in elderly people (Davison and Johnston 1996). Membranous nephropathy is the most common finding on renal biopsy, and is found in over 30 per cent of cases (Murray and Raij 1987; Davison and Johnston 1996). The next most common condition is minimal change disease (10–24 per cent). Other lesions causing nephrotic syndrome are largely untreatable and include amyloidosis (10 per cent), proliferative glomerulonephritis, and focal sclerosis. For minimal change disease effective treatment in the form of steroid therapy is available, but has significant complications and should not be given without accurate diagnosis. Response is slower and less predictable in older people than in the young. Membranous nephropathy follows a remitting and relapsing course. In those over 60 years of age more than 50 per cent may progress to endstage renal failure (Zent et al. 1997). It is important to make a definitive diagnosis as there are many proposed therapeutic, but toxic, regimes of uncertain value for this condition, many of which include large doses of steroids and/or chlorambucil (Cameron 1992). Up to 9 per cent of patients with membranous nephropathy have an underlying malignancy, most frequently lymphomas and leukaemias. Thus the finding of membranous nephropathy in an older patient should stimulate a search to exclude underlying haematological malignancies and a chest radiograph to exclude carcinoma of the lung.

Multiple myeloma

Myelomatosis is a disease of elderly people which occasionally presents with renal failure. The large majority of such cases have 'myeloma kidney', a condition in which the renal tubules are damaged by a high load of filtered light chains. It is commonly believed that patients with severe renal failure and myeloma have a universally poor prognosis but this is not borne out by experience. Many patients live active lives for over 3 years after starting dialysis. Again, rapid diagnosis is important as early institution of fluid repletion, cytotoxic therapy, and sometimes plasmapheresis may reverse the renal failure before fibrosis and permanent damage occur.

Acute renal failure

It is important to understand that 'acute renal failure' is not synonymous with 'acute tubular necrosis'. Many disorders may present as an acute reversible deterioration of renal function (Feest et al. 1993; Pascual et al. 1995) (Fig. 3), including obstruction, rapidly progressive glomerulonephritis and vasculitis, acute interstitial nephritis, and ischaemic lesions. Many of these conditions will not be reversible if not rapidly diagnosed and treated. The increased incidence of severe acute renal failure with advancing age is illustrated in Fig. 1. Prostatic obstruction is a major cause, being responsible for acute renal failure in over one-third of all men. Even if this diagnosis is excluded from the analysis, there is still a marked increase in acute renal failure with age and a male preponderance.

This major contribution of prostatic obstruction to severe renal failure is not widely appreciated. There is no apparent relationship between the severity of prostatic symptoms, prostate size on rectal examination, and the occurrence of renal failure. Many patients undergo tertiary referral before such a simple and treatable diagnosis is made. Although renal failure only occurs in a small minority of the vast numbers of men with prostatic obstruction, this small proportion of a large number is significant. Prostatic obstruction must be considered in all elderly men presenting with renal failure in whom there is not heavy proteinuria and no other obvious cause.

The high frequency of acute renal failure in elderly people is not surprising. As a group they have a high incidence of severe predisposing illness, and as has already been discussed their kidneys are susceptible to circulatory and metabolic insult.

The prognosis of patients with advanced acute renal failure is not significantly worse than that of younger patients. Survival of such patients at 3 months and 2 years is illustrated in Fig. 4. As prostatic disease has been shown to have a particularly good prognosis, the analysis was repeated excluding such patients. Even with this exclusion there is no suggestion that after an episode of acute renal failure survival is significantly decreased with increasing age above 50 years of age, an observation confirmed by many other studies around the world. Thus 70-year-olds as much as 50-year-olds with acute renal failure merit referral for specialist support and treatment. Recovery of renal function after acute renal failure in elderly people may be incomplete in up to 70 per cent of cases (Feest et al. 1993) necessitating long-term follow-up of many of these older patients after recovery from their acute illness.

Approach to the elderly patient presenting acutely with renal failure

The elderly patient presenting acutely with renal failure merits urgent diagnosis and treatment. Renal ultrasound is mandatory. Obstruction will be identified. Many may have acute presentations of chronic lesions and have small scarred kidneys on ultrasound. Asymmetrical kidneys suggesting renovascular disease may be seen. Renal biopsy may be urgently indicated, especially if the kidneys are of normal size

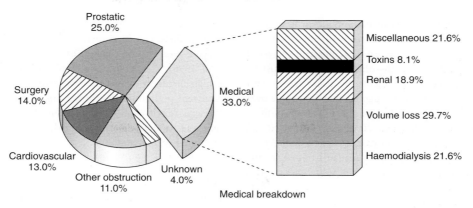

Fig. 3 Causes of acute renal failure. (Reproduced with permission from Feest *et al.* (1993).)

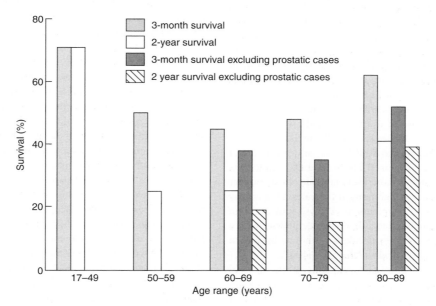

Fig. 4 Acute renal failure: survival by age and effect of excluding prostate disease.

and there is heavy proteinuria and/or haematuria, to exclude rapidly progressive lesions treatable in the early stages such as vasculitis and rapidly progressive glomerulonephritis. In the absence of heavy proteinuria interstitial disease, ischaemia, and myeloma may be found. To achieve such appropriate early diagnosis rapid referral to a renal specialist is frequently indicated.

Chronic renal failure

Renal replacement therapy in elderly people is a challenge. They need more medical and nursing time than younger people, but when successful the results can be very rewarding. Older people acclimatize slowly to new conditions and do not learn about their treatments easily. There is an increased prevalence of comorbidity in an older population, especially cardiovascular disease. The elderly rigid vascular system is very sensitive to fluid changes during haemodialysis, predisposing to dialytic hypotension with rebound hypertension between

dialyses. The old ischaemic heart does not cope with fluid overload and pulmonary oedema easily develops. Elderly people on dialysis are admitted to hospital much more frequently than the young. Many older people are unfit for major surgery and thus transplantation is not a treatment option, as there is a relatively high post-transplant mortality. Overall, therefore, older patients are more difficult and more expensive to treat than younger patients.

Survival of older patients is less than that of younger patients. In Europe the 1-year survival after starting renal replacement therapy for those aged 65 to 74 years is 76 per cent and the 5-year rate is 30 per cent, compared with 81 per cent and 45 per cent respectively for those aged 55 to 64 years (Valderrabano *et al.* 1995). These are significantly better than the survival rates recorded in the United States (Ismail *et al.* 1993). Although this may be due to relatively low doses of haemodialysis being prescribed for elderly people in the United States, the selection of patients probably contributes. The United States treats many more elderly patients with more comorbid conditions and a poorer prognosis from the outset. Even patients over the age of 80 years can have a reasonable prognosis. A study of 50 such patients starting renal replacement therapy noted a 1-year survival of 78 per cent and a 2-year survival of 47 per cent (Neves et al. 1994). Assessment of outcome in the older age groups must be judged against the life expectation of patients of similar age without renal failure. A review of published data suggests that for people over 65 years of age with endstage renal failure mortality is less than three times that expected compared with at least 20 times the expected rate for those starting dialysis at the age of 45 years (Mignon et al. 1993).

Risk factors for elderly people seem to be similar to those for the young with diabetes, significant cardiac comorbidity being most important, and in elderly people left ventricular dilatation is a particularly strong negative predictive factor (Jassel et al. 1996).

As in younger patients cardiac disease is the major cause of death, but discontinuation of treatment is important and increasingly common in this age group. Cultural and religious problems inevitably lead to under-reporting of treatment withdrawal and may also inhibit appropriate care and counselling. A 'good' death can be achieved if appropriate multidisciplinary help is given (Cohen et al. 1995). Treatment withdrawal is recorded as the reason for death in around 7 per cent of older European patients (Valderrabano et al. 1995). In one Dutch centre half the older patients dying in a 5-year period had requested cessation of dialysis. This group had a very high rate of severe comorbidity (Schrander et al. 1995). Treatment withdrawal is the second most common cause of death in Canada (Fenton et al. 1995), is the cause of death of 14 per cent of all Australian patients (Disney 1995), has been estimated to be the cause of death in about 20 per cent of all American patients (Held et al. 1997), and is six times more common in the elderly American dialysands than younger patients (Held et al. 1997). These high rates in the United States may reflect the acceptance policy for treatment. Dialysis outcomes in individuals are difficult to predict. Liberal acceptance policies with a willingness to support patients if they decide to withdraw have been recommended (Port 1994), the so-called 'trial of dialysis'.

Elderly patients can achieve a satisfactory quality of life on renal replacement therapy. The use of erythropoietin to increase serum haemoglobin in elderly people is effective and this drug should not be withheld. A recent British study (Gudex 1995) of 616 adults treated in 40 different renal units showed that elderly patients achieved a good quality of life, perhaps because their expected lifestyle is less altered by dialysis than that of younger patients wanting to travel widely, have children, and participate in sports and other active pursuits.

Choice of modality of dialysis

The problems encountered in dialysing the elderly patient by haemodialysis or peritoneal dialysis are listed in Table 2.

Continuous ambulatory peritoneal dialysis

Elderly patients are generally slower to learn new techniques and training is longer. They need more home support and have more readmissions (Nissenson 1991). A study in Paris (Issad et al. 1996) of continuous ambulatory peritoneal dialysis patients over 75 years of age showed 12 per cent lived in institutions, a further 48 per cent needed private nursing help at home, and only 30 per cent had effective autonomy. Similar results were reported from a small series in New York (Suh et al. 1993). Some centres have been more successful

with elderly continuous ambulatory peritoneal dialysis patients, although there is a high incidence of abdominal surgical events and social reasons causing failure of the technique (Rodriguez-Carnoma et al. 1996). The persistent presence of fluid in the abdomen leads to a high incidence of hernia development. If diverticulitis is present, recurrent peritonitis with bowel organisms will demand cessation of therapy. A self-administered treatment given alone at home often increases the social isolation of elderly people who are already lonely and often relatively immobile.

Haemodialysis

Home haemodialysis can be difficult to learn, and needs significant dexterity and support from a partner. It is rarely useful for elderly people. Older people with their rigid blood vessels are intolerant of fluid change and experience frequent dialytic hypotension. There is an increased incidence of subdural and intracranial haemorrhage related to recurrent heparinization. With cardiovascular disease many patients experience atrial fibrillation related to dialysis. Dialysis access may be difficult to establish, leading to multiple admissions and operations (Feldman et al. 1993; Mignon et al. 1993). As fluid accumulates between dialyses, hypertension and pulmonary oedema are common in elderly people and thrice-weekly dialysis is essential.

Despite these problems, with modern proportionating units using bicarbonate dialysis, control of ultrafiltration during dialysis, and sodium profiling, many of the dialytic complications can be avoided and, in practice, unit-based haemodialysis has become the more attractive and most frequently used treatment for elderly patients, more so than in younger patients.

There have been suggestions that continuous ambulatory peritoneal dialysis in elderly people has a less good prognosis than haemodialysis, but these differences probably reflect selection of patients for different treatments and the difficulty of matching comorbidities in the two treatment groups (Ismail et al. 1993). The choice of treatment must finally depend upon a mix of medical and social factors in each individual case, but around the world the large majority of elderly patients are treated with unit-based haemodialysis (Fig. 5).

Renal transplantation

It is widely accepted that renal transplantation, when it is possible, offers the best renal replacement therapy. In the majority of patients plasma creatinine will fall below 200 μmol/l and there will be few significant continuing metabolic abnormalities. Quality of life with a functioning transplant is better than on dialysis, even in elderly people (Gudex 1995), although initial rehabilitation in older people can be slow (Nyburg 1995a). Despite these benefits renal transplantation is offered to few older people in renal failure. In the United States only 5.8 per cent of patients on renal replacement therapy aged over 65 years have a renal transplant (Held et al. 1997); in Europe the figure is around 5 per cent (Mallick et al. 1996), although in some Scandinavian countries the proportion of older patients with a functioning graft is significantly higher.

A significant number of older dialysands have comorbid conditions, especially cardiovascular disorders, which render them unsuitable for major surgery or transplantation, but this does not necessarily fully explain why so few older patients in Europe have a

Normal filling and continence

Bladder

Urine production is by ultrafiltration in the kidney. The net filtration pressure available is only about 20 cmH$_2$O and back pressure beyond this will stop urine production, so that during filling the smooth muscle (detrusor) in the bladder wall must be able to stretch and rearrange itself to accommodate the volume changes without a significant rise in bladder pressure. At the same time efficient initiation of voiding requires that the shape of the bladder continuously conforms to the minimum surface area–volume relationship available to it (as nearly spherical as possible anatomically), since it is only in this conformation that synchronous contraction of the smooth muscle cells can raise the intravesical pressure and initiate voiding. These two constraints call for unique properties in the smooth muscle in the bladder wall. There must be continuous contractile activity in the smooth muscle cells to adjust their length during filling, and yet this must not result in a rise in intravesical pressure. Therefore the bladder is never floppy, nor is its shape distorted by surrounding organs during filling.

Studies on isolated strips of smooth muscle dissected from normal bladders can reveal some of the unusual properties. The strips frequently exhibit characteristic spontaneous activity that can be shown to be myogenic, since it is not abolished by receptor antagonists, or blockade of neuronal activity with tetrodotoxin, a neurotoxin. The contractions are phasic, rising from and falling back to the baseline, and rarely if ever show the fused tetanic contractions which are characteristic of smooth muscles in which the cells are well coupled electrically. The electrical coupling in normal detrusor cells is relatively poor, so that spontaneous electrical activity spreads ineffectively amongst them. This is supported by electron microscopy of human detrusor cells from normal bladders which show no gap junctions between the cells, but well-developed intermediary junctions between myocytes within the muscle fascicles—small groups of cells surrounded by a thin extracellular matrix that make up the smooth muscle bundles (Elbadawi 1995).

Bladder neck and urethra

The bladder neck and urethra between them prevent urine leakage during bladder filling. Not only must they protect against leakage due to the small intravesical pressure rise whilst the bladder is filling and the gravitational forces during standing, but they must also prevent leakage during intra-abdominal pressure rises, which may be rapid and quite large. The structures involved are complicated, and there is still controversy about the exact mechanisms involved in the maintenance of continence.

The urethra in the male is divided into the preprostatic (bladder neck), prostatic, membranous, bulbar, and penile urethra, with only the first three parts contributing to urinary continence (Fig. 1). In the female, the urethra (3–4 cm long) is closely related to the anterior wall of the vagina and passes through the anterior hiatus of the levator ani to the exterior (Fig. 2). Traditionally, a dual mechanism has been thought to operate, the proximal/distal sphincter or the internal/external sphincter. However, elements of the proximal/internal sphincter extend to involve the distal/external sphincter and vice versa. It is probably more appropriate to consider the sphincter

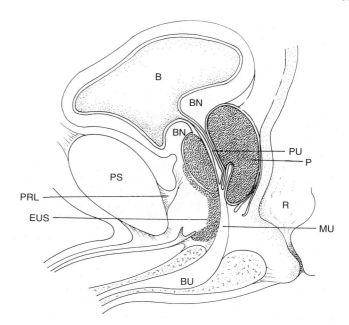

Fig. 1 Male lower urinary tract: sagittal section showing the bladder, bladder neck, prostate, membranous, and bulbar urethra. The bladder neck and membranous urethra are important structures in the maintenance of urinary continence in the male. B, bladder; BN, bladder neck; BU, bulbar urethra; EUS, intramural external urethral sphincter consisting of an outer layer of striated muscle and inner layers of smooth muscle at the membranous urethra; MU, membranous urethra; P, prostate; PPL, puboprostatic ligament; PS, pubic symphysis; PU, prostatic urethra; R, rectum. (Reproduced with permission from Myers (1991).)

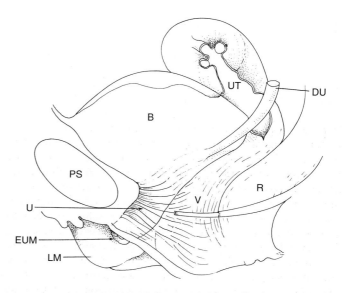

Fig. 2 Anatomy of the female lower urinary tract. B, bladder; DU, distal ureter; EUM, external urethral meatus (arrow); LM, labium minus; PS, pubic symphysis; R, rectum; U, urethra with striated muscle fibres of the intramural external urethral sphincter; Ut, uterus; V, vagina. (Reproduced with permission from Mostwin (1991).)

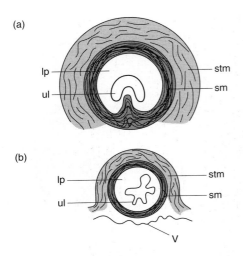

Fig. 3 Schematic diagrams (transverse views) of (a) the membranous urethra in the male and (b) the middle third of the urethra in the female showing layers of muscle and lamina propria. Analogy of structure exists: lp, lamina propria; sm, smooth muscle; stm, striated muscle fibres of the intramural external urethral sphincter; ul, urethral lumen; V, vaginal epithelium.

system in terms of its components, namely the smooth and striated sphincters, and the lamina propria.

In both male and female, the structures surrounding the bladder neck and urethra also play a crucial role in continence. These include the prostate in the male and the vagina in the female, and the fascia and pelvic floor muscles which help to determine the anatomical relationships of the organs and play a role in their correct function.

Smooth sphincter

The bladder neck borders the internal urethral meatus and its structure remains controversial. Gosling *et al.* (1983) have described a complete collar of smooth muscle at the male bladder neck, while others have likened the bladder neck to the shutter of a camera with incomplete loops and slings of detrusor around the internal meatus (Tanagho and Smith 1966; Woodburne and Smith 1968). Elbadawi (1987) has argued that the smooth muscle of the bladder neck and proximal urethra are in continuity, forming a single functional unit.

Structurally both longitudinal and circular smooth muscle are present in the prostatic and membranous urethra in the male (Fig. 3(a)). In the female, a thin layer of circular smooth muscle exists throughout the urethra although there is a more dominant inner layer of longitudinal smooth muscle (Fig. 3(b)). Contraction of the circular smooth muscle will contribute to sphincteric function. The role of the longitudinal smooth muscle is less clear; it may aid coaptation of the mucosa, or contraction of the longitudinal smooth muscle may shorten and open the urethra during micturition. The smooth muscle at the bladder neck in the male serves both as a sphincter for urinary continence and as a sexual sphincter. Its closure during orgasm prevents retrograde ejaculation. In the female, the bladder neck is probably of less importance in the maintenance of continence, as it has been observed to be open in continent nulliparous subjects (Chapple *et al.* 1989).

Striated sphincter

The striated sphincter of the male and female urethras consists of an intramural layer of striated muscle which is separated from the levator ani. In the male, the striated muscle extends from the base of the bladder and the anterior aspect of the prostate to the full length of the membranous urethra. In the female, the striated muscle extends from the proximal urethra distally. The striated sphincter is horseshoe shaped and the muscle cells are smaller than ordinary skeletal muscle, being 15 to 20 µm in diameter. Gosling *et al.* (1981) considered these striated muscles to be composed of slow-twitch fibres (Gosling *et al.* 1981). However, the authors' findings and those of Benoit *et al.* have shown that the striated sphincter is a heterogeneous population (Benoit *et al.* 1988; Ho *et al.* 1997*c*). In the male it consists of 35 per cent of slow and 65 per cent of fast-twitch fibres, and in the female the fibres are intermediate between the fast- and slow-twitch types (Fig. 4). The slow-twitch fibres could be important in developing sustained tone to occlude the urethra, whereas the fast-twitch fibres could be involved in reflex contraction to elevate urethral tone when intra-abdominal pressure rises. There are no muscle spindles in the striated sphincter.

Lamina propria

Within the smooth muscle layers is the lamina propria, comprising the mucosa and submucosal layers. The submucosal layer is highly vascular, and also contains longitudinally arranged smooth muscle cells in the extracellular matrix between the blood vessels, and longitudinally arranged elastic fibres. This structure fills the lumen of the urethra and plays a major role in mediating the pressure generated by contraction of the smooth and striated muscles, and keeping the urethra closed. This is particularly important in the shorter, more direct female urethra. Reduction in blood flow to the lamina propria causes a drop in measured urethral pressure, but recent work in the pig suggests that the vascular filling of the lamina propria, although essential for continence, is not actively regulated but responds passively and reciprocally to changes in the sphincteric tone (Greenland and Brading 1995; Greenland *et al.* 1996). The mucosa is glandular, and mucosal secretions probably aid coaptation and continence, particularly in the female.

Extracellular matrix

The extracellular matrix not only serves as the medium in which the muscular component is embedded and where the blood vessels and nerves ramify, but also contributes to tone and contractility of the organ. Structural and anchoring filamentous proteins are involved in anchoring the contractile elements to the plasma membrane, from which the force of contraction can be transmitted to the extracellular matrix via fibronectin receptors.

Collagen and elastin make up the majority of the fibrillar components of the extracellular matrix, whereas glycosaminoglycans constitute the non-fibrillar component. Collagen provides the extracellular framework of most tissues. Flexible, but allowing movement without stretching, it is synthesized by fibroblasts and bladder smooth muscle cells. Each molecule represents a triple helix of α-chains. Every turn of the helix contains three amino acids, with every third amino acid being proline. A large proportion of the other amino acids are proline and hydroxyproline, the content of which is subjected to post-translational events in the cell. Over 20 types of collagen have

Reduction in urethral pressure

Suppression of the motor input to the urethral striated muscle and its subsequent relaxation plays an important role in the fall in urethral pressure in humans. Relaxation of the human circular urethral smooth muscle may also be important, and is certainly responsible for the drop in urethral pressure in the pig. This relaxation could involve reduction in the excitatory sympathetic input and/or activation of inhibitory nerves. The smooth muscle receives an inhibitory nitrergic innervation, and recent evidence indicates that nerves containing nitric oxide synthase may also contain an haemoxygenase which can synthesize carbon monoxide, another potential inhibitory or neuromodulatory substance (Ho *et al.* 1997*b*).

Neural pathways

Efficient storage and voiding of urine can only occur as a result of complex functional integration of the bladder and urethra. Further control, in an inhibitory or facilitatory manner, is effected by voluntary influences, which in turn depend on the physical and social circumstances. The co-ordination of vesicourethral function depends on a number of reflexes mediated at a spinal and higher level, which are concerned with storage, initiation, continuation, and cessation of micturition.

Afferent pathways

Afferent fibres are important in the perception of pain, temperature, and touch (exteroceptive sensations) and the awareness of fullness (proprioception). The dense plexus of nerves in the subepithelial layer of the urethra and bladder probably subserve sensory function (Dixon and Gosling 1987). Pacinian corpuscles, other encapsulated receptors, and free nerve endings are identifiable in the muscle layers of the urethra and at the vesicourethral junction.

Visceral afferent nerves from the bladder and urethra ascend in the pelvic and hypogastric nerves via Aδ- and C-fibres. Additional afferents from the urethra and the intramural striated urethral sphincter also run in the pudendal nerve. These afferent fibres enter the spinal cord in the thoracolumbar region (T12–L2) via the hypogastric nerve and in the sacral region (S2–S4) via the pelvic and pudendal nerves. Those afferent proprioceptive fibres with long ascending fibres reach the pons via the posterior column, and the exteroceptive fibres interact with secondary neurones in the spinal cord, whose axons contribute to the spinothalamic pathways. The afferent proprioceptive fibres from the striated urethral sphincter and the pelvic floor both ascend to the higher centres, and activate local sacral interneurones involved in the spinal integration of the vesicosphincteric reflexes (pudendal reflex) (Williams and Brading 1992; Zderic *et al.* 1996).

Centres in the brain

Of major importance to bladder and urethral co-ordination is the pontine micturition centre in the brainstem (Fig. 9). This area is responsible for the execution of detrusor contraction and urethral sphincter relaxation during micturition. Lesion below the centre results in dyssynergic action of the bladder and the urethral sphincter (Williams and Brading 1992).

The cerebellum is responsible for co-ordination and fine control of the pelvic floor skeletal muscles. It receives afferent input from both the pelvic floor and bladder, thus helping to maintain contraction of the pelvic floor during the storage phase and facilitates its inhibition

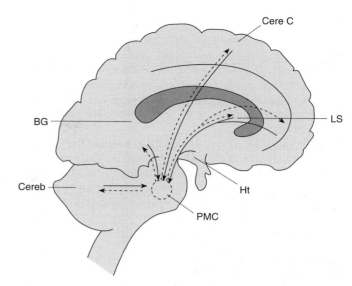

Fig. 9 Central connections for micturition reflex in the cerebrum, midbrain, and brainstem. BG, basal ganglia; Cereb, cerebellum; CereC, cerebral cortex; Ht, hypothalamus; LS, limbic system; PMB, pontine micturition centre. (Reproduced with permission from Torrens (1987*b*).)

during micturition when the bladder contracts. Lesions in the anterior vermis produce detrusor hyperactivity (Zderic *et al.* 1996).

The basal ganglia, thalamic nuclei, and limbic system exert inhibitory influence on the pontine micturition centre. Thus hyperactive detrusor is present in Parkinson's disease, where there is decreased dopaminergic innervation in the substantia nigra of the basal ganglia.

The cerebral cortex provides both facilitatory and inhibitory inputs to the pontine micturition centre. However, transection studies all produce loss of inhibition to the pontine centre. The area of innervation of the striated urethral sphincter is located within the central sulcus of the cortex whereas those of the detrusor originate from the frontal lobe.

Descending and efferent pathways

Amongst the many facilitatory and inhibitory descending pathways there are direct pathways from the motor cortex and via the reticulospinal tract. These pathways influence the motor neurones, innervating the striated urethral sphincter and part of the anal sphincter, which lie in the lateral part of the anterior horn of the grey matter in the second and third sacral segment, also known as Onuf's nucleus.

As described above, both the sympathetic and parasympathetic fibres innervate the lower urinary tract (Fig. 7). The two components converge at the inferior hypogastric plexus, which is formed from the hypogastric and pelvic nerves, lying on the lateral side of the rectum. Nerve fibres converge on a collection of large ganglia at the plexus, or they pass through the plexus to innervate small ganglia in the walls of the bladder and urethra.

Preganglionic sympathetic fibres arise in the intermediolateral column of the spinal cord, and enter the paravertebral sympathetic chain through the ventral spinal nerve roots of T11 to L2. Some of these preganglionic fibres form synapses in the sympathetic chain, from which both pre- and postganglionic fibres travel to the inferior hypogastric plexus via either the inferior mesenteric plexus or the hypogastric nerves. The preganglionic fibres end on the neurones in the ganglia of the inferior hypogastric plexus or the small ganglia in the walls of the bladder and urethra. Therefore the sympathetic ganglia can be located in the sympathetic chain, between the vertebrae and the end organ (as in the inferior hypogastric plexus), or in the wall of the bladder or urethra (peripheral ganglion), with the latter being the predominant form in the lower urinary tract (Williams and Brading 1992).

The preganglionic parasympathetic fibres originate from the sacral parasympathetic nucleus of the intermediolateral column of the spinal cord and emerge from the spinal nerve roots of S2 to S4 in humans. The preganglionic fibres may synapse on neurones in the ganglia in the inferior hypogastric plexus or in intramural ganglia in the bladder or urethra.

Changes with ageing

It is difficult to separate the changes in the lower urinary tract that occur in normal ageing from those that occur as a result of age-associated diseases. Nevertheless, cross-sectional studies (Resnick et al. 1989; Diokno et al. 1992; van Mastrigt 1992; Malone-Lee and Wahedna 1993; Homma et al. 1994) demonstrate age-associated changes in lower urinary tract function. Bladder capacity, maximum flow rate, and the ability to postpone voiding all decline with age in both sexes. The functional urethral length and the maximum urethral pressure decline in women. There is a greater likelihood of residual urine remaining in the bladder after voiding, and there is an increase in the prevalence of unstable pressure rises. These changes reflect alterations in the structure and function of the lower urinary tract. Ultrastructural study of the smooth muscle, interstitium, and intrinsic nerves has greatly enhanced our knowledge about the normal and ageing detrusor.

Changes in the smooth muscle

Elbadawi and coworkers (Elbadawi et al. 1993a, b, 1997; Hailemariam et al. 1997) correlated urodynamic findings in geriatric patients with ultrastructural changes in the bladder wall. In normal adult detrusor, a continuous cell membrane (sarcolemma) confines the content of the muscle cell. Within the sarcolemma, electron-dense zones (dense bands) alternate with less dense zones which are characterized by vesicles (caveolae). As in other cells, organelles such as the nucleus, mitochondria, and endoplasmic reticulum exist, the last two often associated with the caveolae. Myofilaments are anchored at the dense bands. In between the contiguous cells, intermediate junctions of the appearance and width of separation gap are present. These junctions facilitate mechanical coupling of the detrusor cells. Desmosomes and gap junctions are absent. Both the micro- and macrosepta of the interstitium contain collagen and elastin. The identity of the autonomic nerves can be differentiated by the recognition of clear vesicles (cholinergic nerves) or dense vesicles (adrenergic nerves) in the axon terminals.

In elderly people with normal bladder function, the muscle structure, innervation, and interstitium were essentially unchanged, although the spaces between muscle cells were slightly increased. In the sarcolemma, however, considerable depletion of caveolae with elongation of sarcolemmal-dense bands was a dominant feature, probably secondary to a dedifferentiation process associated with ageing. In patients diagnosed as having reduced detrusor contractility, a characteristic but patchy pattern of degeneration of some smooth muscle cells and intrinsic nerves was seen. Patients with unstable (but unobstructed) detrusors showed a disjunction pattern in which close abutments existed between smooth muscle cells and protrusion junctions were commonly seen (Elbadawi et al. 1993c). This pattern would provide a morphological basis for an increased electrical coupling between the cells, and occurred in association with the degeneration pattern in patients with impaired and unstable bladders. Furthermore, in detrusor with obstructive overactivity, often secondary to benign prostatic hyperplasia, a myohypertrophy of the detrusor was recognized, in which hypertrophic muscle cells were apparent, and the intercellular space was much widened with increased amount of collagen deposited within it (Elbadawi et al. 1993d).

Changes in the extracellular matrix

The impact of age on the extracellular matrix is unknown. Nevertheless, oestrogen receptors have been identified in both fibroblasts and tissues for pelvic support. Oestrogen can influence the post-translational events in collagen synthesis by altering the relative content of proline and hydroxyline in the collagen. Thus the hypo-oestrogenic state after menopause can contribute to the synthesis of less stable collagen, resulting in weakened pelvic support and altered compliance of the organs (Klutke and Siegel 1995).

Incontinence in later life

Urinary incontinence is defined as the involuntary loss of urine, which is a social, or hygienic problem that is objectively demonstrable (International Continence Society Standardization Committee 1981). Urinary incontinence is responsible for significant morbidity in the elderly population. It is estimated that 15 to 30 per cent of older people living at home, one-third of those in acute care settings, and half of those in nursing homes are afflicted (Urinary Incontinence Guideline Panel 1992). Urinary incontinence in elderly people is often multifactorial and is generally classified in two groups, transient and established.

Transient incontinence

Resnick and Yalla (1992) have developed the mnemonic **DIAPPERS** for transient incontinence. Delirium (**D**) refers to an acute and fluctuating confusional state due to virtually any drug or acute illness and urinary incontinence is an associated symptom of the underlying illness. Symptomatic urinary tract infection (**I**) with urgency and dysuria predisposes an elderly person to urinary incontinence. Post-menopausal changes secondary to a hypo-oestrogen state leading to atrophic (**A**) vaginitis and urethritis, which causes urinary tract symptoms including urinary incontinence. Pharmaceuticals (**P**) are the most important cause of transient incontinence in elderly people, who often are on multiple medications. Psychological (**P**) causes of incontinence are related to depression or neurosis, and are believed to be less common in elderly people compared with younger groups. Excessive (**E**) urine output may arise from increased fluid intake, diabetic mellitus, or cardiac failure. Restricted (**R**) mobility and reduced manual dexterity can lead to urinary incontinence. Another cause of transient incontinence is stool (**S**) impaction. Up to 10 per

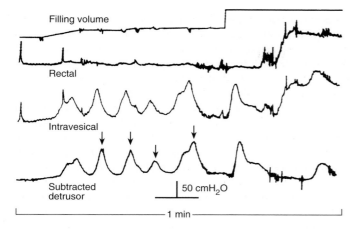

Filling volume

Rectal

Intravesical

Subtracted detrusor

| 50 cmH₂O

— 1 min —

Fig. 10 Urodynamic tracings showing involuntary contractions (arrow) of the detrusor during filling of the bladder. Intravesical pressure minus rectal pressure gives the subtracted detrusor pressure. Urinary incontinence occurs when the subtracted detrusor pressure exceeds the urethral closure pressure during the contractions. (Reproduced with permission from Kelleher and Cardozo (1994).)

cent of elderly patients presenting as acute admissions to hospital or referred to incontinence clinics for urinary incontinence suffer from this. Faecal incontinence is often associated with overflow or urge incontinence in this group. Disimpaction of the stool resolves the urinary incontinence.

Established incontinence

Established incontinence can be subdivided into incontinence secondary to lower urinary tract causes, and functional incontinence which occurs in patients with normal lower urinary tracts. Functional incontinence is often attributed to cognitive impairment, which results in the inability to recognize the bladder is full. However, Resnick and Yalla (1992) have argued that the definition is problematic, in that even in continent and ambulatory institutionalized elderly people, the lower urinary tract is seldom normal. Furthermore, some demented institutionalized elderly people are continent, and their continence rate increases with improvement in their mobility. In addition, those with functional incontinence may also suffer from incontinence due to lower urinary tract causes. Incontinence due to lower urinary tract dysfunction can be associated with detrusor overactivity, genuine stress incontinence, outlet obstruction, detrusor underactivity, or fistulae.

Detrusor overactivity

'Detrusor overactivity' implies uninhibited bladder contraction and can be due to detrusor hyper-reflexia (with central nervous system lesion) or detrusor instability (without central nervous system lesion) (Fig. 10). Central nervous system lesions leading to detrusor hyper-reflexia can occur at the cortical, subcortical, or suprasacral spinal levels, and include Parkinson's disease, Alzheimer's disease, multiple sclerosis, cerebrovascular accidents, cortical atrophy, and spinal cord lesions. It can be difficult to separate hyperactivity and instability as one may superimpose on the other. Furthermore, detrusor instability

can also be secondary to outlet obstruction and outlet incompetence (Resnick and Yalla 1992).

Detrusor overactivity is the leading cause of incontinence afflicting elderly people, and was previously associated with an impaired cognitive status. However, a recent study has, however, failed to find such an association (Resnick *et al.* 1989). Detrusor overactivity is further classified into two subgroups: one with normal detrusor contractility and another with impaired contractility. The latter is the most common cause of incontinence in frail elderly people, and may mimic other causes of urinary incontinence like stress incontinence or urethral obstruction.

It has been suggested that a prerequisite for bladder instability of any cause (i.e. neurogenic, idiopathic, or obstructive) is a change in the smooth muscle properties due to a reduction in excitatory nerve input (Brading and Turner 1994). The changes include an increased excitability of the smooth muscle, and increased coupling between smooth muscles which would allow a focus of activity to spread to cause a myogenic synchronized contraction of the detrusor and an unstable rise in pressure. The ultrastructural changes of the disjunctional pattern seen by Elbadawi in overactive detrusor would provide a morphological basis for this. In support of this hypothesis, patchy denervation has been found in the detrusor of patients with established bladder instability in all types (Speakman *et al.* 1987; German *et al.* 1995; Mills *et al.* 1997), and isolated strips frequently show the fused tetanic contractions that are characteristic of well-coupled smooth muscles and virtually never seen in stable bladders.

Other changes associated with instability that have been clearly demonstrated in animal models are alterations in the afferent pathways (Steers *et al.* 1990; de Groat *et al.* 1993) and changes in the spinal micturition reflex centres. Atropine-resistant contractions of unstable detrusor have also been found in some idiopathic unstable human detrusors (Sjogren *et al.* 1982; C.H. Fry, personal communication).

Outlet obstruction

In elderly men, prostatic hyperplasia is the most common cause of outlet obstruction. For the female, urethral stenosis can occur due to fibrotic changes associated with atrophic vaginitis and decrease in urethral elasticity with age. Rarely, kinking of the female urethra occurs secondary to a large cystocele or following operative bladder-neck suspension.

Obstruction leads to incontinence when it is the cause of detrusor instability, resulting in urge incontinence. It may initially present as postvoid dribbling. If detrusor decompensation occurs, then overflow incontinence may follow.

Obstruction results in hypertrophy of the detrusor, and will inevitably increase the intravesical pressure during micturition, and prolong the time needed for bladder emptying. This has several consequences, including transient periods of bladder wall ischaemia during voiding, and increased substrate utilization. Prolonged obstruction is associated with a patchy denervation of the detrusor, probably caused by death of some of the neurones in the bladder wall due to the ischaemia. This reduced innervation will trigger the changes in the smooth muscle referred to above, which may be a prerequisite for unstable contractions. The hypertrophic changes may also limit the ability to generate forceful contraction, reducing the ability of the bladder to empty efficiently and fully.

Genuine stress incontinence

Stress incontinence is the second most common cause of incontinence in older women. It is usually caused by urethral hypermobility or sphincter incompetence. In the normal female, an increase in intra-abdominal pressure is transmitted equally to the bladder neck and proximal intra-abdominal part of the urethra. If there is pelvic floor muscle laxity, the bladder neck and proximal urethra herniate through the urogenital diaphragm, resulting in transmission of pressure to the bladder alone and not to the bladder neck and proximal urethra. The loss of pressure gradient results in genuine stress incontinence. Conversely, even if the bladder neck and the proximal urethra are in an intra-abdominal position, but the sphincter complex is defective and remains open, a sudden increase in intra-abdominal pressure will result in urinary incontinence. Sphincteric incompetence may be due to diabetes, iatrogenic injury (following radical prostatectomy for example), or injury during childbirth. In elderly women, atrophic changes may contribute to sphincteric incompetence. A less common cause of sphincteric incompetence is urethral instability. This is characterized by abrupt and paradoxical relaxation of the urethral sphincter in the absence of detrusor contraction.

Detrusor underactivity

This is often idiopathic and is characterized by widespread degenerative changes in both muscle cells and axons with no regenerative pattern being recognized. It commonly leads to overflow incontinence.

Fistulas

Fistulas involving the ureter, bladder, or urethra are a rare cause of incontinence in elderly people. There is often associated pelvic or vaginal surgery.

Age-associated disease affecting the lower urinary tract

A wide spectrum of medical conditions can affect elderly people and lead to lower urinary tract dysfunction (DuBeau 1996).

Benign prostatic hyperplasia

The prevalence of benign prostatic hyperplasia increases with age, and when it results in partial obstruction of the urethra is a common cause of urge incontinence in men. Apart from the hypertrophy of the bladder wall, many of the changes to the detrusor seen in benign prostatic hyperplasia also occur with normal ageing. The results of outflow obstruction are described above.

Diabetes mellitus

In late-onset diabetes mellitus, axonal damage followed by segmental demyelination may occur at spinal nerve roots, sympathetic ganglia, peripheral autonomic nerves/ganglia, and intrinsic nerves in the detrusor. Afferent denervation leads to impaired bladder-filling sensation with reduced frequency of micturition. With loss of input to the spinal cord and higher centres, the bladder capacity increases and abdominal straining is required during micturition. Detrusor areflexia may supervene and overflow incontinence may occur (McGuire 1994).

Disorders of the central nervous system

Many central nervous system disorders increase in incidence with age. The most common long-term complication following cerebrovascular accident is detrusor hyper-reflexia, secondary to upper motor neurone damage. This will be accompanied by incontinence if there is no co-ordinated contraction of the striated sphincter. Such urinary tract dysfunction is often transient and improves together with the other symptoms after the incident. Parkinson's disease is associated with urgency, frequency, slow stream, and difficulty with volitional initiation of voiding. The obstructive voiding symptoms can be explained by the bladder contractility and slow urethral sphincter relaxation, which needs to be differentiated from bladder outflow obstruction secondary to prostate hyperplasia in men. Urodynamic studies often demonstrate detrusor hyper-reflexia. Multiple-system atrophy, characterized by degeneration of spinal interomediolateral tract and Onuf's nucleus, is often predated by symptoms of urgency, frequency, and urge incontinence (Beck et al. 1994). Voiding dysfunctions in Shy–Drager syndrome, which embraces features of multiple-system atrophy, consist of incontinence, frequency, and failure to void. In multiple sclerosis, where there is frontal neural degeneration and posterior and lateral columns of cervical spinal cord, urodynamics reveal detrusor hyper-reflexia and striated sphincter dyssynergia. Cystometry reveals a non-functioning bladder neck and proximal urethra and electromyography of the striated sphincter shows a pattern of denervation. Normal-pressure hydrocephalus characteristically produces progressive dementia and apraxia of gait in association with urinary incontinence due to paraventricular compression of the frontal inhibitory centres causing urge incontinence, detrusor hyper-reflexia, and detrusor sphincter inco-ordination. Spinal cord damage due to spondylosis or other conditions may cause incontinence. Detrusor hyper-reflexia can be a consequence of cervical or lumbar stenosis, although the latter can also give rise to areflexia. Spinal cord injury also gives rise to bladder problems and 20 per cent of new spinal cord injury patients are elderly. Voiding dysfunction varies depending on the site of injury and the time from the injury. This is a vast subject outside the parameters of this chapter. Vitamin B_{12} deficiency neuropathy can result in detrusor areflexia with retention and overflow urinary tract incontinence. The relationship of urinary incontinence with dementia is not well understood. Pathophysiology of the lower urinary tract clearly needs to be distinguished from impaired functional ability to maintain continence.

Other disorders

Respiratory diseases with chronic cough may exacerbate stress or urge incontinence. Infectious disease such as herpes zoster, when affecting the sacral dermatome, may precipitate urinary retention. Tertiary neurosyphilis produces neuronal damage at various sites and may be complicated by detrusor areflexia with impaired sensation, or detrusor hyper-reflexia and detrusor sphincter dyssynergia.

Arterial insufficiency secondary to atherosclerotic disease may affect the lower urinary tract. The ischaemic damage to the spinal cord in anterior spinal artery syndrome during thoracic aneurysm rupture or repair is known to produce urinary retention and urinary incontinence.

Treatment of incontinence

Current approaches

This topic is also dealt with in Chapter 15.4. In elderly patients, incontinence often arises from indirect causes and can be improved by common-sense measures, for instance improving access to the toilet and eliminating contributory factors such as the use of various medications. However, more specific treatment for urinary incontinence aims to facilitate bladder filling and urine storage. This can be achieved by inhibiting bladder contractility, decreasing the bladder sensory input, increasing bladder capacity, or raising the outlet resistance. The main treatment modalities can be grouped into behavioural treatment, drug treatment, and surgery (Wein 1992). Behavioural treatments such as bladder training regimes or pelvic floor exercises with or without biofeedback have the advantage of having no serious side-effects, and can be helpful to elderly patients who can comply with the protocols. Drug treatment is usually aimed at reducing bladder contractility with antimuscarinic drugs, or stimulating contraction in urethral smooth muscle with α-adrenoceptor agonists, but the efficacy of such treatment is often poor and side-effects are common. Surgical procedures may be inappropriate for many elderly people, but might include bladder augmentation to improve urine storage and surgical correction for stress incontinence.

Potential pharmacological treatments

A great deal of effort is currently being made by pharmaceutical companies to develop better drugs for the treatment of incontinence. Reduction in the incidence and force of unstable bladder contractions would be beneficial for the treatment of urge incontinence. Two lines of approach are available, firstly reducing the excitability of the bladder smooth muscle itself, and secondly reducing activity in sensory nerves that might be involved in triggering urgency and unstable contractions (Turner and Brading 1997). Potassium-channel-activating drugs show promise in animal models, since they can reduce smooth muscle excitability with minimal interference with the micturition reflex. Currently, the major shortcoming of potassium-channel openers, such as cromakalim and pinacidil, is their effect on other smooth muscles, leading in particular to reduction in blood pressure. Potassium-channel openers with *in vivo* bladder selectivity are currently being tested. Precisely what triggers urgency and unstable bladder contractions is very poorly understood, but the known ability of antimuscarinic drugs to decrease frequency and increase voided volume in urge incontinence suggests that muscarinic receptors may be involved in this aspect of the micturition pathway as well as in initiating voiding contractions. New generations of antimuscarinic drugs, which may have fewer side-effects than those currently available, are about to be released. Drugs acting centrally or more peripherally to reduce sensory activity leading to urgency are also under investigation.

References

Beck, R., Fowler, C.J., and Mathias, C.J. (1994). Genitourinary dysfunction in disorders of the autonomic nervous system. In *Handbook of neuro-urology, neurological disease and therapy* (ed. D.N. Rushton), pp. 281–301. Marcel Dekker, New York.

Benoit, G., Quillard, J., and Jardin, A. (1988). Anatomical study of the infra-montanal urethra in man. *Journal of Urology*, 139, 866–8.

Brading, A.F. and Turner, W.H. (1994). The unstable bladder: towards a common mechanism. *British Journal of Urology*, 73, 3–8.

Bridgewater, M., Davies, J.R., and Brading, A.F. (1995). Regional variations in the neural control of the female pig urethra. *British Journal of Urology*, 76, 730–40.

Chapple, C.R., Helm, C.W., Blease, S., *et al.* (1989). Asymptomatic bladder neck incompetence in nulliparous females. *British Journal of Urology*, 64, 357–9.

Corcoran, M.L., Kleiner, D.E., and Steler-Stevenson, W.G. (1995). Regulation of matrix metalloproteinases during extracellular matrix turnover. In *Muscle, matrix and bladder function* (ed. S.A. Zderic). Plenum Press, New York.

de Groat, W.C. (1990). Central neural control of the lower urinary tract. *Ciba Foundation Symposium*, 151, 27–44.

de Groat, W.C., Booth, A.M., and Yoshimura, N. (1993). Neurophysiology of micturition and its modification in animal models of human disease. In *Nervous control of the urogenital system* (ed. C.A. Maggi), pp. 227–90. Harwood Academic, Chur, Switzerland.

DeLancey, J.O. (1990). Anatomy and physiology of urinary incontinence. *Clinical Obstetrics and Gynecology*, 33, 298–307.

DeLancey, J.O. (1994). Structural support of the urethra as it relates to stress urinary incontinence: the hammock hypothesis. *American Journal of Obstetrics and Gynaecology*, 170, 1713–20.

Diokno, A.C., Brown, M.B., Goldstein, N., and Herzog, A.R. (1992). Epidemiology of bladder emptying symptoms in elderly men. *Journal of Urology*, 148, 1817–21.

Dixon, J. and Gosling, J. (1987). Structure and innervation in the human neuromorphology. In *The physiology of the lower urinary tract* (ed. M. Torrens and J.F.B. Morrison), pp. 3–22. Springer-Verlag, New York.

DuBeau, C.E. (1996). Interpreting the effect of common medical conditions on voiding dysfunction in the elderly. *Urologic Clinics of North America*, 23, 11–18.

Elbadawi, A. (1987). Comparative neuromorphology in animals. In *The physiology of the lower urinary tract* (ed. M. Torrens and J.F.B. Morrison), pp. 23–51. Springer-Verlag, New York.

Elbadawi, A. (1995). Pathology and pathophysiology of detrusor in incontinence. *Urologic Clinics of North America*, 22, 499–512.

Elbadawi, A., Yalla, S.V., and Resnick, N.M. (1993a). Structural basis of geriatric voiding dysfunction. I. Methods of a prospective ultrastructural/urodynamic study and an overview of the findings. *Journal of Urology*, 150, 1650–6.

Elbadawi, A., Yalla, S.V., and Resnick, N.M. (1993b). Structural basis of geriatric voiding dysfunction. II. Aging detrusor: normal versus impaired contractility. *Journal of Urology*, 150, 1657–67.

Elbadawi, A., Yalla, S.V., and Resnick, N.M. (1993c). Structural basis of geriatric voiding dysfunction. III. Detrusor overactivity. *Journal of Urology*, 150, 1668–80.

Elbadawi, A., Yalla, S.V., and Resnick, N.M. (1993d). Structural basis of geriatric voiding dysfunction. IV. Bladder outlet obstruction. *Journal of Urology*, 150, 1681–95.

Elbadawi, A., Hailemariam, S., Yalla, S.V., and Resnick, N.M. (1997). Structural basis of geriatric voiding dysfunction. VI. Validation and update of diagnostic criteria in 71 detrusor biopsies. *Journal of Urology*, 157, 1802–13.

Ewalt, D.H., Howard, P.S., Blyth, B., *et al.* (1992). Is lamina propria matrix responsible for normal bladder compliance? *Journal of Urology*, 148, 544–9.

Ferguson, D.R. and Marchant, J.S. (1995). Inhibitory actions of GABA on rabbit urinary bladder muscle strips: mediation by potassium channels. *British Journal of Pharmacology*, 115, 81–3.

Fowler, C.J. and Fowler, C. (1987). Clinical neurophysiology. In *The physiology of the lower urinary tract* (ed. M. Torrens and J.F.B. Morrison), pp. 309–32. Springer-Verlag, New York.

German, K., Bedwani, J., Davies, J., Brading, A.F., and Stephenson, T.P. (1995). Physiological and morphometric studies into the pathophysiology of detrusor hyperreflexia in neuropathic patients. *Journal of Urology*, 153, 1678–83.

Gosling, J.A. (1986). The distribution of noradrenergic nerves in the human lower urinary tract. *Clinical Science*, 70, 3S–6S.

Gosling, J.A., Dixon, J.S., and Lendon, R.G. (1977). The autonomic innervation of the human male and female bladder neck and proximal urethra. *Journal of Urology*, **118**, 302–5.

Gosling, J.A., Dixon, J.S., Critchley, H.O., and Thompson, S.A. (1981). A comparative study of the human external sphincter and periurethral levator ani muscles. *British Journal of Urology*, **53**, 35–41.

Gosling, J.A., Dixon, J.S., and Humpherson, J.R. (1983). *Functional anatomy of the urinary tract*. Churchill Livingstone, Edinburgh.

Greenland, J.E. and Brading, A.F. (1995). What is the role of the urethral lamina propria? An investigation in a conscious pig model. *Neurology Urodynamics*, **14**, 85–6.

Greenland, J.E., Dass, N., and Brading, A.F. (1996). Intrinsic urethral closure mechanisms in the female pig. *Scandinavian Journal of Urology and Nephrology*, **179**, 75–80.

Hailemariam, S., Elbadawi, A., Yalla, S.V., and Resnick, N.M. (1997). Structural basis of geriatric voiding dysfunction. V. Standardised protocols for routine ultrastructural study and diagnosis of endoscopic detrusor biopsies. *Journal of Urology*, **157**, 1783–801.

Ho, K.M.T., Dass, N., Brading, A.F., and Noble, J. (1997a). Elastin in association with the human male membranous urethral sphincter. *Neurourology Urodynamics*, **16**, 454–5.

Ho, K.M.T., McMurray, G., Brading, A.F., Noble, J., Ny, L., and Andersson, K.-E. (1997b). Co-localisation of carbon monoxide synthesising enzymes in the human female urethral sphincter. *Neurourology Urodynamics*, **16**, 367–8.

Ho, K.M.T., McMurray, G., Mills, I.W., Noble, J., and Brading, A.F. (1997c). The human membranous striated sphincter: does it consist of a homogeneous population of fibres? *Neurourology Urodynamics*, **16**, 453–4.

Homma, Y., Imajo, C., Takahashi, S., Kawabe, K., and Aso, Y. (1994). Urinary symptoms and urodynamics in a normal elderly population. *Scandinavian Journal of Urology and Nephrology*, **157**, 27–30.

Inoue, R. and Brading, A.F. (1991). Human, pig and guinea-pig bladder smooth muscle cells generate similar inward currents in response to purinoceptor activation. *British Journal of Pharmacology*, **103**, 1840–1.

International Continence Society (1981). Fourth report on the standardisation of terminology of the lower urinary tract function. *British Journal of Urology*, **53**, 333–5.

James, M.J., Birmingham, A.T., and Hill, S.J. (1993). Partial mediation by nitric oxide of the relaxation of human isolated detrusor strips in response to electrical field stimulation. *British Journal of Clinical Pharmacology*, **35**, 366–72.

Kelleher, C.J. and Cardozo, L. (1994). Urodynamic assessment. In *Handbook of neuro-urology, neurological disease and therapy* (ed. D.N. Rushton), pp. 129–49. Dekker, New York.

Klutke, J.J. and Bergman, A. (1995). Hormonal influence on the urinary tract. *Urologic Clinics of North America*, **22**, 613–27.

Learmonth, J.R. (1931). A contribution to the neurophysiology of the urinary bladder in man. *Brain*, **54**, 147–76.

McGuire, E.J. (1994). Pathophysiology of incontinence in elderly women. In *Geriatric urology* (ed. P.D. O'Donnell), pp. 221–38. Little, Brown, Boston, MA.

Maggi, C.A. and Meli, A. (1988). The sensory-efferent function of capsaicin-sensitive sensory neurons. *General Pharmacology*, **19**, 1–43.

Malone-Lee, J. and Wahedna, I. (1993). Characterisation of detrusor contractile function in relation to old age. *British Journal of Urology*, **72**, 873–80.

Mills, I.W., Greenland, J.G., McMurray, G., Ho, K.M.T., Noble, J.G., and Brading, A.F. (1997). The *in vitro* and histological properties of bladder from patients with idiopathic detrusor instability indicate that there is partial denervation of the detrusor muscle. *British Journal of Urology*, **79**, 48.

Mostwin, J.L. (1991). Current concepts of female pelvic anatomy and physiology. *Urologic Clinics of North America*, **18**, 175–95.

Myers, R.P. (1991). Male urethral sphincteric anatomy and radical prostatectomy. *Urologic Clinics of North America*, **18**, 211–27.

Resnick, N.M. and Yalla, S.V. (1992). Evaluation and medical management of urinary incontinence. In *Campbell's urology* (ed. P.C. Walsh, A.B. Retik, T.A. Stamey, and E. Darracott Vaughan), pp. 643–58. W.B. Saunders, Philadelphia, PA.

Resnick, N.M., Yalla, S.V., and Laurino, E. (1989). The pathophysiology of urinary incontinence among institutionalized elderly persons. *New England Journal of Medicine*, **320**, 1–7.

Sjogren, C., Andersson, K.E., Husted, S., Mattiasson, A., and Moller Madsen, B. (1982). Atropine resistance of transmurally stimulated isolated human bladder muscle. *Journal of Urology*, **128**, 1368–71.

Speakman, M.J., Brading, A.F., Gilpin, C.J., Dixon, J.S., Gilpin, S.A., and Gosling, J.A. (1987). Bladder outflow obstruction—a cause of denervation supersensitivity. *Journal of Urology*, **138**, 1461–6.

Speakman, M.J., Walmsley, D., and Brading, A.F. (1988). An *in vitro* pharmacological study of the human trigone—a site of non-adrenergic, non-cholinergic neurotransmission. *British Journal of Urology*, **61**, 304–9.

Steers, W.D., Ciambotti, J., Erdman, S., and de Groat, W.C. (1990). Morphological plasticity in efferent pathways to the urinary bladder of the rat following urethral obstruction. *Journal of Neuroscience*, **10**, 1943–51.

Steiner, M.S. (1994). The puboprostatic ligament and the male urethral suspensory mechanism: an anatomic study. *Urology*, **44**, 530–4.

Tanagho, E.A. and Meyers, F.H. (1969). The 'internal sphincter': is it under sympathetic control? *Investigative Urology*, **7**, 79–89.

Tanagho, E.A. and Smith, D.R. (1966). The anatomy and function of the bladder neck. *British Journal of Urology*, **38**, 54–71.

Torrens, M. (1987a). Urodynamics. In *The physiology of the lower urinary tract* (ed. M. Torrens and J.F.B. Morrison), pp. 277–307. Springer-Verlag, New York.

Torrens, M. (1987b). Human physiology. In *The physiology of the lower urinary tract* (ed. M. Torrens and J.F.B. Morrison), pp. 333–50. Springer-Verlag, New York.

Turner, W.H. and Brading, A.F. (1997). Smooth muscle of the bladder in the normal and diseased state; pathophysiology, diagnosis and treatment. *Pharmacology and Therapeutics*, **75**, 77–110.

Urinary Incontinence Guideline Panel (1992). *Urinary incontinence in adults: clinical practice guideline*. AHCPR Publication No. 92–0038.

van Mastrigt, R. (1992). Age dependence of urinary bladder contractility. *Neurourology and Urodynamics*, **11**, 315–17.

Wein, A.J. (1992). Neuromuscular dysfunction of the lower urinary tract. In *Campbell's urology* (ed. P.C. Walsh, A.B. Retik, T.A. Stamey, and E. Darracott Vaughan), pp. 573–642. W.B. Saunders, Philadelphia, PA.

Weiss, R.M., Nangia, A.K., Smith, S.D., and Wheeler, M.A. (1994). Nitric oxide synthase activity in urethra, bladder and bladder smooth muscle cells. *Neurourology and Urodynamics*, **13**, 397–8.

Wellner, M.C. and Isenberg, G. (1993). Stretch-activated non-selective cation channels in urinary bladder myocytes: importance for pacemaker potentials and myogenic response. *EXS*, **66**, 93–9.

Williams, J.H. and Brading, A.F. (1992) Urethral sphincter: normal function and changes in disease. In *Sphincters: normal function—changes in diseases* (ed. E.E. Daniel, T. Tomita, S. Tsuchida, and M. Wantanabe), pp. 315–38. CRC Press, Boca Raton, FL.

Woodburne, R.T. and Smith, D.R. (1968). Anatomy of the bladder and bladder outlet. *Journal of Urology*, **100**, 474.

Yokoyama, O., Mita, E., Ishiura, Y., Nakamura, Y., Nagano, K. and Namiki, M. (1997). Bladder compliance in patients with benign prostatic hyperplasia. *Neurourology and Urodynamics*, **16**, 19–27.

Zderic, S.A., Levin, R., and Wein, A.J. (1996). Voiding function: relevant anatomy, physiology, pharmacology and molecular aspects. In *Adult and paediatric urology* (ed. J.Y. Gillenwater, J.T. Grayhack, S.S. Howards, and J.W. Duckett), pp. 1159–219. C.V. Mosby, St Louis, MO.

15.4 Urinary incontinence

Catherine E. DuBeau

Introduction

Urinary incontinence presents the challenge of a multifactorial syndrome—involving the intersection of specific genitourinary pathology, age-associated changes, and comorbid conditions—that has substantial impact on affected individuals, caregivers, and health-care systems. Significant proportions of older people worldwide are incontinent: 15 to 30 per cent of community-dwelling populations over the age of 65 years (Herzog and Fultz 1990), and up to 50 per cent of people in long-term care (Ouslander et al. 1993). Yet incontinence often remains undetected and undertreated by health-care personnel, leaving incontinent people with unresolved physical, functional, and emotional morbidity. At the same time, total incontinence-related costs in the United States alone exceeded $26 billion for 1995 (Wagner and Hu 1998). Although substantial gains have been made in the last decade in our understanding of incontinence pathophysiology, the effects of ageing on the lower urinary tract, and the impact of incontinence on quality of life, improvements in treatment have yet to progress, especially for frail older people.

Morbidity and impact on quality of life

Considerable medical and psychological morbidity occurs with incontinence: cellulitis and pressure ulcers can result from constant skin irritation by urine and wet clothing; urinary tract infections and urosepsis from urinary retention and indwelling catheters; falls and fractures from slipping on urine; sleep interruption and deprivation from nocturia or incontinence care in institutionalized people; social withdrawal, depression, and sexual dysfunction may develop secondary to the associated embarrassment. Caregiver burden is higher for incontinent elderly people and contributes to decisions to institutionalize such individuals (Ouslander et al. 1990). However, incontinence is not associated with increased mortality (Herzog et al. 1994).

Incontinence may greatly influence quality of life (Wyman et al. 1987), i.e. the complete physical, mental, and social well being of individuals, including their physical, social, and role functions, mental health, and general health perceptions (World Health Organization 1978; Wilson and Cleary 1995). The quality-of-life impact of incontinence appears greatest on coping with embarrassment and activity interference, rather than on actual activity performance (Brocklehurst 1993; DuBeau et al. 1998). While many people find incontinence personally and socially devastating, others describe limited effect on their lifestyle or emotional well being (Jeter and Wagner 1990). Such variability is only partially explained by heterogeneity in severity measures such as frequency of incontinence episodes (Wyman et al. 1990), and probably reflects other factors specific to each individual.

Micturition in older people

Continence depends on both intact micturition physiology (including lower urinary tract, pelvic, and neurological components) and an intact functional ability to toilet oneself, including such factors as the motivation to maintain dryness, sufficient mobility and manual dexterity, and the cognitive ability to recognize and react appropriately to sensations of bladder filling. Thus incontinence, especially in elderly people, frequently reflects multidimensional and often multiple impairments. Although age-associated changes in the lower urinary tract may predispose older people to incontinence, many people with such changes remain asymptomatic and continent (Resnick et al. 1995). Thus age-associated factors do not necessarily cause voiding problems, and voiding symptoms and incontinence are never 'normal ageing'.

Normal micturition

The anatomical components that subserve micturition include bladder smooth muscle (detrusor), which contracts with cholinergic stimulation from parasympathetic nerves arising from sacral spinal cord levels S2–S4, urethral sphincter mechanisms, including proximal smooth muscle that contracts with α-adrenergic sympathetic stimulation from spinal levels T11–L2, and distal striated muscle that contracts with cholinergic somatic stimulation from cord levels S2–S4. Fascial and muscular urethral supports also constitute crucial components of the urethral closure mechanism (DeLancey 1988). In the central nervous system, the parietal lobes and thalamus receive and co-ordinate detrusor afferent stimuli, the frontal lobes and basal ganglia provide modulation with inhibitory signals until one is prepared to void in a suitable location, and a pontine micturition centre integrates these inputs, permitting socially appropriate and co-ordinated voiding (Van Arsdalen and Wein 1991).

Table 3 Drug effects on continence

Function necessary for continence	How drugs impair function	Examples
Cognition	Cause confusion, sedation, decrease motivation	Sedative/hypnotics; antipsychotics; antidepressants; anticonvulsants; alcohol
Mobility	Induce rigidity	Antipsychotics
	Induce orthostatic hypotension	Antihypertensives; tricyclic antidepressants; nitrates
Fluid balance	Fluid retention/pedal oedema, with increased nocturnal diuresis	NSAIDs; dihydropyridine calcium-channel blockers; steroids
	Excess diuresis	Loop diuretics; alcohol; caffeine; theophylline
Bladder contractility	Impair contractility	Anticholinergic agents: antipsychotics, tricyclic antidepressants, antiparkinsonian (trihexylphenidate, benztropine mesylate), antihistamines, antispasmodics, di-isopyramide; calcium-channel blockers; narcotics; vincristine
	Cause constipation, faecal impaction	Anticholinergics; calcium-channel blockers; narcotics; calcium
Sphincter function	Prevent adequate relaxation	α-Adrenergic agonists
	Prevent adequate closure	α-Adrenergic antagonists; misoprostol
	Increase stress manoeuvres (cough)	Angiotensin-converting enzyme inhibitors

NSAIDs, non-steroidal anti-inflammatory drugs.
Adapted from DuBeau (1997).

fluid balance, bladder contractility, or sphincter function can affect continence (Table 3). Many medications may impair several of these functions; for example, the antipsychotic haloperidol can produce confusion, have extrapyramidal effects making ambulation difficult, and, via its anticholinergic action, impair detrusor contraction and cause stool impaction.

Psychiatric causes of incontinence, although not well studied in any age group, are recognizable among people with severe depression and psychotic disorders. Care must be taken to exclude other possible incontinence precipitants—especially the cognitive, anticholinergic, and functional effects of psychoactive medications—before attributing incontinence to psychiatric disease alone. Excessive urine output frequently precipitates or exacerbates geriatric incontinence, and should be particularly looked for when there is associated urinary frequency or nocturia. Causes include excessive fluid intake; diuretics (including caffeine and alcohol); metabolic abnormalities (hyperglycaemia and hypercalcaemia); and disorders of volume overload, such as congestive heart failure, peripheral venous insufficiency, hypothyroidism, hypoalbuminaemia, and drug-induced peripheral oedema (e.g. from non-steroidal anti-inflammatory agents and dihydropyridine calcium-channel blockers).

Restricted mobility may impair the functional ability to toilet, even in people with intact lower urinary tract function. Remediable causes of mobility impairment in older people are legion: physical deconditioning, arthritis, postural or postprandial hypotension, claudication, spinal stenosis, heart failure, poor eyesight, fear of falling, stroke, foot problems, and drug-induced disequilibrium are but a few. Environmental restrictions, ranging from distant bathroom locations to physical restraints, should not be overlooked. Even when the underlying cause of restricted mobility cannot be reversed, use of a urinal or bedside commode may improve or resolve incontinence.

Finally, stool impaction may cause either urge or overflow incontinence; concurrent faecal incontinence is common. Although a well-recognized phenomenon, the association of impaction with incontinence is not well understood; however, disimpaction and reinstitution of bowel function restore continence.

Established incontinence

If leakage persists after transient causes of incontinence have been addressed, the lower urinary tract causes of established incontinence must be considered. The three major clinical types of established incontinence are urge (due to detrusor overactivity), stress (due to failure of sphincter mechanisms to remain closed during bladder filling), and overflow (due to impaired detrusor contractility and/or bladder outlet obstruction). Other types of incontinence, such as extraurethral (from fistula formation) and impaired detrusor compliance (an excessive pressure response to filling, usually due to spinal cord injury), are rare in elderly people.

Urge incontinence

Urge incontinence, the leading cause of incontinence in older individuals, is characterized by abrupt, precipitant urgency with moderate to large leakage, and often urinary frequency and nocturia. The aetiology of urge incontinence is presumed to be uninhibited bladder contractions, termed detrusor overactivity. However, the finding of detrusor overactivity in healthy continent elderly people (Resnick *et al.* 1995) suggests that detrusor overactivity alone is not sufficient to explain urge incontinence, and that a failure of compensatory mechanisms—in both the lower urinary tract and the functional requirements for continence—may have an important aetiological role as well. Detrusor overactivity may be age associated, secondary to impairment of central nervous system inhibitory centres and pathways (e.g. by stroke, cervical stenosis), or secondary to local bladder irritation by infection, bladder stones, inflammation, or neoplasms. Previous classification systems (Abrams et al. 1988) have distinguished between detrusor overactivity associated with a central nervous system lesion (called detrusor hyperreflexia) and detrusor overactivity that is idiopathic or due to other causes (detrusor instability). In older people, however, this distinction is frequently blurred by a multiplicity of comorbid conditions; for example, an elderly man with Parkinson's disease, dementia, and obstructive benign prostatic hypertrophy could have detrusor overactivity on the basis of any one of these conditions, or simply his advanced age, and to date there is no reliable way to differentiate which is responsible. A special subset of urge incontinence that occurs predominantly in (younger) women is interstitial cystitis, characterized by urgency and frequent voiding of small amounts, often with dysuria or pain (Koziol et al. 1993). Unfortunately, a lack of understanding of its pathophysiology has made treatment empirical, difficult and often unsuccessful.

There appear to be two forms of detrusor overactivity in elderly people: in one contractile function is preserved, and in the other it is impaired (Resnick and Yalla 1987). The latter condition has been termed detrusor hyperactivity with impaired contractility (**DHIC**), and it comprises the majority of established incontinence in frail elderly people (Resnick et al. 1989). In DHIC, detrusor overactivity coexists with an elevated postvoiding residual volume (exclusive of outlet obstruction). Detrusor hyperactivity with impaired contractility can mimic other lower urinary tract causes of incontinence. If uninhibited contractions are triggered by or occur coincident with a stress manoeuvre, and the weak bladder contraction (often only 2–6 cmH$_2$O of pressure) is not detected, DHIC will be misdiagnosed as stress incontinence. In men, DHIC shares the symptoms of urinary urgency, frequency, weak flow rate, and elevated residual urine with outlet obstruction and detrusor weakness (Resnick et al. 1996). Furthermore, because the bladder in DHIC is weak, urinary retention may develop, especially if bladder-relaxant therapy is used.

Stress incontinence

Stress incontinence is the second most common cause of incontinence in older women, and may occur in older men after transurethral or radical prostatectomy. Stress leakage occurs with increases in intraabdominal pressure, in the absence of a bladder contraction. In women, stress incontinence most often results from impaired urethral closure due to insufficient support from pelvic endofascia and muscles. Less commonly, leakage is due to complete failure of urethral closure. This condition, which is termed intrinsic sphincter deficiency or type III stress incontinence, usually results from operative trauma and scarring, but also can occur with severe mucosal atrophy in postmenopausal women. Unlike the episodic stress-manoeuvre-related leakage of genuine stress incontinence, intrinsic sphincter deficiency leakage is typically continuous and can occur while sitting or standing quietly. A third but rare cause of stress incontinence is urethral instability, in which the sphincter abruptly and paradoxically relaxes in the absence of an apparent detrusor contraction; older women thought to have this condition may instead have DHIC.

Overflow incontinence

Overflow incontinence occurs with detrusor underactivity or bladder outlet obstruction, either alone or in combination. Leakage typically is small volume, although significant wetting can occur because of its continual nature. The postvoiding residual volume is elevated, and there may be a concomitant weak urinary stream, dribbling, intermittency, hesitancy, frequency, and nocturia. Stress-related leakage may be apparent, reflecting the overwhelming of an otherwise intact sphincter mechanism, rather than true sphincter pathology.

Outlet obstruction is the second most common cause of incontinence in older men, although most obstructed men are not incontinent. Common aetiologies include benign prostatic hyperplasia, prostate cancer, and urethral stricture. Obstruction is uncommon in women, and when present is usually due to previous anti-incontinence surgery or a large cystocele that prolapses and kinks the urethra with voiding. Incontinence associated with obstruction most often presents as postvoid dribbling; urge incontinence may occur in those with associated detrusor overactivity, while overflow incontinence may ensue in those with associated detrusor decompensation. Rarely, obstruction reflects detrusor–sphincter dyssynergia due to a spinal cord lesion; in such cases, interruption of the pathways to the pontine micturition centre leads to loss of detrusor–sphincter co-ordination, resulting in outlet closure during bladder contraction, severe detrusor overactivity, marked bladder trabeculation and diverticula, and often hydronephrosis.

Detrusor underactivity sufficient to cause urinary retention and overflow incontinence occurs in only about 5 to 10 per cent of older people. Intrinsic causes are replacement of detrusor smooth muscle by fibrosis and connective tissue, as occurs in some men with chronic outlet obstruction. Neurological causes include peripheral neuropathy (from diabetes, pernicious anaemia, Parkinson's disease, alcoholism, or tabes dorsalis) or mechanical damage to the spinal detrusor afferents by disc herniation, spinal stenosis, or tumour. In people with arteriosclerotic disease, ischaemia also may contribute to detrusor underactivity, although this is still under investigation.

Evaluation and diagnosis

The multifactorial nature of incontinence in elderly people demands that the diagnostic evaluation be comprehensive, with a careful search for all possible causes and precipitants, and not simply focus on determining a specific genitourinary diagnosis.

History

It is essential that the doctor or nurse initiates discussion about voiding symptoms, because at least half of incontinent individuals do not otherwise report their symptoms to health-care personnel (Branch et al. 1994). Institutionalized incontinent people also may be prone to neglect, especially if staff assume that incontinence is normal in the frail, or if they have limited experience with treatment other than protective garments or time-consuming toileting. An empathic approach and commitment to work over time with the incontinent person (and/or their caregivers) helps correct negative experiences with previous perfunctory or nihilistic incontinence care.

The history should explore the onset of incontinence and its frequency, volume, timing, and precipitants (e.g. medications, caffeinated beverages, alcohol, physical activity, cough). A comprehensive history of medical conditions, symptoms, and medications (prescribed and over the counter) should also be completed. The temporal relationship of these factors to incontinence onset should be explored, to help determine whether such factors are causal or comorbid; for example, dementia of several years duration is unlikely to be responsible for new-onset incontinence.

Although the predictive diagnostic value of individual voiding symptoms varies with how the symptom is defined, and with patient age, sex, and underlying pathology (DuBeau and Resnick 1991), there are several useful general points. For detrusor overactivity, the characteristic symptom is precipitant urgency, the abrupt onset of (or increase in) an overwhelming urge to void, with or without subsequent leakage (Resnick 1990). The length of time one can forestall an intense urge is less useful, as this reflects mentation, sphincter control, mobility, and toilet availability as well as detrusor function. Common precipitants include running water, hand-washing, going out in the cold, and even the sight of the garage or trying to unlock the door when returning home (the 'garage door' and 'key in the lock' syndromes). Leakage with stress manoeuvres (coughing, laughing, bending over, running, changing position) is a sensitive symptom for stress incontinence (Diokno et al. 1990); i.e. if a person denies stress leakage, then stress incontinence is highly unlikely. Genuine stress incontinence leakage occurs instantaneous with the increase in abdominal pressure, whereas a delay between the provocative manoeuvre and the leakage, or the occurrence of a sudden urge before or coincident with the leakage, suggests the provocation of an uninhibited contraction and a diagnosis of stress-induced urge incontinence. Stress leakage with minimal increases in intra-abdominal pressure (e.g. shifting position) and/or continual urine dripping suggests intrinsic sphincter deficiency.

Frequency, nocturia, slow urine stream, hesitancy, interrupted voiding, straining, and terminal dribbling are commonly associated with incontinence, but they lack diagnostic specificity as they occur with detrusor overactivity, DHIC, outlet obstruction, and detrusor underactivity (as well as many medical conditions). Voiding symptom scores, such as the American Urological Association benign prostatic hypertrophy symptom score (Barry et al. 1992), provide useful measures of symptom severity, but they lack specificity and should never be used diagnostically.

In addition to quantifying voiding symptoms, it is crucial to explore their impact and bother with the incontinent person. Patients and health-care professionals often diverge in their assessment of incontinence impact (DuBeau et al. 1998), and interpatient variability is the rule (Jeter and Wagner 1990); the lesson is never to assume, but always to enquire specifically how an individual (or caregiver) is affected. General areas to discuss are activities of daily living, recreational activities, social interactions, emotional coping, interpersonal relationships (including sexual relations), self-concept and perceptions, and general health perception (DuBeau et al. 1997). In addition, it can be important to determine the most bothersome aspect of incontinence for an individual, especially to help target treatment; for example, if daytime leakage is resolved with treatment but the patient is most bothered by nocturia, then the 'cure' will be unsuccessful.

Voiding record

A diary of continent and incontinent voids is a reproducible and reliable method of establishing the baseline incontinence severity against which to assess treatment (Wyman et al. 1988), and often provides useful diagnostic and therapeutic clues. Patients or caregivers are requested to record, over at least 48 h, the time and volume of every continent and incontinent void, pertinent associated activities (e.g. coffee drinking, exercise), and the hours of sleep. In institutional settings, if staff cannot monitor urine output, they should check continence status (dry, damp, soaked) every 2 h. The voiding record reveals the usual timing and circumstances of incontinence, modal voided volume (a proxy for the functional bladder volume), voiding and incontinence frequency, and the total daytime and nocturnal urine output. The voiding record can help to determine whether nocturia is due to an intrinsic problem (such as detrusor overactivity) or an increased nocturnal diuresis. For example, if nocturnal output (amount voided during hours of sleep plus the first morning void) is 800 ml and the functional bladder volume is 200 ml, then the patient must void three to four times during the night ($800/200 = 4$), and causes of nocturnal diuresis such as pedal oedema, congestive heart failure, or an alcohol 'nightcap' should be sought. Occurrence of incontinence at a stereotypical time of day suggests an association with medication, specific beverages, or activity.

Physical examination

A comprehensive—not just 'below the waistline'—examination is necessary to detect contributory factors, and not to miss serious conditions (e.g. multiple sclerosis and bladder cancer) for which incontinence may be the presenting symptom. General evaluation begins with level of alertness, cognition, functional status, and a check of orthostatic vital signs. Limitations in cervical lateral rotation and lateral flexion, interossei muscle wasting, and abnormal Babinski reflex suggest significant cervical spondylosis or stenosis. Dimpling or hair tuft at the spinal cord base suggest occult dysrhaphism (incomplete spina bifida). Volume overload should be evaluated by cardiovascular examination and a check for peripheral oedema. Although insensitive, abdominal palpation may reveal bladder distension. The neurological examination should be thorough, and include evaluation of sacral root integrity by perineal sensation, resting and volitional tone of the anal sphincter, anal 'wink' (visual or palpated anal contraction in response to a light scratch of the perineal skin lateral to the anus), and bulbocavernosus reflex (similar anal contraction in response to a light squeeze of the clitoris or glans penis). All people should be checked for rectal masses and impaction; in men, the prostate consistency and symmetry should be checked (however, estimation of prostate size by digital examination is inaccurate). Uncircumcised men should be checked for phimosis, paraphimosis, and balanitis, with subsequent replacement of the foreskin.

In women, the vaginal mucosa should be inspected for atrophy (thinning, paleness, loss of rugae, narrowing of the introitus by posterior synechia, vault stenosis) and inflammation (erythema, petechiae, telangiectasia, friability, urethral meatal caruncle). To assess pelvic support, remove the top blade of a speculum and hold the bottom blade firmly against the posterior vaginal wall for support; ask the woman to cough, looking for whether the urethra remains firmly fixed or instead swings quickly forward (indicating urethral hypermobility), and for bulging of the anterior vaginal wall (cystocele). Check for rectocele by turning the speculum to support the anterior vaginal wall, and asking the woman to cough again.

Clinical testing

A clinical stress test provides excellent specificity if positive, even in frail institutionalized women (Resnick et al. 1996), although it can be insensitive if the patient cannot co-operate, is inhibited, or the bladder volume is low. Leakage instantaneous with cough is diagnostic of stress incontinence, while a delay of several seconds before leakage suggests stress-induced detrusor overactivity. For best results, ensure that the patient has not recently voided, maintains a relaxed perineum, and gives a single vigorous cough (with multiple coughs, determining whether leakage is instantaneous or delayed is difficult).

Having the patient void provides an opportunity to measure the urine flow rate (when feasible), and most importantly the postvoiding residual volume. A normal flow rate (peak flow of 12 ml/s or more for a void of at least 200 ml) is useful for excluding outlet obstruction in men; low flow rate is non-diagnostic as it can be due to either obstruction or detrusor underactivity (DuBeau 1996a). An elevated postvoiding residual volume (greater than 50 ml) can contribute to frequency (because the bladder refills to its usual voiding volume more quickly), and may exacerbate stress incontinence (because of the constant presence of urine in the bladder). A postvoiding residual volume over 200 ml suggests detrusor weakness or obstruction; potential hydronephrosis should be excluded by ultrasound in men (DuBeau 1996a), but it rarely occurs in elderly women in whom obstruction is unlikely.

Laboratory tests

Renal function and glucose, calcium, and vitamin B_{12} levels should be tested if recent results are unavailable. Urinalysis, and culture if indicated, should be completed for all patients. Urine cytology and cystoscopy are indicated only if haematuria or pelvic pain are present.

Urodynamic testing

The role of urodynamic testing in the routine evaluation of incontinent older people is controversial. Although urodynamics provide a diagnostic gold standard, it is invasive, expensive, requires special equipment and training, and is not widely available outside tertiary centres. Given the multifactorial nature of geriatric incontinence, lower urinary tract pathology is rarely the only aetiological factor, and misplaced focus on urodynamic diagnosis may detract from more relevant precipitants. Moreover, some incontinence therapies—most notably bladder retraining and oestrogen—are effective for several types of incontinence (see below). Precise diagnosis is most important when surgical treatment is considered for stress incontinence and outlet obstruction, because these treatments are invasive and ineffective for detrusor overactivity, DHIC, and detrusor weakness, all of which can mimic stress incontinence and obstruction. Thus, in general, urodynamics should be considered when surgical intervention is desired, if the diagnosis is unclear, or empirical therapy has failed (Resnick 1988). Clinicians should be aware of what information urodynamic tests can and cannot provide (Abrams et al. 1988). Cystometry demonstrates only bladder proprioception, capacity, detrusor stability, and contractility; carbon dioxide cystometry may be unreliable because the gas is compressible and can irritate the bladder. Simultaneous measurement of abdominal pressure is necessary to exclude the effects of abdominal straining and detect DHIC. Fluoroscopic monitoring, abdominal leak-point pressure, or profilometry are required to detect and quantify stress incontinence. Pressure–flow studies are needed if obstruction is suspected.

Bedside cystometric testing was popularized to detect uninhibited contractions and to measure bladder capacity and postvoiding residual volume, especially in frail older patients. It is performed by having the patient void, measuring the postvoiding residual volume by catheterization, and then filling the bladder via a syringe attached to the same catheter; involuntary contractions are identified by a rise in fluid level in the syringe column. Although one study found that bedside cystometry had moderate sensitivity and specificity for detrusor overactivity in ambulatory older patients (Ouslander et al. 1988), its true utility is unclear. Among community-dwelling elderly people, its marginal benefit over history and physical examination is unknown, and in long-term care populations, low pressure DHIC contractions can be missed and it may be difficult to differentiate detrusor overactivity from abdominal straining (DuBeau and Resnick 1991).

Diagnostic approach

In summary, a stepped approach to diagnosis begins with identification and correction of all potential 'transient' precipitants and exacerbating factors. Secondly, if incontinence persists, consider whether detrusor overactivity is likely based on the presence of precipitant urgency. Thirdly, if the stress test is positive, stress incontinence is likely; consider intrinsic sphincter deficiency if there is previous urethral surgery, severe atrophic change, or continuous leakage. Fourthly, consider bladder emptying efficiency based on the postvoiding residual volume; assuming that medication effects have been excluded, in women an elevated postvoiding residual volume suggests DHIC or detrusor weakness, while in men (and women with antecedent pelvic surgery or radiation) outlet obstruction is also possible. When possible, use flow rate to exclude obstruction; otherwise, precise diagnosis, if desired, requires urodynamic evaluation.

Treatment

While identifying the lower urinary tract pathology responsible for incontinence is important, correction of exacerbating factors is always a critical, and should be the primary, component of the treatment plan. Because age-associated changes in the lower urinary tract and other organ systems render elderly people more vulnerable to developing symptoms from additional insults (e.g. medical conditions and medications), correction of these insults alone can often relieve incontinence (Resnick 1988). A multifactorial approach designed to relieve the most bothersome aspects of incontinence for the individual is the key to success. In all cases, a stepped strategy moving from least to more invasive treatments should be used, with behavioural methods tried before medication, and both tried before surgery (Fantl et al. 1996). Treatment aimed at simply decreasing the number of incontinent episodes—the focus of nearly all treatment trials to date—may not be sufficient to improve quality of life for people most bothered by the timing or inconvenience of incontinence, nocturia, or leakage with exercise. Evidence-based evaluation of the efficacy of most incontinence therapy is now available (Fantl et al. 1996) and is summarized in Table 4. A description of diagnosis-based therapy follows below.

Table 4 Evidence-based efficacy of treatments for urge and stress incontinence

Type of incontinence/target population	Treatment	Efficacy	Evidence[a]
Urge incontinence			
	Behavioural		
Cognitively intact	Bladder retraining	⩾50% decrease in UI episodes in 75% of women	A
	Pelvic muscle exercises	Even in conjunction with bladder retraining, efficacy less than that for stress UI (see below); limited data	B
Dependent, cognitively impaired	Prompted voiding	Average reduction 0.8–1.8 UI episodes daily	A
Voiding record available	Habit training	⩾25% decrease in UI episodes in one-third of patients	B
Unable to toilet independently	Scheduled toileting	30%–80% decrease in UI episodes	C
	Medication		
	Oxybutynin	15%–60% decrease in UI episodes over placebo; side-effects common	A
	Tolterodine	12%–18% decrease in episodes over placebo; side-effects approximately 20% less than other muscarinic agents at maximal dose	A
	Propantheline	13%–17% decrease in UI episodes over placebo (NH patient data only); side-effects common	B
	Dicyclomine	42% improvement over placebo	B
	Tricyclic antidepressants	Decrease in nocturnal UI; side-effects common	B
	Hyoscyamine; calcium blockers	Insufficient data	C
	NSAIDs	Limited data in women: 25% decrease in UI episodes over placebo	C
	Flavoxate	Not efficacious	A
Nocturnal enuresis	Vasopressin	Insufficient data in adults	C
Stress incontinence			
	Behavioural		
Women	PME	56%–95% decrease in UI episodes; efficacy dependent on programme intensity	A
	PME and biofeedback	50%–87% improvement	A
	PME and vaginal cones	68%–80% cured or greatly improved (no data on postmenopausal women)	B
Men, postprostatectomy	PME	In conjunction with biofeedback; limited data	C
Women, stress ± urge	Electrical stimulation	50%–94% cure or improvement rate	B
Mixed stress and urge, cognitively intact	Bladder retraining	⩾50% decrease in UI episodes in 75% of patients	A
Mixed stress and urge; dependent, cognitively impaired	Prompted voiding	Average reduction 0.8–1.8 UI episodes daily	A
Mixed stress and urge, voiding record available	Habit training	⩾25% decrease in UI episodes in one-third of patients	B
Mixed stress and urge, unable to toilet independently	Scheduled toileting	30%–80% decrease in UI episodes	C

Table 4 *continued*

Type of incontinence/target population	Treatment	Efficacy	Evidence[a]
	Medication		
Women	α-Adrenergic agonists	0–14% cure, 20%–60% of patients with subjective improvement over placebo	A
Women	α-Adrenergic blockers plus oestrogen	More efficacious than α-agonists alone	A
Women	Oestrogens	30% decrease in UI episodes over placebo; other systemic benefits may exist	B
	Imipramine	Very limited data	C
	Propranolol	Insufficient data	C
	Surgery		
Women	Retropubic suspension	Cure 79%, cure or improvement 84%[b]; complications 18% (range 6%–57%)	B
Women	Needle suspension	Cure 74%, cure or improvement 84%[b]; complications common	B
Women	Anterior vaginal repair	Cure 65% (range 30%–90%), cure or improvement 74% (range 30%–90%)[b]; complication data limited	B
Women with ISD, coexistent hypermobility	Vaginal sling	Cure 78%–84%, cure or improvement 84%–92%[b]; complications less likely with fascial than with synthetic slings	B
Women with ISD	Periurethral bulking injections	Cure 50% (range 8%–100%), cure or improvement 67%	B
Women with ISD	Artificial sphincter	Cure 77%, cure or improvement 80%; high complication rate	B
Men with ISD	Periurethral bulking injections	Cure 20% (range 0–66%), cure or improvement 42% (range 0–80%)	B
Men with ISD	Artificial sphincter	Cure 66% (range 33%–88%), cure or improvement 85% (range 75%–95%); high complication rate	B

ISD, intrinsic sphincter deficiency; NH, nursing home; NSAIDs, non-steroidal anti-inflammatory drugs; PME, pelvic muscle exercise; UI, urinary incontinence.

[a] Evidence strength: A, randomized controlled studies; B, case–control studies; C, case descriptions/expert opinion.
[b] Subjective cure may be less owing to persistent or *de novo* urge incontinence or voiding difficulty.
Data from Fantl *et al.* (1996).

Urge incontinence

Behavioural treatment for urge incontinence is based on two principles: frequent voluntary voiding to keep the bladder volume low, and rehabilitation of central nervous system and pelvic mechanisms to inhibit detrusor contractions. The specific method employed depends on the individual's cognitive and functional status. For cognitively intact people, bladder retraining is used; this comprises timed voiding while awake (with initial frequency based on the smallest modal interval between voids, as noted in the voiding record) and suppression of any intervening precipitant urgency using relaxation techniques (Fantl *et al.* 1991). Patients are instructed to stand still or sit down when a precipitant urge occurs, and to concentrate on making the urge decrease and pass; taking a deep breath and letting it out slowly, or visualizing the urge as a 'wave' that peaks and then falls, may be helpful. Once they feel in control of the urge, they

should walk slowly to a bathroom and void. When the individual can go 2 days without leakage, the time between scheduled voids is increased by 30 to 60 min, and this process is continued until the person voids every 3 to 4 h without intervening leakage. Supplemental biofeedback may be very helpful for some women (Burgio *et al.* 1998). Successful bladder retraining usually takes several weeks; patients need reassurance to proceed despite initial failure to suppress urgency and incontinence.

Alternative behavioural methods for cognitively impaired patients unable to learn urge suppression are habit training (timed voiding with the interval based on an individual's usual voiding schedule, as seen on a voiding record), scheduled voiding (timed voiding using an arbitrarily set interval, usually every 2 to 3 h; Burgio *et al.* 1994), and prompted voiding. Prompted voiding has three components: regular monitoring with encouragement of incontinent people to report their continence status, prompting to toilet on a scheduled basis, and praise and positive feedback when individuals are continent and attempt to toilet. People most likely to respond to prompted voiding are those with who void less than four times every 12 h during the day and who toilet correctly over 75 per cent of the time in an initial trial (Schnelle 1990). Each of these methods requires training, motivation, and continued effort by patients and/or caregivers; special attention and organization is often needed in institutionalized settings, especially to ensure the durability of any treatment success (Schnelle *et al.* 1991).

When behavioural methods alone are unsuccessful, bladder-suppressant medications can be added. Although these medications usually do not ablate detrusor overactivity, they can improve continence (Fantl *et al.* 1996). Choice of drug depends on efficacy, side-effects, and comorbid conditions that may benefit from or be exacerbated by the medication (e.g. tricyclic antidepressants helping both depression and incontinence). Lack of response to one agent does not preclude response to another, and a low-dose combination of agents may work when side-effects from higher doses of single agents are intolerable. Oxybutynin has the best demonstrated efficacy; the initial dosage is 2.5 mg two to three times daily, followed by titration as needed up to 20 mg/day in divided doses. Its quick onset of action makes it useful when protection is wanted at specific times, and it can decrease frequency even if incontinence is not abolished (Szonyi *et al.* 1995). Anticholinergic side-effects can be limiting; constipation and compensatory fluid intake for xerostomia may exacerbate incontinence. Dentulous patients need regular dental care because xerostomia predisposes to caries. The postvoiding residual volume should be monitored, as worsening of incontinence with bladder suppressants can result from subclinical retention and requires lower (not higher) drug dosages.

Other alternative agents are tolterodine (1–2 mg twice daily; efficacy similar to oxybutynin but with less prevalent side-effects), propantheline (15–30 mg three to five times daily; poor bioavailability requires that it be taken on an empty stomach), dicyclomine (10–20 mg three times daily), tricyclic antidepressants (e.g. imipramine 10–25 mg once to four times daily), and oestrogens for postmenopausal women (see below). Hyoscyamine, calcium-channel blockers, and non-steroidal anti-inflammatory agents are also used, but efficacy data are limited. Randomized studies demonstrate that flavoxate is ineffective. Although vasopressin is useful in children with enuresis, initial studies show lower efficacy in elderly people (Seiler *et al.* 1992), and its expense and risks of congestive failure and hyponatraemia argue against routine use in elderly people.

In patients with DHIC, careful monitoring for urinary retention is crucial when suppressant medications are used. Double voiding and a Valsalva or Credé manoeuvre may help improve bladder emptying in such patients. Every effort should be made to prevent and treat constipation. If feasible and acceptable to the patient, another approach is to induce retention with bladder-suppressant medication, and empty the bladder by intermittent clean catheterization several times daily.

The high morbidity of augmentation cystoplasty surgery limits its use to individuals with profoundly severe urge incontinence, usually younger people with poorly compliant bladders secondary to neurological disease (Khoury and Webster 1990).

Stress incontinence

Pelvic muscle exercises are the cornerstone of non-invasive treatment for stress incontinence. The purpose of pelvic muscle exercises is to strengthen the muscular components of the urethral closure mechanism using principles of strength training, that is, small numbers of isometric repetitions at maximal exertion (Wall and Davidson 1992). Unfortunately, much professional and lay misinformation about pelvic muscle exercises is promulgated; people who report 'failing' previous pelvic muscle exercise trials may have used inadequate methods. For best efficacy, pelvic muscle exercises require careful instruction and monitoring by health professionals, and, most importantly, diligent performance by motivated patients; poor compliance occurs even with close monitoring (Wells *et al.* 1991). Pelvic muscle exercise instruction should focus on isolation of pelvic muscles, avoidance of buttock, abdomen, or thigh muscle contraction (Bump *et al.* 1991), moderate repetitions of the strongest contraction possible (typically, repeating sets of ten contractions three to ten times daily), and maintenance of the contraction for progressively longer times (up to 10 s, if possible). Adjuncts to pelvic muscle exercises that may be helpful for some patients include biofeedback monitoring to teach correct muscle contraction and monitor progress, electrical stimulation devices to implement pelvic muscle contractions, and progressively weighted cones that are retained in the vagina during ambulation (Fantl *et al.* 1996). Pessaries may benefit women with stress incontinence exacerbated by bladder or uterine prolapse. The type of pessary chosen depends on the size of the prolapse and whether the patient or others will provide pessary care; cube pessaries are the easiest for older women to insert, but require daily removal for cleaning because of copious vaginal discharge (Zeitlin and Lebherz 1992).

Low-dose systemic or topical oestrogen (0.3–0.6 mg conjugated oestrogen orally daily, or vaginal cream daily) can reduce stress (and urge) incontinence in postmenopausal women (Fantl *et al.* 1994); in addition, oestrogen alleviates dyspareunia and possibly recurrent cystitis, as well as providing possible protective cardiovascular (and perhaps cognitive) effects. Although the intracellular biochemical response may take weeks, the symptomatic response is usually much faster. Assessment of the maturation index of the vaginal epithelium can gauge the epithelial response to oestrogen; with treatment, the percentage of superficial cells should increase while that of intermediate and parabasal cells should decrease. While the duration of therapy has not been well established, one approach is to administer a low-dose daily oestrogen for 1 to 2 months and then increase the dosing interval; after 6 months, oestrogen can be discontinued entirely in some patients, or continued as infrequently as twice to four times monthly (Resnick 1988). With relatively short courses of low-dose oestrogen, the potential carcinogenic effect on uterine and breast tissue should be small. However, if long-term treatment is desired, addition of daily or cyclic progestogen is prudent.

α-Adrenergic agonists are also effective for stress incontinence because they stimulate urethral smooth muscle contraction. Oestrogen can increase α-receptor number and responsiveness, and potentiate α-adrenergic agonist efficacy (Fantl *et al.* 1996). Sustained-release preparations, such as long-acting propanolamine, are preferable. These agents should not be used in patients with hypertension or significant coronary disease. Imipramine, with its dual α-agonist and anticholinergic actions, can be used in women with mixed stress and

Table 5 Probability of voiding symptom improvement with treatments for benign prostatic hyperplasia

Treatment	Median probability (90% CI) (%)
Placebo	45 (26–65)
Watchful waiting	42 (31–55)
α-Blocker	74 (59–86)
Finasteride	67 (54–78)
Balloon dilation	57 (37–76)
Prostate incision	80 (78–83)
Transurethral resection	88 (75–96)
Open prostatectomy	98 (94–99.8)

CI, confidence interval.
Data from McConnell et al. (1994).

urge incontinence, although if the postvoiding residual volume increases stress leakage could be made worse, and efficacy data are lacking.

Surgical correction offers the highest cure rates for stress incontinence even in elderly women (Griffith-Jones and Abrams 1990; Nitti et al. 1993), although at a cost of increased morbidity. The choice of surgery depends on the underlying defect. Bladder-neck suspension procedures, such as the transvaginal Burch colposuspension or minimally invasive needle vaginal suspensions (Pereya, Stamey, and Raz procedures), are used for urethral hypermobility and genuine stress incontinence. Complications include urinary retention and vaginal wall prolapse. Elderly women may be less tolerant of the major abdominal surgery and longer recovery period of the Marshall–Marchetti–Krantz bladder-neck suspension. Anterior colporrhaphy is less effective for incontinence and is not recommended (Fantl et al. 1996). 'Sling' procedures, using autologous or synthetic

material to support the urethra (Blaivas and Jacobs 1991), and periurethral bulking injections with collagen or autologous fat are preferable for type III incontinence. 'Slings' are also used by some surgeons for urethral hypermobility, although long-term efficacy data are lacking.

Unfortunately, curative treatment for men with postprostatectomy stress incontinence is often elusive. For milder cases, pelvic muscle exercises and sometimes bulking injections can be helpful, while severe cases often require supportive management with protective garments or catheters. Cure rates with artificial sphincter replacement are only 50 per cent, even with experienced surgeons, and the morbidity (including reoperation) can be as high as 40 per cent (Montague 1992; Perez and Webster 1992).

Overflow incontinence

Treatment of overflow incontinence depends on its aetiology. For men with outflow obstruction from benign prostatic hypertrophy, a range of medical and surgical alternatives are available, some of which are applicable even in frail people. A summary of benign prostatic hypertrophy treatment efficacy is provided in Table 5; detailed discussion of benign prostatic hypertrophy therapy is available elsewhere (e.g. DuBeau 1996a). In elderly men with obstruction and associated urge incontinence, transurethral resection may lead to decreased incontinence, especially for men with the most severe obstruction (Gormley et al. 1993). Outlet obstruction should be considered in women with previous vaginal or urethral surgery; treatment by unilateral suture removal or urethrolysis (remobilization of adhesions) can restore continence.

For detrusor underactivity, treatment remains supportive. Of course, drugs that impair detrusor contractility and increase urethral tone should be decreased or stopped, and any constipation treated. Bethanachol chloride is ineffective for improving bladder emptying (Finkbeiner 1985), except possibly for patients with overflow incontinence who must remain on an anticholinergic agent (generally, an antidepressant or antipsychotic). With motivated patients and caregivers, intermittent clean catheterization can provide effective

Table 6 Incontinence centres

Country	Address	Telephone
Australia	Continence Foundation of Australia Ltd, 3rd Floor, VACC House, 464 St Kilda Road, Melbourne, Victoria 3004	(03) 820 2396
Denmark	Dansk Inkontinensforening, Post Box 4097, 6715 Esbjerg	(45) 75 1553 53
Germany	Gesellschaft für Inkontinenzhilfe e. V., Friedrich-Ebert-Strasse 124, 3500 Kassel	(05) 61/78 0604
Ireland	The Irish Incontinence Interest Group, 66 Andersonstown Park, Belfast, Northern Ireland BT11 8FG	(0232) 611679
Japan	Japan Continence Action Society, Continence Centre, 9–15 Zenpukuji 1-Chome, Suginami-Ku, Tokyo 167	(3) 3301 3860
Netherlands	Stichting Incontinentie Nederland, University Hospital Maastricht, Department of Urology, PO Box 5800, 6202 AZ Maastricht	(043) 87 65 43
New Zealand	ACA New Zealand, Department of Medicine, Dunedin University, Dunedin	
United Kingdom	The Continence Foundation, The Basement, 2 Doughty Street, London WC1N 2PH	(0171) 404 6875
United States	The Simon Foundation, PO Box 815, Wilmette, IL 60091	(708) 864 3913

management; sterile intermittent catheterization is preferred for frailer patients and in institutionalized settings to minimize infection risk (Fantl *et al.* 1996). Improved bladder emptying may be possible with Credé or Valsalva manoeuvres during voiding, 'double' voiding to empty the bladder as much as possible, or simply unhurried voiding (Root 1979).

Indwelling catheters should be used only for decompression of acute retention, for protection of wounds, or as a last resort in frail patients in whom other treatment is not feasible. In acute retention, decompression should be at least 7 days, followed by a voiding trial initiated by catheter removal, not clamping. Prophylactic antibiotics are recommended only with short-term catheterization because of the otherwise high risk of resistant organisms and secondary infections such as *Clostridium difficile* colitis.

Adjunctive measures

General measures that are useful for most patients include fluid management, especially decreasing evening intake in urge incontinent patients (Griffiths *et al.* 1992). When used, pads and protective garments should be tailored to individuals based on their sex and the type and volume of incontinence leakage (Brink 1990); for example, pads designed for menstrual use are often not sufficiently absorbent for sudden larger-volume leakage, and men with postvoiding dribbling may prefer collection sheaths over more bulky pads. Because of the expense of many of these products, some patients may not change pads frequently enough to escape odour and skin breakdown. Medical supply companies and incontinence patient advocacy groups often publish helpful illustrated catalogues of these products to guide selection.

Incontinence resource centres

Incontinence resource centres in various countries are listed in Table 6.

References

Abrams, P., Blaivas, J.G., Stanton, S.L., and Andersen, J.T. (1988). Standardisation of terminology of lower urinary tract function. *Neurourology and Urodynamics*, 7, 403–27.

Baldassare, J.S. and Kaye, D. (1991). Special problems in urinary tract infection in the elderly. *Medical Clinics of North America*, 75, 375–90.

Barry, M.J., Fowler, F.J. Jr, O'Leary, M.P., *et al.* (1992). The American Urological Association symptom index for benign prostatic hyperplasia. *Journal of Urology*, 148, 1549–57.

Blaivas, J.G. and Jacobs, B.Z. (1991). Pubovaginal fascial sling for the treatment of complicated stress urinary incontinence. *Journal of Urology*, 145, 1214–18.

Borrie, M.J. and Davidson, H.A. (1992). Incontinence in institutions: costs and contributing factors. *Canadian Medical Association Journal*, 147, 322–8.

Branch, L.G., Walker, L.A., Wetle T.T., DuBeau, C.E., and Resnick, N.M. (1994). Urinary incontinence knowledge among community-dwelling people 65 years of age and older. *Journal of the American Geriatrics Society*, 42, 1257–61.

Brandeis, G.H., Baumann, M.M., Hossain, M., Morris, J.M., and Resnick, N.M. (1997). The prevalence of potentially remediable urinary

incontinence in frail older people: a study using the Minimum Data Set. *Journal of the American Geriatrics Society*, 45, 179–84.

Brink, C.A. (1990). Absorbent pads, garments, and management strategies. *Journal of the American Geriatrics Society*, 38, 368–73.

Brocklehurst, J.C. (1993). Urinary incontinence in the community—analysis of a MORI poll. *British Medical Journal*, 306, 832–34.

Bump, R.C., Hurt, W.G., Fantl, J.A., and Wyman, J.F. (1991). Assessment of Kegel pelvic muscle exercise performance after instruction. *American Journal of Obstetrics and Gynecology*, 165, 322–9.

Burgio, L.D., McCormick, K.A., Scheve, A.S., Engel, B.T., Hawkins, A., and Leahy, E. (1994). The effects of changing prompted voiding schedules in the treatment of incontinence in nursing home residents. *Journal of the American Geriatrics Society*, 42, 315–20.

Burgio, K.L. Locher, J.L., Goode, P.S., *et al.* (1998). Behavioral vs drug treatment for urge urinary incontinence in older women. *Journal of the American Medical Association*, 280, 1995–2000.

DeLancey, J.O.L. (1988) Structural aspects of the extrinsic continence mechanism. *Obstetrics and Gynecology*, 72, 296–301.

Diokno, A.C. (1990). Diagnostic categories of incontinence and the role of urodynamic testing. *Journal of the American Geriatrics Society*, 38, 300–3.

Diokno, A.C., Brock, B.M., Herzog, A.R., and Bromberg, J. (1990). Medical correlates of urinary incontinence in the elderly. *Urology*, 36, 129–38.

DuBeau, C.E. (1996a). Benign prostatic hyperplasia. In *Geriatric medicine* (3rd edn) (ed. C. Cassell, H. Cohen, E.B. Larson, *et al.*), pp. 557–69. Springer, New York.

DuBeau, C.E. (1996b). Interpreting the effect of common medical conditions on voiding dysfunction in the elderly. *Urology Clinics of North America*, 23, 11–18.

DuBeau, C.E. (1997). Problems in voiding and diseases of the prostate. In *Geriatric medicine: a case-based manual* (ed. J.Y. Wei and M.N. Sheehan), p. 153. Oxford University Press, New York.

DuBeau, C.E. and Resnick, N.M. (1991). Evaluation of the causes and severity of geriatric incontinence: a critical appraisal. *Urology Clinics of North America*, 18, 243–56.

DuBeau, C.E. and Resnick, N.M. (1995). Urinary incontinence and dementia: the perils of guilt by association. *Journal of the American Geriatrics Society*, 43, 310–11.

DuBeau, C.E., Levy, B., Mangione, C.M., and Resnick, N.M. (1998). The impact of urge urinary incontinence on quality of life: importance of patients' perspective and explanatory style. *Journal of the American Geriatrics Society*, 46, 1118–24.

Elbadawi, A., Yalla, S.V., and Resnick, N.M. (1993a). Structural basis of geriatric voiding dysfunction. I. Methods of a prospective ultrastructural/urodynamic study and an overview of the findings. *Journal of Urology*, 150, 1650–6.

Elbadawi, A., Yalla, S.V., and Resnick, N.M. (1993b). Structural basis of geriatric voiding dysfunction. II. Normal versus impaired contractility. *Journal of Urology*, 150, 1657–67.

Fantl, J.A., Wyman, J.F., McClish, D.K., *et al.* (1991). Efficacy of bladder training in older women with urinary incontinence. *Journal of the American Medical Association*, 265, 609–13.

Fantl, J.A., Cardozo, L., and McClish, D.K. (1994). Oestrogen therapy in the management of urinary incontinence in postmenopausal women: a meta-analysis. First report of the Hormones and Urogenital Therapy Committee. *Obstetrics and Gynaecology*, 83, 12–18.

Fantl, J.A., Newman, D.K., Colling, J., *et al.* (1996). *Urinary incontinence in adults: acute and chronic management.* Clinical Practice Guidelines No. 2, 1996 Update, AHCPR Publication No. 96-0682. Public Health Service, Agency for Health Care Policy and Research, Rockville, MD.

Finkbeiner, A. (1985). Is bethanechol chloride clinically effective in promoting bladder emptying? A literature review. *Journal of Urology*, 134, 443–9.

Gormley, E.A., Griffiths, D.J., McCracken, P.N., Harrison, G.M., and McPhee, M.S. (1993). Effect of transurethral resection of the prostate on detrusor instability and urge incontinence in elderly males. *Neurourology and Urodynamics*, 12, 445–53.

Griffith-Jones, M.D. and Abrams, P.H. (1990). The Stamey endoscopic bladder neck suspension in the elderly. *British Journal of Urology*, 65, 170–2.

Griffiths, D.J., McCracken, P.N., Harrison, G.M., and Gormley, E.A. (1992). Characteristics of urinary incontinence in elderly patients studied by 24-hour monitoring and urodynamic testing. *Age and Ageing*, 21, 195–201.

Herzog, A.R. and Fultz, N.H. (1990). Prevalence and incidence of urinary incontinence in community-dwelling populations. *Journal of the American Geriatrics Society*, 38, 273–81.

Herzog, A.R., Diokno, A.C., Brown, M.B., Fultz, N.H., and Goldstein, N.E. (1994). Urinary incontinence as a risk factor for mortality. *Journal of the American Geriatrics Society*, 42, 264–8.

Jeter, K.F. and Wagner, D.B. (1990). Incontinence in the American home: a survey of 36 500 people. *Journal of the American Geriatrics Society*, 38, 379–83.

Khoury, J.M. and Webster, G.D. (1990). Augmentation cystoplasty. *World Journal of Urology*, 8, 203–7.

Kirkland, J.L., Lye, M., Levy, D.W., and Banerjee, A.K. (1983). Patterns of urine flow and excretion in healthy elderly people. *British Medical Journal*, 287, 1665–7.

Koziol, J.A., Clark, D.C., Gittes, R.F., and Tan, E.M. (1993). The natural history of interstitial cystitis: a survey of 374 patients. *Journal of Urology*, 149, 465–9.

McConnell, J.D., Barry, M.J., Bruskewitz, R.C., *et al.* (1994). *Benign prostatic hyperplasia: diagnosis and treatment*. Clinical Practice Guidelines No. 8, AHCPR Publication No. 94-0582. Public Health Service, Agency for Health Care Policy and Research, Rockville, MD.

Montague, D.K. (1992). The artificial urinary sphincter (AS 800): experience in 166 consecutive patients. *Journal of Urology*, 147, 380–2.

Nitti, V.W., Bregg, K.J., Sussman, E.M., and Raz, S. (1993). The Raz bladder neck suspension in patients 65 years old and older. *Journal of Urology*, 149, 802–7.

Ouslander, J.G., Leach, G., and Abelson, S. (1988). Simple versus multichannel cystometry in the evaluation of bladder function in an incontinent geriatric population. *Journal of Urology*, 140, 1482–6.

Ouslander, J.G., Zarit, S.H., Orr, N.K., and Muira, S.A. (1990). Incontinence among elderly community-dwelling dementia patients. Characteristics, management, and impact on caregivers. *Journal of the American Geriatrics Society*, 38, 440–5.

Ouslander, J.G., Palmer, M.H., Rovner, B.W., and German, P.S. (1993). Urinary incontinence in nursing homes: incidence, remission, and associated factors. *Journal of the American Geriatrics Society*, 41, 1083–9.

Perez, L.M. and Webster, G.D. (1992). Successful outcome of artificial urinary sphincters in men with post-prostatectomy urinary incontinence despite adverse implantation features. *Journal of Urology*, 148, 1166–70.

Resnick, N.M. (1984). Urinary incontinence in the elderly. *Medical Grand Rounds*, 3, 281–90.

Resnick, N.M. (1988). Voiding dysfunction in the elderly. In *Neurourology and urodynamics: principles and practice* (ed. S.V. Yalla, E.J. McGuire, A. Elbadawi, and J.G. Blaivas), pp. 303–30. Macmillan, New York.

Resnick, N.M. (1990). Non-invasive diagnosis of the patient with complex incontinence. *Gerontology*, 36 (Supplement 2), 8–18.

Resnick, N.M. and Yalla, S.V. (1987). Detrusor hyperactivity with impaired contractile function: an unrecognised but common cause of urinary incontinence elderly patients. *Journal of the American Medical Association*, 257, 3076–81.

Resnick, N.M., Yalla, S.V., and Laurino, E. (1989). The pathophysiology of urinary incontinence among institutionalised elderly people. *New England Journal of Medicine*, 320, 1–7.

Resnick, N.M., Elbadawi, A., and Yalla, S.V. (1995). Age and the lower urinary tract: what is normal? *Neurourology and Urodynamics*, 14, 577–9.

Resnick, N.M., Brandeis, G.B., Baumann, M.M., DuBeau, C.E., and Yalla, S.V. (1996). Misdiagnosis of urinary incontinence in nursing home women: prevalence and a proposed solution. *Neurourology and Urodynamics*, 15, 599–613.

Root, M.T. (1979). Living with benign prostatic hypertrophy. *New England Journal of Medicine*, 301, 52.

Schnelle, J.F. (1990). Treatment of urinary incontinence in nursing home patients by prompted voiding. *Journal of the American Geriatrics Society*, 38, 356–60.

Schnelle, J.F., Newman, D.R., Fogarty, T.E., Wallston, K., and Ory, M. (1991). Assessment and quality control of incontinence care in long-term nursing facilities. *Journal of the American Geriatrics Society*, 39, 165–71.

Seiler, W.O., Stähelin, H.B., and Hefti, U. (1992). Desmopressin reduces night urine volume in geriatric patients: implication for treatment of the nocturnal incontinence. *Clinical Investigation*, 70, 619.

Skelly, J. and Flint, A.J. (1995). Urinary incontinence associated with dementia. *Journal of the American Geriatrics Society*, 43, 286–94.

Szonyi, G., Collas, D.M., Ding, Y.Y., and Malone-Lee, J.G. (1995). Oxybutynin with bladder retraining for detrusor instability in elderly people: a randomized controlled trial. *Age and Ageing*, 24, 287–91.

Van Arsdalen, K. and Wein, A. (1991). Physiology of micturition and continence. In *Clinical neuro-urology* (2nd edn) (ed. R.J. Krane and M.B. Siroky), pp. 25–82. Little, Brown, Boston, MA.

Wagner, T.H. and Hu, T.W. (1998). Economic costs of urinary incontinence in 1995. *Urology*, 51, 355–61.

Wall, L.L. and Davidson, T.G. (1992). The role of muscular re-education by physical therapy in the treatment of genuine stress urinary incontinence. *Obstetrical and Gynecological Survey*, 47, 322–31.

Wells, T.J., Brink, C.A., and Diokno, A.C. (1987). Urinary incontinence in elderly women: clinical findings. *Journal of the American Geriatrics Society*, 35, 933–9.

Wells, T.J., Brink, C.A., Diokno, A.C., Wolfe, R., and Gillis, G.L. (1991). Pelvic muscle exercise for stress urinary incontinence in elderly women. *Journal of the American Geriatrics Society*, 39, 785–9.

Wetle, T., Scherr, P., Branch, L., *et al.* (1995). Difficulty with holding urine among older persons in a geographically defined community: prevalence and correlates. *Journal of the American Geriatrics Society*, 43, 349–55.

Wilson, I.B. and Cleary, P.D. (1995). Linking clinical variables with health-related quality of life. *Journal of the American Medical Association*, 272, 59–65.

World Health Organization (1978). *Definition of health from preamble to the constitution of WHO basic documents*. World Health Organization, Geneva.

Wyman, J.F., Harkins, S.W., Choi, S.C., Taylor, J.R., and Fantl, J.A. (1987). Psychosocial impact of urinary incontinence in women. *Obstetrics and Gynecology*, 70, 378–81.

Wyman, J.F., Choi, S.C., Harkins, S.W., Wilson, M.S., and Fantl, J.A. (1988). The urinary diary in evaluation of incontinent women: a test–retest analysis. *Obstetrics and Gynecology*, 71, 812–17.

Wyman, J.F., Harkins, S.W., and Fantl, J.A. (1990). Psychosocial impact of urinary incontinence in the community-dwelling population. *Journal of the American Geriatrics Society*, 38, 282–8.

Zeitlin M.P. and Lebherz, T.B. (1992) Pessaries in the geriatric patient. *Journal of the American Geriatrics Society*, 40, 635–9.

15.5 Benign prostatic disease

Roger C. L. Feneley and Andrea M. Cannon

Introduction

The management of the older man who presents with urinary symptoms can be profoundly influenced by the approach adopted by the medical practitioner at the initial consultation. With advancing years both men and women are liable to develop urinary symptoms as part of the natural ageing process; it has been reported that 85 to 95 per cent of elderly men experienced urinary symptoms to varying degrees (Jensen *et al.* 1986). The ageing population and increased public awareness about diseases of the prostate has led to a rise in the number of patients seeking advice from medical practitioners. Urinary symptoms are common but it is important to know whether they are restricting the individual's quality of life; the amount of bother that they cause the patient (the bother factor) is very relevant (Wasson *et al.* 1995). Some patients simply need reassurance; one study found that 20 per cent of men presenting with urinary symptoms were anxious about prostate cancer, but otherwise were not bothered by their symptoms (Cannon *et al.* 1995).

The bladder has been aptly described as the barometer of the emotions and by increasing the patient's level of anxiety, the practitioner merely exacerbates the symptoms. Diagnostic labels such as 'prostatism' can be highly misleading to the apprehensive patient and should be strenuously avoided because their accuracy is suspect and they seriously erode self-confidence. 'Prostatism' implies that the symptoms are due to prostatic obstruction when alternatively they may be related to impaired detrusor contractility, detrusor instability, or a poor habit; 35 to 40 per cent of men with voiding symptoms suggestive of benign prostatic enlargement have no objective urodynamic evidence of obstruction (Abrams and Feneley 1978; Andersen 1982). The symptoms should be referred to as lower urinary tract symptoms until an accurate diagnosis can be established and a methodical approach is required to achieve that. Lower urinary tract symptoms (**LUTS**) are often variable and are poor indicators of the underlying aetiology; the bladder is well recognized as an unreliable witness.

Definitions

Benign prostatic hyperplasia (**BPH**) is a histological diagnosis characterized by a combination of atrophy and proliferation in prostatic glandular and stromal tissue. Postmortem studies show that the first signs of benign prostatic hyperplasia appear before the age of 40 years followed by a rapid increase in prevalence with age; 80 per cent of 80-year-olds have evidence of benign prostatic hyperplasia (Berry *et al.* 1984). While the onset of benign prostatic hyperplasia is dependent upon age and the presence of circulating androgens, it is probably also more preponderant in certain races and families. Various studies have been performed to assess the prevalence of benign prostatic hyperplasia in different communities; its prevalence in Scotland was found to be higher than that in the United States (Guess *et al.* 1993) which was higher than that in Japan (Tsukamoto *et al.* 1995). However, these studies had different response and prostatectomy rates, and therefore need to be interpreted with caution. Another study evaluated male relatives of men who had undergone a prostatectomy under the age of 64 years and found that they had a greater lifetime risk of having a prostatectomy than control subjects (Sanda *et al.* 1994).

Although almost all men develop benign prostatic hyperplasia with increasing age, only about 50 per cent develop a detectable increase in the volume of the prostate gland, termed benign prostatic enlargement (**BPE**). This can be detected by digital rectal examination or more accurately by transrectal ultrasound of the prostate.

Bladder outlet obstruction (**BOO**) is defined urodynamically by pressure–flow studies; a low flow rate associated with a high voiding pressure is indicative of obstruction. Bladder outlet obstruction may be due to benign prostatic enlargement, when it is called benign prostatic obstruction (**BPO**). However, it can also be due to a urethral stricture, stenosis of the bladder neck, or certain neurological conditions. There is a common assumption that lower urinary tract symptoms, benign prostatic enlargement, and bladder outlet obstruction are synonymous but, as demonstrated in Fig. 1, each can occur in isolation.

Natural history of benign prostatic obstruction

Little is known about the natural history of benign prostatic obstruction and therefore it is difficult to determine the effectiveness of the different treatment options available. This results in differences in clinical practice demonstrated by the regional differences in prostatectomy rates in the United Kingdom; the district rates for transurethral resection of the prostate vary from 2.9 to 29.2 per 10 000 male age-matched population (Donovan *et al.* 1992).

Available data suggest that there is little deterioration in symptoms and urodynamic findings for patients with benign prostatic obstruction over the years, supporting a more conservative approach to

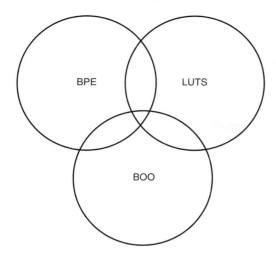

Fig. 1 The association between lower urinary tract symptoms, benign prostatic enlargement, and bladder outlet obstruction, derived from Hald's rings (Hald 1989) by the International Consultation on Benign Prostatic Hyperplasia (Cockett *et al.* 1995).

Table 1 Lower urinary tract symptoms divided into storage and voiding symptoms

Storage symptoms	Voiding symptoms
Frequency	Hesitancy
Nocturia	Poor stream
Urgency	Intermittent stream
(Incontinence)	Terminal dribbling
Suprapubic discomfort	Dysuria
	Straining to void
	Feeling of incomplete bladder emptying

treatment. In a follow-up of 107 patients with symptoms of bladder outlet obstruction 5 years after initial assessment, two developed acute retention and eight underwent elective prostatectomy (Ball *et al.* 1981). The remaining 97 patients were treated conservatively and, of these, 16 considered their symptoms had deteriorated and 31 had noticed an improvement, but the others experienced no change. In the Veterans Affairs Co-operative Study, 600 men with a clinical diagnosis of moderate to severe 'clinical benign prostatic hyperplasia' were randomized to immediate transurethral resection of the prostate or conservative treatment (watchful waiting). Sixty-five (24 per cent) of the watchful waiting group had crossed over to the transurethral resection of the prostate group after 3 years, but only eight developed acute retention, 12 experienced increasing symptoms, and the remainder had deteriorating objective findings such as rising residual volume of urine (Wasson *et al.* 1995). The Olmsted County Study reassessed 1640 patients 18 months after initial presentation with lower urinary tract symptoms, and although there was a minimal increase in urinary symptoms, the bother factor had decreased (Chute *et al.* 1993).

The threat of acute urinary retention is a major cause of anxiety to many elderly men, particularly when a close friend suffers such an outcome. There are no subjective or objective data which lead to its correct prediction, but ongoing prospective studies should produce further information on the natural history of benign prostatic obstruction.

Lower urinary tract symptoms in elderly people

Elderly people visit their doctor for advice for a variety of reasons and it is relevant whether their consultation was initiated by the urinary symptoms or whether these were merely an incidental factor. Although bladder outlet obstruction is common, the clinician needs to be aware of other causes of lower urinary tract symptoms, including detrusor instability, detrusor underactivity, urinary tract calculi, infection, or malignant disease.

Lower urinary tract symptoms indicate a disturbance of bladder/urethral function to store or void urine, and hence they should be considered in two major groups, namely storage (previously termed irritative) symptoms and voiding (previously termed obstructive) symptoms (Table 1).

Storage symptoms

Most elderly men void between six and eight times a day and at least once at night (Carter 1992). Frequency and nocturia can be most accurately assessed by asking the patient to keep a frequency and volume chart, noting the times and the volumes voided.

Urgency is the sudden desire to micturate and can lead to urge incontinence if the individual is unable to reach the toilet in time. This can be exacerbated in elderly people by poor mobility.

In the absence of neurological conditions like dementia, the onset of urinary incontinence at night is invariably a sign of chronic retention with overflow, which can be confirmed by palpation of the distended bladder suprapubically.

Stress incontinence is rare in men, but it may occur in association with a neurological problem or following prostatic surgery if the sphincter mechanism has been damaged or weakened.

Suprapubic discomfort may be related to incomplete emptying of the bladder or intravesical disease, but it is often unrelated to any urinary tract pathology.

Voiding symptoms

Voiding symptoms are commonly described by the patient as variable and are difficult to assess from the history alone.

Hesitancy refers to a delay in initiating micturition and is often most marked in the middle of the night; difficulty initiating voiding after postponing it for a longer interval than usual suggests that the individual may be at risk of acute retention. The long coach journey has an ominous reputation for that!

The urinary flow may be assessed by direct enquiry as to whether the stream 'can hit the wall' or 'splashes the toe-caps of his shoes'. The urine flow rate is closely related to the volume voided and thus a frequency and volume chart, together with a flow rate, is an essential part of the lower urinary tract assessment.

Terminal dribbling is often associated with a poor urinary stream. The patient complains that the urine continues to dribble for some time towards the end of micturition, and is often described as being like a tap that cannot be completely turned off.

Dysuria, a burning discomfort on passing urine, may be associated with a urinary tract infection (cystitis or urethritis).

Straining to void and a feeling of incomplete bladder emptying may be due to bladder outlet obstruction or an underactive detrusor muscle.

Other symptoms

Postmicturition dribble

Many men of all ages are embarrassed by the leakage of urine that occurs down the trouser leg as they walk away from the toilet. This is not a symptom of prostatic obstruction but appears to be a failure of the accessory perineal muscles such as the bulbospongiosum to empty the urethra at the end of micturition. Reassurance that the problem is not indicative of any ominous prognosis and a short demonstration to teach the patient how to compress the bulb of his urethra after micturition can be therapeutic.

Haematuria

Painless haematuria occurring throughout or at the end of micturition is a classic presentation of a bladder tumour and hence demands full investigation with imaging of the urinary tract and a cystoscopy. Initial haematuria is not an uncommon problem in the elderly man. If the history is consistent and clear cut with rapid clearance of blood in the stream or if the blood is noted on the underpants or pyjamas, the problem becomes one of bleeding *per urethram* and invariably arises from veins at the bladder neck or over the prostatic lobes. Under these circumstances urine should be sent for microscopy, culture, and cytological assessment, but it may be wise to postpone an endoscopic examination; the passage of an instrument can precipitate heavy bleeding from the veins which could even necessitate an emergency prostatectomy.

Haematuria is not uncommon after a transurethral resection of the prostate (TURP); Doll *et al.* (1992) reported that 55 per cent of men experienced some haematuria following discharge from hospital. A severe secondary haemorrhage with clot retention is a rare but distressing postoperative complication. Infection should be excluded, but if the haematuria persists it is invariably related to prostatic remnants which may warrant further removal. A transrectal ultrasound examination may provide an accurate estimation of the volume of the residual prostatic tissue.

Haemospermia

Blood-stained or discoloured seminal fluid is another source for alarm amongst elderly men. This is rarely associated with a sinister pathology, but carcinoma of the prostate can occasionally present in this way and a digital rectal examination (DRE) should be performed to exclude this. A urine specimen should be sent for microbiological examination to exclude microscopic haematuria. Transrectal ultrasound has been used to investigate haemospermia but rarely changes

the management of the patient (Andrews *et al.* 1997); it is not recommended as a routine investigation in elderly people, particularly if the digital rectal examination is normal.

Ageing and lower urinary tract symptoms

Elderly men and women can experience similar lower urinary tract symptoms with increasing frequency and urgency of micturition and a variable stream, but women rarely suffer from bladder outlet obstruction. It has been suggested that lower urinary tract symptoms are age associated and may be due in part to habit with frequency dominating the problem. One study compared a group of elderly men presenting with lower urinary tract symptoms thought to be due to benign prostatic hyperplasia with a group of 'normal' elderly men and concluded that those presenting for treatment were similar to the 'normal' group and that obstruction occurred in both groups (Andersen and Nordling 1980). Another study has shown that asymptomatic men experience a reduction in flow rate and increase in detrusor pressure with age (Homma *et al.* 1993).

Age-associated diseases and the differential diagnosis of urinary symptoms

Many diseases can present in the elderly male patient with urinary symptoms, often referred to as 'prostatism'. Neurological conditions such as Parkinson's disease, cerebrovascular disease, or dementia may cause detrusor hyperreflexia or overactivity with loss of cortical inhibition. Diabetes may be associated with either detrusor hyper-reflexia or, if a peripheral neuropathy develops, loss of bladder sensation may lead to overstretching of the bladder and an underactive or acontractile detrusor may result.

Pathology in the sigmoid colon such as diverticulitis or a carcinoma can present initially with urinary symptoms. A low haemoglobin should raise suspicion of gastrointestinal pathology as a potential cause. Injury to the pelvic nerves may occur as a result of radical pelvic surgery, causing temporary or permanent damage to the autonomic nerves supplying the bladder. These patients may present with postoperative retention of urine owing to a failure of detrusor contraction and treatment by long-term or intermittent self-catheterization would be more appropriate than prostatic surgery.

Nocturnal polyuria

Polyuria may be related to a variety of causes such as an excessive fluid intake, diabetes mellitus or insipidus, renal parenchymal disease, or drugs. Several studies have shown that nocturia increases with age (Brocklehurst *et al.* 1971; Barker and Mitteness 1988). Carter (1992) found that nocturia was associated with nocturnal polyuria, the production of more than a third of the 24-h urine output between the hours of midnight and 8 a.m.; mobilization of dependent oedema during sleeping hours may explain the cause in some patients (Guite *et al.* 1988). It is important to recognize nocturnal polyuria from a frequency–volume chart as nocturia is the most persistent symptom following transurethral resection of the prostate (Abrams *et al.* 1979; Doll *et al.* 1992).

If you were to spend the rest of your life with your urinary condition just the way it is now, how would you feel about that	Delighted	Pleased	Mostly satisfied	Mixed about equally satisfied and dissatisfied	Mostly dissatisfied	Unhappy	Terrible
	0	1	2	3	4	5	6

Fig. 2 The quality-of-life question from the International Prostate Symptom Score questionnaire (Cockett et al. 1991).

Assessment of lower urinary tract symptoms

Guidelines for the assessment of lower urinary tract symptoms have been issued by the International Consultation on Benign Prostatic Hyperplasia (Cockett et al. 1996) and include symptom analysis, examination, urine and blood tests, urodynamics, endoscopy, and radiological imaging.

Symptom analysis

Scoring systems can be used to supplement the clinical assessment and to measure the degree of bother experienced by the patient. This has become a popular approach because there is evidence to support the view that patients whose quality of life is most affected respond best to invasive therapy. A number of symptom questionnaires have been produced, such as the Boyarsky questionnaire (Boyarsky et al. 1977) and the Madsen–Iverson questionnaire (Madsen and Iversen 1983), but have not been fully validated. The American Urological Association's seven symptoms index comprises seven questions about lower urinary tract symptoms. It has been fully validated and has been shown to be reliable (Barry et al. 1992), but it does not provide a clear distinction between storage and voiding symptoms. It is also not disease specific; most elderly women do not have bladder outlet obstruction but produce a significant score on the index (Lepor and Machi 1993). This symptom index was adopted at the first International Consultation on Benign Prostatic Hyperplasia, together with a question about quality of life (Fig. 2), and became the widely used International Prostate Symptom Score (Cockett et al. 1991).

Physical examination

Abdominal examination may reveal a palpable bladder due to chronic retention, but a flaccid distension of the bladder can be readily missed. Phimosis, narrowing of the foreskin preventing retraction, may be a simple cause of a poor urinary stream. Digital rectal examination gives an estimate of prostate size and consistency; a normal or 'benign' prostate feels smooth with preservation of the median sulcus between the two lateral lobes, whereas a malignant prostate feels hard and irregular. However, the sensitivity and specificity of digital rectal examination for prostate cancer is only about 30 per cent. As discussed above, it is important to realize that an enlarged prostate does not always account for urinary symptoms and does not always cause obstruction.

Neurological examination may assist in the assessment as a wide range of neurological problems can present with urinary symptoms; perianal sensation and anal tone which are supplied by the same sacral segments (S2–S4) that innervate the bladder can be assessed at the same time as the digital rectal examination. Peripheral oedema and signs of congestive cardiac failure may alert the clinician to the possibility of nocturnal polyuria.

Frequency and volume chart

The simplest and most constructive method of assessing frequency of micturition is to invite the patient to record the time and volume of urine passed on each occasion over a period of 5 to 7 days. A chart of this type provides the most valuable objective record of the patients' problem; combined with a simple instruction sheet about how the bladder functions as a storage tank, the chart can prove to be therapeutic. Bailey et al. (1990) showed that 94 per cent of patients could complete the chart properly prior to their clinic appointment by following written instructions.

Analysis of the chart can provide useful information if interpreted correctly but the terminology requires careful definition; the largest volume of urine passed at one void, for example, is termed the maximum functional bladder capacity and this is usually the first void of urine in the morning after a night of sleep. The structural bladder capacity is the sum of the functional bladder capacity plus the residual urine retained in the bladder after micturition, and the modern hand-held bladder scanner provides a quick way of assessing the latter.

Abrams and Klevmark (1996) correlated the pattern of frequency and urgency with particular types of bladder or urethral pathology; patients who passed reduced or fixed volumes by day or night should raise clinical suspicion of possible intravesical pathology such as carcinoma in situ. A psychosomatic cause of frequency may be suspected when the chart shows that the individual sleeps through the night with minimal disturbance, passes a normal large volume of urine on waking, and then proceeds to pass small frequent volumes throughout the day. A recently bereaved widower may present in this way.

Urine and blood tests

A urine dip-test should always be performed in patients with lower urinary tract symptoms. Haematuria, pyuria, proteinuria, glycosuria, and the presence of nitrites can all be detected by urinalysis, but a false-positive result may be obtained if the patient has a phimosis. Modern urinalysis strips also test for leucocyte esterase which is a sensitive test for a urinary tract infection. If a urinary tract infection is suspected a midstream specimen of urine should be obtained to identify the causal micro-organism. Microscopic haematuria should be investigated appropriately.

Measurement of serum creatinine and urea is recommended by the international guidelines because a significant number of patients with benign prostatic obstruction have renal impairment; one study of patients undergoing surgical treatment for benign prostatic obstruction found abnormal values in 13 per cent of patients (Andersen

Table 2 Age-specific PSA ranges

Age (years)	40	45	50	55	60	65	70	75
PSA (ng/ml)	1.9	2.6	3.2	4.3	5.3	6.0	6.6	7.5

Reproduced with permission from De Antoni et al. (1996).

et al. 1995). A full blood count is important if haematuria is present or gastrointestinal pathology suspected, and a blood glucose estimation is recommended.

Prostate-specific antigen (**PSA**) has been shown to be a useful tumour marker, but it is not a cancer-specific marker; it is produced by normal prostate, benign prostatic hyperplasia, and prostate cancer, and has been detected in women. Various methods have been used to improve the usefulness of PSA in cancer detection including age-specific reference ranges (Table 2), PSA density (PSA concentration divided by prostatic volume), free or unbound PSA, and PSA velocity (the rate of change of PSA with time). Despite the widespread use of PSA in the United States as a screening test for prostate cancer, there is currently little evidence to support such a role. The PSA test lacks sufficient specificity producing a false-positive result in about two-thirds of asymptomatic men (Woolf 1995), and the benefits of the early diagnosis and treatment of prostate cancer are controversial. Two recent reviews by the Health Technology Assessment Programme concluded that there was no role for routine screening for prostate cancer at present (Chamberlain et al. 1997; Selley et al. 1997).

Urodynamic investigations

Uroflowmetry

This is the simplest non-invasive urodynamic test for recording the urinary flow rate, but to represent the patient's normal performance it should be conducted in an appropriate environment. The dedicated flow clinic is to be recommended, with the flowmeter in a room providing privacy and preferably unencumbered by evidence of electronics. Patients should be able to relax in a waiting room where a high fluid intake can be encouraged to establish diuresis. Two or three flow-rate measurements are ideally performed, rather than a single study. The volumes voided during the flow test are compared to those recorded on the patient's frequency and volume chart to ensure that it is an accurate reflection of the patient's normal voiding pattern. Interpretation of a flow trace involves looking at the flow (Q) pattern and determining the maximum flow rate (Q_{max}). A low Q_{max} usually indicates bladder outlet obstruction but can be due to underactivity of the detrusor muscle. A high Q_{max} is less likely to be associated with bladder outlet obstruction but a proportion of patients with a high Q_{max} will have obstruction, as defined by pressure–flow studies (**pQS**).

Measurement of residual urine

Postvoid residual urine (**PVR**) can be readily measured by a hand-held ultrasound in the uroflowmetry clinic (Fig. 3). It can vary considerably in an individual (Birch et al. 1988); two or three measurements are usually taken but it can only be used as a guide for voiding dysfunction. A large postvoid residual urine may suggest bladder outlet obstruction but can also be due to an underactive detrusor.

Pressure–flow studies

Pressure–flow studies are the only accurate method of diagnosing bladder outlet obstruction by measuring the detrusor pressure and flow rate during voiding. The detrusor pressure is the component of bladder or intravesical pressure produced by the bladder wall itself and is derived by electronic subtraction of the rectal pressure from the bladder pressure. Pressure–flow studies are usually preceded by filling cystometry which gives information about bladder capacity, the presence or absence of detrusor instability, and incontinence. Bladder outlet obstruction can be defined by several different methods including the Abrams–Griffiths nomogram (Abrams and Griffiths 1979) or number (Lim et al. 1994), Schafer's linear passive urethral resistance ratio (**L-PURR**) (Schafer 1985), and the group-specific urethral resistance factor (**URA**) (Griffiths et al. 1989); there is good correlation between the methods. Detrusor pressure at maximum flow and Q_{max} are plotted on the Abrams–Griffiths nomogram to determine if the individual is obstructed; a low flow rate and high detrusor pressure are usually indicative of obstruction. Pressure–flow studies should always be considered in the complicated patient, particularly those with neurological disease, or when the diagnosis is doubtful from the flow studies and surgery is contemplated.

Imaging the urinary tract

The ultrasound scan has introduced a straightforward non-invasive method of checking the upper urinary tract for evidence of obstructive uropathy, the bladder for residual urine, and the prostate for size and consistency as well as other pathologies. A plain radiograph of the kidneys, ureters, and bladder is indicated if urinary tract calculi are suspected.

Chronic retention in the elderly man can be of either a low-pressure or high-pressure type; the former is associated with a normal bladder pressure whilst the latter is characterized by a sustained high pressure during the filling phase of the micturition cycle. The high-pressure bladder leads to dilatation of the upper urinary tract and renal impairment with evidence of hydronephrosis and hydroureter whilst the low-pressure bladder protects the upper tract from this outcome.

Endoscopy

Cystoscopic examination localizes the anatomical site of pathological lesions in the lower urinary tract but it is not an accurate method of assessing prostatic size or the degree of obstruction. It is always performed prior to transurethral resection of the prostate, identifying the urethral stricture or the type of prostatic lobe enlargement.

Treatment

The treatment of benign prostatic disease in the elderly man is essentially either reassurance or the relief of obstruction. The initial assessment of the patient should have established a diagnosis, differentiating the symptoms and severity of prostatic obstruction from those conditions masquerading as benign prostatic disease. Acute presentations are rare in comparison; inflammatory conditions of the

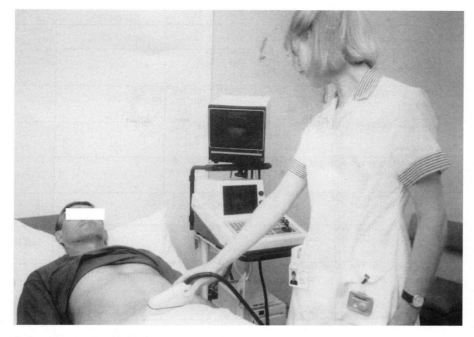

Fig. 3 Measurement of residual urine using a hand-held ultrasound probe.

prostate in this age group are uncommon, but an acute prostatic abscess should be suspected with a history of recurring urinary tract infection and the finding of an acutely tender prostatic lobe.

Acute retention of urine is the most common urological emergency, requiring urgent relief by urethral or suprapubic catheterization. The cause of acute retention is not known; it may occur as a postoperative complication following surgery when acute prostatic infarction has been implicated (Strachan *et al.* 1993) or during the management of an acute medical condition. The volume of residual urine on catheterization should be carefully recorded as it can influence management. If the volume is less than 1 litre, a trial without the catheter may be justified prior to surgery. Failure to re-establish spontaneous micturition or a volume of residual urine greater than 1 litre, signifying a longer standing degree of chronic retention, would be an indication for operative treatment to the prostate.

Chronic retention of urine presenting with overflow incontinence or impaired renal function from obstructive uropathy requires relief of obstruction usually by initial catheterization followed by surgery. A sharp diuresis may follow bladder drainage and the serum electrolytes should be carefully monitored.

The majority of men with benign prostatic obstruction can be reassured that prostatic surgery will not be necessary; objective assessment will be followed by a planned course of management. The options available are watchful waiting, medical treatment, or surgery.

Watchful waiting

Patients with mild to moderate symptoms that are not particularly bothersome should be given a period of conservative management during which they are advised on the amount and type of their fluid intake and instructed on bladder training, particularly if storage symptoms predominate with the passage of small, frequent volumes. The frequency and volume chart (Fig. 4) can be used as a therapeutic

measure. The patient is encouraged to restore the bladder as a storage tank, passing urine by the clock rather than the urge, and gradually extending the intervals between each void. The patient is asked to record a day each week or fortnight on the chart and is encouraged to hold 300 ml or more in the bladder if possible. They are asked to bring the chart back to discuss the results with the clinician and the well-motivated patient will do so.

Drug treatment

Medical treatment of benign prostatic obstruction has transformed the management of elderly people, particularly those who do not wish to undergo surgery but are significantly bothered by their symptoms. There are two main types of medication for benign prostatic obstruction, α-adrenoceptor antagonists (α-blockers) and 5α-reductase inhibitors. Plant extracts (phytotherapy) are a third option but have not been widely used; although some placebo-controlled trials have shown a benefit, several large multicentre randomized trials need to be performed to persuade clinicians of their efficacy.

Alpha-blockers act by blocking the sympathetic adrenergic nerves in the smooth muscle of the bladder neck and prostate. Therefore they act on bladder-neck obstruction as well as benign prostatic obstruction; the smooth muscle around the bladder neck has been termed the preprostatic or sexual sphincter because it is this muscle that closes during ejaculation to prevent retrograde ejaculation of seminal fluid into the bladder. There are two types of α-adreno-receptors, α_1 and α_2, the former being more concentrated in the bladder neck and prostate. Phenoxybenzamine was the first α-blocker to be studied for benign prostatic hyperplasia (Caine *et al.* 1978), but as it blocked both α_1- and α_2-adrenoreceptors, it produced side-effects in 30 per cent of patients because of the wider effect on α_2-adrenoreceptors localized in the peripheral vascular system.

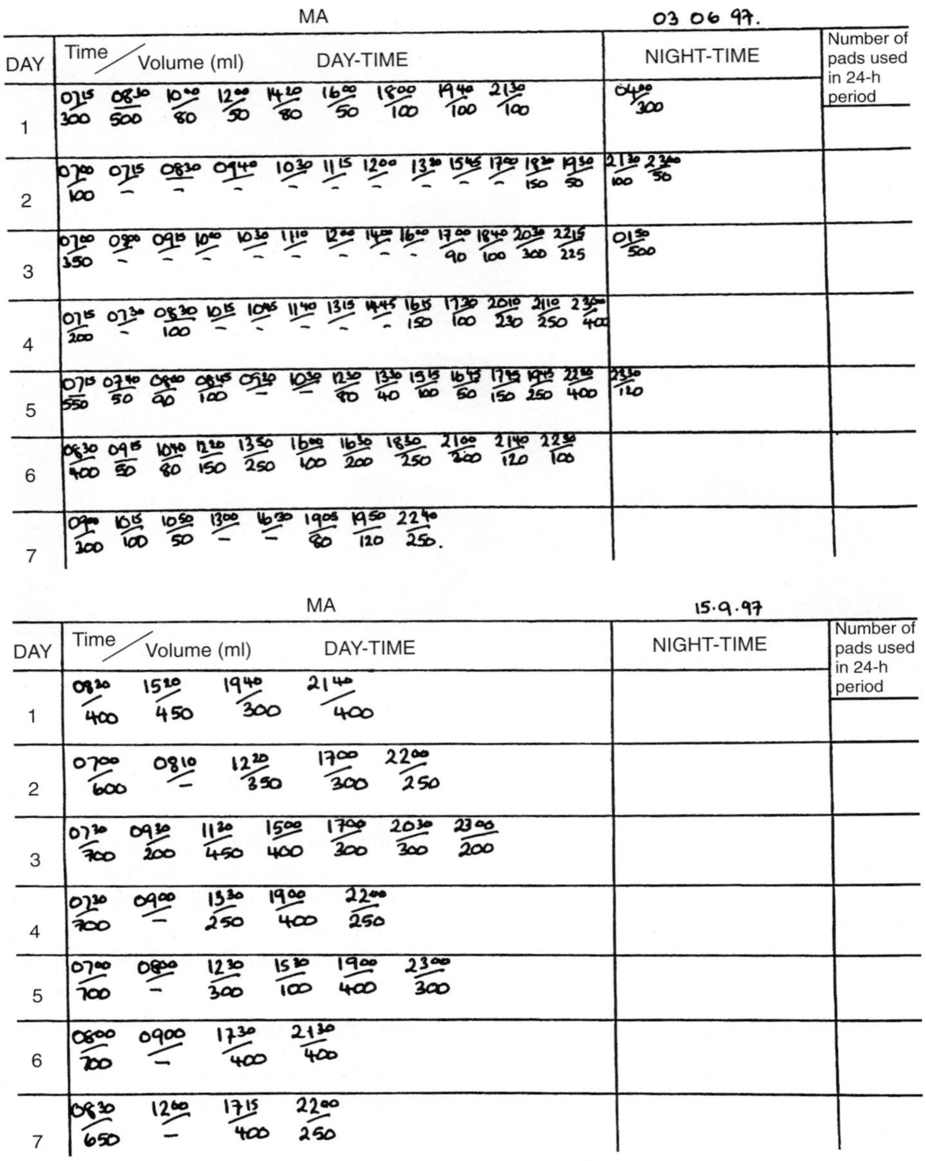

Fig. 4 Frequency and volume chart showing the response of a 72-year-old male patient with lower urinary tract symptoms to bladder training over a 3-month period.

Following this, more selective α_1-blockers have been developed (prazosin, indoramin, terazosin, alfuzosin, and doxazosin), and placebo-controlled studies have demonstrated fewer side-effects than with phenoxybenzamine. All these trials have shown a small improvement in maximum flow rate and a definite symptomatic improvement in patients on active treatment compared with placebo. There is a reported incidence of side-effects in the α_1-blockers in up to 15 per cent of patients, but these are usually mild and do not usually involve withdrawal of the drug. Reported side-effects include headaches, dizziness, drowsiness, and mild postural hypotension.

Tamsulosin is a new drug that is reported to be selective for a subtype of the α_1-adrenoceptor (α_{1A}) and a recent short-term placebo-controlled study (Abrams *et al.* 1995) has shown that it is effective with a side-effect profile similar to that of placebo. The results of a long-term study are awaited.

5α-Reductase inhibitors, such as finasteride, reduce the production of dihydrotestosterone, and act by reducing prostatic growth and may even shrink the prostate. Placebo-controlled trials have shown symptomatic improvement and a reduction in prostatic volume but the patient needs to stay on the drug for at least 6 months to ensure maximum efficacy and this is rather costly. The long-term effects on benign prostatic obstruction are not yet known. The main side-effect is impotence in about 10 per cent of patients (Stoner *et al.* 1994).

Operative treatment

Transurethral prostatectomy remains the gold-standard treatment for benign prostatic obstruction. It has been shown to be effective in both the short term (Doll *et al.* 1992) and the long term (Cannon *et al.* 1996), although up to 25 per cent of patients fail to improve

especially amongst the institutionalized population, will have bacteriuria (Brockleburst *et al.* 1968; Akhtar *et al.* 1972; Boscia *et al.* 1986*a*; Mims *et al.* 1990). In a group of women resident in a geriatric apartment, the frequency of chronic genitourinary or non-specific 'general' symptoms was similar whether or not a woman was bacteriuric (Boscia *et al.* 1986*a*). A prospective randomized blinded study of treatment or no treatment of bacteriuria in institutionalized subjects with incontinence documented no change in degree of chronic incontinence with treatment of bacteriuria (Ouslander *et al.* 1995*b*). Mims *et al.* (1990) reported that frequency, nocturia, urgency, incontinence, and abdominal pain were reported with equal frequency in bacteriuric and non-bacteriuric men. Only dysuria was significantly associated with bacteriuria.

Acute changes in genitourinary symptoms are certainly consistent with symptomatic urinary infection in the elderly population. Such symptoms may be classic lower-tract symptoms such as increased frequency, dysuria, urgency, hesitancy, or suprapubic pain. In addition, new or increased incontinence is a common presentation for acute urinary infection in elderly women. Upper-tract infection may present as a classic pyelonephritis syndrome including fever and flank pain. Individuals with trauma to or obstruction of the urinary tract may present with fever and bacteraemia.

Gross haematuria is frequent in institutionalized populations, but is invariably due to some cause other than bacterial haemorrhagic cystitis (Nicolle *et al.* 1993*b*). However, the majority of subjects with gross haematuria (70 per cent in one study) will be bacteriuric. When gross haematuria occurs, the defect in the mucosal barrier which leads to haematuria may, secondarily, lead to invasive infection and fever. Thus haemorrhagic bacterial cystitis is uncommon, but invasive urinary infection frequently complicates gross haematuria.

The clinical diagnosis of symptomatic infection is frequently problematic in the institutionalized population because of impaired communication and difficulty in identifying symptoms in the presence of the chronic symptoms of multiple comorbid illnesses. It has been suggested that urinary infection may present as subtle changes in resident behaviour or clinical status without findings localized to the genitourinary tract. Currently studies are not available to support this statement, nor identify how frequently this may occur. As the prevalence of positive urine cultures at any time is 30 to 50 per cent in residents of long-term care facilities, individuals with 'subtle changes in clinical status' will frequently have a positive urine culture. Definitive studies which document an improvement in status with antimicrobial therapy have not been reported. Until such studies are reported, a diagnosis of urinary infection should be made with caution in this clinical scenario.

Fever in the institutionalized patient with a positive urine culture, in the absence of localizing genitourinary findings, is seldom due to urinary infection. In fact, less than 10 per cent of such episodes are attributable to a urinary source (Orr *et al.* 1996). The positive predictive value of a positive urine culture for urinary infection in the febrile institutionalized patient is only 12 per cent. Unfortunately, clinical variables which distinguish patients with fever due to urinary infection from those with fever from other causes in the absence of genitourinary signs and symptoms have not been identified. When fever does occur, alternative sources for the cause of fever should be sought, even if the resident is bacteriuric.

Treatment

Asymptomatic infection

Boscia *et al.* (1987) reported a non-significant decrease in the occurrence of episodes of symptomatic urinary infection in a female population resident in a geriatric apartment during the 6 months following treatment of asymptomatic bacteriuria. These symptomatic episodes were not characterized with respect to severity. Prospective randomized comparative trials in elderly institutionalized populations have consistently failed to show any benefits of treatment for asymptomatic bacteriuria (Nicolle *et al.* 1983, 1987*b*; Boscia *et al.* 1987; Abrutyn *et al.* 1994; Ouslander *et al.* 1995*b*). Specifically, treatment of asymptomatic bacteriuria does not improve symptoms of chronic incontinence, does not decrease episodes of morbidity from symptomatic urinary infection, and does not decrease mortality. However, treatment will lead to adverse effects of antimicrobial therapy and promote the emergence of organisms of increased antimicrobial resistance. Thus, for the institutionalized population, asymptomatic bacteriuria should not be treated. This is also probably the case for the non-institutionalized population, but further studies in this group are needed. Following from this, routine screening of elderly populations to identify bacteriuria is not indicated.

Symptomatic infection

Indications for therapy

Symptomatic infection is an indication for treatment with antimicrobial therapy. Urine for culture should be obtained prior to initiating antimicrobial therapy as the wide variety of potential infecting organisms and, especially for the institutionalized population, the likelihood of antimicrobial resistance, mean that optimal therapy requires knowledge of the bacterial isolate and susceptibilities. Diagnostic uncertainty means that a diagnosis of symptomatic urinary infection in institutionalized elderly people will frequently be incorrect. It is not clear, however, how to improve diagnostic accuracy. Currently, the only reasonable approach is to tailor decisions to the individual with respect to empiric antimicrobial therapy for potential urinary infection. Observation and reassessment is the preferred approach where symptoms are not severe and the diagnosis is uncertain.

The selection of an antimicrobial agent for the treatment of symptomatic urinary infection in elderly populations is similar to that in younger populations (Table 3). Antimicrobial pharmacokinetics in elderly people consistently show alterations such as increased volume of distribution and delayed renal clearance. However, these are not of sufficient consistency or magnitude to warrant routine modification in antimicrobial dosing regimens on the basis of age alone (Ljunberg and Nilsson-Ehle 1987). In the presence of renal failure, appropriate dosing modifications should be made.

For oral therapy, nitrofurantoin and co-trimoxazole remain the treatments of choice for susceptible organisms. Several European countries, particularly Sweden and the United Kingdom, have cautioned doctors to avoid co-trimoxazole because of cutaneous side-effects due to the sulpha component. However, there is a long clinical experience with this antimicrobial agent and it is less costly than newer alternatives. It seems premature to argue against using it. Trimethoprim alone is an option where there are concerns about

Table 3 Antimicrobial agents for treatment of urinary infection in elderly people with normal renal function

Agent	Dose
Oral	
Penicillins	
Amoxycillin	500 mg three times daily
Co-amoxiclav	500 mg three times daily
Cephalosporins	
Cephalexin	500 mg four times daily
Cefaclor	500 mg four times daily
Cefadroxil	1 g once or twice daily
Cefixime	400 mg once daily
Cefuroxime axetil	250 mg twice daily
Cefpodoxime proxetil	100–400 mg twice daily
Quinolones	
Norfloxacin	400 mg twice daily
Ciprofloxacin[a]	250–500 mg twice daily
Ofloxacin[a]	200–400 mg twice daily
Enoxacin	200 mg twice daily
Lomefloxacin[a]	400 mg once daily
Fleroxacin[a]	400 mg once daily
Other	
Trimethoprim	100 mg twice daily
Co-trimoxazole[a]	160/800 mg twice daily
Nitrofurantoin	50–100 mg four times daily
Parenteral	
Aminoglycosides (monitor blood levels)	
Gentamicin	1–1.5 mg/kg every 8 h or 4–5 mg/kg every 24 h
Tobramycin	1–1.5 mg/kg every 8 h or 4–5 mg/kg every 24 h
Amikacin	5 mg/kg every 8 h or 15 mg/kg every 24 h
Penicillins	
Ampicillin	1–2 g every 6 h
Piperacillin	3 g every 4 h
Piperacillin + tazobactam	4 g/500 mg every 8 h
Cephalosporins	
Cefazolin	1–2 g every 8 h
Cefotaxime	1–2 g every 8 h
Ceftriaxone	1–2 g once daily
Cefepime	2 g every 12 h
Ceftazidime	0.5–2 g every 8 h
Other	
Aztreonam	1–2 g every 6 h
Imipenem + cilastatin	500 mg every 6 h

[a] These agents may also be given parenterally.

adverse sulpha effects, but some countries report substantial trimethoprim resistance of *E. coli* and other common uropathogens. The quinolones and co-amoxiclav (amoxicillin–clavulanic acid) are effective, but more costly. Intensive quinolone use in nursing homes has led to increased resistance to these agents. They are best reserved for use where resistant organisms or patient intolerance limit other oral antimicrobial agents. Amoxycillin is the therapy of choice for streptococcal infections, including *Enterococcus* species and group B streptococci, but is a second-line agent for Gram-negative organisms

because of the frequency of resistance of organisms to this antimicrobial.

For parenteral therapy, an aminoglycoside remains the initial therapy of choice in subjects with normal renal function because of limited antimicrobial resistance, extensive experience, and documented effectiveness of these agents in the treatment of urinary infection. Ototoxicity or nephrotoxicity are seldom important side-effects if the duration of therapy is limited, with a switch to oral therapy as soon as clinically indicated. Ampicillin may be added for initial empiric therapy if *Enterococcus* is a potential infecting organism. Many other parenteral antimicrobial agents may be effective, but these are more expensive and there is less experience with their use for urinary infection.

Duration of therapy

Optimal duration of antimicrobial therapy varies with sex and clinical presentation. For ambulatory women with acute lower-tract symptoms, 3 days of therapy will be successful in over 50 per cent of episodes. Postmenopausal women, however, have lower success rates with any duration of therapy, and a relatively poorer response with shorter courses (Cardenas *et al.* 1986; Harding *et al.* 1991; Saginur *et al.* 1992). Thus a 7-day course of therapy may be optimal in postmenopausal women, although further studies to define the adverse outcomes and benefits of more prolonged therapy in this population are needed. With upper-tract infection presenting as acute pyelonephritis, 10 to 14 days of therapy should be given. Ambulatory men who present with an initial symptomatic infection should receive antimicrobial agents for 10 to 14 days. If relapse occurs, a prostatic focus of infection is likely and higher success rates will be achieved with retreatment with 6 or 12 weeks of therapy (Gleckman *et al.* 1979; Smith *et al.* 1979).

Prolonged antimicrobial therapy, given for months or years, is seldom indicated for the management of urinary infection in elderly people. More extended therapy for prophylaxis in women with recurrent symptomatic urinary infection or for the treatment of prostatic infection in men is discussed above. Infrequently, prolonged antimicrobial therapy may also be indicated for suppressive therapy (Sheehan *et al.* 1988). Suppressive therapy is given to prevent symptomatic episodes or complications of infection where underlying abnormalities of the genitourinary tract which predispose to urinary infection are present and cannot be corrected. Examples include individuals with infected stones which cannot be removed (Fowler 1996) or with repeated episodes of invasive infection secondary to ureteric strictures or other obstructing lesions. Treatment for suppressive therapy is generally given at higher doses than for prophylactic therapy. The duration is dependent on the clinical response, urine culture results, and the underlying abnormality. A decision to initiate suppressive therapy should be undertaken only in clearly defined clinical situations. Such patients should be reviewed regularly to ensure the therapy remains appropriate and effective.

Outcomes of therapy

Studies have consistently reported a high recurrence rate at 4 to 6 weeks post-therapy following treatment of urinary infection in ambulatory elderly women. Cardenas *et al.* (1986) reported microbiological cure rates with a single dose of cephalexin of 87 per cent for 19- to 24-year-old women, but only 46 per cent for women aged 40 to 70 years. For women treated with either single dose or 3 days of norfloxacin, 91 per cent of those under the age of 40 years were cured, and only 73 per cent of those over 40 years (Saginur *et al.* 1992). For ambulatory men with underlying bacterial prostatitis a recurrence rate of about 70 per cent is anticipated after 10 to 14 days treatment (Gleckman *et al.* 1979; Smith *et al.* 1979).

Early post-treatment recurrence is also characteristic of bacteriuria amongst the institutionalized population. By 6 weeks after therapy at least 50 per cent of men or women treated for either asymptomatic or symptomatic infection have recurrent bacteriuria (Nicolle *et al.* 1983; Renneberg and Paerregaard 1984; Boscia *et al.* 1987; Nicolle 1988*b*; Tzias *et al.* 1990; Flanagan *et al.* 1991; Giamarellou *et al.* 1991; Staszewskia-Pistoni *et al.* 1995). This high frequency of recurrence is similar to the anticipated recurrence rate in populations with complicated urinary infection. Thus prolonged sterilization of the urine is not a realistic goal of treatment for most bacteriuric institutionalized elderly subjects. Therapy should be given to ameliorate symptoms and, in selected circumstances, to prevent complications, but not to sterilize the urine. Following from this, post-therapy urine cultures are not indicated unless urinary symptoms persist or recur.

Long-term indwelling catheters

Indwelling urethral catheters are considered short term if they remain *in situ* for less than 30 days and long term if they are in place for over 30 days. From 5 to 10 per cent of elderly residents in long-term care institutions have long-term indwelling urethral catheters (Kunin 1989; Warren *et al.* 1989). They are used more frequently in women than men, with the principal indications for use being urinary incontinence and retention.

Individuals with long-term indwelling catheters are always bacteriuric, usually with three to five organisms at any time (Warren *et al.* 1987). Organisms gain access to the bladder by both extraluminal and intraluminal routes. A biofilm consisting of bacteria embedded in an extracellular bacterial substance forms along the catheter surface, and organisms within the biofilm survive in a relatively protected environment. The persistent bacteriuria associated with the use of long-term indwelling catheters is not decreased by routine saline or antiseptic irrigation of the catheter, and routine catheter change does not decrease the occurrence of obstruction or complications (Warren 1992). The most effective way to limit bacteriuria associated with long-term indwelling catheters is, of course, to avoid catheter use. Long-term indwelling catheters should only be used in situations where the benefits outweigh possible negative impacts on resident health. Where a decision is made to use a long-term indwelling catheter, this should be reassessed at regular intervals to ensure that the resident still benefits from the intervention.

Infectious complications associated with the indwelling catheter include development of urethritis, periurethral abscesses, obstruction with blockage of the catheter, fever, and bladder stone formation. Bladder stone formation and catheter obstruction occur with urease-producing organisms, particularly *P. mirabilis* and *P. stuartii* (Kunin 1989). The presence of an indwelling catheter is associated with an increased frequency of invasive infection including fever and pyelonephritis compared with bacteriuric residents without indwelling catheters (Warren *et al.* 1987). Some of these episodes are temporally related to catheter manipulation and mucosal trauma. Autopsy studies show an increased prevalence of renal abscess and acute pyelonephritis

in nursing home residents with long-term indwelling catheters compared with those with bacteriuria without catheters (Warren *et al.* 1988). Subjects with chronic indwelling catheters appear to have increased mortality, even following adjustment for other factors which may influence survival (Warren *et al.* 1987; Kunin *et al.* 1992). Thus the resident with a long-term indwelling catheter experiences greater morbidity and, possibly, decreased survival relative to the elderly individual with asymptomatic bacteriuria who does not have an indwelling catheter.

Attempts to treat bacteriuria with antimicrobial agents in an individual with a long-term catheter will not sterilize the urine, but will lead to emergence of organisms of increasing resistance (Alleng *et al.* 1975; Warren *et al.* 1982). The presence of these more resistant organisms will increase the complexity of treatment should symptomatic infection occur. Thus bacteriuria in individuals with long-term indwelling catheters should be treated only if clinical symptoms consistent with urinary infection are identified. Neither the urine culture nor pyuria on urinalysis are useful discriminators to identify symptomatic compared with asymptomatic infection (Steward *et al.* 1985). Some authors have suggested that the catheter should be changed prior to initiation of antimicrobial therapy to remove the bacterial biofilm and limit recurrent infection with the same organism (Grahn *et al.* 1985). This has not yet been documented to lead to improved clinical outcomes. When treatment for symptomatic infection is given, the antimicrobial agent should be selected on the basis of known or expected susceptibilities of the infecting organisms. Assuming clinical response, the duration of antimicrobial therapy should be for as short a period as possible (5–7 days), to attempt to minimize the emergence of resistant organisms.

Future research

Urinary infection is an important problem in elderly populations. The frequency of occurrence and our limited understanding of many aspects of this problem makes further evaluation of the impact, and appropriate management, a priority. Specific needs include population-based studies of the impact of symptomatic infection in community populations, further characterization of the natural history of asymptomatic bacteriuria in non-institutionalized elderly people, and refining our ability to diagnose symptomatic urinary infection in institutionalized populations. Factors contributing to the remarkable prevalence of bacteriuria in older individuals warrant further study, and predictors of symptomatic infection in both institutionalized and non-institutionalized subjects require definition. Finally, the role of asymptomatic bacteriuria as a reservoir for resistant organisms in both catheterized and non-catheterized subjects in the long-term care population needs further assessment. The goals of such studies should be to improve our understanding and management of this very common problem.

References

Abrutyn, E., Mossey, J., Levison, M., Boscia, J., Pitsakis, P., and Kaye, D. (1991). Epidemiology of asymptomatic bacteriuria in elderly women. *Journal of the American Geriatrics Society*, **39**, 388–93.

Abrutyn, E., Mossey, J., Berlin, J.A., *et al.* (1994). Does asymptomatic bacteriuria predict mortality and does antimicrobial treatment reduce mortality in elderly ambulatory women. *Annals of Internal Medicine*, 120, 827–33.

Akhtar, JA.J., Andrews, G.R., Caird, F.I., and Fallon, R.J. (1972). Urinary tract infection in the elderly. A population study. *Age and Ageing*, 1, 48–54.

Alleng, B., Brandberg, A., Seeberg, S., and Svanborg, A. (1975). Effect of consecutive antibacterial therapy on bacteriuria in hospitalised geriatric patients. *Scandinavian Journal of Infectious Diseases*, 7, 201–7.

Avorn, J., Monane, M., Gurwitz, J.H., Glynn, R.J., Choodnovsky, I., and Lipsitz, L.A. (1994). Reduction of bacteriuria and pyuria after ingestion of cranberry juice. *Journal of the American Medical Association*, 271, 751–4.

Bentzen, A. and Vejlsgaard, R. (1980). Asymptomatic bacteriuria in elderly subjects. *Danish Medical Bulletin*, 27, 101–6.

Boscia, J.A., Kobasa, W.D., Abrutyn, E., Levison, M.E., Kaplan, A.M., and Kaye, D. (1986a). Lack of association between bacteriuria and symptoms in the elderly. *American Journal of Medicine*, 81, 979–82.

Boscia, J.A., Kobasa, W.D., Knight, R.A., Abrutyn, E., Levison, M.E., and Kaye, I. (1986b). Epidemiology of bacteriuria in an elderly ambulatory population. *American Journal of Medicine*, 80, 208–14.

Boscia, J.A., Kobasa, W.D., Knight, R.A., Abrutyn, E., Levison, M.E., and Kaye, D. (1987). Therapy vs. no therapy for bacteriuria in elderly ambulatory non-hospitalised women. *Journal of the American Medical Association*, 257, 1067–71.

Boscia, J.A., Abrutyn, E., Levison, M.E., Pitsakis, P., and Kaye, D. (1989). Pyuria and asymptomatic bacteriuria in elderly ambulatory women. *Annals of Internal Medicine*, 10, 404–5.

Brocklehurst, J.C., Dillane, J.B., Griffiths, L., and Fry, J. (1968). The prevalence and symptomatology of urinary infection in an aged population. *Gerontology Clinics*, 10, 242–53.

Brocklehurst, J.C., Bee, P., Jones, D., and Palmer, M.K. (1977). Bacteriuria in geriatric hospital patients: its correlates and management. *Age and Ageing*, 6, 240–5.

Cafferkey, M.T., Falkiner, F.R., Gillespie, W.A., and Murphy, D.M. (1982). Antibiotics for the prevention of septicaemia in urology. *Journal of Antimicrobial Chemotherapy*, 9, 471–7.

Cardenas, J., Quinn, EL., Rooker, G., Bavinger, J., and Pohiod, D. (1986). Single-dose cephalexin therapy for acute bacterial urinary tract infections and acute urethral syndrome with bladder bacteriuria. *Antimicrobial Agents and Chemotherapy*, 29, 383–5.

Dontas, A.S., Kasviki-Charvati, P., Papanayiotou, P.C., and Marketos, S.G. (1981). Bacteriuria and survival in old age. *New England Journal of Medicine*, 304, 939–43.

Duffy, L.M., Cleary, J., Ahern, S., et al. (1995). Clean intermittent catheterisation: safe, cost-effective bladder management for male residents of VA nursing homes. *Journal of the American Geriatrics Society*, 43, 865–70.

Esposito, A.L., Gleckman, R.A., Cram, S., Crowley, M., McCabe, F., and Drapkin, M.S. (1980). Community-acquired bacteremia in the elderly: analysis of one hundred consecutive episodes. *Journal of the American Geriatrics Society*, 28, 315–19.

Flanagan, P.O., Rooney, P.J., Davies, E.A., and Stout, R.W. (1991). A comparison of single-dose versus conventional-dose antibiotic treatment of bacteriuria in elderly women. *Age and Ageing*, 20, 206–11.

Fowler, J.E. Jr (1996). Antimicrobial therapy in the management of infected renal calculi. In *Antibiotic therapy in urology* (ed. S.G. Mulholland), pp. 165–86. Lippincott–Raven, Philadelphia, PA.

Freedman, L.R., Phair, J.P., Seki, M., Hamilton, H.B., and Nefzger, M.D. (1964–65). The epidemiology of urinary tract infections in Hiroshima. *Yale Journal of Biology and Medicine*, 37, 262–82.

Giamarellou, H., Iakovou, M., Pistoni, M., Petrikkos, G., Dontas, A., and Sfikakis, P. (1991) Kinetics and comparative efficacy of ofloxacin versus co-trimoxazole in the asymptomatic bacteriuria of elderly subjects. *Chemotherapy*, 37 (Supplement 1), 19–24.

Gleckman, R., Crowley, M., and Natsios, G.A. (1979). Therapy of recurrent invasive urinary tract infections of men, *New England Journal of Medicine*, 301, 878–80.

Gleckman, R.A., Bradley, P.J., Roth, R.M., and Hibert, D.M. (1985). Bacteremic urosepsis: a phenomenon unique to elderly women. *Journal of Urology*, 133, 174–75.

Grahn, D., Norman, D.C., White, M.L., Cantrell, M., and Yoshikawa, T.T. (1985). Validity of urine catheter specimen for diagnosis of urinary tract infection in the elderly. *Archives of Internal Medicine*, 145, 1858–60.

Harding, G.K.M., Nicolle, LE., Ronald, A.R., et al. (1991). Management of catheter-acquired urinary tract infection in women: therapy following catheter removal. *Annals of Internal Medicine*, 14, 713–19.

Hargreave, T.B., Botto, H., Rikken, G.H., et al. (1993). European collaborative study of antibiotic prophylaxis for transurethral resection of the prostate. *European Urology*, 23, 437–43.

Heinamaki, P., Haavisto, M., Hakulinen, T., Mattila, K., and Rajala, M.S. (1986). Mortality in relation to urinary characteristics in the very aged. *Gerontology*, 32, 167–71.

Hirsh, D.D., Fainstein, V., and Musher, D.M. (1979). Do condom catheter collecting systems cause urinary tract infection? *Journal of the American Medical Association*, 242, 340–1.

Johnson, E.T. (1983). The condom catheter: urinary tract infection and other complications. *Southern Medical Journal*, 76, 579–82.

Kasviki-Charvati, P., Drolette-Kefakis, B., Papanayiotou, P.C., and Dontas, A.S. (1982). Turnover of bacteriuria in old age. *Age and Ageing*, 11, 169–74.

Kunin, C.M. (1989). Blockage of urinary catheters: role of micro-organisms and constituents of the urine on formation of encrustations. *Journal of Clinical Epidemiology*, 42, 835–42.

Kunin, C.M., Douthitt, S., Dancing, J., Anderson, J., and Moeschberger, M. (1992). The association between the use of urinary catheters and morbidity and mortality among elderly patients in nursing homes. *American Journal of Epidemiology*, 135, 291–301.

Lipsky, B.A. (1989). Urinary tract infections in men: epidemiology, pathophysiology, diagnosis, and treatment. *Annals of Internal Medicine*, 110, 138–50.

Ljunberg, B. and Nilsson-Ehle, I. (1987). Pharmacokinetics of antimicrobial agents in the elderly. *Review of Infectious Diseases*, 9, 250–64.

Mims, A.D., Norman, D.C., Yamamina, R.H., and Yoshikawa, T. (1990). Clinically inapparent (asymptomatic) bacteriuria in ambulatory elderly men: epidemiological, clinical, and microbiological findings. *Journal of the American Geriatrics Society*, 38, 1209–14.

Monane, M., Gurwitz, J.H., Lipsitz, L.A., Glynn, R.J., Choodnovskiy, I., and Avorn, J. (1995). Epidemiologic and diagnostic aspects of bacteriuria: a longitudinal study in older women. *Journal of the American Geriatrics Society*, 43, 618–22.

Muder, R.R., Brennen, C., Wagener, M.M., and Goetz, A.M. (1992). Bacteremia in a long term care facility: a five-year prospective study of 163 consecutive episodes. *Clinics in Infectious Diseases*, 14, 647–54.

Nicolle, L.E. (1993). Urinary tract infections in long term care facilities. *Infection Control and Hospital Epidemiology*, 14, 220–5.

Nicolle, L.E. (1997). Asymptomatic bacteriuria in the elderly. *Infectious Disease Clinics of North America*, 11, 647–62.

Nicolle, L.E. and Brunka, J. (1990). Urinary IgG and IgA antibodies in elderly institutionalised subjects with bacteriuria. *Gerontology*, 36, 345–55.

Nicolle, L.E. and Ronald, A.R. (1987). Recurrent urinary tract infection in adult women. Diagnosis and treatment. *Infectious Disease Clinics of North America*, 1, 793–806.

Nicolle, L.E., Bjornson, J., Harding, G.K.M., and MacDonell, J.A. (1983). Bacteriuria in elderly institutionalised men. *New England Journal of Medicine*, 309, 1420–6.

Nicolle, L.E., Henderson, E., Bjornson, J., et al. (1987a). The association of bacteriuria with resident characteristics and survival in elderly institutionalised men. Annals of Internal Medicine, 106, 682–6.

Nicolle, L.E., Mayhew, J.W., and Bryan, L. (1987b). Prospective randomised comparison of therapy and no therapy for asymptomatic bacteriuria in institutionalised women. American Journal of Medicine, 83, 27–33.

Nicolle, L.E., Harding, G.K.M., Kennedy, J., McIntyre, M., Aoki, F., and Murray, D. (1988a). Urine specimen collection with external devices for diagnosis of bacteriuria in elderly incontinent men. Journal of Clinical Microbiology, 26, 1115–19.

Nicolle, L.E., Mayhew, J.W., and Bryan, L. (1988b). Outcome following antimicrobial therapy for asymptomatic bacteriuria in elderly women resident in an institution. Age and Ageing, 17, 187–92.

Nicolle, L.E., Muir, P., Harding, G.K.M., and Norris, M. (1988c). Localisation of site of urinary infection in elderly institutionalised women with asymptomatic bacteriuria. Journal of Infectious Diseases, 157, 65–70.

Nicolle, L.E., Brunka, J., Ujack, E., and Bryan, L. (1989a). Antibodies to major outer membranes of Escherichia coli in urinary infection in the elderly. Journal of Infectious Diseases, 160, 627–33.

Nicolle, L.E., Norris, M., and Finlayson, M. (1989b). Hemagglutination characteristics of Escherichia coli isolates from elderly women with asymptomatic bacteriuria. In Host–parasite interactions in urinary tract infections (ed. B. Kass and C. Svanborg-Eden), pp. 62–5. University of Chicago Press.

Nicolle, L.E., Brunka, J., Orr, P., Wilkins, J., and Harding, G.K.M. (1993a). Urinary immunoreactive interleukin-l alpha and interleukin-6 in bacteriuric institutionalised elderly subjects. Journal of Urology, 149, 1049–53.

Nicolle, L.E., Orr, P., Duckworth, H., et al. (1993b). Gross haematuria in residents of long term care facilities. American Journal of Medicine, 94, 611–18.

Nicolle, L.E., Friesen, D., Harding, G.K.M, and Roos, L.L. (1996a). Hospitalisation for acute pyelonephritis in Manitoba, Canada, during the period from 1989 to 1992. Impact of diabetes, pregnancy, and aboriginal origin. Clinics in Infectious Diseases, 22, 1051–6.

Nicolle, L.E., Strausbaugh, L.J., and Garibaldi, R.A. (1996b). Infections and antibiotic resistance in nursing homes. Clinical Microbiology Review, 9, 1–17.

Nordenstam, G.R., Brandberg, C.A., Oden, A.S., Svanborg Eden, C., and Svanborg, A. (1986). Bacteriuria and mortality in an elderly population. New England Journal of Medicine, 314, 1152–6.

Nordenstam, G.R., Sundh, J., Lincoln, K., Svanborg, A., and Svanborg Eden, C. (1989). Bacteriuria in representative samples of persons aged 72–79 years. American Journal of Epidemiology, 130, 1176–86.

Orlander, J.D., Jick, S.S., Dean, A.D, and Jack, H. (1992). Urinary tract infections and oestrogen use in older women. Journal of the American Geriatrics Society, 40, 817–20.

Orr, P., Nicolle, LB., Duckworth, H., et al. (1996). Febrile urinary infection in the institutionalised elderly. American Journal of Medicine, 100, 71–7.

Ouslander, J.G., Greengold, B., and Chen, S. (1987a). External catheter use and urinary tract infections among incontinent male nursing home patients. Journal of the American Geriatrics Society, 35, 1063–70.

Ouslander, J.G., Greengold, B.A., Silverblatt, F.J., and Garcia, J.P. (1987b). An accurate method to obtain urine for culture in men with external catheters. Archives of Internal Medicine, 147, 286–8.

Ouslander, J.G., Schapira, M., Finegold, S., and Schnelle, J. (1995a). Accuracy of rapid urine screening tests among incontinent nursing home residents with asymptomatic bacteriuria. Journal of the American Geriatrics Society, 43, 772–5.

Ouslander, J.G., Schapira, M., and Schnelle, J.F. (1995b). Urine specimen collection from incontinent female nursing home residents. Journal of the American Geriatrics Society, 43, 279–81.

Ouslander, J.G., Schapira, M., Schnelle, J.F., et al. (1995c). Does eradicating bacteriuria affect the severity of chronic urinary incontinence in nursing home residents? Annals of Internal Medicine, 122, 749–54.

Powers, J.S., Billings, F.T., Behrendt, D., and Burger, M.C. (1988). Antecedent factors in urinary tract infections among nursing home patients. Southern Medical Journal, 81, 734–5.

Raz, R. and Stamm, W. (1993). A controlled trial of intravaginal estriol in post-menopausal women with recurrent urinary tract infections. New England Journal of Medicine, 329, 753–8.

Renneberg, J. and Paerregaard, A. (1984). Single-day treatment with trimethoprim for asymptomatic bacteriuria in the elderly patient. Journal of Urology, 132, 934–5.

Rodgers, K., Nicole, L.E., McIntyre, M., Harding, G.K.M., Hoban, D., and Murray, D, (1991). Pyuria in institutionalised elderly subjects. Canadian Journal of Infectious Diseases, 2, 142–6.

Rubin, R.H., Shapiro, E.D., Andriole, V.T., Davis, R.J., and Stamm, W.E. (1992). Evaluation of new anti-infective drugs for the treatment of urinary tract infection. Clinics in Infectious Diseases, 15 (Supplement 1), S216–27.

Saginur, R., Nicolle, L.E., and the Canadian Infectious Diseases Society Clinical Trials Study Group (1992). Single dose compared with 3 days norfloxacin for treatment of uncomplicated urinary infection in women. Archives of Internal Medicine, 152, 1233–7.

Sheehan, J.G., Harding, G.K.M., Haase, D.A., et al. (1988). Double-blind randomised comparison of 24 weeks of norfloxacin followed by 12 weeks of placebo in the therapy of complicated urinary tract infection. Antimicrobial Agents and Chemotherapy, 32, 1292–3.

Smith, J.W., Jones, S.R., Reed, W.P., Tice, A.D., Deupree, R.H., and Kaijser, B. (1979). Recurrent urinary tract infections in men. Annals of Internal Medicine, 91, 544–8.

Sourander, L.B., and Kasanen, A. (1972). A 5-year follow-up of bacteriuria in the aged. Gerontology Clinics (Basel), 14, 274–81.

Stamey, T.A., Fair, W.R., Timothy, M.M., et al. (1968). Antibacterial nature of prostatic fluid. Nature, 218, 444.

Staszewska-Pistoni, M., Dontas, A.S., Giamorellou, H., and Petrikkos, G. (1995). Controlled 10-day antimicrobial therapy in asymptomatic bacteriuria of old age: relations with localization, mobility and mortality. Gerontology, Nephrology and Urology, 4, 137–43.

Steward, D.K., Wood, G.L., Cohen, R.L., Smith, J.W., and Mackowiak, P.A. (1985). Failure of the urinalysis and quantitative urine culture in diagnosing symptomatic urinary tract infections in patients with long-term urinary catheters. American Journal of Infection Control, 13, 154–60.

Suntharalingam, M., Seth, V., and Moore-Smith, B. (1983). Site of urinary tract infection in elderly women admitted to an acute geriatric assessment unit. Age and Ageing, 12, 317–22.

Tronetti, P.S., Oracely, E.J., and Boscia, J.A. (1990). Lack of association between medication use and the presence or absence of bacteriuria in elderly women. Journal of the American Geriatrics Society, 38, 1199–202.

Tzias, V., Dontas, A.S., Petrikkos, G, Papapetropoulou, M., Dracopoulos, J., and Giamarellou, H. (1990). Three-day antibiotic therapy in bacteriuria of old age. Journal of Antimicrobial Chemotherapy, 26, 705–11.

Walkey, F.A., Judge, T.G., Thompson, J., and Sarkart, N.B.S. (1967). Incidence of urinary infection in the elderly. Scottish Medical Journal, 12, 411–14.

Warren, J.W. (1989). Catheter-associated urinary tract infections. Infectious Disease Clinics of North America, 1, 823–54.

Warren, J.W. (1992). Catheter-associated bacteriuria. Clinics in Geriatric Medicine, 8, 805–19.

Warren, J.W., Anthony, W.C., Hooper, J.M., and Muncie, H.L. Jr (1982). Cephalexin for susceptible bacteriuria in afebrile, long-term catheterised patients. Journal of the American Medical Association, 248, 454–8.

Warren, J.W., Damron, D., Tenney, J.H., Hoopes, J.M., Deforge, B., and Muncie, H.L. Jr (1987). Fever, bacteremia, and death as complications of bacteriuria in women with long term urethral catheters. *Journal of Infectious Diseases*, **155**, 1151–8.

Warren, J.W., Munci, H.L. Jr, and Hall-Graggs, M. (1988). Acute pyelonephritis associated with bacteriuria during long-term catheterisation. A prospective clinicopathological study. *Journal of Infectious Diseases*, **158**, 1341–6.

Warren, J.W., Steinberg, R., Hebel, J.R., and Tenney, J. (1989). The prevalence of urethral catheterisation in Maryland Nursing Homes. *Archives of Internal Medicine*, **149**, 1535–7.

Zhanel, G., Harding, G.K.M., and Nicolle, L.E. (1991). Asymptomatic bacteriuria in diabetics. *Review of Infectious Diseases*, 13,150–4.

16

Disorders of the blood

16 Disorders of the blood

Harvey Jay Cohen

Introduction

Disorders of the blood are very common among elderly people. Debate continues to rage over what proportion of these changes are caused by age-associated alterations in the haemotopoietic system and what proportion by superimposition of the more frequently occurring acute and chronic illnesses of elderly people. The general approach to diagnosis is quite similar to that for younger individuals, although it may be modified by differing levels of expectation for certain processes and disorders. Although management of particular blood disorders may be in general similar to that in younger people, modifications may be required to accommodate the physiological alterations that occur with increasing age. This chapter will concentrate on those areas in which there are issues of particular relevance to age-associated changes, and/or diseases that are particularly prominent in the older age group, and/or have manifestations and management issues that require a different approach in people of advanced age.

History and physical examination

In the history and physical examination certain points should be borne in mind. The symptoms of haematological disorders may be subtle, sometimes chronic in onset, and rather non-specific. Therefore it may be easy for the practitioner to assume that these are simply the changes of 'old age'. In fact, many older patients may themselves assume that changes such as increasing fatigue and weakness are occurring simply because they are 'getting older'. This tendency must be avoided by the doctor and understood by the patient. Because of the increasing frequency of various disease processes with age, symptoms may also be masked by other manifestations of disease. Thus secondary as well as primary haematological disturbances must be considered in the differential diagnosis for elderly individuals. Older patients may also present with manifestations that are rather atypical when compared with those of younger ones. Thus the elderly person who presents with altered mental state, confusion, or delirium may be showing signs of a moderate anaemia that has finally reached the threshold at which function is compromised. In fact, functional alterations rather than specific and definable individual symptoms are often the presentation for elderly patients with disorders of the blood.

Normal blood count

In the absence of disease the stained blood film components are unaltered by age. Whether certain components of the blood are quantitatively altered as a consequence of advancing age *per se,* or whether some of the changes that have been noted over the lifetime are those to which the increasing prevalence of other disease processes contribute, remains controversial. This has been most disputed in defining the 'normal' range for haemoglobin and the haematocrit (O'Rourke and Cohen 1987; Zauber and Zauber 1987). This is of importance because defining the limit at which we begin to consider that an abnormal process such as anaemia is present will naturally affect the number of people regarded as having it. Of general population studies, a number have demonstrated that the mean haemoglobin declines slightly in both elderly men and women, with the mean and the great majority of the people remaining within the 'normal' range (Salive *et al.* 1992). However, most of these studies have included people in varying states of health, and are frequently flawed by being cross-sectional. When the lower limit of normal for haemoglobin is set at approximately 13 g/100 ml for men and 12 g/100 ml for women, there is an increasing prevalence with age of individuals who fall below this and who thus would be defined as anaemic. However, when such low values do occur, they generally appear to be accompanied by processes that can explain them and therefore are not considered a normal concomitant of age (Ania *et al.* 1994; Freedman 1996). In many studies, as many as 20 to 25 per cent of people aged over 65 years will fall into the anaemic range by these criteria. For these reasons an appropriate cut-off point may be approximately 12 g/100 ml of haemoglobin for both men and women, indicating at least a moderate anaemia. Other measurements of red blood cells, such as mean corpuscular volume and mean corpuscular haemoglobin concentration, appear to be distributed normally in elderly subjects. White blood cell counts are largely unchanged, although longitudinal studies have shown a slight decrease in lymphocyte counts in the last 3 years of life, most likely concomitant with the occurrence of other diseases (Sparrow *et al.* 1980). Monocyte and platelet counts are unchanged. The erythrocyte sedimentation rate (ESR) is raised above the usual normal range in 20 to 40 per cent of elderly people. However, most of these changes appear to be associated with various chronic or subacute illnesses or specific abnormalities of plasma proteins. When truly normal healthy elderly people are assessed, the range of ESR is changed very little from that of normal young people (Crawford *et al.* 1987). Thus significant deviations from this range should be assumed to be related to pathological processes. In fact, even grossly elevated ESRs, associated with increased mortality, were associated with significant diagnosis in nearly all patients (Stevens *et al.* 1995).

Bone marrow activity and distribution

Histological studies have suggested that there might be a decline in marrow cellularity from 70 per cent in childhood to 30 per cent in the eighth decade of life (Hartsock *et al.* 1965). In animals, studies of radiolabelled iron distribution do not show marked changes with age in the pattern of marrow distribution (Boggs 1985). Magnetic resonance imaging studies in humans have confirmed a shift from red to yellow marrow in all sites with age, with an age-associated shift of red marrow from the appendicular to the axial skeleton (Richardson and Patten 1994).

Haematopoietic stem cells

Overall, for both pluripotential and committed stem cells, there appears to be little change in the basal level of function with advanced age. Thus the levels of erythroid blast-forming units and granulocyte–macrophage colony-forming units are little changed, although in some cases the latter appear to be decreased somewhat in older animals, perhaps more related to stressful conditions than age *per se.* However, there are age-associated deficiencies in the response of such stem cells to stimuli such as anaemia or infection. Thus the basal function appears to be normal, but the homeostatic reserve appears to be somewhat diminished in response to stress (Cohen and Crawford 1986; Williams *et al.* 1986; O'Rourke and Cohen 1987; Resnitzky *et al.* 1987; Quaglino *et al.* 1996). The erythropoietin response to stress appears to be well maintained (Goodnough *et al.* 1995).

Stem cell disorders

Acute leukaemia

Acute lymphocytic leukaemia is the less common form in elderly adults. It is predominantly a disease of childhood, but has another peak of incidence in late life although it is not clear whether this is the same disease. With approaches to treatment that are similar to those designed for childhood acute lymphocytic leukaemia (prednisone–vincristine combinations as the base, sometimes adding methotrexate, daunorubicin, and/or L-asparaginase), this disorder appears to be much more responsive than acute myeloblastic leukaemia in the adult, but less responsive than the potentially curable forms of childhood acute lymphocytic leukaemia. However, these treatments can produce remissions in as many as 70 to 80 per cent of elderly patients, and this can frequently be achieved without the period of severe marrow aplasia required for the treatment of acute myeloblastic leukaemia. This results in a lower rate of complications and more tolerable induction of remission. Over the long term, survival rates are poor, with as many as 80 per cent of elderly patients relapsing in the first year (Copelan and McGuire 1995; Tiong Ong and Larson 1995).

Acute myeloblastic leukaemia

This disorder is seen predominantly in elderly people, with over half of all patients being over the age of 60 years at presentation (Freedman 1985; Extermann 1997). Presentation is often with non-specific symptoms, such as tiredness, weakness, anorexia, and loss of weight.

Frequently, the haematological findings are rather subtle, with peripheral blood cytopenia and few myeloblasts. These changes should be regarded with suspicion, and marrow examination of bone may reveal hypercellularity with replacement by immature myeloblasts. A further complicating factor is the high proportion of patients (up to one-third) who have had an antecedent preleukaemic or myelodysplastic phase. This might include cytopenia, sideroblastic anaemia, or other smouldering myelodysplastic syndromes. These patients may have a more indolent form of leukaemia that leads to a difficult decision when considering beginning treatment; watchful waiting and symptomatic treatment may be preferable to chemotherapy. In fact, biological marker studies have indicated that even in elderly patients without antecedent myelodysplasia, the leukaemic cells have features, such as unfavourable cytogenetics and expression of multidrug-resistance protein, suggesting that these leukaemias have a common lineage. This may indicate an intrinsic difference in acute myelogenous leukaemia in elderly people, requiring different treatment strategies (Leith *et al.* 1997).

Standard chemotherapy involves a combination of agents, usually including cytosine arabinoside and anthracyclines such as daunorubicin. The goal is complete bone marrow aplasia and normal cellular regrowth without leukaemic cells. In younger adults, there may be remission rates as high as 70 per cent, with improved overall survival. In some studies of elderly individuals, response rates as high as 50 per cent have been recorded, but most studies show lower rates than this (Champlin *et al.* 1989; Extermann 1997). Moreover, there is a high incidence of death during induction, mostly because elderly patients cannot withstand the severe toxicity of the regimens, with resultant infection and bleeding. For this reason, studies have been conducted to assess the utility of colony-stimulating factor support in an attempt to mobilize granulocyte reserves and decrease the period at risk. These studies have generally been disappointing. While the duration of neutropenia is shortened, and in some, short-term mortality reduced, overall mortality is not altered (Dombret *et al.* 1995; Rowe *et al.* 1995; Stone *et al.* 1995). For those who do achieve remission, it may last as long as in the young, but the median survival is only in the general range of 1 year. Thus the likelihood of achieving remission and a somewhat prolonged survival must be set against the high risk of early death, as well as the extensive comorbidity, and time required in hospital for most patients, even those who do not respond. Those with antecedent myelodysplastic syndromes have particularly poor responses. In one study, when this group of poor responders was excluded from the analysis, the remainder had similar responses to those of younger adults (Freedman 1985). However, this has not been uniformly observed (Leith *et al.* 1997).

Because of these poor responses, suggested alternatives are lower doses of cytosine arabinoside, which may produce a similar period of response but with lower toxicity, or supportive care only (Copplestone *et al.* 1989; Powell *et al.* 1989). Some newer agents, such as mitoxantrone and etoposide, appear to have lower toxicities than standard regimens and may produce similar remission rates (Bow *et al.* 1996). This decision should be made with regard to the physiological condition of the patient and the extent of comorbidity as well as to their previous haematological state. It should include a frank discussion with patient and family of the likely short- and long-term outcomes.

Chronic granulocytic and lymphocytic leukaemia

The approach to these disorders in the older patient is little different from that in the younger one, and chronic granulocytic leukaemia tends to occur in younger patients. Chronic lymphocytic leukaemia is chiefly a disease of old age; true cure or complete remission is rarely seen and the aim is to control symptoms. The decision to treat should be based on the current and expected quality of life. In general, treatment is not recommended for the asymptomatic stages where there is no evidence of impingement upon bone marrow function. When treatment is required, a regimen of an alkylating agent plus prednisolone is generally well tolerated by elderly individuals, especially as severe cytopenia and bone marrow aplasia are not goals of therapy (O'Brien et al. 1995; Rai 1997).

Polycythaemia and other myeloproliferative syndromes

These myeloproliferative disorders mostly occur in elderly individuals. Diagnosis demands a high index of suspicion because elderly patients with polycythaemia will often present with rather vague symptoms such as headaches, dizziness, or a thrombosis. Moreover, because of the reduced cerebral blood flow that occurs with haematocrits of above 60 per cent, the elderly patient may present with atypical findings, such as altered mental status or confusion, especially if the haematological disorder is superimposed upon other conditions producing a marginally compensated cognitive state. In these cases, phlebotomy to lower the blood viscosity should first be performed with due caution and not so quickly as to create haemodynamic changes that could further compromise the circulation. In the long run, however, phlebotomy alone is not enough to control the episodes of thromboembolism and bleeding, and specific therapy is required. Radioactive phosphorus (^{12}P) is effective and well tolerated. Hydroxyurea may be an excellent alternative for more rapid lowering of the blood counts; it may be especially useful in states such as primary thrombocytosis when rapid reduction of the platelet count is necessary. However, it probably should not be used for long-term maintenance since it appears to increase the risk of subsequent leukaemia and cancer (Najean and Rain 1997). Myosclerosis and myeloid metaplasia may be even more insidious in onset and overlap with the other myeloproliferative disorders in presentation. As these may be indolent in the older individual, and as chemotherapy may do more harm than good, symptomatic therapy is often the preferred approach.

Aplastic anaemia and other myelodysplastic syndromes

In elderly people, the predominant forms of aplastic anaemia are either idiopathic or presumed to be drug induced. Elderly individuals may be particularly prone to the latter because they use more prescription and over-the-counter medicines than do younger people. As bone marrow transplantation is not at present in general use for patients over the age of 50 years, supportive care, and perhaps attempts at androgenic steroid treatment, are the only options. For the elderly patient with severe aplasia that does not spontaneously remit with drug withdrawal, the outlook is poor.

The myelodysplastic syndromes, including the spectrum of refractory anaemia, sideroblastic anaemia, and refractory anaemia with excess blast cells, are almost exclusively found in elderly adults (Gardner 1987). As mentioned above, they may present insidiously and be a precursor to subsequent myeloproliferative transformation. Supportive care is generally given. Such approaches as low-dose cytosine arabinoside have been used in efforts to achieve differentiation or maturation of cells in patients with myelodysplastic syndromes. However, despite their apparent attractiveness, they are associated with significant toxicity and must be used with caution, especially in elderly patients.

Anaemia

Iron metabolism and deficiency

Iron metabolism generally alters little with age. Although there may be a slight decrease in iron absorption, perhaps conditioned by increased gastric pH, this is rarely enough to create a deficiency state. In general, iron intake is adequate in elderly people. Some, such as those with very low caloric intake among nursing home patients, those who live alone or are disabled, or those of very low socioeconomic status, may have a moderate decline in intake, but even this generally exceeds the minimum daily requirements and dietary iron deficiency is extremely uncommon among elderly people. Deficiency results almost exclusively (at least in developed nations) from blood loss, most commonly from the gastrointestinal tract, because the contribution from menstrual blood loss is absent in postmenopausal women.

The anaemia of iron deficiency is generally microcytic hypochromic, although in earlier phases it may be normochromic. The diagnosis is generally made by laboratory investigation (O'Rourke and Cohen 1987; Babitz and Freedman 1988; Walsh 1989). Unfortunately because of the prevalence of other disorders in elderly people, serum iron and iron-binding capacity are not reliable indicators. There is a tendency for the serum iron to decrease somewhat with advancing age in the absence of iron deficiency, and many chronic illnesses can lower both serum iron and iron-binding capacity. Although the final diagnosis may be made by bone marrow aspiration, stained for storage iron, this procedure is best avoided if possible in the elderly individual. Measurement of serum ferritin may allow one to do so. The normal range of serum ferritin tends to rise somewhat with increasing age, with the concentrations for older men and women converging. A low serum ferritin is diagnostic of iron deficiency and can be accepted without bone marrow examination in some cases. A serum ferritin below 12 µg/l is a false-positive diagnosis in under 3 per cent of cases. A serum ferritin of under 45 µg/l in an elderly individual is highly predictive of iron deficiency, though liver disease and inflammatory disorders may sometimes raise the ferritin into this range (Freedman 1996). In elderly patients, the major differential diagnosis of iron deficiency is the anaemia of chronic disease. Although in its mild stages this is generally normochromic and normocytic, not infrequently it may be hypochromic microcytic. In that case serum ferritin, if low, is the best discriminator. Additional diagnostic information may be contributed by the red blood cell distribution width index, a measurement of anisocytosis made with automatic blood cell counters. This develops early in iron deficiency and generally to a greater extent than in the anaemia of chronic disease. However, there is considerable overlap between the two. The ratio of serum transferrin receptor to ferritin has been suggested as a good discriminant test (Punnonen et al. 1997).

Once the diagnosis of iron deficiency is made, the most important step in an elderly individual is to identify its cause. Because of the frequency of peptic ulceration, colon cancer, diverticulitis, and angiodysplasia, examination of the gastrointestinal tract should be thorough. A common complication is that elderly individuals may be taking various and numerous drugs that may cause gastrointestinal side-effects and bleeding. Nevertheless the cause can be identified in most elderly patients with iron deficiency anaemia (Gordon *et al.* 1996). Treatment is generally by standard methods, but sometimes ferrous sulphate may be poorly tolerated because of increased gastric sensitivity. When this occurs, a paediatric liquid suspension may be considered as an alternative. If parenteral iron therapy is considered, intravenous administration may sometimes be preferable because of the difficulty of deep intramuscular injections in elderly individuals with decreased muscle mass.

Normocytic normochromic anaemias

The anaemia of chronic diseases, especially those known to decrease marrow production (such as renal disease, malignant or inflammatory disorders, or infections to which elderly people are particularly prone), is the most common normocytic normochromic anaemia in this age group. The basic cause appears to be a reticuloendothelial cell block-ade, sometimes complicated by decreased production of erythro-poietin. The anaemia is usually mild but can completely mimic that of iron deficiency. If the serum ferritin is markedly elevated, one can be fairly secure in this diagnosis. Generally a serum ferritin of about 50 µg/l is associated with this type of anaemia. The serum iron and iron-binding capacity are unreliable although, in the equivocal ranges of serum ferritin, very low iron saturation (under 10 per cent) is more suggestive of iron deficiency anaemia.

Megaloblastic anaemia

In elderly individuals, megaloblastic anaemias generally result from deficiency of folic acid or vitamin B_{12} (O'Rourke and Cohen 1987; Freedman 1996). As these disorders are usually correctable, diagnosis should be pursued vigorously. Folic acid deficiency most often results from nutritional deficiency, but other causes, such as malabsorption or increased utilization, can occur. General nutritional surveys show that the average daily folate intake of elderly people is quite sufficient and, in the absence of illness or marked lack of eating, folate deficiency is not a widespread problem among elderly people living in the community in the United States. However, elderly people on low incomes, alcoholics, and elderly residents of institutions are more likely to have decreased intake, and prevalence rates as high as 15 to 20 per cent have been reported in these groups. The serum folate may be helpful in diagnosis but as many as 10 per cent of apparently healthy aged individuals have folate levels below the normal limits. The red blood cell folate is a much more reliable indicator of true tissue folate deficiency and can be used to substantiate the finding of an equivocal serum folate. In elderly individuals, folate deficiency has been associated with neuropsychiatric symptoms, but a direct causal relationship has not been clearly established.

The other major cause of macrocytic anaemia in elderly patients is vitamin B_{12} deficiency. In contrast with folate deficiency, B_{12} deficiency is rarely produced by lack of dietary intake. Because of the large body stores of this vitamin and the high content of vitamin B_{12} in the diet (at least in the United States), deficiency is rarely seen except in the strictest life-long vegans or vegetarians. Other forms of malabsorption, such as those that arise after total gastrectomy or disease of the terminal ileum, may also produce vitamin B_{12} deficiency. However, the most common form in old age is pernicious anaemia, due to impaired secretion of intrinsic factor by the gastric parietal cell, which accounts for two-thirds of cases of vitamin B_{12} deficiency. The lack of intrinsic factor seems to be secondary to chronic atrophic gastritis, a disorder of unknown aetiology that increases in frequency with age. The deficiency can produce a number of neurological changes including degenerative changes in peripheral nerves. Neuropsychiatric symptoms of delirium and confusion are a well-established feature of vitamin B_{12} deficiency, but a clear causal relationship between this deficiency and more fixed, true dementia has not been clearly shown (Crystal *et al.* 1994). Moreover, descriptions of true dementia as-sociated with vitamin B_{12} deficiency in the absence of any haema-tological abnormality are rare.

Measurements of vitamin B_{12} have been used as primary diagnostic tools in the assessment of anaemia, as well as in screening populations for vitamin B_{12} deficiency. There appears to be a progressive fall in the serum B_{12} with advancing age; this generally does not appear to reflect depleted tissue stores of vitamin B_{12}. Some of these low serum levels may be caused by alterations in transcobalamin, the B_{12}-binding protein, in elderly individuals. The diagnosis is established with the Schilling test, which can be done in any elderly individual capable of collecting 24-h urine samples. Whether there is true tissue deficiency of vitamin B_{12} may be determined by measurement of methylmalonic acid in serum or urine (Savage *et al.* 1994). This is frequently normal in borderline cases of low vitamin B_{12}, indicating that, while true vitamin B_{12} deficiency may be prevalent in elderly people (Pennypacker *et al.* 1992), a low vitamin B_{12} is not pathognomonic for tissue deficiency and may require further evaluation rather than immediate treatment (Nilsson-Ehle *et al.* 1989). Correct treatment in older, as in younger, adults should result in a brisk reticulocytosis with both vitamin B_{12} and folate replacement. A complicating feature may be the presence of combined deficiency, for example vitamin B_{12} and folate or one of these plus iron deficiency. If there is an initial response but not full recovery, a combined deficiency should be considered. In particular there may have been a limited amount of iron present in the bone marrow, that has been depleted during the initial rapid erythropoietic response to folate or vitamin B_{12} replacement. These individuals will also require iron replacement, and evaluation of the reason for reduced stores in the first place. Treatment of severe pernicious anaemia should be carried out slowly with very small doses of vitamin B_{12} in elderly patients to reduce the risk of sudden death thought to be due to a massive shift of potassium from the extracellular fluid into red cells released from maturation arrest. Potassium supplements are commonly prescribed although not of proven efficacy.

Disorders of the synthesis or function of haemoglobin

These disorders are largely those of younger individuals. However, it should be remembered that mild forms of thalassaemia may remain undetected and be found for the first time only when an elderly individual presents either for a totally unrelated disorder or when the haemoglobin level falls further than the level at which it has been chronically maintained. In this case, investigations for microcytic anaemia must include the possibility of thalassaemia. It is important to distinguish this process from that of iron deficiency because inappropriate treatment with iron could result in overload. Likewise for the sickling disorders—sickle cell anaemia usually results in death before old age, but those with sickle cell trait appear to have normal survival, and an elderly person with the trait who becomes seriously ill for the first time in late life might be at risk for problems such as deoxygenation during anaesthesia or other stresses. Thus, if not previously done, appropriate investigations would be required in an elderly individual whose racial background predisposes to sickle cell disease.

Sideroblastic anaemias

These disorders are mostly seen in elderly individuals; the idiopathic forms have already been considered. The secondary form may frequently arise because of the number of the drugs that may be potentially responsible for it (such as isoniazid) and because of the prevalence of many systemic diseases that result in ring sideroblasts. These include infections, hypothyroidism, and rheumatological diseases.

Haemolytic anaemias

The inherited haemolytic anaemias are generally thought of as occurring in younger individuals, but these must be considered in older people as well. For example, patients with mild hereditary spherocytosis may well present for the first time with haemolysis under the stress of their first serious infectious disease in old age, after being in previous good health. Likewise, patients with enzyme deficiencies, such as of glucose-6-phosphate dehydrogenase, may not incur enough stress from either diseases or drugs to induce haemolytic manifestations until late in life. Therefore, in an elderly individual with an appropriate racial or ethnic background who presents with an acute haemolytic episode, enzyme deficiencies must be considered if no other apparent cause is found.

Immune haemolytic anaemia, especially the 'warm-antibody' IgG-induced variety, is more common in elderly people. This is especially true of drug-induced immune haemolysis because older people use more drugs. Coombs-positive haemolytic anaemia frequently accompanies, and may be the first presentation of, chronic lymphocytic leukaemia, a disorder of older age, which contributes to its increased prevalence. Chronic cold agglutinin disease, a disorder characterized by both haemagglutination and haemolysis caused by cold-reacting IgM antibodies, occurs almost exclusively in older individuals. This disorder should be particularly considered in differential diagnosis when the Coombs' test is positive but there is no IgG on the cell surface. In many individuals with cold agglutinin disease, symptoms may be more related to the agglutination than to the haemolysis. The explanation for the increase in these types of antibodies with age is unknown. However, there is an increase in a wide variety of autoantibodies among elderly individuals (including rheumatoid factor and antithyroid antibodies), but frequently these do not result in specific disease. Non-immune forms of haemolytic anaemia, such as those related to infections, and both macro- and microintravascular haemolysis occur more often in old age because the primary conditions with which they are associated do so too.

Leucocytes in health and disease

Adequate neutrophil function is largely maintained throughout life. There is some evidence that, in elderly individuals, leucocytes may be less readily mobilized by stressful challenges such as bacteria invasion or steroids. This may be at the root of the clinical observation that infections induce a less vigorous granulocyte response in older people. However, accurate measurements of the maintenance of neutrophil function with age have been complicated by the differing populations studied. Some studies have shown that elderly individuals are less able to phagocytose and kill bacteria and to produce superoxide; other studies of narrowly defined healthy populations have shown more 'normal' chemotaxis, bacterial killing, and oxidative metabolism (Corberand et al. 1986; Nagel et al. 1986; Udupa and Lipschitz 1987; Mege et al. 1988; Rao et al. 1992; Polignano et al. 1994). This is further complicated by the fact that neutrophil function may be impaired secondarily by age-associated disorders such as diabetes, as well as by events more connected with nutritional deficiencies. Neutropenia is not an uncommon finding in elderly individuals, especially in relation to drug use. It may be either immune or non-immune, and may be a mild chronic form or acute and severe. Lymphocytes are functionally compromised with progressive age. The most dramatic aspect of this is the failure of lymphocytes from elderly individuals to respond appropriately to mitogenic stimuli (Cohen 1989). This appears to be predominantly a defect in the T-cell arm of the immune system related to cell-mediated immunity. Altered immunoglobin production by B lymphocytes, when seen, appears to be mainly a secondary outcome of altered T-cell regulation. There are no major quantitative or qualitative changes in other peripheral blood cells such as monocytes, eosinophils, and basophils.

Lymphoproliferative disorders

The lymphomas

Hodgkin's disease has a second peak of incidence in the elderly population. Because of its heterogeneous nature, it is not completely clear if the disease occurring in old age is the same as that in the young adult. Elderly individuals appear to present at a more advanced stage than their younger counterparts, and their histological type is more often lymphocyte depletion. In general, the responses to treatment and survival rates in older age groups are worse than those for younger patients (Freedman 1985; Miescher and Jaffe 1988; Mir et al. 1993). Moreover, treatment-related complications may be more severe. In Hodgkin's disease treated with curative radiation, regeneration of bone marrow activity is considerably delayed in elderly patients, and substantial gastrointestinal toxicity may also occur. In some studies, many elderly patients were unable to undergo full staging of the disease because of difficulty in tolerating laparotomy. However, it is not clear whether this is related more to comorbidity than to age per se. Chemotherapy for Hodgkin's disease is poorly tolerated by elderly patients, with early toxicity and treatment-related deaths (O'Reilly et al. 1997).

Non-Hodgkin's lymphomas are rarely localized in older people and tend to present as disseminated disease from the outset without obvious spread from node to node. It is particularly useful to define the histological type because this will help to define the therapeutic

Miescher, P.A. and Jaffe, E.R. (ed.) (1988). *Seminars in hematology: advances in chemotherapy for Hodgkin's and non-Hodgkin's lymphomas*, Vol. 25, No. 2, Supplement 2. Grune and Stratton, Philadelphia, PA.

Mir, R., Anderson, J., Strauchen, J., *et al.* (1993). Hodgkin disease in patients 60 years of age or older. *Cancer*, 71, 1857–66.

Nagel, J.E., Han, K., Coon, P.J., Adler, W.H., and Bender, B.S. (1986). Age differences in phagocytosis by polymorphonuclear leukocytes measured by flow cytometry. *Journal of Leukocyte Biology*, 39, 399–407.

Najean, Y. and Rain, J.D. (1997). Treatment of polycythemia vera: use of ^{32}P along or in combination with maintenance therapy using hydroxyurea in 461 patients greater than 65 years of age. *Blood*, 89, 2319–27.

Nilsson-Ehle, H., Landahl, S., Lindstedt, G., *et al.* (1989). Low serum cobalamin levels in a population study of 70- and 75-year-old subjects. *Digestive Diseases and Sciences*, 34, 716–23.

O'Brien, S, Giglio, A.D., and Keating, M. (1995). Advances in the biology and treatment of β-cell chronic lymphocytic leukaemia. *Blood*, 85, 307–18.

O'Reilly, S.E., Connors, J.M., Macpherson, N., Klasa, R., and Hoskins, P. (1997). Malignant lymphomas in the elderly. In *Clinics in geriatric medicine* (ed. L. Balducci), pp. 251–63. W.B. Saunders, Philadelphia.

O'Rourke, M.A. and Cohen, H.J. (1987). Anemias. In *Geriatric medicine annual 1987* (ed. R.J. Ham), pp. 237–66. Medical Economics, New York.

Pennypacker, L.C., Allen, R.H., Kelly, J.P., *et al.* (1992). High prevalence of cobalamin deficiency in elderly outpatients. *Journal of the American Geriatrics Society*, 40, 1197–204.

Polignano, A., Tortorella, C., Venezia, A., Jirillo, E., and Antonaci, S. (1994). Age-associated changes of neutrophil responsiveness in a human healthy elderly population. *Cytobios*, 80, 145–53.

Powell, B.L., *et al.* (1989). Low-dose ara-C therapy for acute myelogenous leukaemia in elderly patients. *Leukaemia*, 3, 23–8.

Punnonen, K., Irjala, K., and Rajamäki, A. (1997). Serum transferrin receptor and its ratio to serum ferritin in the diagnosis of iron deficiency. *Blood*, 89, 1052–7.

Quaglino, D., Ginaldi, L., Furia, N., and De Martinis, M. (1996). The effect of age on hemopoiesis. *Aging Clinical Experimental Research*, 8, 1–12.

Rai, K.R. (1997). Chronic lymphocytic leukaemia in the elderly population. In *Clinics in geriatric medicine* (ed. L. Balducci), pp. 245–9. W.B. Saunders, Philadelphia, PA.

Rao, K.M.K., Currie, M.S., Padmanabhan, J., *et al.* (1992). Age-related alterations in actin cytoskeleton and receptor expression in human leukocytes. *Journal of Gerontology*, 47, B37–44.

Resnitzky, P., Segal, M., Barak, Y., and Dassa, C. (1987). Granulopoiesis in aged people: inverse correlation between bone marrow cellularity and myeloid progenitor cell numbers. *Gerontology*, 33, 109–14.

Richardson, M.L. and Patten, R.M. (1994). Age-related changes in marrow distribution in the shoulder: MR imaging findings. *Radiology*, 192, 209–15.

Rowe, J.M., Andersen, J.W., Mazza, J.J., *et al.* (1995). A randomized placebo-controlled phase III study of granulocyte-macrophage colony-stimulating factor in adult patients (> 55 to 70 years of age) with acute myelogenous leukaemia: a study of the eastern co-operative oncology group. *Blood*, 86, 457–62.

Salive, M.E., Cornoni-Huntley, J., Guralnik, J.M., *et al.* (1992). Anemia and hemoglobin levels in older persons: relationship with age, gender, and health status. *Journal of the American Geriatrics Society*, 40, 489–96.

Savage, D.G., Lindenbaum J., Stabler, S.P., *et al.* (1994). Sensitivity of serum methylmalonic acid and total homocysteine determinations for diagnosing cobalamin and folate deficiencies. *American Journal of Medicine*, 96, 239–46.

Solal-Celigny, P., Chastang, C., Herrera, A., *et al.* (1987). Age as the main prognostic factor in adult aggressive non-Hodgkin's lymphoma. *American Journal of Medicine*, 83, 1075–9.

Sparrow, D., Silbert, J.E., and Rowe, J.W. (1980). The influence of age on peripheral lymphocyte count in men: a cross-sectional and longitudinal study. *Journal of Gerontology*, 35, 163.

Stevens, D., Tallis, R., and Hollis, S. (1995). Persistent grossly elevated erythrocyte sedimentation rate in elderly people: one year follow-up of morbidity and mortality. *Gerontology*, 41, 220–6.

Stone, R.M., Berg, D.T., George, S.L., *et al.* (1995). Granulocyte–macrophage colony stimulating factor after initial chemotherapy for elderly patients with primary acute myelogenous leukaemia. *New England Journal of Medicine*, 332, 1671–7.

Tiong Ong, S. and Larson, R.A. (1995). Current management of acute lymphoblastic leukaemia in adults. *Oncology*, 9, 433–50.

Tirelli, U. (1989). Management of malignant lymphoma in the elderly: an EORTC retrospective evaluation. *Acta Oncologica*, 28, 199–201.

Udupa, K.B. and Lipschitz, D.A. (1987). Effect of donor and culture age on the function of neutrophils harvested from long-term bone marrow culture. *Experimental Hematology*, 15, 212–16.

Vericel, E., Croset, M., Sedivy, P., *et al.* (1988). Platelets and aging I. Aggregation, arachidonate metabolism and antioxidant status. *Thrombosis Research*, 49, 331–42.

Vose, J.M., Armitage, J.O., Weisenberger, D.D., *et al.* (1988). The importance of age in survival of patients treated with chemotherapy for aggressive non-Hodgkin's lymphoma. *Journal of Clinical Oncology*, 6, 1838–44.

Walsh, J.R. (1989). Equivocal anemia in the elderly. *Journal of Family Practice*, 28, 521–3.

Williams, L.H., Udupa, K.B., and Lipschitz, D.A. (1986). Evaluation of the effect of age on hematopoiesis in the C57BL/6 mouse. *Experimental Hematology*, 14, 827–32.

Zauber, N.P. and Zauber, A.G. (1987). Hematologic data of healthy very old people. *Journal of American Medical Association*, 257, 2181–4.

17

Skin disease

17 Skin disease

Arthur K. Balin

Introduction

In this chapter the physiological and biological bases for the increased susceptibility to skin disease in older people are reviewed and skin conditions that are particularly prevalent in older people are discussed. Emphasis is given to those conditions that the geriatrician is likely to encounter during the course of daily practice. The reader is referred to several dermatology texts for more detail regarding diagnosis and management of specific skin diseases (Marks 1987*b*; Balin and Kligman 1989; Newcomer and Young 1989).

The expression and treatment of cutaneous disease in older people differ from those applicable to younger adults. Anatomical changes in ageing skin result in altered physiological behaviour and susceptibility to disease. Decreased epidermal renewal and tissue repair accompany ageing. The rate of hair and nail growth typically declines, as well as the quantity of eccrine, apocrine, and sebum secretion. There are alterations in immune surveillance and antigen presentation with ageing. The cutaneous vascular supply is decreased, leading to decreases in inflammatory response, absorption, and cutaneous clearance. Thermal regulation, tactile sensitivity, and pain perception become impaired with ageing. These changes result in altered expression of cutaneous disease and indicate a need for specific modifications in the treatment and prevention of cutaneous disease in older people.

First, the major changes that occur during the intrinsic ageing process of the skin are summarized to facilitate the recognition and treatment of skin disease in the older patient. This is followed by a discussion of the expression of skin disease in older people. Finally, selected specific clinical conditions prevalent in older people are reviewed.

Changes in the skin with age

The skin is composed of the epidermis, dermis, and subcutaneous tissue. The outer layer of the epidermis is the dead stratum corneum that helps provide a barrier between the internal and external world. The viable epidermis is composed of keratinocytes, and contains melanocytes that produce pigment, and Langerhans' cells that provide for immunological recognition and antigen processing. The dermis contains a fibrous support network of collagen and elastic fibres, as well as an interstitial ground substance composed of glycosaminoglycans. An abundant vascular supply permeates the dermis and subcutaneous tissue.

Epidermis

Stratum corneum

There is little change in the number of layers of cells that compose the stratum corneum during ageing. The thickness of the stratum corneum and its resistance to the diffusion of water vapour are similar in young and old people. As a result the barrier function of the stratum corneum is preserved during ageing. However, there is an increased susceptibility to damage of barrier function with age. The moisture content of the stratum corneum of aged skin is less than that in younger adults and as a consequence is somewhat more brittle. There is an age-associated reduction in stratum corneum lipid levels of about 30 per cent. In addition, the corneocytes of aged skin have been found to become larger and less cohesive than those in younger skin.

Turnover of the stratum corneum reflects the renewal time of the epidermis and has been found to take longer in the elderly individual. Thus recovery of damaged barrier function is delayed in aged human skin.

Dry skin and rough skin with aberrant light scattering are consequences of these age-associated changes in the stratum corneum. The longer renewal time means that irritant and sensitizing substances contacting the skin will remain longer, and that substances, including medications, that are placed on the skin take longer to be shed. The treatment time needed to clear superficial fungal infections is increased because of the slower renewal of the stratum corneum.

Keratinocytes

The thickness of the epidermis between the rete ridges remains constant or decreases only slightly during intrinsic ageing (Whitton and Everall 1973). However, there is a pronounced effacement of the rete ridges during ageing. The basal keratinocytes with the highest degree of proliferative capacity and proliferative reserve are located at the bottom of the epidermal rete ridges, and the effacement of these structures reflects the decreased proliferative reserve of the aged epidermis. Fewer basal cells per unit area leads to a decrease in the reproductive compartment and decreased epidermal turnover. Basal cells from light-exposed regions of elderly donors show greater variability in the size, shape, and electron density than similar regions from young donors (Kligman 1979). Basal cells from aged individuals have a paucity of microvilli, and the basal cells are larger and cells in the spinous layer are smaller in elderly individuals (Tosti *et al.* 1987). Certain epidermal functions are decreased in aged epidermis. For example, elderly skin is less responsive to the effect of ultraviolet irradiation in converting provitamin D$_3$ to previtamin D$_3$ (MacLaughlin and Holick 1985).

The decrease in the epidermal rete ridges leads to a decreased area of contact between the dermis and epidermis, resulting in an epidermis that separates from the underlying dermis more easily than in the younger individual. Simple trauma such as application and removal of a plaster or a tightly fitting shoe may peel off the epidermis in older people.

The renewal of the epidermis, like the stratum corneum, is slower in people beyond the age of 60–years: thus epidermal wound healing takes longer. As with the stratum corneum, substances that come in contact with the epidermis remain for a longer time before they are shed.

Cytoheterogeneity of the individual keratinocyte nuclei is observed in aged skin which may reflect some disordered regulation of proliferation and could contribute to the excess cutaneous growths such as seborrhoeic keratosis and skin tags that are nearly universal in older people (Tindall and Smith 1963).

The epidermal response to photodamage differs from that seen in intrinsic ageing. The initial response to ultraviolet light is a hyperproliferative response to injury and a thickening of the epidermis. Late effects of severe ultraviolet irradiation injury result in marked epidermal atrophy.

The number of Langerhans' cells is decreased in aged sun-protected skin and decreases even more in sun-damaged skin, leading to a decreased ability to sensitize with contact allergens. In addition, in experimental animals the ultraviolet-light-induced decrease in Langerhans' cells leads to improper antigen presentation resulting in the production of suppressor T cells that impair tumour rejection.

Most of the studies that have measured the number of melanocytes as a function of age have only employed a small number of subjects and have not adequately controlled for the amount of light exposure that the subject received before measurement. In aggregate, it appears that there is some decline in the number of melanocytes with age (Staricco and Pinkus 1957; Snell and Bischitz 1963). Probably more important, however, are the observations that the function of the remaining melanocytes is abnormal. One consequence of these changes is that ultraviolet exposure produces less effective pigment protection in older people.

Greying of hair is a manifestation of loss of melanocyte function and is one of the earliest changes associated with ageing. In an Australian study of 6000 males, some grey hair was found in 22 per cent of men aged 25 to 34 years, 61 per cent of men aged 35 to 44 years, 89 per cent of men aged 45 to 54 years, and 94 per cent of men older than 55 years. The observation that scattered individual hairs go grey independent of their neighbours illustrates the heterogeneity that is characteristic of ageing.

Dermis

The dermis becomes thinner with age. In addition, it becomes more acellular and avascular. Measurements of the total amount of dermal collagen reveal an annual decrease of about 1–per cent. The remaining collagen fibres thicken, become less soluble, have less capacity to swell, and become more resistant to digestion by collagenase (Shuster and Black 1975). Histologically, the collagen fibres appear to be deposited haphazardly in coarse rope-like bundles rather than in an orderly fashion as in younger skin.

Men have a thicker dermis than women. This may explain why female skin seems to deteriorate more readily with ageing. Actinic damage and trauma more easily damage thinner skin.

Photo-ageing and intrinsic ageing show different changes in elastic tissue. In intrinsic ageing the fine subepidermal oxytalan fibres are lost, eventually contributing to superficial laxity, loss of resilience, and finely wrinkled appearance of the skin. These intrinsic degenerative changes in the elastic tissue begin at about the age of 30 years. As they progress, cystic spaces are seen under the electron microscope as the elastin matrix degenerates. The regression of the subepidermal elastic network permits old skin to be stretched over a large distance at low loads.

The changes of photo-ageing include a great increase in the elastotic material in the dermis. These changes are superimposed upon, and eventually mask, the intrinsic changes of ageing. As the photodamage progresses, the elastic fibres become thicker, more numerous, and tightly coiled (Montagna and Carlisle 1979). Histological sections of these tightly coiled elastic fibres appear as fragmented elastic fibres.

The number of cells in the dermis, including fibroblasts, macrophages, and mast cells, decreases across the entire lifespan. The fibroblast becomes a shrunken narrower fibrocyte that contains decreased cytoplasm, and there is a decrease in the turnover of the dermal matrix components. The decrease in mast cells helps to explain the observation that it is more difficult to raise up wheals by histamine-releasing drugs and the observation that urticaria is uncommon in older people. In addition, heparin, which is found in mast cells, stimulates capillary endothelial cell migration *in vitro* and its relative absence may help contribute to the paucity of vasculature in aged skin (Azizkhan *et al.* 1980).

Microcirculation

Regression and disorganization of small vessels are a prominent feature of aged skin. As the rete ridges flatten, the capillary loops that were present in the dermal papilla disappear. In addition, the small vessels about the cutaneous appendages decrease. This is especially prominent in actinic damage. Vessels in intrinsically aged sun-protected skin become thinner and the surrounding veil cells are decreased (or absent) (Braverman and Fonkerko 1982; Braverman *et al.* 1986). The changes in the microvasculature of photodamaged skin differ from that found in intrinsically aged skin in that photodamaged skin manifests a marked thickening of the postcapillary venular walls.

The minimization of the cutaneous vasculature during ageing has profound clinical consequences. These include a decreased inflammatory response, decreased absorption, decreased clearance, decreased urticarial reactions, decreased sweating, delayed wound healing, impaired thermal regulation, increased susceptibility to bruising, and a muted clinical presentation of many cutaneous diseases.

The superficial blood supply is particularly important for thermal regulation. The decreased vasculature can be observed in the pallor of aged skin. The temperature drop between the groin and the feet is greater. Older people quickly experience coldness when the temperature falls and are more at risk for hypothermia and hyperthermia (see the discussion of impaired sweating below). Even a brief exposure to cold may lead to hypothermia. The hypothermia is due to both the inability to divert blood efficiently and a loss of insulating subcutaneous tissue. Younger people vasoconstrict more, shiver more, and generate more metabolic heat.

It takes longer to absorb substances applied to the skin because of the decreased microvasculature, and it takes longer to clear substances injected into the skin. For example, Balin and Lin (1989) have shown that it took twice as long for 65-year-olds to absorb radioactive testosterone rubbed onto the skin or to resolve an intradermally injected saline wheal than it did for 30-year-olds.

Clinically, this decreased clearance can prolong cases of contact dermatitis. Probably more important, however, is that many skin diseases are distinctive because of their pattern or degree of inflammation. The ability to diagnose disease in older patients can be seriously hampered unless it is recognized that some of the cardinal signs of inflammation, including redness, heat, and swelling, may be absent. Cellulitis, for example, can be much more difficult to recognize without these signs.

The decreased blood supply may also necessitate some modification in therapy. Fewer applications of a topical medication may be appropriate because of the decrease in clearance.

Cutaneous nerves

Cutaneous free-nerve endings are little affected anatomically during ageing although tactile sensitivity is decreased. The number of pacinian corpuscles decreases by about two-thirds from the age of 20 to 90 years. Meissner's corpuscles also decrease in number to a similar extent.

Physiological tests reveal less acuity in pain perception and the pain reaction threshold is decreased; thus older people are less capable of sensing danger and reacting appropriately. One consequence is that burns tend to be more serious and widespread.

Consequences of age-associated changes

Overall, the dermal changes that occur during ageing have a number of disparate physiological consequences including the following:

(1) skin is more easily damaged;
(2) wound healing is delayed;
(3) inflammatory response is decreased;
(4) protection from ultraviolet light is decreased;
(5) urticarial reaction is decreased;
(6) skin wrinkles and sags;
(7) skin easily stretches under low loads;
(8) loss of resilience;
(9) diminished absorption;
(10) altered thermal regulation;
(11) decreased sensitivity to pain and pressure.

Subcutaneous tissue

The subcutaneous tissue serves as a shock absorber and a high calorie storage depot. The subcutaneous tissue also modulates conductive heat loss. Generally, the proportion of body that is fat increases until the age of 70 years but there are great regional differences in the distribution of this fat. For example, the amount of subcutaneous fat is decreased on the face and dorsum of the hands but increased around the abdomen and thighs (Kligman et al. 1985). The subcutaneous tissue protects organisms from blunt and pressure-related trauma and serves as an insulator of heat loss. The loss of this protective padding results in an increase in problems of weight-bearing and pressure-prone surfaces, and other injuries, as well as the risk of hypothermia.

Eccrine sweat

There is a reduction in the overall number of sweat glands in aged skin together with a decrease in the functional capacity of the remaining glands. Recruitment of sweat by thermal stimuli takes longer and the density of actively secreting glands decreases with age. Impairment of evaporative heat loss due to attenuated dermal vasculature and decreased sweating leads to an increased risk of heat stroke during hot weather. There is a decrease in sweating in response to dry heat and to experimentally injected intradermal acetylcholine. However, there are no age-associated changes in either the concentration of muscarinic receptors localized to eccrine sweat glands or to the amount of gland showing receptor binding.

Apocrine sweat

There is a decrease in apocrine secretion with age that appears to be primarily due to the age-associated decrease in testosterone levels. The decreased apocrine secretion results in a decrease in body odour. Therefore the need for antiperspirants and deodorants is decreased.

Sebaceous glands

Sebaceous glands are also androgen dependent. The size of the sebaceous glands increases with age, while the transit time of the individual maturing sebaceous cells is 4 to 6 days longer in the elderly person. The sebaceous pore also becomes larger with age. Despite the increased size of the sebaceous glands, there is a decrease in sebum output by 40 to 50 per cent. Additionally, there is a decrease in the size of the individual sebocyte, smaller cytoplasmic oil droplets within the sebocytes, decreased free cholesterol in sebum, and an increase in the squalene fraction of sebum. The proliferative activity of the sebaceous gland decreases with age. These changes lead to sebaceous hyperplasia which are huge sebaceous follicles. The decrease in sebum secretion may contribute to dry skin.

Sebaceous gland size increases with age in non-sun-exposed sebaceous glands such as the Fordyce spots within the mouth. However, sebaceous gland hyperplasia is worsened by chronic sun damage.

Hair

For scalp hair, the rate of hair growth declines and the diameter of the individual terminal hair decreases with age. There is an increased percentage of hairs in the telogen or resting stages of the cycle. Greying of hairs occurs because of a progressive loss of functional melanocytes from the hair follicle bulb. However, hair growth presents a paradox. Not all hair shows a decrease in growth with age. In women older than 65 years of age there is an increase in hair on the lip and chin, although the same women have a decrease in hair on the head, axillae, and pubis. Men lose scalp and beard hair, but have an increase in the growth of hair over their ears, eyebrows, and nostrils. Understanding the mechanisms that are responsible for the androgen-dependent conversion of vellus hair to terminal hair and vice versa in different body regions at the same time may provide important insights into the processes of differentiation and ageing.

Nail growth

The rate of nail growth declines by an average of 35 per cent between the ages of 20 and 80 years (Hamilton *et al.* 1955; Orentreich and Sharp 1967). Because of the decrease in nail growth rate, treatment for fungal diseases of the nail should be prolonged in elderly people. Nails become brittle and lustreless, and longitudinal striations with ridging and beading form on the nailplate.

Clinical conditions prevalent in elderly people

A number of studies have tried to assess the prevalence of skin disease in elderly people. However, the variables are so numerous that no two populations so far studied are similar. As a result, every statement about age-associated skin conditions must be guarded.

All surveys bear out the high incidence of skin abnormalities in older people. Where sunlight is abundant there will be more solar lentigos, actinic keratoses, solar comedones, etc., which reflect cumulative exposure to radiation (Johnson and Roberts 1977). High concordance is found for such common age-associated lesions as xerosis, angiomas, lax skin, and seborrhoeic keratoses.

The prevalence of less common diseases differs appreciably. For example, Tindall and Smith (1963) observed seborrhoeic dermatitis in a third and rosacea in 12 per cent of subjects. Conversely, a Danish group found seborrhoeic dermatitis in only 7 per cent and rosacea in 0.2 per cent of 587 subjects in a municipal residential home (Weismann *et al.* 1981). Eczematous conditions were not frequent in Tindall and Smith's series, but were noted in 25 per cent in Droller's (1953) study of older people living at home. Young (1965) found that, in the course of 1 year in a chronic care facility in New York, over 65 per cent developed one skin disorder and 50 per cent had two. The Health and Nutrition Survey of a representative sample of all Americans aged 1 to 74 years, conducted by the National Center for Health Statistics between 1971 and 1974, found that 56 per cent of those over 60 years and 66 per cent of those over 70 years had a skin condition that was serious enough to require medical attention (Johnson and Roberts 1977).

The common denominator in all studies is the frequency and multiplicity of skin abnormalities in elderly people. Treatable skin conditions are worsened in the presence of poor general health, emotional deterioration (depression), neurological deterioration (chronic brain damage), and inactivity. In turn, these contribute to inability to provide proper daily skin care including cleaning and grooming; skin health is a function of skin care.

Expression of skin diseases in elderly people

In older people common skin disorders are frequently muted, and are so blurred and morphologically transformed that diagnosis may be delayed or missed altogether.

Dermatitis, whatever its origin—irritation, allergy, stasis, microbial infection, drugs, and others—tends to behave differently than in young people. Unless quickly cleared, it tends to become chronic, to spread widely (a process known as autoeczematization), and to respond sluggishly to treatment (Tindall 1974). Healing is slow and unpredictable (Epstein 1946). Thus speedy diagnosis and treatment

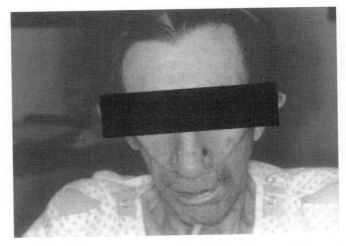

Fig. 1 This patient has severe seborrhoeic dermatitis characterized by yellow greasy scales with erythema of the involved skin. The posterior auricular area is a common location for this disorder.

are exceedingly important to prevent chronicity, extension, and refractoriness.

The failure to react promptly to a toxic stimulus carries with it the danger of continued exposure to noxious agents. Redness appearing shortly after exposure warns a young person to desist. In an older person, because of a long latent period, applications of an irritating agent may continue until suddenly the tissue collapses, sometimes with ulceration. It is only in this sense that older people may be characterized as reacting more vigorously to toxic agents. They should be cautioned regarding self-treatment with home remedies so abundantly at hand.

Some chronic diseases tend to regress in later years. Atopic dermatitis is rare. Plaque-type psoriasis, if not converted to a pustular eruption by overtreatment, usually declines. One might anticipate that hyperproliferative dermatoses would tend to fade as a result of age-dependent declines in mitotic activity. Dandruff, a result of increased production of horny cells, disappears (Leyden *et al.* 1979).

This is counterbalanced to some extent by the emergence of disorders that may achieve prevalence rates considerably higher than in earlier adult life. Seborrhoeic dermatitis (Fig. 1) of the scalp and face, in males particularly, is a striking example. Confinement to bed by severe illness (e.g. myocardial infarction) greatly aggravates seborrhoeic dermatitis and it may generalize (Tager *et al.* 1964). Immobilization generally worsens chronic skin diseases. Rosacea (Fig. 2), starting in young adulthood, may become severe, culminating in such extreme conditions as rhinophyma.

Chronic photosensitivity reactions, especially those of allergic origin, reach their highest prevalence in older people. These are virtually disabling maddeningly pruritic diseases that mainly localize on the faces of older men. The two best known examples are allergic contact dermatitis due to airborne pollen (ragweed) and photocontact allergy due to halogenated salicylanilides (optical bacteriostats) (Fig. 3). These may result in a severe photodermatitis which grotesquely thickens the skin. Such individuals are called persistent light reactors and they are exquisitely sensitive to the entire ultraviolet

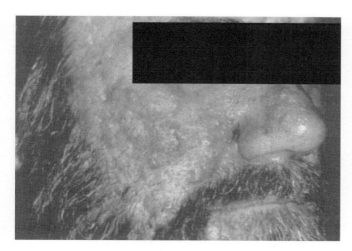

Fig. 2 Rosacea, formerly called acne rosacea, is characterized by erythematous papules, telangiectasia, and pustules on the central face. The condition can also involve the forehead and sides of the face. One form of rosacea can progress to cause enlargement of the nose called rhinophyma.

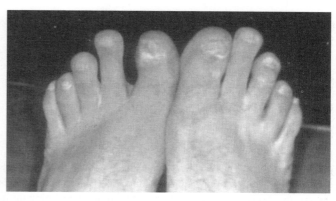

Fig. 4 Tinea pedis which is caused by dermatophyte fungi produces erythema, scaling, and fissuring of the skin of the feet. The infection can spread to involve the toenails. This patient has onychomycosis (fungal infection of the nails) as well as onychogryphosis (thickening and curvature of the nails).

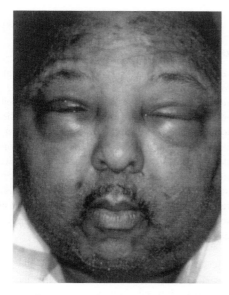

Fig. 3 This patient has a severe contact dermatitis with erythema, vesiculation, and secondary bacterial infection involving the skin around the eyes.

spectrum; the allergen cannot always be identified. Actinically damaged skin with its attenuated blood supply is the substrate in which these photodermatoses develop. Sunlight worsens a number of skin disorders, such as rosacea.

Interdigital athlete's foot (Fig. 4) is common in old age, often extending beyond the confines of the fifth interspace, and is invariably accompanied by onychomycosis. Slower turnover of the horny layer, a depressed inflammatory response, and decreased cellular immunity contribute to chronicity.

The integument is at especially high risk of injury from burns, chemical irritation, and trauma owing to decreased sensory perception and slower reaction times. Particularly telling examples of chemical

toxicity derive from the diminished capacity to mount an inflammatory response promptly. For example, a keratolytic solution of salicylic acid and propylene glycol, often used for dry skin, will incite scaling and redness in a few days if applied twice daily to the face of a young person. In an elderly person, the skin may remain silent for 2 to 3 weeks before suddenly exploding into a severe dermatitis from toxic overload. Household cleaning and disinfectant solutions, often used to stop itching, are a genuine hazard. The sensible safe management of pruritus in older patients requires knowledge and experience (Thorne 1978).

Primary pyodermas due to *Staphylococcus aureus* and β-haemolytic streptococci may not call forth the customary signs of pain, heat, and redness. A furuncle may present as a cold abscess and cellulitis may show only an indolent swelling.

A high order of suspicion is indicated for every widespread eruption that cannot readily be identified. It is surprising how easy it is to miss a diagnosis of scabies which has only maddening pruritus as the signal feature, the lesions being otherwise unrecognizable. These cryptic cases can be the unsuspected source of major epidemics in institutions (Tschin 1982). Also, the expression of skin disease is modified by nutritional deficiencies. Scurvy is more frequent than realized. Many very old people, particularly those living alone or with various disabilities, do not have an adequate diet. Patients with zinc deficiencies suffer exotic rashes which cannot be recognized clinically and which adversely affect cell-mediated immunity (Sandstead *et al.* 1982).

The expression of vitamin or mineral deficiencies is very easily overlooked, being regarded as part of the diverse cutaneous alterations which inevitably come with age (Bienia *et al.* 1982). Thus markedly xerotic skin due to iron deficiency with anaemia arouses no interest since almost all old people suffer from dry skin. Likewise, purpura is so familiar that diagnostic follicular haemorrhages in scurvy are not even seen. Perlèche from a lack of vitamin B will probably be put down to drooling of the corners of the mouth or diagnosed as moniliasis.

Finally, when infections are recognized, exotic organisms, such as yeast-like fungi, unusual Gram-negative organisms, and unfamiliar anaerobes, should be sought. These should not be dismissed as contaminants.

Specific clinical conditions prevalent in elderly people

Pruritus

Pruritus, or itching, is the most common dermatological complaint in older people (Kligman 1979). 'Dry skin' is often credited with causing this incapacitating affliction, and it is true that xerosis is commonly observed. Seborrhoeic dermatitis is also very common in older people, however, and there are numerous other specific conditions that can account for the itching symptoms. It is inappropriate to dismiss pruritus as banal, because the opposite is quite often the case.

The sensation of itching is picked up by various types of nerve endings and transmitted by way of the sensory nerves, located below the dermoepidermal junction, to the posterior nerve roots and spinal cord (Loring 1979). The 'bright and well-localized' sensation of spontaneous itch is transmitted by δ fibres of class A myelinated nerves, which are 10 μm in diameter and conduct at about 10 m/s. The unpleasant and poorly localized itch sensation is transmitted by C fibres of unmyelinated nerves which are 5.5 μm in diameter and conduct at about 1 m/s. Itch and pain are transmitted similarly, but not identically, by C fibres. Heat, for example, blocks itch but spares the sensation of pain. Pain can decrease itch perception. A great deal is unknown about the neurophysiology of itching. An ideal antipruritic agent, antihistamine, narcoleptic, or anti-inflammatory has not been identified (Arnold *et al.* 1979). One problem is the lack of a good model system in human beings in which to study the induction of pruritus and its control. Histamine, proteases, and other agents have been used to induce itching (Hagermark *et al.* 1978).

Clinically, a large number of conditions can cause pruritus, including the following:

(1) xerosis;
(2) infestations (pediculosis corporis, scabies, trichinosis, onchocerciasis, etc.);
(3) metabolic or endocrine problems (hypo- or hyperthyroidism, diabetes mellitus);
(4) malignant neoplasms (lymphoma, leukaemia);
(5) chronic renal disease;
(6) hepatobiliary disease (primary or secondary biliary cirrhosis);
(7) drug ingestion (opiates, codeine, drug hypersensitivity, drugs that cause cholestasis as a side-effect such as erythromycin estolate, chlorpropamide, or chlorpromazine);
(8) haematological disease (iron deficiency anaemia, polycythaemia rubra, paraproteinaemia);
(9) psychiatric problems (chronic depression and agitation, neurotic excoriations, delusions of parasitosis);
(10) many skin diseases (including miliaria, folliculitis, contact dermatitis, and irritant dermatitis from exogenous irritants such as chemicals, hairs, fibreglass, or plant spicules).

Pruritus can be treated symptomatically with antihistamines such as hydroxyzine and topically with Lubriderm with menthol and phenol.

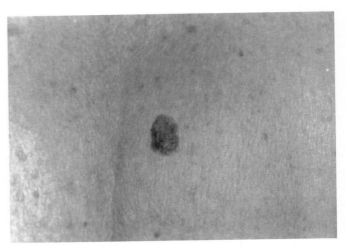

Fig. 5 Seborrhoeic keratoses can vary in colour from dark black to tan or flesh coloured depending on the amount of melanin present. They are sharply demarcated, raised, and have a waxy, stuck-on appearance. This deeply pigmented seborrhoeic keratosis is surrounded by smaller seborrhoeic keratoses and lentigos. Occasionally dark black lesions are mistaken for melanoma.

Seborrhoeic dermatitis

Itching in older people may also be caused by inflammatory dermatoses. Seborrhoeic dermatitis is very common in elderly people, but its cause is unknown (Fig. 5). The prevalence of seborrhoeic dermatitis in parkinsonism, and at times of stress and fatigue, implicates neurological factors. Aetiological roles for sebum and yeast have been proposed for seborrhoeic dermatitis. It does not develop unless the sebaceous glands are active, which probably accounts for its prevalence during infancy and in postpubertal individuals. The standard treatments for seborrhoeic dermatitis involve the use of shampoos containing selenium sulphide, zinc pyrithion, or tar and topical hydrocortisone. Topical ketoconazole or itraconazole has been shown to be effective therapy for seborrhoeic dermatitis.

Xerosis

There is much to be learned about xerosis, which is another cause of itching. Xerosis is due in part to decreases in eccrine sweating, sebum production, water content of the stratum corneum, and cohesion of corneocytes. Changes in the production of sebum may contribute to the development of xerosis because the water-retaining property of the stratum corneum is reduced in old age when the amount of sebum is reduced (Plewig and Kligman 1978). The role played by the keratinization process in determining xerosis is also unclear. Keratinization is partially controlled by age-associated processes.

Xerosis is effectively treated with hydration and emollients such as petrolatum. Lac-hydrin (ammonium lactate lotion 12 per cent) is also very effective.

Cutaneous tumours of epidermal keratinocytes

A number of cutaneous tumours of epidermal keratinocytes are prevalent in older people. Seborrhoeic keratoses, which are benign epithelial neoplasms, occur more frequently as individuals advanced in age. They have been found in up to 88 per cent of people over the age of 65 years; in one study about 50 per cent of those with seborrhoeic keratosis had 10 or more lesions (Tindall and Smith 1963). Seborrhoeic keratoses appear to be dominantly inherited, but they seldom appear before middle-age. They are found on the skin in those areas of the body that are rich in sebaceous glands such as the trunk, face, and extremities. Seborrhoeic keratoses are sharply demarcated, brown, and slightly raised. They look as if they have been stuck on the skin surface. Most have a verrucous surface with a soft friable consistency (see Fig. 5).

The amount of melanin in a seborrhoeic keratosis is variable, and inexperienced observers have been known to mistake them for melanomas (see Fig. 5). If these lesions bleed, become irritated, or change in size, shape, or colour, removal and pathological examination are indicated.

The sign of Leser–Trélat is the sudden appearance and rapid increase in size and number of seborrhoeic keratoses on skin that was previously blemish free. This condition is associated with the development of an internal malignancy which is usually an adeno-carcinoma (Ronchese 1965; Dantzig 1973; Liddell *et al.* 1975; Curry and King 1980).

Several neoplastic conditions that are common in older people are associated with environmental damage to the skin. These include actinic keratoses, Bowen's disease (see below), squamous cell carcinoma, and basal cell carcinoma. The changes that most people equate with ageing of the skin are due to chronic solar damage. Prolonged exposure to ultraviolet irradiation leads to cutaneous atrophy, alterations in pigmentation, wrinkling, dryness, telangiectasia, and solar elastosis. Wavelengths between 290 and 310 nm define the spectral range that produces sunburn, and this is also thought to be the irradiation mainly responsible for actinic damage to the skin (Parish *et al.* 1979). Some of the strongest evidence that implicates ultraviolet light as being important in the aetiology of epidermal tumours comes from epidemiological data correlating the incidence of tumours with the degree of pigmentary protection. The individual principally at risk is light skinned, is easily sunburned, and does not tan. Other strong epidemiological data correlate an increased incidence of skin tumours with decreasing latitude and increasing sun exposure.

Actinic keratoses

Actinic or solar keratoses are composed of clones of anaplastic keratinocytes confined to the epidermis and occur commonly on the sun-damaged skin of elderly individuals (Fig. 6). If left untreated, they may progress and invade through the basement membrane of the epidermodermal junction, thereby becoming invasive squamous cell carcinomas.

Actinic keratoses are extremely common in elderly individuals who have had extensive sun exposure. They usually occur on skin damaged from sun exposure, such as the bald scalp, face, and forearms. They are more common in fair-skinned individuals, and are almost never seen in black people. These observations strongly suggest that chronic exposure to sunlight is an important aetiological factor (see Fig. 6). The carcinogenic property of sunlight resides mainly in the ultraviolet B range and can be adequately screened out by modern sunscreens.

Actinic keratoses occur as well-demarcated scaly rough papules on sun-exposed skin surfaces. The colour varies from tan to red, but

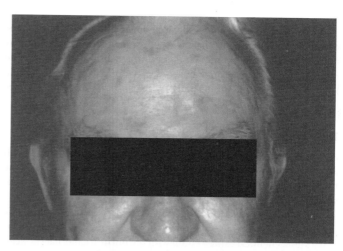

Fig. 6 Actinic keratoses on the cheek and forehead. Each lesion occurs as a discrete, erythematous scaly papule with varying degree of induration. Actinic keratoses can occur on any part of the skin which has been chronically exposed to sunlight.

sometimes they are the same colour as the surrounding skin. As a result, some lesions are more easily palpated than seen. In some cases, known as pigmented actinic keratoses, increased amount of pigmentation renders the lesion a striking brown colour. Actinic keratoses are usually small, measuring from a few millimetres to 1 or 2 cm in size. Depending on the degree of prior sun exposure, a given patient may have one or a few lesions, or hundreds of lesions. There are often other signs of actinic damage in the surrounding skin, including wrinkling, dryness, and yellow discoloration from solar elastosis. Actinic keratoses can occur at the base of cutaneous horns.

Spreading pigmented actinic keratosis is an unusual variant of actinic keratosis. Clinically, they are characterized by large size (over 1 cm), brown pigmentation, and a tendency for centrifugal spread (James *et al.* 1978; Subrt *et al.* 1983). These lesions can mimic lentigo maligna in clinical appearance.

Histologicalally, actinic keratoses are well-demarcated islands of abnormal keratinocytes with overlying parakeratosis. Their nuclei are large, irregular, and hyperchromatic, giving rise to a pleomorphic or atypical appearance. Changes of solar elastosis are invariably present in the underlying dermis.

Progression from carcinoma *in situ* to invasive squamous cell carcinoma

Progression of actinic keratosis to invasive squamous cell carcinoma occurs when buds of atypical keratinocytes extend deep into the dermis, leading to detached nests of abnormal cells capable of autonomous growth. Clinically, the lesion may become thicker, more indurated, and enlarged. Such signs, however, are not always present and are not substitutes for histological confirmation of dermal invasion.

Various studies indicate that, on average, an individual with actinic keratoses would have a likelihood of 1 to 2 per cent per year or 10 to 20 per cent in 10 years of developing an invasive squamous cell carcinoma (Marks *et al.* 1988).

as overall staging. The Global Deterioration Scale stages the progression of Alzheimer's disease cognitively, functionally, and behaviourally. A structured interview is not required, but it needs to be carried out by an experienced clinician who has access to all sources of information about the patient. The Functional Assessment Staging Scale (Reisberg 1988; Sclan and Reisberg 1992) extends the range of the Global Deterioration Scale by expanding the last two stages into 16 for use in more impaired individuals. Other commonly used global rating scales include the Functional Rating Scale (Crockett et al. 1989; Feldman et al. 1995), the Brief Cognitive Rating Scale (Reisberg and Ferris 1988), and the Cambridge Mental Disorders of the Elderly Examination (Roth et al. 1986).

Diagnostic criteria sets

In order to summarize the diagnostic information and to aid in the diagnosis of dementia in particular, the use of diagnostic checklists may be indicated. Currently these are widely used in research, but may have utility in clinical practice to help standardize diagnosis. The three most widely used criteria-based approaches to the diagnosis of Alzheimer's disease are the International Classification of Diseases, 10th revision (ICD-10) (WHO 1992), the Diagnostic and Statistical Manual of Mental Disorders, 4th edition (DSM-IV) (American Psychiatric Association 1994), and the National Institute of Neurological and Communicative Disorders and Stroke–Alzheimer's Disease and Related Disorders Association Work Group criteria (McKhann et al. 1984). In experienced hands these criteria-based diagnoses correlate highly with the pathological diagnosis of Alzheimer's disease (Tierney et al. 1988; Gearing et al. 1995); however, other dementias such as frontal dementia and Lewy body dementia may be misdiagnosed.

In summary, one should approach the use of scales with a caveat. Diagnosis should not be made using the scales alone. They are intended as tools to aid the clinician and should not be used as substitutes for medical knowledge and judgement. Previously these instruments have been primarily used in research; however, with the advent of anticholinesterase drugs for symptomatic treatment of Alzheimer's disease, standardized assessments will be more important. The use of scales will give some objective measurements that can be used as a baseline against which to assess change and hence determine if a given drug is appropriate.

The general neurological examination

Obviously the neurological examination will not be done in isolation and hence the doctor will have to keep in mind how abnormalities in other body systems may affect the nervous system. Signs and symptoms of cardiac disease, hypertension, diabetic complications, and the presence of a carotid bruit may all provide supporting evidence in patients with cerebrovascular disease. Enlargement of the thyroid may indicate a goitre and indicate hypothyroidism which can be associated with cognitive impairment, neuropathy, and reflex changes. Liver enlargement and spider angiomas suggestive of chronic hepatic failure may give clues to a metabolic encephalopathy. Main features of the general neurological examination are shown in Table 3.

Cranial nerves

Abnormalities in cranial nerve examination are rarely associated with normal ageing with the exception of some changes in olfaction, vision,

and hearing (Schaumburg et al. 1983; Walshe 1987; Wolfson and Katzman 1992; Kaye et al. 1994).

Olfaction

Olfaction generally declines symmetrically with age. Kaye et al. (1994) compared a group of younger old individuals (aged 65 to 74 years) with a group of optimally healthy oldest old (aged over 84 years). In the younger group, 7.6 per cent were found to be anosmic, whereas 50 per cent of the older group were similarly impaired. This may be due to non-neurological factors such as chronic mucosal thickening, perhaps secondary to recurrent upper respiratory infections. Asymmetric loss of sense of smell is more likely to have neurological significance. Olfaction is rarely tested as part of the routine neurological examination in younger individuals, but in older patients it should be evaluated as it may provide important clues to underlying pathology. Conditions such as olfactory groove meningiomas, neurodegenerative disorders such as Alzheimer's disease, and head trauma may be associated with disturbances in olfactory function.

Vision

Visual function is often impaired in elderly people (Canadian Task Force on the Periodic Health Examination 1995); 13 per cent have some impairment, while 8 per cent have severe impairment (blindness in both eyes, or inability to read newsprint even with glasses). About 1 per cent of people over the age of 40 years have bilateral blindness. The most common causes of visual impairment in elderly people are presbyopia, cataracts, age-associated macular degeneration, glaucoma, and diabetic retinopathy. Current Canadian guidelines suggest that it is fair to include a visual acuity test by Snellen chart in the periodic health examination, and fundoscopy or retinal photography in patients with diabetes of at least 5 years duration. For patients with a high risk of glaucoma, a periodic assessment by an ophthalmologist is recommended. From the foregoing discussion, it is apparent that decreases in visual acuity from ageing are most often related to abnormalities in the eye and not in the components of the visual system such as the optic nerve, optic tract, and visual cortex. Therefore visual field changes are not likely to be associated with normal ageing, but with underlying central nervous system pathology such as cerebrovascular damage.

Fundoscopic examination is more likely to be abnormal in the older individual. Changes in the retina are often due to systemic diseases such as diabetes or hypertension. Normal ageing does not significantly alter the appearance of the retina. The pupils in elderly patients may be smaller; thus making fundoscopic examination more difficult especially when coupled with changes such as cataracts. The pupillary light reflex and accommodation may be sluggish compared with younger individuals. These pupillary changes are symmetrical and any asymmetry should suggest disease. Problems with ocular convergence and conjugate upward gaze develop more commonly with age; however, other extraocular movement abnormalities would not be expected to occur. In the study by Kaye et al. (1994), upgaze and convergence were limited in the young old (65 to 74 years) by 5.9 per cent and 11.7 per cent respectively, and in the oldest old (over 84 years old) both by 64.7 per cent. Other investigators report upgaze limitation from 9.3 to 25 per cent in elderly people (Galasko et al. 1990; Cosi and Romani 1996; Waite et al. 1996). Nystagmus may be seen in toxic or drug-induced states, for example with anticonvulsant drugs.

Table 3 Main features of the general neurological examination

Domain	Function	Description
General	General physical examination—evidence of systemic processes that may affect the nervous system	Focus on relevant aspects—for example cardiac examination and the presence of carotid bruits may be relevant in cerebrovascular disease
Cranial nerves	Olfaction	Both nostrils
	Vision	Acuity, fundus, visual fields, pupils, extraocular movements
	Hearing	Acuity
Motor (including gait and balance)	Muscle bulk	Assess degree of atrophy or sarcopenia
	Power (strength)	Assess symmetry
	Resting tone	Movement disorders such as tremor (especially non-parkinsonian)
	Gait	Posture, initiation of voluntary movement, speed, stability, stride, turning
	Balance	Standing, walking, heel–toe walking
	Co-ordination	Limb testing—finger–nose and heel–shin
Sensory (including reflexes)	Vibration	Assess other modalities as well; look for symmetry
	Reflexes	Assess symmetry, primitive reflexes

Hearing

Abnormalities of hearing are also associated with advancing age (Gold *et al.* 1996). Hearing loss is present in an estimated 33 per cent of people aged 64 to 74 years, 45 per cent of people aged 75 to 84 years, and 62 per cent of people older than 85 years. It has been shown that the prevalence of hearing loss in older populations with cognitive impairment is even higher than these figures suggest. This factor as well as the previously described visual decline should be taken into account when one is assessing cognitive function, as the cognitive test scores could be erroneously deflated. Labyrinthine function is closely related to hearing. Although problems with dizziness and balance may occur more frequently with ageing, they are not related to the ageing process itself. Rather, they are related to diseases such as benign positional vertigo, Menière's disease, and vascular compromise of the labyrinth, all of which occur more commonly with age.

Motor system, gait, and balance

Changes in the motor system are perhaps the most visible to the casual observer. Muscle wasting or sarcopenia is common particularly in extremely old people (Evans 1995). In ageing, both the number and size of muscle fibres decreases. This loss of muscle bulk is responsible for a mild age-associated decline in muscle strength, and it has been reported that grip strength declines 20 to 30 per cent between the ages of 20 and 80 years. This amount of decline is not usually apparent on routine clinical testing and should not be considered abnormal unless asymmetry is noted.

The ageing process affects gait and posture (Walshe 1987; Wolfson and Katzman 1992). Older individuals tend to have a slightly stooped, forward flexed posture, and a slightly stiff, bradykinetic gait. The study by Kaye *et al.* (1994) shows that there is very little impairment of gait and balance in the young old (65 to 74 years), but in the oldest old (over 84 years old) various abnormalities of gait and balance occur in over 90 per cent of individuals. Galasko *et al.* (1990) examined physical findings in a group of community-dwelling patients with Alzheimer's disease and compared them to non-demented individuals. The prevalence of gait abnormalities in the non-demented group was 22 per cent, while in those with Alzheimer's it was 39 per cent. Stooped posture was reported in 1 per cent of the non-demented group and 16 per cent of the Alzheimer's group. These features are reminiscent of parkinsonism and have been ascribed to basal ganglionic degeneration by some. More likely, in otherwise healthy individuals, these features can be explained by musculoskeletal abnormalities such as osteoarthritis. Deficits in balance have been reported as one of the most significant neurological consequences of ageing; however, others feel that this is just related to an increased burden of nervous system disease in elderly people, and can be explained by a specific disease process rather than ageing itself. Cerebrovascular disease, labyrinthine disease, alcoholism with cerebellar degeneration, and neuropathy with loss of proprioception can all lead to balance problems.

Sensory system and reflexes

With advancing age, vibratory sensation is dulled. This is much more prominent in the lower extremities. Kaye *et al.* (1994) report this in 11.8 per cent of the young old (65 to 74 years) and 67.7 per cent of the oldest old (over 84 years old). Other investigators report dulled vibration sense in the range of 25 to 35 per cent of older individuals (Galasko *et al.* 1990; Waite *et al.* 1996). Other sensory modalities have been reported to be depressed by some and normal by others (Walshe 1987; Wolfson and Katzman 1992). If significant deficits exist in modalities other than vibration sense, they should be considered clinically significant. Structural and functional abnormalities have been reported in the peripheral nervous system; however, most can be accounted for by trauma, disuse, and vascular compromise (Schaumburg *et al.* 1983).

Changes in reflexes are not normally common in elderly people, and asymmetry indicates pathology just as it does in younger individuals. However, the absence of reflexes, particularly the ankle jerks, have been reported to occur with ageing. Kaye *et al.* (1994)

report the loss of the ankle jerk in 29.4 per cent of the young old (65 to 74 years), and in 55.9 per cent of the oldest old (over 84 years old). In the same study there was no loss of the biceps jerk observed in either group. A recent study suggests that although a significant number of normal adults have a unilateral loss of an ankle jerk, the finding is rare enough that it should be considered clinically significant, irrespective of age (Bowditch *et al.* 1996). The suggestion has been made that the loss or reduction in an ankle jerk may be due to inelasticity of the Achilles tendon rather than to changes in the nervous system. It has also been implied that alteration of clinical examination technique may bring out findings felt to be absent. This was demonstrated for ankle jerks by showing that the traditional tendon-strike method of obtaining the reflex did not yield as good a result as the use of a plantar-strike technique in patients seen in a geriatric department (Ipallomeni *et al.* 1984).

Although the presence of an extensor plantar response has been reported as a rare finding in a normal elderly person, it may be difficult to obtain this reflex properly, or to misinterpret a withdrawal response. This may be due to various factors such as thickened plantar skin or calluses, or from deformities due to arthritis. Kaye *et al.* (1994) report an extensor plantar response in 5.9 per cent of the young old (65 to 74 years), and in 11.8 per cent of the oldest old (over 84 years old). In the study by Galasko *et al.* (1990), normal community-dwelling elderly had a prevalence of extensor plantar response of 1 per cent, while in those with Alzheimer's disease it was 9 per cent.

Neuropathy from various causes may also be present, and withdrawal may occur particularly if hyperaesthesia is present. An extensor response should be taken as an indicator of disease and not a normal finding. Superficial abdominal reflexes are often absent in elderly people. The clinical significance of this is not clear. Palmomental and snout reflexes are reported to occur in normal individuals and may increase in frequency with advancing age (Jacobs and Gossman 1980). Certain of the primitive reflexes, particularly the grasp and glabellar response, may be more indicative of neurodegenerative syndromes. Even though the palmomental reflex is non-specific, it may be exaggerated in patients with dementia. One study demonstrated that rigidity, stooped posture, graphaesthesia, neglect of simultaneous tactile stimuli (face–hand test), and snout, grasp, and glabellar reflexes were present significantly more often in patients with Alzheimer's disease than in control subjects (Galasko *et al.* 1990). These findings increased in prevalence with the degree of dementia, and three findings, grasp reflex, graphaesthesia, and the face–hand test were statistically significantly associated with the degree of cognitive impairment.

Conclusion

In summary, the examination of the elderly patient should be approached with the same rigour as one would adopt in a younger individual. The examiner should keep in mind the special needs of the elderly patient, the pattern of disease with advancing age, and the normal involutional changes in the nervous system.

References

American Psychiatric Association (1994). *Diagnostic and statistical manual of mental disorders* (4th edn). American Psychiatric Association, Washington, DC.

Bird, H.R., Canino, G., Stipec, M.R., and Shrout, P. (1987). Use of the Mini-Mental State Examination in a probability sample of a Hispanic population. *Journal of Nervous and Mental Disease*, 175, 731–7.

Bowditch, M.G., Sanderson, P., and Livesey, J.P. (1996). The significance of an absent ankle reflex. *Journal of Bone and Joint Surgery (British)*, 78, 276–9.

Canadian Task Force on the Periodic Health Examination (1995). Periodic health examination, 1995 update: 3. Screening for visual problems among elderly patients. *Canadian Medical Association Journal*, 152, 1211–22.

Cappeliez, P., Quintal, M., Blouin, M., *et al.* (1996). Psychometric properties of the French version of the Modified Mini-Mental State (3MS) in elderly patients evaluated in geriatric psychiatry. *Canadian Journal of Psychiatry—Revue Canadienne de Psychiatrie*, 41, 114–21.

Commenges, D., Gagnon, M., Letenneur, L., Dartigues, J.F., Barberger-Gateau, P., and Salamon, R. (1992). Statistical description of the Mini-Mental State Examination for French elderly community residents. Paquid Study Group. *Journal of Nervous and Mental Disease*, 180, 28–32.

Cosi, V. and Romani, A. (1996). Neurological findings in the normal elderly: prevalence and relationships with memory performance. *Aging (Milan)*, 8, 243–9.

Critchley, M. (1931). The neurology of old age. *Lancet*, i, 1331–6.

Critchley, M. (1956). Neurologic changes in the aged. *Journal of Chronic Diseases*, 3, 459–76.

Crockett, D.J, Tuokko, H., Koch, W., and Parks, R. (1989). The assessment of everyday functioning using the Present Functioning Questionnaire and the Functional Rating Scale in elderly samples. *Clinical Gerontologist*, 8, 3–25.

D'Alessandro, R., Pandolfo, G., Azzimondi, G., and Feruglio, F. S. (1996). Prevalence of dementia among elderly people in Troina, Sicily. *European Journal of Epidemiology*, 12, 595–9.

Dastoor, D.P., Schwartz, G., and Kurzman, D. (1991). Clock-drawing: an assessment technique in dementia. *Journal of Clinical and Experimental Gerontology*, 13, 69–85.

Dautzenberg, P.L., Schmand, B., Vriens, M.T., Deelman, B.G., and Hooijer, C. (1991). Validity of the cognitive screening tests and the mini-mental status examination in a group of elderly hospital patients. *Nederlands Tijdschrift voor Geneeskunde*, 135, 850–5.

Evans, W.J. (1995). Exercise, nutrition, and aging. *Clinics in Geriatric Medicine*, 11, 725–34.

Feldman, H., Schulzer, M., Wang, S., *et al.* (1995). The functional rating scale (FRS) in Alzheimer's disease: a longitudinal study. In *Research advances in Alzheimer's disease and related disorders* (ed. K. Iqbal, J. Mortimer, B. Winbald, and H. Wisiewski), pp. 235–41. Wiley, Chichester.

Folstein, M.F., Folstein, S.E., and McHugh, P.R. (1975). 'Mini-mental state'. A practical method for grading the cognitive state of patients for the clinician. *Journal of Psychiatric Research*, 12, 189–98.

Gagnon, M., Letenneur, L., Dartigues, J. F., *et al.* (1990). Validity of the Mini-Mental State examination as a screening instrument for cognitive impairment and dementia in French elderly community residents. *Neuroepidemiology*, 9, 143–50.

Galasko, D., Kwo-on-Yuen, P.F., Klauber, M.R., and Thal, L.J. (1990). Neurological findings in Alzheimer's disease and normal aging. *Archives of Neurology*, 47, 625–7.

Gauthier, S., Gelinas, I., and Gauthier, L. (1997). Functional disability in Alzheimer's disease. *International Psychogeriatrics*, 9 (Supplement 1), 163–5.

Gearing, M., Mirra, S.S., Hedreen, J.C., Sumi, S.M., Hansen, L. A., and Heyman, A. (1995). The Consortium to Establish a Registry for Alzheimer's Disease (CERAD). Part X. Neuropathology confirmation of the clinical diagnosis of Alzheimer's disease. *Neurology*, 45, 461–6.

Gimenez-Roldan, S., Novillo, M.J., Navarro, E., Dobato, J.L., and Gimenez-Zuccarelli, M. (1997). Mini-mental state examination: proposal of protocol to be used. *Revista de Neurologia*, 25, 576–83.

Gold, M., Lightfoot, L.A., and Hnath-Chisolm, T. (1996). Hearing loss in a memory disorders clinic. A specially vulnerable population. *Archives of Neurology*, 53, 922–8.

Grut, M., Fratiglioni, L., Viitanen, M., and Winblad, B. (1993). Accuracy of the Mini-Mental Status Examination as a screening test for dementia in a Swedish elderly population. *Acta Neurologica Scandinavica*, 87, 312–17.

Hirono, N., Mori, E., Ikejiri, Y., *et al.* (1997). Japanese version of the Neuropsychiatric Inventory—a scoring system for neuropsychiatric disturbance in dementia patients. *No to Shinkei (Brain and Nerve)*, 49, 266–71.

Hughes, C.P., Berg, L., Danziger, W.L., Coben, L.A., and Martin, R.L. (1982). A new clinical scale for the staging of dementia. *British Journal of Psychiatry*, 140, 566–72.

Ipallomeni, M., Kenny, R.A., Flynn, M.D., Kraenzlin, M., and Pallis, C.A. (1984). The elderly and their ankle jerks. *Lancet*, i, 670–2.

Jacobs, L. and Gossman, M.D. (1980). Three primitive reflexes in normal adults. *Neurology*, 30, 184–8.

Jennett, P.A., Hogan, D.B., Crutcher, R.A., Aldous, J., Scott, S., and Kurtz, S.M. (1997). Elderly standardized patients' ratings of physician communication behaviors in office encounters. *Annals of the Royal College of Physicians and Surgeons of Canada*, 30, 211–15.

Kaplan, E., Goodglass H., and Weintraub S. (1983). *The Boston Naming Test*. Lea and Febiger, Philadelphia, PA.

Katzman, R. and Terry R. (1992). Normal aging of the nervous system. In *Principles of geriatric neurology* (ed. R. Katzman and J.W. Rowe), pp. 18–58. F.A. Davis, Philadelphia, PA.

Katzman, R., Zhang, M.Y., Ouang-Ya-Qu, W.Z.Y., *et al.* (1988). A Chinese version of the Mini-Mental State Examination; impact of illiteracy in a Shanghai dementia survey. *Journal of Clinical Epidemiology*, 41, 971–8.

Kaye, J.A., Oken, B.S., Howieson, D.B., Howieson, J., Holm, L. A., and Dennison, K. (1994). Neurologic evaluation of the optimally healthy oldest old. *Archives of Neurology*, 51, 1205–11.

Law, S. and Wolfson, C. (1995). Validation of a French version of an informant-based questionnaire as a screening test for Alzheimer's disease. *British Journal of Psychiatry*, 167, 541–4.

Lawton, M.P. and Brody, E.M. (1969). Assessment of older people: self-maintaining and instrumental activities of daily living. *Gerontologist*, 9, 179–86.

Lazarus, L.W., Newton N., Cohler B., *et al.* (1987). Frequency and presentation of depressive symptoms in patients with primary degenerative dementia. *American Journal of Psychiatry*, 144, 41–5.

Liu, C.K., Lin, R.T., Chen, Y.F., Tai, C.T., Yen, Y.Y., and Howng, S.L. (1996). Prevalence of dementia in an urban area in Taiwan. *Journal of the Formosan Medical Association*, 95, 762–8.

McKhann, G., Drachman, D., Folstein, M., Katzman, R., Price, D., and Stadlan, E.M. (1984). Clinical diagnosis of Alzheimer's disease: report of the NINCDS-ADRDA Work Group under the auspices of Department of Health and Human Services Task Force on Alzheimer's Disease. *Neurology*, 34, 939–44.

Meiran, N., Stuss, D.T., Guzman, D.A., Lafleche, G., and Willmer, J. (1996). Diagnosis of dementia. Methods for interpretation of scores of 5 in neuropsychological tests. *Archives of Neurology*, 53, 1043–54.

Morris, J.C. (1993). The Clinical Dementia Rating (CDR): current version and scoring rules. *Neurology*, 43, 2412–14.

Mulligan, R., Mackinnon, A., Jorm, A.F., Giannakopoulos, P., and Michel, J.P. (1996). A comparison of alternative methods of screening for dementia in clinical settings. *Archives of Neurology*, 53, 532–6.

Murden, R.A. and Galbraith, J. (1997). A Modified Mini-Mental State Examination for use in the poorly educated. *Clinical Gerontologist*, 17, 23–33.

Noser, A., Schonenberger, P.M., and Wettstein, A. (1988). Comparative study between the Folstein mini-mental state and the Zurich variant in demented and non-demented patients. *Schweizer Archiv fur Neurologie und Psychiatrie*, 139, 69–77.

Panisset, M., Roudier, M., Saxton, J., and Boller, F. (1992). A battery of neuropsychological tests for severe dementia. An evaluation study. *Presse Medicale*, 21, 1271–4.

Petersen, R.C. (1995). Normal aging, mild cognitive impairment, and early Alzheimer's disease. *Neurologist*, 1, 326–44.

Reisberg, B. (1988). Functional Assessment Staging (FAST). *Psychopharmacology Bulletin*, 24, 653–9.

Reisberg, B. and Ferris, S.H. (1988). Brief Cognitive Rating Scale (BCRS). *Psychopharmacology Bulletin*, 24, 629–36.

Reisberg, B., Ferris, S.H., de Leon, M.J., and Crook, T. (1982). The Global Deterioration Scale for assessment of primary degenerative dementia. *American Journal of Psychiatry*, 139, 1136–9.

Roth, M., Tym, E., Mountjoy, C.Q., *et al.* (1986). CAMDEX. A standardised instrument for the diagnosis of mental disorder in the elderly with special reference to the early detection of dementia. *British Journal of Psychiatry*, 149, 698–709.

Salmon, D.P., Riekkinen, P.J., Katzman, R., Zhang, M.Y., Jin, H., and Yu, E. (1989). Cross-cultural studies of dementia. A comparison of Mini-Mental State Examination performance in Finland and China. *Archives of Neurology*, 46, 769–72.

Saxton, J. and Swihart, A.A. (1989). Neuropsychological assessment of the severely impaired elderly patient. *Clinics in Geriatric Medicine*, 5, 531–43.

Schaumburg, H.H., Spencer, P.S., and Ochoa, J. (1983). The aging human peripheral nervous system. In *The neurology of aging* (ed. R. Katzman and R. Terry), pp.111–22. F.A. Davis, Philadelphia.

Sclan, S.G. and Reisberg, B. (1992). Functional assessment staging (FAST) in Alzheimer's disease: reliability, validity, and ordinality. *International Psychogeriatrics*, 4 (Supplement 1), 55–69.

Stuss, D.T., Meiran, N., Guzman, D.A., Lafleche, G., and Willmer, J. (1996). Do long tests yield a more accurate diagnosis of dementia than short tests? A comparison of five neuropsychological tests. *Archives of Neurology*, 53, 1033–9.

Teng, E.L. and Chui, H.C. (1987). The Modified Mini-Mental State (3MS) examination. *Journal of Clinical Psychiatry*, 48, 314–18.

Tierney, M.C., Fisher, R.H., Lewis, A.J., *et al.* (1988). The NINCDS–ADRDA Work Group criteria for the clinical diagnosis of probable Alzheimer's disease: a clinicopathologic study of 57 cases. *Neurology*, 38, 359–64.

Vilalta, J., Llinas, J., Lopez Pousa, S., Amiel, J., and Vidal, C. (1990). The Cambridge Mental Disorders of the Elderly Examination. Validation of the Spanish adaptation. *Neurologia*, 5, 117–20.

Waite, L.M., Broe, G.A., Creasey, H., Grayson, D., Edelbrock, D., and O'Toole, B. (1996). Neurological signs, aging, and the neurodegenerative syndromes. *Archives of Neurology*, 53, 498–502.

Walshe, T.M. (1987). Neurologic examination of the elderly patient. Signs of normal aging. *Postgraduate Medicine*, 81, 375–8.

WHO (World Health Organization) (1992). *The ICD-10 classification of mental and behavioural disorders*. World Health Organization, Geneva.

Wolfson, L. and Katzman, R. (1992). The neurologic consultation at age 80. In *Principles of geriatric neurology* (ed. R. Katzman, and J.W. Rowe), pp. 221–44. F.A. Davis, Philadelphia, PA.

Yesavage, J.A., Brink, T.L., Rose, T.L., *et al.* (1983). Development and validation of a geriatric depression screening scale: a preliminary report. *Journal of Psychiatric Research*, 17, 37–49.

Zhang, M.Y., Katzman, R., Salmon, D., *et al.* (1990). The prevalence of dementia and Alzheimer's disease in Shanghai, China: impact of age, gender, and education. *Annals of Neurology*, 27, 428–37.

18.2 **Sleep disorders**

Donald L. Bliwise

Sleep disturbance is one of the most common problems encountered by the geriatrician. In this chapter we summarize the current state of knowledge of the major sleep disorders in old age: sleep apnoea, restless legs (Ekbom's syndrome), periodic leg movements, narcolepsy, sleep disturbance of dementia (sundowning), and insomnia. Firstly, however, the clinical approach to the evaluation of elderly patients with known or suspected sleep disorders is described.

Taking the history

Taking a thorough clinical history of a significant sleep-related complaint in an elderly patient is time consuming, and enough time should be allotted to allow a thorough medical and psychiatric review. Subjective reports of both difficulty in sleeping or daytime sleepiness are characteristically inaccurate and every effort should be made to have the spouse or live-in companion present during some part of the consultation. This informant should be questioned about snoring, irregular breathing, excessive sleepiness, sleep habits, unusual nocturnal behaviours during sleep, changes in cognitive or emotional function associated with sleep disturbance, use of drugs and alcohol, and general psychosocial factors. It must be kept in mind, however, that partners who sleep in separate beds or bedrooms, who may be hearing impaired, who are taking sedating drugs, or who are unusually sound sleepers could be unreliable historians.

The clinical history should be organized as a review of the 24-h sleep–wake cycle, beginning with the night-time routine. Questions should be asked about variability in the daily cycle from day to day, weekday to weekend, home versus travel, and workday versus holiday time. The timing of evening meals and drinks, medications, use of caffeinated products, and the presence of environmental noise or discomfort should be established. Enquiry should be made regarding the extent of typical physical activity and exposure to outdoor sunlight.

Establishing the onset of the complaint and any associated changes in health or psychosocial function that occurred at the time is particularly important. Patients with disturbed nocturnal sleep and/or daytime sleepiness may appear to have symptoms of relatively recent onset, but which, upon further questioning of an informant, may reveal a long-standing and chronic episodic problem that has become more aggravated in the recent past. The presence of a long-standing complaint should neither be discouraging nor imply a functional problem. Individuals with sleep disorders often see many doctors over many years before a definitive evaluation is made.

It cannot be overemphasized that the investigation of sleep complaints in older people must include undiagnosed medical, neurological, and psychiatric conditions. This is particularly true for the latter where elderly patients with a focus on a sleep complaint may be somatizing psychiatric difficulties in a manner similar to that of the patient with a chronic pain or other physical complaint. Conversely, increased recognition in the sleep disorders community of 'primary insomnia' (see below) suggests that poor sleep may occur independently from psychiatric disorders. The role of suboptimal management or exacerbation of pre-existing conditions must also always be considered. The treatment of specific symptoms of known diseases may restore the normal sleep pattern or contribute to an overall improvement along with other interventions. Examples of this would involve the aggressive management of rheumatoid arthritis, congestive heart failure, or chronic obstructive lung disease.

Evaluation of daytime somnolence

The geriatrician must understand that daytime sleepiness is an important medical symptom and should not be dismissed with superficial explanations. Common, erroneous diagnoses of clinically significant sleepiness include ageing, boredom, retirement, leisure, nap behaviour, poor night-time sleep habits, or depression. Patients often deny or minimize clinically significant sleepiness and misinterpret it as lethargy, fatigue, or lack of energy. In all cases of sleepiness, a corroborating history should be obtained. Only in the most obvious cases are direct questions such as 'Are you abnormally sleepy?' likely to provide clinically useful information. History taking should focus on the presence of drowsiness during specific day-to-day activities, as reported by the patients and observed by the informant. Certain clinical cues will identify the seriously sleepy patient. These individuals have drowsiness that is persistent from day to day. Others will see them fall asleep spontaneously in quiet situations such as reading, watching television, or travelling as a passenger. Sleepiness when driving has been shown to be a particularly pernicious problem, particularly for motor vehicle accidents. Sleepy individuals may also take frequent naps during the day, which may be erroneously characterized as a positive habit. Obvious severe pathological sleepiness is indicated by a history of falling asleep while driving, while eating, while on the toilet, during conversation with others, or while waiting on the phone.

It should never be assumed that the presence of clinically severe excessive sleepiness is caused by trouble sleeping at night. In general, patients with severe complaints of being unable to sleep well at night do not have severe excessive sleepiness, although they may complain of fatigue or weariness. A key factor is whether the individual with poor nocturnal sleep is actually able to nap substantially during the daytime. Such patients are seldom able to achieve sound sleep at any point during the 24-h day.

Evaluation of insomnia

The clinical approach to the evaluation of insomnia is made more difficult by the fact that insomnia is a vague term that is used to refer to a variety of sleep-related symptoms. There is even some evidence that an individual's use of the label 'insomnia' may be unrelated to the number of hours he or she typically sleeps at night. Classically, insomnia is broken down into difficulty with falling asleep at the beginning of the night (initial insomnia), difficulty in returning to sleep after nocturnal awakenings, usually during the first two-thirds of the night (middle insomnia), and awakening too early in the morning, usually during the last third of the night (early morning awakening). In practice, many patients have some overlap of these three categories of complaint. Insomnia may also refer to frequent brief awakenings, or complaints of broken, restless sleep, often accompanied by recall of dream fragments. On occasion, a patient may complain of insomnia although there is no subjective sleep disturbance or daytime consequence other than a belief that the sleep period is too short.

Some specific lines of enquiry are worthwhile for each type of insomniac complaint. All patients with initial insomnia should be questioned about specific discomfort in the legs or calves that interferes with sleep onset, characterized by restlessness in the legs and relieved by leg movement. A positive answer suggests that a thorough review of restless leg syndrome and periodic leg movements should be pursued. In the absence of such symptoms, it is important to take care to establish the presence and extent of excessive arousal associated with the process of going to sleep. Arousal refers to a psychophysiological process that results in high levels of mental activity or emotional distress, and may include anxiety and depression or other effects less easily characterized, such as demoralization, hopelessness, and despair. Enhanced somatic sensations may include increased pain, overawareness of normal body sensations such as heartbeat, noise sensitivity, muscle tension, or vague migrating physical discomforts. The development of increased psychophysiological arousal may be secondary to environmental factors or poor sleep hygiene, as well as to conditioned responses of which the patient is unaware. Environmental factors may include noise, disturbing bed-partners, or lack of privacy. Sleep hygiene factors encompass poor bedtime habits, late-night eating and drinking, watching late-night disturbing programmes on television, or personal activities such as arguments, paying bills, or planning for 'the future'. Arousal triggered by conditioning is more difficult to identify, but may be suspected if the sleep disturbance occurs only under certain circumstances and reliably disappears with a change in conditions. More commonly, the patient is conditioned to become aroused by the very process of attempting to sleep, and by repeated failure and apprehension about perceived consequences of sleep loss.

When evaluating a complaint of a middle insomnia, many specific factors associated with or causing awakenings need to be evaluated to establish their relative importance. Conclusions made about causal relationships between specific nocturnal events and nocturnal awakenings can be misleading (i.e. urinary frequency may be secondary to frequent awakenings rather than vice versa). In patients who snore, particular attention should be given to symptoms suggestive of sleep apnoea. In snorers, awakenings associated with snorting, gasping, headache, dyspnoea, choking, chest pain, acid reflux, or night sweats should trigger suspicions of possible sleep apnoea. Broken, fragmented, and restless sleep, with or without leg kicking being reported by the bed-partner or patient, may suggest periodic leg movements. To a lesser extent such movements may be present with sleep-related complaints including unexplained fatigue or drowsiness during the daytime, without the patient having any awareness of a nocturnal sleep disorder.

Early morning awakening has long been considered a hallmark of endogenous affective disorders, but less commonly may also be found in the anxious elderly patient. In practice it is often difficult to distinguish a complaint of middle insomnia from early morning awakening because the patient may remain awake and be unable to return to sleep after awakening at any point during the night. Nonetheless, in patients with this specific complaint, careful consideration should be given to the full range of aetiological factors including sleep apnoea syndrome, which may be substantially aggravated during rapid eye movement sleep in the early morning hours. Complaints of early morning awakening may also be accompanied by early evening sleepiness or early bedtimes. Some physiologists have explained this phenomenon as an advanced phase syndrome (see below).

The duration of the insomnia will have practical, clinical, and therapeutic significance. An insomnia of a few weeks duration suggests a lengthy medical differential diagnosis, while a complaint of chronic insomnia for many years without other associated symptoms may suggest primary insomnia, another primary sleep disorder, or a chronic psychiatric disorder. Organ system function during the nocturnal hours should be reviewed specifically, including gastrointestinal symptoms, muscular or skeletal discomforts, urinary urgency, cramps, breathing difficulties, palpitations, cough, temperature discomfort, nightmares, and anxiety. Episodes of confusion, falling out of bed, falls, and near falls at night should also be specifically sought. Finally, a thorough psychiatric review is essential, including any past history of depression, anxiety, suicidal behaviour, panic, phobia, and previous use of psychotrophic drugs. The review of endogenous symptoms with depression easily follows from open-ended questions about family life, socioeconomic concerns, diet, and daily activity. Sleep disturbance accompanying bereavement often mimics the severity seen in long-term depression. Dementia may be associated with nocturnal sleep disturbance and daytime sleepiness; therefore, memory function should also be investigated. Although the sleep disturbances associated with dementing illness are typically parasomniac in nature (see below), the clinician evaluating insomnia in elderly people should always investigate changes in memory and intellectual function.

Perhaps most crucial in the evaluation of insomnia is a thorough review of current medications, over-the-counter drug use, alcohol, and illegal drugs. In history taking, attempt to establish previous treatments for sleep disturbance as carefully as possible, including drug dosages and regimens, durations, side-effects, and the patient's general response to them. It is necessary to enquire specifically about rebound insomnia or a history suggestive of drug habituation or abuse. A history of alcoholism should be corroborated, if suspected. An ever-growing proportion of elderly patients in the United States have tried melatonin as an over-the-counter 'natural' sleep aid. While

Sleep apnea as a multidetermined condition

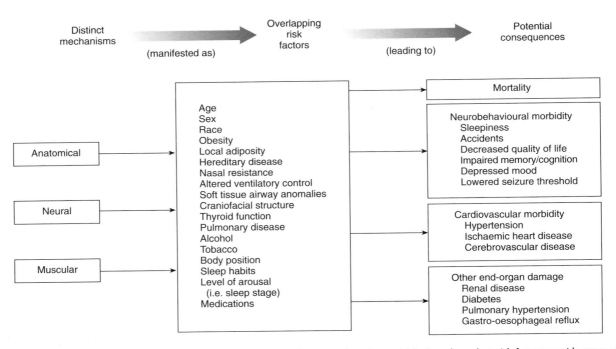

Fig. 3 Heuristic model showing putative mechanisms for sleep apnoea, which are manifested as multiple, interdependent risk factors; a wide range of consequences have been associated with sleep apnoea.

are modulated by anatomical considerations such as the configuration of bony and soft tissues surrounding and otherwise supporting upper-airway patency. A full discussion of the mechanisms controlling upper-airway closure is beyond the scope of this chapter and the reader is directed elsewhere for a description of how these mechanisms may interact to produce sleep apnoea (Dempsey *et al.* 1996; Horner 1996; Strohl and Redline 1996; Weiss *et al.* 1996; Berry and Gleeson 1997; Silverberg and Oskenberg 1997).

On a clinical, descriptive level, mechanisms producing sleep apnoea are manifested as risk factors. Chronological age, sex, race (African-American predominance), and obesity are among the better appreciated risk factors for the condition (Redline *et al.* 1997). As mentioned above, restriction of upper-airway calibre, be it through hypertrophied tonsils, enlarged tongue, deviated septum, or simply redundant oropharyngeal tissue, may all tend to promote airway closure or enhance upper-airway resistance during sleep. The site of obstruction may vary from patient to patient and range from the hypopharyngeal to the oropharyngeal levels. The contribution of craniofacial structure has recently been appreciated (Kushida *et al.* 1997) as affecting the likelihood of such obstruction during sleep. Hereditary diseases involving relative retroposition of the mandible have long been known to predispose to sleep apnoea. Added to these considerations are generalized and localized adiposity to the extent that excess tissue mass may further provide impetus to airway closure during sleep. Both pre-existing restrictive and obstructive pulmonary disease may contribute to sleep apnoea by exaggerating hypoventilation during sleep and reducing effective gas exchange at the alveolar level. Other well-recognized risk factors for sleep apnoea include hypothyroidism (probably involving direct muscosal effects

and central respiratory drive), chronic and acute alcohol use (operating either by elevating nasal resistance and/or decreasing neural output to upper-airway dilators), and smoking (possibly operating by producing airway oedema). Supine body position continues to be recognized as a factor increasing risk for airway closure but probably plays a role in less than half of all cases. Similarly, state dependence (e.g. rapid eye movement sleep) may play a role in some cases (see Fig. 1); however, full or partial airway obstruction may be equally likely in non-rapid eye movement sleep. Medications suppressing central respiratory drive may enhance central and/or obstructive apnoeas, although, fortunately, there is little evidence to suggest that benzodiazepines or imidazopyridines adversely effect sleep apnoea. Sleep habits (e.g. chronic sleep loss) deserves mention as a potential risk factor, though evidence for this is still limited and the pathways by which restricted sleep might impact upon sleep apnoea may be indirect (e.g. sleep loss may promote increased food intake leading to weight gain and subsequent sleep apnoea).

The extent to which age may serve as proxy for any or all of these risk factors, singly or in combination, is exceedingly complicated. For example, because ageing is known to be positively related to changes in pharyngeal resistance, this might explain why elderly people are susceptible to airway collapse during sleep. Such age-associated changes have been reported both in men (White *et al.* 1985) and in men and women (Martin *et al.* 1997). In a rat model, age-associated muscle fatigue was more conspicuous for pharyngeal relative to diaphragmatic muscles (Van Luntren *et al.* 1995).

Age-associated changes in central chemoreceptor drive may also contribute to the development of sleep apnoea in older people. A mild hypoventilation, which results in a small rise in P_{aCO_2} of 3 to

9 mmHg, is known to occur at the onset of sleep. Dempsey and Skatrud (1986) have contended that such hypoventilation results in an unmasking of the hypocapnic apnoeic threshold, thus predisposing to the development of sleep apnoea. Elderly persons, by virtue of their more fragmented sleep and their likelihood for unstable breathing at the onset of sleep, may be more likely to develop such sleep apnoea on this basis. Other factors, such as decreased inspiratory effort in response to airway occlusion, have been noted in older subjects and may also contribute to the development of sleep apnoea (Krieger *et al.* 1997).

Consequences

Seldom has a topic in the field of sleep disorders engendered more controversy than the potential impact and health consequences, or lack thereof, of sleep apnoea. Figure 3 indicates the range and breadth of possible outcomes with which sleep apnoea has been associated (for more recent in-depth reviews see National Institutes of Health 1995; Grunstein 1995; Stradling 1995; Hudgel 1996; Chesson *et al.* 1997; Silverberg and Oksenberg 1997; Stradling and Davies 1997*b*).

In many respects, the controversy involving sleep apnoea has been brought to a head in the United Kingdom by a contested review paper published in the *British Medical Journal* in 1997 (Wright *et al.* 1997). The essence of this paper is that because only one double-blind placebo-controlled trial for the treatment of sleep apnoea has ever been published (Engleman *et al.* 1994), the database conclusively linking sleep apnoea with any adverse outcome is weak and remains a case unproven. Therefore the necessity of patients with the condition to undergo costly nocturnal diagnostic polysomnography and to purchase even more costly nasal continuous positive airway pressure (**CPAP**) equipment (see below) with which to treat it, appears premature and unnecessary. This paper, cosponsored by the North Yorkshire Health Authority, and written by authors who had never performed any research involving sleep apnoea, would appear to represent an obviously tendentious perspective which cannot be disengaged from the funding system which spawned it. Amidst the controversy (Engleman *et al.* 1997; Fleetham 1997; Gibson and Prowse 1997; Pack and Young 1997; Stradling 1997; Stradling and Davies 1997*a*; Walsworth-Bell 1997) caused by this review are numerous commentaries which suggest that, among other points, until the completion of such randomized clinical trials and even large-scale observational epidemiological studies currently under way throughout the world, the existence of descriptive and treatment-derived evidence (single-group designs) should not prevent treatment of what is otherwise clearly recognized as a disease with certain neurobehavioural impact and probable cardiovascular and other end-organ consequences as well. Perhaps the most pithy commentary made in the wake of this paper comes from Kryger (1997) who stated: 'Are the same people who are not funding CPAP systems in the UK also not allowing the use of oxygen in hypoxic patients with pneumonia who are in the hospital? I doubt they will be able to find any placebo-controlled trials to answer this question' (Kryger 1997). It must be recalled that the controversy surrounding sleep apnoea and its treatment has not even specifically involved the aged population in whom, because of comorbid disease and multiple risk factors, might be expected to present a still more complicated picture in so far as morbidity and mortality is concerned (Bliwise 1996*a*).

Of all the outcomes potentially associated with sleep apnoea, none is more dramatic than the possibility that disturbed respiration during the night will lead to death during sleep. So called 'natural' death during sleep has been studied by Bliwise *et al.* (1988) in the Bay Area Sleep Cohort. The data suggest that an individual with respiratory disturbance index of more than 10 events per hour was nearly three times as likely to die within 5 years, though these findings held in only a univariate model. More complex multivariate models could not show the effect, but because the cumulative mortality rate of the cohort of 200 had only reached about 10 per cent, the results may change as the study continues.

Another study of an aged independently living non-patient cohort of over 420 subjects showed similar results, in that respiratory disturbance index was a univariate, rather than a multivariate predictor of mortality (Ancoli-Israel *et al.* 1996), becoming non-significant when chronological age was placed in the model. Elsewhere the author has argued that comparing sleep apnoea to chronological age is probably misleading, since the latter encompasses nearly all other age-dependent disease (Bliwise 1996*a*) and, in fact, when Ancoli-Israel *et al.* included only other disease markers in their model, sleep apnoea was a borderline mortality predictor. A final study, less generalizable because it employed a clinical population and used inappropriate follow-up data analysis methods, concluded that sleep apnoea might even be protective for mortality in old age (Lavie *et al.* 1995), a finding which some have considered biologically implausible (Baltzan and Suissa 1997). Taken together, these results reiterate the need for more careful, descriptive natural history data relating sleep apnoea to health in sizeable aged populations, a situation which has led to the inclusion of substantial numbers of elderly subjects included in the ongoing Sleep Heart Health Study. This study, based in the United States and sponsored by the National Institutes of Health, will be, upon its completion, the largest single effort to document the natural history of sleep apnoea (Quan *et al.* 1997). Results from a study such as this could be important in suggesting relevant parameters for conducting a fully fledged clinical trial (e.g. stratification by age, pre-existing cardiovascular disease, etc.).

Perhaps the most convincing argument that sleep apnoea has adverse effects upon the cardiovascular system is a body of evidence suggesting high levels of sympathetic activation associated with the syndrome. While autonomic involvement has long been recognized accompanying apnoeic events (e.g. cyclic tachycardia/bradycardia) and arrhythmias have been noted to co-occur with such breathing disruptions, a convincing body of evidence including both micro-neurography (Somers *et al.* 1995) as well as plasma norepinephrine levels (Ziegler *et al.* 1997) suggest that sleep apnoea is a major stressor on the cardiovascular system. Studies with transcranial Doppler also suggest that changes in cerebral blood flow may occur during apnoeic episodes as well, thus implying that apnoea could have a crucial role in cerebrovascular disease (Palomaki *et al.* 1992). The existence of such a plausible mechanism suggesting increased vascular resistance and/or increased workload of the left ventricle must be tempered somewhat by clinical studies showing mixed associations between sleep apnoea and particular cardiovascular outcomes. Systemic hypertension, for example, has been the object of intense interest in so far as sleep apnoea is concerned and evidence can be mustered both supporting (Grunstein 1995; Silverberg and Oksenberg 1997; Silverberg *et al.* 1997) and refuting (Stradling and Davies 1997*b*) an association, many of the latter criticisms involving the inability of previous studies to factor out the effects of confounding variables adequately. Future studies with exceptionally large cohorts (e.g. the

Sleep Heart Health Study) will be required to define such effects. In the study generally acknowledged to be the benchmark study of the prevalence of sleep apnoea in middle-aged population (Young *et al.* 1993), sleep apnoea was associated with hypertension (Hla *et al.* 1994).

Regardless of the association of sleep apnoea and such cardio-vascular outcomes, Stradling and others (Stradling and Davies 1997*a*) have contended that the most unambiguous evidence relating sleep apnoea to an adverse outcome involves neurobehavioural measures, namely excessive daytime sleepiness. Such excessive daytime sleepiness can impact upon the aged person in numerous ways by, for example, producing depressed mood, increasing the likelihood of motor vehicle accidents, reducing the quality of life (Kryger *et al.* 1996; Peker *et al.* 1997), and possibly, by playing an additive role in the cognitive loss in old age (Bliwise 1996*b*; Dealberto *et al.* 1996). Intervention studies in middle-aged sleep apnoea patients have demonstrated some improvement in mental function following the use of CPAP (Bedard *et al.* 1993; Valencia-Flores *et al.* 1996) and quality of life measures have also been shown to improve (Jenkinson *et al.* 1997). End-organ damage to other systems may also occur (Fletcher 1993; Rangemark *et al.* 1995; Strohl 1996).

Treatment

Without question the treatment of choice for the vast majority of aged individuals with sleep apnoea is nasal CPAP. This presents a small (2.5 to 15 cmH$_2$O) positive pressure through a mask attached to a blower which the patient wears during sleep. CPAP probably works essentially as a pneumatic splint by simply preventing airway occlusion during negative inspiratory pressure. It is clear that in nearly all cases reported, it is an effective treatment for sleep apnoea. Compliance rates vary between 65 and 83 per cent, depending on the patient population considered (Nino-Murcia *et al.* 1989). Some data suggest that experience during the initial four nights of treatment will predict future use (Weaver *et al.* 1997). The most common side-effects include dry nose and throat, and sore eyes (from mask leakage). Nasal obstruction prevents nightly usage in about a third of the cases. Most of the problems can be countered with humidification, frequent mask replacement, and nasal decongestants. Pretreatment counselling and contact with support staff are essential in overcoming initial reluctance to using the equipment and long-term problems of compliance. To date, few adverse consequences have been reported with nasal CPAP.

Use of oral appliances, worn during sleep to produce a mild mandibular protrusion, represent another treatment option for older subjects. The treatment is relatively effective (Schmidt-Nowara *et al.* 1995; Menn *et al.* 1996) and may afford higher compliance rates than CPAP (Fleetham *et al.* 1996). Of the other treatments for sleep apnoea, surgical options, including uvulopalatopharyngoplasty and maxillofacial restructuring, have received the most attention. The efficacy of the former has been liberally estimated at 50 per cent, based on greater than 50 per cent improvement in the respiratory disturbance index. The maxillofacial approach often involves multiple operations, is a difficult process, and not well suited to elderly people. Gross upper-airway obstruction (e.g. deviated septum, tonsillar hypertrophy) might be possibilities for surgical correction in selected cases. Tracheostomy, the first described treatment for sleep apnoea, is now seldom used, but remains an effective and important option.

Pharmacological treatments, including medroxyprogesterone, protriptyline, and acetazolamide, all received some initially encouraging reports but later accounts were less optimistic. However, there are recent animal data to suggest that serotonin reuptake inhibitors may differentially activate the upper-airway musculature (Fenik *et al.* 1997), and some preliminary work in humans with fluoxetine was encouraging (Hanzel *et al.* 1991).

In mild cases of sleep apnoea, more conservative treatment options can be used. For example, avoidance of the supine position may be helpful in some cases, as may nocturnal administration of nasal corticosteroids. Given the relative importance of body weight, weight loss, even of the order of 4 to 9 kg may have some benefit. Alcohol before bed should be avoided.

Restless legs syndrome/periodic leg movements in sleep

Restless legs syndrome (Ekbom's syndrome) is characterized by paraesthesiae that are difficult for the patient to describe. These are usually in the calves and cause an irresistible urge to move the legs. The patient may use a variety of different words to describe the symptoms, but may mention sensations of restlessness, or creeping and crawling sensations, that are characteristically relieved by leg movement, standing, or walking. The relief of these symptoms by leg movement helps distinguish them from other symptoms related to peripheral neuropathy, vascular insufficiency, or musculoskeletal disease. The symptoms occur most frequently in the evening or in bed and usually disappear during the daytime hours. In more severe cases, the patient is simply unable to sleep and may develop severe emotional disturbance and dysfunction. The restless paraesthesiae may be aggravated by chronic sleep deprivation, apprehension about sleep loss, and expectation of further restlessness, creating a vicious circle. Some medications (e.g. selective serotonin reuptake inhibitors) may also increase symptoms. In the Canadian population over the age of 60 years the prevalence of bedtime leg restlessness has been estimated at 23 per cent and the prevalence of unpleasant leg muscle sensation during sleep has been estimated at 18 per cent, with few, if any, gender differences (Lavigne and Montplaisir 1994). The definition of this syndrome has now been agreed upon by an international panel (Walters 1995), and familial clustering of the syndrome has been described (Montplaisir *et al.* 1997).

Restless legs syndrome clearly overlaps with a polysomnographically defined condition called periodic leg movements in sleep. Most patients with the syndrome also tend to have periodic leg movements but the converse is not necessarily the case, in that many individuals with the leg movements are otherwise asymptomatic. Periodic leg movements are involuntary movements usually limited to unilateral or bilateral extension of the big toe and can include flexion of the foot at the ankle and partial flexion of the knee and the hip. The patient is usually unaware of these movements, which may occur up to 600 or 700 times throughout the night, although often the bed-partner may be aware of the limb movement. The substantial arousal in the central nervous system caused by these leg movements can result in complaints of restless, broken sleep, or, less typically, to daytime fatigue and drowsiness, though some have disputed the strength of these associations (Mendelson 1996). Periodic leg movements have sometimes been referred to as 'nocturnal myoclonus'; however, the term is a misnomer to the extent that the

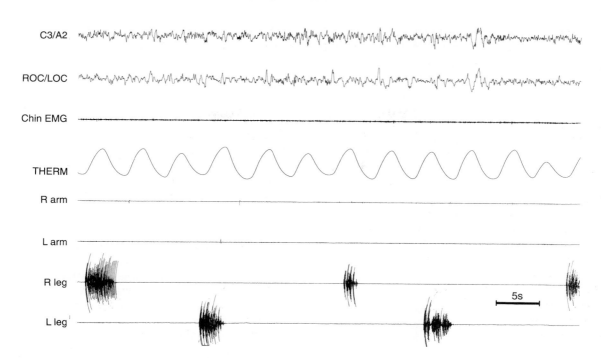

C3/A2

ROC/LOC

Chin EMG

THERM

R arm

L arm

R leg

L leg

5s

Fig. 4 Typical polysomnographic tracing of periodic leg movements in sleep. Notice in this case alternating bilateral movements confined to the lower limbs.

condition is non-epileptiform and occurs in the absence of paroxysmal EEG activity. Figure 4 shows a sample polysomnographic tracing of periodic leg movements during sleep.

These movements have a clear age-associated prevalence into old age and, unlike sleep apnoea, show no obvious drop in the oldest age groups studied to date. Many of these individuals are asymptomatic. In one study, 40 per cent of insomniacs with periodic leg movements reported the experience of leg twitching, but only 18 per cent of insomniacs without leg movements experienced this symptom. However, 60 per cent of elderly insomniacs with periodic leg movements never experienced twitching (Bliwise *et al.* 1985). Despite these findings, periodic leg movements are undeniably associated to some extent with restless legs syndrome. Treatment studies, for example, have often shown reduction in periodic leg movements which parallel lessening of subjective symptoms (Montplaisir *et al.* 1986).

The mechanisms underlying these movements remain obscure, although they appear confined to the lower limbs. This raises the possibility that motor neurone dysfunction may be involved, as larger nerve fibres could be more sensitive to damage, but there is little information to support this idea at present. Another possibility is some type of transient functional suppression of the pyramidal tract. A positive Babinski sign is found in a few patients with periodic leg movements. Some central dysfunction at the pontine level or higher is also likely, given the reported abnormalities in the glabellar reflex (Wechsler *et al.* 1986). Absence of the so-called 'readiness' EEG potential (*Bereitschaftspotential*) during waking dyskinesias in restless legs syndrome patients supports this view of central dysfunction (Trenkwalder *et al.* 1993). Additionally, recent studies with single photon emission tomography have suggested lower D_2-receptor binding in the basal ganglia of periodic leg movement patients (Staedt *et al.* 1993) and functional MRI studies have suggested activation in the

red nuclei and brainstem areas proximal to the pedunculopontine nucleus (Bucher *et al.* 1997). Finally, vascular involvement has also been implicated in that symptoms like cold feet, which are related to poor circulation in the legs, have been associated with periodic leg movements.

Considerable insights into the treatment of restless legs syndrome and periodic leg movements have occurred in recent years. Levodopa–decarboxylase inhibitor combination (e.g. co-careldopa (Sinemet) in relatively low doses of 10–100 or 25–250 mg, one or two tablets at bedtime), may provide relief. Levodopa–carbidopa has also been used successfully in renal failure patients who often have severe restless legs syndrome with or without periodic leg movements (Walker *et al.* 1996).

Use of such medications, while often successful initially, typically results in re-emergence of symptoms later in the night or, in some cases, emergence of the symptoms upon awakening in the morning or afternoon, a phenomenon which has been labelled 'augmentation' (Allen and Earley 1996). Use of continuous release formulations may be helpful in such cases. Alternatively, pergolide or bromocriptine are dopamine agonists which have been reported to be successful (Walters *et al.* 1988; Early and Allen 1996) and may slow development of augmentation type phenomena. Opiates have also been effective in relieving the paraesthesiae, although tolerance can be a problem. In milder cases, non-specific sedating agents such as chlormethiazole or lorazepam allow the patient to ignore the paraesthesiae by producing increased drowsiness. Some have favoured clonazepam, but this must be used in low doses, 0.5 to 2.0 mg, as it may give significant problems with confusion, disorientation, sedation, and behavioural change in elderly patients. Gabapentin at dosages of 300 to 800 mg has been suggested as an alternative treatment of benefit (Mellick and Mellick 1996). A study by O'Keefe *et al.* (1994) suggested that low levels of serum ferritin were associated with restless legs syndrome, and suggests a role for iron replacement as a sole or adjunctive treatment for the condition.

Narcolepsy

Until recently narcolepsy was thought to be one of the few sleep disorders whose prevalence actually decreased with age. Its prevalence has been estimated at 0.02 per cent of the population (Hublin *et al.* 1994). A genetic component has been established in that specific HLA-associated antigens (specifically DRB1*1501 and DQB1*0602 haplotypes) have been associated with the disease in many worldwide populations (Mignot *et al.* 1994) despite some differences in disease prevalence by racial group (Wilner *et al.* 1988). In certain sub-populations (e.g. African-American) DQB*0602 may be a better marker (Neely *et al.* 1987; Rogers *et al.* 1997). While it is useful to rule out narcolepsy, these antigens are too common in the general population (30 per cent) to diagnose the condition. Narcolepsy must be diagnosed polysomnographically, preferably with a nocturnal study and a subsequent day multiple sleep latency test. This test allows the documentation of multiple onsets of rapid eye movement sleep characteristic of this condition. Patients must be free from psycho-active medications before these procedures are implemented.

As is the case for sleep apnoea, the hallmark symptom of narcolepsy is persistent, profound daytime sleepiness. Patients with narcolepsy may also have symptoms of cataplexy (loss of muscle tone with startle, surprise, or strong emotion), sleep paralysis (an inability to move despite being conscious at the beginning or end of the sleep), and hypnagogic hallucinations. It is these extra symptoms that aid in the differential diagnosis from sleep apnoea; however, recent case series (Rye *et al.* 1998*b*) suggest that older cases with HLA subtyping consistent for the disease may present without such accessory symptoms. Additionally, among older patients who carried long-standing diagnoses of narcolepsy, unrecognized exacerbation of cataplexy in their sixties and seventies often led to extensive evaluations for presumed late onset epilepsy and/or cerebrovascular disease including cerebral angiography and MRI (Rye *et al.* 1998*b*). Cases such as these re-emphasize that the geriatrician must be familiar with the varied presentations of cataplexy.

Treatments for narcolepsy include stimulant medication for sleepiness (e.g. pemoline, methylphenidate, amphetamine, and others) and either tricyclic antidepressants (e.g. protriptyline) or selective serotonin reuptake inhibitors (e.g. sertraline, paroxetine) for cataplexy and rapid eye movement-related phenomena. Frequently, concurrent usage of tricyclic agents and stimulants can reduce the required dosage for the latter. For the elderly narcoleptic patient with ischaemic heart disease, dosages of such medications should be kept as low as possible. Rye *et al.* (1998*a*) recently reported that buproprion, an antidepressant with relative specificity for dopamine reuptake blockade, is also useful in narcolepsy. Finally, there is some evidence that regularly scheduled naps can minimize the untoward effects of daytime somnolence and reduce the dosages of such medications.

Sleep–wake disturbance in dementia (sundowning)

The profound sleep–wake disturbance occurring in some demented patients represents one of the most difficult management problems in clinical geriatrics. In fact, several surveys of caregivers have shown this as the single most common reason for a demented family member finally to enter an institution. Such sleep disruption goes beyond the simple inability to sleep in that the demented patient becomes agitated, confused, sometimes aggressive, and disoriented in a temporally specific pattern. The typical time for patients to show such behaviour is at or near sunset and sometimes throughout the night. Such sundowning often has a daytime component of excessive napping and relative docility. While some have contended that this phenomenon in the nursing home is partially related to environmental factors such as nursing shift changes, careful, precise, and objective monitoring of specific disruptive behaviours in the nursing home setting (e.g. loud vocalizations) have confirmed the temporal patterning of such behaviour to occur in the early evening (Burgio *et al.* 1994). Figure 5 shows an example of sundowning-like behaviour in a demented patient, as recorded with a self-contained wrist actigraph for measuring simple activity.

Exactly who sundowns, how long the behaviours actually last, and when in the course of the dementia such behaviours occur are all unanswered questions (Bliwise 1994). There is even contention about what behaviours constitute sundowning. Some have argued that sundowning is essentially nocturnal delirium but because the definition of delirium includes reference to a disturbed sleep–wake cycle such a definition is circular. Nonetheless, prevalence data on delirium in elderly patients may offer some cursory notion as to how common sundowning actually is. In admissions to hospital for acute care in general medical wards, 20 to 30 per cent of older patients are delirious on admission or become delirious in hospital (Gillick *et al.* 1982; Levkoff *et al.* 1986).

It is important to keep in mind that, whether it is called sundowning or nocturnal agitation, delirium in elderly patients may represent a large number of metabolic, toxic, and biochemical abnormalities. Acid–base or electrolyte imbalance, endocrinopathies, liver failure, uraemia, hypovitaminosis, or hypovolaemia can lead to a delirious state in elderly patients, which may then be exacerbated during the night. Medications are another major cause of delirium in these patients including antiarrhythmic, antidiarrhoeal, steroidal and non-steroidal anti-inflammatory, antihistamine, and analgesic agents.

Although there are many such causes of sundowning, demented patients often show behavioural disturbances in the absence of any such factors. The mechanisms underlying this are poorly understood. In as much as the clinical problem is typically manifested across 24 h (excessive daytime dozing and disruptive nocturnal agitation), dysfunction of the circadian timing system is implied. A relevant animal model could be selective deterioration of the suprachiasmatic nucleus of the hypothalamus, because primates with such lesions show loss of circadian rhythms. Because the neuronal degeneration characteristic of Alzheimer's disease frequently involves subcortical structures, such selective deterioration in at least some demented patients appears likely. Based on this hypothesis, other components of 24-h circadian physiology (body temperature, diurnal variation in prolactin, melatonin, luteinizing hormone) might be expected to show marked changes in dementia; some evidence indicates that this has not always been the case (Prinz *et al.* 1984), although certainly these studies have been biased to the extent that the most agitated patients were almost certainly excluded from consideration. There is some suggestion that hyperarousal in the hypothalamopituitary–adrenal axis in dementia (assessed by dexamethasone suppression testing) is related to blunted diurnal variation in cortisol levels, but whether this portends sundowning is uncertain.

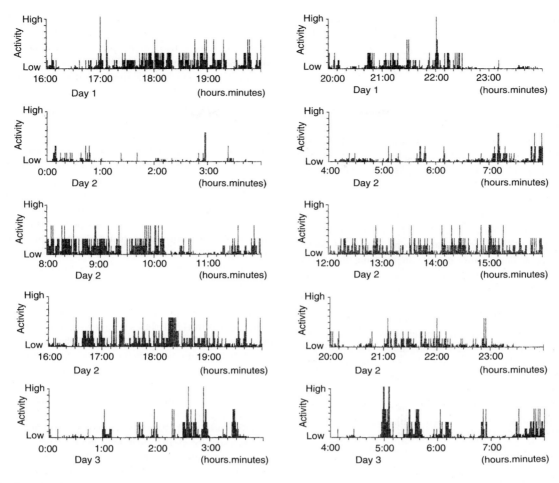

Fig. 5 Example of sundowning in a demented patient recorded with a self-contained wrist actigraph. Notice peaks of activity beginning at 1.00 a.m. on day 3 (last line).

Treatments for sundowning associated with dementia are often inadequate and the condition may be difficult to control. Initial attempts with non-pharmacological management including bright light, restriction of daytime sleep, and even mild physical activity may be worthwhile. Although, in the United States, Federal guidelines for nursing home care require that incontinent patients be awakened frequently during the night to prevent the development of skin lesions, there are some suggestions that such practices are highly disruptive to sleep and may even cause agitation (Bliwise *et al.* 1993; Schnelle *et al.* 1993*a, b*). Melatonin administration at dosages of 2 mg have been shown to be effective as a hypnotic in non-demented nursing home patients (Haimov *et al.* 1995). It remains to be seen whether it is effective in sleep disturbed agitated patients with dementia, though a clinical trial is currently underway testing this hypothesis; dosages of 0.5 and 10 mg have been employed (Singer *et al.* 1995, 1997). Some caution may be advisable in the use of melatonin in frail elderly people, particularly those with cardiovascular disease, since animal models have suggested it may be a potent vasoconstrictor of peripheral vessels (Krause *et al.* 1995).

Use of all psychoactive medications has greatly decreased in nursing homes in the United States over the last 10 years (Shorr *et al.* 1994). Nonetheless, the severely agitated patient in need of nocturnal sedation

often requires that appropriate and judicious pharmacological management be considered. Previously, haloperidol (0.5–1.0 mg) or thioridazine (25–75 mg) were often used and still retain value at present, although side-effects (extrapyramidal symptoms/tardive dyskinesia and postural hypotension, respectively) remain problematic. More recently selective dopamine antagonists such as clozapine (12.5–25 mg), a D_4 selective antagonist, and risperidone (1.0–2.0 mg), a selective D_2 and serotonin type 2 antagonist, have been used (Rabey *et al.* 1995). (Patients receiving clozapine must be monitored carefully for agranulocytosis.) These medications may be particularly useful in treating the dopaminomimetic psychosis of Parkinson's disease and reduce symptoms such as hallucinations and nightmares often accompanying the condition (Wolters *et al.* 1990). Very recently released in the United States, olanzapine, an atypical sedating antipsychotic working on noradrenergic, serotoninergic, and dopaminergic receptors, may also be useful for agitated parkinsonian patients at dosages of 1 to 15 mg (Wolters *et al.* 1996).

A condition described as rapid eye movement sleep behaviour disorder (Schenck *et al.* 1987) may also have some relevance for sundowning. In this, patients (typically elderly men) literally appear to act out their dreams by engaging in apparently complex, purposeful behaviours during rapid eye movement sleep. A recent uncontrolled report indicates that 38 per cent of individuals diagnosed with this condition later developed Parkinson's disease (Schenck *et al.* 1996). Clonazepam has been reported to be a successful treatment at dosages of 0.5 to 1.5 mg at bedtime.

Insomnia

Risk factors, prevalence, and aetiology

Although many specific sleep disorders are encountered in the elderly population, the most common complaint likely to be seen by the geriatrician will be insomnia. As has been stressed in this chapter, primary sleep pathology is often diverse and should never be dismissed. Nonetheless, when the possibility of primary sleep disorders has been eliminated as a cause of nocturnal sleep disturbance and/or excessive daytime sleepiness, the geriatrician is often left with the remaining problem of what to do with the older patient who is unable to sleep.

Numerous physiological factors operate in reducing the depth, quality, and length of nocturnal sleep in older people. These normal age-associated changes include: loss of deep (stages 3 and 4) sleep; an increased proportion of total sleep spent in stage 1 (transitional) sleep; and increased frequency of brief, transient arousals of less than 15 s. Rapid eye movement sleep may change only minimally with ageing. In addition, other factors such as increased sympathetic tone and an elevated auditory arousal threshold (even within stage 2 sleep) may predispose older people to poorer quality sleep. Some have suggested that the pattern for elderly people to become sleepy earlier in the evening and awaken during the night may actually reflect an age-associated change in what is termed a 'phase-advance' of the circadian sleep–wake cycle. Many of these changes are seen even among aged people who sleep well. Because the prevalence of specific sleep disorders such as periodic leg movements and sleep apnoea also increases with age, and the many medical illnesses that disturb sleep are so common in aged populations, these factors combine to predispose the elderly person to insomnia. Pulmonary disease appears especially associated with insomnia in old age (Klink *et al.* 1992; Foley *et al.* 1995) as does chronic pain (Gislason *et al.* 1993). There even may be some specificity in these results in that in one study bronchitis/ bronchial asthma was associated with middle insomnia, diabetes with initial and middle insomnia, and musculoskeletal pain was primarily associated with initial insomnia (Gislason and Almquist 1987). Despite such morbidities, it is important to appreciate that although most elderly people probably experience sleep of poorer quality and duration than when younger, a smaller proportion of these individuals actually complain of insomnia. Insomnia is a symptom and must be evaluated as such, particularly in terms not only of its medical but also its psychosocial implications.

The prevalence of insomnia in the elderly population varies somewhat from survey to survey, depending upon the question asked. In a survey based in Houston, Texas (Karacan *et al.* 1983), about 28 per cent of the men over 65 and about 35 per cent of the women experienced difficulty in falling asleep sometimes, often, or always. These figures were 55 and 65 per cent for difficulty maintaining sleep and 25 and 30 per cent for early morning awakening, respectively. Some polysomnographic studies have suggested a more EEG-definable sleep disturbance in older men than in older women, but data generated from the surveys of the National Institute on Aging and National Center for Health Statistics (Cornoni-Huntley *et al.* 1986) corroborate the self-reported sex differences. These data also suggested

that awakening during the night 'most of the time' afflicts about 25 to 30 per cent of elderly people. There were also some urban–rural differences, with urban elderly people having more trouble falling asleep and awakening too early than rural subjects, who appear to have more difficulty with nocturnal awakenings. In parallel with the age-associated prevalence of all these sleep complaints is the use of hypnotic medication, which also increases with age. Again, estimates vary depending upon the question asked. In the Houston survey, about 12 per cent of the men aged 65 or over used hypnotics at least sometimes, as did about 15 per cent of the women. A Finnish survey (Partinen *et al.* 1983) showed that about 7 per cent of men aged 60 and above and 11.5 per cent of women aged 60 and above used prescription sleeping pills on at least 10 days during the year preceding the survey. Although systematically collected data on the use of melatonin (see below) in the general population are not available, the current popularity of this substance probably would raise these foregoing estimates of medication use prevalence still higher. Typically, sleep maintenance problems predominate in old age although recent data in an American rural population suggested a surprisingly high number of aged sleep latency insomniacs as well (Ganguli *et al.* 1996). Racial differences have also been reported in the prevalence of sleep complaints with elderly black people voicing fewer sleep complaints than elderly whites (Blazer *et al.* 1995; Foley *et al.* 1995).

While for many years the prevailing wisdom has been that most sleep disturbance is caused by psychiatric disorder, a recognition of 'primary' insomnia (American Psychiatric Association 1994) has emerged. This is a diagnostically separate condition which can be reliably diagnosed by experienced clinicians (Buysse *et al.* 1997*b*; Nowell *et al.* 1997). Patients demonstrate internalized stress which becomes somatized as muscle tension and autonomic arousal; these subsequently interfere with sleep. These patients often strike the geriatrician as tense and hypochondriacal. Such patients are often worried over the extent to which their loss of sleep will impact upon their fatigue during the subsequent day. In many cases the insomnia begins concurrently with or subsequent to an acute illness or hospital admission.

Despite the awareness of primary insomnia, it is still likely that many of the elderly insomniac cases encountered in practice will carry a concurrent psychiatric diagnosis (Ohayon 1997). In this regard, a recent focus of research interest has been sleep disturbance following bereavement, a common occurrence for a large segment of the older population. In the United States approximately 800 000 older people lose a spouse annually and depression has been estimated to occur in 10 to 20 per cent of such individuals. Whereas bereavement *per se* is not necessarily associated with poor sleep relative to aged controls (Reynolds *et al.* 1992), several of the biological markers typically considered hallmarks of endogenous depression (e.g. decreases in latency to rapid eye movement sleep) are also seen in depression associated with bereavement. Additionally, depressed bereaved patients showed reductions in total time asleep and time in bed spent asleep (sleep efficiency) comparable to individuals with recurrent depression. A 'subsyndromal' depression related to bereavement has also been described sharing some of these sleep-related markers (Pasternak *et al.* 1992). Sleep disturbance associated with bereavement may respond particularly well to antidepressant medications such as nortriptyline or paroxetine (Pasternak *et al.* 1994; Nowell *et al.* 1998) (see below).

Insomnia complaints, particularly if they are severe and continuous, do not remit. In this regard, it is important to stress that an accumulating database, both in the United States and the United Kingdom, reiterate the importance of actively treating insomnia in old age. Over a period of 10 years, most insomnia complaints did not resolve spontaneously (Klink *et al.* 1992). Natural history data suggest that persistent insomnia over a period of several years may lead to incident depression (Rodin *et al.* 1988; Ford and Kamerow 1989; Livingston *et al.* 1993), and previously a number of large epidemiological studies (Kripke *et al.* 1979; Wingard and Berkman 1983) have shown that insomnia is a significant predictor of all causes of mortality. Not all recent studies have shown such associations between insomnia and mortality (Rumble and Morgan 1992; Foley *et al.* 1995; Ganguli *et al.* 1996), but even in these studies, either daytime sleepiness (Foley *et al.* 1995; Ganguli *et al.* 1996) or use of medications for insomnia (Rumble and Morgan 1992) were predictive of mortality. Of note in the latter study was that the category of medications associated with such adverse outcomes included opiates and codeine-based derivatives rather than benzodiazepines and imidazopyridines. Taken together these results should prompt the geriatrician to treat insomnia in old age actively.

Treatment

Treatments for insomnia can be resolved into pharmacological and non-pharmacological approaches. This does not necessarily mean that the use of medications vitiates the the need for good sleep hygiene. In fact, in selected patients, it may be possible to substitute a programme (see below) of fixed sleep–wake schedule, avoidance of naps, and reduction of alcohol and caffeine once a hypnotic drug has induced a pattern of sound sleep. Before being prescribed sedative hypnotics, a patient should have completed a thorough history for medical and sleep disorders, for the exclusion of a history suggestive of sleep apnoea and restless legs syndrome, and for other specific diagnoses including depression.

The time-honoured question in treating insomnia pharmacologically is whether it is better to employ sedative hypnotics (typically benzodiazepines or imidazopyridines) or antidepressant medications. Substantial evidence exists that all such classes of medications may be helpful to some extent. Among benzodiazepines, medications with intermediate half-lives (temazepam with a starting dose of 15 mg, or estazolam 1 mg) are generally preferred. There is little to recommend the use of antianxiety agents (alprazolam, diazepam) as sleeping pills unless a diagnosis of anxiety disorders has also been made. The imidazopyridines (zolpidem, zopiclone, zaleplon) are benzodiazepine-site-specific (ω_1) binding agents with apparent efficacy in geriatric patients (Shaw *et al.* 1992; Kummer *et al.* 1993), a low side-effect profile, and possible reduced potential for tolerance. Their relatively short half-life (generally less than 4 h) may make them less suitable for sleep maintenance, relative to sleep latency, problems.

Generally, prescriptions for such sedative hypnotics should be accompanied by an overall treatment plan and a time-limited trial. Patients should receive written information outlining possible side-effects and drug interactions, and should be warned about decreased alertness during the day and possible impairment of gait, memory, or cognitive function. The risk of falls should always be considered in a given patient. Use of sleep diaries, to allow an accurate daily record of whether use of medication on a given night actually affects sleep are also encouraged.

Once treatment has been initiated, there may be demands for increases in dose and repeat prescriptions for chronic use. Before the first prescription, patients should be clearly instructed that they are not to increase the dose without at least a telephone consultation. They should also be advised that if the medication becomes ineffective after an initial positive response, increases in dose will not be in their best interest, and that supervised discontinuation of the medication or an alternative treatment plan will be recommended. In general, a previously effective dose should never be increased. Patients should also be encouraged to use medication on an alternate-night or sporadic regimen as much as possible. This may diminish the development of tolerance, allow drug-free nights to normalize sleep patterns, and may encourage some fortitude in coping with sleep disruption.

In contrast to such use of sedative hypnotic medication, anti-depressant medication should be viewed as a more regular, long-term approach to pharmacological management. Such a medication should be considered whenever depressed mood predominates. A long-term trial (1 year) using antidepressant medication (nortriptyline) to treat insomnia associated with depression in geriatric patients has also suggested continued benefit on polysomnographically defined sleep measures (Buysse *et al.* 1997*b*; Reynolds *et al.* 1997). While the so-called activating antidepressants (selective serotonin reuptake inhibitors including paroxetine, fluoxetine, sertraline, venlafaxine) often produce insomnia as a treatment emergent side-effect, roughly at double the incidence rate of placebo, new evidence suggests that even with nocturnal dosing, such medication can actually improve the quality and depth of nocturnal sleep, possibly by reducing electro-encephalographic α-band power (Nowell *et al.* 1999). Some clinicians prefer use of trazadone or nefazodone, as these medications may have fewer activating properties. Finally, it is possible to combine antidepressant and sedative hypnotic medication, even in geriatric patients. For example, adjunctive use of lorazepam together with nortriptyline did not diminish the efficacy of the latter (Buysse *et al.* 1997*a*).

The role of melatonin as a potential hypnotic has received great attention in recent years. Although decade-old data suggested minimal effects when tested in a rigorous double-blind placebo-controlled, sleep laboratory based clinical trial, a burgeoning literature has suggested its utility. A number of such trials, some conducted in aged populations (Garfinkel *et al.* 1995; Haimov *et al.* 1995) have shown impressive results and the popularity of melatonin among Americans has been substantial. Several points should be made regarding these data and also from the standpoint of safety. Although the more recent clinical trials have been generally well done, most have not relied upon the gold standard of measurement of sleep (polysomnography) and instead have relied upon wrist actigraphy on which to infer conclusions regarding sleep. While these estimates may correspond to some degree with polysomnography, there is great potential for error, particularly in older individuals with insomnia (Brooks *et al.* 1993). A very recent polysomnographic study using portable technology, for example, showed no effect of melatonin on classically defined sleep parameters in a group of elderly insomniacs using a variety of dosing schedules (Hughes *et al.* 1998); some reduction of sleep latency, however, was noted. Since elderly subjects typically have sleep maintenance, rather than sleep latency, insomnia, the value of melatonin in such patients may be somewhat diminished.

In so far as safety is concerned, in the United States melatonin is unregulated by the Food and Drug Administration. It is therefore difficult to obtain accurate reporting of adverse events. Nearly all available melatonin is synthesized and, to date, no problems with purity have been documented in the scientific literature. Given the popularity of the substance, its widespread use would imply few, if any, untoward side-effects. Conversely, a series of elegant studies in animals have shown the presence of melatonin receptors throughout the body, most notably on the walls of smooth vessels; these studies show that melatonin may be a potent vasoconstrictor in the rat (Krause *et al.* 1995). These results would at least suggest caution in its use in older patients with cardiac or cerebrovascular disease.

Another preparation becoming increasingly interesting as a hypnotic is valerian root. A modest scientific database on its utility exists (Lindahl and Lindwall 1988) and it is relatively popular in Europe. Rigorous systematic data do not yet exist and, as with any herbal product, some concern over source and manufacture is warranted.

Several non-pharmacological interventions should be specifically noted for use in the older population. Bright light exposure (at intensities of several thousand lux for at least several hours) has been shown to be effective at alleviating sleep maintenance insomnia in elderly subjects (Campbell *et al.* 1993). Timing of exposure is crucial but, for most older people, the typical phase response curve to light would place the optimal timing of such exposure in the evening. The mechanisms of action of bright light probably involve resetting of the endogenously generated biological clock. Physical activity of sufficient intensity to induce a moderate aerobic load has been shown to be a significant treatment intervention for insomnia in later life (King *et al.* 1997), as has strength training (Singh *et al.* 1997). It is important to stress the necessity that such activity be at least modestly rigorous; one intervention study involving very low levels of physical activity in disabled nursing home patients failed to find any effect on sleep (Alessi *et al.* 1995).

Although behavioural treatments (relaxation, autogenic training, biofeedback, self-hypnosis) have been used extensively to treat (primarily initial) insomnia in younger individuals, there have been very few attempts to treat elderly patients with these techniques. The available results are mildly encouraging, although elderly patients with chronic medical conditions were excluded in most studies so the target population may be limited. Sleep restriction therapy (Spielman *et al.* 1987), has also met with some limited success in elderly patients. In this treatment, the usual rules of sleep hygiene (use bed only for sleep, maintain regular bedtime/wake-up hours, avoid alcohol and caffeine) are supplemented by the additional stipulations to avoid all daytime napping (even unintentional 'dozing' and 'resting of the eyes') and drastically curtail the time available in bed for sleep (often to as short as 5 or 6 h). As sleep efficiency improves, the individuals are allowed slightly more time in bed (e.g. an increment of 15 min) every 3 to 5 days. Essentially this treatment uses voluntary sleep deprivation, which has been shown to have consolidating effects on depth of sleep in elderly subjects (Carskadon and Dement 1985), to improve length and quality of sleep. Preliminary findings suggest that elderly people derive some benefits from a 4-week sleep restriction programme with daily contact (Friedman *et al.* 1991). Finally, it is important to stress that regularity of daily routine (not only bedtime and wake-up time but also social contacts, meal timing, and other activities) may have protective effects against the development of poor sleep in old age (Prigerson *et al.* 1994)

References

Alessi, C.A., Schnelle, J.F., MacRae, P.G., *et al.* (1995). Does physical activity improve sleep in impaired nursing home residents? *Journal of the American Geriatrics Society*, 43, 1098–102.

Allen, R.P. and Earley, C.J. (1996). Augmentation of the restless legs syndrome with carbidopa/levodopa. *Sleep*, 19, 205–13.

American Psychiatric Association (1994). *Diagnostic and statistical manual of mental disorders* (DSM-IV), (4th edn). American Psychiatric Association, Washington, DC.

Ancoli-Israel, S., Kripke, D.F., Klauber, M.R., Mason, W.J., Fell, R., and Kaplan, O. (1991). Sleep disordered breathing in community-dwelling elderly. *Sleep*, 14, 486–95.

Ancoli-Israel, S., Kripke, D.F., Klauber, M.R., *et al.* (1996). Morbidity, mortality and sleep-disordered breathing in community dwelling elderly. *Sleep*, 19, 277–82.

Association of Sleep Disorders Centers (ASDC) (1979). Diagnostic classification of sleep and arousal disorders, first edition. *Sleep*, 2, 1–137.

Baltzan, M. and Suissa, S. (1997). Mortality in sleep apnoea patients: a multivariate analysis of risk factors—a response to Lavie and collaborators. *Sleep*, 20, 377–8.

Bedard, M.A., Montplaisir, J., Malo, J., *et al.* (1993). Persistent neuropsychological deficits and vigilance impairment in sleep apnoea syndrome after treatment with continuous positive airway pressure (CPAP). *Journal of Clinical and Experimental Neuropsychology*, 15, 330–41.

Berry, R.B. and Gleeson, K. (1997). Respiratory arousal from sleep: mechanisms and significance. *Sleep*, 20, 654–75.

Blazer, D.G., Hays, J.C., and Foley, D.J. (1995). Sleep complaints in older adults: a racial comparison. *Journal of Gerontology: Medical Sciences*, 50, M280–4.

Bliwise, D.L. (1994). What is sundowning? *Journal of the American Geriatrics Society*, 42, 1009–11.

Bliwise, D.L. (1996a). Chronological age, physiologic age, and mortality in sleep apnoea. *Sleep*, 19, 275–6.

Bliwise, D.L. (1996b). Is sleep apnoea a cause of reversible dementia in old age? *Journal of the American Geriatrics Society*, 44, 1407–9.

Bliwise, D.L., Petta, D., Seidel, W., and Dement, W.C. (1985). Periodic leg movements during sleep in the elderly. *Archives of Gerontology and Geriatrics*, 4, 273–81.

Bliwise, D.L., *et al.* (1987). Risk factors for sleep disordered breathing in heterogeneous geriatric populations. *Journal of the American Geriatrics Society*, 35, 132–41.

Bliwise, D.L., Bliwise, N.G., Partinen, M., Pursley, A.M., and Dement, W.C. (1988). Sleep apnoea and mortality in an aged cohort. *American Journal of Public Health*, 78, 544–7.

Bliwise, D.L., Bevier, W.C., Bliwise, N.G., Edgar, D.M., and Dement, W.C. (1990). Systematic 24-hour behavioral observations of sleep/ wakefulness in a skilled care nursing facility. *Psychology and Aging*, 5, 16–24.

Bliwise, D.L., Nekich, J.C., and Dement W.C. (1991). Relative validity of self-reported snoring as a symptom of sleep apnoea. *Chest*, 99, 600–8.

Bliwise, D.L., Carroll, J.S., Lee, K.A., Nekich, J.C., and Dement, W.C. (1993). Sleep and sundowning in nursing home patients with dementia. *Psychiatry Research*, 48, 277–92.

Brooks, J.O. III, Friedman, L., Bliwise, D.L., and Yesavage, J.A. (1993). Use of the wrist actigraph to study insomnia in older adults. *Sleep*, 16, 151–5.

Bucher, S.F., Seelos, K.C., Oertel, W.H., Reiser, M., and Trenkwalder, C. (1997). Cerebral generators involved in the pathogenesis of the restless legs syndrome. *Annals of Neurology*, 41, 639–45.

Burgio, L., Scilley, K., Hardin J.M., *et al.* (1994). Studying disruptive vocalization and contextual factors in the nursing home using computer-assisted real-time observation. *Journal of Gerontology, Psychological Sciences*, 49, 230–9.

Buysse, D.J., Reynolds, C.F. III, Hoch, C.C., et al. (1996). Longitudinal effects of nortriptyline on EEG sleep and the likelihood of recurrence in elderly depressed patients. *Neuropsychopharmacology*, 14, 243–52.

Buysse, D.J., Reynolds, C.F. III, Houck, P.R., et al. (1997a). Does lorazepam impair the antidepressant response to nortriptyline and psychotherapy? *Journal of Clinical Psychiatry*, 58, 426–32.

Buysse, D.J., Reynolds, C.F. III, Kupfer, D.J., et al. (1997b). Effects of diagnosis on treatment recommendations in chronic insomnia—a report from the APA/NIMH DSM-IV field trial. *Sleep*, 20, 542–52.

Campbell, S.S., Dawson, D., and Anderson, M.W. (1993). Alleviation of sleep maintenance insomnia with timed exposure to bright light. *Journal of the American Geriatrics Society*, 41, 829–36.

Carskadon, M.A. and Dement, W.C. (1985). Sleep loss in elderly volunteers. *Sleep*, 8, 207–21.

Chesson, A.L., Ferber, R.A., Fry, J.M., et al. (1997). The indications for polysomnography and related procedures. *Sleep*, 20, 423–87.

Cornoni-Huntley, J., Brock, D.B., Ostfeld. A.M., Taylor, J.O., and Wallace, R.B. (ed.) (1986). *Established populations for epidemiological studies of the elderly*, NIH Publication No. 86-2443. National Institute on Aging, Washington DC.

Dealberto, M.J., Pajot, N., Courbon, D., et al. (1996). Breathing disorders during sleep and cognitive performance in an older community sample: the EVA study. *Journal of the American Geriatrics Society*, 44, 1287–94.

Dempsey, J.A. and Skatrud, J.B. (1986). A sleep-induced apneic threshold and its consequences. *American Review of Respiratory Disease*, 133, 1163–70.

Dempsey, J.A., Smith, C.A., Harms, C.A., Chow, C.M., and Saupe, K.W. (1996). Sleep induced breathing instability. *Sleep*, 19, 236–47.

Earley, C.J. and Allen, R.P. (1996). Pergolide and carbidopa/levodopa treatment of the restless legs syndrome and periodic leg movements in sleep in a consecutive series of patients. *Sleep*, 19, 801–10.

Engleman, H.M., Martin, S.E., Deary, I.J., and Douglas, N.J. (1994). Effect of continuous positive airway pressure treatment on daytime function in sleep apnoea/hypopnoea syndrome. *Lancet*, 343, 572–5.

Engleman, H.M., Martin, S.E., Deary, I.J., and Douglas, N.J. (1997). Some criticisms of studies are unfounded. *British Medical Journal*, 315, 369.

Fenik, V., Kubin, L., Okabe, S., Pack, A.I., and Davies, R.O. (1997). Differential sensitivity of laryngeal and pharyngeal motoneurons to iontophoretic application of serotonin. *Neuroscience*, 81, 873–85.

Fleetham, J.A. (1997). A wake up call for sleep disordered breathing. *British Medical Journal*, 314, 839–40.

Fleetham, J.A., Ferguson, K.A., Lowe, A.A., and Ryan, C.F. (1996). Oral appliance therapy for the treatment of obstructive sleep apnoea. *Sleep*, 19, S288–90.

Fletcher, E.C. (1993). Obstructive sleep apnoea and the kidney. *Journal of the American Society of Nephrology*, 4, 1111–21.

Foley, D.J., Monjan, A.A., Brown, S.L., Simonsick, E.M., Wallace, R.B., and Blazer, D.G. (1995). Sleep complaints among elderly persons: an epidemiologic study of three communities. *Sleep*, 18, 425–32.

Ford, D.E. and Kamerow, D.B. (1989). Epidemiologic study of sleep disturbances and psychiatric disorders. *Journal of the American Medical Association*, 262, 1479–84.

Friedman, L., Bliwise, D.L., Yesavage, J.A., and Salom, S.R. (1991). A preliminary study comparing sleep restriction and relaxation treatments for insomnia in older adults. *Journal of Gerontology: Psychological Sciences*, 46, P1–8.

Ganguli, M., Reynolds, C.F., and Gilby, J.E. (1996). Prevalence and persistence of sleep complaints in a rural older community sample: the MoVIES Project. *Journal of the American Geriatrics Society*, 44, 778–84.

Garfinkel, D., Laudon, M., Nof, D., and Zisapel, N. (1995). Improvement of sleep quality in elderly people by controlled-release melatonin. *Lancet*, 346, 541–4.

Gibson, G.J. and Prowse, K. (1997). Review was misleading and may deny cost effective treatment to patients. *British Medical Journal*, 315, 368.

Gillick, M.R., Serrell, N.A., and Gillick, L.S. (1982). Adverse consequences of hospitalisation in the elderly. *Social Science and Medicine*, 16, 1033–8.

Gislason, T. and Almqvist, M. (1987). Somatic diseases and sleep complaints. *Acta Medica Scandinavica*, 221, 475–81.

Gislason, T., Reynisdottir, H., Kristbjarnarson, H., and Benediktsdottir, B. (1993). Sleep habits and sleep disturbances among the elderly—an epidemiological survey. *Journal of Internal Medicine*, 234, 31–9.

Grunstein, R. (1995). Obstructive sleep apnoea as a risk factor for hypertension. *Journal of Sleep Research*, 4, 166–70.

Guilleminault, C. (1989). Narcolepsy syndrome. In *Principles and practice of sleep medicine* (ed. M.H. Kryger, T. Roth, and W.C. Dement), pp. 338–46. W.B. Saunders, Philadelphia, PA.

Haimov, I., Lavie, P., Laudon, M., Herer, P., Vigder, C., and Zisapel, N. (1995). Melatonin replacement therapy of elderly insomniacs. *Sleep*, 18, 598–603.

Hanzel, D.A., Proia, N.G., and Hudgel, D.W. (1991). Response of obstructive sleep apnoea to fluoxetine and protriptyline. *Chest*, 100, 416–21.

Hauri, P. and Fisher, J. (1986). Persistent psychophysiologic (learned) insomnia. *Sleep*, 9, 38–53.

Hla, K.M., Young, T.B., Bidwell, T., Palta, M., Skatrud, J.B., and Dempsey, J. (1994). Sleep apnoea and hypertension: a population based study. *Annals of Internal Medicine*, 120, 382–8.

Horner, R.L. (1996). Motor control of the pharyngeal musculature and implications for the pathogenesis of obstructive sleep apnoea. *Sleep*, 19, 827–53.

Hublin, C., Kaprio, J., Partinen, M., et al. (1994). The prevalence of narcolepsy: an epidemiological study of the Finnish twin cohort. *Annals of Neurology*, 35, 709–16.

Hudgel, D.W. (1996). Treatment of obstructive sleep apnoea. *Chest*, 109, 1346–58.

Hughes, R.J., Sack, R.L., and Lewy, A.J., (1998). The role of melatonin and circadian phase in age-related sleep-maintenance insomnia: assessment in a clinical trial of melatonin replacement. *Sleep*, 21, 52–68.

Jenkinson, C., Stradling, J., and Peterson, S. (1997). Comparison of three measures of quality of life outcome in the evaluation of continuous positive airways pressure therapy for sleep apnoea. *Journal of Sleep Research*, 6, 199–204.

Karacan, I., Thornby, J.T., and Williams, R.L. (1983). Sleep disturbance: a community survey. In *Sleep/wake disorders: natural history, epidemiology, and long-term evolution* (ed. C. Guilleminault and E. Lugaresi), pp. 37–60. Raven Press, New York.

King, A.C., Oman, R.F., Brassington, G., Bliwise, D.L., and Haskell, W.L. (1997). Moderate-intensity exercise and self-rated quality of sleep in older adults. *Journal of the American Medical Association*, 277, 32–7.

Klink, M.E., Quan, S.F., Kaltenborn, W.T., and Lebowitz, M.D. (1992). Risk factors associated with complaints of insomnia in general adult population. *Archives of Internal Medicine*, 152, 1634–7.

Krause, D.N., Barrios, V.E., and Duckles, S.P. (1995). Melatonin receptors mediate potentiation of contractile responses to adrenergic nerve stimulation in rat caudal artery. *European Journal of Pharmacology*, 276, 207–13.

Krieger, J., Sforza, E., Boudewijns, A., Zamagni, M., and Petiau, C. (1997). Respiratory effort during obstructive sleep apnoea: role of age and sleep state. *Chest*, 112, 875–49.

Kripke, D.F., Simons, R.N., Garfinkel, L., and Hammond, E.C. (1979). Short and long sleep and sleeping pills: is increased mortality associated? *Archives of General Psychiatry*, 36, 103–16.

Kryger, M. (1997). Sleep apnoea and the misuse of evidence-based medicine. *Lancet*, 349, 803–4.

Kryger, M.H., Roos, L., Delaive, K, Walled, R., and Horrocks, J. (1996). Utilisation of health care services in patients with severe obstructive sleep apnoea. *Sleep*, 19, S111–16.

Kummer, J., Guendel, L., Linden, J., *et al.* (1993). Long-term polysomnographic study of the efficacy and safety of zolpidem in elderly psychiatric in-patients with insomnia. *Journal of International Medical Research*, 21, 171–84.

Kushida, C.A., Efron, B., and Guilleminault, C. (1997). A predictive morphometric model for the obstructive sleep apnoea syndrome. *Annals of Internal Medicine*, 127, 581–7.

Lavie, P., Herer, P., Peled, R., *et al.* (1995). Mortality in sleep apnoea patients: a multivariate analysis of risk factors. *Sleep*, 18, 149–57.

Lavigne, G.J. and Montplaisir, J.Y. (1994). Restless legs syndrome and sleep bruxism: prevalence and association among Canadians. *Sleep*, 17, 739–43.

Levkoff, S.E., Besdine, R.W., and Wetle, T. (1986). Acute confusional states (delirium) in the hospitalised elderly. *Annual Review of Gerontology and Geriatrics*, 6, 1–26.

Lindahl, O. and Lindwall, L. (1988). Double blind study of a valerian preparation. *Pharmacology, Biochemistry and Behavior*, 32, 1065–6.

Livingston, G., Blizard, B., and Mann, A. (1993). Does sleep disturbance predict depression in elderly people? A study in inner London. *British Journal of General Practice*, 43, 445–8.

Martin, S.E., Mathur, R., Marshall, I., and Douglas, N.J. (1997). The effect of age, sex, obesity and posture on upper airway size. *European Respiratory Journal*, 10, 2087–90.

Mellick, G.A. and Mellick, L.B. (1996). Management of restless legs syndrome with gabapentin (Neurontin). *Sleep*, 19, 224–6.

Mendelson, W.B. (1996). Are periodic leg movements associated with clinical sleep disturbance? *Sleep*, 19, 219–23.

Menn, S.J., Loube, D.I., Morgan, T.D., Mitler, M.M., Berger, J.S., and Erman, M.K. (1996). The mandibular repositioning device: role in the treatment of obstructive sleep apnoea. *Sleep*, 19, 794–800.

Mignot, E., Lin, X., Arrigoni, J., *et al.* (1994). DQB1*0602 and DQA1*0102 (DQ1) are better markers than DR2 for narcolepsy in Caucasian and black Americans. *Sleep*, 17, S60–7.

Montplaisir, J., Godbout, R., Poirier, G., and Bedard, M.A. (1986). Restless legs syndrome and periodic movements in sleep: physiopathology and treatment with L-dopa. *Clinical Neuropharmacology*, 9, 456–63.

Montplaisir, J., Boucher, S., Poirier, G. Lavigne, G., Lapierre, O., and Lesperance, P. (1997). Clinical, polysomnographic, and genetic characteristics of restless legs syndrome: a study of 133 patients diagnosed with new standard criteria. *Movement Disorders*, 12, 61–5.

National Institutes of Health (1995). *Sleep apnea: is your patient at risk?* NIH Publication No. 95-3803. National Institutes of Health, National Heart, Lung and Blood Institute, Washington, DC.

Neely, S., Rosenberg, R, Spire, J.P., Antel, J., and Arnason, B.G.W. (1987). HLA antigens in narcolepsy. *Neurology*, 37, 1858–60.

Nino-Murcia, G., McCann, C.C., Bliwise, D.L., Guilleminault, C., and Dement, W.C. (1989). Compliance and side effects in sleep apnea patients treated with nasal CPAP. *Western Journal of Medicine*, 150, 1659.

Nowell, P.D., Buysse, D.J., Reynolds, C.F. III, *et al.* (1997). Clinical factors contributing to the differential diagnosis of primary insomnia and insomnia related to mental disorders. *American Journal of Psychiatry*, 154, 1412–16.

Nowell, P.D., Reynolds, C.F. III, Buysse, D.J., Dew, M.A., and Kupfer, D.J. (1999). Paroxetine in the treatment of primary insomnia: preliminary clinical and EEG sleep data. *Journal of Clinical Psychiatry*, 60, 89–95.

Ohayon, M.M. (1997). Prevalence of DSM-IV diagnostic criteria of insomnia: distinguishing insomnia related to mental disorders from sleep disorders. *Journal of Psychiatric Research*, 31, 333–46.

O'Keeffe, S.T., Gavin, K., and Lavan, J.N. (1994). Iron status and restless legs syndrome in the elderly. *Age and Ageing*, 23, 200–3.

Pack, A.I. and Young, T. (1997). Superficial analysis ignores evidence on efficacy of treatment. *British Medical Journal*, 315, 367.

Palomaki, H., Partinen, M., Erkinjuntti, T., and Kaste, M. (1992). Snoring, sleep apnoea syndrome, and stroke. *Neurology*, 42, 75–82.

Partinen, M., Kaprio, J., Koskenvuo, M., and Langinvaino, H. (1983). Sleeping habits, sleep quality, and use of sleeping pills: a population study of 31 140 adults in Finland. In *Sleep/wake disorders: natural history, epidemiology and long-term evolution* (ed. C. Guilleminault and E. Lugaresi), pp. 29–35. Raven Press, New York.

Pasternak, R.E., Reynolds, C.F. III, Hoch, C.C., *et al.* (1992). Sleep in spousally bereaved elders with subsyndromal depressive symptoms. *Psychiatry Research*, 43, 43–53.

Pasternak, R.E., Reynolds, C.F. III, Houck, P.R. *et al.* (1994). Sleep in bereavement-related depression during and after pharmacotherapy with nortriptyline. *Journal of Geriatric Psychiatry and Neurology*, 7, 71–5.

Peker, Y., Hedner, J., Johansson, A., and Bende, M. (1997). Reduced hospitalisation with cardiovascular and pulmonary disease in obstructive sleep apnoea patients on nasal CPAP treatment. *Sleep*, 20, 645–53.

Prigerson, H.G., Reynolds, C.F. III, Frank, E., Kupfer, D.J., George, C.J., and Houck, P.R. (1994). Stressful life events, social rhythms, and depressive symptoms among the elderly: an examination of hypothesised casual linkages. *Psychiatry Research*, 51, 33–49.

Prinz, P.N. *et al.* (1984). Circadian temperature variation in healthy aged and in Alzheimer's disease. *Journal of Gerontology*, 39, 30–5.

Quan, S.F., Howard, B.V., Iber, C., *et al.* (1997). The Sleep Heart Health Study: design, rationale, and methods. *Sleep*, 20, 1077–85.

Rabey, J.M., Treves, T.A., Neufeld, M.Y., Orlov, E., and Korczyn, A.D. (1995). Low-dose clozapine in the treatment of levodopa-induced mental disturbances in Parkinson's disease. *Neurology*, 45, 432–4.

Rangemark, C., Hedner, J.A., Carlson, J.T., Gleerup, G., and Winther, K. (1995). Platelet function and fibrinolytic activity in hypertensive and normotensive sleep apnoea patients. *Sleep*, 18, 188–94.

Redline, S., Tishler, P.V., Hans, M.G., Tosteson, T.D., Strohl, K.P., and Spry, K. (1997). Racial differences in sleep-disordered breathing in African-Americans and Caucasians. *American Journal of Respiratory and Critical Care Medicine*, 155, 186–92.

Reynolds, C.F. III, Hoch, C.C., Buysse, D.J., *et al.* (1992). Electroencephalographic sleep in spousal bereavement and bereavement-related depression of late life. *Biological Psychiatry*, 31, 69–82.

Reynolds, C.F. III, Buysse, D.J., Brunner, D.P., *et al.* (1997). Maintenance nortriptyline effects on electroencephalographic sleep in elderly patients with recurrent major depression: double-blind, placebo- and plasma-level-controlled evaluation. *Biological Psychiatry*, 42, 560–7.

Rodin, J., McAvay, G., and Timko, C. (1988). A longitudinal study of depressed mood and sleep disturbances in elderly adults. *Journal of Gerontology*, 43, 45–53.

Rogers, A.E., Meehan, J., Guilleminault, C., Grumet, F.C., and Mignot, E. (1997). HLA DR15 (DR2) and DQBI*0602 typing studies in 188 narcoleptic patients with cataplexy. *Neurology*, 48, 1550–6.

Rumble, R. and Morgan, K. (1992). Hypnotics, sleep, and mortality in elderly people. *Journal of the American Geriatrics Society*, 40, 787–91.

Rye, D.B. and Bliwise, D.L. (1997). Movement disorders specific to sleep and the nocturnal manifestations of waking movement disorders. In *Movement disorders: neurologic principles and practice* (ed. R.L. Watts and W.C. Koller), pp. 687–713. McGraw-Hill, New York.

Rye, D.B., Dihenia, B., and Bliwise, D.L. (1998a). Reversal of atypical depression, sleepiness and REM-sleep propensity in narcolepsy with bupropion. *Depression and Anxiety*, 7, 92–5.

Rye, D.B., Dihenia, B., Weissman, J.D., Epstein, C.M. and Bliwise, D.L. (1998b). Presentation of narcolepsy after 40. *Neurology*, 50, 459–65.

Schenck, C.H., Bundlie, S.R., Patterson, A.L., and Mahowald, M.V. (1987). Rapid eye movement sleep behaviour disorder: a treatable parasomnia affecting older adults. *Journal of the American Medical Association*, 257, 1786–9.

Schenck, C.H., Bundlie, S.R., and Mahowald M.W. (1996). Delayed emergence of a Parkinsonian disorder in 38 per cent of 29 older men initially diagnosed with idiopathic rapid eye movement sleep behaviour disorder. *Neurology*, 46, 388–93.

Schmidt-Nowara, W., Lowe, A., Wiegand L., Cartwright, R., Perez-Guerra, F., and Menn S. (1995). Oral appliances for the treatment of snoring and obstructive sleep apnoea: a review. *Sleep*, 18, 501–10.

Schnelle, J.F., Ouslander, J.G., Simmons, S.F., *et al.* (1993*a*). Night-time sleep and bed mobility among incontinent nursing home residents. *Journal of the American Geriatrics Society*, 41, 903–9.

Schnelle, J.F., Ouslander, J.G., Simmons, S.F., *et al.* (1993*b*). The night-time environment, incontinence care, and sleep disruption in nursing homes. *Journal of the American Geriatrics Society*, 41, 910–14.

Shaw, S.H., Curson, H., and Coquelin, J.P. (1992). A double-blind, comparative study of zolpidem and placebo in the treatment of insomnia in elderly psychiatric in-patients. *Journal of Internal Medical Research*, 20, 150–61.

Shorr, R.I., Fought, R.L., and Ray, W.A. (1994). Changes in antipsychotic drug use in nursing homes during implementation of the OBRA-87 regulations. *Journal of the American Medical Association*, 271, 358–62.

Silverberg, D.S. and Oksenberg, A. (1997). Essential hypertension and abnormal upper airway resistance during sleep. *Sleep*, 20, 794–806.

Silverberg, D.S., Oksenberg, A., and Iaina, A. (1997). Sleep related breathing disorders are common contributing factors to the production of essential hypertension but are neglected, underdiagnosed, and undertreated. *American Journal of Hypertension*, 10, 1319–25.

Singer, C., McArthur, A., Hughes, R., Sack, R., Kaye, J., and Lewy, A. (1995). High dose melatonin administration and sleep in the elderly. *Sleep Research*, 24A, 151.

Singer, C.M., Moffit, M.T., Colling E.D., *et al.* (1997). Low dose melatonin administration and nocturnal activity levels in patients with Alzheimer's disease. *Sleep Research*, 26, 752.

Singh, N.A., Clements, K.M., and Fiatarone, M.A. (1997). A randomised controlled trial of the effect of exercise on sleep. *Sleep*, 20, 95–101.

Somers, V.K., Dyken, M.E., Clary, M.P., and Abboud, F.M. (1995). Sympathetic neural mechanisms in obstructive sleep apnoea. *Journal of Clinical Investigation*, 96, 1897–904.

Spielman, A.J., Saskin, P., and Thorpy, M.J. (1987). Treatment of chronic insomnia by restriction of time in bed. *Sleep*, 10, 45–56.

Staedt, J., Stoppe, G., Kogler, A., *et al.* (1993). Dopamine D2 receptor alteration in patients with periodic movements in sleep (nocturnal myoclonus). *Journal of Neural Transmission [Genetic Section]*, 93, 71–4.

Stradling, J. (1995). Obstructive sleep apnoea; definitions, epidemiology, and natural history. *Thorax*, 50, 683–9.

Stradling, J. (1997). Sleep apnoea and the misuse of evidence-based medicine. *Lancet*, 349, 201–2.

Stradling, J.R. and Davies, R.J.O. (1997*a*). Evidence for efficacy of continuous positive airways pressure is compelling. *British Medical Journal*, 315, 368.

Stradling, J. and Davies, R.J.O. (1997*b*). Sleep apnoea and hypertension—what a mess! *Sleep*, 20, 789–93.

Strohl, K.P. (1996). Diabetes and sleep apnoea. *Sleep*, 19, S225–8.

Strohl, K.P. and Redline, S. (1996). Recognition of obstructive sleep apnoea. *Journal of Respiratory and Critical Care Medicine*, 154, 279–89.

Trenkwalder, C., Bucher, S.F., Oertel, W.H., Proeckl, D., Plendl, H., and Paulus, W. (1993). Bereitschaftspotential in idiopathic and symptomatic restless legs syndrome. *Electroencephalography and Clinical Neurophysiology*, 89, 95–103.

Valencia-Flores, M., Bliwise, D.L., Guilleminault, C., Cilveti, R., and Clerk, A. (1996). Cognitive function after acute nocturnal continuous positive airway pressure (CPAP) treatment: sleepiness and hypoxemia effects. *Journal of Clinical and Experimental Neuropsychology*, 18, 197–210.

Van Lunteren, E., Vafaie, H., and Salomone, R.J. (1995). Comparative effects of ageing on pharyngeal and diaphragm muscles. *Respiration Physiology*, 99, 113–25.

Walker, S.L., Fine, A., and Kryger, M.H. (1996). L-Dopa/carbidopa for nocturnal movement disorders in uremia. *Sleep*, 19, 214–18.

Walsworth-Bell, J. (1997). Sleep apnoea and the misuse of evidence-based medicine. *Lancet*, 349, 803.

Walters, A.S. (1995). Toward a better definition of the restless legs syndrome. *Movement Disorders*, 10, 634–42.

Walters, A.S., Hening, W.A., Kavey, N., Chokroverty, S., and Gidro-Frank, S. (1988) A double-blind randomised crossover trial of bromocriptine and placebo in the restless legs syndrome. *Annals of Neurology*, 24, 455–8.

Weaver, T.E., Kribbs, N.B., Pack, A.I., *et al.* (1997). Night to night variability in CPAP use over the first three months of treatment. *Sleep*, 20, 278–83.

Wechsler, L.R., Stakes, J.W., Shahani, B.T., and Busis, N.A. (1986). Periodic leg movements or sleep (nocturnal myoclonus): an electrophysiological study. *Annals of Neurology*, 19, 168–73.

Weiss, J.W., Remsburg, S., Garpestad, E., Ringler, J., Sparrow, D., and Parker, J.A. (1996). Haemodynamic consequences of obstructive sleep apnoea. *Sleep*, 19, 388–97.

White, D.P., Lombard, R.M., Cadieux, R.J., and Zwillich. C.W. (1985). Pharyngeal resistance in normal humans: influence of gender, age, and obesity. *Journal of Applied Physiology*, 58, 365–71.

Wilner, A., Steinman, L., Lavie, P., Peled, R., Friedman, A., and Brautbar, C. (1988). Narcolepsy-cataplexy in Israeli Jews is associated exclusively with the HLA DR2 haplotype: a study at the serological and genomic level. *Human Immunology*, 21, 15–22.

Wingard, D.L. and Berkman, L.F. (1983). Mortality risk associated with sleep patterns among adults. *Sleep*, 6, 102–7.

Wolters, E.C., Hurwitz, T.A., Mak, E., *et al.* (1990). Clozapine in the treatment of Parkinsonian patients with dopaminomimetic psychosis. *Neurology*, 40, 832–4.

Wolters, E.C., Jansen, E.N., Tuynman-Qua, H.G., and Bergmans, P.L. (1996). Olanzapine in the treatment of dopaminomimetic psychosis in patients with Parkinson's disease. *Neurology*, 47, 1085–7.

Wright, J., Johns, R., Watt, I., Melville, A., and Sheldon, T. (1997). Health effects of obstructive sleep apnoea and the effectiveness of continuous positive airways pressure: a systematic review of the research evidence. *British Medical Journal*, 314, 851–60.

Young, T., Palta, M., Dempsey, J., Skatrud J., Weber S., and Badr, S. (1993). The occurrence of sleep-disordered breathing among middle-aged adults. *New England Journal of Medicine*, 328, 1230–5.

Ziegler, M.G., Nelesen, R., Mills, P., Ancoli-Israel, S., Kennedy, B., and Dimsdale, J.E. (1997). Sleep apnoea, norepinephrine-release rate, and daytime hypertension. *Sleep*, 20, 224–31.

18.3   Subdural haematoma

Andrew J. Martin and John R. Bartlett

Introduction

The subdural space is a potential cavity at the junction of the dura and arachnoid mater. It does not communicate with the subarachnoid space. Blood entering the subdural space produces a haematoma which, if small, neither increases the intracranial pressure nor interferes with the function of the brain, and may therefore be symptomless. Acute haemorrhage into the subdural space is most often due to injury. Severe injuries which provide sufficient energy to render the patient unconscious generally produce cortical lacerations, contusions, and/or rupture of cerebral vessels. Brain damage is a prominent feature, so signs of disordered function are present from the outset. In contrast, a trivial injury may rupture one of the fragile bridging veins as it passes from the brain through the meninges to enter the sagittal sinus. This may allow blood to enter the subdural space, particularly in the upright posture when intracranial pressure is low, and this may explain why large chronic subdural haematomas are usually a sequel of trivial injury. There is little or no primary damage to the brain and signs are therefore minimal at this stage.

However, not all acute haematomas are due to trauma. A few are associated with the haemorrhagic diatheses, anticoagulant use, and, rarely, intracranial haemorrhage due to aneurysm or tumour. Like chronic haematomas the effects tend to be those of a large space-occupying lesion within the cranial cavity.

While it is customary to classify subdural haematomas as acute, subacute, and chronic, it is equally important to take account of the extent of the underlying primary brain damage. For the most part, whereas an acute haematoma is associated with severe primary brain damage, a chronic haematoma is not, and the two conditions tend to produce distinct clinical pictures.

Natural history and pathology

A subdural haematoma is a dynamic entity. An initiating factor, usually an injury, allows blood to enter the subdural space. The presence of blood provokes an inflammatory reaction in the overlying dura which leads to the gradual removal of the haematoma. This process is not always successful and an expanding collection may form. Certain factors, which have the common feature of allowing a large volume of blood to enter the subdural space, favour this development. They are conveniently divided into those which increase the potential size of the subdural space and those that reduce the coagulability of the blood. Anticoagulant therapy and the use of

aspirin are increasingly common examples of the latter among older people. Factors that increase the potential size of the subdural space include atrophy associated with age (Creasey and Rapoport 1985), alcohol abuse, parenchymal disease, or vascular insufficiency and hydrocephalus with a functioning cerebrospinal fluid shunt. Bleeding eventually ceases as a result of coagulation and/or the tamponading effect of raised intracranial pressure.

The natural history of haematomas in the subdural space is conveniently divided into three stages: (a) acute, the first week; (b) subacute, the second and third weeks; and (c) chronic, beginning at the fourth week. However, the distinction is not absolute, as each stage merges imperceptibly into the next. Resolution of the haematoma, or death from cerebral compression may occur during any stage.

As soon as the healing process begins the haematoma ceases to be homogeneous. The haematoma capsule, which is the result of a dural and arachnoid reaction, is characterized by capillary ingrowth, the formation of fragile venous sinusoids, and fibroblastic activity. As the haematoma ages the number of capillaries is reduced and the fibroblasts mature. The haematoma may be gradually absorbed and the inner layer adjacent to the pia-arachnoid comes to lie against the outer membrane which is ultimately indistinguishable from normal dura. Not all cases resolve. In some the haematoma increases in size, producing symptoms and signs due to distortion of the brain and raised intracranial pressure. Two theories have been advanced to explain the increase in size of chronic subdural haematomas. Gardner (1932) postulated that the capsule acts as a semipermeable membrane and that as the haematoma is broken down into smaller particles, fluid is drawn in by osmosis. There are several objections to this theory, on which the previous use of osmotic diuretics depended. Fresh erythrocytes are regularly found in the haematoma fluid. Ito *et al.* (1987), using red cells labelled with ^{51}Cr, demonstrated that daily fresh haemorrhage may amount to as much as 10 per cent of the volume of the haematoma and Weir (1980) showed that the osmotic pressure of the haematoma fluid is the same as that of cerebrospinal fluid. Studies of the ultrastructure of the 'membrane' make it clear that it is not a simple semipermeable membrane. Putnam and Cushing (1925) postulated that bleeding occurs intermittently from the delicate granulation tissue that lines the cavity. This theory explains why fresh red cells and albumin are found in fluid aspirated from chronic haematomas and also gives a convincing reason for their growth.

Clearly the development of the vascular membrane or capsule is the means by which blood is removed from the subdural space as well as the source of material for those cases where the haematoma increases in size. What determines why some haematomas enlarge

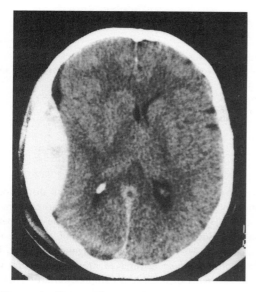

Fig. 1 CT scan of a 63-year-old patient showing the typical lenticular appearance of an acute extradural haematoma. This patient developed a mild left hemiparesis and increasing drowsiness but was able to carry out simple commands immediately before evacuation. She made a full recovery. Extradural haematoma carries a good prognosis, if treated early, and should not be confused with an acute subdural haematoma.

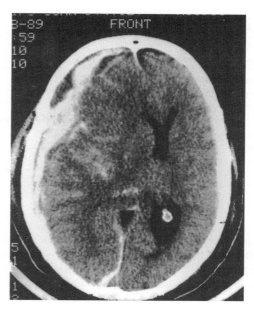

Fig. 2 CT scan of a patient who sustained a severe head injury complicated by extensive right-sided acute subdural haemorrhage. There is marked shift of the mid-line structures which is, in part, due to haemorrhagic contusion and swelling of the cerebral hemisphere. Acute subdural haemorrhage is usually a reflection of a severe primary injury to the brain and carries a grave prognosis.

while others resolve is not clear but there is no doubt that absolute size is an important factor. Apfelbaum *et al.* (1974) pointed out that the larger the volume, the smaller, proportionally, is the surface area. If the rate of absorption is directly related to the surface area of absorbing membrane, then larger haematomas may take longer to resolve. Recurrent haemorrhage could interrupt this process at any time and lead to an increase in size of the haematoma. It is possible that a haematoma must reach a critical size to become chronic and perhaps physical activity on the part of the patient favours recurrent minor haemorrhage. This may explain why the formation of chronic haematomas is rare in patients who have sustained more severe injuries where brain swelling may reduce the potential size of the subdural space. Evacuation of a haematoma through burr holes is never a complete process: the brain does not always expand and a subsequent CT scan may show little initial change. Why evacuation does not precipitate further haemorrhage from the fragile membranes is unclear but removal of fibrinolytic enzymes and fibrin degradation products may be important. Nonetheless, a minor procedure, a burr hole or twist drill drainage, seems to tip the balance back in favour of the healing process.

Acute extradural haemorrhage

Acute extradural haemorrhage, with which subdural haemorrhage may be confused, is rare in elderly people because the dura becomes more adherent to the bony vault with increasing age. On CT the haematoma is lenticular (Fig. 1). This distinction is important because extradural haemorrhage, if treated promptly, carries a far better prognosis as there is typically less associated primary brain damage. In contrast are the chronic haematomas, which are among the largest space-occupying lesions encountered in clinical practice. It is well

known that timely drainage can produce a dramatic recovery and that outcome is chiefly related to the patient's neurological condition at the time of surgery (Van Havenbergh *et al.* 1996). Chronic haematomas exert their pressure over a large area of undamaged brain and with well-directed management the prognosis is excellent and restoration of function is to be expected. Symptoms and signs, confusion and intellectual deterioration often with headache, generally suggest a diffuse disorder of cerebral function and focal signs may be minimal or completely absent. The rise in intracranial pressure responsible for these effects is rarely sufficient to produce papilloedema. Progressive reduction of consciousness with the development of defects of ocular movement and pupillary abnormalities indicate impaired upper brainstem function. These signs are due to the brainstem distortion produced by any large space-occupying lesion within the cranial cavity, and when present to a marked degree, indicate impending death. They are an indication that evacuation of the haematoma is urgent; recovery of function is often incomplete when surgery is delayed to this extent.

Acute subdural haematoma

Acute subdural haematomas due to head injury are generally associated with contusion and swelling of the brain which restricts their size (Fig. 2). Coma and focal signs are therefore prominent. Recovery of function is usually incomplete and fatality is high, particularly in elderly patients.

It is not possible to establish or refute the diagnosis with certainty on clinical grounds alone. The acute haematoma is generally associated with a clear history of head injury. Such patients are usually seen in

Table 1 Indications for admission to a general hospital

All patients with impaired consciousness

Orientated patient

Skull fracture or suture diastasis

Persisting neurological symptoms or signs

Difficulty in assessment (e.g. suspected drugs/alcohol, non-accidental injury, epilepsy, attempted suicide)

Lack of responsible adult to supervise patient

Other medical condition (e.g. coagulation disorder)

Reproduced with permission from Bartlett et al. (1998).

accident and emergency departments where they are assessed for the global effects of the injury. The Society of British Neurological Surgeons (Bartlett *et al.* 1998) has produced guidelines, applicable to adults, for hospital admission (Table 1), skull radiography (Table 2), consultation with a neurosurgeon (Table 3), and CT scanning after admission (Table 4).

Incomplete recovery of consciousness, significant scalp trauma, focal signs, and the presence of a skull fracture are all associated with an increased risk of intracranial haematoma, which may be intracerebral, subdural, or extradural, singly or in combination. As always, the general principles of resuscitation (control of the airway with cervical spine immobilization, oxygenation, and the maintenance

Table 2 Indications for skull radiography after head injury

Patients with impaired consciousness or neurological signs

All patients unless urgent CT is performed or transfer to neurosurgery is arranged

Orientated patient

History of loss of consciousness or amnesia

Suspected penetrating injury

Cerebrospinal fluid or blood loss from nose or ear

Scalp laceration (to bone or >5 cm long), bruise, or swelling

Violent mechanism of injury

Persisting headache and/or vomiting

Reproduced with permission from Bartlett et al. (1998).

Table 3 Indications for consultation with a neurosurgeon and/or urgent CT scan

Coma persisting after resuscitation

Deteriorating consciousness or progressive neurological signs

Fracture of skull with any of the following: confusion or worse impairment of consciousness, epileptic seizure, neurological symptoms or signs

Open injury
     Depressed compound or skull vault
     Fracture of base of skull
     Penetrating injury

Reproduced with permission from Bartlett et al. (1998).

Table 4 Additional indications for CT in a general hospital

Skull fracture or following a fit

Confusion or neurological signs persisting after initial assessment and resuscitation

Unstable systemic state precluding transfer to neurosurgery

Diagnosis uncertain

Reproduced with permission from Bartlett et al. (1998).

of an adequate blood pressure) apply, but a full discussion of the management of trauma is beyond the scope of this chapter.

The sudden development of severe headache in a patient on anticoagulants should arouse the suspicion of an acute subdural haemorrhage (Fig. 3). Because of the coagulation defect, bleeding is usually profuse, and so features of raised intracranial pressure, drowsiness, and signs of brainstem compression are common. The dearth of focal signs generally differentiate subdural from intracerebral haematoma and the relative lack of neck stiffness, photophobia, and the absence of Kernig's sign distinguish the condition from primary subarachnoid haemorrhage. It must be emphasized that acute spontaneous haemorrhage into the subdural space in those with normal blood coagulation is very rare. However, if there is serious doubt about the diagnosis, the matter must be resolved by CT scanning.

Chronic subdural haematoma

In the absence of any history of injury, chronic haematoma may be very difficult to diagnose. Diffuse symptoms of a cerebral disorder such as personality change and intellectual deterioration are common;

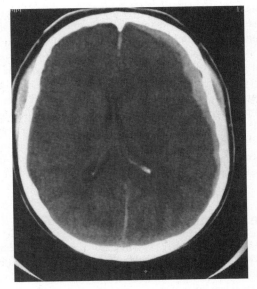

Fig. 3 A CT scan showing an extensive narrow rim of left-sided subdural blood in a patient on anticoagulant therapy. The brain shows no sign of intrinsic damage or pre-existing atrophy. This haematoma produced a degree of life-threatening compression with left-sided pupillary dilatation and required emergency evacuation by craniotomy.

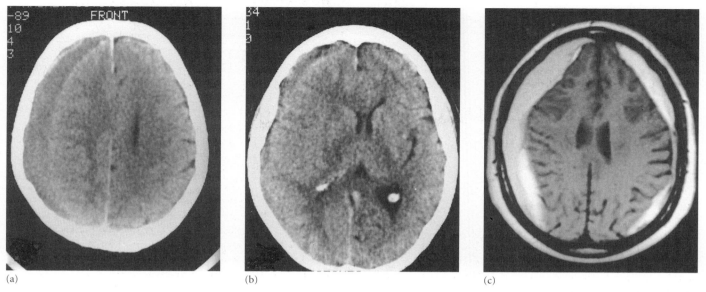

(a)   (b)   (c)

Fig. 4 (a, b) CT scans showing a large, almost isodense, right-sided chronic subdural haematoma. This has caused shift of the cerebral mid-line to the left and has partially effaced the right lateral ventricle. (c). T$_1$-weighted axial MRI scan showing bilateral subdural haematomas of differing ages.

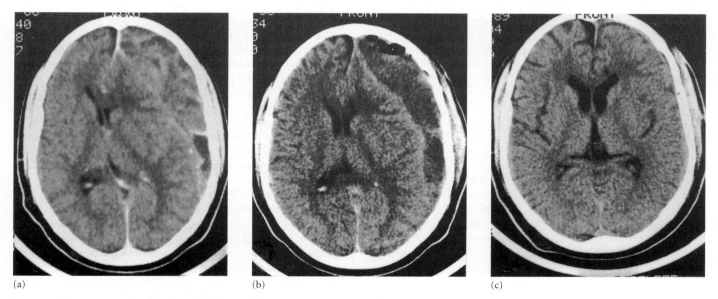

(a)   (b)   (c)

Fig. 5 CT scan of a loculated haematoma presenting with mild headache and, unusually for a chronic haematoma, papilloedema. (a) Before evacuation and (b) after an attempt at burr hole drainage which was later repeated with equal lack of immediate success. (c) Three months later, after several weeks of bed rest followed by restricted physical activity, the haematoma had resolved.

focal signs such as a mild hemiparesis may occur, but dramatic findings such as hemiplegia, hemianopia, or global aphasia are less common. Signs of brainstem compression (altered consciousness, pupillary inequality, and defective ocular movements, particularly reduced upward gaze which is difficult to interpret in elderly patients) are relatively common. Epilepsy is usually a reflection of injury to, or underlying pathology in, the brain. It is more usually associated with acute traumatic haematoma and is relatively rare in the chronic

variety. In any patient with a short history of intellectual deterioration, defects in blood coagulation, or circumstances that are associated with repeated mild injury the clinician should be alert to the possibility of a chronic subdural haematoma. Most patients present with a history of 6 to 8 weeks duration; a history longer than 3 months is unusual.

Many patients have a mild and persistent headache without any physical signs after head injury and only rarely is this due to chronic

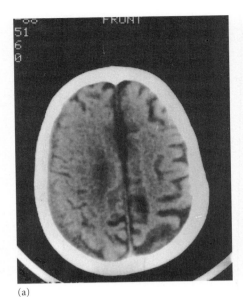

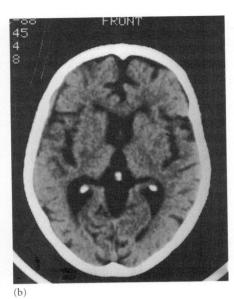

(a)   (b)

Fig. 6 (a) CT scan showing a right-sided surface collection with density a little greater than cerebrospinal fluid and partial obliteration of the cortical sulci consistent with a chronic subdural haematoma or hygroma. (b) A lower section in the same patient shows marked cerebral atrophy and no mid-line shift. There is nothing to be gained from the evacuation of lesions of this kind.

haematoma. Even if a haematoma is demonstrated, it is usually small, and if left alone may absorb without recourse to surgery.

The clinical differentiation of chronic subdural haematoma from diffuse cerebrovascular disease and intracranial tumour may be very difficult. If present, marked fluctuation in the level of consciousness is quite characteristic of chronic haematoma and is possibly due to recurrent haemorrhage. When papilloedema is present, there is a clear indication for further investigation.

Investigation

The definitive investigation is now CT scanning or magnetic resonance imaging (**MRI**) (Fig. 4). Before the introduction of these methods, diagnosis depended on angiography or burr hole exploration of the subdural space. A plain skull radiograph may have revealed a laterally displaced calcified pineal gland. The acute, subacute, and chronic phases in the natural history of subdural haematoma correspond to hyperdense, isodense, and hypodense appearances on a CT scan.

The three stages are equally distinct on MRI: the acute haematoma is isointense with brain on T_1-weighted and hypointense on T_2-weighted images; during the subacute phase, lysis of the red cells and oxidation of deoxyhaemoglobin to met-haemoglobin tends to shorten T_1 and lengthen T_2, which will increase the intensity on these images. The continued breakdown of met-haemoglobin produces compounds that are not paramagnetic and have reduced T_1 values (and thus the signal intensity is reduced). Ultimately the fluid, if it is not fully absorbed, becomes a subdural hygroma behaving similarly to cerebrospinal fluid on MRI (and in this respect analogous to CT). While plain CT has proved a very reliable means of making the diagnosis, it is still possible to miss isodense, bilateral subdural haematomas. In such cases it may be necessary to use intravenous contrast to distinguish the well-perfused cerebral cortex and vascular membrane from the liquid haematoma.

Management

It is almost universally accepted that symptomatic progressive haematomas should be evacuated, whether acute or chronic. Treatment has two aims: (a) to save life when this is threatened by compression of the brainstem, and (b) to remove (sufficient of) the haematoma to tip the balance of the healing process back in favour of the patient. Acute haematomas are usually solid and it is not possible to remove them without craniotomy. Chronic haematomas have a large liquid component, which is easily evacuated through one or more burr holes.

Occasionally the subacute or chronic haematoma cavity becomes loculated; perhaps a reflection of patchy liquefaction. In long-standing haematoma, loculation is more likely, owing to further haemorrhage (Fig. 5).

The importance of loculated haematomas lies in the difficulty in obtaining enough reduction in volume to relieve brainstem compression and raised intracranial pressure through burr holes alone. They may require craniotomy but fortunately such cases are rare. The knowledge that many haematomas resolve spontaneously has led to the exploration of conservative methods of management. Bender and Christoff (1974), who reported 100 cases, demonstrated unequivocally that not all need removal. However, a chronic haematoma with progressive symptoms and signs may have catastrophic effects on the nervous system. Attempts to treat chronic haematoma with infusions of mannitol failed in a controlled trial (Gjerris and Schmidt 1974), despite a report of success in an uncontrolled series (Suzuki and Takaku 1970).

A difficulty still remains. There are patients whose symptoms are a consequence of the underlying conditions that predispose them to the accumulation of fluid similar to cerebrospinal fluid in the subdural space. Such conditions might be demonstrated radiographically, for example wide cortical sulci and atrophy (Fig. 6). Evacuation of such collections does not restore brain function. It is unfortunate that small but insignificant haemorrhages occur into these collections, which are then branded as chronic subdural haematomas possibly requiring surgery. The management of such problems is best resolved by frank discussion of the nature and significance of the findings with the family rather than by ill-considered surgery.

Burr hole evacuation remains the treatment of choice for chronic haematomas with progressive symptoms and signs. Solid, usually acute, haematomas and those chronic haematomas that rapidly and repeatedly reaccumulate require craniotomy. Small haematomas discovered simply because the means of diagnosis is readily available can be managed conservatively in the absence of clinical deterioration.

Further reading

Bartlett, J.R. (1984). Should chronic subdural haematomas always be evacuated? In *Dilemmas in the management of the neurological patient*, (ed. C. Warlow and J. Garfield), pp. 215–22. Churchill Livingstone, Edinburgh.

Maggio, W.W. (1993). Chronic subdural haematoma in adults. In *Brain surgery, complication avoidance and management* (ed. M.L.J. Apuzzo), pp. 1299–314. Churchill Livingstone, Edinburgh.

Markwalder, T.M. (1981). Chronic subdural haematomas: a review. *Journal of Neurosurgery*, **54**, 637–45.

References

Apfelbaum, R.I., Guthkelch, A.N., and Shulman, K. (1974). Experimental production of subdural haematomas. *Journal of Neurosurgery*, **40**, 336–46.

Bartlett, J.R., Kett-White, R., Mendelow, A.D., Miller, J.D., Pickard, J., and Teasdale, G. (1998). Guidelines for the initial management of head injuries. Recommendations from the Society of British Neurological Surgeons. *British Journal of Neurosurgery*, **12**, 349–52.

Bender, M.B. and Christoff, N. (1974). Nonsurgical treatment of subdural haematomas. *Archives of Neurology*, **31**, 73–9.

Creasey, H. and Rapoport, S.I. (1985). The aging human brain. *Annuals of Neurology*, **17**, 2–10.

Gardner, W.J. (1932). Traumatic subdural haematoma with particular reference to the latent interval. *Archives of Neurology and Psychiatry*, **27**, 847–58.

Gjerris, F. and Schmidt, K. (1974). Chronic subdural haematoma—surgery or mannitol treatment. *Journal of Neurosurgery*, **40**, 639–42.

Ito, H., Yamamoto, S., Saiko, K., et al. (1987). Quantitative estimation of haemorrhage in chronic subdural haematoma using the ^{51}Cr erythrocyte labelling method. *Journal of Neurosurgery*, **66**, 862–4.

Putnam, T.J. and Cushing, H. (1925). Chronic subdural haematoma: its pathology, its relation to pachymeningitis haemorrhagica and its surgical treatment. *Archives of Surgery*, **11**, 329–93.

Suzuki, J. and Takaku, A. (1970). Nonsurgical treatment of chronic subdural haematoma. *Journal of Neurosurgery*, **33**, 548–53.

Van Havenburgh, T., Van Calenbergh, F., Goffin, J., and Plets, C. (1996). Outcome of chronic subdural haematoma: analysis of prognostic factors. *British Journal of Neurosurgery*, **10**, 35–9.

Weir, B. (1980). Oncotic pressure of subdural fluids. *Journal of Neurosurgery*, **53**, 512–15.

18.4 Epilepsy and epileptic seizures

Raymond Tallis

Introduction

In many respects, the problem of epilepsy is comparable with that of recurrent falls; although the condition is episodic, the anxiety it causes may be constant. An elderly person may worry, and not without reason, that future fits may lead to injury. The prolonged postictal states seen in old age (Godfrey *et al.* 1982) may add further hazards. Moreover, intermission of consciousness undermines self-confidence at the deepest level; to an elderly person, a fit may seem a harbinger of death. Therefore reassurance, based upon information and education, is crucial.

Definition

Seizures are paroxysmal discharges of cerebral activity, in which a critical mass of neurones fires synchronously. 'Epilepsy' should not be used to refer to a single seizure but to a continuing tendency to epileptic seizures. In epidemiological studies, the term is usually used where a patient has suffered from more than one non-febrile seizure of any type. A diagnosis of epilepsy cannot therefore strictly be made on the basis of a single seizure, especially if the seizure has an external provocation. The distinction, however, is not as sharp as is sometimes implied; the majority of individuals who present with a single seizure will go on to have further seizures (Sander *et al.* 1990).

Epidemiology

Late-onset seizures are very common. Twenty-five years ago Hauser and Kurland reported a rise in the prevalence of epilepsy above the age of 50 years and an even steeper rise in annual incidence—from

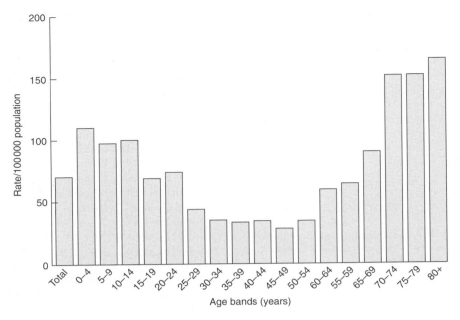

Fig. 1 Age-specific annual incidence of seizures. (Reproduced with permission from Tallis *et al.* (1991).)

12 per 100 000 in the 40 to 59 age range to 82 per 100 000 in those over 60 (Hauser and Kurland 1975). This rise has been confirmed in more recent studies (Hauser *et al.* 1993) and Luhdorf *et al.* (1986*a*) reported a similar annual incidence of 77 per 100 000. A study of a primary care database (Tallis *et al.* 1991) covering 82 practices and nearly 370 000 subjects, 62 000 of whom were over the age of 60 years, revealed a continuing rise in the annual incidence of seizures in old age (Fig. 1): whereas the annual incidence for the overall population was 69 per 100 000, that in the 65 to 69 year age group was 87 per 100 000, in the seventies 147 per 100 000, and in the eighties 159 per 100 000. Over a third of all incident cases placed on antiepileptic drugs were individuals over 60 years of age. Analysis of an expanded primary care database of over 2 000 000 subjects has generated very similar findings (Wallace *et al.* 1998). Recent data from Switzerland (Jallon and Loiseau 1995) have further underlined the dramatic increase in the incidence of seizures in old age: in a population with an overall incidence of initial seizures of 73 per 100 000, the rate increased from 65 for patients in their fifties to just under 200 for those in their eighties. This high incidence is found in definite epilepsy and in both provoked and unprovoked single seizures.

Prevalence studies in epilepsy are complicated by the difficulty of defining active epilepsy. Nevertheless, there is a clear upturn in prevalence at ages over 65 years, and this is even more marked over the age of 75. Hauser (1992) found a prevalence of 14.8 per 100 000 in subjects aged over 75 years, compared with an overall population average of 6 per 100 000. There was a striking secular trend in the prevalence at ages over 75 years between 1940 and 1980, with a rise from 1.9 to 14.8.

Types of seizure

The manifestations of epilepsy are complex and varied, and the methods of classifying seizures correspondingly complex. The revised

1981 International League against Epilepsy classification correlates clinical seizure types with ictal and interictal electroencephalograph features. Table 1 shows those parts of the classification relevant to elderly patients. Jallon and Loiseau (1995) reviewing the recent literature, conclude that at least 75 per cent of elderly onset seizures are focal or focal in origin. They report that simple partial seizures are more frequent than complex seizures. This, however, may be because brief loss or impairment of consciousness may not be observed or reported. Hauser (1992) found that complex partial seizures accounted for nearly 50 per cent of seizures in old age, while simple partial seizures accounted for only 13 per cent. Among generalized convulsive seizures, over 90 per cent are tonic–clonic, myoclonic seizures being exceptionally rare (about 2 per cent of cases). Recent evidence suggests a small second peak of primary generalized seizures occurring for the first time in old age (Luef *et al.* 1996). Epileptologists have increasingly drawn attention to absence status in elderly patients (see below). Not surprisingly, there is a high proportion of unclassifiable seizures in older people (roughly 10 per cent of cases). The proportion of misclassified seizures is probably even higher.

Aetiology

An epileptic fit is the result of an interaction between an individual predisposition, which is constitutional or hereditary, and a provoking cause which may be either an epileptogenic lesion in the brain or a systemic disturbance lowering the convulsive threshold. In elderly patients presenting with fits for the first time, it may be reasonably assumed that the contribution of the provoking cause usually outweighs that of the individual predisposition, since the latter would have already expressed itself earlier in life.

Table 1 Classification of seizures occurring in elderly people

Simple: consciousness unimpaired throughout
With motor symptoms
   Focal motor with or without march
   Versive
   Postural
   Vocalization
With somatosensory or special-sensory symptoms
   Somatosensory
   Visual
   Auditory
   Olfactory
   Gustatory
   Vertiginous
With autonomic symptoms or signs
   Epigastric sensations
   Pallor
   Sweating
   Flushing
   Piloerection
   Pupillary dilation
With disturbances of higher cerebral function
   Dysphasic
   Dysmnestic
   Cognitive
   Affective
Illusions (e.g. macropsia)
Structured hallucinations (e.g. music, scenes)

Complex: consciousness impaired at some point
Beginning as simple partial seizures and progressing to complex seizures
Consciousness impaired from the outset
   Impairment of consciousness only
   Impairment of consciousness with automatism

Partial seizures becoming secondarily generalized (with convulsive manifestations)

Generalized seizures: onset is generalized
Myoclonic seizures
Clonic seizures
Tonic seizures
Tonic–clonic seizures
Atonic seizures

Reproduced with permission from Commission on Classification and Terminology (1981).

Cerebrovascular disease

Cerebrovascular disease is the main cause of epilepsy in older adults, accounting for between 30 and 50 per cent of cases in different series (Luhdorf et al. 1986b; Loiseau et al. 1990; Sander et al. 1990; Forsgren et al. 1996). It accounts for an even higher proportion (up to 75 per cent) of cases in which a definite cause is identified.

There are several ways in which cerebrovascular disease and seizures may be linked.

1. In association with overt stroke:

   (a) early (peristroke, onset, initial) seizures;

   (b) late (poststroke) seizures.

2. In association with otherwise occult stroke disease:

   (a) concurrent CT scan finding of cerebral ischaemia;

   (b) stroke occurring some time after an unexplained seizure.

There have been recent important studies investigating the relationship between overt stroke and early and late seizures. Kilpatrick et al. (1990) found that about 4 per cent of patients had early seizures. Seizures occurred within 5 years of an ischaemic stroke in about 10 per cent of cases in the Oxford Community Stroke Project (Burn et al. 1997). The Oxford Study found a much higher incidence of poststroke seizures in haemorrhagic stroke and this was also observed by Lancman et al. (1993). So et al. (1996) followed 500 patients with ischaemic stroke and found that 6 per cent developed seizures within a week, 78 per cent of these within 24 h. Seizures after a week ('late' seizures) were seen in 5.5 per cent, with 7.5 per cent of subjects developing an initial late seizure by 5 years. An early seizure was a strong predictive factor for late seizures. Late seizures were associated with recurrence in 66 per cent of cases. Overall, ischaemic stroke increased the chances of an individual developing epilepsy by a factor of 17.

The relationship between otherwise occult cerebrovascular disease and seizures is more problematic. It is true that the more carefully cerebrovascular disease is sought in epileptic patients, the more frequently it is found. For example, there is a greater burden of occult ischaemia on CT scanning in older patients who present with otherwise unexplained seizures (Shorvon et al. 1984). Of course, the presence of areas of ischaemia on a CT scan may not mean that they are the primary or even a contributory cause of the seizures. Studies have also shown an excess of previous seizures in patients admitted to hospital with acute stroke compared with controls, suggesting that in a proportion of elderly patients seizures may be the earliest manifestation of cerebrovascular disease (Shinton et al. 1987). The practical significance of this is that any elderly patient with unexplained seizures should be fully screened for cardiovascular risk factors and treatment with low-dose aspirin or other preventative measures should be instituted where appropriate.

The strong relationship between age and the incidence and prevalence of cerebrovascular disease, as reflected in the almost exponential relationship between age and first-ever stroke, underlines the growing importance of this cause of elderly onset seizures, particularly as the elderly population is itself ageing.

Other cerebral disorders

Cerebral tumours

Clinicians are often concerned that elderly onset epilepsy may indicate a cerebral tumour. This, however, applies only to a minority of cases: around 10 to 15 per cent (Luhdorf et al. 1986b; Sander et al. 1990; Forsgren et al. 1996). Tumours are usually either metastatic or (inoperable) gliomas, though a few meningiomas are found. Until there is information on adequately documented, adequately investigated, and sufficiently large population-based series, one cannot be certain what proportion of cases of very late-onset epilepsy are due to treatable and non-treatable tumours. Even less is known of the proportion of patients with seizures due to tumours in which

Table 2 Toxic and metabolic causes of seizures

Pyrexia
Hypoglycaemia
Electrolyte disturbances (including water overload)
Hypoxia with or without respiratory failure
Severe myxoedema
Hepatic failure
Renal failure
Drugs and drug withdrawal

there are no other indicators on history or examination to a space-occupying lesion. These are fairly rare but do occur from time to time.

Non-vascular cerebral disease

A variable proportion of seizures is attributed to non-vascular cerebral degeneration. Again, the data are insufficient and will remain so until large series with uniform access to CT scanning facilities are reported. McAreavy et al. (1992) have suggested that Alzheimer dementia may cause seizures and this has been reiterated by Hesdorffer et al. (1996), who reported a sixfold increased risk of unprovoked seizures. However, in neither study were 'gold standard' criteria used for diagnosing Alzheimer's dementia or differentiating Alzheimer's from multi-infarct dementia or mixed Alzheimer's and multi-infarct dementia. One study (Hauser et al. 1986) reported myoclonus in 10 per cent of patients with autopsy-proven Alzheimer's disease.

Subdural haematoma is a rare but remediable cause (Jones et al. 1989) especially as very elderly patients are prone to this condition because of cerebral atrophy. Direct brain damage due to head injury is itself a relatively uncommon cause of elderly onset epilepsy, except in one series (Sung and Chu 1990) where it accounted for over 20 per cent of cases over the age of 60. This unusually high figure, however, derived from a tertiary referral hospital responsible for head injury.

Seizures may occur during the course of severe cerebral infections (meningitis, encephalitis, or cerebral abscess) but under such circumstances should not strictly be called 'epilepsy'. Following recovery from such infections, however, epilepsy may arise due to scarring. This is a rare cause of epilepsy in older subjects.

Metabolic and toxic causes (Table 2)

Recent series (Loiseau et al. 1990) have underlined the importance of toxic and metabolic causes of seizures in old age. Alcohol is important at any age (Heckmatt 1990; Lechtenberg and Worner 1992). Pyrexia and other acute conditions may precipitate seizures in older people and pneumonia, which in the biologically aged may be more likely to cause hypoxia, may predispose to seizures or precipitate them in an individual who has otherwise well-controlled epilepsy.

A wide range of drugs has been suspected of causing convulsions (Swift 1988) (Table 3). Aminophylline, which has a narrow therapeutic index, and whose disposition may be altered by cigarette smoking, concurrent medication, and comorbidity, is especially prone to cause seizures (Hardy and Smith 1997). Psychotrophic drugs, including

trycyclic antidepressants and phenothiazines, are also important. Benzodiazepines may cause withdrawal fits. Repeated hypoglycaemic episodes due to excessive insulin or oral hypoglycaemics may precipitate recurrent seizures. Strictly, epileptic seizures provoked by metabolic and toxic causes, even if they are recurrent, should not be called 'epilepsy'.

Idiopathic seizures

Occasionally one encounters a patient whose seizures are apparently idiopathic, presenting for medical help for the first time in old age. Such patients may have had a lifetime of untreated epilepsy. Without such a long history, it is difficult to sustain a diagnosis of idiopathic epilepsy, though the possibility of elderly onset idiopathic primary generalized seizures is discussed above (Luef et al. 1996).

Diagnosis and investigation

The diagnostic task when a patient presents with suspected seizures is complex. These are the questions that should be addressed.

1. Are the events seizures?
2. What sort of seizures are they?
3. Why did they occur?
   (a) Was there some unusual precipitant (e.g. a prescribed drug)?
   (b) Is there some continuing underlying cause (e.g. cerebrovascular disease)?
4. Are there other concurrent illnesses?

The most powerful diagnostic tool is a detailed history. In the context of a well-defined aura, clear progression from a tonic to a clonic phase, tongue-biting, incontinence, or focal neurological features during an attack, and stupor or prolonged confusion, headache, and transient neurological signs after the attack, diagnosis is straightforward. Post-event confusion and headache are particularly useful indications of a fit. For obvious reasons, the history from the patient may be unsatisfactory and eye witness reports must be sought. This may be difficult in a patient who lives alone and who has simply been 'found on the floor'. Even evidence from individuals who did not see the event itself but observed the patient's post-event state—neighbours, ambulance driver, casualty staff—may be helpful. The next most powerful tool is a wide-ranging, open-minded, physical examination. The third most powerful tool is time. It is better to wait and see than to initiate inappropriate treatment. Specialist investigations such as the electroencephalograph are only occasionally helpful in positively diagnosing epilepsy, and even less helpful in ruling it out. More useful are tests of cardiovascular function which may positively diagnose syncope as a cause of transient loss of consciousness (see below).

Are the events seizures?

The most common feature of epilepsy in elderly people, as at any other age, is transient impairment or loss of consciousness. Sometimes disturbances of consciousness may be forgotten and the patient will report only a fall. The differential diagnosis will then encompass the numerous other causes of falls in elderly people. A fall occurring in the absence of any obvious environmental cause and which cannot

Table 3 Drugs that may cause seizures

Antibiotics
  Benzylpenicillin
  Oxacillin
  Carbenicillin
  Isoniazid
  Cycloserine

Hormones
  Insulin
  Oral hypoglycaemics
  Prednisone

Local anaesthetics/antiarrhythmics
  Lignocaine (lidocaine)
  Procaine
  Disopyramide
  Anticholinergics in overdose

Psychotrophic drugs
  Chlorpromazine
  Other phenothiazines
  Tricyclic antidepressants
  Lithium

Analeptic drugs
  Aminophylline
  Doxapram

Anaesthetic agents
  Ether
  Methohexitone
  Ketamine
  Halothane
  Althesin

Radiographic contrast media
  Meglumine
  Metrizamide (very rarely)

Withdrawal fits
  Benzodiazepines
  Alcohol

After Chadwick (1991).

be confidently attributed to orthopaedic, cardiovascular, or non-epileptic neurological factors, should raise the suspicion of a fit.

In the case of a classical generalized or partial seizure, the diagnosis can be made readily on the basis of the history. Unfortunately, fits may be difficult to differentiate from a variety of non-epileptic paroxysmal events that also occur in old people (Table 4). Some of these latter may, however, be relatively easily ruled out.

The most difficult differential diagnosis is syncope—transient loss of consciousness due to acute cerebral anoxia secondary to a fall in cerebral perfusion. Even when there is a reasonably good history, the features that characteristically differentiate fits from faints may not be as decisive as in younger adults (Table 5). The diagnosis and management of syncope is covered in Chapter 4.4 and comprehensively reviewed in a recent monograph (Kenny 1996). Therefore it will be touched on only briefly here.

Differentiating fits from faints may be even more difficult when there are coexistent conditions predisposing to both syncope and seizures. And it is well known that transient cerebral anoxia, as for example in vagal hypersensitivity which is now recognized to be more common than previously realized (Macintosh et al. 1993), may itself cause convulsions. Recurrent cardiac arrhythmias are also important; in one series of patients referred to a neurological department with a diagnosis of epilepsy, 20 per cent were found to have cardiac arrhythmias that caused or significantly contributed to their symptoms (Schott et al. 1977). The situation may be particularly confusing, as complex partial seizures affecting the temporal lobes may present with autonomic features and recent attention has been drawn to the ictal bradycardia syndrome, in which episodic bradycardia or even asystole leading to syncope may itself be an ictal event (Reeves et al. 1996).

It may, therefore, prove impossible to determine whether transient cerebral symptoms are cardiac or cerebral in origin. Even ambulatory 24-h electroencephalography, with or without other cardiovascular tests, and prolonged electroencephalograph monitoring may not permit a confident diagnosis. Non-specific abnormalities on an electroencephalograph, or cardiac arrythmias recorded in a 24-h electroencephalograph unrelated to symptoms, may add to the confusion. Head-up tilt for up to 45 min with or without carotid sinus massage may induce bradycardia and/or hypotension and thus help differentiate convulsive syncope from epilepsy (Kenny 1996). However, some genuinely epileptic events may not be appreciated for what they are (Table 6).

In the face of such difficulties, the clinician's primary duty is to acknowledge uncertainty where it exists and, if uncertainty remains after a careful history, examination, and appropriate investigations, simply to wait and see. A 'therapeutic trial' of anticonvulsants as a diagnostic test is not recommended: it will rarely produce a clear answer and will add the burden of possibly unnecessary drug treatment to the patient's troubles. It is important to bear in mind that by interfering with cardiac conduction, some antiepileptic drugs such as phenytoin may make fits due to cardiac standstill more frequent.

Investigations

General investigations

The choice of investigations will, of course, be determined by the history and by the findings on examination as well as by consideration of likely causes. Routine tests should include a full blood count, erythrocyte sedimentation rate, biochemical investigations (including urea, electrolytes, glucose, and liver function tests), ECG, and chest radiography. It is important to rule out metabolic causes (see Table 2) as they will usually be amenable to treatment. An estimate of γ-glutamyl transferase may be a useful marker of recent alcohol consumption. Diabetic control should be reviewed especially where the presenting problem is that of nocturnal seizures in a patient on oral hypoglycaemic agents. A chest radiograph may reveal a relevant primary neoplasm; a skull radiograph is rarely helpful. The choice of other investigations, such as serum tests for syphilis, will be influenced by history and findings on examination.

Table 4 Non-epileptic events that may be confused with seizures

Syncope

Hypoglycaemia

Transient ischaemic attacks

Recurrent paroxysmal behavioural disturbances secondary to organic brain disease

Drop attacks and other non-epileptic causes of falls

Transient global amnesia

Psychogenic attacks
   Panic attacks
   Hyperventilation
   Pseudoseizures

Specialist investigations

The most difficult diagnostic challenge is often to differentiate between fits and faints. If it is thought that the episodes are most probably syncopal, then the patient should be carefully investigated as outlined in Chapter 4.4.

A survey of the management by American neurologists of a single unprovoked seizure (Gifford and Vickrey 1995) showed a wide variation in the use of electroencephalography and neuroimaging. Some neurologists routinely ordered both investigations while some ordered one but not the other, and some requested neither. There is clearly scope here for studies evaluating these different approaches to investigation.

Electroencephalography

Excessive reliance upon an electroencephalograph to make or refute a diagnosis of epilepsy is potentially dangerous. A routine electroencephalograph may support the diagnosis of epilepsy, especially if clear-cut paroxysmal discharges are observed. The absence of such activity on a routine recording does not, however, rule out the diagnosis; after all, most recordings last for only 20 min and ictal or diagnostic interictal activity occurs only intermittently. The range of normality increases with age so that discriminating normal from abnormal is more difficult in an elderly patient. Non-specific abnormalities are more common in old age. In brief, while the electroencephalograph may provide useful supporting evidence for the diagnosis of epilepsy, it should not over-rule the clinical diagnosis nor, with rare exceptions such as non-convulsive status, provide its sole basis. It should also be added that an electroencephalograph, in the older age group as in any other, cannot alone determine the need for a treatment in a newly diagnosed case, establish the adequacy of treatment, or predict the safety of discontinuing therapy.

A focal abnormality on an electroencephalograph may support the clinical diagnosis of a focal origin for fits and suggest a local neurological cause. In those fits where there is an inadequate history or where the focal phase is too brief to be seen clinically, its observation may suggest a focal origin for the first time and guide further investigation. Persistent gross localized abnormalities on an electroencephalograph would strongly support a focal structural lesion. The electroencephalograph may be particularly useful in diagnosing non-convulsive status or epilepsy presenting with recurrent behavioural disturbance or other neuropsychiatric manifestations (Ellis and Lee 1978; Jamal *et al.* 1988; Rowan 1991; Thomas 1996).

Neuroradiology

The older the age of presentation with epilepsy the greater the chance of a positive CT scan: as many as 60 per cent of very late-onset patients with epilepsy may show a structural lesion (Ramirez-Lassepas *et al.* 1984). However, this would be an argument for routine scanning only if identification of such lesions influenced management (Young *et al.* 1982), as in the case of a space-occupying lesion amenable to neurosurgical removal. However, in only a minority of patients with late-onset epilepsy is a neoplasm or subdural haematoma the cause and in only a small proportion of tumour cases would neurosurgical intervention be appropriate. Moreover, the discovery of an otherwise inert meningioma, especially if it is non-operable because of its site or the patient's general condition, may not be of benefit to the patient. Even so, it is sometimes useful to have a definitive diagnosis, though treatment for the underlying condition may not be available or considered inappropriate. Arguable indications for CT scanning are given in Table 7. Magnetic resonance imaging is a powerful and sensitive diagnostic tool; how often the information obtained would alter management in elderly onset epilepsy remains to be seen (Kilpatrick *et al.* 1991).

Management

Doctors tend to think of the care of patients with epilepsy predominantly in terms of drug treatment. Management, however, extends far beyond this.

General measures

Of paramount importance is the reassurance that, in the vast majority of cases, fits do not indicate serious brain damage; that they are unrelated to psychiatric disturbance; and that they can be controlled by medication. Patients should be told that anyone's brain is capable of having seizures if the circumstances are right and that fits are the most common neurological problem after headache.

Patients may want to know whether fits are brought on by any particular activity and whether, for this reason, they should lead restricted lives. The advice in this age group is the same as that given to any patients: avoid only those activities which would mean immediate danger if a fit occurred.

The regulations relating to driving vary from country to country and even, in the United States, from State to State. In the United Kingdom, anyone holding a driving licence diagnosed as having epilepsy must notify the Driver and Vehicle Licensing Authority and stop driving until further directed by the Authority. The onus of responsibility to inform the Authority lies with the patient and not with the doctor. The regulations in the United Kingdom have recently been revised. They have been usefully summarized by Shorvon (1995).

A fit may severely damage confidence and, in individuals who already have locomotor or other disability, this may lead to voluntary restriction of activities and a shrinkage of 'life space' and with initiation of a vicious spiral of reduced mobility. In such patients,

Table 5 Features differentiating seizures from syncopal attacks

Feature	Usual distinction		Modifications in older patients
	Faints	**Fits**	
Posture	Usually occur in the upright position	Not position dependent	Faints in older people are not position dependent because they are often due to significant position-independent pathology
Onset	Gradual	Sudden	Loss of consciousness may be quite abrupt in syncope in an older person; complex partial seizures may have a gradual onset
Injury	Rare	More common	A syncopal attack may be associated with significant soft tissue or bony injury in an older person
Incontinence	Rare	Common	An individual prone to incontinence may be wet during a faint; partial seizures will not usually be associated with incontinence
Recovery	Rapid	Slow	A fit may take the form of a brief ('temporal lobe') absence; a faint associated with a serious arrhythmia may be prolonged
Post-event confusion	Little	Marked	A prolonged hypoxic episode due to a faint may be associated with prolonged post-event confusion
Frequency	Usually infrequent with a clear precipitating cause	May be frequent and usually without precipitating cause	Faints associated with cardiac arrythmias, low cardiac output, postural hypotension, or carotid sinus sensitivity may be very frequent

Table 6 Seizures that may be confused with other conditions

Epileptic event	Possible misdiagnosis
Epilepsia partialis continua (partial motor status)	Extrapyramidal movement disorder
Sensory epilepsy	Transient ischaemic attack
Complex partial seizures	Organic or functional psychosis
Atonic seizures	Drop attacks/hysteria
Epileptic vertigo (due to temporal lobe attacks)	Brainstem/vestibular disease/non-specific dizziness
Todd's palsy	Stroke/transient ischaemic attack
Any kind of seizures	'Falls'

Table 7 Indications for CT in late-onset seizures

Strong
Unexplained focal neurological signs
Progressive or new neurological symptoms especially those of raised intracranial pressure
Progressive or new neurological signs
Poor control of fits not attributable to poor compliance with antiepileptic drugs or continued exposure to precipitants such as alcohol

Less strong
Clear-cut stereotyped focal fits
Persistent marked slow-wave abnormality on EEG

encouragement of mobility, assessment for walking or other aids, and a review of the home circumstances and need for social support services will require input from remedial therapists and social workers. A home visit by an occupational therapist to look for potential sources of dangers—unguarded fires and so on—may be helpful. Where fits are frequent, especially when there is a warning aura, a personal alarm may be useful.

Factors which are known to precipitate fits, such as inadequate sleep or excess alcohol, should be avoided. The patient should be warned that alcohol will increase the side-effects of medication and that other drugs may trigger seizures or interact with antiepileptic drugs. Patients should be encouraged to remind their doctors that they have epilepsy when they are seen about other conditions for which they may receive prescriptions. In any patient presenting with seizures, existing medication should be reviewed and drugs with a known epileptogenic potential or liable to interfere with antiepileptic drugs withdrawn if possible.

Contact numbers for local branches of the national epilepsy associations may be useful, though older patients may find the rest of the membership rather young. With the patient's permission, spouses, relatives, neighbours, and other carers should be advised on how to manage seizures if they occur.

Drug treatment

Most of what we think we know about anticonvulsant therapy in the ageing brain has been extrapolated from studies on younger patients, many of whom do not have the focal lesions that are typical in elderly epileptic patients and all of whom lack the age-associated changes common in older people. Therefore the advice that follows falls rather short of the ideals of evidence-based medicine.

When should antiepileptic drugs be started?

Epilepsy is defined as a tendency to recurring seizures and implicit in treatment with antiepileptic drugs is the assumption that a patient does have such a tendency. A single seizure—especially if it has an obvious precipitating cause such as fever or alcohol—does not count as epilepsy. The correct approach is not antiepileptic drugs but removal of the cause. Where there is a single apparently unprovoked seizure, the decision whether or not to treat with antiepileptic drugs is more difficult. It will be influenced by several considerations: (a) the severity of the index seizure; (b) the clinician's view as to the likelihood of recurrence (estimates range from 27 to 80 per cent; Chadwick 1991; Berg and Shinnar 1991); (c) the estimate of the risks such as injury associated with a recurrent seizure; (d) the possible hazards of antiepileptic drugs; (e) the credence one gives to the notion that 'fits breed fits' so that early treatment may prevent epilepsy becoming chronic or intractable. At present, there is inadequate information upon which to base rational decisions on whether a single unprovoked major seizure in an older person should be treated. Age itself is not a consistent predictor of recurrence although the presence of a clear-cut aetiological factor, such as a focal cerebral lesion, is. The relative dangers of non-treatment (injury due to recurrence) and of treatment (adverse effects of medication) have never been assessed in a systematic population-based prospective manner. Until this has been done, and the results of the long-term outcome of trials comparing the treatment of a single fit with awaiting subsequent fits are available, the decision whether or not a single unprovoked fit should be treated is partly personal prejudice (Reynolds and Chadwick 1995).

At present, it seems reasonable to treat a single unprovoked major seizure only if it is prolonged or if it has a clear-cut underlying cause such as a previous stroke or a cerebral tumour. Late poststroke fits have a high recurrence rate, 66 per cent in one series (So *et al.* 1996). Where there is no such cause, and the fit has not been prolonged, the decision is more difficult. In the case of a short-duration generalized convulsive seizure or a partial or non-convulsive seizure, it is probably best to wait. It is important to emphasize prompt treatment of future problems such as chest infections that might precipitate further fits through hypoxia and the avoidance of drugs with convulsive side-effects. Two or more unprovoked major seizures warrant antiepileptic drug treatment, for then the risk of recurrence is about 70 per cent in the general adult population (Appleton *et al.* 1993) and it will probably be higher in the older adult population, where there is more often a continuing underlying cause.

Treatment of a single minor episode is probably overzealous and it would seem reasonable to wait and see how frequent and how upsetting the episodes are before embarking on drug therapy.

Which antiepileptic drug should be prescribed?

The majority of adult patients with either primary or secondary generalized seizures or partial seizures can be controlled with a single drug (Treiman 1987). Nearly 70 per cent of patients can expect a 5-year remission (Cockerell *et al.* 1997). Phenytoin, carbamazepine, and sodium valproate are equally effective as first-line, broad-spectrum antiepileptic drugs, and this seems to be true of elderly onset patients (Tallis *et al.* 1994). Therefore monotherapy should be preferred to polytherapy. In younger subjects, where monotherapy is unsuccessful, this is very often due to poor compliance or sometimes associated with a serious underlying cerebral condition. Adding a second drug frequently contributes only additional side-effects. If monotherapy with one anticonvulsant agent gives unsatisfactory control, it is worthwhile trying monotherapy with another. Although monotherapy should be the aim, there will be a proportion of patients who will require two antiepileptic drugs (so-called 'rational polypharmacy') but the advice of an expert should be sought. In future, when 'cleaner' drugs whose actions are both more precise and better understood are available, it may be possible to prescribe a combination of drugs with complementary actions, each given in relatively low doses.

Since phenytoin, carbamazepine, and sodium valproate will have approximately equal efficacy in both generalized tonic–clonic and partial seizures, the choice of drug will be greatly influenced by considerations of toxicity and, to a lesser extent, cost. Antiepileptic drugs may cause acute dose-related idiosyncratic and chronic toxic effects. These adverse effects are usefully summarized in Appleton *et al.* (1993) and it is strongly advised to be familiar with them when an antiepileptic drug is prescribed.

The gross neurological side-effects include ataxia, dysarthria, nystagmus, dizziness, unsteadiness, blurring and doubling of vision, reversible dyskinesias, and asterixis. Although some neurotoxic effects may occur more frequently with certain drugs, there is so much overlap that most cannot be regarded as being specific to any one drug. The effects are generally dose related and in the general adult population can usually be avoided or minimized by careful dosage titration. In contrast with the findings from earlier studies, more recent observations have not shown significant differences in the impact of antiepileptic drugs on cognitive function in either the general adult population or elderly patients (Craig and Tallis 1994). If the dose is minimized, adverse cognitive effects are probably not important; and where there are no gross adverse effects, subtle ones are not seen either. Other neurological or neuropsychiatric side-effects—for example, subjective feelings of unsteadiness and tiredness—may, however, still be significant and there may be important differences in the frequency and severity of these. A recent survey of the general population of patients with seizures found that over 80 per cent experienced feelings of tiredness (Brown 1996). These aspects still need systematic study in patients with elderly onset seizures.

Of the many non-neurological side-effects, osteomalacia is more likely to occur in patients whose poor dietary intake of vitamin D and reduced exposure to sunlight already puts them at risk. Phenytoin induces enzymes in the liver, and so accelerates metabolism of vitamin D. There may therefore be a case for routine vitamin supplementation in patients on this antiepileptic drug. Sodium valproate, unlike phenytoin or carbamazepine, does not reduce vitamin D activity. Carbamazepine-induced hyponatraemia increases significantly with age and may occur at very low doses. The risk of hyponatraemia may

18.5 Parkinson's disease and related disorders

Barry J. Snow

Introduction

Approximately 1 per cent of the population aged over 60 years have Parkinson's disease (Tanner 1991). The high frequency and complicated nature of the diagnosis and management of Parkinson's disease means that the disease represents an important problem in geriatric medicine.

Faced with a patient with parkinsonism, the doctor must pursue a logical course. Initially, the parkinsonism must be classified. Is it idiopathic parkinsonism, usually known as Parkinson's disease? Or is the parkinsonism part of the presentation of one of the less common forms of parkinsonism described below? Additional features of the disease such as autonomic disturbance, pain, depression, and dementia must be sought. Once characterized, the doctor must decide on the need for treatment and, if necessary, on the type of treatment. This includes medication as well as the use of other interventions such as physiotherapy. The patient and family need careful education at this and later stages of the illness.

Classification of parkinsonism

Definition

Parkinsonism is a syndrome with the four cardinal features of tremor, rigidity, bradykinesia, and disturbed postural reflexes.

Tremor

Classically, the tremor of Parkinson's disease occurs at rest (Delwaide and Gonce 1993). About 50 per cent of patients also have a postural component, which is revealed when the patient holds the arms outstretched. The postural tremor may lead to a misdiagnosis of essential tremor. More commonly, essential tremor may be misdiagnosed as Parkinson's disease. In most cases, the two conditions can be distinguished by having the patient write. In Parkinson's disease the tremor usually abates, but the writing becomes smaller as the script progresses across the page (micrographia). In essential tremor, the tremor is exacerbated, and the script becomes enlarged and irregular. Occasionally a patient will be encountered who has a long history of postural tremor consistent with essential tremor. After years the patient may develop features of parkinsonism that lead to

diagnostic confusion. Eventually the patient develops more typical Parkinson's disease. This merging of the two diseases is the basis for an ongoing debate about whether or not there is a relationship between the conditions (Jankovic *et al.* 1991).

Rigidity

This is elicited by the examiner passively moving a joint through its compete range. The wrist and elbow are the best joints to examine. There is a continuous resistance that may have a jerky (cogwheel) character. If the patient tenses the opposite hand, the tone in the joint under examination will increase. Increased tone may also be found in the legs. If there is appreciably more tone in the neck than the limbs, then the diagnosis of progressive supranuclear palsy should be considered (see below).

Bradykinesia

Bradykinesia, or slowness of movement, has several manifestations. The earliest is the impassive face (hypomimia). This is so characteristic that the movement disorder neurologist often diagnoses Parkinson's disease in the waiting room. Generalized bradykinesia produces an air of stillness without the usual small changes of posture or spontaneous hand movements. On examination, there is a breakdown of rapid alternating movements. This is best elicited by having the patient alternately tap the palm and dorsum of the hand on the thigh, or tap the foot on the ground. The movements may be normal initially but then become irregular. This is in contrast to a pyramidal disturbance where the clumsiness is relatively constant from the outset.

Postural disturbance

Many patients with Parkinson's disease have abnormal posture and righting reflexes. In the history, ask for difficulty arising from a chair or rolling over in bed. As the disease progresses there may be stumbling and a feeling of poor balance. Falls occur relatively late. If the disease begins with frequent falls, then progressive supranuclear palsy is more likely.

On examination look for difficulty arising from a chair, a stooped posture and a tendency for the patient to take several steps while turning. There may be a disturbance of balance on the 'pull' test: stand behind the patient and pull back on the shoulders. Instead of moving the arms forward and swaying the trunk the parkinsonian patient may take steps backward (retropulsion) or even fall back into the examiner's arms without any attempt to maintain balance.

Parkinson's disease

Clinically, Parkinson's disease can be diagnosed in the following circumstances (Calne *et al.* 1992; Hughes *et al.* 1992):

- there are two of the four cardinal features of parkinsonism present (tremor, rigidity, bradykinesia, and loss of postural reflexes)
- the condition is progressive
- the patient is responsive to levodopa
- there is no alternative cause for the parkinsonism.

Contrary to common belief, Parkinson's disease usually presents asymmetrically—if not, an alternative diagnosis should be considered. Postmortem studies of the accuracy of diagnosis of Parkinson's disease have found that in up to 25 per cent of patients the diagnosis was applied mistakenly (Hughes *et al.* 1992). The increased awareness of the various manifestations of multiple system atrophy in particular (see below) have increased diagnostic accuracy, and now about 11 per cent are misdiagnosed.

Progressive supranuclear palsy (Steele–Richardson–Olszewski syndrome)

Progressive supranuclear palsy was first described in 1964, but it remained a diagnostic curiosity until relatively recently (Steele *et al.* 1964). The mean age of onset is about 62 years, and less than 5 per cent have onset before the age of 50 years. Like Parkinson's disease, the cause is not known; there is no familial tendency.

The clinical presentation is with parkinsonism (Litvan *et al.* 1996). Often the rigidity is distributed more axially than in the limbs, the signs are more symmetrical than Parkinson's disease, and tremor is uncommon. An important diagnostic clue is early falling. This is a common complaint at presentation and very unusual in patients with Parkinson's disease. Frontal lobe, or subcortical dementia is very common. In the early stages a loss of motivation and personality change is frequently described by the family. Early dysarthria and dysphagia is also a strong hint that the patient does not have standard Parkinson's disease.

The disturbance of eye movements is pathognomonic of progressive supranuclear palsy, but it often occurs later into the disease, and experienced movement disorder neurologists will have often considered the diagnosis before the eye movements become diagnostic. Patients often have non-specific visual complaints. Incomplete downward gaze corrected with the oculocephalic reflex is the definitive finding. Before this develops there is often a loss of opticokinetic nystagmus with the stimulus moving upwards and a hesitancy of voluntary downward gaze. Eyelid abnormalities may also be found, especially apraxia of both closing and opening. In the latter, patients may become functionally blind.

The treatment of progressive supranuclear palsy is hampered by the partial or absent response to levodopa. The Parkinson's disease-like components of limb rigidity, bradykinesia, and tremor (if present) often do respond to levodopa, at least in the early stages of the disease. However, the major incapacitating features are the falling, bulbar disturbance, dementia, and abnormal eye movements; and these do not respond to levodopa. Dyskinesias and levodopa-induced psychosis are rare in progressive supranuclear palsy, and therefore it is usually possible to increase the dose to around 1000 mg of levodopa per day. There are reports of improvement with tricyclic antidepressants, methysergide, and perhaps cholinergic agents (Golbe and Davis 1993). These responses may be explained on the basis of the multiple neurotransmitter deficits in progressive supranuclear palsy; however, there is seldom a truly useful response.

The mainstay of treatment of progressive supranuclear palsy is careful rehabilitation. This includes physiotherapy concentrating on safety of gait and transferring. Speech therapy may be useful in the early stages. The family also needs considerable support.

Multiple system atrophy

Multiple system atrophy is the general term for a group of clinical presentations that include striatonigral degeneration, sporadic olivopontocerebellar atrophy, and Shy–Drager syndrome (Spokes *et al.* 1979). These previously separate conditions have been amalgamated under the rubric multiple system atrophy as it is clear that many patients have overlapping clinical features and that the pathology is not discrete (Wenning *et al.* 1997). Despite this, there are patients with classically typical presentations, and an overall understanding of the clinical features of multiple system atrophy is most easily achieved from the viewpoint of the individual subtypes (see also Chapter 18.12).

Striatonigral degeneration is the most difficult to diagnose in life. The pure form presents as symmetrical parkinsonism without tremor and a poor or absent response to levodopa. While the diagnosis may be suspected, it usually only becomes apparent at postmortem or if the patient develops other features of multiple system atrophy. Olivopontocerebellar atrophy is characterized by parkinsonism and cerebellar signs. Shy–Drager syndrome is distinguished by parkinsonism and prominent autonomic failure.

The autonomic failure of multiple system atrophy is indistinguishable from the syndrome of pure autonomic failure (Spokes *et al.* 1979). The autonomic features usually develop first, and the non-autonomic features may take 5 years to become apparent. Genitourinary dysfunction, with impotence in men and then urinary urgency and increased residual urine occurs first. Incontinence develops slowly, and faecal incontinence is a late feature. All patients eventually develop postural hypotension. A feature of postural hypotension in multiple system atrophy is relative supine hypertension. This clue can help distinguish the postural hypotension seen in Parkinson's disease from multiple system atrophy.

Besides the parkinsonism, cerebellar features, and autonomic disturbance there are other distinctive features seen in patients with multiple system atrophy. These include abnormal respiratory patterns with sleep apnoea. Vocal cord paralysis is common, and a crying inspiratory stridor in a parkinsonian patient is almost pathognomonic of multiple system atrophy.

The management of multiple system atrophy is focused on the separate elements of the clinical presentation. The parkinsonism responds variably to levodopa but, like progressive supranuclear palsy, this may not be the major source of disability. The postural hypotension may be controlled for a time by the usual interventions of increased salt intake, fludrocortisone, and other antihypotensive agents, but eventually control is lost and the patient becomes bed bound. The ataxia is not drug responsive and must be approached with physical therapy. The laryngeal disturbance must be monitored closely, and some patients elect to have tracheostomy and percutaneous feeding tubes. The usual duration of disease to death is about 10 years.

Parkinsonism and Alzheimer's disease

A significant proportion of patients with Alzheimer's disease have parkinsonism (Clark *et al.* 1997; Murray *et al.* 1997). This usually presents after the dementia develops, although subtle findings may be present early in the disease (Richards *et al.* 1993). The parkinsonism is usually symmetrical. The most common features are rigidity (62 per cent) and bradykinesia (55 per cent). Tremor develops in only about 4 per cent of patients. Patients with Alzheimer's disease and parkinsonism also tend to have more cognitive impairment than matched patients with dementia alone. It remains unclear whether parkinsonism is a feature of advanced Alzheimer's disease or indicates a second neurodegenerative disorder such as coincidental Parkinson's disease or Lewy body disease.

Postmortem studies have shown reduced numbers of dopaminergic neurones in the substantia nigra, but the pattern of loss in Alzheimer's disease differs from that found in Parkinson's disease (Murray *et al.* 1997). Positron emission tomography studies have not shown convincing evidence for significant nigrostriatal dopaminergic dysfunction in Alzheimer's disease (Tyrell *et al.* 1990). The lack of response to levodopa further indicates that the motor disturbance of Alzheimer's disease does not represent an overlap between the two diseases.

Lewy body disease

At postmortem, the brains of patients with Parkinson's disease are often found to have more widespread Lewy bodies than just in the substantia nigra. In particular, some patients have Lewy bodies distributed throughout the cerebral cortices. Some of these patients have an identifiable clinical syndrome known as Lewy body disease (Hansen *et al.* 1990; Kalra *et al.* 1996). Patients present with parkinsonism and dementia. The cognitive disturbance often fluctuates more than typical Alzheimer's dementia. In addition, there may be characteristic hallucinations that are vivid and often precede the administration of levodopa. The hallucinations are usually much worse with levodopa therapy.

The parkinsonism of Lewy body disease may be indistinguishable from Parkinson's disease. However, there are general differences. These include a lower frequency of tremor, more frequent myoclonus, and a decreased rate of responsiveness to levodopa (Kalra *et al.* 1996).

Patients with Lewy body dementia often come to notice when they develop adverse drug effects. They may develop severe parkinsonism if their hallucinations are treated with neuroleptics. Conversely, if the parkinsonism is treated with levodopa, the hallucinations and confusion may deteriorate.

Drug-induced parkinsonism

Elderly patients are particularly susceptible to develop parkinsonism following exposure to dopamine-blocking drugs. Those on neuroleptics are seldom misdiagnosed. More commonly misdiagnosed, however, are patients who develop parkinsonism on other drugs that are not widely appreciated as causing parkinsonism. The most common offending agent is metoclopramide. Calcium antagonists can also cause parkinsonism.

Special features of Parkinson's disease in elderly people

There appear to be differences in the presentation and progression of the disease between young and old patients (Arevalo *et al.* 1997). Older patients with Parkinson's disease seldom have dystonia before levodopa treatment. The exception is the striatal toe. This is a strongly dorsiflexed toe that is often troublesome in the mornings. It may interfere with putting on socks and stockings and may limit available footwear. There is also a lower frequency of levodopa-induced dyskinesias in older patients with Parkinson's disease.

Parkinson's disease probably progresses more quickly in older people, although this is debated (Lee *et al.* 1994). Some of this apparent faster progression may relate to neurodegenerative changes affecting other neurotransmitter systems. In particular, patients with Parkinson's disease at postmortem are found to have deficits in cholinergic and noradrenergic transmission. Mild cognitive changes and frank dementia are more common in older patients with the disease. Older patients appear also to be more likely to develop autonomic disturbances especially medication-induced postural hypotension and urinary bladder instability.

Management of Parkinson's disease in elderly people

Education

Patients with Parkinson's disease have a strong need for education about their disease and its management. This is reflected by the number and activity of societies and support groups. Patients who have been assigned the diagnosis should be offered help to make contact with one of these service organizations. With elderly patients, the family members should also be offered access to educational material.

Medical management

No treatment has been shown to alter the natural history of Parkinson's disease. There are suggestions, however, that two drugs, selegiline (Deprenyl) and amantadine, may slow the progression of Parkinson's disease.

Selegiline has been the subject of intense scrutiny. Its primary mode of action is as an inhibitor of monoamine oxidation. As such, it prevents the oxidation and breakdown of dopamine in the brain. Selegiline has an undoubted, but mild, beneficial symptomatic effect in Parkinson's disease. This was best shown in the DATATOP study which demonstrated that selegiline delays the need for the initiation of levodopa (Parkinson Study Group 1989). The study was designed on the assumption of a negligible symptomatic effect of selegiline, and the delayed need for further treatment was widely interpreted as indicating a slowing of disease progression. A number of *in vitro* experiments have shown that selegiline may have neuroprotective effects, thus supporting the clinical conclusions (Salo and Tatton 1992).

Subsequent follow-up of the patients in DATATOP has shown that the effect of selegiline is best explained by a symptomatic benefit (Parkinson Study Group 1996). In addition, the delay in the need for levodopa therapy does not result in a long-term delay in either the severity of Parkinson's disease or the development of levodopa-related complications such as dyskinesias (Parkinson Study Group 1996).

Selegiline does prolong and smooth the effect of levodopa, and this remains the primary indication for its use. Selegiline is metabolized to an amphetamine-like metabolite. This metabolite is probably responsible for the main side-effects of selegiline. These include insomnia and confusion, particularly in elderly patients. Selegiline is best prescribed early in the day with the last dose given at noon. As a monoamine oxidase inhibitor, selegiline may have important interactions with other drugs, including pethidine and some selective serotonin-reuptake inhibitor antidepressants.

Amantadine has a number of mechanism of action that contribute to a modest but undoubted antiparkinsonian effect (Fahn and Isgreen 1975). One of these is as a weak inhibitor of excitatory amino acids (Kornhuber *et al.* 1994). A candidate for the pathogenesis of Parkinson's disease is excitatory neurotoxicity induced by cortical glutaminergic nerve endings synapsing with the endings of the dopaminergic terminals. A recent retrospective study suggests that patients on amantadine have a slower progression of disease than patients not on the drug (Uitti *et al.* 1996). This preliminary information awaits further study.

Amantadine can be troublesome in older people. Some patients develop confusion. It can also cause a beefy red discoloration of the limbs. Amantadine is excreted via a renal route, and should be used with caution in renal failure.

Anticholinergic agents have been used for many years for the treatment of Parkinson's disease. They have a modest overall antiparkinsonian effect with an average improvement of around 30 per cent in symptoms (Schwab and Leigh 1949; Schwab and Chafetz 1955). Anticholinergics can be particularly effective for the treatment of tremor (Koller 1986).

Anticholinergics can be difficult to use in elderly people. The most troublesome side-effect is confusion, which can be additive with other antiparkinsonian drugs. Patients may also develop frank hallucinations. Anticholinergics can also produce autonomic disturbances including postural hypotension, urinary retention, and constipation. Generally, they are best avoided in the very old.

Levodopa, combined with either carbidopa (Sinemet) or benserazide (Madopar or Prolopa) to inhibit peripheral decarboxylation, is the mainstay of the treatment of Parkinson's disease. A large proportion of ingested levodopa is destroyed in the periphery by catechol-*O*-methyl transferase, and a large proportion redistributes to muscle (Muenter and Tyce 1971; Nutt *et al.* 1994). In the striatum, the levodopa is decarboxylated to dopamine. Some is stored in vesicles in the nigrostriatal dopaminergic nerve terminals, and some probably

enters a free pool. The dopamine is released by the neurone and stimulates the dopamine receptors on both the next neurone in the dopaminergic pathway and autoreceptors on the nigrostriatal neurone.

In early Parkinson's disease, levodopa produces a clinical response in 80 to 90 per cent of patients. Following a single dose, the response may last about 4 h or more despite a plasma half-life in the order or 90 min (Mouradian *et al.* 1990). Some of this effect may be explained by the storage capacity of the remaining nigrostriatal neurones.

As the disease progresses, and as the duration of levodopa therapy increases, patients experience a progressively shorter duration of response to levodopa (Bravi *et al.* 1994). In addition, the rate of response becomes more rapid, or steeper, and the magnitude of response becomes greater. This combination of effects means that the patient experiences wide swings in the antiparkinsonian effect of levodopa. In addition to these changes, the therapeutic window narrows. This means there is a smaller margin in dose between that which produces an antiparkinsonian effect and that which produces dyskinesias (see below).

The basis for the change in response characteristics to levodopa is not clearly understood (Bravi *et al.* 1994). The traditional explanation for the effect has been a loss of the capacitance of the nigrostriatal neurones and vesicular storage of dopamine. This may not be the case, however, as similar changes can be shown with the direct dopamine agonist apomorphine, which bypasses the nigrostriatal dopaminergic neurones to stimulate the postsynaptic neurone directly (Bravi *et al.* 1994). While degeneration of the nigrostriatal neurones is necessary for the changes in response to occur, the mechanism of the response fluctuations appears to lie in the postsynaptic pathway. The nature of these changes are unclear, but they may involve *N*-methyl-D-aspartate (**NMDA**) receptors. There is experimental evidence that blockade of NMDA receptors can ameliorate the motor fluctuations seen in Parkinson's disease (Papa and Chase 1996).

High doses of levodopa in even early Parkinson's disease may produce dyskinesias (Cotzias *et al.* 1967). These can be divided into two types: choreiform and dystonic (Tolosa *et al.* 1993). Choreiform dyskinesias are writhing, flinging movements more prominent distally. Despite their often gross nature, they produce little in the way of disability for many patients, and they often go unnoticed by the patient with Parkinson's disease. They are very obvious to family members who often find choreiform dyskinesias very irritating.

Dystonic dyskinesias consist of more sustained twisting movements that may be more proximal, especially at the shoulder. These can be painful. They are also often disabling. Patients find dystonic dyskinesias unpleasant and will complain of movements that appear very much less severe than the well-tolerated choreiform dyskinesias.

Dopamine agonists were developed in the hope that direct stimulation of the dopamine receptor might provide a more effective antiparkinsonian action than levodopa, which must be decarboxylated in the degenerating nigrostriatal dopaminergic neurone. Despite the theoretical advantages, dopamine agonists have not proven to be more than adjunctive therapy in the majority of patients (Factor and Weiner 1993).

Bromocriptine (Calne *et al.* 1978), lisuride (LeWitt *et al.* 1982), and pergolide (Lieberman *et al.* 1981) are widely available. Newer orally active agonists include carbergoline (Geminiani *et al.* 1996), ropinerole (Adler *et al.* 1997), and pramipexole (Guttman 1997). Each agonist has a slightly different profile with regard to the relative action on the D_1 and D_2 families of dopamine receptors. In practice, there does not appear to be a great deal of difference in the relative antiparkinsonian effect of these agents, but there is some suggestion that the newer agonists may be superior than the existing agents (Guttman 1997).

Carbergoline is unique in that it has a very long half-life compared to the other agonists, and this may prove beneficial in some patients. Theoretically, smooth, sustained stimulation of dopamine receptors with carbergoline could reduce the frequency of motor fluctuations. This possibility is being explored in a prospective study not yet reported (Rinne et al. 1997).

Ropinerole and pramipexole, in contrast with the other agonists, are non-ergolides. The ergolide-based agonists have all been associated with rare occurrences of hypersensitivity reactions including pulmonary fibrosis. This may not occur with ropinerole and pramipexole.

Apomorphine is a dopamine agonist given parenterally (Frankel et al. 1990; Kempster et al. 1990). It is useful in patients with limited absorption of oral agents. It also has a rapid onset of action. Apomorphine is used in some patients to salvage severe off periods. The patient, or an assistant, injects a preset dose of apomorphine, which usually has an effect within minutes. Some patients also are equipped with automated pumps that inject a continuous subcutaneous dose of apomorphine. Apomorphine is also useful in patients who cannot swallow such as in the postoperative state. A major difficulty with the use of apomorphine is nausea and vomiting, and patients must be pretreated with domperidone before being able to tolerate the apomorphine.

Catechol-O-methyl transferase inhibitors are new agents that retard the metabolism of levodopa (Nutt et al. 1994). They are thus adjuncts to levodopa therapy. Even with decarboxylase inhibitors, only about 20 per cent of a dose of levodopa remains in the circulation after 1 h. The main route of metabolism is via catechol-O-methyl transferase to 3-O-methyltransferase. Catechol-O-methyl transferase inhibitors block this route and increase the availability of a dose of levodopa by 30 to 50 per cent. The peak plasma level of levodopa is not affected, but the duration of effect is prolonged. This has the effect of smoothing out motor fluctuations in patients with predictable motor fluctuations (Rajput et al. 1997). The first catechol-O-methyl transferase inhibitor, tolcapone, has restricted use following reports of fatal hepatic necrosis.

Practical management of the motor disturbance of Parkinson's disease

The mass of information and new therapy available for the treatment of Parkinson's disease can become confusing. It should be kept in mind, however, that no treatment has been shown either to delay the progression of the disease or to hasten the onset of motor complications. There is much theoretical discussion on these points, but none has been proven. Thus the practical management of Parkinson's disease should revolve around replacing the dopaminergic deficit in the simplest and smoothest way possible. This involves treating patients when the symptoms demand control and not before. It also involves regular dosing of levodopa and dopamine agonists in order to provide a relative continuous stimulation of the dopamine receptors. Many of the problems of dealing with Parkinson's disease are related

to special management issues such as cognitive disturbances and alterations in autonomic function.

Special management issues

Cognitive disturbance

The frequency and severity of cognitive disturbances in Parkinson's disease are underappreciated by many doctors (Pollock and Hornabrook 1966). The majority of patients with Parkinson's disease have an alteration of thought processes with a greater degree of rigidity of thought and less spontaneity ('bradyphenia'). Others have more severe disturbances with important clinical consequences. A proportion of patients have an irreversible dementia. Others have treatable cognitive disturbances, namely drug-induced confusion or depression. These possibilities must be actively sought and treated.

Dementia

Estimates vary, but about one-third of patients with Parkinson's disease develop dementia (Pollock and Hornabrook 1966). There may be more than one type. Some patients with Parkinson's disease develop a multifocal cognitive disturbance associated with speech deficits and dyspraxias (Kuhl et al. 1985). This is clinically indistinguishable from Alzheimer's disease. Some of these patients have the neuropathological changes diagnostic of Alzheimer's disease, and this probably represents coincidental diseases. Other patients have diffuse Lewy bodies (and also Alzheimer's changes), and the relationship between the Parkinson's disease and Alzheimer's disease is difficult to determine. A third group of patients develop a greater degree of cognitive slowing, with few if any dyspraxias or language deficits. This form of dementia is consistent with a frontal or so-called subcortical dementia (Kuhl et al. 1985). Some of these patients probably do not have typical Parkinson's disease, and may represent misdiagnosed cases of progressive supranuclear palsy. A frontal lobe pattern of dementia does occur in dementia with Parkinson's disease, however, but the pathological basis for this is unclear.

Drug-induced confusion

All of the antiparkinsonian drugs can cause confusion, often occurring in a patient developing dementia. In demented patients a choice must often be made between maintaining mobility and maintaining cognitive function. The best approach is to stop all medication except levodopa, and then find the lowest possible dose that keeps the patient safely mobile. Slow-release formulations of levodopa may induce less confusion as the peak blood concentrations of levodopa produced by regular-release formulations are eliminated.

Antiparkinsonian medications also induce a distinctive pattern of hallucinations (Young et al. 1997). These are usually visual or cognitive and almost never auditory. Occasionally patients describe vivid hallucinations where they see figures of sometimes recognizable people. At other times the figures take on characteristics more like cartoon characters. Sometimes they may be small animals. They often move about. A common hallucination is a flickering of light in the periphery of the vision. Some patients interpret this as somebody walking back and forth across a doorway. Others believe they have seen a rat or small animal running by. Some patients develop a conviction that there is an unnamed person in the house.

Hallucinations may or may not be disturbing. Some patients recognize them for what they are, and this is not an indication for reducing the dose of antiparkinsonian medication. Other patients become frankly disturbed by the hallucinations. The first step is to simplify the antiparkinsonian medication and usually stop all drugs except for levodopa, which must be administered in low doses. If the hallucinations continue, they may respond to low doses of the atypical neuroleptic clozapine (Factor and Friedman 1997). Clozapine is associated with significant side-effects, including agranulocytosis. The new atypical antipsychotic olanzipine has not been associated with these problems and has also been shown to be effective for the psychosis associated with antiparkinsonian medication (Wolters et al. 1996). Risperidone often exacerbates parkinsonism and is not generally useful.

Electroconvulsive therapy is particularly effective for the drug-induced hallucinations of Parkinson's disease (Hurwitz et al. 1988). The basis for this effect is not known. Electroconvulsive therapy is also very good for the depression associated with Parkinson's disease (see below). Surprisingly, patients who receive electroconvulsive therapy for these indications often experience a marked improvement of their Parkinson's disease, and also of levodopa-associated dyskinesias. This improvement may last several months. Electroconvulsive therapy should not be given to confused patients as this can cause an acute delirium.

Depression

Depression is very common in Parkinson's disease and affects around 40 per cent of patients at some stage during the disease (Cummings 1992). The pattern of depression is somewhat different from that seen in patients without Parkinson's disease, and there is a high frequency of agitation and anxiety and a low frequency of suicidal ideation. Often patients do not appreciate that they are depressed and may complain to the doctor that the antiparkinsonian medication is not working. If there is no measurable difference in motor function from previous assessments, then the possibility that the patient is depressed should be considered. The depression is often difficult to diagnose considering the fact that symptoms commonly associated with depression, such as disturbed sleep, low energy, and a flat affect are also features of Parkinson's disease without depression. The standard antidepressant drugs are often effective in Parkinson's disease. Tricyclic antidepressants are particularly good for patients with associated disturbances of sleep, and hyperactive bladders. Patients with low energy may respond to the selective serotonin reuptake inhibitors, although there have been a few reports of worsening parkinsonism with these medications (Leo 1996).

Sleep disturbances

Patient's with Parkinson's disease often have disturbed sleep. Some effectively invert their sleep–wake cycles, which can be socially disruptive. In addition, many patients find that a good night's sleep improves their parkinsonism (Merello et al. 1997). Standard sleep hygiene issues may be effective, and some patients respond to low doses of tricyclic antidepressants (see Chapter 18.2).

Pain

Pain is common in Parkinson's disease (Goetz et al. 1986). There are two main forms. One is a cramping sensation and the other is an unpleasant dysaesthesia. The cramping sensations may occur at any phase of the treatment cycle. In patients with untreated Parkinson's disease, the cramping often is associated with off-period dystonia. This may be improved with effective antiparkinsonian treatment. Patients with dystonic dyskinesias often find these painful. Other patients develop cramping pains that do not relate to any part of the medication cycle and do not respond to alterations in antiparkinsonian medication. This pain can be very difficult to treat. In some patients pain responds to tricyclic antidepressants, and in others to non-steroidal anti-inflammatory drugs.

Dysaesthetic pain is also common in Parkinson's disease. Patients complain of tingling electric-shock-like sensations. These usually affect the limbs. Tricyclic antidepressants can be effective.

Postural hypotension

Patients who develop prominent postural hypotension, particularly in the early phases of the disease, should be suspected of having multiple system atrophy, particularly of the Shy–Drager type. Autonomic disturbance is common in Parkinson's disease, however, and patients with advanced disease often develop postural hypotension. This is often seen in association with constipation, which can be severe. The postural hypotension is usually exacerbated by antiparkinsonian medication. Occasionally patients do not complain of postural hypotension but instead report a loss of energy or frequent falls. The blood pressure should be taken lying and standing, and again after standing for approximately 3 min, by which time the patient may develop hypotension that was not detectable upon first standing.

The treatment of postural hypotension in Parkinson's disease should start with rationalization of the antiparkinsonian medication. Sometimes patients respond to an increased intake of dietary salt. Few patients tolerate compressive leg bandages or stockings. Occasionally raising the head of the bed by a few centimetres will help maintain compensatory vascular mechanisms. In patients with more severe postural hypotension, fludrocortisone is often effective. Occasionally patients will require more intensive treatment with non-steroidal anti-inflammatory drugs, and the α-agonist midodrine (Jankovic et al. 1993).

Surgical management

The surgical management of Parkinson's disease predates levodopa therapy. Accidental surgical lesions of the basal ganglia, and natural lesions such as those produced by strokes or vascular disease, have long been recognized to improve the signs of Parkinson's disease. Stereotactic thalamic lesions are a well-established treatment for parkinsonian tremors.

In the last 5 to 10 years, attention has moved to other sites of the brain for stereotactic lesions, namely the globus pallidus interna and subthalamic nucleus (Marsden and Obeso 1994). The basal ganglia circuitry consists of serial and parallel circuits with both inhibitory and excitatory pathways. In the state of dopamine deficiency that is Parkinson's disease, the globus pallidus interna and subthalamic nucleus are hypermetabolic. Both of these sites can be lesioned using stereotactic techniques. The major experience to date has been with pallidotomy (Laitinen et al. 1992). The effectiveness of this procedure varies between reports, with at least some of the variations being due to different methods of measurement and reporting, as well as different surgical techniques. There is universal agreement that the pallidotomy is an excellent treatment for contralateral dyskinesias (Laitinen et al. 1992; Kishore et al. 1997). The contralateral parkinsonian features of tremor, bradykinesia, and rigidity also improve in the order of approximately 30 per cent. Surprisingly, there is also an ipsilateral improvement in dyskinesias and the other parkinsonian features. In most series the ipsilateral improvement is not permanent, and some report a return to the baseline state after approximately 1 year. However, other reports have suggested that there is a longer duration of positive effect (Fazzini *et al.* 1997). Bilateral pallidotomies have been performed, but some authorities warn against this procedure in view of a troublingly high frequency of cognitive disturbance and speech arrest similar to that seen with bilateral thalamotomy.

Lesions of the subthalamic nucleus also improve parkinsonism (Limousin *et al.* 1995). With some subthalamic lesions, however, patients become severely dyskinetic, which represents the hemiballismus seen in non-parkinsonian patients with vascular lesions of the subthalamic nucleus. A more controllable method of blocking the overactivity of the subthalamic nucleus is deep brain stimulation. This method involves the placement of electrodes in the subthalamic nucleus, which are then connected via a subcutaneous pathway to a pacemaker, usually inserted below the clavicle. High frequency electrical stimulation blocks the neuronal overactivity of the subthalamic nucleus, and the frequency and intensity of the stimulation can be altered to gain an antiparkinsonian effect without unacceptable dyskinesias.

Future developments

The introduction of the new catechol-*O*-methyl transferase inhibitors and new dopamine agonists may have a substantial impact on the way these patients are treated. As yet the place of these new agents in therapy has not been defined. This is in part because the design of the trials of these drugs tends towards proving an antiparkinsonian effect rather than proving that they are better than the best use of levodopa alone (Hauser *et al.* 1997).

New delivery systems are also being developed for existing and new drugs. In particular, transdermal delivery of dopamine agonists may produce a smoother stimulation of the dopamine receptors.

The success of pallidotomy has focused attention on the pharmacology of the basal ganglia connections. In particular, the excitatory, glutamatergic tract from the subthalamic nucleus to the internal globus pallidus may be responsible for many of the motor disturbances, including drug-induced dyskinesias seen in Parkinson's disease. Animal experiments have shown that this pathway can be blocked using glutamate antagonists (Papa and Chase 1996). As yet these agents are too toxic for human use, but when safe, they may become important for the treatment of parkinsonian tremor and drug-induced dyskinesias in particular.

Transplant therapy is now well established as an experimental treatment of Parkinson's disease (Olanow *et al.* 1996). The successful work to date has used nigral tissue harvested from fetuses aborted around 8 weeks postconception. Patients have generally tolerated the procedure well (Freeman *et al.* 1995). Only minor, or perhaps no, immune suppression is necessary, so the medical care of patients is uncomplicated compared with other transplant therapy. All aspects of parkinsonism improve, but not completely, and most patients still need ongoing antiparkinsonian drug treatment. Double-blind, sham surgical-controlled trials of fetal nigral transplant are currently under way and should give a clear view of the usefulness of the technique. However, the method will probably represent a transitional step. In

particular the ethical and practical issues surrounding procurement of fetal tissue will probably prevent widespread application of the technique. The next step will be the development of new tissue for transplantation. This will probably involve the use of genetically modified tissue (Freese *et al.* 1996).

Summary

Parkinson's disease is the prototype neurological disease of ageing. The basic pathophysiology is well characterized, and, despite ongoing ignorance of the cause of the disease, there are extremely effective therapeutic options available. The disease results in a range of medical, physical, psychological, and social problems. Understanding this mix is the key to successful management of the condition, which is often best treated using the multidisciplinary approach developed by geriatricians.

References

Adler, C.H., Sethi, K.D., Hauser, R.A., *et al.* (1997). Ropinerole for the treatment of early Parkinson's disease. *Neurology*, **49**, 393–9.

Arevalo, G.G., Jorge, R., Garcia, S., Scipioni, O., and Gershanik, O.S. (1997). Clinical and pharmacological differences in early- versus late-onset Parkinson's disease. *Movement Disorders*, **12**, 277–84.

Bravi, D., Mouradian, M.M., Roberts, J.W., *et al.* (1994). Wearing-off fluctuations in Parkinson's disease: contribution of postsynaptic mechanisms. *Annals of Neurology*, **36**, 27–31.

Calne, D.B., Williams, A.C., and Neophytides, A. (1978). Long-term treatment of parkinsonism with bromocriptine. *Lancet*, i, 735–8.

Calne, D.B., Snow, B.J., and Lee, C.S. (1992). Criteria for diagnosing Parkinson's disease. *Annals of Neurology*, **32**, S125–7.

Clark, C.M., Ewbank, D., Lerner, A., *et al.* (1997). The relationship between extrapyramidal signs and cognitive performance in patients with Alzheimer's disease enrolled in the CERAD study. *Neurology*, **49**, 70–5.

Consensus Committee of the American Autonomic Society and the American Academy of Neurology (1996). Consensus statement on the definition of orthostatic hypotension, pure autonomic failure, and multiple system atrophy. *Neurology*, **46**, 1470.

Cotzias, G.C., Van Woert, M.H., and Schiffer, L.M. (1967). Aromatic amino acids and modification of parkinsonism. *New England Journal of Medicine*, **276**, 374–9.

Cummings, J.L. (1992). Depression and Parkinson's disease: a review. *American Journal of Psychiatry*, **149**, 443–54.

Delwaide, P.J. and Gonce, M. (1993). Pathophysiology of Parkinson's signs. In *Parkinson's disease and movement disorders* (ed. J. Jankovic and E. Tolosa), pp. 77–92. Williams and Wilkins, Baltimore, MD.

Factor, S.A. and Friedman, J.H. (1997). The emerging role of clozapine in the treatment of movement disorders. *Movement Disorders*, **12**, 483–96.

Factor, S.A. and Weiner, W.J. (1993). Early combination therapy with bromocriptine and levodopa in Parkinson's disease. *Movement Disorders*, **8**, 257–62.

Fahn, S. and Isgreen, W. (1975). Long-term evaluation of amantadine and levodopa combination in parkinsonism by double blind crossover analysis. *Neurology*, **25**, 695–700.

Fazzini, E., Dogali, M., Sterio, D., Eidelberg, D., and Beric, A. (1997). Stereotactic pallidotomy for Parkinson's disease: a long-term follow-up of unilateral pallidotomy. *Neurology*, **48**, 1273–7.

Frankel, J.P., Lees, A.J., Kempster, P.A., and Stern, G.M. (1990). Subcutaneous apomorphine in the treatment of Parkinson's disease. *Journal of Neurology, Neurosurgery and Psychiatry*, **53**, 96–101.

Freeman, T.B., Olanow, C.W., Hauser, R.A., *et al.* (1995). Bilateral fetal nigral transplantation into the postcommissural putamen in Parkinson's disease. *Annals of Neurology,* 38, 379–88.

Freese, A., Stern, M., Kaplitt, M.G., *et al.* (1996). Prospects for gene therapy in Parkinson's disease. *Movement Disorders,* 11, 469–88.

Geminiani, G., Fetoni, V., Genitrini, S., Giocannini, P., Tamma, F., and Caraceni, T. (1996). Carbergoline in Parkinson's disease complicated by motor fluctuations. *Movement Disorders,* 11, 495–500.

Goetz, C.G., Tanner, C.M., and Levy, M. (1986). Pain in Parkinson's disease. *Movement Disorders,* 1, 45–9.

Golbe, L.I. and Davis, P.H. (1993). Progressive supranuclear palsy. In *Parkinson's disease and movement disorders* (ed. J. Jankovic and E. Tolosa), pp. 145–61. Williams and Wilkins, Baltimore, MD.

Guttman, M. (1997). Double-blind comparison of pramipexole and bromocriptine treatment with placebo in advanced Parkinson's disease. *Neurology,* 49, 1060–5.

Hansen, L., Salmon, D., Galasko, D., *et al.* (1990). The Lewy body variant of Alzheimer's disease: a clinical and pathologic entity. *Neurology,* 40, 1–8.

Hauser, R.A., Zesiewicz, T.A., Factor, S.A., Guttman, M., and Weiner, W.J. (1997). Clinical trials of add-on medications in Parkinson's disease: efficacy versus usefulness. *Parkinsonism and Related Disorders,* 3, 1–6.

Hughes, A.J., Daniel, S.E., Kilford, L., and Lees, A.J. (1992). Accuracy of clinical diagnosis of idiopathic Parkinson's disease: a clinico-pathological study of 100 cases. *Journal of Neurology, Neurosurgery, and Psychiatry,* 3, 181–4.

Hurwitz, T.A., Calne, D.B., and Waterman, K. (1988). Treatment of dopaminimimetic psychosis in Parkinson's disease with electroconvulsive therapy. *Canadian Journal of Neurological Sciences,* 15, 32–4.

Jankovic, J., Beach, J., Schwartz, K., Contant, C., and Lou, J.S. (1991). Tremor and longevity in relatives of patients with Parkinson's disease, essential tremor, and control subjects. Essential tremor: clinical correlates in 350 patients. *Neurology,* 41, 234–8.

Jankovic, J., Gilden, J.L., Hiner, B.C., *et al.* (1993). Neurogenic orthostatic hypotension: a double-blind, placebo-controlled study with midodrine. *American Journal of Medicine,* 95, 38–48.

Kalra, S., Bergeron, C., and Lang, A.E. (1996). Lewy body disease and dementia: a review. *Archives of Internal Medicine,* 156, 487–93.

Kempster, P.A., Frankel, J.P., Stern, G.M., and Lees, A.J. (1990). Comparison of motor response to apomorphine and levodopa in Parkinson's disease. *Journal of Neurology, Neurosurgery and Psychiatry,* 53, 1004–7.

Kishore, A., Turnbull, I.M., Snow, B.J., *et al.* (1997). Efficacy, stability and predictors of outcome of posteroventral pallidotomy for Parkinson's disease: six month follow-up with additional one-year observations. *Brain,* 120, 729–37.

Koller, W.C. (1986). Pharmacologic treatment of parkinsonian tremor. *Archives of Neurology,* 43, 126–7.

Kornhuber, J., Quack, G., Danysz, W., *et al.* (1994). Therapeutic brain concentration of the NMDA receptor antagonist amantadine. Amantadine and memantine are NMDA receptor antagonists with neuroprotective properties. *Neuropharmacology,* 43, 91–104.

Kuhl, D.E., Metter, E.J., Benson, D.F., *et al.* (1985). Similarities of cerebral glucose metabolism in Alzheimer's and Parkinson's dementia. *Journal of Cerebral Blood Flow and Metabolism,* 5, S169–70.

Laitinen, L.V., Bergenheim, T., and Hariz, M.I. (1992). Leskell's posteroventral pallidotomy in the treatment of Parkinson's disease. *Journal of Neurosurgery,* 76, 53–61.

Lee, C.S., Schulzer, M., Mak, E., *et al.* (1994). Clinical observations on the rate of progression of idiopathic parkinsonism and a mathematical model of pathogenesis. *Brain,* 117, 501–7.

Leo, R.J. (1996). Movement disorders associated with the serotonin selective reuptake inhibitors. *Journal of Clinical Psychiatry,* 57, 449–54.

LeWitt, P.A., Gopinathan, G., Ward, C.D., *et al.* (1982). Lisuride versus bromocriptine treatment in Parkinson's disease: a double-blind study. *Neurology,* 32, 69–72.

Lieberman, A.N., Goldstein, M., Leibowitz, M., *et al.* (1981). Treatment of advanced Parkinson's disease with pergolide. *Neurology,* 31, 675–82.

Limousin, P., Pollak, P., Benazzouz, A., *et al.* (1995). Bilateral subthalamic nucleus stimulation for severe Parkinson's disease. *Movement Disorders,* 10, 672–4.

Litvan, I., Agid, Y., Jankovic, J., *et al.* (1996). Accuracy of clinical criteria for the diagnosis of progressive supranuclear palsy (Steele–Richardson–Olszewski syndrome). *Neurology,* 46, 922–30.

Marsden, C.D. and Obeso, J.A. (1994). The functions of the basal ganglia and the paradox of stereotaxic surgery in Parkinson's disease. *Brain,* 117, 877–97.

Merello, M., Hughes, A.J., Colosimo, C., Hoffman, M., Starkstein, S., and Leiguardia, R. (1997). Sleep benefit in Parkinson's disease. *Movement Disorders,* 12, 506–8.

Mouradian, M.M., Heuser, I.J.E., Baronti, F., and Chase, T.N. (1990). Modification of central dopaminergic mechanisms by continuous levodopa therapy for advanced Parkinson's disease. *Annals of Neurology,* 27, 18–23.

Muenter, M.D. and Tyce, G.M. (1971). L-dopa therapy of Parkinson's disease: plasma L-dopa concentration, therapeutic response and side effects. *Mayo Clinic Proceedings,* 46, 231–9.

Murray, A.M., Weihmueller, F.B., Marshall, J.F., Hurtig, H.I., Gottleib, G.L., and Joyce, J.N. (1997). Damage to dopamine systems differs between Parkinson's disease and Alzheimer's disease. *Annals of Neurology,* 37, 300–12.

Nutt, J., Woodward, D.J., Beckner, R.M., *et al.* (1994). Effect of peripheral catechol-*O*-methyltransferase inhibition on the pharmacokinetics and pharmacodynamics of levodopa in parkinsonism. *Neurology,* 44, 913–18.

Olanow, C.W., Kordower, J.H., and Freeman, T. (1996). Foetal nigral transplantation as a therapy for Parkinson's disease. *Trends in Neurosciences,* 19, 102–9.

Papa, S.M. and Chase, T.N. (1996). Levodopa-induced dyskinesias improved by a glutamate agonist in parkinsonian monkeys. *Annals of Neurology,* 39, 574–8.

Parkinson Study Group (1989). Effect of deprenyl on the progression of disability in early Parkinson's disease. *New England Journal of Medicine,* 321, 1364–71.

Parkinson Study Group (1996). Impact of deprenyl and tocopherol treatment on Parkinson's disease in DATATOP subjects not requiring levodopa. *Annals of Neurology,* 39, 29–45.

Pollock, M. and Hornabrook, R.W. (1966). The prevalence, natural history and dementia of Parkinson's disease. *Brain,* 89, 429–48.

Rajput, A.H., Martin, W.R.W., Saint-Hilaire, M.-H., Dorflinger, E., and Pedder, S. (1997). Tolcapone improves motor function in parkinsonian patients with the 'wearing-off' phenomenon. *Neurology,* 49, 1066–71.

Richards, M., Stern, Y., and Mayeux, R. (1993). Subtle extrapyramidal signs can predict the development of dementia in elderly individuals. *Neurology,* 43, 2184–8.

Rinne, U.K., Bracco, F., Chouza, C., *et al.* (1997). Cabergoline in the treatment of early Parkinson's disease: results of the first year of treatment in a double-blind comparison of cabergoline and levodopa. The PKDS009 Collaborative Study Group. *Neurology,* 48, 363–8.

Salo, P.T. and Tatton, W.G. (1992). Deprenyl reduces the death of motoneurons caused by axotomy. *Journal of Neuroscience Research,* 31, 394–400.

Schwab, R.S. and Chafetz, M.E. (1955). Kemadrin for the treatment of parkinsonism. *Neurology,* 5, 273–7.

Schwab, R.S. and Leigh, D. (1949). Parpanit for the treatment of Parkinson's disease. *Journal of the American Medical Association,* 139, 629–34.

Spokes, E.G.S., Bannister, R., and Oppenheimer, D.R. (1979). Multiple system atrophy with autonomic failure. *Journal of the Neurological Sciences*, 43, 59–62.

Steele, J.C., Richardson, J.C., and Olszewski, J. (1964). Progressive supranuclear palsy. A heterogeneous degeneration involving the brainstem, basal ganglia, and cerebellum, with vertical gaze and pseudobulbar palsy, nuchal dystonia and dementia. *Archives of Neurology*, 10, 333–58.

Tanner, C.M. (1991). Epidemiological clues to the cause of Parkinson's disease. In *Movement disorders* (ed. S. Fahn and C.D. Marsden). Butterworths, London.

Tolosa, E., Alom, J., and Marti, M.J. (1993). Drug-induced dyskinesias. In *Parkinson's disease and movement disorders* (ed. J. Jankovic and E. Tolosa), pp. 375–97. Williams and Wilkins, Baltimore, MD.

Tyrell, P., Sawle, G.V., Ibanez, V., *et al.* (1990). Clinical and positron emission tomographic studies in the extrapyramidal syndrome of dementia of the Alzheimer type. *Archives of Neurology*, 47, 1318–23.

Uitti, R.J., Rajput, A.H., Ahlskog, J.E., *et al.* (1996). Amantadine treatment is an independent predictor of impaired survival in Parkinson's disease. *Neurology*, 46, 1551–6.

Wenning, G.K., Ben Shlomo, Y., Daniel, S.E., and Quinn, N.P. (1997). Multiple system atrophy: a review of 203 pathologically proven cases. *Movement Disorders*, 12, 133–47.

Wolters, E.C., Jansen, E.N., Tuynman Qua, H.G., and Bergmans, P.L. (1996). Olanzapine in the treatment of dopaminomimetic psychosis in patients with Parkinson's disease. *Neurology*, 47, 1085–7.

Young, B.K., Camicioli, R., and Ganzini, L. (1997). Neuropsychiatric adverse effects of anti-parkinsonian drugs. Characteristics, evaluation and treatment. *Drugs and Aging*, 10, 367–83.

18.6 Motor neurone disease (amyotrophic lateral sclerosis)

Andrew Eisen

Introduction

In this chapter selected aspects of motor neurone disease (**MND**), more commonly referred to as amyotrophic lateral sclerosis (**ALS**) in North America, and also known as Charcot's disease and Lou Gehrig's disease, are described. Although this disorder is rare it is a prime example of neurodegeneration. Alzheimer's and Parkinson's disease are the other major, and much more common, neurodegenerative diseases. They share many essential features and differ mainly because of the particular selective vulnerability of the neurones and pathways involved. In MND it is the corticomotoneuronal system which is selectively vulnerable and most if not all of the features of MND can be explained by dysfunction or demise of the corticomotoneuronal system. This system comprises colonies of corticomotoneurones which converge to innervate the spinal motoneurones through a single synapse ensuring very rapid conduction to the target cell (Porter and Lemon 1993). However, each colony innervates many different anterior horn cells and each anterior horn cell receives input from different, widely scattered, cortical colonies. The corticomotoneuronal system is well developed only in primates and particularly in humans and underlies the infinite variety of fractionated movements displayed by humans. All the anterior horn cells of all motor neurone pools receive monosynaptic input from corticomotoneurones except the motor neurone pools to the extraocular muscles and those anterior horn cells innervating the bladder wall; both are rarely affected in MND.

These anatomical arrangements and the absence of any naturally occurring or experimental animal models that truly mimic human MND provided the basis for the corticomotoneuronal hypothesis of MND (Eisen *et al.* 1992; Eisen and Krieger 1993; Eisen 1995). This hypothesis postulates that MND is primarily a disease of the corticomotoneurones or their presynaptic terminals and that disease of the lower motor neurones is secondary. The idea that MND might originate in the motor cortex was originally proposed by Charcot (Charcot 1865; Charcot and Joffroy 1869). However, it remains possible that both the upper and lower motor neurones become involved independently of each other. For example, one hallmark of MND is the accumulation of spheroids in the lower motoneurones and similar accumulations called conglomerates in the upper motoneurones (Chou and Norris 1993). Chou *et al.* (1996) have performed experiments suggesting that these accumulations are the result of a shared biochemical abnormality involving peroxynitrite and superoxide. Others have postulated that MND commences in the spinal motor neurones and spreads retrogradely to the upper motor neurones (Pamphlett *et al.* 1995). These concepts are not necessarily mutually exclusive. MND is quite heterogeneous, and it may be that different mechanisms pertain in different phenotypes.

Epidemiological considerations

MND is the least frequent of the three commonly recognized neurodegenerative diseases. The other two, Parkinson's disease and Alzheimer's disease, are respectively about 20 and 100 times more common than MND. MND has a worldwide annual incidence of about 2 per 100 000 population and a prevalence of 4 to 6 per 100 000 population. The incidence of all the neurodegenerative diseases is increasing (Lillienfeld *et al.* 1989, Chancellor and Warlow 1992; Brooks 1996). Age is the only indisputable risk factor for MND (Eisen *et al.* 1993). When this disorder was first described by Charcot, life expectancy was approximately 45 years. Today it is over 80 years. This dramatic increase in longevity together with a decreasing incidence of some diseases, especially heart disease, largely accounts for the increasing incidence of the neurodegenerative diseases. However, there may also be an increasing number of younger-onset cases (under 40 years of age) which if substantiated would suggest that there are unidentified environmental factors of importance in the increasing incidence of MND.

There are few firm data on the specific incidence of MND in people aged 75 years and over (Armon *et al.* 1991; Chancellor *et al.* 1993). An apparent decrease in the incidence of MND after the age of 70 years probably reflects a rising mortality in later life from competing diseases precluding development of MND. Also, progressive loss of strength and difficulty in walking in elderly institutionalized subjects, who are frequently frail, is often disregarded as simply being due to 'old age' and the possibility of MND is easily overlooked.

Aetiopathogenesis

The aetiopathogenesis of MND is complex and incompletely understood (Rowland 1994; Appel *et al.* 1995; Drachman *et al.* 1995). There are four basic elements: ageing, protective and susceptibility genes (yet to be identified), environmental factors (also yet to be identified), and the 'final cascade'. The last consists of an interdependent series of bimolecular steps, some or all of which may be common to a parallel series of events in the other neurodegenerative diseases (Leigh 1994; Al-Chalabi *et al.* 1995; Eisen and Krieger 1998). The terminal cascade is complex, involving glutamate excitotoxicity, oxidative stress, and reactive astrocytosis which is a potential substrate for an inflammatory immunologically mediated cell destruction. Once commenced, these processes seem to proceed relentlessly and appear to be independent of whatever it is that initiates the disease. It is not known when MND begins but this is probably months, if not years, before the onset of clinical deficits. The lack of a biological marker for MND makes the diagnosis impossible in the presymptomatic stage. Ubiquitin-immunoreactive intraneural inclusions are almost pathognomonic of the disease (Leigh *et al.* 1991) and this may be one future avenue of exploration for the development of a biological marker.

About 5 to 10 per cent of MND is hereditary and about 20 per cent of these cases have a mutation of the superoxide dismutase-1 gene. So far more than 60 different mutations of this gene have been identified in more than 200 families throughout the world (Andersen *et al.* 1996; Radunovic and Leigh 1996). When the mutated gene was first discovered it was thought that there would be an underexpression of superoxide dismutase-1 which in turn would result in the accumulation of deleterious oxygen-free radicals. In fact studies in transgenic mice have shown that there is an over expression rather than an underexpression of superoxide dismutase-1. Furthermore, knock-out mice that lack any superoxide dismutase-1 activity do not develop MND. Therefore the role of the mutant gene in MND is not clear (Brown 1996). Other candidate genes for MND are being vigorously sought at the present time. Fundamental to the role that genes play in neurodegeneration are those genes which control the cellular biological clock.

With ageing, genetic information becomes subject to errors as age-associated accumulation of DNA alterations and damage to informational molecules occurs (Osiewacz and Hamann 1997) (see also Chapter 2.2). Some of the changes occur randomly but others result from the differential activity of specific, often subtle, genetic traits. The DNA abnormalities depend upon the rate at which their alterations occur versus the ability to repair them. Ageing cells are more susceptible to a variety of insults which may not otherwise be deleterious. Large ageing cells may be particularly vulnerable to insult and herein may lie the clue to the selective vulnerability underlying MND. The corticomotoneurones and anterior horn cells involved are very large and this may make them particularly vulnerable to insult.

Clinical issues

The diagnosis of MND largely depends upon the recognition of a characteristic clinical constellation with supportive electrophysiological findings. An additional requirement for the diagnosis is the exclusion of disorders which may share similar clinical features. Once the disease has been present for a few months, the diagnosis of MND can usually be made with considerable confidence. The combination of painless, progressive but asymmetrical muscle weakness with wasting, fasciculation (and cramps), in a multimyotomal distribution, associated with upper motor neurone signs, a normal sensory examination, and normal sphincter and ocular function occurring in a middle-aged patient is almost always due to MND. It is necessary to exclude other causes for the symptoms and signs of a cervical cord syndrome such as syringomyelia, arteriovenous malformations, spinal cord tumour, and cervical spondylotic myelopathy. The last disorder is by far the most common and can cause a particular dilemma because some degree of degenerative disc disease is almost invariable at an age when MND has its greatest frequency.

The presenting clinical features of MND are protean and readily misinterpreted (Table 1). Some symptoms are more likely to be ignored in elderly and frail subjects being incorrectly considered to be manifestations of 'normal ageing'. Examples include exercise intolerance, a weak voice, decreasing respiratory reserve, a limp, and clumsiness of hand function. Because of its rarity, primary doctors have a low index of suspicion for MND. It might be argued that early diagnosis of MND in older people is not a major concern given that there is presently very limited treatment for the disorder. However, this nihilistic view must be tempered by the availability of new therapies, and the importance to patients and their families of a diagnosis and prognosis. Certainly, however, it is better to delay the diagnosis a little than to misdiagnose a treatable disease as MND.

Early diagnostic difficulty was an impetus for a classification system, to estimate the probability of MND. The recently developed

Table 1 Presenting features of motor neurone disease (listed in approximate order of frequency)

Clumsy hands
Hoarse voice (dysarthria)
Shoulder dysfunction
Weak foot (foot drop)
Difficulty walking (spastic gait)
Exercise intolerance
Fasciculation
Respiratory insufficiency
Cognitive impairment

El Escorial criteria (Brooks 1994) (Table 2), have been found to be helpful in drug trials and have been validated in a clinicopathological study in which the likelihood of the patient having MND by the diagnostic criteria was correlated with the frequency of ubiquitin-immunoreactive intraneuronal inclusion bodies. These inclusions, although not entirely specific for MND, are a pathological characteristic of the disease (Chaudhuri *et al.* 1995). These criteria are being revised on a regular basis.

In addition to these criteria which are required to make a firm diagnosis of MND, there are several clinical features which are considered as inconsistent with the diagnosis of MND. These include sensory dysfunction, sphincter impairment, autonomic dysfunction, abnormalities of eye movements, movement disorders, and cognitive dysfunction. These exclusion criteria hold true for the majority of patients with MND throughout much of the course of their disease. However, there are well-documented cases of MND with one or more of these 'exceptions'. They are more frequent in elderly patients. An interesting example is bladder dysfunction which is phenotypically

Table 2 The El Escorial diagnostic criteria for motor neurone disease

Definite
UMN and LMN signs in bulbar and two spinal regions
or
UMN and LMN signs in three spinal regions

Probable
UMN and LMN signs in two regions (spinal or bulbar) and UMN signs in a region that is rostral to LMN signs

Possible
UMN and LMN signs in one region (spinal or bulbar)
or
UMN signs in two or three regions (spinal or bulbar)

Suspected
LMN signs in two or three regions (spinal or bulbar)

LMN, lower motor neurone; UMN, upper motor neurone.

characteristic of the D90A Cu/Zn superoxide dismutase-1 mutation (Andersen *et al.* 1996).

There are also clinical clues (Table 3) that should raise concern that the patient does not have MND.

Dementia, extrapyramidal features, sensory findings, or autonomic involvement are well recognized in elderly patients with MND. But it is difficult to determine how many such patients exist. These cases are often identified in large MND clinics where more vigorous case ascertainment is possible. For example, overt clinical dementia occurs in less than 5 per cent of MND patients (Strong *et al.* 1996). But using formal psychometric testing as many as 35 per cent of patients show some evidence of cognitive impairment. Positron emission tomography (**PET**) scanning has revealed abnormalities in dopamine metabolism in a number of MND patients who do not have clinical evidence of Parkinson's disease. Also, functional magnetic resonance imaging (**MRI**) has demonstrated widespread abnormalities outside the primary motor cortex in many MND patients with or without dementia or unusual clinical features. These variations from classical MND raise the question of to what degree the pathogenesis of MND is shared by the other neurodegenerative disorders which might account for the additional clinical features (Calne *et al.* 1986). Alzheimer's disease, Parkinson's disease, and MND certainly share a number of characteristics (Eisen and Calne 1992) (Table 4).

However, with increased attention directed to neuropsychological testing, imaging studies, and neuropathological data, it has become apparent that in most cases the dementia associated with MND is typically of the 'frontal-lobe type' and different from Alzheimer's dementia (Hudson 1991). Other designations include 'frontal-lobe degeneration of non-Alzheimer type', 'dementia of frontal-lobe type', 'frontal lobe-dementia', and, more commonly, 'frontotemporal dementia'. Clinically, the dementia has relatively consistent behavioural and affective features sometimes associated with a speech disorder but with preserved spatial orientation and praxis until late in the disease. Memory is often surprisingly intact and the main behavioural abnormalities of dementia in MND, as summarized in Table 5, are often dominated by erratic and unusual behaviour. Cognitive impairment may follow, but more usually precedes, the other features of MND. These patients are often seen initially by a psychiatrist or in a dementia clinic, and MND is suspected only later because of fasciculation, weakness, or amyotrophy. Conversely, electromyographers may initially make a diagnosis of typical MND, only later to realize that cognition is impaired.

Formerly, in many circumstances, dementia with MND was regarded as a form of Creutzfeldt–Jakob disease, Alzheimer's disease, or Pick's disease (Hudson 1991; Strong *et al.* 1996). However, the disorder had neither the characteristic EEG changes of Creutzfeldt–Jakob disease, nor could it be transmitted to a variety of animal species including non-human primates. Typical Alzheimer plaques and neurofibrillary tangles and Pick bodies were not found at autopsy.

Fasciculation

Fasciculation is seen in many normal older subjects and in a variety of neuromuscular disorders. However, in MND they are particularly striking and often very diffuse, frequently being prominent in clinically strong muscles (Eisen and Krieger 1998). Kennedy's disease (progressive spinobulbar muscular atrophy) may be the only other condition in which fasciculation is so pronounced. When fasciculations

Table 3 Motor neurone disease: the differential diagnosis

Clinical clue	Alternative diagnosis
Symmetrical four-limb weakness/wasting	PMAs, IBM
Absence of diffuse clinical or electrophysiological fasciculation	Spondylotic radiculomyelopathy
Weakness without muscle wasting	MMN
Depressed or absent reflexes in weak myotome	
Depression or loss of reflexes in multiple myotomes	CIDP, Kennedy's disease

CIDP, chronic inflammatory demyelinating neuropathy; IBM, inclusion body myositis; MMN, multifocal motor neuropathy with persistent conduction block; PMAs, progressive muscular atrophies.

Table 4 Shared features of motor neurone disease, Parkinson's disease, and Alzheimer's disease

	MND	PD	AD
Mean age of onset (years)	59.3	61.9	71.9
Mean duration of disease (years)	2.4	10.5	7.3
Incidence per 100 000 per annum	1.2	21	401
Prevalence per 100 000	4.2	300	2155
Age of peak incidence	55–65	70–80	65–75
Male-to-female ratio[a]	1.61:1	1.13:1	1.1:1
Familial occurrence	<10%	<10%	<10%
Twin studies	LC	LC	LC

MND, motor neurone disease; PD, Parkinson's disease; AD, Alzeheimer's disease; LC, low concordance.

[a] Ratio reversed after age 75 years.

Adapted from Eisen and Calne (1992).

Table 5 Some characteristics of dementia in motor neurone disease

Insidious onset with slow progression
Early loss of attention to personal hygiene and grooming
Loss of appropriate social behaviour with frequent misdemeanours
Erratic and unusual behaviour such as shop-lifting
Disinhibition with lack of sexual restraint, violent behaviour, or restlessness

are seen in a multimyotomal distribution and associated with muscle weakness and upper motor neurone signs they invariably mean the patient has MND. Conversely, the absence of clinical or EMG recorded fasciculation makes the diagnosis of MND suspect. Fasciculation may be moderately and sometimes dramatically reduced in patients taking riluzole and other glutamate antagonists such as lamotrigine and gabapentin (Neurontin®). Therefore, before concluding that fasciculation is truly absent, it is necessary to enquire about treatment with any of these recently introduced medications. Fasciculation of the tongue is an important clinical marker of MND, but can be difficult to appreciate unless the tongue is maintained very still. It should not be confused with tongue fibrillation, which has a fine, shimmering appearance. The tongue is the only muscle in which fibrillations can be seen clinically because there is no covering skin.

Fasciculation occurring in the absence of other symptoms, for example muscle weakness or wasting, is usually of little concern. The results of a postal survey in 121 mostly young adults, seen because of fasciculation who had a normal neurological examination, revealed that after a mean time interval of about 7 years, none had developed serious neurological disease, in particular MND (Blexrud et al. 1993). However, the same conclusion should not be reached for patients aged 45 years or older who develop fasciculation for the first time. In the author's experience and that of others, fasciculation may predate other clinical features of MND by many months. There are no definite clinical characteristics to indicate that fasciculation is 'benign' or otherwise. One possible clue is the synchronous occurrence of fasciculation in several muscles of adjoining spinal segments (Norris 1965). This observation suggests that fasciculation in MND may be generated proximal to the anterior horn cell.

Investigating motor neurone disease

Electromyography (EMG) studies, including various types of conduction studies and needle EMG, are of considerable aid in the confirmation of MND (Eisen and McComas 1993; Eisen and Krieger 1998). Indeed, clinical electrophysiological abnormalities have now been incorporated into the El Escorial criteria for MND. Needle EMG is also helpful in documenting early diaphragmatic disease (Bolton et al. 1992), which may be an indication for instituting bimodal passive airway pressure. Nerve conduction studies are essential to exclude some of the disorders that mimic MND but which have a better natural history or are treatable. Needle EMG is also frequently abnormal in clinically strong limbs having normal muscle bulk. Between 50 and 80 per cent of anterior horn cells can be lost before weakness or muscle wasting occur and demonstrating EMG abnormalities in strong muscles helps to identify widespread disease.

Multifocal motor neuropathy with persisting conduction block is a fairly recently delineated clinical entity and can only be confirmed

Lacomblez, L., Bensimon, G., Leigh, P.N., Guillet, P., Meininger, V., and the ALS/Riluzole Study Group II (1996). A dose-ranging study of riluzole in amyotrophic lateral sclerosis. *Lancet*, 347, 1425–31.

Leigh, P.N. (1994). Pathogenic mechanisms in amyotrophic lateral sclerosis and other motor neuron disorders. In *Neurodegenerative diseases* (ed. D.B. Calne), pp. 473–88. W.B. Saunders, Philadelphia, PA.

Leigh, P.N., Whitwell, H., and Garofalo, O. (1991). Ubiquitin-immunoreactive intraneuronal inclusions in amyotrophic lateral sclerosis. *Brain*, 114, 775–88.

Lillienfeld, D.E., Chan, E., Ehland, J., *et al.* (1989). Rising mortality from motoneuron disease in the USA, 1982–84. *Lancet*, i, 710–12.

Martin, D., Thompson, M.A., and Nadler, J.V. (1993). The neuroprotective agent riluzole inhibits release of glutamate and aspartate from slices of hippocampal area CA1. *European Journal of Pharmacology*, 250, 473–6.

Munsat, T.L. (1995). Issues in amyotrophic lateral sclerosis clinical trial design. *Advances in Neurology*, 68, 209–18.

Norris, F.H., Jr (1965). Synchronous fasciculations in motor neuron disease. *Archives of Neurology*, 13, 495–500.

Osiewacz, H.D. and Hamann, A. (1997). DNA reorganization and biological aging. A review. *Biochemistry*, 62, 1275–84.

Pamphlett, R., Kril, J., and Hng, T.M. (1995). Motor neuron disease: a primary disorder of corticomotoneuron? *Muscle and Nerve*, 18, 314–18.

Pioro, E.P., Antel, J.P., Cashman, N.R., and Arnold, D.L. (1994). Detection of cortical neuron loss in motor neuron disease by proton magnetic resonance spectroscopy imaging *in vivo*. *Neurology*, 44, 1933–8.

Porter, R. and Lemon, R. (1993). *Corticospinal function and voluntary movement*, pp. 1–421. Monographs of the Physiological Society 45. Clarendon Press, Oxford.

Radunovic, A. and Leigh, P.N. (1996). Cu/Zn superoxide dismutase gene mutations in amyotrophic lateral sclerosis: correlation between genotype and clinical features. *Journal of Neurology, Neurosurgery and Psychiatry*, 61, 565–72.

Rothstein, J.D., Kuncl, R., Chaudhry, V., *et al.* (1991). Excitatory amino acids in amyotrophic lateral sclerosis: an update. *Annals of Neurology*, 30, 224–5.

Rothstein, J.D., Martin, L., Dykes-Hoberg, M., *et al.* (1995). Selective loss of glial glutamate transporter GLT-1 in amyotrophic lateral sclerosis. *Annals of Neurology*, 38, 73–84.

Rowland, L.P. (1994). Natural history and clinical features of amyotrophic lateral sclerosis and related motor neuron diseases. In *Neurodegenerative diseases* (ed. D.B. Calne), pp. 507–21. W.B. Saunders, Philadelphia, PA.

Shaw, P.J., Forrest, V., Ince, P.G., *et al.* (1995). CSF and plasma amino acid levels in motor neuron disease: elevation of CSF glutamate in a subset of patients. *Neurodegeneration*, 4, 209–16.

Strong, M.J., Grace, G.M., Orange, J.B., and Leeper, H.A. (1996). Cognition, language and speech in amyotrophic lateral sclerosis: a review. *Journal of Clinical Experimental Neuropsychology*, 18, 291–303.

Weber, M. and Eisen, A. (1999). Assessment of upper and lower motor neurons in Kennedy's disease: implications for cortico-motoneuronal PSTH studies. *Muscle and Nerve*, in press.

18.7 Peripheral neuropathy

Pierre Bouche

Peripheral neuropathy is a common feature in elderly people. It is due to involvement of a single nerve or to a more diffuse alteration of the peripheral nervous system. With a few exceptions, the causes of peripheral nerve involvement in elderly people do not differ from those in younger people.

Peripheral nerve diseases are usually classified according to the pattern of distribution of the lesions. Three main types of neuropathy are described: (a) mononeuropathy, a term indicating involvement of an individual peripheral nerve; (b) multiple mononeuropathy, a process due to the simultaneous or multifocal involvement of several peripheral nerves; (c) polyneuropathy, a term designating a generalized process producing widespread and usually symmetrical effects on the peripheral nervous system. These effects may be motor, sensory, sensorimotor, or autonomic and proximal, distal, or generalized in their distribution.

In addition, there are three main types of peripheral nerve fibre lesion.

1. Axonopathy, where the pathological process involves the axon, either in a focal or generalized manner.

2. Myelinopathy, where the pathological process involves the myelin sheath of the axon.

3. Neuronopathy, where the pathological process involves the neurone cell body. A neuronopathy can involve either motoneurones, or sensory neurones (ganglionopathy).

Clinical aspects

Polyneuropathies

The distribution of lesions in polyneuropathies may be distal (often due to an axonopathy), or proximal and proximal/distal (often due to a myelinopathy) and frequently also affecting nerve roots in addition to peripheral nerve (polyradiculoneuropathy).

The onset of distal polyneuropathies is usually insidious and gradual, evolving over several months. Initial findings are frequently in the lower extremities and may be manifested by difficulties in walking, due to a distal motor deficit, or to sensory disturbances (gait ataxia). Sensory symptoms are often present early in the disease process and include cramps, paraesthesiae, burning sensations, or pain of variable intensity. The motor deficit, if present, is localized to the distal muscles of the lower limbs (dying-back degeneration). Muscle atrophy depends on the extent of axonal degeneration. Physical examination shows a stocking–glove sensory and motor loss in a symmetrical distribution with loss of ankle jerks and sometimes loss of knee jerks. Dysautonomia may be present including postural hypotension, sphincter dysfunction, impotence, and sweating abnormalities. Typically, the cerebrospinal fluid protein level is normal, since the pathological changes are usually distal in the nerve and the nerve roots are spared. Recovery is slow, taking many months or years and sometimes never completely occurs, since axonal regeneration is a very slow process and in elderly people it takes much more time.

The onset of proximal or proximal/distal neuropathies may be acute (in days) or chronic and often occurs in a multifocal distribution. Involvement of nerve may be proximal, distal, or include the entire length of the nerve fibre including the root. Often the motor deficit is more evident than the sensory deficit and is usually located in the proximal muscles, although a distal deficit is common. Cranial and thoracic nerves can be involved resulting in respiratory insufficiency. Generalized areflexia is often found without muscle atrophy. The cerebrospinal fluid reveals an elevated protein content without many cells. Recovery is often rapid, consistent with remyelination.

Neuronopathies

In motor neuronopathies the degeneration of the motoneurone in the anterior horn of the spinal cord leads to a pure motor deficit with muscle atrophy, often associated with cramps and fasciculations. The tendon reflexes may be absent but are usually brisk when there is central nervous system involvement.

In sensory neuronopathies degeneration of the dorsal root ganglia leads to a pure sensory neuropathy with generalized areflexia. Gait ataxia is common in this disorder.

Mononeuropathies

The pathological process is localized to a single nerve trunk (median, ulnar, peroneal nerves) and the causes can be trauma or nerve compression (entrapment neuropathies).

Multiple mononeuropathies

More rarely, multifocal involvement of peripheral nerves is seen and in this case the pathological process is usually due to an ischaemic lesion of a number of nerve fibres.

Electromyographic examination

Electromyographic examination is a useful tool in the diagnosis of peripheral nerve diseases (Table 1). The term 'electromyographic' is used in the broadest sense and includes the evaluation of motor and sensory nerve function as well as the function of voluntary muscles.

It may differentiate axonal or demyelinating neuropathies. Voluntary muscles are examined with a needle electrode. In normal muscles at rest, there is usually no spontaneous electrical activity. In diseased muscle, denervation potentials (fibrillation potentials) may occur, indicating active denervation which can be found in axonal degeneration. In demyelinating processes, there is generally no active degeneration of the nerve fibre and consequently no fibrillation potentials. With a progressive muscle contraction, motor units discharge. In a neuropathic process, there is a loss of motor units and a reduction in the amplitude of the motor unit potentials. Measurement of the motor and sensory nerve conduction velocity is also of importance. In axonal degenerations, the motor or sensory conduction velocity is normal or close to normal, but the amplitude of the motor or sensory nerve compound action potential is reduced, corresponding to the amount of degenerated nerve fibres. In a demyelinating process, nerve conduction velocity is markedly reduced with temporal dispersion of the evoked response and sometimes conduction block.

Neuromuscular biopsy

Biopsy of peripheral nerves is sometimes performed. The sural or superficial peroneal nerves are usually biopsied. Sophisticated techniques are used to examine nerve samples and should be left to neuropathological units with relevant expertise. Specific diseases which may call for a nerve biopsy include vasculitis, sarcoidosis, nerve infiltration (lymphoma, leprosy), and amyloidosis. Often, however, the clinical and electromyographic examinations are sufficient for diagnosis in the routine evaluation of a peripheral nerve disorder.

Causes of peripheral neuropathies

Polyneuropathies

Acute polyneuropathies

The symptoms and signs of acute polyneuropathies can evolve in a matter of days. According to the main pathological process outlined above, it is possible to classify neuropathies as follows.

Axonal polyneuropathies

The aetiology of axonal neuropathies includes rare cases of axonal polyradiculoneuritis or axonal Guillain–Barré syndrome, peripheral nerve disorder associated with acute intermittent porphyria, some rare intoxications (thallium salts, arsenic, lithium, triorthocresyl phosphate), some diabetic, uraemic, or alcoholic neuropathies, and polyneuropathic forms of vasculitic neuropathies. In the latter condition, nerve biopsy is indicated.

Demyelinating polyneuropathies

The most frequent is the Guillain–Barré syndrome. The onset may be abrupt or over a few days. The motor deficit may be generalized with generalized areflexia and rare sensory complaints. Cranial nerves are frequently involved and respiratory insufficiency has to be detected rapidly. There is a high level of protein content in the cerebrospinal fluid with few or no cells. Electromyographic examination shows reduced nerve conduction velocity with temporal dispersion and

Table 1 Electromyographic findings in polyneuropathy

	Electromyography			Nerve conduction study					
				Motor				Sensory	
	Spontaneous activity (fibrillation potential)	MUP recruitment	MUP morphology	Conduction velocity	Distal latency	CMAP amplitude	Block/ dispersion	Conduction velocity	SNAP amplitude
Axonopathies									
Acute	+ to + + +	↓↓	N	N	N	↓↓	—	N	↓↓
Subacute/ chronic	(+) to + +	↓↓	PP	N to ↓	N	↓ to ↓↓	—	N to ↓	↓↓
Myelinopathies									
Acute	—	↓↓	N	↓↓	↑↑	↓	+ +	↓↓	↓
Chronic									
CMT	−/+	↓↓	GP or N	↓↓	↑↑	↓	—	↓↓	↓
CIDP	−/+	↓↓	PP	↓ to ↓↓	↑ to ↑↑	↓	+ +	↓↓	↓

CIDP, chronic inflammatory demyelinating polyneuropathy; CMAP, compound muscle action potential; CMT, Charcot–Marie–Tooth disease; GP, giant potential; MUP, motor unit potential; N, normal; PP, polyphasic potential; SNAP, sensory nerve action potential.

conduction block. Recovery may be rapid. Treatment with plasmapheresis or intravenous human immunoglobulin may be effective when administered in the first days of the disease.

The other cause of an acute demyelinating polyneuropathy is diphtheria, but this is quite rare in adult populations.

Neuronopathies

Acute sensory neuronopathies are rare, with the idiopathic form being more frequent.

Subacute polyneuropathies

Axonal polyneuropathies

This is by far the most frequent cause of polyneuropathies. The symptoms and signs evolve in a matter of weeks or months and the causes are usually metabolic or toxic.

Metabolic polyneuropathies Diabetic neuropathies are the most frequent cause of polyneuropathy. The neuropathy is of insidious onset, mainly sensory with absent ankle jerk reflexes. A more diffuse form of neuropathy is sometimes observed, both sensory and motor. The amyotrophic form is rare where the motor deficit and muscle atrophy involve the proximal lower limbs, and is associated with pain and can be of more rapid onset. Diabetic neuropathy may occur in patients with moderately severe diabetes and is therefore difficult to manage. The autonomic nervous system is usually involved in diabetic polyneuropathy. Postural hypotension, sphincter disturbance, and impotence are the most frequent signs and symptoms.

In the late stage of the renal insufficiency, peripheral neuropathy is frequent. Dialysis and renal transplantation are the best therapeutic approaches to such neuropathies.

Peripheral neuropathy in thyroid insufficiency is rare.

Nutritional polyneuropathies Nutritional polyneuropathies are also very frequent. Alcoholic neuropathy is due to a nutritional deficiency and abuse of alcohol. This is a largely axonal polyneuropathy which

may be severe with sensorimotor deficit and muscle atrophy. Treatment includes thiamine administration and correction of nutritional intake.

In elderly people, more diffuse vitamin and nutritional deficiencies are frequent and may account for a complex axonal polyneuropathy.

Toxic polyneuropathies Toxic neuropathies due to environmental hazards and industrial exposure are mainly due to exposure to toxins from industry (acrylamide, carbon disulphide, hexacarbons, lead, organophosphates, thallium, arsenic). These neuropathies are rarely observed in elderly people.

Drug neuropathies are much more frequent in elderly people and are one of the most frequent causes of polyneuropathy after the sixth decade. Amiodarone, a potent ventricular antiarrhythmic drug, causes peripheral neuropathy when prolonged serum concentrations exceed 2.4 mg/l. The neuropathy is sensorimotor. Although the neuropathy is mainly axonal, severe slowing of nerve conduction velocity is characteristic in the advanced stage. Schwann cell lamellar inclusions may be observed along with some degree of segmental demyelination in the nerve biopsy.

Organic gold compounds used to treat rheumatoid arthritis may cause peripheral neuropathy. The neuropathy is sensorimotor and is associated with prominent muscle pain. Segmental demyelination may be observed associated with axonal degeneration in the nerve biopsy.

Metronidazole is an antimicrobial agent used in the treatment of Gram-negative infections and Crohn's disease. It causes distal sensory neuropathy more than motor neuropathy with cumulative doses exceeding 30 g. Misonidazole, a congener of metronidazole, is a cell sensitizer for radiotherapy and the distal axonal neuropathy is similar to that related to metronidazole.

Nitrofurantoin is a broad-spectrum antibiotic used in the treatment of urinary tract infections. A rapidly progressive distal polyneuropathy can occur, especially in patients with renal insufficiency.

Cisplatin is a drug used in the treatment of several cancers. If the cumulative dose exceeds 225 to 500 mg/m², cisplatin causes a large-

Table 2 More common mononeuropathies

Upper limbs
Nerve trunk lesions
    Median nerve at wrist (carpal tunnel syndrome)
    Ulnar nerve at elbow
    Radial nerve
Plexus lesions
    Parsonage–Turner syndrome, brachial neuralgia
    Postradiation plexopathy
    Neoplastic plexopathy
Root lesions
    C5, C6, C7, C8

Lower limbs
Nerve trunk lesions
    Lateral cutaneous nerve of the thigh (meralgia paraesthetica)
    Femoral nerve
    Common peroneal nerve at fibular head
    Posterior tibial nerve (tarsal tunnel syndrome)
Plexus lesions
    Postradiation plexopathy
    Neoplastic plexopathy
Root lesions
    L3, L4, L5, S1

fibre progressive sensory polyneuropathy or neuronopathy (ganglionopathy). The onset of the neuropathy may be delayed up to 4 months after drug withdrawal.

Taxol, a chemotherapeutic plant alkaloid, is a new drug used in the treatment of solid tumours. Doses above 200 mg/m^2 are associated with peripheral axonal and distal polyneuropathy.

Thalidomine is used in the treatment of dermatological conditions such as discoid lupus. An axonal, mainly sensory, neuropathy occurs after a year of treatment at doses of 25 to 50 mg, more rapidly with higher doses.

Vincristine, a chemotherapeutic plant alkaloid is used against a wide spectrum of malignancies. Its use is limited by its neurotoxicity. The neuropathy is a sensorimotor axonopathy which could affect first the forearms and is sometimes associated with dysautonomic signs.

Other drugs may cause distal axonal polyneuropathies such as chloroquine, colchicine, dapsone, new drugs for the treatment of HIV infections (dideoxycytidine, dideoxyinosine, 2′,3′-didehydro-3′-deoxythymidine), disulfiram, isoniazid, and almitrine.

Polyneuropathies in systemic diseases Generally, in systemic diseases, the neuropathy is a multifocal mononeuropathy. A vasculitis affecting the vasa nervorum (blood vessels in the nerves) is usually responsible for the neuropathy. In sarcoidosis, periarteritis nodosa, and rheumatoid arthritis, a distal peripheral sensory neuropathy may develop. Nerve biopsy is useful for an appropriate diagnosis.

Polyneuropathies in lymphoreticulopathies A peripheral distal neuropathy is sometimes observed in some cases of lymphoma.

Polyneuropathies in dysglobulinaemia Dysglobulinaemia is a frequent condition in elderly people. A distal peripheral sensorimotor neuropathy, with a rapid progression and a severe disability, may be observed in multiple myeloma. A less severe and insidious sensory

polyneuropathy is observed in essential mixed cryoglobulinaemia or in cryoglobulinaemia associated with hepatitis C infection.

Infectious polyneuropathy Infectious polyneuropathies are rare. In HIV infections, a painful distal sensory polyneuropathy may be observed in the late stage of the disease. Hepatitis C could be responsible for a peripheral neuropathy even in the absence of cryoglobulinaemia.

Amyloid In primary amyloidosis, a peripheral sensory neuropathy is frequent. Small myelinated and unmyelinated fibres are involved causing a neuropathy characterized by pain and temperature deficit and dysautonomia. The nerve biopsy shows the amyloid deposits stainable by Congo Red dye.

Demyelinating polyneuropathies

Subacute demyelinating polyneuropathies are rare. In idiopathic subacute demyelinating polyradiculoneuropathies the sensorimotor neuropathy occurs over a few weeks and is characterized by motor rather than sensory signs and symptoms, generalized areflexia, a high protein content in the cerebrospinal fluid, and reduced nerve conduction velocity associated with temporal dispersion and conduction block. Treatment by steroids, plasmapheresis, or intravenous immunoglobulins appears to be effective.

In solitary plasmocytoma and the POEMS syndrome (polyneuropathy, organomegaly, endocrinopathy, M protein, and skin changes), a subacute sensorimotor demyelinating polyneuropathy is frequently observed. In some systemic diseases, such as sarcoidosis and systemic lupus erythematosus, a subacute demyelinating polyneuropathy, similar to the idiopathic one can be observed. In the early stage of HIV infections, a subacute inflammatory polyradiculoneuropathy may be observed.

Neuronopathies

Motor neuronopathies are rare but may occur in lymphoma. Sensory neuronopathies are characterized by subacute involvement of large sensory fibres with gait ataxia, generalized areflexia, sometimes pain, and a diffuse distribution of the sensory deficit (face, trunk, and upper limbs more than lower limbs).

Three main associations of sensory neuronopathy are found. The first is the subacute paraneoplastic neuronopathy of Denny–Brown associated with small cell anaplasic carcinoma of the lung. Anti-Hu antibodies are frequently found in the serum of such patients. The neuronopathy may occur several years before the cancer is detectable. The second is a subacute neuronopathy associated with the sicca syndrome or Sjögren's syndrome. The third is idiopathic.

Chronic polyneuropathies

The signs and symptoms of peripheral nerve involvement occur over many years usually with a progressive course. In the older age group inherited neuropathies are uncommon.

Axonal polyneuropathies

In non-hereditary polyneuropathies, some cases are due to dysglobulinaemia (immunoglobulin G), frequently a monoclonal gammopathy.

Inherited polyneuropathies are uncommon. Although rare, it is possible to develop an inherited polyneuropathy after the sixth decade; sometimes patients present with the neuronal form of Charcot–Marie–Tooth disease or type 2 Charcot–Marie–Tooth disease. Rarely,

Table 3 Causes of multiple mononeuropathies

Diabetes: (vascular lesions)
Cranial nerves (oculomotor)
Proximal amyotrophy (lower limbs)
Radiculopathy

Vasculitis (nerve ischaemia)
Systemic necrotizing vasculitis
   Periarteritis nodosa
   Churg–Strauss syndrome
   Rheumatoid arthritis
   Lupus
   Sarcoidosis
Other vasculitis

Dysglobulinaemia
Cryoglobulinaemia
Macroglobulinaemia (Waldenström disease)

Nerve infiltration
Leprosy
Lymphoma

Table 4 Causes of neuropathies in elderly people

	Vital et al. (1992) (%)	Georges and Twomey (1986) (%)
Metabolic neuropathies	22.2	–
Diabetes	–	27
Uraemia	–	3
Nutritional neuropathies (alcohol)	–	3
Dysimmune neuropathies	19.5	–
Guillain–Barré syndrome	–	11
Toxic neuropathies (drugs)	15.1	4
Systemic neuropathies	4.9	4
Neoplastic neuropathies	–	13
Paraneoplastic neuropathies	9.2	–
Haematological neuropathies	9.2	–
Inherited neuropathies	5.4	–
Miscellaneous	3.2	3
Unknown	20	28
Nerve compression	7.6	–

a pure sensory neuropathy may develop. Hereditary amyloidosis usually affects younger people, but with the recent advances in molecular biology, it is possible to detect a peripheral neuropathy due to hereditary amyloidosis in subjects above 60 years of age or more.

Demyelinating polyneuropathies

Acquired polyneuropathies Two main causes of chronic demyelinating polyneuropathies are observed. The first is idiopathic inflammatory polyradiculoneuropathy or chronic inflammatory demyelinating polyneuropathy which is characterized by weakness, sometimes with a sensory deficit, generalized areflexia, a high cerebrospinal fluid protein content, and multifocal abnormalities in nerve conduction studies. These include slow temporal dispersion and conduction block. Treatment of chronic inflammatory demyelinating polyneuropathy is the same as in the subacute form.

Demyelinating polyneuropathy associated with immunoglobulin M monoclonal gammopathy occurs in the older population. Patients can have weakness, or a mainly sensory neuropathy affecting large fibres which leads to an ataxic gait, tremor, and generalized areflexia. There can be a high cerebrospinal fluid protein content. Reduced nerve conduction velocity is seen, sometimes with conduction block. An antimyelin-associated glycoprotein antibody is sometimes found in the sera of these patients.

Hereditary polyneuropathies A late expression of an inherited polyneuropathy is possible. The most frequent form is type 1 Charcot–Marie–Tooth disease. Peroneal atrophy may develop after the sixth decade. The motor nerve conduction velocity is markedly reduced in all nerves. The nerve conduction slowing is homogeneous without temporal dispersion or conduction block. A duplication of the PMP-22 gene is found in chromosome 17 in nearly 75 per cent of patients (type 1A Charcot–Marie–Tooth disease). Other forms of inherited demyelinating polyneuropathies are rare.

Neuronopathies

Chronic neuronopathies are rare with the exception of the inherited neuropathies, either motor (spinal form of Charcot–Marie–Tooth disease) or sensory.

Mononeuropathies

Involvement of a single nerve trunk or root is frequent (Table 2), and these may be due to traumatic injury or nerve compression, particularly in entrapment neuropathies.

Upper limbs

Median nerve (carpal tunnel syndrome) Carpal tunnel syndrome is the most common entrapment neuropathy. It is common in middle-aged women. Patients may complain of intermittent numbness, tingling, and pain in the area of the median nerve distribution. The symptoms worsen at night and may awaken the patient. Examination is usually normal at an early stage but a positive Tinel sign is possible (a sensation of tingling or 'pins and needles' felt in the distal extremity of a limb when percussion is made over the site of an injured nerve). In the advanced stage, patients have persistent symptoms, hypoaesthesia, loss of dexterity and weakness of pinch (thumb abduction). Examination shows weakness and thenar atrophy, as well as sensory loss. At a more advanced stage, patients have marked sensory loss and thenar wasting with a poorer prognosis for recovery. The electromyographic examination shows a focal slowing of motor and sensory nerve conduction across the carpal tunnel and can be used to evaluate the severity of the nerve compression. Non-surgical treatment is advised for mild syndromes using splints and local steroid injections. In more advanced cases, surgical treatment is usually very successful with incision of the transverse carpal ligament. Median nerve compression at the elbow is unusual. The pronator syndrome or anterior interosseous nerve syndrome is rare.

Ulnar nerve Ulnar nerve entrapment at the elbow is a common upper-extremity compression neuropathy. Patients complain of sensory symptoms involving the fourth and fifth fingers. Motor dysfunction is less frequent, but includes weakness of grasp and pinch or a loss of dexterity. Examination reveals some degree of wasting of the first dorsal interosseous muscle, adductor pollicis, and muscles of the hypothenar group. Motor deficits of forearm muscles are less frequent (flexor carpi ulnaris). Electromyographic examination shows slowing of motor nerve conduction at the elbow, and alteration of the distal sensory evoked potential at the wrist with electrical stimulation of the fifth digit. In advanced cases, surgical transposition of the nerve may be indicated. Compression of the ulnar nerve at the wrist or in the palm is rare but may be caused by a ganglion, cyst, by trauma.

Radial nerve The radial nerve is most vulnerable in the upper arm at the level of the spinal groove. The most common cause of compression is external pressure as in 'Saturday night palsy'. The sleeping patient compresses the nerve between the humerus and the back of a chair. A fully developed paralysis is found when the patient wakes up in the morning. Clinically there is a wrist and finger drop. Sensory disturbance over the back of the base of the thumb is inconstant.

Other nerves Compression of other nerves in the upper limbs is less frequent but may involve the axillary, suprascapular, or long thoracic nerves.

Thoracic outlet syndrome The thoracic outlet syndrome involving the lower brachial plexus is rare in subjects over 30 years of age.

Brachial plexus Brachial plexus involvement is mainly due to malignant infiltration of the plexus or a consequence of radiation for breast cancer. Parsonage–Turner syndrome (idiopathic brachial neuralgia) is not rare and is characterized by the acute onset of unilateral shoulder pain followed 8 to 15 days later by weakness and muscle atrophy of the deltoid, infraspinatus and supraspinatus, and serratus anterior muscles. This may follow a viral illness.

Upper-limb radiculopathies Upper-limb radiculopathies are frequent and typically involve the fifth, sixth, seventh, and eighth cervical nerve roots, due to cervical spondylosis.

Lower limbs

In the lower limbs, the L5 and S1 roots are frequently involved. Also, in elderly people, lumbar spinal stenosis is frequent. In this population, compression of the sciatic nerve is uncommon. Involvement of the common peroneal and posterior tibial nerves is more frequent. The common peroneal nerve can be compressed at the fibula head, leading to foot drop. The tarsal tunnel syndrome due to compression of plantar nerves is rare. The femoral nerve can be involved, especially in diabetic patients, but an L3 to L4 root lesion is an alternative diagnosis. Meralgia paraesthetica is due to damage to the lateral cutaneous nerve of the thigh.

Multiple mononeuropathy

Multiple mononeuropathies, or mononeuropathies multiplex, are less frequent (Table 3).

Peripheral neuropathies in elderly patients are summarized in Table 4. The causes differ little from the causes in a younger population.

Further reading

Dyck, P.J., Thomas, P.K., Griffin, J.W., Low, P.A., and Poduslo, J.F. (1993). *Peripheral neuropathy* (3rd edn). W.B. Saunders, Philadelphia, PA.

References

George, J. and Twomey, J.A. (1986). Causes of polyneuropathy in the elderly. *Age and Ageing*, 15, 247–9.

Vital, A., Vallat, J.M., and Bouche, P. (1992). Système nerveux périphérique et vieillissement. In *Neuropathies périphériques* (ed. P. Bouche and J.M. Vallat), pp. 263–70. Doin, Paris.

18.8 Intracranial tumours

Gordon K. Wilcock

Introduction

In this chapter we focus on those aspects of cerebral tumours, and their management in older people, that differ from younger age groups. However, some general features will be included where appropriate, for example in relation to clinical presentation and management.

Intracranial tumours constitute a very small proportion of the neurological disorders that are admitted to departments of geriatric medicine, but this masks the evidence in the literature which indicates that the incidence of primary tumours, in particular in older age groups, is actually rising. In the decade up to 1985 there was a five-fold increase in primary malignant brain tumours in elderly people, but more specifically this appeared to affect mostly those up to the age of 79 years, followed by a plateau and a decline in incidence in people aged 85 years and over (Muir *et al.* 1987; Greig *et al.* 1990). A further and more recent study from Florida, however, reported an increase in incidence of 15 per cent for those aged 65 to 69, 16 per cent in those aged 70 to 74 years, 30 per cent in those aged 75 to 79 years, 36 per cent in those aged 80 to 84 years, and 254 per cent in those aged 85 years or older (Werner *et al.* 1995). These authors also reported that the incidence of anaplastic astrocytoma and glioblastoma in particular had risen, and that this was not the result of an increase in case ascertainment. However, it has been suggested that at least some of this apparent increase in incidence is the result of differential survival. Riggs (1995) investigated age-specific primary malignant brain tumour mortality rates for those aged over 60 years, and suggested that the increase in incidence may reflect differential survival, rather than other factors such as improved diagnosis or an actual increase in the number of people developing cerebral tumours. Further data investigating the trends over the last decade is not yet available, but should indicate whether this trend is continuing. Overall, however, it is important to remember that intracranial tumours occur relatively infrequently in elderly people.

In general terms both the incidence of and likelihood of malignancy in primary brain tumours appears to be a function of increasing age.

Clinical presentation

Generally, the pattern of clinical presentation is not a reliable indicator of whether the underlying neoplasm is likely to be benign or malignant, nor of the histological nature of the pathology, but rather of the location of the tumour and its rate of growth. When considering the significance of clinical signs and symptoms it is also important to remember the importance of the impact of the multiple pathology so often found in older people. Focal pathology, for instance, which might be considered to be indicative of cerebral metastases in a younger person with a primary malignancy elsewhere, may, in an older person with a similar extracranial tumour, result from other neurodegenerative disorders, rather than metastases.

Raised intracranial pressure

Whether or not the symptoms of raised intracranial pressure occur less commonly in older people is unresolved, but in reality it occurs sufficiently frequently to merit consideration when the possibility of a cerebral tumour has been raised. Raised intracranial pressure is not always associated with the typical triad of headache, vomiting, and papilloedema. This may, to some extent, be explained by the involutional processes that occur in most ageing brains, allowing them to accommodate an expanding lesion more easily than would be the case in a younger person. Despite this, in some patients a rapidly expanding lesion can cause a very definite increase in intracranial pressure, and a small number of patients present with a reduced consciousness level of unexplained aetiology. Even at such an advanced stage, the absence of papilloedema does not exclude a cerebral tumour, and the latter should be considered if there are relevant indications, such as focal signs, especially if they have a relatively slow onset.

Focal symptoms and signs

This is probably the most common, or part of the most common, clinical presentation in older patients, especially if the tumour is malignant, but also commonly occurs in benign lesions. Focal signs from hemisphere tumours are very similar to those noted in people with vascular lesions, although the mode of onset is usually more slowly progressive, unless the tumour has precipitated an intracerebral haemorrhage. Tumours situated below the tentorium will affect brainstem and cerebellar functions in particular, again with a relatively slow onset.

Tumours in the prefrontal area particularly affect the intellect, and attention, judgement, and problem-solving ability, sometimes accompanied by other manifestations of frontal lobe damage, such as emotional lability and loss of social inhibition. This may well lead to patients presenting for the investigation of a dementia. Tumours involving Broca's area in the inferior frontal gyrus of the dominant hemisphere, precipitating motor aphasia and lesions of the precentral gyrus, will produce a typical contralateral hemiparesis. Other examples of site-specific presentations include temporal lobe tumours resulting in impediments of hearing, speech, behaviour, and movement, and parietal lesions affecting two-point discrimination and proprioception, whilst tumours of the occipital lobe typically affect vision.

Approximately 3 per cent of patients with a stroke are subsequently found to have a tumour, and conversely the same proportion of tumours may present with a stroke-like picture (Salcman 1992).

Change in mental status

An alteration in mental state, as referred to above, is another frequently occurring presentation of cerebral tumour in older people, as well as in those who are younger. This is usually the result of local damage to the brain parenchyma, in which case there may be clues to the site of the lesion such as the examples cited above. Sometimes, however, a tumour can block the cerebrospinal fluid outflow and result in one or other form of hydrocephalus. In the latter circumstances, focal cognitive features are less prominent than more general signs such as a reduction in intellectual processing speed, vagueness, and disorientation. By this stage of the disease process, however, there is usually also evidence of focal damage, and focal signs will therefore often be present as well as those resulting from hydrocephalus. This is helpful in the differential diagnosis from other parenchymal causes of dementia, or endocrinological or iatrogenic causes of a confusional state. The presence of an organic mental syndrome may indicate involvement of the corpus callosum which is usually associated with a very poor prognosis. The interested reader can explore this aspect of symptomatology in greater depth elsewhere (Harsh and Wilson 1990).

Seizures

Seizures in elderly patients with a cerebral tumour probably occur in less than 20 per cent of cases (Godfrey and Caird 1984). Furthermore, since there are so many other causes of seizure in older people they are not a reliable indicator of cerebral neoplasia, but nevertheless occur sufficiently frequently that the possibility of an intracerebral neoplasm should come to mind when considering their aetiology, especially in the absence of any other potential cause. They are particularly likely to arise when a tumour affects an epileptogenic area of the brain such as the temporal lobe, or the frontoparietal region (Harsh and Wilson 1990). Nevertheless it is true, in general, that whilst seizures are relatively common as a first symptom of cerebral tumour in younger people, this is less often the case in those aged 70 years and over, and they are more likely to be a late rather than an early manifestation. This means, of course, that there will often be other evidence of cerebral tumour before the seizure occurs and it is less likely to be a presenting feature of epilepsy which has apparently arisen *de novo*.

Specific tumours

The features of most specific tumours are probably similar in both younger and older patients, apart from the differential incidence mentioned above. Pituitary tumours, therefore, will present in the characteristic manner with compression of the optic nerve and its chiasm with the typical pattern of visual impairment. The endocrinological manifestations are, however, less likely to be present, as more pituitary tumours in older people are non-functioning such that the typical picture of acromegaly, or Cushing's syndrome, occurs infrequently. Since disease progression is often slow, the early manifestations may be subtle and it is important to undertake a full and careful neurological examination on all patients where a tumour is part of the differential diagnosis, particularly if there are visual symptoms, even though these may appear to result from ocular pathology.

Although impairment of hearing is a very common problem in elderly people, acoustic neuromas are rarely responsible for this. This possibility should, however, at least be considered when there is increasing unilateral deafness associated with tinnitus, vertigo, or other impairment of balance. The insidious nature of the symptoms, and the ease with which it is possible to attribute them to other conditions, can often result in a relatively late detection of an acoustic neuroma (Symon *et al.* 1989). This is particularly likely to be the case in older people.

Investigation and diagnosis

A CT or magnetic resonance imaging (**MRI**) scan is always the investigation of choice, at least initially. Not only will such a scan usually demonstrate the tumour responsible for a patient's symptoms and signs, but it may also give clues to the type of tumour and the extent of its invasion of surrounding parenchyma. It will also demonstrate the presence or otherwise of hydrocephalus. The sensitivity and specificity of CT scanning, with contrast enhancement, will detect the majority of tumours irrespective of site, although those situated below the tentorium are sometimes more difficult to identify.

MRI has an even better record for identifying lesions than CT scanning, especially for those lesions situated in the posterior fossa. Nevertheless, where there is pressure on resources it is difficult to make a case for the routine use of MRI rather than CT scanning, where there is good clinical evidence of a cerebral tumour. Angiography is rarely, if ever, undertaken in most centres for the routine investigation of potential cerebral tumours. There is a significant risk, especially in older people, of both morbidity and mortality compared with the non-invasive nature of more routine scanning. Plain radiography of the skull is of very limited value, except when investigating the possibility of a pituitary tumour. Usually, however, in this case, most doctors would prefer CT scanning where this is available, because of the additional information that such a scan can provide over and above that apparent on a straightforward skull radiograph.

Other investigative techniques such as radionuclide imaging and electroencephalography, although relatively non-invasive, have largely given way to CT and MRI scanning.

Finally, it is important to remember that identifying an intracranial tumour may indicate the need for further investigation. This is fairly obvious when the lesion is an acoustic neuroma or a pituitary tumour, but an isolated mass elsewhere may be a metastasis and limited further investigation may be appropriate, for example a chest radiograph. It is doubtful, however, whether there is much to be gained in most instances by pursuing the site of the primary lesion as this is unlikely to improve the patient's prognosis.

In summary, CT or MRI are the investigations of choice, and should not be withheld on the basis of age, because such neuroimaging technology will demonstrate clinically, and therapeutically, important information such as bleeding or peritumoral oedema.

Management

General principles

The management of elderly patients with an intracranial tumour is guided not by their chronological age, but rather by their general fitness and comorbidities, the nature of the tumour, and the wishes of both themselves and their families. Quality-of-life issues are most important, and as postoperative morbidity and mortality is higher in older patients, this should be considered alongside the effect of surgery.

Little is known about the effect of potentially malignant cerebral tumours on the quality of life of old people, but this area has begun to attract attention as a result of the extended median life expectancy that modern treatment can offer. One case study (Kaplan and Miner 1997) reports significant levels of depression and anxiety, the latter increasing with progression of the tumour. Particular areas of concern expressed included the loss of conjugal closeness and the onset of social inactivity. If, as one may suspect, such feelings are experienced by many people in this situation, this is an important aspect of management that is probably largely overlooked as patients do not always readily express their feelings.

It is easy to assume that limiting certain health-care resources for elderly people will help reduce rising hospital costs when resources are finite. It is sometimes implied that older people overutilize certain resources, but benefit less from them than younger patients. This is an issue that has been specifically addressed in a study of 123 patients undergoing craniotomy for cerebral tumour (Layon et al. 1995). These authors found no differences between patients under the age of 65 compared with those of this age or older, in terms of length of stay in the intensive care unit and hospital, final outcome at discharge, quality of life, or hospital costs, even though the older group underwent a greater number of procedures and suffered more complications.

Neurosurgical intervention

Benign tumours, especially meningiomas in an accessible site, are often the most rewarding to remove, even if a less than complete extirpation is possible. In those tumours where there have been significant symptoms and signs, despite the peri- and postoperative fatality being higher than in younger patients, there is little doubt that such a procedure is worthwhile and may dramatically improve the quality of life of the patient for the remaining lifespan available to them. In general, however, the more severe the neurological dysfunction preoperatively, the less positive the outcome is likely to be. The same principles hold for the removal of an acoustic neuroma, or a pituitary tumour, the latter having relatively low fatality and complication rates, even in older people, if undertaken by the transsphenoidal route.

The advantages of surgical resection of a tumour include decompression of the intracranial cavity where this is relevant, a reduction of the number of malignant cells remaining if radiation and/or chemotherapy is under consideration, and the opportunity for a definitive histological diagnosis. Just as important as the surgical technique is the skill and experience of the anaesthetist. The perioperative and immediate postoperative management is a highly specialized area of medicine which must be given careful consideration.

Technology is now emerging that allows greater accuracy in the localization and removal of brain tumours, tracking the position of instruments during surgery, and displaying their location, in relation to preoperatively obtained images. This allows a greater consistency in achieving adequate exposure and accurate definition of the extent of tumour resection (Maciunas et al. 1996). In many older people, however, it will be more appropriate to limit surgery to a stereotaxic biopsy before deciding on further treatment, unless a decision has already been taken to avoid surgery.

The value of cytoreductive surgery in elderly patients with malignant gliomas requires careful thought. In many, a dual approach such as surgery followed by radiation therapy will be considered inappropriate, but even in those where this is the approach selected, one has to ask very carefully whether it is worthwhile. Frequently, although there is some prolongation of survival in selected patients over the age of 65 years, the benefit obtained is modest and may not be adequate to offset the distress and disruption caused to the patient by the surgery (Ayoubi et al. 1993; Kelly and Hunt 1994).

In general, therefore, brain tumour surgery in older people often has a relatively poor outcome and a high complication rate, but, despite this, well-selected patients can benefit substantially and it is essential to tailor treatment in every case. However, it is probable that the number of elderly people considered suitable for surgery will continue to be a small percentage of those who present with a cerebral tumour, especially if it is malignant.

Radiotherapy

Although there is little doubt that some tumours, for example malignant astrocytomas, are sensitive to radiotherapy with benefit to the patient in terms of prolonged survival, one must nevertheless consider very carefully whether this benefit is sufficient to offset the unwanted effects of radiotherapy, and the increased intrusion of treatment into a patient's remaining lifespan. This is probably true irrespective of the nature of the radiation treatment under consideration.

Where it is decided that a course of radiotherapy is appropriate, evidence is beginning to emerge that relatively short courses in elderly patients with malignant gliomas may confer almost as much benefit as a more radical approach (Hoegler and Davey 1997). Nevertheless the improved duration of life is only of the order of a few months, and it is difficult to infer from the published studies whether the quality of the extended lifespan is adequate to justify such treatment. Again, it is a decision that has to be made on an individual basis for each patient. In another study, involving 103 patients with malignant supratentorial glioma, Meckling et al. (1996) reported that radiotherapy was only associated with an improvement in survival in patients under the age of 80 years, and that neurological status was only rarely significantly improved. These authors concluded that radiotherapy is unlikely to benefit patients who are aged 80 years or older, although it may have short-lived benefit for those who are functionally disabled.

Chemotherapy

A similar debate about the benefits, in relation to duration and quality of life, is under consideration in relation to the use of cytotoxic drugs which have an established usage in the treatment of brain tumours in younger people. Most doctors specializing in the care of older people have a high threshold before recommending chemotherapy in their patients with intracranial neoplasia, and this would seem to be justified from the literature. One has to question whether the increase in duration of life, and its quality, is sufficient to offset the unwanted effects of undergoing courses of cytotoxic agents. In one study of malignant or recurrent astrocytomas only 5 per cent of patients aged 60 or over obtained any response to treatment, and assessment of a number of outcome measures in this retrospective analysis emphasized the poor response of older patients, coupled with an increased risk of complications (Grant et al. 1995).

Whether newer routes of drug delivery, for example using surgically implantable wafers made of biodegradable copolymers impregnated with cytotoxic agents, will change the outcome of cytotoxic treatment in older patients remains to be seen. It is an attractive hypothesis, and in particular may avoid the systemic toxicity that is associated with such treatments. Similarly, we must await the outcome of clinical trials evaluating newer agents, but until it is clear that there are benefits that are meaningful in terms of duration and quality of life, it seems improbable that cytotoxic treatment will have more than a marginal impact upon the management of cerebral tumours in elderly people.

Palliative treatment

It is extremely important that an appropriate professional is identified who will take responsibility for co-ordinating and supervising the palliative measures that will be so important to all those elderly patients in whom a cerebral tumour has been diagnosed, irrespective of whether or not they also undergo other therapeutic measures. Although every patient should have access to careful supervision by an experienced senior doctor, many others provide important aspects of palliative care. Wherever possible this should be undertaken in the community for as long as is practical, and in both contexts involvement of nurse specialists, for example MacMillan nurses in the United Kingdom, provides an invaluable service, as does hospice care in appropriate circumstances.

Rehabilitation is extremely important in those who have undergone neurosurgery and both physiotherapy and occupational therapy advice and support will often make an important contribution to maximizing function, despite a patient's deteriorating physical abilities.

Where it is clear that cerebral oedema surrounding the tumour may be causing or exacerbating focal symptoms and signs, intellectual ability, or conscious level, a trial of high-dose steroids is indicated. Dexamethasone is frequently used in this context, but if there is no improvement after 5 to 7 days it is unlikely that there will be any benefit thereafter. Where it is effective, a high dose should be reduced within 5 to 7 days to the minimum that maintains the level of improvement. Although the use of steroids, especially in high dosage, is associated with unwanted effects and complications, the relatively short time that they are prescribed in this context, varying from a few weeks to several months, means that they are not usually a serious problem. However, they should be avoided if there is any suggestion of intracerebral or other infection. The presence of peritumoral oedema is usually apparent on a CT scan, but rather than subject the patient to further scanning it is often reasonable to undertake a therapeutic trial of dexamethasone instead.

Other aspects of palliative care that are important include the careful use of analgesia and an awareness of the troubles from constipation that some of these drugs may produce. Nausea and vomiting are very distressing symptoms and the judicious use of antiemetics will often be necessary. The control of seizures with anticonvulsant drugs is similarly important, and many, if not all, patients who have recently undergone neurosurgical intervention will be routinely prescribed an anticonvulsant, at least in the short term.

When a patient with a cerebral tumour experiences symptoms that are usually treated in a palliative manner, whether or not they have previously undergone surgery, it is important to remember that there may be other potential causes for distress. The onset of vomiting, for instance, may be a manifestation of a rise in intracranial pressure resulting from hydrocephalus which could be relieved by a simple shunting procedure. Although it is a natural human reaction on the part of those caring for a patient to automatically try to relieve the symptom, and this is important, it is equally necessary to think beyond the symptom itself, and consider whether it may be caused by some alternative underlying aetiology, before finally attributing it to the tumour itself.

Conclusion

Cerebral tumours constitute a small part of the spectrum of neurological disorders that present to those who care for elderly people. It is nevertheless important to make an accurate diagnosis as early as possible, as there is much that can be done to improve the quality of life of the patient. At present, palliative care alone will probably be the mainstay of treatment in the majority, especially the older elderly, but in selected cases surgery, radiotherapy, and, to a lesser extent, chemotherapy may have a role to play. This picture may change in the future, with newer techniques and the emergence of new cytotoxic agents and methods of delivering them.

References

Ayoubi, S., Walter, P.H., Naik, S., Sankaran, M., and Robinson D. (1993). Audit in the management of gliomas. *British Journal of Neurosurgery*, 7, 61–9.

Godfrey, J.B. and Caird, F.I. (1984). Intracranial tumours in the elderly. *Age and Ageing*, 13, 152–8.

Grant, R., Liang, G.C., Page, M.A., Crane, D.L., Greenberg H.S., and Junck, L. (1995). Age influences chemotherapy response in astrocytomas. *Neurology*, 45, 929–33.

Greig, N.H., Ries, L.G., and Yancik, R. (1990). Increasing incidence of primary malignant brain tumors in the elderly. *Journal of National Cancer Institute*, 82, 1621–4.

Harsh, G.R. and Wilson, C.B. (1990). Neuroeithelial tumors of the adult brain. In *Neurological surgery: a comprehensive reference guide to the diagnosis and management of neurosurgical problems* (ed. J.R. Yuoumans) (3rd edn) p. 3040. W.B. Saunders, Philadelphia, PA.

Hoegler, D.B. and Davey, P. (1997). A prospective study of short course radiotherapy in elderly patients with malignant glioma. *Journal of Neuro-Oncology*, 33, 201–4.

Kaplan, C.P. and Miner, M.E. (1997). Anxiety and depression in elderly patients receiving treatment for cerebral tumours. *Brain Injury*, 11, 129–35.

Kelly, P.J. and Hunt, C. (1994). The limited value of cytoreductive surgery in elderly patients with malignant gliomas. *Neurosurgery*, 34, 62–7.

Layon, A.J., George, B.E., Hamby, B., and Gallagher, T.J. (1995). Do elderly patients overutilize healthcare resources and benefit less from them than younger patients? A study of patients who underwent craniotomy for treatment of neoplasm. *Critical Care Medicine*, 23, 829–34.

Maciunas, R.J., Berger, M.S., and Copeland, B. (1996). Techniques for interactive image-guided neurosurgical intervention in primary brain tumors. *Neurosurgery Clinics of North America*, 7, 245–66.

Meckling S., Dold, O., Forsyth, P.A., Brasher, P., and Hagen, N.A. (1996). Malignant supratentorial glioma in the elderly: is radiotherapy useful? *Neurology*, 47, 901–5.

Muir, C., Waterhouse, J., Mack, T., *et al.* (ed.) (1987). *Cancer incidence in five continents*. IARC Scientific Publications, Volume V, No. 88. International Agency for Research on Cancer, Lyon.

Riggs, J.E. (1995). Rising primary malignant brain tumor mortality in the elderly. A manifestation of differential survival. *Archives of Neurology*, 52, 571–5.

Salcman, M. (1992). Intracranial hemorrhage caused by brain tumor. In *Intracerebral hematomas* (ed. H.H. Kaufman), pp. 95–106. Raven Press, New York.

Symon, L., Bordi, L.T., Compton, J.S., Sabin, I.H., and Sayin, E. (1989). Acoustic neuroma: a review of 392 cases. *British Journal of Neurosurgery*, 3, 343–8.

Werner, M.H., Phuphanich, S., and Lyman, G.H. (1995). The increasing incidence of malignant gliomas and primary central nervous system lymphoma in the elderly. *Cancer*, 76, 1634–42.

18.9 Intracranial abscess

Peter Heywood

Introduction

Intracranial abscess may occur within the brain parenchyma, in the extradural or subdural spaces, and occasionally in more than one tissue compartment. Brain abscess is suppurative necrosis of the brain parenchyma caused by infection with one or more organisms. The cranial dura is closely applied to the inner table of the skull—a collection of pus here constitutes an epidural abscess. There is a potential space between dura and arachnoid and pus here is called a subdural empyema.

Diagnosis and management of brain abscess has been improved greatly in recent years by developments in neuroimaging and greater use of identification methods for anaerobic infections; this is illustrated by a fall in overall fatality in an American population from 40 per cent in 1970 to 9 per cent in 1986 (Mamplam and Rosenblum 1988). Brain abscess remains a rare but treatable condition, a diagnosis easily missed especially when prompt access to neuroradiological facilities is not available.

Incidence

There have been no studies specifically examining the incidence of cerebral abscess in an elderly population. McClelland *et al.* (1978) in a community study based in Northern Ireland cite a declining overall incidence from five cases per million per annum in the 1950s to four cases per million per annum in the 1970s. Peak incidence occurred in middle age; 23 per cent of their cases were between the age of 60 and 80 years and there appeared to be a slight decrease in the incidence of cerebral abscess with age. In Olmstead County, Minnesota, between 1950 and 1981 the incidence in all age groups was higher at 11 per million per annum (Nicolosi *et al.* 1986).

Pathogenesis

Experimental work in animal models demonstrates that for abscess formation to take place the presence of an infectious agent is not sufficient—it is also necessary that the blood–brain barrier be breached and that there be some damage to adjacent brain tissue (Molinari *et al.* 1973). Cerebral abscess in the context of meningitis is rare.

Eighty per cent of brain abscesses are solitary. Their distribution in the lobes of the brain is in proportion to the volume of each region (Mamplam and Rosenblum 1988).

Cranial sources of infection

Most abscesses occur as a result of spread of infection to the central nervous system from an extracerebral source. Spread is usually from structures adjacent to the brain: from sinusitis, mastoiditis, or dental infections. Alternatively, there may be haematogenous seeding to the central nervous system, or direct implantation of organisms with a penetrating head injury or neurosurgical intervention. Middle ear and mastoid are now less important sources of infection in the developed world, but are still important sources in the developing world.

From an adjacent site of infection organisms colonize brain either directly through the skull bone (osteomyelitis) or through emissary veins, producing a suppurative vasculitis. Frontal sinus infection spreads to produce frontal lobe abscesses, ethmoidal and sphenoidal sinusitis spreads to frontal or temporal lobes, and ear infection spreads to produce temporal lobe or cerebellar abscesses. Earlier reviews found that 40 per cent of non-traumatic brain abscesses were secondary to a focus of infection adjacent to the brain with one-third due to chronic suppurative ear infection (McClelland *et al.* 1978), but more recent reviews have shown ear infections playing a lesser part in the aetiology of brain abscesses (Mamplam and Rosenblum 1988; Scliamser *et al.* 1988). Abscesses developing from contiguous sites are usually single and adjacent to the focus.

Clearly penetrating head trauma or neurosurgery can cause abscess, which will be localized around the site of injury.

Extracranial sources of infection

Approximately 30 per cent of brain abscesses arise from spread of organisms via the blood stream (McClelland *et al.* 1978; Mamplam and Rosenblum 1988). Haematogenous seeding from a remote site most often produces multiple lesions at the grey–white matter interface, in the territory of the middle cerebral artery. Most commonly in adults, seeding is from pulmonary sources when there is bronchiectasis, empyema, or lung abscess.

Infected heart valves may seed bacteria to produce mycotic aneurysms and septic infarcts with multiple microscopic rather than macroscopic abscesses (Kanter and Hart 1991). Any abnormality that allows blood to shunt the lungs, thus avoiding their filtering effect, predisposes to cerebral abscess; congenital heart disease would be comparatively rare in an elderly population, but elderly patients with pulmonary arteriovenous fistulas, for example in Osler–Weber–Rendu disease, are at increased risk due to their pulmonary shunts.

Cryptogenic abscess

No primary site of infection or predisposing factor can be found in the remaining approximately 25 per cent of patients who have a cryptogenic abscess (McClelland *et al.* 1978; Mamplam and Rosenblum 1988).

Risk factors

Immunosuppression increases the risk of brain abscess. In immunosuppressed patients the primary source of infection is more likely to be unknown, abscesses are more likely to be multiple, and the range of possible causative organisms much wider, including opportunistic organisms such as fungi and parasites. Predisposing conditions include HIV, diabetes, steroids, chemotherapy, immunosuppressive drugs, and sarcoid.

Subdural empyema and epidural abscess usually occur in the context of a sinusitis, otitis media, trauma, or neurosurgery.

Pathology

There are four stages in the development of a brain abscess (Table 1). From early cerebritis to capsule formation takes about 2 weeks. Over

the 2-week development period the necrotic centre and inflammatory surround gradually shrink and fibroblasts in the inflammatory surround produce the capsule. Initially around the necrotic and inflammatory centre there is little gliosis and oedema is maximal. Gradually the oedema settles and there is surrounding gliosis.

Microbiology

The three major pathogens responsible for bacterial meningitis, *Haemophilus influenzae*, *Streptococcus pneumoniae*, and *Neisseria meningitidis*, cause less than 1 per cent of brain abscesses. Streptococci are isolated from approximately 40 per cent of cerebral abscesses. Streptococci are common; most are micro-aerophilic species but anaerobic species also occur. Other anaerobes, especially *Bacteroides* species, are found in 30 per cent. Another important group of pathogens are the aerobic Gram-negative bacilli especially *Proteus*, these tend to be causative in abscesses originating from ear infection. *Staphylococcus aureus* accounts for most abscesses occurring after penetrating trauma. Abscesses seeded haematogenously have mixed flora. A mixture of two or more organisms is found in 30 to 60 per cent of cases. Subdural empyema is almost always streptococcal.

Meticulous technique in storing, handling, and culturing anaerobes is required to obtain a positive culture. Before the use of proper culture techniques, 50 per cent of abscesses were said to contain 'sterile pus'; now by the time abscesses are drained around 20 per cent yield no growth (de Louvois *et al.* 1977).

Intracranial tuberculoma is now rare in developed countries, but is not uncommon in South America and the Indian subcontinent. Tuberculomas are frequently multiple and in 50 per cent of cases there is no evidence of primary tuberculosis elsewhere. In those parts of the world where parasites are endemic cerebral abscess can complicate amoebiasis, schistosomiasis, and hydatid disease. *Taenia solium* may produce cerebral cysticercosis when larvae enter the blood stream from the gut and migrate to the brain. Cerebral cysticercosis is the most common cause of symptomatic epilepsy in South America.

Immunocompromised patients are especially at risk of parasitic and fungal infections. HIV predisposes particularly to *Toxoplasma gondii* abscess, but infection with a wide variety of other opportunistic infections is documented. Fungal infections have usually disseminated haematogenously from the oropharynx or lung to produce multiple abscesses.

Clinical presentation

Presentation of brain abscess is usually subacute; most patients have symptoms over 1 or 2 weeks before the diagnosis is established. Occasionally the presentation is with an indolent illness over several weeks to months; the reverse may be true with patients becoming catastrophically ill in the space of 1 or 2 days.

The symptoms and signs caused by brain abscess are related to the neuroanatomical location of the lesion or lesions and any associated mass effect (Garfield 1979). Raised intracranial pressure, a focal neurological deficit, and fever is the classic triad of cerebral abscess. The triad is present in up to 50 per cent of patients. Raised intracranial pressure presents with headache in 70 per cent of patients who frequently have nausea, vomiting, and altered mental state.

Table 1 Pathological development of brain abscess

	Early cerebritis (days 1–3)	Late cerebritis (days 4–9)	Early capsule formation (days 10–14)	Late capsule formation (day 14 on)
Necrotic centre and its inflammatory periphery	Debris, inflammatory cells, bacteria	Debris, pus; inflammatory cells peripherally	Centre shrinking; fibroblasts and macrophages peripherally	Centre shrinking; fibroblasts
Collagen capsule	None	Reticulin appears	Collagen forming	Collagen increasing
Adjacent cerebritis and new vessels	Cerebritis	Cerebritis maximum; new vessels forming	Cerebritis decreasing; new vessels maximum	Cerebritis immediately outside capsule
Surrounding oedema and gliosis	Oedema	Oedema maximum; gliosis begins	Oedema decreasing; gliosis increasing	Oedema minimal; gliosis continuing

Papilloedema is present in only 25 to 60 per cent; absence of papilloedema cannot therefore be regarded as signifying absence of raised intracranial pressure or that lumbar puncture is safe. Nuchal rigidity is present in 25 per cent. A focal neurological deficit accompanies 65 per cent of abscesses; hemiparesis is most common. A frontoparietal or temporal abscess may present with disturbance of higher function or visual field deficit. A brainstem abscess may present with cranial nerve palsies or cerebellar signs. Fever occurs in 45 to 50 per cent of cases, but is usually less than 38.6°C, unless there is associated meningitis or systemic infection. Seizures occur in 25 to 35 per cent of patients and may be the presenting feature.

Presentation in elderly people may be non-specific with confusion and general malaise, for this reason the diagnosis may be missed and other, more common, conditions considered first such as cerebrovascular disease or toxic confusional state. In a patient presenting with what appears to be a stroke, but whose deficit or conscious level deteriorates, it is important to consider the possibility of a cerebral abscess and obtain a brain scan. The extracerebral source of infection may dominate the clinical picture. In the immunosuppressed patient, systemic signs of infection may be absent. In meningitic presentations with neck stiffness and other signs of meningism, either the abscess is close to the surface of the brain or has already ruptured into the subarachnoid space, or there is impending tonsillar herniation.

The presentation of subdural empyema is similar to brain abscess, with headache, fever, symptoms and signs of raised intracranial pressure, and meningeal irritation; there may be focal neurological deficits. An epidural abscess may be accompanied by redness and swelling of the scalp overlying the abscess; it is unusual to find focal neurological deficits.

Diagnosis

Basic investigations are often unhelpful in brain abscess and therefore normal results do not exclude an abscess. Peripheral leucocytosis is seen in a minority, the erythrocyte sedimentation rate is often normal, and C-reactive protein may be elevated particularly at the stage of cerebritis. Blood culture is positive in only 10 to 20 per cent of cases. Lumbar puncture must not be undertaken because of the risk of brain herniation. If, inadvertently, lumbar puncture is performed, the

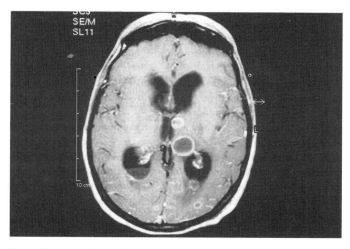

Fig. 1 T$_1$-weighted axial MRI scan with gadolinium enhancement showing multiple ring-enhancing abscesses and pus within the lateral ventricles.

results are characteristic of an aseptic meningitis: a lymphocytic pleocytosis, raised protein, and usually normal glucose. If there is meningitis or ventriculitis after rupture into the ventricles, then there is a reduced ratio of cerebrospinal fluid to blood glucose and organisms are seen in the cerebrospinal fluid.

Chest radiograph may reveal a chronic suppurative condition. A gas bubble or midline shift of a calcified pineal on plain skull radiograph may suggest a mass lesion; this may also reveal changes in the paranasal sinuses, ears, or mastoid bone or a skull fracture. High-voltage delta activity over the hemisphere with the lesion may be seen on electroencephalography, but is not diagnostic. In 95 per cent of patients a radio-isotope brain scan is abnormal revealing an area of increased uptake over the lesion. Where a CT scan or magnetic resonance imaging (MRI) are unavailable, both electroencephalography and radioisotopic brain scan are useful, but not diagnostic.

On brain scan, CT, or MRI, which are the investigations of choice, an abscess appears as a smooth circular thin-walled lesion with low density in the centre and surrounding oedema (Hansman *et al.* 1996) (Fig. 1). A scan will distinguish between an abscess at the cerebritis

18.10 Meningitis and encephalitis

Norman L. Pflaster and John C. M. Brust

Meningitis is not an isolated affliction of only the pia and arachnoid (leptomeningitis); concurrent encephalitis and vasculitis frequently accompany meningitis, and whether the organism is bacterial, fungal, or viral, encephalitic symptoms may predominate (Bell and Sahs 1987).

Epidemiology

Incidence

Bacterial meningitis

Both incidence and fatality rates of bacterial meningitis in adults are highest in elderly people. In 1978 the incidence of bacterial meningitis in the United States in patients over 60 years of age was 1.2 per 100 000, compared with 0.6 per 100 000 in people between 30 and 59 (Centers for Disease Control 1979). Table 1 (Choi 1992) demonstrates both attack and fatality rates for bacterial meningitis based on a Centers for Disease Control-sponsored surveillance study of a population of 34 million people in 1986. Pathogens that cause meningitis in elderly people are summarized in Fig. 1.

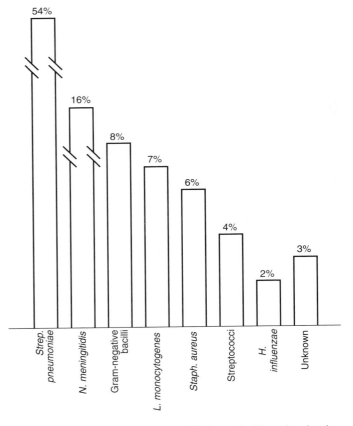

Fig. 1 Causes of bacterial meningitis in elderly people. (Reproduced with permission from Berk (1983).)

Table 1 Surveillance studies of bacterial meningitis in older adults

Organisms	Wenger et al. (1990)		Schlech et al. (1985)	
	AR	CFR	AR	CFR
Strep. pneumoniae	1.5	31	0.50	54
L. monocytogenes	0.5	—	0.10	41
H. influenzae	0.2	—	0.09	24
N. meningitidis	0.1	—	0.20	29
Group B Streptococcus	0.2	51	0.02	23
Others	1.0	—	0.30	62

AR, attack rate per 100 000; CFR, case fatality rate (per cent).

Data from Choi (1992).

Viral meningitis and encephalitis

Most central nervous system viral infections are mild and go undetected. The most common epidemic meningoencephalitis in the United States is St Louis encephalitis (Bale 1991). Two epidemiological patterns occur in the United States: episodic urban-centred epidemics in eastern and central states and cyclic transmission in the western rural areas. The infection there usually occurs from mid-summer to early autumn (Tsai *et al.* 1987). Fewer than 1 per cent of St Louis encephalitis infections are clinically apparent (Centers for Disease

Control 1991). When the older patient is infected with St Louis encephalitis, 85 per cent of the time it manifests as encephalitis, with the rest manifesting as meningitis. Outside the United States, another arbovirus, Japanese B encephalitis, is the most common cause of viral meningitis (Rotbart 1997).

Without seasonality, herpes simplex virus type 1 is the most common cause of non-epidemic, sporadic, acute focal encephalitis in the United States, accounting for 10 to 20 per cent of viral encephalitides (Corey and Spear 1986). At least half of the cases occur in patients over 50 years old (Whitley 1990).

An uncommon cause of encephalitis in the young, varicella zoster virus, does cause encephalitis in elderly people (Whitley 1990). The increasing incidence of symptomatic herpes zoster neuronitis with age (Jemsek et al. 1983) is probably related to the increased incidence of varicella zoster virus encephalitis.

Fatality

There has been a recent improvement in the detection and treatment of bacterial meningitis. A 1963 study of meningitis found a fatality of 50 per cent in patients above 60 years old (Quaade 1963). Data in Table 1 demonstrate more recent case fatality rates of 23 to 62 per cent depending on the organism.

Although the use of antibiotics has had a huge impact on morbidity and fatality from bacterial meningitis, this impact is undermined in elderly people by age-associated debility, concurrent infections, delay in diagnosis, and a susceptibility to particular pathogens.

Gorse et al. (1984) retrospectively reviewed records with discharge diagnosis of meningitis (all types) between 1970 and 1982 at a veterans' hospital and a community hospital. They compared 71 meningitis patients aged 50 years or more to 138 patients aged 15 to 49 years. Bacterial aetiology was more common in the elderly group (54 of 71) than in the younger group (32 of 138). Fatality due to bacterial meningitis was 44 per cent in the older patients (24 of 54), and 8 per cent in the younger patients (four of 32). Behrman et al. (1989) collected data between 1970 and 1985 from an urban hospital and found a 39 per cent fatality from bacterial meningitis in patients over 64 years old. Hodges and Perkins (1976) reported a fatality rate from bacterial meningitis of 40 per cent among patients 60 years or older, 11 per cent in those aged 0 to 19 years, and 37 per cent among those aged 40 to 59 years. A study of 667 cases of bacterial meningitis from Rhode Island hospitals between 1976 and 1985 found a case fatality of 54.8 per cent among 84 patients 65 years of age or more, compared with 10.3 per cent overall (Aronson et al. 1991).

An age of 60 years or above was found to be a risk factor for death in 493 episodes of bacterial meningitis in a large urban hospital reviewed retrospectively from 1962 to 1968 (Durand et al. 1993). Data regarding fatality in viral meningitis in elderly people is scant.

Fatality of herpes simplex type 1 encephalitis (all ages) has been reduced from 70 per cent to about 30 per cent with the use of aciclovir. Increased age was associated with decreased survival in patients with herpes simplex type 1 encephalitis in two studies comparing aciclovir and vidarabine (Skoldenberg et al. 1984; Whitley et al. 1986).

Fatality is also greatest among elderly people with St Louis encephalitis (Riggs et al. 1965; Centers for Disease Control 1979). The higher fatality of St Louis encephalitis in elderly people means that its presentation in older patients will often be confused with the usually more virulent herpes simplex type 1 encephalitis.

Although eastern equine encephalitis causes only 1 per cent of encephalitis cases in the United States, it has the highest fatality rate among the human arboviral diseases in North America (Bale 1991), and although eastern equine encephalitis affects the young more than the old (Bale 1991), unfavourable outcomes and larger lesions on imaging studies are more common in older patients.

Predominantly in tropical and subtropical Asia, Japanese B encephalitis is the most important of the arboviruses from the perspective of worldwide morbidity and fatality. With a 20 to 50 per cent fatality and significant neurological sequelae in survivors, the most vulnerable populations are younger than 10 and older than 65 years.

Pathogens

Massanari (1977) separated pathogens into two groups, the usual (*Streptococcus pneumoniae*, *Neisseria meningitidis*, and *Haemophilus influenzae*) and the unusual (all others). In his review of studies from community and tertiary care hospitals, he found that at least 20 to 25 per cent of elderly patients with bacterial meningitis have unusual pathogens. Berk combined data from seven case series, summarized in Fig. 1, demonstrating that *Strep. pneumoniae*, *N. meningitidis*, and Gram-negative bacilli are the three most common causes of meningitis in elderly people (Quaade 1963; Swartz and Dodge 1965; Weiss et al. 1967; Jensen et al. 1969; Jonsson and Alvin 1971; Massanari 1977; Newton and Wilczynski 1979; Berk 1983).

Fatality associated with particular pathogens has been compared (see Table 1). These data, more recent than those used in Fig. 1, may indicate an increase in the relative number of cases of *H. influenzae* meningitis. Furthermore, neither *Staphylococcus aureus*, nor Gram-negative bacilli are included in the later data. Berk emphasized that the increased frequency of Gram-negative bacilli and *Staph. aureus* in older patients contributes to their poorer prognosis (Berk 1983).

Pneumococcus

In both young and old adults, the most common cause of bacterial meningitis is *Strep. pneumoniae*, representing 60 to 70 per cent of cases (Carpenter and Petersdorf 1962; Swartz and Dodge 1965; Newton and Wilczynski 1979). Pneumonia is most often the primary source of infection; other predisposing illnesses are sinusitis, mastoiditis, and acute otitis media. Carpenter and Petersdorf (1962) found that when there is a pre-existing pneumonia, fatality is higher, perhaps the result of delayed diagnosis in patients with a known source of infection.

Positive blood cultures are found in 20 per cent of patients in hospital with pneumonia attributed to *Strep. pneumoniae* (Musher 1991), and pneumococcal bacteraemia carries a high fatality. In a review of group B streptococcal meningitis in adults, there was a trend for the presence of bacteraemia or advanced age to be associated with an increased fatality rate (Dunne and Quagliarello 1993).

Skull fracture with a dural tear predisposes to meningitis, particularly from *Strep. pneumoniae* (Applebaum 1960; Hand and Sanford 1970). Recurrent meningitis in adults is most commonly associated with traumatic head injury (Schneider and Thompson 1957), and most of these are due to *Strep. pneumoniae*. As at all ages, splenectomy and ethanol abuse predispose elderly patients to *Strep. pneumoniae* meningitis.

Neisseria meningitidis

Compared with younger adults and children, elderly people are infrequently infected with *N. meningitidis*. Because it occurs in epidemics (Young *et al.* 1972), *N. meningitidis* as the cause of meningitis ranges from zero to 34 per cent (Swartz and Dodge 1965; Jensen *et al.* 1969; Geiseler *et al.* 1980). Figure 2 shows that although the incidence of bacterial meningitis increases in elderly people for *H. influenzae*, *Strep. pneumoniae*, group B *Streptococcus*, *Listeria monocytogenes*, and others, this trend is not seen for *N. meningitidis* (Wenger *et al.* 1990).

Staphylococcus aureus

A Mayo clinic study from 1948 to 1958 showed that in patients aged 51 to 80 years, *Staph. aureus* meningitis was the most common pathogen, occurring in 28 per cent of cases; many were associated with neurosurgery (Eigler *et al.* 1961). More recently, *Staph. aureus* meningitis has been shown to occur at a frequency among nosocomial meningitides of about 20 per cent (Hodges and Perkins 1976). Data from the United States (Schlech *et al.* 1985; see Fig. 1) and England (Newton and Wilczynski 1979) show that the frequency is much less among community-acquired meningitides.

Gram-negative bacilli

Frailty, exposure to immunosuppressants or broad-spectrum antibiotics, and invasive procedures increase the risk of Gram-negative infection in elderly people (Berk 1983). Berk (1983) and Durand *et al.* (1993) described an increasing relative frequency of Gram-negative bacillary meningitis in adults. Durand *et al.* (1993), moreover, found Gram-negative bacilli in 33 per cent of nosocomial meningitis, but in only 3 per cent of the community-acquired episodes. The most common predisposing factor is cranial trauma, accidental or neurosurgical (LeFrock *et al.* 1985). Postneurosurgical meningitis occurs in 0.5 per cent of patients and 70 to 80 per cent are due to Gram-negative bacilli (Mangi *et al.* 1975; Buckwold *et al.* 1977). Gram-negative bacteraemia also predisposes older patients in hospital to Gram-negative bacillary meningitis (LeFrock *et al.* 1985).

When Gram-negative meningitis occurs spontaneously, the urinary tract is the primary source of infection. In 60 to 70 per cent of such cases, *Escherichia coli* or *Klebsiella pneumoniae* is responsible (LeFrock *et al.* 1985). Berk and McCabe (1981), reviewing 30 cases of Gram-negative bacillary meningitis, identified retrospectively from 1968 to 1978, found that 40 per cent (12 of 30) were in patients over the age of 60. Seven were non-neurosurgical, non-traumatic Gram-negative bacillary meningitis, five had a urinary source of which three had indwelling Foley catheters, and one had just undergone retrograde catheterization for calculi. These patients had an abrupt onset and a fulminant course, causing death in three. By contrast, postcraniotomy cases are usually of a more insidious onset. As with any form of meningitis, the prognosis is worse if coma or bacteraemia is present (Mangi *et al.* 1975).

Cherubin *et al.* (1981) found an extremely high fatality in elderly people with *E. coli* meningitis. Between 1972 and 1979, of 29 cases occurring in patients over the age of 60, 28 died. They found that the elderly group was more likely to suffer from alcoholism or primary septicaemia; other workers (Mangi *et al.* 1975; Crane and Lerner 1978; Berk and McCabe 1981) described Gram-negative meningitis in

patients with sacral decubiti, chronic osteomyelitis, and prostatectomy (Berk 1983). Cherubin *et al.* (1981) found that *Klebsiella* occurred about half as frequently as *E. coli* among meningitis patients. About a third of such cases were in elderly people, half had septicaemia, and all died.

Listeria

Epidemics have been recorded in newborns in western France and South Africa (Cherubin *et al.* 1981); in the United States *Listeria* meningitis occurs more often in immunosuppressed hosts and elderly people. Diminished cell-mediated immunity is a major risk factor for the development of *Listeria* meningitis (Armstrong and Wong 1982). Although *Listeria* accounted for 0.9 per cent of reported cases of bacterial meningitis in New York City between 1972 and 1979, 77.3 per cent occurred in patients over 50 years of age (Cherubin *et al.* 1981). In about half of these a chronic condition such as renal failure, cancer, a connective tissue disorder, ethanol abuse, or high-dose corticosteroid use was noted. Fatality rate was 83.3 per cent in patients above the age of 70 years, and 17 per cent in patients under the age of 50. In cancer patients, *Listeria* was the most common bacteria causing meningitis, responsible for 22 per cent of the cases (Chernik *et al.* 1973). In the multistate surveillance study (Wenger *et al.* 1990) *Listeria* was responsible in 3.2 per cent of cases of community- and hospital-acquired meningitis.

Streptococcus

The presence of bacteraemia occurs in a large proportion of group B *Streptococcus* infections (Farley 1995), but the organism is an uncommon cause of community-acquired meningitis. Durand *et al.* (1993) reviewed 493 episodes of meningitis in adults and found that group B *Streptococcus* and ungrouped streptococci accounted for 1.6 per cent of community-acquired meningitis and 5.3 per cent of nosocomial meningitis. A review of group B *Streptococcus* meningitis in adults found a bimodal age distribution of patients with this disease: one peak in the mid-twenties and a second observed in the mid-sixties (Dunne and Quagliarello 1993). Dunne and Quagliarello (1993) found group B *Streptococcus* meningitis without comorbid conditions to have a fatality rate of zero; by contrast, fatality was 45 per cent in those with comorbid conditions.

Haemophilus influenzae

H. influenzae meningitis is common in children but rare in elderly people (see Fig. 2). Type B *H. influenzae* is the most common serotype that causes bacteraemia and meningitis. In a multistate surveillance study, Wenger *et al.* (1990) found *H. influenzae* to be the cause of meningitis in less than 5 per cent of patients over the age of 60; the figure is even less in younger adults. The increased susceptibility to *H. influenzae* infection in elderly adults may be related to lower levels of antibody in these individuals (Norden *et al.* 1970). Diabetes mellitus and other debilitating diseases predispose to *H. influenzae* meningitis in adults (Bell and Sahs 1987).

Pseudomonas

An unusual form of meningitis in elderly people is related to malignant external otitis. Most often seen in elderly diabetic patients, a granulomatous inflammatory process extends through the floor of the

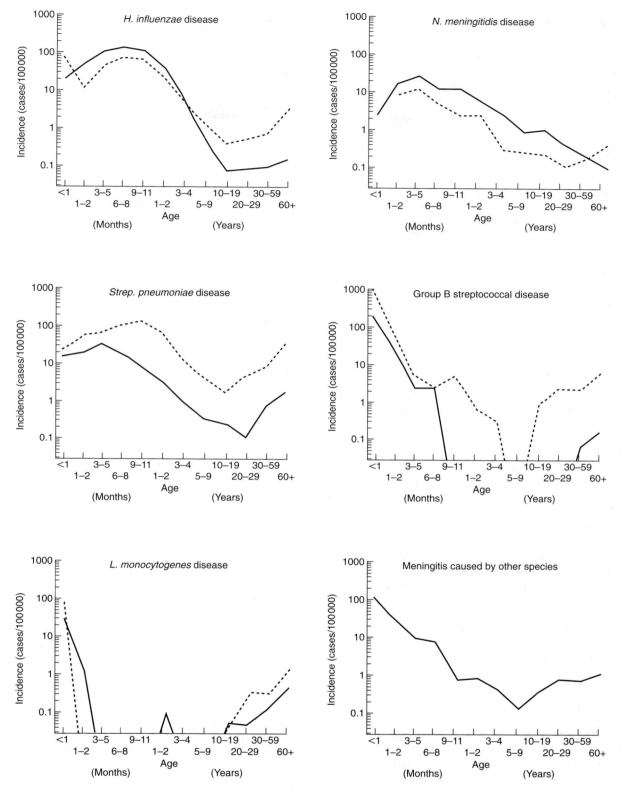

Fig. 2 Age-specific 1986 attack rates of meningitic (——) and non-meningitic (- - -) disease caused by major pathogenic agents of bacterial meningitis. Attack rates for non-meningitic disease caused by *S. pneumoniae* and group B *Streptococcus* are calculated from surveillance and audit data from New Jersey and Oklahoma. All other rates are calculated from surveillance areas in five states: Missouri, New Jersey, Oklahoma, Tennesee, and Washington. (Reproduced with permission from Wenger *et al.* (1990).)

external ear to the parotid gland and from there to the temporo-mandibular joint, the stylomastoid foramen, and eventually the temporal bone. At the site of the stylomastoid foramen, the facial nerve is affected. After osteomyelitis occurs, spread to the skull base may involve cranial nerves 9, 10, or 11; transverse sinus thrombosis sometimes occurs (Zaky *et al.* 1976). *Pseudomonas* meningitis is a late stage of this disorder.

Anaerobes

The immunosuppressed host is prone to anaerobic meningitis. Chronic otitis media and mastoiditis are the most common underlying foci of anaerobic infection leading to anaerobic meningitis. Brain abscess with mixed infection, especially Gram-negative bacilli and streptococci, sometimes occurs. Infection of the sinuses, pharynx, head, or neck as well as cancer, head trauma, and neurosurgery are other sources of infection (Heerema *et al.* 1979).

Spirochaetes

Stroke and dementia affect elderly people (see Chapters 11.1 and 18.20), and neurosyphilis is sometimes a diagnostic consideration. Although an uncommon cause of these illnesses, it is readily treatable. Infectious syphilis can be acquired at any age. In 1979, the Centers for Disease Control found that 3.5 per cent of reported primary infections were in people aged 50 or more (Jaffe and Kabins 1982). Syphilitic infection of the nervous system is often asymptomatic in the young; as patients with neurosyphilis age, the proportion of symptomatic infection gradually increases (Jaffe and Kabins 1982). Both meningovascular syphilis (which causes a multitude of symptoms, including stroke) and paretic neurosyphilis (which causes psychosis or dementia) are often associated with cerebrospinal fluid pleocytosis. General paresis is most common among elderly people (Fiumara 1983).

Although acute syphilitic meningitis, occurring most often within the first 2 years of infection, is rare (Merrit and Moore 1935), acute borrelial meningitis is not. Typically occurring early in infection, it occurs in up to 10 per cent of infected patients; encephalomyelitis probably occurs in no more than 0.1 per cent of patients with Lyme disease (Halperin *et al.* 1990; Hansen and Lebech 1992).

Mycobacterium

Tuberculous meningitis in elderly people is uncommon (see Chapter 12.5). This age group, however, is the largest repository of the tubercle bacillus in the United States (Stead and Lofren 1983). In non-Hispanic white people in the United States, the majority of pulmonary tuberculosis occurs in those between 60 and 90 years old (Stead *et al.* 1985; Iseman 1996). Clusters of elderly Americans in nursing homes have been a source of significant spread of infection (Stead *et al.* 1985). Only 5 to 15 per cent of those infected with the tubercle bacillus get tuberculous meningitis (Bell and Sahs 1987). Occasionally, atypical mycobacteria are encountered (Yamamoto *et al.* 1967). Prognosis is worse in elderly people, ethanol abusers, and those whose treatment is initiated late in the course of the illness (Falk 1962; Barrett-Connor 1967; Haas *et al.* 1977; Ogawa *et al.* 1987).

Fungi

Cryptococcus neoformans, the most common cause of fungal meningitis (Salaki *et al.* 1984), causes a chronic basilar meningitis (like tuberculous meningitis) and a more diffuse meningitis with microscopic and macroscopic clusters of cryptococcomas (Sabetta and Andriole 1985). As with mycobacterial disease, elderly people are predisposed to this and other fungal infections because of decreased cell-mediated immunity (Salaki *et al.* 1984). The two major risk factors are AIDS and corticosteroid therapy (Perfect *et al.* 1983).

Enteroviridae

Aseptic meningitis is a meningeal inflammation in which a bacterial agent cannot be identified. A benign course and lack of encephalitis is implied in this definition (Rotbart 1997). Enteroviral meningitis occurs rarely in adults and even more rarely in elderly people, probably a consequence of immunity due to previous exposure. Nonetheless, the enterovirus is the most common cause of aseptic meningitis in adults, estimated to cause between 60 and 90 per cent of all cases of viral meningitis and meningoencephalitis in the United States (Mosis *et al.* 1977; Kinnunen *et al.* 1987; Rotbart 1997).

Clinical manifestations

Presentation

Carpenter and Petersdorf (1962), observed three distinct patterns of presentation of bacterial meningitis: (a) rapid progression from headache and confusion to lethargy and coma; (b) headache and meningismus gradually worsening over 1 to 7 days (many with accompanying respiratory symptoms); (c) respiratory syndrome preceding the meningitis by 1 to 3 weeks. In elderly people, meningitis can present with any of these patterns (Berk 1983). Contrary to expectation, Carpenter and Petersdorf found that delayed presentation (all age groups) did not predict poor outcome. They postulated that this was due to selection of less fulminant cases. A recent Croatian study of pneumococcal meningitis found that admission to the hospital was often delayed in elderly people. Furthermore, the older patients (fatality 57 per cent) presented in stupor or coma nearly 62 per cent of the time, while the younger patients (fatality 20 per cent) presented in stupor or coma 31 per cent of the time (Barsic *et al.* 1992). In Swartz and Dodge's series (1965), five of 12 patients with pneumococcal meningitis presented in coma and died on the first hospital day.

For more chronic meningitides, delays in diagnosis of either cryptococcal or tuberculous meningitis are associated with increased fatality (Stockstill and Kauffman 1983). Ogawa *et al.* (1987) confirmed that advanced clinical stage predicted a higher fatality in tuberculous meningitis. The presentation of a person with tuberculous or cryptococcal meningitis is less acute, causing many patients to seek medical attention later in the illness. Stockstill and Kauffman (1983) showed that about 25 per cent of patients (all ages) waited until the fourth week of their illness to seek medical attention, although immunosuppressed patients with tuberculous or cryptococcal meningitis may present acutely (Sabetta and Andriole 1985). Some patients with cryptococcal meningitis present after years of untreated symptoms (Campbell *et al.* 1981). Ogawa *et al.* (1987) reported symptoms developing in tuberculous meningitis 2 to 120 days prior to admission (no age data included). The studies do not provide details of these symptoms and the authors believe that these patients have reactivated non-meningitic tuberculosis prior to the development of meningitis and that untreated tuberculous meningitis in adults, as in children, it is usually fatal within 3 weeks (Ogawa et al. 1987).

Patients with herpes simplex type encephalitis often have a non-specific prodrome of headache, fever, malaise, or vomiting. Most untreated patients have a rapidly progressive course with focal signs, focal seizures, or both, and within 1 to 2 weeks, coma and death. A more indolent course with hallucinations, memory loss, or abnormal behaviour can be seen (Baringer 1978).

Fever

Fever is probably the most consistent sign in elderly patients with bacterial meningitis (Behrman et al. 1989), occurring in 90 to 100 per cent of cases; it may be less frequent in younger patients (Gorse et al. 1984). Many elderly patients with hospital-acquired Gram-negative meningitis have a 1- to 2-week history of low-grade fever and lethargy (Berk and McCabe 1981).

Meningismus

Resistance to passive flexion of the neck (nuchal rigidity) is not uncommon in normal elderly people, ranging from 57 to 81 per cent (Gorse et al. 1984; Behrman et al. 1989). Nuchal rigidity was a positive prognostic sign in one study, suggesting its correlation with an immune response (Hojfgaard Rasmussen et al. 1992). In nuchal rigidity there is resistance to forward flexion, but not to passive side-to-side rotation. In cervical osteoarthritis there is resistance to motion in all directions (Roos et al. 1997). Also to be considered is cervical rigidity due to parkinsonism. Kernig's and Brudzinski's signs are often present, although non-specific, with meningeal inflammation. However, they are frequently lost during coma (Berk 1983). In tuberculous meningitis, meningismus is reportedly absent in 25 to 80 per cent of patients (adults, all ages) (Zuger and Lowy 1997).

Altered mental status

Elderly meningitis patients are especially likely to become encephalopathic. Therefore, meningitis and encephalitis enter early into the differential diagnosis of altered mental status in elderly people, whether or not there is any evidence of infection. Interpretation of abnormal mentation is obviously difficult if the baseline mental status is not known. In bacterial meningitis, presentation with severe mental status change is more frequent in elderly people (Gorse et al. 1984). Behrman et al. (1989) found abnormal mentation in 96 per cent of their elderly patients with bacterial meningitis. Durand et al. (1993) reported that 22 per cent of patients responded only to pain at presentation. Predictably, impaired mental status at time of presentation correlates with poor outcome (Carpenter and Petersdorf 1962; Schwartz and Dodge 1965; Hodges and Perkins 1976; Gorse et al. 1984; Behrman et al. 1989).

The neurosurgical patient with altered mental status presents additional problems. Lethargy in the postoperative period can easily be attributed to neurosurgery itself or to medication. The threshold for suspicion of meningitis and cerebrospinal fluid examination in this group must be extremely low.

Stockstill and Kauffman (1983) found that altered mental status and nuchal rigidity were twice as common in patients with tuberculous compared with cryptococcal meningitis. The ages of these patients were not given. The authors' experience is similar. In patients with meningovascular syphilis, Merritt et al. (1946) described a prodrome of headache, vertigo, insomnia, or various psychiatric disturbances weeks or months prior to more fulminant illness, including stroke. Most patients with herpes simplex virus type 1 encephalitis present with a history of altered consciousness, and 64 to 75 per cent have diminished level of alertness at the start of treatment (Skoldenberg et al. 1984; Whitley et al. 1986). Of patients in a recent review of eastern equine encephalitis 44 per cent had confusion on hospital admission (Deresiewicz et al. 1997).

Seizures

Seizures are a non-diagnostic marker of cerebritis. In the series studied by Gorse et al. (1984), seizures (type not stated) occurred in 16 of 54 (30 per cent) of patients with bacterial meningitis in the elderly group and none of the 32 patients in the younger comparison group. Zuger and Lowy (1997) described seizures in up to 13 per cent of adult patients with tuberculous meningitis, and Sabetta and Andriole (1985), studying three pre-AIDS series of adults with cryptococcal meningitis, found seizures in 15 per cent. At least 60 per cent of patients with herpes simplex virus type 1 encephalitis have seizures (Whitley et al. 1982; Skoldenberg et al. 1984), and a National Institutes of Health study found that focal seizures occurred twice as often as generalized seizures in that disease. Half of 36 patients with eastern equine encephalitis had seizures, which were focal in four (Deresiewicz et al. 1997).

Focal signs

When focality is found, abscess must be considered. Fever is absent in almost half of patients with cerebral abscess (Choi 1992). Behrman et al. (1989) found that seven of 57 central nervous system infections were focal (intraparenchymal abscess, epidural abscess, or subdural abscess), and all seven had focal findings on examination. However, about 40 per cent of patients studied by Behrman et al. (1989) and Gorse et al. (1984) series had focal signs without abscesses or empyema. Gorse et al. (1984) found that only 22 per cent (seven of 32) of their younger comparison group had focal signs. Behrman et al. (1989) found that focal signs occurred in 12 of 28 patients with bacterial meningitis, three of three with tuberculous meningitis, and two of two with cryptococcal meningitis.

Focal signs are often the result of stroke, often secondary to vasculitis related to inflammatory tracking along the Virchow–Robin spaces (Igarashi et al. 1984; Hsieh et al. 1992). Cortical vein thrombosis or sagittal sinus thrombosis can occur early or late (weeks) during the course of meningitis and may present with an acute worsening of mental status or seizures (Choi 1992). Subclinical focal cerebral abnormalities that are otherwise inapparent are often seen when there is a toxic or metabolic stressor such as infection.

Over 30 per cent of patients (all ages) with viral encephalitis have hemiparesis on presentation (Whitley et al. 1982). The mechanism is usually focal cerebritis (Zuger and Lowy 1997), which in the case of herpes simplex virus type 1 preferentially affects the temporal lobes (Davis and Johnson 1979); focal seizures may be followed by postictal weakness. Forty-four per cent of patients with eastern equine encephalitis had focal weakness (Deresiewicz *et al.* 1997).

Cranial nerve palsies

Cranial nerve palsies, reflecting basilar meningitis, are present in 15 to 40 per cent of adults with tuberculous meningitis and one-third of patients with cryptococcal meningitis (Sabetta and Andriole 1985; Zuger and Lowy 1997). Gorse *et al.* (1984) found cranial neuropathies in 13 of 86 (15 per cent) patients with bacterial meningitis, with no difference between young and old. One series (Whitley *et al.* 1982) of herpes simplex virus type 1 encephalitis found cranial nerve palsies in one-third of the patients. Cranial nerve palsies were observed in 25 per cent of patients with eastern equine encephalitis (Deresiewicz *et al.* 1997).

Hydrocephalus

Hydrocephalus occurred during treatment in 9 per cent of the older adults but none of the younger adults studied by Gorse *et al.* (1984). In a series of 111 patients of all ages with cryptococcal meningitis prior to the AIDS era, 10 developed hydrocephalus (Diamond and Bennett 1974). In adults, tuberculous meningitis often causes hydrocephalus (Bhagwati 1971).

Laboratory procedures

Although history and physical examination are the cornerstones of diagnosis in bacterial meningitis, the older the patient, the more fragile is this foundation. Cerebrospinal fluid examination makes or breaks the diagnosis of meningitis. However, fever with focality on neurological examination indicates abscess, and, when the patient's condition is permitting, emergency CT scan should be performed prior to lumbar puncture. If papilloedema or signs of transtentorial herniation are present, or if CT scan demonstrates a clinically significant intracranial mass lesion, laboratory procedure (the cerebrospinal fluid examination) may have to be delayed and antimicrobial therapy started immediately.

The role of empirical parenteral antimicrobial therapy prior to laboratory procedure has not been critically analysed; Talan *et al.* (1988), reviewing the literature, found that the data are inadequate to assess the effect on prognosis of a short delay in treatment. However, cerebrospinal fluid white blood cells, protein, and glucose do not change within a few hours of beginning antimicrobial therapy, and the cerebrospinal fluid Gram stain often remains positive. Partial oral antibiotic treatment leads to a 4 to 33 per cent decrease in the number of positive cerebrospinal fluid cultures (Talan *et al.* 1988).

Cerebrospinal fluid opening pressure

In a series of patients of all ages Merritt and Fremont-Smith (1938) found that cerebrospinal fluid pressure is elevated in 90 per cent of patients with purulent meningitis, most often between 200 and 500 mmH$_2$O. In older patients, the opening pressure may be less elevated than expected as a result of decreased brain volume. Acute viral encephalitis is often accompanied by pressures of 200 to 400 mmH$_2$O. Herpes simplex virus type 1 encephalitis causes intracranial hypertension because of its predilection for focal cerebritis and oedema in the temporal lobes. Of 27 patients with herpes simplex virus type 1

encephalitis who died and had autopsies, eight had herniation syndromes and four of eight had cerebrospinal fluid opening pressures above 500 mmH$_2$O (Durand *et al.* 1993).

Cerebrospinal fluid cells

The normal cerebrospinal fluid white blood cell count is less than 5 mononuclear cells/ml (Fishman 1980). Ninety per cent of patients (all ages) with bacterial meningitis have white blood cell count over 100/ml (Roos *et al.* 1997). The white blood cell differential typically shows polymorphonuclear leucocytes in bacterial meningitis, but other diseases such as leukaemic infiltration, postirradiation damage, and parameningeal infection may create a similar white blood cell count profile in the cerebrospinal fluid. Lymphocytes usually predominate in aseptic, mycobacterial, spirochaetal, and fungal meningitis, but neutrophils can predominate. Red blood cell counts are usually not present in the cerebrospinal fluid in bacterial meningitis and raise suspicion for herpes encephalitis, trauma, or subarachnoid haemorrhage. Xanthochromia (yellow supernatant fluid) is from haem pigments and their breakdown products following subarachnoid haemorrhage; cerebrospinal fluid protein greater than 150 mg/dl, bilirubinaemia, and carotenaemia can also cause xanthochromia, and the cerebrospinal fluid of elderly patients sometimes contains chromogens that impart a yellowish tinge (Fishman 1980).

Cerebrospinal fluid microscopy

Gram stain, acid-fast stain, and India ink can help to establish the diagnosis. Behrman *et al.* (1989) described the utility of Gram stain in that 27 of 37 patients (73 per cent) survived when an appropriate antimicrobial was used initially, whereas three of 11 patients (27 per cent) survived when not. It may be difficult to distinguish some Gram-negative bacteria, for example, *H. influenzae* versus *Neisseria* versus Gram-negative enteric bacilli, and some Gram-positive bacteria, for example, *Listeria* versus *Streptococcus* (Stein *et al.* 1969; Berk 1983).

Cerebrospinal fluid protein

Elevated cerebrospinal fluid protein may be the result of many illnesses in elderly people, including diabetic neuropathy and rheumatoid arthritis. Any disruption of the blood–brain barrier will elevate cerebrospinal fluid protein. In isolation, a mild elevation of cerebrospinal fluid protein means very little. If the protein is very high, without cells, one might consider an obstruction to the flow of cerebrospinal fluid. Trauma, including a traumatic lumbar puncture, can lead to an erroneous reading due to mixing of cerebrospinal fluid with blood (Fishman 1980).

Cerebrospinal fluid glucose

Data not specific to elderly people show that cerebrospinal fluid glucose is diminished to 31 per cent of the concurrent serum glucose in 70 per cent of patients with bacterial meningitis (Marton and Gean 1986). The glucose is typically lower in patients with bacterial meningitis than with aseptic meningitis, but cerebrospinal fluid glucose is not useful in distinguishing mycobacterial, treponemal, spirochaetal, or fungal meningitides. Low glucose in the cerebrospinal fluid indicates a poor prognosis in pneumococcal meningitis, especially in elderly people (Weiss *et al.* 1967; Behrman *et al.* 1989). With tuberculous meningitis the glucose is typically moderately reduced, but it is highly variable (Tandon 1978). Cryptococcal meningitis usually causes a cerebrospinal fluid glucose of 10 to 40 mg/dl, but normal levels can be seen (Fishman 1980). With syphilitic meningitis and aseptic meningitis cerebrospinal fluid glucose is normal or moderately reduced; extreme reductions are rare (Merritt and Moore 1935; Rotbart 1997).

Cerebrospinal fluid immunological tests

Coagglutination and latex agglutination tests provide rapid diagnosis of bacterial meningitis. Commercial kits supply antisera to the cell wall or antibacterial antibodies and detect the presence of live or dead bacteria in the cerebrospinal fluid. These tests vary in their sensitivity. Both types are sensitive in detecting *H. influenzae*, *S. pneumoniae*, and *N. meningitidis*, with a specificity of 96 to 100 per cent for all three. Their most effective use is in partially treated meningitis and in patients without organisms on Gram stain. The cerebrospinal fluid Venereal Disease Research Laboratory test is very specific if not contaminated by blood (Simon 1985). When rheumatoid factor and other agglutinins are excluded, latex agglutination detects cryptococcal polysaccharide antigen with over 90 per cent sensitivity and specificity (Roos *et al.* 1997).

Polymerase chain reaction

The cause of acute encephalitis is determined in only 20 to 66 per cent of cases (Sivertsen and Christensen 1996). The polymerase chain reaction is a promising technique that will probably improve diagnostic yield. For herpes simplex virus type 1 encephalitis detection of herpes simplex virus type 1 DNA with polymerase chain reaction carries a sensitivity and specificity of 91 and 92 per cent, respectively (Whitley 1997). For neurosyphilis, tuberculous meningitis, and bacterial meningitis polymerase chain reaction techniques are being refined and will probably be widely used in the future (Hook 1997; Roos *et al.* 1997; Zuger and Lowy 1997).

CT and magnetic resonance imaging

Although of little value in the initial diagnosis of meningitis (except to include mass lesions), neuroimaging is helpful in defining its complications (Table 2). Focal findings on examination, signs of raised intracranial pressure, or seizures should be investigated with CT scan or magnetic resonance imaging (MRI) (Cinnamon *et al.* 1994).

Recurrent meningitis, especially with cerebrospinal fluid rhinorrhoea, would indicate the need for a CT. Cerebrospinal fluid leaks usually begin at the time of head injury, but they may become apparent after an interval of days or weeks. CT scan, combining fine slices in two planes with bone windows, can demonstrate the site of cerebrospinal fluid leakage (Lloyd *et al.* 1994) as well as a parameningeal infection such as osteomyelitis.

Prior to MRI, serial electroencephalographs combined with CT were useful in diagnosing the temporal lobe abnormalities of herpes simplex virus type 1 encephalitis (Vas and Cracco 1990); today, MRI is probably more sensitive. Furthermore, MRI was found to be useful in distinguishing eastern equine encephalitis from herpes simplex virus type 1 encephalitis. MRI abnormalities unique to eastern equine

Table 2 Complications of bacterial meningitis

Central nervous system	Systemic
Infarction	SIADH
Seizures	Shock
Increased ICP	Coagulopathy
Hydrocephalus	Septic endocarditis
Subdural effusions	Arthritis
Subdural/epidural empyemas	Fever
Cortical vein/sinus thrombosis	Bacteraemia
Cerebritis and/or abscess	
Cranial nerve palsies	
Ventriculitis	

ICP, intracranial pressure; SIADH, syndrome of inappropriate ADH secretion.

encephalitis consist of basal ganglia and thalamic changes; and patients with larger lesions tended to be older (Deresiewicz *et al.* 1997). MRI and magnetic resonance angiography are useful in both tuberculous and cryptococcal meningitis, in which basilar arachnoiditis results in endarteritis of the arteries of the circle of Willis and cranial neuropathies (Wilson and Castillo 1994).

Electroencephalography

The electroencephalogram is nearly always abnormal in viral encephalitides; the degree of slowing in acute encephalitis usually parallels the severity of clinical findings. After 2 to 15 days, pseudoperiodic epileptiform discharges often appear. Electroencephalography demonstrates focal abnormalities in up to 81 per cent of patients with clinical features of herpes simplex virus type 1 encephalitis (Vas and Cracco 1990) and a normal electroencephalogram practically excludes the diagnosis of herpes simplex virus type 1 encephalitis in a symptomatic patient (Gasecki and Steg 1991). Non-convulsive status epilepticus carries significant morbidity and fatality, and both the incidence and fatality of non-convulsive status epilepticus are greater in elderly people than in other age groups, including those with meningitis and encephalitis (Barry and Hauser 1993; Krumholz *et al.* 1995). Therefore electroencephalography should be considered in any elderly patient with meningoencephalitis and altered mentation.

Diagnostic approach

Typical signs may be absent in elderly patients with meningitis or encephalitis. Only 18 per cent of the series investigated by Behrman *et al.* (1989) had fever, headache, and meningismus. However, 96 per cent had two or more signs, and half had three signs on admission. When there is any doubt as to the diagnosis, lumbar puncture should be performed.

Treatment

Antibiotics

Antibiotics must penetrate the blood–brain barrier and be present in sufficient concentration in the cerebrospinal fluid to be bactericidal.

Table 3 Antibiotics recommended for empirical therapy in patients with suspected bacterial meningitis who have a non-diagnostic Gram stain of cerebrospinal fluid

	Probable pathogen	Choice of antibiotic
18–50 years	Strep. pneumoniae or N. meningitidis	Broad-spectrum cephalosporin
>50 years	Strep. pneumoniae or N. meningitidis or Gram-negative bacilli	Ampicillin plus broad-spectrum cephalosporin
With impaired cellular immunity	L. monocytogenes or Gram-negative bacilli	Ampicillin plus ceftazidime
With head trauma, neurosurgery, or CSF shunt	Straphylococci or Gram-negative bacilli or Strep. pneumoniae	Vancomycin plus ceftazidime

Adapted from Quagliarello and Scheld (1997).

The possible presence of β-lactamase-producing bacteria (penicillin-resistant *Streptococcus*, or *H. influenzae*), *Listeria*, tuberculosis, fungi, and viral encephalitis must be considered when initiating treatment in any patient with meningitis. Table 3 summarizes the initial therapy of meningitis in adults when a predisposing factor is considered, and Table 4 lists specific therapy of meningitis in adults based on Gram stain or culture.

In patients with community-acquired meningitis and no organism on Gram stain, β-lactamase producing streptococci have led to the use of third-generation cephalosporins, which will cover *H. influenzae* and Gram-negative bacilli, but not *Listeria*. Therefore ampicillin is added, as is vancomycin to cover for possible staphylococcal species (Roos *et al.* 1997).

Corticosteroids

Extrapolation from studies of children and animals have led Quagliarello and Scheld (1997) to recommend that in cases with a Gram stain showing organisms (suggesting a high concentration of bacteria in the cerebrospinal fluid) or in cases with signs of increased intracranial pressure, 0.15 mg/kg dexamethasone be given every 6 h intravenously for 4 days. In elderly people, cerebral atrophy and other central nervous system comorbidity may make detection of elevated intracranial pressure difficult. Imaging studies may be conclusive. In certain cases, intracranial pressure monitoring might be appropriate.

Aciclovir

Neuropsychiatric side-effects have been described in patients receiving aciclovir. Rashiq *et al.* (1993) found in a study of 35 patients that aciclovir neurotoxicity is more common in elderly people, in patients with renal failure, and in the presence of other potentially neurotoxic medications; hallucinations, delirium, agitation, and lethargy were frequent manifestations. Symptoms most often occurred within 2 days of therapy, and discontinuation led to complete resolution. In

Table 4 Recommendations for antibiotic therapy in patients with bacterial meningitis who have a positive Gram stain or culture of cerebrospinal fluid

Bacteria	Antibiotic choice
Gram stain	
Cocci	
Gram-positive	Vancomycin plus broad-spectrum cephalosporin
Gram-negative	Penicillin G
Bacilli	
Gram-positive	Ampicillin (or penicillin G) plus aminoglycoside
Gram-negative	Broad-spectrum cephalosporin plus aminoglycoside
Culture	
Strep. pneumoniae	Vancomycin plus broad-spectrum cephalosporin
H. influenzae	Ceftriaxone
N. meningitidis	Penicillin G
L. monocytogenes	Ampicillin plus gentamicin
Strep. agalactiae	Penicillin G
Enterobacteraceae	Broad-spectrum cephalosporin plus aminoglycoside
Ps. aeruginosa, Acinetobacter	Ceftazidime plus aminoglycoside

Adapted from Quagliarello and Scheld (1997).

patients who were retreated with aciclovir at a lower dose, neurological symptoms did not recur.

Acute complications

In their study of bacterial meningitis, Gorse et al. (1984) found that neurological abnormality occurred in 15 of 54 (28 per cent) of the older patients and six of 32 (19 per cent) of the younger patients. In the older age group, 67 per cent of the patients had complications, and of those aged over 65 years, 85 per cent had complications. Pfister et al. (1993), found that half of 86 adults with bacterial meningitis had some type of acute complication; central nervous system complications developed in 35 patients (40.7 per cent) and systemic complications in 19 (22.1 per cent). Stroke and oedema were the most severe central nervous system complications. Of 13 patients with cerebral infarction, six died. In seven patients, signs of herniation from cerebral oedema, venous sinus thrombosis, or hydrocephalus were detected; three died. Septic shock occurred in 10 patients (11.6 per cent), six of whom died, including three of three patients who also had adult respiratory distress syndrome. Gorse et al. (1984) showed that seizures and hydrocephalus occurred in 30 and 9 per cent of the older patients, but did not occur in any of the younger patients. In a study of patients of all ages, Pfister et al. (1993) found that seizures occurred in 24.4 per cent and hydrocephalus occurred in 11.6 per cent.

Sequelae

Elderly survivors of meningitis are particularly predisposed to sequelae. Gorse et al. (1984) found that, at 5 months after diagnosis, three of 54 patients over 50 years old (5.5 per cent) had persisting mental status deficits and six patients (11 per cent) continued to demonstrate other neurological signs. Jonsson and Alvin (1971) found neurological sequelae in 17 of 39 patients (44 per cent) over age 50 and in one of 21 patients (5 per cent) between 21 and 50 years of age. Of these 17 elderly patients, seven had unilateral or bilateral deafness, six had ataxia, two had mental symptoms, and two had other cranial neuropathy. None had epilepsy. Aminoglycosides were not used in this series. Among children (aged 0–20 years), only five of 213 (2 per cent) had unilateral or bilateral deafness.

References

Applebaum, E. (1960). Meningitis following trauma to the head and face. *Journal of the American Medical Association*, 173, 1818–22.

Armstrong, D. and Wong, B. (1982). Central nervous system infections in immunocompromised hosts. *Annual Review of Medicine*, 33, 293–308.

Aronson, A.M., DeBuono, B.A., and Buechner, J.S. (1991). Acute bacterial meningitis in Rhode Island: a survey of the years 1976 to 1985. *Rhode Island Medical Journal*, 74, 33–6.

Bale, J.F. Jr (1991). Encephalitis and other virus-induced neurologic disorders. In *Clinical neurology* (ed. R. Joynt), Vol. 2, pp. 1–56. J.B. Lippincott, Philadelphia, PA.

Baringer, J.R. (1978). Herpes simplex virus infections of the nervous system. In *Handbook of clinical neurology* (eds P.J. Vinken and G.W. Bruyn), p. 145. North-Holland, Amsterdam.

Barrett-Connor, E. (1967). Tuberculous meningitis in adults. *Southern Medical Journal*, 60, 1061–7.

Barry, E. and Hauser, W.A. (1993). Status epilepticus: the interaction of epilepsy and acute brain disease. *Neurology*, 43, 1473–8.

Barsic, B., Lisic, M., Himbele, J., et al. (1992). Pneumococcal meningitis in the elderly. *Neurologia Croatica*, 41, 131–9.

Behrman, R.E., Meyers, B.R., Mendelson, M.H., Sacks, H.S., and Hirschman, S.Z. (1989) Central nervous system infections in the elderly. *Archives of Internal Medicine*, 149, 1596–9.

Bell, W.E. and Sahs, A.L. (1987). Bacterial meningitis. In *Clinical neurology* (ed. R. Joynt), Vol. 2, pp. 1–100. J.B. Lippincott, Philadelphia, PA.

Berk, S.L. (1983). Bacterial meningitis. In *Infections in the elderly* (ed. R.A. Gleckman and N.M. Glantz), pp. 235–63. Little, Brown, Boston, MA.

Berk, S.L. and McCabe, W.R. (1981). Meningitis caused by *Acinetobacter calcoaceticus* var. *anitratus*. *Archives of Neurology*, 38, 95–8.

Bhagwati, S.N. (1971).Ventriculoatrial shunt in tuberculous meningitis with hydrocephalus. *Journal of Neurosurgery*, 35, 309–13.

Buckwold, F.J., Hand, R., and Hansebout, R.R. (1977). Hospital acquired bacterial meningitis in neurosurgical patients. *Journal of Neurosurgery*, 46, 494–500.

Campbell, F.D., Currier, R.D., and Busey, J.F. (1981). Survival in untreated cryptococcal meningitis. *Neurology*, 31, 1154–7.

Carpenter, R.R., and Petersdorf, R.G. (1962). The clinical spectrum of bacterial meningitis. *American Journal of Medicine*, 33, 262–75.

Centers for Disease Control (1979). Bacterial meningitis and meningococcemia—United States, 1978. *Morbidity and Mortality Weekly Report*, 28, 277–9.

Centers for Disease Control (1991). St Louis encephalitis outbreak, Arkansas, 1991. *Morbidity and Mortality Weekly Report*, 49, 605–7.

Chernik, N.L., Armstrong D., and Posner J.B. (1973). Central nervous system infections in patients with cancer. *Medicine*, 52, 563–81.

Cherubin, C.E., Marr, J.S., Sierra, M.F., and Becker, S. (1981). *Listeria* and Gram-negative bacillary meningitis in New York City. *American Journal of Medicine*, 71, 199–209.

Choi, C. (1992). Bacterial meningitis. *Clinics in Geriatric Medicine*, 8, 889–902.

Cinnamon, J., Sharma, M., Gray, D., Greenberg, R., and Hyman, R.A. (1994). Neuroimaging of meningeal disease. *Seminars in Ultrasound, CT, and MRI*, 15, 466–98.

Corey, L. and Spear, P. (1986). Infections with the herpes simplex virus. *New England Journal of Medicine*, 314, 749–57.

Crane, L.R. and Lerner, A.M. (1978). Non traumatic Gram-negative bacillary meningitis in the Detroit Medical Center, 1964–1974 (with special mention of cases due to *Escherichia coli*). *Medicine*, 57, 197–209.

Davis, L.E. and Johnson, R.T. (1979). An explanation for the localization of herpes simplex encephalitis? *Annals of Neurology*, 5, 2–5.

Deresiewicz, R.L., Thaler, S.J., Hsu, L., and Zamani A.A. (1997). Clinical and neuroradiographic manifestations of eastern equine encephalitis. *New England Journal of Medicine*, 336, 1867–74.

Diamond, R.D. and Bennett, J.E. (1974). Prognostic factors in cryptococcal meningitis, a study in 111 cases. *Annals of Internal Medicine*, 80, 176–81.

Dunne, D.W. and Quagliarello, V. (1993). Group B streptococcal meningitis in adults. *Medicine*, 72, 1–10.

Durand, M.L., Calderwood, S.B., Weber, D.J., et al. (1993). Acute bacterial meningitis in adults: a review of 493 episodes. *New England Journal of Medicine*, 328, 21–8.

Eigler, J.O., Wellman, W.E., Rooke, E.D., Keith, E.D., and Svien, H.J. (1961). Bacterial meningitis. I. General Review. *Mayo Clinic Proceedings*, 36, 357–65.

Falk, A. (1962). US Veterans Administration Armed Forces cooperative study on the chemotherapy of tuberculosis XIII. Tuberculous meningitis in adults, with special reference to survival, neurologic residuals, and work status. *American Review of Respiratory Disease*, 91, 823–31.

Farley, M.M. (1995). Group B streptococcal infection in older patients. *Drugs and Aging*, 6, 293–300.

Fishman, R.A. (1980). *Cerebrospinal fluid findings in diseases of the nervous system*, pp. 168–252. W.B. Saunders, Philadelphia, PA.

Fiumara, N.J. (1983). Diagnosis and treatment of latent and late syphilis: evaluation of the reactive serologic test for syphilis. In *diagnosis and treatment of sexually transmitted diseases* (ed. W.M. McCormack), pp. 127–42. John Wright, Littleton, MA.

Gasecki, A.P. and Steg, R.E. (1991). Correlation of early MRI with CT scan, EEG and cerebrospinal fluid: analyses in a case of biopsy-proven herpes simplex encephalitis. *European Neurology*, 31, 372–5.

Geiseler, P.J., Nelson, K.E., Levin, S., Reddi, K.T., and Moses, V.K. (1980). Community-acquired purulent meningitis: a review of 1316 cases during the antibiotic era, 1954–1976. *Reviews of Infectious Diseases*, 2, 725–45.

Gorse, G.J., Thrupp, L.D., Nudelman, K.L., Wyle, F.A., Hawkins, B., and Cesario, T.C. (1984). Bacterial meningitis in the elderly. *Archives of Internal Medicine*, 144, 1603–7.

Haas, E.J., Madhavan, T., Quinn, E.L., Cox, F., Fisher, E., Burch, K. (1977). Tuberculous meningitis in an urban general hospital. *Archives of Internal Medicine*, 137, 1518–21.

Halperin, J.J., Luft, B.J., Anand, A.K., Roque, C.T., Alvarez, O., and Volkman, D.J. (1990). Lyme neuroborreliosis: central nervous system manifestations. *Neurology*, 39, 753–9.

Hand, W.L. and Sanford J.P. (1970). Post-traumatic bacterial meningitis. *Annals of Internal Medicine*, 72, 869–74.

Hansen, K. and Lebech, A.M. (1992). The clinical and epidemiological profile of lyme neuroborreliosis in Denmark 1985–1990. *Brain*, 115, 399–423.

Heerema, M.S., Ein, M.E., Musher, D.M., Bradshaw, M.W., and Williams, T.W. (1979). Anaerobic bacterial meningitis. *American Journal of Medicine*, 67, 210–27.

Hodges, G.R. and Perkins, R.L. (1976). Hospital acquired bacterial meningitis. *American Journal of the Medical Sciences*, 271, 335–41.

Hojfgaard Rasmussen, H., Toft Sorensen, H., Moller-Peterson, J., Mortensen, F.V., and Nielson, B. (1992). Bacterial meningitis in elderly patients: clinical picture and course, *Age and Ageing*, 21, 216–20.

Hook, E.J. (1997). Syphilis. In *Infections of the central nervous system* (2nd edn) (ed. W.M. Scheld, R.J. Whitley, and D.T. Durack). pp. 669–84. Lippincott–Raven, New York.

Hsieh, L.Y., Chia, L.G., and Shen, W.G. (1992). Locations of cerebral infarctions in tuberculous meningitis. *Neuroradiology*, 34, 197–9.

Igarashi, M., Gilmartin, R.C., Gerald, B., Wilburn, F., and Jabbour, J.T. (1984). Cerebral arteritis and bacterial meningitis. *Archives of Neurology*, 41, 531–5.

Iseman, M.D. (1996). Tuberculosis. In *Cecil textbook of medicine* (ed. J.C. Bennett, F. Plum, and G.L.Mandell), p. 1684. W.B. Saunders, Philadelphia, PA.

Jaffe, H.W. and Kabins, S.A. (1982). Examination of the cerebrospinal fluid in patients with syphilis. *Review of Infectious Disease*, 4, 5842–7.

Jemsek, J., Greenberg, S.B., Taber, L., Harvey, D., Gershon, A., and Couch, R.B. (1983). Herpes zoster-associated encephalitis: clinicopathologic report of 12 cases and review of the literature. *Medicine*, 62, 81–97.

Jensen, K., Ranek, L., and Rosdahl, N. (1969). Bacterial meningitis. *Scandinavian Journal of Infectious Diseases*, 1, 21–30.

Jonsson, M. and Alvin, A. (1971). A 12 year review of acute bacterial meningitis in Stockholm, *Scandinavian Journal of Infectious Disease*, 3, 141–50.

Kinnunen, E., Hovi, T., Stenvik, Hellstrom, O., Porras, J., Kleemola, M., and Kantanen, M-L. (1987). Localized outbreak of enteroviral meningitis in adults. *Acta Neurologica Scandinavica*, 74, 121–5.

Koskiniemi, M., Piiparinen, H., Mannonen, L., Rantalaiho, T., and Vaheri, A. (1996). Herpes encephalitis is a disease of middle aged and elderly people: polymerase chain reaction for detection of herpes simplex virus in the cerebrospinal fluid of 516 patients with encephalitis. *Journal of Neurology, Neurosurgery and Psychiatry*, 60, 174–8.

Krumholz, A., Sung, G.Y., Fisher, R.S., Barry, E., Bergey, G.K., and Grattan, L.M. (1995). Complex partial status epilepticus accompanied by serious morbidity and mortality. *Neurology*, 45, 1499–504.

LeFrock, J.L., Smith, B.R., and Molavi, A. (1985). Gram-negative bacillary meningitis. *Medical Clinics of North America*, 69, 243–56.

Lloyd, M.N.H., Kimber, P.M., and Burrows, E.H. (1994). Post-traumatic cerebrospinal rhinorrhoea: modern high-definition computed tomography is all that is required for the effective demonstration of the site of leakage. *Clinical Radiology*, 49, 100–3.

Mangi, R.J., Quintiliani, R., and Andriole, V.T. (1975). Gram negative bacillary meningitis. *American Journal of Medicine*, 59, 829–36.

Marton, K.I. and Gean, A.D. (1986). The spinal tap: a new look at an old test. *Annals of Internal Medicine*, 104, 840–8.

Massanari, R.M. (1977). Purulent meningitis in the elderly: when to suspect an unusual pathogen. *Geriatrics*, 32, 55–9.

Merritt, H.H. and Fremont-Smith, F. (1938). *The cerebrospinal fluid*. W.B. Saunders, Philadelphia, PA.

Merritt, H.H. and Moore, M. (1935). Acute syphilitic meningitis. *Medicine*, 14, 119–83.

Merritt, H.H., Adams, R.S., and Solomon, H.C. (1946). *Neurosyphilis*, p. 373. Oxford University Press, New York.

Mosis, E.N., Dean, A.G., Hatch, M.H., and Barron, A.L. (1977). An outbreak of aseptic meningitis in the area of Fort Smith, Arkansas, 1975, due to echovirus type 4. *Journal of the Arkansas Medical Association*, 74, 121–5.

Musher, D.M. (1991). Pneumococcal pneumonia including diagnosis and therapy of infection caused by penicillin-resistant strains. *Infectious Disease Clinics of North America*, 5, 509–21.

Newton, J.E. and Wilczynski, P.G.G. (1979). Meningitis in the elderly. *Lancet*, ii, 157–8.

Norden, C.W., Callerame, M.L., and Baum, J. (1970). *Haemophilus influenzae* meningitis in an adult. *New England Journal of Medicine*, 282, 190–4.

Ogawa, S.K., Smith, M.A., Brennessel D.J., and Lowy, F.D. (1987). Tuberculous meningitis in an urban medical center. *Medicine*, 66, 317–26.

Perfect, J.R., Durack D.T., and Gallis H.A. (1983). Crytpococcemia, *Medicine*, 62, 98–109.

Pfister, H.W., Borasio, G.D., Dirnagl, U., Bauer, M., and Einhäupl, K.-M. (1992). Cerebrovascular complications of bacterial meningitis in adults. *Neurology*, 42, 1497–504.

Pfister, H.W., Feiden, W., and Einhäupl, K.-M. (1993). Spectrum of complications during bacterial meningitis in adults. *Archives of Neurology*, 50, 575–81.

Quaade, F. (1963). Meningitis in the aged. *Geriatrics*, 18, 860–4.

Quagliarello, V.J. and Scheld, W. (1997). Treatment of bacterial meningitis. *New England Journal of Medicine*, 336, 708–16.

Rashiq, S., Briewa, L., Mooney, M., Giancarlo, T., Khatib, R., and Wilson, F.M. (1993). Distinguishing aciclovir neurotoxicity from encephalomyelitis. *Journal of Internal Medicine*, 234, 507–11.

Riggs S., Smith, D., and Phillips, C.A. (1965). St Louis encephalitis in adults during the 1964 Houston epidemic. *Journal of the American Medical Association*, 193, 284–8.

Roos K.L., Tunkel, A.R., and Scheld, W.M. (1997). Acute bacterial meningitis in children and adults. In *Infections of the central nervous system* (2nd edn) (ed. W.M. Scheld, R.J. Whitley, and D.T. Durack), pp. 335–402. Lippincott–Raven, New York.

Rotbart, H.A. (1997). Viral meningitis and the aseptic meningitis syndrome. In *Infections of the central nervous system* (2nd edn) (ed. W.M. Scheld, R.J. Whitley, and D.T. Durack), pp. 23–47. Lippincott–Raven, New York.

Sabetta, J.R. and Andriole, V.T. (1985). Cryptococcal infection of the central nervous system. *Medical Clinics of North America*, 69, 333–44.

Salaki, J.S., Louria, D.B., and Chmel, H. (1984). Fungal and yeast infections of the central nervous system. *Medicine*, 63, 108–32.

Schlech, W.F. III, Ward, J.I., Bland, J.D., *et al.* (1985). Bacterial meningitis in the United States, 1978 through 1981. *Journal of the American Medical Association*, 253, 1749–54.

Schneider, R.C. and Thompson, J.M. (1957). Chronic and delayed traumatic cerebrospinal rhinorrhea as a source of recurrent attacks of meningitis. *Annals of Surgery*, 145, 517–29.

Simon, R.P. (1985). Neurosyphilis. *Archives of Neurology*, 42, 606–13.

Sivertsen, B. and Christensen, P.B. (1996). Acute encephalitis. *Acta Neurologica Scandinavica*, 93, 156–9.

Skoldenberg, B., Forsgfen, M., Alestig, K., *et al.* (1984). Aciclovir versus vidarabine in herpes simplex encephalitis: randomised multicentre study in consecutive Swedish patients. *Lancet*, ii, 707–11.

Stead, W.W. and Lofren, J.P. (1983). Medical perspective: does the risk of tuberculosis increase in old age? *Journal of Infectious Diseases*, 147, 951–5.

Stead, W.W., Lofren, J.P., Warren, E., and Thomas, C. (1985). Tuberculosis in an endemic and nosocomial infection among the elderly in nursing homes. *New England Journal of Medicine*, 312, 1483–7.

Stein, J.A., DeRossi, R., and Neu, H.C. (1969) Adult *Haemophilus influenzae* meningitis. *New York State Journal of Medicine*, 69, 1760–6.

Stockstill, M.T. and Kauffman, C.A. (1983) Comparison of cryptococcal and tuberculous meningitis. *Archives of Neurology*, 40, 81–5.

Swartz, M.N. and Dodge, P.R. (1965). Bacterial meningitis—a review of selected aspects. *New England Journal of Medicine*, 272, 954–60.

Talan, D.A., Hoffman, J.R., Yoshikawa, T.T., and Overturf, G. D. (1988). Role of empiric parenteral antibiotics prior to lumbar puncture in suspected bacterial meningitis: state of the art. *Reviews of Infectious Diseases*, 10, 365–76.

Tandon, P.N. (1978). Tuberculous meningitis. In *Handbook of clinical neurology* (ed. P.J. Vinken and G.W. Bruyn), Vol. 33, pp. 195–262. North-Holland, Amsterdam.

Tsai, T.F., Canfield, M.A., Reed, C.M., *et al.* (1986). Epidemiological aspects of a St Louis encephalitis outbreak in Harris County, Texas. *Journal of Infectious Diseases*, 157, 351–6.

Tsai, T.F., Cobb, W.B., Bolin, R.A., *et al.* (1987). Epidemiologic aspects of a St Louis encephalitis outbreak in Mesa County, Colorado. *American Journal of Epidemiology*, 126, 460–73.

Vas, G.A. and Cracco, J.B. (1990). Diffuse encephalopathies. In *Current practice of clinical electroencephalography* (2nd edn) (ed. T.A. Pedley and D.D. Daly), pp. 371–9. Raven Press, New York.

Weiss, W., Figueroa, W., and Shapiro, W.H. (1967). Prognostic factors in pneumococcal meningitis. *Archives of Internal Medicine*, 120, 517–24.

Wenger, J.D., Hightower, A.W., Facklam, R.R., Gaventa, S., and Broome, C.V. (1990) Bacterial meningitis in the United States, 1986: report of a multistate surveillance study. *Journal of Infectious Diseases*, 162, 1316–23.

Whitley, R.J. (1990). Viral encephalitis. *New England Journal of Medicine*, 323, 242–50.

Whitley, R.J. (1997). Arthropod-borne encephalitides. In *Infections of the central nervous system* (2nd edn) (ed. W.M. Scheld, R.J. Whitley, and D.T. Durack), pp. 147–68. Lippincott–Raven, New York.

Whitley, R.J., Soong, S.-J., Tilles, J., and Linneman, C., Jr (1982). Herpes simplex encephalitis: a clinical assessment. *Journal of the American Medical Association*, 247, 317–20.

Whitley, R.J., Alford, C.A., Hirsch, M.S., *et al.* (1986). Vidarabine versus aciclovir therapy in herpes simplex encephalitis. *New England Journal of Medicine*, 314, 144–9.

Wilson, J.D. and Castillo, M. (1994). Magnetic resonance imaging of granulomatous inflammations: sarcoidosis and tuberculosis. *Topics in Magnetic Resonance Imaging*, 6, 32–40.

Yamamoto, M., Ogura, Y., Sudo, K., and Hibino, S. (1967). A study of disease caused by atypical mycobacteria. *American Review of Respiratory Disease*, 96, 779–87.

Young, L.S., LaForce, F.M., Head, J.J., Feeley, J.C., and Bennett, J.V. (1972). A simultaneous outbreak of meningococcal and influenzal infections. *New England Journal of Medicine*, 287, 5–9.

Zaky, D.A., Bentley, D.W., Lowy, K., Betts, R.F., and Douglas, R.G. (1976). Malignant external otitis: a severe form of otitis in diabetic patients. *American Journal of Medicine*, 61, 754–76.

Zuger, A. and Lowy, F.D. (1997). Tuberculosis. In *Infections of the central nervous system* (2nd edn) (ed. W.M. Scheld, R.J. Whitley, and D.T. Durack), pp. 417–44. Lippincott–Raven, New York.

18.11 Mobility disorders—how to evaluate and treat the effects of age and disease

Joy Antonelle deMarcaida and Leslie Wolfson

Mobility is a basic human function, which is necessary for independence, social interaction, and performing the activities of daily living. Loss of mobility, along with the occurrence of falls, is a principal cause of a limited quality of life and increased dependence; therefore both are important factors that cause older people to become inhabitants of long-term care facilities. One-third of older people living at home report a fall in the previous year (Baker and Harvey 1985), and falls occur considerably more often in long-term care facilities (0.67–2.0 falls per bed per year) (Gryfe *et al.* 1977; Rubenstein *et al.* 1988). This is not surprising in view of the prevalence of dementia and frailty, both of which are important risk factors for falls, in older people living in institutions. Falls usually produce minor injury, although their high incidence in older people make them responsible for half of all accidental injuries in this age group (United States Bureau of the Census 1985). The result is 250 000 hip fractures plus numerous other major injuries (e.g. half of all head injuries in 55–65-year-olds) (Cooper *et al*. 1983) as well as 10 000 deaths per year in older Americans.

In addition to sensorimotor function, mobility is dependent on joint function and overall fitness. Arthritis robs the joints of the legs of the ability to support mobility efficiently; deconditioned frail older people become short of breath after walking short distances and their impaired strength lends them only marginal support. Other factors, such as decreased hearing or vision, and orthostatic hypotension or cardiovascular disease producing syncope, are also related to the incidence of falls. Dysfunction of the sensorimotor control mechanism may involve the nervous system at any level, with each locus having characteristic signs and symptoms as well as different pathophysiological mechanisms.

In this chapter we define balance in terms of measurable functional components and then review the effects of age on balance, sensorimotor function, and the brain structures subserving them. An outline is then provided of the diseases that most frequently impair neuromuscular control, and 'idiopathic' dysfunction of gait and balance. Finally, the possible pathophysiology and strategies for treatment are reviewed.

Effects of age on sensorimotor function

'Senile' is defined in one dictionary as 'showing characteristics of old age; weak of mind and body'. This definition demonstrates the misconception that age by itself is inevitably associated with a loss of cognitive and motor function. A vast published record now indicates that most cognitive loss occurs because of age-associated disease and that only mild cognitive changes occur in the absence of these diseases. In the following section we review age-associated loss of sensorimotor function as well as the changes that occur in gait and balance.

Balance

Although balance can be conceptualized from several perspectives, a useful approach should provide a framework for understanding clinical dysfunction and its treatment. Balance is described by the anatomy and structural connections, the physiology of the sensory inputs and their integration into motor responses or by describing its functional components. Aside from a central role of frontal motor/premotor cortex and its subcortical connections, little is known about the anatomy and organization of structures involved in balance. Although there is a significant literature defining the physiology of the long, medium, and short loop components of the balance response, this system does not lend itself to a classification which is meaningful from a clinical or treatment perspective. By contrast, dividing balance into measurable constituent functions provides for quantitative definition of the abnormalities and the treatment strategies to remediate them. Therefore, in this chapter balance is defined in terms of measurable components which are required for the performance of daily activities. For these purposes, balance is divided into the following five components along with their measures:

(1) standing (sway);
(2) ability to use sensory input (loss of balance with limited sensory input);
(3) limits of stability (functional base of support);
(4) response to external perturbations (loss of balance);
(5) stance with a narrowed base of support (single stance time).

While the five categories reflect qualitatively different components, in reality movement is integrated and often can be assigned to more than one category.

Sway during standing increases marginally with age. There is only a 3 per cent difference in the sway amplitude (anteroposterior) of older subjects (average age of 76 ± 5 years) and younger subjects (average age of 35 ± 12 years) (Wolfson *et al*. 1992). The sway differences between old and young people increase when visual input or tactile–proprioceptive input is blocked or inaccurate (Wolfson *et al*. 1992; Schultz *et al*. 1993). Sensory input is redundant and, even in older people, when visual or tactile proprioceptive feedback is shut off there is only a moderate increase in sway. When the vision and tactile–proprioceptive input of older people are both distorted or blocked, balance measures decrease materially in comparison to younger subjects. With this limitation of two sensory modalities, the remaining vestibular input is not sufficient information and 30 to 50 per cent of older subjects have losses of balance during testing (Wolfson *et al*. 1992; Schultz *et al*. 1993) This suggests that in older people the processing of sensory information into a postural response requires more information, which includes visual or tactile–proprioceptive feedback in addition to vestibular input.

Standing requires body mass to be vertically aligned over a support zone (limit of stability) on each foot. When motion and external forces produce weight shifts which leave this zone, a motor response or steps must re-establish vertical alignment. The functional base of support is a measure of this zone of stability in the anteroposterior plane. Measurement requires a force platform to ascertain the per cent of foot length used to uphold body weight with backward and forward leaning. Functional base of support is relatively stable until 60 years of age (60 per cent of foot length), following which it decreases steadily to 40 per cent of foot length at the age of 80 (16 per cent per decade) (King *et al*. 1994).

One-legged stance is necessary for the turning and leaning used in routine activities. Single stance time is a widely used measure of one-legged stance. Single stance time is unchanged from the twenties to the fifties, decreases to 22 s during the sixties and 14 s during the seventies (Bohannon *et al*. 1984). While single stance time is a useful measure in healthy older people, it is usually too difficult for people with motor dysfunction and those above 80 years of age. For these, the ability to hold tandem or semitandem stance are more applicable. Categorical balance is a performance measure of this ability, which determines the narrowest stance a subject can maintain (i.e. parallel, semi-tandem, tandem, and single) (Rossiter-Fornoff *et al*. 1993).

Under conditions with limited sensory input (one modality) older people have much more frequent losses of balance than do young people although both groups adapt effectively during repetitive testing (Wolfson *et al*. 1992). The capacity to make restorative postural adjustments (long-loop reflexes) is critical for avoiding falls and can by assessed by force platforms which produce destabilizing forces.

The response to these forces are different in old and young subjects. In older people vigorous destabilizing forces produce many more losses of balance than in young people although both adapt well during repetitive testing (Wolfson et al. 1992). Many elderly people have EMG evidence of abnormal function in leg muscles during experiments with sudden, horizontal translations of a support platform (Woollacott et al. 1982): response latencies are prolonged, output amplitude is inconsistent, and the timing between distal and proximal muscles is reversed, particularly in perturbations causing posterior sway.

Despite these age-associated changes, under all but stressful circumstances, the balance of older people is effective and improves with repetitive testing. Under conditions which stress balance, limited sensory input, or vigorous perturbation there are frequent losses of balance in older people suggesting that these modest age-associated decrements may be an element in the increased occurrence of falls (Wolfson et al. 1992). In the absence of age-associated diseases known to impair balance, only modest balance decrements can be demonstrated between 70 and 80 + years (Wolfson et al. 1992). By contrast, in a study of nursing home subjects with recurrent falls, half of the subjects had profound deficits of their postural responses as well as impaired gait and lower extremity strength by comparison to the controls (Wolfson et al. 1986). CT scans from subjects with poor balance had an increased incidence of hypodensity suggestive of ischaemic small-vessel disease (Masdeu et al. 1989).

This suggests that balance deterioration of sufficient magnitude to produce impaired mobility is the result of age-associated disease. It is possible to conclude that age-associated balance decrements are analogous to those of other central nervous system dependent functions (e.g. cognition) which do not by themselves lead to significant impairment of function (i.e. immobility).

Data from the literature as well as from the authors' laboratory suggest that major age-associated changes in balance occur as a result of decrements in the central processing of sensorimotor input into an effective postural response (Woollacott et al. 1982). These age-associated changes are amplified by the effects of disease. Although there is no balance centre within the brain, much of the sensorimotor processing occurs in premotor frontal regions. A significant literature suggests that diseases/lesions involving these regions and the subcortical white matter are often associated with poor balance. It is likely that frontal lesions interfere with the parallel processing required for balance.

Gait

Gait velocity remains relatively constant until the sixties and thereafter slows 15 per cent per decade. Decreased walking speed is accompanied by diminished stride length and single support time (one foot on the ground) and increased double support time (both feet on the ground) (Murray et al. 1969; Imms and Edholm 1979). These decrements represent a significant but modest decrease in these quantitative indices of gait. Not surprisingly, walking speed also varies with the level of activity (Imms and Edholm 1979). The gait of elderly individuals who fall is often more compromised than the gait of those who do not, and is characterized by a decreased speed and shorter stride (Imms and Edholm 1979; Guimaraes and Isaacs 1980; Wolfson et al. 1990). Loss of ankle plantar flexor strength in older people may be a factor in the diminished walking speed and stride of older people

(Judge et al. 1996). To assess gait, one can use simple measures of walking (e.g. velocity and stride length) as well as observer-rated analysis of videotaped gait (Wolfson et al. 1990). A study of nursing home residents demonstrated a strong correlation between abnormal gait (stride length, walking speed, and qualitative assessment) and the occurrence of falls (Wolfson et al. 1990).

In the authors' experience there is as wide a range of gait characteristics in older people, as there is in younger individuals (Wolfson et al. 1990). The gait of some older men has been described as small stepped with anteroflexed posture (Murray et al. 1969), but this is by no means universal nor is it clear whether or not many of these individuals have diseases producing these changes.

Motor function

Strength increases through childhood and adolescence, peaks in the mid-twenties, declines modestly until the age of 50, after which a greater decrement is seen (Larsson 1982). Cross-sectional studies have shown a 20 to 40 per cent decrease in strength from the mid-twenties to the seventies (Larsson 1978; Moritani and de Vries 1980). After the age of 40, there is a 1 to 2 per cent decrement of strength per year through the ninth decade (Hurley 1995; Winegard et al. 1996). By contrast, after the age of 60, muscle mass declines annually by 0.5 per cent and 1.0 per cent in men and women respectively. Measurements of strength developed during limb movement (termed isokinetic dynamometry) have demonstrated that these decrements become more prominent at rapid rates of muscle contraction (Larsson 1982). This is consistent with studies of muscle morphology that show a diminished number of fast-twitch type 2 muscle fibres in older people (Tomonaga 1977; Grimby et al. 1982; Larsson 1982). The causes of the atrophy of type 2 muscle fibres are not clear, although there is evidence tying it to both disuse (related to diminished physical activity) (Engel 1970; Larsson 1978), and/or denervation–reinnervation produced by loss of spinal motoneurones (Tomonaga 1977; Grimby et al. 1982; Shields et al. 1984).

Isokinetic dynamometry has shown compromised motor function in specific leg muscles of nursing home residents who fall (Whipple et al. 1987). In particular, the strength of ankle dorsiflexors was profoundly diminished at functional speed of contraction (10 per cent of control strength). The vulnerability of older subjects to defective control of posterior sway and hence backwards loss of balance may be associated with a loss of dorsiflexor strength.

Sensory function and electrophysiology

Many components of sensory function including pain, temperature sensibility (Klawans et al. 1971; Prakash and Stern 1973; Howell 1975; Kokmen et al. 1977) tactile sensitivity (Welford 1980), two-point discrimination (Skinner et al. 1984), joint position sense, and stereognosis (Welford 1980) diminish mildly with age. Prior clinical studies suggest modest decrements in less than one-third of older patients who have abnormalities of these sensory modalities (Klawans et al. 1971; Prakash and Stern 1973; Howell 1975; Kokmen et al. 1977; Carter 1979). Vibratory sensitivity, by comparison, decreases significantly with age. Vibratory threshold increases two- to tenfold in older people (Perret and Reglis 1970; Potvin et al. 1980a, b), and clinically diminished vibratory function is present in two-thirds of older people (Klawans et al. 1971; Prakash and Stern 1973; Howell 1975; Kokmen et al. 1977; Carter 1979). Thus the magnitude of the vibratory decrements are much greater than the other modalities. Neurophysiological indices including nerve conduction velocities, action potential amplitudes, and F-wave latencies decrease mildly from the twenties to the seventies, but not nearly to the extent suggestive of a neuropathy (Buchthal and Rosenfalck 1966; Buchthal *et al.* 1975; Dorfman and Bosley 1979; Schaumburg *et al.* 1983). These mild sensory decrements suggest that changes in lower extremity sensory function are not a primary cause of balance decrements.

Vestibular function

A substantial literature indicates vestibular dysfunction can significantly compromise balance. Vestibular evaluation using oculo-caloric and vestibulo-ocular testing demonstrate minor decrements with age (Bruner and Norris 1971). Another study demonstrates no caloric decrements with age and only modest changes during rotational testing (Peterka *et al.* 1994). There is a reduction in the number of hair cells in the maculae and cristae which may be the anatomical substrate for diminished vestibular function (Rosenhall 1973). The importance of vestibular function in age-associated balance changes remains unclear, although, there are no data to suggest that it is a major factor.

Structural changes

Neural structures serving motor function are affected by age. Cell counting in autopsy material shows a loss of neurones (20–50 per cent) in the motor cortex, substantia nigra, and cerebellar cortex, as well as a decreased dendritic tree in projection neurones of the motor cortex of older subjects compared with children (Shefer 1973; McGeer *et al.* 1977; Nakamura *et al.* 1985). No loss of peripheral nerve cells has been reported, although several studies suggest structural changes (Schaumburg *et al.* 1983). The most relevant to motor function of the numerous chemical changes within the brain is the decrease in striatal dopamine (Carlsson and Winblad 1976) together with a 50 per cent decline in tyrosine hydroxylase activity (rate-limiting in dopamine synthesis) (McGeer 1976). The significance of the structural and chemical changes with age are difficult to interpret, but the magnitude of the decreases is consistent with the decrements of sensorimotor function with age, suggesting the possibility of a relationship between the two. By comparison, autopsy studies of the brains of parkinsonian patients show an 80 per cent decrement in striatal dopamine due to severe loss of dopaminergic projection neurones in the substantia nigra, suggesting (Bernheimer *et al.* 1973) that a higher order of structural change underlies disease states.

The losses of function related to disease are additive to those associated with age and therefore often lead to severe functional incapacity. By comparison, age-associated decrements may weaken and slow responses but reserves are adequate to support motor function. It is therefore reasonable to suggest that significant dysfunction of gait and balance is disease, rather than age associated.

Medical approach to an older patient with a history of falls

Here we focus on the motor dysfunction associated with impaired mobility and falls. Falls have many causes and the details surrounding a fall are critical in determining its cause. The occurrence of altered consciousness, light-headedness, or vertigo suggest transient ischaemic attack, seizure, or cardiovascular causes. Without historical evidence of symptoms suggestive of hemispheric or brainstem ischaemia or the manifestations of epilepsy, one cannot make a diagnosis of transient ischaemic attack or seizure. Furthermore, both have rarely been reported to cause falls (Sheldon 1960; Overstall *et al.* 1977).

If there is no evidence of altered sensorium before a fall, the role of environmental hazards should be explored. In reported series these hazards are related to almost half of all falls (Sheldon 1960; Overstall *et al.* 1977). One must be cautious in evaluating the significance of these hazards. Often older individuals attribute a fall to insignificant hazards (e.g. a crack in the pavement or uneven flooring). The balance reflexes of normal (young and old) individuals are almost always capable of compensating for minor hazards. Thus, while one may stumble over a minor obstacle, a fall should not ensue. The occurrence of multiple falls suggests impaired balance. Usually, cognitively intact older individuals limit their activities to decrease the chance of falling. This fear of falling limits mobility, striking at the quality of life and functional independence. Thus it is important to determine the scope of mobility during the history. Many older people shop daily, use public transport, and walk considerable distances, but others barely leave the perceived safety of their homes.

Cardiovascular dysfunction may result in global cerebral ischaemia of variable magnitude, which may produce light-headedness, black-out of vision, or syncope. The most common cause of these symptoms in older people is orthostatic hypotension (see Chapter 4.4). The diagnosis is suspected if the symptoms occur on standing or after the individual is up for a while. Postprandial and night-time (on the way to the bathroom) symptoms are quite common. Light-headedness, relieved by sitting, is the most common symptom but occasionally, even in the absence of syncope a fall occurs. Reproducing the symptoms in association with a significant drop in blood pressure is evidence for orthostatic hypotension.

Orthostatic hypotension may be produced by autonomic dysfunction within the central (e.g. Shy–Drager syndrome) or peripheral (e.g. diabetic neuropathy) nervous system in elderly subjects. Its prevalence is also widespread in older individuals because of the use of medications. The diagnosis should be considered in all older people with unexplained falls (especially if the gait and balance are satisfactory) and pursued with multiple determinations of blood pressure, supine and immediately after standing up if necessary. Although occasionally difficult to treat, it is often the case that changing antihypertensive drugs or other simple medication manoeuvres produce a 'vast improvement in symptoms'.

Syncope associated with an arrhythmia or valvular heart disease is uncommon as a cause of falls. By contrast with orthostatic hypotension the symptoms frequently occur when lying or sitting, and loss of consciousness is common. Although it may be suspected clinically, the diagnosis is confirmed by specialized cardiological techniques used to provoke arrhythmias. Head turning (flexion–extension or rotation) in older individuals may produce light-headedness, vertigo, or rarely loss of consciousness resulting in falls. Although reportedly common (5 per cent of falls) (Sheldon 1960; Overstall *et al.* 1977), in the authors' experience head turning may sometimes produce light-headedness or vertigo but rarely results in falls. No clear-cut cause for the symptoms is generally accepted, although carotid sinus hypersensitivity, labyrinthine dysfunction, and verte-brobasilar ischaemia due to bony compression have been suggested. An attempt to reproduce the symptoms with head turning is worthwhile. Vertigo induced by head movement (postural vertigo), which is accompanied by nystagmus and nausea, is often produced by vestibular and/or labyrinthine dysfunction, usually lasting for several days. Evaluation of hearing and vestibular function as well as cranial nerve and cerebellar function is warranted, especially if the symptoms persist. In the absence of other symptoms suggestive of a transient ischaemic attack, a diagnosis of vertebrobasilar ischaemia is not warranted. Empirical daily treatment with a soft collar may, however, decrease the symptoms.

Drop attacks are sudden falls produced by a temporary inability of the limbs to support weight. This can be caused by a loss of muscle tone or muscle spasm and is not associated with altered consciousness. These episodes may be either the result of specific diseases (symptomatic) or idiopathic. The causes of symptomatic drop attacks in older people include cardiac disease, cerebrovascular disease, neuromuscular and spinal cord disease producing proximal lower extremity weakness, loss of postural tone due to epilepsy, cataplexy, or myoclonus, structural brain disease (e.g. frontal, medullary, cerebellar), and impaired balance/postural control caused by neurological disease (e.g. Parkinson's disease) (Lee and Marsden 1995). The majority of cases are idiopathic, particularly in older people. The episodes are brief (lasting only 1 to 2 min), usually repetitive, and although they were initially described as involving only women (Stevens and Matthews 1973) they occur often in men. Although reported as a frequent cause of repetitive falls in older subjects, neurologists rarely encounter patients with drop attacks.

Light-headedness, which is a common symptom among older individuals, is also related to the occurrence of falls. Light-headedness may be episodic or continual and is associated with multiple sensory deficits, hyperventilation, and cardiovascular disease, although often a clear-cut cause is not established.

Neurological dysfunction that impairs gait and balance

The examination should determine the extent and type, as well as localize the site(s) of underlying neural dysfunction. Non-neural factors are common, often impairing mobility. Arthritis limits joint function producing pain and limited mobility. Frailty is often associated with weakness and diminished capacity for aerobic work thus compromising gait. Metabolic encephalopathy may be associated with altered sensorium and disturbance of mobility (Larson et al. 1987). Medications, particularly neuroleptics, tricyclic antidepressants, long-acting benzodiazepines, antihypertensive drugs, and alcohol, may impair co-ordination and affect postural reflexes (Sudarsky 1990).

The examination should include observation of the patient arising from a chair, walking, turning, and sitting down. Arising from a low chair (without arm push-off) is an excellent test of the strength of proximal leg muscles (glutei and quadriceps) as well as of the ability to shift the centre of gravity from the chair to a newly established base of support while standing. Standing should be accomplished with one fluid series of movements. Walking is also a series of synchronous automatic movements of the legs, torso, and arms, which have been divided into swing and stance phases. During the swing phase, one foot is lifted and moved forward while the foot in contact with the ground is rolling forward (from heel to toes) in preparation for the next step. During stance, the heel of the swing foot strikes the ground while the other foot prepares for lift-off with a vigorous push from the toes and forefoot. The gait of healthy older individuals appears normal, although it may not be as rapid as in younger subjects. As in younger people, turning in healthy older individuals should result from a smooth pivoting movement rather than a series of small steps. Balance can be tested by creating minor rapid shifts in the centre of gravity using small forward and backward pushes. The healthy older person should easily correct for these without taking steps or losing balance. The examiner should protect the patient from a fall during this test by positioning his or her own body in the direction of the push.

Thus, by observing these key features of a patient's ability to 'get up and go' (Mathias et al. 1986), the clinician is able to study the essential components of gait and balance. The righting reflex is called upon to enable the patient to get from a sitting to an upright position. It requires co-ordination of muscle strength as well as vestibular and proprioceptive reflexes, such that the patient is able to enact this change without falling over or collapsing back. Supporting reactions are then necessary to maintain stance, increasing muscle tone as needed to keep the centre of gravity over a narrow base. When challenged with self- or examiner-initiated shifts in this centre of gravity, anticipatory and postural reflexes are called into play to correct for these changes without having to take steps or losing balance. If the patient fails to correct himself, rescue and protective reactions are then initiated with stretching out of arms or legs to restore equilibrium or break a fall, and stepping reactions to bring the feet back under the shifted centre of gravity. Walking is then initiated, starting with gait initiation which should be fluid and rhythmic, and a normal gait cycle as described above (Nutt et al. 1993).

An experienced clinician uses the type of gait and balance impairment to localize the site of dysfunction within the nervous system. This impression is confirmed by eliciting the appropriate signs during the neurological examination. The sites of dysfunction produce characteristic clinical syndromes, which are discussed below.

Frontal lobe syndrome

The frontal lobe syndrome is a broad term used to encompass a variety of neurological disorders which manifest with a frontal gait disorder. This is a gait pattern characterized by small steps which shuffle and barely clear the ground, as if the feet were magnetically attracted to and just slide along the floor (i.e. magnetic gait) (Denny-Brown 1958; Meyer and Barron 1960; Barron 1967). There is also hesitation and freezing on gait initiation, turns, and changes in movement, moderate disequilibrium on rising from a chair and maintaining stance, a variable base (narrow to wide), and some bradykinesia and rigidity (Sudarsky 1990; Nutt et al. 1993). There may also be associated urinary dysfunction as well as slowed cognitive processing, although dementia, if present, is mild. When it is severe, pseudobulbar speech and swallowing difficulties, blunted, inappropriate, or labile affect as well as frontal lobe release signs with palmar and plantar grasps, paratonia, and pyramidal tract dysfunction (lower extremity spasticity and Babinski signs) may be present.

The disability can be progressive and may become so severe that individuals can no longer correct for minor shifts of weight and so suffer spontaneous falls. Motor manifestations of the frontal lobe syndrome may be difficult to differentiate from Parkinson's disease, perhaps because the output from basal ganglia to the frontal lobes facilitates the same transcortical postural reflexes that are impaired directly by lesions of the frontal lobes. Useful clues, however, are that in frontal gait disorder, truncal posture often remains upright, and there may be preservation of arm swing when walking. Also, a wide-based gait is not usually associated with Parkinson's disease, and festination, retropulsion, or propulsion are more suggestive of this. Often, with frontal lobe syndrome, patients receive an unsuccessful trial of l-dopa.

The differential diagnosis of the bifrontal syndrome includes ischaemic small-vessel disease, structural lesions such as tumours, advanced Alzheimer's disease, and normal pressure hydrocephalus. Visualization of the brain by magnetic resonance imaging (MRI) allows differentiation of small subcortical infarcts, mass lesions, and hydrocephalus.

Ischaemic white matter disease

Small-vessel ischaemic disease produces infarction in the distribution of smaller end arteries feeding subcortical frontal white matter. It may evolve slowly (years), and is associated with increasing age, high blood pressure, and silent cerebral infarction (Longstreth et al. 1996). Prior reports have shown an association between CT or MRI evidence of white matter lesions and gait and balance dysfunction (Masdeu et al. 1989; Baloh et al. 1995). Clinicopathological investigations suggest that leucoaraiosis may denote white matter astrocytosis which is a reaction to focal ischaemia (Baloh and Vinters 1995). Ischaemia has not conclusively been shown to produce these white matter lesions, although previous autopsy studies of patients with bifrontal gait abnormalities have found a high frequency of lacunar infarcts (George et al. 1986; Steingart et al. 1987). MRI has made antemortem detection of small ischaemic lesions feasible.

Normal pressure hydrocephalus

The diagnosis of normal pressure hydrocephalus, currently felt to be an uncommon disease, was made frequently in the years immediately following the description of this syndrome (Adams et al. 1965). Patients with prominent dementia and cortical atrophy, in addition to hydrocephalus, were given shunts. The lack of response and the major complications of shunt surgery produced unsatisfactory results. This diagnosis should be suspected in patients with a frontal lobe syndrome (i.e. the classic triad of gait disturbance, mental deterioration, and urinary incontinence) who on imaging, have severe ventricular dilation and little or no cortical atrophy. Intracranial pressure monitoring to record abnormal fluctuations (Launas and Lobata 1979), as well as clinical response to removal of 40 to 50 cm^3 of cerebrospinal fluid (Fisher 1982; Wikkelso 1982), are often used to predict the success of shunting, although many clinicians rely solely on clinical and imaging features. If appropriate patients are treated, the motor function often improves after the shunt; however, shunt-related complications may occur in as high as 30 to 40 per cent of cases (Vanneste et al. 1992). In many cases, gait disturbance may be the only manifestation of normal pressure hydrocephalus, and thus the sole measure of improvement.

Parkinson's disease

Parkinson's disease is a common age-associated disease with increasing incidence in the sixth to eighth decades. Because it is a syndrome as well as a specific disease state whose primary manifestations involve abnormalities of gait and balance, it is an important cause of impaired mobility and falls. The clinical features and management of Parkinson's disease in later life are discussed in Chapter 18.5.

Briefly, the important features of Parkinson's disease include bradykinesia, rigidity, resting tremor, as well as gait and balance impairment. The bradykinesia manifests as slowness and paucity of use of the arms and hands, an immobile (mask-like) facies, and difficulty initiating movement. The rigidity is characterized as the ratchet-like resistance to passive stretching (i.e. cogwheel rigidity) which is often but not always present in Parkinson's disease. The characteristic 3 to 8 Hz pill rolling resting tremor is likewise an important sign, but not necessarily present in all cases (Quinn 1995). It is most prominent in the arms, but may involve the legs or head. Usually, the gait becomes small stepped, slow, and festinating, with stooped posture and diminished associated arm and torso movement. Turning is done en bloc, with a series of small irregular steps rather than a fluid pivoting movement, and may be preceded by a moment of hesitation or freezing. Similarly, initiation of gait is difficult and marked by hesitation. Arising from a chair may require multiple efforts, with difficulty in establishing a stable standing posture. This is in part due to a fundamental problem of balance as well. The patient is unable to keep the centre of gravity vertical to the base of support, and to make rapid postural corrections after encountering environmental hazards. Postural instability usually occurs in the later stages of idiopathic Parkinson's disease.

Parkinson's disease progresses slowly over many years (5 to 20+ years) and if untreated, often produces severe disability. Treatment provides significant improvement of symptoms at all stages. Gait is usually improved, but imbalance and tremor are not always resolved.

The parkinsonian syndrome includes a number of diseases with features of Parkinson's disease (i.e. impaired gait and balance with motor slowing) which are produced by other mechanisms. These conditions should be differentiated from Parkinson's disease. Features which suggest Parkinson's disease include the resting tremor and a good response to levodopa. Characteristics which suggest other aetiologies include rapid progression of symptoms, early instability or falls, presence of other associated signs such as autonomic failure, cerebellar deficits, pyramidal dysfunction, downgaze palsy, and prominent dementia or bulbar signs (Quinn 1995). Nevertheless, when in doubt, a trial of levodopa/carbidopa is indicated as other diseases producing the syndrome respond poorly to this medication (Newman et al. 1985). Patients receiving phenothiazines or butyrophenones, must have the drugs discontinued for several weeks before a diagnosis of Parkinson's disease can be made.

Pyramidal tract dysfunction

Interruption of the descending corticospinal tract impairs voluntary motor control, resulting in weakness and clumsiness. Unilateral interruption of the tract results in a hemiparesis with a characteristic position of the legs and arms (circumduction at thigh and plantar flexion of the foot). The usual cause of hemiparesis in older patients is stroke, although defining the nature and extent of the infarction as well as evaluating the presence of other causes (e.g. subdural haematoma or tumour) warrants evaluation with CT or MRI. Bilateral corticospinal lesions result in a stiff gait with hyperadduction and spasticity (scissoring) at thighs and feet, which are averted and plantar flexed. Paraparesis results from multiple hemispheric lesions (often lacunar infarcts), mid-line hemispheric lesions, spinal cord compression due to osteoarthritic overgrowth of bony elements within the canal, epidural metastatic lesions, and occasionally amyotrophic lateral sclerosis. Ambulatory elderly patients who develop a progressive paraparesis should be evaluated and a diagnosis established. The possibility of significant benefit with little risk (at least during the investigations) dictates the approach. When paraparesis is secondary to a myelopathy, patients present with pyramidal signs of spasticity and hyper-reflexia, as well as dorsal column deficits in proprioception–vibration, and urinary frequency or incontinence. The spinal cord is well visualized by MRI, while CT allows delineation of bony elements within the canal. Myelography is occasionally required when questions remain. Patients with cervical spondylosis, the most common cause of myelopathy in elderly people, can be treated with a cervical collar. If progression continues, threatening function, healthy symptomatic elderly patients with one or two levels of compression often benefit from surgical intervention. Similarly, patients with epidural spinal cord compression due to metastases, respond to radiation; occasionally a benign tumour (e.g. meningioma, neurofibroma) requires surgery. Vitamin B$_{12}$ deficiency or subacute combined degeneration, is another important and reversible cause of myelopathy in older patients. Response to vitamin B$_{12}$ replacement is usually favourable (Sudarsky 1990).

Progressive supranuclear palsy

Progressive supranuclear palsy, often included within the symptomatic description of parkinsonism, has a prevalence of about 1 per cent of that of Parkinson's disease (Golbe et al. 1987). The disease is progressive, with a mean age of onset at 63 years, and a median survival of 5.6 years (Litvan et al. 1996). The original description called for a constellation of supranuclear ophthalmoplegia, pseudobulbar palsy, dysarthria, neck and truncal dystonia, and dementia (Steele et al. 1964). More recently, it has been described that early postural instability and falls is the most frequent clinical feature of the disease, occurring during the first year in about 58 per cent of cases (Litvan et al. 1996). Vertical supranuclear palsy resulting in impaired voluntary eye movements, particularly on downgaze (Golbe and Davis 1988), is the unique feature of the disease. Symmetric axial rigidity and akinesia, as opposed to the asymmetric limb rigidity–akinesia seen in Parkinson's disease, is often a prominent feature (Collins et al. 1995). The gait is described as shuffling, but more typically wide based. Axial or truncal movements are performed slowly and stiffly, with a classic tendency to move en bloc, to the extent of stiffly dropping onto a chair when attempting to sit. When present, the dementia is mild, and is caused by a subcortical pathology resulting in slow mentation, difficulty in using complex information, forgetfulness, and emotional and personality changes (Maher and Lees 1986; Golbe and Davis 1988) This is usually associated with pseudobulbar and frontal release signs (Litvan et al. 1996) (see also Chapter 18.5).

The pathology of progressive supranuclear palsy is distinct. Postmortem examination demonstrates widespread subcortical neurofibrillary tangles and neuropil threads in the basal ganglia and brainstem (Hauw et al. 1994). The presence of Lewy bodies characteristic of Parkinson's disease, and oligodendroglial inclusion bodies characteristic of multiple-system atrophy, are among the pathological exclusion criteria (Hauw et al. 1994). L-Dopa and synthetic dopamine agonists are ineffective (Golbe and Davis 1988).

Multiple-system atrophy

Another multiple-system degenerative disorder presenting with parkinsonism plus other distinct features is multiple-system atrophy. The presence of any combination of the following clinical syndromes in addition to parkinsonism, suggests this diagnosis: autonomic, cerebellar, or pyramidal dysfunction. Respectively, these correspond to what are specifically called Shy–Drager syndrome, sporadic olivopontocerebellar atrophy, and striatonigral degeneration, depending on which features predominate. Autonomic manifestations of the Shy–Drager syndrome including postural hypotension, impotence, and incontinence have been reported in as many as 97 per cent of patients (Wenning et al. 1995). Cerebellar and pyramidal signs each occur in more than 50 per cent of cases. Therefore gait may be a combination of parkinsonism, ataxia, and spasticity.

Thus, parkinsonian features in a patient with autonomic dysfunction, gait ataxia, dysmetria, postural and action tremor, hyperreflexia, extensor plantar responses, dysarthria, dysphonia, or respiratory stridor, should alert the clinician to the possibility of multiple-system atrophy. Dementia is not usually a feature of this disorder. A trial of levodopa should not result in significant improvement (Quinn and Marsden 1993) (see also Chapter 18.5).

Onset of the disease is usually earlier than that seen in idiopathic Parkinson's disease (range of 33–76 years old, median 55 years), and survival is shortened to a median of 5 to 7 years (Wenning et al. 1995). Establishing the correct diagnosis allows appropriate supportive treatment as well as thoughtful planning based on a realistic prognosis. The cytological hallmark of this complex of syndromes is the presence of oligodendroglial inclusion bodies, in addition to cell loss and gliosis in the substantia nigra, striatum, pons, olives, cerebellum, and spinal cord.

Alzheimer's disease

Alzheimer's disease in its early stages has little obvious effect on motor function, although motor signs become more prominent as the illness progresses. In moderately advanced Alzheimer patients, there are reports (Visser 1983) of diminished stride length, walking speed, and balance (increased sway), and impaired postural reflexes. Some patients may also exhibit extrapyramidal features, particularly rigidity (Tyrell and Rossor 1989) The motor dysfunction may be an important element in the disability in the later stages of Alzheimer's disease, although it is overshadowed by cognitive dysfunction.

Ataxia

A wide-based unsteady gait, with lurching erratic steps and difficulty with postural transitions (turns, standing up, and walking heel to toe), is most characteristic of cerebellar dysfunction. Sensory abnormalities produced by vestibular, propioceptive, visual, and tactile dysfunction may share common features, although they are separable by neurological examination. Ataxia may be produced by mass lesions compressing the mid-line cerebellum or its output, but is more often produced by infarction in older individuals. Structural lesions within the posterior fossa are well demonstrated by MRI. Cerebellar ataxia may be part of an olivopontocerebellar or multiple-system atrophy, as well as a manifestation of alcoholism, hypothyroidism, paraneoplastic syndrome, or vitamin E deficiency.

Vestibular dysfunction due to end-organ problems (vestibular neuronitis) is accompanied by prominent positional vertigo, unsteadiness, with nausea, and gaze-evoked nystagmus. Although the gait is ataxic, no other neurological signs are present unless the symptoms are a result of brainstem ischaemia. Tactile proprioceptive loss results in an unsteady gait with difficulty on uneven surfaces, compensated in part by visual cues. The classic example is the sensory ataxia seen in tabetic neurosyphilis with involvement mainly of the dorsal columns. In older patients with accompanying visual impairment (e.g. glaucoma, cataracts), there may be mild ataxia and unsteadiness perceived as a light-headed sensation. In some cases, difficulties with balance and dizziness arises in fact, simply from a combination of multiple sensory deficits, such as neuropathy from diabetes, proprioception deficits, visual impairment, and vestibular dysfunction. Acute decompensation from any additional stressors is then not an unusual sequela (Drachman and Hart 1972).

Peripheral nerve and muscle dysfunction

As noted above, mild tactile proprioceptive loss in older subjects is presumably related to changes within receptors or sensory nerves. A significant neuropathy is not a part of healthy ageing, and should be evaluated thoroughly. Neuropathy is often the result of systemic illness (e.g. diabetes, vasculitis) but may result from medication or toxic exposure. Conversely, the authors have recently encountered two patients over 70 years with progression of dysfunction, in whom a hereditary sensorimotor neuropathy (Charcot–Marie–Tooth) was the diagnosis. The characteristic steppage gait, with foot slapping, is indicative of weakness of the foot dorsiflexors produced by the neuropathy. Chronic inflammatory demyelinating polyneuropathy may also be seen in the older population; age of onset ranging from 10 to 77 years, mean of about 50 years old (Barohn et al. 1989). It is characterized by progressive (more than 2 months) or relapsing motor and sensory dysfunction with a peripheral nerve distribution, affecting more than one limb (Ad Hoc Subcommittee of the American Academy of Neurology AIDS Task Force 1991). Gait difficulties, similar to other neuropathies, arise as a function of specific weakness and sensory deficits. Diagnosis is made by nerve conduction studies, cerebrospinal fluid showing increased protein with no increase in the cell count, and exclusion of other causes of polyneuropathy. Treatment options include steroids, plasmapharesis, intravenous immunoglobulin, and immunosuppressive therapy (see also Chapter 18.7).

Conversely, myopathy results in proximal weakness with a characteristic waddling gait and difficulty in climbing stairs or arising from a chair. Inflammatory myopathies, osteomalacia, and hypothyroidism are potentially treatable, thereby making evaluation of weakness produced by nerve and muscle problems worthwhile. Muscle enzymes and electrodiagnostic evaluation of nerve and muscle function are essential in making the appropriate diagnosis. In equivocal cases and cases of inclusion body myositis, muscle biopsy may be necessary to make a definitive diagnosis. Inclusion body myositis is worth considering in elderly people. It occurs in the older population,

usually in people above 50 years of age, more commonly in males, and manifests both proximal and distal muscle weakness. Specific muscle groups are predominantly involved (quadriceps, triceps, biceps, and finger flexors) producing selective weakness by comparison with the iliopsoas and other proximal muscles (Griggs et al. 1995). Diagnosis is worthwhile although, unlike the other inflammatory myopathies, response to steroids and immunosuppressive therapy is poor (Dalakas 1991).

Implications of motor dysfunction and age

Alterations in sensorimotor functions that some have associated with ageing are reviewed above. Gait and balance slow modestly with age, and, although these age-associated changes require further definition, the functions remaining are capable of supporting a mobile active lifestyle.

Often patients with ischaemic white matter disease or those with multifactorial impairment of gait and balance who are difficult to place into the diagnostic categories discussed above are said to have a 'senile gait disorder'. This diagnosis does not imply a specific type of gait or pathophysiology and may represent a significant portion of patients with failing mobility that a neurologist will encounter. Moreover, use of this definition implies an age-associated inevitability for motor dysfunction that the facts do not support. It remains for neurologists and geriatricians to broaden their understanding of age-associated diseases that produce this impairment so that a cause can be established for all patients. The importance of ischaemic arteriolar white matter lesions as a mechanism for producing impairment of gait and balance is only now being defined. By avoiding definitions that imply an inevitable deterioration, we may be able to characterize the underlying pathophysiological mechanisms that produce motor dysfunction so as to develop specific disease-oriented interventions.

In older patients without specific remediable diagnoses, treatment should be directed towards improving function. Balance is similar to other motor skills in that training (i.e. repetitive balance challenges) results in improved balance performance. The authors' group accomplished a 3-month intensive (three 1-h sessions per week) balance training programme in healthy community dwellers (mean age 80 years). The intervention which included equilibrium control and centre-of-pressure biofeedback resulted in improvement on multiple indices of balance, analogous to an individual 3 to 10 years younger (Wolfson et al. 1996). Another approach delineates the patient's physical impairments causing poor gait and balance and then remediates them. Therapists capable of this evaluation and remediation programme are available in some communities. This rehabilitative approach may be most appropriate for more severely compromised patients.

Even without such a defined rehabilitative approach, the practitioner can make useful suggestions. Activity should be encouraged, despite the subject's fear of falls. This can be accomplished by the family, friends, or even neighbours who are willing to accompany the patient on daily outings or in the safety of an indoor gym or old people's centre.

The correct choice of shoes may be of help in improving balance by moving the centre of gravity. Individuals who are unable to correct for backwards displacement of their body mass may be helped by heel lifts that move them forward; those who cannot resist forward-directed forces are helped by flat shoes. Shoes with non-slip (but not cleated) soles and a small amount of heel lift are suitable for the remainder of older people with poor balance. A walking stick will broaden the base of support, thereby providing extra security to those with a fear of falling. Selection of an appropriate length (15° of elbow flexion when the stick is in contact with the floor), maximizes support while minimizing interference with gait. Walking frames provide more support but are disruptive to gait efficiency and speed and increase the effort required in walking. This trade-off may be necessary in very unstable older patients. A weighted shopping trolley is effective in providing stability in addition to aiding in important functions that support an independent lifestyle.

Vision is often impaired in older subjects. Visual input may be crucial in individuals with pre-existing tactile proprioceptive or vestibular dysfunction. Therefore, appropriate lenses for medium and far vision may significantly improve balance. Older individuals often live in suboptimal environments surrounded by potentially lethal hazards. Proper lighting, attention to uneven, loose, or stepped surfaces, along with the use of user-friendly environmental aids (grab bars or rails), can be provided with modest cost and effort. Older individuals and their families must also be aware of avoiding hazardous environments where possible (e.g. icy surfaces, tall insecure step-stools, and steep poorly lit stairs).

The realization that disorders of mobility are critical factors in the lives of our elderly populace is already widely accepted. Attention to defining the causes of this dysfunction as well as developing interventions is beginning to effect rapid changes in our approach to this widespread problem.

References

Ad Hoc Subcommittee of the American Academy of Neurology AIDS Task Force (1991). Research criteria for diagnosis of chronic inflammatory demyelinating polyneuropathy (CIDP). *Neurology*, 41, 617–18.

Adams, R.D., Fisher, C.M., Hakim, S., Ojcman, R.G., and Sweet, W.H. (1965). Symptomatic occult hydrocephalus with 'normal' cerebrospinal fluid pressure. *New England Journal of Medicine*, 273, 117–26.

Baker, S.P. and Harvey, A.H. (1985). Fall injuries in the elderly. *Clinics in Geriatric Medicine*, 1, 501–12.

Baloh, R.W. and Vinters, H.V. (1995) White matter lesions and disequilibrium in older people II. Clinicopathologic correlation. *Archives of Neurology*, 52, 975–81.

Baloh, R.W., Yue, Q., Socotch, T.M., and Jacobson, K.M. (1995). White matter lesions and disequilibrium in older people. Case–control comparison. *Archives of Neurology*, 52, 970–4.

Barohn, R.J., Kissel, J.T., et al. (1989). Chronic inflammatory demyelinating polyradiculopathy. *Archives of Neurology*, 46, 878–84.

Barron, R.E. (1967). Disorders of gait related to the aging nervous system. *Geriatrics*, 22, 113.

Bernheimer, H., Birkmayer, W., Hornykiewicz, O., Jellinger, K., and Sertelberger, F. (1973). Brain dopamine and the syndromes of Parkinson and Huntington. Clinical, morphological, and neurocorrelations. *Journal of Neurological Science*, 20, 415–55.

Bohannon, R.W., Larkin, P.A., Cook, P.D., Gear, J., and Singer, J. (1984). Decrease in timed balance test scores with aging. *Physical Therapy*, 64, 1067–70.

Bruner, A. and Norris, T.W. (1971). Age related changes in caloric nystagmus. *Acta Otolaryngological Supplement*, 282, 1–24.

Buchthal, F. and Rosenfalck, A. (1966). Evoked action potentials and conduction velocity in human sensory nerves. *Brain Research*, 3, 1–22.

Buchthal, F., Rosenfalck, A., and Behse, F. (1975). Sensory potentials of normal and diseased nerve. In *Peripheral neuropathy* (ed. P.J. Dyck, P.K. Thomas, and E.H. Lamber), pp. 442–64. W.B. Saunders, Philadelphia, PA.

Carlsson, A. and Winblad, B. (1976). Influence of age and time interval between death and autopsy on dopamine and 3-methoxytyramine levels in human basal ganglia. *Journal of Neural Transmission*, 38, 271–6.

Carter, A.B. (1979) The neurologic aspects of aging. In *Clinical geriatrics* (2nd edn) (ed. I. Rossman), pp. 292–316. J.B. Lippincott, Philadelphia, PA.

Collins, S.J., Ahlskog, J.E., et al. (1995). Progressive supranuclear palsy: neuropathologically based diagnostic clinical criteria. *Journal of Neurology, Neurosurgery and Psychiatry*, 58, 167–73.

Cooper, K.D., Tabaddor, K., Hauser, W.A., Shulman, K., Feiner, C., and Factor, P.R. (1983). The epidemiology of head injury in the Bronx. *Neuroepidemiology*, 2, 70–88.

Dalakas, M.C. (1991). Polymyositis, dermatomyositis, and inclusion-body myositis. *New England Journal of Medicine*, 325, 1487–98.

Denny-Brown, D. (1958). The nature of apraxia. *Journal of Nervous and Mental Diseases*, 126, 9–32.

Dorfman, L.J. and Bosley, T.M. (1979). Age-related changes in peripheral and central nerve conduction in man. *Neurology*, 29, 38–44.

Drachman, D.A. and Hart, C.W. (1972). An approach to the dizzy patient. *Neurology*, 22, 323–34.

Dyck, P.J, Shultz, P.W., and O'Brien, P.C. (1972). Quantification of touch pressure sensation. *Archives of Neurology*, 26, 465–73.

Engel, W.K. (1970). Selective and non-selective susceptibility of muscle fiber types. *Archives of Neurology*, 22, 97–117.

Fisher, C.M. (1982). Hydrocephalus as a cause of disturbances of gait in the elderly. *Neurology*, 32, 1358–63.

George, A.E., De Leon, M.J., Gentes, C.I., et al. (1986). Leukoencephalopathy in normal and pathologic aging: CT of brain lucencies. *American Journal of Neuro-radiology*, 7, 561–6.

Golbe, L.I. and Davis, P.H. (1988). Progressive supranuclear palsy: recent advances. In *Parkinson's disease and movement disorders* (ed. J. Jankovic and E. Tolusa). Urban and Schwarzenberg, Baltimore, MD.

Golbe, L.I., Davis, P.H., Schoenberg, B.S., and Pavoisin, R.C. (1987). The natural history and prevalence of progressive supranuclear palsy. *Neurology*, 37 (Supplement 1), 1031–4.

Griggs, R.C., Askanas, V., et al. (1995). Inclusion body myositis and myopathies. *Annals of Neurology*, 38, 705–13.

Grimby, G., Danneskiold-Sumsoe, B., Huid, K., and Saltin, B. (1982). Morphology and enzymatic capacity in arm and leg muscles in 78–81 year old men and women. *Acta Physiologica Scandinavica*, 115, 125–34.

Gryfe, C.L., Amies, A., and Ashley, M.J. (1977). A longitudinal study of falls in an elderly population. I. Incidence and morbidity. *Age and Ageing*, 6, 201–10.

Guimaraes, R.M. and Isaacs, B. (1980). Characteristics of the gait in old people who fall. *International Journal of Rehabilitative Medicine*, 2, 177–80.

Hauw, J.J., Daniel, S.E., et al. (1994). Preliminary NINDS neuropathologic criteria for Steele–Richardson–Olszewski syndrome (progressive supranuclear palsy). *Neurology*, 44, 2015–19.

Howell, T.H. (1975). Old age—some practical points. In *Geriatrics* (3rd edn), pp. 38–47. H.K. Lewis, London.

Hurley, B.F. (1995). Age, gender and muscular strength. *Journal of Gerontology*, 50A (Special Issue), 41–4.

Imms, F.J. and Edholm, O.G. (1979). Studies of gait and mobility in the elderly. *Age and Ageing*, 10, 147–56.

Judge, J.O., Davis, R.B., and Ounpuu, S. (1996) Step length reductions in advanced age: the role of ankle and hip kinetics. *Journal of Gerontology*, 51A, M303–12.

King, M.B., Judge, J.O., and Wolfson, L. (1994). Functional base of support decreases with age. *Journal of Gerontology*, 48, M258–63.

Klawans, H.L., Tufo, H.M., and Ostfeld, A.M. (1971). Neurologic examination in an elderly population. *Diseases of the Nervous System*, 32, 274–9.

Kokmen, E., Bossemeyer, R.W., Barney, J., and Williams, W.J. (1977). Neurological manifestations of aging. *Journal of Gerontology*, 32, 411–19.

Kokmen, E., Bossemeyer, R.W., and Williams, W. (1978). Quantitative evaluation of joint motion sensation in an aging population. *Journal of Gerontology*, 33, 62–7.

Larson, E.B., Kukull, W.A., *et al.* (1987). Adverse drug reactions associated with global cognitive impairment in elderly persons. *Annals of Internal Medicine*, 107, 169–73.

Larsson, L. (1978). Morphological and functional characteristics of the aging skeletal muscle in man. A cross-sectional study. *Acta Physiologica Scandinavica*, 457 (Supplement).

Larsson, L. (1982). Aging in mammalian skeletal muscle. In *The aging motor system* (ed. J.A. Mortimer, F.J. Pirozzolo and G.J. Maletta), pp. 60–96. Praeger, New York.

Launas, C. and Lobata, R.D. (1979). Intraventricular pressure and CSF dynamics in chronic adult hydrocephalus. *Surgical Neurology*, 12, 287.

Lee, S.K. and Marsden, C.D. (1995). Drop attacks. *Advances in Neurology*, 674, 1–52.

Litvan, I., Mangone, C.A., *et al.* (1996). Natural history of progressive supranuclear palsy (Steele–Richardson–Olszewski syndrome) and clinical predictors of survival: a clinicopathological study. *Journal of Neurology, Neurosurgery and Psychiatry*, 61, 615–20.

Longstreth, W.T., Jr, Manolio, T.A., Arnold, A., *et al.* (1996). Clinical correlates of white matter findings on cranial magnetic resonance imaging of 3301 elderly people. *Stroke*, 27, 1274–82.

McGeer, E.G. (1976). Aging and neurotransmitter metabolism in the human brain. In *Alzheimer's disease, senile dementia and related disorders. Ageing series*, Vol. 7 (ed. R.K. Katzman, R.D. Terry, and K.L. Byck), pp. 427–40. Raven Press, New York.

McGeer, P.L., McGeer, E.G., and Suzuki, J.S. (1977). Aging and extra-pyramidal function. *Archives of Neurology*, 34, 33–5.

Maher, E.R. and Lees, A.J. (1986). The clinical features and natural history of the Steele–Richardson–Olszewski syndrome (progressive supranuclear palsy). *Neurology*, 36, 1005–8.

Masdeu, J.C., Wolfson, L., Lautos, G., *et al.* (1989). Brain white matter disease in elderly prone to falling. *Archives of Neurology*, 46, 1292–6.

Mathias, S., Nayak, U.S.L., and Isaacs, B. (1986). Balance in elderly patients: the 'get up and go' test. *Archives of Physical Medicine and Rehabilitation*, 67, 387–9.

Meyer, J.S. and Barron, D.W. (1960). Apraxia of gait: a clinicophysiologic study. *Brain*, 83, 261–84.

Moritani, T. and de Vries, H.G. (1980). Potential for gross muscle hypertrophy in older men. *Journal of Gerontology*, 24, 169–82.

Murray, M.P., Kory, R.C., and Clarkson, B.H. (1969). Walking patterns in healthy old men. *Journal of Gerontology*, 24, 169–80.

Nakamura, S.I., Akiguchi, M., Kamegama, M., and Mizuno, W. (1985). Age-related changes to pyramidal cell basal dendrites in layers III and V of human motor cortex: a quantitative Golgi study. *Acta Neuropathologica (Berlin)*, 65, 281–4.

Newman, R.P., LeWitt, P., Jaffe, M., Caine, D.B., and Larsen, T.A. (1985). Motor function in the normal aging population treatment with L-dopa. *Neurology*, 35, 571–3.

Nutt, J.G., Marsden, C.D., and Thompson, P.D. (1993). Human walking and higher level gait disorders, particularly in the elderly. *Neurology*, 43, 268–79.

Overstall, P.W., Exton-Smith, A.N., Imms, F.J., and Johnson, A.L. (1977). Falls in the elderly related to postural imbalance. *British Medical Journal*, i, 261–4.

Perret, E. and Reglis, F. (1970). Age and the perceptual threshold for vibratory stimuli. *European Neurology*, 4, 65–76.

Peterka, R.J., Black, F.O., and Schoenfoff, M.B. (1994). Age related changes in human vestibulo-ocular reflexes: sinusoidal rotation and caloric tests. *Journal of Vestibular Research*, 1, 49–59.

Potvin, A.R., Syndulko, K., Tourtellotte, W.W., Goldberg, Z., Potvin, J.H., and Hansch, E.C. (1980*a*). Quantitative evaluation of normal age-related changes in neurologic function. In *Advances in neurogerontology*, Vol. 2 (ed. F.J. Pirozzolo and G.J. Maletta). Praeger, New York.

Potvin, A.R., Syndulko, K., Tourtellotte, W.W., Lemmon, J.J.A., and Potvin, J.H. (1980*b*). Human neurologic function and the aging process. *Journal of the American Geriatrics Society*, 28, 1–9.

Quinn, N. (1995). Parkinsonism—recognition and differential diagnosis. *British Medical Journal*, 310, 447–52.

Quinn, N.P. and Marsden, C.D. (1993). The motor disorder of multiple system atrophy. *Journal of Neurology, Neurosurgery and Psychiatry*, 56, 1239–42.

Rossiter-Fornoff, J.E., Wolf, S.L., Wolfson, L.I., Buchner, D.M., and the FICSIT Group (1995). A cross sectional validation study of the FICSIT common data base balance measures. *Journal of Gerontology*, 50A, M291–7.

Rubenstein, L.Z., Robbins, A.S., Schulman, B.C., Rosada, T., Osterweil, D., and Josephson, K.R. (1988). Falls and instability in the elderly. *Journal of the American Geriatrics Society*, 36, 266–8.

Schaumburg, H.H., Spencer, P.S., and Ochoa, J. (1983). The aging human peripheral nervous system. In *The neurology of aging* (ed. R.K. Katzman and R. Terry), pp. 111–22. F.A. Davis, Philadelphia, PA.

Schultz, A., Alexander, N.B., Gu, M.J., and Boismier, T. (1993). Postural control in young and elderly adults when stance is challenged: clinical versus laboratory measurements. *Annals of Otology, Rhinology, Laryngology*, 102, 508–17.

Shefer, U.F. (1973). Absolute number of neurons and thickness of the cerebral cortex during ageing, senile and vascular dementia and Pick's and Alzheimer's disease. *Neuroscience and Behavioral Physiology*, 6, 319–24.

Sheldon, J.H. (1960). On the natural history of falls in old age. *British Medical Journal*, 5214, 1685–90.

Shields, R.W., Robbins, N., and Verrilli, A.A. (1984). The effects of chronic muscular activity of age-related changes in single fiber EMG. *Muscle and Nerve*, 7, 275–7.

Skinner, H.B., Barrack, R.L., and Cook, S.D. (1984). Age related decline in proprioception. *Clinical Orthopedics and Related Research*, 184, 208–11.

Stalberg, E., Berges, O., Ericsson, M., *et al.* (1989). The quadriceps femoris muscle in 20–70 year old subjects: relationship between knee extension torque, electro-physiologic parameters and muscle fiber characteristics. *Muscle and Nerve*, 12, 382–9.

Steele, J.C., Richardson, J.C., and Olszewski, J. (1964). Progressive supranuclear palsy. *Archives of Neurology*, 10, 333–59.

Steiness, I. (1957). Vibratory perception in normal subjects. *Acta Medica Scandinavica*, 58, 315–25.

Steingart, A., Hachinsk, V.O., Law, C., *et al.* (1987). Cognitive and neurologic findings in subjects with diffuse white matter lucencies on computed tomographic scan (leuko-araiosis). *Archives of Neurology*, 44, 32–5.

Stevens, D.C. and Matthews, W.B. (1973). Cryptogenic drop attacks an affliction of women. *British Medical Journal*, 1, 439.

Sudarsky, L. (1990). Geriatrics: gait disorders in the elderly. *New England Journal of Medicine*, 322, 1441–6.

Tomonaga, M. (1977). Histochemical and ultrastructural changes in senile human skeletal muscle. *Journal of the American Geriatrics Society*, **25**, 125–31.

Tyrell, P.J. and Rossor, M.N. (1989). Extrapyramidal signs in dementia of Alzheimer type. *Lancet*, **ii**, 920.

United States Bureau of the Census (1985). *Estimates of the population of the United States, by age, sex and race, 1980–1984*. Current population reports. Series p-25. No. 965. US Government Printing Office. Washington, DC.

Vanneste, J., Augustijn, P., Dirven, C., Tan, W.F., and Goedhart, Z.D. (1992). Shunting normal-pressure hydrocephalus: do the benefits outweigh the risks? *Neurology*, **42**, 54–9.

Visser, H. (1983). Gait and balance in senile dementia of the Alzheimer type. *Age and Ageing*, **12**, 296.

Welford, A.T. (1980). Sensory perceptual and motor processes in older adults. In *Handbook of mental health and aging* (ed. J.E. Birren and R.B. Swane), p. 192. Prentice-Hall, Englewood Cliffs, NJ.

Wenning, G.K., Ben-Shlomo, Y., et al. (1995). Clinicopathological study of 35 cases of multiple system atrophy. *Journal of Neurology, Neurosurgery and Psychiatry*, **58**, 160–6.

Whipple, R., Wolfson, L.I., and Amerman, P. (1987). The relationship of knee and ankle weakness to falls in nursing home residents. An isokinetic study. *Journal of the American Geriatrics Society*, **35**, 15–20.

Wikkelso, C., Andersson, H., Blomstrand, C., and Lindqvist, G. (1982). The clinical effect of lumbar puncture in normal pressure hydrocephalus. *Journal of Neurology, Neurosurgery and Psychiatry*, **45**, 64–9.

Winegard, K.J., Hicks, A.L., Sale, D.G., and Vandervoot, A.A. (1996). A 12-year follow-up study of ankle muscle function in older adults. *Journal of Gerontology*, **51A**, B202–7.

Wolfson, L.I., Whipple, R.H., Amerman, P., and Kleinberg, A. (1986). Stressing the postural response: a quantitative method for testing balance. *Journal of the American Geriatrics Society*, **34**, 845–50.

Wolfson, L.I., Whipple, R., Amerman, P., and Tobin, J.N. (1990). Gait assessment in the elderly: a gait abnormality rating scale and its relation to falls. *Journal of Gerontology*, **45**, M12–19.

Wolfson, L., Whipple, R., Derby, C.A., et al. (1992). A dynamic posturography study of balance in healthy elderly. *Neurology*, **42**, 2069–75.

Wolfson, L., Whipple, R., Derby, C.A., et al. (1996). Balance and strength training in older adults: intervention gains and tai chi maintenance. *Journal of the American Geriatrics Society*, **44**, 498–506.

Woollacott, M.H., Shumway-Cook, A., and Nashner, L. (1982). Postural reflexes and aging. In *The aging motor system* (ed. J.A. Mortimer, F.J. Pirozzolo, and G.J. Maletta), pp. 98–119. Praeger, New York.

18.12 Autonomic dysfunction

Christopher J. Mathias

Introduction

The autonomic nervous system, through the parasympathetic and sympathetic pathways, innervates and influences the function of every organ in the body. It plays a key role in major integrative processes, such as the control of blood pressure and body temperature. It has numerous pathways, both centrally and peripherally, utilizing an extensive range of neurotransmitters; this results in considerable flexibility and capability. Malfunction of the autonomic nervous system may occur in numerous ways and affect one or more sites, involve single or multiple organs, and disrupt complex integrative processes. Ageing affects both the autonomic nervous system and the target organs it influences, thus impairment may occur even in healthy aged people. A number of autonomic disorders present in the sixth decade and later. Advances in the recognition and therapy of autonomic disorders is contributing to increased longevity, and younger patients with autonomic disorders that are controlled but not cured, will have the added effects of ageing with time. In this chapter we outline the fundamental principles behind the function of the autonomic nervous system and provide a classification of autonomic

dysfunction, followed by a description of clinical manifestations, investigation, and management. Finally there is a brief description of the major autonomic disorders.

Fundamental principles

The autonomic nervous system has two major divisions, the parasympathetic with a cranial and sacral spinal outflow, and the sympathetic with a thoracolumbar spinal outflow (Fig. 1). These efferent pathways are influenced by a variety of afferents, involving virtually every sensory pathway. There are many areas within the brain that control autonomic function, with major centres in the hypothalamus, midbrain, and brainstem. Neurones within the spinal cord include the intermediolateral cell mass in the thoracolumbar segments for sympathetic control, and in the lumbosacral segments for parasympathetic control. Preganglionic efferent pathways from the brain and spinal cord synapse in the ganglia, with postganglionic pathways to target organs; in the parasympathetic system they are usually close to the target organ, unlike the sympathetic system where the ganglia

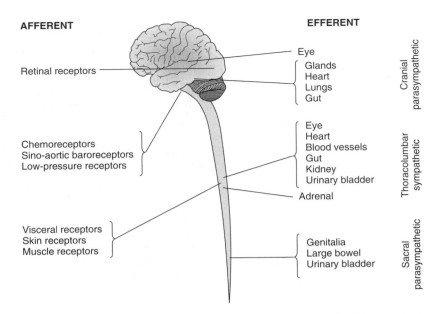

Fig. 1 Diagram to indicate the major afferent pathways that influence the major autonomic efferent outflow (the cranial and sacral parasympathetic and the thoracolumbar sympathetic) supplying various organs.

are paravertebral and thus some distance away. The major neurotransmitters concerned with ganglionic and postganglionic autonomic function are outlined in Fig. 2; additionally there are numerous amines, peptides, and purines involved in neurotransmission and neuromodulation, especially in the enteric nervous system. This is often considered to be the third branch of the autonomic nervous system, and it is adapted to the particular needs of the gastrointestinal system. In addition, within the gut, there is an additional autonomic network of 'intrinsic' plexuses. These consist of the submucous (Auerbach's) plexus and the myenteric (Meissner's) plexus; the transmitters here are predominantly cholinergic and appear similar to those in the intrinsic plexuses in the heart; this may explain why

both organs are targeted in Chagas' disease (*Trypanosoma cruzi* infection).

In humans, the effects of ageing probably have been better studied in relation to the sympathetic than the parasympathetic nervous system. Sympathetic neural activity may be measured in a number of ways: by measurements of plasma noradrenaline, assessment of noradrenaline spill-over, and direct recordings of either muscle or skin sympathetic nerve activity in peripheral nerves using microneurographic techniques. In older people, plasma noradrenaline levels are higher, but this is not due to impaired clearance. There is an increase in muscle sympathetic nerve activity (Fig. 3), but the increase is not generalized, as noradrenaline spill-over studies indicate

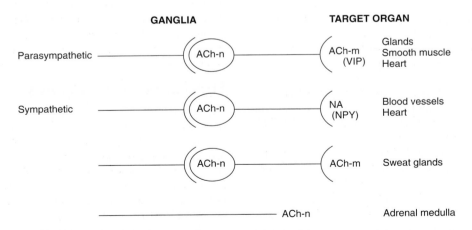

Fig. 2 Outline of the major transmitters at autonomic ganglia and postganglionic sites on target organs supplied by the sympathetic and parasympathetic efferent pathways. The acetylcholine receptors at all ganglia are of the nicotinic subtype (ACh-n). Ganglionic blockers such as hexamethonium thus prevent both parasympathetic and sympathetic activation. Atropine, however, acts only on the muscarinic (ACh-m) receptor at postganglionic parasympathetic and sympathetic cholinergic sites. The cotransmitters along with the primary neurotransmitters are also indicated. NA, noradrenaline (norepinephrine); NPY, neuropeptide Y; VIP, vasoactive intestinal polypeptide.

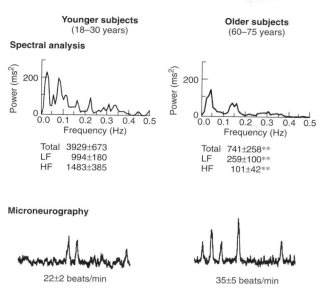

Younger subjects (18–30 years)

Older subjects (60–75 years)

Spectral analysis

Younger subjects:
Total 3929±673
LF   994±180
HF   1483±385

Older subjects:
Total 741±258**
LF   259±100**
HF   101±42**

Microneurography

22±2 beats/min

35±5 beats/min

Cardiac noradrenaline spill-over

11±2 ng/min

21±3 ng/min*

Fig. 3 Influence of ageing on sympathetic nervous system function at rest. Muscle sympathetic nerve firing rate and spill-over of the sympathetic transmitter from the heart were higher in older than in younger healthy subjects. Despite this evidence of sympathetic nervous activation with ageing, spectral analysis of the heart rhythm indicated reduced spectral power at all frequencies, including the low-frequency band associated with sympathetic nervous influence on the heart. Factors include reduced adrenoceptor sensitivity and postreceptor signal transduction in the hearts of older subjects. HF, high frequency; LF, low frequency. (Reproduced with permission from Esler (1995).)

Table 1 Examples of localized autonomic disorders

Holmes–Adie pupil

Horner's syndrome

Crocodile tears (Bogorad's syndrome)

Gustatory sweating (Frey's syndrome)

Reflex sympathetic dystrophy

Idiopathic palmar/axillary hyperhidrosis

Chagas' disease (*Trypanosoma cruzi* infection)[a]

Surgical procedures[b]
   Sympathectomy (regional)
   Vagotomy and gastric drainage procedures in 'dumping syndrome'
   Organ transplantation (heart, lungs)

[a] Listed here as it targets intrinsic cholinergic plexuses in the heart and gut.
[b] Surgery may cause some of the disorders listed above (such as Frey's syndrome following parotid surgery).

a preferential rise in sympathetic outflow to the heart. The reasons for both the increase and the differential changes are not clear; they are unlikely to result from impaired baroreflexes alone and may reflect impaired sensitivity of target organs to the effects of noradrenaline, resulting from mechanisms ranging from subsensitivity of adrenoceptors to impairment of postreceptor signal induction. Thus a variety of causes at neural and non-neural sites may reduce sensitivity to sympathetic stimulation in elderly people.

Classification of autonomic disorders

Autonomic disorders may be broadly classified under localized (Table 1) and generalized (Table 2). The latter include the primary disorders where the cause is not known, and secondary disorders resulting from lesions at known sites, from definitive causes, or with strong disease associations. Two further categories need to be mentioned: neurally mediated syncope where the disorder is usually intermittent, and drug-induced autonomic dysfunction (Table 3).

Clinical manifestations

There is a broad spectrum of clinical manifestations in autonomic disorders (Table 4). Orthostatic hypotension and ejaculatory failure

result from sympathetic adrenergic failure, anhidrosis from sympathetic cholinergic failure, and a fixed heart rate, a sluggish urinary bladder and bowel, and lack of erection from parasympathetic failure. The reverse of autonomic underactivity (autonomic hyperactivity) is also a part of autonomic failure; an example is autonomic dysreflexia in high spinal cord lesions. A combination of both autonomic overactivity and underactivity may occur, as in carotid sinus hypersensitivity, with bradycardia through vagal overactivity and vasodepression through sympathetic withdrawal. The presenting features, especially in the generalized disorders, depend upon which organ or system is initially involved, and the ensuing functional deficit. In progressive neurological disorders such as multiple-system atrophy, and when there is both nerve and target organ damage as in diabetes mellitus, this may result in difficulties with diagnosis, as the clinical features overlap with a number of conditions.

The history and clinical examination are important in providing clues towards the recognition of an autonomic disorder. The description of the abnormality may lead to the diagnosis in localized autonomic disorders. An example is Horner's syndrome with partial drooping of the eyelid, miosis, and warmer skin with cutaneous dilatation and lack of sweating over the affected area of the face. Although localized this may be a harbinger of more widespread autonomic impairment, as it may result from pathological processes involving sympathetic pathways within the brain as in the lateral medullary (Wallenberg) syndrome (attributed to posterior inferior cerebellar artery thrombosis), spinal cord (tumours or syringomyelia), or periphery (Pancoast's apical tumour of the lung). When only the eye is involved with the rest of the face spared, it may indicate dissection of the internal carotid artery (Raeder's syndrome). Another localized disorder where the history is of importance is gustatory hyperhidrosis. In this condition, the ingestion of even mildly flavoured food or drink results in profuse sweating over the head and neck because of aberrant connections between the cholinergic pathways to the salivary glands or stomach, and facial postganglionic sympathetic cholinergic nerves. This may be related to a local lesion (as in Frey's

Table 2 Classification of disorders resulting in autonomic dysfunction

Primary (aetiology unknown)
Acute/subacute dysautonomias
Pure cholinergic dysautonomia
Pure pandysautonomia
Pandysautonomia with neurological features

Chronic autonomic failure syndromes
Pure autonomic failure
Multiple system atrophy (Shy–Drager syndrome)
Autonomic failure with Parkinson's disease

Secondary
Congenital
Nerve growth factor deficiency

Hereditary
Autosomal dominant trait
    Familial amyloid neuropathy
    Porphyria
Autosomal recessive trait
    Familial dysautonomia (Riley–Day syndrome)
    Dopamine β-hydroxylase deficiency
    Aromatic L-amino acid decarboxylase deficiency
X-linked recessive
    Fabry's disease

Metabolic diseases
Diabetes mellitus
Chronic renal failure
Chronic liver disease
Vitamin B_{12} deficiency
Alcohol-induced

Inflammatory
Guillain–Barré syndrome
Transverse myelitis

Infections
Bacterial (tetanus)
Viral (HIV infection)
Parasitic (*Trypanosoma cruzi*, Chagas' disease)
Prion

Neoplasia
Brain tumours (especially of third ventricle or posterior fossa)
Paraneoplastic, to include adenocarcinomas of lung and pancreas, and
    Lambert–Eaton syndrome

Connective tissue disorders
Rheumatoid arthritis
Systemic lupus erythematosus
Mixed connective tissue disease

Surgery
Regional sympathectomy (upper limb, splanchnic)
Vagotomy and drainage procedures ('dumping syndrome')
Organ transplantation (heart, kidney)

Trauma
Spinal cord transection

Miscellaneous
Syringomyelia
Syringobulbia
Systemic amyloidosis

Neurally mediated syncope
Vasovagal syncope
Carotid sinus hypersensitivity
Micturition syncope
Cough syncope
Swallow syncope
Associated with glossopharyngeal neuralgia

Drugs
See Table 3

Adapted from Mathias (1996*a*).

syndrome complicating parotid surgery), or may complicate systemic diseases such as diabetes mellitus.

Other features may indicate a generalized autonomic disorder. A cardinal feature is orthostatic (postural) hypotension (Fig. 4). The symptoms of orthostatic hypotension classically result from impaired perfusion (Table 5), especially to vital organs. In some, non-specific symptoms that include generalized weakness, lethargy, and fatigue may occur; these may be unhelpful or even misleading. In elderly people there may be intermittent confusion, apparent to onlookers but of which the subject may be unaware. There may be transient neurological disturbances (such as speech defects), and an increased tendency to falls. With time, adjustments in cerebral autoregulation may increase orthostatic tolerance, and reduce symptoms. It is now recognized that there are various factors in daily life that influence orthostatic hypotension (Table 6); these are important especially in relation to management strategies. In some subjects, presyncopal symptoms or syncope may be unrelated to postural change, as in carotid sinus hypersensitivity, where there may be a relationship with neck movement. Syncope may be provoked by coughing, swallowing, or micturition; these are rarer causes of neurally mediated syncope. A history of impairment of sweating (and temperature intolerance), urinary disturbances, sexual dysfunction (in the male), and gastro-intestinal abnormalities (such as constipation) especially in combination with orthostatic hypotension, should alert one to the possibility of a generalized autonomic disorder. In elderly people, a detailed drug history is necessary as a variety of medicines can directly or indirectly cause autonomic dysfunction (see Table 3).

The physical examination may provide important clues. With anhidrosis, the palms and affected areas of skin may be dry. In reflex sympathetic dystrophy, sometimes associated with limb surgery (such as median nerve decompression), trauma, or a stroke, the hand or foot may be oedematous, with the overlying skin showing areas of

Table 3 Drugs, chemicals, poisons, and toxins causing autonomic dysfunction

Decreasing sympathetic activity
Centrally acting
Clonidine
Moxonidine
Methyldopa
Reserpine
Barbiturates
Anaesthetics

Peripherally acting
Sympathetic nerve ending (guanethidine, bethanidine)
α-Adrenoceptor blockade (phenoxybenzamine)
β-Adrenoceptor blockade (propranolol)

Increasing sympathetic activity
Amphetamines
Releasing noradrenaline (tyramine)
Uptake blockers (imipramine)
Monoamine oxidase inhibitors (tranylcypromine)
β-Adrenoceptor stimulants (isoprenaline)

Decreasing parasympathetic activity
Antidepressants (imipramine)
Tranquillizers (phenothiazines)
Antidysrhythmics (disopyramide)
Anticholinergics (atropine, propantheline, benztropine)
Toxins (botulinum)

Increasing parasympathetic activity
Cholinomimetics (carbachol, bethanechol, pilocarpine, mushroom poisoning)
Reversible carbamate inhibitors of acetylcholinesterase (pyridostigmine, neostigmine)
Organophosphorus inhibitors of acetylcholinesterase (parathion, sarin)

Miscellaneous
Alcohol, thiamine (vitamin B_1 deficiency)
Vincristine, perhexiline maleate
Thallium, arsenic, mercury

Adapted from Mathias (1996a).

Table 4 Some clinical manifestations in autonomic disorders

Cardiovascular
Orthostatic (postural) hypotension
Lability of blood pressure
Tachycardia
Supine hypertension
Paroxysmal hypertension
Bradycardia

Sudomotor
Hypo- or anhidrosis
Gustatory sweating
Hyperpyrexia
Hyperhidrosis
Heat intolerance

Alimentary
Xerostomia
Gastric stasis
Constipation
Dysphagia
Dumping syndromes
Diarrhoea

Urinary
Nocturia
Urgency; retention
Frequency
Incontinence

Sexual
Erectile failure
Retrograde ejaculation
Ejaculatory failure

Eye
Pupillary abnormalities
Hypo- or alachryma
Ptosis
Abnormal lacrimation with food ingestion

both erythema and pallor (akin to livedo reticularis) and abnormal sweating. Facial findings may be important, as in the syndrome of crocodile tears (gustolachrymal reflex) in which eating causes excessive lachrymal secretion because of aberrant connections between the nerves to the salivary and lachrymal glands; it may complicate facial (Bell's) palsy. Holmes–Adie pupils are large with a sluggish, or absent response to light; they may be associated with tendon areflexia and other autonomic disturbances. A small pupil, together with partial ptosis and the associated facial abnormalities (erythema, lack of sweating, and dryness) characteristically occur in Horner's syndrome. Blood pressure should be measured with the patient lying flat and after standing, to detect orthostatic hypotension (defined as a fall in systolic blood pressure of over 20 mmHg on standing or head-up tilt). A smaller fall on postural change in the presence of relevant symptoms does not exclude significant autonomic dysfunction, as orthostatic hypotension may need to be unmasked or enhanced by other stimuli, such as food ingestion and exercise (Fig. 5). Furthermore, in the presence of vascular disease (such as carotid artery

stenosis), even a small fall in blood pressure may induce cerebral ischaemia. Non-neurogenic causes of orthostatic hypotension also need to be considered (Table 7). In combination with even a mild degree of autonomic failure these can result in severe orthostatic hypotension.

The physical examination may also provide information about diseases such as diabetes mellitus and liver cirrhosis that are associated with autonomic dysfunction. The neurological examination may indicate a specific deficit, such as a peripheral neuropathy in amyloidosis, or parkinsonian and cerebellar signs in multiple-system atrophy. Dipstick testing of urine, for glycosuria in diabetes mellitus or proteinuria in systemic amyloidosis, is important. Accurate measurement of body temperature is necessary, as both hyperthermia or hypothermia may complicate autonomic dysfunction.

Outline of investigational strategies

When an autonomic disorder is suspected, the first step is to determine whether autonomic function is normal or abnormal. Autonomic

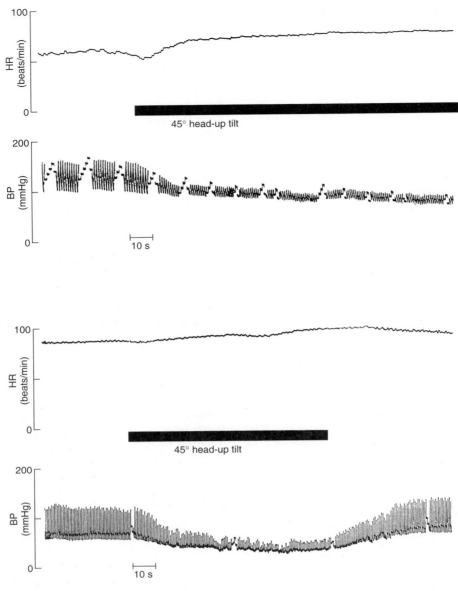

Fig. 4 Continuous blood pressure (BP) and heart rate (HR) measured by a non-invasive technique (the Finapres) in two patients with autonomic failure. In the upper panel, blood pressure falls to low levels; however, the patient could maintain head-up tilt with a low blood pressure for over 20 min with few symptoms. He had autonomic failure for many years and could tolerate such levels, unlike the patient in the panel below, who had to be put back to the horizontal position fairly quickly. She developed severe postural hypotension soon after surgery. (Reproduced with permission from Mathias (1996b).)

screening tests are a useful initial means of assessing autonomic failure, but they have their limitations (Table 8). Tests have mostly involved cardiovascular assessment, using non-invasive approaches (Fig. 6), but a range is now available, or being developed, for other body systems. Cardiovascular autonomic tests usually include measuring the responses of blood pressure and heart rate to stimuli which probe the various components of a baroreflex arc (head-up tilt, standing, and the Valsalva manoeuvre). The use of an electric tilt table is of value, especially in patients disabled with neurological or other disorders, as they can be put back to the horizontal rapidly if the blood pressure falls substantially. In the absence of a tilt table and when standing is not possible, the responses to sitting, with the

legs dependent, is an alternative. An adequate rise in intrathoracic pressure during the Valsalva manoeuvre may be difficult to achieve, especially in those who cannot co-operate or are frail (Fig. 7). A range of stimuli are used to examine efferent sympathetic responses, including isometric exercise, mental arithmetic, and the use of cutaneous cold (with the hand immersed in ice slush). The heart rate responses to different stimuli provide a valuable measure of vagal or sympathetic cardiac function, and ideally should include the responses to deep breathing (Fig. 8), hyperventilation, and either standing or head-up tilt. The responses to a liquid meal challenge and modified exercise testing determine whether such stimuli exacerbate orthostatic hypotension during daily life. This may be of particular value in those

Table 5 Some of the symptoms resulting from orthostatic hypotension and impaired perfusion of various organs

Cerebral hypoperfusion
Dizziness
Visual disturbances
   Blurred (tunnel)
   Scotoma
   Greying out (blacking out)
   Colour defects
Loss of consciousness
Impaired cognition (particularly in elderly people)

Muscle hypoperfusion
Paracervical and suboccipital ('coathanger') ache
Lower back/buttock ache
Calf claudication

Cardiac hypoperfusion
Angina pectoris

Spinal cord hypoperfusion

Renal hypoperfusion
Oliguria

Non-specific
Weakness, lethargy, fatigue

Adapted from Mathias (1995*b*).

Table 6 Factors influencing orthostatic hypotension

Speeds of positional change

Time of day (worse in the morning)

Prolonged recumbency

Warm environment (hot weather, central heating, hot bath)

Raising intrathoracic pressure (micturition, defecation, coughing)

Food and alcohol ingestion

Physical exertion

Physical manoeuvres and positions (bending forward, abdominal
   compression, leg crossing, squatting, activating calf muscle pump)[a]

Drugs with vasoactive properties (including dopaminergic agents)

[a] These manoeuvres usually reduce the postural fall in blood pressure, unlike the others.

Adapted from Mathias (1995).

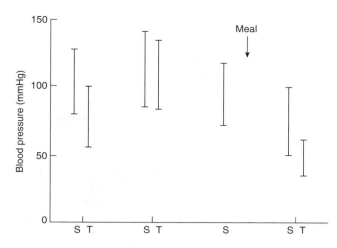

Fig. 5 Systolic and diastolic blood pressure in a patient with multiple-system atrophy while supine (S) and after 45° head-up tilt (T) on three occasions. On the first two, food intake was not controlled; however, the patient had not eaten on the second occasion, when the postural blood pressure fall was smaller. On the third occasion, supine blood pressure was measured while fasting before and 45 min after the meal. Postprandial tilt caused a considerable fall in blood pressure and the patient had to be returned to the horizontal within 3 min. (Reproduced with permission from Mathias *et al.* (1991*a*).)

If the autonomic screening tests are abnormal, further evaluation to determine the site and extent of the lesion, the functional deficit, and whether it is a primary or a secondary autonomic disorder, is needed. An accurate diagnosis is essential for establishing prognosis and anticipation of complications, and for management. The tests used to determine the site and extent of the lesion will depend upon the system involved and the disorder suspected (see Table 8). Assessing the functional deficit may be of importance for therapy; an example is the 24-h non-invasive ambulatory measurement of blood pressure and heart rate to define the effects of stimuli in daily life such as postural change, food ingestion, and exercise (Fig. 10).

A variety of investigations may be needed for diagnosing or excluding underlying diseases causing secondary autonomic dysfunction. These range from neuroimaging studies (such as CT and magnetic resonance imaging) and a sural nerve biopsy (using specific staining with monoclonal antibodies) to a variety of non-neurological investigations, depending upon the disorder suspected.

Management principles

Management will depend upon the autonomic disorder, the functional autonomic deficit, and whether it is the result of primary or secondary autonomic dysfunction. The prognosis, and anticipation of complications, will determine strategies. Management must take into account the underlying condition and non-autonomic deficits in both primary and secondary disorders, as its treatment may worsen or unmask certain autonomic features. Thus the use of L-dopa to reduce parkinsonism in multiple-system atrophy may aggravate orthostatic hypotension. In certain situations simple procedures may help, such as withdrawal of an offending drug, or clearing a blocked urinary catheter to prevent autonomic dysreflexia in high spinal cord lesions.

in whom the history suggests orthostatic hypotension, which is not confirmed by initial tests. Lack of abnormalities on routine screening may not exclude an autonomic disorder, as additional tests may be needed, depending upon the clinical history and examination, and the suspected condition. An example is carotid sinus hypersensitivity, where the response to carotid sinus massage is of particular importance (Fig. 9).

Table 7 Non-neurogenic causes of orthostatic hypotension

Low intravascular volume	
Blood/plasma loss	Haemorrhage, burns, haemodialysis
Fluid/electrolyte loss	Inadequate intake—anorexia nervosa
	Fluid loss—vomiting, diarrhoea, losses from ileostomy
	Renal endocrine—salt-losing nephropathy, adrenal insufficiency
	(Addison's disease), diabetes insipidus, diuretics
Vasodilatation	Drugs[a]—glyceryl trinitrate, antihypertensives
	Alcohol
	Heat, pyrexia
	Hyperbradykininism
	Systemic mastocytosis
	Extensive varicose veins
Cardiac impairment	
Myocardial	Myocarditis
Impaired filling	Atrial myxoma, constrictive pericarditis
Impaired output	Aortic stenosis

[a] A wide variety of drugs can cause excessive vasodilatation, especially when there is a degree of autonomic impairment.

Adapted from Mathias and Bannister (1992).

The maintenance of body temperature may be of crucial importance. The quality of life is often substantially improved by reducing orthostatic hypotension (Table 9), overcoming urinary incontinence, alleviating gastrointestinal disturbances, and if required, treating sexual dysfunction.

Aspects of the management of orthostatic hypotension will be considered briefly. Preventing falls and associated trauma is of special importance for older people. Non-pharmacological approaches should be used first (see Table 9). An important component is advice, and this includes increasing awareness of, and avoiding, factors that will worsen orthostatic hypotension. Many have difficulties with micturition and defecation, and are unaware that straining can precipitate hypotension. In certain situations, such as in narrow toilets, patients who are not able to fall to a horizontal posture and so restore their blood pressure, will be vulnerable to cerebral ischaemia. The degree of vasodilatation induced by heat may not be appreciated, as in those having a hot bath, even in the winter. The possible effects of drugs with vasodepressor properties need special consideration in prescribing for elderly patients.

Valuable non-pharmacological components in management include the introduction of head-up tilt of the bed at night and an increase in salt intake. Postprandial hypotension may be ameliorated by small but frequent meals and a reduction in refined carbohydrates. Regular exercise is advisable for a variety of reasons: exercise while upright will lower blood pressure and supine exercise, including swimming, may overcome this problem. Patients should be advised on manoeuvres that prevent blood pooling and increase venous return, such as crossing the legs, squatting, and activating the calf muscle pump (Wieling et al. 1993). Advice on what to do when symptoms of orthostatic hypotension occur ideally include lying flat, or sitting and lowering the head beneath the knees.

A variety of physical methods have been used, but most of them are either impractical, or have limited value. Antigravity suits can only be used in special situations. There may be a role for abdominal binders, sometimes in the form of corsets; elastic stockings are often unacceptable and do not appear to induce the benefit hoped from them.

Drugs that act in different ways can be used (Mathias and Kimber 1999). The ideal starter drug is the mineralocorticoid, fludrocortisone, usually in a dose of 100 to 200 µg given at night. It causes a degree of fluid and salt retention, and in some may result in ankle oedema or hypokalaemia. The next set of drugs to use are the sympathetic vasoconstrictors. They may act indirectly and an example is ephedrine, which is of value in central autonomic syndromes such as multiple-system atrophy where postganglionic sympathetic pathways are relatively preserved and thus can be activated. In pure autonomic failure with postganglionic sympathetic denervation, agents acting directly on α-adrenoreceptors, such as midodrine, are more effective. The side-effects with higher doses of ephedrine include tremulousness, mild agitation, and appetite suppression. With midodrine there may be itching of the scalp; urinary retention may occur in men because of its effects on the internal urinary sphincter.

An important component in the pharmacological treatment of orthostatic hypotension is individual targeting of therapy. Postprandial hypotension can be a major problem for older people (Jansen and Lipsitz 1995). Caffeine, in the form of strong coffee, may be helpful, although recent studies do not indicate a beneficial effect. The somatostatin analogue, octreotide, prevents the release of vaso-dilatatory gut peptides and has been successfully used for postprandial hypotension. It is often successful in small doses of 25 to 50 µg twice or three times daily prior to meals. Its disadvantage is that it has to be given parenterally by subcutaneous injection, although its low dosage results in few side-effects, unlike those reported in patients with endocrine disorders who often are on considerably higher doses. Drugs with intrinsic sympathomimetic activity such as pindolol and xamoterol that increase cardiac output do not have a role because of their side-effects. For patients with nocturnal polyuria, and especially

Table 8 Outline of investigations in autonomic failure

Cardiovascular

Physiological

Head-up tilt, standing; Valsalva manoeuvre

Pressor stimuli (isometric exercise, cutaneous cold pressor, mental arithmetic)

Heart rate responses (deep breathing, hyperventilation, standing, head-up tilt)

Liquid meal challenge

Exercise testing

Carotid sinus massage

Biochemical

Basal plasma noradrenaline, adrenaline, and dopamine levels

Plasma noradrenaline (supine and during head-up tilt or standing)

Basal urinary catecholamines

Plasma renin activity

Plasma aldosterone

Pharmacological

Noradrenaline (α-adrenoceptors, vascular)

Isoprenaline (β-adrenoceptors, vascular and cardiac)

Tyramine (pressor and noradrenaline response)

Edrophonium (noradrenaline response)

Clonidine (growth hormone response)

Atropine (heart rate response)

Sweating

Thermoregulatory (increase core temperature by 1 °C)

Sweat gland response to intradermal acetylcholine

Sympathetic skin response

Gastrointestinal

Barium studies, videocinefluoroscopy, endoscopy, gastric-emptying studies, anal sphincter electromyography

Renal function and urinary tract

Day and night urine volumes and sodium/potassium excretion

Urodynamic studies, intravenous urography, ultrasound examination, urethral sphincter electromyography

Sexual function

Penile plethysmography

Intracavernosal papaverine

Respiratory

Laryngoscopy

Sleep studies to assess apnoea/oxygen desaturation

Eye

Lachrymal function (Schirmer's test)

Pupillary function (pharmacological and physiological)

Adapted from Mathias and Bannister (1999), from where further details can be obtained.

those with urinary bladder disturbances (as in multiple-system atrophy), the vasopressin analogue desmopressin, at night, reduces urine output. It has the advantage of improving postural hypotension in the morning, when many patients are at their worst, presumably by reducing intravascular and extracellular fluid depletion. Care should be taken, with measurements of electrolytes and osmolality, to ensure that water intoxication does not occur. The effectiveness of vasopressin may be reduced in older patients because of unresponsiveness of the renal tubules to antidiuretic hormone. Erythropoietin is of value in those with refractory anaemia, and when renal failure complicates autonomic failure (as in diabetes mellitus or amyloidosis). Newer agents, including the prodrug dihydroxyphenylserine that is converted to noradrenaline, are currently under evaluation.

The major autonomic disorders

The major autonomic disorders are discussed below, including those that are more likely to be seen in elderly people. Much of the experience is based on patients in their sixth decade and beyond. There may be greater complexities for older patients, as the prevalence of many diseases, especially neurodegenerative disorders, increase with age. Thus a combination of two or more disease processes may coexist, as has been described for multiple-system atrophy and Alzheimer's disease. For clarity, descriptions will be based on the assumption that no other disease processes complicate the clinical picture or investigations.

Primary autonomic failure syndromes

These can be subdivided into the acute/subacute dysautonomias and the chronic autonomic failure syndromes.

Acute/subacute dysautonomias

In these disorders, autonomic features develop over a period of hours or days. They have been reported mainly in children and young adults, and will be briefly described. Although rare, this in part may be because they are not readily diagnosed and thus may be overlooked in elderly people. There are three main varieties: pure cholinergic dysautonomia, pure pandysautonomia, and pandysautonomia with additional neurological features.

In pure cholinergic dysautonomia there are features of widespread parasympathetic failure, with fixed dilated pupils, alachryma, xerostomia, oesophageal dysfunction, constipation, and detrusor muscle failure; there is a tendency to hyperthermia because of anhidrosis, hence the term cholinergic, and not parasympathetic, dysautonomia. The differential diagnosis includes exposure to anticholinergic drugs, poisons, and toxins that have similar effects. A variant of botulism (botulism B) affects cholinergic pathways with sparing of the motor pathways, but substantial recovery often occurs within 3 months unlike pure cholinergic dysautonomia. In the pure pandysautonomias (with no additional neurological defects), both sympathetic and parasympathetic pathways are affected; thus in addition to cholinergic features, postural hypotension is a problem. There are some in whom there are additional neurological features, usually indicative of a peripheral neuropathy. The prognosis is unpredictable and variable; in some there may be substantial recovery. In addition to supportive therapy, immunoglobulin administration has been used with success in a few, favouring the possibility of an immunological basis for some of these disorders.

Chronic autonomic failure

These consist of three groups, two of which (pure autonomic failure and multiple-system atrophy) are well recognized (Fig. 11). There is

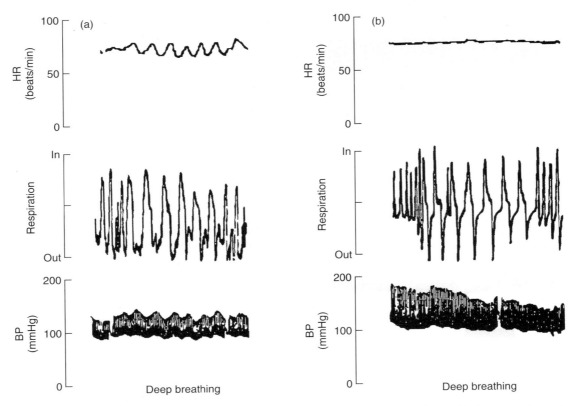

Fig. 8 The effect of deep breathing on continuous heart rate (HR) and blood pressure (BP) (measured by Finapres) in (a) a normal subject and (b) a patient with autonomic failure. There is no sinus arrhythmia in the patient, despite a fall in blood pressure. Respiratory changes are indicated in the middle panel. (Reproduced with permission from Mathias and Bannister (1999).)

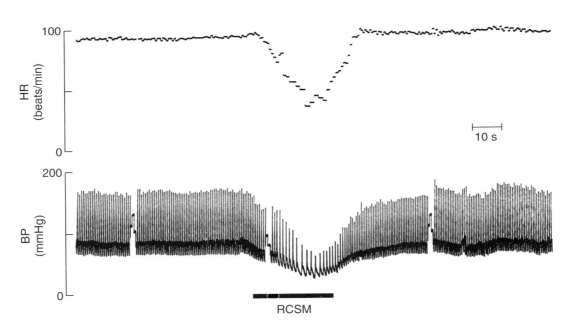

Fig. 9 Continuous blood pressure and heart rate measured non-invasively (by Finapres) in a patient with falls of unknown aetiology. Left carotid sinus massage caused a fall in both heart rate and blood pressure. The findings indicate the mixed (cardio-inhibitory and vasodepressor) form of carotid sinus hypersensitivity. RCSM, right carotid sinus massage.

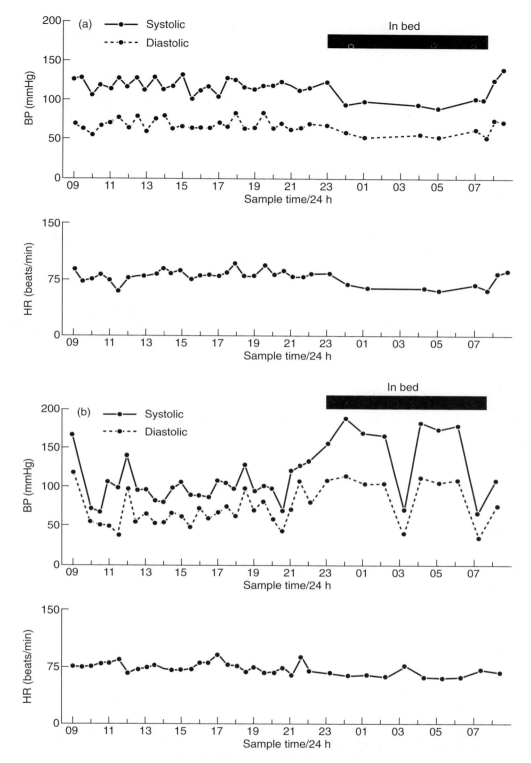

Fig. 10 Continuous (24-h) non-invasive ambulatory blood pressure (BP) and heart rate (HR) profile showing systolic and diastolic blood pressure and heart rate at intervals throughout the day and night. The horizontal axis depicts a 24-h time-scale. (a) Changes in a normal subject; showing an expected circadian fall in blood pressure whilst asleep. (b) Marked fluctuations in blood pressure in a patient with pure autonomic failure. The falls were usually the result of postural changes, either sitting or standing. Supine blood pressure, particularly at night, was elevated, with a reversal of the normal circadian fall in blood pressure. Rising to micturate caused a severe fall in blood pressure (at 03.00 h). There were relatively small changes in heart rate considering the marked fluctuations in blood pressure. (Reproduced with permission from Mathias and Bannister (1999).)

Table 9 Some of the approaches used in the management of orthostatic hypotension, especially in patients with chronic autonomic failure

Avoid
Sudden head-up postural change, especially in the morning
Prolonged recumbency
Straining during micturition and defecation
Heat (warm weather, hot water)
Large meals, especially with carbohydrate and fat
Alcohol
'Severe' physical activity
Drugs with vasodepressor properties

Introduce
High salt intake
Small frequent meals, with less refined carbohydrate
Head-up tilt during sleep
Regular judicious exercise (including swimming)
Manoeuvres that reduce venous pooling and increase venous return

Physical methods
Elastic stockings
Abdominal binders
Antigravity suits

Drugs
Vasoconstrictor (sympathomimetic)
   Directly on resistance vessels (midodrine, phenylephrine)
   Directly on capacitance vessels (dihydroergotamine)
   Indirectly (ephedrine, tyramine with monoamine oxidase inhibitors, yohimbine)
   Prodrug (L-dihydroxyphenylserine)
Vasoconstrictor (non-sympathomimetic)
   Vasopressin-1 agonists (glycopressin, vasopressin)
Preventing vasodilatation
   Prostaglandin synthetase inhibition (indomethacin, flurbiprofen)
   Dopamine receptor blockade (metoclopramide, domperidone)
   β_2-Adrenoceptor blockade (propranolol)
Preventing postprandial hypotension
   Adenosine receptor blockade (caffeine)
   Peptide release inhibitors (somatostatin analogue, octreotide)
Increasing cardiac output (pindolol, xamoterol)
Increasing haemoglobin and blood volume (erythropoietin)
Reducing salt loss/plasma volume expansion
   Mineralocorticoids (fludrocortisone)
Reducing nocturnal polyuria
   Vasopressin-2-receptor agonists (desmopressin)

Adapted from Mathias and Kimber (1998, 1999).

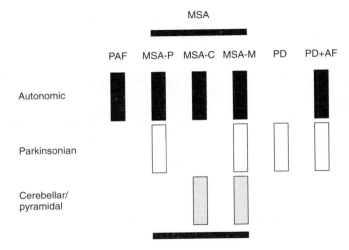

Fig. 11 Schematic representation, indicating the major clinical features in primary chronic autonomic failure syndromes. These include pure autonomic failure (PAF) and the three major neurological forms of multiple-system atrophy (MSA): the parkinsonian form (MSA-P) synonymous with striatonigral degeneration, the cerebellar form (MSA-C) synonymous with olivopontocerebellar degeneration, and the multiple/mixed form (MSA-M) with all features. Included are Parkinson's disease (PD), and the rarer subgroup with Parkinson's disease and autonomic failure (PD + AF). (Adapted from Mathias (1997).)

not known. It may also be abnormal in progressive supranuclear palsy (Steele–Richardson–Olszewski syndrome). A recently developed non-invasive approach that is sensitive, specific, and acceptable to patients for repeated studies, is clonidine growth hormone testing. Clonidine is a centrally-acting α_2-adrenoceptor agonist that normally raises levels of growth hormone through stimulating hypothalamic growth hormone-releasing factor, that acts upon the anterior pituitary to release growth hormone. After clonidine, there is a rise in growth hormone levels in Parkinson's disease (without autonomic failure) and pure autonomic failure (with peripheral autonomic failure), and

the rise is similar to that observed in normal subjects (Fig. 13). After clonidine, however, growth hormone levels remain unchanged in the different forms of multiple-system atrophy (with central autonomic failure). In such multiple-system atrophy subjects, the administration of another growth hormone secretagogue, L-dopa, causes a rise in levels of both growth hormone-releasing hormone and growth hormone, indicating that the clonidine–growth hormone abnormality in multiple-system atrophy is not due to widespread neuronal fall-out and probably indicates a specific deficit involving the α_2-adrenoreceptor hypothalamic–somatotrophic axis (Kimber *et al.* 1997). The clonidine–growth hormone test, therefore, may form the basis of an early test to distinguish multiple-system atrophy from other parkinsonian and peripheral autonomic syndromes, and additionally may provide *in vivo* information on the various central neurotransmitter abnormalities that occur in multiple-system atrophy.

The prognosis for multiple-system atrophy is poor in comparison with Parkinson's disease and pure autonomic failure, as both motor and autonomic systems are progressively impaired. Life expectancy from onset can range from 5 to 20 years, with a mean of about 9 years. Parkinsonian features often become refractory to antiparkinsonian drugs; moreover, side-effects including orthostatic hypotension are more marked in multiple-system atrophy and reduce the therapeutic benefit of these agents. Impairment of mobility and the inability to communicate result from increasing rigidity and speech impairment. In the cerebellar forms, worsening truncal ataxia, the inability to stand upright, and the tendency to falls is compounded by orthostatic hypotension. Lack of co-ordination in the upper limbs, speech deficits, and nystagmus add to the disabilities. In multiple-system atrophy, especially in the later stages, oropharyngeal dysphagia increases the risk of aspiration, especially in the presence of vocal cord abnormalities; this may entail insertion of a percutaneous feeding gastrostomy. Respiratory abnormalities include an obstructive apnoea

Table 10 Some clinical manifestations in patients with primary autonomic failure

Cardiovascular system	Orthostatic (postural) hypotension
Sudomotor system	Anhidrosis, heat intolerance
Alimentary tract	Xerostomia, oropharyngeal dysphagia, constipation, occasionally diarrhoea
Urinary system	Nocturia, frequency, urgency, incontinence, retention
Reproductive system	Erectile and ejaculatory failure in the male
Respiratory system	Stridor, involuntary inspiratory gasps, apnoeic periods
Ocular	Hypolachryma, anisocoria, Horner's syndrome
Other neurological deficits	Parkinsonian, cerebellar, and pyramidal signs

Dysphagia and respiratory symptoms are unlikely to occur in pure autonomic failure, unlike multiple-system atrophy.
Adapted from Mathias (1997).

Table 11 Possible causes of orthostatic hypotension in a patient with parkinsonian features

Multiple system atrophy
Parkinson's disease with autonomic failure
Side-effects of antiparkinsonian therapy to include L-dopa and selegiline
Coincidental disease causing autonomic dysfunction such as diabetes mellitus
Concomitant administration of drugs for an allied condition Examples are antihypertensives, vasodilators, diuretics, and α-adrenoceptor blockers (for benign prostatic hyperplasia)

Adapted from Mathias (1996b).

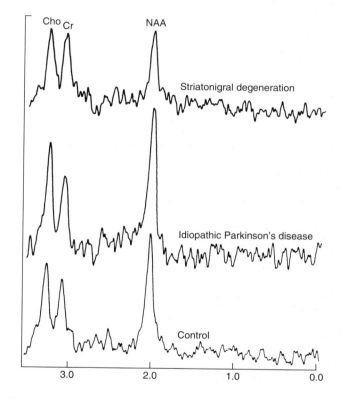

Fig. 12 Proton magnetic resonance spectroscopy in a normal subject (control) (bottom panel), a patient with idiopathic Parkinson's disease (middle panel), and a patient with striatonigral degeneration (the parkinsonian form of multiple-system atrophy) (top panel). The choline (Cho) to creatinine (Cr) ratio in comparison with N-acetyl aspartate (NAA) is different in the patient with multiple-system atrophy. N-acetyl aspartate is a chemical that is selective to neurones. (Reproduced with permission from Davie et al. (1995).)

(due to laryngeal abductor cord paresis) and central apnoea; a tracheostomy may be needed. The neurological decline is not reversible so supportive therapy is required, and should involve both the family and community. Reducing the functional deficits arising from autonomic failure is an important component of management. Orthostatic hypotension, although severe in some and compounded by motor deficits, often responds to therapy. The management of bowel and urinary bladder dysfunction, and if required, sexual dysfunction, are important in improving the quality of life.

Parkinson's disease with autonomic failure

A further group includes mostly elderly patients with idiopathic Parkinson's disease, usually treated successfully with L-dopa for many years, and later develop features of autonomic failure, often with severe orthostatic hypotension. Thus they differ from the majority with Parkinson's disease who usually only have relatively mild autonomic deficits, often compounded by concomitant drug therapy. Pharmacological studies, and more recently PET cardiac scanning (Goldstein et al. 1997), favour the autonomic lesions being peripheral and thus similar in nature to pure autonomic failure. The aetiology is unknown. Whether this disorder is a coincidental association of a common condition (Parkinson's disease) with an uncommon disease

(pure autonomic failure), an indication of vulnerability to autonomic degeneration in a group of those with Parkinson's disease, or linked to increasing age, chronic antiparkinsonian drug therapy, an inherent metabolic susceptibility, or a combination of these factors, remains

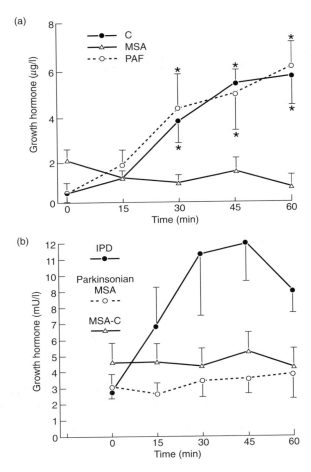

Fig. 13 (a) Serum growth hormone levels before (0 min) and 15, 30, 45, and 60 min after intravenous clonidine (1.5 μg/kg) in normal subjects (control, C), multiple-system atrophy (MSA), and pure autonomic failure (PAF). The error bars indicate ±SEM: * $p < 0.05$. (Reproduced with permission from Thomaides et al. (1992).) (b) Serum growth hormone levels in idiopathic Parkinson's disease (IPD, $n = 14$) compared with multiple-system atrophy (MSA) and with parkinsonian (MSA-P, MSA-M, $n = 15$) and cerebellar (MSA-C, $n = 16$) forms before and after intravenous clonidine. (Reproduced with permission from Kimber et al. (1997).)

unclear. Data on the natural history and prognosis are limited, partly because the age of the patients precludes long-term follow-up. They do not appear to suffer from the recognized complications of multiple-system atrophy, and clinically seem to differ from them in many ways.

Secondary causes of autonomic dysfunction

A variety of diseases, disorders, and lesions may result in secondary autonomic dysfunction. Some listed in Table 2 do not occur in elderly people; examples are the congenital and hereditary disorders that are present and detected at birth (Riley–Day syndrome), diagnosed at the age of 20 years (dopamine β-hydroxylase deficiency), or clinically manifest in the fourth or fifth decade (familial amyloid polyneuropathy). However, some of these may be relevant in due course to geriatricians because of advances in the understanding of pathophysiological processes, development of methods to arrest or reverse

the autonomic dysfunction, and because of overall improvements in management. In the Riley–Day syndrome the previous life expectancy of only a few years has increased to 20 or 30 years, the quality of life in dopamine β-hydroxylase deficiency has been substantially improved by the use of the noradrenaline precursor L-dihydroxyphenylserine, which effectively replaces noradrenaline, and the life expectancy in familial amyloid polyneuropathy is expected to increase because of the promising benefits of hepatic transplantation preventing formation of the abnormal protein transthyrethrin.

Elderly people are prone to various metabolic diseases including diabetes mellitus that may be complicated by autonomic failure. Paraneoplastic syndromes of autonomic failure with orthostatic hypotension can occur. The reverse sympathetic hyperactivity with severe hypertension, may occur in patients with tetanus who are on respirators; recently described diseases, such as the prion disorders fatal familial and sporadic insomnia, may cause autonomic hyperactivity. Certain forms of surgery can cause localized dysfunction. Spinal cord lesions due to trauma, especially cervical and high thoracic transection, result in various forms of autonomic dysfunction. Thus there are many causes of secondary autonomic failure (see Table 2). In this section there will be a brief description of autonomic complications in diabetes mellitus and spinal cord transection.

Diabetes mellitus

There is a high incidence of both peripheral and autonomic neuropathy especially in older and long-standing diabetics on insulin therapy. Their morbidity and mortality is greater than those without a neuropathy. Usually, the vagus is involved initially, with the characteristic features of cardiac vagal denervation (Fig. 14). There may be involvement of the gastrointestinal tract (gastroparesis diabeticorum) and urinary bladder (diabetic cystopathy). Damage to target organs also may occur through non-neuropathic factors, and this can compound the problems caused by the neuropathy. An example is the heart, where the lack of control exerted by vagal denervation may occur in conjunction with partial preservation of the cardiac sympathetic, thus predisposing diabetics, in whom ischaemic heart disease is common, to sudden death from cardiac dysrhythmias. In some, sympathetic failure results in orthostatic hypotension that may be enhanced by insulin (Fig. 15). Other than maintaining normoglycaemia, there is no effective means to prevent and reverse the neuropathy, except possibly by pancreatic transplantation.

Spinal cord lesions

Spinal injury may occur at any age and results in autonomic dysfunction, which is more severe in those with cervical and high thoracic lesions (Mathias and Frankel 1999). Other causes of spinal cord damage include transverse myelitis and syringomyelia. In cervical and high thoracic cord lesions, orthostatic hypotension results because of the inability of the brain to activate efferent sympathetic pathways, despite preservation of baroreceptor afferents and central connections. Orthostatic hypotension may be a particular problem in the early stages of rehabilitation, when recumbency compounds the problem. In the later stages various compensatory mechanisms that include improved cerebrovascular autoregulation, the release of hormones that raise blood pressure (such as renin–angiotensin–aldosterone system and vasopressin), and activation of isolated spinal cord sympathetic reflexes, improve orthostatic tolerance and reduce the fall in blood pressure.

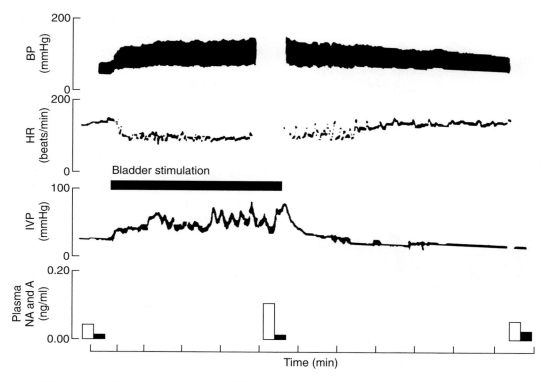

Fig. 14 Blood pressure (BP), heart rate (HR), intravesical pressure (IVP), and plasma noradrenaline (NA) (unshaded bars) and adrenaline (A) (shaded bars) levels in a tetraplegic patient before, during, and after bladder stimulation induced by suprapubic percussion of the anterior abdominal wall. The rise in blood pressure is accompanied by a fall in heart rate as a result of increased vagal activity in response to the rise in blood pressure. Plasma noradrenaline levels rise, but adrenaline levels do not, suggesting an increase in sympathetic neural activity independently of adrenomedullary activation. (Reproduced with permission from Mathias and Frankel (1999).)

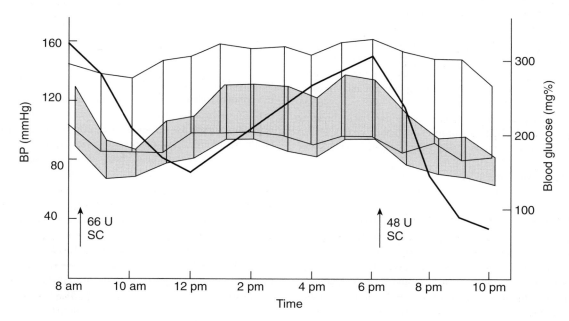

Fig. 15 Variation of lying and standing blood pressures (BP) in a 48-year-old man with severe autonomic neuropathy. Insulin was given subcutaneously (SC) at times shown by the vertical arrows. The unshaded area shows supine blood pressure (upper, systolic; lower, diastolic), the shaded area shows the standing blood pressure, and the continuous line shows the blood glucose. (Reproduced with permission from Watkins and Edmonds (1992).)

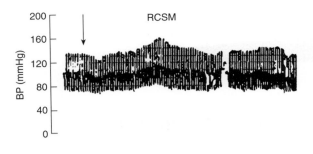

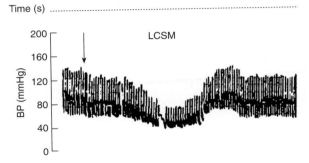

Fig. 16 Continuous non-invasive recording of finger arterial blood pressure (Finapres) before, during, and after carotid sinus massage on the right (RCSM) and left (LCSM) with the subject tilted head-up. Heart rate is not shown separately but can be assessed from the blood pressure trace. The arrow indicates when stimulation began. Stimulation on the right did not lower blood pressure and heart rate. The findings were consistent with the vasodepressor form of carotid sinus hypersensitivity. On the left, carotid sinus massage caused a substantial fall in both systolic and diastolic blood pressure, during which the patient felt light-headed and had greying-out of vision. There was only a modest fall in heart rate. The syncopal attacks were abolished by left carotid sinus denervation. (Reproduced with permission from Mathias *et al.* (1991*b*).)

In the early stages, in the phase of spinal shock when there are absent tendon reflexes and muscle flaccidity, tetraplegics (with C4/5 or higher lesions who are dependent on artificial respirator support), are prone to severe bradycardia and cardiac arrest. Their cardiac vagi are not opposed by the sympathetic nervous system and the pulmonary inflation vagal reflex, and are activated during tracheal suction especially in the presence of hypoxia (Fig. 16). In the early stages, tetraplegics are prone to hypothermia because they lack shivering thermogenesis and the inability to constrict cutaneous vessels. Hypothermia may be missed if a low reading rectal thermometer is not used.

With recovery from spinal shock isolated spinal cord activity returns, resulting in skeletal muscle spasticity, and a neurogenic urinary bladder and large bowel. In this 'chronic' phase autonomic dysreflexia may occur, with paroxysmal hypertension, together with large bowel and urinary bladder contraction as part of the mass reflex, because of isolated reflex activity involving several segments of the spinal cord. A major factor may be the lack of cerebral restraint that would occur normally. A variety of stimuli from below the segmental level of the lesion from skin, skeletal muscle, or viscera can induce autonomic dysreflexia (see Fig. 7). The hypertension can be severe and has the potential to cause cerebral haemorrhage and other neurological sequelae, in addition to myocardial failure. A key factor in management is defining and dealing with the precipitating cause;

if not, various manoeuvres and drugs based on interrupting the spinal sympathetic reflex arc (such as clonidine), or with direct actions on target organs (such as glyceryl trinitrate), may be needed.

Neurally mediated syncope

This group of disorders is characterized by intermittent cardiovascular autonomic abnormalities, resulting in loss of consciousness. An increase in cardiac parasympathetic activity results in severe bradycardia or cardiac arrest, while sympathetic neural withdrawal causes hypotension. There may be no abnormalities detected on routine autonomic testing between episodes. The most common condition causing neurally mediated syncope is probably vasovagal syncope (emotional faints); the onset is usually in the teenage years, it may run in families, and it may be induced by a range of stimuli from fear and the sight of blood to venepuncture and at times even the discussion of venepuncture. The prognosis in vasovagal syncope, especially when precipitating causes can be defined, and prevented or treated (with drugs or behavioural psychological approaches), is extremely good. Although attacks usually diminish with age, they may continue into the seventh and eighth decade. However, in elderly people, carotid sinus hypersensitivity appears to be the more common condition (see Chapter 4.4). Rarer causes of neurally mediated syncope include those induced by swallowing, micturition, defecation, coughing, and even laughing.

Carotid sinus hypersensitivity

This is increasingly recognized in elderly people (see Chapter 4.4). There may be a classical history of syncope induced by head and neck movements (such as neck extension during shaving) or collar tightening, although in many patients the precipitating factors are unclear. Routine autonomic screening tests may show no abnormalities. The diagnosis may be difficult to make, but is of importance, particularly as it is a potentially treatable cause of falls. When suspected, carotid sinus massage should be performed, ideally with the subject also tilted head-up, as hypotension is more likely to occur in situations dependent on sympathetic nerve activation (see Fig. 16). Care is necessary during carotid massage, and ideally patients should be screened for carotid artery stenosis as complications such as thromboembolism may occur. Resuscitation facilities should be on hand in case cardiac arrest occurs. Three forms have been described depending upon the response to carotid massage: cardio-inhibitory (with bradycardia), vasodepressor (with hypotension), and mixed (with both) (McIntosh *et al.* 1993). In recent studies, carotid sinus hypersensitivity accounted for 45 per cent of falls in a syncope clinic; an abnormal response to carotid sinus massage occurred in 17 per cent of elderly people admitted acutely, in 13 per cent in a day hospital, and in 36 per cent admitted with a fractured neck of femur (Kenny 1996).

The management of the cardio-inhibitory forms includes a cardiac demand pacemaker, although there is debate about the precise indications and type of pacemaker. In the vasodepressor form (and the mixed form with syncope due to hypotension despite a pacemaker) the management is unsatisfactory; various pressor agents have been used. Carotid sinus nerve denervation may have a role in the management of syncope in such patients, especially if due to unilateral hypersensitivity.

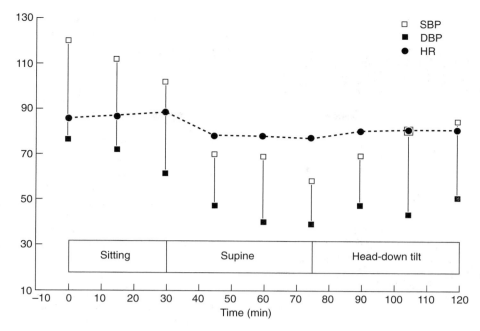

Fig. 17 The effect of a single standard oral dose of L-dopa (250 mg) and a dopadecarboxylase inhibitor, carbidopa (25 mg) given at time zero on the blood pressure of a patient with parkinsonian features. There was a marked fall in blood pressure after 30 min, resulting in the patient being first placed supine and then head-down. On investigation the patient had autonomic failure, with orthostatic hypotension unmasked by L-dopa; the final diagnosis was the parkinsonian form of multiple-system atrophy. SBP, systolic blood pressure; DBP, diastolic blood pressure; HR, heart rate.

Drugs, chemicals, and toxins

Drugs may cause autonomic dysfunction either through their pharmacological effects or by causing an autonomic neuropathy. The latter includes agents such as perhexeline maleate, alcohol, and agents used in chemotherapy, such as vincristine. Autonomic dysfunction may result from their primary pharmacological actions; examples include hypotension caused by sympatholytic agents, and blurred vision due to cycloplegia caused by the anticholinergic effects of oxybutynin, when used to reduce urinary frequency. Autonomic dysfunction may result from the side-effects of drugs such as the anticholinergic effects of antidepressants. Other effects are through unmasking of underlying autonomic deficits, such as the worsening of orthostatic hypotension by L-dopa in multiple-system atrophy (Fig. 17). Drugs may also induce dysfunction through their autonomic actions in susceptible individuals; an example is the anticholinergic property of the antidysrhythmic disopyramide causing urinary retention in benign prostatic hypertrophy.

Elderly people may be prone to drug-induced autonomic dysfunction for a variety of reasons. This includes their increased susceptibility to drugs unmasking a mild to moderate autonomic deficit, and an altered age-associated pharmacokinetic profile. An important aspect is that polypharmacy, sometimes compounded by errors in compliance, is not uncommon with older patients.

Bibliography

Appenzeller, O. and Oribe, E. (1997). *The autonomic nervous system* (5th edn). Elsevier, Amsterdam.

Kenny, R.A. (1996). *Syncope in the older patient. Causes, investigations and consequences of syncope and falls.* Chapman and Hall, London.

Low, P.A. (ed.) (1997). *Clinical autonomic disorders* (2nd edn). Lippincott–Raven, New York.

Mathias, C.J. and Bannister, R. (ed.) (1999). *Autonomic failure: a textbook of clinical disorders of the autonomic nervous system* (4th edn). Oxford University Press.

References

Davie, C.A., Wenning, G.K., Barker, G.J., *et al.* (1995). Differentiation of multiple-system atrophy from idiopathic Parkinson's disease using proton magnetic resonance spectroscopy. *Annals of Neurology,* **37,** 204–10.

Esler, M. (1995). The sympathetic nervous system and catecholamine release and plasma clearance in normal blood pressure control, in ageing and in hypertension. In *Hypertension: pathophysiology, diagnosis, and management* (2nd edn) (ed. J.H. Laragh and B.M. Brenner), pp. 755–73. Raven Press, New York.

Goldstein, D., Holmes, C., Cannon, R.O. III, Eisenhofer, G., and Kopin, I.J. (1997). Sympathetic cardioneuropathy in dysautonomias. *New England Journal of Medicine,* **336,** 696–702.

Jansen, R.W.M.M. and Lipsitz, L.A. (1995). Postprandial hypotension: epidemiology, pathophysiology and clinical management. *Annals of Internal Medicine,* **122,** 286–95.

Johnson, R.H. and Spalding, J.M.K. (1974). *Disorders of the autonomic nervous system.* Blackwell Scientific, Oxford.

Kenny, R.A. (1996). *Syncope in the older patient. Causes, investigations and consequences of syncope and falls.* Chapman and Hall, London.

Kimber, J.R., Watson, L., and Mathias, C.J. (1997). Distinction of idiopathic Parkinson's disease from multiple-system atrophy by stimulation of growth hormone release with clonidine. *Lancet,* **349,** 1877–81.

McIntosh, S.J., Lawson, J., and Kenny, R.A. (1993). Clinical characteristics of vasodepressor, cardioinhibitory and mixed carotid sinus syndrome in the elderly. *American Journal of Medicine*, 95, 203–8.

Mathias, C.J. (1995). Orthostatic hypotension—causes, mechanisms and influencing factors. *Neurology*, 45 (Supplement 5), S6–11.

Mathias, C.J. (1996*a*). Disorders of the autonomic nervous system. In *Neurology in clinical practice* (2nd edn) (ed. W.G. Bradley, R.B. Daroff, G.M. Fenichel, and C.D. Marsden), pp. 1953–81. Butterworth–Heinemann, Boston, MA.

Mathias, C.J. (1996*b*). Disorders affecting autonomic function in parkinsonian patients. In *Advances in neurology*, Vol. 69 (ed. L. Battistin, G. Scarlato, T. Caraceni, and S. Ruggieri), pp. 383–91. Lippincott–Raven, Philadelphia, PA.

Mathias, C.J. (1997). Autonomic disorders and their recognition. *New England Journal of Medicine*, 336, 721–4.

Mathias, C.J. and Bannister, R. (1999). Investigation of autonomic disorders. In *Autonomic failure: a textbook of clinical disorders of the autonomic nervous system* (4th edn) (ed. C.J. Mathias and R. Bannister), pp. 169–95. Oxford University Press.

Mathias, C.J. and Frankel, H.L. (1999). Autonomic disturbances in spinal cord lesions. In *Autonomic failure:a textbook of clinical disorders of the autonomic nervous system* (4th edn) (ed. C.J. Mathias and R. Bannister), pp. 494–513. Oxford University Press.

Mathias, C.J. and Kimber, J.R. (1999). Postural hypotension: causes, clinical features, investigation, and management. *Annual Review of Medicine*, 50, 317–36.

Mathias, C.J. and Williams, A.C. (1994). The Shy–Drager syndrome (and multiple-system atrophy). In *Neurodegenerative diseases* (ed. D.B. Calne), pp. 743–68. W.B. Saunders, Philadelphia, PA.

Mathias, C.J., Holly, E., Armstrong, E., Shareef, M., and Bannister, R. (1991*a*). The influence of food on postural hypotension in three groups with chronic autonomic failure: clinical and therapeutic implications. *Journal of Neurology, Neurosurgery and Psychiatry*, 54, 726–30.

Mathias, C.J., Armstrong, E., Browse, N., Chaudhuri, K.R., Enevoldson, P., and Ross Russell, R. (1991*b*). Value of non-invasive continuous blood pressure monitoring in the detection of carotid sinus hypersensitivity. *Clinical Autonomic Research*, 2, 157–9.

Thomaides, T., Chaudhuri, K.R., Maule, S., Watson, L.P., Marsden, C.D., and Mathias, C.J. (1992). The growth hormone response to clonidine in central and peripheral primary autonomic failure. *Lancet*, 340, 263–6.

Watkins, P.J. and Edmonds, M.E. (1999). Clinical presentations of diabetic autonomic failure. In *Autonomic failure: a textbook of clinical disorders of the autonomic nervous system* (4th edn) (ed. R. Bannister and C.J. Mathias), pp. 373–86. Oxford University Press.

Wieling, W., van Lieshout, J.J., and van Leeuwen, A.M. (1993). Physical manoeuvres that reduce postural hypotension. *Clinical Autonomic Research*, 3, 57–65.

18.13   Temperature homeostasis

Kenneth J. Collins

It is usual for temperature homeostasis to be maintained even in advanced old age, although commonly there are signs of reduced thermoregulatory efficiency and diminished ability to adapt to thermal stresses. Older people react more slowly to the challenge of heat and cold and this is manifest in a wider central nervous hunting pattern of adjustment and often a longer period required to re-establish temperature equilibrium. The pattern of fever, circadian temperature rhythms, and the complex interactions between central cardiovascular and thermoregulatory control are prone to dysregulation in senescence. Age-associated morphological and functional involution influence thermoregulatory effector systems such as vasomotor function, skeletal muscle responses, and sweating. In addition, the effects of physical deconditioning or detraining form part of the basis for deteriorating thermoregulatory control. More obvious changes can occur with pathological conditions associated with old age such as the effects of arteriosclerosis on the compliance of blood vessels and the metabolic effects of hypothyroidism. Medications such as hypnotics and psychotropics may impair the thermoregulatory homeostasis of older patients.

Thermal balance is achieved by adjustments of heat gain and heat loss, and many of the components that maintain thermal equilibrium have been analysed in aged individuals. This chapter considers some of the recent studies that have confirmed and amplified the physiological findings previously described. A relative poikilothermia in the absence of hypothalamic lesions, and the clinical conditions of hypothermia and hyperthermia, represent the more extreme presentations of thermoregulatory dysfunction in elderly people.

Mechanisms of heat gain

There are diminutions in resting metabolic rate, shivering capacity, and non-shivering thermogenesis with age. Impaired neuromuscular co-ordination and loss of motor power in detrained skeletal muscles can lead to minor degrees of hypothermia in cold conditions. These factors may contribute to the increased incidence of falls and proximal femoral fractures during cold weather.

There is a phase of increased thermogenesis after the intake of food and although this effect is small it constitutes a potentially important component of total daily energy production. It varies with a number of factors such as obesity, aerobic fitness, insulin resistance, and meal composition, and is generally lower in older than in younger subjects (Schwartz *et al.* 1990). A reduction in the thermic response to glucose, but not to fructose or protein has been reported in elderly people (Fukagawa *et al.* 1995). Diet-induced thermogenesis is usually found to be lower in older than in younger men, and this can be accounted for by differences in body composition (Visser *et al.* 1995). The variable component of the thermogenic response is associated with the sympathetic nervous response to a meal, which may be reduced as part of a generalized age-associated decrease in autonomic function (Collins 1997) (see also Chapter 18.12).

Mechanisms of heat loss

Many elderly people show a significant decline in the functional capacity of the cutaneous vasomotor and sudomotor systems which regulate heat loss. There is an age-associated reduction in the sensitivity of peripheral blood vessels to vasoconstrictor and vasodilator drugs. Blood vessel compliance also diminishes in elderly patients with arteriosclerosis. The impairment of the constrictor response to cold is due, at least in part, to reduced sensitivity and structural changes in blood vessels rather than to dysfunction of the autonomic nervous system. Cold-induced vasodilatation, a response to the immersion of the extremities in very cold water, is of smaller magnitude and occurs later in older men than in younger (Sawada 1996).

The age-associated reduction in the sudomotor response can also be explained by effector organ changes accompanying atrophy of the skin and peripheral detraining of sweat glands. Immunohistochemical investigations of healthy 80-year-old subjects have shown diminished neurotransmitter activity, with regressive changes in neurone density, as well as target organ atrophy (Abdel-Rahman *et al.* 1992). A small reduction with age in the production of nerve growth factor by the target organ may lead to impairment of transmitter synthesis within the nerve, and a large reduction might produce degeneration of nerve fibres or even nerve cell bodies.

In both young and older individuals, training and physical fitness are correlated with thermoregulatory performance. There have been suggestions that ageing *per se* may have little effect on heat loss responses, and that thermoregulatory changes may be more related to the decline in aerobic capacity with age (Tankersley *et al.* 1991). However, fitness appears to have little effect on measured responses to cold (Budd *et al.* 1991), although ageing, even in middle age, is shown to be accompanied by progressive weakening of the vasoconstrictor response.

Central nervous control

Resting body temperature

Normal resting deep body temperatures have been found to be lower in older than in younger subjects in some surveys but not in others. Disparities can be ascribed to many factors including the method of temperature measurement, differences in habitual activity and energy intake, the environmental conditions, and inclusion of elderly patients with disease or on medication. A fall in normal resting body temperature might be due to a resetting or a change in gain of the

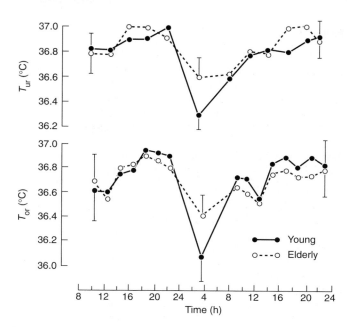

Fig. 1 Circadian changes in oral (T_{or}) and urine (T_{ur}) temperature in elderly and young subjects (mean $\pm$ SD). (Reproduced with permission from Collins *et al.* (1995).)

hypothalamic control centres. Collins *et al.* (1995) studied a group of healthy elderly (61–71 years) and younger (21–31 years) volunteers living together for 48 h during which energy intake, clothing, physical activity, and rest were controlled. Resting levels and day-time rhythms of body temperature were similar in the two age groups, but at night-time body temperatures fell to a lower level in the young (Fig. 1). In the general population, however, diseases common in old age and the effects of medication may lead to lower mean day-time body temperatures in older than in younger adults.

Circadian rhythms

The circadian rhythm of body temperature and the sleep–wake cycle are generated by pacemakers in the brain. When there is deprivation of cues that entrain the pacemakers, the rhythms become desynchronized, with the result that body temperature (and other controlled cyclic functions) become altered. There is evidence that desynchronization of circadian rhythms occur more frequently in old age (Brock 1991). Observed effects of age on the temperature rhythm include reduced amplitude (see Fig. 1) and often a phase advance of the rhythm. It is claimed that temperature rhythm variables may be damped or phase-shifted in patients suffering from Alzheimer's disease or depression (Okawa *et al.* 1991). There are deficits in serotoninergic neurones in Alzheimer's disease, and it is known that serotonin is a key modulator of thermoregulatory control acting in the preoptic region of the hypothalamus. There are also decreases in other neuropeptides which participate in thermoregulatory control. It may be expected that widespread disruption of circadian rhythms can occur in advanced Alzheimer's disease, although entrained temperature rhythms do not appear to be altered in carefully health-screened individuals suffering only mild degrees of the disease (Prinz *et al.* 1992).

Fever

Fever reflects an upward shift in the set-point or an increase in gain of the response to endogenous pyrogens by the preoptic hypothalamic regulators. This leads to a rise in core temperature which is actively maintained at the febrile level by normal autonomic and behavioural mechanisms. In hyperthermia, by contrast, there is no resetting of the set-point nor a pyrogenic response, but an overwhelming of the control system by excessive heat production, failure of heat loss mechanisms, or environmental heat stress. In view of altered autonomic and behavioural mechanisms often found in old age, it is not surprising that there is an age-associated reduction in the fever response. Blunted or absent fever responses to infection have been observed in approximately 30 per cent of elderly bacteraemic patients. Fevers in ill old people are often undetected, however, because body temperatures are inadequately measured (Darowski *et al.* 1991). Conventional mouth and axillary measurements with mercury thermometers are often misleading; rectal measures may be needed although eardrum reflectance can be used to assess core temperature provided the instrument used is regularly and reliably calibrated.

Tumour necrosis factor is a powerful endogenous pyrogen thought to be capable of causing fever by acting on the hypothalamus and by stimulating synthesis of interleukin 1 (IL-1). In old animals, there is an attenuated response to IL-1, and injection of tumour necrosis factor causes a significantly smaller rise in temperature than in younger animals (Miller *et al.* 1991).

Although the association between fever and various infections has been recognized for a long time, there are many other situations in which patients develop fever in the absence of infection. Examples are found in malignancies, connective tissue disease, and non-infective inflammation. Various forms of endogenous pyrogen acting on the thermoregulatory centres are the likely cause.

Poikilothermia

Poikilothermia, the lack of regulated constancy of body temperature, can occur as a 'relative' rather than a primary disorder of the thermoregulatory control system in some elderly patients. The condition reflects lack of adequate central thermoregulatory control, even in normal ambient temperature conditions, and is usually associated with acquired lesions or agenesis of hypothalamic structures. It may also occur as the result of non-specific depression of the central nervous system in deep general anaesthesia. Relative poikilothermia is encountered in elderly people and newborn, particularly premature, infants. Poikilothermic patients demonstrate varying degrees of deficiency or absence of peripheral vasomotor control, shivering, sweating, and metabolic responses. Frequently, lack of thermal discomfort and consequent failure of behavioural thermoregulation contributes to the resulting intermittent episodes of hypothermia or hyperthermia (Mackenzie 1996). Generally, the clinical manifestations are comparable with the signs and symptoms observed in accidental hypothermia and hyperthermia, and the management is similar. It is important to identify any underlying pathology that may be contributing to the poikilothermia if further episodes of hypo- or hyperthermia are to be prevented.

Excess winter mortality

Mortality is greater in winter than in summer in the United Kingdom. Most of the 20 000 to 40 000 excess winter deaths occur among people over 55 years old, but particularly in those over 75 years. For young adults, the seasonal pattern of mortality may be reversed with excess summer deaths due to accidents and violence. There is an association between low environmental temperatures and deaths due to myocardial infarction, stroke, pulmonary embolism, and respiratory disease. Up to 1977, large numbers of winter deaths were caused by epidemics of influenza, but more recent epidemics have been of lower severity. Respiratory deaths are still important, but cardiovascular disease, particularly coronary thrombosis, now causes most of the excess mortality in winter. Hypothermia, once suspected of causing many deaths in elderly people in winter, accounts for less than 1 per cent.

Deaths from coronary thrombosis are maximum 1 to 2 days after the peak of a cold spell; respiratory deaths are more delayed. The early peak of thrombotic deaths can be explained by increases in the concentration in blood of red cells and fibrinogen and increased blood viscosity (Neild *et al.* 1994) and also by other consequences of cutaneous vasoconstriction in the cold such as increased blood pressure (Woodhouse *et al.* 1993). Facial cooling in a cold winter wind, for example, results in a significantly higher arterial blood pressure in healthy elderly than in younger men (Collins *et al.* 1996). The adverse effects of a raised blood pressure in a cold environment include increases in myocardial oxygen demand, ventricular wall stress, and cardiac work. Increased shear forces on the intima of the blood vessels cause epithelial damage predisposing to atheroma and may cause fissuring and rupture of atherosclerotic plaques. Changes in thermoregulatory, cardiovascular, and cardiopulmonary reflex control with age also probably play an important role. Elderly people are at special risk because of age-associated declines in baroreflex sensitivity and ventricular stability when there is imbalance in tonic autonomic control (Schwartz *et al.* 1992).

The causes of the increase in respiratory deaths in winter are less clear, but probably include effects of cold on the respiratory tract, for example inhibition of ciliary movement. There are also a variety of indirect effects such as increases in cross-infection with crowding indoors, and possibly seasonal dietary changes including reduced vitamin C intake. It has been suggested that a high intake of vitamin C provides protection both against respiratory infection and cardiovascular disease (Khaw and Woodhouse 1995).

Excess winter mortality is a worldwide phenomenon in temperate regions, but there are large differences between countries. A number of variables may be relevant including seasonal temperatures, indoor climates, influenza epidemics, nutrition, and various socio-economic and behavioural population characteristics. The severity of winter cold is not the critical factor. Scandinavian countries, the United States, and Canada have low excesses of winter deaths compared with the United Kingdom, Portugal, Israel, and New Zealand. Over the period 1962 to 1995, seasonal mortality ratios have diminished in many of the countries with high winter mortality rates (Fig. 2).

Hypothermia

The susceptibility of elderly people to cold may lead to hypothermia, defined as a deep body temperature below 35°C. The causes and management of this condition are dealt with in Chapter 18.14.

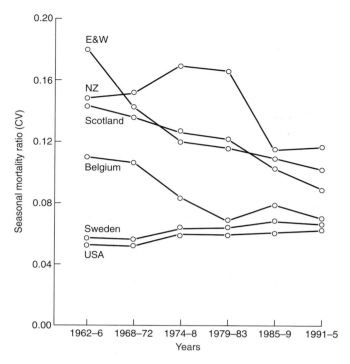

Fig. 2 Seasonal mortality ratios (coefficient of variation (CV) equals standard deviation divided by mean monthly death rate for 5-year periods) for England and Wales (E&W), New Zealand (NZ), Scotland, Belgium, Sweden, and the United States (US). (Data from the *United Nations Demographic Year Books* 1962–1983 and the *United Nations Monthly Bulletins of Statistics* 1985–1995. United Nations, New York.)

Hyperthermia

Medical dangers associated with winter, especially for elderly people, are well recognized, but there is less awareness of the effects of hot summers. Heat-related illnesses are to be expected during heat-waves or prolonged periods of hot weather in urbanized communities in temperate zones, and these mainly affect elderly people, the very young, and those with chronic illness or debility. In the United States, about 4000 deaths each year have been attributed to the effects of heat and 80 per cent involve people aged over 50 years. In the United Kingdom, the annual total of deaths registered as due directly to excessive environmental heat is usually only in single figures, but 37 such deaths were recorded in the prolonged heat-wave of 1976. However, there were 500 excess deaths in the same summer period of 1976, predominantly in those over 65 years of age, and there were also increased hospital admissions of elderly patients suffering from strokes, transient ischaemic attacks, and subarachnoid haemorrhage. The pattern of increased mortality in the elderly population due to heat resembles that for cold winter conditions with peaks in cardiovascular, cerebrovascular, and respiratory deaths.

Predisposing conditions

The extrinsic climatic conditions that lead to heat illnesses are unusually high heat stresses due to high humidity, low air movement, and high radiant heat. The need to increase perfusion of peripheral tissues with cutaneous vasodilatation and increased sweating may not be met in elderly people with diminished thermoregulatory reserve. Diseases that restrict cardiac output, renal disorders which interfere with body fluid balance, skin diseases that impair the ability to sweat, and many commonly prescribed drugs will predispose to heat illness in both young and elderly people (Table 1).

On average, the sweating threshold is raised in elderly people, and lack of adequate sweating is a primary cause of heat illness and increased mortality. As discussed above, sweat glands atrophy and there are regressive changes in the sudomotor nerve endings in old age. The differences between young and old do not appear to be entirely due to a different state of acclimatization to heat. Even when both have been artificially acclimatized to heat, sweat responses are smaller in healthy elderly people than in younger subjects. Increased mortality in the elderly population in urban areas of the United States particularly affects people with pre-existing cardiovascular disease.

Clinical features

The pathological effects of heat arise through four main mechanisms: circulatory instability (heat syncope, heat oedema), heat-induced skin disorders (prickly heat), water and electrolyte imbalance (heat cramps, water and salt deficiency), and hyperthermic failure of thermoregulation (heat stroke).

Syncope can be precipitated in hot conditions by sudden postural change and this is more likely in elderly people with postural hypotension. In urban temperate regions, even during heat-waves, it is unlikely that heat exhaustion due to water or salt deficiency will arise when it is possible to restrict physical activity and to have ready access to fluids. Heat intolerance can, in the extreme, progress to heat stroke, which is characterized by hyperthermia with core temperature reaching 41 °C or above, central nervous system disturbances leading to convulsions and coma, and often a marked anhidrosis. For the majority of unacclimatized people, especially the physically unfit and elderly people, increased cardiovascular strain is the initial threat posed by high environmental temperatures.

The presentation of heat stroke in elderly people is usually not typical of that of young adults (Collins 1996). Classical heat stroke is associated with intolerably hot conditions or heat-waves, without physical exertion, particularly in elderly people. It often occurs in epidemic form and in the presence of predisposing disorders such as ischaemic heart disease, congestive cardiac failure, diabetes mellitus, Parkinson's disease, and recent or old stroke. Exertional heat stroke is generally observed in younger individuals, arising in isolated cases during physical work, and is less frequently associated with an underlying chronic disorder. Prodromal symptoms are not always present but some patients complain of weakness, nausea, vomiting, dizziness, headache, breathlessness, anorexia, and a feeling of warmth. Many of these symptoms can be commonplace in elderly people and may not at first be attributed to heat. Salient clinical features are dehydration with anhidrosis in the majority of patients, coma with complete unresponsiveness to painful stimuli, and signs of pulmonary consolidation, often due to staphylococcal infection. Elderly patients have a diminished ability to combat dehydration because of a reduced thirst sensation and failure of cardiovascular and renal mechanisms for water conservation.

Management

Rapid cooling of heat-stroke patients is essential, and patients should be removed from the warm environment into a cool shaded area

Table 1 Factors contributing to hyperthermia in elderly people

Extrinsic
Exposure to hot indoor or outdoor conditions with high humidity, high radiant temperature, and low air movement
Physical exertion in the heat
High density of living units
Inappropriate clothing
Lack of indoor cooling facilities

Intrinsic
Physiological
Lack of heat acclimatization
Lack of physical fitness
Obesity
Low surface area to mass ratio
Dehydration
Diminished sweating response
Reduced renal efficiency

Clinical conditions

Cardiovascular	Ischaemic heart disease, congestive cardiac failure
Endocrine	Hyperthyroidism, hyperpituitarism, diabetes mellitus
Neurological	Autonomic dysfunction, cerebral haemorrhage, head injury, cerebral tumour or abscess
Mental	Confusional states, dementia
Febrile illness	Respiratory tract, gastrointestinal, tropical infections, septicaemia
Skin disease	Any condition that impairs sweating
Drugs	Anticholinergics, alcohol, psychotropics, hypnotics, antidepressants, amphetamines

and further cooling continued by removing clothing, increasing air movement over the body surface, and sponging with tepid water. Circulatory shock occurs in many heat-stroke patients and intravenous fluids may be required to treat water and/or salt depletion. This should be done with caution for there is a danger of precipitating pulmonary oedema in patients with cardiac or renal failure. The need to avoid vasoconstriction during cooling has led to the development of a body cooling unit for hospital treatment. This method utilizes evaporative and convective cooling from sprays of warm atomized water combined with a powerful flow of warm air to maintain skin temperature above 31 to 32 °C (Collins 1996). The management of classical heat-stroke patients among the Hadj pilgrims at Mecca has proved to be highly successful with this method, the majority of cases being aged over 60 years. As with hypothermia, the prognosis for elderly heat-stroke patients is poor, often owing to the presence of serious associated disease.

Elderly people may be protected in hot environments by restricting physical activity, maintaining fluid intake, wearing light loosely fitting clothing, and avoiding heat stress by appropriate use of air conditioning or ventilating and circulating fans. In general, older people prefer and thrive better in a climate that is warm all the year round, providing that they are equipped to deal with occasional extremes of temperature and humidity that might subject them to thermal stress.

References

Abdel-Rahman, T.A., Collins, K.J., Cowen, T., and Rustin, M. (1992). Immunohistochemical, morphological and functional changes in the peripheral sudomotor neuro-effector system in elderly people. *Journal of the Autonomic Nervous System*, 37, 187–98.

Brock, M.A. (1991). Chronobiology and aging. *Journal of the American Geriatrics Society*, 39, 74–91.

Budd, G.M., Brotherhood, J.R., Hendrie, A.L., and Jeffery, S.E. (1991). Effects of fitness, fatness, and age on men's response to whole body cooling in air. *Journal of Applied Physiology*, 71, 2387–93.

Collins, K.J. (1996). Heat stress and associated disorders. In *Manson's tropical diseases* (20th edn) (ed. G.C. Cook), pp. 421–32. W.B. Saunders, London.

Collins, K.J. (1997). Aging, disease and the autonomic nervous system. *Reviews in Clinical Gerontology*, 7, 119–26.

Collins, K.J., Abdel-Rahman, T.A., Goodwin, J., and McTiffin, L. (1995). Circadian body temperatures and the effects of a cold stress in elderly and young subjects. *Age and Ageing*, 24, 485–9.

Collins, K.J., Abdel-Rahman, T.A., Easton, J.C., Sacco, P., Ison, J., and Doré, C.J. (1996). Effects of facial cooling on elderly and young subjects: interactions with breath-holding and lower body negative pressure. *Clinical Science*, 90, 485–92.

Darowski, A., Najim, Z., Weinberg, J., and Guz, A. (1991). The febrile response to mild infections in elderly hospital in-patients. *Age and Ageing*, 20, 193–8.

Fukagawa, N.K., Veirs, H., and Langeloh, G. (1995). Acute effects of fructose and glucose ingestion with and without caffeine in young and old humans. *Metabolism*, 44, 630–8.

Khaw, K.-T. and Woodhouse, P. (1995). Interrelation of vitamin C, infection, haemostatic factors, and cardiovascular disease. *British Medical Journal*, 310, 1559–63.

Mackenzie, M.A. (1996). *Poikilothermia in man. Pathophysiological aspects and clinical implications*. Nijmegen University Press.

Miller, D., Yoshikawa, T., Castle, S.C., *et al.* (1991). Effects of age on fever responses to recombinant tumor necrosis factor alpha in a murine model. *Journal of Gerontology*, 46, M176–9.

Neild, P.J., Syndercombe-Court, D., Keatinge, W.R., Donaldson, G.C., Mattock, M., and Caunce, M. (1994). Cold-induced increase in erythrocyte count, plasma cholesterol and plasma fibrinogen of elderly people without a comparable rise in protein C or factor X. *Clinical Science*, **86**, 43–8.

Okawa, M., Mishima, K., Hishikawa, Y., Hozumi, S., Hori, H., and Takahashi, K. (1991). Circadian rhythm disorders in sleep-waking and body temperature in elderly patients with dementia and their treatment. *Sleep*, **14**, 478–85.

Prinz, P.N., Moe, K.E., Vitiello, M.V., Marks, A.L., and Larsen, L.H. (1992). Entrained body temperature rhythms are similar in mild Alzheimer's disease, geriatric onset depression, and normal aging. *Journal of Geriatric Psychiatry and Neurology*, **5**, 65–71.

Sawada, S. (1996). Cold-induced vasodilatation response of finger skin blood vessels in older men observed by using a modified local cold tolerance test. *Industrial Health*, **34**, 51–6.

Schwartz, P.J., La Rovere, M.T., and Vandi, E. (1992). Autonomic nervous system and sudden cardiac death. Experimental basis and clinical observations for post-myocardial infarction risk stratification.

Circulation, **85** (Supplement 1), 1–77.

Schwartz, R.S., Jaeger, L.F., and Veith, R.C. (1990). The thermic effect of feeding in older men: the importance of the sympathetic nervous system. *Metabolism*, **39**, 733–7.

Tankersley, C.G., Smolander, J., Kenney, W.L., and Fortney, S.M. (1991). Sweating and skin blood flow during exercise: effects of age and maximal oxygen uptake. *Journal of Applied Physiology*, **71**, 236–42.

Visser, M., Durenberg, P., van-Staveren, W.A., and Hautvast, J.G. (1995). Resting metabolic rate and diet-induced thermogenesis in young and elderly subjects: relationship with body composition, fat distribution, and physical activity level. *American Journal of Clinical Nutrition*, **61**, 772–8.

Woodhouse, P.R., Khaw, K.-T., and Plummer, M. (1993). Seasonal variation of blood pressure and its relationship to ambient temperature in an elderly population. *Journal of Hypertension*, **11**, 1267–74.

18.14 Hypothermia

Peter J. Murphy

Thermoregulation and factors leading to its breakdown in later life are discussed in Chapter 18.13. In humans, core body temperature is maintained between 36.5 and 37.5 °C, 2 to 3 °C above the temperature of the superficial body 'shell' which acts as a variable insulator or heat loss system. Hypothermia is defined as a fall of core body temperature below 35 °C. It can usefully be classified as mild (core body temperature between 35 and 32.2 °C), moderate (between 32.2 and 28 °C), and severe (below 28 °C). Core temperature is most readily measured using a low-reading rectal thermometer; eardrum reflectance is not reliable.

Epidemiology

Fox *et al.* (1973) estimated the prevalence of borderline and actual hypothermia in 1020 randomly selected subjects aged 65 years and over living in their own homes in the United Kingdom. Core temperature was measured by a device allowing the subject to pass urine over a thermometer bulb. Core temperature was between 35 and 35.5 °C in 10 per cent of subjects, and was inversely correlated with age. Only one in 200 of the subjects was actually hypothermic, and only mildly so, at or just below 35 °C. Epidemiological evidence from the United States also suggests that early morning basal body temperatures are rarely low in community-dwelling older people (Rango 1985).

In a hospital-based survey in the United Kingdom, Goldman *et al.* (1977), demonstrated that 3.6 per cent of patients admitted to hospital over 65 years of age were hypothermic on admission. Hislop *et al.* (1995) reported an urban population-based incidence survey from the west of Scotland. The rate of presentation to hospital with hypothermia was 1 per 14 000 people each winter. Extrapolation of these results to the whole of the United Kingdom suggested 4000 hospital admissions with 1000 hospital deaths per annum. Hypothermia is certified as a cause of death for only around 300 deaths in England and Wales per annum. The majority of the 40 000 excess winter deaths in England and Wales are attributed to vascular and respiratory disease. In the United States it is estimated that 60 000 cases of hypothermia are admitted to hospital each annum; with 700 attributed deaths.

Factors predisposing to hypothermia
Pathological factors

Most elderly subjects have intact thermoregulatory function, but may develop conditions and/or take medications that predispose them to hypothermia (Table 1). Diabetes is more common than hypothyroidism in hypothermic subjects. Hypothermia in diabetics most commonly presents with diabetic ketoacidosis. Even excluding diabetic ketoacidotic presentations, elderly diabetic subjects (especially

Table 2 Management of hypothermia

Investigations
Full blood count
Coagulation screen
Urea and electrolytes
Serum creatinine
Blood glucose
'Cardiac' enzymes
Twelve-lead ECG
Serum amylase
Samples for drug screen and alcohol
Regular monitor
   Blood glucose for hypoglycaemia
   Blood urea and electrolytes
   Arterial blood gases
Thyroid function tests
Arterial blood gases
Blood cultures
Urinary culture (if possible)
Chest radiography

Mild hypothermia: temperature 32.2–35 °C
Nurse at a room temperature of 25–30 °C
Monitor rectal temperature every 30 min
Monitor the blood pressure, pulse, and urine output
Cover the patient with two blankets, insulate head and neck
Aim to rewarm at 0.5–1.0 °C/h
Warmed fluids via peripheral intravenous line, as indicated by blood results
Humidified air or oxygen as directed by arterial blood gas results
Intravenous antibiotics
ECG monitoring

Moderate to severe hypothermia: temperature <32.2 °C
Consider referral to intensive care unit where available
Indwelling urinary catheter
Placement of central venous pressure line
Intravenous fluids titrated against blood pressure, central venous pressure, and urine output
Aim to rewarm at 1 °C/h
If rewarming target is not achieved consider active rewarming depending on local facilities, expertise, and whether clinically appropriate

Management of hypothermia

Investigations

Investigations should including a clotting profile (Table 2). Even mild hypothermia may alter the activated partial thromboplastin and prothrombin times. Clotting studies are always measured in the laboratory with the sample warmed to 37 °C. This reverses and can therefore not exclude an *in vivo* hypothermic coagulopathy. However, normal results exclude a consumptive or dilutional coagulopathy which would not be corrected by warming. If there is clinical evidence of bleeding with normal clotting studies, this implies either a hypothermic coagulopathy, the treatment for which is rewarming and/or a separate pathology such as gastric ulceration which may itself complicate hypothermia.

Arterial blood gases should be estimated. These samples are also analysed at 37 °C. In view of temperature-dependent changes in arterial Po_2 which falls approximately 7 per cent with each degree Celsius, there is controversy over whether the results should be corrected for the patient's temperature. In an excellent review of the management of accidental hypothermia, Danzl and Pozos (1994) recommend using uncorrected arterial blood gas values to guide resuscitation. Pulse oximetry may be inaccurate owing to severe vasoconstriction and capillary stasis. Infection, especially pneumonia, commonly precipitates or complicates hypothermia in elderly patients. Intravenous antibiotics should be given empirically to all patients after relevant cultures have been performed.

Moderate hyperglycaemia should be monitored as insulin is only effective at temperatures over 30 °C. Insulin should be used with caution as it may accumulate to become toxic as rewarming occurs. Hypoglycaemia should be identified and corrected aggressively. Samples for screening for drugs and alcohol should be taken.

Rewarming

No prospective randomized controlled trials have been carried out that are large enough to elucidate the impact of different rewarming methods on fatality rates in hypothermia. Hypothermic patients are an extremely heterogeneous group, and it is very difficult to compare the reported clinical series because of variable case mix. Such difficulty is compounded by the influence of improved technology and knowledge of hypothermia, determined by the year of treatment, together with other variables such as access to intensive care support. Larach (1995) has reviewed the clinical studies of rewarming in hypothermia and subsequent fatality rates.

Passive rewarming

Passive rewarming is generally recommended as the management of choice for elderly patients who have developed mild hypothermia gradually. The patient is insulated in blankets in a warm room to minimize heat loss. Rewarming is dependent on effective endogenous thermogenesis. Fatality rates between 5.9 and 82 per cent have been documented for this method.

It has been recommended that elderly hypothermic patients should be rewarmed slowly at rates between 0.5 and 1.0 °C/h. This recommendation seeks to minimize the risk of hypotension complicating rewarming, the so-called after-shock. However, in a North American multicentre survey Danzl et al. (1987) reported rewarming rates for patients aged 60 years and over that far exceeded 0.5 °C/h in the first 3 h of treatment. The fatality rate for the 163 subjects treated with passive rewarming was 16.6 per cent.

Active rewarming

Active rewarming is usually required for subjects with body temperatures below 32.2 °C as endogenous heat production is considerably impaired. Shivering thermogenesis ceases below 32 °C, and metabolic heat production is less than 50 per cent of normal below 28 °C. Other indications for active rewarming are failure of passive rewarming, and impaired thermoregulation from cardiovascular instability, or endocrinological insufficiency.

Active external rewarming

This method fell into disrepute in the 1960s following a number of reports that active external rewarming was associated with a disproportionate fatality attributed to rewarming hypotension (after-shock). A further complication, a drop in temperature during rewarming (the so-called after-drop), is now thought to be of the magnitude of only 0.6 °C and of little clinical significance.

Gautam et al. (1988) reported a study of 86 hypothermic patients (mean age 80.2 years) warmed at 0.5 °C per hour in a purpose built chamber, using slow active rewarming with warm air. The only reported fatality of 36 per cent, was at 48 h. No control group was used. Whilst the non-survivors had a significantly faster rise in temperature than the survivor group, there was no significant difference between the two groups in terms of fall of blood pressure. The complications of after-drop and after-shock were not a problem.

Ledingham and Mone (1980) reported a prospective study of active external rewarming using a radiant heat cradle in 44 patients with a mortality rate of 27 per cent. A comparison group of 89 hypothermic patients enrolled retrospectively had an overall fatality of 60 per cent. However, the active treatment group were younger, were more likely to be hypothermic owing to drug or alcohol ingestion, and were intensively managed in an intensive care unit. Severe hypotension with a systolic pressure below 70 mmHg occurred in 32 per cent of the active group, but was mostly responsive to intravenous fluids.

The only prospective randomized controlled trial between methods of rewarming comes from Steele et al. (1996). Seventeen subjects, aged 40 to 77 years, suffering from moderate to severe hypothermia, were randomized to either passive external rewarming, or active external rewarming using a Bair Hugger Hot Air Jacket. All subjects were treated with warm humidified oxygen, received warmed intravenous fluids, and had their head and neck insulated with blankets. The control group was covered with two standard hospital blankets and rewarmed at 1.4 ± 0.5 °C/h. The active group rewarmed significantly faster at 2.4 ± 1 °C/h). No after-drop in temperature was noted in either group. Hypotension was observed in three of the active group, and in one of the seven control subjects; all responded well to intravenous fluid replacement. There was no significant difference in blood pressure or pulse rate between the two groups. One patient in the active treatment group died of multisystem failure.

It appears that external active rewarming may be undertaken safely, provided subjects are carefully monitored, and receive appropriate fluid replacement, to restore depleted intravascular volume.

Active core rewarming

Humidified and warmed air

Inhalation rewarming requires the air to be completely humidified and heated to 40 to 45 °C. This effectively prevents respiratory heat loss, but heat gain will depend on the efficiency of the subject's ventilation. This is often depressed in hypothermia. This technique is safe and only mildly invasive, but requires specially adapted equipment. Many conventional nebulizers do not heat air to the required temperature.

Core rewarming with heated intravenous infusions is widely used in North America. It is recommended as an adjunct measure for subjects with moderate or severe hypothermia. The infusion should be heated to 40 to 42 °C and given through a central venous line.

Peritoneal dialysis

Whilst gastric, colonic, mediastinal, and peritoneal routes have all been used for rewarming, the peritoneal route is the most applicable. It has the advantage that the equipment and experience of its use are more widely available. An additional benefit is the scope it provides for the management of electrolyte disturbance, uraemia, and poisoning.

General measures

Core body temperature is most realistically monitored with a rectal temperature probe placed 15 cm above the anal margin. Rectal temperature is 0.5° C lower than core body temperature. It lags 30 min behind fluctuations in temperature.

Cardiac dysrhythmias

Atrial fibrillation due to hypothermia often produces a slow ventricular rate and usually reverts spontaneously to sinus rhythm. Digoxin is generally ineffective at low temperatures and should be avoided. Ventricular fibrillation may be resistant to DC cardioversion at temperatures below 30 °C. The most promising antidysrhythmic agent for ventricular fibrillation in this setting is bretylium tosylate infused intravenously.

Endotracheal intubation and assisted ventilation

A comatose hypothermic subject is at high risk of aspiration. Coma or evidence of respiratory failure are indications for endotracheal intubation and possible assisted ventilation where appropriate. Contrary to widespread opinion, endotracheal intubation does not commonly precipitate significant cardiac dysrhythmias (Ledingham and Mone 1980; Danzl et al. 1987).

Miscellaneous therapy

A history of steroid dependency, inexplicable hypotension, or persistent hypothermia during management should prompt consideration of empirical steroid therapy. Patients at a high risk of thiamine deficiency should receive intravenous replacement. Empirical thyroid hormone replacement is not recommended. If opiate overdose is suspected naloxone should be given.

Prognostic factors

The fatality of accidental hypothermia in reported series varies from 0 to over 80 per cent. As noted above, this variation reflects the variable case mix of subjects, the location of treatment, and the period during which the subjects were studied. In general, survival rates from hypothermia have improved over the last 40 years.

Age

Age has been reported as predicting a poor outcome from hypothermia. From a prospective study of 44 patients treated with active external rewarming, Ledingham and Mone (1980) concluded that increasing age was significantly associated with increased fatality for the group as a whole, and for patients presenting with poisoning. For the subgroup of non-poisoned subjects increasing age was not associated with increasing risk of death. Kramer *et al.* (1989) studied the outcome of hypothermic inpatients aged over 60 years (mean age 76, range 60–96 years). Fatality was high at 74 per cent but there was no association between age and fatality. In the large multicentre North American study of 428 hypothermic subjects reported by Danzl *et al.* (1987), fatality was also unassociated with age whatever the form of rewarming employed.

Underlying pathology

The nature and severity of the underlying or precipitating illness may be an important determinant of survival. One suggestion is that patients presenting with alcohol or drug intoxication are more likely to survive. Ledingham and Mone (1980) reported a significantly improved survival in poisoned as compared with non-poisoned hypothermic patients. However, Danzl *et al.* (1987) demonstrated that patients with high ethanol levels on presentation fared neither better nor worse than the other patients. Miller *et al.* (1980) reported an overall fatality rate of 11.9 per cent in a series of 135 cases. Where serious underlying disease was present, the fatality rate was 47.9 per cent.

The degree of hypothermia

The degree of hypothermia is thought to be an important prognostic factor. Intuitively severe hypothermia carries a significant risk of death from complications such as refractory dysrhythmias, whatever the precipitating pathology. Miller *et al.* (1980) argued that survival improved by 1.8 per cent for each rise of 1 °C of presenting temperature. Hislop *et al.* (1995) documented that 20 per cent of mildly hypothermic patients died compared with 50 per cent of moderately to severely hypothermic patients. Danzl *et al.* (1987) showed that although there was no significant difference in physiological or laboratory data between mild and severe hypothermic subjects on presentation, death was more common in the moderate to severe groups.

Danzl *et al.* (1994), in a multivariate analysis, found prehospital cardiac arrest, low or absent blood pressure, elevated urea or creatinine, and the need for endotracheal or nasogastric intubation in the accident and emergency department, as significant predictors of outcome.

Long-term outlook

MacMillan *et al.* (1967) demonstrated persistent thermoregulatory abnormalities in elderly survivors of accidental hypothermia. Darowski *et al.* (1991) emphasized the risk of recurrent clinical hypothermia, with 50 per cent of survivors experiencing recurrent hypothermia within 2 years (two patients having four episodes each). McAlpine and Dall (1987) retrospectively reviewed 81 elderly hypothermic patients. Those suffering from primary hypothermia, for whom no underlying pathology had been identified, were compared with patients with secondary hypothermia due to underlying pathology. The 3-year follow-up fatality was 100 per cent in the primary, and 24 per cent in the secondary group.

Elderly survivors of hypothermia should be assessed for persisting risk factors and advised regarding prevention measures. Such measures will include increased awareness of the avoidable risk factors for hypothermia amongst health and social services professionals and improved education of the general public. Elderly people living in the community might benefit from an assessment of environmental risk factors, such as inadequate insulation and heating of their homes. Advice and financial support for improvements are available from a number of different sources. The high-risk group of elderly people with impaired mobility and cognition who live alone should be visited regularly during cold weather, with attention paid to adequate heating (indoor temperature 21.1 °C) of at least one room of the house, and the use of body worn alarm systems should be encouraged.

References

Clemmer, T.P., Fisher, C.F., Bone, R.C., Slotman, G.S., Metz, C.A., and Thomas, F.O. (1992). Hypothermia in the sepsis syndrome and clinical outcome. *Critical Care Medicine*, 20, 1395–401.

Danzl, D.F. and Pozos, R.S. (1994). Accidental hypothermia. *New England Journal of Medicine*, 331, 1756–60.

Danzl, D.F., Pozos, R.S., Auerbach, P.S., *et al.* (1987). Multicentre Hypothermia Survey. *Annals of Emergency Medicine*, 16, 1042–55.

Danzl, D.F., Pozos, R.S., and Hamlet, M.P. (1994). Accidental hypothermia. In *Wilderness medicine* (ed. W.W. Forguy). I.C.S. Books, Merrillville, IN.

Darowski, A., Nazim, Z., Weinberg, J.R., and Guz, A. (1991). Hypothermia and infection in elderly patients admitted to hospital. *Age and Ageing*, 20, 100–6.

Edelman, I.S. (1974). Thyroid thermogenesis. *New England Journal of Medicine*, 290, 1303.

Fellows, I.W., Macdonald, I.A., Bennett, T., and Allison, S.P. (1985). The effect of undernutrition on thermoregulation in the elderly. *Clinical Science*, 69, 525–32.

Fox, R.H., Woodward, P.M., Exton-Smith, A.N., Green, M.F., Donnison, D.V., and Wicks, M.H. (1973). Body temperatures in the elderly: a national study of physiological, social and environmental conditions. *British Medical Journal*, i, 200–6.

Gautam, P.C., Ghash, S., Mandal, A.R., and Vargas. E. (1988). Hypothermia in the elderly: management in a purpose built chamber. *Gerontology*, 34, 145–50.

Goldman, A., Exton-Smith, A.N., Francis, G., and O'Brien, A. (1977). A pilot study of low body temperatures in old people admitted to hospital. *Journal of the Royal College of Physicians of London*, 11, 291–305.

Hislop, L.J., Wyatt, J.P., McNaughton, G.W., *et al.* (1995). Urban hypothermia in the west of Scotland. *British Medical Journal*, 311, 725.

Kramer, M.R., Vandijk, J., and Robin, A.J. (1989). Mortality in elderly patients with thermoregulatory failure. *Archives of Internal Medicine*, 149, 1521–3.

Larach, M. (1995). Accidental hypothermia. *Lancet*, 345, 493–8.

Ledingham, I. McA. and Mone, J.G. (1980). Treatment of accidental hypothermia: a prospective clinical study. *British Medical Journal*, 280, 1102–5.

McAlpine, C.H. and Dall, J.L.C. (1987). Outcome after episodes of hypothermia. *Age and Ageing*, 16, 115–18.

MacMillan, A.L., Corbett, J.L., Johnson, R.H., Crampton Smith, A., Spalding, J.M.K., and Wollner, L. (1967). Temperature regulation in survivors of accidental hypothermia of the elderly. *Lancet*, ii, 165–9.

Miller, J.W., Danzl, D.F., and Thomas, D.M. (1980). Urban accidental hypothermia: 135 cases. *Annals of Emergency Medicine*, 10, 456–61.

Morgan, R., Blair, A., and King, D. (1996). A winter survey of domestic heating among elderly patients. *Journal of the Royal Society of Medicine*, **89**, 85–6.

Neil, H.A., Dawson, J.A., and Baker, J.E. (1986). Risk of hypothermia in elderly patients with diabetes mellitus. *British Medical Journal*, **293**, 416–18.

Rango, N. (1985). The social epidemiology of accidental hypothermia among the aged. *Gerontologist*, **25**, 424–30.

Slater, D.N. (1988). Death from hypothermia: are current views on causative factors well founded? *British Medical Journal*, **296**, 1643–5.

Steele, M.T., Nelson, M.J., Sessler, D.I., *et al.* (1996). Forced air speeds warming in accidental hypothermia. *Annals of Emergency Medicine*, **27**, 479–84.

Woodhouse, P., Keatinge, W.R., and Coleshaw, S.R.K. (1989). Factors associated with hypothermia in patients admitted to a group of inner city hospitals. *Lancet*, ii, 1201–5.

18.15.1 The eye and senescence

Robert A. Weale

Introduction

A disclaimer

Although the general anatomy and function of the eye are likely to be common to all mankind, this is assumed but not proven. Regional differences, perhaps due to no more than adaptations to the local environment, counsel caution as regards generalizations. Some variations are well known. For example, the African Bantu belong to tribes with relatively narrow lenses, associated with a low incidence of angle-closure glaucoma, the extraocular anatomy of some Asiatics differs from that of Caucasians, there are differences in iris structure amongst Filipinos, and colour vision amongst Brazilian Japanese differs from that prevalent in mainland Japan.

Most of the data accumulated for ocular and visual ageing have been obtained from white Caucasians. This should give us pause for thought before we extend results on ageing rates from one region to another, and from one ethnic group to another. The much admired Mediterranean diet appears to exert preventive effects in cardiac complications; this is likely to affect life expectancy and probably ageing. British brains have been found to contain more lipid and to accumulate it at a faster rate than is true of those of Sri Lankans, a circumstance tentatively attributed to dietary differences. While it is therefore probable that the following outline is generally valid, white is not always right; some published ageing effects may be due to no more than dietary habits peculiar to the United States.

Anatomy and function

The function of the eye is to receive photic information and to transmit it via the optic nerve to the brain (Fig. 1). It achieves this in three sequential ways.

1. Aided by the lens, the cornea produces on the retina a two-dimensional image of the external three-dimensional space.

2. Those light quanta impinging on the retina that are absorbed in its photoreceptors, rods, and cones, elicit a change in the electric potential of their receptor membrane(s).

3. This sets up a chain reaction in the synaptic and cellular network of the retina which ultimately reaches area 17 and other visually responsive areas of the brain. In a somewhat distorted fashion, each retina is projected partly on both sides of the brain, and other areas, thereby permitting the operation of stereoscopic vision.

A variety of optical and spatial filters enable the system to discard information. This may occur following inadequate focusing, or when the fixation reflex or curiosity has not ensured that detail should be imaged on the fovea, the central part of which is referred to clinically as the macula. This retinal region also filters by virtue of being characterized by the highest resolving power, limited only by the laws of physics. It also mediates high-quality colour vision. The pupil also acts as a kind of filter. In addition, the neural system possesses neural filters which subserve the accentuation of contrast, colour, and outline.

The mobility of the eyes is controlled by six extraocular muscles each, and promoted by a virtually frictionless and largely shock-proof environment. This ball-and-socket complex is kept lubricated by an active lachrymal system, which also ensures the maintenance of an optimal optical quality of the exposed cornea. At the same time, the enshrinement of the eyes within the skull provides protection from impact, the lids, lashes, and eyebrows providing additional safe-guards from damage. It may be noted that the blink reflex is one of the fastest reflexes in the whole of the human body.

The cornea

Embryonically, the cornea and the tough sclera are related, but corneal development has remained arrested, hence its transparency. The cornea consists of five layers, the outer epithelium, the monocellular

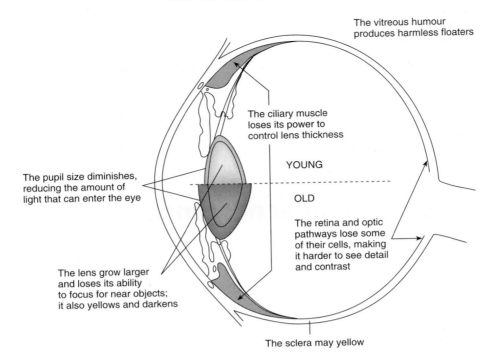

Fig. 1 Young and old eyes compared.

Bowman's membrane, the fibrous stroma which forms 90 per cent of the corneal thickness, Descemet's membrane, and the endothelium. The last two protect the eye from infection, but Bowman's membrane scars if it is damaged. Corneal sensitivity is mediated by nerve fibres carried through from the long and short ciliary nerves; they enter the inner layers of the sclera just outside the corneoscleral junction (the limbus) and ramify under Bowman's membrane. Having lost their myelin for obvious optical reasons they terminate with open endings amongst the epithelial cells.

The endothelial cells form an approximately uniform mosaic in the young eye which can be examined *in vivo* by means of the specular microscope (Laing *et al.* 1979); this makes it possible to study cell number as a function of age (Fig. 2). After the age of around 20 years, there is a rectilinear decline, apparently hitting the ordinate value of zero at about 170 years. The decline of corneal sensitivity to touch declines throughout life, and tends to zero at around 103 years.

The cornea is washed by the lachrymal fluid, which is somewhat more dilute than blood plasma, and contains 0.6 per cent protein and the bacteriostatic lysozyme. Lacrimation decreases systematically throughout life (Fig. 3), and this can lead to the condition of 'dry eye' which requires treatment with artificial tear fluid. The transparency of the cornea rests on the fine regular packing of its constituent fibrils, but does not extend to the far-ultraviolet part of the spectrum (UVC). Since the tissue absorbs this spectral range, transient damage (and considerable pain) can be caused by exposure to high UVC intensities. There is no reliable evidence to suggest that the cornea opacifies with age.

The excellent refraction of the cornea is due to its nearly spherical contour. However, this changes with age (Fig. 4). We are born with the cornea relatively flatter in the horizontal than the vertical meridian ('with the rule'); a reversal to 'against the rule' occurs in later life (Vihlen and Wilson 1983). This is unlikely to be due directly to

senescence, but rather to the continual action of the medial recti muscles which pull on the cornea when making the visual axes converge at a nearby target. There is some evidence to suggest that the cornea is more flexible before than after the age of around 40 years so that, in the absence of a restoring force, elastic or otherwise, the observed deformation would result cumulatively.

The iris

The iris is not usually classed with the ocular image-forming system except in so far as it controls retinal illumination. The pupillary aperture also determines the contrast of retinal images. Under parasympathetic control, the pupillary sphincter responds to a number of reflexes, in antagonism to the weaker and phylogenetically much older dilator which is activated by the sympathetic system. The pupil decreases with age from puberty (Fig. 5); this apparently optical statement rests in fact on a flattening of the iridal tissue. Conventionally attributed to the parasympathetic system winning its tussle with its sympathetic opponent, the age-associated decrease is more likely to be due to the dilator atrophying at a greater rate than is true of its antagonist. This point is of clinical significance. Neurologists use the mobility of the iris as an index of neural integrity. However, small pupils, even if young, are less mobile than large ones so that the relatively low mobility of older pupils is due not to their age but their size. In fact, older pupils have been found to be more mobile than equally sized young ones when judgement was tested by measurement (Schäfer and Weale 1970).

The photometric control exerted by the senescent pupil is without practical consequences in full daylight. But when light is at a premium then the older person is disadvantaged; at the age of 60 years the pupil transmits to the retina only one-third of the amount it used to

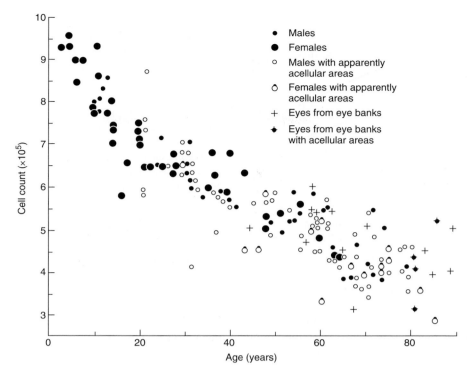

Fig. 2 Individual cell counts in the cornea versus age. (Reproduced with permission from Laule *et al.* (1978).)

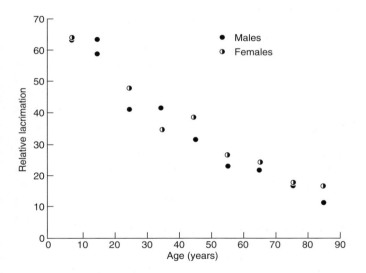

Fig. 3 The decline in tear flow. (Reproduced with permission from de Roetth (1953).)

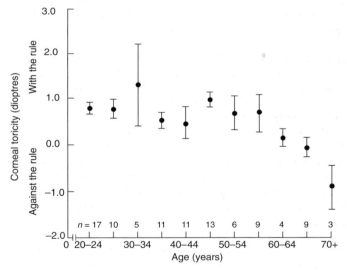

Fig. 4 The change of corneal astigmatism with age. (Reproduced with permission from Vihlen and Wilson (1983).)

send through at the age of 20. Thus elderly people may suffer from misguided parsimony in inadequate illumination of rooms, corridors, and staircases.

The aqueous humour

For the eye to preserve its spherical shape, and the cornea its high optical image-forming ability, the eyeball is inflated to a pressure above that of the atmosphere; an intraocular pressure of not more than 21 mm of mercury is considered normal. Measured by means of a tonometer—according to Sommer *et al.* (1991) 'neither an effective nor an efficient screening tool'—intraocular pressure is maintained by the secretion of the aqueous humour from the ciliary body (which partly engulfs the ciliary muscle); together with the iris and the vitreous humour, the ciliary body encloses the volume of the posterior chamber (see Fig. 1). While the ciliary tissue tends to

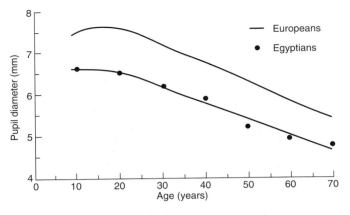

Fig. 5 Age-associated miosis in the United Kingdom and Egypt. (Reproduced with permission from Said and Sawires (1972).)

swell with age, intraocular pressure appears to remain approximately constant; this seems to result from a decline in aqueous secretion being accompanied by a decrease in the outflow of the fluid from the anterior chamber largely via Schlemm's canal. The turnover time of the aqueous in the anterior chamber is about 90 min.

Glaucoma

A rise in intraocular pressure is associated with the age-associated condition of glaucoma. At present, the diagnosis of glaucoma is made only if there is a demonstrable loss in the extent of the visual field and a cupping of the optic disc. Field loss is determined by subjective tests involving the use of perimeters of which a variety are available. In principle, the test requires the patient to maintain firm fixation of a target, while a stimulus of variable intensity is projected into different parts of the retina. The test calls for effort on the patient's part; normative data for the age-associated extent of the field in the absence of glaucoma have been obtained. Mentally disadvantaged patients obviously need special ophthalmic care.

Glaucoma is subdivided into several groups. For example, there is pigmentary glaucoma, associated with the loss of pigment from the iris, in which the particles clog up the aqueous outflow channels thereby causing a rise in intraocular pressure. It is relatively easy to diagnose because melanin particles may also adhere to the inner surface of the cornea.

More fundamentally, there is primary open-angle glaucoma, often associated with myopia, as against narrow-angle or angle-closure glaucoma, which tends to be observed in hypermetropes. The latter can be marked by considerable ocular pain but the former is more insidious. Visual impairment and ultimately blindness may result from a loss of ganglion cells, which manifests as a visual field loss. Glaucoma is treated with drugs which reduce tension, though surgical intervention may be needed, for example, to perforate the iris so that aqueous outflow may be facilitated.

The prevalence of primary open-angle glaucoma rises exponentially from less than 1 per cent during the fifth decade of life to about 10 per cent in the ninth. This simplistic statement disguises a feature of considerable significance namely the ethnic variation of the approximate age of diagnosis of this condition. The prevalence of primary open-angle glaucoma is far greater amongst Afro-Caribbeans than Caucasians (Cowan et al. 1988), and this does not appear to be due essentially to more intense pigmentation. The mean prevalence in Jamaica is 1.4 per cent as compared with 0.47 per cent in Wales, and in the United States the prevalence amongst black people is two to three times greater than amongst whites at all ages (Sommer et al. 1991). In Africa the clinical population reaches a peak in the mid-thirties (Balo et al. 1995), whereas a Caucasian population would reach it some two decades later. Some 7 per cent of the patients surveyed by Balo et al. (1995) were less than 15 years old. Natives of central Africa are liable to present at a much younger age—even in their late teens—than is true of Afro-Caribbeans (Table 1). It is clear that this type of information is only second-best, since screening programmes should be based on age-associated incidence data which alone make comparisons between one population and another meaningful.

Although the aetiology of primary open-angle glaucoma is not understood, glaucoma associated with an anomalous geometry of the angle of the anterior chamber is easier to grasp. Qualitatively it is easy to see that, if the angle is narrow or even closed, drainage of the aqueous out of the eye is likely to be compromised (see Fig. 1). The broad correlation between type of glaucoma and refraction is illustrated with reference to Asia: the Chinese tend to be myopic and there is a considerable prevalence of primary open-angle glaucoma amongst them. Unusually amongst Asians, the Burmese are hypermetropic, not myopic like the Chinese and Japanese, and are at considerable risk from narrow-angle or angle-closure glaucoma rather than from primary open-angle glaucoma.

Table 1 Age and screening for glaucoma (p<0.005)

Country of origin	Average age at presentation		Estimated minimum age for screening (years)	
	Males	Females	Males	Females
Africa	54.9 (13.8)	55.8 (11.2)	13	21
British Isles	70.3 (10.8)	73.3 (10.1)	38	43
Caribbean	64.9 (9.9)	65.5 (10.1)	35	35
Indian subcontinent	64.5 (11.1)	63.5 (13.3)	31	23

Reproduced with permission from Weale (1993).

While the geriatrician may not be in a position to combat either form of glaucoma, prophylactic screening should be as mandatory as measuring blood pressure. One can learn to use the ophthalmoscope so as to view the optic disc—if there is no cataract—and simple field tests are not too difficult to devise, and to teach paramedical collaborators. Experience in everyday clinics shows that a great deal of visual impairment from glaucoma is preventable.

The lens

Unlike the lens of a camera, the lens in the eye acts not as the principal but as an adjuvant image-forming device. The cornea provides two-thirds of the refractive power of the eye and the lens only the remaining third, but it differs from the cornea in that, at least in its young years, its power is variable through the process of accommodation.

An age-associated decline in accommodative power leads to presbyopia, remedied in general by the provision of reading glasses. The unit of optical power is the dioptre (D), which is equal to $1/f$, where f is the focal length in metres. Dioptres are additive, with convex lenses being called plus. If a person focuses a near object sharply at a minimum distance of 1 m (which requires an accommodation of 1 D), but wishes to read at around 30 cm, then the power of the requisite reading lenses is an 'add of $+2$ D'.

The lens matrix is contained within the highly elastic lens capsule. Mitosis of the epithelial cells, underneath the latter and anterior to the lenticular equator, leads to their elongation into fibres, which stretch behind the epithelium anteriorly, and in front of the capsule in the posterior aspect. They are laid down throughout life, and extend from one approximately Y-shaped system of sutures to the other upside-down Y-shaped one. This is accompanied by the loss of their nuclei and organelles, and a corollary disappearance of metabolic potential. Consequently the lenticular nucleus consists of the oldest (antenatal) inert fibres, whereas the superficial cortex is made up of the latest arrivals.

Although complex, the suture system ensures a better optical performance than if the fibres converged onto anterior and posterior knots along the visual axis. The optical homogeneity of the lens is assisted by the existence of small extracellular spaces between adjacent fibres, which assume an almost hexagonal packing.

The proportion of water (two-thirds of the mass) is amongst the lowest in the human body, and, by virtue of the correspondingly high concentration of protein, helps to mediate the strong refracting power of the lens. Thus the refractive index of the lenticular cortex exceeds 1.37, rising along a gradient that varies with age to 1.39 in the central (nuclear) parts (Pierscionek 1995), a matter of significance since refraction is a function of refractive index differences, and the lens is surrounded by water ($n = 1.33$); on the anterior side there is the aqueous humour, and posteriorly the vitreous humour, also consisting of over 99 per cent of water. There is a close parallel between the topographic variation of the refractive index and protein concentration (Siebinga *et al.* 1991).

The lens-specific proteins are α-, β-, and γ-crystallins, so-called because the lens used to be thought of as a crystalline structure, a view that has been challenged (Pierscionek 1993). The relative proportion of the crystallins changes systematically—γ-crystallin decreasing with advancing age—and the proteins tend to form high-molecular-weight

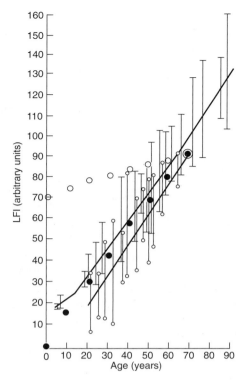

Fig. 6 The age-associated rise in fluorescence of the eye lens, expressed as the lens fluorescence index (LFI), in Atlanta (upper regression line and error bars ending in horizontal dashes) and Oregon (lower regression line and error bars ending in circles). The former has the sunnier environment, which may explain the higher fluorescence values. The large circles are theoretical estimates based on the assumption that (a) the efficiency of fluorescent light being produced per molecule is constant (○) and (b) it rises with age (●). (Reproduced with permission from Weale (1996).)

aggregates, which may account for the increased tendency of the ageing lens to scatter light.

The precise mechanism of this transformation is still being studied. The crystallins are subject to post-translational changes, which include, for example, glycation, phosphorylation, and methionine oxidation which are liable to promote changes in the surface charge of the globular molecules, thereby causing their unfolding (Harding 1972) and exposure to hazards from which they were previously protected. There is notably the oxidation of the initially internal thiol groups. Thus the proteins are under a progressively increasing risk from oxidative stress, but protected from it, at least during early life, by the presence of glutathione, a scavenger of free radicals. Its concentration declines in later life.

Effects of radiation

It is possible that the molecular unfolding is enhanced by the absorption of ultraviolet light acting as a catalyst rather than a directly noxious factor. However, the effect of ultraviolet light on lenticular metabolism and survival is still under debate (Dolin 1994). Several laboratory studies have dealt with mammalian non-human lenses, sometimes obtained from species enjoying a nocturnal lifestyle, and hence not exposed nor adapted to an exposure of significant amounts of ultraviolet radiation. Also the intensities of the radiation used have

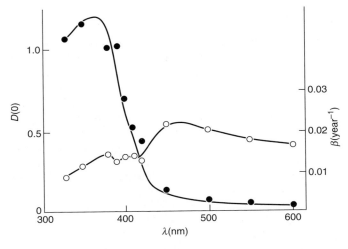

Fig. 7 The neonatal lens absorbance $D(0)$ (●) (UVC part of the spectrum on the left, red on the right) and the exponent β of the annual increase (○). (Reproduced with permission from Weale (1988).)

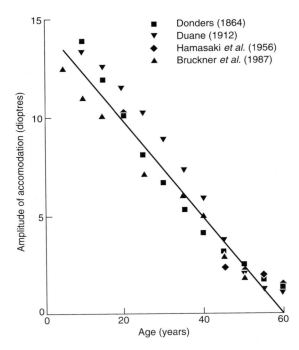

Fig. 8 Amplitude of accommodation versus age.

tended to be unphysiological probably in order to accelerate the experimental procedure. Moreover, short-term laboratory studies are of limited value because possible repair processes are not given a chance to operate.

Recent work on lenticular fluorescence has produced further, if also indirect, information. When an eye is examined with the slit lamp or biomicroscope the lens can be seen to fluoresce. Fluorescence is accentuated in older eyes, but has to be distinguished from light that is scattered (which also increases with age). Lerman (1988) measured the relative amount of fluorescence as a function of age in Oregon and Atlanta. The average annual amount of sunlight in the latter is about 1.6 times greater, and the lenses of the Atlantan population fluoresce with a greater intensity (Fig. 6).

On the simplest of assumptions, there are two ways in which both the age-associated and the geographical increases could be brought about. Senescent lenses could absorb progressively more ultraviolet radiation; they contain at least two pigments, largely confined to the nucleus. One, linked to 3-hydroxykynurenine (van Heyningen 1973), is present from birth. Its absorption (maximal at 360 nm in the ultraviolet A) tends to rise throughout life. Another substance, absorbing maximally at around 470 nm, accumulates after birth, at a greater rate than the former. Consequently lenses appear to become yellower with age. The increase in absorbency of all wavelengths is compatible with an exponential rise in the concentration of at least two chromophores (Fig. 7) and the concomitant yellowing of the lens (Weale 1988). Alternatively, or additionally, there could exist an age-associated increase in the efficiency with which absorbed ultraviolet radiation is converted into fluorescent radiation. This would be expected on the basis of the above-mentioned unfolding of molecules.

Since absorption must precede fluorescence, and there is a fixed relation between absorption and transmissivity, fluorescence characteristics ought to be predictable from the latter. In particular, the variation with age of fluorescence might be derived from that of the transmissivity (T) of the lens, more especially from the absorbency which equals $-\log T$ and is largely proportional to the concentration of lenticular pigments. This has, in fact, been found to be the case

(Weale 1996); however, the observed variation with age of fluorescence is matched by theory only with an additional hypothesis, namely that the efficiency of ultraviolet light conversion into fluorescence is also age dependent (see Fig. 6).

These age-associated changes are significant in that they are probably environmental indices rather than correlates of the processes of senescence *per se*. The lens may be looked on tentatively as a kind of integrating photometer, recording the amount of ultraviolet radiation to which it has been exposed.

Presbyopia

Paradoxically, the best known ocular change associated with ageing, namely presbyopia, appears also largely to result from environmental influences rather than from the ravages of senescence. The reason is that the rate of loss of accommodation is twice that of the average of the majority of senescent processes; in fact, no age-associated phenomenon appears to have been recorded so far to occur faster than, or even equal to, presbyopia (Weale 1995).

Four studies reported over almost a century for Caucasian eyes (Weale 1990) show a rectilinear decline of the accommodative amplitude with age (Fig. 8); at the age at which the ordinate drops below 3 D reading glasses are needed for close work. Figure 9 shows this age to vary systematically with geographical location, the operative variable being temperature (Weale 1963, 1992; Miranda 1979).

The phenomenon is multifactorial. It is explained in terms of changes in the elastic properties of the lens matrix, in the decline of Young's modulus of the capsule (the only relevant factor to change at a rate to be found within the framework of systemic senescence), in changes in lenticular shape (Fisher 1969, 1971, 1973), to a very minor degree in the growth of the lens, and in those involving the

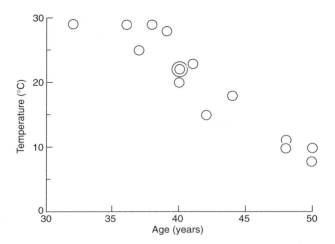

Fig. 9 The mean age of onset of presbyopia as a function of average annual ambient temperature. (Modified from Weale (1983).)

effect of zonular tension on the shape of the lens (Pierscionek and Weale 1995).

For example, Farnsworth and Shyne (1979) observed an age-associated forward shift of the proximal zonular attachments on the anterior lens face. In the unaccommodated state, an increased bending moment is therefore applied to the anterior face of the lens, and zonular tension cannot be reduced in accommodation as much as it could earlier. Therefore the component of zonular tension keeping the lens flat is reduced, but the anterior surface curvature increased; both factors impede the older lens from accommodating when the ciliary muscle is activated. There is, moreover, a concomitant role played by age-associated changes in the refractive index (Pierscionek 1995), counteracting the ametropia which would otherwise arise from the changes in curvature.

It is also likely that the systematic change in the shape of the ciliary muscle plays a role in decreasing the accommodative amplitude (Stieve 1949). We therefore distinguish between lenticular and extra-lenticular factors contributing to presbyopia.

The contraction of this smooth muscle following the arrival of nerve impulses leads to its fibres being pulled inside the eye inward and forward, thereby relaxing zonular tension in a more complicated manner (Rohen and Rentsch 1969) than had been thought earlier in this century. The reduced zonular tension permits the elastic zonule to assume its more nearly unconstrained rotund shape; consequently the power of the lens is increased. An increase in the size of the ciliary muscle, its later hyalinization, and subsequent involution are held to contribute to accommodative failure.

Furthermore, changes in the iris sphincter (Weale 1992) may affect the action of the physiologically relatively stable ciliary muscle (Swegmark 1969; Saladin and Stark 1975). Miosis assists the above-mentioned accommodative increase in lens curvature. Age-associated miosis exerts a pull on the iris root; the force is transmitted to the ciliary tissue causing a centripetal migration of the distal zonular anchors. This view is supported by findings that presbyopia occurs earlier in regions where sunlight is intense and hence pupil sizes are smaller (Weale 1992), although effects of higher temperatures on both pupil size and accommodation cannot be ruled out (see above).

Cataract

Cataract has often been presented as the terminal condition of a tissue wending its way through life first by yellowing, then by becoming presbyopic, and lastly scattering light in its precataractous stage. This blinkered view ignores not only the probability that the first two conditions are, as we have seen, subject to environmental influences, but also the near certainty that a gene exists for at least one type of lens opacity, namely cortical cataract (Heiba et al. 1995).

An understanding of the aetiology of cataract, and probably ultimately of its non-surgical resolution, requires a classification of the different topographically distinguishable types. Thus streaks, clefts, and wedges seen with the slit lamp in the lenticular cortex are grouped together under the term 'cortical cataract'. This is found frequently amongst black people. In contrast, nuclear cataract, involving opacities in the nucleus, occurs frequently amongst those born in the Indian subcontinent. There is also the posterior subcapsular cataract, a condensation located near the visual axis intersecting the posterior lenticular pole. Visually the most disabling of the three, it can result from systemic causes, such as diabetes (but see Miglior et al. 1994), and the ingestion of steroids, and is also associated with radiation damage to the lenticular epithelium.

Mixtures of two or three of the above, called mixed cataracts, also occur. Several risk factors have been established. Except for trauma, they require time to manifest which is why all seven types of cataract tend to be age associated. They take between 4 and 7 years to impair vision completely, but the decision to operate is based on the patient's way of life; if desired activities are hampered the lens will be removed intracapsularly so that the capsule may house within it a plastic implant usually secured with two U-shaped springs. Owing to the proliferation of lenticular epithelial cells, fibroblasts, and iridal pigment cells (Kappelhof and Vrensen 1992), the capsule may opacify not infrequently after some 18 months, a problem easily resolved with a laser beam burning an aperture through it.

In cataract, nuclear cytoplasmic, cytoskeletal, and/or crystallin proteins are liable to manifest post-translational conformational changes (Harding 1991; Young 1991) in the form of an increased aggregation and the creation of cross-linkages and bonds between proteins or between proteins and sugar molecules, leading to proteolysis to low molecular weight polypeptides. These changes alter the size and/or conformation of proteins; proteolytic enzymes reside mainly in the perimembranous cytoplasmic region, and are activated by high Ca^{2+} or low Zn^{2+} concentrations; zinc levels falling dramatically with age in normal eyes (Eichhorn 1979). The short-range order of proteins forming the basis of transparency thus tends to be interfered with, but at a later age than might be postulated on the basis of some of these changes. Thus Horwitz (1992) has suggested that α-crystallin may act as a chaperone, protecting proteins from heat shock and other causes of denaturation. Its bovine form maintains this ability during the first 10 per cent of the estimated lifespan of cattle (around 29 years), although the concentration of the protein is liable to decrease (Carver et al. 1996). If this is applicable to humans, then it is the loss of the protein rather than its degradation which may increase the vulnerability of the lens.

Cortical changes entail the rupture of cell membranes and the consequential random transfer of water, ions, and proteins from cell to cell, resulting probably from oxidative stress (Vrensen 1995). While these changes cause the disorganization of the cortical fibre structure,

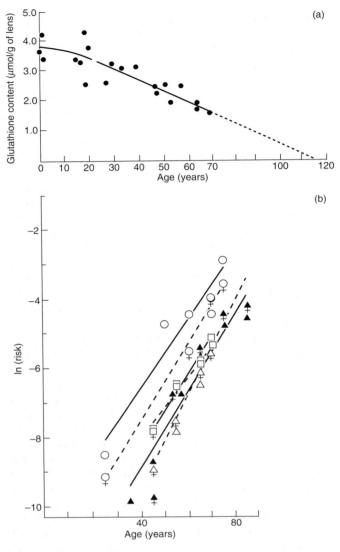

Fig. 10 (a) The decline of the lenticular concentration of glutathione. (Reproduced with permission from Harding (1972).) (b) Logarithmic plots of the cataract risk as reported in a number of studies. (Reproduced with permission from Weale (1983).)

the thickness of the cortex overlying the opacity is translated into years, and so offers a means of estimating when the injury is likely to have occurred. Cholesterol protects deep cortical membranes from oxidative stress (Vrensen 1995), which leaves open the question of why early membrane ruptures and opacities are confined to superficial cortical fibres notably within a narrow equatorial annulus. They do not give rise to any symptoms and can be seen biomicroscopically only when the pupil is dilated; they are sometimes referred to as coronal cataract. Perhaps we are dealing with a phenomenon not of senescence but of wear and tear. This is the region where zonular tension acts when accommodation is relaxed; it is possible that prolonged pulling can lead to local traumatization, creating opacities confined to the equatorial annulus, and never progressing beyond it.

Controllable risk factors are sex and cataract specific. Thus sunlight appears to promote both cortical and posterior subcapsular lesions (Italian-American Cataract Study Group 1991; Hirvelä *et al.* 1995) and to protect from nuclear cataract (Leske *et al.* 1991). Smoking may provoke nuclear cataract (Flaye *et al.* 1989; Leske *et al.* 1991; Hirvelä *et al.* 1995). Multivitamin intake protects men more than women from nuclear cataract (Mares-Perlman *et al.* 1995).

Low educational achievement is a risk for all types of cataract (Leske *et al.* 1991), but, as it does not seem to affect any obvious physiological attribute, it probably correlates with one or more cultural characteristics which do. Thus Pierscionek and Weale (1996) have noted ethnic origin as a risk factor in Australia, the likelihood being that dietary customs are preserved amongst emigrants at least for a generation or two, and that it is diet rather than place of birth that plays a role.

Cataract patients are often told reassuringly that, if we live long enough, we will all suffer from a cataract. It depends on what is meant by 'long enough', but Fig. 10 is informative on this point. Figure 10(a) shows the age-associated decline of glutathione and Fig. 10(b) shows the logarithmic plots (Gompertz 1825) of cataract risks recorded in a variety of studies. The two sections appear to converge after the age of 100 years; thus the exhaustion of a scavenger of free radicals seems to signal that the risk of having a cataract assumes the notion of certainty as distinct from one of probability.

The vitreous humour

The gel of the vitreous humour manifests few, if any, signs of senescence. However, a common sign is the formation of floaters. As the name implies, these are small mobile volumes of material with a refractive index different from that of the surrounding vitreous. Observant patients can find them quite distressing until they are reassured that they are not harbingers of disaster. At the same time, it has to be remembered that the vitreous humour may liquefy with age; this does not imply an increase in its proportion of water, in any case near 100 per cent, but rather that fine strands of mucus which provide a stabilizing scaffolding tend to become disrupted. Myopes have to be alerted to the possibility of the appearance of a cloud, which is a sign of a detachment, possibly of the vitreous humour or, more seriously, of the retina. This symptom does not 'go away'; it needs immediate specialist attention with a minimum of patient movement.

they are retarded by scavengers of free radicals, including glutathione, lysosomal enzymes which remove damaged proteins, and fibre segregation (which may explain the observed streaks). They are joined by superoxide dismutase, the thioredoxin system, catalase, and thiol-transferase. These detoxify superoxide and H_2O_2, and prevent the formation of disulphide bonds.

The topographic location of spokes or streaks, which may be as long as a radius, is not related to the patient's age so that they are unlikely to be due to stress following the relaxation of accommodation. It may be noted in passing that, in some cases, phakochronography (study of the changes of the lens with time) offers instructive information on specific traumatic events. This lenticular archaeology is based on the fact that the cortex of the tissue grows at a fairly constant rate. Suppose now that the lens suffers local trauma which gives rise to the development of a localized opacity. An estimate of

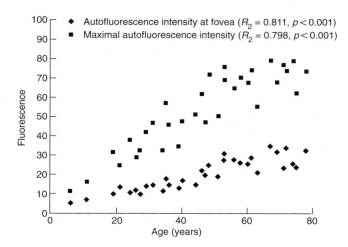

Fig. 11 Age-associated increase in fundus autofluorescence (associated with lipofuscin) in normal eyes, measured (a) in the fovea, and (b) in the region of maximal rod density. (Reproduced with permission from von Rückmann et al. (1997).)

The retina

The retina acts as a transducer, converting radiant energy into molecular events in the photoreceptors. Rods subserve low-intensity vision, and cones daylight vision. Both link synaptically to a variety of bipolar cells which appear to become translocated with age (Gartner and Henkind 1981); in turn, these connect similarly with ganglion cells, the axons of which form the optic nerve and lead to the lateral geniculate bodies. Traversing the optic disc, the axons may suffer damage and death in glaucoma; their loss manifests as an excavation or cupping of the disc. The cones are densest in the retinal centre, the fovea, a thin part of the retina because the higher-order neurones, which overlie the inverted vertebrate retina, have been expelled into the surroundings to reduce the untoward effect of any light they might scatter (or because the blood supply is more abundant there). The fovea forms the centre of the macula.

The macula is yellow in colour owing to the presence of carotenoid xanthophyll, and may serve to provide oxygen to a retinal region which is vascularly undersupplied, so improving performance. It also reduces the effects of chromatic aberration by absorbing blue and violet rays for which the eye is myopic. Contrast, fine detail, and colour are optimally processed by the system subserved by foveal cones; movement is best detected in more peripheral regions of the retina.

In trying to assess the effects of retinal senescence, the same dilemma occurs as with the lens: how much is due to age and how much to lifelong illumination? The cells of the retina and retinal pigment epithelium do not divide postnatally. This is why, in the absence of any pathology, their rate of senescence (Gao and Hollyfield 1992) is three or four times lower than that of tissues made up of dividing cells, such as the capsule or those linked to systemic collagen. Other non-dividing cells, such as cardiac elements, age similarly slowly, and it has been shown that the dividing cells alone are effective predictors of the lifespan just as are measures of DNA activity.

The retinal pigment epithelium abuts Bruch's membrane, an important diffusion barrier separating the retina from the vascular choroid behind it. Bruch's membrane thickens with age and may accumulate debris which can be seen through an ophthalmoscope in the form of 'drusen' after mid-life.

The human retina is liable to be damaged by exposure to solar and other similar energy. The noxious effects of lower intensities are less well known. Intense blue light, in particular, constitutes a hazard, and special precautions should be taken by specialists using lasers in coagulating the retina, or dealing with postoperative capsular problems (Arden et al. 1991).

It is unknown whether age-associated changes in the photo-receptors are primary, or secondary to environmental influences or to changes in the retinal pigment epithelium, which meets their metabolic requirements. Although the continuously renewable fine disc-like composition of the outer limbs of the photoreceptors (some 2 μm in diameter) has been shown to manifest marked age-associated changes, it is not established whether this reflects morbidity or decay. Recent advances in the visualization of individual receptors in the living eye should make it possible to correlate structure with function and to answer this question.

It is not known whether the retinal, as distinct from the choroidal, blood supply diminishes with age. The evidence that it might is largely entoptic; when the blue sky is being viewed one can see blood corpuscles streaking across the visual field. In the largely avascular fovea, they are barely detectable. The method lends itself to a measurement of the avascular area, which is found to increase with age. It could be, however, that it is not the number of capillary vessels that decreases but one's ability to maintain the capability for their detection. This is more than likely for two reasons. Firstly, the age-associated yellowing of the lens reduces the retinal illumination for blue light, thereby lowering the contrast of the blood corpuscles against the background. Secondly, contrast perception also tends to decline with age (Weale 1992). The above-mentioned disc renewal, with a turnover of weeks for rods but months for cones, involves the retinal pigment epithelium in the phagocytosis of discarded discs. In early life this creates few problems. Later the process slows down, leading to an increase in the absorbency of the rod photopigment (rhodopsin) contained in receptor outer limbs (Liem et al. 1991); this is probably due to their elongation, and to the congestion of lipofuscin in the cells of the retinal pigment epithelium (Dorey et al. 1989). In contrast with rhodopsin, cone pigment absorbency declines with advancing years (Keunen et al. 1987).

Lipofuscin is often called an age pigment. However, its rate of accumulation in the retinal pigment epithelium is the subject of debate. Two studies (Feeney-Burns et al. 1984; Wing et al. 1987) report an unmistakably biphasic increase in the retinal concentration of lipofuscin; a rapid early rise following birth slows down to a plateau during the third decade, and resumes its rise during the sixth decade. Conversely, in studies by Delori et al. (1995) and von Rückmann et al. (1997), the latter obtained in vivo with a scanning laser ophthalmoscope, the rise in lipofuscin accumulation with age was almost monotonic (Fig. 11). There is no reason to question the validity of either set of studies and there may be regional, perhaps dietetic, factors involved. For example, lipofuscin accumulates bi-phasically in human stellate and mesenteric ganglia and in the frontal cortex (Koistinaho et al. 1986), and a link between the cerebral concentration of this pigment and diet is possible (Mann and Yates 1982).

Age-associated maculopathy

In the West, age-associated maculopathy is the most serious age-associated affliction. While it is rarely accompanied by total blindness, it involves a failure of central visual function, manifesting by a greatly reduced ability to perceive fine detail and contrast. Reading becomes impossible, and tasks such as watching television become difficult and unenjoyable.

Age-associated maculopathy occurs in two main forms, the wet and the dry. The former involves retinal haemorrhages, which can be partly controlled by laser coagulation of the leaky vessels. Neither cause nor cure is known, but a number of risk factors have been identified. Smoking (in men) and non-specific exposure to chemicals (in men and women) are among the controllable factors. There are important genetic influences, including parental and diagnosed sibling history (Hyman *et al.* 1983), and iris colour, if it entails progressive pallor (Holz *et al.* 1994). Ethnic factors are also known to play a role (Gregor and Joffe 1978). Claims for the existence of inverse prevalence relations between cataract and age-associated maculopathy (van der Hoeve 1919) need to be treated with care; a dense cataract may render age-associated maculopathy invisible.

Conclusion

The question of the extent to which the senescence of the eye is due to general ageing processes remains open. The decline of ocular function occurs at much the same rate as the general age-associated devolution revealed in mortality rates and other forms of functional decline. It certainly seems possible that the ageing process in the various tissues of the eye may give important clues to mechanisms underlying age-associated loss of capacity in other body tissues and organs.

References

Arden, G.B., Beminger, T., Hogg, C.R., and Peny, S. (1991). A survey of colour discrimination in German ophthalmologists. Changes associated with the use of lasers and operating microscopes. *Ophthalmology*, 98, 567–75.

Balo, K.P., Talabe, M., N'Danou, K.H., Agossou, K.A., and Koffi-Gue, K.B. (1995). La papille chez le glaucomateux togolais. *Journal Français d'Ophthalmologie*, 18, 194–9.

Brückner, R., Batschelet, F., and Hugenschmidt, F. (1987). The Basel longitudinal study on aging (1955–1978). *Documenta Ophthalmologica*, 64, 234–310.

Carver, J.A., Nicholls, K.A., Aquilina, J.A., and Truscott, R.J.W. (1996). Age-related changes in bovine α-crystallin and high-molecular-weight protein. *Experimental Eye Research*, 63, 639–47.

Cowan, L.C., Worthen, M.D., Mason, P.R., and Anduze, L.A. (1988). Glaucoma in blacks. *Archives of Ophthalmology*, 106, 738–40.

Delori, F.C., Dorey, C.K., Staurenghi, G., Arend, O., Goger, D. G., and Weiter, J.J. (1995). *In vivo* fluorescence of the ocular fundus exhibits retinal pigment epithelium lipofuscin characteristics. *Investigative Ophthalmology and Visual Science*, 36, 718–29.

de Roetth, A. (1953). Lacrimation in normal eyes. *Archives of Ophthalmology*, 49, 185–9.

Dolin, P.J. (1994). Ultraviolet radiation and cataract: a review of the epidemiological evidence. *British Journal of Ophthalmology*, 78, 478–82.

Donders, F.C. (1864). *On the anomalies of accommodation and refraction of the eye*. New Sydenham Society, London.

Dorey, C.K., Wu, G., Ebenstein, D., Garsd, A., and Weiter, J.J. (1989). Cell loss in the aging retina. *Investigative Ophthalmology and Visual Science*, 30, 1691–9.

Duane, A.J. (1912). Normal values of the accommodation at all ages. *Journal of the American Medical Association*, 59, 1010–13.

Eichhorn, G.L. (1979). Aging, genetics, and the environment: potential of errors introduced into genetic information transfer by metal ions. *Mechanism of Ageing and Development*, 9, 291–301.

Farnsworth, P. and Shyne, S.E. (1979). Anterior zoncular shifts with age. *Experimental Eye Research*, 28, 291–7.

Feeney-Burns, L., Hilderbrand, E.S., and Eldridge, S. (1984). Aging human RPE: morphometric analysis of macular, equatorial, and peripheral cells. *Investigative Ophthalmology and Visual Science*, 25, 195–200.

Fisher, R.F. (1969). Elastic constants of the human lens capsule. *Journal of Physiology*, 201, 1–19.

Fisher, R.F. (1971). The elastic constants of the human lens. *Journal of Physiology*, 212, 147–8.

Fisher, R.F. (1973). Presbyopia and the changes with age of the human crystalline lens. *Journal of Physiology*, 228, 765–79.

Flaye, D.E., Sullivan, K.N., Cullinan, T.R., Silver, J.H., and Whitelocke, R.A.F. (1989). Cataracts and cigarette smoking. *Eye*, 3, 379–84.

Gao, H. and Hollyfield, J.G. (1992). Aging of the human retina. *Investigative Ophthalmology and Visual Science*, 33, 1–17.

Gartner, S. and Henkind, P. (1981). Aging and degeneration of the human macula. 1. Outer nuclear layer and photoreceptors. *British Journal of Ophthalmology*, 65, 23–8.

Gompertz, B. (1825). On the nature of the function expressive of the law of human mortality and on a new mode of determining the value of life contingencies. *Philosophical Transactions of the Royal Society of London*, A115, 513–85.

Gregor, Z. and Joffe, L. (1978). Senile macular changes in the black African. *British Journal of Ophthalmology*, 62, 547–50.

Hamasaki, D., Ong, J., and Marg, E. (1956). The amplitude of accommodation in presbyopia. *American Journal of Optometry*, 33, 3–14.

Harding, J.J. (1972). Conformational changes in human lens proteins in cataract. *Biochemical Journal*, 129, 97–100.

Harding, J.J. (1991). *Cataract: biochemistry, epidemiology and pharmacology*. Chapman & Hall, London.

Heiba, I.M., Elston, R.C., Klein, B.E.K., and Klein, R. (1995). Evidence for a major gene for cortical cataract. *Investigative Ophthalmology and Visual Science*, 36, 227–35.

Hirvelä, H., Luukinen, H., and Laatikainen, L. (1995). Prevalence and risk factors of lens opacities in the elderly in Finland. *Ophthalmology*, 102, 108–17.

Holz, F.G., Piguet, B., Minassian, D.C., Bird, A.C., and Weale, R.A. (1994). Decreasing stromal iris pigmentation as a risk factor for age-related macular degeneration. *American Journal of Ophthalmology*, 117, 19–23.

Horwitz, J. (1992). α-Crystallin can function as a molecular chaperone. *Proceedings of the National Academy of Sciences of the United States of America*, 89, 10449–553.

Hyman, L.G., Lilienfeld, A.M., Ferris III, F.L., and Fine, S.L. (1983). Senile macular degeneration: a case–control study. *American Journal of Epidemiology*, 118, 213–27.

Italian-American Cataract Study Group (1991). Risk factors for age-related cortical, nuclear and posterior subcapsular cataracts. *American Journal of Epidemiology*, 133, 541–53.

Kappelhof, J.P. and Vrensen, G.F. (1992). The pathology of after-cataract. *Acta Ophthalmologica*, 205S, 13–24.

targets on an acuity chart are isolated and static, and in everyday life, objects important for vision are often aggregated and/or dynamic. Vision research confirms the risk of extrapolating from conditions of high-contrast well-illuminated well-spaced static targets to real-life targets with quite different characteristics, especially among older people. Low-contrast, poorly illuminated, aggregated, or dynamic targets disadvantage many older observers much more so than younger observers (Adams *et al.* 1988).

Visual memory

Perception in complex environments requires not only that observers detect and discriminate stimuli presented simultaneously, but also that observers integrate such information accurately across space and time. One index of this ability is short-term memory for purely visual stimuli, such as the spatial frequency of gratings used to assess contrast sensitivity. Many studies have shown that young observers' memory for spatial frequency is high fidelity and relatively long lasting. For example, Bennett and Cortese (1996) found little decline in spatial frequency discrimination as the interval between targets increased from 100 ms to 1 s (a long time for the visual system). Of particular interest is that, although older observers typically perform quite poorly on a wide range of memory tasks, older and younger observers behave similarly in tasks that involve memory for spatial frequency (McIntosh *et al.* 1997). Despite the equivalent level of performance at various ages, results from brain imaging studies using positron emission tomography reveal that the neural systems responsible for this performance are substantially different in young and older observers (McIntosh *et al.* 1997). It seems likely that these differences reflect some general compensatory neural reorganization within the ageing brain. This result also extends to other forms of perceptual memory tasks, including memory for faces (Grady 1996).

Colour vision

Advancing age brings a diminished ability to discriminate subtle differences of hue in the blue-green range, a deficit that is particularly noticeable under conditions of reduced illumination (Knoblauch *et al.* 1987). Although this acquired colour deficit is functionally similar to the genetically determined tritan deficit resulting from abnormally low sensitivity of the eye's short-wavelength system, the age-associated deficit seems to have a different origin, seemingly connected to changes in the density of the ocular media and to changes in receptor sensitivity.

Although receptors for colour vision exhibit diminished sensitivity with age, recent research suggests that the relative cone responses remain constant (Werner and Steele 1988; Knoblauch *et al.* 1995). Such a result is consistent with findings that colour vision is generally quite stable across the lifespan, particularly when the assessment is done using stimuli well above threshold (Werner 1996). For example, older and younger observers have similar colour naming functions (Schefrin and Werner 1993), loci of achromatic points (Werner and Schefrin 1993), and loci of unique hues for yellow and blue (Schefrin and Werner 1990). Thus the visual system seems to take advantage of some as yet unknown mechanisms that continuously recalibrate the strength of colour signals as we age, maintaining colour constancy throughout the lifespan (Werner 1996).

It has been suggested that some subtle changes in colour vision result from sensitivity changes in postreceptor processes (Werner *et al.* 1990). These changes include shifts in the spectral loci of unique hues, wavelengths that produce sensations of elemental blue, green, yellow, and red. The significance of such effects for everyday colour vision remains to be demonstrated.

Binocular vision

Binocular vision depends upon complex neural interactions between separate inputs from left and right eyes. The products of these interactions form the basis for several different computations, which enable a variety of different binocular functions. These interactions produce significant enhancements in binocular vision over its individual monocular origins. Because their magnitude typically exceeds expectations from simple statistical probability summation (Blake *et al.* 1981), these enhancements, which occur first at the levels of the cortex, represent emergent properties.

The best known form of binocular interaction probably is stereopsis, depth perception derived from retinal disparities. The common measure of stereopsis is threshold disparity, the minimum retinal disparity that reliably produces stereopsis (depth). Standard tests of stereopsis, such as those used for screening, include an upper pass–fail stimulus, the maximum disparity available in the test, usually 10 min of arc, several hundred times the minimum detectable disparity for healthy young observers. With age, increasing numbers of individuals are unable to identify the depth represented even with this extreme stimulus. Even disregarding individuals who fail stereoscopic screening tests outright, disparity thresholds for remaining individuals show steady change with age (Bell *et al.* 1974).

Stereopsis certainly depends upon binocular signals, but tells us little about the relative strengths of monocular and binocular signals. This additional piece of information, if it could be obtained, would be useful as an indicator of specific patterns of loss, either in the number of cortical cells or in the efficacy of synaptic connections. To gain the necessary psychophysical information, Pardhan *et al.* (1996) compared binocular and monocular contrast sensitivity in eight young (mean age 23 years) and 18 older (mean age 58 years) subjects. Test targets were either 1 or 6 cycles/degree. The primary measure of interest was the binocular summation ratio, given by the ratio of binocular sensitivity to sensitivity taken with the better single eye. Mean binocular summation ratios were significantly higher for the younger group than for the older group, especially with the target of higher spatial frequency. This frequency dependence was due largely to the older observers' reduced binocular summation at the higher spatial frequency. These measurements of binocular summation were made with central viewing. Pardhan (1997) extended the work by measuring binocular summation ratios for luminance increment presented at various eccentricities, ranging from 0° to 40° eccentricity. For all ages, binocular and monocular sensitivities both declined with eccentricity. But regardless of eccentricity, binocular summation was stronger for younger observers.

Schneider *et al.* (1989) introduced an alternative estimate of the relative strengths of binocular and monocular responses. Their measure, binocular unmasking, represents the binocular advantage in detecting a signal embedded in noise. More particularly, thresholds for detecting a band-limited signal in noise are measured. Both eyes receive the signal, and both eyes receive the noise, but in one condition the noise in one eye's view is shifted relative to the other. This shift introduces retinal disparity, causing noise and the signal to appear to lie in different depth planes. The availability of this disparity information makes the signal far easier to detect. This facilitation is the value added to detectability by cortical neurones sensitive to binocular disparities. Adapting this measure to the study of ageing, Speranza et al. (1995) examined binocular unmasking in two small groups of young and older adults (mean ages 24 and 64 years). For signals at two different spatial scales, older and younger observers enjoyed essentially the same degree of binocular unmasking.

The source of the apparent contradictions between the results of Pardhan (1997) and those of Speranza et al. (1995) is not clear, but could well be related to differences in the tasks used in the studies. For example, it is already clear that all binocular tasks do not show equivalent age-associated changes. For example, the age invariance in binocular unmasking found by Speranza et al. (1995) coexisted, in the same individuals, with appreciable (two to three times) age differences in stereothresholds.

Perception of dynamic displays

Arguably, the most prominent functional decline with age is the visual system's ability to detect temporal change. According to Kline (1987) 'temporally contiguous visual stimuli that would be seen as separate by young observers are often seen as fused or "smeared" by older people'. Kline and Schieber (1982) suggest that age-associated reduction in temporal resolution manifests itself in three ways: reduced critical flicker fusion value, altered temporal extent of visual masking, and increased duration of visual after-images. Other causes, not fully understood, are probably responsible for the well-documented decline in spatial acuity assessed with moving targets. This ability, dynamic visual acuity, may play an important part in everyday vision, particularly in the perception of moving targets.

A moving target, such as a car, is a complex perceptual object. Depending upon the circumstances, observers can extract information about a variety of the moving object's attributes, for example its spatial structure, instantaneous speed, acceleration, direction in three-dimensional space, as well as other attributes. However, little currently is known about possible age-associated changes in the principal responses to a moving object: judgements of speed or direction. The one available set of data on speed perception as a function of age suggests that speed discrimination is not impaired with age. Brown and Bowman (1987) measured speed discrimination thresholds at three different eccentricities, 0°, 4°, and 32°, and found these thresholds were virtually identical for groups of young and old observers (mean ages of 21 years and 67 years respectively). However, the use of just one target size and contrast, and the use of only one standard speed, means that the results cannot be generalized. Equally limited was the first study when comparing direction discrimination in older and younger observers (Ball and Sekuler 1987). When testing with just a single target speed (10°/s), thresholds for discriminating small differences in target direction were measured relative to several different standard directions, for example upward, leftward, and so on. Older observers' direction discrimination thresholds were on

average twice those of younger observers, a result not explicable in terms of optical differences between the groups.

Dengis et al. (1998) recently re-examined this question using directionally broad-band random dot cinematograms, stimuli that contained a wide range of different, spatially intermingled direction vectors. Visual integration of all the directional information contained in these cinematograms gives rise to a percept of global flow approximately along the cinematogram's mean direction. In young observers, the required integration can take several hundred milliseconds for completion. As a result, such stimuli probe not only motion perception per se, but also the efficiency with which motion signals are extracted from the stimulus. Observers ranging in age from 20 to 81 years viewed random dot cinematograms at durations of 75 to 450 ms. Older observers tended to make much larger errors than younger observers in judging the mean direction of motion. This age difference was especially pronounced at the shortest stimulus durations, but at nearly all durations older observers were less efficient in extracting motion signals from the stimuli. In addition, confirming earlier results by Trick and Silverman (1991) and Gilmore et al. (1992), Dengis et al. found that the motion signals of cinematograms were less detectable for older observers. This age effect was especially pronounced for the very oldest observers.

Plasticity

Although practice may not always make perfect, practice certainly does improve many perceptual abilities. Merzenich et al. (1996) recently described some sensory and cognitive domains in which practice-dependent plasticity has been shown. Despite the earlier belief that only immature organisms could reap the benefits of neural plasticity, numerous demonstrations have since established that age is no barrier to practice-dependent plasticity. The ease with which such practice-dependent effects can be generated, together with the persistence of effects once established, suggests that with increasing age, practice-induced plasticity could be of increasing functional significance. In one of the few studies on this subject, Ball and Sekuler (1986) examined the effect of practice on direction discrimination. With repeated testing, direction discrimination improved in both older and younger observers, and at approximately the same rate. With practice, the older observers achieved levels of discrimination that were equivalent to those shown by the younger observers at the start of the study. Also, the older observers retained this gain over a 10-week rest period with no discernible loss and in the absence of further practice. Although Ball and Sekuler could not identify the mechanisms behind the measured improvement in older observers' performance, their results demonstrated clearly that, at least for some tasks, older observers might profit from perceptual training. It is an open question whether such training, on a very simple task, can be applied to more complex, everyday 'uses' of directional information.

As a follow-up to their work on the effective field of view, Sekuler and Ball (1986) gave some of their older observers an opportunity to practice radial localization for several dozen additional trials during each of 5 days. Practice produced a steady improvement in radial localization and, hence, an improvement in the useful field of vision. After rest periods that ranged from 3 to 5 weeks, the older observers were again tested. Despite the lengthy vacations, performance on the retention test did not differ from performance on the last day of practice, suggesting that virtually all the improvement had endured. The potency of the effect of practice can be gauged from an unsolicited remark offered by one older observer. After just 2 days' practice, radial localization had already become so much easier for her that she insisted the researchers must have made the task easier by increasing the duration of the target display.

Lessons and cautions

In an effort to highlight important ideas and in order to provide a stronger framework for future research, it is worth restating the key themes.

1. Vision is not a single unitary function, but a collection of separable ones. This point has been made repeatedly for more than a century (Sekuler and Owsley 1982). The existence of separable processing streams and of multiple maps in the cerebral cortex represents one physiological substrate for some of these separable functions. Clearly, the diversity of visual function in everyday life requires the co-operation of several different visual subsystems.

2. Just as we must respect the diversity of visual functions, we must understand and appreciate the diversity of ageing individuals. After all, 'people do not lose their sight in age cohorts, marching lock step together in obedience to some chronological imperative; people lose their sight as individuals, each in her or his own way and according to a highly individual timetable' (Sekuler 1991).

3. Even when older and younger people perform some visual tasks at equivalent levels, different brain circuits may make that equivalent performance possible (Grady 1996; McIntosh et al. 1997).

4. Except under highly controlled artificial conditions, vision depends not just upon the afferent pathway, but also upon contributions of systems related to memory and cognition (Sekuler et al. 1997). Clearly, when sensory input is diminished, supplementation by cognition becomes increasingly important. Unfortunately, diminished sensory input is likely to be associated with diminished cognition (Lindenberger and Baltes 1994; Salthouse et al. 1996).

References

Adams, A.J., Wang, L.S., Wong, L., and Gould, B. (1988). Visual acuity changes with age: some new perspectives. *American Journal of Optometry and Physiological Optics*, 65, 403–6.

Akutsu, H., Legge, G.E., Ross, J.A., and Schuebel, K.J. (1991). Psychophysics of reading. X. Effects of age-related changes in vision. *Journal of Gerontology: Psychological Sciences*, 46, P325–31.

Ball, K. and Sekuler, R. (1986). Improving visual perception in older observers. *Journal of Gerontology*, 41, 176–82.

Ball, K. and Sekuler, R. (1987). Direction-specific improvement in motion discrimination. *Vision Research*, 27, 953–65.

Ball, K., Owsley, C., and Beard, B. (1990). Clinical visual perimetry underestimates peripheral field problems in older adults. *Clinical Vision Science*, 5, 113–25.

Bell, B., Wolf, E., and Bernholtz, C.D. (1974). Depth perception as a function of age. *Aging and Human Development*, 3, 77–81.

Bennett, P.J. and Cortese, F. (1996). Masking of spatial frequency in visual memory depends on distal, not retinal, frequency. *Vision Research*, 36, 233–8.

Bennett, P.J., Sekuler, A.B., and Ozin, L.A. (1999). The effects of aging on calculation efficiency and equivalent noise. *Journal of the Optical Society of America A*, 16, 654–68.

Blake, R., Sloane, M.E., and Fox, R. (1981). Further developments in binocular summation. *Perception and Psychophysics*, 30, 266–76.

Braak, H. and Braak, E. (1988). Morphology of the human isocortex in young and aged individuals: qualitative and quantitative findings. *Interdisciplinary Topics in Gerontology*, 25, 1–15.

Brown, B. and Bowman K.J. (1987). Sensitivity to changes in size and velocity in young and elderly observers. *Perception*, 16, 41–7.

Burton, K.B., Owsley, C.J., and Sloane, M.E. (1993). Aging and neural spatial contrast sensitivity: photopic vision. *Vision Research*, 33, 939–46.

Cerella, J. (1985). Age-related decline in extrafoveal letter perception. *Journal of Gerontology*, 40, 727–36.

Collins, M. (1989). The onset of prolonged glare recovery with age. *Ophthalmic and Physiological Optics*, 9, 368–71.

Dengis, C., Sekuler, A.B., Bennett, P.J., and Sekuler, R. (1998). Aging affects perceived direction of motion and detection of global flow in random dot cinematograms. *Investigative Ophthalmology and Visual Science*, 39, S1090.

Drance, S.M., Berry, V., and Hughes, A. (1967). Studies of the effects of age on the central and peripheral isopters of the visual field in normal subjects. *American Journal of Ophthalmology*, 63, 1667–72.

Felson, D.T., Anderson, J.J., Hannan, M.T., Milton, R.C., Wilson, P.W.F., and Kiel, D.P. (1989). Impaired vision and hip fracture. *Journal of the American Geriatrics Society*, 37, 495–500.

Gilmore, G.C., Wenk, H.E., Naylor, L.A., and Stuve, T.A. (1992). Motion perception and aging. *Psychology and Aging*, 7, 654–60.

Grady, C.L. (1966). Age-related changes in cortical blood flow activation during perception and memory. *Annals of the New York Academy of Science*, 777, 14–21.

Hakkinen, L. (1984). Vision in the elderly and its use in the social environment. *Scandinavian Journal of Social Medicine*, 35, 5–60.

Higgins, K.E., Jaffe, M.J., Caruso, R.C., and deMonasterio, F.M. (1988). Spatial contrast sensitivity: effects of age, test–retest, and psychophysical method. *Journal of the Optical Society of America A*, 5, 2173–80.

Hirvelä, H., Koskela, P., and Laatikainen, L. (1995). Visual acuity and contrast sensitivity in the elderly. *Acta Ophthalmologica Scandinavica*, 73, 111–15.

Johnson, C. and Keltner, J. (1986). Incidence of visual field loss in 20 000 eyes its relationship to driving performance. *Archives of Ophthalmology*, 101, 371–5.

Johnson, C.A., Adams, A.J., and Lewis, R.A. (1989). Evidence for a neural basis of age-related visual field loss in normal observers. *Investigative Ophthalmology and Visual Science*, 30, 2056–64.

Keltner, J.L. and Johnson, C.A. (1987). Visual function, driving safety, and the elderly. *Ophthalmology*, 94, 1180–8.

Kline, D.A. (1987). Ageing and the spatiotemporal discrimination performance of the visual system. *Eye*, 1, 323–9.

Kline, D.A. and Schieber, F. (1982). Visual persistence and temporal resolution. In *Aging and visual function* (ed. R. Sekuler, D. Kline, and K. Dismukes), pp. 231–44. A.R. Liss, New York.

Kline, D.A., Kline, T.J.B., Fozard, J.L., Kosnik, W., Schieber, F., and Sekuler, R. (1991). Vision, aging and driving: the problems of older drivers. *Journal of Gerontology: Psychological Sciences*, 47, P27–34.

Knoblauch, K., Saunders, F., Kusuda M., et al. (1987) Age and illuminance effects in the Farnsworth–Munsell 100-hue test. *Applied Optics*, 26, 1441–8.

Knoblauch, K., Barbur, J., and Vital-Durand, F. (1995). Development and aging of chromatic sensitivity. *Investigative Ophthalmology and Visual Science*, 36, S910.

Kosnik, W., Winslow, L., Kline, D., Rasinski, K., and Sekuler, R. (1988). Age-related visual changes in daily life throughout adulthood. *Journal of Gerontology*, 43, 63–70.

Kosnik, W.D., Sekuler, R., and Kline, D.W. (1990). Self-reported visual problems of older drivers. *Human Factors*, 32, 597–608.

Legge, G.E., Ahn, S.J., Klitz, T.S., and Luebker, A. (1997*a*). Psychophysics of reading. XVI. The visual span in normal and low vision. *Vision Research*, 37, 1992–2010.

Legge, G.E., Klitz, T.S., and Tjan, B. (1997*b*). Mr Chips: an ideal-observer model of reading. *Psychological Review*, 104, 524–53.

Lindenberger, U. and Baltes, P.B. (1994). Intellectual functioning in old and very old age: cross-sectional results from the Berlin Aging Study. *Psychology and Aging*, 12, 410–32.

McIntosh, A.R., Sekuler, A., Penpeci, C., Rajah, M.N., Grady, C. L., and Sekuler, R. (1997). Effects of aging on neural systems supporting visual perceptual memory. *Society for Neuroscience Supplement*, 23, 1402.

Marshall, J. (1987). The ageing retina: physiology or pathology. *Eye*, 1, 282–95.

Merzenich, M., Wright, B., Jenkins, W., *et al.* (1996). Cortical plasticity underlying perceptual, motor, and cognitive skill development: implications for neurorehabilitation. *Cold Spring Harbor Symposium on Quantitative Biology*, 61, 1–8.

Morgan, M. (1988). Vision through my aging eyes. *Journal of the American Optometric Association*, 59, 278–80.

Nameda, N., Kawara, T., and Ohzu, H. (1989). Human visual spatio-temporal frequency performance as a function of age. *Optometry and Vision Science*, 31, 1623–7.

NRC (National Research Council) (1987). *Work, aging, and vision: report of a conference*. NRC, Washington, DC.

Owsley, C.J. and Sekuler, R. (1984). Visual manifestations of biological aging. *Experimental Aging Research*, 9, 253–5.

Owsley, C. and Sloane, M.E. (1987). Contrast sensitivity, acuity and the perception of 'real-world' targets. *British Journal of Ophthalmology*, 71, 791–6.

Owsley, C., Ball, K., Sloane, M.E., Rosenker, D.L., and Bruni, J.R. (1991). Visual/cognitive correlates of vehicle accidents in older drivers. *Psychology and Aging*, 6, 403–15.

Owsley, C.J., Sekuler, R., and Siemsen, D. (1983). Contrast sensitivity throughout adulthood. *Vision Research*, 23, 689–99.

Pardhan, S. (1997). A comparison of binocular summation in the peripheral visual field in young and older patients. *Current Eye Research*, 16, 252–5.

Pardhan, S., Gilchrist, J., Elliott, D.B., and Beh, G.K. (1996). A comparison of sampling efficiency and internal noise level in young and old subjects. *Vision Research*, 36, 1641–8.

Pelli, D.G. (1990). The quantum efficiency of vision. In *Vision: coding and efficiency* (ed. C. Blakemore), pp. 3–24. Cambridge University Press.

Pfoff, D.S. and Werner, J.S. (1994). Effect of cataract surgery on contrast sensitivity and glare in patients with 20/50 or better Snellen acuity. *Journal of Cataract and Refractive Surgery*, 20, 620–5.

Pitts, D.G. (1982). The effects of aging on selected visual functions: dark adaptation, visual acuity, stereopsis and brightness contrast. In *Aging and visual function* (ed. R. Sekuler, D. Kline, and K. Dismukes), pp. 131–59. Liss, New York.

Post, R.B. and Leibowitz, H.W. (1980). Independence of radial localisation from refractive error. *Journal of the Optical Society of America*, 70, 1377–8.

Salthouse, T.A., Hancock, H.E., Meinz, E.J., and Hambrick, D.Z. (1996). Interrelations of age, visual acuity, and cognitive functioning. *Journal of Gerontology: Psychological Sciences and Social Sciences*, 51, P317–30.

Schefrin, B.E. and Werner, J.S. (1990). Loci of spectral unique hues throughout the life span. *Journal of the Optical Society of America A*, 7, 305–11.

Schefrin, B.E. and Werner, J.S. (1993). Age-related changes in the colour appearance of broadband surfaces. *Colour Research and Applications*, 18, 380–9.

Schneider, B., Moraglia, G., and Jepson, A. (1989). Binocular unmasking: an analogue to binaural unmasking? *Science*, 243, 1479–81.

Scialfa, C.T. and Kline, D.W. (1988). Effects of noise type and retinal eccentricity on age differences in identification and localisation. *Journal of Gerontology: Psychological Sciences and Social Sciences*, 43, P91–9.

Seiple, W., Szlyk, J.P., Yang, S., and Holopigian, K. (1996). Age-related functional field losses are not eccentricity dependent. *Vision Research*, 36, 1859–66.

Sekuler, R. (1991). Why does vision change with age? *Geriatrics*, 46, 96–100.

Sekuler, R. and Ball, K. (1986). Visual localisation: age and practice. *Journal of the Optical Society of America A*, 3, 864–7.

Sekuler, R. and Owsley, C.J. (1982). The spatial vision of older humans. In *Aging and visual function*, (ed. R. Sekuler, D. Kline, and K. Dismukes), pp. 185–202. A.R. Liss, New York.

Sekuler, R., Kline, D., Dismukes, K., and Adams, A.J. (1983). Some research needs in aging and vision perception. *Vision Research*, 23, 213–16.

Sekuler, A.B., Bennett, P.J., and Placenza F.M. (1995). Effects of aging on spatial phase discrimination. *Investigative Ophthalmology and Visual Science*, 36, S912.

Sekuler, A.B., Bennett, P.J., and Mamelak, M. (1997). *Effects of aging and monocularity on the useful field of view*. Technical report 97-01, Vision Laboratory, Department of Psychology, University of Toronto, Canada.

Sloane, M.E., Owsley, C., and Jackson, C.A. (1988). Aging and luminance—adaptation effects on spatial contrast sensitivity. *Journal of the Optical Society of America A*, 5, 2181–90.

Spear, P.D. (1993). Neural bases of visual deficits during aging. *Vision Research*, 33, 2589–609.

Speranza, F., Moraglia, G., and Schneider, B.A. (1995). Age-related changes in binocular vision: detection of noise-masked targets in young and old observers. *Journal of Gerontology: Psychological Sciences and Social Sciences*, 50, P114–23.

Sturr, J.F., Kline, G.E., and Taub, H.A. (1990). Performance of young and older drivers on a static acuity test under photopic and mesopic luminance conditions. *Human Factors*, 32, 1–8.

Sturr, J.F., Zhang, L., Taub, H.A., Hannon, D.J., and Jackowski, M.M. (1997). Psychophysical evidence for losses in rod sensitivity in the aging visual system. *Vision Research*, 37, 475–81.

Trick, G.L. and Silverman, S.E. (1991). Visual sensitivity to motion: age-related changes and deficits in senile dementia of the Alzheimer type. *Neurology*, 41, 1437–40.

Werner, J.S. (1996). Visual problems of the retina during ageing: compensation mechanisms and colour constancy across the life span. *Progress in Retinal and Eye Research*, 15, 621–45.

Werner, J.S. and Schefrin, B.E. (1993). Loci of achromatic points throughout the life span. *Journal of the Optical Society of America A*, 10, 1509–16.

Werner, J.S. and Steele, V.G. (1988). Sensitivity of human foveal colour mechanisms throughout the life span. *Journal of the Optical Society of America A*, 5, 2122–30.

Werner, J.S., Peterzell, D.H., and Scheetz, A.J. (1990). Light, vision, and aging. *Optometry and Vision Science*, 67, 214–29.

Wilkinson, R.T. and Allison, S. (1989). Age and simple reaction time: decade differences for 5325 subjects. *Journal of Gerontology: Psychological Sciences and Social Sciences*, 44, P29–35.

18.15.3 Poor vision

Eleanor E. Faye

When working with older adults who may have a variety of age-associated deficits, the most difficult to evaluate is sight. 'Visual problems' reported by an older person might be a need for new glasses, a normal ageing change, or a pathological change in the eye or brain. The best way to evaluate any visual complaint is with an eye examination, which can be preventive as well as a means of early detection and diagnosis of the disorders that traditionally accompany ageing: cataracts, macular degeneration, glaucoma, and retinopathy of diabetes mellitus.

The tendency of older people (and their families) is to blame changes on ageing, but only a comprehensive eye examination can separate a serious visual impairment from 'normal' ageing changes. Eye care need not be the prerogative of the ophthalmologist. The geriatrician or general practitioner who is aware of the possibility of age-associated vision loss can identify early signs of diminished visual performance.

Symptoms and functional implications

Diagnosis and treatment are traditionally in the realm of the ophthalmologist or optometrist, yet symptoms and their functional implications can be evaluated by any professional involved in the care of the ageing person and lead to a timely referral for diagnosis, treatment, and rehabilitation. In this chapter we review seven normal functions of the eye, and then discusses the normal ageing changes to be expected in each area of function. A history can highlight the difference between normal and pathological changes. A screening examination by the doctor can also provide useful evidence leading to referral for care. Finally, common eye disorders, their typical symptoms, and their natural history are addressed in relation to functional performance; in conclusion, vision rehabilitation and low-vision adaptive devices are discussed.

Normal functions of the eye

The eye has seven functions that normally interact smoothly to transmit a clear image to the brain. Since normal and pathological ageing may exhibit the same symptoms, it is helpful to address normal functions first and follow with a discussion of the significance of changes in these functions.

Visual acuity

The ability of the eye to see detail is historically the most reliable indicator of the integrity of the macula. The macula, which is made up entirely of cones, is responsible for detail vision, daytime (photopic) vision, and colour vision. The cornea and lens bring images into focus on the macula and peripheral retinal receptors. Visual acuity is also related to the refractive state of the eye: myopia, hyperopia, astigmatism, or a combination of these refractive errors that can be improved with corrective lenses. Any reduction in acuity suggests the need for further investigation.

Visual field (see Chapter 18.15.2)

The field of vision encompasses the horizontal and vertical diameter of the area seen binocularly in straight-ahead gaze. Although the acuity of the rods of the peripheral retina is less than that of the macular cones, the function of the periphery is to detect motion, locate gross objects, and see in dim light. The peripheral retina serves both as a warning system and a spatial orientation system.

Accommodation

Until middle age the lens of the eye can assume a convex shape for near vision. In youth the lens of the eye is able to respond promptly to a near object when the muscle of accommodation contracts. This enables the lens to become more convex (stronger) to accommodate for the near range needed for print, computer images, diagrams, and drawings. The lens in combination with the cornea focuses light rays on the macula and peripheral retina.

Colour

The response of pigments in the cones to combinations of wavelengths of blue, red, and yellow light creates the brain's sensation of colour. This is a macular cone function that remains relatively normal throughout life unless there is yellowing of the ageing lens, which can change colour values; for example, pale blue may appear to be aqua. Congenitally colour-blind individuals, predominantly men, confuse colours when they try to match them on tests.

Adaptation to light

Adaptation to light and dark is a function of the rods and cones. The rods of the peripheral retina adapt to dim light or the dark in about

20 min. Cones adapt to daylight, which takes only a few seconds in the normal eye and is not much affected by ageing.

Contrast sensitivity

Contrast sensitivity function is a subtle retinal process involving many retinal channels that transmit high- to low-frequency signals to the brain, which recognizes the frequencies as differences of shading and colour between an object and its background (Ginsburg 1984; Cohen 1993). Black against white is excellent contrast, grey against beige is poor contrast. Colour contrast plays a part in differentiating objects from their surroundings. Tests of retinal sensitivity across a range of frequencies are called contrast sensitivity function tests. A number of tests are available, but the principle of all contrast tests is the same—to measure the eye's ability to distinguish between borders and backgrounds (Bodis-Wollner and Camisa 1980). Although the entire retina is sensitive to contrast stimuli, the fovea is the most sensitive part of the macula. Beyond the macula the sensitivity of the retina diminishes as the cones decrease in number and the rods increase. The potential response of the visually impaired eye to magnification, lighting, and increased contrast can be predicted with contrast sensitivity function tests.

Ocular motility and depth perception

Four rectus muscles for each eye move the eyes in tandem vertically and horizontally, tracking visual stimuli in response to signals from the macula. Each eye also has two oblique muscles that rotate the eye. In a person who has normal binocular vision this function is synchronous regardless of age, resulting in a stereoscopic effect we call depth perception.

Normal ageing (see Chapters 18.15.1 and 18.15.2)

'Normal ageing' of the eye is a term used for decreased visual function unrelated to ocular disease. Individual visual functions do not decrease at the same rate, and ageing does not inevitably result in disease. Although the major eye diseases such as cataract, macular degeneration, glaucoma, and diabetic retinopathy are considered to be age related, age is not the only risk factor; these diseases may occur in children and younger adults as well (Marmor 1995). General health, medications, environmental exposure to toxins (ultraviolet light, chemicals), and genetics may modify the course.

There are many physiological changes in eye tissues that minimally affect visual performance; conversely, there are also eye diseases that do not initially cause a significant level of dysfunction. Since ageing does not affect all people or all systems uniformly or equally, it is important to differentiate between normal ageing and pathology.

The Framingham Study (Leibowitz et al. 1980) dispels the myth that all ageing individuals can expect to develop an eye disease. Of the common conditions such as cataract, macular degeneration, glaucoma, and diabetic retinopathy, only 19 per cent of adults between 65 and 74 years of age have one or more diseases. After the age of 75 the number rises to 50 per cent. With increasing age comes increased prevalence of cataract and macular degeneration (in other words, they are truly 'age associated'), although many older adults remain free of eye disease well into their eighties.

Normal and abnormal function changes in ageing

Decrease in visual acuity (see Chapter 18.15.2)

Visual acuity has been measured for more than 100 years with the graded symbols of the Snellen chart (Pitts 1983). In an elderly person it is difficult to evaluate visual acuity as pure data because many factors are involved in a response. In the normal ageing eye without overt pathology pupil size, clarity of the lens, illumination, and the contrast of the chart letters influence the level of acuity. Faulty visual acuity due simply to uncorrected errors may be corrected with conventional eyeglasses. The average eye tends to become more far-sighted with age (hyperopia), resulting in difficulty focusing a clear image first for near range and eventually for distance, and then a complete dependency on glasses for all ranges.

Most hyperopic individuals wear bifocals or progressive lenses for convenience. A myopic (near-sighted) person sees poorly for distance but focuses clearly at the reading distance, often preferring to read without glasses. Refraction for glasses should be done as part of a comprehensive examination usually at 1- to 2-year intervals to ensure that the older person is wearing optimal eyeglass correction.

Many older people can achieve corrected vision of 20/20 (6/6) to 20/40 (6/12). However, an older person may not achieve 20/20 acuity, even with corrected vision, because of subtle changes in corneal, lens, and vitreous proteins, yet be unaware of any incapacity. If a person expresses concern about 'not seeing as well', refraction and evaluation of the lens and fundus is the next step. It is important in evaluating acuity to remember that a high-contrast letter chart bears little resemblance to the real world. A self-reported change in visual performance is a more significant indication of pathology than an acuity measurement.

During the examination be sure that the person knows which glasses to use for a given activity, that the prescription is current, that the glasses are clean and scratch-free, and that the frame fits properly.

Decrease in near vision (accommodation)

The condition of 'middle-aged sight' (presbyopia) is well known to anyone in the middle to late forties. As the lens becomes more rigid with age, it loses its elasticity and can no longer automatically focus at near range (Carter 1982). The blur of presbyopia can be easily remedied with reading glasses (single lenses, half-eye frames, bifocals, trifocals, and progressive lenses) to compensate for this normal ageing phenomenon. However, blurred vision is also a common early symptom of cataracts, glaucoma, macular degeneration, diabetes, and many systemic medications.

Changes in visual field

There is a gradual apparent reduction of the field of view (peripheral field) as the ageing lens becomes less transparent and the pupil decreases in size (Carter 1982; Ball 1990). Sensitivity is decreased in the peripheral receptors (rods). Although a visual field test may appear to be normal, there may be real-life situations in which the person does not recognize movement or objects at the far edge of the field. An insensitive peripheral field leads in particular to an individual's being less alert to moving objects and other potential hazards while walking or driving (see Chapter 18.15.2). Reaction time may be insufficient to protect the person from a fall or an accident (Tideiksaar 1995). Someone with a peripheral scotomatous defect tends to bump into objects or misplace things easily. If stroke has been diagnosed, hemianopic field loss should be ruled out, particularly in the presence of other sensory or motor defects.

Changes in colour vision

The colour vision function of the retinal cones probably does not change with age (Carter 1982; Marmor 1995). However, changes in the lens may alter colour values, resulting in the loss of contrast and potential errors in colour discrimination (Arditi and Knoblauch 1996). As the ageing lens becomes yellow or amber, it selectively absorbs blue light with the result that light blue may be seen as aqua, yellow as white, and navy blue as black. An older person should be encouraged to label clothing that could be mistaken. Another potentially serious problem for the general practitioner is the patient who identifies pills by colour rather than by shape, size, or the label (which is often printed in pale type). A yellow pill may appear to be white or beige, a red pill brown, and a light blue pill light green. Medications should be labelled plainly by the pharmacist with bold black letters. In diseases that affect the macula there may be a decrease in the perceived intensity of a colour. Complete loss of specific colours does not occur unless there is severe cone damage.

Changes in adaptation to light

One of the most consistent signs of ageing is the way the eye handles light (Rosenberg 1984; Hood and Faye 1995; Marmor 1995). It takes longer for the retina to adapt from light to dark and to adjust to bright light. The pupil does not dilate as briskly in the dark, for instance in a theatre. Even if eye health is excellent, the need for light increases inexorably at the rate of 1 per cent a year after the age of 20 years, or a 10 per cent decrease in light sensitivity every decade. In the late forties through to the fifties a person may suddenly be aware of not seeing well without light. Instead of a prescription for reading glasses, the first prescription could be a good reading lamp and reassurance. A significant part of the quality of vision is dependent on illumination.

Glare

Changes associated with normal ageing of the optical media, namely cornea, lens, and vitreous, cause the sensation of glare. As the clear cornea and lens age, microscopic changes develop in the structure of protein molecules (Marmor 1995). The minute particles absorb light and scatter short-wavelength light rays (blue or ultraviolet light) (Wolf 1960). This reduces not only the quantity of light reaching the retina but also the quality. All these normal corneal and lens changes scatter light from sources such as lamps, headlights, and reflective surfaces, causing veiling and discomfort glare (Rosenberg 1984). This requires more careful placement and selection of general as well as task lighting. When working with older adults, it is important to evaluate what level of illumination and type of lamp provide the most comfort and best contrast; for example, a person may need more light for reading but complain of glare if the intensity is above

the comfort level or if the light is at an angle that reflects from the surface of shiny paper.

Fluorescent and high-intensity light sources, which have a higher proportion of blue light than standard incandescent light sources, may cause fatigue and blur for an older person with no specific eye disorder (Rosenberg 1984). Antireflective eyeglass coatings may be helpful, but attention to lighting and light fixtures is basic. For many older drivers with no overt pathology, the bright headlights in current car models reduce acuity and cause glare.

Glare is also a major symptom of corneal dystrophies, cataracts, miotic pupils, advanced glaucoma, and vitreous opacities (floaters). Floaters result from liquefaction of the normal vitreous gel with condensation of supporting fibrils, which are seen against a light background as floating cells or clumps of translucent fibres. This normally benign condition may be serious if the patient reports a sudden shower of floaters with flashes of light, typical of a vitreal haemorrhage or detached retina.

The role of the pupillary aperture

Another change typical of older people is a reduction in the diameter of the pupil, which may not be able to dilate sufficiently under low light conditions. This slows light and dark adaptation, which for the older person increases the hazards of travelling or driving on cloudy days or at dusk in unfamiliar surroundings. Room and hallway lighting may typically be inadequate for safety. Office (outpatient) appointment scheduling should be sensitive to older people who have difficulty travelling in the dark. They should be given morning or early afternoon appointments.

Patients with glaucoma who were previously on miotic drugs such as pilocarpine may not only have small pupils that do not dilate or react to light but also posterior subcapsular cataracts that further reduce acuity. Opiate drugs cause small pupils, which are also found in individuals with neurological disorders.

Decrease in contrast sensitivity function (see Chapter 18.15.2)

Ageing reduces the ability to discern objects against a plain, textured, or patterned background (Sekuler and Owsley 1982; Owsley et al. 1983; Owsley and Sloane 1986; Marmor 1995). There are several factors at work in the waning of contrast sensitivity such as structural changes in the composition of the cornea and lens, and diminished retinal receptor sensitivity.

Subjective symptoms of decreased vision are of particular significance if the visual acuity is within normal limits. Early stages of neurological disease and subtle optic nerve deterioration in glaucoma affect contrast sensitivity function before reducing the acuity.

The diseases that most affect contrast sensitivity function are cataract and corneal disease, glaucoma, laser-treated diabetic retinopathy, optic nerve disorders, and macular oedema or scars. If the patient's responses fall below the test threshold, the inference is that optical magnification will probably be ineffective.

An activity history from older adults can uncover contrast problems, such as difficulty sewing dark material with dark thread, seeing light-coloured food on a white plate, and reading handwriting, computer print-outs, and print on a television or computer screen. Colours should be selected for maximum contrast (Arditi and Knoblauch 1996), for example dark colours against a light background or vice versa. Black combined with white or yellow offers the best contrast. Contrast can be adjusted on television and computer screens.

Light and dark adaptation change

More time is required for the retina to adapt from light to dark, and to adjust to bright light. The pupil does not dilate instantly in the dark, for instance in a theatre. In several eye diseases (i.e. glaucoma, retinitis pigmentosa, and vitamin A deficiency) night blindness is a common symptom; light sensitivity (photophobia) may be a sign of corneal disease, cataracts, or early retinal cone disease.

Changes in ocular motility and depth perception

Ocular motility and depth perception do not change with age unless a person has suffered direct trauma, head injury, a brain tumour, or a vascular brain accident resulting in diplopia if one or more eye muscles are paralysed. After a period of observation the misalignment of the eyes may be treated with prisms, muscle surgery, or, as many individuals prefer, with occlusion of the deviating eye.

Visual hallucinations

Visual hallucinations are difficult to evaluate; many older people have mild formed or unformed images associated with drugs such as atropine, dopamine agonists, levodopa, antidepressants, anticonvulsants, and cardiovascular and anti-inflammatory agents.

In those who have impaired vision, provided that vascular or malignant disease has been ruled out, the occurrence of hallucinations is presumed to be a release phenomenon due to the reduction of visual acuity (Leporte 1989). A few patients report very clear images of specific scenes or people (Bonnet's syndrome) (Mogk and Mogk 1999). These images are non-threatening and generally occur in bilateral impairment. Patients are often reluctant to reveal their hallucinations unless questioned directly. In one study (Holroyd *et al.* 1992) 80 per cent of the patients who responded affirmatively when they were asked about hallucinations had them following an acute change in vision. Living alone was a significant variable. Patients should be reassured that these phenomena are related to their eye condition and do not indicate a stroke or acute psychiatric condition.

Medications that affect the eye

Although the package inserts for many drugs commonly warn of 'blurred vision', the most significant potential toxicity comes from antimalarials, antidepressants, and anti-anxiety medications (Charles 1995). Antihistamines and antihypertensive drugs can cause blurred near vision from their effect on accommodation. Constricted pupils may be associated with heroin use or with miotic eyedrops for glaucoma (pilocarpine, carbachol).

Retinal toxicity is related to dosage and duration of treatment, particularly the antimalarials used in discoid lupus erythematosus. Long-term oral steroids are associated with cataract formation, and steroid eyedrops with increased intraocular pressure in steroid reactors (often people with a family history of glaucoma). Patients on retinotoxic medication should be told of the potential side-effects of the drug, and should have their vision and visual field measured at intervals suggested by the ophthalmologist. Patients on long-term steroid eyedrops should initially be monitored frequently to establish that there is no rise in intraocular pressure.

History taking for eye health status

In the limited time available for evaluating a systems review, the patient (with help if needed) can answer a brief questionnaire while waiting (Lighthouse 1996; NEI 1996). Questions should reveal problems with specific eye functions and quality of life issues as follows.

1. Do you wear glasses/contact lenses/intraocular lenses/no glasses? How do you rate your vision with your present glasses: good?———adequate?———poor?———
2. Can you see signs?
3. When did you last read a newspaper or periodical?
4. Have you had pain?———redness?———burning?——— itching?———
5. Have you noticed floaters?——— blank areas in your vision? ———
6. Do bright lights cause glare?
7. Do you have difficulty seeing the edge of stairs or curbs?
8. Can you identify a person's facial features?
9. Do you bump into objects off to the side?
10. Are you driving?——— If not, why did you stop?
11. Do you have to rely on others to write cheques?——— shop? ———
12. Have you had to give up a hobby or an interest because of vision?

Each question brings out a different aspect of visual function. Questions 1 and 2 are related to acuity. Question 3 addresses near vision and the answer might suggest an eye disorder as well as a need for new glasses. Question 4 might uncover an infection or allergy. Question 5 might suggest a detached vitreous or retina, or macular degeneration. Question 6 might suggest a cataract or corneal disorder. Questions 7 and 8 relate to contrast. Question 9 relates to the peripheral field. Questions 10 to 12 concern daily living and provide a clue to quality of life.

There are other questions about quality of life that elicit the patient's reactions to the fact that no medical or surgical intervention will bring back normal vision.

1. Are you frustrated with your inability to do customary tasks?
2. Are you depressed? If you are, have you told your doctor?
3. How have you coped with difficulties in the past?
4. Are you afraid you are going to be blind?
5. Have you discovered any techniques or tricks that have helped you?
6. Have you tried using a magnifier of any kind?
7. Do you think you would like to share your experiences with a group of people with similar problems?

Obviously not all of these questions are appropriate, but the psychological state of a patient may be such that the person is afraid to divulge basic concerns about the future lest the doctor has bad news.

The screening examination

Screening tests may reveal essential information that the practitioner thinks warrants a referral to an ophthalmologist. Tests need not require complex equipment to provide useful data.

Vision test

A Snellen chart, symbols, or Landolt C at 6 m can be used if the acuity is at least 20/100 (6/30). If the person does not see the 20/100 line, move the chart in to 3 m, which would change the fraction to 10/letter size, for example 10/70 (20/140) (6/50). If the person cannot see the 100 line at 3 m, move in to 1.5 m using the new distance figure as the numerator: 5/100 (20/400) (3/60). Do not use 'counts fingers'. If people can count fingers, they can see a 9-cm ('200' or '60') letter at a distance closer than 1 m.

A 4-m chart has been developed for use in clinical research (Ferris *et al.* 1982) that is also practical for testing in areas with limited space since it can be used at 1 and 2 m as well (Lighthouse 1998).

If the person has no glasses, test acuity with a pinhole; if the acuity improves two or three lines, it indicates a need for refractive correction. If the person has glasses, test without glasses first and then with correction, making sure that the patient is not wearing reading glasses for the distance test. Test binocular vision first, and then each eye. Frequently the binocular acuity is superior to a monocular acuity. Occasionally the corrected vision may be worse than the uncorrected vision if the eyeglasses are obsolete or scratched.

Test reading vision with a standard reading card, a newspaper, a periodical, or symbols. Near acuity should be at least 20/50 or 1-m print (standard 10-point type). Myopic people often read more efficiently without glasses, although they may wear bifocals for convenience. A small group of patients who develop nuclear cataracts find, to their surprise, that they can read without glasses ('second sight'). They can enjoy this convenience for a while before they need surgery.

Visual field

Peripheral visual field

Test the visual field by confrontation if a peripheral field defect is suspected (stroke, diabetic retinopathy, glaucoma). Occlude one eye at a time. Closing an eye opposite to the patient's occluded eye, the examiner moves an index finger horizontally from an area outside the unoccluded lateral field into the visible field, then in several vertical meridians of the field, noting each time when the patient becomes aware of the target. The patient's field should have approximately the same dimensions as the examiner's field. This method is adequate for finding gross segmental field defects such as a hemianopia or quadrantanopia as well as peripheral constriction typical of retinitis pigmentosa, laser-treated diabetic retinopathy, and advanced glaucoma. The patient can also be asked to state the number of fingers presented in the temporal and nasal fields. A stationary target is more sensitive than a moving one. A field test is most important in stroke to identify a hemianopia because the patient may not be aware of the field loss (spatial neglect).

Central visual field

Test the central visual field with an Amsler grid (Fig. 1). The first presentation of the grid should be at 42.5 cm binocularly. Ask the

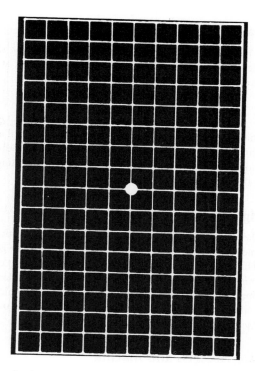

Fig. 1 The Amsler grid measures distortion and scotomas over the 20° area of the macula. The patient is asked to describe the appearance of the grid first binocularly, then monocularly. (Courtesy of Lighthouse International, New York.)

patient to identify the white fixation dot first and then, looking directly at the dot, report distortion or blanks in the grid pattern. Each eye is then tested separately in the same way and the results are compared with the binocular test. Most gross central macular defects can be identified with the grid, or any type of detailed grid-like paper with fine dark lines. If the patient does not report an abnormal grid pattern but complains of seeing distortion or blank areas, the symptoms are more significant than the response to the test. Common visual complaints that may indicate macular degeneration are wavy edges of doors, poles and venetian blinds, missing letters in words, and inability to see facial details of someone 3 m away. The presence of macular pathology can be verified on ophthalmoscopy after pupillary dilation.

Glare test

Shine a penlight at a 45° angle to the pupil while the patient looks at a Snellen chart. Are the letters lost in a haze? If they are, the patient may have either a cataract (most likely) or corneal pathology. Light sensitivity may also indicate a cataract, but in addition it is a common complaint of older people with small pupils.

Contrast

Contrast tests are available (Lighthouse 1998) but are not necessary in a general medical practice. The patient's responses to questions about seeing the edges of stairs or curbs, or not seeing objects against a background of similar colour, are adequate indicators of difficulties with contrast.

External lids

Look at the lid margins for crusting, redness, sties, or skin abnormalities. Patients may have basal cell lesions near or at the lid margin. Look for turned-in eyelashes.

Colour vision

The Ishihara colour test is a test for congenital rather than acquired colour blindness. An older person may see colour less vividly but be able to identify it. Ask if the person has difficulty sorting socks, selecting ties, or matching clothes.

Dilating pupils

Do not hesitate to dilate the pupils, using a weak mydriatic such as tropicamide 0.5 per cent. An acute attack of narrow angle glaucoma is rare. The angle depth can be estimated by shining a light obliquely at the limbus, observing whether the iris appears to be close to the cornea and whether there is a shadow line on the iris, which would indicate a shallow anterior chamber. If in doubt, have the pupils dilated by an ophthalmologist.

The disc, vessels, and macula

Observe the disc for cup size, pallor, vessels (look for nasal displacement, which is a sign of glaucoma), and haemorrhages. A blurred swollen disc with ill-defined margins may indicate hypertension or increased intracranial pressure. Observe retinal vessels for irregular calibre, arteriovenous nicking, small haemorrhages, or microaneurysms. Look at the macula for unusually dark pigmentation, drusen, haemorrhages, or scarring.

Measuring intraocular pressure

Measuring intraocular pressure is now a questionable practice when the technique of measuring pressure accurately requires more elaborate equipment than the old Schiotz tonometer. Unless the tonometer is calibrated and the examiner is skilled, it is probably wiser to evaluate the disc for cupping and pallor, and to encourage the patient to have periodic pressure checks at an eye centre. A normal pressure reading does not rule out glaucoma, particularly normal-tension glaucoma.

Detecting a cataract

To see a lens opacity, stand back about 50 cm from the eye with the ophthalmoscope set at 1 or 2 D of plus (the eye should be in focus) and look at the lens. Cortical cataracts will be seen as dark lamellar spokes at the edge of the pupil. A nuclear cataract will appear as a hazy, dark, or opaque centre surrounded by clear cortex. A small posterior cataract will be seen as a dark dot at the centre of the pupil.

Low vision

There are many remedies available for normal ageing changes: change of glasses, better lighting, employing contrast, large print, wearing tints and filters, slowing down a little, and being more careful with steps and stairs. Age-associated changes, once the person is reassured that there is no eye disease, are perceived as a nuisance rather than an impediment. It is less stressful to adapt to an annoyance than to cope with a permanent impairment that intrudes on daily activities.

When ageing results in actual pathology that cannot be remedied either surgically, medically, or with refraction, the resulting decrease in visual function is called low vision. Low vision is the irreversible loss of one or more visual functions that results in substandard visual performance. In practical terms, there is no single test that describes reduced function; however, an attempt has been made to classify groups of visually impaired people by means of visual acuity and visual field (ICD 1989) (Table 1).

The rehabilitation process

In the course of the rehabilitation process there are four areas that must be addressed as follows:

(1) functional evaluation leading to provision of optical devices and services;
(2) activities of daily living (modification of the environment);
(3) orientation and mobility;
(4) psychosocial adjustment.

There are many levels of impaired vision and many approaches to rehabilitation that may involve ophthalmologists, optometrists, nurses, opticians, educators, occupational therapists, low-vision assistants, vision rehabilitation specialists, physical therapists, social workers, and psychologists, depending on the country, the facility, and the availability of trained personnel. The responsibility for recognition of the person with low vision rests with doctors, particularly primary care ophthalmologists, optometrists, and nurse specialists; the responsibility for rehabilitation may involve many professionals.

The low-vision specialist evaluates the low-vision patient, and later may refer the patient to other support services depending on the evaluation. The results of the history and function tests analysed by the specialist usually provide data for prescribing low-vision lenses or devices, but the patient may need additional specialized training or other types of social or rehabilitation services that can be provided only by a private or state organization.

Each person has a unique pattern of vision loss, level of motivation, and ability to deal with adaptive devices. There is no such thing as a 'routine' low-vision evaluation or prescription. Tests may be performed routinely but the interpretation and application of those tests to the prescription of adaptive devices must be tailored to the person being evaluated.

The low-vision evaluation process

An ideal comprehensive evaluation starts with a series of visual function tests starting with refraction to ensure the best level of visual acuity (Rosenthal 1996). Vision for distance and near is tested with specially designed high-contrast charts (Ferris et al. 1982; Lighthouse 1998). Although the data from a high-contrast chart are not as significant as contrast data, they serve to verify the refraction and level of acuity.

Macular pathology in the central field should be confirmed with the Amsler grid, and the position and the density of central scotomas should be documented, as should areas of distortion that could affect reading skill.

Table 1 Levels of visual impairment from normal and near normal to blindness, including visual acuity and visual field descriptors

Classification		Levels of visual impairment					Additional descriptors which may be encountered
'Legal'	WHO	Visual acuity and/or visual field limitation (whichever is worse)					
	(Near-)normal vision	Range of normal vision 20/10 20/13 20/16 20/20 20/25 2.0 1.6 1.25 1.0 0.8 Near-normal vision 20/30 20/40 20/50 20/60 0.7 0.6 0.5 0.4 0.3					
	Low vision	Moderate visual impairment 20/70 20/80 20/100 20/125 20/160 0.25 0.20 0.16 0.12					Moderate low vision
		Severe visual impairment 20/200 20/250 20/320 20/400 0.10 0.08 0.06 0.05 Visual field: 20° or less					Severe low vision, 'legal' blindness
Legal blindness (USA) both eyes	Blindness (WHO) one or both eyes	Profound visual impairment 20/500 20/630 20/800 20/1000 0.04 0.03 0.025 0.02 Count fingers at less than 3 m Visual field: 10° or less					Profound low vision, moderate blindness
		Near-total visual impairment Visual acuity: less than 0.02 (20/1000) Count fingers at 1 m or less Hand movements: 5 m or less Light projection, light perception Visual field: 5° or less					Severe blindness, near-total blindness
		Total visual impairment No light perception (NLP)					Total blindness

Visual acuity refers to best achievable acuity with correction.
Non-listed Snellen fractions may be classified by converting to the nearest decimal equivalent, e.g. 10/200 = 0.05, 6/30 = 0.20.
CF (count fingers) without designation of distance may be classified to profound impairment.
HM (hand motion) without designation of distance may be classified to near-total impairment.
Visual field measurements refer to the largest field diameter for a 1/100 white test object.

Data from ICD (1989).

If there is evidence of peripheral field defects, they should be mapped to be included in the evaluation for their effect on mobility. If a referral to a professional mobility instructor is appropriate, the visual field diagram is invaluable in planning the mobility programme.

One of the tests to determine retinal sensitivity measures contrast level. In 1984, contrast sensitivity function was introduced as a clinical test for low vision and it has proved to be an invaluable tool; the level of contrast sensitivity indicates the level of retinal sensitivity, which is important in predicting successful rehabilitation with magnifying devices. A subsequent study with low-vision patients demonstrated a correlation between low-contrast results and the need for increased magnification and lighting (Ginsburg et al. 1987; Cohen 1993).

Combining the results of all the function tests, the clinician is able to predict both the dioptric power range of the low-vision optical devices and the patient's lighting, magnification, and contrast requirements. The next step in the rehabilitative process is the introduction of a variety of adaptive and optical devices.

The other consideration before a detailed discussion of the devices in detail is the effect of the eye disease on visual function.

Common eye diseases and visual function

Each of the common eye diseases has functional characteristics and imposes limitations that should be taken into consideration during the rehabilitation process. Prescribing a rehabilitation plan without understanding the role of the eye disease ignores a fundamental fact, namely that the doctor's prescription is limited by the type of eye condition, whereas the patient's response to adaptive devices is limited by the type and degree of damage regardless of motivation and enthusiasm for rehabilitation.

There are three major categories into which most diseases fit. Each category has specific characteristics that affect the design of a remedial plan (Faye 1984, 1990, 1995, 1996, 1997).

1. Defects in the optical media include degenerative, infectious, and postoperative corneal diseases, pupillary abnormalities, cataracts, secondary membranes after surgery, and opacities of the vitreous humour.
2. Central visual field defects include macular degeneration of all types, macular oedema, laser damage to the macula, macular holes and cysts, and neurological scotomas extending from the optic nerve to the macula, and amblyopia.
3. Peripheral visual field defects including advanced glaucoma, advanced retinitis pigmentosa, diabetic retinopathy, either with retinopathy in the peripheral retina or with laser photocoagulation in that area, postsurgical detached retinas, stroke, and any other injury to the optic pathways or brain.

Defects in the media

There are many levels of disability with corneal disease and cataracts, and not all patients require surgery unless the surgeon expects a significant improvement in function. However, with an increasingly long-lived, active ageing population and dramatic improvements in surgical technology and anaesthesia, the risk of anterior segment surgery has become almost a minor consideration. In cataract surgery minimal sedation, corneal incisions, anterior chamber instillation anaesthesia, and flexible intraocular implants have dramatically reduced the morbidity formerly associated with immobilization, anaesthesia, and sedation of older people.

However, the prevalence of underlying age-associated diseases in the ageing eye should introduce a cautionary note into the general euphoria about the low risk of cataract surgery. Although a cataract may not in itself be a low-vision condition, the presence of a cataract or corneal opacities may mask the symptoms of a primary eye disease such as macular degeneration or glaucoma. In addition to the symptoms of the primary condition, a lens or corneal opacity causes haze, photophobia, and reduced vision.

If a patient's condition does not warrant the risk of surgery, or if surgery must be delayed, the patient should be considered a candidate for vision rehabilitation. One of the first questions should explore difficulty with lighting, for a specific task in the home or outdoors. Direct lighting on the task may have to be angled or modified until maximum comfort and illumination levels are achieved. People with cataracts generally prefer conventional incandescent light to intense blue fluorescent or halogen light. If the patient complains of fading vision after reading close to a bright light source, the level must be reduced to prevent photo stress. People who work under fluorescent ceiling light are more comfortable if an incandescent lamp is added at the desk level.

Simple measures include a matt black plastic reading slit (signature guide) to cut glare from shiny paper and a visor to reduce overhead glare. Marking pens, black ink, and large-print telephone numbers provide better print contrast. Light- or medium-grey wrap-around sunglasses filter intense outdoor light.

Two function tests are used by specialists to help differentiate between the effects of the primary condition and the effects of a cataract: (a) a glare test to identify the degradation of vision caused by the cataract, and (b) the potential acuity meter which bypasses the cataract with a pinpoint of light that transmits a vision chart to the macula to obtain an acuity unaffected by the cataract.

Central visual field defects

The macula, responsible for the keenest sight and for colour and daylight vision, occupies at most only 20° of a total field diameter of more than 180°. Eyeglass lenses focus principal rays on the macula for best corrected vision. The two major types of macular disease in older people are atrophic, or 'dry' macular degeneration, for which there is currently no treatment other than foods high in lutein/ zeaxanthine (Seddon *et al.* 1994), and subretinal neovascularization, or 'wet' macular degeneration, for which no effective cure or preventive agent have been substantiated. Some of the new treatments under investigation are antiangiogenesis drugs, photosensitive dyes, cell transplants, and actual relocation of healthy retinal tissue flaps to the damaged macular area.

Regardless of the category of the underlying pathology, if macular cones are damaged by atrophy, haemorrhage, laser treatment, scar tissue, or amblyopia, the sight is blocked centrally to a degree commensurate with cell damage. (Amblyopia is not directly connected with low vision unless the better eye loses vision.) The central loss of vision, whether distortion or scotoma, calls for an adjustment, usually a spontaneous head or eye turn that shifts the vision from the macula to the edge of the lesion (preferred retinal locus). Since the quality of image resolution of this paramacular area is considerably less than that of the fovea, images must be magnified to be identified. The person with a macular defect adapts by looking off centre (up, down, or sideways) and by using magnifying lenses or devices. Patients also need non-optical techniques that they can apply to household activities such as marking dials and thermostats with contrasting tape or raised plastic dots. Because peripheral vision is not affected as a rule, most patients are able to get around by themselves, perhaps using a monocular telescope for signs or asking directions when needed. If these same people are still driving, they need to think of alternative types of transportation before they are no longer able to drive safely. A discussion of driving safety should anticipate the problem before the patient is forced to relinquish their independence.

Very few individuals with macular degeneration need special mobility aids such as a cane because peripheral vision remains intact, unless they feel more secure with a support cane.

Peripheral field limiting disease (see Chapter 7.5)

Defects in the peripheral field are found typically in diabetic retinopathy treated with extensive peripheral photocoagulation, in postsurgical detached retina with scleral buckling, and in degenerative diseases such as retinitis pigmentosa, as well as in neurological damage to the optic nerve, optic pathways, and visual cortex.

Although glaucoma is the most prevalent condition in this category, the average glaucoma patient does not become a low-vision candidate unless the peripheral retinal cells decompensate, leaving only a few degrees of central field. In addition to the loss of peripheral field, the remaining receptors in the central field undergo a gradual decrease in contrast sensitivity, which diminishes subjective vision before it affects the high-contrast chart acuity. Patients often say that they 'see worse every day', yet their chart acuity remains the same. A contrast test would reveal the reason.

Such an advanced stage of glaucoma is unusual in a patient who takes medication faithfully, although susceptible individuals may have progressive disease in spite of maximum medication and/or surgery. This is particularly true of low-tension or normal-tension glaucoma (ischaemic optic neuropathy).

In progressive disease first the peripheral field is obliterated, gradually encroaching on the macula. Night blindness might be an early symptom, but reading does not become difficult until there is actual macular damage. Since magnification is the principal remedy for low vision, glaucoma patients pose a problem in rehabilitation. If there is no healthy peripheral retina to register the image, traditional magnifying lenses are not effective. In late-stage glaucoma, magnification may be limited to closed-circuit television (**CCTV**) reading machines and low-power hand magnifiers. The high contrast of the display on the monitor bolsters the low-contrast sensitivity of the patient, while a low-power magnifier can be moved at varying distances from the page to find the clearest image that fits into the limited field of vision. Eventually no amount of magnification is effective and the person must resort to non-visual techniques, particularly mobility instruction. Patients have three mobility options: a human guide, cane ('white stick') travel, or a guide dog. Most glaucoma patients prefer human guides. The older person may not have the physical strength to manage and care for a guide dog.

The remaining central field in retinitis pigmentosa is generally more useful than the same field in glaucoma. The contrast sensitivity tends to be near normal for many years, although patients are night blind before they are visually impaired. The best low-vision devices are computers with a varied menu of large-print programs, CCTV reading machines, and sunglasses in the yellow–orange spectrum that block blue (ultraviolet) light and enhance contrast (Lighthouse 1998). Most patients with retinitis pigmentosa use mobility aids such as a long cane or a guide dog.

When patients have diabetes with retinopathy, there are additional medical problems to consider. Patients may not be able to tolerate stress, even such a simple task as reading with magnification. Those who have had photocoagulation may be night blind or have reduced contrast. They may be depressed, may be taking multiple medications for other systemic problems, and may lack energy, which the doctor may interpret as lack of motivation. The same considerations should apply to patients who have had brain trauma, particularly stroke. Many seemingly well-functioning people have difficulty concentrating and retaining what they read, and if they have a hemianopia (either right or left), they need special prism glasses and retraining in tracking printed material.

If peripheral field defects decrease the level of contrast perception, patients may use materials that provide maximum contrast, such as black print on a white background, marking pens, enlarged print, CCTV with white letters on a dark background (reverse polarity), and high-level illumination.

When the peripheral field is compromised or blind, a patient can regain independent mobility by taking an instruction course with a mobility specialist generally available through agencies for the visually impaired and blind.

Low-vision rehabilitation

The examiner has to consider the effects of the existing pathology on the patient's performance. All the function tests have to be analysed, and the dioptric power of the magnifying device calculated. Devices in the appropriate range are selected and the rehabilitation begins. Ideally a trained low-vision assistant teaches the patient the correct technique of applying devices to tasks, adjusts lighting, and reviews the need for other skill development such as cooking, shopping, and grooming.

Depending on the complexity of the patient's needs, the rehabilitation team may include (in addition to the ophthalmologist and optometrist) a trained low-vision assistant, a specialist in aids for daily living (vision rehabilitation), an occupational therapist, a nurse specialist or co-ordinator, a mobility instructor, a computer technologist, and a psychologist or social worker.

The skill in applying the low-vision evaluation data lies in recognizing the effects of the visual and physical deficits and guiding the patient's efforts to use residual vision. Once the devices are selected, the patient learns adaptation skills whether reading with magnifiers, mastering a television or computer screen, or using adaptive equipment and a modified environment in the home. Interests, motivation, history of coping, and all the other intangibles that make up the individual are involved in successful vision rehabilitation.

Most people have a satisfactory outcome working with the doctor/optometrist and a low-vision assistant. However, if the prescribed low-vision devices are only a partial solution, the patient can be referred for other rehabilitation services to government and private agencies that provide advanced technology training, mobility, and education or social services.

Types of devices used in low-vision rehabilitation

Basic devices for correcting low vision are optical (magnifying lenses, sunglasses), non-optical (adaptive equipment, large print, reading stands, lighting, voice-output instruments), and electronic technology (large-print computer programs, virtual-reality equipment, reading machines) (Lighthouse 1998).

Optical devices

There are two categories of optical magnification devices: convex lens devices (spectacles, hand-held magnifiers, stand-mounted magnifiers) and telescopic devices.

Convex magnifying lenses

Spectacles

Magnifying lenses mounted in spectacle frames must be used with both hands holding the reading material no more than 32.5 cm from the lens, often as close as 5 or 7.5 cm. Because of these optical restrictions patients may resist reading with high-power spectacles; however, the compensation for the short reading distance is the broad reading field and greater speed than can be achieved with a comparable hand magnifier. A monocular patient will use only the better eye usually at a distance of 5 to 12.5 cm (Fig. 2(a)). A person with binocular vision must use a glass with base-in prism to aid the convergence effort required by reading with both eyes close to the reading material (Lighthouse 1996).

Arranging the illumination so that the light comes from a lamp positioned in front of the face and directed at the page is contrary to most people's habits. Patients must be reassured that this will not

(a)

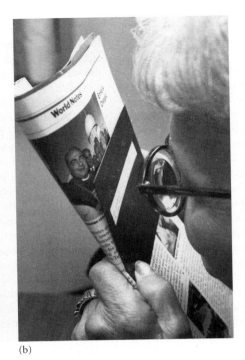

(b)

(c)

Fig. 2 (a) Reading glasses are available in powers of 4 to 80 D. Reading distance in centimetres is related to lens power in dioptres. The working distance of a 10-D lens is $f = 1/D = 100/10 = 10$ cm. A matt plastic mask can serve as a writing guide and to reduce reflected glare. (b) The hand magnifier held at its focal distance is useful for short-term tasks. It can be used either with or without glasses. It is not recommended for patients with a tremor or arthritis. (c) A premounted stand magnifier rests directly on the surface of the page, maintaining the working distance without effort on the part of the patient. An illuminated stand provides excellent lighting for a patient with macular degeneration.

harm their eyes and be shown how to angle the lamp so that there is no glare on the page. Reading skills are relearned, slowly at first, often one word at a time, moving the page slowly past the reading lens or moving the eye along a line of print. People who have been rapid readers are often frustrated by this tedious pace, but usually learn with practice.

Patients with macular degeneration often prefer a spectacle aid for prolonged reading and a hand magnifier for shorter tasks such as reading food labels or addresses on envelopes. If high levels of

illumination are needed, a stand magnifier with a battery or electrical source is an alternative.

The use of spectacle magnification is not as successful in diseases with less than 7° of central field, such as glaucoma, because the magnified image is larger than the available field.

Hand magnifiers

Many people are already familiar with the use of hand-held magnifiers. A person with low vision must use a higher-power lens (12–60 D) than is usually available commercially (3–11 D). Most patients regardless of their eye condition are able to use a hand magnifier for short-term chores such as shopping, looking at dials and thermostats, and reading mail, labels, recipes, and menus. A hand-held lens has the advantage of being held farther from the eye to magnify the object (Fig. 2(b)), although the distance from the reading material is still limited by the power of the lens (the stronger the lens, the closer the working distance). The chief disadvantage is a smaller field of view than a comparable spectacle provides.

For most low-vision patients, a pocket magnifier is easy to use for short-term activities. Macular degeneration patients particularly enjoy being able to read labels in a shop or the menu in a restaurant. If patients have a tremor, orthopaedic restriction of arm motion or neurological deficits of attention or memory, hand magnifiers are not the device of choice because a magnifier must be held in focus.

Stand magnifiers

For patients with restricted arm motion, tremor, arthritis, or other such limitations, a premounted magnifying lens is both stable and manoeuvrable. A stand magnifier is mounted on a base that rests on a page or object. Because the patient does not have to maintain the working distance manually, the stand is easier for the person with orthopaedic limitations to manipulate. Many stands have additional built-in illumination, which makes them the obvious choice for patients who need a uniform bright light source (Fig. 2(c)).

Telescopes

A telescope has an optical characteristic that no other device has—it can magnify at any distance from infinity to near. Spectacles, and hand and stand magnifiers, correct only the near range. Of particular importance in low vision is the intermediate (arm's length) distance, which is beyond the visual range of most low-vision patients. Typical examples of this distance are shelves in a supermarket or library, instrumental music scores, display cases in stores and museums, computer screens, and tools used for repairs in the home.

Telescopes are most often prescribed as a hand-held monocular device. They can also be prescribed mounted in a spectacle frame by low-vision specialists. Telescopes can have a preset focus, be focused by hand, or incorporate an autofocus mechanism. Because of their light weight, spectacle telescopes may be preferable to binoculars for sporting events, movies, lectures, and art exhibitions.

A disadvantage of a telescope is the constricted optical field and critical working distance. Telescopes mounted in a frame block out the peripheral field when the user is looking through them, a potential mobility hazard unless special instruction is offered by the practitioner or agency.

Before computer programs were available in large type and flexible format, telescopes were useful at that intermediate range, although the field limitation was always a drawback that required special training.

Electronic devices

CCTV

A CCTV reading machine designed with a camera either as an integral part of the monitor or as a separate hand unit offers the low-vision patient an alternative to a telescope and computer. With any of the commercially available reading machines it is possible to sit at a relatively normal distance from the screen, or to scan the material with a hand camera while viewing the screen. Recent advances in design have resulted in sets with notepads that allow selected areas of text to be magnified and with other features such as a calculator, calendar, and clock. Many sets have other options such as colour monitors, scrolling, or word-by-word presentation of the scanned material and a variety of contrasting colours for the text. For best contrast, most patients prefer white or yellow letters on a dark background.

CCTV provides the greatest range of magnification (up to 60 ×) and best contrast of any low-vision aid.

Virtual image devices

Virtual imaging is also possible with a head-mounted visor and a hand-held camera that has a small battery pack. The race is on to design sophisticated computers that can select type sizes, scroll the print at any speed, and provide a wide selection of contrasting colours.

Non-optical options

Low vision lenses are appropriate for tasks that require magnification. However, daily living includes many ordinary activities for which the use of optical devices is either impractical or impossible. Many visually impaired individuals need instruction in daily living skills (Williams 1996). Trying to shop, cook, and groom oneself can be more frustrating than the inability to read because it now takes more time and the performance is 'not the same as it used to be'. Practical suggestions include simple adjustments such as moving closer to the television until printed messages on the screen are readable (sometimes as close as 1 m), the use of clocks, timers, and scales with enlarged numerals (Lighthouse 1999), and large-print books. Patients can learn to identify the colour of clothing with labels. In the kitchen, storage jars and canned goods can be labelled with large letters.

Voice-output instruments are welcomed not only by blind people. An auditory signal from a calculator, clock, or scale saves time.

Lighting is a universal problem in the home and office. There are no standards specifically for visually impaired people other than trial and error. General principles and common sense suggest that room lighting should be balanced between the indirect light of sconces and the direct light from floor lamps, and that task lighting should be bright enough to provide maximum contrast without glare. Daylight fluorescent bulbs and incandescent halogen lamps may create a glare source, particularly for people with cataracts, because their spectrum contains more blue light than a standard incandescent bulb. Blue light fluoresces in the cornea and lens of the ageing eye; incandescent light increases contrast and is a comfortable light for most people.

During the rehabilitation process patients should be encouraged to explore new options and re-examine their priorities as they work at home or with an instructor. Not until they have tried the new devices in a variety of activities can they sort out their reactions to their new skills and discoveries.

Support groups

Support groups help visually impaired people to develop a network that can help them to deal with loss of vision and the isolation, that is implicit in the loss of mobility, and increased dependence on others.

Meeting with a facilitator in a group setting helps patients to participate in their own therapy by sharing ideas, expressing anger and frustration, and supporting one another. A group often becomes a powerful advocate for awareness by sponsoring community programmes and influencing local or state legislation for elderly people (Lighthouse 1992).

Conclusion

Concerns about an ageing population are escalating as longevity becomes the rule rather than the exception. A survey in the mid-1990s (Lighthouse 1995a) estimated that there are more than 13 million visually impaired people over 45 years of age in the United States alone. With projected numbers of individuals aged over 65 doubling by the year 2050, there is bound to be a substantial increase in age-associated eye diseases (Benson and Marano 1994; National Advisory Eye Council 1994).

Any professional involved in geriatric care is faced with timely recognition and treatment of age-associated conditions; decision-making and programme planning for placement in elderly care facilities are often based on a patient's functional status. Only a small number of visually impaired older people receive comprehensive vision rehabilitation (Lighthouse 1995). The increasing need for low-vision care may change the inertia within the eye care professions as well as create greater awareness within the other professions involved in general health care. Visually challenged people of the next generation are not going to be satisfied with the doctor's statement that 'nothing can be done' when it is obvious that a judicious combination of low-vision adaptive devices and thorough instruction in their application, together with other rehabilitation techniques, can improve optimal quality of visual function for all low-vision patients.

References

Arditi, A. and Knoblauch, K. (1996). Effective colour contrast and low vision. In *Functional assessment of low vision* (ed. B.P. Rosenthal and R.G. Cole), pp. 129–35. Mosby, St Louis, MO.

Ball, M., Owsley, C., Beard, B. (1990). Clinical visual perimetry underestimates peripheral field problems in older adults. *Clinical Visual Sciences*, 5, 113–25.

Benson, V. and Marano, M.A. (1994). Current estimates from the National Health Interview Survey, 1992. National Center for Health Statistics. *Vital Health Statistics*, 10.

Bodis-Wollner, I. and Camisa, J.M. (1980). Contrast sensitivity measurement, In *Neuro-ophthalmology*, Vol. 1 (ed. G. Lassell and J.T.W. Dolan), pp. 373–401. Excerpta Medica, Amsterdam.

Carter, J.H. (1982). The effects of ageing on selected visual functions: colour, vision, glare sensitivity, field of vision, and accommodation. In *Ageing and human visual function* (ed. R. Sekuler, D. Kline, and K. Dismukes), pp. 124–9. A.R. Liss, New York.

Charles, N. (1995). Medication and vision impairment. In *The ageing eye and low vision* (ed. E.E. Faye and C.S. Stuen), pp. 23–8. Lighthouse, New York.

Cohen, J.M. (1993). Illumination, contrast and glare: problems in poor vision. *Practical Optometry*, 4, 60–6.

Faye, E.E. (1984). *Clinical low vision* (2nd edn), pp. 171–96, 257–325. Little, Brown, Boston.

Faye, E.E. (1990). Low vision. In *Clinical ophthalmology*, Vol. 1 (ed. W. Tasman), pp. 1–14. J.B. Lippincott, Hagerstown, PA.

Faye, E.E. (1995). Low vision. In *General ophthalmology* (14th edn) (ed. D. Vaughn, T. Asbury, and P. Eva-Riordan), pp. 388–95. Appleton and Lange, Norwalk, CT.

Faye, E.E. (1996). Pathology and visual function. In *Functional assessment of low vision* (ed. B.P. Rosenthal and R.G. Cole), pp. 63–75. Mosby, St Louis, MO.

Faye, E.E. (1997). Functional aspects of the eye diagnosis. In *Functional visual behavior: a therapist's guide to evaluation and treatment options* (ed. M. Gentile), pp. 434–7. American Occupational Therapy Association, Bethesda, MD.

Ferris, F.L., III, Kassoff, A., Bresnick, B.H., and Bailey, I. (1982). New visual acuity charts for clinical research. *American Journal of Ophthalmology*, 94, 91–6.

Ginsburg, A.P. (1984). A new contrast sensitivity vision test chart. *American Journal of Optometry and Physiological Optics*, 61, 403–7.

Ginsburg, A.P., Rosenthal, B.P., and Cohen, J. (1987). The evaluation of reading capability of low vision patients using the vision contrast system (VCTS). In *Low vision: principles and application* (ed. G. Woo), pp. 17–18. Springer-Verlag, New York.

Holroyd, S., Rabins, P., Finkelstein, D., *et al.* (1992). Visual hallucinations in patients with macular degeneration. *American Journal of Psychiatry*, 149, 1701–6.

Hood, C.M. and Faye, E.E. (1995). Evaluating the living situation. In *The ageing eye and low vision* (ed. E.E. Faye and C.S. Stuen), pp. 46–54. Lighthouse, New York.

ICD (1989). *International Classification of Diseases* (9th revision), Section 369, *Blindness and low vision*, Vol. 1, pp. 84–5. Practice Management Information, Los Angeles, CA.

Leibowitz, H.M., Kruger, D.E., and Maunder, L.R. (1980). The Framingham Eye Study Monograph. *Survey of Ophthalmology*, 24 (Supplement), 335–610.

Leporte, F.E. (1989). The neuro-ophthalmological case history: elucidating the symptoms. In *Clinical ophthalmology*, Vol. 2 (ed. W. Tasman), pp. 17–19. J.B. Lippincott, Hagerstown, PA.

Lighthouse (1992). *Self-help, mutual aid support group directory and guide.* Lighthouse International, New York.

Lighthouse (1995). *The Lighthouse national survey on vision loss: the experience, attitudes, and knowledge of middle-aged and older Americans.* Lighthouse International, New York.

Lighthouse (1996). *The functional screening questionnaire.* Lighthouse International, New York.

Lighthouse (1998). *Professional products catalog.* Lighthouse International, New York.

Lighthouse (1999). *The Lighthouse catalog.* Lighthouse International, New York.

Marmor, M. (1995). Normal age-related vision changes and their effects on vision. In *The ageing eye and low vision* (ed. E.E. Faye and C.S. Stuen), p. 8–10. Lighthouse, New York.

Mogk, L.G. and Mogk, M. (1999). I see purple flowers everywhere: the many visions of Charles Bonnet. In *Macular degeneration*, pp. 207–23. Ballantine, New York.

National Advisory Eye Council (1994). *Vision research: a national plan 1994–1998. Report of the low vision and rehabilitation panel.* DHHS publication (NIH) 93-3186, pp. 305–321. US Government Printing Office, Washington, DC.

NEI (National Eye Institute) (1996). *Visual functioning questionnaire.* Document 25 (VFQ.25). National Eye Institute, National Institutes of Health, Bethesda, MD.

Owsley, C. and Sloane, M.E. (1986). Contrast sensitivity and the perception of 'real world' targets. *British Journal of Ophthalmology*, 71, 125–36.

Owsley, C., Sekuler, R., and Siemsen, D. (1983). Contrast sensitivity throughout adulthood. *Vision Research*, 23, 689–99.

Pitts, D.G. (1983). The effects of aging on selected visual functions: dark adaptation, visual acuity, stereopsis and brightness contrast. In *Aging and human visual function* (ed. R. Sekuler, D. Kline, and K. Dismukes). Liss, New York

Rosenberg, R. (1984). Light, glare, contrast in low vision care. In *Clinical low vision* (ed. E.E. Faye), pp. 197–212. Little, Brown, Boston, MA.

Rosenthal, B.P. (1991). The structured low vision evaluation. In *Problems in optometry* (ed. B.P. Rosenthal and R.G. Cole), pp. 385–93. Butterworth, St Louis, MO.

Rosenthal, B.P. (1996). The function-based low vision evaluation. In *Functional assessment of low vision* (ed. B.P. Rosenthal and R.G. Cole), pp. 1–25. Mosby, St Louis, MO.

Seddon, J.M., Ajani, U.A., Sperduto, R.D., *et al.* (1994). The Eye Disease Case–Control Study Group. Dietary carotenoids, vitamins A, C, and E, and advanced age-related macular degeneration. *Journal of the American Medical Association*, **272**, 1413–20.

Sekuler, R. and Owsley, C. (1982). The spatial vision of older humans. In *Ageing and human visual function* (ed. R. Sekuler, D. Kline, and K. Dismukes), pp. 185–202. A.R. Liss, New York.

Tideiksaar, R. (1995). Avoiding falls. In *The ageing eye and low vision* (ed. E.E. Faye and C.S. Stuen), pp. 55–60. Lighthouse, New York.

Williams, D.R. (1996). Functional adaptive devices. In *Remediation and management of low vision* (ed. B.P. Rosenthal and R.G. Cole), pp. 71–121. Mosby, St Louis, MO.

Wolf, E. (1960). Glare and age. *Archives of Ophthalmology*, **64**, 502–14.

18.16 Disorders of hearing

A. Julianna Gulya

Introduction

Hearing loss of ageing or presbyacusis (presbycusis) afflicts 10 million elderly citizens in the United States (one-third of people aged 65 to 74 years and one-half of those aged 85 years and older), and can have a profound impact on their lives (USDHHS 1985). The embarrassment engendered by misunderstanding others encourages social withdrawal. Poor hearing breeds the suspicion that others are mumbling or, worse yet, a paranoia that others are conspiring to keep one from overhearing conversations. The victim enters a cycle of suspicion, isolation, loneliness, and depression, certainly an unhappy prospect for one's twilight years.

In this chapter we examine the histopathology of presbyacusis as well as its varied clinical presentations, and conclude with suggestions for the evaluation and management of the individual patient.

Histopathology

Presbyacusis is the term used to describe the clinical manifestations of ageing of the auditory system; the biological mechanisms thought to be involved are discussed in Chapters 2.1 and 2.2. Many factors combine in individually determined permutations to result in the bilaterally symmetric loss of hearing in older people; in the examination of human material, it is exceedingly difficult to separate those histopathological changes of the auditory system associated with hearing loss that are solely attributable to intrinsic ageing from those due to extrinsic factors such as noise exposure, toxins, disease processes, genetic influence, diet, vascular disorders, and climate.

Men generally suffer a greater degree of hearing loss with ageing than women (Matkin and Hodgson 1982).

Changes in the external and middle ears do not appear to contribute significantly to the sensorineural hearing loss of ageing (Etholm and Belal 1974). Thus more attention has been focused on the inner ear.

Those cochlear structures that have been particularly scrutinized for age-associated changes are the organ of Corti, including its sensory cells, the first-order neurones and their afferent dendrites, the stria vascularis, and the basilar membrane (Fig. 1). The significance of the observed 4977 bp mitochondrial DNA deletion found in the cochlea of the elderly people with presbyacusis remains to be determined (Seidman *et al.* 1996). This mitochondrial DNA deletion is thought to be consistent with the membrane hypothesis of ageing, in which senescence is attributed to the additive adverse effects of reactive oxygen metabolites on the function of mitochondria and hence the bioenergy state of the host cell.

Clinical correlation of audiometric configuration with specific patterns of histopathological alteration has been relatively successful, and Schuknecht (1993) has defined four types of presbyacusis: sensory, neural, metabolic, and mechanical (or cochlear conductive).

Sensory presbyacusis

Sensory presbyacusis is defined audiometrically by a bilaterally symmetric, abruptly dropping, pure-tone threshold curve with excellent speech discrimination (Fig. 2). Its hearing loss is generally noticed by those in middle age, although the histopathological correlate, hair cell loss in the basal cochlea, may begin as early as infancy (Fig. 3).

The age-associated degeneration of the organ of Corti progresses very slowly, only affecting a few millimetres of the basal cochlea even

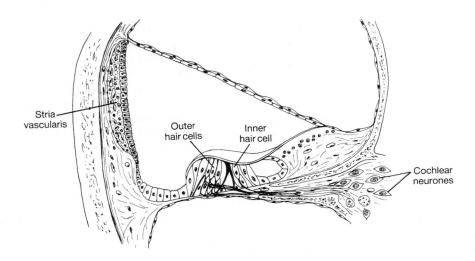

Fig. 1 Normal cochlear structures.

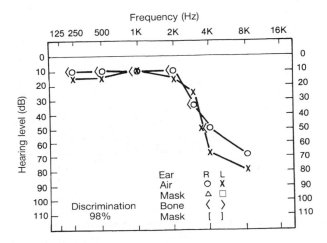

Fig. 2 Sensory presbyacusis, defined audiometrically.

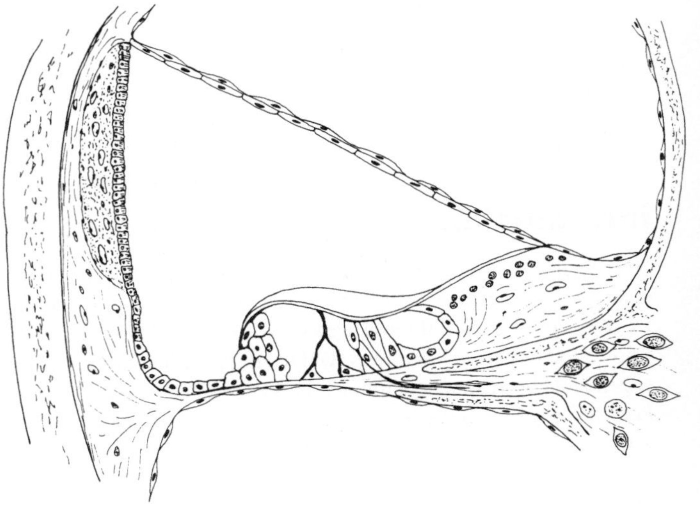

Fig. 3 Hair cell loss in the basal cochlea.

in the very aged (Schuknecht 1993). The outer hair cells, especially those in the third row, are most severely affected, but the degeneration can encompass the first row of outer hair cells, extend to the inner hair cells, and eventually culminate in the disappearance of the entire organ of Corti. A secondary neuronal degeneration occurs as well.

Ultrastructural examination suggests that lipofuscin accumulation and the formation of giant cilia precede cellular loss (Soucek *et al.* 1987). The amount of intracellular lipofuscin found in the cochlear hair cells and spiral ganglion cells has been positively correlated with increased individual age (Ishii *et al.* 1967), tendency to autolysis (Gleeson and Felix 1987), and the extent of hearing loss (Raafat *et al.* 1987).

Neural presbyacusis

The age of onset of neural presbyacusis appears to be determined primarily by genetic factors. Audiometrically, the condition manifests

as a loss of speech discrimination out of proportion to the loss of pure-tone thresholds (Schuknecht 1993) (Fig. 4). Speech discrimination, in comparison with pure-tone perception, apparently requires a greater proportion of surviving neurones to maintain a higher level of signal integration and transmission; this observation accounts for the phenomenon of phonemic regression—loss of speech discrimination while pure-tone thresholds are relatively maintained (Gaeth 1948). Evidence of degenerative changes in the central nervous system, such as memory loss, intellectual decline, and motor incoordination, may be seen in association with particularly rapid progressive neural presbyacusis (Schuknecht 1993).

The histopathological correlates of neural presbyacusis (Fig. 5) lie in the depletion of first-order neurones and their fibres out of proportion to the loss of the organ of Corti, generally most severe in the basal turn of the cochlea (Schuknecht 1993).

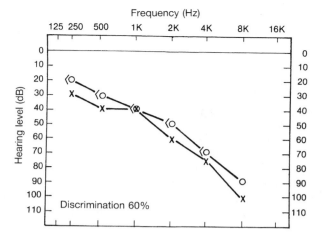

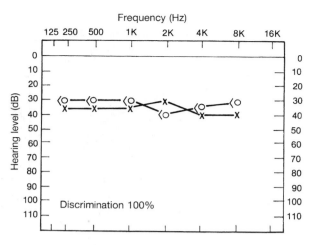

Fig. 4 Neural presbyacusis, defined audiometrically.

Fig. 6 Metabolic presbyacusis, defined audiometrically.

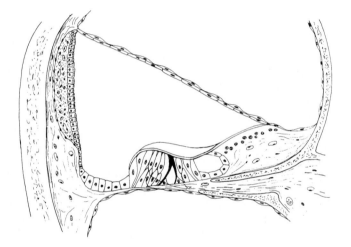

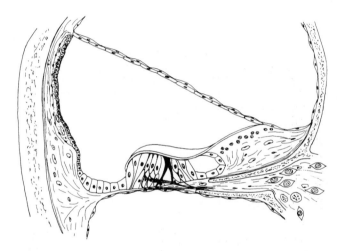

Fig. 5 Depletion of first-order neurones in neural presbyacusis.

Fig. 7 Atrophy of the stria vascularis in metabolic presbyacusis.

Ultrastructural studies have shown lipofuscin accumulation in the ganglion cells, disorganization of the myelin sheath of their dendrites and axons, and loss of synapses at the hair cell bases (Nadol 1979). Presumably, the alterations in the myelin sheath are sufficient to disrupt normal saltatory conductive mechanisms, with consequent delay and energy loss as transmission of impulses occurs through cell bodies.

Metabolic presbyacusis

Metabolic presbyacusis has its onset in the third to sixth decades of life, is slowly progressive, and appears to have a familial tendency (Schuknecht 1993). The audiogram typically has a flat configuration, with speech discrimination scores remaining normal until the pure-tone thresholds exceed 50 dB (Fig. 6).

Histopathological examination (Fig. 7) has correlated atrophy of the stria vascularis—the metabolically active electrophysiological generator of the cochlea—with this type of presbyacusis (Schuknecht 1993). Computer-aided morphometric techniques have been able to

establish a statistically significant relationship between the degree of strial atrophy and the extent of hearing loss (Pauler *et al.* 1988). The degeneration of the stria has been variably attributed to vascular changes in the cochlea (Johnsson and Hawkins 1977) or to a genetically determined tendency for early cellular degeneration (Pauler *et al.* 1988). Although the marginal cells (those cells that face the fluid space of the cochlear duct) are most markedly affected, the entire stria may be reduced to a mere layer of basal cells (Kimura and Schuknecht 1970).

Cochlear conductive presbyacusis

Cochlear conductive (mechanical) presbyacusis describes a downward-sloping threshold curve (Fig. 8) associated with speech discrimination scores that are inversely proportional to the steepness of the slope of the curve (Schuknecht 1993).

Typically, histopathological examination of the cochlea is unable to reveal any alteration in the hair cells, neurones, or stria vascularis that could account for the hearing loss. It has been suggested that

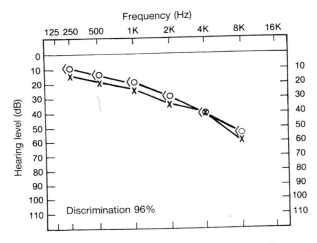

Fig. 8 Cochlear conductive presbyacusis defined audiometrically.

some alteration in the motion mechanics of the cochlea, centring particularly on the basilar membrane, underlies this type of presbyacusis (Schuknecht 1993). Some support for this explanation comes from the light microscopic demonstration of hyalinization (Crowe *et al.* 1934), calcification (Mayer 1919–20), and even a lipidosis of the basilar membrane (Nomura 1970). More convincingly, a marked thickening of the basilar membrane in the basal 10 mm of the cochlea has been found by electron microscopy in a patient with audiometric findings typical for cochlear conductive presbyacusis (Nadol 1979).

Other pathological changes

Although 'pure' forms of the four types of presbyacusis are described above, various combinations can occur and result in differing audiometric configurations (Schuknecht 1993).

Alterations in the central auditory pathways have also long been suspected as being affected in ageing (Schuknecht 1993), but it has been difficult to obtain conclusive evidence. Findings which suggest that there is a loss of cells from the superior temporal gyrus (Brody 1955), ventral cochlear nucleus (Kirikae *et al.* 1964), dorsal cochlear nucleus (Hansen and Reske-Neilsen 1965), medial geniculate body (Kirikae *et al.* 1964), superior olivary nucleus (Kirikae *et al.* 1964), and inferior colliculus (Hansen and Reske-Neilsen 1965) with ageing have been contradicted (Konigsmark and Murphy 1972). Nonetheless, there is evidence that accumulation of lipofuscin and degeneration of myelin occur in the central auditory structures (Hansen and Reske-Neilsen 1965).

Correlation of specific functional deficits with specific central structural alterations is extremely difficult, particularly as peripheral auditory dysfunction/alteration nearly uniformly presents as an important confounding variable.

In a similar fashion, although vascular alterations, including atrophy with devascularization and an increased incidence of periodic acid–Schiff-positive thickening of capillary walls have been found in cochleas from elderly subjects (Jorgensen 1961), correlating such changes with degenerative changes in cochlear duct structures and hearing loss remains a formidable task.

The influence of depletion of neural transmitters in age-associated hearing loss warrants further investigation.

Evaluation

Presbyacusis may begin insidiously; usually the higher frequencies are involved first, but with progression, the frequencies of the upper range of human speech are affected, interfering particularly with consonant discrimination. Patients complain especially of difficulty with understanding high-pitched women's voices, children's voices, and conversations in crowded environments. Key factors to elicit in the history are the time course of the hearing loss, its progression, and any associated symptoms such as tinnitus, aural fullness, or fluctuation in hearing. Questioning should uncover any history of exposure to excessive noise or ototoxic drugs, as well as any family history of hearing loss or past history of ear infections or surgery. Asymmetric, sudden, rapidly progressive, or fluctuating hearing losses are not consistent with presbyacusis and demand full evaluation with referral to an otolaryngologist/otologist.

The examination of any complaint of hearing loss comprises a pneumatoscopic examination of the ears with initial assessment of the hearing deficit by the Weber, Rinne, and whisper-threshold tests. In general, in the Weber test, the 512-Hz tuning fork lateralizes from the central forehead location to the poorer hearing ear in the case of a conductive hearing loss, and to the better hearing ear in the case of a sensorineural hearing loss. The Rinne test is positive (air conduction greater than bone conduction, when comparing mastoid process to ear canal positions) in normal hearing or in the case of a sensorineural hearing loss, and negative in the case of a conductive hearing loss. Accumulated cerumen, which may interfere with hearing and/or auditory testing, must be removed before testing.

The complete audiogram, including pure-tone (air and bone conduction) threshold testing, determination of speech discrimination, and tympanometry is an integral part of evaluation and management. As discussed above, presbyacusis is bilaterally symmetric; hence, any significant asymmetry, as well as any suggestion of retrocochlear disease (e.g. acoustic neuroma), demands further testing, which may include auditory brainstem response testing and structural evaluation of the central auditory structures by gadolinium-enhanced magnetic resonance imaging. Otolaryngological/neuro-otological consultation is indicated in such cases.

Management

The evaluation and fitting of hearing aids, speech reading, auditory training, and assistive listening devices can be used in various combinations to help the hearing-impaired person.

Hearing aids (Stach and Gulya 1996)

Hearing aids are amplification devices that vary in size, power, and sophistication, yet have in common certain basic elements. A microphone is used to detect the incoming sound signals and convert them into electrical energy. An amplifier then boosts the energy of the signal by a factor, the 'gain' of the particular device. The output from the aid is then channelled to the ear canal by the ear mould part of the device.

Individuals with conductive, sensorineural, or mixed hearing losses may benefit from appropriate evaluation and fitting of a hearing aid. In general, those hearing losses with relatively good discrimination scores are expected to perform better with hearing aids than those with poor speech discrimination; however, some individuals with poor discrimination do better than expected with a hearing aid, indicating that only a trial of a properly fitted hearing aid can determine its potential benefit in the individual case.

Hearing aids range from tiny, completely in-the-canal (CIC) devices to bulky 'body' aids. The hearing aid professional should work with the patient to determine the appropriate device and special features for each individual.

The contralateral routing of signals (CROS) aid is designed for individuals with a unilateral, profound hearing loss, but normal hearing in the opposite ear. A microphone worn on the 'bad' side transmits, by cord or FM signal (cordless), incoming signals to the normal ear. The bi-contralateral routing of signals (biCROS) aid is a similar device but appropriately amplifies the crossed signal to accommodate for a hearing impairment in the 'good' ear.

It may be wise to recommend either a body aid, with its more easily manipulated controls, special geriatric moulds, or 'remote controlled' hearing aids, because of the limitations of fine motor dexterity in some elderly people.

There are other modifications of hearing aids. Use of a telephone with the aid is facilitated by the 't' (for telecoil) switch. Automatic gain control circuitry appropriately modifies incoming soft or loud stimuli; it is especially helpful for the patient with the 'recruiting' ear, i.e. an ear in which there is an abnormally rapid rise in the perceived loudness of, and discomfort associated with, an incoming sound signal. Automatic and multiple signal processing describes modifications of the circuitry that are geared to improving the signal-to-noise ratio—improving human speech perception in the presence of competing environmental noise.

The oscillator of a bone conduction hearing aid is placed in direct contact with the skull, most commonly held firmly at the mastoid by a headset. Patients with uncontrollable otorrhoea, canal atresia, or other conditions that preclude the use of an air conduction aid may derive substantial benefit from a bone conduction aid. The bone-anchored hearing aid (Nobel Biocare, Goteborg, Sweden) is an 'implantable' bone conduction device. In an outpatient surgical procedure, an osseointegrated anchoring screw is placed in the bone of the skull posterior to the ear to be amplified; the portion of the screw which penetrates the skin serves to anchor the aid (Gulya and Stach 1996).

The evaluation of a patient for a hearing aid is conducted by a qualified audiologist who carefully assesses the individual's thresholds and discrimination scores to the recommended aid. In addition to the appropriateness of the selection and settings of the aid, other factors, such as motivation, the need to communicate in the patient's environment, and realistic expectations, combine to determine whether the individual is a good hearing aid candidate. Patients with recruiting ears tolerate amplification within a relatively narrow range before reaching uncomfortable levels of loudness, while others, with discrimination reduced out of proportion to pure-tone averages, may not derive much benefit from a hearing aid.

Training in the proper cleaning, maintenance, and operation of the device is a necessary part of the evaluation and fitting. Often it is helpful to have an interested family member participate in such training to help prompt the memory of the senior citizen.

The cochlear implant

The cochlear implant is a major advance in the management of individuals with severe to profound sensorineural hearing losses who derive little or no benefit from optimal hearing aid fitting. The implanted electrode array conveys electrical impulses from an external receiver across the skin to stimulate directly the surviving neural population of the cochlea. Somewhat reminiscent of a hearing aid, signals are perceived by a microphone and specifically altered by a signal processor before being transmitted down the intracochlear array.

Candidacy for cochlear implantation is determined by careful audiological, radiological, and surgical evaluation; the implantation of the device by mastoidectomy can be done on an outpatient basis. The cost of the device is high; nonetheless, the benefit perceived by appropriate recipients is substantial, who note a diminished sense of isolation, and both improved speech-reading ability and voice modulation.

Vibrotactile devices

Vibrotactile devices are devices designed to help profoundly deaf people perceive sound. Vibrators placed on the wrist, sternum, or waist transform environmental sound and speech into skin vibrations. After appropriate training, patients can use these devices to localize and identify sounds, in addition to improving communication skills.

Speech reading

Speech reading is the term used to describe the perception of linguistic information by observation of the speaker's facial expressions and gestures as well as lip movements. Speech reading may be used in conjunction with, or as an alternative to, a hearing aid. Poor visual acuity as well as failing short-term memory may impede the acquisition of this skill by some elderly people.

Auditory training

Auditory training attempts to educate the patient to discriminate differing sound stimuli, especially speech sounds, progressing to finer and finer distinctions. The awareness of subtle auditory cues thus developed should always be considered in conjunction with amplification.

As with hearing aid care, the participation of an interested family member provides support for the elderly patient, as well as a memory aid.

Assistive listening devices

Assistive listening devices non-specifically help hearing-impaired people in special circumstances, such as hearing in an auditorium or church, listening to the television or radio with people with normal hearing, or group conversations.

Many public facilities, such as churches and concert halls, provide some type of assistive listening device, either by 'looping' or installing an infrared transmission system. Hearing impaired individuals can 'tune' their hearing aids in to the looping system or can borrow the special receiver for the infrared system. With an infrared system, a hearing-impaired person can hear the television or radio while others present can continue to enjoy normal listening levels. Telecaptioning of television programmes may require a special decoder, although many televisions have this capacity built in.

For conversations in small groups, small easily portable systems, consisting of a microphone, amplifier, and earphone, are available at a modest cost.

Alerting devices, either boosting the alarm signal or using alternative stimuli, such as flashing lights or vibrations, are available to permit the perception of doorbells, alarm clocks, and so on.

General guidelines

Communicating with any hearing-impaired individual can be a frustrating experience for both speaker and listener. A few simple guidelines can help alleviate some of the frustration (Matkin and Hodgson 1982). It is important to be sure that one has captured the listener's attention and that the face of the speaker is well illuminated. The elimination or reduction to an absolute minimum, of any competing noise is essential. Shouting is not necessary; rather, one should speak slowly and clearly, favouring the better ear and maintaining an optimal distance of about 1 m. If a statement is not understood, try an alternative wording, rather than simply repeating the misunderstood phrase.

Conclusion

Although hearing impairment, to a certain extent, is inevitable for many elderly people, there is much that can be done to reduce the impact it has on an individual's ability to communicate. It is the responsibility of every health-care professional who works with elderly people to have a basic understanding of the psychosocial problems that hearing impairment presents and of how to initiate appropriate evaluation and treatment. By keeping elderly people in communication with their world, the aim is to make the later years of life less lonely and frustrating.

References

Brody, H. (1955). Organization of the cerebral cortex. III. A study of ageing in the human cerebral cortex. *Journal of Comparative Neurology*, **102**, 511–56.

Crowe, S.J., Guild, S.T., and Polvogt, L.M. (1934). Observations on the pathology of high tone deafness. *Bulletin of the Johns Hopkins Hospital*, **54**, 315–79.

Etholm, B. and Belal, A.A. Jr (1974). Senile changes in the middle ear joints. *Annals of Otology, Rhinology and Laryngology*, **83**, 49–54.

Gaeth, J. (1948). Study of phonemic regression in relation to hearing loss. Thesis, Northwestern University, Chicago, IL.

Gleeson, M. and Felix, H. (1987). A comparative study of the effect of age on the human cochlea and vestibular neuroepithelia. *Acta Otolaryngologica (Stockholm)*, **436** (Supplement), 103–9.

Gulya, A.J. and Stach, B.A. (1996). Hearing aids: state of the art review. Part II. implantable hearing aids. *Archives of Otolaryngology, Head and Neck Surgery*, **122**, 363–7.

Hansen, C.C. and Reske-Neilsen, E. (1965). Pathological studies in presbyacusis: cochlear and central findings in 12 aged patients. *Archives of Otolaryngology, Head and Neck Surgery*, **82**, 115–32.

Ishii, T., Murakami, Y., Kimura, R.S., and Balogh, K. Jr (1967). Electron microscopic and histochemical identification of lipofuscin in the human inner ear. *Acta Otolaryngologica (Stockholm)*, **64**, 17–29.

Johnsson, L.-G. and Hawkins, J.E. Jr (1977). Age-related degeneration of the inner ear. In *Special senses in ageing: a current biological assessment* (ed. S.S. Han and D.H. Coons), pp. 119–35. University of Michigan Press, Ann Arbor, MI.

Jorgensen, M.B. (1961). Changes of ageing in the inner ear. *Archives of Otolaryngology*, **74**, 164–70.

Kimura, R.S. and Schuknecht, H.F. (1970). The ultrastructure of the human stria vascularis. II. *Acta Otolaryngologica (Stockholm)*, **70**, 301–18.

Kirikae, I., Sato, T., and Shitara, T. (1964). A study of hearing in advanced age. *Laryngoscope*, **74**, 205–20.

Konigsmark, B.W. and Murphy, E.A. (1972). Volume of the ventral cochlear nucleus in man: its relationship to neuronal population and age. *Journal of Neuropathology and Experimental Neurology*, **31**, 304–16.

Matkin, N.D. and Hodgson, W.R. (1982). Amplification and the elderly patient. *Otolaryngology Clinics of North America*, **15**, 371–86.

Mayer, P. (1919–20). Das anatomische Substrat der Altersschwerhörigkeit. *Archiv für klinische und experimentelle Ohren-, Nasen-, und Kehlkopfheilkunde*, **105**, 1–13.

Nadol, J.B. Jr (1979). Electron microscopic findings in presbycousic degeneration of the basal turn of the human cochlea. *Otolaryngology, Head and Neck Surgery*, **87**, 818–36.

Nomura, Y. (1970). Lipidosis of the basilar membrane. *Acta Otolaryngologica (Stockholm)*, **69**, 352–7.

Pauler, M., Schuknecht, H.F., and White, J.A. (1988). Atrophy of the stria vascularis as a cause of sensorineural hearing loss. *Laryngoscope*, **98**, 754–9.

Raafat, S.A., Linthicum, F.H. Jr, and Terr, L.I. (1987). Quantitative study of lipofuscin accumulation in ganglion cells of the cochlea. *Association for Research in Otolaryngology Abstracts*, **10**, 205.

Schuknecht, H.F. (1993). *Pathology of the ear* (2nd edn), pp. 416–37. Lea and Febiger, Philadelphia, PA.

Seidman, M.D., Bai, U., Khan, M.J., et al. (1996). Association of mitochondrial DNA deletions and cochlear pathology: a molecular biologic tool. *Laryngoscope*, **106**, 777–83.

Soucek, S., Michaels, L., and Frohlich, A. (1987). Pathological changes in the organ of Corti in presbyacusis as revealed by microslicing and staining. *Acta Otolaryngologica (Stockholm)*, **426** (Supplement), 93–102.

Stach, B.A. and Gulya, A.J. (1996). Hearing aids: state of the art review. Part I. Conventional hearing devices. *Archives of Otolaryngology, Head and Neck Surgery*, **122**, 227–31.

USDHHS (United States Department of Health and Human Services) (1985). *Vital and health statistics*, Series 10, No. 160. National Center for Health Statistics, Rockville, MD.

Table 2 Representative medical conditions that impair taste or smell sensations

Nervous
Alzheimer's disease
Bell's palsy
Damage to chorda tympani
Epilepsy
Head trauma
Korsakoff's syndrome
Multiple sclerosis
Parkinson's disease
Tumours and lesions

Nutritional
Cancer
Chronic renal failure
Liver disease including cirrhosis
Niacin (vitamin B$_3$) deficiency
Vitamin B$_{12}$ deficiency
Zinc deficiency

Endocrine
Diabetes mellitus
Hypothyroidism

Other
Allergic rhinitis, atopy, and bronchial asthma
Sinusitis and polyposis
Xerostomic conditions including Sjögren's syndrome
Viral infections

detection losses are independent of cognitive status. In Alzheimer's disease, cognitive deficits do not impair the ability to detect odours until fairly advanced stages of the disease. The odour thresholds for older people are between two and 15 times higher than a younger cohort with the losses tending to be uniform across compounds with different structures (Cain and Gent 1991); this is unlike threshold losses for taste where degree of loss tends to be more structure specific. Olfactory losses at threshold (and supra-threshold) levels are exacerbated by malnutrition and wasting (Schiffman and Wedral 1996).

Impairment of supra-threshold odour perception

Supra-threshold functioning of olfaction (Schiffman 1979; Stevens and Cain 1985; Schiffman and Warwick 1991), and the chemaesthetic sense in the nose (e.g. CO_2 which stimulates the trigeminal nerve) (Stevens et al. 1982) are both diminished in older people. Most older individuals have reduced capacity to discriminate the degree of difference between odour qualities when compared with younger individuals (Schiffman 1979; Schiffman and Warwick 1991). The ability to identify odours is especially impaired in healthy older people (Schiffman 1979) but there is heterogeneity among individuals. Older people have reduced ability to identify foods on the basis of smell (and taste) (Schiffman 1979). A study that evaluated performance on an odour identification task found that more than 75 per cent of older people over 80 years of age had major difficulty perceiving and identifying odours. Odour identification is especially impaired in

Alzheimer's disease and in patients with other neurodegenerative diseases (Schiffman et al. 1990).

Aetiology of olfactory losses

There are many reasons for loss of olfaction in older people including normal ageing, diseases, medications, viral insult, cumulated exposure to toxic fumes, and head trauma (see Tables 1 and 2). Perceptual losses parallel anatomical and physiological changes in the structure of the upper airway, the olfactory epithelium, olfactory bulb and nerves, hippocampus and amygdaloid complex, and hypothalamus; these alterations include damage to cells, reduced cell numbers, and diminished levels of neurotransmitters (Schiffman 1983). Anatomical and physiological changes are especially profound in neurodegenerative conditions such as Alzheimer's and Parkinson's diseases (Doty 1991). Post-traumatic olfactory dysfunction is correlated with damage to the olfactory bulbs and tracts and the inferior frontal lobes (Yousem et al. 1996). Medications or environmental toxins that are mitotic inhibitors can cause loss of olfactory function. Age-associated losses in olfactory perception do not appear to be related to reduced odorant responsivity of olfactory receptor neurones as measured by Cs^{2+} imaging techniques (Rawson et al. 1997), but rather to losses in the total number of receptors as well as changes in the levels of neurotransmitters.

Impact of chemosensory losses on food intake, digestion, and immunity

The taste and smell losses that occur in older individuals can contribute to malnutrition and impaired immune status (Schiffman 1992; Schiffman and Warwick 1993; Schiffman and Wedral 1996). When taste and smell perception are compromised, chemosensory signals cannot serve as cues for the metabolic consequences of food ingestion. This can be troublesome for older people in hospital or nursing homes who no longer have control over food choices. Their perceptual losses make it difficult for them to learn associations between the taste and smell sensations of an unfamiliar food and its post-ingestive effects. That is, learning the expected satiation from food and associating it with taste and smell cues is more difficult for older people with reduced chemosensory perception (see Young and Corwin (1997) for data on impaired food intake and body weight regulation in aged rats). Altered chemosensory perception may also contribute to food neophobia (reluctance to try or dislike of the flavour of novel foods) sometimes seen in older patients in hospital. Olfactory decrements may also contribute to losses in the ability to manipulate and swallow food since olfaction is strongly involved in tongue reflex regulation (Mameli et al. 1995).

Clinical evaluation of chemosensory disorders

Clinical evaluation of chemosensory complaints usually includes four steps: (a) medical history, (b) physical examination, (c) psychophysical testing, and (d) medical imaging (Snow et al. 1991). The medical history is important because it provides information about the events associated with the onset of the loss. Some patients can associate their taste and smell losses with use of a new medication, for example, or with a viral infection. However, most older individuals cannot associate their losses with a particular event mainly because the changes have been gradual and progressive over the years. The physical examination generally includes examination of the head (including nasal airways/upper respiratory tract and ears) and neck. Nasal mucous membranes are examined often using a vasoconstrictor to improve visualization. The olfactory epithelium itself is difficult to visualize even with small modern instruments. A neurological examination generally includes a mental status examination, memory testing, and motor and gait evaluation, as well as evaluation of cranial, peripheral, and autonomic nerve functioning. Memory testing is especially important for the diagnosis of Alzheimer's disease while evaluation of motor and gait are helpful for the diagnosis of Parkinson's disease. A variety of quantitative psychophysical tests are generally performed by a chemosensory specialist trained to evaluate patients with taste and smell complaints. These tests include both threshold tests as well as supra-threshold tests that measure the ability to discriminate and identify tastes and smells (Schiffman 1993). Medical imaging of the head is often used to assist in diagnosis when structural causes are suspected in chemosensory loss; however, the results of medical imaging are negative in the majority of cases, in spite of functional losses (Yousem et al. 1996).

Treatment of chemosensory losses in older people—use of flavour enhancement

Age-associated chemosensory decrements are seldom treatable by pharmacological methods (Schiffman 1983), and prognosis for recovery of smell and taste sensations experienced by older people is poor. Dysgeusia caused by medications sometimes remits upon substitution of another drug for a medical condition. Addition of elevated concentrations of flavour can compensate for losses in taste and smell. That is, complaints of hyposmia (but not anosmia), can be reduced by adding simulated food flavours to meats, vegetables, and nutritious foods to amplify the odour intensity. For example, beef can be marinated with beef flavour to amplify its aroma. A variety of other flavours (e.g. cheese or bacon flavour) can be added to soups and vegetables. Simulated flavours are mixtures of odorous compounds that are extracted from natural foods or are synthesized after chemical analysis of the target food. They are comparable in odour intensity to extract of vanilla or concentrated orange juice. Flavours should not irritate the stomach like spices which is important because gastric intolerance to spices is a common complaint in older individuals (Schiffman and Covey 1984). For people with chronic complaints of bitter taste, addition of flavours such as coffee and chocolate to foods or medications can be helpful since these odours are compatible with bitter taste.

Experimental data indicate that amplification of flavour to levels preferred by older people can improve food enjoyment, have a positive effect on food intake, and foster appropriate nutritional intake (Schiffman 1979, 1992; Schiffman and Warwick 1993). When flavours were added to the nutrient-dense food of wasting patients, there was an increase in total intake (Schiffman 1979, 1983, 1992;

Warwick et al. 1993; Schiffman and Wedral 1996). For relatively healthy older people who resided in a retirement home, flavour amplification of food produced increased plasma level of T and B lymphocytes and improved physical strength, but did not alter total dietary intake and other biochemical measures (Schiffman and Warwick 1993).

Interventions in addition to flavour enhancement have been used to increase appetite in people with taste and smell losses. Firstly, providing meals with a variety of tastes and flavours, and then alternating intake of different foods on the plate at a meal, can reduce sensory adaptation or fatigue as well as improve intake (Schiffman 1983; Hetherington 1996). Secondly, ensuring that the temperature of food is high enough is important to increase the concentration of volatile compounds. (However, care must be taken that the food is not too hot since sensitivity to temperature declines with age, predisposing older people to oral damage from boiling foods.) Increasing textural variety, combining creamy, crispy, and chewy foods, can also improve intake. Monosodium glutamate has been reported to increase palatability of foods for older people (Bellisle et al. 1991). Dietary supplementation with vitamins and minerals has been used over the years, but evidence for their effectiveness in enhancing flavour is not compelling (Schiffman 1983).

Although taste and smell perception is impaired in many older individuals, sensory interventions are not always warranted. Many older people are simply not aware of losses of smell that result from ageing (Nordin et al. 1995). Some older people are content with monotonous diets (Rolls 1993). Older people report fewer food aversions probably due to reductions in the sense of smell perception (Schiffman and Covey 1984; Pelchat and LaChaussee 1994). The relative degree of chemosensory loss is not always correlated with the degree of reduction of pleasure obtained from food nor does it predict changes in intake (Drewnowski et al. 1996). Thus psychological factors as well as sensory losses both play a role in the eating behaviour of the older person.

Conclusion

Losses of taste and smell are common in the older population. These not only reduce the pleasure and comfort from food but can contribute to malnutrition and weight loss. In addition, older people with chemosensory losses are more vulnerable to food poisoning or overexposure to environmentally hazardous chemicals which are otherwise detectable by taste and smell. Enhancing food flavours can increase enjoyment of food and improve food intake and immune status.

References

Bartoshuk, L.M., Desnoyers, S., Hudson, C., et al. (1987). Tasting on localised areas. *Annals of the New York Academy of Sciences*, 510, 166–8.

Beauchamp, G.K., Bertino, M., Burke, D., and Engelman, K. (1990). Experimental sodium depletion and salt taste in normal human volunteers. *American Journal of Clinical Nutrition*, 51, 881–9.

Bellisle, F., Monneuse, M.O., Chabert, M., Larue-Achagiotis, C., Lanteaume, M.T., and Louis-Sylvestre, J. (1991). Monosodium glutamate as a palatability enhancer in the European diet. *Physiology and Behaviour*, 49, 869–73.

Booth, D.A. (1985). Food-conditioned eating preferences and aversions with interoceptive elements: conditioned appetites and satieties. *Annals of the New York Academy of Sciences*, 443, 22–41.

Breer, H. (1994). Odour recognition and second messenger signalling in olfactory receptor neurons. *Seminars in Cell Biology*, 5, 25–32.

Cain, W.S. and Gent, J.F. (1991). Olfactory sensitivity: reliability, generality, and association with ageing. *Journal of Experimental Psychology and Human Perception Performance*, 17, 382–91.

Doty, R.L. (1991). Olfactory capacities in ageing and Alzheimer's disease: psychophysical and anatomic consideration. *Annals of the New York Academy of Sciences*, 640, 20–7.

Drenowski, A., Krahn, D.D., Demitrack, M.A., Nairn, K., and Gosnell, B.A. (1995). Naloxone, an opiate blocker, reduces the consumption of sweet high-fat foods in obese and lean female binge eaters. *American Journal of Clinical Nutrition*, 61, 1206–12.

Drenowski, A., Henderson, S.A., Driscoll, A., and Rolls, B.J. (1996). Salt taste perceptions and preferences are unrelated to sodium consumption in healthy older adults. *Journal of the American Dietetic Association*, 96, 471–4.

Duffy, V.B., Backstrand, J.R., and Ferris, A.M. (1995). Olfactory dysfunction and related nutritional risk in free-living elderly women. *Journal of the American Dietetic Association*, 95, 879–84; quiz 885–6.

Friedman, M.I. (1989). Metabolic control of food intake. *Boletin—Asociacon Medica de Puerto Rico*, 81, 111–13.

Gilmore, M.M. and Murphy, C. (1989). Ageing is associated with increased Weber ratios for caffeine, but not for sucrose. *Perception Psychophysics*, 46, 555–9.

Hetherington, M.M. (1996). Sensory-specific satiety and its importance in meal termination. *Neuroscience and Biobehaviour Review*, 20, 113–17.

Höfer, D., Puschel, B., and Dreckhahn, D. (1996). Taste receptor-like cells in the rat gut identified by expression of alpha-gustducin. *Proceedings of the National Academy of Sciencess of the United States of America*, 93, 6631–4.

Kasper, J. (1982). *Prescribed medicines: use, expenditures, and sources of payment*. National Health Care Expenditures Study Data Preview 9. DHHS No. (PHS) 82-3320. National Center for Health Services Research, Hyattsville, MD.

Kettenmann, B., Hummel, C., Stefan, H., and Kobal, G. (1996). Multichannel magnetoencephalographical recordings: separation of cortical responses to different chemical stimulation in man. *Electroencephalographic Clinics and Neurophysiology*, 46 (Supplement), 271–4.

Kinnamon, S.C. and Margolskee, R.F. (1996). Mechanisms of taste transduction. *Current Opinions in Neurobiology*, 6, 506–13.

Lewis, I.K., Hanlon, J.T., Hobbins, M.J., and Beck, J.D. (1993). Use of medications with potential oral adverse drug reactions in community-dwelling elderly. *Special Care in Dentistry*, 13, 171–6.

Mameli, O., Melis, F., Caria, M.A., et al. (1995). Olfactory influence on tongue activity. *Archives of Italian Biology*, 133, 273–88.

Mattes, R.D. and Cowart, B.J. (1994). Dietary assessment of patients with chemosensory disorders. *Journal of the American Dietetic Association*, 94, 50–6.

Mistretta, C.M. (1984). Ageing effects on anatomy and neurophysiology of taste and smell. *Gerodontology*, 3, 131–6.

Mori, I. and Yoshihara, Y. (1995). Molecular recognition and olfactory processing in the mammalian olfactory system. *Progess in Neurobiology*, 45, 585–619.

Murphy, C. (1993). Nutrition and chemosensory perception in the elderly. *Critical Review of Food Science and Nutrition*, 33, 3–15.

Nordin, S., Monsch, A.U., and Murphy, C. (1995). Unawareness of smell loss in normal ageing and Alzheimer's disease: discrepancy between self-reported and diagnosed smell sensitivity. *Journal of Gerontology B*, 50, P187–92.

Pelchat, M. and LaChaussee, J.L. (1994). Food cravings and taste aversions in the elderly. *Appetite*, 23, 193.

Physicians' Desk Reference (49th edn) (1995). Medical Economics, Des Moines, IA.

Rawson, N.E., Gomez, G., Cowart, B., Lowry, L.D., Pribitkin, E.A., and Restrepo, D. (1997). Cell biology of human olfaction: changes with age. Presented at the Society for the Study of Ingestive Behaviour Annual Meeting, 16–20 July 1997. Johns Hopkins University, Baltimore, MD.

Rolls, B.J. (1993). Appetite, hunger, and satiety in the elderly. *Critical Review of Food Science and Nutrition*, 33, 39–44.

Schiffman, S. (1979). Changes in taste and smell with age: psychophysical aspects. In *Sensory systems and communications in the elderly*. Vol. 10, *Ageing* (ed. J.M. Ordy and K. Brizzee), pp. 227–46. Raven Press, New York.

Schiffman, S.S. (1983). Taste and smell in disease. *New England Journal of Medicine*, 308, 1275–9, 1337–43.

Schiffman, S.S. (1991). Drugs influencing taste and smell perception. In *Smell and taste in health and disease* (ed. T.V. Getchell, R.L. Doty, L.M. Bartoshuk, and J.B. Snow), pp. 845–50. Raven Press, New York.

Schiffman, S.S. (1992). Food acceptability and nutritional status: considerations for the ageing population in the 21st century. In *For a better nutrition in the 21st century* (ed. P. Leathwood, M. Horisberger, and W.P.T. James), pp. 149–62, Vol. 27. Nestlé Nutrition Workshop Series. Raven Press, New York.

Schiffman, S.S. (1993). Perception of taste and smell in elderly persons. *Critical Review of Food Science and Nutrition*, 33, 17–26.

Schiffman, S.S. (1994). The role of taste and smell in appetite and satiety: impact of chemosensory changes due to ageing and drug interactions. In *Nutrition in a sustainable environment* (ed. M.L. Wahlqvist, A.S. Truswell, R. Smith, and P.J. Nestell), pp. 728–31. Smith-Gordon, London.

Schiffman, S.S. and Covey, E. (1984). Changes in taste and smell with age: nutritional aspects. In *Nutrition in gerontology* (ed. J.M. Ordy, D. Harman, and R. Alfin-Slater), pp. 43–64. Raven Press, New York.

Schiffman, S.S. and Erickson, R.P. (1993). Psychophysics: insights into transduction mechanisms and neural coding. In *Mechanisms of taste transduction* (ed. S.A. Simon and S.D. Roper), pp. 395–424. CRC Press, Boca Raton, FL.

Schiffman, S.S. and Warwick, Z.S. (1991). Changes in taste and smell over the lifespan: effects on appetite and nutrition in the elderly. In *Chemical senses*. Vol. 4, *Appetite and nutrition* (ed. M.I. Friedman, M.G. Tordoff, and M.R. Kare), pp. 341–65. Marcel Dekker, New York.

Schiffman, S.S. and Warwick, Z.S. (1992). The biology of taste and food intake. In *The science of food regulation: food intake, taste, nutrient partitioning, and energy expenditure* (ed. G.A. Brayand and D.H. Ryan), Vol. 2, pp. 293–311. Pennington Center Nutrition Series. Louisiana State University Press, Baton Rouge, LA.

Schiffman, S.S. and Warwick, Z.S. (1993). Effect of flavour enhancement of foods for the elderly on nutritional status: food intake, biochemical indices and anthropometric measures. *Physiology and Behaviour*, 53, 395–402.

Schiffman, S.S. and Wedral, E. (1996). Contribution of taste and smell losses to the wasting syndrome. *Age and Nutrition*, 7, 106–20.

Schiffman, S.S., Lindley, M.G., Clark, T.B., and Makino, C. (1981). Molecular mechanism of sweet taste: relationship of hydrogen bonding to taste sensitivity for both young and elderly. *Neurobiology of Aging*, 2, 173–85.

Schiffman, S.S., Clark, C.M., and Warwick, Z.S. (1990). Gustatory and olfactory dysfunction in dementia: not specific to Alzheimer's disease. *Neurobiology of Aging*, 11, 597–600.

Schiffman, S.S., Graham, B.G., Vance, A.R., Gaillard, K., Warwick, Z.S., and Erickson, R.P. (1992). Detection thresholds for emulsified oils in young and elderly subjects. *Chemical Senses*, 17, 693.

Scott, T.R. (1992). Taste: the neural basis of body wisdom. *World Review of Nutrition and Diet*, **67**, 1–39.

Scott, T.R., Yan, J., and Rolls, E.T. (1995). Brian mechanisms of satiety and taste in macaques. *Neurobiology*, **3**, 281–92.

Snow, J.B., Jr, Doty, R.L., and Bartoshuk, L.M. (1991). Clinical evaluation of olfactory and gustatory disorders. In *Smell and taste in health and disease* (ed. T.V. Getchell, R.L. Doty, L.M. Bartoshuk, and J.B. Snow Jr), pp. 463–7. Raven Press, New York.

Spielman, A.I., Huque, T., Whitney, G., and Brand, J.G. (1992). The diversity of bitter taste signal transduction mechanisms. *Society of General Physiologists Series*, **47**, 307–24.

Stevens, J.C. and Cain, W.S. (1985). Age-related deficiency in the perceived strength of six odorants. *Chemical Senses*, **10**, 517–29.

Stevens, J.C., Plantinga, A., and Cain, W.S. (1982). Reduction of odour and nasal pungency associated with ageing. *Neurobiology of Aging*, **3**, 125–32.

Sullivan, S.L., Ressler, K.J., and Buck, L.B. (1994). Odorant receptor diversity and patterned gene expression in the mammalian olfactory epithelium. *Progress in Clinical Biological Research*, **390**, 75–84.

Tuorila, H., Hellemann, U., and Matuswewska, I. (1990). Can sodium contents of foods be reduced by adding flavours? Studies with beef broth. *Physiology and Behaviour*, **47**, 709–12.

Van Buskirk, R.L. and Erickson, R.P. (1977). Odorant responses in taste neurons of the rat NTS. *Brain Research*, **135**, 287–303.

Warwick, Z.S. and Schiffman, S.S. (1991). Flavour–calorie relationships: effect on weight gain in rats. *Physiology and Behaviour*, **50**, 465–70.

Warwick, Z.S., Hall, W.G., Pappas, T.N., and Schiffman, S.S. (1993). Taste and smell sensations enhance the satiating effect of both a high-carbohydrate and a high-fat meal in humans. *Physiology and Behaviour*, **53**, 553–63.

Young, M. and Corwin, R. (1997). Impaired food intake and body weight regulation in aged rates. Presented at the Society for the Study of Ingestive Behaviour Annual Meeting, 16–20 July 1997. Johns Hopkins University, Baltimore, MD.

Yousem, D.M., Geckle, R.J., Bilker, W.B., McKeown, D.A., and Doty, R.L. (1996). Post-traumatic olfactory dysfunction: MR and clinical evaluation. *American Journal of Neuroradiology*, **17**, 1171–9.

18.18 Memory and ageing

Lars Bäckman, Brent J. Small, and Maria Larsson

Introduction

A common opinion in society is that memory functioning deteriorates as one becomes older. This belief is articulated not least by elderly persons themselves (Dixon and Hultsch 1983). The purpose of this chapter is to review the scientific underpinnings of this belief. The review is principally focused on the way in which the normal ageing process affects different forms of memory. In addition, prominent theoretical views attempting to account for age-associated changes in memory performance will be highlighted, and salient individual-difference variables that are related to memory proficiency in old age are discussed. Finally, current attempts to improve memory functioning in old age through various types of intervention procedures are discussed.

A recurrent debate in cognitive psychology during the last decades has been whether human memory should be conceptualized in terms of systems or processes (Nyberg and Tulving 1996; Shanks 1997). In brief, proponents of the memory systems view argue that memory may be divided into several different, but interrelated, systems. One example of this orientation is the framework developed by Tulving and associates (Tulving 1993). In this framework, five forms of memory are distinguished:

(1) procedural memory, which refers to memory for skills and procedures;

(2) perceptual representation system, which is involved in the identification of objects and underlies the phenomenon of perceptual priming;

(3) semantic memory, which concerns acquisition and use of general knowledge;

(4) short-term memory, which involves retrieval of information from consciousness;

(5) episodic memory, which refers to memory for personal events encoded in a particular temporal–spatial context.

This ordering of systems corresponds to their presumed developmental sequence in both a phylogenetic and an ontogenetic sense; procedural memory is conceived of as the earliest system to develop and episodic memory the latest. The ordering also reflects the assumed relations among the systems; many operations of subsequently evolved systems are assumed to be dependent on and supported by the operations of earlier systems, whereas earlier systems can operate essentially independently of the later ones.

Empirical evidence in favour of the memory-systems view involves studies that have found that one form of memory (e.g. episodic) may be grossly impaired in various clinical populations (such as amnesics), although other forms of memory (e.g. semantic, short-term) are relatively well preserved (Nyberg and Tulving 1996). Other evidence supporting this perspective includes dissociations between different experimental variables (such as retention interval, repetition) and forms of memory (e.g. episodic memory versus priming) (Nyberg and Tulving 1996).

Another way of subdividing human memory is the distinction between explicit and implicit memory (Graf and Schacter 1985). In this view, explicit memory (e.g. episodic memory) involves conscious recollection of information, whereas implicit memory (e.g. priming) does not require deliberate retrieval of the study episode.

By contrast, advocates of the process-oriented view (Blaxton 1989) maintain that dissociations of the above kind may be explained by the different processes that individuals engage in while performing different memory tasks (such as data-driven processing versus conceptually driven processing; conscious recollection versus familiarity). Other important points made by proponents of this view are that (a) the degree to which the cognitive operations carried out during encoding match those engaged in during retrieval is a major factor in accounting for patterns of memory performance in normal and impaired populations (Blaxton 1992), and (b) different forms of memory are not 'process pure', in the sense that they draw on separate cognitive operations (Jacoby et al. 1993).

As is true with the systems view, the process view is supported by a wealth of data, and it may be difficult, if not impossible, to conduct the critical experiment that would adequately discriminate between the two positions. The literature is full of studies in which the empirical outcome can, in fact, be handled by both views. Moreover, it may be argued that whether human memory should be conceptualized in terms of systems or processes is not the most productive question. This is because processes, by necessity, need to operate within a particular structure and, at the same time, a memory system without processes would not seem to serve any adaptive purpose.

With these issues in mind, the current chapter is organized in terms of the classificatory scheme for memory systems devised by Tulving and colleagues (Tulving 1993). However, the review of how different memory systems are affected by the ageing process will be supplemented with a discussion of the influence of human ageing on various memorial processes.

Memory systems

Procedural memory

Procedural memory is a form of memory underlying acquisition of skills and other aspects of knowledge that are not directly accessible to consciousness and whose presence can only be demonstrated indirectly by action (e.g. walking, skating). Procedural memory may have appeared early in evolution and is shared in various forms by most living organisms (Tulving 1993). It involves the acquisition of motor, perceptual, or cognitive operations that occur gradually as a function of practice. Unlike semantic and episodic information that can be acquired quickly, acquisition of most procedural skills occurs slowly. At an early point, the acquisition of any skill poses demands on other types of memory, but practice will transfer the performance of the skill to procedural memory (e.g. learning to drive, learning to type). In contrast to other types of knowledge, procedural knowledge is little influenced by the passage of time, which is reflected in the fact that we may adequately perform skills that we have not done in years.

Perhaps the best evidence for the unique features of procedural memory comes from studies of patients with the amnesic syndrome who exhibit severe impairment in explicit memory tasks. Yet these patients show generally preserved procedural knowledge, and also procedural learning in the absence of any conscious recollection of its previous occurrence (Nyberg and Tulving 1996).

The literature is very sparse with regard to the relationship between different categories of procedural learning and ageing, although it is commonly held that procedural memory is largely unaffected by age, particularly when contrasted against explicit memory (Light and La Voie 1993). However, evidence is somewhat mixed as to whether ageing affects procedural memory negatively, and there are indications that age differences may vary as a function of the complexity of the task. Age deficits have been reported in partial word identification (Hashtroudi et al. 1991), the pursuit rotor task (Ruch 1934), and in learning to read inverted sentences (Moscovitch et al. 1986).

However, Hashtroudi et al. (1991) demonstrated that age differences were present only when stimuli were presented at a short presentation rate or at a high degree of degradation. Age-associated deficits in visual acuity and basic visual processing (Lindenberger and Baltes 1994) may partly underlie the observed deterioration in skill learning with advancing age. Evidence in favour of the robustness of skill acquisition in old age was recently reported by Schugens et al. (1997). In this study, perceptual skill acquisition within the context of a mirror reading task was unaffected by age, whereas explicit recall of verbal and visual materials declined steadily with increasing age.

Further research is needed in order to obtain a more precise picture of the effects of age on various aspects of procedural memory. One reason for the mixed evidence may be differences among studies with regard to the requirement of strategies, which may draw on cognitive abilities other than procedural memory (e.g. semantic memory, visuospatial skill, and reasoning).

Perceptual representation system

In recent years, there has been a great deal of interest among memory researchers for the phenomenon of priming (Graf and Masson 1993). In part, this interest has been sparked by findings indicating that measures of priming can behave very differently from standard explicit tests of memory such as recall and recognition. As is true with procedural memory, amnesics who show little evidence of conscious memory when tested by recall and recognition, typically perform at normal or near-normal levels on tests of priming (Nyberg and Tulving 1996).

Priming tests can be categorized into those involving mainly perceptual processes or conceptual processes. In perceptually based tests, the emphasis is on the physical characteristics of the items. For example, in word-stem completion, subjects are required to complete a word stem (e.g. TRU—) with the first word that comes to mind. Prior presentation of a valid completion (e.g. truck) for a stem enhances the probability of its generation, implying a form of memory for the initial presentation. By contrast, conceptually based tests rely on the semantic meaning of the study items. For example, in a fact completion test, subjects may be presented with factual knowledge questions (for example, 'What small vessel supplies oxygen and nutrients to cell tissue?'). Prior presentation of the answer to such questions (i.e. 'capillaries') increases the likelihood of the question being answered successfully. The facilitation of task performance in these tests is called priming.

The general pattern of age differences in priming is one of small advantages in favour of younger adults. Often, these differences are not reliable (Russo and Parkin 1993), but in some studies they are statistically significant (Hultsch *et al.* 1991). In a recent meta-analysis of the literature, LaVoie and Light (1994) evaluated age differences on a number of perceptually based priming tests, and concluded that there were small, but statistically reliable age differences in this class of tests. However, several studies using conceptually based priming tests reveal no age differences in performance (Isingrini *et al.* 1995).

Two recent studies further complicate attempts to characterize age differences in perceptually or conceptually based priming tests as favouring one group or another. Small *et al.* (1995) reported age deficits in a perceptually based task (word-stem completion), but not in a conceptually based task (fact completion). In contrast, Jelicic *et al.* (1996) found age deficits in a conceptual task (category production) but not in a perceptual task (word-fragment completion). In general, the likelihood of obtaining significant age differences in these tests probably reflects the interaction between processes invoked at study and the method by which memory is assessed at retrieval. Systematic research, using perceptually and conceptually based priming tests, should clarify the existence of age differences on these measures. However, irrespective of whether age differences are statistically reliable or not, the group differences that are present in these tasks are much smaller than those observed with explicit tests of memory.

Although the work on age differences in implicit tests of memory is informative, it has also been criticized for being susceptible to contamination by explicit memory processes (Jacoby 1991). For example, age differences could be observed on implicit memory tasks because the younger group of adults may use their superior explicit memory to improve performance. In response to this dilemma, Jacoby (1991) devised the process dissociation procedure to separate the relative contributions of automatic (implicit) and consciously controlled (explicit) processes. Using this methodology, the influences of automatic and conscious processes are put in opposition in order to derive unbiased estimates of performance. In one such study, Jennings and Jacoby (1993) reported no age differences in automatic influences of memory for younger and older adults, which contrasted against reliable age differences for the consciously controlled processes.

Another method by which the influence of conscious and unconscious memory processes have been contrasted is the know–remember paradigm (Gardiner and Parkin 1990). In this case, at retrieval, individuals are asked to describe whether they consciously remember (R) having seen an item before, or they do not have a specific remembrance of the item but know (K) that it was presented earlier. These two responses are assumed to reflect the influence of conscious and unconscious retrieval processes, respectively. Several studies have reported that, in contrast to large age deficits in the R component, the ability to retrieve memories linked to K responses is relatively well preserved across the adult lifespan (Parkin and Walter 1992).

Taken together, irrespective of whether automatic influences of memory are measured by priming tests, or by more sophisticated methodologies such as the process dissociation procedure and the know/remember paradigm, it is clear that the age differences in performance which exist here are much smaller than those evident from explicit tests of memory, such as recall and recognition.

Semantic memory

Semantic memory or generic memory refers to our general knowledge of the world. It encompasses meanings about words, concepts, and symbols, their associations as well as rules for manipulating these concepts and symbols (Tulving 1993). The information in semantic memory is stored without reference to the temporal and spatial context present at the time of its storage. Semantic memory also involves knowledge about one's own memory proficiency and one's own memory processes. This aspect of semantic memory has been termed metamemory (Flavell and Wellman 1977).

In general, age differences in semantic memory tasks tend to be highly selective and often negligible. This is illustrated in a number of studies which indicate an increase in vocabulary and general knowledge from youth to middle age, and only slight declines from middle age to older ages (Bäckman and Nilsson 1996). There is also evidence that older people are equally proficient as young people in the metamemorial skill of knowing what they know and what they do not know (Lachman *et al.* 1979).

The most studied component of semantic memory is what has been referred to as the internal lexicon or mental dictionary. The internal lexicon is thought of as consisting of a network of nodes that represents words, concepts, and associations between different representations (Collins and Loftus 1975). It is assumed that the information is organized hierarchically, following a top-to-bottom structure. The superordinate category (e.g. fruit) is represented at the top of the hierarchy, its more specific attributes (e.g. yellow, sour) are located further down the hierarchy, followed by lower-order categories (e.g. banana, lemon).

Several lines of evidence suggest that the organization and associative structure of the internal lexicon remain stable across the adult lifespan (Laver and Burke 1993). For example, young and older adults do not differ in the types of word associations emitted (Burke and Peters 1986), and access categorical information alike (Balota and Duchek 1988). Furthermore, Howard *et al.* (1986) reported similar semantic priming effects across age in a lexical decision task. In this task, subjects have to decide whether a string of letters makes up a meaningful word or not. Both young and old adults showed priming, but differed in that young subjects showed priming at shorter latencies (150 ms), whereas elderly subjects required half a second or more in order to show priming. This outcome suggests that the semantic network is intact, but that lexical access may be slower in old age. Small or non-existent age differences have also been reported in other tasks assessing semantic memory, including object descriptions (Stine 1986) and release from proactive inhibition (Puglisi 1980).

However, not all aspects of semantic memory are immune to the ageing process. In addition to lexical slowing, older adults have been found to exhibit more temporary blockages of lexical information than do younger subjects. This phenomenon is illustrated by difficulties among older adults in remembering proper names (Crook and West 1990), in generating items in tests of verbal fluency (Bäckman and Nilsson 1996), and in a reduced ability to name common objects as recorded by the Boston Naming Test (Albert *et al.* 1988).

In sum, the available evidence suggests that it is unlikely that age deficits in accessing semantic memory information are related to a true loss of representations of the names or words, given the stability, or even performance increments, observed in priming and vocabulary tests across the adult lifespan. Rather, age deficits in retrieving semantic information may be related to problems in accessing lexical information rapidly (Howard *et al.* 1986; Albert *et al.* 1988). In addition, age decrements in semantic memory appear to be most likely to occur when the task is highly effortful.

Short-term memory

Short-term memory can be divided into two components: primary memory and working memory. Both types of memory are indices of short-term memory, because the to-be-remembered items reside in consciousness. Where they differ concerns whether additional processing operations are performed on the to-be-remembered information. Specifically, items in primary memory are maintained passively, whereas items in working memory are manipulated in some fashion (Baddeley 1986). The Digit Span Test of the Wechsler Adult Intelligence Scale can be used to provide an example of this distinction. Forward digit span requires individuals to recall a series of digits in the same order as they were presented. Thus subjects need only to rehearse the items relatively passively, and this task represents a measure of primary memory. By contrast, backward digit span requires that subjects recall a series of digits in the reverse order of that in which they were presented. Thus, not only do individuals have to remember the items, they also have to manipulate them. Specifically, they have to reverse the items based on the original input format, in order to produce them in the correct order, and hence, we can consider this task to be an index of working memory.

Evidence regarding the existence of age-associated performance decrements in primary memory is somewhat mixed. For example, there is research showing that primary memory abilities decline across the adult lifespan (Botwinick and Storandt 1974). In contrast, other authors have contended that the ability to store information temporarily in a relatively untransformed fashion is not affected by the ageing process (Craik and Rabinowitz 1984). Methodological variations may account for differences between studies as to whether age differences in primary memory are statistically reliable or not. Nevertheless, the ability to maintain information in an untransformed manner is a skill that is relatively well preserved across the adult lifespan.

Although the existence of relatively small age differences in primary memory is under some debate, there is an overwhelming consensus that when the material is to be manipulated in some way, there are substantial age differences in functioning. Examples of working memory tasks used in this research include word and computation span (Salthouse and Babcock 1991) and reading span (Hultsch et al. 1990). Moreover, several reports have indicated that, as the complexity of working memory tasks increases, so does the magnitude of age differences in performance (Craik and Rabinowitz 1984).

Some research has attempted to isolate the source of age differences in working memory. Salthouse and Babcock (1991) divided working memory into three components: storage, processing, and executive function. They concluded that deficits in the processing component of the tasks was the prime source of age differences in functioning.

In the future, working memory will continue to be a very important concept in cognitive research, because its role is seen as crucial in many everyday tasks. For example, as discussed below, the role of working memory in age differences in other varieties of memory (e.g. episodic) is a topic that has received considerable empirical attention. Studies directed at isolating the source of age differences in performance, as well as determining whether working memory is a general resource or is represented by a number of specific abilities, will be helpful in understanding the source of age deficits in functioning.

Episodic memory

Episodic memory involves retrieval of information that is acquired in a particular place at a particular time (Tulving 1993). In the laboratory, episodic memory is typically assessed by having subjects recall or recognize information encountered in the experimental setting (e.g. lists of words, pictures of faces). This is the form of memory that has been examined most systematically in cognitive ageing research over the years. Generally, it is also clear that the magnitude of age-associated performance differences is greater in episodic memory tasks compared with tasks assessing other forms of memory (Craik and Jennings 1992).

The sensitivity of episodic memory to ageing is interesting to view in light of the fact that numerous other more or less severe conditions (e.g. ischaemia, hypoxia, Korsakoff's syndrome, depression, alcohol intoxication, sleep deprivation) have negative repercussions for episodic memory functioning, while leaving other varieties of memory intact, or at least less affected. The vulnerability of episodic memory may reflect that this form of memory evolved late phylogenetically and also evolves late ontogenetically (Tulving 1993). Episodic memory draws on a widespread network of brain structures, including the hippocampal formation and related cortical structures, diencephalon, anterior cingulate gyrus, precuneus, prefrontal cortex, and cerebellum (Nyberg and Tulving 1996; Bäckman et al. 1997; Cabeza et al. 1997), possibly because of its advanced nature, evolutionally as well as ontogenetically. Thus the susceptibility of episodic memory to ageing and other conditions may result from the fact that changes at multiple sites in a large distributed network are capable of disrupting performance.

In research on ageing and episodic memory, a popular research strategy has been to manipulate one or several variables experimentally, the purpose being to identify processes that are more or less affected by ageing. Often this strategy has involved manipulations of the level of cognitive support provided to the subject. Cognitive support refers to aspects of the task conditions that may facilitate encoding and subsequent retrieval of information. For example, objects are richer in terms of the features available for encoding than words, and hence offer a more supportive encoding environment. Relatedly, instructions to organize a semantically related word list provide more guidance for encoding than merely providing intentional learning instructions. As a final example, providing cues at the time of memory testing (e.g. category cues, copy cues) increases the retrieval support relative to free-recall conditions.

An interesting finding from research in which the degree of cognitive support has been manipulated in episodic memory tasks is that older adults may benefit more than young adults as task conditions become more supportive. Results conforming to this pattern have been obtained manipulating variables such as encoding cues, context relatedness, number of input modalities, spatial organization, item richness, and retrieval cues (Bäckman 1989; Bäckman et al. 1990). Interaction patterns like those described above can be viewed from two different perspectives. Firstly, they suggest that older adults are able to use compensatory task conditions for remembering, whereby age-associated memory deficits may be attenuated. Secondly, an analysis of the processing requirements involved in the less supportive conditions in which age differences are magnified, may help delineate age-sensitive cognitive operations. Along these lines it has been suggested that age-associated deficits in recoding (Bäckman 1989) and distinctiveness of encoding (Mäntylä and Bäckman 1990) may underlie age decrements in episodic remembering.

However, other evidence indicates that the pattern of disproportionate increases of memory performance in old age from the provision of cognitive support may represent only a special case in a complicated interaction sphere involving various subject-related and external factors that jointly determine the size of age-associated deficits in episodic memory (Bäckman *et al*. 1990; Craik and Jennings 1992). For example, there is now compelling evidence that the most common outcome in research varying the degree of cognitive support across the lifespan is one of parallel gains from support in early and late adulthood (Rabinowitz and Craik 1986; Cohen *et al*. 1987; Johnson *et al*. 1989; Bäckman 1991; Larsson and Bäckman 1993). Finally, there is evidence that young adults, under certain conditions, may profit more than older adults from cognitive support in memory tasks (Craik and Rabinowitz 1985; Kliegl *et al*. 1989), suggesting decreases in cognitive reserve capacity with advancing age.

Thus, although there is some evidence that ageing may affect certain memorial processes selectively (e.g. recoding, distinctiveness of encoding), the bulk of research suggests that the age-associated episodic memory deficit is global. Illustrative evidence for this point comes from research indicating that the deficit applies across a variety of materials (Cohen *et al*. 1987; Bäckman 1991), sensory modalities (Bäckman 1986; Larsson and Bäckman 1998), and retrieval conditions (White and Cunningham 1982; Craik *et al*. 1987). In addition, the size of the age-associated episodic memory deficit appears to be equally large in traditional laboratory-based tasks (e.g. word recall, paired-associate learning) and tasks that approximate more closely to the memory demands of everyday life (e.g. face recognition, text recall) (Bäckman *et al*. 1990).

The research on episodic memory and ageing reviewed hitherto has involved retrospective memory for content information. In recent years, there has been increasing interest in two related, but different, aspects of episodic memory, namely memory for future actions or prospective memory, and memory for the context in which the information was acquired or source memory. Relevant research addressing the effects of ageing on these forms of memory are discussed below.

Prospective memory

Prospective memory failures (e.g. to forget to take medicine or to pay the rent) have obvious repercussions in everyday life. The upsurge of interest in examining the influence of ageing on prospective memory seen in the last few years may have been prompted, in part, by some initial findings indicating small or non-existent age differences in prospective memory. Such results were documented employing both laboratory-based (Einstein and McDaniel 1990) and naturalistic (Dobbs and Rule 1987) tasks. Indeed, if the effects of ageing on prospective memory is minimal, this may suggest that the real-life implications of growing older for memory functioning would be less debilitating than previously thought. However, more recent laboratory-based as well as real-life studies have revealed clear age-associated impairments in prospective memory (Maylor 1993; Mäntylä 1994; Einstein *et al*. 1995)

An interesting observation is that the size of age differences in prospective memory may be greater for some tasks than for others. For example, it appears that older adults may do as well as young adults in remembering future actions when they can rely on external reminders, but not when internal reminding has to be used (Maylor 1990). In a related vein, there is some evidence that age-associated deficits may be more easily observed in time-based (e.g. remembering to call the doctor next Monday) compared with event-based (e.g.

remembering to tell your daughter to read a particular book the next time you meet her) prospective memory tasks (Einstein and McDaniel 1990; Einstein *et al*. 1995).

However, some research indicates that ageing may also negatively influence performance in event-based tasks (Maylor 1993; Mäntylä 1994). Conceivably, the crucial factor is not whether the task is time based or event based, but rather the requirement of self-initiated monitoring and retrieval operations. Typically, an event-based task involves some form of external event that cues retrieval, whereas time-based tasks require more self-initiated processing for successful performance.

Varying the demands of self-initiation in an event-based task, Mäntylä (1994) found that the magnitude of age differences increased with increasing demands of self-initiation. This result, together with findings that age differences in prospective memory are generally larger in time-based than in event-based tasks, suggests an interesting similarity between prospective and retrospective remembering across the adult lifespan. For both types of episodic memory, the degree of self-initiation required for successful performance appears to be related to the size of age-associated performance deficits (Craik and Jennings 1992; Mäntylä 1994).

Source memory

Trying to remember who told us something or in which newspaper we read a news item are examples of source memory tasks. Some of our memories are externally derived, i.e. experienced and encoded by our senses, and may include information that we have heard other people say, events that we have witnessed, or acts we have performed. Other memories originate from internal sources and may be generated from our imaginations, dreams, plans, and so on (Johnson *et al*. 1993). Thus, in current conceptualizations of source memory, the term source refers to the specific conditions that were present when a certain memory was acquired (for example, the temporal, spatial, and social context of the event, or the modality through which it was perceived). Although testing of episodic memory has traditionally involved item information, recollection of source would appear to be at the heart of episodic memory (i.e. recollection of information acquired in a particular place at a particular time) (Tulving 1993).

Principally, three types of source monitoring discriminations can be made (Johnson *et al*. 1993). The first type, the process of distinguishing between internally generated and externally derived information in memory (e.g. to discriminate between fantasy and perceived experiences), has been referred to as reality monitoring. The second type is related to discriminations between internally generated memories (internal source monitoring; for example discriminating one's thoughts from what one says). The third type is related to discriminations between externally derived sources (external source monitoring; for example discriminating statements made by one person from statements made by another).

Older adults are typically less able than younger adults to specify the sources of events (Hashtroudi *et al*. 1989; Spencer and Raz 1994), but there is some evidence suggesting that the magnitude of the age deficit depends on the type of source monitoring task a person confronts. Hashtroudi *et al*. (1989) showed that older adults were particularly impaired in external and internal source monitoring decisions, but performed as well as the younger subjects in reality monitoring decisions.

A number of studies indicate that older adults have more difficulties than younger adults in discriminating between sources of externally derived information, such as the sex of the presenter (Kausler and Puckett 1981), the colour of the materials (Park and Puglisi 1985), or the input modality (Larsson and Bäckman 1998). Interestingly, Ferguson et al. (1992) showed that the rate of source confusions in elderly subjects increased as a function of increasing perceptual similarity. In that study, older adults had difficulty with source monitoring when perceptual cues were similar, i.e. when the source was one of two women. However, this age deficit was overcome when perceptual cues were made more distinctive, in this case when the information was presented by a man or a woman. This outcome not only indicates that older adults have more difficulties than younger adults in encoding perceptual cues to discriminate between sources, but also that age-associated differences can be ameliorated or exacerbated by varying the similarity between sources.

A further issue of interest is whether source memory is selectively impaired in ageing relative to item memory. Most studies addressing this issue report disproportionate age differences when recollection of source is required (Hashtroudi et al. 1989; Ferguson et al. 1992; Schacter et al. 1994).

It is important to note that, even though source memory may be selectively affected by ageing, item and source memory may not draw on qualitatively different processes. Johnson et al. (1993) argued that different memory tasks require different degrees of differentiation such that, for example, a recognition task requires less perceptual and cognitive differentiation than a source monitoring task. Empirical evidence in favour of this view comes from research indicating that source decisions require more processing time than recognition decisions (Johnson et al. 1993). This suggests that source monitoring processes incorporate and require more complete and differentiated information than item recognition processes. Thus the finding of a selective age deficit in source memory may reflect the fact that older adults have greater problems than the young in integrating perceptual features with target information at encoding, and in reconstructing this source information and its association with target information at retrieval (Schacter et al. 1994).

Theoretical accounts

A number of theoretical accounts for these deficits have been proposed because to account for age-associated deficits in episodic memory functioning. For the present discussion, the explanatory models are divided into three types: (a) speed of processing, (b) working memory capacity, and (c) inhibitory functioning.

One hypothesis that has received considerable empirical attention focuses on whether age-associated differences in memory are due to a reduction in the speed with which information is processed in the cognitive system (Salthouse 1991). Support for this contention comes from research indicating that controlling for speed of processing greatly reduces the age-associated variation in several cognitive tasks (Salthouse 1991; Park et al. 1996). However, significant age-associated decrements in performance typically exist after statistical control of processing speed (Hultsch et al. 1990; Bryan and Luszcz 1996). Thus, although speed may account for a sizeable portion of the age-associated variance in cognitive performance, it does not explain all of the age-associated variation.

A hypothesis that has also received a great deal of attention concerns the role of working memory as a predictor of episodic memory performance. In this view, age differences in episodic memory functioning can be linked to the capacity of working memory declining with age. Similar to the research on speed of processing, statistical control of working memory results in the attenuation of the age-associated variation in functioning (Morrell and Park 1993). However, it is often the fact that a reliable portion of age-associated variance in the criterion variable still remains that is independent of working memory functioning.

Another theoretical account of age deficits in memory functioning focuses on a specific aspect of working memory functioning. Hasher and Zacks (1988) proposed that older adults have poorer inhibitory control abilities, resulting in irrelevant information entering working memory and compromising retrieval. Evidence for this view has come from several sources. For example, Hartman and Hasher (1991) reported that performance in older adults on implicit tests of memory was similar for words that were irrelevant to the task as compared to relevant words. In contrast, younger adults showed implicit memory only for those words that were relevant to task performance. They interpreted these results as indicating that older adults had implicit memory for both types of words because they had difficulty in inhibiting the task-irrelevant information. However, support for this hypothesis has been equivocal, with other studies finding no evidence for age-associated deficits in inhibitory mechanisms (Stine and Wingfield 1994). Moreover, concerns have surfaced recently over the reliability of tasks used to measure this construct (Park et al. 1996).

Taken together, it is clear from this brief review that no single theoretical account can adequately describe all of the age differences that appear in human episodic memory functioning. However, the search for such an explanatory 'holy grail' may be an endeavour that is doomed to fail. Given the inherent complexity of the subject matter in question, it may be more reasonable to borrow from a number of theoretical accounts in order to explain the age-associated variation in memory performance. Furthermore, because studies focusing on memory in old age exhibit considerable variability with regard to sample selection, participant composition, as well as criterion tasks, perhaps we should focus on overall patterns of results across studies, rather than dismissing an account based on a minority of discrepant findings.

Individual differences

The use of variables such as processing speed, working memory, and inhibition to account for age differences in memory performance can be subsumed under a larger domain of enquiry that seeks to identify additional individual-difference predictors of memory performance. The individual-difference perspective has been a very useful heuristic method and has resulted in the explication of several potential sources of variation in complex memory tasks. Furthermore, this domain can be subdivided to include those variables that are related to age differences in performance, and those that contribute to the performance in memory tasks independent of age.

Age-associated individual-difference predictors of memory

Other attempts to account for age-associated variation in memory functioning have focused on additional cognitive factors that may be related to performance. Hultsch *et al.* (1990) reported that measures associated with verbal ability and general knowledge accounted for significant portions of the age-associated variance in word and text recall that were independent of processing speed and working memory. Moreover, after the influence of these variables was accounted for, the effect of age on word recall was no longer statistically reliable.

Researchers have also examined the role of physical health in memory functioning. It is entirely reasonable to expect a relationship between health and cognition given that increased age is associated with impairments of health (Elias *et al.* 1990). Hultsch *et al.* (1993) found that 10 per cent of the age-associated variance in story recall was accounted for by differences in self-reported health. In addition, interest has focused on the role that environmental complexity, such as activity lifestyle, has on cognitive functioning. Hultsch *et al.* (1993) reported that lifestyle factors accounted for 26 per cent of the age-associated variance in word recall, and 54 per cent of the variance in text recall. Similarly, Hill *et al.* (1995) found that not only was social activity related to overall episodic memory functioning in old age, but it was also associated with the ability to benefit from cognitive support for remembering.

Perhaps the most interesting non-cognitive predictors of cognitive performance in recent years are measures associated with sensory functioning (e.g. hearing and vision). Lindenberger and Baltes (1994) reported that over 90 per cent of the age-associated variance in intellectual performance in samples of very old adults was accounted for by individual differences in vision and hearing. Extending these results to adults with a greater range of ages (18–80 years) Salthouse *et al.* (1996) found similar relationships between visual acuity and cognitive functioning. These results have led investigators to posit a 'common cause' explanation for the observed predictive relationships. In this hypothesis, there is a common cause that is related to age-associated variance in cognitive measures, and also to variance in more basic biological parameters such as vision and hearing. Although this hypothesis may be consistent with the data patterns that are observed, the theoretical value of such a hypothesis may be somewhat questionable. Future research will need to explore what this common factor actually represents and may benefit from the inclusion of brain-based indices (e.g. morphological parameters, cerebral blood flow, receptor density).

General individual-difference predictors of memory

Although several individual-difference factors are associated with age-associated variance in memory functioning, other factors contribute variance to the criterion measures independent of the influence of age. This section describes a number of memory-relevant factors that apply across the adult lifespan, including demographic characteristics, biological parameters, and genetic factors.

Demographic characteristics such as sex (Herlitz *et al.* 1997) have been found to be related to episodic memory functioning, whereby women outperform men on these tests. Social, hormonal, and evolutionary factors have been proposed to account for the female advantage in episodic memory (Herlitz *et al.* 1997). Another demographic characteristic that exerts a strong influence on memory performance is years of formal education. Numerous studies have reported a positive influence of education on memory functioning in old age (Inouye *et al.* 1993); this effect may be linked to a variety of factors, including genetic selection, neuronal growth during critical periods in life, cognitive stimulation in the work place, physical health, and use of memory strategies (Hill *et al.* 1995).

Another class of general individual-difference variables are measures of biological functioning. How variations in self-reported physical health can account for age-associated variations in memory performance are discussed above; these variations are also related to memory functioning independent of age (Hultsch *et al.* 1993). In addition, the role of several vitamins in episodic memory functioning has recently been identified. For example, Wahlin *et al.* (1996) examined the influence of vitamin B_{12} and folic acid on memory functioning. They found that older people who had low levels of folic acid (less than 11 nmol/l) as well as those with low levels of vitamin B_{12} (less than 200 pmol/l) and folic acid performed more poorly on tests of free recall than individuals whose vitamin status was not compromised. A similar predictive relationship between thyroid-stimulating hormone and episodic memory in old age has recently been discovered (Wahlin *et al.* 1998).

A final class of variables that has been found to be related to episodic memory functioning independent of age are genetic factors. For example, a number of studies have attempted to identify the role of hereditary factors versus environmental factors in cognitive functioning, by examining twin pairs who are monozygotic or dizygotic. In one study, Finkel *et al.* (1995) compared the heritability of memory functioning in two samples of twins from Minnesota or Sweden. They reported that the average heritability estimate for a general memory factor ranged between 49 and 60 per cent across the two countries. Thus genotypic variation may contribute strongly to individual differences in memory functioning.

Additional evidence for a link between genotype and memory comes from studies that have examined the influence of specific genes on cognitive performance. For example, there has been a great deal of interest in recent years in the gene coding for apolipoprotein, a plasma protein involved in the transportation of cholesterol. The gene coding for apolipoprotein is located on the long arm of chromosome 19 and has three alleles, ε2, ε3, and ε4 (Wahley 1988). There is growing consensus that the presence of the ε4 variant of apolipoprotein is associated with an increased risk of developing Alzheimer's disease (Strittmatter *et al.* 1993). However, relatively little is known about this gene in terms of its role in cognitive performance of non-demented adults. For example, are individuals with the ε4 allele not only susceptible for developing Alzheimer's disease, but are they somehow genetically inferior in terms of their overall cognitive functioning as well? The evidence regarding this relationship suggests slight decrements in cognitive performance among non-demented individuals with the ε4 allele (Bondi *et al.* 1995). In a recent study, Small *et al.* (1998) examined this relationship and found no apolipoprotein-related differences in baseline memory functioning. However, longitudinal differences were observed, whereby the ε4 group declined at a more rapid rate on some memory measures than those with other alleles. These differences might be related to a greater representation of individuals in a preclinical phase of dementia in the ε4 group, rather than to apolipoprotein-related memory changes in normal ageing.

Brain imaging

Cognitive accounts of age deficits in memory are extremely valuable in enhancing our understanding of how the ageing process affects memory

lobe. The behavioural consequences of the other neurotransmitter deficiencies are not well defined.

All individuals with Down syndrome develop pathological evidence of Alzheimer's disease if they live past 35 years of age. Clinical evidence of dementia is evident in perhaps half of Down subjects at this age. The neuropathological and neurochemical features of Alzheimer's disease are identical in people with or without Down syndrome. Triplication of the amyloid precursor protein gene on chromosome 21 in Down syndrome leads, by an as yet unknown mechanism, to overexpression of amyloid precursor protein and increased levels of Aβ and amyloid deposition (Rumble et al. 1989).

Vascular dementia

A second common cause of dementia in Western countries is vascular dementia which is responsible for up to 15 to 20 per cent of cases. In another 10 to 15 per cent of cases, vascular dementia is found in coexistence with Alzheimer's disease. Until recently the term 'vascular dementia' was often used synonymously with 'multi-infarct dementia'. However, there are many different causes of vascular dementia and the reader is referred elsewhere for a more formal review (Amar and Wilcock 1996). In addition to multiple areas of infarction vascular dementia can also be associated with single strategically placed infarcts, and white matter ischaemia (also known as leukoaraiosis).

The infarctions that characterize vascular dementia may be superficial or deep, small or large, and many involve large, intermediate, or small vessels. Strokes that are associated with this state are generally bilateral. Small infarctions, called lacunae (2 to 15 mm in diameter) may be distributed throughout the basal ganglia, internal capsule, and corona radiata and are associated with vascular lipohyalinosis, hypertension, and dementia (lacunar state). Clinical features associated with multi-infarct dementia include abrupt onset, history of strokes, focal symptoms and signs, stepwise deterioration, fluctuating courses, and history of hypertension. These symptoms and signs form the Hachinski ischaemia scale (Hachinksi et al. 1975). Patients with Alzheimer's disease, without evidence of cerebral infarction, generally do not show these symptoms.

One form of vascular dementia with severe incomplete infarction of deep white matter has been known as Binswanger's disease (subcortical arteriosclerotic encephalopathy). In Binswanger's disease, dementia is often accompanied by gait disturbance and pseudobulbar palsy (emotional incontinence, dysarthria, facial weakness). The identity of Binswanger's disease as a separate entity is becoming less clear as the role of leukoaraiosis is increasingly investigated. This shows up on CT and magnetic resonance imaging (MRI) scans as areas, usually in the periventricular region, of low attenuation (i.e. white matter rarefaction) similar to Binswanger changes. Binswanger's disease was originally considered to be uncommon but the advent of brain scanning has shown that this rarefaction of the white matter occurs much more frequently than was previously realized, in up to 10 per cent of normal elderly subjects and possibly even as many as 30 per cent at the age of 85 years. It was originally a pathological rather than a clinical diagnosis. White matter changes on neuroimaging are linked to advancing age and hypertension, but a consistent pattern of clinicopathological correlation has been difficult to define. Pathologically it is characterized by demyelination and reactive gliosis accompanied by arteriosclerotic changes, increased Virchow–Robin spaces, and hyalinization or fibrosis of the walls of small penetrating arteries or arterioles. Binswanger's disease may occur without hypertension in a familial form called cerebral autosomal dominant arteriopathy with subcortical infarcts and leukoencephalopathy (CADASIL), which has been linked to a gene on chromosome 19 (Fig. 1).

The distribution and severity of white matter changes is to some extent reflected in the clinical findings on neuropsychological assessment when it occurs in conjunction with Alzheimer's disease (Amar et al. 1996a), suggesting that it may be an entity in its own right, even perhaps representing the occurrence of coincidental Alzheimer's disease and vascular pathology.

The presence of vascular dementia should lead to an assessment of vascular risk factors, including those usually associated with cerebrovascular disease, for example hypertension, heart disease, diabetes mellitus, carotid vessel disease, abnormal serum lipids, and smoking. Less commonly other factors should be sought, for example where there is a clinical indication or a relevant family history. These include arteritides and coagulation abnormalities although they are less frequently relevant in older people.

The diagnosis of vascular dementia is often made with the assistance of the Hachinski Ischaemia Scale (Hachinski 1975) but its poor inter-rater reliability (O'Neill et al. 1995) and other practical issues have led to attempts to improve upon it and more recently two newer scales have been proposed. These are the State of California Alzheimer's Disease Diagnostic and Treatment Centres (ADDTC) criteria and the NINDS-AIREN criteria (Chui et al. 1992; Roman et al. 1993). They require the presence of dementia and cerebrovascular disease, and a relationship between the two, for example the onset of dementia shortly after a stroke. These criteria are a step forward, and there is evidence suggesting that the ADDTC criteria in particular may be more sensitive than the Hachinski scale (Amar et al. 1996b).

The mainstay of treatment centres on managing the underlying risk factors where these are detected. In many older people this may seem like shutting the stable door after the horse has bolted, but it is nevertheless important as it may be possible to reduce further vascular damage. There are in addition newer strategies under evaluation, including the use of neuroprotective mechanisms to block postischaemic damage from excitatory amino acids. If successful, these will be complementary to existing therapeutic approaches rather than a replacement for them.

Lewy body dementia and dementia in Parkinson's disease

Although dementia is found in 25 to 40 per cent of patients with Parkinson's disease a considerably more frequent dementia in elderly people is that known as Lewy body dementia. This is not Parkinson's disease with dementia, but a different entity that shares some common features with Alzheimer's disease, for example diffuse or neuritic plaques and similar neurotransmitter deficits. It differs from Parkinson's disease as the Lewy bodies usually affect, initially at least, predominantly cortical structures. Some regard this as a Lewy body variant of Alzheimer's disease, but many consider it a dementia in its own right, comparable in frequency with vascular dementia. It is part of a spectrum of dementias associated with Lewy bodies and, despite the nosological debate, deserves careful consideration at a clinical level.

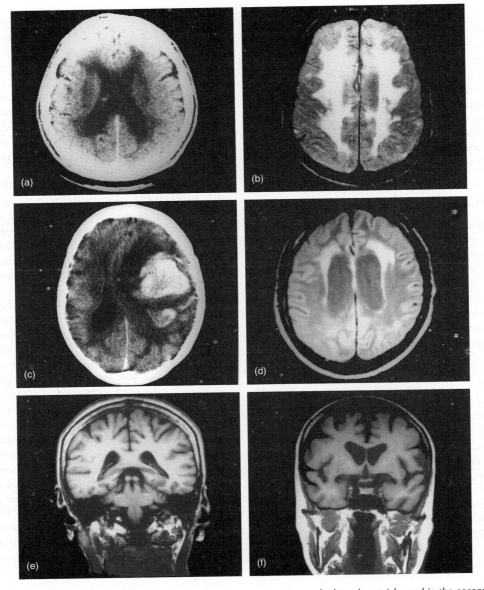

Fig. 1 CT and MRI images in dementing illnesses. (a) Severe white matter lucency anterior to the lateral ventricles and in the corona radiata (CT scan), reflected in the abnormal darkness of the deep white matter, in a case of CADASIL. (b) CADASIL: severe white matter hyperintense lesions on MRI which are deep and confluent in vascular dementia. (c) Large fatal intracerebral haemorrhage in a patient with severe cerebral amyloid angiopathy and mild Alzheimer's disease. (d) Preoperative MRI images showing periventricular increased signal in a case of normal pressure hydrocephalus (marked improvement found after shunting). (e) Progressive supranuclear palsy. Note severe atrophy of the midbrain. (f) Atrophy of the head of the caudate nuclei in Huntington's disease.

It usually presents as a dementia rather than a movement disorder although extrapyramidal features frequently develop as the disease progresses. Early and prominent neuropsychological abnormalities include attentional deficits and problem-solving and visuospatial difficulties. Early features also include fluctuation in cognitive function, persistent well-formed visual hallucinations, and the spontaneous motor features of parkinsonism already mentioned. These and other features have been incorporated into consensus guidelines following an international workshop which also considered the pathological diagnosis (McKeith *et al.* 1996). Many patients with this condition are extremely sensitive to phenothiazines which can precipitate severe

extrapyramidal signs or even the potentially fatal neuroleptic malignant syndrome. The cholinergic deficit which this condition shares with Alzheimer's disease is leading to the evaluation of similar cholinergic strategies to those now available for treating Alzheimer's disease but the outcome of these trials is awaited.

In Parkinson's disease significant cognitive impairment usually occurs later in the course of the illness, although there are features that overlap with the Lewy body dementias and also, to a lesser extent, Alzheimer's disease. Neuronal loss is seen in the dopaminergic substantia nigra pars compacta and ventral mesencephalic tegmentum, the cholinergic basal forebrain, the noradrenergic locus ceruleus, and the serotonergic dorsal raphe nucleus. Dementia in Parkinson's disease is associated with cell loss in these important projection systems, without intrinsic pathology in the cortex. In a proportion of cases of Parkinson's disease there may be the concurrent presence of Alzheimer's disease. Conversely, features of parkinsonism (bradykinesia, rigidity, masked facies) may also be found in some patients with Alzheimer's disease, usually in the later stages.

Creutzfeldt–Jakob disease

Creutzfeldt–Jakob disease is a rare form of dementing illness found throughout the world which occurs with an incidence of approximately one in 1 million per year. It is characterized by a very rapid course, usually with death occurring within 1 year of onset. It occurs relatively infrequently in older people when the course may be less aggressive than is usually seen in younger subjects. Five to ten per cent of all cases of Creutzfeldt–Jakob disease are familial.

Most patients have associated neurological deficits in addition to marked dementia, and there may be a prodromal illness which is often rather non-specific in nature. These additional features include weakness, spasticity, abnormal movements, myoclonus, seizures, and occasionally, fasciculation. Myoclonus is found in more than 80 per cent of patients and is often associated with characteristic abnormalities on the electroencephalogram tracing. Electroencephalography reveals periodic sharp wave complexes appearing synchronously at regular intervals, often with burst suppression.

The diagnosis of the disease is usually apparent because of the rapid course and abnormal electroencephalogram. Findings on CT or MRI do not differ significantly from the abnormalities seen in Alzheimer's disease or healthy ageing.

Creutzfeldt–Jakob disease is known to be caused by an unusual transmissible agent that is similar to the agent of a disease found in New Guinea called kuru, and also to scrapie, a disease of sheep and goats. These conditions are transmitted only by direct contact with brain or other infected tissue. The brain contains small vacuoles in the neuropil, producing a spongiform encephalopathy. The responsible agent is called a prion, which stands for 'proteinaceous infectious agent'. It is believed to have no nucleic acid, and the fundamental event is thought to be a dramatic conformational change in the prion protein (Telling et al. 1996).

Several instances of iatrogenic transmission of the disease have been reported. These have occurred through dural grafts, corneal transplants, contaminated electroencephalograph depth electrodes, and therapeutic use of human growth hormone derived from human pituitary glands postmortem. There is no effective treatment for the condition, although the associated seizure disorder and myoclonic abnormalities may be amenable to symptomatic medication.

An epidemic of an infection very similar to other prion-related diseases is occurring in cattle in the United Kingdom, although it is now on the wane. It is believed that this infection (bovine spongiform encephalopathy or mad cow disease) was spread through the use of cattle feed containing material from scrapie-infected sheep. The recent recognition of a new variant of Creutzfeldt–Jakob disease in younger people in the United Kingdom supports the hypothesis that the infection can spread from cows to humans. Many believe that it is reasonable to avoid eating beef products from areas where bovine spongiform encephalopathy is endemic.

The treatable dementias

The treatable dementias are a large and multifaceted group of illnesses. Many of the treatable dementias are clinically identical or very similar to Alzheimer's disease. It is estimated that as many as 10 to 20 per cent of all cases of dementia are due to potentially treatable illnesses. Clarfield (1988) has concluded from a review (chiefly of studies done in referral centres) that 11 per cent of patients with dementia had illnesses that partially or fully reversed with treatment. The true incidence of treatable dementia in the community may actually be higher but to some extent depends upon the definition. For example, when does a condition induced by medication or an infection become a dementia rather than being described as a 'toxic or acute confusional state' or 'delirium'? Prompt recognition and appropriate treatment for these conditions is of great importance, because delays in treatment can produce death or permanent disability. Conditions causing treatable dementia are listed in Table 2.

Toxic states, most often due to drug effects, are the most common cause of treatable dementia. The overall incidence of adverse drug reaction in patients in the older age groups is two to three times that found in young adults (Montamat et al. 1989). Older patients have numerous features that make them more sensitive than younger people to the toxic effects of drugs on the central nervous system: polypharmacy, poor compliance, greater severity of disease, reduced blood volume, reduced lean body mass, diminished renal clearance, decreased cardiac output, lowered hepatic metabolism, poor nutritional status, and neuronal loss. For example, diazepam and nitrazepam have prolonged action in older patients because of an increased volume of distribution of these lipid-soluble agents and possibly because of increased penetration into, or diminished clearance from, the brain. Furthermore, older patients are especially sensitive to cognitive impairment induced by psychoactive and other drugs with anticholinergic properties.

Cardiovascular disorders may cause dementia by causing chronic global impairment of cerebral blood flow (e.g. congestive heart failure, cardiomyopathy) or multiple episodes of acute impairment of the cerebral circulation (e.g. endocarditis, cardiogenic embolization). Disorders of any organ system can cause dementia by interfering with the metabolic homoeostasis of the brain. Particularly important systemic disorders that may cause dementia include hypothyroidism, Cushing's disease, liver failure, uraemia, pulmonary insufficiency, anaemia, pellagra, hypoglycaemia, disorders of calcium metabolism (in particular hyperparathyroidism), and vitamin B_{12} deficiency.

Depression is a common illness among the older age groups. It is associated with cognitive loss in many cases, and mental impairment may be the initial complaint. Depression may be masked, without subjective recognition of depressed affect. Vegetative signs of depression (e.g. anorexia, weight loss, sleep disturbances), anhedonia, and past history of depressive illness may assist in recognition of the diagnosis. Depressed patients with cognitive impairment are usually quite vocal in their complaints concerning their problems. Hypomanic patients may also perform poorly on psychometric tests because of distractibility and restlessness. The dementia of depression has been referred to as 'pseudodementia' but this term is not appropriate as the cognitive insufficiency of these patients is real, and not an artefact of their affective state. Depression with dementia is a treatable condition, with good response to antidepressant medication in many cases. However, Alzheimer's disease or another dementia may also

Table 2 The treatable[a] dementias

Cardiovascular disorders
Cardiac disorders
Multi-infarct dementia
Vasculitis
Subarachnoid haemorrhage (late effects)
Delayed effects of radiation
Vascular malformation

Systemic and metabolic disorders
Thyroid, parathyroid, pituitary, adrenal, liver, pulmonary, kidney, or blood
    disorders
Sarcoidosis
Porphyria
Systemic lupus erythematosus
Fluid and electrolyte abnormalities
Hypoglycaemia
Nutritional deficiency (vitamin B_{12}, thiamine, niacin)
Diabetes mellitus (hypoglycaemia, ketosis)
Hyperlipidaemia

Toxic disorders
Drugs
Alcohol
Industrial agents
Pollutants
Metals (arsenic, thallium, lead, bismuth, magnesium, manganese, aluminium,
    mercury)
Carbon monoxide

Affective disorders
Depression

Trauma
Subdural haematoma, hygroma

Seizure disorders

Infectious disorders
Meningitis
Encephalitis (including HIV infection and Lyme borreliosis)
Brain abscess
Syphilis
Whipple's disease

Neoplastic disorders
Direct and indirect effects of primary and metastatic tumours

Hydrocephalus
'Normal' pressure hydrocephalus
Obstructive hydrocephalus (aqueductal stenosis)

Genetic diseases
Wilson's disease
Cerebrotendinous xanthomatosis

Hysteria

Sensory deprivation

[a] All these disorders are considered to be treatable because there is the potential for slowing the rate of disease progression or reversing the behavioural deficit. For example, in multi-infarct dementia, control of the risk factors for stroke may slow the progress of the disease. While many of these disorders produce dementia in only a minority of patients, they are all capable of producing the dementia syndrome.

present with coexisting depression, and conversely cases of depression with cognitive impairment at times go on to develop Alzheimer's disease (for more detailed discussion of depression see Chapter 20.1). Alzheimer patients with depression may have improved performance after treatment with antidepressants, although the dementia will remain. Wherever possible, tricyclic antidepressants should be avoided as they may worsen the patient's memory impairment because of their anticholinergic effects.

Alcohol can produce dementia by many mechanisms: head trauma, anoxia, ischaemic infarction, hepatic encephalopathy, malnutrition, and direct toxic effects. Neuronal loss in the Wernicke–Korsakoff syndrome may include the basal forebrain and locus caeruleus. Wernicke's encephalopathy is an important and often unrecognized cause of cognitive impairment. All debilitated alcoholic patients given intravenous fluids should receive parenteral thiamine upon admission.

In older patients, chronic subdural haematoma may develop without a clear history of trauma. Dementia may be present in patients with subdural haematoma without marked disorders of consciousness or signs of increased intracranial pressure. Recurrent complex partial seizures can mimic dementia, and are suggested by a history of olfactory hallucinations or other episodic disturbances. Meningitis caused by fungi or the tubercle bacillus can also cause treatable dementia.

In the United States, HIV infection (AIDS–dementia complex) is the most common cause of dementia among young adults in some urban areas. AIDS–dementia can also occur in older people, especially in homosexual men. AIDS–dementia complex may be clinically similar to Alzheimer's disease, and is suggested by a history of blood transfusion, drug addiction, or sexual activity with partners infected with the virus. However, it rarely develops *de novo*, and in most cases there is pre-existing evidence of an HIV-related illness.

Chronic meningoencephalitis, for example caused by infection with the tick-borne organism *Borrelia burgdorferi* (Lyme borreliosis), may also cause dementia, at times with cerebrospinal fluid pleocytosis and lesions of the deep cerebral white matter on MRI. Dementia is also caused by the direct and indirect effects of neoplasms. Space-occupying lesions (such as meningioma of the olfactory groove, colloid cyst of the third ventricle) can present with dementia. Dementia also occurs as a remote effect of systemic malignancy (e.g. hypercalcaemia, 'limbic encephalitis').

So-called normal-pressure hydrocephalus is another uncommon cause of treatable dementia (Petersen *et al.* 1985). In normal-pressure hydrocephalus there is a disturbance of circulation of the cerebrospinal fluid with hydrocephalus and normal fluid pressure on lumbar puncture but an episodically elevated pressure is found on monitoring intracranial pressure. Neuroimaging shows large ventricles in the disease with or without cortical atrophy, often with white matter intense lesions on MRI (see Fig. 1). The disorder is suggested by the clinical triad of dementia, gait disturbance (without an obvious underlying cause such as signs of an upper motor neurone lesion indicating cerebrovascular disease), and urinary incontinence presenting early in the course of the illness. It may develop as a late complication of intracranial bleeding from trauma or rupture of an aneurysm, or as a complication of intracranial infection. It may also develop idiopathically. In normal-pressure hydrocephalus, placement of a shunt diverting the flow of cerebrospinal fluid from normal channels may cause resolution of the dementia.

Other dementias

There are many other causes of dementia in older people, but they occur less frequently than those described in this chapter. Some will be familiar to the reader (e.g. Huntington's disease) and others will be less well known (see Fig. 1). As it is beyond the scope of this chapter to describe these in detail, the reader is referred to alternative texts, for example Burns and Levy (1994), when necessary.

Case evaluation and differential diagnosis

Patients with dementia require a comprehensive evaluation of the social, psychological, medical, psychiatric, and neurological factors that contribute to the observed decline. It is not possible to evaluate a case of dementia properly without viewing the patient in the context of his or her lifestyle and family environment. It is essential to include the family in interviews with patients suspected of having dementia, as the loss of insight that is frequently seen in dementia may obscure important aspects of the clinical picture. Separate interviews with patients alone, and family members alone, may also be of value. The history should provide a view of the cognitive deterioration. Of particular importance is information concerning hobbies and occupation, because of the opportunity to learn about the effects of the disease on the patient's performance and to uncover possible toxic exposures. The drug history is also crucial, as older patients are often taking many medications, sometimes with incorrect dosing.

General physical examination is important for systemic illnesses that may affect cognitive function. The examination is designed to uncover signs and symptoms of systemic illness, and toxic or metabolic states. In particular, evidence of the adverse effects of drugs should be ascertained, including urinary retention, syncope, falls, postural hypotension, dyskinesias, extrapyramidal dysfunction, and sedation.

The neurological and psychiatric examinations focus on the patient's mental status and evidence of disturbance in awareness, orientation, insight, general behaviour, general information, memory, language function (spontaneous speech, repetition, comprehension, naming of object parts), praxis, visuospatial function, topographical orientation, problem-solving ability, judgement, calculations, and affect (including vegetative signs of depression). The presence of hallucinations, illusions, and delusional beliefs should be investigated. It is helpful to retain copies of the patient's actual performance (e.g. clock drawing) in order to facilitate comparisons at a later date. In this regard it is also crucial to undertake standardized tests for the quantitation of the cognitive deficit, such as the Mini-Mental State Examination (Folstein et al. 1975) although these should be interpreted carefully.

Formal neuropsychological testing is often helpful in the evaluation of performance abilities. However, neuropsychological testing does not replace the mental status examination, which should be made by the doctor. The remainder of the neurological examination evaluates other possible evidence of involvement of the central or peripheral nervous system that may be of diagnostic importance (e.g. fundoscopy, ocular motility, other motor abilities, distal superficial and deep sensibility, Babinski signs, gait, carotid bruits).

Laboratory tests necessary in the evaluation of demented patients include complete blood count, erythrocyte sedimentation rate, serum electrolytes, vitamin B_{12} and folate, liver enzymes, syphilis serology, and thyroid function tests. Many doctors would also consider urinalysis, chest radiograph, and ECG important, and at the very least these should be arranged whenever there is any evidence that they are clinically indicated.

CT (without contrast) or MRI of the brain is desirable. Brain imaging, although not available everywhere, is a crucial step in excluding the presence of brain tumours or other space-occupying lesions and should always be undertaken when clinically indicated. On MRI, findings of severe, diffuse, deep lesions of white matter, with or without other evidence of cerebral infarction, are helpful in suggesting the diagnosis of vascular dementia. Either X-ray CT or MRI, without contrast infusion, are adequate for the evaluation of most patients with dementia. Ideally brain imaging should be undertaken in all cases, regardless of clinical features or history, because evidence of intracranial mass lesions may be masked in slow growing lesions. Where it is not routinely available there should be clear guidelines as to when it should be arranged.

Electroencephalography is also helpful in grading the severity of the encephalopathy. The tracing is often normal or only mildly impaired in Alzheimer's disease, while it is usually markedly disturbed in toxic or metabolic disorders, and usually has characteristic changes in Creutzfeldt–Jakob disease. Electroencephalogaphy is not indicated in all cases of dementia.

Genotyping for apoE is of great interest in research studies of Alzheimer's disease. However, the clinical value of apoE genotyping is controversial (Growdon 1999). As many as 50 per cent of cases of Alzheimer's disease do not have any copies of apoE ε4, and many people with one or two doses of apoE ε4 may live to advanced ages and not get the disease (Lendon et al. 1997). Patients with vascular dementia also have an increased frequency of the apoE ε4 genotype (Slooter et al. 1997) and this has also been reported in Lewy body dementia (St Clair et al. 1994). If apoE genotyping is provided it should be linked to pre- and post-test counselling, education, and psychosocial support (NIA 1996).

Tests of cerebrospinal fluid are indicated in the evaluation of patients who have atypical illness or are suspected of having infectious conditions. These tests should include cerebrospinal fluid total protein and glucose assays, cell count, syphilis serology, culture, and fungal antigen tests, when indicated. A cerebrospinal fluid protein associated with Creutzfeldt–Jakob disease may also be assessed. Lumbar puncture is not necessary in all cases.

The diagnostic process in dementia should focus on uncovering potentially treatable causes for the patient's illness. As Alzheimer's disease is currently a diagnosis of exclusion, it is not possible to rely on any specific abnormality to secure the diagnosis: it can only be concluded that a patient has the disease after the tests listed above have failed to demonstrate the presence of other illnesses that could be responsible for the dementing process. Cases with unusual features, such as incontinence in early disease, should raise suspicions that alternative disease processes are present. The term 'definite Alzheimer's disease' is reserved for those cases with histological evidence of the diagnosis provided by biopsy or autopsy (McKhann et al. 1984). 'Probable Alzheimer's disease' is used in those cases where there is no evidence of other illness that could account for the impairment, and in the presence of dementia with a typically progressive course. 'Possible Alzheimer's disease' is used when there are variations in the course, onset, or clinical features of the disease, or when a second

Table 3 Basic principles of geriatric psychopharmacology

Use low doses, especially initially
Watch out for drug interactions
Do not use drugs with long-term complications (such as major tranquillizers) unless absolutely necessary
Try behavioural methods before prescribing drugs with serious side-effects
Always obtain a history from family members, as well as from the patient, when evaluating complaints and responses to drugs
Beware of inaccurate compliance
Side-effects are more severe in older patients. Be on guard for them
Use side-effects to advantage (e.g. trazodone is a sedating antidepressant which helps patients who cannot sleep)
Avoid drugs with anticholinergic effects, especially for patients with cognitive impairment
Review treatment regimens regularly. Drugs which have beneficial effects may no longer be needed at a later date
Check compliance at every visit by asking open-ended questions regarding what medications the patient is taking. Check the labels and contents of drug vials
Ask patients about over-the-counter medications and home remedies
Use treatment appropriate for the situation. Do not try to make behaviour conform to an ideal standard

systemic or brain disorder is present which could be responsible for the illness but is not considered to be the cause. The diagnostic accuracy in cases of probable Alzheimer's disease is in the region of 90 per cent.

The diagnosis of vascular dementia is suggested by a score of 7 or more on the Hachinski scale, or by the use of one of the more recent protocols mentioned above, and by the presence of prominent lesions in white matter or multiple infarctions on CT or MRI. While the Hachinski and other scales are helpful in patient evaluation, they alone should not be relied upon to make the diagnosis of vascular dementia. A careful history and examination are essential and will serve as a context within which to assess the results obtained from the scales.

Follow-up is often helpful in detecting the presence of dementing illnesses other than Alzheimer's disease. It should be understood that it is crucial to recognize the treatable dementing illnesses, even though the likelihood of their presence in an individual case of dementia is small. It is a grave error to miss the diagnosis of a potentially treatable process or a treatable comorbid condition.

Treatment and management

Currently there is no treatment that can reverse the effects of Alzheimer's disease or vascular dementia on memory or cognition. Trials of treatment with choline, lecithin, physostigmine, and related compounds has failed to provide evidence for sustained significant therapeutic effects in patients with Alzheimer's disease. So-called nootropic agents with effects on cerebral blood flow and metabolism have also been found to be of no significant benefit to patients with Alzheimer's disease, vascular dementia, or related illnesses.

The acetylcholinesterase inhibitors tetrahydroaminoacridine (tacrine), donepezil, and rivastigmine increase effective concentrations of acetylcholine through blocking acetylcholinesterase and have been demonstrated to have modest effects in improving function in up to

40 per cent of patients with mild or moderate Alzheimer's disease. Improvement equivalent to perhaps 6 to 12 months of disease progression has been reported (Knapp et al. 1994; Burns et al. 1999). Tetrahydroaminoacridine is poorly tolerated and is no longer indicated. Many other agents are being evaluated for possible therapeutic value, including oestrogen, newer acetylcholinesterase inhibitors, prednisone, non-steroidal anti-inflammatory drugs, and growth factors. Vitamin E is an effective antioxidant which may have some beneficial effects in Alzheimer's disease in high doses (2000 IU/day) (Sano et al. 1997). Intensive work is underway around the world to develop agents which will alter the important processes of amyloid β protein production, aggregation, and metabolism, and to reduce the diversion of tau into neurofibrillary tangle production. The recent development of lines of transgenic mice expressing the mutations found in Alzheimer's disease should enhance the development of drugs for this condition.

Despite the absence of curative therapy at present, there are many clinical features of dementing illnesses that can benefit from appropriate non-pharmacological as well as pharmacological interventions. Among the most important aspects of care for these people, which family members as well as the professional staff of institutions must learn, are initially to adapt the approach to the previous, established preferences and routines of the patient. A regular familiar daily routine is most important, together with learning which responses may ease the individual's tensions. Often snacks, or a stroll, or other diversions, can be quite effective. At times the cautious use of drugs may be indicated to help treat otherwise uncontrollable agitation and hostility, depression, and sleep disturbances. It is important to use psychoactive agents in small dosages, as demented patients, especially those with Lewy body dementia, are sensitive to unwanted central nervous system effects of the drugs. In addition, drugs with anticholinergic activities should be used cautiously, in order to avoid deleterious effects upon primary memory and cognitive function.

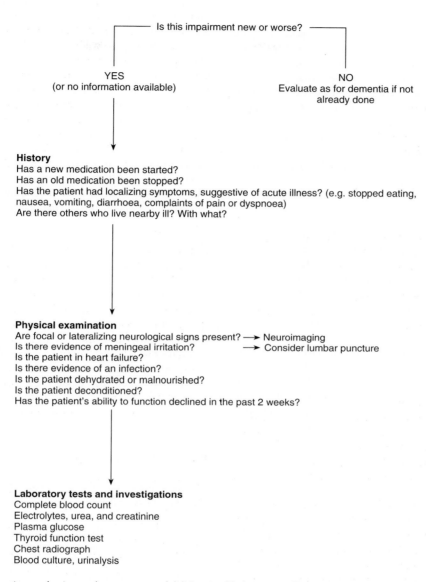

Does the patient appear confused or vague?
Has the patient been labelled as a 'poor historian', 'gomer', or 'social admission'?
Has someone said, in the absence of focal signs or neuroimaging, that the patient 'must have had a stroke'?
Document cognitive impairment (e.g. Mini-Mental State Examination, Abbreviated Mental Test)

Is this impairment new or worse?

YES
(or no information available)

NO
Evaluate as for dementia if not already done

History
Has a new medication been started?
Has an old medication been stopped?
Has the patient had localizing symptoms, suggestive of acute illness? (e.g. stopped eating, nausea, vomiting, diarrhoea, complaints of pain or dyspnoea)
Are there others who live nearby ill? With what?

Physical examination
Are focal or lateralizing neurological signs present? ⟶ Neuroimaging
Is there evidence of meningeal irritation? ⟶ Consider lumbar puncture
Is the patient in heart failure?
Is there evidence of an infection?
Is the patient dehydrated or malnourished?
Is the patient deconditioned?
Has the patient's ability to function declined in the past 2 weeks?

Laboratory tests and investigations
Complete blood count
Electrolytes, urea, and creatinine
Plasma glucose
Thyroid function test
Chest radiograph
Blood culture, urinalysis

Fig. 1 Algorithm for the detection, evaluation, and management of delirium in elderly patients. The term 'gomer' is sometimes applied pejoratively to a frail elderly patient with an atypical disease presentation, and is said to stand for 'get out of my emergency room'.

(Folstein *et al.* 1975) and the Abbreviated Mental Test (Jitapunkul *et al.* 1991). The latter has been endorsed by the British Geriatrics Society in its clinical practice guidelines for the detection and management of delirium.

The presence of delirium can be re-established in accordance with the DSM-IV or similar criteria, and distinguished from other causes of cognitive impairment in elderly people including depression, deafness, and dementia. The chief guide to the presence of delirium and the best questions to ask, once the presence of cognitive impairment has been established, is whether the impaired cognition is new or worse.

A more specific screening instrument for delirium is the Confusion Assessment Method which may be especially helpful in research studies. In its short form, the Confusion Assessment Method screens with four criteria: acute onset and fluctuating course, inattention, disorganized thinking, and altered level of consciousness (Inouye *et al.* 1990). Several other instruments have been used as formal approaches to diagnosing delirium, as opposed to screening for it, and have been reviewed elsewhere (Inouye 1994).

In addition to the Confusion Assessment Method, the most widely used such instrument to date is the Delirium Rating Scale (Trzepacz *et al.* 1988). The Delirium Rating Scale operationalizes and quantifies many of the DSM-IIIR criteria for delirium, although it has no category for inattention.

Management

The management of delirium chiefly requires management of the underlying cause, which is the most specific therapy available. Non-specific therapy is directed towards symptomatic management. Few controlled trials of these treatments are available, although there are a number of case reports, case series, and uncontrolled studies, particularly of antipsychotic agents. However, most of these studies are directed towards the treatment of non-specific agitation, or agitation in the setting of alcohol withdrawal (delirium tremens), again illustrating the particular problem of semantics and definitions in this area, and are irrelevant to the treatment of frail elderly patients who are acutely confused.

Supportive care

The recognition of danger is a highly conserved aspect of animate existence, and whatever groundless fears a patient with delirium may have, few delirious patients are so unresponsive as to be unable to distinguish calm skilled care from unskilled anxiety. Delirious patients will react badly to the latter, and to its attendant threats, so that poor care promotes aggression. Cole *et al.* (1994) studied supportive care as an aspect of a systematic intervention for patients with delirium. Those in the intervention group received a consultation by a geriatrician or geriatric psychiatrist, with follow-up by a liaison nurse. The nursing intervention focused on creating an appropriate environment, reality orientation, familiarity of objects and people in the room, enhanced communication techniques, and the promotion of self-care, with freedom from restraint. The benefits were small, but did include improved cognitive function and behaviour in the intervention group.

The elements of supportive care which appear to work best are a calm carer, who provides continuous reassurance through voice, carriage, and touch, and a quiet well-lit room which has a visible clock and calendar. Patients should be allowed to sleep without interruption. Care should be taken to check for incontinence and, in patients tending towards stupor, for incipient pressure ulcers. When patients are delirious and exhibit psychomotor agitation, it is the author's practice to have family members take shifts in a bedside vigil, where they can keep the patient reassured and prevent unwarranted nosocomial insults. Perhaps the most noxious of these insults is the physical restraint, which is most commonly ineffective (Powell *et al.* 1989) and sometimes harmful (O'Halloran and Lewman 1993).

Pharmacological therapy

There are no randomized placebo-controlled trials of psychoactive medications for the treatment of delirium in frail elderly patients who are acutely ill. One recent report from the management of delirium in patients with AIDS suggested that lorazepam alone was associated with more adverse outcomes than haloperidol alone (Breitbart *et al.* 1996) but the extent to which these data can be applied to elderly patients is unclear. In two studies of delirium in patients across a range of ages, those who received haloperidol and a benzodiazepine had better outcomes than those who received haloperidol alone (Adams 1988; Menza *et al.* 1988).

The author has used the following regimen for the management of delirium with psychomotor agitation. It is based on the observations that (a) dementia and frailty are the most common predisposing factors, (b) very low doses of medication are effective in such patient; in the great majority of cases, the abolition of symptoms is achieved only with significant side-effects, and (c) most of the agitation will settle in a few days as treatment is put in place (Rockwood 1993). Patients who require sedation over that period are prescribed haloperidol (in a tailored dose, usually 0.5, 1.0, or 1.5 mg) given intramuscularly every 8 h, and mixed in the same syringe with lorazepam 1.0 mg. This order is written as 'every 8 h for 3 days; do not add to or adjust this dose in any way without calling me first'. Coupled with tailored but vigorous education of the responsible house staff and auxiliary health professionals, the need to adjust the dose is rare, and satisfactory patient outcomes are usually achieved. Such a regimen avoids the tragic and otherwise not uncommon error of neuroleptic-induced akathisia being mistaken for ineffectiveness, with a resulting cycle of agitation and increasing drug doses, in the extreme cured only by extrapyramidal rigidity.

Prognosis

The validity of conclusions about the prognosis of delirium is confounded by the varied methods by which delirium has been diagnosed in studies to date. This is important, as some patients with delirium probably have an underlying dementia, and unless care has been taken to ensure that this is not the case, wrong associations will be made. Similarly, as delirium is a marker of both underlying frailty, and illness severity, the failure to adjust for these factors will result in the adverse impact of delirium being overstated. Cole and Primeau (1993) have conducted an overview analysis of eight studies, and concluded that in the short term, delirium adversely affects prognosis. Hospital stays were longer (21 versus 9 days) and a higher proportion of patients with delirium were newly discharged to nursing homes (43 per cent) than those without delirium (8 per cent). Patients with delirium also had a higher death rate in the short term (14 versus 5 per cent at 1 month). These associations have been confirmed and extended (Jitapunkul *et al.* 1992; Kolbeinsson and Jonsson 1993) and the relative risk of delirium remains when adjusted for illness severity and other confounders. (Murray *et al.* 1993; Pompei *et al.* 1994; Jarrett *et al.* 1995; O'Keeffe and Lavan 1997).

There are few longer-term studies of the adverse impacts of delirium beyond 6 months. Francis and Kapoor (1992) reported that patients with delirium had higher rates of death (relative risk 1.82, 95 per cent confidence intervals ± 1.04–3.19), worse function, and lower Mini-Mental State Examination scores 2 years after hospital discharge, even after adjusting for other important confounders.

Conclusion

Delirium is a common presentation of acute illness in elderly patients, particularly those who are physically frail or have dementia. Much of the earlier work on the occurrence and outcomes of delirium, and the effect of various types of treatment is of limited use as estimates cannot be generally applied with precision due to the variability in diagnostic criteria. More recently, research on delirium has benefited from the use of standard definitions and protocols.

Delirium is common, and associated with many adverse health outcomes both in the near and longer term. Nevertheless it is often not recognized by doctors.

The care of patients with delirium can be particularly rewarding, as the delirious state provokes anxiety from all concerned. A careful evaluation has a high diagnostic yield, and despite the absence of specific therapy beyond treatment of the underlying problem, it is clearly possible to provide effective assistance.

References

Adams, F. (1988). Emergency intravenous sedation of the delirious, medically ill patient. *Journal of Clinical Psychiatry*, 49, 22–7.

American Psychiatric Association (1994). *Diagnostic and statistical manual of mental disorders* (4th edn). American Psychiatric Association, Washington, DC.

Breitbart, W., Marotta, R., Matt, M.M., *et al.* (1996). A double-blind trial of haloperidol, chlorpromazine, and lorazepam in the treatment of delirium in hopitalized AIDS patients. *American Journal of Psychiatry*, 153, 231–7.

Cole, M.G. and Primeau, F. (1993). Prognosis of delirium in elderly hospital patients. *Canadian Medical Association Journal*, 149, 41–6.

Cole, M.G., Primeau, F.J., Bailey R.F., *et al.* (1994). Systematic intervention for elderly inpatients with delirium: a randomised trial. *Canadian Medical Association Journal*, 151, 965–70.

Cole, M.G., Primeau, F.J., and McCusker, J. (1996). Effectiveness of interventions to prevent delirium in hospitalized patients: a systematic review. *Canadian Medical Association Journal*, 155, 1263–8.

Farrell, K.R. and Ganzini, L. (1995). Misdiagnosing delirium as depression in medically ill elderly patients. *Archives of Internal Medicine*, 155, 2459–64.

Fisher, B.W. and Flowerdew, G. (1995). A simple model for predicting postoperative delirium in older patients undergoing elective orthopedic surgery. *Journal of the American Geriatrics Society*, 43, 175–8.

Folstein, M.F., Folstein, S.E., and McHugh, P.R. (1975). 'Mini-Mental State': a practical guide for grading the cognitive state of patients and clinicians. *Journal of Psychiatric Research*, 12, 189–98.

Francis, J. and Kapoor, W.M. (1992). Prognosis after hospital discharge of older medical patients with delirium. *Journal of the American Geriatrics Society*, 40, 601–6.

Harwood, D.M.J., Hope, T., and Jacoby, R. (1997). Cognitive impairment in medical inpatients. II. Do physicians miss cognitive impairment? *Age and Ageing*, 26, 37–9.

Inouye, S.K. (1994). The dilemma of delirium: clinical and research controversies regarding diagnosis and evaluation of delirium in hopitalized elderly medical patients. *American Journal of Medicine*, 97, 278–88.

Inouye, S.K. and Charpentier, P.A. (1996). Precipitating factors for delirium in hospitalized elderly persons. Predictive model and interrelationship with baseline vulnerability. *Journal of the American Medical Association*, 275, 852–7.

Inouye, S.K., van Dyck, C.H., Alessi, C.A., Balkin, S., Siegal, A.P., and Horwitz, R.I. (1990). Clarifying confusion: the confusion assessment method. A new method for detection of delirium. *Annals of Internal Medicine*, 113, 9418.

Jarrett, P.G., Rockwood, K., Carver, D., Stolee, P., and Cosway, S. (1995). Illness presentation in elderly patients. *Archives of Internal Medicine*, 155, 1060–4.

Jitapunkul, S., Pillay, I., and Ebrahim, S. (1991). The Abbreviated Mental Test: its use and validity. *Age and Ageing*, 20, 332–6.

Jitapunkul, S., Pillay, I., and Ebrahim, S. (1992). Delirium in newly admitted elderly patients: a prospective study. *Quarterly Journal of Medicine*, 300, 307–14.

Kolbeinsson, H. and Jonsson, A. (1993). Delirium and dementia in acute medical admissions of elderly patients in Iceland. *Acta Psychiatrica Scandinavica*, 87, 123–7.

Levkoff, S., Evans, D.A., Liptzin, B., *et al.* (1992). Delirium: the occurrence and persistence of symptoms among elderly hospitalized patients. *Archives of Internal Medicine*, 152, 334–40.

Liptzin, B., Levkoff, S.E., Cleary, P.D., *et al.* (1991). An empirical study of diagnostic criteria for delirium. *American Journal of Psychiatry*, 148, 454–7.

Menza, M.A., Murray, G.B., Holmes, V.F., and Rafuls, W.A. (1988). Controlled study of extrapyramidal reactions in the management of delirious, medically ill patients. Intravenous haloperidol versus intravenous haloperidol plus benzodiazepines. *Heart and Lung*, 17, 238–41.

Murray, A.M., Levkoff, S.E., Wetle, T.T., *et al.* (1993). Acute delirium and functional decline in the hospitalized elderly patient. *Journal of Gerontology*, 48, M181–6.

O'Halloran, R.L. and Lewman, L.V. (1993). Restraint asphyxiation in excited delirium. *American Journal of Forensic Medicine and Pathology*, 14, 289–95.

O'Keeffe, S. and Lavan, S. (1997). The prognostic significance of delirium in older hospital patients. *Journal of the American Geriatrics Society*, 45, 174–8.

O'Keeffe S.T. and Ni-Chonchubhair, A. (1994). Postoperative delirium in the elderly. *British Journal of Anaesthesia*, 73, 673–87.

Plum, F. and Posner, J. (ed.) (1982). *The diagnosis of stupor and coma* (3rd edn). F.A. Davis, Philadelphia, PA.

Pompei, P., Foreman, M., Radberg, M.A., Inouye, S.K., Brand, V., and Cassel, C.K. (1994). Delirium in hospitalized older persons: outcomes and predictors. *Journal of the American Geriatrics Society*, 42, 809–15.

Pompei, P., Foreman, M., Cassel, C.K., Alessi, C., and Cox, P. (1995). Detecting delirium among hospitalized older patients. *Archives of Internal Medicine*, 155, 301–7.

Powell, C., Mitchell-Pedersen, L., Fingernote, E., and Edmund, L. (1989) Freedom from restraint: consequences of reducing physical restraints in the management of the elderly. *Canadian Medical Association Journal*, 141, 561–4.

Rockwood, K. (1993). The occurrence and duration of symptoms in elderly patients with delirium. *Journal of Gerontology*, 48, M162–6.

Rockwood, K., Cosway, S., Stolee, P., *et al.* (1994). Increasing the recognition of delirium in elderly patients. *Journal of the American Geriatrics Society*, 42, 252–6.

Trzepacz, P.T. (1996). Delirium. Advances in diagnosis, pathophysiology, and treatment. *Psychiatric Clinics of North America*, 19, 429–48.

Trzepacz, P.T., Baker, R.W., and Greenhouse, J. (1988). A symptom rating scale for delirium. *Psychiatry Research*, 23, 89–97.

Tune, L., Carr, S., Cooper, T., Klug, B., and Golinger, R.C. (1993). Association of anticholinergic activity of prescribed medications with postoperative delirium. *Journal of Neuropsychiatry and Clinical Neurosciences*, 5, 208–10.

18.22 Head injury

G. P. Malcolm

Introduction

The treatment of head injury in the older person presents a challenge. The pathophysiological disturbances in the injured brain differ significantly from those seen in the younger patient as do the surgical pathologies encountered. Older patients have a higher prevalence of coexistent disease than the young and, even with aggressive management, morbidity and mortality remain disproportionately high. It must also be remembered that standard management guidelines for head-injured patients have been devised from studies involving younger adults and so cannot always be applied to elderly people. The limited clinical studies of head injury in the older population make decisions in this age group particularly difficult.

In this chapter we review some of the published data relating to head injury in elderly people as well as discussing intensive care management of the severe head injury. Severity of head injury is measured using the Glasgow Coma Scale (GCS) which scores eye, verbal, and motor responses as an assessment of depth of impaired consciousness and coma (Teasdale and Jennett 1974). Patients are scored between 3 and 15, with severe head injury defined as a GCS score of 3 to 8, moderate head injury as a score of 9 to 12, and mild head injury as a score of 13 to 15. Coma is defined as a state of unconsciousness in which the subject lies with eyes closed (Plum and Posner 1980), lacking cycles of sleep and awareness (Multi-Society Task Force on PVS 1994). In the GCS definition such patients fail to open their eyes, obey commands or use intelligible words (maximum GCS score of 8).

Age and incidence of head injury

Calculated incidences vary according to whether the data relate to deaths, admissions, or hospital attendance. Reliable statistics are difficult to derive from routinely collected data, but age-specific hospital admission rates and mortality rates show a rise in elderly people (Jennett 1996).

Sex

Men outnumber women two to one if head injuries of all ages and severity are taken together (Teasdale 1995). In most series there is an increasing percentage of women in the head-injured population with increasing age. Women over 65 years comprised 50 per cent of patients (Becker et al. 1977) in one series, and in another 60 per cent of patients over 80 years were female (Amacher and Dybee 1987). This

trend is not confirmed in all reports (Rakier et al. 1995; Schiller et al. 1995).

Causes of head injury

The most common causes of head injury are road traffic accidents, falls, and assaults. In the younger population motor vehicle related accidents predominate as the cause of head injury (Alberico et al. 1987; Bring et al. 1996). The proportion of injuries secondary to falls increases markedly with age and in most series of elderly patients the most common cause of head injury is falls (Luerssen et al. 1988; Vollmer et al. 1991). In one series of 263 consecutive head-injured patients over 65 admitted to hospital a fall was the cause of injury in 70 per cent (Rakier et al. 1995).

Presence of systemic disease

The majority of elderly patients sustaining head injury have a history of significant systemic disease (Vollmer et al. 1991; Rakier et al. 1995). This is relevant in terms of increasing the likelihood of falls and resultant head injury (Zwimpfer and Moulton 1993), although its contribution to poor outcome is debated (Vollmer et al. 1991).

Anticoagulants and intracranial haematoma

The risk of intracranial haematoma is increased 10-fold in patients on warfarin (Hylek and Singer 1994) and in a proportion there will be a history of head trauma (Wintzen and Tijssen 1982). All elderly patients on warfarin should be considered for CT scanning even if a head injury is apparently minor (Saab et al. 1996). Any risk related to the use of aspirin remains undefined.

Pathology of head injury

Of patients seen in hospital with a head injury 40 per cent have a scalp laceration which may lead to shock (Teasdale 1996); 1.5 per cent of patients have a skull fracture and such a finding is of particular significance in an elderly person, indicating a significant head injury.

Primary brain injury

Damage to the brain at the time of non-missile injury is termed primary traumatic brain damage and involves two main pathological processes: diffuse axonal injury, and contusions and lacerations.

Diffuse axonal injury

Diffuse axonal injury has been defined as axonal damage not associated with an intracranial mass lesion and is the single most important lesion in traumatic brain damage (Adams *et al.* 1989). The effect in the acute phase may vary from transient loss of memory to prolonged coma. Pathologically there is scattered damage and divisions of axons throughout the white matter.

Contusions and lacerations

Contusions and lacerations are found predominantly in the cerebral cortex of the frontal and temporal lobes (Fig. 1). Contusions occurring in eloquent brain may cause a focal deficit, while those in the frontal and temporal lobe may lead to changes in personality and mental state or the onset of epilepsy.

Secondary brain damage

This develops following the primary injury and is thought to result from cerebral ischaemia (Graham *et al.* 1978). Head injury treatment aims to limit this secondary damage which in its most dramatic form may be manifest as the patient who 'talks and dies'. Such patients have led some to argue that secondary insults may be more important than the primary brain injury in determining the extent of disability after head injury (Miller 1992). Prominent among 'avoidable' factors that lead to secondary brain injury are intracranial haemorrhage, brain swelling, seizures, and infection.

Intracranial complications

Haematomas

Extradural haematomas

These occur when there is bleeding between the skull and dura, and there is often an associated skull fracture. These collections are uncommon in elderly people due to the tight adherence of dura to skull. They have a characteristic lentiform appearance on CT scan (Fig. 2).

Acute subdural haematomas

These collections lie between the dura and brain surface, and commonly arise without a skull fracture. They are common in elderly people and arise from damage to bridging veins or cortical vessels. These collections spread extensively in the potential space between dura and cortical surface and may reach a considerable size. They have a characteristic crescentic appearance on CT scan (Fig. 3).

Intracerebral haematomas

These collections arise within the brain substance, commonly in the frontal or temporal lobe. Such collections represent one end of a spectrum which extends from small petechial haemorrhages (just visible on scan) through haemorrhagic contusions to large haematomas.

Haematomas in elderly people

Head-injured patients over the age of 60 years have a significantly increased incidence of traumatic intracranial haematomas (Pentland

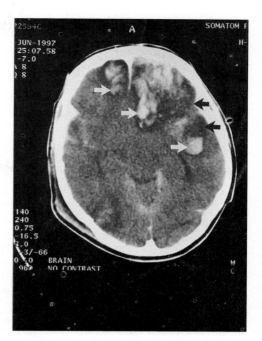

Fig. 1 CT scan demonstrating extensive contusions of both frontal lobes and a temporal lobe (white arrows). There is associated oedema (black arrows).

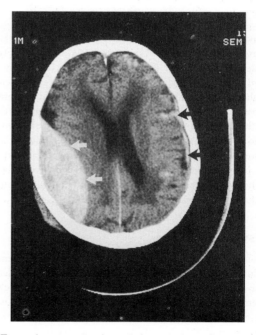

Fig. 2 CT scan demonstrating the typical appearances of an acute extradural haematoma. This is seen as a biconvex lentiform mass lesion (white arrows). There is a small contralateral subdural collection (black arrows).

et al. 1986; Jeret *et al.* 1993). In one series patients over 60 had twice as many mass lesions as subjects below this age (Zwimpfer and Moulton 1993). This high incidence of haematomas is in part related

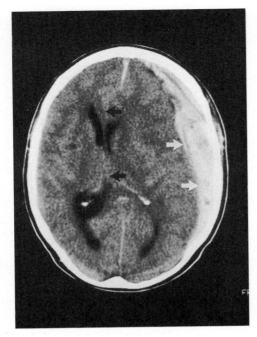

Fig. 3 CT scan demonstrating the typical appearances of an acute subdural haematoma. This is seen as a crescentic extra-axial mass lesion (white arrows), causing mass effect manifest by sulcal effacement, ventricular compression, and midline shift (black arrows).

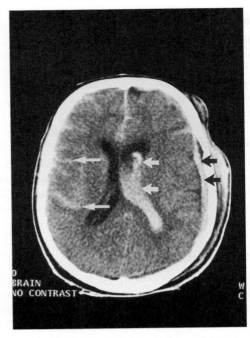

Fig. 4 CT scan demonstrating traumatic subarachnoid blood (large white arrows) and intraventricular haemorrhage (small white arrows). There is a small acute subdural haematoma (black arrows)

to the high incidence of falls in elderly people, a known risk factor for traumatic haematomas (Alberico *et al.* 1987). Age itself is also an independent risk factor for operable intracranial haematomas (Gutman *et al.* 1992). The majority of haematomas are intracerebral or in the subdural space. Extradural (epidural) haematomas are rare in elderly patients because the dura is densely adherent to the inner table of the skull. Poor outcome with extradural haematoma is said to be due to the considerable force needed to generate such lesions. Brain atrophy and hypertensive and amyloid cerebral vascular damage, and the higher frequency of anticoagulant use in elderly people, may all help to explain the increased risk of traumatic intracranial haemorrhage (Zwimpfer and Moulton 1993) (Fig. 4).

Brain swelling

Local brain swelling occurs around contusions following head injury, and is thought to be due to microvascular compromise leading to progressive cytotoxic (ischaemic) oedema with resultant cell death (Schroder *et al.* 1995).

Diffuse brain swelling is less common in adults than children (Zimmerman and Bilaniuk 1981) and can occur in one or both hemispheres. The mechanism is uncertain, but in part is related to excessive blood flow (hyperaemia), a result of disturbed cerebral autoregulation. The clinical significance of hyperaemia is not clearly defined. Bruce *et al.* (1973) suggest it is the primary cause of raised intracranial pressure although other studies dispute this (Robertson *et al.* 1992).

Vollmer *et al.* (1991) demonstrated convincingly that in traumatic coma, mass lesions (i.e. extradural, subdural, or intracerebral haematomas) were the major factor in the fatal outcome of older patients

in contrast to diffuse injury with or without swelling in younger patients.

Infection

Base of skull fractures may be associated with cerebrospinal fluid leak from ear or nose with associated risk of meningitis. Most cerebrospinal fluid leaks resolve spontaneously, but if they persist beyond a week neurosurgical advice should be sought as surgical repair is sometimes necessary. In general, prophylactic antibiotics are not advised. If symptoms of meningitis develop the diagnosis can be rapidly established by lumbar puncture and appropriate antibiotics given. *Pneumococcus* remains the most common pathogen.

Resuscitation of people with head injuries

All patients should be resuscitated according to the Advanced Trauma Life Support Programme guidelines (American College of Surgeons 1989). Ensuring an adequate airway (with cervical spine control) is critical as hypoxia correlates with poor outcome in head trauma (Gentleman 1992). It is also extremely important to avoid hypoxia as patients with a single episode of hypotension (systolic blood pressure less than 90 mmHg) have a doubled fatality and increased morbidity (Chestnut *et al.* 1993). Patients must be adequately resuscitated with satisfactory oxygenation and blood pressure before consideration of head injury treatment. Initial neurological assessment will include pupillary response, GCS assessment, and a brief neurological examination. In the patient with a significant head injury it is important to consider whether altered conscious level may be due to causes other than the head injury.

Patients who remain comatose after resuscitation are intubated. Cervical spine injuries occur in up to 15 per cent of patients with severe head injuries and are managed as appropriate.

Elderly patients are difficult to resuscitate. In one study elderly patients had twice the transfusion requirements of younger patients as well as a high incidence of cardiac dysrhythmias (Schiller et al. 1995). This latter problem may be an indication of pre-existing coronary artery disease, chronic electrolyte disturbance, and volume depletion.

Assessment of head injuries

Mild head injuries

The definition of mild head injury is unsatisfactory because this group will include patients with a GCS of 15 who have a very low risk of complications in the acute stage (Mendelow et al. 1983; Teasdale et al. 1990), as well as patients with a GCS of 13 and 14 who may have a very significant injury (Hsiang et al. 1997). The degree of brain damage and the probability that a patient will require neurosurgical intervention increases significantly as the GCS diminishes from 15 to 13 (Culotta et al. 1996). This has led to further subdivisions of this category being suggested although none has yet gained widespread acceptance (Stein 1996; Hsiang et al. 1997).

Elderly patients with an altered conscious level (i.e. GCS 13 or 14) should undergo a CT scan and in general be admitted for observation until their conscious level has returned to normal. Headache is an unreliable clinical feature, vomiting has no relationship to acute radiographic abnormality (Hsiang et al. 1997), and loss of consciousness has no relationship to CT scan abnormalities (Lucchi et al. 1995). In younger patients the presence of a fracture on skull radiography contributes to triaging patients as the risk of an intracranial haematoma in a confused patient rises from one in 120 to one in four if a fracture is present (Teasdale 1996). However, age over 65 is considered an independent risk factor in most head injury classifications which again emphasizes the need to CT scan elderly patients with an altered conscious level.

A difficult category are those elderly patients with evidence of a head injury, but no loss of consciousness or amnesia, normal alertness and memory, and a GCS of 15. In patients under 65 the risk of an intracranial (or surgical) lesion is almost zero and management consists of emergency room evaluation and discharge. In such elderly patients with persisting headache, nausea, or vomiting the risk of a surgical lesion has been estimated at 0.2 per cent (Stein 1996) as opposed to 0.08 per cent in the total patient group (Borczuk 1995). It may not be appropriate simply to discharge these patients.

The increasing use of CT scanning has revolutionized the management of mild head injury. Such an approach is safe and may well be justifiable in financial terms, saving on hospital admission as well as missed pathology (Stein 1996).

Moderate and severe head injuries

Once resuscitation has been completed (including cervical radiography) patients should undergo urgent CT scanning. If a large subdural (or extradural) haematoma is identified treatment for raised intracranial pressure begins immediately with administration of mannitol (1.0 g/kg body weight) while the patient is being transferred to the operating theatre for craniotomy. The decision on whether to operate on a large intracerebral haematoma in an elderly person is difficult and will depend on the GCS and neurological deficit prior to intubation. Jamjoon et al. (1992) reported a series of elderly patients who underwent surgery for traumatic intracranial haematomas. They noted that elderly patients had a worse outcome than younger patients, with a very high probability of poor outcome in elderly patients with preoperative pupillary dilatation or an extensor motor response. If surgery is to be performed, it should proceed without delay.

There are no precise rules about which haematomas should be treated by immediate surgery. The association of an extracerebral haematoma with midline shift of over 5 mm, depression of conscious level or even severe headache or vomiting are indications for surgery (Miller 1992).

Smaller collections may be managed conservatively. If a patient is obeying commands he is carefully observed on the ward with regular charting of GCS, pupillary reaction, and limb power. If deterioration occurs CT scanning should be repeated to assess any possible change in the size of the haematoma that might necessitate surgery. If brain swelling rather than clot enlargement is seen consideration should be given to ventilation and intracranial pressure monitoring.

If no surgical treatment is necessary comatose patients should have an intracranial pressure monitor inserted and be transferred to the intensive care unit for ventilation. The preferred technique of intracranial pressure monitoring is by intraventricular catheter which allows cerebrospinal fluid drainage if necessary as a means of controlling intracranial pressure.

In 1991 the results of a prospective study of 661 patients that analysed the relationship between patient age and clinical outcome following traumatic coma was published (Vollmer et al. 1991). The data analysed were entered into the Traumatic Coma Data Bank. These high-quality data provide much of the basis for the subsequent discussion.

CT findings in severe head injury (Vollmer et al. 1991)

The percentage of patients with lesions on CT scanning increases with age, with extracerebral haematomas showing a marked age relationship both in frequency and size. There is also a trend with increasing age to more frequent and larger intracerebral haematomas. Of patients 26 per cent have a collection greater than 15 cm^3. Traumatic subarachnoid haemorrhage (see Fig. 4), shift of midline structures, and ventricular asymmetry also increase in frequency with increasing age. Interestingly compression of the mesencephalic cistern does not follow this trend.

Surgical rates in severe head injury (Vollmer et al. 1991)

The proportion of patients with haematomas increases with age although there was in this series no difference between age groups in the frequency of evacuation of intracranial haematomas.

Intensive care management of severe head injuries

Patients who are comatose prior to surgery or who are in coma without a surgically treatable pathology are managed so as to avoid secondary (ischaemic) insults to the damaged brain. The patient remains intubated to maintain satisfactory oxygenation and is administered sedatives and analgesics to prevent episodes of agitation or combativeness that might raise intracranial pressure. Neuromuscular blockade is associated with complications and is avoided if possible (Bullock *et al.* 1996).

Patients remain ventilated and their intracranial pressure monitored until it is apparent that the latter is controlled and the cerebral perfusion pressure stabilized at a satisfactory level (see below).

Cerebral perfusion pressure and intracranial pressure monitoring

Cerebral perfusion pressure is the physiological parameter that determines the pressure gradient for cerebral blood flow, and as such is the critical determinant of cerebral ischaemia.

Cerebral perfusion pressure is defined as follows:

cerebral perfusion pressure =
    mean arterial pressure – mean intracranial pressure.

It cannot be calculated without monitoring intracranial pressure. Effective head injury treatment aims to maintain a cerebral perfusion pressure above 70 mmHg (Chan *et al.* 1992) while keeping intracranial pressure below 20 mmHg (Marmarou *et al.* 1991). Cerebral perfusion pressure may be increased by raising arterial pressure or lowering intracranial pressure.

Treatment of inadequate cerebral perfusion pressure

Poor cerebral perfusion pressure (less than 70 mmHg) may be due to hypotension, raised intracranial pressure, or a combination of these factors.

General manoeuvres

It is first established that the patient is well oxygenated (check position of endotracheal tube, treat retained sputum, chest infection, and so on), and has an adequate haemoglobin and central venous pressure. Pain relief and sedation must be appropriate, pyrexia treated, and fits controlled (electroencephalographic monitoring may be necessary in the paralysed patient).

Treatment of inadequate mean arterial pressure

Inotropes are administered to raise the mean arterial pressure to above 90 mmHg.

Treatment of raised intracranial pressure

If intracranial pressure is above 20 mmHg and hypotension has been corrected (i.e. mean arterial pressure is at least 90 mmHg) specific treatment for raised intracranial pressure is begun.

Hyperventilation

Previously, aggressive hyperventilation was one of the mainstays of treatment of severely head-injured patients (Kerr 1993). However, there is now evidence that the cerebral vasoconstriction provoked by hyperventilation can lead to cerebral anoxia (Raichle and Plum 1972), and this has lead the American Trauma Brain Foundation to warn specifically against prolonged hyperventilation in the treatment of raised intracranial pressure. Hyperventilation is used briefly to control surges in intracranial pressure.

Mild hyperventilation may also be employed to control intracranial pressure if an assessment of adequacy of cerebral blood flow is available (see below).

Cerebrospinal fluid drainage

If ventricular size allows, a ventricular catheter is inserted for intracranial pressure monitoring. This will also enable controlled drainage of cerebrospinal fluid which is often an extremely effective way of lowering intracranial pressure.

Mannitol

Mannitol acts to lower intracranial pressure by two mechanisms. The immediate effect is due to reduced haematocrit and blood viscosity with increased cerebral blood flow, and the delayed action due to an osmotic diuresis (Pickard and Czosnyka 1993). Mannitol is administered intermittently when necessary as determined by intracranial pressure. Plasma osmolality must be monitored and mannitol administration stopped if plasma osmolarity exceeds 330 mmol/l because of the risk of renal failure. It is important to maintain an adequate circulating volume and to monitor for hypokalaemia and hypernatraemia.

Barbiturates

If 30° head-up tilt, maintenance of normocapnia, cerebrospinal fluid drainage, and mannitol fail to control intracranial pressure a repeat CT scan is performed to exclude a surgically treatable collection. If no such lesion is found barbiturate therapy with thiopentone may be instituted. Thiopentone acts to depress cerebral oxidative metabolism and hence lower cerebral blood flow, cerebral blood volume, and thus intracranial pressure. Its use is not recommended prophylactically and it is of limited use in elderly people because of the potential serious side-effects of haemodynamic instability and infection.

Surgery for uncontrolled intracranial pressure

There is no place in the elderly patient for brain or calvarial resection as a means of controlling intracranial pressure. Occasionally unilateral frontal or temporal lobe contusions are resected if they are causing marked local mass effect. However, it must be emphasized that in the older patients such procedures are rarely appropriate.

'Targeted therapy' and jugular venous oximetry

The treatment regime discussed above for raised intracranial pressure reflects the so-called 'staircase approach'. However, attempts have been made to select therapies that target the varying causes of raised intracranial pressure in different patients (Miller and Dearden 1992). For this so-called 'targeted therapy' an assessment of the adequacy of cerebral blood flow is needed. The most commonly used technique involves measurement of jugular venous oxygen saturation. A catheter is passed into the jugular bulb allowing continuous measurement of jugular venous oxygen saturation with figures of between 50 and 70 per cent considered normal. A value above 70 per cent indicates a relative excess of blood flow in relation to metabolic demand, so-called luxury perfusion or 'hyperaemia', while a level below 50 per cent is thought to indicate hypoperfusion with cerebral ischaemia. Higher figures are more commonly found in the younger patient who may be treated with hypnotic agents or hyperventilation to diminish blood flow and lower intracranial pressure. The patient with low jugular venous saturations (and thus inadequate blood flow for metabolic demand) is treated differently with manoeuvres that improve blood flow such as mannitol or perhaps an elevation of CO_2 level.

Other treatments

Steroid use in head injury

There is no indication for the use of steroids in the treatment of head injuries.

Anticonvulsants and head injury

Post-traumatic seizures are divided into early seizures, which occur within 7 days of injury, and late seizures which occur after this time (Temkin *et al.* 1991). Phenytoin may be used to treat early post-traumatic seizures in those at high risk, but because of its unproven benefit in late seizures, and the potential side-effects, it should not be continued after the first week.

Hypothermia

This has been shown to be of benefit in a subgroup of severely head-injured patients. Clinical trials are continuing (Mannon *et al.* 1997).

Delayed surgery for subdural collections

Elderly patients may present following head injury with a small acute subdural collection which does not require surgical evacuation. Most of these collections will resorb spontaneously and if the patient remains well no intervention is necessary. However, in a proportion of patients these collections will enlarge and can be associated with increasing symptoms of raised intracranial pressure (Fig. 5). Such patients may be treated by burrhole drainage of the collection. It is important to repeat the CT scan if an elderly person has persisting symptoms after significant head injury.

Outcome of head injury in older people

Elderly patients who suffer head injuries have a higher fatality and survivors are much less likely to return home. The correlation between outcome and age is high for patients over 60 years of age. Age affects outcome from head injury independent of GCS, pupillary reflexes, the presence of mass lesions, or associated systemic injuries. Age is a powerful independent predictor of outcome both in terms of morbidity and mortality (Vollmer *et al.* 1991). Interestingly there is no increase in the frequency of vegetative survival with increasing age (Vollmer *et al.* 1991).

Mortality

Severe head injuries

The adverse effect of increasing age after head injury among the adult population has been verified in numerous series (Hernesniemi 1979; Jennett *et al.* 1979; Teasdale *et al.* 1979; Overgaard *et al.* 1981; Luerssen *et al.* 1988; Aalst *et al.* 1991; Vollmer *et al.* 1991; Jamjoon *et al.* 1992). Although early investigators attributed excess fatality in elderly people solely to a higher incidence of complications, subsequent studies have indicated a deleterious effect of ageing *per se*, which expresses itself in a uniform fashion across the entire adult age range (Vollmer *et al.* 1991).

For severe head injuries the figures are particularly grim. Jamjoon *et al.* (1992) reported 100 per cent fatality in 11 patients with a mean age of 73 years, with GCS scores of 3 to 5. They all died in hospital. Ross *et al.* (1992) reported 95 patients with a mean age of 75 years and GCS of 3 to 8. There was a 91 per cent fatality in the 6-month follow-up. The same fatality figure was reported by Pennings *et al.* (1993) in 42 patients with a mean age of 74 years and GCS of 3 to 5.

Zwimpfer and Moulton (1993) reported a cumulative fatality exceeding 90 per cent for patients with a GCS below 5 in their seventh decade, 6 in their eighth, and below 8 in their ninth. The majority of deaths were a direct consequence of the head injury and not a result of extracranial complications. Elderly patients are at a greater risk of systemic complications such as pulmonary embolus, respiratory failure, sepsis, myocardial infarction, and multisystem failure, yet such conditions are the main cause of death in fewer than one-third of such patients (Amacher and Dybee 1987).

Comparison of fatality between age groups is difficult. Pentland *et al.* (1986) reported a fatality of 77 per cent in severe head injuries in those over 65 years of age compared to 39 per cent in the younger age group. Schiller *et al.* (1995) reported figures of 31 and 17.1 per cent, respectively.

When mortality is examined with respect to time after injury, deaths within 48 h of admission are not significantly more frequent in older age group than the young. However, late mortality (over 48 h) was observed significantly more commonly in the older age group. Survival curves have demonstrated continued fatality in the older age group which persists well beyond the first week postinjury while the curves for the younger age groups tend to level off (Vollmer *et al.* 1991).

Age is an independent predictor of outcome from traumatic coma and the effect of age is most likely related to alteration in the pathophysiological response of the ageing nervous system to severe trauma (Vollmer *et al.* 1991).

Moderate head injuries

Pentland *et al.* (1986) reported a fatality of 9 per cent in moderate head injuries over the age of 65 years as opposed to 1 per cent in younger patients.

Mild head injuries

Pentland *et al.* (1986) reported three deaths in 377 mild head injuries in those over the age of 65 years and one death in 1324 younger patients. Hsiang *et al.* (1997) reported 1360 patients of all ages with mild head injuries. Four deaths occurred, all in patients over 65 years of age.

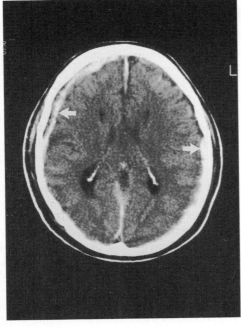

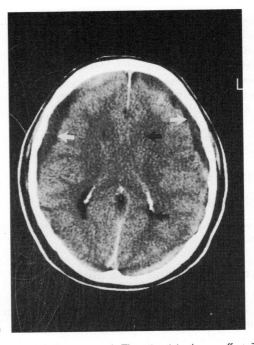

(a)   (b)

Fig. 5 CT scans on the same patient. (a) Admission CT scan small bilateral acute subdural haematomas (white arrows). There is minimal mass effect. The patient was relatively well and managed conservatively. (b) CT scan performed 2 weeks after admission. The subdural haematomas have increased in size and have become largely hypodense with respect to the brain (white arrows). There is now mass effect manifest by sulcal effacement and ventricular compression (black arrows).

Morbidity

Elderly patients who survive severe head injury almost never recover to their premorbid state and consequently are often unable to return to independent living. Kilaru *et al.* (1996) reported a series of survivors of severe head injuries over 65 years of age. At long-term follow-up, less than one in four survivors were living at home in functional independence while the rest were dependent on nursing home care. These survivors had not shown any significant improvement since discharge from hospital and these outcomes were in a group of patients who were independent prior to their injury. In another study fewer than 10 per cent of patients over the age of 60 made a good recovery or were left with only a moderate disability following head injury (Teasdale *et al.* 1979).

Elderly patients with severe head injuries have a fivefold increase in cardiac dysrythmias and a twofold increase in chest complications, infections, and thrombophlebitis. These differences are highly significant and in one series accounted for much of the increased hospital stay and fatality (Schiller *et al.* 1995).

A group of patients with pre-existing systemic disease includes significantly more fatalities and vegetative outcomes after severe head injury. However, when outcome with or without systemic disease is examined in these patients according to age there appears to be an independent age effect. Systemic disease does not therefore completely account for the age effect on outcome after head injury (Vollmer *et al.* 1991).

Moderate head injuries

In the study by Pentland *et al.* (1986) 57 per cent of survivors over 65 years of age made a good recovery or were left with moderate disability as assessed by the Glasgow Outcome Scale (Jennett and Bond 1975). Of younger patients, 86 per cent achieved this outcome (Pentland *et al.* 1986).

Mild head injuries

These patients have a significant fatality (see above). However, in the survivors outcome is generally good with the majority of patients of all ages making a good recovery or being left with moderate disability (Pentland *et al.* 1986).

Neurobehavioural consequences of closed head injury in the older population

Various methods have been used to assess the outcome in older adults after head injury including global measures such as level of independence, length of hospital stay, and discharge disposition (Goldstein *et al.* 1994). Using the Glasgow Outcome Scale it has been demonstrated that the probability of resuming preinjury activities with mild or no neurological deficit declined with advancing age (Alberico *et al.* 1987).

Studies of cognitive function in older closed head injury patients are more limited. One study (Mazzuchi *et al.* 1992) found that 50 per cent of patients exhibited generalized deterioration and dementia whereas only 25 per cent had minimal or no deterioration. Moreover, patients with mild head injuries were no more likely to have a better outcome than those with severe injuries. Generalized deterioration and dementia were common in both groups with mild and moderate to severe injury. This was important research indicating that closed head injury produced cognitive defects across the injury severity spectrum. A further study by Goldstein et al. (1994) looked at specific cognitive features in the 7 months after mild to moderate closed head injury. Compared with demographically similar normal controls, the patients exhibited significantly poorer functioning in the cognitive domains. Naming and word fluency under time conditions, verbal and visual memory, and the ability to infer similarities were especially vulnerable. However, at variance with the findings of Goldstein et al. (1994) is the study of Aharon-Peretz et al. (1997). Word fluency, memory, and reasoning were compared in elderly patients who had survived closed head injury, orthopaedic trauma patients, and healthy age-matched volunteers. No differences in outcome were found between head-injured and orthopaedic patients.

Alzheimer's disease after head injury

Head injury with loss of consciousness has been implicated as a possible risk factor for Alzheimer's disease in several case–control studies and by a combined reanalysis of previous case–control studies (Mortimer et al. 1991). A recent cohort study from Manhattan provides further strong evidence of this association (Schofield et al. 1997). There are several possible mechanisms by which head injury might increase the risk of Alzheimer's disease. Firstly, head injury might cause cerebral damage and thereby lower the reserve against the cognitive consequences of subsequent, entirely unrelated cerebral pathology (including Alzheimer's disease). Secondly, head injury might be particularly damaging when it occurs in the presymptomatic phase of Alzheimer's disease. Thirdly, head injury might function as a catalyst to trigger or promote some critical early event in the pathogenesis of Alzheimer's disease. Susceptibility to Alzheimer's disease as conferred by apolipoprotein ε4 does not appear to increase the risk associated with head injury (O'Meara et al. 1997).

Prediction of outcome after severe head injury

The accurate prediction of outcome after head injury is notoriously difficult and attempts continue to find reliable prognostic indicators. The Leeds scale (Gibson and Stephenson 1989) was reported to predict fatal outcome after head injury accurately in 100 per cent of cases; however, its reliability has now been seriously questioned (Feldman et al. 1991).

Quigley et al. (1997) recommends a simple combination of age and admission GCS to predict the limits of functional survival (non-vegetative) after severe head injury in those patients with a GCS of 3 to 5. In their series the oldest survivor with a GCS score of 3 was aged in their thirties, a score of 4 in their forties, and a score of 5 in their fifties. There were no functional survivors in patients above 60 years of age with an admission GCS of 5 or less.

Namelak et al. (1996) has reported that age is the most important independent predictor for survival 24 h following severe head injury (GCS 3 to 8), followed by best motor score, pupillary reactivity, and extraocular motility. These predictors were combined and are claimed to predict outcome reliably at 6 months postinjury.

Kilaru et al. (1996) in a further retrospective study found that admission GCS and heart rate were predictive of long-term functional outcome after severe head injury.

There is no doubt that to date the admission GCS score remains the single most useful predictor available for outcome in an elderly person with a head injury; however, the significance of the above studies is greatly (perhaps critically) diminished by their retrospective nature without prospective validation. The need to establish multi-centre, longitudinal databases with long-term data on the functional outcome of elderly survivors of severe closed head injury seems as great as ever.

Prevention of head injury in elderly people

Elderly people have an increased incidence of falls, as well as an increased risk of sustaining head trauma from those falls (Teasdale et al. 1979; Vollmer et al. 1991). The risk of falling can be reduced by modifying known risk factors (Tinnetti et al. 1994), and strategies to achieve this may well offer the best chance of head injury reduction in elderly people.

Continued educational efforts concerning road safety may also be beneficial in the older patient. In one series of severe head injuries only 17 per cent of drivers were wearing seat belts and 14 per cent had positive blood alcohol levels (Schiller et al. 1995).

References

Aalst, J.A., Morris, J.A., Yates, H.K., et al. (1991). Patients return to independent living: a study of factors influencing function and independence. Journal of Trauma, 31, 1096–102.

Adams, J.H., Doyle, D., Ford I., et al. (1989). Diffuse axonal injury in head injury: definition, diagnosis and grading. Histopathology, 15, 49–59.

Aharon-Peretz, J., Kliot, D., Amyel-Zvi, D., Tomer, R., Rakier, A., and Feinsod, M. (1997). Neurobehavioural consequences of closed head injury in the elderly. Brain Injury, 11, 871–5.

Alberico, A., Ward, J., Choi, S., et al. (1987). Outcome after severe head injury. Journal of Neurosurgery, 67, 648–56.

Amacher, A.L. and Dybee, D.E. (1987). Toleration of head injury by the elderly. Neurosurgery, 20, 954–8.

American College of Surgeons (1989). Advanced trauma life support program. Committee on Trauma, American College of Surgeons, Chicago.

Becker, D.P., Miller, J.D., Ward, J.D., et al. (1977). The outcome from severe head injury with early diagnosis and intensive management. Journal of Neurosurgery, 47, 491–502.

Borczuk, P. (1995). Predictors of intracranial injury in patients with mild head trauma. Annals of Emergency Medicine, 25, 731–6.

Bring, G., Bjornstig, G., and Westman, G. (1996). Gender patterns in minor head and neck injuries: an analysis of casualty register data. Accident Analysis and Prevention, 28, 356–69.

Bruce, D.A., Langfitt, T.W., Miller, J.D., et al. (1973). Regional cerebral blood flow, intracranial pressure, and brain metabolism in comatose patients. Journal of Neurosurgery, 38, 131–44.

Bullock, R., Chestnut, R., Clifton, F., et al. (1996) Guidelines for the management of severe head injury. Brain Trauma Foundation, New York.

Chan, K.H., Miller, J.D., Dearden, N.M., Andrews, P.J.D., and Midgely, S. (1992). The effect of changes in cerebral perfusion pressure upon middle cerebral artery blood flow velocity and jugular bulb venous oxygen saturation after severe brain injury. *Journal of Neurosurgery*, 77, 55–61.

Chestnut, R.M., Marshall, L.F., Klauber, M.R., *et al.* (1993). The role of secondary brain injury in determining outcome from severe head injury. *Journal of Trauma*, 34, 216–22.

Culotta, V.P., Sementilli, M.E., Gerold, K., *et al.* (1996). Clinicopathological heterogeneity in the classification of mild head injury. *Neurosurgery*, 38, 245–50.

Feldman, Z., Contant, C.F., Robertson, C.S., *et al.* (1991). Evaluation of the Leeds prognostic score for severe head injury. *Lancet*, 337, 1451.

Gentleman, D. (1992). Causes and effects of systemic complications among severely head injured patients transferred to a neurosurgical unit. *International Surgery*, 77, 297–302.

Gibson, R.M. and Stephenson, G.C. (1989). Aggressive management of severe closed head trauma: time for reappraisal. *Lancet*, ii, 369.

Goldstein, F.C., Levin, H.S., Presley, R.M., *et al.* (1994). Neurobehavioural consequences of closed head injury in adults. *Journal of Neurology, Neurosurgery and Psychiatry*, 57, 961–6.

Graham, D.I., Adams, J.H., *et al.* (1978). Ischaemic brain damage in fatal non missile injuries. *Journal of Neurological Science*, 39, 213–34.

Gutman, M.B., Moulton, R.J., Sullivan, I., *et al.* (1992). Risk factors predicting operable intracranial haematomas in head injury. *Journal of Neurosurgery*, 77, 9.

Hernesniemi, J. (1979). Outcome following head injury in the elderly. *Acta Neurochirurgica*, 49, 67.

Hsiang, J.N.K., Yeung, T., Yu, A.L.M., and Poon, W.S. (1997). High risk mild head injury. *Journal of Neurosurgery*, 87, 243–8.

Hylek, E.M. and Singer, D.E. (1994). Risk factors for intracranial haematoma in patients taking warfarin. *Annals of Internal Medicine*, 120, 897–902.

Jamjoon, A., Nelson, R.J., Stranjalis, G.A., *et al.* (1992). Outcome following surgical evacuation of traumatic intracranial haematomas in the elderly. *British Journal of Neurosurgery*, 6, 27.

Jennett, B. (1996). Epidemiology of head injury. *Journal of Neurology, Neurosurgery and Psychiatry*, 60, 362–9.

Jennett, B. and Bond, M.R. (1975). Assessment of outcome after severe brain damage. A practical scale. *Lancet*, i, 480–7.

Jennett, B., Teasdale, G., Galbraith, S., *et al.* (1979). Prognosis of patients with severe head injury. *Acta Neurochirurgica*, 28 (Supplement), 149.

Jeret, J.S., Mandell, M., Anziska, B., *et al.* (1993). Clinical predictors of abnormality disclosed by computed tomography after mild head trauma. *Neurosurgery*, 32, 9–??.

Kerr, M.E. (1993). Hyperventilation and head injuries. *Heart and Lung*, 22, 516–22.

Kilaru, S., Garb, J., Emhoff, T., *et al.* (1996). Long term functional status and mortality of elderly patients with severe closed head injuries. *Journal of Trauma, Injury, Infection and Critical Care*, 41, 957–63.

Lucchi, S., Giuia, G., Bettinelli, A., *et al.* (1995). The role of computerised tomography in the management of mild head injury patients. *Reviews of Neuroradiology*, 8, 415–28.

Luerssen, T., Klauaber, M., and Marshall, L. (1988). Outcome from head injury related to patient's age. *Journal of Neurosurgery*, 68, 409–16.

Mannon, M.W., Penrod, L.E., Kelsey, S.F., *et al.* (1997). Treatment of traumatic brain injury with moderate hypothermia. *New England Journal of Medicine*, 336, 540–6.

Marmarou, A., Anderson, R.L., Ward, J.D., *et al.* (1991). Impact of ICP instability and hypotension on outcome in patients with severe head trauma. *Journal of Neurosurgery*, 75, S159–66.

Mazzuchi, A., Cattelani, R., Missale, G., *et al.* (1992). Head injured patients over 50 years: correlations between variables of trauma and neuropsychological follow up. *Journal of Neurology*, 239, 256–60.

Mendelow, A.D., Teasdale, G.M., Jennett, B., *et al.* (1983). Risks of intracranial haematoma in head injured adults. *British Medical Journal*, 287, 1173–6.

Miller, J.D. (1992). Evaluation and treatment of head injury in adults. *Neurosurgery Quarterly*, 2, 28–43.

Miller, J.D. and Dearden, N.M. (1992). Measurement analysis and the management of raised intracranial pressure. In *Current neurosurgery* (ed. G.M. Teasdale and J.D. Miller), pp. 119–56. Churchill Livingstone, Edinburgh.

Mortimer, J.A., van Duijn, C.M., Chandra, V., *et al.* (1991). Head trauma as a risk factor for Alzheimer's disease: a collaborative re-analysis of case control studies. *International Journal of Epidemiology*, 20, S28–35.

Multi-Society Task Force on PVS (1994). Medical aspects of the persistent vegetative state. *New England Journal of Medicine*, 330, 1572–9.

Namelak, A.N., Pitts, L.H., and Damron, S. (1996). Predicting survival from head trauma 24 h after injury: a practical method with therapeutic implications. *Journal of Trauma: Injury, Infection and Critical Care*, 41, 91–9.

O'Meara, E.S., Kukull, W.A., Sheppard, L., *et al.* (1997). Head injury and risk of Alzheimer's disease by apolipoprotein E genotype. *American Journal of Epidemiology*, 146, 373–84.

Overgaard, J., Hansen, O.H., Land, A.M., *et al.* (1981). Improved confidence of outcome prediction in severe head injury. *Journal of Neurosurgery*, 54, 751.

Pennings, J.L., Bachulis, B.L., Simons, C.T., *et al.* (1993). Survival after severe brain injury in the aged. *Archives of Surgery*, 128, 787.

Pentland, B., Jones, P.A., Roy, C.W., *et al.* (1986). Head injury in the elderly. *Age and Ageing*, 15, 193–202.

Pickard, J.D. and Czosnyka, M. (1993). Management of raised intracranial pressure. *Journal of Neurology, Neurosurgery and Psychiatry*, 56, 845–58.

Plum, F. and Posner, J.B. (1980). *The diagnosis of stupor and coma*, pp. 5–6. F.A. Davis, Philadelphia, PA.

Quigley, M.R., Vidovich, D., Cantella, D., *et al.* (1997). Defining the limits of survivorship after severe head injury. *Journal of Trauma: Injury, Infection and Critical Care*, 42, 7–10.

Raichle, M.E. and Plum, F. (1972). Hyperventilation and cerebral blood flow. *Stroke*, 3, 566–75.

Rakier, A., Guilburd, J.N., Soustiel, J.F., Zaaroor, M., and Feinsod, M. (1995). Head injuries in the elderly. *Brain Injury*, 9, 187–93.

Robertson, C.S., Contant, C.F., Narayan, R.K., *et al.* (1992). Cerebral blood flow, arteriovenous oxygen saturation difference, and neurologic outcome in head injured patients. *Journal of Neurotrauma*, 9 (Supplement 1), S349–58.

Ross, A.M., Pitts, L.H., Lobayashi, S., *et al.* (1992). Prognosticators of outcome after major head injury in the elderly, *Journal of Neurosurgical Nursing*, 24, 88.

Roy, C.W., Pentland, B., and Miller, J.D. (1986). The causes and consequences of minor head injury in the elderly. *Injury*, 17, 220–3.

Saab, M., Gray, A., Hodgkinson, D., and Irfan, M. (1996). Warfarin and the apparent minor head injury. *Journal of Accident and Emergency Medicine*, 13, 208–9.

Schiller, W.R., Knox, R., and Chleboard, W. (1995). A 5-year experience with severe head injuries in elderly patients. *Accident Analysis and Prevention*, 27, 167–74.

Schofield, P.W., Tang, M., Marder, K., *et al.* (1997). Alzheimer's disease after remote head injury: an incidence study. *Journal of Neurology, Neurosurgery and Psychiatry*, 62, 119–24.

Schroder, M.L., Muizelaaar, J.P., Bullock, M.R., Salvant, J.B., and Povlishock, J.T. (1995). Focal ischaemia due to traumatic contusions documented by stable xenon-CT and ultrastructural studies. *Journal of Neurosurgery*, 82, 966–71.

Stein, S.C. (1996). Management of minor closed head injury. *Neurosurgery Quarterly*, 6, 108–15.

Teasdale, G.M. (1996). Head injuries. In *Oxford textbook of medicine* (3rd edn) (ed. D.J. Weatherall, J.G.G. Ledingham, and D.A. Warrell), pp. 4044–50. Oxford University Press.

Teasdale, G.M. (1995). Head injury. *Journal of Neurology, Neurosurgery and Psychiatry*, **58**, 526–39.

Teasdale, G. and Jennett, B. (1974). Assessment of coma and impaired consciousness: a practical scale. *Lancet*, ii, 81–4.

Teasdale, G.M., Skeen, A., Parker L., *et al.* (1979). Age and outcome of severe head injury. *Acta Neurochirurgica*, **28** (Supplement), 140.

Teasdale, G.M., Murray, G., Anderson, E., *et al.* (1990). Risks of traumatic intracranial haematoma in children and adults: implications for managing head injuries, *British Medical Journal*, **300**, 363–7.

Temkin, N.R., Dimken, S.S., and Winn, H.R. (1991). Post-traumatic seizures. *Neurosurgical Clinics of North America*, **2**, 425–35.

Tinetti, M.E., Baker, D.I., McAvay, G., *et al.* (1994). Controlled trial of a risk abatement strategy for fall prevention among community elderly person. *New England Journal of Medicine*, **331**, 821–7.

Vollmer, D.G., Torner, J. C., Jane, J.A., *et al.* (1991). Age and outcome following traumatic coma: why do older patients fare worse? *Journal of Neurosurgery*, **75**, S37–49.

Wintzen, A.R. and Tijssen, J.G.P. (1982). Subdural haematoma and oral anticoagulant therapy. *Archives of Neurology*, **39**, 69–72.

Zimmerman, R. and Bilaniuk, L. (1981). Computed tomography in pediatric head trauma. *Journal of Neuroradiology*, **8**, 257–71.

Zwimpfer, T.J. and Moulton, R.J. (1993) Neurologic trauma concerns. *Critical Care Clinics*, **9**, 727–39.

18.23 Headaches and facial pain

James Howe

Backache and headache are the most common symptoms that people suffer (Crook *et al.* 1984). While backache is common in elderly individuals, people seem to complain less about headaches as they grow older. Zeigler *et al.* (1977) found that only 1 per cent of a population sample aged over 65 years had started to complain of severe headache in the previous year, although 18 per cent of the men and 29 per cent of the women over 65 years old complained of disabling or severe headaches. There are three causes of head pain that become more common with increasing age: temporal arteritis (see Chapter 13.5), trigeminal neuralgia, and post-herpetic neuralgia. Elderly people are subject to pain caused by other pathological processes in the head and neck as are younger people but migraine and tension headache are much less common.

In many studies the prevalence of both migraine and headache declines after middle age (Goldstein and Chen 1982); Leviton *et al.* (1974) reported a slightly higher risk of death before the age of 70 for migraine sufferers. However, migraine does not disappear altogether; Whitty and Hockaday (1968) reviewed a group of patients who had attended a hospital outpatient clinic up to 20 years before and found that half of them were still having migraine attacks after the age of 65.

When formulating a differential diagnosis of headache or facial pain for an elderly patient, it is useful to have a simple mental picture of the pain-sensitive structures in the head and sensory pathways, and to analyse the time course of the pain. It is particularly helpful to imagine and review all the tissues and organs in the solid part of the head that would be transected by a coronal cut from the vertex to the chin, remembering that they are all innervated by the trigeminal nerve. This means that pain from supratentorial intracranial structures and the sinuses is referred to the front of the head. The meninges and blood vessels are the intracranial tissues that contain pain-sensitive nerve endings. In humans, stimulation of the first cervical dorsal root refers pain to the frontal and orbital regions (Kerr 1961), but most disease of the upper cervical spine refers pain solely to the occiput and upper part of the neck (Edmeads 1979*a*). Degenerative arthropathy in the neck is universal in older people, yet neck pain is not a common complaint in geriatric wards and clinics. When severe neck pain does occur in an elderly person, malignant disease must be excluded (Edmeads 1979*a*).

Depressed patients may complain of headache, and patients with chronic headaches may become depressed (Romano and Turner 1985). In elderly people, depression is more likely to generate somatic complaints, being associated with an increase in hypochondriasis (Anonymous 1984), and the present generation of elderly people, at least in the United Kingdom, are much more likely to present to doctors with somatic complaints rather than emotional problems. This feature of the medicine of old age in the United Kingdom is likely to change over the next decade.

Atypical facial pain is not a diagnosis that should lightly be made in elderly patients. Frazier and Russell (1924) appear to have been the first to use this term to distinguish trigeminal neuralgia from other kinds of facial pain. Since then it has been used in the neurological literature to describe chronic facial pain in middle-aged people, especially women, with no evidence of an organic cause, and psychological factors have usually been blamed (Lascelles 1966; Friedman 1969). In dental practice similar patients are diagnosed as suffering from the temporomandibular joint pain–dysfunction syndrome (Feinmann and Harris 1984; Yusuf and Rothwell 1986). Problems like this sometimes bring patients to geriatricians.

It is uncommon for rheumatoid or degenerative arthritis to cause pain in the temporomandibular joint (Cawson 1984). Pain in the jaw precipitated by talking or chewing can be caused by ischaemia in cranial arteritis, so-called 'jaw claudication'. Hayreh *et al.* (1997) provide evidence that this symptom is strongly suggestive of giant cell arteritis.

Headache is also less common in elderly patients with cerebral tumours. Godfrey and Caird (1984) found that only 10 per cent of their series of patients had headache and only 2.5 per cent had papilloedema. In contrast, up to 43 per cent of patients with subdural haematoma report headache (Cameron 1978) but it is rare in patients with ischaemic stroke (Edmeads 1979*b*). Facial or head pain is usually a prominent feature with tumours involving bones, sinuses, and meninges (Wasserstrom *et al.* 1978).

Paget's disease of the skull can cause headache, cranial nerve palsies, and ataxia and spasticity if there is craniovertebral distortion due to basilar invagination (Friedman *et al.* 1971).

Carbon monoxide poisoning and carbon dioxide retention in chronic obstructive airways disease both cause headache. Old people with faulty gas appliances are at risk of carbon monoxide poisoning which, if not fatal can cause headache and confusion (James 1984).

Painful diseases involving the eyes, teeth, and sinuses are usually obvious but in a confused or dysphasic patient who appears to have head pain, such possibilities should be systematically considered, as should parotitis. This is more likely to occur in a frail dehydrated old person on an anticholinergic drug such as a tricyclic antidepressant.

Investigation

The erythrocyte sedimentation rate or plasma viscosity and C-reactive protein should be measured in all elderly patients with headache (Hayreh *et al.* 1997). Plain radiographs of the skull, sinuses, or neck bones may be needed. CT or magnetic resonance imaging may be indicated, as palliative treatment of tumours and hydrocephalus can be successful in elderly patients, subdural haematomas can be removed, infections cured, and Paget's disease treated (Cameron 1978; Godfrey and Caird 1984).

Specific conditions

Giant cell arteritis is dealt with in Chapter 13.5. Two other conditions that are particularly important in elderly people will be discussed here: trigeminal neuralgia and post-herpetic neuralgia.

Trigeminal neuralgia

This is a cause of severe pain, which becomes more common in older age groups. Disease or damage to the trigeminal nerve is presumed to cause increased firing in the nerve as well as impaired efficiency of central inhibitory mechanisms and leads to paroxysmal bursts of neuronal activity which cause sudden excruciating paroxysms of facial pain (Fromm *et al.* 1984). The lightning explosions of pain are often triggered by minimal cutaneous stimuli at particular places and patients may be unable to eat, shave, wash their faces, or blow their noses because of it. The pain rarely attacks all three sensory divisions of the nerve and the first division is less often affected than the other two. The presence of sensory loss or motor weakness should arouse suspicion of a progressive structural lesion affecting the nerve or nucleus, as should signs of involvement of neighbouring cranial

nerves. Many different lesions appear to be able to cause the chronic irritation that results in trigeminal neuralgia, including chronic oral and dental disease, tumours, plaques of multiple sclerosis, and, most commonly of all, tortuous blood vessels (Fromm *et al.* 1984). Progressive elongation and tortuosity of arterial loops with advancing age and atheroma seem to account for the increased prevalence of trigeminal neuralgia in old age.

Glossopharyngeal neuralgia is much less common. The pattern of pain is similar to trigeminal neuralgia but it is triggered from, and felt in, the throat, sometimes radiating to the ear. Involvement of vagal fibres may cause autonomic symptoms such as syncope or bradycardia (Rushton *et al.* 1981). Similar features, including cardiac arrest, have been reported in trigeminal neuralgia (Gottesman *et al.* 1996).

The pain of trigeminal neuralgia can be suppressed with anticonvulsant drugs such as carbamazepine, phenytoin, and clonazepam. Clobazam is effective and easier to use in frail, elderly patients who are often intolerant of the other drugs because of ataxia. Baclofen has also been used, with some success (Fromm *et al.* 1980). Newer anticonvulsants such as gabapentin and lamotrigine which are reported to have fewer side-effects may find a place in the management of neuralgia. In elderly patients, a low starting dose and gradual increases in dose are essential with carbamazepine and phenytoin if dangerous ataxia is to be avoided.

When drugs are ineffective, surgery should be considered and a number of options are open depending on the fitness of the patient. Peripheral nerve injection, followed if necessary by avulsion of the nerve to denervate the trigger area, can be worthwhile. Where this is not successful, radiofrequency lesions of the nerve root or ganglion can be tried. This is a safe technique and has a relatively low risk of side-effects but the pain can recur (Tew 1979). Neurosurgeons seem to be performing this procedure less and less (E. Ballantyne, personal communication). Microvascular decompression of the trigeminal nerve is said to be effective in over 90 per cent of patients (Richards *et al.* 1983). Long-term follow-up has shown that 30 per cent of patients develop recurrence of symptoms after microvascular decompression but second operations are possible. Ten years after surgery 70 per cent of patients in one series (Barker *et al.* 1996) were pain free without medication. These authors report very low complication rates. As a result of improvement in anaesthetic and surgical techniques elderly patients in severe pain should not be denied a neurosurgical opinion just because they are frail.

Post-herpetic neuralgia

Half of those who reach the age of 85 can expect an attack of herpes zoster (Hope-Simpson 1965) and the number of patients still suffering pain 1 year after the acute attack rises with increasing age. More than 60 per cent of those aged over 70 with involvement of the trigeminal nerve, which is the dermatome most commonly affected, and nearly half of those over 70 who have shingles elsewhere on the body, report persisting pain 1 year after the acute attack (de Morgas and Kierland 1957). The severity and duration of the pain, which is felt in the dermatome where the vesicles appeared, is worse in elderly people. It can be agonizing and persistent, is usually described as 'burning', with increased, painful and abnormal sensitivity to any stimulus in the affected area. Stabbing neuralgic-type pain can also occur and sufferers quickly become demoralized and depressed. Portenoy *et al.*

(1986) provide an authoritative account of the pathophysiology and management of post-herpetic neuralgia and recommend that pain continuing 2 months after the onset of the rash should be labelled post-herpetic neuralgia in order to compare therapeutic regimens.

Oral and intravenous aciclovir and oral famciclovir (De Greef 1994) have been shown to speed resolution and reduce the pain of the acute attack. Oral prednisolone in addition to acyclovir has been shown to reduce acute symptoms (Wood *et al.* 1994) and in frail elderly patients with severe pain should probably be used (Portenoy *et al.* 1986; BSSI 1995). So far there is still no evidence that this drug reduces the prevalence or severity of post-herpetic neuralgia (McKendrick *et al.* 1986). Antiviral drugs should definitely be used in all elderly patients with trigeminal herpes zoster, and when the neck, limbs, or perineum are involved. It has not yet been shown that other antiviral agents are superior to aciclovir (BSSI 1995).

The scheme recommended by Portenoy *et al.* (1986) for the management of post-herpetic neuralgia can be followed at a day hospital. They recommend the simultaneous prescription of a tricyclic antidepressant, physiotherapy, and occupational therapy to increase activity, build confidence, and improve function, and transcutaneous electrical nerve stimulation. Small portable stimulators are inexpensive, reliable, and useful in other pain syndromes but the response is variable and different electrode placements and stimulation protocols should be tried before transcutaneous electrical nerve stimulation is abandoned. If triggering of painful paroxysms is a feature, then anticonvulsants may be helpful. Hoffmann *et al.* (1994) report success with oral ketamine where other treatments had failed. Portenoy *et al.* (1986) emphasized the importance of psychological, functional, and social approaches to management from the start. Putting the patient back in control of at least some aspect of their problem is helpful in post-herpetic neuralgia as in any chronic disorder. Other simple measures including the use of cling film to protect sensitive areas, local anaesthetic cream, capsaicin ointment, and cold packs should be tried (BSSI 1995).

Instruction in methods of relaxation and distraction, and encouraging the patient to keep a diary to demonstrate increasing levels of physical and social activity, are all helpful. Neurolytic and surgical techniques should be avoided in post-herpetic neuralgia as they are generally unhelpful.

Conclusion

Headache may not be common in elderly people and diagnosis can be made more difficult by problems with communication and multiple pathology. Where pain develops rapidly and increases in severity, especially when associated with neurological signs, prompt and full investigation is needed. The pattern of pain in the more common conditions is usually characteristic and successful treatment is possible in most patients.

References

Anonymous (1984). Headache and depression (Editorial). *Lancet*, i, 495.

Barker, F.G. II, Janetta, P.J., Bissonette, D.J., Larkins, M.V., and Jho, H.D. (1996). The long term outcome of microvascular decompression for trigeminal neuralgia. *New England Journal of Medicine*, **374**, 1077–83.

BSSI (British Society for the Study of Infection) (1995). Special report. Guidelines for the management of shingles. *Journal of Infection*, **30**, 193–200.

Cameron, M.M. (1978). Chronic subdural haematoma: a review of 114 cases. *Journal of Neurology, Neurosurgery and Psychiatry*, **41**, 184–9.

Cawson, R.A. (1984). Pain in the temporomandibular joint. *British Medical Journal*, **188**, 1857–8.

Crook, J., Rideout, E., and Browne, G. (1984). The prevalence of pain complaints in a general population. *Pain*, **19**, 199–314.

De Greef, H. (1994). Famciclovir Herpes Zoster Clinical Study Group. Famciclovir, a new oral anti-herpes drug: results of the first controlled clinical study demonstrating its efficacy and safety in the treatment of uncomplicated herpes zoster in immunocompetent patients. *International Journal of Antimicrobial Agents*, **4**, 241–6.

Edmeads, J. (1979a). Headaches and head pains associated with diseases of the cervical spine. *Medical Clinics of North America*, **62**, 533–44.

Edmeads, J. (1979b). The headaches of ischaemic cerebrovascular disease. *Headache*, **19**, 345–9.

Feinmann, C. and Harris, M. (1984). Psychogenic facial pain. *British Dental Journal*, **156**, 165–8.

Frazier, C.H. and Russell, E.C. (1924). Neuralgia of the face. An analysis of 754 cases with relation to pain and other sensory phenomena before and after operation. *Archives of Neurology and Psychiatry*, **11**, 557–68.

Friedman, A.P. (1969). Atypical facial pain. *Headache*, **9**, 27–30.

Friedman, P., Sklaver, N., and Klawans, H.L. (1971). Neurological manifestations of Paget's disease of the skull. *Diseases of the Nervous System*, **32**, 809–17.

Fromm, G.H., Terrence, G.F., Chatta, A.S., and Glass, J.D. (1980). Baclofen in the treatment of refractory trigeminal neuralgia. *Archives of Neurology*, **37**, 768–71.

Fromm, G.H., Terrence, G.F., and Maroon, J.C. (1984). Trigeminal neuralgia: current concepts regarding aetiology and pathogenesis. *Archives of Neurology*, **41**, 1204–7.

Godfrey, J.B. and Caird, F.I. (1984). Intracranial tumours in the elderly: diagnosis and treatment. *Age and Ageing*, **13**, 152–8.

Goldstein, M. and Chen, T.C. (1982). The epidemiology of disabling headache. In *Headache, advances in neurology*, (ed. M. Critchley, A.P. Friedman, G. Schiffman, and F. Sicuteri), Vol. 33, pp. 377–90. Raven Press, New York.

Gottesman, M.H., Ibrahim, B., Elfenbein, A.S., Mechanic, A., and Hertz, S. (1996). Cardiac arrest caused by trigeminal neuralgia. *Headache*, **36**, 392–4.

Hayreh, S.S., Podhajsky, P.A., Raman, R., and Zimmerman, B. (1977). Giant cell arteritis: validity and reliability of various diagnostic criteria *American Journal of Ophthalmology*, **123**, 285–96.

Hoffmann, V., Coppejans, H., Vercauteran, M., and Adriaensen, H. (1994). Successful treatment of post-herpetic neuralgia with oral ketamine. *Clinical Journal of Pain*, **10**, 240–2.

Hope-Simpson, R.E. (1965). The nature of herpes zoster: a long term study and a new hypothesis. *Proceedings of the Royal Society, London (Biology)*, **58**, 9–20.

James, P.B. (1984). Carbon monoxide poisoning. *Lancet*, ii, 810.

Kerr, F.W.L. (1961). A mechanism to account for frontal headache in cases of posterior fossa tumour. *Journal of Neurosurgery*, **18**, 605–9.

Lascelles, R.G. (1966). Atypical facial pain and depression. *British Journal of Psychiatry*, **112**, 651–59.

Leviton, A., Malvea, B., and Graham, J.R. (1974). Vascular disease, mortality and migraine in the parents of migraine patients. *Neurology*, **24**, 669–72.

McKendrick, M.W., McGill, J.I., White, J.E., and Wood, M.J. (1986). Oral acyclovir in acute herpes zoster. *British Medical Journal*, **293**, 1529–32.

Portenoy, R.K., Duma, D., and Foley, K.M. (1986). Acute herpetic and post-herpetic neuralgia: clinical review and current management. *Annals of Neurology*, **20**, 651–64.

Richards, P., Shawdon, H., and Illingworth, R. (1983). Operative findings on microsurgical exploration of the cerebello-pontine angle in trigeminal neuralgia. *Journal of Neurology, Neurosurgery and Psychiatry*, **46**, 1098–101.

Romano, J.M. and Turner, J.A. (1985). Chronic pain and depression: does the evidence support a relationship? *Psychological Bulletin*, **97**, 18–34.

Rushton, J.G., Stevens, J.C., and Miller, R.H. (1981). Glossopharyngeal (vagoglossopharyngeal) neuralgia: a study of 217 cases. *Archives of Neurology*, **38**, 201–5.

Tew, J.M. (1979). Treatment of trigeminal neuralgia. *Neurosurgery*, **4**, 93–4.

Wasserstrom, W.R., Glass, J.P., and Posner, J.B. (1978). Diagnosis and treatment of leptomeningeal metastases from solid tumours. *Cancer*, **49**, 759–72.

Whitty, C.W.M. and Hockaday, J.M. (1968). Migraine: a follow up study of 92 patients. *British Medical Journal*, i, 735–6.

Wood, M.J., Johnson, R.W., McKendrik, M.W., Taylor, J., Mandal, B.K., and Crook, J. (1994). A randomised trial of acyclovir for 7 days or 21 days with and without prednisolone for the treatment of acute herpes zoster. *New England Journal of Medicine*, **330**, 896–900.

Yusuf, H. and Rothwell, P.S. (1986). Temporo-mandibular joint pain—dysfunction in patients suffering from atypical facial pain. *British Dental Journal*, **161**, 208–12.

Ziegler, D.K., Hassanein, R.S., and Couch, J.R. (1977). Characteristics of life headache histories in a non-clinic population. *Neurology*, **27**, 265–9.

18.24 Dizziness

W. J. MacLennan

Introduction

Dizziness is a common symptom in old age which confronts the clinician with major problems in diagnosis and management. Patients use the term to describe sensations that may include unsteadiness, light-headedness, anxiety, vertigo, or even syncope. Even detailed questioning may fail to elicit their exact nature. A further difficulty is that physical examination may reveal a whole series of abnormalities, and it is difficult to determine which of these is responsible for the symptom. Finally, the patient may present to a neurologist with little experience of geriatric medicine, to a geriatrician with little experience of otolaryngology, or to an otolaryngologist with little experience of cardiology. A wide-ranging medical education and effective rapport with specialist colleagues is thus a prerequisite for the effective management of this condition.

Epidemiology

At ages over 65 years, between a quarter and a third of men and 30 to 40 per cent of women report some form of dizziness with only a minor increase with age (Grimley Evans 1990; Colledge *et al.* 1994). It is more common in individuals with vascular disease such as angina, a previous stroke or hypertension. Rotatory vertigo and non-rotatory dizziness may differ in their implications. In one epidemiological study, vertigo was associated with an enhanced risk of subsequent stroke but not with a history of falls. For non-rotatory dizziness the opposite was found (Grimley Evans 1990).

Aetiology

Ageing

Ageing has an adverse effect on most of the end-organs and neuronal pathways concerned with balance. An example is the decline in peripheral position sense. A further cause of ataxia is damage to neuronal pathways within the midbrain. Experimental lesions of the posterior vermis of the cerebellum in animals, and damage to this site in humans produce a truncal ataxia, a picture that is found in many elderly people who are unsteady on their feet, but who have few other focal neurological signs.

Ageing is associated with a reduction in the number of hair cell receptors within the vestibular apparatus, and a concomitant reduction in the number of fibres in the vestibular nerve. There is no clear relationship between these changes and clinical evidence of vestibular dysfunction or ataxia in old age.

Vision also has an important part to play in regulating balance, so that old people whose balance is already compromised by proprioceptive defects, midbrain damage, and, possibly, vestibular degeneration are at particular risk if they suffer from one of the range of eye defects common in old age.

Cerebral function is dependent upon an adequate blood supply and this may be compromised by postural hypotension. This is fairly

Table 1 Causes of dizziness in old age

System	Disorder
Neurological	Vertebrobasilar insufficiency
	Carotid artery stenosis
	Subclavian steal
	Cerebellar ischaemia
	Drop attacks
	Epilepsy
	Anxiety neurosis
	Depression
Cardiovascular	Carotid sinus hypersensitivity
	Cardiac arrhythmias
	Aortic stenosis
	Postural hypotension
Metabolic	Hyperventilation
	Diabetes/hyperglycaemia
Otological	Positional nystagmus
	Vestibular neuronitis
	Infection
	Vascular damage
	Menière's syndrome
	Acoustic neuroma
	Drug side-effects
Other	Ocular
	Cervical spondylosis
	Cough syncope
	Anaemia
	Micturition syncope

common, even in healthy old people, but is often not associated with symptoms (see Chapter 18.12).

Disease in old age

A wide range of disorders common in old age may be responsible for dizziness. It is important to recognize, however, that in many cases even detailed investigation may fail to reveal a specific cause. Thus, a survey of 740 old people presenting to an otological clinic with dizziness revealed that only 21 per cent had diseases specifically associated with the symptom (Belal and Glorig 1986). The remainder were disabled by one or more of the degenerative processes associated with ageing, and were labelled as suffering from 'presbyastasis'.

Table 1 lists possible causes for recurrent episodes of dizziness in elderly people. This is not comprehensive in that many less common disorders have been omitted. However, it forms a useful framework on which a history, physical examination, and investigation can be based. A single episode of dizziness may be the first manifestation of one of these disorders. Alternatively, it may herald a brainstem infarction or haemorrhage, or may indicate a sudden fall in the intracranial perfusion pressure resulting from haemorrhage, dehydration, or a cardiovascular catastrophe.

Dizziness in old people usually occurs in the context of multiple pathology so that the cause for the symptom is often multifactorial. It is also often of such severity that it is responsible for general misery and a poor quality of life (Grimby and Rosenhall 1995).

Assessment

History

Assessment of dizziness is simplified if a systematic approach is taken to history taking, physical examination, and investigation. An attempt should be made to distinguish the rotational symptom of vertigo from other sensations. Information on the time course, duration, and frequency of symptoms is important, as is a history of precipitating factors such as neck movements, or exposure to drugs. Symptoms of deafness and dizziness increase the likelihood of the lesion being central, whilst those of diplopia, weakness, and ataxia indicate that it is peripheral. Nausea and vomiting are common where vertigo is related to vestibular dysfunction, but rare in other conditions. Vertigo of central origin is more likely to be associated with diplopia, dysarthria, incoordination, numbness, or weakness.

If there is no clear history of vertigo, then symptoms of imbalance in the lower limbs, light-headedness, or blackouts, may indicate the aetiology. Again, the association of any of these with a particular medication may be relevant. Questions relating to mental health should also be asked and, where appropriate, scales relating to anxiety or depression administered (Sullivan *et al.* 1993).

Physical examination

A full examination of the cardiovascular and neurological systems is essential. In relation to the first of these, particular attention should be paid to identification of the cardiac rhythm, to palpation of the carotid arteries, and to auscultation of the heart valves and over the subclavian, carotid, and subclavian arteries. Lying and standing systolic and diastolic blood pressures should be recorded, the latter being estimated immediately and 2 min after the patient has assumed an erect position. Neurological signs of particular relevance include nystagmus, intention tremor, past pointing, and abnormalities of the corticospinal tract. Eyesight is tested with a near-vision chart. Adequate evaluation of position sense is difficult, but one way of quantifying this is to score out of 20 the ability of patients to identify correctly five movements each for the right and left halluces and ankles. Balance should be tested by asking the patient to stand with feet comfortably apart, first with eyes open and then with eyes closed. A more accurate evaluation of balance may be obtained by asking the patient to assume a series of positions ranging from standing with legs comfortably apart with eyes open, to standing with one foot in front of the other ('tandem standing') with eyes closed (Gabell and Simons 1982).

Where appropriate, a more detailed examination should include testing for positional nystagmus. In summary, the patient is seated on a table, the head is turned 45° to one side, and then lowered to an angle 30° below the horizontal; the test is then repeated with the head turned to 45° in the opposite direction; the test is finally repeated with the head looking forwards. With each manoeuvre a careful evaluation is made of any eye movements (Venna 1986*a*).

Balance may also be compromised by locomotor problems so that the feet and ankles, hip and knee joints should be examined. The range of movement within the cervical vertebrae should also be tested.

Investigations

Simple baseline investigations of dizziness should include haemoglobin, blood urea and electrolyte levels, a random blood glucose

Table 2 Causes of syncope in elderly patients[a]

	Percentage
Cardio-inhibitory carotid sinus syndrome	5
Vasodepressor carotid sinus syndrome	26
Mixed carotid sinus syndrome	14
Orthostatic hypotension	32
Vasodepressor vasovagal syncope	11
Cardiac arrhythmia	21
Epilepsy	9
Cerebrovascular disease	6
Others	12.5

[a] Many patients had more than one pathology.

Reproduced with permission from McIntosh et al. (1993).

concentration, an ECG, and a chest radiograph. Although cervical spondylosis may cause dizziness or ataxia in a variety of ways, osteoarthritic changes are almost universal in the necks of old people so that radiography is of no diagnostic value (Adams et al. 1986). Balance can be quantified by measuring the magnitude and velocity of sway with an individual standing on a force platform, but there is no relationship between these and the causes or frequency of falls (Baloh et al. 1995).

If dizziness is associated with other symptoms such as syncope further investigations may be appropriate. These include ambulatory ECG, carotid sinus massage, and a reaction to prolonged head-up tilt (McIntosh et al. 1993). Diagnoses made as a result of these investigations on a group of elderly patients are detailed in Table 2 (see also Chapter 4.4).

Cardiovascular investigations

Sensitivity of the carotid sinuses is tested by lightly massaging in turn the right and left common carotid arteries for 5 s each. A sinus is diagnosed as hypersensitive if massage causes a cardio-inhibitory pause of more than 3 s, or a drop in blood pressure of more than 50 mmHg. The pulse rate is measured on an ECG, and the blood pressure recorded by continuous non-invasive monitoring. Complications are uncommon but do occur. In a review of 5000 investigations it was found that seven patients had developed neurological signs consisting of five with pyramidal signs and two with visual field defects (Munro et al. 1994). In one case with pyramidal signs the changes were permanent.

Ambulatory ECG monitoring should be run for at least 24 h, but periods of up to 7 days may be necessary if an arrhythmia is particularly elusive. Continuous-loop ECG recording is usually needed for such long periods of monitoring. There should be a system whereby the patient records symptoms to identify a temporal link between symptoms and arrhythmias since these are frequently found in elderly people without dizziness.

Lesions of the subclavian, vertebral, and carotid arteries can be identified by retrograde transfemoral or brachial angiography.

However, the techniques are invasive, and are associated with a significant though low incidence of serious morbidity. Less invasive tests include Doppler angiography, intravenous digital subtraction angiography, and magnetic resonance imaging (**MRI**) (Wentz et al. 1994).

Neurological investigations

Electronystagmography is particularly useful in defining lesions suspected of involving the peripheral parts of the vestibular system, whereas a test involving vestibular autorotation is more helpful for the investigation of a lesion thought to be central in origin such as a head injury (Murphy 1994).

Electrophysiological tests are of value in pursuing the possibility of epilepsy (see Chapter 18.4). They are also useful in monitoring the course of transient ischaemic attacks. An example is that brainstem, auditory-evoked responses separate out different parts of the labyrinthine pathway and have been used to identify and monitor temporary neurological damage after vertebrobasilar, transient ischaemic attacks (Factor and Detinger 1987). The test is also useful in distinguishing an acoustic neuroma from Ménière's disease. Computed force platforms and more elaborate posturography equipment have been widely used as research tools in defining the roles of vision, position sense, and vestibular function in controlling balance (Harcourt 1995). Clinical experience has established that they are of limited value in defining diagnoses in individual patients.

Although CT is often of value in defining a cerebral lesion, it is less sensitive than MRI in identifying abnormalities of the midbrain and cerebellum. The technique has identified cerebellar atrophy associated with ageing but there was no correlation between these changes and ataxia. Truncal ataxia may be associated with changes in the vermis and CT is insufficiently sensitive to identify these. MRI is of value in this context.

Even if a clinician takes a full history, makes a detailed examination, and organizes appropriate tests he or she may be left with no convincing explanation for dizziness, or with several minor abnormalities, any one of which or any combination could account for the symptom. Although a well-designed algorithm is useful, particularly in general practice, a considerable amount of frustration, compromise, and empiricism is inevitable in dealing with this difficult area (Colledge et al. 1996).

Vertebrobasilar insufficiency

This condition may present as recurrent, non-specific episodes of dizziness (Venna 1986b). Eventually, however, there are the additional symptoms of midbrain ischaemia, which include limb numbness or weakness, facial paraesthesia, dysarthria, diplopia, and visual impairment. These may or may not be accompanied by clinical signs of permanent damage to the midbrain, cerebellum, or occipital cortex. The condition is usually associated with atheroma of the vertebral or basilar arteries. Contrary to earlier opinions, 71 per cent of cases of vertebrobasilar deficiency are due to combined carotid and vertebral artery stenosis, with only 13 per cent due an isolated vertebral lesion (Delcker et al. 1993). There are even a few patients in whom stenosis is confined to the carotid artery. The extent to which emboli cause vertebrobasilar symptoms is uncertain. Emboli from the stenotic ostia

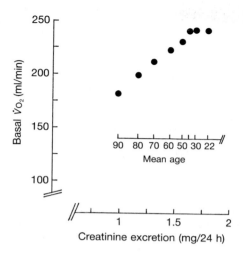

Fig. 1 The decline in total muscle mass with increasing age (as reflected in 24-h creatinine excretion) is associated with a reduced basal metabolic rate (basal oxygen consumption). Data from male volunteers. (Redrawn from Tzankoff and Norris (1977).)

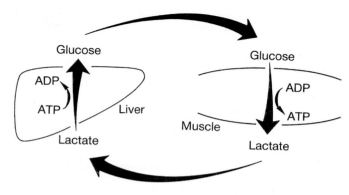

Fig. 2 The Cori cycle, viewed as a substrate cycle. More ATP is used to convert lactate to glucose than is synthesized in converting glucose to lactate; the result is that the overall cycle converts chemical energy into heat.

age. The progressive reduction in creatinine excretion described by Tzankoff and Norris (1977) corresponds to a 45 per cent reduction in total muscle mass between 23 and 90 years of age (Fig. 1). In frail and/or chronically malnourished elderly patients, the loss of muscle mass may be even more dramatic. The changes in drug pharmacokinetics which result from this change in body composition are well known, with a greatly prolonged half-life for fat-soluble drugs and an elevated peak plasma level following the administration of a water-soluble drug. The metabolic consequences of the reduced muscle mass are less well known although it seems likely that some may be at least as important, limiting the elderly patient's ability to mount and sustain an adequate metabolic response in times of stress due, for example, to sepsis, trauma, surgery, other severe illness, or cold.

Sarcopenia and survival from severe illness

Age alone has only a modest impact on survival from critical illness (Mahul *et al.* 1991; Kass *et al.* 1992; Rockwood *et al.* 1993). What matters is the severity and duration of illness, extent of organ dysfunction, and previous health status; it is the physiological reserve of the patient to cope with both the extent and the duration of the insult that is important. Skeletal muscle, accounting for some 40 per cent of a young man's body weight and 50 per cent of his body protein, is a major physiological reserve which is called upon in critical illness.

Metabolic events in severe illness

Cuthbertson's hypermetabolic 'flow' phase—after major surgery, trauma, or sepsis—starts with increased circulating concentrations of adrenaline, glucagon, cortisol, and glucose followed by elevated insulin levels. Increased glucocorticoids and glucagon induce muscle wasting

by decreasing protein synthesis. Disturbances of the actions of insulin and insulin-like growth factor 1 (IGF-1), coupled with reduced protein intake, impair protein synthesis in muscle. Glucose turnover is increased, with increased gluconeogenesis from lactate and alanine and with a major contribution from glutamine. The rates of efflux of alanine and glutamine from skeletal muscle are increased and their levels in muscle are depleted. Increased uptake of alanine and glutamine occurs in the liver, intestine, and immune system. Thus there is an increase in the body flux of nitrogen with a net loss from muscle. The role of skeletal muscle in illness can be seen as providing a pool of amino acids that can be mobilized, not only for hepatic gluconeogenesis but also for the hepatic synthesis of acute-phase proteins, enzymes, metal-binding proteins, and antioxidants such as glutathione. In particular, the increased nitrogen flux, sustained by the consumption of muscle protein, ensures a plentiful supply of glutamine, essential for the function of macrophages, lymphocytes, and cells involved in repair (Newsholme *et al.* 1988), as discussed below.

Sympathetic stimulation is partially responsible for the elevation in metabolic rate and core temperature after injury. At least part of this increased thermogenesis results from increased rates of substrate cycling. For instance, in severely burned patients there is increased activity of the intracellular triacylglycerol–fatty acid cycle and the glycolytic–gluconeogenic cycles in the liver (Wolfe *et al.* 1987). Indeed, the Cori cycle (Fig. 2) can be considered to be another large substrate cycle. It acts as a dynamic buffer to provide adequate amounts of circulating glucose and/or lactate for tissues which may need to use them at high but variable rates during illness (e.g. lymphocytes, macrophages, fibroblasts, endothelial cells) (discussed below).

Skeletal muscle and survival

The metabolic responses to the increasingly severe challenges imposed by elective surgery, multiple trauma, sepsis, and burns can be seen as 'purposeful and ultimately beneficial' (Beisel 1986), but the cost is high and they cannot be sustained indefinitely. In particular, prolonged or particularly serious illness severely depletes the labile store of nitrogen in the muscle. Over a 21-day period after trauma or sepsis critically ill patients have average losses of 17 per cent in extracellular water, 17 per cent intracellular water, 16 per cent total body protein,

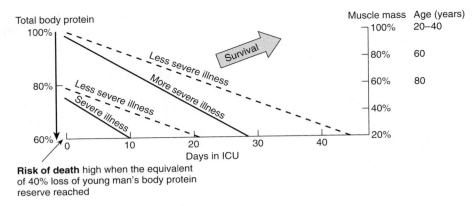

Fig. 3 Diagram illustrating protein consumption in the critically ill and the relationship between total body protein, muscle mass, and age with potential days of survival in the intensive care unit. The rates of loss of muscle and protein are consistent with current evidence. The elderly or malnourished patient starts with a reduced protein and muscle reserve, and so the days of potential survival will be reduced. Any therapy that can reduce the consumption of protein will buy time for the patient, by reducing the slope or bending the curves out to the right and so extending their survival time. However, once 40 per cent of total body protein depletion has occurred (equivalent to an 80 per cent loss of skeletal muscle) there is a high risk of death.

and 19 per cent total body potassium (Finn *et al.* 1996). Such staggering losses of lean body mass (whole-body water and protein) of almost 1 per cent per day of illness are far greater than can be accounted for by bed rest alone. Even the weightlessness of a long space flight produces losses at only one-tenth of this rate. A rough calculation shows that losses sustained at this rate over 40 days in an initially healthy young man would produce the same critical loss of 40 per cent lean body mass (or of total body protein) seen historically (Winick 1979) in those dying from starvation.

Skeletal muscle accounts for about half of the total body protein. Muscle biopsies from very sick patients show a loss of fibre area of some 2 per cent per day averaged over 21 days (Helliwell *et al.* 1991), indicating that most of the loss of lean body tissue has occurred from skeletal muscle. Thus, a 40 per cent fall in lean body mass implies a 70 to 80 per cent loss of muscle.

In a healthy 60-year-old (the median age for general intensive care admissions) the skeletal muscle mass has already been reduced by 20 per cent from that of a young adult. This is equivalent to the loss of some 10 days of 'protein reserve' and so shortens the projected survival time to 30 days. The oldest 20 per cent of admissions (average age approximately 80 years) might expect an average projected survival time of only 20 days (Fig. 3).

A small muscle mass not only shortens but also weakens the metabolic defence which can be mounted: the smaller the muscle mass before the illness, the less the mobilization of muscle protein and the worse the impact of the illness on the patient (Allison 1986). For example, the remaining amount of skeletal muscle mass is an important determinant of life expectancy in cancer (Heymsfield *et al.* 1982), the extent of malnutrition (based on a combination of indicators, including arm muscle circumference) is a major predictor of mortality in elderly medical patients, notably those with heart failure (Cederholm *et al.* 1995), and there is even the much earlier observation that the greater the preoperative weight loss the greater the mortality associated with surgery for peptic ulcer (Studley 1936).

Cachexia, as judged from anthropometric indices, is closely linked with death rates after femoral fracture. In a study in Nottingham of 744 elderly women with fractures of the neck of the femur, the 47 per cent who had triceps skinfold thickness (fat) and mid-arm muscle circumferences similar to a reference population had only a 4.4 per cent fatality, the 34 per cent with values between 1 and 2 standard deviations below the reference means had a doubling of fatality, while the remaining 19 per cent who were even thinner had a fatality of 18 per cent (Bastow *et al.* 1983*a*). Supplementary nasogastric feeding of the two thinner groups increased their total caloric intake, improved their anthropometric indices, and shortened the time to independent mobility. Fatality in the very thin group was reduced to 8 per cent, although this difference was not statistically significant (Bastow *et al.* 1983*b*). A Swiss study also suggests that supplementary nutrition is beneficial for elderly patients with femoral fracture (Delmi *et al.* 1990).

There is a role for supplementary feeding in helping to meet the heavy metabolic demands imposed by trauma and surgery and, in so doing, to reduce the amount of muscle tissue sacrificed to meet those metabolic requirements. The recommendation (Allison 1986) for 'per- and postoperative feeding to mimic the substrate mobilization of injury in the patients who have no substrate to mobilise' applies with particular force to frail elderly patients and deserves to be practised more widely.

Glutamine and survival

Characteristically, critically ill patients experience an inflammatory response resulting from tissue injury or infection and involving endocrine and paracrine effectors, immune system activation, the release of inflammatory mediators, and the generation of oxidants and free radicals. This has profound pathophysiological effects on the heart, vasculature, and organs and can result in the syndrome of multiple organ failure.

Muscle provides a massive dynamic reservoir of proteins, minerals, and other intermediate metabolites which is 'cannibalized' to meet the needs of tissues activated and involved in the inflammatory response. Glutamine is the most abundant amino acid in the body, accounting for nearly two-thirds of the free intracellular amino acid pool. The glutamine concentration in intramuscular water is typically some 30 times that in plasma. This is a vast free pool. Glutamine is released from skeletal muscle through a specific transport system

(system N) (Rennie *et al.* 1994) whose activity is increased in times of stress. It is a precursor for protein synthesis and donates nitrogen for the synthesis of purines, pyrimidines, nucleotides and amino sugars, and glutamate for the synthesis of glutathione, an important antioxidant. It is an important fuel for the small intestine (Windmueller and Spaeth 1974) and some cells of the immune system (Newsholme *et al.* 1985), and is used at a high rate by these cells. It is also important in the kidney in acid–base balance. In the critically ill patient, plasma and intracellular depletion of glutamine occur and this predisposes to impaired tissue healing, poor immune function, and reduced survival. The elderly patient's reduced muscle mass before the illness implies that this state of critical glutamine deficiency will occur sooner than in a younger person.

Until recently, commercially available amino acid solutions used for intravenous parenteral nutrition did not contain glutamine because of technical difficulties. Glutamine administration can counteract the fall in muscle protein synthesis following surgery, but if supplements are discontinued prematurely intracellular glutamine falls again (Hammarqvist *et al.* 1989). Therefore there was the potential for the supply of glutamine from muscle to be critically limiting in severely ill patients dependent on parenteral nutrition. In a prospective block-randomized double-blind clinical study, survival at 6 months was significantly better with a glutamine-supplemented feed (57 per cent) than with an isonitrogenous isoenergetic control feed (33 per cent) (Griffiths *et al.* 1997). The glutamine-supplemented feed also led to a 50 per cent reduction in the total hospital cost per survivor. The excess deaths with the glutamine-deficient control feed all occurred after 21 days, by which time, following the preceding discussion, it might be expected that due to progressive skeletal muscle loss, endogenous glutamine supply had become critical to survival. It is unlikely that functional muscle mass was preserved but rather the survival advantage may have been because exogenous glutamine supplemented the limited endogenous glutamine available from a greatly reduced muscle mass, so ameliorating some of the immediate consequences of a low plasma level of glutamine. This beneficial effect of glutamine may last as long as the elderly patient has sufficient remaining cardiac or respiratory muscle mass for cardiorespiratory function. The older the patient, the earlier in the course of severe illness will the lack of available glutamine become critical. Therefore it seems likely that with increasing age the need for supplementary glutamine will occur sooner, in a higher proportion of patients, and after less severe insult. Fortunately, some new formulations of amino acid solutions now include dipeptides which contain glutamine. (See also Chapter 23.7.)

Other potential interventions

Other approaches have been at least tentatively explored. Potentially beneficial interventions might attempt to enlarge the muscle mass before major surgery, spare muscle during the catabolic phase of illness, or hasten the restoration of muscle mass after the catabolic phase has run its course. In all of them the net gain or loss of skeletal muscle is ultimately determined by the balance between protein synthesis and degradation (Gizard *et al.* 1995). While much is known about the mechanisms and control of protein synthesis less is understood about proteolysis and its control in muscle.

If we accept that the breakdown of muscle in critical illness is part of an integrated set of responses which are essentially life preserving, it would seem foolish to try to prevent muscle breakdown without ensuring an adequate alternative source of the most important products of muscle catabolism. Once again, the administration of glutamine appears to offer exciting possibilities; it may combine both elements. As discussed above, glutamine may well be one of the most important products of muscle breakdown. In addition, work on the hydration state of liver cells indicates cellular hydration as a signal and regulator of proteolysis. Cellular dehydration has been implicated as a mechanism influencing the extent of catabolism in disease (Häussinger *et al.* 1993). Since amino acids, and in particular glutamine, can induce cell swelling they may be antiproteolytic.

Growth hormone

It is possible that treatment with recombinant human growth hormone might counteract the loss of muscle mass associated with injury or critical illness. This has been explored from all three directions: improving muscle mass before elective surgery, as an anticatabolic agent, and as an anabolic agent.

The first approach was studied with older patients undergoing elective hip-replacement surgery (Weissberger *et al.* 1996). A month's treatment with recombinant growth hormone produced 5 per cent preoperative muscle growth. Although this is unlikely to be of major clinical benefit in the context of the relatively good preoperative muscle mass of such patients and the relatively mild metabolic insult of their surgery, preoperative recombinant growth hormone may yet prove to have a role in preparing patients for more severe elective operations, such as for an abdominal aortic aneurysm.

It is the potential role of recombinant human growth hormone as an anticatabolic agent that has received the greatest attention (Ross *et al.* 1993). Numerous studies have shown improved nitrogen retention in catabolic patients treated with supraphysiological doses of growth hormone. Few, however, have demonstrated clinical benefit although there are some promising indications. The main problem limiting the use of growth hormone as an anticatabolic treatment seems to be that the more severely ill the patient, the poorer the IGF-1 response to the administration of growth hormone. Several research groups are now examining the effectiveness of using IGF-1 itself, either alone or in combination with growth hormone, as an anticatabolic agent.

Growth hormone therapy during convalescence, when catabolism has ceased, may have more potential. It has its origins in the observation that young adult patients with growth hormone deficiency have a low muscle mass and that treatment with recombinant human growth hormone increases muscle mass, muscle strength, and aerobic exercise performance (Cuneo *et al.* 1991a, 1991b). Indeed one study observed that the gain in quadriceps strength was proportional to the peak IGF-1 level (Rutherford *et al.* 1994). Although healthy elderly men do not appear to gain any additional benefit when treatment with recombinant growth hormone is added to strength training (Yarasheski *et al.* 1995), there may be some very frail patients for whom strength training is impractical. Encouraging results have been reported from an open study of treatment with recombinant growth hormone for patients who are proving difficult to wean from a ventilator (Knox *et al.* 1996). A blinded study of the treatment of HIV-associated cachexia reported gains in lean body mass and treadmill exercise performance (Schambelan *et al.* 1996). Unfortunately, however, the circulating IGF-1 response to treatment with recombinant growth hormone after surgery to repair hip fracture is inversely proportional to the severity of cachexia (Yeo *et al.* 1996); the response is least in those most in need of an anabolic boost. Whilst the possibility remains that circulating IGF-1 is of less importance for muscle growth than its local production in muscle, it is clear that the efficacy of recombinant growth hormone as a treatment for sarcopenia in frail, cachectic elderly patients cannot be assumed.

Testosterone and anabolic steroids

Despite their popularity amongst unethical athletes, the evidence, from adequately controlled studies, that these agents improve muscle size and strength is surprisingly limited. Such evidence as exists is for testosterone. A well-designed study showed that treatment of healthy young men with testosterone increased muscle cross-sectional area and strength by about 10 per cent (Bhasin *et al.* 1996). Moreover, the gains were in addition to gains achieved by strength training. In androgen-deficient men with AIDS-related cachexia (Grinspoon *et al.* 1998) and in older men receiving prolonged prednisolone treatment (Reid *et al.* 1996), testosterone produced a treatment advantage of 14 per cent in total muscle mass and of 5 per cent in lean body mass, respectively. An uncontrolled study of older men also suggests the possibility of testosterone-induced improvements in strength, coupled with increases in intramuscular messenger RNA for IGF-1 and an increased fractional synthetic rate for muscle protein (Urban *et al.* 1995).

β_2 agonists

β_2 adrenoceptor agonists (e.g. clenbuterol) promote muscle growth in laboratory and agricultural animals, where their effects include counteracting the generalized muscle wasting associated with experimental femoral fracture or scalding (Choo *et al.* 1990; Martineau *et al.* 1993). However, evidence of their efficacy in humans remains sparse, being limited to one study of healthy young men, one of young men with quadriceps wasting after open meniscectomy, and one of young men with spinal cord injury (Martineau *et al.* 1992; Maltin *et al.* 1993; Signorile *et al.* 1995).

Exercise and stretch

Use and stretch both stimulate muscle growth. Even elderly people can increase muscle protein synthesis with strength training (Yarasheski *et al.* 1993), with a 10 per cent increase in muscle size (Frontera *et al.* 1988; Fiatarone *et al.* 1990) or perhaps a 5 to 6 per cent increase in total muscle mass (Nelson *et al.* 1994). Although strength training may be impossible for ill patients, passive stretching of muscles may still be possible. In critically ill patients passive stretch reduces protein loss and muscle fibre atrophy, probably by reducing proteolytic activity (Griffiths *et al.* 1995). Mechanical forces are now recognized as powerful influences for muscle growth with a number of cellular changes linking mechanical stimulation to gene expression, and mediated by the autocrine–paracrine action of IGF-1 (Millward 1995; Yang *et al.* 1996). However, it remains unclear to what extent it is the synthesis of contractile or non-contractile proteins that is stimulated through each mechanism.

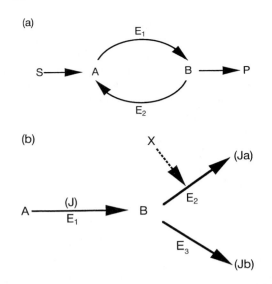

Fig. 4 (a) A hypothetical substrate cycle. A substrate cycle is produced when a non-equilibrium reaction in the forward direction (A→B) catalysed by enzyme E_1 is opposed by another non-equilibrium reaction in the reverse direction (B→A) catalysed by enzyme E_2. The highest sensitivity is achieved when the cycling rate is high compared with the flux through the pathway (S→P). (b) The regulation of flux through a branch in a branched pathway. A branched pathway is produced when the flux (J) divides into two separate fluxes (Ja) and (Jb) The overall response of Ja to X is most effective when Jb is much greater than Ja, i.e. when Ja is much smaller than the total flux (J).

Other metabolic functions of muscle

In order to understand metabolic changes that may depend on changes in elderly muscle, it is necessary to appreciate the mechanisms that may enhance sensitivity in the control of metabolic processes, permitting the flux in a metabolic pathway to undergo a rapid and considerable increase. (The theory and principles underlying this concept are discussed by Crabtree *et al.* (1999).) The rates of many processes change hugely in response to physiological stimuli (e.g. walking upstairs requires an increase in the rate of glycolysis of several hundredfold). Such large changes in flux may be mediated by mechanisms which increase sensitivity, for example 'substrate cycles' (Newsholme 1980) and 'branched-point sensitivity' (Newsholme *et al.* 1988). These mechanisms may become less effective in old age.

Substrate cycles

A substrate cycle exists if a reaction which is non-equilibrium in the 'forward' direction of a pathway operates simultaneously with an opposing reaction which is non-equilibrium in the reverse direction of the pathway and which is catalysed by a different enzyme (Fig. 4(a)). A substrate cycle is an energy-consuming and heat-producing process. Catecholamines increase the rate of cycling. There are several examples of tissues and reactions where responsiveness to both adrenaline and noradrenaline is decreased in old age, even though the plasma levels may be elevated.

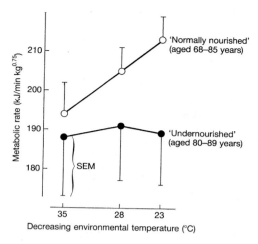

Fig. 5 Effect of nutritional status on the ability of elderly women to increase their metabolic rate in response to a cold challenge. (Redrawn from the data of Fellows *et al.* (1985).)

Branched-point sensitivity

The increased sensitivity in metabolic control provided by the branched-point mechanism is similar in principle to that achieved in the substrate cycle; a continuous high flux in one branch of a pathway provides optimal conditions for the precise regulation of the (much smaller) flux in the other branch (Fig. 4(b)).

Heat production

Even healthy elderly subjects seem to be less able than young adults to maintain their core temperature when exposed to a low ambient temperature (Collins *et al.* 1985). Amongst elderly subjects, those who are thinnest are most at risk, showing a fall in core temperature (and therefore in muscle temperature) after only a mild degree of cooling. This is not merely because of their poorer insulation but because they are less able to mount a protective increase in their metabolic rate (Fig. 5) (Fellows *et al.* 1985). This may be due, in part, to their smaller total muscle mass but it seems likely that there is also a qualitative change which results in a decreased ability to stimulate substrate cycles in muscle and other tissues (especially adipose tissue). Perhaps the catecholamine sensitivity of thermogenic cycles is even lower in cachectic than in well-nourished elderly people. However, this has yet to be confirmed.

Glucose tolerance

It is well known that old age is accompanied by impairment of the ability to correct the hyperglycaemia produced by an oral glucose load. As muscle is the major site of uptake, it is not surprising that a diminished total muscle mass should result in a decreased rate of glucose disposal. However, the decrements in insulin responsiveness and sensitivity are too great for this to be an adequate explanation on its own; the sensitivity of muscle to insulin is also decreased (Leighton *et al.* 1989). There is evidence that chronic elevation of the plasma level of adrenaline increases the sensitivity of muscle to insulin. Thus a decrease in the sensitivity of elderly muscle to the effects of

catecholamines may contribute to its decreased insulin sensitivity (Newsholme 1989).

Immune function

Glutamine and glucose are important fuels for lymphocytes and macrophages. Both fuels are only partially oxidized and their rates of utilization are high, even in relatively 'quiescent' cells. These processes provide not only energy but also intermediates for biosynthesis, for example glutamine, ammonia, and aspartate (from glutaminolysis) for synthesis of purine and pyrimidine nucleotides, and glucose-6-phosphate (from glycolysis) for synthesis of ribose-5-phosphate. However, the rates of glutaminolysis and glycolysis in lymphocytes are hugely in excess of the apparent maximal capacity of the biosynthetic processes (Szondy and Newsholme 1989). This is an example of branched-point sensitivity; the high rates of glutamine and glucose utilization in lymphocytes and macrophages allow high precision in the control of the rates of synthesis of purine and pyrimidine nuc-leotides at specific times during the cell cycle. This allows a rapid rate of successful cell division.

The major role of muscle may be to provide glutamine at a sufficiently high rate to allow branched-point sensitivity to operate in cells of the immune system and cells involved in repair, thus enabling them to respond with rapid and effective proliferation and biosynthesis.

References

Allison, S.P. (1986). Some metabolic aspects of injury. In *The scientific basis for the care of the critically ill* (ed. R.A. Little and K.N. Frayn), pp. 169–83. Manchester University Press.

Bastow, M.D., Rawlings, J., and Allison, S.P. (1983*a*). Undernutrition, hypothermia, and injury in elderly women with fractured femur: an injury response to altered metabolism? *Lancet*, i, 143–6.

Bastow, M.D., Rawlings, J., and Allison, S.P. (1983*b*). Benefits of supplementary tube feeding after fractured neck of femur: a randomised controlled trial. *British Medical Journal*, **287**, 1589–92.

Beisel, W.R. (1986). Sepsis and metabolism. In *The scientific basis for the care of the critically ill* (ed. R.A. Little and K.N. Frayn), pp. 103–22. Manchester University Press.

Bhasin, S., Storer, T.W., Berman, N., *et al.* (1996). The effects of supraphysiologic doses of testosterone on muscle size and strength in normal men. *New England Journal of Medicine*, **335**, 1–7.

Cederholm, T., Jägrén, C., and Hellström, K. (1995). Outcome of protein-energy malnutrition in elderly medical patients. *American Journal of Medicine*, **98**, 67–74.

Choo, J.J., Horan, M.A., Little, R.A., Rothwell, N.J., and Wareham, A. (1990). Anabolic beta-2-agonist clenbuterol fails to modify muscle atrophy due to femur fracture. *Circulatory Shock*, **32**, 165–71.

Collins, K.J., Easton, J.C., Belfield-Smith, H., Exton-Smith, A.N., and Pluck, R.A. (1985). Effects of age on body temperature and blood pressure in cold environments. *Clinical Science*, **69**, 465–70.

Crabtree, B., Newsholme, E.A., and Reppar, N.B. (1999). Principles of regulation and control in biochemistry: a pragmatic, flux-oriented approach. In *Handbook of physiology*, Section 14, *Cell physiology* (ed. J.F. Hoffman and J.D. Jamieson). Oxford University Press, New York.

Cuneo, R.C., Salomon, F., Wiles, C.M., Hesp, R., and Sönksen, P.H. (1991*a*). Growth hormone treatment in growth hormone-deficient adults. I. Effects on muscle mass and strength. *Journal of Applied Physiology*, **70**, 688–94.

Cuneo, R.C., Salomon, F., Wiles, C.M., Hesp, R. , and Sönksen, P.H. (1991b). Growth hormone treatment in growth hormone-deficient adults. II. Effects on exercise performance. *Journal of Applied Physiology*, **70**, 695–700.

Delmi, M., Rapin, C.-H., Bengoa, J.-M., Delmas, P.D., Vasey, H., and Bonjour, J.-P. (1990). Dietary supplementation in elderly patients with fractured neck of the femur. *Lancet*, **335**, 1013–16.

Fellows, I.W., Macdonald, I.A., Bennett, T., and Allison, S.P. (1985). The effect of undernutrition on thermoregulation in the elderly. *Clinical Science*, **69**, 525–32.

Fiatarone, M.A., Marks, E.C., Ryan, N.D., Meredith, C.N., Lipsitz, L.A., and Evans, W.J. (1990). High-intensity strength training in nonagenarians. Effects on skeletal muscle. *Journal of the American Medical Association*, **263**, 3029–34.

Finn, P.J., Plank, L.D., Clark, M.A., Connolly, A.B., and Hill, G.L. (1996). Progressive cellular dehydration and proteolysis in critically-ill patients. *Lancet*, **347**, 654–6.

Frontera, W.R., Meredith, C.N., O'Reilly, K.P., Knuttgen, H.G., and Evans, W.J. (1988). Strength conditioning in older men: skeletal muscle hypertrophy and improved function. *Journal of Applied Physiology*, **64**, 1038–44.

Gizard, J., Dardevet, D., Papet, I., *et al.* (1995). Nutrient regulation of skeletal muscle protein metabolism in animals. The involvement of hormones and substrates. *Nutrition Research Review*, **8**, 67–91.

Griffiths, R.D., Palmer, T.E.A., Helliwell, T., MacLennan, P., and Macmillan, R.R. (1995). Effect of passive stretching on the wasting of muscle in the critically ill. *Nutrition*, **11**, 428–32.

Griffiths, R.D., Jones, C., and Palmer, T.E.A. (1997). Six month outcome of critically-ill patients given glutamine supplemented parenteral nutrition. *Nutrition*, **13**, 295–302.

Grinspoon, S., Corcoran, C., Askari, H., *et al.* (1998). Effects of androgen administration in men with the AIDS wasting syndrome. *Annals of Internal Medicine*, **129**, 18–26.

Hammarqvist, F., Wernerman, J., Ali, R., von der Decken, A., and Vinnars, E. (1989). Addition of glutamine to total parenteral nutrition after elective abdominal surgery spares free glutamine in muscle, counteracts the fall in muscle protein synthesis, and improves nitrogen balance. *Annals of Surgery*, **209**, 455–61.

Häussinger, D., Roth, E., Lang, F., and Gerok, W. (1993). Cellular hydration state: an important determinant of protein catabolism in health and disease. *Lancet*, **341**, 1330–2.

Helliwell, T.R., Coakley, J.H., Wagenmakers, A.J.M., *et al.* (1991). Necrotizing myopathy in critically-ill patients. *Journal of Pathology*, **164**, 307–14.

Heymsfield, S.B., McManus, C., Stevens, V., and Smith, J. (1982). Muscle mass: reliable indicator of protein-energy malnutrition severity and outcome. *American Journal of Clinical Nutrition*, **35**, 1192–9.

Kass, J.E., Castriotta, R.J., and Malakoff, F. (1992). Intensive care unit outcome in the very elderly. *Critical Care Medicine*, **20**, 1666–71.

Knox, J.B., Wilmore, D.W., Demling, R.H., Sarraf, P., and Santos, A.A. (1996). Use of growth hormone for postoperative respiratory failure. *American Journal of Surgery*, **171**, 576–80.

Leighton, B., Dimitriadis, G.D., Parry-Billings, M., Lozeman, F.J., and Newsholme, E.A. (1989). Effects of ageing on the sensitivity and responsiveness of insulin-stimulated glucose metabolism in skeletal muscle. *Biochemical Journal*, **261**, 383–7.

Mahul, P., Perrot, D., Tempelhoff, G., *et al.* (1991). Short-term and long-term prognosis, functional outcome following ICU for elderly. *Intensive Care Medicine*, **17**, 7–10.

Maltin, C.A., Delday, M.I., Watson, J.S., *et al.* (1993). Clenbuterol, a β-adrenoceptor agonist, increases relative muscle strength in orthopaedic patients. *Clinical Science*, **84**, 651–4.

Martineau, L., Horan, M.A., Rothwell, N.J., and Little, R.A. (1992). Salbutamol, a β_2-adrenoceptor agonist, increases skeletal muscle strength in young men. *Clinical Science*, **83**, 615–21.

Martineau, L., Little, R.A., Rothwell, N.J., and Fisher, M.I. (1993). Clenbuterol, a beta 2-adrenergic agonist, reverses muscle wasting due to scald injury in the rat. *Burns*, **19**, 26–34.

Millward, D.J. (1995). A protein-stat mechanism for regulation of growth and maintenance of the lean body mass. *Nutrition Research Review*, **8**, 93–120.

Morley, J.E., Perry, M.H., Kaiser, F.E., *et al.* (1993). Effects of testosterone replacement therapy in old hypogonadal males: a preliminary study. *Journal of the American Geriatrics Society*, **41**, 149–52.

Nelson, M.E., Fiatarone, M.A., Morganti, C.M., Trice, I., Greenberg, R.A., and Evans, W.J. (1994). Effects of high-intensity strength training on multiple risk factors for osteoporotic fractures. *Journal of the American Medical Association*, **272**, 1909–14.

Newsholme, E.A. (1980). A possible metabolic basis for the control of body weight. *New England Journal of Medicine*, **302**, 400–5.

Newsholme, E.A. (1989). A common mechanism to account for changes in thermogenesis and insulin sensitivity. In *Hormones, thermogenesis and obesity* (ed. H. Landy and F. Statman), pp. 47–58. Elsevier, New York.

Newsholme, E.A., Crabtree, B., and Ardawi, M.S.M. (1985). Glutamine metabolism in lymphocytes, its biochemical, physiological and clinical importance. *Quarterly Journal of Experimental Physiology*, **70**, 473–89.

Newsholme, E.A., Newsholme, P., Curi, R., Challoner, E., and Ardawi, M.S.M. (1988). A role for muscle in the immune system and its importance in surgery, trauma, sepsis and burns. *Nutrition*, **4**, 261–8.

Reid, I.R., Wattie, D.J., Evans, M.C., and Stapleton, J.P. (1996). Testosterone therapy in glucocorticoid-treated men. *Archives of Internal Medicine*, **156**, 1173–7.

Rennie, M.J., Tadros, L., Khogal, S., Ahmed, A., and Taylor, P.M. (1994). Glutamine transport and its metabolic effects. *Journal of Nutrition*, **124**, 1503S–8.

Rockwood, K., Noseworthy, T.W., Gibney, R.T.N., *et al.* (1993). One-year outcome of elderly and young patients admitted to intensive care units. *Critical Care Medicine*, **21**, 687–91.

Ross, R.J.M., Rodriguez-Arnao, J., Bentham, J., and Coakley, J.H. (1993). The role of insulin, growth hormone and IGF-I as anabolic agents in the critically ill. *Intensive Care Medicine*, **19**, S54–7.

Rutherford, O.M., Beshyah, S.A., and Johnston, D.G. (1994). Quadriceps strength before and after growth hormone replacement in hypopituitary adults: relationship to changes in lean body mass and IGF-1. *Endocrinology and Metabolism*, **1**, 41–7.

Schambelan, M., Mulligan, K., Grunfeld, C., *et al.* and Serostim Study Group (1996). Recombinant human growth hormone in patients with HIV-associated wasting. *Annals of Internal Medicine*, **125**, 873–82.

Signorile, J.F., Banovac, K., Gomez, M., Flipse, D., Caruso, J.F., and Lowensteyn, I. (1995). Increased muscle strength in paralyzed patients after spinal cord injury: effect of beta-2 adrenergic agonist. *Archives of Physical Medicine and Rehabilitation*, **76**, 55–8.

Studley, H.O. (1936). Percentage of weight loss. A basic indicator of surgical risk in patients with chronic peptic ulcer. *Journal of the American Medical Association*, **106**, 458–60.

Szondy, Z. and Newsholme, E.A. (1989). The effect of glutamine concentration on the activity of carbamoyl-phosphate synthase II and on the incorporation of [3H]thymidine into DNA in rat mesenteric lymphocytes stimulated by phytohaemagglutinin. *Biochemical Journal*, **261**, 979–83.

Tenover, J.S. (1992). Effects of testosterone supplementation in the aging male. *Journal of Endocrinology and Metabolism*, **75**, 1092–8.

Tzankoff, S.P. and Norris, A.H. (1977). Effect of muscle mass decrease on age-related BMR changes. *Journal of Applied Physiology*, **43**, 1001–6.

Urban, R.J., Bodenburg, Y.H., Gilkison, C., *et al.* (1995). Testosterone administration to elderly men increases muscle strength and protein synthesis. *American Journal of Physiology*, **269**, E820–6.

Weissberger, A., Anastadiadis, A., Smith, M., Sönksen, P., and Sturgess, I. (1996). The effects of growth hormone on body composition in elderly subjects undergoing total hip replacement (abstract). *Age and Ageing*, **25** (Supplement 2), 14.

Windmueller, H.G. and Spaeth, A.E. (1974). Uptake and metabolism of plasma glutamine by the small intestine. *Journal of Biological Chemistry*, **249**, 5070–9.

Winick, M. (ed.) (1979). *Hunger disease: studies by the Jewish physicians in the Warsaw ghetto.* John Wiley, New York.

Wolfe, R.R., Herndon, D.N., Jahoor, F., Miyoshi, H., and Wolfe, M. (1987). Effect of severe burn injury on substrate cycling by glucose and fatty acids. *New England Journal of Medicine*, **317**, 403–8.

Yang, S., Alnaqueeb, M., Simpson, H., and Goldspink, G. (1996). Cloning and characterization of an IGF-1 isoform expressed in skeletal muscle subjected to stretch. *Journal of Muscle Research and Cell Contractility*, **17**, 487–95.

Yarasheski, K.E., Zachwieja, J.J., and Bier, D.M. (1993). Acute effects of resistance exercise on muscle protein synthesis rate in young and elderly men and women. *American Journal of Physiology*, **265**, E210–14.

Yarasheski, K.E., Zachwieja, J.J., Campbell, J.A., and Bier, D.M. (1995). Effect of growth hormone and resistance exercise on muscle growth and strength in older men. *American Journal of Physiology*, **268**, E268–76.

Yeo, A., Levy, D., Martin, F.C., Sönksen, P., Wheeler, M., and Young, A. (1996). Physical frailty and the response to growth hormone in elderly women with hip fracture (abstract). *Age and Ageing*, **25**, 6.

19.4 Muscle disease

Archie Young

Introduction

The neuromuscular diseases which present as muscle weakness in old age are well described in conventional accounts of muscle disease (Engel and Franzini-Armstrong 1994; Weatherall *et al.* 1996). The reader is referred to these texts for detailed accounts of polymyositis and dermatomyositis, cancer-related myositis, myopathy and neuropathy, metabolic and endocrine myopathies, alcohol-induced and drug-induced myopathies, motor neurone disease, myasthenia gravis, the limb girdle syndrome, facioscapulohumeral dystrophy, distal myopathy, and oculopharyngeal dystrophy. In this chapter we highlight selected aspects of particular conditions and draw attention to some of the potential pitfalls in the diagnosis of muscle pathology in elderly patients.

As always in geriatric medicine, it is crucial that a thorough search is made for any potentially reversible contributory factors. The most important of these are the metabolic and endocrine causes of muscle weakness, external agents such as drugs or alcohol, and the inflammatory myosites (despite the rising prevalence of associated carcinoma).

Drug-induced muscle weakness

Excessive exposure to diuretics (a common problem for elderly people) may produce a severe generalized weakness and lassitude, probably related principally to the loss of potassium. This is readily reversible. So too is the common complaint of fatigue experienced by patients taking a β-blocker. Conversely, the myasthenic syndrome occasionally resulting from treatment with D-penicillamine may prove irreversible.

Treatment with steroids is probably the best known, and the most common, example of drug-induced weakness. Because the fluorinated steroids are more liable to cause weakness, they are usually avoided. Nevertheless, weakness from high-dose or prolonged treatment with non-fluorinated steroids may be severe. As in Cushing's syndrome, the weakness is due principally to muscle atrophy, possibly aggravated by hypokalaemia. The loss of muscle tissue on exposure to high-dose steroids may be profound. As Fig. 1 illustrates, a study of metabolic balance in a 64-year-old man starting a trial of 60 mg of prednisolone daily (to determine the reversibility of his chronic airflow obstruction) suggested a loss of some 250 g of muscle per day, starting within the first 4-day balance period and continuing at that rate of loss for four more 4-day periods until the prednisolone was stopped.

Osteomalacia

Osteomalacia is common in old age and muscle weakness is common in osteomalacia. The weakness has a predominantly proximal distribution and may be the presenting symptom of the disease. The severity of the weakness has no relation to the degree of hypocalcaemia or hypophosphataemia. The presence of weakness is associated with reduced mean levels of muscle ATP and

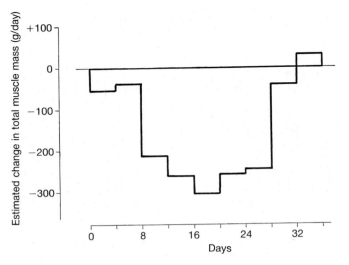

Fig. 1 Changes in total muscle mass (g/day) calculated from data on calcium, phosphorus, and nitrogen balance for successive 4-day periods. The patient is a 64-year-old man with chronic airflow obstruction on a 4200 kJ (1000 kcal) reducing diet throughout and taking 60 mg prednisolone daily during periods 3 to 7 inclusive. (Patient of Professor R.H.T. Edwards.)

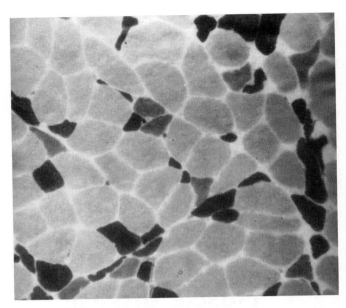

Fig. 2 Transverse section of a needle biopsy specimen from the quadriceps muscle, stained to show the activity of myosin ATPase (pH 9.4) and demonstrating marked preferential atrophy of the type II fibres. The patient is a 60-year-old East African Hindu woman with nutritional osteomalacia, who presented with a 9-month history of being confined to bed, unable to walk (see also Fig. 3). (Patient of Dr L.C.A. Watson.)

phosphocreatine, but its severity bears no relation to the muscle's concentration of these high-energy phosphates. Some authors have reported a high prevalence of 'myopathic' electromyograms, i.e. with short-duration polyphasic potentials often of low amplitude, but this has not been a universal finding and a normal electromyogram is by no means uncommon. The plasma concentration of creatine kinase is normal.

Needle biopsies of muscle from patients with osteomalacia (including five aged between 60 and 71 years) showed no evidence of replacement of muscle by fat or fibrous tissue, nor of denervation, inflammation, or necrosis (Young *et al.* 1981). Mean fibre size was reduced, its variability was increased, and there was often a severe degree of preferential type II fibre atrophy (Fig. 2). Relaxation of the quadriceps muscles from electrically stimulated contractions is slow but neither the cause nor the relevance of this slowing is known. It is not as pronounced as in hypothyroidism and is not clinically evident. There are some animal studies which suggest that it may be related to impairment of calcium uptake by the sacroplasmic reticulum.

The anabolic influence of vitamin D on vitamin-D-deficient muscle probably starts promptly on the initiation of treatment. Nevertheless, the recovery of strength is a slow process, measured in weeks or months (Fig. 3). It is associated with growth of muscle fibres, especially of the type II fibres, and the rate of recovery appears similar during treatment with vitamin D_2, vitamin D_3, or 1α-hydroxycholecalciferol. After 4 weeks of treatment, the subject of Fig. 3 was showing a daily nitrogen balance equivalent to an increase in total body muscle of some 0.5 per cent per day, associated with a similar or slightly faster rate of increase in quadriceps strength.

A feature of patients receiving treatment for osteomalacia may be a disparity between the rates of recovery of objectively measured muscle strength and of subjective well being and general physical ability. Even a small increase in strength may result in a large increase

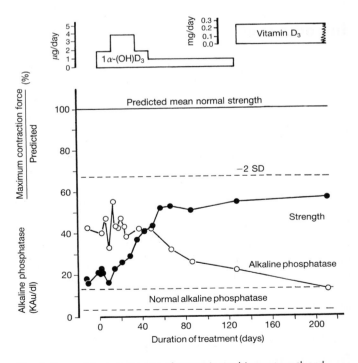

Fig. 3 Sequential measurements of isometric quadriceps strength and plasma alkaline phosphatase in a patient (same patient as in Fig. 2) with nutritional osteomalacia treated with 1α-hydroxycholecalciferol and then vitamin D_3. The normal range for quadriceps strength is age matched not racially matched. (Patient of Dr L.C.A. Watson.)

in a patient's functional ability. Changes in strength occur on a continuous scale but functional changes are quantal. It may need only a small gain in strength to take a patient from being 'just unable' to being 'just able' to perform some functionally important activity (see discussion of 'thresholds' in Chapter 19.1).

Hyperparathyroidism

Occasionally, muscle weakness is a prominent feature in patients with primary hyperparathyroidism. Plasma creatine kinase is normal, muscle biopsy may show type II atrophy, and a variety of moderate electromyographic abnormalities have been reported. The mechanism is unknown.

Thyroid disease

Muscle weakness and fatigue are common features of thyrotoxicosis. The weakness is associated with atrophy of muscle fibres of both fibre types. In hypothyroidism, muscle stiffness, aching, and mild weakness are common and a wide range of mildly myopathic microscopic features have been described. Muscle cross-sectional area may be increased without a corresponding increase in strength.

It is well known that hypothyroid muscle relaxes slowly. Thyrotoxic muscle relaxes rapidly, but this is more difficult to demonstrate as there is a greater overlap with the normal range. These changes in muscle speed are associated with changes in fibre-type composition, with hypothyroid muscle commonly showing a predominance of type I fibres and thyrotoxic muscles showing a tendency to type II predominance. However, the changes in muscle speed are much greater than can be explained merely on the basis of altered fibre-type composition as judged histochemically. It is not yet known whether they are due to histochemically undetectable changes in the myosin isoforms expressed or to changes in function of the sarcoplasmic reticulum.

Alterations in the relaxation rate of muscle are probably unimportant for the expression of maximal strength. In submaximal contractions, however, the increased relaxation rate of thyrotoxicosis means that a higher stimulus frequency is required to achieve tetanic fusion. Also, the increased rate of turnover of ATP means that the length of time for which a submaximal contraction may be sustained is reduced.

Unlike the other metabolic and endocrine myopathies, the plasma level of creatine kinase is often abnormal in patients with thyroid disease. It may be greatly elevated in hypothyroidism and tends to be towards or even below the lower limit of normal in thyrotoxicosis.

'Late-onset' muscular dystrophy

In 1885, Landouzy and Dejerine examined the relatives of their original case of facioscapulohumeral dystrophy. One was an 8-year-old girl with facial weakness. She lived until she was 86, although bed-bound from about 70 years of age (Justin-Besançon

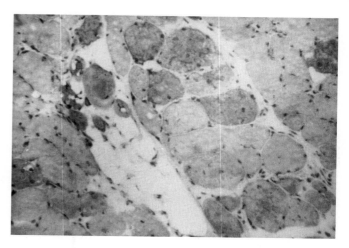

Fig. 4 Transverse section of a needle biopsy specimen from the quadriceps muscle, stained with haematoxylin and eosin, and demonstrating evidence of muscular dystrophy, namely increased variation in fibre size, central nuclei, moth-eaten and whorled fibres, ring fibres, increased endomysial connective tissue, and fat infiltration. The patient is a 78-year-old man who presented with an 18-month history of progressive muscle weakness, culminating in 5 weeks of difficulty in dressing and feeding, and 'bottom-shuffling' on stairs. He had a severe kyphoscoliosis, weakness, and wasting, worse in the upper limbs and worse proximally, and was unable to whistle. Plasma creatine kinase was normal and electromyograms of an upper limb (Dr G. Rushworth) showed a population of brief polyphasic low-amplitude single motor units, typical of a muscle fibre disease. When aged 33, he had had some spinal curvature but had been passed A1 for wartime military service. (Patient of the late Dr R.A. Griffiths.)

et al. 1964). Patients with limb girdle dystrophy (Shields 1994) or facioscapulohumeral dystrophy (Munsat 1994) may achieve a normal lifespan. Rarely, they may even present to medical attention for the first time in old age. Perhaps this is because the steady loss of strength is not apparent until the patient crosses a functionally important 'threshold' and is suddenly unable to perform an important everyday activity (see Chapter 19.1). Alternatively, the patient who is losing strength may unconsciously develop compensatory trick movements which, for a time, maintain function and so conceal deterioration. Nevin (1936) described a blacksmith with dystrophy mainly of the upper limb girdle who presented aged 60 with a history of symptoms for only 3 years. On questioning his family, however, there was evidence for weakness from the age of 27.

Patients with oculopharyngeal dystrophy (Tomé and Fardeau 1994) may present in old age with life-threatening dysphagia, but with a progressive ptosis dating back to their forties. In its later stages, the disease may also involve other external ocular muscles and proximal limb muscles. Family details may reflect its autosomal dominant inheritance.

Although the muscle biopsy and electromyographic appearances may be unmistakably myopathic, the plasma creatine kinase may be within the normal range (Fig. 4). This is because the underlying dystrophy is relatively benign and, as the patient is elderly, the total muscle mass is small.

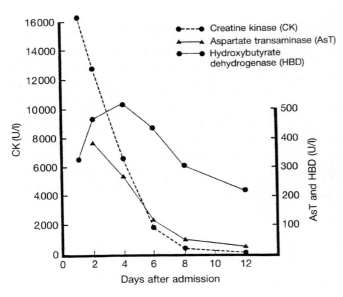

Fig. 5 Plasma creatine kinase, aspartate transaminase, and hydroxybutyrate dehydrogenase in an 81-year-old woman with parkinsonism and cardiac failure, admitted to hospital after lying undiscovered for some 7 h after a fall. (Reproduced with permission from Mallinson and Green (1985).)

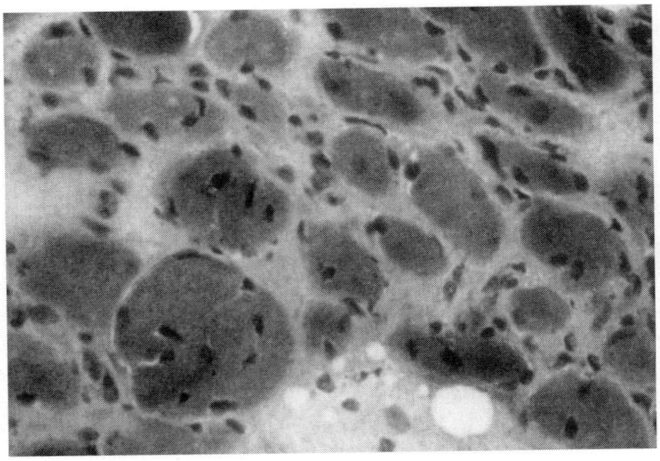

Fig. 6 Transverse section of a needle biopsy specimen from the left anterior tibial muscle, showing extensive muscle necrosis with macrophage infiltration and regeneration. The patient is an 82-year-old man, admitted as a medical emergency, confused, pyrexial, dehydrated, and with a swollen left calf. He had lain on a stone floor for several hours before discovery. Plasma aspartate transaminase was over 500 IU/l (normal 5–35 IU/l); plasma creatine kinase was over 17 000 IU/l (normal less than 100 IU/l); peak plasma urea was 68 mmol; peak plasma creatinine was 1041 mmol/l. Treatment included haemodialysis. The patient made a good recovery and was discharged home. (Patient of the late Dr R.A. Griffiths; see Ratcliffe et al. (1983).)

Rhabdomyolysis

Much the most common cause of rhabdomyolysis in old age is pressure necrosis of muscle in the patient who has lain for several hours after a fall. In most cases, the muscle damage is of little clinical significance except as a biochemical diagnostic 'red herring'. Elevated levels of plasma creatine kinase, aspartate transaminase, and hydroxybutyrate dehydrogenase do not necessarily imply damage to myocardial muscle (Fig. 5).

Not only are enzymes such as creatine kinase, aspartate transaminase, and hydroxybutyrate dehydrogenase released from damaged muscle, but myoglobin is also released. Myoglobin is normally cleared rapidly from the circulation by the kidney, but particularly high circulating levels may cause acute tubular necrosis and consequent acute renal failure. This is a life-threatening condition (Fig. 6). Urine, if there is any, will be positive for 'blood' on strip testing but microscopy will show no red cells. The damaged muscle tissue takes up calcium and releases potassium, phosphate, creatine, and purines. Therefore, for a given degree of renal failure, the plasma calcium is unusually low and plasma levels of potassium, phosphate, creatinine, and urate are unusually high. Treatment is by careful forced alkaline diuresis and close monitoring of plasma levels of calcium and potassium. A period of dialysis may be required (Firth and Winearls 1996).

Polymyalgia rheumatica and arteritis

Polymyalgia rheumatica is three times as common in women over 80 years of age as in those aged 60 to 69 years. It is also quite possible that many cases are not brought to medical attention. The predominant symptoms are pain, aching, and stiffness of the limb girdle musculature, especially in the neck and shoulders. Morning stiffness, generalized malaise, fatigue, and anorexia are common features. There may be a low-grade fever, mild anaemia, and elevation of the plasma alkaline phosphatase. The most striking laboratory abnormality is elevation of the erythrocyte sedimentation rate (ESR), sometimes to a considerable degree. (It is important not to be misled by this as only a minority of elderly patients with a greatly elevated ESR prove to have polymyalgia rheumatica.) Although the symptoms appear predominantly myalgic, the true pathology is probably joint synovitis, bursitis, and tenosynovitis. Electromyography, muscle biopsy, and plasma creatine kinase are all normal. Diagnosis rests primarily on the history.

There is a considerable overlap of polymyalgia rheumatica with the arteritides, particularly temporal arteritis. This, and the treatment of the conditions, is discussed in greater detail in Chapter 13.5 and by Salvarani et al. (1997). A further potential source of diagnostic confusion is the fact that an elderly patient with a connective tissue disease, especially one producing inflammation of the joints, may experience myalgia of the limb girdle and stiffness in the early morning for some months before the true nature of the underlying condition becomes apparent. Conversely, about a third of patients with polymyalgia rheumatica experience at least one episode of distal joint synovitis.

Arthrogenous amyotrophy

Pathology in a joint is often associated with weakness and wasting of muscles acting across the involved joint. Much of this is due to 'reflex inhibition', i.e. a reflexly mediated inhibition of anterior horn cells by afferent stimuli arising in or around the joint (Young 1993). Reflex inhibition is well seen in the patient with knee pathology. In particular, an acute effusion of the knee may result in profound weakness of the quadriceps, even in the absence of perceived pain. Not only are voluntary contractions inhibited, so too is reflex activation of the muscle (as indicated by the reduced size of its H reflex). Long-standing reflex inhibition may result in severe atrophy, seemingly resistant to treatment, and microscopic changes indistinguishable from those of denervation.

Experimental evidence indicates that the severity of inhibition may be much greater when the knee is in full extension. It is tempting to speculate that a sudden increase in inhibitory afferent activity may explain some 'drop attacks', in which the patient's knee suddenly buckles without any alteration in the level of consciousness.

Postpoliomyelitis syndrome

Patients with a history of previous poliomyelitis, whose clinical status has been stable for many years sometimes present in late middle-age or later with complaints of profound fatiguability, progressive weakness and/or increasing disability (Agre 1996; Grimby 1996). The principal cause is probably decompensation precipitated by the age-associated loss of motor units. The difference from the normal age-associated loss of motor units (see Chapter 19.1) is that the surviving motor units in a muscle previously affected by poliomyelitis are fewer, are greatly enlarged, and are probably unable to adopt any further muscle fibres. As a result, the consequences of the age-associated loss of surviving motor neurones may be dramatic. Additional factors in individual cases may include deconditioning due to coincidental illness or arthrogenous weakness due to damage caused to joints by years of biomechanically abnormal loading. There may also be subtle abnormalities in myocellular function (Sharma et al. 1994), but their significance is still uncertain.

Table 1 Data from muscle biopsies of elderly patients

Pathological 'diagnosis'	Neuromuscular patients[a]	Other patients[b]
Denervation, neuropathic	18	17
'Myopathy'	11	15
Type II atrophy	14	25
Myositis	17	0
Other	8	15
Normal	1	?

[a] Data from a review of muscle biopsies performed between 1971 and 1985 as part of an investigation of neuromuscular symptoms in 63 patients aged 65 years and over (mean age 73 years) (Squier 1987).
[b] Data from biopsies taken from the trunk and thigh muscles of 63 patients (mean age 75 years) undergoing surgery but without apparent neuromuscular disease (Tomonaga 1977).

Interpretation of muscle biopsies

As discussed in Chapter 19.1, slowly progressive denervation is a feature of aged muscle. Clearly, therefore, evidence of denervation in muscle biopsies from elderly patients must be interpreted with great caution. There is a risk of overdiagnosing pathological denervation in elderly muscle. This risk may be even greater if the patient is not only elderly but also cachectic as a result of some other underlying disease (Tomlinson et al. 1969).

This may not be the only potential pitfall. It seems that biopsies from elderly patients without apparent neuromuscular disease may show other changes which might usually be interpreted as indicating neuromuscular pathology (Table 1).

References

Agre, J.C. (1996). Rationale for treatment of new fatigue. *Disability and Rehabilitation*, **18**, 307–10.

Engel, A.G. and Franzini-Armstrong, C. (ed.) (1994). *Myology* (2nd edn). McGraw-Hill, New York.

Firth, J.D. and Winearls, C.G. (1996). Acute renal failure. In *Oxford textbook of medicine* (3rd edn) (ed. D.J. Weatherall, J.G.G. Ledingham, and D.A. Warrell), pp. 3279–94. Oxford University Press.

Grimby, G. (1996). Symptoms, disability, muscular structure and function, and electromyographic evaluation of post-polio individuals at 4–5 years of follow-up. *Disability and Rehabilitation*, **18**, 306–7.

Justin-Besançon, L., Péquignot, H., Contamin, F., Delauvierre, P., and Rolland, P. (1964). Myopathie de type Landouzy-Dejerine. Présentation d'une observation historique. *Revue Neurologique*, **110**, 56–7.

Mallinson, W.J.W. and Green, M.F. (1985). Covert muscle injury in aged patients admitted to hospital following falls. *Age and Ageing*, **14**, 174–8.

Munsat, T.L. (1994). Facioscapulohumeral disease and the scapuloperoneal syndrome. In *Myology* (2nd edn) (ed. A.G. Engle and C. Franzini-Armstrong), pp. 1220–32. McGraw-Hill, New York.

Nevin, S. (1936). Two cases of muscular degeneration occurring in late adult life, with a review of the recorded cases of late progressive muscular dystrophy (late progressive myopathy). *Quarterly Journal of Medicine*, **5**, 51–68.

Ratcliffe, P.J., Berman, P., and Griffiths, R.A. (1983). Pressure induced rhabdomyolysis complicating an undiscovered fall. *Age and Ageing*, **12**, 245–8.

Salvarani, C., Maccioni, P., and Boiardi, L. (1997). Polymyalgia rheumatica. *Lancet*, **350**, 43–7.

Sharma, K.R., Kent-Braun, J., Mynhier, M.A., Weiner, M.W., and Miller, R.G. (1994). Excessive muscular fatigue in the post-poliomyelitis syndrome. *Neurology*, **44**, 642–6.

Shields, R.W. (1994). Limb girdle syndromes. In *Myology* (2nd edn) (ed. A.G. Engel and C. Franzini-Armstrong), pp. 1258–74. McGraw-Hill, New York.

Squier, M.V. (1987). The pathology of neuromuscular disease in the elderly. In *Degenerative neurological disease in the elderly* (ed. R.A. Griffiths and S.T. McCarthy), pp. 119–29. John Wright, Bristol.

Tomé, F.M.S. and Fardeau, M. (1994). Oculopharyngeal muscular dystrophy. In *Myology* (2nd edn) (ed. A.G. Engel and C. Franzini-Armstrong), pp. 1233–45. McGraw-Hill, New York.

Tomlinson, B.E., Walton, J.N., and Rebeiz, J.J. (1969). The effects of ageing and of cachexia upon skeletal muscle. A histopathological study. *Journal of the Neurological Sciences*, **9**, 321–46.

Tomonaga, M. (1977). Histochemical and ultrastructural changes in senile human skeletal muscle. *Journal of the American Geriatrics Society*, **25**, 125–31.

Weatherall, D.J., Ledingham, J.G.G., and Warrell, D.A. (ed.) (1996). *Oxford textbook of medicine* (3rd edn), Section 25. Oxford University Press.

Young, A. (1993). Current issues in arthrogenous inhibition. *Annals of the Rheumatic Diseases*, **52**, 829–34.

Young, A., Edwards, R.H.T., Jones, D.A., and Brenton, D.P. (1981). Quadriceps muscle strength and fibre size during the treatment of osteomalacia. In *Mechanical factors and the skeleton* (ed. I.A.F. Stokes), pp. 137–45. Libbey, London.

20

Psychiatric aspects of the medicine of later life

20.1 Depression

Robert C. Baldwin

Introduction

It is a surprising fact that as recently as the 1950s depressive disorders in older people were thought to be linked to senility in general and dementia and 'arteriosclerosis' in particular. The classic study was that of Roth (1955) who demonstrated clear differences in outcome for dementia, persecutory psychosis in later life, and affective disorders.

It is also not well known that depression, and not dementia, is the most common mental health problem of later life. Although it is more readily treatable, it has received scant attention compared with dementia. In this chapter we address the classification of depression in later life and its prevalence, presentation, aetiology, management, and prognosis.

Nomenclature

Depression in elderly people is not a unitary clinical entity. Beekman (1996) cited 15 prevalence studies of depression in the primary care of people over the age of 55. For major depression (depressive illness) the weighted average was 1.7 per cent (range 0.4–10.2). However, when a broader concept of 'clinically significant depression' (sometimes known as 'pervasive depression') was used, the weighted average was 13.4 per cent (range 9–18 per cent). Thus, although depressive illness/major depression is probably no more and no less common in older than in younger people, depressive symptoms are far more common. Pervasive depression has been validated with structured psychiatric schedules in community elderly subjects (Copeland *et al.* 1987; Livingston *et al.* 1990) and it is certainly not trivial depression. Rather, the concept captures many of the distressing mood disorders of older people which are not recognized in modern classificatory systems because they are relatively rigid.

Both the American classificatory system DSM-IV (American Psychiatric Association 1994) and the ICD-10 system used in Europe (World Health Organization 1993) have focused on the more severe types of depression, such as are seen commonly from mid-life onwards. These are termed major depressions or depressive episodes. When psychiatrists refer to depressive illness they mean the following.

For a 'major depressive episode' in DSM-IV, five or more of the following symptoms must have been present during the same 2-week period and represent change from previous functioning:

(1) depressed mood most of the day, nearly every day, as indicated by either subjective report (e.g. feels sad or empty) or observation made by others (e.g. appears tearful);

(2) markedly diminished interest or pleasure in all, or almost all, activities most of nearly every day (as indicated by either subjective account or observation made by others);

(3) significant weight loss when not dieting or weight gain (e.g. a change of more than 5 per cent of body weight in a month), or decrease or increase in appetite nearly every day;

(4) insomnia or hypersomnia nearly every day;

(5) psychomotor agitation or retardation nearly every day (observable by others, not merely subjective feelings of restlessness or being slowed down);

(6) fatigue or loss of energy nearly every day;

(7) feelings of worthlessness or excessive or inappropriate guilt (which may be delusional) nearly every day (not merely self-reproach or guilt about being ill);

(8) diminished ability to think or concentrate, or indecisiveness, nearly every day (either by subjective account or as observed by others);

(9) recurrent thoughts of death (not just fear of dying), recurrent suicidal ideation without a specific plan, or a suicide attempt or a specific plan for committing suicide.

The equivalent criteria for a 'depressive episode' in ICD-10 are outlined in Table 1. Clearly, there is a good deal of overlap. The ICD-10 system is used in the United Kingdom, but the North American DSM-IV system is probably easier to commit to memory.

In this chapter, the unqualified term 'depression' refers to the above important clinical syndrome. Pervasive depression is not recognized within these two major classifications. Recently, however, DSM-IV has allowed a research category of 'minor depression', which is similar.

Whatever terminology is used, the negative impact of depression is well established. At primary care level, the Medical Outcomes Study found that the level of functional impairment and interference with quality of life associated with depression was comparable with or worse than that of eight major chronic medical conditions, including diabetes, arthritis, and severe coronary artery disease (Wells *et al.* 1989). In another United States study, older patients with the most depressive symptoms averaged four times more visits to their general practitioners than the least depressed (Waxman *et al.* 1983). In the United Kingdom, the Gospel Oak study (an epidemiological catchment area study in London) found that individuals identified as 'pervasively depressed' were more likely to have visited their general practitioner in the previous month, and to have visited hospital departments, required a district nurse and a home help, and attended a day centre (Livingston *et al.* 1990).

Table 1 Criteria for a depressive episode in the ICD-10 system

A. The syndrome of depression must be present for at least 2 weeks, no history of mania, and not attributable to organic disease or psychoactive substance

Mild depressive episode

B. At least two of the following three symptoms must be present
  1. Depressed mood to a degree that is definitely abnormal for the individual, present for most of the day and almost every day, largely uninfluenced by circumstances, and sustained for at least 2 weeks
  2. Loss of interest or pleasure in activities that are normally pleasurable
  3. Decreased energy or increased fatiguability
C. Additional symptoms from the following (to give a total of at least four)
  1. Loss of confidence or self-esteem
  2. Unreasonable feelings of self-reproach or excessive and inappropriate guilt
  3. Recurrent thoughts of death or suicide, or any suicidal behaviour
  4. Complaints or evidence of diminished ability to think or concentrate, such as indecisiveness or vacillation
  5. Change in psychomotor activity, with agitation or retardation (either subjective or objective)
  6. Sleep disturbance of any type
  7. Change in appetite with corresponding weight change

Moderate depressive episode

As above but at least six symptoms overall with at least two from B

Severe depressive episode

All three symptoms from B and at least five from C (eight symptoms in total)
Severe cases may be further subdivided according to the presence or absence of psychosis and/or stupor

Prevalence

It is important not to overstate the prevalence of depression in older people. Health professionals see, in the main, just those elderly people most susceptible to depression—frail individuals with acute or chronic medical illness. This may result in one of two errors: believing that depression is inevitable in older people, particularly when ill, and, as a result, overlooking serious life-threatening depression in such individuals. Ironically, sometimes only the depression can be remedied in older people with multiple irreversible system pathology.

Furthermore, prevalence is influenced by location and comorbidity. Figures for the community have been quoted above. Although pervasive depression is present in only 10 to 15 per cent of elderly people at home, in a United Kingdom study it was detected in a third of elderly patients attending their general practitioner (MacDonald 1986). In elderly hospital patients the prevalence of (major) depression is high, with a range of between 12 and 45 per cent (Jackson and Baldwin 1993). Perhaps most disturbing of all is the discovery of severe depression in almost two-fifths of local authority home residents (Ames et al. 1988). Sometimes depression occurs together with another psychiatric disorder. Allen and Burns (1995) have recently calculated this comorbidity in patients with Alzheimer's disease to be 20 per cent, which is considerably higher than in age-matched community residents. Depression is probably more common in vascular than in Alzheimer-type dementia (Allen and Burns 1995). It is important not to take an 'either/or' approach to patients with dementia, as they frequently have both depression and cognitive impairment.

Depression and physical illness commonly occur together, and this topic is explored in a later section. Physicians should have a low threshold for diagnosing depression among their elderly physically unwell patients.

Table 2 Presentations of depression particular to old age

Overlap of physical and somatic psychiatric symptoms

Minimal expression of sadness

Somatization or disproportionate complaints associated with physical disorder

Neurotic symptoms of recent onset

Deliberate self-harm (particularly medically 'trivial')

'Pseudodementia'

Conduct disorder

Accentuation of abnormal personality traits

Late-onset alcohol dependency syndrome

Presentation

One reason why depression may not always be diagnosed in practice is because it often presents differently in older people. Table 2 illustrates some of the pitfalls.

A common difficulty arises from associated physical ill health leading to overlapping symptoms. DSM-IV criteria require that if symptoms can be attributed to associated physical illness, they cannot be counted as symptoms of depression. In practice this is not always easy. An individual with active rheumatoid arthritis may experience insomnia, fatigue, and poor appetite equally from his or her physical illness or an associated depression. However, matters can usually be clarified if attention is paid to the following. First, on closer enquiry

done to prevent death), retardation, and 'mummification' (maintaining grief by keeping everything unchanged) suggest the presence of depressive illness.

Tricyclic antidepressants have been available for over 30 years. Although newer antidepressants are advocated enthusiastically for geriatric depression, it would be premature to dismiss tricyclics as first-line agents in older patients unless there is intolerance or a contraindication. Arguments for the virtual abandonment of tricyclics in favour of newer drugs which are safer in overdosage (Beaumont 1989) seem to place drug profiles ahead of clinical considerations. This may lead to a complacent attitude to suicide risk, which must be properly managed. Nevertheless, the point is well made that casual, often half-hearted, and poorly supervised prescribing of potentially lethal drugs is to be deplored (Beaumont 1989). Unfortunately, however, non-psychiatrists quite often tend to use insufficient dosages of tricyclic drugs.

Efficacy

There have been numerous trials of antidepressant drugs which have demonstrated their superiority over placebo, but most of these have been conducted on younger patients. Studies of newer antidepressants have involved comparison against established drugs, such as the older tricyclics, mianserin, or trazodone. Few have included a placebo arm. The results suggest that they are as effective as the established drugs. However, research sponsored by drug companies usually fails to include the typical patient seen by old-age psychiatrists and geriatricians—the very old and frail. The perceptive remark of Gerson (1985) still holds true: '. . . the choice of drug is based on side effect profiles and potential drug–drug interactions rather than on degree of therapeutic efficacy'. In other words, given that no antidepressant is more effective than another, non-psychiatrists are advised to become familiar with one or two antidepressants from each class so that treatment can be matched to the patient: for example, amitriptyline (old) and lofepramine (new) or imipramine (old) and dothiepin (new) from the tricyclic class, and fluoxetine, paroxetine, sertraline, or citalopram (selective serotonin reuptake inhibitors) and moclobemide (a reversible inhibitor of monoamine oxidase) or venlafaxine (a serotonin/noradrenaline reuptake inhibitor) from the newer antidepressants.

Efficacy in special patient groups

Elderly patients with dementia Reifler et al. (1989) reported improvement in depression in 28 elderly patients with underlying Alzheimer's disease in a trial of imipramine lasting for 8 weeks, but comparable improvement was also noted in a placebo group! The average dose was 80 mg. Of the newer drugs, Hebenstreit et al. (1991) demonstrated highly significant therapeutic efficacy of moclobemide (400 mg) over placebo in 726 elderly patients with unspecified dementia who were also depressed.

Depression associated with general systemic disease Antidepressants can be helpful when given to older patients with concurrent medical illnesses, but intolerance occurs in about one-third of cases (Lipsey et al. 1984; Katz 1990). To emphasize the point, Koenig et al. (1989) had to abandon a proposed drug trial using nortriptyline in physically ill older patients because virtually all had contraindications or were intolerant of the drug.

Table 7 Side-effects of tricyclic antidepressants

Anticholinergic	Antihistaminic	Adrenergic
Dry mouth	Oversedation	Postural hypotension
Blurred vision	Weight gain	
Constipation		
Urinary retention		
Cardiotoxicity		
Delirium		

If the newer antidepressants have anything to offer, it is surely in the area of patients seriously compromised by physical illnesses which preclude treatment with traditional drugs. Yet there is virtually no systematic evaluation of them in this setting. Physically ill depressives have been treated in an open trial for one up to a year with fluoxetine 20 mg daily (Evans 1993). The drug was tolerated well in a range of serious medical disorders, many grave. More recently, Roose et al. (1994), found that 22 depressed patients with heart disease with a mean age of 73 years responded less well to fluoxetine than 42 comparable patients treated with nortriptyline (mean age 70). Indeed only five of the 22 fluoxetine-treated patients responded; those with a melancholic subtype of major depression (the majority) did particularly poorly. The number of dropouts in each group was similar. Therefore, although the newer antidepressants appear to have a niche here, the evidence for their efficacy over established antidepressants is not convincing and it is surprising how little evaluation of them there has been in this context.

Side-effects

The cardiotoxicity of tricyclic drugs has probably been exaggerated. Minor electrocardiographic ischaemia, an uncomplicated myocardial infarct more than 3 months old, or even heart failure, provided that it is stable (Glassman et al. 1983), are not in themselves definite contraindications. Nevertheless, a tricyclic should not be given to patients with a known tendency to either tachy- or bradyarrhythmia, with bundle branch block, with abnormal QT interval syndromes (Cohen-Cole and Stoudemire 1987), or with poorly controlled heart failure. Newer drugs have been shown to be safer in healthy subjects, but some trials exclude elderly patients and very few studies have been conducted on people with heart disease. In the absence of such information it is unwise to assume uncritically that newer antidepressants are totally safe in patients with heart disease.

The main problem that occurs when tricyclics are given to elderly people is that they often cause postural hypotension, which may lead to unpleasant dizziness or dangerous falls. Secondary amine tricyclics are generally safer in this respect than tertiary drugs. Those with poor left ventricular function are most at risk, as are patients taking diuretics, on antihypertensive medication, and with left bundle branch block. Ideally, lying and standing blood pressure should be measured before starting treatment. Delirium is an occasional problem, more so in medically compromised patients.

The main side-effects of the older tricyclics are summarized in Table 7.

Table 8 Side-effects of selective serotonin reuptake inhibitors

Nausea (around 15%)
Diarrhoea (around 10%)
Insomnia (5%–15%)
Anxiety/agitation (2%–15%)
Headache
Weight loss

Lofepramine has minimal anticholinergic effects and a good safety record, although there has been some concern about occasional disturbance of liver function (Committee on Safety of Medicines 1988).

The side-effects of the selective serotonin reuptake inhibitors are given in Table 8. The main metabolite of fluoxetine is clinically active and remains so for approximately a week, possibly longer for older patients. Some members of the selective serotonin reuptake inhibitor category (thus far fluoxetine, fluvoxamine, paroxetine, and to some degree citalopram) have proved to be inhibitors of hepatic enzymic oxidation (cytochrome P-450 2D6, debrisoquine hydrochloride) (Crewe et al. 1992)). These drugs can alter the pharmacokinetics of other drugs which are hepatically oxidized, leading to drug interactions. Drugs metabolized by this enzyme, and hence likely to be affected by these new antidepressants, are tricyclic antidepressants and trazodone, neuroleptics, lipophilic β-blockers (e.g. metoprolol), some antiarrhythmics, and triazolobenzodiazepines such as alprazolam.

Behavioural toxicity (affecting vigilance, reaction times, etc.) has been largely ignored among elderly people. Now that so many older people drive and pursue other activities demanding high levels of vigilance, this must be taken more seriously. Sherwood and Hindmarch (1993) found that, among five commonly prescribed antidepressants, lofepramine, fluoxetine, and paroxetine had more favourable profiles with respect to measures of skilled performance, believed to reflect everyday activities, than amitriptyline and dothiepin.

A profile of side-effects classified by three biochemical systems for the main antidepressants in use in the United Kingdom is shown in Table 9.

The adage 'start low, go slow' is particularly appropriate for tricyclics. Suggested starting doses, in accordance with *British National Formulary* guidelines, are given in Table 9. The effective dose of tricyclic antidepressants for elderly patients is roughly half the adult dose (Table 9). Some of the newer antidepressants, such as mianserin, the selective serotonin reuptake inhibitors, and moclobemide, often require no dose adjustment for elderly people. Patients and relatives should be warned that the antidepressant effects may not be apparent for 10 to 14 days, otherwise compliance is less likely.

A successful outcome is unlikely if no response at all has occurred within 6 weeks, assuming adequate dosage and compliance. Most responders will have improved within 3 to 4 weeks of being on a therapeutic dosage of the chosen antidepressant.

Electroconvulsive therapy

Since its introduction in 1938, electroconvulsive therapy has remained the most effective treatment for depression. In all, a recovery rate from depressive illness of around 80 per cent can be expected, with no evidence that this response rate is any lower for elderly patients. Electroconvulsive therapy is the treatment of choice for patients whose lives are threatened by food and/or fluid refusal, profound retardation, or suicidal behaviour. Of course the administration of electroconvulsive therapy is for the specialist, but geriatricians are often called upon to advise on anaesthetic risk. However, the contraindications to electroconvulsive therapy are all relative, as the risks must be offset by those of death from severe depression.

Pharmacological treatment of resistant depression

Around one-third of patients fail to respond to monotherapy, usually defined as 4 to 6 weeks of a single antidepressant in therapeutic dosage (Dinan 1993). There are a number of questions that the clinician should ask when faced with a patient who fails to respond. The diagnosis should be reviewed, with special reference to subtle neurological or systemic disease (e.g. thyroid disorder) or alcoholism. The psychiatric diagnosis may also be wrong; for example, on rare occasions a psychotically depressed patient may conceal depressive delusions. Treatment adequacy, duration of treatment (at a therapeutic dose), compliance with treatment, psychosocial reinforcers, and side-effects should all be re-evaluated.

Various strategies have been recommended, such as changing from one class of drug to another (e.g. from a tricyclic to a selective serotonin reuptake inhibitor), lithium augmentation, combination of a tricyclic with low-dose neuroleptic, combination of a selective serotonin reuptake inhibitor and a tricyclic, electroconvulsive therapy, or *in extremis* psychosurgery. However, data pertaining to older patients are very limited. By this time the help of a psychiatrist will have been sought, since all these strategies require special expertise. This topic has been reviewed by Baldwin (1997).

Psychological approaches to management

Counselling

Counselling may well be more appropriate for depressive symptoms accompanying change, stress, threat, or loss to the individual. A good example is bereavement. However, depression should be properly treated first.

Psychotherapy

Psychotherapy can be given to elderly people with benefit, either individually or in a group setting (Steuer 1982; Yost et al. 1986). Cognitive–behavioural therapy is the most widely advocated approach for elderly patients, although there is little systematic evaluation of it. Jarvik et al. (1982) studied two groups with a mean age of 67 years. One was treated with standard tricyclic antidepressants and the other was given either dynamic or cognitive–behavioural therapy, both in groups. Although both groups fared better than a third placebo group, more of those treated with antidepressants enjoyed complete remissions. The style of individual work with older patients may need some modification. Given the decline in semantic processing which

Table 9 Side-effect profiles and dosages of the main antidepressants available in the United Kingdom

Drug	Side-effects			Starting dosage (mg)	Average daily dose (mg)
	Anticholinergic	Antihistaminic	Adrenergic		
Amitriptyline	+ + + +	+ + + +	+ + + +	25–50	75–100
Imipramine	+ + +	+ +	+ + +	10	30–50
Dothiepin	+ + +	+ +	+ +	50–75	75
Mianserin	0/ +	+ + +	0/ +	30	30–90
Lofepramine	+	+	+	70–140	70–210
Trazodone	0	+ + +	+	100	300
Fluvoxamine	0/ +	0/ +	0	50–100	100–200
Sertraline	0/ +	0	0	50	50–100
Fluoxetine	0/ +	0	0	20	20
Paroxetine	0/ +	0	0	20	20–30
Citalopram	0/ +	0	0	20	20–40
Moclobemide	0/ +	0	0	300	300–400
Venlafaxine	0/ +	0	0/ +	75	Up to 375

Symbols + to + + + + indicate increasing degree of effect.

occurs with ageing, the frequent occurrence of deafness, and proportionately greater memory problems associated with old-age depressions, it may be necessary to rely more on repetition and writing things down.

Similar considerations apply to group therapy, although there is little systematic evaluation. Some believe this approach to be better than individual work with older patients. In one study (Steuer *et al.* 1984), two groups of patients with depressive illness were compared. One received a psychodynamic approach and the other received cognitive–behavioural therapy. At 9 months both groups had improved by an equivalent amount, suggesting little to choose between the treatment types.

Anxiety management

Another behavioural approach which can be helpful in depression is anxiety management. This is more relevant when patients are recovering or have recovered from depression but are left with residual anxiety. Techniques may involve progressive relaxation, either alone with a commercial tape or in groups. Another problem, which is probably under-recognized, is phobic avoidance of normal activities after a prolonged bout of depression. Specific graded tasks under the supervision of an occupational therapist or psychologist can be extremely helpful. These patients are also encountered occasionally on geriatric wards where they may be labelled as having 'lost confidence'.

Family work

'Far and away the most important agency supporting the psychogeriatric patient at home is the family' (Pitt, 1982). Not only may a dysfunctional family contribute to the onset of depressive illness but the family is often critical in ensuring a successful outcome in treatment.

Interventions with families vary in complexity. Often the first step is to give straightforward information about the nature of the illness. Given that clinicians in the past have tended to link affective disorder with dementia, it is hardly surprising that relatives often jump to the same conclusion. Simple behavioural techniques to modify negative thoughts or behaviours, such as perpetual remarks related to hopelessness or constant demands for attention, can take some of the pressure off families and, likewise, graded activity aimed at countering withdrawal may lessen the family's own sense of despair. Sometimes the roles adopted by different family members can subtly undermine recovery or unwittingly collude with the patient's more maladaptive behaviours.

Marital therapy utilizes skills from several of the therapies described above and it may become a more delineated form of family work, in which case it is best if therapists work in pairs. Unresolved conflicts may be resurrected by a depressive illness. Fear of a future relapse and the responsibilities that go with suicidal ideation may also be a focus of therapy.

Prognosis

There is no evidence that the prognosis is worse for older patients with depression than for younger ones. Rather, depression in all age groups is prone to relapse, recurrence, and chronicity. Cole (1990), in a review of studies involving almost 1000 subjects, found that only a quarter of patients can be expected to remain completely well. The majority (60 per cent) fell into the category of either well or well with prior relapses over an average follow-up period of 32 months.

Mortality

Although rates for relapse and chronicity vary quite considerably, there is a little more uniformity regarding mortality. Although one might expect increased morality due to suicide, there is an excess beyond what might be explained by suicide alone. In one study (Rabins *et al.* 1985), it exceeded that expected by a factor of 2.5 and was chiefly due to cardiovascular causes; a similar excess was reported by Murphy *et al.* (1988). The common-sense explanation, that those with higher mortality had worse initial health, is unlikely to be the whole answer. In the study by Murphy *et al.* (1988), a group with depression was compared with an age- and sex-matched control group from the community. The groups were then matched for levels of physical illness, with the finding that the depressed group still had statistically higher mortality.

O'Brien and Ames (1994) postulate several possible mechanisms for the increased mortality in depression: comorbid physical illness, occult illness, illness effects (e.g. related to psychomotor retardation), treatment effects, and biological effects such as abnormality of the hypothalamic–pituitary–adrenal axis or endocrine abnormalities. Undertreatment is another possible factor. Undertreated depression is associated with increased mortality (Baldwin 1991).

Prognostic factors

Which variables best predict outcome? As a generalization they can be divided into general factors and factors more closely related to characteristics of the illness. Adverse general factors are the presence of organic cerebral pathology, either coarse (Post 1962) or more subtle (Jacoby *et al.* 1981) changes, initial and supervening serious physical ill health, and ensuing major adverse life events. Surprisingly few features of the illness itself can be directly linked with a poorer prognosis. The following have been suggested (Baldwin 1991): a slow recovery, three or more previous episodes, severity of illness, and duration of onset exceeding 2 years, all of which predict a poorer outcome.

Prevention

Helping personnel who have regular contact with elderly people at high risk of depression might be useful in prevention. These include home helps, wardens, district nurses, the staff of residential care facilities, and nurses on geriatric wards. The Defeat Depression campaign of the United Kingdom Royal College of Psychiatrists included an initiative with elderly patients, with a special leaflet for carers and patients. Awareness of relevant organizations and how they can be contacted is also important.

Secondary prevention

Whether one regards the summary prognostic figures above as good, poor, or indifferent is a matter of opinion. What is undisputed is that major depression at any age is prone to recur. There are three ways to improve outcome. The first is treatment adequacy. An antidepressant must be given in adequate dosage over a period of up to 6 weeks, with compliance. The second aspect of secondary prevention is prophylaxis. Depression treatment is conventionally subdivided into acute phase, relapse prevention (continuation phase), and prevention of recurrence (prophylaxis). With regard to continuation-phase therapy, Flint (1992) calculated the maximum risk period for relapse and recurrence to be 2 years. In a double-blind placebo-controlled trial, it was found that maintenance dothiepin 75 mg daily was associated with a reduction of a factor of 2.5 in relapse/recurrence over 2 years (OADIG 1993).

Given these findings, is there an argument for indefinite prophylactic treatment of major depression in elderly patients? Some would say unequivocally 'yes', for a significant reduction in the risk of either relapse or recurrence might enable a 75-year-old with a life expectancy of 5 years to be spared from misery for 6 months, or 10 per cent of that lifespan. However, a counterview is that, since some of those in the placebo group in the OADIG study remained well, there would be a risk of overtreatment if there were to be a blanket policy of prophylaxis. This could be dangerous to a group ageing quickly, and hence exponentially prone to drug side-effects. The last word on this has not been written, but it is a sobering thought that in the more than 30 years since antidepressants were introduced, there has not been any demonstrable further improvement in the outcome of major depression (Baldwin 1995). Therefore the emphasis must be on early detection and prevention.

Medical, i.e. drug, prophylaxis is not the only means of prevention. For example, Ong *et al.* (1987) were able to demonstrate that a support group for discharged elderly depressives, run by a social worker and a community psychiatric nurse, resulted in a significant reduction in relapses and readmissions over a 1- year period.

Third, without planned aftercare relapses and recurrences are likely to go undetected (Sadavoy and Reiman-Sheldon 1983) even though further treatment is often successful. It is important to arrange appropriate aftercare. Most United Kingdom Health Authorities have old-age psychiatric mental health teams who should be involved in following up patients.

Suicide and attempted suicide

Major depression is the most frequent context for both these tragic behaviours. In general, what is true of suicide in old age is also true of attempted suicide. There are some differences (Lindesay 1991), although in practice these are not marked. In the United Kingdom, official mortality statistics for 1992 reported 3675 suicides, of which 688 (20 per cent) were aged over 65. Approximately 14 per cent of the population are of retirement age. Whereas successful suicide is over-represented among elderly people, the reverse is true of attempted suicide where the elderly contribute a mere 5 per cent to the number of recorded attempts.

It is unusual for elderly attempters to take 'manipulative' overdoses, so that the term 'deliberate self-harm' is potentially misleading. A related issue is the incorrect assumption that there is a direct relationship between the medical severity of an overdose and its psychiatric significance. This is both erroneous and dangerous. Thus, whereas young people may overdose themselves fatally (e.g. on paracetamol) with no evident serious psychiatric disorder, elderly people may take medically trivial overdoses yet be seriously depressed. Some of these differences are presumably generational. The assessing doctor is usually from a generation closer to the non-psychiatrically ill younger person and may fail to make these distinctions, sometimes with fatal consequences. It is safer to assume that depressive illness is likely to be present in any older person who harms him- or herself and insist on a psychiatric opinion.

The story of the reduction of suicides in the 1960s in the United Kingdom is well known. The credit for this goes to the Gas Board, who introduced non-toxic natural gas, rather than to doctors. Unfortunately, recent trends suggest that gas intoxication is on the increase again, at least for elderly men, this time from car exhaust poisoning.

The links between depression and physical ill health have already been emphasized, together with the adverse effects for the prognosis of both. It is not surprising that the prevalence of physical illness in elderly suicides is much higher than expected (Barraclough 1971; Cattell and Jolley 1995). Of concern is the notion that such suicides are 'understandable', when in fact the emphasis should be on careful evaluation of the mental state.

Prevention

Can suicide be prevented? For those suffering from depressive illness the main risk factors—isolation, a bereavement, physical illness, and previous attempts—do not, apart from the last, allow individual predictions. Suicide is a complex personal event. For the individual patient the first step is to diagnose depression correctly and manage the suicide risk, always taking care to clarify the exact state of mind. Those most at risk have illnesses marked by agitation, guilt, pervasive feelings of hopelessness, persistent insomnia, and hypochondriasis. The latter is very important since the majority of elderly people who kill themselves are known to have visited their family doctor within the previous 3 months. The implication is that their somatic preoccupations divert attention away from the underlying depression. Another vulnerable period is the anniversary after a bereavement, and of course the latter may serve as a trigger for both depression and suicide. In addition, families and doctors must be educated to take statements concerning self-harm seriously, remove any means of committing the act, and be aware of the importance of behaviours such as suddenly altering wills, giving away possessions, or sudden changes in religious interest. Attention to medical ailments is important and control of any painful conditions is paramount. Finally, it is important to have the patient's confidence. Talking about suicide does not increase its likelihood; most people harbouring such ideas are relieved when they are brought out into the open.

Depression and physical symptomatology

Physical symptoms arising out of depressive illness

Excessive concern with health may be associated with physiological changes due to ageing or disease, with physical disease in peers or peer expectations (e.g. concerning the regularity of bowel habit), as an illness behaviour to maintain certain roles and patterns, or as part of a psychiatric disorder such as depressive illness. Hypochondriasis—a morbid fear of bodily illness—is common in depressive illness.

Sometimes these preoccupations can become delusional, occasionally achieving grotesque proportions. For example, one patient on a geriatric ward dismissed the author and instead requested an undertaker, for she believed herself already dead and was convinced that her flesh had rotted.

Sometimes a known physical illness, previously tolerated, becomes unbearable when depressive illness develops. Particular difficulties arise in treatment when patients fail to comply with psychotropic medication because of persistent attribution of all symptoms to physical illness. Time must be set aside to explain carefully the nature and extent of any actual physical illness present and its likely effects. Sometimes it is also necessary to examine the ways in which both the patient and his or her family understand illness and its consequence in order to understand what might be the rewards of invalidism. An elderly patient may use physical illness and physical symptomatology to foster dependence, often in the face of social isolation. Sometimes, after the depressive component has been treated adequately, these issues linger and impede functional recovery. Such cases demand a consistent approach from all staff who come into contact with the patient and a behavioural programme with appropriate rewards, or at the very least a carefully structured day to promote useful activity.

Physical illness leading to depressive symptoms

In recent years much energy has been expended on demonstrating links between depression and particular physical illnesses. In fact the literature is growing in a manner which suggests that a great many illnesses, both acute and chronic, are associated with depressive symptoms. In only a minority does this reach the intensity of a depressive illness/major depression. Most research has been conducted on patients with stroke and idiopathic Parkinson's disease, both of which are particularly relevant to elderly people in whom they reach their maximum incidence.

A number of stimulating articles concerning post-stroke depression has emerged from the Johns Hopkins School of Medicine in the United States. One of the many findings was an association between the incidence of depression, including depressive illness, and the proximity of the destructive lesion to the anterior pole of the left hemisphere (Robinson et al. 1984). Although intriguing, the work has been criticized on the grounds of patient selection and location, the way in which rating instruments were used, and the fact that lesions close to the left anterior pole cause a minority of strokes if patients from the community and not just those in hospital are included (House 1987). Also, although between one-third and one-fifth of post-stroke survivors may suffer depression of all grades of severity, it is not agreed that this is higher than in other patients with equally chronic disabling illnesses (House 1987).

A number of other neurotransmitter systems besides the dopamine pathways are disrupted in Parkinson's disease. In relation to depression, which is the most frequent mental change in Parkinson's disease, it has been suggested that serotonin deficiency may be an important predisposing factor (Mayeux et al. 1986). However, although depressive symptoms occur in about 40 per cent of patients with the disease, probably only a minority amount to depressive illnesses and there is disagreement as to whether, in any case, the frequency of depressive illness is above that found in other disabling conditions such as rheumatoid arthritis (Gotham et al. 1986). Parkinson's disease serves as a useful model for exploring the links between psychiatry and physical illness. For example, the manner in which electroconvulsive therapy benefits not only lowered mood but also the motor changes of Parkinson's disease is of considerable neurobiological interest.

Organic depressions have been discussed earlier and clearly a number of illnesses, some of which are not obvious at first presentation, may be involved in triggering depression. Furthermore, even for manifest diseases, treatment may sometimes precipitate depression. Nowadays steroids and non-selective β-blockers are probably the main offenders, and alcohol abuse should always be considered.

The headings used in this section are not meant to imply fixed causal relationships. An association undoubtedly exists between depression and physical illness which is not based on chance alone (Murphy and Brown 1980). Strict divisions along the lines of physically induced depression or psychologically induced physical disorder have not proved very helpful in the past. They risk a rehearsal of the sterile mind–body dualism of earlier times. A model based on interactions rather than causal relationships lends itself to multivariate analysis (Eastwood and Corbin 1986) and also fits in with modern eclectic medical practice.

References

Abrams, R.C., Alexopoulos, G.S., and Young, R.C. (1987). Geriatric depression and DSMIIIR personality disorder criteria. *Journal of the American Geriatrics Society*, 35, 383–6.

Allen, N.H.P. and Burns, A. (1995). The non-cognitive features of dementia. *Reviews in Clinical Gerontology*, 5, 57–75.

American Psychiatric Association (1994). *Diagnostic and statistical manual version IV*. American Psychiatric Association, Washington, DC.

Ames, D., Ashby, D., Mann, A.H., and Graham, N. (1988). Psychiatric illness in elderly residents of part III homes in one London borough: prognosis and review. *Age and Ageing*, 17, 249–56.

Baldwin, B. (1991). The outcome of depression in old age. *International Journal of Geriatric Psychiatry*, 6, 398–400.

Baldwin, R.C. (1993). Late life depression and structural brain changes: a review of recent magnetic resonance imaging research. *International Journal of Geriatric Psychiatry*, 8, 115–23.

Baldwin, R.C. (1995). Antidepressants in geriatric psychiatry: what difference have they made? *International Psychogeriatrics*, 7 (Supplement), 1–14.

Baldwin, R.C. (1997). Treatment resistant depression in the elderly: a review of treatment options. *Reviews in Clinical Gerontology*, 6, 343–8.

Barraclough, B.M. (1971). Suicide in the elderly. In *Recent developments in psychogeriatrics* (ed. D.W.K. Kay and A. Walk), pp. 87–97. Headley, Kent.

Beaumont, G. (1989). The toxicity of antidepressants. *British Journal of Psychiatry*, 154, 454–8.

Beekman, A.T.F. (1996). Depression in later life: studies in the community, pp. 18–24. Unpublished Ph.D. Thesis, Vrije Universiteit, Amsterdam.

Bergmann, K. (1978). Neurosis and personality disorder in old age. In *Studies in geriatric psychiatry* (ed. A.D. Isaacs and F. Post), pp. 41–75. Wiley, Chichester.

Cattell, H. and Jolley, D.J. (1995). One hundred cases of suicide in elderly people. *British Journal of Psychiatry*, 166, 451–7.

Cohen-Cole, S.A. and Stoudemire, A. (1987). Major depression and physical illness: special considerations in diagnosis and biologic treatment . *Psychiatric Clinics of North America*, 10, 1–17.

Cole, M.G. (1990). The prognosis of depression in the elderly *Canadian Medical Association Journal*, 143, 633–40.

Committee on Safety of Medicines (1988). *Current Problems*, 23 September 1988. Medicines Control Agency.

Copeland, J.R.M., Dewey, M.E., Wood, N., Searle, R., Davidson, I.A., and McWilliam, C. (1987). Range of mental illness among the elderly in the community: prevalence in Liverpool using the GMS-AGECAT package. *British Journal of Psychiatry*, 150, 815–23.

Crewe, H.K., Lennard, M.S., Tucker, G.T., Woods, F.R., and Haddock, R.E. (1992). The effect of selective serotonin re-uptake inhibitors on cytochrome P4502D6 (CYP2D6) activity in human liver microsomes. *British Journal of Clinical Pharmacology*, 34, 262–5.

Dinan, T.G. (1993). A rational approach to the non-responding depressed patient. *International Clinical Psychopharmacology*, 8, 221–3.

Eastwood, M.R. and Corbin, S.L. (1986). The relationship between physical illness and depression in old age. In *Affective disorders in the elderly* (ed. E. Murphy), pp. 177–86. Churchill Livingstone, Edinburgh.

Evans, M.E. (1993). Depression in elderly physically ill inpatients: a 12 month prospective study. *International Journal of Geriatric Psychiatry*, 8, 587–92.

Flint, A.J. (1992). The optimum duration of antidepressant treatment in the elderly. *International Journal of Geriatric Psychiatry*, 7, 617–19.

Folstein, M.F., Folstein, S.E., and McHugh, P.R. (1975). 'Mini-Mental State': a practical method for grading the cognitive state of patients for the clinician. *Journal of Psychiatric Research*, 12, 185–98.

Georgotas, A. (1983). Affective disorders in the elderly: diagnostic and research considerations. *Age and Ageing*, 12, 1–10.

Gerson, R.H. (1985). Present status of drug therapy of depression in late life. *Journal of Affective Disorders*, Supplement 1, S23–31.

Glassman, A.H., Johnson, L.L., Giardina, E.V., Walsh, B., Roose, S.P., and Couper, T.B. (1983). The use of imipramine in depressed patients with congestive heart failure. *Journal of American Medical Association*, 250, 1997–2001.

Gotham, A.-M., Brown, R.G., and Marsden, C.D. (1986). Depression in Parkinson's disease: a quantitative and qualitative analysis. *Journal of Neurology, Neurosurgery, and Psychiatry*, 49, 381–9.

Hebenstreit, G.F., Baumhackl, U., Chan-Palay, V., et al. (1991). *Proceedings of the 5th Congress of the International Psychogeriatric Association, Rome*, p. 31.

Hickie, I., Scott, E., Mitchell, P., Wilhelm, K., Austin, M.P., and Bennett, B. (1995). Subcortical hyperintensities on magnetic resonance imaging: clinical correlates and prognostic significance in patients with severe depression. *Biological Psychiatry*, 37, 151–60.

House, A. (1987). Mood disorders after stroke: a review of the evidence. *International Journal of Geriatric Psychiatry*, 2, 211–21.

Jackson, R. and Baldwin, B. (1993). Detecting depression in elderly medically ill patients: the use of the Geriatric Depression Scale compared with medical and nursing observations. *Age and Ageing*, 22, 349–53.

Jacoby, R.J., Levy, R., and Bird, J.M. (1981). Computed tomography and the outcome of affective disorder: a follow-up study of elderly patients. *British Journal of Psychiatry*, 139, 288–92.

Jarvik, L.S., Mintz, J., Steuer, J., and Gerner, R. (1982). Treating geriatric depression: a 26 week interim analysis. *Journal of American Geriatrics Society*, 30, 713–17.

Katz, I.R., Simpson, G.M., Curlik, S.M., Parmelee, P.A., and Muhly, C. (1990). Pharmacologic treatment of major depression for elderly patients in residential care settings. *Journal of Clinical Psychiatry*, 51 (Supplement 4), 41–7.

Koenig, H.G., Goli, V., Shelp, F., et al. (1989). Antidepressant use in elderly medical patients: lessons from an attempted clinical trial. *Journal of General Internal Medicine*, 4, 498–505.

Lindesay, J. (1991). Suicide in the elderly. *International Journal of Geriatric Psychiatry*, 6, 355–61.

Lipsey, J.R., Robinson, R.G., Pearlson, G.D., Rao, K., and Price, T.R. (1984). Nortriptyline treatment of post-stroke depression: a double-blind study. *Lancet*, 333, 297–300.

Lishman, W.A. (1987). *Organic Psychiatry* (2nd edn). Blackwell Scientific, Oxford.

Livingston, G., Hawkins, A., Graham, N., and Blizard, B. (1990). The Gospel Oak study: prevalence rates of dementia, depression and activity limitation among elderly residents in Inner London *Psychological Medicine*, 20, 137–46.

MacDonald, A.J.D. (1986). Do general practitioners 'miss' depression in elderly patients? *British Medical Journal*, 292, 1365–7.

Massey, E.W. and Bullock, R. (1978). Peroneal palsy in depression. *Journal of Clinical Psychiatry*, 287, 291–2.

Mayeux, R., Stern, Y., Williams, J.B.W., Cote, L., Frantz, A., and Dyrenfurth, I. (1986). Clinical and biochemical features of depression in Parkinson's disease. *American Journal of Psychiatry*, 143, 756–9.

Mendelwicz, J. (1976). The age factor in depressive illness: somogenetic considerations. *Journal of Gerontology*, 31, 300–3.

Murphy, E. (1982). Social origins of depression in old age. *British Journal of Psychiatry*, 141, 135–42.

Murphy, E. and Brown, G.W. (1980). Life events, psychiatric disturbance and physical illness. *British Journal of Psychiatry*, 136, 326–38.

Murphy, E., Smith, R., Lindesay, J., and Slattery, J. (1988). Increased mortality rates in late-life depression. *British Journal of Psychiatry*, 152, 347–53.

OADIG (1993). How long should the elderly take antidepressants? A double blind placebo-controlled study of continuation/prophylaxis therapy with dothiepin. *British Journal of Psychiatry*, 162, 175–82.

O'Brien, J.T. and Ames, D. (1994). Why do the depressed elderly die? *International Journal of Geriatric Psychiatry*, 9, 689–93.

Ong, Y.-L., Martineau, F., Lloyd, C., and Robbins, I. (1987). Support group for the depressed elderly. *International Journal of Geriatric Psychiatry*, 2, 119–23.

Peterson, P. (1968). Psychiatric disorders in primary hyperparathyroidism. *Journal of Clinical Endocrinology and Metabolism*, 28, 1491–5.

Pitt, B. (1982). *Psychogeriatrics* (2nd edn). Churchill Livingstone, Edinburgh.

Post, F. (1962). *The significance of affective symptoms in old age*, Maudsley Monographs 10. Oxford University Press.

Post, F. (1972). The management and nature of depressive illnesses in late life: a follow-through study. *British Journal of Psychiatry*, 121, 393–404.

Post, F. (1982). Functional disorders. In *The psychiatry of late life* (ed. R. Levy and F. Post), pp. 176–221. Blackwell Scientific, Oxford,

Prince, M., Lewis, G., Bird, A., and Blizard, R. (1996). A longitudinal study of factors predicting change in cognitive test scores over time in an older hypertensive population. *Psychological Medicine*, 26, 555–68.

Rabins, P.V., Harvis, K., and Koven, S. (1985). High fatality rates of late-life depression associated with cardiovascular disease. *Journal of Affective Disorders*, 9, 165–7.

Rapp, S.R. and Davis, K.M. (1989). Geriatric depression: physicians' knowledge, perceptions, and diagnostic practice. *Gerontologist*, 29, 252–7.

Reifler, B.V., Teri, L., Raskind, M., *et al.* (1989). Double-blind trial of imipramine in Alzheimer's disease patients with and without depression. *American Journal of Psychiatry*, 146, 45–9.

Robinson, R.G., Kubos, K.L., Starr, L.B., Rao, K., and Price, T.R. (1984). Mood disorders in stroke patients: importance of location of lesion. *Brain*, 107, 81–93.

Roose, S.P., Glassman, A.H., Attia, E., and Woodring, S. (1994). Comparative efficacy of selective serotonin reuptake inhibitors and tricyclics in the treatment of melancholia. *American Journal of Psychiatry*, 151, 1735–9.

Roth, M. (1955). The natural history of mental disorder in old age. *Journal of Mental Science*, 101, 281–301.

Sadavoy, J. and Reiman-Sheldon, E. (1983). General hospital geriatric psychiatric treatment: a follow-up study. *Journal of the American Geriatrics Society*, 31, 200–5.

Schneider, L.S. (1992). Psychobiologic features of geriatric affective disorders. *Clinics in Geriatric Medicine*, 8, 253–65.

Sherwood, N. and Hindmarch, I. (1993). A comparison of five commonly prescribed antidepressants with particular reference to behavioural toxicity. *Human Psychopharmacology*, 8, 417–22.

Steuer, J.L. (1982). Psychotherapy for depressed elders. In *Depression in later life* (ed. D. Blazer), pp. 195–200. Mosby, St Louis, MO.

Steuer, J.L., Mintz, J., Hammen, C.L., *et al.* (1984). Cognitive–behavioral and psychodynamic group psychotherapy in treatment of geriatric depression. *Journal of Consulting and Clinical Psychology*, 52, 180–9.

Veith, R.C. and Raskind, M.A. (1988). The neurobiology of aging: does it predispose to depression? *Neurobiology of Aging*, 9, 101–17.

Waxman, H.M., Carner, E.A., and Blum, A. (1983). Depressive symptoms and health service utilisation among the community elderly. *Journal of the American Geriatrics Society*, 31, 417–20.

Wells, K.B., Stewart, A., Hays, R.D., and Burnam, M.A. (1989). The functioning and well-being of depressed patients. Results from the Medical Outcomes Study. *Journal of the American Medical Association*, 262, 914–19.

World Health Organization (1993). *The ICD-10 classification of mental and behavioural disorders: research criteria*. World Health Organization, Geneva.

Yesavage, J.A., Brink, T.L., Rose, T.L., *et al.* (1983). Development and validation of a geriatric depression screening scale: a preliminary report. *Journal of Psychiatric Research*, 17, 37–49.

Yost, E.B., Beutler, L.E., Corbishley, M.A., and Allender, J.R. (1986). *Group cognitive therapy: a treatment approach for depressed older adults*. Pergamon Press, New York.

20.2 Anxiety, paranoid, and manic disorders

Kenneth I. Shulman

Introduction

In this chapter we focus on three disorders that have received considerably less attention than the classic '3 Ds' (dementia, delirium, and depression) which have dominated the field of geriatric psychiatry. Anxiety disorders have only recently attracted significant interest although they represent a relatively common disorder in old age, ranging in prevalence from 5 to 15 per cent (Flint 1994; Manela *et al.* 1996). Methodological problems such as a lack of uniform diagnostic criteria contribute to the discrepancies reported. Nonetheless, these are clinically important conditions, particularly because of their high comorbidity with medical and other psychiatric disorders.

There has also been renewed interest in the paranoid disorders, with particular focus on neurobiological developments. Although they are relatively uncommon and 'exotic' disorders in geriatric psychiatry, as pure syndromes they have heuristic value in the understanding of the schizophrenic syndrome and paranoid symptomatology in general. Recent advances in neuroimaging are providing a stimulus for better characterization of the neuropathology associated with this subgroup.

Manic disorders, like paranoid psychoses, are relatively uncommon but have a theoretical relevance to our understanding of bipolar conditions at all ages. Physicians interested in the care of elderly people must be familiar with the full range of psychiatric disorders in old age and their particular association with many underlying medical and neurological conditions. We are forced to develop a truly integrated model that incorporates genetic predisposition with early development, life course, psychosocial stressors, and late-life neurobiological changes. Here, we provide an overview of recent developments as well as conceptual and theoretical issues that can inform our formulations of these disorders.

Anxiety disorders

Determining the epidemiology and prevalence of anxiety disorders in old age is complicated by the fact that anxiety is a symptom of most psychiatric and many medical conditions in old age. In this chapter we focus on those conditions defined as 'anxiety disorders' in the DSM-IV classification (American Psychiatric Association 1994). These disorders include generalized anxiety disorder, phobias, obsessive–compulsive disorder, post-traumatic stress disorder, and anxiety disorder due to general medical conditions.

Flint (1994) has recently reviewed the epidemiology and co-morbidity of anxiety disorders in later life, as well as the methodologies and instruments used to determine their prevalence. The Epidemiologic Catchment Area study in the United States over-represented older age groups, as up to 30 per cent of their sample were over the age of 65 (Regier *et al.* 1988). In the Edmonton study (Bland *et al.* 1988), 10 per cent of the sample were over 65, and Copeland *et al.* (1987*a*, 1987*b*) studied elderly populations in London, Liverpool, and New York using the Geriatric Mental State and computer-generated AGECAT. The Guys/Age Concern Survey (Lindesay *et al.* 1989) studied 890 persons over the age of 65 in inner London using the Present State Examination, the Geriatric Mental State, and the Comprehensive Assessment and Referral Evaluation (**CARE**) schedule. Similarly, Manela *et al.* (1996) surveyed an elderly population in inner London using a shortened version of CARE and the Anxiety Disorder Scale.

Generalized anxiety disorder

Generalized anxiety disorder is characterized by chronic anxiety and apprehensive expectation during most of the waking time. The individual finds it difficult to control this anxiety and the condition is associated with three or more of the following symptoms: restlessness, fatigue, poor concentration, irritability, muscle tension, and sleep disturbance (American Psychiatric Association 1994).

Prevalence of generalized anxiety disorders in old age ranges from 1.4 per cent (Copeland *et al.* 1987*b*) to 7.1 per cent (Myers *et al.* 1984). Lindesay *et al.* (1989) reported a prevalence of 3.7 per cent, but almost all suffered from comorbid depression. Manela *et al.* (1996) determined a prevalence of 4.7 per cent for generalized anxiety disorder. They also found a high comorbid level of depression at 70 per cent and noted that more than half were taking psychotropic medications, mainly hypnotics.

In the Epidemiologic Catchment Area study only 3 per cent of generalized anxiety disorders began after the age of 65 and they tended to be comorbid with depression throughout the life span (Blazer *et al.* 1991). Generalized anxiety disorder may overlap with depression in up to two-thirds of elderly patients (Parmelee *et al.* 1993; Manela *et al.* 1996). Conversely, Flint (1997) noted that 20 to 40 per cent of older people suffering from major depression may have generalized anxiety disorder. If subsyndromal anxiety symptoms are included, then the majority (up to three-quarters) of elderly depressed patients report comorbidity. Other comorbid conditions include dementia, in which almost one-third of a sample met criteria for generalized anxiety disorders (Ballard *et al.* 1994). In a long-term

memory. Although MRI abnormalities were found in 40 per cent of the patients, the majority had no clinical suspicion of structural brain disease.

In summary, late-onset paranoid disorders appear to have a multifactorial basis including a subgroup with a modest genetic predisposition similar to schizophrenia. However, other factors, including social isolation, sensory deficits, and particularly neurobiological factors, appear to be contributory particularly in paranoid syndromes without schizophrenia-like symptomatology. While many younger schizophrenics continue to be symptomatic into late life, the late-onset group appears to be qualitatively different and there is some evidence that dementia occurs more frequently in older schizophrenics. The DSM-IV category of 'delusional disorder' is neutral with respect to aetiology (American Psychiatric Association 1994).

Treatment options

There are few new data on the treatment of late-life paraphrenia and schizophrenia (Jeste et al. 1993). Neuroleptics remain the most effective treatment for schizophrenia in later life, although much lower doses are required than for younger patients. The risk of tardive dyskinesia is significant, occurring at an annual incidence of 26 per cent in middle-aged and elderly subjects, almost six times as high as reported in young schizophrenics. Therefore extreme caution needs to be exercised in the prolonged use of neuroleptics in elderly patients, and trials of neuroleptic discontinuation are recommended whenever feasible. Studies of the newer atypical neuroleptic agents, such as clozapine, remoxipride, and risperidone, are now necessary with particular regard to extrapyramidal side-effects and tardive dyskinesia.

Manic syndromes

Bipolar disorders are relatively uncommon in old age but have theoretical and clinical relevance to mood disorders of earlier onset. Their prevalence in community surveys decreases from 1.4 per cent in young adults to 0.1 per cent in old age (Weissman et al. 1988). However, first admission rates for mania appear to increase at the extremes of old age (Eagles and Whalley 1985). Since mood disorders tend to confer a lifelong vulnerability, these conflicting findings suggest that the epidemiological study of bipolar disorder in old age may shed light on the long-term course of early-onset bipolar disorders while elucidating the relevant factors in the emergence of late-life mania. In this section we focus on the pathogenesis of late-onset cases and their medical management.

Generally, elderly manic patients have a late average age of onset in middle age (Shulman 1996) with a bimodal distribution. The first group are those whose first episode is depression, usually occurring in middle age, followed by a long latency (15 years on average) before mania becomes manifest. The second cluster are first-episode late-onset manias usually associated with a medical or neurological disorder (Snowdon 1991; Shulman et al. 1992).

Manic patients have been shown to have a significant degree of cognitive impairment (Stone 1989; Broadhead and Jacoby 1990) but relatively few appear to go on to a clinically significant dementia. It has been postulated that cerebrovascular disease is particularly common in the manic syndromes of late life (Berrios and Bakshi 1991). Indeed,

neurological comorbidity appears to be a common feature of late-life mania (Shulman 1997).

Neurological comorbidity (secondary mania)

The term 'secondary mania' was coined by Krauthammer and Klerman (1978) who defined it as mania associated with a variety of organic and medical aetiologies; family history tends to be negative with a general lack of any prior history of mood disturbance. This term has now been revised under DSM-IV as a 'mood disorder secondary to an underlying medical condition' (American Psychiatric Association 1994). The concept of secondary mania has been reviewed extensively (Strakowski et al. 1994; Verdoux and Bourgeois 1995) and the literature consists of a large number of individual case reports and small case series.

Cerebrovascular lesions have been most prominently associated with mania in late life (Robinson et al. 1988; Starkstein et al. 1990). A series of reports have consistently found a predominance of right-hemisphere lesions in the cortical and subcortical areas but also involving the basal region of the right temporal lobe and the orbito-frontal regions of the cortex. The consistency of right-sided cerebro-vascular lesions comes from a heterogeneous group of case reports including those by Jampala and Abrams (1983), Cummings and Mendez (1984), Kulisevsky et al. (1993), and Fawcett (1991). Associated clinical conditions include postoperative consequences of cardiac surgery, mitral valvuloplasty, and other heterogeneous central nervous system disturbances including vitamin B_{12} deficiency with gait disturbance (Jacobs et al. 1990). Two cases of neuroendocrine disturbance have been described, including a case of Addison's disease (Ur et al. 1992) and a reported mania associated with thyrotoxicosis (Lee et al. 1991).

Head trauma also appears to be an important risk factor for the development of mania in late life (Shukla et al. 1987; Miller et al. 1992; Burnstein 1993; Jorge et al. 1993). In one study (Jorge et al. 1993), 9 per cent of head trauma patients met diagnostic criteria for a manic episode within the first year following the trauma.

Neuroimaging studies

With the advent of improved neuroimaging technology, bipolar disorder has been associated with a high frequency of pathologies on both structural (MRI) and functional (single-photon emission CT) neuroimaging. In particular, subcortical hyperintensities have been found in deep white matter (McDonald et al. 1991). Migliorelli et al. (1993) used single-photon emission CT to study a small number of patients with mania and noted a general decrease in cerebral blood flow in the basal portion of the right temporal lobe.

Of particular interest, is the finding by Japanese investigators of a preponderance of silent cerebral infarctions associated with mania (Fujikawa et al. 1995). These investigators used MRI to determine the prevalence and location of silent cerebral infarctions in late-onset compared with early-onset mania and found a preponderance in the late-onset group. Kobayashi et al. (1991) also showed an increased incidence of silent cerebral infarctions with age, ranging from less than 10 per cent in patients who were in their forties to over 20 per cent in manic patients who were in their sixties. A decreased family history of mood disorder is associated with silent cerebral infarctions and mania. Not surprisingly, they showed a higher prevalence of risk factors for cerebrovascular disease such as hypertension.

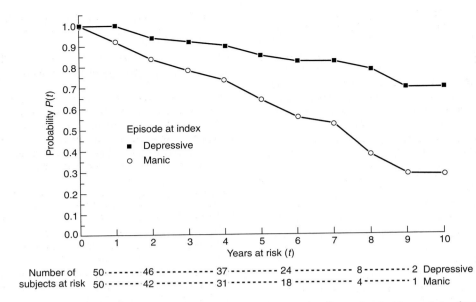

Fig. 1 Cumulative probability of survival for patients with index manic and depressive episodes. (Reproduced with permission from Shulman *et al.* (1992).)

Outcome studies for mania in old age are of particular importance in patients with high neurological comorbidity. There is now evidence that mania in old age carries a significant morbidity and mortality even when compared with age- and sex-matched elderly depressives who in turn have been shown to have high rates of both recurrence and mortality (Shulman *et al.* 1992). Figure 1 shows the survival analysis in a follow-up study of elderly manics compared with age- and sex-matched unipolar depressives. At a mean of 6.2 years follow-up, 50 per cent of the manic patients had died. This is not surprising in light of the association with the heterogeneous group of neurological disorders, particularly cerebrovascular disease.

The factors associated with mania in old age suggest that a very careful search for an underlying neurological disorder is indicated, particularly in late-onset first-episode manias. The nature of the underlying lesions may help to shed light on the pathophysiology of bipolar disorders in younger patients. Similar to the high comorbidity of panic disorder with medical illness, many psychiatric syndromes such as anxiety, paranoid, and manic disorders may be signals of underlying medical and neurological pathology. The clinician must be aware of this association and perform a careful evaluation before diagnosing primary psychiatric illness.

Treatment

There are no controlled studies of the treatment of bipolar disorder in old age. Clinical experience suggests that mood stabilizers and neuroleptic agents are equally efficacious in older patients, although the usual cautions with regard to side-effects and toxicity are applicable. The recent emergence of divalproex as a mood stabilizer has been a welcome addition to our armamentarium given that lithium carbonate has such a narrow therapeutic index at older ages (Emilien and Maloteaux 1996). Indeed, clinicians are now using combinations of lithium and divalproex when single mood stabilizers are insufficient to control the disorder (Solomon *et al.* 1997). Atypical neuroleptics such as clozapine and olanzapine may be useful in refractory bipolar

disorders or schizoaffective disorders (Zarate *et al.* 1995). Further systematic studies of both treatment and outcome are now indicated.

References

Almeida, O.P., Howard, R.J., Levy, R., David, A.S., Morris, R.G., and Sahakian, B.J. (1995). Clinical and cognitive diversity of psychotic states arising in late life (late paraphrenia). *Psychological Medicine*, **25**, 699–714.

American Psychiatric Association (1994). *Diagnostic and statistical manual* (4th edn). American Psychiatric Association, Washington, DC.

Andreasen, N.C. (1987). The diagnosis of schizophrenia. *Schizophrenia Bulletin*, **13**, 9–22.

Ballard, C.G. Mohan, R.N.C. Patel, A., and Graham, C. (1994). Anxiety disorder in dementia. *Irish Journal of Psychological Medicine*, **11**, 108–9.

Berrios, G.E. and Bakshi, N. (1991). Manic and depressive symptoms in the elderly: Their relationships to treatment outcome, cognition and motor symptoms. *Psychopharmacology*, **24**, 31–8.

Bland, R.C., Newman, S.C., and Orn, H. (1988). Prevalence of psychiatric disorders in the elderly in Edmonton. *Acta Psychiatrica Scandinavica*, Supplement 338, 57–63.

Blazer, D., George, L.K., and Hughes, D. (1991). Generalised anxiety disorder. In *Psychiatric disorders in America: the Epidemiological Catchment Area study* (ed. L.N. Robins and D.A. Regier), pp. 180–203. Free Press, New York.

Broadhead, J. and Jacoby, R. (1990). Mania in old age: a first prospective study. *International Journal of Geriatric Psychiatry*, **5**, 215–22.

Burnstein, A. (1993). Bipolar and pure mania disorders precipitated by head trauma. *Psychosomatics*, **34**, 194–5.

Calamari, J.E. Faber, S.D., Hitsman, B.L., and Poppe, C.J. (1994). Treatment of obsessive compulsive disorder in the elderly: a review and case example. *Journal of Behaviour Therapy and Experimental Psychiatry*, **25**, 95–104.

Castillo, C.S., Starkstein, S.E., Fedoroff, J.P., *et al.* (1993). Generalized anxiety disorder after stroke. *Journal of Nervous and Mental Disease*, **181**, 100–6.

Christenson, R. and Blazer, D. (1984). Epidemiology of persecutory ideation in an elderly population in the community. *American Journal of Psychiatry*, 141, 1088–91.

Cohen, C.I. (1990). Outcome of schizophrenia into later life: an overview. *Gerontologist*, 30, 790–7.

Copeland, J.R.M., Dewey, M.E., Wood, N., Dearle, R., Davidson, I.A., and McWilliam, C. (1987a). Range of mental illness among the elderly in the community: prevalence in Liverpool using the GMS-AGECAT package. *British Journal of Psychiatry*, 150, 815–23.

Copeland, J.R.M., Gurland, B.J., Dewey, M.E., Kelleher, M.J., Smith, A.M.R., and Davidson, I.A. (1987b). Is there more dementia, depression and neurosis in New York? A comparative study of the elderly in New York and London using the computer diagnosis AGECAT. *British Journal of Psychiatry*, 151, 466–73.

Cummings, J.L. and Mendez, M.F. (1984). Secondary mania with focal cerebrovascular lesions. *American Journal of Psychiatry*, 141, 1084.

Eagles, J.M. and Whalley, L.J. (1985). Ageing and affective disorders: the age at first onset of affective disorders in Scotland, 1969–1978. *British Journal of Psychiatry*, 147, 180–7.

Emilien, G. and Maloteaux, J.M. (1996). Lithium neurotoxicity at low therapeutic doses. Hypotheses for causes and mechanism of action following a retrospective analysis of published case reports. *Acta Neurologica Belgica*, 96, 281–93.

Fawcett, R.G. (1991). Cerebral infarct presenting as mania. *Journal of Clinical Psychiatry*, 52, 352–3.

Flint, A.J. (1994). Epidemiology and comorbidity of anxiety disorders in the elderly. *American Journal of Psychiatry*, 151, 640–9.

Flint, A.J. (1995). Treatment of late-onset agoraphobia secondary to depression. *Canadian Journal of Psychiatry*, 40, 568.

Flint, A.J. (1997). Epidemiology and comorbidity of anxiety disorders in later life: implications for treatment. *Clinical Neuroscience*, 4, 31–6.

Flint, A.J., Cook, J.M., and Rabins, P.V. (1996). Why is panic disorder less frequent in late life? *American Journal of Geriatric Psychiatry*, 4, 96–109.

Forstl, H., Dalgalarrondo, P., Riecher-Rossler, A., Lotz, M., Geiger-Kabisch, C., and Hentschel, F. (1994). Organic factors and the clinical features of late paranoid psychosis: a comparison with Alzheimer's disease and normal ageing. *Acta Psychiatrica Scandinavica*, 89, 335–40.

Fujikawa, T., Yamawaki, S., and Touhouda, Y. (1995). Silent cerebral infarctions in patients with late-onset mania. *Stroke*, 26, 946–9.

Goenjian, A.K., Najarian, L.M., Pynoos, R., *et al.* (1994). Post traumatic stress disorder in elderly and younger adults after the 1988 earthquake in America. *American Journal of Psychiatry*, 151, 895–901.

Herrmann, N. and Eryavec, G. (1994). Delayed onset post-traumatic stress disorder in World War II veterans. *Canadian Journal of Psychiatry*, 39, 439–41.

Howard, R. (1996). Raymond Levy and paranoid states of late life. *International Journal of Geriatric Psychiatry*, 11, 355–61.

Howard, R., Almeida, O., Levy, R., Graves, P., and Graves, M. (1994). Quantitative magnetic resonance imaging volumetry distinguishes delusional disorder from late onset schizophrenia. *British Journal of Psychiatry*, 165, 474–80.

Hymas, N., Naguib, M., and Levy, R. (1989). Late paraphrenia—a follow-up study. *International Journal of Geriatric Psychiatry*, 4, 23–9.

Jackson, C.W. (1995). Obsessive–compulsive disorder in elderly patients. *Drugs and Ageing*, 7, 438–48.

Jacobs, L.A., Bloom, H.F., and Behrman, F.Z. (1990). Mania and a gait disorder due to cobalamin deficiency. *Journal of the American Geriatrics Society*, 38, 473–4.

Jampala, V.S. and Abrams, R. (1983). Mania secondary to left and right hemisphere damage. *American Journal of Psychiatry*, 140, 1197–9.

Jenike, M.A. (1991). Geriatric obsessive–compulsive disorder. *Journal of Geriatric Psychiatry and Neurology*, 4, 34–9.

Jeste, D.V., Harris, M.J., Pearlson, G.D., *et al.* (1988). Late-onset schizophrenia: studying clinical validity. *Psychiatric Clinics of North America*, 11, 1–14.

Jeste, D.V., Lacro, J.P., Gilbert, P.L., Kline, J., and Kline, N. (1993). Treatment of late-life schizophrenia with neuroleptics. *Schizophrenia Bulletin*, 19, 817–30.

Jorge, R.E., Robinson, R.G., Starkstein, S.E., Arndt, S.V., Forrester, A.W., and Geisler, F.H. (1993). Secondary mania following traumatic brain injury. *American Journal of Psychiatry*, 150, 916–21.

Kay, D.W.K. and Roth, M. (1961). Environmental and hereditary factors in the schizophrenias of old age ('late paraphrenia') and their bearing on the general problem of causation in schizophrenia. *Journal of Mental Science*, 107, 649–86.

Kidson, M.A., Douglas, J.C., and Holwill, B.J. (1993). Post-traumatic stress disorder in Australian World War II veterans attending a psychiatric outpatient clinic. *Medical Journal of Australia*, 158, 563–6.

Kobayashi, S. Okada, K., and Yamashita, K. (1991). Incidence of silent lacunar lesions in normal adults and its relation to cerebral blood flow and risks factors. *Stroke*, 22, 1379–83.

Krauthammer, C. and Klerman, G.L. (1978). Secondary mania: manic syndromes associated with antecedent physical illness or drugs. *Archives of General Psychiatry*, 30, 74–9.

Kulisevsky, J., Berthier, M.L., and Pujol, J. (1993). Hemiballismus and secondary mania following a right thalamic infarction. *Neurology*, 43, 1422–4.

Lee, K.A., Vaillant, G.E., Torrey, W.C., and Elder, G.H. (1995). A 50-year prospective study of the psychological sequelae of World War II combat. *American Journal of Psychiatry*, 152, 516–22.

Lee, S., Chow, C.C., Wing, Y.K., Leung, C.M., Chiu, H., and Chen, C. (1991). Mania secondary to thyrotoxicosis. *British Journal of Psychiatry*, 159, 712–13.

Lindesay, J. (1991). Phobic disorders in the elderly. *British Journal of Psychiatry*, 159, 531–41.

Lindesay, J., Briggs, K., and Murphy, E. (1989). The Guy's/Age Concern Survey: prevalence rates of cognitive impairment, depression and anxiety in an urban elderly community. *British Journal of Psychiatry*, 155, 317–29.

McDonald, W.M., Krishnan, K.R.R., Doraiswamy, P.M., and Blazer, D.G. (1991). Occurrence of subcortical hyperintensities in elderly subjects with mania. *Psychiatry Research Neuroimaging*, 40, 211–20.

Magni, G. and De Leo, D. (1984). Anxiety and depression in geriatric and adult medical inpatients: a comparison. *Psychological Reports*, 55, 607–12.

Manela, M., Katona, C., and Livingston, G. (1996). How common are the anxiety disorders in old age? *International Journal of Geriatric Psychiatry*, 11, 65–70.

Migliorelli, R., Starkstein, S.E., Teson, A., de Quiros, G., Vazques, S., and Leiguardia, R.G. (1993). SPECT findings in patients with primary mania. *Journal of Neuropsychiatry*, 5, 379–83.

Miller, B.L., Lesser, I.M., Boone, K., Hill, E., Mehringer, C.M., and Wong, K. (1991). Brain lesions and cognitive function in late-life psychosis. *British Journal of Psychiatry*, 158, 76–82.

Miller, L.S., Garde, I.B., Moses, J.A., Zipursky, R.B., Kravitz, K., and Faustman, W.O. (1992). Head injury and mood disturbance. *Journal of Clinical Psychiatry*, 53, 171–2.

Myers, J.K., Weissman, M.M., Tischler, G.L., *et al.* (1984). Six-month prevalence of psychiatric disorders in three communities. *Archives of General Psychiatry*, 41, 959–67.

Naguib, M. and Levy, R. (1987). Late paraphrenia: neuropsychological impairment and structural brain abnormalities on computed tomography. *International Journal of Geriatric Psychiatry*, 2, 83–90.

Naguib, M., McGuffin, P., Levy, R., Festenstein, H., and Alonso, A. (1987). Genetic markers in late paraphrenia: a study of HLA antigens. *British Journal of Psychiatry*, 150, 124–7.

Parmelee, P.A., Katz, I.R., and Lawton, M.P. (1993). Anxiety and its association with depression among institutionalized elderly. *American Journal of Geriatric Psychiatry*, 1, 46–58.

Post, F. (1966). *Persistent persecutory states of the elderly*. Pergamon Press, Oxford.

Rabins, P., Pearlson, G., Jayaram, G., et al. (1987). Increased ventricle-to-brain ratio in late-onset schizophrenia. *American Journal of Psychiatry*, 142, 557–9.

Regier, D.A., Boyd, J.H., Burke, J.D., Jr, et al. (1988). One-month prevalence of mental disorders in the United States: based on five Epidemiologic Catchment Area sites. *Archives of General Psychiatry*, 45, 977–86.

Rickels, K. (1981). Limbitrol (amitriptyline plus chlordiazepoxide) revisited. *Psychopharmacology*, 75, 31–3.

Robinson, R.G., Starkstein, S.E., and Price, T.R. (1988). Post-stroke depression and lesion location. *Stroke*, 19, 125.

Rogers, M.P., White, K., Warshaw, M.G., et al. (1994). Prevalence of medical illness in patients with anxiety disorders. *International Journal of Psychiatry in Medicine*, 24, 83–96.

Schneider, L.S. (1996). Overview of generalized anxiety disorder in the elderly. *Journal of Clinical Psychiatry*, 57 (Supplement 7), 34–45.

Sherbourne, C.D., Wells, K.B., Meredith, L.S., Jackson, C.A., and Camp, P. (1996). Comorbid anxiety disorder and the functioning and well-being of chronically ill patients of general medical providers. *Archives of General Psychiatry*, 53, 889–95.

Shukla, S., Cook, B.L., Cook, S., Mukherjee, C., Godwin, C., and Miller, M.G. (1987). Mania following head trauma. *American Journal of Psychiatry*, 144, 93–6.

Shulman, K.I. (1996). Recent developments in the epidemiology, co-morbidity and outcome of mania in old age. *Reviews in Clinical Gerontology*, 6, 249–54.

Shulman, K.I. (1997). Neurologic co-morbidity and mania in old age. *Clinical Neuroscience*, 4, 37–40.

Shulman, K.I., Tohen, M., Satlin, A., Mallya, G., and Kalunian, D. (1992). Mania compared with unipolar depression in old age. *American Journal of Psychiatry*, 149, 341–5.

Snowdon, J. (1991). A retrospective case-note study of bipolar disorder in old age. *British Journal of Psychiatry*, 158, 484–90.

Solomon, D.A., Ryan, C.E., Keitner, G.I., et al. (1997). A pilot study of lithium carbonate plus divalproex sodium for the continuation and maintenance treatment of patients with bipolar I disorder. *Journal of Clinical Psychiatry*, 58, 95–9.

Starkstein, S.E., Mayberg, H.S., Berthier, M.L., Fedoroff, P., Price, T.R., and Robinson, R.G. (1990). Mania after brain injury: neuro-radiological and metabolic findings. *Annals of Neurology*, 27, 652–9.

Steinberg, J.R. (1994). Anxiety in elderly patients. A comparison of azapirones and benzodiazepines. *Drugs and Ageing*, 5, 335–45.

Stone, K. (1989). Mania in the elderly. *British Journal of Psychiatry*, 155, 220–4.

Stoudemire, A. and Moran, M.G. (1993). Psychopharmacologic treatment of anxiety in the medically ill elderly patient: special considerations. *Journal of Clinical Psychiatry*, 54 (Supplement 5), 27–33.

Strakowski, S.M., McElroy, S., Keck, P., and West, S. (1994). The co-occurrence of mania with medical and other psychiatric disorders. *International Journal of Psychiatry*, 24, 305–28.

Ur, E., Turner, T.H., Goodwin, T.J., Grossman, A., and Besser, G.M. (1992). Mania in association with hydrocortisone replacement for Addison's disease. *Postgraduate Medicine*, 68, 41–3.

Verdoux, H. and Bourgeois, M. (1995). Manies secondaires à des pathologies organiques cerebrales. *Annals Médico-Psychologiques*, 153, 161–8.

Weinberger, D.R., Jeste, D.V., Wyatt, R.J., and Teychenne, P.F. (1987). Cerebral atrophy in elderly schizophrenia patients: effects of ageing and of long-term instutionalization and neuroleptic therapy. In *Schizophrenia and ageing* (ed. N.E. Miller and G.D. Cohen), pp. 109–18. Guilford Press, New York.

Weissman, M.M., Leaf, P.J., Tichler, G.L., et al. (1988). Affective disorders in five United States communities. *Psychological Medicine*, 18, 141–53.

Wise, M.G. and Griffies, W.S. (1995). A combined treatment approach to anxiety in the medically ill. *Journal of Clinical Psychiatry*, 56 (Supplement 2), 14–19.

Zarate, C.A., Tohen, M., Banov, M.D., Weiss, M.K., and Cole, J.O. (1995). Is clozapine a mood stabiliser? *Journal of Clinical Psychiatry*, 56, 108–12.

20.3 Alcoholism

Thomas P. Beresford

Until recently alcoholism has been regarded as a condition that afflicted persons in the second to the fifth decades of life (Beresford and Gomberg 1995). Uncontrolled drinking of alcohol was reported to taper off considerably beyond that age, resulting in fewer and fewer alcoholics reaching the elderly decades and a minute number, if any, beginning problem drinking in late life. It has not been unusual to hear clinical colleagues say that alcohol use among the elderly is a 'non-problem' and that we need not be concerned about this age group. The opposite case is argued in this chapter. We begin by reviewing clinical and epidemiological studies that indicate the scope of the problem and its likely course over the next decades, including a discussion of the nosology of alcoholism as it applies to elderly individuals. Next, we move to both standard and more recent data on the age specificity of ethanol metabolism and intoxication. We then review what is known about ethanol and the health problems of older persons as well as the prognosis of and treatment for alcohol dependence in the elderly age group. Finally, ways in which clinical and research disciplines might make use of present knowledge in a search for better ways of preventing elderly alcoholism and of caring for those who suffer from it in late life are briefly described.

Early studies

Nearly 20 years ago, a few investigators had the foresight to begin questioning the belief that alcoholism, a condition reputedly confined to late adolescence through middle age (Atkinson 1990), would be rare among the burgeoning elderly population because of the early deaths of affected individuals or the unlikely occurrence of new cases. Rathbone-McCuan *et al.* (1976), in a community survey of 695 persons age 55 and older, provided a first look at the extent of drinking in later life. In her sample, a total of 8 per cent of subjects reported problem drinking defined as a score of between 1 and 6 on the Michigan Alcohol Screening Test (**MAST**) (Selzer 1971); this test, standardized on much younger subjects, probably resulted in an underestimate as noted below. Another 4 per cent of her sample reporting 'alcoholic drinking' with a score greater than 6. This called into question earlier data from a national telephone survey (Cahalan 1970) which reported only 6 per cent (or half as many) of persons over 60 as heavy drinkers.

Subsequently, Barnes (1979) conducted a cross-sectional probability study of over 1000 adults in western New York State and obtained similar findings to those of Rathbone-McCuan *et al.* (1976); as many as 24 per cent of males aged between 60 and 69 years could be classified as heavy drinkers. She used a range of phenomena to define heavy drinking: from those who drank two or more drinks three or more times a day to those who drank twice or more a month but consumed more than five standard beverages at a time. She also noted that heavy-drinking males aged more than 60 were almost equally likely to be married (17 per cent), widowed (14 per cent), or never married (13 per cent)—all of which differed from the non-heavy-drinking sample and suggested social isolation as a co-occurring factor in late-life alcohol abuse. Similarly, heavy-drinking elderly males were slightly more likely to be employed (22 per cent), than to be retired or unemployed (13 per cent), suggesting that work or economic stress was related to late-life alcohol use.

Roughly contemporaneous with these studies were reports by Rosin and Glatt (1971) and by Zimberg (1974) suggesting that up to one-third of problem drinkers aged over 65 may have begun their pathological drinking in late middle age or after. Taken together, these early studies provided the first evidence that alcohol dependence affected elderly Americans in large numbers and that new cases of alcoholism after age 65 were not rare.

Recognition and diagnosis

Early human studies of alcoholism were hampered by the lack of standardized criteria for alcohol dependence and abuse. This was rectified in 1980 with the publication of standard clinical criteria in the third edition of the *Diagnostic and Statistical Manual* (American Psychiatric Association 1980) and its subsequent revisions (American Psychiatric Association 1987, 1994). While standard definitions were a welcome improvement generally, their specific application to the

elderly group seemed more problematic. For example, the authors of DSM-III wrote 'In males, symptoms of alcohol dependence or abuse rarely occur for the first time after age 45' (American Psychiatric Association 1987; Atkinson 1990).

Part of the problem lay in the fact that the diagnostic criteria had been standardized on relatively young alcoholic and non-alcoholic samples. Current thought suggests that the three general areas of diagnostic importance (Beresford *et al.* 1991)—physical dependence which includes both tolerance to alcohol and withdrawal from its effects, impaired control of alcohol use once drinking begins, and impaired or lost social functioning due to excessive use—can be expressed, at least partially, in age-specific phenomena.

Tolerance

A daily ethanol dose regarded as moderate in a younger person may signal an ability to handle an increased ethanol load when presented to the central nervous system of an older person. For example, an increase to three rather two standard drinks daily might not be considered a profound change for a 25-year-old but may represent a striking increase in a septuagenarian (Beresford *et al.* 1988). However, there have been no studies addressing whether tolerance to alcohol may be acquired more rapidly and with less total alcohol exposure among elderly persons than among younger persons simply as a function of central nervous system age. A related question is whether the same amounts of alcohol have measurably more debilitating effects in normal non-alcoholic elderly persons than in younger persons (Chermack *et al.* 1996; Fink *et al.* 1996), something considered below. For present purposes, the 50 per cent increase in regular alcohol intake above a historical baseline—a requirement for tolerance in the standard criteria (American Psychiatric Association 1994)—is probably a useful sign when evaluating elderly drinkers. This may be true even if the regular daily amount of alcohol taken at baseline use is small.

Withdrawal

Similarly, very preliminary studies have suggested that withdrawal symptoms may be more severe and longer lasting in elderly than in younger alcoholics (Liskow *et al.* 1989; Brower *et al.* 1994). Whether this is a result solely of the quantity of alcohol drunk over a lifetime or of exposure to repeated withdrawal episodes, along the model of central nervous system kindling, or whether it is merely the interaction of a toxin with an elderly central nervous system is unknown. One animal study of ageing and withdrawal supports the latter explanation; older rats trained to drink alcohol showed more severe withdrawal signs than did younger animals given the same length of exposure to ethanol. (Maier and Pohorecky 1989) The fact that ethanol is more powerfully toxic to older animals was demonstrated long ago when researchers noted that the lethal dose (LD_{50}) for ethanol decreased as the animals aged (Wiberg *et al.* 1970).

Only brief retrospective reports exist in the literature on the question of alcohol withdrawal phenomena and their severity in elderly persons. Liskow *et al.* (1989) measured withdrawal in young and old subjects and found that withdrawal symptoms were more severe and required more chlordiazepoxide for their control in the elderly subjects. Brower *et al.* (1994) reviewed the records of older and younger adults in a rehabilitation facility and obtained the same results. Neither study controlled for length and regularity of exposure to alcohol, the frequency of previous withdrawal episodes, or the timing of the onset of alcohol addiction. There have been no comparisons of withdrawal phenomena in samples of early-onset versus recent-onset alcoholic elderly. For the purposes of diagnosis, what little is known suggests that withdrawal symptoms may occur after less frequent or less heavy alcohol use among elderly persons, a possibility that must be accounted for in the clinical history.

Impaired control

In contrast with the symptoms of ethanol tolerance and withdrawal, those of the impaired control phenomenon, which is defined as an inability to predict the extent or amount of alcohol used in a consistent fashion from one drinking episode to the next, may appear very much the same in elderly dependent drinkers as in their younger counterparts. There are no present studies suggesting that alcoholic elderly subjects are any less likely to experience characteristic symptoms. When control of alcohol use has been lost, dependent drinkers struggle to stop drinking after exposure to alcohol, may report many attempts at cutting down or stopping alcohol use, and often engage external means of trying to control this internally driven behaviour such as using alcohol only at certain times of the day, in certain beverage forms, or within the constraints of a limited money supply. While the nature of the impaired control phenomenon continues to elude those searching for its neural mechanisms, its presence as a phenomenological entity remains at the centre of our present conceptions of dependent drinking.

Social and physical problems due to alcohol

Like the symptoms of physical dependence, social decline resulting from uncontrolled drinking appears to be manifested in age-specific phenomena. For example, while fist fights, one of the items in MAST, may be a clue to uncontrolled alcohol use in a 25-year-old male, most 65-year-old male alcoholics would not report this as a frequent symptom. Conversely, present data suggest that the threatened loss of a driver's licence due to drinking carries a far greater impact at age 65 (Atkinson et al. 1990) because of the loss of personal autonomy often already compromised by age. Researchers have only just begun to identify which age-specific phenomena might be useful when attempting to understand the social effects of uncontrolled drinking in an elderly person.

Age-specific screening for alcoholism

Experience with elderly alcoholics given MAST, the CAGE questions (Cutting down, Annoyance by criticism, Guilty feeling, Eye-openers), and other screening tests have led us to conclude that an age-specific instrument was needed (Beresford et al. 1990). For example, we found that the sensitivity of the CAGE questions, the most effective of the current screening devices for elderly people seen in health-care settings, drops rapidly from 77 per cent for 60-year-olds to 52 per cent for octogenarians whereas specificity remains above 90 per cent irrespective of age (Blow et al. 1992). In response to this, we have developed an age-specific alcoholism screening test which attempts to list those phenomena most likely to reflect pathological drinking in the elderly age group (Blow et al. 1992). This is known as MAST-G (see Chapter 27). It was developed from contact with a series of elderly alcoholic individuals and, during early field testing, was shown to be significantly more sensitive and specific than other standard screening instruments such as MAST or the CAGE questions. Some of its age-specific items, for example reluctance of the family to allow a grandparent to care for his or her grandchildren, may be instructive for clinicians in evaluating drinking elderly persons. While this test offers a promise of increased effectiveness, it requires further validation in large studies using more detailed instruments such as Finney's Drinking Problems Index (Finney et al. 1991). One recent study comparing CAGE and MAST-G found them essentially equivalent in a male nursing home subject group (Joseph et al. 1995). Whether age-specific screening can be established remains to be seen.

Recent clinical and population studies

Armed with more sophisticated clinical recognition schemes and with a greater appreciation of age-specific phenomena, researchers in the last 10 years have given much improved clarity to our understanding of the shape and course of alcoholism as it occurs in persons who live beyond age 60.

Epidemiology

Viewed from an epidemiological perspective, the problem of elderly alcoholism may become even greater than the early researchers had suggested. One example of this lies in the effect of values held by the cohort that comprises the American elderly population of today. Most were raised in the 1920s and 1930s when alcohol use carried the stigma of association with illegality and organized crime. This negative effect could be predicted to reduce alcoholism prevalence rates among those currently living in old age. In contrast, the large number of persons born after the Second World War, who will comprise the doubling of the aged population forecast to occur between 1980 and 2030, experienced their formative years in the 1960s and 1970s when either no social stigma or a positive social value was associated with drinking. This cohort can be predicted to show a significantly higher prevalence of alcohol use disorders when they reach old age. Early evidence to support both predictions has come from the Veterans Administration Normative Ageing Study (Glynn et al. 1985), in which alcohol prevalence is higher among Vietnam veterans than among their Second World War predecessors.

At the same time, the concerns of early investigators who sensed the presence of a large number of elderly Americans who begin their alcohol abuse and dependence in late life have been borne out in systematic studies. For example, the Epidemiologic Catchment Area study reported the incidence of alcohol use disorders, as defined by DSM-III (American Psychiatric Association 1980), in relation to age (Eaton et al. 1989). Although the group aged 65 and above showed a low overall incidence, about 20 per cent of that seen in the younger groups, there was a steady frequency of new cases throughout the elderly cohort with a mild upswing in incidence after age 75. Reviewing these data, Atkinson (1992) noted that their true importance was in the continued incidence figures throughout late life, suggesting that the risk for alcohol dependence does not disappear after age 65.

A second community study, this time of prevalence of drinking problems among elderly persons, was based on telephone interviews with over 1800 persons aged between 55 and 65 (Moos et al. 1991). The investigators found one or more current alcohol problems in 37 per cent of the respondents in this age range, and about one out of every three of the positive respondents reported that they had not had alcohol problems prior to 2 years before the survey. These data again point to the likelihood of an increase in drinking among some persons in late middle age and early old age, an often subtle phenomenon that may escape ordinary monitoring in health-care centres.

Comparison of the relative prevalence of alcohol-dependent persons in clinical settings appears to give credence to the notion first articulated by Atkinson that recent-onset elderly alcoholics are likely to have more social and economic resources and therefore are more likely to be seen in private treatment facilities. For example, his group reported that 24 per cent of a sample of 54 patients seeking treatment in a veterans alcohol clinic who were over 65 years of age had begun drinking within the previous 5 years (Atkinson et al. 1990). In contrast, Finlayson et al. (1988) reported that 41 per cent of a sample of 211 elderly alcohol-dependent patients seen at the Mayo Clinic had begun drinking after age 60 and, in an earlier study, Wiens et al. (1982) found that 68 per cent of a sample of 68 alcoholic persons over the age of 65 in a private alcohol rehabilitation facility had begun drinking after the age of 60. Atkinson commented that the increasing frequencies of recent-onset alcohol dependence in the three studies reflected a trend from lower to middle and upper-middle class subjects. This agrees with the notion of a downhill progressive course of alcoholism, outlined by Jellinek (1960) and subsequently by others (Vaillant 1995), that predicts a loss of personal resources as the effects of uncontrolled alcohol use become more serious.

Biological effects of age and ethanol

There is increasing evidence to suggest that the biological effects of ethanol may differ between elderly and younger persons. For example, epidemiological surveys have shown that absolute amounts of alcohol drunk decrease with age for light and moderate as well as for heavy drinkers (Mishara and Kastenbaum 1980; Nordstrom and Berglund 1987). Early studies of the age-associated effects of a standard ethanol dose suggested a possible reason: elderly persons may be more sensitive to ethanol that their younger counterparts (Vogel-Sprott and Barrett 1984; Jones and Neri 1985) A more recent study found that older subjects performed significantly worse than younger subjects in driving simulation when given the same alcohol dose (Roehrs et al. 1994). Table 1 lists other studies of the age-associated biological effects of ethanol that have been conducted in humans, either clinically using chemical or radiological probes or in vitro by studying tissues obtained at autopsy.

However, the question of which effects can be attributed to age alone, which to ethanol exposure alone, and which to a demonstrable interaction between the two has provided a new and necessary degree of complexity to the puzzles surrounding ethanol and ageing. Table 2 lists those studies which, to the best of our knowledge, have addressed the relative contributions of each variable in manifesting specific ethanol effects. Probably the only conclusion that can be drawn from the few studies listed is that no clear pattern exists. However, it is likely that an ageing nervous system will be seen as a significant variable in managing an ethanol load affecting such variables as sleep or cognition.

A prior challenge to researchers seeking to study the effects of age–ethanol interactions has been to identify the contributions to

Table 1 Human studies of alcoholism and ageing

Affected by ethanol

Performance impairment among older pilots (Morrow et al. 1990)

Lessened cognitive abilities compared with non-alcoholics (Schuckit 1982)

Stress results in increased drinking in elderly drivers (Wells et al. 1983)

Association with decreased bone mineral density in older women (Laitinen et al. 1991) and in older alcoholic men (Karantanas et al. 1991)

Normalizing of pattern-reversal visual evoked potentials slowed or lost in elderly alcoholics in withdrawal (Kelley et al. 1984)

Large muscle group impairment in old alcoholics only (Pendergast et al. 1990)

Altered T_1 relaxation (magnetic resonance) during withdrawal related to age (Agartz et al. 1991)

Increased cerebral atrophy and increased hypointense lesions related to alcohol use associated with increased age (Hayakawa et al. 1992)

Decreased hippocampal muscarinic receptors in older alcoholics only (Hughes and Davis 1983)

Decreased putamen muscarinic receptors in alcoholic brains; little age effect (Freund and Ballinger 1989b)

Decreased hippocampal muscarinic and benzodiazepine receptors in alcoholic brains; little age effect (Freund and Ballinger 1989a)

Decreased serotonin receptor density in cortex, hippocampus, and raphe nuclei in alcoholics related to age (Dillon et al. 1991)

Unaffected by ethanol

Age-associated decrease in male hormone production (Simon et al. 1992)

Relationship between magnetic resonance scan changes and alcohol in elderly women (Kroft et al. 1991)

Change in stomach/duodenum prostaglandin concentration (Cryer et al. 1992)

Putamen benzodiazepine receptor density from brains of alcoholics (Freund and Ballinger 1989b)

ethanol's effects on the nervous and other systems depending on whether these originate from altered ethanol pharmacokinetics (absorption and metabolism) or altered ethanol pharmacodynamics (sensitivity and tolerance) or both. This has led to studies of whether elderly persons absorb or metabolize ethanol differently from younger persons or whether, at similar circulating levels of ethanol, elderly persons notice more severe or more frequent intoxication effects than do their younger counterparts.

Clinical metabolic studies

Only a few investigators have attempted to elucidate either the metabolic or pharmacodynamic effects of ethanol in elderly subjects. Vestal et al. (1977) studied the association between age and ethanol metabolism in a group of 50 healthy non-alcoholic subjects, aged from 21 to 81 years, who were given a 1-h infusion of ethanol in a dose of 0.57 g/kg body weight. While age had no effect on observed rates of ethanol elimination, peak ethanol concentration in blood at the end of the infusion period correlated directly with age. Comparing ethanol levels and estimates of body water, Vestal and coworkers concluded that a smaller volume of distribution, associated with decreased lean body mass among their elderly subjects, explained the higher peak ethanol concentrations.

Vogel-Sprott and Barrett (1984) studied a range of 41 male social drinkers aged between 19 and 63 years. Their subjects performed

Table 2 Differential and interactive effects of age and alcohol use

	Age	Alcohol	Both
Sleep			
O$_2$ desaturation episodes (Vitiello et al. 1990)	×		
Cognitive tasks			
Lack of contextual priming (Cermak et al. 1988)	×		×
Recognition of emotional themes (Oscar et al. 1990)	×		
Dichotic listening patterns (Ellis 1990)	×		×
Neuroreceptors			
Muscarinic receptors decrease (Hughes and Davis 1983)	×	×	
D$_2$ receptors decrease (Govoni et al. 1988)	×		
Serotonin receptors decrease (Dillon et al. 1991)		×	

balance-beam and bead-stringing tasks after receiving a single ethanol dose of 0.57 g/kg served in halves given 20 min apart and taken after a 4-h fast. When individual differences in peak blood alcohol level were controlled statistically, alcohol-induced impairment in task performance increased during peak ethanol exposure and in association with age in this non-stratified sample. The authors concluded that the reduction in the volume of distribution for alcohol that Vestal and coworkers had observed and 'an intensified behavioural effect' of alcohol, i.e. a postulated increase in sensitivity to ethanol, may together explain the lessening of alcohol use among elderly non-alcoholic people. However, they noted that their estimates of the proportion of body water accounted for only 25 per cent of the variance in peak blood ethanol levels.

Jones and Neri (1985) studied subjective intoxication in four groups of healthy non-alcoholic men stratified by decades: twenties, thirties, forties, and fifties (12 per group). After a 12-h fast, each of the subjects drank 0.68 g/kg of ethanol within 20 min. The subjects' degree of self-reported feelings of intoxication rose in association with age. At the same time, it was noted that the distribution volume of ethanol per kilogram body weight decreased by only 8 per cent in subjects in their twenties compared with those in their fifties.

However, these workers did not separate subjects into young and old cohorts and compare the average area under the curve (**AUC**) for blood ethanol concentration; neither did they compare male and female subjects by age, investigate the effects of varying administration routes (one way of studying volume of distribution as noted below), or account for fasting versus feeding states. Noting these concerns, we studied total of 57 subjects (28 male, 29 female) in four age-by-sex cohorts (Lucey et al. 1999). All subjects received a low dose of ethanol (0.3 g/kg) on three occasions: orally after an overnight fast, orally after a standard breakfast, and intravenously after a standard breakfast. The blood ethanol response was represented by the AUC over 240 min. In all cohorts, there was a hierarchy of blood ethanol AUC responses: oral fasted were greater than intravenously fed who were greater than oral fed. Within sexes, blood ethanol AUCs among males were significantly greater in older subjects than younger subjects in the oral fasted and intravenously fed states but not in the oral fed state. Among female subjects, the difference between old and young was striking in the oral fasted state alone. The average magnitude of the difference in AUC between the elderly and young male groups given alcohol orally in a fasted state was 13 per cent; the same figure

for elderly versus young females was three times greater (39 per cent). In contrast with other reports (Frezza et al. 1990), we found no ethanol AUC sex differences when comparing sex cohorts matched for age. Nor do our data support the suggestion of a reversal of putative first-pass metabolism sex differences due to age (Pozzato et al. 1995) These data support an influence of age on ethanol metabolism, particularly in the fasting state, for both sexes. However, the previous explanation of reduced volume of distribution accounting for higher peak ethanol levels among elderly subjects does not appear to fit our data.

Clinical studies of age and intoxication

Route of administration and feeding status appear to be important factors not only in metabolism but also in the intoxication that follows exposure to alcohol. Lucey et al. (1999) asked subjects to rate their subjective sense of intoxication and fatigue, to perform pencil and paper tasks of perceptual motor functioning, and to perform a test of reaction time after a standard ethanol dose of 0.3 g/kg given intravenously after a standard breakfast. Over the course of the experiment young and old subjects demonstrated similar changes from baseline functioning on objective intoxication measures, and there was an age-independent increase in subjective intoxication in both groups. Among elderly subjects, there was a clear age-associated worsening of perceptual motor test performance at baseline that continued throughout the experiment, but there was no added component of objectively measurable loss of function that indicated an age-plus-ethanol effect unique to the older subject group. These data suggest that at a low dose the magnitude of the toxic effects of ethanol among elderly subjects, when compared with their baseline performance, are no greater that those seen among younger persons relative to their baseline. This is similar to a recent report by Jones and Neri (1994), apparently based on their 1985 study, in which little difference was found in the effect of ethanol in subjects aged between 20 and 59.

To pursue these findings further, we administered the same measures of intoxication to split groups of subjects who had ingested the same dose of alcohol orally after either a 12-h overnight fast or a standard breakfast. Elderly subjects of both sexes achieved greater degrees of subjective intoxication over baseline at the ethanol peak in the fasted state when compared with the same perceptions in a fed state. The increased perception of intoxication in the non-fed state was still significantly higher than baseline when assessed again after 100 min. The data suggested that recovery from an intoxicated state occurred at a significantly slower rate among the elderly subjects than among their younger counterparts.

Possible clinical characteristics of age-associated differences

Perhaps the first conclusion that can be drawn is that, from a metabolic point of view, a 'standard drink' for an elderly person probably contains about 20 per cent less ethanol than that for a younger person.

Second, a low dose of ethanol results in considerable subjective feelings of intoxication among elderly subjects of either sex and the effects are longer lasting among the elderly than among the younger subject groups.

Third, considering only the objective intoxication data, non-alcoholic elderly subjects begin with lessened perceptual–motor capability at baseline and may experience a similar magnitude of impairment after ethanol, measured as change from baseline, as their younger colleagues. At commonly used doses, age rather than alcohol appears to account for most of the differences in activities such as walking, driving, or writing.

Finally, our study suggests that both subjective and objective intoxication are worsened by fasting. Although ethanol absorption is markedly increased when subjects of any age have not eaten, the difference between young and old women was particularly striking and may be a factor in the drop in ethanol consumption reported among elderly women in population surveys. While the metabolic mechanism for this is unclear at present, its elucidation may afford some useful insight into the biology of ethanol metabolism that might be applicable to old and young alike.

Table 3 Basic studies of alcoholism and ageing

LD$_{50}$ for ethanol decreases as animals age (Wiberg et al. 1970)
Older animals exhibit more severe withdrawal (Wood et al. 1982; Maier and Pohorecky 1989)
Increased intoxication but less tolerance in older mice (Wood et al. 1982)
Increased sleep time after ethanol in older mice (Wood et al. 1982)
Less change in body temperature after ethanol in older mice (Wood et al. 1982)
Older rats reawaken at lower blood and brain ethanol concentrations (Ritzmann and Springer 1980)
Lower brain ethanol concentrations causes sleep in older rats (Ott et al. 1985)
Slowing of neuronal membrane functions with age and alcohol exposure (Bunting and Scott 1989)
Decreased membrane fluidization with age after ethanol in vitro (Armbrecht et al. 1983)
Increased polyphosphoinositide in young but not old mice after ethanol (Sun et al. 1987, 1993)
Decreased inhibition of GABA release by ethanol in older mice (Strong and Wood 1984)
Decreased glutamine release after ethanol in old rats (Peinado et al. 1987)
Ethanol depolarizes old but hyperpolarizes young rat neurones (Niesen et al. 1988)
Increased muscarinic receptor density in young but not old rats after ethanol (Pietrzak et al. 1989)
Increased serotonin reuptake and decreased serotonin-2a receptor concentration in rats (Druse et al. 1997)

Basic research on ethanol toxicity and age

Researchers have only recently begun animal studies aimed at elucidating the mechanisms of the age–ethanol interactions seen in or hypothesized from clinical experience. In the past, basic studies of the neuropharmacology and neurophysiology of alcoholism were often avoided because of the many effects of ethanol in tissue or cellular preparations. Recent research, generally conducted without reference to ageing processes, has attacked this biological complexity through several lines of parallel study of both specific neuroreceptors and intracellular second-messenger signalling systems. However, only a few studies have considered ageing as a variable. Most of those that have done so point to a lessened resilience or responsiveness of the ageing nervous system after a toxic insult from ethanol (Table 3).

In a series of studies of possible mechanisms of the age–ethanol interaction, Wood et al. (1982) reiterated the clinical truism that an ageing brain responds to a toxic insult differently, usually with less resilience, than a young brain. For example, they found that the adaptation in depolarized release of the neurotransmitter GABA found in young rats exposed to ethanol (both acute and chronic models of drinking) was missing in aged rats. The same lack of adaptation to ethanol was observed for the activity of polyphosphoinositide, a prime

transmitter in receptor-mediated transduction systems. Interestingly, animal studies to date have not linked changes in molecular mechanisms such as these to age differences in measurable phenomena such as the severity of withdrawal from alcohol, noted above, or to changes in sleep time or thermal regulation. While some of the basic studies occasionally offer contradictory explanations, the general trend among them is to suggest a lessened responsiveness in managing the cellular and molecular effects of ethanol as an organism ages.

Age-associated loss of nervous system resilience was the conclusion of a recent study by Bickford et al. (1995). Their data on the mechanism of lessened central nervous system response to ethanol in older animals suggested that some neurophysiological processes mediating the pharmacodynamic effects of ethanol may be reversed through the processes of normal central nervous system ageing. This phenomenon, if borne out in other investigations, may result in a pharmacological armamentarium for elderly alcoholics that differs qualitatively from that for younger patients.

It is clear that there is a need to define the mechanisms of age-specific ethanol responses, particularly with the goal of devising new pharmacological treatment approaches. To some, ageing neurophysiology is regarded largely as an extension of that seen in younger persons but with lessened functional efficacy. Surprises may be in appear to be partially reversible with abstinence. However, the changes in cerebral volume, as in the case of neuropsychological deficits, appear to be correlated with advancing age rather than with the amount of alcohol consumed. In a comprehensive study (Ron *et al.* 1980) both neurocognitive and brain volume lesions were positively correlated with IQ. This phenomenon, together with a divergence in vocabulary scores cited by other investigators (Bowden 1987), has drawn research attention to the confounding factor of premorbid intelligence in assessing the effects of alcohol. Despite the continued controversy in this field, it seems appropriate to conclude that persons with dementing illnesses may worsen their dementia by regular ingestion of alcohol. At the same time, while social drinking appears to have a negligible effect on age-associated changes in cognition, the effects of chronic heavy drinking have yet to be elucidated adequately.

More recent studies have led to more cause for concern about the relationship between ethanol and direct injury to the ageing brain. One group found that elderly alcoholics demonstrated a greater loss of grey matter than a group of younger alcoholics who reported about the same duration of heavy drinking (Pfefferbaum *et al.* 1997); there was also volume loss in the anterior hippocampus that did not occur in the younger group (Sullivan *et al.* 1995). Further elucidation of the interaction between ethanol and the ageing brain awaits studies using techniques in which physiology and morphology can be linked, as in evoked potentials (Biggins *et al.* 1995; Pollock *et al.* 1995).

Sleep problems

Acting as a central nervous system depressant, ethanol adversely affects sleep in vulnerable younger individuals. This occurs in at least two ways: reduced stimulation of the hypoglossal nerve resulting in upper-airway instability (Krol *et al.* 1984) and impairment of the hypercapnic–hypoxic respiratory drive in the brainstem (Remmers 1984). Both conditions worsen sleep apnoea, fostering more frequent apnoeic episodes, longer-lasting apnoeic spells, or both. At the same time, the body's adjustment to the absence of alcohol can result in insomnia. This is demonstrated most clearly in the interrupted sleep patterns manifested during alcohol withdrawal, and generally reported in clinical populations of younger individuals drinking heavily for a month or more.

Consider the same effects of alcohol in the context of an older, more sensitive, and less resilient nervous system. Smaller doses or less frequent use, well short of the quantities and frequencies seen among alcohol-abusing or alcohol-dependent patients, become important. In the case of sleep apnoea, for example, ageing alone results in an instability of the upper airway reflected in the increase in snoring with age (Webb 1982). It has also been noted that the hypercapnic respiratory drive decreases in elderly people while the hypoxic respiratory drive does not appear to be affected. (Kronenberg and Drage 1973); however, the hypercapnic–hypoxic synergy is reduced. In this context, the addition of a central nervous system depressant, such as ethanol, can be particularly troublesome in vulnerable individuals.

Insomnia, the most frequent sleep complaint among elderly persons, also has an etiological basis in physiological ageing (Dement *et al.* 1982). Sleep efficiency, i.e. the time asleep as a proportion of the time spent in bed, is decreased in normal elderly persons. At the same time, wakefulness is increased in older persons, particularly in response to external stimuli. For many, the use of small doses of alcohol to help fall asleep results in rebound wakefulness later during the sleep cycle. Although poorly elucidated, this wakefulness appears to be a less formidable variant of the sleep continuity disorder seen in alcohol withdrawal. In an effort to reset itself after a dose of depressant drug, the elderly nervous system appears to become more active and more likely to resume wakefulness. The common practice of prescribing small doses of alcohol to aid sleep in older persons may worsen the sleep problem for many and could be dangerous for individuals susceptible to sleep apnoeic episodes.

While changes of this nature have been noted in normal elderly persons given alcohol, the effects of drinking among active elderly alcoholics remains to be understood. For example, the effects of tolerance to large doses of alcohol on the sleep–wake cycle is not clear. It is possible that, as long as tolerance is maintained, it protects against sleep apnoea. Whether a reverse tolerance, resulting in greater sensitivity to alcohol after a prolonged period of abstinence, renders upper-airway obstruction more likely is unknown. Similarly, whether chronic heavy drinking results in effects like those in milder withdrawal from alcohol remains to be studied. Based on present evidence, however, we can conclude that the interaction of ageing and alcohol use in the setting of alcohol dependence is probably deleterious.

Prognosis of alcoholism in late life

No discussion of alcoholism in late life can exclude prognosis, and the significance of environmental strengths and supports in sustained abstinence from ethanol among those who are dependent on it. The now classic longitudinal study by Vaillant (1983, 1995) of early-onset middle-aged alcoholics (mean age, 45 years, ± 10 years) identified four prognostic factors that were associated with continued abstinence from alcohol beyond 3 years:

(1) one or more substitute activities with which to structure the time previously spent drinking;

(2) a significant relationship with a caring person who is capable of placing knowledgeable limits on drinking behaviour;

(3) a source of hope or improved self-esteem that serves to counterbalance guilt due to drinking or related problems;

(4) an immediate consequence of drinking that is both certain and noxious.

Whether and to what extent these factors apply to elderly alcoholic persons remains an important question.

In a study of treatment of late-life alcoholic persons, Atkinson *et al.* (1993) demonstrated that the last of Vaillant's factors was useful when they showed that the revocation or impending revocation of a driver's licence was one of the best predictors of treatment compliance in their sample of elderly outpatient alcoholics in the Veterans Affairs system. Similarly, in the short-term remission study by Moos's group noted earlier (Moos *et al.* 1991, 1994*a*, *b*, *c*; Brennan *et al.* 1993, 1994; Schutte *et al.* 1994; Brennan and Moos 1996; Mertens *et al.* 1996) it was reported that late-life problem drinkers who remitted within 1 year of initial contact consumed less alcohol, reported fewer drinking problems, had friends who approved less of drinking, and were more likely to seek help from mental health practitioners. While the first two factors may appear somewhat academic, the disapproval of friends and seeking help from another person both appear congruent with Vaillant's idea of a knowledgeable significant other whose

Table 4 Putative characteristics of late-onset problem drinkers

Higher socio-economic status (Glynn *et al.* 1988; Atkinson 1990)

Married (Glynn *et al.* 1988)

Stressful life events trigger drinking increase (Wells *et al.* 1983; Finlayson *et al.* 1988)

May affect women more frequently than men (Holzer *et al.* 1984)

May affect minorities more frequently (Gomberg 1994)

May be related to social pressure among some elderly groups (Atkinson *et al.* 1990; Brennan *et al.* 1993; Brennan and Moos 1994)

Better prognosis compared with early onset (Moos *et al.* 1991, 1994*a, b, c*)

Lower frequency of family positive alcohol histories (Atkinson 1990)

May have a more severe withdrawal syndrome than younger drinkers with similar alcohol exposure (Alling *et al.* 1982)

Problem drinking begins in late life (Eaton 1989; Atkinson *et al.* 1990; Moos 1991)

Female spouse dissatisfied with marriage (Epstein *et al.* 1997)

concern is balanced by clear limits to tolerating drinking. In the study by Moos's group, late-onset problem drinkers were also more likely to remit over the follow-up period than were early-onset problem drinkers.

While at first glance this might be ascribed to the brevity of problem drinking, it may also be the case that, if recent-onset elderly dependent drinkers remit more easily than younger recent-onset dependent drinkers, the intransigence of uncontrolled drinking, characteristic of alcohol dependence at a young age, may itself be altered in ways that might be traceable to the alterations of an ageing physiology. Moos and coworkers used very general language to conclude that late-onset problem drinkers might be 'more reactive to physical health stressors and to social influences' than persons with long-standing alcoholism (Moos *et al.* 1994*c*). While present data suggests that late-life recent-onset alcoholism may be less severe and more treatable than early-onset alcoholism (Table 4), they do not offer a view of a path to recovery as much as a list of the possible resources to be used to that end. The course differentiating those who recover from those who do not is unknown at the present time. The best approach to recent-onset versus early-onset elderly alcoholism, if indeed a differential approach is required, has yet to be determined systematically.

Vaillant (1983, 1995) has reported a longitudinal study of a large group of elderly drinkers, who began drinking well before old age and had long lives despite this. He studied two male cohorts from differing social backgrounds. With the telescoping of time provided by a 50-year follow-up study of the same cohorts (Vaillant 1996), he sought to answer three unanswered questions.

1. Is alcohol abuse progressive over the life course?

2. When does either abstinence or controlled drinking become a stable pattern of behaviour?

3. Does long-term remission, high mortality, or poor case finding explain the decline in alcoholism rates seen with increasing age?

Following 202 of the subjects who had fulfilled the DSM-III criteria for alcohol dependence, Vaillant noted that the severity of alcohol abuse, if it was present after age 45, did not increase as most of the progressive theories of alcoholism would have predicted. This appears congruent with data from Nordstrom and Berglund (1987), suggesting that heavy drinking wanes with the passage of the decades. Second, even after 2 years of stable abstinence, the observed relapse rate to uncontrolled drinking was still 35 per cent. Abstinence for 5 years resulted in stable long-term remission among elderly alcoholics. 'Controlled-drinking' subjects fared worse; five of the 15 subjects in this category maintained controlled drinking for 10 or more years, while seven of the remaining 10 relapsed to chronic abuse and three opted for total abstinence. In agreement with the survey and cross-sectional data noted above, Vaillant found that 8 per cent of the men in his sample first abused alcohol after age 50. By the age of 65, 18 per cent of the total alcohol-dependent sample were actively abusing alcohol. Nearly a third of the sample (29 per cent) had died through a combination of alcohol and cigarette abuse, a death rate three times that of the non-dependent subjects. One-fifth of the group (19 per cent) were abstinent, another 15 per cent drank socially, and the fate of the remaining 19 per cent was listed as 'uncertain outcomes'. From these results, Vaillant concluded that three factors—abstinence, a high death rate, and socially less problematic use—combined to reduce the frequency of alcohol abuse as the subjects entered old age. From these and other such data it is reasonable to consider age itself as a good prognostic sign with respect to alcohol dependence, a stance contrary to most of the stereotypes of both alcoholics and elderly persons. At the same time, it is clear that morbidity and mortality could be substantially reduced by careful attention to identifying and treating this specific group of alcohol-dependent persons.

Treatment

We must care for the alcoholic elderly patients of our day with the methods at hand. Present knowledge suggests that they must be identified and diagnosed using active age-specific means, that the physical sequelae of extended heavy alcohol use may be severe and must be treated appropriately, that intercurrent medical illnesses are probably more frequent and must be identified and treated, and that prognostic assessments leading to treatment must be carried out. Having done all this, treatment of the underlying alcohol dependence must be provided in ways that elderly persons will accept.

There is good preliminary evidence to suggest that treatment programmes for elderly alcoholics should be tailored to address age-specific needs. Atkinson (1990) has been a pioneer in this line of inquiry. Perhaps his two greatest contributions have been in recognizing first that treatment settings must be tailored to the comfort of individual patients, as when he established that some older alcoholics prefer treatment with their own age group while others prefer to be in settings with younger patients, and second that, while treatment settings may be a matter of preference, treatment approaches are remarkably similar; elderly alcoholics do not do well with an aggressive, probing therapist but respond positively to a patient supportive interpersonal style. We have Atkinson's group (Atkinson *et al.* 1990) to thank for researching and highlighting the idea that prognostic patterns appear to differentiate recent-onset from early-onset elderly drinkers. This may serve to increase optimism in treating both groups; it has been recognized that the recent-onset drinkers will respond because of relatively intact social resources, and that those early-onset drinkers with little in the way of resources will depend more heavily on treatment facilities and public and health-care social support networks. Neither group should be overlooked or viewed passively. Treatment must entail longitudinal contact, particularly in the cases of those who are most destitute and least likely to follow through with either alcoholism treatment or medical treatment of life-threatening conditions.

The last point was recently emphasized by Willenbring et al. (1995) who found that active follow-up care among ageing alcoholics in a Veterans Affairs facility saved lives. They demonstrated that only one in 28 alcoholic patients of the least compliant type died during the course of a year of active follow-up compared with eight of 28 patients in a matched control group who did not receive active follow-up care. At the same time, care significantly lessened the use of costly emergency and intensive care services for the treatment group compared with the control group. A brief translation of their outcome data into dollars saved illustrates the point: the average annual costs of hospital treatment for each patient in the follow-up care group would have dropped from $7000 to about $4000, saving about $3000 per patient or about $84 000 per year on average for the 28 patients. At the same time the cost per patient for those left in ordinary care would be expected to rise from the treated patient's yearly health bill of $4000 to $10 250 annually, an increase of $6250 per patient or $175 000 on average for the 28 patients in the control group. This increase in expense would obtain even though more than one in four of the control patients could be expected to die during the year. The cost savings from providing the service plus the added expense of not providing it yields an estimated total of $252 560 annually, on average, for the 56 patients in this study. A common tendency in some quarters is to ignore ageing, seriously ill, and homeless alcoholics. However, mortality figures, cost estimates, and the dictates of human concern all converge to argue for better, cheaper, and more humane care for even the most difficult group of elderly alcoholic patients.

Conclusions

There is little doubt that alcoholism and its attendant effects will be a growing problem over the next several decades as the populations of industrialized nations age (Beresford and Gomberg 1995). Uncontrolled alcohol use will worsen the health problems associated with advanced age and this will threaten the provision of health services on a large scale. It will provide a sizeable challenge to the health-care budgets of most countries. We are learning to recognize both alcoholism in older persons and the roles of health-care providers in the prevention and treatment of this very serious condition. It is also clear that very little of the biological aetiology of alcoholism as it relates to ageing is understood and that there are no age-specific pharmacological interventions. We know a little more about psycho-social interventions and how they might be tailored to the elderly alcoholic, but outcome studies are few and cost–benefit studies of the treatment of elderly alcoholic persons are all but non-existent. The same can be said for both primary and secondary studies of alcoholism prevention among elderly people. The challenges are clear. The question is whether we shall meet them.

References

Agartz, I., Saaf, J., Wahlund, L.O., and Wetterberg, L. (1991). T_1 and T_2 relaxation time estimates and brain measures during withdrawal in alcoholic men. *Drug and Alcohol Dependence*, 29, 157–69.

Alling, C., Balldin, J., Bokstrom, K., Gottfries, C.G., Karlsson, I., and Langstrom, G. (1982). Studies on duration of a late recovery period after chronic abuse of ethanol. A cross-sectional study of biochemical and psychiatric indicators. *Acta Psychiatrica Scandinavica*, 66, 384–97.

American Psychiatric Association (1980). *Diagnostic and statistical manual* (3rd edn). American Psychiatric Association, Washington, DC.

American Psychiatric Association (1987). *Diagnostic and statistical manual* (3rd edn revised). American Psychiatric Association, Washington, DC.

American Psychiatric Association (1994). *Diagnostic and statistical manual* (4th edn). American Psychiatric Association, Washington, DC.

Armbrecht, H.J., Wood, W.G., Wise, R.W., Walsh, J.B., Thomas, B.N., and Strong, R. (1983). Ethanol influenced disordering of membranes from different age groups of C57BL/NNia mice. *Journal of Pharmacology and Experimental Therapeutics*, 226, 387–91.

Ascherio, A., Hennekens, C., Willett, W.C., et al. (1996). Prospective study of nutritional factors, blood pressure, and hypertension among US women. *Hypertension*, 27, 1065–72.

Atkinson, R.M. (1990). Ageing and alcohol use disorders in the elderly. *International Psychogeriatrics*, 2, 55–72.

Atkinson, R.M. (1992). Epidemiology of late onset problem drinking in older adults. Presented at the Annual Scientific Meeting of the Research Society on Alcoholism, San Diego, CA.

Atkinson, R.M., Tolson, R.L., and Turner, J.A. (1990). Late versus early onset problem drinking in older men. *Alcoholism: Clinical and Experimental Research*, 14, 574–9.

Atkinson, R.M., Tolson, R.L., and Turner, J.A. (1993). Factors affecting outpatient treatment compliance of older male problem drinkers. *Journal of Studies on Alcohol*, 54, 102–6.

Baker, S.P. and Harvey, A.H. (1985). Fall injuries in the elderly. *Clinics in Geriatric Medicine*, 1, 501–12.

Barnes, G.M. (1979). Alcohol use among older persons: findings from a Western New York State general population survey. *Journal of the American Geriatrics Societyc*, 27, 244–50.

Basen, M. (1977). The elderly and drugs—problem overview and program strategy. *Public Health Reports*, 92, 43–8.

Beresford, T.P. and Gomberg, E.S.L. (ed.) (1995). *Alcohol and ageing*. Oxford University Press, New York.

Beresford, T.P., Blow, F.C., Brower, K.J. (1988). Alcohol and ageing in the general hospital. *Psychosomatics*, 29, 61–72.

Beresford, T.P., Blow, F.C., Hill, E., Singer, K., and Lucey, M.R. (1990). Comparison of CAGE questionnaire and computer-assisted laboratory profiles in screening for covert alcoholism. *Lancet*, 336, 482–5.

Beresford, T.P., Blow, F.C., Hill, E.M., and Singer, K. (1991). When is an alcoholic an alcoholic? *Alcohol and Alcoholism*, 26 (Supplement 1), 487–8.

Bickford, P., Lin, A., Parfitt, K., and Palmer, M. (1995). The effects of ageing on the interaction of ethanol with chemical neurotransmission in the brain. In *Alcohol and ageing* (ed. T.P. Beresford and E.S.L. Gomberg), pp. 150–68. Oxford University Press, New York.

Biggins, C.A., MacKay, S., Poole, N., and Fein, G. (1995). Delayed P3A in abstinent elderly male chronic alcoholics. *Alcoholism: Clinical and Experimental Research*, 19, 1032–42.

Blow, F.C., Brower, K.J., Schulenber, J.E., et al. (1992). The Michigan Alcoholism Screening Test–Geriatric Version (MAST-G): a new elderly-specific screening instrument. *Alcoholism: Clinical and Experimental Research*, 16, 372.

Bowden, S.C. (1987). Brain impairment in social drinkers? No cause for concern. *Alcoholism: Clinical and Experimental Research*, 11, 407–10.

Brennan, P.L. and Moos, R.H. (1996). Late-life problem drinking: personal and environmental risk factors for 4-year functioning outcomes and treatment seeking. *Journal of Substance Abuse*, 8, 167–80.

Brennan, P.L., Moos, R.H., and Kim J.Y. (1993). Gender differences in the individual characteristics and life contexts of late-middle-aged and older problem drinkers. *Addiction*, 88, 781–90.

Brennan, P.L., Moos, R.H., and Mertens, J.R. (1994). Personal and environmental risk factors as predictors of alcohol use, depression, and treatment-seeking: a longitudinal analysis of late-life problem drinkers. *Journal of Substance Abuse*, 6, 191–208.

Brower, K.J., Mudd, S., Blow, F.C., Young, J.P., and Hill, E.M. (1994). Severity and treatment of alcohol withdrawal in elderly versus younger patients. *Alcoholism: Clinical and Experimental Research*, 18, 196–201.

Bunting, T.A., and Scott, B.S. (1989). Ageing and ethanol alter neuronal electric membrane properties. *Brain Research*, 501, 105–15.

Cahalan, D. (1970). *Problem drinkers: a national survey*. Jossey-Bass, San Francisco, CA.

Cermak, L.S., Bleich, R.P., and Blackford, S.P. (1988). Deficits in the implicit retention of new associations by alcoholic Korsakoff patients. *Brain Cognition*, 7, 312–23.

Chermack, S.T., Blow, F.C., Gomberg, E.S.L., Mudd, S.A., and Hill, E.M. (1996). Older adult controlled drinkers and abstainers. *Journal of Substance Abuse*, 8, 453–62.

Cryer, B., Lee, E., and Feldman, M. (1992). Factors influencing gastroduodenal mucosal prostaglandin concentrations: roles of smoking and ageing. *Annals of Internal Medicine*, 116, 636–40.

Cutting, J.C. (1988). Alcohol cognitive impairment and ageing: still an uncertain relationship. *British Journal of Addiction*, 83, 995–7.

Dement, W.C., Miles, L.E., and Carskadon, M.A. (1982). 'White paper' on sleep and ageing. *Journal of the American Geriatrics Society*, 30, 25–50.

Dillon, K.A., Gross, I.R., Israeli, M., and Biegon, A. (1991). Autoradiographic analysis of serotonin 5-HT1A receptor binding in the human brain post-mortem: effects of age and alcohol. *Brain Research*, 554, 56–64.

Di Sclafani, V., Ezekiel, F., Meyerhoff, D.J., *et al.* (1995). Brain atrophy and cognitive function in older abstinent alcoholic men. *Alcoholism: Clinical and Experimental Research*, 19, 1121–6.

Druse, M.J., Tajuddin, N.F., and Ricken, J.D. (1997). Effects of chronic ethanol consumption and ageing on 5-HT2a receptors and 5-HT reuptake sites. *Alcoholism: Clinical and Experimental Research*, 21, 1157–64.

Eaton, W., Kramer, M., Anthony, J.C., Dryman, A., Shapiro, S., and Locke, B.Z. (1989). The incidence of specific DIS/DSM-III mental disorders: data from the NIMH Epidemiological Catchment Area program. *Acta Psychiatrica Scandinavica*, 79, 163–78.

Ellis, R.J. (1990). Dichotic asymmetries in ageing and alcoholic subjects. *Alcoholism: Clinical and Experimental Research*, 14, 863–71.

Epstein, E.E., McCrady, B.S., and Hirsch, L.S. (1997). Marital functioning in early versus late-onset alcoholic couples. *Alcoholism: Clinical and Experimental Research*, 21, 547–56.

Feitelberg, S., Epstein, S., Ismail, F., and D'Amanda, C. (1987). Deranged bone mineral metabolism in chronic alcoholism. *Metabolism*, 36, 322–6.

Felson, D.T., Kiel, D.P., Anderson, J.J., and Kannel, W.B. (1988). Alcohol consumption and hip fractures: the Framingham Study. *American Journal of Epidemiology*, 128, 1102–10.

Feuerlein, W., Heesch, D., Schmidt, L., Werner, H.P., Bethge, H., and Gortelmeyer, R. (1984). Alcohol misuse and abuse among the elderly. *Drug Intelligence and Clinical Pharmacy*, 18, 649–51.

Fink, A., Hays, R.D., Moore, A.A., and Beck, J.C. (1996). Alcohol-related problems in older persons. *Archives of Internal Medicine*, 156, 1150–6.

Finlayson, R., Hurt, R.D., Davis, L.J., and Morse, R.M. (1988). Alcoholism in elderly persons: a study of the psychiatric and psychosocial features of 216 inpatients. *Mayo Clinic Proceedings*, 63, 761–8.

Finney, J.W., Moos, R.H., and Brennan, P.L. (1991). The Drinking Problems Index: a measure to assess alcohol-related problems among older adults. *Journal of Substance Abuse*, 3, 395–404.

Fratiglioni, L., Ahlbom, A., Viitanen, M., and Winblad, B. (1993). Risk factors for late-onset Alzheimer's disease: a population-based, case-control study. *Annals of Neurology*, 33, 258–66.

Freund, G. and Ballinger, W.J. (1989a). Loss of muscarinic and benzodiazepine neuroreceptors from hippocampus of alcohol abusers. *Alcohol*, 6, 23–31.

Freund, G. and Ballinger, W.J. (1989b). Neuroreceptor changes in the putamen of alcohol abusers. *Alcoholism: Clinical and Experimental Research*, 13, 213–18.

Frezza, M., di Padova, C., Pozzato, G., *et al.* (1990). High blood alcohol levels in women: the role of decreased gastric alcohol dehydrogenase activity in first-pass metabolism. *New England Journal of Medicine*, 322, 95–9.

Gerbino, P.P. (1982). Complications of alcohol use combined with drug therapy in the elderly. *Journal of the American Geriatrics Society*, 30 (Supplement 11), S88–93.

Glynn, R.J., Bouchard, G.R., LoCastro, J.S., and Laird, N.M. (1985). Ageing and generational effects on drinking behaviors in men: results from the normative ageing study. *American Journal of Public Health*, 75, 1413–19.

Gomberg, E.S.L. (ed.) (1994). *Older women and alcohol: use and abuse*. Plenum Press, New York.

Govoni, S., Rius, R.A., Battaini, F., Magnoni, M.S., Lucchi, L., and Trabucchi, M. (1988). The central dopaminergic system: susceptibility to risk factors for accelerated ageing. *Gerontology*, 34, 29–34.

Grabbe, L., Demi, A., Camann, M.A., and Potter, L. (1997). The health status of elderly persons in the last year of life: a comparison of deaths by suicide, injury, and natural causes. *American Journal of Public Health*, 87, 434–7.

Grinker, J.A., Tucker, K., Vokonas, P.S., and Rush, D. (1995). Body habitus changes among adult males from the normative ageing study: relations to ageing, smoking history and alcohol intake. *Obesity Research*, 3, 435–46.

Grisso, J.A., Chiu, G.Y., Maislin, G., Steinmann, W.C., and Portale, J. (1991). Risk factors for hip fractures in men: a preliminary study. *Journal of Bone and Mineral Research*, 6, 865–8.

Hayakawa, K., Kumagai, H., Suzuki, Y., *et al.* (1992). MR imaging of chronic alcoholism. *Acta Radiologica*, 33, 201–6.

Heller, D. and McLearn, G. (1995). Alcohol, ageing and genetics. In *Alcohol and ageing* (ed. T.P Beresford and E.S.L. Gomberg), pp. 99–116. Oxford University Press, New York.

Hemenway, D., Colditz, G.A., Willett, W.C., Stampfer, M.J., and Speizer, F.E. (1988). Fractures and lifestyle: effect of cigarette smoking, alcohol intake, and relative weight on the risk of hip and forearm fractures in middle-aged women. *American Journal of Public Health*, 78, 1554–8.

Hernandez-Avila, M., Colditz, G.A., Stampfer, M.J., Rosner, B., Speizer, F.E., and Willett, W.C. (1991). Caffeine, moderate alcohol intake, and risk of fractures of the hip and forearm in middle-aged women. *American Journal of Clinical Nutrition*, 54, 157–63.

Hingson, R. and Howland, J. (1987). Alcohol as a risk factor for injury or death resulting from accidental falls: a review of the literature. *Journal of Studies on Alcohol*, 48, 212–19.

Hingson, R. and Howland, J. (1993). Alcohol and non-traffic unintended injuries. *Addiction*, 88, 877–83.

Holzer, C.I., Robins, L.N., Myers, J.K., *et al.* (ed.) (1984). *Antecedents and correlates of alcohol abuse and dependence in the elderly*. NIAAA/US Government Printing Office, Rockville, MD.

Hughes, G.J., and Davis, L. (1983). Changes in cholinergic activity in human hippocampus following chronic alcohol abuse. *Pharmacology, Biochemistry and Behavior*, 1, 397–400.

1020

1024
1026
1030

ALCOHOLISM

CARE FOR ELDERLY PEOPLE WHO EXHIBIT DISTURBING BEHAVIOUR

CARE FOR ELDERLY PEOPLE WHO EXHIBIT DISTURBING BEHAVIOUR

SEXUAL ACTIVITY

question respondents on the frequency of petting to orgasm. This was a rare activity which reached its maximum in the late thirties.

The Wellcome survey in the United Kingdom (Wellings *et al.* 1994) excluded subjects over the age of 60 years but confirmed the decline of intercourse with age with a median frequency of intercourse per 4 weeks of seven at 20, five at 40, and three in the fifties, all much lower than the figures obtained by Kinsey in the United States. Cultural bias in response to interviews, in addition to bias in sample selection and response rates, may have contributed to these differences.

The menopause

Hallstrom (1977) studied the sexual activity of 800 subjects in Gothenburg. This study focused on the activity of women aged 38 to 54 years, a total of 586 subjects. It detected a loss of sexual interest which seemed related more to the menopause than to age itself. The same conclusion applied to coital frequency and change in capacity for orgasm. Conversely, the decline in sexual interest was much more marked in the lower social classes suggesting a powerful cultural influence. Hawton *et al.* (1994) studied 436 women aged 35 to 59 years living in Oxford and with partners. There was a clear decline with age in the frequency of coitus; 73 per cent of the sample aged 35 to 39 years had coitus one or more times a week compared with only 23 per cent of the women aged 55 to 59 years. There was a similar decline in the frequency of orgasm with their partner. To examine the effects of the menopause they compared two groups of 34 women who had ceased or continued to menstruate, but matched for age. There were few significant differences except that the postmenopausal group contained eight subjects who had no enjoyment of sexual activity. There was a slight trend in the expected direction for sexual interest, satisfaction, and frequency of orgasm with a partner. However, in this English sample it would appear that the effects of age were stronger than those of the menopause.

Cutler *et al.* (1987) studied 155 volunteers around the time of their menopause. They found little effect of the menopause, except for 25 per cent of the sample with the lowest levels of oestradiol who had a lower frequency of coitus. The direction of causality underlying this association is not clear; reduction in sexual activity might reduce oestrogen secretion as well as vice versa.

The senium

Persson (1980) studied a random sample of 166 men and 226 women aged 70 years living in Gothenburg. Fifty-two per cent of married men and 36 per cent of married women were still engaging in regular coitus. Active men may have had better mental health and a stronger sex drive in their twenties, whilst the activity of women related more to better health, youth, and happier marriage. In other words the coital frequency of women is probably governed by their spouse. This study reached similar conclusions to a study of French managers whose age at giving up sexual intercourse followed an exponential curve and whose continued activity related to health and early loss of virginity (Vallery-Masson *et al.* 1981). Perhaps the most surprising study looked at the activity of healthy 80- to 102-year-olds living in upper-class retirement facilities in California (Bretschneider and McCoy 1988). Less than a quarter of the sample were currently

married. Sixty six per cent of men and 39 per cent of women indulged in heterosexual petting at least several times a month. The figures for masturbation and coitus were 41 per cent and 13 per cent respectively for men, and 29 per cent and 10 per cent respectively for women. Sexual activity was related to higher income, less sexual guilt in the past, and, not surprisingly, more previous enjoyment of sexual activity and being married.

All these studies were cross-sectional and leave the reader in doubt as to whether the lower activity in the older groups is due to age or cohort factors such as style of upbringing. Two longitudinal studies have been reported by groups from Duke University. The first (Pfeiffer *et al.* 1968) showed that decline in activity was not inevitable; 6 per cent of subjects reported an increase in sexual activity over 2 years, and 3 per cent an increase in sexual interest. For men, sexual activity was related to youth, good health, and upper class; for women the variables were being married, youth, and education.

A direct comparison of longitudinal with cross-sectional estimates of age-associated trends was provided by a study of 170 men and 108 women which necessitated four interviews at 2-yearly intervals over a period in which they remained married (George and Weiler 1981). In contrast with the study by Pfeiffer *et al.* (1968), participants were not volunteers but were randomly selected from a health insurance programme. In men coital frequency at ages 46 to 55 years fell over 6 years from 2.03 times per week to 1.94. The predicted fall on cross-sectional data would have been to 1.69. The figures for women showed a similar pattern, with coital activity of the younger group declining from 1.70 to 1.66 over 6 years, whilst the prediction would have been to 1.42. Thus the cohort effect was greater than the age effect for both sexes, and predictions based on cross-sectional data are unreliable.

Age-associated changes and hormone replacement therapy

Age-associated changes in sexual function, as derived from the data of Masters and Johnson (1966), are summarized in Table 1. The female volunteers were largely prostitutes which must cast some doubt on the findings, and certainly not everyone was so affected. The introduction of hormone replacement therapy (see Chapter 7.3) has demonstrated the ability of oestrogens to halt the physical changes in the female genitalia after the menopause. Hormone replacement therapy helps to prevent vaginal atrophy and seems to preserve libido in many women, although this action may be secondary to the prevention of dyspareunia. It is now widely used, although unbiased assessment of its long-term benefits and hazards must await the results of the randomized trials that are only just being launched.

The role of testosterone in female libido remains uncertain. Undoubtedly a testosterone supplement to oestrogen replacement after oophorectomy increases sexual interest (Sherwin *et al.* 1985) but it may increase the proceptive approach of the male rather than receptivity. Dow *et al.* (1983) found no benefit in adding testosterone to oestrogen in a double-blind study of postmenopausal women.

The place of sex hormone replacement therapy for the ageing male is not yet established (Bagatell and Bremner 1996). In contrast with the ovarian failure which underlies the menopause, the testes of most men continue to secrete adequate levels of testosterone into old age. 'Adequate' in this context merely implies that the pituitary is

Table 1 Age-associated changes

	Male	Female
Unaffected	Nil	Engorgement of nipples and clitoris (with direct stimulation) and retraction of clitoris
Reduced	Penile erection (often only complete at orgasm), nipple erection, testicular elevation, power and frequency of ejaculation, and number of contractions	Vasocongestion with lengthening of inner vagina, uterine elevation, vaginal lubrication, engorgement of areolae, and anterior vagina, Bartholin's secretion, orgasmic contractions
Lost	Sexual flush, re-erection, scrotal engorgement, ejaculatory inevitability, prostatic contractions	Sexual flush, engorgement of breasts and labia majora

not stimulated to respond with increased levels of luteinizing hormone. In short-term experiments involving men with demonstrated hypogonadism, improvements in well being and muscle mass have been reported, but properly conducted long-term randomized trials are needed. It has been suggested that dihydrotestosterone, an active metabolite of testosterone, may be preferable in that, unlike testosterone, it does not induce prostatic hypertrophy and prostatic carcinoma in rats, and may not promote baldness in human males (De Lignieres 1993).

Davidson *et al.* (1983) and Schiavi *et al.* (1991) found that age was a much more important factor in relation to sexual activity than testosterone though as the two correlate closely it is possible that some of the effects of ageing can be due to the reduction in free testosterone. Thus Davidson *et al.* (1983) found that sexual activity with orgasm had a correlation of 0.2 with free testosterone but −0.34 with age, while Schiavi *et al.* (1991) found no significant correlation of coital frequency with free testosterone, despite a strong negative correlation with age (−0.42), but the frequency of sexual desire correlated equally highly with both (0.52). This fits well with other evidence that testosterone is more important in promoting desire than erectile function (O'Carroll and Bancroft 1984), and yet it is erectile response which appears to be deficient (Rowland *et al.* 1993).

Conditions which present in the form of an exponential curve are likely to be multifactorial or due to a single defect consequent on multiple chance defects. Rowland *et al.* (1993) related the erectile response to fantasy and erotic videos (in 39 males aged 21 to 82 years) to penile sensitivity, sensory evoked potentials to electrical stimulation of the penis and ankle, ischaemia-induced vasodilatation, and total testosterone. There were strong correlations between penile tumescence and sensory threshold to electrical stimulation ($r = -0.45$, $p < 0.05$), but as both varied with age the nature of the relationship remains unclear.

The author has recently looked at several measures which might differ between 28 elderly men with erectile failure and an age-matched group of 26 who retained their potency. The measures included body mass index, age at first coitus, current level of sexual interest, ratio of pulse variation on deep breathing and the Valsalva manoeuvre, brachial and penile blood pressure, skin collagen, hormone levels (including testosterone, sex hormone-binding globulin, prolactin, luteinizing hormone, and thyroxine), blood glucose, intake of alcohol and tobacco, and a general blood screen. With 40 such measures one would expect two to distinguish the groups at the 5 per cent level of significance by chance alone. Only two measures separated the groups both in the expected direction and at high levels of significance. They

were a measure of sweat glands activated by pilocarpine (more glands in the potent), and a composite measure of vascularity based on the history of hypertension and ischaemic heart disease. The significance of the sweat test was 0.0001 and the vascular factor 0.008. These results are difficult to interpret as the two factors appear unrelated to each other, unless foot ischaemia causes a reduction in sweat gland sensitivity.

Social factors

Whilst the strong libido of early adulthood is likely to overwhelm most taboos, the gentler drive of the older person is more subject to social pressure. Even the failure to enquire about sex life gives the message that it is either absent or unimportant. The media promote the sexuality of the young whilst the sexuality of elderly people is more likely to be portrayed as a joke, as in the infatuations of Falstaff in *The Merry Wives of Windsor* for example, or as contemptible or even a threat, as in the stereotype of the 'dirty old man'. Although some authors of romances may be elderly (e.g. Barbara Cartland), their subjects are always in the first flush of youth. Sexuality in later life may be curtailed by religious dogma. For example, a Muslim schoolmaster was unable to satisfy his wife when erectile failure developed as Islamic teaching forbids masturbation.

The importance society confers on sexual consummation can often result in all intimacy being abandoned when penetration fails. The genital stimulation necessary to complete the male arousal phase may be avoided by a wife brought up to believe that such active participation in sexual intercourse is the *métier* of a prostitute. Forbidden to masturbate and deprived of a potent partner, the 50-year-old woman may decide to suppress her sexual needs and devote her affection to her cat. From the age of 60 years the woman is increasingly likely to be without a partner of any kind, and her sexuality may express itself in condemning the sexuality of others or resorting to the comfort of the romantic novel. A striking feature of the paranoid illness of the elderly female is the presence of sexual fantasy and envy. For example, two spinsters in their eighties complained of nightly rapes by an unknown intruder, although the complaint was somewhat muted, and another was incensed by the belief that her 60-year-old neighbour was scaling her 7-foot fence, during the night, to cross her garden and gain access to the female neighbour on the other side of her house.

The doctor can be a potent reinforcer of social mores. Actions which deny the sexual life of the patient, such as the use of a vaginal pessary for prolapse or an indwelling catheter, a failure to address sexual issues when counselling a patient after a myocardial infarct or mastectomy, or the separation of sleeping arrangements owing to difficulties with the stairs can all convey the message that sexual activity in later life is taboo. Other examples are the lack of privacy granted to spouses visiting their partners in institutional care, and the frequency of the term sexual abuse applied to consenting sex (of course abuse can occur and the notion of consent in a demented patient is confused).

Pharmacological factors

Atherosclerosis of the pudendal arteries is a common cause of erectile failure and can be made worse if the blood pressure is rapidly reduced by antihypertensive medication even though the long-term effects may be to increase potency. This is particularly likely to follow the use of drugs such as β-blockers and thiazides rather than vasodilators such as calcium antagonists and angiotensin-converting enzyme inhibitors. As α-blockers tend to promote erections there may a particular use for prazosyn in patients troubled by uncertain potency. Alternatively, it might be sensible to miss out a drug causing impotence if coitus is planned. Erectile failure is also reported as a side-effect of digoxin. Atherosclerosis of the common iliac arteries may induce a femoral steal syndrome whereby exercise of the legs diverts blood from the pudendal arteries and prevents erection (Michal et al. 1978). The patient presents with a history of having a normal erection during foreplay which fails when thrusting begins, when gluteal pain may also appear. This syndrome may be misinterpreted as psychogenic in origin.

Sexual arousal is mediated by the parasympathetic system for which reason it is commonly assumed that impotence is a feature of cholinergic blockers. Whatever other reservations one may have about the use of these drugs for older patients (Potamianos and Kellett 1982), they rarely cause erectile failure since this is largely mediated peripherally by other neurotransmitters including nitric oxide, prostaglandins, and vasointestinal peptide.

Psychotropic drugs are particularly likely to affect sexual function. Dopamine blockers, the traditional antipsychotics, reduce libido (by reducing the effect of testosterone) and possibly erections, as well as increasing levels of prolactin. Even mild degrees of parkinsonism reduce the non-verbal signals which play such an important part in sexual communication. The blank stare as opposed to the twinkle in the eye will quickly freeze sexual desire in the partner, and inhibit the formation of new sexual bonds after widowhood. The newer atypical antipsychotics may be free of these effects at least in low doses, and their ability to block 5-HT$_2$ receptors could facilitate ejaculation and increase libido. The benzodiazepines have a dose-related effect in reducing libido (Riley and Riley 1986) but rarely cause the condition to present because they also induce complacency. Less predictable is the effect of antidepressants. All except viloxacine, trazodone, and nefazodone reduce sexual activity largely by their effect on libido. The selective serotonin reuptake inhibitors, despite suppressing libido, may very rarely cause a bizarre state of hypersexuality independent of mania.

Not surprisingly, drugs which antagonize testosterone like cyproterone acetate and gosrelin, reduce libido, and may be prescribed for this purpose. Opiates reduce sexuality possibly by swamping the brain with endorphins and thereby preventing any additional pleasurable effects from orgasm. Most other social drugs like alcohol and cannabis increase sexuality in small doses but decrease in large doses as sedative effects take over. Even drugs like cocoa when first introduced were thought to threaten the moral fibre of the nation by increasing libido, perhaps an early example of a drug exerting an effect through its reputation.

Effects of disease

Malaise from whatever cause will reduce sexual activity. Sometimes, however, the breathlessness of orgasm is misinterpreted as straining the respiratory and cardiac systems, and leads to an unnecessary curtailment of coitus. The hyperventilation associated with orgasm causes a respiratory alkalosis which may help to establish the erotic qualities of the partner, thereby facilitating subsequent sexual encounters. Nevertheless the physical activity associated with coitus can tire the weak, and by suitable choice of posture the fitter partner can play the more active role. Pain can be a problem, often due either to arthritis or to changes in the genital system (see below). A non-opiate analgesic taken before coitus together with the use of cushions placed under the lumbar curve and buttocks of the lower partner is usually sufficient, bearing in mind that the endorphins released by orgasm should reduce the pain further.

Diabetes mellitus is particularly likely to reduce sexual performance. Chiefly this is because of autonomic neuropathy; parasympathetic damage impairs mechanisms of arousal in both sexes, while sympathetic neuropathy can abolish orgasm. As already described, vascular disease may reduce blood supply to the genitalia. The degree of control of the diabetes also has effects; hyperglycaemia causes malaise and hypoglycaemia inhibits erection due to induced sympathetic stimulation. It is important to check for the presence of diabetes in any older person presenting with sexual dysfunction.

Other diseases which damage the autonomic nervous system are also likely to cause sexual dysfunction, and include Parkinson's disease, motor neurone disease, and multiple sclerosis. Most dementias, like Alzheimer's disease, result in a reduction of libido in their early stages, possibly owing to a fall in levels of luteinizing hormone-releasing hormone (Oram et al. 1981). The retention of libido in dementia can cause problems. This is particularly likely to occur in frontal lobe syndrome where the loss of social skills, combined with disinhibition, can lead to criminal prosecution. The bonding effect of sexual activity can transcend the alienation of dementia. It has been observed that men who continue to make love to their demented wives make better carers (Morris et al. 1988).

Conditions leading to a reduction in testosterone cause loss of libido in men and may be due to testicular damage (for example from mumps, trauma, myotonia dystrophica) or from pituitary failure (as with tumours or haemochromatosis). The excess of oestrogen found in cirrhosis suppresses luteinizing hormone-releasing hormone. Prolactinomas increase in frequency with age and also inhibit gonadotrophin release, although prolactin may reduce sexual drive directly. Hypothyroidism may also present with low libido. A common mistake is to estimate total testosterone rather than recording the level of sex hormone binding globulin and calculating the free and active component. Alternatively, testosterone may be assayed in the saliva where only the free hormone is present. As with most steroid hormones, testosterone shows circadian rhythm, with a twofold variation, the maximum level being in the early hours of the morning. The interpretation is made yet more difficult by the pulsatile release of testosterone, causing the blood level to vary from minute to minute. A marginal result with a raised luteinizing hormone-releasing hormone is an indication for a trial of replacement where clinically appropriate.

Genital disease

Benign prostatic enlargement is not in itself associated with sexual dysfunction but prostatectomy may result in retrograde ejaculation and erectile failure. The cause of the latter is often unclear and certainly erectile nerves are most unlikely to be damaged by a transurethral resection. However, the processes of catheterization and perineal pain may exacerbate the changes of ageing. The National Prostatectomy Audit has analysed questionnaires from 3965 patients who had undergone transurethral resection of the prostate. One-third were potent, one-third had erectile problems, and one-third were impotent at the time of surgery. Although there was a slight decline in potency after surgery the striking finding was its effect on ejaculation. Seventy-seven per cent of those who were sexually active after surgery reported diminished or absence of ejaculation and half reported a change in the sensation of orgasm, mostly a complete loss of sensation. Not surprisingly most of these patients lost sexual satisfaction. Interestingly, more patients reported being sexually active after surgery than before (36 versus 26 per cent) (Dunsmuir and Emberton 1996). The parasympathetic nerve plexus is closely applied to the rectum and is often damaged by rectal surgery, as well as by the cancer which is so often the cause for excision. Even such simple procedures as sclerotherapy for piles may occasionally result in erectile failures (Bullock 1997). The penis is not immune to the effects of disease and may be thrombosed in sickle cell disease, fibrosed by Peyronie's disease or multifocal fibrosis, and damaged during coitus or through intracavernosal injections.

The female has to cope with a fall in oestrogens leading to atrophy of the vaginal epithelium and, often, reduced vaginal lubrication. The vagina is more vulnerable to infection by *Candida* or other agents. Obesity and weakness of the muscles of the pelvic floor lead to prolapse, stress incontinence of urine, including during orgasm, and irritation of the bladder neck by penile thrusts. Disorders of the rectosigmoid colon can cause pain on deep thrusting and may be a presenting symptom of carcinoma. Even constipation can reduce sexual enjoyment. Infection and malignant changes in the cervix or body of the uterus are also causes of dyspareunia. Pain on penetration at the introitus is more likely to have a psychological component, when it is commonly accompanied by lack of sexual arousal and lubrication. Clearly there can be a vicious circle, with low arousal leading to a dry vagina leading to pain leading to fear of penetration leading to low arousal. The simple remedy of using artificial vaginal lubricants can break this cycle, as can ensuring that foreplay is adequately skilled and prolonged. At ages over 60 years at least 20 min is often needed.

Psychological factors

Probably the most important inhibitor of sexual expression in old age is the perception that sex is only for the young as discussed above.

The strong libido of youth can overcome social inhibitions, but the sexuality of elderly people is a delicate flower more easily killed by the first frost of disapproval. Other inhibitory factors include embarrassment over an ageing body which prevents the individual appearing naked, upbringing which discouraged sexual practices such as fellatio and cunnilingus, and a lack of privacy, which may be a problem when sharing a house with younger family members. The visual stimulus of his naked partner is especially important for the ageing male who is likely to have difficulty responding when modesty denies this to him.

Psychiatric illness like depression may present with loss of libido and usually causes a cessation of coitus. It may be difficult to decide whether marital conflict is the cause or the result of the depression. Mania, a much underdiagnosed condition in elderly people, may be associated with an increase in libido and expose an affected patient to rejection. The neuroses are less likely to affect sexual function. However, marked loss of weight caused by dementia or physical disease does inhibit pituitary function and release of luteinizing hormone-releasing hormone and follicle-stimulating hormone. The general effects of dementias are discussed above but focal features of dementing or cerebrovascular diseases may occasionally present as sexual dysfunction. Prosopagnosia can be interpreted as coldness or rejection to a spouse. A patient with Capgras' syndrome may become convinced that his or her spouse has been replaced by an impostor. In the later stages of dementia sufferers may regress to an earlier age and misidentify their spouses as belonging to an older generation.

Institutional life

Normally, limitations on funding ensure that old people admitted to institutions are very frail and unlikely to retain libido. Sexual intimacy requires privacy which is often lacking in institutions. Residents may, however, strike up new relationships and this may be resented by families, not least because of the threat it may present to their inheritances. Unless both partners are cognitively intact there is also a danger of exploitation. These concerns aside, most staff in old people's homes are now more liberal in their attitudes than the residents (Kaas 1978; Damrosch 1984). There is a need for residential and nursing homes to be able to provide for married couples who are unable to cope in the community but wish to remain together.

Treatment

There are many different approaches to the treatment of sexual dysfunction. 'Dynamic' approaches lay stress on the individual and the tendency to transfer feelings from prominent figures in childhood. Interpretive psychotherapy helps the patient to gain insight and also to relate to the partner free of prejudices. Such systems held sway until Masters and Johnson (1966) publicized a behavioural method first described by John Hunter in 1786. It was based on the simple notion that a fear of being unable to perform the sexual act inhibits the process of arousal, so predisposing to further failures. An authoritative ban on genital sex removes this fear, allowing sexual arousal to grow unhindered by performance anxiety and aided by instructions into foreplay technique. If the genital failure is primary, due for example to autonomic neuropathy, this treatment will not bring about a cure, but it allows the couple to make the most of their physical intimacy and is a valuable addition to organic therapies.

The process begins by taking a sexual history. This involves an accurate description of the presenting problem, freed from ambiguous terms used by anxious patients, identification of possible causative factors, and enquiry about previous sexual problems and therapies. The counsellor also needs to assess the quality of the marital relationship and establish long-term intentions. One may find, for example, that a similar problem has arisen in all previous relationships after a year of intimacy and may require more deep-seated psychotherapy. Usually the couple are advised to stop attempting intercourse, and to set aside three 30-min sessions a week to practice foreplay in the technique of 'sensate focus'. Starting with non-erotic and non-threatening caressing involving the face, hair, and hands the couple re-establish an ability to relax during intimacy. They are advised to take turns to stroke each other, to avoid distraction using the body of their partner as a mantra, and concentrating more on receiving than giving pleasure. As confidence returns the restrictions are gradually removed over a period of weeks to back massage and torso massage excluding the breasts and genitalia. Before penetration is attempted the couple are told to use mutual masturbation.

Not only do these exercises desensitize the couple to aspects of foreplay but they learn a repertoire of sexual acts which they can use if for any reason genital sex is excluded. A female with vaginitis may still wish to masturbate her spouse, and a tired male may still wish to share in the pleasure of his wife's orgasm without having to take an active part.

A woman with loss of interest is more likely to respond if she has pride in herself, a pride which may be increased by a new hair style, pretty underclothes, a diet, and the use of make-up. She can be taught to like her body by focusing on positive aspects and by education, removing feelings of revulsion.

Common causes of failure are a reluctance to do the exercises, attributed to insufficient time or forgetfulness, and, as in any process of desensitization, fear will inhibit progression to the most difficult areas. Sometimes the programme has to be arranged in advance specifying times, places, and activities.

Other psychological techniques include masturbatory shaping based on the notion of using the image at orgasm to alter sexual orientation and vaginal dilators to desensitize the woman to penetration. However, elderly people with an organic defect often have its effects made worse by their psychological response.

Sex manuals and educational videotapes not only aid treatment but can be effective on their own (Greengross and Greengross 1989), and there are now Internet sites concerned with sexual activity in later life.

Organic remedies

There are a number of organic approaches to the treatment of erectile failure. They include oral drugs like yohimbine, oxpentifylline (for vascular insufficiency), mesterolone and testosterone undecanoate (for hormonal deficiency), and bromocriptine for hyperprolactinaemia. Intracavernosal injections of papaverine, phentolamine, and alprostadil can be effective. Drugs may also be delivered intraurethrally or transdermally to the penis or scrotum. Means are available to deliver intracavernosal drugs from a reservoir in the scrotum.

Not surprisingly there is a demand for an effective oral remedy, which is likely to be filled by sildenofil (Viagra®). This drug uses the vasodilating properties of the naturally released cyclic guanosine monophosphate by inhibiting its conversion to the less active non-cyclic variant, thereby intensifying a normal erectile response rather than creating an artificial one. It needs to be taken between 1 and 10 h before coitus and like most vasodilators causes mild flushing, dyspepsia, and headaches. There is also evidence that it increases physiological arousal in females. It is less effective in vasculogenic failure.

Mechanical approaches to erectile failure include vacuum systems to engorge the penis and maintain this with a tight rubber ring, and silastic penile implants of varying degrees of sophistication. The choice of system depends on the couple. Generally, oral remedies are often ineffective, intracavernosal injections produce a more natural response but have a high incidence of side-effects, vacuum systems are cumbersome but are ideal for a long-term relationship, and implants, though effective, are often an expensive last resort.

Another common problem for the older man, and his partner, is premature ejaculation. This can be improved by most of the selective serotonin reuptake inhibitors like sertraline and paroxetine. Anorgasmia is sometimes helped by an α-agonist like midodrine. Low libido, especially if associated with Parkinson's disease, may respond to dopamine agonists.

Sexual deviation

Sexual deviations are culturally defined. In Western societies concern for the autonomy of individuals is emphasized in social and legal proscription of coercive or intrusive sexual practices. Loss of inhibition due to frontal-lobe dysfunction or alcoholism may lead to old people expressing sexual proclivities which they had held in check during earlier life. By the time people reach old age their sexuality is well imprinted and there is little to be gained by attempts at sexual reorientation. There may be scope for advice over more discrete outlets for socially unacceptable impulses, though this might come more appropriately from family and friends than from a medical adviser. An alternative approach, with the patient's consent, is to reduce libido by pharmacological means. Drugs most commonly used for this purpose are benperidol, cyproterone, and gosrelin, in ascending order of efficacy.

Conclusion

The danger with any pleasurable activity is that it can become an addiction, displacing other rewarding activities, and becoming a source of conflict between those who have different demands and expectations. The male who complains that his erection is too poor to enable penetration more than once a night is just as unreasonable as his wife who cannot understand why anyone aged over 50 should want to indulge in sexual activity. The doctor has a duty to foster marital harmony, recognizing the power of the sexual act to facilitate this. Perhaps in the present cultural climate one of the more valuable activities of the doctor for older patients is to encourage a change of emphasis from penetrative coitus to more general continued intimacy (Kellett 1987).

References

Bagatell, C.J. and Bremner, W.J. (1996). Drug therapy: androgens in men—uses and abuses. *New England Journal of Medicine*, **334**, 707–14.

Bretschneider, J.G. and McCoy N. (1988). Sexual interest and behaviour in healthy 80 to 102 year olds. *Archives of Sexual Behavior*, **17**, 109–29.

Bullock, N. (1997). Impotence after sclerotherapy of haemorrhoids. *British Medical Journal*, **314**, 419.

Cutler, W.B., Garcia, C.R., and McCoy, N. (1987). Perimenopausal sexuality. *Archives of Sexual Behaviour*, **16**, 225–34.

Damrosch, S.R. (1984). Graduate nursing students' attitudes toward sexually active older persons. *Gerontologist*, **24**, 299–302.

Davidson, J.M., Chen J.J., Crapo L., Gray G.D., Greenleaf W.J., and Catania J.A. (1983). Hormonal changes and sexual function in aging men. *Journal of Clinical Endocrinology and Metabolism*, **57**, 71–7.

De Lignieres, B. (1993). Transdermal dihydrotestosterone treatment of 'andropause'. *Annals of Medicine*, **25**, 253–41.

Dow, M.G.T., Hart, D.M., and Forrest, C.A. (1983). Hormonal treatment of sexual unresponsiveness in post menopausal women; a British comparative study. *Journal of Obstetrics and Gynaecology*, **90**, 361–6.

Dunsmuir, W.D., Emberton, M., and Neal, D.E. (1996). There is significant sexual dissatisfaction after TURP. *British Journal of Urology*, **77**, 161A.

George, L. and Weiler, S. (1981). Sexuality and middle and later life. *Archives of General Psychiatry*, **38**, 919–23.

Greengross, W. and Greengross, S. (1989). *Living, loving, and ageing: sexual and personal relationships in later life*. Age Concern, Mitcham.

Hallstrom, T. (1977). Sexuality in the climacteric. *Clinics in Obstetrics and Gynaecology*, **4**, 227–39.

Hawton, K., Gath, D., and Day, A. (1994). Sexual function in a community sample of middle aged women with partners: effects of age, marital, socio-economic, psychiatric, gynecological, and menopausal factors. *Archives of Sexual Behavior*, **23**, 375–95.

Hunter, J. (1786). *Venereal disease*. London.

Kaas, M.J. (1978). Sexual expression of the elderly in nursing homes. *Gerontologist*, **18**, 372–8.

Kellett, J.M. (1987). Treatment of sexual disorder: a prophylaxis for major pathology? *Journal of the Royal College of Physicians of London*, **21**, 58–60.

Kinsey, A.C., Pomeroy, W.B., and Martin, C.E. (1948). *Sexual behaviour in the human male*. W.B. Saunders, Philadelphia, PA.

Kinsey, A.C., Pomeroy, W.B., Martin, C.E., and Gebhard, C.H. (1953). *Sexual behaviour in the human female*. W.B. Saunders, Philadelphia, PA.

Masters, W. and Johnson, V. (1966). *Human sexual response*. Churchill Livingstone, London.

Michal, V., Kramar, R., and Pospichal, J. (1978). External iliac 'steal syndrome'. *Journal of Cardiovascular Surgery*, **19**, 255–7.

Morris, L.W, Morris, R.G., and Britton, P.G. (1988). The relationship between marital intimacy, perceived strain, and depression in spouse caregivers of dementia sufferers. *British Journal of Medical Psychology*, **61**, 231–6.

O'Carroll, R.F. and Bancroft, J. (1984). Testosterone for low sexual interest and erectile dysfunction in men. *British Journal of Psychiatry*, **145**, 146–51.

Oram, J., Edwardson, J., and Millard, P. (1981). Investigation of cerebrospinal fluid peptides in idiopathic senile dementia. *Gerontology*, **27**, 216–23.

Persson, G. (1980). Sexuality in a 70-year-old urban population. *Journal of Psychosomatic Research*, **24**, 335–42.

Pfeiffer, E., Verwoerdt, A., and Wang, H. (1968). Sexual behavior in aged men and women. *Archives of General Psychiatry*, **19**, 753–8.

Potamianos, G. and Kellett, J. (1982). Anticholinergic drugs and memory: effects of benzhexol on memory in a group of geriatric patients. *British Journal of Psychiatry*, **140**, 470–2.

Riley, A. and Riley, E. (1986). The effect of single dose diazepam on female sexual response induced by masturbation. *Sexual and Marital Therapy*, **1**, 49–53.

Rowland, D.L., Greenleaf, W.J., Dorfman, L.J., and Davidson, J.M. (1993). Aging and sexual function in men. *Archives of Sexual Behavior*, **22**, 545–7.

Schiavi, R.C., Schreiner-Engel, P., White, D., and Mandell, J. (1991). The relationship between pituitary-gonadal function and sexual behavior in healthy aging men. *Psychosomatic Medicine*, **53**, 363–74.

Sherwin, B.B., Gelfand, M.M., and Brender, W. (1985). Androgen enhances sexual motivation in females: a prospective cross-over study of sex steroid administration in the surgical menopause. *Psychosomatic Medicine*, **47**, 339–51.

Vallery Masson, J., Valleron, A.J., and Poitrennaud, J. (1981). Factors related to sexual intercourse frequency in a group of French preretirement managers. *Age and Ageing*, **10**, 53–9.

Wellings, K., Field, J., Johnson, A.M., and Wadsworth, J. (1994). *Sexual behaviour in Britain*. Penguin, Harmondsworth.

21

Perioperative assessment and management

21 Perioperative assessment and management

Diane G. Snustad and Richard W. Lindsay

As the population ages and surgical techniques are improved, surgery on elderly people is becoming more common. Currently, 25 per cent of all surgery in the United States is performed on those aged 65 years or older. By the year 2055, it is estimated that 40 per cent of surgical patients will be elderly (Mangano 1990). Age is often listed as a risk factor for surgical morbidity and fatality (Goldman *et al.* 1977), but studies that control for other variables such as disease severity, show that severity of illness is much more important than age in predicting complications of surgery (Dunlop *et al.* 1993). When carefully selected and monitored, even very elderly patients can face acceptable levels of risk for surgery (Burns-Cox *et al.* 1997).

This chapter reviews preoperative assessment and care in older patients, as well as selected aspects of perioperative and postoperative care, with special attention to some of the physiological changes of ageing that can affect management. It is primarily aimed at the medical practitioner in his or her role as consultant throughout the patient's time in the hospital.

Preoperative assessment

The role of the medical consultant who is asked to evaluate an elderly surgical patient should involve both preoperative assessment and assistance in postoperative care. The consultant should identify and assess the magnitude of any risk factors, as well as establish a baseline with which to compare any postoperative changes. He or she needs to establish a plan to decrease these risks, and to discuss the risks and prognosis with the patient, family, and surgeon. Postoperatively, the consultant can assist in the early identification of complications and aid in their management.

Preoperative assessment includes a history and physical examination, as well as certain laboratory investigations. In the history, special attention should be paid to pulmonary or cardiac symptoms. A history of anorexia or recent weight loss can suggest the need for nutritional evaluation and possible supplementation before elective surgery.

A careful drug history, including non-prescribed medications and allergies, should be taken, and degree of compliance should be ascertained. Not uncommonly, patients who may be only partially compliant with their medications at home develop complications when given full doses in hospital. Alcohol abuse is often a hidden problem, and so relatives as well as the patient should be questioned about alcohol consumption. A smoking history is important in predicting pulmonary complications.

A complete functional assessment is invaluable for several reasons. Present functional status and potential changes anticipated as a result of surgery should be considered both in making the decision to operate, and in deciding how to manage the patient postoperatively. One needs to consider if the proposed surgery may cure the disease but leave the patient with diminished functional status and quality of life. Cognitive impairment and emotional problems such as depression may adversely affect the patient's willingness and ability to give consent or be co-operative with the procedures necessary for the operation and in the recovery period. A preoperative test of mental status is essential to help predict these problems as well as to serve as a baseline against which to judge any postoperative changes. It can also help predict the risk of delirium, as patients with dementia are more likely to develop this complication in the postoperative period. Testing mental status using, for example, the Mini-Mental State Examination (Folstein *et al.* 1975) often detects decreased cognitive function even in patients who do not appear to be demented, and so should be done on most elderly patients preoperatively. Information from the family regarding any recent decline in cognitive function is also very valuable.

Social factors should be considered, such as where the patient will convalesce and what supports are available, as these factors may influence how long the patient needs to stay in the hospital. If home supports seem inadequate for the convalescence, then early assistance from social workers can help in making the arrangements for additional support in the home or temporary placement in a nursing home or other facility.

In the physical examination, particular attention should be paid to hydration and nutritional status. Pulmonary examination is especially important, as abnormal findings should prompt consideration of pulmonary function tests. A careful search for signs of congestive heart failure, especially a third heart sound or jugular venous distension, is essential, although one should remember that basal rales on chest examination may indicate atelectasis rather than pulmonary congestion, and that pedal oedema may be related to venous insufficiency rather than fluid overload. The assessment of aortic stenosis, a predictor of operative risk, is often difficult without echocardiography because of the absence, on physical examination alone, of the classical findings.

Table 1 American Society of Anesthesiologists physical status scale

Class	Description	Fatality within 1 month for patients over age 80 years
I	Healthy patient	0.5 ($n=87$)
II	Mild to moderate systemic disease	4 ($n=256$)
III	Severe systemic disease	25 ($n=56$)
IV	Severe systemic disease that is a threat to life	100 ($n=1$)
V	Moribund patient unlikely to survive 24 h with or without operation	
E	Added to class if emergency surgery	

Other parts of the physical examination that are especially pertinent in the older patient include a screening for hearing and visual problems, a careful skin examination for signs of impending or actual breakdown, and a screen for signs of Parkinson's disease or other neurological disorders that may predispose to immobility and its complications postoperatively.

The value and content of preoperative laboratory testing is controversial. Preoperative blood tests should include electrolytes, glucose, blood urea nitrogen, serum creatinine and albumin, and a complete blood count. Prothrombin time and partial thromboplastin time need to be ordered only if there are signs or symptoms of a bleeding diasthesis. An ECG is commonly recommended for all patients over the age of 55 years. The need for a preoperative chest radiograph remains the subject of much debate; it should certainly be taken in those who have pulmonary or cardiac signs or symptoms or who are scheduled for thoracic or upper abdominal procedures. However, even among those elderly patients without a specific indication, many have unsuspected but significant findings on chest radiography and some may need a postoperative film, for which a baseline examination is invaluable. In some cases, further testing of cardiac or pulmonary function may be warranted (see below).

Surgical risk can further be assessed by using the physical status scale devised by the American Society of Anesthesiologists (Dripps *et al.* 1982) (Table 1). This has been shown to be well correlated with surgical fatality in the elderly patient (Djokovic and Hedley-Whyte 1979).

Assessment of specific organ systems and states

Cardiovascular system

Cardiac complications are one of the major risks to elderly patients undergoing surgery. Studies have indicated a cardiac fatality rate of between 0.5 and 11 per cent in elderly patients undergoing noncardiac surgery. Cardiac morbidity is also high, with reports of recognized postoperative myocardial infarction of 1 to 4 per cent, and congestive heart failure in 4 to 10 per cent (Seymour 1986). Nearly half of postoperative deaths are cardiovascular.

All the above complications have a higher rate in older than in younger patients. Whether this is due to the effects of age alone or to the increased incidence of cardiovascular disease is controversial. There are changes in the heart and vascular system with age that may in themselves increase risk. Although in an elderly person free of atherosclerotic disease, cardiac output is maintained at levels equivalent to those of a young person at any given level of exertion, the maximum exercise that can be accomplished is less in the older patient (Rodeheffer *et al.* 1984). In addition, elderly patients have, on average, a decrease in cardiac output and cardiac index. Baroreceptor responses are impaired, increasing the danger associated with hypotension. These factors make even a healthy elderly patient more susceptible to problems during and after surgery. But these are most likely to be minor compared with the risk imposed by the atherosclerotic and other cardiac diseases that are present in many older surgical patients.

The stresses imposed on the heart by surgery are multiple. Cardiac output is increased, elevating myocardial oxygen consumption. Anaesthetic agents can depress myocardial function, increase myocardial irritability, and cause vasodilatation. Intraoperative hypotension and hypertension can both occur, especially in hypertensive patients. The cardiac risks extend beyond the actual time of surgery, with the risk of congestive heart failure from mobilization of fluids given intraoperatively lasting at least 2 days postoperatively, and the risk of myocardial infarction being present for at least 4 days (Shah *et al.* 1990). The fact that up to a quarter of these infarctions are silent suggests the need for close monitoring with serial ECG or cardiac isoenzymes in high-risk patients.

Initial assessment of cardiovascular risk should include history, physical examination, and ECG, focusing on identification of evidence of serious cardiovascular disease, including coronary artery disease, congestive heart failure, and arrhythmia. The stability and severity of these conditions should also be assessed, in addition to functional capacity, comorbid conditions, and type of surgery.

Several methods have been proposed for assessing cardiac risk preoperatively. The Goldman cardiac risk index (Table 2) is one of the most commonly used. This index was developed for use in patients over the age of 40 years, and assigns a point value to various risk factors. The total number of points is then used to predict risk of cardiac morbidity and fatality (Table 3). More recent work by Goldman indicates that premature ventricular contractions in a healthy heart do not increase a patient's risk, and that elective abdominal aortic surgery actually carries a 40 per cent greater cardiac risk than indicated in the original index (Weitz and Goldman 1987).

Table 2 Cardiac risk index

Criteria	Points
Historical	
Age over 70 years	5
Myocardial infarction previous 6 months	10
Examination	
S3 gallop/jugular venous distension	11
Significant aortic valvular stenosis	3
ECG	
Premature atrial contractions or rhythm other than sinus	7
More than five premature ventricular contractions per minute	7
General status	
$PO_2 < 60$ or $PCO_2 > 50$ mmHg ($PO_2 < 8$ or $PCO_2 > 6.7$ kPa)	3 (each factor)
or $K < 3.0$ or $HCO_3 < 20$ mmol/l	
or BUN > 50 or creatinine > 3.0 mg/100 ml	
or liver disease	
or bedridden from non-cardiac causes	
Operation	
Emergency	4
Intraperitoneal, thoracic, aortic	3
Total possible	**53**

Adapted with permission from Goldman *et al.* (1977).

Table 3 Correlation of cardiac risk points and postoperative cardiac problems

Point total	Life-threatening complications (%)	Cardiac deaths (%)
0–5	0.7	0.2
6–12	5.0	2.0
13–25	11.0	2.0
Greater than 26	22.0	56.0

Adapted with permission from Goldman *et al.* (1977).

The estimate of the operative risk in patients with recent myocardial infarcts has also been revised. The risk of surgery can be reduced by improving the cardiac status as much as possible preoperatively through use of invasive monitoring and by active treatment of any haemodynamic abnormality. Using this approach, Shah *et al.* (1990) showed an incidence of reinfarction of 5.5 per cent in those over the age of 65 years who had a myocardial infarction in the 6 months prior to surgery. However, when possible, surgery should be delayed until at least 6 months after a myocardial infarct.

In a study comparing the usefulness of the American Society of Anaesthesiologists physical status scale, the Goldman cardiac risk index, history and physical examination, ECG, and pulmonary function tests in patients over the age of 65 years, the most sensitive

indicator of cardiac and pulmonary risk was the inability to do 2 min of bicycle exercise in the supine position to a heart rate above 99 beats/min (Gerson *et al.* 1990). Those who were unable to do this had a sixfold increase in perioperative cardiac complications.

Predictors of increased postoperative cardiovascular risk have recently been reviewed by the American College of Cardiology and the American Heart Association and are listed in Table 4. If the major predictors are present, then intensive management is essential, which may result in delay or cancellation of surgery. Intermediate predictors are markers of increased perioperative cardiac risk. If these are present, the patient's current cardiac status should be carefully assessed. Minor predictors are markers for cardiovascular disease but have not been shown independently to predict cardiovascular perioperative risk.

The type of surgery can also predict risks. Table 5 lists types of surgery by risk category. The following groups of patients should undergo non-invasive testing before surgery: patients with intermediate clinical predictors who have poor functional status or are being considered for high-risk surgical procedures, and patients with minor or no clinical predictors who have poor functional status or are facing a high-risk surgical procedure. The need for invasive testing would then be determined by the results of the non-invasive testing. The most commonly used non-invasive testing would include an exercise stress test for patients with good functional status, or pharmacological stress testing. If the patient has evidence of congestive heart failure, then he or she should undergo electrocardiography to ascertain the aetiology for the congestive heart failure and medical treatment to optimize the patient's status before surgery. Indications for coronary artery bypass graft or coronary angioplasty are the same as if the patient were not in the preoperative period.

Mild to moderate hypertension with a diastolic blood pressure less than 110 mmHg by itself is not a major risk factor (Goldman and Caldera 1979). However, hypertension does increase the risk of both hypertension and hypotension during surgery, each occurring in a quarter of hypertensive patients whether or not the hypertension is adequately treated preoperatively. Other studies indicate that intraoperative lability of blood pressure is decreased when hypertension is under good control preoperatively (Prys-Roberts *et al.* 1971). Any antihypertensive agent that the patient had been taking, with the possible exception of diuretics, should be continued up until the morning of surgery, and resumed immediately postoperatively.

Patients with valvular heart disease should be evaluated and treated in the same way, whether in the preoperative period or in the non-operative setting. Symptomatic stenosis is associated with risks of congestive heart failure or hypotension in the postoperative period and consideration should be given to treatment before non-cardiac surgery. Similarly, recommendations for treatments of arrhythmias are similar, whether or not the patient is in the perioperative period.

In patients who have or are at high risk of coronary artery disease, and who undergo non-cardiac surgery, treatment with β-blockers during the perioperative period has been shown in some studies to reduce mortality. This effect has continued for as long as 2 years after surgery (Mangano *et al.* 1996).

The need for invasive monitoring of the elderly surgical patient has been much debated. Del Guerico and Cohn (1980) found that only 13.5 per cent of older patients cleared for surgery had normal results on invasive monitoring; many had abnormalities that affected preoperative care, and 23 per cent had findings that made them

Table 4 Clinical predictors of increased perioperative cardiovascular risk (myocardial infarction, congestive heart failure, death)

Major

Unstable coronary syndromes
   Recent myocardial infarction[a] with evidence of important ischaemic risk by clinical symptoms or non-invasive study
   Unstable or severe[b] angina (Canadian class III or IV)[c]
Significant arrhythmias
   High-grade atrioventricular block
   Symptomatic ventricular arrhythmias in the presence of underlying heart disease
   Supraventricular arrhythmias with uncontrolled ventricular rate
Severe valvular disease

Intermediate

Mild angina pectoris (Canadian class I or II)
Prior myocardial infarction by history or pathological Q waves
Diabetes mellitus

Minor

Advanced age
Abnormal ECG (left ventricular hypertrophy, left bundle branch block, ST-T abnormalities)
Rhythm other than sinus (e.g. atrial fibrillation)
Low functional capacity (e.g. inability to climb one flight of stairs with a bag of groceries)
History of stroke
Uncontrolled systemic hypertension

[a] The American College of Cardiology National Database Library defines 'recent myocardial infarction' as greater than 7 days but less than or equal to 1 month (30 days).
[b] May include 'stable' angina in patients who are usually sedentary.
[c] Campeau (1976).

Reproduced with permission from the American College of Cardiology/American Heart Association Task Force Report (1996).

Table 5 Cardiac risk[a] stratification for non-cardiac surgical procedures

High (reported cardiac risk often >5%)
Emergent major operation, particularly in elderly people
Aortic and other major vascular surgery
Peripheral vascular surgery
Anticipate prolonged surgical procedures associated with large fluid shifts and/or blood loss

Intermediate (reported cardiac risk generally <5%)
Carotid endarterectomy
Head and neck surgery
Intraperitoneal and intrathoracic surgery
Orthopaedic surgery
Prostate surgery

Low[b] (reported cardiac risk generally <1%)
Endoscopic procedures
Superficial procedures
Cataract surgery
Breast surgery

[a] Combined incidence of cardiac death and non-fatal myocardial infarction.
[b] Do not generally require further preoperative cardiac testing.

Reproduced with permission from the American College of Cardiology/American Heart Association Task Force Report (1996).

unacceptable risks for surgery. Because of this, they suggested that all elderly patients should undergo Swan–Ganz catheterization before surgery. The results of this invasive monitoring were not compared with a non-invasive evaluation of cardiac risk, other than the Dripps' classifications. Many doctors prefer to use this technique only for patients found to be at high risk by other methods or in those with obvious haemodynamic alterations (Tuman *et al.* 1989), or in those who have risk factors and are undergoing high-risk procedures (American Society of Anesthesiologists Task Force on Pulmonary Artery Catheterization 1993).

The risk that asymptomatic stenosis of a carotid artery will lead to an intraoperative stroke is a matter of some controversy. Some studies do not show an increased incidence of cerebrovascular accidents in the asymptomatic patient with a carotid bruit undergoing elective surgery, while others do, particularly during cardiac surgery. Current guidelines do not recommend further testing in asymptomatic patients regardless of the type of surgery planned (Feussner and Matchar 1988). However, patients with symptoms of transient ischaemic attacks should be fully evaluated before surgery. Significant carotid stenosis can be operated on at the same time as cardiac surgery.

Pulmonary system

Respiratory complications cause between one-sixth and one-third of the deaths in elderly surgical patients. Twelve to 46 per cent of older surgical patients suffer some postoperative pulmonary problem (Seymour 1986). As with cardiac risk, pulmonary risk is due to a combination of the normal changes of ageing and pre-existing disease, with the latter being the most significant.

Those changes in pulmonary function that are common with age and that might increase surgical risk include a decrease in most static lung volumes, flow rate, pulmonary clearance mechanisms, compliance, and partial pressure of oxygen (Po_2), and increased closing volume. These changes tend to promote atelectasis and decrease protective mechanisms. Elderly patients also have decreased sensitivity of the respiratory centre and a blunted response to hypercapnia and hypoxia. Impaired laryngeal reflexes contribute to the risk of aspiration pneumonia.

Abdominal (especially upper abdominal) and thoracic operations may cause further decreases in vital capacity, forced expiratory volume in 1 s (FEV_1), functional residual capacity, and protective reflexes, increasing the risk of respiratory complications. The incidence of these abnormalities is maximal on the first and second days after the surgery, but can remain high for as long as 14 to 21 days. General anaesthesia also affects respiratory function by impairing oxygenation and elimination of carbon dioxide, and by decreasing functional residual capacity, laryngeal reflexes, and hypoxic drive.

In general, elderly patients have the same risk factors for postoperative respiratory complications as do younger patients. The major factors are lung disease, smoking, and surgery on the thorax or upper abdomen. Other factors that may predict problems include obesity, decreased albumin, and longer operative procedures. Age is sometimes listed as an independent risk factor, but others have found that this is no longer significant when controlled for site and duration of surgery.

Preoperative assessment of pulmonary risk begins with the history and physical examination. A history of smoking or previous lung disease doubles the risk of respiratory complications. Preoperative pulmonary function tests have been found to predict respiratory complications in those undergoing lung resection and may be helpful in coronary artery bypass patients. In patients with a history of tobacco use and dyspnoea, it may be prudent to include pulmonary function tests as part of the preoperative evaluation before upper abdominal procedures. In other types of surgery the role of pulmonary function tests in non-smoking asymptomatic patients remains unclear (American College of Physicians 1990). When pulmonary function tests are indicated, simple spirometry, measurement of maximal

ventilatory volume, and arterial blood gases constitute a reasonable assessment. An FEV_1 of less than 1 litre (less than 2 litres in patients undergoing lung resection), a maximal ventilatory volume below 60 per cent of predicted, or a Pco_2 above 45 mmHg indicate a significant risk. As mentioned previously, pulmonary and cardiac risk was found in one study of patients 65 years of age or older to be best predicted by inability to do 2 min of supine bicycle exercise, raising the heart rate to more than 99 beats/min. Patients who were unable to do this had a sevenfold increase in pulmonary complications (Gerson et al. 1990).

Several steps should be taken to improve lung function before surgery in those at risk. Primary among these is the cessation of smoking for at least 2 months prior to surgery (Warner et al. 1989). Bronchodilators can be used in patients with obstructive lung disease, and any infection should be treated appropriately. Incentive spirometry, which promotes maximal inspiration, will help prevent postoperative atelectasis, and patients should be instructed in its use preoperatively (Hall et al. 1996).

After the operation, the patient should be encouraged to use the incentive spirometer frequently. Early mobilization should be a goal, as the supine position worsens the decrease in lung volumes that predispose to atelectasis and infection.

Renal system

Renal function in older patients is extremely variable, with some showing normal function as they age, and others having significant decline in creatinine clearance. It is important to remember that because of a concomitant decline in muscle mass, the serum creatinine is often not a good reflection of renal function, and the use of a nomogram or, ideally, determination of 24-h creatinine clearance is necessary to ascertain true renal function. Fluid and electrolyte homeostasis may also be impaired, necessitating close attention to these aspects throughout the hospital stay. This is especially important because volume depletion, as well as overload, can significantly increase surgical risk. Older patients are more susceptible to urinary tract infections, especially if indwelling catheters are used. They are also at higher risk for the nephrotoxic effects of drugs.

Hepatic system

Hepatic function is also variably affected in older people. The most consistent change is a decrease in the mixed-function oxidase capacity, changing the metabolism of some medications, most notably some of the benzodiazepines such as diazepam and chlordiazepoxide. This change is not reflected in liver function tests, but should be assumed to be present, and drug dosages and choices should be adjusted accordingly. Many anaesthetic agents are metabolized and excreted by the liver, and can themselves affect hepatic function by decreasing hepatic blood flow.

The immune system—antimicrobial prophylaxis

Impaired immunological function with age causes the elderly patient to be more susceptible to infective complications from surgery. Antimicrobial prophylaxis has been shown to decrease the incidence of postoperative infection in a variety of surgical procedures.

One of the major uses of prophylactic antibiotics is in the prevention of endocarditis. The incidence of infective endocarditis in

Table 6 Other procedures and endocarditis prophylaxis[a]

Endocarditis prophylaxis recommended

Respiratory tract
   Tonsillectomy and/or adenoidectomy
   Surgical operations that involve respiratory mucosa
   Bronchoscopy with a rigid bronchoscope
Gastrointestinal tract[a]
   Sclerotherapy for oesophageal varices
   Oesophageal stricture dilation
   Endoscopic retrograde cholangiography with biliary obstruction
   Biliary tract surgery
   Surgical operations that involve intestinal mucosa
Genitourinary tract
   Prostate surgery
   Cystoscopy
   Urethral dilation

[a] Prophylaxis is recommended for high-risk patients; optional for medium-risk patients.

Adapted with permission from Dajani *et al.* (1997).

elderly people has been rising. The primary predisposing conditions include prosthetic heart valves, valvular degeneration, and mitral valve prolapse. Indications for prophylaxis and the antibiotics used are the same as in the younger patient (Tables 6–9) (Dajani *et al.* 1997). (See also Chapter 9.13.)

A variety of other procedures require prophylaxis against wound infection and sepsis, even in the absence of a cardiac abnormality (Kroenke 1987). Any elderly patient undergoing cholecystectomy should receive antibiotics as they are likely to have bacterial contamination. Patients undergoing other gastrointestinal procedures such as appendicectomy and colonic surgery should also be given antibiotics. Orthopaedic procedures that introduce a prosthesis or involve an open fracture are also associated with risk of infection, as are vascular procedures and hysterectomy. Urological surgery in the absence of infected urine does not usually require prophylaxis. The use of prophylactic antibiotics and the agents to be used should ideally be subject to regular review as part of the local policy for control of hospital infection.

Nutrition

The state of nutrition is an important consideration both before and after surgery. Studies of elderly patients in hospital have indicated between 17 and 65 per cent are malnourished (Sullivan *et al.* 1999). Hypoalbuminaemia in the elderly surgical patient has been shown to double the risk of sepsis and increase fatality 10-fold (Seymour 1986). Wound healing is also impaired in such patients, and the risk of postoperative infections and decubitus ulcers increased. A weight of less than 80 per cent of the ideal for the patient's height, decreased albumin and transferrin, anergy to skin testing, and reduced triceps skinfold thickness are indications of malnutrition and predictors of poor surgical outcome in studies done in younger patients. All of these variables may be affected by age and concomitant medical conditions, and malnutrition may be more difficult to diagnose accurately in the elderly patient. Despite this, the above indicators combined with a careful dietary history and clinical judgement can serve to alert one to the possibility of malnutrition.

Table 7 Cardiac conditions associated with endocarditis

Endocarditis prophylaxis recommended

High-risk category
   Prosthetic cardiac valves, including bioprosthetic and homograft valves
   Previous bacterial endocarditis
   Complex cyanotic congenital heart disease (e.g. single-ventricle states, transposition of the great arteries, tetralogy of Fallot)
   Surgically constructed systemic pulmonary shunts or conduits
Moderate-risk category
   Most other congenital cardiac malformations (other than above and below)
   Acquired valvar dysfunction (e.g. rheumatic heart disease)
   Hypertrophic cardiomyopathy
   Mitral valve prolapse with valvar regurgitation and/or thickened leaflets[a]

Endocarditis prophylaxis not recommended

Negligible-risk category (no greater risk than the general population)
   Isolated secundum atrial septal defect
   Surgical repair of atrial septal defect, ventricular septal defect, or patent ductus arteriosus (without residua beyond 6 months)
   Previous coronary artery bypass graft surgery
   Mitral valve prolapse without valvar regurgitation[a]
   Physiological, functional, or innocent heart murmurs
   Previous Kawasaki disease without valvar dysfunction
   Previous rheumatic fever without valvar dysfunction
   Cardiac pacemakers (intravascular and epicardial) and implanted defibrillators

[a] See Dajani *et al.* (1997) for further discussion of mitral valve prolapse and endocarditis prophylaxis.

Reproduced with permission from Dajani *et al.* (1997).

Table 8 Prophylactic regimens for dental, oral, respiratory tract, or oesophageal procedures

Situation	Agent	Regimen
Standard general prophylaxis	Amoxycillin	2.0 g 1 h before procedure
Unable to take oral medications	Ampicillin	2.0 IM or IV within 30 min before procedure
Allergic to penicillin	Clindamycin or	600 mg orally 1 h before procedure
	Cephalexin[a] or cefadroxil[a] or	2.0 g orally 1 h before procedure
	Azithromycin or clarithromycin	500 mg orally 1 h before procedure
Allergic to penicillin and unable to take oral medications	Clindamycin or	600 mg IV within 30 min before procedure
	Cefazolin[a]	1.0 g IM or IV within 30 min before procedure

IM, intramuscular; IV, intravenous.

[a] Cephalosporins should not be used in individuals with immediate-type hypersensitivity reaction (urticaria, angioedema, anaphylaxis) to penicillins.

Reproduced with permission from Dajani et al. (1997).

Table 9 Prophylactic regimens for genitourinary gastrointestinal (excluding oesophageal) procedures

Situation	Agents	Regimen
High-risk patients	Ampicillin plus gentamicin	Ampicillin 2.0 g IM or IV plus gentamicin 1.5 mg/kg (not to exceed 120 mg) within 30 min of starting the procedure; 8 h later, ampicillin 1 g IM/IV or amoxicillin 1 g orally
High-risk patients allergic to ampicillin/amoxicillin	Vancomycin plus gentamicin	Vancomycin 1.0 g IV over 1–2 h plus gentamicin 1.5 mg/kg IV/IM (not to exceed 120 mg); complete injection/infusion within 30 min of starting the procedure
Moderate-risk patients	Amoxycillin or ampicillin	Amoxycillin 2.0 g orally 1 h before procedure, or ampicillin 2.0 g IM/IV within 30 min of starting procedure
Moderate-risk patients allergic to ampicillin/amoxicillin	Vancomycin	Vancomycin 1.0 g IV over 1–2 h; complete infusion within 30 min of starting the procedure

IM, intramuscular; IV, intravenous.

Adapted with permission from Dajani et al. (1997).

Although intuitively it would seem that improving a patient's nutritional status would decrease postoperative complications, studies of this question have produced mixed results (Cooper 1987). Preoperative total parenteral nutrition has been shown to improve outcomes only in severely malnourished patients (Veterans Affairs Total Parenteral Nutrition Cooperative Study Group 1991). The costs of delaying surgery, both in monetary terms and terms of the possible progression of, or further complications from, the disease must also be weighed.

Nutrition is also an important concern postoperatively and supplementation needs to be considered early in the patient who is not meeting his or her own needs owing to anorexia, medical complications, or the inability to take food by mouth.

Intraoperative concerns

The choice of specific anaesthetic agents for the geriatric patient should be made by the anaesthetist. The medical consultant and surgeon may, however, assist in the decision to use local, regional, or general anaesthesia. The advantages and disadvantages must be weighed in each individual case. Local anaesthesia is generally safe, and may be used in procedures such as cataract or dental/oral surgery, or surgery involving the extremities. Regional anaesthesia is often used for hernia repair, hip surgery, vaginal hysterectomies, and transurethral resection of the prostate. Despite common belief, there is no evidence of a decrease in respiratory complications with regional as opposed to general anaesthesia. Regional anaesthesia can also be associated with significant haemodynamic effects, including hypotension and decreased cardiac output, which may be less controllable than with general anaesthesia. Studies comparing postoperative mental changes between patients after regional or general anaesthesia vary in their conclusions; some have found less confusion after regional anaesthesia and others have shown no difference. Epidural anaesthesia and analgesia have been associated with decreased vaso-occlusive events in high-risk patients, and decreased thromboembolism in a variety of types of surgery (Liu *et al.* 1995).

General anaesthesia should be used in major abdominal and thoracic procedures, when control of the airway is essential and when the patient cannot comply with instructions. Most general anaesthetics will depress myocardial function to a greater or lesser degree, with variable effects on heart rate and the peripheral vasculature. Some of these effects are influenced by medications, such as β-blockers and antiarrhythmic agents.

The effects of general anaesthesia may be prolonged if the patient becomes hypothermic in the operating room. This is a dangerous occurrence in elderly patients, as they are more susceptible both to the development of hypothermia and its consequences. Anaesthetized patients of any age become poikilothermic and at risk for hypothermia in a cold operating room. The risk is heightened with increasing age as there is an associated decrease in basal metabolic rate, muscle mass, and vasomotor response to cold, all of which predispose to the development of hypothermia. Other risk factors for hypothermia include operations longer than 3 h, exposure of the major body cavities, or major vascular surgery. Hypothermia can be protective against brain ischaemia but the hypothermic patient is more susceptible to cardiac arrhythmias, congestive heart failure, pneumonia, coagulopathy, and decreased resistance to wound infection (Sessler 1997). Peripheral vasoconstriction during hypothermia can cause hypertension in the operating room, and the vasodilatation that occurs when the patient is rewarmed can cause significant hypotension. Shivering as the patient awakens from anaesthesia can also be dangerous, as it dramatically increases oxygen demand. Hypothermia can be avoided by careful monitoring of core temperatures, warmer operating rooms, warming blankets, and intravenous fluids given at body temperature.

Another risk to the elderly patient is development of decubitus ulcers while lying on a hard operating table for a long time without movement. This risk is particularly high in the presence of malnutrition, anaemia, and vascular disease. Proper padding of the table and intermittent relief of pressure on bony prominences can avoid this problem.

Postoperative concerns

Pain control

Adequate pain control should be a goal both for the comfort of the patient, and to prevent postoperative complications by facilitating early mobilization, coughing, and deep breathing. Adequate treatment of pain can also decrease potentially detrimental sympathetic responses. Assessing the need for medications against pain may be difficult in demented or delirious patients, as they may not remember or know how to ask for medication. Pain in these patients may be manifested by agitation or increased confusion rather than by complaints of discomfort. Conversely, overmedication can also be

manifested by increased agitation and confusion, and the doctor and nurses must use judgement to determine which is actually the problem in the individual case.

There are many analgesics available for use in postoperative pain. Narcotics are very effective, but their prolonged half-lives in the elderly patient can lead to accumulation. Constipation and nausea are common side-effects. They should initially be given regularly rather than on demand, as this will improve pain relief and reduce the total dose needed. The same results can be obtained in those who are mentally intact by patient-controlled analgesia, which allows them to administer their own medication through a bedside pump and has been shown to be useful even in the frail elderly patient (Egbert *et al.* 1990). Epidural analgesia can be very effective, with fewer systemic effects. For less severe pain, non-steroidal anti-inflammatory agents either parenterally or orally (watching for gastrointestinal or renal side-effects) or paracetamol (acetaminophen) can be helpful. Another option is a transcutaneous electrical stimulation unit, which has been used successfully on elderly patients and avoids the many untoward side-effects of medication.

Prophylaxis against venous thrombosis

Patients of any age undergoing surgery, particularly orthopaedic cases, are at risk of developing deep venous thrombosis. Fibrinogen scanning has detected thrombosis in the legs in a quarter of general surgery patients, with 1.6 per cent developing clinically significant pulmonary embolism (Clagett *et al.* 1995). The risk is highest in hip surgery and knee reconstruction, with 45 to 70 per cent of these patients developing deep vein thrombosis, and 20 per cent of patients for hip surgery developing a pulmonary embolism. The incidence of both these conditions increases with age. Predisposing medical conditions include heart failure, acute myocardial infarction, cancer, obesity, stroke with weakness of the legs, prior deep venous thrombosis, varicose veins, oestrogen use, and congenital or acquired abnormalities of the coagulation system. There are various ways of preventing deep venous thrombosis and pulmonary embolism; their use should be routine in elderly patients in whom there are no contraindications. The incidence of both conditions in the general surgical patient has been significantly reduced by the use of low-dose subcutaneous heparin. Giving heparin 2 h before surgery and every 8 to 12 h after cuts the incidence of deep venous thrombosis to 10 per cent and of embolism to 0.8 per cent (Clagett *et al.* 1995). Heparin-induced thrombocytopenia is a rare complication, and there is an increased risk of postoperative haematoma, but in most patients, this regimen does not significantly increase serious bleeding complications.

Low-molecular-weight heparin is only slightly better than standard heparin in preventing venous thromboembolism in most settings, but may cause fewer bleeding complications. It is considerably more expensive. In hip and knee surgery, it has been proved superior to standard heparin. Low-dose heparin combined with dihydroergotamine is effective, but this combination has been withdrawn from the American market.

Warfarin is effective in preventing deep venous thrombosis in hip surgery. It is usually begun the night before surgery and adjusted to maintain the international normalized ratio between 2 and 3. Table 10 contains the current recommendations for prophylaxis against deep venous thrombosis in various settings.

Table 10 Prevention of deep venous thrombosis

Type of surgery	Preferred method (when started)	Alternative	Adjunctive
General surgery (moderate risk patient)	ES (IO), LDUH (PR), or IPC (IO)		
Major general surgery (additional risk factors)	LDUH every 8 h (PR) or LMWH	IPC	
Major general surgery (high-risk patient)	LDUH (PR), LMWH (PR), or dextran (IO), and IPC (IO)	Warfarin	
Total hip replacement	LMWH (PO), warfarin (PR), adjusted-dose unfractionated heparin (PR)		ES or IPC
Total knee replacement	LMWH (PO) or IPC (IO)		
Hip fracture	LMWH (PR) or warfarin		
Intracranial neurosurgery	IPC (IO)	LDUH	LDUH or ES
Multiple trauma	IPC, warfarin, or LMWH	Vena cava filtration	Serial DVT screening

PR, preoperative; PO, postoperative; IO, intraoperative; LMWH, low-molecular-weight heparin; LDUH, low-dose unfractionated heparin; IPC, intermittent pneumatic compression; ES, elastic stockings.

Adapted with permission from Clagett *et al.* (1995).

Non-pharmacological methods of prophylaxis are also available. Properly fitted graduated elastic compression stockings improve venous return and can be used in combination with other therapies. The use of external pneumatic-compression stockings is also an effective prophylactic measure, and should be begun before surgery and continued at least 3 days or until the patient is fully ambulatory. This may be the preferred approach in patients who are at significant risk from bleeding with anticoagulation.

Delirium

Delirium is a common complication in surgical patients, with an average incidence of 36.7 per cent (Dyer *et al.* 1995). Age is a consistent risk factor in studies of postoperative delirium. Studies of elderly patients with hip fractures have shown that up to 60 per cent develop postoperative confusion (Gustafson *et al.* 1988). The occurrence of delirium is associated with prolonged stays in hospital, more need for long-term care after discharge, a decreased ability to walk, falls, and a higher incidence of postoperative complications and death. Besides age, risk factors include dementia, depression, Parkinson's disease, impaired hearing or vision, anticholinergic drugs, hypoxaemia, emergency surgery, previous psychiatric conditions, and medical problems. A knowledge of preoperative mental status is important in order to detect subtle changes that may indicate the presence of delirium. The causes and treatment of delirium are discussed further in Chapter 18.21.

Other postoperative concerns

There are a variety of postoperative complications that may be less common and less dramatic than events in the cardiac, pulmonary, or central nervous systems, but that can nevertheless cause considerable discomfort and inconvenience. These include urinary incontinence or retention, constipation, and decubitus ulcers. Being aware of the risk factors and instituting preventive measures may decrease the frequency with which these occur.

Urinary incontinence is common in elderly patients in the hospital, with a prevalence of 17 per cent on the general surgical ward in one study (Sullivan and Lindsay 1984). Medications, immobility, faecal impaction, and sedation, all common factors postoperatively, can each increase the incidence of incontinence. Adverse consequences include decubitus ulcers, falls, and the insertion of indwelling catheters with their attendant risk of infection. The chances of a patient remaining continent can be enhanced by the provision of a urinal and/or bedside commode, regular toileting, and avoidance of constipation, oversedation, and unnecessary use of drugs that might induce incontinence. Indwelling catheters should not be used for the management of incontinence unless there is skin breakdown or urine output needs to be monitored closely.

Postoperative urinary retention is also a common problem. Many anaesthetic agents can induce retention by altering the effect of the autonomic nervous system on the bladder and urethra. Older men are especially at risk owing to a high prevalence of urethral narrowing from prostatic hypertrophy. Indwelling catheters are commonly used intraoperatively and when used for 24 h after orthopaedic surgery have been shown to decrease the incidence of postoperative retention as compared with intermittent catheterization (Michelson *et al.* 1988). Unless absolutely necessary for management of fluid status, they should be removed 24 to 48 h after surgery.

Both urinary incontinence and retention can be induced by faecal impaction. Constipation is extremely common after surgery, owing to the direct effects of surgery on the bowel, drugs, dehydration, poor intake of dietary fibre, immobilization, pain, anxiety, bedpans, and lack of privacy in the hospital. Early mobilization, adequate hydration, and the judicious use of pain medications and prophylactic stool softeners and laxatives can all minimize this problem.

Early mobilization

Many of the above complications, including pulmonary infections, thrombophlebitis, urinary problems, constipation, pressure sores, and delirium, are associated with immobility and can be prevented or treated with early mobilization. Attempts to mobilize an elderly patient may be affected by poor preoperative functional status, arthritis, orthostatic hypotension, confusion, and pain. These should be seen not as reasons to stay in bed, but as factors that must be addressed and included in the plan for mobilization and rehabilitation. Physical and occupational therapists, as well as the nursing staff, can be invaluable in developing and instituting a rehabilitation plan, which should include an early use of usual dress, frequent visits by family and friends, and avoidance of the use of bedside rails or other restraints.

Conclusion

As the elderly population continues to increase, and surgical techniques and management continue to improve, the number of elderly surgical patients will continue to grow. An understanding of the physiology of ageing and an awareness of concomitant diseases, in combination with careful selection, monitoring, and preoperative and postoperative assessment and care, can ensure a satisfactory outcome for the vast majority of these patients.

References

American College of Cardiology/American Heart Association Task Force Report (1996). Guidelines for perioperative cardiovascular evaluation for noncardiac surgery. *Circulation*, 93, 1278–1317.

American College of Physicians (1990). Preoperative pulmonary function testing. Position paper. *Annals of Internal Medicine*, 112, 793–4.

American Society of Anesthesiologists Task Force on Pulmonary Artery Catheterization (1993). Guidelines for pulmonary artery catheterization. *Anesthesiology*, 78, 380–94.

Burns-Cox, N., Campbell, W.B., Van Nimmen, B.A.J., Vacaeren, P.M.K., and Lucarotti, M. (1997). Surgical care and outcome for patients in their nineties. *British Journal of Surgery*, 84, 496–8.

Campeau, L. (1976). Grading of angina pectoris. *Circulation*, 54, 522–3.

Clagett, G.P., Anderson, F.A., Heit, J., Levine, M.N., and Wheeler, H.B. (1995). Prevention of venous thomboembolism. *Chest*, 108, 312S–29S.

Cooper, J.K. (1987). Does nutrition affect surgical outcome? *Journal of the American Geriatrics Society*, 35, 229–32.

Dajani, A.S., Taubert, K.A., Wilson, W., *et al.* (1997). Prevention of bacterial endocarditis: recommendations by the American Heart Association. *Journal of the American Medical Association*, 277, 1794–801.

Del Guercio, L.R. and Cohn, J.D. (1980). Monitoring operative risk in the elderly. *Journal of the American Medical Association*, 234, 1350–5.

Djokovic, J. and Hedley-Whyte, J. (1979). Prediction of outcome of surgery and anesthesia in patients over 80. *Journal of the American Medical Association*, 242, 2301–6.

Dripps, R.D., Eckenhoff, J.E., and Vandam, L.D. (1982). *Introduction to anesthesia: the principals of safe practice* (6th edn). W.B. Saunders, Philadelphia, PA.

Dunlop, W.E., Rosenblood, L., Lawrason L., Birdsall, L., and Rusnak, C.H. (1993). Effects of age and severity of illness on outcome and length of stay in geriatric surgical patients. *American Journal of Surgery*, 165, 577–80.

Dyer, C.B., Ashton, C.M., and Teasdale, T.A. (1995). Postoperative delirium. A review of 80 primary data-collection studies. *Archives of Internal Medicine*, 155, 461–5.

Egbert, A.M., Parks, L.H., Short, L.M., and Burnett, M.L. (1990). Randomized trial of postoperative patient-controlled analgesia vs intramuscular narcotics in frail elderly men. *Archives of Internal Medicine*, 150, 1987–2003.

Feussner, J.R. and Matchar, D. (1988). When and how to study the carotid arteries. *Annals of Internal Medicine*, 109, 805–18.

Folstein, M.F., Folstein S.E., and McHugh, P.R. (1975). Mini-Mental State: a practical method for grading the cognitive state of patients for the clinician. *Journal of Psychiatric Research*, 12, 189–98.

Gerson, M.C., Hurst J.M., Hertzberg V.S., Baughman, R., Rouan, G.W., and Ellis, K. (1990). Prediction of cardiac and pulmonary complications related to elective abdominal and noncardiac thoracic surgery geriatric patients. *American Journal of Medicine*, 88, 101–7.

Goldman, L. and Caldera, D.L. (1979). Risks of general anaesthesia and elective operation in the hypertensive patient. *Anaesthesiology*, 50, 285–92.

Goldman L., Caldera, D.L., Nussbaum, S.R, *et al.* (1977). Multifactorial index of cardiac risk in noncardiac surgical procedures. *New England Journal of Medicine*, 297, 845–50.

Greenfield, S., Blanco, D.M., Elashoff, R.M., and Ganz, P.A. (1987). Patterns of care related to age of breast cancer patients. *Journal of the American Medical Association*, 257, 2766–70.

Gustafson, Y., Berggren, D., Brännström, B., *et al.* (1988). Acute confusional states in elderly patients treated for femoral neck fracture. *Journal of the American Geriatrics Society*, 36, 525–30.

Hall, J.C., Tarala, R.A., Tapper, J., and Hall, J.L. (1996). Prevention of respiratory complications after abdominal surgery: a randomised clinical trial. *British Medical Journal*, 312, 148–52.

Hosking, M.P., Warner, M.A., Lobdell, C.M., Offord, K.P., and Melton, J. (1989). Outcomes of surgery in patients 90 years of age and older. *Journal of the American Medical Association*, 261, 1909–15.

Kroenke, K. (1987). Clinical reviews: preoperative evaluation: the assessment and management of surgical risk. *Journal of General Internal Medicine*, 2, 257–69.

Liu, S., Carpenter, R.L., and Neal, J.M. (1995). Epidural anesthesia and analgesia: their role in postoperative outcome. *Anesthesiology*, 82, 1474–97.

Mangano, D.T. (1990). Perioperative cardiac morbidity. *Anesthesiology*, 72, 153–84.

Mangano, D.T., Layug, E.L., Wallace, A., and Tateo, I. (1996). Effect of Atenolol on mortality and cardiovascular morbidity after noncardiac surgery. *New England Journal of Medicine*, 335, 1713–19.

Michelson, J.D., Lotke, P.A., and Steinberg, M.E. (1988). Urinary-bladder management after total joint-replacement surgery. *New England Journal of Medicine*, 219, 321–6.

Prys-Roberts, C., Meloche, R., and Foex, P. (1971). Studies of anesthesia in response to hypertension. *British Journal of Anaesthesia*, 43, 112–37.

Rodeheffer, R.J., Gerstenblith, G., Becker, L.C., Fleg, J.L., Weisfeldt, M.L., and Lakatta, E.G. (1984). Exercise cardiac output is maintained with advancing age in healthy human subjects: cardiac dilatation and increased stroke volume compensate for a diminished heart rate. *Circulation*, 69, 203–13.

Sessler, D.I. (1997). Mild perioperative hypothermia. *New England Journal of Medicine*, 336, 1730–7.

Seymour, D.G. (1986). *Medical assessment of the elderly surgical patient*. Aspen Publications, Rockville, MD.

Shah, K.B., Kleinman, B.S., Sami, H., Joyoti, P.L., and Rao, T.L.K. (1990). Re-evaluation of perioperative myocardial infarction undergoing noncardiac operations. *Anesthesia Analgesia*, **71**, 231–5.

Sullivan D. and Lindsay, R. (1984). Urinary incontinence in the geriatric population of an acute care hospital. *Journal of the American Geriatrics Society*, **32**, 646–50.

Sullivan, D.H., Sun, S., and Walls, R.C. (1991). Protein-energy undernutrition among elderly hospitalized patients. A prospective study. *Journal of the American Medical Association*, **281**, 2013–19.

Tuman, K., McCarthy, R.J., Spiess, B.D., *et al.* (1989). Effect of pulmonary artery catheterization on outcome in patients undergoing coronary artery surgery. *Anesthesiology*, **70**, 199–206.

Veterans Affairs Total Parenteral Nutritional Cooperative Study Group (1991). Perioperative total parenteral nutrition in surgical patients. *New England Journal of Medicine*, **325**, 525–32.

Warner, M.A., Offord, K.P., Warner M.E., Lennon, R.L., Conover, M.A., and Jansson-Schumacher U. (1989). Role of preoperative cessation of smoking and other factors in postoperative pulmonary complications: a blinded prospective study of coronary artery bypass patients. *Mayo Clinic Proceedings*, **64**, 609–16.

Weitz, H.H. and Goldman, L. (1987). Noncardiac surgery in the patient with heart disease. *Medical Clinics of North America*, **71**, 413–32.

22

Legal and ethical issues in geriatric medicine

22 Legal and ethical issues in geriatric medicine

Heather MacDonald, Charles Weijer, and Peter Singer

Ethical issues present themselves daily in the practice of geriatric medicine. Therefore, it is critically important that doctors caring for elderly people have a working knowledge of these issues. Guided by case examples, this chapter explores the most common ethical issues confronted—consent and capacity, substitute decision-making and advance care planning, euthanasia and assisted suicide, resource allocation and 'futility', truth-telling, confidentiality, research ethics, and genetics and ethics.

Consent and capacity (competence)

Mrs A is an 81-year-old patient with angina, osteoarthritis, and severe angiodysplasia of the colon. She has had several hospital admissions for colonic bleeding. She has always been treated with supportive care and transfusions, and the bleeding stopped spontaneously. She has now been readmitted with bleeding and has required multiple transfusions. The bleeding is not stopping. She is informed that a bowel resection is the only treatment that will save her life. She refuses surgery. Her family and doctor question her capacity to make such a decision.

Doctors should seek consent before providing diagnostic tests or treatment because capable (competent) adults have the legal right to choose or refuse recommended diagnostic tests or treatment (Faden and Beauchamp 1986). This includes the right to forego (not start or stop) life-sustaining treatment such as cardiopulmonary resuscitation, mechanical ventilation, dialysis, antibiotics, and artificial nutrition and hydration, even if this decision results in death. This right is grounded in the ethical principle of respect for patient autonomy and protected by the legal doctrine of informed consent. The elements of consent include (a) disclosure, (b) capacity, and (c) voluntariness (Etchells *et al.* 1996*b, c, d*).

Disclosure

The doctor should inform the patient about any proposed diagnostic tests and treatments. The key elements of such disclosure include the risks and benefits of the proposed test or treatment as well as any alternative tests or treatment (Etchells *et al.* 1996*b*).

Although standards for disclosure vary from one jurisdiction to another, the doctor should disclose all the information that a reasonable person in the patient's situation would want or need to know before making a decision. This would include information about any risks that were likely or serious. Moreover, it is prudent for the doctor to explain any benefits, risks, or alternative tests or treatments that may have special significance for the particular patient. For example, any risk of upper extremity peripheral neuropathy should be disclosed to a concert violinist, and the alternative of delaying a surgical procedure should be disclosed to a person who is only a few months away from receiving his or her pension.

Effective communication skills are essential to the process of obtaining informed consent. The doctor must spend sufficient time to ensure that the patient has the opportunity to understand the information provided and to have his or her questions answered. This is particularly important for elderly patients, and often doctors may need to present the information in different ways and over more than one visit. Compensating for perceptual deficits, which are common in older people, by using a hearing aid or large print books, may also be necessary.

Capacity (competence)

The assessment of capacity plays a pivotal role in patient care (Etchells *et al.* 1996*c*). If the patient is deemed capable, the doctor should seek consent from the patient; if the patient is incapable, the doctor should seek consent from the appropriate substitute decision-maker. (At present in the United Kingdom, consent by proxies has no legal standing. The clinician has the responsibility for making decisions in the patient's best interest but is expected to make conscientious enquiries of the patient's family and friends in identifying that best interest.)

Capacity can be defined as the ability to understand information relevant to a decision and appreciate the consequences of a particular decision or lack of decision. Unfortunately, there are no widely accepted clinical measures to assess patient capacity in practice. The Aid to Capacity Assessment is a decision aid to help clinicians assess patient capacity to consent to treatment (full text available at the University of Toronto Joint Centre for Bioethics website at http://www.utoronto.ca/jcb). Sample questions from the Aid to Capacity Assessment are shown in Table 1.

It is important to distinguish between the concepts of cognitive impairment and incapacity. Cognitive impairment is a syndrome, and does not imply capacity or incapacity. Cognitively impaired people are often capable of making many decisions regarding their health care. Capacity must be assessed on the basis of the decision in hand.

identifiable without actually using his or her name) when presenting cases at educational rounds.

Despite the importance of maintaining patient confidentiality, this principle is not absolute and does admit of exceptions. Although the justifiable exceptions to confidentiality arose initially in the context of psychiatric cases of patients who threaten violence against a third party, other examples of such cases include the person infected with HIV who continues to have sexual intercourse and refuses to disclose the risk of HIV infection to his or her sexual partner(s), other reportable infectious diseases, child abuse, and people who are unfit to drive. In cases where there is a reasonably high likelihood that the patient will cause serious harm to a specific, identifiable person, this harm may be averted through disclosure of confidential patient information to the third party, and the person is unlikely to discover the information through other means, it may be permissible, even required, to violate patient confidentiality and disclose patient information to a legally authorized third party.

The justification for violating patient confidentiality in such cases is based on the ethical principle of beneficence (promoting good) and non-maleficence (avoiding harm). Many jurisdictions have specific legislation, usually requiring disclosure, regarding such cases.

In the case of Mr F, the doctor was obliged to report the patient to the Ministry of Transport as unfit to operate a motor vehicle. Because of legislation governing medical conditions and driving, the doctor met with Mr F before doing this. At the meeting, the doctor explained the legislation, and his legal obligation to report. He also empathized with Mr F as it would now be more difficult for Mr F to get to work, and together they discussed safe transportation alternatives that would allow Mr F to maintain his job as long as he was able to work.

Research ethics

Mrs G accompanies her 59-year-old husband to the geriatrician asking if he can be given experimental treatment for his Alzheimer's disease. Mr G developed early-onset Alzheimer's disease 2 years ago and has experienced rapid deterioration in his cognitive abilities. A trial of tacrine failed to slow the progression of his symptoms. Mrs G has legal power of attorney for her husband and makes health-care and financial decisions on his behalf.

Clinical research provides a solid foundation for high-quality medical care. Experiments involving humans help determine the aetiology of disease; clinical trials ensure that new medical interventions are safe and effective. Important as research is to the advance of medical care, past abuses highlight the need for ethical principles and regulations to guide the conduct of research. One well-known research scandal involved elderly research subjects (Katz 1972; Levine 1988). In 1963, doctors at the Jewish Chronic Disease Hospital in Brooklyn, New York, injected 22 chronically ill patients with live cancer cells in order to study the immune response to cancer (the investigators believed, but did not know, that the cancer cells would be destroyed by the body's immune system). Problematically, patients were not informed that the injections contained cancer cells, written

consent was not obtained, and some of the research participants may have been incapable of providing informed consent.

The Belmont Report principles

What ethical principles guide the conduct of human experimentation? In the *Belmont Report*, the members of the American National Commission for the Protection of Human Subjects of Biomedical and Behavioural Research (1979) set out three ethical principles for research: respect for persons, beneficence, and justice. The principle of respect for persons requires that the choices of autonomous individuals be respected and that people incapable of autonomous choice be protected. Respect for persons establishes the requirement for informed consent to research participation. The principle of beneficence entails that participation in research must be associated with a favourable balance of benefits and risks. Justice demands that researchers neither prey upon vulnerable people nor exclude without good reason those who may benefit from research participation. Each of these principles finds expression in the regulations and guidelines that govern research in the United States (Department of Health and Human Services 1991), Canada (Medical Research Council of Canada 1987), and the United Kingdom (Royal College of Physicians 1990).

Informed consent

Older people are a heterogeneous group and investigators should be sensitive to diversity in ability. A number of characteristics of later life pose challenges to obtaining informed consent in the research setting: cognitive deficits are more common with advancing age (nonetheless only 5 to 10 per cent of people over the age of 65 years show signs of dementia), perceptual deficits are more common, and older people tend to be more risk averse than the young (Office for the Protection from Research Risks 1993). Taub and Baker (1984) have suggested a two-part consent process for research involving elderly subjects: subjects are informed and then given a multiple choice test. Not only does testing provide an opportunity to exclude from participation those who cannot provide valid consent, but repeat testing was found to improve comprehension of consent information. In another study, Taub (1987) found that a substantial proportion of poor comprehension is explained by perceptual rather than cognitive defects. Thus, the simple measure of using a large typeface in a consent form may improve comprehension in prospective research subjects. Finally, Levine (1988) recommends that risk information in the consent process ought to be expressed in day-to-day terms whenever possible.

People incapable of giving consent

What of subjects who, owing to incapacity, are unable to consent to research participation? Can they ever be enrolled legitimately in research? If yes, how much risk may they be exposed to in research? A policy restricting research participation to those capable of giving consent would result in harm: groups within society, including those with dementia (and for that matter, children), would become 'therapeutic orphans' and be deprived of medical advances that derive from research. Furthermore, individuals would be denied direct benefits associated with research participation. A research study may enrol older people who cannot give informed consent if (a) the research cannot be done on another population, (b) the study addresses an issue of importance to this population, (c) the subject's proxy (where these are legally recognized) consents to research participation, and (d) the research involves non-therapeutic research risks that do not exceed a minor increment above minimal risk (Office for Protection from Research Risks 1993). 'Minimal risk' is risk comparable to that 'ordinarily encountered in daily life or during the performance of routine physical or psychological tests' (Freedman *et al.* 1993). Examples of research interventions associated with minimal risk include drawing a small amount of blood or the administration of a mental status examination. Researchers should comply with local legal standards regarding proxy consent.

There is substantial heterogeneity among jurisdictions as to who may provide proxy consent to research participation and the types of research to which the proxy may consent. In some jurisdictions, consent to research participation may be effected by an advance directive in which the now incompetent subject set out, when competent, a clear desire to participate in research (Keyserlingk *et al.* 1995).

Unjust inclusion and exclusion

The Jewish Chronic Disease Hospital Study is a clear example of unjust inclusion of elderly people in research. Participants were selected for the experiment because institutionalization made them convenient research subjects, and, in some cases, because incapacity made them accommodating ones as well. Recent interest has focused on the unjust exclusion of groups of subjects—particularly older people, women, and members of racial and ethnic minority groups—from research. When subjects are unjustly included in research, they are exposed to the risks associated with research; when subjects are unjustly excluded from research, other harms may be incurred: insufficient information may exist to ensure that members of excluded groups receive effective medical care (Weijer 1999).

The omission of elderly people from clinical trials of treatments for cancer provides a clear illustration of harms associated with unjust exclusion. Older people are excluded from cancer clinical trials by eligibility criteria that set an age cut-off (for example 70 years of age), establish a life-expectancy requirement (for example 10 years excluding the diagnosis of cancer), or forbid coexisting disease in participants (Fuks *et al.* 1998). The existence of such criteria has lead to under-representation of elderly people in clinical trials, including those funded by the United States National Cancer Institute (Trimble *et al.* 1994). The failure to include older people in cancer trials has lead to a lack of information on proper treatment of cancer in elderly people and puts them at risk of being undertreated (Mor *et al.* 1985). Other examples include the treatment of myocardial infarction (Gurwitz *et al.* 1992) and Parkinson's disease (Mitchell *et al.* 1997). Investigators must not exclude older patients from clinical research unless a compelling justification is provided to (and accepted by) the relevant funding agency and institutional review board.

In the case of Mr G, the geriatrician discussed with Mrs G several clinical trials of prospective Alzheimer treatments for which Mr G may be eligible. Each of the studies suggested by the geriatrician involved a different novel agent as well as some added laboratory and cognitive tests. The studies have been reviewed and approved by a local research ethics committee. After careful consideration of the risks, benefits, and

alternatives, she selected a study for her husband. After further testing to establish eligibility for study participation, Mr G began treatment on the clinial trial.

Genetics and ethics

Mrs H, a 73-year-old woman with late-onset Alzheimer's disease, and her daughter Mrs K, a 35-year-old mother of four, present to Mrs H's geriatrician both requesting the genetic test for Alzheimer's disease that they recently read about in the newspaper. Mrs K is worried that she or one of her children may eventually develop the disease.

The discovery of genes associated with the development of Alzheimer's disease has generated tremendous interest in both the scientific and lay community. Mutations in three genes—β-APP, Presenilin 1, and Presenilin 2—are rare and associated with early-onset Alzheimer's disease. Polymorphisms in the fourth gene, apolipoprotein E (apoE), are associated with the common late-onset variant of Alzheimer's disease. Inheriting one or two apoE4 alleles in a dose-dependent manner both increases the odds of developing the disease and decreases the age of onset.

At the time of writing, genetic tests for Alzheimer's disease are predominantly conducted within the research setting. As a result, ethical issues in genetic testing are largely subsumed under the Belmont principles—respect for persons, beneficence, and justice—and research regulations and guidelines discussed above. Glass and colleagues provide a comprehensive discussion of ethical issues in (and ethics committee review of) gene localization and identification studies (Glass *et al.* 1996), genetic screening and diagnostic tests (Glass *et al.* 1997), and gene therapy studies (Glass *et al.* 1999).

Informed consent

Genetic testing for Alzheimer's disease presents a number of challenges for the informed consent process. Firstly, genetic testing often involves highly technical test procedures and stochastic information regarding the meaningfulness of test results. Researchers must find ways to convey complex information to subjects in a comprehensible fashion. Secondly, new categories of information must be relayed to subjects compared with other types of research studies and, thus, the disclosure process (and consent documents) will be lengthier. For example, Weir and Horton have proposed a detailed disclosure process for all genetic studies that involve DNA banking (Weir and Horton 1995*a*, *b*). Given the complexity and mass of information involved, it is strongly recommended that researchers involve genetic counsellors in the conduct of any study involving genetic testing for Alzheimer's disease.

Insurance and employment

Genetic tests for Alzheimer's disease not only involve unfamiliar procedures and complex information, they carry with them risks to health insurance, life insurance, and employment for study participants. Indeed, it is typical in genetic studies for social risks to participants to outweigh the risks to subjects associated with study procedures (e.g. venepuncture, psychometric testing). How common is discrimination against those who carry mutations associated with genetic disease? Lapham *et al.* (1996) surveyed individuals affiliated with genetic disease support groups and asked them about their experiences with insurers and employers. Forty per cent of respondents indicated that they had been asked about genetic disease by insurers; 22 per cent said that either they or family members were denied insurance because of a genetic condition within the family. Fifteen per cent of those surveyed reported that they had been asked about genetic diseases on job applications; 13 per cent revealed that either they or a family member were refused a job or fired from one because of genetic disease in the family.

How can research subjects be protected? Risks involving health insurance, life insurance, and employment must be disclosed to prospective research subjects in any study involving genetic testing for Alzheimer's disease. Research subjects—and, for that matter, patients in the clinical setting—must be fully apprised of the risks associated with genetic testing if they are to make an informed decision. Some degree of protection may be conferred if researchers record only clinically relevant information in the patient's chart and relegate other information to a separate research file. While no step undertaken by researchers can guarantee protection from discrimination (the mere fact of study participation, apart from test results, may result in discrimination), 'certificates of confidentiality', available to American-based research studies, may represent the best protection available (Earley and Strong 1995). The certificate of confidentiality is obtained by applying to the United States Office of Health Planning and Research in Washington and prevents the researcher from having to identify a research subject in 'any Federal, State, or local civil, criminal, administrative, legislative, or other proceedings'.

Clinical use of tests

Despite a lack of agreement on the proper clinical use of genetic testing for apoE, at least one test is available commercially (Mayeux and Schupf 1995). Genetic testing for apoE and Alzheimer's disease may occur in three settings: a screening test for unaffected individuals (including family members), a diagnostic test for symptomatic people, and a test to guide therapy. Most people with Alzheimer's disease do not carry the relevant apoE allele and many people who carry the allele will not develop Alzheimer's disease. As a result of this, and the absence of any effective preventive intervention, apoE screening is not recommended for asymptomatic individuals (American College of Medical Genetics 1995; Relkin *et al.* 1996; Post *et al.* 1997). The use of apoE testing as a diagnostic test is controversial. The pretest probability of Alzheimer's disease for an older patient with memory impairment is 66 per cent; conventional tests typically result in post-test probabilities of 75 to 85 per cent. ApoE testing may increase diagnostic accuracy in this situation by as much as 14 per cent (Relkin *et al.* 1996), but not all agree that the added certainty is of clinical value (American College of Medical Genetics 1995). In the future, apoE testing may have a role in guiding therapy. For instance, tacrine therapy may be less effective in patients with Alzheimer's disease who carry the apoE4 allele (Roses 1996), and this lack of effect may be more pronounced in women (Farlow *et al.* 1996).

The geriatrician explained to Mrs H and Mrs K that the genetic test for Alzheimer's disease is unlikely to be helpful to either of them. Mrs H's diagnosis of Alzheimer's disease is already clear and genetic testing to guide therapy is currently experimental.

In Mrs K's case, too much uncertainty surrounds the meaning of test results in asymptomatic individuals for the test to be of any use. When the risks of genetic testing are explained, including risks to employment and insurance, Mrs K agreed with the doctor that genetic testing would not be advisable.

References

American College of Medical Genetics/American Society of Human Genetics Working Group on ApoE and Alzheimer disease (1995). Statement on use of apolipoprotein E testing for Alzheimer disease. *Journal of the American Medical Association*, **274**, 1627–9.

Angell, M. (1991). A new kind of 'right to die' case. *New England Journal of Medicine*, **325**, 511–12.

Asai, A., Fukuhara, S., and Lo, B. (1995). Attitudes of Japanese and Japanese-American physicians towards life-sustaining treatment. *Lancet*, **346**, 356–9.

Buchanan, A.E. and Brock, D.W. (1989). *Deciding for others: the ethics of surrogate decision making.* Cambridge University Press, New York.

Buckman, R. (1992). *How to break bad news: a guide for health care professionals.* University of Toronto Press, Toronto.

Callahan, D. (1987). *Setting limits: medical goals in an aging society.* Simon and Schuster, New York.

Department of Health and Human Services (1991). Protection of human subjects. Title 45. *Code of Federal Regulations*, part 46. Revised 18 June 1991.

Drickamer, M.A. and Lachs, M.S. (1992). Should patients with Alzheimer's disease be told their diagnosis? *New England Journal of Medicine*, **326**, 947–51.

Earley, C.L. and Strong, L.C. (1995). Certificates of confidentiality: a valuable tool for protecting genetic data. *American Journal of Human Genetics*, **57**, 727–31.

Emanuel, L.L. (1995). Advance directives: do they work? *Journal of the American College of Cardiology*, **25**, 35–8.

Emanuel, L.L. and Emanuel, E.J. (1989). The medical directive: a new comprehensive advance care document. *Journal of the American Medical Association*, **261**, 3288–93.

Emanuel, E.J. and Emanuel, L.L. (1990). Living wills: past, present, and future. *Journal of Clinical Ethics*, **1**, 9–19.

Emanuel, L.L., Barry, M.J., Stoeckle, J.D., Ettelson, L.M., and Emanuel, E.J. (1991). Advance directives for medical care: a case for greater use. *New England Journal of Medicine*, **324**, 889–95.

Emanuel, L.L., Danis, M., Pearlman, R.A., and Singer, P.A. (1995). Advance care planning as a process: structuring the discussions in practice. *Journal of the American Geriatrics Society*, **43**, 440–6.

Etchells, E., Sharpe, G., Walsh, P., Williams, J.R., and Singer, P.A. (1996*a*). Bioethics for clinicians. 1. Consent. *Canadian Medical Association Journal*, **155**, 177–80.

Etchells, E., Sharpe, G., Burgess, M.M., and Singer, P.A. (1996*b*). Bioethics for clinicians. 2. Disclosure. *Canadian Medical Association Journal*, **155**, 387–91.

Etchells, E., Sharpe, G., Elliott, C., and Singer, P.A. (1996*c*). Bioethics for clinicians. 3. Capacity. *Canadian Medical Association Journal*, **155**, 657–61.

Etchells, E., Sharpe, G., Dykeman, M.J., Meslin, E.M., and Singer, P.A. (1996*d*). Bioethics for clinicians. 4. Voluntariness. *Canadian Medical Association Journal*, **155**, 1083–6.

Faden, R.R. and Beauchamp, T.L. (1986). *A history and theory of informed consent.* Oxford University Press, New York.

Fallowfield, L. (1993). Giving bad and sad news. *Lancet*, 341, 476–8.

Farlow, M.R., Lahiri, D.K., Poirier, J., Davignon, J., and Hui, S. (1996). Apolipoprotein E genotype and gender influence response to tacrine therapy. *Annals of the New York Academy of Sciences*, 802, 101–10.

Freedman, B., Fuks, A., and Weijer, C. (1993). *In loco parentis*: minimal risk as an ethical threshold for research upon children. *Hastings Center Report*, 23(2), 13–19.

Fuks, A., Weijer, C., Freedman, B., Shapiro, S., Skrutkowska, M., and Riaz, A. (1998). A study in contrasts: eligibility criteria in a twenty-year sample of NSABP and POG clinical trials. *Journal of Clinical Epidemiology*, 51, 69–79.

Glass, K.C., Weijer, C., Palmour, R., Shapiro, S.H., Lemmens, T.M., and Lebacqz, K. (1996). Structuring the review of human genetics protocols: gene localisation and identification studies. *IRB: A Review of Human Subjects Research*, 18, 1–9.

Glass, K.C., Weijer, C., Lemmens, T.M., Palmour, R.M., and Shapiro, S.H. (1997). Structuring the review of human genetics protocols. Part II. Diagnostic and screening studies. *IRB: A Review of Human Subjects Research*, 19, 1–11, 13.

Glass, K.C., Weijer, C., Cournoyer, D., *et al.* (1999). Structuring the review of human genetic protocols. Part III: Gene therapy studies. *IRB: A Review of Human Subjects Research*, 21, 1–9.

Gordon, M. and Singer, P.A. (1995). Decisions and care at the end of life. *Lancet*, 346, 163–6.

Grimley Evans, J. (1997). Rationing health care by age. The case against. *British Medical Journal*, 314, 11–12.

Gurwitz, J.H., Col, N.F., and Avorn, J. (1992). The exclusion of the elderly and women from clinical trials in myocardial infarction. *Journal of the American Medical Association*, 268, 1417–22.

Halevy, A. and Brody, B.A. (1996). A multi-institution collaborative policy on medical futility. *Journal of the American Medical Association*, 276, 571–4.

Hébert, P.C., Hoffmaster, B., Glass, K.C., and Singer, P.A. (1997). Bioethics for clinicians. 7. Truth telling. *Canadian Medical Association Journal*, 156, 225–8.

Holroyd, S., Snustad, D.G., and Chalifoux, Z.L. (1996). Attitudes of older adults' on being told the diagnosis of Alzheimer's disease. *Journal of the American Geriatrics Society*, 44, 400–3.

Jecker, N. and Pearlman, R.A. (1989). Ethical constraints on age-based rationing of medical care. *Journal of the American Geriatrics Society*, 37, 1067–75.

Jecker, N. and Pearlman, R.A. (1992). An ethical framework for rationing health care. *Journal of Medicine and Philosophy*, 17, 79–96.

Jecker, N.S. and Schneiderman, L.J. (1992). Futility and rationing. *American Journal of Medicine*, 92, 189–96.

Katz, J. (1972). *Experimentation with human beings*, pp. 9–65. Russell Sage Foundation, New York.

Keyserlingk, E.W., Glass, K., Kogan, S., and Gauthier, S. (1995). Proposed guidelines for the participation of persons with dementia as research subjects. *Perspectives in Biology and Medicine*, 38, 319–62.

Kleinman, I., Baylis, F., Rodgers, S., and Singer, P.A. (1997) Bioethics for clinicians. 8. Confidentiality. *Canadian Medical Association Journal*, 156, 521–4.

Lapham, E.V., Kozma, C., and Weiss, J.O. (1996). Genetic discrimination: perspectives of consumers. *Science*, 274, 621–4.

Lavery, J.V., Dickens, B.M., Boyle, J.M., and Singer, P.A. (1997). Bioethics for clinicians. 11. Euthanasia and assisted suicide. *Canadian Medical Association Journal*, 156, 1405–8.

Lazar, N.M., Griener, G.G., Robertson, G., and Singer, P.A. (1996). Bioethics for clinicians. 5. Substitute decision making. *Canadian Medical Association Journal*, 155, 1435–7.

Levine, R.J. (1988). *Ethics and regulation of clinical research* (2nd edn). Yale University Press, New Haven, CT.

Levinsky, N.G. (1984). The doctor's master. *New England Journal of Medicine*, 311, 1573–5.

McKneally, M.F., Dickens, B.M., Meslin, E.M., and Singer, P.A. (1997). Bioethics for clinicians. 13. Resource allocation. *Canadian Medical Association Journal*, 157, 163–7.

Martin, D.K., Thiel, E.C., and Singer, P.A. (1999). A new model of advance care planning: observations from people with HIV. *Archives of Internal Medicine*, 159, 86–92.

Mayeux, R. and Schupf, N. (1995). Apolipoprotein E and Alzheimer's disease: the implications of progress in molecular medicine. *American Journal of Public Health*, 85, 1280–4.

Medical Research Council of Canada (1987). *Guidelines on research involving human subjects*. Minister of Supply and Services, Ottawa.

Mitchell, S.L., Sullivan, E.A., and Lipsitz, L.A. (1997). Exclusion of elderly subjects from clinical trials for Parkinson's disease. *Archives of Neurology*, 157, 1393–8.

Molloy, D.W., Silberfeld, M., Darzins, P., *et al.* (1996). Measuring capacity to complete an advance directive. *Journal of the American Geriatrics Society*, 44, 660–4.

Mor, V., Masterson-Allen, S., Goldberg, R.J., Cummings, F.J., Glicksman, A.S., and Fretwell, M.D. (1985). Relationship between age at diagnosis and treatments received by cancer patients. *Journal of the American Geriatrics Society*, 33, 585–9.

Morreim, E.H. (1995). *Balancing act: the new medical ethics of medicine's new economics*. Georgetown University Press, Washington, DC.

National Commission for the Protection of Human Subjects in Biomedical and Behavioral Research (1979). The Belmont Report: ethical principles and guidelines for the protection of human subjects of research. *OPRR Reports*, 18 April, 1–8.

Office for Protection from Research Risks (1993). *Protecting human research subjects: institutional review board guidebook*. United States Government Printing Office, Washington.

Pellegrino, E.D. (1995). Is truth telling to the patient a cultural artefact? In *Health care ethics in Canada* (ed. F. Baylis *et al.*), pp. 55–8. Harcourt Brace, Toronto.

Post, S.G., Whitehouse, P.J., Binstock, R.H., *et al.* (1997). The clinical introduction of genetic testing for Alzheimer disease: an ethical perspective. *Journal of the American Medical Association*, 277, 832–6.

Relkin, N.R., Kwon, Y.J., Tsai, J., and Gandy, S. (1996). The National Institute on Ageing/Alzheimer's Association recommendation on the application of apolipoprotein E genotyping to Alzheimer's disease. *Annals of the New York Academy of Sciences*, 802, 149–71.

Roses, A.D. (1996). Apolipoprotein E and Alzheimer's disease: a rapidly expanding field with medical and epidemiological consequences. *Annals of the New York Academy of Sciences*, 802, 50–7.

Royal College of Physicians (1990). *Guidelines on the practice of ethics committees in medical research*. Royal College of Physicians, London.

Schneiderman, L.J. and Jecker, N.S. (1995). *Wrong medicine: doctors, patients, and futile treatment*. Johns Hopkins University Press, Baltimore, MD.

Siegler, M. (1982). Confidentiality in medicine—a decrepit concept. *New England Journal of Medicine*, 307, 1518–21.

Singer, P.A. (1994). Disease-specific advance directives. *Lancet*, 344, 594–6.

Singer, P.A., Robertson, G., and Roy, D.J. (1996). Bioethics for clinicians. 6. Advance care planning. *Canadian Medical Association Journal*, 155, 1689–92.

Singer, P.A., Martin, D.K., Lavery, J.V., Thiel, E.C., Kelner, M., and Mendelssohn, D.C. (1998). Reconceptualizing advance care planning from the patient's perspective. *Archives of Internal Medicine*, 158, 879–84.

SUPPORT Principal Investigator (1995). A controlled trial to improve care for seriously ill hospitalised patients: the Study to Understand Prognoses and Preferences for Outcomes and Risks of Treatments (SUPPORT). *Journal of the American Medical Association*, **274**, 1591–8.

Taub, H.A. and Baker, M.T. (1984). A re-evaluation of informed consent in the elderly: a method of improving comprehension through direct testing. *Clinical Research*, **32**, 17–21.

Taub, H.A., Baker, M.T., Kline, G.E., and Sturr, J.F. (1987). Comprehension of information by young-old through old-old volunteers. *Experimental Aging Research*, **13**, 173–8.

Teno, J.M., Nelson, H.L., and Lynn, J. (1994). Advance care planning: priorities for ethical and empirical research. *Hastings Center Report*, **24** (Supplement), S32–6.

Thomsen, O.Ø., Wulff, H.R., Martin, A., and Singer, P.A. (1993). What do gastroenterologists in Europe tell cancer patients? *Lancet*, **341**, 473–6.

Trimble, E.L., Carter, C.C., Cain, D., Freidlin, B., Ungerleider, R.S., and Friedman, M.A. (1994). Representation of older patients in cancer treatment trials. *Cancer*, **74** (Supplement), 2208–14.

Weijer, C. (1999). Selecting subjects for participation in clinical research: one sphere of justice. *Journal of Medical Ethics*, **25**, 31–6.

Weijer, C., Singer, P.A., Dickens, B.N., and Workman, S. (1998). Bioethics for clinicians. 16. Dealing with demands for inappropriate treatment. *Canadian Medical Association Journal*, **159**, 817–21.

Weir, B. and Horton, J.R. (1995a). DNA banking and informed consent. Part 1. *IRB: A Review of Human Subjects Research*, **17**(4), 1–4.

Weir, B. and Horton, J.R. (1995b). DNA banking and informed consent. Part 2. *IRB: A Review of Human Subjects Research*, **17**(5,6), 1–8.

Williams, A. (1997). Rationing health care by age. The case for. *British Medical Journal*, **314**, 8–9.

23

Services

23.1 Principles of care

John Grimley Evans

The essential properties of a system of care for older people include the following: comprehensiveness in range; easy accessibility; co-ordination to ensure that it is a system and not a loose collection of separate services; continuity in the sense of avoiding gaps both in content and in time. To these must be added respect for the autonomy of patients and concern for the welfare of their carers.

The characteristics of disease in later life that need to be taken into account in the design of health-care services and in the delivery of care to individual patients are summarized in Table 1. The first four of these characteristics establish a need of older patients who become ill to have timely access to the best facilities of modern health care. The cardinal feature of ageing is loss of adaptability, and attenuation of the conventional symptoms and signs of disease is a manifestation of this. Many of the clinical and diagnostic features of disease are due to the body's inflammatory responses which are often slowed, and may be reduced in intensity, in the older patient. In particular, the response to infection may be cryptic and the localizing signs of inflammation may not appear until later. In the older patient, pneumonia may present with general malaise, perhaps with mental confusion, and the only localizing indication of lung infection may be a rise in the respiratory rate. The febrile response is often reduced, although a fever may be missed through inadequacies in technique of measuring body temperature (Darowski *et al.* 1991), and failure to allow a patient time to warm up after a cold journey to the doctor's office or hospital.

A second example lies with intra-abdominal catastrophes. With acute appendicitis or even gastrointestinal perforation, localizing signs in the abdomen may be lacking and pain may be absent or apparently trivial. Abdominal radiography and ultrasound may be required to reveal disease that in a younger patient would be dramatically obvious from clinical examination. In general therefore, older patients need more investigations than younger patients in order to achieve comparable levels of diagnostic accuracy.

Age-associated loss of adaptability also underlies the rapid deterioration of older people if disease is not diagnosed and treated promptly. Furthermore, because an older person's physiological reserves may be low, recovery may be compromised by delays in treatment. Complication rates in illnesses of later life tend to be high, again because of loss of adaptability, but also because of interactions between multiple illnesses and their treatments. This aspect of disease in later life calls for vigilance and frequent, regular, reviews by skilled staff.

The second group of characteristics in Table 1 indicate the requirement for care to be deployed within the context of a broad approach not only to the presenting disease but also to the social circumstances and future needs of older patients. In particular, loss of adaptability means that the older patient is more likely to need a programme of active rehabilitation to restore physical, mental, and social function following illness from which a younger patient might be expected to recover spontaneously. The rehabilitative phase must be seen and provided as an integral part of acute care.

The aim of care for older people is most often to return them to life in their community. The caring team needs to be aware of details of their patient's home circumstances and to be able to deal with the often complex arrangements for providing an appropriate mix of medical and social domiciliary after-care. Doctors also have a responsibility to ensure that the care they offer is the most cost-effective way of dealing with the problems presented, and that the care is provided in such a way that all those who could benefit from it have access to it. Rationing is the responsibility of politicians not clinicians.

Table 2 outlines the four-stage geriatric process. The first stage of assessment includes an accurate diagnosis and estimation of prognosis. In addition to knowing what diseases the patient is suffering from it is essential also to make a functional assessment in the broad domains of physical, mental, and social abilities. To facilitate audit and ensure an adequate basic review, standardized measures of functional abilities form an important part of this process, but should not be regarded as sufficient in themselves. Patients are being assessed, not processed. Resources available for care from family, neighbours, and friends need to be identified, including an appraisal of whether that care is likely to be available in the future. Some illnesses in later life herald the breakdown of informal systems of care and it is important to identify this situation as early as possible. Appraisal of the patient's educational and cultural background contributes to an understanding

Table 1 Characteristics of disease in old age

Calling for rapid access to high-quality medical care
Multiple disease
Non-specific or cryptic presentation
Rapid deterioration if untreated
High incidence of complications (of disease and treatment)

Calling for specialist expertise
Need for active rehabilitation
Importance of environmental factors
Complexity of community care
Economic management of resources

Table 2 The process of geriatric care

Assessment
Health (diagnoses, prognosis)
Function (physical, mental, social)
Resources (culture, education, social, economic)

Agree objectives of care
What does the patient want?
What is feasible?

Specify the management plan
To close the ecological gap between what the patient can do and what the environment demands
    Therapeutically—improve the patient
    Prosthetically—reduce environmental demands

Regular review
Is progress as expected?
Does the plan need changing?

Table 3 The geriatric team

Core members
Doctor
Nurse
Occupational therapist
Physiotherapist
Social worker

Other contributors
Carers
Chiropodist
Clergy
Dietitian
Pharmacist
Psychogeriatrician
Speech therapist
Voluntary agencies

of what they may hope to attain from treatment and also facilitates communication. It is important for the doctor and other members of the care team to use language that the patient can understand and sufficient empathy so that they in turn can understand the patient. Difficulties in this area are obvious enough where patient and doctor differ in religion or race, but it is also necessary to be sensitive to cohort differences in value systems and use of language between older and younger members of the same cultural group.

The second stage of care, the setting of care objectives, is the phase that is often omitted with younger patients. With younger patients it is usually assumed, not always appropriately, that care has the single objective of prolonging life. Older patients may have other priorities. They may fear disability, and the dependence and indignity that disability may bring, more than they fear death. Conversely, they may have some very specific objectives that they wish to attain within what they know is likely to be a short time remaining to them.

Setting objectives for care therefore requires a dialogue between the doctor who knows what could be done and the patient who must decide what should be done. Particular problems arise where for one reason or another the patient is unable to take part in this dialogue, for example because of confusion or aphasia. The legal and ethical aspects of this situation differ between countries. The use of valid and relevant advance directives varies from country to country. In the United States family members have the right and duty to act as proxies for the patient. Several studies have shown that proxies may not accurately understand the patient's wishes even when that proxy is someone the patient thinks will understand him or her (Ouslander *et al.* 1989). Until recently in the United Kingdom proxy decisions on behalf of adults had no legal standing and the responsibility for decisions about treatment rested with the clinician acting in the patient's 'best interests' but always having ascertained the opinions of family members and friends. The advantages of this approach include less use of intensive but futile care demanded by families not wishing to be thought insufficiently caring, and less risk of families carrying a burden of guilt in later years from anxiety over whether or not they had made the right decision. The skill and tact with which clinicians conduct these often complex negotiations are important to

the success of this approach which, unfortunately, may become obsolete under pressure for more legalistic procedures.

Having agreed objectives of care with the patient, the caring team then has to translate objectives into a management plan. Table 3 lists the members of the core team who need to work in concert with each other and with other professionals listed in the table, and in continuous dialogue with family and other informal carers. The plan needs to specify what care is to be given and by whom, and expectations for the timing of intermediate goals.

In many situations, for example with a patient who has suffered a stroke, the aim has to be to reduce residual disability by closing the ecological gap between what a patient's environment is going to demand and what the patient is capable of doing. Therapeutic interventions are aimed at improving the patient's function. Prosthetic interventions aim at reducing the demands of the environment. Therefore the management plan has to consider both aspects. Prosthetic interventions include physical modifications to a patient's home, or even rehousing, and the provision of domiciliary care of various forms. The programme of prosthetic care has to be thought about early in setting the management plan to ensure that when the patient's function has been improved therapeutically to its best, there is then no delay while the home is prepared. The planning of prosthetic care can often be aided by an early visit by the occupational therapist and physiotherapist to the patient's home to identify what future problems there are likely to be. Prior to discharge, it is often beneficial for therapists to accompany the patient on a further home visit so that he or she can try out various aspects of daily living under observation. Any remaining gaps between environmental demands and the patient's capabilities can thereby be identified and rectified. Ideally a further visit 2 weeks after discharge is desirable to ensure that the plan was realistic and that all the domiciliary services that were expected have indeed been put in place and are effective. Although this example relates to a patient in hospital with a stroke, the same principles should govern the approach to a patient with any disability, whether in hospital, at home, at the outpatient clinic or in the day hospital.

Regular review of the patient's progress is also an essential part of geriatric care. At least once a week the patient's progress should be reviewed by the team to make sure that progress is as expected and that no new problems have arisen. If progress is not as expected the situation needs to be reviewed to see if something was overlooked in the initial evaluation, whether the plan was unrealistic, or whether something new has intervened. A common example of the latter is of the stroke patient who makes good progress to begin with but then 'stalls' owing to an intercurrent depressive reaction. Sometimes the problem may not lie so much with the patient as with the informal carers who are perhaps communicating to the patient their own anxieties about their ability to continue caring or, indeed, even their own depression.

The design of services

These principles of care can be applied whether the older patient's problems are to be dealt with in primary or secondary care. In practice the more seriously ill older people will need access to hospital care. The need to combine the best of modern high-technology medicine with specific geriatric expertise, has led to a range of designs of hospital-based services for older people. In the United Kingdom, where geriatric medicine has been developed from a base in secondary care, three basic models have evolved (Royal College of Physicians 1994). The first, so-called 'traditional' model is of a separate service for those older people selected for referral to it by general practitioners or other doctors. Since the referring doctors may or may not be sufficiently knowledgeable about the functions of the geriatric service, referrals may not be appropriate or timely. This model is now largely obsolete in England and Wales. In the 1970s two models were developed that aimed to bring geriatric expertise to bear on the acute as well as the rehabilitative phase of care for older people. In the 'age-defined model', parallel medical services are set up, a general medical service for patients below a specified age, and geriatric services for patients above that age (O'Brien et al. 1973). Resources are not always equitably distributed between the two services, and this arrangement can lead to older patients having poorer access than younger patients to specialist services such as cardiology or nephrology. This is a pervasive problem in the United Kingdom; one survey found that as a matter of policy, 19 per cent of British coronary care units had an upper age limit for admission ranging as low as 65 years (Dudley and Burns 1992). In the 'integrated model', doctors with special responsibility for elderly patients join their colleagues in other medical specialties in providing acute general medical services, in addition to being responsible for the rehabilitation and community liaison work needed by a proportion of older patients coming to hospital (Grimley Evans 1983). One aim of this model is to ensure that older people have access to the full range of modern medical specialties from which they can benefit. There has been no formal comparison of these two modern models but both aim at providing a service characterized by comprehensiveness and continuity from a patient's acute admission to his or her return home. Geriatric services in the United Kingdom have evolved in the context of a universal primary care system deployed by general practitioners who are responsible for the medical care of patients living in the community but who do not usually have care of hospital beds. The United Kingdom also benefits from a formal specialty of psychogeriatrics, based in hospital but working largely and increasingly with patients in their own homes.

In North America, specialist geriatric expertise has been provided to older patients in hospital and ambulatory clinics by geriatric evaluation units and visiting teams. Most depend on referral from non-geriatric sources and therefore are subject to the limitations of the traditional model in the United Kingdom. The practice of geriatric medicine was developed empirically by the specialty in the United Kingdom from its foundation in 1948, but has only been adequately evaluated in the United States. Overall, randomized controlled trials in the United States indicate that geriatric inpatient units and outpatient services are more effective than conventional care in improving patient function and in returning them to their own homes and maintaining them there (Williams et al. 1987; Boult et al. 1994). In some circumstances at least, geriatric services may also reduce mortality and health-care costs (Rubenstein et al. 1984, 1988). It seems that to be effective, geriatric teams must be able to implement their recommendations directly. Purely advisory services are generally not successful; a meta-analysis suggesting a beneficial effect (Stuck et al. 1993) was probably subject to publication bias (Egger et al. 1997).

Worldwide, there is a great diversity of models of geriatric care. Several countries in continental Europe do not yet recognize geriatrics as a medical specialty. In some instances this is because of fears that geriatricians would take money as well as work from other specialties, especially primary care. This may change as sufficient nations that do recognize geriatrics have now joined the European Union for the specialty to have an official European existence. In the United Kingdom geriatric medicine is now the largest hospital specialty of adult medicine. Given present demographic trends this is logical, but it is probably a development made uniquely possible by the conditions of medical practice under the British National Health Service.

In the developing world, where more than half of the world's population of older people now live (Chapter 1.3), models of geriatric care from the developed world are unlikely to be directly relevant for at least another generation. There the emphasis has to be on the development of primary care (often not health care) built on locally identified resources. A recognition at governmental level of the special needs of older people coupled with the principles of care for them can inform the gradual growth of a rational structure of health and social support (Expert Committee on Health of the Elderly 1989).

However, there are many problems still to be solved. Governments may not perceive, or may be unwilling to acknowledge, that traditional forms of family support for older people are no longer effective or appropriate. Economics may outweigh humanity in presenting old people as unproductive and therefore of low social value. In a better world, aid-giving nations would insist that part of their donations should be used to provide the services needed to substitute for the destruction of traditional social structures by economic development. Such a world has yet to be born.

References

Boult, C., Boult, L. Murphy, C., Ebbitt, B., Luptak, M., and Kane, R.L. (1994). A controlled trial of outpatient geriatric evaluation and management. *Journal of the American Geriatrics Society*, 42, 465–70.

Darowski, A., Najim, Z., Weinberg, J., and Guz, A. (1991). The febrile response to mild infections in elderly hospital inpatients. *Age and Ageing*, 20, 193–8.

Dudley, N.J. and Burns, E. (1992). The influence of age on policies for admission and thrombolysis in coronary care units in the United Kingdom. *Age and Ageing*, 21, 95–8.

Egger, M., Smith, G.C., Schneider, M., and Minder, C. (1997). Bias in meta-analysis detected by a simple graphical test. *British Medical Journal*, 315, 629–34.

Expert Committee on Health of the Elderly (1989). *Health of the elderly*. Technical Report Series 779. Geneva, World Health Organization.

Grimley Evans, J. (1983). Integration of geriatric with general medical services in Newcastle. *Lancet*, i, 1430–3.

O'Brien, T.D., Joshi, D.M., and Warren, E.W. (1973). No apology for geriatrics. *British Medical Journal*, i, 277–80.

Ouslander, J.G., Tymchuk, A.J., and Rahbar, B. (1989). Health care decisions among elderly long-term care residents and their potential proxies. *Archives of Internal Medicine*, 149, 1367–72.

Royal College of Physicians (1994). *Ensuring equity and quality of care for elderly people. The interface between geriatric medicine and general (internal) medicine*. Royal College of Physicians, London.

Rubenstein, L.Z. Josephson, K.R., Wieland, G.D., English, P.A., Sayre, J.A., and Kane, R.L. (1984). Effectiveness of a geriatric evaluation unit. A randomized clinical trial. *New England Journal of Medicine*, 311, 1664–70.

Rubenstein, L.Z., Wieland, G.D., Josephson, K.R., Rosbrook, B., Sayre, J., and Kane, R.L. (1988). Improved survival for frail elderly inpatients on a geriatric evaluation unit (GEU): who benefits? *Journal of Clinical Epidemiology*, 41, 441–50.

Stuck, A.E., Siu, A.L., Wieland, G.D., Adams, J., and Rubenstein, L.Z. (1993). Comprehensive geriatric assessment: a meta-analysis of controlled trials. *Lancet*, 342, 1032–6.

Williams, M.E., Williams, T.F., Zimmer, J.G., Hall, W.J., and Podgorski, C.A. (1987). How does the team approach to outpatient geriatric evaluation compare with traditional care: a report of a randomized controlled trial. *Journal of the American Geriatrics Society*, 35, 1071–8.

23.2 Institutional care

Gabriel Gold and Vincent Marchello

Unlike acute care, institutional care varies greatly from country to country, both in its organizational structure and financial support. Although many equate it with long-term care, the two terms are not equal. In fact, a large portion of long-term care is community based. Institutional care can involve both young and old disabled individuals. The goals of care and expectations are quite different for these two age groups. This chapter addresses institutional care for older people.

Demographics, costs, and payers

The continued expansion of the older population and the high prevalence of chronic disease and disability in elderly people have led to a dramatic increase in institutional care. Institutionalization rates vary greatly from country to country (Fig. 1). In 1964 approximately half a million people lived in nursing homes in the United States (National Center for Health Statistics 1970). By 1987, this number had grown to nearly 2 million people representing 6.7 per cent of the American population aged 65 years or more (Freiman and Murtaugh 1995).

It has been estimated that 43 per cent of people who turned 65 years of age in 1990 will enter a nursing home at some time before they die (Kemper and Murtaugh 1991).

In 1993 in the United States, nursing home expenditures reached $70 billion and accounted for 8 per cent of health-care spending. With the continuing growth of the elderly population this expansion is very likely to continue. Approximately 40 per cent of institutional care expenditures were paid for out of pocket by residents and their families and the rest by public funds. Although private long-term care insurance is available, this option has not proven very popular. In 1995 only 2.9 million policies had been sold for a population aged over 65 years of more than 31 million (Temkin-Greener and Meiners 1995).

Institutional care should not be viewed as an isolated system; its important interactions with acute care should be understood (Freiman and Murtaugh 1995). In fact, long-term care residents account for a significant portion of acute health-care costs. In 1987, 816 000 people were transferred from nursing homes to hospitals representing 8.5 per cent of all Medicare hospital admissions for people over 65 years of age in the United States (Freiman and Murtaugh 1995). Furthermore, in many instances the acute hospital is the portal of entry into long-term care. Cost shifting from acute to long-term care can also occur. After the introduction of the diagnosis-related groups based prospective payment system in the United States, the number of patients in hospital discharged back to their homes decreased and the number of prolonged nursing home stays increased (Khan *et al.* 1990). Modifications in long-term care policies such as increasing the number of direct admissions from home to institutions or providing on-site appropriate treatment of acute decompensations within the nursing home can have a significant impact on both acute and long-term care costs (Zimmer *et al.* 1988).

Risk factors for institutionalization

Many studies have sought to identify individuals at high risk of institutionalization. Some risk factors such as functional impairment,

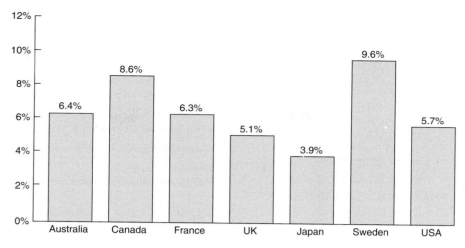

Fig. 1 Percentage of elderly people living in institutions (mid-1980s or early 1990s data depending on the country). (Data from Taeuber (1993), Grundy (1996), and Hoskins (1996).)

previous institutionalization, and living alone seem universal and have been reported in the United States, Europe, and Japan (Wachtel *et al*. 1987; Ishizaki *et al*. 1995; McCormick *et al*. 1995). For other risk factors, results vary depending on the methodology and the population investigated.

Nursing home patients tend to fall into two groups. Residents who stay for a short period of time include individuals admitted for rehabilitative or terminal care while those who stay longer usually suffer from more chronic disease and are no longer able to live in the community. In the United States, approximately one-third of lifetime nursing home risk applies to stays of 90 days or less (Liu *et al*. 1994). Risk factors for institutionalization may be different in short stay residents. In one study that specifically addressed this issue, cognitive impairment, dependency in activities of daily living, and prior nursing home use which are strongly associated with long-term stays were not significant predictors of short stay admission (Liu *et al*. 1994).

Financial status may also be an important factor. In one study of over 50 000 elderly people living in Monroe County, New York, the risk of nursing home admission was markedly lower for private-pay elderly people than for poorer individuals who were on Medicaid. The impact of risk factors, such as hospitalization for dementia, was 10 times greater in the latter group (Temkin-Greener and Meiners 1995).

Risk of institutionalization is influenced by patient character-istics, but also depends on supports available and caregiver characteristics. In a study from Baltimore, Maryland, individuals already receiving community-based long-term care were more likely to be admitted to a nursing home if their caregivers lived separately from them, had job-related time conflicts, or were stressed by caregiving (Tsuji *et al*. 1995). In a New Haven, Connecticut, study of a population sample, risk of institutionalization was 41 per cent lower for those with a living spouse than for those without, 27 per cent lower for those with at least one daughter than for those without (sons conferred no benefit), and 21 per cent lower for those with at least one living sibling than for those without (Freedman 1996).

Evaluation and care of the institutionalized patient

Institutionalization is usually the result of marked functional or cognitive impairment and the absence of adequate social supports in the community, but beyond this common admission pathway nursing home residents represent a very heterogeneous population. Clearly, the evaluation and management of an individual with severe cognitive impairment and behavioural symptoms and that of a functionally dependent cancer patient with a few months left to live have little in common. The goals of care must be tailored to the individual and it is impossible to recommend a common approach to all nursing home residents. Some general guidelines can nevertheless be proposed. These are discussed below.

The admission evaluation should go beyond the traditional history and physical examination, and requires a team approach. It should include a comprehensive assessment, using validated tools (Table 1), and should lead to the establishment of an appropriate plan of care. The goals of care for each resident need to be well defined upon admission and reviewed on a regular basis.

Goals of care in an institutional setting may differ from those of the acute hospital. The emphasis is placed on maximizing function and quality of life rather than curing disease. In the United States a standard Minimum Data Set is required to be prepared and peri-odically updated on all residents of all nursing homes; this data set is then used to guide therapeutic services and to trigger steps for control/improvement of quality of care. It is important to spend time with the resident's family, to address their fears and feelings of guilt, when present, and to enlist their participation as allies in the development of the plan of care. Follow-up care includes interventions to handle acute events, periodic reassessments of the patient's status, and regular re-evaluation of the plan of care. Regular visits, for example monthly (or at a minimum bi-monthly) provide an opportunity to review the resident's and nurses' concerns, monitor vital signs in-cluding weight, identify changes in the physical examination, re-examine the medication list, and review the care plan. Yearly as-sessments are more comprehensive (Table 2).

Table 1 Admission assessment of nursing home residents

Assessment components	Proposed assessment instrument or intervention
Functional status	Activities of Daily Living Scale (Katz *et al.* 1963) Instrumental Activities of Daily Living Scale (Lawton *et al.* 1982) Functional Independence Measure (State University of New York 1994)
Mental status	Mini-Mental State (Folstein *et al.* 1975)
Affective status	Geriatric Depression Scale (Yesavage and Brink 1983)
Continence	History and observation Bladder and bowel incontinence record
Mobility, gait, and risk of falls	Get Up and Go Test (Mathias *et al.* 1986) Performance-oriented assessment of mobility (Tinetti 1986)
Nutritional status	Mini Nutritional Assessment (Guigoz *et al.* 1996)
Hearing	Screening with an audioscope and referral to audiology if abnormal
Vision	Referral to optometry/ophthalmology
Dental status	Referral to dentist
Disease prevention	Date of last influenza and pneumococcal vaccines Purified protein derivative status
Advance directives, hospital admission and resuscitation preferences	See text

Nutrition

Malnutrition is particularly common in nursing homes (Abbasi and Rudman 1993). Nutritional status should be evaluated upon admission and then once a year, and also following episodes of acute illness. The Mini Nutritional Assessment (Guigoz *et al.* 1996), which has been validated in elderly populations, is a useful screening tool for this purpose (see Chapter 27). Monitoring a resident's weight on a monthly basis can also help detect weight loss in a timely fashion.

The management of malnutrition should include identification and correction, if possible, of the cause. Meals should be served in a pleasant environment that provides an opportunity for socialization. Individual preferences should be taken into account. Frail and dependent residents should be assisted with feeding. Enteral tube feeding can sustain weight and maintain or improve nutritional status in such conditions as advanced dementia or swallowing disorders which are common in institutions (but note the importance of advance directives, as discussed below).

Nasogastric tubes are relatively easy to insert but they are of smaller calibre and residents often repeatedly attempt to remove them. Gastrostomy and jejunostomy tubes are generally better tolerated. Endoscopic insertion of a gastrostomy tube is a relatively simple procedure with few complications.

Few decisions in long-term care are as difficult as those dealing with artificial nutrition. Although enteral tube feeding can improve nutritional status, its effect on quality of life is less clear. While some feel that the provision of artificial nutrition is basic humane care it is regarded by most as medical treatment with its potential risks and complications (Hodges and Tolle 1994). As such, it must conform to the patient's wishes. This can be relatively straightforward when the patient has the capacity for making decisions; if not it can be quite complex. Advance directives can be of particular help in these situations.

Autonomy and advance directives

Nursing home residents are rarely consulted about medical decision-making; their fears regarding illness and dying are infrequently explored, and their wishes regarding resuscitation, admission to hospital, and medical interventions are rarely discussed. A recent audit of 241 residents in 17 nursing homes in the United Kingdom revealed that in only 39 per cent of the cases had residents or their representatives contributed to the care plan. Furthermore, only 17 per cent of those unable to articulate their choice had a named independent advocate (Brocklehurst and Dickinson 1996).

Institutionalized elderly people often suffer from cognitive impairment and are unable to express their wishes or participate fully in their own care. Advance directives such as living wills or proxy appointments, where these have legal standing, can facilitate decision-making that respects a resident's values and wishes.

A living will enables a competent adult to leave written instructions regarding future care. A health-care proxy appointment enables a competent adult to appoint an agent for health-care decisions in case of future incapacity. Individuals entering nursing homes have frequently already lost the ability to participate in medical decisions. Ideally, community-dwelling individuals should be encouraged by their doctors to designate a proxy or write a living will (in countries where these have legal standing) at a the time when they are competent (Meier *et al.* 1996).

Restraints

Physical and chemical restraints have long been a controversial yet frequently employed modality in the care of nursing home residents in the United States. They are used in an effort to promote safety, prevent falls, and control violent behaviour. Unfortunately, restraints

Table 2 Suggested format for annual physician review of long-term nursing home residents

---

Active medical problem list
....

Medical history
Description of acute medical conditions that have occurred in the past year
Comment on results of laboratory tests to monitor active medical problems
Summarize symptoms relevant to active medical problems
List current medications
....

Symptom review
Review symptoms common in nursing home residents
....

Physical examination
Note any new physical findings
....

Functional status
Briefly summarize current status, highlighting changes in
   (a) ability to perform basic activities of daily living
   (b) mobility
   (c) continence
   (d) cognitive function
   (e) affective status (including behavioural disturbances)
Assess rehabilitation potential (if relevant)
....

Social status
Review any family involvement, family concerns, or problems
....

Health maintenance
Review the results of screening evaluations, including
   (a) audiological
   (b) ophthalmological/optometric
   (c) dental
   (d) podiatric
   (e) tuberculosis testing
....

Advanced directives
Existence of directive
Identification of proxy
Can the resident still make or participate in decisions about his or her health care?
Intensity of care (no cardiopulmonary resuscitation etc.)
....

Plans
Summarize overall goals for care
List specific plans related to findings from the entire review

---

Reproduced with permission from Ouslander and Osterweil (1994).

may actually increase the risk of injury producing falls (Tinetti *et al.* 1992). Physical restraints have not only been associated with increased injury, but also increased mental impairment, decubitus ulcers, nosocomial infections, and increased agitation (Burton *et al.* 1992). Surveys performed in the 1970s and 1980s in the United States revealed a physical restraint prevalence as high as 75 per cent in some facilities and psychotropic drug use as high as 90 per cent (Tinetti *et al.* 1991; Harrington *et al.* 1992). A more recent study showed a 43 per cent prevalence of physical restraint use in nursing homes in Sweden (Karlsson *et al.* 1996). In a recent clinical trial of interventions aimed at reducing the use of restraints in nursing homes, Capezuti *et al.* (1998) showed that restraint removal did not lead to increases in falls or fall-related injuries.

Many factors such as a better understanding of the risks related to restraints, an increase in public awareness, and dignity issues led towards a concern regarding the appropriateness of physical and chemical restraints. This culminated in the United States in a detailed regulatory framework governing the use of such restraints, as contained in the Nursing Home Reform Amendments of the Omnibus Budget Reconciliation Act of 1987 (Anonymous 1995). This Act placed freedom from restraint within the broader context of residents' rights and quality of life. According to these regulations, when a physical restraint is employed, the facility must demonstrate consultation with physical and/or occupational therapy and documentation that less restrictive measures were considered. These and other requirements are listed in Table 3.

The challenges put forth by this new legislation, which was enacted in 1991, entailed reformulation of policy, re-education of staff, exploration of alternatives to restraint use, and, most importantly, adoption of new attitudes. Restraints should be avoided. Antipsychotic drugs should only be given to treat specific conditions such as psychotic symptoms and specific behaviours that cause residents to

Table 3 Requirements for the use of physical restraints (Omnibus Budget Reconciliation Act 1987)

Consultation with physical and/or occupational therapy
Documentation that less restrictive measures were considered
Doctor's order
Consent of the resident or family
Documentation that the restraint enables the resident to maintain maximum functional and psychosocial well being

endanger themselves or others. They should not be prescribed to control resident behaviour for the convenience of the facility.

Preventive care in the nursing home

Preventive care in the nursing home presents philosophical, scientific, and ethical problems. Is there a role for preventive interventions in frail and very elderly institutionalized population whose life expectancy may be reduced to just a few years? Is it important and cost-effective to screen for conditions that may not become clinically significant for several years and for which effective treatment may not be available or feasible?

Although prevention of the diseases and disabilities of old age should begin early in youth and middle age, some interventions, such as the treatment of isolated systolic hypertension, have been shown to remain quite effective even in very old patients (SHEP Cooperative Research Group 1991).

Unfortunately, much of the clinical and laboratory screening performed annually and upon admission to nursing homes is derived from the study of younger and healthier individuals and may be of limited value (Wolf-Klein et al. 1985; Kim and Berlowitz 1994). The most appropriate preventive interventions in the nursing home are those directed at preservation of function and quality of life.

Tertiary prevention, which is aimed at preventing the complications of disease, should be emphasized. Screening for hearing and visual problems, cognitive disorders, mobility impairment, malnutrition, incontinence as well as optometry, podiatry, and dental needs is recommended (Ouslander and Osterweil 1994).

Prevention of contagious diseases is also important. Tuberculosis can be endemic and epidemic in nursing homes and remains a major concern (Narain et al. 1985; Stead et al. 1985). Purified protein derivative skin testing should be performed on all entering residents who are not known to have had a positive result or who have had tuberculosis. When the initial test is negative, a two-step testing procedure should be performed (second skin test 1 to 2 weeks after a negative first test) to check for a booster phenomenon. This occurs when waning skin reactivity is boosted by the initial purified protein derivative injection resulting in a positive response to the second test (Finucane 1988). A vaccination programme should be in place with policies and procedures for each individual vaccine. These include influenza vaccine annually and pneumococcal vaccine upon admission (if not already vaccinated within the last 6 years). Tetanus and diphtheria immunization are recommended in the absence of a clear vaccination history (US Preventive Services Task Force 1995). Influenza is a major cause of excess death in institutions. Influenza vaccine is highly effective in preventing complications, hospital admission, and death from both influenza A and influenza B.

Despite strong recommendations to vaccinate elderly people, particularly those living in residential care, many institutions do not have effective policies. In a recent study of 49 old people's homes in the United Kingdom, vaccine uptake was only 39.6 per cent (Warren et al. 1995). Amantadine and rimantadine are effective in the early treatment and prevention of influenza A but not influenza B. Their use has been advocated for the control of influenza outbreaks in nursing homes (Gomolin et al. 1995). Unfortunately, both drugs have adverse side-effects which are more prominent in elderly people and drug resistance can develop. Vaccine remains the most effective and best tolerated prophylaxis against influenza (Nicholson 1996).

Infection control

Institutionalized older people are at particularly high risk for infection because their immunity may be impaired by age and comorbidities while at the same time they live in a closed environment. New arrivals from the acute hospital setting may bring virulent and resistant organisms which are difficult to treat. The average incidence rate in American long-term care facilities is between one and two infections per resident per year (Yoshikawa and Normal 1995). These infections are responsible for a significant portion of acute hospital transfers and mortality. In 1 year, more than half of a nursing home's residents receive at least one course of antibiotics (Warren et al. 1991).

The major elements of a successful infection control programme include, a rational approach to prevention and screening (including a vaccination programme), a procedure for identifying and investigating infections, treatment of infections, and supervision of epidemics.

The facility must educate its staff in proper preventive measures including the use of universal precautions, the importance of simple hand washing, aseptic technique, and proper disposal of contaminated materials and solutions. A procedure for reporting infections should be developed.

Patients from hospital may cause concern over potentially infectious agents such as methicillin-resistant Staphylococcus aureus, vancomycin-resistant Enterococcus, or Clostridium difficile. Awareness of these infections and appropriate precautions are important in minimizing spread to other nursing home patients.

Most facilities have specific policies and procedures for identifying and investigating infections. Infections are classified according to location, such as urinary tract, respiratory tract, skin, and soft tissue. The infection control co-ordinator, usually a registered nurse, works closely with the medical director tracking and following infections in the facility ensuring proper treatment protocols and responses. Routine committee meetings are scheduled to review statistics and rates of infection. Quality assurance reports are discussed. The information from these meetings is used to educate staff and improve the quality of care rendered in these facilities. Epidemics in nursing homes are a serious matter with potentially devastating results. Fortunately outbreaks are infrequent. An interdisciplinary team effort is critical in containing outbreaks when they occur.

Quality assurance

Quality assurance programmes which began in the 1970s comprised the first attempts to measure health-care quality. The conceptual framework for quality assurance was first described by Donabedian (1978), who stated that quality assurance is defined by structure, process, and outcome. Structure refers to the material elements used to provide care such as staff, space, equipment, etc., process includes the actual delivery of care, and outcome refers to specific changes in health status which result from that care.

Quality improvement (also known as continuous quality improvement or total quality management) represents an advance on quality assurance because it incorporates specific principles of system change which had originally been devised and tested for industry. These principles, originally described by Edwards-Deming, include both philosophical and statistical methodologies (Berwick 1989; Kritchevsky and Simmons 1991).

The push to introduce principles of quality assurance and quality improvement into nursing homes is relatively recent. A major barrier to the implementation of these principles has been the identification of valid quality indicators. Most authorities now agree that these can include structural indicators such as staffing ratios, process indicators such as use of restraints, and outcome indicators such as decubitus ulcers (Institute of Medicine 1986).

Quality assurance and quality improvement programmes in long-term care require committees. Successful approaches necessitate facility-wide participation involving the administrative staff and the direct primary care providers. The concept of quality improvement evaluates and addresses all areas, not only those where a problem exists, thereby improving the overall system of care.

Medical education and long-term care

Medical education is traditionally oriented towards hospital-based acute care. This provides little exposure to the natural course of chronic illness.

With the modern trend towards ever shorter hospital stays, students and house staff in traditional programmes are more rarely exposed to follow-up care. In extreme cases, trainees essentially shepherd patients through medical tests while most of the decisions are made both before and after the hospital admission. Another model, a multisite medical school which includes not only hospitals but also such settings as home care, hospices, and nursing homes, can provide a unique understanding of the natural course of illness (Butler 1992). In their report on medical education, the Institute of Medicine recommended that medical students and resident doctors gain experience in long-term care facilities (Dans and Kerr 1979). In 1983 the Association of American Medical Colleges departed from its traditional reticence in addressing categorical subjects in medical school curricula and published a guideline for geriatrics curriculum assessment, outlining ways in which courses in basic science and

clinical medicine could be strengthened in the areas of geriatrics and gerontology (Executive Council of the Association of American Medical Colleges 1983). The Association of American Medical Colleges indicated that medical schools should accept responsibility for offering a variety of clinical settings (including ambulatory, long-term institution, and home care experiences) through which students can learn special arrangements for the care, diagnosis, and treatment of older patients. Although efforts at implementing geriatric training in nursing homes have been hampered by a lack of qualified teachers, most medical schools now offer training in geriatrics and long-term care.

These programmes allow students to develop their fund of geriatric knowledge further, learn specific geriatric skills, and develop into comprehensive practitioners who can apply the team approach to address all the medical, functional, psychosocial, and ethical aspects of caring for elderly people (Gold 1993). Continuing professional education in geriatrics for doctors and other professionals already in practice is also receiving increasing attention.

Research is another major responsibility of the academic nursing home. Chronically ill elderly people, particularly the very old, have often been excluded from scientific studies (Bene and Liston 1997). Long-term care institutions offer significant advantages for the study of this population and also represent the most appropriate site for research into costs and quality of nursing home care. Nursing home based studies have increased in quantity and quality over the past decade (Katz *et al.* 1995). Unfortunately, many barriers need to be overcome: administrators may be reluctant to bear the increased cost and paperwork, research may disrupt the daily routines, the staff may be unwilling to participate, the selective nature of an institutional population may not be appropriate for some studies, families may be unwilling to co-operate with investigators, and informed consent may be difficult to obtain. Ethical issues must be carefully addressed since study participants are often mentally and functionally impaired and represent a particularly vulnerable group.

Role of the medical director

The role of the medical director encompasses not only clinical oversight of the medical care rendered, but also administrative functions such as policy development and quality assurance. The role of the medical director can be classified into several different areas.

Organizing the medical staff

There are two models of primary-care coverage in nursing homes. The closed system model involves full- or part-time employment of the medical staff by the nursing facility. In an open system, doctors practising in the community carry a panel of patients in the nursing home. Doctors and, in some countries, other personnel such as physician assistants and nurse practitioners, are employed to deliver medical care to nursing home residents. The medical director is responsible for appointing and checking the credentials of all doctors and other equivalent personnel, and ensuring that the medical coverage meets the needs of the nursing facility. He or she must serve as an opinion leader and a role model, and must educate caregivers and provide specific feedback to all doctors.

Overseeing policies and procedures

The medical director is responsible for participating in the co-ordination and development of policies and procedures relating to patient care in the nursing home. These policies and procedures must accurately reflect statutory regulations, and doctors and other staff must be educated by the medical director about the value of following them. The medical director must also help to implement procedures and evaluate their effectiveness.

Establishing and using committees effectively

Most nursing homes now include many committees addressing such issues as infection control, ethics, pharmacy, safety, emergency pro-cedures, and quality assurance. Establishing committees and using them effectively is an important role for the medical director. Par-ticipation in committees represents an opportunity to interact with other institutional staff, help direct care, and affect change.

Overseeing employee health programmes

The medical department in nursing facilities is responsible for de-veloping and implementing an employee health programme within the institution. Components of employee health include the following:

- ensuring that employees are physically and mentally capable of performing their duties;
- ensuring appropriate handling of occupational injuries;
- ensuring the safety of the workplace;
- encouraging personal health by utilizing periodic assessments such as medical questionnaires.

Direct patient care

Many medical directors are the primary doctor for a portion of the residents in their facility. They may also be called upon in emergency situations. This provides the opportunity to function as a role model and to become fully familiar with the system of care. In one study, 19 per cent of medical directors indicated that direct patient care and acting as a doctor of last resort were the most important tasks they performed (Elton 1993).

Leadership

The role of the medical director is currently being redefined. The medical director is a key player in improving the quality of care in the facility, disseminating information, educating staff, and promoting research. Frail institutionalized elderly people residing in nursing homes deserve to be cared for by dedicated and knowledgeable professionals, and to receive high quality, individualized care. It is the responsibility of the medical director to ensure that this occurs.

Conclusion

Residents in long-term care institutions should receive the best possible care available and should be allowed to benefit from continued advances in the body of knowledge of geriatrics. At the same time, it should be recognized that the institution is also their home. It must meet their social needs and respect their privacy and autonomy. A multidisciplinary team of dedicated and knowledgeable professionals is essential to address the multiple medical, psychiatric, rehabilitative, and social aspects of caring for institutionalized elderly people.

References

Abbasi, A.A. and Rudman, D. (1993). Observations on the prevalence of protein-calorie under-nutrition in VA nursing homes. *Journal of the American Geriatrics Society*, **41**, 117–21.

Anonymous (1995). *The OBRA'87 Enforcement Rule: implications for attending physicians and medical directors*. American Medical Directors Association, Columbia, MD.

Bene, J. and Liston, R. (1997). The special problems of conducting clinical trials in elderly patients. *Reviews in Clinical Gerontology*, 7, 1–3.

Berwick, D.M. (1989). Continuous improvement as an ideal in healthcare. *New England Journal of Medicine*, **320**, 1424–5.

Brocklehurst, J. and Dickinson, E. (1996). Autonomy for elderly people in long-term care. *Age and Ageing*, **2**, 329–32.

Burton, L.C., German, P.S., Rovner, B.W., and Brant, L.J. (1992). Physical restraint use and cognitive decline among nursing home residents. *Journal of the American Geriatrics Society*, **40**, 811–16.

Butler, R.N. (1992). Education and research: key components of healthcare reform. *Geriatrics*, **47**, 11–12.

Capezuti, E., Strumpf, N.E., Evans, L.K., Grisso, J.A., and Muslin G. (1998). The relationship between physical restraint removal and falls and injuries among nursing home residents. *Journal of Gerontology*, **53A**, M47–52.

Dans, P.E. and Kerr, M.R. (1979). Gerontology and geriatrics in medical education. *New England Journal of Medicine*, **300**, 228–32.

Donabedian, A. (1978). The quality of medical care. *Science*, **200**, 856–64.

Elton, R. (1993). The nursing home medical director role in transition. *Journal of the American Geriatrics Society*, **41**, 131–5.

Executive Council of the Association of American Medical Colleges (1983). Preparation in undergraduate medical education for improved geriatric care—a guideline for curriculum assessment. *Journal of Medical Education*, **58**, 501–26.

Finucane, T.E. (1988). The American Geriatrics Society statement on two-step PPD testing for nursing home patients on admission. *Journal of the American Geriatrics Society*, **36**, 77–8.

Folstein, M.F., Folstein, S.E., and McHugh, P.R. (1975). 'Mini-Mental State': a practical method for grading the cognitive state of patients for the clinician. *Journal of Psychiatric Research*, **12**, 189–98.

Freedman, V.A. (1996). Family structure and the risk of nursing home admission. *Journal of Gerontology*, **51B**, S61–9.

Freiman, M.P. and Murtaugh, C.M. (1995). Interactions between hospital and nursing home use. *Public Health Reports*, **110**, 547–54.

Gold, G. (1993). Education in geriatrics: a required curriculum for medical students. *Mount Sinai Journal of Medicine*, **60**, 461–4.

Gomolin, I.H., Leib, H.B., Arden, N.H., and Sherman, F.T. (1995). Control of influenza outbreaks in the nursing home: guidelines for diagnosis and management. *Journal of the American Geriatrics Society*, **43**, 71–4.

Grundy, E. (1996). Population review: (5) The population aged 60 and over. *Population Trends*, **84**, 14–20.

Guigoz, Y., Vellas, B., and Garry, P. (1996). Assessing the nutritional status of the elderly: the Mini Nutritional Assessment as part of the geriatric evaluation. *Nutrition Reviews*, **54**, S59–65.

Harrington, C., Tompkins, C., Curtis, M., and Grant, L. (1992). Psychotropic drug use in long-term care facilities: a review of the literature. *Gerontologist*, **32**, 822–33.

Hodges, M.O. and Tolle, S.W. (1994). Tube-feeding decisions in the elderly. *Clinics in Geriatrics Medicine*, **10**, 475–88.

Hoskins, I. (1996). *Combining work and elder care: a challenge for now and the future.* International Labour Organization, Geneva.

Institute of Medicine (1986). Committee on Nursing Home Regulation. *Improving the quality of care in nursing homes.* National Academy Press, Washington, DC.

Ishizaki, T., Kai, I., Hisata, M., *et al.* (1995). Factors influencing users' return home on discharge from a geriatric intermediate care facility in Japan. *Journal of the American Geriatrics Society,* **43**, 623–6.

Karlsson, S., Bucht, G., Eriksson, S., and Sandman, P.O. (1996). Physical restraints in geriatric care in Sweden: prevalence and patient characteristics. *Journal of the American Geriatrics Society,* **44**, 1348–54.

Katz, S., Ford, A.B., Moskowitz, R.W., *et al.* (1963). Studies of illness in the aged: the index of ADL. *Journal of the American Medical Association,* **185**, 914–19.

Katz, P., Karuza, J., and Counsell, S.R. (1995). Academics and the nursing home. *Clinics in Geriatric Medicine,* **1**, 503–13.

Kemper, P. and Murtaugh, C.M. (1991). Lifetime use of nursing home care. *New England Journal of Medicine,* **324**, 595–600.

Khan, K.L., Keeler, E.B., Sherwood, M.J., *et al.* (1990). Comparing outcomes of care before and after implementation of the DRG-based prospective payment system. *Journal of the American Medical Association,* **264**, 1984–8.

Kim, D.E. and Berlowitz, D.R. (1994). The limited value of routine laboratory assessments in severely impaired nursing home residents. *Journal of the American Medical Association,* **272**, 1447–52.

Kritchevsky, S.B. and Simmons, B.P. (1991). Continuous quality improvement. Concepts and applications for physician care. *Journal of the American Medical Association,* **66**, 1817–23.

Lawton, M.P., Moss, M., Fulcomer, M., *et al.* (1982). A research and service-oriented multilevel assessment instrument. *Journal of Gerontology,* **37**, 91–9.

Liu, K., McBride, T., and Coughlin, R. (1994). Risk of entering nursing homes for long versus short stays. *Medical Care,* **32**, 315–27.

McCormick, W.C., Imai, Y., and Rubenstein, L.Z. (1995). International common denominators in geriatric rehabilitation and long-term care. *Journal of the American Geriatrics Society,* **43**, 714–15.

Mathias, S., Nayak, U.S.L., and Isaacs, B. (1986). The 'Get Up and Go' test: a simple clinical test of balance in old people. *Archives of Physical and Medical Rehabilitation,* **67**, 387–9.

Meier, D.E., Gold, G., Mertz, K., *et al.* (1996). Enhancement of proxy appointment for older persons: physician counselling in the ambulatory setting. *Journal of the American Geriatrics Society,* **44**, 37–43.

Narain, J., Lofgren, J., Warren, E., *et al.* (1985). Epidemic tuberculosis in a nursing home: a retrospective cohort study. *Journal of the American Geriatrics Society,* **33**, 258–63.

National Center for Health Statistics (1970). *Arrangements for physician services to residents in nursing and personal care homes, United States, May to June 1964. Vital and health statistics.* PHS Publication No. 1000, Series 12, No. 13. Government Printing Office, Washington, DC.

Nicholson, K.G. (1996). Use of antivirals in the elderly: prophylaxis and therapy. *Gerontology,* **42**, 280–9.

Ouslander, J.G. and Osterweil, D. (1994). Physician evaluation and management of nursing home residents. *Annals of Internal Medicine,* **120**, 584–92.

SHEP Cooperative Research Group (1991). Prevention of stroke by antihypertensive drug treatment in older persons with isolated systolic hypertension: final results of the Systolic Hypertension in the Elderly Program (SHEP). *Journal of the American Medical Association,* **265**, 3255–64.

State University of New York (1994). *Guide to the use of the Uniform Data Set for medical rehabilitation including the Functional Independence Measure.* Version 4.0. State University of New York, Buffalo, NY.

Stead, W.W., Lofgren, J.P., Warren, E., and Thomas, C. (1985). Tuberculosis as an endemic and nosocomial infection among the elderly in nursing homes. *New England Journal of Medicine,* **312**, 1483–7.

Taeuber, C.M. (1993). *Sixty five plus in America.* Malta International Institute on Aging, United Nations – Malta.

Temkin-Greener, H. and Meiners, M.R. (1995). Transitions in long-term care. *Gerontologist,* **35**, 196–206.

Tinetti, M.E. (1986). Performance-oriented assessment of mobility problems in elderly patients. *Journal of the American Geriatrics Society,* **34**, 119–26.

Tinetti, M.E., Liu, W.L., Marottoli, R.A., and Ginter, S.F. (1991). Mechanical restraint use among residents of skilled nursing facilities: prevalence, patterns and predictors. *Journal of the American Medical Association,* **265**, 468–71.

Tinetti, M.E., Liu, W.L., and Ginter, S.F. (1992). Mechanical restraint use and fall-related injuries among residents of skilled nursing facilities. *Annals of Internal Medicine,* **116**, 369–74.

Tsuji, I., Whalen, S., and Finucane, T.E. (1995). Predictors of nursing home placement in community-based long-term care. *Journal of the American Geriatrics Society,* **43**, 761–6.

US Preventive Services Task Force (1995). *Guide to clinical and preventive services* (2nd edn). Williams and Wilkins, Baltimore, MD.

Wachtel, T.J., Fulton, J.P., and Goldfarb, J. (1987). Early prediction of discharge disposition after hospitalization. *Gerontologist,* **27**, 98–103.

Warren, J.W., Palumbo, F.B., Fitterman, L., *et al.* (1991). Incidence and characteristics of antibiotic use in aged nursing home patients. *Journal of the American Geriatrics Society,* **39**, 963.

Warren, S.S., Nguyen-Van-Tam, J.S., Pearson, J.C.G., and Madeley, R.J. (1995). Practices and policies for influenza immunization in old people's homes in Nottingham (UK) during the 1992–1993 season: potential for improvement. *Journal of Public Health,* **17**, 392–6.

Wolf-Klein, G.P., Holt, T., Silverstone, F.A., Foley, C., and Spatz, M. (1985). Efficacy of routine annual studies in the care of elderly patients. *Journal of the American Geriatrics Society,* **33**, 325–9.

Yesavage, J.A. and Brink, T.L. (1983). Development and validation of a geriatric depression screening scale: a preliminary report. *Journal of Psychiatric Research,* **17**, 37–49.

Yoshikawa, T.T. and Normal, D.C. (1995). Infection control in long-term care. *Clinics in Geriatric Medicine,* **11**, 467–80.

Zimmer, J.G., Eggert, G.M., Treat, A., Brodows, B., and Hyg, M.S. (1988). Nursing homes as acute care providers. a pilot study of incentives to reduce hospitalizations. *Journal of the American Geriatrics Society,* **36**, 124–9.

23.3 The geriatric day hospital

Irene D. Turpie

Geriatric day hospitals grew with the development of geriatric medicine in the United Kingdom. At the time of their first development, there was a national drive to prevent institutionalization of older people and to reduce the overall numbers of hospital beds. They were designed to be sited in a geriatric facility and to be part of a system of geriatric services which included inpatient beds and a home consultation service. At this time of rapid growth in the United Kingdom, health services for older people were mainly separate from adult medicine. Day hospitals were part of an system of care for elderly people which provided health care for most adults over the age of 65 years. They quickly became an important focus for the delivery of health care to frail older people and have remained so to the present.

As population ageing has become an issue in North America, Australasia, and elsewhere, day hospitals and programmes designed specifically for frail older adults have developed throughout the world. In many of these countries the day hospital models developed in Western Europe have been adopted. Conversely in the United States, day programmes providing both assessment and management, similar in some ways to day hospitals, are developing as 'day health centres' in integrated health systems for frail elderly people (Eng *et al.* 1997). Despite ongoing controversy as to the function and effectiveness of geriatric day hospitals, they continue to proliferate and develop.

This chapter examines the structure of day hospitals, their function, and the types of people who are managed in them, and evidence for their effectiveness in the published literature. Finally, it will close with a discussion of the present and potential future place of the day hospital in the health-care delivery system.

General features of day hospitals

Most day hospitals are on sites where there are a range of diagnostic and other health programmes, but a few have developed in different settings—in shopping centres (e.g. in Winnipeg, Manitoba) and community health centres (e.g. in Hamilton, Ontario). They often have been developed from existing conventional hospital structures but there are a few which have been custom built to suit the ambulant frail individual.

Day hospitals need large open indoor spaces for communal activities and an adequate number of toilets with adapted facilities, bathing facilities, and facilities to assess activities of daily living. Easy access from the exterior is very important as people often come in wheelchairs, special transport, or ambulances and have to be helped into the day hospital by staff or volunteers (Fig. 1). Day hospitals usually provide midday meals. In Canada there is a charge which is the same rate as for Meals on Wheels delivered daily by local agencies.

The day hospital, like other forms of geriatric management, focuses on restoring function in older adults, especially those who are not only frail but have complex health problems which require the services of a number of health-care professionals (Fig. 2). The first day hospital models in the United Kingdom provided diagnostic, rehabilitative, and therapeutic services during the day for some part of the week under the supervision of medical and other health professionals, and social workers (Brocklehurst 1978). This definition has been interpreted in Ontario, Canada, as allowing the admission of people who require the services of two health professionals apart from a doctor or nurse (such as physiotherapy, occupational therapy, or speech pathology), and implies the presence of a physical disability in each person admitted. Most geriatric day hospitals focus on medical and functional problems, although there are day hospitals designed for patients with dementia and other psychiatric disorders.

In the United Kingdom, geriatric day hospitals based on general hospital sites are being increasingly used as acute assessment and treatment centres for older people at risk of emergency hospital admission. Such day hospitals require high levels of medical staffing, and immediate access to diagnostic facilities and treatment including intravenous therapy. In order to provide an acute service they must maintain less than complete occupancy, and so require active management and a high turnover. Given the rising emergency admission rates for older people in the United Kingdom, this type of day hospital is thought to fulfill an important function for a comprehensive geriatric service, but there have been no adequate studies of its cost effectiveness.

Day hospital staffing consists of an interdisciplinary team of specialists from medicine nursing, physiotherapy, social work, and occupational therapy. Some day hospitals have recreational therapists who assess and provide advice regarding leisure, hobbies, and activities for patients to help re-establish them in their community. Other therapists such as speech and language pathologists, psychologists, or nutritionists are available as required. Medical care is usually provided by either a primary care doctor or a geriatrician. In some programmes, a nurse practitioner serves as care manager and develops a treatment plan with the geriatrician and other members of the team (Evans *et al.* 1995). The staff of a day hospital may be part of a hospital department and able to work elsewhere at times when the day hospital is not functioning. If the day hospital is part of a large hospital corporation the staff may rotate from other departments in the

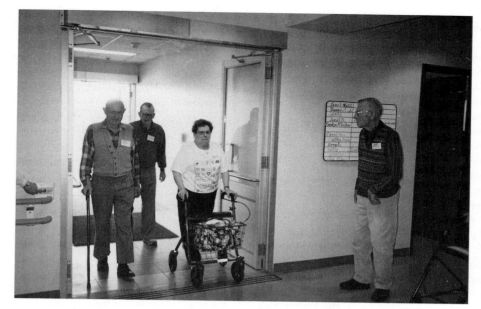

Fig. 1 Day hospital entrance with wide doors, good lighting, level floors, and direct access from outside.

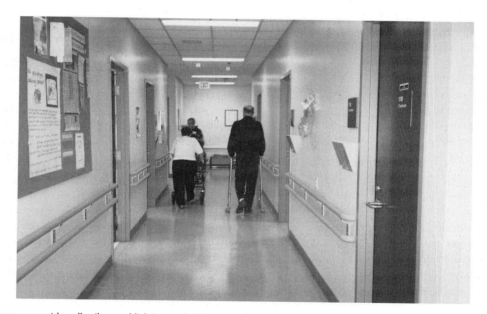

Fig. 2 Daily walking programme with wall rails, good lighting, and ability to walk two abreast (many friendships start here).

hospital. Other day hospitals have developed with a programme management structure where staff report to a programme manager rather than a department head.

Patients are referred to a day hospital by their family doctor, home care personnel in discussion with the family doctor, or a hospital team or medical consultant. It is important that the family doctors are aware of day hospital admissions and each management change which occurs, as they are responsible for a patient's care when not in the day hospital. Few referrals come from medical specialists apart from geriatricians, despite the high prevalence of appropriate problems (Royal College of Physicians 1994).

In North American day hospital programmes, the decision to admit a patient to the day hospital is often not made by the doctor but by the members of the day hospital interdisciplinary team who meet to discuss each referred patient on completion of an interdisciplinary assessment. After medical and functional assessment, a member of the team, usually not a doctor, may act as care manager. The care manager co-ordinates the person's care with other team members and liaises with family, family doctor, and home care workers involved at the time of admission and at discharge from the day hospital when the family doctor will continue the care or home care provided as necessary. Goals for attendance are usually mutually agreed upon by the patient, family, and team and are related to the functions of the day hospital—rehabilitation, maintenance, recreational activities, family counselling, and education, and in some facilities medical and nursing procedures.

In some day hospitals, there has been a move away from the traditional medical model of care in which the doctor hears the opinions of other members of the team but is still responsible for decisions on management. Instead, there is a recognition of the important roles of other members of the interdisciplinary team in management. In some day hospitals the care manager is a nurse but in others it is the professional who is felt to be most involved in achieving the treatment goals and could be any member of the team.

People usually attend for part of a day for 4 or 5 h, have their midday meal in the day hospital, have individual and group programmes depending on the agreed management plan, and return to their own homes at night. Transport is usually arranged by the day hospital. Attendance is often 2 days a week, but may be up to 5 or (rarely) 6 days. Numbers attending each day vary from 20 to 40 people. Smaller programmes (six to eight patients attending daily) are managed by geriatric nurse practitioners in the United States (Evans et al. 1995).

There are few descriptions of specific patient eligibility criteria. Usually patients admitted to day hospitals fall into the general category of frail elderly (Rockwood et al. 1994) and have a measurable disability or handicap. Often they have strokes, Parkinson's disease, hip fractures, or arthritic problems, impairing their ability to perform the activities of daily living, but are able to live in their own home (Royal College of Physicians 1994). Some may have had a prolonged illness with physical deconditioning; many patients also have a dementia but all are considered to have rehabilitation potential by the team who consider cognition, ability to learn, and tolerance as well as medical problems. They also consider the ability and willingness of the patient to come to the site.

As noted below, in the United States the Programmes for All-Inclusive Care of the Elderly are health- and social-orientated day programmes combined with home care designed to maintain very frail people in their homes who otherwise would need nursing home care. Attendance is often defined by the geographical area in which an attender lives because of travel convenience. Transport to the facility is usually arranged by the day hospital or by a regional transport service designed for disabled people. People who live too far away may be unable to attend. A few mobile day hospitals are described where day hospital staff travel to different locations on different days (Royal College of Physicians 1994).

Day hospitals have been carefully differentiated from day centres which are designed for socialization and caregiver relief (Currie et al. 1995). Some day centres work in close relationship to day hospitals but others are quite separate and often people are referred to day centres after attendance in a day hospital to maintain the level of activity which had been achieved in the day hospital. Generally, day care centres are staffed with different professionals, and there is likely to be a social flavour to the activities and a lower staff-to-patient ratio (Table 1). There are no studies comparing the effectiveness of day hospitals and day centres.

The geriatric day hospital provides a link between hospital and community care (Evans 1995). The purposes of a day hospital were described in a literature review (Eagle 1987), and included rehabilitation for patients in their own homes, improved function and

Table 1 Differences between day hospitals and day care centres

Day hospital	Day care centre
Medical assessment and focus	Social and recreational function
Larger staff-to-patient ratio	Smaller staff-to-patient ratio
Diagnostic facility	Maintenance of function/other abilities
Assessment	Caregiver relief
Rehabilitation	May provide activity programme
Education	
Individual therapy	
Counselling	

quality of life for the person attending, facilitation of early hospital discharge, reduction of the caregiving burden on families, and staff preferences for working in a day hospital setting (Royal College of Physicians 1994).

Day hospital trials in the literature

The evidence for either the achievement of the goals outlined above or of cost-effectiveness is less than impressive if one examines the few reported randomized controlled trials which have been published. The studies emphasize the difficulty of undertaking health service research in this heterogeneous population of frail elderly people with complex medical problems.

An early randomized controlled trial (Tucker et al. 1984) examined a New Zealand day hospital in its start up stage. Relatively young people over the age of 55 years (average age of 72 years) were referred from hospital at discharge (40 per cent of total referrals) or by their family doctors (60 per cent). Dementia patients and those referred only for caregiver relief were excluded. People were randomized at the time of the first activities of daily living assessment (dressing, toileting, washing, walking). The day hospital was 55 per cent occupied during the period of the trial and the average attendance of the day hospital patient was 23.4 days at 2 days per week (Table 2).

Participants were randomized to either day hospital attendance or usual care (which could include attendance for physiotherapy at the hospital, domiciliary services, a day care centre, or follow-up from their general practitioner). Activities of daily living, mood, mental status, and social support (Northwick Park activities of daily living assessment, Zung self-rating depression instrument, depression index, 10-question abbreviated mental status test) were assessed by an 'independent' occupational therapist who was blinded as to treatment group. More physiotherapy and occupational therapy in hours was given to the day hospital patients than to the control patients but the authors did not describe what other professional time was devoted to day hospital patients or how many patients were discharged from the day hospital programme prior to completion of the 5-month study. Home care use was measured, and the costs of staffing and transport (by ambulance) were calculated. During the trial period, only study patients were admitted to the day hospital

Table 2 Summary of published randomized controlled trials of day hospitals

Name of study and population	Number of persons involved	Average age (years)	Population	Intervention attendances	Intervention (therapy received)	Outcomes
People referred on hospital discharge or from the family doctor, mixed diagnosis (Tucker *et al.* 1984)	62 in treatment group and 58 in control group	72	Referred by GPs or on hospital discharge	Newly established day hospital, 23.4 attendances twice weekly for duration; control group received usual care	Day hospital group: median 398 h PT, 543 h OT. Control group: 103 h PT, 20 h OT	Improved at 6 weeks but not sustained at 5 months; more inpatient days in control group
People referred for geriatric assessment (Eagle *et al.* 1991)	55 in treatment group and 58 in control group	79	Frail elderly people referred to a geriatrician for assessment Multiple medical diagnoses Moderate disability	Newly established day hospital versus usual care	Trial group attended day hospital—both groups had home care	Treatment group had fewer hospital days but no difference in function, quality of life, general health, or mortality; day hospital cost more
Trial randomized at time of hospital discharge after stroke (Young and Forster 1992)	52 in study group and 56 in home treatment group	Over 60	31 visits versus 15 visits to home rehabilitation group (mostly PT) Moderate disability	Day hospital care versus home care	Day hospital group: 15 h PT, 15 h OT Home group: 6.5 h PT, 10 h OT	General health, walking, caregiver stress similar in both groups; home groups were better able to walk outside after 6 months
Day hospital admission on discharge from health care for the elderly wards (Gladman *et al.* 1995)	162 home rehabilitation and 165 hospital-based	77	Equal numbers of men and women Stroke patients with moderate disability	Day hospital was part of the established health care for the elderly programme	Home rehabilitation versus day hospital	IADL scores in the day hospital group were better than in the home treatment group
Stroke patients in New Territories, Hong Kong (Hui *et al.* 1995)	59 day hospital and 61 controls	74	Stroke patients with moderate to severe disability	Usual care in outpatient clinic versus day hospital	Day hospital versus outpatient clinic. No home care	Initial improvement in day hospital at 3 months which was not sustained at 6 months

GP, general practitioner; IADL, instrumental activities of daily living; OT, occupational therapy; PT, physical therapy.

which did not run at full occupancy at this time, although this was adjusted in the final cost calculation. The day hospital group showed improved initial function (approximately one category on the chosen activities of daily living score) but this was not maintained at 5 months. A sustained improvement in mood in the day hospital patients was measured at 5 months. Day hospital treatment proved more costly in the analysis.

A Canadian study from an urban health sciences centre compared day hospital care by geriatricians with 'usual' care by the same geriatricians (inpatient, home care, and clinic care) as the control therapy. This study took place at an early stage in this day hospital's development and the team was new to day hospital care. The patient population consisted of frail elderly people with impairment in the activities of daily living who had been referred to the study geriatricians for assessment. There was no targeting of any specific disease for admission. If after geriatric medical assessment, people were considered appropriate for day hospital admission by the geriatricians, they were then randomized into treatment or control groups.

The day hospital staff is described but not the hours of therapy each person received while attending either the day hospital or from

home care. Outcomes were measured at 3, 6, and 12 months. Outcomes measured were activities of daily living and quality of life (Barthel Index, geriatric quality of life, RAND health measurement questionnaire). Not all study participants (60 per cent study group, 64 per cent control group) were able to complete the geriatric quality of life questionnaire, mainly because of their cognitive limitations (Guyatt *et al.* 1993). The day hospital group attended the day hospital twice weekly for half a day for 3 months. This group spent less days in hospital than the control group. There was no significant difference in outcome on any of the measurements used including mortality. Furthermore, the overall costs of day hospital attendance were higher.

Stroke is a common day hospital diagnosis (Royal College of Physicians 1994), and day hospital attendance for stroke survivors has been examined in several studies. The first (Young and Forster 1992) compared day hospital attendance with home physiotherapy for relatively young stroke survivors (average age was 70 years) who were randomized at hospital discharge either to attend day hospital for 15 weeks or to have home physiotherapy. General health, walking ability, disability, and caregiver stress were measured and there was no difference between the groups in any of the measurements at the end of 6 months.

A second British study of stroke patients (Gladman *et al.* 1993) following hospital discharge compared home rehabilitation with 'usual care'. In addition to patients admitted to the stroke unit and general medical beds, the study included day hospital care for those older people who had been admitted to health care for the elderly beds and for whom attendance at a day hospital following discharge was the 'usual care'. This study was stratified by site from which the patients were discharged as follows: (a) to a stroke unit (younger, mean age 60 years) with little previous ill health; (b) admitted to general medical beds (mean age 65 years); (c) health care for the elderly beds (mean age of 77 years, poor antemorbid mobility, more likely to be living alone).

There was no significant difference in outcome overall but the group of older frailer patients (the group who attended the day hospital) had better extended activities of daily living scores at 6 months and 1 year than those who were treated at home. More day hospital randomized patients did not attend for treatment compared with the home treatment group.

A positive effect of the day hospitals in treating older stroke survivors with more comorbid illness was reported in another study from the New Territories in Hong Kong where 120 stroke patients with an average age of 74 years were randomized to care in a stroke unit or a geriatric ward (Hui *et al.* 1995). The geriatric patients were subsequently discharged from the geriatric wards to a day hospital, again as part of the 'normal practice'. Patients had comparable neurological deficits. Improvement in Barthel score was more marked in the day hospital group at 3 but not at 6 months. In this study, there was no home care available for the control group who attended an outpatient clinic for treatment.

A retrospective cohort comparison study from the United States, using care in a geriatric outpatient clinic as control, describes a trial of a different day hospital model (Sui *et al.* 1994). This day hospital had a wider focus than the traditional day hospital and was defined as an outpatient facility where frail older patients can receive subacute or acute medical, nursing, social, or rehabilitative services over any portion of the day. The day hospital was used for gastrointestinal tests, intravenous therapy, biopsies, and diagnostic imaging, facilities now available in some modern British day hospitals. Patients were assessed by the geriatrician, nurse practitioner, and social worker, and had a mean of one or two visits to the day hospital in total. Only 24 per cent of the patients visited the day hospital more than four times. Both day hospital and clinic groups were equally likely to receive follow-up care or rehabilitative services although the day hospital group was more likely to have psychiatric or social work intervention. Return was arranged as necessary. The authors retrospectively compared all patients seen for geriatric assessment in this day hospital, with a similar group who were assessed in a university or community geriatric assessment clinic. They compared day hospital attenders with a similar group of people who received usual care: the characteristics of this group included age over 65 years, people with one activities of daily living restriction, and problems identified with gait instability, malnutrition, incontinence, severe depression, or dementia. General well being, mood, and level of satisfaction were measured in addition to services received, hospital admission, family doctor visits, and community service use after 6 months. There was no difference between day hospital users and clinic attenders. However,

the day hospital group had a higher level of dementia and were more functionally impaired than the control group, and there was lack of randomization into two equivalent groups. The patients referred to day hospital may have been more impaired than those referred to clinics.

Another study of extended community geriatric assessment in the United States (Boult *et al.* 1994) took the form of a controlled trial of outpatient geriatric assessment of specifically identified high-risk senior citizens. They were assessed, seen at 2 to 3 week intervals in the clinic over a 3 to 4 month period, and followed by the programme with the permission of the patients and their primary care doctors. There was much telephone consultation with home care and other agencies involved with the patients' care such as day centres. The average number of visits paid to the programme by each patient was 6.4; the number of telephone calls made by staff was not documented. After the 3- to 4-month assessment period was completed the person was returned to the care of the primary care doctor and followed over the next 10 to 12 months. The trial group had a lower mortality, higher satisfaction, and reduced acute care utilization.

Programmes for All-Inclusive Care of the Elderly in the United States are showing promise in terms of delivering effective care to frail, elderly, nursing home eligible patients maintained in the community. Care for this group is delivered within an integrated system of care funded by Medicare and Medicaid. A day health centre forms the central focus of this programme. Both primary and specialist medical care is available and patients are followed by the same staff whether they are at home, in hospital, or in a nursing home. Home care and outreach programmes run from the same site. The programmes seem to be providing effective interdisciplinary care and are also cost-effective (Eng *et al.* 1997). The health centre forms a central focus for an integrated system of care for that population. Patients are assessed initially at the centres and community care is directed from the one central site. All skilled professional care is delivered in the day health centre

Discussion

Day hospitals can form a link between patient care in the hospital and care in an individual's own home, and in many parts of the world, they have an important place in health-care delivery systems for the frail older person. Whether this place is justifiable is still being debated. Reported randomized controlled trials to guide practitioners are few, and there are good reasons for challenging the outcomes of those studies which do exist (Table 3).

The randomized controlled trials may not have been effective for several reasons. The trials took place before the day hospitals had been fully operational and often before the interdisciplinary group forming the team had become accustomed to working together. Teams take time to develop their assessment, communication, and co-operative skills.

In health services research, randomized controlled trials cannot be blinded. Participants and practitioners alike are aware of the group to which the individual has been assigned. The twentieth century has resulted in many population shifts and older populations have multiple ethnic backgrounds. Many immigrants have not been able to learn to speak the main language of the country to which they have come. People who cannot communicate in English are often excluded from

Table 3 Difficulty in health services research in the frail elderly population

Randomized controlled trials usually take place at the start of a service, before a team has formed or the difficulties ascertained or ironed out (Tucker *et al.* 1984; Eagle *et al.* 1991), and before the day service is fully utilized
Outcome measures may not be fully tested
Different perspectives on necessary outcome measures from consumers, care providers, administrators, staff
Different populations from study to study—affects generalizability
Different interventions in different studies—affects generalizability
Patients or staff cannot be 'blinded' to intervention
Patients with dementia excluded
Patients who cannot speak the local language excluded
Patients with communication difficulties excluded

randomized controlled trials. These people may benefit from a day hospital owing to their increased social isolation and difficulties in communication.

The assessment tools which were used in the published trials may not have been the ideal tools. For example, disability may not change as a result of rehabilitation but handicap may. (A woman attending the day hospital may not be able to increase the strength of a stroke affected limb but may be able to learn to use an aid confidently, and this may allow her to go out to enjoy her usual leisure activities.) A measure of disability (e.g. the Barthel score) would not show any change in this instance; whereas, a measure of handicap would (Wood 1980).

In the trials quoted, outcome measures were chosen from the perspective of the service providers such as mortality, hospital admission, and institutionalization. Few studies considered the quality of life for either the patient or the caregiver. Measurement of quality of life is difficult in this population, especially in those who have an aphasia or cognitive impairment. Only 50 per cent of people in one study were able to complete the measure (Eagle *et al.* 1991). Improved patient and carer satisfaction are important outcomes which may determine an individual's independence and should be considered in such studies.

Day hospitals may be providing 'too much' therapy. Despite similar outcomes in the studies which have documented their interventions (see Table 2), patients receiving home therapy actually received very much less in terms of therapists' individual time than those in the day hospitals. However, the key consideration should be to provide day hospital care at the frequency, which may be several times a week, determined to be most beneficial for each individual patient. We need to consider whether less time spent in individual therapy can achieve the same outcomes. Weekly day hospital attendance may be sufficient. A combination of home therapy and day hospital attendance, using both the home environment and the equipment, facilities, and peer therapy of the day hospital, may provide an acceptable alternative to those who find twice weekly day hospital attendance too much (see above).

Day hospitals are often completely separate from day centres which are seen to serve 'a social purpose'; however, people who have attended a day hospital often 'graduate' to a day centre on discharge. We need to challenge the perception that such programmes should be completely separate. Both serve a similar population and there may be efficiencies in terms of common programming which could be achieved by having them in closer proximity.

Different programmes and trials cannot be compared until there is better standardization of assessment instruments and descriptions of the patients admitted. Use of standardized evaluation schemes such as those suggested by the Royal College of Physicians (1992) will allow better comparison and programme evaluation.

Global predictions indicate increasing numbers of older adults and little decrease in disability associated with that increase. Older people have made it clear that they prefer living in their own homes to institutionalization whenever possible. Day hospitals are probably most effective where they are part of a health-care system directed at frail elderly people such as is suggested by the evidence of the Programmes for All-Inclusive Care of the Elderly. This system can be contrasted with most countries, where it is possible for a frail elderly person to be cared for by several different components of the system—home care, the regional geriatric programme, and the acute care system—with much duplication and little communication between each component.

Medical students and other health professionals can learn about the management of frail older adults in a day hospital. There is increasing understanding of the importance of research initiatives in community and long-term care settings. Practitioners need to learn more about the community care of older adults (Turpie *et al.* 1997). Most students will eventually practice in environments outside health science centres; yet their education is still focused in those institutions. The day hospital provides an endless source of interesting learning opportunities for students. The people who come to a day hospital are usually medically relatively stable and often very patient and tolerant with learners of all disciplines.

Conclusion

There is a growing appreciation of the urgent need to develop integrated systems of care for the older person incorporating smooth and efficient flow from community to hospital care, appropriate and integrated use of specialist care, and co-ordinated interprofessional services. The shifting emphasis from institutional long-term care to community long-term care makes further examination of the usefulness of the day hospital a priority in the delivery of specialist services to frail elderly people.

The traditional day hospital primarily serves a rehabilitative purpose for medically stable people already assessed either as inpatients or in an outpatient clinic. There are some indications of effectiveness. Older people with more physical limitations may do better in a day hospital after they have had a stroke (Gladman 1995; Hui *et al.* 1995); more rapid restoration of function (Tucker *et al.* 1984; Hui *et al.* 1995) may be important outcomes for older individuals struggling to maintain their independence at home, and day hospitals seem to achieve this. The acute day hospital on the modern British model also various aspects of the effectiveness of stroke unit care in general before looking at the evidence supporting different approaches to the delivery of stroke unit care. Particular emphasis will be given to how clinicians might use this information in the planning and delivery of services.

The central question is whether patients receiving care from services which can be broadly defined as a stroke unit enjoy better outcomes than those receiving the contemporary conventional care. In order to answer this question the collaborative review approach incorporated input from the co-ordinators of each of the original randomized trials (Stroke Unit Trialists' Collaboration 1997) to achieve the following:

(1) to identify all relevant randomized trials of stroke unit care;
(2) to obtain standardized descriptive information about service characteristics;
(3) to obtain standardized outcome information comparable across trials;
(4) to synthesize the information to draw appropriate conclusions about the effectiveness of stroke unit care.

This process identified 19 randomized trials of which 18 were complete and able to provide data. These 18 trials were carried out in seven different countries and included over 3000 patients. The broad comparison was between organized inpatient (stroke unit) care and the contemporary conventional care. The definition of a stroke unit trial (i.e. any trial where there is an attempt to improve the organization of inpatient stroke care) was deliberately broad to ensure that all services approximating to a stroke unit would be included.

Can deaths be prevented?

The first analysis examined the chances (odds) of death for patients receiving organized inpatient (stroke unit) care as opposed to the contemporary conventional care. In order to rule out the possibility that deaths might be temporarily delayed rather than prevented in the long term, results at the end of scheduled follow-up (a median of 1 year after the index stroke) will be reported. The summary results are presented as a meta-analysis plot in Fig. 1. The odds of death were reduced (odds ratio 0.82; 95 per cent confidence interval, 0.69 to 0.98; $2p < 0.05$) within the stroke unit setting; a result which was essentially unchanged when the analysis was carried out in different ways, for different periods of follow-up, and after the exclusion of less methodologically rigorous trials. However, the observed reduction in case fatality is not statistically robust and we cannot exclude the possibility of publication bias in that a small number of unpublished negative trials might exist which would overturn these conclusions.

This result was surprising because an intervention such as co-ordinated multidisciplinary care which is not directed at the patho-physiological process of stroke was not expected to influence the risk of death after stroke (although there is an interesting parallel with trials of organized geriatric medical care where a reduction in death has also been noted; Rubenstein 1990; Stuck et al. 1993). The authors therefore set out to explore these observations in greater detail. The first question was at what stage after stroke were deaths prevented? A secondary analysis of the case fatality data (Stroke Unit Trialists'

Collaboration 1996) indicated that the apparent reduction in the number of deaths occurred between 1 and 3 weeks after the index stroke. Thereafter the death rates were very similar between the stroke unit and conventional care groups.

The second question was what causes of death were being reduced by stroke unit care? The reduction in death was seen across all the main causes of death but was most apparent for those causes considered to be secondary to immobility (e.g. chest infection, urinary tract infection, venous thromboembolism) and cardiovascular causes (myocardial infarction, heart failure, arrhythmia). These conclusions were based on a rather limited amount of data and were largely based on the certified causes of death and only tentative conclusions can be drawn (Stroke Unit Trialists' Collaboration 1996). The available information suggests that the reduction in deaths within the stroke unit care setting was largely due to the potentially preventable complications of stroke occurring predominantly in the postacute period.

Can disability be prevented?

Although the apparent reduction in the risk of death after stroke seen in the stroke unit groups is encouraging, it is of borderline statistical significance and may not be the most relevant outcome for stroke disease where the burden of disability is so great. Preventing deaths may be of dubious value if it merely reflects an increase in the chances of a patient surviving in a severely disabled state (Donnan 1993). For this reason it is important to look at the totality of patient outcomes, that is, evidence that patients receiving stroke unit care were more likely to not only survive but also to regain independence and return home. Two primary outcome measures were used to examine this question, both of which have their limitations. The first is the combined adverse outcome of death or requiring long-term institutional care. Institutionalization is a robust outcome which is unlikely to be subject to differences in interpretation (observer bias) and approximates to the level of disability (Barer et al. 1993). However, the absolute institutionalization rates will vary from place to place and the results may be difficult to interpret. In addition institutionalization could in theory be reduced by more aggressive discharge planning or imposition rather than through improving patient recovery after stroke. A further analysis is therefore needed of the combined adverse outcome of death or dependency (disability). Clearly, this is a more direct measure of patient outcome but it has two major drawbacks. Firstly, a variety of measures of dependency (disability) were used in different trials and so some standardization of data was required. Secondly, the assessment of dependency is subject to observer bias and unless the outcome assessor who measures dependency is 'blinded' to the treatment that a patient has received there is a danger of bias occurring in the scoring of the level of dependency.

Figure 2 presents the results for the odds of a combined adverse outcome of death or requiring long-term institutional care (Stroke Unit Trialists' Collaboration 1997). In this case the summary results (odds ratio 0.75; 95 per cent confidence intervals 0.65 to 0.87; $2p < 0.0001$) was highly significant and unlikely to be overturned by unpublished data. The conclusions were unchanged if the analysis was carried out in different ways such as different periods of follow-up and with the exclusion of less methodologically sound trials. The

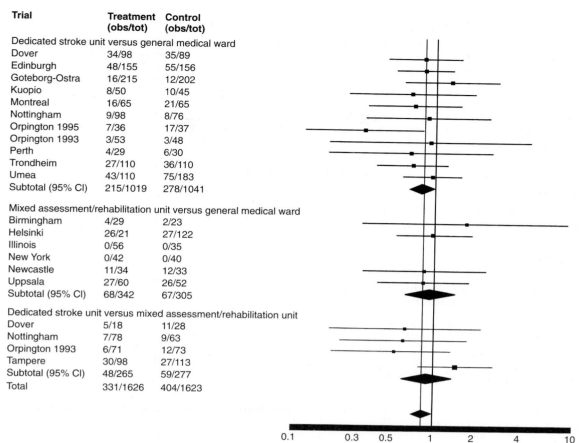

Fig. 1 Organized (stroke unit) care versus conventional care: death by the end of scheduled follow-up. Results are presented as the odds of death occurring by the end of scheduled follow-up (median 1 year; range 6 weeks to 1 year) in the stroke unit versus conventional care settings. The odds ratios and 95 per cent confidence intervals (CI) of individual trials are presented as a black box and horizontal line. The pooled odds ratio and 95 per cent confidence interval for a group of trials is represented by a diamond. The definitions of service characteristics are as follows: dedicated stroke unit, accepting only stroke patients; mixed assessment–rehabilitation unit, managing stroke patients within a mixed disability setting; general medical ward, specializing in acute medical care but not subsequent rehabilitation. O − E denotes 'observed minus expected' and 'var' denotes variance.

results do not appear to be due to unreasonable hospital discharge policies because the reduction in the need for institutional care was sustained for a period of up to 1 year.

If the observed reduction in the need for institutional care is due to a reduction in the number of patients remaining physically dependent, then an examination of the number of patients who were dead or dependent in activities of daily living at the end of scheduled follow-up should indicate a similar trend. Figure 3 presents results for this analysis of all available trials (Stroke Unit Trialists' Collaboration 1997). The overall odds ratio for being dead or dependent if exposed to stroke unit care as opposed to the contemporary conventional care was 0.71 (95 per cent confidence intervals, 0.61 to 0.82; 2p < 0.0001). This result is statistically very robust and not substantially altered by different methods of analysis, exclusion of trials using poor randomization procedures, or exclusion of trials where there was no unequivocal blinding of the final assessment of outcome. These conclusions (and those regarding death or institutionalization results) are unlikely to be affected by publication bias. Therefore, within the randomized trials patients who receive stroke unit care were more likely to survive, regain independence, and return home than those

who were managed in a conventional manner (usually in general medical wards).

What do these results mean?

The methods used to analyse the results of the stroke unit trials are statistically robust but are not easy to interpret in a clinical sense. It is useful to examine the results in terms of the absolute outcome rates. Table 1 presents results in terms of the proportion (per cent) of patients within the stroke unit and conventional care groups who were observed to be in each outcome category at the end of scheduled follow-up. The relative change in that outcome is also presented together with the 95 per cent confidence interval which can be used to calculate the number needed to prevent a particular bad outcome (Sackett et al. 1996). The apparent benefits of stroke unit care were seen across all four outcome categories (see Table 1). There was a small but potentially important reduction in the proportion of patients who died and in those who required institutional care, and a sub-stantial increase in the number who returned home in a physically

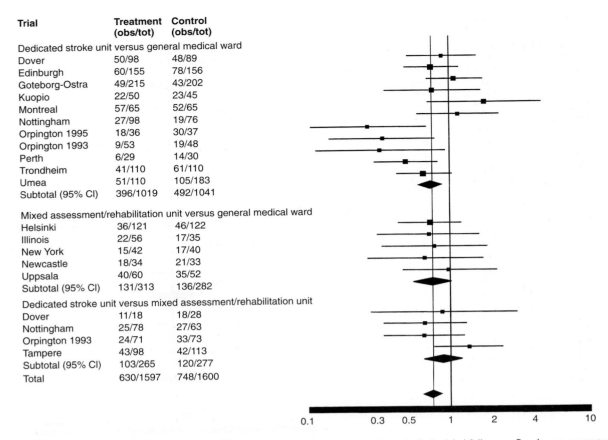

Trial	Treatment (obs/tot)	Control (obs/tot)
Dedicated stroke unit versus general medical ward		
Dover	50/98	48/89
Edinburgh	60/155	78/156
Goteborg-Ostra	49/215	43/202
Kuopio	22/50	23/45
Montreal	57/65	52/65
Nottingham	27/98	19/76
Orpington 1995	18/36	30/37
Orpington 1993	9/53	19/48
Perth	6/29	14/30
Trondheim	41/110	61/110
Umea	51/110	105/183
Subtotal (95% CI)	396/1019	492/1041
Mixed assessment/rehabilitation unit versus general medical ward		
Helsinki	36/121	46/122
Illinois	22/56	17/35
New York	15/42	17/40
Newcastle	18/34	21/33
Uppsala	40/60	35/52
Subtotal (95% CI)	131/313	136/282
Dedicated stroke unit versus mixed assessment/rehabilitation unit		
Dover	11/18	18/28
Nottingham	25/78	27/63
Orpington 1993	24/71	33/73
Tampere	43/98	42/113
Subtotal (95% CI)	103/265	120/277
Total	630/1597	748/1600

Fig. 2 Organized (stroke unit) care versus conventional care: death or institutionalization at the end of scheduled follow-up. Results are presented as the odds ratio (95 per cent confidence interval (CI)) of the combined adverse outcome of being dead or requiring institutional care at the end of scheduled follow-up (median, 1 year; range, 6 weeks to 1 year). Abbreviations and terms as in Fig. 1.

Table 1 Outcome in stroke unit trials

Outcome	Stroke unit (%)	Control (%)	Odds ratio	95% confidence interval
Home (independent)	42	36	1.31	1.09–1.56**
Home (dependent)	19	18	1.09	0.87–1.37
Institutional care	20	22	0.86	0.70–1.05
Dead	20	24	0.78	0.65–0.92*

The table shows the proportion of patients in the stroke unit and control groups who were in each outcome category at the end of scheduled follow-up (median, 1 year). Also shown is the odds ratio (95% confidence interval) of a particular outcome occurring in the stroke unit versus control group. The term 'independent' is equivalent to a Rankin score of 0–2 and 'dependent' is equivalent to a Rankin score of 3–5. Tests of significance are based on the z-statistic of the odds ratio where * denotes $p < 0.05$ and ** denotes $p < 0.01$.

independent state. Based on these figures it was possible to calculate that the number of patients who need to receive stroke unit care to prevent one death is 22. The number needed to receive treatment to allow one additional patient to return home in a physically independent state is 16. These are impressively positive results which compare favourably with many conventional medical and surgical interventions.

Will all patients obtain benefit?

The results available at present indicate that stroke unit care can be beneficial in terms of a number of outcomes. However, can we be confident that these observations are applicable to the majority of stroke patients, particularly the older and frailer stroke patient groups often seen by geriatricians? In considering this question the Stroke

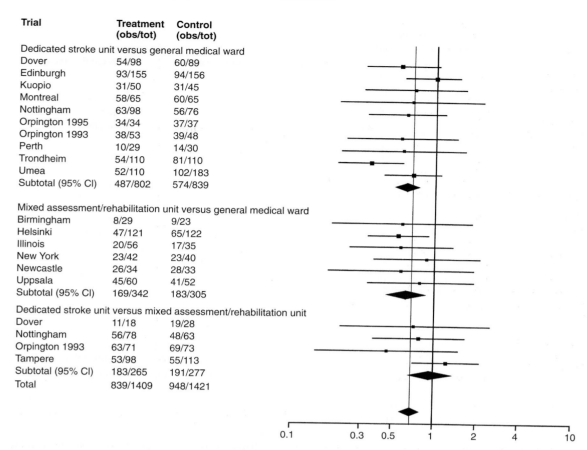

Fig. 3 Organized (stroke unit) care versus conventional care: death or dependency at the end of scheduled follow-up. Results are presented as the odds ratio (95 per cent confidence interval (CI)) of the combined adverse outcome of death or dependency at the end of scheduled follow-up (median, 1 year; range, 6 weeks to 1 year). Abbreviations and terms as in Fig. 1.

Unit Trialists' Collaboration Group carried out several prespecified subgroup analyses based on patient age, sex, and stroke severity. Stroke severity was defined as follows:

(1) mild stroke—patient able to mobilize (with or without assistance) at the time of randomization;
(2) moderate stroke—intermediate severity between mild and severe;
(3) severe stroke—patient has no sitting balance (frequently with reduced consciousness) at the time of randomization.

It was apparent from this analysis (Fig. 4) that there was no clear association of patient age, sex, or stroke severity with the effectiveness of stroke unit care. It is important to recognize that a relatively small number of patients are represented in each subgroup and so the statistical power of this analysis is rather limited. Also, many of the randomized trials employed some selection criteria to exclude the most mild and the most severe stroke patients. Moreover, subgroup analyses have well-recognized problems and must be interpreted cautiously (Oxman and Guyatt 1992). However, the available information does seem to suggest that there are no good grounds to exclude patients from organized stroke unit care on the basis of age, sex, or stroke severity.

Although it appears that patients with a range of stroke severities can benefit from stroke unit care there is some evidence to suggest that the degree of benefit they enjoy depends on the severity of the

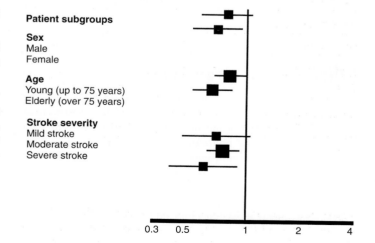

Fig. 4 Organized (stroke unit) care versus conventional care: analysis of various patient subgroups. Results are presented as the odds ratio (95 per cent confidence interval (CI)) of the combined adverse outcome of death or requiring long-term institutional care. Definitions of stroke severity are given in the text.

Table 2 Outcomes within stroke severity subgroups

	Stroke unit (%)	Control (%)	Odds ratio	95% confidence interval
Mild stroke				
Independent	78	71	1.42	0.98–2.08
Dependent	12	19	0.56	0.36–0.89*
Dead	10	10	1.07	0.61–1.88
Moderate stroke				
Independent	37	31	1.29	1.01–1.64*
Dependent	43	43	1.04	0.80–1.36
Dead	20	25	0.76	0.57–1.01
Severe stroke				
Independent	10	7	1.50	0.74–3.03
Dependent	43	37	1.30	0.87–1.94
Dead	46	56	0.74	0.48–1.12

The table shows the proportion of patients in the stroke unit and control groups (subdivided by initial stroke severity) who were in each outcome category at the end of scheduled follow-up (median, 1 year). Data are presented as in Table 1.

initial stroke (Stroke Unit Trialists' Collaboration 1996). Table 2 shows the absolute outcome rates in patients with a mild, moderate, or severe stroke. These data can then be used to calculate the number needed to be treated to allow one extra patient to benefit. Overall, mild stroke patients did not appear to benefit in terms of a reduction in case fatality (which was very low in the first place) but only 14 such patients needed to be treated to ensure that one additional patient regained physical independence. Within the moderate stroke group there was an apparent reduction in deaths and once again an impressive increase in the number of individuals who regained physical independence. The greatest reduction in deaths occurred within the severe stroke group but the number needed to be treated to produce independent survivors was higher at 33. These analyses are limited by the relatively small amounts of data and the difficulties in reliably recording physical dependency which have been described above. However, they do indicate that many patients' chances of avoiding an adverse outcome depend on their baseline risk of experiencing that outcome.

What kind of stroke unit?

The analysis presented above compares two types of 'black box'. This is a reasonable approach to the broad question of whether stroke units can improve patient outcomes. However, if we wish to apply the results of the stroke unit trials, we need to look in more detail at the different models and components of stroke unit care included within the systematic review bearing in mind the methodological problems with such analyses (Oxman and Guyatt 1992). The components of the different approaches to stroke unit care, and the evidence to support these individual models need to be outlined.

Acute stroke units

Acute stroke units were initially developed in the United States and modelled on coronary care and neurological intensive care units (Langhorne et al. 1995). The rationale for these units was that many

of the early deaths following stroke are due to potentially modifiable causes such as infections, venous thromboembolism, and cardiac disease, and by improving the quality of care during the first few days these modifiable complications could be reduced. A number of early non-randomized trials were carried out (Millikan 1979) which suggested that the quality of stroke care may well be improved but there was no measurable effect on case fatality. Only one randomized trial has evaluated an acute stroke unit which intervened in the immediate poststroke period (Ilmavirta et al. 1993). This trial found no significant difference in patient outcomes between the acute stroke unit and the conventional care provided by a multidisciplinary team in a mixed neurological ward. At present these units appear to offer a model for improving the organization and delivery of acute stroke care but there is no evidence that this alone will improve patient outcomes. This conclusion could change if effective acute treatments which require closely monitored acute care are developed.

Rehabilitation stroke units

Another approach has been to focus on a later phase of the illness; accepting patients 1 to 2 weeks after their initial stroke and continuing their care for many weeks or even months thereafter. Eight randomized trials have compared this model of care with general medical wards. These units appeared to improve aspects of the process and delivery of care (Langhorne et al. 1995) and also appeared to improve patient outcomes in terms of reducing death, disability, and institutionalization. Therefore there is evidence to support this model of care although it would not allow clinicians to exploit any new developments in acute stroke care.

Combined acute and rehabilitation stroke unit

An alternative model which has been particularly common in Scandinavia (Strand et al. 1985; Indredavik et al. 1991) is to combine acute stroke management with a period of rehabilitation lasting several weeks if required. This approach has been the subject of 12 randomized trials and appeared to reduce case fatality, dependency, and institutionalization. The main practical limitation to this form of stroke unit is that larger hospitals with large patient numbers would have practical difficulties in providing all stroke care within one unit.

Stroke teams

There has been some interest in developing organized stroke care based on a mobile stroke team rather than an architecturally defined unit. This approach may be able to provide a more flexible form of care although there are often practical difficulties in co-ordinating care across a large number of wards (Dennis and Langhorne 1994). Only one randomized trial (Wood-Dauphinée et al. 1984) has specifically evaluated this form of care so there is a lack of sufficient evidence to come to a reliable conclusion.

Disease-specific versus disability-specific units

One question which frequently arises in geriatric medical practice is whether the benefits of a stroke unit can also be achieved through improvements in stroke care within a mixed disability setting such as a geriatric medical assessment and rehabilitation unit. Descriptive studies (Stroke Unit Trialists' Collaboration 1997) indicate that the organization of care is very similar within these two types of stroke unit setting. The information available from the randomized trials (Stroke Unit Trialists' Collaboration 1997) strongly suggests that both disease-specific (stroke only) and disability-specific (mixed disability) services can improve stroke patient outcomes in comparison with conventional care in general medical wards. Information from the three randomized trials (Stevens et al. 1984; Kalra et al. 1993; Juby et al. 1996) which have directly compared the two forms of organized stroke care indicated trends towards improved outcomes within the disease-specific (stroke only) type of unit. However, these results are not statistically significant and this remains one of the main unresolved questions about how best to organize the delivery of care for stroke patients.

What are the components of a stroke unit?

A basic practical question when planning services for stroke inpatients is what are the important components of an effective stroke unit? The information from the randomized trials can be used to construct a basic template of a stroke unit which has been shown to be effective in clinical trials.

1. Staff—medical, nursing, physiotherapy, occupational therapy, speech and language therapy, and social work staff are required in any basic multidisciplinary team.
2. Co-ordination—the multidisciplinary team should be involved in the planning and delivery of individual patient care and should be co-ordinated through weekly team meetings in which each member of the team can contribute.
3. Interests of staff—units will be staffed by individuals who have an interest and expertise in stroke and/or rehabilitation.
4. Size—stroke units have varied in size from between six and 30 beds. The larger units will be able to cope with fluctuations in patient load; however, practical difficulties can arise in managing larger patient numbers.

5. Protocols—there was no clear trend in the use of investigation or treatment protocols within the stroke unit trials but these are often developed according to the interests of the rehabilitation staff.
6. Involvement of relatives—almost all units reported that they routinely tried to involve relatives in the rehabilitation process at an early stage.
7. Education and training—most units reported that they had programmes of ongoing education and training for staff in the subject of stroke disease. The majority of units also routinely provided information for patients and carers.
8. Specific treatments—no routine medical therapies have yet been proven to be of benefit in the management of acute stroke (Counsell and Sandercock 1994). There was no clear pattern of the use of specific medical, nursing, physiotherapy, occupational therapy, or speech therapy interventions within the stroke unit trials.

Future developments

Considerable information is available from randomized trials to conclude that organized inpatient (stroke unit) care centred around a co-ordinated multidisciplinary team with an interest in stroke can improve patient outcomes in comparison with conventional practice in general medical wards. However, a number of questions remain and indicate areas in which development could occur in future.

1. What is the best form of stroke unit care? We do not know which type of unit can produce the best outcomes.
2. Can acute care alone improve outcomes? Information is lacking on whether acute stroke units can improve outcomes in their own right.
3. Care after discharge from hospital. A number of trials have looked at rehabilitation in the longer term to support elderly stroke patients, but to date no clear consensus has emerged (Langhorne 1995).
4. Alternatives to hospital-based care. A few randomized trials are examining systems of care to prevent admission to hospital or to accelerate discharge from hospital. At present these systems of care remain unevaluated and it is unknown whether they can provide equivalent patient and carer outcomes to stroke unit care.
5. Can mobile stroke teams provide similar care to stroke wards? It is unclear at present if mobile stroke teams can replicate the benefits of stroke unit care provided within a specific location such as a stroke ward. There are practical difficulties in providing mobile team care and the main costs (i.e. staff costs) are probably similar to that of a stroke ward.

Conclusion

A number of randomized trials have indicated that organized inpatient (stroke unit) care is more effective than conventional care in a general medical ward. Patients managed in the stroke unit setting were more likely to survive, regain independence, and return home. These benefits were seen across a range of stroke patients and a range of stroke unit settings. The challenge is to implement the systems of care evaluated in these trials and improve the care of stroke patients in general.

References

Barer, D., Gibson, P., Ellul, J., and the 'GUESS' Group (1993). Outcome of hospital care for stroke in 12 centres. *Age and Ageing*, 22 (Supplement 3), P15–P16.

Bonita, R. (1992). Epidemiology of stroke. *Lancet*, 339, 342–4.

Bonner, C.D. (1973). Stroke units in community hospitals: a how to guide. *Geriatrics*, 28, 166–70.

Counsell, C. and Sandercock, P. (1994). The management of patients with acute ischaemic stroke. *Current Medical Literature: Geriatrics*, 7, 99–104.

Davenport, R.J., Dennis, M.S., and Warlow, C.P. (1996). Effect of correcting outcome data for case mix: an example from stroke medicine. *British Medical Journal*, 312, 1503–5.

Dennis, M. and Langhorne, P. (1994). So stroke units save lives: where do we go from here? *British Medical Journal*, 312, 1503–5.

Donnan, G.A. (1993). Lifesaving for stroke. *Lancet*, 342, 383–4.

Ebrahim, S. (1990). *Clinical epidemiology of stroke*. Oxford University Press.

Feigensen, J.S., Gitlow, H.S., and Greenberg, S.D. (1979). The disability orientated rehabilitation unit—a major factor influencing stroke outcome. *Stroke*, 10, 5–8.

Garraway, W.M. (1985). Stroke rehabilitation units: concepts, evaluation and unresolved issues. *Stroke*, 16, 178–81.

Ilmavirta, M., Frey, H., Erila, T., and Fogelholm, R. (1993). Does treatment in a non-intensive care stroke unit improve the outcome of ischemic stroke? Presented at 7th Nordic Meeting on Cardiovascular Diseases, Jyvaskyla, Finland.

Indredavik, B., Bakke, F., Solberg, R., et al. (1991). Benefit of stroke unit: a randomised controlled trial. *Stroke*, 22, 1026–31.

Isaacs, B. (1977). Five years experience of a stroke unit. *Health Bulletin*, 35, 93–8.

Juby, L.C., Lincoln, N.B., and Berman, P. (1996). The effect of a stroke rehabilitation unit on functional and psychological outcome. *Cerebrovascular Disease*, 6, 106–10.

Kalra, L., Dale, P., and Crome, P. (1993). Improving stroke rehabilitation. A controlled study. *Stroke*, 24, 1462–7.

King's Fund Forum Consensus Conference Statement (1988). Treatment of stroke. *British Medical Journal*, 297, 126–8.

Langhorne, P. (1995). Developing comprehensive stroke services: an evidence-based approach. *Postgraduate Medical Journal*, 71, 733–7.

Langhorne, P., Dennis, M.S., and Williams, B.O. (1995). Stroke units: their role in acute stroke management. *Vascular Medicine Review*, 6, 33–44.

Langton Hewer, R. (1990). Rehabilitation after stroke. *Quarterly Journal of Medicine*, 76, 659–74.

Lindley, R.I., Amayo, E.O., Marshall, J., et al. (1995). Hospital services for patients with acute stroke in the United Kingdom: the Stroke Association survey of consultant opinion. *Age and Ageing*, 24, 525–32.

Millikan, C.H. (1979). Stroke intensive care: objectives and results. *Stroke*, 10, 235–7.

Oxman, A.D. and Guyatt, G.H. (1992). A consumer's guide to subgroup analysis. *Annals of Internal Medicine*, 116, 78–84.

Rubenstein, L.Z. (1990). The efficacy of geriatric assessment programmes. In *Improving the health of older people; a world view*, (ed. R.L. Kane, J. Grimley Evans, and D. MacFayden), pp. 417–39. Oxford University Press.

Sackett, D., Rosenberg, W., Richardson, S., et al. (1996). *How to practise and teach evidence-based medicine*. Churchill Livingstone, Edinburgh.

Stevens, R.S., Ambler, N.R., and Warren, M.D. (1984). A randomised controlled trial of a stroke rehabilitation ward. *Age and Ageing*, 13, 65–75.

Strand, T., Asplund, K., Eriksson, S., et al. (1985). A non-intensive stroke unit reduces functional disability and the need for long-term hospitalisation. *Stroke*, 16, 29–34.

Stroke Unit Trialists' Collaboration (1995). What is a stroke unit? A survey of the randomised trials. *Cerebrovascular Disease*, 5, 228.

Stroke Unit Trialists' Collaboration (1996). Why are stroke units effective? A systematic review of the randomised trials. *Cerebrovascular Disease*, 6, 24.

Stroke Unit Trialists' Collaboration (1997). A collaborative systematic review of the randomised trials of organized inpatient (stroke unit) care after stroke. *British Medical Journal*, 314, 1151–9.

Stuck, A.E., Siu, A.L., Wieland, G.D., et al. (1993). Comprehensive geriatric assessment: a meta-analysis of controlled trials. *Lancet*, 342, 1032–6.

Warlow, C., van Gijn, J., and Sandercock, P. (1997). *The stroke module of the Cochrane Database of Systematic Reviews*. BMJ Publishing, London (CD-ROM updated quarterly).

Wood-Dauphinée, S., Shapiro, S., and Bass, E. (1984). A randomised trial of team care following stroke. *Stroke*, 5, 864–72.

23.5 Memory disorders clinics

Gordon K. Wilcock

Introduction

The increasing number of people with dementia and other memory-related disorders has had an impact, at an international level, on the development of services to advise about the detection and management of these conditions. This is becoming increasingly important with the availability of treatment programmes for a number of the underlying conditions that cause dementia, and the need for early recognition and diagnosis. Many of these approaches are multidisciplinary in nature, and the staff involved are frequently available in the context of a hospital clinic, which allows the back-up facilities of a secondary care setting to be made more easily available. Nevertheless, many

Test' (Baddeley *et al.* 1993) which utilizes the ability to choose between 50 pairs of words and non-words as an estimate of premorbid ability.

Computer assessment

Computerized neuropsychological test batteries have been developed for use in a number of contexts, including a memory clinic setting. They are not an alternative to the standard approach, but are complementary. Their strengths include reducing the subject–rater interaction, or at least going some way towards standardizing this, and a rapid calculation of the results of the outcome of the test procedures. They can perform sophisticated statistical analyses very rapidly, and there is emerging evidence that they may be of value in the early detection of dementia (Fowler *et al.* 1997). They are also useful in a context of sequential assessment as most of them have alternative versions that have been cross-validated against each other, minimizing the learning effect.

Assessment of function

The loss of functional ability in social and occupational activities that accompanies the cognitive decline in dementia is an important part of the disease process. Its assessment does not always receive the same interest and attention as that of cognitive impairment. In many instances, however, it is an inability to undertake normal day-to-day activities that first alerts relatives or professional colleagues to the fact that there may be something wrong. This is especially the case for those dementias that do not present with a prominent memory loss in the early stages. Functional decline does not always mirror that in cognition, and it is therefore often impossible to extrapolate from one to the other. For this reason it is important to use a standardized assessment of functional ability whenever this is feasible. Establishing a baseline and monitoring the progression of this type of impairment may be more relevant to assessing a person's ability to remain at home than neuropsychological testing.

The most usual and useful forms of functional assessment are centred on the activities of daily living. These are often divided into two categories: the basic activities of daily living, including self-care (dressing, bathing, feeding, etc.), and the more complex instrumental activities of daily living such as shopping, cooking, jobs around the house, using the telephone, etc. Unlike basic activities of daily living, instrumental activities of daily living are influenced by a number of personal factors, such as cultural and educational background, whether male or female, and the development of professional skills. The importance of functional assessment is now enshrined in many of the definitions of dementia which require that the intellectual deficits are sufficient to cause significant impairment in social and occupational functioning.

A number of scales have been developed to measure functional ability, and those that are most practical involve third party report, for example from a spouse or caregiver, rather than direct observation. The score obtained from a rating scale may depend upon the ability to undertake and complete a task but often of more value are those scales that provide a qualitative measure, that is how well the task is undertaken, and/or how much help is needed to complete it (Lawton and Brody 1969; Linn and Linn 1982; Bucks *et al.* 1996*b*). More recent developments in this field include the development of process scales which concentrate on assessing the process of performing an activity instead of measuring whether it is successfully performed.

The skills that are assessed in this context include those that we often take for granted, such as the ability to organize and plan an activity, whether the sequence of events in a complex activity such as dressing are undertaken in a logical order, etc. The activity itself is less important in this measure of assessment than the process, and how the latter is undertaken (Carswell *et al.* 1995).

When choosing an instrument for use in a particular context, such as a memory disorders clinic, it is important to remember that there are a number of factors that should be considered before a final decision is made. This includes the context in which the instrument was first developed and the population at which it was targeted, its validity in terms of the relevance of the information gained to assessment of the patient in a clinic setting, and more practical aspects such as the time that it requires and whether it is administered by direct observation or caregiver report. One of the most important considerations is to question whether or not it was developed for use with people who have a dementia, rather than the less specific task of assessing elderly people in general.

Differential diagnosis

The findings on history and examination play a major role, as already described, in arriving at the most likely diagnosis. For the majority of patients the diagnosis is usually that which is most probable, for example probable Alzheimer's disease, probable vascular dementia, rather than a more definitive decision. Nevertheless, the accuracy of such probable diagnoses in clinics with experience and relevant expertise is of the order of 90 per cent, when confirmed by autopsy examination of the brain. A more reliable diagnosis can be achieved where there is definitive laboratory evidence for a particular underlying disorder, which occurs infrequently, or where there is a genetic element, for instance familial dementia, in which the aetiology of the disease has been established at autopsy in members of the family previously affected. The difficulty in making a diagnosis for the majority of elderly people who develop a dementia has led to the establishment of standardized criteria, which have proved invaluable in both the clinical and research setting. Nevertheless, they must not be regarded as absolute. Examples include the National Institute of Neurological and Communicative Diseases and Stroke/Alzheimer's Disease and Related Disorders Association (NINCDS-ADRDA) criteria for Alzheimer's disease (McKhann *et al.* 1984), the Hachinski Ischemia Scale (Hachinski *et al.* 1974), and the more recently developed diagnostic instruments for vascular dementia, the State of California Alzheimer's Disease Diagnostic Treatment Centres (AD-DTC) test (Chui *et al.* 1992) and the NINDS-AIREN test (Roman *et al.* 1993). These newer criteria are reviewed by Amar *et al.* (1996). A similar approach has been adopted for the diagnosis of dementia associated with Lewy bodies (McKeith *et al.* 1996).

Management of dementia

The principles of the management of dementia and some of the different conditions that are responsible are covered in Chapter 18.20. As well as the traditional approach to treating behavioural disturbance, that is the judicious and sparing use of pharmacological treatment where behavioural modification and management fails, attention to risk factors that predispose to the development of vascular dementia, and the need to very carefully use phenothiazines in those with Lewy body dementias, a whole host of new and exciting developments have appeared for the specific treatment of Alzheimer's disease, some of which may also be relevant for dementia associated with Lewy bodies. These include the cholinesterase inhibitors, muscarinic agonists, strategies to retard the basic pathological processes such as the formation of amyloid and neurofibrillary tangles in Alzheimer's disease, and the emerging importance of anti-inflammatory medication, hormone replacement therapy and antioxidants such as vitamin E. Despite these developments, it is important not to forget that most of the 'treatment' for dementia sufferers and their families is presently still borne by carers. Much of this can be initiated through the clinic, if this is part of its brief, or by recommendations back to the referring agency if that is more appropriate.

References

Alexopoulos, G.S., Abrams, R.C., Young R.C., and Shamoian, C.A. (1988). Cornell Scale for Depression in dementia. *Biological Psychiatry*, 23, 271–84.

Amar, K., Wilcock, G.K., and Scott, M. (1996). The diagnosis of vascular dementia in light of the new criteria. *Age and Ageing*, 25, 51–5.

Baddeley, A., Emslie, H., and Nimmo-Smith, I. (1993). The Spot the Word Test: a robust estimate of verbal intelligence based upon lexical decision. *Journal of Clinical Psychology*, 32, 55–65.

Ballard C.G., Bannister, C., and Oyebode, F. (1996). Depression in dementia sufferers. *International Journal of Geriatric Psychiatry*, 11, 507–15.

Beattie, L.B., Bucks, R.S., and Matthews, J. (1998). Administration and organisational aspects. In *Diagnosis and management of dementia: a manual for memory disorders teams* (ed. G.K. Wilcock, K. Rockwood, and R.S. Bucks), pp. 13–28. Oxford University Press.

Bucks, R.S. and Loewenstein, D. (1998). Neuropsychological assessment. In *Diagnosis and management of dementia: a manual for memory disorders teams* (ed. G.K. Wilcock, K. Rockwood, and R.S. Bucks), pp. 102–23. Oxford University Press.

Bucks, R.S., Scott, M.I., Pearsall, T., and Ashworth, D.L. (1996a). The short NART: utility in a memory disorders clinic. *British Journal of Clinical Psychology*, 35, 133–41.

Bucks, R.S., Ashworth, D.A., Wilcock, G.K., and Siegfried, K.S. (1996b). Assessment of activities of daily living in dementia: development of the Bristol activities of daily living scale. *Age and Ageing*, 25, 113–20.

Carswell, A., Dulberg, C., Carson, L., and Zgola, J. (1995). The functional performance measure for persons with Alzheimer's disease: reliability and validity. *Canadian Journal of Occupational Therapy*, 62, 62–9.

Chui, H.C., Victoroff, J.I., Margolin, D., Jagust, W.J., Shankle, R., and Katzman, R. (1992). Criteria for the diagnosis of ischemic vascular dementia proposed by the State of California Alzheimer's Disease Diagnostic and Treatment Centres. *Neurology*, 42, 473–80.

Costa, P.J., Jr, Williams, T.F., Albert, M.S., *et al.* (1997). Early identification of Alzheimer's disease and related dementias. *American Familiy Physician*, 55, 1303–14.

Folstein M.F., Folstein, S.E., and McHugh, P.E. (1975). 'Mini-Mental State': a practical method for grading the cognitive state of patients for the clinician? Mini-Mental State Examination. *Neurology*, 40, 1894–6.

Fowler, K.S., Saling M.M., Conway, E.L., Semple, J.M., and Louis, W.J. (1997). Computerised neuropsychological tests in the early detection of dementia: prospective findings. *Journal of the International Neuropsychological Society*, 3, 139–46.

Graham, J.E. and Agg, M. (1998). In *Diagnosis and management of dementia: a manual for memory disorders teams* (ed. G.K. Wilcock, K. Rockwood, and R.S. Bucks), pp. 29–47. Oxford University Press.

Hachinski, V.C., Lassen, N.A., and Marshal, J. (1974). Multi-infarct dementia: a cause of mental deterioration in the elderly. *Lancet*, ii, 207–10.

Lawton, M.P. and Brody, E.M. (1969). Assessment of older people: self-maintaining and instrumental activities of daily living. *Gerontologist*, 9, 179–86.

Linn, M.W. and Linn B.S. (1982). The Rapid Disability Scale—2. *Journal of the American Geriatrics Society*, 30, 378–82.

McKeith, I.G., Galasko, G., Kosaka, K., *et al.* (1996). Consensus guidelines for the clinical and pathologic diagnosis of dementia with Lewy bodies (DLB): report of the Consortium on DLB International Workshop. *Neurology*, 47, 1113–24.

McKhann, G., Drachmann, D.A., Folstein, M., Katzman, R., Price, D.L., and Stadlan, E.M. (1984). Clinical diagnosis of Alzheimer's disease. Report of the NINCDS-ADRDA Work Group under the auspices of the Department of Health and Human Services Task Force on Alzheimer's Disease. *Neurology*, 34, 939–44.

Morris, J.C., Heyman, A., Mohs, R.C., Hughs, J.P., van Belle, G., Fillenbaum, G., and the CERAD Investigators (1989). The Consortium to Establish a Registry for Alzheimer's Disease (CERAD). I. Clinical and neuropsychological assessment of Alzheimer's disease. *Neurology*, 39, 1159–65.

Nelson, H.E. and Willison, J. (1991). *National Adult Reading Test (NART) test manual including new data supplement*. NFER-Nelson, Windsor.

Reisberg, G., Borenstein, J., Salob, S., *et al.* (1987). Behavioural symptoms in Alzheimer's disease: phenomenology and treatment. *Journal of Clinical Psychiatry*, 48 (Supplement 5), 9–15.

Roman, G.C., Tatemichi, T.K., Erkinjuntti, T., Cummings, J.L., Masdeu, J.C., and Garcia, J.H. (1993). Vascular dementia: diagnostic criteria for research studies. Report of the NINDS-AIREN International Workshop. *Neurology*, 43, 250–60.

Smith J.S. and Kiloh L.G. (1981). The investigation of dementia: results in 200 consecutive admissions. *Lancet*, i, 824–7.

Wilcock, G.K. and Skoog, I. (1998). Medical assessment. In *Diagnosis and management of dementia: a manual for memory disorders teams* (ed. G.K. Wilcock, K. Rockwood, and R.S. Bucks), pp. 48–61. Oxford University Press.

Wright, N. and Lindesay, J. (1995). A survey of memory clinics in the British Isles. *International Journal of Geriatric Psychiatry*, 10, 379–85.

23.6 Home care: issues and innovations

Bruce Leff and Knight Steel

Introduction

The images of a physician, talismanic black bag in hand, or a nurse making a house call are powerful ones. They evoke the dedication and caring of those health professionals who know their patients within the more complete context of their lives. Providing care on the patient's own 'turf' makes human the recipient of care and facilitates assessment of 'non-medical' aspects of care: social support systems, environment, and functional abilities of individuals. It encourages the appropriate use of the history and physical examination as a tool for clinical decision making. Home care can strengthen the relationship between a health-care provider and patient, and reinforce the need for health-care providers to be educators and advocates for their patients. Furthermore, providers are required to work in teams which often include family members (Burton 1985). All of these features of home care provide a unique opportunity for health-care professionals to make a significant contribution to the lives and well being of their patients.

Quite understandably, home care is popular with elderly people, and in many places, utilization of services has increased substantially in recent years. In the United States, spending on home health services by Medicare, which funds most health care for older Americans, increased from $2 billion in 1988 to $16.7 billion in 1996 and now accounts for 8 per cent of Medicare expenditure (Welch *et al.* 1996). This growth is a function of demographic, social, and technological factors, as well as economic incentives within the system. The number of older people, especially the oldest old, is increasing sharply in societies throughout the industrialized world. Although many in this segment of the population prefer home-based care, especially when it comes to long-term care, demographic projections suggest that there will be fewer family members close at hand to assist in the care of this frail group of individuals. Improvements in medical technology have helped move progressively more complex care from the hospital, long-term care, and ambulatory sites to the home. As pressures mount to reduce the use of high cost hospital care individuals will need to be more acutely ill to gain admission to hospitals and will remain there for progressively shorter periods of time thereby assuring that home care will increasingly be directed to a larger and more medically unstable population. These forces place enormous evolutionary pressures on home care and it is fairly certain that in the year 2010, home care will be more expansive, perhaps even with subspecialties targeted to special needs.

This chapter focuses exclusively on home care as it relates to the care of older people. Most of the data come from the United States and Europe, and though many of these care models may be system specific, it is likely that elements of these systems could be adapted to other settings and health-care systems. Such an examination should permit rational judgements to be made within a specific societal and cultural context and should prevent the tendency to romanticize home care. The chapter concludes with a discussion of problems related to home care as well as recent innovations in the field.

Semantics

The term home care is quite vague and may refer to any of a number of health-care services provided in the home. It most often refers to nursing, hygienic, or social support services provided to older people in need of chronic care with the explicit goal of maintaining them in the community. Such care usually is provided by one or more members of an interdisciplinary team under the general direction of a physician. Home care may also refer to postacute hospital care, geriatric assessment services, prevention health strategies, formal rehabilitation services, and high-technology programmes. Often, these services overlap and it may be difficult to put one simple label on an intervention. For example, a study of home-based geriatric assessment provided to older people upon discharge from the acute hospital that provides physician-led community-based long-term care and rehabilitation with an interdisciplinary team may be difficult to categorize.

Utilization of home care

Irrespective of the country where research is conducted, functional disability is a major predictor of the use of home care services. This is found across many studies, examining different health systems, with different measures, samples, and comparison groups (Chappell 1994). In the United States, the 1987 National Medical Expenditure Survey (**NMES**-2) described the characteristics and number of functionally impaired people over the age of 65 years. Those most likely to use home health services were aged 75 years and older, female, living alone, and had limitations in three or more activities of daily living (Short and Leon 1990). Other data suggest that utilization may be predicted by the supply of services. A study examining the differences in rural and urban community mental health care in The Netherlands found that supply of services, not need, was the major predictor of utilization (Gerritsen *et al.* 1990). In the United States the significant geographic variation in home care utilization is probably not explained by differences in disease burden and may relate more to local reimbursement policies or the result of business practices (Welch *et al.* 1996).

Community-based long-term care

Community-based long-term care entails the provision of health or personal care services to older people in their homes. Such care programmes include in-home nursing, interdisciplinary team care, home aide care, adult day health care, hospice care, respite care, and programmes that provide combinations of these and other services. The explicit goals of such care are to maintain elderly people in the community, maintain or improve function, prevent hospital admission or nursing-home placement, and reduce costs. As of 1994, the 32 well-designed studies of community-based long-term care were reviewed (Hedrick and Inui 1986; Weissert and Hedrick 1994).

The largest and most ambitious study of community-based long-term care was the Channeling National Long Term Care Demonstration project carried out in the United States. This massive undertaking, carried out in 10 states, compared case management with and without an infusion of a broad array of purchased services. The trial served a very frail population; 22 per cent of subjects were dependent in five of six activities of daily living. The results of this study were similar to other community-based long-term care studies. Despite state-of-the-art screening, targeting community-based long-term care to frail older people failed to identify people who would end up in nursing homes. The intervention failed to lower hospital use or nursing-home placement or affect the functional abilities of patients. There was no major effect on the provision of informal caregiving, and there was increased use of formal community services. The comprehensive assessment and follow-up did decrease unmet care needs, produced a transient improvement in life satisfaction, and appealed to caregivers (Kemper 1988; Weissert 1988).

The Adult Day Health Care Evaluation Study had two components: a randomized controlled trial of adult day health care compared with usual care in eight veteran's administration medical centres, and a prospective cohort study comparing community-based adult day health care with veteran's administration-based adult day health care and usual care. In this well-designed and well-implemented study, there were no differences in health outcomes between groups, and costs were generally higher in the intervention groups. One subgroup of patients, those with severe disabilities, had lower nursing home, clinic, home care, pharmacy, and laboratory costs. Patients with moderate and low levels of disability and few behavioural problems had significantly higher costs (Hedrick *et al.* 1993).

These trials contain lessons for clinicians and policy makers (Weissert and Hedrick 1994). Clinicians need to improve their ability to predict risk so as to target patients who will most likely benefit from specific interventions. They must also appreciate that less care may be as beneficial to functional outcomes as more care. Policy makers must incorporate consumer preference to remain at home into their decision to support community-based long-term care in the absence of data suggesting that there will be significant economic savings associated with its use.

Recent evaluations of the Programs for All-inclusive Care of the Elderly (**PACE**) in the United States, combined day programmes and home care for very frail elderly people, have shown significant economic savings consisting of reduced hospital admissions and less use of nursing homes (Eng 1997).

Postacute hospital home care— interventions to reduce hospital readmissions

Home care following an acute hospital admission has become increasingly common as hospital stays in the United States and other nations are truncated. Individuals are increasingly discharged 'sicker and quicker' (Shaughnessy and Kramer 1990) in response to economic pressures to reduce acute hospital costs. This trend has been facilitated by the growing capabilities of home care to provide types of care that were formerly available only in the acute inpatient setting.

Certain postacute hospital home care interventions have been shown to be beneficial. These interventions have been undertaken in various countries and have resulted in improvements in function, reduction in acute hospital utilization, and even some economic savings. Each of the successful trials have targeted interventions to individuals at risk: those over the age of 75 years or those with specific chronic conditions, such as congestive heart failure, commonly associated with early readmission to hospital. Unlike many home care programmes typical of community-based long-term care, these interventions have included substantial medical management, had much of the care delivered by nurse practitioners and nurse specialists, and have been relatively inexpensive (Campion 1995). A variety of interventions have been demonstrated to be successful.

In Denmark, 404 patients over the age of 75 years upon discharge from the acute hospital were randomly assigned to usual care or to visits by a nurse on the day of discharge from hospital. The nurse who made these visits was instructed to identify and solve new problems. Two weeks later, a general practitioner made a home visit to follow-up on hospital treatment and make any other required adjustments in the patient's care plan. At 1 year, the intervention group had significantly fewer nursing-home admissions, though no change in mortality or number of readmissions to the acute hospital (Hansen *et al.* 1992). In England, 903 subjects over the age of 75 years were randomly assigned at the time of discharge from hospital to support from a care attendant who could provide up to 12 h of care per week for a period of 2 weeks. The care attendant provided practical care, help with rehabilitation, and assisted in organizing social help from family, friends, and statutory services. There was no difference between the intervention and control groups in their abilities to perform activities of daily living or in mortality. However, at 18 months, patients in the control group spent significantly more time in hospital and were twice as likely to be readmitted to hospital more than twice (Townsend *et al.* 1988). In Israel, patients with severe congestive heart failure, were enrolled in an intensive home surveillance programme. The intervention consisted of weekly home visits by a physician and a trained paramedical team. In a preintervention/postintervention analysis, there was a significant reduction in the rates of hospital admissions for both cardiac causes and all causes as well as a decrease in hospital length of stay and improved function (Kornowski *et al.* 1995). A trial in the United States which also focused on older patients with congestive heart failure randomly assigned patients at the time of hospital discharge to an intervention consisting of the following: intensive education of patients by nurses regarding their illness, dietary assessment and instructions by a dietitian, discharge planning by a social worker, review and consolidation of the medical regimen by a geriatric cardiologist, and intensive follow-up by nurses by phone and home visits. The intervention resulted in a significant reduction in the number of readmissions for heart failure and in the number of multiple readmissions. Quality of life measures improved in both groups, though significantly more in the intervention group. It is unknown which element or combination of elements of this intervention were most important in producing these beneficial effects (Rich et al. 1995).

A recent English randomized trial of home hospital compared with acute hospital treatment suggested that there were few clinical differences in treatment groups for patients recovering from hip replacement or hysterectomy, patients with chronic obstructive airways disease, or elderly patients with medical problems (Coast et al. 1998; Shepperd et al. 1998). In addition, costs for home hospital patients were lower, most patients preferred home hospital, and there was no increase in caregiver burden. Another randomized trial of home hospital in Australia, for older adults with medical problems, found that it was at least as effective, safe, and acceptable as acute hospital; reduced rates of common iatrogenic complications such as confusion, bowel complications, and urinary complications were demonstrated in the home hospital group (Caplan et al. 1999).

Home geriatric assessment and prevention models

The home is an ideal environment in which to implement geriatric assessment and prevention strategies. Patients can be examined in their usual surroundings where the realities of their daily living and function are more obvious than in the office or hospital setting (Ramsdell et al. 1989). Studies examining home geriatric assessment and prevention strategies have demonstrated beneficial effects.

The strategies reported from American and European studies have employed a variety of types of interventions targeted to different populations among elderly people. A common thread among these studies is assessment, surveillance, and the making of specific recommendations to patients or their physician or initiating referrals to appropriate community services. Some studies have targeted older people at enhanced risk of future problems while others have simply used an age criterion. Controlled trials of such interventions, many of which were randomized studies, have demonstrated a variety of beneficial outcomes.

There have been several interventions targeted at older patients immediately following discharge from the acute hospital. In-home assessment, by a nurse practitioner with interdisciplinary back-up, of people with risk factors for functional decline has demonstrated an ability to detect significant problems after recent hospital discharge and high compliance with recommendations made to primary physicians based on assessment findings (Kravitz et al. 1994). A randomized study of a home assessment for patients over the age of 75 years by a nurse on the day of hospital discharge and a physician visit 2 weeks later demonstrated a decreased rate of nursing-home admissions among those patients receiving the assessment (Hansen et al. 1992).

However, regular health visitor visits which did not result in a significant number of referrals or recommendations being made had no significant benefit (Williams et al. 1992).

Community-based in-home assessment programmes of varying complexity and expense have demonstrated varying degrees of benefits. Low-intensity interventions such as regularly scheduled home visits by unskilled volunteers to assess activities of daily life and make referrals for medical and social services resulted in reductions in long-term institutional admissions and quicker referrals to community supports (Carpenter and Demopoulos 1990). Health visitors have also been shown in urban settings to have a benefit on mortality rates (Vetter et al. 1984). Interventions by nurses who perform assessments, educate patients, and make referrals to appropriate medical and social services are more costly than health visitor interventions but have been shown to improve the morale of patients (McEwan et al. 1990), improve survival (Hendriksen et al. 1984; Hall et al. 1992; Pathy et al. 1992), and decrease the number of hospital admissions and hospital days (Hendriksen et al. 1989). Such interventions usually result in an increase in the use of community services among intervention groups, though the financial impact for the health system is usually neutral. Higher intensity home assessment programmes consisting of initial assessment by a nurse, review with a geriatrician, recommendations to the primary physician, and scheduled nursing follow-up have been shown to result in higher function, decreased admission to nursing homes (Stuck et al. 1995), increased likelihood of having a primary physician, and the maintenance of function (Fabacher et al. 1994).

Physician house-call programmes

Physician house-call programmes designed to provide longitudinal care for frail older people at home have been described in several countries. These programmes provide an important service for those truly housebound patients for whom going to an ambulatory clinic is a significant physical or logistical hardship. In addition to providing a needed service, they provide an excellent training ground for physicians. They promote positive attitudes towards home care (Finucane and Burton 1994). This latter attribute may be especially important in that it has been found that whether a physician values making a house visit is associated with the likelihood that he or she will make them as part of their practice (Boling et al. 1990).

Such programmes have been described the literature in several countries (Galinsky et al. 1983; Steel 1987; Finucane and Burton 1994). Some are associated with large medical centres and teaching hospitals while others are associated with primary care clinics. Successful programmes share certain key features. An explicitly articulated mission to provide care to frail older people at home and a multidisciplinary team of physicians, nurses, home health aides, social worker, and therapists dedicated to the programme are critical to success. The linchpin of many such programmes is a patient or programme co-ordinator whose function it is to orchestrate the function of this team. Team meetings occur on a regularly scheduled, often weekly, basis to allow group discussion of active patients. Although it is sometimes difficult to differentiate between community-based long-term care programmes and these physician-led house-call programmes in the literature, there have been studies which demonstrate the effectiveness of the latter. A physician-led house-call programme in Sweden targeting patients dependent in one to five activities of daily life, but excluding demented patients and patients totally dependent in activities of daily life, demonstrated in a randomized controlled trial improved function in the instrumental activities of daily life, fewer active diagnoses, decreased medication use, and reduced costs compared with conventional treatment (Melin et al. 1993). In a randomized trial of a physician-led house-call programme for terminally ill and severely disabled American veterans (with more than two deficiencies in the activities of daily life), there was improved satisfaction with care and a reduction in care costs (Cummings et al. 1990). Another randomized trial of this type of care model demonstrated fewer hospital admissions, nursing-home admissions, and outpatient visits compared with usual care (Zimmer et al. 1995).

Home rehabilitation care

Providing rehabilitation care for older people in their home allows individuals to avoid prolonged stays in inpatient rehabilitation settings and appropriately personalizes the approach to maximize function. One home physical therapy programme in the United Kingdom, which was compared with a compatible programme provided in a geriatric day hospital was shown to have a slight advantage in improving activities of daily life (Young and Forster 1992). However, another study in England comparing home physical and occupational therapy with hospital-based services found no difference in outcome (Gladman et al. 1993). When these studies were examined in a pooled analysis, a small advantage was found for home rehabilitation in reducing disability at 6 months (Gladman et al. 1995). An Australian study of home rehabilitation for older people with femur fractures, using historical controls, demonstrated a significant reduction in the length of hospital stay, no change in morbidity or mortality, and a 15 per cent cost savings (Sikorski and Senior 1993).

Problems in home care

Home care policy in any nation must be understood in the context of its particular health and social system and its specific policy aims. To a varying degree most countries are concerned with reducing hospital costs and rates of institutionalization, and all wish to improve the quality of life of their older citizens and their caregivers. In some nations, such as Denmark and the United Kingdom which have tax-funded national health systems, home care services consist predominantly of help with personal care and home making, rather than skilled nursing. Care is often provided on a long-term basis and services, based on professionally defined needs, are available without a physician's prescription. In other nations, such as Germany and the United States, where an insurance principle dominates health-care funding, home care is not automatically recognized as a matter for public provision. This results in the significant 'medicalization' of patient problems in order to obtain home care and may be followed by administrative efforts to reduce care (Jamieson 1992). For example, the chief administrator of the Health Care Finance Administration in the United States recently wanted to tighten the definition of 'homebound' to forestall elaborate treatment plans for people not sick enough to need them (Anders and McGinley 1997). All policy-makers will need to reconcile the great popularity of home care and

growing political influence of older people with economic exigencies by deciding how to value home care especially in those circumstances when its benefit in a strictly economic sense may be marginal or non-existent.

In most countries, the vast majority of physicians are not involved in nor have been trained to provide home care. The major reasons cited for this lack of involvement are the inconvenience and inefficiency of making home visits, lack of adequate reimbursement, and concerns about the ability to deliver quality medical care in the home with attendant liability concerns (Keenan and Fanale 1989). In addition, medical education, at least in the United States, essentially ignores home care to the extent that almost half of all medical schools did not devote a single hour to home care over the 4-year curriculum (Steel et al. 1994). As a result, academic interest in the field is generally lacking and the ensuing dearth of qualified faculty staff to teach home care compounds the problem.

Problems related to the issue of caregivers transcend geography. In the United States, family caregivers provide at least 80 per cent of home health care received by community-dwelling frail elderly people (Council on Scientific Affairs 1991). Caring for a family member at home is often extremely demanding and due to factors related to the demographics of ageing and societal habits, caregiving burdens fall disproportionately on women—spouses of chronically ill husbands, and adult daughters or daughters-in-law of elderly parents (Arras and Dubler 1994). Despite economic pressures that may reduce at-home care for patients, the number of older people maintained in the community will increase and the continued availability of informal caregivers will be necessary.

Concerns regarding the quality of home health care and the measures of quality of care delivered in the home are prevalent among providers, policy makers, and academics. Although issues related to quality are challenging in the traditional settings of the hospital and ambulatory clinic (Blumenthal 1996; Brook et al. 1996), in the home these issues become more complex (Applebaum and Phillips 1990). Needs for home services may be determined by other than strictly medical considerations. Cognitive and functional limitations of patients and even caregivers become important considerations. Furthermore, there are frequently administrative issues when a variety of medical and social services are provided by multiple agencies and corporations each with different procedures and incentives to provide care. This can result in fragmentation of care and a lack of accountability for care (Jette et al. 1996). A recent study examining the quality of over 4000 episodes of Medicare-reimbursed home health care, using process indicators, found that 57 per cent of all home health-care episodes had no quality problem, but nearly 15 per cent of episodes had a quality deficiency with potential for or actual adverse impact on the patient. The likelihood of quality problems increased with the level of frailty of the patients. Interestingly, there was no detectable difference in this American study in the quality of care delivered between agencies providing care on a prospective payment basis compared with those on a fee-for-service basis. It should be noted that such process-oriented quality studies do not address outcomes or the effectiveness of the care provided.

Although home care is often preferred to long-term institutional care or hospital care, ethical and social problems may result when substantial quantities of care are provided in the home. Even non-technological home care for older people can be a complex phenomenon in terms of what it requires from caregivers. There is a tendency for home care to use higher levels of technology, such as the use of feeding tubes, parenteral medications or nutrition, or special beds to 'medicalize' the home environment. This may alter the view of the patient and the family of the meaning of the word 'home'. As one philosopher argued, 'illness and treatment can transform even spacious quarters and caring family relationships into hospital-like conditions. Rooms may lose their comforting familiarity, and families may lose their familial intimacies and mutual trust' (Ruddick 1994). This reminds us that home care is not necessarily suited to all people and situations and that home care should not be romanticized as 'the worst home is not necessarily better than the best hospital' (Arras and Dubler 1994).

Innovations in home health care

The rapid growth of medical capabilities as well as economically driven changes in medical systems in the industrialized world have sparked significant innovations in models of home health-care delivery, types of care able to be delivered at home, quality measures for home health care, and educational efforts to improve home health care.

The development of home hospitals has been an important innovation in home health care. Care shifted from the home to the hospital in the second half of the twentieth century with an explosion of biomedical knowledge and technology, support from third-party payers, and heightened liability concerns. However, in time, patients, some physicians, and many payers have come to realize that the acute hospital is not the ideal care environment for all medical problems. This is especially true for older people who, in hospital, suffer significant functional decline and are more susceptible to iatrogenic illness and a cascade to dependency (Creditor 1993). To help certain patients avoid or abbreviate inpatient hospital stays, home hospitals are being developed in the United States (Leff *et al.* 1999), United Kingdom (Shepperd and Iliffe 1996), Canada (Ferguson 1993), and Israel (Stessman *et al.* 1996). In this model of care, critical elements of hospital care, physician and nursing care, medicines, and technology, are brought home to the patient. There are significant problems related to the issue of patient selection for this care model. Patients must be neither so sick that intensive care is required nor so well that home hospital simply provides extra care to those who should be treated in a less expensive and expansive manner (Leff and Burton 1996). To resolve this dilemma, some home hospital models have focused on specific illnesses such as myocardial infarction (Mather *et al.* 1976) or deep venous thrombosis (Koopman *et al.* 1996; Levine *et al.* 1996), which most physicians believe requires hospital admission. Other models have focused on older people with common illnesses such as community-acquired pneumonia or heart failure. The Israeli model provides home hospital without a specific diagnostic criterion. To date, specific home hospital models have been found to be feasible, safe, effective, and economical (Stessman *et al.* 1996). A similar study demonstrated that the benefits of this type of intervention in patients with heart failure may be sustained for at least 18 months (Stewart *et al.* 1999). More recent studies suggest that similar home-based interventions for patients with chronic illnesses following acute hospital stays can result in fewer unplanned readmissions, lower fatality, fewer emergency department encounters,

fewer total days spent in hospital, and lower cost of care (Stewart *et al.* 1998; Naylor *et al.* 1999).

Apart from specific new models of home health care, there has been a veritable explosion in the development of new portable medical technology available for home care. Mobile diagnostic units and emergency rooms have been developed. Many diagnostic tests once only available in the hospital or imaging centre such as ultrasound, radiography, ECG, etc. are now available for home use. Together with the movement of advanced diagnostic technology into the home there has been the movement of treatments into the home that previously would have required institutional long-term care such as enteral feeding tubes, parenteral nutrition, and wound care. With the increasing sophistication of home health agencies and pressures to reduce hospital costs, such treatments may be encouraged in the home although there are few data about their merits or disadvantages.

Recently, new quality measures have been developed and are being evaluated. Quality indicator groups have been developed for home health care and have been based on the premise that it is important to combine focused outcome and process indicators, and to a lesser extent structural measures, to assure quality. Quality indicator groups stratify home care recipients according to homogeneous care needs and for each of the 16 quality indicator groups, there are specific and appropriate outcome and process indicators. Quality indicator group proponents suggest that home health agencies may be profiled on the quality of care provided, and that such a schema of stratification will allow appropriate examination of case-mix issues, thereby improving care (Kramer *et al.* 1990).

The Outcome Assessment Information Set, currently being field-tested in the United States, represents an attempt to develop appropriate outcome measures for home care. It covers 79 specific items in several domains and for each domain the Outcome Assessment Information Set presents a very specific multiple choice format. It is hypothesized that the specificity of the questions will help with consistency between nurses assessing patients and define what care accomplishes (Carr 1996).

Another quality measurement tool is the Resident Assessment Instrument–Home Care System. This is a comprehensive, standardized instrument for evaluating the needs, strengths, and preferences of elderly clients of home care agencies. It was developed by an international group of researchers and has been designed to be compatible with the congressionally mandated Resident Assessment Instrument used in nursing homes in the United States and several other countries. Such compatibility can promote continuity of care through a 'seamless' geriatric assessment system across multiple health-care settings, and will promote a person-centred evaluation as opposed to site-specific assessment. The system is composed of a minimum data set for home care which is a screening tool. Items from the minimum data set for home care have 'triggers' which link the data set to 30 client assessment protocols which contain general guidelines for further assessment and individualized care planning. The average patient will trigger on 10 to 14 of the client assessment protocols. The instrument has high reliability and has been tested in many racial and ethnic groups (Morris *et al.* 1997).

All physicians should know the capabilities and limits of home care. Recently, there have been increasing efforts to improve the education of physicians in home health care with the goal of increasing their involvement as practitioners and leaders in this field. In the United States, the Council on Scientific Affairs of the American

Medical Association recommended that training in home health care be incorporated into the undergraduate, graduate, and continuing education of physicians and identified specific educational competencies and goals for physicians (Council on Scientific Affairs 1991). In addition, the American Medical Association developed it own programme of continuing medical education for physicians. At the postgraduate level there have been efforts to expand home care into academic medicine.

Conclusion

As the number of older people continues to increase, professionals within health-care systems throughout the industrialized world will need to make choices about the types of care they provide. For frail older people, home care is often preferable to most types of long-term institutional care and certain types of traditionally hospital-based acute care. Such preferences will need to be weighed carefully by researchers and policy makers alike. Home care can clearly benefit certain people though targeting appropriately and evaluating these interventions is difficult and complex.

References

Anders, G. and McGinley, L. (1997). Medicare home visits are a boon for entrepreneurs; costs explode 30 per cent a year; nurses pushed to add work. *Wall Street Journal*, 5 March 1997, p.1.

Applebaum, R. and Phillips, P. (1990). Assuring the quality of in-home care: the 'other' challenge for long-term care. *Gerontologist*, 30, 444–50.

Arras, J.D. and Dubler, N.N. (1994). Bringing the hospital home: ethical and social implications of high-tech home care. *Hastings Center Report*, 24 (Special Supplement 5), S19–S28.

Blumenthal, D. (1996). Quality of care—what is it? *New England Journal of Medicine*, 335, 891–4.

Boling, P.A., Retchin, S.M., Ellis, J., and Pancoast, S.A. (1990). The influence of physician specialty on housecalls. *Archives of Internal Medicine*, 150, 2333–7.

Brook, R.H., McGlynn, E.A., and Cleary, P.D. (1996). Measuring quality of care. *New England Journal of Medicine*, 335, 966–70.

Burton, J.R. (1985). The house call: an important service for the frail elderly. *Journal of the American Geriatrics Society*, 33, 291–3.

Campion, E.W. (1995). New hope for home care? *New England Journal of Medicine*, 333, 1213–14.

Caplan, G.A., Ward, J.A., Brennan, N.J., Coconis, J., Board, N., and Brown, A. (1999). Hospital in the home: a randomized controlled trial. *Medical Journal of Australia*, 170, 156–60.

Carpenter, G.I. and Demopoulos, G.R. (1990). Screening the elderly in the community: controlled trial of dependency surveillance using a questionnaire administered by volunteers. *British Medical Journal*, 300, 1253–6.

Carr, P. (1996). Get ready for OASIS. *Home Healthcare Nurse*, 14, 61–2.

Chappell, N.L. (1994). Home care research: what does it tell us? *Gerontologist*, 34, 116–20.

Coast, J., Richards, S.H., Peters, T.J., Gunnell, D.J., Darlow, A., and Pounsford, J. (1998). Hospital at home or acute hospital care? A cost minimisation analysis. *British Medical Journal*, 316, 1802–6.

Council on Scientific Affairs (1991). Educating physicians in home health care. *Journal of the American Medical Association*, 265, 769–71.

Creditor, M.C. (1993). Hazards of hospitalisation of the elderly. *Annals of Internal Medicine*, 118, 219–23.

Cummings, J.E., Hughes, S.L., Weaver, F.M., *et al.* (1990). Cost-effectiveness of Veterans Administration hospital-based home care. *Archives of Internal Medicine*, 150, 1274–80.

Eng, C., Pedulla, J., Eleanor, G.P., *et al.* (1997). Program for All-Inclusive Care of Elders (PACE): an innovative model of geriatric care and financing. *Journal of the American Geriatrics Society*, 45, 223–32.

Fabacher, D., Josephson, K., Pietruszka, F., Linderborn, K., Morley, J.E., and Rubenstein, L.Z. (1994). An in-home preventive assessment program for independent older adults: a randomized controlled trial. *Journal of the American Geriatrics Society*, 42, 630–8.

Ferguson, G. (1993). Designed to serve: the New Brunswick Extra-mural Hospital. *Journal of Ambulatory Care Management*, 16, 40–50.

Finucane, T.E. and Burton, J.R. (1994). The Elder Housecall Program at Johns Hopkins. *Pride Institute Journal*, 13, 29–36.

Galinsky, D., Schneiderman, K., and Lowenthal, M. (1983). A home care unit: geriatrically oriented and hospital-based with the active involvement of the family physician. *Israeli Journal of Medical Scientists*, 19, 841–4.

Gerritsen, J.C., Wolffensperger, E.W., and van den Heuvel, W.J.A. (1990). Rural–urban differences in the utilisation of care by the elderly. *Journal of Cross-Cultural Gerontology*, 5, 131–40.

Gladman, J.R.F., Lincoln, N.B., and Barer, D.H. (1993). A randomised controlled trial of domiciliary and hospital-based rehabilitation for stroke patients after discharge from hospital. *Journal of Neurologic, Neurosurgery and Psychiatry*, 56, 960–6.

Gladman, J., Forster, A., and Young, J. (1995). Hospital- and home-based rehabilitation after discharge from hospital for stroke patients: analysis of two trials. *Age and Ageing*, 24, 49–53.

Hall, N., Beck, P.D., Johnson, D., Mackinnon, K., Gutman, G., and Glick, N. (1992). Randomized trial of a health promotion program for frail elders. *Canadian Journal of Aging*, 11, 72–91.

Hansen, F.R., Spedtsberg, K., and Schroll, M. (1992). Geriatric follow-up by home visits after discharge from hospital: a randomized controlled trial. *Age and Ageing*, 21, 445–50.

Hedrick, S.C. and Inui, T.S. (1986). The effectiveness and cost of home care: an information synthesis. *Health Services Research*, 20, 851–80.

Hedrick, S.C., Rothman, M.L., Chapko, M., *et al.* (1993). Summary and discussion of methods and results of the adult day health care evaluation study. *Medical Care*, 31, SS94–103.

Hendriksen, C., Lund, E., and Stromgard, E. (1984). Consequences of assessment and intervention among elderly people: a 3-year randomised controlled trial. *British Medical Journal*, 289, 1522–4.

Hendriksen, C., Lund, E., and Stromgard, E. (1989). Hospitalisation of elderly people a 3-year controlled trial. *Journal of the American Geriatrics Society*, 37, 117–22.

Jamieson, A. (1992). Home care in old age: a lost cause? *Journal of Health Politics, Policies and Law*, 17, 879–98.

Jette, A.M., Smith, K.W., and McDermott, S.M. (1996). Quality of Medicare-reimbursed home health care. *Gerontologist*, 36, 492–501.

Keenan, J.M. and Fanale, J.E. (1989). Home care: past and present, problems and potential. *Journal of the American Geriatrics Society*, 37, 1076–83.

Kemper, P. (1988). The evaluation of the national long term care demonstration. 10. Overview of the findings. *Health Services Research*, 23, 162–74.

Koopman, M.M.W., Prandoni, P., Piovella, F., *et al.* (1996). Treatment of venous thrombosis with intravenous unfractionated heparin administered in the hospital as compared with subcutaneous low molecular-weight heparin administered at home. *New England Journal of Medicine*, 334, 682–7.

Kornowski, R., Zeeli, D., Averbuch, M., *et al.* (1995). Intensive home-care surveillance prevents hospitalisation and improves morbidity rates among elderly patients with severe congestive heart failure. *American Heart Journal*, 129, 762–6.

Kramer, A.M., Shaughnessy, P.W., Bauman, M.K., and Crisler, K.S. (1990). Assessing and assuring the quality of home health care: a conceptual framework. *Milbank Quarterly*, 68, 413–43.

Kravitz, R.L., Reuben, D.B., Davis, J.W., *et al.* (1994). Geriatric home assessment after hospital discharge. *Journal of the American Geriatrics Society*, 42, 1229–34.

Leff, B. and Burton, J.R. (1996). Acute medical care in the home. *Journal of the American Geriatrics Society*, 44, 603–5.

Leff, B., Burton, L., Guido, S., Greenough, W.B., Steinwachs, D., and Burton, J.R. (1999). Home hospital program: a pilot study. *Journal of the American Geriatrics Society*, 47, 697–702.

Levine, M., Gent, M., Hirsh, J., *et al.* (1996). A comparison of low-molecular-weight heparin administered primarily at home with unfractionated heparin administered in the hospital for proximal deep-vein thrombosis. *New England Journal of Medicine*, 334, 677–81.

McEwan, R.T., Davison, N., Forster, D.P., Pearson, P., and Stirling, E. (1990). Screening elderly people in primary care: a randomised controlled trial. *British Journal of General Practice*, 40, 94–7.

Mather, H.G., Morgan, D.C., Pearson, N.G., *et al.* (1976). Myocardial infarction: a comparison between home and hospital care for patients. *British Medical Journal*, i, 925–9.

Melin, A.-L., Hakansson, S., and Bygren, L.O. (1993). The cost-effectiveness of rehabilitation in the home: a study of Swedish elderly. *American Journal of Public Health*, 83, 356–62.

Morris, J.N., Fries, B.E., Steel, K., *et al.* (1997). Comprehensive clinical assessment in community setting—applicability of the MDS-HC. *Journal of the American Geriatrics Society*, 45, 1017–24.

Naylor, M.D., Brooten, D., Campbell, R., *et al.* (1999). Comprehensive discharge planning and home follow-up of hospitalized elders. *Journal of the American Medical Association*, 281, 613–20.

Pathy, M.S.J., Bayer, A., Harding, K., and Dibble, A. (1992). Randomised trial of case finding and surveillance of elderly people at home. *Lancet*, 340, 890–3.

Ramsdell, J.W., Swart, J.A., Jackson, J.E., and Renvall, M. (1989). The yield of a home visit in the assessment of geriatric patients. *Journal of the American Geriatrics Society*, 37, 17–24.

Rich, M.W., Beckham, V., Wittenberg, C., Leven, C.L., Freedland, K.E., and Carney, R.M. (1995). A multidisciplinary intervention to prevent the re-admission of elderly patients with congestive heart failure. *New England Journal of Medicine*, 333, 1190–5.

Ruddick, W. (1994). Transforming homes and hospitals. *Hastings Center Report*, 5 (Special Supplement), S11–14.

Shaughnessy, P.W. and Kramer, A.M. (1990). The increased needs of patients in nursing homes and patients receiving home health care. *New England Journal of Medicine*, 322, 21–7.

Shepperd, S. and Iliffe, S. (1996). Hospital at home: an uncertain future. *British Medical Journal*, 312, 923–4.

Shepperd, S., Harwood, D., Jenkinson, C., Gray, A., Vessey, M., and Morgan, P. (1998). Randomised controlled trial comparing hospital at home with inpatient hospital care. I: Three month follow-up of health outcomes. *British Medical Journal*, 316, 1786–91.

Short, P. and Leon, J. (1990). *Use of home and community services by persons aged 65 and older with functional disabilities. National Medical Expenditure Survey Research Findings 5.* United States Department of Health and Human Services, Rockville, Maryland.

Sikorski, J.M. and Senior, J. (1993). The domiciliary rehabilitation and support program. *Medical Journal of Australia*, 159, 23–5.

Steel, K. (1987). Physician-directed long-term home health care for the elderly—a century-long experience. *Journal of the American Geriatrics Society*, 35, 264–8.

Steel, R.K., Musliner, M., and Boling, P.A. (1994). Medical schools and home care. *New England Journal of Medicine*, 331, 1098–9.

Stessman, J., Ginsberg, G., Hammerman-Rozenberg, R., *et al.* (1996). Decreased hospital utilisation by older adults attributable to a home hospitalisation program. *Journal of the American Geriatrics Society*, 44, 591–8.

Stewart, S., Pearson, S., Luke, C.G., and Horowitz, J.D. (1998). Effects of home-based intervention on unplanned readmissions and out-of-hospital deaths. *Journal of the American Geriatrics Society*, 46, 174–80.

Stewart, S., Vandenbrock, A.J., Pearson, S., and Horowitz, J.D. (1999). Prolonged beneficial effects of a home-based intervention on unplanned readmission and mortality among patients with congestive heart failure. *Archives of Internal Medicine*, 159, 257–61.

Stuck, A.E., Aronow, H.U., Steiner, A., *et al.* (1995). A trial of annual in-home comprehensive geriatric assessments for elderly people living in the community. *New England Journal of Medicine*, 333, 1184–9.

Townsend, J., Piper, M., Frank, A.O., Dyer, S., North, W.R.S., and Meade, T.W. (1988). Reduction in hospital re-admission stay of elderly patients by a community based hospital discharge scheme: a randomised controlled trial. *British Medical Journal*, 297, 544–7.

Vetter, N.J., Jones, D.A., and Victor, C.R. (1984). Effect of health visitors working with elderly patients in general practice: a randomised controlled trial. *British Medical Journal*, 288, 369–72.

Weissert, W.G. (1988). The national channelling demonstration: what we knew, know now, and still need to know. *Health Services Research*, 23, 176–87.

Weissert, W.G. and Hedrick, S.C. (1994). Lessons learned from research on effects of community-based long-term care. *Journal of the American Geriatrics Society*, 42, 348–53.

Welch, H.G., Wenneberg, D.E., and Welch, W.P. (1996). The use of Medicare home health care services. *New England Journal of Medicine*, 335, 324–9.

Williams, E.I., Greenwell, J., and Groom, L.M. (1992). The care of people over 75 years old after discharge from hospital: an evaluation of timetabled visiting by health visitor assistants. *Journal of Public Health Medicine*, 14, 138–44.

Young, J.B. and Forster, A. (1992). The Bradford community stroke trial: results at 6 months. *British Medical Journal*, 304, 1085–9.

Zimmer, J.G., Groth-Juncker, A., and McCusker, J. (1995). A randomized controlled study of a home health care team. *American Journal of Public Health*, 75, 134–41.

23.7 Intensive care units

Barry J. Goldlist

General considerations

Epidemiology

People over 65 years of age comprise a significant proportion of patients admitted to critical care units. Many conditions resulting in critical illness are simply more common in elderly people. These include ischaemic heart disease, chronic lung disease, pneumonia, and gastrointestinal bleeding. Also, elderly people are much more frequently the victims of trauma than are those under the age of 65. In 1993 in Ontario, Canada, 36 per cent of all injury deaths were in the over 65 age group (Ontario Trauma Registry 1995). This group only constitutes about 10 per cent of the Ontario population. A similar pattern has been demonstrated in the United States, where the injury rate is 57 per 100 000 people in all age groups but rises to 93 for those aged 65 to 74 years, and to 625 per 100 000 people for those over 85 years old (Oreskovich *et al.* 1984). Thus, trauma deaths are disproportionately high in elderly people. Similar data are available from the United Kingdom where elderly people, although representing less than 20 per cent of the population, account for more than a third of all deaths due to injury and poisoning. In this database, traffic accidents are the most common cause of death from injury in the youngest old (aged 65 to 74 years), whereas falls account for over half of all accidental deaths in men over 84 years of age, and almost three-quarters of all accidental deaths in women over 84 years (Lilley *et al.* 1995).

As a result of the increase in specific diseases and trauma in elderly people, people aged 65 years or older are over-represented in intensive care unit (**ICU**) admissions. In one Canadian study (Rockwood *et al.* 1993), 46 per cent of admissions to an ICU (excluding self-induced poisoning) were over the age of 65. American data confirm that approximately 50 per cent of all patients admitted to ICUs are over the age of 65 (Adelman *et al.* 1994). This is approximately a fourfold increase over the proportion of elderly people in the population as a whole.

Outcomes

There are three key issues about the outcomes of elderly patients in the ICU: how age affects fatality; the quality of life of elderly people after their ICU stay; and the cost of the ICU intervention.

These issues are difficult to quantify, primarily because of the complex reasons for ICU admissions. Patients are admitted to the ICU because of their physiological status, not because of a unifying diagnosis. Studies looking at ICU outcomes generally use prognostic scoring systems such as the Acute Physiology and Chronic Health Evaluation (**APACHE**), which has evolved through various iterations, the Mortality Prediction Model (**MPM**), and the Simplified Acute Physiology Score (**SAPS**) (Chelluri *et al.* 1995). Research using hypothetical case scenarios suggested (rather than confirmed) that when age is the only differing variable, doctors favoured admitting the younger patient to the last critical care bed by a wide margin (Nuckton and List 1995). However, when further differences in case scenarios were introduced, the impact of age was reduced, and only 5 per cent of doctors in this American sample felt there should be a cut-off age limit for critical care admission.

In a prospective study performed in Canada (Rockwood *et al.* 1993), a significantly different survival between ICU patients over 65 and under 65 was demonstrated, both during ICU admission and at 1 year follow-up. However, almost all the difference could be explained by differences in initial physiological assessment (APACHE II score), length of stay, prior ICU admission, and respiratory failure. A retrospective American study (Wu *et al.* 1990) also showed a greater fatality in elderly people that could be accounted for by different premorbid physiological scores. Of interest, omitting the points awarded for age in traditional physiological scales (APACHE II), did not impair the predictive power of the resulting scale (APACHE IIM). However, the construction and interpretation of predictive models for ICU outcomes is a complex undertaking (Ruttimann 1994) and for the average clinician, it is quite apparent from the prior studies, and numerous others (McClish *et al.* 1987; Sage *et al.* 1987; Horn 1997) that ICU fatality increases with advancing age. There is some evidence to suggest that prior functional status can also help predict ICU outcomes (Mayer-Oakes *et al.* 1991). In this retrospective American study the combination of functional impairment and advancing age was a particularly potent predictor of in-hospital fatality. Recently, Roche *et al.* (1999) in a prospective observational cohort study using convenience sampling showed that older people had worse functional ability at ICU admission and this was a major determinant of recovery while the APACHE II at admission was the main correlate of fatality. They concluded that the functional and physiological measures were complementary information for clinically relevant outcomes for ICU admissions. However, in a validation study of the APACHE III prognostic system, Knaus *et al.* (1991) found that, when all other variables were entered into the predictive equation, age accounted for only 3 per cent of the variance in survival.

Health-related quality of life can be difficult to define and difficult to measure. Some factors that influence quality of life include functional status, mobility, cognitive function, and pain. The study by Rockwood *et al.* (1993) showed minimal differences in functional capacity between young and old ICU survivors (where 75 per cent of the patients had follow-up) and more positive health attitudes among those over 65 years of age. Sage *et al.* (1987) demonstrated only minor differences in quality of life among elderly ICU survivors compared with elderly non-ICU controls.

Total ICU costs, and costs as a proportion of total hospital costs, are rising in most industrial countries (Chelluri *et al.* 1995; Horn 1997). Data to determine whether the cost per ICU case is influenced by age alone are difficult to obtain. Many studies do not differentiate between costs and charges, and differing fatality rates skew costs as well (Chelluri *et al.* 1995). Wu *et al.* (1990), found no evidence that elderly people are denied major interventions in comparison to younger ICU patients. One review (Chelluri *et al.* 1995) found no support in the literature for the concept that older patients receive more ICU resources than younger patients. Unfortunately, most of the data additionally are flawed by the lack of follow-up costs after hospital discharge (Chelluri *et al.* 1995).

In summary, clinicians should base their estimate of the likely benefit of intensive care on a carefully conducted review of the patient's previous health and physical independence (Sage *et al.* 1987; Rockwood *et al.* 1993). When a clear decision is not possible, a trial of ICU therapy, with frequent reassessment, is probably the most prudent course.

General issues of care

The two elements that differentiate care of elderly people on hospital wards and outpatient services, namely impaired physiological reserve and significant comorbidity, are also apparent in the ICU setting. Impaired vision and hearing are much more common in elderly people, making effective communication a tremendous challenge (Adelman *et al.* 1994). The use of physical restraints is very common in the ICU setting (Lever *et al.* 1994), as is the use of sedating medications. Unexpectedly prolonged or severe effects secondary to the use of sedating medications are commonly caused by a combination of pharmacokinetic and pharmacodynamic factors (Hammerlein *et al.* 1998). Both physical and chemical restraints are believed to increase the risks of skin ulceration (Evans and Strumpf 1989), presumably by further reducing mobility (Patterson and Bennett 1995). While development of a pressure ulcer is correlated with a large increase in 1-year fatality, this difference is largely explained by differences in baseline nutritional and functional status, APACHE II score, and other indices of disease severity (Thomas *et al.* 1996). Monitoring devices and support devices (for example intravenous lines), ubiquitous in the ICU, are significant predictors of restraint use (Robbins *et al.* 1987). Predicting and preventing pressure ulcers, while difficult in an ICU setting, are important in preventing both morbidity and increased hospital stays (American Geriatrics Society Clinical Practice Committee 1996). One study, in an ICU setting consisting predominantly of trauma patients, suggested that even well-established scales such as the Braden Scale, should have different cut-off scores to predict risk for ICU populations compared with scores for risk for medical geriatric ward populations (Jiricka *et al.* 1995).

Critical illness results in a severe catabolic state for all patients. The high prevalence of underlying nutritional deficiency makes this particularly problematic in elderly people (Opper and Burakoff 1994). It has been difficult to show benefit for prophylactic enteral alimentation in mixed ICU populations, although benefit has been demonstrated with specific types of formulae (Opper and Burakoff 1994; Bower *et al.* 1995). Enteral alimentation has been shown to counteract the effect of various agents in preventing gastric colonization with potential pathogens, but the significance of this finding is not clear (Atkinson *et al.* 1998). It is likely that adequate protein intake helps to prevent and heal decubitus ulcers (Pinchcofsky-Devin and Kaminski 1986; Breslaw *et al.* 1993; Bonten *et al.* 1994). Many of the problems that impair provision of proper nutrition by nasogastric tube can be avoided by percutaneous endoscopic insertion of a gastrostomy tube (Norton *et al.* 1996). There is some evidence that an education and quality improvement programme for nutritional support in ICU settings will increase the proportion of patients fed enterally versus parenterally (Schwartz 1996).

As we age, our diversity in all spheres, including physiology increases (Comfort 1979). This can result in problems when care is delivered by algorithms (Sickbert 1989) and 'rules must be followed'. Care of elderly people, regardless of the venue, requires a flexibility of approach that can accommodate the broad heterogeneity of the pathophysiology in elderly people. Involving families in the care of their elderly relatives can be a help in this process (Adelman *et al.* 1994; Krieger 1994). To ignore the psychosocial needs of the critically ill elderly patient can result in outcomes distressing to both the patient and the family (Krieger 1994).

Specific diseases and syndromes in the ICU

Respiratory failure

In an ICU setting, respiratory failure requiring mechanical ventilation is most frequent among very elderly patients (Krieger 1994). This is probably due to age-associated effects on pulmonary physiology, respiratory drive, muscle performance, and cardiac function. Most cases of respiratory failure in elderly ICU patients are not due to primary pulmonary diseases. It is estimated that in the ICU only 7 to 26 per cent of elderly patients requiring mechanical ventilation do so for primary pulmonary pathology while the remainder develop respiratory failure secondary to other systemic problems, such as sepsis (Troche and Moine 1997). The duration of mechanical ventilation is dependent on the type of disease and the extent of physiological derangement. Age is not an independent risk factor for prolonged mechanical ventilation (Seneff *et al.* 1996; Troche and Moine 1997). Early detection of recovery from respiratory failure by daily trials of spontaneous breathing in one elderly (but not exclusively so) cohort of patients resulted in shorter duration of mechanical ventilation, decreased ICU costs, and fewer complications than usual care (Ely *et al.* 1996). Non-respiratory factors that impair weaning include serum albumin level at the time of weaning (Sapijaszko *et al.* 1996) and neuromuscular disorders (Maher *et al.* 1995). Where non-ICU weaning centres are available, the proportion of patients with primary lung pathology as the cause of respiratory failure is, not surprisingly, very high, often exceeding 50 per cent of total admissions (Scheinhorn *et al.* 1997). One large regional weaning centre reported on over 1000 patients with a mean patient age of 69 plus or minus 13 years; the most common diagnosis in these patients requiring prolonged weaning was acute pneumonia superimposed on underlying chronic obstructive pulmonary disease (Dardaine *et al.* 1995).

Age is not an independent factor in predicting short-term outcome of respiratory failure in the ICU. One retrospective French study involving 110 consecutive ICU patients over the age of 70 years requiring mechanical ventilation found that fatality in the ICU depended on the presence of shock and the use of major therapeutic interventions rather than age. Six-month survival could be predicted by admission in shock, prior health status, and marital status. By 18 months most elderly survivors were living in the same residence and had the same health status and autonomy as before their admission to the ICU (Dardaine *et al.* 1995). An American retrospective study reviewing 1860 ventilated patients, including 282 patients 80 years of age and older, also concluded that short-term survival was not age dependent. However, this study identified a group of patients over the age of 80 years with a particularly poor prognosis. These patients had one or more of the following prior to ICU admission: liver disease, urea nitrogen over 17.8 mmol/l, systemic illness (such as lupus erythematosus or rheumatoid arthritis), cancer, or gastrointestinal disease with malnutrition. Short-term survival in this group was only 7 per cent, in comparison to an overall survival of 31 per cent in the total group aged over 80 years, and 44 per cent in those under the age of 80. In this study mechanical ventilation for more than 15 days in those over 80 years of age resulted in only a 9 per cent short-term survival, in comparison with 36 per cent for younger patients (Swinburne *et al.* 1993). One small study, which included several older patients, found that the daily administration of recombinant growth hormone had no effect on shortening the duration of mechanical ventilation despite promoting significant nitrogen retention (Pichard *et al.* 1996).

Although primary lung pathology is not the most common cause of respiratory failure in ICU patients, management of these patients can be quite difficult, although many can be managed quite successfully. One retrospective Australian study on 100 consecutive ICU patients with acute exacerbations of chronic obstructive pulmonary disease (average age 68 years), revealed an 11 per cent reduction in hospital fatality. This was not influenced by whether mechanical ventilation was used or not. Six-month and 2-year survival rates were also reasonable (Moran *et al.* 1998). Selection bias for patient referral to an ICU can be a partial explanation for these favourable results.

The increasing use of non-invasive positive pressure ventilation by facemask has important implications for elderly people, who are less likely to suffer from 'age discrimination' if non-invasive measures are available. It is likely that non-invasive positive pressure ventilation is effective in a wide range of patients with hypercapnic acute respiratory failure or hypoxaemic acute respiratory failure who are haemodynamically stable and who have a condition that can be reversed in 48 to 72 h (Meduri *et al.* 1996).

One study of nasal mask ventilation in a very elderly group (mean age 76 years), also revealed very promising results, even in very ill patients (Benhamou *et al.* 1992). Nava *et al.* (1998), in a prospective randomized trial of non-invasive mechanical ventilation in the weaning of patients with respiratory failure due to chronic obstructive pulmonary disease, revealed positive results. Weaning time, length of ICU stay, and the incidence of nosocomial infection were reduced, while 60-day survival was improved. The average age in this study was approximately 69 years (Nava *et al.* 1998).

Nosocomial pneumonia is a major problem in hospital admitted patients, with elderly patients particularly vulnerable (Harkness *et al.* 1990). Tracheal intubation is a clear risk factor for nosocomial pneumonia. Poor nutrition and neuromuscular disease, common problems in the ICU, are also risk factors for nosocomial pneumonia (Hanson *et al.* 1992). It is possible that nasogastric tubes also represent a risk factor for nosocomial pneumonia (Hanson *et al.* 1992). It has been postulated that higher gastric pH (as associated with use of H_2-blockers) is also associated with increased incidence of nosocomial infection. However, a large multicentre randomized blinded placebo-controlled trial of sucralfate versus ranitidine to prevent upper gastrointestinal bleeding in patients requiring mechanical ventilation showed no difference in the rates of ventilator-associated pneumonia. The rate of bleeding was much less in the ranitidine group, making the use of H_2-blockers the clear choice to prevent haemorrhage (Cook *et al.* 1998).

The successful use of mechanical ventilation in specific disease states such as cirrhosis (Singh *et al.* 1998) or stroke depend on the specific factors causing respiratory failure. One small observational study from the Mayo Clinic suggested that the outcome from mechanical ventilation in ischaemic stroke is reasonable if the indication for ventilation was uncontrolled seizures or pulmonary oedema, but poor if progressive brain swelling impairing respiration was the cause (Wijdicks and Scott 1997).

Trauma

Comparing survival and cost in elderly trauma victims with similarly injured to younger patients is made difficult by deficiencies in the methods being used (Murphy *et al.* 1990; Rutledge *et al.* 1997; Demetriades *et al.* 1998; Rutledge and Osler 1998). The Injury Severity Score (**ISS**) was developed to express the overall effect of injuries to various body systems, and when combined with age is used to stratify patients by severity (Suarez-Alvarez *et al.* 1995). The Trauma and Injury Severity Score (**TRISS**) takes the information from the ISS and provides a calculation for predicting probability of survival and is widely used in studies. However, some studies suggest that there is a significant likelihood of misclassification with TRISS, particularly in cases of severe trauma (Murphy *et al.* 1990). TRISS is not helpful in predicting resource utilization (Demetriades *et al.* 1998), and alternative methodologies, such as those using the injury diagnosis codes from the *International Classification of Disease, Version 9, Clinical Modification*, are being developed (Demetriades *et al.* 1998; Rutledge and Osler 1998). One Spanish study demonstrated some benefits, but also limitations, in the use of TRISS in a 2-year prospective study in a tertiary care trauma ICU (Suarez-Alvarez *et al.* 1995). A Canadian study suggested value in developing regional norms for TRISS as a better tool to assess trauma hospital performance (Lane *et al.* 1996). This requires ability to collect data on a regional basis in a standardized manner. Regardless of the overall benefits of TRISS, one Brazilian study has suggested that intensive study of deaths which are unexpected according to TRISS can serve as an excellent method of quality assurance and quality improvement (Coimbra *et al.* 1996).

Many of the current trauma scoring systems were at least partially based on information derived from the Major Trauma Outcome Study sponsored by the American College of Surgeons Committee on Trauma. One early paper deriving from this study analysed data from 3833 patients over the age of 65 and compared this with data

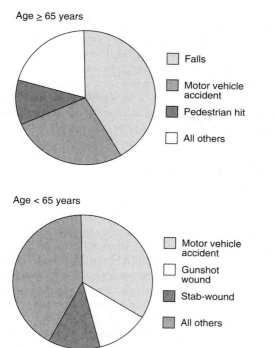

Age ≥ 65 years

- Falls
- Motor vehicle accident
- Pedestrian hit
- All others

Age < 65 years

- Motor vehicle accident
- Gunshot wound
- Stab-wound
- All others

Fig. 1 Mechanism of injury in those aged 65 years and over compared with those aged under 65. (Adapted from Champion *et al.* (1989).)

from over 40 000 patients under the age of 65. The elderly group did not differ from the younger group in terms of ISS, but their fatality rate was much higher—19.0 per cent versus 9.8 per cent in the younger group (Champion *et al.* 1989). This differential mortality held for every cause of trauma and at every level of ISS. Also, elderly people had higher complication rates and longer hospital stays than those under 65. There were also major differences in the most common causes of trauma in elderly people compared with the young (Fig. 1). These American data do not necessarily reflect causes of trauma in other countries.

A retrospective American study, using a regional trauma registry, confirmed that elderly people had a higher fatality (Smith *et al.* 1990). The ISS associated with a 10 per cent fatality in elderly people was much lower than in those under 65 years of age. The cause of trauma and the number of complications influenced fatality, but pre-existing disease did not. A more sophisticated prospective study of trauma further explored the increased fatality of the very old (aged 75 and over) (Shabot and Johnson 1995). The study revealed that in this very old cohort, despite an identical Trauma Score, the ISS was significantly higher. Also, for identical injury severity scores, the very old group had greater physiological derangements as measured by the SAPS. The conclusions would seem to be that very elderly people suffer greater injury from given degrees of trauma than do younger individuals, and that they suffer greater degrees of physiological disruption for similar degrees of injury.

A prospective study from the United Kingdom examining factors relating to fatality from blunt trauma found that age was an independent risk factor (Jones *et al.* 1995). An interesting discovery in this study was that trauma occurring in the home was independently associated with higher fatality than trauma from a motor vehicle

accident. There were not enough data from this study to generate hypotheses, but one would suspect that prior functioning or physiological status was worse in patients suffering injury in the 'friendly' confines of home.

Delayed death from trauma (after 24 h), is much greater in elderly people than in younger patients, and is generally ascribed to pre-existing disease and complications (after correction for initial ISS) (Perdue *et al.* 1998). However, one American retrospective cohort analysis suggests that long-term survival of elderly trauma victims is decreased as compared with age-matched controls (Gubler *et al.* 1997). Specifically even elderly people, who had survived 3 years after the trauma, have poorer survival at the 5-year point than controls. The reasons for this are unclear, but it suggests trauma care for elderly people may need to focus on long-term rehabilitation and care as well as immediate hospital care. This large study (9424 elderly patients, 37 787 controls), also found pre-existing disease to be a risk factor for mortality in elderly people, in contrast to other studies (Jones *et al.* 1995; Shabot and Johnson 1995).

The question of relative cost of trauma in the young and old is hard to study. True costs can be very difficult to calculate, in most hospitals. One study of head-injured patients demonstrated that injury severity predicted costs, and that age was not a factor (Saywell *et al.* 1989). However, there is no attempt in this study to determine costs after the acute hospital stay, and such a reductionist view of health care is not really helpful. The complications introduced by funding systems is clearly demonstrated in one American analysis (Young *et al.* 1998). In this study per capita costs for elderly people were lower than for younger patients, but reimbursement was higher. This was a result of almost universal coverage of elderly people by the Medicare system, which adequately covered costs for elderly people patients. The authors of this study suggested that universal insurance coverage for all trauma patients would be desirable. This paper suggests that in the United States it is more economically prudent to treat trauma patients over the age of 65.

Clearly the fact that trauma rates increase with advancing age makes elderly people major beneficiaries of well-organized trauma programmes. Although complication rates, for example venous thromboembolism (Geerts *et al.* 1994) and pulmonary embolism (Tuttle-Newhall *et al.* 1997), and fatality are age dependent, it is unclear whether changes in triage or specific management will alter outcomes. At the same time severity of injury, however it may be measured, is a far greater predictor of fatality than age (Murphy *et al.* 1990; Knaus *et al.* 1991; Jones *et al.* 1995; Suarez-Alvarez *et al.* 1995; Demetriades *et al.* 1998; Rutledge and Osler 1998).

Myocardial infarction

Difficulties in management of myocardial infarction in elderly people are heightened by its frequent atypical presentation, such as confusion, syncope, or shortness of breath in the absence of chest pain (Bayer *et al.* 1986; Day *et al.* 1987; Montague *et al.* 1992; Tresch 1998). In fact, most retrospective studies underestimate how frequently the presentation of myocardial infarction is atypical in this group, presumably because the most atypical cases are not as often diagnosed (Wroblewski *et al.* 1986). Older studies that observed the impact of coronary care unit admission on outcome, cannot be meaningfully interpreted because of the bias introduced by non-randomized patient selection for coronary care unit care (Berman 1979; MacDonald *et al.* 1983; Sagie *et al.* 1987). In any event, modern studies suggest that it is the specific therapeutic interventions available in the coronary care unit that improve outcome (Daida *et al.* 1997). It is thus particularly concerning that age discrimination may limit the admission of elderly people to coronary care units in both the United Kingdom and the United States (Fleming *et al.* 1991; Dudley and Burns 1992). Also, advanced age is probably a determinant of delayed hospital presentation (Gurwitz *et al.* 1997). This further limits the ability to provide proven effective therapy.

It is almost certain that age is an independent risk factor for death in acute myocardial infarction, both in the early postinfarct period and at 1 year follow-up (Rich *et al.* 1992; Herlitz *et al.* 1993; Devlin *et al.* 1995). Since most effective interventions for myocardial infarction have the same relative risk reduction in both young and old patients, the absolute risk reduction, and hence the number needed to treat, are both more favourable in elderly people. One cost-effectiveness study (comparing tissue plasminogen activator and streptokinase) highlighted the greater cost-effectiveness of treating older rather than younger patients (Mark *et al.* 1995). Streptokinase itself is known to be a cost-effective method of improving outcome after myocardial infarction in elderly people (Krumholz *et al.* 1992).

Despite the proven efficacy of most standard treatment modalities for acute myocardial infarction in elderly people, there is persuasive evidence that β-blockers, thrombolytic agents, and even aspirin are underused in elderly people (Gurwitz *et al.* 1992, 1996; Rosenthal and Fortinsky 1994; Krumholz *et al.* 1995, 1996, 1998; McLaughlin *et al.* 1996; Soumerai *et al.* 1997; Aronow 1998; Gottlieb *et al.* 1998). The benefit of these therapies has been clearly shown to be generalizable to the elderly population as a whole by analysis of databases that consistently show an improvement in outcome with the use of current treatment modalities for acute myocardial infarction (Pashos *et al.* 1993; McClennan *et al.* 1994; Gottlieb *et al.* 1997). Thrombolytic therapy has been shown to be safe for very elderly people even outside the confines of a clinical trial (Kafetz and Luder 1982). It must be remembered, however, that relatively few data from clinical trials exists for patients over the age of 80 (Rich 1998).

Therefore it seems that, because of their higher baseline risk of fatality, elderly patients can benefit more from effective treatment modalities for myocardial infarction than younger patients (Gotsman *et al.* 1998). However, there is a possibility that this will result in a higher prevalence of heart failure in the elderly population (Gotsman *et al.* 1998). This will make proper detection and management of heart failure in elderly people an increasingly important issue in the future (Havranek *et al.* 1998). Also, preventing further cardiac events, by such means as cholesterol-lowering therapy, should become more common (Miettinen *et al.* 1997).

Gastrointestinal bleeding

Gastrointestinal bleeding is a common occurrence at any age, but particularly so in elderly people (Segal and Cello 1997). Severe bleeding episodes are frequently managed in ICUs, but less severe bleeds can safely be triaged to less intensive monitoring. One American study found no independent relationship between age and outcome from gastrointestinal bleeding. Rather, objective clinical criteria were capable of predicting low-risk gastrointestinal haemorrhage that did not require ICU admission (Kollef *et al.* 1995). This predictive tool was then further validated in a prospective cohort of 465 patients at two

separate university-affiliated teaching hospitals (Kollef *et al.* 1997). It thus seems reasonable to apply similar criteria to elderly patients in the emergency room: ongoing bleeding, low systolic blood pressure, elevated prothrombin time, erratic mental status, or unstable co-morbid disease predict a high-risk gastrointestinal bleed. Patients meeting one or more of these criteria, regardless of age, are significantly more likely to develop additional organ system dysfunction, require a greater number of transfusions, and have a prolonged hospital stay (Cappel 1995). A retrospective study of 200 patients admitted with upper gastrointestinal bleeding (100 patients under 60 years of age, 100 patients over 60 years of age) also failed to reveal any age-associated difference with regard to need for intensive care, transfusion requirements, duration of hospital stay, or fatality (Kollef *et al.* 1995). This study did suggest some differences in the causes of upper gastrointestinal bleeding in the old versus younger individuals. Elderly patients are more likely to be bleeding from peptic ulcers, and probably less likely to be bleeding from varices or Mallory–Weiss tears. Also, this group of elderly people with upper gastrointestinal bleeds was less likely to have a history of dyspepsia or excessive alcohol use. However, there was a significant increase in the presence of coronary artery disease in the elderly group. Thus, in those patients with simultaneous upper gastrointestinal bleeds and myocardial infarction, the mean age is quite high (Cappel 1995). In patients who suffer concurrent myocardial infarctions with their upper gastro-intestinal bleeds, the clinical presentation is usually dominated by the gastrointestinal findings. In addition to the severity of the bleed, symptoms such as syncope, dizziness, or confusion increase the risk of a concurrent myocardial infarct (Cappel 1995). Such patients should clearly be managed in an ICU setting at least until the presence or absence of a myocardial infarction has been confirmed.

Guillain–Barré syndrome

Guillain–Barré syndrome is an acute autoimmune demyelinating inflammatory neuropathy that increases in incidence with advancing age. The average annual incidence in the United States is 3 cases per 100 000 of population, but reaches 8.6 cases per 100 000 in the 70 to 79 year age group (Prevots and Sutter 1997). Smaller studies in different geographical areas confirm an increased incidence with advancing age (Winner and Grimley Evans 1990; Emilia-Romagna Study Group 1997; Hughes and Rees 1997; Rees *et al.* 1998). Severe cases frequently require ICU admission, particularly for ventilatory failure (Ng *et al.* 1995). Other common reasons for ICU admission include bulbar weakness, autonomic dysfunction, or serious general medical problems. Management generally requires the presence of an experienced neurologist, and specific therapy now includes plasma exchange and intravenous immunoglobulin therapy, as well as the usual supportive measures (Sheth *et al.* 1996). Although it is not clear whether age is an independent risk factor for death in Guillain–Barré syndrome, it is clear that age is the major risk factor that determines severity (Sheth *et al.* 1996; Rees *et al.* 1998). Thus most Guillain–Barré syndrome deaths occur in elderly people (Sheth *et al.* 1996; Hughes and Rees 1997; Meythaler *et al.* 1997; Rees *et al.* 1998). It is estimated that in the United States, well over half of Guillain–Barré syndrome deaths occur in elderly people (Rees *et al.* 1998). It is unclear if age is a factor in rehabilitation outcome of patients with Guillain–Barré syndrome, but at least one study has suggested that initial disease severity (specifically need for ventilation) is a factor (Meythaler *et al.*

1997). As elderly people are more likely to have severe disease, they tend to have poorer rehabilitation outcomes. Health status after Guillain–Barré syndrome is affected by psychosocial factors as well as by neurological recovery (Bernsen *et al.* 1997).

Futile treatment of elderly people in the ICU

Difficult clinical decisions are an everyday occurrence in the care of elderly people, but the issue of 'futility' is particularly prominent in the ICU because of the high use of life-sustaining technology (Jonsen 1994). The debate about futility has now entered the medical administration literature, where one can read quotations such as this: 'We need therefore to look at our ICU treatments for the older patients to determine if we can decrease or avoid expenditures for futile treatments' (Frezza *et al.* 1998). Futility should be defined more in terms of medical values, such as proven lack of efficacy and avoidance of cruel or painful treatment at the end of life (Braithwaite and Thomasma 1986; Dubowitz 1997; Weijer *et al.* 1998). However, in the ICU the specific issues of stopping ventilation or not providing cardiopulmonary resuscitation seem at least qualitatively different from other examples of medical futility (e.g. treating viral infections with antibiotics) because failure to provide these interventions can be a self-fulfilling prophecy (Truog *et al.* 1992; Veatch 1994; Waisel and Truog 1995). Most articles advise doctors to enter into a dialogue with the patient or family in order to reach a consensus, but this is not always successful (Veatch 1994). It has been suggested that the concept of futility faces an insurmountable barrier if there is an absence of trust between doctor and patient (Caplan 1996). The reporting in the popular press of significant controversy concerning the right of patients or family to demand cardiopulmonary resuscitation (*Globe and Mail* 1998) suggests to this author that there must be a broader societal consensus as to what constitutes futility in cardiopulmonary resuscitation, ventilation, and other immediate life-saving interventions before this trust between doctor and patient can be gained.

General principles of care of elderly people in the ICU

The same principles of care that pertain to care of elderly people in general also apply in the ICU. However, the hectic pace in such units at times seems to conspire against elderly people. While it is clear that severity of illness or injury is the prime determinant of ICU outcome, at times it seems to those involved in geriatrics that there is still active age discrimination for admission. Some intensive care specialists may not appreciate the slower rate of recovery characteristic of frail elderly patients. This sometimes results in disproportionate attention given to younger patients who seem to be improving more rapidly, and are thus felt to be more deserving of care.

The incidence of delirium is clearly age associated, and the presence of agitated confused patients disrupts normal patterns of care. Communication is more difficult, and collaborative information gathering assumes great importance. If confusion is not recognized, the likelihood of poor clinical decision-making increases. Impaired vision and hearing, common in elderly people, further complicate effective communication.

The multiplicity of concurrent medical problems frequently seen in elderly people also increases the complexity of care. Frequently, the correction of seemingly minor medical problems are crucial for the recovery of elderly patients. It becomes difficult to concentrate on a large number of chronic conditions at one time (Redelmeier *et al.* 1998). It is clear that there should be more formal geriatric consultations in the ICU than currently occur. This would also facilitate the difficult issue of post-ICU care for elderly people.

In conclusion, ICU outcome is more dependent on illness or injury severity than age itself for older patients. Attention to management of confusion, nutritional support, psychosocial issues, multiple comorbid diseases and prevention of decubitus ulcers is critical for effective management. Effective treatments in younger patients are also effective treatments in elderly patients and are often more cost effective.

References

Adelman, R.D., Berger, J.T., and Macina, L.O. (1994). Critical care for the geriatric patient. *Clinics in Geriatric Medicine*, **10**, 19–30.

American Geriatrics Society Clinical Practice Committee (1996). Pressure ulcers in adults: prediction and prevention. *Journal of the American Geriatrics Society*, **44**, 1118–19.

Aronow, W.S. (1998). Underutilization of aspirin in older patients with prior myocardial infarction at the time of admission to a nursing home. *Journal of the American Geriatrics Society*, **46**, 615–16.

Atkinson, S., Siefert, E., and Bihari, D. (1998). A prospective, randomized, double-blind, conrolled clinical trial of enteral immunonutrition in the critically ill. *Critical Care Medicine*, **26**, 1164–72.

Bayer, A.J., Chadha, J.S., Farag, R.R., *et al.* (1986). Changing presentation of myocardial infarction with increasing old age. *Journal of the American Geriatrics Society*, **34**, 263–6.

Benhamou, D., Girault, C., Faure, C., *et al.* (1992). Nasal mask ventilation in acutre respiratory failure. Experience in elderly patients. *Clinical Investigations in Critical Care*, **102**, 912–17.

Berman, N.D. (1979). The elderly patient in the coronary care unit. I. Acute myocardial infarction. *Journal of the American Geriatrics Society*, **27**, 145–50.

Bernsen, R.A.J.A.M., Jacobs, H.M., deJager, A.E.J., *et al.* (1997). Residual health status after Guillain–Barré syndrome. *Journal of Neurology, Neurosurgery and Psychiatry*, **62**, 637–40.

Bonten, M.J.M., Gaillard, C.A., van Tiel, F.H., *et al.* (1994). Continuous enteral feeding counteracts preventive measures for gastric colonization in intensive care unit patients. *Critical Care Medicine*, **22**, 939–44.

Bower, R.H., Cerra, F.B., Bershadsky, B., *et al.* (1995). Early enteral administration of a formula (Impact) supplemented with arginine, nucleotides, and fish oil in intensive care unit patients. Results of a multicenter, prospective, randomized, clinical trail. *Critical Care Medicine*, **23**, 436–49.

Braithwaite, S. and Thomasma, D.C. (1986). New guidelines on foregoing life-sustaining treatment in incompetent patients. An anti-cruelty policy. *Annals of Internal Medicine*, **104**, 711–15.

Breslow, R.S., Hallfrisch, J., Guy, D.G., *et al.* (1993). The importance of dietary protein in healing pressure ulcers. *Journal of the American Geriatrics Society*, **41**, 357–62.

Caplan AL. (1996). Odds and ends. Trust and the debate over medical futility. *Annals of Internal Medicine*, **125**, 688–9.

Cappel, M.S. (1995). A study of the syndrome of simultaneous acute upper gastrointestinal bleeding and myocardial infarction in 36 patients. *American Journal of Gastroenterology*, **90**, 1444–9.

Champion, H.R., Copes, W.S., Buyer, D., *et al.* (1989). Major trauma in geriatric patients. *American Journal of Public Health*, 79, 1278–82.

Chelluri, L., Grenvik, A., and Silverman, M. (1995). Intensive care for critically ill elderly: mortality, costs, and quality of life. *Archives of Internal Medicine*, 155, 1013–22.

Coimbra, R., Razuk, A., Pinto, M.C.C., *et al.* (1996). Severely injured patients in the intensive care unit. A critical analysis of outcome and unexpected deaths identified by the TRISS methodology. *International Surgery*, 81, 102–6.

Comfort, A. (1979). *The biology of senescence* (3rd edn). Churchill Livingstone, London.

Cook, D., Guyatt, G., Marshall, J., *et al.* (1998). A comparison of sucralfate and ranitidine for the prevention of upper gastrointestinal bleeding in patients requiring mechanical ventilation. *New England Journal of Medicine*, 338, 791–7.

Daida, H., Kottke, T.E., Backes, R.J., *et al.* (1997). Are coronary-care unit changes in therapy associated with acute myocardial infarction? *Mayo Clinic Proceedings*, 72, 1014–21.

Dardaine, V., Constans, T., Lasfargues, G., *et al.* (1995). Outcome of elderly patients requiring ventilatory support in intensive care. *Aging Clinical Experimental Research*, 7, 221–7.

Day, J.J., Bayer, A.J., Pathy, M.S.J., *et al.* (1987). Acute myocardial infarction: diagnostic difficulties and outcome in advanced old age. *Age and Ageing*, 16, 239–43.

Demetriades, D., Chan, L.S., Valmahos, G., *et al.* (1998). TRISS methodology in trauma: the need for alternatives. *British Journal of Surgery*, 85, 379–84.

Devlin, W., Gragg, D., Jacks, M., *et al.* (1995). Comparison of outcome in patients with acute myocardial infarction aged > 75 years with that in younger patients. *American Journal of Cardiology*, 75, 573–6.

Dubowitz, V. (1997). Withdrawing intensive life-sustaining treatment—recommendations for compassionate clinical managment. *New England Journal of Medicine*, 336, 651–2.

Dudley, N.J. and Burns, E. (1992). The influence of age on policies for admission and thrombolysis in coronary care units in the United Kingdom. *Age and Ageing*, 21, 95–8.

Ely, E.W., Baker, A.M., Dunagan, D.P., *et al.* (1996). Effect on the duration of mechanical ventilation of identifying patients capable of breathing spontaneously. *New England Journal of Medicine*, 335, 1864–9.

Emilia-Romagna Study Group (1997). A prospective study on the incidence and prognosis of Guillain–Barré syndrome in Emilia-Romagna region, Italy (1992–1993). *Neurology*, 48, 214–21.

Evans, L.K. and Strumpf, N.E. (1989). Tying down the elderly. A review of the literature on physical restraint. *Journal of the American Geriatrics Society*, 37, 65–74.

Fleming, G., D'Agostino, R.B., and Selker, H.P. (1991). Is coronary-care-unit admission restricted for elderly patients? A multicenter study. *American Journal of Public Health*, 81, 1121–6.

Frezza, E.E., Squillario, D.M., and Smith, T.J. (1998). The ethical challenge and the futile treatment in the older population admitted to the intensive care unit. *American Journal of Medical Quality*, 13, 121–6.

Geerts, W.H., Code, K.I., Jay, R.M., *et al.* (1994). A prospective study of venous thromboembolism after major trauma. *New England Journal of Medicine*, 331, 1601–6.

Globe and Mail (1998). Patient's beloved deserve a say (Andrew Sawatzky case). 17 November, Toronto, Canada.

Gotsman, M.S., Admon, D., Zahger, D., *et al.* (1998). Thrombolysis in acute myocardial infarction improves prognosis and prolongs life but will increase the prevalence of heart failure in the geriatric population. *International Journal of Cardiology*, 65, S29–S35.

Gottlieb, S., Goldbourt, U., Boyko, V., *et al.* (1997). Improved outcome of elderly patients (over 75 years of age) with acute myocardial infarction from 1981–1983 to 1992–1994 in Israel. *Circulation*, 95, 342–50.

Gottlieb, S.S., McCarter, R.J., and Vogel, R.A. (1998). Effect of beta-blockade on mortality among high-risk and low-risk patients after myocardial infarction. *New England Journal of Medicine*, 339, 489–97.

Gubler, K.D., Davis, R., Koepsell, T., *et al.* (1997). Long-term survival of elderly trauma patients. *Archives of Surgery*, 132, 1010–14.

Gurwitz, J.H., Goldberg, R.J., Chen, Z., *et al.* (1992). β-blocker therapy in acute myocardial infarction: evidence for undreutilization in the elderly. *American Journal of Medicine*, 93, 605–10.

Gurwitz, J.H., Gore, J.M., Goldberg, R.J., *et al.* (1996). Recent age-related trends in the use of thrombolytic therapy in patients who have had acute myocardial infarction. *Annals of Internal Medicine*, 124, 283–91.

Gurwitz, J.H., McLaughlin, T.J., Willison, D.J., *et al.* (1997). Delayed hospital presentation in patients who have had acute myocardial infarction. *Annals of Internal Medicine*, 126, 593–9.

Hammerlein, A., Derendorf, H., and Lowenthal, D.T. (1998). Pharmacokinetic and pharmacodynamic changes in the elderly. *Clinical Pharmacokinetics*, 35, 49–64.

Hanson, L.C., Weber, D.J., and Rutala, W.A. (1992). Risk factors for nosocomial pneumonia in the elderly. *American Journal of Medicine*, 92, 161–6.

Harkness, G.A., Bentley, D.W., and Roghmann, K.J.H. (1990). Risk factors for nosocomial pneumonia in the elderly. *American Journal of Medicine*, 89, 457–63.

Havranek, E.P., Abrams, F., Stevens, E., *et al.* (1998). Determinants of mortality in elderly patients with heart failure. *Archives of Internal Medicine*, 158, 2024–8.

Herlitz, J., Karlson, B.W., and Hjalmarson, A. (1993). Prognosis of acute myocardial infarction in relation to age. *Cardiology in the Elderly*, 1, 23–8.

Horn, J. (1997). Intensive care and the elderly. *Archives of Gerontology and Geriatrics*, 25, 101–10.

Hughes, R.A.C. and Rees, J.H. (1997). Clinical and epidemiologic features of Guillain–Barré syndrome. *Journal of Infectious Diseases*, 176 (Supplement 2), S92–8.

Jiricka, M.K., Ryan, P., Carvalho, M.A., *et al.* (1995). Pressure ulcer risk factors in an ICU population. *American Journal of Critical Care*, 4, 361–7.

Jones, J.M., Maryosh, J., Johnstone, S., *et al.* (1995). A multivariate analysis of factors related to the mortality of blunt trauma admissions ot the North Staffordshire Hospital Centre. *Journal of Trauma: Injury, Infection, and Critical Care*, 38, 118–22.

Jonsen, A.R. (1994). Intimations of futility. *American Journal of Medicine*, 96, 107–9.

Kafetz, K. and Luder, R. (1992). Safe use of streptokinase in myocardial infarction in patients aged 75 and over. *Postgraduate Medical Journal*, 68, 746–9.

Knaus, W.A., Wagner, D.P., Draper, E.A., *et al.* (1991). The APACHE III prognostic system. Risk prediction of hospital mortality for critically ill hospitalized patients. *Chest*, 100, 1619–36.

Kollef, M.H., Canfield, D.A., and Zuckerman, G.R. (1995). Triage considerations for patients with acute gastrointestinal hemorrhage admitted to a medical intensive care unit. *Critical Care Medicine*, 23, 1048–54.

Kollef, M.H., O'Brien, J.D., Zuckerman, G.R., *et al.* (1997). BLEED: a classification tool to predict outcomes in patients with acute upper and lower gastrointestinal hemorrhage. *Critical Care Medicine*, 25, 1125–32.

Krieger, B.P. (1994). Respiratory failure in the elderly. *Clinics in Geriatric Medicine*, 10, 103–19.

Krumholz, H.M., Pasternak, R.C., Weinstein, M.C., *et al.* (1992). Cost effectiveness of thrombolytic hterapy with streptokinase in elderly patients with suspected acute myocardial infarction. *New England Journal of Medicine*, 327, 7–13.

Krumholz, H.M., Radford, M.J., Ellerbeck, E.F., *et al.* (1995). Aspirin in the treatment of acute myocardial infarction in elderly Medicare beneficiaries. *Circulation*, 92, 2841–7.

Krumholz, H.M., Radford, M.J., Ellerbeck, E.F., *et al.* (1996). Aspirin for secondary prevention after acute myocardial infarction in the elderly: prescribed use and outcomes. *Annals of Internal Medicine*, 124, 292–8.

Krumholz, H.M., Radford, M.J., Wang, Y., *et al.* (1998). National use and effectiveness of β-blockers for the treatment of elderly patients after acute myocardial infarction. *Journal of the American Medical Association*, 280, 623–9.

Lane, P.L., Doig, G., Mikrogianakis, A., *et al.* (1996). An evaluation of Ontario trauma outcomes and the development of regional norms for trauma and injury severity score (TRISS) analysis. *Journal of Trauma: Injury, Infection, and Critical Care*, 41, 731–4.

Lever, J.A., Molloy, D.W., and Eagle, D.J. (1994). Use of physical restraints and their relationship to medication use in patients in four different institutional settings. *Humane Medicine*, 10, 17–27.

Lilley, J.M., Arie, T., and Chilvers, C.E.D. (1995). Special review—accidents involving older people: a review of the literature. *Age and Ageing*, 24, 346–65.

McClennan, M., McNeil, B.J., and Newhouse, J.P. (1994). Does more intensive treatment of acute myocardial infarction in the elderly reduce mortality? *Journal of the American Medical Association*, 272, 859–66.

McClish, D.K., Powell, S.H., Montenegro, H., *et al.* (1987). The impact of age on utilization of intensive care resources. *Journal of the American Geriatrics Society*, 35, 983–8.

MacDonald, J.B., Baillie, J., Williams, B.O., *et al.* (1983). Coronary care in the elderly. *Age and Ageing*, 12, 17–20.

McLaughlin, T.J., Sumerai, S.T., Willison, D.J., *et al.* (1996). Adherence to national guidelines for drug treatment of suspected acute myocardial infarciton. *Archives of Internal Medicine*, 156, 799–805.

Maher, J., Trutledge, F., Remtulla, H., *et al.* (1995). Neuromuscular disorders associated with failure to wean from the ventilator. *Intensive Care Medicine*, 21, 737–43.

Mark, D.B., Hlatky, M.A., Califf, R.M., *et al.* (1995). Cost effectiveness of thrombolytic therapy with tissue plasminogen activator as compared with streptokinase for acute myocardial infarction. *New England Journal of Medicine*, 332, 1418–24.

Mayer-Oakes, S.A., Oye, R.K., and Leake, B. (1991). Predictors of mortality in older patients following medical intensive care. The importance of functional status. *Journal of the American Geriatrics Society*, 39, 862–8.

Meduri, G.U., Turner, R.E., Abou-Shala, N., *et al.* (1996). Non-invasive positive pressure ventilation via face mask. First-line intervention in patients with acute hypercapnic and hypoxemic respiratory failure. *Chest*, 109, 179–92.

Meythaler, J.M., DeVivo, M.J., and Braswell, W.C. (1997). Rehabilitation outcomes of patients who have developed Guillain–Barré syndrome. *American Journal of Physical Medicine and Rehabilitation*, 76, 411–19.

Miettinen, T.A., Pyorala, K., Olsson, A.G., *et al.* (1997). Cholesterol-lowering therapy in women and elderly patients with myocardial infarction or angina pectoris. *Circulation*, 96, 4211–18.

Montague, T.J., Wong, R.Y., Burton, J.R., *et al.* (1992). Changes in acute myocardial infarction risk and patterns of practice for patients older and younger than 70 years, 1987–90. *Canadian Journal of Cardiology*, 8, 596–600.

Moran, J.L., Green, J.V., Homa, S.D., *et al.* (1998). Acute exacerbations of chronic obstructive pulmonary disease and mechanical ventilation: a re-evaluation. *Critical Care Medicine*, 26, 71–8.

Murphy, J.G., Cayten, C.G., and Stahl, W.M. (1990). Controlling for the severity of injuries in emergency medicine research. *American Journal of Emergency Medicine*, 8, 484–91.

Nava, S., Ambrosino, N., Clini, E., *et al.* (1998). Noninvasive mechanical ventilation in the weaning of patients with respiratory failure due to chronic obstructive pulmonary disease. *Annals of Internal Medicine*, 128, 721–8.

Ng, K.K.P., Howard, R.S., Fish, D.R., *et al.* (1995). Management and outcome of severe Guillain–Barré syndrome. *Quarterly Journal of Medicine*, 88, 243–50.

Norton, B., Homer-Ward, M., Donnelly, M.T., *et al.* (1996). A randomized prospective comparison of percutaneous endoscopic gastrostomy and nasogastric tube feeding after dysphagic stroke. *British Medical Journal*, 312, 13–16.

Nuckton, T.J. and List, D. (1995). Age as a factor in critical care unit admissions. *Archives of Internal Medicine*, 155, 1087–92.

Ontario Trauma Registry (1995). *Injury in the elderly (aged over 65)*, Vol. 4. Ontario Ministry of Health, Don Mills, Ontario.

Opper, F.H. and Burakoff, R. (1994). Nutritional support of the elderly patient in an intensive care unit. *Clinics in Geriatric Medicine*, 10, 31–49.

Oreskovich, M.R., Howard, J.D., Copass, M.K., *et al.* (1984). Geriatric trauma: injury patterns and outcome. *Journal of Trauma:* 24, 565–72.

Pashos, C.L., Newhouse, J.P., and McNeil, B.J. (1993). Temporal changes in the care and outcomes of elderly patients with acute myocardial infarction, 1987 through 1990. *Journal of the American Medical Association*, 270, 1832–6.

Patterson, J.A. and Bennett, R.G. (1995). Prevention and treatment of pressure sores. *Journal of the American Geriatrics Society*, 43, 919–27.

Perdue, P.W., Watts, D.D., Kaufmann, C.R., *et al.* (1998). Differences in mortality between elderly and younger adult trauma patients. Geriatric status increases risk of delayed death. *Journal of Trauma: Injury, Infection, and Critical Care*, 45, 805–10.

Pichard, C., Kyle, U., Chevrolet, J.C., *et al.* (1996). Lack of effects of recombinant growth hormone on muscle function in patients requiring prolonged mechanical ventilation: a prospective, randomized controlled study. *Critical Care Medicine*, 24, 403–13.

Pinchocofsky-Devin, G.D. and Kaminski, M.V. (1986). Correlation of pressure sores and nutritional status. *Journal of the American Geriatrics Society*, 34, 435–40.

Prevots, D.R. and Sutter, R.W. (1997). Assessment of Guillain–Barré syndrome mortality and morbidity in the United States: implicaitons for acute flaccid paralysis surveillance. *Journal of Infectious Diseases*, 175 (Supplement), S151–5.

Redelmeier, D.A., Tan, S.H., and Booth, G.L. (1998). The treatment of unrelated disorders in patients with chronic medical diseases. *New England Journal of Medicine*, 338, 1516–20.

Rees, J.H., Thompson, R.D., Smeeton, N.C., *et al.* (1998). Epidemiological study of Guillain–Barré syndrome in south east England. *Journal of Neurology, Neurosurgery and Psychiatry*, 64, 74–7.

Rich, M.W. (1998). Therapy for acute myocardial infarction in older persons. *Journal of the American Geriatrics Society*, 46, 1302–7.

Rich, M.W., Bosner, M.S., Chung, M.K., *et al.* (1992). Is age an independent predictor of early and late mortality in patients with acute myocardial infarction? *American Journal of Medicine*, 92, 7–13.

Robbins, L.J., Boyko, E., Lane, J., *et al.* (1987). Binding the elderly: a prospective study of the use of mechanical restraints in an acute care hospital. *Journal of the American Geriatrics Society*, 35, 290–6.

Roche, V.M.L., Dramer, A., Hester, E., and Welsh, C.H. (1999). Long-term functional outcome after intensive care. *Journal of the American Geriatrics Society*, 47, 18–24.

Rockwood, K., Noseworthy, T.W., Gibney, R.T.N., *et al.* (1993). One-year outcome of elderly and young patients admitted to intensive care units. *Critical Care Medicine*, 21, 687–91.

Rosenthal, G.E. and Fortinsky, R.H. (1994). Differences in the treatment of patients with acute myocardial infarction according to patient age. *Journal of the American Geriatrics Society*, 42, 826–32.

Rutledge, R. and Osler, T. (1998). The ICD-9-Based illness severity score: a new model that outperforms both DRG and APR-DRG as predictors of survival and resource utilization. *Journal of Trauma: Injury, Infection, and Critical Care*, **45**, 791–9.

Rutledge, R., Hoyt, D.B., Eastman, A.B., et al. (1997). Comparison of the injury severity score and ICD-9 diagnosis codes as predictors of outcome in injury: analysis of 44,032 patients. *Journal of Trauma: Injury, Infection and Critical Care*, **2**, 477–89.

Ruttimann, U.E. (1994). Statistical approaches to development and validation of predictive instruments. *Critical Care Clinics*, **10**, 19–35.

Sage, M., Sage, A.B., Hurst, C.R., et al. (1987). Intensive care for the elderly: outcome of elective and non-elective admissions. *Journal of the American Geriatrics Society*, **35**, 312–18.

Sagie, A., Rotenberg, Z., Weinberger, I., et al. (1987). Acute transmural myocardial infarction in elderly patients hospitalized in the coronary care unit versus the general medical ward. *Journal of the American Geriatrics Society*, **35**, 915–19.

Sapijaszko, M.F.A., Brant, R., Sandham, D., et al. (1996). Non-respiratory predictor of mechanical ventilation dependency in intensive care unit patients. *Critical Care Medicine*, **24**, 601–7.

Saywell, R.M., Woods, J.R., Rappaport, S.A., et al. (1989). The value of age and severity as predictors of costs in geriatric head trauma patients. *Journal of the American Geriatrics Society*, **37**, 625–30.

Scheinhorn, D.J., Chao, D.C., Stearn-Hassenpflug, M., et al. (1997). Post-ICU mechanical ventilation. Treatment of 1123 patients at a regional weaning center. *Clinical Investigations in Critical Care*, **111**, 1654–9.

Schwartz, D.B. (1996). Enhanced enteral and parenteral nutrition practice and outcomes in an intensive care unit with a hospital-wide performance improvement process. *Journal of the American Dietetic Association*, **96**, 484–9.

Segal, W.M. and Cello, J.P. (1997). Hemorrhage in the upper gastrointestinal tract in the older patient. *American Journal of Gastroenterology*, **92**, 42–6.

Seneff, M.G., Zimmerman, J.E., Knaus, W.A., et al. (1996). Predicting the duration of mechanical ventilation. The importance of disease and patient characteristics. *Clinical Investigations in Critical Care*, **110**, 469–79.

Shabot, M.M. and Johnson, C.L. (1995). Outcome from critical care in the 'oldest old' trauma patients. *Journal of Trauma: Injury, Infection, and Critical Care*, **39**, 254–60.

Sheth, R.D., Riggs, J.E., Hobbs, G.R., et al. (1996). Age and Guillain–Barré syndrome severity. *Muscle and Nerve*, **19**, 375–7.

Sickbert, S.F. (1989). Coronary care unit visitation and summary of the literature. *Journal of the American Geriatrics Society*, **37**, 655–7.

Singh, N., Garowski, T., Wagener, M.M., et al. (1998). Outcome of patients with cirrhosis requiring intensive care unit support. Prospective assessment of predictors of mortality. *Journal of Gastroenterology*, **33**, 73–9.

Smith, P.D., Enderson, B.L., and Maull, K.I. (1990). Trauma in the elderly: determinants of outcome. *Southern Medical Journal*, **83**, 171–7.

Soumerai, S.B., McLaughlin, T.J., Spiegelman, D., et al. (1997). Adverse outcomes of underuse of β-blockers in elderly survivors of acute myocardial infarction. *Journal of the American Medical Association*, **277**, 115–21.

Suarez-Alvarez, J.R., Miquel, J., Del Rio, F.J., et al. (1995). Epidemiologic apsects and results of applying the TRISS methodology in a Spanish trauma intensive care unit (TICU). *Intensive Care Medicine*, **21**, 729–36.

Swinburne, A.J., Fedullo, A.J., Bixby, K., et al. (1993). Respiratory failure in the elderly. Analysis of outcome after treatment with mechanical ventilation. *Archives of Internal Medicine*, **153**, 1657–62.

Thomas, D.R., Goode, P.S., Tarquine, P.H., et al. (1996). Hospital-acquired pressure ulcers and risk of death. *Journal of the American Geriatrics Society*, **44**, 1435–40.

Tresch, D.D. (1998). Management of the older patient with acute myocardial infarction: difference in clinical presentations between older and younger patients. *Journal of the American Geriatrics Society*, **46**, 1157–62.

Troche, F. and Moine, P. (1997). Is the duration of mechanical ventilation predictable? *Clinical Investigation in Critical Care*, **112**, 745–51.

Truog, R.D., Brett, A.S., and Frader, J. (1992). The problem with futility. *New England Journal of Medicine*, **326**, 1560–4.

Tuttle-Newhall, J.E., Rutledge, R., and Hultman, S. (1997). Statewide, population-based time series analysis of the frequency and outcome of pulmonary embolus in 318,554 trauma patients. *Journal of Trauma: Injury, Infection, and Critical Care*, **41**, 90–9.

Veatch, R.M. (1994). Why physicians cannot determine if care is futile. *Journal of the American Geriatrics Society*, **42**, 871–4.

Waisel, D.B. and Truog, R.D. (1995). The cardiopulmonary resuscitation-not-indicated order: futility revisited. *Annals of Internal Medicine*, **122**, 304–8.

Weijer, C., Singer, P.A., Dickens, B.M., et al. (1998). Bioethics for clinicians: 16. Dealing with demands for inappropriate treatment. *Canadian Medical Association Journal*, **159**, 817–21.

Wijdicks, E.F.M. and Scott, J.P. (1997). Causes and outcome of mechanical ventilation in patients with hemispheric ischemic stroke. *Mayo Clinics Proceedings*, **72**, 210–13.

Winner, S.J. and Grimley Evans, J. (1990). Age-specific incidence of Guillain–Barré syndrome in Oxfordshire. *Quarterly Journal of Medicine*, **77**, 1297–304.

Wroblewski, M., Mikulowski, P., and Steen, B. (1986). Symptoms of myocardial infarction in old age: clinical case, retrospective and prospective studies. *Age and Ageing*, **15**, 99–104.

Wu, A.W., Rubin, H.R., and Rosen, M.J. (1990). Are elderly people less responsive to intensive care? *Journal of the American Geriatrics Society*, **38**, 621–7.

Young, J.S., Cephas, G.A., and Blow, O. (1998). Outcome and cost of trauma among the elderly, A real-life model of a single-payer reimbursement system. *Journal of Trauma: Injury, Infection, and Critical Care*, **45**, 800–4.

23.8 Symptom management and palliative care

Mary J. Baines and Nigel P. Sykes

I conceive it the office of the physician not only to restore the health but to mitigate pain and dolours; and not only when such mitigation may conduce to recovery but when it may serve to make a fair and easy passage.

(Francis Bacon 1561–1626)

The nurses battled on heroically. They emerged with far greater credit than we (the doctors) who are still capable of ignoring the conditions which make muted people suffer. The dissatisfied dead cannot noise abroad the negligence they have suffered.

(Hinton 1967)

The doctor, in Bacon's time, could do very little to 'restore health'; not surprisingly he concentrated on mitigating 'pains and dolours'. But, with the advent of scientific medicine and the study of diseases rather than their symptoms, this situation has radically changed. The successful treatment of tuberculosis relieved cough; vitamin B_{12} prevented the lethargy and dyspnoea of pernicious anaemia.

With the increased availability of diagnostic tools and therapeutic options there was the inevitable tendency to institute active therapy even for patients with very advanced or incurable disease, often associated with extreme old age. Such endeavour could easily mean that the relief of symptoms and the support of patients and family became low priorities. It was the lack of appropriate care for the dying that resulted, in the 1960s, in a number of influential reports (Hinton 1967) and the advent of the modern hospice movement.

The medical specialty of palliative care has its origin in the hospice movement. It has now spread worldwide and is involved with patients at home, in general hospitals and in nursing homes as well as inpatient hospice units. Palliative care requires a team approach with nurses playing an important role. They are responsible for the regular evaluation of pain and symptom control and for much of the counselling and support. Other members of the multiprofessional team include social workers, physiotherapists, occupational therapists, and clergy.

Palliative care is the active total care of patients whose disease is not responsive to curative treatment. The goal of palliative care is the achievement of the best possible quality of life for patients and their families. According to the World Health Organization (**WHO**) palliative care has the following functions (WHO 1990):

- it affirms life and regards dying as a normal process
- it neither hastens nor postpones death
- it provides relief from pain and other distressing symptoms
- it integrates the psychological and spiritual aspects of care
- it offers a support system to help patients live as actively as possible until death
- it offers a support system to help the family cope during the patient's illness and in their own bereavement.

The diagnosis of dying

The decision that treatment aimed at prolonging life is no longer appropriate must always be difficult. The common respiratory or cardiovascular diseases may have fluctuating courses with unexpected but worthwhile improvements following treatment. In such diseases the diagnosis of dying is made by exclusion, after a patient has failed to respond to standard therapeutic and rehabilitative endeavours. Experienced nursing staff are often the first to recognize the situation (Blackburn 1989).

In advanced malignant disease the decision to abandon active treatment is often easier, with the expectation of a steadily deteriorating situation. It is partly for this reason that hospices were founded initially for cancer patients. However, most hospices have extended their care to other people with diseases whose trajectories or symptoms resemble those of cancer, particularly motor neurone disease and AIDS. Many cancer patients die with cardiac failure, pneumonia, renal failure, or organic brain disease, and it has become recognized that many people with these or other progressive, incurable, non-malignant conditions can also benefit from palliative care.

Perhaps the distinction between active treatment and palliative care should not be clearly defined, for they can occur together.

treated. Fortunately, the situation is now improving and, in the developed world, most patients with cancer should be assured of good relief of pain with the range of treatments now available.

In the developing world, where the majority of patients present with advanced disease, the control of pain is also improving. This is due to the initiative of the WHO in promoting the wide availability of oral morphine for cancer patients, and to the spread of palliative care.

Diagnosis of pain

It is important to make a diagnosis as to the cause of pain or, more often, pains. Most patients with advanced cancer have more than one pain, some caused directly by the tumour, others resulting from treatment, debility, or concurrent illness.

Most cancer pain is nociceptive, in that it is caused by mechanical or chemical stimuli in the bone, viscera, or soft tissue, and is conducted along intact somatosensory pathways. However, a significant proportion of cancer pain is neuropathic, caused by damage to the central or peripheral nervous system. Neuropathic pain is felt in the relevant dermatome, it is often described as 'burning' or 'shooting', and is associated with motor, sensory, or autonomic changes.

Management of pain

Treatment for pain should be started immediately, based on the presumptive diagnosis of its cause. Sometimes the response to treatment will make the diagnosis clearer or allow further investigations to be made. Occasionally, the patient is confused or too ill for a full assessment to be made, and in this situation adequate analgesia must not be withheld.

For most patients, a combination of the following methods will be required:

- analgesic drugs
- adjuvant analgesic drugs
- psychological and emotional support
- palliative radiotherapy
- anaesthetic techniques.

The last two methods should always be considered, but in the majority of terminally ill patients the correct treatment is with the skilled use of drugs and the support of patient and family.

Analgesic drugs

The criterion for giving analgesia, and especially opioids, is the presence of pain—not the expected length of life. Unfortunately, many patients and doctors still feel that if morphine is started early 'it will lose its effect'. The reverse is nearer the truth, and the really intractable pain, seen occasionally at the end of life, has often been preceded by months of inadequate control leading to depression, anger, and fear.

Paracetamol (acetaminophen)

A dosage of 650 to 1000 mg every 6 h is recommended for the treatment of mild pain. If this proves ineffective, the choice is between adding a weak opioid, for example dextropropoxyphene with paracetamol (co-proxamol) or codeine with paracetamol (co-codamol), or a low dose of a strong opioid. With escalating pain or

a very sick patient, it is advisable to change directly from paracetamol to morphine.

Morphine

Morphine is well absorbed when given by mouth, through the buccal mucosa, or rectally. It is rapidly distributed throughout the body. Metabolism mainly occurs in the liver, where morphine is broken down into glucuronides, and it is in this form that most renal excretion occurs. The plasma half-life of morphine and its active metabolites is about 3 h.

Preparations of morphine

1. Morphine sulphate solution or tablet given every 4 h. The solution is also sometimes given sublingually.
2. Slow-release morphine sulphate tablet: preparations are available for administration every 12 h or every 24 h.
3. Morphine injections given every 4 h. Parenteral to oral potency ratio is about 3:1 in patients receiving regular morphine. Diamorphine is identical in action to morphine. If it is available (as in the United Kingdom) it is preferred for injection because of its greater solubility and so smaller volume. Diamorphine or morphine is given by injection or subcutaneous infusion only if the patient is unable to take oral drugs. There is no evidence that these routes improve pain control except for rapidity of action, in an emergency.
4. Epidural morphine is given every 12 h or by infusion. The ratio of epidural dose to oral dose is 1:10.
5. Morphine suppositories are given every 4 h but are rarely used now.

Clinical use of morphine Oral morphine must be given regularly, with the dose interval depending on the preparation used. The correct dose is the lowest which achieves pain control. If pain has escaped control with regular paracetamol, then morphine 5 mg every 4 h or an equivalent dose of a longer-acting preparation is suggested. Morphine 10 mg every 4 h is usually needed if the patient has been receiving dextropropoxyphene or a similar weak opioid. This dose should be increased by 50 per cent increments every 24 h until pain relief is obtained, using top-up doses for breakthrough pain as often as necessary. The majority of patients require less than 150 mg daily but occasionally 1000 mg daily, or even higher, is needed.

This pattern of morphine administration, with a careful titration of dose against the patient's pain, allows for individual variation in age, weight, and renal function.

Problems with morphine About one-third of patients feel nauseated on starting morphine, and so an antiemetic such as metoclopramide should be given to prevent this. It can usually be stopped after a week. Constipation should be anticipated and laxatives prescribed routinely. Respiratory depression is not a clinical problem if the morphine dose is titrated against the pain, for pain is a respiratory stimulant. A dry mouth is common and requires regular mouth care.

Tolerance, although widely feared, is a minor problem. When an increasing dose of morphine is needed, this is usually due to increased pain from an enlarging malignancy. Addiction—an overpowering drive to take a drug for its psychological effects—does not appear to occur in patients with pain. Physical dependence does develop, but if the pain lessens, for example after radiotherapy, it is possible to reduce the dose of morphine slowly without producing withdrawal symptoms.

Table 2 Alternatives to oral morphine

Name	Preparation	Dose interval (h)	Dose required to give equivalent analgesic effect to morphine 10 mg every 4 h	Comment
Buprenorphine	200 µg 400 µg	6–8	300 µg every 8 h	Given sublingually; probable ceiling effect at 3–5 mg/24 h
Dextromoramide	5 mg 10 mg	2	5 mg (short-lived peak efect)	Too short acting for regular use
Fentanyl patch	25 µg/h, 50 µg/h, 75 µg/h, 100 µg/h	72	25 µg/h every 72 h	Titration difficult; expensive
Hydromorphone	Normal release: 1.3 mg, 2.6 mg Slow release: 2 mg, 4 mg, 8 mg, 16 mg	Normal release: 4 Slow release: 12	1.3 mg every 4 h	Similar properties to morphine
Methadone	5 mg	12	10 mg (single dose); probably about 2 mg with repeated administration	Long plasma half-life, thus accumulation occurs; may be used if morphine toxicity arises
Pethidine	50 mg	2–3	100 mg every 2–3 h	Weak oral analgesic; short acting
Phenazocine	5 mg	8	2.5 mg every 8 h	Useful alternative to morphine; sublingual administration possible
Tramadol	50 mg	4–6	50 mg every 4 h	Should be considered an alternative to codeine

Myoclonic jerks are a sign of opioid toxicity and may occur with a stable dose of morphine if renal function is deteriorating. A reduction in morphine dose usually lessens the problem. Drowsiness may occur when morphine is started or the dose increased, but patients on a stable dose have unaltered cognitive function and are allowed to drive (Vainio 1995).

Alternatives to morphine Although morphine is the recommended strong analgesic, there are a few patients who complain of severe nausea or drowsiness which they attribute to the drug, and others who refuse to have it. For such patients it is necessary to have alternatives to oral morphine. Fentanyl patches are sometimes used as an alternative to morphine. The patch is placed on a convenient area of skin and the dose should be adjusted to maintain pain control. It needs to be replaced every 72 h and dose titration may prove difficult. Table 2 lists alternative strong analgesics, and it can also be used in converting to morphine from other drugs.

Adjuvant analgesic drugs

The correct use of adjuvants for analgesia may mean that morphine is not required, or it may be possible to give it in a lower dose. Response to adjuvant treatment is variable, so it is recommended that, unless delayed response is likely, the drug is discontinued after a week if there is no improvement.

Other treatment

Radiotherapy may be helpful during the last weeks of life provided that it is given without delay and with the minimum number of treatments. The most common indication is the development of a painful bony metastasis, and worthwhile pain relief is achieved in 80 per cent of patients, often with a single fraction (Needham and Hoskin 1994).

The value of anaesthetic techniques will depend on the availability of an anaesthetist specializing in pain control. Epidural steroids, morphine, and bupivacaine have proved valuable, as have some peripheral or autonomic nerve blocks. Transcutaneous electrical nerve stimulation is occasionally useful for the control of cancer pain. Acupuncture has rarely been found to be effective. The use of adjuvant drugs and other treatments is summarized in Table 3.

Chronic non-malignant pain

Unfortunately, chronic pain is common in older people. There are many causes, which include osteoarthritis and rheumatoid arthritis, trigeminal and post-herpetic neuralgia, ischaemic legs, back problems, bedsores, and the pain of immobility from stroke or severe disability. The principles of treatment for non-malignant pain are the same as those for cancer pain. It is important to make a clear diagnosis, institute specific treatment if possible, use analgesic drugs regularly in adequate doses and give appropriate psychological support. Non-opioids (paracetamol, non-steroidal anti-inflammatory drugs) and weak opioids (codeine and dextropropoxyphene) are preferred. However, there has recently been a re-evaluation of the use of strong opioids in patients with a variety of non-malignant pains including back pain, phantom pain, and neuropathic pain. This suggests that

Table 3 Adjuvant therapy in cancer pain

Type of pain	Adjuvant drug	Other treatment
Bone pain	Diclofenac 150 mg daily or other NSAID	Palliative radiotherapy; immobilization, e.g. surgical fixation
Refractory bone pain	Bisphosphonates, e.g. pamidronate 30–60 mg by intravenous infusion	
Neuropathic pain	Amitriptyline 25 mg at night with increasing dose for dysaesthetic pain Carbamazepine 200 mg daily with increasing dose for lancinating pain Flecainide 100–200 mg daily	Epidural steroids; epidural bupivacaine (in lumbar region)
Pancreatic or liver pain	NSAID	Coeliac plexus block
Intestinal colic (from inoperable obstruction)	Hyoscine butylbromide 60–200 mg daily	
Headaches (from raised intracranial pressure)	Dexamethasone 16 mg daily, reducing dose as possible	Cranial irradiation
Chest wall pain	NSAID	Intercostal or thoracic paravertebral block
Lymphoedema		Compression bandaging

NSAID, non-steroidal anti-inflammatory drug.

a proportion of patients gain partial or good sustained analgesia without major side-effects (Portenoy 1996). With severe pain, such as from gangrene, it is essential that morphine should be given without delay and in adequate doses.

Psychotropic drugs have a major role in the management of many types of chronic non-malignant pain. Tricyclic antidepressants and anticonvulsants are used for post-herpetic pain and trigeminal neuralgia, diabetic neuropathy, and phantom limb pain. Nerve blocks include the infiltration of trigger areas with local anaesthetic, epidural steroids for root irritation, and sympathetic blocks for ischaemia.

Physical methods such as local anaesthetic sprays, transcutaneous electrical stimulation, and acupuncture seem of greater value in chronic non-malignant pain than in the pain caused by cancer.

Confusion

The differential diagnosis and treatment of confusion are two of the most difficult problems facing a doctor who is caring for dying patients. Whereas pain, or perhaps incontinence, is the symptom most dreaded by the patient, confusion is probably the symptom that most distresses the family. Causes and management of delirium are discussed elsewhere (Chapter 18.21). In practice, confusion is usually of mixed aetiology. For example, an elderly cancer patient with a mild degree of dementia may be 'just about' coping at home. The development of a chest infection necessitating hospital admission tips the balance and precipitates an acute confusional state.

Reversible causes for confusion should be sought and treated appropriately. Non-drug methods of management are most important. These include the provision of a familiar routine, if possible in home surroundings. Hearing aids and glasses should be checked. Many patients value a simple explanation of the cause of their confusion and the steps planned to help with this.

The 'quietly muddled' patient with dementia requires no medication and sedative drugs may worsen the confusion. Psychotropic drugs are used to reduce the agitation sometimes associated with confusion. Thioridazine is widely used in this situation; haloperidol gives less sedation but extrapyramidal side-effects are common and can be severe.

Constipation

The great majority of patients with terminal illness become constipated. This may be due to a specific, potentially reversible, condition such as hypercalcaemia, intestinal obstruction, hypothyroidism, or depression. Much more often the constipation is caused by a combination of inactivity, a diet low in roughage, general weakness, confusion, and constipating drugs such as opioids and tricyclic antidepressants.

Unless the patient is very frail, an attempt should be made to increase activity, add fibre to the diet, and maintain a good oral fluid intake. Assistance with mobility should be available so that the patient can use the lavatory rather than a commode or bedpan. However, in spite of these measures, constipation often remains a problem and, in practice, laxatives and rectal measures are required.

Laxatives are often divided into those that stimulate bowel peristalsis and those that soften and bulk the stool. This is not pharmacologically tenable, as increased stool size in itself causes increased peristalsis, but the division remains useful in the clinical choice of laxatives. Faecal softeners retain water in the bowel by osmosis or increase water penetration of stool. These include magnesium hydroxide or sulphate, lactulose, docusate, and poloxamer. Stimulant laxatives such as senna, bisacodyl, and danthron increase colonic muscle activity.

Constipation in terminally ill patients is best managed with a combination of both types of laxative. This will avoid either painful colic or a bowel loaded with soft faeces, problems that arise if a stimulant or softening laxative is given alone (Sykes 1996). Examples include the following.

- Codanthramer (danthron and poloxamer): available in two strengths, both available as suspension or capsule.
- Magnesium hydroxide and liquid paraffin emulsion with senna tablets.

The dose should be gradually increased until a regular soft bowel action is obtained. Suppositories, an enema or manual removal may be needed if a patient presents with a loaded rectum or if the laxative regimen is ineffective. It is a good general rule to perform a rectal examination on the third day if the bowels have not opened, inserting a glycerin or bisacodyl suppository if the rectum is loaded.

Cough

Cough receptors are found at all levels of the respiratory tree and can be stimulated by mechanical or chemical means. Common causes of cough include bacterial or viral infections, primary or secondary tumours involving the respiratory tract, cardiac failure, asthma or chronic obstructive pulmonary disease, angiotensin-converting enzyme inhibitor therapy, and smoking.

Specific treatment aimed at relieving the cause of coughing should be given unless the patient is too ill. Such treatments include antibiotics, diuretics, bronchodilators, corticosteroids, and radiotherapy. If specific treatment is inappropriate or ineffective, symptomatic treatment must be offered including the following.

1. Simple linctus (a simple syrup): this seems to soothe the pharynx and reduce coughing. Proprietary preparations offer no advantages.
2. Steam inhalations or nebulized saline aid the expectoration of viscid sputum, especially if they are followed by physiotherapy.
3. Opioids such as codeine, morphine, and methadone suppress the cough reflex centrally. They should be reserved for those with a dry cough, those too weak to expectorate, or occasionally at night if cough disturbs sleep. Codeine 30 to 60 mg every 4 h is often effective, but with an intractable cough, usually caused by lung cancer, morphine is needed. Morphine 5 mg every 4 h is the starting dose; this can be increased until relief is obtained.
4. Nebulized local anaesthetic using 5 ml of 2 per cent lignocaine (lidocaine) every 4 h has occasionally been used with benefit but many patients find it unacceptable.

Depression

Appropriate sadness is a natural reaction to declining strength or the approach of death and most people, from time to time, find themselves unable to concentrate, fearful of the future, and sleeping poorly. This situation is normally treated with short-term psychological help; giving information, helping the patient find practical steps in adjusting to the circumstances, and emphasizing past strengths and coping mechanisms.

The diagnosis of clinical depression in a patient with terminal illness is difficult as the normal biological indicators, such as poor appetite and loss of energy, are of little value. The diagnosis must depend on psychological symptoms, especially a loss of interest and enjoyment in all, or almost all, activities. Studies have shown that about 10 per cent of terminally ill cancer patients become clinically depressed. This level tends to fall as death approaches (Hinton 1994). The prevalence of depression in other life-threatening illnesses is not known.

Depressed patients are treated with a combination of antidepressants and psychological measures. Tricyclics and selective serotonin reuptake inhibitors are equally effective as antidepressants, so the choice will normally depend on their differing side-effects. Many patients already suffer with a dry mouth, drowsiness, and constipation, so often a serotonin reuptake inhibitor such as paroxetine is preferred.

Dysphagia

Difficulty in swallowing can be caused by malignant or benign obstructive lesions involving the pharynx or oesophagus. Neurological causes include cerebrovascular disease, cerebral tumours, and motor neurone disease. Dysphagia can be caused, or exacerbated, by pain on swallowing, a dry mouth, and anxiety.

Having diagnosed the cause of dysphagia, specific treatment may be possible. Thrush infections of the mouth or oesophagus should be treated with nystatin or fluconazole. Oesophageal cancer can be treated with radiotherapy, laser therapy, bouginage, an indwelling flexible oesophageal tube, or alcohol injection. Radiotherapy should be considered for mediastinal lymphadenopathy but, if the patient is not fit enough, the dysphagia may respond temporarily to corticosteroids (dexamethasone 8 mg/day), which cause shrinkage of peritumour inflammatory oedema.

If such specific treatment is inappropriate or inadequately effective, then dietary modification is required. In general, patients with obstructive lesions need a nourishing but fluid diet, whereas those with neurological problems prefer semisolid food. Correct positioning and adequate time for feeding is important.

Nasogastric tubes are considered by many patients as uncomfortable and undignified, and parenteral nutrition is not appropriate in those with advanced and irreversible disease. Endoscopically or radiologically placed percutaneous gastrostomy feeding has proved valuable for selected patients with motor neurone disease. It should also be considered in those with head and neck cancers if there is minimal residual disease. However, the implementation of any alternative route of feeding should only occur after most careful consideration, as their use may simply prolong the process of dying.

Patients with severe dysphagia will need drugs for symptom relief to be given by subcutaneous infusion or, perhaps, rectally. Most will, sooner or later, develop an aspiration pneumonia which should usually be treated symptomatically.

Dyspnoea

Dyspnoea is defined as a distressing difficulty in breathing. It is therefore a subjective symptom (like pain) and its severity may be poorly related to tachypnoea or to pulmonary pathology. Breathing is under the control of the respiratory centres, and these are stimulated by chemical changes in the blood ($P\text{co}_2$, $P\text{o}_2$, H^+), by afferent impulses from the lung, heart, chest wall, diaphragm, and from higher centres.

It is important to seek a diagnosis of the cause (or causes) of breathlessness in a terminally ill patient. Such causes include infection, primary or secondary lung tumour, chronic obstructive airways disease, cardiac failure, pleural effusion, pulmonary embolus, and anxiety. In most patients these should, in the first instance, be treated actively, provided that necessary symptomatic measures are used as well. For example, low-dose oral morphine will ease the dyspnoea and pain from a chest infection; it can be withdrawn later if the infection resolves with antibiotics and physiotherapy.

However, as the disease progresses, the place for active treatment becomes less. The patient may not improve following pleural aspiration or a course of antibiotics and it may be decided that the side-effects of a treatment, such as anticoagulation, outweigh its possible benefits.

A significant number of terminally ill patients will express to their families, or to medical and nursing staff, their 'readiness to go' or their hope that 'things won't be dragged out'. Such wishes must be respected when a decision about active treatment is made. The patient and family should be reassured that dyspnoea and pain will be relieved even if, for example, antibiotics are not prescribed.

Symptomatic treatment of dyspnoea

Non-pharmacological measures

Severe dyspnoea is frightening and the resultant anxiety exacerbates the symptom. Medical and nursing staff should encourage patients to express their fears, usually of choking or suffocating, and give careful explanation and reassurance. Simple measures such as an open window, a fan, or a backrest in bed often help.

Physiotherapists have an important role; they can help with breathing retraining, relaxation, and the expectoration of secretions through light percussion on the chest. A nurse-led dyspnoea clinic using counselling and breathing retraining, and teaching coping and adaptation strategies, has been reported to provide significant improvement in lung cancer patients (Corner et al. 1996).

Morphine

Oral morphine has been used for many years in the symptomatic management of breathlessness. Its mechanism of action remains unclear; it reduces the sensitivity of the respiratory centre to stimuli but, when opioids are administered over a period of time, tolerance to this occurs. Morphine appears to reduce the sensation of dyspnoea more than it reduces the level of ventilation. Clinical experience indicates that regular oral morphine, starting with 2.5 to 5 mg every 4 h and increasing slowly if needed, is safe and often effective.

However, in spite of long experience with oral morphine in dyspnoeic patients, there are, as yet, no good controlled trials showing benefit, and further research is needed. There has also been interest in the use of nebulized morphine, but it appears that this is no more effective than nebulized saline.

Anxiolytic drugs

As dyspnoea is exacerbated by anxiety, it is logical to use anxiolytic drugs. Diazepam, with its long half-life, can be conveniently given as a single nightly dose of 2 to 10 mg. Lorazepam 1 mg is used sublingually for a rapid onset of action in patients with acute anxiety and dyspnoea.

If benzodiazepines prove too sedating, buspirone 5 to 10 mg twice daily can be helpful. Serotonin agonists have been shown to have a ventilatory stimulant effect in addition to their anxiolytic properties (Craven and Sutherland 1991).

Hyoscine (scopolamine) and glycopyrronium

These drugs reduce exocrine secretions and relax smooth muscle. Hyoscine hydrobromide is sedative, although it can occasionally cause paradoxical excitation. Glycopyrronium bromide is less able to penetrate the blood–brain barrier and cause central effects. These drugs are used to reduce bronchial secretions that accumulate in the last hours of life causing the 'death rattle'. In this context, the sedative effect of hyoscine may be desirable. The dose of hyoscine is 0.4 mg every 4 h, or up to 2.4 mg over 24 h by subcutaneous infusion. Glycopyrronium is more potent, and so the dose is half that of hyoscine. Either drug can be combined with morphine or diamorphine in the syringe drive. As with all anticholinergic agents, hyoscine may thicken secretions to a degree that can be troublesome in anything but short-term use.

Oxygen

The use of oxygen in the dyspnoea of terminal illness is controversial, as is the role of hypoxia in causing this symptom. Both oxygen and air, administered using nasal cannulae, can cause a significant but equal improvement in dyspnoea. This response does not correlate with the level of hypoxia (Booth et al. 1996). As an oxygen mask or nasal cannulae often present barriers between patient and family, it is recommended that non-pharmacological and drug treatments are tried first, only using oxygen if the response is inadequate.

Respiratory emergencies

These include a major haemoptysis, pulmonary embolus, or acute tracheal compression. Intravenous or intramuscular midazolam 10 to 20 mg should be given slowly. An alternative is an injection of diamorphine 5 mg with hyoscine 0.4 mg.

Insomnia

Many patients with advanced disease sleep poorly owing to unrelieved physical or mental distress. Before prescribing a hypnotic it is necessary to enquire if sleep is disturbed by pain or discomfort, sweats or cramps, fear of incontinence or any other physical symptom for which appropriate relief can be given. More often, anxiety, depression, or a fear of dying in the night prevent normal sleep. A careful enquiry will usually uncover such factors and they can be helped by counselling with, occasionally, the addition of psychotropic drugs. However, in spite of these measures, many patients request a hypnotic which can be administered as follows.

1. Chlormethiazole one to two capsules (192–384 mg): a useful hypnotic for older people, even if confused. It has a very short half-life.
2. Zopiclone 3.75 to 7.5 mg: a non-benzodiazepine with a half-life of about 5 h.

3. Temazepam 10 to 20 mg: a benzodiazepine with a half-life of 6 to 8 h, but which may have undesirable prolonged effects in some elderly patients.

Intestinal obstruction

The overall incidence of intestinal obstruction in patients with advanced cancer is about 3 per cent, but those with advanced ovarian cancer have a risk of 25 to 40 per cent. Patients with metastatic abdominal or pelvic malignancy often have both mechanical and functional causes for obstruction and this may occur at more than one site.

There are now a number of treatment options for the patient with advanced cancer who develops intestinal obstruction. It is rarely an emergency, so there is usually time to discuss the situation with the patient and family so that they can make an informed choice about treatment.

Palliative surgery

This should be considered in every case. However, operative fatality is high, mean survival is short, and there is a high incidence of enterocutaneous fistulas. Many elderly patients do not want another operation if it is only palliative, and none should be referred for surgery simply to prevent a distressing death from obstruction; the correct use of drugs can prevent this.

Nasogastric intubation

There is no evidence that this leads to a sustained relief of obstruction. It should only be used for patients who are being considered for surgery and for those, principally with a high obstruction, who respond poorly to pharmacological treatment. In this group, percutaneous venting gastrostomy should be considered as a better tolerated alternative.

Pharmacological treatment

Continuous subcutaneous infusion, using a portable syringe driver, is the preferred route of drug administration. A combination of drugs can be given to control symptoms of colic, continuous abdominal pain, nausea, and vomiting, so that the patient maintains mobility and independence. If a syringe driver is unavailable, the drugs can be given by bolus injection or rectally. Colic should be treated by stopping stimulant laxatives and prokinetic antiemetics. Opioids are sometimes effective alone, but usually an antispasmodic such as hyoscine butylbromide 60 to 300 mg daily is required. Continuous abdominal pain is treated by titrating the dose of diamorphine or morphine in the syringe driver.

Haloperidol or cyclizine may be used as first-line treatment for nausea and vomiting. The somatostatin analogue, octreotide, and hyoscine butylbromide reduce gastrointestinal secretions and motility; they are therefore effective antiemetics in this situation. Methotrimeprazine is also used in refractory vomiting. Pharmacological treatment offers good control of pain and colic although most patients continue to vomit about once a day, but with little nausea. Patients eat and drink as they choose (Baines 1998).

Nausea and vomiting

Vomiting results from impulses reaching the vomiting centre in the medulla, which contains both histamine and muscarinic cholinergic receptors. It can be stimulated in the following ways:

- from the chemoreceptor trigger zone where dopamine and serotonin receptors are concentrated
- from vagal afferents from the gastrointestinal tract
- from the vestibular apparatus: this, like the vomiting centre, contains both histamine and muscarinic cholinergic receptors
- directly, from raised intracranial pressure
- from psychological causes, especially anxiety.

Thus nausea and vomiting have a large range of potential causes originating in many parts of the body.

Assessment

The causes of vomiting in the patient who is terminally ill can usually be determined from a careful history and clinical examination. Note should also be taken of the volume, content, and timing of vomits. A biochemical profile may be needed, but other investigations are rarely necessary or appropriate.

In many patients, the predominant cause of vomiting can be identified and an antiemetic drug selected that is relatively specific for the mechanism involved. Other patients have vomiting with multifactorial causation, and need a combination of antiemetics and other treatment.

Antiemetic drugs

A large number of antiemetic drugs have been found useful and research is continuing, with the development of new agents. Table 4 lists recommended antiemetics, with their site of action, dosage, and available routes.

It may be possible to treat nausea with oral medication, but alternative routes are needed for patients with severe vomiting. An antiemetic injection is suitable to control a single episode but, with a persistent problem, it is preferable to give drugs by subcutaneous infusion, using a syringe driver. Antiemetics in suppository or tablet form can also be given rectally.

Management

Suggested treatment for some causes of vomiting is as follows.

1. Opioid-induced vomiting: about one-third of patients starting morphine feel nauseated during the first week of treatment. Metoclopramide should be given prophylactically.

2. Cytotoxic chemotherapy: the use of ondansetron, granisetron, or tropisetron (the 5-HT$_3$ receptor antagonists), has greatly improved the control of emesis. The effect is enhanced by adding dexamethasone. Lorazepam is used to reduce anticipatory anxiety and nausea.

3. Renal failure: haloperidol is usually effective. Methotrimeprazine is sometimes needed for intractable vomiting.

4. Hypercalcaemia: this should usually be treated actively with intravenous rehydration and a bisphosphonate. If this is inappropriate, antiemetics should be given as for renal failure.

Table 4 Recommended antiemetic drugs

Antiemetic	Dose/24 h	Use in syringe driver	Main site of action
Phenothiazines Methotrimeprazine	5–100 mg	Yes	Blocks dopamine and serotonin receptors at CTZ; also effective at vestibular and vomiting centres
Butyrophenones Haloperidol	1.5–10 mg	Yes	Blocks dopamine receptors at CTZ
Antihistamines Cyclizine	150 mg	Yes	Vestibular and vomiting centres
Anticholinergics Hyoscine butylbromide	60–300 mg	Yes	Reduces gastrointestinal secretions and motility
Prokinetics Metoclopramide Domperidone	30–80 mg 30–80 mg	Yes No	Increase peristalsis in upper gut; also dopamine antagonists
5-HT$_3$ receptor antagonists Ondansetron	8–16 mg	Yes	Blocks serotonin receptors at CTZ and in gut
Corticosteroids Dexamethasone	8–20 mg	Yes	Reduces inflammatory oedema; also central effect
Somatostatin analogues Octreotide	0.3–0.6 mg	Yes	Reduces gastrointestinal secretions and motility

CTZ, chemoreceptor trigger zone.

5. Raised intracranial pressure: if dexamethasone is contraindicated or ineffective, cyclizine is the antiemetic of choice.
6. Gastroduodenal obstruction: this occurs with pancreatic or pyloric cancer. Metoclopramide may be effective if the obstruction is partial. Dexamethasone can shrink inflammatory oedema around an obstructive lesion. Octreotide may reduce the volume of vomit, otherwise venting gastrostomy or intubation will be required.
7. Intestinal obstruction (see above).
8. Constipation (see above).
9. Vestibular disturbance: both hysocine hydrobromide (scopolamine) and cyclizine are used.
10. Anxiety (see above).

Pressure sores

The breakdown of skin in pressure areas is a major problem both in terms of the suffering it causes and the cost of prevention and treatment. Poor general condition due to advanced disease, immobility, incontinence, inadequate nutrition, and impaired consciousness predispose to skin breakdown.

Pressure sores, especially superficial ones, are usually exquisitely painful. Less often recognized are the psychological effects on the patient, family, and nurse, of discharging and offensive wounds. Traditionally, the care of the skin has been a nursing issue and it is only in more recent years that research has been done to assess the effectiveness of the treatment used. This has shown that poor equipment, lack of knowledge associated with an element of folklore,

and delays in the process of care all contribute to the formation of pressure sores.

Prevention

1. Assessment of risk factors (see above) so that vulnerable patients start treatment immediately.
2. Skin care, avoiding overfrequent washing (removes sebum) or massaging. An occlusive dressing can prevent damage from friction and shearing stresses.
3. Relieve pressure by rotating the patient through different positions.
4. Use appropriate appliances, if available, such as pressure-relieving mattresses, sheepskins, bed cradles, and low pressure profile beds.

Treatment

In addition to the measures used to prevent skin breakdown, it is necessary to apply dressings which provide optimum conditions for healing. The following factors are important:

- maintenance of a warm moist environment at the wound–dressing interface
- absorption of exudate
- allowance of gaseous exchange
- ease of removal without trauma
- hypoxia under occlusive dressing stimulates healing and contributes to pain relief.

There are a growing number of proprietary preparations which meet many of these criteria. If the nurse has both time and enthusiasm it is usually possible to improve patient comfort and reduce odour, even if complete healing is not achieved.

Sore or dry mouth

A dry or painful mouth is common in terminally ill people. Causes include drugs with anticholinergic effects, dehydration, thrush, and poorly fitting dentures.

Good oral hygiene is most important. Teeth and dentures should be cleaned regularly. Mouthwashes with chlorhexidine 0.2 per cent moisten and cleanse the mouth. Salivary stimulants, such as citrus sweets and chewing gum, are usually more effective than artificial saliva. Some patients benefit from pilocarpine 5 mg three times daily.

Thrush infections are common and should be treated with nystatin suspension or fluconazole. Buccal analgesics include benzydamine, a non-steroidal anti-inflammatory drug absorbed through the mucosa, and choline salicylate which can be applied to ulcerated areas before meals. Hydrocortisone pellets are used for painful aphthous ulcers.

Urinary incontinence

A degree of incontinence is not uncommon in the elderly population. It is a frequent complication of neurological or pelvic disease and so, inevitably, it will often occur in those who are terminally ill. Patients find incontinence deeply humiliating, it is a major cause of breakdown in home care, and its management occupies a vast amount of nursing time in geriatric wards and nursing homes.

As with any other symptom, a diagnosis of the cause should be made if possible. Unfortunately, in this group of patients, few causes are reversible, though occasionally incontinence is due to urinary infection, faecal impaction, diuretics, depression, or simple inaccessibility of toilet facilities, all of which can be treated or ameliorated.

Drug treatment with oxybutynin or imipramine is only rarely successful and the great majority of patients require a urinary catheter. A latex or silicone catheter with a 5 ml balloon is used, and bladder washouts with saline are given if there is a lot of sediment. Urinary infection is treated if symptomatic. While it is acknowledged that long-term catheterization leads to many problems, they are irrelevant in this group of patients, for whom comfort and dignity are paramount.

The last days

The correct management of the last few days of life involves the care of both the patient and family. The way in which the death is handled will influence the family's grief, bereavement, and their ability to cope with the future. Those who visit the bereaved will be only too aware how the last hours become imprinted on the memory with unanswerable questions such as 'I wonder if she was trying to say something to me?' or 'Do you think he was in pain?'

Medical management

As death approaches there is usually a gradual increase in drowsiness and weakness, but it is often the experienced nurse who will recognize that this is not a temporary deterioration but represents the imminence of death. This 'diagnosis of dying' needs to be confirmed by the doctor who should then review the medication, stopping all drugs except those for symptom relief. Drugs to withdraw include antibiotics, diuretics, antihypertensives, antidepressants, and laxatives. Corticosteroids and non-steroidal anti-inflammatory drugs are usually continued until the patient cannot swallow.

Studies have shown that two-thirds of patients continue to take some oral medication until the last day of life, but essential drugs must be charted so that, if swallowing becomes impossible, they can be given regularly by injection or suppository. These essential drugs are as follows.

1. Morphine or diamorphine: the oral dose should be converted to the dose for injection and given either by subcutaneous infusion or every 4 h (see above).
2. Anticonvulsants should be replaced by diazepam suppositories 10 to 20 mg twice daily or by midazolam by subcutaneous infusion.
3. Hyoscine hydrobromide or glycopyrronium may be needed for the 'death rattle' (see above).
4. Psychotropic drugs: while most patients become more drowsy and lapse into coma, some become restless and agitated. This may be due to unrelieved pain, a distended bladder or rectum, or morphine toxicity, especially if renal function is deteriorating. However, usually no cause can be identified. The following drugs are used:

- midazolam 30 to 100 mg/24 h by subcutaneous infusion
- methotrimeprazine 25 to 100 mg/24 h by subcutaneous infusion
- diazepam suppositories 10 mg as needed.

Medication, although important, is not the only way of managing a restless dying patient. Staff often notice that the presence of the family or nurse sitting by the bedside, holding the hand or speaking quietly to an apparently unconscious patient, has a remarkable calming effect.

Ethical issues in terminal illness

The principal ethical issues of current concern in palliative care are the use of artificial means of hydration and nutrition, the position of advance directives, and calls for legalization of euthanasia. All these are relevant to the care of terminally ill elderly people.

Rehydration

A recognition of the value of fluid and nutritional support in general medicine and surgery led to the application of the same methods to the terminally ill. The aims of such treatments are to sustain life, relieve distressing symptoms, and make 'an affirmation of the doctor's role as a caring individual [and provide] a nurturing and symbolic act that avoids any appearance of abandoning of the patient' (Siegler and Shiedermayer 1987). The resultant medicalization of dying appears to be a factor in the appearance, particularly in the United States, of advance directives, or living wills, which usually attempt to limit the types of treatment to which individuals may be subjected should they fall incurably ill and be unable at that time to make their wishes known.

In palliative medicine it has become common practice not to rehydrate routinely dying patients when they are no longer able to take oral fluids, on the basis that a drip is an intrusion upon the patient and family at a precious time and the absence of fluids causes no discernible symptoms save possibly a dry mouth which is best dealt with by local measures. This stance has been questioned by some geriatricians on the grounds that there is a risk of missing correctable causes of deterioration and the policy is a potent cause of distress to families, who have a strong need to feel that their loved one is still receiving sustenance (Craig 1994).

There are undoubtedly reversible causes of food refusal which must not be overlooked: a painful mouth, persistent nausea, malaise secondary to infection, or depression, for instance. However, dying patients become tired and drowsy days or weeks in advance of cessation of fluid intake, not as a result of it. In those with advanced cancer there is no evidence that aggressive nutritional support, either enterally or intravenously, prolongs life or significantly alters the distinctive metabolic abnormalities of the cachectic state.

Analysis of blood and urine chemistry in terminally ill patients has demonstrated that, even without artificial hydration, the majority of patients in the last 48 h of life are not dehydrated (Oliver 1984). In a prospective study of such patients (median time to death, 2 days), the symptoms of dry mouth and thirst were not correlated with the level of hydration (Ellershaw et al. 1995). Conversely, rehydration in hypoalbuminaemic terminally ill patients can lead rapidly to pulmonary and peripheral oedema. A valid indication for artificial hydration would be a patient who is unable to take enough oral fluid for his needs and complains of thirst. An effective, safe, and non-intrusive method of rehydration is to give 1 litre of saline overnight subcutaneously, removing the infusion set during the day (Bruera et al. 1990).

However, the distress of families can be marked, and whilst this is not a reason for clinicians to embark on inappropriate treatment, it is a reason to pay careful attention to a process of communication which preferably should have begun well before a patient reaches the point of not being able to eat or drink. Carers have a strong instinctive desire to give food, and need help in translating a concept of 'she won't eat and therefore she will die' into the more realistic one of 'she is dying and therefore won't eat'. The urge to care can be harnessed in assisting with practical tasks like mouth care to prevent dry mouth, and in washing and turning the patient. Relatives can find it helpful to be reminded that hearing and touch appear to be the last senses to survive, so that their physical contact and speech can continue to bring comfort.

Most medication ceases to be relevant in the closing hours or days of life, but drugs essential for symptom control, most often opioid analgesia, an antiemetic, and sometimes a sedative, can be continued by subcutaneous infusion from a portable syringe driver, by injection through a subcutaneous cannula left in situ, or rectally.

Advance directives

By their nature, advance directives or living wills are likely to impinge more on geriatric services than on most areas of medicine. They are an attempt to inform the attending doctor of what an incompetent patient, when mentally capable, would have wanted to be done (or, more often, not done) in the situation that has now arisen. The motivation is usually a desire to avoid treatment which would be seen as inappropriately life-prolonging in someone who is frail and probably incurably ill. The British Medical Association has published a code of practice to advise on the use of living wills (British Medical Association 1995).

In the United States there is a general policy to encourage strongly and expect written advance directives together with health-care proxies for every adult, as a matter of record for his or her own protection, in the same sense as having a will. Many states require that advance directives and health-care proxies be completed, if not already available, at the time of admission to hospital or any long-term care institution or service.

Such directives can be an aid to constructive dialogue between the patient and doctor regarding the future pattern of care if certain circumstances arise, and are certainly never a substitute for it. However, concern has arisen that their terms may be so widely drawn as to inhibit treatment of reversible conditions: for instance, would a prohibition on life-sustaining treatment in a patient with Alzheimer's disease mean that insulin could not be given if he developed diabetes and a consequent hyperglycaemic coma? Or, similarly, would a ban on operations in such circumstances prevent repair of a fractured hip? It is clear that people's treatment wishes change as they move from health into illness, and whilst vaguely drafted documents might have undesired results, attempts to foresee the exact situation that might arise are unlikely to succeed. In the United Kingdom, a Practice Note on the Vegetative State delivered on 26 July 1996 from the Official Solicitor (Harris 1996) merely stated that they will be an 'important component' in the decisions of doctors and courts if they apply to the circumstances which have actually arisen. Therefore at present in the United Kingdom doctors are not legally bound by advance directives, but would be expected to consider them in the formulation of treatment plans. However, in 1997 the Law Commission issued the consultation document Who Decides? (Lord Chancellor's Department 1997), which proposes that advanced directives should be legally enforceable and also that health-care decisions for incapable adults could be taken by a person appointed by the court or given a continuing power of attorney by the patient.

Euthanasia

Legalization of euthanasia, or 'doctor-assisted suicide' is under discussion in many countries around the world. In the debate, the withholding of treatments such as antibiotics from frail or incurably ill patients is sometimes unhelpfully described as 'passive' euthanasia. It has long been recognized that knowing when to stop a line of treatment is good medical practice, not an abandonment of the patient. As Osler wrote over a century ago: 'Pneumonia may well be called the friend of the aged. Taken off by it in an acute, short, not often painful illness, the old man escapes those cold degradations of decay so distressing to himself and to his friends' (Osler 1898). Inappropriate use of antibiotics and other therapies can foil the old man in his escape. Conversely, it would be equally inappropriate not to give such treatments to someone who still has a prognosis of some months, affairs to settle, or even further work to accomplish in order to come to terms with dying.

The resolution of dilemmas regarding the interpretation of living wills, and professional attitudes towards euthanasia, have no easy answers. Both types of measure are seen to have particular relevance to patients who can no longer exercise their autonomy. Thus they require as much thought from geriatricians as from palliative doctors, since through age or illness both specialties have particular numbers of such people in their care. The well being of this group in the future will be strongly influenced by the participation of members of these specialties in the ongoing ethical debates that will shape public policy.

Speaking of death

It has been shown that patients are less anxious or depressed in situations where open discussion about the illness is welcomed. Many patients will want to ask questions, not just about the diagnosis but about future symptoms that they fear, chiefly pain, incontinence, and confusion. Many elderly patients dread the prospect of the final stages of life being prolonged 'artificially', and are reassured that this will not be done. Some have major fears about the actual process of dying and the surprisingly common terror of being nailed into the coffin while still alive. A question such as 'What worries you most?' will often bring such fears to light. Talking about death cannot be hurried; it will not fit easily into the busy outpatient clinic or large ward round. Medical and nursing staff need time to see the patient alone so that there is ample opportunity for these issues to be raised. They need to record a summary of what is said so that other members of the team can continue to help the patient in his or her individual journey of understanding and acceptance.

Support for the family

Much of the distress of dying is due to the fear of separation from other family members and the anxiety about how they will manage in the future. Such fears will be increased if the spouse is very old or ill or isolated, or if there is a conspiracy of silence so that conversation avoids the main issues. Unfortunately, doctors sometimes abet this by telling important facts about the illness to the spouse or patient on their own.

Experience has shown that many couples and families are greatly relieved when encouraged slowly to share the truth. This may require the presence of a doctor, nurse, or social worker as a third party, helping the family to talk openly to each other. Families may be reluctant to talk to the patient about important problems—where the surviving spouse will live, or how he or she will manage financially. They believe that this will add to the burden whereas, in fact, the reverse is often true. Discussing these practical issues reaffirms the importance of the patients in their families and brings them closer together.

There is often an irrational guilt felt by the relatives of the dying. This is sometimes because they feel themselves responsible for the illness—''He was so busy looking after me he didn't go to the doctor in time'. More often, they feel guilty about being unable to care at home until the end, especially if this was the patient's wish. These feelings need exploring gently, going over the history of the disease and emphasizing that the time often comes when full-time professional help is needed.

Nurses can often involve the spouse in simple practical care. The best preparation for the process of bereavement is done before death, by involving the family in the physical and emotional care of the dying.

Spiritual pain

Faced with serious illness or impending death, many patients will begin to think more deeply about their life and its meaning. Some will have a profound sense of guilt and failure about the past, things left undone, or failed relationships. Others feel deeply the meaninglessness of life, and that there has been no point or purpose in it. A few are troubled by the fear of what happens after death. These, and many other considerations, are aspects of spiritual pain and are very real to many terminally ill patients. Doctors working with dying people need to be aware of these issues. They should be informed of the patient's religious beliefs so that specific religious practices of the Jew, Moslem, Hindu, Buddhist, or Christian can be adhered to. If the patient has even a vague church connection he or she will probably appreciate the offer to contact the priest or minister.

However, the burning questions that start 'Why me?', 'If only . . . ', and 'What is the point of it all?' cannot wait until the chaplain is summoned. They arise during a physical examination or following an enquiry about last night's sleep. Sometimes all that the doctor can do is to listen and share. Surprisingly, quite often, the doctor will be asked, 'What do you think?' and the opportunity comes to say something about a God who loves and cares.

Staff pain

Doctors and nurses working with elderly and dying people may need considerable support, especially when they start in such work. They may wonder if everything possible was done, they grieve with the families, and the work can be physically and emotionally exhausting.

Some form of group support needs to be planned. This will often occur in the context of the ward report, especially if the ward doctor and social worker are present. At least as important is the spontaneous conversation, in the dining room or on the stairs, when an individual's anxiety or anger or sadness can be expressed. But the greatest support comes from the work itself; giving effective pain and symptom control is very satisfying. It is rewarding to see anxious and denying patients come to terms with their illness and share this with their family. The dying have much to teach us about the meaning of life, for it is at this time that people are at their most mature and their most courageous.

References

Baines, M.J. (1998). The pathophysiology and management of malignant intestinal obstruction. In *Oxford textbook of palliative medicine* (ed. D. Doyle, G.W.C. Hanks, and N. MacDonald) (2nd edn), pp. 526–34. Oxford University Press.

Blackburn, A.M. (1989). Problems of terminal care in elderly patients. *Palliative Medicine*, 3, 203–6

Booth, S., Kelly, M.J., Cox, N.P., Adams, L., and Guz, A. (1996). Does oxygen help dyspnoea in patients with cancer? *American Journal of Respiratory and Critical Care Medicine*, 153, 1515–18.

British Medical Association (1995). *Advance statements about medical treatment.* BMJ Publishing, London.

Bruera, E., Legris, M.A., Kuehn, N., and Miller, M.J. (1990). Hypodermoclysis for the administration of fluids and narcotic analgesics in patients with advanced cancer. *Journal of Pain and Symptom Management*, 5, 218–20.

Table 2 Manoeuvres which should be included in clinical preventive health care

Counselling	Tobacco avoidance
	Prudent diet
	Regular exercise
	Safe driving
	Oestrogen replacement
Vaccinations	Influenza
	Pneumococcus
	Tetanus
Early detection	Hypertension
	Atrial fibrillation
Malignancies	Breast cancer (mammography)
	Cervical cancer (cervical smear)
	Colorectal carcinoma (faecal occult blood testing)
Special senses	Visual loss: sight card
	Hearing loss: whisper test or audioscope
Miscellaneous	Problem drinking
	Injury prevention

groups for increasing the cessation rate (Taylor and Dingle 1994). Nicotine replacement therapy must be used with caution in older individuals who may suffer from coronary artery disease or peripheral vascular disease. Counselling should be complemented by public policy restricting smoking in enclosed areas.

Diet

Historically, modification of diet represented a common approach to disease and its prevention, and ways in which dietary recommendations have altered over the years are intriguing. There is evidence that diets rich in saturated fats are associated with increased risk of cardiovascular disorders, which remain the most common cause of death in the developed world. Although lipid modification reduces the incidence of symptomatic coronary artery disease in those with established risk factors, there is presently no compelling evidence that specific diets reduce cardiovascular morbidity or mortality in symptom-free older people with or without hyperlipidaemia (Sih 1995). Case–control studies show that diets high in saturated fat increase the risk of carcinomas of the breast and colon, but there is no evidence that reduced fat diets modify the risk of malignancy in older individuals. Thus, recommendations for dietary change rely on non-randomized trial evidence and conventional wisdom. It is presently believed that the total fat intake should not exceed 30 per cent of daily caloric intake. In view of the association between diets low in dietary fibre and increased risk of diverticular disease and colonic malignancy, it is recommended that dietary fibre should be increased (20 g/day). There is case–control but no randomized clinical trial evidence to support this recommendation (Howe *et al.* 1992). The recommended dietary intake of calcium should be 1200 to 1500 mg/day in postmenopausal women to help reduce the risk of osteoporosis (Cumming 1990). Moderate dietary sodium restriction is encouraged owing to the association between high dietary sodium intake and hypertension in some (but not all) individuals. While vitamin supplementation is commonly recommended, there is no evidence of benefit to healthy older people who consume a balanced diet. A diet rich in carotene-containing vegetables may be associated with a lower risk of malignancy (Johnson 1995). Epidemiological evidence indicates that hyperhomocysteinaemia is a risk factor for arterial and venous vascular disease, and that blood levels of homocysteine rise with age (Ubbink 1998). Enhanced folate intake will reduce high blood homocysteine levels (Jacques *et al.* 1999), but there has not yet been a randomized controlled intervention trial to prove that raising folate intake by supplementation or fortification reduces the incidence of vascular disease in later life. Folate supplements should not be prescribed for a patient whose vitamin B_{12} status has not been established.

Simple educational techniques such as counselling and brochures may increase compliance with dietary advice by as much as 30 per cent (Patterson 1994*a*). Older individuals at special risk of inadequate nutrition include alcoholics and those living alone.

Exercise

Regular aerobic exercise has many benefits. These include an improved sense of well being, aerobic fitness, muscle strength, and bone mass. These benefits continue even into advanced age in the most frail elderly people, where lower limb strengthening by weight-training substantially improves physical activity (Fiatarone *et al.* 1994). A high threshold of exercise is not necessary. Even gentle aerobic activity such as walking 30 to 60 min/day benefits cardiovascular fitness. Longitudinal and case–control studies have shown that an increase in fitness level is associated with a decrease in all causes of mortality (Blair *et al.* 1989). One must be cautious about interpreting longitudinal studies because self selection, motivation, and presence or absence of disease strongly influence the ability to exercise. With that proviso, there remains sufficient evidence to recommend counselling for the individual regarding avoidance of a sedentary lifestyle and engagement in regular aerobic activity.

Motor vehicle driving

Clinicians should know whether an older patient drives or not. The risk of motor vehicle injuries rises with the age of the driver after middle age. Nonetheless, most older drivers have fewer accidents than young males, as they tend to drive more slowly, travel shorter distances, and avoid night driving and high volume roads. In addition to counselling older individuals to avoid alcohol when driving, and to use seat belts for all journeys, the doctor should remain alert for illnesses that may place the individual at higher risk of unsafe driving. These include many cardiovascular, neurological, and locomotor disorders. In many jurisdictions doctors are required to report potentially unsafe drivers to authorities. Doctor assessment of safety in driving is a poor predictor of safety, unless a disability is obvious. In cases of doubt, a comprehensive driving assessment is necessary (see Chapter 26.1)

Vaccination

Influenza

Both incidence of and mortality from influenza are significantly reduced by annual inoculations with strain-specific influenza vaccine. Individuals with comorbid disease and those residing in institutions are at increased risk of mortality from influenza, and may thus benefit more from inoculation; however, evidence favours the use of annual influenza inoculation for all individuals over the age of 65 years (Elford and Tarrant 1994). Improved compliance with this manoeuvre is obtained with health education programmes for clinicians and senior citizens. Influenza inoculations for health-care workers in institutions reduce the mortality of the residents by improving 'herd' immunity (Potter *et al.* 1997).

Pneumococcal vaccine

There is good evidence that one-time inoculations reduce the incidence of pneumonia in individuals living in institutions (Gaillat *et al.* 1985). Evidence for benefit in older individuals living in the community is less clear. General use for all those over 65 is recommended by some panels (US Preventive Services Task Force 1996) but is limited to those residing in institutions by others (Canadian Task Force on the Periodic Health Examination 1991). Population-based studies of the incidence of pneumonia and invasive pneumococcal disease are underway in Ontario, Canada, where pneumococcal inoculation has recently been introduced for all senior citizens.

Tetanus inoculation

Although tetanus is a rare disease, its fatality is extremely high in older individuals. Immunity from tetanus is maintained by inoculations at 10-year intervals throughout life. A single booster inoculation at the age of 65 confers similar benefit at greatly reduced cost (Balestra and Littenberg 1993).

Secondary prevention

The purpose of secondary prevention is to prevent disability by early detection of subclinical disease through screening or case finding.

In developed countries the most common causes of morbidity and mortality are cardiovascular diseases, malignancies, and cerebrovascular disease. Manoeuvres to prevent these diseases have received high priority in recent years.

Hypertension (see Chapter 9.5)

The prevalence of hypertension rises with age, and in some surveys the prevalence of hypertension (160/95 mmHg or greater) is in excess of 70 per cent (Working Group on Hypertension in the Elderly 1986). The prevalence is highest in black women, but may be as high as 40 per cent in males between 65 and 74 years of age. Both systolic and diastolic hypertension are associated with cardiovascular and cerebrovascular diseases. With increasing age the risk of cerebrovascular events increases dramatically for the same level of blood pressure. Large-scale randomized controlled trials have proved that treatment of both systolic (160 mmHg or greater) and diastolic (90 mmHg or greater) hypertension leads to substantial reductions in the incidence of stroke, death, and cardiac events. The most compelling evidence comes from the Swedish Trial of Old People with Hypertension which demonstrated that only 14 hypertensive older individuals have to be treated for 5 years to prevent one stroke or death (Dahlof *et al.* 1991). For isolated systolic hypertension approximately 40 people must be treated for 5 years to prevent one stroke (SHEP Co-operative Research Group 1991). In none of these studies do adverse effects of treatment detract from proven benefits. Specifically, there was no increase in injuries due to falls (historically

a concern raised by geriatricians that treatment may induce orthostatic hypotension leading to excessive falls) neither was there any increase in myocardial infarctions (actually a decrease) which had also been suggested based on the fear of reduced coronary artery perfusion pressures. While there is no conclusive evidence of benefit to individuals over the age of 84, and data from one observational study showed an inverse relationship between level of blood pressure and mortality in the very old (Rajala *et al.* 1983), it now seems reasonable to continue judicious treatment of systolic and diastolic hypertension into advanced age.

Malignant diseases

Carcinoma of the breast

Carcinoma of the breast is the most common carcinoma in women. The incidence increases with age, and there is no evidence that the disease becomes less malignant with onset in later life. Surgical and adjunctive treatment in the early stages improves life expectancy. Seven randomized controlled trials have demonstrated survival benefit for individuals screened with mammography and clinical examination in women between the ages of 50 and 69 (Morrison 1994a). Breast cancer mortality reduction has now been shown to age 75 (Van Dijck *et al.* 1997). Despite increasing prevalence above this age, there is insufficient evidence to continue mammographic screening, although it would appear prudent to do so. An alternative approach in women above the age of 75 is to continue with an annual physical examination of the breasts (which should detect approximately two-thirds of the tumours detected by both physical examination and mammography), at a cost of detection approximately one-tenth that of both procedures. In those with a family history of breast cancer or other risk factors (e.g. carcinoma in the contralateral breast) many authorities recommend continued annual mammography. However, the risk of false-positive results rises to nearly 25 per cent after 10 annual examinations (Elmore *et al.* 1998). Women should be made aware of this risk.

Carcinoma of the cervix

While this condition is often regarded as a disease of young women, the incidence remains high into old age, with 41 per cent of deaths and one-quarter of new cases occurring over the age of 65 (Mandelblatt *et al.* 1986). Participation in cervical screening programmes has reduced the incidence of invasive disease. For these reasons, screening should continue in older women who have been sexually active. Although the evidence is open to interpretation, it should be continued at least up until the age of 65, and discontinued only if previous smears have been consistently normal (US Preventive Services Task Force 1996). A more conservative recommendation is to continue screening every 3 years up until the age of 69, before discontinuing if consecutive smears have remained normal (Morrison 1994b).

The caution about previously normal smears is particularly important. Many older women have not been screened earlier in life. In one American survey only one-quarter of women over the age of 65 had been screened regularly, and one-quarter had never had a Papanicolaou test (Mandelblatt *et al.* 1986).

Screening for colorectal cancer

The incidence of colorectal cancer rises steeply with age in both sexes. It is the second most common cancer in most developed countries.

Early detection and treatment lead to improved outcome. Therefore colorectal cancers fulfil many of the criteria appropriate for a screening intervention. Of the available detection manoeuvres, tests for faecal occult blood, sigmoidoscopy, and colonoscopy have all been considered. Both colonoscopy and rigid sigmoidoscopy are relatively expensive as they require physician expertise and time. They are not always acceptable to asymptomatic patients, and adequate preparation for the procedure may be difficult in older people. Faecal occult blood testing has been widely recommended for screening. Four large randomized controlled trials have shown that faecal occult blood testing results in a decrease of about 15 per cent in fatality from colorectal cancer, although no improvement in overall mortality has occurred. A meta-analysis of these studies revealed that screening 10 000 individuals for 10 years would save about 8.5 lives (Towler *et al.* 1998). The relative insensitivity of the test (approximately 50 per cent) and the high cost of screening are potential drawbacks. Colonoscopy is a superior test as the sensitivity and specificity for carcinoma are extremely high, and precancerous lesions such as polyps can be removed by the procedure. Therefore, in individuals who have not undergone colonoscopy, regular screening with faecal occult blood testing is now recommended by most authorities. Individuals with familial adenomatous polyposis and hereditary non-polyposis colon cancer (multiple family members affected with colorectal, endometrial, gastric, small-bowel, pancreatic, ovarian, and urinary tract cancers) should be identified early in life and undergo regular colonoscopy.

Oestrogen replacement

Differences in morbidity and mortality from cardiovascular diseases between men and women converge after the menopause. Reduced protection from oestrogenic hormones is suggested as one mechanism. A meta-analysis of prospective cohort studies suggests that the relative risk of cardiovascular death or morbidity is substantially reduced in women who have used oestrogen replacement therapy (Stamper and Colditz 1991). However, all the observational studies are subject to volunteer bias, and a definitive conclusion must await publication of long-term randomized controlled trials. Fractures of the hip, vertebrae, and radius are common in postmenopausal women, accounting for the huge burden of morbidity and cost attributable to osteoporosis (see Chapter 14.1). Oestrogenic hormone replacement therapy prevents bone loss and may reduce the risk of osteoporotic fractures in women up to 10 years postmenopausal and possibly beyond (Lindsay 1987). Thus the benefits of hormone replacement therapy include reduction in cardiovascular and skeletal disease, and possibly Alzheimer's disease (Yaffe *et al.* 1998), as well as improving well being and menopausal symptoms. Balanced against the benefits is the posibility of an increased risk of breast cancer. A large case–control study indicates that the use of hormone replacement therapy increases that the risk of breast cancer by a factor of 1.023 for each year of use (Collaborative Group 1997). This is biologically plausible in being equivalent in magnitude to the effect of delaying menopause. After therapy has stopped, risk returns to baseline within 5 years. The increased risk of carcinoma of the body of the uterus in those given unopposed oestrogen hormones is pevented by concurrent progesterone use. Rather than recommending hormone replacement therapy to all postmenopausal women, individual counselling should be based on the risks and benefits to each woman.

Special senses

Diminished visual acuity (see Chapters 18.15.1–18.15.3)

The prevalence of all common causes of reduced visual acuity (presbyopia, cataracts, open angle glaucoma, age-associated macular degeneration, diabetic retinopathy) all increase dramatically with age. At least 13 per cent of older people have significant visual problems. Many older people do not appreciate the severity of their visual loss. Community screening studies have revealed that much unrecognized visual loss is remediable. In screening studies using a Snellen type sight card, when visual disability is detected, simple interventions such as changing the prescription for eye glasses, lead to a significant improvement in vision in half of those screened abnormal. In the case of cataracts, extraction with lens implantation produces a satisfactory result in over 95 per cent of cases, and has been shown to improve physical and psychological functioning.

The value of fundoscopy is highly dependent upon the observer. In skilled hands, the sensitivity of detection of glaucomatous optic discs, macular degeneration and diabetic retinopathy is in the range of 70 to 90 per cent. In less skilled hands the diagnostic accuracy of fundoscopy is likely to be much less. Thus a case can be made for regular examination by an eye specialist for diabetics, those at increased risk for age-associated macular degeneration (positive family history, smokers, blue eyes), and those with a family history of glaucoma. Primary care screening methods for glaucoma are unsatisfactory; Schiotz tonometry is no longer recommended for screening. The high false-positive and false-negative rate, and the lack of convincing evidence that early treatment of ocular hypertension influences the outcome, argues against this form of screening. Automated perimetry may offer a better alternative in the future when it is more widely available, as loss of peripheral vision is a highly sensitive (but not specific) indicator of glaucoma. All older individuals should be regularly tested with a Snellen type sight card (Patterson 1994*e*).

Hearing loss (see Chapter 18.16)

Many of the one-third of older people who suffer from hearing loss are unaware of their disability. Complaints that others are mumbling, or of difficulty hearing in the presence of background noise often indicate high frequency loss. Counselling to avoid factors such as excessive noise, and ototoxic drugs are recommended to preserve hearing in earlier life. When hearing loss is present, hearing aids improve not only the quality of life, but also cognitive performance and capacity in daily activities (Mulrow *et al.* 1990). About one-quarter of people do not use their hearing aids. In those that do, screening in primary care has revealed a surprisingly high prevalence of faulty or inappropriate hearing aids (Sangster *et al.* 1991). Hearing loss may be detected by enquiry (e.g. about mumbling or loss of discrimination) but is more accurately detected by whisper test (whisper six test words at a set distance from the patient's ear and out of the field of vision, and ask the patient to repeat the words). The sensitivity of this test (80–100 per cent) approaches that of the audioscope (Welsh–Allyn) which delivers pure tone frequencies at 500, 1000, 2000, and 4000 Hz at thresholds of 25 or 40 dB. Older individuals should be regularly screened for hearing loss (Patterson 1994*b*).

Problem drinking (alcohol)

A modest consumption of alcohol (one or two drinks daily) reduces cardiovascular mortality (Marmot and Brunner 1991). Excessive alcohol use is reportedly the third most common mental health disorder among elderly men. Denial and concealment complicate the detection of alcoholism. An intermediate condition defined as 'problem drinking' may precede serious alcoholism and be amenable to appropriate counselling. Problem drinking can be detected by enquiry or the use of brief questionnaires such as the CAGE questions (Ewing 1984):

C   Have you ever felt the need to cut down on your drinking?

A   Have you felt annoyed by criticism of your drinking?

G   Have you ever felt guilty feelings about your drinking?

E   Have you ever taken a morning 'eye-opener' drink?

A score of two positive responses detects alcoholism with a sensitivity of 75 to 89 per cent and a specificity of 68 to 96 per cent.

Injury prevention

Injuries, particularly falls, rank within the top seven causes of death in most developed countries. The causes of falls are multiple, and reviewed elsewhere. Assessment of an individual following a fall reduces subsequent falls both in the community (Tinetti *et al.* 1994) and in institutional settings (Rubenstein *et al.* 1990). Risk factors for falls and their management should be reviewed regularly in the older adult (Elford 1994).

Atrial fibrillation (see Chapter 9.6)

Atrial fibrillation is a common cardiac arrhythmia which increases in prevalence with age. Regardless of aetiology, this arrhythmia increases the risk of embolic stroke, with an overall incidence of approximately 5 per cent per year. Additional risk factors (e.g. hypertension, older age, left ventricular dysfunction, enlarged left atrium) further increase the risk of stroke. Five randomized controlled trials have now convincingly demonstrated that anticoagulants substantially reduce the risk of embolic stroke (Cairns and Connolly 1991). With careful anticoagulant control the risk of significant haemorrhage is 1 to 2 per cent. With close monitoring, this risk is not substantially higher in older individuals who are carefully selected for treatment. The finding of an irregular pulse in an older individual should be followed by an ECG in those individuals for whom anticoagulants would be considered. Anticoagulants are not appropriate in those with a high risk of falls or other injury, increased risk of haemorrhage, or an inability to comply with or monitor closely an anticoagulant prescription.

Secondary prevention: another definition

Another use of the term secondary prevention (which is distinct from that used in this chapter) is the prevention of recurrence of illnesses such as myocardial infarction and stroke. There is substantial evidence that acetylsalicylic acid and β-adrenergic blockers reduce the risk of recurrent myocardial infarction. Platelet antagonists and control of hypertension reduce the risk of recurrent stroke. These strategies for secondary prevention are discussed elsewhere (see Chapter 11.2).

Tertiary prevention

Tertiary prevention is defined as the prevention of morbidity or mortality from established disease. As this is equivalent to therapeutic care it will not be further considered here, except to give two examples relevant to geriatric medicine. The first is rehabilitation of people who have suffered from a fractured hip, to reduce disability and

Table 3 Manoeuvres to consider where evidence is insufficient for firm recommendation

Abdominal aortic aneurysm	Palpation, ultrasound
Cognitive impairment	Assessment of function or mental test score
Abuse of elderly people	Questionnaire
Frailty	Questionnaire: physical performance measures
Depression	Single question
Carcinoma of prostate	Serum prostate-specific antigen, rectal digital examination

improve their ability to care for themselves. A second example is stroke rehabilitation to reduce disability by multidisciplinary intervention. Viewing these interventions as 'preventive' helps to place them within the broader context of improving health rather than simply addressing specific diseases.

Controversies in preventive health care

There are some areas where evidence is insufficient for firm recommendations (Table 3).

Prostate cancer (see Chapter 10)

This is the most common cancer in older males in the developed world. Large-scale randomized controlled trials are underway in Europe and North America to determine whether early detection influences survival. Of the available detection methods, rectal digital examination is relatively insensitive (33–58 per cent) although highly specific. Prostate-specific antigen appears to be highly sensitive, but has a low positive predictive value. At a cut-off of 4 μg/l the positive predictive value for biopsy-proven cancer is only 8 to 33 per cent. This means that at best 67 per cent and at worst as many as 92 per cent of patients with a 'positive' test will undergo unnecessary biopsy. Early treatment in asymptomatic men with radical prostatectomy or radiotherapy does not influence survival and is associated with significant morbidity. While screening remains a controversial area, there is insufficient evidence to recommend the procedure at this time (Feightner 1994b; Anonymous 1997).

Abdominal aortic aneurysm

Increasingly common in older men, especially smokers and those with hypertension, aneurysms increase in size at a predictable rate. The risk of rupture rises substantially after the aneurysm reaches 5 cm in diameter (approximately 25 per cent at 8 years). Elective replacement graft carries a surgical fatality well under 5 per cent. Ruptured aneurysm is fatal without surgery but emergency surgical fatality is 30 to 50 per cent. Early detection therefore appears desirable. Ultrasound screening followed by elective surgery reduces ruptured aortic aneurysm by 55 per cent and death from ruptured aneurysm by 42 per cent (Scott *et al.* 1995). In this English study there was no all-cause mortality reduction after 5 years of follow-up as ruptured aneurysm accounts for only a little more than 1 per cent at all deaths in older men. Several large multicentre trials are currently under way to determine whether these encouraging results will be replicated. In the meantime, the prudent doctor may include a targeted abdominal aneurysm examination in males over the age of 60, as most aneurysms of 'surgical' size are detectable on physical examination (Patterson 1994c).

Cognitive impairment

Knowing that an individual suffers from cognitive impairment may facilitate planning for power of attorney, advance directives, and supportive care. Balanced against this must be weighed the negative effects of labelling and the uncertain natural history of cognitive impairment in the absence of dementia. With the prospect of effective medications for treatment of dementing disorders (particularly Alzheimer's disease) there may be a stronger case for the early detection of cognitive impairment. At present there is insufficient evidence to recommend for or against this manoeuvre (Patterson 1994d).

Nevertheless, clinicians should be sensitive to and follow up on any symptoms suggesting cognitive loss, including observations of family members (Costa et al. 1996).

Abuse of elderly people (see Chapter 26.2)

The prevalence of abuse of elderly people may be as high as 10 per cent. Difficulties in definition, and uncertainty whether treatment is effective (except for the withdrawal of a physically abused individual from an abusive situation), complicate the decision over recommending case finding. In many jurisdictions (most states in the United States and several provinces in Canada) the reporting of abuse of elderly people is mandatory. Despite this only a small percentage of abused individuals are reported to the authorities and doctors' knowledge of legal requirements is often lacking. Except where reporting is mandatory, the evidence is insufficient to recommend formal case finding, although a high index of suspicion should be maintained in cases of unexplained or unusual injury (Patterson 1994f).

Depression (see Chapter 20.1)

Depression is a common illness in older people. The community prevalence of major affective disorder is 1 to 2 per cent, 6 per cent in those attending medical outpatient clinics, and as high as 21 per cent in institutions. Mortality rates are increased in depression, but pharmacological treatments are usually effective. While randomized controlled trials of screening questionnaires have failed to show any benefit to younger individuals (Feightner 1994a), the prudent doctor should have a high index of clinical suspicion in older individuals. The single question 'Do you often feel down hearted and sad?' has the same sensitivity and specificity as the Geriatric Depression Scale (Mahoney et al. 1994).

Screening for frailty

Frailty is best thought of as a breakdown in the dynamic balance between an individual's strengths and deficits (Rockwood et al. 1994). Deficits in physical and cognitive functioning threaten the autonomy of individuals as reflected in performance of basic and instrumental activities of daily living. Development of better methods to measure function (mental, physical, and social) in elderly people was recommended as a high priority for screening before providing activities and assistive devices to enhance quality of people's lives (WHO 1983). The prevalence of frailty rises with age due to the presence of chronic disabilities. Longitudinal studies are identifying factors which predict the onset of frailty. These factors include self perception of health, various diseases (such as stroke, osteoarthritis, hip fracture), mental abilities, and physical factors such as muscular strength and endurance (Kaplan et al. 1993). Functional decline can be predicted by a surprisingly simple range of activities. For example, timed manual performance of activities (such as simulated eating, stacking checkers, turning cards) can identify those at increased risk of hospital admission and death (Williams et al. 1994). Lower limb performance such as standing balance, timed walking, and five repetitions of rising from a chair and sitting down, can identify those at risk of later functional decline (Guralnik et al. 1995). Simple questionnaires can help detect those who will experience subsequent physical deterioration (Hébert et al. 1996). Exercise programmes can improve muscular strength, endurance, and physical functioning.

It is not yet known whether screening for frailty or potential frailty, identifying those at risk and targeting them for interventions (which might include exercise), will prevent the onset of frailty and disability. This remains an important priority for further research. Simply reporting details of functional impairments to primary doctors does not produce measurable benefit (Rubenstein et al. 1989). The evidence is presently insufficient to recommend questionnaires or performance-based measures as a screen for future frailty. The prudent doctor will look for difficulties in performing daily activities and should consider modifying the history and examination to adopt a more function-based approach (Lachs et al. 1990).

Site of preventive health-care interventions

Preventive health-care interventions can be initiated in doctors' own premises, other health-care facilities or in the place of residence. While the above measures can be instituted in any location, considerable interest has been devoted to interventions in the home. The British Department of Health has stipulated that all individuals over the age of 75 should be offered a home visit and specific examinations annually (Royal College of General Practitioners 1990).

Community surveys have identified various unrecognized (and presumably unmet) conditions in older people. Even though most older people have contact with their family doctors at least once per year (e.g. in the United Kingdom and urban Canada) few would doubt that an assessment in the home provides potentially useful additional information. Numerous randomized controlled trials have examined the impact of contacting community-dwelling older people by means of questionnaires and home visits by a nurse or health visitor. While, in general, individuals who do not visit their family doctors do not differ in their health status from those who do (Ebrahim et al. 1984), home visits have certain benefits. There is evidence that those who have received an assessment at home experience a lower mortality and admissions to hospital or other institutions have been reduced. In some studies improvement was

Table 4 Costs of some preventive health-care manoeuvres

Manoeuvre	Cost per life year gained (1993 US dollars)
Influenza vaccination (all citizens)[a]	141
Pneumococcal vaccination[a]	1769; 2008
Tetanus vaccination[b]	
Single booster at age 65	4527
Booster every 10 years	153 138
Nicotine gum and smoking cessation advice for men aged 65–69[a]	9072
Cervical cancer screening every 3 years for women aged 65 +[a,c]	≤0; 2778; 41 376
Mammography for breast cancer (age 65–74)[d]	92 412
Physical examination for breast cancer[d]	9597
Abdominal palpation for aortic aneurysm	28 741
Ultrasound examination for aortic aneurysm[e]	41 550
Mandatory seat belt use law[a]	69

[a] Tengs et al. (1996).
[b] Balestra and Littenberg (1993).
[c] Costs vary widely due to different assumptions.
[d] Eddy (1989).
[e] Frame et al. (1993).

evident in quality of life. Conversely, a number of randomized controlled trials have failed to show benefit in functional status as measured by activities of daily living (Patterson and Chambers 1995). Home visits appear to identify the need for additional services, and generally increase the utilization of health-care services. It may be that benefit is due to the involvement of additional services and agencies which help address personal handicap rather than disability.

Costs of prevention

Prevention is not cheap. It cannot be assumed that preventive health care will reduce the subsequent cost of curative or palliative treatment, although this remains an area of substantial debate. Comprehensive manoeuvres that detect preclinical illness will identify new cases which require confirmatory diagnosis and some will require treatment. Depending upon the specificity of the detection manoeuvre, many cases of 'disease' thus detected will be false-positive cases and will not require treatment.

Cost-effectiveness analysis takes into account indirect expenses such as loss of productivity and transport for investigation and treatment. For senior citizens who are no longer in the work-force, prolonging life can be seen as a net societal expenditure (Avorn 1984). Estimating only direct health-care costs simplifies analysis, and Table 4 cites some representative costs of preventive health-care manoeuvres.

There is some evidence that programmes of true health promotion do reduce costs. For example in one study, retired people were randomized into three groups: one received a health promotion programme, one group a questionnaire only, and the third group received regular care. The health promotion programme costing $US30 per participant per year appeared to reduce direct health-care costs by $US142 per participant in the subsequent year (Leigh et al. 1992).

True health promotion

If we accept that health promotion is 'the process of enabling people to increase control over, and to improve, their health' (WHO 1986) lay people (consumers) must be consulted and involved. Setting priorities according to these views becomes more important as health-care resources are constrained. There are many examples of priority setting by involving consumers of health care. The best known is the Oregon Health Decisions, a grass roots organization which consulted widely concerning health-care priorities (Crawshaw et al. 1985; Crawshaw 1994). Interestingly members of the public surveyed in London, England, ranked preventive services ninth, below hospice care for the dying (ranked second), high technology surgery (third), medical research (fourth), community care at home (fifth), surgery to help people with disabilities (sixth), therapy for people with disabilities (seventh), and long stay care for elderly people (eighth). Treatment for children with life-threatening illness was ranked first. Preventive services were ranked sixth by London general practitioners (Bowling et al. 1993). In an American community survey, health-care professionals ranked smoking as the most important health concern, whereas consumers ranked health-care insurance as first, accident prevention fifth, physical fitness eleventh, and smoking thirteenth (Lichtner et al. 1986). For many older people, fear of leaving their homes because of the risk of assault and robbery is an important health concern (Kauffman and Sharps 1996).

Thus, health concerns of individuals vary widely, and health promotion programmes must take into account local concerns prior to any implementation. One planning strategy begins with a community diagnostic process which includes surveys, focus groups, and epidemiological and administrative reviews involving local consumers and professionals in a comprehensive plan leading to behaviour change and influence on environmental factors (Green and Kreuter 1991). Examples of successful empowerment of senior citizens include the organization of local merchants to visit an apartment building as a 'market' to enable those afraid to leave the building to purchase fresh produce. Another is the use of a symbol which older individuals at home place in the window upon arising, so that neighbours or visitors (e.g. postal delivery worker) can see that no help is needed that day. Examples such as these offer low cost and innovative solutions that go far beyond traditional health care while helping to preserve the autonomy of older individuals.

Conclusion

Improving the health of our older people requires a collaborative effort involving health-care workers, planners, politicians, and older individuals themselves. The doctor, the most common point of contact for health-care services has an important role in initiating and guiding preventive health-care manoeuvres, while also acting as an advocate for better living conditions.

References

Anonymous (1997). The prostate question unanswered still (editorial). *Lancet*, **349**, 443.

Avorn, J. (1984). Benefit and cost analysis in geriatric care. *New England Journal of Medicine*, **310**, 1294–1301.

Balestra, D.J. and Littenberg, B. (1993). Should adult tetanus immunisation be given as a single vaccination at age 65. *Journal of General Internal Medicine*, **8**, 405–12.

Blair, S.N., Blair, P.E.D., Kohl, H.W. III, *et al.* (1989). Physical fitness and all-cause mortality. A prospective study of healthy men and women. *Journal of the American Medical Association*, **262**, 2395–401.

Bowling, A., Jacobson, B., and Southgate, L. (1993). Health service priorities: explorations in consultation of the public and health professionals on priority setting in an inner London Health District. *Social Science and Medicine*, **37**, 851–7.

Cairns, J.A. and Connolly, S.J. (1991). Nonrheumatic atrial fibrillation risk of stroke and role of antithrombotic therapy. *Circulation*, **84**, 469–81.

Canadian Task Force on the Periodic Health Examination (1991). Update 2. Administration of pneumococcal vaccine. *Canadian Medical Association Journal*, **144**, 665–71.

Collaborative Group on Hormone Factors in Breast Cancer (1997). Breast cancer and hormone replacement therapy: collaborative reanalysis of data from 51 epidemiological studies of 52 705 women with breast cancer and 108 411 women without breast cancer. *Lancet*, **350**, 1047–59.

Costa, P.T. and Williams, T.F. (co-chairs) (1996). *Quick reference guide for clinicians: early identification of Alzheimer's disease and related dementias.* Publication no. 97-0703. United States Department of Health and Human Services, Agency for Health Care Policy and Research, Rockville, MD.

Crawshaw, R. (1994). Grass roots participation in health care reform. *Annals of Internal Medicine*, **120**, 677–81.

Crawshaw, R., Garland, M.J., Hines, B., and Lobitz, C. (1985). Oregon health decisions—an experiment with informed community consent. *Journal of the American Medical Association*, **354**, 3213–16.

Cumming, R.G. (1990). Calcium intake and bone mass: a quantitative review of the evidence. *Calcified Tissue International*, **47**, 194–201.

Dahlof, B., Lindholm, L.H., Hansson, L., Scherston, B., Ekbom, T., and Wester, P.O. (1991). Morbidity and mortality in the Swedish Trial in Old People with Hypertension (STOP Hypertension). *Lancet*, **338**, 1281–5.

Ebrahim, S., Hedley, R., and Sheldon, M. (1984). Low levels of ill health among elderly non-consulters in general practice. *British Medical Journal*, **289**, 1273–5.

Eddy, D.M. (1989). Screening for breast cancer. *Annals of Internal Medicine*, **111**, 389–99.

Elford, R.W. (1994). Prevention of household and recreational injuries in the elderly. In *The Canadian guide to clinical preventive health care* (ed. R. Goldbloom), pp. 912–20. Canada Communications Group, Ottawa.

Elford, R.W. and Tarrant, M. (1994). Prevention of influenza. In *The Canadian Guide to clinical preventive health care* (ed. R. Goldbloom), pp. 744–51. Canada Communications Group, Ottawa.

Elmore, J.G., Barton, M.B., Moceri, V.M., Arena, P.J., and Fletcher, S.W. (1998). Ten year risk of false positive screening mammograms and clinical breast examination. *New England Journal of Medicine*, **338**, 1089–96.

Feightner, J.W. (1994*a*). Early detection of depression. In *The Canadian guide to clinical preventive health care* (ed. R. Goldbloom), pp. 450–4. Canada Communications Group, Ottawa.

Feightner, J.W. (1994*b*). Screening for prostate cancer. In *The Canadian guide to clinical preventive health care* (ed. R. Goldbloom), pp. 812–23. Canada Communications Group, Ottawa.

Fiatarone, M.A., O'Neill, E.F., Ryan, N.D., *et al.* (1994). Exercise training and nutritional supplementation for physical frailty in very old people. *New England Journal of Medicine*, **330**, 1769–75.

Frame, P.S., Fryback, D.G., and Patterson, C. (1993). Screening for abdominal aortic aneurysm in men aged 60 to 90 years: a cost effectiveness analysis. *Annals of Internal Medicine*, **119**, 411–16.

Gaillat, K., Zmirou, D., Mallaret, M.R., *et al.* (1985). Essai clinique du vaccin antipneumococcique chez des personnes âgées vivant en institution. *Revue d'Epidemiologie et de Santé Publique*, **33**, 437–44.

Goldbloom, R.B. (ed.) (1994). *The Canadian guide to clinical preventive health care.* Canada Communications Group, Ottawa.

Green, L.W. and Kreuter, M.W. (1991). *Health promotion planning. An educational and environmental approach.* Mayfield Publishing, Mountainview, CA.

Guralnik, J.M., Ferrucci, L., Simonsick, E.M., Salive, M., and Wallace, R.B. (1995). Lower-extremity function in persons over the age of 70 years as a predictor of subsequent disability. *New England Journal of Medicine*, **332**, 556–61.

Hébert, R., Bravo, G., Korner-Bitensky, N., and Voyer, L. (1996). Predictive validity of a postal questionnaire for screening community-dwelling elderly individuals at risk of functional decline. *Age and Ageing*, **25**, 159–67.

Howe, G.R., Benito, E., and Castelleto, R. (1992). Dietary intake of fibre and decreased risk of cancers of the colon and rectum; evidence from the combined analysis of 13 case–control studies. *Journal of the National Cancer Institute*, **84**, 1887–96.

Jacques, P.F., Selhub, J., Bostom, A.G., Wilson, P.W.F., and Rosenberg, I.H. (1999). The effect of folic acid fortification on plasma folate and total homocysteine concentrations. *New England Journal of Medicine*, **340**, 1449–54.

Johnson, L.E. (1995). Vitamins and aging. In *Annual review of gerontology and geriatrics* (ed. J. Morley, D. Miller, and M. Lawton), pp. 143–86. Springer, New York.

Kaplan, G.A., Strawbridge, W.J., Camacho, T., and Cohen, R.D. (1993). Factors associated with change in physical functioning in the elderly: a 6-year prospective study. *Journal of Aging and Health*, **5**, 140–53.

Kauffman, K.S. and Sharps, P.W. (1996). 'Urban fear syndrome' among elderly among elderly black women living in an inner-city known for dangerous public spaces. *Gerontologist*, **36** (special edition), 321.

Lachs, M.S., Feinstein, A.R., Cooney, L.M., *et al.* (1990). A simple procedure for general screening for functional disability in elderly patients. *Annals of Internal Medicine*, **112**, 699–706.

Lacroix, A.Z. and Omenn, G.S. (1992). Older adults and smoking. *Clinics in Geriatric Medicine*, **8**, 69–87.

Leigh, J.P., Richardson, N., Beck, R., *et al.* (1992). Randomized controlled study of a retiree health promotion program. *Archives of Internal Medicine*, **152**, 1201–6.

Lichtner, M., Arens, P.L., and Reinstein, N. (1986). Oakwood Hospital community health promotion program. *Health Care Management Review*, **11**, 75–87.

Lindsay, R. (1987). Oestrogen therapy in the prevention and management of osteoporosis. *American Journal of Obstetrics and Gynecology*, **156**, 1347–56.

McCormick, J. (1994). Health promotion: the ethical dimension. *Lancet*, **344**, 390–1.

Mahoney, J., Drinka, T.J.K., Abler, R., *et al.* (1994). Screening for depression: single questions versus GDS. *Journal of the American Geriatrics Society*, **42**, 1006–8.

Mandelblatt, J., Global, I., and Wisterick, M. (1986). Gynaecological care of elderly women. *Journal of the American Medical Association*, **256**, 367–71.

Marmot, M. and Brunner, E. (1991). Alcohol and cardiovascular disease: the status of the U-shaped curve. *British Medical Journal*, **303**, 565–8.

Medical Research Council Working Party (1985). MRC trial of treatment of mild hypertension: principal results. *British Medical Journal (Clinical Research Edition)*, **291**, 97–104.

Mills, K., Verboncoeur, C., McLellan, B., *et al.* (1996). Determinants of interest in a physical activity program. *Gerontologist*, **36** (special issue), 108.

Morrison, B.J. (1994a). Screening for breast cancer. In *The Canadian guide to clinical preventive health care* (ed. R. Goldbloom), pp. 788–95. Canada Communications Group, Ottawa.

Morrison, B.J. (1994b). Screening for cervical cancer. In *The Canadian guide to clinical preventive health care* (ed. R. Goldbloom), pp. 884–9. Canada Communications Group, Ottawa.

Mulrow, C.D., Aguilar, C., and Endicott, J.E. (1990). Quality of life changes and hearing impairment: a randomized trial. *Annals of Internal Medicine*, **113**, 188–94.

Patterson, C. (1994a). Nutritional counselling for undesirable dietary patterns and screening for protein/calorie malnutrition disorders in adults. In *The Canadian guide to clinical preventive health care* (ed. R. Goldbloom), pp. 586–99. Canada Communications Group, Ottawa.

Patterson C. (1994b). Prevention of hearing impairment and disability in the elderly. In *The Canadian guide to clinical preventive health care* (ed. R. Goldbloom), pp. 954–63. Canada Communications Group, Ottawa.

Patterson C. (1994c). Screening for abdominal aortic aneurysm. In *The Canadian guide to clinical preventive health care* (ed. R. Goldbloom), pp. 672–78. Canada Communications Group, Ottawa.

Patterson C. (1994d). Screening for cognitive impairment . In *The Canadian guide to clinical preventive health care* (ed. R. Goldbloom), pp. 902. Canada Communications Group, Ottawa.

Patterson C. (1994e). Screening for visual impairment in the elderly. In *The Canadian guide to clinical preventive health care* (ed. R. Goldbloom), pp. 932–42. Canada Communications Group, Ottawa.

Patterson C. (1994f). Secondary prevention of elderly abuse. In *The Canadian guide to clinical preventive health care* (ed. R. Goldbloom), pp. 922–9. Canada Communications Group, Ottawa.

Patterson, C. and Chambers, L.W. (1995). Preventive health care. *Lancet*, **345**, 1611–15.

Potter, J., Stott, D.J., and Roberts, M.A. (1997). Influenza vaccination of health care workers in long-term-care hospitals reduces the mortality of elderly patients. *Journal of Infectious Diseases*, **175**, 1–6.

Rajala, S., Haavisto, M., Heinkinheimo, R., and Mattila, K. (1983). Blood pressure and mortality in the very old. *Lancet*, **ii**, 520–1.

Rockwood, K., Fox, R.A., Stolee, P., Robertson, D., and Beattie, L.B. (1994). Frailty in elderly people: an evolving concept. *Canadian Medical Association Journal*, **150**, 489–93.

Royal College of General Practitioners (1990). *Care of old people: a framework for progress*. Occasional paper 45. Royal College of General Practitioners, London.

Rubenstein, L.V., Calkins, D.R., Young, R.T., *et al.* (1989). Improving patient function: a randomised trial of functional disability screening. *Annals of Internal Medicine*, **111**, 836–42.

Rubenstein, L.Z., Robbins, A.S., Josephson, K.R., Schulman, B.L., and Osterweil, D. (1990). The value of assessing falls in an elderly population. *Annals of Internal Medicine*, **113**, 308–16.

Sangster, J.F., Gerace, T.M., and Seewald, R.C. (1991). Hearing loss in elderly patients in a family practice. *Canadian Medical Association Journal*, **144**, 1981–4.

Scott, R.A.P., Wilson, N.M., Ashton, H.A., and Kay, D.N. (1995). Influence of screening on the incidence of ruptured aortic aneurysm 5 year results of a randomized controlled study. *British Journal of Surgery*, **82**, 1066–70.

SHEP Co-operative Research Group (1991). Prevention of stroke by antihypertensive drug treatment in older persons with isolated systolic hypertension. *Journal of the American Medical Association*, **265**, 3255–64.

Sih, R. (1995). Cholesterol and the healthy senior. In *Annual review of gerontology and geriatrics* (ed. J. Morley, D. Miller, and M. Lawton), pp. 229–55. Springer, New York.

Stamper, M.J. and Colditz. G.A. (1991). Oestrogen replacement therapy and coronary heart disease: a quantitative assessment of the epidemiological evidence. *Preventive Medicine*, **20**, 47–63.

Taylor, M.C. and Dingle, J.L. (1994). Prevention of tobacco-caused diseases. In *The Canadian guide to clinical preventive health care* (ed. R. Goldbloom), pp. 500–11. Canada Communications Group, Ottawa.

Tengs, T.O., Adams, M.E., Pliskin, J.S., *et al.* (1996). Five-hundred life-saving interventions and their cost-effectiveness. *Risk Analysis*, **1**, 131.

Tinetti, M.E., Baker, D.I., McAvay, G., *et al.* (1994). A multifactorial intervention to reduce the risk of falling among elderly people living in the community. *New England Journal of Medicine*, **331**, 821–7.

Towler, B., Irwig, L., Glasziou, P., Kewenter, J., Weller, D., and Silagy, C. (1998). A systematic review of the effects of screening for colorectal cancer using the faecal occult blood test, Hemoccult. *British Medical Journal*, **317**, 559–65.

Ubbink, J.B. (1998). Should all elderly people receive folate supplements? *Drugs and Aging*, **13**, 415–20.

US Preventive Services Task Force (1996). *Guide to clinical preventive services* (2nd edn). Williams and Wilkins, Baltimore, MD.

Van Dijck, J.A.A.M., Broeders, M.J.M., and Verbeek, A.L.M. (1997). Mammographic screening in older women. Is it worthwhile? *Drugs and Aging*, **10**, 69–79.

Wagner, E.H., LaCroix, A.Z., Groth, L., *et al.* (1994). Preventing disability and falls in older adults: a population-based randomized trial. *American Journal of Public Health*, **84**, 1800–6.

WHO (World Health Organization) (1983). *Services to prevent disability in the elderly*. Euro Reports and Studies 83. WHO, Geneva.

WHO (World Health Organization) (1986). *Ottawa charter for health promotion*. WHO, Health and Welfare Canada, Canadian Public Health Association, Ottawa.

Williams, M.E., Gaylor, S.E., and Gerrity, M.S. (1994). The timed manual performance test as a predictor of hospitalisation and death in a community-based elderly population. *Journal of the American Geriatrics Society*, **42**, 21–7.

Woolf, S.H., Battista, R.N., Anderson, G.M., Logan, A.G., Wang, E.E.L., and Dingle, J.L. (1994). Methodology. In *The Canadian guide to clinical preventive health care* (ed. R. Goldbloom), pp. xxv–xxxv. Canada Communications Group, Ottawa.

Working Group on Hypertension in the Elderly (1986). Statement on hypertension in the elderly. *Journal of the American Medical Association*, **256**, 70–4.

Yaffe, K., Sawaya, G., Liberburg, I., and Grady, D. (1998). Estrogen therapy in postmenopausal women: effects on cognitive function and dementia. *Journal of the American Medical Association*, **279**, 688–95.

24

Exercise and lifestyle

24 Exercise and lifestyle
Sarah E. Lamb

Introduction

In many countries, participation of most older people in physical activity and exercise is at a level below that recommended by public health guidelines for the maintenance of physical fitness, health, and function (Killoran *et al.* 1994). Physical fitness determines the capacity of an individual to perform physical work. It depends on four attributes: cardiovascular stamina, muscle strength/power, flexibility, and psychomotor skill. These attributes tend to decline with advancing age, but it remains unclear to what extent this is the result of a sedentary lifestyle, chronic diseases (either subclinical or clinical), or the intrinsic biological processes of ageing. Although we do not understand the complex relationships between inactivity, disease, and ageing, we do know that engaging in regular activity and exercise is one of the most important predictors of optimal ageing in the short and long term (Guralnik and Kaplan 1989; Mor *et al.* 1989; Berkman *et al.* 1993). Conversely, inactivity reduces physical fitness and when it is sufficiently impaired, loss of function and disability can ensue.

The combination of the high prevalence of inactivity in the older population, and the high risk of ill-health and disability associated with inactivity, suggests that programmes that are successful in increasing levels of activity and exercise in significant numbers of older people could have a great impact on population health in later life. In the United States, fewer than 10 per cent of women aged over 75 years old smoke, whereas 70 per cent of women are inactive, leading some to suggest that inactivity is the primary lifestyle risk factor in old age (Buchner 1997). Similar observations can be made in other countries.

Benefits of physical activity and exercise in later life

There is an important distinction between the terms 'physical activity' and 'exercise'. Physical activity is any body movement produced by skeletal muscle that results in energy expenditure, and includes activities such as dressing, walking to the shops, and gardening. Exercise is a subset of physical activity defined as planned, structured, and repetitive movement aimed at improving or maintaining one or more components of fitness (Casperson 1985).

The benefits of physical activity and exercise in later life are protection against disease, promotion of health, and prevention of disability (detailed in Table 1). The beneficial effects of physical activity and exercise are not limited to the young elderly, to older

Table 1 Some reported benefits of physical activity and exercise in older people

Improvements in aerobic capacity, muscle strength, flexibility
Improvements in physical performance and function
Prevention of falls
Improvements in sleep quality
Improvements in mood and well being
Improvements in psychomotor skill
Reduction of anxiety and depression
Increased longevity
Decreased risk of cardiovascular disease

people in good health, or those who have been active throughout their lives. People who are physically frail, have chronic diseases, or cognitive impairments can also experience significant benefits. Advice to increase activity and exercise should not exclude people purely on the basis of frailty and poor health status. This raises concerns and challenges to medical and health-care practitioners who provide advice and encouragement to increase activity and exercise. Published recommendations focus on the prevention of coronary heart disease in healthy, younger age groups. Few address the problems of exercise prescription when chronic disease, medications, and poor fitness impair exercise tolerance and capacity.

There are only a few absolute contraindications to increasing physical activity, and these are detailed in Table 2. A useful starting point in recommending physical activity and exercise to older people,

Table 2 Contraindications to exercise in older adults

Severe coronary artery disease, unstable angina pectoris, acute myocardial infarction
Decompensated congestive cardiac failure
Uncontrolled ventricular arrhythmias
Uncontrolled atrial arrhythmias (compromising cardiac function)
Severe valvular heart disease including aortic, pulmonary, and mitral stenosis
Uncontrolled systemic hypertension (e.g. 200/105 mmHg)
Pulmonary hypertension
Acute myocarditis
Recent pulmonary embolism and deep vein thrombosis

Adapted from Heath (1993).

Table 3 Intensity of effort of some physical activities

Light intensity	Moderate intensity	Hard/vigorous intensity
Walking slowly (1–2 m.p.h.)	Brisk walk (3–4 m.p.h.)	Brisk walk uphill or with a load
Cycling on an exercise bike	Cycling (≤10 m.p.h.)	Cycling (>10 m.p.h.)
Fishing (sitting)	Fishing (casting/standing)	Fishing (walking/wading)
Gardening (e.g. weeding)	Home keep-fit exercises	Running
Dancing	Jogging	Hockey
Golf	Swimming	Volleyball
Light housework	Tennis	
	Digging/heavy labour	
	Heavy housework	
	Heavy gardening	

is the health fitness gradient adapted here from World Health Organization (**WHO**) recommendations (WHO 1996). This considers older people in three broad groups as follows.

Group 1: older people who are physically fit, disease free, and independent in function.

Group 2: older people who are physically unfit, may have chronic diseases, but are independent in function.

Group 3: older people who are physically unfit, may have chronic diseases, and are unable to function independently.

The needs of the people in each group will differ, partly because the emphasis of activity will progress from prevention of disease (group 1) to that of disability (group 3), and the capacity to engage in physical exercise without supervision will change.

Group 1

In this group, the important motivation for participating in regular physical activity is to prevent the onset of diseases for which a sedentary lifestyle and lack of fitness are strong risk factors. Sufficient evidence exists to support a causal link between a sedentary lifestyle and the subsequent onset of cardiovascular disease. Other diseases in which a causal link has been suggested include colon cancers, non-insulin-dependent diabetes, osteoporosis, anxiety and depression, and stroke (American College of Sports Medicine 1995).

Physical activity of at least moderate intensity is indicated for the primary prevention of cardiovascular disease (Pater *et al.* 1995). The American Centers for Disease Control and American College of Sports Medicine (American College of Sports Medicine 1995) suggest that people who have no chronic diseases or risk factors for disease, should participate in moderate-intensity physical activities, for 30 min/day, to experience worthwhile improvements in health. These are similar to the recommendations made by the Health Education Authority in the United Kingdom. The emphasis is on moderate intensity activities that raise the heart rate sufficiently to make the subject feel warm and slightly out of breath (Killoran *et al.* 1994). Examples of light, moderate, and high intensity activities and exercise are given in Table 3.

An important consideration is that even for fit older people, the intensity of activity required to produce increases in heart rate and a sweaty breathlessness will be lower than in younger people. Recommendations to increase activity and exercise should be correspondingly conservative. For older adults, the intensity of activity should be monitored on perceptions of effort and not on calculations of age-predicted maximal heart rate (American College of Sports Medicine 1995). The Borg Scale of Perceived Exertion is recommended (Noble *et al.* 1983), and activities or exercises should be perceived as being 'moderately difficult'.

The published recommendations emphasize the importance of regular physical activity as opposed to specific exercises. This is an attempt to develop a single general message about the benefits of simple changes in lifestyle, that can be conveyed to the whole adult population. Some activities which enhance cardiovascular fitness may not be effective in improving other aspects of fitness, such as strength. With fit, older people it may also be prudent to encourage the use of exercises to maintain strength and flexibility as well (American College of Sports Medicine 1995).

Group 2

People in this group will have some degree of musculoskeletal frailty and/or chronic disease, and an important motivation for exercising is the prevention of disability. In general, these people will have the capacity to exercise safely without supervision. Chronic and acute disease can result in a generalized loss of physical fitness unless premorbid levels of activity are quickly reinstated. Specific deficits in fitness occur where the pathological process is limited to one or more of the physiological systems of the body. For example, osteoarthritis is associated with a localized loss of muscular strength around the affected joint. Although the prescription of exercise and activity is complicated by these factors, people who fall into this category are likely to experience significant gains in health and function from exercise.

Activities and exercises which improve strength, such as light resistance training, seem to be the most effective in restoring, maintaining, or improving function in frail older adults. The disease preventive effects of strengthening exercises are not known, and strengthening should be supplemented by light or moderate intensity activities to enhance cardiovascular fitness. An overview of current research suggests that strength training should be undertaken two or three times a week, using either light resistance elastic exercise bands, strap-on cuff weights, or more traditional gymnasium equipment for resistance.

Muscle mass and the ability to contract muscles quickly decreases with age (see Chapter 19.1). Older people are likely to be weaker than their younger counterparts, to tire more quickly, and to recover more slowly from strengthening exercises. They may experience more difficulty in recruitment of motor units to achieve maximum force in a graded, smooth way. Correspondingly the resistance used in strength training should be adjusted to the strength of the individual, contractions should be fewer in number, and with sufficient time for force to be generated slowly and relaxation to occur between contractions. High-intensity contractions should be avoided as these can result in fatigue specific to low-frequency firing motor units (Woods et al. 1987). This can interfere with muscle activity during simple activities of daily living, and may persist for several days (Newham et al. 1987).

Advice to exercise and maintain activity is an essential component of the management of any chronic disease including stroke, osteoarthritis, diabetes, and cardiovascular disease. However, these disease processes affect tolerance to exercise in different ways, and recommendations need to take this into account. Maximum gains in function will occur if pathology-linked deficits of physical fitness are addressed. The reader is referred to Skinner (1987) and Bouchard (1990) for a comprehensive review of exercise physiology and prescription in different diseases.

Joint pain and osteoarthritis are common in later life, and may be one of the reasons why many older people choose not to exercise. If people have mild or moderate symptoms, they should be reassured that strengthening exercises and cardiovascular activities will not exacerbate pain, can result in improvements in function, and can prevent further deterioration in disability. Low resistance, low repetition strength training and regular walking are effective modalities (Kovar et al. 1992; Coleman et al. 1996; Ettinger et al. 1997). If people have acute or intense symptoms of joint pain, they should be encouraged to be active and exercise, but weight-bearing activities should be replaced by non-weight-bearing exercise such as cycling and water-based exercise (Heath 1993; Routi 1994). Static strengthening exercise, in which the joint is held in a fixed position whilst contracting the surrounding muscles, may minimize discomfort.

Exercise and activity have important roles in controlling cardiovascular disease processes, and limiting the effects of cardiovascular disease on function. In general, people with mild to moderate symptoms and who have stable responses to exercise, can exercise safely without medical supervision (Painter and Haskell 1993). A key factor is to identify those people who have severe or acute cardiovascular disease, are at high risk of developing exercise complications, and who, therefore, need expert supervision. People who report a history of cardiovascular disease should obtain medical clearance prior to increasing physical activity or participating in an exercise programme. Moderate to low intensity, symptom-limited activities are indicated, for example walking and slow cycling (Heath 1993). If patients are hypertensive, strength training should be limited to low-intensity low-repetition dynamic movements and avoid static muscle work

(Heath 1993). There is encouraging evidence regarding the benefits of different types of activity and exercise after stroke (Potempa et al. 1995; Duncan et al. 1998; Kwakkel et al. 1999). People who have had a stroke present with a range of problems that will affect exercise tolerance and ability to exercise safely and without supervision. Balance and sensory problems should be accommodated by suggesting exercises in the sitting position, or with standing support. Fatigue will occur quickly if limbs are paretic, and excessive effort may serve only to increase spasticity. Loss of motor co-ordination and asymmetry of muscle strength render swimming and other complex activities difficult.

In the case of diabetes, symptoms and caloric intake should be carefully monitored. Moderate intensity cardiovascular activities, flexibility, and low-resistance high-repetition strength training are indicated (Heath 1993). If participants are dizzy, ataxic, or have orthostatic hypotension, exercises in the sitting position may be preferred, and exercises which involve changing postures, for example from sitting to standing, should be avoided.

Group 3

This population is characterized by frailty, disability, high levels of chronic disease, comorbidity, and often dependence on others for assistance in simple everyday activities. Several studies have demonstrated that supervised exercise can stimulate significant improvements in the physical function and mood of people who live in residential or nursing homes (Fiatarone et al. 1994). Improvements in flexibility and strength may reduce the burden of care by improving transfer skill, and pertain to people who have cognitive and physical impairments. In most cases, physical fitness will be poor, and the intensity of exercise needed to stimulate increases in heart rate and strength will be low. General recommendations are to encourage people to be as independent as possible in their activities of daily living, to walk, and to perform exercises to maintain range of movement and strength daily. Generally, exercises require supervision, either in a group setting or on an individual basis.

Safety and avoidance of complications

The risk of cardiovascular complications and injury as a consequence of physical activity and exercise are small, provided that an adequate history of medical conditions has been taken and accounted for. The American College of Sports Medicine (1995) suggests that all older people should be screened for the possibility of cardiac and other complications using a simple questionnaire, such as the Readiness for Physical Activity Questionnaire (Thomas et al. 1983). If there are any doubts about a person's capacity to increase their levels of physical activity, they should be referred to their doctor. A simple test of postural control, such as the tandem stand or tandem walk test (Tinetti 1986) should be used to test stability before recommending complex exercises and activities.

All exercise or vigorous physical activity should be preceded by a warm-up to minimize the risk of injury. Age-associated changes in thermoregulation mean that older people are more susceptible to dehydration and heat intolerance during moderate intensity activities, and regular intake of fluids is important. People should feel no more than pleasantly tired after activity. Facilities where exercise or physical activities are undertaken should be well ventilated and have good lighting, and people must wear adequate clothing and shoes. Over the last few years, private and public fitness facilities have turned their attention to the needs of older people. Low-cost supervised programmes are becoming available. Whilst supervision is not strictly necessary for many older people, it does offer several safety advantages. These include access to accredited fitness trainers, and a secure and safe environment in which to exercise.

Effectiveness

From a population perspective, effectiveness is the product of two factors:

- the number of people who receive the advice/programme
- the advice/programme results in a sustained change in exercise or physical activity that is associated with the desired health benefits.

Research has focused on documenting effectiveness in terms of the adherence, behavioural change, and the physiological/health benefits of different types of programmes. Long-term follow-up studies are rare. Studies which target low income, low participation groups are also rare. Very little is known about those people who choose not to participate in the programmes, and therefore it is difficult to estimate the impact on the population.

Strategies which seem to be successful in encouraging large numbers of older people to increase their activity levels are those targeted to situations where concentrations of older people can be found. This includes senior and community centres, and residential or other institutional settings. Many older people seem to enjoy the social aspects of group exercise or activity programmes. Other components of successful community-based programmes include assurances about personal safety, transport, cost, time commitment, disruption to usual routine, and fear of injury or medical complications. A sense of community ownership, for example that the programme has been designed to meet the needs of local people, seems to be important, as does information regarding the benefits of exercise. A number of effective low-cost programmes have been devised in the last few years in the United States, notably supervised outdoor or mall-walking programmes.

Older people have high levels of contact with primary care and hospital-based health-care professionals, and the approval or recommendation of their doctors is a strong factor in motivating older people to take up exercise, or participate in specific programmes (Haug 1979). An efficient method for health-care professionals to promote physical activity and exercise participation is to have a good knowledge of the programmes available in their community, social services, and hospitals so that appropriate suggestions can be made (Elward and Larson 1992). Programmes are not always available locally and do not suit the needs of all older people. Doctors and health professionals are then reliant on their expertise and experience in exercise and activity prescription. Successful exercise prescription in older people draws on a large body of knowledge from the fields of exercise and behavioural science, as well as medicine. Software and desktop packages have been developed to assist in exercise prescription. These have been successful in helping doctors promote suitable activities for people at high risk of cardiac disease (for example Long et al. 1996) but have not until recently addressed the problems of older people. Some primary care practices and hospitals

Table 4 Summary of key points in recommending physical activity and exercise to older people

Simple assessment of baseline fitness, including postural stability and risk of cardiovascular complications

Explain benefits in simple terms of health and functional gain

Assess current participation in exercise and attitudes/barriers to exercise

Consider the implications of comorbid disease

Select intensity, duration, and frequency of exercise with attention to the above

Prescribe exercises which utilize simple known movements, provide written/visual instructions, demonstrate exercises, and allow time for practice

Seek assessment from doctor/physiotherapist if cardiovascular response to exercise is unstable or there are any concerns regarding safety or effectiveness of prescription

Maximize enjoyment, minimize cost and inconvenience, attention to safety, enlist supervision when required, inform about community resources

Regular follow-up and reinforcement of exercise principles, progression of prescription to maintain training intensity and minimize boredom

employ fitness trainers or physiotherapists to provide physical conditioning programmes and advice.

Medical and health-care professionals can maximize the likelihood of people taking advice and changing their physical activity habits in a number of ways (summarized in Table 4). The reader is referred to Killoran et al. (1994) for a more detailed review of behavioural techniques used to encourage people to change their lifestyle behaviours. The benefits of activity and exercise should be described in a simple way. They should be related to the fitness, health, and function of the individual (e.g. using the Health Fitness Gradient), in terms of individual risk of disability and disease. Reassurance should be given that the activity will not pose an increased risk of illness, pain, or injury.

People should be encouraged regularly, even if progress seems slow. In middle-aged people, the transition from being sedentary to regular participation in exercise takes on average 1 year (Marcus et al. 1992). Older people may take even longer to build up their confidence to participate in moderate intensity activities. Programmes or suggestions which offer people a range of activities to choose from are likely to be most successful in facilitating long-term adherence to exercise programmes (Thompson and Wankel 1980). Enjoyment is a critical factor. Progress needs to be reviewed regularly to prevent boredom, and new targets set. Simple tests to self-monitor improvements in fitness help to maintain motivation, as do regular face-to-face or telephone contacts with programme or health centre staff. Unless exercise and activity is of sufficient intensity and frequency, health, function, and fitness benefits will not accrue. However, care must be taken to avoid symptoms of muscle soreness, and excessive breathlessness and sweating which can occur if the training target is set too high, or the programme progresses too quickly. Printed visual materials are helpful in recalling exercise instructions and should be accompanied with simple instructions. Exercises or activities which use simple or known movement patterns should be used; the exercises should be demonstrated and repeated under supervision to ensure that the method is correct and understood.

Conclusion

Physical activity and exercise is crucial to the maintenance and improvement of function, and mental and physical health in later life. Many older people are sedentary. If health-care professionals routinely provide advice to increase physical activity and exercise as part of their consultations with older people, this could be an effective method of promoting health and preventing disability and chronic disease in later life. Medical, nursing, and allied professions need to be educated about the effects of activity and exercise, and importantly, in the practical skills of simple exercise and activity counselling and prescription. Future research should concentrate on identifying the types and threshold of exercise intensity that are associated with different health benefits in later life, and factors and behavioural strategies which motivate older people to become more active.

References

American College of Sports Medicine (1995). *ACSM's guidelines for exercise testing and prescription* (5th edn). Williams and Wilkins, Baltimore, MD.

Berkman, L.F., Seeman, T.E., Albert, M., et al. (1993). High, usual and impaired functioning in community dwelling older men and women: findings from the MacArthur Foundation Research Network on Successful Aging. *Journal of Clinical Epidemiology*, 46, 1129–40.

Bouchard, C., Shephard, R.J., Stephens, T., Sutton, J.R., and McPherson, B.D. (1990). *Exercise, fitness and health. A consensus of current knowledge.* Human Kinetic Books, Champaign, IL.

Buchner, D.M. (1997). Physical activity and quality of life in older adults. *Journal of the American Medical Association*, 227, 64–6.

Casperson. C.J. (1985). Physical activity, exercise and physical fitness. Definitions and distinctions for health-related research. *Public Health Reports*, 100, 126–30.

Coleman, E.A, Buchner, D.M., Cress, M.E., Chan, B.K., and DeLatuer, B.J. (1996). The relationship of joint symptoms with exercise performance in older adults. *Journal of the American Geriatrics Society*, 44, 14–21.

Duncan, P., Richards, L., Wallace, D., et al. (1998). A randomised controlled pilot study of a home-based exercise programme for individuals with mild to moderate stroke. *Stroke*, 10, 2055–60.

Elward, K. and Larson, E.B. (1992). Benefits of exercise for older adults. *Clinics in Geriatric Medicine*, 8, 35–50.

Ettinger, W.H., Burns, R., Messier, S.P., et al. (1997). A randomized trial comparing aerobic exercise and resistance exercise with a health education programme in older adults with knee osteoarthritis. *Journal of American Medical Association*, 227, 25–31.

Fiatarone, M.A., O'Neill, E.F., Ryan, N.D., et al. (1994). Exercise training and nutritional supplementation for physical frailty in very elderly people. *New England Journal of Medicine*, 330, 1769–75.

Guralnik, J.M. and Kaplan, G.A. (1989). Predictors of healthy aging. Prospective evidence from the Alameda county study. *American Journal of Public Health Medicine*, 76, 703–8.

Haug, M. (1979). Doctor–patient relationships and the older patient. *Journal of Gerontology*, 34, 852–60.

Heath, G.W. (1993). Exercise programming for the older adult. In *American College of Sports Medicine resource manual for guidelines for exercise testing and prescription* (2nd edn), pp. 418–26. Lea and Febiger, Philadelphia, PA.

Killoran, A.J., Fentem, P., and Casperson, C. (ed.) (1994). *Moving on. International perspectives on promoting physical activity.* Health Education Council, UK.

Kovar, P.A., Allegrante, J.P., MacKenzie, C.R., Peterson, M.G., Gutin, B., and Charlson, M.E. (1992). Supervised fitness walking in patients with osteoarthritis of the knee. A randomised controlled trial. *Annals of Internal Medicine*, 1, 529–34.

Kwakkel, G., Wagenaar, R.C., Twisk, J.W., Lankhorst, G.J., and Koetsier, J.C. (1999). Intensity of leg and arm training after primary middle-cerebral-artery stroke: a randomised controlled trial. *Lancet*, 354, 191–6.

Lamb, S.E. (1993). Physical fitness and the importance of exercise in the third age. In *Health and function in the third age* (ed. J. Grimley Evans, M.J. Goldacre, M. Hodkinson, S. Lamb, and M. Savory), pp. 137–53. Nuffield Provincial Hospitals Trust, London.

Long, B.J., Calfas, K.J., Wooten, W., et al. (1996). A multisite field test of the acceptability of physical activity counselling in primary care: project PACE. *American Journal of Preventive Medicine*, 12, 73–81.

Lowenthal, D.T., Kirschner, D.A., Scarpace, N.T., Pollock, M., and Graves, J. (1994). Effects of exercise on age and disease. *Southern Medical Journal*, 87, 5–12.

Marcus, B., Rossi, J., Sleby, V., Niaura, R., and Abrams, D. (1992). The stages and process of exercise adoption and maintenance in a worksite sample. *Health Psychology*, 11, 368–95.

Mor, V., Murphy, J., Masterson-Allen, S., et al. (1989). Risk of functional decline among well elders. *Journal of Clinical Epidemiology*, 42, 895–904.

Newham, D.J., Jones, D.A., and Clarkson, P.M. (1987). Repeated high-force eccentric exercise: effects on muscle pain and damage. *Journal of Applied Physiology*, 63, 1381–6.

Noble, B.J., Borg, C.A.V., Jacobs, I., Ceci, R., and Kaiser, P. (1983). A category-ratio perceived exertion scale: relationship to blood and muscle lactates and heart rate. *Medicine and Science in Sports and Exercise*, 15, 523–8.

Painter, P.L. and Haskell, W.L. (1993). Decision making in programming exercise. In *American College of Sports Medicine resource manual for guidelines for exercise testing and prescription* (2nd edn), pp. 311–18. Lea and Febiger, Philadelphia, PA.

Pater, R.R., Pratt, M., Blair, S.N., et al. (1995). Physical activity and public health. A recommendation for disease control and prevention and the American College of Sports Medicine. *Journal of the American Medical Association*, 273, 402–7.

Potempa, K., Lopez, M., Braun, L.T., Szidon, J.P., Fogg, L., and Tincknell, T. (1995). Physiological outcomes of aerobic exercise training in hemiparetic stroke patients. *Stroke*, 26, 101–5.

Province, M.A., Hadley, E.C., and Hornbrook, M.C. (1995). The effects of exercise on falls in elderly patients: a pre-planned meta-analysis of the FICSIT trials. *Journal of the American Medical Association*, 273, 1341–7.

Ruoti, R.G., Troup, J.T., and Berger, R.A. (1994). The effects of non-swimming water exercise on older adults. *Journal of Sports and Orthopaedic Physical Therapy*, 19, 140–5.

Skinner, J.S. (1987). *Exercise testing and exercise prescription for special cases. Theoretical basis and clinical application.* Lea and Febiger, Philadelphia, PA.

Thomas, S., Reading, J., and Shephard, R.J. (1992). Revision of the Physical Activity Readiness Scale (PAR-Q). *Canadian Journal of Sports Science*, 17, 338–45.

Thompson, C.E and Wankel, L.M. (1980). The effects of perceived activity choice upon frequency of exercise behaviour. *Journal of Applied Social Psychology*, 10, 436–43.

Tinetti, M.E. (1986). Performance orientated test of mobility problems in elderly patients. *Journal of American Geriatrics Society*, 273, 1348–53.

WHO (World Health Organization) (1996). *The Heidelberg Guide lines for promoting physical activity among older adults.* Ageing and Health Programme, Division of Health Promotion, Education and Communication, WHO, Geneva.

Woods, J.J., Furbush, F., and Bigland-Ritchie, B. (1987). Evidence for a fatigue-induced reflex inhibition of motorneurone firing rates. *Journal of Neurophysiology*, 58, 125–37.

25

Assessing quality of life

which to judge to what extent individuals with disorders such as dementia and other forms of severe cognitive impairment can provide appropriate, reliable, and valid information about their quality of life. In such circumstances consideration has to be given to reliance on the judgements of proxies such as carers or health professionals. The problem is that proxy informants are always a 'second best' source because of the consistent evidence, summarized in a systematic review (Sprangers and Aaronson 1992), that proxy informants are not accurate judges of others' quality of life. Additional complexities arise from the likelihood that carers' own quality of life may be jeopardized by caring for individuals with disorders such as dementia.

A balance has to be found in quality-of-life assessment between the principle that older individuals are normally best placed to provide judgements of their health-related quality of life and realistic recognition of practical limitations.

References

Aaronson, N., Bullinger, M., and Ahmedzai, S. (1988). A modular approach to quality of life assessment in clinical trials. *Recent Results in Cancer Research*, 111, 231–49.

Beckett, L., Brock, D., Lemke, J., *et al.* (1996). Analysis of change in self-reported physical function among older persons in four population studies. *American Journal of Epidemiology*, 143, 766–78.

Bergner, M., Bobbitt, R., Carter, W., and Gilson, B. (1981). The Sickness Impact Profile: development and final revision of a health status measure. *Medical Care*, 19, 787–805.

Bowling, A. (1995). *Measuring disease*. Open University Press, Buckingham.

Bowling, A., Formby, J., Grant, K., and Ebrahim, S. (1991). A randomised controlled trial of nursing home and long-stay geriatric ward care for elderly people. *Age and Ageing*, 20, 316–24.

Browne, J., O'Boyle, C., McGee, H., *et al.* (1994). Individual quality of life in the healthy elderly. *Quality of Life Research*, 3, 235–44.

Carabellese, C., Appollonio, I., Bianchetti, A., Frisoni, G., Frattola, L., and Trabucchi, M. (1993). Sensory impairment and quality of life in a community elderly population. *Journal of the American Geriatrics Society*, 41, 401–7.

Cella, D. and Tulsky, D. (1990). Measuring quality of life today: methodological issues. *Oncology*, 4, 29–38.

Coleman, P. (1984). Assessing self-esteem and its sources in elderly people. *Ageing and Society*, 4, 117–35.

Dorevitch, M., Cossar, R., Bailey, F., *et al.* (1992). The accuracy of self and informant ratings of physical functional capacity. *Journal of Clinical Epidemiology*, 45, 791–8.

Ebrahim, S., Brittis, S., and Wu, A. (1991). The valuation of states of ill-health: the impact of age and disability. *Age and Ageing*, 20, 37–40.

Farquhar, M. (1995). Elderly people's definitions of quality of life. *Social Science and Medicine*, 41, 1439–46.

Fitzpatrick, R., Davey, C., Buxton, M., and Jones, D. (1998). Evaluating patient-based outcome measures for use in clinical trials. *Health Technology Assessment*, 2, 1–73.

Fletcher, A., Dickinson, J., and Philp, I. (1992). Review: audit measures: quality of life instruments for everyday use with elderly patients. *Age and Ageing*, 21, 142–50.

Fries, J., Spitz, P., and Young, D. (1982). The dimensions of health outcomes: the Health Assessment Questionnaire, disability and pain scales. *Journal of Rheumatology*, 9, 789–93.

Gallagher, D., Nies, G., and Thompson, L. (1982). Reliability of the Beck Depression Inventory with older adults. *Journal of Consulting and Clinical Psychology*, 50, 152–3.

Gill, T. and Feinstein, A. (1994). A critical appraisal of the quality of quality of life assessments. *Journal of the American Medical Association*, 272, 619–26.

Gurland, B., Copeland, J., and Kelleher, M. (1983). *The mind and mood of ageing: the mental health problems of the community elderly in New York and London*. Haworth Press, New York.

Institute of Medicine (1996). *Health outcomes for older people*. National Academy Press, Washington, DC.

Katz, J., Phillips, C., Fossell, A., and Liang, M. (1994). Stability and responsiveness of utility measures. *Medical Care*, 32, 183–8.

Kazis, L., Callahan, L., Meenan, R., and Pincus, T. (1990). Health status reports in the care of patients with rheumatoid arthritis. *Journal of Clinical Epidemiology*, 43, 1243–53.

Kurtzke, J. (1983). Rating neurologic impairment in multiple sclerosis: an expanded disability status scale (EDSS). *Neurology*, 33, 1444–52.

Kutner, N., Ory, M., Baker, D., Schechtman, K., Hornbrook, M., and Mulrow, C. (1992). Measuring the quality of life of the elderly in health promotion intervention trials. *Public Health Reports*, 107, 530–9.

Lyons, R., Perry, H., and Littlepage, B. (1994). Evidence for the validity of the Short-form 36 Questionnaire (SF-36) in an elderly population. *Age and Ageing*, 23, 102–4.

McEwen, J. (1988). The Nottingham health profile. In *Quality of life: assessment and applications*, (ed. S. Walker and R. Rosser), pp. 95–111. MTP, Lancaster.

Mahoney, F. and Barthel, D. (1965). Functional evaluation: the Barthel Index. *Maryland State Medical Journal*, 14, 61–5.

Nelson, E. and Berwick, D. (1989). The measurement of health status in clinical practice. *Medical Care*, 27, S77-S90.

Ory, M. (1988). Considerations in the development of age-sensitive indicators for assessing health promotion. *Health Promotion*, 3, 139–50.

Patrick, D. and Erickson P. (1993). Assessing health-related quality of life for clinical decision-making. In *Quality of life assessment: key issues in the 1990s* (ed. S. Walker and R. Rosser), pp. 11–63. Kluwer, Dordrecht.

Pearlman, R. and Uhlmann, R. (1988). Quality of life in chronic diseases: perceptions of elderly patients. *Journal of Gerontology*, 43, 25–30.

Peto, V., Jenkinson, C., Fitzpatrick, R., and Greenhall, R. (1995). The development of a short measure of functioning and well being for individuals with Parkinson's disease. *Quality of Life Research*, 4, 241–8.

Powell Lawton, M. (1975). The Philadelphia Geriatric Centre Morale Scale: a revision. *Journal of Gerontology*, 30, 85–9.

Reuben, D., Rubenstein, L., Hirsch, S., and Hays, R. (1992). Value of functional status as a predictor of mortality: results of a prospective study. *American Journal of Medicine*, 93, 663–9.

Rothwell, P., McDowell, Z., Wong, C., and Dorman, P. (1997). Doctors and patients don't agree: cross-sectional study of patients' and doctors' perceptions and assessments of disability in multiple sclerosis. *British Medical Journal*, 314, 1580–3.

Schag, C., Heinrich, R., and Ganz, P. (1984). Karkofsky Performance Status revisited: reliability, validity and guidelines. *Journal of Clinical Oncology*, 2, 187–93.

Schumacher, M., Olschewski, M., and Schulgen, G. (1991). Assessment of quality of life in clinical trials. *Statistics in Medicine*, 10, 1915–30.

Siu, A., Reuben, D., Ouslander, J., and Osterwell, D. (1993). Using multidimensional health measures in older persons to identify risk of hospitalisation and skilled nursing placement. *Quality of Life Research*, 2, 253–61.

Sprangers, M. and Aaronson, N. (1992). The role of health care providers and significant others in evaluating the quality of life of patients with chronic disease: a review. *Journal of Clinical Epidemiology*, 45, 743–60.

Steinbrocker, O., Traeger, C., and Batterman, R. (1949). Therapeutic criteria in rheumatoid arthritis. *Journal of the American Medical Association*, 140, 659–62.

Testa, M. and Simonson, D. (1996). Assessment of quality-of-life outcomes. *New England Journal of Medicine*, 334, 835–40.

Tugwell, P., Bombardier, C., Buchanan, W., Goldsmith, C., Grace, E., and Hanna, B. (1987). The MACTAR Patient Preference Disability Questionnaire—an individualised functional priority approach for assessing improvement in physical disability in clinical trials in rheumatoid arthritis. *Journal of Rheumatology*, **14**, 446–51.

Wagner, E., LaCroix, A., Grothaus, L., and Hecht, J. (1993). Responsiveness of health status measures to change among older adults. *Journal of the American Geriatrics Society*, **41**, 241–8.

Wells, K., Stewart A., Hays, R., *et al.* (1989). The functioning and well-being of depressed patients: results from the Medical Outcomes Study. *Journal of the American Medical Association*, **262**, 914–19.

26

Special problems

26.1 Driving and mobility

Desmond O'Neill

Driving: a 'basic' instrumental activity of daily living

Functional assessment is a core element of geriatric medicine. With the development of the specialty, an initial emphasis on assessment of basic activities of daily living has matured into increasing recognition of the importance of instrumental activities of daily living. This is particularly true of driving and other mobility issues which are critical to ensuring independence in the community. Maintaining social contacts, getting to appointments, and access to health care and shopping are among the primary functions of driving in older age groups; 77 per cent of drivers over the age of 55 perceive driving as essential or very important (AA Foundation for Road Safety Research 1988). At the White House Conference on Ageing in 1971, transportation was ranked third in importance after income and health as priorities in later life (Carp *et al.* 1980). Loneliness, lower life satisfaction, and lower activity levels are linked with the loss of driving ability among elderly people (Berg *et al.* 1981; Gonda 1982).

Public transport has figured in some guides to geriatric care (Roper and Mulley 1996) and is often mooted as a solution to the transportation needs of older people. However, it is unsatisfactory for many reasons. Older people do not consider that public transport is adequate or efficient, and it poses problems of security and convenience (Rabbitt *et al.* 1996); in the United States public transport accounts for less than 3 per cent of trips by older people (Eberhard 1996) and its use by older people has been steadily declining in both Europe and the United States.

Older drivers: a growing population

Carl Benz, one of the pioneers of motor manufacturing, foresaw no more than 1 million cars on the road, as this number represented those suitable to be trained as chauffeurs! He would have been surprised by the exponential rise in the proportion of older drivers among the driving population in the Western world. In the United Kingdom there has been an increase of 200 per cent and 600 per cent, respectively, in the number of men and women drivers over the age of 65 between 1965 and 1985 (Department of Transport 1991). In the United States, the number of women drivers over the age of 65 was 2.9 million in 1970 and 10.8 million in 1990, an increase of 269 per cent (Stamatiadis 1993); this trend is expected to continue.

One of the key questions about the ageing of the driving population is whether older drivers add significantly to hazard on the roads. The word accident has fallen out of favour among researchers into traffic safety. They argue that accident may convey a sense that the losses are due to fate and are devoid of predictability, whereas crash is a descriptive term which does not imply a cause *per se* (Evans 1991). This distinction is helpful as it focuses on risk factors for crashes. The overriding contribution of human factors to motor crashes is well established (Council on Scientific Affairs 1983).

The crash rate for older drivers for a given period of time is considerably lower than for the driving population as a whole (Gebers *et al.* 1993). Many safety experts defend older drivers as a relatively safe group (Evans 1988) and in some road tests healthy older drivers perform better than younger controls (Carr *et al.* 1992). Conversely, an increase in the crash rate per miles driven has been noted in elderly populations in comparison with middle-aged controls. In 1984, drivers over the age of 70 comprised 7.9 per cent of all drivers and 9.2 per cent of those involved in fatal crashes in the United States; by 1994, these rates were 8.9 per cent and 13.3 per cent respectively (National Center for Statistics and Analysis: National Highway Traffic Safety Administration 1995). If accident-rate and injury-severity data obtained among elderly people are normalized for exposure, they approximate the data for 15 to 25-year-olds (OECD 1985).

Some of this apparent risk is due to a reduction of long-distance driving, leaving almost all of their mileage on local roads and streets. This exposes them to more dangers per mile than high-mileage drivers as they encounter disproportionately more intersections, congestion, confusing visual environments, signs, and signals (Janke 1991). Crashes involving elderly people are also more likely to be fatal, by a factor of 3.5 in two-car accidents (Klamm 1985). Opposing these trends is the fact that the accident rates for young adults often arise from behaviour that leads to high-risk situations; accident rates in older drivers occur despite a trend to avoid high-risk situations (Planek *et al.* 1968) and the lowest proportion of crashes while under the influence of alcohol (National Center for Statistics and Analysis: National Highway Traffic Safety Administration 1995).

Janke (1994) has suggested a reasonable interpretation of these apparently contradictory findings. A group's average crash rate per year may be considered as an indicator of the degree of risk posed to society by that group, whereas average accident rate per mile indicates the degree of risk posed to individual drivers in the group when they drive, as well as their passengers. The increased risk to individual drivers is most likely due to age-associated illnesses, particularly neurodegenerative and vascular diseases (O'Neill 1992; Sjøgren 1994; Johansson *et al.* 1997*a*).

Medical aspects

Despite an early paper expressing concerns about older drivers (those over the age of 40) (Da Silva 1938), the medical literature on medical fitness to drive is mostly recent. Several themes are perceptible:

- a relative unawareness among doctors and the rehabilitation disciplines of the functional and medical importance of fitness to drive;
- an overemphasis on selecting those who should not drive rather than on enabling older drivers;
- increasing pressure for screening programmes for older drivers.

Doctors are unaware of the driving habits of their patients when prescribing drugs which may affect driving (Cartwright 1990), are not aware of fitness to drive regulations (Miller and Morley 1991; Strickberger *et al.* 1991; O'Neill *et al.* 1994), and do not give appropriate advice to patients with many illnesses (O'Neill *et al.* 1992; MacMahon *et al.* 1996). There may also be an element of ageism by which doctors may assume that older patients do not drive. Finally, in the rehabilitation environment, disabled drivers and stroke victims are not offered appropriate advice and rehabilitation about driving (Legh-Smith *et al.* 1986; Barnes and Hoyle 1995).

A further concern is that many older drivers cease driving for health reasons, and it is possible that remediation strategies have been insufficiently explored in a proportion of these. In one study, one in four older drivers stopped driving over a 6-year period (Marottoli *et al.* 1993). Medical factors which predicted those who would not drive included neurological disease (Parkinson's disease or stroke) and cataract, but interestingly not cognitive impairment. In Florida, health factors accounted for about half of decisions to stop (Campbell *et al.* 1993) and in Europe, medical and financial reasons were rated equally in importance by those who had stopped driving in later life (Rabbitt *et al.* 1996).

Enabling strategies

The role of health in driving cessation demands that emphasis on negative rather than enabling aspects of medical fitness to drive needs to be challenged. Many illnesses present opportunities for interventions which directly or indirectly will improve driving safety and comfort (Table 1). A typical illness with potential for enabling is arthritis. Not only do patients experience many difficulties in driving (Thevenon *et al.* 1989), but there is also evidence to show that appropriate intervention may improve driving ability and comfort (Jones *et al.* 1991). Many patients do not return to driving after a stroke (Legh-Smith *et al.* 1986), and rehabilitation and specialized driving re-education may return some of these to independence (van Zomeren *et al.* 1987). Lack of an enabling strategy may negatively influence the relationship between doctor and patient.

Other forces shaping the driving assessment

Patients attend their doctors in the hope of remaining healthy and retaining maximum function, particularly in later life. Ideally, a doctor should be considering whether or not patients are fit to drive with a view to correcting any physical or functional deficits and enabling

Table 1 Sample diseases for which appropriate assessment and remediation may be of benefit

Neuropsychiatric	
Stroke	Driving-specific rehabilitation (van Zomeren *et al.* 1987)
Parkinson's disease	Maximizing motor function, treatment of depression, assessment of cognitive function (Anonymous 1990)
Delirium	Treatment and resolution
Depression	Treatment: if antidepressant, choose one with least potential of cognitive/motor effects (Rubinsztein and Lawton 1995)
Mild dementia	Assess, treat depression, reduce/eliminate psychoactive drugs, advise not to drive alone (O'Neill 1996*a*)
Cardiovascular	
Syncope	Advice pending investigation: treat cause (O'Neill 1996*b*)
Respiratory	
Sleep apnoea	Treatment of underlying disease (Haraldsson *et al.* 1992)
Vision	
Cataract	Surgery, appropriate corrective lens and advice about glare (Munton 1995)
Metabolic	
Diabetes	Direct therapy to avoid hypoglycaemia (Frier 1992)
Musculoskeletal	
All arthritides	Driving-specific rehabilitation programme (Jones *et al.* 1991)
Iatrogenic	
Polypharmacy	Rationalize medications (Ray *et al.* 1993)
Psychoactive medication	Rationalize, minimize (Ray *et al.* 1992)

the patient to be independent. Several societal responsibilities and processes militate against this positive approach to driving assessment.

An overwhelming emphasis on detection of those who should not drive is implicit in legislation, official manuals on fitness to drive as well as much of the scientific literature. This confers a policing role on doctors, a role which is further developed in legislation for mandatory reporting by doctors of certain illnesses in some jurisdictions in the United States for instance, such as California. This poses a clinical and ethical dilemma as a policing mentality may instil negative attitudes to older drivers. It may also deter patients from attending their doctors if they fear that disclosure of illness may result in limitation of driving.

A different pressure comes from patients and their families who may feel aggrieved by advice to stop driving or indeed to continue driving; in cases such as these, threats of litigation are not unknown. Failure to advise compliance with current regulations may also lead to a claim of negligence (Retchin and Annapolle 1993). There may also be a clear conflict between patient confidentiality and concern about risk to third parties; in most countries, it is considered reasonable to breach confidentiality if (a) there is clear evidence of dangerous driving and (b) the patient refuses to curtail driving despite discussion with the patient and family. Finally, insurance companies require that customers report any illness to them which may affect driving, and non-disclosure will usually invalidate motor insurance. Clearly, there is a difficulty in illnesses with cognitive impairment and poor insight, where advice to inform the insurance company cannot be complied with.

Ethically, doctors need to keep the interest of their patients to the fore, and to consider professional responses to legislation, and mandatory reporting in particular; reporting in California runs well below the estimated prevalence of drivers with dementia. The legal and insurance aspects of driving make it prudent to advise all patients and their carers about driving and mobility, and to document the advice given.

Models of driving behaviour

While the geriatrician is aided in the assessment and rehabilitation of problems with balance and gait by an understanding of the underlying mechanisms, driving is a complex task, and there has been a marked lack of progress in developing a comprehensive model of driving behaviour. There are almost no universally agreed guidelines for fitness to drive for any one illness, and there is a wide range of regulations in North America (Retchin and Annapolle 1993) and the European Union. This lack of consensus reflects not only a paucity of literature but also the absence of a unitary model of driving behaviour. At least five main types of model have been explored: psychometric, motivational, hierarchical controls, information processing, and error theory.

Owing to the relative ease of measuring cognitive function, clinicians may look to psychometric measures as a means of assessing older drivers. At a practical level, one test battery which has been proposed for driving assessments in dementia fails over 40 per cent of controls, raising doubts over its usefulness (Mitchell *et al.* 1995). A preliminary emphasis on psychometric measures relating to accident-causing behaviour has been faulted for having been conducted without the benefit of a process model of driving, for focusing primarily on accident-causing behaviours and not on everyday driving, and on relying heavily on *post hoc* explanations (Ranney 1994). Some of the problems with using such *post hoc* research measures are restricted range of criterion and/or predictor variables (e.g. as might be due to the death of the worst drivers before they can be tested), the potential effect on motivation or test performance of knowledge by the driver or having been placed in a special category due to accident involvement, and the questionable assumption that skills or attributes

measured by the individual variables are highly reliable and do not change over time.

Motivational models which distinguish between drivers' performance limits and on-road driving offer a different perspective. For example, a pioneering Swedish study showed that when drivers are asked to remember road signs, the accuracy ranged from 17 to 78 per cent, depending on the subjective importance of the sign, that is, the amount of risk involved in ignoring the sign (Johansson and Backlund 1970). Early models assume risk to be a primary motivating factor; second-generation motivational models have given emphasis to motives other than risk, such as pleasure in driving, traffic risks, driving time, and expense (Rothengatter and de Bruin 1988). They also factor in concurrent activity at operational, manoeuvring, and strategic levels and portray the driver as an active decision maker rather than as a passive responder implicit in early information-processing models. The driver's allocation of attention depends on the immediate driving situation and the driver's motives which include the level of risk and other motives relating to the purpose of the trip. The main research interest is in identifying factors that influence the drivers allocation of attention among the tasks of the different control levels.

Much of routine driving is done automatically and automaticity, which is fast effortless cognitive processing, can occur at all three levels of control, and contrasts with control processing which is demanding of attention and resources. This automaticity can develop as a response to several types of stimuli and underlies much of experienced driving behaviour until knowledge-based problem solving is required. A combined model of a control hierarchy and an automaticity/controlled processing scheme is illustrated in Table 2.

A practical hierarchical approach

One practical scheme has been outlined, with an emphasis on a hierarchy of strategic, tactical, and operational factors (Table 3) (Michon 1985). Strategic performance includes the planning of choice of route, time of day (avoiding rush hour), or even the decision not to drive and to take public transport. Tactical decisions are those aspects of the driving style which are characteristic of the driver and are consciously or unconsciously adopted for a great range of reasons, for example decisions on whether or not to overtake, go through amber lights, or signalling in good time before turning. Operational performance is the response to specific traffic situations, such as speed control, braking, and signalling. Driving a car requires organization of action at and between all three levels.

Clinical assessment up to now has tended to dwell on deficiencies on the operational level, that is whether an illness affects the subject's appreciation of distracting stimuli or the reaction time to a hazardous

Table 2 Classification of selected driving tasks by Michon's control hierarchy and Rasmussen's skill–rule–knowledge framework

	Strategic	Tactical/manoeuvring	Operational/control
Knowledge	Navigating in unfamiliar area	Controlling skid	Novice on first lesson
Rule	Choice between familiar routes	Passing other vehicles	Driving unfamiliar vehicle
Skill	Route used for daily commute	Negotiating familiar intersection	Vehicle handling on curves

Reproduced with permission from Ranney (1994).

Table 3 Hierarchical scheme of driving assessment

Level of task performance	Level of risk
Strategic	Accepting risk
Tactical	Taking risk
Operational	Dealing with acute danger

situation. This emphasis is misguided; reaction time (a measure which is an integral part of operational tasks) is shortest in the 15 to 25 year age group, the group with the highest accident rate. It is very likely that decisions at a strategic and a tactical level are much more important in causing accidents. Older drivers are known to use strategic and tactical measures widely to avoid delay, stress, and risk by driving less at night and during bad weather, avoiding rush hour and unfamiliar routes, and so on (AA Foundation for Road Safety Research 1988; Michon 1989).

The application of these three levels of function can be of practical help in decision-making. This is illustrated by studies of drivers with acquired brain damage, particularly stroke (van Zomeren et al. 1987). Evidence for impairment at all levels may be collected by discussion with patient and relatives as well as by clinical observation. At a strategic level we would look for evidence of inappropriate planning of trips or lack of selective use of cars. Poor planning, poor judgement, lack of insight, and impulsivity affect both strategic and tactical levels. Impulsivity is attributed to disinhibition and/or cognitive impairment. Factors which interfere with the operational level include inadequate visual scanning of the environment, poor visual tracking, slowness in acting, and confusion when more complex acts have to be carried out. Right hemisphere lesions seem to produce a more adverse effect on driving skills, possibly relating to visuospatial deficits and inattention (Quigley and DeLisa 1983).

Assessment

The uncertainties underlying models of driver behaviour also affect the art/science of risk assessment. It is better to live with uncertainty and a considered individualized clinical approach than to prematurely adopt guidelines with apparent face validity. Risk assessment in older drivers is affected not only by the understanding of models of driving behaviour as well as by empirical studies of disease and crash risk but also by clinical attributes common to the assessment of function in older patients. A schedule for the assessment of older patients who drive is outlined in Table 4.

Interindividual variability is extremely important and implies a case-by-case approach. Factors relating to age-associated diseases include not only a different spectrum of illness to younger people, but also the presence of multiple illnesses. In any one patient, is it the arthritis, the dementia, the visual acuity, or even the multiple medications which is affecting driving? Within the rubric of one illness there may be multiple influences on driving skills. For example, there is an increased risk of crashes with Parkinson's disease (Dubinsky et al. 1991; Lings and Dupont 1992). The illness may involve problems of motor function, depression, and impaired cognitive function.

Rather than stating that Parkinson's disease is dangerous for driving, it is vital to take a phenomenological approach. The depression and the motor function must be treated, psychoactive medications minimized, and cognitive function assessed and managed before any decisions are made about fitness to drive.

Interdisciplinary approach

An interdisciplinary approach (Carr 1991) is probably useful with emphasis on the doctor, occupational therapist, neuropsychologist, and if possible a specialized driving assessor. A social worker may be very helpful if driving is no longer permitted. However, while it is fair to say that no one (or indeed any) member of the team may be able to predict driving safety accurately (Reuben 1993), a team approach has been shown to improve general health and functional status. In the academic department it also provides a focus for interdisciplinary research; much of the research to date has involved at most only two disciplines, either doctors and psychologists, or occupational therapists and specialist driving assessors. A cascade of assessments is appropriate; many drivers can be classed as fit to drive, unfit to drive, or appropriate for driver rehabilitation at a clinical assessment, and on-road driving assessments should be reserved for when a patient does not clearly fall into one of these patterns.

Most reviews on driver assessment published since 1992 include a common core (Underwood 1992; Carr 1993; O'Neill 1993a; Reuben 1993) (Table 5). One of the most important final common pathways of concern in driving is cortical function, when disrupted by syncope, cognitive function, inattention, neglect, or personality change. Perception is probably more important than vision. The relative ease of screening for cognitive dysfunction (O'Neill 1993b) may conceal the difficulties of interpreting mild to moderate degrees of deficit; functional measures may be more important as a predictor of diminished driving skills (O'Neill et al. 1992). This has the useful effect of diverting attention from cognitive measures (easily measured but of uncertain value) to either functional or behavioural measures as surrogates for driving ability.

Age-associated diseases and risk assessment

An ever-increasing list of illnesses may affect driver competency; recent additions include sleep apnoea (Haraldsson et al. 1992) and HIV infection (Näthke 1989). Assessment of risk due to an illness requires careful scrutiny of the relevant literature. The study sample is one of the most critical factors, particularly if it came from a specialized clinic; there are issues around whether or not the study was large enough and if the results on levels of risk are generalizable. The study of Hansotia and Broste on diabetes, epilepsy, and risk of crashes (Hansotia and Broste 1991) illustrates some of these points. Epilepsy and diabetes are both illnesses that have been very clearly defined in many fitness to drive manuals, often with stringent licence restrictions and/or punitive insurance loadings. This large-scale community study demonstrated that the increased risks were in fact quite small. If a more selected group are studied, for example people over 65 in a health maintenance organization, the relative risk for diabetes and crashes may be higher (Koepsell et al. 1994). As in any application of the medical literature, the doctor has to relate the sample population

Table 1 American Medical Association definitions of elder mistreatment

---

Physical abuse involves acts of violence that may result in pain, injury impairment, or disease

Physical neglect is characterized by a failure of the caregiver to provide the goods or services that are necessary for optimal functioning or to avoid harm

Psychological abuse is conduct that causes mental anguish such as threatening, berating, infantilizing, or isolating the older person

Psychological neglect is the failure to provide a dependent elderly individual with social stimulation

Financial or material abuse involves misuse of the elderly person's income or resources for the financial or personal gain of a caretaker or advisor

Financial or material neglect is failure to use available funds and resources necessary to sustain or restore the health and well being of the older adult

Violation of personal rights occurs when caretakers or providers ignore the older person's rights and capability to make decisions for him- or herself

---

Reproduced with permission from American Medical Association (1992).

or who locks a parent in a room as punishment. Neglectful behaviour is characterized by withholding physical, psychological, or financial resources that the older person needs to be happy and healthy. Neglect can be an active or passive process. For example, a daughter may make a conscious decision that she is too busy to take her mother to the doctor's surgery. In the case of passive neglect, the daughter may not take her mother to see the physician because she attributes urinary incontinence to old age and does not realize that it may be caused by a treatable urinary tract infection. Exploitation occurs when an older person's property or financial resources are used by another person, for that person's benefit, without the consent of the older adult. An example would be pressuring the older person to sign over assets or change his will in favour of the exploiter. Violation of rights occurs when the older person's rights and capability for self-determination are overridden. A common example is involuntary nursing home placement, but other examples, which may be more subtle, include not permitting the older person to make choices about his or her socialization, marriage or divorce, or living situation.

The variety of definitions is only one problem that researchers in this field face. Denial, by many members of our society, of the possibility that elder abuse exists is another barrier to progress. Ageist viewpoints cause people to dismiss signs and symptoms of mistreatment as part of ' normal ageing'. Even in situations in which victims and/or abusers admit there is a problem, either or both may be unwilling to discuss it for fear of repercussions. In the United States, legislative efforts to help victims of abuse by mandating reporting of suspected cases to public agencies have ended up hindering research, since many potential research subjects wish to maintain their privacy. Furthermore, while politicians may publicly decry elder abuse, they have done little to provide funding for research on the problem of elder mistreatment or for those agencies charged with prevention and management of the problem. The limitation in funding for studies of elder mistreatment has resulted in a vicious circle. The paucity of research data and repeated critiques of the methodological

quality of existing research have allowed the public and funding agencies to minimize the magnitude of the problem and to justify continued underfunding of those researchers and clinicians who are attempting to make an impact on this major problem for senior citizens.

Prevalence of elder mistreatment

Nonetheless, there is now research from at least 17 countries that testifies to the ubiquity of the problem of elder mistreatment and gives us some appreciation of its magnitude (Kosberg and Garcia 1995). These studies have taken the form of direct interviews with older people asking about different forms of elder mistreatment and interviews with health care professionals to determine whether they have encountered mistreatment or have themselves mistreated older persons. Despite the geographic and definitional diversity that characterizes these studies, a surprisingly stable estimate of mistreatment has emerged. The consensus from these studies is that 2 to 6 per cent of people aged over 60 years suffer some form of mistreatment annually. This means that the prevalence of elder mistreatment rivals that of many common chronic 'organic' medical conditions.

We are also beginning to accumulate data on the distribution of harm types. In the United States, all the states have laws on elder abuse and Adult Protective Service (APS) agencies charged with investigation of suspected cases of abuse and management of substantiated cases. Tatara (1993) has analysed reports from the state APS agencies and found that slightly over half of the cases are self-neglect. The distribution of harm types in the other half of the cases was as follows: physical violence, 20 per cent of reported cases; psychological abuse, 13 per cent, sexual abuse, 0.6 per cent; financial abuse, 17 per cent; neglect by others, 46 per cent. Generalization from the APS data has been criticized as these represent only the cases which have come to official attention. It is thought that APS cases represent 'the tip of the iceberg' and that the there may be a different distribution of harm types (i.e. less violence) in the cases that go unreported. But even in Tatara's APS dataset 65 per cent of the cases involve either neglect or self-neglect. On the other side of the Atlantic, a small study by Ogg and Bennett (1992) in the United Kingdom found a 5 per cent incidence of verbal abuse, 2 per cent incidence of physical abuse, and 2 per cent incidence of financial abuse. These authors did not investigate the problem of neglect. While neglect and self-neglect are not as dramatic as 'granny bashing', they can result in equally poor outcomes for the victim. The high prevalence of neglect must be addressed by all those seeking to prevent, diagnose, and manage elder mistreatment. A wider United Kingdom perspective on abuse of older people has been provided by Bennett *et al.* (1997).

Proposed aetiologies of elder mistreatment

In order to address the problem of elder mistreatment it would be helpful to develop an aetiological framework. Sociologists have proposed a number of theories which are outlined in Table 2 (Lachs and Pillemer 1995). The theory of transgenerational violence suggests that if parents use violent ways of dealing with their children, the

Table 2 Proposed theories for the aetiology of elder mistreatment

Theory	Proposed risk factor
Symbolic interactionism	Caregiver stress
Situational theory	Victim isolation
Exchange theory	Dependency of the victim on the caregiver, and the caregiver on the victim
Social learning theory	Transgenerational violence
Psychoanalytic theory	Psychopathology in the victim or caregiver

Adapted from Lachs and Pillemer (1995).

children learn to use violence as a coping mechanism. The children may then employ violence against their parents when they are placed in the caregiving role. The caregiver psychopathology hypothesis suggests that elder mistreatment occurs when the caregiver has psychological or substance abuse problems. The caregiver dependency hypothesis posits that when caregivers are dependent on the older person, they may use mistreatment as an equalizing strategy. This may overlap with abuser psychopathology theories, as many adult children who remain dependent on their parents have psychological or substance abuse problems. The social isolation hypothesis suggests that older people without support networks are more easily victimized. Another theory that has received major attention in the literature is that of caregiver stress. This is an appealing model in terms of conceptualizing prevention and intervention.

A particularly clinically relevant framework had been provided by Fulmer and O'Malley (1987), who suggest viewing the problem of elder mistreatment as one of unmet needs of both the caregiver and the older person. This fits well with the paradigm of geriatric assessment and case management. Physicians may be more comfortable viewing the problem of elder mistreatment within a 'disease model', and feel more competent to deal with it than when the problem is cast as one of psychodynamic or psychopathological origin. This model also fits well with the fact that primary care physicians are often the gatekeepers for services, such as visiting nurses, home health aids, physical therapy, and referral to specialists, which are needed by elderly people and their caregivers. With the growth of the managed care paradigm, there will be increased emphasis on the physician's role as gatekeeper, and an increased need for physician awareness of patient and caregiver requirements and for physician advocacy to obtain the services needed to prevent and manage elder mistreatment.

Risk factors for elder mistreatment

The physician's ability to diagnose a problem is based on having a group of signs and symptoms associated with that specific problem and an awareness of characteristics that put patients at risk for it. Table 3 lists some of the risk factors for which physicians have been advised to check (Lachs and Pillemer 1995). There has been some effort to combine the various hypotheses of the aetiology of elder

mistreatment with patient profiles suggestive of high risk. Initially, it was thought that the typical victim was a frail older woman with mild cognitive impairment and moderate chronic disease burden. Further work has revealed the limitations of this stereotype and suggests that those most at risk are people who cohabit, since the most common perpetrators of mistreatment are spouses, children, and grandchildren. The roles of physical frailty and cognitive impairment have not yet been clarified. These problems may increase the risk of mistreatment, decrease the victim's ability to escape, or reflect the outcome of mistreatment—or all of the above. In truth, we do not have a robust identification of risk factors because there are probably different risk factors for different harm types and many older people are subjected to more than one type of mistreatment. To extend the disease model, elder mistreatment is probably many different 'diseases', each with different aetiological factors, which warrant different remedial strategies. The notion of a 'typical victim' should be abandoned because the problem of elder mistreatment crosses all socio-economic and cultural boundaries. Physicians must screen all older patients to determine whether they are being victimized or are self-neglecting.

Detection of mistreatment

Because there are no clear risk factor profiles, the clinician must rely more on screening techniques, recognition of signs, and elicitation of symptoms. Geriatricians frequently use screening instruments such as the Mini Mental Status Examination for cognitive status (Folstein et al. 1975), the Geriatric Depression Scale for affective status (Brink et al. 1982), and the Activities of Daily Living scale for functional status (Katz et al. 1963). Unfortunately for the clinician, while various research protocols have been developed for interviewing subjects to detect possible mistreatment, there is a notable absence of instruments geared for clinical use in detecting mistreatment in the office or hospital setting. Furthermore, it is still unclear what should serve as the gold standard for evaluating these protocols. The American Medical Association has suggested that physicians ask the questions listed in Table 4, but the efficacy of these questions has never been tested in comparison with research protocol interviews. There are a number of protocols which have been published for use in the emergency room setting (Jones 1990), but most of these are for use after case detection (i.e. the collection of information in a confirmed case) rather than for screening.

This means that the clinician must depend on his or her own skills and initiative. Maintaining a high index of suspicion is important, since the majority of cases will not be obvious. Rather, it will be up to the clinician to build a rapport with the patient and caregiver and to take the initiative in eliciting whether there are problems. Suggestions for taking a history are listed in Table 5. It is suggested that the clinician always speak to the patient and the caregiver separately. This is important if the older person is being mistreated but fears retaliation from the caregiver. It is also important to obtain the caregiver's version of what is happening, since with cognitively impaired or psychiatrically disturbed elders, their perception of the situation may not agree that that of others.

It is also important to observe the older person's affect. Is he or she anxious, depressed, withdrawn, or displaying mood liability? What are the characteristics of the interaction between the patient and the caregiver? Is

Table 3 Mechanisms for determining risk factors for elder mistreatment

Risk factor	Mechanism
Poor health and functional impairment in the elderly person	Disability reduces the elderly person's ability to seek help and defend him- or herself
Cognitive impairment in the elderly person	Aggression towards the caregiver and disruptive behaviour resulting from dementia may precipitate abuse. Higher rates of abuse have been found among patients with dementia
Substance abuse or mental illness on the part of the abuser	Abusers are likely to abuse alcohol or drugs and to have serious mental illness, which in turn leads to abusive behaviour
Dependence of the abuser on the victim	Abusers are very likely to depend on the victim financially, for housing, and in other areas. Abuse results from attempts by a relative (especially an adult child) to obtain resources from the elderly person
Shared living arrangement	Abuse is much less likely among elderly people living alone. A shared living situation provides greater opportunities for tension and conflict, which generally precede incidents of abuse
External factors causing stress	Stressful life events and continuing financial strain decrease the family's resistance and increase the likelihood of abuse
Social isolation	Elderly people with fewer social contacts are more likely to be victims. Isolation reduces the likelihood that abuse will be detected and stopped. In addition, social support can buffer the effects of stress
History of violence	Particularly among spouses, a history of violence in the relationship may predict abuse in later life

Adapted from Lachs and Pillemer (1995).

Table 4 American Medical Association screening questions

Has anyone at home ever hurt you?

Has anyone ever touched you without your consent?

Has anyone ever made you do things you did not want to do?

Has anyone taken anything that was yours without asking?

Has anyone ever scolded or threatened you?

Has you ever signed any documents you did not understand?

Are you afraid of anyone at home?

Are you alone a lot?

Has anyone ever failed to help you take care of yourself when you needed help?

Table 5 Checklist for screening for mistreatment

Watch for 'red flags' of missed appointments, 'doctor hopping', unexplained delays in seeking treatment, unexplained or repeated injuries

Always talk to the patient alone

Assess patient affect working for depression, anxiety, withdrawal, or confusion

Always take a careful sexual history

Ask the patient directly about mistreatment

Assess the quality of the interactions between the patient and the caregiver

Ask the caregiver if he or she is experiencing any problems in providing care

Assess the social support system

it warm and caring, or does the patient appear to be afraid of the caregiver? Is the caregiver indifferent, angry, overly concerned with treatment costs or unwilling to permit the physician to speak to the patient alone? These findings are suggestive of an underlying problem that needs further investigation. Other 'red flags' in the history include patterns of physician hopping, missed appointments, unexplained delays in seeking treatment, previous unexplained injuries, explanations of injury inconsistent with medical findings and reports of previous similar injuries. It is important that the physician always includes a sexual history in the routine questions. Assessment of the patient's social support system is also crucial. Lastly, the physician must be comfortable asking directly about mistreatment. Posing the questions in the course of a routine history, and framing the questions as inquiries into whether either the patient or the caregiver has unmet needs or is suffering from physical or emotional stress, is a non-judgemental and non-threatening way of tackling this difficult topic. Delineation of unmet needs can also help in the development of a care plan.

Physical examination

Signs to check for on physical examination are listed in Table 6. Trauma in the form of fractures, dislocations, lacerations, abrasions, burns, or bruises is usually quite obvious, although the clinician must make it a practice for the patient to be fully undressed to check for skin lesions. A pelvic examination to check for trauma in the genital area or the presence of sexually transmitted disease may be the only

Table 6 Physical findings in cases of abuse

Fractures or dislocations

Lacerations, abrasions, burns

Bruises (especially old and new bruises)

Sexually transmitted disease, or pain or bleeding in the genital area

Signs of overuse, underuse, or misuse of medications

Poor personal hygiene

Table 8 Developing a care plan

Is mistreatment occurring?

What type of mistreatment is it?

Has this happened before?

Has the patient received help for the problem previously?

Is the abuser present?

Is it safe for the patient to return home?

What services are necessary to ensure patient safety and meet victim and abuser needs?

What does the patient want to happen?

Is it necessary to report the case to the appropriate authority?

way to uncover a history of sexual abuse. The clinician must also be prepared to question the pathogenesis of any traumatic findings, rather than assuming that 'old people fall and break their hips'.

Less obvious signs which are suggestive of neglect include poor hygiene, malnutrition, dehydration, urine burns, decubiti, contractures, and faecal impaction (Table 7). Under- or overuse of medications can also suggest possible mistreatment.

Laboratory and radiological studies should be guided by the findings from the history and physical examination. In the United States, where elder abuse has been criminalized and physicians are mandated to report putative cases to APS agencies, laboratory and radiological tests have become a part of the formal documentation process. Clinicians are also encouraged to photograph findings consistent with abuse or neglect or to make elaborate sketches documenting their findings.

Care management

In the United States most states mandate that physicians report possible cases of elder mistreatment to APS agencies. Workers from these agencies then investigate and decide if mistreatment is taking place. If the evidence is substantiated, the worker must decide whether

Table 7 Physical findings in cases of neglect

Cachexia

Poor hygiene

Inappropriate dress

Mobility impairment

Sensory impairment

Absence of assistive devices (spectacles, hearing aid, teeth, cane or walker)

Communication impairment (sensory or cognitive barrier)

Debilitation

Decubiti

Urine burns

Contractures

Adapted from Fulmer and O'Malley (1987).

the victim is 'vulnerable' based on 'physical or cognitive impairment' and therefore unable to protect him- or herself from mistreatment. If this is the case, the agency then intervenes with an appropriate treatment plan.

In actuality, most APS agencies are understaffed and underfunded. Therefore investigations are often less than optimal. Less than half of referred cases are substantiated and deemed eligible for intervention, and agency resources for making interventions are often very limited due to budget and personnel constraints.

This means that physicians in the United States must be prepared to help all those patients who are not eligible for APS services and to supplement APS efforts for the patients who can receive APS assistance. In the United Kingdom and other countries without mandatory reporting and formal APS agencies there is an even greater need for the physician to know how to manage cases of elder mistreatment. Key points for care assessment are listed in Table 8. It is important to determine if the problem is an isolated incident or a long-standing problem. How serious are the consequences of the mistreatment? Is it safe for the mistreated older person to return to the same setting? What does the patient think and what does he or she want to happen? If the patient is competent, than it is up to him or her to decide what to do. For example, an older woman may choose to return to an abusive husband, especially if the marriage has always been abusive. However, it is clearly incumbent on the physician to provide the patient with alternative choices. If the patient is incompetent, the physician must intervene to protect him or her.

The non-abusing caregiver of the elderly abuse victim may also require supportive services. The psychological impact of witnessing family violence in all its forms is established; in so far as elder mistreatment can be linked to chronic disease, the caregiver of the older adult with any chronic disease is at risk. Here, too, support groups and other carefully tailored interventions may be helpful.

To do this, the physician must know about the patient's social and financial support system, what resources are available in the community and how to access them, and how to use the legal system to gain protection for the patient when necessary. For many physicians this will mean acquiring expertise in areas often considered to be the province of social work or other disciplines. This effort will pay off not only in organizing care for mistreated older patients but also in caring for all frail older persons who may need similar services. If caregiver stress is truly a contributor to elder mistreatment, then thorough assessment and care management that meets the patient's and caregiver's needs may have a major role in primary prevention of elder mistreatment.

Ethical issues for the physician

No physician can regard elder mistreatment as acceptable. Nevertheless, dealing with elder mistreatment can raise a number of ethical issues for the physician. Physicians are taught to maintain patient confidentiality. Mandatory reporting laws override traditional concepts of doctor–patient confidentiality. Doctors are also taught to respect and maintain patient autonomy. Again, mandatory reporting laws require that all possible cases of elder mistreatment be reported to the authorities. It is role of the APS, not the physician, to decide if the patient is competent, and therefore has the right to choose to remain in an abusive situation, or incompetent, and therefore compelled to accept assistance. In the absence of mandatory reporting, doctors still cannot impose their own value systems to intervene 'to help' competent patients they deem to be mistreated. Yet another issue for physicians is the dictum *primum non nocere*. It may seem extremely difficult to address possible elder mistreatment and still maintain a relationship with the patient and caregiver so that they will continue to come to the physician for services. It is also essential that the physician's intervention be carried out in a way that does not place the victim at increased risk by upsetting or angering the caregiver. This may be particularly tricky when mandatory reporting laws force the physician to hand the case over to an agency whose workers may be undertrained and overloaded and who lack the resources needed to remedy the situation. It will be an ongoing challenge for physicians to care for mistreated patients effectively and to maintain traditional medical ethical values while meeting legislatively imposed societal imperatives.

Roles for the physician

This chapter has focused on the role of the physician in the diagnosis and management of elder mistreatment, but physicians potentially have roles to play in other areas as well. There is a great need for physician participation in research. Only with physician participation in the research process will data be generated that are directly applicable to medical practice. Physicians also have a role in teaching about elder mistreatment both within the medical community and in the community at large. Studies have shown that physician knowledge about elder mistreatment is at best limited (Blakely and Dolan 1991). We must raise the level of consciousness about the problem as well as the level of expertise in its recognition and management. Physicians can play a role in prevention of elder mistreatment. Although we still lack formal research data, it is intuitively obvious that the frailest old people are at risk for mistreatment and are probably the least able to escape it. A full geriatric assessment of cognitive, affective, functional, and social status may help to identify those patients potentially at risk. Putting in place those services needed to maximize the older person's autonomy and minimize caregiver stress may

significantly reduce the risk of elder mistreatment in the community setting. In the chronic care setting, physicians have the opportunity, as nursing home directors and care providers, to educate staff and to initiate quality assurance programmes that will reduce the likelihood of elder mistreatment. Lastly, physicians can be advocates for their older patients. Only through active advocacy will we achieve the funding needed for further research into this complex problem and to create the programmes and services needed for prevention and treatment of elder mistreatment.

References

American Medical Association (1992). *Diagnostic and treatment guidelines on elder abuse and neglect.* Chicago, IL.

Bennett, G., Kingston, P., and Penhale, B. (1997). *The dimensions of elder abuse.* Macmillan, London.

Blakely, B.E. and Dolan, R. (1991). The relative contributions of occupation groups in the discovery and treatment of elder abuse and neglect. *Journal of Gerontological Social Work*, 17, 183–99.

Brink, T.L., Yesavage, J.A., Lum, O., Heersema, P., Adey, M., and Rose, T.L. (1982). Screening tests for geriatric depression. *Clinical Gerontologist*, 1, 37–43.

Burston, G.R. (1975). Granny-battering. *British Medical Journal*, 3, 592.

Folstein, M.F., Folstein, S.E., and McHugh, P.R. (1975). 'Mini-Mental State': a practical method for grading the cognitive state of patients for the clinician. *Journal of Psychiatric Research*, 12, 189–98.

Fulmer, T.T. and O'Malley, T.A. (1987). *Inadequate care of the elderly: a health care perspective on abuse and neglect.* Springer, New York.

Jones, J.S. (1990). Geriatric abuse and neglect. In *Geriatric emergency medicine* (ed. G. Bosker, G.R. Schwartz, J.S. Jones, and M. Sequeira), pp. 533–42. C.V. Mosby, St. Louis, MO.

Katz, S., Ford, A.B., Moskowitz, R.W., Jackson, B.A., and Jaffe, M.W. (1963). Studies of illness in the aged. The index of ADL: a standardized measure of biological and psychosocial function. *Journal of the American Medical Association*, 185, 914–19.

Kinston, P., Penhale, B., and Bennett, G. (1995). Is elder abuse on the curriculum? The relative contribution of child abuse, domestic violence, and elder abuse in social work, nursing, and medicine qualifying curricula. *Health and Social Care in the Community*, 3, 353–63.

Kosberg, J.I. and Garcia, J.L. (ed.) (1995). *Elder abuse—international and cross-cultural perspectives.* Haworth Press, Binghamton, NY.

Lachs, M.S. and Pillemer, K. (1995). Current concepts: abuse and neglect of elderly persons. *New England Journal of Medicine*, 332, 437–43.

McCreadie, C., Bennett, G., and Tinker, A. (1998). General practitioners' knowledge and experience of the abuse of older people in the community: report of an exploratory research study in the inner London borough of Tower Hamlets. *British Journal of General Practice*, 48, 1687–8.

Ogg, J. and Bennet, G. (1992). Elder abuse in Britain. *British Medical Journal*, 305, 988–9.

Tatara, T. (1993). Understanding the nature and scope of domestic elder abuse with the use of state aggregate data: summaries of key findings of a national survey of state APS and ageing agencies. *Journal of Elder Abuse and Neglect*, 5, 35–57.

Wolfe, R.S. (1988). Elder abuse: ten years later. *Journal of the American Geriatrics Society*, 36, 758–62.

26.3 Failure to thrive

B. Lynn Beattie and Jason Francoeur

In his 1914 textbook on geriatrics, Nascher described Grawitz's cachexia as 'a fatal cachexia without discernible anatomical cause' (Nascher 1979). The introduction to Nascher's early book on geriatrics was written by the paediatrician Jacobi, and he indicated the need to acknowledge geriatrics as a specialty: 'the study of advanced age will enhance the competency of the doctor to the same degree to which it was advanced by the closer knowledge of the physiology and pathology of the infant and child' (Nascher 1979). In Hodkinson (1973), in a paper on non-specific presentation of illness in old age, borrowed the term 'failure to thrive' from paediatrics and described how illness in the aged often presented as insidious and progressive with loss of appetite, weight loss, diminishing social competence, and a decline of initiative, concentration, and drive. There has been increasing attention to describing failure to thrive and some insight into pathogenesis (Verdery 1997) but a full understanding remains elusive. Is failure to thrive a syndrome or is it a marker for dysfunction or increasing dependence? Is failure to thrive in elderly people a stimulus for further evaluation or a negative term provoking indifference? Is it a term for clinical medicine or one that should be reserved for research?

Definitions

Frailty has been defined as a dynamic concept for elderly people, with more frail elderly people being more vulnerable to circumstances making them more functionally dependent. Frail elderly people are those in whom the assets maintaining health and the deficits threatening health are in precarious balance (Rockwood *et al.* 1994). It is generally assumed that failure to thrive is a phenomenon more likely to occur in frail elderly people who are at extreme risk for dependency.

Failure to thrive may be considered a syndrome presenting in a frail elderly person with weight loss, decreased appetite, and increasing dependence in the activities of daily living where the underlying reason for this change is not obvious. The *International Classification of Diseases, Ninth Revision* (ICD-9) (WHO 1979) describes 'senility without mention of psychosis' as the condition of physical and mental deterioration associated with old age, and uses synonyms such as old age, senescence, senile asthenia, senile debility, and/or exhaustion. The proposed coding for ICD-10 (R54) is similar (WHO 1992). In these coding systems, the term failure to thrive (ICD-9 783.4) applies to paediatrics, although in some jurisdictions it is applied to elderly people (Verdery 1996). This should provoke, not prevent, a systematic approach to the components of the disorder in the aged. The elderly person may be at home in the community (often living alone), in the acute care hospital emergency department, or at various assessment venues including the doctor's office, outpatient clinics, or geriatric day hospitals. Generally these individuals are not recognized as being acutely ill but are seen as 'bed blockers' in acute care, nuisance patients in the acute care emergency room, or difficult patients in community settings because the presentation is non-specific, for both the patient and the assessor. The astute health-care worker or family member may observe that over time the individual seems to 'dwindle', is 'off her feet', or just not doing as well as she used to do. There may be identified trigger events (Verdery 1995) such as hip fracture or pneumonia. In a number of circumstances, after assessment, the underlying reason for the deterioration in function may be understood, for example when a diagnosis of infection is made (Norman *et al.* 1996). In other circumstances, despite assessment, no specific diagnosis/diagnoses are made and the deterioration continues with subtle evolution from the failure to thrive state to the pre-death state (Isaacs *et al.* 1971) and, ultimately, death.

There is an interest in failure to thrive in the medical and nursing literature. In a study on peritoneal dialysis in elderly people (Suh *et al.* 1993) failure to thrive in one elderly person was the reason for transfer from peritoneal dialysis to inpatient haemodialysis. In the medical literature there are attempts to elucidate the definition, pathophysiology, and management of the patient with failure to thrive although there are few prospective studies (Katz *et al.* 1993; Fox *et al.* 1996). In the nursing literature, there is a clear attempt to understand the concept, origin, and nursing care roles in failure to thrive. Table 1 summarizes the basis for the definitions of failure to thrive and the working definitions used by various authors.

Incidence and prevalence

The incidence and prevalence of failure to thrive are uncertain since there is variability of the definition and multiple factors to consider. Verdery (1995) suggested that it is important to distinguish between frailty (the risk of deterioration), failure to thrive (the process of deterioration), and pre-death. Longitudinal evaluation may help to distinguish them, though the time taken for this varies substantially.

Fox *et al.* (1996) reviewed the prevalence of failure to thrive and noted it to be common in older institutionalized people and those in hospital. Again, the definition is important. It may be 1 per cent as an annotated diagnosis in a Massachusetts hospital or up to 35 to

Table 1 Summary of literature on failure to thrive with basis for definition and working definition of the syndrome

Author	Basis for definition	Failure to thrive definition
Hodkinson (1973)	Used the paediatric term failure to thrive to describe insidious and progressive physical deterioration in older people	Decline comprises deteriorating social competence, weight loss, loss of appetite, increasing frailty, and diminishing initiative, concentration, and drive
Messert et al. (1976)	Clinical observation and related case reports in people with central nervous system disorders at age range 24–67 years to describe adult failure to thrive. Autopsy information was available in some cases but neuropathological correlation with clinical features was elusive	Clinical course with the following features: irreversible relentless weight loss refractory to a high caloric intake; wide temperature swings, both above and below normal, unrelated to the presence or absence of infection; decrease in the level of consciousness; rapid onset of decubitus ulcerations not usually seen in a good nursing setting; sudden death
O'Malley et al. (1983)	Unexplained trauma, neglected medical problems, failure to thrive, malnutrition, and misuse of medications	A component of abuse and neglect of elderly people
Braun et al. (1988)	Literature review and derivation of concept from paediatric experience	Physical and psychosocial atrophy: a broad-symptom complex originating, perhaps, from varied physiological, psychological, or combined sources where the older person loses weight, declines in physical and cognitive function, and often exhibits signs of hopelessness and helplessness
Berkman et al. (1989)	Acute care descriptive study, retrospective chart review of 85 patients over 65 years of age admitted with a diagnosis of failure to thrive (out of 11 000 admissions) (14 cases of failure to thrive were <65 years of age and admitted during the same period but excluded)	A diagnosis used when the elderly patient's functional ability to live with multisystem diseases, cope with the ensuing problems, and manage his or her care are remarkably diminished and no longer responsive to medical and non-medical interventions. There is a tolerance or threshold level for the failure to thrive diagnosis
Palmer (1990)	Case report and literature review	A gradual decline in physical and/or cognitive function of an elderly patient, usually accompanied by weight loss, reduced appetite, and social withdrawal that occurs without immediate explanation
Lonergan (1991)	Part of a national research agenda on ageing	Syndrome of weight loss, decreased appetite, poor nutrition, and inactivity, often accompanied by dehydration, depressive symptoms, impaired immune function, and low cholesterol
Newbern (1992)	Review in conceptual context of failure to thrive in infants and related syndrome in elderly people	Decline in cognitive and physical function, consistent unplanned weight loss, inadequate nutritional intake, signs of depression, giving up or taking to bed, and helplessness
Egbert (1993a, b)	Case example, literature review, and concept discussion. May also be the manifestation of alcoholism in the older patient	Functional decline in elderly people as a non-specific symptom of physical, psychological, or social dysfunction; suggests this is a clinical clue to dysfunction in any of several domains rather than a specific syndrome
Groom (1993)	Literature review and diagnostic model for failure to thrive	Proposed a three-dimensional model of failure to thrive based on depression, delirium, dementia, and malnourishment presuming there are interactive physical, predisposing, and psychosocial factors
Katz et al. (1993)	Prospective longitudinal study of elderly individuals living in a nursing home and a resident congregate apartment facility; mean age 84.12 years and mean length of residence 30.8 ($\pm$42.4) months	Incorporated Braun et al. (1988) concept and measurable variables such as physical deterioration, disability, cognitive decline, depression, and undernutrition. Concluded that hypoalbuminaemia and anaemia were associated with decreased survival and disability, cognitive impairment, depression, and summary measures of disease

[cont.]

Table 1 *Continued*

Author	Basis for definition	Failure to thrive definition
Osato *et al.* (1993)	Retrospective chart review of 62 patients admitted with a diagnosis of failure to thrive and 2-year follow-up at two California medical centres; mean age 71 years, but range from 37 to 104 years (26% <65 years)	Failure to thrive described the acutely ill patients with numerous hospital admissions in which diagnosis had been established and treatment options were limited to 'care' rather than 'cure' (patients with AIDS, cancer). Subgroup of people over 80 were more independent in ADL<IADL with lower death rate than those with AIDS, cancer
Newbern and Krowchuk (1994)	Conceptual analysis as it applies to nursing practice using the interactionist model including case examples bringing antecedent behaviours, including those from birth and childhood, to the failure to thrive concept in older individuals	Failure in the human–environmental interaction including social relatedness (disconnectedness, inability to give of oneself, inability to find meaning in life, inability to attach to others) and physical/cognitive dysfunction (consistent unplanned weight loss, decline in cognitive function, signs of depression)
Verdery (1995)	Literature review and evaluation of the concept	The progressive loss of function that occurs in frail people, leading to cachexia and death. A process marked by loss of weight, strength, and the ability to perform personal and IADLs
Kimball and Williams-Burgess (1995)	Case studies and review of assessment, intervention, and implications for (psychiatric) nursing emphasizing psychosocial issues	Complex of non-specific symptoms that often leads to increased disability and premature death
Fox *et al.* (1996)	Prospective study of patients admitted to acute care with hip fracture followed for 24 months after fracture. There were 252 patients who survived 1 year and had a self-report assessment at 6 and 12 months	A decline in walking ability from 6 to 12 months after the fracture after some recovery of mobility had been obtained
Sarkisian and Lachs (1996)	Review of concept and recommended a measurement-oriented approach	Four contributing domains: impaired physical functioning, malnutrition, depression, and dementia for systematic evaluation
Verdery (1997)	Background questions related to understanding and managing failure to thrive to determine if it is due to starvation, undiagnosed disease, or underlying process uniquely associated with ageing	A syndrome related to classical nutritional abnormalities including nutritional marasmus, hypoalbuminaemia, inflammation-associated malnutrition and immune activation, the physiological stress response, involutional changes in anabolic hormones, and the chronic–acute phase response

ADL, activities of daily living; IADL, instrumental activities of daily living.

50 per cent of medical-surgical patients if malnutrition and weight loss are used as markers.

Recognizing failure to thrive and the predisposing factors

Palmer (1990) suggested that there were age-associated and socio-demographic factors predisposing elderly people to failure to thrive. The most common are dementia, depression, delirium, drug reactions, and a few chronic diseases.

Fox *et al.* (1996) described markers of failure to thrive among older hip fracture patients. For their study they prospectively reviewed patients who were living in the community and subsequently admitted to hospital for hip fracture. Follow-up was to 24 months after the fracture. They argued that hip fracture could impose immobility and deconditioning that could put elderly patients at risk for failure to thrive. There were 252 subjects in their study. These had survived to 24 months and the decliners were defined as those with decreased ability to walk one city block (approximately 150 m) from 6 to 12 months after the fracture. There were no differences in admission characteristics between the groups of decliners and non-decliners from 6 to 12 months after the fracture though there was a tendency for those who declined to be slightly older, weigh less, and more likely to be female and living alone than those who did not decline in walking ability. Their decliners had poorer functioning throughout the 24 months, had more cognitive impairment, and increased health-care utilization as they declined further. The authors suggested markers for decline included impaired function in physical activities of daily living at 6 months after the fracture, high glucose, calcium, and carbon dioxide at admission, low blood urea nitrogen, serum

Table 2 Categories for failure to thrive including diagnoses and problems which may be detected in the investigation leading to appropriately directed interventions

---

Previously unrecognized disease
Malignancy
Chronic infection, e.g. tuberculosis
Use of multiple medications (prescribed, borrowed, over the counter)
Alcoholism

(New) illness with related functional disability
Stroke
Arthritis
Heart failure
Impaired senses, deafness, blindness

Mental illness
Depression
Dementia
Other psychiatric disorders

Social status
Isolation
Poverty
Abuse and neglect
Loss of, or burden for, caregiving spouse, relative, or friend

Dying
The biological clock is slowly stopping
Pre-death and death

Table 3 Triggers or markers for failure to thrive

Falls and fractures
Social circumstances such as loss of a spouse or other loved one(s)
Diseases including chronic obstructive lung disease, heart failure, cancer, diabetes, infections
Delirium
Alcohol and substance abuse
Drug effects and side-effects including over/undercompliance
Neurological disorders such as Parkinson's disease
Sensory deficits including impaired hearing, impaired vision
Abuse and neglect
Repeated hospital admission
Institutionalization

These markers may lead the clinician to review the care plan and the approach to investigation and treatment.

glutamate pyruvate transaminase, and creatinine at hospital admission as well as arthroplasty repair.

Causes of failure to thrive

There are five main categories for failure to thrive including previously unrecognized disease, relatively new illness with related functional disability, mental illness, social status, and dying (Table 2). In each category there are specific problems which may be ascertained and lead to specific interventions.

Presenting features

In failure to thrive there appears to be a downward spiral of deterioration and the challenge is to identify remediable factors. Components include anorexia, weight loss, malnutrition, depression, cognitive dysfunction, social withdrawal, isolation, giving up, and, ultimately, death. Depending on the underlying problems and physiological status in terms of nutrition, immunocompetence, and endocrine and metabolic factors, it may or may not be possible to stop the decline. If a non-skin malignancy is identified for which there is no specific treatment, palliative care is indicated. Katz *et al.* (1993) observed that depressed individuals in residential care who had hypoalbuminaemia and self-care disability (markers of failure to thrive) were less likely to respond to nortriptyline therapy. It was considered this was possibly an effect of undernutrition or related stresses from chronic illness and self-care deficits.

In frail elderly people, there may be triggers or markers for failure to thrive, or these markers may occur (and even be more likely to occur) in individuals experiencing the process of failure to thrive. These are included in Table 3.

Thus failure to thrive is a complex situation in elderly people, with many factors contributing over time and potential triggers or markers along the way. Understanding the markers may lead to definitive interventions which may alter the patient's course and lead to more appropriate care.

Diagnosis

The diagnosis of failure to thrive at this stage in our understanding is probably related to the information and education of the health professional seeing the elderly individual. The recognition of anorexia and weight loss together with deterioration in functional capacity in a frail elderly individual would raise awareness. If the elderly person has fallen or has presented in acute care, the diagnostic label may be fall, fracture, or weight loss, not failure to thrive. Katz *et al.* (1993) have suggested that failure to thrive may be more relevant as a research concept than as a clinical diagnosis and effective problem solving for the patient may be aimed at close dissection and management of the specific components of the syndrome. In this vein Sarkisian and Lachs (1996) suggest abandoning failure to thrive as a diagnostic term and focusing on understanding and measuring the components of the disorder and instituting rational appropriate interventions for remediable problems.

The term failure to thrive may have negative connotations and its use may be discouraged as a diagnosis (Berkman *et al.* 1989) in order to avoid reinforcing negative stereotypes about the frail elderly. Conversely, in some venues such as the nursing home, recognition of insidious change in status by nursing personnel may be very helpful in triggering evaluation and establishing a more suitable care plan. Furthermore, acknowledging failure to thrive may stimulate systematic intervention and evaluation of a critical path in the care of elderly people.

Management

The availability of a skilled geriatric team may be very helpful in the management of failure to thrive and its many components. Interventions may be targeted to nutrition, swallowing, physiotherapy, socialization, self-care deficits, and vigorous treatment of depression. Clearly, diagnostic assessment and directed medical treatment is fundamental to the treatment plan. Ongoing follow-up is critical and team meetings may be required including family members to assess progress and also to ascertain when death is imminent and palliative care is appropriate.

Fiatarone et al. (1990), using the premise that muscle dysfunction and associated mobility impairment increase the risk of falls, fractures, and functional dependency showed that high-resistance weight training leads to significant gains in muscle strength, size, and functional mobility in frail residents of nursing homes up to 96 years of age. Sloan et al. (1992) designed a randomized placebo-controlled trial of nandrolone in elderly patients with hip fractures and although it was safe at the doses given, it was of minimal benefit. Strategies such as these and others need to be explored further to provide interventions particularly targeted with known trigger events (Table 3).

Social policy issues

Serious consideration about failure to thrive as a valid clinical syndrome is required. The definition is evolving and the information available about the components including weight loss, impaired function, and death is available but the population described to date with failure to thrive is heterogeneous. Perhaps at this time it is sufficient to acknowledge that there is a permanent group of patients with impaired nutrition, decreased appetite, and weight loss with functional deterioration and contributing psychosocial factors. Ascertaining these patients and active evaluation of their status may reveal remediable elements. Sarkisian and Lachs (1996) suggest that there are often multiple contributors at work some of which are unmodifiable, some easily modifiable, and some potentially modifiable but only with the use of resource-intensive strategies. There are ethical, policy, or resource issues to consider. The data are as yet unavailable to help in the understanding of the components and predict outcome when failure to thrive is diagnosed.

Research

The definition of failure to thrive, its course, and its outcome are poorly understood. This is a ripe area for further research (Verdery 1996, 1997). In the meantime, astute clinical evaluation and management of frail elderly people with change in their functional status remains imperative. As Nascher has argued, recovery from new diseases is affected by the tissue changes due to previous accidents or ailments: 'there are few people of advanced years without a permanent blemish—one or many—which make the diagnosis of any additional illness or morbid condition more difficult, treatment more uncertain, and complete recovery more doubtful' (Nascher 1979, p. xviii).

References

Berkman, B., Foster, L.W.S., and Campion, E. (1989). Failure to thrive: paradigm for the frail elder. *Gerontologist*, 29, 654–9.

Braun, J.V., Wykle, M.H., and Cowling, W.R. (1988). Failure to thrive in older persons: a concept derived. *Gerontologist*, 28, 809–12.

Egbert, A.M. (1993a). 'The dwindles'. Failure to thrive in older patients. *Postgraduate Medicine*, 94, 199–212.

Egbert, A.M. (1993b). The older alcoholic: recognising the subtle clinical clues. *Geriatrics*, 48, 63–9.

Fiatarone, M., Marks, E.C., Ryan, N.D., et al. (1990). High-intensity strength training in nonagenarians. *Journal of the American Medical Association*, 263, 3029–34.

Fox, K.M., Hawkes, W.G., Magaziner, J., Zimmerman, S.I., and Hebel, J.R. (1996). Markers of failure to thrive among older hip fracture patients. *Journal of the American Geriatrics Society*, 44, 371–6.

Groom, D.D. (1993). A diagnostic model for failure to thrive in the elderly. *Journal of Gerontological Nursing*, 19, 12–16.

Hodkinson, H.M. (1973). Medicine in old age—non-specific presentation of illness. *British Medical Journal*, 4, 94–6.

Isaacs, B., Gunn, J., McKechan, A., McMillan, I., and Neville, Y. (1971). The concept of pre-death. *Lancet*, 709, 1115–19.

Katz, I.R., Beaston-Wimmer, P., Parmelee, P., Friedman, E., and Lawton, P. (1993). Failure to thrive in the elderly: exploration of the concept and delineation of psychiatric components. *Journal of Geriatric Psychiatry and Neurology*, 6, 161–9.

Kimball, M.J. and Williams-Burgess, C. (1995). Failure to thrive: the silent epidemic of the elderly. *Archives of Psychiatric Nursing*, 9, 99–105.

Lonergan E.T. (ed.) (1991). *Extending life, enhancing life. A national research agenda on aging*. National Academy Press, Washington, DC.

Messert B., Kurlanzik, A.E., and Thorning D.R. (1976). Adult 'failure-to-thrive' syndrome. *Journal of Nervous and Mental Disease*, 162, 401–9.

Nascher, I.L. (1979). *Geriatrics: the diseases of old age and their treatment*. Arno Press, New York. (First published 1914.)

Newbern V.B. (1992). Failure to thrive: a growing concern in the elderly. *Journal of Gerontological Nursing*, 18, 21–5.

Newbern, V.B. and Krowchuk, H.V. (1994). Failure to thrive in elderly people: a conceptual analysis. *Journal of Advanced Nursing*, 19, 840–9.

Norman, D.C. and Yoshikawa, T.T. (1996). Fever in the elderly. *Infectious Disease Clinics of North America*, 10, 93–9.

O'Malley, T.A., Everitt, D.E., O'Malley, H.C., and Campion, E.W. (1983). Identifying and preventing family-mediated abuse and neglect of elderly persons. *Annals of Internal Medicine*, 98, 998–1005.

Osato, E.E., Stone, J., Takano, P., Steven, L., and Winne, D.M. (1993). Failure to thrive in the elderly. *Journal of Gerontological Nursing*, 19, 28–34.

Palmer, R.M. (1990). 'Failure to thrive' in the elderly: diagnosis and management. *Geriatrics*, 45, 47–55.

Rockwood, K., Fox, R.A., Stolee, P., Robertson, D., and Beattie, B.L. (1994). Frailty in elderly people: an evolving concept. *Canadian Medical Association Journal*, 150, 489–95.

Sarkisian, C.A. and Lachs, M.S. (1996). 'Failure to thrive' in older adults. *Annals of Internal Medicine*, 124, 1072–8.

Sloan, J.P., Wing, P., Dian, L., and Meneilly, G. (1992). A pilot study of anabolic steroids in elderly patients with hip fractures. *Journal of the American Geriatrics Society*, 40, 1105–11.

Suh, H., Wadhwa, N.K., Cabralda, T., Dolamu, S., and Solomon, M. (1993). Peritoneal dialysis in elderly end-stage renal disease patients. *Advances in Peritoneal Dialysis*, 9, 134–7.

Verdery, R.B. (1995). Failure to thrive in the elderly. *Clinics in Geriatric Medicine*, 11, 653–9.

Verdery, R.B. (1996). Failure to thrive in older people. *Journal of the American Geriatrics Society*, **44**, 465–6.

Verdery, R.B. (1997). Failure to thrive in old age: follow-up on a workshop. *Journal of Gerontology: Medical Sciences*, **52A**, M333–6.

WHO (World Health Organization) (1979). *International classification of diseases, ninth revision*. WHO, Geneva.

WHO (World Health Organization) (1992). *International classification of diseases and related health problems, tenth revision*. WHO, Geneva.

26.4 Consequences of immobility

W. O. Seiler

Introduction

Immobility and related complications of patients in nursing homes and acute hospitals are major problems with profound health-care and financial implications. The most common risk factors associated with immobility are contractures, severe dementia, osteoporosis, pressure ulcers, poor vision, and history of hip and leg fractures (Selikson *et al*. 1988). The chronically ill, aged, and disabled populations are particularly susceptible to complications of prolonged bed rest, immobilization, and inactivity (Bonner 1969). Initially, immobility impairs the functional capacity in a single organ and later causes a wide range of organ complications and metabolic changes (Table 1). This chapter reviews some of the most common complications of immobility in elderly people.

Causes of immobility

Any illness and condition in aged people can cause immobility (Table 2). Degenerative joint diseases and social isolation are the most common risk factors that lead to immobility in elderly community-dwelling populations. Depression, fear of falling, lack of appropriate aids, alcohol, blurred vision, and self-ordered wheelchair use also contribute to impairment of mobility.

Dementia, cerebrovascular diseases, drugs, and inappropriate restriction to bed are the leading causes of immobility in acute care hospitals and nursing homes. Prevention and remobilization solely are feasible when the cause of immobility is apparent.

Drug-induced impairment of mobility is very frequent and often not identified. Therefore, careful regular control of the medication of each patient is mandatory.

Consequences and prevention of immobility

Inactivity and bed rest produce a variety of alterations in several organ systems and in metabolic functions (Tables 1 and 3).

Pathophysiological changes occur during immobility in both healthy and ill people. Even a normal healthy person with prolonged immobilization will develop complications including wasting of the musculature, osteoporosis, negative nitrogen balance, constipation, weakness, and psychological alterations. Elderly patients with few organ reserves and with pre-existing multimorbidity or a decline of cognitive functions will develop these complications at a faster rate. In addition, when functional capacity decreases and mobility reaches a low level, new complications appear and the vicious circle of inactivity begins.

Muscle wasting

The normal physiological mechanisms during standing in an erect position increase the energy expenditure by more than 20 per cent over that seen during bed rest. The metabolic rate of muscle may surpass up to 50 or 100 times that at rest during physical activity or locomotion (Greenleaf and Kozlowski 1983). The resulting cardio-pulmonary response leads to a 20-fold increase in muscle blood circulation.

In the supine position pathophysiological mechanisms significantly decrease blood supply to the musculature. In addition, trophic muscle stimulation by the nervous system decreases. Additional factors that cause muscle atrophy include biological changes of ageing in itself, the accumulation of acute and chronic diseases, and malnutrition.

The histological changes of the musculature after prolonged immobilization reveal muscle fibre degeneration and an increase in fat and fibrous tissue (Booth and Gollnick 1983). Muscle mass shrinks to half the initial size after 2 months of complete inactivity. Muscle mass mostly decreases from the lower limb and trunk muscles. Inactivity triggers a negative nitrogen balance resulting in an increased urinary nitrogen elimination.

The result of prolonged bed rest and malnutrition is profound muscle atrophy with significant decrease in muscle strength and size. Muscle weakness in immobilized elderly people is prevalent and morbid, and closely linked to frailty, to functional decline, and to additional immobility, falls, and injuries.

Table 1 Metabolic changes during bed rest compared with normal physical activity

Organ, hormones	Metabolic changes during prolonged bed rest
Muscle wasting[a]	50- to 100-fold decrease of the metabolic rate Decreased cardiopulmonary response 20-fold decrease in muscle blood supply Longer accumulation of lactic acid
Bone resorption[b]	Bone loss: initial rapid loss and equally rapid reversal Bone loss after 12 weeks: slower loss and reversal Hypercalcaemia starts in the 4th week in young subjects Calcium level normal in elderly subjects
Skin[c]	Pressure-induced localized ischaemia Pressure-induced localized lactic acid accumulation Ischaemic skin necrosis, pressure ulcer
Nitrogen[a]	Urinary excretion increased to 2.0 mg daily Reconditioning: 1 week of retraining needed Contribution to hypoproteinaemia
Antidiuretic hormone[d]	Decreased secretion Increased diuresis; urinary incontinence Weight loss
Cortisol[e]	Increased urinary excretion Contribution to catabolism
Androgen hormones[f]	Decreased levels Contribution to catabolism
Carbohydrates[g]	Increased intolerance during entire bed rest period Contribution to hyperglycaemia

[a] Data from Greenleaf and Kozlowski (1983); [b] data from Donaldson et al. (1970); [c] data from Seiler and Stähelin (1985); [d] data from Halar and Bell (1990); [e] data from Melada et al. (1975); [f] data from Cockett et al. (1970); [g] data from Wirth et al. (1981).

Table 2 Cause and risk factor of immobility in elderly people

Cognition impairment and sensory factors
Dementia of any degree
Delirium
Impaired vision

Drug effects and side-effects
Drug-induced postural hypotension (i.e. tricyclic antidepressants)
Drug-induced sedation (e.g. hypnotics, tranquillizers, opiates)
Drug-induced extrapyramidal effects (e.g. antipsychotics)
Drug-induced ataxia (any drugs with central anticholinergic effects)
Drug-induced blurred vision (any drugs with central anticholinergic effects)
Drug combinations (e.g. tricyclic antidepressants with tranquillizers)

Central nervous system
Cerebrovascular diseases
Cerebellar dysfunction
Parkinson's disease
Multiple sclerosis
Paraplegia
Neuropathies

Metabolism
Severe obesity
Failure to thrive, catabolic state
Hypothyroidism
Malnutrition
Specific deficiencies (e.g. vitamin B_{12}, folic acid, zinc)
Cachexia
Widespread malignancy

Musculature, joint, and skeleton
Disuse muscle weakness
Arthritis, acute and chronic
Degenerative joint disease
Osteoporosis
Fractures
Polymyalgia rheumatica
Osteoporosis

Heart, lung, and circulation
Any severe systemic illness
Chronic obstructive lung disease
Severe heart failure
Chronic coronary heart disease
Peripheral vascular disease

Psychological and social factors
Depression
Isolation
Fear of falling
Pain of any localization
Anxiety states
Forced immobilization (restraint use)

Other factors
Alcohol
General weakness after prolonged bed rest
Severe illness of any type

Prevention and treatment of immobility includes shortening the periods of immobility and inactivity, and lowering severity and frequency of complications. Although prevention of immobility is not always possible in elderly patients, early recognition of complications and routine institution of preventive measures minimize these complications. Even small improvements in mobility reduce the number and severity of complications. The best treatment of disuse muscle atrophy and weakness is early prevention. Regular positioning and turning is always feasible, even in the most immobile patients. Efficient preventive measures include therapeutic exercises in patients lying in bed, early mobilization out of bed, transfer to the chair, and finally functional training. A 30 per cent daily muscle contraction of its maximal strength will maintain muscle strength. In addition, appropriate interventions reverse inactivity and malnutrition at least partially. Similarly, appropriate modality of physical activity and nutritional support that have positive effects on muscle physiology is to be considered on an individual basis.

Joint and muscle contractures

Up to 50 per cent of very disabled elderly people present at least one contracted joint. The prevalence of joint contractures is very high and results in functional impairment. Those patients with upper limb contractures are nearly twice as likely to be unable to feed themselves as those without contractures. The presence of at least one lower

Table 3 Common consequences of prolonged bed rest in elderly people

---

Psychological and social impairments
Isolation, loneliness
Depression
Delirium
Dementia
Sensory deprivation

Musculoskeletal system
Muscle wasting
Contractures
Muscle pain
Bone resorption, osteoporosis
Skeletal pain

Metabolic impairments
Nitrogen loss, weight loss
Catabolism
Decreased glucose tolerance
Elevated cortisol levels
Decreased plasma volume

Gastrointestinal tract
Constipation, faecal impaction
Anorexia, weight loss

Pulmonary complications
Hypoventilation, retention of mucus secretion
Atelectasis
Increased frequency of pneumonia, mainly aspiration pneumonia

Cardiovascular system
Postural hypotension
Stimulation of baroreceptors in the atrium
Decreased cardiac stroke volume and output
Venous thromboembolism
Lung embolism

---

limb contracture represents a high risk of immobility (Yip *et al.* 1996).

Pathophysiological changes seen in contracted muscle, in the connective tissue surrounding the joint, and in the bony part of the joint are similar to that after inactivity. In addition, muscle masses shrink because of decreased microcirculation and lack of trophic nervous stimulation. The result is the degeneration of muscle and the proliferation of new connective tissue and subsequent muscle shortening.

Inactivity or immobility during bed rest always dramatically diminishes the frequency of joint motions both in healthy and ill people. The single most common risk factor leading to contractures is the reduction or absence of joint movement. Contractures may result from pathological changes in the bony part of the joint, in the muscle itself, or in the connective tissue surrounding the joint.

The causes of muscular contractures include spasticity, cerebrovascular events with paralysis, or the mechanical and pharmacological restriction of motion by use of tranquillizers, analgesics, and neuroleptics. Positional and mechanical factors also often lead to contractures in bedridden and immobile elderly patients. Even in healthy elderly people the muscles tend to shorten.

Immobilization of any additional joint that becomes necessary because of pain or a fracture increases the immobility of other joints.

Prevention of muscular contractures is an important goal in bedridden patients. To hinder the formation of muscular contractions in healthy but inactive people, flexibility exercises for only 15 min three times a week are sufficient. However, to avoid progression of contractures the aged patients need application of passive motions at least once or twice a day for 20 min.

Arthrogenic contractures often result from inflammation, degenerative joint lesions, infection, and trauma. All these conditions are painful and lead to joint immobilization. The collagen of the joint capsule and the surrounding soft tissue will shrink. The resulting contracture hinders joint motions and passive mobilization and thus worsens contractures. Poor nutritional state, long duration of immobilization, and inadequate positioning of the limbs and arms, may intensify the complications of bed rest. Mobilization of unaffected joints and frequent changes of body position are favourable in preventing the development of contractures.

Early recognition, prevention, and treatment of the causes of arthrogenic contractures that include treatment of inflammation, pain, and infection will decrease the risk of contractures or can diminish their severity. In addition, two basic methods are commonly helpful in the prevention of arthrogenic contractures: early joint mobilization under an adequate pain treatment and optimal positioning of the involved extremity. Specifically designed devices to provide continuous passive motion to the upper and lower extremities significantly maintain joint motion even in immobile and frail elderly patients. These methods are becoming increasingly popular on hospital geriatric wards (Bentham *et al.* 1987).

Osteoporosis (see Chapter 14.1)

Osteoporosis, the result of an imbalance between bone resorption and bone formation, occurs in about 30 per cent of elderly people. Osteoporosis that develops during immobilization of elderly patients is much more frequent and is a severe condition. Bone density of less than 1 g/cm^3 represents a high fracture risk. Bone fractures, pain, disability, and immobilization are the main complications of osteoporosis.

Main risk factors for osteoporosis and fractures are long-term immobility, increasing age, female sex, removal of the ovaries at an early age, white race, and chronic use of corticosteroids. Obesity and use of oestrogen replacement therapy are protective. Factors that may increase risk in postmenopausal white females include a low calcium intake, cigarette smoking, and use of long half-life psychotrophic drugs and heavy alcohol consumption (Kelsey 1989).

Bone loss in elderly people is often clinically silent, and routine radiographs reveal the presence of osteoporosis only when a 40 per cent loss of the bone density has occurred. Often it takes a fracture of the hip, wrist, or lower thoracic and upper lumbar vertebrae to bring the diagnosis of osteoporosis to light. The major factor in bone loss during immobilization is an increased bone resorption. Bone mass decreases as a whole but the ratio of inorganic to organic matrix components remains unchanged. The concentration of calcium, phosphorus, and hydroxyproline in the urine increases during the initial weeks of immobilization. Total body calcium decreases up to 4 per cent during a 7-month period of bed rest (Donaldson *et al.* 1970).

Radiography and history taking normally reveals the osteoporosis. Additional laboratory studies usually show normal values for calcium, phosphorus, magnesium, alkaline phosphatase, and thyroid and parathyroid hormone.

Prevention has to start early in life and aims at increasing peak bone mass at young ages, preventing bone loss in postmenopausal women, and preventing fractures and their negative consequences in older people with osteoporosis.

Treatment strategies for osteoporosis include exercise, oestrogen, high doses of dietary calcium, vitamin D, fluoride, and calcitonin. Daily calcium intake of more than 1000 mg and vitamin D supplementations in a dose of 800 IU efficiently prevent hip vertebral fractures (Chapuy et al. 1992). High degrees of osteoporosis requires treatment with calcitonin and fluoride. The most common and efficient treatment is oestrogen when it starts early, because it prevents bone loss and reduces the incidence of fractures. However, contraindications and potential side-effects including endometrial cancer and vascular complications, are to be considered despite the beneficial effect of oestrogen.

Pressure ulcer (see Chapter 4.3)

The bedridden and completely immobile patient does not move during the night because involuntary and voluntary movements are absent and nursing activities lack. The sacral motility score in these immobile patients is equal to zero movements per hour, resulting in increased interface pressure acting continuously on the same skin area (Seiler et al. 1992). Pressure has an impact on the sacral skin region when in the supine position. The blood flow ceases in the compressed skin area, producing tissue anoxia and eventually necrosis. The interface pressure acts on skin tissue until mobilization by the nursing staff occurs, that is the turning of the patient into the 30 degree lateral position.

The amount of interface that is able to occlude the skin microcirculation ranges around 25 mmHg in elderly patients and 32 mmHg in young subjects. The interface pressure exceeds 80 mmHg on the skin region covering the ischial bony prominence in both healthy young and elderly ill people. However, the crucial difference between the immobile elderly patient at high risk and a healthy young person not at risk is immobility. Immobility means a pathologically prolonged pressure duration for perhaps over 2 h due to immobility (Seiler et al. 1992).

Pressure of more than 25 mmHg that acts continuously on skin or soft tissue for a long enough period leads even in healthy subjects to complete capillary vessel compression. Long periods of blood vessel compression produces intra-arteriolar thromboses and fibrin clots that permanently maintain skin ischaemia. Pressure relief at this time does not open the blood vessels, and pressure sores will form despite pressure relief.

Mobility steadily diminishes with increasing age and is lowest during sleep since there are no voluntary movements. In addition, nursing attendance is lacking at night and involuntary movements become very rare. Therefore night time presents a significant increased risk for pressure ulcers (Exton-Smith et al. 1961).

Pressure sores are the most frequent complication in immobile elderly patients. The risk factors or predisposing factors include any condition or disease that greatly decreases frequency of voluntary and involuntary movements. These factors extend the duration of pressure to the skin. In addition, risk factors lower the critical arteriolar closing pressure or decrease the resistance to the amount of interface pressure.

Risk factors most frequently seen in elderly people include fever, comatose states, cerebrovascular accidents, infections, anaemia, malnutrition, cachexia, oversedation, hypotension, shock, dehydration, surgical intervention, neurological diseases with paralysis, lymphopenia, immobility, decreased body weight, dry sacral skin, and nonblanchable erythema (Allman et al. 1995). When risk factors appear it is crucial to implement the prevention plan without delay.

To prevent pressure ulcers in patients at risk, it is important to eliminate the cause of ulcer formation, that is the relief of continuous pressure on skin areas over bony prominences. Therefore, the relief of pressure on skin areas over bony prominences is the primary goal of prevention and treatment of pressure ulcers. Two simple techniques of soft foam supports and 30° oblique positioning are very successful and decrease both the amount and the duration of interface pressure (Seiler et al. 1986).

A simple standardized treatment plan achieves healing more effectively than trial-and-error approaches, and simplifies selection of drugs and other remedies. The treatment originates from the pathophysiological findings that impair wound healing. Ulcers can heal only if the treatment methods restore normal physiological wound conditions as far possible.

Five treatment principles corresponding to pathological findings have been established (Seiler et al. 1985):

(1) complete pressure relief;
(2) debridement of necrotic tissue;
(3) treatment of local infection with systemic antibiotics;
(4) wet wound dressings using Ringer's solution;
(5) elimination of risk factors and evaluation for possible surgical intervention.

Postural hypotension (see Chapter 18.12)

Common complications of complete immobility and prolonged bed rest, mainly in geriatric patients, are disruption of normal cardiovascular postural responses, decreased cardiac efficiency, and thromboembolic diseases.

The definition of postural hypotension is a decline in main blood pressure of over 20 mmHg in response to head-up tilt. In addition, clinical symptoms of cerebral ischaemia, most commonly lightheadedness and syncope, must be present. An increase in heart rate of more than 10 beats/min indicates the sympathetic type of postural hypotension whilst a rise in heart rate of less than 10 beats/min is the asympathetic type.

It is imperative to understand the pathogenesis of the postural hypotension phenomenon to provide efficient preventive and supportive care for patients suffering from postural hypotension.

In the standing position normally 600 to 800 ml of blood fluid shifts into the inferior part of the body, mainly into the legs. This redistribution of body fluid causes an initial 20 per cent reduction of cardiac output, a 35 per cent reduction of heart stroke volume, and a 30 per cent acceleration of the heart frequency. In normal healthy subjects compensatory mechanisms leading to vasoconstriction and an increase in heart rate makes the blood pressure fall. Blood pressure, thus, remains unchanged or slightly elevated on acute arising. Complete bed rest for as little as 3 weeks strongly impairs the ability to adjust to the upright position even in healthy subjects, and this effect is more pronounced in elderly patients.

In the supine position, normally 600 to 800 ml of plasma volume returns to the lungs and the heart, and by stimulating the baroreceptors, heart rate, cardiac stroke volume, and cardiac output increase. Antidiuretic hormone release diminishes during the initial weeks of immobilization leading to increased diuresis and a significant decrease of plasma volume. The loss of plasma volume reaches 10 per cent during the first 2 weeks of bed rest and more than 20 per cent thereafter.

In addition, prolonged bed rest and lying in the supine position stimulate baroreceptors in the atrium and reverse the initial normal cardiovascular responses. The final state results in a significant decrease in cardiac stroke volume and cardiac output. Abnormally low cardiac output may cause postural hypotension in elderly people after long-term immobilization, because usually an increase in cardiac output rather than vasoconstriction protects elderly subjects from postural hypotension (Luutonen et al. 1995).

Symptoms and signs of acute postural hypotension include decreased systolic blood pressure on arising by more than 20 mmHg, sweating, pallor, dizziness, light-headedness, increased or unchanged heart rate, fainting, and, in severe cases, falls, which possibly result in further complications such as fractures, soft tissue haematomas, or cerebral bleeding.

Besides immobility, diseases and drugs also impair the ability of the cardiovascular system to maintain blood pressure in the upright posture (Table 2). Among these the most dangerous include autonomic neuropathies, hypovolaemia, Shy–Drager syndrome, and degenerative disorders such as parkinsonism, Huntington's chorea, syringomyelia, and basilar artery disease. Drugs that often cause postural hypotension are tricyclic antidepressants, monoamine oxidase inhibitors, diuretics, antihypertensive agents, β-blockers, α-blockers, dopamine agonists, nitrates, and sedative neuroleptics.

Preventing acute orthostatic hypotension after prolonged bed rest entails careful assessment of the status of the sympathetic reflexes before the patient leaves the bed. Supportive care during the patient's early experiences out of bed involves measures to reduce the likelihood of acute orthostatic hypotension. Monitoring postural blood pressure and pulse rate in bedridden elderly people should be done in the routine assessment when the patient leaves the bed for the first time.

Prevention and treatment of postural hypotension may also focus on the cause. Withdrawal of drugs that lower blood pressure and early mobilization of bedridden patients are mandatory measures. Strengthening exercise to the major muscles and contraction of the abdominal and leg musculature promotes venous blood return most efficiently. Supportive garments, such as full-length elastic stockings and abdominal binders, represent the treatment of choice for postural hypotension.

Treatment of reversible non-autonomic causes, reduced blood volume, dehydration, and underlying diseases such as diabetes mellitus is important. The goal of therapy is to relieve symptoms. Non-pharmacological approaches include increasing sodium intake, avoiding rapid postural changes, and wearing elastic garments.

Pharmacological treatments often become necessary. The drugs of choice for all types of postural hypotension are fludrocortisone acetate and prostaglandin synthetase inhibitors. Sympathomimetics with or without monoamine oxidase inhibitors, β-adrenergic antagonists, and ergot alkaloids are efficient for patients with postural hypertension of the sympathetic type. Midodrine, yohimbine, and desmopressin are not free of side-effects but are useful for the treatment of severe refractory postural hypotension. Often a combination of non-drug and drug therapies can increase blood pressure (Stumpf and Mitrzyk 1994).

Deep venous thrombosis and lung embolism

Deep venous thrombosis and lung embolism are the most acute and serious complications of bed rest. Immobile patients need prophylactic anticoagulation using low molecular heparin.

Constipation and faecal impaction

Constipation, faecal impaction, and bowel obstruction are common problems for immobile elderly patients during bed rest. Prolonged bed rest significantly lowers the colon transit time. The longer the transit time of stool in the large intestine, the greater the fluid absorption and the harder the stool becomes. If stool does not pass on a regular basis (generally, once a day to several times a day), faecal impaction with partial or complete blockage may occur.

Faecal impaction refers to the collection of dry hardened faeces in the rectum or colon. An elderly patient with faecal impaction rarely presents typical gastrointestinal symptoms. Instead they show circulatory, cardiac, and respiratory symptoms, or they may present with delirium. If the signs and symptoms of stool impaction persist or progress severe risk of death results.

Common factors that cause constipation are diet, altered bowel habits, and lack of exercise. In addition, functional disorders such as inactivity, immobility, and bed rest, and psychological conditions including depression and anxiety, mainly contribute to the development of constipation. In the immobile elderly patient, typically inadequate fluid intake, dehydration, frailty, and medications cause constipation.

Regular assessment of stool habits in immobile patients is important. At least three stools per week and no more than three per day is a normal bowel pattern. The evaluation should also include assessment of associated symptoms such as distension, flatus, cramping, or rectal fullness. A digital rectal examination often rules out faecal impaction when constipation occurs.

Physical assessment will determine the presence or absence of bowel sounds and flatus, or of abdominal distension. The knowledge of the dietary habits, fluid intake, activity levels, and use of narcotics is important.

Comprehensive management of constipation in immobilized patients includes continuous prevention and elimination of causative factors. A programme for prevention of constipation first has to define the goal. In geriatric patients the monitoring of fluid intake, mobility level, and diet is mandatory. The goal of prevention is to avoid faecal impaction and ileus.

The intervention plan includes increasing fluid intake, with a goal of drinking eight glasses of fluid daily and regular exercises. In addition, to execute exercise in bed or to mobilize patients from bed to chair, if possible, is very important. If the patient has not had a stool in 3 days stool softeners may stimulate bowel voiding. Constipation under morphine treatment requires stool softeners in combination with a stimulant laxative. Stimulant laxatives increase motor activity of the bowels by direct action on the intestinal nervous system.

The high osmolarity of saline laxatives attracts water into the lumen of the intestines. The fluid accumulation alters the stool

Table 4 Causes of constipation and faecal impaction

Prolonged immobility and inadequate exercise
Insufficient fibre or bulk in diet
Inadequate fluid intake
Excessive use of laxatives
Fatigue and weakness
Anticholinergic medications
Opiates or sedatives
Antiparkinsonism agents
Tricyclic antidepressants
Phenothiazines
Calcium- and aluminium-based antacids
Diuretics
Tranquillizers and sleeping medications
Chemotherapeutic medications
Hypothyroidism
Uraemia
Dehydration
Hypercalcaemia
Hypokalaemia
Hyponatraemia
Depression
Malnutrition, cachexia
Anaemia
Carcinoma
Dementia
Autonomic neuropathy

consistency, distends the bowel, and induces peristaltic movement. Lubricant laxatives lubricate intestinal mucosa and soften stool.

Lactulose, the most often used and safest laxative in geriatric immobile patients, is a synthetic disaccharide that passes to the colon undigested. Lactulose produces lactic acid, formic acid, acetic acid, and carbon dioxide in the colon. These products increase the osmotic pressure, thus increasing water in the stool, which softens the stool and increases frequency. Excessive amounts may cause diarrhoea with electrolyte losses.

Metabolism and endocrine system

Immobility-induced changes impair function of the metabolic and endocrine system (Table 4). Typically, these changes have a slow and insidious onset, and are often recognized only when the patient starts remobilization.

Old age and immobility significantly reduce protein turnover. Plasma cortisol levels are higher in immobile elderly people as compared to healthy older subjects. These higher plasma cortisol levels transform the metabolism into a catabolic state and thus may be partly responsible for the lower protein turnover found in immobile elderly patients (Lehmann et al. 1989).

A 7-day period of inactivity and bed rest only increase the excretion of urinary nitrogen. The increase of urinary excretion peaks with an average loss of 2 mg/day. Hypoproteinaemia, oedema, and weight loss are the consequences. The daily nitrogen loss increases up to 12 g in the presence of malnutrition, trauma, hip fracture, or infection. The exact cause of the increase in nitrogen loss over that seen during sole inactivity is not yet clear. However, interleukin stimulates tumour necrosis factor-α. The latter and cortisol contribute to the formation of a catabolic metabolism. Hepatic protein synthesis decreases and lean body mass proteins (muscle proteins) rather than fat tissue are wasting to produce glucose.

Suppression of antidiuretic hormone secretion during bed rest increases diuresis and leads, together with muscle breakdown, to a significant loss of body weight. Urinary incontinence may also result (Halar and Bell 1990).

Psychological disturbances

Depression, isolation, and anxiety are risk factors for elderly people for becoming immobile. Prolonged bed rest and inactivity contribute to the development of depression and isolation, thus maintaining a vicious circle.

Prolonged immobility and chronic depression predispose to pressure neuropathies due to postures such as leg crossings, resting arms on elbows, and resting chin on hyperextended wrist (Riley et al. 1980).

Immobile patients often lack environmental stimulation that prevents delirium and sustains cognitive functions. Routine clinical assessment of mental stress and the institution of preventive measures, and psychological and medical treatment, can diminish these complications and increase the quality of life of elderly patients.

Conclusion

Immobility and risk factors for immobility increase with advancing age (Exton-Smith and Sherwin 1961). Complications of inactivity and prolonged bed rest are frequent and tend to present greater problems than the original cause of immobility. Initially, immobility impairs the functional capacity in a single organ and later causes a wide range of adverse effects on multiple organs.

Thus, immobility per se may behave as a disease that produces further illness and complications, mainly in elderly patients.

Immobility-related medical complications and disability can be substantially reduced by identifying risk factors and applying preventive measures. Periods of required immobilization and bed rest must be as short as possible. Providers of acute and chronic medical care for elderly patients should devise, as a routine procedure, a preventive care plan to avoid complications of immobility in all patients. The plan is beneficial on patient outcome, and stops immobility becoming an autonomic disease.

References

Allman, R.M., Goode, P.S., Patrick, M.M., Burst, N., and Bartolucci, A.A. (1995). Pressure ulcer risk factors among hospitalised patients with activity limitation. *Journal of the American Medical Association*, **273**, 865–70.

Bentham, J.S., Bereton, W.D.S., Cochrane, I.W., and Lyttle, D. (1987). Continuous passive motion device for hand rehabilitation. *Archives of Physical Medicine and Rehabilitation*, **68**, 248–50.

Bonner, C.D. (1969). Rehabilitation instead of bed rest? *Geriatrics*, **24**, 109–18.

Booth, F.W. and Gollnick, P.D. (1983). Effects of disuse on the structure and function of skeletal muscle. *Medicine and Science of Sports and Exercise*, **15**, 415–20.

Chapuy, M.C., Arlot, M.E., Duboeuf, F., *et al.* (1992). Vitamin D$_3$ and calcium to prevent hip fractures in elderly women. *New England Journal of Medicine*, 327, 1637–42.

Cockett, A.T., Elbadawi, A., and Zemjanis, R. (1970). The effects of immobilization on spermatogenesis in subhuman primates. *Fertility and Sterility*, 21, 610–14.

Donaldson, C.L., Hully, S.B., Vogel, J.M., *et al.* (1970). Effect of prolonged bed rest on bone mineral. *Metabolism*, 19, 1071–84.

Exton-Smith, A.N. and Sherwin, R.W. (1961). The prevention of pressure sores: the significance of spontaneous bodily movements. *Lancet*, ii, 1124–6.

Greenleaf, J.E. and Kozlowski, S. (1983). Reduction in peak oxygen uptake after prolonged bedrest. *Science of Sports and Exercise*, 14, 477–80.

Halar, E.M. and Bell, K.R. (1990). Rehabilitation's relationship to inactivity. In *Handbook of physical medicine and rehabilitation* (ed. F.J. Kottke and J.F. Lehmann), Vol. 4, pp. 1113–33. W.B. Saunders, Philadelphia, PA.

Kelsey, J.L. (1989). Risk factors for osteoporosis and associated fractures. *Public Health Reports*, 104 (Supplement), 14–20.

Lehmann, A.B., Johnston, D., and James, O.F. (1989). The effects of old age and immobility on protein turnover in human subjects with some observations on the possible role of hormones. *Age and Ageing*, 18, 148–57.

Luutonen, S., Antila, K., Erkko, M., Raiha, I., Rajala, T., and Sourander, L. (1995). Haemodynamic response to head-up tilt in elderly hypertensives and diabetics. *Age and Ageing*, 24, 315–20.

Melada, G.A., Goldman, R.H., Leutscher, J.A., and Eager, P.G. (1975). Hemodynamics, renal function, plasma renin, and aldosterone in man after 5 to 14 days of bedrest. *Aviation, Space, and Environmental Medicine*, 46, 1049–55.

Riley, T.L., Pleet, A.B., and Stewart, C.R. (1980). Multiple entrapment neuropathies in depression. *Journal of Clinical Psychiatry*, 41, 214–15.

Seiler, W.O. and Stähelin, H.B. (1985). Decubitus ulcers: treatment through five therapeutic principles. *Geriatrics*, 9, 30–44.

Seiler, W.O., Allen, S., and Stähelin, H.B. (1986). Influence of the 30 degree laterally inclined position and the 'super-soft' three-piece mattress on skin oxygen tension on areas of maximum pressure. Implications for pressure sore prevention. *Gerontology*, 32, 158–66.

Seiler, W.O., Stähelin, H.B., and Stoffel, F. (1992). Recordings of movement leading to pressure relief of the sacral skin region: identification of patients at risk for pressure ulcer development. *Wounds (USA)*, 4, 256–61.

Selikson, S., Damus, K., and Hamerman, D. (1988). Risk factors associated with immobility. *Journal of the American Geriatrics Society*, 36, 707–12.

Stumpf, J.L. and Mitrzyk, B. (1994). Management of orthostatic hypotension. *American Journal of Hospital Pharmacology*, 51, 648–60, 697–8.

Wirth, A., Diehm, C., Mayer, H., *et al.* (1981). Plasma C-peptide and insulin in trained and untrained subjects. *Journal of Applied Physiology*, 50, 71–7.

Yip, B., Stewart, D.A., and Roberts, M.A. (1996). The prevalence of joint contractures in residents in NHS continuing care. *Health Bulletin (Edinburgh)*, 54, 338–43.

26.5 Frailty

Gary Naglie

Introduction

The bulk of ageing research has emphasized age-associated deteriorations in health and functioning (Seeman 1994). Cross-sectional studies have demonstrated a significant decline in many physiological variables with increasing age (Shock *et al.* 1984; Rowe and Kahn 1987). Studies have also shown an increase in functional and mobility impairment with increasing age, especially in cohorts over 80 years of age (Schneider and Guralnik 1990; Strawbridge *et al.* 1992). However, longitudinal studies of ageing populations have demonstrated that ageing is a highly variable process, with some elderly individuals having little or no change in physiological variables over time (Shock *et al.* 1984). There is also evidence of considerable variability in physical activity and functioning, with some elderly subgroups exhibiting levels similar to those seen in younger age groups (Berkman *et al.* 1993; Seeman 1994). In addition, prospective studies have shown that some individuals with impairments in function can demonstrate improvement over time (Branch *et al.* 1984; Strawbridge *et al.* 1992).

Rowe and Kahn (1987) introduced the terms 'usual' and 'successful' ageing to characterize the heterogeneity within the population of elderly people who are free of disease. 'Usual' ageing refers to elderly people who exhibit the typical age-associated physiological losses, while 'successful' ageing refers to older people who experience minimal or no physiological losses. At the opposite extreme to the concept of successful ageing is the notion of 'frailty'. The term 'frail' includes those who depend on others for the activities of daily living or are at high risk of becoming dependent (Rockwood *et al.* 1994).

Given the heterogeneity of the elderly population, how can primary care doctors identify patients who require special attention, and patients who may benefit from care by specialists in geriatric medicine? These questions are very important to the care of elderly people, but the answers have been far from clear. The National Institutes of Health Consensus Development Conference on Geriatric Assessment

(National Institutes of Health Consensus Development Panel 1988) stated that comprehensive geriatric assessment methodologies are particularly suited to frail elderly people. However, the terms 'frail' and 'frailty' have remained poorly defined (Rockwood *et al.* 1994).

Several definitions of frailty have been proposed. Buchner and Wagner (1992) defined frailty as a 'state of reduced physiological reserve associated with increased susceptibility to disability'. The National Institutes of Health Consensus Development Conference on Geriatric Assessment (National Institutes of Health 1988) defined the frail elderly as individuals who 'tend to exhibit great medical complexity and vulnerability; have illnesses with atypical and obscure presentations; suffer major cognitive, affective, and functional problems; are especially vulnerable to iatrogenesis; are often socially isolated and economically deprived; and are at high risk for premature or inappropriate institutionalisation'. Speechley and Tinetti (1991) used factor analysis to identify nine variables which correlated strongly with frailty: age over 80 years, balance and gait abnormalities, infrequent walking for exercise, decreased knee strength, lower-extremity disability, decreased shoulder strength, decreased near vision, depression, and sedative use. Winograd *et al.* (1991), in trying to target frail elderly patients in hospital who could benefit from geriatric consultation, used the term frail to include any one of the following criteria: stroke, disabling chronic illness, confusion, dependence in activities of daily living, depression, malnutrition, polypharmacy, sensory impairment, socio-economic/family problems, impaired mobility, falls, incontinence, pressure sores, prolonged bed rest, and restraint use.

Brocklehurst (1985) suggested that the objective of geriatric care is to 'meet and overcome breakdown in independent living among old people'. He identified the following variables which tend to cause a breakdown in independent living in elderly people: the decremental effects of ageing, the accumulation of pathologies, the untoward effects of many medications, and underlying social deprivation. He also identified several factors which tend to offset the breakdown of independence in older people including networks of support from family members, neighbours, and social services, physical and mental health, and the innate desire of individuals to retain their independence. Brocklehurst went on to state that the balance between these factors determined whether senior citizens remain independent or not, and that the addition of negative factors, such as acute illness, or the removal of positive factors, such as loss of social support, could shift the balance towards dependence.

Rockwood *et al.* (1994) refer to this balance between biomedical and psychosocial components as the dynamic model of frailty in elderly people. On one side of the balance are assets which help a person maintain their independence, and on the other side are deficits, which threaten independence. Table 1 summarizes the combined list of assets and deficits proposed by Brocklehurst (1985) and by Rockwood *et al.* (1994). The model is dynamic in that changes in the assets or deficits can tilt the balance from favouring independence to favouring dependence. Using this model, Rockwood *et al.* (1994) divide the elderly population into three groups: (a) those in whom the assets heavily outweigh the deficits, such as the well elderly; (b) those in whom the deficits outweigh the assets, so that they cannot maintain their independence in the community, such as the institutionalised frail elderly; (c) those in whom the assets and deficits are in precarious balance, such as the frail community-living elderly.

Those involved in the care of elderly people attempt to maximize the assets and minimize the deficits of older people, to promote independent community living. This chapter reviews some of the important predictors of adverse outcomes in elderly people, as well as some of the predictors of successful ageing. A better knowledge of these predictors can enhance the understanding of frailty, help to identify older people at risk for adverse clinical outcomes, and provide clues about interventions that can prevent or minimize adverse outcomes.

Sociodemographic factors

Several sociodemographic factors have been found to be associated with poor outcomes in elderly people, such as decreased functioning and institutionalization. These include advanced age, low income, low level of education, living alone, and absence of a caregiver (Shapiro and Tate 1988; Jette *et al.* 1992; Berkman *et al.* 1993; Dooghe 1994; Boaz and Muller 1994; Rockwood *et al.* 1996). The MacArthur Studies of Successful Aging are community-based studies of men and women aged 70 to 79 years from three population samples in the United States (Berkman *et al.* 1993). They compared those functioning in the top third of their age group with those functioning in the middle and lowest third. Individuals in the low functioning group were much more likely to have an annual income of less than $5000, to have less than 12 years of education, and to be non-white. These findings were corroborated by the Alameda County Longitudinal Study of Aging (Strawbridge *et al.* 1992) which looked at the predictors of successful ageing. This study prospectively followed a cohort of community-living men and women aged 65 to 95 years between 1984 and 1990. The investigators defined successful ageing as needing no assistance, nor having any difficulty performing any of 13 activity and mobility measures, plus having little or no difficulty on five physical performance measures. Among the factors that were found to be predictive of successful ageing were income above the lowest quintile, more than 12 years of education, white ethnicity, and having five or more close personal contacts. Foley *et al.* (1992) studied the 3-year incidence of nursing home admission for community-dwelling residents aged 65 and over in communities in three American States. They found that the use of nursing homes was highest among people with the lowest incomes. They also noted that people most likely to be institutionalized were living alone, while those least likely to enter a nursing home were living with a spouse. A 12-year prospective study (1971–1983) of a representative cohort of elderly people in Manitoba, Canada, revealed that the odds of successful ageing decreased if one's spouse died or was placed in a nursing home (Roos and Havens 1991).

The associations between poverty, lower levels of education, non-white race, and poor function are very consistent in the literature. The reasons for this association have not been clearly elucidated. Hypotheses include poorer access to health care, more medical illness, different patterns of lifelong health behaviour, and limited psychological and/or social resources (Berkman *et al.* 1993). The reasons for the association between poor function and factors such as living alone and absence of a caregiver or social contacts are probably multifactorial. The importance of caregivers and social contacts may include the availability of encouragement to follow positive health behaviour and avoid risky behaviour, the provision of material support, the encouragement to seek health care, or the enhancement of self-perception and quality of life (Strawbridge *et al.* 1992). In older

Table 1 The dynamic model of frailty: assets favouring independence and deficits threatening independence

Assets	Deficits
Social supports	Ageing changes
Caregiver	Ill health
Physical health	Medication effects
Mental health	Disability
Functional capacity	Dependence on other(s) for activities of daily living
Desire to retain independence	Social isolation
Positive attitude towards health	Burden on caregivers
Other resources (social, spiritual, financial, and environmental)	

people with a caregiver, high caregiver burden is an important predictor of institutionalization (Colerick and George 1986; McFall and Miller 1992). Further research is needed to determine more clearly how sociodemographic factors impact on function and outcomes in elderly people.

Self-rated health

Kaplan *et al.* (1988) noted that health status involves a 'complex relationship between the physical and psychological aspects of health and illness and between the objective and subjective aspects of these states'. For many years, researchers have used self-rated health assessments as a measure of health status. Self-rated health refers to a subjective evaluation by an individual of their overall state of health. Self-rated health is measured by asking people to rate their health as excellent to poor on a scale with three to five levels (Greiner *et al.* 1996). For example, participants may be asked to respond to one of the following questions: 'At the present time, would you say that your health in general is excellent, very good, good, fair, or poor?'; 'Compared to other people your age, would you say your health is excellent, good, fair, or poor?' (Dasbach *et al.* 1994). This simple approach to health status assessment has gained increasing acceptance in the social and health sciences as a reliable measure of health status (Greiner *et al.* 1996).

Numerous epidemiological studies in the United States, Canada, Europe, and Japan have found that self-rated health in community-living elderly is an important predictor of mortality (Mossey and Shapiro 1982; Jagger and Clarke 1988; Idler and Kasl 1991; Wolinsky *et al.* 1994; Appels *et al.* 1996). This relationship between self-rated health and mortality remains even after correcting for demographic factors, socio-economic status, psychosocial factors, and for a variety of measures of physical health and functional status (Idler and Kasl 1991; Wolinsky *et al.* 1994). Results from the MacArthur Studies of Successful Aging (Schoenfeld *et al.* 1994) suggested that self-rated health was even more predictive of mortality in individuals with a maximum of one chronic disease than it was in those with more than one chronic disease. In the Manitoba prospective study of elderly people (Roos and Havens 1991), self-rated health was found to be a strong predictor of successful ageing. Several studies have also suggested that self-rated health is an independent predictor of the use

of health services (Hulka and Wheat 1985; Wolinsky and Johnson 1992; Chi *et al.* 1995).

Several hypotheses have been suggested to explain the relationship between self-rated health and mortality. These include (Schoenfeld *et al.* 1994) (a) negative subjective health status may result in neuro-hormonal changes which suppress the immune system and increase susceptibility to disease, (b) poor subjective health may reflect self-detection of physiological problems which have not yet become clinically evident, and (c) poor self-rated health reduces the likelihood of pursuing health protective behaviour. Unfortunately, the studies available to date cannot shed further light on the actual mechanisms responsible for the association between self-rated health and mortality. Despite the lack of a clear explanation for this finding, many have suggested that the consistent finding of a relationship between poor self-rated health and mortality has important clinical implications. Idler and Kasl (1991) have stated that 'the knowledge that expressions of subjective health status are sensitive indicators of survival length should engender new respect among health professionals for what people, especially the elderly people they treat, are saying about their health'. Wolinsky *et al.* (1994) go even further, recommending that 'when older adults perceive their health to be poor, regardless of the presence or absence of confirming signs or symptoms, further investigation by their doctor is warranted'. This recommendation requires further study before it can be widely recommended. Future randomized studies should investigate whether conducting a more comprehensive assessment in people who rate their health as poor can result in improved outcomes.

Functional status

The National Institutes of Health Consensus Development Conference on Geriatric Assessment (National Institutes of Health Consensus Development Panel 1988) stated that the assessment of functional status was an important element of comprehensive geriatric assessment. Functional status was defined as the ability to carry out the basic activities of daily living independently (e.g. dressing, bathing, toileting), as well as the instrumental activities of daily living (e.g. financial management, meal preparation, grocery shopping). These are traditionally measured by self-report or proxy-report functional status instruments (Applegate *et al.* 1990).

The assessment of functional status has become a cornerstone of geriatric assessment and a major outcome measure in geriatric research because it has been demonstrated to be a consistent predictor of adverse outcomes in elderly people. Dependency in activities of daily living has been shown to be predictive of the following outcomes in elderly people: (a) admission to hospital (Evashwick et al. 1984; Freedman et al. 1996); (b) prolonged hospital stays (Narain et al. 1988; Roos et al. 1988); (c) worsening of function in hospital (Incalzi et al. 1992; Sager et al. 1996); (d) greater home care use (Evashwick et al. 1984; Branch et al. 1988); (e) nursing home placement (Branch and Jette 1982; Manton 1988; Shapiro and Tate 1988; Foley et al. 1992; Rockwood et al. 1996); (f) death (Manton 1988; Narain et al. 1988; Incalzi et al. 1992; Reuben et al. 1992; Wolinsky et al. 1993).

Physical performance measures

Physical performance measures are objective tests of an individual's performance of standardized tasks that are required for carrying out common daily activities (e.g. strength, balance, real and simulated functional tasks). A review of physical performance measures (Guralnik et al. 1989) describes an objective performance measure as 'one in which an individual is asked to perform a specific task and is evaluated in an objective, uniform manner using predetermined criteria'. Physical performance measures are usually evaluated by timing the task (e.g. time taken to walk a fixed distance), or by counting the number of repetitions of the task that the individual can carry out, usually in a fixed time period (e.g. number of times a person can rise from a chair and sit back down in 5 min). Guralnik et al. (1989) have recommended that physical performance measures be used to supplement the traditionally used self-reports or proxy-reports of functional ability. They suggest that the objective nature of physical performance measures can overcome some of the short-comings of traditional functional status measures, such as respondent reporting bias associated with perceptions of socially acceptable or desirable responses. In addition, they point out that physical performance measures are less likely to be influenced by culture, language, and educational level. These assertions about the purported benefits of physical performance measures over traditional self-report and proxy-report functional status assessments will need to be validated by further research.

A wide variety of physical performance measures have been used in geriatric populations, including tests which assess upper-extremity, lower-extremity, and trunk functions. Some of the commonly used physical performance measures include grip strength, self-selected gait speed (Bassey et al. 1976), time to walk a fixed distance (Guralnik et al. 1994), distance walked in a fixed period of time (Guyatt et al. 1985), time to rise from a chair (i.e. timed chair stand) (Guralnik et al. 1994), the timed 'get up and go' test (time to rise from a chair, walk 6 m, and sit back down) (Podsiadlo and Richardson 1991), functional reach (a test of balance by measuring the furthest distance a person can reach forward while standing and not taking a step) (Weiner et al. 1991), timed 360° turn (Guralnik et al. 1994), and ability to maintain feet in side-by-side, semi-tandem, and tandem positions for 10 s (Guralnik et al. 1994).

In addition to individual physical performance measures, several assessment instruments have been developed which incorporate multiple physical performance measures. The Timed Manual Performance Test (Williams et al. 1982) is a comprehensive measure of upper-extremity manual ability, involving the timed opening and closing of nine door fasteners, and the timed performance of five hand skills. The Bed Rise Difficulty Scale (Alexander et al. 1992) is a 12-item quantitative scale of bed mobility. The Physical Performance Test (Reuben and Siu 1990) is a nine- or seven-item scored measure of physical performance. The nine-item scale includes writing a sentence, simulated eating, turning 360°, putting on and removing a jacket, lifting a book and putting it on a shelf, picking up a penny from the floor, a 50-foot walk test, and climbing stairs (two items). The seven-item scale excludes the two stair climbing items. The Physical Performance and Mobility Examination (Winograd et al. 1994) is a scored measure assessing six domains of physical functioning and mobility for elderly people in hospital. The domains include bed mobility, transfer skills, multiple stands from a chair, standing balance, climbing one step, and ambulation. The Physical Capacity Evaluation (Daltroy et al. 1995) is a scored measure of 13 tasks, including five measures of hand function, two measures of ability to dress, three measures of shoulder range of motion, one measure of lower-extremity function, one measure of walking, and one measure of balance. The Physical Disability Index (Gerety et al. 1993) is a scored 54-item measure for frail elderly people.

The first physical performance measures were introduced in the 1960s, but it was not until much later that physical performance measures became broadly recognized in the field of geriatrics. Williams et al. (1982) demonstrated that upper-extremity manual ability was an important marker of dependency in elderly women. Subsequent studies of timed manual performance have confirmed its correlation with the degree of independence in various living situations (Ostwald et al. 1989), and, in addition, its ability to prospectively identify elderly individuals likely to require long-term care services (Williams 1987).

Numerous studies have now been published which emphasize the importance of physical performance measures as predictors of clinically important outcomes in elderly people. In populations of community-living elderly people, physical performance measures have been shown to predict outcomes such as increased dependency in activities of daily living and instrumental activities of daily living, falls, institutionalization, and death, after correcting for other important predictors (Tinetti et al. 1988; Reuben et al. 1992; Rozzini et al. 1993; Wolinsky et al. 1993; Guralnik et al. 1994; Gill et al. 1995; Judge et al. 1996). Two more recent studies of cohorts of exclusively non-disabled community-living elderly people demonstrated that baseline performance on physical performance measures of lower-extremity function was highly predictive of the subsequent development of functional and mobility impairment (Guralnik et al. 1995; Gill et al. 1996). The many studies of physical performance measures have helped to establish the reliability and validity of these measures, and have suggested that physical performance measures may be more sensitive to change than self-report and proxy-report functional status instruments (Guralnik et al. 1989). A recent study has also suggested that physical performance measures can be reliably used, with some modifications, in cognitively impaired individuals (Tappen et al. 1997). Future research will have to help clarify the normative ranges for the physical performance measures, which individual physical performance measures or which combination of physical performance measures most reliably and accurately identifies community and hospital populations at risk, and whether interventions which attempt to improve physical performance measures (e.g. exercise) can prevent adverse outcomes in elderly people.

Mental status

Cognitive impairment is an independent risk factor for the development of functional dependence (Gill *et al.* 1996). Dementia leads to progressive functional impairment, institutionalization, and death (Brodaty *et al.* 1993; Gill *et al.* 1996). Delirium has been shown to be a risk factor for prolonged hospital stays, prolonged functional impairment, prolonged cognitive impairment, institutionalization, and mortality (Francis *et al.* 1990; Cole and Primeau 1993; Murray *et al.* 1993; O'Keefe and Lavan 1997). Unfortunately, we do not have very good empirical evidence to date for the benefits of interventions used to prevent delirium or to improve the outcomes of patients with delirium (Cole *et al.* 1994, 1996).

Studies have suggested that individuals with depressive symptoms are less likely to be physically active (Ruuskanen and Parkatti 1994; Ruuskanen and Ruoppila 1995). Other studies have noted that depression in elderly people is associated with impairment in activities of daily living and psychosocial functioning (Bruce *et al.* 1994*b*; Alexopoulos *et al.* 1996). Alexopoulos *et al.* (1996) found that in older patients with major depression, impairment in instrumental activities of daily living was significantly associated with the severity of the depression. The MacArthur Studies of Successful Aging (Bruce *et al.* 1994*b*) examined the relationship between depressive symptoms and functional status in senior citizens aged between 70 and 79 years who were functioning in the top third for their age group. Approximately 2.5 years after the baseline interview, disability in activities of daily living developed in 5.7 per cent of men and 4.1 per cent of women. For both men and women, high levels of depressive symptoms in the baseline interview were associated with increased risk for the development of dependence in carrying out activities of daily living. In the Alameda County Longitudinal Study of Successful Aging (Strawbridge *et al.* 1996), the absence of depression was a significant independent predictor of successful ageing. Other studies have found that older people with depression have an increased risk of mortality (Bruce and Leaf 1989; Bruce *et al.* 1994*a*).

Chronic disease

The risk of chronic disease increases rapidly with increasing age. American studies suggest that about 80 per cent of community-living elderly people have at least one chronic condition, and 30 per cent have three or more (Soldo and Manton 1988). The most common conditions reported are heart disease, arthritis, hypertension, hearing, and visual problems. A study of a non-institutionalized Finnish population aged 65 years and older revealed that the most common chronic conditions were circulatory system disease, followed by musculoskeletal disorders and diabetes (Bourliere and Vallery-Masson 1985). The most common cause of death in elderly people in the West is heart disease (Bourliere and Vallery-Masson 1985). Other important causes of death in elderly people include cancer, cerebrovascular disease, chronic obstructive pulmonary disease, pneumonia, influenza, diabetes mellitus, and accidents (Rossman 1986). The two chronic diseases that studies have most commonly identified as risk

factors for hospital admission in elderly people are cardiovascular disease and diabetes (Incalzi *et al.* 1992; Boult *et al.* 1993; Freedman *et al.* 1996). In the MacArthur Studies of Successful Aging (Seeman *et al.* 1994), declines in physical performance between 1988 and 1991 were predicted by the presence of diabetes and lower peak expiratory flow rates. In the Alameda County Longitudinal Study of Successful Aging (Strawbridge *et al.* 1996), the presence of diabetes, chronic obstructive pulmonary disease, and arthritis were associated with decreased odds of subsequent successful ageing (Strawbridge *et al.* 1992). In the Manitoba Longitudinal Study of an elderly population, individuals who did not have diabetes were more likely to age successfully (Roos and Havens 1991).

Polypharmacy

Studies in the United Kingdom, Canada, and the United States have demonstrated that people over 65 years of age are prescribed disproportionately large numbers of medications compared with younger individuals (Williams and Rush 1986; Anonymous 1988; Nolan and O'Malley 1988*b*). In the United States, people over 65 years of age fill an average of 12 prescriptions per year, compared with slightly more than five per year for people aged 25 to 44 years (Williams and Rush 1986). There is some controversy as to whether there is an increase in the incidence of adverse drug reactions with increasing age (Nolan and O'Malley 1988*a*; Gurwitz and Avorn 1991). However, it has been consistently shown that in hospital-admitted and community-living senior citizens, the incidence of adverse drug reactions increases significantly with the number of medications taken (Nolan and O'Malley 1988*a*). In fact, it has been suggested that the incidence of adverse drug reactions rises exponentially with the number of medications taken (Nolan and O'Malley 1988*a*). Williams and Rush (1986) reported that when up to five medications are taken concurrently, the incidence of reported adverse reactions is 4 per cent. The incidence of reported adverse reactions rises to 24 per cent when 11 to 15 medications are taken. Taking multiple medications has also been shown to be an important risk factor for medication non-adherence, falls, and mortality in elderly people (Tinetti *et al.* 1986; Morrow *et al.* 1988; Incalzi *et al.* 1992; Melin *et al.* 1995). Many medications have been implicated in causing adverse outcomes in elderly people, but sedative-hypnotics, especially the long-acting benzodiazepines, are the most common medications associated with adverse events (Lamy 1990).

Sensory impairment

Cross-sectional studies have suggested a relationship between visual impairment and functional dependence (Jette and Branch 1985; Bergman and Sjostrand 1992; Dargent-Molina *et al.* 1996; West *et al.* 1997). Longitudinal studies have shown an association between visual impairment and the development of limitations in activities of daily living, mobility, and physical performance (Mor *et al.* 1989; La Forge *et al.* 1992; Rudberg *et al.* 1993; Salive *et al.* 1994). Data from the Established Populations for the Epidemiologic Studies of the Elderly, involving three American communities, was used to examine the association of visual function with physical function during an average follow-up of 15 months (Salive *et al.* 1994). Study participants with severe visual impairment (distant vision worse than 20/200) were noted to have a threefold higher incidence of limitations in activities of daily living and of limitations in mobility than those with visual acuity of 20/40 or better, after adjusting for demographic factors and disease history. A prospective study of patients undergoing cataract surgery revealed that 4 months after surgery there were significant improvements in visual acuity as well as in subjective and objective measures of function (Applegate *et al.* 1987). (See also Chapter 18.15.3.)

The results from studies evaluating the relationship between hearing impairment and functional impairment have conflicting results, with an association being found in some cases (Bess *et al.* 1989; Carabellese *et al.* 1993; Dargent-Molina *et al.* 1996) but not in others (Jette and Branch 1985; Rudberg *et al.* 1993). Some studies have suggested a relationship between hearing impairment and cognitive impairment (Herbst and Humphrey 1980; Uhlmann *et al.* 1989). Mulrow *et al.* (1990) randomized 194 elderly individuals with hearing impairment to receive a hearing aid or to join a waiting list. Those receiving a hearing aid had significant improvements in social, emotional, and cognitive function compared with those on the waiting list. Further studies will be needed to clarify the relationship between hearing impairment and adverse outcomes in elderly people. (See also Chapter 18.16.)

Malnutrition

Observational studies have found protein energy undernutrition to be an independent predictor of death in nursing home patients and in hospital-admitted elderly patients (Frisoni *et al.* 1994; Sullivan *et al.* 1995). Studies have also suggested that malnutrition is associated with longer hospital stays and higher hospital complication rates, such as infection, pressure sore development, and primary disease relapse (Sullivan 1995). The clinical markers for which these correlations have been strongest include the following: a history of significant involuntary weight loss, anthropometric measurements, hypoalbuminaemia, hypocholesterolaemia, and anaemia (Sullivan 1995). A prospective study of community-living senior citizens in the United States revealed that low body mass index was an independent predictor of the development of functional impairment (Galanos *et al.* 1994). Recent findings from the Nun Study, a longitudinal study of ageing involving Catholic sisters in the United States, indicate that an annual weight loss of 3 per cent or greater carries a significant risk of becoming dependent in a basic activity of daily living (Tully and Snowdon 1995).

Despite the growing evidence that malnutrition is an important risk factor for mortality, morbidity, and functional decline, caution must be taken in interpreting the available evidence. Weak study designs and the presence of numerous potential confounding factors have raised questions about the validity of some of the findings. Although some studies have suggested that nutritional supplementation can enhance clinical outcomes in surgical patients (Bastow *et al.* 1983; Delmi *et al.* 1990), many others have not (Sullivan 1995). Randomized trials studying the effectiveness of nutritional supplementation in malnourished elderly people will be needed to prove the benefits of such interventions. (See also Chapter 6.1.)

Hospital admission

Several studies have demonstrated that for older people, prior hospital admission is a potent risk factor for subsequent hospital admissions (Boult *et al.* 1993; Tierny and Worth 1995; Stearns *et al.* 1996). In older people, hospital admission is an important risk factor for functional decline (Hirsch *et al.* 1990; Inouye *et al.* 1993b; Sager *et al.* 1996). In a prospective cohort study of 1279 community-dwelling senior citizens aged 70 years and older admitted to acute wards, 31 per cent exhibited a decline in activities of daily living at the time of discharge (Sager *et al.* 1996). Patients at greatest risk of adverse functional outcomes at discharge were older and had preadmission disabilities in instrumental activities of daily living. Inouye *et al.* (1993b) identified four independent risk factors for functional decline in hospital: the presence on admission of a decubitus ulcer, functional impairment, cognitive impairment, and low social activity level. Functional decline in hospital-admitted elderly people has been shown to be predictive of poor outcomes including longer hospital stays, and higher rates of institutionalization and death (Narain *et al.* 1988; Inouye *et al.* 1993b). Reasons suggested for the functional decline of hospital-admitted elderly people include loss of physiological reserve associated with ageing, consequences of the illness itself, adverse effects of treatment, and the deconditioning effects of immobilization (Hoenig and Rubenstein 1991; Creditor 1993).

Geriatric syndromes and shared risk factors

Delirium, falls, immobility, urinary incontinence, and pressure sores are health conditions which are often referred to as geriatric syndromes, which are usually experienced by frail elderly people (Winograd *et al.* 1991; Rockwood *et al.* 1994; Tinetti *et al.* 1995). Although these syndromes can develop from distinct abnormalities within discrete organ systems, they often result from the accumulated effect of multiple impairments which overwhelm the individual's compensatory abilities and make them vulnerable to additional insults (Tinetti *et al.* 1995). Tinetti *et al.* (1995) suggest that the 'increased vulnerability resulting from impairments in multiple systems defines frailty, thus explaining why the subset of frail elderly people are at particular risk of experiencing geriatric syndromes'. This theory is supported by epidemiological evidence that the incidence of delirium and falls increases with an increase in the number of risk factors present (Tinetti *et al.* 1988; Inouye *et al.* 1993a; Francis *et al.* 1990).

Tinetti *et al.* (1995) conducted a longitudinal study of community-living elderly people over the age of 70 years to determine whether a set of predisposing factors could be found that were associated with falling, incontinence, and functional impairment. One-year follow-up was completed for 927 participants, and during the year of follow-up, 20 per cent reported functional dependence, 10 per cent reported the occurrence of two or more falls, and 16 per cent reported urinary incontinence. Adjusted stepwise logistic modelling was used to identify variables measured at baseline which were associated with falls, urinary incontinence, and functional dependence. Upper-extremity impairment (measured by shoulder abduction and grip strength), lower-extremity impairment (measured by chair stands), vision and hearing impairment, and anxiety were found to be associated with the development of falls, incontinence, and functional impairment.

Patient Code

3. The following questions are about activities you might do during a typical day. Does *your health now limit you* in these activities? If so, how much?

(circle one number on each line)

Activities	Yes, limited a lot	Yes, limited a little	No, not limited at all
(a) **Vigorous activities**, such as running, lifting heavy objects, participating in strenous sports	1	2	3
(b) **Moderate activities**, such as moving a table, pushing a vacuum cleaner, bowling, or playing golf	1	2	3
(c) Lifting or carrying groceries	1	2	3
(d) Climbing **several** flights of stairs	1	2	3
(e) Climbing **one** flight of stairs	1	2	3
(f) Bending, kneeling, or stooping	1	2	3
(g) Walking **more than a mile**	1	2	3
(h) Walking **half a mile**	1	2	3
(i) Walking **one hundred yards**	1	2	3
(j) Bathing or dressing yourself	1	2	3

4. During the *past 4 weeks*, have you had any of the following problems with your work or other regular daily activities *as a result of your physical health*?

(circle one number on each line)

	Yes	No
(a) Cut down on the **amount of time** you spent on work or other activities	1	2
(b) **Accomplished less** than you would like	1	2
(c) Were limited in the **kind** of work or other activities	1	2
(d) Had **difficulty** performing the work or other activities (for example, it took extra effort)	1	2

5. During the *past 4 weeks*, have you had any of the following problems with your work or other regular daily activities *as a result of any emotional problems* (such as feeling depressed or anxious)?

(circle one number on each line)

	Yes	No
(a) Cut down on the **amount of time** you spent on work or other activities	1	2
(b) **Accomplished less** than you would like	1	2
(c) Didn't do work or other activities as **carefully** as usual	1	2

6. During the *past 4 weeks*, to what extent has your physical health or emotional problems interfered with your normal social activities with family, friends, neighbours, or groups?

(circle one)

Not at all 1

Slightly 2

Moderately 3

Quite a bit 4

Extremely 5

7. How much *bodily* pain have you had during the past *4 weeks* ?

(circle one)

None 1

Very mild 2

Mild 3

Moderate 4

Severe 5

Very severe 6

Patient Code

8. During the *past 4 weeks* how much did *pain* interfere with your normal work (including both work outside the home and housework)?

(circle one)

Not at all	1
A little bit	2
Moderately	3
Quite a bit	4
Extremely	5

9. These questions are about how you feel and how things have been with you *during the past 4 weeks*. For each question, please give the one answer that comes closest to the way you have been feeling. How much of the time during the *past 4 weeks*.....

(circle one number on each line)

	All of the time	Most of the time	A good bit of the time	Some of the time	A little of the time	None of the time
(a) Did you feel full of life?	1	2	3	4	5	6
(b) Have you been a very nervous person?	1	2	3	4	5	6
(c) Have you felt so down in the dumps that nothing could cheer you up?	1	2	3	4	5	6
(d) Have you felt calm and peaceful?	1	2	3	4	5	6
(e) Did you have a lot of energy?	1	2	3	4	5	6
(f) Have you felt downhearted and low?	1	2	3	4	5	6
(g) Did you feel worn out?	1	2	3	4	5	6
(h) Have you been a happy person?	1	2	3	4	5	6
(i) Did you feel tired?	1	2	3	4	5	6

Patient Code

10. During the *past 4 weeks*, how much of the time has your *physical health or emotional problems* interfered with your social activities (like visiting friends, relatives, etc.)?

(circle one)

All of the time	1
Most of the time	2
Some of the time	3
A little of the time	4
None of the time	5

11. How TRUE or FALSE is each of the following statements for you?

(circle one number on each line)

	Definitely true	Mostly true	Don't know	Mostly false	Definitely false
(a) I seem to get ill more easily than other people	1	2	3	4	5
(b) I am as healthy as anybody I know	1	2	3	4	5
(c) I expect my health to get worse	1	2	3	4	5
(d) My health is excellent	1	2	3	4	5

Thank you very much for taking the time to complete this form.

Geriatric Depression Scale

1. **Are you basically satisfied with your life?** .... Yes **No**

2. **Have you dropped many of your activities and interests?** .... **Yes** No

3. **Do you feel that your life is empty?** .... **Yes** No

4. **Do you often get bored?** .... **Yes** No

5. Are you hopeful about the future? .... Yes **No**

6. Are you bothered by thoughts you can't get out of your head? .... **Yes** No

7. **Are you in good spirits most of the time?** .... Yes **No**

8. **Are you afraid that something bad is going to happen to you?** .... **Yes** No

9. **Do you feel happy most of the time?** .... Yes **No**

10. **Do you often feel helpless?** .... **Yes** No

11. Do you often get restless and fidgety? .... **Yes** No

12. **Do you prefer to stay at home, rather than going out and doing new things?** .... **Yes** No

13. Do you frequently worry about the future? .... **Yes** No

14. **Do you have more problems with your memory than most?** .... **Yes** No

15. **Do you think it is wonderful to be alive now?** .... Yes **No**

16. Do you often feel downhearted and blue (sad)? .... **Yes** No

17. **Do you often feel pretty worthless the way you are now?** .... **Yes** No

18. Do you worry a lot about the past? .... **Yes** No

19. Do you find life very exciting? .... Yes **No**

20. Is it hard for you to get started on new projects? .... **Yes** No

21. **Do you feel full of energy?** .... Yes **No**

22. **Do you feel that your situation is hopeless?** .... **Yes** No

23. **Do you think that most people are better off than you are?** .... **Yes** No

24. Do you frequently get upset over little things? .... **Yes** No

25. Do you frequently feel like crying? .... **Yes** No

26. Do you have trouble concentrating? .... **Yes** No

27. Do you enjoy getting up in the morning? .... Yes **No**

28. Do you prefer to avoid social gatherings? .... **Yes** No

29. Is it easy for you to make decisions? .... Yes **No**

30. Is your mind as clear as it used to be? .... Yes **No**

The questions for the shortened (15-item) version are shown in bold type.
Score 1 for each shaded answer: 0–1, not depressed; 5–15, depressed.

J.A. Yesavage *et al.* (1983). Development and validation of a geriatric depression screening scale: a preliminary report. *Journal of Psychiatric Research*, **17**, 37–49.

Frenchay Aphasia Screening Test
Administration Form

Materials required
Picture card with attached reading cards, pencil and paper, stop watch.

Check
Patient is wearing spectacles, if needed. Patient can hear you adequately (raise voice if necessary).

Comprehension
Show patient card with river scene. Say: 'Look at the picture. Listen carefully to what is said and point to the things I tell you to.' Score 1 for each correctly performed. If instructions require repeating, score as error. Unprompted self-correction may be scored as correct. Score range 0 – 10.

Instructions
(a) *River scene*
  1. Point to a boat
  2. Point to the tallest tree
  3. Point to the man and point to the dog
  4. Point to the man's left leg and then to the canoe
  5. Before pointing to a duck near the bridge, show me the middle hill

(b) *Shapes*
  1. Point to the square
  2. Point to the cone
  3. Point to the oblong and the square
  4. Point to the square, the cone, and the semicircle
  5. Point to the one that looks like a pyramid and the one that looks like a segment of orange

Expression
(a) Show patient the river scene and say 'Tell me as much about the picture as you can'. If patient does not appear to understand, say: 'Name anything you can see in the picture'. Score range 0–5.

Score
0 Unable to name any objects intelligibly
1 Names 1–2 objects
2 Names 3–4 objects
3 Names 5–7 objects
4 Names 8 or 9 objects or uses phrases and sentences, but performance *not* normal (e.g. hesitations, inappropriate comments, etc.)
5 Normal—uses phrases and sentences, naming 10 items

(b) Remove picture card from view and inform patient that you are now going to attempt something a little different. Then ask him to name as many animals as he can think of in 1 minute. If patient appears doubtful, explain that you want the names of any kind of animal, wild or domestic, and not just those which may have been seen in the picture. Commence timing as soon as patient names first animal and allow 60 seconds. Score range 0–5.

Score
0 None named
1 Names 1–2
2 Names 3–5
3 Names 6–9
4 Names 10–14
5 Names 15 or more

Reading
Check that the patient is wearing correct spectacles for reading purposes. Show patient river scene and first reading card. Ask him to read the sentence to himself, not aloud, and do whatever it instructs him to do. Proceed in the same manner with the remaining four reading cards. Score range 0–5.

Score 1 for each correct.

Writing
Show patient river scene and say: 'Please write as much as you can about *what is happening* in the picture'. If he does not appear to understand say: 'Write anything that you can see in the picture'. If dominant hand is affected ask patient to attempt with non-dominant hand. Encourage if he stops prematurely. Allow a *maximum* of 5 minutes. Score range 0–5.

Score
0 Able to attempt task but does not write any intelligent or appropriate words
1 Writes 1 or 2 appropriate words
2 Writes down names of 3 objects or a phrase including 2 or 3 objects
3 Writes down names of 4 objects (correctly spelled), or 2 or 3 phrases including names of 4 items
4 Uses phrases and sentences, including names of 5 items, but *not* considered 'normal' performance, e.g. sentence not integrating people and actions
5 Definitely normal performance, e.g. sentence integrating people and actions

Interpretation
The presence of aphasia is indicated if the patient scores below the following cut-off points. (Referral to speech therapy for full assessment is suggested.)

Age	Raw score
Up to 60	27
61+	25

P. Enderby *et al.* (1986). *Frenchay Aphasia Screening Test*. Whurr, London.

River scene

Shapes

Reading cards

1. Point to the dog
2. Show me the bridge
3. Point to the man standing in the barge
4. Touch the left-hand corner of the card
5. Touch the bottom of the card and then the top of it

Michigan Alcoholism Screening Test—Geriatric Version (MAST-G)

	Yes (1)	No (2)
1. After drinking have you ever noticed an increase in your heart rate or beating in your chest?	1. —	—
2. When talking with others, do you ever underestimate how much you actually drink?	2. —	—
3. Does alcohol make you sleepy so that you often fall asleep in your chair?	3. —	—
4. After a few drinks have you sometimes not eaten or been able to skip a meal because you didn't feel hungry	4. —	—
5. Does having a few drinks help decrease your shakiness or tremors?	5. —	—
6. Does alcohol sometimes make it hard for you to remember parts of the day or night?	6. —	—
7. Do you have rules for yourself that you won't drink before a certain time of the day?	7. —	—
8. Have you lost interest in hobbies or activities you used to enjoy?	8. —	—
9. When you wake up in the morning, do you ever have trouble remembering part of the night before?	9. —	—
10. Does having a drink help you sleep?	10. —	—
11. Do you hide your alcohol bottles from family members?	11. —	—
12. After a social gathering, have you ever felt embarrassed because you drank too much?	12. —	—

	Yes (1)	No (2)
13. Have you ever been concerned that the drinking might be harmful to your health?	13. —	—
14. Do you like to end the evening with a night cap?	14. —	—
15. Did you find your drinking increased after someone close to you died?	15. —	—
16. In general, would you prefer to have a few drinks at home rather than go out to social events?	16. —	—
17. Are you drinking more now than in the past?	17. —	—
18. Do you usually take a drink to relax or calm your nerves?	18. —	—
19. Do you drink to take your mind off your problems?	19. —	—
20. Have you ever increased your drinking after experiencing a loss in your life?	20. —	—
21. Do you sometimes drive when you have had too much to drink?	21. —	—
22. Has a doctor or nurse ever said they were worried or concerned about your drinking?	22. —	—
23. Have you ever made rules to manage your drinking?	23. —	—
24. When you feel lonely does having a drink help?	24. —	—

Scoring: five or more 'yes' responses indicative of alcohol problem

Index

Page numbers in **bold** refer to main discussions in the text. Page number in *italics* refer to tables.
Index entries are arranged in letter-by-letter alphabetical order.
Abbreviations used in subentries (without explanation):
COPD chronic obstructive pulmonary disease
CPR cardiopulmonary resuscitation
NSAID non-steroidal anti-inflammatory drug
PTH parathyroid hormone
TSH thyroid-stimulating hormone